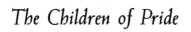

The Children of Pride

Books by
ROBERT MANSON MYERS

HANDEL'S MESSIAH: A TOUCHSTONE OF TASTE (1948)
FROM BEOWULF TO VIRGINIA WOOLF (1952)
HANDEL, DRYDEN, AND MILTON (1956)
RESTORATION COMEDY (1961)
THE CHILDREN OF PRIDE (1972)

The Children of Pride

A TRUE STORY OF GEORGIA
AND THE CIVIL WAR

EDITED BY

Robert Manson Myers

NEW HAVEN AND LONDON

Yale University Press

4-13-76
79-998344

Designed by John O. C. McCrillis
and set in Granjon type.
Printed in the United States of America by
The Colonial Press Inc., Clinton, Massachusetts.

Published in Great Britain, Europe, and Africa by
Yale University Press, Ltd., London.
Distributed in Canada by McGill-Queen's University
Press, Montreal; in Latin America by Kaiman & Polon,
Inc., New York City; in Australasia and Southeast
Asia by John Wiley & Sons Australasia Pty. Ltd.,
Sydney; in India by UBS Publishers' Distributors Pvt.,
Ltd., Delhi; in Japan by John Weatherhill, Inc., Tokyo.

IN MEMORIAM M. M. M.
OBIIT MCMLXII

*He beholdeth all high things: he is a
king over all the children of pride.*

JOB 41:34

Contents

Preface

In preparing this book for publication I have been guided by a single purpose: to select from the voluminous family papers of the Rev. Dr. Charles Colcock Jones (1804–1863), of Liberty County, Georgia, letters which, when brought together in chronological order without editorial links, would form a coherent, independent narrative related entirely in the words of the characters themselves. What has emerged is a true story told in letters—something akin to an epistolary novel: a leisurely account of family life in coastal Georgia before, during, and after the Civil War. It is a story of intelligent, perceptive, well-to-do plantation people remote from the public eye—people who lived out their lives with little feeling that they were making history or changing destiny, and who went to their graves with no suspicion that their letters, written in the heat of the moment and posted without delay, would ultimately see print. It is a quiet story of births and marriages and deaths, of daily joys and sorrows, of the response of a proud people to one of the great crises of American history. For fourteen years (from 1854 to 1868) we follow their fortunes and misfortunes in multifarious detail—from prewar plenty through wartime privation to postwar ruin. As the story mounts to its terrible climax we see a whole generation caught in the grips of a national tragedy.

Nothing so graphically conveys the essence of an age as its letters. Momentous events, recorded impersonally on the page of history, start vividly to life when delineated in human terms. A young Georgian, a law student at Harvard, witnesses abolition riots in Boston in 1854: "Do not be surprised if when I return home you find me a *confirmed disunionist.*" Two years later he rejoices with trembling at the election of Buchanan: "The next issue will doubtless be purely sectional in its character. . . . We of the South must and will be prepared to meet it bravely and without concession." In November 1859 the rumblings of Harpers Ferry reverberate in far-off Georgia: "Let them know that the fortunes of the American republic are embarked in one vessel, and neither stem nor stern shall be broken up without damage and loss of the whole." And so on through that calamitous sequence of events now known to every schoolboy: Lincoln's election ("We are on the verge of Heaven only knows what"); secession ("How do you feel now, dear Mother, that *we* are in a foreign land?"); coercion ("I confess I have no idea that we shall have war; if so, but one or two battles, and then peace we shall have on our own terms"); Lincoln's inaugural ("What does it mean? It means this, and it means that; and then it may mean neither"); First Manassas ("For miles around the air was awful—so many men either unburied or partially covered, and such numbers of dead horses upon the field"); inflation ("Think of giving three dollars per pound for ordinary beef, and choice pieces from four to five dollars per pound!"); gathering gloom ("If we have not the power to prevent the enemy from occupying our strongholds, how are we ever to dislodge them and drive them out when once they have gained possession?"); pride in defeat ("I can look extinction for me and mine in the face, but *submission* never!"); Lincoln's assassination ("One sweet drop among so much that is painful is that he at least cannot raise his howl of diabolical triumph over us").

Here is an old story, universally familiar and often repeated; its countless retellings have stirred hearers and readers for more than a century. With each retelling what is old becomes new: the well-known plot, heightened by fresh details, is transmuted into something rich and strange. History is miraculously brought to life by a rehearsal of the particulars of every day— what Ivy Compton-Burnett has called "those little things which are more important than big ones, because they make up life." It is unfortunate that statesmen and generals tend to monopolize the page of history: the texture of daily experience is to be found not so much in accounts of laws and battles as in the records of ordinary people leading ordinary lives and facing ordinary problems. By means of letters we can reconstruct the quality of such ordinary lives; by means of the letters in this book we can reconstruct the quality of ordinary lives in coastal Georgia a century ago. The wealth of detail is enormous; at a thousand points we see how people lived. We see their dress, their food and drink, their homes, their family life, their manners and morals, their social customs, their pastimes and amusements, their modes of travel, their medical practices, their financial transactions. We meet the individuals who people their world: judges, bankers, dentists, soldiers, constables, steamboat captains, railroad conductors, slave traders, plantation overseers, carpenters, bakers, grocers, apothecaries, postal clerks, commission merchants, college professors, planters, governesses, dressmakers, nurses, country doctors, gentlemen of leisure. We share their lives from day to day: we purchase Central of Georgia Railroad stock; we visit Niagara Falls and Mammoth Cave and Lookout Mountain; we survive the yellow fever epidemic of 1854; we attend a Negro wedding; we vacation at the fashionable Virginia springs; we hear Thackeray lecture on *The Four Georges;* we buy a bonnet; we sit for a daguerreotype; we join the throng of mourners at a mayor's funeral; we witness an appalling train wreck; we visit a Confederate hospital; we hear a wartime sermon. We see mid-nineteenth-century Georgia in all its range and variety; in the company of the Joneses and their relatives and friends we virtually enter another world.

Their story unfolds in a series of letters passing from town to country, from country to town, from plantation to plantation; as the correspondents exchange their news and opinions we catch revealing glimpses of the contemporary Southern scene. A sensitive youth becomes "completely deranged" and dies far from home in a Northern "asylum." A runaway Negro house servant named Jane is arrested in a private house in Savannah where she has been masquerading for more than a month as a hired girl named Sarah. A doctor spends several weeks at Andersonville Prison "investigating the most dreadful diseases amongst those infamous Yankees." A Negro mother murders her infant; another dies of fever, leaving five orphaned children ("We feel those losses more than the Northerners think"). A clergyman's wife reads *The Marble Faun* ("Mr. Mallard has been laughing at me for reading a romance"); a spinster friend reads *Jane Eyre* ("I must say, although I know it displays great want of taste, that I was never more disappointed in my life"). A favorite aunt dies of cancer; a sister-in-law dies of puerperal fever; an acquaintance, "probably in a fit of lunacy," plunges to her death from a second- or third-story window. A mother enjoins her daughter to secure a proper escort ("I do not like to see *young ladies* traveling alone in a public stage"). A housewife regrets the distance of a friend ("There is at least a mile between us, so that it would be impossible for us to be really sociable"). A baby is born on an isolated plantation during a Yankee raid. A dissolute cousin contracts a degrading second marriage. A matron has nine teeth extracted and collapses in the dentist's chair "from nervous exhaustion and loss of blood." A Negro man is sold for six hundred dollars cash ("a very good sale for him, as he was about fifty and rather complaining. We sold him at half price, as we could not warrant him sound").

This is the stuff of history; it is the very essence of historical data. The life of the Joneses evolves so simply and naturally that we tend to forget that we are reading documents of fundamental interest to the social historian. And the record is all the more valid because it is *immediate*. It is firsthand, not retrospective. It is the response to an event dashed off while it is happening, the sensation of an experience captured the moment it is felt. "The mosquitoes are fairly putting out the lamp, and I am covered from ankle to knee with fleas." "The cat has jumped upon the table, and for the last ten minutes has been watching my pen with great interest." "Your dear mother is sitting by me at her work, and we have no sounds in our little chamber but the racing of my pen over the paper, and the rustle of the silk and the drawing of her stitches and the occasional click of her scissors as she plies the work on her new dress." Through such incidental glances we come to feel that we are present as events transpire, participating in the action and sharing the emotions of the characters.

As I write, the campfires are all dead save that which burns brightly still in front of the guard tent, where "the watchers keep their vigils sharp"; and the stillness is unbroken save by the lazy flap of the tent curtains, the soft ripple of the tide as it gently chafes with the shore, and the occasional note of some waking songbird among the overshadowing branches. All else is hushed. Not a sound from the stables. No challenge from the sentinels. They are keeping their posts, however; for every now and then I can detect the clank of the scabbard against the slings as they come to the about. Even the quiet breathing of the captain, whom I can touch with my hand as he lies sleeping behind me on his camp cot, I cannot hear. And I am holding silent converse with you, my dear parents; and my heart is going forth in warmest love towards you and my sweet little daughter. May a kind Providence prove ever near you to bless and keep you from every harm!

Here is a moment in a Confederate camp, realized with startling immediacy; suddenly, through the miracle of words, the years vanish and we are living a century ago. No narrative device so fully communicates this sense of actuality as the letter form. The interval of time between the writer and the event he describes is reduced to nothing; the future, still undetermined, has yet to issue from the present; the writer's experience is therefore tentative, inconclusive, immediate. Such immediacy is scarcely possible in an account of action already completed. With the elapse of time passions cool, animosities soften, perspectives blur: a memoir written months or years after the event is apt to be stale and distorted. Two centuries ago the novelist Samuel Richardson saw the advantage of writing "to the moment, while the heart is agitated by hopes and fears on events undecided." "Much more lively and affecting," he wrote in his preface to *Clarissa,* "must be the style of those who write in the height of a present distress; the mind tortured by the pangs of uncertainty (the events then hidden in the womb of fate); than the dry, narrative, unanimated style of a person relating difficulties and dangers surmounted, can be; the relater perfectly at ease; and if himself unmoved by his own story, not likely greatly to affect the reader."

But there are hazards in writing "to the moment," and the reader of familiar letters must accept the liabilities of the form along with its many assets. The correspondence reproduced in this book is private, set forth frankly and without reserve; scarcely a letter can be said to have been written for publication. If it is spontaneous, it is also impromptu; if it is unselfconscious, it is also unrehearsed; inevitably it must bear the marks of day-to-day extemporaneous prose. Three universal notes seem rather too frequently struck: weather, religion, and health. "Disquisitions upon the weather," says one character, "are, I am aware, rather uninteresting; yet you know one is very apt to speak first of that which most engrosses his attention—of that upon which he *feels most.*" Religion is a constant theme. A strain of Calvinism runs through the book, and the didactic tone is pronounced; the parents' concern for their son's spiritual state becomes a strand of the plot. Clergymen and clergymen's wives abound; their letters are liberally sprinkled with "D.V." (*Deo volente,* God willing) and "D.G." (*Deo gratias,* Thanks be to God). Even more conspicuous, perhaps, is the general preoccupation with health. Disease is ever-present and often frightful, and death is a daily visitor. Quite understandably the correspondents tend to luxuriate in medical particulars. Their account of prescriptions and

cures is often illuminating; their fascination for lingering illnesses and protracted deathbed scenes strikes us as excessive if not bizarre. But this at least
can be said: the frequency of their talk of weather, religion, and health is
part of the historical record. It completes the picture; it enhances verisimili-
tude; it sharpens our sense that we are in the midst of life.

The same might be said of the general quality of the prose. In a correspondence touching the problems of every day, struck off by members of a
family and never designed for the public eye, it is hardly surprising to find
occasional passages that are flat and commonplace. The diction, to be sure,
is sometimes pedestrian, and now and then letters seem inordinately prolix.
There is a bothersome tendency to repeat certain epistolary formulas: "I
am in receipt of your esteemed favor of the 18th inst., and sincerely rejoice
to know that all at home are well." "Howdy for the servants, and kind remembrances for all relatives and friends." Several correspondents are given
to pompous rhetoric, and at least one has a weakness for eccentric word
order: "It is a nut when fresh and well boiled of which I am very fond."
"The peaches and melons in delightful order arrived safely." But on the
whole the level of English is remarkably high. If it is not always distinguished, it is generally disciplined and workmanlike. At its worst it is competent and sensible; at its best it has power and charm:

Montevideo looks beautifully—all day long vocal with the sweet voices of nature bursting from every tree and cover, the little squirrels playing about, the
lawn lighted aslant by the evening sun spread with green and covered with
sheep and calves and poultry, and Mother's garden looking as if a rainbow had
been broken and showered down and its beautiful and varied fragments had
caught on all the plants and shrubbery.

A keen northwester is sweeping over the lawn and whistling among the trees,
from the branches of which the long gray moss is waving. The pall of death is
suddenly thrown over our once cheerful and happy home. Not a living creature
stirs in garden or yard, on the plain or in the grove. Nature wears a funereal
aspect, and the blast, as it sweeps through the branches, is sighing a requiem
to departed days.

A most lovely night it is. A bank of clouds toward the north breaks the continuity of the otherwise clear sky, while a full moon pours down its silver radiance from its lofty throne. I plucked from the vine in our flower garden a few
jessamines—the first I have seen. The green leaves glistened in the moon's rays
and were wet with the dew. I send the flowers, and as I am ignorant of their
language and have some misgivings about their carrying the proper message,
will just say that they are intended as a little offering of love to her who has not
lost the sweetheart in the wife.

Here we have extemporaneous prose at its best. With no self-consciousness,
with no thought of readers beyond the immediate family circle, the corre-

spondents capture fleeting moments in fresh, unrehearsed language. Fortunately they appreciate the importance of little things in the texture of daily experience; they show an eye for significant detail; and they possess the power to convey their impressions in firm, vivid English.

One of the most striking features of writing "to the moment" is the segmented structure inherent in the epistolary form. The story proceeds in letters; it holds together, as it were, by continual splicing. At each new letter we must pause and adjust our stance: Who is speaking? To whom? Where? When? Soon we sense that we are reading in effect an extended dialogue, in which characters vent letters instead of speeches and in so doing forward the plot of a vast drama. A variety of actors speak; the interplay of their voices is sometimes quiet, sometimes animated and tense; in their exchanges they reveal themselves and their friends and their world. The revelation is kaleidoscopic: character comes out in flashes, and plot develops not so much in conventionally ordered scenes as in glimpses. Gradually we form a synthesis, and ultimately all the flashes and glimpses merge into one perfected vision.

Among the merits of this narrative approach is a great expansion of our point of view. From a number of characters writing out of a variety of backgrounds we gain a fuller comprehension of the contemporary social scene than would be possible in a journal or diary or memoir, where the vision is commonly limited to one sensibility. In this book the viewpoint shifts continually from character to character; we hear from old and young, from male and female, from married and single, from rich and poor; sometimes several voices contribute to the development of a single episode. Together the characters unfold a diverse but unified panorama. Our interest is accordingly stirred; our focus is broadened; and our experience is immeasurably enriched.

How fully, we ask, do the characters reveal themselves? To what extent is self-revelation submerged in self-disguise? How much is suppressed, how much evaded, how much camouflaged? In considering these questions we cannot ignore the natural human barrier against full exposure of the self; writing "to the moment" does not guarantee complete self-revelation. Moreover, the art of letter-writing a century ago was an exacting business: formalities and restraints were punctiliously observed. But we need not read far in this book to note that formalities and restraints are observed to varying degrees and in varying styles by different correspondents. One son's prose, for instance, is conspicuously formal, even rhetorical and inflated, and it waxes more so as tension mounts; in this respect he is like his mother. Another son's prose is forthright and plain, strictly disciplined but far less rhetorical; in his prose, as in his character, he is more nearly akin to his father. A cousin's prose is loose, rambling, disjointed—in keeping, we sense, with her charming but erratic nature. In each case character appears not only in *what* is said but also in *how* it is said; the correspondents are individualized by the distinctive tone of their letters; their manner is sometimes as revealing as their matter. As Samuel Richardson recognized, "Styles differ, too, as much as faces, and are indicative generally, beyond the power of disguise, of the mind of the writer."

But people are more than faces, and character revelation is more than prose style. The great virtue of the epistolary form is its power to probe the human heart. The familiar letter is a plausible medium whereby our innermost sensibilities may be candidly revealed; it explores particularities of thought and feeling on terms of intimacy scarcely to be equaled by any other literary form. Through letters we gain access to emotions and responses not normally verbalized; this access deepens our comprehension of the writer's total being and heightens our identification with his consciousness. Even if a correspondent reveals himself but partially in his letters, it is tempting to speculate on the basis of the hints we are given. The hints may be scattered; the shadings may be subtle; but soon the correspondents begin to breathe, and by the end of the book they seem intensely alive.

Character portrayal is one of the chief fascinations of *The Children of Pride*. On a canvas that is broad and densely peopled we find a number of full-length portraits: the Joneses together with their relatives and friends make up a sizable Southern "connection." It is exciting to follow their fortunes and misfortunes through fourteen anxious years. We know their fate from the start; the actors in the drama do not. They cannot sense that theirs is a pivotal moment, that a way of life is about to be swept from the earth. They grope, dazed and bewildered, while we from the perspective of a later day look back with Olympian eyes, absorbed, astonished, horror-struck. The collapse of a civilization is a momentous thing, and it is our privilege in this book to pursue its course from day to day.

The publication of *The Children of Pride* has been made possible by a combination of circumstances that is rare if not unique. Countless collections of family letters have been published before; but none to my knowledge has been so shaped as to tell an independent story, complete with beginning, middle, and end, entirely in the words of the participants themselves, without the distraction of footnotes, bracketed emendations, and explanatory links. Such a feat is the result of a number of chances, all favoring a happy issue; if any *one* of the following conditions had not prevailed, this book might never have been published: (1) the events herein recorded actually occurred; (2) the events are of historical significance; (3) the events are of human interest; (4) the correspondents lived precisely *where* the events occurred; (5) the correspondents lived there precisely *when* the events occurred; (6) the correspondents were sufficiently perceptive to *observe* the events in accurate detail; (7) the correspondents were sufficiently cultivated to *record* the events in disciplined, effective English; (8) the correspondents were sufficiently separated to necessitate written communication; (9) their letters, once posted and delivered, were recalled and collected; (10) the letters thus collected, passing from generation to generation and suffering the vicissitudes of time, were not misplaced, lost, or destroyed; (11) the collection thus preserved is so complete that a continuous story covering a period of fourteen years may be fashioned by assembling selected letters in chronological order without the intrusion of editorial links; (12) the story thus fashioned carries sufficient impact to move the sensitive reader. Such a combination of fortunate conditions is remarkable indeed: taken singly the conditions may be usual enough; taken together they are extremely rare. Few collections of letters are at once so comprehensive and various in their presentation of significant and stirring historical events, so strategically fixed in place and time, so fully preserved, and, finally, so rich in narrative appeal as to make possible a self-contained work of the character and scope of *The Children of Pride*.

Why were the letters saved? By whom were they collected? How were they preserved intact? And what was their ultimate fate? The odyssey of the Jones papers over the course of a hundred years constitutes a story full of drama, pathos, and mystery. Evidently someone in the family felt an irresistible compulsion to collect and preserve the letters as they were written, even recalling letters from their recipients. As early as January 18th, 1860, the Rev. Dr. Charles Colcock Jones, father of the household, noted in his journal: "We brought up old letters and papers of every description to cull and save and destroy." At the height of the war, on September 24th, 1863, Mrs. Jones, by then a widow, wrote to her son, a lieutenant colonel encamped near Charleston: "I am keeping all your letters—especially at this period—for your little daughter; if her life is spared I know she will have a head and heart to appreciate them." These very letters were among the papers searched by a marauder from Sherman's army during a plantation raid in December 1864:

He went into the attic and instituted a thorough search into every hole and corner. He opened a large trunk containing the private papers of my dear father, and finding a tin canister, he tried to open it. Mother could not immediately find the key, and as he spoke insolently to her about getting the key, she told him he had better break it, but she could assure him it contained only the private papers of her husband, who was a minister of the gospel.

When Mrs. Jones was forced to flee from the Yankees in March 1865, she grieved that the one-horse cart conveying her baggage to Southwest Georgia allowed no room for the papers of her deceased husband: "I cannot even take Mr. Jones's papers that I value above all things. My heart is very sad." And when, in January 1868, she left her plantation and went to live with her daughter in New Orleans, she insisted that the family papers accompany her: "I must bring on your father's papers; I could not leave them. All else—books, pictures, bedding, etc., etc.—must remain." On her deathbed in April 1869 Mrs. Jones bequeathed the papers to her daughter, Mrs. Robert Quarterman Mallard; at Mrs. Mallard's death in August 1889 they passed to her daughter Georgia (later Mrs. William Kimsey Seago). In

Mrs. Seago's possession they remained, for the most part stored in trunks and boxes and canisters in her New Orleans attic, until her death in December 1952, when they became the property of her four children, Mrs. Mary Seago Brooke, Miss Dorothy Wilson Seago, Mrs. Georgia Seago Fischer, and Mr. Robert Quarterman Mallard Seago. This collection, comprising some five thousand items, chiefly letters, was presented to Tulane University in New Orleans in 1962.

Meanwhile another collection of Jones papers, equally significant though somewhat less voluminous, was following its separate course in a distant state. On May 28th, 1866, the elder son of the family, then a lawyer in New York City, wrote his mother, Mrs. Jones, who was still residing on her Georgia plantation:

I have promised the Georgia Historical Society to prepare an account of the fortifications erected around, and of the military operations connected with, the city of Savannah during the last war. Have you any journal or newspaper or written accounts or memoranda with the loan of which you could favor me? I have thought that perhaps my letters to yourself and Father from 1860, or say 1859, to the close of the war would prove of some value to me, and enable me to fix certain dates which otherwise I might find trouble in doing. May I ask the favor of you at some early leisure moment to gather up those letters and memoranda of every sort and kind in your possession and send them on to me by express at your early convenience? I will be greatly obliged to you if you would do so. The express freight on the package I will pay here.

Mrs. Jones promptly executed her son's request; but in withdrawing from the family papers the letters written by her son from 1859 to 1865 she reduced the size and altered the character of the original collection, and at the same time unwittingly brought about a division of the family papers that has obtained to the present time. The "loan" of letters sent to New York in 1866 remained in the possession of the son, Charles Colcock Jones, Jr., until his death in July 1893, when, together with numerous other family papers, they passed to his daughter, Mrs. Samuel Barstow Carpenter. At her death in July 1934 the collection became the property of her two daughters, Mrs. Earll C. Waller and Mrs. Harcourt E. Waller, of Augusta, Georgia. A substantial portion of these papers, chiefly those concerning the postwar public career of Charles Colcock Jones, Jr., were subsequently acquired by Duke University in Durham, North Carolina. Papers of a more private and personal character, including many letters reproduced in this book, remained in the Waller family until 1960, when most (some thirteen hundred items) were acquired by the University of Georgia in Athens. A few items of special family interest were retained by the Wallers at the time of sale.

It will thus be seen that the Jones papers having marked family interest are now to be found in three places: Athens, Augusta, and New Orleans; and that these three collections were originally one, divided by chance a century ago. The division bears little if any relationship to the narrative structure of *The Children of Pride*. One letter may be found in Athens, its reply in New Orleans; read separately the two letters may seem to lack relevance; read together they may be charged with meaning. In view of the fact that what is essentially one uniform collection is now perhaps forever divided, it has seemed fitting to represent the three collections as generously as possible within the limits of a single book. Much of the richest material in the three collections is reproduced here; some twelve hundred letters have been printed from a total of approximately six thousand. Something more than half of these letters are drawn from New Orleans, something less than half from Athens, a small but essential group from Augusta. In the present text the source of each letter is indicated at the end of its title line by the appropriate superior character: *g* (University of Georgia, Athens); *t* (Tulane University, New Orleans); *w* (Waller Collection, Augusta).

Brought together, the three collections form a homogeneous unit that is remarkably complete. The Joneses were ideal collectors: they kept virtually everything; they did not ask: "Is this important?" Perhaps the very letters which they might have discarded as the least "important" would seem to us the most so; as we have already observed, the trifles of ordinary life, which most people take for granted and few consciously record, often assume great significance for the social historian of a subsequent day, and may well prove to be more useful (as well as more elusive) than the so-called "important" events of battlegrounds and legislative halls. Fortunately the Joneses did not discriminate; everything went into the trunk, and most of what they saved has come down to us intact.

There are, to be sure, occasional gaps; and these tend to occur at crises. Weddings, for example, are not vividly realized, perhaps because the correspondents usually came together for such family events and hence saw little necessity to describe them in letters. Or perhaps the important moment occasioned an account of such peculiar interest that the prized letter was circulated among family and friends, and from carelessness or inadvertency was never restored to its proper place in the collection. Actually there are few if any serious gaps in the sequence of letters reproduced in this book; and even the occasional gaps that may be apparent should serve to pique our interest. Silences sometimes limit the narrative viewpoint and thereby sharpen psychological focus: we do not have, for example, the letter of February 1858 in which Charles Colcock Jones, Jr., informs his parents of his engagement to Miss Ruth Berrien Whitehead; but we have his mother's reply, which reflects more or less fully the contents of the son's missing letter. Similarly, in the long courtship of the Rev. Robert Quarterman Mallard and Miss Mary Sharpe Jones, we have only the letters of the suitor; none of the young lady's letters to her fiancé have survived. (*She* kept *his* letters, but *he* evidently did not keep *hers;* or were they kept and later misplaced or lost—or perhaps deliberately destroyed?) It is intriguing to have this one-sided view of the romance, to surmise from *his* letters what *she* has written;

and to add to the intrigue, we hear frequently from *her* throughout the courtship, but never when she speaks to *him*.

In shaping the story I have of course sought to avoid as far as possible any sense of gaps in the correspondence; if an episode is not fully or clearly developed in the letters, I have usually eliminated it altogether. The extraordinary completeness of the collection has allowed me the luxury of choice, and I have felt free to include and exclude precisely as my taste and narrative instinct directed. For the resulting bias in shape and tone I must assume full responsibility: in a real sense I have "written" every word of this book myself, confined strictly to the unrehearsed English placed at my disposal by a family who wrote impromptu letters a century ago. From the beginning I have aimed to produce a story that is at once readable, informative, and moving. Though the letters treat the daily concerns of a normal, active family and are therefore as varied and miscellaneous as normal, active days are apt to be, I have attempted to arrange the letters in chapters reflecting at least to some extent a pattern of plot development. In several instances a wedding serves as the termination of a chapter; an extended journey to Kentucky, Ohio, and Virginia forms a natural unit; the events of a household during a mother's absence mark a logical division and are set apart as such. At times, regrettably, I have been forced to include letters of little distinction simply because they act as links in the story sequence; at times, too, I have been forced to omit excellent letters that plainly interrupt the flow of events. I have sometimes excluded minor episodes in order to strengthen the impact of major ones; I have dropped a number of peripheral characters whose presence seemed distracting or irrelevant; and I have deleted dozens of passages which could only be described as tedious.

But whatever appears on the pages of *The Children of Pride* I have reproduced with painstaking fidelity to the manuscript text. To facilitate reference I have regularized all datelines, supplying at the head of each letter the name of addressor and addressee, together with place and date of writing; within letters I have retained all dates in their original form. A few undated and misdated letters I have correctly dated on the basis of internal evidence; datelines so altered I have terminated with an asterisk. Obvious discrepancies in dates I have silently corrected wherever possible. Readers will note that a few letters begin on one date and continue on another without indication of change of date, thus causing apparent (but not actual) discrepancies between date and text; as, for example, in the letter of Charles Colcock Jones, Jr., beginning Friday, October 27th, 1854, and ending with a reference to "tomorrow" (that is, Sunday) as "the day of holy rest." Such seeming discrepancies I have allowed to stand.

The Joneses and their friends wrote extraordinarily careful English, but for ease of reading it has seemed wise to reduce a varying text to a consistent standard. To this end I have normalized all spelling, capitalization, punctuation, and paragraphing. I have retained the italics of the original letters; in addition I have silently italicized titles of books, names of ships, and foreign phrases in accordance with modern usage. I have ignored the erratic and apparently meaningless italics of one correspondent (Miss Mary Eliza Robarts), who underlined every second word on the average, evidently out of nervous habit. I have expanded abbreviations at will. A few clear inadvertencies I have set right without notice. On rare occasions, to prevent misreading, I have silently introduced a pronoun or a conjunction or an article or a form of the verb *to be*. A journal kept jointly by Mrs. Mary Jones and her daughter, Mrs. Mary S. Mallard, I have sectioned according to author on the basis of internal evidence. Throughout I have employed suspension points to indicate all cuts; in the few instances where postscripts are deleted I have disregarded the omission. From beginning to end I have done everything possible to render the text uniform, clear, and smooth without sacrifice of textual integrity.

Thus I have sought to make *The Children of Pride* a happy blend of accuracy and readability—a reliable sourcebook for the scholar as well as an engaging story for the layman. In my determination to keep scholarly apparatus to a minimum I have stoutly resisted all temptation to intrude upon the text with explanatory notes, feeling that any interruption of the narrative flow would prove more a distraction than an aid. As Dr. Johnson observed two centuries ago, "Notes are often necessary, but they are necessary evils. . . . The mind is refrigerated by interruption; the thoughts are diverted from the principal object; the reader is weary, he suspects not why; and at last throws away the book which he has too diligently studied." In editing the letters I have preferred to keep the reader in the nineteenth century rather than force him to shuttle between the nineteenth and twentieth. I have let the story speak for itself. At the same time I have felt the need of some form of annotation; I have accordingly included at the end of the narrative a complete "Who's Who," presenting in alphabetical order a biographical sketch of every individual mentioned in the text. In this way I trust I have made the documentation unobtrusive yet readily accessible: it is possible to read the whole of the narrative without once resorting to the "Who's Who"; it is also possible to satisfy one's interest conveniently at any point without having to seek out a footnote lost on some preceding page.

Unearthing precise and trustworthy biographical data on more than a thousand individuals, many of them obscure, who lived in urban and rural Georgia a century ago has proved a stupendous task. The research involved in establishing reliable birth and marriage and death dates for plantation overseers and railroad conductors and postal clerks; in tracing the nebulous careers of nurses and dressmakers and carpenters and constables and daguerreotypists; in verifying the dates of college and university degrees earned by lawyers and physicians and clergymen; in putting flesh on the bones of aunts and uncles and cousins and neighboring friends; in expanding initials and ascertaining middle names and correcting misspellings and discrediting unfounded traditions and sifting gossip for essential truth—the research involved in settling such problems as these has required some seventeen years of intensive study and travel, and has often taxed my detective powers to the utmost. For months on end I have tangled in genealogical mazes. In Washington I have exploited to the full the generous resources accessible to the student of Americana: I have scrutinized the Federal Census and pored over compiled military service records at the National Archives; I have leafed through decades of newspaper files at the Library of Congress on the chance that a microscopic obituary notice might catch my eye. I have written hundreds of letters of inquiry; I have examined scores of marriage licenses and death certificates; I have ransacked telephone directories for names of elusive descendants. In Georgia I have worked for weeks with the public records of Atlanta, Augusta, Macon, and Savannah; I have deciphered yellowing documents in remote county courthouses; I have sat on village porches sipping tea as I listened to reminiscences of the past. I have risked rattlesnakes (and mosquitoes and poison ivy) in the rank growth of forgotten graveyards; I have transcribed tombstones beneath a merciless August sun; I have even spent a darksome evening groping for markers in a private burial ground by the light of a flickering candle. In my pursuit of biographical data I have journeyed to Kentucky and Tennessee twice, to Georgia, Alabama, and Florida ten times. I have had innumerable adventures, some of them amusing, a few of them harrowing, most of them gratifying. And wherever I have turned I have met with kindly assistance.

To name all those who have contributed in one way or another to the completion of this book over the course of many years would be impossible; I regret that space does not permit my thanking individually the hundreds of persons who have answered my letters, who have granted personal interviews, who have provided access to materials in public institutions, and who have willingly paused in their daily duties to ease my path in various ways. Of these hundreds of persons I can here specify only a few. I record with pleasure my appreciation of the energy and enthusiasm of that great archivist, the late Mrs. Mary Givens Bryan, director of the Georgia State Department of Archives and History until her untimely death in 1964; I am also grateful to the present director, Miss Carroll Hart, and her staff, particularly Mr. J. Harmon Smith. In Athens I was offered every assistance by Mr. John W. Bonner, Jr., special collections librarian at the University of Georgia, and his staff, particularly Mrs. William Tate, whose resourcefulness led to the solution of some of my most baffling problems. In Macon I enjoyed a number of conferences with Miss Catherine Stewart Jones, who shared her intimate acquaintance with Jones family history and put at my disposal a number of documents pertaining to her grandfather, Henry Hart Jones. In Savannah I had the guidance of that excellent historian, Mrs.

Lilla M. Hawes, director of the Georgia Historical Society. At the Savannah Public Library I received substantial help from Miss Geraldine Le May, director, and her cooperative staff, particularly Miss Margaret Godley. At the Chatham County Department of Health Mr. Champion McAlpin, registrar of vital statistics, extended me every courtesy on numerous visits. In Liberty County Miss Josephine Bacon Martin, hostess of the Midway Museum, arranged introductions, provided research materials, and drew on her broad knowledge of local history. For special assistance in Liberty County I wish also to thank Mr. Ernest Meldrim Brewton, Mrs. J. F. Browning, Mr. J. W. Griner, Mr. Charles Berrien Jones, Mrs. Wallace Fleming Martin, Sr., Mrs. Floyd E. Miller, Mrs. Hugh C. Norman, Mrs. Henry I. Rahn, and Miss Alma Stacy. At the Historical Foundation of the Presbyterian and Reformed Churches at Montreat, North Carolina, I was most courteously received by the Rev. Dr. Thomas Hugh Spence, Jr., director, and by Mrs. M. N. Lane, of his staff, who graciously and efficiently addressed herself to the problems of my book.

For prompt response to my queries and for kind manifestations of interest in my work I feel much indebted to the late Hon. Richard Brevard Russell, United States senator from Georgia, and to his sister, Mrs. Hugh Peterson, and his brother, Dr. Fielding D. Russell. For friendly counsel I am grateful to Miss Marjorie Gray Wynne, of the Beinecke Rare Book and Manuscript Library of Yale University. To Mrs. Connie G. Griffith, director of the Manuscripts Division and Rare Book Room of the Tulane University Library, I am obligated for cooperation in supplying photocopies of documents in the Tulane collection of Jones papers. For assistance beyond the call of duty I should like also to thank the following: Mrs. C. B. Almon, Dr. William T. Avery, Dr. Stanhope Bayne-Jones, Mrs. Rose C. Betts, Mrs. Margaret Davis Cate, Mr. Milton K. Chamberlain, Miss Anna King Clark, Mr. Joseph B. Cumming, Mr. Waymon Dekle, Mrs. Harold M. DeLorme, Mrs. Corinne Demetropolis, Mr. Ralph W. Donnelly, Miss Tallulah Dowse, Mrs. Vivian Schley Earnest, Mr. Herbert A. Fierst, Judge Joseph T. Grice, Miss Jeanne Hollis, Miss Isabel Howell, Mrs. Sara D. Jackson, Miss Annie Kate Jenkins, Mrs. Raymond L. Johnson, Miss Bessie Lewis, Mr. Harold W. McRae, Dr. Charles C. Mish, Mrs. Eleanor Drake Mitchell, Miss Elizabeth J. Nelson, Mrs. Virginia G. Palmer, Mr. Elmer O. Parker, Mrs. Gertrude Parsley, Mr. Benjamin K. Phipps, Miss Leonora Quarterman, Mr. Luther H. Quarterman, Mrs. Michael Roblyer, Miss Anne Houstoun Sadler, Mrs. F. M. Scott, Mr. M. L. Sharpe, Miss Katherine Simpson, Mrs. Annette McDonald Suarez, Mr. Douglas Richard Taylor, Miss Lucia M. Tryon, Mr. Samuel Carpenter Waller, Mr. and Mrs. Herbert Wilcox, Mr. Earl J. Witmer, and Mr. Michael J. Zajic.

In conducting my research I have received courteous consideration from the authorities of the Library of Congress, the National Archives, the D.A.R. Library, the National Library of Medicine, the Atlanta Public Li-

brary, the Augusta Public Library, the New York Public Library, the
Philadelphia Public Library, the Alabama State Library, the Tennessee State
Library, the Virginia State Library, the Bibb County Courthouse (Macon),
the Chatham County Courthouse (Savannah), the Fulton County Courthouse (Atlanta), and the Richmond County Courthouse (Augusta). I am
particularly obliged to the authorities of the Tulane University Library
and the Library of the University of Georgia, as well as to the Seago family
of New Orleans and the Waller family of Augusta, for permission to publish the letters contained in this book.

ROBERT MANSON MYERS

Washington, D.C.
January 29th, 1971

The Children of Pride

A Note on the Letters

A superior character terminating a title line indicates the source of the letter:

^{g} = University of Georgia, Athens
^{t} = Tulane University, New Orleans
^{w} = Waller Collection, Augusta

An asterisk (*) terminating a dateline indicates that the date has been supplied or corrected.

An extended dash (——) following the title *Mr.* indicates the name of a man who for prudential reasons must remain anonymous.

The Principal Characters

At Maybank, Montevideo, and Arcadia

Rev. Dr. Charles Colcock Jones, *a retired Presbyterian clergyman*
Mary (Jones) Jones, *his wife*
Charles Colcock Jones, Jr.
Joseph Jones } *their children*
Mary Sharpe Jones

At Social Bluff (Point Maxwell), Lambert, and White Oak

Susan Mary (Jones) (Maxwell) Cumming, *twice-widowed sister of the Rev. Dr. C. C. Jones*
Laura Elizabeth Maxwell, *her daughter*

At the Cottage and Springfield

Colonel William Maxwell, *a planter*
Elizabeth (Jones) Maxwell, *his wife, half-sister of the Rev. Dr. C. C. Jones*

At Woodville, Yellow Bluff, and South Hampton

Roswell King, Jr., *a planter*
Julia Rebecca (Maxwell) King, *his wife*
James Audley Maxwell King
George Frederick King
William Henry King
Roswell King III
Isabel Couper King } *their children*
Julian Clarence King
Bayard Hand King
John Butler King
Dr. Charlton Henry Wells, *a physician*
Mary Elizabeth (King) Wells, *his wife, eldest daughter of Roswell King, Jr.*

At Lodebar, the Retreat, Malvern, and Cuthbert

Henry Hart Jones, Esq., *a planter, half-brother of Mrs. Mary Jones*
Abigail Sturges (Dowse) Jones, *his wife*
Ella Sturges Jones
Eliza Low Jones } *their daughters*
Abby Augusta Jones

In Savannah

Dr. Charles William West, *a physician, cousin of the Rev. Dr. C. C. Jones*
Eliza Alice (Whitehead) West, *his wife*
William Whitehead West ⎤
Charles Nephew West   ⎬ *their children*
Laura Maxwell West   ⎦

In Savannah, Walthourville, Washington, Rome, Newton, and Griffin

Rev. John Jones, *a Presbyterian clergyman, brother of Mrs. Mary Jones*
Jane Adaline (Dunwody) Jones, *his wife*
James Dunwody Jones ⎤
John Carolin Jones ⎬ *their sons*
Joseph Henry Jones ⎦

In Marietta

Eliza Greene (Low) (Walker) (Robarts) Robarts, *thrice-widowed half-aunt of the Rev. Dr. C. C. Jones*
Mary Eliza Robarts ⎤
Louisa Jane Robarts ⎦ *her daughters*
Joseph William Robarts, *her son, a widower*
Mary Sophia Robarts   ⎤
Elizabeth Walton Robarts ⎬ *children of Joseph William Robarts*
Ellen Douglas Robarts   ⎥
Joseph Jones Robarts   ⎦

Friends in Various Places

General John Hartwell Cocke, *of Bremo, Fluvanna County, Virginia: a country gentleman*
Rev. Dr. George Howe, *of Columbia, South Carolina: professor at Columbia Theological Seminary*
Rev. Dr. I. S. K. Axson, *of Greensboro, Georgia: president of Greensboro Female College*
Thomas Cooper Nisbet, Esq., *of Macon: an iron manufacturer*
Hon. William Law, *of Savannah: a lawyer*
Hon. John Elliott Ward, *of Savannah: a lawyer*
Eliza Caroline Clay, *of Richmond-on-Ogeechee: a lady of leisure*
Rev. David Lyman Buttolph, *of Dorchester: a Presbyterian clergyman*
Rev. Robert Quarterman Mallard, *of Walthourville: a Presbyterian clergyman*
Ruth Berrien Whitehead, *of Bath*
Eva Berrien Eve, *of Augusta*
Caroline Smelt Davis, *of Augusta*
Katherine Clay (Kitty) Stiles, *of Savannah*
Matilda Jane Harden, *of Jonesville*
Mary Jones Taylor, *of Philadelphia*

Prologue

SOUTH OF SAVANNAH the Georgia landscape stretches broadly to the sea. Long, low islands, crowned with cedar, myrtle, and palmetto, fringe the coast and beat back the thundering surf; wide, waving salt marshes, everywhere broken by sluggish streams, spread to the encircling sandy bluffs; here and there bold estuaries reach their giant fingers past the shore to the boundless green beyond. The growth is rank and wild: dense forests of long-leaf pine are intersected by dark, languid cypress swamps, where the gray moss floats from every branch and twig like the beard of some hoary patriarch, and the yellow jessamine wreathes itself in clusters amongst the tangled vines, and the butterflies flit eternally in the mysterious half-light. Overhead the sun shines as it seems to shine only in a southern sky; and everywhere the soft sea breeze mingles with the fragrance of jessamine and magnolia and pine.

To the motorist speeding south along the coastal highway linking Savannah and Jacksonville this semitropical landscape offers little that is striking or dramatic. His route passes through a monotonous expanse of swampland and primeval undergrowth; on built-up causeways and modern bridges he traverses a maze of ponds and creeks and branches and drainage canals, with now and then a glimpse of a farmer's shack, or perhaps in a clearing a majestic avenue of live oaks calling up the grace of a day that is dead. From Chatham County he crosses the Great Ogeechee River into Bryan; from Bryan County he soon passes into historic Liberty; then suddenly, some thirty miles out of Savannah, he finds himself irresistibly drawn to a commanding structure on the left. A white frame church, reminiscent of a New England meetinghouse and now venerable with age, stands facing south in a grove of pines and moss-draped oaks a short distance to the east of the highway at the fork of two roads. Shuttered, small-paned windows line each clapboarded side in a double row; two small circular openings adorn the pedimented front gable; rising from the roof is a slender square tower surmounted by an open belfry and a tall hexagonal spire. Inside the church the same chaste mood is sustained. Stiff pews with old-fashioned hinged doors stand on a wide-planked floor in three sections, separated by aisles. Eight sturdy wooden columns support a circular gallery designed expressly for the use of Negro slaves. A high pulpit, superbly paneled and approached on either side by a flight of steps, occupies the north end and places the clergyman in equal touch with his hearers above and below. Altogether it is a strict, solemn place—beautiful in its restraint and touching in its evocations of a noble past.

A bronze tablet to the left of the entrance identifies this imposing landmark as Midway Congregational Church, erected in 1792, but organized some forty years before by descendants of an English colony which had migrated to Massachusetts in 1630, to Connecticut in 1635, to South Carolina in 1695, and to Georgia in 1752. The church has been called "the cradle of

Revolutionary spirit in Georgia": two of its sons, Lyman Hall and Button Gwinnett, were signers of the Declaration of Independence; two others, Daniel Stewart and James Screven, became brigadier generals in the Revolutionary army. In recognition of the marked patriotism of the Midway community during the Revolutionary War the county of which the parish later became a part was honored by the name of Liberty. Six counties in Georgia today bear the names of Midway sons: Lyman Hall, Button Gwinnett, Daniel Stewart, James Screven, John Baker, and Augustus Octavius Bacon. Four sons of Midway became early governors of Georgia: Lyman Hall, Button Gwinnett, Richard Howley, and Nathan Brownson. Among distinguished Midway pastors were Abiel Holmes, father of Oliver Wendell Holmes, and Jedidiah Morse, father of Samuel F. B. Morse. The scientist Louis LeConte, world-famed for his botanical gardens, was a communicant of Midway Church; his two sons, John and Joseph LeConte, also distinguished scientists, were instrumental in founding the University of California, and John LeConte served for a time as its president. Descendants of the Midway community have found their way even to the White House: Theodore Roosevelt was a great-grandson of General Daniel Stewart, of Revolutionary fame; and Ellen Louise Axson, the first wife of Woodrow Wilson, was a granddaughter of the Rev. Dr. I. S. K. Axson, for seventeen years pastor of Midway Church. It would be impossible to name or even to number here the countless clergymen, doctors, lawyers, professors, teachers, scientists, judges, legislators, and soldiers who have left this tiny church to assume positions of influence and distinction throughout the nation and the world. For a rural community which at no time boasted more than a few hundred souls, and which was dispersed only a little more than a century after it was settled, such a record is indeed astonishing if not unique.

When the first colonists removed from South Carolina in 1752, they emigrated in a body under their pastor and officers and established themselves in a district some thirty miles south of Savannah and some ten miles west of the sea islands at the headwaters of the Medway and Newport Rivers, two short tidewater streams draining what was afterwards known as St. John's Parish and what ultimately became Liberty County. These hardy settlers were sober, pious, God-fearing Calvinists of English, Scottish, and French Huguenot extraction; they found the low swamplands readily adapted to the culture of rice, and the rich, alluvial soil of the higher lands ideally suited to the culture of cotton and corn. Their first concern was to provide for the services of religion. For a time they met in private houses, but early in 1754 they built a temporary log meetinghouse three-quarters of a mile east of the spot where the present structure stands. This first church was called Midway, its situation being midway between Savannah and Darien, or midway between the Savannah and Altamaha Rivers. Here the first sermon was preached on June 7th, 1754, and here the colonists convened on August 28th, 1754, to frame articles for the civil and religious government of their community. On this historic occasion the people formally instituted the Midway

Church and Society, a governing body consisting of two coordinate branches: the Church, comprising all male communicants, was to administer spiritual affairs; the Society, comprising all male residents whether communicants or not, was to administer temporal affairs. Annual meetings of the Midway Church and Society were to be held on second Wednesdays in March, when a pastor, a clerk, and three or more selectmen were to be chosen. Though nominally Congregational, the church was from its incorporation essentially Presbyterian; it was so understood and so universally styled, and every pastor in its history was Presbyterian with but two exceptions.

Plans for a permanent structure were drawn up at the organizational meeting in August 1754. The first rude meetinghouse was accordingly replaced by a frame building, thirty-six by forty-four feet, with pitched roof hipped at one end, facing the Sunbury road on the site of the present structure; here services were first held on January 2nd, 1757. This building was not destined to survive long. After twenty-one years, on November 27th, 1778, it was burned by the British; the community was overrun, and the congregation was for a time scattered. A third structure, a "coarse meetinghouse" designed to be temporary, was erected near the site of the second church in 1784. Finally, on August 23rd, 1791, the Midway Church and Society agreed on specifications for a fourth church:

Voted, that the selectmen contract with some person or persons to build a meetinghouse. Voted, said house be built sixty feet by forty; also agreed it shall be twenty feet in the stories. Voted, that the form of the roof be as our old meetinghouse was; that is to say, a pitched roof hipped at one end, and a steeple at the other; and also to stand in the same manner as the former house did. Voted, that the number of lights in said house be left to the selectmen to determine. Agreed also the above house be built of the best wood. [James Stacy, *The Published Records of Midway Church* (Newnan, Georgia, 1894), p. 51]

This handsome meetinghouse, weatherboarded in cypress and fashioned with hand-wrought nails, was completed in 1792. Originally there were three doors, one opening north, one opening west, and one opening south. A high pulpit stood on the east side with a great sounding board overhead; a gallery extended across the south end with two flights of steps providing access directly from the outside. In 1849 the pulpit was removed to the north end, its present position; and the gallery was extended to the three sides opposite. At the same time two of the three doors were closed, thus confining access to the south—a measure intended, it is said, to encourage members of the congregation to mingle as they passed out. Adjacent to the church at convenient distances were thirty or more little houses, something like booths or pavilions, to which the various families retired for rest and refreshment during the intermission between morning and afternoon services.

The district settled by the South Carolina colonists in 1752 abounded in swamps and stagnant pools; it was an insalubrious region, and the culture of rice, with its system of canals and ditches and dams and backwaters,

multiplied the hazards of disease. In an age of primitive hygiene malaria
was a menace against which only the Negro was proof, and the mortality
rate among the early settlers was appalling. To escape the exposures of the
sickly months the planters soon sought healthier spots on higher ground,
where it became their custom to live through half the year in summer retreats. To these retreats, clustered in villages among the pine forests, they
withdrew with their servants late in the spring; almost without exception
they visited their plantations at least twice a week during the summer
months; in late autumn, after the first killing frost, they returned in safety to
their winter homes. As the community grew, the retreats prospered. In the
early days a number of planters resorted to Sunbury and Colonel's Island,
where the pleasures of social life and the sport of angling and the cool sea
breeze brought relief from the scorching suns. But the coast was distant and
hence inaccessible to many plantations, and in time it became necessary to establish retreats contiguous to the outlying districts. As early as 1795 a rich
planter, Andrew Walthour, settled some fifteen miles southwest of Midway
Church in an area known as the Sand Hills, afterwards called Walthourville
in his honor. By 1814 several families were summering eleven miles northwest of Midway Church at Gravel Hill, later renamed Flemington after its
first settler, William Fleming. Meanwhile the people in the neighborhood of
Riceboro had penetrated the piney woods below Bulltown Swamp and had
joined Samuel Jones, the first settler, in establishing a village called Jonesville some eight miles south of Midway Church. And in 1843, with the decline and eventual abandonment of Sunbury as a result of its increasing un-
healthiness, a group of planters nearer the coast withdrew to form the village
of Dorchester some six miles east of Midway Church on the Sunbury road.
With the passing of years a number of these families came to find their semi-
annual migration from plantation to retreat, from retreat to plantation, both
expensive and inconvenient; and inevitably some of them chose to reside
permanently at their summer homes.

Throughout the antebellum South the Midway people were justly known
for their remarkable way of life. No planting community could boast deeper
religious convictions, higher intellectual cultivation, gentler social refinement,
or greater material wealth. The church was the very cornerstone of their being; their piety was orthodox, practical, unpretending, and exalted. Education was second only to religion: in each of the four retreats—Walthourville,
Flemington, Jonesville, and Dorchester—an academy was promptly established, and schools also flourished from time to time at Sunbury, Newport,
Riceboro, Hinesville, and Taylor's Creek. Often parents engaged private
tutors to live in their households and instruct their children; and promising
sons were sent to the state university in Athens if not to Princeton or Yale
or Harvard. In a society thus fixed on the things of the mind and the spirit
the people were virtuous and accomplished. If few were extravagantly rich,
all were comfortably disposed; equality of rank and fortune generally prevailed, and social life was leisurely, gracious, and polite. Describing this

world in an *Address Delivered at Midway Meetinghouse in Liberty County,
Georgia, on the Second Wednesday in March 1889,* Charles Colcock Jones,
Jr., distinguished Georgia historian and himself a son of Midway, recalled
the society he had known so well as a youth:

When the centennial was celebrated in 1852 everything relating to this congregation and county was in a prosperous and satisfactory condition. While there
were few who could lay claim to large estates, the planters of this community
were in comfortable circumstances. They were industrious, observant of their
obligations, humane in the treatment of their servants, given to hospitality, fond
of manly exercise, and solicitous for the moral and intellectual education of their
children. The traditions of the fathers gave birth to patriotic impulses and encouraged a high standard of honor, integrity, and manhood. The military spirit
survived in the person of the Liberty Independent Troop; and on stated occasions
contests involving rare excellence in horsemanship and in the use of the saber and
pistol attracted the gaze of the public and won the approving smiles of noble
women. Leisure hours were spent in hunting and fishing, and in social intercourse.
Of litigation there was little. Misunderstandings, when they occurred, were
usually accommodated by honorable arbitration. Personal responsibility, freely
admitted, engendered mutual respect and a most commendable degree of manliness. The rules of morality and of the church were respected, acknowledged, and
upheld. The community was well-ordered and prosperous, and the homes of the
inhabitants were peaceful and happy. Of all the political divisions of this commonwealth none was more substantial, observant of law, or better instructed
than the county of Liberty. Enviable was her position in the sisterhood of counties.
In bringing about this satisfactory condition of affairs the influence of Midway
Church and its congregation was very potent. [pp. 14–15]

Till the coming of the Civil War the fortunes of the Midway people continued to rise. Their economy was founded on Negro slavery, and they were
reputed to be among the largest slaveholders in the South. Some four thousand Negroes lived and toiled in Liberty County alone. The concern of the
Midway community for the spiritual state of these Negroes was sincere and
active; the efforts of masters to instruct their servants in religious matters
became nationally and even internationally known. That veteran traveler,
Frederick Law Olmsted, journeying on horseback through the seaboard
slave states in the 1850s, observed the religious instruction of the Negroes in
Liberty County firsthand; in his two-volume work, *The Cotton Kingdom,*
published in New York and London in 1861, he gave a picture of the conditions surrounding Negro slavery in the South that had great influence on
British as well as American opinion during the critical years to follow:

In the county of Liberty, in Georgia, a Presbyterian minister has been for many
years employed exclusively in laboring for the moral enlightenment of the slaves,
being engaged and paid for this especial duty by their owners. From this circumstance, almost unparalleled as it is, it may be inferred that the planters of

that county are as a body remarkably intelligent, liberal, and thoughtful for the moral welfare of the childlike wards Providence has placed under their care and tutorship. According to my private information, there is no body of slaveowners more, if any as much so, in the United States. I heard them referred to with admiration of their reputation in this particular even as far away as Virginia and Kentucky. I believe that in no other district has there been displayed as general and long-continued an interest in the spiritual well-being of the Negroes. It must be supposed that nowhere else are their circumstances more happy and favorable to Christian nurture. [II, 215]

In promoting the spiritual welfare of the Negro population in Liberty County and throughout the South no man was more active or zealous than the Rev. Dr. Charles Colcock Jones, "Apostle to the Blacks," a lifelong member of Midway Church, who now lies buried in the historic graveyard directly across the way. This extraordinary man, father of the Georgia historian quoted above, was a rich planter, a gentleman of liberal education, and a Presbyterian clergyman of radiant Christian character, aptly described by his son-in-law as "one of the noblest men God ever made." He was born in Liberty County at his father's plantation, Liberty Hall, on December 20th, 1804. His paternal grandfather, Major John Jones (1749–1779), a native of Charleston, South Carolina, had migrated shortly before the Revolutionary War to coastal Georgia, where he had purchased a plantation in St. John's Parish and commenced the cultivation of rice. A few years later, at the siege of Savannah, he had met a patriot's death in a bloody and futile assault upon the British lines on the morning of October 9th, 1779. Jones Street in Savannah was named in his honor. He left a widow, Mary (Sharpe) Jones, who in 1783 married Major Philip Low, a cousin of General Nathanael Greene, and had one daughter, Eliza Greene (born September 29th, 1785); he also left two sons: John (born November 25th, 1772), who became the father of Charles Colcock Jones; and Joseph (born November 26th, 1779), who became the father of his wife, Mary Jones.

The elder son, Captain John Jones, a successful planter in Liberty County, was said to be an admirable type of the English country gentleman; he was fond of everything English, and he imported everything possible from England—his horses and hounds and his guns and pistols as well as his pictures and books. He represented Liberty County in the state legislature in 1796, 1797, and 1798. In 1793 he married Elizabeth Stewart, sister of General Daniel Stewart, by whom he had one daughter, Elizabeth (born September 11th, 1794); soon after the death of his first wife in 1801 he married Susannah Hyrne Girardeau, daughter of John Girardeau, of French Huguenot descent, by whom he had two living children, Susan Mary (born October 22nd, 1803) and Charles Colcock (born December 20th, 1804). In his early thirties this generous, attractive, popular man was thrown from his horse while chasing a deer; he died from the effects on March 28th, 1805, leaving his two infants to the care of his widow, a woman of singular piety and great strength of character, and to the guardianship of his younger brother, Captain Joseph Jones, a gentleman of large wealth, known throughout Liberty County as "the guardian of widows and orphans." His grandson, Charles Colcock Jones, Jr., later characterized Captain Joseph Jones as "a man of imperious will, of great personal courage, quick in quarrel, impatient of restraint, intolerant of opposition, and of mark in the community." He married three times and fathered twenty-six children, the youngest born in his sixty-fourth year. He died on October 18th, 1846, from injuries sustained when he was thrown from his buggy three days before.

Fatherless at three months, the boy was also motherless at five and a half years. Susannah (Girardeau) Jones died on July 1st, 1810; on her deathbed she committed her two young children, Susan and Charles, to the custody of her deceased husband's half-sister, Eliza Greene Low, then Mrs. Robarts, widow of James Robarts. In November 1810 Captain Joseph Jones carried the two children to Mrs. Robarts at her home in Greene County, eight miles from the village of Greensboro. Some weeks later, following the marriage of Mrs. Robarts to her deceased husband's cousin, David Robarts, she removed to Greensboro, where Susan and Charles attended school until late in 1811, when Captain Joseph Jones brought the children back to Liberty County to live with their half-sister, Elizabeth, recently married to Colonel William Maxwell. In December 1813 Mrs. Robarts, following the death of her third husband, returned to Liberty County with her three small children, Mary Eliza, Joseph, and Louisa Jane. Thereafter for several years the Jones children, Susan and Charles, divided their time between their half-sister, Mrs. Maxwell, and their half-aunt, Mrs. Robarts: they summered with Mrs. Robarts and her children at Sunbury; they wintered with Colonel and Mrs. Maxwell, a childless couple, at Yellow Bluff on Colonel's Island; and at frequent intervals they visited their uncle and guardian, Captain Joseph Jones, at his plantation home, the Retreat. These kind relatives—Aunt Eliza Robarts, Sister Betsy Maxwell, and Uncle Joseph Jones—were the three mainstays of Charles's orphaned childhood; to him they ever stood *in loco parentis,* and to them he ever looked with respect, obedience, and cherished affection.

Upon their return to Liberty County Susan and Charles were placed at the Sunbury Academy, then one of the finest schools in Georgia, where they mastered the rudiments of an English education under the tutelage of the Rev. Dr. William McWhir. Early in 1819 Charles was sent to Savannah, where at the age of fourteen he became a clerk in the countinghouse of William Neff, a prosperous commission merchant. Here for four years he prepared himself for a mercantile career; and such were his energy, integrity, and practical gifts that his services were soon in demand and his prospects for business were bright. Noting his extraordinary powers, the Hon. John Elliott, United States senator from Georgia and a warm friend of the family, urged Captain Joseph Jones to send his ward to West Point Military Academy, and volunteered his influence in securing him a place. But the versatile young man was ordained to nobler work: a near-fatal illness had proved the instrument of his spiritual awakening. When nearly eighteen, on the fourth Sunday of November 1822, he became a member of Midway Church along with some forty others, including his sister, Susan, and his cousin, Mary Eliza Robarts. The Rev. Murdoch Murphy, then pastor at Midway, urged him to study for the ministry; he at once became active in the Sunday school and church, and after profound and prayerful deliberation he felt the call to preach. In May 1825, having already passed his twentieth birthday, he entered Phillips Academy, Andover, Massachusetts, where for the first time he took up a Latin grammar. Two years later he proceeded to Andover Theological Seminary, where he remained till October 1829. Without graduating from Andover he went on to Princeton, and there he received his diploma from Princeton Theological Seminary on September 27th, 1830, having been licensed to preach the gospel the preceding spring. Returning to Liberty County, he was married at Retreat plantation on December 21st, 1830, by the Rev. Dr. William McWhir, to his first cousin, Mary Jones, an intelligent and pious young lady of twenty-two years (born September 24th, 1808), daughter of Captain Joseph Jones, his uncle and guardian.

Thus opened the public career of the Rev. Dr. Charles Colcock Jones. In May 1831 he was called to the First Presbyterian Church of Savannah, where he labored earnestly and successfully for eighteen months. But the cry of the Negroes of his native county was too urgent for him to resist; to their needy spiritual state he had been drawn while a student at Princeton, and he now felt constrained to devote himself to their evangelization as well as to their moral and social uplift. With some regret he resigned from the Savannah church in November 1832: his first pastoral charge was destined to be his last. Returning once more to Liberty County, he gave himself body, mind, and soul to the great work of his life. His brother-in-law, the Rev. John Jones, later recalled his missionary efforts in some detail; he wrote from intimate family acquaintance, and his account is worth quoting at length:

Although he commenced his work in the most favorable location in Georgia, yea, in the entire South, he nevertheless encountered opposition, both open and secret, demanding a spotless personal reputation, a strong social position, and unwavering decision, combined with a patient manly prudence, and all animated and controlled by love to the Lord Jesus and lifelong consecration to His service. These qualifications were wonderfully combined in Charles Colcock Jones. By nature and by grace he seemed to be called of God to meet a new, most difficult, and delicate emergency: to personally open and occupy an almost untried field. As a good brother, in allusion to his work among the colored people, once said, he seems to be the apostle to that portion of the gentiles. And he succeeded to a remarkable extent in awakening an interest in this neglected people, not only in his own county, but by his extensive correspondence, his writings, and annual reports of his labors he under God did more than any other man in arousing the whole church of this country to a new interest in the spiritual welfare of the Africans in our midst.

And how abundant, self-sacrificing, and untiring were his personal labors for that people! He had three principal stations: Midway, Newport, and Pleasant Grove. Midway was hard by the old mother Midway. There was another station, Hutchison, where he occasionally preached. Three of these houses of worship were erected very much through his agency. His work commenced in the closet and study. His preparations for Sabbath were made most carefully, with critical examinations of the original Scriptures. His sermons were often expository, and uniformly instructive and impressive. He generally rode to the stations on horseback. The labors of the Sabbath were introduced by a prayer meeting and a watchman's meeting; then followed the regular services of the morning, himself leading the music. The third service was a patient inquiry meeting, to which all were invited to come who desired personal instruction. This meeting, to which many responded, was highly prized by him, having faithfully tested its value. The closing exercise was the Sabbath school, in which he taught hymns and his catechism. Into these schools hundreds of all ages gathered, but especially children and youth. All recited together. These schools illustrated the efficiency of oral instruction. They were remarkable for their animation, proficiency, and accuracy, and their scriptural instructions received the special sanction of God the Holy Spirit.

Such were the Sabbath labors of this beloved missionary. He literally worked whilst it was day! The sun was usually in the tops of the trees, and the shadows of evening fast gathering, before turning his face homeward. In addition to Sabbath labors he had, during seven months of the year when at his winter home, his plantation meetings from once to thrice a week. These were at night. He would ride in the saddle from three to ten miles to some plantation, preach and return home, however late the hour or long the distance. This part of his work was very useful, but a great draught on his constitution.

His labors were confined to a warm, damp, and exceedingly depressing climate. The plantation work was particularly drastic. Frequently he would return home in midwinter, and at midnight, with feet and clothing thoroughly soaked from watery roads and night dews. From such exposures and unremitting toil his constitution received a shock which resulted in a premature decay of vigor and the going down of his sun even before the autumn of old age.

But he was permitted to see the pleasure of the Lord prospering in his hands in the happy results and abundant fruits of his labors. These were manifest in the increased intelligence, good order, neatness, and general morality of the colored people; their elevated regard for marriage vows, and attention to the morals and manners of their children. Scripture knowledge abounded in comparison with the past; and the Blessed Spirit sealed the Word in the conversion of many souls. The good seed was continually watered; and there was one season particularly distinguished by a marked and protracted refreshing from the presence of the Lord. It commenced in 1838 and continued until the close of 1842; and the fruits were an addition to the churches of the county of three hundred members. And the general results of his labors were seen in other communities and regions beyond: a decided attention to the physical as well as the moral condition of the race; the erection of neighborhood and plantation chapels; the multiplying of family and plantation schools, in which Jones's catechism was taught; a greater devotion of time to the Negroes by pastors and churches; and an emphatic awakening throughout the South to the duty of systematic religious instruction to the blacks. [*Memorial Volume of the Semi-Centennial of the Theological Seminary at Columbia, South Carolina* (Columbia, 1884), pp. 197–199]

Nothing contributed more to Dr. Jones's success in the spiritual elevation of the Negro race than his *Catechism of Scripture Doctrine and Practice,* first published in Savannah in 1837. This volume, designed chiefly for "the oral instruction of colored persons," was used extensively in families and schools throughout the antebellum South; it was translated into Armenian and Turko-Armenian by the Rev. John Bailey Adger, missionary at Smyrna, in 1842; it was also translated into Chinese by the Rev. John Winn Quarterman, missionary at Ningpo, in 1853. A second volume, *The Religious Instruction of the Negroes in the United States,* published in Savannah in 1842, considerably augmented the usefulness of the first.

Through his publications as well as through his labors among the blacks Dr. Jones won nationwide recognition. In November 1836 he was elected professor of ecclesiastical history and church polity at the Presbyterian Theological Seminary in Columbia, South Carolina. Early in 1837 he removed with his family to Columbia, where he remained till December 1838, returning at that time to resume work among the Negroes of Liberty County. For nine consecutive years—from January 1839 to the close of 1847—he continued his chosen work, devoting the prime of his manhood to the cause nearest his heart. In November 1847 he was again elected professor of ecclesiastical history and church polity at the Columbia seminary; again he accepted the call, and early in 1848 he returned to Columbia to remain for two more years. Then came the challenge of his life. In the spring of 1850, at a time of peculiar national tension over the slavery issue, he was elected corresponding secretary of the Board of Domestic Missions of the Presbyterian Church, a position bringing him conspicuously before the whole church both North and South, and necessitating his removal to Philadelphia. It was a distinction altogether fitting and deserved. As *The Southern Presbyterian* noted on July 25th, "There is probably no other minister in our connection whose thorough knowledge of the state of things at the South, whose personal experience in missionary life, whose sound judgment and conciliatory manner are calculated at once so effectually to check the rabid zeal of Northern fanatics and secure the confidence and hearty cooperation of the South in sustaining missions among our own people, as is our highly esteemed and long-tried brother, Dr. Jones."

To Philadelphia Dr. and Mrs. Jones removed in October 1850. Their two sons, Charles Colcock and Joseph, were taken from the South Carolina College in Columbia and entered as undergraduates at Nassau Hall, Princeton; their only daughter, Mary Sharpe, was placed at a seminary for young ladies in Philadelphia conducted by the Misses Gill. In his new and most responsible position Dr. Jones manifested all his executive talents: his untiring energy and zeal, his common sense, his systematic business habits, his manly independence, his unfailing tact, and his thorough comprehension of the field. And his efforts were crowned with success: he infused new life into the operations of the Board of Domestic Missions, and he awakened the national church to the religious plight of the Negro. But he was not to continue long in the North: his constitution, never vigorous and now debilitated by the shock of his missionary labors, declined appreciably under the incessant demands of his office. As a boy at play he had accidentally fallen against a stick and pierced his lungs; an abscess had developed, and for a time he had been desperately ill. From this injury he had never fully recovered; his lungs had always been delicate, and in consequence he had suffered increasingly from a mystifying "inaction" or "paralysis affection"—a phenomenon considerably aggravated by cold and often accompanied by an overwhelming sense of weariness in his vocal cords. To his already enfeebled condition the burdens of his Philadelphia post measurably contributed, and after three years of unremitting labor he collapsed. There was no alternative: he was compelled to resign his secretaryship and seek restoration in the quiet of his Georgia home. In October 1853, leaving his two sons in the North, he returned with his wife and daughter to Liberty County to live out his days as a semi-invalid, teaching and preaching as his strength permitted, but growing progressively weaker with the months and years. His disease was known as the "wasting palsy"; it gradually but fearfully consumed his frame, leaving his mind untouched to the end. As his daughter wrote to a friend in 1860, "His inaction increases, so that it is with difficulty that he gets about at times. . . . He seldom preaches now, and is always compelled to sit while doing so. There is one great comfort: the nervous inaction has never affected his lungs or his head."

It was in many respects an agreeable and gracious world to which Dr. Jones returned in the autumn of 1853. He was a man of large property, chiefly in land and slaves. In the Federal Census of 1850 he was recorded as the owner of 107 slaves; by 1860 the number had increased to 129. In addition he and his wife were joint owners of three plantations. The largest of these, Arcadia, was also the farthest from the coast; it stretched from Midway Church to McIntosh Station and comprised 1996½ acres. Evidently Arcadia was never a favorite residence; although the Joneses visited the "long-deserted mansion" from time to time and actually wintered there in 1855, they occupied it as a settled home only in 1862, when its distance from the coast seemed to render it safe from Yankee raids. Dr. and Mrs. Jones deeded Arcadia to their three children, to be held by them jointly, early in 1857.

Far dearer to the Joneses was their fixed winter residence, Montevideo, a rice and sea-island cotton plantation comprising 941 acres, situated on the south bank of the North Newport River about a mile and a half below Riceboro. The first house at Montevideo was built in 1833; some twenty years later it was substantially altered and enlarged, and in November 1856 the Joneses first occupied the remodeled structure. It was, as Mrs. Jones wrote at the time, "a double two-story house, new, nicely painted and finished throughout"; there were fifteen rooms, with four large corner rooms on each of the two main stories. The dining and drawing rooms, each twenty-one feet square, communicated by means of a large folding door; from the drawing room projected a wing for a library eighteen feet square; from the dining room projected a corresponding wing "fitted up with closet and locked and open cupboards and all the appointments of a pantry and eating room." On the same floor there were two chambers seventeen feet square, separated by an "entry" or hall; on the floor above there were four more chambers and a laundry. As Mrs. Jones went on to say, in an undated note preserved at Tulane University:

The house is beautifully located, on one side fronting a lawn of twenty or thirty acres covered with live oak, magnolias, cedars, pines, and many other forest trees, arranged in groves or stretching out in lines and avenues or dotting the lawn here and there. On the other front passes the North Newport River, where all the produce of the place may be shipped to Savannah and water communication obtained to any point. In the gardens will be found both sweet and sour oranges and the myrtle orange, pomegranates, figs, the bearing olive, and grapes. . . . Attached to the house lot are a brick kitchen, brick dairy, smokehouse, washing and weaving rooms, two servants' houses, a commodious new stable and a carriage house and wagon shed, various poultry houses and yards attached, a well of excellent water, and a never-failing spring. On the plantation settlement are a two-story cotton house, gin and ginhouse, barn, cornhouse, ricehouse, winnowing house, millhouses, and fifteen frame houses, a brick shed and yard of excellent clay, and a chapel twenty by thirty feet.

Through the lawn or park in front of the house a straight avenue led approximately a mile from the chapel to the plantation gates. Midway Church was six and a half miles away; McIntosh Station was ten, Flemington fourteen, Walthourville thirteen, and Dorchester four. To the Jones family Montevideo ever remained "a happy, happy home." At the height of the war the widowed mother found consolation in returning to its welcoming embrace: "This precious home," she wrote on December 21st, 1863, "had always peculiar charms for me. Your beloved father often asked if I was conscious of always singing as I came in sight of the house."

From Montevideo the Joneses removed each year, late in May or early in June, to the healthier climate of their summer retreat, Maybank, a sea-island cotton plantation comprising 700 acres, situated fifteen miles to the east of Montevideo and overlooking the mouth of the Medway River at the northwest end of Colonel's Island. This picturesque island, actually an elevated tract of land surrounded by low salt marshes and hence free from malaria-bearing mosquitoes, lay between St. Catherines Island and the mainland, to which it was connected by means of a causeway. It was originally known as Bermuda Island, having been settled prior to the Revolutionary War by emigrants from the Bermudas; it was renamed Colonel's Island about 1778 because, it is said, as many as six colonels had established their summer retreats on a tract not more than three miles wide. To the Joneses and their friends it was known simply as "the Island." The soil there was exceedingly fertile, and the oyster beds were extraordinarily fine. Maybank had been bequeathed to Dr. and Mrs. Jones, together with some thirty Negro slaves, early in 1834 by Major Andrew Maybank ("Uncle Maybank"), a brother of Mary Maybank, the first wife of Mrs. Jones's father, Captain Joseph Jones. The original house, known as the Hut, had been the Joneses' residence for seven summers; in 1840 a new house had been built on an adjacent site and the Hut had been demolished; the Joneses had first occupied the new house in the summer of 1841. "We must ever hold Uncle Maybank in grateful remembrance," wrote Dr. Jones in his journal on June 2nd, 1860, "for bestowing upon us this quiet and healthful retreat, where we reared and educated our children until prepared for college, and where we have experienced unnumbered mercies from above." It was a house with many happy associations; for years the Jones children looked back nostalgically upon its simple domestic pleasures. Charles Colcock Jones, Jr., wrote thus on October 10th, 1857:

Some of the pleasantest recollections of youthful days are connected with the first fall fires on the Island, shedding their cheerful rays around the parlor while the rude northeast wind came dashing its watery gusts against the windows. Well do I remember the first gathering of the little basket- and net-makers around the genial hearth and the delights there experienced. Oh, the happy days of youth— they come not again!

On one occasion Mrs. Jones described Maybank as an unpretentious place, offering "such comforts as a plain country residence can furnish"; but her son Charles Colcock, writing to his only daughter, Mary Ruth, on May 11th, 1888, recalled that the plantation houses were "ample and very comfortably furnished" both at Maybank and at Montevideo:

These were generous homes, and the hospitality there extended was profuse and refined. Daddy Jack was the majordomo. Patience and Lucy were the chambermaids. Phoebe and Clarissa were the seamstresses. Marcia was the cook. Gilbert was the carriage driver. Flora and Silvy were the handmaidens. Jupiter and Caesar were the gardeners, and sundry younger servants were commissioned to sweep, scrub, brush flies, and run on errands. Niger was the fisherman, and there was a lad to bring the triweekly mail. There was no lack of service, and everything about the establishment was conducted upon the most liberal scale. . . .

That my sister, my brother, and myself might be well instructed, Father engaged the services of private tutors who resided in the family. At Maybank and also at Montevideo schoolhouses were built by Father. At the former the children of our neighbor, Mr. Roswell King, united with us, and at the latter were also convened the children of Mr. John Barnard. The teacher was generally the graduate of some approved college. The general direction of our studies was indicated by Father, and he not infrequently gave his personal attention to the manner and scope of our studies. The school hours were from eight in the morning until two o'clock P.M. in summer, and from nine until three in winter. Saturday was a holiday, and was devoted to hunting and fishing. Every Monday morning we read compositions and declaimed. Very rarely the tutor was absent, and then my dear father took upon himself the burden of our instruction. . . . The 4th of July, the 22nd of February, and three days at Christmas constituted our only vacations during the year.

The country abounded in deer, wild turkeys, ducks, squirrels, rabbits, raccoons, quail, woodcock, doves, ricebirds, fishes, alligators, and crabs, and we enjoyed every opportunity for hunting and fishing. We had our sailboat also; and that we might be encouraged in the art of riding and in swordsmanship, a little cavalry company was formed which paraded weekly at home and at the residences of our neighbors. . . . Fourth of July celebrations were held under the great live oak on the lawn at Maybank, the speeches of the youngsters being preliminary to a generous spread to which the neighbors were invited. On the 22nd of February we always repaired to the parade ground of the Liberty Independent Troop to listen to the oration and to witness the prize contest with saber and pistol. . . . I look back upon this boyhood period with unalloyed pleasure and gratitude. No son could have had kinder or more indulgent parents, or fuller opportunities for indulging in those pastimes which a plantation life afforded.

It was at Maybank, "the house that has been so dear to us," where "the climate is so healthy, and the advantages of the salt water so great," that the Jones family were settled in May 1854, when the story of *The Children of Pride* begins. The elder son, Charles Colcock, "the Judge," born in Savannah on October 28th, 1831, and now in his twenty-third year, was a student at Dane Law School, Harvard University, having graduated from Nassau Hall, Princeton, in 1852 and spent the following academic year in Philadelphia reading law in the office of Samuel H. Perkins, Esq. The second son, Joseph, "the Doctor," born in Walthourville on September 6th, 1833, and now in his twenty-first year, was a student at the Medical College of the University of Pennsylvania in Philadelphia, having graduated from Princeton the preceding June. The youngest child, Mary Sharpe, born at Lodebar, the plantation of Colonel and Mrs. William Maxwell near Dorchester, on June 12th, 1835, and now in her nineteenth year, was residing with her parents at Maybank and leading the life of a young lady at home, having attended the Philadelphia seminary of the Misses Gill from 1850 to 1852. It was generally agreed by family and friends that Charles Colcock and Joseph were exceptional young men destined to brilliant public careers. As their uncle, the Rev. John Jones, wrote in 1856, "I am acquainted with no young men who have had equal advantages and who have made so diligent improvement of them. They bring to their professions minds not only well stored but (what is better) well disciplined. With patience of investigation and persevering purpose they are bound to excel." And Mary Sharpe was felt to be equally promising in the private sphere to which young ladies were then confined; a family friend remembered her as "a sprightly, intelligent, well-informed young woman . . . bright, quick, merry, joyous." Typical was the response of Laura Elizabeth Maxwell, first cousin and lifelong friend of the Jones children, who wrote pleasantly in 1855: "I am proud of my cousins, and have every reason to be. To my mind none are *more polished;* and I must hide my diminished head, having never had the advantages of a *polished Philadelphia* school."

Few friends were as well qualified to assess the merits of the Jones children as Laura Elizabeth Maxwell, daughter and only living child of Dr. Jones's beloved sister, Susan, now Mrs. Cumming. As a girl Susan Mary Jones had attended the Sunbury Academy for several years with her brother, Charles; in 1818 she had proceeded with her cousin, Mary Eliza Robarts, to Charleston to attend a select boarding school for young ladies. Returning to Liberty County in 1819, she had resided with her half-sister, Elizabeth, wife of Colonel William Maxwell, until her marriage in September 1823 to James Audley Maxwell, grandson of Colonel James Maxwell, one of the first settlers of the Midway community. Three children blessed this union: Laura Elizabeth (born July 20th, 1824), who survived all three of her Jones cousins and lived past the turn of the century; Charles Edward (born May 18th, 1826), who when about to graduate from the Medical College of the University of Pennsylvania was stricken with dysentery and died tragically in Morristown, New Jersey, on April 3rd, 1852; and Georgia (born March 7th, 1828), who died in infancy. On December 1st, 1828, Mrs. Maxwell had been left a widow with three small children; ten years later (on November 21st, 1838) she had married Joseph Cumming, a Savannah widower with four children: William Henry, Mary Cuthbert, Montgomery, and Wallace. She had been widowed a second time on December 5th, 1846. Although she owned two plantations in Liberty County—Lambert and White Oak—she had preferred to live much of the time between her first and second marriages in the household of her brother, where her two surviving children, Laura and Charles, had come to feel toward the Jones children more as brother and sister than as cousins. After the death of her second husband in 1846 she had again lived at intervals in her brother's family; in October 1850 she and her daughter, Laura, had accompanied the Joneses to Philadelphia, where her son, Charles, was then studying medicine; and in the spring of 1854, still mourning the untimely death of her son two years before, she was living with Laura in the Jones household at Maybank pending the rental of a residence in Savannah.

Between Mrs. Cumming and Dr. Jones there existed from the first "an affection not often witnessed and never transcended." So wrote Charles Colcock Jones, Jr., years later in an obituary of his aunt. And the Jones letters provide ample evidence of this deep and abiding devotion which through the years brought the two families to feel virtually as one. "I have never known any difference between your interest and my own," wrote Dr. Jones to his sister in 1855; "and *yours* have always been to me as mine own children." "Your dear children," wrote Mrs. Cumming in 1864: "dear to me as my own, they are constantly on my heart." Living for many years in the same household, Laura and Mary Sharpe were brought up as sisters, and they ever regarded each other as such, despite a difference in age of nearly eleven years. "She is *my* little *sister*," Laura once said; and her affection was fully reciprocated. "When I am with Aunt Susan and yourself," wrote Mary Sharpe to her cousin in 1856, "I feel as though I were in another home." Mary Sharpe was to name one of her children for Mrs. Cumming's deceased infant, Georgia Maxwell; Mary Sharpe's children were to call Laura "Aunt Laura" and Mrs. Cumming "Grandma Susan"; and eventually Mary Sharpe was to say to her cousin: "I feel to your children as though they were my sister's children."

From her father, James Audley Maxwell, Laura had inherited the Maxwell place, Social Bluff, or Point Maxwell as it was later called, occupying the northeast portion of Colonel's Island. In May 1854 this beautiful retreat was the residence of Laura's half-aunt, Mrs. Maxwell, and her husband, Colonel William Maxwell; it was described by Mrs. Adam L. Alexander during a visit the preceding year: "The house is on a bluff overgrown with magnificent oaks and cedars, and surrounded on three sides by a fine wide river (Newport), which opens off at two points to St. Catherines Sound, and where you can see the Florida boats pass and repass, and from whence they have the sea breeze in perfection." The Maxwells she found to be "two charming old people" whose "warm hospitality and friendly manners" made them great favorites with all. Colonel Maxwell was a retired officer of the United States navy; he had commanded a gunboat during the War of 1812 and was known to his friends as "Gunboat Billy." With the exception of one year he had served as captain of the Liberty Independent Troop from 1815 to 1832; he had also served for a time as collector of the port of Sunbury; and he had been a selectman of Midway Church from 1842 to 1844. He was a prosperous planter, one of the respected citizens of Liberty County, and "a most elegant gentleman of the olden time," moving about, as Dr. Jones observed, with "dignified air and martial step, prepared to command an army." On June 10th, 1811, he had married Elizabeth Jones, half-sister of Susan Mary and Charles Colcock Jones. In time the childless pair had come to regard Dr. and Mrs. Jones as their own children: it was at Yellow Bluff, their retreat on Colonel's Island, that young Charles had spent a part of his orphaned boyhood; it was at Lodebar, their plantation near Dorchester, that Mary Sharpe Jones had been born on June 12th, 1835; and later the aging couple had grown so intimately attached to the three Jones children that "Aunty" and "Uncle" were referred to affectionately without their Christian names. "I am indebted to them for unnumbered kindnesses in sickness and in health," Dr. Jones once wrote; and Mrs. Jones spoke of "Sister Betsy" as a relative "who almost occupied a mother's place in our hearts." She was greatly beloved by all her friends. "None who knew her," said her cousin, the Rev. John Jones, "can ever forget the intense humanity that pervaded her whole nature—her bold generous heart, her willing helping hand, her transparent candor, her quenchless zeal in all good works, her ardent devotional spirit, and her unshrinking piety." On May 1st, 1854, Colonel Maxwell celebrated his sixty-ninth birthday; his wife was then in her sixtieth year.

Also summering on Colonel's Island was the family of Roswell King, Jr., a "kind friend and good neighbor," whose two plantations, Yellow Bluff and Woodville, occupied the east and southeast portions of the island overlooking the waters of St. Catherines Sound. The Kings divided their year between Woodville, their pleasant summer retreat high on Half Moon Bluff, and South Hampton, their handsome winter residence a few miles east of Montevideo. Roswell King sprang from long-established New England stock. His father, also Roswell King, had come to Georgia from Windsor, Connecticut, in the 1780s and settled at Darien, then an important mercantile center, where he had commenced a thriving business in lumber, rice, and sea-island cotton. In the 1830s he had founded a village in Upper Georgia called Lebanon, where he had established flour mills, and another village called Roswell, where he had established cotton mills and erected a splendid mansion, Barrington Hall. Three of his sons figured in the lives of the Joneses: Roswell (born 1796), their near neighbor and intimate friend; Barrington (born 1798), a coastal planter who had removed to Upper Georgia in 1837 and engaged in manufacturing at his father's village of Roswell; and William (born 1804), a Savannah merchant, in whose household Dr. and Mrs. Jones had resided during his brief pastorate of the First Presbyterian Church in 1831–1832.

For many years the two Roswell Kings, father and son, had jointly or separately supervised the vast Georgia estates of Pierce Butler in Glynn County, where the English actress Frances Anne Kemble had lived briefly in the 1830s; and her famous *Journal of a Residence on a Georgian Plantation in 1838–1839,* published in New York and London in 1863 in an effort to influence British opinion against Negro slavery in the South, painted a vivid if somewhat biased portrait of the younger Roswell King. "He is a remarkable man," she wrote, "and is much respected for his integrity and honorable dealing by everybody here. His activity and energy are wonderful; and the mere fact of his having charge of for nineteen years, and personally governing without any assistance whatever, seven hundred people scattered over three large tracts of land at a considerable distance from each other certainly bespeaks efficiency and energy of a very uncommon order." Miss Kemble detailed "a most interesting conversation" with Roswell King in which they discussed the institution of slavery:

You may be sure I listened with infinite interest to the opinions of a man of uncommon shrewdness and sagacity, who was born in the very bosom of it, and has passed his whole life among slaves. If anyone is competent to judge of its effects, such a man is one; and this was his verdict: "I hate slavery with all my heart; I consider it an absolute curse wherever it exists. It will keep those states where it does exist fifty years behind the others in improvement and prosperity. . . . As for its being an irremediable evil—a thing not to be helped or got rid of —that's all nonsense; for as soon as people become convinced that it is their interest to get rid of it, they will soon find the means to do so, depend upon it."

Miss Kemble then went on to relate how "the all-efficient and all-satisfactory Mr. King" took Betty, a married Negro, as his concubine and fathered by her a son "whose straight features and diluted color, no less than his troublesome, discontented, and insubmissive disposition, bear witness to his Yankee descent." Elsewhere she spoke of a lad "whose extremely light color and straight, handsome features and striking resemblance to Mr. King had suggested suspicions of a rather unpleasant nature to me, and whose sole acknowledged parent was a very black Negress of the name of Minda. I have no doubt at all now that he is another son of Mr. King, Mr. Butler's paragon overseer."

Whatever the truth of Miss Kemble's assertions, the gravestone of Roswell King in Midway Cemetery pronounces him to have been "a good citizen, an upright man, and a most devoted husband and father." In 1825 he had married Julia Rebecca Maxwell (born 1808), a sister of James Audley Maxwell, the first husband of Susan Mary Jones. Mrs. King was therefore sister-in-law to Mrs. Cumming and aunt to her daughter, Laura Maxwell; and by easy extension she became "Aunt Julia" to the three Jones children, who looked on Laura as a sister. The Joneses and the Kings were the closest of neighbors and the dearest of friends. In crises they were quick to come to each other's aid; in joy as well as in sorrow they were often united; and at Maybank and Montevideo their children attended the same school. As Mrs. Jones observed in 1858, "the many, many years of kind intercourse and unbroken friendship we have enjoyed make them all especially near and dear."

There were nine living children. The eldest, Mary Elizabeth (born 1827), was characterized by Mary Sharpe Jones as "a very amusing person," though "very odd in some things." She was known for her merry laugh and lively repartee, and was said to be "as gay as a lark and at the head of all mischief and fun," even though she had "little health to enjoy anything" and suffered continually from headaches. In 1849 she had married Dr. Charlton Henry Wells (born 1822), a South Carolinian who had graduated from the College of Physicians and Surgeons, Columbia University, in 1846. He was described as "a truly lovely young man," "a most gentlemanly and amiable person," and "one of the best husbands in the world." In May 1854 he was residing with his wife, "Cousin Mary Wells," in Savannah, where he enjoyed a growing practice. In the absence of the eldest sister much responsibility devolved upon the second child, James Audley Maxwell (born 1829), universally known as "Audley," "a most dutiful and affectionate son," "a great comfort, and invaluable to his parents." By 1851 he was reported by Mrs. Jones to be "an established planter" who "fills admirably a useful position in the family, not only governing the plantation but all the little folks at home. His services could not well be dispensed with." Joseph LeConte remembered him as "the pink of gentility, neatness, and propriety"; but his father, conceding that he was "Mother's main man," found him to be "too much a man of rules: if a thing cannot be done according to rule, it cannot be done at all. He does not enjoy his breakfast unless his hair is perfectly brushed." The next son, George Frederick (born 1831), usually called "Fred," had attended Yale College for a few months in the autumn of 1850 and had then returned to Georgia and established a tannery two miles from his grandfather's village of Roswell. William Henry (born 1833), the fourth child, affectionately called "Willie," was said by his cousin, Laura Maxwell, to be "the most promising and most loved" of all the Kings. He had attended Yale College and the Sheffield Scientific School from 1850 to 1853; late in 1853, without graduating, he had gone on to Philadelphia, where in May 1854 he was clerking in the drugstore of Edward Parrish while attending lectures in pharmacy at the Medical College of the University of Pennsylvania. His younger brother, Roswell III (born 1836), usually called "Ross" or "Rossie," was somewhat less of a student; in April 1854 he had gone to Roswell to work in his brother's tannery. Of the five older Kings—Mary, Audley, Fred, Willie, and Rossie—only one, Audley, was still living at home in May 1854; and it was Audley's responsibility to supervise the four younger Kings, to whom he was almost a father: Isabel Couper, or "Belle" (born 1842); Julian Clarence, or "Clarence" (born 1844); Bayard Hand, or "Bayard" (born 1846); and John Butler, or "Johnnie" (born 1848). "Audley exercises a good influence over them," his mother wrote. "He is very gentle and kind, yet they never disobey him. To Isabel 'My little sister, you must not do so' is always sufficient, and has the desired effect."

These were the neighbors of Dr. and Mrs. Jones on Colonel's Island; a number of other friends and relatives resided elsewhere in the county. The Jones family constituted a typical Southern "connection," brought by marriage, remarriage, and intermarriage to a state of almost bewildering complexity. Of the twenty-six children of Captain Joseph Jones eleven were still alive in May 1854; and all but two (Mrs. Mary Jones and the Rev. John Jones) were children of his third wife, Elizabeth Screven Lee Hart: Charles Berrien (born 1820); Henry Hart (born 1823); James Newton (born 1825); Emma Adelaide (born 1827), wife of Dr. Stephen Nathan Harris; Hetty Augusta (born 1829), wife of George Troup Maxwell; Andrew Maybank (born 1831); Edwin West (born 1833); Josephine Elizabeth Caroline (born 1839); and Helen Louisa (born 1841). Most of these half-brothers and half-sisters were living in Liberty County, and two were associated on terms of particular intimacy with the family at Montevideo and Maybank. Henry Hart Jones, a planter residing at Lodebar plantation near Dorchester, had graduated from Franklin College (Athens) in 1844; his prime interests were agriculture, journalism, and politics, and he had served as a delegate to the Democratic National Convention in Baltimore in 1852. On May 21st, 1846, he had married Abigail Sturges Dowse (born 1828), of Burke County, known to the Jones children as "Aunt Abby." His younger brother, James Newton Jones ("Uncle Jimma"), a planter residing at Retreat plantation a mile or so southeast of Riceboro, was a man of uncommon usefulness to his family. At the death of Captain Joseph Jones in October 1846 he had assumed his father's place as head of a large household of young children; and although still a youth himself he had managed their numerous and varied interests with eminent success. On November 27th, 1851, he had married Sarah Jane Norman (born 1827), of Liberty County, known to the Jones children as "Aunt Sarah Jane."

Even closer to Mrs. Jones than her numerous half-brothers and half-sisters was her one full brother, the Rev. John Jones (born November 15th, 1815), son of Captain Joseph Jones by his second wife, Sarah Anderson. John Jones and his sister, Mary, were the only surviving children of their father's second marriage; their mother had died in September 1817, when Mary was almost nine and John was not yet two. From the beginning the younger brother had cherished a peculiar tenderness for "one who has been to me not only a kind sister but also has acted the part of an affectionate mother." He had graduated from Franklin College (Athens) in 1836 and from Columbia Theological Seminary in 1839. On February 18th, 1841, he had married Jane Adaline Dunwody (born October 10th, 1820), of McIntosh County. For the next twelve years he had served churches in Bryan County (1841–1843), Darien (1843–1847), and Marietta (1847–1853). In January 1854, then in his thirty-ninth year, he had become pastor of the First Presbyterian Church in Savannah. "John is really an excellent minister," his cousin, Mary Eliza Robarts, had written from Marietta in 1851; "and the only thing which militates against his usefulness is his habit of procrastination, which seems incurable." His "criminal procrastination," as he himself called it, was a source of great family concern. "It is sad," his sister once wrote, "when the influences of a noble character are marred by the prevalence of one bad habit."

His wife, Jane, aged thirty-three, "truly a lovable woman, and little, and very amusing," suffered from "extreme reserve" and perennially feeble health. She had inherited large holdings in McIntosh County, which, together with her husband's planting interests at Bonaventure, his plantation in Liberty County, necessitated frequent visits to the coast. Their eldest son, James Dunwody, known to all as "Dunwody," was born in McIntosh County on May 1st, 1842. Before he was ten years old the boy had become a problem to his parents: his father had written as early as 1850 that Dunwody was "progressing slowly in his books" and "requires much management"; and in 1853 he had described his son as "rather a hard boy," causing his parents "much anxiety" and "many painful feelings." In January 1854 Dunwody had been entered at the Chatham Academy in Savannah; but by April he was already vacationing at Maybank with the Joneses, who were, his father once said, "more to him as parents than as uncle and aunt." During that April visit Mary Sharpe Jones had reported that "Dunwody is very fond of a gun, and has many exploits to relate; and he is really quite a successful little marksman." On May 1st, 1854, Dunwody celebrated his twelfth birthday; by then two younger brothers, both "handsome and manly children," had enlarged the family to five: John Carolin (born June 30th, 1852), "a noble little son"; and Joseph Henry (born April 21st, 1854), "a beautiful boy with dark eyes resembling his mother."

While living in Marietta the Rev. John Jones had enjoyed daily association with the best-loved and most highly esteemed relative in the Jones family connection: Mrs. Eliza Greene (Low) (Walker) (Robarts) Robarts. (Members of the Robarts family stressed the second syllable of their surname.) "Dear old lady," the Rev. John Jones had written in 1850: "as years multiply, she increases in affection and tenderness. If you have a relative on earth whose affection for you all is pure and constant and above the fluctuations of feeling and superior to absence and distance, that relative is Aunty." Before her twenty-eighth birthday this indomitable woman had been widowed three times. She had married first (on January 20th, 1802) Charles Walker, who had died ten months later without issue. She had married second (on March 1st, 1804) James Robarts, a Sunbury merchant, to whom she had borne one daughter, Mary Eliza (born February 1st, 1805). James Robarts had died at Greensboro, Georgia, on April 4th, 1807. His widow had continued to reside in Greene County with her one small daughter; and three years later (on December 20th, 1810) she had married her second husband's cousin, David Robarts, a cotton factor and commission merchant, to whom she had borne two children: Joseph William (born November 1811) and Louisa Jane (born September 1st, 1813). A few days after the birth of his second child David Robarts had died, and late in the same year his wife, then thrice a widow, had returned to her former home in Liberty County. For many years "Aunt Eliza Robarts" had resided with her three small children in Sunbury; later she had joined the household of her half-brother, Captain Joseph Jones, at the Retreat. After his death in October 1846 she had returned to live temporarily in Sunbury while she cast about for a suitable permanent residence.

Meanwhile her son, Joseph William Robarts, always something of a ne'er-do-well, had married (on December 21st, 1837) Sophia Louisa Gibson, a young woman without beauty or fortune; she had borne him four children: Mary Sophia (born November 29th, 1838), Elizabeth Walton, or "Lilla" (born December 7th, 1840), Ellen Douglas (born March 12th, 1843), and

Joseph Jones (born June 1845). Two years later (on July 24th, 1847) Sophia
(Gibson) Robarts had died suddenly of lockjaw, leaving her four small children (ranging in age from two to eight and a half) to the care of their paternal grandmother, Mrs. Robarts, and their two maiden aunts, Mary Eliza
and Louisa Jane Robarts. With this sizable addition to her household, and
with practically no addition to her already meager income, Mrs. Robarts had
found herself in a strait; on the recommendation of her nephew, the Rev.
John Jones, then pastor of the Presbyterian church in Marietta, she had removed to that thriving up-country village in May 1849, believing it to be both
healthier and cheaper as a place of residence than Liberty County. Four
years later she had resolved to establish a permanent home in Marietta, "a
pleasant and growing village containing about fifteen hundred inhabitants";
she had purchased for twenty-five hundred dollars "a comfortable two-story
house" (though "not quite as large as I could wish") situated on "a pretty
lot" with trees, "in a good neighborhood," and "near the new church." And
here she had settled with her flock in October 1853, leaving her widowed son
to fend for himself in Savannah, where, coincidentally, he had that very
month been elected city treasurer.

It was certainly an improbable establishment—dominated by an impe-
cunious matriarch then in her sixty-ninth year, managed by her two spinster
daughters, half-sisters aged forty-nine and forty respectively, and shared by
four motherless grandchildren, aged eight and a half to fifteen, who had
been virtually abandoned by their trifling father. Money, of course, was a
chronic concern, and the family exchequer was repeatedly exhausted. "The
same epidemic prevails here as in the low country: a want of money." "I assure you I have been many times without a dime in my purse." "My purse
at this time is very low; if I can get it replenished by the last of December or
first of January, I will try and come." So wrote the "venerated aunt" again
and again in her "tedious scrawl." ("Excuse the nervous hand of your
aunt.") But somehow the household always survived, to the infinite relief
of anxious relatives. "It is indeed a matter of astonishment how Aunty supports her large family so well on her small means," wrote the Rev. John
Jones in 1856. "She and her daughters are the best economists I have ever
known."

Her daughters were indefatigable—"cheerful, charitable, and kind," as Joseph Jones later said, "and the best of daughters and housekeepers." Dunwody Jones remembered them as "two of the most lovable women I ever
knew." Mary Eliza, the elder, was invariably "engrossed in the fleshpots" and
could "think of nothing else"; but she found time also to serve as the family's
chief correspondent, though her spidery scratch is almost indecipherable, and
though she was, as she herself conceded, "a poor scribe." "I am simply a lady
of good intentions," she once wrote, "but fail miserably in all my endeavors
at excellence." To the Jones children she was an "affectionate and sympathizing" aunt, "full of mischief" and "just as fat and good-natured as ever"; to

Charles Colcock Jones, Jr., she was an "estimable godmother, who recently sent her 'fat little Charlie' a paper of sugared apples and plums"; to Dr. and Mrs. Jones she was "Lady Mary Wortley Montagu," holding sway in "her own mansion of hospitality and wit." "I should never choose her as a very intimate friend," Dr. Jones had written his fiancée in 1829. "I must say this, relationship to the contrary notwithstanding. I love Cousin Mary, but could never repose that confidence in her judgment and fidelity that I have often wished I could. . . . She has much art in pumping out things of a private nature. I think she loves us both, and on my part as well as on yours that love is reciprocated."

To her half-sister, Louisa, had fallen the general care of their brother's four children; and Louisa was eminently suited both in character and in temperament to the responsibilities of her task. As Mrs. Jones observed, "Her piety, energy, and capacity all fit her for great usefulness." In the spring of 1854 the three Robarts girls were attending a school conducted by Miss Cornelia Hansell in Marietta. "I think they are three as affectionate, self-sacrificing sisters as I ever knew," their Aunt Mary wrote. "Lilla looks on nature with a poet's eye; she has a taste for the beautiful. The other two are more matter-of-fact, and grass is only green with them, and clothed with no particular or sentimental interest." The education of the two older girls, Mary Sophia and Lilla, was apparently the responsibility of Mrs. Robarts; and she was happy to report that "They are all fond of their books; every morning after breakfast they read history or practice sums in algebra." The two younger children, Ellen and Joe, were evidently the special wards of their aunts. Mary Eliza had taken her niece Ellen as her own daughter; and it became her custom to speak of "my baby Ellen, the darling of my heart," as a "daughter," and to speak of herself as a "mother"; later she was to refer to Ellen's husband as her "son-in-law." "Ellen inherits her grandmother's skill at her needle," she had written in January 1852, when Ellen was not yet nine. "She has made herself two chemises very neatly, two sunbonnets, and has taught herself to darn stockings, so that she darns her own, sometimes Joe's, and last week a pair for me." Joe, the youngest child, named for his great-uncle, Captain Joseph Jones, had become the adopted "son" of his Aunt Louisa, who was, her sister wrote, "as devoted to him as an own mother could be, and he as fond of her." On a visit to Marietta in November 1851 Dr. Jones had described the six-year-old Joe as "a chatterbox—and the most industrious fellow in these parts." Two years later, in February 1854, his Aunt Mary had written that "our little boy is very active and sweet in sawing wood, receiving our things at the depot, paying the freight, and having a dray to haul them up; but he has no love for books, though Louisa is very faithful and regular in teaching him every day."

Such was the world of the Rev. Dr. Charles Colcock Jones in May 1854. There were, of course, numerous other relatives and friends both far and near. In Fluvanna County, Virginia, at Bremo, a James River mansion designed by

Thomas Jefferson, there was General John Hartwell Cocke, friend of Jefferson, Randolph, Madison, and Monroe, co-founder with Jefferson and Cabell of the University of Virginia. In Columbia, South Carolina, there was the Rev. Dr. George Howe, Massachusetts-born educator and historian who in 1830 had resigned his professorship at Dartmouth College for reasons of health and moved South to become professor of Biblical literature at Columbia Theological Seminary. In Greensboro, Georgia, there was the Rev. Dr. I. S. K. Axson, formerly pastor of Midway Church (from 1836 to 1853), then president of Greensboro Female College, and soon to become pastor of the Independent Presbyterian Church in Savannah, where he was to remain for the rest of his life. In Macon there was Thomas Cooper Nisbet, Esq., a flourishing iron manufacturer, who in 1847 had married the delightful Miss Mary Cuthbert Cumming, stepdaughter of Dr. Jones's sister by her second husband. In neighboring Bryan County there was Miss Eliza Caroline Clay, witty and outspoken mistress of Richmond-on-Ogeechee plantation, where she headed a household consisting of five young nephews and nieces and their widowed mother. And in Savannah there were many friends and family connections: the Hon. William Law, celebrated jurist and advocate at the bar; the Hon. John Elliott Ward, distinguished attorney and legislator, in 1854 to be elected mayor of Savannah and in 1858 to be appointed first United States minister to China; Dr. Charles William West, a cousin of the Joneses, a practicing physician whom Dr. Jones described as "a man of remarkably sober and fine private and public character"; and Miss Kitty Stiles, a "great friend" of the Lee family of Arlington, Virginia, and almost a sister to Mary Sharpe Jones.

By all these relatives and friends Dr. Jones was cordially esteemed; by those in his intimate family circle he was greatly beloved. Members of the Jones family felt bound together by ties of extraordinary affection—partly, perhaps, because first cousins had married; and the center of that affection was Dr. Jones: beloved as nephew, cousin, brother, father, husband. "The anguish of my heart is great, for I have indeed lost a son," wrote Mrs. Eliza G. Robarts at the time of her nephew's death. "This day the tears of a mother and sisters are shed for one who has ever been to them a son and brother," wrote Miss Mary Eliza Robarts. "To *me* he ever stood more in the relation of a parent than a brother," wrote Henry Hart Jones; "from early childhood he was my counselor and guide, and I can truly add that no mortal man ever wielded such influence over me for good." "I loved him more than any man on earth," wrote the Rev. John Jones; "he came very near to my own father." "The memory of my father is the richest legacy I have on earth," wrote Charles Colcock Jones, Jr.; "and I can never be sufficiently grateful for all his goodness and example, for all his precept and principle." "For thirty-two years," wrote Mrs. Mary Jones, "it pleased the Lord to honor me with his companionship—with his guidance, his support, his spiritual instruction, his wise counsels, his intellectual light and knowledge, his daily example, his prayers and his precepts, and all that tender and affectionate intercourse which as a wife I felt was the cherished boon of my life. Oh, that I had been found worthy of such a blessing!"

Mrs. Jones was indeed found worthy, and by no one more feelingly than her husband, who was ever articulate in sounding the praises of his "model wife." On October 19th, 1859, writing to his son Charles, he enlarged on a favorite theme:

Her industry, her economy, her prudence, her foresight, her resolution, her intelligence are uncommon. She has done her husband good all the days of his life, and has never stood in the way of his advancement, but has taken the liveliest interest in his office and duties, and made sacrifices for it, and kept up her mental improvement, and been at home in all circles in which she has moved and in all the company we have so numerously entertained. And how she manages her household, and how she discharges her duties therein, and above all what a mother in all respects she has been to her children, they best know. And so she continues to be and will ever be. And so you can well understand how my esteem and admiration and affection for her continues and grows.

It was a mutual happiness which husband and wife bestowed: their relationship was one of selfless interdependence. "My anxiety knows no abatement when I am separated from you." So wrote the wife to her husband. And the husband responded in kind. On June 21st, 1851, sojourning briefly at Maybank, he wrote to his wife, then far away in Philadelphia, of the peace of their summer home:

I am upstairs in my old quiet pleasant study. Not a sound about the house. Perfect quiet within. But the whole world without is filled with the melody and notes of a hundred birds. Their voices are not silent a second of time. They seem to have entered in and taken possession more perfectly than when we were here. The calmness, the quiet is delightful. The lot looks so grown, so fresh and green. The house all open, so clean and pleasant from top to bottom. Everything just as you left it, and all reminding me of my love, my sweet Mary. If I look out on the flowers and smell their fragrance, she planted and trained them with her own hands; if I look at the trees and the garden with its fruits, its oranges and figs and pomegranates, its pears and peaches and plums and apples, they were all set out under her eye and pruned and fostered by her care; if I walk in the piazza, in imagination she is at my side, and we are leaning in the cool breeze upon the shaded banister, sharing our thoughts and our love together. In the parlor, in the passage, in our chamber, her image is before me. There is not a part of the dwelling—no, not a single part of it—which does not furnish some scene of affection, some moments of love between us. Oh, if you were here, you would know how my heart beats towards you, my own, my dearest Mary!

Book One
Many Mansions
(1854–1860)

I

Rev. C. C. Jones *to* Mr. Charles C. Jones, Jr.[g]

Maybank Plantation, Liberty County, Georgia
Monday Morning, May 22nd, 1854

I do not think, my dear son, that anyone wrote you last week. I did not, it having been a busy week. Mother is always busy, you know, and has had company. She is remarkably well, and was never so fleshy. I must give you a sketch of her daily life.

She rises about six in the morning, or now half-past five; takes her bath, reads, and is ready for family worship about seven; then breakfasts with a moderate appetite and enjoys a cup of good tea. Breakfast concluded and the cups, etc., washed up and dinner ordered, Little Jack gathers up his *"weepons,"* as he calls them—the flower trowel, the trimming saw, the nippers and pruning shears and two garden hoes—and follows his mistress, with her sunbonnet on and her large India-rubber-cloth working gloves, into the flower and vegetable gardens. In these places she spends sometimes near two hours hoeing, planting, pruning, etc., Little Jack and frequently Beck and several other little fellows and Gilbert in the bargain all kept as busy as bees about her—one sweeping, another watering, another weeding, another planting and trimming, and another carrying off the limbs and trash. Then she dismisses the forces, and they go off in separate detachments to their respective duties about the house and premises, and she takes a walk of observation and superintendence about the kitchen yard and through the orchard and lawn, accompanied by any friends she may have with her and who may be disposed to take a walk of a quiet domestic nature.

About ten her outdoor exercise is over, and she comes in, sets aside her bonnet, draws off her gloves, and refreshes herself with a basin of cool water, after which she disposes of her seamstresses and looks that the house has been well put to rights and in point and in perfect order—flowerpots dressed, etc. She now devotes herself to cutting out, planning, fitting, or sewing, giving attention to the clothing department and to the condition of the furniture of chambers, curtains, towels, linens, etc. The wants of the servants' wardrobe are inquired into, and all the thousand and one cares of the family attended to.

Meanwhile the yards have been swept, the walk sanded, and Patience has her culinary world all in neat order. The two milk-white cats have had their breakfast, and are lying in each other's paws in the shade on the green grass in the flower garden; and the young dog *Rex,* having enjoyed his repast, has stretched himself at full length in the sun, and ever and anon rolls over and wallows and kicks his feet into the air. The old turkey hen has spread her young ones like scouts around her, and is slowly picking along the green, and the gobbler is strutting with two or three idle dames in another direction. The fowls have scattered themselves everywhere in the lot, crowing and cackling and scratching; the sheep have finished their early browse, and are lying down beneath the great hickory tree; and overhead and all around is one general concert of birds.

The glorious sunlight, the soft south wind, and the green earth and the blue heavens—Mother sees and enjoys it all; but she is too busy now to come out and take a view. If she has visitors, she is sitting at work and in conversation with them, or for an hour or two before dinner takes her book or pen in hand. But sometimes she indulges in a quiet little doze, and gets up refreshed just before we are called to dinner. This meal she usually enjoys, but is never much of an eater; enjoys her food, but in much moderation.

For an hour or two after dinner she retires, and about the middle of the afternoon makes her appearance dressed for the evening. Then she is full of her uniform cheerfulness, and attracts everybody to her—husband, children, servants, visitors, old and young. The sea breeze is blowing sweetly. Our friends have driven over; the horses have been taken from the carriage, and the drivers have gone to pay their calls in the servants' quarters. The chairs are set out in the piazza, and here we spend a social hour and take tea. Our friends take leave, and then we have family worship. Sometimes they unite with us before they go. We all retire now to our study or rooms, and when the business of the day is over, then Mother enjoys the quiet, and loves to sit up reading and writing and conversing. She says this is the pleasantest part of *the day* to her.

You will recognize all this as very natural—what you have seen many times. Surely our hearts should be full of gratitude to God for all His unnumbered and undeserved favors to us as a family. May we all through riches of grace be saved in a brighter, better, and more enduring world than this! . . . All in the house—Mother, Brother, Sister, Aunt Susan, and Cousin Laura—send much love. I hear Mary Sharpe and Laura singing at the piano, and your brother talking to Mother. He is all the time quite busy. The Lord be with and bless you, my dear son!

Your ever affectionate father,
C. C. Jones.

Mr. Charles C. Jones, Jr., *to* Rev. C. C. Jones[t]
Harvard University, Cambridge, Massachusetts
Tuesday, May 30th, 1854

My dear Father,

Your very welcome letter, presenting me in such charming colors with all the pleasures which you are all now enjoying at home, and especially with the engagements and recreations of dear Mother, was yesterday morning received. To me the picture, always so attractive, is rendered even more dear in consideration of the endless confusion, turmoil, and bloody scenes which are now hourly transpiring in our very midst.

Mob law, *perjury,* free-soilism, and *abolitionism* are *running riot.* Never before in all my life have my feelings been so severely tried as they have been during these past and present occurrences. For two days I have been present in the courthouse attending this trial. The room is filled with armed men; even the counsel at bar have their revolvers and bowie knives. The passages are strictly guarded night and day by the military, of whom over one hundred marines from the navy yard are garrisoned in the courthouse proper, besides two other companies, while the city hall contains four volunteer companies ordered out by the mayor. All the military of Boston are under arms, ready at a moment's notice to appear at any given point. Hourly are the streets opened around the courthouse and cleared of the mob by companies marching in solid columns for that purpose. The drum and fife, the challenge of the guards, the commands of the officers, the shouts of the mob, all mingling in such confusion, often prevent you, although even within a few feet of counsel arguing at the bar, from hearing them. The halls of justice are literally thronged with armed men. Singular and I may say awful sight!

I will not enter upon any account of the proceedings. These you will find contained in the papers, which I will send you daily. Nor will I speak of the causes of this disturbance, or mention the infernal machinations of such men as Theodore Parker, Wendell Phillips, Ellis, and others. I will not burden you with descriptive epithets of their characters and actions—epithets which, to be true, must necessarily be of such a character as would neither be befitting in me to utter or you to see.

It is yet quite doubtful whether the Negro will be sent back or not. The commissioner, Judge Loring, one of our professors, wants firmness. The case is as clear as the noontide sun. Six witnesses have been introduced today in the defense, who testify that they saw Burns in Boston *more than three weeks* before ever he left Virginia, while he was yet in the employ of Mr. Brent, who hired him from Colonel Suttle, and who is now with the latter in Boston. *Flat perjury.* My blood boiled at this Negro testimony, at the vile epithets heaped up upon Colonel Suttle and his friend hourly in the courthouse by counsel.

Colonel Suttle is a perfect Virginia gentleman, of high standing, well educated, of fine, commanding, prepossessing appearance. For two days have I sat at his side, conversed with him freely in and out of court, and consequently entertain for him not only such sentiments of regard as a highminded, generous person should claim and receive from anyone, but also such an attachment as only a Southerner can know for his brother Southerner when he finds him in a land of abolitionists, conspiring not only against his property but his *life.* Believe no statement in the papers derogatory to such honor and character, as well as actions, as you know does characterize a gentleman of the *first class*.

Excuse this meager letter. I am tired, downhearted, and vexed at the scenes and opinions which are running rife in our midst. Hope that the matter will be settled in a day or two. With warmest love to you, dear Father, dear Mother, Sister, Brother, and all relatives, I remain, in haste,

Your ever affectionate son,
Charles C. Jones, Jr.

That Colonel Suttle is the proper and legal owner of Burns is denied by no one. His claim is perfect; naught but flat palpable perjury instigated by abolitionism can hold the contrary for an instant. Secret meetings are held by abolitionists with the avowed purpose of finding persons who will appear as witnesses and swear to anything which they are instructed to do. Do not be surprised if when I return home you find me a *confirmed disunionist*.

George Helm wrote me in such warm and pressing terms that, D.V., if it meets your views and convenience, I will visit Kentucky in July.

Rev. C. C. Jones *to* Mr. Charles C. Jones, Jr.[g]

Arcadia Plantation, Liberty County, Georgia
Wednesday, June 7th, 1854

My dear Son,

We have received your last letter, and yesterday Matt. F. Ward's trial and several Boston papers containing the recent mobs in behalf of the fugitive slave from Virginia.

I have not had time to read Ward's trial. The pamphlet is reviewed as *ex parte;* the presumption is that it is so. He is a *scape-law,* and I cannot approve the efforts of the lawyers through whose ingenuity and talents he has been cleared. I never wish to see *you* figuring in a pamphlet in a similar way.

If blood had not been shed and poor Batchelder, one of the U.S. officers, killed, the Boston riots would have been a *storm in a teapot.* The effect over the Union will be adverse to the cause of abolitionism and disunion. It is a pity the *instigators* of rebellion and of murder could not be reached and punished. Boston is a remarkable city, and seems to be in a fair way of working out fame of some sort.

We had last week a very cold northeaster, and fires for several days were not only comfortable but necessary. Such a June storm is not unusual. And it has been followed up by daily and copious rains, which have retarded planting operations and thrown crops into the grass, and so everybody has his hands full in that line. Our own prospects are tolerable, and could we have a week's dry weather matters would look well. But a kind Providence knows what is best.

Niger Senior was bitten by a snake (he says a rattlesnake) last week. Mr. Allen called in a new physician—a Dr. Alexander Duke, from Albemarle, Virginia. He treated the case promptly and efficiently, and Niger is doing very well. The poison did not get into the circulation. My idea is, if it was not a *moccasin*, it was a *small* rattlesnake. He with much presence of mind on being bitten took out his knife and scarified the wound and put his foot into cold water and bound up the leg.

The dysentery which was so prevalent among the Negroes last year, and of which many died, still lingers. Mr. Barnard, our neighbor, has lost four lately; and Mr. King told me that one-third of his efficient force was laid up with it. The type is milder than last year. We have reason for gratitude that so far we have been spared so afflicting a visitation.

A man by the name of Haymans in the upper part of the county stabbed another by the name of Moody to death last week (Saturday) *at church!* Mr. Barnard's carpenter boy, who I wrote you was drowned, it is now fully believed *was killed*. Suspicion seems to rest upon some Negro on Mr. Barnard's own place! No arrests as yet. You see I give you all local news, bad and good.

Your uncle and aunt are about *moving to the Sand Hills*. They have rented Mr. Joseph Anderson's house and his plantation for a term of years. *They* remove at once; their people next year. The reason is your aunt's *health*. She has for a long time been dissatisfied with the Island, and desirous of a removal from it. We shall be glad if her health is improved, but we shall miss them very much out of our limited circle of friends on the seaboard.

Your Aunt Susan and cousin will spend the summer at Maybank with us. They expect to go to housekeeping in Savannah in the fall.

Midway Church has given a call to Rev. Mr. Buttolph, assistant now to Dr. Smyth of Charleston. Mr. Palmer declined coming. The people on the Sand Hills at their recent annual meeting resolved to hold on to Midway till *January;* then they will call Mr. Axson, draw off peacefully, and organize a *Presbyterian church*. So I understand. The interests of religion demand it of them; if so, no man should object. Your Uncle James Newton was anxious that I should attend the meeting, but Niger's snakebite and indisposition and rain all together prevented. Suffered a good deal last week from this incipient paralysis affection; preached too much on our Communion Sabbath.

Have been elected president of *Oakland College, Mississippi*, about five miles inland from *Rodney,* which is immediately on the Mississippi River. A noble field for doing good, but I have no physical power for such an arduous undertaking. I feel grateful for the honor conferred, but I do not see my way clear to accept it. Mother says if I had not strength to stay in Philadelphia, I have not strength to go to *Mississippi*.

I shall, D.V., write this mail to Mr. Cumming to forward you a check for two hundred and fifty dollars. Your trip to Kentucky no doubt will be pleasant and improving; and your mother and I think you had better go by the way of Niagara and see the falls, as you may not go that way again for some time. And you can then see the lakes. Take the railroad to Cincinnati, and thence you can cross the river to Kentucky and so go on to Mr. Helm's. It would be well for you to write your friend and learn your best route to his house should you go that way. *You had better avoid traveling on the Ohio*

River in the boats at that season. The railroad running from the lake to Cincinnati passes directly by *Yellow Springs,* said to be a delightful spot, in one of the most beautiful portions of Ohio. And there my old friend *Mr. William Neff* resides in the summer. I lived in his counting room four years in Savannah, as you know. *I wish you particularly to stop and see him.* I think he will be glad to see you, and you will be amply repaid for so doing. I enclose a letter of introduction to him. Also one to Dr. John S. Law, formerly of Liberty County, an old neighbor, schoolmate, and friend, who lives in *Cincinnati.* He will be glad to see you.

Mother wishes me to say that your box of clothing will leave here on *next Tuesday* the 13th and go on by express to you, either by Harnden's or Adams'. So you must keep a bright lookout for it. She has hurried to get it ready. Your brother says the alligator must not go with the clothing, but be sent afterwards. There is too much mush about the bones. They are nearly dry enough.

You can take the notes of introduction out and put them in neat envelopes, should you use them. You will write us before you leave, and frequently when you are on your excursion. I pray that your life may be preserved from all danger and harm, and that God may keep you from all evil and grant you a pleasant and profitable summer. You will travel much alone. Guard against strangers and all the dissipating influences of travel. And "Remember the Sabbath Day to keep it holy"; do not travel, on any pretext whatever, on that day.

My dear son, I have continued anxiety of mind in relation to your spiritual state. What will all that this world is to you avail if you lose your own soul? I pray God to send His Holy Spirit into your heart to incline you to repentance towards God and faith in our Lord Jesus Christ.

I came from Maybank this morning. All well, and Mother, Brother, and Sister send much love.

Your affectionate father,
C. C. Jones.

Thursday, June 8th, 1854. All well. Just going to Montevideo.

Mrs. Mary Jones *to* Mr. Charles C. Jones, Jr.ᵍ

Maybank, *Monday,* June 12th, 1854

My dear Son,

The last stitch has been taken, the last garment folded and laid away in the box, the little household gifts all gathered up and placed side by side, the musk-cluster roses and verbena scattered throughout, by their sweet odors reminding you as you use each garment of the sweet love and tender remembrance ever cherished at home for the loved absent son and brother. I hope they may all reach you safely and contribute to your comfort. I am sorry to find that the linen buttons do not promise durability on the shirt bosoms; if they break off, you must get some *small* pearl buttons and have them sewed on. And if you please you can purchase a small neat pin for the bosom; if you do so, let it be *plain and genteel*. Enclosed in the little box is a pair of sleeve buttons and a gold piece from your mother. The buttons are so poorly marked you must have them cut over.

I wish you, my dear child, every proper enjoyment in your present visit. I wish you could go through New Haven and see Mrs. Clay, Mrs. and the *Misses McAllister,* who have been there all winter, and our friends Dr. and Mrs. Wells. Your father desires you to go by the way of Niagara, and visit his old friend Mr. Neff at Yellow Springs, and Dr. Law. But he has already written. You will remember our caution about a certain *young lady,* should you see her; I assure you when you know all you will feel as much surprised as we have been at her treatment of your brother, but it would not do to say more until we meet. Should you have any old clothing, you can put them aside for the servants, as they are always acceptable to them. I send your little Testament for your traveling companion. I wish we were all going to the Mammoth Cave; when there you must remember and bring me some curiosity of your own gathering.

It would do your dear father and sister good to travel, but he does not feel disposed, unless there is an absolute necessity for it, to leave home this summer. Perhaps your sister may go to Marietta in the fall. . . . We hear frequently from our dear relatives in Marietta. All well, and always send love to you.

You will be surprised to know that your aunt and uncle have by a sudden determination gone to live on the Sand Hills in Brother Joe Anderson's house, renting also his plantation. To move his servants in January. Your Aunt Susan and Cousin Laura will be with us during the summer; they have rented a house in Savannah from the 1st of next November, when they expect once more to go to housekeeping. We all feel very badly at your aunty and uncle's leaving us, for we shall miss them very much, but hope the move will result in good to Sister Betsy, for she was very thin and very unwell.

Our good neighbors are at Woodville. They have had a great deal of sickness in the family and on the plantation: scarlet fever and cholera. We have been mercifully dealt with—far more than we deserve—up to this period. Cassius, who came down on Saturday, reports *Maria* as having scarlet fever and very sick. We hope to go up early in the morning. Old Niger is quite relieved from the effects of the snakebite; Young Niger suffering still from bad medical treatment. Dr. Duke from Virginia has recently settled at the Boro, and has been attending our people. We know little of him as yet, but he appears to be a gentleman.

We have received the Matt. Ward trial and all the papers about the Boston riots. My dear child, I cannot tell you the deep anxiety I have felt on your account, exposed as you have been to scenes that were calculated to exasperate your feelings. I am thankful that, if Providence permits, you will soon be removed from such an atmosphere of abolitionism and every evil work.

Today I asked Joe if he knew where your *pistol* was; he said you had carried it. I hope, my dear child, you will never carry arms about you. This *awful and cowardly practice,* from the evidence in the Ward trial, seems to be very common in Kentucky. I think the man who carries concealed weapons places himself beyond the divine protection, and is in the broad road to the commission of some rash if not murderous act. Your grandfather always regarded it as a never-failing sign of a *coward*—and a *"dastardly one,"* as I have frequently heard him express it.

For three or four days I have been suffering from an attack of acute rheumatism, and have written this in great pain, not only from that cause but also from a mustard plaster on the back of my neck, which has blistered. Your dear father does not seem to feel that he is radically better, although I can but hope that he is improving. I believe Brother and Sister have each a word to send for themselves, so I will close. A pleasant and happy trip to you, my dear son! Write often and particularly. The servants all send howdies. With love from us all. The Lord bless and save you!

Ever your affectionate mother,
Mary Jones.

P.S. I forgot to say your brother cannot send the alligator at this time. Am sorry I have no better seeds to send you; five years' absence has made sad havoc with the flowers. Will try and send the verbena and magnolia when the bones are sent on.

Ever your mother.

Contents of box: 8 shirts, 6 cravats, 6 collars, 1 nightshirt, 3 pair drawers, 4 pair socks, 1 box sleeve buttons, *etc.,* 1 pincushion, soap and tooth powder, 1 Testament and tracts, 2 bunches feathers, flower seeds.

Rev. C. C. Jones *to* Mr. Charles C. Jones, Jr.ᵍ

Maybank, *Monday,* June 12th, 1854*

My dear Son,

Your box of clothing, with sundry notes and little matters, is just nailing up (8½ P.M.), and we hope to send it down by the stage tomorrow to Mr. Cumming to be forwarded by express immediately. It is directed "Charles C. Jones, Dane Law School, Cambridge, Massachusetts. At Mrs. Blake's, Main Street." And hope you may receive it early and safely, as it will add much to your comfort.

Your last letter was one of great interest to us, and I am glad that you were with Colonel Suttle and gave him sympathy and support. Although he appears to be a gentleman capable of any emergency, yet as a gentleman he would and no doubt did appreciate your attentions and those of other young gentlemen from the law school. . . . I agree with you that the conduct of the abolitionists was infamous. They demonstrate themselves in this case to be fanatics of the worst sort, setting at defiance all laws human and divine, the constitution of their country, all truth, all decency, without one redeeming quality—not even the common courage of men! However, I think the Bostonians *deserve credit for the execution of the law. They did execute it,* and the whole matter will do good in our country, even in New England itself. And your worthy professor came out with flying colors. The creatures of the law school hissed him as he came into his lecture room! They should have been *expelled* by the college authorities. The Southern and right-minded students did well to *cheer him.*

I do not at all regret that you have been an eye- and ear-witness to all this matter. You will see what human nature is under fanatical influences, what nerve is required of men in facing public excitement and mob violence, and how necessary is calm resolution and self-possession for the vindication of right and for the accomplishment of just purposes. You will see also the silent, potent majesty of the law, executed to the letter in open day in the face of twenty thousand persons assembled to witness it, a very small part of whom were disposed to risk an attempt at a rescue. You will learn also the nature and tendencies of abolitionism in its pure unadulterated infidel form; the New Englanders will drink their fill of it. And you will see also that there is *power* in our government. Gather experience from all these things; make your observations; and learn self-control, calm self-possession under circumstances of excitement and danger. This gives a man vast advantages, and enables him to act wisely and successfully.

The report of Matt. Ward's trial I have looked over. It is meager: a poor showing of so important a trial. The reported evidence and speeches are slim. Speeches *weak:* Governor Crittenden's I have not read; if not better reported than the rest, not of any great account. An *ex parte* affair: my opinion remains unchanged. Be careful when you visit your young friend not to make any remarks on the trial that would be wounding. Governor Helm's speech seems less obnoxious than others, and he seems to have been involved in the trial from strong personal and family feeling and friendship.

Sister's birthday! She is now playing "Lilly Dale" most sweetly. Mother is giving Gilbert orders to have the carriage at the door by sunrise; she goes up with me to Montevideo in the morning, D.V. The family are waiting for evening worship, and I must close. Love from all. May the Lord have you in His holy keeping!

Your ever affectionate father,
C. C. Jones.

Remember me to Dr. Albro. Tell him I have no letter from him yet!

MR. CHARLES C. JONES, JR., *to* REV. *and* MRS. C. C. JONES[w]
Cambridge, *Tuesday,* June 13th, 1854

My dear Mother and Father,

I have delayed a little longer than usual in writing you, yet I know you will readily pardon this silence when you hear that I have been recently incapacitated for the discharge of that which to me has always been the most pleasing of social duties by a severe cold, which for five or six days has so encompassed me on every side as to prevent any effort requiring a clear head or a quiet hand. The fever has, however, left me, and I hope, with the blessing of God, will not return. It is well that I have a pen, for should I raise my voice, your ears would be saluted with sounds by no means euphonious and decidedly of the *basest* sort. The weather has for the past few weeks been of such a variable character that the system has momentarily been subjected to many liabilities to cold—a kind of cold also which not only converts your head into a confused ball of lead but sets your ears to ringing, your neck to aching, your temples to throbbing, while the "big manly voice," at one moment "turning toward childish treble, pipes and whistles," at another indulges in tones not unlike those which are frequently heard from the depths of a Georgia swamp at eveningtide. Last Sabbath, confined to my room all day, I was unable to attend any place of worship. This is the first Lord's Day since I left you that I have spent without being found in the sanctuary.

The excitement in reference to the rendition of Burns, Colonel Suttle's slave, which for so many days kept Yankeedom in perfect commotion, is ceasing. The war of words is heard in more subdued tones, the mobs have dispersed, and we are flooded with pamphlets purporting to be "sermons of the times" and "lessons for the day"—incendiary in their character, bitter against the South, Southern men, Southern institutions, and particularly vehement upon topics of "Chains and Slavery," Nebraska Bill, Fugitive Slave Law. And what will appear most remarkable to the sober, pious mind is that they all come as emanations from the respective *pulpits* of this vicinity—promulgated, moreover, upon a day which the Lord has consecrated for His especial service. Strange and enormous must be the stupefying fanaticism of that man who, professing to be called of God for the revelation of holy things unto men, can so far forget his sacred office, and the solemnities of the season, as to indulge openly in vituperations against his country and fellow man, not only unbecoming a minister but unworthy a sensible person upon a secular occasion. It is really surprising to what an extent a person becomes an actual *fool* who, possessed of one prejudice, one misconceived idea, surrenders himself a total slave to its miserable influence. I have recently from observation formed an estimate of the elements of fanaticism more vivid and real than ever before, and willingly subscribe to the old rule: "Never dispute or argue with fools or bigots either in religion or politics."

Our professor, Judge Loring, deserves the approbation of the entire country for the manly, open, and determined manner in which he conducted himself during the entire trial and finally disposed of the case. You have no idea what he endured and what indignities he is still forced to suffer at the hands of the thousand miserable monomaniacs by whom he is surrounded. He has, as Professor Parsons remarked to me, acted as well as mortal man could, regarding only the laws of his country, upheld by a stern sense of justice and an approving conscience. The voices of a misguided community may be unpleasant as they are raised in impotent sneers, but they cannot seriously affect the equanimity of a *mens conscia recti,* as the old Roman would and has expressed it. Some of the abolition ladies of Boston, I understand, sent him *thirty three-cent pieces;* and upon the package in which they were enclosed was written: "The *price of blood.*" You will understand at once the blasphemous allusion. In our lecture room at Cambridge several of the viler species of abolitionists, members of the law school, so far forgot even such gentlemanly bearing as belonged to them (although I must confess as a general thing very little obtains in the genus *abolitionist*) as to indulge their anserine propensities in hissing. For a second only could the notes of these geese be distinguished, and then old Dane Hall shook to the very center with the thunders of welcome and shouts of approval to him who had in such trying times sustained the honor of the school, his city, his state, his country. I could scarcely refrain from leaving my seat and forcibly ejecting from the room, by a stout application of boot leather, a puny scoundrel who was hissing in one corner of the room. But respect for the school and myself forbade such a course.

You have, I hope, received the papers which I forwarded containing a minute account of all the incidents of trial, the excitement in Boston, and final rendition of the fugitive. Therefore I will not indulge in any account of the scenes which then and there transpired, but will merely remark that due praise must be given to the officers both of the state and city as well as of the United States for the promptitude with which they conducted themselves in all arrangements requiring decision, accuracy, firmness. The powerful military force on the ground and the efficient disposition of the soldiers is all that prevented Boston from becoming one miserable arena of riot, blood, and lawlessness.

We—that is, the trees and shrubs—have recently been literally eaten up with worms and bugs. In fact, many of them are in a denuded state, presenting very much such an appearance as a cotton field would if caterpillars should take up their abode therein for several days or a week—and that only with the proviso that they operate very industriously upon everything green. Plenty of mosquitoes of the finest lungs and respectable proportions.

Am now reading Story on partnership—a work well written but diffuse, with many repetitions. Judge Story's writings are daily growing, in the estimation of many of us, of less and less repute. The truth is, he wrote *too rapidly,* and consequently without sufficient care and consideration. He is most profuse also in quotations from every source. I have heard it remarked by persons who are well informed on the subject that Justice Story has been known to embody an entire English treatise in one of his works, that in others the amount of original matter contributed would not constitute one-fourth of the volume. His works are, however, models in the way of style; and there is no doubt but that while he is voluminous he still sheds a greater amount of light, collecting its rays from every quarter, upon a given topic than almost any other text-writer. He and Chief Justice Marshall certainly accomplished more for the advancement and improvement of American jurisprudence than any persons who preceded or have followed them. For my part, I do by no means agree with those who speak so slightingly of his productions. I have read several of them, always with great pleasure, and I hope with profit. There is no doubt, however, that had Justice Story written with greater deliberation and succinctness, his legal commentaries would have been far more valuable. In this respect Professor Greenleaf is vastly his superior, although by no means the lawyer of that vast erudition which Justice Story possessed in such a remarkable degree.

Have another case in moot court to be heard in a few days. My senior counsel in the case has left Cambridge, so that I am compelled to argue it alone in the defense. These hot days are not as favorable for the study of the law as the colder hours of winter. . . . Hoping, my dear father and mother, that you are both in the enjoyment of every blessing, I remain, with warmest love to selves, Sister, Brother, and all relatives and friends,

Your ever affectionate son,
Charles C. Jones, Jr.

Howdy for all the servants.

Mr. Charles C. Jones, Jr., *to* Rev. C. C. Jones[g]

Cambridge, *Tuesday,* June 20th, 1854

My dear Father,

Your last two favors have been duly received, and for them let me return you my sincere thanks. The mail of Saturday also brought me a letter from Mr. Cumming containing a check for two hundred and fifty dollars, which was duly cashed at the Charles River Bank of this city. For this also, my dear father, I am exceedingly obliged to you, and will try and make a good and judicious use of it. I acknowledged the receipt of the same to Mr. M. Cumming on the day of its arrival.

The box which my dear mother and yourself have sent has not arrived, but is daily expected. The receipt for the same has been handed to the expressman of Cambridge, who will bring it out so soon as it reaches Boston. I know how much I will be obliged to you for it, and how glad I will be to see its contents, coming as they do from home. But I anticipate, and will defer a letter of acknowledgment until its arrival and an examination of its contents.

Am happy to hear that Niger has suffered so little from the effects of the snakebite. His presence of mind was remarkable for a Negro; no one could have acted more deliberately or efficiently on such an occasion. Hope that he will be entirely relieved. . . .

Regret to hear that Aunt and Uncle will leave you so soon. From your little circle on the Island their presence will be sadly missed, and I know how much they will lose in this remove from your immediate neighborhood, now that the shadows of age are lengthening and the attentions of relatives are rendered hourly more and more necessary. Moves are always attended with inconveniences and disadvantages, greater or less, especially at their time of life. Hope as they have determined to leave the Island that the change will be for the better.

Liberty seems to be forfeiting her right to the good name for peace, morality, and order which she has so long and emphatically enjoyed. One person stabbed—and that at church! And a Negro supposed to have been murdered by his fellow servant! I hope that all guilty parties may be made to suffer the just penalty prescribed by law for such aggravated offenses, and that due means will be employed to ascertain the truth or falsity of the suspicions resting upon the occurrence upon Mr. Barnard's plantation. When they are brought to trial, let Liberty show a more reliable jury than that recently collected in Hardin County!

I must congratulate you, Father, upon the honor recently tendered for your acceptance. Oakland College occupies a very prominent position among the institutions of the South, and you would indeed, as you truly remarked, have a noble field for doing good. The office at your disposal is one of much responsibility, not only in a literary but a moral and religious point of view. No one appreciates the importance of collegiate years until he has passed through them and afterwards calmly recurs to them and recalls the influences for good or evil then and there exerted, with the effect which they have individually exerted. As the spirit of a military corps is dependent in a great degree upon the courage and daring of its officers, so is the moral and religious tone of a college molded in accordance with the character and example of its president and professors. I have known several graduates of Oakland College, and they all speak in affectionate terms of their alma mater. They have made a wise choice, for I am certain they cannot elsewhere secure the services of so able a president. I know that you, Mother, also would know exactly how to *keep the boys straight,* and would sustain the dignities and courtesies of the president's house in a manner not to be equaled. I regret that ill health should prevent you, if you saw your way clear, from accepting the appointment. I know your admirable qualifications for such a position, and I think that it would be one in many respects suited to your tastes. The duties are not burdensome, and you would consequently have a very good opportunity of prosecuting your literary labors. He who forms and directs the mental, moral, and social education of young men at that important period does indeed occupy a position whose influence cannot be overrated. Especially is the *social* condition of collegians neglected. We need standard institutions at the South, conducted by minds of the finest cast. This want is daily becoming more and more apparent as repulsive action is on the increase between different sections of our country.

D.V., I hope in two weeks to leave Cambridge for Kentucky, and my only regret is that my journey will not lead me to Liberty, where I might meet my dear parents, Sister, Brother, and all relatives. Expect, however, to be with you in December. Thank you, Father, for the letters of introduction, which I shall make it a point to deliver. To make and retain friends is one of the pleasantest and most important duties in this life. I anticipate much enjoyment from my contemplated trip, and you may rest assured you shall share with me its pleasures so far as my pen can depict them.

Next Tuesday I expect to argue a case in moot court, and am quite busy in its preparation.

I agree with you in your remarks with reference to the report of Ward's trial. The jury should *at least* have returned a verdict for homicide in the second degree.

Last week I sent Mother a catalogue of the Society of Christian Brethren in Harvard University. I was not aware of the existence of such an institution until a few days since I received a note acquainting me of my election as a member. From the catalogue you will see the ends and aims of the society. It has been in existence more than fifty years, and has, I doubt not, accomplished much good. Its existence in college is as a general thing known only to its members, and they are elected only by a unanimous vote. I was pleased with the honor, and shall try and profit by its advantages. It meets every Tuesday evening for reading of the Scriptures, prayer, and the discussion of religious topics. No Unitarianism about it.

Last Saturday evening one of my young friends called for me in a buggy, and we had a delightful ride through some of the adjacent towns to Boston. It was the anniversary of the battle of Bunker Hill. The military was out, and the common crowded to see the evolutions and witness the firing of the flying artillery.

Have mailed to you a copy of an address of Professor Peirce, the distinguished mathematician of Harvard. In his department he is said to be second to none in the world.

I see from *The Southern Presbyterian* that the members of Midway Church have at length secured the services of a pastor. May they be pleased with him, and may his ministrations of the Word be blessed to the spiritual good of all hearers! Many, many happy returns to my dear sister of her birthday, each finding her wiser and better. Will write her soon. With warmest love, my dear father and dear mother, to you both, Sister and Brother, Aunt Susan, Aunt Betsy, Cousin Laura, Uncle, and all relatives and friends, I remain

Your ever affectionate son,
Charles C. Jones, Jr.

Howdy for the servants.

Mr. Charles C. Jones, Jr., *to* Mrs. Mary Jones[t]

Cambridge, *Thursday,* June 22nd, 1854

My very dear Mother,

The box with its precious contents has arrived and has been opened. How shall I thank you all for this most kind token of remembrance? You know, dear Mother, how much I am obliged to you. You can appreciate my feelings, and therefore I will not attempt a portrayal of them at this distance merely with my pen. Unless you have enjoyed similar good fortunes you cannot duly appreciate the pleasant emotions which filled my breast, causing the eye to sparkle, the heart to throb, as article by article, package after parcel was successively removed from the position of order in which your own hand had so recently placed them. A happy home and its beloved inmates were brought to mind in a manner so emphatic, so agreeable, that while I looked upon these tokens, each bearing the impress of your own hand, I seemed to breathe an atmosphere of that dear native spot redolent of the balmy air of love and affection. How much did I wish to be with you all in order that I might *in propria persona* return you my sincerest thanks, not only for these renewed favors themselves, but also for the delightful emotions and glimpses of home which they afforded.

My dear father and mother, never did any boy have such kind, indulgent, pious, and noble parents. Each hour calls for new gratitude from me to God and yourselves. Should an hundred winters sprinkle their frosts upon my head, never could I discharge one tithe of that debt of love, respect, and gratitude which I owe to you. Every day that I live do I feel this more and more sensibly. In the very appreciation of this, while it brings many a pang of remorse for past shortcomings, accompanied with a hope and knowledge of pardon, there exists a refined, pure pleasure quietly cherished, which he alone knows and can experience who has such parents, and appreciates the intimate and tender relation existing between them and himself. Cicero, my old master, has in a word summed up much that is embraced in the term *filial obligation,* and if you will allow me I will quote a little from him. *Parentes carissimos habere debemus, quod ab illis nobis vita, matrimonium, libertas, civitas, tradita est. Quisquis in vita sua parentes colit, hic et vivus et defunctus diis carus est. Contra, contemptus parentum eius generis peccatum est, quod et ab hominibus odio habetur, et in viventibus ac mortuis a diis damnatur ac punitur.*

The musk-cluster roses and sprigs of verbena did indeed remind me of many past pleasures at home, as pure and delightful as they, while their sweet perfume was but an index, a representative, of that atmosphere fragrant with love and tender remembrance ever cherished there—an atmosphere undisturbed by the whirlwinds of passion or discord. The sleeve buttons, my dear mother, are beautiful. With the gold piece I will at some time add another to the already long list of presents from you. All of the shirts, drawers, and collars fit exactly, and are, I can assure you, a welcome addition to my wardrobe. Even the piece of soap was seasonable and acceptable, and reminded me forcibly of home; for one of the earliest literary attainments of which I have any distinct recollection was the deciphering both as to spelling and pronunciation of the word *almond* upon the cake of soap. I am very glad that you sent my Testament. My Bible is rather large to carry about with you in traveling, and I was thinking only a day or two since that I should have to procure a smaller one as a traveling companion; for a person upon a journey without a Bible (morally considered) is like a ship destitute of her rudder.

Thanks to Sister for her remembrance of me in the pincushion, a very appropriate present for a young bachelor. I shall carry it near my heart—that is, in my left vest pocket—where it shall always be at the service of the ladies who may perchance have lost a pin.

Brother's feathers are before me, unruffled and reminding me of many an *ardea* that has breathed his last before our guns and rifles. I would give a great deal now to take a good hunt. At present my venatic sports all lie in *hunting* up cases in digests and reports, and many a hard one do I find. . . .

The flower seeds I shall give to some ladies of Cambridge who will plant them and see if they will grow in this vicinity. When Brother sends the alligator skeleton, I will be much obliged if he will have placed in the box some cotton, cotton seed, and cotton bolls, with a few leaves, some rough rice, seminole pease, and the common cowpea, with a joint of sugarcane and a piece of arrowroot if the latter is sufficiently matured, and a few pods of the popinac. Persons in this vicinity who have never seen such products of a Southern clime view them as great curiosities, and esteem them very valuable presents. I have several lady and gentleman friends here to whom I would like to give specimens of them.

I anticipate much pleasure from my contemplated Kentucky trip, and you shall certainly hear from me with reference to all the scenes of attraction and objects of interest with which I shall come in contact. The Mammoth Cave shall be ransacked for its hidden treasures, and I shall endeavor to procure as many specimens of its curiosities as I can. Would that we could all visit it together; how much would the enjoyment be enhanced! I shall remember your injunction with regard to a certain young lady; as I do not intend visiting that part of the state, I shall not probably see her. Shall try and pay a short visit to Mrs. Clay and the Misses McAllister in New Haven; it would afford me much pleasure to see them. . . . As soon as my argument has been made in moot court, I hope to leave for Kentucky.

My cold still continues, and my regret was upon opening the box that I could not detect the sweet perfume that lingered there. However, I knew that the perfume was delightful, and the memory of the past furnished me with pleasant sensations for the present.

There is nothing of interest with us now. A few cases of cholera in Boston, but as yet confined to the filthy localities of the city. Wishing you, my dear mother and father, every enjoyment and blessing, with an hundred thanks and love to selves, Sister, Brother, and all relatives, I remain, as ever,

Your affectionate son,
Charles C. Jones, Jr.

Shall, D.V., write Sister and Brother soon.
Howdy for all the servants.

Mr. Charles C. Jones, Jr., *to* Rev. *and* Mrs. C. C. Jones[t]
Cambridge, *Tuesday,* July 4th, 1854

My dear Father and Mother,

Mrs. Blake has just sent me up a large pitcher of ice water, and never was the presence of that delightful beverage more apropos. The winds are dead, and the sun "with vengeful wrath imbued" seems determined to torture us with "agonies of heat." Never have I felt such weather before. In an open cotton field during some sultry day in the month of August, with no friendly shade tree to cast its shadow over your warm brow, you have experienced the *wilting* influence of the noontide ray. Still I verily believe that even that temperature, burdened as it is with the dead heat of the season, can be more easily endured than this which at present surrounds us. In this Northern climate the extremes of heat and cold seem emphatically to meet. Probably the changes are so rapid that the physical system is not gradually and sufficiently prepared to endure them comfortably. Pocket handkerchiefs are too small to remove the perspiration which gathers so thickly and rapidly upon the brow and neck. Coatless, vestless, I am trying to keep as cool as possible while penning these lines; and yet I am compelled every few moments to resort to a large towel at my side, else this would be a blistered sheet. Disquisitions upon the weather are, I am aware, rather uninteresting; yet you know one is very apt to speak first of that which most engrosses his attention—of that upon which he *feels most.*

Last Wednesday my case was argued in moot court. It was novel in its character and rather complicated, but withal interesting. Spoke a little over an hour. Have not received judgment as yet.

Thursday morning June 29th I left Cambridge and paid a flying visit to our friends in New Haven. Reached that city at 2 P.M. Stopped at the Tontine Hotel, just opposite the green, and very near Mrs. Clay's residence. After a good wash, ridding myself of the dust of the cars, my regimentals brushed, and having partaken of a very good dinner, I walked to Mrs. Clay's and presented my card. There I found Mrs. McAllister, Mrs. Clay, Misses Clem, Rosa, and Emma McAllister, Miss Black of South Carolina, and Miss Aborn of Savannah, with the boys Joe and Tommy and the little children. They all appeared very nearly as much pleased to see the subscriber as he was to meet them. It was next thing to seeing home and family. That word *"Charlie"* sounded so prettily and affectionately from the lips of the ladies, especially since for the past ten months I have known myself only as "Mr. Jones," "Georgia Jones," "Judge," "General," etc. There were the warm hearts, the pleasant smile, the hospitable bearing, the delicate and refined deportment, all of which brought vividly to mind the attractions of a Southern home—in striking contrast, I may truly say, to the "belongings" of a Northern residence. We spoke often of you all.

There I obtained, Father, much to my rejoicing, a *daguerreotype* of you. Mrs. Clay has a very fine one which you may remember. From this the artist Mr. Wells of New Haven succeeded in taking a capital picture. So that now I have, Mother, *your shadow* upon my finger, the most precious *vade mecum* that a son can have, and your likeness, Father, upon my table or in my trunk. You cannot imagine, my dear parents, what a source of gratification it is for me to have these likenesses of you with me in this distant land, where I have not a single relative within a thousand miles and can find sympathy of soul only with a few friends endeared by the social intercourse of a few months only.

It is at such an institution as this, under such circumstances as these, that one learns to appreciate aright the true value of firm friends, entertaining for you not merely an ephemeral esteem but a warm, growing regard. My social disposition has, I may safely say, undergone a great change, and that for the better, since my sojourn in this region. Once I entertained ideas—boyish notions—of living independent of friends. Such selfish conceits have all been discarded, and every day am I learning more and more the delightful enjoyments which flow from a communion of kindred spirits. I have also learned that there are comparatively very few whom you can actually regard as *friends* in the strict, intimate application of that term, while there may be many agreeable companions. My rule is to treat everyone in a gentlemanly manner, and thus, while I have my own choice friends, secure if possible the esteem of all.

But I am wandering from my account of my visit to New Haven. On Thursday evening Miss Clem and myself called upon Dr. and Mrs. Wells. They inquired particularly after you. Scarcely ever have I seen a more accomplished and agreeable family. Upon invitation I dined with them the next day, and I can assure you enjoyed the literary and social feast prepared much more than the physical, which was itself very fine. Miss Wells is a highly educated young lady, and converses very intelligently. The entire family, with the exception of the two eldest sons, leave for Europe in August, where they contemplate remaining a year or two. Dr. Wells says that a trip there would, Father, accomplish more for the rapid restoration and establishment of your health than anything you could possibly do. He wrote you to that effect once, and desired me in presenting his kind regards to Mother and yourself to refer you again to the advice contained in that letter, accompanying his reference with the promise to add a few more lines of like import if you will allow them to have any influence in impelling you to such a step.

Visited the college library and the Trumbull Gallery. The latter is quite interesting, as it contains the original illustrations of Colonel Trumbull of some of the most prominent Revolutionary engagements of our country. The illustrious author has indeed contributed his pen, pencil, and I believe his sword in dignifying the honor of his country. The library and buildings of Yale do not compare very favorably with those of Harvard.

Friday evening I placed carriages at the disposal of the ladies, and we rode out to a beautiful lake some four miles from New Haven. The sun was just sinking in the west; the shadows of the surrounding hills, covered with their dark green array, rested noiselessly upon the unruffled bosom of the lake, imaging each leaf, tree, and rock. Every object seemed enjoying the calm repose of the hour—that repose which nature delights to impart just before the curtains of night are falling upon her manifold beauties, and the evening star is beginning to twinkle in the sky. The entire scene was one of refined beauty, and we all enjoyed the prospect. The name of the lake is, I believe, Salkenstall. (Pardon the spelling if it has not been rendered correctly; having never seen the name in print, I have attempted to give you by letters the sound as I remember it.)

The ladies are all well. Miss Clem looks thin, having some time since suffered severely from an attack of scarlet fever. Tommy Clay was unwell, his indisposition probably occasioned by imprudent bathing. Joe and Tom are now attending a military school under the superintendence of Mr. Russell. From all I learned and saw of its purposes and regulations, I am disposed to regard it as a fine institution. I am a little afraid that those boys are not quite as fond of their books as they might be. They are good boys, conscientious, mindful of their mother's wishes, and perhaps as studious as boys generally are at their ages. Spent most of my time, and took several meals, at Mrs. Clay's. She enjoined it upon me never again to stop at the hotel when I came to New Haven. Her house, I knew, was filled, and I thought it better to do so.

Returned to Cambridge on Saturday. Should have reached Boston at 5 P.M., but our train did not arrive at the depot until after ten. Were thus delayed five hours. A freight train had that morning been thrown off the track in consequence of the breaking of the axle of the locomotive. The track was much injured and needed repairs. As we passed in the afternoon the scene of the morning's accident, broken cars were lying in every direction, dead hogs all mangled and bloody, while the locomotive was all in fragments. Two engineers were severely injured, one of whom has, I believe, subsequently died.

My little trip to New Haven was, as you may well imagine, extremely pleasant.

Today is the 4th of July, and I have been celebrating it by writing you a long letter, which I fear will tire you. Hardly slept a wink last night. There was one continual discharge of firecrackers, guns, pistols, rockets, etc. The most uncouth sounds also proceeded from a band who style themselves the Calathumpian Band. Horns, drums, tin pans, and other rowdy instruments, accompanied with unearthly yells, composed their nightly serenade. Here I must tell you that the clock has struck 12 M., and from four quarters the brazen-mouthed cannons are proclaiming the return of our nation's natal day by salutes. They will fire one hundred guns from Cambridge Common, Boston Common, Cambridge port, the United States arsenal morning, noon, and night. The bells all ring also at the same seasons. The attempt of the abolitionists to prevent a celebration of the day has signally failed. Tonight a series of splendid fireworks will be given on the Boston Common. The patriotism of these Yankees seems, however, to manifest itself only in smoke. I hear of no orations commemorative of the day, but merely of fireworks, floral processions, etc. For my part, I prefer some other more intellectual celebration. Would like to see the old Liberty Troop parade.

Tomorrow morning, D.V., I shall leave Cambridge for Kentucky. Shall try and deliver the letters of introduction which you, Father, so kindly sent me. Hope to have a pleasant visit there. Shall secure as many specimens of the wonders of the Mammoth Cave as possible. . . . Hoping, my dear mother and father, that this will find you all in the enjoyment of every blessing, I remain, with warmest love to you both, Sister, Brother, Aunt Susan, Cousin Laura, and all friends and relatives,

Your ever affectionate son,
Charles C. Jones, Jr.

Howdy to all the servants. All well.

II

Mr. Charles C. Jones, Jr., *to* Mr. Joseph Jones *and* Miss M. S. Jones[t]
American Hotel, Buffalo, New York, *Thursday,* July 6th, 1854
My dear Brother and Sister,

Your affectionate letters have remained unanswered much longer than I had anticipated, or could have desired. For your kind remembrance of me in the tokens which you placed in the box I returned my sincere thanks in a letter of acknowledgment to my dear mother. Let me here reiterate them. In writing you at the present time I can hardly do better (as you will perceive from the date of this letter that I am on the wing) than to give you a running account of my trip thus far.

July 5th a young friend from Kentucky, Mr. McHenry, and myself left Boston at 9 A.M. for Albany. The morning was intensely hot, and during the day we suffered much from the dust and heat. The thermometer in Boston upon the day previous ranged at intervals in the shade from 96° to 100°. Between Boston and Springfield the road skirts along the shores of several beautiful little lakes. One of these, preeminent for its artificial as well as natural advantages, is Lake Cochituate, which supplies the city of Boston with water. Although some eighteen miles distant from that place, its pure and healthy water is conducted thither, being first received into an admirably constructed reservoir in Brookline and subsequently into another just behind the capitol near the common, whence it is distributed generally through the city. Some of these little sheets of water presented really a poetic appearance—at one time embosomed among hills richly wooded, their glassy surfaces reflecting their forms distinctly and so accurately that every tree and shrub that grew upon their sides and summits could be seen imaged there; at another filled with small islands, fit retreats for water nymphs or parties of nature-loving persons. Upon some of them the hand of art had erected residences and bowers replete with taste, while the tiny sail seen in the distance imparted an air of vivacity to the scene. We had, of course, only a bird's-eye view of them, and you will excuse further description.

Reached Springfield at 12 M. Crossing the Connecticut River there (comparatively shallow, filled with rapids, and affording ample facilities for the carrying on of the various and extensive manufacturing establishments which there abound), we soon found ourselves nearing the tall hills (perhaps you might more appropriately call them mountains) extending through the northwest portion of Massachusetts. A heavy uphill grade impeded our progress essentially, although two powerful locomotives were in the lead. On this account a finer opportunity was afforded of observing the scenery, which was truly in many places of the wildest character. Some persons would call it grand. A cool breeze fresh from the green mountain tops invigorated our drooping spirits, and relieved us in a great measure from the dust which hitherto in perfect clouds had mercilessly settled upon us, to the great discomfiture of eyes, noses, ears, and lungs. Many times did I envy the ladies with their protective veils. Sometimes we would seem completely shut in by the surrounding hills, now presenting a barren, rocky front, again sides robed in forests which appeared in their native luxuriance; and you would certainly expect a tunnel, when suddenly, after a rapid curve around the base, a narrow passage would open through which the iron horse plunged joyfully, confidently, as if relieved in spirit at the unexpected removal of obstacles which seemed insurmountable. Often did a foaming streamlet rush across our way, and the noise of our wheels thundered through the little valleys over bridges many, many feet above the noisy brooks. For many miles few were the residences of man among these wild hills, and even these deserved (many of them) only the appellation of miserable huts. So poor is the soil, so rocky and so shallow, that few can be the rewards of the agriculturalist. (You have here a practical exemplification of seed sown upon rocky ground.) Here and there you see small fields of corn and Irish potatoes struggling into life.

Having passed through this range of mountains, we emerged into a more level and richer tract of country, more thickly inhabited. Reached Albany at half-past five. Having performed various ablutions, which he can best appreciate who has been covered with dust and incommoded by the heat in close cars for eight or nine hours, and having done full justice to the supper of our host of Peter Delavan Hotel, we walked through State Street and viewed the shipping on the Hudson. The evening was, however, so sultry, and the streets so full of Dutch and Irish emigrants, that we soon returned to the hotel, and at an early hour retired. Albany at this season of the year is not, I should imagine, a very pleasant place—rather filthy, and the side streets narrow. The distance from Boston to this place is two hundred miles.

This morning we took passage in the early express train for Buffalo: $7\frac{1}{2}$ A.M. Still very warm. Depot thronged with Dutch emigrants for the West. The appearance of the country presented a pleasing contrast to that of yesterday. Soil generally fertile, especially along the river bottoms. Surface of the country quite level. Observed many ploughing with oxen. Saw for the first time a reaping machine in active operation. Passed rapidly through Schenectady. At Utica we were completely besieged by throngs of little boys, whose little lungs tired not with repeated boisterous cries of "Here's lemonade—ice cold!" "Cherries right sweet!"

Rome is a flourishing town, or rather I should dignify it perchance with the name of city. On every hand from an hundred chimneys rose curls of smoke, and the hum of machine shops was everywhere to be heard. Judging from the number of drinking shops, I should suppose that the Maine Liquor Law would receive many opponents in New York.

The cars upon this New York Central Road are remarkably fine; the locomotives large and powerful. Train after train, both passenger and freight, repeatedly passed us. It is astonishing what an amount of business is here carried on. Our road lay for much of the time along the Erie Canal—that monument of the skill and enterprise of De Witt Clinton. I thought of our trip upon that canal in 1839, and as I saw here and there bridges spanning it, elevated just enough to allow the boats to pass under, my memory brought to mind "Bridge ahead! All hands below!" etc. The distance which at that day it required ten days to accomplish can now be passed over in almost as many hours.

Just beyond Chittenango a beautiful Indian squaw with an infant in her arms entered the cars. She was dressed in fanciful robes and displayed to the passengers many bead bags, moccasins, etc., curiously and artistically wrought. Tall, finely formed, and graceful in her movements, she seemed, at least in person, a fit representative of the American aborigines. But the dauntless spirit was not there. I felt deeply interested in her. Her babe was a really pretty youngster of perhaps eight months. It is singular how the love of display lingers with all savages, even after they have lived for some time under the influence of civilization. In her it was prominently manifested in the silver ornaments, scarlet shawl, bright robe, and variegated moccasin. You remember how Tacitus describes the same love of dress in the Germans, especially those of the interior, who had not learned to barter their choice robes to the Romans in commerce.

Near Syracuse, that nest of abolitionism and all the "isms" you may choose to name, the cars skirted a small lake with sandy shores. It did not compare favorably, however, with those of yesterday.

Twenty minutes past four found us in Rochester, the abode of Spiritual Rappists. The trade of this place must be very large, as on both sides of the river a factory appeared wherever a place could be found upon which to locate it. The waterpower is fine.

From this point until we reached Buffalo at every place of stopping we were beset with clamorous runners for the lake boats. Arrived at Buffalo at a quarter before seven. Am now sitting in my room, No. 17 American Hotel. Have seen nothing as yet of the city. Tomorrow, D.V., shall leave for Niagara.

My dear sister and brother, you must excuse this dry detail of travel, as I have thus far had no opportunity for noting "free jottings by the way." You will also excuse the style and chirography as well as the typography when you remember that your brother has ridden in the cars two hundred and ninety-eight miles today, is consequently tired, and has all the time while writing had the notes of his friend's violin singing in his ear, to say nothing of his frequent questions and jokes. Twelve o'clock. Good night. Warmest love to dear Mother and Father, selves, Aunt Susan, Cousin Laura, and all relatives from

Your ever affectionate brother,
Charles C. Jones, Jr.

Howdy for the servants.

MR. CHARLES C. JONES, JR., *to* REV. *and* MRS. C. C. JONES[g]

Galt House, Louisville, Kentucky, *Wednesday,* July 12th, 1854

My dear Father and Mother,

I had hoped long before this to have written you at length, but a succession of novelties, each attracting attention, and also the daily routine of travel, each evening finding me wearied with the dust and fatigue of the day, have thus far prevented. Before retiring this evening, however, I am resolved to send you at least a few hasty lines, acquainting you with my journeyings hitherto.

You will perceive from the date of this letter that I am again on Southern soil, and although many hundred miles away from you, feel more at home than I have done for some time. From the bird's-eye view of Louisville which we had in crossing the river from Jeffersonville and in passing through to this hotel, it is not the elegant city which I had anticipated. Probably this is the most unfavorable season of the year for one to form his ideas and gather first impressions of the thrift, business, and neatness of the place. The river is quite low, business matters seem quite dull, and there is very little activity in the streets. On my right, through an open window, I have a fine view of the Ohio and the Indiana shore. Ferryboats are crossing and recrossing, and the heavy cough of large steamers is heard now and then ascending and descending the river. It must be a noble stream in the spring of the year, when its swollen waters are even with the banks. Louisville is situated upon a sandy bluff of perhaps some fifteen feet in height, seems to be pretty regularly laid out, but many of the buildings present an old and dingy appearance. Tomorrow morning, D.V., I expect to leave at four o'clock in the stage for Elizabethtown, near which place Governor Helm and family reside.

Let me recur to a few of the scenes and localities through which I have passed since leaving Cambridge. From Buffalo I wrote Brother and Sister, just after I reached the city, before I had noted its situation and appearance, giving them a running account of my trip thus far. The next morning my young friend and myself hired a buggy and rode all over the city. It is, you may say, regularly laid out, and advantageously situated upon Lake Erie, whose waters, like those of the sea, stretch far away in the distance until they seem limited by the horizon alone. Upon its broad bosom the white sails of commerce were widely spread, and were you not intellectually apprised of the fact that this was indeed a lake, you could not otherwise have refrained from believing that you were indeed viewing the blue waters of the Atlantic.

The wharves were crowded with steamers for all parts of its enlarged domains, while canalboats without number, with vessels of every description, were discharging their respective cargoes and receiving others. Dutch and German emigrants seem now to form a principal article of import and export. You are surrounded with them on every hand, and sometimes it is with difficulty that you can under some circumstances address yourself to an assemblage with any degree of certainty that you will receive an English reply.

This influx of foreign population forms a prominent and in some respects a dangerous feature in the present history and condition of the West. I have seen in the past week a far greater number of Germans, Dutch, Irish, and other emigrants than in all the former portion of my life. It is among this class principally that the cholera occurs on the lakes and rivers here. And no wonder that they are affected with that terrible disease. Often, debilitated with the sea voyage, they land in some large city, are huddled together in narrow quarters by hundreds, indulge to an enormous extent in salt cabbage and other kindred cheap articles of food, sleep in rooms badly ventilated, thence spend days and sometimes weeks upon steamboats where they are generally treated no better than so many beasts. And thus in consequence of bad food, bad air, and bad attention, hundreds of them fall victims to disease while seeking their fortunes and a home in this western world. I have been among them and observed their habits, their modes of travel, of diet, etc., and can well comprehend the hardships and inconveniences which induce this mortality among them. The only wonder is that more do not perish. They can thank Heaven, however, for their originally excellent constitutions.

Buffalo in that part which looks towards the lake must be rather unhealthy. The shores are low, and that portion of the city is intersected by numerous canals, which are filled with water by no means the clearest and purest in the world. Here also are large manufacturing establishments, ironworks, tanyards, etc. Its commercial relations must be extensive. In the suburbs and in the country part of the city there are many beautiful residences with fine open lots and luxuriant trees and gardens. The National Hotel there is well kept, and is the best in the city.

At 5 P.M. took the cars for Niagara. Had a fine view of the river, the railroad running parallel with its shores for nearly the entire distance (twenty-four miles). The omnibus from the depot deposited us at the International, which is decidedly the pleasantest and neatest hotel that I have seen during my trip. Having washed and dressed, we crossed the bridge which passes over the American Rapids, and remained upon Goat Island long after the sun had sought his western couch in admiring the ten thousand beauties and sublimities that are embraced in that complex wonder of all natural wonders, Niagara Falls. It were vain for me to attempt a description of them. Words descriptive of them would prove as idle as the winds which ever and anon sport with the falling waters. You have witnessed this astonishing natural scene, have contemplated it in its manifold bearings and phases, and therefore know full well the terribly awful conceptions of sublimity and power which fill the soul, the ideas imparted of the might of Him who laid the foundations of earth and formed all her wonders. This visit to the falls of Niagara has been one of the profoundest pleasure and profit to me. It has awakened emotions and imparted conceptions which hitherto lay almost dormant. Upon my memory they are engraven as with a pen of iron, and should my life be spared until my head is silvered with the weight of years, they will only increase in power and effect. Viewed the rapids and both falls from all points from which they can be regarded on Goat Island and the American shore. Nor did I study the sublimity of the scene by daylight alone. A bright moon at night illumined the entire prospect, imparting a beauty even more attractive and affecting than that revealed by the stronger light of the "King of Day." Until twelve o'clock at night you might have found me moistened with the never-ending spray, drinking in the beauties and sublimities, catching the spirit of Niagara that dwells forever in that ceaseless war that sports amid that "hell of waters."

Saturday morning I made the descent to and visited the Cave of the Winds. It underlies the American Falls, and in order to reach it you pass under the descending waters. Divested of your clothing, and dressed sailor-fashion in red flannel jackets, blue pantaloons, and black oilcloth caps, attended by a guide, you make the descent. So powerful is the force of the falling waters, so blinding the madly rolling spray as it rises in confused masses from the rocks upon which the river has been dashed, that many are unable to endure it, and return without seeing the Cave of the Winds. To me the descent was delightful. So invigorating was the effect of the water, so animating and novel the occasion, I felt I could remain hours underneath the falls. In going far into the cave I found a very fine specimen of a petrified worm—the first that has been seen in that immediate locality, as the guide informed me. It is interesting in itself, yet rendered doubly so considering the circumstances and the remarkable position. I will preserve it for you.

Thence we crossed over the suspension bridge to the Canada shore, reported ourselves as having no contraband articles aboard, and proceeded to the Horseshoe Falls. Every hack, carriage, or wagon, immediately upon its crossing the bridge, has to report itself at the customhouse; otherwise the driver is liable to have his carriage and horses sold. The object is the prevention of smuggling goods. No examination, however, is made, and the word of the driver is usually taken unless some suspicions be excited. Often do the drivers, as I learned from one of them, carry articles from one country into the other without paying the duty established by law, boldly approaching the customhouse and crying out: "Nothing aboard!" When the officer came out to the carriage, I asked him whether a person coming for the express purpose of *spying* out the land was not a contraband article. He smiled and said: "Not in a time of peace."

Having obtained fine views of the American and Horseshoe Falls from the English shore, I made the descent and again clad as a sailor went under the Horseshoe Falls. The prospect there of the waters falling over you from Table Rock is beautiful and sublime. There with a hammer I obtained some beautiful specimens of gypsum, pure as the falling snow, and also a few quartz crystals of a yellow hue. There is a satisfaction in knowing that you secured these specimens yourself. We also visited the battleground and heard the old soldier recount the scenes of that eventful day. The Whirlpool and the Devil's Hole each received our attention, and well do they deserve careful consideration, especially the former. From the battleground I purchased of the keeper a grapeshot, a bullet, and the lock of a pistol. At the Whirlpool, far down among the rocks, I found some fossil shells, and also brought with me some rattlesnake vertebrae and ribs from a celebrated den which long proved a source of terror to the inhabitants and visitors.

On Sabbath I attended in the morning a meeting of the Tuscarora tribe. The occasion was interesting, and the exercises solemn. As I wish to give you an account of the services at length, you will excuse me from doing so now, as I fear you are already wearied with this protracted letter. . . .

Leaving Niagara at a quarter past seven on Monday morning, I returned to Buffalo, and thence at half-past eleven proceeded to Cleveland, which seemed beautiful indeed as the last rays of the sun fell upon its pretty houses and the deep blue expanse of the lake, which extended far away in the distance as far as the eye could reach, blue as the azure vault of heaven, calm and quiet in the evening air, the white sail contrasting charmingly with its placid bosom. The cars for some distance just before we entered Cleveland skirted along the edge of the lake, thus affording us an admirable view of its beautiful expanse. "The lake! The lake!" involuntarily burst from the lips of the passengers, and that side of the cars which was nearest to it was thronged with persons eager to gaze upon the attractions of the scene.

Cleveland stands upon a high bluff, and you do not see much of the city until you ascend from the level of the lake. As we passed up the bluff, numbers were sitting upon benches upon the edge, watching the last rays of the sun as they sported with a few fleecy clouds in the sky and kissed the glassy bosom of Erie. Cleveland is well laid out, and appears to be a very thriving place. In fact, its happy location would insure it much business in a commercial point of view. Put up at the Weddell Hotel. Did not find it the hotel I expected, or was led to believe it from report. Food covered with flies, waiters inattentive, and house dirty. Should I pass through Cleveland again I should stop at the American or Angier. The latter, I think, would be the preferable one of the two.

During our ride from Buffalo to Cleveland the road ran for many miles parallel with the lake, every now and then affording us a most beautiful glimpse of its blue waters through opening trees and the streets of the towns at which the iron horse paused to drop his passengers, or himself to take his frugal yet substantial meal of wood and water. Hence the road from Buffalo to Cleveland is called the "Lake Shore Railroad Route," passing through Erie, etc.

Left Cleveland for Cincinnati at 8 A.M., and arrived at the latter city at 6 P.M. The country through which we passed this day is the most beautiful I have ever seen in my life if viewed with reference to agricultural purposes. Level, rich, and thickly wooded, it apparently possesses a fertility which will richly repay the labors of the farmer; and judging from the character of the crops, such is undoubtedly the case. Ohio is indeed a noble state in her internal resources. The road between Cleveland and Cincinnati via Columbus is also the finest I have ever traveled upon. The cars themselves are well furnished and softly cushioned, and there is no motion at all, so accurately are the rails laid. The speed is also rapid. I was much pleased with Ohio, and am happy that I have had an opportunity of acquainting myself with the character of this part of our country.

Arrived at Cincinnati, and having dressed and supped at the Burnet House, which by the way is one of the finest hotels I have ever seen, I called upon Dr. Law. He was unfortunately not at home. Conversed with Mrs. Law, however, for more than an hour. She seemed pleased to see me, and inquired very particularly concerning you both, my dear parents. Gave her all the Liberty news of which I was possessed. Much that was very old was quite new to her. . . . Dr. Law is in the insurance business and succeeds well. Mrs. Law is pleased with Cincinnati, and feels perfectly at home. Returned to the hotel before ten. Horrible smells in some parts of the city: cholera among the Irish and emigrants.

Leaving Cincinnati at six this morning, we took the cars for Louisville, which city we reached at one o'clock. Road miserable: almost jolted to death. Indiana a poor state except along the river bottoms. Corn there not tasseling as yet. The railroad runs from Cincinnati to Seymour; there you change cars and come to Jeffersonville opposite Louisville on the Indiana shore.

And now, my dear father and mother, regretting that my letter has necessarily been so hastily penned, I must bid you good night as, D.V., I have to be up at three o'clock tomorrow morning for the stage. With warmest love to you both, Aunt Susan, Sister, Cousin Laura, Brother, and all relatives and friends, I remain

Your ever affectionate son,
Charles C. Jones, Jr.

Howdy for the servants.

Mr. Charles C. Jones, Jr., *to* Rev. *and* Mrs. C. C. Jones[t]
　　　　Helm Station, Kentucky, *Wednesday,* July 19th, 1854
My dear Father and Mother,

For the past week I have been so much indisposed that it has been out of my power practically to embody those communings which mentally I have had often with you. Am happy, however, in being able this morning to accomplish my wishes.

I left Louisville the morning succeeding the evening upon which I wrote you, at four o'clock. The air was delightful. The corn and clover fields, bending joyfully beneath the thousand dewdrops which clustered thickly upon each leaf and stem, filled the morning atmosphere with a fresh and delightful aroma. It was a pleasant change from the confinement and heat of railroad cars. Stagecoach traveling, when a person is in no hurry and feels in a good humor with himself and all the rest of mankind, is in some respects preferable to the more expeditious modes of the present day. You certainly enjoy a finer opportunity of seeing the country through which you are passing, of noting its peculiarities, and of learning its advantages. Fortunately for us, the road between Louisville and Elizabethtown is a hard rock turnpike, and consequently we were delivered from the presence of that unpleasant companion, dust. The sun also for the most of the time was obscured, only now and then looking down in his might, affording us a foretaste of what we might have anticipated had not kindly clouds intervened for our protection.

A stagecoach is a place whose social atmosphere is more dependent upon the particular conduct of each individual than any other vehicle of public travel. It is always a happy circumstance when you have a day's ride before you to find that you are with those who can enjoy a laugh and converse intelligently. Misanthropic and idiosyncratic individuals have no business here, and should by general consent be excluded, or forced to ride on the top, where they may undisturbed indulge their man-hating reveries, or under the influence of a summer's sun be induced to forget for a season their peculiar tempers for once, in consideration of more pressing and moving circumstances of time and place.

Fortunately for us, we were troubled with none such. There was only one who seemed out of place, and she was a Yankee schoolmistress who was accompanying a gentleman and lady from Atlanta, Georgia, home to act in the capacity of a governess. The rest of us were all good lively Southerners, and she with heroic (and I may say stoic) resignation held her peace, marring the harmony of the circle in no other manner than by her simple silence, which probably was all for the best. If you may infer anything from physical and forehead development, I should not stand in fear of contradiction in venturing the assertion that from all appearances two ideas never at once appeared within the scope of her mental horizon; and no one seemed to regret the absence of the soft tones of her voice, as in giving utterance of that she would necessarily have been compelled to make prospect of a set of teeth which were certainly formed not of the most brilliant or regular ivory you ever saw. Upon the back seat were two beautiful young Kentucky ladies, with whom I had much pleasant conversation; for you know after two hours or so a stagecoach becomes quite a sociable place.

Breakfasted some nine or ten miles from Louisville at a regular country house, where hot biscuits, corn bread, eggs, fried chickens, milk, etc., were served up in true Southern style and abundance. In the piazza, which appeared to be a general resort for all the neighbors of the vicinity, sat the famous *Kentucky Giant,* who is over eight feet high. He is decidedly the tallest curiosity in human form I have ever seen. He has, I understand, exhibited himself not only in this country but in Europe. Now, however, he has retired from public life, and is engaged in the ordinary avocation of grocery-keeping.

The road between this place and Elizabethtown for some eight miles winds along the very brink of the Ohio. The scenery here is truly attractive. On either bank of the broad stream rise bluffs varying from thirty to eighty and perhaps an hundred feet; while beyond, in both states, Kentucky and Indiana, rolling hills covered with foliage stretch away in the distance, occasionally springing from the very edge of the bank, with the waters of the Ohio washing their northern and southern flanks respectively. By a ferryboat we crossed *Salt River,* a stream of political celebrity, emptying its turbid waters into the Ohio. General Scott is said to have explored its headwaters more thoroughly than any aspirant for popular favor. He would undoubtedly be an invaluable assistant to any party which would have for its object an investigation of its courses and rise.

About one o'clock the stage neared Elizabethtown. Governor Helm's residence is handsomely situated upon a hill a mile and a quarter from the village. George Helm was ready to receive me at the head of his avenue with a buggy, and gave me the warm welcome of a brother. Since that time I have been staying with them, and never have I found a kinder or more pleasant family. They all possess the happy faculty of making a visitor feel as if he really was at home. Governor Helm is a gentleman of the first standing, has filled every post of honor in his state, and is far-famed for his legal and oratorical powers. He is in appearance, manner, and physical conformation much like Grandfather, and reminds me of him continually. Mrs. Helm is one of the most literary ladies you ever saw, and converses admirably. There is nothing in English or foreign literature with which she does not seem familiar. Her love for letters seems to have been very generally inherited by her children, of whom there are eleven. Two of the Misses Helm are grown, and are truly interesting and pretty young ladies. While I am writing, the piano downstairs is discoursing sweet music.

Since my sojourn with this delightful family, however, I have been sorely afflicted, much to my sorrow. The second day after my arrival I was seized with the severest fever I have ever had in my life. It raged with such violence that for nearly a half of a day I could not think or speak coherently. Through the kindness of a benignant Providence, however, the remedies applied were blessed to my speedy restoration. Dr. Slaughter was called in, who dosed me pretty severely, and the fever was broken. No sooner, however, had it made its exit than the erysipelas appeared in all its power, covering my mouth from nose to chin and nearly from ear to ear with its eruption of fiery acrid humor. The why and wherefore of its presence I have been unable to discover. It would amuse you could you only see the comical appearance that I present. You would be at once reminded of Lazarus. Have been living very lightly for four or five days upon bread and water or milk, without exercise, with a plenty of smartweed tea, two Seidlitz powders a day, and a constant wash of the sugar of lead. The vesicles are now drying up, and I hope in about a week they will all more or less disappear. You may realize my situation in the presence of the young ladies and their two cousins about the same age, who arrived a day or two since. What cannot be helped, however, must be endured, and one must make a virtue of necessity. The ladies here are not those who look merely upon the outward face, and thereby hangs my consolation.

The weather has been uncommonly warm, but inasmuch as I have not been hardly out of the house since here, the heat has not been felt. Took a short ride with the ladies yesterday evening just before sundown upon horseback. Delightful, reminding me of home and old times.

While writing you from Louisville I promised that I would give you an account of the Indian meeting on Sabbath near Niagara. Understanding that the services were interesting, and being desirous of seeing the practical operation of the missionary efforts among the Indians, I determined to attend. Left the hotel about nine in the morning, and after a ride of seven miles found myself entering upon what is termed the Indian reservation. This includes some six or eight thousand acres of very good land. A liberty pole marks one corner of it near the road. Upon this tract of land some three hundred and fifty of the Tuscarora tribe reside. Some of them even now subsist principally by venatic exercises, making excursions into the forests upon the upper waters of Lake Ontario, the care of their cabins being delegated to their squaws, who engage in a little tillage and in fancy work, which is disposed of at the falls to visitors. The majority, however, devote their attention to, and derive their support from, agriculture. Many farms belonging to them on either hand of the road, although seemingly in a prosperous condition, did not present that high degree of improvement which many manifest in the hands of the white man.

Passing through the reservation for a mile or two, we reached the church, a plain wooden building, beautifully situated upon a hill commanding a fine view of Lake Ontario and of the Niagara River in some of its windings. The congregation was collecting and the hour for service was at hand. The squaws were all dressed in flaming colors of scarlet, yellow, blue, etc., with large broadcloth blankets thrown over their shoulders. In vain did I look for that beauty which we have from infancy thought to find in the Indian maiden. The majority of the females were truly ugly. Several with hoary heads and feeble footsteps were seen wending their way across the fields to the House of God. Others had arrived, and were seated in groups near the church, playing with their children or conversing in low tones. I asked one of the old women if it was near the season for the exercises to commence; in a characteristic manner she looked up at the sun and replied: "Soon."

At a given signal the little church was peopled almost to overflowing, for its capacities are not very great. On the right of the church sat the squaws, on the left the men, while the space near the pulpit and immediately in front was filled by some thirty whites and children. The choir is composed entirely of Indian singers. An old Indian with a violin acted as the leader. The hymn, read in English by the pastor, Rev. Mr. Rockwood, was sung in the Tuscarora tongue. Prayer in English. Mr. Rockwood opens the Bible and reads from one of the last chapters of Revelation. The Indian interpreter, William Mount-Pleasant, is at his right, and translates verse by verse as the minister reads. That good old hymn, "There is a Land of Pure Delight," etc., is given out, and sung in the Tuscarora language by the choir in good time and with feeling. They appeared fond of solos and duets. The music was in some passages really plaintive and excellent. All the several parts were distinctly carried. Fine bass voices. The air was conducted by the two prettiest Indian maidens in the room. The sermon followed. Subject: the song of the hundred and forty and four thousand who were redeemed and washed white in the Blood of the Lamb. The discourse was pronounced in short sentences, which were successively translated into Indian by the interpreter. Thus both the whites and the Indians who were unacquainted with English could hear the gospel preached intelligently. The sermon was pretty good, although in some respects not entirely suited to the circumstances of the occasion. Never have I witnessed a more attentive congregation. The natural taciturn, silent disposition of the Indian in a great degree, I have no doubt, tends to render him a good listener.

Of the three hundred and fifty members of the tribe, as I learned from John Mount-Pleasant, another of the chiefs, about one hundred are in regular connection with the church—a large proportion for any community. This John Mount-Pleasant is very rich, his property being valued, as I was informed, at not less than one hundred thousand dollars. He is a very successful farmer, and always employs white labor upon his farms. The appearance of the Indians and their places generally did not indicate much thrift, although we did not see the finest part of their settlement.

Spent that Sabbath morning in an interesting manner, and hope not without profit, as there are many wholesome lessons to be drawn therefrom. While the poor Indian as to this world's honors and wealth is indigent indeed, it is a happy thought that they who have taken from him his temporal possessions are offering to him those treasures which are eternal.

I must ask pardon for the length of this letter, as I fear lately they have become quite serious visitations. Expect in the course of a few weeks to join a large party to visit the cave. Will there collect as many specimens as I can, and together with those which I now have, deposit them in a box and forward by Adams' Express to Savannah. I will probably be able to procure many which will prove interesting and valuable. The whole of this part of Kentucky is a limestone formation, and immediately in the vicinity of Mr. Helm's house I have found several fine specimens of petrifactions, such as fossil shells, etc.

Father, I will be much obliged to you if you will send me *fifty dollars*. I am sorry to have to write for this after so much that you have sent me this year, but circumstances have been such that I could not avoid it. In the first place, one of my friends in Cambridge was sick and without money, and I had to lend him of my store. Then the doctors have recently partaken of my substance, both in Cambridge and here. My trip also has and will cost me more than I had anticipated. I like to travel intelligently, and see all that is to be seen. Hence in doing this I spend more than a casual observer. I have now money enough to take me through the trip to the cave, but will need some to return to Cambridge, etc.

The young ladies are on the eve of a horseback ride, and Ben Hardin Helm and George have just insisted upon my joining. Have not been out of the house today, and the exercise will help me. With warmest love, my dear father and dear mother, to you both, Sister, Brother, Aunt Susan, Cousin Laura, and all relatives and friends, I remain, as ever,

Your affectionate son,
Charles C. Jones, Jr.

Howdy for the servants.
Direct: Elizabethtown, Hardin County, Kentucky.

Mr. Charles C. Jones, Jr., *to* Rev. *and* Mrs. C. C. Jones[t]
Helm Station, *Saturday,* August 5th, 1854

My dear Father and Mother,

Four weeks have elapsed since I have received any letter from you or from home, and you may well appreciate my anxiety to learn your welfare and the items of interest in Liberty.

The visit which I am now paying to Governor Helm's family is the most delightful that I have ever made in my life. It is unnecessary for me to mention the many pleasures or enumerate the various sources of enjoyment which are daily and hourly experienced. When we meet, you shall know them all. Suffice to say that among them literary tête-à-têtes, music, walking, and riding stand preeminent. I have been reading aloud to the ladies from some standard author for several days, since the state of my mouth was such as to permit easy and distinct enunciation. I never have met a family circle in which the members were more attached to each other, one that presented more attractions to the visitor, adopting him at once as a friend and an additional member, making him feel perfectly at home. In the vicinity are many agreeable families, and pretty ladies, whose acquaintance I have formed.

Some five miles from Elizabethtown there is a tunnel through Muldraugh's Hill now in process of construction. It will when completed be two thousand feet through the solid rock, and forms a part of the Louisville & Nashville Railroad. . . . This tunnel we visited a few days ago. Three shafts have been sunk in the hill, and about seven hundred feet have already been excavated from the solid rock. . . . The approaches to the tunnel are nearly finished. After ascertaining at what angle the road will enter the hill, and its direction, instead of beginning at the sides and tunneling through, shafts are sunk from the top of the hill to the level of the road; and at the bottom of each shaft workmen are placed who excavate along the line of the road both backwards and forwards. By this method a larger number of hands can be located, and the tunnel more rapidly completed. . . . The hill is composed of blue limestone and shell rock.

At the base of the hill there is one of the most singular formations I have ever seen. The rocks are composed entirely of shells and the vertebrae of small seafish, and evidently evince the action of water at some distant period. Some of them are completely worn away at the base, and present the appearance of a series of inverted sugar loaves on a grand scale; others seem to have been broken from their foundations with the force of the waves, and to have been tossed about until worn completely round. I wish that you could have seen them, for I regard this spot as invested with peculiar interest to everyone, and especially to the geologist. This formation was revealed by the excavation for the railroad, just where it enters the hill. Obtained some very good specimens of fossil shells, fish vertebrae, etc., which I shall preserve for you.

The geological formation of Kentucky is quite a novel one to me, and very interesting. . . . Upon Governor Helm's farm there is a small cave which we visited last week. The mouth was, however, filled with water, and we could not enter. Kentucky abounds with such, and I believe they are always found in rotten limestone formations.

Next week we expect to visit the Mammoth Cave, and I look forward to the trip with the greatest pleasure. Our party will be a delightful one. I expect to escort Miss Lizzie Helm, the governor's eldest daughter, about Sister's age. Shall write you particularly, D.V., upon our return.

For a few days past an agreeable young gentleman has been spending his time here who plays beautifully upon the guitar. He and I serenaded the ladies every night vocally and instrumentally, the subscriber playing upon his flute.

As dinner is ready, my dear parents, I must close. Hoping that you are both in the enjoyment of every blessing, and that I will hear from you soon, I remain, with warmest love to selves, Sister, Brother, Aunt Susan, Cousin Laura, and all relatives,

Your affectionate son,
Charles C. Jones, Jr.

Howdy for the servants.

Rev. C. C. Jones *to* Mr. Charles C. Jones, Jr.[g]

Maybank, *Monday,* August 7th, 1854

My dear Son,

We were relieved of great anxiety by the receipt of your letter from Governor Helm's. We were confident something had happened to prevent your writing. Now we are sure of it, and return thanks to God for His great mercy in restoring you from so severe and dangerous an attack. We were fearful of the effects of travel in such warm weather upon you, being in so high health, and the country generally sickly. . . .

We have had much sorrow in our little circle since we last wrote you. Our old and kind friend and neighbor Mr. King is *no more!* He was taken violently ill with inflammation of the stomach, and after three days' illness (the last of which he was in a comatose state) he died on the evening of July 1st. You may picture to yourself the distress of his family. Your brother and myself performed the last sad office of friendship, preparing him for his grave. Your Aunt Susan made his shroud. It has created a great vacuum in our little community. I performed his funeral service at Woodville on Sabbath afternoon the 2nd, and he was interred in Midway on Monday the 3rd. Your dear mother will write you circumstantially of this and many other things transpiring with us.

The summer has been of unusual warmth. The county generally healthy, with the exception of the epidemic, which has not yet subsided. Through divine favor our places have not yet been visited except with very light cases, if any at all. The crops on the different places so far are favorable, and we feel specially grateful for the continued health of the people. Our relations and friends generally well at this time.

I have just drawn a check and enclosed it to Mr. M. Cumming, Savannah, requesting him to purchase a check *on New York in your favor for one hundred dollars,* which he will forward you; and you can *cash it* either in Elizabethtown or Louisville. This is the best mode of forwarding funds to you, and hope you may receive the check immediately.

I think, my son, as there is so much cholera at Cincinnati and the places along the western route back to Cambridge that perhaps your better route back may be *through Virginia via the springs* and so on north. The Northern cities now all have cholera and are sickly; but hope it may pass off before you are ready to return. *Take the most favorable route back.* Let us know your movements when you next write.

I trust your residence with your friends will be a happy and agreeable one. I am assured you will be gentlemanly and considerate and upright in all your conduct and bearing. Your mother and I feel grateful to them for their hospitable and kind attentions to you, especially during your recent illness. Express the same to them for us. We all send much love. Mother expects to write you by this mail also. God be with you, my dear son!

Your ever affectionate father,
C. C. Jones.

Mrs. Mary Jones *to* Mr. Charles C. Jones, Jr.[g]

Maybank, *Monday,* August 7th, 1854

My dear Son,

Our hearts were filled with gratitude to our Heavenly Father this afternoon upon the receipt of your letter for all His goodness and mercy in rebuking your disease and restoring your health. The past week has been one of peculiar anxiety to us on your account; it has been two weeks today since your last letter was received. We have talked over and over the exposures in traveling at this season, particularly the liability of contracting that awful disease the cholera, of which the papers contain such distressing accounts. The circumstances and afflictions of friends around us—as you will learn ere I close—have all tended to very sad reflections and feelings, so you may conceive that I was prepared to receive tidings of sorrow. But "Bless the Lord, O my soul, and all that is within me bless His holy name!" My dear child, although in a land of strangers, was surrounded by friends, and had the timely attentions of a physician. Erysipelas in the West is often alarming and dangerous. Truly can I sympathize with you in the mortifying affection of your face. But it is a mercy that it appeared upon the surface. I am happy to know that your friends will not judge by present and outward appearances. To Governor and Mrs. Helm and your friend Mr. George Helm please tender our most grateful acknowledgments, not only for the favor conferred by their polite invitation to visit them but also for their kind attentions to you in sickness. You and we too, my dear boy, would shrink from embarrassing them with any care or trouble; therefore do we warmly appreciate the kindness so hospitably bestowed, and hope that in the good providence of life it may be our happiness to acknowledge it beneath our own roof. We shall feel most anxious to know, my dear son, that you are entirely restored to your usual health. And may the Lord sanctify it to your best good!

I must tell you now what I have longed to do so many, many times: the joy and comfort that little pamphlet you sent from Cambridge brought us. To see your name registered with those "Christian Brethren" who for so long a time have been lights in the midst of darkness! It was after night before our mail arrived; your father and myself had retired. When it arrived, a light was brought to our bedside. My eye fell upon that precious little pamphlet. There stood the name of our beloved child! We wept for joy. We arose and knelt at the bedside, and your dear father poured out his soul in prayer and thanksgiving that you were thus associated. *"I have no greater joy than to hear that my children walk in truth."* Oh, for the *full assurance* that you have embraced with *your whole heart* the truth as it is in Christ Jesus! *Tell me, my dear child, is it so? Have you sought and found the gracious Saviour?*

Your dear father has just handed me his letter to you. You will perceive the sad affliction which is laid upon our friends at Woodville and has fallen upon our little social circle. Mr. King came from South Hampton Wednesday night sick; on Saturday his reason departed; that night at half-past ten o'clock his soul passed from time to eternity! Our poor friend Mrs. King has been almost distracted. She says: "Oh, if there was but one word of comfort!" My son, I must forbear all descriptions of this heartrending sorrow until we meet; I have no inclination or power to relate them. His family are all sadly afflicted. Upon Audley will rest their care, and a great mercy it is that they have one so excellent and qualified to become their guide and protector. . . .

Your dear sister was very unwell soon after Mr. King's decease. We obtained medical advice of Dr. Wells for her, and she is now looking remarkably well. . . . Your sister has learned the music you sent for the guitar. "Ah, for Wings to Soar" is beautiful. . . . Your friends all inquire particularly of you, and desire to be remembered. So do all the servants. . . . Our new minister, Mr. Buttolph, has arrived several weeks. All pleased with him. . . . I must now close; my paper is gone, and it is verging to midnight. Everything is magnificent without: the full-orbed moon is riding mid-heavens, a cool southeasterly breeze waving the long gray moss and softly sighing amid the boughs of the oaks before the door. . . . May the blessing of our Covenant God rest upon you this night and evermore!

Ever your affectionate mother,
Mary Jones.

Mr. Charles C. Jones, Jr., *to* Rev. *and* Mrs. C. C. Jones[t]

Helm Station, *Saturday,* August 19th, 1854

My dear Father and Mother,

How much do I long to receive some token of remembrance from you! Five long weeks have been numbered with the past since my eyes have rested upon lines traced by your hands. Never before in all my life that I can remember have so many days elapsed without my having a letter from you. In the absence of positive knowledge I sincerely hope that God has kindly granted to you all health and enjoyment this summer.

I have never spent a vacation as pleasantly as the present, and never been treated with more marked courtesy, attention, and affection. I shall always revert to this visit to Governor Helm's family as one of the pleasant passages in my life. Providence favoring, I anticipate leaving Kentucky for Cambridge next week, with the brightest hopes for the accomplishment of many advances in my profession. These relaxations are admirably adapted to the advantageous pursuance of a subsequent and severe course of study. At least I have generally found it thus with myself. I enjoy pleasure and play as much as anyone; my strong nervous temperament inclines me to a vigorous appreciation of whatever attractions are before and around me. Still when the hour of social and festive excitement is past, it is always with avidity, and an appetite increased and not blunted by the respite, that I again court the society and converse of my books. My impression is that knowledge acquired immediately after a vacation is apt in many cases to be more clearly defined and more accurately remembered than that obtained at periods when for weeks the mind has been engaged in consecutive and exhausting study. The reason is evident. I hope to accomplish much this coming session at Cambridge; and my purpose is to communicate with Mr. Ward so soon as I reach the university and learn from him the legal studies and branches upon which I had best bestow particular attention.

The brightest anticipation toward which my heart is ever fondly turning is the expectation of being with you in December. Both your likenesses, my dear parents, are before me; and many are the pleasant moments passed in looking upon those shadows of you whom I love more and more as each day shows new cause for increased affection, which is already as intense and pure as it can be. God grant that these cherished anticipations of a reunion in person may be surely realized!

Last week we paid our willing adorations to the beauties, attractions, and I may say sublimities of the Mammoth Cave of Kentucky. Our party consisted of Mrs. Preston Pope and two nieces, the Misses Rogers of Louisville, Miss Lizzie Helm, Miss Hardin, Ben Hardin Helm, George Helm, and myself. In two carriages we left Governor Helm's at half-past two in the morning, and after a pleasant ride of fifteen hours, including one delay upon the road, reached the Cave Hotel just as the shades of evening were settling upon all things, and the country candles shining brightly upon a table well furnished with young chickens, corn bread, and fresh butter for the benefit of those who may have lingered long in the cave. The distance traveled was fifty-four miles. In consequence of the roughness and length of the road we drove a pair of fine black mules, whose endurance of heat and fatigue at this season of the year far exceeds that of the horses. We had some amusing scenes with them, at one time halting and positively refusing to move further, again seeming of a mind to lie down in the water as we were crossing Green River. The governor remarked as we left that he presumed we would have rather a merry time with them, and that their conduct would serve to supply perchance some interregnums of conversation.

The country between Elizabethtown and the cave does not exhibit many signs of extraordinary fertility. Especially is this the case at the present season. Scarcely a drop of rain has fallen in this section since my sojourn in the state, and during the month of July they had hardly so much as a heavy dew. You may readily imagine, then, the diminutive and dying appearance of the corn crops. The tobacco seemed to flourish better than any of the products of the soil. As far as the corn crop is concerned, you may say there will be almost a famine in this portion of Kentucky. Our road wound along the turnpike between Louisville and Nashville, in full view of many pretty small mountains known as Muldraugh's Hills, and for some nine miles, just before we reached the cave, upon the summit of a high level ridge. This part of our way reminded me often of the road leading to Tallulah Falls, which we traveled several summers ago. The scenery was of that calm, regular, and pleasing character which, while it does not impress the mind very forcibly, still engages the attention and delights the beholder with its exhibitions of tranquil beauty.

The Cave Hotel we found embosomed in trees, constructed of wooden buildings of different dates, these having been increased from time to time to meet the demands for accommodation made by the yearly increasing number of visitors. The main hotel is about two hundred feet long, with piazzas above and below. On the right runs a long row of connected cottages, built of logs, of at least two hundred feet. These are one story in height, with colonnades and piazza, affording an admirable opportunity for promenading with ladies, which you know amid the cool pleasant hours of twilight after the fatigues of the day is a delightful occupation. The proprietor, Mr. Miller (by the way, a very gentlemanly and obliging person), soon accommodated us with agreeable quarters, where we prepared ourselves for the evening entertainment and our debut in the parlor. After supper the ladies of our party soon found many of their acquaintance, and our numbers increased rapidly.

After a sound repose in the arms of Morpheus (for the temperature of the night was cool and favorable for sleeping) we arose early the next morning with eager hopes for a speedy introduction into the mysterious windings of the underground temple appropriately designated *Mammoth* Cave. We determined the first day upon taking what is called the "short" trip, nine miles in length. In order to this, leaving the hotel immediately after breakfast, we passed down a beautiful ravine embosomed in overarching trees some two hundred yards, and approached the entrance to the cave. Green River flows some four hundred yards beyond, at the foot of the hill through which the cave extends.

Before proceeding further, however, let me tell you how fancifully we were arrayed for our trip. The ladies were all dressed in bloomer costume, Miss Lizzie Helm and Miss Sallie Hardin in yellow flannel, tastefully trimmed with black velvet, the upper garments gracefully confined around the waist by a sash, and wearing light blue turbans with black plumes upon the head. The costume was really pretty, and Turkish in appearance. The Misses Rogers were dressed in Scottish plaid made after the same fashion. George Helm and myself wore scarlet flannel coats, with collars, pocket flaps, and edges lined and trimmed with black cotton velvet. Our pants were of light green color of the same material. Around my waist I wore Hardin Helm's dragoon belt. Large Byron collars, which Mrs. Helm kindly made for us, and small caps completed our fanciful costume. The ladies are compelled to adopt this mode of dress as that best adapted to promote that freedom of action which is indispensable among the rocks and uneven surfaces of this subterranean region. You may readily imagine the fantastic appearance presented by some thirty tourists, each one arrayed in garments such as his or her taste may suggest as most becoming the occasion.

Opposite the mouth of the cave, at the distance of not more than thirty feet, stands the residence of Dr. Croghan, whose heirs now own the cave. It is situated in an artificial atmosphere, the wind constantly issuing from the mouth of the cave being many degrees cooler than that which moves upon the surface of the earth. It was, however, found an unhealthy location and has been for several years deserted.

At the mouth of the cave we were provided with lamps and a guide (Matt by name), who carries on his arm a large basket of provisions, and swung round his back a canteen of lamp oil. Your way now leads down some thirty feet of rude stone steps, kept continually moist and slippery by little streams of water falling from the sides of the opening. The crowning rock is wild and unequal, and on every side the mouth is surrounded by large forest trees.

In a moment you have entered and are treading the main avenue. The lamps flicker in the strong breeze, and seem on the point of being blown out. You feel chilled almost to the heart, an unearthly sensation fills your breast, all is utter gloom beyond, while the massive rocky sides give back a hollow funereal sound at your every tread. But this feeling endures but for a moment. The merry lights are glancing on every hand, illuminating the chaotic darkness of the scene; you have recovered from the chilly sensation at first produced, and feel completely exhilarated by the cool pure atmosphere circulating so freely; every sensation of wonder, delight, and interest at the novelty of the situation is awakened; you are escorting a beautiful young lady, who sympathizes deeply in the excitement of the scene; and thus every circumstance tends at each new moment to keep you ever on the *qui vive*. I was favored during the whole of our wanderings in the cave with the especial guardianship of Miss Lizzie Helm, one of the most agreeable and accomplished young ladies I have seen for many days.

The first objects of interest that attract your attention are the wooden pipes which conducted water to the hoppers and vats on either hand when this part of the cave was used for the manufacture of saltpeter. The period at which these works were carried on was during the War of 1812. Tracks of oxen are still distinctly visible in the hard clay; and the pipes, as well as the woodwork of the vats, are still as sound and perfect as they were the day they were first used. This at once bespeaks the purity and dryness of the atmosphere.

Some distance beyond, the main avenue widens into a large hall, on the left of which stands a rock platform. This is called the Church, and not unfrequently is divine service performed here. There is no place of worship near the cave, and truly nature has here erected a strange and impressive underground temple for the worship of the Most High God. The ceiling of the Church is sixty-three feet high, while its diameter is not far from one hundred. Older by far than any cathedral that man has ever framed, devoid of all the tinsel and ornament with which man has seen fit to adorn those edifices erected to the God of Heaven, with no "dim religious light" stealing through stained windows, it stands a rough rock-bound temple of nature's own handiwork fit for the worship of nature's God. Logs and the old water pipes spoken of serve as seats for the congregation. Anxiously did I crave the opportunity of listening to some able divine who in this strange place, inspired by the occasion, should break the Bread of Life in fervency and in power. I can imagine the feelings which would pervade the breasts of preacher and hearer, but I would wish in reality to feel them.

The Kentucky Cliffs passed (so called from the supposed resemblance to the high bluffs on that river), you have a view of the Giant's Coffin on the right. This stands a solid rock detached from the wall—a stone coffin sixty feet in length. The resemblance is striking, and you can scarcely avoid believing that within repose the remains of some noted father of giants in former days.

Many are the halls through which you pass, and many the objects of interest which engage the attention—far too numerous for me even to mention. You will therefore pardon me if I merely allude to some of the most striking. The walls of the cave are often covered with beautiful incrustations of gypsum and lime in this vicinity. Here also are those incrustations which, varied in their appearance, interest you not unfrequently with their fanciful delineations. Thus at one time you trace the perfect image of a great anteater; again of an Indian chief, feathers in his hair, his blanket around him, seated in his canoe; again the image of an elephant with eyes, trunk, and tusks, etc. On Audubon's Avenue you are struck with the beauty of the walls and ceiling. Here it was that several mummies have been found in a state of remarkable preservation with numerous articles of wardrobe and warfare around them. Many, many years and perhaps centuries have elapsed since these discolored remnants of mortality moved about the earth possessing feeling and sensibility like ourselves, and now they are but so many *specimens* of interest for the examination of the antiquary. Fearful manifestation of the frailty of man! Louisa's Bower and Vulcan's Furnace are now passed. They are marked by heaps of something similar in appearance to cinders. The Register Rooms are completely disfigured by the vain egotism of hundreds who have with the smoke of their lamps traced their obscure names upon the pure walls, originally of unsullied white.

After passing through these, the guide collects all the lamps and bids the party wait a few moments. During this interval he has disposed the lights here and there among the rocks in such a manner as to give you at once an illuminated view of the Gothic Chapel, and truly it is an interesting and beautiful place. The Chapel, elliptical in form, is eighty feet long by fifty wide. Columns of stalagmites extend from the ceiling to the floor. Many of these pillars which seem supporting the massive roof are very large, some presenting the appearance of two truncated cones with their smaller ends united; others are slight and covered with delicate tracery; while from the ceiling hang innumerable stalagmites in process of formation, which as yet have not reached the floor. This serves as a natural and becoming drapery to the Gothic Chapel. The place is well named, and an air of sacred mystery seems to pervade it in every part. One or two marriage ceremonies have been performed at the request of certain very romantic young lovers in this chapel.

The next object of interest which engages the visitor's attention is the Devil's Armchair. This consists of a huge stalagmite formation, or rather series of columns, in the center of which is formed a spacious seat which they regard as having been made for the especial purpose of affording all due comfort to His Satanic Majesty when wearied with his perambulations amid the gloomy shades of this region of darkness. Doubtless, had the Roman gazed upon it, he would have regarded it as the throne of Pluto. Truly this is an Avernus even more terrible in blackness of darkness and other particulars than that described by the poets and sages of antiquity.

Napoleon's Breastwork, the Elephant's Head and Lovers' Leap, the Ballroom, the Sickroom are all passed, and we proceed to the Star Chamber, which affords one of the most engaging sights in the whole cave.

One word, however, with reference to the Sickroom. The row of cabins built for consumptives presents a singular appearance as they stand revealed by the light of your lamp. You question the right of man to dispose specimens of his handiwork amid such exhibitions of grandeur. Two of them are built of stone, the rest of wood. The air of the cave is regarded as favorable to consumptives, and as being exceedingly healthy. In proof of this it is said that the niter diggers were a remarkably healthy set of men, that some of feeble constitutions who were engaged in this avocation were restored to health and strength, while the men engaged in hauling the nitrous earth after a month or two became in as fine a condition for the shambles as if fattened in the stall. The visitor, although rambling for hours over paths of the roughest and most difficult kind, is seldom conscious of fatigue until he returns to the upper air; and there it does indeed seem to him that he has exchanged the atmosphere of paradise for that of a charnel house filled with unpleasant odors. All without is so heavy, so dead, so mephitic. At least, this seems to be so in the summer season.

The Star Chamber has been justly regarded as one of the greatest and most beautiful curiosities in the cave. The side rocks are of a light gray color and contrast strikingly with the perfectly black ceiling, which is studded with innumerable sparkling substances resembling very nearly the canopy of the heavens seen in a dark night. On approaching this chamber the guide extinguished all our lamps, and disappearing from the main room left us seated in perfect darkness—a darkness so thoroughly Egyptian in its character that you could sensibly feel its presence. Soon, however, a faint ray from the left was thrown upon the ceiling, and the stellar illusion became most manifest. The side rocks do not apparently reach the top of the chamber; no connection can be perceived between the sides and the ceiling, and hence the latter appears to be at an immense distance; and after regarding it for a moment, you can scarcely divest yourself of the belief that you are indeed beneath the open canopy of heaven. Thousands of stars are twinkling above; there is seen the reflection of an erratic comet, strangely and truthfully delineated; and there just at the edge of the horizon the rising moon. We lingered long in this part of the cave, admiring its beauties and impressed with the skill of our guide in his disposition of light and shadow to give a pleasing effect to the whole.

Fairy Grotto, a place that is a perfect realization of its name, is fancifully pretty—just such a place as the Bard of Avon might imagine when in "frenzy fine" he had his wanton dream, where Titania might move in beauty and Puck his frolics play. Stalactites by thousands are seen in every direction. Of various shapes and sizes, their variety of appearance can scarcely be excelled by the kaleidoscope. The incrustations, many of them transparent, illuminated by the lamps disclose a scene of rare and astonishing beauty. The Grotto is much disfigured by having many of its most attractive ornaments broken off by strangers.

The Sidesaddle Pit and the Bottomless Pit are fearful, rayless apertures in the solid rock sinking far, far below, apparently without bottom, for the ray of your lamp will not penetrate the gloom. It is, however, relieved by the strong light thrown down by the guide.

Louisa's Dome is a grotto of some fifteen feet in diameter by twenty in height.

Gorin's Dome is one of the most striking localities in the cave. It rises to the height of three hundred feet. You approach and look upon it through an aperture nearly midway. The guide has thrown up his light; the sides of the fluted walls, the brilliant Corinthian columns, the apparent gulf beneath, the dome towering to a height which you cannot exactly comprehend, the translucent incrustations of gypsum, the fantastic group of admiring beholders— all unite in forming a scene beautiful and impressive.

Our path lay over broken rocks, through narrow defiles, wide avenues, to various localities too numerous to mention. After wandering in the cave for five hours, we returned in time for dinner. What transpired the next day, when we made the long route and crossed Echo River, together with my opinion of the origin of the cave, I must reserve for a future letter, for I will not weary you too much at once.

With warmest love to you both, my dear parents, Sister, Brother, Aunt, Cousin, and all friends, I remain

Your ever affectionate son,
Charles C. Jones, Jr.

Howdy for the servants.

Mr. Charles C. Jones, Jr., *to* Rev. *and* Mrs. C. C. Jones[t]

Helm Station, *Thursday,* August 24th, 1854

My dear Father and Mother,

Your two favors reached me a few days since, and I need not assure you that their presence was welcomed with the warmest of hearts. Several weeks had elapsed since I had heard from you, and as my eyes fell upon your well-known autographs, my bosom swelled with joy, and I thanked God for having guarded and prolonged your lives.

It was with the profoundest sorrow, however, that I perused the melancholy tidings conveyed that death had invaded your Island circle and borne away one who had for many long years been a companion, a neighbor, and a friend. I could scarcely appreciate the truth of the event. It is hard to endure the stroke when the tender plant of a few days is plucked from its parent stem; severer still when it is putting forth the bright leaves of promise and blossoms in the springtime of life; but when the full-grown tree, with its infant shoots clustering around it, its head weighty with the fruits of age—it is truly terrible when this bows its head and sleeps in the dust. The hopes of a family, the thousand social relations incident to the situation of father, master, citizen, neighbor, are thus in a moment sundered, and a blank dreary void exists which for a season at least nothing earthly can fill. I know the keen anguish that must and will for a long time remain with the bereaved of Woodville. My heart is in the grave with them, and I hope that you will tell them how much I sympathize with them in this their weightiest of afflictions. Truly a heavy cloud must hang over your spirits, for I know how sincerely you rejoice with those that do rejoice, and weep with those that weep. It is doubtless a mournfully pleasant gratification to you, as well as the bereaved family, that you all were so near, could administer to his wants during the last hours of fading life, and perform those sad and final offices, the last tokens of regard and affection to the departed friend. I would have esteemed it a great privilege to have served at his bedside, and mingled my tears with those that flowed so freely at the absence of one who fills so prominent a place in my remembrance of early social relations. Sad is the situation of a large family without a male head. Much responsibility now devolves upon Audley. I know his affectionate character, and feel persuaded that he will do all that lies in his power to fill the position from which his father has thus suddenly been snatched by death. . . .

About four o'clock this morning we were all aroused from profound slumbers by the most piteous shrieks proceeding from the room occupied by four of the young ladies at present here. Two of them, the Misses Hardin, were preparing to leave in the early stage for Louisville, when the elder, Miss Sallie Hardin, suddenly fell fainting upon the floor. The cries of her sister were heartrending. For some time it appeared impossible to revive her, and she was to all intents and purposes dead. The remedies employed, however, for her restoration were blessed, and she is now sleeping very quietly. We hope that she will be entirely relieved. You may readily conceive the circumstances of the case—how they would conspire at that early hour, when everyone was in a moment roused from sleep, and by such cries from a sister calling for help, to cause alarm and anxiety.

Last week Mrs. Helm gave us a very handsome party, which we all enjoyed exceedingly. . . . The neighborhood here is in many respects a pleasant one, and the family with whom I am staying one of the most delightful I have ever seen.

On next Monday, D.V., I leave for Cambridge. Through the good providence of God my health is, I trust, fully restored; and as I am anxious to renew my studies, I have concluded to return directly to Cambridge. The check, Father, was duly received, and for it let me return you my warmest thanks. I will get it cashed in Louisville. With warmest love, my dear mother and father, to you both, Sister, Brother, Aunt, Cousin, and all friends, I remain, as ever,

Your affectionate son,
Charles C. Jones, Jr.

The receipt of the check I acknowledged to Mr. Cumming upon its arrival.

I had purposed in this letter to have given you a further account of the cave, but I must crave your indulgence for this until I reach Cambridge.

Kentucky is sorely afflicted by the absence of rain. Corn crops in this section are all lost. Governor Helm expected certainly to have made at least ten thousand bushels, and now says that he will deem himself fortunate if he gathers two thousand. All the creeks are dried up, and in many localities it is with the greatest difficulty that drinking water can be obtained.

I have a box of specimens from the cave and this vicinity, as well as some from Niagara, which I shall send to you from Louisville, care of Adams & Company's Express. Shall write you when they are placed in the hands of the express company and to the care of Mr. Cumming. Hope that they may prove interesting to you. So many specimens have been by each visitor obtained from the cave that it is a very difficult matter to secure them. Fishes are very scarce. I paid one of the guides, however, to try and obtain some of them for me one night, and he succeeded in securing two, besides several crawfish and crickets. With love,

Your affectionate boy,
Charles C. Jones, Jr.

Mr. CHARLES C. JONES, JR., *to* REV. *and* MRS. C. C. JONES[t]
Cambridge, *Monday,* September 4th, 1854

My very dear Mother and Father,

By the kind favor of a superintending Providence I have been conducted and guarded in my wanderings, and have at length in safety been returned to this my temporary home of professional study. For all these continued mercies which have ever attended my pathway by night and by day, by land and upon the water, I desire sincerely to thank the God of Heaven.

In returning from Kentucky I pursued a somewhat different course of travel from that which I adopted upon leaving Cambridge. From Louisville I took the cars for Indianapolis, thence to Galion, Cleveland, Erie, Dunkirk, there taking the Great New York & Erie Railroad for New York. I was thus enabled to see more of the states of Indiana and Ohio.

We failed in making the connections at several places, and were thus detained much longer than we should otherwise have been. For example, we left Indianapolis at 12 M. and were due at Cleveland at 1 A.M. Between the former city, however, and Galion, we met with an accident which delayed us fourteen hours. The cars were moving at the rate of perhaps thirty miles per hour. It was between eight and nine at night, and I was standing up in the hindmost car by one of the lamps, which you know are suspended at the sides, reading the life of Madame Roland. Deeply interested in the history of the Girondist and Jacobin parties, in the eventful scenes and acts of this prominent lady and her tragic fate, I was *totus in illis* when suddenly we were startled by the shrill scream of the iron horse. The next moment we were off the track, and were bouncing at a violent rate over the crossties of the road. The car rocked to the right and left alternately, as if uncertain on which side of the embankment finally to fall. I sprang out into the aisle of the car, ready to jump out of that window which should eventually be uppermost if the car did turn over. In this manner we rolled forty yards, when the cars finally jumped with a heavy jerk off the track, yet still on the embankment.

Leaping out of the door, I ran to the front of the train, where we found the engine at the bottom of an embankment some ten or fifteen feet high, completely shattered. The boiler was broken by the fall, and from it the steam issued with terrible roaring. The whole engine was turned bottom upwards and presented a miserable wreck. For a moment the fearful belief pervaded our minds that the engineer was lying beneath the burning, boiling mass. In an instant, however, we found him covered with blood; he had been thrown some fifteen feet, and struck upon his head against the hard clay embankment. Although his head was badly bruised and his shoulder seriously hurt, you may be assured of our happy relief when we found him by no means dangerously wounded. The fireman was also somewhat injured.

Some of the passengers were thrown upon their back in the floor of the cars, but through a kind Providence no one was killed, and no limbs were broken. . . . Never have I witnessed a more manifest interposition of Providence in the preservation of human life. Had the passenger cars passed over the embankment, we would certainly have had many broken legs and arms, and perhaps lives may have been lost. Our car, when it buried its wheels in the ground, was partially off of the embankment, and the advance of a few feet would have precipitated us to the bottom. I lifted up my heart in grateful thanks to the Giver of All Good for His kind salvation of us all. This accident, as I said, delayed us fourteen hours.

The New York & Erie Railroad is the finest in the country. Leaving Dunkirk at nine on Thursday evening, we ran through to New York, a distance of four hundred and sixty miles, in sixteen hours excluding stoppages. . . . Arrived in New York on Friday evening and remained there until Monday morning, when I left for Boston. . . . Am again at Cambridge, having just passed through one of the pleasantest recreations of my life.

Refreshed both in body and mind, I hope during the few remaining months that I shall tarry here to devote myself with renewed assiduity to the acquisition of my profession; and when these in the hurried march of time shall have winged their way and been numbered with the months that were, how happy shall I be once more to see you, my dear parents, my sister, brother, and relatives in my own loved home!

From Louisville I sent, care of Adams & Company's Express, a box of specimens for Brother. . . . The box was packed as carefully as possible, and my hope is that it will reach you in safety, its contents uninjured. It will reach Savannah about the 10th of September. I did my best in endeavoring to secure the finest specimens I could, but as I said in a former letter, the most beautiful have already been removed. Hope that you will be pleased with them. The greatest curiosities, the eyeless fish and crawfish, together with the crickets, I have with me, and shall send soon. I was afraid to risk them with the rocks. It is extremely difficult to secure these now, as they are rare and wild. You will therefore prize them the more.

I regret exceedingly to see the prevalence of the yellow fever in Savannah, and my prayer is that God will mercifully preserve our friends and the city at large from the effects of that fearful malady. With warmest love to you both, my beloved parents, Brother, Sister, and all relatives, I am ever

Your affectionate son,

Charles C. Jones, Jr.

Have just received Sister's letter, and will reply to her interesting and welcome communication at earliest opportunity.

Our lectures commenced today. Many new students.

III

Arcadia, *Wednesday,* September 6th, 1854*

My dear Son,

It is some time since I have written you. We received your long and interesting letter on the *Mammoth Cave,* one of the *"seven* wonders" of the world surely. Your descriptions were graphic. Am glad you have had so delightful a visit to Kentucky. Governor Helm and family have done everything to render your stay under their hospitable roof agreeable and pleasant. You have of course extended an invitation to your friend Mr. George Helm and also to his brother to return your visit at your own home in Georgia. Do so in *your mother's name and also in my name;* and it will afford us great pleasure to see any or all the members of the family and make them welcome. They have treated you so kindly, your mother has felt almost fully resolved to write Mrs. Helm a note of acknowledgment.

The summer has passed—the hottest in many years (so said to be); nor has the sun abated much of his fervor yet. Our cotton crop, which was very fine at Montevideo and Arcadia, has fallen off *greatly* from the rains and heat. Shall not realize more than half our first promise at this place, from present appearances. Provision crops good. We have the men from Montevideo here this week helping Stepney to get in his rice. Gilbert is just taking down a great trencher of boiled rice and bacon for the men in the ricefield. The wind is northeast and tolerably cool.

We have been mercifully dealt with on the places this summer. The epidemic dysentery has not as yet, except perhaps in mild cases, visited us. The severest case is that of Daphne, Stepney's wife. She was taken sick last week, and has been very ill with peritonitis and other inflammation. Our new doctor, *Duke,* has been in attendance and dismissed the case this morning, although she is yet by no means out of danger. Came up on Monday and have been here ever since. If she continues brave all day, will ride to Maybank this evening and see Mother and return in the morning. We have whooping cough among the children at Montevideo.

The carpenters are now getting out a frame for the repair and for an alteration in the Montevideo house. Your mother wishes to spend the winter there, but fear the house will be longer in repairing, etc., than we would wish. The plantations have gone out of repair a great deal during our absence, and it takes time to bring things up. We committed a great error in not building with *brick* from the start: *homemade.*

Cato has lost his wife, Betsy. Died of the epidemic on the Sand Hills. Great loss to him.

At Maybank we keep trimming up and improving in little things, and keep up our interest and spirits. Joe has been a great comfort to us. His time for departure back to study draws near. He has been not only industrious but laborious in study this summer—too much so for vacation. His health is good. Leaves latter part of this month.

Your sister intended going with him to Marietta on a visit to Aunt Eliza and your Uncle John, but the yellow fever is very bad in Savannah, and we do not think it right to expose them to it. Shall try and get Joe to the railroad without going to Savannah—cut across a back way from this county. Numbers of the citizens have left Savannah. Several families have come out to Liberty—but families originally from the county. Captain Williams, who ran a small sloop from Sunbury to Savannah, returned from Savannah week before last and died of *yellow* fever in Sunbury.

Rode up on Monday with Mrs. King and Audley to Hinesville from this place. Mrs. King qualified as executrix of her husband's estate and appointed Audley her attorney. Assisted them in getting their papers, etc. The gentlemen appointed executors with Mrs. King all are nonresidents of the county. The estate is to be kept together until the youngest child is twenty-one—a period some fifteen years off! Will made in *1840*; children *then* all *young*. The case is altered now, and the *will* should have been altered; and I understand Mr. King *intended* to alter it. *Business matters of moment should never be left for the morrow!* The children all draw a support from the estate, but nothing more.

In a spiritual point of view Mr. King's death is a very melancholy one! He died as he lived. My dear son, *do not put off making your peace with God.* You stand in danger of eternal ruin every hour you live without repentance and faith in the Lord Jesus Christ!

Your Aunt Susan goes to Savannah in November to keep house. She and Laura are staying chiefly at Woodville. All relatives and friends well. By this time you must be (if God has prospered you) in Cambridge, and so I direct my letter, hoping it may meet you there in good health, prepared for your studies. Present me kindly to Dr. Albro.

Your ever affectionate father,
C. C. Jones.

Mr. Charles C. Jones, Jr., *to* Rev. *and* Mrs. C. C. Jones[t]
Cambridge, *Saturday,* September 9th, 1854

My dear Father and Mother,

Two letters were this day received from the loved ones of home—one from you, Mother, the other from Brother. They came to hand via Elizabethtown, whence they were forwarded to Cambridge by my friend George Helm.

Happy am I to learn that you are all in the enjoyment of health. Of late, ever since the prevalence of the yellow fever in Savannah, my solicitude for you all has been very great, and also for those of our friends and relatives who are in the city, especially such as in the discharge of professional duties will be called to administer to the immediate wants and serve around the bed of many who are suffering from this fearful disease. . . . I hope that the city council will use every exertion to keep the place clean and thus prevent as much as possible the increase of the fever, if they cannot remove the cause. I see it is also on the increase in New Orleans.

The fact is, our ports are so completely thrown open to the vessels of the world, so many in consequence of our commercial relations are flocking hither from every nation and at all seasons of the year, that we may expect the transportation and importation of every kind of malignant disease, and that this, when once introduced, will continue as a settled sickness of the country. You have a positive illustration in the yearly appearance of the cholera in the West and in some portions of the Southern states. Now, this was formerly an exotic; and yet at present it seems scarcely credible that an epidemic not indigenous, so to speak, should so rapidly and securely have maintained and retained its hold. Probably not many years and perhaps months will elapse before we are visited with the ravages of the Persian black plague or with some foreign disease of which we are at present in person ignorant. . . .

Our term opens with a goodly number of new students. The right hand of fellowship has been cordially extended to those who were co-laborers with us during past sessions and also in welcoming others who for the first time have sought this seat of learning. May a like friendly feeling characterize all our intercourse during the present term!

On last Friday I was highly honored by the assembly of Dane Law School in being elected the *first speaker of the senior class for the present session*. The duties of the presiding officer are responsible where there are an hundred and fifty young lawyers to be ruled. We are organized after the fashion of the House of Representatives in Washington. In order to fill the office of speaker then properly, you have to render yourself familiar with all the rules of parliamentary practice; and in order to this the manuals of Jefferson and Cushing are to be not merely read but studied. It is a fine position to familiarize one with proceedings of this character, and I have no doubt but that I shall derive much benefit from the experimental knowledge and practice thence gathered. This honor was the more pleasing to me in that in its inception and final consummation it was in a great degree unexpected and wholly unsolicited. Therefore I esteem it the more as an expression of the confidence and free will of my fellow students. Honors and offices purchased are satisfactory to neither party, whereas they are always pleasing to both parties when merit alone is regarded as the standard of availability. I tell these appointments to you because I believe that you will be pleased to hear of them; and I must confess, my dear parents, in all such cases the satisfaction I experience is tripled when I think that they will prove satisfactory to you, and that in them you will infer indications of improvement.

The first lecture that I attended this session my name was announced as senior counsel on a moot court case to be heard on the 19th of this month; so you see they have put me right to work.

Am happy to hear from Brother himself that his hand is so nearly relieved. The sting of a catfish is, I am aware from personal experience, often quite severe, and sometimes accompanied with danger. He must be quite an adept with the hook and line. Should like to share the sport with him. Next time that he chases wounded gannets in the marsh, he had better look before he leaps.

I have never, I believe, completed my description of our second day's trip in the cave. This I will try and do in my next, Providence and time permitting. Hope that the box of specimens sent you from Louisville will reach you in good condition, for I think you will be pleased with them. I have some other little matters of even greater interest which I shall dispatch before long. With warmest love, my dear father and mother, to you both, Sister, Brother, Aunt, Cousin, and all relatives and friends, I remain

Your ever affectionate son,
Charles C. Jones, Jr.

Howdy for all the servants. I am happy to think and learn that they sometimes inquire after me.

REV. C. C. JONES *to* MR. CHARLES C. JONES, JR.ᵍ

Maybank, Monday, September 11th, 1854

My dear Son,

I wrote you from Arcadia on the 6th and came to Maybank the same evening. Returned Thursday the 7th. About eleven o'clock the northeast wind which had commenced blowing lightly on Tuesday began to come in with scuds of rain and thunder and heavy puffs of wind—a sure evidence of an approaching gale. Rice could not be taken in. Towards evening looked heavy towards northeast. Squally: heavy dashes of rain. Had the horses put to the carriage and left after sundown; arrived at Maybank a little before ten. Every appearance of a gale. Moon just past the full. Made windows and doors all tight. Wind increased to a gale during the night. When we rose in the morning we were in the midst of it. Not a spear of marsh to be seen. A clear rolling sea all around us and reaching away to Bryan, Sunbury, and Palmyra, the whitecaps keeping it in a foam and the driving spray and mist shutting the distant shores from the sight.

It brightened up a little after breakfast, and Joe and I put on our thick coats and sallied out to view the scene. We had to go above the upper spring in the drain before we could cross going to the Negro houses. The spring was some three feet under water, and the tide rose up some distance in Andrew's garden—the highest tide I ever saw. The bluffs washed and caving rapidly. The poor marsh hens in numbers sitting on the drifted sedge alongshore. At Betsy's Bluff facing the north the waves were dashing high, and the sheets of spray and foam combing over the top of the bluff!

On our return we picked up a wood ibis at the foot of a tree, just dashed down by the wind and dead, but still warm. So large and unwieldy a bird if blown from the perch can do but little in the gale. There—there is one! See him in the mist! He beats to windward, but is driven rapidly away. Now the wind catches him. His head is turned down, and he falls with the rapidity of a stone right into the trees upon the margin, killed no doubt by the fall.

We started a kingfisher. He flew out over the water into the wind. He beats the air for dear life; just holds his own, close down to the waves. Ah, that puff! He drives back, but head to the storm. He dares not turn or tack. He must give over—a desperate struggle. He dips. Up again. Dips. He is growing faint! He slowly gives back with a slight inclination to the lee of the bluff. He is sheltered. Ah, how he bounds up! The danger is passed. There he goes into the wood! Happy fellow!

We came back well drenched. By the time we had changed our clothes, the trees in the yard and lot began to fall and to lose their branches. The rain drove into the house under the shingles, through the plastering. All hands securing the windows, tying them hard and fast. Servants with tubs swabbing up the water as it pours into the entry and rooms.

The wind veers northwest. It blows a hurricane! There goes another tree! The top of the grand old hickory is off! I was upstairs fastening the windows. A loud jar and explosion below! "What's that?" I rushed down, and a perfect upstir. Both shutters of the two large windows opening into the front piazza, although fastened back, suddenly and at the same moment blown to with a loud report, shivering many panes of glass in each. Your Aunt Abby for a moment much frightened. Servants picking up the glass in both rooms. Rain driving through the broken panes. Waiters, sheets, etc., crammed in and water shut out. All the pride-of-India trees in the front yard down but two. Two of the poplars snapped off. Three locust trees torn up. There goes the old cedar on the lawn! Poor old fellow, riven from top to bottom, split in two. How the wind roars! The trees are in an agony. Their limbs are torn and twisted off. The earth is strewed with leaves and twigs and boughs.

"Well, Andrew! What's it?"

"Came over, sir, to see how you all fared."

"Where are the people?"

"Every soul came over with me. Would not stay behind. All in Patience's house. Master, is this a storm or a *harrycane?*"

"*Harrycane,* Andrew, sure."

"The carriage-house door has blown off, and some of the weatherboarding."

Dispatched Gilbert, who made all tight again.

The wind veers again to southwest. Blows as fiercely as ever. Night comes on. Some little appearance of lulling. At 10 P.M. storm going down. Saturday morning, September 9th: storm over. A fresh gale still from southwest. Fences flat universally. All hands righting. Trees down the avenue rent and torn and blown down everywhere.

At breakfast your Uncle Henry came, cutting his way as far as Mr. Dunham's Myers field. There left his carriage and took it afoot. Finds his wife and child, through a kind Providence, both well. Our causeway bridge gone. Causeway impassable: cut deep and wide by tide flowing over. No leaving the Island in wheels till repaired. Reports the storm terrible in the country. Roads blocked up; fences leveled; houses of various kinds blown down on almost every plantation heard from; crops of cotton nearly annihilated; every kind of crop greatly damaged. . . . Have not heard further; but destruction of houses, crops, and timber in the woods very great.

The storm has been more serious than that of 1824—more than any since 1804, so far as we have heard in our neighborhood. How the upper part of the county and the seaboard generally has fared we know not. The tide was so high at Woodville that they drew the boats from the river on the top of the bluff. The wind was prodigious, and instead of going east and south about as is the usual course in northeast storms, it went north and west about, and finally blew itself into a gentle breeze from southwest, where it now holds, and a tolerably sunny day.

Your Uncle Henry came back last night, and took your Aunt Abby on horseback as far as Mr. Stevens' Springfield, and little Ella on horse with him. He goes on to Lodebar and returns with his carriage for them. All the beautiful trees at Lodebar, he says, are down, and you would not know the place.

Maybank looks bald enough. Every tree in the front (except the line of water oaks—they stood, with loss of limbs and leaves only) is gone. All cut and split up and taken out of the yard this morning. And when the only two pride-of-India trees which did not fall, but are so denuded of limbs and old that they must be cut down, are removed, there will not be any left but the two small live oaks in the back yard; and one of them has lost nearly every limb. We shall plant no more trees *near* the house. This storm has taught us a lesson. And wonderful to tell, the only two which would have seriously injured the house in providence did not fall.

But how merciful has the Lord been in this fearful visitation! Not a life lost of man or beast, so far as we have learned. The storm is a great calamity and affliction in temporal affairs and prospects. May we profit by it, and learn not to trust in our uncertain possessions, but in the Living God, who gives us all things richly to enjoy. By these strokes of His hand he rebukes the presumption and idolatry of men, and makes them know verily that there is a God, and calls them to consider their ways and seek His forgiveness and favor.

Our county has been and is now greatly afflicted. Old Dr. Harris went down to Savannah and contracted the yellow fever and was extremely ill yesterday. The epidemic in Savannah, they say, is fearful! On the last Sabbath (not yesterday) not a bell struck in the whole city for church, so occupied were the inhabitants with the sick and dying and dead. Mr. Ward fills his station as mayor with noble courage and success. Cousin Joseph Robarts is in the city, and is city treasurer. He takes his meals with Mr. Ward. The affliction of the city is very great. It must affect its prosperity for some time to come. The visitation has come upon it like a clap of thunder in a clear sky. It has indeed been a year of remarkable visitations over our *whole country*. Every section of the Union has been chastened.

Everybody busy today. Mother having the house cleaned and everything sunned. Your sister has overhauled her piano. Your brother has had all your books and his rubbed clear of damp and mold, and Phoebe is now going over the books in my library. I have been superintending the cleaning off the trees and litter in the yard and writing you this letter. Our losses in crops and expenses in repairs will be heavy, so we must make economy the order of the day.

Write us regularly and let us know how you are getting on in every particular. All friends and relatives well, so far as we know. Mother, Sister, and Brother send much love. The Lord bless and keep you from all evil, my dear son!

Your ever affectionate father,
C. C. Jones.

Mrs. Mary Jones *to* Mr. Charles C. Jones, Jr.[g]

Maybank, *Thursday,* September 14th, 1854

My dear Son,

For the last hour I have been roaming about our silent dwelling from room to room, now below stairs, then above, like one whose anxious and sorrowful spirit could not rest. Not that individually (thank God for His mercy to us!) I have any cause for this state of feeling; but my heart is weighed with tenderest sympathy for suffering and bereaved friends.

Our Father in Heaven has seen best to repeat the blow so recently fallen upon the family at Woodville. Another (we may say) head has been removed, for in all that was useful, tender, affectionate, and devoted he was emphatically such. One month since, Dr. Charlton Wells returned from a delightful visit to all his relatives at the North, bidding farewell to his father and family in the bay of New York on their way to Europe. In his absence Mary remained with her mother. After his return he looked the picture of health, and stayed one week on the Island. The report of yellow fever in Savannah had reached us, and we all felt anxious at the thought of their going back; but he was desirous to be doing something in his profession, and said in times of sickness the physician's post of duty claimed him. Since their return to the city the epidemic has been raging with fearful and awful results. Night and day has he been engaged, attending the sick, the most of whom were poor people. He said he knew he would never receive any compensation, but yet it was his duty and he would do it. Keeping no horse and buggy, he was worn with fatigue. During the storm of last week he got wet several times, was taken with yellow fever, and night before last at nine o'clock he expired.

A messenger was sent out yesterday, arriving just before sunset. Mr. Dunham, who was working on the causeway, considerately sent one of our boys up to inform us of the fact. We had just ordered our horses saddled (for we could go over in no other way, as our bridge is gone and the road blocked up) when Cain rode up to ask that we would come speedily to his mistress. We did so as fast as we could. The shadows of evening had fallen around, and every object seemed shrouded in gloom. The lofty and beautiful trees lay uprooted in every direction around the house, and there stood upon the steps the heart-stricken family, nature without seeming to sympathize with the torn and lacerated bosoms within. . . . It was indeed the house of mourning. We remained until a late hour, and returned with Cain to pilot us over the marsh and creek. Audley was at South Hampton; a boat was dispatched immediately to him.

Your father and brother have gone to meet the *body,* which was to be brought out by ten o'clock this morning to Midway graveyard. Mrs. King and your Aunt Susan have gone also to meet poor Mary, who will come out in the stage of today if she is well enough to ride. Your sister went over to stay with Laura and the children until their return.

Poor Mary! God alone can comfort and sustain her! They were all in all to each other, devotedly attached. Some very interesting things mark their intercourse. One I will name, it is so lovely and remarkable. From the time of their engagement it was their habit before separating for the night to read a chapter in the Bible together and kneel side by side in silent prayer. Since their marriage nothing has been suffered to interrupt this exercise together twice a day. . . . We have seen a good deal of him this summer, and a more lovely character is seldom met with: talented and accomplished in his profession, pure-minded, gentle, and affectionate, tender and devoted in all the relations of life, reflecting peace and happiness. Who could fail to love and admire one so truly amiable, accomplished, and gentlemanly? Long will his many virtues be cherished in the hearts of his friends and relatives. Poor Mary will now, I presume, make her home with her mother.

The city of Savannah has suffered beyond description. The Angel of Death has visited and swept every class. Five physicians are reported as dead. *Mr. Ward, the mayor,* has stuck to his post nobly; by last accounts he too was sick. On the last Sabbaths not a church-going bell broke the stillness; the living were all with the dead and dying. All have left the city that could, and still the bill of mortality is not diminished in numbers, such is the increasing malignity. In the midst of all this suffering and death the besom of destruction has swept over the city, prostrating houses, uprooting trees, blocking up the streets, and filling them with additional causes of disease in the decaying vegetation. If anything could heighten the scene of woe, it was the horror of darkness which for several nights brooded over the city. The gasworks were so much damaged that their lights were all put out. Only a few little shops remaining open, a supply of candles and oil could not be had. Only think of the poor sufferers under such circumstances—the sick, the dying, the dead, all shrouded in darkness; not a ray of light with which to administer medicine or to catch the farewell look of affection or perform the last sad offices! With what feelings must they have watched for the breaking morn! I never heard of more distress in my life. Cousin Charles West has been sick, but has recovered. . . . Your Uncle John was so ill before leaving Savannah that he has not recovered sufficiently to return.

Your dear father gave you a graphic account of the storm. Never has a more desolating one passed over this county. Our individual losses have been very heavy. The new cotton house, the barn, a large shuck house put up last year, and the millhouse destroyed at Montevideo; a corn- and old ricehouse at Arcadia. The crops a wreck. We had a beautiful rice crop at Arcadia which must be almost destroyed. As I look out of the study window where I am writing, the cotton looks like December had fallen on it. Your Uncles Henry and Maybank lost no buildings; your Uncles John and Newton several valuable ones. Your aunt and cousin did not suffer any loss of houses either at the Point or on their plantations. Neither has Audley, but his rice and cotton much injured. In all the destruction of property I have not heard of one life lost. There is great mercy in this!

During the early period of the storm your Aunt Abby (who was with us and little Ella) with your sister enjoyed the grand and majestic whirl of the clouds with the tossing of the trees "against the stormy sky." But when they began to fall in every direction—some uprooted, others broken off and pitched away—it became too serious for pleasure. Your sister went around, teaspoon in hand, dosing everybody from a bottle of ginger syrup. As night came on, Andrew brought all the people over. I had a large boiler of strong coffee made and gave them all some, so that although most of them were drenched, nobody took cold. It was as much as we could do to preserve yours and your brother's books from injury. The wind drove the rain through the featheredge boards, and it fell in a shower through the plastering. Joe hid his iconographic encyclopedia under the bed, piling on bolster, pillows, bed clothing, etc. Over the shelves were hung coats, overcoats, pants, vests, blankets, crumb cloths, spreads, etc., etc.—everything his ingenuity could invent or lay hands upon. The books, piano, and pictures were the most precious things in the house, and everything went to preserve them. I have had them all rubbed thoroughly over, and none are damaged. A few were wet in the study. We had a fine prospect of pomegranates, some of which I hoped to send you; but they are all thrashed off, only a few small ones remaining. We have cut away fifteen trees from the yard, and are living in an appalling glare of sunlight. It makes me sorrowful to look out, for I know it is not probable that *I* shall ever again enjoy the pleasant shady trees which were so much my delight. But God's will be done! Oh, that my spiritual house may be founded upon the Everlasting Rock, which neither rain nor storms can beat upon or destroy!

It has been a great source of happiness to us, my dear son, that you have enjoyed your vacation so much. I feel so grateful to Mrs. Helm for her kind attentions to you, particularly during your sickness, that I have been half inclined to write her a letter of acknowledgment. *Would it be a matter of propriety?* You never made any allusion to the *religious character of the family.* Are any of them professors of religion? Your brother and sister both wrote you, and I another letter which perhaps you did not receive before you left.

To give you some idea of the storm, I have just come up from the cellar, where I found *fiddlers* crawling. They are all over the lot, driven up by the wind. Poor fellows, they are quite out of their element.

Afternoon. Father and Brother returned. Dr. Wells's body was not brought out. *Impossible.* Mr. and Mrs. William King sent a dispatch. *Poor Mary* herself too sick to come out, and her friends here forbidden to go to her, as they say it will amount to death for anyone to go into Savannah.

16th. Mary is reported better. Dr. Stephen Harris died yesterday. Poor Emma came out today, her children having been previously brought out to Dorchester. It is a season of unexampled distress and darkness. Will forward two Savannah papers with this letter.

Your letter, my dear son, of the 4th did not reach us until this afternoon. With grateful hearts we would acknowledge the goodness and mercy of the Lord to you in all your journey, and especially in your recent preservation. When I look around at my poor suffering bereaved friends, Lord, what are we that Thou shouldst be mindful of us and visit us with such mercy and blessing? In the day of prosperity let us consider, and may His goodness lead us to repentance! Thank you, my dear good child, for remembering to obtain so many interesting things for us at home. We shall duly prize them if the box reaches us; but there is so much distress and confusion in Savannah I would not be surprised if it never arrives.

On Monday the 25th our dear Joe expects to leave us in company with our minister, Mr. Buttolph, who is going on to see his mother. Your brother and sister intended to have made a visit to Marietta, but the sickness has prevented. It would be dangerous for Mr. Buttolph and himself to go through Savannah. They will take private conveyance to the thirty-mile station and reach the cars. . . . The thought of seeing you so soon is a delightful one to us all. Do take care of yourself as fall comes on, and put on flannel early. . . . Your aunt and cousin and Uncle Henry and Aunt Abby all send love. Father, Brother, and Sister unite with me in tenderest love. Servants all send howdies. Good night, my dear boy! May the coming day be to you a pleasant and profitable *Sabbath!*

Ever your affectionate mother,
Mary Jones.

Mr. Charles C. Jones, Jr., *to* Rev. *and* Mrs. C. C. Jones[t]

Cambridge, *Monday,* September 18th, 1854

My dear Father and Mother,

Although very busily engaged, I must not forget my regular habit of writing you upon the first of every week.

Since my last, my attention has been enlisted in the preparation of a moot court case involving considerable difficulty, assigned for a hearing on the 19th of the present month. As it is the first of the session, and I am one of the senior counsel, I have felt somewhat solicitous as to the preparation and final argument. In consequence of the unsettled condition of the law school and the presence of many who for the first time have approached this temple of learning, and necessarily look to us who are initiated to introduce them to its professors and assist them in locating themselves, I have not enjoyed as uninterrupted an opportunity of investigating my case as I could have desired. Finally, however, I believe the light dawns, and I see my way and line of argument pretty clearly defined.

Last week I had the pleasure of meeting General Cocke. Arrived in Boston, he wrote me a note, stating his location, and that he would be happy if I would call and see him. This I of course and with pleasure did. He was at the Marlboro Hotel, conducted upon cold water principles; and there, strange to say, morning and evening prayers at a certain hour are regularly held in the public parlor. Grace also is pronounced at the table before a single plate is turned. This is the first public house I have ever seen where such regulations are openly and systematically observed. The first morning that I called, General Cocke was not in his room, having other engagements in the city. Upon my second visit, however, I succeeded in meeting him, and passed the evening very pleasantly, taking tea with him and a young friend of his from Virginia, who is his traveling companion. His inquiries concerning you both, Sister, and Brother were very special. He says, Father, that you are in debt a letter to him, and that he is anxious to enlist your interest in an enterprise mentioned therein of a character, if I remember correctly, relative to the moral and social education of the Negro population. An answer he hopes to find awaiting him on his return to Virginia. From Boston he proceeded to Hartford to attend a convention there assembled. Thence he purposed a visit to Mrs. Clay in New Haven. The general is looking remarkably well, and remarked that he never was in the enjoyment of better general health. His kindest regards he desired me to present to you all.

It is with great anxiety and sorrow that I have daily noticed the ravages of the yellow fever in Savannah; and this the more, my dear parents, on account of the proximity of your present situation to the infected city. I have observed numerous instances where persons having left Savannah to escape the epidemic have after the lapse of several days or a week been attacked at the house of friends and fallen victims to the fever. I know not but that the Island home may be a resort, and that thus indirectly you may be brought within the sphere of its influence. My prayer is that God will mercifully preserve you all from this and every other calamity. The mortality in Savannah is truly terrible—proportionately as large, or very nearly so, as that of New Orleans last summer. Have seen an account of the treatment of the fever by Dr. Wildman which, if as successful as represented, must redound to his advantage and entitle him to the thanks of the community and country. The last steamer brings the intelligence that he is lying at the point of death. I wish that some of this cool weather could visit the city; for the past week fires have been not only comfortable but quite necessary.

Our assembly has now under discussion the Greytown question. The friends of the administration are decidedly in the minority.

We have recently had an addition to our numbers in the law school in the shape of a Georgian from Elbert County, Colonel Rucker by name. He made his appearance in full uniform, being, as he informed us, an aide to Governor Johnson with rank of colonel. For several days he has persisted in wearing it in town, at meals, and in the law school. Now that his rank is known, much amusement is caused among the natives at this introduction of Georgia militia uniform into the staid puritanic habits of Massachusetts. This love of military display has afforded merriment to all, the Georgia delegation excepted, who have added to the former much chagrin at the evident greenness and bad taste of their new companion. By the advice of *a friend,* he has concluded finally to defer for the present all further military demonstrations.

Do persuade Brother as he comes on to Philadelphia to take the New York boat for New York and come thence to Boston. You cannot imagine how much I wish to see someone from home. With warmest love, my dear mother, father, sister, and brother, to you all, with kind regards to all relatives and friends, I am, as ever,

Your affectionate son,
Charles C. Jones, Jr.

Mr. Charles C. Jones, Jr., *to* Rev. *and* Mrs. C. C. Jones[t]
Cambridge, *Wednesday,* September 27th, 1854
My very dear Mother and Father,

For some days past I have been so continuously occupied that I have been compelled to defer an immediate reply to your kind and interesting letters. Moot and club court cases have engaged my attention to the exclusion of almost every other duty. On Monday I have a decision to make in a case of agency by no means well defined or capable of ready solution in its intricacies. My hope is, therefore, that you will excuse an earlier answer.

Upon the perusal of your favors my heart grew sad—very sad—at the mention of so many sorrows with which the God of Heaven has in His wisdom seen fit to afflict not only the community at large but also families of our immediate neighborhood with whom we have so long been on terms of friendship and intimacy. . . . With Dr. Wells I had never formed an extended acquaintance, because we had never enjoyed the opportunity of doing so; but

from the little that I saw of him I fully concur with you in the high estimate
of his character, talents, accomplishments, and affectionate disposition which
you express in your letter. For Aunt Julia and Cousin Mary I feel deeply.
. . . I can appreciate in a great measure the situation of Cousin Mary, because she and I are nearly the same age, and from early years I have been
with her and know her disposition, her feelings. Please tell her how much I
sympathize with her, how deeply I feel for herself and Aunt Julia. . . . I
have been very much gratified at the conduct of Cousin Charles West in
Savannah. He has remained, quietly yet nobly discharging the arduous duties
of his profession, while the pestilence has driven away many from their
avocations. May God preserve him safe from disease amid his labors of love!

The situation of Savannah has been, and I regret to see from the morning
paper still is, awful. Probably the relative mortality has been greater than almost any city in our Union that has been afflicted with similar visitations.
The appearance of the city must have been terrible during the hurricane.
Truly the Angel of Death was very near, hovering over its devoted precincts,
from his sable wings shaking dire contagion. The conduct of Mayor Ward
has been such as to entitle him to the highest respect and thanks of everyone.
An occasion like this proves the true man of nerve and the philanthropist.

The storm on the Island must have been terrible, and extremely grand.
Your description, Father, was so graphic that it appeared distinctly before
me in all its power and effects. It is truly melancholy to see the crop at this
season of the year already made, you may say, thus in a moment destroyed.
There also are the beautiful shade trees and the improvements—the labor of
years—thus in a short hour overturned. Singular must be the appearance of
the Island house; it makes me sad to think of its present denuded situation.

Before this reaches you, Brother will probably be in Philadelphia. There I
hope to meet him in December if not before. Nothing of interest has transpired, and therefore, my dear father and mother, I must bid you for the
present farewell. With kindest love to you both, Sister, and all relatives and
friends, I remain, as ever,

Your devoted son,
Charles C. Jones, Jr.

Howdy for the servants.

Mr. Charles C. Jones, Jr., *to* Rev. *and* Mrs. C. C. Jones[t]

Cambridge, Wednesday, October 4th, 1854

My dear Father and Mother,

Although there is nothing whatever of interest with us, still I feel that in
compliance with a cherished habit I must not allow the week to pass without
spending at least a moment in converse with those I love best. The north
wind with its boisterous breath is blowing the yellow leaves from the trees,
and nature is reluctantly casting off the bright green livery of summer in
anticipation of the approaching severities of winter. Fires and overcoats

have some time since proved comfortable, and the long evenings, so favorable and pleasant for the student, are already with us. To me this season of the year is at once one of the pleasantest and most suggestive. Nothing do I love better than to walk and meditate in the woods amid the falling and eddying leaves. There are lessons for man taught by nature, and to be gathered from her ever-varying phases at every season; but now the peculiar lesson for the day seems most impressive and wholesome. It is that which reminds him of his own changing, frail existence, as shadowed forth in the sere and yellow leaf. Beautifully has Shakespeare in his inimitable manner portrayed and embodied this lesson drawn from analogy:

> This is the state of man: today he puts forth
> The tender leaves of hope; tomorrow blossoms
> And bears his blushing honours thick upon him;
> The third day comes a frost, a killing frost,
> And when he thinks, good easy man, full surely
> His greatness is a-ripening, nips his root,
> And then he falls, as I do.
> (*Henry VIII,* Act III, Scene ii)

Yesterday I received a letter from George Helm. The drought still continues to an alarming extent in Kentucky. In some of the towns water is so exceedingly scarce that clothes have not been washed for two or three weeks, and a guard is maintained at the public pump to see that no household obtains more than two buckets of Adam's ale per diem. I should not think that it would be a favorable time for pressing the Maine Liquor Law. The corn crops are all lost, and planters are trying to dispose of their mules and horses to avoid the expense of supporting them, while the hogs have all been turned into the woods to sustain themselves as best they may upon acorns, nuts, etc.

I notice the death of Hon. P. Ewing from Kentucky from cholera at the Mammoth Cave. I saw him last summer in Elizabethtown on his return from Washington, where during the past session he had taken an active part in the discussions upon the Nebraska Bill. He was a young man of promise, and was a distant relative of Governor Helm.

On the 2nd of this month Charleston was annexed to Boston. The result of the popular vote on the question was not known until about 10 P.M., and thereupon a tremendous discharge of artillery from both cities was continued for about an hour in honor of the event. My roommate, John Sale, and myself were at a loss to imagine the cause, as every discharge was distinctly heard in Cambridge, as the booming of the cannon was transmitted along Charles River. We imagined that news from Europe may have been received, and that perhaps the Allied forces had been successful in the bombardment of Sebastopol.

The law school this session is quite well attended, as the catalogue will show. This will probably be ready about the first of next week, when you shall have a copy. . . . I am happy to see from the papers that the yellow fever is decreasing in Savannah. May the terrible scourge rapidly abate! Hoping, my dear father and mother, that you will excuse the dearth of interesting matter in this letter, I remain, with warmest love to selves, Sister, and all friends,

Your ever affectionate son,
Charles C. Jones, Jr.

Howdy for all the servants.

P.S. I have recently been reading with great pleasure Humboldt's *Kosmos*.

The studies of this term are possessed of much interest. The laws of agency, mercantile insurance, and of wills are all now the subject of lectures from our professors. Before club court I delivered on Monday a long decision in an important case of agency, which required considerable investigation.

In regard, Father, to my expenses here this term I will leave it with your convenience at what time they shall be paid. If it is most convenient, I will let them remain until the end of the session, as my credit is good; for I know that you have not as yet found a market for any of the crop. Before leaving Cambridge I would like to purchase a hundred dollars' worth of books, which will be absolutely necessary for me to prosecute my studies.

I am counting already the days which must elapse before I, if Heaven permit, will again be with my dear mother and father at home. Let them pass as rapidly as they will, and I will in the meantime try and improve them.

Your own son,
Charles C. Jones, Jr.

Rev. C. C. Jones *to* Mr. Charles C. Jones, Jr.ᵍ

Maybank, *Thursday,* October 5th, 1854*

My dear Son,

Your last letter has been received, and I presume ere this you have received ours to you.

Your appointments are certainly very complimentary, and must be of great advantage if you succeed in improving them, which I know you are desirous of doing. The appointment of speaker to your assembly is one of great value; and if you now make yourself familiar with the duties of the *chair* in a deliberative body, it will be an accomplishment, and if you are spared to enter into life, will be of great advantage to you. What you need, of course, in the first place is *knowledge* of rules and forms and usages; this you will get from the *manuals,* and have at command from practice. And in the second place, *personal qualifications,* such as *close attention* to the business before the house, *respectful attention* to the speakers on the floor, *perfect impartiality and justice* to everyone, *promptness* in indicating and enforcing rules, and *calmness and self-possession* and *dispatch* in conducting the business, that it be not inanimate and drag its slow length along. Of course your bearing must be *uniformly conciliatory and gentlemanly, connected with self-respect and dignity.* It will be a good training to you, and you must endeavor to make the best speaker you can. Let us know how you succeed. Your election took us rather on a surprise, you being a Southerner and there being so much anti-Southern feeling in that region of country. May it all perish in a short time!

Your dear brother left us on Monday the 25th September. He took the carriage, and at Dorchester was joined by our new minister, Mr. Buttolph, and Robert Q. Mallard in another carriage. They attempted to go through Bryan County to the railroad (as we did not wish them to go through Savannah); but the bridges had been carried away, as they learned, and they turned back, crossed Ogeechee bridge, and went as far as Mr. Anderson's plantation, there stayed overnight, and took the cars six miles above Savannah on Tuesday the 26th. Our horses performed well: traveled fifty-two miles on Monday. Gilbert got back to Maybank on Wednesday noon, full of his travel and of the sight of a railroad and the wonderful "steam cars." We miss Joe very much. He has been, with his sister, the life of the house, and has attended to a great many little domestic matters for me. He has exposed far more than I desired, but went away in fine health and spirits. He has devoted almost all his time to professional pursuits: reading, preparing on his thesis, and comparative anatomy. He possesses one element of success, which is *devotion* to his profession. Our constant prayer is that God may spare you both and make you useful men in the high and noble professions you have chosen, and bring you to *glorify Him* in them by calling you both into His Heavenly Kingdom. Mr. Buttolph will be Joe's traveling companion to Philadelphia. This is very pleasant. Mr. Mallard turns off for Columbia Seminary, where he stays one year more.

The late hurricane, as we call it, was followed by a second blow some time after, which followed up the damage previously done. Crops necessarily short, and gathered in a damaged state. Montevideo never before had such a look of desolation. We are trying to put things to rights again, but it is slow work. There is a quantity of water on the ground, and the swamps are offensive. Thus far the county has continued generally healthy. I have not spent a night on the plantations since the gale, not deeming it prudent. Our people have been much favored on the whole, though we have the whooping cough at Montevideo, and have lost two children, Gilbert's little Nanny and Rose's little Nat; and Betty's infant I left on Thursday *ill* with it. I sent Dr. Duke to it.

Mrs. Wells, who you know has lost her husband, Dr. Wells, by yellow fever in Savannah, has come out and is at Woodville convalescing. She was very ill with the yellow fever after his death. I never knew such a year of general affliction and sorrow! Cousin Joseph Robarts has had it and is recovering. Young Dr. West also. He had sent his wife and family to Bath, and a few days ago was sent for to his wife, who had been taken with yellow fever! My paper is out. Mother and Sister send much love.

Your ever affectionate father,
C. C. Jones.

Rev. C. C. Jones *to* Mr. Charles C. Jones, Jr.ᵍ

Maybank, *Monday Evening,* October 9th, 1854

My dear Son,

I made an appointment, D.V., to preach in Sunbury yesterday particularly to the Negroes. I was out pretty early, before breakfast, giving out feed for the horses when I observed a horse hitched at the front gate. On returning to the house, your sister handed me a brief note from your Uncle Henry saying your Uncle Jimma had come to his house on Friday evening after dark, and was taken with a chill followed by fever; and so fearfully had been the progress of his disease that we must come immediately up if we *wished to see him alive!*

We hurried breakfast after family worship, and reached Lodebar about 9 A.M., meeting one of the attending physicians, Dr. Way the younger, who gave us to understand there was no hope. We found your uncle in the shed room off the parlor *pulseless,* his hands blackened, the blood settling under the nails, perfectly calm and conscious when roused, then falling into sleep. He turned over and gave me his hand, saying: "What do you think of my case?" He had taken much quinine, and was then taking brandy at intervals; his hands and feet rubbed with brandy and pepper, and blisters applied on legs, thighs, stomach, breast, and arms and back of the neck. Every effort made to bring on reaction. Your dear mother rubbed his hands and arms incessantly; others his feet.

Shortly your uncle and aunt and Aunt Susan and Cousin Laura arrived. We found his wife, Mrs. Jones, Mrs. S. N. Harris, and Miss Newell there with your Uncle Henry and Aunt Abby. West came; and some time after, your Uncle Berrien and Mr. Joseph Anderson and several gentlemen from Dorchester came over. Dr. Duke, one of the attending physicians, was very sick upstairs, and could not come down. He boards with your Uncle Henry. Dr. Way came.

But your Uncle Jimma continued *to sink!* He said to your mother: "Now, Sister, you will make yourself sick." His wife, who lay at his right side, said: "Jimma, do you not wish your brother to pray with you?" He replied "he would be glad for me to do so," and turned his face to the front of the bed. We prayed, and he endeavored to accompany us; but although the prayer was short, he was asleep when we rose from our knees. He repeated the first two verses of the 103rd Psalm audibly to himself with his hands clasped on his breast. "Bless the Lord, O my soul: and all that is within me, bless His holy name. Bless the Lord, O my soul, and forget not all His benefits." Your Uncle Henry had a most satisfactory conversation with him on Saturday evening, in which he expressed his firm reliance upon the Lord Jesus Christ, whom he had professed, and his resignation to the divine will.

The last words he spoke were in answer to his afflicted wife. She said, putting her hand on his cheek and bending over him: "Jimma, Jimma, my dear Jimma, speak to me once more. Do you know me? Who am I?" He replied:

"My own dear Sallie." Said she, bending her face nearer still: "What do you say?" *"My own dear Sallie."* And his last act of consciousness was to turn over to her and fix his dying eyes upon her!

Between 1 and 2 P.M. your dear Uncle Jimma *ceased to breathe!* Alas, my dear son, it is too true! *He is dead!* Oh, it is like a thunderclap to us all in the family—to the whole community! Your Uncle Henry, Captain Winn, and myself laid him out—in full flesh, in the prime of manhood. Had in September last completed his twenty-ninth year. Snatched from a position of uncommon usefulness to his father's family (a second father), from the head of his own little family, and from a commanding station in society, and one of increasing influence. There was no man of his age to compare with him in this community in many respects. The blow is sudden, the affliction great; the loss seems irreparable. Sorrow clothes us all! Rapid was his disease, and terribly did it do its work.

You may be anxious to know of *what he died.* He died of *yellow fever!* He went down most imprudently some eight or nine days ago to Savannah with his widowed sister, Mrs. Stephen Harris, to get some papers out of her house. He went into her house—every room in it—*in which her husband died of yellow fever,* and went also about the streets. Was in the city four or five hours. And *this is the fearful and sad result!* It is supposed that the confined air of the infected house must have done the work. It was his kind feeling but erroneous judgment. He went, too, without the knowledge either of his wife or mother! Both had protested against his going on a previous occasion, and had prevented his doing so. There have been a number of cases similar to this. Persons have gone into the city as your uncle did, and stayed only a few hours in the day, contracted the disease, and have returned to their homes in the country and died! He is the first person your dear sister ever saw die! I will leave her to tell you her own feelings.

We came back last evening (your Uncle Henry's house being very full) and returned early this morning. When we arrived, your Uncles William and Henry had already left with the body for the Retreat. Dr. Duke recommended that it be kept as short a time as possible, as injurious effects might ensue. Decomposition is rapid in such cases. The funeral was appointed at Lodebar at 12 M., and I did not follow on, there being no one but myself to superintend the arrangements. There was a large concourse of the citizens from every part of our district, from all the retreats, and a universal expression of unfeigned sorrow. Rev. Messrs. John and Sumner Winn conducted the services in a solemn and impressive manner. The troop turned out in uniform, of which you know he was a prominent and active member. The Negroes from Laurel View and your Uncle John's place and Lodebar were present also.

My dear son, this is a sudden and great affliction to us all. May we be enabled to improve it! In order to this we should seriously consider it in all its affecting lessons and appeals! How empty and transitory is *life,* the *pur-*

suits of life, the *possessions* of life! How near are we to *God and eternity with all its amazing realities!* How *necessary*—how *preeminently important* —that we be *the children of God by faith in the Lord Jesus Christ!* Do not, I entreat you, let this renewed warning and call of God be neglected by you. Turn to God. Pray for salvation in the Blessed Redeemer's name, and do not cease until you obtain peace in believing. For what are you living? What will be your end if you are a mere man of the world when death comes? Your dear mother, your dear sister, your father—we all daily pray for your conversion. Pray for yourself, and may God in mercy hear and answer your prayers!

This afternoon we returned to Maybank, sad and weary. And this evening I have taken my pen to convey to you this sad intelligence, which I know will grieve you most deeply, as it does us. And as I cannot get another letter for your brother under my own hand ready in time for the mail in the morning, I have begged your sister to copy this, that I may direct it to him also. . . . Write us soon. Mother and Sister send much love.

From your ever affectionate father,
C. C. Jones.

Little Andrew has just come with *the jersey* which was used to convey your uncle to his last resting place! Half-past eight. You remember it was used for my dear nephew—your Cousin Charles Edward—from Savannah!

REV. C. C. JONES *to* MR. CHARLES C. JONES, JR.[g]

Arcadia, Wednesday, October 18th, 1854

My dear Son,

I wrote you last week giving you an account of the sad death of your Uncle Jimma. As he went to Savannah with his sister, Mrs. Harris, she and her kindred on her deceased husband's side have stoutly denied in the face of the clearest evidence that he died of *yellow fever*. It is a purely selfish act on their part to avert blame from themselves for being the occasion of his death by taking him to Savannah on their business, which might have been postponed for weeks. Whenever afflictions fall upon us it seems to be the time for Satan and our own depravity to bring in some disturbing cause to blunt if not paralyze its designed and happy effect. We say nothing, but adhere to the truth and mourn his early and sudden demise! Although I closed his eyes and performed the last sad offices for him, it all appears a misty and troubled vision. He died Sunday, October 8th, between one and two o'clock P.M. . . .

I preached at Dorchester last Sunday for the first time for a long, long time, and have an engagement, D.V., for Sunbury the coming Sabbath. . . . Came up here on Monday. We are breaking in corn. Turns out light, and damaged by the storm. Hope from one thing to another that through God's mercy to us we shall make provisions. We are relying much upon the *pea crop,* which will require for its maturity a late frost. The weather has been, since the close of the storm, *most delightful:* cool mornings and evenings, and almost cloudless skies day and night, and gentle airs all the day long.

I shall enclose a check to your brother in Philadelphia for two hundred dollars, which I will get him to forward to you in a check on Boston from Philadelphia. Mr. Cumming is not in Savannah, and do not know how long he may be away. Business cannot fairly open there before frost, although the yellow fever has much abated. Will send Joe the check by the mail that takes this letter to you.

I wish you to make up your accounts and let me know *precisely how much more* you will need to settle everything in Cambridge and buy your books and come home, that I may make arrangements; for funds are nearly exhausted, and it will be some time before we can get anything to market.

Your mother and sister were quite well on Monday. Your Aunt Betsy suffering from her old complaint. Rest of our relatives and neighbors well. Our people generally well. Your Uncle John has been dangerously sick in Marietta; by last accounts he was better. I remain, my dear son,

Your ever affectionate father,
C. C. Jones.

MRS. MARY JONES *to* MR. CHARLES C. JONES, JR.[g]
Maybank, *Saturday,* October 21st, 1854

It appears to be a long, long period, my very dear child, since I have sent you a line from my own pen; and the interval to my own mind appears trebly long, occupied as it has been with great sorrow and affliction.

Your dear father wrote immediately to your brother and yourself all the particulars of your Uncle James's death. Not sick over forty hours! I know it was an afflictive stroke to your warm and affectionate heart. . . . It has been my earnest prayer that your father's letters to your brother and yourself might prove not simply the messenger of sad tidings but the monitor of serious and solemn warning to you both. . . . "Be ye also ready, for in such an hour as ye think not the Son of Man cometh." Sudden and awful have been the visitations of Providence to us as a family for years past. And shall we continue to neglect the great salvation? Shall we forget God? Shall we harden our necks against reproof and thus invite for ourselves sudden destruction? . . . Few in life have ever filled with more fidelity the duties assigned in providence than your Uncle James. And few have gone to the grave so much beloved and lamented as a son, a husband, a brother, a relative, a friend, a master, a member of the church, and a citizen. Long will there be cause to mourn his absence.

Your Uncle Henry now takes charge of the business of the family. James has left no will. His wife and child are of course his heirs. It will give Henry a great deal to do, and I almost fear his health will fail under it. He has

looked and felt better this summer than he has done at all for many years.
. . . Your father hopes to preach tomorrow, and as it is Saturday night, I
must close until Monday. Good night, my child. May the Holy Sabbath
be a delight unto you!

Monday Morning. We had a delightful day yesterday. Your dear father
was enabled to preach with great feeling and power from 1 John 3:1-2. A
large congregation of Negroes. I trust some good was done. I felt that it was
good to be there myself. Sometimes I have hope that your father is improving; then again I am much discouraged. He has certainly gained flesh, but
the nervous inaction continues. Dr. Wells advised blistering the spine for
six months. For nearly *two* they have been kept just below the neck. As
soon as they dry up I apply fresh ones each side of the spine and dress with
an irritative ointment. This treatment is painful, but he thinks it beneficial.
If Providence permits, he hopes to attend the meeting of Synod at Macon
on the 27th of next month.

When, my dear son, may we look for you? My heart scarcely dares allow
itself the delightful anticipation of seeing you so soon—now nearly fourteen
months since we parted! The catalogue was received by the last mail. I see
you have changed your boarding place, and are associated with a fellow
Georgian. This is pleasant—if he is an improving companion, one of good
character and gentlemanly manners. And I feel assured that my son would
associate himself with none other.

The weather is now the most delightful that you can imagine: cool enough
for a little fire nearly all day. We have had no frost. Charming harvest if
there were much to gather, but such general destruction I have scarcely ever
known. . . . *Economy* will be a practical virtue with us all this year. I feel
thankful, my dear son, that we have thus far been enabled to afford your
brother and yourself the best advantages our country affords in obtaining
your professions without running in debt.

I have had great anxiety and distress on your Uncle John's account. He has
had an attack of typhoid pneumonia: twenty-two days in bed. By the last
letters his fever had left him, he rested well at nights, and was taking
quinine, but was so weak that the physicians forbid his being informed of
James's death. We are just sending up for the mail, and *I hope* for good
tidings. The yellow fever has visited our whole coast: Charleston, Beaufort,
Savannah, Darien, St. Marys.

Your uncle and aunt have returned to the Island, and seem very happy.
All friends at Woodville well, and desire love to you whenever I write. Also
your Uncle Henry and Aunt Abby. The sweet music has been received,
and Sister will know it all ere you come. . . . Father and Sister unite in best
love to you. We hear with *great pleasure* of the honor conferred by your
election as speaker of the assembly.

Ever, my dear boy, your own affectionate mother,

Mary Jones.

Servants all send howdies.

Your brother left a skeleton of an alligator for you. Shall it be sent on with the other things you desired? The bones are all apart, but perfect. Write and let me know.

Mr. CHARLES C. JONES, JR., *to* REV. *and* MRS. C. C. JONES[w]
Cambridge, *Friday,* October 27th, 1854

My dear Father and Mother,

Your letter, Father, of October 18th reached me yesterday, and today was followed by one from Brother containing a check for $196, the receipt of which I have just acknowledged to him. For the same, my dear parents, I am much obliged to you. So serious have been the damages sustained by the plantations in consequence of the recent storms, and so deleterious has been the influence of the awful epidemic upon the market and fiscal affairs in general, that I fear my expenses here fall more heavily than they should. I am trying to make good use of my time and opportunities, however, and hope that the sum here and now invested in the acquisition of my profession will at no distant period, with the blessing of God upon subsequent efforts, yield an interest if not large at least by no means meager. Brother, with the assistance of Mr. Powel, sold the check to a broker at a discount of two percent, and enclosed the aforementioned check, which was duly cashed at the Charles River Bank of this place.

I regret to hear that your sorrowful hearts should have been wounded by the conduct of one who has already proved the cause of much trouble in our family—one who, if dealt with according to her deserts, will be found to have forfeited all claim of relationship and regard. Certainly in all human probability, and to human eyes, she was the proximate cause of Uncle Jimma's death. It betrays thoughtlessness (to say the least) in the highest degree reprehensible thus to have insisted upon his presence in Savannah, under circumstances the most dangerous in their character, merely to attend to a little business which might readily have been postponed for weeks. And then when the positive nature of the disease from which he died admits of no doubt, when it is also certain that this was contracted in consequence of his visit to that city, to deny stubbornly that he died of yellow fever, and that his sickness was not contracted in the attention to their business, argues badly for the state of mind in which she and her husband's family now are —a state strangely at variance with that which we have a right to expect at this time, when the tender grass has not yet overgrown his new-made grave. . . . The account of his death was to me as troubled tidings which I must believe, the full import of which, however, I could not fully appreciate. Heaven grant, nevertheless, that this be not lightly pondered or speedily dismissed from my thoughts.

I presume never before has such a season of universal mourning been known in Georgia, and especially in our portion of the state. It reminds us of the weeping and lamentation in Rama when Herod slew all the children in Bethlehem and the coasts thereof from two years old and under, or of that dread night of sorrow when the Death Angel passed over and smote all the firstborn in the land of Egypt, from the firstborn of Pharaoh that sat on his throne unto the firstborn of the captive that was in the dungeon; when there was a great cry in Egypt, *for there was not a house where there was not one dead*. Many are the serious reflections suggested by such a state of things, and it becomes us solemnly to consider the purposes and designs which the Almighty has in view in these terrible dispensations.

I am happy to see that the yellow fever is rapidly disappearing from Savannah. Unprecedented have been its ravages in that city. Regret to hear of Uncle John's continued indisposition, and earnestly hope that he may speedily be restored to his accustomed health and field of labors.

For a week or two past we have been here enjoying all the glories of an Indian summer, which you know here at the North forms almost a distinct season of the year. Most of the trees, under the influence of the late frosts, are completely denuded; while others still retain their foliage either in whole or in part, exhibiting a change in color at once varied and you may say gorgeous, contrasting strangely with their former appearance and that now presented by the evergreen pines and cedars. Mount Auburn is an impressive spot, especially at this season of the year, when nature seems dying with man. The sun for the past few days has shone with a brilliancy and power that causes us fairly to forget the near approach of winter. Yet so variable is the climate here that probably before this letter shall have been read by you the east wind will be sweeping mournfully through the streets, ruffling the now smooth surface of Charles River, and we who are now enjoying the pleasant sunshine in open air be forced to seek shelter from a dripping, freezing sky.

I am now busily engaged in reviewing some of the branches of law which have formed subjects of study during my course here. This I find both pleasant and improving. In proportion as the time draws near when I hope to see you, my beloved mother and father, sister and all relatives, does my anxiety increase duly to improve the interim and return more worthy of you all.

You wish me, Father, to state precisely how much more money I will need to settle up my accounts in Cambridge, purchase necessary law books, and defray expenses home. I have estimated the same, and will state the sum at four hundred dollars. Everything in Cambridge ever since my stay here has been steadily advancing in price. Thus board which at first could be obtained at three dollars per week cannot now be had under five, and rooms which the first session were worth only two dollars or two and a half are now three dollars and over. Washing, fuel, and everything has proportionably advanced. It seems to be the determination of Cambridge and its inhabitants to support itself and them almost entirely from gains derived from students.

Law books can be more reasonably procured here than in Savannah, and there are some forty volumes which it will be necessary for me at the time of leaving Cambridge to have. Law books are, you know, the most expensive of all professional works, the uniform price per volume ranging from three to six dollars. I wish also before returning home to get some clothes, and on my way to Georgia shall spend a short time with Brother in Philadelphia. I will be sorry, my dear parents, to have you believe that I have been extravagant. My greatest passion is for books, and somehow or other a bookstore has such an attraction that I am tempted to visit it perhaps rather too often, my purse suffering meanwhile. I hope that it will not put you to inconvenience to send me this, as I shall not need it before the *15th* of *December*. Please let me know, Father, if you will be able to let me have it by that time, as I shall make my arrangements accordingly.

The weekly Bible classes at Dr. Albro's, which I regularly attend, have of late been unusually interesting. We are now studying the latter part of John, with reference to the Crucifixion of our Saviour, than which, you know, no portion of the sacred Scriptures can be more solemn, instructive, or suggestive.

As the hour of midnight approaches, and tomorrow will be the day of holy rest, I will bid you, my dear father, mother, and sister, a good night, hoping that God will ever preserve you and all our family in safety and health.

From your ever affectionate son,
Charles C. Jones, Jr.

Howdy for the servants.

MRS. MARY JONES *to* MR. CHARLES C. JONES, JR.^g

Maybank, *Saturday,* October 28th, 1854

This, my very dear son, has been your *twenty-third* birthday, and I cannot resign myself to the repose of the night without telling you that amidst its passing hours my heart has been going forth to you in thoughts of tenderest affection, best wishes, and poor but I trust fervent supplications to my Father in Heaven that He would bless our firstborn with saving love and mercy. . . . When I think of you in the past as our own affectionate, dutiful, and upright child, the review is very pleasant. Such you have ever been. As my mind stretches on to the future, anxiety increases. The period of childhood and youth, of study and preparation, is soon to cease. You are now to come forth as a man amongst men. Your character, your principles, your conduct in every respect will indicate your future position in society, your usefulness, and your happiness. *Would, my child, that as your mother I had been more faithful to you in example and in precept! The Lord forgive all my neglect and failures in duty!*

We received by the last mail your affectionate letter. I knew it would grieve you as it has done us to be informed of your uncle's death. How sudden! How awful! Although I saw his manly, noble form cold in death and helped to shroud him for the grave, it seems impossible! I long to go and weep beside his grave. . . . I feel thankful to say that your Uncle John is better; but he has been extremely ill, and fears he will not be able to preach this winter. . . . I asked Mrs. King to let Belle and the three little boys spend the day with us, as it was your birthday. They came early, and begged that I would say for each of them that they sent love and wished you many happy returns. They are good children, and we feel a special interest in them now they are fatherless. . . . Willie King is expected on a visit home; returns in company with Mr. Buttolph, our minister. . . . The fever in Savannah somewhat abated, but dying still from three to five a day. The city in a most desolate state from the epidemic and the storm. Many, many houses unroofed up to this time. Your aunt and cousin will not probably go down before December. When may we look for you, my dear son?

Father is shaving and preparing for bed, so I must close. He said just now: "I really believe I have improved some." He and Sister unite in best love to you. Friends at the Point and Woodville desire the same. And all the servants send howdies. May the best of blessings ever rest upon you, my dear son!

Your ever affectionate mother,
Mary Jones.

P.S. Read with interest the address of Professor Peirce. And *thanks* for the other pamphlets.

MR. CHARLES C. JONES, JR., *to* MRS. MARY JONES[t]

Cambridge, *Saturday,* November 4th, 1854

My dear Mother,

The mail favored me a day or two since with a precious letter from your own pen, and you well know how highly an attached son prizes such a memento of affection from a beloved parent. This regular receipt of a letter from either Father or yourself does indeed to me, away from the home circle, form the pleasantest epoch of the week, and to its arrival I ever look forward with zealous anticipation. Still, hearing from you is not equal to positive conversation; seeing these lines, traced although they be by your hand, is not equivalent to beholding the form that dictated them; and my thoughts are ever running beyond the present and resting upon that bright expectation, for many days ardently cherished, in a few short weeks of seeing you all face to face, when we may all gather again around the home hearthstone— around the family altar from whose holy influence I have been in person for more than a year a wanderer. Never before have I looked forward with such pleasure to any future event as I now do to the hour when I shall once again be united to those I love best. It would be impossible to delineate the delightful visions which are ever stealing over me of the thousand enjoyments in anticipation.

The past week, whose hours are now almost numbered, has been one of much study. I have devoted myself to law alone, daily, for eleven hours on an average, and am employed in reviewing my course, thus locating more particularly the knowledge which I have been endeavoring here to obtain. So extensive is the range of law, so varied its applications to meet every emergency, every want of man, as well as to afford a remedy for every wrong done, so intricate many of its branches, that it is one of the most difficult matters in the world to preserve what knowledge you have obtained in a legal and orderly manner. Unless the chambers of the brain are thus occasionally arranged and the furniture properly disposed, the head becomes a thesaurus of notions and opinions, dicta and rules, without system, and consequently (in their confused state) almost wholly unfit for immediate use and application. . . . I have a little plan on foot in regard to my legal studies here, which I have not as yet consummated, and of which I shall not now speak. Perhaps I shall be able to surprise you and Father a little—and perchance agreeably—in a week or two.

The skies during the week have been dark and dripping—at times quite warm, but with a decided tendency for the past forty-eight hours to a cool change. Upon rising this morning we found the air filled with eddying flakes of snow—the first of the season. You have no idea what an exhilarating influence is exerted by the first snowstorm, slight although it be. This, however, soon vanishes when the fields have for weeks been concealed from view, when the continued glare becomes painful to the eye, when even dead nature seems longing for life enough to break the icy chain and throw aside this dreary mantle. Then the stern realities of winter, completely divested as they are of all the poetic novelties which first accompanied them, become terrible and tiresome. The wind has now shifted, and a bright full moon with her attendant starry train is beaming beautifully upon a frozen earth. John Sale and I are seated near the stove enjoying its pleasant heat.

I believe I have never described my roommate minutely to you. He is six feet three inches high, straight as an arrow, handsome, and a good student. His heart fills his whole breast. He is one of the kindest and most amiable gentlemen I have ever met. We became mutual friends soon after our meeting in Cambridge, and the warmest attachment, ripening every day, has grown up between us. You know, there are some persons toward whom you feel instinctively drawn almost upon first acquaintance. Such are, however, very rare. . . . I know it will be recommending John Sale highly in your estimation when I say that he has always a due regard to the wishes of his parents, entertaining for them the warmest affection, and that although not a member of the church, he is a regular reader of the Bible and not unmindful of his private devotions. In this we both agree. Besides, he is a Georgian, and here there is magic in that name—a magnetic influence which unites us "to the manner born" in a common bond of brotherhood. We expect this intimacy here formed to be coextensive with the remainder of our days. John expects to settle in Augusta.

I regret, my dear mother and father, that there are no topics of interest in my possession with which to entertain you. It is law, law; and when I turn from my book to write, I feel almost as the mariner who sails without his chart, although the needle is ever pointing homeward. . . . With warmest love, my beloved parents, to you both, Sister, and all relatives, I remain

Your ever affectionate son,

Charles C. Jones, Jr.

I do not think that I will wish the alligator sent until my return. Howdy for all the servants.

IV

Arcadia, *Wednesday,* November 8th, 1854

My dear Son,

The South Carolina Railroad and Mr. Secretary Campbell have got into a dispute about carrying the mails, and the railroad has discontinued since the 1st. Consequently we are some six or eight mails behindhand, and in this way we account for our not receiving letters from yourself and your brother last week.

I was anxious to hear from you, to send on what additional money you might need before going up the country. Our presbytery meets at Gravel Hill on the 16th. We shall, D.V., all come up here and attend its sessions and religious services every day and return home in the evenings. This will be our best arrangement. The week after, God willing, your mother, sister, and self go up to Macon to attend our synod, which meets on the 23rd. When it closes, our expectation is to visit Burke for a few days. So we may be absent near three weeks in all. The trip will be pleasant and refreshing to us after the summer's confinement. My hope is that your dear mother and sister will enjoy it. I feel anxious to meet my brethren once more.

We are at present, through God's mercy, all well. All well this morning when I left. Mrs. King moves up to South Hampton tomorrow. Your aunt and cousin stay with us until next Wednesday, and then go up to South Hampton, and from thence from the 23rd to the 26th to Savannah. We have had no frost yet, but the yellow fever has disappeared, and the citizens are invited to return. The county is generally healthy.

Our harvests have been greatly cut off by the storm—the cotton crop *two-thirds,* rice more than that. Provisions abundant at Montevideo; *here* quite short; the same at *Maybank.* Our neighbors have all shared in the affliction.

The box of specimens from Kentucky came on Monday, and yesterday your mother and sister took them out and washed them off and were much pleased with them. Some are beautiful. They will get you to go over them when you return, God willing. Mother thought at first it was the box with her dresses, etc., which Joe was to send from Philadelphia; but she was disappointed—but agreeably so.

Be sure and bring your diploma from the law school. We are looking forward with fond anticipations to your return, and are counting the weeks. Write us precisely your movements. And the Lord grant us the desires of our hearts! You will of course pass through Philadelphia and spend some days with your brother. You might ship your books and baggage direct from Boston to Savannah if you like.

In relation to your settlement in life, my dear son, I wish you to exercise your preference and discretion. Do not confine yourself to the South if any other part of the Union is more agreeable to you. And I wish to make the impression upon you with the point of a diamond *that you never can succeed and attain to any eminence in your profession if you have anything at all to do with the management of Negro property. No man in any profession* within my knowledge ever has—and for the obvious reason that no man can succeed in either profession who follows *two*. I am certain my necessary and unavoidable connection with the management of Negroes and the conduct of planting has been a most serious drawback to me in a professional point of view; and nothing but the most industrious habits and indomitable perseverance ever kept me up at all; and I have rid myself of the drawback several times in accepting calls out of this county. Planting requires such a consumption of time, and the property you manage makes such a draft upon your attention, etc., etc., that no student and professional man can prosper under it all. I wish you to profit by my experience, if nobody's else, and make up your mind to *live by your profession and to be totus in illis.* We shall endeavor to render you every assistance in our power. Nor shall your patrimony—whatever we have to give you, in the kind providence of God—be any way endamaged by your having nothing to do with any other pursuit than that of your profession. We trust and believe that with perseverance and uprightness and proper attention, by God's favor, you will succeed. I express the sentiments and wishes also of your dear mother. May God ever be your guide and your portion!

Please remember me to Dr. Albro. Write soon. The people are much pleased to hear that you are expected home in a few weeks.

Your ever affectionate father,
C. C. Jones.

Rev. C. C. Jones *to* Mr. Charles C. Jones, Jr.ᵍ

Maybank, *Tuesday,* November 14th, 1854

My dear Son,

Your letter of October 27th was received by the mail yesterday—a long passage, owing to the interruption of the mails.

I have enclosed checks to Mr. M. Cumming, Savannah, and requested him to forward you a check on Boston, if possible, for four hundred dollars, the amount which you say you will need to get books and clothing and bring you home. Your expenses have been greater than I anticipated, but presume you have been economical and put your funds to good use. Have you kept an account of your expenses?

You must write us *definitely* what time you will get your diploma and leave

Cambridge, and about what time you may be expected home. Your Aunt Susan goes to Savannah between the 20th and 25th of this month, and will be housekeeping when you arrive, God willing, in Savannah. Her house is in *Jones Street*. Your books you had better take to her house. She expects you to stay with her. She and your cousin go over to your uncle's this afternoon, and from thence to South Hampton on Thursday.

Your mother has just received her things from Philadelphia, and is very busy preparing to go up to Macon with me next week. Your sister also, Providence permitting. Frost and ice last night for the first time. We feel the sudden change. Cold is a depressing agent with me, and the *inaction* is increased by it.

Our friends, relatives, and people are all well at present, so far as I know. Your Uncle John is improving fast, as we learn by a letter from Marietta yesterday, and comes down the country in a short time.

I wish you to purchase *Romaine on Faith:* the Life, Walk, and Triumph of Faith, *Carter's Edition,* New York. Two copies: one *for yourself,* a present from *your father;* and the other *present to Dr. Albro with my fraternal regards.* Tell him it is a humble volume, but one which he will read with improvement and delight if he has never read it. I do not remember to have been more benefited by any book I have read. I recommend it to your serious perusal. I have given a copy to your dear mother, sister, and brother, each, and one to your Aunt Susan. Your brother commenced reading his before he left us.

You must be sure and stay a few days with your brother. . . . While in Philadelphia, if you think of it, call at Smith & English's and stir them up about my books. Aunt Susan, Cousin Laura, Mother, and Sister unite in much love to you. All the people well. Cannot write more now: do not feel very bright. May God bless and keep you, my dear son, through this present life and unto life eternal!

Your ever affectionate father,
C. C. Jones.

Rev. C. C. Jones *to* Mr. Charles C. Jones, Jr.^g

Macon, *Tuesday,* November 28th, 1854

My dear Son,

We left home on the 21st in the carriage, came through to the twenty-mile station on the Central Road, and took the cars on the 22nd and arrived here the same evening. We are staying with Mr. Thomas C. Nisbet, who you know married Miss Mary Cumming. They have received and entertained us with all the confidence and affection of relatives.

Your dear mother and sister have enjoyed the visit to Macon very much; and our meeting of Synod, which closed last evening, has been a delightful one. It was pleasant to meet with my brethren once more after some five years' absence. Today Mother returns her calls, and tomorrow, God willing, we go on to Perry, Houston County, to spend a few days with Cousin Charles West. He was much affected at meeting us here. Saturday we return here, and leave for home on Monday.

Your Uncle John arrived here on Saturday afternoon, stayed over Sunday, and left Monday for Savannah. He is improving fast, and I think before long he will be able to resume his pulpit duties. His last son, Joseph Henry, is a remarkably fine infant. . . . I think we wrote you that your Uncle Henry *lost his little daughter and only child on Saturday last (week) of croup.* A sad affliction. Your mother, sister, and I were with them in their distress. The little thing suffered a great deal, but finally died tranquilly. Thus are our afflictions continued. . . . Have you received your draft from Mr. Cumming? Time permits me to write no more at present. Mother and Sister send much love. Every blessing attend you, my dear son!

Your ever affectionate father,
C. C. Jones.

Mrs. Mary Jones *to* Mr. Charles C. Jones, Jr.⁸

Arcadia, *Thursday,* December 7th, 1854*

My dear Son,

After a delightful visit of two weeks to our friends in Macon and Perry, we reached our home on last Tuesday at half-past two o'clock—a distance of thirty-six and a half miles from the twenty-mile station, where Gilbert met us the day previous. Your dear father was much benefited by the change and the cheerful society of his friends and Christian brethren; but he has contracted a violent cold, and is now scarcely able to speak. I hope, however, it is passing off. I am plying him with some delicious syrup of our own boiling.

Yesterday Jimmie the mule was hitched on to the pole of the sugar mill, Robin and Gilbert acting as tenders, Charles and Lucy engineers at the furnace and boilers, *myself* superintendent general, Father and Sister tasters and lookers-on. And I am happy to say the result of the experiment is a perfect and successful demonstration of the art of syrup-boiling. More beautiful I never saw. I always thought it so much in the line of *preserve-making* as to come fairly into the ladies' department of cookery. The only regret is that we had so little cane; another year we hope to have enough planted to secure an abundant supply for the people.

The thought, my dear child, that you are to be so soon with us seems more than I dare anticipate. May the Lord bless and bring you safely to us, and fill our hearts with love and gratitude for all His goodness and mercy towards us as a family! What are we that He should be mindful of us? I am very glad that you have acknowledged your aunt and cousin's letter and accepted their very kind invitation, made as I know it is with the most generous and affectionate feelings. I know of no situation where you would be more happily located; and I rejoice in your being with her, and feel assured that you will do everything in your power to promote their comfort and happiness.

Our house at Montevideo is so much out of repair that we have concluded to move *here* (Arcadia) until it can be rendered comfortable, and shall do so in a week or two. You will have fine sport with the wild ducks; Stepney has kept us supplied with the finest I ever saw.

Audley has gone on to Philadelphia, and I hope you may return together. Write us exactly when to look for you. . . . Remember us to all friends in Philadelphia. . . . Our united love to your dear brother and yourself. . . . The servants all send howdies to you both.

Ever, my dear son, your affectionate mother,
Mary Jones.

Rev. C. C. Jones *to* Mrs. Susan M. Cumming[t]

Arcadia, *Thursday,* December 7th, 1854

My dear Sister,

We know not what shall be on the morrow—first the storm, then the flood, and now fire. I deeply regret to inform you that Lambert cotton house was burnt down this morning. It took fire from the skirt of Big Sarey's frock. She went out to warm her fingers at the fire some distance from the cotton house; on her return the fire was communicated to cotton which she was moting. I heard of the calamity immediately after breakfast. On reaching Lambert I found Mr. Fleming and Captain Winn on the ground with all the hands and hands from Mr. Fleming's and Judge Fleming's plantations hard at work extinguishing the fire. The roof and all the sides of the house were burnt clean away and left a huge pile of charred seed cotton. We took off the outer burnt coating and bore away the good cotton. I am happy to say that you will probably save one-half if not more of the crop in the house, which amounted to forty bags and over. I hope you will save from twenty to twenty-five bags. Five or six packed were under the ginhouse shed and were not injured at all. Judge Fleming's carpenters, Sharper and William —also Mr. Fleming's driver, Prime—rendered very essential service, and I requested Mr. Fleming to make some suitable return to them for it. Big Sarey made no concealment, and her statement is confirmed by Charlotte and Susan, who were in the house with her. The Negroes all worked with good will and seemed to regret the occurrence. Mr. Fleming, I presume, will write you particularly. The cotton will require close handling, and he will be thrown back considerably in getting out the crop.

You have met with a great loss. Cotton is low, and you must *practice economy to keep out of debt.* If you feel like making any alteration in your arrangements for keeping house in Savannah the present year, remember that our house and home are always open to yourself and my dear niece. I hope we may recognize the hand of God in this event and have grace given us to profit by it.

All well saving myself. I returned from our most pleasant visit to Macon and Perry with a very bad cold. Brother and Sister and all friends well. We are at present at Arcadia. Heard from Charles and Joe this week; both in good health, through a kind Providence. Charles expects to leave Cambridge, God willing, from the 12th to 15th of this month, and may be in Savannah about Christmas. My dear wife and daughter unite with me in much love to yourself and Laura and sympathy in your great loss. I am, my dear sister,

Your ever affectionate brother,
C. C. Jones.

My dear daughter has acted as my amanuensis.

Mrs. Susan M. Cumming *to* Rev. C. C. Jones[t]

Savannah, *Saturday,* December 9th, 1854

My dear Brother,

Your most affectionate sympathizing letter through dear Mary confirmed the intelligence received that morning from Mr. Nevitt of the burning of the Lambert cotton house. Your statement is far better than I could have expected, as I heard the loss of house and cotton was entire. And another most agreeable feature in the case is that it was *not design*. And I feel particularly grateful for the kind and efficient aid afforded by all our friends, both white and colored, and heartily concur with you in desiring that some suitable return be made them. We ask our Heavenly Father to dispose of us and ours as seemeth Him good; and if He lay His hand upon anything, shall we not say: "Even so, Father"? I do pray to have that spirit. May there be no self-delusion!

Again we return you and Sister M. our heartfelt thanks for your reiterated offers of kindness to us in the event of our wishing to make any alteration in our arrangements. Your house has always afforded us a pleasant, happy home, and the time passed with you of great enjoyment. I think that it will not be necessary to make any change in our plans at present, and that we will remain here. We shall endeavor to be prudent in the management of the finances and not involve ourselves unnecessarily. We hope to go to housekeeping in the course of a week or two—so soon as we can get gas admitted, which is promised next week. It was impossible to have it done earlier.

We had a most affectionate letter from Charles Colcock in which he says: "I will cheerfully and gladly accept your invitation, and hope that I may in all things prove an obliged, obliging, and serviceable nephew to you."

I heard through Mary Nisbet of your pleasant visit to her, which she says she enjoyed so much, and regretted that her sickness should have deprived her of any part of it. I am truly sorry to hear you took cold. Hope it may be temporary; and so soon as we get settled shall expect you, Sister Mary, and Mary and Charlie. . . . Cousin Charles West's family are all well. The little stranger-lady who arrived on last Sunday morning bears the name of Laura Maxwell, and by a striking coincidence Laura was the first lady to see her.

. . . Our affectionate love to Sister Mary and Mary, and a great share for yourself. And believe me, my dear brother,

Your affectionate sister,
S. M. Cumming.

Miss Laura E. Maxwell *to* Rev. C. C. Jones[t]

Savannah, *Saturday,* December 9th, 1854

My heart is filled with gratitude to you, my ever kind uncle and aunt, for your continued and renewed kindness to Mother and my unworthy self. All we claim in this life, as you once so beautifully remarked, is only *lent* us, and our Heavenly Father has a perfect right to take it when He sees best. . . . Rejoice greatly that no precious lives were lost at the fire! Dear Aunt Mary and yourself have a realizing sense of that word *fire.* How small our loss when compared with yours!

Am too sorry you took cold returning from Macon. . . . Mary Nisbet seems to have enjoyed your visit *exceedingly.*

Tell Mary we have such a nice little room for her, and a large one for Charlie, and a fine light for him to study by. I am proud of my cousins, and hope they will reach the topmost round of the ladder: not only great but good. I hope dear Aunt Mary and yourself will come and see us so soon as we are fixed. I have missed you so much already, and long to see you all. I think I will be able to have a little garden at Mother's house, and in my imagination it is filled with flourishing plants. Wallace and Montgomery unite with me in much love to your dear selves and Mary.

Your ever affectionate niece,
Laura E. Maxwell.

Miss Mary Sharpe Jones *to* Miss Laura E. Maxwell[t]

Maybank, *Monday,* December 25th, 1854

Dear Cousin Laura,

It is now time, as Father would say, that "all honest folks had gone to bed"; but as this is a season when the young ones are permitted to "sit up" a little longer than usual, I suppose that I may be excused if I am not found one of the aforesaid class tonight, for I feel that I cannot retire without spending a short time with your dear self.

This morning before six my slumbers were disturbed by Dunwody's "Merry Christmas! Merry Christmas, Cousin Mary! I've caught you!" I really enjoyed seeing his delight, for I well remember the great pleasure I used to feel in being the first to announce this season of festivity. I hope that this has been a "merry" Christmas to my dear aunt and yourself; or if I may not wish you a *merry* Christmas, I can at least a *very happy* one. We have passed the day pleasantly; Uncle and Aunty dined with us; also Dr. Duke.

I was so nicely caught this morning that I must really tell you of it. This morning when I met Aunty in Mother's room, she wished me a Merry Christmas and hoped that the next would find me married. I replied: "I hope so too!" And much to my confusion Father answered from behind the screen: "You *do,* do you? Tired of the old folks, are you?" "Oh!" said I (for I had nothing else to say), "Father, I really did not know that you were behind the screen!" Aunty seemed to be greatly amused. . . .

As you may have imagined, Brother Charlie's unexpected arrival surprised us very much. Mother and myself were on our way to the Sand Hills to see Aunt Marion and Aunt Gus, but concluded to wait at Montevideo until the stage came, in order that we might get our letters and possibly learn the exact time of his arrival. Judge then our surprise and delight when, as we turned the corner at the Boro, I discovered C. C. J., Jr., upon a trunk! Our direction was immediately changed, and we went to South Hampton—of course much to the astonishment of Aunt Julia, who received us with all her accustomed cordiality. Brother Charlie had so recently parted from Willie that we thought it would gratify her to learn of him through one who had just seen him. We had a delightful visit and remained until Wednesday. The children were greatly pleased to see Brother Charlie and were unwilling to have him leave.

I think with you that there is some resemblance between Mr. Buttolph and Mr. Sale, though I think the latter handsomer. By the way, Dame Report says that you are to *be* Mrs. B. one of these days! And while this topic is under consideration, I will just give you a leaf from the dame's recent publication, *Facts Relative to Matrimony.* Laura Jones's engagement with Mr. Bowman is broken off. *They say* because *she* could not be married immediately, *he* would not wait. I do really think that any young minister who acts in this way and breaks engagements ought to be disciplined in some way, for I think that in many cases there must be something wrong in the gentleman! (I do not mean to confine this remark to clergymen alone.) Young Dr. Way is to be married on Wednesday evening to Miss Martin, a very pretty girl. Miss Amanda Baker is said to be engaged to Mr. Peter Fleming, and will ere long be married. I cannot vouch for the truth of this last statement, but I believe the others are really true.

Uncle Henry received a letter from Aunt Eliza last week, and she mentions that she does not expect to come down before February.

You cannot think how much pleasure our trip to Macon and Perry afforded us. Cousin Mary is as lively, attractive, and affectionate as ever. Mr. Nisbet treated us with great kindness and hospitality. The children, Eliza and Hattie, are very interesting and good. Cousin Mary manages them admirably. Eliza is one of the most winning and gentle children I have ever seen. She is very timid. Hattie is a mischievous little beauty. She persisted one morning in using her father's shaving brush as a hearth broom. Cousin Mary finally took it from her, saying: "I cannot allow you to do so." Eliza with much emphasis said: "*That's right,* Ma!" (She usually calls her mother

"Miss Mary.") Cousin Maria Gilbert is a fine housekeeper, and moves about her cottage quite in matron style—and actually had the impudence to commiserate my condition! Of course she is an advocate for matrimony.

I must now bid you good night, my dear cousin, for I feel that it is time for me to be enjoying myself in another land. So good night!

December 27th. My dear cousin, I had no opportunity of sending this to the mail yesterday, and I am afraid that when you receive it you will be tempted to regard its contents as rather stale.

Audley came down this evening and reports all well at South Hampton. Mr. Buttolph dined with them on Christmas. In the evening they had a Christmas tree for the children; I suppose that someone of the family will write you a description of it. . . . This Christmas has passed off very quietly down here; it seems to me that persons do not make as much noise at this season as they formerly did. I in honor of the occasion made some cheesecakes. If you had been only a little nearer I might have sent you one in order that you might judge of their excellency.

You say that you are already almost tired of city life. When you feel wholly and entirely tired, you must return and visit your "woodsy" cousin, who will, I can assure you, be most happy to have you.

Brother Charlie goes out gunning in his cave costume: coat of bright scarlet flannel trimmed with black velvet, pantaloons of green. Altogether it is quite a fanciful affair, and at a distance has quite a picturesque appearance. . . . Brother Charlie is reading aloud downstairs, and I must join the circle, so please excuse me. . . . Do write me all about your little namesake; I should like to have a description of her. Give our love to Cousin Eliza and Cousin Charles. . . . I hope that you are now comfortably located in your own house. We feel very much obliged to my dear aunt and yourself for your kind invitation to Brother Charlie. Has Sarey recovered from her fright yet? Mother, Father, and Brother Charlie unite with me in warmest love to Aunt Susan and yourself.

Your ever affectionate cousin,
Mary S. Jones.

How are your birds? Mine are very flourishing. Willie is so pleased with Belle's appearance that he cannot sing in her presence, so I am obliged to keep her out of his sight when I want him to sing. I am still in doubt whether Belle is a lady or a gentleman, for sometimes she sings a little, or rather attempts to do so.

MISS MARY E. ROBARTS *to* MRS. MARY JONES[t]

Marietta, *Friday,* January 5th, 1855

My dearest Cousin,

I have been expecting a letter from you for some time, but have concluded to wait no longer, and send you and my dear cousin our congratulations that your valuable lives have been spared to see another new year, and that its rising and setting suns may find you and yours the special objects of divine favor. After the sad providences of the past year it would seem like mockery to pay the usual compliments of the season; but if it finds us with resigned and submissive spirits and grateful hearts for remaining mercies, it is all that we can expect.

We spent the Christmas and the New Year far away from friends and kindred, and our thoughts strayed away to find a home among them, each loved face passing before our mind's eye. But I will not consume my paper by telling what I thought you were all doing; will wait to hear it from you.

The new year will be an eventful one to us, for it will bring about a very remarkable event in our family—even the marriage of my dear and only sister Louisa. And if it were not that she is about to bestow herself on a man every way worthy of her, it would cause us serious anxiety. But on this point we are at rest. I must now tell you who it is: Dr. Tennent. He has been for three years our family physician, which gave us an opportunity of becoming very well acquainted with him. He is a good physician, in fine practice, a pious man (member of our own church), a liberal supporter of the gospel, an honorable and high-minded man, a very good property (not wealthy), and permanently settled in Marietta. The only objection that could possibly be urged against him is that he has eight children. Louisa does not think this an insurmountable obstacle (though an objection), and she feels that her happiness will be increased by marrying him. She desires her best love to you and our dear cousin, and says she would like to have consulted you both, had you been acquainted so as to be able to advise her. Having gained Mother's consent and mine, she has asked no one else, as she felt that she was the best judge of what would promote her own happiness. She is about to assume great responsibilities, but has had eight years' experience in the ways of children and the care of them; and I think if anyone is fitted to discharge the duties of a stepmother kindly and judiciously, she is the one. For proof of this I would cite the faithful part she has acted to little Joe.

It is useless to say more: it is a thing that is to be. And while the doctor will gain a good wife, Mother will lose a good, dutiful daughter, I a kind sister, and the family a useful, energetic member. But these selfish considerations do not weigh a moment with me when her happiness is involved; and though your poor old cousin will be left alone like a sparrow on the housetop, yet I would not for the world say one word against it.

I know you will feel anxious to know how Mother stands it. It came like a clap of thunder in a clear day, for she never dreamed that either Louisa or myself would ever marry, nor did she desire it. Although it grieves her to part with Louisa, and she feels all the solicitude natural to a mother's heart about the step she is about to take, she has acquiesced. But when we come down, I will tell you some funny things. Poor little Joe cried all the first night, and every time he awoke he would say: "My dear mama, I cannot spare you!" But when these young widows get matrimony in their head the babies are always second. Little Joe will fall to me, and in case of my dear mother's death I would be left with quite a charge, and no one to share my cares. But I am thankful that I have a comfortable home, and will trust the care of that kind Providence who has always cared for me.

And now you will desire to know something about when the event is to be consummated. The doctor, like all young lovers, is very anxious that it should be immediately; but this we cannot assent to, as Louisa must go and see her friends in Liberty, as it will be a long time before she could go after she becomes the head of such a family. We expect to leave here about the 5th of February for Savannah, remain there ten days, then go to Liberty for a couple of months. Neither the doctor nor herself wishes a wedding, and I have thought that if she could be privately married in the low country (as she earnestly desires Cousin Charles to perform the ceremony) that it would be best. What think you of it? The weddings folks have in the present day are not worth summoning friends and kindred from a distance to attend; and yet I could not bear the idea of her being married without our beloved relative present. Please write me your views on the subject by return of mail.

Louisa sends her best love to you, and says she longs to see you, but she is so afraid of you and me that she dreads to go down the country! But you don't know how prettily I behave to her. I make a bright fire in the drawing room every evening and have it in point for her to receive her beau, while I keep the children in the parlor and read aloud for their amusement and Mother's. And yesterday I went out and purchased materials for under-garments, and the young widow is now industriously at work. . . . Dr. Tennent came over last night and brought his two daughters to see Louisa. One has been her Sabbath school scholar for several years; the other, his eldest daughter, is a lovely girl and very amiable. When they came in they went immediately up to Louisa and kissed her most affectionately. I could see that it was very gratifying to him. *I* carried on the conversation of the evening, had some cake handed, and after a pleasant evening they left. We were always very sociable with this family, and Mrs. Tennent always professed the greatest friendship for us.

For further particulars of the doctor I would refer you to John; he knows him intimately. I will write him next week. Would have done so this week, but thought he was at Mount Zion. Do you know what his plans are for the present year?

I must now beg, my dear cousin, that you will keep this secret profoundly till we meet. I will write Cousin Betsy next week and tell her of it; and do beg her not to hint it to anyone. It will be time enough to tell the rest of our relatives when we come down. It would be very painful to us to have it talked of in the county.

I suppose by this time Sam has got to Liberty and you have seen him. Mother expects him to leave about the last day of January so as to be up here by the 4th of February, which will be the day we leave. When we come out we will come to your house first, my dear cousin, if you are at Arcadia. We are obliged to bring the children with us, as we cannot leave them; but as our visit will be short, we will divide them among our friends so as not to let them be a burden long to any *one*. After I hear from you I will write you again before we leave.

Mother and Louisa desire much love to Cousin Charles and yourself, Mary, and Charles Colcock. I long to see you all, and hope a kind Providence may spare us to meet. . . . I have not heard from Cousin Susan and Laura since they have been in Savannah; was truly grieved to hear of the loss they met with by fire. . . . Farewell, my dear cousin. Believe me

Most affectionately yours,
Mary E. Robarts.

Mr. Joseph Jones *to* Rev. *and* Mrs. C. C. Jones[t]
University of Pennsylvania, Philadelphia, Pennsylvania
Tuesday, January 9th, 1855

A Happy New Year to you, my dear parents! Nothing could have given me more pleasure than to have been home and completed our little family circle upon your wedding day and this occasion, and upon your birthday, dear Father. May God spare your lives and give you health to enjoy many happy returns!

Brother must have taken you upon as great a surprise as he did us in Philadelphia. Willie King had stepped over and informed me of the arrival of his brother, and we were sitting around a large stove in Mr. Parrish's store talking about home, when who should walk in but Brother! I had not received his letter, and did not expect to see him for two weeks. I was rejoiced to see him in such good health and spirits. Law students appear to be happier and heartier fellows than medical students. The contrast between us was very striking: he looked like Shakespeare's alderman and I like an anatomical preparation. I was very much pleased with Mr. John Sale, his roommate; he appeared to be a very amiable and gentlemanly young man.

After Audley left, Willie was quite unwell for two weeks with an attack of bronchitis. I am glad, however, to say that he has entirely recovered. He has determined to return home in a week or ten days. I think that it is a wise arrangement, because he has been closely employed during the summer and winter. The drug business requires close confinement and attention, and a store of this character in a large city is of all places the most unsuitable for the recovery of lost strength. Willie is very attentive to his business and anxious to improve his time to the best advantage, and I have no doubt that if he continues to pursue his studies with his accustomed diligence he will rise to eminence in his profession. Since his determination to return home he has attended several lectures at the university with me every day. They are interesting and at the same time instructive to him, for every druggist should know as much as possible about the practice of medicine.

During the last three weeks I have been busily occupied in preparing a paper upon my investigations of last summer. They embrace fifty pages of closely written foolscap and two large plates containing over forty figures. I hoped to have had them ready to read before the Academy of Natural Sciences last month. Although I improved every leisure moment between lectures and at night, it was impossible to accomplish this. I showed the paper to Dr. Jackson, who appeared very much pleased and offered to pay the expenses himself of their publication. I told him that I could not think of trespassing so far upon his kindness. He then presented it to Dr. Isaac Hays, the editor of *The American Journal of the Medical Sciences*. He will publish the investigations in the next number of his journal, which will come out the first of next April. I feel under many obligations to Dr. Jackson for his kindness. There are very few men that would have made so liberal an offer, for the expenses of publication with the plates would have amounted to sixty or seventy dollars. This morning I corrected the proof sheet of the paper upon endosmose, and it will be printed tomorrow. The Academy of Natural Sciences are poor, and I had to bear the expenses of the publishing and the lithographing of a handsome plate.

I had intended writing you a much longer letter, my dear parents, but I was interrupted yesterday by a severe toothache, which is beginning to return with some violence, and I must close. Willie King sends his kind regards. With much love to you, Brother, and Sister, I remain

Your affectionate son,
Joseph Jones.

Mrs. Mary Jones *to* Mrs. Susan M. Cumming[t]
Arcadia, *Thursday,* January 11th, 1855

A Happy New Year to you, my dear sister and niece! May the blessing of our Father in Heaven, which maketh rich and addeth no sorrow, abide with you both!

I have been waiting a long, long time for a leisure moment to sit down and write, but it is all in vain: I am evidently one of the working class. On last Monday we packed up, and moved here on Tuesday. Yesterday and today I have been as busy as I well could be, cleaning up this long-deserted mansion. Terrible would be the shock if the shade of Old Isaac could gaze upon the darkened walls and stained floors!

The evening before we left Maybank Sister Betsy and Brother William took tea with us. Also Mr. William Stevens, who spent the night. Brother William has been very unwell with that same pain and affection which he had all summer; sometimes he wakes up with cramp in the stomach, which causes great suffering and requires immediate relief. Sister Betsy is in her usual health, and has been very busy doing up her old dresses. You will be quite surprised to see how smart and fashionable the old lady is with her flowing bishops!

We saw Julia and Mary at church on Sabbath with all the family but Johnnie; he was a little unwell with cold. . . . Audley appears to have enjoyed and improved his trip North. Willie is in bad health; has been confined to his chamber, and now has blisters on his chest.

We have not heard from our boy Joe for several weeks; I presume he thinks his brother's presence relieves him of several letters.

Charles took us quite by surprise. I desire to feel most grateful to God for his return to us, and in such health of body. He begins to feel a little anxious to get to his studies, and talks of going sometime next week to Savannah. And here, my dear sister and Laura, I would take the opportunity of telling you how gratefully I appreciate your kindness to our child in inviting him to become a member of your household. And I bless God for giving him a home with those who love him, and where only the best influences will be exerted upon his character. I trust that he will prove an agreeable inmate of your family. In going to Savannah he seems to realize the fact that he will be a stranger in the midst of strangers so far as his business relations extend. We can only commend him to the favor of God and pray that he may be made useful in his day and generation.

Mr. Jones asked that I would leave a space for him in my letter, so I will close, with our united love to dear Laura and yourself. Remember us to Mr. and Mrs. Cumming, Major and Mrs. Porter, Captain and Mrs. Gilmer. I hope you find yourselves comfortably located in your new abode. Believe me, as ever,

Your affectionate sister,
Mary Jones.

Rev. C. C. Jones *to* Mrs. Susan M. Cumming[t]

Arcadia, *Thursday,* January 11th, 1855

My dear Sister,

I saw Mr. Allen yesterday and engaged him for you to attend to your business at White Oak for the present year. It is the best arrangement that can be made; I would attend to it for you, but really have not the physical power. Mr. Allen has, I think, no more to do this than the last year. I saw all the people at White Oak. Mary has another boy. All well.

Tell Mr. Montgomery Cumming that I hope he will do his best to sell our cotton speedily, as we have to pay people what we owe.

You may possibly have our dear daughter to visit you when Charles goes down next week. Aunt is coming in February, and if Mary Sharpe goes to see you this winter, she had better go before Aunty comes. Hope our children will always be affectionate and dutiful to you; we have tried to bring them up to be so. As my good wife has given you all the news, I will add no more; but with much love to Laura I subscribe myself

Your ever affectionate brother,

C. C. Jones.

Mrs. Susan M. Cumming *to* Mrs. Mary Jones[t]

Savannah, *Wednesday,* January 17th, 1855

My dear Sister,

Sincerely do I thank you for all your kind wishes to me and mine on this opening year. May they all be realized by you and yours a thousandfold! . . . Since I came here I have often felt sad that I could not go as *usual* and see all of your dear faces and exchange our cordial greetings and enjoy the pleasant intercourse we have so long enjoyed. The older people grow the more the heart yearns and turns to their own kindred.

I am sorry to hear that Brother William has been so much more unwell and suffering from that cramp. I wish he and Sister would come here; a trip would do them good. We have written to ask them to do so.

We had no reason to expect Mary and Charles Colcock on any particular day, but yesterday I expected them certainly. But Henry came in after tea and told us Charles had been sick. I hope it was only temporary, and shall expect Mary and himself certainly, Providence permitting, on Friday, as Henry told us that was the day appointed. And you and Brother must not remain long after them. Let Mary come to stay a long time with us. We want to have her. Aunt is to be down in about two weeks, and Mary can see them all here. They will be in wedding haste. Are you not surprised?

We shall be too glad when Charles comes. The first night we came here Laura had frightful dreams and said she could not sleep. I read the 127th Psalm to her, and told her to take that for her meditation. Charles will be a great comfort to us. You need not thank us; it is quite a selfish feeling to wish to have so agreeable an inmate, and one of our own family. We will do all we can to make his home pleasant to him, and I hope he will make many friends here who will do him good and not evil all the days of his life. He has had faithful and judicious parents to warn and watch over him, and I think they will continue to see their reward.

We have been at home nearly two weeks, and are now fairly at housekeeping, though it all seems to me entirely new—though I have seen a great many of my old acquaintances. Mr. Palmer preached on Sabbath: everyone much pleased. The people are greatly disappointed at Cousin John's resignation. I hope Jane will be able to live on the Sand Hills; I do not think she was satisfied here. Laura unites with me in love to you, Brother, Mary, and Charles. Your friends here all inquire after you and Brother. Believe me

Your affectionate sister,

S. M. Cumming.

Mrs. Susan M. Cumming *to* Rev. C. C. Jones[t]

Savannah, *Wednesday,* January 17th, 1855

My dear Brother,

Thank you kindly for engaging Mr. Allen for another year to attend to our concerns.

I have not seen Monty to deliver your message about the cotton, but hope he will be able to sell soon for us all. Monty recommends most strongly that we purchase seed in Carolina to plant our crop. He says Mr. Gibbons purchases every year and plants every third now with Carolina seed; that the fiber is longer and stronger than ours grown on the same kind of land and brings a far better price; that anyone would be struck with the difference of the cotton.

I know and feel assured that you would do more for us, but thank you, and shall always feel grateful for all you have done and all you continue to do. I am truly glad you are going to send your children to us. Will try and take the best care of them we can.

Your ever affectionate sister,
S. M. Cumming.

Mr. Joseph Jones *to* Rev. C. C. Jones[t]

Philadelphia, *Wednesday,* January 17th, 1855

My dear Father,

Your valued letter of the 11th was last evening received, and I am sorry that my neglect should have caused any anxiety and led you to think that my not writing was the result of carelessness and inattention. After Brother left Philadelphia every leisure moment between and after lectures has been employed in preparing the investigations of last summer, and I was unconscious that so long a time had elapsed. They are now finished, and I will make it a point to write every week.

My duties this winter have been very numerous and confining, and I have been compelled to pay a corresponding degree of attention to my diet and exercise. I have given up the use of tea and coffee, and take regular exercise at the gymnasium. . . . Last Saturday evening I called upon your old friends Mr. and Mrs. Newkirk—the first social visit that I have paid for a month. They asked to be remembered to Mother and yourself in the warmest terms of friendship. Mr. Newkirk did not exhibit his usual vivacity, but appeared low-spirited. I have heard several reports that his pecuniary affairs are in an embarrassed condition. He is a man of great energy of character, and engages in many enterprises. Such men always suffer when there is a sudden tightness in the money market, because their extended operations require the investment of all their capital, and they have nothing to fall back upon.

Last Sabbath was the anniversary of the Sunday school of the Central Church. Several excellent addresses were delivered. The infant school, composed of a hundred and fifty little children from three to five years of age, sang a long hymn, which added great interest to the exercises. I would rather listen to such music than to that of the best organ and choir in the world.

I was very much surprised to hear the news from Marietta, and am glad that Cousin Louisa Robarts has found one so worthy of her affections. I hope that he may prove a useful and dutiful son to Aunty, and relieve her of much care and anxiety in her old age.

It was also a matter of surprise that Uncle John would lend a favorable ear to the call from the Sand Hills church. Such a situation appears favorable for vegetation and not for the development and maintenance of pride and commanding influence.

I was very sorry to learn from a former letter that the crops at the different places had fallen so short, and also that the sale of cotton was so slow and dull in Savannah. My expenses this winter have been necessarily heavy. My tuition bills to Dr. Leidy and the university amount to nearly two hundred and fifty dollars. Board, lights, washing, and fuel cost seven dollars per week. This is as cheap as can be obtained in any respectable house. Not being able, on account of the yellow fever, to bring on my books, I have bought about twenty volumes of standard works by authors different from those at home. The conduction of my experiments and the publication of my investigations have also been expensive. I will therefore have to ask you for the sum which Brother mentioned: two hundred and fifty dollars. I am at present short of funds, and would be very much obliged if you could send as soon as convenient thirty or forty dollars.

If Providence permits, I hope to leave Philadelphia about the middle of March. With best love to yourself, Mother, Sister, and Brother, I remain

Your affectionate son,
Joseph Jones.

Miss Mary E. Robarts *to* Mrs. Mary Jones[t]

Marietta, *Thursday,* January 18th, 1855

My dearest Cousin,

I received your kind and prompt reply to my last letter on Monday, and would have answered it the same day, but had company. Next day I had a sick headache, and this is the reason that you will have to wait till Monday for my reply. Your busy day at Maybank, the early tea, Cousin Betsy and Cousin William—oh, how vividly they carried me back to the past and made me wish almost to get over the intervening weeks and be with you at once! That little scene in the piazza—how it made us all laugh! I thought I could almost see the different countenances and hear the exclamations.

But to business. Many and united thanks from every one of us to each of you, our dear cousins, for the very kind offer contained in your letter. We consider you our very best friends, and to you we would go for counsel and sympathy either in joy or sorrow; and this will only be an additional proof of your disinterested kindness and affection. And we accept with heartfelt pleasure the hospitalities of your house for the occasion, and are glad that Maybank is the place you have selected. I do so love the seaboard. Do not think, my dear cousin, that we meant to sponge upon you in involving you in expense and trouble about this affair. Our idea is this. We expect to order cake enough made in Savannah for the evening—a little to send out, and two cakes for Louisa to take home with her; get Cousin Susan to attend to it and have that and the fruit sent out at the proper time. As for the guests, we only wish Aunt Elizabeth, Charles Berrien, Cousin Harriet Handley, Jane Harden, Henry and Abby, Cousin Susan, Laura, and my brother, of course, our dear Cousin Betsy and Cousin William. These are all the guests we wish invited, including our dear John and Jane. We know that you will make all things as pleasant and nice as possible, but be sure not to take too much trouble. We expect to do Louisa's shopping in Savannah, have her dresses cut and basted, and finish them in the country. We expect to be out on the 15th, Providence permitting, spend a fortnight at Arcadia, then the first of March make a short visit to the Sand Hills, then go to Henry's (and Louisa will visit Jane Harden), then go to the Island and remain till we leave the county. I forgot to say that the very last Thursday in April is the day appointed. Dr. Tennent is very much pleased at the idea of going down to Liberty, and I was induced to suggest this plan so that he could become acquainted with Louisa's relatives. I always think a gentleman respects a lady more when he knows the family he marries into, particularly when they can boast of such relatives as we can. Say to our dear cousin that Louisa desires her best thanks to be expressed in *prose* by her *prosy* sister for the kind offer expressed so *poetically*. She gratefully accepts it, but feels as if she cannot write her thanks. I agree with my Cousin Mary about the fee, not only because I am "of a frugal mind," but I think a good wife is worth paying for. So pray pocket the fee if offered; it might rouse the high Carolina blood to refuse it!

We leave here on Monday fortnight. Hope to be in Savannah on Tuesday evening. Will write you from there when to meet us at Midway. We think of leaving Mary Sophia and Lilla to spend the month of February with Mrs. LaRoche. Immediately after the wedding—at least on Tuesday—the doctor and Louisa will leave in the stage for Savannah. Mother and the children will come on in the next stage, and then we will return home.

What has become of John? He has not written me a line since he left. I wrote him last week and told him of this affair, but have received no answer. I suppose they will soon make you a visit. That call to the Sand Hills does not strike me favorably, but of course I can give no advice. . . . If he and Jane are with you, do give our love to them. I hope she has not been sick, as she has not written me.

I must again enjoin secrecy on the subject we have been writing about.

Louisa has not even written Jane Harden; and we hope it may be kept secret. Mother and Louisa unite in best love to you and our dear Cousin Charles. Oh, how I long to see you both, and Mary and Charlie! He is in Savannah by this, I suppose. . . . Cousin Susan and Laura were much pleased with the news I wrote them, and Cousin Susan says Louisa would be thrown away on any other than a widower with children. . . . Nothing new in our community. We have dined out several times, and are making calls before leaving, which with the work we have to do keeps us quite busy. And various are the regrets expressed at our leaving; but they have no idea of the change about to take place in our family. . . . I must close.

Your ever affectionate cousin,
Mary E. Robarts.

Mr. Charles C. Jones, Jr., *to* Rev. *and* Mrs. C. C. Jones[g]

Savannah, *Saturday,* January 20th, 1855

My dear Father and Mother,

Although it is rather late Saturday night, I must before retiring at least acquaint you with our safe arrival in Savannah and the health of all our relatives and friends here. Our ride from Riceboro was very pleasant both as to temperature, convenience, and companions. . . . Found Aunt Susan and Cousin Laura expecting our arrival and happy to see us. She and Cousin are both looking remarkably well, and are in fine spirits. . . . Today I called upon Mr. M. Cumming; he has executed your commissions and written Brother.

Have seen Mr. Ward. He is very busy. Received me kindly, and I commence operations on Monday morning. He advises me to study until May before applying for admission. This I will do, if life be spared. On Monday morning, then, bright and early I begin my preparatory labors in Savannah. Upon these I enter with firm determination to do my best. Will write you more fully when I am more settled.

Your ink, Father, I will send out on Wednesday if not before.

I am delightfully located here at Aunt Susan's, and feel under many obligations to her for her many kindnesses. My books I unpacked and arranged this evening. They arrived safely and in good order. My next step is to find more fully what is in them.

Sister appears to be enjoying herself very much. Her throat, although still sore, is better, and I hope will soon be relieved. . . . As the hour of midnight is almost at hand, and this is but one of three letters I have written since tea, I must bid you good night.

Your affectionate son,
Charles C. Jones, Jr.

Delivered the letters of introduction to Mr. Ward. So busy he could not read them while I was in his office, which was full of clients.

Rev. C. C. Jones *to* Mr. Charles C. Jones, Jr.ᵍ

Arcadia, *Thursday,* January 25th, 1855

My dear Son,

Your letter was received by Monday's mail, and we were glad to hear of your safe arrival, and that you would enter upon your office duties so early, and when Mr. Ward's business is so pressing. You will be *in medias res.* I have no doubt that if you are patient and apply yourself as I know you can, and adhere by God's assistance to a life of integrity and virtue, you will succeed in your profession. I would urge upon you a due attention to exercise, diet, and regimen. A person of your full habit must have exercise and temperance in all things in order to secure and to preserve health. All that is left for your parents now is to commend you constantly to the merciful care of God, and to invoke for you every blessing at His hands. You can never cease to be to them an object of fond and earnest solicitude, and we shall ever take the liveliest interest in everything that relates to your welfare. We hope that you will ever consider us your best friends, and as such freely and fully communicate with us at all times and on all subjects that you may desire.

We can but enjoin upon you a continuation of those good habits formed in your childhood, and which we believe you have continued to the present hour, of daily secret prayer and careful reading of God's Holy Word. And choose a favorable time for it. And of a regular attendance upon the public worship of God on the Sabbath Day, and a strict observance of that holy day. I have never known a man in my life who was an habitual Sabbath-breaker, or who frequently absented himself from the House of God, who was not deficient in some of the fundamental virtues which make up the character of a sober, honest, and virtuous man. I can never give a Sabbath-breaker my confidence. However fair he may appear to the eyes of men, a close inspection will almost invariably discover some special defect in principle or practice. In your own profession you have names of the highest repute who have been distinguished for their rigid observance of the Sabbath. Knowing Savannah well, and the social habits of the people, I do hope you will be careful of the intimacies you form, and depart not from the principles of total abstinence. You will never see reason to regret it, whatever little crosses you may be subjected to on account of them. I feel assured you will avoid the evening resorts of idle and intemperate men. *There is much gained in the labor of life by a proper beginning, and upon right principles.*

Say to my dear daughter that her mother will write her by the next mail, and that she must *tell her aunt at once the request which she made of her,* and that she take good care of her health. . . . I remain, my dear son,

Your ever affectionate father,

C. C. Jones.

N.B. The *up-country event* in which we feel a deep interest will take place *the last Thursday in April;* and *through Savannah* the blaze of the news has shined into every corner of Liberty County. Alas for the keepers of secrets— or rather for those who have secrets to keep! Our offer has been accepted.

Miss Mary Sharpe Jones *to* Mr. Joseph Jones[t]

Savannah, *Friday,* January 26th, 1855

My dear Brother Joe,

I wrote you some time ago, and as I have received no reply will send you another epistle, concluding that you have been too much occupied with your studies to have much time for anything else.

I left home just a week since, and am now staying with our dear Aunt Susan and Cousin Laura. They have a very nice house on the corner of Jones and Abercorn Streets. It is perfectly new, and they have the satisfaction of knowing that they are the first occupants. Brother Charlie will remain with them, having already commenced his studies in Mr. John Ward's office. Mr. Ward has a very fine library and an extensive practice, and I think Brother Charlie will be much pleased. He expects his friend Mr. George Helm about the 15th of February, and has written to Mr. Sale inviting him to come at the same time. As they expect to remain some weeks, I hope that you will come home before they leave.

We hope to have Aunt Eliza and family with us in a few weeks, to remain two or three months. We were all very much astonished a short time since by a letter from Aunt Mary Robarts announcing the engagement of Aunt Lou to Dr. Tennent of Marietta. It was written to us as a great secret which we must on no account divulge; but on coming to Savannah I found that so many of our friends had been written to and were so generally acquainted with the fact that it ceased to be any longer a secret. I presume that by this time Father and Mother have written to you informing you of it. They have invited them to come down and have their nuptials celebrated in our house —at Maybank, I expect. We have received no answers yet, so I cannot say what they will do. Dr. Tennent is a widower with eight children, not very wealthy but in comfortable circumstances, and has a fine practice, a professor of religion, and they think everything they could desire. As you may suppose, we were very much astonished at the news; and for a half of an hour after the letter arrived there was almost a row in our house—Mother, Aunt Betsy, and myself all jumping up and capering over the piazza.

Young Dr. Way was married a short time since to Miss Martin.

Dr. Duke expects to leave Liberty County very soon and come to Savannah to be associated with Dr. John Barnard. Dr. Duke says that he cannot stand the country practice, although I have no doubt but that he is doing much better in the county than he will be able to do here in the same length of time. Notwithstanding, Mr. Barnard says that John "booked" four hundred dollars in three months without formally announcing himself as a practitioner.

Uncle John has resigned his pastoral charge here and has accepted a call to the Sand Hills church. He enters upon his duties there about the 1st of February. I am very sorry that he could not remain here and build up this little church—particularly, too, as they have passed through so much affliction this summer.

Mr. Sumner Winn has resigned at Midway, so that now we will have Mr. Buttolph to preach for us all the time.

I have seen Cousin Joe West several times since I came, and he mentioned a day or so ago that he had received your pamphlet and had read it. He seemed to have been very much interested in it. I congratulate you upon your success, and hope that your labors may always be crowned with success, and that your most sanguine hopes may be realized. Dr. Jackson has written a letter to Dr. Duke in which he compliments you very highly. He says that you ought not to think of preparing yourself to remain in the country, but fit yourself for a professorship. Cousin Charles West has a plan for you. He says that after you graduate he wishes you to come to Savannah, become acquainted with the faculty and people here, interest yourself in the college, and then he will give you his professorship. This year, notwithstanding the fever last summer, they have fifty medical students. This is indeed very encouraging. He is very anxious to get you here if possible.

I shall be very much obliged to you, my dear brother, if you will get me six of the upper E strings for my guitar. Also five B strings. Please get them from Mr. William Schubert. He lives in 7th Street above Vine, just the other side of the square. His strings are the best in the city, and if he has none please request him to procure some for you. Just say you want them for Miss Jones who lived in 13th Street, and I think you will find him very accommodating.

It is growing so dark that I can scarcely see. Last night we had a most delightful serenade—intended for your sister, they say! Aunt Susan, Cousin Laura, and Brother Charlie unite with me in much love to yourself. Write soon. And if you see Mrs. Mary Gaul, do give my love to her.

Your ever affectionate sister,
Mary S. Jones.

When you come on, you must be sure to stop and see Aunt Susan and Cousin Laura.

Mr. Charles C. Jones, Jr., *to* Rev. *and* Mrs. C. C. Jones[g]

Savannah, *Saturday*, January 27th, 1855

My dear Father and Mother,

The closing hours of my first week of study in Savannah are nearly ended. As a final act I will pen you a few lines, although I have little else of interest to communicate than the daily routine of office duties.

Your letter, Father, was this morning received, and for the good advice and tender solicitude for my conduct and success here I sincerely thank you. It shall be my endeavor to meet your wishes in every respect, as far as may lie in my power. Am happy to find that Mother is well, and hope that you may more rapidly than heretofore be restored to that health which you so much need in order that you may again enter upon those duties which appertain to your calling.

Savannah, as far as I have had an opportunity of judging, appears to be a pleasant city for residence. There seems to be a spirit of comity prevailing among the members of the bar, and there are many lawyers here who will compare favorably with any I have ever seen. Mr. Ward I find a very agreeable gentleman: exceedingly companionable, ready to answer and satisfy any inquiry, and also one well read in the principles of law, and admirably informed as to the statute law and conduct of courts in this state. He has been a member of the bar now just *twenty years.*

I am endeavoring to make due use of my time, and turn everything to advantage by improving every opportunity presented. The statute law at present appears somewhat dry, and especially so when compared with my past readings in the text-writers. This must for a short time necessarily be the case, in consequence of its novelty and the want of that connection of topic which obtains in regular systematic treatises. After a week's study, however, I find the difficulty in a measure abated, while repetition begets familiarity with the various enactments. Here at least the old motto fails: "Familiarity breeds contempt." Am now engaged in studying the judiciary. Mr. Ward's practice being large, I have had an opportunity already of seeing several petitions, etc., and intend watching the progress of the suits thus instituted. Have had a good deal of writing the past week. Mr. Owens (George), the other partner in the firm, in my intercourse with him I have found a pleasant person, ready also to give me an item in practice.

Mr. Ward advises that I apply in May at the session of the superior court in this city. Between that time and the present I have much to accomplish, and will have to devote myself regularly and earnestly to the task. It is an easy matter to be admitted, but not quite such an easy matter to be actually and intelligently prepared for the bar. It shall be my endeavor to prepare myself, so far as time and circumstance will permit, for the proper and scientific discharge of all those duties (and their name is legion) which may appertain to the profession. Nor am I ignorant that in order to this, many long months and years of continued investigation are requisite. Still it is the profession of my choice; upon it I have staked my reputation and my hope of support; and my life, whether long or short, must be devoted to its acquisition and mastery.

Mr. Ward was tendered a few days since the captaincy of the Chatham Artillery and accepted the same. . . . Have called upon Major Porter, Mr. Hutchison, and the lawyers; they all received me very kindly and invited me to visit them ad libitum. . . . Aunt Susan, Cousin Laura, and Sister are all well, and unite with me in warmest love.

Your affectionate son,
Charles C. Jones, Jr.

Cousin Charles West's infant is better. The bottle of carmine ink I sent out by Thursday's stage, to be left at Stebbins' store. Am much obliged for the letters forwarded. Please let me know, my dear parents, whenever and in what respect I can be of service to you here.

Mrs. Mary Jones *to* Miss Mary Sharpe Jones[t]

Arcadia, *Monday,* January 29th, 1855

My dear Daughter,

We were happy to hear from your brother and yourself this day week. Your father replied to his letter, and I intended writing you by last Friday's mail, but as usual was prevented. With the exception of one day I believe we have not been without company since you left. Your Uncle John spent nearly all of last week with us; has concluded to go to the Sand Hills, and will board with Mr. Henry Stevens. Whilst your father reads the news to your uncle and aunty in the parlor I have slipped off to write you a few lines.

Yesterday was a cold and rainy day; we did not go to church. About one o'clock all the people large and small assembled in the vacant upper chamber, and your father gave them a practical discourse with the usual services. They were all attentive and interested. Just before the close we heard a step below. One of the servants went down and coming back informed me that your aunt and uncle had arrived. We went down after the close of the meeting; I excused myself to them and returned to the school, which was held about an hour. All the children and young persons were present and answered very well. I have always delighted in the work of teaching the Negroes.

We took our usual dinner, and tea just before sunset. . . . The windows were closed, the candles lighted, the books were placed before your father, and he was just about to commence family worship when we heard a rap at the door, and who should come in but Brother Troup and Augusta with their two children and Maybank! The rain had prevented their attendance at church. Maybank left us this morning, and expects to go to Savannah tomorrow. Troup and Augusta and the children went this afternoon to South Hampton. Gilbert brings word that all are well there; we hope to spend a night with them soon.

Dr. Duke spent last Thursday night with us, making himself very pleasant.

We went to Maybank last week. Your japonicas had several flowers open on two of the bushes: very brilliant, and double; never saw any more beautiful. You must try and secure a double white one from some of the horticultural establishments in town.

We are happy to hear that your aunt and cousin are so pleasantly settled in their new house. Aunt Betsy sends much love to them and both of you; says she wants to come down and see them. . . . I received a letter from your Aunt Mary last week accepting our invitation and appointing the time for the last Thursday in April. She again enjoins secrecy; but through *Mrs. Winn and Henry* the news has spread far and wide. . . . Your uncle begs Sister Susan to send out by the first stage to Mr. Stebbins' care the *cassaba* cuttings sent him from Florida, now in her possession. He values them highly, and is much interested in his new garden. . . . I hope your brother is pleased with his situation in Mr. Ward's office. A kind Providence has greatly favored him in finding a home with your good aunt, who has ever manifested such true and affectionate interest in you all.

I am very weary tonight, as you will see from this poor scrawl. Your father, aunt, and uncle unite with me in best love to your aunt and cousin, your brother, and yourself.

Ever, my darling child, your affectionate mother,
Mary Jones.

Mr. CHARLES C. JONES, JR., *to* REV. *and* MRS. C. C. JONES[t]

Savannah, *Saturday,* February 3rd, 1855
My dear Father and Mother,

Audley King reached Savannah yesterday evening from Liberty, and through him we are glad to hear of you, and at the same time sorry to learn that you, Father, are suffering from a cold and not so well as you were when we left.

The week has passed rapidly away, and my time has been so fully occupied that I scarcely have preserved an accurate account of its flight. Have enjoyed the opportunity of examining two important cases, both as to the facts and preparatory papers and also their subsequent conduct in the courtroom. Have nearly finished the Judiciary Act of 1799, and will soon take up the penal code. It is a hard matter to remember all the acts passed, they are so numerous and various in their character. Their study involves rather an exercise of memory than any exertion of the reasoning powers. Repetition and practice alone can fix them accurately and readily in the mind.

On Thursday of this week we took tea at Major Porter's by invitation. Spent a pleasant evening there. They all desire their kind regards to be presented.

Mrs. Davis and her daughter Miss Anne from Augusta came from that place on Friday and have been with Aunt Susan since. Mrs. Davis requests me to express the kindest remembrances of Dr. Davis and herself to you.

On Tuesday of next week we are expecting Aunt Eliza and family from Marietta. We will then see how the young bride in expectancy bears her blushing honors! I fear she will find that the *family secret,* so carefully entrusted to a chosen few, has become the property of many not within the limited circle intended. The circumstances of the whole affair are so unexpected and novel in their character that they can scarcely fail of attracting attention and remark wherever known.

Sister appears to be enjoying herself very much, and I think you will be pleased with the improvement in her health. Last evening she looked prettier than I ever saw her before. Her sore throat has been entirely repudiated. Aunt Susan and Cousin Laura are both well, and seem satisfied with their city residence. . . . Sister speaks of returning sometime next week, although I do not believe that she has fixed upon any definite time. With kindest love from Sister, Aunt, and Cousin, I remain, as ever, my dear parents,

Your affectionate son,
Charles C. Jones, Jr.

Miss Mary Sharpe Jones *to* Mrs. Mary Jones[t]

Savannah, *Saturday,* February 10th, 1855

My dear Mother,

I had appointed next Thursday as the time for my departure, but Aunt Susan and Aunt Eliza have insisted upon my remaining until the following Monday, as that is the day upon which the latter expects to be with you. So on Monday the 19th you will, if nothing prevents, see Aunt Eliza, Aunts Mary and Lou, Ellen, Joe, and myself. Nancy will come out at the same time. Aunt desires me to say to you that they have so many trunks that it will be necessary for you to engage a steamboat to transport them from place to place! She begs that you will inform Aunt Betsy of their advent and request her to meet them at Arcadia. I sincerely hope, my dear mother, that we will not be disappointed in our present arrangements, for I can assure you that I want to see my dear father and yourself very, very much. My visit here has been longer than I had anticipated, but my time has fled pleasantly and rapidly away. Aunt Susan and Cousin Laura have treated me with the same affection which they have ever manifested toward me.

Aunt Lou is in great trouble. She left Dr. Tennent quite sick, and has heard but once from his daughter, and she mentioned that he was no better (has inflammation of the stomach), so of course Aunt Lou has the worst attack of "the blues" that ever I saw. I really feel sorry for her, for she is so desponding that it is with difficulty that she can be persuaded to make her purchases. Aunt Mary is just as full of mischief as ever, and amuses us greatly, often at Aunt Lou's expense.

I did not receive your memorandum until Thursday afternoon. I immediately sent to Mr. Hutchison's, but found that Uncle John had left the city; so your things could not be sent by his wagon. I have purchased everything you desired except the ginghams, and I did not get them because they were all remarkably ugly and coarse. In a few weeks they expect a new supply, and if any are received before I leave I will look again. If there is anything else that you wish me to do for you, dear Mother, please let me know. I did not get the boots, for I was undecided as to whether you had erased them from the list or not. . . .

The young ladies here have been very polite in calling to see me. Miss Richardsone came for me last evening, and we took quite a long walk together. I am quite pleased with her. She brought me a beautiful bouquet of japonicas. Miss Anna McIntosh (the same who was in Liberty last winter) desired me to present her kind regards to Father and yourself; her sisters and herself have all been to see me. On next Tuesday evening Cousin Laura and myself are engaged to take tea with Miss Maria Footman.

Mrs. Dr. Screven has returned home. Her mind has not been entirely restored, but she is much better and perfectly harmless; takes quite an interest in her grandchildren. For some time she imagined that she had charge of an asylum, and she regarded the family as inmates. Consequently she took great interest in keeping everything in good order about the house.

Aunt Mary Robarts says that I must tell you that they have arrived here in safety, but feel anxious about some of the Marietta *beaux,* one of whom they left in bed, and says that you must know that it is impossible for such young maidens as they are to feel lighthearted under such circumstances. It really seems to me as though they were all in love. I sincerely hope that they may hear something favorable this evening, for if they do not, I am afraid that Aunt Lou will be sick herself, so great is her anxiety and so many her fears.

In a week I hope to be with my dear father and yourself, my own dear mother. I was truly sorry to hear that Father had not been well. Aunt Susan is very anxious for him to spend some time here and place himself under Cousin Charles's care. Aunt Eliza and Aunt Mary are staying here, and send much love; also Aunt Susan, Cousin Laura, and Brother Charlie. Accept, dear Mother and Father, all that is affectionate from

Your child,

Mary S. Jones.

MISS LAURA E. MAXWELL *to* MRS. MARY JONES[t]

Savannah, *Saturday,* February 10th, 1855

My very dear Aunt,

Thank you most kindly for your last favor, which should have had an immediate reply, but unfortunately never reached my eyes until the afternoon of the day the stage left; and this is the very first opportunity I have had since. I desired to write and beg you to request your darling daughter to remain longer with us. We do esteem it a privilege to have Mary and Charlie with us. I am proud of my cousins, and have every reason to be. To my mind none are *more polished;* and I must hide my diminished head, having never had the advantages of a *polished Philadelphia* school.

Mother says that Aunt Robarts and Cousins Mary and Louisa, Ellen and Joe are coming out on Monday week the 19th. Will spend one week with you, then go up to the Sand Hills, then come down to Henry's; and then the latter part of the time is spent between you and Aunt Betsy. . . . Mary Sophia and Lilla are to remain here with their aunt Mrs. LaRoche until Abby returns from the up country. . . . Cousin Lou is sojourning with Cousin Eliza and feels very sad, as Dr. Tennent is quite sick in Marietta, and no tidings today. "Darkness shows us worlds of light we never saw by day." I hope glad tidings are in store for her. . . . May his life be spared to take care of her and the eight interesting *steps!* It will give me great pleasure to accept of your kind invitation and be present at *the* wedding. Aunt Eliza and Aunt Mary are quite in the spirit of the wedding; the latter has amused us not a little, and will make you merry when she arrives.

Am glad to hear such a good account of "our good Timothy." I must first know the *right* the "gent" has to ask such searching questions before I can answer them. He has not made his appearance in these regions yet.

On Sabbath Cousin John's resignation was read to the church, and the letter sent him by the session. A very sad, sad day it seemed to all present, and a sadder silence prevailed. . . . I've been interrupted again and again, my dear aunt, by company, and beg that you will excuse an extra quantity of ink upon this page. . . . Give our love to Aunt Betsy and Uncle William; I will write Aunty very soon. Mother, Charlie (Mary is writing for herself), Aunt Eliza, and Aunt Mary unite with me in warmest love to my dear Uncle Charlie and yourself.

Ever affectionately your niece,
Laura E. Maxwell.

Mr. Charles C. Jones, Jr., *to* Rev. *and* Mrs. C. C. Jones[t]
Savannah, *Sunday,* February 11th, 1855

Enclosed you will find, my dear mother and father, a letter, this hour received from Marietta, containing very melancholy intelligence with reference to the health of Dr. Tennent. Aunt Lou is, as you may imagine, very much distressed; and in this she receives deep sympathy from Aunt Eliza and Aunt Mary. We all feel for her. Her affections seem all concentered upon him to an unusual degree, and I fear in case of his death it will go very hard with her. At the request of Aunt Mary I enclose this, which will be deposited in the mail in time, I hope, for the morrow's mail.

Aunt Mary is packing her carpetbag, and I accompany her immediately to Cousin Charles West's, where Cousin Louisa is staying. She expects that it will be her purpose to leave Savannah for Marietta tomorrow morning, and therefore goes prepared to accompany her. When we reach Cousin Charles's I will ascertain their determination and pencil the same to you in this note.

We heard Mr. King twice today. His evening's discourse had reference to the necessity of erecting a new place of worship, the reasons for doing the same, and the means whereby it may be accomplished. Rather an inappropriate topic, I think, for several reasons.

All well, and unite in warmest love to you both, my dear parents.

From your affectionate son,
Charles C. Jones, Jr.

At Cousin Charles West's. Cousin Louisa is much distressed. Aunt Mary thinks they will go up tomorrow to Marietta. Not positive, but probable.

Mrs. Mary Jones *to* Miss Mary Sharpe Jones[t]
Arcadia, *Thursday,* February 15th, 1855

My dear Daughter,

It was with great sorrow that we received the sad tidings conveyed to us by last Monday's mail, and we are awaiting with deep anxiety the news of today. God grant to spare dear Lou the heavy affliction which we fear from Mrs. Petrie's letter may await her! We presume that Cousin Mary and herself went up on Monday. Our tenderest love and sympathy to her and to our dear aunt and cousin. We shall hope to meet them all at Midway Church on Monday, and shall be prepared for all the trunks they bring.

We would have written by Tuesday's mail, but received the letters on our way to spend the night with Mrs. Harden, which we did very pleasantly on Monday last. Matilda looks bloomingly, and sends much love to you. Says she wants to see you very much. Expects to spend her next summer at the North.

We met Maybank and West at the Boro, and they ask that you will stay to the squadron parade, which commences on Monday. We leave these arrangements to your own pleasure. Next Sabbath week is our Communion, and we are to have services on Friday and Saturday previously; I think you would find it pleasant and profitable to be here at that time.

I feel very grateful to your aunt and cousin for all their kindness to your brother and yourself, and I know you have enjoyed your visit. Will write dear Laura when I have time to sit down and tell her all the news. And will write your brother very shortly; I am happy to learn that he is making friends in the city with those whose friendship is worth valuing. Has he heard from Mr. Helm lately? We expect to return to Maybank the first week in March, according to arrangement, and await their coming. It will give us great pleasure to receive them.

I am just about starting for Maybank to spend the night with your aunt and uncle. Your father does not accompany me, as he is engaged at home. Your Uncle John may be with him tonight. I am going down to see after *little matters* which it was useless for him to take the ride for. I think he seems better this week. I want him (when all things suit) to spend a little while with Sister Susan; it would cheer him up and amuse him.

Do get me in addition to the articles sent for at Lathrop's a sufficient quantity of *white brillante* for two basques of different patterns, one piece of fine good quality cotton shirting *for shirts, six yards* fine linen for bosoms (at seventy-five to eighty-seven cents), and some *whalebones.* Perhaps if they do not have the *ginghams* they would get them elsewhere for you; I would rather *wait* than get an *inferior article.*

I must now close, as my time is gone. With best love to aunts and cousins, your brother and yourself,

Ever, my dear child, your affectionate mother,

Mary Jones.

Excuse my hand: it is very tremulous today.

MISS MARY SHARPE JONES *to* MISS LAURA E. MAXWELL[t]

Arcadia, *Thursday,* February 22nd, 1855

Dear Cousin Laura,

The sad intelligence of Dr. Tennent's death reached us today. Our dear aunt is much afflicted, and sympathizes deeply with Aunt Lou. This we all do, for I do really think it a peculiarly melancholy case. Many had been our arrangements and great our pleasure in the anticipation of *the* event, but their laughter has been turned into sorrow. Yet it is pleasant and comforting to feel that "He doeth all things well." I doubt not but that the issue of *this,* dark though it may be to those most intimately concerned, still is ordered for some wise end. Aunt Mary mentioned that they would be with us on Monday, and I suppose that you have already seen them.

After our hasty departure in the stage we had frequent and hard showers upon us, but by keeping the curtains buttoned and the windows up we suffered no ill effects from the exposure. The extra shawl proved quite useful in keeping some of us dry. We were favored in having only eight passengers as far as Bailey's; there two got out and Mr. Edward Stevens got in. We were very much interested in his conversation. When we reached Midway we found Father with Gilbert, Charles, carriage, buggy, and cart waiting for us, and upon driving up to the house found Mother, Aunty, and Uncle ready to welcome us.

Tell Aunt Susan that it suited exactly, for I immediately handed Aunty the work, and she says that she will endeavor to complete it if possible before she leaves for Savannah. Uncle and herself hope, if nothing prevents, to be with you next week. Uncle says that he expects that you will make his wife spend half of his money getting fixed up to walk with your fine selves! I hope that they may not be prevented, as they seem to anticipate much pleasure in spending some time with you.

Aunt Eliza bore the journey out much better than I had expected, though she has been very unwell ever since her arrival—so much so as to render her unable to be downstairs at all. Her anxiety has been so great that *that* alone is sufficient to make her sick. She says that I must tell you that she has been quite sick since she left you, and that she has missed the singing of the "nuns" at night; their chanting lulled her to rest while in Savannah. . . .

Mother was so much pleased with the calicoes that she has taken the two brown ones for herself, and begs that you will be so kind as to get a yard and a quarter more of each. Also two dark patterns for the servants. . . . Please get also five yards of the brillante, as we think that will be sufficient for two basques. We will be very much obliged to you if you will purchase these and send them by Aunt Mary on Monday.

There will be preaching at Midway tomorrow. We anticipate a very pleasant season. Dr. Palmer is not here, and does not expect to be present at all, for he is now in Natchez. Mrs. Palmer is still here; I have not seen her yet. . . . Uncle John is with us at present, and will remain the rest of the week, as he expects to take part in the meeting. Father hopes to preach tomorrow morning; he does not look well, and I fear that he is not able to exert himself at all. I expect to go out in the morning with the children. Mother will remain with Aunt Eliza and go out on Saturday. Aunty is too feeble to attend herself. Aunt Betsy and Uncle William will remain with us during the meeting.

How is Cousin Eliza and your baby? Do give much love to them all, and kiss the little ones. . . . Aunt Eliza desires much love to be given to Aunt Mary and Aunt Lou, and says that she longs to see them and hopes that nothing will prevent their coming on Monday. Do give our united love to them, and say that we will certainly meet them at Midway. . . . Tell Aunt Susan that my velvet basque is nearly finished, and I shall take great delight in wearing it, and always think of her. My visit in Savannah to you was so pleasant, and the time flew so rapidly, that I can scarcely realize that I spent one month away. I feel very much obliged to my dear aunt and yourself for your kindness and attention to me while there. . . . Do write soon, and be particular in directing to Father's care; for since Laura Jones and family have returned, several mistakes have been made with our letters. . . . It is growing late, and I must bid you good night. . . . Mother and Father unite with me in much love to Aunt Susan, Brother Charlie, and yourself.

Your affectionate cousin,
Mary S. Jones.

Howdy for the servants.

Mr. Joseph Jones *to* Rev. C. C. Jones[t]

Philadelphia, Saturday, February 24th, 1855

My dear Father,

I was very sorry to learn from your letter that you felt no better. I am assured that you do not give your mind and body sufficient rest. Dr. Jackson in all his lectures upon the nervous system recommends this as the great remedial agent in cases of exhausted nervous force. Dr. Hodge concurs with him in this opinion. When the forces of the animal economy have been worn down by long-continued mental and physical exertions, nature requires time to restore these losses. The process is analogous to that which takes place after a long and wasting disease. We all know how slow and tedious a recovery is in these cases. The laws of nature, as far as the power of man extends, are fixed and immutable; the physician can assist and in a measure direct her operations, but he can never by all his skill or learning cause nature to act contrary to her established laws.

Drs. Hodge and Jackson recommend you to pursue all your studies and reading in the recumbent posture. They concur with Dr. Duke in his prescription of the iodide of potassium, and advise in conjunction with it the use of one of the preparations of iron in small doses. Both of these medicines act slowly upon the constitution—the former as an alterative, the latter as a tonic. They must therefore be persevered in for a length of time.

I have procured a very handsome galvanic battery, which I hope will be beneficial if used cautiously. Electricity acts as a nervous stimulant; it excites the muscles to contract. If, therefore, it be applied too often and too violently, it will exhaust the remaining nervous force and counteract the great treatment, which consists in allowing the physical and mental man to remain quiet whilst nature repairs her damages.

You should not stand up to study. When the body is in the erect position, an immense amount of muscular and nervous force is expended. This should be economized. For this reason Dr. Jackson has this winter delivered all his lectures in the sitting posture. You know that he was once in a dilapidated state of health; his forces were broken down from excessive mental and physical exertions, and he was upon the very verge of paralysis. By a careful attendance to this great rule of rest, however, he is now heartier than nine-tenths of his fellow men of the same age.

It gave me great pleasure to know that you were pleased with the article upon endosmose, and I am much obliged for your valuable suggestions. . . . The article was published in *The Proceedings of the Academy of Natural Sciences,* and the pamphlets which I sent you were extra copies which I had struck off for my friends. Dr. Hays, the editor of *The American Journal of Medical Sciences,* requested me to allow him to publish it in his journal. It will appear in the April number, together with my investigations upon the kidney and its excretions in different animals. In this there will be many woodcuts; of these I send you two specimens. I have corrected the proof sheets and find that it will occupy about forty-five pages of his journal.

If Providence permits, I hope to leave Philadelphia in the Savannah steamer *Keystone* on the 7th of March. Our lectures close on the 10th of this month, so that I will lose only a few lectures. It will give me great pleasure to fulfill any commissions for you, Mother, Sister, and Brother in Philadelphia. I have called several times at Mr. Smith's bookstore and inquired about your books; he says that he has not yet been able to procure them in England. Yesterday I sent you three papers containing documents which I hope may prove of some interest. With best love to you, Mother, Sister, and Brother, I remain

Your affectionate son,
Joseph Jones.

Miss Mary Sharpe Jones *to* Miss Laura E. Maxwell[t]

Arcadia, *Thursday,* March 1st, 1855

My dear Cousin Laura,

After vigorous exercise today on horseback I feel very much like retiring to rest, but cannot resist a desire to dispatch an epistle to yourself.

And now to the business part first: namely, Mother requests me to thank you very much for the purchase of the gingham; thinks it beautiful and says that she would have been hard to be pleased indeed had she been dissatisfied with this. You need not get any of the calicoes; these that we have will be sufficient. I am very much obliged to you for the samples; they are neat, but I did not expect to get anything for myself just now, though you are very kind in offering to purchase anything for us; and when we wish a new dress, will gladly avail ourselves of your kindness.

We were very much disappointed this afternoon in not having Aunty and Uncle with us. They promised to spend tonight with us, and expected to go to Savannah tomorrow. As they have not come, I fear that they have been prevented by something. Uncle was not very well on last Sabbath. We had hoped to have sent another "offense" by them to Aunt Susan in the form of a fat roasting pig.

Aunts Mary and Lou arrived quite safely on Monday after a very cold ride. We deeply sympathize with the latter. She has been very unwell ever since she came, but today came down to dinner. Oh, hers is a sad, sad affliction! They all expect to go to the Sand Hills on Monday, and we hope to go to the Island next week.

As had been appointed, there was meeting at Midway. Mother remained with Aunt Eliza; I attended with Father and Uncle John and had the pleasure of hearing them both preach. On Saturday I remained and Mother went out; Mr. John Winn and Mr. Baker preached. On Sabbath we all attended. The weather was rather unpropitious, but Aunt Eliza ventured out and suffered no evil consequences. The day was a most interesting and pleasant one. Before service there was an inquiry meeting and a prayer meeting, the latter conducted by my dear father. . . . Uncle John preached in the morning; Father and Mr. Buttolph made addresses at the Communion table. There were six additions, all of colored persons. . . . After service, as Aunty was quite feeble, Mother, Ellen, and myself returned home. Father and Uncle John remained and heard an admirable sermon from Mr. Baker. . . . Father says he possesses uncommon talents. At present he is spending a few days with Aunt Julia, but his trunk is still here, and I think he regards this as headquarters. He is awfully stiff, and shows in every action, word, and look from what portion of the country he came. But he is an admirable preacher, and I wish that I could always hear sermons like that delivered by himself on Sabbath. . . . Mr. Buttolph seems to be very much interested indeed in these meetings. I think that there is no doubt of his making an excellent pastor.

Tallulah Cassels is now very feeble, and Mrs. Cassels has requested the prayers of the church in her behalf. She is, you know, not pious. It is very sad to see one so young fading and hastening rapidly to the tomb. Consumption has given peculiar brilliancy to her eye, and the bright red spot on her cheek but too surely marks her as the victim of this flattering disease. Hers is to me a peculiarly sad and interesting case. Mrs. Cassels is now here.

We received a letter from Brother Joe by the last mail, and he expects to leave Philadelphia on the 7th, so you may expect to see him very soon. . . . I hope that your baby is growing and improving every day; I hear that she

has grown prettier and fatter since I last saw her. . . . Dr. Duke has, I understand, gone to Savannah, so tell Aunt Susan that she may expect the
promised "peep" before very long. It is growing quite late, and I must close,
as I am told it is not right to sit up at night. . . . Father and Mother unite
with me in much love to Aunt Susan, Brother Charlie, and yourself. Good
night.

Your affectionate cousin,
Mary S. Jones.

Miss Laura E. Maxwell *to* Mrs. Mary Jones[t]

Savannah, *Sunday,* March 11th, 1855

My dear Aunt Mary,

We are too sorry that the days for the leaving of the Philadelphia steamer
have been changed; consequently, as the steamer left on Saturday, she will
not arrive here before Tuesday. So you will be disappointed in not seeing Joe
on Monday. And so were we, until we found out the reason. We had a room
all fixed for him, which we hope he will occupy on Tuesday. And when Mr.
Helm comes, Mother says Charlie must bring him to stay with him until he
goes into the country, and we will try and be as civil to him as he was to
Charlie when he was in Kentucky.

Am sorry to say that Charlie has been suffering with a cold for a week
past. On Wednesday night he had quite a hot fever, and as our good friend
Cousin Charles was too sick to be called out, Charlie decided to have Dr.
Duke, who accordingly came and gave him some pills. "Believe me, madam,
I have pills." On Thursday he gave him some tartar water, which had a
usual effect; Friday he ate oranges and flax tea; Saturday took two Seidlitz
powders; today dressed and came down to dinner; feels better than he has
done for a week. . . . He is thinner than he was when he came to town—
owing to *much study,* I suppose. Mother says she tries to take the best care
of him she can. . . . I can only say that Charlie has not been singular with
his cold; Mrs. Porter, Mrs. Gilmer, Mother, and myself and almost everybody I know has suffered from it more or less. And the reason why Mr.
Hutchison did not call to see Mary was that his cold fell on his side and he
was afraid to expose himself to the night air.

Mother sends a great deal of love to you and Uncle Charlie and Mary, and
her special thanks for the pig, which was roasted on Saturday with the expectation that Joe would dine with us upon it. Aunty and Uncle William
enjoyed it very much. . . . How do you think Mr. Baker would suit for our
church? *We fear* they will call Mr. King. . . . Sorry Uncle leaves us in the
morning; glad Aunty remains. Hope she will enjoy her visit. Mother asks
when you and Uncle Charlie and Mary are coming to see us. Believe me

Your affectionate niece,
Laura E. Maxwell.

Mrs. Susan M. Cumming *to* Rev. C. C. Jones[t]
Savannah, *Tuesday,* March 20th, 1855

My dear Brother,

I received your letter by Sandy, who arrived safely, though he had some disasters by the way. . . . Joseph gave us an agreeable surprise after all our expectations; and presume Mr. Helm will also. Should he arrive today or tomorrow, Charles desires me to say you may expect them on Thursday. . . . I hope nothing will disappoint your expectation of having all your children with you on Thursday.

A meeting is to be held this evening to take into consideration the calling of a pastor to our church. I fear Mr. King will be the one called. He has a call elsewhere and wishes to ascertain if he will be called here before he decides. . . . The building of the lecture room has been commenced, and Mr. King has been very active in proposing plans for raising the money to pay for it. Perhaps he is the one to build it, but I hardly think he will please as minister long, though I may be mistaken in my judgment. If all the prayers were answered which have been put up for that church, I think its prosperity would equal and greatly surpass any church in our denomination. The Great Head of the Church accomplishes His plans by His own instrumentality, however weak or feeble it may appear, that the honor may be all His own.

Sister you have seen ere this. She and Brother William made us a very pleasant visit; I wish they could have remained longer. When are you and Sister coming? Certainly to Charles's examination the first of May if not before. . . . He has been applying himself very closely; a little recreation will do him good. After Joe gets fixed, he and Mary must come in and make us a visit.

Mr. Baker preached for us on Sunday; I was not only pleased but trust profited. I would give him my vote as pastor on that specimen. I understand he has accepted a call to a professorship in Austin College. He is too young for that; he should preach some years first—get more experience and have his judgment matured. I wish we had such a pastor as Mr. Buttolph.

Charles and Laura unite with me in love to you, Sister Mary, Mary, and Joe—and Aunt and cousins if with you. . . . I have great expectations that Joe's battery and Sister Mary's mustard will cure you; do let them practice on you. Believe me

Your affectionate sister,
S. M. Cumming.

Mr. Charles C. Jones, Jr., *to* Rev. C. C. Jones[t]
Savannah, *Wednesday,* March 21st, 1855

My dear Father,

My friend Helm has not as yet arrived. He is behind his time, having assigned as the days of his arrival in Savannah from the 15th to the 20th of this month inclusive. I have received no communication from him since he left Kentucky, and therefore am ignorant at what stage of his journey he now is. I am daily expecting him. I am sorry to give you the trouble of sending to Midway, and wish that I could say positively at what time Helm will be here; but you see exactly in what uncertainty the matter lies. My hope is that he will either be with us in person before next Monday or else communicate the cause of his delay.

This evening we have a decided change of weather, the sky being overcast and the wind very cool. . . . Sandy left Savannah this morning, and from him you will receive a letter from Aunt Susan.

The Presbyterian church held a meeting for the election of a pastor on last Tuesday, but adjourned for further consideration without proceeding to an election. The meeting was, in my humble opinion, poorly conducted. I attended, and were I a member should have indulged in a short speech on the occasion. But I will tell you of it when we meet, which I hope will be in a short time.

Am now prepared for admission, and wish that I could now stand my examination, but will have to wait until the second Monday of May next. We are all well, although I learn from the physicians that there is much sickness at present in the city. Saw several Liberty County gentlemen in the streets this morning. With warmest love to you both, my dear father and mother, to Brother, Sister, and all relatives, I am, as ever,

Your affectionate son,
Charles C. Jones, Jr.

I hope that Helm will be here in time to take the stage out on next Monday.

Rev. C. C. Jones *to* Mrs. Susan M. Cumming[t]

Maybank, *Saturday,* March 31st, 1855

My dear Sister,

Your letter of 20th came safely to hand. Our friends, passing and repassing from you to us and from us to you, have been our links of communication this winter.

Sister and Brother have returned much improved and in good spirits; Aunt and family are with them now. All dined with us on Thursday. Aunt feeble; Lou the same. Poor thing, how sad, how deep that wound! Yet mercy shines in it too. They will come to stay at Maybank shortly.

Mr. Helm and Charles came Monday, and we gave them a hearty welcome. Mr. Helm is an interesting and sensible young gentleman, and it affords us great pleasure to entertain him and extend to him our warmest hospitalities. We have tried to render his stay pleasant. If we can charter a small vessel they will spend a few days marooning at Blackbeard.

Our meeting, we hope, has done good, and Mr. Buttolph thinks the seriousness continues. He has established a prayer meeting every morning before service at Midway—an excellent thing. He has been and is now much engaged. Mr. Baker has been invited as his assistant (salary: eight hundred dollars), and it is believed he will accept for the year (not permanently). The field for two ministers is very circumscribed (not above three hundred people); and now, adding John at Walthourville, they have three ministers for about five hundred people! Surely they are highly favored. But these ministers are not required to attend to the Negroes at all! This I deem wrong.

Your own church labors under trials still. You have only to wait patiently the issue. Of the merits of your present supply for a pastor I have no means of judging. You need a good and efficient man. . . .

We are now having a northeaster and considerable rain. The rain much needed, but the cold has been great. *Winter*—not *spring!* Neither Joe's battery nor anything else seems to remove the nervous inaction. His lozenges of iron have given me a good appetite. You see my handwriting is no better. Julia's family are all well. The county healthy. Mr. Fleming is putting Lambert in fine order. Mr. Allen says he is doing pretty well at White Oak. We all send much love to you and to Laura.

Your ever affectionate brother,
C. C. Jones.

Mrs. Susan M. Cumming *to* Mrs. Mary Jones[t]

Savannah, Saturday, April 7th, 1855

My dear Sister,

I first thought I would write to my dear brother; but as second thoughts are sometimes best, and as this letter would find more favor in your eyes than in his, because it contains a new prescription from our cousin for him— It is the application of iodine on his spine, where he used to apply the blisters. He thinks it will benefit him. It acts by absorption. But Joe can explain all that more satisfactorily than I can. Try it two weeks, and if any perceptible benefit, continue it two months.

The other recipe is for those pills for Mary. Have they benefited at all? If so, Joe must make up a supply; he can do it as well and better and cheaper than the apothecary. And let her continue them. Should Joe not have the ingredients, by writing to Cousin Charles or myself they shall be gotten and forwarded immediately.

I congratulate you that you have all your family once more together with you. Though few, you have been widely separated.

I am sorry to say that Laura has been quite sick the past week: confined to bed with a cold and fever and most distressing, troublesome cough, but no pain in her breast or side. Cousin Charles has been visiting her, and has prescribed the iodine applied three times a day to her throat and chest, with the happiest results in checking the cough. She says she can testify to its beneficial and painful effects. It is like a shovel of burning coals, causing the whole body to sympathize with the afflicted part. . . . You will have to apply the iodine with a camel's-hair pencil. Laura says it gives me great pleasure to exercise my skill in painting her, and thinks I widen the space each time. It just forms a cross on her.

We were quite pleased with Mr. Helm, and shall be glad to see him again. Laura unites with me in much love to you, Brother, Mary, and *the boys.* . . . Our church had an election for pastor. Twenty-nine present. Twenty-two voted for Mr. King; seven voted blanks—on the strength of which a call with a salary of twelve hundred dollars is to be made him. Some think he will refuse it. The lecture room of the church progresses. . . . Be sure to let Mary come back with Charles: we miss her too much.

Your affectionate sister,
S. M. Cumming.

Dr. Joseph Jones West *to* Rev. C. C. Jones[t]

Savannah, *Wednesday,* June 6th, 1855

Dear Cousin,

Could you experience for but a short time the state of mind under which I am now existing, and which has almost rendered me unfit for any duty for months past, you would receive this communication with some allowance for what there may be wrong in it, and pardon a former act which I know you consider unkind if not absolutely disrespectful—the manner in which I opened my heart to your daughter. Respect for you as her parent, and the affection with which I have always regarded you as a man and a relative, demanded that I should have first obtained your consent. Against these were arrayed the usages of society and the deep, soul-absorbing passion which subdued my better judgment. And can you blame me for doing what I see done every day, and by men universally esteemed, and when I have never known an objection raised but by your immediate family? That you are right I must acknowledge. But you have not forgotten the ardor of your younger days, and can pardon what you deem wrong when you consider the strong feeling which urged me on.

My cousin has given me no encouragement to continue my addresses, but I cannot conquer my love without making another attempt, the first step of which she must approve. Have I your consent? May I seek a happiness without which life would be protracted wretchedness?

It is right that I should say something of my prospects. They are good. My practice is good and increasing, and with the little property which fell to me last winter it will be enough to support a wife in comfort. I have heard you say that it was your desire that Cousin Mary should not marry for several years. Should I gain her consent and yours, I am willing to wait as long as you desire. Only let me live knowing that she will one day be mine!

It is needless for me to write any more. You know my heart and can destroy my every hope with a word. Decide; but in deciding remember that my love is founded upon an esteem which has been growing all my life and will last as long as that life does.

Should my suit meet with favor, will you give the enclosed note to Cousin Mamie? If not, let me know speedily: suspense is torture. With love to Cousins Mary, Mamie, and Joe, I remain

Sincerely yours,
Joseph J. West.

REV. C. C. JONES *to* DR. JOSEPH JONES WEST[t]

Maybank, *Monday,* June 11th, 1855

Dear Joseph,

I received your note by the last mail, and agreeably to your request handed its enclosure to my daughter, and now return you her answer, which is the result of her own judgment in the matter. We appreciate your feelings of friendship towards us, and hope they may ever remain unchanged. Wishing you every success and blessing in life, I am

Very truly yours,
C. C. Jones.

REV. C. C. JONES *to* MR. CHARLES C. JONES, JR.[g]

Maybank, *Monday,* June 11th, 1855

My dear Son,

Your two last letters are at hand. . . . Your appointment is a very pleasant one, and for which I am much obliged to Mr. Ward. I think it will be well for you to meet it, as by so doing you will visit *our Athens,* and make acquaintances which not only may prove agreeable but profitable to you in time to come. Enclosed is a check for fifty dollars which will cover your expenses; and would send you more, but you are aware we are living upon borrowed money this year, and I must beg you to be economical. It is my impression that your expenses as a visitor to the university of the state are provided for and will be paid you by the state. Mine were paid by South Carolina when I was appointed visitor to the state college in Columbia. If the state pays your expenses, as it certainly should do, then do not be too wise and independent to refuse taking the money. You will receive also a few letters of *introduction* to some of my friends and acquaintances whom you will have opportunity of seeing, and hope you will deliver them.

Say to your aunt and cousin that we are happy to hear of their coming, and will have the carriage and cart at Midway on *Thursday week the 21st inst.* to bring them down to Maybank, bag and baggage, where we will give them a hearty welcome.

Your brother also received a very pleasant letter from Mr. Helm. He writes much pleased with his visit to us. Be sure when you reply to present to him our kindest regards.

The "Know-Nothing" skies have become overcast with the shadows of abolitionism; and while I could not enter their body because it is a *secret political organization,* which the times do not exactly justify, I certainly can wish them no success whatever while stained with a connection with those who are not only enemies of our own section of the Union but even of the Union itself. Let us have the flag at the masthead, declared principles, an open sea, and a fair fight. That is the best way in everything.

Will you call at Mr. Lincoln's drugstore and request him to send out for me to Riceboro *by the Thursday's stage* a box of *fresh Saratoga water.* I wish the water for your mother. Let the bottles be the *"magnum bonum."* Direct care of C. Stebbins. *One dozen bottles.*

Preached at Dorchester yesterday: morning to whites, afternoon to blacks. All pretty well. Your dear mother took too long a ride last week, had fever two days, was much indisposed, is better. All at Social Bluff and Woodville pretty well. Love from all to your aunt and cousin and to yourself.

Your affectionate father,
C. C. Jones.

P.S. Be careful how you visit young ladies in and about *Augusta,* or anywhere else. I trust you have the bump of prudence well developed.
C. C. J.

Send out to me Mr. Ward's *Digest of the Census of 1850,* if you can get the use of it for me for a while. It is a congressional document. Am needing it particularly.

Mr. Charles C. Jones, Jr., *to* Rev. *and* Mrs. C. C. Jones[t]

Augusta, *Saturday,* June 16th, 1855

My dear Father and Mother,

You will see from the date and location of this letter that I am now in Augusta with my warm friend J. S. Sale, Esq.

My visit to this city has been exceedingly pleasant in its character. The supreme court was in session on Thursday and Friday. Have seen Judge Lumpkin, who desires his kind remembrance to you. He inquired very particularly concerning your health, Father. I was much pleased with his society, for he appears to be a temperate Christian gentleman, and one of the old school in manners and conversation. Mr. Alexander Stephens delivered an eloquent appeal for a new trial before the court in the Keener murder case. This application upon argument was subsequently allowed by the court. I was agreeably surprised in the eloquence of Mr. Stephens. Have you ever heard him? Upon my return I hope to give you its characteristics. As you know, he is one of the prominent men of our state.

Augusta now wears a beautiful appearance, and the retreat upon the Sand Hills is one of the pleasantest summer resorts I have ever seen in Georgia. The society also is in keeping with the location. I have already formed the acquaintance of the young ladies of beauty and standing, through the introduction of my friend Mr. Sale and the Misses Davis. I have been especially pleased with Miss Emma Cumming, a daughter of Colonel Cumming. . . . Mrs. and Dr. Davis and the young ladies of the family have been very kind to me. They desire their regards to be presented to you and Sister, and hope that they will be favored with a visit from you this summer. I have been somewhat amused with some of the compliments paid, and their great interest in me. The society of the family is, however, of a very interesting character. The young ladies are all well educated, intelligent, and studious in their habits, with fine conversational powers. . . . It is a pity that I am not a more susceptible young man; although extravagantly fond of ladies' society, it appears that my admiration is too general, and not personal in its kind.

My old friend John is just the same that he ever was, and our present union after the lapse of half a year is as the meeting of brothers. He is very comfortably located, and with his winning ways and general popularity, if attentive to business, will succeed admirably here.

My visit to Augusta has been delightful to me in every respect, and I am happy to have enjoyed the opportunity of forming so many agreeable acquaintances, especially among the ladies. On Monday morning I anticipate leaving Augusta for Athens. Tomorrow, I understand from Mrs. Harriss, Rev. David Porter will preach in the Presbyterian church. I feel anxious to hear him, as he is an old collegemate; and from the high opinion entertained of his talents by many, I am induced to believe that his sermon will be an excellent one.

I hardly think that I will be able to reach Liberty by the 25th of the present month. Will try and let you know positively from Athens what my arrangements will be. Leaving many occurrences of interest untold, I will give you an account of everything when we meet, D.V. With much love to you, my dear mother and father, to Sister, Brother, and all relatives, I am, as ever,

Your affectionate son,
Charles C. Jones, Jr.

Mrs. Susan M. Cumming *to* Rev. C. C. Jones[t]

Savannah, *Saturday,* June 16th, 1855

My dear Brother,

Thank you most kindly for arranging to meet us on next Thursday, when, Providence permitting, we hope to have the great pleasure of meeting you and all of our friends on the Island.

Charles Colcock left us at nine o'clock on Wednesday night in good health and spirits for Augusta, where he would probably stay with his friend Mr. Sale until Monday, and then go on to Athens to attend the examination of the students. It was quite an honorable appointment, and as he is just from the seats of learning, can propose the most puzzling questions. We have missed him very much. . . . Hope he will occupy his rooms the next winter. I have no doubt Savannah will afford him as sure a field for success as any other place—more so, for he has many friends here. . . . And when Joe is ready for the professor's chair, we will have a place for him too.

Give our warmest love to Sister Mary and Mary. . . . Laura unites with me in all love.

Your affectionate sister,
S. M. Cumming.

Rev. C. C. Jones *to* Mrs. Susan M. Cumming[t]

Maybank, *Thursday,* June 21st, 1855*

My dear Sister,

After much and most serious and wise consideration of the question, "Shall I or Joe go up to meet you at Midway today?" the conclusion has been arrived at that our room for the short journey to this place might be I do not say more agreeable but more *convenient* than our company, since there may be a goodly number of boxes, bundles, and all so forth that might be snugly disposed in the said seat which we should occupy. Added to all this is the impressive fact that the weather is warm, the horses not as fat as common, dinner will be waiting for you, and a lighter load would expedite your appearance here below. So if our wisdom and prudence have overcome our gallantry, you will consider us as making some valuable advances. And after all it is but gallantry in a judicious exhibition of itself, for we are consulting what we believe to be the comfort and convenience of the ladies. If we have erred, please give us credit for the very best intentions, and we shall certainly adopt another course another time.

We have been fixing up for you and Laura, and hope to be ready with everything—even with a dinner, which we shall try and prepare for town ladies. And tomorrow it is decreed that we will slay a savory animal and do better. We all send love, and shall give you a hearty welcome—and with much gratitude to receive you back again in health and mercy.

Your affectionate brother,
C. C. Jones.

V

Maybank, *Friday,* August 31st, 1855

My dear Daughter,

We have felt very lonely since your aunt and cousin and yourself have left us. Your father and myself are now entirely alone. Yesterday afternoon your brothers, accompanied by Willie in the buggy and pair, with Gilbert to drive, left us for Dorchester to pass the night with your Uncle Henry and go up to Hinesville today to hear Mr. Ward's address to the people of Liberty. Your uncle also goes up, leaving Sister Betsy in Dorchester.

This morning before I was out of bed Mrs. King's servant came over with the mail and a basket of the finest red potatoes that I have seen for many a day. I wished that I could have forwarded them to Marietta. We were very happy to receive your letter and hear of your safe arrival in Savannah. The day you left was very hot, and I feared the ride might give fever.

I trust you are all beyond the reach of the mosquitoes. They have poured in upon us the three past nights, owing to the rain and northeast winds. It is still lightning in the east, which betokens unsettled weather. I trust it may not end in a storm, which would prove most disastrous to the hopes of the planters, already blighted.

In the absence of your own dear voice, the sound of the piano and guitar, your little Willie has been cheering us all day long with his sweet song, while Lady and Moses and Rex have redoubled their attentions, Duchess and Jet proving indifferent. . . . By the time this reaches you I trust you will be with our dear relatives. I know how happy you will feel with those who have ever loved and treated you so kindly and affectionately. . . . Sister Betsy rode over the morning you left and carried the birds, etc., etc., to the Bluff; they will interest "the old folks at home". . . . We expect Willie and Joe home tomorrow; Charles may remain a day or two longer on the Sand Hills. . . . I am sorry there is nothing new or interesting to communicate. You will have to cheer and interest us by your letters. Your father unites with me in best love to our dear and venerated aunt. Our best wishes attend her on her forthcoming birthday! Love to Sister Susan and Laura and to Cousin Mary and dear Lou and to each of the girls and Joe. . . . Tell the servants howdy for us. Wishing you, my beloved child, every blessing spiritual and temporal,

Ever your affectionate mother,
Mary Jones.

Rev. C. C. Jones *to* Miss Mary Sharpe Jones[t]

Montevideo, *Thursday,* September 6th, 1855[*]

My dear Daughter,

I left Mother and your brothers at Maybank yesterday morning—all, through divine mercy, quite well. Maybank was on a visit to his nephews, and he and they with their rods in their hands were just off for the river. Joe had rigged his uncle in a suit of his clothes, which fitted him well all to the length of the legs of the pantaloons! Mother was as busy as usual, now getting your brother ready for Philadelphia. He has secured some valuable contributions to his menagerie, which, however, are disappearing day by day as his time grows shorter.

Your brother the Judge went to a political meeting back of the Sand Hills with Banky last week, and a justice's court being in session at the same place and time, he unexpectedly was called upon to appear as an advocate. And he then and there obtained his first case, and made his first speech in court. I tell him he should enter it upon his journal, and that minutely. He refused a fee from his client, who promised to do all he could for him in these parts. Charles is to send him some of his *cards,* which he will faithfully set up in conspicuous places for his benefit and behoof. This is a beginning, and I like it very much. He aided a poor and honest man and charged him nothing.

I must leave your brothers to tell you the political news: some movements in our quiet waters. You may see something of it in the *Georgian* of this week. . . . All well on the Island. Remember us affectionately to your aunt and Cousin Laura, and to Aunty and Lady Mary Wortley Montagu, and to Lou and the children. . . . Make yourself useful, my dear child, wherever you are. Let us hear from you often.

Your ever affectionate father,

C. C. Jones.

Mrs. Mary Jones *to* Miss Mary Sharpe Jones[t]

Maybank, *Monday,* September 10th, 1855

My dear Daughter,

We sent up for the mail today, directing the boy to come on to Woodville, where we were "taking tea," and were very happy to receive your letter. I am afraid, my dear child, that you are not well. Be sure and write us particularly about your health. I shall feel very anxious until I know that you are well again. Your brother Joseph received also your cousin's kind and interesting letter, and will reply shortly to it. He leaves us in the course of two weeks to be in time for the opening term. It would have given both of your brothers great pleasure to visit our dear relatives in Marietta this summer, but it was not convenient in the money line. If you need any more do not fail to write and let us know. Your kind aunt has indeed presented you with a handsome bonnet!

Tomorrow your brother Charles expects to start for Savannah to engage an office. I trust a kind Providence will favor and direct him. Your father wrote you of his "maiden speech"; he has another application from a poor man to defend his cause. I repeat to him: "*Blessed* is he that considereth the poor: the Lord will deliver him in time of trouble." I would rather have the good will of the poor than the flattery of the rich.

Mr. Buttolph rode down for a short time to see us on Friday. He is looking remarkably well, and I gave him a fresh supply of lozenges. . . . Your uncle and aunt are well: quite interested in politics. . . . Your maid has improved so much that I have not had occasion to reprove her for nodding since you left; the promise of that new dress stimulates her to overcome the habit. She is a good child. She and all the servants send howdies except Jack; he only wants me to tell you "how good he takes care of your flowers." I must now close, with our united love to all your aunts and cousins. Write us often. May the Lord bless and keep you, my dear child, ever prays

Your affectionate mother,
Mary Jones.

Mrs. Mary Jones *to* Miss Mary Sharpe Jones[t]

Maybank, *Tuesday,* September 25th, 1855

My dear Child,

Up to this moment I have been as busy as I could be to get your brother ready. Whilst we are waiting for breakfast I write these few lines to enclose with Matilda's letter, which I opened knowing who it was from, and that I might know when she was coming home. Your dear father was *very* sick all last week—in bed from Tuesday to Saturday. He was three days in the country the previous week, which I think was the cause of his sickness. He says he now feels better than he has done for a long time. . . . The bell rings. Love to all.

Ever your affectionate mother,
Mary Jones.

Your brother will be off for Midway immediately.

Mrs. Susan M. Cumming *to* Rev. C. C. Jones[t]

Marietta, September 1855

My dear Brother,

After all you saw the past summer, you will not be surprised to hear that Mr. D. L. B. has commenced a correspondence with Laura which has been favorably received, though nothing definite or decided has occurred. He wishes to know when we will visit the Lookout Mountain, and would like to be our escort to Savannah. He has been informed that we will do so, D.V., on the 15th or 16th of October, and come down to Macon on the 24th to remain a few days before returning to Savannah. This matter I inform you of, my dear brother, knowing your interest in us and all that concerns us. I think it a matter of prudence that the matter be private; of course you will acquaint Sister Mary of it.

We are all well. I have begged a corner of Mary's letter for this. Believe me

Your affectionate sister,
S. M. Cumming.

REV. C. C. JONES *to* MRS. SUSAN M. CUMMING[t]
Montevideo, *Thursday,* September 27th, 1855*

Your enclosure in Mary's letter, my dear sister, came safely to hand. The arrangement you intimate, so far as I can see and know, meets my approbation. Of course the proof of its wisdom experience only can decide; and pretty much everything in the present instance must be left to those who are of age and can answer for themselves. I have never known any difference between your interest and my own, and *yours* have always been to me as mine own children. We must in this, as in all things, look up and live upon the text: "Except the Lord build the house, they labor in vain that build it."

Mary and myself came from Maybank this morning, leaving Charles Colcock and all friends on the Island quite well. . . . We spend the night here, and are now writing opposite each other at the table and in a salubrious atmosphere of tar smoke.

A young friend of mine wishes me to supply his pulpit for one or two Sabbaths soon, as he wishes to make a short excursion for a vacation after the labors of the summer. I promised him before I was sick that I would endeavor to do so, but *now* cannot tell how it will be. Am much pulled down.

County generally healthy. . . . Your people at both places, I believe, are all pretty well. . . . Am just about writing my dear child, and Mary is writing dear Aunty, so between all the letters you will have some news. Mary sends you much love. As ever,

Your affectionate brother,
C. C. Jones.

REV. C. C. JONES *to* MISS MARY SHARPE JONES[t]
Montevideo, *Thursday,* September 27th, 1855*

My dear Daughter,

I have not been as sick since 1840; but through God's mercy the fever left me on Friday last and has not returned. It has left me considerably reduced, and all I had previously gained is apparently lost, and am below where I was when I came home. It seemed that perhaps I had reached the measure of my days, and that the Lord intended to remove me from the land of the living. And now that He has been pleased to bring me so far up again, it is like taking new hold of life once more. My constant prayer is that the Lord would prepare me for His coming, and suffer me not to live that That Day may overtake me as a thief and find me unprepared! It is our duty and our privilege to walk *by faith* and not *by sight*. Here is the warfare; and it is grace only that can give us the victory.

Your dear brother Joe left us on Tuesday. Your brother rode up with him to Midway and saw him safe in the stage, and I presume he went right on that evening for Augusta and so on. Your mother and I, after he left, went into his room and then into the cotton house (his laboratory) and picked up his little matters which he had not time to put away; and Mother made Flora go in and wash up everything. His thermometer I hung up inside the entry alongside the front door, and his bellows were carried into my study, and his scales into your room. So in one way and another we put everything snugly away, and we felt so melancholy we were often very nigh if not quite in tears. His visit home has been so pleasant and refreshing, and now that he is gone we do not recollect the least unpleasantness of any kind. He was busy up to the last moment, and it was not until twelve at night Monday night that we got through, Mother and Brother Charlie and all the servants packing and fixing; for my sickness had thrown everything back, and Mother barely got all his wardrobe ready. He had a great box of *skeletons,* etc., for Dr. Leidy, and the steamboat took all his boxes at Woodville the morning he left. Dear child, may God watch over and bless him, and make him His own child and an instrument for good on earth! You must direct your letters to him, as heretofore, *care of Dr. Joseph Leidy.* Widgeon he gave to Lafayette; and Moses is where he was, privileged either dog or cat according to his association. Your canaries are both in good health and spirits.

We miss Joe and yourself very much, but your dear brother tries to do all he can to help us and fill up your places. He is very fat and hearty.

Mother and I came up this morning, and the ride is so long we are staying overnight. The new part of the house is creeping on, and our plan is, God willing, so soon as it is weatherboarded in, to put in repair the old part so that we can move up in the fall. This will be best for us and for the work too. The lot, and indeed the whole plantation, needs a world of fixing. It will take time to do all.

You will observe in the *News* of this week communications in which your Uncle Banky is involved. The affair has been badly—or injudiciously —managed from the beginning, and is mortifying in all its aspects. Hope there may be some peaceful and honorable issue to it. Men should never *write;* it is not the best mode of securing speedy and peaceful relations. The Lord restrain and control all!

Our people are generally very hearty. We have had Harriet's *little Betsy* about two weeks at Maybank for a change of air and medicine. The child is not yet out of danger. We all take a hand at prescribing for it because it is young.

It would much gratify us to visit Marietta, but as we are now circumstanced, we have no hope of it. Try and enjoy your vacation, and pleasant scenes and kind friends; and may God add His blessing and restore you to us in improved health! My love to Lady Mary Wortley Montagu; I hope yet to visit her in her own mansion of hospitality and wit and be a partaker thereof. And let me hear no more messages of such *old sort of people* and *old sort of clothes* and *old sort of doings;* we'll have none of it. Mother is writing a very long letter to dear Aunty, and I will stop after sending love to everybody in the house. I remain, my dear child,

Your ever affectionate father,
C. C. Jones.

Mrs. Mary Jones *to* Mrs. Susan M. Cumming[t]
Montevideo, *Thursday,* September 27th, 1855*

Your letters, my dear sister and niece, were thankfully received by us, and we rejoice to find you all enjoying yourselves so much. I knew it could not be otherwise with "such charming society," as *our friend* said. You must not imagine the hot weather located at the foot of the mountains; it has pervaded even these balmy plains, and September has poured down a torrid ray of heat. Mr. John Stevens says the sun was so hot he told his Negroes to go in from the field. . . . We had a pleasant visit from him and Mr. William last evening. Indeed, our friends have all been sociable and kind. Still they do not fill your places; they are vacant, and we miss you very much. I hope our dear child will improve in health. We do so long to see her.

Charles was favored in securing an excellent office in Gaudry's building (lately occupied as the telegraphic office). In times past it has been used by many illustrious predecessors in the legal profession. I hope the dear child will find employment.

Joseph appreciated your kind letter, dear Laura, very highly, and nothing but constant work prevented his replying before he left. . . . Mr. Jones has retired, weak and weary; I must not keep him awake, so good night to you all, with a bundle of love to be equally divided. Do remember us to our friends at Roswell.

Ever your sincerely attached
Mary Jones.

Miss Mary Sharpe Jones *to* Rev. *and* Mrs. C. C. Jones[t]
Marietta, *Monday,* October 1st, 1855

My dear Father and Mother,

We were *all* very much favored this morning in receiving letters from you both. I am very, very sorry, dear Father, to hear that you have been so sick, and feel truly grateful to our kind Heavenly Father for His mercy in restoring you to health, and hope that you will speedily recover all that you have lost.

Matilda's letter was unexpected but very welcome. She had neglected writing so long that I had despaired of her doing so, and left her direction at home; but I will answer her soon and enclose the letter to Mrs. Harden. She is a warmhearted girl; I am glad to find her so strongly in favor of Presbyterianism. . . .

Saturday was Aunt Eliza's seventieth birthday. The children brought their offerings: Joe a pig, and the girls a toasting fork, Aunt Susan a napkin ring, Cousin Laura a fruit knife, and I a dressing gown. She is a very active lady for one of her age—a pattern of industry.

Recently she has been very much disturbed in regard to the difficulty between Mr. McConnell and Uncle Banky. From the newspapers (our only source of information) we can learn nothing very definite or satisfactory. I understand that Captain McConnell has gone to Liberty for the purpose of settling the affair, so I presume he will insist upon less writing and more action.

This is election day, and thus far everything has passed off very quietly, though some of the citizens are fearing that King Alcohol will bear rule this evening.

Tomorrow we expect to go to Roswell, and will return, D.V., on Friday.

We saw Mr. Goulding a few evenings ago, and he said that he felt so badly about having gone to sleep in the cars that he came very near writing us a letter of apology. Aunt Mary said she hoped he had waked up. "Why," he said, "he hoped in a short time to awake to some very pleasant realities!" His marriage will take place on the 18th of this month.

Aunt Mary is just going to preside at a meeting of the Benevolent Association, and says that I must tell you she is acting upon your hint and has risen a little, having gotten out of the pantry today. . . .

Mr. Petrie preached last evening upon the state of the soul between death and the Judgment. He is preaching a series on Sabbath evening. A few of the members of his Bible class presented him with twenty dollars on Saturday as a small token of their regard and affection.

I am very glad to hear that we will be able to move up to Montevideo this fall; it will be very pleasant to spend a winter at the old place once more. . . . I must now close, dear Father and Mother, as we expect to take tea this evening with Mrs. Petrie. . . . You must indeed be lonely without Brother Joe; I will write him soon. Aunt Susan and Cousin Laura are quite well, and send much love to you; also to Brother Charlie. My best love to him. Accept, dear Father and Mother, a large portion of love from

Your ever attached child,

Mary S. Jones.

Mrs. Mary Jones *to* Miss Mary Sharpe Jones[t]

Maybank, *Wednesday,* October 3rd, 1855

Your letter, my darling child, reached us by the last mail, and we are happy to find that you are enjoying yourself so much. But *I am distressed* to know that your cough still lingers. You must use *rubbing* and *irritants* to your *chest* and *between your shoulders night and morning;* and get immediately a bottle of *Cherry Pectoral* and *take it faithfully.* You know it has done you good on a former occasion, and you must use every means to get rid of the cough at once. No doubt it is the remains of the whooping cough; it has been very common with those who have had it here this season. Be sure and put on your flannels early.

You judge rightly why I have not written you oftener of late. I was very much worn down nursing your dear father the week he was so sick, and at the same time occupying every spare moment in work for Joe. If your aunty had not very kindly assisted me he would not have had his wardrobe completed; but he has left us with a full supply, and all new and good. We do miss the dear child sadly. In the morning I almost instinctively tap at his door to wake him, or order the bell rung in the end of the piazza to call him from his laboratory. My heart has risen up in grateful thanks to our Father in Heaven for permitting us all, an unbroken family, to be together this summer. Oh, that through His grace we might attain to the blessedness of those who shall dwell in His presence eternally!

I ripped up your silk dress and sent it on to be dyed, and your brother carried on with his articles a small jar of limes for your friend Miss Taylor. We shipped his boxes at Woodville by the steamer who now wakes up our long-slumbering waters once a week, as she comes steaming as high up the Newport as Melon Bluff. (Mr. Busby and all his family, I am told, contemplate a trip down in her as far as Woodville, their carriages going around *by land* to meet them!)

We had a very interesting day last Sabbath at Dorchester. Mr. Mallard preached two admirable sermons, one of them to the children. He certainly possesses eminent gifts as a preacher. Mr. Buttolph and himself spent last night with us, and your brother and Mr. Mallard went out early this morning fishing. They returned about eleven o'clock with over a hundred, the best of which I made him take home, giving also your aunty and uncle a fine string. They had just called up on their way home.

I will leave your brother to give you all the political news, and tell of the Democratic triumph!

After the election your uncle went up to Walthourville on Maybank's business. No doubt you have seen the *last* piece from the pen of J. D. McConnell. It could not be exceeded for insolence and prevarication. If they will pursue the course marked out by your uncle, I hope the affair will soon be settled. It has caused us much unhappiness. We pray God to overrule it all. We hope the *demon* of which you have heard so much will now be exorcised, and his reign of confusion and every evil work will come to an end.

Your Uncle John has decided to accept the call to Washington. Has sent in his resignation to the Sand Hills church, which has been accepted. They part with him with regret; some of his members say they fear that they will never get another pastor like him. I am told they will present a call to Mr. Mallard. This may decide him to remain in the county for the present, and not to go West immediately as he seemed desirous of doing. . . .

Would you not like to attend Julia Fisher's wedding? You mentioned she was to be married the last of November. Your father says he would like you to do so, and perhaps it might suit him to make a visit there at that time. He said this afternoon he wanted to attend the meeting of our synod. He has been very much reduced in flesh and strength by his recent sickness, and a little change would do him good. You remember how much he enjoyed it last fall.

On next Tuesday Audley and Mrs. King expect to leave for Atlanta, Marietta, and Roswell. Mr. Buttolph also expects to make a *short visit* to the up country.

4th. We took tea at Woodville this evening. Audley had not arrived when we left, but the mailbag has just been handed in. Letters from our dear aunt and yourself and from Joe. He arrived in Philadelphia half-past twelve at night on the 29th. Met Dr. Leland on the Charleston Road; he wanted to know if you were married! Thanks to our dear aunt for her valued letter. Our best wishes and prayers for the best of Heaven's blessings to crown the evening of her valuable life! I trust she may be long spared to us all. . . .

I must close to send a line to Philadelphia by the morning's mail. Your father and brother Charles unite with me in best love to Aunt and cousins, Sister Susan, Laura, and yourself and the children. I hope to hear that your cough has entirely left you. May the Lord bless and keep you, ever prays

Your own affectionate mother,
Mary Jones.

The servants all send howdies.

I will be glad of some rose cuttings or any flowers; would like a root of the jessamine that runs on Aunt's porch.

Mrs. Mary Jones *to* Miss Mary Sharpe Jones[t]

Maybank, *Tuesday,* October 9th, 1855

You know, my dear child, that I am a great advocate for flannels and keeping warm. Fearing that you might suffer from the cool change, I have this moment finished your petticoats to take over to your Aunt Julia, who very kindly offers to convey them to you. I thought at first of taxing our good pastor, who leaves tomorrow for the Lookout Mountain. But perhaps he only carries a portmanteau and would not like such encumbrances *for the present*. By and by he may appreciate their necessity!

We have now the most charming weather, and your father went to Montevideo today. I tried hard to persuade him to let me accompany him, but he thought it best that I should not do so. We are trying to get the old part of the house comfortable for us to maroon in by the first of November, when we hope to go up. Of course, there will be very little moving, excepting for the servants, until the house is done, which will not be for some time yet.

Tell our dear aunt that your father and myself felt most highly flattered at her remembrance of us on her seventieth birthday. Our best wishes ever attend her, with our poor prayers for her continued life and health and happiness!

What do you think I did this morning? Turned out with all hands and burnt up the trash on the lawn. It now looks like a newly shaved beau. In the midst of smoke up rode *Willie* with net and fishing rods trailing behind; and he and Charles immediately rigged themselves in red flannel shirts, and off they went, looking as though they were just ready to ship before the mast. I sent them down a large pan of dinner, and they have not yet come back. The fish have been very fine and abundant. We often wish we could place the fine sheepshead on Aunt's table, or exchange them for a dish of your fine peaches.

Our county has been and continues to be blessed with great health.

Miss Lizzie Helm sent you not long ago a wild lily (pressed); it looks like the fragrant one that blooms in our yard here by the althea tree. I put it away so carefully that I cannot find it now. Will keep it for you. *Mr. George* has sent us three kinds of grass from Kentucky. Can you get me seeds of the vanilla grass in Marietta? Or any vernal grass? . . .

Best love to aunts and cousins, Laura and yourself, and the children. May you all enjoy the contemplated trip and return in safety! Your birds and flowers are doing well. The servants all send howdies. Your aunty has been quite sick with her cold; is now better.

Ever, my darling child, your affectionate mother,
Mary Jones.

MISS MARY SHARPE JONES *to* MRS. MARY JONES[t]

Marietta, *Saturday,* October 13th, 1855

My dear Mother,

I did not write you on Thursday as I usually do, for I wished to see some of our friends from Liberty before doing so. Aunt Mary says I have been waiting for the "Express Mail" (alias Mr. Buttolph). We expected him on Wednesday night, but owing to a collision which took place seventeen miles from Savannah, and their getting too late to the cars in Macon, he did not arrive until last night, and consequently did not make his appearance here until this morning. His nonarrival caused some anxiety with some of our party, who were evidently at the seat of expectation! I felt thankful to learn that you were all quite well, and dear Father improving. Aunt Julia stopped in Atlanta; we hope, however, that she will come up on Monday and join our party to the Lookout. Aunt Susan is now writing and urging her to do so. We expect to leave the first of next week.

Mr. Buttolph says he has a bundle for me, and I suppose it contains my flannel. I am very much obliged to you, dear Mother, for thinking of me. I think I shall need them on the mountain, as all our friends say it will be very cold there. But I hope the air there will take away my cough entirely, as it is said to be peculiarly efficacious in removing colds and coughs. I am taking the Cherry Pectoral, and am beginning to feel the benefit of it. . . .

I have written this very hastily, dear Mother, as the mail will close in a very short time, and if this does not go now you will not receive it before Thursday. The family are all quite well, and send much love. Aunt Susan and Cousin Laura unite with me in best love to Brother Charlie, dear Father, and yourself. I am, as ever,

Your affectionate child,
Mary S. Jones.

Give a great deal of love to Aunty and Uncle.

Miss Mary Sharpe Jones *to* Rev. *and* Mrs. C. C. Jones[t]

Marietta, *Monday,* October 15th, 1855

My dear Father and Mother,

We are surrounded by so many of our Liberty friends that we can almost fancy ourselves there. Aunt Julia, Audley, and Johnnie came up this morning, and intended to have gone directly to Roswell, but Aunt Mary laid violent hands upon them and insisted upon their remaining at least one night. They expect to leave tomorrow morning. We had hoped to have them of our party to the Lookout, but they have declined for want of time. We expect to leave tomorrow at ten, our party consisting of Mr. Buttolph and ourselves.

Mr. Buttolph preached for Mr. Petrie yesterday morning: an excellent sermon on the Atonement. He begs me to present his kindest remembrances to you, and hopes that you feel no inconvenience, dear Father, from filling his pulpit yesterday.

This morning I read with mingled feelings of pain and gratitude an account of the poisoning of Dr. Leland's family. One of the ladies, in mixing some biscuits for tea, put in two teaspoonfuls of arsenic by mistake. The paper states that the bread was prepared by one of the daughters, and Mrs. Leland had purchased the arsenic without her daughters' knowledge for the purpose of destroying rats. Mrs. Leland, her two daughters, a granddaughter, and a part of the servants partook of the bread. They were seized with great pain and nausea, and discovered the cause about an hour after. Drs. Fair and Crane were immediately called in, prompt remedies were used, and all with the exception of Mrs. Leland were relieved in a short time. Mrs. Leland took violent emetics, but it was not until five hours after that she succeeded in vomiting the fetid mass. She was dangerously ill, but is now convalescent. Dr. Leland was absent at the time. I am inclined to think that it was Mary who made the mistake, though I do not know. I felt truly grateful to think that they were all so mercifully spared, for it would have been awful if any one of them had died. I think I shall be very careful hereafter to ascertain the nature of powders before putting them in bread! . . .

Aunt Julia says I must tell you that she sees quite an improvement in my appearance. I begin to feel much stronger. She begs that you will tell Cousin Mary of her arrival here, as she may be prevented from writing before going to Roswell. Johnnie is quite well except a slight cold. He is very much amused in the yard "knocking down chestnuts"—the favorite amusement of the boys at this season. Indeed, some parts of the street are so filled with the burrs that it is worse than walking through a bed of cockspurs.

The weather has moderated very much, and we hope to have a continuance of mild weather on the mountain. The public house there is now closed, but we expect to stop at a farmhouse. . . .

Card playing is a favorite amusement in the evening at the hotel, and professors of religion do not scruple to engage in it. It really seems to me that persons who leave home for the summer often leave their principles at home. I have been surprised to hear of some ladies who have been seen evening after evening seated around the card table. There is something revolting in the idea of any female who has any pretensions to refinement being found night after night at the card table. They say there is no harm in playing, as they do merely for amusement. . . .

The family here are all quite well. Aunt Eliza's cough is very troublesome at times; she coughs a great deal in the morning. All send love. Aunt Susan and Cousin Laura are both well. Mr. Buttolph is staying with Mr. Ardis, but he takes almost all of his meals here. When will Brother Charlie go to Savannah? My love to him. I hope my little birds are well. With much love, dear Father and Mother, I remain

Your affectionate child,
Mary S. Jones.

MISS MARY SHARPE JONES *to* REV. *and* MRS. C. C. JONES[t]

Marietta, *Saturday,* October 20th, 1855

My dear Father and Mother,

Our anticipated excursions to the Lookout and Stone Mountains have been made, and we are once again with our kind aunt and family. To say that we have been much pleased and gratified conveys but little impression of the real enjoyment we have had; and in sitting down to write you of some of the scenes we have seen, and of our various adventures, I scarcely know where to commence or what to say. But presuming that you would like to know all, and trusting to your clemency if I weary you, I will begin from the beginning.

On Tuesday morning at 10 A.M. we—that is, Aunt Susan, Cousin Laura, Mr. Buttolph, and myself—seated ourselves in the cars and were soon on our way to Chattanooga. I amused myself a part of the way with *Star Papers,* a book recently published by Mr. Henry W. Beecher. The country through which we passed was rolling and pleasing, but there was nothing of much interest until we came to the Etowah River and bridge, which is the highest I have ever crossed except the suspension bridge over the Niagara River. The next object of interest was the tunnel, the terror of nervous and old ladies. Between Dalton and Chattanooga we crossed fourteen bridges, twelve of them covered; and ten of them were over the Chickamauga River. This name signifies *death,* and I learned from a Mr. Freeman on the mountain that its banks were unhealthy, and owing to the frequent risings of the river the fording is difficult, and many persons have been drowned in the attempt. Hence the name.

At 5 P.M. we arrived in Chattanooga and stopped at the Crutchfield House, which is just by the railroad. Chattanooga is a very flourishing town of nearly five thousand inhabitants, and rapidly increasing in population. The Presbyterian church is quite a fine one—brick, occupying a very conspicuous place. At present they are without a pastor, their minister having recently gone to Nashville. There are Baptist, Methodist, Episcopal, and Catholic churches in the place, the last two very small and not in a flourishing condition. We had not time to explore the town for ourselves, but learned as much as we could from persons resident there. Soon after tea Mr. Buttolph made all necessary inquiries respecting our intended trip to the mountain, and engaged a hack to convey us to the top the next morning, we agreeing to be ready at half-past seven, an hour which most of us thought quite early enough!

When we awoke on Wednesday morning our eyes were not greeted with the bright rays of the sun. On the contrary, everything was enveloped in a dense fog. However, with the hope that this would soon disappear, we were ready at eight o'clock to set out for the mountain, which is five miles from Chattanooga—that is, two and a half to the foot and the same to the summit. There is a very good road all the way up—in some places pretty steep, but for the greater part the ascent is easy. The road winds up through the trees along the sides of deep and immense ravines, while large masses of rock jut out all around you, above and below, sometimes apparently threatening to come down and send to destruction everything that might chance to be in their way. The mountain is so thickly wooded that a view of the surrounding country is quite impracticable while one is ascending. At first I felt impatient for a sight, but afterwards was glad that the whole view burst upon us at once.

The first point we visited when nearly on the summit was the Brow, from which you get the first good view. Just below is the Leonora Spring. In order to reach this we descended quite a number of steps built of wood against the side of the rock. The spring was discovered by a young lady named Leonora Whiteside, and it now bears her name. It flows from under the rocks on the side of the mountain, forming a kind of miniature cave into which you can look for six or eight feet. The water is not allowed to flow down the rocks as it pleases, but is conveyed by pipes to the top of the mountain. A portion of it passes a short distance through a small wooden trough to a tub which answers the purpose of a reservoir, and by means of a bucket which runs up and down on a wire it is carried to another part of the mountain. The scenery just around the spring is wild. Large perpendicular rocks hang above, in some places projecting out so far as to form "quite a church," as one of our party suggested, the fallen rocks answering very well for seats.

After spending some time here, and as we walked along and ascended the steps, pausing involuntarily to glance at the names carved on the rocks with a vague hope of recognizing the initials of some acquaintance, we seated ourselves on the Brow and again feasted our eyes upon the landscape below. Of this view I shall not say much, for if I begin to express my feelings I shall have no words left through which to convey to you my admiration of *the view*. This "brow" overlooks the Chattanooga Creek, and as far as the eye could reach there was one unbroken sea of mountains. It was exceedingly hazy, and this rendered our view much more circumscribed than it would otherwise have been. Mr. Powers, our driver, a young man of sixteen or seventeen, said "he reckoned it was what he would call a considerable of a hazy day; 'twon't common to have so much fog on yon mountains." We lingered here as long as we could, though by no means as long as we desired. The day was advancing, and we had much of interest before us.

From this we rode about two miles on the top to another point, from which we took an observation, and then proceeded to the North Point or Lookout. This is *the view* on the mountain. I wish I could convey to you some impression of the scene below, but I have no language. All that I can say is that I *felt* it. From this point you look into six states and, I am told, fifteen counties. On every side mountains—on the right, far in the distance, the Blue Ridge; Chattanooga valley and the town beautifully situated on the Tennessee River, which threads its serpentine course below, forming in front the "Moccasin Bend." This is a large piece of land shaped by the windings of the river into a huge shoe or moccasin. The form strikes you immediately, and requires no stretch of the imagination. The river and state are said to derive their name from this, as *Tennessee* is said to be the Indian for "moccasin." Here you can count six or eight distinct bends in the river. Chattanooga (or Ross's Landing, as it was formerly called) looks like a toy village, the cultivated portions of the surrounding country like a succession of gardens, men like ants. In a meadow below on the "moccasin" were some horses and cows feeding, and they were no larger than mice. The railroad track scarcely appeared as wide as an ordinary footpath. The forest on the mountains and in the plains presented a most brilliant and beautiful appearance. Nature had decked the trees in every imaginable shade of scarlet, orange, and green, and their gay dresses seemed to scorn the idea of decay. I never before realized the full beauty of the forest in autumn, and felt that it was the most appropriate season for our visit. The temperature was so delightful—cool but not sufficiently so to make a shawl necessary.

The view from this "north point" is one of the grandest and most beautiful I have ever seen. I never expect to see one surpassing it. *Beautiful, grand,* and *sublime* are terms too inadequate to describe it. When the time came for us to leave this spot I felt so reluctant to go that I wished that I could become ethereal and just float above the scene until my soul was satisfied. There is nothing, I think, which so convinces man of his own insignificance as a sight of God's wonderful creation, himself only as the dust in the balance. I felt deeply excited, but it was that excitement which sealed my lips and chained me to the spot. It does take a great deal from the romance of one's feelings when, just as they are admiring some beautiful spur of mountains, to be told: "That is Raccoon Ridge." What a descent! One comes immediately down from the clouds and finds themselves standing on mother earth.

From this point we turned our faces towards Mr. Freeman's, two miles distant. Here we stopped for dinner and gained all the information we could. Found out that it was altogether out of the question to visit the lake that afternoon, as it was six miles off, and most of the road very rocky and steep. (You will have some idea of the size of the mountain when I tell you that it is from six to nine miles in length; you ride over this distance in passing from one point to another.) The lake, when full of water, is quite an interesting object, for the water falls over a precipice six hundred feet in height. At this time there is very little water there, and we were told that there was not much to be seen. So we occupied the rest of the afternoon in visiting the Rock City.

This is one of the greatest curiosities I have ever seen. You recollect the appearance of the stone church in Dover Plains? Just imagine rocks fifty feet in height, piled against each other, forming as it were underground passages; or rather I felt as though I was wandering among the ruins of some giant's castle. Not that the rocks at all assume any regular forms, but there are these long passages between them—sometimes covered, narrow, and then suddenly widening into large halls. I will tell you all about it when we meet. I wished for you all the time, and felt that I should have enjoyed it so much more if you had only been there. These passages are (some of them) carpeted with beautiful green moss, and I presume from their appearance that in wet seasons streams of water must flow through them.

Everyone that can ought to visit this mountain. I fear that I have long since wearied you with my long epistle, so I will cease and run hastily through the rest.

After wandering through this "rock city" we returned by way of the Elephant, taking this curiosity last. This is a large piece of sandstone in the shape of an elephant. The stone is soft, and the trunk has unfortunately been broken off, but still the resemblance is very strong.

After seeing the Elephant we bade farewell to the summit and commenced to descend. We lingered on our way to see the sun sink to rest behind the mountain, thus giving a beautiful close to our day on the mountain—one of great pleasure, and long to be remembered. I never expect to spend one of greater interest. My only regret was that you, together with my dear brothers, were not with us; but I hope that at some future day you will all visit it. The mountain is said to be twenty-eight hundred feet high. There are twenty-five families who spend their summers on it, and twelve reside permanently. There is a small church there, but they have no regular preaching and frequently go to Chattanooga on Sabbath.

We spent Wednesday night in Chattanooga, and on Thursday morning at eight took the cars for Marietta, but determined after we had ridden a few hours to pass on to the Stone Mountain, as we had none of us seen that. At Marietta we saw Joe, and through him made known our plans to Aunty. Aunt Julia, Audley, and Johnnie got in here, and we rode together as far as Atlanta. But of this they will tell you. We spent Thursday night at the Stone Mountain, ascended it Friday morning, and returned that evening.

My letter is too long already, so I will reserve the narration of our adventures here until I see you. . . . We hope to leave on Wednesday for Macon, remain there until the Monday or Tuesday following, and then go to Savannah. I wish to remain there a few days to have my teeth attended to, and will write from there and say just when I will come home—probably today two weeks, which will be the 5th of November. . . . With affectionate love, dear Father and Mother, I remain

Your attached child,
Mary S. Jones.

Rev. C. C. Jones *to* Miss Mary Sharpe Jones[t]

Arcadia, *Monday,* October 22nd, 1855

My dear Daughter,

A letter came by the mail this evening from Columbia, and I forward it with this note to you to Macon, where we suppose you now to be on your way down homeward. Your mother and I have felt happy at your enjoyment of your visit to the up country, and your improvement in health, and hope, God willing, you will return to us in perfect health.

I left your mother and brother at Maybank this morning. Both well.

We heard Mr. R. Q. Mallard preach two excellent sermons at Dorchester yesterday. He has accepted the call to the Walthourville church, soon to be vacated by your Uncle John: eight hundred dollars per annum. I suppose it is a temporary arrangement with him, as there is not sufficient field there for a young and ardent man. So I should suppose; I know nothing.

We had a fine rain yesterday, and it has refreshed everything. The drought has been excessive. A letter is just at hand from your brother Joe. Quite well and quite busy, and all our friends in Philadelphia well. Am up here attending to business, but feel not very bright. Just waiting for the people to come in to prayers. A brilliant night! Remember me affectionately to your Aunt Susan and Cousin Laura and to Mr. and Mrs. Nisbet. Kiss their little ones for me. Excuse this hasty letter; would write more but must stop. The Lord bless and keep you in all your ways, my dear child, and make you a blessing!

Your ever affectionate father,
C. C. Jones.

Mrs. Sarah A. Howe *to* Mrs. Mary Jones[t]

Columbia, South Carolina, Wednesday, October 24th, 1855

My dear Friend,

I received your letter on Saturday evening, and lest that "thief of time" should make me appear ungrateful for your favor, I take up my pen to give you an immediate acknowledgment. Mr. Howe and myself have been talking much of you of late, and he has intended writing Dr. Jones; but his pressing duties at home and frequent calls for ministerial labors abroad have made him delay doing what would have been a pleasure to him. I assure you I was delighted to hear from you once more, especially as you give the pleasing intelligence that our dear friend is improving in health. God grant that he may be restored so as to labor many years in the Master's vineyard! "For the harvest *is* plenteous and the laborers few."

It was perhaps as great a disappointment to me as to Mary Leland that Mary Sharpe did not come up to the wedding, for I had been led to hope that she would do so, and should have claimed her as my guest. However, as you say she has another invitation, I may still have the pleasure of a visit from her. It has, too, suggested to my mind a plan which I propose to you. Why cannot the doctor and yourself accompany her? We would enjoy your society so much, and you have been stationary now for some time. A little excursion would do you both good. Can you not accomplish it? I think Julia is to be married in November. Perhaps it would be pleasant to Dr. Jones to come over in time to attend the meeting of our synod in Camden. Talk it over and let me know. At any rate, should Mary Sharpe come up, if you will give us timely notice we will meet her at the depot and take care of her as long as she will be pleased to remain in Columbia.

I am glad to hear that Charles is about establishing himself in his profession so near you. I trust that both Joseph and himself will be useful men, not only in the world but in the church. We want Christian men in both professions; and they can accomplish much, if they have the right spirit, for the advancement of the Redeemer's Kingdom. Joseph has sent us twice a copy of his printed essays, which show to what an unusual extent he has prosecuted his studies. I think he is destined to take a high stand in science.

The escape from death of Dr. Leland's family was indeed miraculous!

They have entirely recovered, and seem deeply affected by the goodness of God in sparing them. Eliza and Mary are both at home at this time. They have married excellent men, and I think will be *useful* men.

Mr. Howe is absent from home attending a meeting of Presbytery at Beech Island. . . . Dr. Thornwell is still at the college; will not leave until commencement is over. Cannot say who will be his successor. . . . Our seminary has opened with pretty fair prospects. I cannot tell you the exact number, they have come in so irregularly. . . . I am pleased to hear that Mr. Mallard is so acceptable a preacher; *I* think him a *remarkably* promising young man. Liberty County has no representative here this term—the first time in *twenty years*. Why is it? . . . I hear that Mr. Buttolph is soon to be your nephew. I am glad of it: the parties are worthy of each other.

I am sorry to hear that "Sister Betsy" is so unwell. It is a long time since I have seen her, but I love her still. Remember me affectionately to her and the colonel. Among the reminiscences of the past are pleasant days spent beneath their roof enjoying their society, always so full of sunshine.

Columbia is now a city, and you will see when you come that she deserves the rank. The march of improvement goes on. I only wish that the church progressed in the same ratio. But the ways of Zion mourn. . . . Our ministers preach the same truths elsewhere and a blessing comes, but here it is like water spilt upon the ground. . . . My children—Willie, Emily, and George—are quite well, and are industriously employed at their studies. At the advice of our physicians we have taken Walthour from school and placed him on a farm in Vermont with his Uncle Matthews. It was a sore trial to us and to him, but we have done it for the best. He writes that he is quite well and happy, and we cannot but hope he will be entirely restored and return to us with both mind and body invigorated.

Dear friend, I have almost filled my second sheet. Excuse me. Much love to Dr. Jones and each of the children. And believe me

Affectionately your friend,
Sarah A. Howe.

Mr. George Helm *to* Rev. C. C. Jones[t]

Helm Station, *Sunday,* October 28th, 1855

Mr. Jones,

I was truly gratified on receiving yesterday your interesting letter—one which at once awakened the philosophy of the mind and the better feelings of the heart. . . . The tract which you speak of has not come yet, but Ma asked me to return her thanks for your kindness, and says she will be much obliged to you for it. I gave a copy of your catechism to one of our Negroes who is studying to be a minister, and he was very much delighted with it. He uses it constantly.

In my last letter to Charlie I told him I would leave the ensuing week for Memphis, but the yellow fever has detained me thus far and will perhaps a week longer. Tell Charlie I congratulate him upon his first cases. Joe seems the most indefatigable student I ever saw, but distinction will certainly be his reward.

I sent Mr. Maxwell a paper of plum seed—a very large kind that I promised him before leaving Georgia. Did he receive them? I would like for Georgia soil to bear some mementos from Kentucky, for my visit there was not only delightful but has been since a source of great pleasure to me in recollections. Your quiet yet cheerful and happy life gave me its lesson. My grandfather, father, and uncles have always lived in the excitement of the bar or politics, and of course they have been constantly before me as examples, until that has seemed to me to be certainly the most pleasant life to lead. By a close observance of your habits and feelings during my visit I have seen how unnecessary such excitements are. I hope it will be a lasting lesson, notwithstanding the opinion of the author of *Rasselas* to the contrary.

I wish it was so that Charlie and Joe could pay me another visit at my Kentucky home. I would be so glad to see them. But I am going away soon to struggle for myself and make a new home—I fear none so dear as the one I leave. If they will come any summer, though, and let me know, I will meet them if it is possible. If not, they will always find a hearty welcome with the family, who will still live at the old place. So will you, Mr. Jones and Mrs. Jones and Miss Mary, if ever you could honor us with a visit.

Give my regards, if you please, to Mrs. Jones and Miss Mary, also to Charlie and the Doctor, to Mr. and Mrs. Maxwell, Mr. Henry Jones and Banky, and all with whom I had the pleasure of being introduced. And accept for yourself the warm esteem of

Your friend,
George Helm.

Mrs. Mary Jones *to* Miss Mary Sharpe Jones[t]

Maybank, *Monday,* October 29th, 1855

Your long and deeply interesting letter, my very dear daughter, was received by the last mail; and most gladly do we welcome you all home, and only wish your aunt and cousin would come out with you, for we long to see you all. I wrote a note to meet you in Savannah by Willie, but he had left in the steamer ere we reached Woodville. Next Friday, Providence permitting, your brother Charles expects to come in the same way to town. Were it not for the meeting of Presbytery on the 8th of November in Bryan, your father would come down for you; but it would be inconvenient for him to do so, as he must be at the meeting. How would you like to return in the steamer and land at Woodville, bringing all your baggage? I am told some young ladies from Dorchester are going down on Friday and will be coming out next week. We will write you further by Charles.

I think, my dear, you had best get your winter bonnet at once. And let it be something pretty—and "neat, not gaudy." How do you like the black-lace or lace-and-velvet bonnets? But I do not know anything of the fashions; only please yourself and you will please me. I would only advise before deciding that you look around at the ready-made bonnets. I see *Lathrop* advertises handsome dress goods; if there is anything you would like to have in the way of a silk or delaine or anything else, get it. Whatever you do get, let it *be handsome,* for you have a plenty of secondhand and common dresses already. If you get anything in the way of worked collars, let it be a set. I would like *one* neat morning collar, and two yards of wash blonde for underkerchiefs, six papers pins (two of them small), one pair of black kid gloves (you know the size), and a piece of cotton shirting (good quality). I will write and send you a memorandum, perhaps by Charles. If you wish shoes, we have an account at Verstille's. I want you to bring me out a pair of gaiters; get them easy-fitting for yourself: light soles.

Your dear father preached a searching and deeply interesting sermon yesterday in Sunbury: "Follow peace with all men, and holiness, without which no man shall see the Lord." In the afternoon he gave an exposition of the Ten Commandments to the Negroes. . . . I have just finished a long letter to Joe, and must close, as it is late. Your father is at Montevideo tonight. Charles unites with me in best love to your aunt, cousin, and yourself. I do long to see you all and to have my own dear baby once more at home.

Ever your affectionate mother,
Mary Jones.

P.S. Your aunty is still very unwell with cold. Uncle well. The family at Woodville move up on Thursday.

REV. C. C. JONES *to* MISS MARY SHARPE JONES[t]
Maybank, Thursday, November 1st, 1855

My dear Daughter,

We received your letter after we came home about your going to Columbia, and we will endeavor to make arrangements for you to go, as the visit will be very pleasant to you and agreeable to your friend.

Mother sent for you to Midway today; your brother went up for you. But I told them after you received my letter that you would not be out. You missed a good dinner and a potato pone by not coming. Mother wants to add a line. Love to your dear aunty and cousin.

Your affectionate father,
C. C. Jones.

MRS. MARY JONES *to* MISS MARY SHARPE JONES[t]
Maybank, Thursday, November 1st, 1855

My dear Child,

You had best write your friend immediately and let her know that, Providence permitting, you will wait on her. Thinking that you would like to have the brocade dress sent you, I have done so that you may have it cut and basted at least. If you need any articles for the occasion, you must get them at Lathrop's, as we have not the money to send you at this time. Consult your aunt: she will tell you what would be best. How would blonde flounces do, put to your *gros de Paris?* But you can do as you think best.

Please get me two yards of brown linen for binding; *and* if Lathrop has any of that cheap black velvet (I mean the *silk* and *cotton*), I would like enough for a basque. I have so many old skirts, and do not expect to get any new ones, that I must have something of the kind.

It is late, and I must close, for I am very tired. Hoping to see you very soon, with love to your dear aunt and cousin and all friends,

Ever your affectionate mother,
Mary Jones.

Charles will hand you six dollars.

Mr. Charles C. Jones, Jr., *to* Rev. *and* Mrs. C. C. Jones[t]

Savannah, *Sabbath Evening,* November 4th, 1855

My dear Father and Mother,

I do not wish to violate the sanctity of the day, nor do I think that I will do so if I pen a few lines to you. We arrived in Savannah this afternoon, safe and sound, at half-past two. Would have been here yesterday evening, but the wind died away when we had just entered Wassaw Sound, and again it became calm with head tides as we neared Thunderbolt. There we remained until eleven today. The passage has been quite pleasant; but I will not at this season enter upon any descriptions or incidents.

Arrived at Aunt Susan's residence. Found them all at lunch. Surprised them on their return. Sister, Aunt, and Cousin all look remarkably well—especially the young ladies—and are in fine spirits, highly pleased with their trip. . . . Much love from all. Sister will, D.V., be out on Thursday next. We are just going to attend monthly concert at the new chapel. Hoping, my dear parents, that every blessing will attend you, I am, as ever,

Your affectionate son,
Charles C. Jones, Jr.

Mr. Charles C. Jones, Jr., *to* Rev. *and* Mrs. C. C. Jones[t]

Savannah, *Wednesday,* November 7th, 1855

My dear Father and Mother,

By a singular mistake you did not receive a letter from me by Monday's mail. On Sabbath evening, just before we attended monthly concert, I penned a few lines to you, and in directing the letter inserted "Savannah" instead of "Riceboro." The consequence was that on Monday morning the letter which I supposed to be in Liberty was handed me by the postmaster. It was a singular mistake—one which I scarcely imagine I will make again.

After parting with you at Woodville and trying to see, as we sailed down the river, whether with the glass I could recognize anyone in the piazza at Social Bluff, we had a pleasant and favorable passage until we reached Wassaw Sound. There the wind died away just as we were rounding a point of marsh, and in consequence of a rapid head tide we were forced to come to anchor for an hour or two. In consequence of this delay, instead of sleeping in Savannah on Saturday night as we confidently expected to have done, we were forced to anchor, with a lost tide and calm, a mile or two the other side of Thunderbolt. There we spent the night, reaching Savannah the next day at half-past two. The passage was to me very pleasant, the captain kind and social, the mate ditto. I believe we settled every doubtful point in theology, government, demonology, the destiny of the Russians and the Allied forces, etc. . . . George made the acquaintance of Prince, the cook, first and foremost, and might be found near him at almost any hour of the day with a cup of coffee and sailor bread. . . . The trip I would not have missed.

My office is undergoing repairs, and meanwhile I am occupying an office on the same floor. My card will be up tomorrow. Have purchased a desk and half a dozen chairs from Mr. Morrell; he is also making for me an office table.

George is considerably bewildered; says so many roads turn off he cannot keep the path—that he lives at "Miss Abby Jones's corner" (corner of Jones and Abercorn). But I will not write more, as Sister is going out tomorrow and will give you all the news. Hoping, my dear parents, that every blessing will attend you, with much love to selves, Uncle, Aunty, and all friends, I am, as ever,

Your affectionate son,
Charles C. Jones, Jr.

Tell Uncle, if you please, that his watch is not quite regulated. Will send it out by earliest opportunity.

Selected your order; hope everything was of the proper kind and reached the Island safely on Tuesday.

MR. CHARLES C. JONES, JR., *to* REV. *and* MRS. C. C. JONES[t]
Savannah, *Sunday,* November 11th, 1855

My dear Father and Mother,

I only write today to let you know that my office was this morning seriously burned and all my books and furniture almost entirely destroyed. The fire was doubtless the work of an incendiary, and originated in the room above. My books are (many of them) badly burned, not only on the backs but also within. All are completely soaked: covers nearly all off. There are some of them which can be rebound. All the sufferers are insured, I am told, but myself. The desk and chairs which I purchased from Morrell really present a melancholy, dilapidated appearance. The building will probably not be repaired before spring, as there will be much to be done. I am legally responsible for the rent for one year. Meanwhile Mr. Montgomery Cumming very kindly invites me to remain with him in his office until repairs are made. It is Sabbath, and of course I will enter upon no secular arrangements before tomorrow.

The morning was very rainy, and the pattering of the rain upon the pavements and tin roof prevented us from hearing even the alarm of fire. It originated between 5 and 6 A.M. Dr. Duke, who happened to be in that vicinity about half-past eight, sent me word by a fireman. I went down immediately, but the mischief was all done. Robert Grant kindly offered me the use of his office, and there I have removed the remains of my late handsome little law library—worth pecuniarily nearly three hundred dollars, and to me much more. Joe West kindly ordered his horse and cart for that purpose. The loss is heavy, but there is an old saying: "What can't be helped must be endured." I am perfectly satisfied; there may be some good yet to grow from this.

Aunt and Cousin are both well. Uncle John will preach for us this afternoon. He called to see us yesterday evening and spent a very pleasant social hour. As he was leaving, I agreed to call for him at nine o'clock on Monday morning and show him how nicely I was located. This morning he came over for a moment into the burnt building, but very changed was that office in appearance. Hoping that you do not feel any the worse for your visit to Bryan, Father, and that you, Mother and Sister, are well, with warmest love, I am, as ever,

Your most affectionate son,
Charles C. Jones, Jr.

Mr. Charles C. Jones, Jr., *to* Rev. *and* Mrs. C. C. Jones^t

Savannah, *Wednesday,* November 14th, 1855

My dear Father and Mother,

In my last letter I mentioned to you the burning of my office and the loss of most of my books and furniture. Mr. Montgomery Cumming very kindly offered me the use of his office and books; I am there for the present. Mr. Sorrel will have the building repaired, he hopes, in about three months; the workmen are already engaged. My books are now open in Robert Grant, Jr.'s, office drying, and there will be some of them which when rebound will answer every purpose. My present position is a pleasant one in many respects. Mr. Cumming, being a justice of the inferior court, has men on legal business very frequently in his office. Thus I am learning somewhat of the practice, and also am forming acquaintances—by no means the least important matter to a lawyer. Mr. Cumming is one of my best friends in this city. I pay Mr. Sorrel no rent until the repairs are completed. Am on the lookout for a room for a classmate, and if I succeed, we may occupy the same until Sorrel's building is repaired, when I will resume my office. You will find my card in the *Daily News.*

Am happy, Father, to learn through a letter from you, Mother, to Aunt Susan that you will take Sister under your protection to Columbia. The trip will, I doubt not, be very agreeable, and you will there revive pleasant associations of the past. Tell Sister that she must beware of the *third* time she makes her appearance as a bridesmaid. The old saying is: "Thrice a *bridesmaid,* then you will surely be an *old maid*." In the latter state I hope I shall never see her—unless she will agree to be a second edition of my estimable godmother, who recently sent her "fat little Charlie" a paper of sugared apples and plums. If no untoward circumstance intervenes to prevent, we will have one bridal occasion in the family this year, and perchance it may be followed by another. . . . Mother, cannot you spend the few days of Father's absence with us here? You know how glad we would be to see you. Aunt Susan, Cousin Laura, and all friends are well, and unite with me in much love.

From your ever affectionate son,
Charles C. Jones, Jr.

Sister's matters will be sent out by the stage tomorrow.

Aunt Susan has just called to me from her room and says: "Tell Brother and Mary that we will be very glad to see them on Friday week; and tell Sister Mary that she must come too and stay with us until their return."

Rev. C. C. Jones *to* Mrs. Mary Jones[t]

Columbia, *Tuesday,* November 27th, 1855

We arrived here, my dearest wife, this morning at eight o'clock after a comfortable and successful journey, through the kind providence of God. We took a hack and drove up to Dr. Howe's, and lo, a fine carriage at the door, the tongue lying on the ground and the harnesses cut and scattered about! The good Dr. and Mrs. Howe were on the steps to welcome us, and said: "We were just sending for you, but we have had a trouble. We borrowed Mrs. Macfie's horses, and as we were driving off, one of them reared up and then kicked up and got one leg over the tongue and fell over on his match, who in turn got scared, cut capers, and down he went and scuffled under the carriage; and the doctor had to jump out, and he and Mr. Campbell Bryce cut the animals loose from the carriage." No damage beyond cutting the traces, reins, and breast straps. We were grateful that it all happened *where* and *as* it did, for it would have been dreadful for the horses to have run away with Dr. Howe. So much for having fine horses and not keeping them gentle by use! Since Dr. Howe had his horses burnt up he has not been able to replace them.

They are both looking remarkably well. Both more gray. Are so sorry you did not come with us.

Daughter's cold is no worse, and we have had breakfast, and she has gone to Miss Fisher's to see what is to be done, and soon returns and will then rest awhile. We got some very smart dozes of sleep during the night.

All friends well. Legislature in session. Town lively. . . . Daughter sends love with me to Sister and Laura and Charles Colcock. Send you this hasty line; hope you may be able to read it. Will write again in a day or two.

From your ever affectionate husband,

C. C. Jones.

Dr. and Mrs. H. send much love to all.

Rev. C. C. Jones *to* Mrs. Mary Jones[t]

Columbia, *Friday Evening,* November 30th, 1855

My dear Wife,

We have called upon our old neighbor Mr. Zimmerman. He and his lady were happy to see us. "Welcome! Welcome!" said he. "*Doobly* welcome!" He promises to send you by us a collection of *bulbs:* hyacinths and perhaps tulips. Dr. and Mrs. Trezevant received us with great kindness, and made special inquiries after yourself and Charles and Joseph; and the doctor promises to send you cuttings of the cloth-of-gold and other fine roses, of which Mrs. Trezevant has a variety, and also cuttings and roots of other kinds of flowers. Mrs. Howe is also to make you up a parcel, and so I hope we may be able to bring you a good contribution. . . . Mrs. and Miss Crawford have called; they invited us to tea this evening, but we were too tired to go. Mrs. and Miss Macfie have called, and the Misses Brumby and Mr. Brumby. Dr. Howe had some gentlemen to dine with him today.

Last evening Mrs. Thomson gave a bridal party. Daughter went about eight. Dr. Howe and I went to the statehouse and heard the notable General Cary lecture on temperance. A *capital* lecture. A great crowd. After the lecture I went to Mrs. Thomson's. Spent about half an hour, and as we do not dance and have no special liking for supper at twelve midnight, Daughter and I came home at ten. She was pretty tired.

This morning we went to hear General Cary lecture in the Baptist church. Full house. Good lecture. He has many striking and excellent qualities as a public speaker, and must accomplish much good. They called on me to open the meeting with prayer.

Dr. Thornwell has been called to see his brother, who is extremely ill, and may not be here to deliver his commencement and valedictory sermon nor to preside at the commencement. The trustees of the college are in great straits: they know not whom to elect as president in his place. Many are talked of; election on next Wednesday. It is doubtful if Dr. Thornwell has done right to leave his position in the college. Time alone can show. . . . Called to see Mrs. Thornwell last evening. All well. There I met Mr. Robert W. Barnwell. Our meeting was cordial. He inquired particularly after you; and when he learned that you were not in Columbia, said he: "How is that? I thought you never separated, and wherever you went Mrs. Jones was with you." I told him I was sorry it was not so at this time. He promised to call and see me.

We hope to finish our calls tomorrow, and see the legislature, and dine at Dr. Leland's. Am engaged to preach on Sabbath morning, God willing. The commencement is on Monday, and they insist that I stay to it. We have consented to do so, and will leave here on Tuesday sometime in the day, and if prospered be in Savannah on Wednesday sometime. . . . Am wishing to return. Our visit has been very pleasant, but everybody has something to do, and I am idle. . . . My love to all. Every blessing attend you, my dearest wife!

Your ever affectionate husband,
C. C. Jones.

P.S. Mrs. Howe says: "Tell Mary I am sorry she is not here, for then, besides the pleasure of seeing her, we might keep you longer."

MISS MARY SHARPE JONES *to* REV. *and* MRS. C. C. JONES[t]

Savannah, Wednesday, December 12th, 1855

My dear Father and Mother,

We were very glad to hear of your safe arrival at home, and thank you for sending my letter. It contained the sad news of Anna Wilson's death. Poor girl, a victim to that terrible disease consumption. Maggie is the only member of the family left, and I am afraid she too will fall a victim to the same disease. . . .

Aunt Susan says that you must be in no hurry to send for me, and wishes to know if you would not think it a matter of great impropriety for me to go out with "that young gentleman." He will, I believe, spend Christmas here.

We were truly sorry to hear of Laura Jones's loss; a letter from Mr. Fleming to Aunt Susan states that most of their furniture and clothing was saved. This morning Brother Charlie insured six hundred dollars more on Aunt Susan's furniture, and I think he insured his library also.

Have you heard from Brother Joe? I suppose Matilda Harden still has his likeness.

Aunt Susan and Cousin Laura are quite well, and send much love to Aunty, Uncle, and yourselves. I am pretty well, though I feel weak. Am taking quinine. I have not yet seen Dr. Parsons; will do so as soon as it is convenient for Aunt Susan to accompany me. How do you feel, dear Father, after all your recent fatigues?

It is very cold: ice yesterday and today. The tickets which were presented by the keeper of the wild men have been given to Joe and George, and this afternoon they have gone down to see them. Aunt Susan concluded this would be the best use to make of them. . . . Accept, dear Father and Mother, the affectionate love of

Your attached child,
Mary S. Jones.

Mrs. Mary Jones *to* Mr. Charles C. Jones, Jr.[5]

Arcadia, *Tuesday,* December 18th, 1855

My dear Son,

I do not think that even eighteen months at Cambridge has made you Yankee enough to guess what were the first sounds that saluted our ears this morning: a serenade at sunrise by a traveling minstrel on a hurdy-gurdy or hand organ—a young French refugee escaped from his country with his brothers to our *happy land* to avoid a draft for Russia. He speaks English "little"; says last night he slept in "the bush" between this and Hinesville. And we had full proof that he must have gone to bed supperless by the ample justice done to breakfast. The plantation all assembled in delighted wonder to hear "Susannah," "Yankee Doodle," etc., and to gaze upon the "great show" of Napoleon laid out in state with his military cap upon his breast. A soldier has raised the pall; an officer stands by gesticulating very solemnly; another keeps guard; whilst at the threshold is a *Negro* with plate in hand inviting contributions. These figures move with the music, shake their heads and roll their eyes about, and as a piece of money falls into the plate, Congo bobs, turns round, and it disappears in a box behind. This will certainly be an event long to be remembered by the Arcadians.

Robert and Mary Ann, who were quite sick last week, have both recovered. We have reason for great gratitude to our Heavenly Father for our continued health and lives and that of our servants.

Your dear father has suffered much from inaction since his return home, and I am glad that he has come to the resolution of living in the open air and exercising on horseback. Confinement will never restore vigor to his frame. He has an invitation to visit the Orange Spring in Florida, thirty miles from Palatka, where Rev. Joseph Quarterman is now settled. I wish he could try that climate and those waters for a month or two. They have proven very beneficial in nervous diseases.

Last evening we received a letter from your brother. He sympathizes deeply with you in the loss of your books, and thinking it your literary as well as law library, begs that we will send to you from his collection such works as you might find useful, regretting that he had so few of a literary character to give. He says this will be a very expensive year to him. His experiments on the action of medicines will be published in the January number of *The American Journal of Medical Sciences.* He says *I* must not expect a copy, as they might appear to be the result of great cruelty, and not designed for refined ladies! By Mr. Buttolph I will forward his likeness, which we think excellent, but retain the Bible until your sister comes home.

Your uncle has purchased Mr. Allen's place near us for thirteen hundred and fifty dollars—six hundred dollars paid this year—and I am told will remove his men shortly. We have not seen them since this arrangement has been made.

We are now in the midst of sugar-boiling. Daughter can tell you how zealous I am on the subject, thinking it akin to preserve-making. Shall reserve a good stock of cane for private use when you come out.

Shall I send you by Captain Russell the box for your friend with the limes, etc.?

We felt very sorry to leave the Island, but present duty lies this way.

Your man William came last night to ask leave to "take a wife," and that you might be informed of the fact. And Sister Susan and Laura have a right in the matter, for the fair one is the daughter of Hannah, the sister of Driver William: Kate by name. He says she is very clever and a member of the church and lives near home—all worthy considerations.

The last of the present week we look for Brother John and his family to visit us, and next week we hope to enter our winter quarters at Montevideo and do the best by ourselves and our friends who come to see us until we have the house finished. . . . Your father unites with me in best love to your aunt and cousin, to your sister and yourself. . . . I hope your business prospects brighten. Do not be discouraged; you as well as others must expect a season of trial. God grant you a spirit of filial submission to His sovereign will, and a heart renewed and sanctified and led to repentance by His goodness, ever prays

Your affectionate mother,
Mary Jones.

The servants all send howdies.

MR. CHARLES C. JONES, JR., *to* REV. *and* MRS. C. C. JONES[t]
Savannah, *Wednesday,* December 19th, 1855
My dear Father and Mother,

We hoped yesterday to have received a letter from you. In the absence of intelligence to the contrary, the fair presumption is that you are both well. This we sincerely trust is the case.

On Saturday last, as you will observe from the papers of the present week, the bar as a body attended the funeral services of one of its members, the late Robert H. Griffin. . . . It were ungenerous to mention anything unkind with regard to the character of one dead, but I have heard it said by many who were capable of knowing that he was his own enemy; that during the past few years he was in the habit of drinking freely, and especially *at night,* the very worst period for indulgence of that kind. His funeral was largely attended: by the bar in a body, the Blues in uniform, the Masonic and Odd Fellow orders, and by a large number of citizens. He dies in the prime of life—in the thirty-fourth year of his age—and leaves a widow and children.

Mr. Mallard preached two excellent sermons for us last Sabbath. He was more deliberate and quiet in his manner than usual.

Cousin Laura is in anxious expectation of the coming of the pastor from Liberty on Friday. I never have known a more communicative lover: letters by every mail. . . . Tomorrow is, I believe, your birthday, Father, and the day after, the anniversary of your marriage. Let me congratulate you, Father, and you both, my dear parents, upon the recurrence of these occasions, with the hope that you may be spared to see the happy return of many more, and that the same kind Providence which has hitherto supported you may still continue to watch over and protect you. . . . Joe West is said to be engaged to one of the Misses Rogers. . . . With much love from Sister, Aunt, and Cousin, I am, as ever,

Your affectionate son,
Charles C. Jones, Jr.

Received this week interesting letters from Hon. William F. Colcock and Mr. J. N. Dickson in reply to notes enclosing my professional card. They kindly promise their influence and recommendations in the legal line. George Helm writes that he is located in Memphis, and sends me a number of cards for distribution.

Everyone seems anticipating the arrival of a happy Christmas. The little boys are popping away with their firecrackers in every direction.

C. C. J., Jr.

MRS. MARY JONES *to* MISS MARY SHARPE JONES[t]

Arcadia, *Monday,* December 24th, 1855

My dear Daughter,

I am just up from Maybank; went down this morning to "give out Christmas" to the people whilst your father went to Montevideo. Your white japonica had two beautifully expanded flowers and a bud just bursting. I am very tired, but must send you a line. . . . I do long, my darling child, to see you, but leave it entirely to yourself to come out when you please. Your dear aunt and cousin are so kind to our children that we feel very grateful to them.

As soon as the holidays are over we shall go to Montevideo, Providence permitting. . . . We expected your Uncle John this week with his family; they have not come; neither have we heard a word from them. I hope you have written your brother in Philadelphia; he is afar, and we should not forget him. Your father unites with me in best love to Sister Susan and Laura, Charles and yourself, and to our good friend Mr. Buttolph. A happy Christmas to you all!

Ever, my dear child, your affectionate mother,
Mary Jones.

REV. C. C. JONES *to* MISS MARY SHARPE JONES[t]

Arcadia, *Tuesday,* January 1st, 1856

Happy New Year to you, my dear daughter! The Lord bless you and cause His face to shine upon you evermore! Happy New Year to your dear brother and to your aunt and cousin. Mother joins with me.

We are all well—white and black—through divine mercy. Still at Arcadia. Hoped to have been at Montevideo this week, but your Uncle John did not get to see us till the last of last week, and we shall not perhaps move before next week. Your uncle and aunt came up yesterday, and are also with us. Do not know how long they will stay.

Your mother says: "Thank Laura for her note to us." Mr. Buttolph got home safe in a great rain. Great exposure of health!

Tell your aunt your Uncle William has an excellent new canoe boat: $17.50. Worth it. If Mr. Oliver Stevens does not take it, I think she had better buy it on the spot. And she will need it; that is, I so suppose. She will want *grass* and *fish!* Tell her: *grass and fish!*

Rain! Rain! Rain! More than for six months all put together. Liberty County looks like itself again: ditches, canals, ricefields, ponds, puddles, and swamps all full of water.

Ask your brother to say to Mr. Montgomery Cumming that he will receive by Captain Russell (*Fort George Packet*) twelve bales white cotton and two stained, which he must sell. Captain Russell has a letter for Mr. Cumming.

Stay as long as you wish—that is, as long as your aunt will let you. We are moving and fixing and fixing and not fixed. Our love to all.

Glad to hear your brother has another case. He must make a learned and able speech and win his case, and make a powerful impression on Mr. Justice Raiford. He must carry the superior court in due time by sapping—sapping through the justice's courts; and every chance he gets, be powerful; and push on his works.

No news from Joe—not even a paper. Enclosed is a letter from Miss Taylor, received today.

Your aunt and uncle much pleased at their new purchase. Several names: "*Galeberry Flat*," "*Hickory Hill*," "*Cottage*"; the second the *true* name, the last the name it is to have. Their people left the Island on their move up—that is, the field hands—not with drums beating and colors flying but with waving of hats, swinging of arms, hurrahing, and oxen on a trot! We are having moving scenes here as elsewhere.

Nobody went to church from this place Sunday. Worship at home morning and night. Mother had Sunday school. Excuse bad writing: can't do better this morning.

Your ever affectionate father,
C. C. Jones.

P.S. Your uncle wishes to sell twenty-five head of his cattle at the Island. Ask your Aunt Susan if she wishes any or all of them. They may be a convenience to her, being on the place, if she has the money to pay for them. There is *no necessity for her to buy*, as cattle may be driven down from *Lambert* for her use for milk. But she can if she will. Answer by Thursday's mail.

C. C. J.

MISS MARY SHARPE JONES *to* REV. *and* MRS. C. C. JONES[t]

Savannah, *Wednesday,* January 2nd, 1856

A happy, happy New Year to you, my dear father and mother! May our Heavenly Father long spare your useful lives and make us a blessing to you! Another year will, I hope, dear Father, find you enjoying perfect health.

Thank you for the letter sent by Uncle John; presume I shall see him before he leaves the city.

On Monday Aunt Susan and I sat up until the old year had departed. With the dawning of the new passed away one of Georgia's most distinguished statesmen. Judge Berrien is dead. He had been ill for a week; returned from the "Know-Nothing" meeting in Milledgeville sick. His funeral will take place on Friday; it is delayed with the hope that his daughters will reach Savannah in time to see their father's face once more. They are at school in Philadelphia. There will be a meeting of the bar today.

There was less visiting yesterday than usual; the custom is not as scrupulously observed as formerly. Brother Charlie did not go out at all, but spent the day in his office. He had studied his case thoroughly, thought out his speech, and felt himself prepared to astonish the superior court—when, lo and behold, yesterday the Irishman came and informed him that the difficulty had been settled! One of the parties was aged, and "it was hard to swear against the old man." On Brother Charlie's account I am sorry they succeeded in settling it so easily, for it is quite a disappointment; though he laughs and says he always knew the Irish were not to be trusted.

We are glad to learn that our friend Mr. Buttolph arrived in safety, and presume that the flame was so warm that it would be quite impossible for him to have taken cold!

I am glad to know that Uncle and Aunty are so much pleased with their purchase. Do they think of moving up themselves to live this winter? "The Cottage" will, I think, be a very pretty name for it.

We have had continued rain for nearly a week past; we have been unable to leave the house since last Thursday. So wet on Sabbath that none of us attended church. . . . On Sunday afternoon Joe and George attended the Methodist chapel, and during the sermon a woman wept aloud, shouted, and clapped her hands. George in great alarm begged that he might be taken out of the church, for he said "they were licking that woman, and they would lick all round, and soon come and lick me too." This was quite original—a country Negro's first impression of shouting.

Cousin Maria Gilbert has determined to defer her visit to us for a month or two; the weather has been so cold and rainy that she could not come at the time appointed for fear of making the baby sick. . . . Little Laura West is better; the poor little thing is cutting all of her teeth at once, and looks very feeble. . . . Mr. Porter is expected back with his bride this week. . . . I have not heard from Brother Joe, though I have written him twice since the reception of his last letter. I suppose he must be laboring under the hallucination that his ambrotype speaks to me.

You say stay as long as I wish. Aunt Susan and Cousin Laura are very kind in inviting me to stay, and it is very pleasant for me to do so, but I think it is now nearly time for me to be returning home. I do want to see you both very much. . . . Aunt Susan will fill up the other page and answer your inquiries. Please give a great deal of love to Aunty and Uncle; I hope their new place will suit them in every respect. Give love to Aunt Julia, Cousin Mary, and the children. Willie called here last evening and is quite well. Brother Charlie is busy at his office, Cousin Laura downstairs practicing, and Aunt Susan and I writing. All unite in love.

Your attached child,
Mary S. Jones.

Howdy for all the servants.

Mrs. Susan M. Cumming *to* Rev. *and* Mrs. C. C. Jones[t]

Savannah, *Wednesday,* January 2nd, 1856

Thank you, my dear brother and sister, for your kind wishes on this opening year. May they be multiplied to you a thousandfold, both temporal and spiritual!

I shall certainly want grass and fish, and a boat must be at hand to get them, and I will take the boat at $17.50. Shall have to beg someone to keep it safe till I want it. Two good milch cows I should like to have on the spot and used to the range for milk, but *do not want* the twenty-five; in fact, have not the money to pay for them if I did. What do you think of my making arrangements to build a stable there? One is wanted there, whether or no.

I am glad Brother and Sister seem pleased at the prospect of a removal from the Island. I hope they will do as well off of it as they have done on it. Brother can get someone up there no doubt to manage his people, which he could not do on the Island; and he is too infirm to do it himself. I rejoice in all that promotes their happiness.

I thank you so much for letting Mary stay with us. I give you warning that I shall keep her as long as I can. I tell her you are too much occupied to want her just now. We have had an abundance of rain, but it is all best. Laura unites with me in love to you both. Believe me

Your affectionate sister,
S. M. Cumming.

Rev. C. C. Jones *to* Miss Mary Sharpe Jones[t]

Montevideo, *Thursday,* January 10th, 1856

My dear Daughter,

Your letter and one from your brother came today, and we are much distressed to hear of your dear aunt's sickness. I pray God she may have speedy relief and restoration to health. Do not by any means come out while your aunt is so sick; stay and wait upon her and do all you can for her in our stead as well as from your own affection and duty. Should she be in danger, send out immediately and let me know, and we will come down without delay. *Be sure to write us on Monday,* and then you can better decide whether you will come out on Thursday or not, God willing.

Mother would write, but she is very tired, having been on her feet all day seeing after her domestic concerns—cutting up bacon, etc., etc. She can do no more tonight than write to your brother Joseph. We had a letter from him last Thursday. He was quite well, and very busy preparing his summer work for the press. In Dr. Smith's recent edition of Carpenter's *Physiology* (the textbook on that subject in the University of Pennsylvania Medical College) Dr. Smith has introduced your brother's experiments (as he published them) on endosmose *entire*. Quite a great compliment.

By Tuesday's stage Mother will send down your brother Charlie's box for Cambridge, and perhaps something on the top of it for your aunt's table. . . . Your little birds are up here, and both in good health and spirits. . . . Our people generally well. Have commenced my old regular plantation meetings with them. It is old times come back again. . . . We shall be very happy when you return. Mother says she is constantly looking about the old house for her *little* children. Everything within doors and out-of-doors brings you all to our remembrance. . . . Mother unites in love to your aunt and cousin and to your brother. We are glad to learn that he continues to be pleased with his present situation. The Lord bless and keep you both unto His Heavenly Kingdom!

Your ever affectionate father,
C. C. Jones.

Rev. C. C. Jones *to* Mr. Charles C. Jones, Jr.^g

Montevideo, *Thursday,* January 17th, 1856

My dear Son,

Through divine favor we received your sister in health and safety today, and were happy to hear through her of your aunt's recovery and that your cousin and yourself were well.

This note is on business. Will you call on Mr. W. Wright, the real and personal estate broker, and learn from him: (1) Whether he receives and sells Negro property, and on what commissions and expenses? (2) Whether he buys on his own account? (3) Whether he is able to sell without delay to persons in the up country? (4) What would be the probable value sold in the up country of a family consisting of father, mother, and five children—father forty-three, mother forty-six, two girls nineteen and fourteen, and three boys twenty-one, sixteen, and twelve; all healthy and good-looking; the mother a superior house servant and seamstress? (5) Whether all could be sold to *one master* without separation?

You know the family I allude to. We feel that there is a limit to patience, and perhaps they may do better—*some, not all* of them—in other hands. We do not wish to separate them, and let all go together. In conversing with Mr. Wright mention no names, and of course enter into no agreements. Let me have the result of your inquiries. There may be other and better brokers in town of whom you might also inquire. And another question: (6) Could they be easily sold in Savannah to one man, and at what probable value?

We are all pretty well at present. Mother and Sister unite in love to Aunt, Cousin, and yourself.

Your ever affectionate father,
C. C. Jones.

Let me hear from you by Monday's mail, D.V.

VI

Mrs. Mary Jones *to* Mr. Charles C. Jones, Jr.ᵍ

Montevideo, *Thursday*, January 31st, 1856

My dear Son,

We were rejoiced to welcome our daughter home, and to learn of your well-being and well-doing. The Lord hath ever dealt mercifully with you. May He give you a heart to recognize all His providential dealings with feelings of love and gratitude, and may all His goodness lead you to repentance and consecration to His service!

I regret to say that your father has been very unwell recently. I hope it is to be attributed to the continued cold and wet weather, which always increases the inaction. And seven years' nonresidence on this place increases the care of management in every department. And the extremely severe season retards all labor, especially the carpenter's work. But we must patiently work on. "There remaineth a rest" for those who truly love and serve the Blessed Master.

We have not yet determined what we shall do in reference to *that* family. We wish to act aright. They have always been unprincipled. *Jane* gives constant trouble. Much as I should miss the *mother,* I will not separate them if I can help it. It is a painful and harassing business.

Your Uncle John came home with us on Sabbath from Midway and remained until Wednesday. He seemed hurt that you had not called to see him once during his stay of *ten* days in Savannah. It surprised me to hear this. He is your *mother's brother* and your only own uncle. I hope you will find time to call and see him and his family as he passes through next week. He expects to be at the Pulaski House on Tuesday evening. Your sister says he may be at Mr. Shackelford's.

Old Mr. Varnedoe continues very sick. No prospect of recovery. Your father has been twice to see him. His children are all around him and very attentive.

I believe I have never mentioned the marriage of your man William. It was soon after we moved here, and during that dreadful spell of weather. When he left Saturday morning, your father charged him to be in time at night. As the weather was so cold and rainy, and himself so unwell, after tea the carriage was brought to the door and Flora and Kate allowed seats. He reached Lambert and waited and waited, but no groom appeared—when he left for home. The next morning bright and early, before we had left our chamber, the young couple were announced as below, awaiting the ceremony.

We went down and had them brought into the parlor—bride and brides-maid in *swiss muslins* with white wreaths on their heads, Sam and William in broadcloth and white gloves. A number of witnesses crowded in. The nuptials being over, I invited the bridal party to retire to the kitchen and partake of a hot breakfast. It was a freezing, shivering morning, and I thought they had displayed a great deal of principle in coming over to be married in the proper manner. The poor fellow had been disappointed the night before by his father, who promised to bring his coat and failed to do it in time. You must not forget the one you promised. I gave him a pair of pants, shirt, etc.

Your father wishes to know when he will get the *boots*. He and your sister unite with me in best love to your aunt and cousin and yourself. All are well at South Hampton. As ever,

Your affectionate mother,
Mary Jones.

Mr. Charles C. Jones, Jr., *to* Mrs. Mary Jones[t]

Savannah, *Friday,* February 1st, 1856

My dear Mother,

Yesterday's mail brought a letter for each of us. We are always very glad to hear from home, and my only regret is to hear you say that Father's health has not been as good as usual the past week or two.

The weather recently has been trying to everyone, and especially to the indisposed. Today, however, the atmosphere is delightful, and we seem to feel the first breathings of spring. If it be true that an unfavorable season is followed by a pleasant one, we may reasonably anticipate a delightful spring. The orange trees in the city, I observe, have all been severely injured, and not a few of the younger killed in consequence of the cold, both protracted and severe for this latitude. There is an old saying that a cold winter will cause a fruitful summer and an abundant autumn. I sincerely hope that it will be verified the present year.

The social pulse of this city has been beating quite freely of late. Last winter all were clad in the habit of mourning, and consequently very few indulged in the usual festivities. Now, however, party-givings are numerous, party-goers lively, and everything and every person is gay. I have only attended two parties—one at Mr. Stoddard's, the other at the Warings'. It is not a very easy matter to work hard and attend to business all day, prepare for the party at nine, be in attendance until an early hour in the morning, and then be prepared to resume your duties in the morning at the usual hour. It becomes me, however, inasmuch as I am a newcomer in the city, to im-prove the opportunities offered for social intercourse. At the same time it is more important to be ever ready and actually engaged in business.

I was not aware that Uncle John was in Savannah more than a few days, and during the time I knew him to be here I was prevented by engagements from calling upon him. This will account for my seeming neglect.

Aunt Susan tells me that she was informed by Mr. Buttolph that Father would deliver an address before the Liberty Independent Troop on the 22nd of February next. I am happy to hear it, and hope that Father will honor them by appearing. . . . Am glad to hear from Aunt Susan that it is Father and not myself.

Received a letter from Brother a few days since. He has been in Washington recently, and presented his observations of last summer to the Smithsonian Institute. You doubtless, however, know the particulars.

Our city is quiet. Cotton advanced half a cent yesterday upon receipt of the peace news from the continent. Some think that England will be glad to close her war-gates against Russia in order that she may open her batteries against us. This I am inclined not to believe.

I am sorry that Father's boots have not been repaired before this. Two bootmakers have promised and failed to mend. I will try again and another, and send them out so soon as they are repaired. We are all well. Please excuse defects in the present, as I write under pressure of business, and in the office. With much love, dear Mother, to self, Father, and Sister, I am, as ever,

Your affectionate son,

Charles C. Jones, Jr.

Howdy for all the servants.

REV. C. C. JONES *to* MR. CHARLES C. JONES, JR.[g]

Montevideo, *Monday,* February 4th, 1856

My dear Son,

The troop has invited me to deliver an address on the 22nd inst., D.V., its anniversary. Have consented. May do some good by it. I wish to know *when* the troop was organized. It was organized *shortly after the Chatham Artillery.* Could you find out by referring to the acts of the legislature, laws of Georgia, or in any other way and let me know? Also I wish to know *who* was its *first* commander, if that anywhere appears. And *when* was the *Chatham Artillery* organized? Any facts you can gather from the books respecting the troop, would be glad to have them. The old files of the *Georgia Gazette* in the Historical Society might furnish some notices. The *oldest records* of the troop are lost.

We are all pretty well this very cold day. Our united love to you and to your aunt and cousin. Please answer as soon as you can.

Your affectionate father,

C. C. Jones.

When was *McIntosh County set off from Liberty?* They once were *one.*

Tuesday Morning. Received your letter last night, and Mr. Buttolph sent the gloves and tea. Glad to hear you are getting acquainted in a pleasant way with the good people of Savannah. But you are right to remember business and duty. The world is not all pleasure. Excuse my writing. Would write better, but cannot now. Good writing comes to me now only at times. Love to all.

Your affectionate father,
C. C. J.

REV. C. C. JONES *to* MR. CHARLES C. JONES, JR.ᵍ

Montevideo, *Thursday,* February 14th, 1856*

My dear Son,

My boots are worn out, and if our good friend from France has not fixed up those left with him, please take the enclosed measure to Butler's and get me not a *fine* but a *good substantial* pair, not high priced, and send out by Audley, who promises to bring them. If Robider has not fixed the boots, just let George bring them home and let them lie till I come down, D.V.

Our friend and neighbor Mr. Varnedoe was buried on Wednesday. His sufferings were very great. I regret his loss: he was a good citizen, and one of the best of neighbors. Mrs. Varnedoe has been ill, and is still so by last accounts.

Send by Captain Russell this trip fifteen bales from Arcadia and four from other place to Mr. John W. Anderson. Hope we shall have better sales. The loss on the sale of the last twelve bales was over two hundred dollars.

We have not heard from your brother for *three weeks*. Have you had any letters lately? Children ought never to be too busy to write their parents. We feel uneasy about him. All well. Mother and Sister unite in much love to your aunt and cousin with me, and to yourself.

Your ever affectionate father,
C. C. Jones.

MR. CHARLES C. JONES, JR., *to* REV. C. C. JONESᵍ

Savannah, *Saturday,* February 16th, 1856*

My dear Father,

I am almost ashamed to mention anything respecting your boots, as you have good presumptive evidence to imagine neglect on my part. The fact of the matter, however, is simply this. Not only our old friend from France, but another, a Dutchman, have both had their repair under contract with divers promises at sundry times for the completion of the same, all of which have been signally broken. I had a great mind to file a bill in equity praying for a specific performance. A third has, however, finished one, which Audley will carry out with him. The excuse given upon every occasion was the quantity of new work, while the standing complaint of the French artist was: "My workman, he git trunk, en vat ne kin do?" In your letter you state that *if* the boots are not yet repaired, I must send you another pair from Butler's. I have sent this pair to you, and if you wish the new pair, will send it out so soon as I hear from you.

On Thursday last, was summoned to be and appear at 9 A.M. at the arsenal to perform military duty as required by law. At the appointed hour a motley group assembled, and we entered upon the drill on the common. The captain, Mr. Buker, so soon as I arrived at the place of rendezvous, was so struck with my personal bearing and military appearance that he offered me the rank of second lieutenant, which of course was readily accepted. Independently of the honor it was a delightful relief to exchange a heavy sixteen-pound musket for an officer's sword. In the afternoon he met me in the streets with the request that I should allow my name to come before the company at the next election as a candidate for a lieutenancy; that he was highly gratified at my knowledge of military tactics and soldierly bearing; that he hoped I would suffer my name to be brought forward by him; and that I would always parade, as it *gave an air of respectability to the company when such men appeared*. Of course I was highly pleased and agreeably surprised to find myself so much more of a soldier than I had hitherto supposed. I do not know but that Company F may apply, when well officered, for the position of a *forlorn hope* in the Russian army. Doubtless under its intrepid and *competent* leaders the fortunes of Sebastopol would be improved.

We are all well again. Thackeray lectures tonight, and we attend. His subject: the Georges of England. We wish that you were all here to attend. Have not heard from Brother for three weeks. Have written him since. With warmest love to self, Mother, and Sister, I am, as ever,

Your affectionate son,

Charles C. Jones, Jr.

Father, I wish very much that I could be present next week and hear your oration, but we are all so very busy that it will be out of my power. The least the troop can do will be to publish it, and then I can read it, which will be some amends.

We regret to learn the death of Mr. Varnedoe.

Mrs. Mary Jones *to* Mr. Charles C. Jones, Jr.[g]

Montevideo, *Monday,* February 18th, 1856

My dear Son,

We were happy to receive your letter today, and the description of your military promotion amused us greatly, especially your father. It caused him several hearty laughs, and did him good.

We wish it was compatible with your engagements to be out on the 22nd. The address will, I trust, not only interest but benefit the corps and the citizens. It has caused much labor and quite too much exertion to collect and arrange and write out the past history of the troop. You know your father can never do anything by halves. *This,* added to preaching every Sabbath for the past six weeks, has had a decidedly exhausting effect. His perseverance and energy are most astonishing!

Maybank came home with us from church last night. He is in good spirits, and looks much better. On Saturday *Henry's* case was reported upon by the committee of investigation, his statement and acknowledgment of error received, and he was restored to the fellowship and communion of the church. We are thankful for the termination.

I spent this morning with our afflicted friend Mrs. Varnedoe. It is a truly melancholy sight to behold the effect of sorrow and anxiety. Her mind seems paralyzed; she has not spoken *a sentence* since Mr. Varnedoe's death. Sits calm and immovable, uttering every now and then a sigh, or giving some evidence of a weary and worn heart. Her pulse is low, and she takes no nourishment except as you feed her. This morning her son James was sitting by her as I went in and feeding her with a little bird he had killed to tempt her appetite. As I spoke to her a faint smile stole over her face. She kissed me; afterwards took my hand and held it and kissed it; but I could not rouse her to say anything but yes or no. Mrs. Axson arrived in today's stage. I went for and carried her to Mrs. Varnedoe, but would not remain to see the effect of the interview. I trust it will do her good.

Your uncle and aunt are now at the Cottage. In consequence of the rain and cold they have had very unpleasant times moving, but appear satisfied. I spent one day last week with Gilbert helping her to get the house in order. . . .

We are happy to hear that Sister Susan will be out early in April. Do say to her if there is anything I can do for her I hope she will let me know it. And I am expecting her to send me some sewing work. I hope she will not fail to call upon me for anything within my power.

We heard from your brother today. He is quite well, but very busy as usual. As I wish to write him tonight I must now close, with our united and best love to your aunt and cousin and yourself.

> Ever your affectionate mother,
> Mary Jones.

Miss Mary Sharpe Jones *to* Mr. Charles C. Jones, Jr.[g]

Montevideo, *Monday,* February 18th, 1856

Dear Brother Charlie,

Please get for me two pounds of mixed canary seed. It can be had at any of the grocers'. Goodrich has very good seed—almost opposite to Lathrop's store. . . . If you will do this I shall be very much obliged to you, for my little birds will very soon need more food. Mother says you have some money belonging to herself, so if you are moneyless or do not think my credit good, you will know what course to pursue. Only don't forget to send the seed.

I wish very much you could be present on the 22nd. Can you not arrange your business so that you may be able to come in Thursday's stage? Father has been at a great deal of trouble in procuring facts respecting the organization and history of the troop, and I think his address will be one of peculiar interest. It has been necessarily a laborious undertaking, and I only wish he had the health and strength to warrant all he undertakes.

We received two letters from Brother Joe today; but dear Mother is writing you, and I know she has told you of them. My eyes burn me from drawing, so I must bid you good night. With much love to Aunt Susan, Cousin Laura, and yourself,

Your affectionate sister,
Mary S. Jones.

Miss Mary Sharpe Jones *to* Miss Laura E. Maxwell[t]

Montevideo, *Saturday,* February 23rd, 1856

Dear Cousin Laura,

I had intended writing yesterday, but we were so late at the parade ground that supper came soon after our return, and some engagements afterward prevented my sending you a long epistle. I am writing before breakfast, and if you discover many deficiencies in this you must conclude that they are in consequence of a decided "goneness" right—you know where!

We had yesterday a most interesting day, and of course the chief interest consisted in Father's address, which was historical in its character and on this account peculiarly interesting, as it contained valuable information unknown, I presume, not only to some of the corps but to the majority of the citizens. Brother Charlie will tell you all about it, and I rather think you will receive a full account of all the proceedings from the "Express Mail." Our friend was there, and his idea (or rather that which seemed uppermost in his mind) was: "The ladies ought to have come out; they have missed a great deal"—no doubt secretly thinking: "I would have gained a great deal if they had come out."

He looks very well, and begs me to go back to Savannah with him. I tell him it is impossible for me to leave home until my piece is finished; and he is so obliging that he will wait as long as I desire, which I think will be for some weeks, as my piece progresses slowly, it being the most trying piece to my eyes I have ever attempted. I am glad to hear that you are succeeding with your sailor-boy. I have sent you a white crayon and another which I do not think you have; they were imported and given to me by Mr. Miller.

Aunty and Uncle came here on Thursday, and will remain with us until their house is habitable. They engaged some carpenters to repair it, and they have turned them out, so we will have them some days with us. They are both quite well, and Aunty quite delighted with your proposal. I think it is a capital idea. Uncle, however, disclaims any agency in the making of the match. He says: "Betsy, I tell you I did not make the match." She humors the joke.

All are well at Aunt Julia's. Mrs. Varnedoe continues in the same state. Mrs. Axson came out on Monday. Breakfast is ready, so I must close, with much love from us all to my dear aunt and yourself. I was very much obliged to you for sending out the cactus; I think it has grown since I last saw it.

Your affectionate cousin,
Mary S. Jones.

There will be Communion at Midway tomorrow. We expect to attend the preparatory service there today. Mr. B. preaches.

Mrs. Mary Jones *to* Mr. Charles C. Jones, Jr.[g]

Montevideo, *Thursday,* March 6th, 1856

My dear Son,

We were happy to receive your letter today and to hear of the well-being of your dear aunt and cousin and self. I trust this mild weather may arrest the progress of scarlet fever and measles.

I regret to learn the decease of Mrs. McAllister. She was a lovely Christian lady, and through all her protracted sufferings I am told has been comforted and sustained by Him in whom she trusted. Her life was a life of faith, and I doubt not her end was peace, and she has entered into the joy of her Lord. How striking the contrast with that of our poor friend and fellow citizen so recently deceased! He had lived all his life in the sound and sight almost of the House of God, yet seldom seen within as a worshiper. Born of pious parents and blessed with religious training and every means of grace, he has gone down to the grave without hope. His end was very awful.

Mr. Allen continues very ill. Today we hear there is but slight hope of recovery. His disease is inflammatory rheumatism.

Your aunt and uncle have left us for the Cottage, but I fear they are scarcely comfortable. Your aunt is complaining very much of her arm, which is not only very painful but looks inflamed. I wish some physician could see it soon, for if not taken in time, it promises to give trouble. We tried to persuade them to go down in their carriage to Savannah this week and obtain medical advice. She would be glad if Cousin Charles could be informed of the increasing size and pain of the tumor.

Say to Sister Susan that Matilda is quite well again. She came over to see me recently, and seems rejoiced at the prospect of her mistress' moving into the country.

Audley spent the afternoon with us. All well at South Hampton. . . . Your father rode on horseback to Arcadia today and has retired. . . . Mr. Axson is with us, and has also gone to his room, having preached in the chapel for the people tonight. . . . I had a short letter from Joe by Monday's mail. He is very busy; his examinations must have commenced by this time. . . . We heard of our good pastor today; he is well, and has invited Daughter to accompany him to Savannah. . . . And now, my dear child, good night. . . . Our united love to your aunt, cousin, and self. God bless and save you, my child, ever prays

Your affectionate mother,
Mary Jones.

Mr. Charles C. Jones, Jr., *to* Mrs. Mary Jones[t]

Savannah, *Saturday,* March 8th, 1856

My dear Mother,

Your kind favor of March 6th was yesterday evening received, and we are happy to know that all at home are well. I will see Cousin Charles West and inform him of the present condition of Aunt Betsy's arm, although it would be much better and more satisfactory to both parties if physician and patient could meet and consult in person.

In about six weeks Aunt Susan expects to leave this city for Liberty. On Thursday she sent two painters out to Social Bluff with directions to prepare the family mansion in the most approved style for the reception of the bride-elect.

Speaking of brides, I am reminded of a note which I received a day or two since from Kentucky, inviting my presence at the marriage feast and the attendant ceremonies of my friend and quondam classmate Ben Hardin Helm. He is, according to the announcement, on the 26th of March next

To quit the freedom he enjoyed
And run his neck into a noose

prepared by Miss Emilie Todd of Frankfort. I presume Ben Hardin marries on the strength of his present responsibilities as the representative of Hardin County, upon the established rule that the more numerous and urgent the responsibilities we are called to meet, the more likely are we to incur new and still more important ones. I wish him joy in his present union, and hope that his proposed companion for life may possess a disposition as genial and pleasant as his own. . . .

Does Brother expect to return home this summer? He owes me a letter now, and has, I presume, been prevented from replying by his engagements —although he is not very fond of letter-writing.

We are happy to hear that Sister will pay us a visit during the latter portion of the present month. Cousin Laura receives letters every week—or rather twice a week—from the Rev. D. L., but from her we gather little or nothing of Liberty County items. Her reply to interrogatories relative to the same is always the same: "All well, and no news; his letter is filled with his own thoughts." With much love from all, I am, my dear mother, with love to Father and Sister,

Your ever affectionate son,
Charles C. Jones, Jr.

The responsibilities of the office now all devolve upon me, as both Mr. Ward and Mr. Owens are absent from the city on professional business.

Mrs. Susan M. Cumming *to* Rev. C. C. Jones[t]

Savannah, *Wednesday,* March 12th, 1856

My dear Brother,

We were very glad to hear last evening that you were all well and that Mary will come in with our friend on the 18th. When are you and Sister Mary coming to pay your farewell visit? For the time passes, and in little more than one month we shall, Providence permitting, take our leave of this place and go to live near you, where we can see you every day. I am sorry to leave Charles, but hope he may be able to get a pleasant lodging place. The office gives him employment enough; he has no waiting time now. We shall miss him very much.

I have just had a letter from Mr. Fleming in which he says Mr. Allen is improving and that Mr. Girardeau has been attending to White Oak. If Mr. Allen cannot attend to White Oak the ensuing year, I must get someone else. Can you suggest anyone in the event of that being the case?

Captain Russell is to bring the Lambert cotton next trip—in all, twenty bags and three packets, and ten from White Oak. I have written to apprise Mr. J. W. Anderson that it will be sent to him. I shall hope for a high price. Our crop is short this year, but we have made a plenty of provisions and some to spare; no fatal sickness among our people; and things have moved on as smoothly as we could expect—for all of which I desire to be sincerely grateful and thankful to the Giver of All Good, our kind Heavenly Father, who dispenses His favors upon the evil and the good.

Our friends here are all well. . . . Dr. West has had one case of measles in his family: Willie White. Mrs. Whitehead is still there, suffering from disease of the heart, but was more comfortable yesterday. Presume she is incurable.

Miss Clay made us a short visit, and asked if I thought it would be inconvenient to you for her to visit you—that you would let her occupy with Mary. I told her I thought she would be welcomed warmly by Sister Mary and yourself.

You see we are fixing up at the Point for the new neighbors. Audley King kindly offered to give some supervision to matters and things there, and we thankfully accepted. Will Joseph spend his summer on the Island? It would be so pleasant to have him there. He did not exhaust all the fishes in the sea last season; he might find more work there than at the North.

There is a good deal of feeling here among the colored people about despoiling the graves of their friends. A colored woman was disinterred, and the body found in the new medical college—*not* Dr. West's. A white infant has been taken from the white cemetery. These are outrages that ought to be punished—and will be if the perpetrators can be discovered.

There is a fine building in sight called the Massie School. You remember Mr. Peter Massie; he left a sum for educational purposes. It has been accumulating, and the trustees are putting up a building, and can support a teacher. His name will be perpetuated in a most useful and honorable way.

I am very glad to hear that your address will be published by the troop, for Charles and I determined to publish it on our own account. Laura and Charles unite with me in affectionate love to you, Sister Mary, and Mary. Believe me, dear Brother,

Your affectionate sister,
S. M. Cumming.

Miss Mary Sharpe Jones *to* Miss Laura E. Maxwell[t]
Montevideo, *Thursday,* March 13th, 1856

My dear Cousin Laura,

The last mail brought your pleasant letter, with your kind invitation for me to visit you once more before you leave for another home. This I purpose to do; and I understand from one of your friends that you are expecting me on Monday or Tuesday. Now, let me say that you must not expect us to be with you on Monday, for if all of my plans are successful we will not see you before Tuesday.

Day before yesterday our good friend Miss Eliza Clay came, and is still with us. Yesterday Mother, Miss Eliza, and myself set out on a visiting expedition. We went to Mrs. Harden's, and there saw Mrs. John LeConte, who is now visiting the county; her dress and appearance I will describe when we meet. Mother invited Mrs. Harden to accompany us to Woodmanston, as Miss Eliza never had seen the japonicas growing there. So she ordered her carriage and went with us, and thanks to her generosity gave us a large and beautiful bouquet of red and variegated japonicas, the white being all over. The garden is shamefully neglected, rare flowers blooming in the midst of fennel and broom grass. No one takes any care at all of it now. From Woodmanston we went to Aunt Julia's, and found her alone, Cousin Mary having gone to the Sand Hills to see Aunt Howe and bring Anna King home. I had intended and engaged to go up with Cousin Mary, but the reception of a note announcing Miss Eliza's coming prevented my doing so. We have not yet seen Aunt Howe.

Miss Eliza, hearing that we intended going to Savannah on Monday, has invited us to spend that night with her. I have not seen Mr. B. yet and do not know what he will say, but I think he will like the arrangement, as it is the only opportunity he will have of seeing the place, for Miss Eliza expects to leave the 29th of this month. If he accedes to the proposition, you need not expect to see us before Tuesday. Miss Eliza intended to have left us this morning, but has been prevented by the rain—a most delightful circumstance to us; and from a selfish motive I hope something will detain her again tomorrow. . . .

I hear the house at the Bluff is going to look quite new. Aunt Julia and Mother are beginning to think their houses look very shabby, and wonder the folks from the newly painted regions will condescend to visit in such dingy habitations. . . .

I have not quite finished my piece. My interruptions have been many, varied, and continued; and added to these, my eyes have not been very strong. But I hope to complete it and bring it with me in order to get it mounted and framed. Mother, too, is anxious that Mr. Miller should see it. I am glad to hear of your success, and am very anxious to see your picture. I suppose you will soon finish it.

Aunty and Uncle are now settled at the Cottage. Aunty complains very much of her arm, and begins to feel very anxious about it; and I think she has just cause for feeling so. The tumor has grown very much, and causes her a great deal of pain. Uncle looks pretty well, and says he believes moving about suits him.

I understand there is another freshet in the Ogeechee River and that the causeway is again under water—a pleasant prospect to those of us who expect to pass over it in a few days!

Mr. Baker has sent in his resignation. The annual church meeting was held, and the Rev. D. L. Buttolph reelected; and they resolved to get an assistant, but who that will be no one knows yet. . . .

Our garden is beginning to look very prettily. The roses and shrubs are all budding, and there is every indication of approaching spring. The jessamines, owing to the severity of the winter, are just putting out.

I understand that the measles are all over Savannah. You must find out whether it is dangerous for country folks to come to town. . . . It is growing late, so I must bid you good night. Father and Mother unite with me in much love to Aunt Susan, Brother Charlie, and yourself. Hoping to see you soon, I remain

Your affectionate cousin,
Mary S. Jones.

Miss Mary E. Robarts *to* Rev. C. C. Jones[t]

Marietta, *Tuesday,* March 18th, 1856

My very dear Cousin,

I have not written to you for so long a time that it is not strange that you should find a difficulty in reading my letters, if I were not even a poor scribe. I should consider myself much to blame in not having written you, my dear cousin, if it were not for the frequent interchange of letters with the ladies of your household, almost as dear to me as they are to you. I know that letter-writing must have become burdensome to you; and that is the reason why you are not oftener addressed in your own proper person. But while this outward silence has been maintained, our hearts have not been silent in their deep affection toward you, whom we all have so much reason to love and reverence. . . . We often pine for your society, and the days when we were wont to take sweet counsel together are often recalled. I feel that I am losing much in being deprived of the latter part of your ministry. I say *latter,* my dear cousin, because it is not noon with either of us; the twilight is fast approaching, and if the evening of our days should be brightened by a more spiritual light, we shall have no reason to mourn the declining sun. . . . The ministry of my present pastor has not only been delightful but truly edifying to me. His constant aim seems to be that his church members should be active, growing Christians; and with such precept and example as we have in him, and such teaching too, we ought to be all that he could wish us. . . . We hope to increase his salary this year; he deserves all his people can give him.

I hope the troop in Liberty may publish your address; I hear from private letters that you touched them up about public spirit. I do wish we had it here, for we feel the want of it very much. And how can a community live without it? Our prosperity as a town is rather at a stand; the losses by fire have been felt, and the burnt districts have not been repaired. Some new brick stores on the burnt lots are going up, and a very fine new flour mill; but property does not meet with a ready sale. When are you and Cousin Mary coming to see us? Shall we expect you in strawberry, cherry, or peach season? At either you would be most gladly welcomed.

We heard yesterday from my Cousin John through a letter to Mr. Petrie. He was well, and so were his family. Dunwody recovered from scarlet fever. Hope he may find Washington a pleasant home, and the field, though small, a useful one.

We have not much family news to give you. My dear mother sits in her chair by the window writing. I often think if all aged persons had her resources the listlessness of old age would seldom be complained of. Her mind is as much interested in reading as any person I know, and she has the same skill with her needle and her pen she ever had. Goes to church generally twice every Sabbath, visits her neighbors and friends in fine weather, and sets all an example of cheerfulness and content. Louisa is upstairs instructing her boy in the mysteries of the spelling book and grammar, to prepare for his teacher tomorrow. The young ladies of the family retired from the breakfast table to don their school bonnets and shawls, with satchels on their arms, to repair to their seat of learning. And I heard them rejoicing this morning that the rye in their yard was so beautiful and green. Lilla looks on nature with a poet's eye; she has a taste for the beautiful. The other two are more matter-of-fact, and grass is only green with them, and clothed with no particular or sentimental interest.

And now what shall I say to you of your old friend Lady Mary? Well, she arises in the morning and soon commences the active duties of the day. Provides food convenient for her household, and after the departure of the juveniles to school spends an hour with the cups and saucers. Then repairs to the yard on her morning rounds, receives (as any housekeeper does) a welcome from her family of ducks, turkeys, and chickens, attends to their present wants, and decrees their life or death as circumstances may require. Then hears the whistle of the car and sends to the post office, from whence she is often refreshed with tidings from absent friends. Then seats herself either to write, sew, or read. And then in the afternoon walks round in her ward and takes up the monthly collections if it is the time for it; if not, visits, walks, talks, laughs (if anything amuses her), then comes to her home, takes tea, after which she reads aloud for the entertainment of the family. Thus day after day passes, and night finds her ready for repose. And this is all I can tell you of her ladyship—and this is not much, you will say.

The presbytery will meet here in April, when we shall be "on hospitable thoughts intent," and have invited our good friends Mr. Dunwody and Dr. Pratt to stay with us. . . . My mother, Louisa, and myself desire warmest love to my dear Cousin Mary and Mary Sharpe, who if I mistake not has gone to Savannah today. . . . We hear constantly of the health and success in their professions of your dear sons. . . . Farewell, my dear and highly esteemed cousin; hope your health may be improving as the spring advances. Please remember us to your servants, and tell Rosetta our faithful Sam is well.

Your ever affectionate cousin,
Mary E. Robarts.

I shall prize a letter from you much if it will not tire you to write.

Mr. Charles C. Jones, Jr., *to* Rev. *and* Mrs. C. C. Jones[g]

Savannah, Wednesday, March 19th, 1856

My dear Father and Mother,

I have but a moment, and that I improve by setting your minds at ease upon a subject which must have enlisted your anxiety. The difficulty between Banky and McConnell is settled, and has been settled through arbitration. It seems that the place and time of meeting were both known before Maybank reached Savannah, and as soon as he arrived propositions were made to lift the challenge until four o'clock today. In the meantime Judge Law, Colonel Lawton, Edward Anderson, Mr. Ward, Joseph Bryan, and others entered into an examination of the matter; and this evening, I understand, the propositions submitted as the basis of a settlement have been mutually accepted. I am now (9 P.M.) going to the Pulaski House to learn the particulars. Mr. Ward said that there had been a mutual retraction of all that had been said and done by both parties. Not knowing the particulars, of course, I cannot give you any satisfactory information; and my sole object in writing is to relieve your minds of the anxiety which must be resting upon them. This entire difficulty has learned me two lessons: first, in all difficulties have nothing to do with newspapers; secondly, if you wish to *fight, keep clear* of *cities.*

Mr. Buttolph and Sister arrived yesterday before dinner. Both well. By

Mr. Buttolph, Father, I will send your book, watch, and trowel. All unite in love. With warmest affection, I am, as ever, my dear father and mother, in haste,

Your ever affectionate son,
Charles C. Jones, Jr.

REV. C. C. JONES *to* MR. CHARLES C. JONES, JR.[g]

Montevideo, *Friday*, March 21st, 1856

Am happy to learn, my dear son, through your note of yesterday that matters have been adjusted. Your inferences are both good, and I would suggest another, which I think better than either: get into no difficulty at all. It has been a mismanaged affair from the beginning, and am grateful that it is terminated.

Boston will show you a paper I have drawn up for him. He says everybody tells him he is free. I have not seen the passage of the bill. Did it pass? If so, can you get a copy of it and draw out what he calls his *free papers* for him? That will be your subscription to his paper.

Mrs. Howe is with us; goes today to Mrs. King's. Your mother has had a bad cold (some fever), but is up and brave today. Our love to your aunt and cousin and dear sister. We received her letter yesterday; will answer it soon.

Your ever affectionate father,
C. C. Jones.

MRS. SUSAN M. CUMMING *to* REV. C. C. JONES[t]

Savannah, *Saturday*, March 22nd, 1856

My dear Brother,

Seeing Mary was next to seeing you and Sister M. We were glad to welcome her and your good pastor. I am surprised to hear such reports of measles here; there have been and still are a good many cases of it, but generally mild. . . . I do not know why people will exaggerate so much.

I received a letter from Mrs. Allen last mail enclosing Mr. Allen's account for his last year's wages ($130) and a list of thirteen hands as he rates them. I did not know that it was *usual* to put quarter-hands in the field; and who Lucy is (a quarter-hand) I do not know. I have enclosed the letter; please read it and tell me what you think of it. I paid Mr. Allen $100 last year for 1854, and have never received any intimation that I was to pay him $130 for 1855. If he is entitled to it, I shall pay him; but he should have told me of the increased salary at the beginning of the year. But I never see him except on Sunday, and he never writes. I wish I could get someone to manage that place. Prince, I think, has been sole manager a long time. I am truly sorry to hear of his continued illness, but when he was well he undertook too much. If Mr. Allen had been well I would have written to him, but did not like to do it, as he continues so ill and his account may be correct.

Did you see Mr. Cunningham? Who would have supposed that our little church would have felt able to pledge five hundred dollars! But so they did. . . . Mr. Cunningham is a most interesting preacher; his manner is peculiarly his own. . . . We are all well, and shall keep Mary as long as she will stay. . . . Laura unites with me in love to you and Sister Mary. Mary and Charles have written their own remembrances. Believe me, dear Brother,

Your affectionate sister,
S. M. Cumming.

MISS MARY SHARPE JONES *to* MRS. MARY JONES[t]

Savannah, *Saturday,* March 22nd, 1856

My dear Mother,

I am very sorry to hear that you have been unwell, but hope you will have no return of fever. If you do, please let me know, and I will come out immediately.

I have been to the stores today for the first time, and have gotten the small brown plaid gingham you desired, but I am quite at a loss to know what to select among the bareges. Enclosed you will find some samples. The light one (marked sixty-two and a half cents) is very pretty, and I think would please you. There are very few good figured bareges except the robes, and they are generally gaudy, and I do not think would please you. I purchased a barege for myself, and have gotten a pretty mantle at seven dollars—the cheapest I could find. The American ginghams are not very pretty this season—not equal to those Lathrop had last year.

Mr. Sam Stiles and Carrie Rogers were married on Thursday evening in the Independent Church. Mr. Rogers performed the ceremony, and I believe Mr. Joseph Stiles assisted. The latter is here now with his daughter Josephine. Anne Rogers is, I hear, not to be married for a year; in the meantime Cousin Joe is going to Paris to prosecute his studies there. . . .

I saw Mr. Hutchison a few evenings since, and he desired his kind regards, wishing as usual that Father could go to England. He is very attentive to Carrie Shackelford, but thinks the idea of an engagement preposterous. He loves the young lady dearly as a daughter.

I have had my daguerreotype taken for Brother Joe. It is not so good as that one on the Island, but Cary says he cannot take a better one, as this is the tenth attempt. I do not know why he finds such difficulty, for Broadbent seemed to find none in Philadelphia.

Please let me know, dear Mother, if any of these samples please you by Tuesday's mail. We are all quite well. Cousin Laura has been engaged all morning in drawing. My piece has been much admired; have not shown it yet to Mr. Miller. Aunt Susan, Cousin Laura, and Brother Charlie unite with me in much love to dear Father and yourself.

Your affectionate child,
Mary S. Jones.

Mrs. Mary Jones *to* Miss Mary Sharpe Jones[t]

Montevideo, *Monday,* March 24th, 1856

My dear Daughter,

Your affectionate letter was received today, and we are happy to know that your dear aunt and cousin and brother are well. You must not feel anxious on my account. I have not felt well for some time, but believe my recent fever was produced very much by distress of mind. We have reason to bless the Lord for the termination of that difficulty. I regard duelling as a sin of awful enormity, meriting the indignation of every civilized (not to say Christian) person, and which not only merits but will surely receive the just displeasure of a holy God. I cannot tell you what we suffered from Monday to Thursday! Oh, that our unconverted ones were all united by faith to our gracious Redeemer! I know of no safeguard for my dear sons amid the sins and temptations, the conflicts and the sorrows of life but the *love* and the *fear* of God ever abiding uppermost in their hearts.

We have had a delightful visit from your Aunt Howe. She found me in bed, but I was able to get up before dinner, and we enjoyed ourselves as in former days. She brought Emily and George and Alice Walthour with her. The young ladies each sued for the hands of my sons. Alice said she must have Mr. Charles, and Emily said she must have Cousin Joe, for she loved him dearly; and her parting request was that I would write and beg Joe not to get tired waiting for her. At night she took his likeness and put it under her pillow. She was very much disappointed at not seeing you, and so was your Aunt Howe. She will go to Savannah on her return to Columbia next Tuesday (*tomorrow week*). I hope your brother will make it a point to see her; she is anxious to see him, and is one of our dearest friends. . . . Your Aunt Howe received the intelligence whilst here that *Mary Edmunds* has a daughter. I wish you could find time to make and send her up a little sacque.

I am obliged for the bareges. The light one is very pretty, but too much like the tissue I now have. I think the barege at fifty cents will answer my purpose better. Get twelve yards, with sewing silk to suit, and two yards of paper cambric for the sleeves. . . . Bring me *four yards* of brown linen for a skirt, eight yards of dowlass for cup towels, and in place of the American gingham choose four patterns of neat dark calico *that will wash* (eight yards in three of them, nine in Patience's).

Do let me know by Thursday's mail what you can find pretty for *my present*. Are there any handsome *china vases* like Cousin Eliza's? And what do they cost? Price silver candlesticks and cake baskets. I am quite puzzled, and have not yet written Joe.

I must close, for I am very weary. Your father joins me in love to your aunt and cousin, brother and self. Do not be in any hurry to come out; I can attend to your society business if you will send your book and collections.

Ever, my dear child, your affectionate mother,

Mary Jones.

Rev. C. C. Jones *to* Miss Mary Sharpe Jones[t]

Montevideo, *Thursday,* March 27th, 1856

My dear Daughter,

Mother received your letter today, and we are happy to learn that you are well, and all at your dear aunt's. Tell your Aunt Betsy that we called to see your uncle today and found him quite well. It was the dinner hour, and he enjoyed his nice dinner and was in excellent spirits, and says he will be in Savannah, D.V., on next Tuesday. We think it the best arrangement for you to remain and come out with them on Thursday, and are glad you have determined so to do. Mother will add a line after I have finished.

Our friend and neighbor Mr. Allen died on Tuesday morning at eight, and was buried yesterday afternoon at Midway with military honors by the troop, of which he was an active and useful member. We attended his funeral at 12 M. Mr. Buttolph delivered an excellent address to quite a large assembly, and called on me to conclude with prayer. He was a very public-spirited and useful and pleasant man in the sphere in which he moved, and is a loss to our little community. He leaves a wife and some five children, and not much for their support, I fear. Who will act for them I do not know.

Say to your Aunt Susan that I saw Mr. John Girardeau today and got the only key he had belonging to White Oak, which was the cornhouse key. I will see to matters until other arrangements can be made. She need not be uneasy. Mr. Girardeau said he would have a bill against her for attending to the business at White Oak for two or three months during Mr. Allen's sickness. I told him Mrs. Cumming would be out before long, and he could then make out his bill. I moreover told him that she had received Mr. Allen's account for managing for 1855, and that she would pay it so soon as there was anybody authorized to receive it for his estate. So she must *keep the money until she knows who to pay it to.*

Enclosed is a check on the state bank for $23.74 of date in favor of your brother, which I wish him *to draw from the bank and pay over to Mr. Montgomery Cumming.* It is the balance which I owe him in account which he has forwarded to me today, and he must take Mr. Cumming's receipt for it. Say to your brother I received his note and Boston's free papers today. I will try and see that his owners pay the expense attending the business: ten dollars. They should pay it.

Your dear mother, am happy to say, looks, and I think she feels, much better than before she was sick. We are both about as busy as usual. Our people all well, through divine mercy. We shall be truly glad to see all your young friends at Maybank when that time some folks are looking for arrives, and will do all in our power to make them happy. We have just returned from Arcadia; stayed there last night. Love to your aunts and cousin and brother. Must leave a space for Mother. The Lord bless and keep you, my dear child!

Your ever affectionate father,
C. C. Jones.

Mrs. Mary Jones *to* Miss Mary Sharpe Jones[t]
Montevideo, *Thursday,* March 27th, 1856

My dear Daughter,

If it is putting your Aunt Susan to no inconvenience, we prefer your coming out with your aunt and uncle. I do not like to see *young ladies* traveling alone in a public stage. Write me by *Monday's stage* about your missionary collections, and I will act for you at the meeting on *Wednesday next.* I hope you will not expose yourself directly to measles, as there is no necessity for your doing so.

I wish you to get a *pretty summer bonnet,* and admire the crepe. How would it do for you to write and enclose Mary Taylor the sum you would be willing to give and request her to send you a bonnet by your brother? Also six dollars for one for myself? (Such an one as would suit her mother: close to the face and plainly trimmed with white, and a neat cap within.) They could both come in one small box. Get all my articles at Lathrop's, and whatever you want for yourself, and have them charged. Do bring out some summer sleeve patterns, and six yards nainsook muslin like your dress to make a baby frock for Augusta and Sister Abby.

Belle and Willie have been at enmity for several days, she flogging him terribly. On looking into the nest not an egg was to be found. All eaten up, shell and all! What must be done with such little sinners? Phoebe thinks Willie ate them and Belle whipped him for it.

Duchess has three beautiful kittens, of which she is very proud.

I must now close to write Joe. Our united love to your aunts and cousin, brother and self. It would give us great pleasure to see *Rev. Mr. Joseph Stiles.* Please remember us *to him.*

Ever your affectionate mother,
Mary Jones.

Please ask your brother to forward Sam's letter.

Do not forget my tea.

Mr. Charles C. Jones, Jr., *to* Rev. C. C. Jones[g]
Savannah, *Saturday,* March 29th, 1856

My dear Father,

Enclosed please find receipt of Mr. Cumming for the amount sent per check in Sister's letter: $23.74.

I hope that you will say nothing to the former owners of Boston with regard to the amount expended by me in obtaining his manumission; and this for the simple reason that I was never employed by them in the premises, it being a matter purely *ex gratia* on my part, and consequently have no claim upon them either upon agreement or *in foro justitiae.* The amount expended and services rendered form my individual contribution to him, and as such I desire they should be regarded. I hope, therefore, that you will say nothing about the matter to any of his former part-owners.

We are all well, and are glad to hear that dear Mother is quite well again. With warmest love to Mother and self, I am, in haste,

Your affectionate son,
Charles C. Jones, Jr.

Mr. CHARLES C. JONES, JR., *to* Mrs. MARY JONES[t]

Savannah, *Saturday,* March 29th, 1856

My dear Mother,

I this morning wrote Father a few lines, and now improve a momentary calm in business matters to tell you that we are happy to know that you are again well and in the enjoyment of usual health.

Dr. Bulloch and Cousin Charles West this morning (as I learned at dinner) had an examination of Aunt Betsy's arm, but have reserved their decision until Uncle William arrives on Tuesday, when they will confer with him as to time and place for performing the operation. It is their impression, I understand, that the tumor should be removed as soon as convenient, as delay will only increase the existing difficulty. They prefer, however, operating in the city, as their professional engagements are of such a character as to preclude the thought of going to Liberty County and of remaining there as long as they would wish in care of the case and recovery. No definite arrangements have, however, been formed.

We regret to learn the death of Mr. Allen. His loss will be severely felt in his family circle and also in the sphere which he filled in the county. Politically his death is serious to the Democratic party, for he was a man of much influence among the citizens of the pine-barren portion of our county.

A Kansas meeting will this evening be held in the exchange; hope to attend if I am at leisure in time for the same. We are all well, and unite in warmest love to dear Father and self.

From your ever affectionate son,
Charles C. Jones, Jr.

You must excuse these short letters, as I write in a hurry, and when I have the opportunity.

Mrs. MARY JONES *to* Mrs. SUSAN M. CUMMING[t]

Montevideo, *Monday,* March 31st, 1856

My dear Sister,

Our children hold the pens of such ready writers and are such faithful scribes that the "old folks" feel themselves very much exonerated from their former duties in that line.

We rejoice, my dear sister, that the time draws near when you will be with us. If there is anything I can do for you, I hope you will let me have the pleasure of knowing and doing it. I can never cease to feel grateful to you and dear Laura for all your kindness to our child. I know that you have been a mother to him, influencing him in every right way. I trust he has appreciated and profited by all the good received at your hands. I hope Charles may be enabled to secure a *good* boarding place when you leave. I am very anxious on that point. May the Lord direct!

By today's mail *Daughter* received a letter from Joseph. We were so anxious to hear from him that we opened it, and as she is to be at home so soon, will not send it. He announced the fact that he had received a notice of his being an accepted M.D., and was to have received his diploma in the Musical Fund Hall at their commencement on last Saturday the 29th. Drs. Jackson and Leidy paid him the compliment of *"passing him"* without an examination. He had also received a letter from Professor Henry, informing him of the acceptance of his article for publication by the Smithsonian Institution. This will keep him a week or two longer in Philadelphia.

We are happy to know that Sister Betsy has had the advice of the physician about her arm. We have felt very uneasy about it for some time, and urged that it not be delayed. . . . I hope Brother William will go tomorrow, as I want to send you a little roaster.

Tell Daughter be sure and bring the tea out with her. We will meet her, Providence permitting, on Thursday. Mr. Jones unites with me in much love to yourself and Laura, Sister Betsy, and our children.

Ever your affectionate sister,

Mary Jones.

I will write Charles by the next mail.

Mrs. Susan M. Cumming *to* Mrs. Mary Jones[t]

Savannah, *Saturday,* April 5th, 1856

My dear Sister,

Accept of my very sincere thanks for your kind letter and the acceptable present, which has been lodged in the icehouse for an emergency.

I anticipate great pleasure in being with you and all our kind friends this summer. It has been a great satisfaction to us to have had Charles Colcock with us, and he has proven a very pleasant and agreeable inmate. I hope success will attend him in all his lawful undertakings, for next to my own child I feel interested in the welfare of yours, and am always glad to have them with me. We shall be very sorry to part with Mary on Monday, but she thinks she is missed and can be useful to her dear father and mother at home.

We were very glad that Sister and Brother concluded to have that operation performed here. It was far more painful and serious than was anticipated. The tumor was deep-seated. Sister bore it with great fortitude, and is wonderfully well after it. She has had fever, but not more than was expected. And the doctor says the wound looks healthy and well, and thinks it will heal very soon. She is very comfortable today, and spirits good.

I am always glad to hear from Joe. Have just written him, and hope he will arrive while we are here, that he may tarry with us. . . . Sister and Laura unite with me in much love to you and Brother. . . . Love to all inquiring friends. Believe me, dear Sister,

Your affectionate sister,
S. M. Cumming.

MRS. LUCINDA B. HELM *to* REV. C. C. JONES[t]

Helm Station, *Monday,* April 7th, 1856

Sir,

I received with grateful pleasure some three weeks since your kind note promising me your article on slavery. I did not answer it then, as I wished to read the document first; and that did not come until I had left home to attend my son's marriage. On my return after an absence of two weeks, I read it with much interest. Mr. Helm is now in New York; when he comes home he will gladly read and preserve it, as I know it meets his wishes for a scriptural view of slavery; for not long since (not having time himself) he requested me to mark out for him every text in the Bible that had any bearing on slavery. I was delighted, on reading your article, to see it so fully done.

You speak of the severe winter in Georgia; our winter exceeded in continued and intense cold anything ever known in this state. I walk through my yard and grieve over my losses: roses, honeysuckles, and almost all my shrubbery killed to the ground.

Though my flowers suffered, I am thankful my family have enjoyed excellent health. George is now in Kentucky; he sends his love to yourself and family. Present my kindest regards to Mrs. Jones and Miss Mary; to your sons—particularly Charles, whom we all hold in pleasing remembrance. My little boy Jimmie said to me yesterday morning: "Ma, comb my hair like Charlie Jones's. I wish I could hear him play the flute, don't you, Ma?" So you see, the little fellows have not forgotten him.

Most respectfully yours,
Lucinda B. Helm.

VII

Miss Mary Sharpe Jones *to* Miss Mary Jones Taylor[t]

Montevideo, Tuesday, April 8th, 1856

My dear Mary,

What will you say when I tell you that your letter found me again in Savannah! I have been spending three weeks there very pleasantly—the last I shall spend there for some time, as my Cousin Laura expects to be married in June and will then reside in this county, as our pastor is the gentleman-elect.

I am very much obliged to you for the poetry sent, and agree with you in thinking it beautiful. The style is somewhat peculiar. Where did you find it? . . . You speak of that little jessamine as a faint smile of spring; if you were only here you might revel in their sweet odors: the forest is wreathed with them. The air is delightfully freighted with Spring's sweet perfumes. Nature is now yielding to her beautiful sway and bursting forth into new life at the touch of her magic breath, though stern old Winter, reluctant to yield his dominion, sometimes returns, wreathes his shaggy brow with a frozen diadem, then retires with dripping locks and tardy steps. But what have I been betrayed into? . . . I will send you some flowers, which will convince you more than language can of the sweets of yellow jessamines.

Now what shall I say to interest you? I have drawn a snow scene and took it to Savannah to have it framed; and I must tell you that it has been much admired. I have another model loaned me by a drawing teacher there, and I am encouraged to copy it, notwithstanding the formidable appearance of four mules and some pedestrians! And I do not think that my talent for animal-drawing is very remarkable. Do you ever indulge in this amusement now? How do you progress in oil painting? Or are you stationary in oil? You used to draw very prettily.

Whilst I am writing I am serenaded by the screaming of two young owls. You will think, I expect, that we have a strange collection of pets! We have not had the owls quite two days. They are not yet fledged, and I do not know whether we shall succeed in raising them. They are the funniest-looking things you ever saw. What say you to my having two cats and seven kittens? Don't you want some of them sent on to you by express? However, you must not suppose I am to be burdened with all these; I have already promised five of them to various individuals.

Has Matilda Harden written Sallie yet? I do not think either of them need say anything about our correspondence until they do better themselves! I

have not seen Matilda since my return, but I understand she is quite blooming, and expects to spend a portion of her summer in Athens, Georgia. She
has an uncle who is a professor in the college there, and also a brother who is
a student. So she has many attractions there.

I should have liked to have been with you on that pleasant evening you
passed at Sue Dickson's. I was quite sure you would like Anna Bulloch. Give
my love to her and to all my friends—Paulina, Sue, and Maggie Wilson not
excepted. Where is Maggie Wilson staying now? And how is her health? I
hope that she shows no consumptive tendencies.

My love to Sallie; and tell her I should like to know what she is doing
these days. Where will you spend your summer? Are you going to Maryland? We expect to have Brother Joe with us in about a month. Mother
unites with me in love to you. Mine to your mother.

Your affectionate friend,
Mary S. Jones.

Mrs. Susan M. Cumming *to* Rev. C. C. Jones[t]

Savannah, Wednesday, April 9th, 1856

My dear Brother,

I was truly glad to hear that Mary arrived safely, for the stage has been
upset twice recently, and I always feel anxious whenever any of my friends
go in it now. We missed Mary so much; and while Laura was taking her
last nap I had no one to chat with me. Several of her acquaintances have
called since she left.

I am glad to say that Sister had a comfortable night and felt better this
morning. The dressing of the wound was very painful, for Dr. Bulloch
found it necessary to take three or four stitches to close the upper part of it.
Sister bore it remarkably well, and is quite comfortable this evening. She is
taking ale. The wound suppurates well now, and the doctor allows her to
eat anything she wishes. Tell Sister Mary that the little roaster was brought
from the icehouse yesterday and nicely roasted, and Sister dined and breakfasted on it very heartily. It was delicate and delicious to all our palates. Tell
Mary I did not have it cooked before she left because I wanted to let her
aunt eat of it when she was able. I hope it will heal very soon. We will take
the best care of her that we can. The doctor does not allow her to see company, for he says very little talking on her part will irritate the muscles and
nerves.

Thank you kindly for getting Mr. Barnard to attend to my planting interest at White Oak. I have just written him that it meets with my entire
satisfaction and concurrence. I know full well your interest in me and mine;
have had too many proofs of it to question it for a moment. I only wish you
had the ability to do even a fourth of what you desire to do. God give you
strength for all His will, and us hearts to acquiesce in that will under all circumstances!

I wrote Joe last week and addressed my letter to *Dr.* Joseph Jones.

Charles is quite well. I think George is getting measles. He slept all yesterday, but is up today eating as usual. Says he is better. Shall look for measles Sunday. Eliza West has been very sick with measles, and all the children have had and are having it: nine cases. . . . Glad to hear all well at Julia's; our love when you see them. Charles and Laura unite with me in love to you, Sister Mary, and Mary. Shall be glad to see you and Sister Mary on any terms. Believe me, dear Brother,

Your affectionate sister,
S. M. Cumming.

Miss Mary Sharpe Jones *to* Miss Laura E. Maxwell[t]

Montevideo, *Thursday,* April 17th, 1856

Dear Cousin Laura,

Thank you for your affectionate and pleasant letter, and your invitation too. How much pleasure it would give me to accept it! When I am with Aunt Susan and yourself I feel as though I were in another home. I should like to see the Judge in his uniform, but this sight must be reserved for some future day, as I cannot go to Savannah again this spring—notwithstanding, too, the pleasant opportunity of going I have had offered me by a kind friend. . . . He has, however, commended me to a better mind, and warns me against not following the advice of my parents and pastor.

But self has occupied space enough in this letter, so *I* will cease and tell you of something more interesting. Mother and I went on last Friday afternoon to the Sand Hills to attend the meeting of Presbytery. . . . On Saturday evening the elders (Mr. Samuel Mallard and Mr. John B. Mallard) were ordained. Mr. Porter preached a very interesting sermon, and Mr. Buttolph made the ordaining prayer and delivered the charge to the elders. . . . On Sabbath morning Father preached Mr. Mallard's ordination sermon. Mr. Buttolph made the prayer and propounded the questions; Mr. Fraser delivered the charge to the newly ordained bishop and pastor, and Mr. Porter the charge to the people. Mr. Fraser's charge was one of the most beautiful and touching I ever listened to. In the afternoon Mr. Porter preached, and the Lord's Supper was administered. This latter service Mr. Mallard conducted, and admitted one colored woman. In the evening Mr. John Winn preached, and with this sermon closed the public exercises of the presbytery, though it did not adjourn until 3 P.M. on Monday. Mother and I returned in the morning, and Mr. Buttolph and Father came down in the evening. . . . This is the first visit I have made to Walthourville in twelve years. . . . Tell Aunty Aunt Marion says her little namesake is the handsomest child she has.

Last evening we waited tea until after nine o'clock, hoping to see Mr. Ward; and I and indeed we all thought Brother Charlie might come with him. But our waiting did not bring the lawyers.

We are very glad to hear that Aunty is doing well, and hope she will not fatigue herself too much with company. . . . You speak of a beautiful branch of spirea. We have a fine bush of it growing in the garden, and it has bloomed abundantly this spring. I think it grows from the cutting, so you can have some when you come out. . . . I am sorry George should have taken the measles and thereby brought you some additional trouble. I hope Joe and Sarey will not take them. I am told they have "been through Sunbury" and now are at Dorchester. . . . Father and Mother unite with me in best love to Aunty, Aunt Susan, and yourself.

Your affectionate cousin,
Mary S. Jones.

I picked two ripe strawberries yesterday.

Mrs. Susan M. Cumming *to* Rev. C. C. Jones[t]

Savannah, *Thursday,* April 17th, 1856

My dear Brother,

About twelve o'clock today Drs. West and Bulloch came and removed the tumor on Sister's neck. The operation was painful, of course, but Sister bore it with her usual fortitude. It required about five minutes to remove it, after which she took half a glass of wine, then two eggs, a nap, and ate a hearty dinner. She is now sitting in the rocking chair in our room (four o'clock). I do sincerely hope that this will be the last, and that Sister will soon recover her usual strength. . . . Sister sends any quantity of love to you, in which we all unite.

Your affectionate sister,
S. M. Cumming.

Mrs. Mary Jones *to* Mr. Charles C. Jones, Jr.[g]

Montevideo, *Tuesday Morning,* April 22nd, 1856

My dear Son,

We were happy to hear from you yesterday, but grieved to learn that your aunt had suffered so much from the removal of the second tumor. Brother William was at church on Sabbath and quite well—only complaining a little of the long rides. He hopes that Sister Betsy will be able to come out during the coming week. He no doubt will write of his arrangements.

We were much disappointed at not having the pleasure of Mr. Ward's company on last Wednesday night. We had taken it into our heads that *you* were coming too. We had a *hot supper* and one of my best arrowroot cakes in waiting until ten o'clock, when we gave you out. Mr. Ward was at Midway on Sabbath afternoon.

Our friend and pastor is quite well again, and expects to visit Savannah this week. Your sister received her *invite* to your *picnic* by the mail yesterday, and you must not be surprised if she accepts it.

Your father requests you to call on Mr. Anderson and ask if he will be good enough to send him account sales of the *fine cotton,* as he has some bills that ought to be discharged immediately. *Mr. Anderson* wrote him that the cotton was sold.

We have all been a little unwell since our visit to Walthourville. It was excessively warm for *this* season whilst there. Last night we had frost. Mary is expecting Miss Harden to see her today. Rev. Mr. Mallard spent the night with us. The family are all getting up, and I must close to be in time. With our united love to your aunts and cousin and yourself, as ever,

Your affectionate mother,

Mary Jones.

I am glad to hear that George is over the measles. They are in the county.

Mr. Charles C. Jones, Jr., *to* Mrs. Mary Jones[t]

Savannah, *Wednesday,* April 23rd, 1856

My dear Mother,

Your kind favor of yesterday was duly received. . . . I am sorry to learn that you were all more or less unwell after the meeting of Presbytery, and hope that the same may be the result of fatigue only and not of any permanent indisposition.

I am happy to tell you that Aunt Betsy appears decidedly better today. She has suffered more than we had anticipated, but the first and large wound has healed almost entirely, and the second promises a speedy reunion of the severed parts. Operations are always more serious, and a subsequent recovery more protracted, in a person of advanced age than in the case of one young in age with active recuperative powers.

Today I spoke to Mr. Jackson, Mr. Anderson's head clerk, in relation to Father's request. He replied that account sales had to the best of his recollection been sent already, but that he would examine the letter book and see that the same were forwarded by the present mail.

We will be very happy to see not only Sister but yourself and Father on the 1st of May. The celebration of that day will be conducted pleasantly and agreeably, and our hope is that the ladies will by their presence impart a softening, refining influence to the festivities. Once in ten years the artillery indulge in a commemoration of this character. The Chatham Artillery and the Liberty Independent Troop have always reminded me of twin brothers, antedating as they do all other companies, and embracing in their numbers so many who were prominent in past generations and reliable in the present. Seldom do we find volunteer companies sustained with so much interest for so long a period. The use of such associations was emphatically portrayed by Father in his late address. I think it a duty which every citizen owes in our citizen-soldier state of society—and especially in our section of the country— to connect himself if possible with one of these military companies. It is certainly a police service very necessary in its character, and one, moreover, quite light—especially if we remember the army and civil requisitions made upon the citizens of the nations of Europe. Each company in this city has its alarm posts, and at a moment's warning, in obedience to a given signal, the members repair thither. It will at once appear how well adapted such an arrangement as this is to quell sudden insurrection or domestic lawlessness in case of emergency.

I will be very much obliged to you, Mother, if you will have my thin summer clothes sent in at your earliest convenience. The weather is growing rather warm again, and I shall need some white pants for parade on the 1st of May. I believe some of those left on the Island are in rather a dilapidated condition.

After July, D.V., I hope we shall have more leisure, when I will try and spend a few weeks on the Island; and am anxious also to read a few works on criminal law during the interval of business.

Brother, I presume, will return home early in May. He has not replied to my last two letters. Perhaps his engagements are pressing.

Cousin Eliza West, I learn from Aunt Susan, left the city this morning for Burke. Her mother and father are both quite sick.

Savannah is looking beautifully. The foliage of the trees is very rich. Never in a southern clime have I seen vegetation more rapid in its growth. I hope the late frosts have been too slight to injure materially the crops.

Do say to Father that any matters which need attention I will be happy to see to for him. It is useless for me to say this, however. Aunts and Cousin unite in warmest love to you, dear Mother, to Father, and to Sister.

From your ever affectionate son,
Charles C. Jones, Jr.

Mrs. Mary Jones *to* Mr. Charles C. Jones, Jr.^g

Montevideo, *Monday,* April 28th, 1856

My dear Son,

We were happy to learn through your letter today that your aunt was improving so decidedly. Your uncle spent the day with us; seemed very cheerful and enjoyed his dinner. Mr. Buttolph also dined with us, and your sister is very much obliged to your cousin for the articles. Brother William will not come down before next week in the carriage. As Mrs. Porter kindly offered your aunt the use of her carriage, your uncle hopes she will accept it and test her strength before she takes her journey homeward.

Your father thought of going to Savannah tomorrow, but he has been suffering for several days with a pain in the left side. Today he is measurably relieved, and may come down in Friday's stage. But you must not expect him until you see him. He had an appointment to preach at Midway on Sabbath, but we persuaded him to keep silence, he was so unwell. He complains at times of debility, and I think he needs some tonic. I feel thankful your brother, if Providence permits, will be with us so soon.

I am sorry, my son, to send you so meager a summer supply, but this is all I can find of yours. The new vest is without buttons; I had not one in the house. Thought you might like to wear your agate set with it; if not, you can get the *tailor* to put on such as you fancy. It wants also a buckle on the strap. Any articles for yourself or your man George that you wish made up, you must get and send out to me.

Where will you board when your kind aunt leaves? I feel very anxious on this point, and trust you will be able to spend the summer months at home on the Island. . . . It is late, and I must close. Your father and sister unite with me in much love to your aunts and cousin and self. I hope your brother will be with you shortly. Do take care of yourself on the 1st of May; I hope you will have a pleasant time.

Ever, my dear son, your affectionate mother,
Mary Jones.

P.S. The *bundle* with your clothes comes in by *this stage* (*Tuesday's*). You had best inquire for it, as the driver does not leave usually at the house. Will send your trunk by the carriage.

Mr. Charles C. Jones, Jr., *to* Mrs. Mary Jones[t]
Savannah, Wednesday, April 30th, 1856

My dear Mother,

Your very kind favor of the 28th inst. and the package per stage were both duly received, for which please accept my hearty thanks. We regret to hear that Father has not been feeling as well as usual during the past week, and are glad that you prevailed upon him to remain a listener on Sabbath last. We shall be very happy to welcome him if he comes in on Friday. Why cannot you and Sister also make at least a flying visit to Savannah? Brother may be here on Saturday. We had hoped that you would all have been with us on the 1st of May.

Aunt Betsy continues to improve rapidly. Today she rode out with Mrs. Porter, and seemed favorably impressed with the exercise. She expects to be able to leave for Liberty next week.

Tomorrow we have our celebration, and we hope that everything connected with the same will be conducted to the satisfaction of our guests and fellow soldiers. At half-past seven in the morning we are to fire a salute of seventy guns, this being our seventieth anniversary. At Thunderbolt there will be a contention for a prize: distance eight hundred yards. But I will not anticipate, as you shall, if nothing happens, have a full account of the proceedings of the day.

As I write at the eleventh hour, having been very busy all day, I hope, dear Mother, that you will excuse this short and unsatisfactory letter. With best love to self, Father, and Sister, in which all here unite, I remain, as ever,

Your affectionate son,
Charles C. Jones, Jr.

Miss Laura E. Maxwell *to* Mrs. Mary Jones[t]

Savannah, *Saturday,* May 3rd, 1856

My dearest Aunt Mary,

We were so sorry that you did not come too yesterday—and still more sorry today, when your most acceptable present was served up as strawberry ice cream, that you were not here to enjoy it with us. Uncle Charlie wished that he could place it before you. Mother says I must return her best thanks for your bounty. We dined on the roaster today, and regretted that we had not sent it to the icehouse, as Aunty had an unfavorable turn last night and could not partake of it today, and it is a dish of which she is so fond. Aunty has not improved within the last two or three days; seems debilitated and is very weak.

Can you not come this week with Uncle and make us a visit? We have another cook, and Sarey is getting better and better, and the rest quite well, and we would be so glad to see you.

I was surprised to hear that Mary had finished the piece she took with her already. My dear aunt, I am very much obliged to you indeed for your kindness in lending me your beautiful picture, and will return it to you in good order. Mine is not quite so beautiful, but it is pronounced a good copy, and Mother is so much pleased with it. Mary Screven offered me Raphael's "Madonna and Child" to copy yesterday evening, but Mother says I will not have time to copy it; and I am very sorry I will not, as it is a study for crayon, and her face is so lovely. . . .

I did wish you could have seen your son in his uniform! He looked *finely,* and although his was the first fire, he placed the ball within three feet of the bull's-eye in a direct line; and had those who were more experienced not altered the direction he gave the gun, the prize would have been his. The person to whom it was given did not even fire his own gun; someone else fired for him when his number was called out. Good luck simply! The day was so dusty, and I did not have an offer of a drive to Wassaw, so I remained in Aunty's sickroom. Some of the company told Charlie to keep his mouth closed and brace himself back when he touched off the guns in the morning, and others to open his mouth to avoid the effect. So my first question was: "Did you keep your mouth open or shut?" And he replied he was so much excited that he did not know; that he liked the excitement, and it has not the slightest effect upon him. The artillery is a grand old company; I am so glad that he belongs to it. And he looks so handsomely in his uniform! He took Joe on the steamboat to take care of his knapsack, and his face was beaming with delight. And George tired himself out looking at the soldiers.

Uncle Charlie has been invited to preach in the Independent Church tomorrow, and I am so glad that he is not going to preach *anywhere.* I hope he will not feel the injury of his fatiguing ride. His old friend Mr. Hutchison is entertaining him now downstairs. By the way, I hear Dan Elliott is going with him to Europe this summer, and they leave very soon. Mr. Stoddard informed Mr. Hutchison the other day that "Lucy Sorrel would marry any man as rich as he was." It seems that Miss Stoddard and Miss Sorrel are rival singers, and it is "diamond cut diamond" with them just now. . . . Mr. Hutchison says he leaves in the steamer of the 12th on his way to the North and Europe, and made me many good wishes, *and* promises to think of me very affectionately on *that day,* for which I thanked him.

Tell Mary Gertrude leaves in the steamer this week for New York, and she alone will be there to stand by me unless she objects, and then Kitty Stiles will have to be asked to stand with her and wait with Charlie, though I am not careful about that. Mary is more to me than anyone else, and I've never been very intimate with Kitty, though she is a very lovely girl, and it has just happened so that we have not seen much of each other.

My dear Aunt Mary, I wish I could do something for you, you have always been so kind to me. Aunty is sleeping sweetly, and seems more comfortable this evening. The doctor has just left her. With a deal of love to you and Mary from Mother, Aunty, Uncle, Charlie, and all,

Your affectionate niece,
Laura E. Maxwell.

Rev. C. C. Jones *to* Mrs. Mary Jones[t]

Savannah, *Saturday,* May 3rd, 1856

My dear Wife,

Our ride yesterday was very dusty, so that I was like a miller, only browner. . . . Sister has been very unwell today; in bed all day, but is better this evening. Unless she recruits considerably, I think it doubtful if she will be able to ride out home next week. However, we can say nothing to the contrary. Should you hear nothing tomorrow (Sabbath), you may conclude she continues to improve. She has had a severe time, but is calm and in a pleasant state of mind.

Saw Cousin Charles W. West this afternoon in relation to Joe's professorship. He says the pecuniary condition is not necessarily connected with the matter, and arrangements may be made to offer him the situation independent of it. So it may turn out in favor of his settlement here, at least for a time. I will learn more of it yet.

Cousin Charles's family are all well of the measles, but Cousin Eliza has taken a cold up the country and is not so well. Mr. and Mrs. Whitehead are exceedingly unwell. Their friends watch over them with great solicitude from day to day. Both have heart disease!

Have been invited to preach in First Presbyterian and in the Independent Churches tomorrow, but have had so much inaction today that I declined both invitations, and hope I have not done wrong. Mr. Sorrel called to invite me to preach in the Independent Church, and Mr. Rogers also wrote me a note. Mr. Hutchison called.

Charles is very hearty. Sister and Laura also. Should you need anything, write by *Tuesday's mail.* . . . All unite in much love to you and Daughter.

Kiss my dear child for me. And may God watch over and keep you both in the hollow of His mighty hand! I am, as ever, my dear wife,

Your true lover and devoted husband,
C. C. Jones.

Mrs. Mary Jones *to* Rev. C. C. Jones[t]

Montevideo, *Monday,* May 5th, 1856

Your letter, my dearest husband, was most welcome today. I have thought most anxiously of you since you left, and hope you will not only enjoy but be benefited by your trip. I am sorry to know that our dear sister has not improved in the past week. Brother William was at church yesterday; I have not heard from him today, and am just going to send Gilbert off. Enclosed I send Joseph's letter. How much happiness it would give me to have our dear child settled in Savannah!

I went to the Island on Saturday and found all well and moving on well. But the drought is most distressing. We had a sprinkling of rain last night —not enough to appear this morning. I trust we may be remembered in mercy soon, or the labor of the husbandman must fail. Our people are all well. Henry is better, but looks badly. And our good pastor has had a slight return of his dyspeptic symptoms. I hope he will be with us tonight. He gave us two most interesting sermons yesterday.

Thank dear Laura for her kind letter. I am so sorry my dear boy missed the prize. He will point his gun himself next time. Had he won the prize it would have been a pleasant memorial of their seventieth anniversary and his first parade. I feel exceedingly gratified that he has connected himself with that ancient and honorable corps.

Will you be good enough to get me *six* tin boxes of *sugar lemon?* They cost *fifteen* cents apiece and are to be had, Henry says, only at *Rodgers'* (formerly Crane & Rodgers'). He keeps their grocery store, and I presume it would be a nice place to deal at, for I was always pleased with articles sent us by them.

I must now close, as I wish to send in this envelope a note to Joe, which you will please send on at the same time that you do the draft. Daughter unites with me in love and kisses to dear Father, Aunts, Cousin, and Brother.

Ever your attached
Mary.

Be sure and get a *summer vest;* I have given the old one away.

Miss Mary Sharpe Jones *to* Miss Laura E. Maxwell[t]

Montevideo, *Friday,* May 9th, 1856

Dear Cousin Laura,

Thank you for your note, which I did not deserve, for I have been in your debt for two weeks; but you must excuse me, for I really have not had much time for writing lately. I was very much obliged to you for the things you sent by Mr. Buttolph, though I am tardy in expressing my thanks.

Mr. Buttolph called here this afternoon, and I am sorry to say looks badly; he has been suffering very much recently, and is still, with dyspepsia. I am very glad to hear that you are coming out in two weeks, though we had hoped you would have been able to have been with us sooner. Aunt Julia and family have moved down; went today. We will not go for two weeks or more, though on account of my music I would like to go as early as possible.

I attended the May party; Isabel and Mr. McClellan went up with me. We spent the night with Aunt Marion. I enjoyed it as much as I generally do a party; it was a pleasant one. Isabel enjoyed herself very much; was greatly amused with the dancing: the first party she had ever attended. A Mrs. Lockett danced, and I presume she was nearsighted, as she wore spectacles. This was an amusing thing to Isabel; she concluded, of course, that she was an old woman and as such she ought not to have been engaged in such amusements. I had not attended a May party there for ten years. Isabel looked very prettily; she will be very handsome, I think.

I am very much obliged to you for ordering my frame. I had to work very rapidly to finish the piece—too much so to do it full justice, though Mr. Buttolph said this evening that it was a much handsomer piece than he thought it would be.

We are rejoiced to hear that Aunty has borne the ride out so well. Gilbert has returned and reports her walking about the house and sitting in the piazza. We will go and see her tomorrow morning.

Mother and I were very much surprised by our handsome present. We think the silks beautiful and very appropriate and becoming; we are very much obliged to Aunt Susan for her agency in their purchase.

Dear Cousin, I have written this so hastily that I fear you will be quite tired of it. I scarcely know what I have said, for Uncle John and myself have been writing and talking all the time; so you must excuse all defects. Mother, Father, and Uncle John unite with me in much love to Aunt Susan and yourself. We are so glad to have dear Father at home again. He says your piece is splendid. Good night.

Your affectionate cousin,
Mary S. Jones.

Miss Laura E. Maxwell *to* Mrs. Mary Jones[t]
Savannah, *Wednesday,* May 14th, 1856
My dear Aunt Mary,

We are very much obliged to you indeed for your kind offer to meet us at the Boro and take us to your beautiful Montevideo; and on Monday the 26th, D.V., we will be there in the stage.

We enjoyed dear Uncle Charlie's visit so much, and if wishes could have brought yourself and Mary, our enjoyment would have been greatly increased by your actual presence. We wished so much that you would come, as the time was so near for our final departure from Savannah. I never saw this place looking more beautifully than at the present time, notwithstanding the want of rain. I hope by this time that you have been visited by refreshing showers, and that your gardens are as beautiful as ever.

I would not be surprised if we brought you your long-absent son Joe. It will grieve us to leave Charlie here. He is a noble, industrious fellow and will, I am persuaded, distinguish himself in the world. Indeed, you have reason to be proud of your sons, and of your daughter too. And I am proud of my cousins. Willie and Charlie are more devoted to their business than any other young gentlemen here among my acquaintance.

Dr. Palmer's sermons on Sabbath were very fine; he preached three times in the Independent Church. . . . He told me he had accepted the call to the church in New Orleans, and was going there in the fall. I fear the climate may shorten his days of usefulness. While on this subject, I have just heard that the Independent Church here are going to send a delegation to Dr. Palmer to call him to this church: Mr. John Anderson, Mr. George Anderson, Mr. Duncan, and two others. "He says he has calls from five churches now in his hands, and is not yet committed to any of them, and is open to a call from this church." So they say. They are going to offer him five thousand dollars and a parsonage. Mrs. Porter has just come from the meeting and told us all this. And Mr. Alexander thinks they ought to have a talk with *Mrs.* Palmer, and then they might hope to secure *Mr.* Palmer.

I am *exceedingly obliged to you, my dear aunt*, for the use of your picture. I hope you will find it quite improved by its trip to town. It has on it a "contribution frame" from some of your dear friends—Mother, Charlie, and your niece. If Louisa can contrive to carry it in the stage tomorrow, we will send it together with Mary's picture frame.

If we can bring anything out for you on the 26th, please let us know. Mother and Charlie unite with me in warmest love to you, dear Uncle Charlie, and Mary.

> Ever affectionately your niece,
> Laura E. Maxwell.

Mrs. Mary Jones *to* Miss Laura E. Maxwell[t]

Montevideo, *Monday,* May 19th, 1856

My very dear Laura,

I intended to send yourself and Charles a long letter this evening, but *company* has come unexpectedly for the night, and I leave Mr. Jones and Mary for the entertainment whilst I send you these lines to thank you for your kind favor, and to express my gratitude to all parties for the picture frame. I must congratulate you on your success; everyone pronounces your piece most beautiful. *One gentleman* told me it was *magnificent!* Your Uncle Charlie (who is a judge) bestowed the highest praise upon it.

We shall meet you at the Boro on next Monday, Providence permitting. And I wish you, dear Laura, to say *to all your friends* in Savannah whom you intend inviting to the joyful occasion that we shall be most happy to entertain them at Maybank. Our hearts and home will be open to them all. I do hope our good friends Major and Mrs. Porter will be of the number.

Sister Betsy and Brother William spent last week with us. She is regaining her strength; I thought I could perceive an improvement daily. But we fear her sufferings are not over. Five or six of those tumors have appeared in different parts of her person. They are very small as yet. This week she expects to visit Mrs. Winn, who has a *fine son*.

Please say to my dear son Charles that I have shipped by Captain Russell all the articles he desired. A list of them will be found in the top of the trunk, which he can keep. If he has no use for the sheet around the bedding, he can send it out, as it is one we have for moving; and perhaps your mother might find it useful in packing her things, and it could come in that way. He will have to get a key to the trunk; I did not have one to send.

Our good pastor preached twice on Sabbath very interestingly. The next will be our Communion season, and Mr. Jones, without my *knowledge* or *consent*, has *volunteered* to assist in one sermon. He is really too unwell to do so, but felt that Mr. Buttolph needed help. We want him to be quite well again before the 10th of June.

I must now close, as it is very late. Mr. Jones and Mary unite with me in best love to Sister Susan and yourself and Charles. I will write him by the next mail. Believe me, as ever,

Your attached aunt,
Mary Jones.

Miss Laura E. Maxwell *to* Mrs. Mary Jones[t]
Savannah, *Wednesday,* May 21st, 1856

My very dear Aunt Mary,

I am so much obliged to you for your continued acts of kindness to me. I hope the pictures have arrived safely.

Your absent son will cheer your heart tomorrow. Dr. Joseph Jones surprised us all on Monday morning. The gun of the steamer awakened Mother, but Charlie and Laura were not even dreaming. You have reason to be proud of your sons. The Doctor likes the college and all of the professors, and seems quite pleased with his professorship. He is a genius, and will leave his mark upon the world. Here comes Dr. Bulloch inquiring again and again for Dr. Jones already. And here comes Willie the poison-grinder to take tea with the young professor two evenings in succession. . . .

It grieves me to hear of Aunt Betsy's sad prospect for the future; I hope she will have the six tumors removed speedily, before they attain to any size. Fortunately she possesses great fortitude, but it is sad to see one at her time of life suffering so much pain.

Mrs. Porter has gone to Washington with her brother, and Major Porter informed me that Mr. Tefft would go away and he would be obliged to remain in the bank, so I doubt if they come. Captain and Mrs. Gilmer and Mr. and Mrs. Lawton seem very anxious to be present on the 10th, though I am not certain that they will be there, the ride is so long. And Wallace cannot leave his bank; and of course Hattie has to remain and take care of her children. I presume some few of my friends from this place will be there, but who they are I will not be able to say. I've just invited Hamilton Couper. And Cousin Charles West says he would like so much to attend and pay you all a visit, but Cousin Eliza is expecting daily a call from her parents and cannot be out of the way. (They were more comfortable when last heard from.) I am so much obliged to you for your kind offer, and would not be surprised if some of our friends availed themselves of it.

I will give Mary's message to Kitty Stiles. I am so sorry that my dear uncle is going to preach on Sabbath, and that Mr. Buttolph requires help. I hope he will not suffer. . . . It is very late, and I desire to see Joe off in the morning. The things you sent Charlie by the vessel arrived safely. . . . Mother and Charlie unite with me in warmest love to you, Uncle Charlie, and Mary.

Your affectionate niece,
Laura E. Maxwell.

Mrs. Eliza G. Robarts *to* Rev. C. C. Jones[t]

Marietta, *Monday,* June 2nd, 1856

Dear Charles,

You see your old aunt will be troubling you sometimes with her tedious scrawl, which is now so bad I think you will find it difficult to read; but when distance prevents my having a personal interview with dear friends that I love to see and converse with, I must resort to my pen, although I hold not one of a ready writer.

It is with much regret we hear your health has not improved, and I write to beg you, Mary, and Mary Sharpe will come up this summer and spend some time with us. Perhaps the change might benefit and strengthen your general health if no more; and you could try some of our celebrated springs, whose waters are said to be very efficacious. You and Mary can select your own time for coming; any part of the summer we will be happy and glad to see you all. A hearty welcome, pure air, good water, and a plenty of fruit are the only luxuries we can offer.

Last week I received a letter from my dear Betsy. You can't think how glad I was to see her handwriting once more. I have been and still am very anxious about her. Her sufferings are truly great—and more of those tumors forming! Do beg her not to have any more taken out: she cannot stand such operations. The doctors no doubt give her medicine to produce an alteration in her system; this, with the blessing of God, I rely upon more than the cutting out. You recollect my woman Harriet (Peggy's mother), who had the scrofula for many years. Dr. West tried many remedies; she took panacea and catholicon; all failed. Mr. Roswell King recommended the simple remedy of eight grams of tartar emetic in a quart of water, a tablespoonful taken twice a day. This I tried, and it cured her ulcers entirely, and she was able to walk from Hickory Hill to Sunbury to meeting, and lived many years after.

Tell Dr. Joseph Jones he must excuse my daring to recommend anything when such an Aesculapius was near as him. I truly hope he will benefit his father and his aunt. We were truly pleased to see his appointment in the papers by the medical college. You have two such talented and popular sons, I fear they will be forgetting their poor Cherokee relations.

Last Thursday night Mrs. Dr. Dunwody and her little children from Darien spent the night with us on her way to Roswell. On Friday the Rev. James Dunwody dined with us, preached for Mr. Petrie at night, then took the cars for Carolina, and will be married on the 4th of June to a Miss Martin; returns with his bride to Roswell in three weeks; then they travel North. His mother (Mrs. Dunwody) is much better. Marion Glen says I must tell you she wants you to try the homeopathic system; it has done her mother good. The people in Roswell are all in favor of it, there has been so many cures of rheumatism by its use.

Yesterday was our Communion day. Our good pastor gave us a great and solemn sermon. He is truly a faithful and active man. . . . Last week he received two invitations to visit Savannah. He goes down the last of this week, and we fear the next week will end in a call to the Independent Church. We can only pray God will direct his footsteps; then all will be right, and we must submit to His unerring will. There will be a church meeting on Wednesday to raise the pew rent so the minister's salary may be increased from one thousand to twelve hundred dollars per annum. Mr. Petrie is much beloved by his flock, as John was.

I suppose this week Susan, Mary, and Julia will all be busy as bees on the Island, as Laura's suit at court will be ended on the 10th. We wish her and Mr. Buttolph all the happiness attendant on a married state. It would have afforded us pleasure for some of us to attend, but distance and the warm season prevent. You must give love to the bride- and groom-elect; tell them my best wishes and prayers attend them. Poor Betsy, how she would have enjoyed the festive scene had she been well enough to help with the preparations! I hope she will be strong enough to be present on *the* night.

Our weather in the last fortnight has been very cool: every morning with east winds, which caused severe colds and some sickness in the town. . . . The weather today just begins to feel like summer. . . . I suppose you are all at Maybank enjoying the sea breeze and crabs, fish, and shrimp. . . . Mary and Louisa and the girls unite in love to all. . . . Tell Rosetta Sam is well and true as the sundial to his work. . . . Believe me

Your affectionate aunt,
Eliza G. Robarts.

Mrs. Eliza G. Robarts *to* Mrs. Susan M. Cumming[t]

Marietta, *Monday,* June 23rd, 1856

Dear Susan,

I write you a few lines this morning first to congratulate you on the marriage of your daughter, giving you a son who no doubt will contribute much to the happiness of your little family. We thought of you all much on *the* night. The moon shone brightly with us, and we all hoped it was emblematical of the pure happiness dear Laura would enjoy. Next I must thank you for the beautiful cake you sent us; it arrived safely the Saturday after Laura's marriage. It looked so beautiful we sent over for Mr. Ardis' family and Mr. Petrie's to come over at five o'clock and take a slice with a glass of lemonade. . . . This morning I was much disappointed we did not get a letter from Mary Sharpe Jones or some of the family giving us a particular description of Laura's wedding. How many guests you had, who they were, how the bride was dressed, how many handsome presents she had, etc. —all those, you know, interest your Cherokee aunt and cousins, who are so old-fashioned.

I am very anxious to hear from dear Betsy. Was she strong enough to attend the wedding? Where is she now? . . . Do some of you write us soon.

Much love to Laura; we shall be glad to hear from her whenever she can write. Mary and Louisa send love to you both. . . . I don't know how I should get along without two such energetic daughters, I am so worthless. . . . Our love to Julia's family and Charles's.

Your ever affectionate aunt,

Eliza G. Robarts.

Excuse the nervous hand of your aunt.

Rev. John Jones *to* Mrs. Mary Jones[t]

Washington, *Wednesday,* June 25th, 1856

My dear Sister,

I have somewhat against thee! Why so silent to thy brother? After—very soon after—returning home, my delightful visit to Montevideo still lingering in my memory and on my tongue, I wrote you and requested an early answer, particularly that I might learn the condition of Cousin Betsy and Brother Charles in point of health. I have looked anxiously, though vainly, for an answer. Perhaps you did not receive my letter. Or perhaps you have been very much occupied in moving, and in various preparations and doings for the happiness of the newly married pair. Then my Sharpe niece, who wields a ready pen, might have come to your relief. But wedding times have a wonderful effect even on the Sharpest girls, and *just then* all things and all persons out of sight are apt to be out of mind. (Wonder if said niece has any idea of pairing off with one Mallard of the duck tribe? She is of age; let her answer for herself!)

How are Cousin Laura and Cousin David? They both owe me a letter apiece. And now, as they are no longer twain, a letter from one of them would discharge the obligations of both. But they are so happy now that they have forgiven their enemies and forgotten their friends. My best wishes and kindest feelings are with them both. And I trust Cousin Susan may find another son to fill in some measure that sad blank which can never be perfectly filled again.

My dear wife and little boys are well, although we are all suffering from hot weather both by day and night. . . . I have carried Dunwody back to Dr. Beman's; he went back very cheerfully and was received very kindly. The teacher of this place is absent at the North. . . . Jane unites in best love to Brother Charles, Mary, Charles, and Joseph, and all at Social Bluff and Woodville, and to Cousin Betsy and Cousin William wherever they are.

Your affectionate brother,
John Jones.

MRS. MARY JONES *to* MR. CHARLES C. JONES, JR.^g

Montevideo, *Wednesday,* June 25th, 1856

My dear Son,

We left Maybank at half-past five this morning, hoping by an early start to secure a cool ride, but before we reached Montevideo it became intensely warm. *Yesterday* was the warmest we have experienced this summer. Your sister and brother rode in the morning to Dorchester to see your aunt, and returned between two and three o'clock worn out with the intense heat.

Your dear aunt has been suffering very much from her arm recently. She is now confined to her room. Your brother thinks her situation a very critical one. The disease is evidently invading her whole system. She is as cheerful as could be expected from her bodily sufferings, and her mind is calm and resigned to the will of her Heavenly Father, but we feel most anxious on her account. We were very anxious for Brother William and herself to spend the summer with us, but he says on account of the distance from his plantation that it would be impossible. They are pleasantly located with Captain and Mrs. Winn, and everybody is very kind and attentive, calling and sending little delicacies.

We have had a deluge of rain up here. It is almost impossible from the saturated state of the ground to kill the grass or work successfully. We have a good prospect for corn, but the cotton is very poor. However, we have no reason to murmur or repine; God's mercies are *infinitely* beyond our deserts.

We enjoyed Miss Stiles's visit so much; we would gladly have detained her longer. The evening before she left, our friends all came over from the Point and Woodville. . . . The bride and groom seem to be in the enjoyment of every earthly happiness and blessing. Mr. Buttolph has improved astonishingly in health, and says he will nevermore return to the use of tobacco. I am glad his resolution has survived the transition period. I am sure he will be a healthier man for the change.

Your brother will soon be very busy in his preparations for the winter term. The Smithsonian is publishing his last article in elegant style. . . . Your dear father has improved under your brother's treatment, with God's blessing on the means. I wish he could change the climate, for a short period at least, a little later in the season. At present he feels too anxious on your aunt's account to leave.

As you are the *absent one,* our thoughts are constantly with you. May God preserve you, my dear son, from the many temptations that I know surround your path! Read your Bible daily and prayerfully. This morning before leaving I read the *7th Chapter of Proverbs.* "Wherewithal shall a young man cleanse his way? By taking *heed unto thy Word.*" It *grieves my heart* to know that you are not a Christian; but it would *break it* to hear of you or your brother what is said of most young men in cities.

Your father requests you to see *Mr. Isaac Brunner,* corner of Jones and Barnard Streets, and request him to send out *twenty bushels of hair* with the laths for plastering. And will you, my dear son, get the dividend of the Central Railroad and send it out by the first opportunity.

Yesterday in amusing myself with some old numbers of *The Magnolia* I found an extended description of Mr. Smets's library and an account of Savannah containing a list of all the mayors and aldermen from the first election down to the period in which the sketch was drawn, with the origin of the names of the streets, both of which I will keep for you, as they may interest you. It would be a treat to you to spend some of your leisure hours (if you have any) in visiting Mr. Smets's library.

Thursday Morning. The sun is pouring down a stream of burning rays. We are just starting for Arcadia. Mr. Martin is to meet your father there. He seems to be a good man, and has the reputation of being a good manager. I wish we could secure someone for this place; it would relieve your father of much care and exhaustion from these long rides. I am so anxious when he is absent from me that I cannot consent to his staying a night here alone. Your father unites with me in best love to you. Remember us to Dr. West and family. And best regards to Miss Stiles when you see her.

Ever, my dear son, your affectionate mother,
Mary Jones.

REV. C. C. JONES *to* MR. CHARLES C. JONES, JR.[g]

Maybank, *Wednesday,* July 2nd, 1856

We have thought much of you, my dear son, this hot weather. Hope you will be prudent and avoid as much as possible the hot sun and the night air. The sea breeze which comes every day is a great blessing to us. The rains have not fallen now for four or five days. Generally all well.

Your dear aunt, we fear, is destined to great suffering. Dr. West says there is no hope in her case, and she may not continue longer than three or four months! How sad it is! Yet, my dear son, to this we too must come. And may we have as sure a hope as your aunt has when our last hour arrives! You ought not—you must not—defer the great duty of repentance and reconciliation with God through our Lord Jesus Christ. All is loss and ruin without this.

The addresses came safely, and are well printed. Saw but two errors: not important. But ninety-five dollars! That is heavy. You sent out three hundred copies to Captain Fleming. I presume you will send out the remaining hundred and fifty. Five hundred Mr. Cooper was to print.

I saw a notice that the Savannah & Albany Railroad had called in a fifth installment, but could find no advertisement in the paper to that effect. If it be so, will you ask Mr. Anderson to hand you fifty dollars on my account and pay it up for me? I have not money enough in bank to pay taxes and the installment too. And if you can sell or *have sold* the five shares held by me I will be glad for you to do so, and place the amount to my credit in the state bank. If the fifth installment is paid in, then *one-half* will have been paid in: two hundred and fifty dollars. See what can be done with it. It would help us out to have something like that amount in cash at this time.

The young married folks are very happy. All well. Have just learned that Willie King has come. Mother, Brother, and Sister send much love. Do hand Cousin Joseph Robarts a copy of the address for me; I omitted his name when your sister wrote.

Your ever affectionate father,
C. C. Jones.

MRS. MARY JONES *to* MR. CHARLES C. JONES, JR.[g]

Maybank, *Saturday,* July 5th, 1856

My dear Son,

Willie called to see us this morning, and tells us he will return to Savannah early Monday morning. I cannot permit him to do so without sending you a line from home.

Your father and myself have just returned from spending the evening at Woodville. Your sister and brother have remained to witness some *fireworks* in honor of the 4th. Soon after tea we had family worship. The gathering together of the little ones always reminds us most touchingly of our departed friend and neighbor as he used to sit in the rocking chair with one of them in his lap. Immediately after, a bonfire of the remains of the old kitchen, which has recently been removed, was lighted up, blazing high amidst the tall oaks, deepening in the distance the dark shadow of the grove around. The old folks and young ones all assembled upon the bluff, when Mr. McClellan sent up a beautiful blue and white balloon. The ascent was very direct and gradual, as we had little or no breeze. Just as it was reaching the point of admiration from the spectators below, and receiving the farewell shouts from the boys, it suddenly fired up and soon vanished into thin air. At this point your father and myself left, leaving the young folks to enjoy the fireworks.

Yesterday your father and myself went up to Montevideo, and were thankful to find all well. In returning called to see your aunt at Dorchester. She was cheerful, but suffers greatly, and without any prospect of relief in this world. Her friends are all kind and attentive, and everything is done to alleviate her sufferings.

We have had it extremely warm for the Island. I do not now recollect ever to have passed hotter weather here. But the Lord blesses us with health throughout the county. . . . I hope, my dear child, you will soon be released from your duties in town and come out to your Island home. . . . It is Saturday night, and I must close. . . . May you rest beneath the shadow of the Almighty, and be prepared in body and spirit to welcome the Holy Sabbath Day! . . . Love from Father, Sister, Brother, in which unites

Your affectionate mother,
Mary Jones.

The servants send howdies. *Patience* has a *son*.

Mrs. Mary Jones *to* Mr. Charles C. Jones, Jr.^g

Maybank, Thursday, July 10th, 1856

My dear Son,

We were happy to learn through your letter to your father by the last mail that we might hope to see you about the middle of August.

The Doctor's little office under the *southwest* end of the piazza is now completed, and he has quite an array of medicines, chemicals, apparatus, and instruments upon his shelves. I charged him this morning to put in no explosive substance to blow us all up! Poor fellow, he was so much worn down by his winter's work that he is just beginning to improve.

I am sorry, my dear son, to announce to you the sad failure of the watermelons. The hot suns and rains have destroyed the vines. Andrew has planted some late seed, and hope you will yet have them. It always did me good to see you eat them, it was with such a relish.

I wish *Willie* King could come out too. He looked very thin and badly, I thought, and have no doubt he needs rest and country air.

This morning I let your father go alone for the first time this season to the plantation, but he promised to return this afternoon; and your sister accompanied him to Dorchester to spend the day with your aunt. Sister Susan is now staying with her, and is a great comfort to her, for she needs the attention of a female relative. To obtain ease and rest from her pains she is obliged to take anodynes; when the stimulus dies out she is left prostrated, and often nearly faints away. At such times she needs prompt attention. The state of your dear father's health does not permit me to leave him to nurse her. We try to be with her as often as we can. Her mind is very calm, and her hope and confidence firm in her Lord and Saviour. . . . How blessed to have the *light* that has guided and sustained us through all our Christian pilgrimage *shine* even unto the closing hour, and throw its bright beams along the dark valley and shadow of death as we are passing through to our happy home above!

I have a little secret to tell you, and you must write me as soon as you can what *your* views and feelings are. A certain reverend whom you saw not long ago on the Island has been very marked in his attentions for several months. The matter has ended in a proposal, to which no answer has yet been given; and I cannot say what will be the result. What is your opinion of the matter? Would it meet your approbation? When you write, put in a private slip with your answer. I am anxious to know your view of him as a gentleman and a Christian minister, and how you would like the matter.

Only Joe and myself are at home today. *Patience* had a fine little boy on the 1st, named Robin after his grandpa. We have it cool and pleasant now. Your man George has been stung by a *wasp,* and has his jaws swollen and in addition a large poultice tied on. Friends all desire love to you, and howdies from the servants.

Ever your affectionate mother,
Mary Jones.

Mr. Charles C. Jones, Jr., *to* Mrs. Mary Jones[t]
Savannah, *Saturday,* July 12th, 1856

My dear Mother,

Your kind favor of the 10th inst. was duly received. I am happy to know that through the continued mercies of a kind Providence all on the Island are in the enjoyment of wonted health.

You mention the failure of the watermelon crop; the absence of this fruit in a warm climate is sincerely felt by all. . . . Mrs. Caruthers for the past three weeks or more has been supplying her table very bountifully with an excellent kind of melon, both water and musk. She gets a good many of them from her brother's (Mr. Gibson) plantation on Whitemarsh Island.

Our city continues, I believe, generally healthy, although in the report of last week I notice several deaths from fever.

I regret very deeply to hear of Aunt Betsy's enfeebled condition and her protracted sufferings. By the last stage I sent her some oranges, lemons, and coconuts, which I hope she may be able to relish.

My letter of last Thursday has, I trust, been received, as its contents were far more valuable than any you have had from me for a long time. Forty dollars, the amount of the dividends declared on eight shares Central Railroad stock, were enclosed, and the letter duly registered in the post office.

The Doctor must have a pleasant office under the house, and I should have exacted from him, before permission was granted to enter the same, a written obligation to the effect that not only explosives but also combustibles, gases of an unpleasant character, and also all remnants of birds of the air, fish of the sea, and all creeping things should be positively excluded from this new sanctum and the vicinage. Otherwise the summer air may perchance be robbed of its sweet perfume.

Saw Miss Stiles a few days since. She is quite well, and enjoyed her visit to the Island very much. She is, I think, a pleasant lady. . . . With warmest love, dear Mother, to self, Father, Sister, the Doctor, and all friends, I am, as ever,

Your affectionate son,
Charles C. Jones, Jr.

REV. C. C. JONES *to* MR. CHARLES C. JONES, JR.*

Maybank, *Thursday,* July 17th, 1856

My dear Son,

Your Aunt Betsy is no better, but on the contrary gradually declines. Her mind is calm and we trust resting upon the only and sure foundation in view of approaching death and judgment, the Lord Jesus Christ. We saw her late last evening. Your Aunt Susan is with her all the time—her devoted sister. In her affliction we are all afflicted. Rest of us, through divine favor, in good health.

Will you be good enough to see Messrs. Palmer & Son and get from them a coarse wire sifter of good size such as masons use *for sifting lime,* and send it out by Monday's stage, care of C. Stebbins. Also request Messrs. Palmer & Son to send me *another keg of lathing nails by the first vessel.* Also Mr. Brunner, corner of Jones and Barnard Streets, to send *me by first vessel:*

4000 laths more

30 bushels hair for plastering

12 barrels stone lime, *fresh and good for finishing.* Ask Mr. Brunner if he will do me the favor of seeing that the barrels are in strong and good order. If not, I would prefer having them in full and perfect order and pay something extra for them.

4 barrels plaster of Paris

Captain Thomson (schooner *William Totten*) I presume is about ready to return. If not, Captain Russell will be in Savannah the last of this or the next week. Mills the mason will commence lathing next Wednesday, and we are in a great hurry for all things. Have two boats bringing shells for lime on every tide (for first coat) and two oxcarts bringing wood for kilns. So we are busy. Providence permitting, we hope the house will be drawing to a finish in a couple of months.

Provision crops at Montevideo and Arcadia good. Cotton ditto improving. Your sister has just left us for Dorchester to spend a few days with your aunt. She, Mother, and Brother unite in much love. The matter concerning which your mother wrote you seems to be coming to an issue. About what time do you suppose you may be able to come out, D.V.? And how long will you stay? Your Aunt Betsy asked me these questions yesterday.

Your ever affectionate father,
C. C. Jones.

Rev. John Jones *to* Mrs. Mary Jones[t]

Washington, Friday, July 18th, 1856

My dear Sister,

Your welcome letter was received last week. . . . I regret most truly that Brother Charles had that attack of fever. . . . It must have been a great comfort to have had your own dear Joseph at home; and thus his father enjoyed the combined attentions of son and physician.

I wish it were possible for my dear brother to leave home this summer and pass a few months in the refreshing climate of the mountains, and in the immediate neighborhood of strong iron waters. Just such a location may be found at the Gordon Springs, a quiet retreat, the resort of sober people, and owned and managed by an excellent Presbyterian. I expect to take my dear wife and children up to said springs early in August to remain at least a month. . . . On our way we will stop a few days in Marietta to see our dear aunt and cousins. Oh, that it were possible to have yourself and Brother Charles and Mary as members of our party—for his sake and yours and ours!

The reason given in your letter for remaining at home this summer seems insuperable. How sadly do I feel in regard to our dear Cousin Betsy! Every letter speaks of her as growing worse and worse, without a single ray of hope for recovery. . . . And dear Cousin William—how dark must be the cloud that now hangs over his path! May God's grace abound unto him and prepare him for the future!

You have no doubt learned before this of the death of Mrs. John Dunwody. Thus our oldest friends are fading away like morning stars into the light of heaven. We have sent a letter of sympathy to Mr. Dunwody, but have not received an answer. To him the remaining pathway of life will be very lonely, for he was a most tender and confiding husband. His wife was his right arm.

My dear sister, I rejoice with you in the prospects of your sons. I am acquainted with no young men who have had equal advantages and who have made so diligent improvement of them. They bring to their professions minds not only well stored but (what is better) well disciplined. With patience of investigation and persevering purpose they are bound to excel. I think Joseph has more patience of application than any young man I have ever known; and his labors have been eminently crowned with success and rewarded with honors. It is a rare fact that a young man should be elected to a professorship in a medical college before attaining his twenty-third year. It will be a peculiar comfort to Brother Charles and yourself to have your sons settled so near you. . . .

Jane unites with me in best love to yourself, Brother Charles, Joseph, and Mary—and Charles by letter if he is still in Savannah—and to all at the Point and Woodville.

                              Your affectionate brother,
                              John Jones.

REV. JOHN JONES *to* MRS. MARY JONES[t]

                    Washington, *Thursday,* July 24th, 1856

My dear Sister,

I have just this evening received your note of the 21st and 22nd from Dorchester; it fills my heart with tender agony. I had no doubt that our dear relative was certainly declining under her fearful disease, but I had no conception of such rapid advances. And now that the reality draws near—oh, how sad! Her sufferings must be indescribable. . . . The thought of never looking again upon her loved familiar face, nor listening to her kind words again on earth, is indeed painful beyond expression. Most truly do you remark that her place will never be filled in our social circle. . . . And poor Cousin William, what will he do if called to walk alone to the end life's pilgrimage? . . . If our precious cousin is still spared when this reaches you, do give her again the warmest assurances of love and tender and constant regard from my dear Jane (who loves her truly) and myself, and the same to Cousin William.

I thank you again and again for your note. Do let me hear again very shortly. Jane unites with me in best love to you, Brother Charles, and all at Maybank.

                              Your affectionate brother,
                              John Jones.

REV. JOHN JONES *to* REV. C. C. JONES[t]

                    Washington, *Monday,* August 4th, 1856

My dear Brother,

I send this line to acknowledge the receipt of your kind note conveying to us the sad intelligence that our dear cousin would meet us no more on earth. We will look every day for the account of her last days and her dying testimony.

Excuse the brevity of this letter, as we leave very early in the morning for Gordon Springs via Marietta. Should you write after receiving this, please direct up to the 20th inst. to Gordon Springs, Whitfield County, Georgia. My dear Jane unites with me in most affectionate regards to Sister, yourself, and all at Maybank and at the Point, and especially to our afflicted Cousin William. I will write him from the springs.

                              Your affectionate brother,
                              John Jones.

VIII

Rev. R. Q. Mallard *to* Miss Mary Sharpe Jones[t]
Walthourville, *Monday*, August 11th, 1856

My dear Friend,

I occupy a position new to me, and one of pleasure before unknown. I have had regular lady-correspondents, but they were those of my own kin, to whom I was drawn by the ties of consanguinity. But now I am to commence a correspondence with one who stands in no such relation to me, and yet to whom I feel the mysterious tide of my affections gushing forth with a sweetness and power never before experienced. And is it true that my Mary has honored me with this mark of her confidence—that she is willing to entrust in a measure her happiness to my keeping? May our Heavenly Father give me grace so that I may never betray this trust! It is a reflection of indescribable sweetness that my affections are given to one "beloved of God." In life and in death I trust we shall be united. I regard you as God's gift, and trust I am grateful to the Giver of All Good.

Does it bode well or ill to the preservation of our future "peace relations" that in this my first letter to my nearest earthly friend I shall have to ask pardon for offenses committed? Miss Mary, do you know you have put confidence in one who is—shall I say it—a thief? In the dead of night, had you been on the watch, you might have seen one issuing cautiously from his chamber, casting quick glances around him, advancing softly into a certain parlor, seizing and hiding about his person precious treasure, and as quickly seeking the shelter of his chamber. And dreadful to say, not then nor now has he felt any compunctions of conscience, nor does he now feel rebuked by the mild eyes of that same *"precious treasure"* as they beam upon him from the stolen case. Will you condemn? The temptation was great, the offense so easily perpetrated, the gain to me so great, the loss to you so inconsiderable. Remember your own conduct under much less trying circumstances and be lenient. I'll take it for granted that I am forgiven, and hope you will make my peace with the owner of the stolen property.

My other offense is this (I fear I will have to call it a violation of promise): my watch-guard ornament I occasionally transfer to my finger. Not when I appear in public, but at home and among my relatives. And now that my crime is fully confessed, listen to my defense. You will say it is a very lame one, I fear, when I tell you that my only apology is—the pleasure it affords me! This ring, when I wear it, is ever by its gentle pressure reminding me of *you* and of our plighted troth. Now this being so, will you wonder that I love to see and to feel it encircling my finger—a pledge that I have with it been made *rich* with my Mary's love? I know that yours is a gentle nature, and will therefore take it for granted that I am forgiven.

How pleasant it would be to me were I now in Dorchester looking forward with high anticipations to an evening's ride toward the sea! But another week must intervene ere I shall enjoy that happiness. Some of the good folks up here seem to have imagined that I pay weekly visits to my parents. One asked Mrs. Quarterman yesterday: "Why, *isn't* Mr. Mallard going down tomorrow?" I only wish it were possible that I could do so without interfering with my labors. . . . I write not expecting an answer until after my next week's anticipated visit, until which time I must bid *my dearest* Mary adieu.

With sincere affection yours,
Robert Q. Mallard.

Rev. R. Q. Mallard *to* Miss Mary Sharpe Jones[t]

Walthourville, Monday, August 25th, 1856

My dearest Mary,

You have correctly said that I do not follow out my impulses. Were I to give the rein to them, they would hurry me now into such expressions as might possibly tend to create in you skepticism as to the depth of my affection. Deep waters, you know, are still; shallow brooks noisy.

My own, how strange the pleasure I feel in telling you again what I have so repeatedly uttered before: *I love you.* I have sometimes been disposed to think that I was not gifted with too warm a heart, but a loved voice has awakened its slumbering capacities, and I now believe that I can love tenderly and deeply. . . . What a command that is: "Husbands, love your wives, even as Christ loved the Church and gave Himself for it." Christ's self-sacrificing love to His Church the model! Where could a nobler one be found? . . . A passage directly enjoining upon the wife the duty of her loving her husband I believe cannot be found. One has beautifully assigned as a reason for this omission that she needs no such admonition.

Have you ever noticed that Scripture usually speaks of the sacrifice as made by the husband? "Therefore shall a *man* leave his father and his mother and shall cleave unto his wife." The circumstances of our times are certainly different. With us, in the process of obtaining an education, the young man is gradually weaned from home, until with the completion of his literary training he is prepared, without any great violence being done to his feelings, to make for himself a home elsewhere. But it is not so with the mass of our ladies. They grow up under the rooftree, seldom away long enough to weaken in the least their attachment for their parents' home. Hence it costs them sometimes a severe struggle to sever these ties and to form attachments for a new home. Do you know that when I was calculating the probabilities of success, I feared that this would be a great obstacle—your love for your own happy home? I believe that you have the qualities for making a happy home wherever you go, when once you have left what is now your home. I assure you it will not lead me to doubt your affection if you should manifest the warmest attachment to it and great reluctance to leave it. And yet while I say this, I hope my Mary will be ready to overcome at some early period this natural reluctance and *be mine* in a yet nearer sense than now.

I cannot yet make any definite arrangements for the future, as my movements depend upon the actions of some who are still undecided what *they* will do. Of this we may speak another time.

Perhaps you would like to know something of my health. I have not yet had a return of fever, and am still continuing the quinine. I preached twice yesterday and attended my Bible class at night; I don't think I felt after these exercises more than usually fatigued. After the close of the morning's service, while I was still in the pulpit, I was startled by my sister Mrs. Quarterman coming to me with the question: "Do you feel badly?" She had noticed that my face was much flushed.

Yesterday was a warm day—Mr. John Mallard says warmer, according to his thermometer, by several degrees than any other day this summer. I fear you had it unpleasantly warm at Midway. Brother Sam was down. He tells me that Mr.—Brother—Buttolph preached two sermons. In his present state of ill health it must have been a severe task to him. I am glad that he received some assistance in serving the tables, but am almost sorry that it was rendered by your father. I hope that he has received no injury from it. I understand that a meeting of the church and congregation was called after service to take some steps in reference to releasing him (Mr. B.) for a time from his labors, but have not heard the result. Mr. Buttolph's absence will, I fear, place great temptations in your father's way. You will have to form a "triple alliance" (yourself, mother, and brothers) and forbid his encroachments upon his own health and strength.

I spent this morning in visiting among my people. Mondays when in the village I usually devote to that work. This, together with one other day, or rather the evening of another day, enables me to visit them quite frequently. Two of my visits were to the good old sisters Mrs. Bacon (alias "Aunt Polly") and Mrs. Oliver Stevens. Strictly pastoral visits, such as these were, I have some satisfaction in reviewing; but many of my visits (owing to peculiar circumstances and sometimes, I fear, to a sinful backwardness in myself) are purely social. However, I do not think these, if conducted with sobriety, are without their use.

I have heard some very sad intelligence recently concerning a family we both love: Dr. Howe's. Walthour, his eldest son, has become completely deranged. You remember he has for several years past been subject to fits. These became so frequent of late that the doctor and Mrs. Howe hurried on to the North to be with him. Since then through Mr. Walthour we have heard that he has lost his reason. They were consulting what disposition to make of the poor boy—whether to leave him in a Northern asylum or to bring him to Columbia. What a dreadful affliction! I feel for them, and hope and pray a kind Providence may sustain them under this heavy stroke.

I am admonished by the lessening space of this sheet that it is time to close. Present my kind regards to your dear parents and brothers, already becoming dear to me for my Mary's sake. I shall be much disappointed if Thursday's mail brings me no tidings from you. May Heaven's richest blessings rest upon you and yours, is the prayer of

Your own

R. Q. Mallard.

REV. R. Q. MALLARD *to* MISS MARY SHARPE JONES[t]

Walthourville, *Thursday,* September 4th, 1856

My dearest Mary,

As it wants an hour of my usual time for retiring, I have concluded to spend it in a manner most pleasant to me. In accordance with my promise, I shall endeavor to send you a letter by Monday's mail. Whenever I take my pen to write you, I feel a strong disposition to repeat my assurances of attachment and to lavish upon you terms of endearment. But *my dearest Mary* is, I doubt not, convinced of the sincerity of my love, and the only apology (if one be needed) which I have to offer is that just as it is natural for the sun to shine, so is it natural for affection to seek to express itself in the weak symbols which human ingenuity has invented. . . . My hour has expired, and I must lay down my pen for the present; and though I may not speak, I will write a "good night" to my love.

Saturday Evening. I commenced writing you two nights ago, as I feared I might be somewhat pressed for time today. I am now pretty nearly prepared for Sabbath and can devote a few moments to sweet converse with a dear absent friend (?)—a term all too cold. (There it is again. "But out of the abundance of the heart," etc.) I have some indistinct recollection of somewhere meeting with a caution to this effect: that young people in our fix (a glorious fix to me) should be guarded in their epistolary intercourse; that what is said may be forgotten, but what is written is thrown into durable form; and that in the event of the engagement ceasing by the will of either party, these "love letters," or *duplicates,* might prove inconvenient. As for me, in this matter I care not to look to the possibilities of the future. It is too cold a prudence, to my notion, to put ever a rein on feeling and say "Miss" when I *feel "Dear."* I have no fear that anything in either of us hereafter shall make it painful to read these expressions of attachment.

What a strange life is this upon which we have entered! In my plans for the future I move not alone, nor yet with an indistinct ideal by my side, but with one whose *voice* and *face* and *form* are familiar to me—*my own loved Mary.* I hope a kind Providence (who I am confident has this far guided me) will grant me a realization of these anticipations. What an hour will that be when I shall (as I hope) lead from the altar my own loved bride! The future will have its joys and its griefs, but with another I hope to enjoy the one and to bear the other.

I met your mother in a ride a few evenings ago, and called to see her yesterday evening. I am afraid what you said of my reserve may not benefit me in my intercourse with her. I do not wish to be; and the effort to avoid it may only make matters worse.

Your father wished me to procure for him Dr. Howe's address. It is this: Middlebury, Vermont, care of Rev. Mr. Matthews. Mr. Walthour did not remember his given name. This is his direction until the 15th or 16th of this month.

I am tempted to take another sheet, but I forbear. You may look for me on Monday a week.

Your affectionate
R. Q. Mallard.

Miss Mary Sharpe Jones *to* Mrs. Susan M. Cumming[t]
Maybank, Saturday, September 13th, 1856

My dear Aunt Susan,

Nearly two weeks have elapsed since your departure, and as yet we have heard nothing from you; but presuming that you are now in Williamstown, I have determined to write, knowing that you will be anxious to hear of my dear father's health.

The morning after you left, Mother was summoned to Walthourville. Uncle Berrien wrote quite in a state of excitement announcing the birth of another daughter—his sixth living child. Mother remained nearly a week, and left Aunt Marion very well, and says that the baby is very pretty, and I think must be remarkable, for she sent me a beautiful lock of her soft brown hair. Mother was favored in having very cool weather during her visit; and indeed it has been so cool here that we *might* have enjoyed a little fire. But it is warm again—though I suppose you are experiencing a very different temperature.

For the past two Sabbaths Father has preached in Sunbury, and consequently has not been very well. Has had some fever this week, and we think it almost entirely due to his exertions on Sabbath. And I believe he is convinced of it himself, for he has recalled the appointment made for tomorrow; and you know he seldom does this. On last Sabbath there was the largest congregation present that I have seen at all this summer, so that the temptation to preach another Sabbath was peculiarly strong.

After bidding you farewell we—that is, those of us who were in the buggy —extended our ride to Point Maxwell. We met Joe with Charlie at the gate, on their way to Lambert; and they were the only living creatures we saw. Everything about the house and lawn seemed to say that no one was at home. You always say that it is a satisfaction to feel that you are missed, and I can assure you that it is yours to enjoy now, for we all feel your absence very much. I should have liked to have accompanied you; and I am sure Cousin Laura must sadly feel the want of two such efficient persons to move and rearrange the furniture in her room so as to form corners entirely one's own with a chair and trunk in each!

This reminds me of our Marietta and Washington friends. They have returned from the springs—not, however, very much pleased. Aunt Jane did not improve at all: found the journey one of fatigue and not one of benefit or pleasure. So she is glad to be quietly located in Washington again.

During Mother's absence I spent a night at Woodville. . . . Cousin Mary is pretty well, and at present Mr. McClellan and herself are very much interested in vinegar-making. They think they are succeeding "splendidly."

Brother Charlie thinks of leaving for Savannah next week. We shall miss him very much. In a few weeks we shall lose Brother Joe also, for he will go in October. Thus far they have made no definite arrangements in regard to their housekeeping, as they do not yet know that they will be able to rent the house they desired.

Joe has been quite a good neighbor to us; has twice brought butter, for which we must thank you. He reports all the servants as being well, and says Augustus and himself are very busy clearing up the grove. I am sorry Dr. Duke is not in the county to give an account of your prospects in the crop line. If *he* were here, I might be able to tell you something about the result of your harvest. I believe almost everyone is thus engaged at this season.

I wish that my dear father and mother could join you in Williamstown. It is useless for Father to be anywhere without Mother, for even during her short stay on the Sand Hills he was the same disconsolate lover he always is when she is not with him. . . . I hope that Cousin Lyman's health is improving, and that he will speedily be restored to his accustomed vigor. Do you still think of remaining all the time in Williamstown? . . . Father, Mother, and Brothers Charlie and Joe unite with me in affectionate love to Cousin Laura, Cousin Lyman, and yourself. Tell Cousin Laura I will write her soon. If you wish anything done that I can do, please let me know and I will be happy to do it.

> Your affectionate niece,
> Mary S. Jones.

MRS. SUSAN M. CUMMING *to* MRS. MARY JONES[t]

New York, *Monday,* September 15th, 1856

My dear Sister,

You have no doubt imagined us flying at railroad speed over the country from this place to Albany and Pittsfield and Williamstown. But not so. Laura has been very ill for eight days past: violent cold and inflammation of the kidneys. We sent for Dr. Francis immediately; he was absent, but his associate, Dr. Kissam, came and administered various things which afforded temporary relief. On Wednesday Dr. Francis came with Dr. Kissam, and they bled her largely, which relieved her more than any previous remedy. Gave calomel and anodyne. On Friday ten leeches were applied to the lower part of her stomach, and they acted like a charm, relieving the pain greatly, and she was able to sleep. She has suffered *intensely*. Poultices, cloths wrung out of hot water, chloroform, laudanum, camphor—all have been used; and I am most thankful to say last night she slept comfortably, and today is decidedly better. The swelling has subsided; and the doctor says should she continue to improve the next twenty-four hours as she has done the last, she will be able to go on her way, we hope, on Wednesday or Thursday. . . . Mr. Buttolph and myself have been up with her day and night for eight days, scarcely sleeping; but last night we took off our clothes and all slept comfortably.

Mr. Buttolph is improving. Laura says her illness has "aroused him like a shower bath." He feels much better. Dr. Francis and Kissam have been visiting Laura twice a day, but think her better decidedly today. We now think of going to Trenton to visit Mr. Buttolph's cousin and remain there until Laura is well enough to go to Williamstown. We can go to Trenton in a few hours, and with far less fatigue than to Williamstown.

The physicians have been much interested in Laura's case, and have been as kind and attentive as possible. We have everything we call for, and the housekeeper and chambermaid are very attentive; but a hotel is a poor place to be ill in, as you well know experimentally. I cannot begin to tell you how kind and helpful Mr. Buttolph has been. In addition to the fatigue of the journey I think we all slept in damp sheets the first night we came. These are some of the delights of traveling!

I wish you could see our bright, cheerful, thankful faces today, Laura is so much better. . . . We hope to be able to leave here for Trenton on Wednesday or Thursday, Providence permitting. . . . Laura and Mr. Buttolph unite with me in much love to you, my dear brother, Mary, Joe, and Charles, and Brother William and all of Julia's household. Tell her she must take some of this letter to herself.

Your affectionate sister,
S. M. C.

I would have written before, but Laura was too sick; and I did not like to excite your fears, as you could not come to us.

Miss Mary Sharpe Jones *to* Mrs. Susan M. Cumming[t]
Maybank, *Thursday,* September 25th, 1856
My dear Aunt Susan,

About two weeks ago, supposing that you had safely reached Williamstown, I sent you a letter directed to Dr. Cumming's care. Your letter to Mother received on Monday made us feel very sad, but truly grateful to our Heavenly Father for His mercy in sparing our dear cousin. She must indeed have been very ill; I wish I could have been with you to have helped in nursing her.

We have all been pretty well since you left except my dear father; and he has had some fever once or twice—in consequence, we think, of preaching. He has been resting for two Sabbaths, and expects to preach again on next Sabbath in Sunbury. The presbytery meets next week in Mount Vernon, but the journey is so fatiguing that Father has concluded not to attend.

Tell Cousin Laura Mother and I spent Tuesday in Dorchester returning the calls of the ladies who "found Mr. Mallard seated in the piazza ready to entertain company." I spent Monday night at Lodebar. . . . Last evening the family from Woodville—children and all—came over. It seemed strange not to see you in our midst. It was so cold that we all gathered around the fire; and we are now enjoying winter weather, for last night it was almost cold enough for frost, which Father says would be a great calamity to the planting community.

Mother has proposed to Father that we all go up to Washington and Marietta a short time before the meeting of Synod, which will be in Atlanta; and I think we will do so about the last of October. Brother Joe will go to Savannah about the 15th, and in a week or two after, I suppose, we will take our flight. And I have no doubt Father will be much benefited. Brother Charlie returned to Savannah last week, pleading business as his excuse for going so early.

Mother says I must leave some space for her, and as Lafayette is waiting, I must close. I hope sincerely that Cousin Laura is quite well; we are glad to hear of Cousin Lyman's improvement. Accept a great deal of love for them both and yourself, dear Aunt. And believe me

Your affectionate niece,
Mary S. Jones.

Mrs. Mary Jones *to* Mrs. Susan M. Cumming[t]

Maybank, *Thursday*, September 25th, 1856

Most deeply, my dear sister, have we sympathized with you and Mr. Buttolph and our dear Laura in her severe and sudden illness. From experience I know what such an attack is; her sufferings must have been intense. . . . We shall look with great interest for some tidings from you by this evening's mail. Supposing that you were all in Williamstown, Mr. Jones had just directed our *postmaster* to forward your letters. . . . He forgot to say they must be directed to Dr. Cumming's care, so if you fail to receive them immediately you had best institute special inquiries.

I rode over a few evenings since to Point Maxwell and found all well and cheerfully employed at their duties. Sawney and his gang were harvesting the corn. Joe has trimmed the left side of the grove, and it looks beautifully. Sarey called up the Shanghaies, and they are quite grown. . . . Excuse haste to be in time for the mail. Mr. Jones, Mary, and Joe unite with me in best love to you, dear Sister, and Laura and Mr. Buttolph. Do let us hear often from you.

Ever your affectionate sister,
Mary Jones.

Miss Mary Sharpe Jones *to* Mr. Charles C. Jones, Jr.^g

Maybank, *Thursday,* September 25th, 1856

Dear Brother Charlie,

Your letter to Father and Mother informing us of your safe arrival was received on Monday. Thank you for sending the cake to Kitty, which she acknowledged very pleasantly in a letter to me; also mentioned that you had spent an evening with her. Father has been pretty well since you left, and will preach, Providence permitting, on next Sabbath in Sunbury. He requests me to say that he would have written you, but has not had time; will do so very soon.

Brother Joe and Mr. McClellan took a short hunt last evening, but as the tide was low were not as successful as you were. By the way, have you quite recovered from the effects of that hunt? I am glad on your account that the weather is so cool. We have been enjoying fire for two days past. Lafayette is waiting to take this to the mail; only write to tell you of our well-being and how much we have missed you. Father, Mother, and Brother Joe unite with me in much love to you.

Your affectionate sister,
Mary S. Jones.

Mrs. Mary Jones *to* Mr. Charles C. Jones, Jr.^g

Maybank, *Thursday,* September 25th, 1856

I trust, my dear child, that you will take special care of your health until there is settled cool weather. I have often heard that October was the most trying month in the year for health in Savannah. I feel daily anxiety on your account, and hope you will be prudent.

By a recent letter your aunt informs us that your Cousin Laura had been very ill for eight days in New York—the effect of fatigue and cold taken from sleeping in *wet sheets* at the great *Metropolitan*. She was relieved and decidedly better when she wrote. They expected in a day or two to leave for Trenton, New Jersey, on a visit to Mr. Buttolph's relatives, Dr. and Mrs. Buttolph, who had both been to New York to see them. How wisely ordered it was for your aunt to accompany Laura!

Please, my son, ask Mr. Lathrop if he has not yet sent the dowlass to forward at the same time the articles on the enclosed memorandum. We miss you very much. Father and Brother and Sister unite in best love to you with

Your ever affectionate mother,
Mary Jones.

MR. CHARLES C. JONES, JR., *to* MRS. MARY JONES[t]

Savannah, *Saturday,* September 27th, 1856

My dear Mother and Sister,

Your joint favor of the 25th inst. was this morning received. I am truly happy to hear that all are well at home.

It was indeed a fortunate circumstance that Aunt Susan accompanied Cousin Laura in her Northern trip. Her situation would have been pitiable indeed away from home without any female friend to administer to her wants. Does Mr. Buttolph's health improve?

The dowlass went out in the last stage. The present order will be filled by Mr. Lathrop, and together with the tea will be sent, D.V., in Thursday's stage.

There is nothing at all of interest with us. The city is about as full of politics as I am of work, and that is brimful. No house yet, I am sorry to say. It is next to an impossibility to obtain one in the central part of the city. With much love to selves, Father, the Doctor, and all friends,

Your affectionate son and brother,
Charles C. Jones, Jr.

Willie quite well.

MR. CHARLES C. JONES, JR., *to* REV. C. C. JONES[g]

Savannah, *Wednesday,* October 1st, 1856

My dear Father,

Jane was yesterday afternoon about six o'clock arrested by Jones, a constable of this city, and is now in confinement in Wright the broker's yard. She has been in Savannah more than a month, and is known by the name of Sarah. She was arrested in the house of Mrs. Dunham, a sister-in-law of old Mr. William Dunham of Liberty County. Mrs. Dunham is now absent on a visit to some of her relatives in Screven County. Mr. John S. Baker, whom perhaps you know as a son of the Mr. Baker of McIntosh County from whom Uncle John purchased a number of Negroes (Charity and Brutus among others) several years since, lives with her. So soon as I heard that Jane had been arrested at that house, I requested an interview with him, he being at the time of the arrest absent from the house. He came immediately, and the following is the statement made by him.

About a month since, Mrs. Dunham was in want of a house servant to act in the capacity of chambermaid, and requested Nelson, Dr. West's house servant, who had a wife in the yard, to make inquiry for her and see if he could not get a woman whom she could hire to do the work above described. On the following day Nelson brought Jane (or Sarah, as she called herself) into the yard to Mrs. Dunham. Jane represented herself as belonging to a gentleman in the up country who allowed her to find work and pay wages— a very common thing in this city. She declared herself able to do housework, and agreed to work for Mrs. Dunham for $6.50 per month. Mr. Baker states that she behaved herself very well, attending ordinarily well to her duties, but that she was greatly inclined to be lazy, and at times somewhat impudent in answering back when spoken to with reference to her work. A few days since, Jane told Mr. Baker, who acted with his wife in the management of Mrs. Dunham's house and household matters during her absence, that her master was in the city and had told her that she must go back with him up the country, and that she wished he would pay her her month's wages, as she must leave. Mr. Baker says he said to her: "Go to your master and get from him a receipt for your month's wages, and I will pay you. Also ask him to let you stay a day or two longer in order that I may have time to get another servant." After this she said nothing further about wages or about leaving, and was in the yard until yesterday afternoon arrested.

Mr. Baker assures me that Mrs. Dunham was honestly deceived in the girl, and took her at her representations, not suspecting at all that she was a runaway. He also begged me to take no legal steps in the premises. I find upon inquiry that Mrs. Dunham is a very upright, good, easy old soul who would do no one any harm, hard-working and suspecting no wrong in another. I am convinced that she was deceived by the representations of the girl, and did in no way harbor or secrete her knowingly and maliciously. She was wrong, however, in hiring the girl without a written permit from her master to find an employer. There are, you may say, hundreds of Negroes in this city who go about from house to house—some carpenters, some house servants, etc.—who never see their masters except at pay day, live out of their yards, hire themselves without written permit, etc. This of course is very wrong, and exerts a most injurious influence upon the relation of master and servant. Servants who thus hire their own time and pay wages, as the common saying is, are very frequently employed without any expression of the will of the master manifested by written permit, etc. Such a person did Mrs. Dunham think she was employing, and thus was deceived.

I told Mr. Baker under his statement and the circumstances of the case I would institute no legal proceedings against Mrs. Dunham, and I had no doubt but that when informed of the facts you would sanction my course. The fact is, Father, not only from Mr. Baker's statement but also from other and good authority, I am persuaded that there was no intention in the case to harbor the Negro in any manner, shape, or form. A prosecution would be unpleasant, tending to make the matter notorious, and would in every probability be unaccompanied by conviction. Unless there be an obligation resting upon one for purposes affecting the general good, order, and well-being of society, the less said and done in cases of this kind the better. Mrs. Dunham lives next door but one to Judge Berrien's dwelling, so that Jane was living on Broughton Street in one of the thickly peopled parts of the city for over a month, and just in the capacity which above all others would be least likely to excite suspicion.

Learning that Nelson was the person who brought her to Mrs. Dunham's yard, I went to Dr. West's, told him the facts of the case, and requested him to send for Nelson in order that he might be examined in the presence of both of us, and if found guilty of harboring the Negress in any manner that he might be properly punished. The doctor very kindly and gladly consented, and Nelson was sent for. His tale was told in a straightforward and consistent manner, and agrees with that of Mr. Baker. Nelson says after being requested by Mrs. Dunham to look out for a house servant for her, he had been making inquiries for a day or two, and one evening just after dinner he was met in Broughton Street by Jane (calling herself Sarah), whom he says he had never seen before and knew nothing of. She accosted him and asked if he knew anyone who wanted to hire a woman about a house; that she belonged to a gentleman in the up country, but was living in Savannah, hiring her own time and paying wages. Nelson then carried her to Mrs. Dunham, who employed her as above narrated. I cross-questioned him very closely, but found no ground even for suspicion in his conduct.

Jane is just as fat as she can be, with fine ear- and finger-rings, etc. I consider the place in which she now is as safe and comfortable as any in which she can be placed until I hear from you as to what disposition shall be made of her. Wright charges twenty-five cents per diem for board, etc. I have instructed him to keep her under strict watch, and to allow no liberties or privileges of the yard or of any other kind. She would be worth in this market eight or nine hundred dollars. It is a question with me, Father, whether she should be allowed to come on the plantation again. Her tales of Savannah and of high life in the city would probably not have the most beneficial effect upon her compeers. But of this you will be the judge.

I shall hope to hear from you on Friday. Will you also be good enough to send me a draft for the money to be paid as a reward to Jones, the arresting constable. You will remember the reward offered was twenty-five dollars. Jones told me he had been at an expense of fifteen dollars' spy money, and had had much trouble in watching an opportunity to arrest her. Whether you can believe a tale of this kind or no is a matter of great doubt. These constables are themselves notorious rascals. It would not be amiss, I think, Father, to give him thirty dollars, as rewards are running quite high. Will you please make the check payable to my order, that I may in person pay the sum and take receipt therefor. I shall try and learn more of the premises and see if I cannot find facts tending to convict anyone of harboring, etc., in a quiet way. Savannah is the last place in the world for servants inclined to evil.

I yesterday succeeded in renting a house. It is the only one after a diligent inquiry and search of two weeks that I have been able to find in any part of the city. It is situated on State Street, just next door to Major Porter's, west. Has two parlors below and three bedrooms above; good kitchen in the yard, and servants' apartments; also stable. Rent: four hundred and sixteen dollars per annum. This was my only chance. Upon consultation with friends was advised to close the bargain, and have done so. Rent begins today. The sooner, therefore, we get into the house the better. Will you please let me know, Father, what arrangements will be made regarding servants, etc.? Shall I purchase furniture for the same, etc.?

The watches are now in fine order and keeping excellent time. Will send them out by earliest opportunity. All friends well. With love to all,

From your affectionate son,
Charles C. Jones, Jr.

Willie quite well.

Rev. C. C. Jones *to* Mr. Charles C. Jones, Jr.ᵍ

Maybank, *Thursday,* October 2nd, 1856

My dear Son,

Yours of yesterday reached us this evening, and am glad matters have come to a favorable issue. I agree with you that *no legal steps be taken in the premises.* I hope we may yet discover *in what conveyance* and *by whom* she was taken to Savannah. One or the other of the vessels may have had to do with the matter. Nelson ought to be honest enough to tell you what man or men were in the habit of visiting Mrs. Dunham's yard. This would afford some clue.

If there is the least probability of her escape from her present place of confinement, have her safely lodged in jail. If closer confinement be necessary at Wright's for security, let it be resorted to. We have had trouble enough, and I wish to have no more. She is no more to return to the plantation nor to the county. Her family out here are privy to her movements, and are in good spirits and consider her gone for good. They will not be informed of her arrest, nor any others on the places for the present. We have concluded to dispose of the whole family, but not in Savannah nor in the low country. They must be sold up the country, where they will not come back. It is very painful, but we have no comfort or confidence in them, and they appear unhappy themselves—no doubt from the trouble they have from time to time occasioned. Enclosed is a list of them—to which *Titus* is added—with your mother's estimate, which cannot be far from a correct one. You can copy the list without the sums annexed and show it to Wright, and if you think best to Montmollin also, and learn what their estimate would be, and if they have orders from the up country, and could dispose of the whole family to one owner; for we cannot consent to separate them. If the thing can be done, we will close the matter at once. Should you hear of anyone willing to purchase, you might come to some understanding about it. Make no final contract without consulting us.

I think your idea a good one about the constable's fee; and enclosed you will find a check for thirty dollars payable to yourself which you can endorse and pay over to him and take his receipt.

The renting of the house pleases all round—the Doctor especially. He hopes, D.V., to be in Savannah on next Tuesday week. Meanwhile we will put our wisdom together and determine what servants shall be sent down, and get bedding and all such matters ready; provisions also. And Mother says she will accompany your brother to town and will then aid you in furnishing and putting to rights. Sooner than this arrangements could not be made. So the house must be tenantless for a short time. If you are responsible for the rent in case it burns down, you had better have it insured if the owner has not done it. Remember your office! We think the location fine. The house we take to be a wooden one. Hope it is in good repair.

Let us hear from you. You can keep the watches till Mother comes down, unless you have a *good and safe* opportunity of sending them out. Heard from your aunt this evening; your Cousin Laura is better still. Mother, Brother, and Sister send much love.

Your ever affectionate father,
C. C. Jones.
List

C. Sr.	Father. Age 45. Good field hand, basket-maker, and handy at jobs (I put him at that; Mother thinks it too low)	$800
P.	Mother. Age 47. Accomplished house servant in any and every line: good cook, washer and ironer, and fine seamstress	1000
C. Jr.	Son. Good field hand. Age 20	1000
J.	Daughter (in town). Age 18. House servant, good seamstress, and field hand	900
P.	Son. Field hand. Handy fellow. Age 16	800
V.	Daughter. Age 14. Smart, active field hand	800
Lf.	Son. Age 12. Smart, active boy	800
T.	Man. Age 29. Field hand and good oxcart man	600
		6700

All Cassius and Phoebe's family with themselves have excellent constitutions and are in good health. Titus is well now and improving!

MRS. MARY JONES *to* MR. CHARLES C. JONES, JR.[g]

Maybank, Thursday, October 2nd, 1856

My dear Son,

We were happy to hear from you by the last mail, and I received the roll of dowlass from Messrs. Lathrop & Company. The other articles will doubtless be forthcoming in due time.

We have now the most charming weather: frost for the two past nights, and some report of ice! Vegetation has assumed the appearance of advanced autumn. This with the recent drought will very much curtail our prospects of a cotton crop.

Your father and myself spent night before the last at Arcadia. The servants all well, and rice and corn harvested. The *rice* gives a *poor* yield; *corn* abundant for provisions; cotton late but promises fair. Mr. Martin seems very much pleased.

On our return met your uncle at Midway, attending a church meeting for calling an assistant pastor. Rev. Frank Bowman, I am told, has been proposed. Your uncle is not well: looked feverish and has been suffering from an affection of his bowels to which he is subject. Stays much at his plantation. The old gentleman is very sad and lonely now. I feel most truly for him, and hope you will find time to write him occasionally.

Since your absence the fish have returned to our waters in accumulated numbers. Late yesterday afternoon Niger and Lafayette went down to the river, and all told must have caught a hundred by teatime. We had the finest and fattest yellowtail for supper, and this morning large trout, bass, and yellowtail for breakfast.

Thank you, my dear son, for the last *Harper*. It is a very interesting number. I have read aloud the greater part of it to your father, and he has listened with great interest. . . . Your sister is very busily engaged helping your brother to draw and paint anatomical diagrams for his forthcoming lectures in the medical college. . . . Did you give my invitation to Cousin Joseph Robarts? . . . The united love of Father, Sister, and Brother with that of

Your affectionate mother,
Mary Jones.

All well at Woodville. Love to Willie.

Mr. Charles C. Jones, Jr., *to* Rev. C. C. Jones[g]

Savannah, *Saturday*, October 4th, 1856

My dear Father,

Your favors of the 2nd inst. and also the enclosed note from my dear mother have all been duly received, and I am truly happy to know that all at home are well, and also that the arrangements made with reference to the house and the fugitive are satisfactory. Jane still remains in Wright's yard, where I think she is as safe and as well taken care of as in any other place in Savannah.

Enclosed please find estimates of the respective value of each of the Negroes mentioned in the list contained in your last letter; also original valuation by Mother, and receipt of Jones the constable for thirty dollars in full of all claim for reward for the apprehension of Jane.

Montmollin states that these Negroes can be sold in Southwestern Georgia in nine or ten days to one owner without further expense than the trouble of getting them here and food until sold.

Wright thinks a more ready market can be had a month later. The estimates given must necessarily be subject to greater or less modification. The size, soundness of teeth, etc., are all to be considered. So soon as a positive order is received by these gentlemen I have requested them to acquaint me with the fact.

I shall be very happy indeed to see Mother, and shall feel very much obliged to her for her trouble in seeing the two young bachelors fairly settled in their new home. Am glad that all are pleased with the location. Regret to hear of Uncle William's indisposition, and hope that he is before this entirely relieved. With a great deal of love to self, Mother, Sister, the Doctor, and all friends, I am, as ever,

Your affectionate son,
Charles C. Jones, Jr.

Willie well, and doing well. Please say to Mother that I delivered her invitation to Cousin Joseph W. Robarts. He says he is too busy, but would be very glad to accept. In much haste,

C. C. J., Jr.

Montmollin's Estimate

1. Negro man, aged 45, good field hand, basket-maker, and handy at jobs 500
2. Woman, aged 47, accomplished house servant in every line, good cook, washer and ironer, and fine seamstress 600
3. Man, aged 20, fine field hand 950
4. Woman, aged 19, house servant, good seamstress, and field hand 800
5. Lad, aged 16, field hand, handy fellow 800
6. Girl, aged 14, smart, active in the field 700
7. Boy, aged 12, smart, active fellow 600
8. Man, aged 29, field hand, and good oxcart driver 800

5750

Must be sold out of this city, and in the up country or in Southwestern Georgia. Must all be sold together.

Wright's Estimate

1. Negro man, aged 45, good field hand, basket-maker, and handy at jobs 600 to 650
2. Woman, aged 47, accomplished house servant in any line, good cook, washer and ironer, and fine seamstress 650 to 700
3. Negro man, aged 20, good field hand 950 to 1000
4. Woman, aged 19, house servant, good seamstress, and field hand 825 to 850
5. Lad, aged 16, field hand, handy fellow 800 to 850
6. Girl, aged 14, smart, active in the field 675 to 700
7. Boy, aged 12, smart, active boy 600 to 650
8. Man, aged 29, field hand, and good oxcart driver 900 to 950

6000 to 6350

Must be sold out of this city, and in the up country or in Southwestern Georgia. Must all be sold together.

The above estimates are in consideration that the Negroes are all sound, healthy, and likely.

Mr. Charles C. Jones, Jr., *to* Rev. *and* Mrs. C. C. Jones[g]
Savannah, *Wednesday,* October 8th, 1856

My dear Father and Mother,

Politics forms the all-absorbing topic at present in our city. Both parties are sanguine, but it requires nothing less than a prophetic vision to foresee the result. The Americans are moving "heaven and earth," as the expression runs, to compass the reelection of the present incumbent, Mayor Anderson. Monday next will determine the contest. I wish it were all over, and the issue such as we desire.

Buchanan's prospects seem by no means as encouraging as they were at first. The union of the Fillmore and Frémont men in Pennsylvania will, it is seriously feared, cause the old Keystone State to deviate from her hitherto unshaken adherence to Democratic principles. What a shame it will be if she repudiates her noble, trueborn son for such a miserable offspring of fanaticism as Frémont "the Pathfinder"! Fillmore is not in the race. The whole aim of the combination is to defeat Buchanan; and regarding Frémont as the most available of the two to accomplish that purpose, regardless of all principles and sound national considerations, the masses are declaring allegiance to him.

The Union, in the event of Frémont's election, will, at least in this section of the state, be decidedly below par. Disunion sentiments are already entertained to a very general extent. Our country was probably never before to such a degree disturbed by factions at home, and those of a purely sectional character. To what this will all lead, time only will reveal. It is to be sincerely hoped that every true lover of his country, of the liberties guaranteed under the Constitution, will come to the rescue.

The other evening, returning home, I observed two sable sons of Nigritia in close confab beneath a lamp in the streets. As I passed I heard a short political dialogue, during which the profession was mutually made that they were "Know-Nothings." I thought: "Surely for once we have an example of the fact that profession and practice, the ideal and the real, are not always at variance!" If Negroes are talking politics in the streets, you may imagine to what an extent the whites are engaged.

Jane is still in safe custody and well. Very few purchasers in the market. Two from Southwestern Georgia last week would make no offer without seeing the Negroes. If they are to be sold, Father, in this market, they will have to be sent to Savannah. It will be best, at any rate, to wait until the present municipal election is over. . . .

Will be very happy to see you, dear Mother, next week. Will you stop while in the city with Cousin Charles West? If you do not, the pleasantest public place will be the Pavilion House, just opposite the Independent Church. With warmest love, my dear parents, to selves, Sister, Brother, and all friends, I am, as ever,

Your affectionate son,
Charles C. Jones, Jr.

Willie quite well.

Did the frost injure the cotton seriously?

Howdy for the servants.

MRS. MARY JONES *to* MR. CHARLES C. JONES, JR.g

Montevideo, *Thursday,* October 9th, 1856

My dear Son,

Your father and myself are here for the day, and expect to return immediately. Your last favor was received on Monday, and we are happy to know you continue well. Our arrangements about that family will remain until further information is obtained. I hope there is no probability of Jane's escape.

Providence permitting, we expect to send down by Captain Russell's vessel, which will probably leave in the early part of next week, your brother's books, etc., bedding, provisions of various sorts, etc., etc., with *Titus* and Lafayette; and if you desire George to come down, will send him also. Joe and myself with Sue, Lucy, and Gilbert will come *by land* in the carriage. I presume Mrs. Caruthers can accommodate me with a room for a day and night. After that, with such efficient help as I will bring, hope to see you established in your own hired house.

Upon consultation we decided that you could not do well without a *man* about your house and yard and office, and as Titus was the only one, your brother concluded to take him. He seems much pleased, and professes to know all things. His mother now has him in tow, teaching him to *cook and wash,* so that he may help Sue and serve any emergency. *Patience* is much pleased at the choice, and says he is able to do all you want him to. I am sure he and Sue will give no trouble as to fidelity. Lafayette will attend upon the office and college duties, etc., etc.

I am going to bring Lucy to make your carpet and any little work necessary and to clean and put to rights. She will return with me. We thought as there is a stable on the lot to bring down corn for our horses and save the expense of the livery stables. It would be well to have the house opened and aired if you can get anyone to do it; and if any whitewashing, Titus can do it at his leisure. We may come down on Tuesday. Will write if not. With much love, in haste,

Your affectionate mother,

Mary Jones.

Your father requests you to see Mr. Brunner and ask him to send by the first vessel three barrels of stone lime (good barrels like those he sent) and one barrel of plaster of Paris. Captain Thomson is now in town. . . . He wishes to know by the *next mail* when the vessel will come out. If it does not return next week, we will have to try and get the lime by railroad, as it will certainly be wanting next week for the house.

Mr. CHARLES C. JONES, JR., *to* Mrs. MARY JONES[t]
Savannah, *Saturday,* October 11th, 1856

My dear Mother,

Your kind favor of the 9th inst. was yesterday received. I feel deeply obliged to dear Father and yourself for your kindness and interest in making such admirable arrangements with reference to our present intention of house-keeping. I shall be very happy to see you on Tuesday of next week or any day that may be most convenient for you to visit Savannah.

With reference to the place of stoppage while in the city, I would say that just at the present time there are several persons sick at the house of Mrs. Caruthers; her table is also full, the places being occupied by gentleman boarders; and moreover she is not in the habit of accommodating any others than regular boarders. Under these circumstances you would not find it pleasant to stop there; and I do not think she will be able to accommodate you, because to my knowledge her rooms are all occupied and engaged. The most comfortable and agreeable location will be the Pavilion Hotel—if you do not tarry with Cousin Charles West. If you do not come in on Tuesday, please let me know by return mail, and I will see that a pleasant room is in readiness for you at the Pavilion.

The arrangement with regard to the servants to be sent to town is, I think, the best that could be made. . . . With regard to the disposition of the horses while in the city, the stable is small, and with only one stall, and room enough to accommodate only a buggy. If the carriage and horses can be accommodated, it will be best to place them there, and of this we can judge when you come.

There is nothing of interest in the city with the exception of the election, and this is attracting the undivided attention of both parties. The election takes place on Monday next; will be glad when it is all over. With much love to all at home,

Your ever affectionate son,
Charles C. Jones, Jr.

Willie in good health, and doing a fine business.

P.S. Since writing the above, dear Mother, I have seen Cousin Eliza and family, and she desires me to say to you that if you are not otherwise engaged, she will be very happy to have you make her house your home while you are in the city; that your room is all in readiness for you. This I think will be decidedly your pleasantest arrangement, and I hope you will accept her invitation.

Miss MARY E. ROBARTS *to* Mrs. MARY JONES[t]
Marietta, *Monday,* October 13th, 1856

I received your last a fortnight since, my own dear cousin; but like yourself I often have to let such favors lie over to attend to the more imperative duties of everyday life, which will be attended to in their time. We have had a large family most of the summer, and though I feel at night as if I had accomplished very little, am conscious of being all the time employed. Dr. West's two little boys spent a week with us. They and Joe were the happiest little fellows I have seen for a long time. Gathering chestnuts was a great amusement to them, as they had never been where they grew before. They left us on Thursday, and we were sorry to part with them. They are very fine little boys, and seemed to me like little grandsons, I had so often played with their father in the way I did with them. They look fatter than I have ever seen them. The children of beloved relatives are very dear to me, and it always gives me pleasure to have them around me.

And is it possible you mean to give away your baby? Why, what will you and my reverend cousin do without one child at your fireside? We heard the rumor from the low-country people up here even while it was yet in prospect. Such a thing as the marriage of a young minister cannot be kept secret, particularly when so many of his flock are up here. I congratulate you on giving your only daughter to a young man of unblemished character—not only so, but a talented Christian minister of pious parentage, nothing to be found out about them or him, but each already and long known to you. The only possible objection is his being rather largely connected; this is often an infelicity in a congregation, but even this can be regulated. I have not the pleasure of the gentleman's acquaintance; have not seen him since he went to college, I think. You must ask him to come up and see us from Atlanta if he goes to Synod. By coming up the day before, he could make us a visit and then go to Synod.

I cannot tell you, my dear cousin, how happy we feel at the prospect of seeing our dear cousin and yourself here. And now for the preliminaries. Do beg him to give us a Sabbath in his visit; I long to hear him preach. By leaving Washington in the morning you would get here ten o'clock at night. Just specify the time you will be with us, and we will meet you at the depot. And a more than warm welcome! We are truly happy at the prospect. Don't let the visit be too short. As you could not be here on Mother's birthday, she will have it over again, cheered by the presence of her nephew, niece, and grandniece. The up country will be dismantled of her summer dress and perhaps look desolate to you, but our hearts will be as warm as ever. . . .

I cannot yet think with composure that we shall never again see our dear Cousin Betsy. It is too recent to be realized yet. Should we ever go to Liberty again, then we shall feel that she is indeed gone. Do give our love to Cousin William. We think of him daily. Do not wonder that he realizes his loss every hour of his life; and when he goes to his lonely cottage it will be worse.

Mr. Henry M. Stevens purchased John's house in Marietta, and we felt that the last link was broken which bound him here. Mr. Stevens requested Mr. Petrie to occupy it for the winter, as he wished to change his residence, not liking the house he was in. So he has moved there, and will rent another house in the spring. I only wish our church could have purchased it for a parsonage; but they did not feel able.

We have some new buildings going up in Marietta, and some families from Carolina have purchased here, but they are strangers, and we do not know if they will improve our society. One family is Presbyterian. . . . Laura Jones wrote to Mr. Petrie to inquire the price of house rent; wishes to make a home here. I hear Mrs. McConnell wishes to sell her house and come here to be near her son; trust they will bring a peaceable spirit if they come. . . . We have heard another rumor which surprised us more than the one about Mary: that Mary Wells was to be married to Mr. McClellan. I did not know till I heard this that Julia's teacher was a gentleman. Thought she had a governess. Can this be true—this match? . . . Poor Dr. and Mrs. Howe are deeply afflicted at Walthour's derangement; and surely it is one of the sorest trials which could visit a parent. . . . Regret to hear that there has been frost in the low country.

Tell Mary I have forgotten whether I have answered her last letter; that I will leave it to her honor to say. Hope she will write me soon. Unless she tells me, as Laura did, she is "so engaged," I will not take this excuse from her. Charlie and Joe, I suppose, are both in Savannah, so love to them would have to go via Liberty County and then back to Savannah. I should like to know when Mary is to take orders, and when the ceremony will take place.

Mary Sophia left school last week, and now begins the life of a young lady at home. Ellen says she wishes to be a very intelligent young lady; that she is studying very hard, but thinks traveling would improve her very much, and that I had better send her to Mount Holyoke. I tell her she must make the best use of the opportunities she has and learn domestic duties at home. . . . Sam is quite well; sends howdy to his wife and children. . . . Much love from Mother, Louisa, and myself to my dear cousin, yourself, and Mary. We feel so happy at the thought of seeing you so soon.

Your ever affectionate cousin,
Mary E. Robarts.

Rev. R. Q. Mallard *to* Miss Mary Sharpe Jones[t]
Walthourville, *Monday,* October 20th, 1856
My dearest Mary,

I had set apart this morning for pastoral visitation, but as there is appearance of rain, I have concluded to wait a half hour before I venture out. (Something to that effect I had commenced writing when, the weather clearing, I laid aside my pen and spent the morning as I had anticipated. I have just returned, and would now employ the few moments between this and our dinner hour in a work always anticipated by me with pleasure. Pardon me for using a term associated commonly with the tiresome; I use it in no such sense. It is not properly a work, but a joy and a delight, even to *cor-respond* with one who occupies no second place in my heart.)

My last visit, although an exceedingly pleasant one, left me no leisure time between it and the Sabbath. If I were to be in this "fix" seven years (and even considerably less), I should be compelled to substitute *letters* for *visits*. I find no great difficulty in preparing for the Sabbath, but am not furnishing my mind with knowledge as rapidly as I could desire. At the rate of two discourses every Sabbath and a lecture weekly, you will see that unless some recuperative process be kept up, I run the risk of a speedy exhaustion.

Do you know that I feel great reluctance in allowing my mind to dwell upon the period yet to "drag its slow length along" ere March appears? You talk of *my* "filial piety"; did modesty forbid allusion to your own? But I will not be impatient. I honor you for your attachment to your parents. Your obligations to them can never be discharged; and if the delay of which I have spoken contributes anything to their happiness, I am willing that mine remain in abeyance for a time. Fearing that I might be forestalled, I made some inquiries this morning of Mr. McConnell in reference to his mother's house. The family have not yet fully decided on leaving; but should they go, I am to have the refusal of their house. I did not mention *when* I should need it, but simply said that I supposed I should have use for it at some future time. You perceive how wonderfully prudent and trustworthy I am, don't you? No one knows from me the "evil day" (so your mother, by a strange perversion of language, called it) but my mother, Sister Lou, and Brother Sam. I *think* no one else. . . .

The "sacred concert" last week was, so far as the music is concerned, an excellent thing. The selection of pieces manifested a fine taste, so far as I am a judge. The solos, duets, and quartets were particularly fine. A quartet called "Hallelujah to the Father" I admired very much. Mrs. Anne Stevens sang as a solo "I Know that My Redeemer Liveth." I was anxious to hear that celebrated piece, and it was, to my ear, rendered beautifully by the singer. She has a fine and well-cultivated voice. Miss Kitty's "Ave Maria" was Protestantized by the words "O Holy Father." The choir were not repaid for their trouble by either the number or the character of the audience. There were about sixty-four persons present, the most of them children and young people who, if they had the capacity to appreciate good music, did not exercise it much. As I wished to hear, I went up in the gallery. I am more than ever disposed to question the propriety of these "oratorios" when held in churches, as is customary other places besides this. While I would not go to the length of *The New York Churchman* in its superstitious veneration for the house of worship, and particularly for certain parts of it, as the chancel, it seems to me that the church should be recognized as a place for strictly religious purposes and protected from profane associations.

After all I have said of the performance of the choir, I would have much more enjoyed some piano or guitar music—providing, as always, that the keys of the one and strings of the other had been touched by my Mary's hand. When shall I enjoy again that pleasure? I hope next Monday evening— although this visit must be a shorter one than the last. It is a hard contest where the heart and duty are antagonists. . . .

I have an engagement this evening, and must now close. Candidly, don't you think it is time? It is not night, or I would send a "good night." Accept, therefore, in its stead the deepest love of

Your own
R. Q. Mallard.

Miss Mary Sharpe Jones *to* Mrs. Mary Jones[t]

Maybank, *Monday,* October 20th, 1856

My dear Mother,

You cannot imagine how much Father and I have missed Brother Joe and yourself. The house has been as still as possible. But we both hope you will remain some days after getting the young bachelors fixed and take a little recreation.

On Friday afternoon we called upon the Walthourville ladies: Mrs. Fleming, Mrs. Walthour, Kate, and Augusta. It rained so much the first day of their visit that they had no opportunity of seeing the Island. Augusta spent most of her time in the boat, with Mr. McClellan (Cousin Mary says) as her devoted attendant. They all left early on Saturday morning.

One event of that morning will, I fear, be afflicting to Brother Joe. Father went up to Montevideo, and as the buggy was starting, poor little Baby ran under the wheel and got his leg broken. It is broken so near the body that we could devise no means of setting it, but I hope it will get well without deforming him much. I believe I would almost rather have had one of the large cats injured! Daddy Andrew says it will soon be well, because "varmint is not like human."

Mr. Joseph Maxwell came to Woodville on last Thursday. We expect him to dine with us today. Niger has caught some fine fish, so we will be able to give him a fish dinner.

Yesterday my dear father preached a very solemn sermon in Sunbury from Romans 3:23-24: "For all have sinned," etc. There was a fine white congregation, but not so large a colored one as on last Sunday. . . . I have been searching in vain in the pantry for Bath brick; just after you left, Jack reported that he had none. We want also a box of table salt. . . . Father wishes to add something to this, so I must close, with affectionate love to Brothers Charlie and Joe and yourself. Mom Phoebe sends howdy for all, with many charges to Lafayette and George not to wrestle on the Sabbath Day.

Your affectionate daughter,
Mary S. Jones.

REV. C. C. JONES *to* MRS. MARY JONES[t]

Maybank, *Monday,* October 20th, 1856

My dear Wife,

Daughter has been scribe today. Gilbert goes up for the letters directly, and I will wait to hear from you this evening, and will, D.V., return you an answer tomorrow. Feel pretty well after preaching yesterday. Nothing new with us. Tell Charles hurry Thomson off; we are waiting for the lime and plaster. The house is *creeping* along: lathing the garret. We send you Cousin Mary's letter. Love to Charles and Joe. Hope they will be pleasantly fixed, and very grateful to you for all your trouble and kindness. Excuse a very unsteady hand this morning.

From your ever affectionate husband,

C. C. Jones.

Do bring out from Cooper's a ream of *good* letter paper and a plenty of *good envelopes.*

REV. C. C. JONES *to* MRS. MARY JONES[t]

Maybank, *Monday Evening,* October 20th, 1856

My dear Mary,

We were much disappointed on emptying the mailbag this evening to find no letter from anybody in Savannah, and concluded that you were all too busy to write, and that you were all well. Thinking that you might have written and the letter in some way miscarried, and perhaps an appointment in it to come out, I now write to say that no letter has been received, and of course you will have to defer your appointment, if made, till you get us word in another letter.

Mr. Joseph E. Maxwell, Mr. John Stevens, and Mrs. Wells did us the honor of dining with us today. Niger succeeded in procuring some fine fish for two dishes; we had also an excellent oyster pie and roasted chicken and a dessert. So that Daughter acquitted herself handsomely, and our friends enjoyed the good cheer we gave them. The gentlemen particularly relished the fish and oysters. After an early tea they left us.

Letters from Sister and Mr. Buttolph. All improving. Sister and Laura at Williamstown, and Mr. Buttolph at Norwich with his father. They expect very shortly to set their faces homeward.

Please ask Joe if he finds a number of *The Princeton Review* among his books (January or April number) send it to me. . . . Daughter unites in love to you and to her brothers. May the presence and blessing of God be with you!

Your affectionate husband,

C. C. Jones.

I hope you will not make your visit to Savannah one of fatigue and hurry. Take your time to arrange things, and after you get through, then stay and enjoy some quiet and leisure and see your sons well settled in housekeeping. . . . The change will be agreeable, and do you good after your close confinement and constant occupation at home. Consult your own convenience and wishes about returning; do not come back on our account. We will cheerfully forego the pleasure of your return so long as we know you are enjoying yourself. . . . We would be glad to hear from you by Thursday's mail should you have time to write.

C. C. J.

REV. C. C. JONES *to* MRS. MARY JONES[t]
Maybank, Thursday Evening, October 23rd, 1856

My dear Mary,

Your welcome letter reached us an hour or two since, and we were happy to learn your good success in locating our sons in their own hired house to your satisfaction. No doubt everything is in excellent taste and order. Miss Kitty Stiles calls it "Castle Dismal." A dreadful name: pray alter it! When there are so many pleasant names in the world, why give unpleasant ones? Do remember us with sincere affection to Cousin Charles and Cousin Eliza. They are kind relatives, and I feel grateful to them for their attentions to you.

The notices of Joe and his lectures are such as to encourage him, but I hope he will have the good sense modestly to pursue the even tenor of his way, and to remember that his success as a lecturer remains to be proved, and that his reputation as a professor must be based upon solid and progressive learning and improvement in his department. . . . One notice in the papers states that a number of students have matriculated; you say the prospect is small as yet. My own opinion is that, considering the number of medical colleges in the state and the recent establishment of the one in Savannah, a large number of students cannot reasonably be expected. If the college pays its expenses it will do well.

I thought we had determined to part with the whole family, and were only waiting, upon recommendation, a month later for a better sale, until within a few days of your leaving for Savannah, when you appeared to hesitate on account of the inconvenience and trouble that would ensue upon the loss of an efficient house servant and seamstress. Our determination to sell the whole family was based, I believe, on these considerations: (1) An indisposition to separate parents and child, no matter how evil their conduct had been in the premises. (2) The unreliable character of the family, the trouble the mother has always given, and the moral certainty that whenever occasions offer, the same rebellious conduct will appear again. (3) And in case of the sale of the present incorrigible runaway apart from her family, although they have sent her away never to return, the effect upon them in all probability will not be for the better. (4) And lastly, a change of investment would be more desirable than otherwise.

I do not wish to influence you in the least degree beyond your own convictions, nor to have you subjected to any inconveniences in your domestic arrangements whatever, and therefore cannot assume the sole responsibility of a decision. *It is the second or third time we have had it in contemplation to sell this family*. The sale of one may prove beneficial to the character and subordination of those that remain. Time only can show. If not, they may be sent after her. Certainly both she and her parents have settled the matter, so far as they could, of her final removal of herself from us and them; and it would be no special injustice to let her go. They could, I am certain, have brought her back, and they did not. And they have sold all her clothing, plainly intimating that she is no more expected or desired back. Had she or they cause for all this, I should feel differently. But I think they have not. Jane has been treated as our other servants have been, and every effort has been used to reclaim her—and without effect. If, therefore, you wish the whole family sold, I have not the least objection. If not, then Jane may be sold and we may wait and see the effect. If for good, we shall be glad; if for evil, then we must meet the evil as best we may. But I have very little hope of any improvement. The *main* objection to the sale of the family, so far as I can see, is the loss of the services of a servant who has given us more trouble, and even now and always has required more watching, than all our servants twice put together. However, I am willing to keep her and do all I can to make her profitable to you—as much so as in times past. I have no objection.

The titles are easily made. Our joint signatures with Brother's, the summary trustee of your property, will be sufficient. And have the change of investment entered on the marriage settlement.

I do not know that the width of the fireplaces here and at Montevideo are the same. I send you the width here as desired. Tomorrow, God willing, Daughter and I ride up to Montevideo and will measure those there, and if there be any very material difference, will write you by Tuesday's mail. . . . Pray do not get *solid brass fenders* (they are *offenders*) but *high open-wire fenders*—to keep in wood and sparks. And you had better get *six fenders*—or *eight: one for every fireplace in the Montevideo house*. The two stoves will require none.

Daughter encloses a note, and sends much love to you and her brothers. My love to my dear sons. We will send for you to Way's Station, with all the articles we can collect for the housekeepers, on *next Thursday,* Providence permitting: the 30th.

From your ever affectionate husband,
C. C. Jones.

Width of Maybank fireplaces within woodwork of mantelpieces: *two feet; twenty inches* in parlor and chamber below stairs.

Mr. Charles C. Jones, Jr., *to* Rev. *and* Mrs. C. C. Jones[g]

Savannah, Saturday, November 1st, 1856

By the return trip of the cars which bore you, my dear parents, back to Liberty we received a coop of twenty-five excellent fowls and a nice pan of butter. The feathered tribe are already quite used to the yard, and impart to it quite an air of life and animation. The butter is peculiarly acceptable to the Doctor, who very gravely stakes his professional reputation upon the fact that oily matters are positively necessary to the full and energetic sustentation of life and health, and that his system especially needs this sort of food. Sue has already been playing the part of the executioner, and three fowls have been rendered headless by her hand. She makes us an excellent servant, and seems perfectly satisfied with her new avocation and location. In fact, they all appear pleased. Many thanks to you, dear Mother, for your kindness in thus comfortably and pleasantly establishing us in our new home.

We are now getting along in absolute freedom and quiet. Last Friday evening we had a large political meeting in St. Andrew's Hall. . . . On Tuesday next, you know, the election for President is held, and the Democrats are rallying their forces. . . . With much love to selves, my dear parents, Sister, and all friends, I am, as ever,

Your affectionate son,
Charles C. Jones, Jr.

The Doctor is quite well, and unites in love.

Rev. C. C. Jones *to* Mr. Charles C. Jones, Jr.[g]

Maybank, *Saturday Evening,* November 1st, 1856

My dear Son,

Mr. Joseph Jackson has been engaged to take Cassius and his family (five in all) to Savannah on Monday, Providence permitting. Stepney goes down with him with the jersey and two horses—to divide the load and expedite the journey. They will carry provisions for the horses, and Jackson says he will put them in a yard and feed them where he usually stops, and they will be safe and at a trifling expense. Stepney will stay in your yard for the night, and will leave with Jackson on Tuesday morning for home. On reflection I thought this the least public way and most speedy. Have directed Mr. Jackson to call at your house on his way in, and you would go around with him and see the people located. Circumstances since we returned home have decided this step on our part, and we believe it to be right. They have taken their own clothing, and can put on what they like and appear well. Mr. Wright must see to this. We have had no time to make any special preparations for them.

Montmollin's estimate for six, throwing out Lafayette, is an average of $725; including him, $707. (Titus is altogether excluded.) Wright's estimate for six, throwing out Lafayette—his *lower* estimate—is $750 round; including Lafayette is $733. His *higher* estimate, throwing out Lafayette, is $791; including him, $771. We will take nothing under $800 round for the *six;* and *if* Lafayette is added, it ought to make no difference: he ought to be reckoned in at the same rate. You can give Mr. Wright your views, and he can get more if he can. And let him consult you before he closes the sale. We do not wish them sacrificed. You can advise us of any offers made, and give your judgment of them.

We have had a sad day of it, as you may suppose—the first of the kind in our lives. We could not conscientiously part the family, and therefore send all. *The original instruction as to the sale to be adhered to*—that is, sold out of the city, all together, to one owner (not a speculator), and in the up country or Southwest Georgia. When sold, give a bond for titles, or make what arrangement you think best to this end. Draw the titles and send them out, and we will execute and return them. Deposit the proceeds to my credit in the state bank, and send certificate of same. Would be glad of a *speedy* close to this trying business.

Mother is now writing to your brother and yourself, and will give you another of the sad events of the day! Tell your brother I will hand our good neighbor Dr. *Joseph* Way, of Dorchester, one of his Smithsonian books in his name. Dr. Stevens has written me a very handsome acknowledgment of the copy he received. Our united love to you both.

Your ever affectionate father,
C. C. Jones.

Monday Morning, 4 A.M. All well, D.G. Tell Joe his three boxes are on board Captain Thomson; he left the Boro on Saturday.

Do try and have the sale made as *soon* as may be.

C. C. J.

REV. R. Q. MALLARD *to* MISS MARY SHARPE JONES[t]

Walthourville, *Monday,* November 3rd, 1856

My own dear Mary,

I am all alone—sole occupant of a house of eight rooms. My sister and niece left during my absence for Savannah, expecting to return on next Friday. I am not lonely, however; for what time I spend here is in the company of my books. I spend my nights and take my meals at my brother's. This is my recreation day, usually spent in visiting and correspondence.

My correspondents are not numerous; can that be the only reason I so highly prize them? We are confidants, are we not? As a proof of my belief that we have tacitly entered into some such arrangement, I will tell you my private reasons for the opinion that there are other grounds besides the one specified for my very natural attachment to my correspondents. To explain: there is Harris and Porter, young men of noble natural qualities, of decided piety, of similar tastes with myself, and pursuing the same occupation. My other correspondent is not yet a minister, nor will ever be one—unless considerable alterations are made in the established usages of society. The nearest approach to it possible to this friend will be the minister's ——. There, the secret is out. A lady! Yes, and a lady who has promised to be *mine* at some future day. Need I tell you that although no minister this is my most valued, my *dearest* correspondent? . . .

My dearest love, you must bear with me if I seem to transcend the bounds of decorum in my correspondence with one who is yet only my affianced. Perhaps it *would* be well to be more cautious. But when I sit down to write you, my heart warms, and straightway words find their way to the sheet—words which a cold prudence might condemn, but which love finds it not in his heart to chide. . . . No phantom fear with finger on his lip shall warn me into silence when I would pour into my Mary's ear the sweet soft words of love.

But I must now to duty. My hour for morning visits has arrived, and I must away. . . .

Tomorrow will be, no doubt, an eventful day. Some seem disposed to regard it as a day decisive of the question between union and disunion. But whatever the result of the election—whether Fillmore or Buchanan or Frémont takes his place in the White House—I trust there is, in the honesty and virtue of the mass, conservative element sufficient to falsify the predictions of traitors to the Union, North and South.

Don't you think that in a crisis like this such patriots as the ladies are apt to be should be allowed the right of suffrage? Just to think what a revolution in that event would be made in the scenes around the ballot box! Enters the courtroom, elbowing her way through the crowd at some risk to her apparel, a blooming miss of twenty-and-one summers, her color heightened by exercise and the presence of so many men. "Susan Ann Hopkins!" cries the freeholder. A delicately written, neatly folded, sweetly scented note touches lightly the broad extended palm and is lost in the more masculine "Buchanan's," etc., already crowding the ballot box. The youths at the table beneath snatch for a moment their admiring eyes from Miss Susan Ann Hopkins to "check" her name upon the growing list. One, you observe, has written that name as if he had seen it before. Hark! A screech, a rush, a cry: "A fight! A fight!" There they are, locked in close embrace—two patriotic amazons! Alas for silk and lace! Are they rending their garments and tearing their hair because of Frémont's defeat? No: the votes are not yet counted. But they are in this manner endeavoring, in a neighborly way, to settle a difference of opinion as to the result.

What think you of the picture? No, the courtroom is not the place for gentle woman. Home—that is her empire; there she governs (?) with sweet and all but despotic sway. As mother, sister, wife she moves gracefully in the domestic circle, and there wields (sweet enchantress) the mystic scepter, love. Somebody has said: "Man was made of dust refined, woman of dust doubly refined." Let us put the china in the drawing room; the delft will answer for the common parlor.

I have determined to go to the meeting of Synod, if nothing occurs to prevent. I hope to see you on next Monday. As I will probably go in to

Savannah on Tuesday, I will not be able to enjoy as much of your company as usual—unless indeed (which would be fine) you conclude to visit the up country yourself. Mr. John Mallard will, I think, go as elder from this church.

I believe I have no "news" to communicate. It is time indeed I were done. Brother Sam is below, and we expect in a few moments to take a ride together. I told him as I came up that I wished to finish a letter for the mail. He desired the privilege of reading it; and as he is my brother and I can make very free with him, and as he is withal a very prudent man, I will—*not* grant his request, except with your permission. Present my best regards to your dear parents, and allow me to subscribe myself, my dearest Mary,

Your affectionate
Robert Q. Mallard.

MISS MARY SHARPE JONES *to* MISS MARY JONES TAYLOR[t]

Maybank, *Wednesday,* November 5th, 1856

My dear Mary,

I did not conclude, as you supposed, that you were either dead or married, as I am in the habit of looking over the lists of marriages and deaths recorded in the Philadelphia paper, and your name appeared in neither column. I did, however, begin to think that laziness or a dearth of ideas had taken possession of your soul, and still think the former had something to do with the delay of your reply! But I must tell you that your letter was truly welcome and fully appreciated.

And now let me ask you what did you mean by writing me that you had been "so much *engaged,*" underscoring the word in the most special manner? Engaged? When? How? Or to whom? If you have a secret, please do not be quite so obscure in your hints, but candidly make confession to a friend!

I do indeed sympathize with you in your anticipated move to Maryland; and I believe my feeling is not wholly unselfish, for it will grieve me greatly to know that my only Philadelphia correspondent is no longer a resident of that city. Cannot you possibly persuade your father to remain? I do not like to think of your living anywhere else. . . .

You ask what has become of Matilda Harden. Tell Sallie I should like to know where their flourishing correspondence is! I have not seen her for several months, but heard of her a week since; she is quite well. We never see much of each other in summer, as we each move to our respective summer retreats, and do not move about much during the hot season. We will soon be at our winter residence, and then I hope to see her often, as we shall be only four miles distant.

Have you seen Anna Bulloch recently? I think you called to see her—or have I imagined the latter fact? I am under the impression you wrote me so.

You cautioned me in your last not to omit returning answers to all of your inquiries. Now, I feel that I can to *some* but not to *all*. For instance, I can give name and residence, but I am doubtful as to a full description! I do not exactly feel called upon to give it. His name is Rev. Robert Q. Mallard, a Presbyterian minister. Does that meet your approbation? I told him that one of my friends said she would not give her consent until she had heard more particularly concerning him; he replied that he was not aware that there was yet another to be consulted! He is settled in Walthourville, a village located in this county. And now for his appearance. Black hair and dark complexion; some say handsome, but I do not think so. He is above medium height. And now I won't tell you anything more, but leave his qualities to your imagination.

I do not exactly know when the consummation will take place, but whenever it does I want to have you present. Perhaps it will be just about the time you are leaving Philadelphia for Maryland, so cannot you extend your journey to Georgia and be one of my attendants on that occasion? I know I am asking quite a favor, but it would give me and all of us a great deal of pleasure to have you with us. Do say to Sallie I do not mean to exclude her: she must come with you too.

(Don't say anything about what I have written you. I believe all my friends know the fact, for you know it is impossible ever to keep such a thing secret, and I do not approve of telling stories on such occasions.)

Do write me very soon. My brothers are keeping bachelor's hall in Savannah. My dear father has not been well for some weeks past. Do give my love to all inquiring friends, to your mother and Sallie. Mother unites with me in love to yourself.

Your attached friend,
Mary S. Jones.

Mr. Charles C. Jones, Jr., *to* Rev. *and* Mrs. C. C. Jones[t]

Savannah, *Saturday,* November 8th, 1856

My dear Father and Mother,

Since last writing you the people of this country have met and decided an important issue, boldly and broadly presented; and happy am I that we are able to congratulate ourselves upon the result. For at least four years, under the administration-elect, may we hope for peace and prosperity. Beyond that period we scarce dare expect a continuance of our present relations. Unless there be a material reaction in the sentiments of at least a portion of our common country at the expiration of the term of office of the President- and Vice-President-elect, it is to be feared that the cohorts of fanaticism will claim one of their own persuasion as the officer-elect to preside over the destinies of this great republic. Whence that reaction will arise, and whether there is the least probability of its occurring, is more than problematical. Buchanan and Breckinridge are elected, and owe their election to the South mainly; while the vote of the North with but few exceptions has been cast for Frémont. The next issue will doubtless be purely sectional in its character. The prospect is fearful, but everything indicates such a future condition of affairs. And when it does come, we of the South must and will be prepared to meet it bravely and without concession. You have observed in the papers that the Democratic majority in Chatham is four hundred. Well done also for Liberty!

Peace will now, I hope, again spread her white wings over our land; the angry and excited passions of men be calmed; and everyone, dismissing the excitement of this late political struggle from the mind, attend once more to the more quiet yet not less important duties of life. Our Fillmore friends are entirely nonplussed, and are now prepared to admit, if honest, that in Buchanan's election rested the hope of the South and our country, and that every vote cast for Fillmore under the circumstance was polled in violation of the duty of a Southern man, or in culpable ignorance.

The people at Wright's are now all well. No sale as yet. . . . The Doctor is quite well. Twenty students in attendance. . . . With much love, my dear parents, to you both and to my sister, I am, as ever,
                              Your affectionate son,
                                    Charles C. Jones, Jr.
Ask Sister to read "Orion" in the *Ledgers,* weekly sent.
Howdy for the servants.

Mrs. Eliza G. Robarts *to* Mrs. Mary Jones[t]
                         Marietta, *Monday,* November 10th, 1856
My dear Mary,

This morning brought me your affectionate letter, and although I was rejoiced to receive it, still it brought us disappointment, and we ate our breakfast with a heavy heart. You cannot imagine how disappointed we were to read you and Mary Sharpe would have to defer your visit. And the weather up here is now so cold I fear it will not suit Charles to attend Synod, for his health might suffer more, if he is like his old aunt; she feels like a wilted collard leaf in extreme cold. If he should go to Synod, it will rejoice our hearts to see him, and I certainly shall expect him.

I think you have fitted up your boys under very favorable circumstances for housekeeping. If they don't take care, before the year is out some of the girls will be trying to break up that bachelor establishment.

Mr. Petrie went on Thursday to Athens to assist Dr. Hoyt in the dedication of their new church; consequently there was no preaching in our church. Mary, Louisa, the girls, and Joe all went to the Episcopalian church to hear Mr. Scott, formerly of Savannah and this place, now bishop of Oregon. At night he preached on the subject of missions in Oregon. The girls liked him very much. The day was so cold I did not venture out at all.

This morning old Mrs. Smith called for me in her carriage, and we rode out and made four calls. Don't you think that was smart for two old ladies, one seventy-one, the other eighty-two years old? And here I am trying to finish my letter; but it will be too late for today's mail.

I am sorry to hear of the death of your servant Eve. We feel those losses more than the Northerners think; the tie is next to our relatives. . . . The few days you spent in Dr. West's family must have been pleasant; and to see the likeness of their dear father and mother so perfect must have been gratifying. I have an excellent likeness of my dear brother; perhaps you could get a good ambrotype taken from that. . . . James West on his way back to Kentucky spent a day with us. He is really an interesting man—so affectionate. . . . Henry made us a short visit; I suppose by this he and Abby are quietly settled at home.

Now about our coming down. As you can't come to see us, I feel a stronger desire than ever to see you all. But the same epidemic prevails here as in the low country: a want of money. My purse at this time is very low; if I can get it replenished by the last of December or first of January, I will try and come. . . . Mary Sophia and Lilla are anxious to go to Savannah about the last of December to spend some time with their aunt. . . . If the girls do go to Savannah, they will certainly go to Liberty and make Mary Sharpe a visit. . . . Sam wishes me to let him go down before Christmas, and I shall do so. If there was any chance of hiring him for two months at Riceboro, I would do so to avoid the cold winter. He is now quite old, and I must favor him. It would not be good for him or me to be idle so long.

Mary says I must ask Mary Sharpe what makes her so close about her love matters. If she was to be married, she would tell everybody all about it. . . . I have some nice preserves to send you, Susan, and Laura. I will put them up in a box next week and send them to the care of Charles Colcock, Savannah, by the express, so they may not be delayed on the way as common freight. Will write to Charles before we send them. . . . Although I anticipate much in seeing you all, I know the visit will be a sad one. The death of my dear Betsy is always in my mind. How I shall miss that dear one! Poor Mr. Maxwell, I feel truly for him in his desolate home. . . . Mary, Louisa, the girls, and Joe all join in affectionate love to you, Charles, and Mary. Joe says he has an appointment at Christmas with Charlie and Willie West and he must be there. Ellen says she wishes to travel for the improvement of her mind. Adieu.

Your aunt,

E. G. R.

Rev. C. C. Jones *to* Mr. Charles C. Jones, Jr.[g]

Montevideo, *Monday,* November 17th, 1856

My dear Son,

We received your letter today enclosing the bills of sale, which will be executed the first opportunity, D.V. *I would be very glad on many accounts if*

Mr. Wright could effect a speedy sale. You did right in procuring the shoes, and I wish you would get of Mr. Lathrop striped Negro winter cloth the same as we bought for the people: six and a half yards apiece, and three yards of cotton homespun apiece, and some buttons and thread, and have it given to them. Phoebe and Jane can make it up in a few days. Your mother says you had better have it cut off in six-and-a-half-yard pieces. I do not know what the price of this property now is, or is likely to be, and $800 round may be *over* the market value. You can see and let us know. The offer of $4000 was $666⅔ each. Some 180 or 200 are advertised by Montmollin. The weekly expense is $10.50.

Mills has left his bill ($340) for work done on the house. If he calls, tell him that he must wait a little until we are in funds, and that his bill is something over my anticipations. Will settle with him the first opportunity when it is in my power, and hope it may not be long. Please say the same to Mr. Brunner should you meet him. Am sorry my expectation to pay him through Mr. Anderson failed. Will you ask Mr. Anderson if there is any sale for *rough rice?* Please ask Claghorn & Cunningham to send by Russell fifty pounds good Rio coffee and one box *adamantine* candles (*short sixes*) not to exceed the *usual price* (from twenty-eight to thirty-one cents per pound).

It gives us great pleasure to learn that you and your brother are getting along so pleasantly in your new mode of life. Am sure you must find it more independent and compatible and more favorable to your studies than boarding out, and I hope not more expensive, if as expensive. Your sister expects to pay you a visit ere long.

We have just moved up here, and shall have much fixing and cleaning and clearing up to do. The masons finished on Saturday. Am sorry my strength is so feeble for work; have been much weakened within a few days from causes beyond my control. Mother has been all the way to Maybank today to arrange the loads for the oxcarts tomorrow, and did not get back till 8 P.M. I was unable to go. Tell Joe the box came today, and I will open it tomorrow, and will faithfully follow his prescriptions myself and see that Niger does also. Niger is about the same. Will write him particularly in a few days. With my necessary cares and anxieties I see but little prospect of amendment. Am decidedly retrograding. I cannot control my circumstances to relieve myself. However, the will of the Lord be done!

Sina is quite sick; feel uneasy about her case. Sandy Maybank is also sick. All well at Arcadia and the Island. Your sister is spending a couple of days with your Uncle William. Both well.

The election has ended well. May it be the first act of divine goodness in our deliverance from the political and religious heresies which have been disorganizing and destroying the country! Mother unites in much love to you and your brother. Tell Joe am much gratified that he is succeeding in his lectures, and that the class is increasing. I remain, my dear son,

Your ever affectionate father,
C. C. Jones.

Mrs. Mary Jones *to* Mr. Charles C. Jones, Jr.ᵍ
                    Montevideo, *Thursday,* November 20th, 1856

My dear Sons,

Although there has been no public recognition of this day as one of thanksgiving according to the recommendation of our governor, in this county, as has always been your father's arrangement when we have been at home, all business and plantation arrangements have been suspended and religious services observed with the people. It has rained the whole day, and the chapel service has been a sad one: the funeral of our poor servant-woman Sina.

Thus have we a second time very recently been made to see and feel the power of God! She has had chill and fever for some time, but would miss it; and on Sabbath as we returned from church we found her in bed with fever. The usual remedies not succeeding, we called in young Dr. Way, who did not consider her case dangerous. Yesterday morning she lost an infant. The doctor was with us all day, and when he left just before sunset he did not express any special fears about her situation. I had been with her until two o'clock, and went over after the doctor left. After tea your sister and myself were engaged giving out Negro cloth. Your father rode over at nine o'clock and said he saw no change except a profuse perspiration. She was perfectly sensible, but drowsy from the influence of opiates, and her pulse numbered 100. He returned to the house but a short time when he was summoned back; and she died at ten o'clock without a struggle. Your father rode and I walked over. She was no more when I reached her.

Her family seem much distressed. Eve left four children, and she leaves five. Nine motherless ones now to be cared for!

You know the tenderness of your father's feelings, and his ceaseless anxiety when the servants are sick. They tell most sensibly, and he is more unwell than for a great while: the nervous inaction greatly increased. He is now taking the medicines sent by you, my dear son Joseph, and I trust the Lord will bless them. I cannot tell you how anxiously I feel. . . .

Niger we think on the improving order. He walks out every day, but complains of great pain in the joints, and there is a rising on one elbow. His skin is becoming quite smooth.

Your father says *if you can do so* with ease to yourself you had better accept the invitation to address the Young Men's Christian Association. And let them appoint you *late* in their course, that you may have time to prepare something useful and creditable to yourself. Nothing so much delights my heart as to feel that your brother and yourself are casting your individual influence in society into the right scale. In life's great battle there can be no neutral ranks.

Your letter, my dear son Charles, was received today. Your father and myself think with you that if $4300 can be realized for that family, you had best close the bargain; for their present expense is very great, and increasing. Of course, as we are compelled to sell, we would like to realize their value, but are willing to let them go for less in view of selling all together. We are now much in want of funds to meet our liabilities in bank and for the house. I know that you will do the best for us in this matter. It will be a relief to have the business closed. It has caused me great distress.

Your father requests you to say to Mr. Palmer that we want the common-sized *mortised locks* with *white knobs*. And if Falligant has not the doors on hand, perhaps Shaffer may have them. We want them immediately if they can be procured.

Rev. *R. Q. M.* is here tonight. Thanks for the *Ledger;* it interests your father and all of us. Our united love to you both, in which Sister joins. Howdy for the servants. Tell Sue take care of everything.

Your affectionate mother,
Mary Jones.

Mr. Charles C. Jones, Jr., *to* Mrs. Mary Jones[t]

Savannah, *Saturday,* November 22nd, 1856

Your kind favor, my dear mother, of Friday last was duly received. The death of Sina is indeed sad—especially so in view of the family now mother-less, and the fact of Eve's recent demise. There is this to be said, however: that with kind masters the orphans are always cared for, which is more than can be affirmed of many poor persons not occupying a similar relation in life. Their children are left to public charity, which is too often meager and beggarly.

I am very sorry to hear that Father is feeling so badly, and sincerely hope that he may be benefited by the medicines sent by the Doctor.

Aunt Susan, Cousin Laura, and Mr. Buttolph returned today at half-past one. Not learning their arrival until teatime, after tea the Doctor and myself called at Dr. West's residence, where they are staying, to see them. Cousin Laura, feeling fatigued, had retired; Aunt Susan and Mr. Buttolph look re-markably well, and excepting the illness of Cousin Laura have found noth-ing to mar the pleasure of the trip. They will all leave the city on Thursday, and will be obliged to Father and yourself if you will direct the carriage to meet them on that day at Riceboro. They expect to pay you a short visit at Montevideo.

The weather now is very warm and damp—by no means healthy, I should think, for this season of the year.

The sale of the Negroes I will effect so soon as possible, and to the best ad-vantage. Uncle Henry and Aunt Abby have returned from Bath, and expect to leave this city on Wednesday for Liberty. Brother quite well, and busy as usual. Fred King is here; will be in Riceboro next week, and purposes spend-ing the winter at home. With much love, my dear mother, to self, Father, Sister, and all friends, I am

Your affectionate son,
Charles C. Jones, Jr.

Mr. Charles C. Jones, Jr., *to* Rev. C. C. Jones*ᵍ*

Savannah, *Saturday,* November 29th, 1856

My dear Father,

I am in treaty with General Harrison for the sale of the Negroes, and had hoped for a reply by Friday's mail to my letter written and favored by Aunt Susan. He will make a good master, and is a gentleman of high respectability. Being anxious to purchase such a family as that now offered, he is prepared to give perhaps a better price than any other purchaser. It is also a satisfaction to know into whose hands they will pass, and to believe that they will be well cared for. He will pay some $2000 in cash and the balance of the purchase moneys by note with good endorser, payable at twelve months with interest from date. The family sold as a family will not command as high a price as when sold separately. From all I can gather (and there have been a number of purchasers in the market) the present, if consummated, will be the most advantageous arrangement that can be made. He will give, I am led to believe (both from a conversation with him), $4200 or $4250 for the six. He anxiously awaits a reply from me; and if convenient, please let me hear by return mail. General Harrison lives on the line of this county and Effingham. He wishes Phoebe and Jane as house servants, and gives on that account a much better offer than any hitherto made. I do not think, after the delay already experienced in effecting a sale, and all things considered, that there can be any objection to the purchaser or the terms of the sale. But of this you will judge. My own opinion is that the sale had better be effected upon the terms proposed.

Received a letter from Aunt Mary Robarts yesterday. All friends in Marietta well. Aunt Eliza and family anticipate a visit to the low country in December next. By Harnden's Express Lady Mary will send in a few days a box of preserves for Mother and Aunt Susan. So soon as it arrives in the city I will forward the *box,* but it may perhaps be divested of its *contents* in consequence of its "stoppage *in transiter*" in Savannah. It is a dangerous piece of business to entrust to the care of two young bachelors anything that can be eaten, and especially a jar or jars of preserves endorsed by the fact that they come from the hand of so notable a housewife as Aunt Mary. . . . Please advise Mother and Aunt Susan of this my avowed purpose, and when an action for "larceny after a trust delegated" is brought against the subscriber, do tell them that they cannot engage my valuable professional services for the prosecution, inasmuch as I am already retained counsel for the defense.

Mills came to see me today, and I told him he must wait for a while.

The weather is very unusual for this period of the year. We have had no fires for two weeks, and summer clothing would be much more comfortable to one's feelings than the winter garb. The change, however, would not be prudent.

By Mr. Buttolph I sent for Sister to read aloud to Mother and self the best modern poem I have found for many days: *Bothwell,* by Aytoun. The scene well laid, and the period one of the most interesting in Scottish history. So soon as Mr. Buttolph has read it he will send it to Montevideo. Sister can remind him of his promise.

The weekly *Ledger* is in the mail for Monday's stage. Rough rice is still at a discount, and can scarcely or not at all be sold. All friends well in Savannah. Law business unusually dull for this season of the year. Hoping, my dear father, that you are better than you have been of late, with much love to self, dear Mother, and Sister, I remain, as ever,

Your affectionate son,
Charles C. Jones, Jr.

The Doctor quite well, and unites in love. Our black family well, and send howdy.

REV. C. C. JONES *to* MR. CHARLES C. JONES, JR.ᵍ

Montevideo, *Saturday,* November 29th, 1856
My dear Son,

Your favor by your aunt of the 26th did not reach us till Friday night. . . . We prefer the Negroes sold at a distance, as already intimated. If that be an *impossibility,* then the next farthest distance; but not in Savannah, and as far from this county as possible.

We prefer the sale *to be cash.* Or if credit be allowed for one year, then the security must be ample, with *a responsible city acceptance,* and the paper *bankable* so that we may get it discounted, and without our own endorsement. This will put us in funds which we need, and save all the trouble of future collection. *One-half* paid down at *the least; two-thirds* if possible. A credit sale, of course, should be for a larger amount than a cash sale. We should be glad to know the offers made, so that we might determine whether to take them or not—if such notice be practicable.

The expenses are large keeping the Negroes in town, and Mr. Wright's entire bill if sold now will not be far from two hundred dollars. They may manage to keep them on hand long enough to make a good profit. If not sold very shortly, I must make an effort in some other way—by sending them out into the Southwest by a responsible individual in this county. If you can sell for four thousand dollars clear of all expenses, do so at once.

You have drawn out the bill of sale *"warranting the Negroes sound."* Now, this I am not able to do, not having seen them for weeks; and can only do so at any time and under any circumstances *to the best of my knowledge and belief.* The purchaser must take the risk after the day of sale. We can go nothing beyond that day. We sell what we honestly believe to be sound, but we give *no warrant which allows of after abatements or reclamation.*

I will have the bills of sale copied off with this amendment and signed and sent to you, D.V., on Tuesday next, December 2nd, and will sign the bills you sent also and send them, which you can use if you prefer it, *but with the correction made in them.* The matter occasions your mother a great deal of anxiety, and am therefore very anxious to close it, and hope Mr. Wright will use his best exertions. I am well aware you will do *your* best.

December 1st. I had written thus far on Saturday. Your letter of 29th November reached us today. You will receive the bills of sale with this letter by tomorrow's mail. Your mother and I after consultation agree with you that the sale should be closed with General Harrison at the price named: $4200 or $4250. You must *look well to the security,* and *if possible* have the note drawn so that we may get it *discounted,* as suggested on the other page, if we wish to do so. The endorser should be a responsible *city* endorser. I think a mortgage on the property would make the matter still more secure. I am thus particular because the property is *all your mother's* but one, and I would not like to run any risk about it. You might mention this fact to the purchaser if you should deem it necessary. *The property is in trust.* Your mother desires the mortgage if possible; but in the event of not being able to secure a mortgage, do not let that prevent the sale if you have undoubted security. We now leave the matter with you, and you can let us know the issue. We are gratified to know that the Negroes will have the prospect of a good master. We hope all parties may do well.

Your supplies will reach you by railroad on Thursday evening. No mutton to be had, but you will receive a *fine porker.* Mother recommends you to *corn the hams.* The rest you do not use immediately will keep, but in the icehouse. A small package will be sent down at the same time for *Dr. West.* Send it to him, Mother says, immediately. Mother and Sister send much love to you. As ever,

Your affectionate father,
C. C. Jones.

IX

Richmond-on-Ogeechee, *Wednesday,* December 10th, 1856

My dear Mother,

We reached this place about sunset last evening after a pleasant and comfortable ride. Father read aloud and finished Dr. Kane's book on the way. We found good Miss Eliza expecting us, with nice fires in the parlor and chambers. She says she can't tell you how much disappointed she is that you did not come, for she certainly thought you would have done so. And this morning we had some delightful venison which she had reserved in view of your coming.

My dear father is pretty well this morning, though very inactive, it is so cold. Miss Eliza has kindly offered to take us to the railroad, so Gilbert will return this morning. We have learned nothing further in reference to the cars running to Lane Station, but presume we shall hear something today, and will write you by Thursday's mail.

Richmond looks as beautifully as ever, and Miss Eliza is in such good spirits. Father has walked out to have a little talk with Mr. Ulmer. Betty has just come in, and says with great warmth: "If you are writing to your mother, do give my best love to her, and tell her I want to see her." Miss Eliza says she had quite set her heart upon your coming, and hopes you will do so yet, and sends you some more oranges with her love. Dear Father unites with me in all that is affectionate, dear Mother.

Your attached child,
Mary S. Jones.

Rev. C. C. Jones *to* Mrs. Mary Jones[t]

Savannah, *Wednesday,* December 10th, 1856

My dear Wife,

Daughter wrote you this morning from Richmond. Miss Eliza accompanied us to the cars. We had a pleasant run, arrived safely, and found all well.

Charles has effected a sale: $4500 cash, Joe's little man *included,* making $642.85 each, expenses to be deducted. The best sale that could be effected at present. Some four hundred now in the market; money scarce and hard to be obtained. They have all been sold to one person—not to be separated, but remain on his own farm in the vicinity of *Macon.* General Harrison did not purchase; his offer in the end not as advantageous. They have been sold as we desired, and of this we should be glad, although more might have been obtained had they been sold separately. Conscience is better than money. Have not seen Charles yet, and the letter must go at once to the office.

The cars will run *to the Lane Station* (*Mr. Thomas W. Fleming's*) on Monday and every day after. So if we are all alive and well, you can please send Gilbert for me there *on Tuesday next*. I say Tuesday, as starting on Monday may not be so well for me, especially should I preach on Sunday. You can write us by Friday and let me know what further I shall do for you.

Miss Eliza sent the boys some oranges, ten nice *doves,* and a plate of *fresh butter!* She says her young housekeeping friends ought to be encouraged. Was well pleased with her plantation affairs. She was much disappointed at your not coming.

Let me beg you not to work too hard, as work you will. I shall stay no longer than is necessary, and am sorry to have to leave you at all. Daughter and Joe send a great deal of love. Sue is quite well. Titus' face is becoming as round and full as if he had been stung with a bee on each side. George is well. Lafayette went with the rest yesterday or today. The Lord watch over and be with you, my dear wife!

Your ever affectionate husband,
C. C. Jones.

Charles has just come in. Quite well, and sends much love.
The *shoes* are on board Captain Thomson. Please send for them.

Rev. R. Q. Mallard *to* Miss Mary Sharpe Jones[t]
Walthourville, *Wednesday,* December 10th, 1856

My dearest Mary,

Shall I write the absent and loved friend tonight or not? It is late, and I feel somewhat fatigued from last night's dissipation, and the soft sound of falling rain is wooing me to rest. But I obey a sweeter influence: love. I must not leave home without dispatching a messenger to console my beloved, even now, perhaps, imprisoned in "Castle Dismal." Could I only share your captivity, like a true knight, I should soon fancy your prison a palace, and the fair prisoner (no fancy this if the heart be the empire) *my queen. . . .*

Tomorrow evening, D.V., I leave for Montgomery. I had hoped that I might have my cousin Mr. Mallard's company, but the weather is rather unpromising, and I do not think he will go. I gave John Baker this evening an invitation to accompany me, but the proposition does not seem to meet with much favor from him. He is, however, excusable, and I felt no disposition to press the matter, as he has some business to transact in the earlier part of the week which imperatively demands his presence in the village.

But I have not written a line in regard to *the wedding,* which you recollect was to console me for your absence. I confess to a feeling of sadness when our roads separated, although mine was leading me to the merry gathering. I will acknowledge, too, that I would willingly have foregone the anticipated festivity for the pleasure of a seat by my Mary's side, with one of her soft hands in mine and my eyes making acquaintance with hers. But notwithstanding all this, I did enjoy myself at the wedding party very well indeed. . . . Brother B., as was expected, performed the ceremony (I mean your Cousin Lyman). The bride looked well, as did her attendants, who supported her in number, I should say, amply sufficient (seven). I suppose the gentlemen looked their prettiest. In the course of the evening I took occasion to enforce by sundry arguments the exhortations of Brother B. upon the newly married wife, especially calling to her notice those words *subjection, obey,* etc. I left at a pretty late hour in company with Brother Bowman, who spent the night with me at Leander V.'s. "Cousin Lyman" had returned earlier in the evening to Montevideo to console your "disconsolate" mother.

Now, Miss Mary, I fear you will exclaim, "You mean thing!" when I tell you that, under the *strict* injunction of secrecy, I let Brother Bowman know in general terms about what time I hope to be made happy by you. This, as your good nature will lead you to perceive, was almost a necessary consequence of my request that he should hold himself in readiness to do me a service at some future day. He will take great pleasure in assisting me in the capacity specified.

Thursday. I did not finish my letter last night, as I might have done with this page, for I wished to say some more "last words." I have concluded to start for Mount Vernon tomorrow morning. Mr. J. B. Mallard, owing to the indisposition of one of his children, has declined going; so I, as you see, will have a lonely ride, without even a *picture* to cheer me. But do I need one to bring my *heart's own* before me? Not altogether; yet still I should highly prize one, especially now in my Mary's absence. I wish you all enjoyment in the city, but hope that its attractiveness may not keep you longer than anticipated from the country.

I have just finished the composition of a marriage ceremony, and hear sounds which make it very probable that it will be required before long. Several young ladies are with us this morning, and I judge some of them must at this moment be engaged in preparations for "cake fixin's," such as beating of eggs, etc. What a difference there would be in my feelings were there a slight change made in the program! If, for example, instead of being the officiating minister I should be one party to the deed. . . . But old Winter must be buried and its ghost well laid before the happy hour. Perhaps April inconstant—"inconsistent" April, with its smiles and tears—will inaugurate our married life. Well, I have all confidence in her to whom I have entrusted the keeping of my affections that she will have sufficient reasons for any course she may pursue. "Cunning speech," do you call it? I won't discuss the question, but send you by letter that which you will not (yet) receive in person: a —— with love from

Your loving and (I believe) loved friend,
R. Q. Mallard.

My regards to the family. Remember the promised daguerreotype, and be sure *you* don't look "stern"! Wear the curls (insolent, am I not?) and look as you always do when I have seen you—*sweet*. . . . I expect to return to the village on Tuesday next. Why may not I find awaiting—or at least receive by next mail—a letter from (forgive me) my darling?

Mr. Charles C. Jones, Jr., *to* Mrs. Mary Jones[t]
Savannah, *Saturday,* December 13th, 1856

My dear Mother,

We are all around the table, and will soon be taking our evening repast around the *bachelor* table. Would that you were here! Miss Kitty, upon the strength of Father's and Sister's being here, has ventured into "Castle Dismal," and would have complimented us with her presence at dinner today had she not been prevented by other engagements.

Father expects to preach tomorrow in the First Presbyterian Church. We shall be very glad to hear him, and hope that he may have strength to support him comfortably in the effort.

The Southern Commercial Convention adjourned on last evening, and the numerous strange faces have disappeared like magic. The effort to reopen the slave trade—as far as an expression of the will of the convention could effect that object—has, I am glad to say, been voted down by a handsome majority of the members. The only wonder is that any should have been found advocating such a measure.

Father promises to add a postscript. . . . With much love from all,
Your affectionate son,
Charles C. Jones, Jr.

Rev. C. C. Jones *to* Mrs. Mary Jones[t]
Savannah, *Saturday,* December 13th, 1856

My dear Wife,

Charles has left a page for me. Have been much interested in the commercial convention. Adjourned last night. The abominable resolution on reviving the slave trade was rejected decidedly. It is thought to owe its paternity to South Carolina, and to be a measure looking towards *disunion*. Governor Adams of that state recommended the reopening of the slave trade in his message to the legislature! Much talent in the convention.

Have visited nowhere as yet but at Cousin Charles West's. Have gotten through pretty much with our little commissions. Will bring the barrel of flour with me on Tuesday, D.V.; so the jersey may come along with Gilbert —or the *small oxcart*. This will save waiting for the vessel.

Miss Stiles and Daughter have entered into an alliance offensive and defensive. Mr. Brunner has just called, and shall have to close. Am very anxious, my dear wife, to return to you, and am sorry to leave you alone a day. Mr.

Porter wishes me to preach tomorrow, and may do so. We all send much love. I remain, my dear wife,

Your ever affectionate husband,
C. C. Jones.

REV. C. C. JONES *to* MR. CHARLES C. JONES, JR.ᵍ

Montevideo, *Thursday,* December 18th, 1856

My dear Son,

With great thankfulness I found your dear mother in excellent health, having done a world of work since my absence. Had things moved over from Arcadia. Went down to the Island, spent the night with your aunt, had the oxcarts at Maybank next day, and moved up Sister's piano and all the tables and chairs, etc. And the parlors in the new part of the house here are all fixed and furnished, and we have moved into them. And the chambers are fixed and fixing, and the pantry soon will be. There is nothing like her energy. We hope to be to rights, Providence permitting, ere long. Yesterday I sent by railroad to Savannah for *two doors* for the wings, and they are now (today) in the house, safe and sound, to be hung tomorrow. This is the convenience of the railroad.

Our people are all well at all the places—a matter of great thankfulness.

Judge Law was fellow passenger out and gave me some of his early history. Dr. McWhir and Mr. Boggs were his only preceptors; what else he learned was by himself. Had no patrimony, married early, came to Savannah, was admitted to the bar, used to copy Mr. Joseph S. Pelot's writs at a quarter of a dollar each. Pelot was the solicitor general, and too lazy and pleasure-loving to do it himself. He would also go around to the lawyers' offices and get papers to copy or writings to do, if they had any to give him. And again he would go into the justices' offices and look over their dockets, and now and then they would give him a case. Thus he spent his winters eking out a living; and when summer came he would take the place of some of the teachers in the academy going North and teach till they returned, then go back to his profession in the winter. . . . I mention this to show you what are the beginnings of many distinguished men. Judge Law has been rewarded for his patient and untiring application and industry. He is now at the head of the bar, and is as studious and laborious as ever. I told the judge that I had pointed him out to you as a self-made man, as an illustration of that success which crowns indomitable perseverance and industry. He considered your situation in Messrs. Ward and Owens' office as one of great value to you professionally, and complimented the handsome manner in which you sent out all the papers from the office. I mention this for your encouragement, and that you may know that the eyes of men in the city take notice of you as well as of other men.

Mother would write tonight, but she is so tired you must all excuse her. She says: "If you can, do come out on Christmas; she wishes to see yourself and brother at home. But do not neglect your business." We shall expect you, my dear son Joe, on Saturday, D.V.; and you must bring any friends out with you you like. The carriage will be at the depot, and you will reach home by 2 P.M. to dinner. And I will thank you *to pay Mr. Fulton, the conductor, the freight for the doors* which came today, and his *commission* for his trouble. I sent him a bill, but he could not change it.

My dear daughter, your room is all nicely fixed by Mother, your little maid as busy as a bee, and Mother insists upon my occupying the opposite room as my study on account of its warmth. If your neighbor should grow troublesome, you must get your brother to issue a writ of ejectment for you, and I will clear out before it is served, to save expenses.

We have had an invitation to the wedding on the Sand Hills tonight, but you see we have not gone.

I hope, my son, you went through your duties as judge advocate to the satisfaction of your commander. I pray the Lord to be with and bless you all for time and for eternity. Mother sends much love; has retired.

Your ever affectionate father,
C. C. Jones.

No letters came from any of you today. What about the *pants?* Am happy to see the action in relation to reelection of Judge Fleming.

Mr. CHARLES C. JONES, JR., *to* REV. C. C. JONES[t]
Savannah, *Friday,* December 19th, 1856

My dear Father,

Your kind and interesting letter was this afternoon duly received. I am glad to learn that dear Mother is so well. She must, from the changes noticed on your return in the household arrangements, have been very busily occupied during your absence. I hope you feel as well as the steadiness of your hand indicates. The penmanship of your present letter reminds me of your writing in years past.

Judge Law told me today that he had the pleasure of meeting and riding out with you on the cars as far as Way's Station, and that you had a delightful chat all the way. He is an accomplished gentleman of the old school, remarkably uniform and urbane in his manners, and noted for his courtesy to brother members of the bar. His experience must have been interesting to you, coming as it did as a concise autobiography. His experience is that of many of the prominent men of our country, who, without the assistance which wealth and family afford, have pursued their studies and accomplished great purposes despite early disadvantages. He is, as you very well say, now at the head of the Savannah bar. We young members may take courage and profit by his example. I shall preserve the little sketch of the early efforts at the bar of the judge, which you have thus perpetuated, as an interesting item in the history of our bar.

The judge appears to be yielding more sensibly now to the influence of age than at any time since I have known him. This I could but observe today as I noticed him walking through the square. The rude cold wind was lifting his thin hair from either side of his head; his face appeared wan and colorless; and his step was more feeble than usual. He has been of late very busily engaged in preparing an important case for argument before the supreme court of Florida. Sickness and moral obliquities in his family also exert a depressing influence upon him. Life is a singular thing, viewed in the abstract: full of trouble, labor, sorrow; and one-half, and more, spent in mere preparation; and when reason is matured, and experience has inculcated its valuable lessons, and man seems just best fitted to accomplish the ends of life, age and disease hurry him to the grave. Judge Law is now the only one left of the older members of the bar, and in the course of human life cannot survive many years.

On the first day of January next, D.V., I expect to open an office for myself—with what success remains to be proven. The past year has been a pleasant one to me in very many respects, and I hope has been spent not without profit. There is no more sure way, and in fact the only way to acquire an accurate and practical knowledge of the profession is to enter at once *in medias res;* and this can only be done in an office of large business. Having thus acquired much of the knowledge requisite for accurate conveyancing and for the preparation of various legal papers, I hope again to return to the study of the theory, and will also have more time to watch the conduct of courts. The greatest trouble with me is the absence of a legal library, having lost those books—or most of them—carefully selected which composed my library at first.

Mr. Owens has had during the past year some idea of retiring from practice. In that event Mr. Ward offered me the position of a copartner with him. . . . Mr. Owens, however, has concluded not to abandon the practice of the law. We part the best of friends, and I think Mr. Ward will take pleasure in assisting me. . . . I must beg that you will say nothing of this matter of copartnership or of Mr. Owens' retiring from the practice, as they are private matters and known only within the office. To speak of them would be to place me in an unpleasant position, as they were confidential communications. Where I will find an office I know not as yet. Lawyers are paying one hundred and fifty dollars for rooms about ten by eight. Perfect extortion.

I wish very much that I could accompany the Doctor tomorrow. I long for the freedom of the country and the open air. The Doctor will tell you of the military parade and the appearance of the judge advocate. Sister leaves us tomorrow for Mrs. Stiles's. With much love to dear Mother and self, I am, as ever,

Your affectionate son,
Charles C. Jones, Jr.

I wrote you by the last mail, but it appears that you never received my letter.

Mrs. Mary Jones *to* Mr. Charles C. Jones, Jr.[g]
Montevideo, *Monday,* December 22nd, 1856

My dear Son,

Many thanks for your *sweet remembrancer* by your father. We have enjoyed it together. I felt very much disappointed at your not coming out with your brother on Saturday. Although you did not say that you would come, I still had an impression that you would do so. I really think you ought to have a few days' holiday at Christmas.

Your father was much improved by his trip to Savannah. I only wish he could have remained longer. . . . I was glad to see that the *infamous proposition* to the commercial convention for the revival of the slave trade was promptly rejected. It was a perfect disgrace to the body to present such a subject for consideration.

We were very much pleased to hear of your honorable appointment as judge advocate. The Lord blesses you, my son, with health and strength and worldly prosperity. I pray that He may not withhold "His favor, which is life, and His loving-kindness, which is more than life." It gives me great happiness to hear from various sources of the respect and esteem in which your brother and yourself are held, professionally and socially. *Character* is everything to a young man.

Old Daddy Tony and Rosetta return you "tousand tanks" for the tobacco. It was a cold damp evening when I took it around to the old man. He had not left his house in consequence of the cold for several days, and was sitting over the fire when I entered and told him I had brought him a present from his young master. When I handed it over, he rose from his seat, his eye kindling, and exclaimed: "God bless my young master! He never forgets the old man! Do, Missis, write and give him tousand tanks. Tell him *I can do nothing for him, but the Lord can do everything for him;* and I pray the Lord to bless him and make him a good Christian." They pride themselves upon the fact that the tobacco is put up in a paper. I have never the least toleration for the weed except in cases of happiness conferred upon some old mama or daddy.

Wishing to send your sister a line also, I must close. Father unites with me in much love to you, and so does your brother. I wish you could come out on Thursday with Mr. Buttolph. As ever, my dear son,

Your affectionate mother,
Mary Jones.

Mrs. Mary Jones *to* Miss Mary Sharpe Jones[t]
Montevideo, *Monday,* December 22nd, 1856

My darling Child,

Your brother has just remembered that his pocketbook contained letters for your father and myself from your brother and yourself. Many thanks for your interesting favor. I am happy to know that you are enjoying yourself; I know your visit to Mrs. and Miss Stiles will be a delightful one. Be sure and go to see Mrs. Mackay; we have long entertained for her and all the ladies of the family feelings of sincere affection and respect. You must hold Kitty to her promise of returning with you.

The box for Miss Dunning will be surely sent by the Doctor, Providence permitting.

I wish that you would get some mantua-maker to cut you a good low-neck dress pattern such as we could send on to Philadelphia.

Please inquire how much the sewing machines cost, and where and how they may be obtained. I hear such various accounts about them that I am quite puzzled.

I rode today to South Hampton. Your Aunt Julia is full to overflowing. Your aunt and cousin will spend the week between us. Laura has been suffering from toothache, but looks remarkably well.

Please, my child, say to Sue that I was surprised to see your brother's shirts so badly done up after having made Lucy show her how to wash and iron them. She must use grists for starch and put a little *tallow* or candle grease. She ironed them with *dirty irons.* Tell her from me that *they must be properly done up,* and she must not depend upon Titus, but do the washing herself, making him help with the coarse things and his own and George's clothes. And when she breaks off the buttons, she must sew them on again. Even the new shirts are nearly ruined. Tell her I expect to come down and see after things, and your brother's clothes must look very much improved or I shall be very much displeased. . . .

It is so late and cold I must close, with our united affectionate regards to Mrs. Stiles and Kitty and Mrs. and Misses Mackay. Love from Father and Brother and Mother to you, my dear daughter. Howdies from Kate and Flora and Jack to Missy and Aunty, Young Master and Joe and George.

Ever your own loving mother,
Mary Jones.

MR. CHARLES C. JONES, JR., *to* MRS. MARY JONES[t]

Savannah, *Wednesday,* December 24th, 1856

My dear Mother,

Your kind favor was yesterday afternoon received at the hands of Mr. Buttolph. The bundle accompanying I supposed was for Sister, and sent the same with your note to her to Mrs. Stiles's, where Sister now is, in whose presence the package was opened, who laughed when the same was opened; and the attendant circumstances (probably of an amusing character) I know not, as I have not seen Sister today. Of this much, however, I am sure: that the sausages were returned, that Mr. Buttolph and myself this morning discovered at breakfast that they were delightful, and that I am truly obliged to you for your kind remembrance.

Aunt Eliza and family arrived last night. Have not seen them as yet, but purpose doing so after supper. The weather is very cold, the thermometer being this morning 18° above zero. The mercury in our latitude seldom indicates such severity.

Please say to Father that Mills came to see me today, and says if convenient that he should very much like some money, as he has to pay the workmen's wages. I told him I would write and probably receive an answer by Friday's stage.

Sister quite well. How much do I wish that I could have been with you during Christmas! But the Doctor must enjoy himself twice as well to make up for my absence. With much love to self, Father, the Doctor, and all friends. In haste,

Your ever affectionate son,
Charles C. Jones, Jr.

Miss Mary Sharpe Jones *to* Mrs. Mary Jones[t]
Savannah, *Wednesday,* December 24th, 1856
My own dear Mother,

Your welcome letter was handed me last evening, and I was quite surprised to find Cousin Lyman's name upon the back of it. I am glad to hear that you are all well, and hope this cold weather will not make dear Father sick. For the past three days it has been almost impossible to keep warm.

I went this morning to see Aunt Eliza and family, all of whom (except Mary Sophia and Lilla) are staying with Cousin Charles West. Aunt Eliza looks remarkably well, and so does Aunt Lou. And Aunt Mary is in her usual good spirits. They will probably remain a week or two here, then go to Uncle Henry's. . . .

In regard to the low-neck dress pattern, I can have that cut; but I think it would be better to get a high-neck pattern to send away, as all my dresses are made in that way. We are so unfortunate in getting things from the North that I think it would be safer to have things made here if it could be done. And Kitty says illusion flounced upon tarlatan for a foundation makes a beautiful and by no means an expensive dress. It has a very light, airy appearance.

Mrs. Stiles and Kitty—and indeed all the family—have been very kind to me, and I find my time here very pleasantly spent. Mrs. Stiles is suffering from headache today in consequence of excitement. Two nights since, there was a cry of fire. Brother Charlie was here at the time, and Mr. Stiles and himself, being both on the alarm squad, hastened out. The former ran very fast, and upon reaching the spot found that the stable in which he kept his horse was in flames, and his pet not out. This of course excited him very much, but after standing a moment he felt such a violent pain in his chest that he turned immediately, and with difficulty reached home. As soon as he came in, everyone observed his paleness, and he asked for brandy or wine. As he was afraid he had broken a blood vessel, Dr. Read was sent for; and he remained with him an hour or two until he grew better, and found that no vessel was ruptured. Today he is quite well again. His lungs are exceedingly delicate, and the whole family seem continually to be fearful lest something should affect them seriously. They have all been mourning over the loss of their little pony Robin; Mr. Stiles trained him and has won two prizes with him.

I will go and see Mrs. Mackay; she lives next door, and there is almost hourly communication between the two families.

I have spoken to Sue about her washing, and shall make it a point to go and deliver your message to her.

Kitty says I must give you a great deal of love, and that I am not going home for a long time; but I do not think I shall be able to stay with her as long as she wishes, as she says I must be with her at least two weeks longer. . . . Tell Father that Sidney's beautiful cat Malta has gone off, and nothing can be heard of it, though she has sent in every direction. It was one of the prettiest cats I have ever seen. . . . It is so dark that I can scarcely see, and have written the greater part of this more by faith than sight. . . . Please give love to Aunt Susan and Cousin Laura, and to Aunt Julia's family. With any quantity of love to dear Father, Brother Joe, and yourself, dear Mother, I am

Your affectionate child,
Mary S. Jones.

Howdy for all the servants.

Rev. R. Q. Mallard *to* Miss Mary Sharpe Jones[t]

Walthourville, *Wednesday,* December 24th, 1856

My own Mary,

Do you believe in dreams? *I* do not in *all;* for I dreamed on Monday night that I was disappointed in not hearing from you as I expected, but found on my return from Dorchester a letter awaiting me. My sister, in answer to my inquiry, said that there were a number of letters for me; but I found upon examination that one was a circular, two invitations (one to a party at Mr. Baker's tomorrow night and the other to a temperance celebration on Taylor's Creek), and only one of value (epistolary): from my sweet friend. To the celebration I do not expect to go, but hope to attend the party, where perhaps I shall dispose of my remaining stock of "reserve." What say you? Shall I part with all, or *reserve* enough to keep me modest? . . . Hereafter I shall plead guilty and throw myself upon the mercy of the court.

But I must tell you something of the wedding. At the hour appointed I looked into the room where the ceremony was to be performed, and it quite puzzled me to know how a parlor already full could receive seventeen more persons. But the occupants of the room were principally ladies, and the dear creatures rather than miss the ceremony packed themselves closely for a few moments into corners and other available spaces, leaving a vacant place for the couple and their attendants. Stepping into the area (with some trepidation, I will admit, yet concealed, I hope, from most persons), I married them, using a ceremony which I will show you as you wish at some future day. Several persons were pleased to congratulate me on the performance. At the close of the ceremony I used an uncle's privilege and with hearty good will, I assure you, for I *like* it, kissed the bride. . . . Guess what young lady (I used to carry married ladies) I took to the table. Why, a very pleasant young lady indeed, and a friend of mine from whom, I am sorry to say, I am to be instrumental on the last day of this month in effecting a separation: Miss Julia Cay. I heard it said that we could sympathize with each other: I suppose in being alike *engaged;* certainly not in being alike near to our weddings.

I did one little thing innocently which I would not under certain circumstances knowingly have done. I produced from the recesses of the sideboard what I supposed to be blackberry wine, and helped a young lady to what was in fact Madeira. She wished it, however, as I afterwards learned, for her sister, who felt unwell.

Our guests seemed to enjoy themselves very well, I thought. Sister had three tables set—one in the back piazza, and two some three or four feet below in a shed thrown off from the piazza and floored for the occasion. It was a new and pretty arrangement, furnishing something like an illustration of "the highest and lowest rooms at the feast" of Scripture. One would have supposed, from the tendency to remain at the upper table, that it *was* considered the place of honor. . . . But enough of the wedding.

I took John over to see his father next day (that is, we went together), as someone had remarked that he looked *homesick*. (Query: Will *I* under the same circumstances?) John and Lizzie seem now to be enjoying a quiet kind of happiness; and do you know that I sometimes feel almost envious? Well, I suppose I have to content myself with an occasional letter and a visit and a daguerreotype. Could you not send the latter to me by mail?

My own, when am I to see you again? You do not say in your letter how much longer you will remain in the city. Let me know in your next; it may influence me in deciding upon a visit to Savannah. After the annual meeting of our church on (I think) the first Saturday in January, I will have a good excuse to visit you. But do I need one? Not if you are away much longer.

I did not finish my letter yesterday, and must now add a few more words with a pen which has traveled (I like that better) through a number of pages of sermon paper since I wrote the above. . . . Present me kindly to your brothers and to Miss Kitty. What Christmas present shall I send my own dear friend? What my prudent friend I hope will accept sent by letter if not delivered in person: a kiss with love from

Your affianced,

Robert Q. Mallard.

P.S. Your suggestion about being provoked to write by Thursday's mail on one condition was not received in time. Do you prefer me to write shorter letters but oftener?

Miss Mary Sharpe Jones *to* Mrs. Mary Jones[t]

Savannah, *Saturday,* December 27th, 1856

My dear Mother,

Since writing you last I have heard of another sewing machine—made by Hunt. Dr. Parsons, the dentist, told Mrs. Stiles that he used one of these in his family and found it very useful not only for coarse but fine shirt work. At present there are none of these machines in the city. Most persons prefer Wilson & Wheeler's machine, and quite a number of this make are now in use here. Cousin Eliza's is of this make. I have heard of but one being used of Singer's make, and they say it is rather clumsy, though I have not seen anyone who has actually tried it. I should think you would not be disappointed in getting either Hunt's or Wilson & Wheeler's. I do not know the cost of Hunt's, but such an one as Cousin Eliza has can be obtained for a hundred dollars, and for twenty more a box for covering and protecting the machine. I have not yet seen Cousin Eliza's in operation; as she has so much company with her at present, she has no time to prepare work for it.

I dined with them all yesterday. Aunty is quite well, and will not probably go to Liberty until week after next, though if she hears from Uncle Henry, she may leave sometime next week. She requested him to say when it would be convenient for him to meet her.

I hope you have all had a pleasant Christmas. We all went to hear the bishop preach, and he gave us an interesting sermon from the text, "Who hath believed our report?" After sermon the Communion was administered, and it was the first time I had ever seen this in the Episcopal Church. Christmas was remarkably quiet. No noise at all in the streets, as all firing of crackers was prohibited. Brother Charlie went out to King's bridge and was very successful; and he sent a large portion of the birds to Mrs. Stiles, and we dined upon them today.

Brother Joe has just arrived safely—as he says, with all his plunder. I am very much obliged to you for the box, dear Mother, and will take it to Miss Gertrude. I had my likeness taken, and when Cousin Lyman was here he begged that I would send it out to dine with you on Christmas Day; and Brother Joe says he does not believe you have received it yet, so please ask him for it and keep it until I come.

I do not know how long I will be here; Kitty says I must remain with her on New Year's Day, as she expects to receive company then. They are all very kind to me, and seem to enjoy themselves very much with their relatives, some of whom come to see them every day. The Misses Mackay both desire their love to dear Father and yourself. If there is anything that I can do for you, dear Mother, please let me know of it. Brother Charlie is quite well.

Kitty sends much love to Father and yourself. Please give love to Aunt Susan and Cousin Laura; also to Aunt Julia's family. And accept all that is affectionate from

Your attached child,
Mary S. Jones.

Howdy for all the servants.

Miss Mary E. Robarts *to* Mrs. Mary Jones[t]

Savannah, *Sunday,* December 28th, 1856

My dearest Cousin,

We arrived last Tuesday night after a very cold and fatiguing journey; but the cordial welcome and many appliances of comfort we received at the house of our hospitable kinsman and his lovely wife soon thawed us out. Mother stood the journey about as well as the rest of us. Louisa is not well today, having an attack of bronchitis; but I hope she will soon be better.

We found it impossible to make definite arrangements about the time and manner of going to Liberty till we got here. Therefore Mother wrote Henry and requested him to write her to Savannah naming the place he should meet us at the terminus of the railroad. We received a long and kind letter from him, and mentioning his plans for moving, but that they would certainly receive us at Lodebar, if only for a night till we could get to the Island or to Banky's. Banky's wife is a stranger to us; and we would not wish to take our baggage to the Island or the Sand Hills, those being the most remote points, but deposit it at some central point and visit from there. Of course this move of Henry's was a thing that neither he nor we expected, and we find ourselves in a strait. So, my dearest cousin, if you could receive us for a day or two on our first arrival, we could then talk over our plans and go to the Island. We are sorry to put you to this inconvenience, knowing your house is not yet completed; but if you will just entertain the travelers in camping style we shall be satisfied. We shall leave here for Liberty on Monday week the 5th of January. Shall go to the end of the railroad and go with whoever is there to claim us. Please confer with Henry and write us to Savannah, care of Dr. C. W. West.

I worshiped with all three of your children at church today. All well. Mary Sophia and Lilla will remain in Savannah a month longer, so will not be with us. Love to our dear cousin from all of us. And believe me, as ever,

Your affectionate cousin,
Mary E. R.

Rev. R. Q. Mallard *to* Miss Mary Sharpe Jones[t]

Walthourville, *Monday,* December 29th, 1856

"I shall expect a letter on Friday, and it would be very pleasant to receive one on Tuesday; that might provoke me to write on Thursday." So pleasant is the thought of writing you, as well as that of hearing twice in one week from my own sweet Mary, that I am tempted to provoke you to the performance of the threatened act.

Only less pleasant is the employment in which I am now engaged than that which I should prefer: *talking to you face to face*. If in my power, distance should be no obstacle to the indulgence of such a desire; but I fear I may have to wait for my Mary's return to indulge this most *reasonable* wish. Next Wednesday night I have, as you know, a marriage ceremony to perform, so that it is impossible for me to leave this week. Sabbath after next is the time for our Communion, and such occasions, unassisted as I usually am, require more than ordinary preparations. I mention these facts because I would not have you suppose that it is any want of inclination that keeps me from the city at this time. I will see what intelligence your expected letter will bring this evening, and shape my movements accordingly.

Have you shared in the general uneasiness as to the apprehended troubles during "Christmas holidays"? Some persons here strongly suspected some strolling organ-grinders who passed through the county some weeks past of tampering with our Negroes. I thought that it was very well that our citizens should be on their guard, although *I* did not feel much apprehension. In the event that these anticipations, or rather fears, should be realized, I am glad that you were in the city. The excitement seems to have subsided.

I attended another party (but not a wedding) last week. Mr. Baker gave one in honor of the newly wedded pair. I can't say that I enjoyed myself a great deal. I much prefer a cozy chat by the fireside with only *one* to talk at a time and *one* to hear. Brother Bowman was present. What do you think? (Now, don't you breathe it to a soul, for you see it is quite an evidence of my vanity to mention it.) A lady (Mrs. Harden) was heard to say that both the *officiating minister* and the groom were better-looking than the reverend attendant.

The evening of Mr. B.'s party, a dancing party was given by Augustus Quarterman, and some of the guests of the former adjourned to it at the close. They kept up the latter, I understand, until four o'clock A.M. Your friend Miss Matilda Harden was one of the number. Herself together with Colonel Quarterman's two daughters and Mr. T. Quarterman's were, I believe, the only professors of religion who danced. I don't think they were as happy next day as they might have been. The world claims this amusement for its own, and seems astonished that Christians should participate with them in it. . . . Mrs. Lockett and her husband, I was sorry to hear, both danced, although Mrs. L. apologizes for both by saying that they did it simply to "complete a set."

There are quite a number of strangers at present in the village. Several young ladies are here from Florida, one from Savannah. . . . We had an unusual number of strangers in our congregation yesterday. The subject of my morning's discourse was the Judgment. The attention with which it was listened to was encouraging. I endeavored to be very plain, and have found that the "closest" sermons are the best liked. From a want of suitable preparation I was deservedly mortified in the afternoon. There is such a temptation to slight one's subjects when he expects to *extemporize* that I feel of late like abandoning it altogether. What do you think of the two methods of preaching? My efforts with "notes" are so much superior to those made without that the contrast is to me painful. I suppose, however, that the best speakers have generally been compelled to pass through just such a mortifying discipline. (You see I am availing myself of your request to write about *myself.*)

I have lately received a beautiful letter from Dr. and Mrs. Howe in reply to a letter of sympathy which, at the suggestion of my mother, I wrote to them a few weeks ago. They are in great affliction, but I doubt not bear it with Christian fortitude and resignation. I should judge from the tenor of some of his remarks that the doctor is aware of our engagement. "You are just commencing life," he says, "with many anticipations of earthly joy. But," he adds, "there is sorrow in every lot: griefs and joys strangely commingled." I do not believe that either of us have those high-wrought unearthly anticipations of life which doom the possessor to certain disappointment. With you I hope and believe I shall be happy; yet I do not expect such joy as shall make me wish earth was my heaven. My Mary will, I know, learn to concede much to the infirmities of fallen human nature. If I know my own heart, it is my solemn purpose, with God's help, to meet every reasonable expectation of yours. I will not, if it is in my power, give you occasion to repent the step which you have taken. *I* will not expect *perfection* in her who has now the custody of my affections, for none are perfect in this life. But I believe those same affections are in the keeping of one who will not disappoint my expectations—in whom my heart may safely trust.

But I must leave room for a postscript after the arrival of the mail.

I have just finished a second reading of a long, interesting, and valued letter received by this evening's mail. Can Miss Mary guess from whom? I will tell you: from one I only love less than—myself. (You see, I am waiting until a certain occasion before I feel at liberty to obey the command: "Nevertheless let everyone in particular so love his wife even *as* himself.")

You say nothing definitely as to the probable time of your return; I hope you may be able to say by Thursday's mail. (You see, I expect the fulfillment of your threat.) I must confess that I begin to feel quite anxious to see you. It has been a long time since I parted with you at your father's gate. So many things have transpired since to make the time appear longer. It seems to me that I have seen you very little alone since you moved from that great old place, Colonel's Island.

About that daguerreotype: I suppose it is useless to say a word, as the thing is already done; but I *should* like to have received it a little earlier than I shall. I am sorry to hear of the losses which have befallen the kind family where you are at present domiciliated. The pet Malta I happened to have seen. So you had so much of a "Sunday feeling" on Christmas that you wouldn't receive my present. Are you a descendant of the Puritans who placed beer under interdict because it *worked* on Sabbath? You see how at a loss I am to know why my present should have been, if not *returned*, sent back untasted. Well, I won't risk another just now, for fear it too will be returned (?), but send you the best respects, kind regards, (out with it) and love of

R. Q. Mallard.

Rev. C. C. Jones *to* Miss Mary Sharpe Jones[t]
Montevideo, *Monday,* December 29th, 1856
My very dear Daughter,

We were glad to hear from you and from your brother this evening, though he mentioned that you were not well, while you said nothing about it. Be sure and let us know if you are at all sick. You are in a most pleasant and kind and affectionate family, and I have no doubt they will make you happy in your visit. We feel grateful to them for their kind attentions to you. Remember your dear mother and myself most sincerely to Mrs. Stiles and Miss Stiles and her sister and to Mrs. Mackay and her amiable daughters, our old friends. Has Mr. Stiles recovered from his overexertion the night of the fire?

Please say to Cousin Mary that your mother received her letter this evening; and that we will send to meet them at the railroad station (No. 2, the present terminus) on Monday next, agreeable to the wish expressed in her letter; and that Mother, who is as usual very busy tonight, will write her by Friday's mail, Providence permitting. Give our united love to dear Aunty and to Cousins Mary and Louisa and the children.We shall be glad to see them all.

Audley, Fred, Willie, and Mr. McClellan called in last week to see you, but you were not at home.

And now I send you an invitation to Miss Cay's wedding. And my friend Mr. Cay sent *us* an invitation also. If the ride was not so long, I should be tempted to step in and see the ceremony. Above twenty years ago I performed Mr. Cay's ceremony, and it was on the Sand Hills too. Quite stirring times in Liberty: three weddings in as many weeks!

We enjoyed your brother's visit, but it was so short, and so many things occurring, it seems like a dream. . . . Your Aunt Susan and Cousin Laura and Mr. Buttolph came on Friday from Mrs. King's, and your uncle met them here. He was very cheerful, and left us Saturday. The Christmas has been a very quiet one; we were at home all the time. All went to church Sunday but your cousin: riding does not agree with her. . . . Mrs. J. N. Jones has sold out all her people and her interest in the Retreat, and the little girl's property also. Negroes bought by Messrs. Cay, P.W. and T.W. Fleming, and the Retreat by your Uncle Henry. He has sold Lodebar to Mr. Smith

Hart. . . . Mother has accomplished a world of work, and is working, working from morning to night, and late at night, every day. I do long to see the time when she will take some rest. She wishes to add a postscript, so I will leave some space for her.

You must stay as long as it is agreeable to you to do so. We have heard and seen nothing whatever of anybody Walthourville side. We think your likeness a good one, but not equal to the one taken with your brother Joe in Philadelphia. The Lord be with and bless you, my dear child!

Your ever affectionate father,
C. C. Jones.

Mrs. Mary Jones *to* Miss Mary Sharpe Jones[t]
Montevideo, *Monday,* December 29th, 1856
My dear Child,

Your likeness cheered our Christmas dinner. Your brother was absent at the time; did not come home until dark, and company so divided his attention that the picture was forgotten. I do not think it equal to the one I have. I will keep it safely until you come.

Have not heard or seen anything of a certain gentleman since you left.

Please see Mr. Sp—— (the *piano tuner,* I mean) and ask if he can come out and tune your piano. Appoint a time for us to meet him at the railroad, and be sure to let him know that your instrument is of Schomacker's make, and he must bring a hammer of proper construction: large and strong.

I do long to see you, my own dear child; but you must not shorten your visit, but stay as long as you please. How much did Mrs. Gilmer's sewing machine cost? A hundred dollars is a great deal to invest in an uncertainty. I am rejoiced to know that our dear aunt and cousins are in town, and we will send to meet them on Monday next, Providence permitting. Please hand them the enclosed note from Sister Susan and myself. Our best regards to Mrs. Stiles and Kitty, and shall certainly expect her promised visit. Hope her sister will accompany her; and should be very happy to see her brother also, and he might indulge his sporting propensities if he has any. Love to your brothers.

Ever, my darling child, your affectionate mother,
Mary Jones.
Be sure *to invite Mary and Lilla to visit you.*

Miss Mary Sharpe Jones *to* Rev. *and* Mrs. C. C. Jones[t]
Savannah, *Wednesday,* December 31st, 1856
My dear Father and Mother,

Your affectionate letters were received this afternoon, and I am truly glad to learn that you are both quite well.

I did not know Brother Joe had written you I was unwell. I have been suffering from a severe cold, which they tell me makes me look pale; but it is much better now, and I think would be quite well could we have a little fair weather. It has been a long time since I have had such a severe cold. Kitty and I were both in the same plight, and Mrs. Stiles says she thinks we must have done something special to get them. But now she and her son both have colds. Mrs. Stiles seems to be exceedingly delicate, and Kitty thinks more so than usual this winter.

I think Mrs. Gilmer's sewing machine cost a hundred dollars; and Kitty says that she thinks Wilson & Wheeler's machine will suit, and says she is sure it would be no risk for you to get one, and says, moreover—and this, I think, is very, very kind—that if you do get one and her mother is well enough for her to leave home, she will go out to Montevideo and teach us how to sew upon it. Hunt's machine, of which I spoke in my last letter, is more expensive; it costs, I think, fifty dollars more than Wilson's. . . . Kitty has just come in and says do let her beg you to get a machine, and if you wish it she will write on for you at any time, as she knows for what little accompaniments to write, such as sizes of needles, etc. Mrs. Low, she says, writes constantly; so they know all about it.

Aunt Eliza and family expect to go out on Monday, and want me to go with them; but as they are so soon going to the Island, I think I will wait a few days longer. Miss Gertrude Dunning says she wishes to go out with me to pay Cousin Laura a visit, and I think I will be with you on Wednesday or Thursday next. I will write again on Monday and say definitely.

The weather has been so damp that we have not been able to go out very much. Brothers Charlie and Joe are both quite well. I took tea with Mrs. John Ward on Monday evening; Brother Joe went also. Aunts Mary and Lou and the young ladies were there. Kitty sends much love to you. Do give a great deal of love to Uncle William and Aunt Susan and Cousins Laura and Lyman. Love to Aunt Julia's family. With affectionate love to you both, my dear father and mother, I am

> Your attached child,
> Mary S. Jones.

MR. CHARLES C. JONES, JR., *to* REV. *and* MRS. C. C. JONES[g]
> Savannah, *Wednesday,* December 31st, 1856

My dear Mother and Father,

Messrs. Ward and Owens have very kindly offered me the position of a copartner with them in the practice of the law, which, as you may easily imagine, I have accepted. . . . I have to leave the city on business for Brunswick on Saturday next, but will write you again, D.V., before I go. All well, and unite in love. . . . As ever,

> Your affectionate son,
> Charles C. Jones, Jr.

Mrs. Mary Jones *to* Mr. Charles C. Jones, Jr.ᵍ
Montevideo, Wednesday, December 31st, 1856

My dear Son,

Old Father Time is making rapid strokes from the grave of 1856, and hasting to welcome the light of a newborn year. Amid the hurry and cares of life I would gladly pause and with memory's lamp linger amid the fading shadows of the past. Were I alone, I could pass this whole night in communion with my departed hours, but this would not be duty. My thoughts, however, must dwell with grateful remembrance upon the goodness and mercy of my God and Saviour during the past year. It is true that one tenderly beloved, who almost occupied a mother's place in our hearts, has been removed from our family circle; and we have been called to part by death with faithful servants, and by removal with others, and have not been exempt from the ordinary cares and trials of life. Yet how beyond compare do our privileges, our mercies, our blessings abound!

In putting away some old books, etc., this afternoon I came across many little mementos of your own and your brother's and sister's childhood, amongst them this *little book,* the gift of your Cousin Marion Dunwody when you were a very little boy. Well do I remember how much you prized it. As each Sabbath came, you would fold it in your little white handkerchief, put it into your pocket, and bear it away to church. It may speak to you of the past. May it not also have a warning voice for the present! . . .

January 1st, 1857. A Happy New Year to you both, my dear sons! Unexpectedly we were informed this morning as your father was on his way to the Island that Maybank would deliver the address to the Agricultural Society at the parade ground. He returned for me, and we went there immediately. A large number of the citizens were present, with many strangers; and he gave us an excellent address, well written and handsomely delivered. We did not stay for the exhibition or the dinner, as it was cool and damp, and I did not wish your father to expose himself.

On our return we took your letter, my dear son Charles, from the mail; and I need not say that your father and myself are very much pleased at the offer made and accepted. We find today's *News* confirming the copartnership. If ever one had cause to love and bless God, it is yourself.

It is late, and I must close. Will try to send you a little package by Monday's cars; you can make Titus inquire for it. With love to you both and your dear sister and all friends,

Ever your affectionate mother,
Mary Jones.

Mrs. Mary Jones *to* Miss Mary Sharpe Jonesᵗ
Montevideo, Thursday, January 1st, 1857

A happy, happy New Year to you, my beloved child! And should it bring over your life changes of vast importance, may they be only those of increasing happiness and usefulness! I cannot feel that anyone is able to love you much more than Father and Mother have done and still do; and if in God's providence we shall ever see you leave your own home to form a new one, our best blessing will go with you and rest upon you, for you have ever been to us a dutiful and loving daughter.

Thank you for all the information about the sewing machine. And do thank Kitty most kindly. If we had the money, would most gladly accept it at once; but having many liabilities to meet, your father has disposed of all ready money, and we shall now have to wait until the crop is sold.

As Aunt will come out on next Monday, you had best wait until that day week, for our carriage will have to take them to the Island on Wednesday or Thursday. We shall be most happy to see Miss Dunning; please say so to her. Could you bring me some cuttings of the *white banksia* and any other roses or plants? Do not forget about your piano; I want you to practice when you come out. Tell Kitty I shall really be grieved if she does not come with you. I regret to hear that Mrs. Stiles's health is so feeble. Our united love to them. Your brother will tell you about the address. Our united love to Aunt and cousins and Cousins Charles and Eliza. Sister Susan and Laura left us yesterday. With the exception of the time your father was in Savannah we have been scarcely a day alone. Please bring me out four or five loaves of bread; your father enjoys milk toast.

Ever, my daughter, your affectionate mother,
Mary Jones.

The severe cold has killed your beautiful moss.

Mr. Charles C. Jones, Jr., *to* Rev. *and* Mrs. C. C. Jones[t]

Savannah, *Friday,* January 2nd, 1857

A Happy New Year to you both, my dear mother and father, with many pleasant returns!

The old year passed gloomily away, and no sunlight dawned upon the morning of the new. The 1st was nevertheless a merry day in Savannah. The streets were filled with numbers on foot and in vehicles of every description, paying their New Year visits in obedience to what is now a well-established custom. Being in Rome, I would not be found negligent of Roman manners, and consequently with a companion "went the rounds," accomplishing in the space of some five hours and a half forty or fifty "pop calls." The ladies were all in pleasant humors, ready to receive; and the day was delightfully spent —a cheerful episode in the experience of the laborious businessman. Thus— for the present, at least—I am square with all the good folks in Savannah. To make amends for the day's amusement, after a late dinner I repaired to the office and there remained, pen in hand, until about eleven o'clock. Could not prevail upon the Doctor to accompany us in our social tour.

Your kind favor, Mother, with its little memento of bygone years, was this afternoon received. Thank you for both, and the accompanying kind wishes. I shall preserve the little book with care, and hope to derive profit from its precepts.

I had a conversation, Father, with Major Porter with reference to your note in bank. He says under the present circumstances existing in relation to monetary affairs in general and the fiscal matters of the bank, he would request you to extend the note for five hundred dollars for sixty days. That will bring it to the 17th/20th of March, when he promises a renewal for the year. You said in your last letter that you wished no further renewal. I will have another interview with the major so soon as I return from Brunswick and let you know the result.

Aunt Eliza and family expect to leave the city for Liberty on Monday next. . . . The new firm of Ward, Owens & Jones is in active operation. Tomorrow morning I expect to leave this city for Brunswick on professional business. This will be my first experience on the circuit. Sister still with Miss Kitty. She and all friends quite well and uniting in love.

Your ever affectionate son,
Charles C. Jones, Jr.

Miss Mary Sharpe Jones *to* Mrs. Mary Jones[t]

Savannah, Saturday, January 3rd, 1857

My dear Mother,

Your much valued note I received last evening on my return from a lecture delivered by Dr. John LeConte before the Young Men's Christian Association. This lecture was on galvanism, and I think was particularly dry. Dr. LeConte's manner is not very pleasant, and that in a measure detracted from the interest of what he said. Mrs. John and Mrs. Joe LeConte were both there. Kitty did not attend, as she was not very well.

For a week past the weather has been so dark and rainy that we have been confined to the house nearly all the time. This morning I spent with Dr. Parsons, and had five teeth filled. I had no idea that he would have had more than two, but I am very glad now that it is all over. This afternoon I went to look at some plants advertised for sale. They were Northern plants (spruce trees, azaleas, japonicas, etc.), but they were so expensive that I did not get any of them. Small azaleas four or five inches high were a dollar. I found some nice celery seed, and send you a paper; also one of nasturtium seed.

On Thursday Kitty received visits from the gentlemen; and cake, wine, and hot chocolate were handed, and the chocolate was by far the most popular. . . . We spent the evening with Mrs. Low in her magnificent house. It is beautifully furnished. I saw there a work which interested me very much; it contained handsome engravings of the pictures in the Dresden Gallery. There are four volumes, and I think Mr. Low told me *two* of them cost five hundred dollars. Mrs. Low has a beautiful collection of pressed ferns made by herself this summer while in England.

Aunt Mary is going out on Monday, and she will tell you all the news. Brother Charlie left this morning for Brunswick on business. I suppose you have seen the notice in the *News* of his being associated as a copartner with Messrs. Ward and Owens.

Mrs. Stiles has not been well for more than a week. Her health is feeble at best, but of late it has seemed even more delicate than usual, which makes them all feel very uneasy about her; and Kitty says she cannot come out to see us until her mother is better. She is often unable to come downstairs. I saw Mrs. Mackay this evening, and she says she always remembers you with pleasure and interest.

Brother Joe dined with us today. Kitty sends love to Father and yourself. If nothing prevents, I hope to be with you on Monday week. It seems to me I have been absent a long time. Good night, dear Mother. With affectionate love to dear Father and yourself,

> Your attached child,
> Mary S. Jones.

Miss Mary Sharpe Jones *to* Mrs. Mary Jones[t]

> Savannah, *Wednesday,* January 7th, 1857

My dear Mother,

I forgot until this moment that the mail goes out tomorrow, and it is now nearly eleven, and Brother Joe and myself have just returned from Mrs. Neely's, where we have been spending the evening. I hope to go out on Monday next, and Miss Gertrude Dunning will accompany me, and will go to Montevideo unless Cousin Lyman meets her at the cars. Kitty has declined going at this time, as her mother's health still continues delicate; however, she will be with us as soon as she is well enough for her to leave.

I was quite surprised on Monday evening to see one of my Walthourville friends enter the room.

I am now with kind Cousins Charles and Eliza. Brother Charlie has not returned yet. Brother Joe is quite well, and I was glad to draw him out this evening. Hoping to be with dear Father and yourself, dear Mother, very soon, I am, as ever,

> Your attached child,
> Mary S. Jones.

Rev. R. Q. Mallard *to* Miss Mary Sharpe Jones[t]

> Walthourville, *Thursday,* January 8th, 1857

My own dearest Mary,

The thought struck me a few minutes ago that I might spend the time I usually devote to rest after my morning's labors in a very pleasant way—in writing you just a note to say that I have arrived safely, etc. It is possible that you may slightly expect to hear from me by this mail, and I do not wish to disappoint you nor to deprive myself of the pleasure.

My visit to Savannah I assure you was one of the pleasantest I ever made, but has made me a more hopeless captive than I ever was before. To your account I place that last item. These moonlight walks as well as rides and these interviews only disturbed occasionally by a devoted husband "seeking Eliza" are, as I know, very dangerous to freedom. However, I don't mean to complain, but resign myself *cheerfully* to my fate. But while I am tabling charges against you, bear with me while I bring forward one more. I charge you with defrauding me of time on my way out from the city. There I left you, as you remember; but you would persist in accompanying me to the country. It is true I did not very strenuously resist, if at all: that wouldn't have been polite, would it? You see, I was making the comparison between actual enjoyment and the *memory* of it. My next trial will be of the comparative merits of memory and *anticipation*. . . .

I have a little item of news that I have a half mind to tell and a half mind to keep. Which? "Tell!" Well, it is this. Mr. J. B. M. will not take *the house* as he somewhat expected. Let me see: has that intelligence kindled a smile in my Mary's eye or heaved her bosom with a sigh? Perhaps both: a smile (may I hope it?) for me, a sigh for "the old folks at home." I shouldn't be surprised if the latter alone. Never mind; I'll bide my time. When my Mary loves me as deeply (did you put that?) as I do her, such news will add a softer hue to the gentle light of love which I have sometimes fancied I saw in her eye of blue.

My time is nearly gone, and lo, my note has become a letter to one fondly, deeply loved by

Her own
Robert.

Rev. R. Q. Mallard *to* Miss Mary Sharpe Jones[t]

Walthourville, *Thursday,* January 15th, 1857

My own dearest Mary,

Am I to have the pleasure of hearing from you by this evening's mail? We said nothing about corresponding, as our parting was in the presence of a third person; but I hope if at home you have written. Perhaps you have gone to the Island, and I had better not expect a messenger this week from *my darling*. Well, if I should be disappointed, I have a good representative of my Mary at hand. Although a mute, I can converse with her by signs. I can look into those eyes so softly beaming upon me and —— those unresisting sweet lips. I thank you for that picture; it is only less attractive than the original.

How short the time we were together in my last visit—I mean, not with others around us, but alone. Miss Dunning was kind indeed, and my Mary kinder, after her day's fatigue to allow me the privilege of seeing her alone. I wanted to have a talk with you about matters in which you and I are, perhaps, more interested than anybody else.

And so you begin to think "it looks serious"! Our people up here are certainly expecting that my rented house is ere very long to have a fair occupant. Being a single man, they offered me, when called to take charge of this church, a salary of eight hundred dollars. At their annual meeting yesterday they raised it to a thousand, besides punctually paying me my last year's salary. They have also very kindly appropriated two seats to the pastor's use. Inasmuch as it is possible you may some day as a friend of mine occupy one of these seats, I will tell you that they are in one of the side pews, the remaining seats being taken by John Baker and Mrs. Quarterman. As John and his lady belong to the choir, we will have a plenty of room for your father and mother and such other friends as may favor us with their company. As another indication of the views of the people, a gentleman called on me yesterday to engage to me some furniture which he expects to dispose of. . . .

I thought I should have a fine time this week for preparing some sermons for emergencies, but was in part disappointed. . . . I wish very much to have four or five sermons prepared beforehand, as I desire to have a little holiday sometime in *April*. Just to think—January is already nearly half gone! For once I am satisfied with the swiftness of time. I hope nothing will occur to delay *the event*. . . . I have been asked a number of times of late when I am to be married, and I have to answer: "The public don't know yet." How long do you mean it kept a secret?

(Excuse my digression, but did you notice how well your eyes were taken in your daguerreotype? They look lifelike. And that hand half-buried in the snowy folds of your handkerchief, with its little memorial of our plighted love—how I should like to press it in my own!)

I must close. Remember me affectionately to your dear parents, and receive a kiss with love from

Your own
Robert.

P.S. Mr. Buttolph returns on Saturday to preach for me on Sabbath.

I hope now that you have got back in the country to breathe its pure air you will reap the benefit of your visit to the city. You must not get any thinner. What do you think? *I* weighed in Riceboro on Tuesday and weighed more than I ever did before in my life.

REV. R. Q. MALLARD *to* MISS MARY SHARPE JONES[t]
Dorchester, *Tuesday,* January 20th, 1857

My dearest Mary,

According to your request, I have made inquiry in reference to the *pianos,* and find that there are *two*—Mr. Delegal's and Mr. Busby's—which the own-

ers wish tuned. I hope these, together with yours, will offer sufficient inducement to bring Mr. S—— (I can't spell his name) out. If he has any gallantry
in his soul, your solicitations *should* be sufficient. Certainly such would be
the effect on me.

"Uncle Banky" overtook me after I left Riceboro, and we rode in company
to Dorchester. He, like many others, would like to know *when* "I am to be
made happy." My answer was as usual: "The public don't know." He thinks
that he does not come under that general head. Banky says that it was only
his relationship to you which prevented his recommending you to me when I
asked him to select a young lady for me.

Mr. Shackelford called at the house of Mr. Ladson lately, I understand,
and spoke highly of a certain lady of my acquaintance. The reply modesty
should forbid my reporting. There is a surprising unanimity of opinion, so
far as I have heard any expression of it, in regard to *our affair.*

If my Mary could have burst in (as I did yesterday upon your mother) un-
announced, I wonder what she would have thought of my employment this
evening. Fancy me seated with pen and paper, writing neither a sermon nor
a letter but a memorandum of articles ranging from the sofa down to a
strainer. Don't think, however, that I have been unassisted; my mother and
sister have dictated what I have written. These same articles, having only
this far an ink-and-paper existence, I hope will at no very distant day start
into (furniture) life. And then too a bright dream will, I trust, be fulfilled:
a queen will occupy and rule the realm of my home, swaying none other
scepter but that of love.

I have written only a note. Yet some notes are valuable—for example, to
both a *bashful* and *needy* clergyman. So valuable do I esteem this: a *note* so
evidently in *tune* that I shall expect to be paid in *kind* by my Mary; at least
I'll *let-her.* Pleasant dreams to you, my own!
From your attached
Robert Q. Mallard.

P.S. My sister also wishes *her* piano tuned. . . . Her piano is not so much
out of tune, but the cloth which keeps the strings in place is moth-eaten. Mr.
S. should know this, that he may come prepared.

Mr. Charles C. Jones, Jr., *to* Rev. *and* Mrs. C. C. Jones[t]
Savannah, *Saturday,* January 24th, 1857

My dear Father and Mother,

The weather is so intensely and continuously cold for our section of the
country that the oldest inhabitants have now, I believe, reluctantly acknowledged that even in their long and varied experience they cannot recall a
parallel. The little boys have been sliding all about the streets upon the little
ponds formed by the heavy rains which ushered in this severe spell. Groups
of young and old are often seen collected at some corner, watching with

eagerness the many mishaps which attend the first attempts to slide of those who seldom or never before have seen ice capable of supporting their weight. Now one little fellow will take a running start and slide beautifully and smoothly over the icy path. Another follows—and down he goes, heels over head. And now a half dozen or more in quick succession spring upon the ice. Perhaps the first trips; and now here they come—white boys and black boys, Irish boys and yellow boys—falling one upon the other in a confused merry heap. At which the assembled crowd indulge in loud cheers, which each moment attract passersby and swell the numbers in attendance, until all passage along the sidewalk and through the street is precluded. Everyone enjoyed the novelty of the scene. I hope, however, that the worst is over, and that Boreas will now hie him to his Northern home. This is one disadvantage accomplished by Captain Kane: he has put us in too direct communication with those far-off storehouses of snow and ice. This temperature, Father, must especially upon you exercise an unpleasant and depressing influence.

The Doctor is succeeding capitally with his lectures. His audience at the medical college in attendance upon his first two lectures numbered about one hundred and fifty. In consequence of the inclemency of the weather, his lecture before the Young Men's Christian Association, advertised for yesterday evening, was postponed until Wednesday of next week. The audience at the medical college has been composed of the most intelligent ladies and gentlemen in the city, and I hope the interest will continue.

On Thursday of this week a large fancy party was given at the residence of Miss Waring. It was a novel thing to me, and the evening was delightfully spent: a plenty of good cheer, good music, good dancing, and very many pretty ladies. There were costumes of every variety: ladies of the court of Louis XIV, French and Neapolitan peasants, countesses, queens, nights, mornings, seasons, Folly, Jewesses, gypsy girls, and Shakespearean ladies. Then among the gentlemen we had the Emperor Napoleon himself, counts, Hamlets, monks, friars, brigands, country crackers, Turks, Greeks, Arabs, and a host of impersonations too numerous to mention. Many of the dresses were magnificent, and the characters capitally sustained. The scene presented was gay and unusual. Your subscriber appeared as Colonel Morier, the hero of Lodi, etc. (The character, you know, is from *The Lady of Lyons.*) My staff uniform with slight modifications suited very well.

> A little folly now and then
> Is relished by the wisest men.

Mills has not yet called for the check. I am retaining it for him. The Doctor begs me to say to you that he would answer your kind favors, but he is very busy preparing for his Monday's lecture. With much love, my dear parents, to you both, to Sister, and all friends, as ever,

Your affectionate son,
Charles C. Jones, Jr.

In the mail are two *Ledgers.*

We sent Titus to the railroad depot today, and he reports that there is no package there for us. We regret to miss those fine sausages and spareribs.

Rev. R. Q. Mallard *to* Miss Mary Sharpe Jones[t]
Walthourville, *Monday,* January 26th, 1857

My own Love,

I have sat down to write merely a "note" to explain my regretted absence from you this evening. Some of my first, if not the very *first,* waking thoughts this morning were of you, and in connection with the fear that my anticipated visit would be prevented. I awoke suffering with I suppose what might in these days be termed "neuralgia," but to use old-fashioned phraseology, "stiffness in the neck." I hoped that it would wear away or at least yield to vigorous treatment, but have been confined to the house all day with it. After the use of various remedies I have only succeeded in alleviating the pain, but hope that a little more "doctoring" tonight will effect a perfect cure. I will endeavor to see you tomorrow evening if I am able, for I feel as if I can scarcely go with a good heart to my weekly toil without the much-prized pleasure of an interview with you.

Disappointed in making my Monday calls, and unwilling to enter immediately upon the labors of the week, I have been dissipating today—I mean, intellectually. I accompanied Catherine Sinclair a good way in a tour through Scotland. *Scotland and the Scotch* is the name of her book: quite a readable affair. Sailed—no, I must rather say *steamed*—up several of Scotia's noble lakes. Then I looked over the columns of a literary paper, reading a part of a tale (and disgusted by its unnaturalness), and finishing another from Mrs. Caroline Lee Hentz's last publication. I finished up my miscellaneous foray with a dozen or more of the first chapters of *The Southern Matron,* by Mrs. Caroline Gilman of Charleston. With the last I am very much pleased. The pictures of Southern manners are drawn to the life. She read me some lessons upon the feelings proper to the minister of the gospel.

But I have only promised a "note," and if I wish to give a *visit,* as I earnestly wish I may be able, it is time I had signed my name. With my kind regards to your parents, accept the reiterated assertion of love to yourself, my own sweet Mary.

R. Q. Mallard.

Rev. R. Q. Mallard *to* Miss Mary Sharpe Jones[t]
Walthourville, *Thursday,* February 19th, 1857

My darling Mary,

On my return home from my visit to you I found a letter from Mr. Buttolph, calling a meeting of Presbytery in Dorchester next week. This induces me to change my arrangements. I will not visit you next Monday as I expected, but will spend *Wednesday night* at Montevideo. If you do not expect to be at home then, write me a note by the Riceboro mail, and I will get it in passing through.

My visits to you are always pleasant, not only in anticipation but in fruition. That last was a delightful one, and long to be remembered. At last my sweet Mary has allowed my hopes and happy anticipations to be fixed upon a definite date as the period for their consummation. The 16th of—nobody will see it—of April, if nothing occur to prevent my union with my heart's best beloved, will find me the happiest of men. And will I not have abundant reason? Am I not to be wedded to the sweetest girl I ever knew or expect to know? My own love, I *do think* myself one of the most fortunate of men; for from my heart of hearts I say it: I would not have *my* Mary to change in a *single* particular with any lady I have met with *anywhere*. I love you, my own darling, for your own sweet self; and I have the deep joy to know that I am loved—tenderly and deeply, I believe. Would you know how I have ascertained this? Why, partly by inference, and more by my own experience of it. My Mary would not wed one she did not love, and where she loves it is her nature to love deeply and tenderly; that is the inference. Then I have felt it and seen it: I have felt it in the gentle pressure of her dear hand; I have seen it beaming from her gentle eyes as they exchanged signals of love with mine. I long to press you to my heart as my own sweet wife. . . .

The boy has come to my room for letters to take to the mail, and I close. My kindest regards to your dear parents. I am, my love, as ever,

Your own

Robert Q. Mallard.

Mrs. Mary Jones *to* Mr. Charles C. Jones, Jr.ᵍ

Montevideo, *Thursday,* February 19th, 1857

My dear Son,

Our visit to your brother and yourself was most pleasant to your father and myself, and we have seldom taken our seats at table since our return home without his remarking: "How much I miss our boys!" To hear your brother lecture was a source of great gratification to us. We stopped and dined with your uncle, bringing Sister home. Her stay with the old gentleman seemed to be a comfort to him. He is now so lonely; says when it grows warm he will come to see you. We felt grateful to God that all had been kept in health and peace during our absence. And your dear sister looked much improved.

Today, as *previously arranged,* we sent two oxcarts to Fleming Station for the furniture which Mr. Morrell had been requested to send. They returned this evening bringing only the box of crockery from Hasbrouck and a bag of salt from Claghorn & Cunningham. *The bag of things for the servants did not come. Was it sent?* We have written Mr. Morrell to send our furniture by Captain Thomson, as it will save hauling thirteen miles. If the bag for the servants is sent out, please send a line requesting Mr. Fleming to take charge of it. There are frequent opportunities, and he might forward it to the Boro.

My dear son, the awful occurrence on Monday previously to our leaving Savannah is ever in my thoughts. God grant that it may be a warning to the young men of the community—commencing in a gambling saloon and ending in eternal death! The testimony of the *courtroom* and this awful event prove the truth of God's word: *"The wages of sin is death."* All sin is hateful in the sight of a holy and just God; but oh, there are some which mark so plainly the broad road which leads to destruction that it is wonderful that men will dare to commit them. And it is the *insidious beginnings* of these things that need to be guarded. The *drunkard*—the *gambler*—commenced with his social glass or social game of cards at the hospitable board or perchance around the evening fireside of some polite friends; he talks only of innocent pleasure, of harmless amusement, and dreams not that he has entered the arena of vice. With every indulgence his perception darkens, his principles weaken; and it is a miracle of grace if he is not left to go the whole descending scale of infamy and ruin. My beloved child, shun these things in their beginnings: they bring only misery, disgrace, and eternal destruction.

I have not felt very well since returning, and last night your father prescribed a dose of blue mass, followed this morning by Sampson; so you may conclude I feel like bed. Father and Sister unite with me in much love to Brother and yourself. The servants send a thousand thanks to Brother and yourself for remembering them so kindly. The Lord bless and save you, ever prays

Your affectionate mother,
Mary Jones.

Mr. CHARLES C. JONES, JR., *to* Mrs. MARY JONES[t]
Savannah, *Saturday,* February 21st, 1857

My dear Mother,

Your kind favor of the 19th inst. was duly received. The visit of Father and yourself to us was exceedingly pleasant, and our regret is that you were unable to remain longer in the city. Its ameliorating influence upon our domestic arrangements is still quite perceptible. We hope that you may soon find it convenient to repeat your visit, and that you will then find more leisure to remain.

I regret to learn that after so much trouble you were disappointed in not receiving the articles of furniture from Mr. Morrell as expected. The morning that you left the city, your note to him was carried by me to his store and there delivered to his clerk, with verbal instructions to have the articles sent out by the cars on Thursday, and also with the request that the note be handed to Mr. Morrell when he came in. All of which the clerk promised faithfully to do. I will see him in person and learn the cause of the nonperformance of his engagement, and will enjoin upon them to have the furniture sent as requested.

The servants' bag was also duly marked and sent, and I cannot imagine the cause of its detention. Will make due inquiries respecting it.

This afternoon we received the Light Dragoons from Charleston in grand style; and at the collation given at St. Andrew's Hall, among other celebrated military worthies the judge advocate was called upon for a speech and a sentiment. On Monday a contention will be had between the two companies for a very handsome saddlecloth elaborately worked by several of the ladies of Savannah and offered as the prize of the occasion.

Cousin Charles West, this morning upon rising from bed to dress himself, had a slight hemorrhage, from the effects of which he is at present confined to his bed. He hopes that nothing serious will result.

We have written Aunt Susan, asking her to make our house her home while in the city, and will do all we can to make her stay as comfortable as possible under the circumstances. She has been so very kind to us—and especially to me—that I am very happy to be able even in a slight degree to reciprocate.

We are sorry to hear, Mother, that you have been unwell since your return, and sincerely hope that you are before this entirely relieved. With much love to self, Father, Sister, and all friends, as ever,

Your affectionate son,
Charles C. Jones, Jr.

Rev. C. C. Jones *to* Mr. Charles C. Jones, Jr.[g]

Montevideo, *Tuesday,* February 24th, 1857

My dear Son,

It gratifies your mother and myself that you and your brother have made an offer of your house to your aunt and cousin, and we feel assured that you will both do all in your power to render their stay pleasant. Your quarters will necessarily be close, as your room is not ample. I suppose you will continue to occupy your own room, and Joe take the little one next to it; and he will have to do his studying in his office, which he may well do now, as the weather is warm. Am glad his lectures are drawing to a close, and that he will have more leisure. Should it be at all necessary for you to vacate your room at any time and for a time, which indeed may not be necessary, we suppose you will go to Mrs. Caruthers' in preference to any place else: more preferable than the Pulaski.

Since my return I have cast up my accounts, and we shall be about a thousand dollars short—provided our remaining crop sells as well as what has gone to market. I mean *my own personal* accounts. Major Porter was so kind as to offer his aid should we need anything when we were in Savannah. I wrote him last week and received a most kind and friendly letter from him. He has nothing on hand for a private loan at present, but may have as an executor some sixty days hence; and he says if I will send in my note made payable at the Bank of the State of Georgia in Savannah at sixty days for a thousand dollars, he will have it discounted for me; and he says "my son the lawyer" can endorse it, and if need be, he will endorse it himself. He certainly could do no more for me. I replied to him today, saying I would see to the drawing and forwarding of the note in a few days. If he is able to let me have the thousand dollars on private loan at the expiration of the sixty days, then we will pay up the thousand-dollar note in the bank and let the five hundred dollars go on. If not, both notes must run till the next crop comes in. Will send you a note, D.V., by Thursday's mail—or *Friday's,* rather.

The articles all arrived from the railroad yesterday in good order, and the servants' bundle is safe and has been distributed according to order. We are sorry to hear of Cousin Charles's attack; hope it may not prove serious. Our united love to your brother and yourself; Mother is now writing him. All well at present, D.G. Send me *Payne* by Mr. Buttolph; I forgot it.

Your ever affectionate father,
C. C. Jones.

Miss Mary E. Robarts *to* Mrs. Mary Jones[t]
Montevideo, *Thursday,* February 26th, 1857

This will inform the Rev. Mrs. Jones that her house has been entered during her absence—not by a robber but her own dear cousin, who came with peaceable intent to receive and give pleasure. But not finding the proprietors at home, she took the liberty of walking in and going to her own trunks with her own keys to get some things therefrom, taking no other liberty but walking into the chamber which contained them, and leaving the house without purloining anything except this piece of paper. In short, my dear cousin, I am sorry not to find you at home. Henry was going to the Boro, and said he would drive through if I wished to come; so, glad of a little chat with my well-beloved cousin, I came, but saw nothing but a deserted mansion and your handmaids all busy at work.

If you get any news from Savannah this evening, please send it over to us. We feel anxious to know if Laura stood the ride well. . . . Mother and Abby desire love—in which I unite—to His Reverence, Mary, and yourself.

Your affectionate cousin,
Mary E. Robarts.

When is John coming down?
I took the note and letter on the mantelpiece directed to me.

Mrs. Laura E. Buttolph *to* Mrs. Mary Jones[t]

Marshall House, Savannah, *Thursday,* February 26th, 1857

My dear Aunt Mary,

We had a very comfortable ride to the railroad station, and I experienced less fatigue than I expected, though I was very, very tired last night and am very weary this morning. Joe very kindly met us at the depot, and said Charlie and himself were expecting us and had a plenty of room. But as our stay is so uncertain, we concluded to come here, fearing it might be more inconvenient to them than they supposed. We got a comfortable room here on the first floor, and could be comfortable here, but not as quiet as at Mrs. Savage's, who now has a vacant room, which Mr. Buttolph engaged; and we are to remove to it this afternoon.

Dr. West was out yesterday for the first time, and poor Cousin Eliza feels very anxious about him. She is so devoted as a wife, and so lovely in every respect, I trust she may be long shielded from sorrow—though I know her heart aches when she thinks of her father's state too.

If we can do anything for you while here, please let us know, and it will give us pleasure. Gertrude Dunning has sent me an affectionate note already, and desires to be very specially remembered to you and Mary and my Liberty friends; Aunt Eliza, Aunt Mary, and Cousin Lou come in for a large share, and dear Uncle Charlie. Mother and Mr. Buttolph unite with me in much love to you and Uncle Charlie and Mary Sharpe.

Yours affectionately,

Laura E. Buttolph.

Mrs. Mary Jones *to* Mr. Charles C. Jones, Jr.[g]

Montevideo, *Monday,* March 2nd, 1857

My dear Son,

We were happy to be informed of the safe arrival of your aunt and cousin, and to know that your uncle would pay you a visit this week. We hope to send you by the railroad tomorrow a nice roasting piece of beef, and a piece for steaks, which we hope will reach you in good condition. It will be placed under the care of Mr. Fulton, the conductor. If you do not receive it when the cars come in, you had best send to the depot and inquire for it.

Has your brother received the shirts and collars sent by your aunt? By the first good opportunity I will send you four also, worked with buttonholes for studs. If you should not like them so, a common button can be put on.

Your sister has just written Miss Stiles. To make matters suit all around, the *event* is deferred until the *22nd of April* (*Wednesday*), and we shall wish your brother and yourself to ask as many of your personal friends as you desire. However, there is time enough for preliminaries.

Your Uncle John and family will be in Savannah on the 5th inst., Providence permitting, and leave on the 7th for Darien. . . . Your father preached

with his usual interest a most excellent sermon at Pleasant Grove yesterday.
. . . It is late, and I must say good night, with best love from Father, Mother,
and Sister to Brother and yourself. Our love to Brother William. Howdies
for the servants.

Ever your affectionate mother,
Mary Jones.

Miss Mary Sharpe Jones *to* Miss Mary Jones Taylor[t]

Montevideo, *Monday,* March 2nd, 1857

My dear Mary,

Your kind letter was received a few days since, and I am truly sorry to
find that there is a prospect of my being disappointed in regard to your being
with me in April. And yet I cannot chide you, even should you determine
positively not to come, for I felt in inviting you that I was asking a great
favor—one which I should have been most happy could you have granted it,
for aside from the occasion which would have been the immediate cause of
your coming, we should have been glad to welcome you in Georgia at our
Southern home. If you do not come this time, I shall still hope for this
pleasure, and trust it will be realized at some future day.

And now, in regard to your kind invitation to me, I thank you for it, but
am very sorry that I cannot accept it. Not from any want of inclination, I can
assure you, for there is no place that I would rather visit than Philadelphia.
I should like very much to see my friends there, and yourself in particular.
Your likeness lies upon my table, and I often look at it. It is an excellent picture.

I have one favor to ask of you, and that is for you to look in a directory for
Martin Gaul's name and send me his direction. He married Miss Mary Carroll, a friend of mine, and I would like to have their direction. I do not even
know that they are now in Philadelphia; they were living there when we left,
but I have heard nothing from them since we left.

You are an odd girl! Invite me to visit Philadelphia and at the same time
tell me that the city has increased so much in wickedness that it is scarcely
safe to walk the streets alone! I am very sorry to hear such accounts, for I
have always regarded it as the most quiet and well-ordered of our Northern
cities. I think the attack upon your cousin was one of the most outrageous
things I ever heard of. I should think this state of things would in a measure
reconcile you to your anticipated removal.

Have the Misses Gill all left Philadelphia? And if so, what is their direction? Also Maggie Wilson's? You can easily divine my reason for asking
these questions. The 22nd of April is *the* day, and when my friends are invited, I do not wish to forget my Northern ones. Sue Dickson's address is,
I suppose, Philadelphia.

I wish you were here now. The forest is wreathed with yellow jessamines, and the air is fragrant with their delicious odor. For some weeks past we have had delightful spring weather, but we are again thrown back into winter. March has come in blustering and cold, and I am afraid breathing blight if not death upon the tender buds just ready to burst into life.

My father's health does not seem to improve much; he preaches occasionally, and this does not benefit him. Mother sends love to you. Mine to your mother and to saucy Sarah Ann. Accept a portion for yourself. Write soon!

Your affectionate friend,
Mary S. Jones.

MR. CHARLES C. JONES, JR., *to* MRS. MARY JONES[t]

Savannah, *Saturday,* March 7th, 1857

Your kind note, my dear mother, enclosed in your letter to Brother, was duly received on yesterday. The beef arrived in safety, and for your kind thought of us, and practical remembrance, we would return our warmest thanks. The shirts also for the Doctor were duly welcomed by him. Those for me with buttonholes I shall be very happy to receive, and shall be thankful for.

As we are on the subject of garments, would it be convenient, Mother, for Lucy or someone else of the servants to make my little "general" a suit or two? I notice that his robes indicate the effects of the "tooth of decay" quite plainly, and I shall be compelled to find means to supply the deficiency. I think he must *sit down* too much, as most of the rents indicate!

Uncle John and Aunt Jane left today for Darien. On last evening they honored us with a call, and we enjoyed their society very much. The little folk we did not see. After spending some time in McIntosh, they purpose a visit to Liberty. Their furniture is all packed up, and the change to Rome is contemplated so soon as Uncle John returns. They both appear very well, and unite in much love.

Robert Mallard also was with us several times. He has been visiting the city with his sister in order to make all due arrangements for housekeeping. The fellow appears as happy as a lark. If coming events cast so pleasant a shadow before, I hope that the reality will prove even more delightful than the anticipation. With a very self-satisfied smile he said to me: "Charlie, I believe I have got everything." My reply was: "Bob, I will venture anything you have forgotten a pair of pothooks." And sure enough, such was the fact. So that whenever Sister looks upon that humble but very necessary culinary article, she must remember my friendly suggestion to her worthy lord.

Uncle appeared to enjoy himself while with us, and we hope he will find it both convenient and agreeable to repeat his visit.

Aunt Susan and Cousin Laura are both quite well, and very comfortably located at Mrs. Savage's boardinghouse, where they are constantly receiving attentions and calls from kind friends.

The postponement will be a source of gratification to Miss Kitty, inasmuch as it will afford her an opportunity of being present at both marriage festivals.

Mr. Speissegger expects to leave Savannah for Liberty on Thursday next, and I hope he will put the piano in fine tune for the wedding. There is nothing of interest with us in the city. With much love, my dear mother, to self, Father, Sister, and all relatives, as ever,

Your affectionate son,
Charles C. Jones, Jr.

P.S. Have just received a letter from General Cocke. He writes from Alabama, is quite well, and unites in kind remembrance.

MRS. SUSAN M. CUMMING *to* REV. C. C. JONES[t]

Savannah, *Friday,* March 13th, 1857

My dear Brother,

You have heard of our safe journey and pleasant location here. All things continue as they were, and we with patience wait.

Mr. Buttolph was the escort of Gertrude Dunning and myself to Joseph's lecture last evening. We were very much gratified: he lectured with so much ease to himself, and succeeded in all his experiments; never referred once to his notes. I wished you and Sister Mary could have been present. You are reaping the reward of your labor in your children. We see them very often. They are very attentive to us, and desire us to call on them for any service they can render us, which we shall most assuredly do. . . . Laura unites with me in love to you, Sister Mary, and Mary. And believe me

Your affectionate sister,
S. M. Cumming.

MRS. MARY JONES *to* MR. CHARLES C. JONES, JR.[g]

Montevideo, *Wednesday,* March 18th, 1857

My dear Son,

Please send us *without fail* on Saturday by *Sandy Maybank,* who comes out on the railroad, Providence permitting, to No. 3 on that day, ten pounds of best butter, for which I send a bucket, and one box of stearine or adamantine candles. Please examine and see that these are a clear, white, and firm article. The last box sent us from Savannah was very inferior. Get them at *Goodrich's* or anywhere you think best—only *not* at Claghorn & Cunningham's.

Send a bill of the same, and we will send a check immediately for the amount. We do not wish to open an account. . . . With love to your brother, aunt, and cousin,

Your affectionate mother,
Mary Jones.

Candles short sixes.

REV. C. C. JONES *to* MR. CHARLES C. JONES, JR.[g]

Montevideo, *Wednesday,* March 18th, 1857

My dear Son,

Enclosed is Cassius' account. Have delayed until we could sell his mare. Sold last week. Balance to his credit: $84.75, for which you will find a check within of date, the space left blank for the name to whom the check shall be paid. *Insert the name of Cassius' master,* to whom you will please send *the account and check.* But *first* write to him to *ascertain if Cassius and his family are still with him,* so that there may be a certainty of Cassius' getting his money. Keep copies of your letters, and *register* the letter enclosing the check when you send it. We must use every precaution to get his money to him.

Referring you to our dear cousins for all news of the family, I am, my dear son,

Your ever affectionate father,
C. C. Jones.

MR. CHARLES C. JONES, JR., *to* REV. C. C. JONES[t]

Savannah, *Friday,* March 20th, 1857

My dear Father,

Your favor of the 18th inst. was yesterday duly received at the hands of Sandy Maybank. I write today to the purchaser of Cash and family, and so soon as the necessary information is received, will remit the amount of the enclosed check ($84.75), which I hope will reach the owner in safety. I will also send a copy of the list of articles and personal property sold, with the prices obtained. . . .

Aunt Mary and Cousin Louisa arrived last evening, and are now with Dr. West. Aunt Susan and Cousin Laura are both quite well. Cousin Laura never looked better in her life. Every attention is paid them by kind friends and acquaintances, so that their stay is as pleasant as it could be under the circumstances.

May I trouble you to give my rifle in charge to Titus in order that he may bring it with him to Savannah on his return Tuesday next? Nothing but the rifle. With much love to dear Mother, self, Sister, and all friends, as ever,

Your affectionate son,
Charles C. Jones, Jr.

MR. CHARLES C. JONES, JR., *to* MRS. MARY JONES[t]

Savannah, *Friday,* March 20th, 1857

My dear Mother,

Your note and the accompanying bucket of clothes were both duly received on yesterday evening, for both of which please accept my sincere thanks. The "general's" garments fit him admirably, and he emphatically looks a little Corporal Trim.

By Sandy you will receive the ten pounds butter and box adamantine candles, both purchased from W. W. Goodrich. The butter is the best that can be had in the city—pure Goshen. The candles are perhaps not so white as you may have anticipated, but Mr. Goodrich assures me that no better article can be had; that they have given universal satisfaction, and burn evenly, brightly, and cleanly. I hope they will both prove satisfactory. Enclosed is a receipted bill, sent as desired.

The Doctor, I understand from those who were in attendance, delivered a capital lecture last night. Was so busy at the office that I did not leave until too late to attend.

Miss Kitty is now, I believe, with you. Remember me kindly to her, if you please.

What did you think of the personal appearance of our majordomo? He expects to excite by his fine raiments quite the jealousy of his own sex, and the admiration of the fair sex of kindred extraction. He is a good boy, and attends cheerfully to his business. . . . With much love to you, dear Mother, Father, Sister, and all friends, as ever,

Your affectionate son,
Charles C. Jones, Jr.

DR. JOSEPH JONES *to* REV. C. C. JONES[t]

Savannah, Friday, March 20th, 1857

My dear Father,

Many thanks for your letter. . . . Our college has recently received a most valuable mineralogical and botanical collection from Mr. Hodgson of this city. The specimens were collected by a distinguished German naturalist, and the collection as a whole is perhaps more valuable than any similar one in the United States. The labels are all in German and not attached to the specimens, and as no one of the faculty will undertake the labor, it has fallen to my lot to translate and arrange them. It will require eight months of hard labor before the collection will be in complete order. There are more than three thousand minerals and between ten and fifteen thousand plants. If my present plans are carried out, each mineral will be labeled not only with the technical name but also with its chemical constituents. This method will render the collection invaluable to students, and will, I hope, promote the development of the mineral resources of our state by showing not only the appearance but also the chemical constitution of nearly every mineral upon the face of our globe. The specimens have not been unpacked since they left Germany, and had they remained much longer, the plants would have been seriously injured by the insects. I have been busily engaged in unpacking the plants and killing the insects.

With best love to Mother, Sister, and yourself, I remain

Your affectionate son,
Joseph Jones.

P.S. I would be much obliged if you would send me as soon as convenient the German dictionary. This was presented to me by Aunt Susan, and is, I think, at Social Bluff on the Colonel's Island.

Your affectionate son,
Joseph Jones.

MISS MARY E. ROBARTS *to* MRS. MARY JONES[t]

Savannah, *Sunday,* March 22nd, 1857

My dear Cousin,

I am thankful to say to you that dear Laura is safely over her trouble, and has a very fine large boy, born at seven o'clock on Saturday evening.

Her first premonitions were at twelve o'clock in the day Friday, but nothing decided till in the night. They called up the doctor; we knew nothing of it till we went down to breakfast. When we inquired for him, Eliza told us that he was with Laura. He came in when we were nearly through breakfast, looking like a man who had been on a spree. So I said: "Monsieur, how is your patient?" "Suffering, madame, but not relieved." So I went over to beguile the tedious hours of Lady Susan; so I sat there all the morning. The doctor went round, visited some other patients, but never left Laura's room after eleven o'clock.

At two matters seemed approaching a consummation, so I proposed coming home and sending the surgeon's mate, to which he assented. I came home and said "Come," and told Eliza it was her watch now. She went immediately and cheerfully over, and I stayed several hours, then went back and sat in the entry upstairs, but came home between six and seven. At eight the doctor and Eliza came and reported a fine little son, and Laura doing well. Hattie Cumming came over, and she and Eliza and the doctor were in the room. Cousin Susan proposed taking charge of her grandson, so all came away by nine. The baby is really a fine large infant—a sturdy Scotch Presbyterian, a ruddy complexion, and a real Maxwell; looks like his great-grandfather Maxwell. A young lawyer was at hand and recorded his birth and name in his book: "Charles Maxwell Buttolph." So he is written down. Mr. Buttolph by advice betook himself to an upper chamber, where Dr. Joe and Counselor Charles bore him company frequently through the day. But what they discoursed of I know not.

Eliza and myself both offered to stay with Cousin Susan today, take charge of Laura and the baby, and let her rest. But she said she could not sleep, so we left her alone, no doubt returning thanks that it was so far well with her dear and only child. Laura did not sleep last night, and the doctor enjoins perfect quiet; his orders exclude all but the necessary nurses. Mr. Buttolph could not go to Bryan yesterday, but left at six this morning in a hired buggy. He said when he saw the baby: "Why, what a precious little thing!"

Cousin Susan begs you will let Cousin William know about Laura, and she requested me to write a note to Julia, which I will do. . . . Please give our united love to Cousin Charles and all with you. Our present expectation is to come out on Thursday week, but will write again by Henry or the mail on Thursday. Suppose Miss Stiles and Mary will soon come in now. . . . Cousin Susan and Laura desired love. I was pleased to find them so comfortably fixed: a large, well-furnished, cheerful front chamber, the doctor just round the corner, and friends just at call for either day or night service. Anything I can do for you, just command my services, my dear cousin.

Your ever affectionate cousin,
Mary Eliza Robarts.

REV. C. C. JONES *to* MR. CHARLES C. JONES, JR.ᵍ

Montevideo, *Thursday,* March 26th, 1857

My dear Son,

We were happy to hear today of your own and your brother's good health. . . . Enclosed you will find a letter received today which will be as great a surprise to you and Joe as it has been to us. The man Lilly who writes the letter is evidently a Negro trader, and not the permanent owner of the Negroes! The internal evidence of the letter proves it. In addition, I have learned that *Lyons* at the Boro received a *friendly* letter from Old Cassius this evening in which he speaks of not yet being *at home*—dated in New Orleans. My opinion is that they are there on sale! *Lilly* says *he bought them in Savannah.* This was not the *name* of the man who appeared in the purchase, nor was *New Orleans* his home. Was it not a *planter* near Macon who bought for his *own use* and not to sell again? Here seems to be deception—a wheel within a wheel!

So soon as you hear from the ostensible purchaser you will know more about it—should he answer your letter. Do not let him know of Lilly's letter. He may request you to send him the money for the people. Do not do so. It will be a roundabout way, and they may never get it. All we wish to learn of him is to know how the game has been played. If we have been deceived by Wright and the purchaser, we have been deceived. We were endeavoring to do the best we could.

Rev. Dr. Palmer is now in New Orleans, and we might enclose the money to him; and at our request, stating our fears that the people have fallen into the hands of a trader, he would pay it over to Cassius and Phoebe himself and then inform us of the fact. This, I think, my son, will be the safer course. You can write him at my request as the only friend I have in New Orleans upon whom I could confidently call in the matter. If you can get no draft for the amount on New Orleans, a draft on New York sent to New Orleans in favor of Dr. B. M. Palmer will answer the purpose. It will be best to write in this way to Dr. Palmer without delay. The list sent in Lilly's letter you see is different from the one given me by Cassius himself. Send a copy of the account I sent you to Dr. Palmer.

Am truly sorry to learn the death of poor Jane! How soon and unexpectedly has she been cut off—the cause of all that has been done! Would that she had lived and died at home in peace with God and with the world! I have prayed for those people many, many, very many times. I wish them well.

Your sister and Miss Stiles left us today for Richmond, and hope to be in Savannah Saturday afternoon. Miss Stiles is an excellent and very pleasant lady; we have enjoyed her visit. Your sister goes to her house. Please ask Messrs. Claghorn & Cunningham to send me their bill for 1856. Am hoping to hear of the sale of our remaining produce in Mr. Anderson's hands daily. Mother sends much love to you and to your dear brother. And the same from

Your affectionate father,
C. C. Jones.

MR. CHARLES C. JONES, JR., *to* REV. *and* MRS. C. C. JONES[t]
Savannah, *Saturday,* March 28th, 1857

My dear Father and Mother,

Your kind favor, Father, has been duly received. The news contained in the enclosed communication was as unexpected as it was unpleasant. The death of Jane is sad. I hope she may have made some preparation for the great change, but the probabilities under the circumstances are unfavorable. The revelation confirms me in the hitherto unshaken conviction that no confidence whatever can be placed in the word of a Negro trader. It is the lowest occupation in which mortal man can engage, and the effect is a complete perversion of all that is just, kind, honorable, and of good report among men. The plan you propose with regard to the transmission of the money realized from the sale of Cassius' property is without doubt the best, and I will see that a check is duly purchased and forwarded on Monday.

Sister quite well, and with Miss Kitty. Cousin Laura recovering as rapidly as may be expected, and the little infant lively and growing finely. . . . Nat Pratt and Brother are busily engaged in arranging the minerals recently presented to the college—an undertaking of no little moment, involving much labor and expenditure of time. . . . Nothing novel or interesting in the city. With much love, my dear mother and father, to you both, and kind remembrance to all relatives, as ever,

Your affectionate son,
Charles C. Jones, Jr.

MRS. MARY JONES *to* MISS MARY SHARPE JONES[t]
Montevideo, *Monday,* March 30th, 1857

My dear Child,

Your Uncle Henry called on his return from Savannah on Friday and delivered into my charge a beautiful tea set of gilt and white china for you.

From the size of the box it must be a very complete set. I feel grateful for such a mark of affection, and hope you will acknowledge it kindly.

Your Uncle John and Aunt Jane and their noble little boys are now with us, and will leave on Wednesday. They will stop with Mr. Shackelford, and leave on Thursday. I write to inform you, that you may know where to find them. You had best call on Wednesday afternoon. . . .

I think it probable that I will come down early next week to make arrangements for the wedding. I wish your brother Charles to attend to the printing of the cards for us, and will let him know what number is requisite. Ask him to inform me what time is required for printing them.

Enclosed is one dollar. Please lay it out in candy for the little boys and hand it to them. . . . Do give our best regards to Mrs. Stiles and Kitty. I do feel most grateful for all their kindness to you. Love to your brothers, Aunts Susan and Mary and Lou. Love to Cousins Eliza and Charles and dear Laura. Kiss the baby. I do hope they will be with us on the 22nd of April. I must now close, for it is late, and all are abed but myself.

Ever, my dear child, your affectionate mother,
Mary Jones.

Mrs. Mary Jones *to* Mr. Charles C. Jones, Jr.ᵍ

Montevideo, *Thursday,* April 2nd, 1857

My dear Son,

Our time of preparation is drawing to a close, and I have so much to do to be ready for the forthcoming event that I scarcely know where to begin. My time and thoughts have been so wholly taken up otherwise for the past month that I will now have to be most diligent and to trouble my friends to help me—at least in those things that I cannot do myself.

I will thank you, my son, to have the cards printed as early as possible and in the *usual* way. I presume cards for two hundred invitations will be amply sufficient; we shall not want over a hundred and fifty. Your brother and yourself must invite whom you please of your friends. I presume two hundred will cover the whole.

It will be necessary for me to visit Savannah next week to get articles for *the entertainment* and make arrangements for the wedding. I cannot remain over two days, and think, *Providence permitting,* of coming in on Monday and bringing out the *needfuls* on Thursday by the cars. It is so fatiguing to your dear father that I expect to come alone. Aunt and family also being with us, someone must remain at home. If permitted to come on Monday, will bring the *list for invitations;* also the *items* for your sister's marriage settlement, which we wish you to draw up.

I have been to Maybank and returned today. The weather has been cold, windy, and rainy, and I feel quite stupid and tired from its effects and packing up little matters at Maybank. Tomorrow we expect to dine with your uncle at the Cottage. Your father unites with me in best love to your sister, brother, and yourself and all friends. The servants all send howdies.

Your affectionate mother,
Mary Jones.

MISS MARY JONES TAYLOR *to* MISS MARY SHARPE JONES[t]

Philadelphia, *Saturday,* April 4th, 1857

My dear Mary,

I have been waiting and hoping that something would happen by which I might decide that it was necessary for me to go to Georgia this month; but alas, all my hoping has been of no avail, so I suppose I must be content with bidding Mary Jones good-bye by letter only. Indeed, Mary, you don't know what a disappointment it is to me. But it is what we all have to expect. So never mind: you must come on and pay us a visit in Maryland. We expect to move this month, and then there will be enough to do to drown thought. If I should happen to hear of a right good opportunity, I may pack up in a hurry and take you by storm. But there is not the least danger of that.

We have been paying flying visits to our friends preparatory to our departure, and returned this morning from Florence, New Jersey, where we have two uncles. And a merrier set than that house contained yesterday I think would be really hard to find. My uncles' houses are most beautifully situated on the Delaware. They have cleared away the woods immediately around the house, but have left groups of the native trees still standing, and quantities of the rhododendron, so that in summer the place is perfectly lovely. It is about six miles above Burlington, and boats are constantly passing, so that there is plenty of life and constant facilities for reaching the city. Oh, if Winchester were only on the Delaware!

Now I must answer your inquiries. Mr. Gaul's address is No. 55 North 4th Street. Miss Dickson's: care James N. Dickson, No. 80½ Walnut Street. Maggie Wilson is living with her uncle, Dr. Wilson, Newark, New Jersey. Misses Sidney and Emily Gill are there also, and the others are still at the corner of Spruce and Juniper. They expect to move to Newark this summer. . . . I think I have now answered your queries; and hoping soon to hear from you, and wishing you all possible happiness in the path you have chosen, believe me, as ever, dear Mary,

Sincerely your friend,
Mary J. Taylor.

MR. GEORGE HELM *to* REV. C. C. JONES[t]

Helm Station, *Tuesday,* April 7th, 1857

Dear Sir,

I was very much gratified on the reception of your kind letter today, and regret exceedingly that I cannot respond *in persona.* My courts will be coming on about that time, and I am in a heavy practice for this part of the country; so you see I would be false to my clients should I follow the bent of my inclination and accept your kind invitation. You must present to Miss Mary my congratulations and warmest wishes for her happiness. I should have liked to have seen her again before she joined that *order ancient* indeed but destructive of vernal charms. I must send her the first rose that blooms as a token from Kentucky. Father is not at home, but Ma and Sister Jenny express great desire to accept your invitation, but find it impossible. They ask to present their warm congratulations.

Ma joins with me in saying that we consider you now committed, and we shall insist upon your giving us the honor of a visit in May. We will expect you certainly, and be perfectly delighted to see you. Bring the bridal couple with you on a tour; I think Kentucky's bright land will enhance the delights of the honeymoon more than any other the sun shines on. So present the bridal pair a pressing invitation from Mother and Sister, and come with them time enough to pay us a visit before the assembly meets.

I have been intending to write to you some time, and take this opportunity to ask the favor of a paper of those watermelon seed that you (and I with you) prize so highly. All the family unite in love to you and all the family. I am, as ever,

Most truly your friend,
George Helm.

Ma asks to be specially remembered to Mrs. Jones, and says she will of course expect her to come with you to Kentucky and give us the additional honor and pleasure of her company.

Mrs. SARAH A. HOWE *to* Mrs. MARY JONES[t]

Columbia, *Friday,* April 10th, 1857

My dear Friend,

Your letter of the 20th of March was duly received. I am always glad to hear from you, no matter what the occasion may be; and be assured that I feel a deep interest in whatever concerns the welfare of yourself and family.

I thank you for your timely invitation to attend the wedding of your dear daughter. Few things in this world would give me more pleasure than to witness the *union* of two young friends whom I not only esteem *but love*. Mary Sharpe has always seemed very near to me, and I can give her *my* blessing with all the feelings of a mother's heart. We are so situated that it will not be practicable for any of us to attend. Emily would be delighted to go down, but we know of no one with whom we would be willing to trust her. She received your message with her usual girlish glee, and said: "Now, Mother, when you write, be sure and give Aunty Jones a great deal of love, and tell her I *wish* I could be at Cousin Mary's wedding." Poor thing, it is difficult to keep her buoyant spirits within bounds, and it is not always easy to know how far to control her.

I am truly glad to hear of "the arrival of Master *Charles Maxwell Buttolph*," and hope he will live to comfort his grandmother and be a blessing to his parents. . . . I thank you, dear friend, for your tender sympathy with us in our severe affliction. I cannot express what I felt nor describe the state of mind I was in for several months last summer and fall. It was long before I could *feel* that *acquiescence* in the divine will which our holy religion teaches, and which is the legitimate fruit of a faith in God. I think I can say "Thy will be done" in all sincerity; and yet the thought of my poor exiled boy embitters every enjoyment and keeps me in the dust. . . . Warmest regards to my friend Dr. Jones. My best wishes to dear Mary. May she be as happy as she *can* be in this world, and *do much good!* Love to the boys, Mrs. Robarts, the girls. And believe me

Your truly attached
Sarah A. Howe.

REV. JOHN JONES *to* MRS. MARY JONES[t]

Rome, *Thursday,* April 16th, 1857

My dear Sister,

This will inform you of our safe arrival at Rome. It has been uncomfortably cold in this region, and continues. On Sabbath last I walked to church through a snowstorm and preached to more than one hundred hearers. Yesterday there was ice, and today another snowstorm which continued for two hours. As we have been so recently in the low country, ourselves and servants feel the change most sensibly. . . .

We received yesterday a pleasant letter from Dunwody, and another from Dr. Beman giving an encouraging account of our son. It is hard to realize that he will be fifteen years old in a few days.

This evening we received the invitations to the wedding to be on the 22nd inst. It is a sad thing to look at the cards and know I shall not be present on that interesting occasion. It is indeed a disappointment to me. Duty to church and family forbids my absence now and perhaps for weeks. We are daily watching for measles; we have three servants and two children to have them. I know it will be a great trial to see your dear child leave your home for another; but she will be near you, and her new relation will be, I doubt not, an increasingly happy one. It is a matter of thankfulness to see a daughter well married—that is, to one who commands our confidence. . . . Jane unites with me in much love to all.

Your affectionate brother,
John Jones.

P.S. As soon as you can write, do send us a line and tell us all about the evening of the 22nd.

Will Brother Charles attend the General Assembly?

J. J.

X

Mrs. Mary S. Mallard *to* Miss Kitty Stiles[t]

Montevideo, *Monday,* May 4th, 1857

My dear Kitty,

This is the first time since my marriage that I have taken a pen to write a letter, and I feel that you have the best claim to this. . . . I am glad you went to the party, and hope you enjoyed yourself. Doubtless it would have been a great calamity to have had "so delightful a member of the family" absent. By the way, a few days ago someone remarked to me that they were very much struck with the stylish appearance of my friend, and asked her name; for she thought she was not only stylish in her black dress but looked very prettily in her evening dress.

After you left on Friday we had a number of visitors. All of our neighbors have called, and Mr. Mallard and I have in reserve the pleasure of returning these visits. Mr. Mallard preached at Midway on Sabbath, and Mr. Buttolph supplied his pulpit in Walthourville. He thought it rather a hard case that he could not rest the first Sabbath after his marriage. . . . On last Monday we went to Dorchester to see Mr. Mallard's parents, and spent one night with them. They received me very kindly, and I had a very pleasant visit, though I did feel rather awkward for a time, as I had never been in their house before. His mother asked me some funny questions, and if you will promise not to tell, here they are. "Mary, do you know how to keep house?" I told her no. Sometime afterwards she was speaking of sewing, and asked me if I knew how to make a vest, and I said no, and moreover that I knew nothing about making gentlemen's apparel. So she did not question me further. Notwithstanding my professed ignorance, she seemed quite pleased with her new daughter-in-law. She is a remarkably pious old lady, but is almost blind, so that she is unable to read for herself, which she feels is a great privation.

On last Friday Father and Mr. Mallard went to Bryan to attend a meeting of Presbytery and stayed at Richmond. Mrs. Clay was at Strathy Hall. Mr. Mallard returned on Saturday evening, as he had to preach in Walthourville yesterday. Father remained, as he was appointed to take part in Dr. Bowman's installation. We expect him this afternoon. Mr. Mallard preached in Walthourville yesterday, and has not returned yet. I did not go with him, as the day was dark.

Father and Mother will, I think, go to the General Assembly, and I am delighted at the idea, for I know it will benefit Father very much to leave home; and indeed it will do Mother good too, for she needs rest. The assembly meets in Lexington, and Cousin James West lives only six miles from that place, so they will find it pleasant to go on more accounts than one. And then, too, I think if they go away they will be induced to visit the Virginia springs. If they go, they will leave next week, and I presume Mr. Mallard and I will go to Walthourville a few days before. And then I shall be duly installed as housekeeper, and shall have an opportunity of displaying my ignorance! Won't you come sometime and see me there? I shall be too happy to see you. And then you know the railroad stops only a mile from us, so it will be very convenient to come from Savannah.

Dr. Duke said he meant very early to pay his respects to me after I went to housekeeping, but I do not think much that he will come quite as soon as he said he would, as physicians do not have a great deal of spare time. . . . Cousin Laura and Aunt Susan are still with us, but expect soon to go to South Hampton to see Aunt Julia. The baby is a dear little fellow—very good, and grows prettier every day. Some persons say he resembles his father, but he does not seem to me to be particularly like anyone. . . . Do give much love to your mother and Sid, and to Mr. Eddie too, and write me whenever you can. With a deal of love,

Your affectionate friend,
Mary S. Mallard.

Mr. Charles C. Jones, Jr., *to* Rev. *and* Mrs. C. C. Jones[t]
Savannah, *Thursday,* May 21st, 1857
My dear Father and Mother,

You are doubtless now in the garden spot of Kentucky—with improved health, I sincerely hope, and in the enjoyment of many pleasures. I trust the journey was accomplished with ease to yourselves, and that you experienced much both in the companionship of friends and the novelty and beauty of the localities through which you have and are passing. . . . From a letter received a few days since from Uncle John, I was glad to learn that you had concluded to take a steamboat from Nashville. Travel on a boat, and on the water, is much more convenient, less fatiguing, and affords a finer opportunity for enjoyment of the scenery than the close, confined, and dusty rides on railroad cars, with but confused glimpses of passing objects. Whenever I have a choice, my preference for many reasons is the boat.

Do you feel, Father, much fatigued by the travel? And do you mark any tendency to improvement as yet? The season for real improvement will be, however, when you have rested and are free from undue exercise and confinement—or, as the Siamese say, "when you can find a green spot under a shady tree, where you can recline in quiet, without heat and without motion." Among the many delegates to the General Assembly, convened as they will be at Lexington from all parts of our country, it will be pleasant, after an interval of several (and perhaps many) years, to meet with friends and acquaintances—men of intelligence, position, and talent—and renew agreeable acquaintances formed in bygone days. I hope, Mother, that among the ladies of "the dark and bloody ground"—forbidding though the name may be—you will find congenial spirits. The Louisville Hotel is, I understand, a better hotel than the Galt House, although when in Louisville I tarried at the latter house. The visit to Helm Station must be paid if it does not seriously interfere with other arrangements. They will all welcome you there.

There is very little of interest with us in this city. Yesterday, last night, and this morning the temperature was unseasonably cold. The degree of cold, however, was not sufficient to injure the crops. Until the comet be overpassed, some wiseheads say, we will be subjected to these continued changes. . . . The Doctor quite well, and engaged from morning till night in the pursuit of his professional studies. He is making a beautiful collection of the reptiles of this section of our state, and has many little boys in his employ who daily search the neighboring woods and ponds, and not infrequently invade even the sacred confines of the Old Burial Ground, in order to secure new specimens.

Hoping, my dear parents, that every blessing will attend you, with much love, in which the Doctor unites, I am, as ever,

Your affectionate son,
Charles C. Jones, Jr.

Mrs. Mary Jones *to* Mrs. Mary S. Mallard[t]
Broadway Hotel, Lexington, Kentucky, *Friday,* May 22nd, 1857
My dear Daughter,

Through the goodness and mercy of God you will perceive that we have reached our place of destination. I feel it a cause for very special gratitude that your dear father has been preserved amidst the fatigues of our long journey. Could I have in any degree foreseen how much exhausted he would have been, I would never have consented to his coming on to the assembly, but have gone immediately to the Virginia springs. However, now that he has been spared to reach here, I think he is much better today, and I can see already the reviving influence of meeting "brethren beloved." We arrived here about seven o'clock last evening; this morning he has taken his breakfast and is off for the assembly. I preferred to remain and send some letters home.

On Wednesday we left Savannah and ran entirely through to Marietta. Your Uncle John came from Rome and was there to welcome us in the cars, with Joe and a carriage to take us up to Aunt's, where we found them all awaiting our arrival, and a nice cup of hot tea to cheer our weary bodies. After a sweet night's rest we left with your uncle the next morning, arriving at Rome to dinner. Sister Jane and the dear little boys were all ready to welcome us. I said to Johnnie: "Were you looking out for Papa?" He replied: "No, I was looking for Uncle Charles, and I knew him at first sight." (These are his exact words.) Two more lovely boys I never saw, and very good children. Rome is a beautiful spot. But I will not have time for any descriptions in this letter.

We arrived at Chattanooga before sunset, and whilst taking our tea, whom should we discover at our right hand but our old friend of seminary memory, Mr. Foster! He has devoted himself to your father, and we have had no charge of our baggage since. He relieves us of all care of that; also in procuring tickets and making arrangements from place to place. I feel under great obligations to him. Also to a Mr. Curry, delegate from the Florida Presbytery. He is a large, stout man, and your father leans upon him for support whenever it is necessary. You have no conception, my dear child, how feeble your dear father is. I am convinced if ever he is to be permanently benefited, the effort must now be made; and if he improves, our absence from home may be protracted for several months. His life and health are beyond every other consideration to me.

Cousin James and Cousin Belle West have just called. They appear delighted to see us, and say all they have—time, carriage and horses, home, and all—are at our disposal, and we must stay with them. But I fear it will be too far for us; we must wait until the assembly adjourns and then visit them. Belle has grown to be a splendid-looking woman; and as some lady remarked in the parlor, they are considered here a model couple. They seem so much disappointed at not seeing you; thought Robert and yourself would surely come on and make a bridal visit at this time.

I wish indeed, my dear child, that you were both with us. It is a very full assembly. Dr. Van Rensselaer has been elected moderator, and New Orleans the next place of meeting. Many of the great and good men of our church are here. I have wished for you a hundred times to enjoy all that I am enjoying, but I must think of you now as happy and trying to promote happiness in a new sphere. It was very sad to me to leave you as I did—so hurriedly. I had no time to think of or prepare many little comforts which I intended for you.

I hope you did not leave anything in the pantry of a perishable nature. I scarcely know what there was myself. If you have time, do ride down and take whatever you wish. And if you need the butter, tell Patience to send it to you; if not, she must use the rock salt and put it carefully away in the tub; and after the weather becomes warm she must melt it in a bucket in hot water and put it down in jars. That is, if we do not return and you have no use for it. I hope you get it regularly from Arcadia every other week.

I would be glad if you could ride down and see after little matters for me before it gets too warm. When Patience gets through house-cleaning, etc., with Flora, I want her to go to Arcadia and pick all the geese carefully (also those at Montevideo) and have the feathers put into bags and sunned regularly. We want Gilbert to shear the sheep at both places now at once, and then Patience and Flora must pick and wash the wool until it is free from all grease or smell of any kind, and then have it all carded up ready to be made into mattresses. They must card in the washroom after having it well cleaned out, and keep the carded wool in the locked part where it will be free from dust. Patience and Flora must take care of everything about the house and watch that the carpets and blankets are not injured by moths. And when Niger goes to the Island, they must take care of the poultry. Do charge them about the cats and Jet. If they are at any loss for work, they must help in the gardens. Tell Flora she must weed around all the flowers in the garden; I am afraid to trust the old man. If the japonicas look badly, have them covered from the sun. Cato can find employment for Miley and Kate. Please, my darling, tell the servants whatever you may see to be done. The little basket of work you can have done at your leisure, and not at all if Lucy is busy. Please put up the piece of shirting for me until I come; it is for use in another way. Tell all the servants howdy for us. I hope you have a *comfortable house* for your servant Lucy. You must not forget her welfare, for she is an excellent woman, and I think will be faithful to you. Tell Kate I hope to hear good accounts of her. . . .

We are meeting acquaintances constantly. Everyone looks happy and interested in the assembly. I wish every moment for Robert and yourself. He would be much gratified to make the acquaintance of the many truly good and great men assembled here. . . . I must now close. Father joins me in best love to you both. Howdy for Lucy and Kate. . . . In haste and confusion,

Ever your own affectionate mother,
Mary Jones.

Mrs. Mary Jones *to* Messrs. Charles C. Jones, Jr., *and* Joseph Jones[g]
Lexington, *Monday,* May 25th, 1857

My dear Sons,

Through the goodness and mercy of God we were permitted to reach this place last Thursday between six and seven o'clock. The journey has been one of great anxiety to me, for at times your dear father has been greatly exhausted by the fatigue. Had we known how little strength he really had, we should have declined the undertaking of attending the assembly and gone directly to the Virginia springs. I am more and more convinced that if ever he is to be benefited by a change of climate and removal from all care, it must be done at once.

At Chattanooga we met with our old friend *Mr. Foster* of seminary memory, coming on as a commissioner from his presbytery in Alabama. He has devoted himself to your father, taking care of the baggage, obtaining tickets, and making all arrangements as we would change boats or cars. A relative could not have been kinder or more considerate of our comfort, and I feel very gratefully to him. We had also the kind assistance, whenever it was necessary, of Mr. Curry from the Presbytery of Florida. He is a large, strong man; your father would lean upon his arm. And there were occasions when we had to move hurriedly; once particularly in the night we had to change from the *Alida* on the Cumberland River to the *Woodford*, a splendid New Orleans steamer, on the Ohio. We have received kindness and attention from everyone.

On Friday your father handed in his commission and took his seat in the assembly, which is said to be one of the largest that has ever been convened. I did not attend that day. Stayed at the hotel to write your sister, expecting also to write you both, but company prevented. Cousin James West and his wife called, and would scarcely take a denial that we should go immediately home with them. But on account of the distance at which he lives we have concluded to remain here for the present and visit him afterwards. We are really proud to see the position he and his family occupy in this community. He is universally respected. After he had left the parlor a stranger turned to me and said: "Is that Mr. James West? He is a model man here, and he and his wife are considered a *model couple*."

On Saturday we had the pleasure and honor of an introduction to our Vice-President, Mr. Breckinridge, who spoke of Cousin James as a personal friend and man of highest-toned honor and integrity. We were very much pleased with Mr. Breckinridge's appearance and urbanity of manners. He paid me the compliment of saying that Mrs. Breckinridge would certainly call and make my acquaintance.

I wish it were so, my dear sons, that you could be with us and form the acquaintance of the many, many good and great men of our church now assembled here. The more I see of the order, intelligence, and piety of the Presbyterian Church the more confirmed do I feel in my faith and attachment to it. Oh, that you both, my dear sons, were numbered with the professed disciples of the Lord Jesus Christ! To feel that your influence in life is not yet upon the side of truth and godliness is very heartrending to us. How long shall it be thus?

Our old friend and teacher Mr. Dubuar is here, and inquired particularly after you both. Mr. Baker is also here, and told me Mrs. Pratt had written him that *Nat* was studying German and French to prepare himself for the professorship at Athens. Your pamphlet was handed to Dr. Eve in Nashville, and I want to give some away here. Your father is at the assembly, but left best love for you both.

> Ever your affectionate mother,
> Mary Jones.

Will write you of our intended movements soon.

REV. JOHN JONES *to* REV. *and* MRS. C. C. JONES[t]

> Rome, *Monday,* June 1st, 1857

My dear Brother and Sister,

We have been looking every day for a line from you, that we might be assured of your safe progress and arrival at Lexington. The reports of the assembly did not reach us until last Friday, and then for the first time we knew that you had a prosperous journey.

Your visit to us was most refreshing, and I returned from Kingston jack-in-the-doldrums. Our dear little boys remember you and talk of you and say it is time for you to come back again. And the dear little hearts are the echoes of our own. We shall be truly happy to see you here in our cottage and have you make it your summer home. Don't forget the installation on the second Sabbath of July.

And now a word about Joseph. I received a letter from him today in answer to one I wrote just after you left to inform himself and Charles of your progress, etc. He and Charles are well. And I have today a letter from Mr. W. L. Mitchell of Athens, in answer to one I wrote him about the professorship of natural science. He says that there will be an announcement in the papers of the vacant professorship. He mentions a letter just received from Henry, and was expecting from Henry's letter a copy of the Smithsonian publication, which I had also mentioned to him and would have sent him; but he has no doubt received it before this. He says that N. A. Pratt, Jr., will be a candidate for the same chair, and then adds in the next sentence: "Be sure and urge Dr. Jones, your nephew, to be at commencement and form as many acquaintances among the trustees as he can." Such is the substance of the letter: friendly, without pledge or committal, on the whole favorable, I think. Charles Colcock wrote me on the subject some days since; I will send Mr. Mitchell's letter to him and Joseph. I will suggest that Charles may accomplish something through Major Porter, who can move through his nephew, young Hull, and through him upon his father, Asbury Hull, a very influential trustee, and secretary of the college for thirty years. If Judge Law will be in Athens at commencement, he would be the man to introduce Joseph. And if I can help him personally, I will, D.V., meet him in Athens at or a little before commencement and do my best for him. I shall in all probability have to go to the low country in this month on business of the Sidon estate, and will see Joseph personally.

Jane and the little boys unite with me in much—yea, very much—love to you both.

Your affectionate brother,
John Jones.

Please give our affectionate remembrance to Cousin James West, wife, and children. I thank you for the journal of the assembly.

Rev. C. C. Jones *to* Mrs. Susan M. Cumming[t]
Russell's Cave, Kentucky, Thursday, June 4th, 1857

My dear Sister,

The General Assembly adjourned on Monday evening the 1st inst. after a harmonious and excellent session of ten days—the largest perhaps we have ever had. The people of Lexington were hospitable without limit, and left nothing undone that might contribute to the comfort and success of the assembly. The impression has been *good*. A report of the proceedings I ordered sent to my nephew daily, and hope he has regularly received the paper.

We came *here* to Cousin James N. West's Tuesday afternoon, where we now are and hope to remain until Monday or Tuesday next; then, God willing, go and pay Governor Helm and family a visit at Elizabethtown; and then go on to Cincinnati and visit our old friend Dr. John S. Law, who has written us a polite invitation so to do; and afterwards move on to the springs in Virginia. . . . Cousin James has a beautiful place. The country around Lexington is uncommonly fine and beautiful—the boast of the Kentuckians. . . . We are now, measuring the way we came, 1265 miles from Montevideo. The journey fatigued me *greatly;* the constant attendance on the assembly added somewhat to it. . . . My dear wife is quite well, and has enjoyed her trip very much, which has given me great pleasure. . . . We have received three letters from home—one from Charles Colcock and two from Daughter.

Do say to my dear nephew that I will be truly obliged if he will give an eye to our affairs at Maybank for me for the present. I failed in getting someone to superintend until I should return. Andrew must *keep his plow moving,* and thin his cotton as soon as possible, and keep the grass down. His corn, I suppose, is all thinned out, and the earth brushed around it, and the Baden corn manured. Have his early peas hauled up so soon as they are ready to draw out, and remember to put in his cornfield peas the last of this month: dark nights in June. Little Andrew must plow up the old field, as he did for early peas, *for close peas*—plant all he can of these; and have his *slip ground plowed* and *ready in time* to plant slips so soon as he has vines; and *plant every chance the rain gives him.*

I know my nephew is no planter. He can read this to Andrew and tell him I shall have to depend upon him mainly to carry on his work till I get back, God willing. I did not have an opportunity of seeing Audley to inquire if he could take charge of Maybank till I should return. Will you see him and ask him if he will do so for me *as a business matter,* for which I will expect him to make a regular charge? I would be very glad if he would do so.

Give our love to him and to our dear friend Mrs. King and Mrs. Wells and to all the children. . . . Our love to our dear nephew and niece; kiss Charlie for us. . . . Our love to Brother; will write him soon. . . . Love to Henry and Abby if you see them. Remember our dear child at Walthourville, and Robert. Tell Andrew and all the people at Maybank and Montevideo and Arcadia howdy for us. Mary sends much love to you. . . . It is doubtful if we go to Governor Helm's; it is a hundred and thirty-five miles from here. Direct to us *care of Colonel John Strother, Sir John's Run, Berkeley Springs, Virginia.* The Lord be with and bless you, my dear sister!

Your ever affectionate brother,
C. C. Jones.

Rev. C. C. Jones *to* Messrs. Charles C. Jones, Jr., *and* Joseph Jones[g]

Russell's Cave, *Monday,* June 8th, 1857

My dear Sons,

Mother wrote you week before last from Lexington. I have been so much occupied and withal so weary that this is but my second letter home: the first a few days since to your Aunt Susan. We are now, measuring railroad and river, 1265 miles from Montevideo, and the cost, including both of us (fare and stoppages), $87.20. Mother enjoyed the travel very much. The scenery ever varying and interesting; that on the Chattanooga & Nashville Road through the mountains and across the Tennessee River uncommonly fine and imposing.

That we might be near the place of meeting of the General Assembly, and not put Cousin James West to the trouble of sending us in daily a distance of six miles, we put up at the Broadway Hotel, kept by a large landlord named Didlake. A number of commissioners to the General Assembly, forming for us a most agreeable society, put up there also. I attended the morning and afternoon sessions of the General Assembly, and went out to the evening sermons and meetings but once, and that was to hear the sermon on behalf of the Board of Domestic Missions. All the sermons appointed to be preached before the assembly were *very long!* It is the fullest assembly we have ever had: some 275 or 280 commissioners, gathered from the Atlantic to the Pacific and from the Gulf of Mexico to the lakes, from the Indian tribes on the West and from India and China. For learning, talent, dignity, and piety a body of men unsurpassed by any in our land and perhaps by any in any other land. The utmost harmony and good feeling prevailed throughout. Our discussions were at times animated and interesting, and all the business of the church was dispatched successfully. . . . The question of slavery came up in no way, shape, or form. Our correspondence with all the foreign bodies of Congregationalists North was discontinued with but one dissenting voice. The assembly felt it was time to shut out these self-appointed reprovers and disturbers of the peace.

I subscribed for the daily report of our proceedings and directed them mailed to you from Louisville, and hope you received them regularly. Sent you also a roll of the assembly. I did not take an active part in the deliberations of the assembly or its business beyond the conduct of the business committed to me as chairman of the standing committee on the Board of Missions, for I was worn down and too weary. The brethren received me with great cordiality and treated me with marked respect. I met and renewed many old friends and friendships. It is a sort of jubilee in our church. Believing that the assembly would not close its sessions until Tuesday morning June 2nd, I did not attend the session Monday night. The body then finished its business and dissolved, and I missed what I specially desired to participate in—the solemn and affecting close. It is always an hour of deep impression and of many tears.

The citizens of Lexington and vicinity were unbounded in their hospitality and attentions, and left nothing to be desired. They paid the bills of all commissioners and *their wives* who put up at the hotels—wholly unexpected on their part; and the day after the assembly dissolved, carriages were put at the disposal of the members to ride around and see the country and its curiosities. I heard a gentleman incidentally say that the cost of the assembly which the citizens assumed was a thousand dollars. They say: "This is old Kentucky." The impression made by the assembly has been most excellent. Our Northern and Western commissioners were specially pleased with this trip into a slave state.

Your old teacher Mr. Dubuar ate at the hotel, and was with us every day. He has grown older, and was as glad to see us as we were to see him. He made every inquiry after his old pupils, and expressed great pleasure at hearing from you, and desired to be remembered affectionately to you all. He has a wife and five children, and is well located at Northville, Michigan. Mr. G. Foster was also with us a great deal, and sent love to you.

Tuesday afternoon June 2nd Cousin James West came into Lexington and brought us out to this place—his rich, extensive, and beautiful Kentucky farm and home. He has been confined to his house nearly all the time since we have been here by indisposition. The physician has been in attendance, and he is much better today, and at no time dangerously sick. Hopes to be about in a few days. He has an admirable wife and four fine children, and is as well situated as most mortals are in this world.

The situation itself is beautiful, and lies in the beautiful country around Lexington, which is considered the pride and garden spot of Kentucky. I have seen in the United States in *my* travels, on the whole, no country superior to it. The foundation is cavernous limestone, I believe, which presents a rolling country without being broken. The stone crops out occasionally on the surface, and shows itself in cuts in the roads or on broken hillsides along the streams. The swelling hills are perfectly green, with the celebrated and wonderful *"blue grass"* and with crops of grain. The "wooded land" is much thinned out by the use of years, and all the fallen limbs and trunks are piled up or removed. Not a sprig of underbrush of any kind appears. The surface is entirely covered with the blue grass, upon which the finest stock of every kind is luxuriating, and what they thus term their "wooded land" resembles a gentleman's park kept in perfect order. These grounds are all pastured. In vain you look for dense forests and tangled thickets. This peculiarity strikes the eye of the stranger immediately. Wheat, hemp, rye, oats, and corn are the chief productions; the first two the principal market and cash crops.

It is, as you well know, a land for stock-raising: horses, mules, and cattle. Much money is made in this way—nay, a great deal; it is a regular business. The stock of cattle in this region is the short-horn Durham. No finer in the United States. Mr. Hughes, Cousin James's father-in-law, showed us a *male calf three years old* on Saturday—the finest specimen of the ox race I ever saw. He weighed him for our satisfaction, and he weighed *2195 pounds on the foot.* This is an example.

A Mr. Alexander, who lives between Lexington and Frankfort, a distinguished stock-raiser, invited the members of the General Assembly to visit his farm last Wednesday and see his stock of cattle and witness the annual sale which he has. He is a man of great wealth—a subject of Her Majesty Queen Victoria. Kentucky-born; however, of Scotch descent. Large estate in Kentucky; and his estates in Scotland yield him, *they say,* some $80,000 or $100,000 annually. Cousin James and I went. A car chartered by Mr. A. for the members of the General Assembly, a free ticket, carriages in waiting at the railroad to take them to his farm, and an entertainment for the thousand persons on the ground—all done after the manner of a prince. His cows and horses beyond anything in the United States. Never saw such. His sales amounted to between $18,000 and $20,000. Calves sold from $300 to over $700 apiece, and cows from over $300 down to $100, etc., etc. Had a fine view of the Kentucky yeomanry: bronzed, healthy, sober, calm, self-possessed, self-reliant, respectful, frank, sociable, well-dressed, working, businesslike men. Mr. Alexander exhibited his horse "Lexington," for which he gave $15,000, and his imported horse "Scythian," for which he gave $7,000. These are some of the things we have seen. Cousin James and I were late going to the feast, and the tables were cleared. We succeeded in securing a part of a leg of roasted mutton, and one of my brethren shared a small piece of bread with us. We came home fagged out.

Cousin James's friends have been very kind in calling to see us. Mother and I have made the acquaintance of our *Vice-President and lady.* Mrs. Breckinridge called to see Mother, and she returned Mrs. B.'s call. He is a fine-looking man, universally esteemed and respected, deemed and taken to be a son of fortune, destined to rise. He resides in Lexington, a little out of town: a handsome cottage residence.

The medical college in Lexington has a very capital and large brick building, but the school has dwindled down to about twenty students. Louisville first, and Nashville next, have pretty nearly finished it. Lexington has about six thousand white inhabitants; does considerable business; lies in a valley, the parallel ridges around with handsome residences that melt away into the adjacent beautiful country. Excellent churches. We have not yet visited Ashland.

Yesterday we went to *Horeb Church:* three miles; an ancient country church; Cousin James an elder in it; and I enjoyed the privilege of preaching to an excellent congregation.

Tomorrow, God willing, we hope to leave for Cincinnati to pay Dr. John S. Law a visit, who has kindly invited us to do so. The distance is so great to Governor Helm's (a hundred and forty miles) and the fatigue of getting there so great, we have concluded not to go there; and I wrote George to that effect last week. We much regret it, but think it prudent not to go. We will go a hundred and forty miles out of our way. We intended to take the stage at Nashville and stop as we came along, but I was from fatigue obliged to take the boat.

Direct to us at *Berkeley Springs, Sir John's Run, on Baltimore & Ohio Railroad, care of Colonel John Strother.* We hope to stop there a short time before going to the Hot Springs.

Mother is hearty and is getting fleshy. She is sitting opposite me writing your Uncle Henry, and she has a fine double chin, rosy complexion, and full face. She sends much love to you both. Write us all the news about yourselves and friends and home. Our kind regards to Major and Mrs. Porter and Cousin Charles West and family. Our kind relatives here send much love.

When you have read this letter please send it out to your dear sister and Robert. Mother has written them twice, and I will write them next. . . . If Mr. Anderson has sold our cotton, would be glad to receive the account sale of it. And at any rate do enclose me the *sale of all the Arcadia cotton,* that I may close the year's account and render in my own. The Lord be with and bless you, my ever dear sons, and my ever dear daughter and son!

Your affectionate father,
C. C. Jones.

Mrs. Mary S. Mallard *to* Miss Mary Jones Taylor[t]

Walthourville, *Thursday,* June 11th, 1857

My dear Mary,

My eyes were quite refreshed by the sight of your well-known and always welcome hand, though it did look rather queerly directed—to Mrs. Mary S. Mallard instead of Jones—which last I tell Mr. Mallard is decidedly the prettiest when written.

We all regretted exceedingly your not being able to come to my wedding. Matilda Harden and my friend Kitty Stiles were my only attendants. My dear father performed the ceremony; Brother Charlie and Rev. Mr. Bowman were groomsmen; and the company generally seemed to think we were a pretty respectable-looking party. Three weeks after my marriage Father and Mother left for the General Assembly; and as soon as they left we commenced preparations for our departure, and a day or two after came to this place, which is situated about twelve miles from my parents' winter home and about twenty-six from their summer retreat. But our roads are so good that even this distance is not as long as it would be in some sections of the country. I can assure you that I rejoiced greatly at Father's and Mother's leaving before we did, for that made it a little less like leaving home.

Mary, can you realize that I am a minister's wife, and am actually keeping house and trying to feel the importance of my station? Sometimes when I think of it I sit down and laugh heartily! Mr. Mallard generally spends his evenings with me and reads aloud, which makes the time pass very pleasantly. How I should like to see you in my own house! And I flatter myself you would enjoy a visit—especially at this time, as I am quite a novice in the housekeeping art, though Mr. M. declares we are getting on swimmingly, and that I know all about it; and as long as I can keep him convinced of this fact, I shall be quite satisfied. Imagine me standing, receipt book in hand, giving directions to one of the colored society, who says she has never cooked for "white folks" and knows nothing about it! To do her justice, however, she is doing very well.

I have been wishing for some weeks past to write you, but knew not where to direct, and was quite rejoiced to learn your whereabouts from your letter. I cannot bear the idea of your living anywhere except in Philadelphia; I feel as though one of my strongest ties to that place had been broken. . . . I hope by this time all of your family have moved down, and I doubt not you are having a pleasant time. . . . I should like to see you very much, and often wonder if you have changed since I last saw you. I think *I* have somewhat: I am thinner and imagine I look a few years older. I think we will have to exchange likenesses again. . . . Tell Sarah Ann I ask her if it is true she is engaged to be married, or only flirting. How did Miss Mary Gill get her information in regard to my residence near Richmond, Virginia? I was quite amused; do inform her I am still in Liberty County, Georgia. Has she given up the school yet?

The Savannah, Albany & Gulf Railroad, now being made, passes within two miles of this village, so it will be quite convenient for you to make me a visit, which I hope you will be able to do at some future time. Do write soon and direct to the care of Rev. R. Q. Mallard, Walthourville, Liberty County, Georgia. Give love to your mother and Sarah Ann. Mr. Mallard is sitting by me and says: "Give my love to Miss Taylor."

Your affectionate friend,
Mary S. Mallard.

REV. C. C. JONES *to* REV. *and* MRS. R. Q. MALLARD[t]

Cincinnati, Ohio, *Friday,* June 12th, 1857

My very dear Son and Daughter,

We received your letter in Lexington, from which place your mother wrote you. I will not say anything more of the assembly, as I directed the daily report to be forwarded to you, and wrote a long letter to your brothers in Savannah and requested them to send it out to you also, as it was meant for you all.

Cousin James West was sick all the time we were at his house, which was the only drawback to the pleasure of our visit. We left his house on Tuesday the 9th in his carriage, William driving us. We took a note of introduction from Cousin James to Mr. James B. Clay, who now resides at Ashland, the celebrated home of his father, Henry Clay. Mother wished to see the place and the house. It is about a mile or so out of Lexington. We drove up to the door. The house is entirely newly built of brick and is a fine mansion. The old one was taken down, and it is said the old lumber was sold by J. B. Clay to make snuffboxes, walking canes, etc., etc., as memorials of the illustrious dead! William rang, and our card was taken in by the servant-boy that came to the door. Very soon a square-built fat Irish woman with great big naked arms, just from the kitchen or the washtub, in complete working trim, came down the steps and said: "*Meester* Clay is gone away from home, and *Misthress* Clay is *vary* unwell and begs you will *plase* excuse her." We laughed outright. This was the end of our visit to see Ashland, and we drove off as wise as we went. Report says the dignitaries at Ashland are not very complaisant to visitors in common. They have a great many, and it must be a sore tax to receive them all. And to crown all, James B. Clay, heir of *Henry Clay,* is now running on *the Democratic ticket* in his district for Congress!

Mother insisted upon my going to the new cemetery. We drove through the grounds, and we were amply repaid. They are beautiful. The "blue grass" carpeted the whole. The snowy monuments of every size and variety, many of exceeding taste and costliness, shot up from this green ground, which put them in perfect relief. The clear sun brightened the hills and the valley and the dell, and dappled the green with the shade of the many beautiful trees with which both the hand of nature and of art had adorned this city of the dead. We left the carriage and walked to the grave of Henry Clay's mother. Her monument, erected by him, stands not over but nearby her grave, which is a green mound, shaped coffin-fashion. Within the plot is another grave of the same form; the mower had just shorn it smooth. It was of a bright mellow green. To be certain, we said to him: "And whose grave is this?" He answered: "That is Mr. Clay himself: that is his grave." Stretched in darkness and decay beneath this little mound of earth reposed the remains of that great man. We were disposed to silence and to reflection. To this all flesh must come at last. And where now is that spirit? And what of the world to him? "The mighty forest waves on, reckless that a leaf has fallen." On the slope of the hill, not fifty yards off, some twenty workmen were cutting stone and laying the foundations for a monument to his memory, which is to be some forty feet high. The structure was just level with the ground, and the opening was made in the center, where that body was to be put which lay at our feet. The monument is erected by the State of Kentucky. Webster in Massachusetts, Calhoun in South Carolina, and Clay in Kentucky: "the first three."

Mother pointed out a monument of singular character and effect. A smooth pole of marble fifteen feet high or more rose from a pedestal, and an entwining serpent was sculptured, its head shooting along the pole and pointing upward near the top. There it stood adhering to the pole, high up. What can be the meaning of it? Look at the inscription below: "And as Moses lifted up the serpent in the wilderness, even so must the Son of Man be lifted up: That whosoever believeth in Him should not perish, but have eternal life" (John 3:14-15). And whose monument is it? Look around. It seems to be the monument for a minister and his family—a Christian family. The simple inscription and testimonial for them is: *"These all died in the faith."* The conception was singular, the impression tender and impressive.

We dined at our old quarters, the Broadway Hotel, took the cars on the Lexington & Covington Road, which runs most of the way along the banks of the Licking River, and reached Covington, opposite Cincinnati, at 7 P.M. We took the omnibus and drove down into the ferry steamboat, with three or four more, and retaining our seats drove out on the other side. Dr. and Mrs. Law were expecting us, and gave us a genuine Southern greeting. The doctor and his boys laid hold of our baggage, and we were soon in our room, three stories up (alas, for my legs), preparing for tea. (This is an old friend whom you have never seen, but of whom you have, my dear daughter, heard us frequently speak. I mentioned at table today that I was writing you both, and Dr. and Mrs. Law begged me to present their kind regards to you, although they have never had the pleasure of knowing you.)

This is our third day here. Mother and Mrs. Law have been out shopping and seeing the great city of the West, as it once was. Mother is very busy today with a dressmaker downstairs, making up a beautiful black poplin dress. She came up into our room a short time since, and says she: "Speak quick—I have no time to stay." And she left in two seconds.

You recollect Laura said Mother could go into no store in Philadelphia without the people consulting her on some important matter or telling her some special occurrence. Her fortune attends her here. She went out to buy something the dressmaker needed, and after the merchant-woman served her, she related the following affecting story. A pious mother of several children dependent upon her for support, yesterday feeling unwell, took what she supposed was a dose of salts, and in fifteen minutes was dead! Two of her female friends and members of the same church came in the evening to sit up with the corpse and prepare all for the burial today. Having occasion to go into a chamber, the floor gave way; one sprang forward and escaped, the other fell through. The alarm was given, and not until three o'clock this morning was the body of the unfortunate woman recovered. She was taken up out of twenty feet of water *dead!* The minister was sent for, and he broke the sad intelligence to her old mother, and she has not spoken since! How wonderful are the dealings of God with His people! How are we perpetually reminded to live in readiness for death! It is a blessed state to be delivered from the fear of death through faith in our Divine Redeemer and to be always prepared for His coming.

I preached last Sunday at Horeb Church, Cousin James West's church, and was glad to do so.

You must read my letter to your Uncle William, and read this to him and to your Uncle Henry. . . . Mother says I must leave some space for a line from her. We send much love to you both; and it makes us happy to hear that you are happy and doing well. *Robert, be tender to my precious child, and love her, and take care of her.* God bless and keep you both unto His Heavenly Kingdom!

From your ever affectionate father,
C. C. Jones.

Love to all relatives and friends, and howdy for all the servants at all the places. Write to the Hot Springs, Virginia.

Monday, June 15th, 1857. I left this page open for your mother to fill up, but she has been so much occupied that she has not found time to do so, and now sends enclosed a half-sheet written in pencil. We are, through divine favor, well today, and have made our arrangements to leave here in a steamboat for Charleston, Virginia, on the Kanawha River, and thence by stage to the *Hot Springs.* We leave, D.V., tomorrow.

P.S. Has our friend Mr. Thomas W. Fleming handed you the marriage settlement? I begged him to have it recorded for me, and in my absence to hand it to you. You need not inquire about it.

Mrs. Mary Jones *to* Mrs. Mary S. Mallard[t]

Cincinnati, *Friday,* June 12th, 1857

My darling Daughter,

The rising sun is just gilding the hilltops that environ this great city; the bell of the cathedral is calling the faithful to morning devotions; and the hum of the multitude, as they awake to the life and duties of another day, rises up like the sound of many waters. I expect, as we have been every day, that I shall have no time on this ever dear and memorable one to me even so much as to send you a letter, for Dr. Law has engaged a hack to take us everywhere both in and without the city. My earliest thoughts are of you, my precious child, on your birthday; and I have been trying to commend you for your every interest and relation before our Father's throne. May He whose salvation cannot fail, "having loved you, love you unto the end," and grant you the daily constant guidance and comfort of His Blessed Holy Spirit, and make you faithful to all things, that you may live to the praise and glory of His great name! My heart goes out in tenderest love to you.

But I must close. God bless you, my child! With much love to dear Robert,
Ever your affectionate mother,
Mary Jones.

Mr. Audley King *to* Rev. C. C. Jones[t]

Riceboro, *Thursday,* June 18th, 1857

Dear Uncle,

For some time past I've thought to write Aunt and yourself and give the outline of our circle (tangent, cotangent, etc.), but an uncertainty in relation to your address has been *the* obstacle. I was glad by last mail to see a letter to Aunt Susan in your hand, and quite pleased to peruse its pages.

I am glad that I can serve you in any way, and that you've called upon me to do so, which I shall endeavor to do. I saw Andrew this morning; took an account of his force, crop, etc. Servants pretty well. Some cotton very good; parts that are shaded and some veins of lighter land not so good. Corn has suffered for want of rain, which has been much needed, but since 11 A.M. to 8 P.M. it has fallen gently, with prospect of continuing through the night. Your cattle at Maybank look well. In my next, after a closer view, I shall probably give further particulars.

Some two weeks since I spent a night and Sabbath following with your good children at Walthourville, and real pleasure it was. They are nicely located: an airy spacious lot, surrounded by the kindest neighbors; and Mr. Mallard much beloved and his labors esteemed by our good friends under his care. Oh, he is a most excellent man. I listened with pleasure to his morning sermon, a continued address on family government. . . . I asked Cousin Mary if there had not been a consultation on some points; Mr. Mallard laughingly said he believed they had discussed some points.

A few days after, they came to the Island, arriving in the afternoon previous to Mother and Sister's leaving for Savannah on their way North; and as I saw them to the station, I lost sight of your children, being with them but a few moments. Sister Mary had been quite sick, and suffered so much that on her illbed she consented to try a change of scene and air. So accordingly dear Mother accompanied her to New York in the steamer *Florida* on Saturday last (13th inst.). I saw them safely off that morn, and we hope soon to learn of their safe arrival. Dear Mother will return, Providence permitting, in a week or two; Sister will tarry until fall. She improved very much before she left Savannah, and there said she must cease speaking of going on for her health, everyone saying how well she looked. Hers is a wonderful constitution to have borne all it has. Faith in an all-wise Providence is one main support: I believe she is a true child of God. To bear pain as she does, and speak about subjects tearing my heartstrings with such composure as she does, argues a higher support than human.

We trust that after the fatigue of travel and the duties of the assembly you will recover general composure and receive much benefit from the springs and change of air. I do not know where the Berkeley Springs are, but almost any spot in the Old Dominion bears a charm sufficient at all events to restore an ex-Virginian. How proud they are of their state! I presume the recent Jamestown celebration has awakened sparks of patriotism perhaps long since grown dim. I see G. W. P. Custis' name among the number.

Our household arrangements are so enfeebled by our dear mother's and sister's absence and Isabel's spending the nights with Aunt that we feel broken up, and shall be glad to see our head return. How much depends on *one!* May our dear mother's useful life and example be long spared to us! All are pretty well; and with our united love to Aunt and yourself, I am

Very truly,

J. A. M. King.

Mrs. Susan M. Cumming *to* Rev. *and* Mrs. C. C. Jones[t]

Point Maxwell, *Friday,* June 19th, 1857

My dear Brother and Sister,

You can scarcely imagine the pleasure your letters gave us in our lonely home now that you, Sister Mary and Mary and Julia and Mary Wells are all gone. Mr. Buttolph wrote you to Lexington, but I thought that I would postpone until hearing where you actually were. When Sister Mary's letter reached us the assembly had adjourned, and then I did not know where to direct; but your welcome letter leaves me without excuse. Sister Mary's letter gave us the first intelligence we had of you, and we were grieved to hear you suffered so much from the fatigue of the journey; but it did not seem so, for the papers stated that you were on the Committee for Domestic Missions and made "a most thrilling appeal" to the churches. . . . We are very glad to hear that you have decided to go to the Virginia springs. You must give them a fair trial—that is, stay long enough to test their virtues. And do not get discouraged too soon. Your return, you say, will depend on your improvement; although we miss you every day, we hope you will remain away at least until cool weather. It would not be prudent to return after this.

Laura and Mr. Buttolph have ridden very often to Maybank, and Mr. Buttolph has attended to the wants of the people. They have all continued well, and attending to their work. Audley says he will give his attention to your business there with pleasure, and is glad he has it in his power to serve you. He took your address and will write to you.

Mary and Mr. Mallard were with us a day and night on the 10th, the anniversary of the wedding. We talked much of you and Sister Mary. Mary looks better, and says she feels better. And they both were very cheerful and happy; said their horse could hardly be persuaded to pass Maybank road. Mary says she has experienced a great deal of kindness and attention at Walthourville.

Charles Colcock came out to Montevideo to refresh himself for a day or two, but had not time to extend his visit here. I saw Patience at Midway at Communion; reported all getting on well.

I went up on Saturday before Communion with Mr. Buttolph and stayed with Brother William. He was at Dorchester on Sunday at church, but was not well: had taken cold from sleeping in the wind after walking, and suffered very much from his back; was scarcely able to sit up. Says he will remove to Dorchester in July; he says it is too far to stay on the Island with us, and seems to be very happy with Mr. Winn's family.

Mary Wells became so much worse after they removed to the Island that it was determined she should go North; and as she was too sick to go alone, Julia accompanied her. Julia will remain two or three weeks, and then Audley will go on for her. Mary will remain all summer. Isabel and Johnnie stay with us at night and go over to school every morning. Mr. McClellan and Fred take care of the rest. Audley is commander in chief.

Only think—I have written thus far without writing of Charlie, our sun-beam! He grows finely, and interests us more and more. He lies down in his bath, enjoys it so much, and yesterday pulled my glasses off my face. By the time you return, if spared to us, he will almost talk to you. He occupies all the spare minutes, and if it were not for Charlie now that you are all gone, I do not know what we should do.

Gilbert brought all our things safely, and has been busy at Maybank whitewashing—though I hope Brother will improve and that you will not need the house this summer. Sister Mary must leave that pain in her side at the springs. Mr. Buttolph is quite enlivened by Charlie. He and Laura unite with me in much love to you both.

Your affectionate sister,
S. M. Cumming.

Rev. D. L. Buttolph *to* Rev. C. C Jones[t]

Point Maxwell, Friday, June 19th, 1857

Dear Uncle,

Your letter to Mother was duly received. We were all rejoiced to hear from you, but were sorry to learn that you suffered so much fatigue in your journey to Lexington. Now that the General Assembly has closed its session, I hope you will begin to receive the benefit of the change. The reports of the General Assembly came duly to hand. Accept my thanks for the same. We were all interested in the perusal of them.

Cousin Robert and Mary spent the 10th of June with us, which was the an-niversary of our wedding day. They were both well, and looked remarkably happy.

Aunt Julia and Cousin Mary Wells left Woodville on the 10th inst. for Savannah, and sailed for New York on the 13th. Cousin Mary's health seemed to be failing previous to her departure. Belle and Johnnie are with us; the rest of the family stay at Woodville.

Laura and I have ridden over to Maybank frequently. I have given out al-lowance for three weeks. I wish I understood planting, so that I could attend to your interests there. But Audley will overlook matters, and I hope that all will go on well during your absence. The people are all well.

There is no news of special interest in the county. Our little household are in the enjoyment of excellent health. Charlie is growing fatter and more lovely and engaging every day. He finds a great source of amusement in pulling off his grandmother's spectacles. The little fellow takes a bath every morning in his bathing tub, and splashes the water with his hands and feet. He is a dear boy, and I hope he will grow up and be useful in the world.

I wrote to you at Lexington, but I fear the letter arrived after your de-parture. If there is anything I can do for you here, please let me know. I trust Aunt Mary enjoyed the meeting of the assembly; it must have been a very harmonious and edifying meeting. Mother and Laura unite with me in warmest love to yourself and Aunt Mary, and little Charlie sends a kiss to both.

Your affectionate nephew,
D. L. Buttolph.

Mrs. Laura E. Buttolph *to* Rev. *and* Mrs. C. C. Jones[t]

Point Maxwell, *Saturday,* June 20th, 1857

My dear Aunt and Uncle,

You will not be greatly surprised to hear that we have all missed you very much indeed since your departure. Still we would think of your good, and rejoice that you are breathing the air of a more invigorating clime and bathing in strengthening waters. It does one good to change the air and scene even when one has been ill, and I am so glad that you are away enjoying yourselves. I sometimes amuse myself by imagining where you are and what you are doing. I know you will form many pleasant acquaintances, not to say friends, while you are away, besides renewing old friendships. May you both return feeling greatly refreshed in mind, body, and spirit!

Mr. Buttolph and myself take a little drive almost every morning, and have ridden up to Maybank to ask after your people. The trees on your lawn are looking very fresh, and at one time there were a great many flowers blooming in your garden, but recently rain has been much needed. On Wednesday Mr. Buttolph went to Dorchester to lecture in the face of a very dark cloud, and I remarked it and hoped he would be either behind or ahead of the thunderstorm; and he said he would rather take a wetting than not get the rain, it was so much needed for the corn. And sure enough, he did get very wet, and had to preach in wet garments, and returned home about nine or ten o'clock quite chilled, and took a slight cold. Since that we have had several full-pond showers, and the roads well beaten; and I presume the corn is laughing with delight.

Andrew is eloquent on the fine watermelons he is going to make this summer; I am eloquent on the subject of our dear little Charlie, who with the exception of colic has not been sick a day; and some afternoons he escapes that entirely. He is as fat as a ricebird, and has grown very much. He is called handsome now, and I often wish we could place him before you, he is so lovely and bewitching. Yesterday he tried his best to pull off Mother's glasses, and did at last do so. He lies down in his bath and kicks his feet and seems to enjoy it greatly, but keeps his eyes all the time fixed on Mother's face, as if he did not quite understand it. Yesterday he was learning to touch things, and today he seems to be measuring distances. Mother is so good to him I feel that he is her child and I am his nurse; and all of her wishes are as strictly carried out as if they were her commands to me. And he knows her and almost leaps from Rachel's arms to go to her, and will leave me as readily if Mother talks to him. Mr. Buttolph can keep him for a very short time, but he likes him so much that in a little while he will cry to go to the study, I suppose.

Aunt Julia and Cousin Mary Wells have gone to the North, and we miss them very much, but feel that they will both be benefited, and they required the decided change. Belle and Johnnie spend their nights here in Mother's room. Fred and Mr. McClellan take care of the children at Woodville, and send the buggy quite early for Belle and Johnnie to go over to school.

But my little Charlie is the earliest *awaker* on the Island. He insists on being walked about at four o'clock in the morning, and I indulge him, as he only wakes me at twelve or one during the night and goes to sleep *usually* at sunset.

Mother is writing you, and I know she will say all that is new and pleasant. . . . I find that Mr. Buttolph has also written you, and if we were to wait a month I do not know that our letters would contain more interesting items. . . . Fanny Habersham is engaged to Mr. Manigault of South Carolina: very rich and respectable. She is the youngest daughter of old Dr. Habersham.

Ever affectionately your niece,
Laura E. M. Buttolph.

Rev. C. C. Jones *to* Messrs. Charles C. Jones, Jr., *and* Joseph Jones[g]
White Sulphur Springs, Virginia, Tuesday, June 23rd, 1857

My dear Sons,

I wrote you last from Cousin James West's in Kentucky. We took leave of him and his interesting family on the 9th, and reached Cincinnati (ninety-nine miles by the Lexington & Covington Railroad), and were received by our old friend and schoolmate Dr. John S. Law and his amiable wife with open and hearty greeting. And we passed a most agreeable week under their hospitable roof. He was very happy to welcome his old Liberty County friends. His older boys declare themselves *true Southerners,* and mean to see Georgia.

The city contains some two hundred thousand inhabitants, and is remarkably well built—perhaps better built than Philadelphia for its size. It has some fine public buildings. The Ohio Medical College is one of them—a flourishing school to which we presented one of your Smithsonian numbers, *in the name of the author,* through Dr. Law. The doctor took it down to his insurance office and exhibited it to a number of his friends as a specimen of what Southern young men could do and were doing, and made quite a speech over it.

The site of the city is good: it occupies a bend of the Ohio on the right bank, and the plain is in the form of a crescent ascending from the river to a level which extends above a mile back and rests upon an encircling range of high hills crowned with houses, forests, and fields. This range bathes its feet at each horn of the crescent in two streams running inland and emptying in the Ohio. The eastern stream flows in blood in pork-killing season. The western, Deer Creek, is called the Rhine, and along its banks the Germans have their quarters. The hills on the back are a continuation of the Kentucky hills that are here cut in two by the Ohio.

Every effort is made to advance the mercantile and manufacturing interests of the city, and it is undergoing much improvement now in the way of pulling down old buildings and putting up new and splendid modern ones. Population a hodgepodge of all classes and peoples. Much education. Many churches, and Sabbath well observed. The many furnaces and factories cover the city all the week with smoke, and coal dust discolors the roofs and endamages furniture. Not a sewer for drainage. City depends upon scavengers and rains to clean and wash off. A filthy custom prevails of depositing all the offal of the yards in the middle of the street! Here it is kneaded by horses' hoofs, nuzzled by the swine, gnawed by dogs, and ground in between the stones by the wheels of carriages! The consequence is, the streets and lanes smell—and often *look*—awfully. And I do not see why cholera may not be a constant visitor. It must occasion sickness. Opposite, the Licking River empties into the Ohio, having the town of Covington on the left bank and Newport on the right. Mother was much pleased with the city. I was not able to walk much, and saw less of it than she did in that way. But we saw much in our rides.

On the 16th we parted with our kind friends and took the stern-wheel boat *Quarrier* for Charleston, Virginia, on the Kanawha River (385 miles). Arrived after a pleasant passage, saving the wickedness of the boat (the worst I ever voyaged in) at twelve midnight Thursday 18th. Took stage at 4 A.M. 19th for Lewisburg (100 miles) and thence by hack ten miles to the White Sulphur, reaching here at 9 A.M. Saturday 20th. I took a hack from Lewisburg to avoid traveling in the stage on Sunday. This delightful and romantic ride I must not describe, but leave it for your dear mother to do for you. We enjoyed it exceedingly.

You thus perceive we have changed our route. We first intended to go up to Wheeling and take the Baltimore & Ohio Railroad and tarry at the Berkeley Springs and so come down here. But it was like going *round* the house at a wide distance to go *through* it. I wrote yesterday requesting the proprietor of the Berkeley Springs to forward what letters may go there for us to the *Hot Springs, Virginia.* You must write us immediately at *the Hot Springs.* Am anxious to hear from the plantations. Not a word since we left. . . .

Mother is well and I think much improved by her trip, and is enjoying the sulphur water and sweet climate of this beautiful place. Judge Wayne and his lady are here. He is improving, he tells me. Age begins to make its mark upon him. My own health is *in statu quo.* I see and feel no change for the better; rather a decline. The fatigue of travel has been too great. Mother says I am better. Your good pills, my dear son, are nearly out. Have thought they did me good. No effects on the nerves perceptible. Hope to go to the Hot Springs, God willing, this week and give them a fair trial.

Enclosed, my son, is my note in place of the sixty-day one at renewal—for twelve months. Have left the date to be filled up by you. Also a check for the amount of discount to be paid, which you can fill up. And let me know how much it is. I did not return your taxes for property in Savannah (*exclusive* of your servants) nor for your *possessions,* supposing you would be called on in Chatham. All else I have returned; and I now enclose a check for seventy-five dollars, which I think will be sufficient to pay our entire taxes—yours and your sister's and ours—for the present year. I do this in case I should not be at home in time—if I should live. You can write Mr. Martin to let you know from the tax collector how much it is, and you can then settle with the collector through Mr. Martin or in any other way that may be most easy and convenient. I wish you would forward to me the account sale of the last Arcadia cottons from Mr. Anderson. I want to close up the year's account. Has he sold the last from Montevideo and Maybank?

Your dear mother unites in much love to you both. We think of our dear children constantly, and pray for them morning and evening in our devotions together and every time we bow our knees in secret. Oh, how we desire the best blessings for you! And how do we pray and long for your conversion to God, my dear, dear sons! We pray that you may be preserved from the paths of the Destroyer and kept from vice in every form and from every shadow of infidelity, and that you may be virtuous, upright, and honorable men, and be the sincere and humble disciples of our ever blessed and glorious Redeemer. You have never reached the great end of your existence until you come to Him.

From your ever affectionate father,
C. C. Jones.

Mrs. Mary Jones *to* Mrs. Mary S. Mallard[t]
Hot Springs, Virginia, *Friday,* June 26th, 1857

My dear Daughter,

It seems an age since we have heard from our dear children, our friends, and home. Whilst in Lexington our purpose was to have gone directly to the Berkeley Springs, where we requested our letters to be directed, so we have not received a line for over three weeks. We have written Colonel Strother to forward them to this place, where we hope to remain for several weeks, that your dear father may make a fair trial of the waters. Whilst I am writing, he is in the piazza of our little cottage (or *cabin,* as they style them here) consulting Dr. Crump, the resident physician, and who married the daughter of Dr. Goode, the proprietor, upon his case and the proper method of using the waters.

Leaving the White Sulphur Springs at two o'clock yesterday morning, we arrived here by eleven o'clock—a distance of thirty-five miles. Our driver, stage, and horses were good, but the road very rough. The early hour and incessant jolting fatigued us both—especially your dear father—and I think produced some fever last night. But we retired early, and he feels better today. I cannot as yet perceive any decided improvement in his strength; there has been in his appetite. My hope and daily prayer is that a special blessing may rest upon his use of these wonderful waters—these fountains which an all-wise and gracious Providence has opened here for the suffering and afflicted. Springing from depths unknown, they have a living heat which seems to penetrate the whole system, and exert an astonishing influence in removing old and chronic diseases, liver affections, rheumatism, neuralgia, dyspepsia, etc., etc. A pious lady today, as we stood by the hot flowing tide, when I asked her where did this come from, replied: "The Lord's ways, you know, are past finding out; and this is one of them." Dr. Crump advises that your father commence with the temperate bath once a day. The hour has now arrived for bathing.

Afternoon. At eleven we took a temperate bath, which stands at 100°. The ladies and gentlemen have, of course, separate houses. The vats are filled about four feet deep, into which is constantly falling one or two spouts of the hot water, which runs off as fast as it comes in, so that it is kept constantly pure. You go down by steps and stand in the water and let the spout pour upon whatever part of the body is affected. They do not usually advise you to remain over twenty-five minutes. The feeling is perfectly delightful: the water buoyant, and having a peculiarly softening effect upon the surface, making it feel like satin. After returning to our cabin we lay down for more than an hour until the excitement (which is very great) passed off. Your father slept; I could not, for warm baths are always so stimulating they keep me awake. The doctor told your father the bath would probably create a febrile excitement with him, which has been the case. His pulse, from between 80 and 90, has risen to 110.

Today whilst Mrs. Gilchrist and myself were taking a survey of the baths, I discovered a *large* black hairy spider like those horrible ones we sometimes see at home in the boiler, the heat of which stands at 106°. I watched the monster whilst she fled out for a stick, and soon returned with a plank, with which I broke off one or two of the feet, when away it darted into the hot water! What should we do? The thought of allowing it to remain in the ladies' bath was dreadful: perhaps it might kill someone.

"Do call one of the waiters!"

In comes a very respectable-looking *uncle,* and in the name of the ladies we besought him to kill the spider. After several attempts he brought it out upon the end of the plank.

"Now, do take him to the doctor; I am sure he will be a great curiosity." (He was at that moment passing the bathhouse.) "Doctor! See what we have found. Would you not like to preserve it? Where could it have come from? I thought that I had got beyond the reach of such monsters!"

"Why, *madam,*" he said, in true Virginia accent, "you have just got in their region. For these mountains abound in all such things, and plenty of rattlesnakes. This fellow, I presume, had the gout or rheumatism and has come in for the benefit of the waters."

We returned, and lo, another and another! We had them all killed, and broke up their nest. To my horror, when I went to bathe myself in the temperate bath, the first object was one of a similar kind! I called loudly to my attendant, who came and soon dispatched it and two others. I *warned* her if she let one get on me I might have a fit in the water, and she would have to answer for it. She has been very watchful ever since. . . . Do you recollect Gough in describing one of his awful impressions during a fit of delirium tremens? Says he thought large black hairy spiders were crawling all over his body.

Saturday, June 27th. Your dear father was feverish all night, and slept but little. At eleven, his usual hour, he has taken the bath, and the effect has been decidedly favorable. He has come up and gone to sleep in a profuse perspiration; awoke refreshed.

We have had our dinner. Everything is bountiful and delightfully prepared: beef, mutton, ham, venison, the best bread, butter, and milk. Our pastry is superior: straw- and gooseberry pies, puddings, and plenty of strawberries gathered on the mountains. They are small but finely flavored. Yesterday *William Judah,* our head waiter, placed before the *sick ladies* and your father and myself a saucer; and when your father inquired what was in it, he said very graciously: "In old times we used to call it *sallybub.*" It proved to be very nice blancmange, with a little of the "sallybub" over it.

We have not over ten boarders, all invalids. None but such come to these waters: no pleasure-seekers are here, as at the White Sulphur, where fashion and display abound. But I must reserve descriptions for another sheet.

Monday Morning, June 29th. I trust my dear daughter and son are well this morning, and enjoyed all the blessings of a peaceful Christian Sabbath yesterday. Dr. Crump has *positively forbidden* your father to preach or exert himself in any way whilst under his treatment and the use of the waters. I thanked him personally for the prohibition, as his authority could not be set aside. He said yesterday all the *"old women"* got at him about it; but he told them he must keep silence, for preaching was the worst thing he could do. The doctor is a very intelligent and pleasant gentleman, and seems interested in your father's case. There was preaching in a schoolhouse about three miles distant by the Methodists, but none here. We spent our Sabbath in our cottage, and tried to employ its sacred hours profitably. After dinner two little colored girls (*both free*) came to me, and I taught them. *Tell Kate* they did not know a word of the Lord's Prayer, or their Commandments, or any of the catechism. They seemed very anxious to learn, and I think will improve fast. They are to come every Sabbath whilst I am here.

I dreamed of *you,* my dear child, last night. I hope Robert is taking good care of you. We were very happy to receive a page from his pen in your last, and to know that you are a useful wife. You must not allow your domestic duties to absorb all your time, but give a *due share to mental culture*. And do not neglect your music. We long to hear you play and sing. I look back with great pleasure to the early years of our married life, when we read a great many valuable works together; and your father's constant effort and habit was to impart knowledge to his family. How degrading to the intellect is the way in which *young females particularly* spend their time! With the mass of mankind there seems very little conscientious appreciation or improvement of the talents—for which they will have to render an account.

Your dear father wrote Robert and yourself a long letter from Cincinnati. After spending a week very pleasantly with our kind friends Dr. and Mrs. Law and their truly polite children (six in number: Hugh, Ben, Frank, Charles, Wallace, and *Sissy*—Sarah Elizabeth, I think) we parted from them in the afternoon of Tuesday, June 16th. At the levee we got on board the steamer *A. W. Quarrier* (Captain Johnston) and proceeded up the Ohio. A parallel ridge of hills—not very high, but well wooded and sometimes rocky and precipitous—runs along the course of the river on both the Kentucky and Ohio sides. Frequently fertile valleys, well cultivated, lie between the shores and the hills. The country is poorly improved, and you see no handsome settlements, and all the villages are inferior in appearance —some of them dilapidated, particularly where the railroads have diverted the trade. And such has been their effect upon travel that all the first-class steamers are now withdrawn from the Ohio. At Point Pleasant we passed into the Kanawha and entered the Old Dominion. The meeting of the waters of these two rivers is very marked for some distance; they flow side by side, the limpid waters of the Kanawha apparently loath to mingle its crystal drops with the turbid and muddy waves of the Ohio. But as "evil communications corrupt good manners," after they have shaken hands they are soon lost to sight and borne away by the overwhelming flood.

We reached Charleston Thursday night at eleven o'clock. On the boat we had the pleasure of meeting Bishop Meade. . . . Your father and Bishop Meade enjoyed the interview very much, and he presented me with several tracts on the Eighth Commandment written by a lady of his family for *colored persons*.

I wanted to write you a description of our journey onward, but must reserve it for another time, as I must now talk of some domestic matters.

You know I left home so hurriedly that my wardrobe was in a poor condition, and will be worse ere I return. The basket sent you, my dear child, from Savannah contained, as well as I can remember, six undergarments cut out, and two petticoats with bindings which I shall very much need by the time I get home, and the remainder of the piece of shirting, which you can keep for me. Have you seen anything of my maid Peggy? Do find out and let me know from Mrs. Quarterman if she knows anything about her trade and has any idea of cutting and fitting. I wish her to know how to cut out men's clothes; I mean plantation work. I am very anxious to hear something from Patience and Flora—what they are doing. Should you at any time ride down to Montevideo, please examine the trunk with my dresses; but you must not expose yourself in going there. And do be sure and make use of the garden and anything you want in our absence. When we shall return to our dear home is a matter of uncertainty, and will be regulated entirely by your father's improvement. Do tell Patience and Flora to take care of everything and pick the weeds from the flowers. I hope the japonicas and azaleas have been shaded. And Niger must take care of the poultry, and Jack of Jet. I do long, my darling child, to see you. You must write me particularly of yourself and all home news.

Remember us most affectionately to Sister Marion and the children. We feel the deepest sympathy for her in her sad bereavement. I hope you will go to see her frequently.

Tuesday, June 30th. (My own dear mother's birthday, wedding day, and birthday of her last child!) The office is opened, and we have just received a letter from your brother Charles via the Berkeley Springs. Also one from Audley, in which he very kindly gives us an account of his visit to Walthourville, and promises to take charge of Maybank for us. A great relief to our anxieties about that place. Please remember us affectionately to all friends, especially your Uncle Henry and Aunt Abby. Tell Lucy and Kate howdy for us. I hope Kate is a good girl and improving in her sewing. Your father joins me in best love to our dear daughter and son. May God's blessing ever abide with you!

Your own affectionate mother,
Mary Jones.

Mrs. Mary Jones *to* Mr. Charles C. Jones, Jr.[g]

Hot Springs, Tuesday, June 30th, 1857

My dear Son,

If I had only the power, I would this moment transport your brother and yourself and sister and Robert from the toil and weariness of professional labor, and the heat and dust of a low-country climate, to this charming valley, where you might sit as I am now doing to breathe the cool mountain air, bringing as it does strength and vigor with every inspiration, and where your souls would expand with all that is beautiful and grand in nature around —these lofty summits ever pointing upward to Him who hath weighed the mountains in scales and laid the foundations of the everlasting hills. We see not, feel not, enjoy not anything that is delightful without the immediately expressed desire: "Oh, that our dear children were here to enjoy this with us!" I hope you will all one day see all and much more than we have ever done. But above all earthly delights may the blessing of God in Christ rest upon your souls and fill you with that joy and peace in believing which the *world* can *neither give nor take away*.

Leaving the White Sulphur at two o'clock in the morning of the 25th, we reached these springs about 11 A.M., much fatigued (especially your dear father) by the early hour and rough road. I persuaded him before using the waters to consult Dr. Crump, who married the daughter of Dr. Goode, the proprietor, and has for six years acted as resident physician, and whom we have found a most intelligent and agreeable gentleman. He has entered fully and with interest into your father's case, and I cannot but hope with God's blessing that these fountains opened by Infinite Wisdom and Beneficence for the healing of the sick and afflicted will be blessed to his recovery.

He has been using only the temperate bath, which stands between 98° and 100°, and has found it decidedly beneficial. There is certainly an improvement in his locomotive powers and strengthening of his throat, or rather entire relief from that distressing tendency to spasm. His bath is taken about eleven o'clock A.M. Remains about fifteen minutes, then comes up to our cottage or cabin, lies down between two blankets, and sleeps for an hour or more, and rises in time to dress and read a little before dinner. I usually go at the same time to the ladies' pleasure or temperate bath, which is a room (with dressing rooms attached) of twelve feet by fourteen into which is constantly falling two spouts of hot water retained to a depth of four feet, and then as constantly passing off in the opposite direction, so that it is kept fresh and pure all the time as it runs in from the spring on one side and passes immediately out on the other. Springing as these fountains do from depths unknown, there is a living heat which cannot be counterfeited; and they have proven most efficacious in innumerable instances, some almost miraculous.

It is the resort almost exclusively of invalids; few mere pleasure-seekers come here, from reasons they are now trying to obviate. We have not more than twelve or fifteen here at this time. Our fare is excellent: good beef, mutton, venison, butter, and milk, the best of corn and wheat bread, strawberries from the mountainsides, and fine pastry.

Whilst at the White Sulphur Springs we had the pleasure of seeing Judge and Mrs. Wayne frequently. The judge is there for the relief of something like erysipelas. He remarked to your father one day that upon all constitutional questions he had studied the *large edition* of Marshall's *Life of Washington* more than any other work. Mrs. Wayne is a lady of rare intelligence and dignity of manners. I was pleased to hear her say that in the many places she had lived in she regarded the tone of morality (particularly with the young men) in Savannah as high if not higher than in most places; and she instanced the observance of the Sabbath, attendance upon divine worship, and freedom from the common practices of amusement such as pleasure rides, walks, etc., etc. Oh, that we could all feel that in the keeping of God's law there is great reward!

Whilst in Kentucky we had the pleasure of seeing one of your Princeton collegemates, Mr. Peyton Harrison of Virginia. He is an elder in the Presbyterian church where he lives, and was sent as a delegate to our General Assembly. I heard him spoken of with the greatest respect and affection as a most worthy and useful Christian man. He is married and has one child, and inquired very kindly after you.

It was with great regret (I may say deep sorrow), my dear son, that I have heard the opposite character of another of your friends. Such statements are reported of his principles and practices as have shocked my feelings; and knowing the intimacy and friendship which seemed to exist between Mr. Sale and yourself, I can only account for your regard for him upon the supposition that he was not what he is now said to be, or that you are totally ignorant of his character and habits as common fame now represent them to be. It is said that Mr. Toombs, with a father's feelings for a daughter's happiness, could not do otherwise than prevent the marriage. Withal Mr. Sale is spoken of as a young man of *fascinating manners and address.*

Yesterday we received your affectionate letter via Berkeley Springs—the first we have had for over three weeks. Also a very kind one from Audley. Your father requests me to say that he has already forwarded to you the note duly executed, and will write you in a few days. How long we shall tarry here will be determined by his improvement.

I hope, my dear son, your brother and yourself will soon both be at Maybank enjoying your Island home. At Montevideo you will find all necessary stores of bacon, flour, sugar, lights, tea, etc. Not much coffee left, I believe, but you can order whatever you want from Wood & Claghorn. And make Patience and Flora move down with Gilbert whenever you please with bedding, etc., etc. Do be sure and make the servants provide for your wants. They are so much accustomed to my direction I fear you may want many comforts. I hope you will also have some good fruit. Be sure and remember that your dear sister is within a few hours of you, and you must not neglect her. Do tell all our servants howdy, and write us particularly of everything and everybody at home. I will write my dear son Joseph in a few days. Our love to Cousin Charles and Cousin Eliza West. Remember us affectionately to Mrs. and Miss Stiles. Your father unites with me in best love to you both.

Ever, my dear son, your affectionate mother,

Mary Jones.

Tea bell is ringing. Howdy for Sue, Titus, and George.

Mrs. Mary S. Mallard *to* Rev. *and* Mrs. C. C. Jones[t]

Walthourville, *Thursday,* July 2nd, 1857

My dear Father and Mother,

The last mail brought us a great treat—your letter, Father, written from Cincinnati, and also one written from the White Sulphur Springs to

Brothers Charlie and Joe, which they kindly sent out for our perusal. Supposing that you would spend some days at the Berkeley Springs, I wrote you a long letter, which I presume will be forwarded. I think of you now as enjoying the delightful baths at the Hot Springs, and sincerely hope you may, my dear father, derive great benefit from them. I want to see you very much, but hope you will not return until your health is decidedly better. I only wish I could be with you.

Last week I had an attack of fever, which made me feel very homesick. I wished often for Father and Mother. Mr. Mallard sent for Dr. Stevens, and he thought I must have taken cold. The fever lasted a day and night, and since then I have had no return.

The day after I was sick, before I had left my room, I heard the sound of wheels, and Kate came running up to say "Young Massa Joe" had come. I do not know that I ever felt more glad to see anyone. He stayed with us from Friday until Monday afternoon, when we sent him to the Cottage; and he spent the night with Uncle William and returned to Savannah the next day, to be in time to commence his hospital duties on yesterday. He looks quite thin but well, and enjoyed his visit to us very much; said he felt as though he had gained several pounds in those few days. With characteristic zeal he inquired of all the servants and country people if they would not catch him some gophers and leave them at "the parson's." Charles Marion caught three for him while he was with us; these he took with him.

Cousin Joe West has returned from Paris, and expects to be married in a short time, and has invited both Brothers Charlie and Joe to be his attendants. It will be Brother Joe's first appearance in this capacity.

Two nights ago Mr. Mallard and I rose at two o'clock to see the comet. It has no tail, and presents the appearance of a very large star. At times it would be exceedingly luminous, and then for a moment or two fade and become small, very much resembling the light of a flickering candle when seen at a distance. This may have been due in part to the state of the atmosphere, for in the main the light was steady, like that of the planets. I have heard some persons say they could discover the tail, but I think this must be imagination, for the night was very clear upon which we saw it, and neither of us could discover any appearance of its tail. I do not know whether it has affected the weather or not, but we have had a great deal of rain and cool weather. The nights are sometimes chilly, though the middle of the day is quite warm.

Our friends and neighbors still continue kind to us, and I have not yet wanted vegetables. It really seems that whenever I give out the last I have, someone sends a fresh supply. Mrs. Colonel Quarterman has sent me some very generous waiters of vegetables—almost a week's supply at a time. . . . Aunt Marion is better, and rides out; she asked Brother Joe to send her some tonic, which he has done. . . . I heard last week from the Island. All well there. Cousin Lyman lectures on Romans weekly at Dorchester. . . . Mr.

Thomas Fleming has not handed us the marriage settlement. Both his good lady and himself have been to see us.

In reply to your charge, Father, Mr. Mallard says you may rest satisfied he will try. And he promises this the more freely because he knows that the same feeling which dictated the charge will secure his obedience—namely, love for your "precious child." He is quite well, and has a plenty of work to do; his lecture, prayer meeting, and Bible class, beside his Sabbath exercises, keep his time fully occupied. He unites with me in much love and many good wishes for your enjoyment and benefit. The servants send howdy.

Your ever affectionate daughter,
Mary S. Mallard.

Rev. John Jones *to* Rev. C. C. Jones[t]

Rome, Friday, July 3rd, 1857

My dear Brother,

Your affectionate letter from the White Sulphur was received on Monday last the 29th June, and this answer has been delayed a few days by the examination and commencement of Rome Female College, which exercises closed last night. They were all highly satisfactory, and the prospects of the infant institution are promising.

We were truly interested in your visits and journeyings, and I wish I could have been present in all. How long will you remain in the mountain and spring country of Virginia? Can you give me any information of the Rockbridge Alum Springs, so famous for curing dyspepsia and dyspeptic sore throats? I am trying to persuade my dear Jane to let me take her over to the Alum Springs in August, D.V. She suffers very much, from one-half to three-fourths of the time, with dyspeptic sore throat.

My people seem very willing for us to go. I have not been absent a Sabbath since my coming here. Our congregations are growing constantly, and the attendance at night services on Sabbath and Thursday, I am told, is unusually large. I hope it may not be like the new broom. We have commenced a colored Sunday school, which opened with about twenty and has gone up to 110, and still they come. It would fill your heart with joy to see yourself represented by your catechism. We have sent for five dollars' worth, not only for teachers but also for some of our larger scholars at their request. . . . Next week our meeting for Communion and installation commences, and will embrace the second Sabbath of July. I am anxious for the presence of yourself and my dear sister, but presume you will not leave Virginia so soon. I know you will both remember me on the second Sabbath inst.

July 4th. This day carries me back into the regions of the past, and pleasant and painful memories gather around me. Alas, the changes—how many, how sad! The friends and relatives who have gone like leaves in wintry weather! Surely I am growing old! This has been a day of cold, of cloud and showers. This morning between 5 and 6 A.M. the mercury stood at 56°; at 2 P.M. at 64°; then rose to 66°; and now at 10 P.M. it stands at 60° —the coolest 4th of July I have ever known. . . .

You inquire if I had heard from Mr. Mitchell. I did, and wrote to yourself and Sister to Lexington, and sent a copy of a portion of Mr. Mitchell's letter. It was noncommittal, though not unfavorable. He mentions that N. A. Pratt, Jr., was a candidate for the same chair. He mentions the importance of Joseph's coming up to Athens before the election and forming the acquaintance of as many trustees as possible. Brother Pratt, Sr., will be here this week to attend the installation, and I will in a quiet way learn from him the prospects of his son. I have had a correspondence with Charles Colcock on the above subject. Will write you again if I gather anything worth communicating.

Do write us your plans and movements for the summer. Should you remain in Virginia through August, we may come to you and bring you home with us. If you return before August, then remember that your room and an affectionate welcome is here for you, my dear sister and brother. Do not think of Liberty before "the fall of the leaf." Our dear little boys remember you very distinctly, and say it is time you came back again. I asked Johnnie: "What sort of a coat did Uncle Charlie wear?" He said: "White." And Josie said: "He had a black coat under the white, and the tail of the black coat was cut in two." Today Joseph said he did not like Satan because he would burn him. "But," said he, "I will take his own tongs and punch him and burn him." Precious little fellows, they are a joy to us forever.

Dunwody spent ten days with us and returned to his old master. He has grown considerably and is quite well, and desired much to have seen you both. Jane unites with me in best love to you both. Write soon to

Your affectionate brother,
John Jones.

P.S. Johnnie and Josie send love to Aunt Mary and Uncle Charles, and say you must soon come back.

J. J.

Mrs. Mary Jones *to* Mrs. Mary S. Mallard[t]

Hot Springs, Friday, July 10th, 1857

My dear Daughter,

Your affectionate favor, with our dear son Robert's postscript, and also your letter of the 2nd, have both reached us. . . . Your last letter, my darling, has made us feel anxious about you. What could have caused the fever? Had it any connection with your visit to the Island? I know persons on the Sand Hills always feel suspicious of the seaboard. Do write us candidly if you are sick. I shall feel very anxious to return on your account. How I do wish Robert and yourself were with us! It would add so much to our enjoyment; and these warm baths might be beneficial.

Your dear father has not derived the advantage we anticipated. It was two weeks yesterday since we arrived here. The effect upon his system, especially the acceleration of his pulse, made Dr. Crump advise him to refrain from the bath for a few days and substitute dry cupping, which he has submitted to under the hands of Dr. Billy Moody, the doctor's servant, a most valuable man, reminding me of our faithful old servant Jack. The cupping is very soothing, and your father usually falls asleep. . . . I think we will leave as soon as we receive a reply from your brother Charles to a business letter which we must receive before we can leave this place. I am anxious for your dear father to try the Rockbridge Alum Springs; they are *now* most relied on. (But in forming an opinion of these various fountains I am quite bewildered, for they are all recommended for the same diseases, and the analysis of one may well pass for the whole.)

If it is the Lord's will to favor our present intentions, we shall return through Tennessee, down to Marietta, where we will see our dear relatives, and your Uncle John at Rome, and perhaps our friends at Roswell before we come *home,* which, if the travel does not prove more beneficial than it has yet, is certainly the best place for your father. Being unable to exercise by walking, he needs the daily use of *Jerry.* His case is certainly a very peculiar one, that seems not to yield to the usual remedies. At times he appears very despondent in reference to his future recovery. In all our hours of darkness and sorrow how precious is the truth that if we are indeed the children of God, *loving* Him, all things shall work together for our good! Here rests our faith and hope.

It gratifies us to know that you receive such kind attentions from your friends and neighbors; and I hope, my dear child, that you will not be wanting in any conduct or feeling that will entitle you to respect and affection as a minister's wife. Be kind to all. Neglect none, especially those who rank amongst the poor and humble. I know that the congregation admits of as few distinctions of that kind as almost any I ever knew; indeed, equality of rank and fortune prevails more generally in Liberty County than any place I have seen. I do not think it any disadvantage that you have gone almost a stranger into your husband's congregation. *Indulge no prejudices. Form no intimacies.* If you seek to do good, the way will ever be opened to you.

Until within a few days we have not numbered over ten (almost entirely invalids) at one time. I felt myself the only well one at table. Now we number nearly fifty, and have a band of music that seeks to charm us a half hour before dinner and again after tea. But I can assure you they are by no means an Orphean band moving hills and groves. . . . Father asks for a little space, so I will leave the next page for him. He unites with me in all that is affectionate to Robert and yourself. Remember us to all relatives and friends. Howdies for Lucy and Kate. Good night, my dear children. That the best of Heaven's blessings may rest upon you both ever prays

Your affectionate mother,
Mary Jones.

Rev. C. C. Jones *to* Mrs. Mary S. Mallard[t]

Hot Springs, *Friday,* July 10th, 1857

I intended writing you, my dear child, myself, but Mother has got ahead of me. We are keeping house down in the vale in a room in the east end of the last cottage on Bath Row West—about eighteen feet by eighteen. Scant! Our furniture consists of a small pine single washstand stained red, two basins and ewers, and two tumblers. And as Mother cannot do without *flowers,* one is converted into a flowerpot, which stands on a high mantel filled with kalmias, roses, lilies, and wild flowers gathered in our walks. Next: two small tables of plain country walnut, covered with oilcloth—one a dressing, the other a writing-and-work table. A great country-made arm-chair (which we call "Daniel Lambert") with rockers; two of the same manufacture without rockers; and one stick-backed, wooden-bottomed chair painted green. And in the piazza stands a country-made chair with an arm fastened to each side, and extending a good way front and rear, to carry sick people to the baths. A piece of carpet to dress on; a low red-stained pine bedstead; a straw broom and a straw dustbroom; a small pair of iron andirons (one broken); and the most diminutive pair of shovel-and-tongs imaginable. Nothing more. If we have an uncommon run of company, when our chairs are exhausted we take to our two trunks and a bonnet box.

We have, too, many conveniences. We have five wooden pegs along the walls to hang things on; and two small closets—one with shelves and one with nails to hang up dresses, etc.; and a corn-shuck doormat, pretty far gone to decay. Our library is partly on the mantelpiece and partly on the table; and papers and books and letters lying scattered about give us a *literary* air. And several vials filled with sirens and lizards in alcohol give a *scientific* air to our apartment. My bag of shaving things hangs on one peg by one window (two we have); and Mother's bag with combs and brushes (and stuck all over with pins outside) hangs by the other. We have white cotton curtains. And our most important piece of furniture I forgot to mention, not having as much use for it as some others: a small square looking glass. No paint in the room: walls plastered and whitewashed.

Here we keep house. Rise between five and six, dress, have family worship, read until the bell rings, go to breakfast. Sometimes sit a few moments in the parlor before coming down to our cottage. A morning's walk for exercise. Returned, Mother gets out her work and sews; I read to her or write till the bathing hour comes: 11 A.M. From eleven to twelve or one: bathing, including a lull after bathing of twenty or thirty minutes. Dress. Dinner at 2 P.M. From three to five reading aloud or writing, if nobody calls. Tea at six. Then a walk until seven, and if we have any calls to make, make them on our return. Family worship and bed from nine to ten. This the general routine. The *sick* are much occupied with themselves, and the *well* make the most amusement they can for themselves. Those who choose roll ninepins, play backgammon or draughts or chess (and some *cards*), ride or walk about, and dance, dress, and show off, etc.

This is *spring life*. You will say it is a poor one for all the great ends of life. True. It is a phase of life. There are *times* which men must devote to the acquisition of health, and there are *places* to which they must go for it; and we must make the best of it. I long to be at work regularly, if it may ever be. Tell Robert if there are books in the library he wishes, to take them. We hope to have preaching tomorrow—the first in a month: Rev. Mr. Broadus, Baptist minister of Charlottesville, Virginia. My love to Robert. I remain, my dear daughter,

Your ever affectionate father,
C. C. Jones.

Rev. R. Q. Mallard *to* Rev. C. C. Jones[t]

Walthourville, *Monday,* July 13th, 1857

Dear Father,

I expected to have been differently employed this evening—conversing with, instead of writing to, my honored parents. Not that I anticipated being in Virginia tonight, but in Dorchester with my other parents. This afternoon I had set apart for this visit, but the aspect of the weather was so threatening that I was constrained to defer it until tomorrow. So here we are—Mary and I—keeping each other company with the cheerful music of our pens. Womanlike (shall I say it?) hers is rapidly coursing along the unwritten page and fast converting the blank sheet into the all-but-speaking letter, while mine more leisurely tramps along, leaving at least heavier marks.

It was not Mary's expectation to go with me to Dorchester this time. Aunt Susan, who (as you will learn from Mary's letter) has been staying with us nearly a week, requested her not to run the risk of a visit even to the Island. She thinks the change and the ride in the sun necessary would be far from proving beneficial. I should like to know your opinion in regard to it. One would not have suffered as much in traveling from the heat this season as usual. The weather which we have been having is certainly uncommon. If I remember correctly, it was on the 4th cold enough to require for comfort the closing of doors and windows; a fire would not have been uncomfortable. Speaking with Mr. Richard Axson a few days ago in regard to it, I was told that there was in Augusta on the same day in 1836 *a frost*. Indeed, he said that one of his servants had according to his account observed frost a few mornings ago.

The heavens have been dripping and at intervals literally *pouring down,* water upon us for some time past. One day last week there was, in addition to the rain, a heavy fall of hail. Not a morsel of ice fell just here, but in sufficient quantity at Mr. Miller's in the village to be gathered by the quart to furnish old Mrs. Stevens with ice enough for Sunday consumption, and on Dr. Stevens' crop of cotton to riddle and destroy it. Some persons perhaps will be disposed to attribute the unusual coolness and moisture of the season to the influence of the *comet*. I think it was the opinion of Sir Isaac Newton that one office which these mysterious visitants to our system discharge is to supply it with moisture. While I write, the rain is playing an appropriate symphony upon the roof above us.

But I must let the weather alone, as it will not be induced to "take up" by my words, and give you some account of what transpires in our little world, which has proved itself thus far independent of outside influences. I believe I may speak for two of the inhabitants and say *they are happy*. For this I must thank you and our good mother. My mornings, after a ride for exercise, I devote sacredly to my books, not suffering visitors (unless on special business) to interfere. Frequently we spend the afternoons together reading some work both entertaining and profitable; the evenings generally in the same pleasant employment. I have been recently reading a book which would interest you, and *on your plan:* Borrow's *Bible and Gypsies in Spain*. Almost every place I have traced out on the map, and its physical geography I have learned from an excellent article on Spain in *The English Encyclopedia*. This is a practice which I intend pursuing in the perusal of books of this character, and is one of the benefits which I have derived from my intercourse with you. As marriage fees come in rather slowly, I have made but small additions to my library of late—Bengel's *Gnomon*, however, and Augustine's *De Civitate Dei* being among that number. The latter work seems to treat briefly of almost every subject relating to the sublimest of all sciences, theology. I rejoice that I am not one of those who think human learning incompatible with piety. "Covet earnestly the best gifts." It is a good motto for the student. To preach the glorious gospel of the Blessed God is indeed pleasant work, and no pains should be spared which may fit one for the work.

I feel for you in your affliction (for such I know you esteem it): your not being able to proclaim a Saviour's grace. And yet, my dear father, I must rejoice that your physician has positively forbidden your preaching. Your ultimate restoration to health does seem to depend upon your complete silence. At least it is worth the trial. May God bless to you the rest and other means which you are using, and give you a sweet and quiet submission to His will! Some Christians God calls to be heroes in doing, others heroes in suffering.

The hour is late, and I must close. In regard to your message (which has indeed been already answered), let me say that if you only remember the love you bear to your partner and then recollect that your dear child sustains the same near and endearing relation to me, you will feel that the only request necessary is: "Follow the suggestions of love, and take the Holy Bible as the manual of your married life." My love (and I would add Mary's, but she has written by the same mail) to Mother. Mary enjoys good health, to which I think her domestic habits no little contribute.

Affectionately yours,
Robert Q. Mallard.

Mrs. Susan M. Cumming *to* Mrs. Mary Jones[t]

Point Maxwell, *Wednesday,* July 15th, 1857

My dear Sister,

It gives me great pleasure to tell you that I have just spent a week with dear Mary and Robert, and returned on Monday, leaving them both quite well. Mary has had a light attack of fever, but has recovered and looks as well if not better than before she had it. We feared that the ride down here had made her sick, but it was three weeks after it, and Joseph said "it was very slow *pison*." She is very comfortably fixed, and is a very industrious and notable housewife. Her neighbors are kind and attentive; each day that I was there was marked by some act of kindness. Curds, cream, potatoes, loaf bread, and various kinds of vegetables were sent to her. And all have visited her with, I believe, but one exception; and they apologized on account of want of conveyance, being too far to walk. I told her I should write you that Mr. M. would not let her feet touch the ground, but took her up and brought her from the buggy into the house. They read together a part of each day. . . .

Mary received while I was with her your letter from the Hot Springs, and I read Brother's received before I went up. They were the first I had seen from either of you since you left Kentucky, and I really feel hopeful that the water of the Hot Springs will benefit you both. You must give them a fair trial and not get discouraged too soon. I am glad you are in such a pleasant region of country, and you must enjoy it very much. Mr. Buttolph received and answered Brother's letter to him. I feel encouraged about Brother; his writing is really very good, and that rest must do him good.

As far as I could hear, all of your people are well. As they say, "No much complaint." As one of the people from White Oak told me, "All well at Maybank." Since Audley received your letter, Mr. B. has resigned the key to him. He and Laura have ridden over a number of times, and the people are told to call on us for any thing or help they may require from us. Some of them come over on Sunday and during the week with chickens. Andrew has let us have some nice little roasters. . . . It has been very cool and rainy —perhaps too much rain for the crops, but good for slip-planting.

You can scarcely imagine how much we have missed you, but console ourselves by thinking how much you are enjoying, and that your health will be so much improved. Charlie beguiles our time; he is more interesting each day. He recognized me when I returned home. I came to that conclusion, as he cries when strangers take him, and he smiled on me. You will find him, I hope, much grown and changed. He is very well pleased with Rachel for a nurse. Give our affectionate love to my dear brother; thank him for his letter very much, which I answered and directed to Berkeley Springs. Laura and Mr. B. unite with me in love to you both, and best wishes for your health and happiness. And believe me

Your affectionate sister,

S. M. Cumming.

Mrs. Laura E. Buttolph *to* Mrs. Mary Jones[t]

Point Maxwell, *Wednesday,* July 15th, 1857

My dear Aunt Mary,

I write to inform you that nothing remains unless I pick up a few fragments and send them to entertain you; for my dear mother in very few words generally informs her friends on all points.

We continue to miss your society, and will be delighted to welcome you back, hoping that you will return with fine health and spirits to cheer us up. Whenever our little Charlie looks particularly pretty, or does or *says* some new and smart things, we wish that his Aunt Mary and Uncle Charlie could see him. I generally understand his baby talk, and translate for the benefit of friends. Rachel is singing him to sleep, and I send you the words of her song:

> By oh baby go sleepy!
> Maumer ketch one raaaabit,
> Bile um sweet for baby!
> Rock um by baby go sleepy,
> All de bread an' de cheese I git,
> Put um up for de baby!
> Maumer ketch one raaaabit,
> Bile um sweet for baby!

I wonder what his grandfather would say if he could hear the lullaby of his grandson. . . . Charlie now cries after his father, laughs aloud at the sight of his bathtub, and almost springs out of my lap when I put him in. Sometimes he cries when taken out, and keeps looking over the side of the tub into the water as if he would like to go back.

Mother desires me to say that she spent a day with Cousin Marion, and found her as much composed as you could expect and attending to the affairs of her family. . . . Aunt Julia was very kind in staying with me at night while Mother was on the Sand Hills. . . . I hope your efforts after health will be crowned with success, and that the hot baths will invigorate you both. I rather think you will like the Hot Springs best, though presume you are going through the whole course. Mother and Mr. Buttolph unite with me in *more* love to you and Uncle Charlie.

Your niece,
Laura E. M. B.

Mr. Audley King *to* Rev. C. C. Jones[t]

Riceboro, *Tuesday,* July 21st, 1857

Dear Uncle,

Your esteemed letter of 9th inst. we received but a few days since, and by your bidding I "write soon" with a most cheerful spirit; for to read the items of interest is almost equal to seeing you. Aunt Susan read the greater part of your letter to the colonel on last Sabbath, and the dear old gentleman (in his way) says he does not believe at all that you've laid labor aside. We really hope that you have, and that you'll be much benefited by relaxation and the change. You've certainly traveled far enough for one excursion, and in various manner sufficient to decide on choice, etc.

Our dear mother only accompanied Sister Mary to Brooklyn, spent a fortnight, and is with us again, invigorated by the trip. Sister writes often and in good spirits. . . . Our Island circle so far have enjoyed our usual share of blessings. The health of Liberty has been good, though death has been once, twice, three times before us, almost in the twinkling of an eye, taking away the young and the aged with its impressive language, "Be ye therefore also ready."

I hope you'll feel easy about Maybank and your library. All are well there. I've directed Sarah Ann to attend to the books. And Andrew is such an intelligent man—and one of principle—it is a pleasure to see to his work. The cotton is good: some quite large, and all well fruited. Corn suffered for want of rain; was in good order when I first saw it, and now all laid by. . . . Andrew inquires particularly of Aunt and yourself, as though I'd just left your side; sends howdy for himself and the other servants. The old man has had two rattlesnake adventures since you left—too long to tell now.

Colonel Maxwell says he is still at the Cottage. He looks remarkably well, and is to be in Dorchester soon. He received one letter and expects the other to be at Riceboro. . . . Do accept of our *united* love to Aunt and yourself. And believe me

Yours very truly,
J. A. M. King.

Mrs. Mary S. Mallard *to* Rev. *and* Mrs. C. C. Jones[t]
Walthourville, *Monday,* July 27th, 1857

My dear Mother and Father,

A letter from Brother Charlie received this evening informed us that you are now at the Alum Springs. I did not write last week because I did not know your address. I am very sorry, dear Father, that you have derived no benefit from the hot baths. Brother Charlie says you speak of returning home soon, but I hope you will not, for I think a quiet month in the up country would do you a great deal of good. If I were to consult my own wishes, you would be with us now, for it seems to me you have been absent twice the length of time you really have.

Brother Joe is spending a little time with us. He has been quite sick in Savannah, and came out last Friday in search of a little strength. He is very thin, but has a good appetite, and has improved since his stay with us. Today he went out gopher-hunting, and this evening reports eighty-seven caught today with the aid of Gilbert and James. He is quite delighted with his success, and hopes to take as many more with him. All of these were caught within a quarter of a mile of the house. He found the skeleton of one beautifully prepared and perfect except the head.

Brother Joe sent for Gilbert and the carriage, and tomorrow we expect to go to see Uncle William. Will dine with him and then go to the Island. It is such a good opportunity for me to go down in the carriage that I will embrace it, as I don't think it would be quite prudent for me to go later. Mr. Mallard cannot accompany us, and I do not like to leave him; but if I do not go now, I cannot again this summer.

I will try and keep Brother Joe with us as long as possible. His attack was brought on by his own imprudence—performing experiments at the hospital all day and neglecting to eat his dinner, sometimes remaining until nine or ten at night. I believe he begins to feel that he can work too much.

Cousin Joe West was married on the 16th of this month to Anne Rogers. They left the day after for the up country. Brothers Charlie and Joe were both attendants.

Aunt Abby and Uncle Henry are both well, and send much love to you. . . . All well at Aunt Marion's. . . . You must excuse this short letter, dear Father and Mother, as it is growing late, and we expect to leave early in the morning. Mr. Mallard is quite well, and unites with me, and Brother Joe also, in warmest love to you both.

Your affectionate daughter,
Mary S. Mallard.

Rev. C. C. Jones *to* Mrs. Mary S. Mallard[t]

Rockbridge Alum Springs, Virginia, *Tuesday,* July 28th, 1857
My dear Daughter,

Mother says she would have written you today, but her wardrobe is so rundown that she is obliged to put it in repair and get a new dress in readiness for wear. She and Mrs. Roper of Charleston and Mrs. Reid of Augusta are the plainest dressers among all the hundred and fifty ladies here: low-country gentility, you know. The "spring" custom with the ladies is: first, a morning dress for breakfast and a walk after; second, a dinner dress, more precise and perfect; and third, a tea and evening dress, in the fashion, more elaborate, and the person well adorned; and fourth (for those who like it) a real ball dress. (These go to the evening dances, which break up about ten or half-past ten.) Poor invalid people dress as they can and look on. The gentlemen dress every sort of fashion, and we have seen no exquisites nor indeed bucks of any kind. There are more young ladies here than young men.

The place is a pretty one: a campus of green grass intersected by walks and adorned with shade trees and surrounded by brick cottages with piazzas on two sides of the circle. The upper side is occupied by the hotel proper and dining rooms, and the lower side by a two-story brick building for sleeping rooms, in which is the post office. And this building is flanked on the west by a wooden cottage, and just beyond, at the foot of the precipice, *the spring,* with a stone and wooden covering, temple-fashion. And on the east it is flanked by the *barroom,* and (across the road farther on) by the ballroom and bachelors' hall. We room in this central brick building at the lower side of the campus—a corner room; and just across a narrow lane is the said barroom, so we get the benefit of any racket at night created by too free a use of mint juleps, sherry cobblers, and hailstorms (names we have learned here). We have the benefit also of the music in the ballroom every evening; and at our distance from it it sounds almost all the time like the whinny of young animals whose name may not be mentioned, with the accompaniment of Pandean pipes. It does not disturb us.

The visitors are very sociable and agreeable, and spend much time in calling upon each other. We have made many pleasant and profitable acquaintances, and they are almost all truly pious Christian people. Indeed, you would be surprised at the number of professors of religion here of all denominations, and what a marked sobriety there is on the face of the community, and with what remarkable propriety the Sabbath is observed. An Episcopal minister preached on Sabbath and carried out his service, and nearly one-half the visitors appeared of that persuasion. It would be a blessing to these resorts if the proprietors would employ a minister for the season so as to *secure* services every Sabbath. Most visitors would gladly contribute to his support if it could not be otherwise provided. But if the proprietors can afford to pay from three hundred to nine hundred dollars for music, and have barrooms and ninepin alleys and billiard rooms and gambling dens, they might, with a better conscience, I am sure, have *regular* religious services for their visitors.

It is quite a lively scene: children playing on the green; persons sitting in their piazzas and on the benches under the trees; ladies and gentlemen out promenading, and a constant stream going to and from the spring; stages arriving and departing; and music vocal and instrumental lending its aid; green mountains around, and the bright sun and deep blue sky above all. This is the scene before me now while I write. Your dear mother is sitting by me at her work, and we have no sounds in our little chamber but the racing of my pen over the paper, and the rustle of the silk and the drawing of her stitches and the occasional click of her scissors as she plies the work on her new dress. She is looking as well as I ever saw her, and it affords me great satisfaction that our travel has been so agreeable and beneficial to her. But she is continually saying: "Oh, I want to see my dear children so much! My dear precious child—I do want to see her so much!" And I am saying the same thing. And when we read your letter about your sickness and your joy at your brother's coming, we both said "The dear child!" and cried.

We expected to leave here yesterday, Monday the 27th, but Mother thought that I had improved a little and we might remain till Thursday, making two weeks. It matters not where we stay, if we could only see improvement. General health good; inaction much the same. Have been praying for some decided indications of the Lord's will respecting my restoration to wonted strength, but have received no decided answer yet. Mother says I am not to expect miracles but a gradual improvement, and that will be the answer. I long to be at work again, if it is the Lord's will. There is so much to be done in the world.

We expect, as we have already mentioned, to take the Virginia & Tennessee Railroad to Knoxville (some fifty miles' staging), and thence to Chattanooga, and so on to Rome and Marietta. It is our nearest and best route. We long to be at home; and yet I am afraid to go back, on account of cares and work, which will be sure to come on me. Must be very resolute and cast all off and give myself a chance for a while.

Tell my dear son I received his long and affectionate and interesting letter a few days ago, and will answer it soon. He must not overtask himself. Take regular and sufficient exercise, eat moderately, and do not sit up late at night studying.

Do, my dear child, write to your Uncle William and beg him to come up and see you, and omit no attentions to him. A year ago this month your dear aunt left us for her heavenly rest, and he is all alone now, and we must do all we can to make him happy. I wrote him a short time since. Always let us know how he is when you write.

We feel grateful to your Aunt Susan for her kindness in spending a week with you. Perhaps you ought not to expose yourself in too long rides. You should exercise daily, and a ride out in some pleasant part of the day will much refresh you. Tell Lucy and Kate howdy for us, and that we are glad that they are useful to you. Send howdy by Charles to all the people at Arcadia for us; and always make him come in every week on his visits to Lucy and give you an account of everything on the plantation.

July 29th. Not so well today. Fever last night. Went to Dr. Davidson to buy some quinine (twenty grains). "What is the price, doctor?" "Nothing: never charge ministers anything." *This is a custom all through Virginia.* . . . We think we shall leave here tomorrow for the Rockbridge Baths, another watering place, between here and Lexington, right on our way, where we shall remain until Monday, D.V., and so move on. . . . Do not write till you hear from us again, unless you write us to Rome or to Marietta.

Write your dear aunt in Marietta. She will be glad to hear from you, and it is an attention you owe her. We received a long and affectionate letter from her last night in which she says she has heard but very seldom from Liberty. Says she: "I miss the faithful correspondence *of my dear Betsy.*" "Thou shalt rise up before the old and gray-headed" is our Lord's command in the Old Testament. And how much more should we show reverence and attention to the old and gray-headed when they are our own kindred according to the flesh! Robert, my dear son, preach a sermon to the youth of your church and congregation from *that text*. It will do great good; our children and young people need it everywhere and at all times.

Mother sends with me much love to you both. Fear God, love, and be happy.

Your ever affectionate father,
C. C. Jones.

Our love to all our dear relatives on the Sand Hills, and to Uncle William when you see him.

MRS. MARY JONES *to* MRS. MARY S. MALLARD[t]

Rockbridge Baths, Virginia, *Saturday,* August 1st, 1857

My ever dear Daughter,

Leaving the Rockbridge Alum, where we spent two weeks very pleasantly in a choice circle of Christian friends, but where your dear father improved, *he thought,* but little, we came over to this watering place day before yesterday. And he has written so graphic and truthful a description of our journey here (back to some friends at the Rockbridge Alum) that I will just transcribe that portion of his letter, for I conceive that it will deeply interest you:

"The rain ceased yesterday, and our ride was delightful, and for the distance one of the most interesting we ever made. Did you ever hear or know anything of the passage of the North River through the North Mountain? No? Then let me tell you something of it. Our drive up the valley between the Mill and North Mountain extended some six or eight miles, when our prospect opened: on the left the Mill Mountain stretching away north, in front a rolling valley; and mountains beyond that turned across and met the North Mountain going down on our right. We turned south and east at right angles from our road, and before us the mountain broke down, and there was the first gap—a level meadow and farm on our left. A shower passed before us on the mountains. We stopped at a spring, and while there the sun, which was high, shone out and threw a brilliant and perfectly defined rainbow, one foot resting on the plain; and the arch, coursing up the mountain, swept over into the heavens and bent down along the brow, where it descended at the gap; and the other foot was set in the very track before us —the whole valley, the mountain forests (wet with the shower and shining through the watery veil), and the crest of the mountain from one side of this glorious arch to the other crowned with a milk-white vapor. Our admiration was extreme. How beautiful! We got down upon our knees in the carriage and gazed out of the windows at this vision—the first we had ever seen of a rainbow on the mountains.

"The sun gradually withdrew his shining, and the vision faded. The rain fell heavily on the mountain; it smoked with boiling vapor; and we drove into the gap. The road runs on the right bank of the river, and is cut into the face of the mountains; in many places is walled up with stones next the river for support. And as it follows the serpentine course of the stream, it ascends and descends, now elevated twenty, forty, sixty feet, or at times (it seems) a hundred, and now descending to the level of the water. And so it runs until it reaches the other side in the great Valley of Virginia.

"The first gap is imposing, with the roaring river below and mountains on either side. But when you enter the second gap (one continuation), the scenery rises into the picturesque and reaches the grand. In the chasm far below, the swollen waters brawl and rush and foam through shoals of great rocks thrown down from the overhanging cliffs; and lifting your eyes, you see the chasm opening hundreds of feet above to the tops of the mountains. Great masses of rock open on the face of the mountains; there the strata lie as when 'the foundations were laid'; they come out on the crown of the huge pile and lie along like a great fortification. The river winds, and at every turn new views present themselves; and the scenery engages the whole attention until you emerge into the valley. The recent rain had saturated the mountain along whose face our road lay, and springs gushed in jets from the rocks, and little cascades fell, mingling their glad voices with the roar of the river to which they were speeding. We turned this way and that; we changed our seats; now we were on the floor; now we were on our seats again—admiring every change, and discovering new beauty in rocks and streams and forests. All this is worth a trip from Georgia to see."

August 3rd. My dear child, on Saturday our kind and attentive landlord, Mr. Jordan, rigged up his "pleasure wagon" (which is a kind of light omnibus on springs, without a top), and your father and myself, one lady and four gentlemen took a drive about half way through the mountain gorge, which lost nothing by a second sight of its grandeur and magnificence. When we stopped to turn, most of the party ascended to a rocky height overlooking a scene of peculiar wildness: rocks of every size and shape piled upon each other in every direction. Through the trees and rocks we caught glimpses of a beautiful mountain cascade of about fifty feet fall, but broken in its descent. It was said to be very charming by two of the gentlemen who clambered down to the bottom. Your father and a gentleman from New Orleans (affected much like himself) could ascend but a short way; they sat and rested until we came down.

Yesterday we enjoyed the privilege of hearing the gospel preached twice. In the morning your father went in the buggy and attended the Sabbath school and spoke to the children. At the usual hour I went with the ladies in the "pleasure wagon." The church is an ancient brick edifice with galleries on three sides, divided in the middle: half for whites and the other for blacks. The pulpit alone was painted. It is located on a lofty ridge surrounded by the native forest trees, and very near by flows the North River with its ever-murmuring sounds rushing along its rocky bed. The congregation came pouring in from every direction, some in carriages, some in buggies. Here would be a man and his wife on horseback; there two ladies riding the same horse; now a father with his wife or daughter or little son behind holding tightly on as they straightened up the hill. . . . Whilst we were sitting, a servant brought in a large wooden pitcher (very much like a churn with a handle and top), and placing a tumbler on the lid, put it on a bench beneath the pulpit. And immediately a number of little thirsty urchins rose and refreshed themselves. The congregation assembled in a most quiet and reverential manner; they appeared to realize the fact that God was in His holy temple. Eight young men (teachers of the Sabbath school) occupied the front seat and formed the choir. At the right moment the venerable pastor, Rev. *Mr. Trimble,* ascended the pulpit. The invocation was most appropriate. Then was sung

> Through every age, eternal God,
> Thou art our rest, our safe abode—

the congregation joining with heart and voice. Then the chapter (II Corinthians 5): "For we know that if our earthly house of this tabernacle were dissolved," etc. The chapter ended, the congregation rose; and the man of God broke forth in the language of Moses: "Lord, thou hast been our dwelling place in all generations," etc. Most humble, penitent, fervent, and believing was his prayer. His text was chosen from the chapter he had read (II Corinthians 5:20), and most faithfully did he as an ambassador for Christ deliver his message of truth and mercy. We enjoyed the precious Word. This church is called Bethesda, and is one of that number that has long blessed this land so early favored with the godly teaching and influence of devoted Presbyterian ministers. . . . In the afternoon we heard Rev. Mr. Huff, a Baptist minister. He preached in the ballroom of our hotel, and gave us a very good sermon. He is a young man, not long in the ministry, but bore marks of decided talent.

The bathing is very pleasant. The spring is simply limestone water. The pool is twenty feet square and about four and a half feet deep—perfectly clear and rising constantly in bubbles to the surface, the water not very cold but invigorating. Your dear father has not derived any perceptible benefit from their use, and tomorrow, *God willing,* we expect to leave for Lexington on our way home. . . . We hope to spend a little time with your uncle in Rome and friends in Marietta. . . . We do so long, my dear child, to see you and be near all our dear children. . . . Best love to Robert and yourself. Remember us kindly to all relatives and friends. . . . May God's blessing ever rest upon you!

Your own affectionate mother,
Mary Jones.

REV. C. C. JONES *to* MR. CHARLES C. JONES, JR.^g

Rome, *Monday,* August 10th, 1857

My dear Son,

We arrived here at your uncle's, through divine mercy, on Saturday last at two to dinner. We came by the Virginia & East Tennessee Railroad via

Knoxville, and had to ride one entire night and the half of a night in the stage. And the entire night's ride was forty-two miles—the gap between the termini of the railroad in Tennessee. The distance from the Virginia line (Bristol) to Knoxville is some hundred and twenty miles. From Bristol we took the cars twenty-one miles to Jonesboro, and then the stages forty-two over as rough a road as any man need travel, and then took the railroad again fifty-seven miles to Knoxville. Here we stepped from one car to another and ran down to Dalton, and next day came here. The half night's ride was on our way from Lexington, Virginia, to the Virginia & Tennessee Railroad.

Your dear mother was most decidedly affected by the *forty-two miles'* staging—so rough and jolting—and passed an uncomfortable night at Dalton. Yesterday she went to church, and last night was taken with very severe pain, similar to her attack at Maybank two years ago. She rose and took a good dose of blue mass and magnesia, and after some two hours of suffering she was enabled to sleep, and feels much better this morning, and has just taken a dose of Sampson (the old standby), and says she hopes soon to be entirely relieved. I was much distressed last night, remembering her extreme illness at Maybank, but pray that she may now have no severe return of that sickness. She has been so remarkably fat and hearty, and has enjoyed her trip so much that I was hopeful she would reach home without any drawback. That forty-two miles! Enough to make a robust man sick—and not one wink of sleep possible.

We met your Uncle John at Kingston (the place he parted with us) on his way home from Athens, where he had expressly and most kindly gone to forward your brother's interests. And it was well that he was there to represent him and answer inquiries. He did good service, and in a candid and gentlemanly manner, and had the satisfaction (in which we all share) of learning, when the election was declared, that your brother had received *a unanimous vote*. He has much amusing matter to relate of things said and done in one way and another on the occasion. I feel truly grateful to him for his kindness. He has done everything he could. Joe owes much—very much —to him, and also to his Uncle Henry, who originated the matter. And we owe a great deal to our old friend *Judge Law*. Your uncle says he used all his influence for Joe, and made a speech before the trustees almost an hour long in his favor. But we will talk it all over when we meet, D.V. Am sorry to hear your brother has been so sick. Will write him in a day or two. *He must make his arrangements leisurely to remove to Athens, and not go until he has fairly recovered and is able to resume study to advantage.*

Your uncle and Aunt Jane are quite well. Your aunt's health, we think, is better. Johnnie and Joe are two as interesting and beautiful boys as you will see in a thousand. We hear their little voices now. We enjoyed your uncle's sermon yesterday morning on the text: "Behold, I lay in Zion a cornerstone," etc. It was a very fine sermon. I went with him in the afternoon to his black Sabbath school. We did not go out at night on account of the distance.

Our present plan is to stay here a few days, and a few days with Aunt at Marietta, and then go down home. Will write you what day to expect us. If you can, send this letter out to your dear sister, and Joe will see it also. All in the house unite in a great deal of love to you. Mother and I are very anxious to see our dear children once more. It seems an age since we parted. The Lord be praised for His tender mercies towards us! Tell Sue and the boys howdy for us. Have written this before breakfast in my nightdress to be in time for the morning's mail. I remain, my dear son,

Your ever affectionate father,
C. C. Jones.

REV. C. C. JONES *to* DR. JOSEPH JONES[t]

Rome, Monday, August 10th, 1857

My dear Son,

I wrote your brother this morning, which letter you will see, giving a short account of our travel and arrival here at your uncle's on Saturday the 8th, and of Mother's sickness. Am happy to say she continues to improve, and hope she will be in a few hours wholly relieved.

Your election was unanimous, and you owe very much to your Uncle Henry for the origination of the matter, and to your Uncle John for his deep interest in your success, and for his own presence and personal efforts in Athens on your behalf. He conducted the affair in a candid and gentlemanly and at the same time an independent manner, and did nothing which was not consistent with honor and truth. And I am specially pleased that he acted in a generous and kind and friendly manner towards the other candidate, towards whom we all entertain none other than kind feelings. And had he been elected, I should have felt a sincere satisfaction in it. Your uncle's presence in Athens was of special advantage, for he was enabled to answer many important inquiries and give information which was of material importance. He is well pleased at the result, and will write you himself. Your own dear brother has acted the part of a brother, and has done everything that lay in his power for you. I hope and believe you will ever cleave to each other and be helpful to each other as affectionate and devoted brothers through all the scenes of life so long as you are spared on earth. Your mother and father have ever desired that both of you and your dear sister may be one in affection and interest always. We also owe much—very much —to our old friend Judge Law, who took the warmest interest in your election and actually spoke for an hour before the board of trustees in your favor, and at the same time said not a word to the disparagement of our young friend's claims, but everything in his favor.

Under the circumstances, the vote's being *unanimous* is particularly gratifying; and my sincere hope is that if our friend has had any unkind feeling arising from wrong impressions, that when he comes fully to understand that at the time he was at Montevideo and in Savannah you had not the most remote idea of the office; and that it was some time *after* when the suggestion was first made by your Uncle Henry and urged by him and others upon you; and that you did not consent to it until all hope of a profitable continuation in your professorship in the medical college in Savannah was at an end; and that you had entered into no pledges with anyone, nor with himself, to support him, and no pledges that you yourself would not offer for the appointment; and that the appointment was public, open to the whole literary world, and candidates were invited to present their claims—nor were you under any obligations of friendship or otherwise to prefer his claims to your own; I say, when he comes to consider these things, I hope he will not feel improperly towards you or your friends. He had the same access to the office that you had, and made all the interest in his power. The whole matter was open, in the daylight, and the board decided according to their best judgment. It is decided, and let it be so. We must now *say nothing to anyone on the subject*. We have no triumphs to celebrate. We did not go into the matter with feelings of opposition to our friend, nor with desires to defeat him as a thing specially gratifying to us. We did nothing whatsoever to prejudice his election; but all we did was of the contrary character. We looked upon him as a friend, and the competition was open and friendly on our part. Say nothing further. If any statements come to our personal knowledge that need correcting, we can quietly make the correction. But let no one *volunteer* to set you right. There is no need of it, and it would be not only highly improper but decidedly injurious.

Your parents feel grateful to all your kind relatives and friends who have aided you. We prayed over the whole thing and endeavored to leave it wholly with our Heavenly Father, and whichever way it should by Him be decided, to feel satisfied that all would be right.

And now through His great goodness, my dear son, He has given you an honorable, a useful and valuable position—one in which you may be eminently useful to your state and country, and in which you will after a while have ample time to prosecute your favorite branches of science. You will have the great advantage of a good climate, an agreeable and literary society and abundant religious privileges, a sufficient pecuniary support, and a vacation of some three months in the year. And now your *physiological investigations must be suspended for a while,* and your attention be given to a thorough preparation on the different branches of natural science which you are required to teach in the college. It is essential to your success and good standing, and to your character, that you be *a good professor.* Your success in the medical college last season in Savannah I trust may be an earnest of your success in Athens. I have a strong belief that you will be successful. But I must caution you—and as your father lay my positive commands upon you

—to moderate your application to study. You have, I am confident, pushed your application too far; and your recent sickness is a result of it. And unless you alter especially the habit of night studies and late sleeping, my dear son, you cannot last, but must bring on an enfeebled constitution and premature decay. Nor will you be under any necessity for such excessive application in your new position. You are young, especially in the branches (or some, at least) you will teach; and the faculty and trustees will give you time to grow. You must not attempt too much, but go on faithfully and carefully and gradually, and bring your classes on as fast and far and fundamentally as you can. Avoid mental excitement in your pursuit after knowledge, and take exercise and plenty of early and refreshing sleep. You need this more perhaps than you are aware of.

And as you have been sick with fever, you must enter into no engagements to be at your post at any particular time near at hand, but write Dr. Church how it is with you: that your sickness has been unexpected and providential; and that you will go to Athens so soon as you are able to assume, with hope of health, your office there; and meantime you trust he and the faculty will consent to spare you. They are shorthanded in the college and need you, but you must not go before you are able to resume work. I have no fears but that you will conscientiously discharge *all the duties* devolving upon you as an officer of college, and that, *treating the president and professors with every official and personal respect,* you will secure their confidence and esteem. May God grant you His grace and favor and make you an ornament and blessing to the institution!

We intend, God willing, to remain a few days with your uncle and aunt here, and a few days with Aunty in Marietta, and so come on down home. You must by no means leave before we reach home. We wish to see you very much, and Mother says "she will have to fix you up before you go."

I will here mention through your Uncle John that my friend *Mr. William L. Mitchell* of Athens, one of the trustees of the college, took a lively interest in your election, and requested that you would on reaching Athens *go immediately to his house,* and remain with him until you could arrange for your location, board, etc. This is an offer of sincere friendship, and I wish you to accept it, and make Mr. Mitchell your friend. He is one of the best of men.

Your Uncle John and Aunt Jane send much love, and little Johnnie and Josie say: "Tell Cousin Joe howdy for us." And Johnnie says: "Tell Cousin Josie that I had the *monia,* and me and Josie had the measles; and the doctor took a fedder, and put it in salt and water and bitter, and poked it down Josie's throat, and mine too, three times, and gave me and Josie brandy three times, and I liked the brandy." Mother sends much love. Love to Sister and Brother Robert, and to all our relatives in Liberty. Howdy for all the servants.

Your affectionate father,
C. C. Jones.

Mrs. Mary S. Mallard *to* Miss Mary Jones Taylor[t]

Walthourville, *Wednesday*, August 12th, 1857

My dear Mary,

You say it takes two weeks, judging from dates, for a letter to travel from Georgia to Berlin. I think the distance is a little longer from Berlin to Georgia! I intended to have answered your interesting letter upon the same night that I received it, but I believe company prevented; and you must know from experience that if one is disappointed in the first attempt, a letter is apt to lie unanswered a long time. But there is no use in filling this sheet with such trash, so will proceed to answer some of your surmises and queries.

You say: "How much your mother must miss you!" My mother and father are not at home at present. I think I mentioned in a former letter that they left home, much to my joy, before I did, and went to Kentucky to attend the General Assembly. After the adjournment of the assembly they remained a week near Lexington with a relative, then went to Cincinnati and spent a short time with an old friend residing there. From this place they passed into Virginia, stopping a few days at the White Sulphur Springs, and then went to the Hot Springs for the benefit of Father's health. They remained three weeks at this place, and as Father had not been at all benefited, went to the Rockbridge Alum Springs, Virginia. Here they remained two weeks, and now, I presume, are on their way home via Marietta and Rome. We have relatives in both of these places, and I presume they will spend a short time in each. So you see, Mother has hardly had time to feel that I have left home. In winter they will be twelve miles from us, and their summer residence is twenty-six miles distant—quite a journey for a warm day!

I entirely agree with you that housekeeping in the city is not worthy the name. It really is not—especially in Philadelphia. I think *it* quite a paradise for housekeepers—provided they have a long purse! In answer to your question, I keep my own house and visit the smokehouse *occasionally;* also make my fingers acquainted with the ingredients of loaf bread, undertake to whip eggs, wash cups, see that the servants thrust their brooms into dusty corners, buy beef, pickle cabbage and other vegetables, besides many other fascinating little amusements connected with this wonderful science called housekeeping. . . . The best of it is, Mr. Mallard approves all my culinary performances, and does all he can to take away cares; often reads aloud to me. In between whiles I practice a little on my piano and read to myself. Mr. Mallard and I have a good deal of visiting to do, and of course some calls to receive, so you see we try to occupy our time. He is in his study in the mornings, and this morning I am there too, writing at the same table. He is composing a sermon from the text: "For it must needs be that offenses come, but woe unto that man by whom the offense cometh," while I am running on to you about worldly cares. (It is well my pen does not speak aloud, for if it did, I do not think his would move along as quietly as it is now doing!)

You want to know something about our house, congregation, and church.

Well, to begin at our dwelling place (for I do not call it home), it is a rented house—wood, and plain in exterior (used to be painted). Within, it is comfortably and neatly furnished, and we think our drawing room is as pretty, saving the papering on the wall, as any we could desire. (When you are married and have a companion to share your cares and pleasures, you will know how to make allowances for any expressions I may use in speaking of matters and things in general.) But to return to the drawing room. There stands my piano, whose tones you heard in Philadelphia. I sometimes neglect it, and I ought to say often. Until a week or two past I have had no new pieces to learn. Good ballads are rare. Whenever you hear a pretty one, do send me the name. Your likeness has a place, together with Mr. Mallard's and mine, on our bureau. Mr. Mallard says I ought to give them a place on the whatnot, so I think I will. I am sorry you are so situated as not to be able to have another likeness taken for me. I wish you would whenever you can; and tell Sarah Ann I wish she would deign to place her countenance upon the same plate, as I hear it has grown to be quite pretty. How flourishes her correspondence with Matilda Harden? This latter young lady resides about eight miles from this place; I have seen her once this summer, and then she looked thin.

It seems to me, my dear Mary, that as soon as I begin to say anything about the house, so many other thoughts obtrude that I will have to content myself by saying it is situated in the midst of what we call a "pine barren." You have been amongst Jersey pines, so know something about such a region of country. The community is composed chiefly of planters. The society is pleasant; I believe almost everyone in the village has called upon us. The church is in sight of our house: a neat wooden building. I have received a great deal of kindness from persons here; we have been supplied with vegetables, and I have beautiful flowers sent me. Speaking of flowers, I shall be most happy to receive some seeds of that vine I admired so much in Philadelphia, and will plant them and think of you. As to your Georgia acorn, I am afraid it is too old to germinate, as acorns seldom do after becoming dry. I knew of a box of earth being placed under an oak tree by a gentleman who wished to take some live oaks to the up country; the experiment succeeded very well, for a number of the acorns fell in the box and soon germinated. If I ever get an opportunity to Berlin, I will send you a small tree; or still better, if ever I am called near that region, will bring one. By the way, how could I get there, supposing I were in Baltimore?

I am fast coming to the conclusion that I ought to stop, but before I close must tell you a little piece of news. You recollect my Cousin Joe West, who used to be with us in Philadelphia? He was married the other day to a Miss Rogers of Savannah. He has been in Paris for more than a year, attending the medical lectures there, and now has returned home; and the next step I have told you. . . . Do write soon and let me know anything of Philadelphia friends you may hear. Give love to your mother and Sallie. Mr. Mallard says he has seen your picture, so feels acquainted with you and sends his kind regards. Accept much love from

Your affectionate friend,
Mary S. Mallard.

Mrs. Mary S. Mallard *to* Mrs. Mary Jones[t]
Walthourville, *Thursday,* August 13th, 1857

My dear Mother,

On Monday I received your interesting letter written from Rockbridge Baths. Today's mail brought Mr. Mallard a long letter from dear Father, in which he speaks of your sickness. We are truly sorry to hear it, and sincerely hope you will have no more of it. I am glad you will have no more stage rides to take.

I think I shall be almost beside myself when you return. Do you think there is no risk in coming back so soon? Thus far the summer has been remarkably cool, but now the August suns are beginning to beam upon us with great power.

Since I last wrote our household has been increased by the addition of another canary and two kittens. The former was given me by Cousin Mary Wells, and I call him Charlie Wells. The kittens belong to Duchess, and she is as proud as mothers in general.

I wrote Aunt Mary last week telling her all the news, and suppose you have seen that letter. You will probably see Uncle Henry and Aunt Abby, and they will give you a full detail of all interesting items. . . . Mom Patience and family have been moved to the Island; they were all sick at Montevideo. Gilbert's poor little Nancy died about three weeks ago; she had a recurrence of those spasms which she used to have, and I believe died in one of them. Maria has lost her infant: born dead. With these exceptions the people have been pretty well; and they say Mr. Barnard is very kind and attentive. When there is sickness he sometimes goes twice a day to the place. . . . Mr. and Mrs. Walthour have gone to Columbia, where Dr. and Aunt Howe will join them and go to Philadelphia to see Walthour. I am afraid there is but little hope of his recovery. . . . Brother Joe's election is very gratifying, but I do not think he is strong enough to undertake the duties at present.

Mr. Mallard says he is very glad to hear you are so near home, and that you are coming directly here. Please give our love to all of our dear aunts and cousins, for I suppose you will be in Marietta when this reaches you. Mr. Mallard unites with me in warmest love to dear Father and yourself.

Your attached child,
Mary S. Mallard.

XI

Maybank, *Wednesday,* September 2nd, 1857

My dear Daughter,

It was eight last night when your brother's arrival was heralded by Rex and Jet. The wind had been blowing briskly from the northeast all day, and did not subside as night set in. The windows and doors were closed, and I was in the entry reading to your dear father, who reclined on the couch. We had been watching his coming since sunset, and knew not until we heard the bark of the dogs and his step in the piazza that he had arrived. You know, old Aunt Ellen used to say "she loved Mr. Charles, he was so heartsome." And we are cheered by the presence of the dear child. Today he is not very well: I prepared some crabs for his supper, which he ate, and drank sweet milk after them, which did him harm last night. But he is now off rigging his beautiful sailboat.

I am so delighted, my darling child, to know that Robert and yourself will soon be with us. I sent your note over to your aunt this morning, and Gilbert has just returned with her answer: "Mr. Buttolph will exchange with Mr. Mallard." So I presume the brethren will make their own arrangements. I want you to write *us certainly* by next *Monday's* mail what day we shall send the carriage for you. You must not come in the buggy, for the carriage is at your service, and there will be less fatigue in coming in it. I am grieved to know of your indisposition, and think a little change will do you good. I cannot begin to tell you how much we miss you. I try to console myself with the reflection that the happiness of my children should be my happiness, but this philosophy does not always still the heart's yearning.

The work I will send up when the carriage goes. . . . Our friends on the Island are all well, and desire a great deal of love to you and Robert. . . . Little Charlie is cutting his fifth tooth, and is indeed a fine babe. . . . Please when you come bring my workbasket that was sent out from Savannah. . . . Your dear father has not been well since Sabbath; he spoke twice on that day to the servants, and has been fatiguing himself arranging and putting his study in order. I trust he may not lose what he has gained. . . . Father and Brother unite with me in best love to Robert and yourself. The Lord bless you, my dear child!

Ever your affectionate mother,
Mary Jones.

Excuse a broken steel pen.

Rev. C. C. Jones *to* Mrs. Mary S. Mallard[t]

Maybank, *Wednesday,* September 2nd, 1857

When we left you, my dear daughter, last Monday week, it was the first time I realized that I could not take my dear child home with me, and I was excessively sad all day. But you are now acting a woman's part in life, and a Christian's part, and I know the Lord will be with and bless you. And I feel assured that you and Robert will be happy in each other, and helpful to each other in all your interests for time and for eternity.

When you feel weak or unwell you must not exert yourself as much as usual. And do not tax your strength to go to four services on the Sabbath (including your Sunday school) when you are feeling badly.

We anticipate your visit with great pleasure; and a little relaxation will do Robert no harm. Gilbert will come up the night before the day you shall name for leaving Walthourville, and then you can take an early start, stop at Dorchester to dinner if you choose, and reach Maybank to tea.

The weather has been cool and pleasant: wind northeast for two days. Have been wearing my thick coat. . . . Your Aunt Susan and Cousin Lyman rode up while we were at dinner, on their way to Dorchester to lecture. It looking like rain, she remained and he went on; and the rain did come. She sends a great deal of love to you and to your good husband, and says "she will let her son exchange with her nephew, and then you can come and pay us all a visit."

We have letters from Marietta. All well. Much love to my dear son. *Numbers 6:24–26.*

From your ever affectionate father,
C. C. Jones.

Rev. R. Q. Mallard *to* Mrs. Mary S. Mallard[t]

Walthourville, *Monday,* September 21st, 1857

My darling Wife,

"Last not least" my pen has written for *you* the *fifth* "Walthourville, September 21st," etc. I almost hope this letter will miscarry—that before it reaches the Island my arms will enfold my Mary. I requested Charlie at parting to tell you that in compassion upon the horses you had better remain at Maybank until Friday; but I am sure I shall be disposed to treat Jerry and his friend very handsomely if they should strain a point and bring you back on Thursday. The house is lonesome without you, and I have been counting the days until you shall return. This separation is far from being a pleasant business. The first night (I will confess it sub rosa) that I slept in our room I was a "leetle" nervous. This evening, as the shadows of approaching night were falling, and the pattering rain dripping from the piazza eaves, I wished very much that the vacant chair by my side was occupied by my sweet Mary. And inasmuch as this wish could not be gratified, I sent her a kiss. Away, away let it go—through pine top, over swamp and marsh—

until it gently presses those lips for which mine are now longing. I hope that nothing will keep you much longer away.

I have given all the directions to the servants as you requested. The pipe clay is now sucking most lustily at the grease spots of the much-abused pantry. The unusual crown of pan-and-shucks resting this morning upon the unostentatious head of the step-post gives—or gave—proof that the costermonger has been about. The cloth is fast assuming under the manipulations of Lucy form and shape; at least, so I infer. The staring bars of a skeleton bedstead proved today for its usual covering an alibi. I have not invaded the culinary department, and trust that personal inspection may not be necessary. The shower left nothing to be desired for your garden pets. Thus you see that your memorandum was not forgotten.

Today I began "breaking in corn." Was interrupted too soon by the rain to form any good estimate of the probable yield. Hope to make more than "four acres to the bushel."

This is mail day. No letters for you, but one for me from Brother Porter, another from Smith & English. D. H. P. thanks us very heartily for our invitation, but is afraid to leave the city to return before frost. Mrs. Porter, he says, is far from being well. Smith & English regret the miscarriage of my book, and offer to send me another for half price. I have remitted to them the full amount. I had this evening both a disappointment and surprise. Seeing James approaching with two books from the mail, I at once concluded that the missing book had turned up and had become traveling companion to another sent by Smith & English. Breaking open the packages, I found that some unknown friend had sent me the two volumes of *Theodosia Ernest,* a Baptist religious novel. . . .

Pussy's darlings are in good health and quite frolicsome. They clamber up on me at meals in a manner that sometimes gives me a feeling sense of the keenness of their claws. When I passed through the piazza on my way upstairs, I found them very lovingly stowed away in my opened umbrella.

It is now nearly ten o'clock (since —— your hour for retiring), and I must hasten to give you a kiss before you are off and far away in the land of dreams. A pleasant rest to you, my love! And may our Heavenly Father bless you and keep you, is the constant prayer of

Your loving husband,
R. Q. Mallard.

Mr. Charles C. Jones, Jr., *to* Rev. *and* Mrs. C. C. Jones[t]

Savannah, *Saturday,* September 26th, 1857

My dear Father and Mother,

So completely am I again immersed in customary office duties that I can hardly persuade myself that the ordinary routine has even for a moment been interrupted. But the pleasant recollection of my recent delightful sojourn with you on the Island is often present, and never remembered except with much regret that the stay should have been shortened, and that in all probability the obligations of business will not permit a repetition for many days. The duties of an attorney in full practice are very engrossing, and demand uninterrupted attention. In fact, the same is true of every profession if its calls are faithfully met. I am now alone in the office, and consequently much occupied. And it is to me a source of pleasure and congratulation that the opportunity is afforded of enjoying the delights and profits of a large practice. Thanks to early education, I am not afraid of work.

Our city is now very quiet, although it is feared the pressure in the money market at the North will have an unfavorable effect. You have doubtless observed in what an unfortunate condition the banks in the principal Northern cities now find themselves.

Cousin Charles and Cousin Eliza are at present unwell. Nothing serious. Charlie, their little son, also has fever.

Can you not prevail upon the Doctor to remain longer with you than he purposed when leaving the city? I think he owes it to himself, in consideration of past and future engagements, to improve the opportunity for relaxation. But with him it is emphatically the case, "like father, like son." Hoping that his medical skill may prove of great benefit to you both, my dear parents, I remain, with much love,

Your affectionate son,
Charles C. Jones, Jr.

MR. CHARLES C. JONES, JR., *to* REV. *and* MRS. C. C. JONES[t]

Savannah, Wednesday, September 30th, 1857

My dear Father and Mother,

On Monday last the sad intelligence was conveyed, through a letter written by Jackson Maxwell to his brother Thomas, of the death of Josephine. The particulars Jackson does not minutely detail. He says he is very desolate. . . . A bride but six short weeks since, and now in the bosom of the damp earth! You will observe a notice of the death of Aunt Augusta—herself and little Elliott—in the *News* which reaches you tomorrow.

Our city is full of political excitement. Mr. Ward has serious opposition at the hands of the disaffected and a portion of the "Know-Nothing" party (that party having made no nominations), who support the claims of one John Cooper, who appears as an independent candidate for the Senate. Cooper is a shopkeeper—a man of no qualifications for the position sought, and is supported by a faction, by no means small, composed of men of his own and worse stamp, who are opposed to strict city regulations, etc., etc. The opposition is not to be despised, and much will have to be done to secure Mr. Ward's election as matters now stand. He will get the vote of all respectable men. We hope for a change for the better in the mind of the *vulgus commune.*

The Doctor quite well, and all at Cousin Eliza's recovered. I write in pain. My head aches violently, and I must bid you good evening. With warmest love to you both, my dear parents, I am, as ever,

Your affectionate son,
Charles C. Jones, Jr.

Thanks, Mother, for the Indian darts. The potatoes are excellent. Love to all friends and relatives, and howdy for the servants. If Old George brings an Indian pipe to Maybank for me, please pay him twenty-five dollars and keep it for me. And if you have an opportunity, please remind him of his promise to bring it.

MR. CHARLES C. JONES, JR., *to* REV. *and* MRS. C. C. JONES[t]
Savannah, *Thursday,* October 8th, 1857

My dear Father and Mother,

Many thanks to a kind Providence, I am again up, and I hope over my attack, having yesterday and today thus far missed my fever. I am still, however, as you may imagine, very weak, and compelled to remain quiet. This morning I wrote some half-dozen business letters, and brought a few writs for the court that demanded immediate attention. Tomorrow, I hope, if the weather is favorable, to ride to the office and see how matters and things have progressed without me. . . . As glad as I would have been to have seen you both, my dear parents, I was happy that you did not fatigue yourselves by coming to the city. I have been in good hands—in the care of Drs. West and Jones.

You will see by the papers that our election on Monday was all that we could have desired. How badly Mr. Bartow will be defeated throughout the district! I myself was unable to vote. This I regretted, but of course under the circumstances it could not be otherwise.

I regret very much, Father, to hear of your serious fall. Hope you have recovered entirely from its effects. Your note, Mother, and the basket safely arrived. For both of them we are much obliged to you. The eggs are excellent—just the article of diet I craved. The butter also comes just in time, as our supply was exhausted. . . . All friends well. The Doctor is at the hospital, busied with the care of his hundred patients. With much love to you both, my dear father and mother, and kind regards to all friends on the Island, I am, as ever,

Your affectionate son,
Charles C. Jones, Jr.

MRS. MARY JONES *to* MRS. MARY S. MALLARD[t]
Maybank, *Friday,* October 9th, 1857

My dear Daughter,

I received your note by your uncle, who returned from the Sand Hills greatly pleased with his visit to Robert and yourself.

Thank you, my dear child, for the finished garments. You have done me a great service in having them made, for my arm continues so painful and weak in the muscles I know not when I shall be able to use it again. It now hangs in a sling whilst I am writing. Joe says it must be supported, and has sent me a bottle of palm oil for rubbing. This damp and stormy weather increases the pain; at times I hardly feel able to sit up.

I feared, my dear daughter, you would be alarmed at hearing that your father had fallen from his horse. I have had no opportunity of writing you an account of how it occurred. His riding horse (Jerry) was in the country, and he used one of the blacks, who is gentle and easy under the saddle. On returning he called George to take the horse; at the moment that he threw his feet from the stirrup and was rising on the saddle to dismount, George rushed up in haste and frightened the horse, who jumped and threw your father violently down on the back of his head and small of the back. The jar was so great as to deprive him of consciousness for a moment, but he soon recovered, and when I ran to him was standing, and walked immediately from the cornhouse (where it occurred) to the dwelling. I bathed his face with cold water and put a wet towel on his head, and he sat for some time in the cool breeze in the front piazza. That was Friday morning. On Saturday and Sunday there was such a sense of soreness and pain throughout his whole person that I persuaded him to keep quiet and not go to church. I rubbed his spine freely with chloroform liniment, and although he is much better, he still feels the effects. *Surely we have reason to bless and praise the Lord for this merciful deliverance!* I was never more alarmed in my life.

On Tuesday we received Joseph's letter saying that Charles was sick. I determined to go immediately to him; Patience volunteered to wean Robin and accompany me. Your father said he would go too—at least as far as the depot. So we got ready and started soon as we could after breakfast. At the depot we met a letter saying he was better. We wrote that we would spend the night at Montevideo and await the letter of the next day, and if Charles had a return of fever we would come down. Joseph's letter was received the next day by us at Arcadia, where we had gone to be in time for the cars, assuring us that his brother was so much better as to be considered almost well. I dispatched to them a little basket of eggs and butter, and we returned, grateful to God for His mercy to our child and to us. I am often filled with wonder and amazement when I look at our unworthiness and His great goodness and long-suffering toward us as a family. . . .

Your Aunt Julia had an anxious time last week and part of this. Mr. Parsons and Fred both quite sick with fever. Mr. Parsons took cold from sleeping with all the windows open one of those cold nights. Fred, Old George, and Israel went fishing; the sailboat upset; neither of the servants could swim. Fred had to jerk out the mast and sails that the boat might right, then assist the servants and swim after his trunk that had floated off, and then after every article (fish and all) that had floated from the boat, recovering almost everything through his perseverance and presence of mind.

He was a long time swimming; the exertion was very great without any assistance; and he was four hours in wet clothing before they reached Woodville at night. And all this in the cool weather of last week! It is no wonder he was taken sick. Through a kind Providence both are much better and up again.

Our friends at Social Bluff are quite well. They spent last Monday with us. Indeed, we have been alone but few days since our return home. . . . I will now leave this until Monday morning. For weeks the winds have prevailed from northeast: almost a hurricane tide for several days past; a sea between this and Sunbury. We hope the wind is changing this evening. A poor prospect for church tomorrow.

Monday Morning. How are you, my dear child, today? I trust well, and having enjoyed the privileges of God's Sabbath and sanctuary, feel refreshed for the duties of another week. We did not go out yesterday. It was damp and cloudy, with occasional scuds from the sea; but we should have ventured out if not detained by the lameness of one of the carriage horses. Your father sent a kind note to the minister expressing our regrets at not hearing him. We expect to send Gilbert for the buggy early this week.

A letter just from the mail from Charles. Am thankful he has missed his fever. Complains of weakness, but is again at business. How great is God's mercy and goodness to us as a family! . . . We have no further tidings from Key West; I hear that Dr. Jackson Maxwell is expected by the next steamer. . . . Father says he wants to see you every day. He unites with me in best love to Robert and yourself.

Ever, my dear daughter, your affectionate mother,

Mary Jones.

Mr. Charles C. Jones, Jr., *to* Rev. *and* Mrs. C. C. Jones[t]

Savannah, Saturday, October 10th, 1857

My dear Parents,

The wind still continues from the northeast, and the consequence is, the health of our city is materially impaired. The patients are (most of them) suffering from fevers and colds, which, although troublesome to those affected with them, generally yield readily to medical treatment. These northeast winds, coming as they do across the river and newly cut ricefields, are the most unhealthy that we have. It is fortunate that our city is situated on the southern bluff; were it located on the other side of the river, in all probability it would be anything else than a healthy city.

Today for the first time I ventured out of the house, and have attended to considerable business. I hope that my fever is thoroughly broken, and that with a little care there will be no recurrence.

The Doctor is very much occupied with his hospital engagements. He has now one hundred patients under his charge—an unusually large number, many of them seamen suffering from the effects of exposure on the river. It is astonishing the amount of exposure and consequent suffering which they as a class undergo.

I send by this mail a *Union* containing some interesting India items.

Our city labors at present under the effects of the great pressure in the money market. It is hoped that our banks will remain firm. The news has just reached us that the Bank of South Carolina has suspended specie payment. You have already noticed the condition of the Northern banks. There is now on the way a large quantity of specie both from France and England. The equilibrium will, it is hoped, soon be restored. There has been of late such a wild spirit of extravagance and reckless speculation in our country that this result can scarcely be wondered at.

Have just sent Mr. Martin amount necessary to pay all taxes, which I hope will safely reach him.

Cousin Charles and family and all friends well. Fires are comfortable. How I would like to be with you now and enjoy some fine oysters! Some of the pleasantest recollections of youthful days are connected with the first fall fires on the Island, shedding their cheerful rays around the parlor while the rude northeast wind came dashing its watery gusts against the windows. Well do I remember the first gathering of the little basket- and net-makers around the genial hearth and the delights there experienced. Oh, the happy days of youth—they come not again! But their pleasant recollections will be cherished while Memory holds her seat.

On Monday we have our municipal election. Brother unites with me in warmest love to you both, my dear parents. As ever,

Your affectionate son,
Charles C. Jones, Jr.

Kind remembrances to all friends on the Island. Willie quite well. Howdy for the servants.

DR. JOSEPH JONES *to* REV. C. C. JONES[t]

Savannah, *Thursday,* October 15th, 1857

My dear Father,

Your valued letter has been received, and we are glad to know that you will be so soon with us. Brother has had no return of fever, and is now enjoying his usual health. This morning he argued and gained a case in court against Colonel William B. Gaulden and Judge Harden.

My duties at the Savannah marine hospital and poorhouse have been arduous during the last month and the present. We have had over one hundred patients. We have now sixty-five seamen—a larger number than has ever been in the recollection of Dr. Arnold and Mr. Duncan. Many of the cases have been very severe, especially those of congestive fever. Notwithstanding the large number, I have been, through a kind Providence, much favored, thus far losing only one seaman out of one hundred and fifty cases of remittent and intermittent fever; and this man was brought to the hospital in a delirious state and could not be roused by any means in my power. Out of the poorhouse I have in the last five weeks lost but four patients out of more than one hundred cases. Two of these were consumptives, and the other two suffered from a combination of pneumonia, pleurisy, and bilious remittent fever.

The extraordinary amount of sickness amongst the seamen is readily explained. The wind has been from the northeast for nearly one month. The miasmatic poison from the swamps and newly cut ricefields and low grounds of South Carolina is blown directly into the city. The seamen, of course, receive the strongest dose, because they all live either on the river or else on Bay Street. More than one-half of all the seamen who have been in this port three weeks are now, or have been, sick at the hospital. We have whole crews all sick. The worst cases occurred amongst those who slept or worked on board the ships. The long line of warehouses along the bluff protects the city in great measure from the malaria. The cases which have occurred amongst the residents of the town have generally been mild, and have yielded readily to treatment.

This has been a golden season for improvement; I have never spent in my life a more profitable season. My great design in analyzing the blood of various animals has been to fit myself for investigations in the diseases of man. I have full notes of the symptoms and treatment of all the interesting cases, and have investigated as far as my time and strength would allow the changes in the blood and different organs and encretions.

If it will not be too much trouble, we will be very glad to have the assistance of Patience. With best love to yourself and Mother, I remain

Your affectionate son,
Joseph Jones.

Mr. Charles C. Jones, Jr., *to* Rev. *and* Mrs. C. C. Jones[t]

Savannah, *Thursday,* October 15th, 1857

My dear Father and Mother,

We shall be truly happy to see you on the 20th prox., which will be on Tuesday next, and we will endeavor to have the bachelor apartments set in order against your coming.

Our city is busied with the present condition of the "monetary crisis," as it is generally called. All the banks of the city suspended specie payments this morning with one consent, acting upon the advice of the merchants, who held a meeting in the exchange yesterday. So long as the banks are regarded as solvent, their bills will pass as they hitherto have done. We must, however, be affected in the matter of exchange. It is deemed generally a wise step in the banks to suspend. They thus keep in their vaults what specie they have, and will be able at an earlier date to resume specie payment.

Am sorry to see that the yellow fever is in Charleston, and sincerely hope that it will not be communicated to Savannah. It is now so late in the season that it is scarcely to be expected that it will prevail to any very general extent before frost. Its ravages, however, might be very terrible even in the course of a few weeks.

The news has just reached the city of the death of Mr. Robert Mackay, whom you know—or knew in days past. His life has been a blank. For several years he has suffered from paralysis, having lost the power of speech almost entirely, and being quite feeble. This is all to a very great degree the result of his habits.

All friends well. With much love to you both, my dear parents, in which the Doctor unites, I remain, as ever,

Your affectionate son,
Charles C. Jones, Jr.

Kind regards to all friends. Howdy for the servants. Titus will be very happy to see his mother.

Mr. Charles C. Jones, Jr., *to* Rev. *and* Mrs. C. C. Jones[g]

Savannah, *Friday,* November 6th, 1857

My dear Father and Mother,

Having been all alone in the office during the past week, I have had so much to engage attention that my usual letter to you has been postponed.

We have at length finished our packing. The Doctor left yesterday at 6 P.M. for Athens, which place he doubtless reached today about three o'clock. He was very much fatigued in consequence of his extensive preparations for a safe removal of all his specimens, etc. Most of them being in glass, they had to be arranged and packed with great care. I hope that they will all reach their destination safely, and that in his new home he will find both honor and friendship. The thumb of his right hand, recently cut during a postmortem, has caused him much pain, especially under the circumstances of the past week, having been obliged to use it constantly. His removal was no small undertaking.

Gilbert has been of great assistance to him and to us. He seems very anxious to return to his "Liberty home," and has not realized the enjoyments of a city life which his imagination had pictured. Most sadly does he lament the fact that there have been no shows and parades during his sojourn here. The first day the Doctor had him employed at the medical college; Tom, the janitor, introduced him to all the mysteries of the building, and especially to the objects of interest in one apartment, best known to the demonstrator of anatomy. The boy did not recover from his fright the entire evening. After breathing the atmosphere of the hospital his imagination led him to believe that he was certainly liable to the contraction simultaneously of some half-dozen diseases. Well do I remember my visit to the sick wards in the Blockley Hospital, and how for a week or more after leaving its precincts every finger ache forebode the commencement of some severe indisposition whose fearful effects I had there seen portrayed in living reality.

My rooms I find quite comfortable, and the house and inmates very quiet, orderly, and cleanly.

Brother expects to return next week, and on his return purposes remaining in the city for a few days in order to examine the bills of mortality for many years.

By this mail I send you, Mother, this week's *Home Journal,* and to you, Father, some papers containing the message of our governor, an account of the organization of the legislature, Mr. Ward's election, his speech, and also a paragraph commemorative of Stepney's recent exploit in deer-catching. I one day mentioned the incident in conversation, one of our editors being present, and he remarked he would give it a notice, and you see he has done so.

Miss King was on yesternight married. Mr. Bowman insisted upon my appearing as one of his attendants. Miss Lou Neely and myself waited together. The ceremony was performed in the Independent Church, the father of the groom officiating. The evening was pleasantly spent at the home of the bride after leaving the church. The bridal party left the city this morning to spend a few weeks in Upper Georgia. Every happiness attend them!

The United States court is now in session, and our city court sits on Monday next.

Do you, my dear parents, purpose attending the session of Presbytery next week? I am truly sorry that our bachelor doors are closed. If you stop at a hotel, I think you will find the Screven House as pleasant a place as any in the city.

All friends well. The boys go out tomorrow morning. With warmest love, I am, as ever, my dear parents,

Your ever affectionate son,
Charles C. Jones, Jr.

Howdy for all the servants. Saw Mr. Buttolph last evening. Quite well. Enclosed, Father, I send notice of note for one thousand dollars falling due 15th/18th November. Will you send renewal note? If you attend Presbytery, the matter can then be all arranged.

REV. JOHN JONES *to* REV. C. C. JONES[t]

Rome, Wednesday, November 11th, 1857

My dear Brother,

I send a line to express our regret that you will not be with us at Synod. My dear sister informs me that you will not come up. We had arranged for yourself and son Robert. Please give him our kind regards and invitation to come immediately to our house should I miss him when he comes, although I expect to meet the brethren generally at the depot.

We have made special arrangements for the brethren, clerical and lay, and expect to "do things up brown." Our people anticipate the meeting of Synod with pleasure and spirit. We have obtained the pledge of three railroads to pass the delegates at half price. Please mention this to Brother Porter, that he may speak to the superintendents of the Central and Waynesboro Railroads. I have written both to Augusta and Macon in reference to those roads, but have received no answer.

My dear Jane and our three boys (all at home) unite with me in much love to you and Sister when you see her.

Your affectionate brother,
J. Jones.

Mr. Robarts wishes Mr. Mallard to carry a small bundle to Marietta for Mrs. Robarts.

MRS. MARY JONES *to* REV. C. C. JONES[t]

Montevideo, Thursday, November 12th, 1857

My dearest Mr. Jones,

Our dear child arrived about dusk, quite bright and cheerful, and does not appear particularly fatigued by the ride. Our limekiln was prepared, and I had it fired up just before she came in honor of her arrival. Servants, Jet, and Lady all gave her a hearty welcome home. We have been chatting of all things in general and particular, and it is now near bedtime.

I have discovered your memorandum on the mantelpiece, and thinking you would be at a loss without it, will forward it tomorrow. . . . A letter from our dear Joe says he hopes to leave Athens on the 11th. Will pay a visit to his Uncle John if his funds hold out; says the move has been very expensive. . . . I must now bid you good night. Daughter unites with me in love to you and Robert and Charles. Do take care of yourself; I shall feel anxious until you return. God bless and keep you, ever prays

Your affectionate
Mary.

MR. CHARLES C. JONES, JR., *to* MRS. MARY JONES[t]

Savannah, Friday, November 13th, 1857

My dear Mother,

I write for Father, who feels rather tired after considerable fatigue endured today. Will you be so kind as to have the carriage at the depot (McIntosh Station) on Monday next, and also direct an oxcart from Arcadia (the light cart) to be there at the same time? Father and Brother will be with you on that day. The Doctor has made very pleasant arrangements in Athens, and will now rusticate a little at home before entering upon the regular discharge of his professional duties.

Last night Father spent at the Screven House, but he is now with Cousin Charles and Cousin Eliza, where he will remain during the session of the presbytery. Robert preached an excellent sermon last evening, although I only heard the end of it. By this mail I send the *Home Journal*. With much love from Father, Brother, and self to yourself and Sister, I remain, as ever,

Your affectionate son,
Charles C. Jones, Jr.

Rev. R. Q. Mallard *to* Mrs. Mary S. Mallard[t]

Savannah, *Saturday,* November 14th, 1857

My own darling Wife,

I have much to say and little time in which to say it. Pretty much the whole of yesterday was occupied by the session of our presbytery. The afternoon, short as you know it is at this season, I devoted to a little business. Last night I was rather afraid to sit up writing you, as I feared it would renew my cold. It has not yet advanced beyond the sneezing point, and I think pretty well destroyed by the quinine prepared by a loved hand. So you perceive that I have not had much time unemployed. Now, if I should be egotistical, you will pardon me, will you not?

Our trip to the city was a pleasant one to me, and we reached our destination in ample time for the services of the evening. Judge Law got on in Bryan; he had been *dining,* and was very affable. . . . I preached the opening sermon as expected, and to a very good congregation, Porter says. . . . Brother John Bowman and Rev. Rufus Porter are here, and staying with me at Brother Porter's. R. P. preached last night on the subject of "Holding the Truth in Unrighteousness." Not as good an effort as I *have* heard from him.

By invitation I took tea last evening at Mr. William King's. Made Mr. Norwood's acquaintance; he has no substantial claims in the way of personal attractions. Mrs. Norwood is looking very well; she as well as many other persons asked after you. . . . Dined today at Rev. Mr. Rogers'; enjoyed myself very well indeed. Your friend Joseph West asked after you; his lady begs to be remembered to you. The family had on exhibition at the table one of the plumpest little mortals I 'most ever saw: Miss Carrie Stiles.

Speaking of babies, Helen Porter has been practicing her lungs just now. Am glad to find that such efforts do not disturb me. Query: Why?

I have just returned from a visit to Miss Kitty. She has received your letter; seems to be quite well. . . . What do you think? Miss C. Sha—— was at this morning's session in company with the Rogerses. Why, she is not so pretty after all, and I don't believe is anything great comparatively. . . . Your brothers are both well; I have not seen much of them yet, as I have been so much employed.

Well, by dint of abridging sentences I believe I have said all that I had to communicate. I wish I had time to talk with my heart's darling more leisurely, but I must wait until my return. I wish I could press those dear lips of yours to mine tonight before I resign myself to my slumbers. A likeness is no substitute at all; it can give no warm answering pressure. . . . Give my love to our dear mother, and tell her that I am sorry that I have not been able to give Father the attention that I would have done if entertained at the same house. . . . Write me at Rome and to care of your uncle; he has written Father and invites me directly to his house. Of my movements after the adjournment of Synod I will let you know from Rome. . . . My love, good night.

Your lover and husband,
Robert Q. Mallard.

P.S. I expect you will think I should have signed myself "Juvenis," packing together, as I have done, so heterogeneous a mass. But I have written *currente calamo.*

REV. R. Q. MALLARD *to* MRS. MARY S. MALLARD[t]

Kingston, *Tuesday,* November 17th, 1857

My own dearest Wife,

Here I am, detained overnight in sixteen miles of Rome. I might have taken a hack for that place, but the character of the country forbids the expectation of turnpike roads. I would have stopped in Marietta, but thought I could pass immediately through to my place of destination, and preferred making my visit on my return. However, I am very comfortable at a plain hotel, of which I seem to be the only boarder, and certainly most pleasantly employed writing to one dearer to me than the whole world beside.

Well, my darling heart, shall I arrange my thoughts logically, or shall I follow the chronological order and *journalize* a little? Do you say the latter?

Monday I saw your father and mine off in the omnibus. Took breakfast and went downtown with Brother Porter. We strolled into the lecture room of a Baptist church in which the Sunbury Association was sitting. We were *not* invited to sit as corresponding members. . . . When we entered, a Mr. Cassidey was delivering himself of an earnest exhortation in behalf of the Baptist cause in Brunswick. At the close a collection was taken up to further the enterprise, during which a hymn was sung.

Finishing our business downtown, we returned to Porter's. Mr. Buttolph having neglected to invite me to tea at Mr. Wallace Cumming's as requested, I made a call, and a pleasant one, in the morning upon Mrs. Cumming. By this time a pair of new boots began to remind me in the most feeling manner that they were not the thing for the *seven hills* of Rome. So off I sped downtown to get another and larger article of the kind. This brought me back to Mr. William King's, where I was invited to lunch just in time to overtake in a measure the slow performers.

John Bowman, Miss Annie, and myself, in the midst of a falling shower, stowed ourselves away in a closed carriage, and were safely settled in our rolling home in ample time. The ride up to Atlanta I found extremely pleasant. Miss Anna I like very much: she is so openhearted and *unreserved*. (As to this latter expression, I don't doubt if asked she would also apply it to me.) By the way, somebody else seemed to like our young traveler. He was there to see her off. "Who?" Why, he of the royal line who sits behind the counter and wields a pestle as his scepter.

On our way up several things occurred which made us think of "Juvenis." For instance, a gentleman who to my knowledge swore more than once—and took, I believe, quite as many drinks—I heard, sometimes above the din and sometimes in the intervals, engaged in quite a religious conversation with one who proved to be a minister. As I thought, the minister's effort was towards a personal application, which was by his companion warded off.

Speaking of noises, let me throw in here a parenthesis to tell you that I am writing with a young beginner fiddling away on a violin just at my left, and the voices of childhood quite numerous—and as pleasant.

The supper bell! Fare pretty good, but table furniture (I don't mean the stiff-backed chairs but stiff-backed people) intolerably stiff.

But to return. I parted with my traveling companions at Atlanta with regret, but soon made up a new acquaintance after this style. A gentleman and I were compelled to guard our baggage on the platform; after seeing this matter attended to, we adjourned to the gentlemen's sitting room and entered into conversation. Finding he was from Milledgeville and that he seemed conversant with the affairs of the Senate, I asked him from what county he was the senator. He was not a representative. Continued talking about the legislature, etc., about the appropriation for Athens. Spoke myself pretty freely about Mr. McCay and the other old professors and new. Spoke neither in praise nor blame, fortunately, of the mathematical professor, Mr. Rutherford. He replied: "I am he." Quite a lesson on ruling the tongue, was it not?

At Atlanta a mishap befell me. In crossing the railroad track (which was wet) I slipped, and in recovering my balance sprained my ankle. It is not, I hope, badly strained; and by cold applications I hope to reduce the slight inflammation produced.

On the cars to this place I met with my old teacher Dr. Church, with Rev. William Baker and his father-in-law Mr. Barrington King, the reverend on his way to Staunton, Virginia, on an invitation. So you see, I have met with pleasant friends all the way.

At Marietta I saw Joseph; said that they were all well, and laid an injunction against my passing them by without a visit. . . . I will write you again, my darling, from Rome, where I hope to hear from you. Love to all. God bless my own!

Your own loving husband,
Robert Q. Mallard.

Rev. R. Q. Mallard *to* Mrs. Mary S. Mallard[t]

Rome, *Saturday,* November 21st, 1857

My own precious Wife,

Cold! Cold! (But my heart is warm, and beats with fondest love to my Mary.) The mercury stood this morning about 19°. Rome, unless my opinion alters, will not directly get my vote as a place of meeting for Synod, at least at this late date. From the night sessions my lameness furnished me with a dispensation, so that I have not been as much inconvenienced by the weather as others. Lest you should be uneasy, I would say before I forget it that my ankle is nearly if not quite well. I have walked today to and from the church, a distance of three-quarters of a mile, four times.

This is Saturday evening, and I have only a few moments to spend in finishing this letter begun this morning. There is a good prospect of adjournment tonight. On Monday I shall probably leave for Marietta—in company, I hope, with Mr. Jones (Uncle John), he being on his way to McIntosh. How long I shall remain, I can't say. Inclination—love, I should say—is drawing me powerfully toward the seaboard. I have much to talk with you about, and would prefer to defer it until, with the blessing of God, I am permitted once more to see and press my darling to my heart.

Your uncle's family are all doing well, as doubtless you have inferred from what I have said about his leaving on Monday. His little boys are certainly remarkable children; I am sorry that I have not seen more of them. . . . If possible I will keep you advised of my movements. Mr. Jones (Uncle John) desires me to send "their united love" to you. And now, my darling heart, good night.

Your own
Robert.

Mrs. Mary S. Mallard *to* Miss Mary Jones Taylor[t]

Walthourville, *Monday,* December 14th, 1857

My dear Mary,

You must not interpret my long silence as a returning evil for evil. I have no such intention. Your letter found me upon a sickbed, suffering from the influenza, which has, I believe, prevailed through the whole Union. You have doubtless experienced the same in Maryland. I had it quite severely, and this must account for two weeks of my silence. Soon after I recovered, I went home to visit my father and mother, and remained there nearly three weeks. During this time Mr. Mallard was absent attending Presbytery and Synod. He laughs and says I was so glad of an opportunity of spending some time at home that I did not wish him to return at all. It was indeed most delightful to be there, but I don't think my feelings were quite such as he described.

I think my father's health has improved a little, and I hope he will to a greater degree reap the benefit of his past summer's travel. Returning home, they had an awful stage ride of forty miles. Mother was in high health, and it made her very sick, and her arm was seriously injured. She says the road was so rough, and the speed of the coach so rapid, that it was with great difficulty she could retain her seat, being in danger of touching the top one moment and the next of being thrown on the front seat. Imagine this for forty miles! In order to keep her seat and preserve her body from as many bruises as possible, she held the strap of the middle seat, and the continuous jerking (the physicians say) tore the ligaments of the shoulder. And they say she would have recovered much sooner had the bone been broken. Fine consolation, this! She is obliged to carry her arm in a sling, and finds it exceedingly difficult to carry out the prescription of the physicians, which is entire rest. I tell her she makes the hand and arm do half a day's work daily. It is almost impossible for a housekeeper to do otherwise.

You spoke in your letter of having visited West Chester. Did you become acquainted with Mrs. Cresson Stiles? She was a Miss Wells. Mr. Stiles and herself were married in Europe. If you became acquainted with her, you probably saw Mrs. Wells, a sister of Willie King, whom you knew in Philadelphia. Cousin Mary Wells is spending some months with Mrs. Stiles, and I hope you saw her. She is a very amusing person—very odd in some things. She has carried on her maid (a colored person), and she is constantly entreating her mistress to return, as she is "sick and tired of the Norrud." Speaking of Willie King, I must tell you he is settled in Savannah and keeps a drugstore, and is doing very well.

My brother Joe expects to leave his professorship in the Savannah Medical College in January. He has been elected to a professorship in our state university at Athens, and will go there. I am a little sorry he will leave Savannah, as he will be much farther from us; but it is unreasonable to suppose we will always be located near each other.

The spirit of enterprise has at length reached this place, and we now have a daily train of cars passing through this county, and in this village we are now enjoying the blessings of a daily mail. Quite an improvement upon the old arrangement, by which our mail was brought twice a week by a stage. I verily believe we prized papers more then because they were a greater rarity.

How has your winter in Maryland been? We have enjoyed pleasant weather, generally mild, having had but one very cold spell. In this climate the changes are so frequent that cold never lasts very long. I was quite surprised yesterday to find a yellow jessamine blooming. The single bright little flower looked lonely upon the vine, and yet I felt as though it were scarcely right to pick; but it was laden with such sweet perfume I could not resist the temptation. Jessamines do not bloom before February, and for several years past our winters have been so cold they have bloomed much later.

Have you been reading anything interesting recently? And have you heard any pretty songs? Mr. Mallard often reads to me in the evening. Our readings have been various of late: sometimes history, at others theology, interspersed occasionally with Shakespeare, etc.

But it is time for me to close. Do give love to your mother and Sallie, and accept the same for yourself. Mr. Mallard desires to be remembered.

Your affectionate friend,
Mary S. Mallard.

The cat has jumped upon the table, and for the last ten minutes has been watching my pen with great interest. If I were not already married you would call me "old maid"!

Rev. John Jones *to* Rev. *and* Mrs. C. C. Jones[t]

Rome, Friday, January 1st, 1858

My dear Sister and Brother,

I arrived home on Tuesday evening of this week and found my dear Jane in a most prostrate condition. I was shocked at her weakness. She was alone excepting her little children and servants. I wrote immediately for our esteemed Cousin Mary, and she came next day through torrents of rain. That night (the 30th) the fever, which I think is typhoid, went completely off, and the depression was so great that my dear wife seemed to be sinking away. We sent at 1 A.M. for the doctor, and used diligently mustard and brandy. She revived, and yesterday seemed better. Today she is not so well. . . . Cousin Mary is all to us now that mortal friend could be. I will write you again and shortly.

Ever your affectionate brother,
J. Jones.

P.S. I give you many thanks for your prompt kindness in aiding me to reach Savannah. My time with you was most pleasant.

Rev. John Jones *to* Rev. *and* Mrs. C. C. Jones[t]

Rome, Thursday, January 7th, 1858

My dear Brother and Sister,

It is indeed difficult to give you a proper idea of the condition of my dear Jane. Yesterday she acknowledged in the morning for the first time that she felt better, and our hearts rejoiced with trembling hope. But at 2 to 3 P.M. there came on flushing and great mental depression, and there succeeded a night of extreme weakness and copious perspiration, and she seemed more ill than ever. . . . She has typhoid fever, is weak beyond anything I have ever witnessed in her, and requires the most careful and constant watching. Says herself that her life is like a candle that may be snuffed out in a moment. . . . Cousin Mary is invaluable to us. She unites with me in best love to you both. Our dear boys are well.

Ever your affectionate brother,
John Jones.

N.B. My dear Jane has relished more than any other nourishment the arrowroot given her by Sister, and she says: "When I drink this, I think of Sister." Excuse the pencil. Will write again. Do send us a line.

J. J.

REV. JOHN JONES *to* REV. *and* MRS. C. C. JONES[t]

Rome, *Tuesday,* January 12th, 1858

My dear Brother and Sister,

My dear Jane is better. I could say this yesterday for the first time with confidence. But she is so weak she needs constant medical care and nursing. I know you will unite with me in giving thanks to God for His tender mercy in sparing my dear wife. . . . I cannot sufficiently thank you for your joint letter of sympathy and love and encouragement. And my dear Jane, to whom it was read, also thanks you, and unites with me in tender love to you both, and dear Mary when you see her, and kindest regards for Mr. Mallard. Do write again. Dunwody and the little boys send love to Uncle Charles and Aunt Mary.

Your affectionate brother,

John Jones.

Our dear Cousin Mary Robarts unites in love to you; she has been cousin, sister, friend, everything to us.

J. J.

MRS. ELIZA G. ROBARTS *to* REV. *and* MRS. C. C. JONES[t]

Marietta, *Saturday,* January 16th, 1858

Dear Charles and Mary,

You see your old aunt's scrawl will be coming along to remind you she is still living and thinking often of you. I began yesterday to write you, but was so nervous I had to quit. For three months I have not had a perfect day of health. . . . Judge Hale (Sarah Pynchon's husband) sent me a bottle of the balsam of wild cherry and wood naphtha, prepared by a Dr. Williams of Huntsville, Alabama. A teaspoonful night and morning has relieved my cough more than anything I have ever taken, and my cough is now better than it has been for four years. I have sent to Huntsville for another bottle; if you can procure it in Savannah, I think it would be excellent for your servants. Price: one dollar.

For two weeks past we have suffered great anxiety about dear Jane, who has been dangerously ill; but thank God, she is now better. . . . Mary Robarts would have come home this week, but it has rained every day but last Monday; she wrote she would come the first bright sunny day. . . . I don't know when I have seen such a rainy winter; we scarce have two bright days together. My yard is so wet I have not walked out for three weeks.

The winter thus far has been very mild: no severe cold but once in November for a few days. But I fear we may have a cold spring, which might kill the fruit again. . . . I regret to hear of so many deaths from Midway Church. How sad it makes me to hear of so many friends departed! . . . Old Mr. Harris, who lived just beyond our church, on Christmas Day walked into his yard, and a short time afterwards was found speechless, and died that night. He was a good old man, and will be missed in the Methodist church, to which he belonged.

Our pastor, Mr. Palmer, seems to be generally liked; has been kindly received by the people. Some of the ladies furnished his study nicely; the rest supplied his pantry with many good things toward housekeeping. His wife is a pleasant little woman; resembles Augusta Palmer on a smaller scale. . . . They have two interesting little girls six and four years of age. . . . Mr. Petrie has made me a present of his ambrotype. It is like him, but on rather too large a scale. This present is the first compliment of the kind I have ever had paid me.

Mrs. Sadler and Mrs. Pynchon live so far I do not see them often. They always inquire after Charles and yourself. Mrs. Sadler is all alone this winter; her daughters are away—one at school, the other in Florida. . . . Rev. John Baker, formerly of Milledgeville, has opened a school for boys and girls. Commenced last Monday. Opened with fifty scholars this week and expects more. He has a young gentleman by name of Smith to assist him—a graduate of the military institute. Joe goes to him. I think he will make a good teacher.

Poor Charlie McDonald (governor's son) has been sent, we hear, to the lunatic asylum—I believe in Columbia. Poor fellow, it seems he is deranged on the subject of religion. About three weeks ago he called here and invited myself and the family to go the next Sunday to the pool to see him baptized. Thinking he was deranged, the Baptist church did not receive him. . . .

I have told you all the Marietta news I can think of, but fear you will not be able to read this poor scrawl. I will now say a word about hard times. If you all in the low country feel it, what must we do who have everything to buy and nothing to buy with? I assure you this year has been the hardest year to get along, provisions of every kind has been so high and money so scarce. I assure you I have been many times without a dime in my purse. . . . Not that we have spent so much money, but my income has been less, for I have lost some by my Negroes in Savannah by sickness and loss of time. . . . I have fallen short two hundred dollars, which I owe mostly in Savannah for things bought last spring for the family. . . . I must now thank Charles for hiring Katy and Lucy; I feel that it is a great favor. . . . I am quite satisfied with the present arrangement, and hope now Katy is with her husband they will be satisfied and give no trouble. As Katy complains of rheumatism, she may not be worth more than forty dollars per year. Fifty-five is what Henry allowed for Lucy, which is as little as I can afford to take. . . . I am really very sorry to hear your crop is so short, particularly this pressing year; but I believe it is the general complaint. . . . Self-denial and economy has so long been our watchword we scarce know anything else; but this year it will have to be practiced more closely. Not an article in the way of dress has been bought since last spring.

Lilla has completed her term of education. Ellen goes to Miss Green. They are all fond of their books; every morning after breakfast they read history or practice sums in algebra. I hope they will make good and useful children.

Mary arrived on Saturday night from Rome; left our dear Jane better. She will write you a little note. . . . What a pleasure it is to receive letters from absent friends and be remembered by them! As I grow older my heart clings closer to my dear relations, and I feel low-spirited when I don't hear from them. . . . Sam sends howdy for Rose. Tell her he is so smart: he comes in every morning at six o'clock, makes the fire in the parlor, sweeps the carpet, rubs the sideboard, then milks the cow; sometimes in fair weather scours the porch, cleans brasses, whitewashes the chimney, and cuts wood. . . . All unite in love. . . . Excuse this scrawl of your old aunt's.

Truly yours,
E. G. Robarts.

MISS MARY E. ROBARTS *to* MRS. MARY JONES[t]

Marietta, *Monday,* January 18th, 1858

My dear Cousin,

I returned from Rome on Saturday and left dear Jane decidedly better. She had had no fever for a week, and gained a little, I think, in strength every day, though but a little. She had lost so much that the gain was scarcely perceptible. She cannot yet rise up or lie down or turn over without assistance. It is a long time since I have seen anyone so ill or so much reduced. I think if John had not returned at the time he did, she would have been too far gone to recover. The Saturday before he came she had got out of bed; when she attempted to get in again, she fainted and lay across the foot of the bed, for some time insensible. Patty and Lavinia were both in the room, but did not know what was the matter, and did not touch her till she came to and told them to call Nancy to put her in bed. Her head was so much affected that she said she believed she had not been in her senses for two weeks. Indeed, the great danger in her case was the tendency to the brain, and she was so nervous she could not bear the slightest noise or the least ray of light.

You may imagine how shocked your dear brother was to find his wife in that situation. He sat down immediately and wrote me, and in twelve hours from the time he wrote I was with them. The night I got there she sank so low it was doubtful if she would live till morning; but thinking it might be the decline of the fever or the crisis of the disease, we applied mustard and stimulated her with brandy and sent for the doctor. She said her very throat was failing, and said: "My dear cousin, don't let the doctor deceive Mr. Jones; my life is like the snuff of a candle: it will soon be out. Do watch me;

I will pass off before you know it." I told her I would. When the doctor came he requested me to apply cloths wet in brandy to her throat. I did so, and kept up the stimulants. She revived in a few hours, but her brain continued so much affected that he applied blisters behind her ears, which with his other treatment had a happy effect. These blisters had to be repeated after a few days. She will now, without a very unexpected relapse, recover.

Thus, my dear cousin, Jane came near falling a victim to her extreme reserve. She did not write John, thinking he would be busy and come as soon as he could; and she did not let her neighbors know, for she did not feel free to call upon them. When John returned they all seemed mortified to think she was so sick without their knowing it, but they really were not to blame. His residence is very remote, and they knew she was busy moving; and the weather being bad, few had been to see her. They were kind in sending after I went there and offering to do anything they could; but I nursed her entirely, as I had a bed in the room. It was only two nights that John and myself sat up with her all night. I hope now she will in a few weeks be able to come here and rest on her way to the low country. I should dread the cold winds of spring in her delicate state. Mrs. Dunwody and Mary are with her, or I should not have left.

Johnnie and Josie called me Aunt Mary *Jones* when I first went there, and said: "Aunt Mary Jones, you must take Brother Dunwody in hand: he sticks us with pins." Farewell, my dear cousin. Will write you soon. Love to Cousin Charles.

Your ever affectionate cousin,
Mary E. Robarts.

My dear mother is quite well again. We were very unhappy about her the first of the winter.

Rev. John Jones *to* Rev. *and* Mrs. C. C. Jones[t]

Rome, *Thursday,* January 21st, 1858

My dear Sister and Brother,

Although very much engaged today with company calling to see my dear Jane, and also in seeing Dunwody off to school, I must send you a short line.

I know you will rejoice with me in learning that my dear wife was able today for the first time to sit up. I took her in my arms and placed her in the rocking chair, and she sat up an hour or two. She has improved astonishingly in the last ten days, and has a wonderful appetite. Thus God has been wonderfully merciful to us. Our excellent Cousin Mary Robarts has returned home, and I have heard from her and all at Aunty's. All well.

I received yesterday a most kind sympathizing letter from your (our) dear Joseph. It made the tears start—to know that so young a man, and one so near to me, was so considerate and mindful of others. It is not common; it is rare. He writes as follows: "My dear uncle, I was exceedingly sorry to hear of Aunt Jane's sickness. If it had been in my power, I would have come immediately up to Rome and assisted you in nursing. I have thought of you and your dear little boys a thousand times, with the hope that their dear mother might be spared." Can I help loving such a nephew? I will answer him to-morrow. He also mentioned that an arrangement had been made of the studies agreeable to himself.

Yesterday Dunwody received Aunt Mary's kind letter, and it had more effect on him than anything said to him of late. It seemed to make him pause and think. The truth is, Dunwody is a bad boy; and I am truly thankful to you both for your interest in him, and your prayers for his salvation. Nothing but the grace of God will ever make anything of him, even for this world. . . . But I will cease.

Ever your affectionate brother,
John Jones.

My dear Jane, Mrs. Dunwody, and Sister Mary Dunwody send much love to you both. Remember us to Mary Sharpe and Brother Robert. . . . Do write soon again.

Miss Mary Sophia Robarts *to* Mrs. Mary Jones[t]

Marietta, Sunday, January 31st, 1858

Dear Cousin Mary,

Aunt Mary begged me to write Cousin Susan and yourself and let you know that dear Grandmother is as low as she possibly can be. Dr. Hardy says he has such a faint hope that he does not like to express it; and I fear, dear Cousin, before this reaches you I will have no grandmother to love and take care of me. And I have no mother; what shall we do?

Last week Grandmother appeared to be better than she has been all winter. Monday night she said she thought she had a chill, which was succeeded by a hot fever. The next morning she vomited a great deal of bile; but we thought she would be better until Friday night, when she fainted, and we thought it was all over with her; but after a time she revived, and since that time we think that she has gradually grown worse. She had a very bad night last night, but is a little more comfortable this morning. Complains of pains in her side and stomach. Tomorrow will be Aunt Mary's birthday, but I fear she will have a sad time. All of our friends have been very kind and sympathizing. Mrs. Pynchon and Mrs. Fraser were with her all night, and Mrs. Sadler spent yesterday and today with us.

Grandmother is very anxious to see Father and Cousin John. I wrote for them, but they will not arrive for a day or two. Grandmother told Mr. Palmer that she was perfectly resigned to God's will. He then asked if she would prefer to live or die; she said: "I prefer to live, for I have strong ties—my children and grandchildren; they have no mother." How could we do without her? Home would not be home to one of us without our mother and dear grandmother. I hope God may see fit in His great mercy to spare us this very great trial. Pray for us that we may be willing to submit to His will.

Please let our other friends know of dear Grandmother's illness. Do excuse this badly written letter, but I am in haste to finish it. Much love to Cousin Charles and yourself.

Your affectionate cousin,
M. S. E. Robarts.

Miss Mary E. Robarts *to* Mrs. Mary Jones[t]

Marietta, *Sabbath Afternoon,* January 31st, 1858

I add a line with an aching heart to tell my dear cousins that my beloved mother seems to be at the very gates of death; and perhaps the next you hear may be a request to meet her precious remains and find them a resting place in the graveyard at Midway near your own enclosure. She has enjoined it upon me, in sickness and in health, not to let her be buried up here. . . . Just now, seeing me writing, she said: "Tell Charles and Mary they must find some little spot in the graveyard to squeeze me in; I will not take up much room."

Last night we did not think she would see the light of day. The difficulty seems now to be congestion of the liver and kidneys; she has had no action from the kidneys for twenty-four hours, and suffers great pain. This morning she has slept several hours at a time; it is either a sign that she is a little better or fearfully worse. Oh, my cousin, pray for us! Louisa and I have not closed our eyes or taken off our clothes for three nights and days; though we have a number of kind friends to watch with us, we never leave the room. We have written for my brother, for my Cousin John, and Mr. Rogers from Atlanta. If the worst happens, will get Mr. Rogers to telegraph Charles to Savannah so that he can write you. Harriet Pynchon said Mr. Pynchon would write Cousin Charles today.

Your afflicted cousin,
Mary.

Please let our other friends know how ill she is.

Mr. E. E. Pynchon *to* Rev. C. C. Jones[t]

Marietta, *Sunday Night,* January 31st, 1858

Dear Sir,

At the request of Miss Mary Robarts I write to you to inform you of the health of Mrs. Robarts. You are aware that the old lady has long suffered from a cough, and that her health, in consequence of that, and of increasing years perhaps, has been feeble for some time past. This fall and winter, however, she has been using some medicine recommended to her by my daughter's husband with decidedly good effect, and she thought she was going to get freed entirely from her cough. On Monday last she was up all day, and said she felt better than she had for many months. After retiring at about eight o'clock she had a very severe chill, which was followed by a fever which lasted two or three days. On Thursday, her physician says, her symptoms indicated congestion of the liver and a *total* inaction of the kidneys. Her condition is considered extremely critical. Mrs. Pynchon watched with her last night, and thinks it *extremely doubtful if she can recover.*

Miss Mary and Miss Louisa are much overcome by this sudden and severe illness of their mother; and they feel it the more as they are so far separated from their male relatives, on whom, at this trying moment, they seem to feel the necessity of relying. Mr. John Jones and Mr. Joseph Robarts have been written to, and it is hoped they will both arrive tomorrow. The family are receiving largely the sympathies of the community, and nothing will be wanting that can be done by the kindness of friends and neighbors.

Mrs. Pynchon unites with me in kind regards to yourself and family.

Very respectfully yours,
E. E. Pynchon.

REV. JOHN JONES *to* REV. *and* MRS. C. C. JONES[t]

Marietta, Monday, February 1st, 1858

My dear Brother and Sister,

At the request of Cousin Mary I send a brief line to inform you that our dear aunt is a little better. The doctor and all cherish some hope that she may recover. But she is exceedingly weak and nervous. Cousin Mary says that her (Aunty's) great difficulties proceed from the liver and the kidneys, the former causing a constant nausea and frequent vomitings of bile. And the kidneys are in an excessively irritated state. Her mind is clear. She remembers everyone, and asks after everyone. She seems desirous of living for the sake of her children and grandchildren, but prays to be resigned to the will of God.

I received a letter calling for me late Saturday evening, and left by first train (three o'clock) this morning. (No Sabbath train.) Left my dear Jane much better, but I am anxious that she is alone: her mother and sister came down with me. . . . Do inform Cousin Susan and Henry of the news you receive, as we cannot write each one.

Ever your affectionate brother,
J. Jones.

All send best love to you both.

Robert's letter came to Aunt today and was read to her.

J. J.

MRS. MARY JONES *to* MR. CHARLES C. JONES, JR.[g]

Montevideo, Thursday, February 4th, 1858

My very dear Son,

The contents of your favor by last Tuesday's mail I must confess took your father and myself quite by surprise! Your representations of the young lady are such as to command our entire approval, and our heart's desire and prayer to God is for His blessing to rest upon your engagement. May she indeed be to you a gift from God—one that will do you good and not evil all your days! What a blessing to have won the affections of a pious, intelligent, and prudent lady, whose example and loving influence will ever be leading you heavenward whilst she shares and lightens the cares and duties as well as sorrows that must ever attend our mortal state! I believe that your social and affectionate disposition could never be truly suited in your present isolated position; and it will greatly increase our happiness to see you happily married. How long will the lady remain in Savannah? If we can possibly do so, I should like to come down and pay our respects to her, for I feel that she already occupies a warm corner in my heart. I have heard your sister and aunt and cousin speak very flatteringly of her. I am happy to know that she resembles Cousin Eliza, for you know how much we all love and admire her. . . .

Tonight our hearts are very sorrowful. Today's mail brought us alarming intelligence of our beloved and venerated aunt. We fear she may be no longer in the land of the living. Our only hope is based upon the fact of your not writing. Cousin Mary said if she was no more, they would telegraph you immediately, and her remains, at her oft-repeated request, would be brought down and buried at Midway. They all are filled with deepest sorrow. We received letters from Mary Sophia and Cousin Mary and a very kind one from Mr. Pynchon.

Our dear friend Mr. Dunwody too is failing very fast; Marion writes us he is longing to depart and be with his precious Saviour. Old Mrs. Mallard has been and still is very sick, and the old gentleman quite unwell. Thus the ancient and venerable ones are all passing away. Your father and myself will soon stand in the *front ranks*—if not taken away before they fall! . . . Daughter is with us, and sends much love.

From your ever affectionate parents,
C. C. and Mary Jones.

REV. C. C. JONES *to* MR. CHARLES C. JONES, JR.ᵍ

Montevideo, *Friday,* February 12th, 1858

My dear Son,

We received a pleasant letter from your dear brother yesterday. He writes in good spirits, and is as busy as usual. He has taken a pew in Dr. Hoyt's church, and Mr. Cobb and Mr. Mitchell, superintendents of the Sunday school, collected a large and interesting class of men (the youngest, Joe says, could not have been under thirty years of age), and would take no excuse from him, but he must become the teacher. His modesty forbade this, and he compromised with all interested by becoming a kind of chairman of the class and conducting it on the plan of *mutual instruction.* He had had a conversation with Mr. Mitchell upon some lectures which he intended to deliver to the students on natural theology; and he thinks Mr. Mitchell took the idea of giving him a class from this conversation. It makes us very happy to find him associating with the wise and the good and attempting to make himself useful in the highest form to his fellow men. I pray continually that you both may be brought to an open and sincere profession of the Lord Jesus, and never be ashamed to be employed in any and in every way in promoting His honor and glory on the earth. No man fully attains the end of his being until he reaches, through divine grace, this point.

One special matter of thankfulness—and which indeed supersedes all others—in your anticipated change in life is that your friend is a professor, and I trust a possessor, of religion, and belongs to our own denomination. "Whoso findeth a wife"—that is, a real pious and accomplished woman in that station—"findeth a good thing, and obtaineth favor of the Lord" (Proverbs 18:22).

Your brother requested me to enclose you Dr. Henry's letter to him, which you will read with pleasure, as we have. It is encouraging and flattering. Return it to your brother when you have read it. *DeBow* is interesting Mother, who sends much love. In some haste for the mail,

Your ever affectionate father,
C. C. Jones.

Mr. CHARLES C. JONES, JR., *to* REV. C. C. JONES[t]

Savannah, *Saturday,* February 13th, 1858

My dear Father,

Your kind favor of the 12th inst. enclosing letter of Dr. Henry and also containing such pleasant intelligence from the new professor at Athens, was yesterday received. Professor Henry's letter I have read with much interest, and I doubt not the favorable notice therein contained of the Doctor's investigations during the past summer will be fully justified when those investigations, and the results therefrom arising, shall have been arranged with system and thrown into some permanent, accessible form.

Returned from Brunswick, I saw upon my table in the office a newspaper folded and to my address. Casually opening it, you may imagine my surprise and sorrow when my eye, glancing over the items, was arrested by an obituary notice of my friend and former roommate George Helm. For months we lived together in the same apartment upon the most intimate terms of friendship, engaged in the acquisition of a common profession. And now he is taken away, his foot on the threshold of life. And why he and not the companion of his student days? The paper containing the obituary notice I have already sent you. Nothing has for many days affected me so much as this sad intelligence. I will write a letter of sympathy to Governor and Mrs. Helm.

Saw Cousin Joseph Robarts yesterday. Aunt Eliza, thanks to a kind Providence, continues to improve, although still quite weak and unable to rise from her couch. Aunt Jane is also better, and expects soon to visit the low country.

Our superior court is still in session, and there are several important civil cases and all on the criminal docket yet to be tried.

Miss Ruth is quite well, and desires her kind and respectful remembrance. She leaves the city in a week, but returns again in April. With warmest love, my dear mother and father, to you both, I am, as ever,

Your affectionate son,
Charles C. Jones, Jr.

I enclose Dr. Henry's letter to Brother.

Kind regards to all friends, and howdy for the servants.

MRS. MARY JONES *to* MR. CHARLES C. JONES, JR.[g]

Montevideo, *Tuesday,* February 16th, 1858

My dear Son,

On Saturday last we received the paper announcing the death of our young friend George Helm. It came very near our hearts. He was *your friend, your classmate!* He was in a peculiar sense associated with you. And then came the recollection of the pleasant time he passed with us on the Island. His voice, his look, his manner—all were so familiar: his gentlemanly deportment, his kind and respectful feelings and conduct. There was everything about him in that visit to impress us favorably and to draw our sympathies and kindest regards to him. And he is gone from this world of hope and promise! Would that I could know how he died. I have often thought of his spiritual state. Did he return to the Ark of Safety? Had he an opportunity to seek his Saviour's face? We may never know. Your father and myself gave him at parting a little token of our interest in his spiritual welfare. Why was he taken and you are left? God's sovereignty has so ordained it, but for some wise design. My dear son, I pray the Lord to open your eyes and open your heart by this stroke to see and feel your need of a precious Saviour. Oh, to live without Christ and to die without Christ is to be lost forever! Poor, lost, and guilty as we are, we must have an Advocate with the Father—divine and all-sufficient Jesus Christ the Righteous! Do you know if George ever married? No allusion is made to his being married in the paper sent.

Our friends are generally well. Your aunt has had a slight attack of sore throat. Your uncle seems quite cheerful and happy at Arcadia. He spent a night with us last week. You have had an addition to your servants there: *Clarissa* has a very large *daughter.* I have supplied all her wants but *a blanket,* and have not one on hand, unless *I* give her one of the pair sent out from Savannah. We have for many years made it a practice to give a new blanket to every newborn infant as a kind of bonus to the mother. If you say so, I will give her one of the blankets, for I presume when you go to housekeeping again you would not look at the *bachelor stores.*

Your uncle is delighted to hear *the news.* Have not seen your Aunt Susan to tell her. *May I tell your Aunt Mary and your Uncle John?* But I'll leave *you* to do it.

Willie drove *Miss Bowman* from Midway to Dorchester on Sabbath; I really suspect he is engaged.

Your father and I truly regret to hear that Miss Whitehead will leave Savannah so soon; we wanted to pay our respects in person to her. Present us affectionately to her. Love to Cousin Charles and Cousin Eliza. Father says he will write you soon. Did you get a package by *Mrs. Axson?* As ever, my dear son,

Your affectionate mother,
Mary Jones.

MR. CHARLES C. JONES, JR., *to* MRS. MARY JONES[t]

Savannah, Friday, February 19th, 1858

My dear Mother,

Your kind favor of the 16th inst. was yesterday received, and I am truly happy to know that all at home are well.

The death of my friend and former companion and roommate George Helm is indeed very sad, and has filled my heart with sorrow. Whether he ever married or not, I do not know. He, you may recollect, invited me to act as his first groomsman in December last, when he expected to have married a lady in Louisville. From the fact that I never received any reply to my letter (expressing my regrets that circumstances would not permit a compliance with his friendly request), and from the further facts that we never received any invitations (which would certainly have been sent had the union been consummated at the season at first contemplated), and that no notice of his recent marriage and desolate young bride was made in the papers announcing his death, I am led to infer that he never married. And the sad inference, drawn from the circumstance of his removal to Memphis, induces the belief that he possibly may have been disappointed in his love affair. You know he once before settled in Memphis with a view to the practice of the law, and after remaining there for a few months returned again to Kentucky. Poor fellow, I deeply sympathize with him and his bereaved family. May the lesson not be lost in its effect upon me! I have been so much occupied that I have had no suitable opportunity as yet for writing Governor and Mrs. Helm. I will do so this evening if I possibly can.

I am deeply obliged to you, Mother, for your kind interest in Clarissa, and will be glad if you will direct that one of the blankets sent out be given to her. Has she named her baby yet?

In regard to the engagement, I certainly can have no objections to your

telling it to anyone you think proper, and would be glad if you would tell
Uncle John and Aunt Mary of it.

Willie, I think, is deeply in love with Miss Bowman; but from a bird's-eye
glance I am almost afraid that she will show him her heels if he presses the
suit too closely. She is young, and like many young ladies thinks the future
more inviting than the present.

Miss Ruth is quite well, and desires her affectionate remembrance, thanking you and Father for your kind consideration of her. . . . This afternoon
a thunderstorm reminds us of the approach of spring. . . . With much love,
my dear parents, to you both, I am, as ever,

Your affectionate son,
Charles C. Jones, Jr.

I am exceedingly obliged to you, dear Mother, for the package received at
the hands of Mrs. Varnedoe's son, and in my forgetfulness omitted to mention its receipt in a former letter.

Mrs. Mary S. Mallard *to* Miss Mary Jones Taylor[t]
Walthourville, Thursday, March 4th, 1858

My dear Mary,

I was quite amazed this evening, on looking at the date of your last interesting favor, to find it had been in my possession so long. How is it with you?
Time flies so rapidly with me that I find if a letter is not answered immediately upon its receipt, weeks and even months glide by before an opportunity
offers for writing.

I am very much obliged to you for the seeds, and in order to insure as far
as possible some of them growing, I have divided them with Mother and one
of my friends. I have always found it good policy to give away plants and
seeds, for I have sometimes lost mine and had them replaced by those to
whom I had given cuttings.

Until the first of March we have had remarkably mild weather—indeed,
scarcely any that could be properly placed in the winter months. But for a
few days past, the cold has been unusually severe, not only by contrast but
actually so. The jessamines and roses that were blooming so luxuriantly are
now hanging their heads, looking in utter despair at the idea of having winter instead of spring ushered in at this stage of their existence.

I was quite interested in your statement in regard to the condition of your
church, but am afraid neither Mr. Mallard nor myself can help you. A congregation without a pastor is indeed in a deplorable condition; and I am
afraid you will find it rather difficult to secure a "talented" minister for six
hundred dollars, unless living is so cheap in your section that this will comfortably support a minister and his wife—or probably you expect to provide
him with the latter commodity after his arrival. You say your congregation
is next to the wealthiest in the state. Now, judging from the salary, I must

either conclude the churches generally must be very poor, or else yours does not contribute as liberally as they might. I am afraid you will think I have grown very mercenary, but I don't think I am; I only have a slight fellow feeling since entering into the fraternity. I hope your church will not continue long vacant. Especially is it desirable for a people to have stated preaching at this time, when our Heavenly Father seems to be pouring out His Spirit and reviving His cause throughout our whole country. You have of course seen accounts of the numerous revivals in New Jersey, Pennsylvania, New York, and other places. This good work has begun, I hope, in our own state; there is some interest in the Presbyterian church in Macon.

You ask about Mother's arm. It is not well yet, though she is able to take it out of the sling now, and is gradually recovering the use of it. Many months will elapse before it will become as strong as it was before. Mr. Mallard and myself expect in a week or two to go home and spend some time with them. These visits home are so pleasant, when I get there I feel like staying altogether.

Sarah Ann wishes to know if I am still "Mary Sharpe." Tell her I am, for that portion of my name (for which my attachment is known) fortunately remains unchanged. From this message I perceive that she is still "Sarah Ann."

You want to know what has become of Matilda Harden. She is in the county and quite well, though I have seen very little of her this winter. She does not live near this village, nor does she attend this church, so I have only seen her when I have been in the lower portion of the county. Sallie's correspondence with her must long since have perished!

I believe you are skilled in the art of bread-making. I have made good bread too, but the other day I was too amused: I "set some leaven," and it rose three days after! I thought it a fortunate circumstance the satisfying of our hunger did not depend upon that loaf of bread. I am not an experienced housekeeper, so any nice receipts you may have will be thankfully received. I use only those that have been proven by the experience of my friends.

Do give my love to Sue Dickson when you write. What has become of Paulina and Lizzie Paul, Maggie Wilson, and the Misses Gill in particular? Do write something of them. Give love to Sarah Ann and your mother. Mr. Mallard desires to be remembered to you. With much love,

Your affectionate friend,
Mary S. Mallard.

Mr. Charles C. Jones, Jr., *to* Mrs. Mary Jones[t]
Savannah, Friday, March 12th, 1858
My dear Mother,

I had hoped that this evening's mail would have made me happy in the receipt of a letter from yourself or dear Father; and perchance that pleasure is reserved for the morrow, as the Liberty mail arrived so late that it was not distributed when the office closed.

Tomorrow you will receive several copies of "Georgia's" communication, and also a package which I forward at the request of Mrs. Grant. Of the contents you may perhaps have been made aware by letter from her. I have not gratified my curiosity by prying into it.

This week has been one of unusual labor. Night after night until a late hour have I been engaged at the office; and the consequence is, I feel considerably fatigued, and shall look forward to the coming Sabbath as an actual day of rest.

May I ask the favor of you, Mother, to have my summer clothes "overhauled," as the sailors would say? They need repairs, I have no doubt. And when a suitable opportunity occurs, please send them to the city.

All friends well, and unite in much love. My "Lady Bird" (to borrow a term of endearment from the old Nurse in *Romeo and Juliet*) has flown, and I am obliged to console myself only with the companionship of my professional engagements. The cold, blustering winds of March appeared yesterday to have sought their northern homes, but this evening we are reminded that Winter will not resign his dominion without a struggle. With much love, my dear father and mother, to you both, I am, as ever,

Your affectionate son,
Charles C. Jones, Jr.

Kind regards to all friends, and howdy for the servants.

Rev. C. C. Jones *to* Mr. Charles C. Jones, Jr.[g]

Montevideo, *Monday,* March 15th, 1858

My dear Son,

Last week was a week of travel, and therefore you did not hear from us. We went to your sister's on Friday the 5th. Saturday paid some calls at Walthourville. Left Mother there and proceeded to Flemington. Called to see Mr. C. Hines, and spent the night at Mr. Martin's. His little son Charles Jones is a fine little fellow. Preached twice on Sunday at Flemington—*sitting.* Night at Mr. Ezra Stacy's. Made three calls Monday morning, and reached Walthourville to dinner. Tuesday came home. Wednesday all day at Midway attending the annual meeting of the Society. Called our two ministers again: eight hundred dollars each. Thursday, with your Aunt Susan in company, went to Miss Clay's. Friday there. Preached in the evening. Saturday returned to Montevideo *via* Arcadia, leaving your uncle well, and well pleased with a fine *roed shad.* Sunday church at Pleasant Grove. Today Mother has gone down to the Island for diverse intents, carrying one dozen Washington heads for the Mount Vernon Association, to be sold *there* if possible—that is, by the way at *Dorchester.* I embrace the leisure to overhaul domestic affairs, and to square off some of my last year's accounts (that my friends may be kept friendly), and to write to you and do many other things. . . .

Enclosed is one of the most affecting letters I have ever received. It is from our afflicted friend Mrs. Helm. You will read it with deep interest and (like your mother and myself) with many tears, as well for the living as for the dead! I hope and we pray that this deep affliction may not only be savingly improved by poor George's brother and sisters but by you, my dear son, and by your brother, to whom I wish you to enclose the letter after you have read it and finished with it. And request him *to return it to me;* I would not lose it on any account.

How clearly do you see in our young friend's early and unexpected and painful death the necessity of an immediate repentance toward God and faith in our Lord Jesus Christ, that you may fulfill your obligations to God your Saviour and render to Him the glory due unto His holy name and stand prepared both for life and for death? My son, you ought not to defer in the manner you do your solemn attention to the salvation of your immortal soul.

Tuesday, March 16th. We had no letters from abroad today. When quietly seated to my desk anticipating a day of profitable study, your Uncle Banky and lady were announced. We have spent a pleasant day with them. Their little boy is a cheerful, fine infant. They have just left. So far had I written when your Uncle Henry was announced. His good lady has been quite unwell yesterday and today, but is better. After an agreeable hour he left us as supper was coming on table. Supper is over, and we have had family worship, at which we always remember our dear children; and again I sit down to finish my letter.

Mother desires me to say that she will fix up your clothing and send it to you as soon as possible, and will write you shortly. The carriage goes up in the morning for Daughter. Robert and I hope, D.V., to go to Presbytery in St. Marys next week; start about Wednesday. Mother sends much love. Servants at all the places well. I remain, my dear son,

Your ever affectionate father,
C. C. Jones.

Thank Mr. Ward for a copy of his address for me.

Mrs. Mary Jones *to* Mr. Charles C. Jones, Jr.[g]

Montevideo, *Monday,* March 22nd, 1858*

I have but a moment, my dear son, to inform you that I will send by the railroad tomorrow under Mr. Buttolph's care a bundle with your thin clothes. Your father and Robert are just starting for Darien, expecting to take the boat for St. Marys this evening. I will write you longer tomorrow, Providence permitting. With our united love to you and all friends,

Ever your affectionate mother,
Mary Jones.

MRS. MARY JONES *to* MR. CHARLES C. JONES, JR.^g

Montevideo, *Monday,* March 22nd, 1858*

My dear Son,

I hope you will find buttons and strings all in order, and that your summer garments will reach you safely tomorrow. I have sent all saving the two pair of coarse pants which I reserve for hunting and fishing.

Sister is dozing quietly in the rocking chair, her open book in hand; Jack and Kate and Tom have all run off for a play in the moonlight; and I am solus. Our pasture is on fire (intentionally), and every now and then a loud report is heard from the popping canes, and the lurid flames mount upward. Your dear father and Robert are now, I presume, on board the boat for St. Marys. The Lord bless and keep them! Oh, how precious is a realizing faith and trust in a special Providence! If my Heavenly Father knoweth the sparrow that falls to the ground, and clothes with beauty the lily of the field, surely I may resign to His care my mortal body and my immortal soul and all that I hold dear.

I received the package of Washington portraits which you sent me from Mrs. Grant safely, and am trying to dispose of them for the Mount Vernon cause. It is really surprising how little sympathy *we* (I mean the *ladies*) meet with in this cause. People seem to have money for every other call. In Savannah the interest which Professor Fowler creates is a fair specimen. I really hoped the good sense which has hitherto characterized the Southern mind would not be laid aside. He seems to have done more toward turning their heads than he ever will to expanding their common sense. I really thought the phrenological mania had died out years since. It is purely infidel in its tendency.

Thank you, my dear son, for the papers with the piece from "Georgia." If she does nothing more than appear in print, she will have done very little. The lightest feather from your plumes would turn the scale in our favor—and not diminish aught of your chivalry or patriotism!

In your bundle I have sent two vials. Please give them to Willie and request him to have them filled, and send me at the same time the articles on the enclosed memorandum. I will thank you also to hand the enclosed memorandum to Mr. Lathrop. And will you, my dear son, be kind enough to send me two pounds currants, one pound ginger, one pound hyson tea, and ten pounds of Passover bread from Borchert's the baker. Mr. Lathrop frequently offers to pack any articles I want sent, and if he would *put Willie's package with these other things* in his box of dry goods and send them all out on next Saturday to No. 3 (McIntosh Station), it would be a great accommodation. I will thank Willie to send me the *six jars ordered* by Captain Charlie's next trip. Please let me know by Thursday's mail if the things will come on *Saturday.* Enclosed are the memorandums; please hand to Messrs. Lathrop & Company and to King & Waring.

It is late, and I must say good night. Do not fail to present my love when you write Miss R. And much love to Cousins Eliza and Charles, in all of which Sister unites. And a large share for yourself from us both. God bless and save you, my child!

Your affectionate mother,
Mary Jones.

Miss MARY E. ROBARTS *to* Mrs. MARY JONES[t]

Marietta, *Monday,* March 22nd, 1858

It has been several weeks, my dearest cousin, since I received your last affectionate and interesting letter, which I resolved and *re*-resolved to answer but never did. When I received another token of your remembrance this morning, I determined not to let the day pass without writing; so after washing up the cups, giving out dinner, and hurrying over the arrangements for the day, I came into Mother's room and took my desk on my lap without even looking at a piece of work. So I have made a fair start for a letter, and hope to be able to finish without interruption.

Before speaking of other matters I will tell you how it has been with my dear mother since I last wrote. She remained in her room seven weeks, sitting up first one, then two or three hours, then five or six a day, amusing herself in reading and knitting. On Monday last she walked into the parlor with Louisa and myself and spent several hours in her usual seat. . . . On Wednesday she requested us to invite Mrs. Fraser to spend the day with her, which she did; and when I came into her room after giving out dinner, I found her dressed in her alpaca, with her dress cap on, looking as well, I thought, as she did before she was taken sick. She went into the drawing room and stayed till four o'clock. Fearing the effort was too much for her, we persuaded her to return to her room and lie down, which she did. . . . We are very careful of her, and never leave her alone for an hour. Either Louisa or myself are with her all the time, and we feel thankful that we have been able to render her such attentions.

Twelve o'clock. Interruption No. 1. . . . I had to put by my writing for an hour or so, but now resume it. And first let me say how delighted I was to hear such pleasant news of my dear boy Charlie. . . . I knew the young lady when a little girl. The Bath ladies are all kind, social, affectionate in their dispositions, good housekeepers, and make devoted wives; are energetic and enthusiastic in all they undertake. These are their most striking characteristics; and if in addition to this she is an earnest Christian, what more could a young man ask? Surely Charlie will get value received for what the young lady will get in him: a noble and true heart, talents, position, true nobility of soul. And if he can only get his father's recipe for making a good husband, his wife will be a happy woman. You must congratulate him for me; I do not like to write him till he writes me first. Tell him I feel perfectly satisfied; and this is saying a great deal, for I was so much afraid of being disappointed in the lady of his choice. If he knew his Aunt Mary as she knows herself, he would not want a wife like her. I am simply a lady of good intentions, but fail miserably in all my endeavors at excellence. And now, my dear cousins, let me congratulate you on the choice of your son. I trust your daughter will be a Ruth indeed to you, as was her namesake of Scripture memory to her mother-in-law. Tell Charlie if he cannot make a more interesting bridal trip, he must make me a visit. I shall be happy indeed to see them.

Do you recollect that I showed you a gold piece which my godson gave me? Well, I kept it, and every time I could spare a little money added to it, and sent to Charleston by Mrs. Sadler for a nice carpet for our drawing room. She brought me a beautiful Brussels at $1.12½ per yard, and we have just finished making it. I spent the money in this way not only because it would perpetuate the gift a long time, but because it was an article we very much needed; and Mother never can spare anything from family expenses to buy articles of furniture for the house. The times have been indeed tight to those of us who have large families and small incomes. But I thought when I was in such great affliction that if God would only spare my dear mother to us, all other trials would be light; so I must not complain after all His goodness to us.

I am glad to hear that Cousin Charles has a manager; it is indeed too much for him to attend to plantation matters. He is not able to undergo the bodily fatigue, much less the mental excitement. Am much obliged to him for receiving Katy and Lucy; our Negroes have never been satisfied at the Retreat since poor James died. . . . This is little Charlie Buttolph's birthday. Dear little fellow, how I would like to see him! If he is with you, kiss him for me. And give much love to Cousin Susan, Laura, and Mr. Buttolph. And much love to Cousin Charles and dear Mary, and best wishes for her. We hope to have a little contribution to a tiny wardrobe from the Cherokee relatives. . . . Please give our love to Julia and Mary.

Your affectionate cousin,
Mary E. Robarts.

I must now tell you what a loss we are to meet with in the removal of Mr. Pynchon and Harriet to Huntsville, Alabama. They have always been kind friends and neighbors to us, and we shall miss them very much. They leave the middle of April. . . . Farewell, my dear cousin. Do write soon. . . . Sam is quite well, and sends love to his family; also Katy and Lucy.

Rev. R. Q. Mallard *to* Mrs. Mary S. Mallard[t]

St. Marys, Wednesday, March 24th, 1858

My darling Wife,

Your father has just observed to one of the young ladies at our house that "married people are constantly writing love letters." This is all just and proper, is it not? For who can know so well what love is as those who sustain toward each other the tenderest earthly relation? I wished this morning that I could fly home with telegraphic speed and see how my—family—is. Or are?

We reached Darien after a pleasant ride in ample time. On the way we were quite amused with the satisfactory answer given to Father's question by a boy riding a horse.

"Well, John, whose horse is that?"

"Da massa horse, sir!"

And on he rode with the air of one who had given all reasonable information to the questioner.

We arrived in the city of Darien early in the evening—say, half-past four o'clock—and went immediately to the *little homeopathic* doctor's residence; but not finding him at home, we turned our horse's head to Mr. Mitchel's. As we rode up, Father spoke to a little Negro boy.

"Howdy, John."

"My name is Norman, sir."

"Ah, yes—Norman!"

As we passed, someone asked Norman who we were.

"I don't know," was his reply, "who he is. *But he know me.*"

Mr. and Mrs. Mitchel we found well, and we were very pleasantly entertained by them. The doctor and Mr. Goulding came over in the course of the evening and took tea with us. I walked down to the boat with Mr. Goulding, calling at his residence on our way, and thus made Mrs. Goulding's acquaintance. Mr. Mitchel kindly sent his buggy down with Father. . . . Our St. Marys party was rather a small one, Mr. Mitchel being the only delegate to Presbytery beside ourselves.

About eight o'clock we steamed away from the town. The night was a beautiful one for navigation. After a rather uncomfortable endeavor at rest, which for me was broken by almost every sound, morning dawned upon us. Just as the light of the lighthouse was put out at the approach of "the greater light made to rule the day," Father went up on deck, and I soon followed him. We were just steaming around the ample curve in the river which forms a graceful entrance to the port of St. Marys. We were soon alongside of the wharf, which rises but a few feet above high watermark. We breakfasted at a boardinghouse on the bay kept by a Roman Catholic family. . . . We are but a *short* distance from the church; of this I am very glad for Father's sake.

In company with Mr. Mitchel on the day of our arrival I visited the cemetery. It is a very pleasant place, neatly fenced and shaded by a number of live oaks, the most of which do not appear to be very aged. A new-made grave with a wreath of cedar and a few flowers resting upon it (affection's offering) was pointed out to us as the last resting place of our deceased brother Rev. Mr. Fleming. From all that I have learned he was an excellent and laborious servant of God. He was quite young, and has left a wife and four children in very dependent circumstances. They are at present in this

place. This instance coming under my notice impresses me favorably with
one of the charities of our church not on our cards—the fund for the relief
of superannuated ministers and the *families* of deceased ministers.

We commenced the services of the meeting by preaching last night (Tuesday). We thought that it would be well thus to employ our time until the
meeting of the presbytery. I preached then; Father expects to preach tonight.
He has been very much fatigued from the journey and "the sitting up for
company" on the first day. I hope that he will feel better with the quiet of
today.

I can't say positively, my darling, when we will be at home. I *hope* on
Tuesday next, although Mr. Goulding, not having been able to attend in St.
Marys, would probably like an adjourned meeting in Darien to receive him
into our presbytery. This may detain us a day longer. Give my love to
Mother, and accept a warm kiss from

Your own
Robert.

REV. C. C. JONES *to* MRS. MARY JONES[t]

St. Marys, *Wednesday,* March 24th, 1858

My dearest Wife,

We had a pleasant ride and reached Darien on Monday about 4½ P.M.
Dr. Dunwody was out in the country on his practice, and we drove on to
Mr. Mitchel's and were received with great kindness. Mrs. Mitchel inquired
particularly after you. She is looking well, and retains her identity in all
respects. Her flower garden is in excellent order; she has some uncommon
varieties of the heartsease both in color and in size. Her aviary is well stocked,
and there are a few rare birds in it from abroad. But the space is too limited,
and the *building* birds are sadly interrupted. They get into violent family
quarrels and into pitched battles with their neighbors. Their nests are often
broken up and their eggs stolen, and the poor mates droop in disappointment
and sorrow. Yet true to the instincts of nature, the male renews his song of
love and cheers his companion. And she forgets her grief, and with her little
heart throbbing with joy and happy anticipations she renews her labors. The
animated world never ceases to interest me.

Brother Goulding called over to see us. In good health and spirits. Getting
a little bald. Keeps a select school every day till 2 P.M. His wife a most active
minister's wife, making herself useful in every way, and is well reported of
for good works. Dr. Dunwody called also. Reports his family well. Gives a
sad account of his father; says he is a *perfect skeleton,* and cannot bear to be
spoken to about recovery. . . . You would scarcely know Darien. Every
church newly painted. Courthouse also. And a new town hall. New hotel
building. And the lots generally brushed up.

Brother Goulding and the doctor took tea and went down to the boat with
us. Mr. Mitchel and I rode. . . . Robert and myself occupied the same state-

room. Mr. Mitchel not far off. Pulled off our coats and boots and turned in, covering with our cloaks. Room hot from the vicinity of the boilers. Up at daylight. Reached St. Marys about sunrise. Put up at the *newest* hotel. . . . Mr. Mitchel and Robert made their toilets; I was pronounced by both of them "well enough looking surely for the day." A great relief, as dressing is no pleasure. The two gentlemen walked out to see the graveyard; I sat down and read in a fine large Bible presented by the St. Marys Female Bible Society to a division of the Sons of Temperance. . . . Tell Daughter Robert makes a good roommate and a dutiful and attentive son, and thinks he is the most favored man in the world, having a wife that is uncommon. He preached an excellent sermon last night to a good congregation. This afternoon we have, if the weather permits, a prayer meeting in the church, and preaching again tonight. . . . We hope and pray the Lord may graciously visit and bless us in our meeting. Many men here do not go to church at all!

Heavy rain, wind northeast, and very cool. Prevented from calling on Mrs. Fleming this morning. . . . Save the paper (the last) containing Mr. Fleming's obituary.

Robert is writing and will report himself at headquarters. Says he: "I've finished before you." "Yes," I answer, "you have; my letter has much more in it than yours." So much for being an old and true lover. Kiss my dear child for me. Hope you will both be well and happy. We will come home, God willing, sometime next week. Howdy for all the servants. Respects to Mr. McDonald; hope he has had a good rain. It is near dinner time, and the steamer will come for the letters soon. The Lord be with and bless you, my dear wife!

Your ever affectionate husband,
C. C. Jones.

Mr. Charles C. Jones, Jr., *to* Mrs. Mary Jones[t]

Savannah, *Monday,* March 29th, 1858

My dear Mother,

The bundle of summer clothes was not received until Saturday. Upon opening it, your note was first received. This will explain to you why the articles ordered were not forwarded on Thursday, the day named for their being sent to No. 3. The commissions have all been executed, and the respective parcels go out tomorrow morning to No. 3, where they will await your pleasure. You had better send for them at your early convenience, as I have (in the box from Brown) sent you and Sister a few oranges, lemons, etc., which I hope will reach you in good order.

All friends well. With warmest love to self, Sister, Father, Robert, and all friends, I am, as ever,

Your affectionate son,
Charles C. Jones, Jr.

Howdy for the servants.

I am very much obliged to you for your kind care of my summer suits; they are much improved by the keeping.

I almost forgot to tell you what I intended saying first of all: that I have had the pleasure of seeing Mr. Dickson and Miss Margie from Philadelphia. They leave the city this afternoon on their return home, and desire kindest remembrance. Their time is so limited (Mr. Dickson being the president of the Bank of North America) that they cannot enjoy the pleasure of a visit to Liberty, which they very much regret. All friends in Philadelphia well.

MRS. MARY JONES *to* MR. CHARLES C. JONES, JR.ᵍ

Montevideo, *Tuesday,* March 30th, 1858

My dear Son,

Your father and Robert have just arrived, having passed a very interesting time at Presbytery. We are all delighted to see them, and they to get home. I think the little change has done your father good.

Today I received your kind favor, and am much obliged by your attention to my requests. You must send me a bill of the articles bought. And your sister and myself return many thanks for the fruit; we shall enjoy it when it arrives. I am glad to know that your summer clothes have arrived; I began to feel uneasy about them.

Your aunt and cousin and Charlie are with us. I am so happy to know that you will be with us next week. Bring as many friends as you please; there is room in our hearts and room in our home for all. I will try and have some fine oysters for you when you come. Your aunt and cousin, Sister and Robert and Father unite in best love to you with

Your ever affectionate mother,
Mary Jones.

The servants send many howdies.

Thanks to Captain Anderson for the *Paris plums. Friends* have remembered me very kindly recently. In my *professional line* I have now, in addition to the Paris plums, *gourd seed* from the *wilderness of sin, feather grass* from Switzerland, and some curious-looking seeds from *Egypt.* Anything agricultural or horticultural is always prized: I am a "tiller of the ground."

Father says he will write soon.

REV. C. C. JONES *to* MR. CHARLES C. JONES, JR.ᵍ

Montevideo, *Wednesday,* March 31st, 1858

My dear Son,

Robert and I returned home yesterday afternoon from our attendance upon a pleasant meeting of our presbytery in St. Marys. We left Monday morning the 22nd at ten and reached St. Marys next morning at *sunrise.* Returning, we left St. Marys Monday morning the 29th at nine o'clock and reached home Tuesday afternoon at six o'clock. But we lay at New Fernandina near four hours, and spent twelve hours in Darien. The trip and work ashore have been fatiguing, but on the whole refreshing. Found your dear mother, sister, aunt, and all *well*. People also. *Deo gratias!*

Saw St. Marys at a stand: low down. New Fernandina going up. Brunswick at a standstill. If the railroad from Alligator to Jacksonville is finished which *crosses* the Fernandina Railroad, and Dr. Screven will run to the Florida line in a point to meet the Jacksonville Railroad when it runs to the line, he will cut off the neck of the Fernandina Railroad. Savannah will then get the main business of the road. This will be better than running to St. Marys to connect with Fernandina by *ferry*. The doctor no doubt will fix it to the best advantage. Am glad to see our seaboard improving.

Both your letters have come to hand. The bills and accounts all right. Enclosed is an order on Mr. Anderson for $98.66, favor of Claghorn & Cunningham. Please hand it to them and take receipt for their bill up to January 1st, 1858, as rendered against me. Will the bank *discount on* for the year? You have deposited enough nearly to pay six months' interest.

Have received a long letter from your brother in explanation of his views and reasons for leaving Athens. He has given the change due consideration. His letter is clear and conclusive. You will see the letter when you come out, which will be next week, D.V., much to our great pleasure. He returned Mrs. Helm's letter.

I was greatly shocked on learning the death of Mrs. Hutchison! Every way a most sad—yea, distressing—affliction. I understand she was not a professing Christian. My poor friend has passed and is passing through deep waters! I do most deeply feel for him.

Mother begs for the rest of the sheet.

Your ever affectionate father,
C. C. Jones.

MRS. MARY JONES *to* MR. CHARLES C. JONES, JR.[g]
Montevideo, *Wednesday,* March 31st, 1858

My dear Son,

The articles ordered were all received yesterday. Accept many thanks from your sister and myself for the delicious fruit. I have not tasted such sweet oranges for a long time. We have been enjoying them.

I have written Mr. Lathrop for a few more articles for your aunt and cousin, and requested him to hand them to you if you are coming out soon; if not, he can send them to Riceboro.

Last night the wind blew a gale, and the rain fell in torrents. Our friends, with Miss Dunning, left for the Island this morning. My space is fitted. Our love to Cousins Charles and Eliza. Affectionate regards to *Miss R.* Sister, Father, and Robert unite with me in best love to you.

Ever your affectionate mother,
M. J.

Willie made a mistake. *I did not wish the ether and chloroform mixed.* I will thank him to send *two vials—the one with ether,* the other with chloroform *as marked—when you come out.*

By the last mail we have letters from your Aunt Mary and your brother. He has been quite unwell, but was better. Your aunt is much pleased to hear of your engagement; says she rejoices but cannot write, as you have not written her yourself. She has always been one of your most attached relatives. I will keep her letter for you to see her high opinion of you.

I am told they have commenced a daily prayer meeting for businessmen in Savannah. God grant that they may be as signally blessed there as elsewhere! There has certainly been a remarkable outpouring of God's Spirit throughout our whole land. Let me entreat you, my dear child, if these meetings are held, to attend them and use the means of grace; they may be for the saving of your soul—*your immortal soul!* Surely it is time for you to be in earnest! Your mother's heart yearns to know that your peace is made with God through Jesus Christ our Saviour.

MR. CHARLES C. JONES, JR., *to* REV. *and* MRS. C. C. JONES[t]

Savannah, *Saturday,* April 3rd, 1858

My dear Father and Mother,

In consequence of my absence from the city, your kind favors were not until this morning received. I have just returned from Augusta, where I have been spending a day or two in the companionship of my dear Ruthie, whom I found as well and lovely as ever.

The first person I saw as I entered the Planters' Hotel was Mr. Dickson, and the second, Dr. Joseph Jones! He was looking very thin, having but just recovered from a pretty severe attack of fever. He improved the opportunity offered by his *weakness* (is it not characteristic of him?) to visit Augusta, become acquainted with the professors, and inquire into the condition of the college, etc. He was warmly welcomed by the members of the faculty, who received him with marked attention and kindness. He was dining and supping out all the time he was in Augusta. As you may imagine, it was a very pleasant surprise to meet so unexpectedly. We roomed together and spent many delightful moments in each other's society. The change from Athens to Augusta will be in every respect favorable for him. He will there be in the regular line of professional engagements and occupations well suited to his natural tastes. The salary is about the same, and all made in three or four months, affording an opportunity for uninterrupted pursuit of such subjects and investigations as taste may indicate during the remaining eight months of the year. His relations with the members of the faculty will also be of a very pleasant character.

It is a source of untold pleasure to me to find my ladylove so happy and well.

Enclosed I send receipt of Claghorn & Cunningham for $98.66, the same being amount of draft on John W. Anderson, Esq.

This morning's papers announce the death of Mr. Dunning, Miss Gertrude's father. The intelligence will be unexpected and deeply affecting to her.

I hope to see you about the 17th of this month, and may bring a brother chip or two with me to enjoy the pleasures of home for a day or so. I am glad to see that there is a good prospect this evening for a clear day again—and that without frost. The orchards in the up country are in beautiful bloom, and the prospect for fruit charming. All friends in Savannah well, as far as I have seen or heard. With much love to you both, my dear mother and father, and my dear sister, and Robert if he is with you, I am, as ever,

Your affectionate son,
Charles C. Jones, Jr.

The ether and chloroform will be attended to.

Howdy for the servants.

XII

Mrs. Mary Jones *to* Miss Kitty Stiles[t]

Montevideo, *Saturday,* April 24th, 1858

My dear Kitty,

The gentlemen have debated if they should be allowed the honor of writing to inform you of the arrival of a little stranger in our household, but I believe they conclude it most becoming the newly made grandmama to do so. *Daughter* desired that you should be informed immediately, but numerous occupations have prevented to the present moment. As an assurance that she has truly a sweet, precious little daughter she sends you the enclosed hair, of which the little lady can boast but a small quantity at present. *She* made her appearance on last Sabbath night at nine minutes past ten o'clock. As *you may* (or rather I should say *your mother* would) be assured, it has been a season of intense anxiety to us, and we desire to bless the Lord for His goodness and mercy to her and to us. She is doing well in every respect, and nothing would gratify us more than to receive a visit from you at this *anniversary season.* Strange contrast of the past and present 22nd!

I hope never to forget, dear Kitty, the kind and affectionate interest manifested by your dear mother and yourself in our dear child. I would be glad for time to write you a long and *circumstantial* letter, but I am sole nurse, and my little charge does not permit me to be absent long. I cannot close, however, without imparting to you one other source of rejoicing which now fills our hearts with joy and our mouths with praise: the *conversion of our beloved son in Athens!* We think constantly and strive to pray especially for the young men of Savannah. May the Lord bless your own dear brother with His saving grace!

Daughter and Mr. Jones unite with me in best love to you. Present us affectionately to your mother and venerated grandmother and to your aunts. Mr. Mallard is away at Walthourville attending to his duties. In haste,

Sincerely and affectionately your friend,

Mary Jones.

Miss Mary E. Robarts *to* Rev. C. C. Jones[t]

Marietta, *Monday,* April 26th, 1858

We tender our united and heartfelt congratulations to our ever dear cousins on the birth of their dear little granddaughter, and that your dear daughter has been spared through her season of peril. Mother says she is very glad to hear that she is a little *lady,* and she sends her a little pair of slippers and her blessing; and we all send her a great many kisses. . . . Mother thanks you for your graphic description of the little lady's arrival. She certainly had friends enough there at the old homestead to welcome her, and is the first of the family that can claim it as her birthplace. Hope she may spend many anniversaries there with her beloved grandparents. And is it possible that His Reverence had to turn housekeeper on the occasion? What a pity his friend Lady Mary had not been there to relieve him of the key basket!

My dear mother says she is not able to write now, and thanks you for your kind wishes in regard to her health. . . . She seems so much better that I think she will have a comfortable summer when the weather becomes settled and these cool changes, so unfriendly to an invalid, pass off. . . . I hope Cousin Mary, yourself, and Cousin Susan will come up sometime in the summer to see her. The times are so hard I should dislike to put you to the expense unless you felt that you could come conveniently. I hope you are not quite as bad off as we are, for trips of this kind would be to us impossible on account of the scarcity of money.

On Friday John and Jane and their little boys arrived here on their way to Rome. They left Dunwody much better. He must have been extremely ill, having been delirious from Monday till Saturday. We feel grateful that his life has been spared, and trust he may be led to repentance and become a new creature. John had such a severe sick headache that he had to go immediately to bed. They arrived here at one o'clock in the day, and left at noon the next day, so that we saw very little of him. Jane is entirely restored: looks well, and the little boys very fat and lively. John will return here on the 15th May to Mr. Palmer's installation. . . .

I have not space to write more. Mr. Pynchon and family left for Huntsville on Thursday. We shall miss them very much. Give love from everyone of us to dear Mary, yourself, Cousin Mary. And tell her I hope her little granddaughter will not make her write so seldom as Cousin Susan does.

Your ever affectionate cousin,
Mary E. Robarts.

Our love to Cousin Susan, Laura, Mr. Buttolph, and Charlie. What is the baby to be named? I say Mary Jones; Louisa says Mary Elizabeth. . . . Much love to Cousin William. Tell Rosetta Sam is quite well.

Hon. Joseph H. Lumpkin *to* Rev. C. C. Jones[t]

Athens, *Monday,* April 26th, 1858

Allow me, my dear brother, to congratulate you that he who was yours by natural generation is God's son by regeneration. I allude to our noble young professor, Dr. Jones. He has, I doubt not, informed you of the fact. It having been my privilege as an elder of the church to welcome him yesterday within the fold of Christ and to tender to him (with others) the emblems of the broken Body and shed Blood of the Saviour, I could not forego the pleasure of tendering to you my congratulations.

Yesterday, my brother, was one of the happiest days of my life, notwithstanding my bodily infirmity. With your son and some forty others, three of my own children and three grandchildren entered into a covenant with God and His people that, His grace enabling them, the lives which they shall in the future live shall be by faith on His Son. Our town has been highly blessed with a gracious season of refreshing from the presence of the Lord. Between one hundred and fifty and two hundred have been hopefully converted and are rejoicing in the light and liberty of God's children. Included in this number is more than one-half of the students of the college. Every member of the faculty—president, professors, and tutors—engaged actively and with their whole hearts in the work, and the result is a most delightful state of feeling between teachers and scholars.

Everyone has been deeply impressed with the childlike simplicity of manner and godly sincerity of your son. Not the smallest or feeblest lamb in the flock behaved with more guilelessness and truthfulness of character. He and Tutor Wash propose to embark immediately on the Sabbath instruction of the people of color in the place. I would not flatter you, my dear brother, for worlds; but you may well feel all of a father's pride in your son. No one has ever made a more favorable impression upon anybody than Dr. Joseph has in this community; he is universally beloved and respected. Tomorrow he leads by invitation the twelve o'clock prayer meeting in my son's law office. Oh, you know not how we dislike to give him up! That the change may be better for him is possible; that he can ever go where he will be more fully appreciated I do not believe. It was a beautiful incident to see his boy marching up with his young master to join the church, and commemorating together with him for the first time the New Testament Passover. He said his "old master's religion was good enough for him."

In sincerity and in the fellowship of the gospel,
Jos. Henry Lumpkin.

Mrs. Mary C. Nisbet *to* Rev. *and* Mrs. C. C. Jones[t]

Macon, Friday Afternoon, April 30th, 1858

Our dear Friends,

I am deputed "scribe" this time because of unusual pressure of business engagements with Mr. Nisbet today; and the joyful tidings reached us only last night of the arrival of the little stranger. We offer our congratulations and best wishes to the mama, papa, and grandparents; and as it is the first time any of the party assume their relations, we most heartily hail you all in each one. We desire all earthly good for the little one: blessings of every name and kind, of body, mind, soul, and spirit, blessings for this world and the next, that she may be all you desire her to be, mentally, morally, and physically. . . . May her little life be spared to bless you all; and as she grows in stature may she grow in grace and in favor with both God and man. . . . Will not one or the other or both of the grandparents write and tell us "all about everything"—how it all is? And give us every minute fact: the shade of the hair and of the eyes, the skin, the resemblances, the noticeable things that I know have already shown themselves. Tell us of the mother, and how the father sustains his new honors and dignities. And leave nothing untold. Will you not?

And while, dear friends, we rejoice with trembling over this accession to your joys, cares, and responsibilities, allow us to offer our heartfelt sympathy and rejoicing over that other new birth in your family; I mean your son Joe. Can you not say: "I have seen Thy salvation"? . . . I have thought that this is no new thing with Joe: the leaven has been hid, but it has been working. And behold and see what God has wrought! . . . With loving remembrance to your friends and ours—Mother, Laura, Mr. Buttolph, Colonel Maxwell, and Mrs. King—accept for yourselves, dear friends, the love and sympathy of

Your affectionate friends,
Mary C. Nisbet for herself
and for T. C. Nisbet.

Kiss the baby for me. And don't forget to tell its name.

Rev. John Jones *to* Rev. C. C. Jones[t]

Rome, *Tuesday,* May 4th, 1858

Dear Brother Charles,

We found your welcome letter on our return home. Thank you again and again for all that affectionate interest you constantly cherish for our dear Dunwody. He has been extremely ill, but has been spared in tender mercy— I would humbly believe to repent and embrace a precious Saviour. Another student died of the same disease (typhoid pneumonia) whilst we were at Brother Reid's. His closing hours were most painful, leaving almost no hope in his death. He made a confession to Brother Reid a few hours before death of having committed murder in Louisiana a few months ago. He fled to Georgia (to some relatives in Telfair County), whence he came under an assumed name to the quiet and secluded village of Woodstock and entered the Philomath school of Brother Reid. It was a dreadful case, developing human depravity, the power of conscience, and the overruling providence of God. The details I will give you when I see you. We can never forget the prompt visit of dear Joseph in our distress. I was glad even to tears. He is a wonderful young man.

And now, dear Brother, let me hasten to rejoice with you and my dear sister in the birth of your little granddaughter, and the second birth of your dear Joseph. These two events must have been near together; I thus judge from a message received on Sabbath from Mr. Newton, an elder of the Athens church, that Joseph and his servant Titus had with others (thirty-eight in all) united with the church on Sabbath the 25th of April. I thank God every time I think of it. . . . But I must not forget the precious little baby—another little Mary. That will be the name: the sweetest of names. Blessings on its little head, and joy to the young parents, and special thanks that the young mother is so well. May mother and babe be blessed and strengthened day by day, and may the little creature live to be a wellspring of joy to its parents and grandparents! There's nothing like a baby—nothing so humanizing, so concentrating, so softening, so peacemaking. My dear Jane and myself long to see the little wonder.

I may make a short visit the last of this month to the low country—not so much on account of my own private affairs as for business in McIntosh. I have to preach the installation sermon of Brother E. P. Palmer in Marietta on the third Sabbath of this month, and will come on then if at all to Liberty. Do send a line to Marietta informing me where you will all be the last of May or after the third Sabbath, that I may shape my movements accordingly. . . . Jane and the little boys unite with me in best love to dear Sister and yourself, Mary Sharpe, Robert, and Baby, and all relatives who may be with you, and all who are not, always including Cousin William and the Island friends and relatives.

> Ever your affectionate brother,
> John Jones.

Mrs. Mary Jones *to* Dr. Joseph Jones[t]

Montevideo, *Thursday,* May 13th, 1858

My dear Son,

Scarcely have I had a moment in the last three weeks in which I could sit down to write you. You will understand this, knowing that I have been the sole nurse of your dear sister and the little baby—and in addition company to be provided for almost every day. I have longed to tell you the joy and happiness which have flowed into my soul through God's mercy and goodness in bestowing upon you "the gift of eternal life through Jesus Christ our Lord," and enabling you and your faithful boy Titus to profess Him before men, and to avouch the Lord Jehovah to be your God and Saviour. May the Lord ever bless you, my dear child, and make your path that of the just! . . . Your dear brother appears to feel very great pleasure at your profession of religion. Oh, that in this time of special gracious visitation he too might be brought into the Ark of Safety! . . . Today we received an interesting letter from Miss Clay. Both Joseph and Tom have recently professed conversion during the season of revival in Yale College. They write as those who have been truly born again.

We wish daily that you could see your sweet little niece just as she is. We have thought at times that she resembled *you* in your infancy. She is not large, but well formed (particularly her head), and fat as a ricebird, is strong and healthy, has never had a colic, and has the best appetite you can imagine.

And your dear sister has such an abundance of nourishment that she has had to nurse one of the little Negroes. I have tried to do all I knew, with God's blessing, to secure her sure restoration to health and strength. I have not allowed her yet to have any care of the baby at night. She will be four weeks old next Sabbath night. I observed the nine-days rule in bed *strictly,* and as you suggested, kept her very quiet for over two weeks. She now takes a short ride every morning, and dined with us for the first time today, Mr. and Mrs. Busby being here. I do not want her to leave us under two weeks, for she looks very pale, and I think is not strong enough to undertake household duties.

I am now giving the medicines you sent to your father daily, but there has not been time to test their efficacy. He complains of great weakness, but is nevertheless at work all the time. . . . Your sister, father, and Robert join me in best love to you, with a kiss from your little niece. Porter and Patience and all the servants want to be remembered to you and to Titus. I have not time or space for more.

Ever your affectionate mother,
Mary Jones.

Rev. D. L. Buttolph *to* Rev. C. C. Jones[t]

Point Maxwell, *Monday,* May 17th, 1858
Two o'clock A.M.

My dear Uncle,

Our little Charlie has left us. God has taken him. "The Lord gave, and the Lord hath taken away; *blessed be the name of the Lord.*" Charlie grew much worse after I left home. The doctor arrived at 12 M. As soon as I saw him this evening, I perceived a very great change in him, but did not anticipate his death. Between ten and eleven o'clock he was taken with convulsions, in which he died at $1\frac{1}{2}$ A.M.

The doctor is still with us, and so is Aunt Julia. Our hearts are crushed, but we try to bow submissively to the will of God. I know we have your prayers and deepest sympathies. May God give us grace to support us in this trying hour! Mother and Laura unite with me in warmest love to you, Aunt, and Cousin and Robert and Baby.

Your affectionate nephew,
D. L. Buttolph.

Mr. Charles C. Jones, Jr., *to* Rev. C. C. Jones[t]

Savannah, *Tuesday,* May 18th, 1858

My dear Father,

I cannot tell you how much I was shocked and grieved to hear of the death of dear little Charlie. I did not even know of his indisposition; and it is hard to believe that I will never again look upon his noble little face and form.

How deep the shadows that must now be lying upon that threshold from whence the light of the household has gone forever! Oh, the loneliness and sorrow that must encircle their dwelling! I have this day written Aunt Susan, Cousin Laura, and Mr. Buttolph a letter of sympathy. But they know where to look for support and comfort under this affliction so sad to them and to us all.

When will you and dear Mother visit Savannah? All friends well. With warmest love, I am, as ever,

Your affectionate son,
Charles C. Jones, Jr.

Mr. Charles C. Jones, Jr., *to* Rev. C. C. Jones[g]

Savannah, *Monday*, May 24th, 1858

My dear Father,

I was deeply pained a few moments since to learn from Judge Law that you suffered while in the cars on Saturday morning last from another of those distressing attacks, and sincerely hope that you are now feeling no inconvenience from the same alarming cause. Did you get a particle of coal or of dust down your throat?

Miss Ruth highly appreciates with me your kind and pleasant visit to Savannah; and we very much regret that dear Mother in consequence of her engagements could not find it in her power to accompany you.

The sea breeze after a delightful day is stealing with its soft refreshing influence over our city. The square in front of our office is filled with numbers of merry-hearted little children amusing themselves upon the greensward. What a source of positive health and comfort, as well as of beauty and pleasure, these public squares are in any—and especially in a Southern—city!

All friends well, and unite in kind remembrance. Miss Ruth leaves the city for Bath on Monday next. How I shall miss her pleasant companionship! With warmest love to dear Mother, self, Sister, Robert, and my little niece, I remain, as ever,

Your affectionate son,
Charles C. Jones, Jr.

Rev. C. C. Jones *to* Mr. Charles C. Jones, Jr.[g]

Montevideo, *Wednesday*, May 26th, 1858

My dear Son,

We were happy to hear from you yesterday.

Not having had an attack of the spasm of the glottis for months, I began to hope the affection had passed away. The attack in the car arose from a small cinder which I inhaled. It stuck to the glottis, and the difficulty was protracted. Have never had but one severer paroxysm. Your Uncle Henry was with me, and quickly got a tumbler of water. He was very kind, and I do not know what I should have done without him. I trace the attack to exhaustion from two day's exertion in town and sitting up late at night. We are reminded that we know neither the day nor the hour when we shall be called into eternity. A daily preparation for that solemn event is our duty and privilege.

My visit to Savannah is one of the most agreeable I have ever made; and we have found another friend to love and pray for, and we hope that the lapse of time will but make perfect our confidence and affection. Mother joins in love to Miss Whitehead and to yourself and to Cousin Eliza and Cousin Charles. Your aunt and Cousins Lyman and Laura have been with us since Saturday; they leave for the Island this morning. All send love to you, with Sister and Robert. The little baby grows finely.

Your ever affectionate father,
C. C. Jones.

MRS. MARY S. MALLARD *to* MR. CHARLES C. JONES, JR.[g]
Montevideo, Thursday, May 27th, 1858
Dear Brother Charlie,

Accept from Robert and myself many thanks for the beautiful spoon you so kindly sent to our little Mary. She used it tonight for the first time. I wish you could see her now; she has grown very much, and we imagine her store of knowledge and attractions daily increase.

Aunt Susan and Cousins Laura and Lyman remained with us until yesterday. They have passed through deep waters, but I trust they do receive comfort and support from Him who alone can heal their wounds. . . . We expect to go to Walthourville on Saturday. I do not know what I shall do when I go away from Father and Mother, especially now that I have a little baby to take care of.

Father was very much pleased with Miss Ruth, and I have no doubt we will all love her. Father is not very well, and Mother still suffers from the rheumatism in her arms. If able she will add a few lines to this tonight. You must excuse my not writing more, but I am very weary and sleepy. Baby has had a hearty cry, and has just composed herself for the night, I hope. If she were old enough, she would send her own thanks for the spoon. With love from Father, Mother, and myself, I remain

Your affectionate sister,
Mary S. Mallard.

P.S. Mr. Mallard is in Dorchester.

MRS. MARY JONES *to* MR. CHARLES C. JONES, JR.[g]
Montevideo, Thursday, May 27th, 1858
Thanks, my dear son, for the many nice things sent us by your father. We have all enjoyed them, and shall do so for many days to come.

When are you coming out to be with us on the Island? I long to have you a little while at least at home with us.

It was a matter of sincere regret that I could not accompany your father in his visit to Savannah, which was especially designed to meet Miss Whitehead, with whom he was very much pleased.

Your dear sister and our little pet think of leaving us on Saturday. I shall feel lost without my precious charge, but know it is best they should not remain longer below. We think of moving next week.

Everything is suffering from the excessive drought.

I have not time or space to add more at this time. Present us affectionately to Miss Whitehead, with love to Cousins Eliza and Charles. Good night, my dear child. May the Saviour's love and blessing rest upon you!

Your affectionate mother,
Mary Jones.

The servants always wish to be remembered.

MR. CHARLES C. JONES, JR., *to* MRS. MARY JONES[t]

Savannah, Monday, May 31st, 1858

Your kind note, my dear mother, was duly received, and it makes me very happy to know that all at home are well, and that the little articles kindly carried out by Father you found pleasant and agreeable.

Sister, Robert, and the little niece have left you, and you and Father are all alone. How I wish that I could leave my office and spend at least a few days in the quiet delightful enjoyment of the thousand pleasant associations that cluster around my early home—associations that every year renders more and more sacred! I hope the weeks are not far distant when I may find it in my power to realize this happy anticipation.

Cousin Charles may visit you about the second or third week in June. He expects much pleasure in the enjoyment of your society, in the quiet relaxation from engagements, in fishing and feasting upon the good things from the salt water. He cannot say, however, as yet whether his professional duties will permit an absence.

Miss Lucy Sorrel on tomorrow evening expects to espouse the name of Elliott. I wish her joy, but fear a disappointment. Were I a lady, I would certainly be very loath to marry one who had the guilt of homicide upon his skirts. The marriage is not, I am told, very warmly approved by her parents.

The weather has been very warm today, but a pleasant rain yesterday has relieved us from the dust which usually accompanies a burning sun. . . . All friends well, and unite in love. Miss Ruth desires her special remembrance. Excuse this letter: I have written in haste, and a crowd in the office. With warmest love to dear Father and self, I am, as ever,

Your affectionate son,
Charles C. Jones, Jr.

Howdy for all the servants.

Mrs. Mary Jones *to* Mr. Charles C. Jones, Jr.[g]
                              Montevideo, *Thursday,* June 3rd, 1858*
My dear Son,

This is our meeting night, and when your father left for the chapel, I intended to devote an hour to you, but have been clearly caught *napping*. All day I have been busy preparing to move, which, Providence permitting, we hope to do the early part of next week. I presume we shall get down ourselves about Wednesday.

Your affectionate favor was received by Tuesday's mail. Please say to Cousin Charles that we shall be most happy to welcome him at Maybank, and the enjoyment would be more than twofold if he would only bring Cousin Eliza and the children.

It is quite time that we had moved, although everything around us here is very pleasant: the atmosphere cool, no stagnant water, and very few mosquitoes.

Your sister, Robert, and the dear baby left us on last Saturday; and tomorrow, God willing, we expect to go up to Walthourville. They wish your father to baptize the baby on Sabbath. . . . My paper ends, and so must I. Your father unites with me in best love to you and all friends.

              Ever, my dear child, your affectionate mother,
                              Mary Jones.

Miss Mary E. Robarts *to* Mrs. Mary Jones[t]
                              Marietta, *Friday,* June 4th, 1858*
My dearest Cousin,

Your long, interesting, and affectionate letter I received some weeks since, and having at that time the bishop of Rome, his dear family, and Major Minton and his little lady, I had to be "on hospitable thoughts intent"; put the letter in my pocket while I carried its contents about with me to think on in pantry and storeroom while engaged in the active duties of housekeeping. After that your note arrived confirming the distressing intelligence, brought us by Elizabeth Stevens, of dear little Charlie's illness and death. I know not which of my dear cousins to weep most for—Cousin Susan, Laura, or Mr. Buttolph. It is indeed a case of peculiar sorrow, and I pray that they may be sanctified and comforted by the Holy Ghost the Comforter. Have written them; please give our united love to them when you see them.

Suppose your dear daughter and granddaughter have left you for their summer home. No doubt Grandmother went up with them to see them safely at home and to assure herself that the little girl's crib was just in the right place—away from the draft of the opening door and not too near the reflection of that sunny window. Dear little creature, I just wish I could take her in my arms and hug and kiss her. Tell her grandfather that Lady Mary feels so maternal in her feelings that she thinks she has a large family of children and grandchildren. . . .

I could shed tears of grateful joy with my dear cousins in the conversion of their dear son. Do tell him so. And beg him to spend his August vacation with us; we do long to see him at our house. It was really interesting to hear that master and servant acknowledged themselves servants of Christ at the same time. May the Great Shepherd keep them till they shall be gathered with all the redeemed into the fold above! "Where He is, there shall His servants be." Dear Charles! My constant prayer for him is that he may not choose this world as his portion, but seek at once the Kingdom of Heaven and its righteousness, and be delivered from the snares of prosperity—that is, worldly ambition; not to be satisfied with the honor that comes from men. When will he be married?

My dear mother sat at my right hand at breakfast this morning at seven o'clock—the first time in many months. She says the warm summer weather and the strawberries have cured her, and I doubt not they have. If you and Cousin Charles were only here now, we could give you raspberries for breakfast, cherry and apple pies for dinner. The trees are loaded with fruit. . . . Our united thanks to our dear cousins for their acceptable present of rice and the beautiful rice flour. My up-country neighbors will see what nice bread we have!

Our girls made a visit to Roswell last week; enjoyed it very much. Mrs. King sent her carriage for them. . . . They had a week of pleasure (walks, rides, strawberries and ice cream), and as the folks over there tell us, were very much beloved and admired—even pronounced handsome and interesting young ladies, who honored by their deportment those who had trained them. All flattery, perhaps you may think. . . . Mother and Louisa desire much love, in which I unite, to all at Maybank, Maxwell, and Woodville. Tell Julia Willie passed through on his way to Atlanta (did not stop) last night; he has been to Mr. Waring's wedding. Mrs. William King, Anna, and Baby also left last night.

Your ever affectionate cousin,
Mary E. Robarts.

Hope my dear Cousin Charles feels better in this warm weather. If someone would only give each of us a hundred dollars we could go to the Warm Springs in Meriwether. . . . Tell Katy Hannah is to be married on Sunday evening to a very good man. . . . Nancy desires many thanks for the dress for her baby. . . . Farewell, my dear cousin. Paper is too short for all the love I have in my heart for you and yours.

REV. C. C. JONES *to* MR. CHARLES C. JONES, JR.[g]

Montevideo, Tuesday, June 8th, 1858

We were glad to hear from you today, my dear son, and to learn that if we are all spared we may hope to see you at Maybank sometime this summer. We are just moving down this week; sent the first loads today.

Went up to Walthourville on last Friday to see your sister and our little granddaughter. Your sister not as strong as we could wish. The baby growing nicely. On Sunday morning before sermon baptized the dear child and your Uncle Henry's little girl: *Mary Jones* and *Eliza Low*. (Named Eliza Low after Aunt Eliza, whose maiden name, you know, was *Low*.) It was one of the most interesting and impressive services. The little things were unconscious of the mercies of God descending upon them. The water falling upon their heads startled them, but they did not awake, and not a sound was heard. It was simply beautiful in the House of God. . . . We wished much for you and your brother.

Robert is doing well in his church. It is growing, and the people appear much united in him.

When you see Messrs. H. Lathrop & Company please say to them the bundle came safely to hand and is all right and satisfactory; and to Mr. Anderson that the sale of the stained cotton is also satisfactory.

Season pleasant. Some favorable showers. More needed. Crops doing pretty well. People generally in good health. . . . Mother sends much love. Remember us to Cousin Charles and Cousin Eliza *and to the absent one*.

Your ever affectionate father,
C. C. Jones.

Mr. Charles C. Jones, Jr., *to* Rev. C. C. Jones[t]

Savannah, *Friday,* June 11th, 1858

My dear Father,

Your kind favor was duly received. The baptismal service of my dear little niece must have been exceedingly interesting. It would have afforded me much pleasure to have been present. The ceremony no doubt was invested with a peculiar interest to dear Mother and self, and it must have been very gratifying to Sister and Robert to have the seal of the covenant imposed by yourself. It will also be a pleasant fact for her to learn and appreciate—that her little forehead was besprinkled with the consecrated water at the hands of her own grandfather. May God in His mercy spare this tender one, make her the light of the household, and endow her plenteously with every grace, virtue, and attraction! What a source of joy, of affectionate solicitude, of lively pleasure she must be to Robert and Sister! Is Lucy her nurse? Or does Kate assume that responsibility?

I have been for some time expecting a letter from the Doctor, but presume he is so much occupied with his professorial engagements that he cannot find time for writing. You may have noticed my appointment by the governor as one of the board of visitors to attend the examination of the graduating class on the 22nd inst. I once visited Athens under similar auspices and enjoyed myself. The pleasure of a repetition of that visit would of course be now very materially enhanced, my dear brother being there. How much I wish to see him! My fear is, however, that my duties here will prevent an attendance. This is certainly the prospect as at present advised. The supreme court holds its summer session in the city next week, and having five cases before that honorable body, we are busied with the preparation of briefs, etc.

There is nothing of interest with us. Temperature cool, and a plenty of rain. With warmest love to you both, my dear parents, and kind regards to all at Social Bluff and Woodville, I am, as ever,

Your affectionate son,
Charles C. Jones, Jr.

Rev. C. C. Jones *to* Mrs. Mary S. Mallard[t]
Maybank, Tuesday, June 15th, 1858

My dear Daughter,

Last Saturday was your birthday, and Mother and Father remembered you particularly and your husband and your dear little one. There were no blessings for the soul and for the body, for the life that now is and for that which is to come, which we did not implore our Heavenly Father to grant to you and to all yours.

The baptismal service of our little granddaughter and of our little niece was one of the most interesting and impressive I have ever had anything to do with. The ordinance was beautiful in the courts of the Lord! Our Sabbath was pleasant to us.

We came down to the Island on Thursday, and for the first time in so many moves an oxcart was upset, much to Jackson's chagrin. It was a sudden rush of the oxen after water. No very great damage: Mother had a considerable part of her tea drawn too soon—and not with the best water; and of course some of the sugar went with it. All friends here welcomed us down; and some of them sent us a piece of mutton to begin housekeeping upon, to which Andrew added some fresh fish and shrimp and eggs. The pile of trash removed from within and around the premises was amazing. Mother had every hand that could chop and sweep and bear burdens employed. The monument of their careful labors was consumed to ashes today. We begin to look more natural.

We rode over on Saturday evening to the Point and brought your aunt and cousin home with us and took them to church on Sunday. They returned home on Sunday evening. . . . Today the mail brings a letter from your brother Charles. He is quite well and busy. . . . Today we learn the death of our dear friend Cousin John Dunwody. Took the sacrament the Friday before; died Saturday night. He is at rest with his Saviour. . . . Much love to yourself and Robert, and many kisses from us both to our sweet little granddaughter. How are you? *Take care of yourself.* The Lord have you in His holy keeping, my dear child!

Your ever affectionate father,
C. C. Jones.

Mrs. Mary Jones *to* Mr. Charles C. Jones, Jr.ᵍ

Maybank, *Saturday,* June 19th, 1858

My dear Son,

It gave us great pleasure to receive your last affectionate favor and to know that we might anticipate having you with us early in July. I hope it will be for all summer. You cannot think how much your father and mother miss their dear children. They are the sources of our greatest earthly comfort and happiness; and although we rejoice that they are filling stations of usefulness in the spheres allotted them by our Father in Heaven, still home is scarcely home without them. I keep some little memento of each daily in sight. Whilst writing I can look up and see the three little chairs you occupied in childhood, and to my eye they are almost fashioned into images of yourselves.

We saw with much satisfaction your appointment as one of the examining committee for Franklin University, hoping it might suit you to attend. How much pleasure it would give your dear brother! I wish it was in our power to attend the commencement—or I should say to go and see him this summer. It appears so long before we shall see him if he has to go immediately to Augusta.

Your father has been very feeble since we came down. I hope it is only the effect of fatigue in moving. You know every book must find its place from his own hand. I too have not been well, but am better today.

Last evening our three families met at Woodville. We have agreed to alternate at the different houses and spend every Friday evening together, closing always with family worship. Your father conducted last evening most interestingly; he read and explained the 17th Chapter of Genesis. All of our loved ones—especially the *absent*—were remembered before the throne of grace. We are but two or three gathered together, but our Father's promise is with us, and I believe that He will yet gather into His fold all our wandering ones. Your father's faith, my dear son, is very strong in reference *to you.* Oh, how much my heart feels, not only for *you, my beloved child,* but also for the unconverted children of my kind friend Julia—for dear Willie and Fred and Rossie and the younger ones! The many, many years of kind intercourse and unbroken friendship we have enjoyed make them all especially near and dear.

Our bereaved relatives at the Point are greatly sustained under their heavy affliction.

Have you, my dear son, any thought of going North before winter?

I have commenced some household matters for you. I wish I could talk with you for an hour. Can *fine* good linen bosoms for shirts be got in Savannah? I have eight shirts nearly done for you—all to the bosoms; and my eyes have failed so much I am not able to *tuck* as once I did. *When will the bank dividend* be due? *Please let me know,* for when it is, I would like to come down and make a few purchases of such articles as you will need made up during the summer.

Our servants are well at both places, and always inquiring about you. Recently we have had some pleasant showers, and crops look well. Mr. McDonald is quite attentive to our business, and I hope will do well. Did you hear of the death of our dear and valued friend Mr. Dunwody? A joyful release from pain and suffering. The *sea breeze* has just flirted over my paper and blotted this page. Excuse it! Father unites with me in best love to you, and all the servants send howdies. Love to all friends.

Your ever affectionate mother,
Mary Jones.

Mr. Charles C. Jones, Jr., *to* Mrs. Mary Jones[t]

Savannah, *Wednesday,* June 23rd, 1858

My dear Mother,

Your very kind favor was duly received. Regret to learn Father's indisposition, and sincerely hope that the fatigue of moving may have been the cause of his unusual weakness.

I was very sorry the other day that I could not prolong my stay in the county. It made me sad to think that I was within sixteen miles of my dear parents and unable to see them. My engagements in Savannah, however, rendered a return absolutely necessary; so that my absence was only for a few hours, and then entirely on business. The truth is, there are so many things to be done in the office, so many postponed duties to be met, that I see but very little prospect now of any considerable vacation during the summer. You may be sure the first leisure moment at my command I will be with you on the Island. . . .

You are very kind, Mother, in having the shirts made; and by tomorrow's stage I send eight bosoms, which you will, I am sure, think quite neat. My measure around the chest is forty inches, around the neck about sixteen and a half or seventeen. . . . I find that the decay of time is passing over and leaving marked traces upon several shirts now in my drawer, so that the present of these new ones will be acceptable indeed.

All friends well, and unite in much love. Our mayor, Dr. Wayne, is very ill. With warmest love, my dear mother, to self and dear Father, and kind regards to all relatives and friends on the Island, I am, as ever,

Your affectionate son,
Charles C. Jones, Jr.

The Central Railroad dividend is now due.

Mrs. Mary S. Mallard *to* Mrs. Laura E. Buttolph[t]

Walthourville, *Thursday,* June 24th, 1858

My dear Cousin Laura,

I wish you could have a glimpse of our dear little baby's face peeping out of the beautiful bonnet you made for her! I am truly obliged to you; it is very becoming. I put it on her a few evenings since and carried her to see Mrs.

McCollough; and much to my satisfaction, she behaved like a little lady, although there were persons enough around—and talking to her—to have frightened her. I believe some of the good folks here think me quite notional when I tell them I am afraid to send my baby visiting; but I do not think it right or safe to send babies about, particularly when so young. . . .

I often think of you all on the Island, and only wish I were near enough to see you often. What a pity the railroad does not run nearby; it would be so convenient to us! I hope we will be able to come down in July—that is, if Baby continues as well as she now is. Persons hardly believe me when I tell them she has never had a colic. As she is now more than two months old, I hope she never will.

It is nearly time to send to the mail, so I must close. I intended to have written you a long letter, but Baby stole away a large part of the time I had devoted to writing. Whenever she wants anything she will have it as soon as possible. I find my time is a good deal at her disposal. . . . Do give love to all, and accept for Aunt Susan, Cousin Lyman, and yourself a great deal of love from Mr. Mallard and myself. Yesterday afternoon ice cream was brought around for sale: ten cents a glass. I would like to send you some. Cannot you come up and see us? I should be so glad to have you.

Your affectionate cousin,
Mary S. Mallard.

Mr. Charles C. Jones, Jr., *to* Rev. *and* Mrs. C. C. Jones[t]
Savannah, *Wednesday,* June 30th, 1858
My dear Father and Mother,

What would I not give for the privilege of your dear society and the pleasures of the sea breeze this afternoon! The sultry atmosphere of our city is motionless and dead. A few hours since, distant rumblings betokened the approach of a thunderstorm, and we confidently anticipated the coming of those refreshing influences which always accompany its presence. But the expectation has resulted in positive disappointment, and the skies, clear and dry, are again looking down upon a parched city.

Never before has Savannah witnessed such funeral honors as those paid on Monday last to the memory of the late mayor, Dr. Wayne. The entire Volunteer Regiment, the Georgia Hussars, the major and his staff, the white fire companies, the Masonic fraternity, the Odd Fellows, the Sons of Malta, the Irish societies, and other kindred associations united with the friends of the deceased, and the citizens generally, in a funeral procession which when in line and under way must have been more than half a mile in length. South Broad Street and in fact all the streets through which the procession moved were densely thronged—sidewalks, steps, stoops, windows all filled. So general was the determination of the population to these given points that the other portions of the city appeared silent and deserted. All day long the large flag at the city hall hung drooping at half-mast, while the bell of the exchange with melancholy, measured stroke tolled the sad requiem. As the procession moved from the late residence of Dr. Wayne to Laurel Grove Cemetery, all the bells of the respective churches united in tolling the solemn farewell. At the grave the usual Episcopal burial service was read by Bishop Elliott, after which the peculiar ceremonies of the Odd Fellows and the Masons were performed around the open grave, the last tribute being paid by the Republican Blues (of which company the deceased had been a member), who fired the customary salute.

But to me, my dear parents, by far the most interesting and affecting incident connected with the afternoon's ceremonies was the *singing of the Negroes* in the cemetery. All the members of the choirs of the various colored churches in the city (probably a hundred or more in number) had repaired to the necropolis in advance of the funeral cortege, and had taken position along one of the principal avenues. As the procession entered, they commenced singing that beautiful and solemn funeral hymn, "We Are Passing Away." All the parts were admirably sustained, and there was a depth of feeling, a harmony, a propriety in voice and manner, that rendered the tribute exceedingly touching. One could but be affected—and that deeply. With feeling emphasis did those solemn words, "We are passing away," tremble upon their lips and awake a sad echo in every breast.

The dead yet speaking witness of the fearful truth was at hand. That afternoon four of the well-known citizens of Savannah were lying in the cold embraces of death. Mournful lesson touching the frailty of human life. Striking confirmation of the fact that "flesh is grass, and earthly things are mist." And yet how soon by the living are these practical teachings forgotten! How true these lines from *Tancred and Sigismunda*:

> The death of those distinguish'd by their station
> . . . . awakes the mind
> To solemn dread . . . .
> . . . . And yet the best
> Are by the playful children of this world
> At once forgot, as they had never been.

How few are this day reflecting upon the scenes of last Monday! And the dead in their new-made graves lie already forgotten by all save those whose sorrow-stricken hearts still melt at thought of the loved and the lost.

Although the procession was in motion at five o'clock, it was eight before we reached the city; and the ceremonies concluded by the dismission of the regiment. I was out as judge advocate of the regiment. This, I understand, is the first time that a mayor of the city of Savannah has died while in office.

By this mail, Mother, I send you a copy of Mr. Dawson's Mount Vernon oration, which you will pronounce quite a curiosity in its way. He has said it is the result of *twenty years'* thought, reflection, and reading! If this be so, he may very properly (could he so persuade himself) enter upon his diary a much more serious lamentation than the "*Diem* perdidi."

To you, Father, I send a copy of *The Eclectic* containing a steel engraving and an accompanying biographical notice of General Havelock, whose conduct in the East has so much attracted the attention of the world.

Nothing new in the city. Our city court commences its session on next Monday. The following Monday I have to be in Brunswick. It seems to me that every day brings its engagements, so as to preclude almost all hope of future relaxation. . . . With warmest love, my dear parents, to you both, and kind regards to all friends, I remain, as ever,

Your affectionate son,
Charles C. Jones, Jr.

Howdy for all the servants. Will you please keep George, if convenient, with you on the Island, about the house, as I do not wish that he should forget his training. I want him to acquire a *house look*, which you know is not the acquisition of a day. He may have to be my little majordomo in the fall. Where will I find a cook?

Your affectionate son,
Charles.

Mrs. Mary Jones *to* Mr. Charles C. Jones, Jr.^g

Maybank, *Wednesday,* July 7th, 1858

My dear Son,

This afternoon it ceased raining, and Mr. Buttolph with Mr. —— from the Point, *Willie* with Mr. Stewart from Woodville, called and took a cup of tea with us. Willie tells me he leaves for Savannah tomorrow, and I embrace the opportunity of sending you a line.

Your last two affectionate favors, with the papers and periodicals and Mr. Dawson's address, were received by yesterday's mail; and many thanks, my dear child, for them all. They serve to interest us very much. I have intended whenever I wrote to thank you for sending the *Literary Messenger* and *Home Journal;* I will keep them filed away.

The incident you so beautifully describe of the Negroes' singing at Dr. Wayne's funeral was one of the most touching I ever heard of. I told your father I wished to copy it for the Philadelphia *Presbyterian*. He thinks Dr. Leyburn would prize it. I must find time to do so. If it be dreadful to have the cry of the poor and the oppressed rising up to God against us, how sweet like incense poured forth their tributes of gratitude and affection, their prayers and benedictions! One of the precious recollections of my own dear mother was her unvarying kindness to the poor and needy, which to their dying day embalmed her memory in their hearts.

Yesterday morning I left Maybank at five o'clock for Montevideo. The rain met me on the causeway and poured down in straight lines until I reached home. After looking at my garden, etc., I returned and reached Maybank after four and a half hours on the road—wind and rain blowing and falling almost like a hurricane, the marshes all covered, and the water quite high up the sides of the causeway. Your father was delighted to see me back; but I had enjoyed the day very much, having your *Life of Schiller* for a traveling companion.

The rain is a great blessing. Our provision crop was on the verge of ruin. . . . Our melons are small and few here, but fine at Montevideo. I wish, my dear child, I could set one that I brought from Montevideo before you and see you enjoy it. I have sent the fellow to it to *Willie.* Do come out before they are all over. We long to have you at home. I really think it time for you to take a little holiday.

I will send and have George brought down. Having so little to employ him, he was left at Montevideo; but I will put him to training for the house when he comes. We will try and arrange about a cook when we meet.

The shirt bosoms have been received, and are *very beautiful.* I am now engaged upon them. Should you wish to have some of them to take to Burke, *write me certainly about them* by the next mail, and I will, Providence permitting, have four ready for you to wear with the *beautiful buttons.* Please say, too, *how I must direct,* and *where,* in sending them, and *at what time.*

Do, my dear child, be careful of your health in going to Brunswick. . . . I hope your sister and Robert and our dear baby will be with us shortly. . . . Your father has retired, and I must close. He unites with me in best love to you, and Miss Whitehead when you write.

> Ever your affectionate mother,
> Mary Jones.

Mr. Charles C. Jones, Jr., *to* Mrs. Mary Jones[t]

> Savannah, *Friday,* July 9th, 1858

My very dear Mother,

Your kind favor of yesterday was this morning handed me by Willie, who brings pleasant news from all friends on the Island. I avail myself of the courtesy of Mr. Maxwell, who goes to the Island tomorrow morning, to send this little note to you. Having been in the courtroom almost the entire day— and a warm one it indeed has been—and with rather an important legal question coming up tomorrow morning upon which I have to gather some new views tonight, you will excuse this brief reply to your esteemed favor.

Am happy to know that the refreshing rains of heaven have at length exerted their sweet influences, imparting new life and vigor to drooping vegetation, and cheering the heart of the anxious planter. A letter from Mr. Martin states that there is still hope for a fair crop. I certainly hope that we may realize an abundant yield and have fair prices, as (if my present pleasant anticipation is realized) I shall need every dollar that I can command.

In regard to the shirts, my dear mother, which you are so kindly having made for me—if you are not inconvenienced by the early request, I would be very happy to have a few of them by Friday's stage, in order that they may be worn while at Bath. I promised Ruthie to see her on *next* Monday, but am compelled by engagements in Glynn to delay my visit until the Monday following. A few days after my return from Bath, I hope to be with you on the Island—a pleasure the enjoyment of which I can assure you I sincerely covet.

Mr. Maxwell's coming will be very agreeable, and you will all appreciate the pleasant addition to the society on the Island. Nothing of interest in our city. If you conclude to send the shirts on Friday next, be pleased to direct them to me care of William P. Clark, Pavilion Hotel. With warmest love, my dear father and mother, to you both, I am, as ever,

Your affectionate son,

Charles C. Jones, Jr.

Kind regards to all friends at Social Bluff and Woodville. Howdy for the servants.

Mr. Charles C. Jones, Jr., *to* Mrs. Mary Jones[t]

Savannah, *Saturday,* July 17th, 1858

Many thanks, my dear mother, for the shirts, which I this morning received from the depot. As yet I have had no opportunity to examine them, but I make no doubt that they will fit admirably and look very nicely.

I returned from Brunswick on Thursday. Monday, in passing through St. Catherines Sound, we encountered a heavy thunderstorm, which prevented me from obtaining a very satisfactory view of the Island. The rain was falling in such torrents, and the clouds so shut out the sunlight, that only the outline of the Island could be discerned. There is a sad pleasure in obtaining even a distant view of home.

In consequence of the sickness of Judge Cochran, Glynn Superior Court was adjourned after a session of only a few hours; and our business unfinished, we were compelled to amuse ourselves as best we might in the uninteresting little town of Brunswick until the return of the *Darlington.* That place is evidently on the decline; the retrograding tendency is clearly perceptible. City lots that during the New York sales a year or two since would have commanded five hundred or even a thousand dollars are now sold under the sheriff's hammer for five and ten dollars. The spirit of enterprise is dead. There is no capital wherewith to operate, and I am credibly informed that there are numbers and numbers of the present occupants who would willingly leave the place if they only possessed the means of getting away. It is a mutual marvel with everyone in Brunswick how, and upon what, his next-door neighbor manages to live. A strange fatality appears to attend every effort made to inaugurate a city on our seacoast. The reason, however, is obvious.

While in Brunswick I read Hugh Miller's last work, entitled *The Cruise of the Betsy.* It is interesting, and I will soon, D.V., bring it out with me for your perusal, my dear parents.

There is a strange and unfortunate impression resting upon the minds of the members of the Independent congregation in regard to a sermon preached by Mr. Bowman some time since from the Independent pulpit on the subject of "Moses' Death." He is believed to have appropriated large passages, and even pages, from Melvill's sermon on that subject—and that without the slightest acknowledgment. I myself heard the sermon delivered, and have since read Melvill's discourse, and must, I am sorry to say, confess that I cannot divest myself of the conviction that Mr. Bowman's sermon was not only modeled from but composed largely of passages, thoughts, and expressions derived immediately and without acknowledgment from Mr. Melvill's sermon. It is in truth the town talk, and cannot fail to affect the professional standing of Mr. Bowman. He never can preach again in the Independent Church. I had this morning a long talk on the subject with Mr. Axson, the result of which it may not be best for me to commit to paper, as I will see you soon. This occurrence is to be deeply regretted, and I should think would affect him unfavorably in the eyes of his own congregation. Olcott, of the firm of John M. Cooper & Company, told me he had sold more copies of Melvill's *Sermons* since Mr. Bowman's discourse than he had done for the past six years; that the work was really in demand. The ministry is such an exalted and holy office that it makes me feel very badly whenever I find even a shadow falling upon one wearing the sacred robe. You know, too, how prone human depravity is to see only the mote in the sunbeam—to harp upon the casual defect while all the excellencies, the true virtues, are forgotten.

Monday morning early I expect to leave for Bath, where I purpose spending a few days in the companionship of the queen of my affections. All friends are well, and unite in kind remembrance. With warmest love, my dear parents, to you both, and thanking you again, Mother, for your kind and acceptable present, I am, as ever,

Your affectionate son,
Charles C. Jones, Jr.

Love to all friends on the Island. Howdy for the servants.

REV. C. C. JONES *to* MR. CHARLES C. JONES, JR.[g]

Maybank, *Tuesday Evening,* July 20th, 1858

My dear Son,

We received your very interesting letter while at tea, and were happy to learn your safe return from Brunswick and your good health. We had at tea Miss Katy Fleming, Miss Isabella King, Mrs. Wells, and Robert and Daughter (who are now with us), and Mr. McDonald. Your sister is very thin, with an indifferent appetite, and we hope she will stay some little time and recruit. Her infant is a sweet little thing—very good, and fat and growing, and of course the pet of the house. Their coming has enlivened us. We have the perfection of weather.

Mother says *you must write her when you intend coming out,* and *she will go down to Savannah and do a little shopping and return under your escort.* And lest I forget it, let me here request you to bring out from Cooper's for me a large bottle of Maynard & Noyes' ink; also a bottle of David's carmine ink.

Shall be glad to read Miller's *Cruise of the Betsy*. It is highly spoken of. He was a marvelous man, and his powers of description surpassingly fine. You do well in traveling to carry a good book as a companion. It beguiles many a weary hour, and redeems the time. And I think you should at least occasionally read scientific works.

The occurrence to which you painfully allude in your letter was made known to the families at Point Maxwell and Maybank (and to them alone) some time since, and we were hoping the best until your letter came. We have and shall for proper reasons keep the matter close, and not let it get out through ourselves. We have told it to Robert and your sister, and they have read your letter; but to none others. It must come into the county. The effect cannot be otherwise than injurious—highly so! We have been and are distressed about it. I have always looked upon such an act as a great transgression, and as inflicting a heavy wound upon the Saviour in the house of His friends! We know that He is infinite excellence, and His way is perfect and His religion truth and holiness, whatever men may say or do.

All friends, through divine mercy, well; and the people generally so on the different places. We wish you an agreeable trip on one of the most agreeable errands that can take you away from your business. Mother, Daughter, and Robert unite in much love to you; your little niece would do the same if she were able. Heard from your brother last week. Quite well, and busy as usual. We are anticipating great pleasure from your visit, and hope, God willing, you may come soon and stay a long time. The Lord be with and bless you, my dear son!

Your ever affectionate father,
C. C. Jones.

Wednesday Morning, six o'clock. A most lovely morning. The air is refreshingly cool; the landscape the richest green; the sunlight gentle and bright; and the birds are uttering their sweet songs to the Great Author of All Being. Be sure when you go to Burke to remember Mother and myself in the kindest manner to Miss W. Good morning!

Mr. CHARLES C. JONES, JR., *to* REV. C. C. JONES[t]

Savannah, *Monday,* July 26th, 1858

My dear Father,

In consequence of my absence from the city, your very kind favor of the 20th inst. was not until this morning received. I did not reach Savannah until ten o'clock on Saturday evening.

My visit to Bath was, as you may well imagine, exceedingly pleasant, and I shall always remember the kind courtesy and uniform hospitality extended to me during my brief sojourn in that delightful summer retreat. The incidents and particular pleasures I will recount *in extenso* when we meet on the

Island, which I sincerely hope will be very soon. I would come out this week, but Mr. Ward expects to leave with his family on Wednesday next, and it will not do to have the doors of the office closed.

Please say to Mother that even if I cannot accompany her fairly home, I will be happy to meet her any afternoon that she may suggest as most convenient at the depot, and will at least on her return form her escort as far as No. 3, and will hope to be able to see her all the way safely home.

The ink will be brought out when I come, or will be sent any day that you may name if you need it for immediate use.

Am sorry to hear that Sister is looking thin and feeling rather weak. She ought to spend at least a few weeks with you on the Island and try the benefits of the pure salt air. Give her my love, and kiss my sweet little niece for me.

We are having a regular northeast blow today—not violent, but remarkably cool.

The crops in Middle Georgia are finer than they have been for years. And such an abundance of the finest fruit you never saw. I have some seeds of Burke watermelons that I must freely confess are finer than any I have ever seen. Will bring them out, that you may give them a fair trial next season.

Ruth desired me to present her affectionately to yourself and dear Mother. All friends well, and our city generally healthy. With warmest love, my dear father, to self, dear Mother, Sister, Robert, and little Niece, I am, as ever,

Your affectionate son,
Charles C. Jones, Jr.

Kind regards to all friends, and howdy for the servants.

Mr. Charles C. Jones, Jr., *to* Mrs. Mary Jones[t]

Savannah, *Wednesday,* July 28th, 1858

My dear Mother,

Somehow or other the impression had taken possession of my mind that we would have the pleasure of your promised visit to Savannah this afternoon. But the cars have arrived, the mail has been distributed, and not even a letter from home! Cousin Eliza begs me to say to you that she will certainly expect you to remain with her while you are in the city. What day do you purpose coming?

We have nothing now either new or interesting. Everything very quiet, and business exceedingly dull. The truth is, all things indicate the positive advent of the summer *solstice,* taken in its most literal acceptation. Do give warmest love, my dear mother, to Father, Sister, Robert, and little Niece. And think of me always as

Your devotedly attached son,
Charles C. Jones, Jr.

Kind regards to all friends on the Island, and howdy for the servants. Mosquitoes are biting so badly that I have sent you but a very brief note.

Rev. C. C. Jones *to* Mr. Charles C. Jones, Jr.ᵍ

Maybank, *Friday,* July 30th, 1858

My dear Son,

Your letter was received yesterday, and one also from your dear brother; and we were happy to hear of the good health of both of you.

Your sister's health is not what we could wish it, and think if she could remain a longer time at Maybank she would be much benefited. I think she has improved; and the little baby has certainly grown in mind and body, and is a most engaging infant—at least to her grandparents. Robert goes up for good to Walthourville this afternoon, but Daughter remains until sometime next week. Consequently Mother will not be able—in connection with some other circumstances—to visit Savannah before next Tuesday week, God willing, *which will be the 10th day of August.* So she requests me to advertise you, and to convey to Cousin Eliza West her kindest regards, and to say that she will accept her invitation with the certainty that her visit will prove one of great pleasure to her. Remember us also to Cousin Charles.

We are sorry you cannot be with us at this time. Excellent melons and superb peaches. Not as much cream and butter as common, since our milch cows have—at least the great majority of them—had the sore mouth, black tongue, or murrain, as people term it differently. And the climate, though a little warm from the prevalence all day of the southwest winds, cannot well be improved. Robert amused himself two days in the river, and secured each day a respectable dish of both fried and boiled fish.

I never saw your dear mother in fuller health, except last summer at the springs, though I am inclined to believe she must weigh as much now as then. For this I desire to be specially grateful.

All on the Island at present well. Mrs. King lost on the 28th her old and valuable and most respectable and I trust *Christian* servant Phillis. Dr. Harris thinks she died of typhoid fever. Mr. Buttolph and myself both visited her in her illness. She is Flora's grandmother. All in the three families—black and white, field people and all—attended her funeral at Woodville yesterday afternoon. I conducted the services. The death of old and valued members of our families and households creates losses that never can be repaired. We ought to cherish the spark of life in the aged to the last hour, and pay them every attention, and add all we can to their comfort and happiness. God's command is: "Thou shalt rise up before the old and gray-headed." How comprehensive! How beautiful!

Abram was down from Arcadia this week with another load of corn. I have received in all forty-six bushels. *Make a note of this.* He reports all well. Crop good. Cattle getting over the disease. They did *nothing;* we here and at Montevideo swabbed out their mouths twice a day with the copperas and turpentine, and gave one good dose of salt and water. Lost none at Arcadia, none at Montevideo, so far one here (the first taken). . . .

Mother and Sister and Brother Robert and your little niece (we undertake to speak for her) unite in much love to you. May God be with and bless you and bring you, my dear son, into His Heavenly Kingdom—and that speedily! And may you not resist the stirrings of His Holy Spirit! Remember us, when you write, to Miss Whitehead always.

Your ever affectionate father,
C. C. Jones.

MR. CHARLES C. JONES, JR., *to* REV. C. C. JONES[t]

Savannah, *Monday,* August 2nd, 1858

My dear Father,

Your very kind and interesting favor of the 30th ult. was this moment received. I am truly sorry to know that Sister's health is not what we could wish. My hope is that she will prolong her visit on the Island. The pleasure of being with yourself and dear Mother cannot fail of exerting a beneficial influence. Can you not persuade her to remain at least during my intended visit? It will be a sad disappointment for me, when I come out on Thursday, to find that she has returned.

Will you be kind enough to send the buggy on that day to No. 3 (McIntosh Station)? I hope to be with you for several days, and will return with Mother on Tuesday, the day fixed upon for her visit to Savannah. Cousin Eliza will be most happy to see her, and a room will be in readiness.

Did you ever feel warmer weather?

As I expect the pleasure of seeing you, my dear parents, so soon, I will now bid you good night, as I have some little matters claiming attention. With warmest love to you both, my dear father and mother, Sister, little Niece, and all friends, I am, as ever,

Your affectionate son,
Charles C. Jones, Jr.

REV. C. C. JONES *to* MR. CHARLES C. JONES, JR.[g]

Maybank, *Wednesday,* August 4th, 1858

My dear Son,

We send up Gilbert with the buggy to meet you early at the station tomorrow morning, God willing. Would ride up to meet you if I were able. Please inquire of Mr. Augustus Fleming for some scythes and handles sent out by Mr. Anderson for me. You must exercise your pleasure in coming down to dinner, as you may like to stop at Arcadia. But the afternoons, while pleasant to ride, are sometimes uncertain from rain.

Am sorry to say your dear sister did not go to the Sand Hills on Tuesday as she intended on account of fever from fatigue on Sunday. She is, I hope, clear of it this afternoon. She and Mother send much love, and we shall all be very glad to see you.

Your affectionate father,
C. C. Jones.

XIII

Maybank, *Friday,* August 27th, 1858

My dear Son,

We were happy to hear through your favor of Saturday last of your safe return to the city. Your visit, although short, must have been one of peculiar enjoyment. I am glad you saw our dear relatives in Marietta.

Your brother's visit was most refreshing to us. Oh, how precious it was to hear his voice lifted up in prayer around our family altar, especially for us his parents and for his dear brother and sister! The recent visits of our dear children have cheered our hearts. Oh, that we could see you all daily! But we bless the Lord for calling you all—if in His providence we must be separated—to fields of usefulness and influence.

Your father and myself rejoice to know that, *God willing,* you will be married in November. Our hearts are open to receive the loved one of your choice as a dear and cherished daughter. We truly regret that she does not concur with you in the wish to go immediately to housekeeping. To have your own quiet home, we are persuaded, would greatly promote your happiness, and give you a position in society which you cannot have as boarders. Moving, too, creates such an unsettled feeling, and is expensive and troublesome, although you may not have much more than a wardrobe and library to move. I know housekeeping brings cares; but they must come, and it is well for us "to bear the yoke in our youth." Today I quilted a comforter for you, and shall go on with your household preparations hoping they will yet be wanted.

Your dear sister's health has not strengthened as we desired, and today she writes me they think of being in Savannah on Monday week on their way to the up country for a change of climate. I may accompany her as far as Savannah. Enclosed, my dear son, is a check for the amount due in the Central Railroad Bank. *Please draw it out in bills of the Central Railroad Bank,* and keep fifty dollars subject to your *sister's order should she come to town on her way to the up country.* You can hand it to her.

Your uncle spent yesterday and last night with us. We had prayer meeting at the Point this afternoon. All well but Mary Wells; she has been very ill with one of her old attacks of headache. Your father has been very feeble this week. He joins me in best love to you.

Ever, my dear son, your affectionate mother,

Mary Jones.

Mr. Charles C. Jones, Jr., *to* Rev. *and* Mrs. C. C. Jones[t]

Savannah, *Saturday,* August 28th, 1858

My dear Father and Mother,

I had hoped that I should have received a letter from you this week in relation to the matters contained in my letter of the 20th inst.; but I presume that the long distance you are removed from the office has rendered a reply inconvenient.

Sister wrote me on Thursday that she had enjoyed your visit to Robert and herself very much. She seems inclined to go to Upper Georgia this fall, and I have urged her to do so. Cousin Charles West thinks that the trip will be of much benefit. In Rome, Marietta, and Atlanta she will find the kindest relatives and friends, who will contribute everything in their power towards rendering her stay pleasant. The Walthourville congregation should favor their pastor with at least a few weeks' vacation; his earnest, continued, and devoted services merit at their hands such indulgence. And even if he cannot tarry with Sister and little Niece all the time, he can leave them with those who will take delight in seeing that every attention and kindness are bestowed.

I wrote you in my last an account of friends in Marietta, and communicated the further fact that it was our pleasant anticipation to be married in November next. The precise day has not yet been appointed; I hope in a day or two to have the definite time agreed upon. I also told you that at her request I had concluded to board, at least for a few months after our marriage. A pleasant room can be secured at the Pavilion, although at rather a high figure. The truth is, everything in this city is so inflated that the prospect of assuming new and important responsibilities almost frightens me.

Our city enjoys its accustomed degree of health, as far as I can ascertain; and we hope that we shall have a total exemption from that fearful epidemic that is even now prevailing in our sister city. . . . What effect has this recent northeast weather had upon the crops in Liberty? I understand they are suffering very materially in many portions of the state. . . . Hoping, my dear father and mother, that every blessing will attend you, I am, with warmest love, as ever,

Your affectionate son,

Charles C. Jones, Jr.

Kind regards to all friends on the Island, and howdy for the servants.

Mr. Charles C. Jones, Jr., *to* Rev. C. C. Jones[t]

Savannah, *Saturday,* August 28th, 1858

I forgot, Father, to ask, in the letter which I have just placed in the post, that you will oblige me by *sending George here* as soon as he conveniently can be spared at Maybank. I am now all alone, sole occupant of Eckman's house, with not even a servant in the yard, and am at times at a loss for fresh water, etc., and in case of sickness have no one upon whom I could call for assistance. . . . The family will be absent for a month or six weeks.

All friends well, and unite in kindest remembrance. With warmest love to dear Mother and yourself, I am, as ever,

Your affectionate son,
Charles C. Jones, Jr.

MR. CHARLES C. JONES, JR., *to* MRS. MARY JONES[t]

Savannah, *Thursday,* September 2nd, 1858

My dear Mother,

Your kind favor of the 27th ult. was duly received. I am truly sorry to know that Father has been so feeble, and sincerely hope that he now feels stronger. Am happy to hear that Sister has determined to try the benefit of the air of Upper Georgia, and have no doubt but that the pleasant temperature, the change of incident and scenery, and the kindnesses of friends will all exert a beneficial influence upon her health.

The hundred and fifty dollars (the same being amount of dividend of Central Railroad Bank stock) has been paid, and I now hold that amount subject to your order.

A letter just received from Ruth announces her acquiescence in my proposal to render memorable the 9th November next by our marriage. So we will, D.V., be married at Bath on that day. I regret myself that she does not feel inclined to go at once to housekeeping; but I think she ought to be indulged in her preference, at least for a time—especially as I am persuaded she will tire of the Pavilion or of any public house in a very short time. We can then mutually select our household furniture and arrange everything together.

Cousin Eliza will expect you at her house if you come in on Monday next. The room will be all in readiness. Our city still continues in the enjoyment of health. All friends well, and unite in kind remembrances. With warmest love, my dear father and mother, to you both, and kind regards to all friends on the Island, I am, as ever,

Your affectionate son,
Charles C. Jones, Jr.

REV. C. C. JONES *to* MR. CHARLES C. JONES, JR.[g]

Maybank, *Thursday,* September 2nd, 1858

My dear Son,

We were happy to learn by your last letter your continued health, and hope it may please God to preserve it for time to come. Should you get sick, send out for us.

Your dear mother, not anticipating your early call for George, is obliged to keep him a few days to fix up his wardrobe. He will be down, however, God willing, on *Monday next.*

Your sister and Robert and Mrs. King and family and Mrs. Wells all hope to take the cars *on Monday* for the up country via Savannah, where you will have the pleasure of seeing them. We trust Daughter's health will be improved, and the little baby suffer nothing by the change. Mrs. King goes on account of Mrs. Wells's health; she has been very sick lately.

Your Catoosa trip must have been very pleasant indeed; but I cannot say that I admire your arrangements in the matter of boarding. It is postponing housekeeping without any advantage in the end towards a beginning. But on the contrary boarding at so high a figure will leave you as dry and bare to begin housekeeping, and a great deal more so than at first. If you have determined to make Savannah your home, then decidedly I would try and get a home in it at once. And in that home your convenience, comfort, and independence will far exceed anything the Pavilion or any other hotel can give you. Putting off, if it would enable you to meet expenses when you commence housekeeping, would be very well. But there is no probability that it will do that. What you should avoid is going to too much expense in house rent and furniture. Good sense and prudence ought to direct in such matters. Our object in life should be not to equal others and make a show, but to live, and live within our income—at the least, try for it. Many begin life as they should leave it off. If you cannot do all you would like to do at first, you will have room to amend it afterwards. However, you are of age and must judge for yourself; and if the decision is fixed that you *must board* and nothing else after the happy event, then it must be so. In either event, you know, my dear son, we will do all in our power to aid you. My regret is that I am not able to do more for my children.

Your mother hopes you received her letter with the draft sent last Monday, and begs that you will hand fifty dollars to your sister, and says "maybe —perhaps—you may see her Monday too, as she has a great notion to go down and get some things for your future use anyhow." Your brother dissuaded her from going to Savannah this season of the year unless there should be a necessity. She is now in excellent health.

We had a letter from him last mail. Presume you heard from him also. He has wisely rented a small brick house in Augusta next to Dr. Eve's—a good arrangement to one in his profession. Books to move, and specimens to fix, etc. Where will you put your books, etc., etc., at the Pavilion?

All well at present on the Island except Mrs. Wells; she is better. Our love to Cousin Charles and Cousin Eliza. People at all the places generally well. Cotton crops fallen off much from excessive drought in August and rains—in some places a great deal. Hear that Arcadia holds on tolerably well, but injured. Mother sends a great deal of love. May the Lord ever watch over and keep you, my dear son!

Your ever affectionate father,
C. C. Jones.

Mr. Charles C. Jones, Jr., *to* Rev. C. C. Jones[t]

Savannah, *Saturday,* September 4th, 1858

My dear Father,

I have the pleasure of acknowledging the receipt of your kind favor of the 2nd inst. We will be very happy to see dear Mother, Sister, and Robert on Monday evening next. The change to the up country will doubtless have a beneficial effect upon Sister's health. Removed as she will be from the influence of our autumnal sun, interested by the change of scene and incident, and experiencing the cool mountain atmosphere of that elevated region, as well as the kind attentions of friends and relatives, with the consequent diversion of mind and pleasant exercise, she must improve.

I have noted carefully your remarks in regard to our boarding after marriage, and agree with you fully in every particular. I have already stated that it is no wish of mine, but simply a compliance with the express request of one who perhaps under the circumstances should be gratified in her desires. It is and will be, I am persuaded, only a very temporary arrangement. My own disposition has always been to meet a question and overcome a trouble at once. Any shift only postpones the evil day. That we would be more independent in every respect in our own house, that more real quiet pleasure would be there experienced, I am well aware. Besides, the capability of seeing dear relatives and friends, and of entertaining them beneath one's own vine and fig tree, is thus excluded. The position in society is not the same under both circumstances. My own design was to have assumed at once the duties that appertained to an independent household. There is a great satisfaction in being master of the establishment, ordinary though it be. While boarding you do not accumulate as you do while housekeeping. There is not the same feeling of home. But again I have thought that I could not resist a direct expression of the will of her who will be equally interested with myself, or refuse the request made in all earnestness. That we will be the inmates of the Pavilion but a comparatively short time I have no question. The expense of boarding will certainly not be greater than that of housekeeping, and after the lapse of a few months we will be in as good a condition as we now are to assume the duties of regular housekeeping. She will then, moreover, have a voice in the selection of the furniture, etc. You may rest assured that I will take advantage of the earliest opportunity to begin in earnest the duties of the household. With reference to the trouble of moving, I myself have only my books and clothing to remove from my present apartment. The most of my library I will put in my room at the Pavilion.

Regret to hear, my dear father, that you have recently been feeling so unwell. I wish from the bottom of my heart that I could exchange health with you. I would esteem it in truth a privilege, for in your keeping it would be used to so much greater advantage and profit. We hope that you will perform our marriage ceremony in November. The 9th is the day set apart for the solemnization of the engagement.

Today the heat of summer is with us. The "falling off" in the cotton crops is said to be very general all over the country. What the result will be, time only can show. Planting is at best, like all other human occupations, uncertain in its issues. Mr. Ward will return, I hope, in a few days. Our city still enjoys its usual health. All friends well, and unite in kind remembrance. With warmest love, my dear father, to self, Mother, and all friends, I am, as ever,

Your affectionate son,
Charles C. Jones, Jr.

Our captain being away leaves me in command of the Chatham Artillery. The hundred and fifty dollars are subject to your wishes.

Hope that my sending for George will not inconvenience; and I am very much obliged to Mother for her kindness in having him fitted for his city entrée.

MR. CHARLES C. JONES, JR., *to* REV. C. C. JONES[t]

Savannah, *Monday,* September 6th, 1858

My dear Father,

I have just received a letter from Ruth, in which she asks me to effect just such arrangements as I may deem best in regard to our future manner of life, and that she will be perfectly satisfied with such as shall be perfected; that if I prefer, she will willingly do her best in the line of housekeeping as soon as we are married. Your views in the matter can now be met, and I will have to try and secure the best house that my circumstances will warrant. And this, by the way, is not a very easily accomplished matter. Rents are high, and very few houses vacant.

We hope to see Mother this evening, as I would be very glad to have a talk with her and Cousin Eliza together. Will write you again soon. As ever,

Your affectionate son,
Charles C. Jones, Jr.

MR. CHARLES C. JONES, JR., *to* REV. *and* MRS. C. C. JONES[t]

Savannah, *Wednesday,* September 8th, 1858

My dear Father and Mother,

Sister, Robert, Baby, and her nurse Lucy left us yesterday at noon in the midst of a dripping rain for the up country. I fear they will find an inclement welcome as far as the dripping skies and northeastern winds are concerned. Sister is evidently stronger than when I saw her on the Island, and I sincerely hope that she will soon experience decided benefit from a change of air and scene.

George has been at my heels ever since his arrival. He is decidedly the most indifferent Negro to local attractions and the supposed fascinations of home I have ever seen. Enclosed please find his passage money (one dollar), which it entirely escaped my mind to send before asking you to commit him to the care of the conductor. I am very much obliged to you, Mother, for your kind care of his wardrobe, and also for the Indian specimens. These I will prize highly. They are valuable.

Have been trying to find a suitable house—by the way, not a very easy task. The rents are enormously high in consequence of the tremendous taxes of our city, and most of the houses offered for rent are either at a figure too high for me or are in such out-of-the-way neighborhoods that I could not reconcile it with my own inclination to inhabit them as gifts. Will, however, do my best, and this done, will rest content.

Our city has been completely deluged with rain for the last forty-eight hours. Today has presented as dull and gloomy an aspect as I have ever seen. It is sometimes a hard matter to shake off the feeling of loneliness and almost sadness suggested by such weather. Dr. Johnson used to say that it was the evidence of a weak mind to yield to the depressing influences of weeping skies and wailing winds; but he was rather more of a stoic than most men. The truth is, I have not heard from Ruthie for several days, and this has almost given me what I suppose is technically termed "the blues."

Mrs. King, Mrs. Wells, and family left yesterday also. All friends well, and unite with me in kind remembrance. With best love, my dear parents, I am, as ever,

Your affectionate son,
Charles C. Jones, Jr.

Mr. Charles C. Jones, Jr., *to* Rev. *and* Mrs. C. C. Jones[t]

Savannah, *Saturday,* September 11th, 1858

My dear Mother and Father,

Although there is nothing of interest in our city, it would not be a difficult matter for me to tell you why I have taken my pen. . . . The truth is, I am writing simply because I am thinking of you, and loving you, and wishing that it were consistent with my engagements here for me to leave the city and enjoy at home with you those quiet pleasures, those pure and holy influences, that are felt and enjoyed scarce anywhere else. As year after year is numbered with the past, how do I find my heart knit closer and more closely still to you whom God and nature and every kind act and good deed have made so very dear!

One of the greatest pleasures I have in anticipation when Ruthie and myself are married and quietly located in our own home is that of welcoming you, my dear parents, beneath our own roof, and of contributing in any and every way in our power to your comfort and happiness. When I think of the pure enjoyments that I fain would believe are now in store in the future, how my soul longs for their realization! And until the 9th of November time will, I fear, exchange its light and airy pinions for leaden wings.

She leaves now the arrangements for the winter entirely to me, and will be perfectly satisfied and happy, she says, whatever they may be. She is a noble specimen of a young woman of the most generous impulses, and of remarkably good judgment. I have often found that her heart is always in the right place, and her plans and purposes all ultimately well considered and correct. I presume at first the reason why she intimated a preference for boarding was simply because she shrank a little from the responsibilities that would immediately attach so soon as she entered her own house. But this has all passed away; her mind is made up, and without my having persuaded her to the change.

My greatest trouble now is to obtain a suitable location. . . . The rents are so high that one or two houses (the best for rent) are above my figure. Expect in a week or so that other houses will be on the market, and then we may be suited. Will let you know the selection so soon as it is made.

Brother writes me today that he is well and will soon leave Athens for Augusta.

Abram is in Wright's office for sale, and in a very distressed frame of mind, not knowing who will be his purchaser, and with the probability staring him in the face of his being carried far away from his wife and children, to whom he appears to be sincerely attached. It is a hard case, and I would in a moment purchase and send him to the Island were such a thing practicable. As it is, we can only regret the sad fact of his being thus parted without the means of preventing the separation.

Cousin Eliza, Cousin Charles, and family are all well. Considerable anxiety exists in our city with reference to the yellow fever, but we sincerely hope that a kind Providence will avert its pestilential influences and spare us a repetition of those fearful scenes that so affrighted this devoted city in 1854. It would not be very prudent for strangers to visit the city and remain here any length of time now.

Mr. Ward I am expecting daily. With warmest love, my dear father and mother, to you both, and kind regards to all relatives on the Island, and hoping that every blessing will attend you, I am, as ever,

Your affectionate son,
Charles C. Jones, Jr.

Howdy for all the servants.

Miss Mary Jones Taylor *to* Mrs. Mary S. Mallard[t]

Winchester, Berlin, Maryland, *Tuesday,* September 14th, 1858

My dear Mary,

You do not know how really glad I was to receive your letter. I had been intending for more than a month to write to you, for I had heard of the advent of a little one, but one thing after another prevented. And I see by the date of your letter it must have been a long time on the route, for it arrived only a few days ago.

First of all, I must send my greetings to Miss Mallard, and a host of kisses—if babies like old maid's kisses, Mary, for I assure you I am more devoted than ever to spinsterhood. I do congratulate you most sincerely, my dear Mary, on the treasure you have received, and rejoice with you that she is so good and healthy. No doubt her name brought its own benefits with it, for did you ever hear of one who bore the illustrious cognomen of *Mary Jones* who was not a blessing to society at large? Although your child is named for her grandma, I shall consider her my especial namesake and leave her a silver spoon in my will in memory of her old-maid cousin. Mary, do you know I really think Mr. Mallard would have been jealous if he had seen your letter? Baby Mary crowded him almost out of its pages! However, I have no doubt he is an extremely sensible man. (Now, do not read that aloud, or I shall receive a clerical admonition, which is more than I can stand!)

I have not written to you for so long a time I must travel back. Here I have been the whole summer, part of the time with the house as full as it could be, and then again for three weeks almost entirely alone. So you see I have had variety on a small scale. I think I wrote to you that Lizzie Grier was coming to make us a visit. She spent nearly two months with us. . . . She appeared to enjoy herself, and I think really did so. Of course we had no parties, but we have a number of intimate friends who did all in their power to entertain her. Her opinion of the Eastern Shore is raised decidedly. You know it is considered the most "God-forsaken" spot in America. At least, so a Philadelphian informed me!

A few weeks after Lizzie's departure I induced Ma, by dint of urgent entreaties, to pay a visit North; so she with Sarah and Pa went down to Atlantic City. . . . You will doubtless think I had a fine time for reading and practicing. So I had, but of course I did not improve it as I should have done. I had frequent visitors and numerous interruptions, so that I fear my intellect suffered from neglect. I have never read *The Conquest of Peru*, but have read *The Conquest of Mexico*, and intend embracing the first opportunity of reading the former. I have read this summer *The Rise of the Dutch Republic*, by Philip Motley, and if you want delightful reading, Mary, I advise you to get it. I should qualify that remark, though, by assuring you your blood will run cold at the horrors of the persecutions the poor Dutch suffered from those unrelenting Spaniards. But the sturdy, stubborn resistance with which the Spaniards were met and *foiled* does my heart good to read of. And for William of Orange my admiration knows no bounds.

I suppose you have read Bayne's *Christian Life*. I consider that a wonderful book. Some of his essays I like much; the second series I prefer to the first. I am just now reading Robertson's *History of Scotland*, which I ought to have read years ago. And whenever I have a spare hour or two (not that they are so particularly scarce), I devote it to Macaulay's essays. Have you ever read *Hypatia*, by Kingsley? I think that would entertain you; a most brilliant succession of pictures, differing from anything you remember in other writers, attests the brilliancy of his imagination. *Quito*, a novel by the author of *The Tribals*, I like better than any novel I have read for some time.

I wish I were near enough to send you these books if you have not read them. Have you seen *A Woman's Thoughts About Women,* by Miss Mulock? That is really excellent, although as you are married you do not need its advice much.

I read *Jane Eyre* a long time ago—so long that I had forgotten it entirely—and reread it this summer, and *Shirley* also. And I must say, although I know it displays great want of taste, that I was never more disappointed in my life. Some passages in both I admire exceedingly; some descriptions equal anything I ever read written by a woman. But it makes me furious for a woman deliberately to describe her heroines as loving so desperately and displaying their feelings so that the heroes were perfectly aware of the state of their minds before they offered themselves. I consider it a perfect outrage on female delicacy. I think I can hear you laugh at me, Mary; but really I have been so disgusted by seeing gentlemen met halfway in their addresses I have to condemn everything that tends to encourage it. There is plenty of pure love in the world that will make itself known without any help, and I think that was what was intended. It is a great pity so much should be wasted. . . .

Now, my dear Mary, do let me hear from you as soon as you can. I suppose I must be content with letters when I can get them now, thanks to Miss Mary! But I shall always look for them. Ma and Sarah send their love; and do give mine to your mother when you write. I hope your health is quite restored by this time, and that your father will improve with cold weather.

Affectionately yours,
Mary J. Taylor.

Miss Mary E. Robarts *to* Rev. C. C. Jones[t]

Marietta, *Friday,* September 17th, 1858

My very dear and reverend Cousin,

Two letters and a dispatch came to my care yesterday for the Rev. R. Q. Mallard. On the outside of one was a request from you that I would see that those letters reached their destination. So I write a line to tell you that, expecting Mr. Mallard to pass down last night on the ten o'clock train, my little nephew buttoned on his overcoat (the air being frosty) and went down to the cars. I put the letters in an envelope and told him to say to Mr. Mallard that he had better pass the night with us, as there would be hardly time for him to read the letters while the cars stopped. In a few moments Joe came back accompanied by your reverend son-in-law. We were all in bed, but he sat by the lamp in the parlor and read them, and Joe then showed him to his room. Next morning after prayers he read them to us, and though we all regretted the cause of his detention, we were glad that your letters came in time to prevent his passing through Savannah, and that he could pass another Sabbath in the up country. We had urged him to do so before, but he said his conscience would not allow him to do so. But after reading your letter and Cousin Mary's, all things seemed so pleasant at home, and you were so faithfully performing the duties of "senior pastor," that he felt quite satisfied to remain. After an early dinner he left to join Mary and the baby in Rome, pleasantly remarking that you had sent a kiss for Mary and the baby, and he would have to go back to deliver it. By the way, I would just appoint you a committee of one to return our thanks to Laura and Mary Sharpe for adding two such pleasant relatives and interesting ministers to our family as Mr. Buttolph and Mr. Mallard.

But to go on with my story. . . . Julia King and her boys spent a week in Marietta. She, Mary, and Isabella stayed with Mrs. Fraser; the boys stayed with us, and Joe was glad to have them. Julia and Mary and Isabella dined with us twice. Mary walked up here both times (Mrs. Fraser lives near the Methodist church), so that I think Mary must have improved some, though she looks thin and delicate. The boys weighed and said they gained a pound a day. All left for Roswell yesterday in Mr. Barrington King's carriage.

I hope my godson is with you ere this. . . . Hope a kind Providence may preserve you in health, and that the pestilence may be stayed in Savannah. Am glad to hear that Dr. West's family have left. . . . Mr. Mallard expects to be in Liberty on Saturday the 25th; has written for his buggy to meet him at the twenty-mile station. He desired love; would have written you, but had not time, so I thought I would have a good excuse for inflicting a few lines on you. Much love to my dear cousin. Tell her I fear she will not find time to write me till both of her sons are married!

Your ever affectionate cousin,
Mary E. Robarts.

I fear you have had quite a spell of northeast weather. It has blown from the east for several days up here, and for three days past we have had fire.

MRS. MARY S. MALLARD *to* MRS. LAURA E. BUTTOLPH[t]

Rome, *Saturday,* October 2nd, 1858

My dear Cousin Laura,

This month three years ago we were in Marietta together, and contemplating a visit to Lookout Mountain. It has been my pleasure to take the same trip again this summer, though under very different circumstances. I thought very often of Aunt Susan and yourself and Cousin Lyman (then Mr. Buttolph). The ride from Marietta to Chattanooga brought everything vividly to my remembrance. The dust was not sufficient to produce the same effect upon my hair that it did on a former occasion. Do you remember the famous puffs? We stopped at the Crutchfield House, and almost the first person I saw was the same chambermaid that had waited upon us. The Crutchfield House has been enlarged and greatly improved. Tell Cousin Lyman when I went to the tea table there were some of the veritable batter cakes which so many waiters were in pursuit of three years ago.

I was reminded of you all the way up the mountain. You recollect the hotel on the top of the mountain was just finished when we were there. Now it is surrounded by a number of small cottages and other buildings for the accommodation of visitors. We went to the Leonora Spring, but alas, what a change has come over this beautiful spot! The spring is roughly boarded up, and a small circular house stands in front, or rather a little to the side of it. In this is tied a mule whose business it is to go round and round two or three times a day, pumping up the water to the summit of the mountain. I looked in vain for the spot which might have been called the "anxious point" and for the rock upon which I climbed and took a view.

The "lookout point" remains unchanged. Even the little bush upon which you sat while someone else enjoyed a seat nearby still grows and looks as though it had borne the weight of many travelers. We saw the Elephant, but whether it was that it does not bear a second sight or not I do not know, but it did not bear the strong resemblance to that animal it did when we saw it. In the Rock City I searched in vain for the little mossy dell from which we collected that beautiful moss. (We did not take a guide with us.) I wanted to have gathered some of the same moss. We visited the lake and falls, and I now regret very much that you did not do so too. They are, I think, among the most interesting objects on the mountain. I will describe them to you when we meet again. I hope I have not already wearied you by recalling so many familiar scenes, but I thought you might be amused. . . .

I wish you could see Aunt Jane's little boys. They are handsome and manly children. Josie has been very much interested in watching the "conic" (comet), as he calls it, and every evening announces its appearance. A few evenings ago it was very dark, and he called to Johnnie: "Come out, my brother Johnnie, and see the conic. I'll be your guide; nothing shall hurt you. Here—take my hand." Though the younger of the two, he often takes Johnnie under his protection. I am often amused to see with how much coolness he takes possession of Johnnie's playthings. "I want it! Give it to *me!* Let me have that first to play with, and then you may have it." These seem to be sufficient reasons why he should have his brother's things. Johnnie has a gentle disposition and often kindly yields. . . .

My dear little baby has not been perfectly well since I came here, though she is getting better. She is very lively, and is so fond of being out-of-doors that she manifests the most decided disapprobation when she is brought in. She reaches out her little hands and takes up her bonnet and then looks towards the door in the most eager and cunning way.

If you feel able, please answer this. I would be so glad to have a letter from you. Give a great deal of love to dear Father and Mother and Brother Charlie. Uncle John and Aunt Jane send love. Accept for Aunt Susan, Cousin Lyman, and yourself much love from my little darling and myself.

Your affectionate cousin,
Mary S. Mallard.

The thermometer is 84° in the entry today; I cannot think the weather warmer with you.

Rev. R. Q. Mallard *to* Mrs. Mary S. Mallard[t]
Walthourville, *Monday,* October 4th, 1858

My darling Wife,

Through a kind Providence I have reached home safely, but find, alas, no loved one here to greet me with her sweet smile of welcome. I think, were you and my precious babe here, I should be as happy as one can well be on earth.

I am very glad to get back, and received a cordial greeting from my people. James says on the Saturday when he returned without me a number of persons sent out to him as he passed to know if I had come. "Aunt Polly" longed to see the buggy with the white horse. Almost everyone inquired kindly after you. . . . James has just returned from the post office. He has brought me the papers and letters which have accumulated during my absence. One letter for you, which I will forward by this mail. Nothing of consequence for me.

I must now go out visiting, or I would write more. . . . The worst news I have heard since my return is the probability that we will have to play "move house" sometime in the course of three or four months. I do not know how true it may be, but should it be so, I must be on the alert and try to procure some other place. Let me know your preferences as to locations, etc.

Kiss my sweet baby and yourself for me. I pray that a kind Providence may ever preserve us and permit us again to meet under this roof. Love to Brother Jones and family. God bless you, my darling!

Your husband,
Robert Q. Mallard.

P.S. Your likeness slept under my pillow Saturday night.

Last night I spent at Lizzie's.

Rev. R. Q. Mallard *to* Mrs. Mary S. Mallard[t]
Walthourville, *Thursday,* October 7th, 1858

My own sweet Wife,

I was quite disappointed today. I looked long and anxiously for the mail-bag, and had nearly concluded that, there being nothing for me, the boy had not taken the trouble of coming to announce it, when Bucer gave notice there was someone below, and Harriet brought me in her hand several papers and letters. I ran my eye over the latter, but did not recognize the handwriting dearest to me of all others on earth. I think my letter is on the way, however, and I will get it tomorrow. One I wrote to Brother Sam took five days to come. Many thanks, my darling, for the letter which traveled behind me, and which was received on Monday. I must say it was not altogether un-expected, although *highly appreciated.*

I feel more uneasy about our dear little one since I have been removed so far from you, and am anxious to hear from or of her. Her sweet smiles and merry capers when present with her would scarcely allow me to think that she was more than slightly indisposed. Brother Sam says such occasional irregularities are not uncommon with babies. May a kind Providence restore the health of both my Marys! My love, do for my sake spare yourself as much as possible, and allow your constitution a chance to recruit.

Baby's likeness almost if not everyone pronounces capital. Sister S. M. Q. thinks it very good and like you; did not know Baby looked so much like you. I showed it to Harriet and asked her if she knew the picture. She exclaimed with energy: "Miss Mary, Baby, and Aunt Lucy! Ih"—how shall I abbreviate *it is?*—"very putty!" I would not take something handsome for it. The one sent to Mother Jones has been received and highly prized, Charlie writes me.

I am a premium number-one housekeeper for a male—an improvement upon former exploits in this line. I designate the *amount,* the *quality* of flour, and the *kind* of bread. Harriet responds very well, and has been doing up things brown. I not only "give out" but also "take in" my meals, and with an appetite wonderful for a solitaire. I will not say how much I miss you, and how long it already seems since I was with you. I want you to stay as long as it may be for the benefit of your health.

I would willingly continue this pleasant employment, but I must prepare for prayer meeting, so adieu for the present, my ———— (My pen has paused long, but I find no words but seem feeble and trite. Fill it up as your heart dictates.)

Thursday Night, five minutes to eleven o'clock. This was your night for correspondence. Wonder if you are so engaged now. I hope you are writing to me. I wish I could hear from you every mail, but will not exact so much.

Have just returned from lecture. A very good attendance and attention. . . . I made inquiry of Captain Fleming this evening in regard to the rumor that we are to be deprived of this house next year. He says he knows nothing of it except through report—"that from what the children say, they are going to wind up matters this winter." I gathered that there would be not much danger of losing the house unless they called for a division, and then the house might not fall to them. He will keep me posted. . . . I fed and foddered my own horse tonight.

Inez is a mother again. She is endeavoring to raise to doghood three fine puppies, severally for Old Bacchus, Charles, and Gilbert. She has got back her natural disposition (snappishness), and Bucer imitates her as a dutiful son. Four deedies waddle about garden and yard after querulous mama. I write these particulars because they are about home and may interest you.

Hope to visit Dorchester next week and perhaps the Island. Think we will go to Mount Vernon last Sabbath in the month. My paper admonishes me to close. Good night, my heart's beloved. A kiss and a fervent "God bless you" to you both!

Your affectionate lover and husband,
Robert Q. Mallard.

Remember me to your uncle and family.

Rev. R. Q. Mallard *to* Mrs. Mary S. Mallard[t]

Walthourville, *Monday,* October 11th, 1858

My dearest Mary,

I write from the depot, having terminated my Monday morning round here in time to send you a hurried note. . . . Your letter was a great treat, I assure you. I cannot understand why it has been so long on the way. . . . I am sorry that I am so hurried; I would like to have a longer talk with my sweet wife, and would like to tell her the old yet ever new tale: how much I love her. Kiss my precious little one for me. Love to Uncle John and family. The blessing of Heaven rest on you, my heart's best earthly treasure!

Your own husband,

Robert Q. Mallard.

P.S. I will write you as often as I can, and hope that you will write frequently. You do not know how I prize your letters.

R. Q. M.

Will send the *News* and *Presbyterian* by tomorrow's mail.

Rev. R. Q. Mallard *to* Mrs. Mary S. Mallard[t]

Maybank, *Wednesday,* October 13th, 1858

My darling Wife,

As you will perceive, I am tonight at your old and cherished home. . . . I reached Dorchester a little after dark last night. The fog was rising when I passed the bay near the place, and my overcoat became so damp that Sister Lou asked me if I had been in a rain. I do not care about riding at night in this section. Just as I threw on my overcoat this morning to go out to my buggy on my way to the Island, your father's carriage drove up the road. Father and Mother were on their way to Montevideo. I remained consequently in Dorchester and came here after lecture this evening. Your parents were very glad to see me, and would have been much more so had I brought with me one whom we all love very tenderly—your own darling self.

Your father is suffering from a cold, although the painful symptoms have left him. A "tickling in the throat" inconveniences him at present. He seems to attribute his sickness not to the labor in Walthourville but to something in his food disagreeing with him. Would that we could see him in the enjoyment of robust health! Mother seems well and in fine spirits, and making preparations for the approaching nuptials of her firstborn. Charlie is here, having just returned from a short and last visit to *Miss* Ruth. Says that *he* will not be troubled with a baby at night. Won't it be funny to see him going into ecstasies over his own one of these days!

Baby's likenesses please everyone. They (that is, Father Jones and Mother) think the likeness sent them the best. I am very glad that they think so, but prefer as more accurate the other. Charlie says our baby's feet in the picture look like bear's claws. Better say that when you are two or three hundred miles distant!

Your letter written to your mother on the 5th has been received, so I have had the pleasure of reading two letters from you written on that date. I think Cousin Laura had also received hers. Mr. Buttolph tells me that he will not be able to go to Synod; cause you may guess.

Mr. Buttolph went up to Walthourville to see Mr. Fleming and left at our house a small bundle for me. I opened it and found a new coat like your father's neatly folded up, with my name pinned on: a present from your mother. I was very much obliged to her indeed, and wore it as an expression of my thanks, which, however, were also spoken.

I hardly think I will be able to go to the wedding. Write, however, and let me know your arrangements, as it may determine me. Had I time, and did duty permit, I would rejoice to take the cars for Rome tomorrow, and shall feel much like meeting you as early as possible at Bath or Augusta. If I cannot go to Bath—and can scarcely say I have any intention of doing so—and if no way for your return before that date be open, perhaps you had better return to Augusta, and, Providence permitting, I will be with you the week following the wedding on Tuesday evening. Let me know your views and plans.

Charlie and Mr. McDonald are busily engaged on the other side of the table preparing fishing tackle for a fishing tomorrow. I have been invited to join them, but am compelled to decline. . . . Good-bye, my dearest wife. A dozen kisses for both my Marys! Mother and Sister Lou send love for yourself and kisses for Baby.

Your own husband,
Robert Q. Mallard.

P.S. I forgot to give your father's love, and should perhaps have said, "in which all unite". . . . What would I not give for one long sweet kiss from lips of all others I love best! Remember me to Mr. Jones and Mrs. Jones.

Your
Robert.

Rev. R. Q. Mallard *to* Mrs. Mary S. Mallard[t]

Walthourville, *Monday,* October 18th, 1858

My darling Wife,

I find that I will not be able to write you by this day's mail unless I send, as I did last Monday, a hurried note. So you must wait one day longer for this letter, and attribute the delay not to the want of love, but to that love which disinclines me to a short interview—even if it be only through letter—with the sole object of my strongest earthly affection. I long to fold you to my heart, my own, and time moves but slowly in your absence.

Today our little darling reaches her sixth *monthly* birthday. I was reminded of this at table this morning by Sister. She said that Lizzie's baby was seven months old today and still without a tooth, and Lizzie remarked that this was also the birthday of our little one. Six months old! "Time and tide," etc. You know the proverb. How I would like to see her today and give her Papa's blessing and congratulations! Although it may be late, give her *six* kisses from me.

I believe we shall have to abandon the honorable titles of "Mr. and Mrs. Blifkins" in favor of John and Lizzie. John was roused partially out of his sleep last night by a pricking sensation in one of his legs. He drew up that member, but his hand failed to discover the cause. Again was it stretched out, when he felt another sharp prick. "Ah, it is a bedbug," thought our friend; "I will get him now." So he slyly slid his hand down to the spot and seized —Lizzie's hand. She had had some dream about the baby, and finding in her sleep a pin somewhere in her own clothing, had been very industriously endeavoring to "pin up"—J. E. B. Not long since, she very affectionately patted John's foot; whether she succeeded in getting it to sleep, deponent saith not. We haven't near come up to that yet, and I think we must resign the name and honors thereunto attached.

It would appear from what I have recently heard that mishaps at night are not confined to married men. Mr. P. Henry Woodward has been victimized by some designing persons or person. It seems that he has been in the habit of retiring at night without a light to prevent dreaming that he is in the "mosquito country." Some nights since, he went up to his room, disrobed himself in the dark, and prepared for bed. Taking a certain garment, he deliberately thrust his arm into the sleeve, when (ugh!) his hand came in contact with—a *frog*. His exclamation of surprise and terror, they say, was tremendous. Obtaining a light, he got rid of the unwelcome intruder (which, by the way, had no way of egress, the sleeve being sewed up); and once more in array for the night he sprang into—and *out of*—bed in double-quick time. A strange crop of cockleburs had grown up in the day. I hear he is very much excited, and no doubt on the watch to ward against the stratagems of those cunning folks, *girls*. He has nailed up one door and keeps the other locked.

Mr. Woodward expects to leave in a few more weeks. Brother Sam and Mr. Gignilliat have engaged the services of another graduate of Yale, to teach both winter and summer. So you perceive the Gignilliat house will not be for rent next summer.

I am sorry to say that my fears in regard to our leaving this house have been realized. Miss Mary Eliza expects to keep house in January, her brothers living with her. She is tired of being driven from pillar to post. The marriage is to take place in the spring, I understand. Willie Winn has engaged the house for another year. . . . John Baker told me last night that he and Edgar Way intended carrying round a paper soon to obtain subscriptions to the building of a parsonage. For the winter, if no other arrangement can be made, we can live at Arcadia. I hope a home will be provided when needed.

By today's mail I have received your much-prized favor of the 14th inst. I am rejoiced to hear that you are feeling better again, and that Baby has improved in her behavior at night. I think if you could secure more unbroken sleep, your strength would return. . . . Tomorrow, I hope, you will make the distance between us a little less than it has been. You don't know what a pleasant emotion thrilled my heart at the mere announcement that you were *coming* to Marietta. Our letters then, I hope, will not be such slow travelers. Your letters are all highly appreciated, anxiously expected, and read and reread with interest.

Along with your letter there came a note from Brother Bowman, declining to go to Mount Vernon. . . . He is engaged to officiate about that time at a wedding ceremony. Whose he does not state, although from Leander Varnedoe's acquaintance with Mr. Bowman's movements I have surmised it must be somebody in Jonesville. . . . To show you what other folks think of other folks' babies I will transcribe a sentence or two of his. "Little Fannie grows fast and improves rapidly. She is just six weeks old tonight, and she already coos and laughs aloud, and very attentively watches everything that goes on around her, and sometimes makes great efforts to talk a little and express her opinion about what she sees, etc., etc., etc. But the fact is, she is a very *remarkable*—indeed, *wonderful*—child."

His letter is very pleasantly written. . . . But I am drawing near the end of another sheet, and must leave a little space for personal matters. . . . As soon as I hear what arrangement you have made about getting home, I will determine. If I go to Charlie's wedding, my going to Synod is doubtful. I can go to the wedding and get back on the day Presbytery opens, or the day after. Could you return with me on the morning after the affair? Or would you prefer to remain in Augusta until Synod convenes? Do, my dearest, act freely in the matter, and let me know as soon as you have determined.

I am doing pretty well in housekeeping, but long for the return of the housekeeper. Bucer and the cats give me some company. The former comes up in the morning to greet me before I leave the room. . . . I have been writing with two daguerreotypes open before me. Guess whose they are. . . . Do give my best love to all. Howdy for Lucy. Tell her I showed her likeness to Charles. . . . Howdy for Mr. Jones's servants. My dear heart, good-bye.

> Yours,
> R. Q. Mallard.

MRS. MARY S. MALLARD *to* REV. R. Q. MALLARD[t]

> Marietta, *Wednesday,* October 20th, 1858

My own dear Husband,

Your precious letter of the 18th was received today. It was a valued treat—such a long chat with my own. I am very glad to be here, and really feel a great deal nearer to you than I did when in Rome. That place seemed a long, long distance from friends.

Uncle John very kindly brought me to Kingston last evening, and there he met your old friend Mr. Newton Russell, who was on his way to Marietta. This suited exactly, and I was put under his care. I found him very pleasant and attentive. He seemed quite pleased with our baby, who behaved admirably. He said his second child was a most interesting little girl thirteen months old, just beginning to walk and talk. He has a heavy sorrow in his first child, a son. He is now four years old and has never noticed anything, is unable to walk, and is a mere skeleton. There is something wrong about his head. Mr. Russell said he had an injury upon it, and he had consulted many physicians to know if any operation could be performed. Some thought he ought to risk it, even if the operation destroyed the child; but this of course he could not do. From what he said I gathered that there must have been some malformation or perhaps injury at the birth. (I have heard since that the child is an *idiot*.) I could but feel how very thankful we ought to be to our Heavenly Father for having given us a perfectly formed child possessed of a sound mind. It is indeed a great cause for thankfulness. It made me sad to hear Mr. Russell talk of his poor little boy.

When I reached Marietta last evening, I found Aunts Mary and Lou, Ellen and Joe all kindly waiting for me at the depot; also Daddy Sam with his wheelbarrow to take the baggage. . . . All friends here think Baby has grown and improved very much. Joe says she is better-looking.

While I am speaking of Joe, I want to make a request of you. Aunt Lou says during Joe's serious impressions she would have given anything to have had him converse with you; and today she said she would be so glad if you would even write him a note, for he is exceedingly fond of you. He has expressed a hope, and there evidently is a change. Do write him a letter of advice and encouragement; and do write it at your earliest convenience. It would be highly appreciated by both Aunt Lou and Joe. . . . The revival here in the Methodist and Baptist churches has been very extensive.

I have very little time for writing this evening, so must talk of some home affairs. I want you to look in the closet in the parlor, and there you will see a square tin caddy on the shelf, and in it you will find some arrowroot. Please put it up either in a small pasteboard box or parcel and send it immediately to me by mail. The expense of sending through the mail will be less than to purchase it at the drugstores, and then I am sure of the baby's having a good article. Do, darling, do this as soon as you receive this letter, for Baby wants it now.

In regard to my going to Augusta, I think Aunt Mary and myself will go down to Brother Joe's a day or two before the wedding. I am very anxious for you to be there, and if you desire it, think I could come down the morning after. I should be very sorry to have you miss the meeting of Synod. If you do not come to the wedding and I get an opportunity, I will come home as soon after as possible. I will do, however, just whatever you would prefer.

It is time for the mail to close, so I must put aside my pen, for I want this to go tonight. . . . All our kind relatives here are quite well, and send a great deal of love to you, and say they are glad to get me here and will take good care of me. I wish I could send Baby to see you for a little while. And now, my darling, you must accept all the love of

Your own wife,
Mary S. Mallard.

The ink is so miserable that I have written with difficulty.
Kiss my dear Robert for me.

MRS. MARY JONES *to* MRS. MARY S. MALLARD[t]

Maybank, *Thursday,* October 21st, 1858

My dear Daughter,

Does it not seem strange for a mother to be so busy working for one child as scarcely to find time to write another? This has literally been my case. Charles has so recently determined to go to housekeeping that I have very little time left to prepare even the necessaries. Yesterday I received a bundle of sheets, etc., etc., from Savannah, and today the last rays of the sun found me still cutting out. . . . The yellow fever preventing my going to Savannah, I have not as yet half the articles required for Charles. I have had samples sent out, but only a very few are such as I would select.

I find your little maid very useful, and I think you will say she is quite a seamstress when you return. Patience has been in such ill health all summer that she has not been able to do any work scarcely. Flora has become my washer; she complains so much today that I feel frightened, and have ordered the jersey up tomorrow to take her to Montevideo on Saturday for her confinement. I trust the Lord will bring her safely through.

Dear Laura looks very large, and we think her time of trial cannot be far off. I hope it will be over before we leave. Old Lady Norman is to escort Mr. Buttolph home on Monday next. Laura has been working herself two most beautiful infant's waists—equal to *French* today. Patience made her a little down pillow, and Kate has made and frilled the case very nicely.

Last week we had a very pleasant visit from our son Robert, and caught a gleam of our dear daughter and sweet baby, with Lucy's ebony face. Oh, how I long to see the precious little darling! I hope you will be able to attend your brother's wedding. Robert says he wants to come up at that time and take you home.

Our plans are very undecided. Your father wants to attend Synod, and I presume we will remain with Joe until it closes. He has spoken of a visit to Dr. Howe of *consultation* about his *History.* I would be glad to return home, that Charles and Ruth might spend some time with us. Cannot speak positively of any future arrangement.

I presume by this time you are with our dear relatives in Marietta. I hope we shall have them all with us this winter. . . . The yellow fever still continues in Savannah, and absentees ought not to return before frost. . . . It is now very late; I have received *several calls* and *messages* and must close.

Kiss my dear old aunty and cousins for us, with our united and best love to each one of the household. We rejoice to hear that dear little Joe hopes that he is a Christian. A dozen kisses for our baby. Good night, my dear child. The Lord bless you!

Your own mother,
Mary Jones.

Howdies from the servants for Lucy, Sue, Peggy, Nancy, and Hannah.

REV. R. Q. MALLARD *to* MRS. MARY S. MALLARD[t]

Walthourville, *Thursday,* October 21st, 1858

My own darling Mary,

In the few minutes intervening between the present moment and my solitary meal I can at least begin a letter, to be finished on my return from lecture. My anxiety to see you does not diminish, I assure you, as the time of our expected separation shortens. . . . I have not heard from you since Monday's mail, and suppose from this that you went to Marietta on Tuesday as you anticipated. As I frequently take a trip in imagination to the up country, I will not now have to travel quite so far.

Have just returned from lecture. A most lovely night it is. A bank of clouds toward the north breaks the continuity of the otherwise clear sky, while a full moon pours down its silver radiance from its lofty throne. I plucked from the vine in our flower garden a few jessamines—the first I have seen. The green leaves glistened in the moon's rays and were wet with the dew. I send the flowers, and as I am ignorant of their language and have some misgivings about their carrying the proper message, will just say that they are intended as a little offering of love to her who has not lost the sweetheart in the wife.

Speaking of the moon and the heavens, have you seen the star in the day? At about half-past four o'clock last Friday evening I very distinctly saw Venus. The sky was beautifully blue, and the star shone like a diamond —small but silvery bright. I am sorry to see that our comet is fast receding from our system. It has been a source of great enjoyment to me, and certainly was one of the most magnificent objects upon which I ever looked.

On the way to the Island I paused with your father and mother on the causeway leading to the main, and we saw one of the grandest and most beautiful spectacles I ever witnessed. You know the view there is entirely unobstructed. There was the moon "walking in brightness"; not far from her the evening star shone large and lustrous; and near to both the comet with its head of fire almost burrowing in the western horizon, and its train of light sweeping with a graceful curve the starlit corridors of the sky. Your father, as you may well suppose, enjoyed the scene most keenly. How wonderful and unsearchable the Great Architect! With what delight must He gaze forth upon the immense with its million suns and revolving worlds! . . .

My candle is burning short, and I must close. I have written to get the refusal of the old parsonage for three weeks. In reference to Charlie's wedding, I hope to hear whether you will have any opportunity of getting home and when, or how much longer you would like to remain. This will decide me. All friends are well. Spent last evening at Mr. H. H. J.'s; you were kindly remembered by all. Mrs. West was very glad to hear of your improvement. Love to all. God bless my wife and child!

Your own
Robert.

Friday Morning. I add one or two jessamines wet with the *morning* dew. Do give my kind remembrances to the Marietta friends. A morning kiss. And now, my love, good-bye.

R. Q. M., your own.

Rev. R. Q. Mallard *to* Mrs. Mary S. Mallard[t]

Walthourville, *Monday,* October 25th, 1858

My own darling Mary,

I have just returned from my Monday morning's round, and find to my great satisfaction a letter from you. As I cannot at this distance kiss your sweet lips for the favor, I must e'en bestow that endearment on your representative. But, alas, the picture is mute: unresisting but not responsive! The time of our separation is shortening. Tomorrow afternoon, Providence permitting, I leave for Montgomery; that day a week I hope to return; and one week from that day I hope, through the blessing of God, to press to my heart my precious wife and babe.

It is my present expectation to attend your brother's wedding. I think I will be able to get back in time for Presbytery on Thursday morning by having my horse to meet me at Mr. Thomas Fleming's station. I will not insist on your returning then if it should be inconvenient. In that case you can return with me after Synod. It is probable, I see from the papers, that the railroads will pass us to and from Augusta for one fare. If so, the trip will be attended with very little expense, and at any rate the expenditure of means will not be very great. I think, then, we may consider our arrangements as definitely made. What do you suppose is the chief attraction which carries me to Bath? To witness a marriage ceremony? Pshaw! *You* can guess.

But I mustn't fill up my letter with that old but to me ever new and sweet song. I must give you the news of the village and "surroundings." And what easier transition than to pass from one wedding to another? Tomorrow night Mr. William Winn leads to the altar Miss Claudia Varnedoe! Perhaps you will see this notice: "Married, on the night of the 26th of October, Mr. William Winn to Miss Claudia Varnedoe, by *Rev. F. H. Bowman.*" I suppose we shall have to let them do as they please. *I* certainly, with my present understanding of the Confession of Faith, to say nothing of the Bible, could not have performed the ceremony. "The man may not marry any of his wife's kindred nearer in blood than he may of his own, nor the woman," etc. Our General Assembly, while it has refrained from a dogmatic statement, has by several acts pronounced such unions inexpedient, and recommends that they be discouraged. I am sorry the whole affair has occurred. "Aunt Polly" thinks it will have a bad effect.

Her name is suggestive. The old lady, I am sorry to say, has been sick and is quite feeble, although walking about. I went to see her this morning. She inquired kindly after you. As I walked from the house she asked me if I expected to dine at home, and upon my replying that I did, she said she would send me some pies: "She expected company tomorrow." Sure enough, I found Sammy's horse hitching at the gate when I returned. He had brought me several very large potatoes, a saucer of nice peach preserves, and two apple pies. I have a good friend in this dear old lady.

I made five visits this morning, three social and two pastoral. . . . It would appear that two of our doctors, unwilling to wait the slow approach of disease to kill them or allow them to kill, went of late to the field of honor to kill or be killed: Drs. Stuart and Sabal, the latter the challenger. The matter, I understand, was "settled amicably and *honorably*" on the ground. So goes the world. Mr. J. B. Mallard says he is opposed to anti-duelling societies, and would rather see in their stead a public sentiment created which would stigmatize a duel in which both parties have come off with their lives.

But enough of this. . . . Satan is mustering his forces. A dancing party is upon the tapis. . . . "Aunt Polly" thinks I ought to step forward and interfere. Her policy is decidedly coercive.

There is also on hand an exhibition to take place in a week or two. William Handley is to act one of the characters. The play is *Rip Van Winkle*. The evil results of the latter will affect, I suppose, the immediate participants in the affair. The public will talk a little of it before and after, and be amused on the night of it, and then are done with it. I do not know the "cast" (I believe they call it) of the play excepting the principal actor, and I believe Axson Quarterman and Josiah Fleming. I do not see anything wrong in the mere acting of a play, provided it is not immoral in character, but fear it may engross too much thought. . . .

I am rejoiced to hear of our little darling's improvement. I fear she will outgrow her remembrance of me. That I long to see her I need not tell *you*. Her little carriage I long to see once more with its dear little occupant, and her crib, too, with the little sleeping beauty in repose. Her likeness by common vote is a capital one. . . . In regard to Miss Louisa Robarts' messages, tell her that when she talks about a "smart sweet baby" I assent to it all, but can't listen to any proposal to keep in the up country either her or her "smart sweet mama"; that we men-kind are so selfish and *cruel* that I shall be compelled to rob her of both child and grandchild, unless Grandmama by a change of residence prevents the separation.

I shall not go through Savannah if the yellow fever continues. You must make up your mind about coming back with me, in order that I may make arrangements about carriages should it be unsafe to pass through the city. Do, my love, consult your own wishes about this. About servants' clothing I can say nothing just now; I will make the best arrangement I can. Do remember me very kindly to our friends. I will write Joe by the same mail with this. Good night, my own love. May the Keeper of Israel preserve you and my dear little treasure! So prays

Your ever loving husband,
Robert Q. Mallard.

REV. C. C. JONES *to* MISS MARY E. ROBARTS[t]

Maybank, *Tuesday,* October 26th, 1858

My dear Cousin,

You were so kind a short time since to write me a long and an affectionate letter, which I am sure His Reverence did not in the least deserve, and for which he thinks it his duty to return you his humble thanks—and that without delay.

You know that there is a young couple keeping house at the place my letter is dated from, and it seems they awoke pretty early on last Sunday morning the 24th. And the young groom said to his spouse: "Good morning, my dear. A pleasant and profitable Sabbath to you!"

Said she: "Thank you, my dear. And I do wish I could take the world and cast it away from me on Sunday. But the more one tries to keep one's thoughts aright, the more worldly things rush in and multiply."

He answered: "Do you know the reason? Dr. Owen in his book on spiritual-mindedness lays down the evidence of a spiritual mind to be that the general and habitual tendency and flow of the meditations and feelings and thoughts of the soul are on spiritual things, and worldly and vain thoughts and desires are the exception. Hence the reason why we feel it so difficult to keep the heart in a spiritual frame on Sunday is because we do not try to keep it in a spiritual frame all the six days of the week, but it runs wild, and we take little account of it."

As the conversation reached this point Little Jack tapped softly at the door.

"Come in!"

And he came in with a softly voice. "Miss Susan sends you this note, ma'am, by Uncle Sawney."

"Hand me my spectacles!"

The note acted like an electric shock. Hastily throwing me the note, the fair lady sprang to the floor. "I must go right over to Sister Susan's. Call Flora. Tell her get me a cup of tea in a minute. Here—Little Kate! Run tell Cook Kate to get some breakfast quick for Joe: he has to go immediately off to Gravel Hill for Mr. Buttolph. Peggy! Peggy! Have you brought water? Come, I must be dressed at once."

And by this time the excitement ran through the house from top to bottom. Doors were locking and unlocking, servants flying up and down stairs and through the yard to the kitchen, scattering cats and fowls and ducks on the way.

The note produced a brisk movement on the part of the groom, and he said: "I will get up and go with you, my dear."

"No," said she. "Why should *you* go? You will only be *in the way*."

It's a time, you know, when women bear rule (if there be any time when they never rule at all), and so he meekly sank back into a state of quiescence. It was a damper to his zeal in so commendable a cause. He, however, mustered up courage to say: "I only thought in case there should be any difficulty, there would be no gentleman about the house, and I might be able to assist you in some way."

"Well," said she condescendingly, "if you *choose* to go, you may. You *might* be needed."

Joe got his breakfast, mounted the mule, and pushed. We took our tea. Jerry was put in the buggy, with a harness that fit him like Saul's armor did David; and we whipped up for Maxwell, wondering and conjecturing and hoping and fearing more things than it would be proper to mention, bound on a work of necessity most manifestly. Jerry seemed to consider it an unusually rapid and forced journey for Sunday morning.

Out we jumped at the gate. The lady went upstairs at the call of Lady Susan, and the other visitor went into the parlor.

Down comes Sister. "Must send for Dr. Harris right off. Not a moment to spare! Write him a note."

Down I sat and wrote in a minute.

"Saddle Jerry, Jacob! Go the nigh way for Dr. Harris. Be in a hurry. But don't kill the horse!"

Pretty soon here he comes on horseback, very prompt and smiling. We exchange salutes, and he disappears to parts unknown.

I take the Bible and try to look up for a blessing. And lo, before 11 A.M. I was invited upstairs to see a fine young nephew of mine that I had never seen before—nor anyone else—all dressed and ready to receive the congratulations of his friends on his happy arrival among them! Quite a scene of joy in that chamber. The doctor pronounced the little fellow "a very fine fellow." And then everyone present thought he looked like it was impossible to say exactly who. But one thing was certain: he had light hair tolerable and blue eyes and was very fat and tall and had a "powerful big" hand. The doctor left us for home, and shortly after we returned thanks in the room, and I read the 127th Psalm for Laura and the 128th for Mr. Buttolph.

Late in the evening—nine o'clock, beautiful moonlight night—here came the bishop and *Mrs. Norman!* It was my duty to announce the pleasing intelligence to the newly arrived party. Both were delighted.

"Oh, what an anxious day I have passed!" said Mr. Buttolph. "What a load is taken off my mind!"

"I am glad to hear it," said Mrs. Norman; "it will be so sometimes."

"We were away at the camp meeting eight miles beyond Gravel Hill. Joe came to us there."

And so Joe and his mule had a ride of about sixty-four or sixty-eight miles going and returning! There are certainly some pretty moving times occurring occasionally in these low grounds of sorrow.

I forgot to mention that all day at Maxwell the settlement was in an ominous ferment. The Negroes ran about in a still, anxious hurry, looking round and behind, and running in and out of the house so often. The cats and dogs in the piazza and the poultry in the yard were so disturbed that they cleared out altogether. I passed most of the day in the drawing room with the Best of Books. . . . Other things occurred on this interesting occasion which, as I did not witness and hear myself, it would be venturing too much for me to narrate, and so you must wait for reports from other hands.

Now, all that I have so freely communicated is not by any means matter of secrecy, but of family and general interest; and you will be conferring a favor on all concerned to spread the news in your own homestead.

We are moving up this week, as next week, God willing, we hope to take up the line of march for Bath via Augusta; and we fondly hope to see you and all our dear relatives who can come, and our dear daughter, at the nuptials of your godson. He is here with us, and is looking forward to the occasion with serious and happy anticipations. Mary and he unite in abundance of love to dear Aunty and Lou and Cousin Joe and the young ladies and little Joe, and to our dear daughter, who we suppose is now with you. And kisses for *little Mary*. Howdy for Lucy and all the servants. Robert is quite well, and I think goes to Mount Vernon (Montgomery County) this week. All friends and relatives well down here. Brother pretty well. County healthy. I remain, my dear cousin, as ever,

Most affectionately yours,
C. C. Jones.

The yellow fever still continues in Savannah, though somewhat less. We have had northeast wind and light rains off and on for about two weeks. Still continues, and no prospect of clearing. A shift of the wind into the northwest would in all probability give us *frost*—a blessing now much looked for and hoped for for our afflicted *cities!*

A letter from Joe by today's mail. Quite well. But no letter from Daughter!

XIV

Miss Mary E. Robarts *to* Mrs. Mary Jones[t]

Columbia, *Thursday*, December 9th, 1858

My dearest Cousin,

I have not written you before, as I had nothing new to tell you of myself, having so lately seen you, so waited to see something of Columbia. I arrived safely, but felt almost used up from my cold; and the journey increased the pain in my side which troubled me so much in Augusta. I congratulated myself that I did not come over in the night train, as the engine gave out and they did not arrive till twelve the next day.

Dr. and Mrs. Howe gave me their usual kind and cordial reception. Their children all met me and kissed me and called me Aunt Mary. I was surprised to find them so much grown, not having seen any of them for eight years. Mrs. Howe looks remarkably well in the face, I think, but the night I arrived she suffered very much from her throat; felt almost like quinsy. Dr. Howe looks remarkably well. But the image of their poor afflicted boy Walthour so haunted me that I could not get rid of it for days. Dr. Howe and Willie went to see him last summer, but he did not know them—took no notice of his father and brother; and they could not interest him by telling him of his mother and home. He seems to become more and more imbecile, but is quiet and docile. My dear cousin, is not this a heart trouble—to have a child in this situation? They bear it with resignation, and are more cheerful than could be expected; but I have no doubt an aching heart is constantly borne about them even while in discharge of the active and Christian duties of life.

Dr. Howe has been very much occupied ever since I have been here. Dr. Adger, you recollect, told us he was going to Charleston to attend his father's funeral; they went on Thursday and were detained there till day before yesterday. And Dr. Thornwell has gone to the Synod of Alabama. This makes double duty for Dr. Howe. Mr. John Crawford told me that old Mr. Adger had left ten thousand dollars apiece to twenty-three grandchildren, and a hundred thousand dollars to each of his children. I did not hear of any bequests to religious institutions; no doubt there are some. Ask my Cousin C. C. how much he is going to leave his children and grandchildren, and how much to his old friend Lady Mary!

I find Columbia so much improved that I did not know the place. Will not particularize, as it would not be so striking to you as to me. . . . I have enjoyed riding about the town very much and looking at the beautiful gardens and hedges. . . . Mrs. Hampton's beautiful garden is left hospitably open, that all may walk in and refresh themselves with its beauty and verdure while the proprietors are away for health and education. . . . I find "the Presbyterian meetinghouse" a very elegant building; suppose you have often worshiped in it. Have heard Dr. Thornwell with great pleasure, but with neither more pleasure nor profit than I heard my own cousin in Augusta. The Presbyterians are thinking of building a second Presbyterian church; have some twenty-five hundred dollars for the purpose. . . . I have been to the statehouse, seen all the great men, attended commencement, and heard the speeches of the graduating classes, and seen the diplomas given and the prizes awarded. . . . The Drs. LeConte saw me at commencement with Mrs. Howe; they both bowed to me from the stage, and soon as the exercises were over came down from the stage and greeted me very cordially. They are very highly esteemed here, and Dr. Joseph LeConte is called "the idol of the college". . . . Dr. Leland and his daughter Mrs. Edmunds called to see me; the old gentleman looks quite well.

Give my love to Julia King, and tell her I heard her praises sounded from the isles of the sea by a Presbyterian minister from Edisto Island—a Mr. ——, the father of the gentleman who taught school at Flemington. He said his son wrote him that he had been invited by Mr. King to visit him on the Island, and there he saw three of the kindest and most interesting families he had ever met: Mrs. King's, Dr. Jones's, and Mr. Buttolph's family. The old gentleman then entered into a description of the place and people. I told him I could endorse all his son said of them, as I had often been there, and those families were my relatives and friends. He was very much surprised to find I knew anything of them; said they had been so kind to his son.

This old gentleman came up here on a very mournful errand: he has a daughter in the lunatic asylum. Spent several days here; spent every morning and afternoon with her and stayed here at night. Dr. and Mrs. Howe feel a peculiar sympathy for him. It seems to me I never heard of as many cases of derangement. . . .

I believe I have now told you all I know of Columbia, except the love of Dr. and Mrs. Howe to you and Cousin Charles. Dr. Howe regrets that he did not go to Synod so that he might have seen you. Emily says she is afraid you will let Joseph serve her as Charlie did Alice—that you promised your sons to them!

I have not heard from Augusta since we left, but how often I have thought of the kind friends there; and our pleasant sojourn among them will long be remembered. I hear from home twice a week. Mother writes that my furlough is almost out—that she cannot spare me much longer; so I expect to be at home by Christmas. Shall stop a day or so in Augusta, as it will be a long, long time before I get there again. . . . I suppose Charlie and his bride made you their promised visit. In "Christian confidence," how did you like your new daughter, and my goddaughter? When you make them a visit, you must write me how they are fixed—all about their house. They will be old married people before I see them. . . . Farewell, my dear cousin. Trust you may have a pleasant and happy winter. . . . Dr. and Mrs. Howe regret that you could not come over; they hope you will soon.

Your ever affectionate cousin,
Mary E. Robarts.

Louisa writes that my daughter Ellen is a lady in my absence.

Mrs. Mary Jones *to* Mrs. Mary S. Mallard[t]

Montevideo, *Thursday,* December 9th, 1858

My dear Daughter,

I have been so busy since I reached home—or rather since my work came from Savannah (it was nearly a week before we got the bundle left at the depot the day we came out)—that I have scarcely had time to *think.* Yesterday we dispatched all Charles and Ruthie's articles for housekeeping with Gilbert and George. And Sue is to follow as soon as they are ready for her, which I presume will be before long, as they are anxious to get into their own house.

We had a delightful visit from them; I wished you and Robert could have been with us too. Ruthie is a most affectionate, warmhearted, and confiding young person. We were very much pleased with her. She is a staunch Presbyterian, and I hope a true Christian. It was a great disappointment that you could not come down; all day she was looking out for the baby. You know not how much your father and I have missed our little darling.

Do write us what your plans are for the winter. I am sorry we cannot come to see you this week. Sister Abby and the children are to be with us this afternoon. Henry and Dr. West have gone out to the southwest in this state looking at lands, and she will pay me a visit at this time. . . . Father unites with me in tenderest love to you and Robert, and kisses for our little darling. In haste,

Your affectionate mother,
Mary Jones.

Mrs. Laura E. Buttolph *to* Mrs. Mary Jones[t]

Point Maxwell, *Saturday,* December 11th, 1858

My dear Aunt Mary,

We are glad to hear of your safe return home, and long to see dear Uncle Charlie and yourself and to show you the little boy to whom you were so kind, as we think he has grown in loveliness. He makes many sounds that seem like talking, and looks about very inquiringly. Every day he looks more like our little Charlie, for which we feel very grateful. He sleeps *day* and night, and has only an occasional twinge of the colic. He is getting fat, and his legs seem to be *growing shorter* and his neck growing longer. His eyes are very deep blue and very bright, and he is the pet and comfort of the household. My heart bounds—and then a sudden check is felt, and I feel that he is a lent treasure, not given, though he may be lent to us all the days of our lives.

I long to see little Mary Jones Mallard, and trust her cold has entirely passed away. Has she any teeth yet, and can she say "Mama" or "Papa"? It must have been a disappointment to you all not to see her and her dear mother on the day you expected them.

We were charmed with your new daughter, and sorry when Charlie came to carry her home, as we anticipated one day more. They are a handsome couple, and I trust will be a blessing to each other. We have had no visitors since their departure, and I am sorry I cannot send you a more interesting note. . . . Mr. Buttolph and myself take a walk daily, and I enjoy the cool weather and feel better and better. This morning we walked a mile. This is my first note or letter, as my eyes have not been strong enough to read or write much. . . . Mother, Mr. Buttolph, and James unite with me in love to you and Uncle Charlie.

Yours affectionately,
Laura E. Buttolph.

Mrs. Laura E. Buttolph *to* Mrs. Mary Jones[t]
Point Maxwell, Tuesday, December 21st, 1858
My dear Aunt Mary,

We are very much obliged to you—also to Uncle Charlie—for your kind invitation to spend Christmas with you, and are sorry that we will not be able to accept it. The weather has been so unfavorable most of the time that our little baby has never taken a ride; and he is not yet over with the thrush, though it seems to be passing away. He grows and thrives and is very good. He will be glad to see his little Cousin Mary Jones, and will greet her with a smile. Can she not come and spend New Year's Day with him and bring her father and mother and grandmother and grandfather? We long to see Cousin Mary and her sweet little daughter and all of your household with your own self, to whom I can now talk as much as I please.

Jimmie returns his thanks through me to his cousin in Augusta and to his Cousin Mary too, and will try and write her a remarkable letter thanking her for the elegant sacque she made and sent to him. I thought his father had written one until he informed me this week that he had not, as he thought I had written.

When will the Doctor make you a visit? I am so curious to hear his "message," and imagine it is some of his fun. It will do me good to have a hearty laugh. Is it a "usual" message? Little Mary is smart to cut her teeth already. Precious little thing, my heart goes out to her with peculiar tenderness. May she *ever* be the light of your dwelling and the comfort of your hearts! . . . Mother and Mr. Buttolph unite with me in much love to you and Uncle Charlie, Cousin Mary and Robert, and to little Mary. Many kisses from little James.

Ever affectionately your niece,
Laura E. Buttolph.

MRS. MARY S. MALLARD *to* MISS MARY JONES TAYLOR[t]

Walthourville, *Thursday,* December 30th, 1858

My dear Mary,

I will not abuse your clemency, so embrace the earliest opportunity for replying to your last valued favor.

First let me offer you sincere thanks for your beautiful present to my little daughter. The case containing the fork and spoon preceded your letter by two or three mails. Mr. Mallard opened the package and handed it to me, saying that some of my friends had sent me a Christmas present. But upon closer inspection we found the initials were M. J. M. and not M. S. M. It was very kind in you to think of our little baby. You promised to bequeath a spoon to her in your will, but I am glad you thought it proper to allow her the use of it during your life.

While I am on this subject, I must tell you a little about this baby. She has improved very much: sits alone and has a remarkable faculty of amusing herself. She can boast of one tooth, and her accomplishments are "blowing the fire," saying "bow wow" when the dog barks, etc. My friends now think her strikingly like my father and myself. She has lost the resemblance to Mr. Mallard almost entirely. But this is enough about the baby. (But I will tell you for your comfort that Mr. Mallard speaks of having her likeness taken to be sent to you; so one of these days when she is a little older, you may expect to find her little face in a letter. I have an ambrotype of her taken at five months which is very good.)

I was very glad to learn something of our old teachers the Misses Gill. How I should like to see them! You must excuse Miss Sidney's forgetfulness, for you know the period of teething is always a trying one, though I don't think my name so very hard to be remembered. Did you ever succeed in convincing Miss Mary that Georgia is my home and not Virginia? I am glad, too, to hear of Paulina. Has she made an agreement with you to devote herself to spinsterhood? Where are Maggie Wilson and Lizzie Paul? Are either of them married? I have not heard anything of them for a long time. Do write something about Margie Dickson's health. What is the matter with her? I heard neuralgia.

After these many questions I must give you a little time to breathe and tell you where I have been since I last wrote. (This will account for my long silence.) I did not recover my strength after the birth of my baby. Indeed, my health became so feeble that my physician recommended a change as the only thing to speedily benefit me, and so sent me off to the upper portion of our state. Mr. Mallard, Baby, and myself left home about the 6th of September, and I did not return home until the latter part of November. Mr. Mallard left home intending only to take me to the up country and then return immediately; but in the meantime the yellow fever broke out in Savannah, thus rendering it unsafe for him to pass through, so he had to stay away three weeks. Of course I was delighted at his detention, though sorry for the cause.

We went first to the Lookout Mountain, which is situated in the northern part of this state—indeed, on the line, for a portion of the mountain is in Tennessee. The air there is delightful, and the scenery as fine, I presume, as any in the United States. There are also many curiosities to be seen on the mountain. I witnessed a sunrise from the summit. Mr. Mallard and myself rose just as the gray morning began to dawn, at least an hour before the appearance of Old Sol. We stood upon the brow of the mountain. To our left the Tennessee River threaded its way through eight bends and then lost itself behind the mountain. On its banks was situated Chattanooga, looking more like a collection of toy houses and blocks than a town. In the far distance, bounding our horizon, lay Taylor's Ridge and the Cumberland Mountains, and nearer, members of smaller ranges. That sunrise scene was one of peculiar beauty. At first the whole landscape was veiled in darkness, but as the King of Day approached, sending forth his gray beams, shading them into purple and violet, then brightening their hue and changing it to orange and gold, one after another the mountains rose with the mist of the valley hanging like hoary locks around their summits, spreading silvery mantles over their dark sides, and hiding itself in the luxuriant foliage. In the valley, too, the dimly traced outlines of the cottages surrounded by cultivated farms contributed their share of beauty to the scene. In addition were all the sweet sounds peculiar to early morning. I do not recollect ever to have enjoyed scenery more. I wish you could have been with us.

We remained nearly a week on the mountain and then went to Rome, Georgia. I have an uncle living in this place, and I spent a month there. After leaving Rome I remained some time with relatives in Marietta, and purposed returning home at the end of my visit there; but my brother Charlie fixed his wedding day on the 9th of November, and would take no excuse for nonappearance at the wedding. He was married at Bath (near Augusta) to Miss Ruth Whitehead, a very sweet girl; and I think I shall love her very much as a sister.

After the wedding Father, Mother, and myself returned to Augusta and paid a visit of three weeks to my brother Joseph, who is keeping bachelor's hall in that city. He is one of the professors in the medical college located there. He has but recently moved to Augusta. While in Augusta our synod convened, and we had an opportunity of seeing many old friends. Mr. Mallard was with us during most of our visit in Augusta, and after the adjournment of Synod we returned home. The only drawback to my pleasure was Mr. Mallard's absence for a portion of the time. It was impossible for him to leave his people. My health improved very much; I feel like a different person.

Whilst in Augusta I met Kate Lampkin (formerly) and her husband, whose name does not occur to me at present. Kate informed me that she had two children—both boys, I think. She is living in Augusta, and invited me to spend Sabbath evening with her, as that was the only leisure time her husband had. Of course I declined, as I am opposed to Sunday visiting. I saw Kate for such a short time that I had no opportunity of finding out anything about her husband. He seemed to be a very large, fine-looking man, and I think she introduced him as a Dr. Harker (or Dr. Something Else). They have been married four years. Kate looks pretty much as she did when at school, saving a more matronly air and an increase of flesh.

Since my return home I have had a quantity of work to do, such as cutting and making drawers, shirts, and nightshirts, shortening Baby's dresses, etc., etc. Making gentlemen's garments is something quite new to me, and being an entire novice, I am not very expeditious, and am longing for a sewing machine, which I hope to have one of these days.

Now, my dear Mary, I think this long letter will atone for my past delinquency; so do forgive me and write soon, and I think I will do better. We are just on the eve of moving to another house in the village; the owner of this house wants it, so we have to move. Do give love to your mother and *Sarah Ann*. My father's health is pretty much the same. Mother is quite well. Mr. Mallard desires to be remembered to you. With much love,

Your affectionate friend,
Mary S. Mallard.

REV. D. L. BUTTOLPH *to* REV. C. C. JONES[t]
Point Maxwell, Thursday, December 30th, 1858
My dear Uncle,

I have just returned from Savannah, where I went on Monday last. I was most hospitably and agreeably entertained while in the city by Cousins Charlie and Ruth at their pleasant residence in Harris Street. They have a delightful *home* in every sense of the word. Cousin Ruth not promises to make but *is* a most capital housekeeper. She is agreeable everywhere, but especially in her own house.

I left Cousin Charlie this morning quite sick. He came home yesterday to dinner with a severe headache and some fever. He sent for Dr. West, who prescribed for him. The doctor thought that his sickness proceeded from a cold, and that a day or two's rest would make all right again. I left him this morning in bed, with a very severe headache and some fever still on him. I hope, however, that his sickness will be slight.

I found our little Jimmie suffering from a cold. His mother sent for Dr. Harris this morning, who called before I got home. Dr. Harris thinks he will soon be well again.

The news of most importance in Savannah at present respects the *Wanderer* and crew. The examination of prisoners is still going on, but with little success, I should think. Cotton dull, and likely to be for some time to come, so I learn.

Mother and Laura unite with me in much love to yourself and Aunt Mary. Jimmie sends kisses.

Sincerely and affectionately yours,
D. L. Buttolph.

REV. C. C. JONES *to* MR. CHARLES C. JONES, JR.^g

Montevideo, *Thursday,* December 30th, 1858

My dear Son,

We duly received your two last. . . . We will do ourselves the pleasure of paying *you* a bridal visit (*we* celebrated our twenty-eighth wedding day on the 21st) so soon as we possibly can, but are not able to fix the time just now. . . . Am sorry to say your mother has not been at all well for several days. Has been suffering a good deal, and we have feared an attack similar to the one she had on the Island when you remember she was so ill. Poor George Helm was with us. May God restore her to her usual health!

Robert, Sister, and Baby are quite well, and move next week into your grandfather's house for the coming year, which they have rented.

Write your Uncle William. He took Christmas dinner with us, and is tolerably well.

Is this infamous slave trade to be tolerated in our state and in South Carolina? Did ever mortal simplicity deliver such a speech as Thompson puts in his paper this week from a *Mr. Spratt* of the South Carolina legislature? He certainly belongs to the school of the smallest and most common fishes that swim the ocean. Thompson deserves a leather medal for his discernment. I am much disgusted with his ridiculous remarks and excerpts on the slave trade. Are there no good and true citizens who will oppose this matter in the prints? Am happy to learn the *Republican* speaks decidedly against it. I am strongly tempted to write on the subject. What do the thinking and respectable portion of your community say about the matter?

Mother unites with me in much love to our new and dear daughter and to yourself. Hope you are getting on most happily and successfully in your own home. Gilbert reports all things in excellent order, and his young mistress "same like Mistress—turn her hand to everything." May God ever dwell under your roof and bless you both!

Your affectionate father,
C. C. Jones.

P.S. Mail you a letter opened without observing the direction.

Mrs. Mary Jones *to* Mr. Charles C. Jones, Jr.ᵍ

Montevideo, *Friday,* December 31st, 1858*

Tomorrow will be January 1st, *1859!* May it bring a Happy New Year to our dear children in Savannah! We wish you could spend it with us. We shall think of you, and pray that it may be signalized by blessings spiritual and temporal to you both.

Thanks, dear Ruthie, for your affectionate favor and the articles sent out by Gilbert. We enjoyed the fruit—especially the *pineapples*—and wished for you both on Christmas. Our friends were prevented from coming from the Island, as the weather was damp, and Laura and the babe had not left home before. We had Robert, Sister, and the dear baby, Brother William, and Mrs. James Jones and her little daughter Ellen. They all remained several days, and we had a quiet, happy Christmas—only I felt sad that all our children were not at home. I like the old custom of a family gathering on that day.

The boy waits, and Father calls for his letter. In haste,

Your affectionate mother,
Mary Jones.

Mr. Charles C. Jones, Jr., *to* Rev. *and* Mrs. C. C. Jonesᵗ

Savannah, *Monday,* January 3rd, 1859

Your very kind letters of the 31st ult., my dear father and mother, were not until this morning received. For all your good wishes Ruth and myself are sincerely grateful, and we hope that with the opening year every happiness will continually attend you, our dear parents.

Today is the first day since last Wednesday that I have left the house, and until yesterday since I could raise myself from my bed. The attack of cold and fever was quite severe; and although the former has, I believe and hope, left me, the latter still continues giving me no little pain and uneasiness. Hope, however, that a kind Providence will soon grant a restoration to wonted health.

It was with much sorrow, my dear mother, that we learn your threatened indisposition, and sincerely hope that all pain and apprehension are now overpassed, and that you are remitted to the enjoyment of your accustomed degree of health.

The examination of the persons charged with being implicated in the transportation of slaves from Africa was today for the present concluded, and resulted in the accused being remanded to jail to answer at the next term of the United States court to the charge of piracy. A happy termination surely—one which should call for rejoicing at the mouths of all humanity-loving and law-abiding citizens. Thompson of the *News* is a drunken fool, and that is all I have to say either for him or his paper. Sneed of the *Republican* pursues a proper course. The tone of feeling in the city is to a great extent extremely at fault; and such men as C. A. L. Lamar, Tucker, etc., run riot without let or hindrance. And this will continue until they are guilty of some flagrant outrage, at which the feelings of even their hangers-on, in obedience to the indignant voice of the community, will revolt. Lamar is a dangerous man, and with all his apparent recklessness and lawlessness a cautious one too; for he never ventures in the presence of any save those whom he may regard as followers, or whom he may readily intimidate. The great difficulty in cases of this character is to procure testimony sufficient to procure conviction. Parties all who are interested refuse to testify on the ground that the testimony which they would give would criminate themselves. The lesson in the present case will be a very good one; and if the government will proceed as vigorously in every instance, the importation will soon become very unprofitable and will necessarily be discontinued.

My dear Ruth is quite well, and unites with me in warmest love. We will anxiously await your promised visit. As ever, my dear father and mother,

Your affectionate son,

Charles C. Jones, Jr.

Rev. C. C. Jones *to* Mr. Charles C. Jones, Jr.ᵍ

Montevideo, *Monday,* January 10th, 1859

We were happy to hear from you, my dear son, on Saturday, and that you were out and improving, and that our dear daughter was well. Hope you will be speedily restored. Certain it is, for your health you will be obliged to take more exercise daily. *Take it;* you will lose no time by it. Every now and then you have to take time for headaches, etc. I would prefer taking it in good wholesome exercise.

Mother says she would come down and hear your essay on "Indian Remains" this evening were she able; but she is much indisposed, and confined to her chamber. She has not been well since Christmas; indeed, has suffered a great deal, though generally up during the day. And yesterday—Sabbath as it was—I sent for Dr. Stevens. He came to the moment and prescribed, and hopes that the attack will yield readily to his prescriptions. Mother is suffering from what is called hepatitis (pronounced hep-a-*te*-tis), an affection of the liver. She had a comfortable night on the whole, and felt so well that this morning she must needs get up and dress, which has brought on the pain in the right side again, and so has obliged her to be recumbent once more. She has been (as well as myself) much cheered by the coming yesterday of your sister and the baby. So soon as she heard that Mother was sick and the doctor sent for, she got your Aunt Marion's carriage and came down, without waiting for us to send for her if necessary. You need not feel overanxious; if your dear mother does not improve, I will directly let you know. Dr. Stevens anticipates no difficulty; and may God so ordain! The weather is clear and cold and favorable for her.

I write in some haste for the mail this morning. Mother and Sister unite in much love to yourself and Ruthie. Nephew Buttolph has returned filled with praises of your pleasant home and of Cousin Ruthie's accomplishments as a housekeeper. My daily prayer for you both is that you may both be God's dear children, and have resting upon you both the mercies of the earth and the mercies of heaven.

Your ever affectionate father,

C. C. Jones.

Rev. C. C. Jones *to* Mr. Charles C. Jones, Jr.[t]

Montevideo, *Friday,* January 14th, 1859

My dear Son,

Am happy to inform you that your dear mother is, we hope, recovering from her severe attack. But she has to be very careful, and it will require time. She has been much cheered up by the company of your sister, and by the unexpected visit of your brother, who took us by a great and agreeable surprise. They both leave us today; and if Mother should not continue to improve, will let you know. Your brother is looking much better, and will speak in person for himself.

This is the year to give blankets to our people at all the places. Will you look at Mr. Lathrop's stock and request him to send us sixty-five by the *William Totten* (Captain Thomson), which vessel will be in Savannah this week. Mr. Martin can let you know how many you will need at Arcadia. Getting all together, Mr. Lathrop may give us a good bargain. Please request Claghorn & Cunningham to send by the *William Totten:* 50 pounds La Guayra coffee; $\frac{1}{2}$ barrel good quality B sugar; 2 pounds hyson tea; 5 gallons lard oil (can to be sent for this by *Fort George Packet*); $\frac{1}{2}$ barrel rye flour; 1 bushel Irish potatoes *for planting* (either the *white* mercer or the *pinks*). Say to Mr. Anderson that he will receive by the *Fort George Packet* four bales more of the fine cotton. . . . The *Packet* leaves Riceboro tomorrow. We will not limit him in the sale of this lot; but if he is offered fifty cents, he need not refuse it.

Providence permitting, Mother and I will do ourselves the pleasure of hearing your address before the Georgia Historical Society on the 12th prox. Your "Indian Remains" will be much more agreeable than a high-flying oration unless it be *uncommon,* and I have no doubt you can prepare such a one.

Your mother and myself beg you particularly to present our kindest regards to Mr. and Mrs. Ward, and our sincerest wishes and prayers for their safe voyage and successful and agreeable sojourn in foreign lands, and also for their safe return. We unite in much love to dear Ruthie and yourself, and will come and see you so soon as we are able.

Your affectionate father,

C. C. Jones.

P.S. Blankets from $1.25 to $1.37 apiece.

Rev. C. C. Jones *to* Mr. Charles C. Jones, Jr.ᵍ

Montevideo, *Monday,* January 17th, 1859

My dear Son,

Your dear mother, am happy to say, is gradually improving, although it will be some time before we can expect perfect restoration.

As Sam is on his way to Marietta, Mother has sent you and Ruthie some nice Maybank oysters just opened raw from the shell this morning, which you two must eat for her sake and your own for your supper.

We unite in much love to you both.

Your affectionate father,
C. C. Jones.

Sam just off!

When you order the blankets, send with them a *half piece common red flannel* (*all wool*) for us.

Rev. C. C. Jones *to* Mr. Charles C. Jones, Jr.ᵍ

Montevideo, *Wednesday,* January 19th, 1859

Your kind favor, my dear son, and basket of nice fruit reached us yesterday, brought from Arcadia by your Uncle William, who spent last night with us. Mother enjoyed an apple last night, and thinks it did her good. Am glad to say she is convalescing and looking like herself again.

Your uncle thinks he will join our party, D.V., down to Savannah to call on the bride and groom and hear the anniversary address before the Georgia Historical Society if he thinks there will be room for him.

We must try and reduce the note this time, and more the next if we can; and have requested Mr. Anderson to sell our cotton and pay you four hundred dollars for that purpose. Please send me *by return of mail a blank note* to sign—blank as to date and amount, as I have lost the special wording of it.

Hope you delivered our kind wishes to your good friend Mr. Ward before he left. The honors done him are very proper and complimentary, and I shall ever feel grateful to him for his kindness to you. Our united love to Daughter and yourself.

Your ever affectionate father,
C. C. Jones.

Mrs. Mary Jones *to* Mr. Charles C. Jones, Jr.ᵍ

Montevideo, *Wednesday,* January 19th, 1859

Many thanks, my dear son, for your kind remembrance of me. If any parents have reason to be grateful to God for affectionate and attentive children, we surely have! Your sister and brother came to us as soon as possible. She remained nearly a week to nurse me, which was a great comfort to your father as well as myself. Through the divine goodness and mercy I am relieved of suffering, but still weak and under medical treatment. This is my first attempt to write, and I find both head and hand unsteady.

We desire most truly to see you and our dear Ruthie, and if our lives are spared, D.V., anticipate being with you on the *12th of February*. And your old uncle says the same. He has a great desire to hear your address, and asked me if I thought Ruth and yourself would have a *little room* for him. This you can answer to him.

Your sister and Robert and Baby propose a visit to you on Saturday, I believe; and by them I will return your basket with a few country articles that I hope will prove acceptable.

The fruit is especially so to me at this time, as I am kept on very plain diet, and not much of that: no meat, no milk, no eggs, a little toast and tea or dry hominy. I am venturing a few oysters, but I am so much better under the retrenchment system that I hope I may not be tempted to return to a more luxurious course. You must forgive me for illustrating the law of invalids, writing and talking of nobody but myself!

Wishing Heaven's best blessings for you, my dear son, and your dear wife,

Ever your affectionate mother,
Mary Jones.

Mrs. Eliza G. Robarts *to* Rev. C. C. Jones[t]
Marietta, *Saturday,* January 22nd, 1859
Dear Charles,

Sam arrived safely on Friday in the midst of a hard rain. Will and Willis gave the news, and the whole yard was soon in motion, all were so glad to see him. I wish you could have seen how glad we were at the sight of the oysters. Mary began directly to prepare some on the chafing dish with butter and pepper, and soon we were all seated with a saucer, and ate so many we had little appetite for dinner. The oysters were very good, although Sam let the cars leave him a day longer than he was expected. I thank Mary very much for the oysters. And many thanks to you for the rice and rice flour; it is a great present. The rice had to be sent by the freight; will arrive in a day or two.

We were very sorry to hear Mary had been so sick; Susan wrote me about it. You will have to take her next summer to Saratoga to cure her liver complaint. . . . On Christmas Day I was taken with a chill and fever; was one day in bed. After that every day I had such sick turns and such prostrations of strength and nerves, this is the first week I have been able to work.

As regards the sale of my Negroes, I have no desire to sell them on a rice plantation. My women would not suit Mr. Gignilliat's work. Of those in Savannah Charles is the only one who would; if I sold the others I could not support my family, my income would be so small. As it is, with the many drawbacks of unexpected expenses and losses for the two last years, I have not cleared them, although Joseph pays Ellen and Joe's schooling and furnishes the two large girls with the most of their clothing. The expense of wood, state and city taxes (all high), insurance on my house, besides pew rent and doctor's bill, take away more than a hundred dollars from my income of eight hundred. I am very much obliged to you for keeping Katy and Lucy this year. You and Henry can fix the amount of their hire, as I feel assured you will do what is right. I am sorry to trouble you with them, but it is too late to make other arrangements. But in the fall I will get Henry to sell or hire them in the neighborhood for next year.

I shall write Henry on Monday. I suppose he will be at home by the time my letter gets there. I know when he was in Baker he had a multiplicity of business to attend to. I think Henry is right to move his Negroes to Baker; the Retreat lands are much worn. But it makes my heart sad to think of it: the old homestead of my mother and my brother, with other associations, endears it to me; and I would hate to see it pass into strange hands.

I hope Banky will realize all his anticipations in going to Jacksonville. I wrote him it was late in life to begin the study of law, but hoped he would be like the great Patrick Henry of Virginia, who began late in life the study of law, and his eloquence was compared to a mighty torrent which swept everything before it.

We have not had a very cold winter yet, but rain every week and at times very damp, so my cough increases every wet spell. Although the winter has been mild so far, I have already paid thirty dollars for wood. . . . John wrote they would be down the first of February, stop a day or two, and then go to the low country. . . . Give a great deal of love to Mary for us all. I hope she was well enough to go to Savannah with you to see her son and daughter. The visit will do her good. . . . I must now close.

Your affectionate aunt,
E. G. Robarts.

I shall be glad to get the hire whenever convenient for you to send.

Mrs. Eliza G. Robarts *to* Rev. C. C. Jones[t]

Marietta, *Monday,* February 21st, 1859

Dear Charles,

I received your kind letter last Monday with the enclosed check of ninety-five dollars, for which I thank you very much; for I had several bills due which I was anxious to pay. I am very well satisfied to have Katy and Lucy hired at the rates you mentioned, as last year. I would have written and sent the receipt before this, but for three or four days there was no mail. The constant and hard rains of last week swept off a small bridge between Cartersville and Kingston; and there was another wreck in the road five miles above, which prevented the cars from running for several days. But this morning they are busily passing.

It has rained nearly all the week; it was warm and like spring weather.

Last night it cleared off, and it is quite cold today, but clear. I expect March will be colder than February. Hope our fruit will not be killed.

I hope you and Mary had a pleasant visit to Savannah and heard Charlie's fine speech. I saw a notice of it in the Savannah papers, and hope when it is published I shall get a copy.

I hope John and Jane were with you last week. If it rained as constantly and hard as it did here, they would have had but little opportunity of going about. . . . Has Maybank gone to Jacksonville? Has he sold Laurel View?

I am sorry to hear Mr. Maxwell is so unwell. Please give our kind love to him, and ask him if he won't come up and see us this summer. Perhaps the change will strengthen him.

We hope to see you and Mary this summer unless you conclude to go to Saratoga, which I think would benefit you both. And you can now go the whole way by land route. I was trying to persuade John and Jane to go. I think they need a change—particularly Jane, after being so ill last winter and sick again this winter.

My own health is better than it was about Christmas, but every cold and wet spell renews my cough. . . . It has been a dull winter: the roads are so bad the wagons can scarcely get on. . . . Mary, Louisa, and the girls with Joe all join in love to you and Mary. Give our love to Mr. Mallard and Mary when you see them, and many kisses for the dear little baby. I long to see her smiling face again. Our love to Henry and Abby. And believe me

Your ever affectionate aunt,
Eliza G. Robarts.

Mrs. Eliza G. Robarts *to* Mrs. Mary Jones[t]

Marietta, Monday, March 14th, 1859

My dear Mary,

I have been indebted to you some time for two letters. As nothing of interest has occurred with us, I deferred from time to time to write; and even now I have nothing to write about but some rain.

We have had a very unusual winter: mild, and some days warm spring weather, every week three or four days of very rainy weather. We have not had more than three spells of freezing weather, and one little dash of snow, which melted as fast as it fell. Today is very rainy, but everything is looking like spring. Our trees (plum and peach) are now in full bloom, and we have every prospect of an abundance of fruit. If the frost should come in April, I fear the prospect would be cut off.

Notwithstanding the constant rain and damp, my health has been much better than in very cold weather, which is great cause of gratitude with me that I am not burdensome to my family; for I can amuse myself by reading, knitting, sewing, and sometimes by scribbling a letter. . . . On Saturday I was reading over old letters, and oh, how sad it made me to think I was so far separated from those I love! . . . My dear Betsy I miss more and more.

. . . And my dear brother's family—what sad changes have come over them!
. . . Dear Henry and Abby! . . . I hope they will spend the summer in Marietta; it will be a great comfort to me to have them here.

Now let me ask, Mary, where will you and Charles spend the summer? At Maybank as usual? You were so sick this winter I felt as if I wanted you both to spend a few weeks at Saratoga, for the water is said to be excellent for liver complaint. The change might improve Charles's health. If you don't go North, you must come up and see us and try the Meriwether Springs. . . . Where do Charlie and Ruthie intend spending the summer, and dear Mary Sharpe and Mr. Mallard? . . . Is your son Joseph with you? Do give our love to him. Tell him Augusta is not too far for him to pay us a visit whenever there is a vacation in college.

You must write me what you are all doing. You see my letter is made up of trifles. . . . Mary, Louisa, the three girls, and Joe all send much love to you and Charles. The girls and Joe have just had a flower garden laid out at the bottom of the yard on the left-hand side of the drawing room. Louisa begs if you have any flower seeds, please send her some by Jane. . . . Be sure and give my love to Mr. Mallard and Mary, and kiss the dear little baby. Can she walk? Tell Rose Sam is well and quite active; he sends howdy for her and his children. Our servants send howdy for all of yours. Write soon. And believe me

> Ever your affectionate aunt,
> Eliza G. Robarts.

Miss Mary E. Robarts *to* Mrs. Mary Jones[t]

> Marietta, *Sunday,* April 10th, 1859

My dearest Cousin,

It has been a long—very long—time since we have heard from you. I have regretted to hear that you were not well, and fear that the constant fatigue you undergo is not good for you. Some are pining away for lack of effort and energy, some for taxing their energies too severely; so what can be done to help the overindustrious? I know life is full of pressing cares, and only the indolent find little to do. Your dear father said once laughingly a man has to exert himself when he has a grandchild born every other day. (That was when Bessie and Charles Marion were born.) I suppose you will tell me a lady has to be busy when she has a daughter married one year, a granddaughter born the next, and a son married on two successive years!

Having rejoiced with you in person on the pleasant occasion of our dear Charlie's marriage, I must now offer my congratulations on the engagement of your other dear son, communicated to me in a letter from his sister at his request. He will have a large share of happiness if he is as happy as he deserves to be. One so noble and generous-hearted as he is—so kind to all his relatives, so sympathizing with the distressed and afflicted—will make one of the best of husbands, and will, I hope, get a real warmhearted loving wife.

I have never had the pleasure of seeing the lady, but Mrs. Walker spoke of the Misses Davis as very interesting young ladies. And if she is the lady of his choice, of course she is the one for him, and will no doubt appreciate him as a literary man, being intelligent herself.

I hear that our friend Willie King was smitten with Miss Morris. Is it so? And has she smiled on him? . . . I have not time to say more. . . . Do write us soon; we long to hear from you. Best love from Mother, Louisa, and the girls.

Your ever affectionate cousin,
Mary E. Robarts.

I must write dear Mary next week. She sent me some nice groundnut macaroons by Jane; I never ate any better.

Mrs. Mary S. Mallard *to* Miss Louisa J. Robarts[t]

Walthourville, Saturday, April 30th, 1859

My dear Aunt Lou,

I am afraid you have almost concluded that I have forgotten that I am in your debt. I will not, however, waste time and words upon apologies, as I have something more important to communicate.

A wedding took place in our neighborhood two nights ago. You must guess the parties concerned: Aunt Marion and Mr. Thomas King. The wedding was very private. No formal invitations were sent out; only a *very few* friends were invited informally. Mr. Mallard performed the ceremony. Mother and myself called upon the bride this morning; she seems to be very happy, and I doubt not Mr. King will do everything in his power to promote her comfort and happiness. I must tell you about the wedding. The table was spread in the common parlor; Mrs. Dr. Stevens, Aunt Sarah Jane, and myself arranged the good things upon it; Mrs. Stevens made a beautiful pyramid of cedar and roses for the center. As the company was small, of course the table was of corresponding size; but it was very prettily arranged and looked very nicely. Aunt Marion wore a lawn dress and illusion veil. She really looked very prettily. I hope her marriage will be for her good, for she has wanted some protector. You know her brother is not one upon whom she can depend. Her marriage was, I may say, a very sudden one; for as soon as she determined to marry him she did it; for she said she would have no engagement. Situated as she was, I think it was the best plan. She has seen much trouble, but I hope she will have some bright days yet.

The young people of the village have been very busy practicing for the May party for some weeks past. The party will take place on the 5th of May. Ellen Fleming, Captain Fleming's daughter, is to be the queen. She is not pretty, but will, I think, make a fine-looking queen. The invitations are sent out for the 5th and 6th of May.

I wish you could see our dear little baby now, she is such a cunning little thing running about. She walks very well, but like all other children is so frisky she cannot be trusted very far by herself. She says a good many little words; "Daddy" is one of the last she has learned, and she is very fond of saying it on all occasions. Not long since she was at Montevideo. Mother's dress had some purple spots which of Baby's own accord she thought flies, and when Mother would come near her, she would put her little fingers on the spots and say: "Shoo! Shoo!" She has eight teeth, and I feel that I am blessed in her teething without sickness. She is very much like Father, and is perfectly devoted to him. He says she has his head exactly. It is remarkably like his.

Father has not been very well for some weeks past. He attended the meeting of Presbytery in Darien, and has not recovered from the fatigue. Mother's health has improved very much. Last week they paid Brother Charlie and Ruth a visit.

Mr. Mallard and myself have been very much interested in gardening this spring, and thus far we have had much to encourage us. Notwithstanding the cow ate all our green peas just as they were ready to bloom, and the birds helped themselves to many of our seeds, still we have a pretty good garden left. We have nice beds of Irish potatoes, beans, beets, lettuce, tomatoes, and squashes. They are all growing finely, and I hope will fulfill their promise. Gardening is a new thing with us, for we had no suitable spot upon the lot we first occupied.

I had a pleasant visit from Mrs. Clay and Miss Eliza. They wrote me if I would appoint the time, they would come by railroad and spend the day with me and return by the afternoon train. I appointed a day, and they came. I enjoyed having them here exceedingly. Mrs. Clay looks remarkably well. She brought her second daughter, Emma. Anne, her eldest, is not yet fourteen, and she measures five feet eight inches in height! It is to be hoped she will cease growing. Tom Clay has been very much interested this winter in the religious instruction of the Negroes on the plantation, and has been instrumental in the conversion of thirty or forty. I suppose you know the family have all been South this winter.

I had a visit of ten days from my friend Kitty Stiles this spring. It is very pleasant to have one's friends in one's own house. I wish you were all near enough to come and see us sometimes. I hope, however, to have that pleasure next winter, if we are all spared; for I hope at least a part if not all of you will come to the low country then. . . . Cousin Laura paid me a visit about a month ago—the first since my marriage.

I heard from some source that your health is not good. I am very sorry to hear it, and hope you will soon recover. Do give a great deal of love to Aunty, Aunt Mary, and all your household, reserving a large portion for yourself. I suppose Joe and Ellen are both hard at their studies. Baby sends kisses. You would be amused to see her bowing her head for "good morning" and kissing her hand. Tell Aunt Mary she is still "Patty Pry."

Yours very affectionately,
Mary S. Mallard.

Tell Aunt Mary she owes me a letter.

Mr. Mallard expects to go to the General Assembly on next Wednesday week. You know the assembly meets in Indianapolis. He will be gone one month.

REV. C. C. JONES *to* REV. R. Q. MALLARD[t]

Montevideo, *Monday,* May 9th, 1859

Dear Robert,

I send you a few notes of introduction, and would have multiplied them, but find by the commissioners appointed that you will find many prominent men with whom you are already well acquainted. The note to Dr. Leyburn you can hand to him; it may be of consequence for you to know the stated clerk personally. . . . Also the note to Mrs. Helm. Should you not call, mail it to her as directed. Call on Dr. Edgar so soon as you reach Nashville.

Keep a daily journal of all you see and hear, and of all your impressions, and send it off to your wife every chance you can get. It will interest her and be a paper for pleasant review in after times, if you live. And should you find time to do more, you can write to all your other friends. Keep your eyes and ears open, and see and hear and learn and improve all you can. Do whatever is required of you in the assembly; take your share in public duties; preach whenever you are asked to do so. . . . Love to my ever dear daughter, and many kisses for *Little* Daughter. Mother unites with me.

Your affectionate father,

C. C. Jones.

May 10th, 1859. Have to send this by Tom to No. 3. . . . You will have ninety miles' staging after running out forty miles on railroad from Nashville. *You will not have time to stop at the Mammoth Cave going;* at least, I think so. Take time if you wish to see it.

C. C. J.

Mother says: "*No!* Send Tom up on Jerry this afternoon. Decidedly the best way. And Daughter can write me when to send for her." So Tom goes! Again farewell. And the Lord carry and bring you back in peace!

C. C. J.

REV. R. Q. MALLARD *to* MRS. MARY S. MALLARD[t]

Atlanta, *Friday,* May 13th, 1859

My darling Wife,

We have reached this place safely, and I embrace the opportunity of a delay here to send you a few lines.

I was much reminded of you and Baby at the depot in Savannah. Mr. Holcombe parted with his young wife and two interesting little children, who were on their way to Alabama to visit Mrs. Holcombe's mother, as I learned by remarks overheard. Both husband and wife, I thought, seemed to feel quite sad. The youngest child, a little girl fourteen months old, although not as pretty as our little treasure, reminded me very much of her. Her little exclamation of admiring wonder—"OO!"—could not have been more like Baby's. You may be sure that I felt drawn toward the little creature.

Our trip had the usual amount of incident: departure and entrance of new faces, those worn by your sex frequently frightening out of sleep and sleeping postures the more unfortunate sex. I was amused by one family party. Evidently their experience in railroad traveling was not extensive. The mother (as I supposed), with her bonnet assuming almost the vertical of a man's hat, established herself in the center of a seat and was supported by her two little daughters, one on each side. I overheard the father contrasting the speed of the Columbus train and that on which we were at that time traveling. He "allowed" that the Columbus train had "a better driver."

Last night seemed as long as three ordinary ones at home, and as long as two extraordinary ones when Baby keeps Papa awake! You and my little darling were often in my thoughts. . . . We leave at ten o'clock today, reaching Chattanooga at 6½ o'clock P.M. . . . We have not as yet met with any commissioners to the assembly. . . . Kiss my little Mary for Papa, and be assured that your husband's deepest, strongest love is yours. God bless my precious ones!

Your husband,
Robert Q. Mallard.

Rev. R. Q. Mallard *to* Mrs. Mary S. Mallard[t]

Chattanooga, *Monday,* May 16th, 1859

My darling Wife,

Before the above date I expected to be in Nashville; but while "man proposes, God disposes." Cousin J. B. Mallard was taken sick on the cars on Friday last, and we have remained in this city in consequence until the present time. His disease: an affection of the bowels. I think he is better, and I trust through a kind Providence will be soon restored. He has pretty much abandoned the notion of going on, even if he should be well enough to travel. I think I shall accompany him a part of his way homeward, should he get well enough to stand the fatigue. My movements, however, are very uncertain, and will depend entirely upon the state of Cousin John's health. We are staying at the Crutchfield House.

I wrote you from Atlanta. Had I there known that Mr. Rogers was a commissioner, I would have sought him out if in the city.

Our ride by rail from Atlanta to this place was exceedingly unpleasant for the most part. It was hot—summer heat. To add to our discomfort, the cars were much crowded with delegates on their way to Dalton to attend a meeting of the Georgia Baptist Convention. The delegates were very respectable in appearance, and seemed to enjoy themselves very much. We concluded that at Dalton we should discharge most of our live freight and would then have more room. But no! The places of the Baptists were filled by passengers from the North who had come by the way of the East Tennessee Road. A party of ladies with one gentleman in attendance came in our car and found some little difficulty in procuring seats. I am sorry to say that I did not give up my seat as they passed. I selfishly concluded they would find room elsewhere. A gentleman—or gentlemen—immediately in our rear gave up to them their seats. I was much prejudiced against the party by the remarks which one of them made. She seemed to be a very bold piece, venturing all sorts of observations for the benefit of the travelers in general. She said that if it continued as hot, that before they reached Nashville nothing of her would be left but a grease spot. Denounced hoops as hot; said to "Cousin Morris" gentlemen are "great conveniences," etc. I was disgusted. But my opinion was somewhat changed by their subsequent conduct. If coarse, they were certainly kind. For when Cousin John was taken sick in the cars, they manifested a great deal of sympathy; and the gentleman rendered essential service by furnishing some brandy and getting ice for me to apply to Cousin John's head, which latter relieved him somewhat. I think hereafter I will be more polite to lady travelers. But enough of this.

I spent yesterday (Sabbath) in the hotel, not wishing to leave J. B. M. by himself. In conversation with a carpenter who is working on a building a few rods off, I learned that there was and is quite a revival in progress in the churches of this city. As elsewhere, the union of denominations is a characteristic feature of the revival here. There is no Old School Presbyterian church in the place.

Mr. John Bowman and Mr. Gresham of Macon, commissioners to General Assembly, passed through Chattanooga on last Saturday. The arrival and departure of the trains affords me some amusement. What astonishes me is the number of faces altogether strange to me. I was glad to see that the trains on Sunday were not as crowded as usual on other days of the week. It is an indication that as a nation we are Sabbath-observing.

Lookout Mountain is in full view from our chamber windows, and reminds me of the loved ones many a mile away with whom I ascended its rocky sides. God bless my precious wife and child! The time of my absence from you is measured not by the speed of the locomotive but by the miles over which it has so swiftly borne me. Would you believe it—an age seems to intervene between this time and the time of our parting in Savannah. If there be anything of which I am more certain than of others, it is this: I love my own dearest Mary and my precious little lamb—so much so that I am inclined to announce it as a general proposition that no disappointment in my plans is grievous which carries me back to you.

I wonder where this letter will find you. I imagine it will be at the sewing machine, where the cloth with a "click-click-click" slides rapidly over the burnished plate as Mrs. Mallard with a smile on her face exclaims: "Grover

& Baker's is the best!" Kiss my little darling one hundred times (more or less) for me. Give my best love to your parents and mine, and (should you see them) my parents and yours. Oh, for one long sweet kiss from lips I love more than I can tell!

Your still lover-husband,
Robert Q. Mallard.

Tuesday. Cousin J. B. not so well this morning, but I think upon the whole is improving.

R. Q. M.

Rev. R. Q. Mallard *to* Mrs. Mary S. Mallard[t]

Chattanooga, *Wednesday,* May 18th, 1859

My darling Mary,

As you perceive from the above, I am still in Chattanooga. I have scarcely any idea as to the time when I will be able to get away; my movements are utterly uncertain. I am very uneasy about Cousin John. His disease is not entirely checked, although the more unfavorable symptoms have ceased. You may be sure that I feel very great responsibility, as I am here alone with him. One other friend present would greatly relieve my mind. Cousin John certainly is much better than he has been, but he is at times so low-spirited that I can't help catching the infection and feeling very blue. But enough of this.

I saw a day or two ago a newspaper extract very complimentary to your brother Joe. I have copied it into my blankbook, and will show it to you when I return—or rather will now send it to you. It is from the Louisville *Courier*: "Dr. Jones of Georgia gave a very interesting verbal abstract of a treatise submitted by him to the Committee on Voluntary Communications on the subject of changes of the solids and fluids in malarial fever. Dr. Jones, though a young man, was listened to with profound attention by the large number of gentlemen present. He is an eloquent and forcible speaker, and his happy mode of simplifying a subject would indicate his superior fitness as a lecturer and teacher." When I read anything like the above, my heart swells and my eyes fill. I know not why, except it be that I rejoice in the rewarding of sterling merit and feel a deep interest in your brother.

We have had recently two severe thunderstorms occurring at night, and it is now raining and thundering. A heavy shower is falling on Lookout. For several mornings white clouds have been sweeping across its brow, and I judge it must be exceedingly damp up there. The Lookout House has been enlarged—that is, the accommodations on the grounds increased, I think, two-thirds. It will be open for visitors on the 1st of June. How would you like to spend another week in our corner room?

I was much interested, and yet at the same time shocked, by a spectacle which I witnessed two nights ago. Hearing singing in the neighborhood of the hotel, I went to the church from which it proceeded. It belongs to the white congregation of a Cumberland Presbyterian church. I stood at the door and looked in—and such confusion of sights and sounds! The Negroes were holding a revival meeting. Some were standing, others sitting, others moving from one seat to another, several exhorting along the aisles. The whole congregation kept up one loud monotonous strain, interrupted by various sounds: groans and screams and clapping of hands. One woman specially under the influence of the excitement went across the church in a quick succession of leaps: now down on her knees with a sharp crack that smote upon my ear the full length of the church, then up again; now with her arms about some brother or sister, and again tossing them wildly in the air and clapping her hands together and accompanying the whole by a series of short, sharp shrieks. I was astonished that such proceedings were countenanced in even a Cumberland church. One of the women servants at this hotel, I understand, kept up her shouting after she returned from the meeting the entire night, and was not quieted until next day at nine o'clock.

I looked in at the meeting again last night. The demonstrations were not so violent as before, and the prayers with which the exercises were interspersed were seemingly earnest and appropriate. With one I was particularly struck. The leader knelt near the pulpit with his face toward the congregation, and offered up a well-composed prayer in very good language. As he prayed he waxed more earnest. Finally he lifted his clasped hands above his head. Then, disengaging them, he held his right arm aloft and shook his open hand until it quivered like an aspen. Nor was he the only one who prayed audibly. Beneath his distinct utterance I could hear a deep bass tone and a really musical treble, interrupted by an occasional shout of "Amen" and a keen shriek. The leader brought his prayer to a sudden close, and up sprang the congregation to their feet, and up rose another tune or chant.

Considering the mere excitement manifested in these disorderly ways, I could but ask: What religion is there in this? And yet I could scarcely doubt the sincerity and even piety of some who offered prayer. Some allowance, of course, must be made for the *excitability* of the Negro temperament. What better, indeed, could we expect of those who only imitate (somewhat exaggerating it, of course) the conduct of some of their masters, who should know better? This is, I believe, almost if not exactly the region of that wonderful phenomenon "the jerks," which many years ago accompanied what seemed to be a genuine work of grace.

I have made the acquaintance of Mr. Bradshaw, the New School Presbyterian minister.

Write me soon, and direct to Chattanooga. As soon as I can determine my movements, I will let you know. Remember me affectionately to Father and Mother Jones. Kiss my sweet babe, and don't allow her to forget Papa. My darling precious wife, with unchanging love I remain

Your husband,

Robert Q. Mallard.

Rev. R. Q. Mallard to Mrs. Mary S. Mallard[t]

Chattanooga, *Monday,* May 23rd, 1859

My precious Wife,

Our sick friend is still improving, and I trust through the mercy of God will soon be out of danger. Much to my satisfaction and joy, last evening's train brought Sarah and Tony and, to my agreeable surprise, John Baker. The horizon is growing brighter. I have been so anxious, and have felt so heavily my responsibility, that I have scarcely been able to think connectedly of the assembly, or even of home and home folks. It seems to me that I am many months older than when I saw you last. I trust I have obtained some experience in nursing the sick which will be of profit.

We have received much kindness and attention. The servants have been the most obliging I have ever met with. Mr. Bradshaw has called frequently. Some of the ladies have also called. Cousin J. B., previous to the last-mentioned calls, said one day to the doctor: "I would rather see one lady than all the men in Tennessee." The physician in attendance is a very pleasant man—a Presbyterian, and said to be by the minister a skillful practitioner.

Providence continuing to favor us, I trust it will not be long before I fold to my heart the dearest earthly object, my own Mary. Cousin John continuing to improve, I hope to return sometime this week. . . . It is too late to go to the assembly. . . . I would write more, but fear I may lose the mail. My love to Father, Mother, and Brother Joe. Kiss Baby for Papa. And accept what is already yours—the heart of

Your own
Robert.

XV

Montevideo, *Tuesday,* May 24th, 1859

My dear Son,

We received your affectionate letter today, and I am happy to think you will visit Nashville next month. It is not only a high compliment but will prove a delightful trip, and I hope will benefit your health. No doubt you will all pay your tribute of respect to the old hero who sleeps in the bosom of his own home at the Hermitage. Do bring a little blade of grass or leaf as a memento for me from his grave. I hope dear Ruthie will come and spend the time you are away with us. We will meet her any time you will appoint. We are moved *halfway,* and expect to leave here on Thursday.

Your father and I rode to Jonesville today and called upon Mr. and Mrs. Way, our missionaries from China. They presented me with some specimens of embroidery (floss silk) and painting upon rice paper, and a beautifully carved picture frame in wood. Called also to bid our friend Mrs. Harden good-bye. *Matilda* is now in Savannah, and will be for ten days. She called to see Val whilst she was here, and I thought she might wish to return the visit.

I am grieved, my dear son, to hear that your thumb is still so painful. Your brother says if you do not take some rest and use constantly *iodine* to reduce the inflammation that you will suffer seriously. Get *Willie* to prepare you a vial of *iodine and glycerine* and rub with it at least twice a day. I am sure Ruthie will not only remind you of it but rub your thumb for you. If you are not careful, it will affect your whole arm.

Last Sabbath was our Communion at Midway. Six Negroes and one young man (John Quarterman) united. *Stepney* from Arcadia was among the number. He has been for some time an inquirer, and I trust he has found a *precious Saviour!* . . . Father unites with me in best love to Ruth and yourself. . . . God bless and save you, my own dear child!

Your affectionate mother,
Mary Jones.

Savannah, *Wednesday,* May 25th, 1859

My dear Mother,

Your very kind favor of the 24th inst. has just been received, and we are happy to know that all at home are well.

The trip to Nashville, although fatiguing, will, I hope, prove as pleasant as such excursions can be. I will certainly remember your wish and obtain the memento from the grave of the hero of the 8th January 1815. It has been told me that in the capitol at Nashville there is, among other curiosities, a small collection of aboriginal remains. This will prove interesting, and I will certainly improve the opportunity afforded for examining the specimens carefully. We hope to carry sixty men in uniform, and a battery of six pieces, two of which will be our Washington guns, which you will remember were presented by General Washington in person to our company. Letters received privately from Nashville assure us that we will meet with a generous reception.

Adeline arrived from Arcadia last evening by the Savannah, Albany & Gulf Railroad, looking remarkably well and in fine spirits. She will, I hope, make us a good cook and a faithful servant. Sue's health was so bad that we were obliged to this arrangement. She would be unfit for any and all duties at least three or four days of every week; and consequently our washing would be neglected, our washerwoman having to leave her task and attend to the cooking. Such constant interruptions are serious inconveniences to the housekeeper. Sue will remain for a short time longer, that she may impart her experience in the culinary art to Adeline. It makes us sad to part with Sue, she is so faithful, so honest, so respectful, so careful of the interest of her superiors, and so much attached to us. But she should leave Savannah. Dr. West says her days will be materially shortened if she remains. It is a fact that persons liable to attacks of asthma cannot live with any comfort or health in Savannah. Will give you notice when she goes out.

On Friday of this week I expect to go to Baker to look out for a plantation. To hire Ruth's Negroes another year would be ruinous. I think a location in Southwest Georgia promises more advantages than any other. I will do my best.

We have been and are enjoying the delightful chipped beef which you sent us. Our only regret is that it will not daily recover from the nightly depredations which we commit. Am glad to hear the good news of Stepney. All friends well, and unite in kind remembrance. Ruth joins me in warmest love to self, dear Mother, Father, Brother, Sister, and little Niece.

From your ever affectionate son,
Charles C. Jones, Jr.

MR. CHARLES C. JONES, JR., *to* REV. C. C. JONES[t]

Savannah, *Friday,* June 3rd, 1859

My dear Father,

I returned on Wednesday morning from Southwest Georgia. While there I looked at several places, and finally purchased in the lower part of Baker, near the edge of Miller. The plantation contains twelve hundred and fifty acres; lies on the direct road running between Newton and Bainbridge, distant about thirty miles from Albany, twelve from Newton, and eighteen from Bainbridge. It is well watered—cypress creek running directly through the tract, and the Ichawaynochaway bounding it on the east. A post office is located a mile and a half from the settlement. Two saw- and gristmills in the neighborhood, distant, respectively, half a mile and one mile and a half. Improvements on the place consist of an overseer's house, six large Negro houses, a meat house, a cornhouse (all of sawn timber, well made and white-washed), a well, and seven hundred acres of deadened land. The terms of the sale are seven dollars and a half per acre, four thousand dollars to be paid in cash next February, and the balance of the purchase moneys to be paid in three equal installments, to be due, respectively, January 1st, 1862, January 1st, 1863, and January 1st, 1864. . . . I forgot to mention that a church, where they have preaching every other Sabbath, stands a little over a mile from the settlement. . . . I think—and others agree with me—that the purchase is an advantageous one, and I hope with proper attention will prove a valuable investment. I am put in possession of the place in January next.

Ruth expects to go with Charlie Whitehead, her brother, who is now with us, to Florida (Tallahassee) next week to attend the wedding of a very dear cousin whom she regards in the light almost of a brother.

Uncle Henry, whom I had the pleasure of meeting yesterday, and who will see you in a day or two, can give you definite information in regard to the location and character of my place. I find it named "Fair View."

All friends well, and unite in kind remembrance. Sue goes out tomorrow morning. She cannot continue well for any length of time in Savannah. We regret exceedingly that we have to part from her, and feel deeply obliged to you both, my dear parents, for her services. My dear Ruth, who is quite well, unites with me in warmest love.

From your affectionate son,
Charles C. Jones, Jr.

Rev. C. C. Jones *to* Mr. Charles C. Jones, Jr.[g]

Maybank, *Tuesday,* June 7th, 1859

My dear Son,

We have received your two last favors, and were happy to learn your safe journey to and from the Southwest. . . . As you have determined to keep the property in the Southwest *as it is,* your arrangements appear to have been made with prudence and foresight; and I hope you will be able to meet your engagements as they come to maturity. I wish I had the means of paying up the whole for you at once. The *stocking* of the plantation will be a serious item, and the procuring of a reliable manager all-important. You must advance by degrees, and see your way before you. My objection to the country is its godlessness! The condition of society is wild; the rush is for accumulation; the game played at is speculation; and the weather becomes very foul to the poor craft that falls astern! And there is little sympathy for the *laborers* in the race. The gentlemen surrounding you may unite and create a healthy tone of public sentiment and inaugurate a milder system of treatment.

To prosecute your profession, as I trust you will, you can never become a real planter. It is impossible to be of two professions. The question was between selling out and investing or keeping and planting. The first would simplify, and leave more freedom for professional duties and advancement; the second might be more gratifying to personal feelings and family habits. You have decided on the latter. There is much inflation at present in the value of Negro property. The prices of produce are high. But such times have been before. The fall of a few cents in cotton would change the face of affairs materially. *"I, Wisdom, dwell with Prudence."*

The weather is delightful, but the drought is becoming excessive. Your brother is hard at work. Mother busy as usual, and looking remarkably well. A very pleasant visit from Sister and Robert last week; now gone to the Sand Hills. The little baby is an uncommonly interesting child; runs all about and begins to say anything. Friends and neighbors and people all well. Sorry Sue's health has failed. Your Uncle William not yet moved to Maybank. Let us know if you go to Nashville and *when*. Mother and Brother unite in much love to dear Ruthie and yourself.

Your ever affectionate father,
C. C. Jones.

REV. C. C. JONES *to* MRS. RUTH B. JONES[g]

Maybank, *Thursday*, June 16th, 1859

My dear Daughter,

We were happy to learn that you did not go to the marriage in Florida, because of the length and exposure of the journey, and above all the heat of the weather. Your good kinsman must be satisfied with your excellent intentions and hearty congratulations.

And another piece of information affords us great pleasure—namely, that our dear son and yourself intend, God willing, to spend the second week in July with us. We hope our fruit, such as it is, may be ripening at that time, and that the river may abound with fish to afford your husband recreation. We shall do all in our power to render your visit agreeable and to induce you to protract it as long as possible. Thus far the summer has been delightful: but few warm days, and for the most of the days refreshing sea breezes.

The Doctor is with us, hard at work on his prize essay, which will require some two or three weeks' more close application to complete it. His hope is that it may prove a valuable contribution to the science and practice of medicine. He is at work downstairs, and I am at work upstairs, and Mother is at work upstairs and downstairs both, but not at the same time. She is generally in her chamber opposite the study, where I hear her now at her avocations. So you see we try to practice upon the great secret of happiness in life, which is to be always usefully employed. This keeps mind and body active and the spirits cheerful, and adds pleasure to the seasons of relaxation. When you come we shall still be busy and have relaxation too, and a part of our business will be to see that you are happy. I hope our sweet birds will not have ceased their songs by that time. Since we moved down, not a moment from early dawn to the twilight of evening has been without their various and pleasant songs.

The excursion to Nashville is truly a handsome and interesting affair, and we wish the party every pleasure and a successful end of their journey. Mr. Cuyler has gotten it up in the most creditable style, and it will make a favorable impression in both states. Charles will be highly gratified. Of course the entire party will perform a pilgrimage to the tomb of President Jackson, but a few miles out of Nashville. President Polk's grave and monument is immediately in the town itself—in front of his residence, now occupied by his widow.

Mother says she is glad you will be out so soon. She is anxious to see you, and sends a great deal of love. The Doctor adds his. We beg to be kindly remembered to your sisters, Miss Whitehead when you write her, and to Mrs. Neely, and to Cousins Charles and Eliza and family. Wishing you every blessing, my dear daughter, I am

Your affectionate father,
C. C. Jones.

Give our love to our dear son on his return. Hope you will receive him back in good health and spirits.

Mr. Charles C. Jones, Jr., *to* Rev. *and* Mrs. C. C. Jones[w]

Savannah, *Tuesday,* June 21st, 1859

My dear Father and Mother,

Our company returned yesterday morning, having during the entire trip experienced not the slightest accident or untoward circumstance of any character whatsoever. The reception extended to us by the military and citizens of our city was generous and flattering in the extreme. This excursion will long be remembered as a bright incident in the history of our time-honored corps, and we will ever cherish in lively recollection the many kindnesses and acts of courtesy extended.

From the moment of our leaving Savannah until our return, the excursion was in fact a perfect ovation. At Macon we were received with a salute from the artillery company newly formed, were escorted by the Macon Volunteers, the Floyd Rifles, and the Bibb County Cavalry to a fine hall, where a magnificent and costly repast was already spread for our entertainment. There we spent an hour and a half in social intercourse, indulging in speeches and mutual compliments. Midway between Macon and Atlanta we were met by a delegation from the Gate City Guards, who escorted us to Atlanta, where we were received by the entire company and welcomed to a capital entertainment. As we passed through Marietta the cadets from the military institute gave us a salute with a small battery of six-pounders. At every station and town the citizens flocked to see the streaming banners as they floated at all points from our train, to hear the report of a little four-pounder which we carried in the forward car as it time and again rang out loud and clear its honest salutations, and to look with eagerness at the Washington guns posted on an open car in the forefront of our battery. Upon these they gazed with expressions that spoke of unqualified admiration and veneration. Many were the patriotic and complimentary remarks which their presence called forth. Our battery consisted of six six-pounders, guns, carriages, limbers, harness, ammunition all carried in perfect order. The train consisted of four elegantly furnished passenger cars, two baggage cars, two open cars in which our guns were carried, and a locomotive that would have proved an ornament to any workshop in this or any other country—all made at the workshops of the Central Railroad in Savannah. Our music consisted of a brass band of ten pieces from Augusta, and our own field music of six pieces. We numbered some fifty-three officers and men, besides invited guests and servants.

You know the beautiful scenery that greets the eye all along the road from Chattanooga to Nashville, and I will not pause to describe its physical features or the pleasant emotions awakened.

Arrived at Nashville early on Wednesday morning, all in good health and buoyant spirits. In the beautiful grounds of the female institute near the depot we were received by the German Yagers, the Shelby Guards, and the cadets from the military institute. Thence we were escorted through the principal streets in the city to the City Hotel, where in the presence of a vast concourse we were received by the mayor of the city. Throughout the entire line of march the streets were thronged with citizens of every class, every age, every color. One of the most beautiful and impressive incidents connected with the march of that morning was our reception and welcome at one point by some fifteen hundred little boys and girls, all of them dressed uniformly in white, with bouquets in their hands. These they showered upon us until the very street became a pathway of roses. These little friends were formed on both sides of one of the principal thoroughfares, their little feet dressing in line upon the curbstones so that we almost touched them as we passed. Cheer after cheer rose from the full hearts of our men. They gathered the fragrant offerings as they fell at their feet, stuck their belts full of them, ornamented the guns, and seemed rather a floral procession than a warlike company. We now have many of these bouquets, and will preserve them in happy remembrance of the occasion and of the kind little donors who extended this unique and beautiful welcome.

The mayor's reception over, we marched to the capitol; and from the brow of that commanding eminence, upon which the statehouse stands in all its fair proportions a modern Parthenon, in the presence of the assembled thousands we fired a national salute of thirty-three guns. Returning, we saluted the grave of James K. Polk. You have visited it, are familiar with its location and appearance, and therefore I will not pause to describe it. We saluted with "present swords" as we marched down the street, passing immediately in front of it. It is a remarkable coincidence that this salute was given on the anniversary of his death.

Returning to our quarters at the City Hotel, we were dismissed. The afternoon was spent in driving about the city, in visiting the statehouse, the penitentiary, etc. By the way, Mother, I have for you a beautiful cedar dipper made by one of the convicts which I will send or bring at the earliest opportunity. It will serve as a little memento of the excursion.

At nine o'clock we formed and marched to the residence of Mrs. Polk. She was prepared for us, and gave us a very pleasant reception. We were individually presented to her, and spent a few pleasant moments in her company. Her rooms were filled with many beautiful and interesting ladies. Her own appearance and manners are very prepossessing. She is said to have presided at the White House with a grace and dignity surpassed perhaps only by the elegant Mrs. Madison. Our excellent brass band serenaded her and her company for nearly an hour, playing several appropriate pieces with becoming taste and expression. I have brought home several flowers plucked from the garden, some of them growing nearest the tomb.

Thursday was assigned for a visit to the Hermitage. At nine o'clock A.M., in company with the military of the city, we embarked on board two riverboats lashed side by side and soon were moving amid the booming of cannon, the sounds of our reliable brass band, and the huzzahs of the assembled multitude upon the bosom of the beautiful Cumberland. A journey of twenty-three miles brought us to the Hermitage landing. There we left our boats, and after a march of a mile and a half in the shade of the stately trees and upon a carpet of soft green grass such as can only be found in Tennessee and Kentucky, reached that consecrated spot which every patriot regards as a national mecca.

Our battery had been sent by land a distance of some eleven miles, and was already in line awaiting our arrival. We filed into the garden, and there in silence and with uncovered heads paid our heartfelt homage at the tomb of one whom the nation will ever delight to honor. It is republican in its simplicity. At his side reposes his wife, whom that man of iron nerve tenderly loved. The inscription is singularly appropriate and touching, and was penned by himself. He sleeps in his own garden, in silence and apparent neglect. A weeping willow bends mournfully over the tomb. The garden paths are tangled, and the summerhouses are falling into decay. A commentary on human greatness! And yet he needs no tomb, for the memory of his great name and great deeds lives in every breast. I was shocked to observe the air of neglect and decay that pervaded the Hermitage in all its grounds. The explanation I find in the fact that it has passed out of the hands of the Jackson family, having been purchased by the State of Tennessee at a cost of fifty thousand dollars. By the State of Tennessee the Hermitage is now offered to the general government upon condition that a Southern military academy, to be preparatory to that at West Point, be established there. As yet, however, no action has been taken by the general government in the premises.

Returning from the garden, we fired thirty-three minute guns in front of the mansion and then entered the dwelling, where we were shown the room in which he died, the very bed upon which the old hero fought his last great battle, his carriage made from the wood of the frigate *Constitution,* his favorite armchair, his books, the portraits of his officers, etc., etc. Upon them all the impress of the great man still lives; and his spirit appears still to dwell in silent, unseen, yet felt majesty in those deserted halls. It is a national shame that the graves of our great men, and the favorite seats which they have dignified and consecrated, do not receive that attention, that respectful care, which they so richly deserve.

I did not forget your memento, Mother; and I have brought for you, Father, a hickory stick cut from the adjacent grove.

I forgot to state in the proper connection that while at the tomb of Jackson the photographic likeness of the artillery was taken. The artist designs it for publication in one of the illustrated papers of the North. I do not think from the specimen exhibited to us subsequently that he succeeded very well.

Our return to Nashville was not accomplished until nearly eight o'clock. Ten o'clock found us just entering Germania Hall, whither we were invited by the German Yagers to a military ball in honor of the Chatham Artillery. There we amused ourselves with the German beauties and the mazes of the dance until an early hour in the morning, when we retired not a little leg-weary to our quarters—to sleep only, however, until roll call at six in the morning.

Friday morning we devoted to a dress parade, which had been duly announced in the public prints. It appeared to me that all Nashville was in the streets. After passing through the principal streets, we marched beyond the sulphur spring out upon the plain, the only locality near the city suitable for artillery evolutions. The hill near the spring, the housetops, the valley, every foot of land in the vicinity, even the far-off steps and porches of the statehouse, were peopled to overflowing with the citizens of every age and class. It was a handsome sight to the eye, and a felt compliment to us. For three hours and more we performed various evolutions (by the flank, in column, in line, in battery), and fired with all the actions (now by piece, now by section, and then by battery). We sent the deep blue smoke curling among the spectators like a war cloud, and shook to their center those solid hills upon which the city stands.

At three o'clock P.M. we sat down to a sumptuous dinner given by the city authorities. Wit, humor, intellect, friendship—all were there. I will send you notices of the same, and of all the incidents connected with our sojourn in the "City of Rocks" as contained in the Nashville papers. Some of them you have doubtless already noticed, copied in our daily papers.

Saturday morning at five o'clock we bade farewell to the kind city that had entertained us so hospitably, and turned our faces homeward. Sabbath we spent in Macon, attending church in a body, and arrived in Savannah at $7\frac{1}{2}$ A.M. Monday morning. The Guards, the Blues, the Oglethorpe Light Infantry, and the Irish Jasper Greens were all out in full ranks to meet us. It was a compliment we sincerely appreciated, because it came from those who were friends at home. All the old members of the artillery were also at the depot formed in two detachments, with black coats, white pants, and side arms, to meet and welcome us. These detachments were commanded by Colonel William T. Williams, our oldest ex-captain; Mr. Sorrel, William Duncan, and such men filled the ranks of this veteran corps, part and parcel of ourselves. The military escorted us to our hall, and then dismissed to assemble at the Blues drill room at 6 P.M. There at that hour were assembled over four hundred men, all in full uniform, to meet and welcome to their homes and friends again the members of the Chatham Artillery. It was an exceedingly gratifying and flattering expression of friendship and high regard, which we can never forget. And so ended amid fine speeches, glad welcomes, and loud huzzahs our Nashville excursion.

Think of it: an excursion of twelve hundred miles by a military company in the same train without a single change of cars accomplished within a week—and that without the slightest accident or untoward occurrence of any kind. Our thanks are due to a kind Providence for His superintending care and manifold kindnesses. This excursion stands without a parallel in the history of military companies (volunteer, I mean) in our country. Facilities for making such a trip must necessarily be very seldom enjoyed.

Our visit to Nashville inaugurated a new spirit, a perfect enthusiasm in the military line. Artillery practice was a branch of the service entirely unknown experimentally to them; and yet such was the influence of the presence and conduct of our corps that the day before we left Nashville an artillery company had been formed with ninety names on the muster roll and one hundred dollars subscribed by each member to defray the primal expenses of the organization of the corps. The most respectable citizens of Nashville are members. This company we will ever regard as a legitimate offspring of our own, as the firstfruits of this interchange of friendship between respectively the two principal cities of sister states. Our reception by Mayor McGavock at his private residence was easy, hospitable, and pleasant. He has a charming wife, and is himself a gentleman of accomplished manners, of travel, of education, of intelligence, and of thought. I have a bouquet now presented me by Mrs. McGavock. St. Clair M. Morgan, a prince of good fellows, also endeared himself to us. In fine, the hospitalities extended to us by everyone were most profuse, liberal, and heartfelt in their character. We now owe a debt of gratitude which it will be our pleasure to discharge so soon as occasion may offer. I have been in most instances the spokesman of my company, and must have made at least a dozen speeches, besides toasts and sentiments of which I have no account. This excursion will and has proved of benefit. It has enlarged my acquaintance—and that in a very pleasant and honorable way.

In Nashville I saw an old collegemate, Robert McEwen, now a man of family and in good practice. His welcome and unremitting attentions were of the most hospitable character. He gave me an entertainment at his house, placed his carriage at my disposal, and did everything in his power to render our visit agreeable. He regrets not having seen the Doctor on his return from Louisville; says that he waited for him at the hotel until one o'clock A.M. Desires his kindest remembrances.

Had the pleasure of meeting Dr. Paul F. Eve and daughter. The doctor called to see me immediately after our arrival in the city, my answer to the reception speech on behalf of the military having put my name in everybody's mouth. He spoke very kindly of Brother.

In Macon I saw Judge Nisbet and Cousin Mary Nisbet. She has quite recovered her health, and looks remarkably well. You have her kindest regards.

But I fear that you are already weary with this long letter. Ruth desires me to say to you, Father, that your kind letter has been received, and that she will answer it in a very few days. She has been quite unwell for several days, but is now better. All friends well. We hope to be with you, my dear parents, at no distant day. Enclosed you have the mementos from the tombs of Jackson and Polk. With warmest love to you both, my dear parents, and to the Doctor, in which Ruth cordially unites, I am, as ever,

Your affectionate son,
Charles C. Jones, Jr.

Kind regards to all friends and relatives, and howdy for the servants.

Mr. Buttolph brought me a very fine specimen of an Indian hatchet. Ruth has forgotten the name of the party who was kind enough to send it to me. Please ask Aunt Susan or Cousin Laura if they know from whom it comes, that I may write a letter of acknowledgments.

Rev. C. C. Jones *to* Mr. Charles C. Jones, Jr.[g]

Maybank, *Saturday,* June 25th, 1859

We were very happy, my dear son, to receive your long and interesting and handsomely drawn up letter giving us an account of your Nashville excursion, which I think ranks among the most interesting events—if not the most so—of the kind we have any knowledge of. A princely affair in its conception, and a princely manifestation to it in its existence from beginning to end. It becomes a chronicled event. We take great pleasure in knowing that you met all the duties devolving upon you as a soldier and a man in right gentlemanly and gallant style. It furnished an excellent occasion of extending your acquaintance—and that in the most agreeable manner. It will not be without profit to you individually, and the profit will be shared by all in the excursion, and in both cities. The reception of the artillery on its return to

Savannah, and the close given to the whole affair in the military and civic meeting of the evening, could not have been more grateful to the ancient and honorable corps, nor more graceful on the part of the military and citizens. It ended handsomely. We look beneath the surface and admire the generosity and citizenship and friendliness and patriotism which gave warmth and color and life and captivating energy to the whole; and we run the hazard of lavish encomiums upon a people capable of these things.

You were remembered, my dear son, in family worship and our closets daily, together with your company and party, and God's protection and blessings invoked upon you. He has dealt mercifully and kindly to you all, and we desire to be grateful. We felt from the beginning great anxiety how and where you would spend the Holy Sabbath, and were happily relieved when we learned that you lay over in Macon and attended public worship! This gave dignity and consistency and impression to your character as men and good citizens. Your Uncle William said this last was best of all—who listened, and at times with tears in his eyes, with great delight to your letter. He has just left us for Dorchester, and is very unwell with his back.

You must come out and bring our dear daughter as soon, and stay as long, as you can. We will send for you at any appointed time. And do not forget that you and Ruthie have not yet been to pay your sister a visit. She and Robert will be very happy to see you under their own roof. I wish my children to esteem each other their best friends, and visit and be as much with each other as possible, and omit no attentions of respect and affection. And I am sure it will always be so with you.

The Doctor says he will drop you a line, and with dear Mother unites in much love to Ruthie and yourself. I remain, my dear son,

Your ever affectionate father,

C. C. Jones.

P.S. Your company *lacked one thing* in the completeness of its organization and the entireness of its impression in the excursion—namely, *a chaplain* —that you might have sought God's blessing on your departure and during your absence, and returned thanks on your return. *"In all thy ways acknowledge Him"*—individually, socially, privately, publicly—*"and He shall direct thy paths."* Correct this the next time.

Rev. C. C. Jones *to* Mrs. Mary S. Mallard[t]

Maybank, *Saturday,* June 25th, 1859

My dear Daughter,

Mother has determined to pay you a visit on Monday, God willing—to start early in the morning—and has, moreover, determined that I shall not accompany her as I desired to do, saying: "The ride will be too long and fatiguing to you. Joe will be left all alone. And I want to have a quiet time!" "Well, my dear, when may I expect you back?" "When the *flies* are *gone!*" (They have been very bad; if she persists in this determination, the prospect of seeing her at Maybank for a long, long time to come is very small.) You perceive how matters stand with me, and you and Robert will have to take the will for the deed.

Mother bears all the news with her from these regions. Give my love to Robert, and many kisses for Little Daughter, whom I wish to see very much. I send some gumdrops for her, but I doubt if she will be able to learn from what quarter they came. Hope to pay you a visit before long. Joe encourages me that my health is improving. Am not preaching now. The Lord be with and bless you, my dear child, and all yours!

From your ever affectionate father,
C. C. Jones.

Corrigendum: Mother says she never said one word about having "a *quiet time*." Consequently an error has crept into the text, which you will carefully observe and duly correct. It is one among a large class of errors which appear from time to time in both ancient and modern manuscripts, and give much perplexity and trouble to the learned, but wonderful employment to their ingenuity and scholarship. I derive much satisfaction from the fact that the present grave error has been so splendidly and satisfactorily corrected, although I candidly confess it to be very difficult now to determine what the true reading should be. It must be left to conjecture.

Mrs. MARY JONES *to* Mr. CHARLES C. JONES, Jr.[g]

Walthourville, *Monday,* June 27th, 1859

My dear Son,

Leaving Maybank at five o'clock this morning, I reached here about eleven, and found Daughter and Robert at the foot of the hill on their way to pastoral visitations. The weather is so warm, and the journey so fatiguing, that I persuaded your dear father to let me come alone. I wanted to see my dear little baby so much I could not stay longer away. I find her covered with heat and some of Job's comforters, which of course renders her fretful and disfigured. The Doctor promises to take good care of Father in my absence.

Your letter, my dear son, descriptive of your Nashville trip, has not only interested but delighted us. I read it to the friends on the Island, and have brought it up with me for your sister and Robert to read, and shall preserve it most faithfully as amongst our treasures. Thanks especially for the mementos from the graves of the honored dead.

I am delighted to think that our dear Ruthie and yourself will so soon be with us. How would it suit you to come directly here and see your sister and let the carriage meet you here? But you must do just as you please. Only write us at what point we shall send to meet you. I expect to return home on Wednesday morning, Providence permitting.

Notwithstanding my refusal, I find *The Mount Vernon Record* announces my name as "Lady Manager" for Liberty County. I will consequently have to try and do something for the cause, and am just going to send a note to Captain Fleming asking if the Independent Troop and Liberty Guards will not contribute something to our cause on the 4th of July. One dollar a member is all we ask. Fresh from the field of your honors, has the Chatham Artillery nothing to bestow?

It was no less a personage than *Dr. Samuel Way* who sent you the Indian hatchet, and I know you will duly acknowledge the favor.

I write in great haste for Gilbert to take this to the mail. Our friends Mrs. King with Mary and Belle, the latter on their way North, will be in town this evening. Sister and Robert unite with me in best love to Ruth and yourself and to Cousin Charles and Cousin Eliza.

Ever, my dear son, your affectionate mother,
Mary Jones.

Mr. Charles C. Jones, Jr., *to* Rev. *and* Mrs. C. C. Jones[t]
Savannah, *Wednesday,* June 29th, 1859
My dear Father and Mother,

Both of your kind favors have been received, and are sincerely appreciated.

The Nashville excursion has been the theme of encomium in the mouth of everyone. It was without doubt an achievement; and now that it is cleverly over, and has become a matter of record, we can appreciate its objects and character in all their bearings. I will ever remember it with pleasure and satisfaction, and it will be a source of pride for me to recollect that I had the honor of representing my time-honored corps upon every occasion of note during that trip. Many acquaintances formed will, I trust, be matured into friendships of a profitable and pleasant character.

Above all, our thanks are due to a kind and superintending Providence for watching over, preserving, and returning us all again to our homes in health and safety. You will observe by the enclosed slip that in framing the acknowledgments of our company I did not forget or omit to render thanks to Him who is the Giver of All Good. The resolution, although somewhat unusual upon occasions of that character, I felt to be of the first importance, and so soon as I submitted it, met with the hearty sanction of every member of the corps. You could not have observed carefully our company roll, for upon examination you will find we had a *chaplain*—by the way, a very clever and pious man: Mr. Bogart.

We are daily receiving letters of friendship from the citizens of Nashville. Two companies in that city will owe their existence to our visit, and there is no doubt but that others will be formed in obedience to the military enthusiasm engendered by our presence. The notices of our visit, as they appeared in the Nashville and other papers, I have collected and pasted in a blankbook, to be preserved *in memoriam*. This I will bring with me when we come, that you may judge of the attention elicited and the courtesies extended. William T. Thompson ("Major Jones") is writing an account of the excursion to be published in pamphlet form. He can do it well if he has a mind; and I presume he will, for he accompanied us, was the recipient of many favors, and consequently has somewhat of a debt to discharge. Our company have selected two elegant silver pitchers and waiters to be suitably engraved and sent as testimonials—one to the mayor of Nashville, the other to St. Clair M. Morgan, a gentleman of wealth and standing, who was preeminent in his attentions and princely hospitalities.

One of our members, who accompanied us on our late excursion, was drowned on last Sabbath. We buried him on Monday afternoon.

Judge Law's daughter Emily died on Monday evening and was buried yesterday. It is a very sad affliction; but they have, if I may judge from Mr. Axson's remarks at the funeral, hope in her death. The judge himself is looking badly, and I am afraid will not live very long unless there be a change for the better. These recent and severe attacks have affected him very seriously. He leaves in a short time, however, for the up country, and thence expects to cross over the country to the Virginia springs.

All friends well, and unite in kindest remembrances. With warmest love to you both, my dear parents, and to the Doctor, from Ruth and myself, I am, as ever,

Your affectionate son,
Charles C. Jones, Jr.

MR. AUDLEY KING *to* MRS. MARY JONES[t]
Woodville, *Thursday,* June 30th, 1859
Dear Aunt,

Thank you for the perusal of Charlie's long, *interesting,* and remarkably well-written letter. You enjoy a twofold pleasure in the matter: first, having visited many of the scenes noticed; and second, the grateful pleasure (I might say justifiable pride) in the writer; for I will venture to say no other parent or friend has received such account of so pleasant and fortunate an excursion. It is really wonderful—the comfort, facility, and safety of such a number, traveling so many miles, and under the circumstances when pleasure so often relaxes vigilance.

With kind and affectionate remembrance to Uncle and yourself,
Yours truly,
J. A. M. King.

REV. C. C. JONES *to* REV. R. Q. MALLARD[t]
Maybank, *Wednesday,* July 6th, 1859
Dear Robert,

Gilbert got home this morning, and we were glad to receive Daughter's note informing us of your health in the family, although having much anxiety for the issue of the case of Mr. Britton, the stranger. I knew nothing of his illness until the day your mother returned from her visit to you. Mr. McDonald told me of it just before her arrival, and we were casting in our minds what we should do for him, when we learned that you had written for him to be sent to your house. Although it involves great care and responsibility, yet I would not have had you do otherwise. "I was a stranger and ye took me in." For Christ's sake I have no doubt you did it; and God will bless it to you and yours, and bless the example of Christian and ministerial charity set before your people. It was much better for him to go to the Sand Hills than come to Maybank, inasmuch as he would be nearer medical advice and in the midst of many willing to aid in nursing him. I pray that he may yet be spared, and that the sickness may result in his eternal gain. Speak cheerfully to him, that the mind may not overburden the body. (Of course I mean not *levity*.)

I have directed Mr. McDonald to send up Sam to you in the morning to aid you in nursing. He is the handiest and best man we can command for the service. He can relieve James. If you want him, keep him; and if not, he can return home. Am sorry we are so far away and not able to aid you as we would, and that my inactive and weak body does not permit me to go and help you. Be not overanxious. Cast this care upon God, doing for the poor stranger what you can. Am glad to know everybody is so kindly disposed towards him.

Mother unites in much love to you and our dear child. Take good care of your wife, my son, and love her. Kiss Little Daughter. I long to see her. Will visit you as soon as I can.

Your affectionate father,
C. C. Jones.

Mrs. Mary Jones *to* Mrs. Mary S. Mallard[t]

Maybank, Monday, July 11th, 1859

My dear Daughter,

Your letter about the sick stranger interested us deeply, and we have constantly sympathized with Robert and yourself in the care and responsibility devolving upon you both. We trust your strength will be equal to your day, and that the poor man may be spared, and that you may be the instruments of ministering to both soul and body. We knew not how to help you except in sending someone to assist in nursing, and your father requested Mr. McDonald to send you Sam on last Thursday. I hope he proves serviceable. Of course he is without experience, but is strong and willing. We have heard nothing definite from him since your letter—only a line on Saturday to say that he was living but still very ill. Where did he come from? And has he a family?

I am sorry your brother and dear Ruthie's visit will be at such a sorrowful time. He requested the carriage to meet him at No. 3 tomorrow afternoon, but we have thought it best to send it to Walthourville tonight, and then he can make what use he pleases of it—either in going to Arcadia or coming immediately down. We do not want them to expose to the night air. The desert road he will find a cool and shady one. I wish, my darling, Robert and yourself could come down and be with us too. We long to see our little baby.

Laura has been suffering with toothache, but your aunt and Jimmie are quite well. Also all at Woodville. Mr. Maxwell is now there. Julia has received a letter from Mary. The steamer *Star of the South* broke her machinery on the passage, and they had to depend upon their sails. Whilst under sail, during a thunderstorm, she was struck by lightning! Two remarkable providences! They did not reach New York until Sabbath night. I have not read the letter, so cannot state particulars. . . . I write in haste for this to be off. Your father unites with me in best love to Robert and yourself, and the same to Ruthie and your brother. We are very happy to know that they will so soon be with us. A dozen dozen kisses from Grandpapa and Grandmama for their little darling. Our servants send howdies; and *Patience* says she made the *baby* and *snake* for *Little Missy*.

Ever your affectionate mother,
Mary Jones.

Grandpapa sends the gumdrops for Baby.

Rev. C. C. Jones *to* Mrs. Mary S. Mallard[t]

Maybank, *Friday,* July 15th, 1859

My dear Daughter,

Mother received your interesting letter by your brother, and we have sympathized with you and Robert in your recent cares and anxieties in watching over so peculiar and in some respects very painful a case as that of Mr. Britton. Poor stranger, he has gone unexpectedly to himself, leaving no encouraging hope behind that his last great change has been a favorable one to him!

I would not have had you do otherwise than you have done, and I am sure God will give you both a rich blessing in it. In striving to do our duty, the Lord among other blessings teaches us how duty should be done. Our Saviour says: "Do good, and lend, hoping for nothing again; and your reward shall be great, and ye shall be the children of the Highest: for He is kind unto the *unthankful* and *to the evil*" (Luke 6:35). You will understand this Scripture better than you ever did before, and understand how *for* Christ and *like* Christ we must do all things. We ought to bless God for every opportunity He gives us of doing good to our fellow men—of doing good in any form. Good works develop character. They only are enduring; they glorify our Father in Heaven and beneficially impress mankind. This wayfaring man has been sent into your church and congregation to awaken your Christian sympathies and efforts; and from the pastor down—elders and people, male and female—you have done well, and all you could, to minister to the afflicted. And I hope you will all—the whole church—ever stand prominent for activity and charity. We often hear it said: "Take care or beware of *strangers*." But strangers are commended to us in Scripture. "Do good to strangers." "Ye were once strangers." (I quote the sense.) "Be careful to entertain strangers." The Samaritan was neighbor to him that fell among thieves. "I was a stranger and ye took me in." The kind attentions and care we bestow upon strangers in their desolation and want is what is required of us. This is very different from taking them to our confidence unknown and making them inmates of our families.

It is all over now. Say no more than is necessary about the departed. Do not let the sad sights and sounds of his sick chamber tarry in your memory to disturb you. You have done all your work, and he is gone, and not with you any more. Throw open the chamber. Say as you pass by or through it: "Here he passed away; we can do no more for him. We felt for him while he lived. It has pleased God to take him. He is no longer here, and we leave all now with God. Let us go forward with the duties of life." Am sorry I could not have been with you.

We regretted to hear of Mrs. Bacon's death, although I expected it from what Mother told me. You have lost a good and kind friend, and the church an old and valued member. She is the last of your Uncle William's schoolmates.

The visit of your brother and sister has been very pleasant to us, as it was to you. They have taken tea at Woodville and spent a night at Maxwell, and return tomorrow. Your brother has suffered part of the time from headache. We are now enjoying what fruit the orchard affords, and regret that you are not with us. Had I known that Mr. Britton was no more when Gilbert went up, I would have urged your coming down in the carriage also. Will visit you so soon as I can. Mother had a very severe headache yesterday; better today. All unite in much love to Robert and yourself, and many kisses for dear Little Daughter. All friends at present well. The Lord be with you and bless you and all yours, my dear child!

Your affectionate father,
C. C. Jones.

Rev. C. C. Jones *to* Mr. Charles C. Jones, Jr.[g]

Maybank, *Saturday*, July 23rd, 1859

My dear Son,

We were happy to hear of your safe arrival and pleasant circumstances and continued health. You were here in a cool season compared with what it was after you left. The change in the temperature took place the day you went into town. The day after (Sabbath) was hot, Monday hotter, and Tuesday hottest: 96° in the entry, Dorchester 97°. In my recollection the thermometer has never been at Maybank 96° before. It was *hot:* wind all the time due southwest day and night. Since Tuesday we have not gone over 90°, and pleasant summer weather has come back.

Your sister and Robert came down on Tuesday. Robert returned Thursday, and your sister and Little Daughter this morning: a pleasant visit. But the dear little one, from some imprudence in diet (*fruit*), was made seriously unwell; and for fear she might continue so at a distance from their physician, it was thought best that she be carried home without delay. She has been weakened by the attack, but we thought her better this morning. She amused us with her little tricks, and left us in good spirits. We hope it may please God to grant her sound and constant health. She is a most winning and interesting child.

You saw a notice of Dr. Davis' escape and preservation from sudden death in the streets of Augusta, and his boy also. This may have kept the Doctor a day or two longer.

All well on the Island. Uncle William and Mother unite in much love to dear Ruthie and yourself. God bless you and keep you both from all evil, my dear children!

> Your ever affectionate father,
> C. C. Jones.

MRS. MARY JONES *to* MR. CHARLES C. JONES, JR.ᵍ

> Maybank, *Monday,* July 25th, 1859

My dear Son,

Louisa's husband John is just leaving for Savannah, and I send a line to say that through a kind Providence we are all in usual health excepting colds with the servants. Your sister spent last week with us. Dear Baby was unwell—probably from eating fruit—and she returned on Saturday. The Doctor reached home at one o'clock today, leaving her better. He is much improved by his visit, and I hope will now rest.

The visit of dear Ruthie and yourself was very cheering to us—only far too short. I hope your headaches have left you ere this. The little articles from Mr. Lathrop's sent for last week can be reserved for any private opportunity, as we do not send often to the depot. With our united and best love to you both, and all friends. In haste,

> Your ever affectionate mother,
> Mary Jones.

REV. C. C. JONES *to* MR. CHARLES C. JONES, JR.ᵍ

> Maybank, *Monday,* July 25th, 1859

Please add to the little articles to come by private opportunity a quart bottle of Maynard & Noyes' ink; for the learned writers in this establishment require an additional supply. I say *quart:* the largest size. From Cooper's. The articles might be sent by *stage* to Lyons & Trask, Riceboro.

> C. C. J.

MR. CHARLES C. JONES, JR., *to* REV. C. C. JONES[t]

Savannah, *Friday,* July 29th, 1859

My dear Father,

Your kind favor of the 23rd inst., and also Mother's note by John, have both been received. We are truly happy to know that all at home are well, and hope that Baby has quite recovered from her recent indisposition.

The articles ordered by Mother, and the bottle of Maynard & Noyes' ink, were yesterday sent as requested to Riceboro, care of Lyons & Trask, and will, I trust, reach you in convenient season and in good order.

The note in bank was this morning renewed for ninety days. This extends it in its present form to 1st November. Cost of renewal ($17.84) paid by me.

The news of peace was as unexpected as it was gratifying to many. Napoleon certainly has his own way of managing his affairs. The advance in cotton consequent upon this announcement has brought a smile of satisfaction to the faces of many on the Bay whose countenances were indicative of fearful apprehension of heavy losses. Some have already suffered greatly.

Our city, through a kind Providence, still remains healthy, and we hope that we will escape a recurrence of the yellow fever. Ruth suffered from the heat of the past week, but the present pleasant weather has quite restored her. Judge Jackson is absent, attending the commencement at Athens. All friends well. With warmest love to you both, my dear parents, to the Doctor, Uncle William, and all friends from Ruth and myself, I am, as ever,

Your affectionate son,

Charles C. Jones, Jr.

REV. C. C. JONES *to* MR. CHARLES C. JONES, JR.[g]

Maybank, *Tuesday,* August 9th, 1859

No letter from you today, my dear son; but a paper, which signifies that yourself and dear Ruthie are both well, for which we thank the Lord, and pray a continuance of health and every blessing for you both.

The box and ink came safely, and we owe you thanks for it. Mother is obliged to return a part of what Messrs. Henry Lathrop & Company sent, and which I believe Mr. J. E. Maxwell takes in tomorrow, and through whom you will receive this letter. His pleasant annual visit closes tomorrow, and we part with him with regret. He told me he expected to put up at the Pulaski, and would remain a day in Savannah to see his son Audley. Do not fail to call on him.

Am happy to inform you that your little niece was very much better of her late sickness, if not entirely relieved, last week on Thursday, for we were on a visit to her and her parents. Having heard nothing since, hope she is restored.

As a specimen of travel in our present weather, I give you the following for our trip to Walthourville. Started from Maybank in carriage at 7 A.M.;

reached Walthourville at 2 P.M. Time: seven hours; distance: about twenty-five miles. Returning, left Walthourville 8 A.M.; reached Montevideo, including stoppage in the Boro, half-past 12 M. Distance: thirteen and a half miles. Left Montevideo 5 P.M.; reached Maybank 10½ P.M. Time: five and a half hours; distance: about fifteen and a half miles. Not much of the pleasure of a visit in extremely warm weather lies *in transiter*.

Your dear mother is better than she was some time back, but still suffers at times, and cannot expose to the heat of the sun nor take as much active exercise as she formerly did. I trust it will all pass off, and her usual good health be granted to her again. She is very busy getting your brother ready for the coming event. He forwarded his manuscript when in Augusta, and has heard nothing from Philadelphia concerning it yet. He and your Uncle William and all on the Island are quite well.

Considerable rain lately—enough for the present, we suppose, but not too much. Our people well generally at the different places, and good promise in the fields. Robert's church moving in the matter of a parsonage; hope the matter will be carried through. Mr. Buttolph has been attending a two days' meeting at Flemington; had not returned this morning.

Your old friend and instructor Dr. Lieber, now of New York City, has published an enlarged edition of his work *On Civil Liberty and Self-Government* (8vo, 624 pp.). It is most highly commended in *The Princeton Review*. It says: "We welcome the book as the most opportune as well as valuable political present which literature has ever given to our country," etc. It ranks high in Europe and America. Are you acquainted with it?

Write and let us know how you are, and how the summer wears with you both. It would afford us great happiness to have you with us, but duty and desire do not and cannot always correspond. I pray that it may please God to grant to your city and all in it a deliverance from any epidemic this season. The health of all Southern cities so far has been excellent.

Last Sabbath we spent at home (no preaching near); and in the evening we remembered you particularly at a throne of grace at family worship. I am listening every day, my dear son, to hear the glad tidings that you have sought your Saviour and found Him. Mother, Brother, and Uncle William unite in much love to Ruthie and yourself.

Your ever affectionate father,
C. C. Jones.

Enclosed is a letter received today. You will know how to answer it—if you can *read* it.

Mr. CHARLES C. JONES, JR., *to* REV. C. C. JONES[t]

Savannah, *Thursday,* August 11th, 1859

My dear Father,

Your kind favor of the 9th inst. has just been received. It was left upon my table by Mr. Maxwell during my temporary absence from the office. I have therefore not seen him yet, but will take an opportunity to pay my respects to him this afternoon.

We regret to learn that dear Mother has been not as well as usual, and hope, as you suggest, that she will be soon relieved.

The recent "rate of travel" mentioned by you reminds me of the speed accomplished by Egyptian oxcarts in the days of the sojourn of Herodotus in that land of mysteries. The trip to the Sand Hills must have been very fatiguing to you. A recent letter from Robert states that Sister and Baby are both quite restored.

Is it not decidedly strange that the Doctor does not hear from his manuscript? I sincerely hope it has not miscarried. The loss will be a very severe one. I presume, however, he will soon ascertain the fact that it is safe, and that the delay must be imputed to the tardy printer. By the way, I am preparing a small manuscript for the Liberty County Historical and Library Society, in the shape of an address to be presented the latter part of the present month.

I have the first edition of Dr. Lieber's work *On Civil Liberty,* and have read it with great interest. The notice of *The Princeton Review* is not undeserved.

The enclosed letter I will answer by sending a copy of the address.

Sol and Pluvius have during the present month been waging a daily warfare in our city, and I think—certainly at the present time—the former must confess himself fairly vanquished. Many of our streets seem converted into canals, and we almost imagine in some localities that we have exchanged Savannah for Venice. My dear Ruth enjoys excellent health; in fact, all our friends and acquaintances are well. May a kind Providence avert the summer pestilence! Ruth unites with me in warmest love to you both, my dear parents, to the Doctor, Uncle William, and all friends. As ever,

Your affectionate son,
Charles C. Jones, Jr.

The bundle for Mr. Lathrop will be handed to him today.

Mrs. Mary Jones *to* Mr. Charles C. Jones, Jr.[g]

Maybank, *Saturday,* August 13th, 1859

My dear Son,

We were happy to receive your favor by the last mail and to know that dear Ruth and yourself, through God's goodness, were preserved in health. I have watched with great anxiety from week to week the official reports of the health of the city. They present a striking contrast to this time last year. We hope and pray that it may be so unto the close of summer; but there are certainly grounds for fear from the protracted rains.

How could you ask if it would "trouble us" to have you with us? Is it not your home, and do we not want Ruthie to feel that it is hers too? Come as soon as you please, and stay just as long as you please. Your room is ever at your service, and such comforts as a plain country residence can furnish, with Father's and Mother's welcome ever ready for you.

I am glad you have accepted the invitation of the Library Society at Walthourville. Please let us know exactly when you will be out, and when we shall send for you.

There are a few little items of business which I will give on the next page which I will be glad for you to attend to for me. . . . You have here a check for twenty dollars; please get it in small sums for housekeeping. And I will thank you to get if you can, and pay for them from the twenty dollars, one dozen panes of glass like those bought by your brother at Falligant's establishment. They are very thick glass measuring twenty by fourteen inches, and he gave twenty-five cents a pane. Do not get them unless he will let you have them at this price, and are the same kind and size as Joe's. Any other would not do. If you cannot obtain a whole dozen, I would be glad of six or eight panes.

Your father says he has been fixing up the buggy in style for you and Ruthie to ride in, and wants you to *bring* or send a piece of oilcloth (good quality, *bright colors,* forty-four inches long, forty inches wide) to cover the floor of the buggy. You can get it at Lathrop's. Father says send it by the stage and railroad, care of Lyons & Trask. I have a few articles to come from Lathrop's; they might send them at the same time. And if you can get the glass, bring them when you come.

Friends are all well on the Island. *Willie* and his friends took a tripe supper with us night before last. Father and Uncle unite with me in best love to Ruth and yourself. Remember us to all friends. Howdies for Adeline, George, and Grace.

Ever your affectionate mother,
Mary Jones.

Mrs. Mary Jones *to* Mrs. Mary S. Mallard[t]

Maybank, Tuesday, August 16th, 1859

My dear Daughter,

We were so happy to hear of you through your brother, and as Abram from Arcadia will go up in the morning, I send a line for Charles to take up to you with a few red potatoes for dear Baby.

I hope she has passed through her *great trial,* and that Robert is no longer under the necessity of singing *"Happy Day"* all night long. *Your uncle* laughed very heartily at your brother's description of Robert's vigilance. He is always so much interested in everything concerning the baby. . . . My darling, do not let her kiss the little dog: it is dangerous. You know dogs may have symptoms of hydrophobia before we know it. I do long to see her. Now she is weaned, you can spare her to us for a little while.

Charles writes that his address is all ready. Ruth and himself will then come out and be with us, I hope, until cool weather.

How sad the intelligence of Mr. Walthour's death! Truly do we sympathize with Mrs. Walthour and the family.

Friends on the Island are all well. Mary and Belle are now at Pittsfield, Massachusetts. Willie and two gentlemen have been at Woodville for a week. They both took tea with us on last Friday *evening,* and enjoy themselves upon the river in *fancy costume.*

Laura and Sister Susan both use the sewing machine admirably—*without* basting. Mr. Buttolph learned all about it, and they have a description and plates of every part. It makes a stitch like Mary Wells's, but is not a shuttle machine: sews in front, not at the side. Is not cased, but has a large top folding back on hinges from the table. All of black walnut. It is a nice article and costs fifty-seven dollars (the full price: seventy-five dollars). Laura says it is the easiest thing in the world. I think it will prove a great comfort.

Many thanks, my dear child, for the drawers. Joe has now ten pair finished, and with your good help I am getting along finely. . . . Why did you not send for Sue? She is at your service whenever you want her. . . . It is late, and I must close. Father, Uncle, and Brother unite with me in best love to Robert and yourself. Kisses for Baby. Write soon to

> Your ever affectionate mother,
> Mary Jones.

Mrs. Mary S. Mallard *to* Rev. C. C. Jones[t]
> Walthourville, *Wednesday,* August 17th, 1859

My dear Father,

Whilst I am waiting for Mr. Mallard's return I will employ the time in writing home. Mr. Mallard went to Midway with Mr. Walthour's family.

This has been a sad day to us and to our village. Mrs. Walthour, Augusta, and Dr. Walthour and Mr. Lowndes Walthour arrived last night between twelve and one with the remains of Mr. Walthour. Dr. and Aunt Howe had been telegraphed, so they met them in Savannah and came out with them. In order that there should be no delay Mr. Walthour's sons engaged an express train to bring the family out as soon as the steamer should arrive. Mr. Mallard conducted the funeral exercises this morning at eleven. Dr. Howe took no part; he said he could not. There were a large number present—all from the village, and very many from abroad. I do not think I have ever seen more general heartfelt sorrow and sympathy manifested. All seemed to feel that their friend had been taken away. After the funeral the box containing the coffins was opened. He was placed first in a lead and then in a mahogany coffin. In the lead coffin was inserted a glass, and through this we all took a farewell look. There he lay dressed in a black suit, looking almost as though he were sleeping. This was such a comfort to his children and to his sister.

The captain of the *Florida* (in which the family had sailed, and which brought them back) showed every mark of respect and attention that a man could. In New York he attended to *every* arrangement: had everything prepared, kept the body in ice until just before leaving, then himself carried it and placed it on board. He did what he could in Savannah, and came out to the funeral. I could not think who the stranger could be; but I was more than ordinarily struck with the delicacy and kindness which he showed in relieving the family today. . . . Mrs. Walthour appreciates the captain's kindness most highly.

I have not heard any of the particulars of Mr. Walthour's illness and death excepting that he never recovered his speech, though he did consciousness, and would take his wife's hand and place it upon the paralyzed arm and make her understand he wished her to rub it. The family are deeply afflicted. . . . Dr. Howe and Aunt Howe will be here all this week and a part of next. I wish Mother and yourself could come up and see them. They are very anxious to see you. If you should come, do make your arrangements so that you can spend some time and recover from the fatigue of the long ride. . . . Robert has returned from Midway. He says all of the servants were there. The coffin was opened for them; their grief was great and very loud. Robert made a little address and prayed at the grave.

Our dear little baby is quite well again and gaining flesh. But her first great trouble commenced night before last. She fretted so much after me and woke so often during the night that we thought she would improve if she was weaned. After a night of frequent wakings Mr. Mallard determined "the baby must be weaned, and I will begin this night." Sure enough, he did, and has stuck to it manfully, singing "Happy Day" in a most doleful manner. It has the desired effect. Last night he had a pretty hard and long contest. The poor little thing called for Mama so disconsolately that I could hardly resist going to her. We have commenced, and it won't do to lose what we have gained. She is very fond of potatoes, and very often wakes up at midday and calls: "Tata tater!" She cannot understand why I should neglect her so much.

We were very glad to see Brother Joe. Dr. Howe is very anxious to see you, and says after he went to Columbia (the last visit he paid here) he reproached himself very much for not having remained a day or two longer and made an extra effort to see you. It is growing late, so I must bid you good night, dear Father. I will send this to Mr. Cay in the morning, and if he is going down I hope you will get this tomorrow. We are all quite well. Harriet has a little baby. I think it would weigh between five and six pounds, clothes and all. She seems perfectly healthy and has a fine appetite, so I suppose size will come in due time. Do give love to Aunt Susan and Cousins Lyman and Laura; also to all at Woodville. Love to Brother Joe and Uncle. Mr. Mallard unites with me in warmest love to dear Mother and yourself. Baby sends her kisses. You would be amused to hear her say *pantry* and take the key and try to open the door. Howdy for the servants.

Your ever attached daughter,
Mary S. Mallard.

Rev. C. C. Jones *to* Mr. Charles C. Jones, Jr.^g

Maybank, *Friday,* August 19th, 1859

My dear Son,

Through divine favor, all well. Enclosed are two communications (identical) for the papers, which Mother begs you will hand on for publication. There is a sly reflection upon your honorable companies in the city.

Mr. Walthour's death was a shock to our community, and is universally regretted. My old friend and schoolmate, though several years my senior. I truly feel his sudden departure. A great loss to his family, to the Baptist church of which he was a member, and to our county. Dr. and Mrs. Howe came down and met the body in Savannah and attended the funeral, conducted by Robert on Wednesday. Buried at Midway. We did not go. No notice; and so distant I suppose they did not think to send beyond Dorchester. We (Mother and I) prepare, D.V., to go up to Walthourville tomorrow to see our afflicted friends Dr. and Mrs. Howe and Mrs. Walthour and family, and remain over Sabbath. So warm I fear the ride.

What a vanity is all earthly wealth and distinction as a portion to the immortal soul! Verily "there is but one thing needful." I hope I may be prepared for my last and great change when it comes, for it is a fearful thing to die.

Mother and Brother and Uncle William unite in much love to dear Ruthie and yourself. We are happy at the prospect of having you with us. All well at Robert's.

Your affectionate father,
C. C. Jones.

Mrs. Mary Jones *to* Mr. Charles C. Jones, Jr.^g

Walthourville, *Monday,* August 22nd, 1859

My dear Son,

In our customary oriental style of travel we reached this village at nine o'clock Saturday night, having divided the journey by stopping at Montevideo, where we were detained by rain until near sunset. Your sister, Robert, and Mr. Axson were at meeting, so we made ourselves at home until their return. Our object in visiting the Sand Hills at this time was to see our very dear friends Dr. and Mrs. Howe, and to offer our sympathies to them and the recently bereaved family of Mr. Walthour.

The Sabbath was a day of precious privilege, and we enjoyed all the services. Dr. Howe preached one of the best sermons I ever listened to in the morning, and your father in the afternoon. The prayer meetings have been especially interesting. Mr. Axson's remarks this morning were very encouraging, and we can but hope that much good will be the result of these religious services. At Flemington there has been a remarkable interest and many hopeful conversions. We do trust that the divine blessing which has been so richly shed upon other portions of our country may now be granted unto us!

Today we received your letter telling us of your appointment for the 26th, and we most deeply regret, my dear son, that we shall not be present. We left your uncle at home with the intention of returning today or tomorrow, and your father and myself are not able to come back, for he is very feeble, and I have been quite unwell from the long ride. Your uncle said he would certainly come up, and your brother also.

I hope dear Ruthie and yourself are now coming out to remain with us the rest of the summer. We certainly understood from your letter before the last that you would do so, and have all felt so happy at the prospect. She must bring any work she may have to do, and I will assist her with it. And it will give us pleasure to have Charlie West make us a visit. I am sure he would enjoy himself with the young Kings, and a little change would do him good. Please write us *certainly by Thursday* when and where we shall send to meet you.

I did not know about the bank arrangements, and will enclose a check for the whole amount. Please get me a few gold dollars, and bring when you come. I did not care to have the glass unless it was exactly *like Joe's,* as it would not answer our purpose.

It is now late, my dear son. The rain prevented us from going to church tonight. Your father has retired, and I must follow, as we expect to leave early in the morning. Good night, dear Son and Daughter! With our united love to you both, and affectionate remembrance to all friends,

Ever your affectionate mother,
Mary Jones.

MR. CHARLES C. JONES, JR., *to* MRS. MARY JONES[t]

Savannah, *Wednesday,* August 24th, 1859

My dear Mother,

Your kind favor of the 22nd inst. has just been received. Ruth and myself had promised ourselves the pleasure of seeing you at Walthourville on Friday the 26th inst., hoping as you were already there that you might find it convenient to remain. It would be very fatiguing for you now, however, to return. We regret to know that you and dear Father are so unwell, and sincerely hope that you will both be soon restored to wonted health.

Charlie West will accompany us on Friday, and expects to return to the Island with Brother, who promised to be on the Sand Hills at that time. We would most gladly ourselves be with you on the Island were a visit in our power. This, however, being Ruth's first summer in Savannah, it becomes us to be very careful and not subject her to an attack of fever by changes of air. Besides, Judge Jackson is now absent from the city, and should I leave, our office would be unrepresented. Unless there be a recurrence of the yellow fever, I expect we are fixtures here for the fall.

The glass has gone out, with some articles forwarded to Father's address by King & Waring. The price was a trifle above that named, but the panes themselves you will, I think, find exactly what you wish. The dividend I will collect and deposit to Father's credit in the Bank State of Georgia, deducting $23.60—$3.60 to cover cost of glass, and $20.00 to be sent in change as requested. This I will hand to Brother at Walthourville.

We were this morning and all last night deluged with rain, our yard becoming so overflowed that the water could not be kept out of the entry, kitchen, and one of the servants' rooms downstairs. By this mail I send the city papers of yesterday containing communications in reference to the action of the Liberty Independent Troop in reference to the Mount Vernon cause. Hope that our volunteer associations here will follow the example. My dear Ruth, who is quite well, unites with me in warmest love to self, dear Father, Brother, and Uncle. As ever,

Your affectionate son,
Charles C. Jones, Jr.

REV. C. C. JONES *to* MR. CHARLES C. JONES, JR.ᵍ

Maybank, *Friday,* August 26th, 1859

My dear Son,

Your favor was received last evening, and I send up a buggy for our young friend Charles West, Jr.—the only arrangement I could make. Please request him in returning tomorrow to bring the mail for all on the Island—Rev. D. L. Buttolph and family, Mrs. King, Dr. Joseph Jones and ourselves—and to bring *whatever bundles,* etc., which may come for us by the stage.

It was impossible for us to return to Walthourville this week, much as we desired to do so, and then go to Midway on Sabbath to Communion. Our faithful Omar and Sultan could not stand it. Nor could we remain for the week while up there. Your brother was obliged to be in readiness for the proofs of his book. We are now all in addition confined at home by the sickness of your Cousin Laura and her little boy. We found them quite sick when we got down (climate fever), and your brother has been in constant attendance twice a day; and other cases in the same family among the servants on hand. He greatly regrets his disappointment at not being with you this evening.

It seems impossible for him to secure any rest. The first part of the season was spent in the closest application day and almost night, and he is sent for to the sick constantly. And now he has the opening address of his college to prepare, and but a few weeks to prepare it in. He has done practice enough this summer to net him a handsome sum, and all for the honor and love of it. He is thin, and I feel anxious that he should have some uninterrupted time before he goes back to Augusta.

While it would have afforded us great pleasure to have received a visit from Ruthie and yourself, yet I think your decision in the matter is judicious. It is Ruthie's first summer below, and it is best to be careful; and with due care I trust through divine favor you will both enjoy a healthy season. The health of the Southern seaboard as far as New Orleans has been so far remarkably fine.

Your brother has written you a note, and so speaks for himself. Mother unites in much love to our dear Ruthie and yourself; and you can convey our love to her in a kiss if you like. Love to your dear sister and Robert, and a kiss for Little Daughter. Mother sends some knickknacks in the buggy for Daughter. Your uncle has been unwell with one of his constitutional attacks, but is better and I presume well, though I have not seen him yet this morning.

Your ever affectionate father,
C. C. Jones.

P.S. If you can find time, I would be very glad if you would call and see Mrs. Walthour in her affliction. She would esteem it highly, and it would be a gratifying attention for the sake of my old friend and schoolmate, whose death I greatly lament.

Mrs. Mary Jones *to* Mr. Charles C. Jones, Jr.[5]

Maybank, Tuesday, August 30th, 1859

My dear Son,

Thanks for the twenty dollars sent by Charlie West, who arrived in good time and quite well. It was a sore disappointment to us all that we could not hear your address, of which your sister writes most flatteringly. Sorry your audience was so small; various circumstances conspired to make it such.

Our God, wise and merciful, orders all things well. Had your brother, who was detained by sickness at the Point, been absent, *Clarence King,* so far as we can see, must certainly have died. He was taken extremely ill, and received from your brother the most energetic treatment. He has not left him, excepting to ride over and change his clothes and dine with us yesterday, for three days and nights. I could not pretend to describe the case, saying only that the mechanical difficulty is removed. But he is still in a critical situation. Yesterday morning your brother left him for a short time to see the sick at the Point; he was sent for, and found him speechless and apparently dying. He made use of powerful stimulants, internally and externally, which were blessed to his restoration. Joe has just come—whilst we are at breakfast—and says Clarence had a good night, slept well, and is decidedly better. Hopes with the divine blessing and close attention that he will recover. All are better at the Point—Laura and Jimmie and the sick servants.

Your brother has recently had a flattering invitation from a prominent gentleman connected with the establishment of a university in Missouri to allow him to place his name for the occupancy of the chair of physical sciences. The *professorship* has been recently endowed with twenty or thirty thousand dollars by Mr. Charless' daughter as a tribute to the memory of her father, who was much interested in the institution. She was the young lady who interested your father and Uncle John when they visited St. Louis, Missouri, in 1851. And her father was killed last spring by a young man whom he had largely befriended. He was one of the most influential, wealthy, and excellent men in that great city.

The oilcloth and boxes from King & Waring have all come safe to hand. I write in haste by John, who is just leaving. Our trees bore a few quinces, and I send dear Ruth and yourself a few preserved for your tea this evening or tomorrow. Eat them and think of home. Charlie West has gone to Woodville this morning; John bears a letter from him to his father. Remember us to the doctor and Cousin Eliza. Your father, brother, and uncle unite with me in much love to Ruth and yourself.

Your affectionate mother,
Mary Jones.

Father says the *call* is to one of the finest institutions in the West. The gentleman who wrote said they had heard of him during the meeting of the Medical Association of the Union, and presumed he was the son of Rev. C. C. J., D.D.

Mr. Charles C. Jones, Jr., *to* Mrs. Mary Jones[t]
Savannah, *Friday,* September 2nd, 1859
My dear Mother,

Many thanks for your kind favor of the 30th ult. It was duly received at the hands of John, a faithful and good servant, who came burdened with ducks, chickens, and eggs for Ruth, and also brought your delightful remembrance, for which she desires me to present her sincere thanks.

Your note was the first intimation we had received of the severe illness of Clarence. We had heard that he was indisposed, but supposed that the attack was simply the result of imprudence and not of a serious character. It gives us great pleasure to know that he is so much relieved, and our hope is that he soon will be entirely restored.

The kind, valuable, and unremitted attentions of the Doctor will be long and gratefully remembered. Am happy to know that he has been recently flattered by so honorable an application as that coming from St. Louis. Does he contemplate an acceptance? If so, what does his fair Dulcinea say to a removal from her home circle in Augusta?

You would have been amused with the personal appearance of the subscriber during the past week. A cold in the face, an entire row of aching teeth, and a countenance so swollen that the left eye was at one time quite closed and the point of my immense nose barely discernible! Everyone on the street, as I passed along, seemed to regard me with a suspicious air, as some poor fellow who had been engaged in an Irish shindy and "come out second best," as the saying is. As it was, I had to bear a stiff upper lip and fall back upon my known reputation. I verily believe that Hogarth would not have begrudged a ten-pound note for one good squint at my phiz. At present, however, my appearance is much more tolerable. The pain has in a measure subsided, and I am chiefly disturbed by the prospect of a general rising and bursting near the right nose, midway between mouth and eye. Speaking in the courtroom this morning did my physical feelings no good.

Remember me to Charlie West. Tell him to write me and let me know what progress he is making in shooting, fishing, swimming, and Latin. All friends well. Our city, through a kind Providence, continues in the enjoyment of an unusual degree of health. Ruth, who is quite well, unites with me in warmest love to self, dear Mother, Father, Brother, Uncle, Charlie, and in kind remembrances to all relatives and friends on the Island. As ever,

Your affectionate son,
Charles C. Jones, Jr.

Did you observe the beautiful appearance of the aurora borealis on Sunday night and also on last night?

REV. C. C. JONES *to* REV. *and* MRS. R. Q. MALLARD[t]

Maybank, Friday Evening, September 2nd, 1859

My dear Son and Daughter,

A chance by Mr. Cay tomorrow morning: embraced. First, *sickness:* your Cousin Laura and her little son have had an attack of climate fever. Clarence King extremely ill: obstruction. Physician: Dr. Joseph Jones. Second, *result:* all cured and well. Third, *gratitude* to our Heavenly Father for these recoveries, and for the general health we are all now permitted to enjoy, and for unnumbered mercies temporal and spiritual.

Fourth, *Communion at Midway last Sabbath:* eleven whites, two blacks on profession. Rev. Donald Fraser preached a good sermon—best I think I ever heard from him. He and Rev. R. Q. Way at the table. Large congregation white and black. Rev. C. C. Jones conducted prayer meeting in the afternoon. A day of much interest in the old church. Your mother and brother not present: Mother too unwell on that day to take the long ride; Brother could not leave Clarence. Regretted by both.

Fifth, *occupation: Mother:* busy getting the Doctor ready for October and happiness. To mark tomorrow some hundred and fifty pieces of all sorts and kinds. In her spare moments copying a piece for me for *The Southern Review.* And keeps the whole house in activity and order. *Brother:* preparing his address for opening of his college in Augusta. Hope it may be something *extra.* Making entomological collections—Little Harry and Ebenezer his industrious "bug-catchers," as they style themselves. And mail days writing Carrie. *Uncle:* a smoke after breakfast, reading all day, conversation, and a visit to his plantation at stated times. *Charlie West:* gunning, fishing, feeding his pet young raccoon, studying languages, and reading. *Father:* Hebrew in morning, Greek at night, *History* all the day, reading, a ride after breakfast and a sort of walk in evening, and much time lost one way and another, and little accomplished. Bedtime: a rubbing, and closed with shocks from electrical battery. And we all sleep at night. *Servants:* everyone at some regular business, and get along on the whole pretty fair. . . .

Sunday night and last night the most brilliant auroras I ever saw in these latitudes. Did you see them? Hope you did.

Sorry your brother had so poor an audience: what I anticipated. Mother, Brother, and Uncle all unite in love to you both, and many kisses for our dear Little Daughter. All well at Dorchester Wednesday. Write soon.

From your ever affectionate father,
C. C. Jones.

Your brother's skill in treating Clarence's case *uncommon.* Will tell you of it when we meet, D.V.

Mrs. Mary S. Mallard *to* Rev. *and* Mrs. C. C. Jones[t]

Walthourville, Monday, September 5th, 1859

My dear Father and Mother,

Mr. Mallard thinks of going to Dorchester this afternoon, so I will embrace the opportunity and send the bonnet Kitty made for you, dear Mother. I think you will be very much pleased with it.

We were very glad to receive your letter on Saturday, dear Father. It was *multum in parvo.* I hope Clarence will continue to improve. I suppose Charlie West gave you a doleful account of the audience Brother Charlie had. Had his lecture been delivered a little earlier or later, he would have had a fine attendance. There were several circumstances that hindered many families from coming out. There were six families who did not come on account of Mr. Walthour's death, and several others remained at home on their children's account: they were so deeply impressed that they felt but little interest in any other subject. So you see, we can readily account for the absence of at least ten families. Add to these our absentees, and you will see there were not many to come. I was very sorry it should so have happened, for the lecture was one of more than ordinary interest. And then Brother Charlie delivered it so handsomely. . . .

We are all quite well; Baby a little fretful from teething, but full of life. She told me this morning: "Mama—Papa—bed—heeping" (sleeping). She is beginning to connect words very well. This morning she would put her greasy hands on the slab, and I slapped them whenever she put them there. She went to her father holding up her little hand: "Mama knock." Do give love to Aunt Susan, Cousin Laura, and Cousin Lyman; also to all at Woodville. Mr. Mallard unites with me in much love to Uncle, Brother Joe, and yourselves, dear Father and Mother. Love to Charlie West.

Your affectionate child,
Mary S. Mallard.

Mrs. Mary Jones *to* Mr. Charles C. Jones, Jr.^g

Maybank, *Thursday,* September 15th, 1859

My dear Son,

We have all spent the day very pleasantly at the Point—your brother's farewell visit. He begins to pack up tomorrow, and asks me to say to you that, Providence permitting, he hopes to pass next Thursday night with you and leave in the midday train on the following day, which will be Friday the 23rd. He will then tell you all his future arrangements. He will take Phillis and her family up with him.

Today's mail brought me your note enclosed in your father's letter, and I hasten to assure you, my dear son and daughter, that as you desire it, if God spares my life and health, I will certainly be with you in November, and trust I may be enabled to render to one whom I tenderly love the sympathy and kindness which should flow from a mother's heart and hand in such an hour of trial.

We received your letter last week. . . . We shall feel very sadly when our dear son leaves us. He has devoted himself to your father, and I think the results are evident in his decided improvement. It is late, and I must now close, with our united love to dear Ruth and yourself and all friends. Charlie is quite well. The servants send howdies, especially Sue.

Ever your affectionate mother,
Mary Jones.

Mr. Charles C. Jones, Jr., *to* Mrs. Mary Jones^t

Savannah, *Saturday,* September 17th, 1859

My dear Mother,

Your very kind letter of the 15th inst. has just been received, and Ruth and myself are a thousand times obliged to you for your tender expressions of such affection as a parent alone can know, feel, and express, and also for the promised compliance with our request. Father, of course, will come also, unless his engagements otherwise prevent. We will use every exertion to render your sojourn with us agreeable and comfortable.

Miss Lizzie Bowen comes this evening to remain some time with us. She is without a home, and divides her time among her friends. Mrs. Bowen has returned from the North. Old Major Bowen, I understand, went on to Philadelphia and induced if not compelled a return. He is a drunken vagabond, and the only wonder is that he is permitted to live—an annoyance to his family and a miserable incubus upon society.

Tell the Doctor that we will be happy to welcome him and his on Thursday next, and hope that he may be prevailed upon to protract his short stay in Savannah beyond the time specified. All friends well. . . . I am, as ever,

Your affectionate son,
Charles C. Jones, Jr.

Mr. Charles C. Jones, Jr., *to* Rev. C. C. Jones[g]
Savannah, *Wednesday,* September 21st, 1859

John has called for a ticket to pass him to Maybank tomorrow, and I improve the moment, my dear father, to assure you of our continued health and to send the warmest love of dear Ruth and myself.

Sam will hand you a little volume by the author of *Two Years Before the Mast,* etc., which, giving as it does some interesting views of Cuba, may give you pleasant occupation for an after-dinner hour.

All friends well. We look for the Doctor tomorrow afternoon. With best love from Ruth and self to dear Mother, self, Uncle, and kind regards to all friends, I am, as ever,

Your affectionate son,
Charles C. Jones, Jr.

Mr. Charles C. Jones, Jr., *to* Rev. *and* Mrs. C. C. Jones[g]
Savannah, *Thursday,* September 22nd, 1859

My dear Father and Mother,

We are anxiously expecting the arrival of the Doctor this evening. Within a few moments the whistle of the train will be heard, and by the time I reach the house I presume and hope he will be there. He always, however, gives us the go-by, tarrying at best only a half day or so.

By this mail I send for your perusal Mr. Everett's oration on the occasion of the inauguration of the Webster statue at Boston, as reported in the *Herald* of today. You will find it upon the last page. May I ask the favor of you to preserve it, and after a perusal please return by mail or other favorable opportunity. Mr. Everett is, I presume, the most accomplished occasional orator of his age.

The city continues, through a kind Providence, in the enjoyment of a remarkable degree of health. In the morning and evening air one can already denote the approach of fall weather. . . . All friends well. The summer birds are not yet returning from their Northern migrations. . . . My dear Ruth, who is quite well, unites with me in warmest love to you both, my dear parents, and to Uncle William, and in kind regards to all relatives and friends on the Island. As ever,

Your affectionate son,
Charles C. Jones, Jr.

Dr. Joseph Jones *to* Mrs. Mary Jones[t]
Augusta, *Saturday,* September 24th, 1859

My dear Mother,

Through a kind Providence I have arrived in Augusta with my servants safely, and find all friends well.

In Savannah Brother and Sister Ruthie were looking remarkably well. I do not know that I have ever seen Brother in better health and spirits. He was very kind, and assisted me greatly in my business arrangements. Yesterday morning Willie King took breakfast with us; he is looking a little thin, but says that he is in good health. After breakfast I transacted my business on horseback, and was thus enabled to have all my articles delivered before the 12 M. train left.

I have just received a letter from Dr. Austin Flint of New York, requesting me to allow him to present my name as a candidate for the chair of physiology and chemistry in a summer school of medicine to be started in Brooklyn. Dr. Flint is one of the most celebrated American medical writers and teachers, and is a professor in the New Orleans School of Medicine, and has upon two occasions received the first prize of the American Medical Association. . . . Dr. Flint says: "As to remuneration, it is of course impossible to give any definite idea of what the ticket fees will afford, inasmuch as the school is an experiment as yet untried. It would not, however, be proper to ask you to come from such a distance without some guaranty as to the amount of compensation. If you are favorably disposed, will you name a sum which you would like to have guarantied to you? The friends of the enterprise are willing to assume a moderate pecuniary responsibility. Should you take a place in this school, it would not interfere with your present relations in Augusta. Perhaps it would be useful, and at all events it would be agreeable, to form associations in this part of the world." You see from this, my dear mother, that the friends of the enterprise are liberal.

As far as I have considered the call, I am decided *not* to go—for several reasons. First, it is a summer school, and I am opposed to them on the ground that they shorten the term of medical education. As, however, Dr. Flint does not state the requirements of the school for graduation, it may not thus injure the profession. Second, two courses of lectures during the year would, unless greatly remunerative, be too much labor. Third, the distance is so great that it would give an unsettled condition to my life and studies. Fourth, the enterprise is problematical, and might prejudice me in the eyes of older and more staunch institutions, as the University of Pennsylvania. I think, however, that I will before returning an answer consult Dr. Samuel Jackson of Philadelphia and my colleagues in the Medical College of Georgia. I would be very much obliged to you, my dear mother and father, for your advice. The call comes from such a high professional source that it demands careful consideration.

Carrie says that she is afraid that it would give me too much hard work. Our wedding will probably take place on the 25th of October. We will put it off to as near the beginning of the session as possible. . . . With warmest love to yourself, Father, and Uncle William, I remain

Your affectionate son,
Joseph Jones.

Rev. C. C. Jones *to* Mr. Charles C. Jones, Jr.^g

Maybank, *Saturday,* September 24th, 1859

My dear Son,

We embrace the opportunity of a line by the bishop of Midway, who pays your city a visit next week, D.V. He will see and communicate to you all the local news of Bermuda Island and St. John's Parish. And there is some news of interest.

Your brother's departure caused a fall in our social atmosphere of many degrees. His summer—and the last, I suppose, he will ever spend with us—has been pleasant to his parents and to all his friends. He has been closely occupied the whole time, and the last day was about the only leisure day he had. I believe professionally he has been the means of saving the lives of some three people, all *in extremis,* in our neighborhood.

We are much obliged to you for the treat of Dana's *To Cuba and Back.* I read nine chapters to your mother last evening. His compliments to Captain Bulloch are delicate, handsome, and just, and am glad our friend is doing so well in the world. Dana describes finely; he paints. And one feels that he has taken a voyage to Cuba and seen the island himself. His *Two Years Before the Mast* is a capital work of the kind. His father was a man of taste and a poet, and has left his worthy representative behind him, who I think bears his name also.

What a religion for the masses is popery! All the work going on on Sunday: churches closed at 10 A.M., bishop dining with a select party, and the hours consecrated to promiscuous conversation and pleasurable indulgence! It is a religion that takes away the key of both worldly and heavenly knowledge from the people, rules them by superstition and brute force, sanctifies them in sin, and gives them rigorous lords temporal and lords spiritual, and no redemption save by revolution. And what an eternity lies before all!

Enclosed is the advertisement for *dyeing and staining wood,* which Mother requests you to show to Messrs. Solomons & Company, druggists. They told her some time ago they should like to have it, and would get the article. *Keep the advertisement* when they have used it, and let your mother know if they have the article or will get it.

Mother will be obliged to you to send her "that piece of *long lawn*" by Mr. Buttolph. And please send me by the same a red and a blue of the newfangled Faber pencils from Cooper's, if to be had separately. I understand they are sold in boxes.

Weather and temperature as near perfection as we can conceive. A time of general health. The Lord's mercies are unbounded to us. May He grant us hearts of gratitude and obedience! . . . Our united love to our dear daughter. Glad you both continue so well.

Your ever affectionate father,
C. C. Jones.

P.S. Mother is very busy today cutting out some very pretty *little* work, after a hard summer's work for the Doctor. One generation goeth and another cometh.

Mrs. Mary Jones *to* Mr. Charles C. Jones, Jr.ᵍ

Maybank, *Monday,* September 26th, 1859

My dear Son,

As I was seating myself for the usual employments of the day I found upon my worktable the following, which your father says is his epigram for Monday morning. And as I was going to send you a line by John, he permits me to copy it:

> Two sorts of men must surely come to naught,
> And soon in life are justly sold and bought.
> One is known: the *favored man of leisure;*
> The other, the *happy man of pleasure.*

I will only add that I do not think he or his sons will be found in either category.

By the last mail I received a long letter from our valued friend Miss Clay. She says: "Tell Charles if he is with you there is another trespass on our land, and I *must* prosecute this time." Says she was about writing you to move in the cases in your hands; presume you will understand all about it when she does. Said she had just had a *law talk* with Judge Jackson previous to a *war talk* with someone else.

This morning we received your affectionate letter, and rejoice to know that dear Ruth and yourself continue well. We are much obliged to you for sending Mr. Everett's oration, and will preserve and return the papers.

Also one from your Uncle Henry. . . . Our venerable aunt was very feeble when he wrote: frequent fever and troublesome cough. The death of Mrs. Stevens, her early friend and companion, will, I doubt not, be keenly felt by her.

But few remain of those whom we consider *aged.* I begin to realize that your father and myself will soon be in the front ranks, pressing onward to the grave! Last Saturday was my birthday, and I have numbered my half century! The past has nothing to rest in; the future, only a trembling hope through the merits and righteousness of a Divine Redeemer.

Our friends on the Island are all quite well at this time. Charlie West has been spending the past week at Woodville, and looks very hearty. Julia's boys are excellent children.

As the captain of the *William Totten* was just loading for Savannah, I hastened Gilbert over with a bag of red potatoes for you, sending also the money for the freight. But Captain Charlie returns it, saying that "you are too good a friend to him for him to think of charging you." And he promises to send them safely as soon as he arrives. Tell dear Ruthie to make Adeline *roast* them in *hot ashes;* they are so much better than cooked in any other way. I hope the Doctor remembered to give the pomegranates to her.

Father and Uncle unite with me in best love to Ruth and yourself. The servants all desire to be remembered. Howdies for your servants. Kind remembrances to all friends.

Ever your affectionate mother,
Mary Jones.

MR. CHARLES C. JONES, JR., *to* REV. C. C. JONES[g]
Savannah, *Tuesday,* September 27th, 1859

My dear Father,

We were last evening favored with your kind letter of the 24th inst. Not being myself at home last night when Mr. Buttolph called, I lost the pleasure of his visit. He promised Ruth, however, to dine with us today. The "long lawn" will be committed to his charge. The pencils also which you desired I will trouble him to carry to you from me.

In the matter of the preparations for staining wood, I called upon Messrs. A. A. Solomons & Company, but they have not the article. They can and will, however, procure it at any moment from the North. One of the co-partners is now in the city of New York, and will give his personal attention to any order with which he or they may be entrusted. Enclosed please find advertisement returned as requested.

I am happy to know that Dana's little book gave Mother and yourself so much pleasure. He is the only abolitionist for whom I ever entertained any profound respect. While in Cambridge I frequently saw him and often had occasion to admire him, not only as a lawyer and a scholar but also as a gentleman and a man of high-toned feeling and honor. His conduct during the Burns trial, and upon the occasion of the impeachment of Judge Loring, I will ever have cause to remember. I read his "vacation trip" with much interest.

We are now busy with our local elections, and no little feeling is enlisted. The result you will know in a few days. Mr. Buttolph will give you all the items of interest. Do thank dear Mother sincerely for her kind and tender remembrance of Ruth. With warmest love from us both, I am, as ever,

Your affectionate son,
Charles C. Jones, Jr.

MR. CHARLES C. JONES, JR., *to* MRS. MARY JONES[t]
Savannah, *Thursday,* September 29th, 1859

My dear Mother,

We were last evening favored with yours of the 26th inst., and are truly happy to know that all at home are well. Father's epigram is excellent.

You have our best wishes on the recurrence of your birthday, with many fervent hopes for its oft-repeated and happy returns. Fifty years: a long period if we look forward to its coming, but short—very short—when it has actually passed.

The red potatoes will be a great treat, and I hope that my generous friend Captain Charlie will not tarry too long in Romney Marsh. The pomegranates were duly received, and were highly prized by Ruth. They were the finest she had ever seen.

Am expecting Judge Jackson next week; he has had a regular summer vacation.

Local politics are running quite high for a small town. You will observe by the papers the bad faith with which Gordon has acted towards Colonel Lawton. Matters are just at this moment all at seas. I have refused to take any part as a *candidate* or *otherwise,* except in a general way, and in such manner and to such degree as every citizen should interest himself for his friends and the good of the community.

Ruth is quite well, and unites with me in warmest love to self, dear Mother, dear Father, and Uncle. Kind regards to all relatives and friends on the Island. As ever,

Your affectionate son,
Charles C. Jones, Jr.

REV. C. C. JONES *to* MR. CHARLES C. JONES, JR.[g]

Maybank, *Monday,* October 3rd, 1859

My dear Son,

Thank you for your two last favors and the papers sent. All very interesting. Dana's paragraph about the Jesuits is a real piece of Yankee trimming and indifference to truth! He knows better.

Mr. Ward is in Peking, I hope. Admiral Love (or Hope—which is it?) acted in great rashness and ill judgment, and has met a fearful retribution, and complicated affairs with the English and French and Chinese more than ever, and opened the gates of war and death! Captain Tattnall went a little too far for a neutral: he helped in the battle. His sympathy and visit as a friend to the wounded admiral was noble. If Mr. Ward has gone to Peking (unless Captain Tattnall has knocked the matter up), it will clearly demonstrate the good faith of the Chinese and the unwarrantable and offensive steps of the British admiral.

Your brother has received another and most flattering and honorable call to a lectureship in a newly projected summer medical school in Brooklyn, New York. Not to interfere with his present position; he to retain both. He has, as far as advised, in his own judgment come pretty much to the conclusion not to accept; and as far as I see into the matter, I approve the decision. It is not settled definitely yet. I enclose his note about it, which you can read and return to us.

You have acted perfectly right in the recent political troubles in Savannah, and just what I should have anticipated from your good judgment and prudence. If you desire *place,* you can afford to wait for it. My friend Colonel Lawton has my best wishes for his election, and especially as I know him to be a determined opponent morally and politically of the infamous and abominable slave trade.

An irritative fever (pulse 120 all day) has confined me at home today, and consequently have not gone to the polls. Poor showing for state and national legislature! Fever induced from preaching at Dorchester yesterday and the ride to and from there for two days and the consequent confinement in attendance on meetings. Mr. Buttolph had two days' preaching, most of which was done by Rev. Donald Fraser, now of Jacksonville, Florida. He has been spending the summer in the county, and has been abundant in labors and blessed in his preaching; and the people of Midway congregation owe him much. The religious interest in the county continues. The meeting at Dorchester was attended by all the regular congregation there with much attention. There were two interesting cases at the inquiry meeting Sunday morning. Mr. Buttolph has another inquiry meeting on Wednesday afternoon and preaching at night. When, my son, will you seek the Lord? *Why are you not a Christian?*

Mother sends much love to your dear wife and yourself along with myself. All well, through God's great mercy.

Your ever affectionate father,
C. C. Jones.

Mr. Charles C. Jones, Jr., *to* Rev. C. C. Jones[g]

Savannah, *Thursday,* October 6th, 1859

My dear Father,

I am this morning favored with your interesting and kind letter of the 3rd inst. with enclosure as stated. We sincerely regret to hear of your indisposition, and hope that rest and quiet have relieved you from the irritative fever. The religious condition of Liberty County at present is deeply interesting, and I trust nothing will interrupt the free and complete operation of the blessed influences of the Holy Spirit.

Brother's letter I have read with pleasure and pride. The question presented, I take it, can best be determined by himself. But if he has any reasonable expectation of position in the medical school in Philadelphia it seems to be the best policy to avoid countenancing any policy which may be in itself problematical or questionable. . . . Dr. Jackson's advice in the premises I should deem very valuable. Whatever his determination may be, I sincerely trust that everything will eventuate in his every good.

We are in the midst of an exciting canvass. The main question at issue is: Shall law and order prevail in our community? The present administration of the city government is obnoxious to every good citizen whose eyes are not blinded by party professions and personal or friendly interests. You see at once, however, that we have to oppose officeholders, not a few of them men devoid of principle. The entire patronage of the city is against us. But we have our "quarrel just," and it is a mere matter of time, for truth is mighty and will prevail. We may be defeated in the present conflict, but a day will come when men will see the error of their ways, when the violators of public law and order will be subjected to a merited rebuke and condemnation. In questions of right there is always a conservative element in every community which may safely be depended upon.

Under the present administration the Sunday ordinance has become almost a dead letter; the police is unsustained in executing the internal regulations affecting public peace and order. They may report offenders, but the cases are not unfrequently, even after they are placed upon the mayor's docket, *never called*. The rum shops are filled with Negroes drinking at all hours of the day and night. Gambling is rampant. In fine, the present condition of the city is anything but desirable. Our object, then, is to inaugurate if possible a new and a more auspicious era. We wish an effective mayor: a man of honor, principle, determination; not a man of straw, a nose of wax. We wish a change of city officers, and desire to place in positions of responsibility and emolument men who will dignify the office and discharge the duties appertaining thereto with candor and honesty. Monday will determine the matter. Colonel Lawton desires his sincere acknowledgments for your sympathies in his favor.

I think with you that Captain Tattnall did violate the strict rules of neutrality in towing the British vessels into action; but although an error, it was a generous error. The Chinese have certainly treated us with marked favor, and every effort should be made to perpetuate and not interrupt the friendly relations now existing. The English and French have acted rashly and imprudently, and dearly have they atoned for their indiscretion. "Never presume upon the weakness or the inferiority of your adversary" is a rule that should obtain as well in war as in debate.

My dear Ruth is quite well, and unites in warmest love to you both, my dear parents. All friends well. Our city in the enjoyment of a remarkable degree of health, for which we owe many thanks to a kind Providence. As ever,

Your affectionate son,
Charles C. Jones, Jr.

Our love to Uncle William if he is still with you, and to all friends on the Island. Howdy for the servants.

MR. CHARLES C. JONES, JR., *to* REV. *and* MRS. C. C. JONES[g]
Savannah, *Tuesday,* October 11th, 1859
My dear Mother and Father,

You see by the papers that notwithstanding all my protestations I was finally obliged to dabble personally in the local politics of the city. We met the enemy yesterday and they are ours. It was a contest of law and order, honesty and respectability against misrule. The principle involved was a good one, and worth contending for, and we are more than pleased with the result. The next duty is to discharge the duties devolved upon us with impartiality and fidelity. You will see that Wallace Cumming and myself led the ticket.

Today everything is quiet—the quiet that follows the storm. My dear Ruth is quite well, and unites in warmest love to you both, my dear parents. When do you go to Augusta? As ever,

Your affectionate son,
Charles C. Jones, Jr.

Rev. C. C. Jones *to* Mr. Charles C. Jones, Jr.ᵍ
Maybank, *Saturday,* October 15th, 1859

My dear Son,

I embrace the opportunity by our young friend C. N. West to acknowledge your last favors; to congratulate you on your new dignity; to wish you success in the faithful and honorable discharge of its duties; to caution you against the pleasant taste of popular favor; to advise you of the marriage of your brother on the 26th inst., God willing; to answer your question, that we hope to be in Savannah by the cars Monday the 24th; to ask your company with us on Tuesday the 25th by the midday train to Augusta; to inform you of the good health of all around us; and to express to dear Ruthie and yourself the united love of your affectionate mother and

Your affectionate father,
C. C. Jones.

Rev. C. C. Jones *to* Mr. Charles C. Jones, Jr.ᵍ
Maybank, *Wednesday,* October 19th, 1859

My dear Son,

Yours of 17th came last evening, and we were happy to hear from you. All well. We have never seen the poll for aldermen. Friend Sneed ought to record all such matters, if for no other end than that his paper might be a faithful chronicle of events. And one of the annually great events in a city is its change of dynasty. Integrity, impartiality, and independence of popular fear or favor are the virtues of a good alderman. The office is one of high honor and of real and extensive responsibility. . . .

Am glad to know you will go, D.V., to your brother's wedding. Your sister, Robert, Mother, and myself are all from these regions who are anticipating the pleasure. Your Uncle John writes he cannot go; and Aunt Eliza's health is at present so feeble that Cousin Mary says she cannot go. The match is purely a love match on his part, I am sure, and believe it is equally so on the other side. And from all I can learn, Carrie will take a great interest in his pursuits and pride in his advancement, and will exert herself to render his home happy. And I am glad to learn also that she is both industrious and economical and fond of reading, which in my experience are invaluable traits in a wife.

Your own dear mother is a model wife in all these and many other particulars too numerous for me to mention. Her industry, her economy, her prudence, her foresight, her resolution, her intelligence are uncommon. She has done her husband good all the days of his life, and has never stood in the way of his advancement, but has taken the liveliest interest in his office and duties, and made sacrifices for it, and kept up her mental improvement, and been at home in all circles in which she has moved and in all the company we have so numerously entertained. And how she manages her household, and how she discharges her duties therein, and above all what a mother in all respects she has been to her children, they best know. And so she continues to be and will ever be. And so you can well understand how my esteem and admiration and affection for her continues and grows.

And now, upon the ground that the world is getting better, my hope is that my *three daughters*—Daughter, Ruthie, and Carrie (I take them in the order of their marriage)—will even surpass their mother in all her excellencies, and that my *three sons* will far surpass their father in their character as husbands. And I will frankly acknowledge that it will not be difficult for my sons to do so. Of one thing I am certain: your parents have the strongest affection for you all, and know no difference between you, and stand ready to aid you at all times, and constantly remember you before God, and desire that your three families may always be united in closest intimacy and affection, and that you may always prove generous and true friends to each other under all circumstances. We render special thanks to our Heavenly Father for His great goodness and mercy in sparing all our lives, and in permitting us to see you all grown and respectably and successfully settled in life. May He in continuation of His mercy be your God and Saviour, and of all yours, and unite us an unbroken family before His throne in the Heavenly Kingdom!

This is our last day of a summer of great mercy at Maybank. Servants and movables all left this morning for Montevideo. We spend the night at Maxwell, taking tea at Woodville, and go up in the morning, D.V. . . . Our united love to Ruthie and yourself.

Your ever affectionate father,
C. C. Jones.

Montevideo, Friday Morning, October 21st. All well! Fill up the blank in the check with the amount you deposited of Mother's money in the Savannah bank and draw it out and have it ready for her Monday, D.V. Think Brother Buttolph will go to the wedding.

XVI

Montevideo, *Monday,* November 7th, 1859

My dear Son,

Your three last favors have been received. We will try and reduce the note to nothing if possible at its next maturity; and it was thoughtful in you to renew for ninety days and give time to get something to market. Cato has in about thirty-seven bales, and estimates the crop here, if no loss in the field occurs from storms and rain, at fifty. Andrew will make between ten and twelve; so through a kind Providence I hope we may be able to pay up all our accounts. . . .

We are glad to hear from you so frequently. Do not fail to write Mother in time. The Lord be with and bless you both! Read the Psalms I read for you on your birthday morning—the 127th and 128th. To have the true comfort of them you must be "one that feareth the Lord, and that walketh in His ways."

The Harpers Ferry affair proves to be more serious than at first it appeared to be—not in reference to the Negro population, for that had nothing to do with it; but in reference to the hostility of large numbers of men of all classes in the free states to the slaveholding states, even unto blood, and their readiness to aid and abet such attempts with counsels and money, and to employ reckless agents to carry them out. There is a covert, cowardly, assassin-like heart in these men. Why do they not arm and come to the field in open day? From the tone of the abolition press in the free states, both secular and religious, there is great sympathy for the prisoners at Harpers Ferry. Some go so far as to justify the act, and only condemn the time and manner of it! The whole abolition crusade which has been preached for thirty years *ends in the sword*. The volunteering of counsel for the prisoners from the free states is another proof of sympathy in their crime, and an insult to the justice of the South.

Some of the papers friendly to the South hope that the South will be forbearing and magnanimous! Against the miserable lives of these men who have plotted arson, robbery, murder, and treason over a vast portion of our country, who may weigh millions of property, millions of lives, the virtue, the order, the peace and happiness of our people, the majesty of the laws, the sacredness of religion, our Constitution and our Union? There is no place left for forbearance—no ground for compromises. The magnanimity of the South must not be exercised towards public criminals of the deepest dye, but towards herself in all her greatest and best interests, and towards our common country. Such sparks as these, struck to produce a universal conflagration, should be stamped out immediately. Such enemies should be met and overwhelmed without quarter in a moment. A decision of this sort is demanded by our circumstances, and brings the free and the slave states to a perfect understanding on the whole subject.

These are my sentiments, and I believe they are the sentiments of every intelligent and truehearted citizen in the Southern states. And I am sure they will not only be entertained but acted upon whenever there may be occasion for it. If the conservative and loyal men of the free states, who we believe do now possess the power, are willing and ready to rule down this spirit of treasonable and violent aggression upon an unoffending and invaluable section of our country, we shall be most happy to see them do it. But if not, then let them know that the fortunes of the American republic are embarked in one vessel, and neither stem nor stern shall be broken up without damage and loss of the whole; and that they, secure as they may esteem themselves to be, will surely, and to their heart's content, come in for a full draught of the cup of political ruin!

Mother unites in love to Ruthie and yourself, and begs to add a line.

Your affectionate father,
C. C. Jones.

The infant has been found—the twelfth day after its birth and secretion! Exposed—yet preserved, *in providence,* to establish beyond doubt the guilt. Dead: partially decomposed, of course. Full maturity. Tied up in a piece of cloth! The guilty mother now confesses all, with the reservation that it was *stillborn!* . . . Will write you more particularly in a few days.

Mrs. Mary Jones *to* Mr. Charles C. Jones, Jr.ᵍ

Montevideo, *Monday,* November 7th, 1859

My dear Son,

Upon your father's reading his letter to me I felt that it was so perfectly adapted to the present state of affairs that I asked if a *publication* of it at this time might not do good throughout the country. He says if you think so, you are at liberty to do what you please with it; says it contains his honest sentiments, and he is perfectly willing to have them appear with his signature attached. I have never realized before that the malicious fanaticism of the North could extend to such organized and practical results. It is no longer a war of words.

I trust our dear Ruthie continues well. I shall await her wishes at a moment's warning. Have been very busy with the winter clothing this week. Gilbert and Jacob have commenced painting. Robert goes to Presbytery in Bryan next week, and your sister and Little Daughter will be with us. . . . Love to dear Ruthie and yourself.

Ever your affectionate mother,
Mary Jones.

Miss Mary E. Robarts *to* Mrs. Mary Jones[t]

Marietta, *Tuesday,* November 8th, 1859

Many thanks, my dear cousin, for your kind and affectionate letter, and your still kinder and cordial invitation to visit you this winter. If my dear mother continues to improve as she has done for the last three weeks, we will accept it with pleasure. She is better—far better—than I ever expected to see her again. Her cough is much less distressing, and though still there, yet the spells are not so long or violent, and the expectoration much less. Dr. Stewart thinks she can undertake the journey without any risk; so, Providence permitting, we expect to be down about the 1st December. Of course we will consult the weather and Mother's feelings at the time; a few days earlier or later we would not regard. We had two reasons for postponing our journey till then: the month of November is generally a mild pleasant month up here; and we thought it would be best to remain as long as we could up here so as to include the month of March in our visit to the low country. As it is, we have a long spell of loafing on our friends! Another reason: we have been so much hindered in our family work by Mother's sickness and Nancy's having a sore finger that we have to be very busy to get ready. You will hear often from us before we go down. Will go either to Mary's or Henry's first; they must settle that between them. Then we expect to go to the Island, and leave you for the last.

I must now tell you what a surprise we had in Mr. Buttolph and Cousin Susan's arrival. It was indeed kind in them to come up to see my dear mother, and if she had not been so much better than Cousin Susan expected to find her, she would have remained with us longer. We shall long remember her kindness in coming.

We also had a most agreeable surprise in seeing your dear son and his bride. I never should have had the vanity to suppose a bridal trip could be made agreeable in the up country after the 1st October, when everyone is turning their thoughts to the low country, so should have been too diffident of the attractions of our mountain home to have proposed a visit at this season. Was therefore quite surprised when Cousin Susan told us she had left them at the Stone Mountain. And on Monday they came up and spent the day with us, and an agreeable one it was—to us, at least. No bride could have deported herself with more affability or sociability, more kindness and affection, than she did, ushered into a family of strange relatives. We were all quite pleased with her, and are glad that we made her acquaintance just as we did—at our own house, and in that impromptu manner. The young doctor looks, as Mr. King would have said, "as happy as a clam at high water." Tell my reverend cousin that I congratulate him on having a daughter-in-law who can talk to him; think Carrie very sociable.

I trust that your visit to Savannah may be very pleasant, and that dear Charlie and Ruth may be fortunate in welcoming a fine little babe. I shall think often of them. . . . Mother, Louisa, and the girls desire much love to you and our dear Cousin Charles, and Mary if she is with you. . . . And give much love to Henry and Abby and little Eliza Low. . . . The girls thank you kindly for your cordial invitation to them; they will come in the course of the winter. Expect they will remain in Savannah a month or two with their aunt. . . . Farewell, my ever dear cousin. . . . Tell your servants and ours howdy for us. Tell Rosetta I expect we will bring Sam to see her this winter.

> Your ever affectionate cousin,
> Mary.

Dr. Joseph Jones *to* Rev. *and* Mrs. C. C. Jones[t]
Augusta, *Tuesday,* November 8th, 1859

My dear Parents,

The time has flown so rapidly since our marriage that I was not aware of my neglect in not writing you until I counted the days and found that upon the morrow two weeks will have passed without sending you an account of our prosperity, good health, and happiness.

Our visit to the up country, and especially to Marietta, was very pleasant. Aunt Eliza and Cousins Mary and Louisa and the young ladies received Carrie and myself with great affection and hospitality. Carrie is greatly pleased with the kind manner in which my relatives have received and adopted her. She has spoken frequently of your affectionate reception.

A few hours after our arrival in Augusta I was summoned to a meeting of the trustees and faculty of the medical college, which had been called in response to a communication from the trustees of the University of Georgia. The trustees and faculty decided that I should represent them at Milledgeville during the meeting of the board of trustees and senatus academicus of the University of Georgia. It seemed to be, under all the circumstances (my recent marriage and the coming introductory lecture and preparations for the course), rather an ungenerous request. Nevertheless, as I had advocated the measure strongly, and as they placed their request upon the ground that I was acquainted with the trustees personally, I felt it to be my duty to go. My dear Carrie accompanied me, and after traveling all night and waiting patiently all day in the statehouse, I was informed by the board of trustees that they had concluded to abandon the scheme of connecting the Medical College of Georgia with the university.

I was surprised and disgusted with their plans and time-serving talk. Amongst other things they propose to establish a summer school of medicine at Athens similar to that at Atlanta, and attempt to obtain one professor from each one of the medical schools of the state. The plan of cutting the institution in two, and of converting the two lower classes into a high school under the direction of the tutors, has been adopted after much and powerful opposition. They call this ridiculous plan "The University." The immense labors of these mountains have not resulted even in the production of a little mouse, but rather in the stinting and starving and mutilation of the poor little mouse which has been declining under their care for many years.

Yesterday I delivered the introductory; the audience was large and attentive. My table is covered with proofs from Philadelphia. On the morrow my regular lectures commence. With best love, I remain

Your affectionate son,
Joseph Jones.

REV. C. C. JONES *to* MR. CHARLES C. JONES, JR.ᵍ

Montevideo, *Thursday,* November 10th, 1859

My dear Son,

We received yours of yesterday today, and one also from your brother, and we are glad to hear of your health and happiness in your families. Your sister is with us, and she and the "baby" (as the little chatterbox calls herself) are well. Robert left this morning for Bryan to attend Presbytery. Did not feel able to go and undertake the necessary fatigue.

Your dear mother is not so well, and is suffering from a long ride to Sunbury on Tuesday and back the same day. Hope it will soon pass off. We went down to see Joseph Anderson, who has been at *death's door*—for sufficient cause! Is out of danger, and will (humanly speaking) get well—if he does not put himself back by his own act! As years increase, my dread and abhorrence of the use of spirituous liquors and opium do also increase. Death is smiting with a perpetual stroke with these means!

What an unexpected and afflicting death is that of Mr. John A. Thomas! Buried on Monday. About forty-five. Leaves a wife and six or seven fine children! What warnings have we had in this county! My son, *obsta principiis:* touch not, taste not, handle not. Men in public life are particularly exposed and therefore require to be doubly on their guard.

The newspaper containing the speech alluded to has been sent us. The marvel not only is that such men are permitted to live and disturb the country, but also that there are such numbers who go to hear their infamous speeches and not only tolerate but approve them. The Harpers Ferry affair is something for such men to gloat over. I hope it may be overruled for good. Time only will show.

Does Colonel Jackson accept the presidency of Franklin College? The changes adopted in the college are peculiar, problematical, and by no means make it a university, nor give it much of a step in that direction. They have declined uniting the medical college in Augusta in the program, and propose a summer school of medicine in Athens conducted by a professor from each of the medical schools in the state! Verily there is a head wanted somewhere in that region. If Colonel Jackson goes there, he will have to take the college, trustees, senatus academicus, legislature all upon his back and fix matters as they should be fixed. Your brother was sent up by the medical college in

Augusta to meet the trustees in Milledgeville; and lo, the proposition to the Augusta school, made by themselves, was withdrawn, and the remarkable project of the summer school devised in lieu of it! This is enough to warrant the convocation of an indignation meeting on the part of the medical faculty in Augusta.

Will take your advice in the case referred to, and enclose you a memorandum which you can preserve if we proceed, as I suppose we must. Mother and Sister unite in much love to dear Ruthie and yourself.

Your ever affectionate father,
C. C. Jones.

Mother says she will be down on Tuesday the 15th, God willing.

Let me hear from you about *the case* so soon as you decide, as I am anxious to be relieved of it.

[Enclosure]

Facts Respecting the Case of Infanticide on Montevideo Plantation[t]

The woman Lucy known to be in a family way by driver, midwife, and generally by all on the plantation. Directed driver and midwife to tell her to take care of herself and see that nothing happened to the child some three weeks before its birth. She denied strenuously being in that way, and told the driver that if she was, neither *he nor anyone else should ever see the child*.

Tuesday October 11th laid up in her house under color of having a *bad bile*. Manager directed the midwife and nurse to attend to her. Midwife several times in her house between 11th and 15th (from Tuesday to Saturday). Her mother was in the house with her (Lucy lived with her mother); said she saw and attended to the bile. Friday night (14th) midwife sent for; says she saw something, but not the child; never saw *it*. Her mother says *she* never saw it. Both endeavored to make the impression that she never had a child, and could not have been in a family way. Monday morning October 17th examined the woman; clear evidence of having been delivered of a mature child. *She positively denied it.* October 22nd had the woman thoroughly examined by a physician; he pronounced that she had unmistakably been delivered of a mature child. *Woman positively denied it.* Search ordered to find the child since 17th. Tuesday the 25th *child found, tied up in a piece of cloth, secreted in grass and bushes!* Dead: in process of decomposition. Physician brought to see it; pronounces it a child come to its maturity. Sensible Negro women and men saw it; said it was full-grown.

Confession. The wretched mother on the finding of the child confesses. She laid up Tuesday October 11th: had a bile in truth. Thursday (13th) midday, *alone in her house, had the child: dead born!* She then tied it up in the cloth, carried it down into the bottom, and hid it. Was afraid to disclose it, as she had all along denied it. The child by her own confession of her peculiar situation last January or February proves the child to have come to its full time.

The question arises: Was the child alive or dead at its birth? If dead, why should she conceal it? The midwife, she confesses, was called to her Friday night by her mother, and saw what came from her, which she says was the *afterbirth. And the midwife said it was*—and that in presence of her mother. Midwife and mother *accessories to the concealment,* and should be prosecuted as such.

Mr. Charles C. Jones, Jr., *to* Rev. C. C. Jones[g]
Savannah, *Friday,* November 11th, 1859

My dear Father,

I am this moment in receipt of your favor of the 10th inst., and regret to know that dear Mother is not so well as usual. Sincerely hope that her indisposition is but temporary, and that she may soon be restored to her wonted health. It must be a great pleasure both to yourselves and to Sister to be again united, even for a limited period, beneath the generous roof of the old homestead.

There are more suicides in this world than one who does not reflect would be inclined to imagine. The death of Mr. Thomas is emphatically *a warning.* What a prostitution of time, talent, parental responsibility, and of life!

The case of Joseph Anderson is sad in the extreme. His conduct places him beyond the bounds almost of pity and sympathy.

Judge Jackson will probably not accept the appointment recently tendered by the senatus academicus. The views which you express in reference to the present status of Franklin College and the proposed changes are heartily reciprocated by him. The truth is, the spirit of legislation alive in our state is to be sincerely deprecated. Ignorant men are sent to deal with measures which are above their comprehension, and while in the legislature are busied rather with the passage of acts which conduce to local interests and personal advantage, to the exclusion of graver matters, the obligations of which they either wholly neglect or but partially consider.

The recent election of Mr. Lyon as a judge of the supreme court is to be heartily regretted. He brings to the discharge of his duties scarcely a single qualification of a respectable judge, owing his success simply to the efforts of a political faction whose avowed object was the defeat of one of the incumbents, Henry L. Benning. Think of electing such a man in preference to Charles J. Jenkins, who was also a candidate! The supreme court as originally constituted was entitled to all respect. Lumpkin, Nisbet, and Warner were all good and true men, above reproach, elected by virtue of individual merit, and of excellent legal education. There was a uniformity about their decisions which gave rest to legal inquiries and inspired confidence. Those decisions were then respected not only in our own but in sister states. But the times are changed. The judgeship has become a matter of political intrigue. The bench changes, and decisions with it. The consequence is that confidence is to a very great degree shaken—and very reasonably, too, when you remember that the court now at pleasure reverses its own decisions, thereby placing it out of the power of an attorney, on many points, to give an opinion which either satisfies himself or will prove valuable to his client. It is now a fact that the supreme court has degenerated almost into a petit jury, trying each case upon its peculiar merits and their own notions of right and wrong, to the interruption of well-established rules and the disregard of settled authority. *Stare decicis* has with those judges long since ceased to be a leading motto.

Pardon this crusade against the court. I have occasion to speak feelingly, for several times of late have we been the victims of their hasty, incorrect decision. As now constituted, the court had best, I should say, be abolished, and suitors left to their chances before a circuit judge, and a convention of them who will constitute a court of errors and sit annually at some central point within the state. The recent legislation in reference to Franklin College and the medical institution is another case in point. The idea seems to be to break down all barriers, all the safeguards to education, professional or otherwise, and open a broad road in which the ignorant and foolish may rush heedlessly along.

In the matter of the infanticide, it seems to me that your proper course would be to prepare a statement of the facts connected with the case and submit the same to the solicitor general, to be used by him as he may deem best. He is the public officer representing the state in all matters of this character; and when you have made known the circumstances to him, and placed the case in his hands for further action, it seems to me that you will have discharged your every duty. This can be done at the next term of Liberty Superior Court, which sits early in December. An examination before magistrates would result only in a commitment, which would involve costs and accomplish ultimately no more than the other course suggested. Enclosed I send statement already furnished, that you may insert names of witnesses to prove the facts respectively therein set forth. I can then prepare the statement in due form and submit it to the solicitor general for further action in the premises. Will write you again.

We will be more than happy to welcome dear Mother on Tuesday next. Will you not come also? Ruth is pretty well, although now grievously burdened with the primal sorrow of her sex. Accept our united love for self, dear Mother, Sister, and Baby. And believe me ever

Your affectionate son,

Charles C. Jones, Jr.

The *Wanderer* case will probably be commenced on Tuesday next.

Rev. C. C. Jones *to* Mrs. Mary Jones[t]

Walthourville, *Wednesday,* November 16th, 1859

My dear Wife,

Little Daughter was nauseated yesterday after you left. Dr. Stevens prescribed again, and after a fair night's rest she is quite bright this morning; and her little tongue has been going, as her dear aunt would say, "thirteen to the dozen." We hope, through divine favor, she will now be restored. . . .

Breakfast is just in, with Kate and Tom in active employ. A nice broiled chicken, fried bread, and all other good dishes, crowned by the refreshing fragrance of the tea upon the tray. Hope to leave for Montevideo after breakfast, to hurry forward the embellishments of the old homestead, within and without. We all unite in love to Mother and Sister, Ruthie and Brother Charlie. I leave the amount you may need blank, which you can fill up as you like.

Your ever affectionate husband,
C. C. Jones.

Mr. CHARLES C. JONES, JR., *to* REV. C. C. JONES[g]
Savannah, *Thursday,* November 17th, 1859
6:30 A.M.

My dear Father,

Your kind favor of the 16th inst. was yesterday afternoon duly received by dear Mother, who arrived safely, and in most opportune season, the day previous. We are happy to know that you are well, and that Baby is so much better.

My dear Ruth has been suffering severely ever since eleven o'clock Tuesday night, and is not yet relieved: a case of protracted labor, very burdensome to her and trying to all of us, that has already continued more than thirty hours! Think of the amount of pain and anguish involved—and no respite yet! Dr. West, who has been in attendance all the time, extending every care and kindness, says that everything is right, and we will have to await the action of nature. God grant her relief at the earliest possible moment! Cousin Eliza and Philo have been with us all the past day and night. We will never forget the kindness of dear Mother and of them.

I purposed before this writing you more fully in reference to the infanticide, but have been prevented hitherto. Will do so at the earliest possible moment. You may expect a letter from us tomorrow, directed to No. 3 (McIntosh Station). I hope before the receipt of this that all will be well. Dear Mother unites in much love.

Your affectionate son,
Charles C. Jones, Jr.

Mr. CHARLES C. JONES, JR., *to* REV. C. C. JONES[w]
Savannah, *Friday,* November 18th, 1859
5 A.M.

My dear Father,

Ruth was an hour ago delivered of a well-formed little infant, whom we shall soon hope to have the pleasure of presenting to you as your second granddaughter. My dear Ruth has for the past *fifty-three hours* suffered intensely, and as a consequence, now that relief and reaction have supervened, is exceedingly feeble. She is, however, as well as we have any cause to expect.

We will never be able to express all the thanks we owe to dear Mother and to Dr. West and Sister Eliza.

Hoping, my dear father, that you are well, and that we may soon have the pleasure of seeing you and of placing this little stranger in the arms of her grandfather, I am, with sincerest love, in which dear Mother and all unite,

Your affectionate son,
Charles C. Jones, Jr.

With the exception of necessary fatigue, Mother is quite well.

REV. C. C. JONES *to* MRS. MARY JONES[t]

Montevideo, *Friday,* November 18th, 1859

My dear Wife,

Rode to the Boro this morning, after sending Tom to the depot, to see Mrs. Trask. Quite sick. Said: "Mr. Jones, I have felt Christ precious to me this morning." Had just been bled: not proper to protract the conversation to any length. Prayed with her and left. Mr. Britt, whom I met in the entry, helped me downstairs and down the steps; and he and Mr. Lyons together helped me on Jerry. Very inactive.

Set the painters to the inside first in your room, that it may be thoroughly dry for you when you return. Left the doors and those of the study unpainted, thinking on the whole you might prefer to have all the doors in the new part of the house stained and varnished. Can be easily altered if you wish it. Wrote about five pages in *History*.

At half-past two o'clock Tom came with a letter from Charles Colcock, giving the happy intelligence that Ruthie and himself were parents, and we were grandparents, of a living and a perfect child—a *little daughter!* I sincerely rejoice with them, and unite in special thanksgiving to our Heavenly Father for this precious gift and great mercy. May it be spared to its parents, and parents to it, for mutual happiness and blessing! It is another immortal spirit added to our number to be prayed for and to be trained up for heaven. Hope Charles has written his sister and brother, as they will be glad to hear without delay. The servants all appear delighted to learn the good news, and send congratulations. Cato says: "The news is good indeed; I *told* Marse Charles he would have a girl-baby." Will write Charles and Ruthie.

Caesar came in after tea. Says he wishes to go with me in joining the church. Appears in spirit very well, but deficient in clear views of the plan of salvation. Recommended him to wait another Communion for further instruction. Perfectly willing. The amount of ignorance among the Negroes is great, and am surprised how little our own people seem to know of the Way of Life. I wish every one of them had access to the Word of Life; it surely would much relieve our responsibility. What can be done for the better religious instruction of our Negro population?

Saturday Evening. In morning's ride called to know how Mrs. Trask was.

Measurably better, but not relieved altogether. Did not request to see her, as she was desirous of sleeping. Conversed with Mr. Trask on his own spiritual state. Seemed tender and grateful.

Paid a sort of pastoral as well as friendly visit to our neighbors Mr. and Mrs. Chapman. Very glad to see me. A long conversation with both together on their spiritual interests; were precisely on the same ground they occupied (at least he) some two years ago! Reasoned the case, explained the Way of Life as well as I was able, urged a reception of it, and prayed with them. They have nine children, the oldest fifteen: a girl.

Have spent the remainder of the day in writing letters. Wrote Carrie an answer to her letter, which I have not; you must have it. Wrote Charles and Ruthie also on the birth of their little daughter. The evening sky beautiful. A lonely walk. Discovered *Venus* just falling into the tops of the trees, brilliant as a diamond. Tea. Wrote tickets. Sent the wedding cake by Dan to Audley to South Hampton to send to his mother and cousin, and a sugarplum apiece for the little boys to let them know Cousin Joe was really married and happy. Family worship. Read the *Wanderer* trial as reported in the *Republican*. And now write up my letter to my dear wife. May you have peaceful rest and a quiet and profitable Sabbath! Love to Ruthie and Charles, and many kisses for my little granddaughter. . . . All well.

Your ever affectionate husband,
C. C. Jones.

Rev. C. C. Jones *to* Mr. *and* Mrs. Charles C. Jones, Jr.[g]

Montevideo, *Friday,* November 18th, 1859

My dear Children,

My relief and my joy were great today when I received the intelligence that through the tender mercy of our Heavenly Father you were made *this morning* the happy parents of a living and a perfect child—a tender little daughter. I unite with you in rendering thanks to God for this precious gift to you, and pray that it may be spared to you a source of comfort and happiness, and that God may early convert and bring it into His Kingdom for usefulness here and glory hereafter, and that you both may adequately feel the responsibility of parents and be enabled to train it up in the fear of the Lord. I cannot wish for you and for the little one better things; and I shall not fail, I trust, to remember it in constant prayer with our loved ones. It will afford me real joy to behold its face and give it a welcome to my heart, and shall come to see you as soon as possible—although I suppose it may be well to let the little stranger have the quiet of a few days, that she may be a little more at home in the world and with her friends. You can each of you give it a kiss for its grandfather as an earnest, God willing, of a kiss of welcome from himself.

Patience begs to "send you much joy, and hopes through sparing mercy the baby may be made a comfort to you." Sue also begs "to present her congratulations; that she was in distress all the time till all was well, and sends howdy for all, but more for the baby."

Take good care of Mother for me. Hope you will write your sister and brother; they will be happy to hear directly from you. Wishing you and your little one every mercy, I remain, my dear son and daughter,

Your ever affectionate father,
C. C. Jones.

Mrs. Mary Jones *to* Rev. C. C. Jones[t]
Savannah, *Monday,* November 21st, 1859
My dear Husband,

You have been constantly in my mind since we parted, although I have not had one moment to write you. You have been informed of the happy termination of Ruth's protracted sufferings.

You know I arrived here on Tuesday afternoon. We retired that night about eleven o'clock. Soon after, I heard her coughing violently, and went into her room and applied a bit of cloth saturated with camphor to her chest, which relieved her in part. I had scarcely composed myself in bed before Charles called me. I went in, and he went for the doctor (Cousin Charles); and from that hour, day and night, excepting when we left to eat a mouthful or to refresh ourselves, we stood or sat around her bed until Friday morning at four o'clock, when a little voice gave forth a feeble cry of existence. Cousin Eliza came over on Wednesday morning and did not leave until all was over. If they had been Ruth's own father and mother, they could not have been kinder or more devoted.

I have been constantly engaged ever since. Tonight Ruth is suffering from her bosoms, and the little babe not as well as I could desire. I sent for Cousin Charles; he has prescribed and left. But I shall not sleep tonight. You know my feelings: I should be miserable if any neglect on my part resulted in injury to mother or child. It is a sweet little babe. We hope to secure a nurse soon which will be competent to her business. This will relieve me much; the one we now have is not much removed from an ordinary plantation nurse. But I have been supported beyond my expectations—but feel as if I shall never sleep again. If a good nurse is obtained, I will return home immediately. Anyhow I hope to be with you next week *early*—say Tuesday. Will write you certainly.

I hope our dear Little Daughter is better.

The *Wanderer* trial is in the most interesting time. Judge Jackson spoke four hours and a half today: Charles says the most powerful effort he ever heard. But it nearly cost him a severe attack—something like the spasmodic affection of your throat. Such was the alarm at his situation that the judge on the *bench* called out: "Bring brandy!" Charles has taken down his speech; I hope it will be published. He is an honor to his state and country. I would be delighted to hear him.

What can I do for you in town? Do make Gilbert sleep every night near you—within call. Friends are all well in town. It is almost midnight, and I must close to go up to my charge above. Charles unites with me in best love. Howdies for all the servants. Dr. Wilson from Augusta preached here on Sabbath; I did not go out. Good night!

Ever your affectionate wife,
Mary Jones.

Rev. C. C. Jones *to* Mrs. Mary Jones[t]

Montevideo, *Tuesday,* November 22nd, 1859

My dear Wife,

On my way to church Sunday saw Mrs. Trask. Still very sick. . . . Brother Buttolph preached two excellent sermons: "Ye are the salt of the earth" and "The Lord shall descend from heaven with a shout." Good congregation and attention. . . . He gave out a sermon for Thursday (Thanksgiving Day in the state) and urged the people to observe it, and I believe they will. . . . Had Sunday school for you in the evening at home. . . . Monday Henry rode over; sat till dinner time. . . . Says John and his family comes out on Thursday. . . . Tuesday rode over all the plantation with Stepney. Will make about thirty-five bales cotton. Plenty of corn, but potatoes very short. Rice short—perhaps three hundred bushels. Peas yet to pick. . . . Ordered beef for the people Thanksgiving Day. . . . Received a letter from Daughter, dated 19th, mailed 21st. Little Daughter has been quite sick since we left. Doctor called in again; better when she wrote. . . . Mr. Cassidey undecided about giving up the academy. Daughter thinks the academy pretty much out of the question!

Took your kind letter from the post office. Am thankful to learn that you have been sustained in your anxiety and fatigue better than you expected. Be not overanxious to make yourself sick. I think, now the trouble is over, you might take some hours to rest and get sleep to refresh you. I do not like to hear you say "you feel as if you shall never sleep again." I hope you will, and be refreshed, and then spend some days in town enjoying the company of your little granddaughter, and rejoicing with your friends and children. The house-painting will be hardly ready for you by next Tuesday, and I would not wish you to come home after your fatigue to have the confusion and uncomfortableness of the house as it is at present, and get sick from the paint and want of good accommodations. Am hurrying it on as fast as possible; and my presence is equal to two additional workmen.

Had you not better order from Claghorn & Cunningham what articles you will need for house supplies while you are in Savannah and let them be sent round by Captain Charlie, who is now in Savannah? We shall need a sack of Turk's Island salt.

I am in need of nothing but a suit of gray clothes, which I shall have to procure in person. I wish also to visit our little granddaughter, and may do so, and you return home with me when you can do so. Thursday is Thanksgiving, Saturday is preparatory lecture, and Sabbath is Communion; and if I live to be there, it will be the *thirty-seventh anniversary of my membership with Midway Church.* (Received *November 1822.*) I wish to be there, God willing. For these reasons I desire to put off my visit to the "sweet little babe" (as you say she is, and I have no doubt of it) until next week. But will come this week if you think I had better do so. Have you drawn on Mr. Anderson? If so, do send me a five-dollar bill to pay my way down, for I am as dry as a bone.

It will be a lasting regret that I could not hear Judge Jackson's speech. I hope sincerely he will write it out; and then it must be published, not only in the newspapers but in a pamphlet form. It ought to go before the people.

Give my love to Ruthie and Charles. Kiss my granddaughter for me, and tell her Grandpapa is coming to see her. Through divine favor the people are all well. I sleep, eat, and study in the old common parlor. Jack sleeps in there also at night. The Lord be with and bless you, my dear wife!

Your ever affectionate husband,
C. C. Jones.

Wednesday Morning, eight o'clock, 23rd. All well, D.G.

Rev. C. C. Jones *to* Mrs. Mary Jones[t]

Montevideo, *Thursday,* November 24th, 1859

My dear Wife,

Thanksgiving Day. Had a small beef killed and some rice given out for the people last evening for their dinner today, which most of them stayed at home to eat, very few going to Midway, the only place of worship open. We had, as Mr. Thomas W. Fleming said, an uncommon turnout for Midway—an excellent congregation of whites and of blacks. The observance of the day is a new thing under the sun in our congregation, to our shame be it spoken! But it was a noble beginning, and such was the interesting character of Mr. Buttolph's sermon and of the exercises generally that there will be a better attendance another year. . . . Called on my return to see Mrs. Trask. Improving, the doctor thinks, but weak.

Much typhoid fever in the upper part of the county; they say some thirty cases. Mr. Nathaniel Martin, uncle to our Mr. W. G. Martin, and one of the oldest men and members in Midway Church, died this week with it. . . . Mr. McDonald's brother, the young man who married Mrs. George McDonald (Miss Powell that was), is very ill, and our Mr. McDonald fears he will die. Had been sick, got better, was baptized that rainy cool Sunday in Darien, relapsed, and so lies very low. Our *mode* might have been less injurious.

Received yours of 23rd as I came home from Midway. Glad to hear that you are all well, and the baby too, and that sleep visits you again. It has always been a good and constant friend to you; and I believe you have cherished the friendship, and with good advantage. The charge of Judge Wayne to the jury when they were impaneled is a noble one. I wish it was printed in a pamphlet form and circulated through the whole state. It does the judge honor. His last charge I have not read. The speech of Judge Jackson I sincerely hope he will be at the pains of writing out; and if printed, it may go far to correct public sentiment and fix the hand of infamy upon the miscreants who have escaped, to the disgrace of the state, the just vengeance of the law. It is abominable. Am glad they are again indicted. Would that some of the principals that go at large in the streets could be laid hold of! We can only pray that "Justice may not fall in the streets."

As there cannot be room at Charles's to accommodate Aunt and her family and yourself also, God willing, I will come down for you on Monday (if you will come out) *and return on Tuesday.* I cannot at present stay later. John did not come out today; comes next Tuesday. No doubt Aunt comes with him to Savannah, and if the synodical steamer touches at Darien, will put his family on board on Wednesday morning and leave his visit to Liberty till his return. So Henry informed me today.

Have not heard this week from Daughter; consequently conclude the dear child is better. All well, through divine mercy, around us. . . . I am very much afraid the paint will make you sick. *It is very strong through the whole house.* Tomorrow the second inside coat begins to go on, which I believe dries very quick. Every blessing attend you, my dear wife! Love to Charles and Ruthie, and a kiss for Baby. Thank Charles for his letter of instructions. Shall not act before I communicate with Aunt and Cousin Mary, as the matter will in all probability go before the justice's court.

Your ever affectionate husband,
C. C. Jones.

Friday Morning, eight o'clock, 25th. Let me know by *tomorrow's* mail, D.V., if the arrangement for coming out *Tuesday* suits you. Do just as you like. If you wish to stay and see John, which no doubt you desire, do so. I will conform to your arrangements. Beautiful morning. All well.

Mrs. Mary Jones *to* Rev. C. C. Jones[t]

Savannah, *Friday,* November 25th, 1859

Your most welcome favor, my dear husband, was this evening received, and I rejoice to know that I will so soon have the pleasure of seeing you. If it suits you best to come on Monday, then do so, and I will be ready to go home with you on Tuesday.

On Tuesday night Brother John and family will be here in Savannah; also Aunt and family. Only Cousin Mary will stay with Charles. Brother John wrote for Charles to engage a room for him at the Pulaski House, saying as the boats did not touch at Darien he would go on in the steamer, and Sister Jane and the little boys would go out to Liberty. Charles says the boat *will* touch at Darien, and he expects to go in her himself on Wednesday to attend the southern courts. So I presume Brother John may take all his family with him. It would be a great pleasure for me to see them, and if it suits equally well to come for me on Wednesday, we could return on Thursday.

This is the *first* day I have put my feet upon the front steps since I came in; consequently have done no shopping, and there are a few little matters I should like to attend to. Yesterday the *black* nurse was dismissed, and a very clever white one has taken her place. She is very competent, and I am now relieved of all care of mother and infant, who are doing as well as possible. The babe is a sweet little creature, and I have given her Grandpapa's kisses. Last night we all had uninterrupted sleep, and hope to enjoy the same tonight.

Thanksgiving Day was observed in some of the churches here, but did not go out myself. Tried amidst many interruptions to lift up my heart in grateful thanks to my God and Saviour for all His mercies.

I am glad you defer the case until Aunt and Cousin Mary come down. Charles thinks she ought not to be trusted on the plantation, but removed to Hinesville jail, as she is capable of any deed, incendiary or otherwise. He thinks if it takes the regular course of law, that not only she but also the *nurse* and any others that are proven as partakers of her crime will be likely to suffer the death penalty. The law is very stringent.

Should you conclude not to come on Monday, do be sure and write. Charles and Ruth unite with me in best love to you, with kisses from your granddaughter.

Ever your own affectionate
Mary.

REV. C. C. JONES *to* MRS. MARY JONES[t]
Montevideo, *Saturday,* November 26th, 1859
My dear Wife,

Your welcome letter came by today's mail, and am happy to know grandmother, mother, father, and baby are all well.

It will suit me just as well to come for you next Wednesday, if I live and am enabled to do so, as on Monday. You will enjoy seeing John and family and Aunt and family. Do your shopping, and we will get on a little further with the painting. You will find it very uncomfortable to be at home just now, for the house is in confusion from top to bottom, and only one room (reserved to sleep in) not painted; and the smell of the paint, I fear, will make you sick. We push on as fast as the two workmen can without hurting themselves; but there is a great deal of surface to be gone over, and it takes time. So if you prefer to remain longer, I can conform to your wishes; and you can write me by *Tuesday's mail* whether you will stay longer or I shall come for you on Wednesday.

Had a pleasant letter from our dear child today, dated the 24th. She says: "Baby is much better, though still feeble. She has been coughing a good deal for a day or two, but I hope she will continue to improve. She only seems to need care now, though it is very hard to get her digestion right; and I am afraid that will not be regulated till her teeth are out. I shall have to keep her very quiet until she gets entirely over this attack. She is feverish at night, and I am often waked by her little call, 'Mama, want water.' I give her flax tea: she drinks so much I am afraid to give her water altogether." Dear child, I trust it may please God to restore her to health.

The children are married and settled in families; we can no more be with them to help them except occasionally, for which we desire to be thankful. We can do no more than commit them and theirs to the constant and kind care of Him who has always watched over us and ours. And when we are gone, the Lord abides; and I lay hold upon His precious promise that "He will be a God to us and to our seed after us."

Write by Tuesday's mail. Love to Charles and Ruthie. Kisses for the baby. Thank Charles for his letter. Save change to bring us out with. You had better get two locks like the one on the front door next the flower garden for the door leading out of the old common parlor towards the vegetable garden, and for the door leading from the old drawing room into the pantry. They must have new locks. Tell Mr. Palmer how they open, and he will suit the locks to them. We are all pretty well. Do give love to Aunt and Cousins Mary and Lou and the children. I remain, my dear wife,

Your ever affectionate husband,
C. C. Jones.

Monday, 8 A.M., November 28th, 1859. A very interesting and trust profitable day at Midway yesterday. Large congregation of whites and blacks. Mr. Buttolph preached an admirable morning sermon from our Saviour's agony in the garden. *Ten* white additions, all in the covenant; two colored. Assisted at the Communion, and made an address to the young converts at the afternoon prayer meeting. Too tired to hold Sunday school for you last night.

Niger and Sue their old attacks; all the rest, I believe, well. Love to all.

Your affectionate husband,
C. C. J.

MRS. MARY JONES *to* REV. C. C. JONES[t]

Savannah, *Monday*, November 28th, 1859

Your most welcome letter, my dear husband, reached me this afternoon and brings me the joyful anticipation of seeing you on Wednesday. Although the paint may be unpleasant, I cannot think of leaving you longer alone. My anxiety knows no abatement when I am separated from you, and now that the object for which I left you through God's mercy has been accomplished, and Ruth and the dear baby are so well and have the watch and care of a competent white nurse, I must return at once.

I have thought of this plan. You know the *kitchen* is perfectly tight and comfortable. Could you not order the cooking utensils removed into the washroom, and have it thoroughly whitewashed and cleaned, and the pantry carpet laid down on the floor, and the trundle bed put into it for our sleeping apartment? I think it could be made perfectly comfortable, and would relieve us of the paint. Please have this done, and we will maroon together there for a few weeks.

Tomorrow night our friends will all be down, D.V. Aunt, Lou, and Joe will stay with Cousin Charles; Cousin Mary here; and the young ladies with their aunt. I presume Brother John and Sister Jane will go on the day after. The Chatham bar will be also on board as far as Darien. Charles says they will have to be on their best behavior.

Yesterday I attended Mr. Porter's church twice. In the morning Mr. Schenck, secretary of our Board of Publication, preached a solemn and impressive sermon. Rev. Joseph Porter preached at night.

Several of my friends have called, and I hope to return their visits tomorrow.

As it is late, I must bid you good night. My son takes the best care of me, and does everything to render my stay pleasant. Today the little baby presented her grandmother with a silver goblet. She is a little darling, and improves every day. . . . Charles has just come in from his aldermanic duties. He has not been well for several days, and wants *rest, rest*. Again good night! Love from Charles and Ruth. Yesterday I took the first volume of your Scott from the *whatnot* and asked them to begin the reading of it together, which they did. Oh, that he were a true child of God!

Ever your loving wife,
Mary Jones.

REV. C. C. JONES *to* MR. CHARLES C. JONES, JR.ᵍ

Montevideo, Saturday, December 10th, 1859

My dear Son,

Your favor of yesterday came to hand this evening, and we are happy to hear of your safe arrival and the health of Ruthie and Miss Julia Berrien, who will soon, I trust, give promise of a stout and handsome young lady.

Mr. Joseph Ashmore called very politely yesterday and made arrangements for the trial of the woman Lucy today, which trial to my great relief was issued today. The sentence of the magistrates (Darsey, Quarterman, and Ashmore) was eight days' imprisonment in the county jail and corporal punishment to the amount of ninety stripes, inflicted at intervals of two and three days, one-third at a time—the lightest punishment for so great a crime (concealment, etc.) the court said it could decree. Conceiving the ends of justice would be met and a due example made by this decision, by permission of the court I withdrew the prosecution of the accessories, Rosetta and Katy, who were brought up and reprimanded and warned by the court, after which, for the sake of impression, the constable by my direction gave them a few stripes over their jackets. And so the matter ended. The trial was conducted with fairness, deliberation, and gravity. The court, in the absence of counsel for the criminals, requested your Uncle Henry to act for them, which he did in a proper manner. It is my impression that if owners would more frequently refer criminal acts of their servants to the decision of the courts, they would aid in establishing correct public sentiment among themselves in relation to different kinds of crimes committed by the Negroes, give better support to their own authority, and restrain the vices of the Negroes themselves.

Mother thinks the dividend uncommonly fine. She requests you to pay *yourself* your bill for cash advanced to your *mother and father* for discount paid on note in bank, etc., etc. Then send Bailie & Brothers the amount of their bill, which you will find enclosed, with a request that they would let you know what they paid on the carpets in the way of expenses, railroad freight, etc.; and when you know, enclose the amount in bills to them. Let them send you receipts for all. *The balance* you can send out to Mother in some safe way. We understand that the dividend declared for the *past six months,* by your letter, is ten percent, which makes up three hundred dollars on your mother's stock. . . . Mother unites in love to Ruthie and yourself, and kisses for the baby, and in prayers for God's every blessing on you and yours.

Your ever affectionate father,
C. C. Jones.

Mrs. Mary Jones *to* Mr. Charles C. Jones, Jr.[g]
Montevideo, Saturday, December 10th, 1859
My dear Son,

You did not mention your eyes. I have felt very uneasy about them. You should not trifle with them. I really consider them in a serious condition. If not *entirely* relieved, ask Cousin Charles to prescribe for them. And *be sure to use* the preparation he promised to order for your throat.

My dear child, God has blessed you with so much health and strength from your infancy to the present time that I fear you fail to realize the fact that it is all *His gift,* for the right use and *care* of which you are accountable. Your *life* and *health* are precious gifts. Excuse my solicitude. With love to dear Ruth and yourself, and kisses for my baby,

Your affectionate mother,
Mary Jones.

Mr. Charles C. Jones, Jr., *to* Rev. C. C. Jones[g]
Savannah, Monday, December 12th, 1859
My dear Father,

Let me congratulate you upon the correct termination of the legal proceedings against Lucy. The judgment of the court was proper; you have discharged your duty as every good and true citizen is bound to do; and I am happy that your mind is now relieved from the burden of the prosecution. The effect upon Rose and Katy is probably better than it would have been had actual punishment have been inflicted. The power of the law is brought to bear, they made to realize the fact of a misdemeanor committed, and a new element of mercy and forbearance impressed upon them. The recognition of this will be a pledge of future amendment. Mr. Ashmore deserves our thanks for his prompt and obliging conduct. I fully agree with you in the views expressed with regard to the duties of masters in cases where the penal laws of our state are infringed.

The enclosures were safely received. The dividend in Central Railroad & Banking Company is not due until the 15th inst. I will then present the order and see to the execution of all your commissions with pleasure. Do oblige me by having the enclosed forwarded to Mr. Jackson at your early convenience. With much love, I am

Your affectionate son,
Charles C. Jones, Jr.

Mr. Charles C. Jones, Jr., *to* Mrs. Mary Jones[g]

Savannah, *Monday,* December 12th, 1859

My dear Mother,

Your kind note of the 10th inst. was with Father's esteemed favor of same date duly received, and I thank you sincerely for your tender solicitude. My eyes are better, although they still trouble me somewhat if I read or write much at night. Wet towels around my throat at night have given me considerable relief. Cousin Charles promises to prepare the prescription for me.

Your little granddaughter improves daily, especially in her *vocal powers*. Aunt and family, with the exception of the young ladies, left Savannah for Liberty this morning. All friends well. Ruth hopes to attend church and render thanks on Sabbath next. With warmest love, I am, as ever,

Your affectionate son,
Charles C. Jones, Jr.

The dividend on the stock is three hundred dollars.

Mr. Charles C. Jones, Jr., *to* Mrs. Mary Jones[t]

Savannah, *Monday,* December 12th, 1859

My dear Mother,

I omitted in my note of this evening to beg that you would send to Arcadia on Friday of this week the covering for the wagon which you so kindly promised to let me have. I hope to start my carts from this place for Southwest Georgia on Saturday morning. They will rest at Arcadia over Sabbath and commence the journey in earnest on Monday morning. My purpose is in person to inaugurate the commencement of my planting operations in

Baker about the 27th inst. It is a grievous undertaking, involving great outlay and expense, but will, I trust, with the favor of a kind and superintending Providence, eventuate in good and profit.

Ruth, the baby, and Mrs. Hall are all asleep. Hoping, my dear mother, that you and Father will both enjoy the refreshing influences of "tired nature's sweet restorer," I am, as ever,

Your affectionate son,
Charles C. Jones, Jr.

¼ *to 12 Midnight.*

Mrs. Mary Jones *to* Mr. Charles C. Jones, Jr.[g]
Montevideo, *Thursday,* December 15th, 1859

My dear Son,

This afternoon your father and myself rode over to the Retreat to welcome our dear aunt and cousins to the county. Found Aunt looking much better than could have been anticipated, the family well, and your Uncle Henry going to Savannah tomorrow.

On our return home your kind note was received, and I will see that the covering for the wagon goes over in time to Arcadia. What can I do for you? If anything, please let me know by Saturday's mail. As your brother and yourself are professional men, we have desired that you should never be involved in planting or the management of Negroes. Properly attended to, it brings great care, great anxiety, expenses that must be met, means or no means, and responsibilities not only for time but for eternity. All these you will realize more and more if your life is spared, especially if you are an enlightened, conscientious master, which I pray the Lord to make you.

When do you leave? I wish our home was in such a situation of comfort as to allow dear Ruth and our sweet baby to spend the period of your absence with us. I long to see the little darling. Do request Ruthie if she feels able to go out to church on Sabbath to be very prudent that she does not take cold. Be sure to dress warmly.

If the dividend has been received, after paying the bill of Bailie & Brothers and yourself please send out the remainder by your Uncle Henry. We have several expenses here to be met immediately, for which it will come in play. The expenses upon the servant Lucy will be at least twenty dollars; we do not wish Aunt to bear any part of them.

Your father sent your *note* immediately to Mr. Jackson; the boy returned saying he was in Savannah. I presume you saw him.

Your crib, my dear son, is subject to your order whenever you wish it. But I have thought as it is so large and high for your present room, if you will let it remain for the present, then I wish you to go to Mr. Morrell's and select one like the one I gave my little granddaughter Mary Jones and present it to my other little granddaughter Julia Berrien. You can select it either of black walnut or mahogany as Ruth pleases; and ask Mr. Morrell to charge the same to us. Be sure and do this at once, unless you prefer me to send in your old one.

It is late, and I must close. Your father unites with me in much love to Ruth and yourself, kisses for Baby, and kind regards to Mrs. Hall. May the Saviour bless and include you in His everlasting covenant, ever prays

Your affectionate mother,
Mary Jones.

MR. CHARLES C. JONES, JR., *to* REV. *and* MRS. C. C. JONES[g]

Savannah, Thursday, December 15th, 1859

My dear Father and Mother,

I have this morning drawn amount dividend from Central Railroad & Banking Company, and have remitted check to Messrs. James G. Bailie & Brother, and have also, as you desired, deducted amount due me. On the other page please find statement.

I am on the eve of negotiating for the sale of Ruth's Negroes. The heavy expenses which must necessarily be incurred in planting in Southwest Georgia, my inability to give my personal attention at such a distance, and the conflict between the duties of a planter and of a professional man—all induce me to look to a change of investment. I expect to go to Baker next week with a view to a sale to Dr. Martin of this city, who will if he purchases remove them at once to his plantation in Alabama just across the Georgia line. There will be no separation of members of families; they will all go together, and to a good owner.

We are all well. Ruth hopes to be downstairs tomorrow, to ride out on Saturday, and to attend church on Sabbath. With warmest love from Ruth, self, and Baby, I am, my dear parents, as ever,

Your affectionate son,
Charles C. Jones, Jr.

To and received by me from Central Railroad & Banking Company dividend of thirty shares capital stock held by C. C. Jones, trustee Mrs. Mary Jones		$300.00
By cash remitted Messrs. J. G. Bailie & Brother		147.75
		152.25
By cash paid self for two renewals in bank on note of C. C. Jones $17.84 each	$35.68	
and for cash loaned	10.00	45.68
Balance due by me this day		$106.57

Charles C. Jones, Jr.

Savannah, December 15th, 1859.

Mrs. Mary Jones *to* Mr. Charles C. Jones, Jr.[g]

Montevideo, *Monday,* December 19th, 1859

My dear Son,

As I was engaged as usual on Sabbath night teaching the young people and children, your good and trusty man William came in last night and joined in the service. At the close he handed me your letter. I judged of its contents by the size and laid it aside for Monday morning, and now write to acknowledge its receipt and to thank you for your prompt attention to my many little troublesome requests.

Our dear little granddaughter was a month old yesterday. We thought and spoke of you all! Rev. James Stacy preached for us at Midway. Friends all present from the Point, but your uncle too unwell to be out. He has again fared with a heavy loss from fire. Last week his cotton house was burnt! All the packed cotton (consisting of four or five bales) was saved, and seed cotton amounting to three more; but a large part of his crop must be gone. He had made a very fine crop. I feel deep sympathy for him. We are just sending Tom to inquire how he is this morning.

Breakfast waits. Father unites with me in love to Ruth and yourself. *Kiss* our dear baby for us. Remembrance to Mrs. Hall, and howdies for the servants. In haste,

Your affectionate mother,
Mary Jones.

William says: "The baby looks same like Massa."

Rev. *and* Mrs. C. C. Jones *to* Their Three Children[g]

Montevideo, *Wednesday,* December 21st, 1859

Our very dear Children,

This is *the twenty-ninth wedding day* of your father and mother, and we could not let it pass without sending you a line in memorial of it—to let you know that we are as happy today as we were this day twenty-nine years ago, and certainly are twenty-nine times deeper in love with each other. But we desire especially to record the goodness and mercy of the Lord, who has led us by the hand all these years, and blessed us with dear and dutiful children, and permitted us to train them up and to educate and see them happily married and reputably and successfully settled in life, and even granted us the sight of our children's children! He has also bountifully provided for us and ours temporally, and has suffered us to want no earthly good, and remarkably preserved the lives and increased the number of our servants. And our connection, with but few exceptions, has been kind and pleasant with them. We have traveled much, and changed our residence several times, and have passed through afflictions and losses; and yet we continue to the present hour, so far as we now know while writing, an unbroken family, and a family provided for, and having many affectionate relations and kind friends.

And more particularly we record that you, Charles Colcock, Joseph, and Mary Sharpe, had the prayers of your parents offered for you before you saw the light. You were born children of God's everlasting covenant, and in your infancy had the sign and seal of that covenant placed upon you in the House of God by His faithful minister, your father and mother then and there standing with you in their arms and presenting you to the Lord. And what thanks do we render to Him that two of you, as we truly hope and believe, have been called by His grace into His Kingdom, and that you have embraced that covenant for yourselves; and that the one yet remaining is not insensible to the claims of his God and Saviour upon him, and for whose speedy conversion we do daily and earnestly pray, and have faith in God that he too will be brought in. And how happy we are that you, Robert and Ruthie and Carrie, are our children, that you are tenderly loved by your companions, by us, and by each other, and we are all one family; that your three families hold each other in love and in honor and in reputation; and that you will ever continue to do so and be mutually assisting to each other in all the sunshine and shade that may fall upon you in life.

On this our wedding day we send you our blessing, and a blessing upon the little ones, and pray that your lives may be more useful to your families, to the Church of God, and to the world than ours have been, and that in the retrospect of years you may have far less of sin and of evil to deplore, and more of the riches of God's grace and the comforts of His salvation to rejoice in. Ever remember that while we have a home in this world, it is your home; and you and yours will be always welcome to it, and to our warmest embraces.

It has been a quiet and happy day with us, and after rendering thanks to God, and praying for pardon, and commending ourselves and ours to His mercy, through Jesus Christ our Saviour, in all time to come, we retire on our twenty-ninth wedding night with hearts of gratitude and love.

Your ever affectionate parents,
C. C. Jones
Mary Jones.

Mr. Charles C. Jones, Jr., *to* Rev. *and* Mrs. C. C. Jones[t]

Savannah, *Monday,* December 26th, 1859

My dear Father and Mother,

Upon my return home on Saturday last I found your valued favors of the 19th and 21st inst. awaiting my coming.

I cannot tell you how sincerely we appreciate your letter penned on the anniversary of your twenty-ninth wedding day; and heartily do we thank you for all your kind blessings and good wishes. To tell you, my dear parents, that your tender affection is reciprocated with all the warmth of a heart sensibly alive to all the precious memories of the past, to all your unchanging acts of kindness and forbearing charity towards the many faults of an erring but not ungrateful son, to your unceasing care and Christian counsel and example from my earliest infancy, would be to express not a moiety of all I feel. The past, as to you, is consecrated. Never did child have better parents; never was he blessed by a good God with a kinder or more perfect father and mother. The only misgiving is that the advantages—religious, intellectual, and secular—which you have ever extended with such ceaseless and lavish care have not been by me improved to better purpose. . . . The highest enjoyment I can expect in this world, my dear parents, will be found in staying your hands when age and infirmity draw near. God grant that you may long be spared—ornaments to the church, the esteemed of all in the community in which you dwell, the delight of your children and your children's children! We wish you many, many happy returns of your wedding day, and a merry, pleasant Christmas.

Last week I spent in Baker County. Upon reflection I came to the conclusion that it would be unwise for me to plant in that section. The character of the region, the semi-barbaric tone in morals and religion, the character of the treatment to which Negroes are there subjected, the esteem in which they are held, the remove from my place of residence, the inability to extend to my people and planting interests that attention and careful consideration which they deserve for mutual comfort and profit—all induced me to look to a change of investment. I accordingly offered my Negroes to Dr. Martin of this city, a planter in Alabama about thirty miles from Columbus, and a kind, considerate master. He purchased them, and has removed them to his plantation. Thus is my mind relieved of a burden. Not a single separation occurred; not a single family tie was sundered. I could, by separating them, have made the sale more profitable, but what is profit in the light of a compensation for the recollection of having interrupted natural affection, and sundered ties which at least in the eye of God and of enlightened humanity are as sacred with the Negro as with those who stand higher in the scale of civilization? The price was a fair, honest price—about $770 apiece. I never could have consented to a hiring of the Negroes for another year. Three have died during the last twelvemonth, and the treatment has in all probability not been of that character which should have been extended. I still hold the land I purchased, and hope to realize a profit.

The Central Railroad, in addition to their semi-annual dividend of ten percent, have declared a stock dividend of twelve and a half percent. Thus every owner of eight shares will now have nine. Twenty-seven and a half percent in one year is uncommon. Would that we all owned a hundred thousand dollars' worth of the stock, and that a like dividend could be realized every year!

Ruth and little Julia are both quite well, and unite with me in warmest love to you both, my dear parents. Do let me know whenever I can be of any service to you. As ever,

Your affectionate son,
Charles C. Jones, Jr.

Mrs. Mary Jones *to* Mr. *and* Mrs. Charles C. Jones, Jr.ᵍ

Montevideo, *Saturday,* December 31st, 1859

I intended to have consecrated *this day,* the last of *1859,* to communings with my dear absent children; but alas for the interruptions which seem at times to invade almost every moment of my life! Here I am, late Saturday evening, excusing myself *to company* and seeking a moment's retirement to send a line of love to you, my beloved children, and a kiss for you, my sweet little granddaughter, whom I long to see.

Thanks, my dear son, from your father and mother for your deeply interesting and affectionate letter to us. The love, the respect, the care of our dear children in our declining years makes up our greatest earthly happiness! We were rejoiced to know that you had succeeded in arranging your business to your satisfaction. I believe you will never regret it. When will you come out to see us? We hope in a short time to complete the painting, all to the blinds and one more coat on the outside. Did you get my letter about the crib?

Dear Ruthie, by Titus I send you a little jar of *yellow orange* preserves. *Robert* brought them from Jacksonville, Florida. And I must ask the favor of you to have the dresses which he brings sent for me to Miss Hyde, with the request that she will alter them immediately for me. They are so short in the waist I cannot wear them. I wish her to insert the belts at the bottom of the waists, tightening them a little where they hook, and shortening the skirts just as much as she lengthens the waist.

Your sister returned on Thursday to Walthourville, and they intended moving immediately into the *academy,* which is the best arrangement they can make at present.

Night, dark and rainy, closes in, and I must stop. Father unites with me in tenderest love to you both, and kisses for our little Julia. Wishing you, my dear children, a happy, happy New Year, and the divine favor and blessing crowning all your days and years,

Ever your affectionate mother,

Mary Jones.

Howdy for the servants. Tell *George Washington* his mother has a fine son, remarkably large; and we will name him, as she wishes us to do so, *Edward Everett.*

Have you received the portrait of Mr. E. yet?

Rev. C. C. Jones *to* Mr. Charles C. Jones, Jr.ᵍ

Montevideo, *Tuesday,* January 10th, 1860

My dear Son,

Your mother and father wish dear Ruthie, yourself, and the little one a truly happy New Year—happy in the best and highest sense: in the saving love and mercy of God our Saviour upon each of you personally and upon all collectively and upon all your household. This we do sincerely and prayerfully.

Your last favors have all come to hand, and we thank you for your kind and filial wishes and your careful attentions to our many little commissions. The arrangement which you have made with your personal interests in Southwest Georgia meets my approbation for the reasons stated in your letter which moved you thereto; and it was the view which your mother and myself entertained at the first. And I trust that you may never see occasion to regret the step you have taken. My own experience assures me that a professional man, if he means to continue one, must be *totus in illis* and avoid any business that diverts him from his one pursuit, and in our country from *planting especially;* for there is no business, if it be of any reasonable extent, which involves more responsibility and consumes more time and gives more care to a conscientious person than it does. You made a fair sale, and you were properly influenced by humane motives in seeking no more. Your friend Dr. Martin has reason to congratulate himself, as such property is now selling at a much higher rate. The next duty is to seek an economical, safe, and profitable investment. Keep *the principal intact.*

We sent down week before last ten bales cotton by the Savannah, Albany & Gulf Railroad to Mr. Anderson, and have not heard from it, but hope he has sold it, for January bills are coming in. Have sent by Captain Thomson, now in the river near the house on his way down, five bales more. If Mr. Anderson will sell this lot at a fair price, we will reduce our note five hundred dollars and pay off some of our more pressing bills. Meanwhile will send in as fast as we get out the crop, and hope through a kind Providence we may be successful in paying off everything we owe this year.

I requested Robert to beg you to get me a *good substantial carriage harness at Mr. Knapp's,* but not an *expensive* one, and ask Mr. Knapp to send it out *with Robert.* And I wish you would send me out, *put up in the same bundle with the harness,* a ream of just such letter paper *as this* I now write on, and a copy of Cobb's *Walker's Dictionary* from Mr. Cooper's. I leave yourself and Robert to select the harness, and I promise to be satisfied with your choice. The old harness is so worn that I fear to use it.

You will have a pleasant visit from your sister and brother Robert. Sister has special intent of paying her visit to Ruthie and the baby. Hope it is growing finely. Tell Daughter Little Daughter is perfectly happy and seems at home and is quite well and is a great source of interest in our quiet home; nor must she feel uneasy about her.

Mother unites in much love to Ruth and yourself, and we send kisses for our little granddaughter. Love to Robert and Daughter. Servants on the places as far as heard from generally well.

Your ever affectionate father,
C. C. Jones.

Mother says: "Don't sacrifice your land; you can get more than you gave."

Mr. Charles C. Jones, Jr., *to* Rev. C. C. Jones[g]

Savannah, *Wednesday,* January 11th, 1860

My dear Father,

Your kind letter of the 10th inst. was this afternoon received—too late, however, to comply strictly with your request to have the writing paper and dictionary enclosed in the same package with the harness. The harness had been sent to the depot before your favor was taken from the post. Robert, however, will carry the paper, etc., to Walthourville on the morrow. I have placed in the bundle two pencils of a new description which you may find convenient. The harness was the best that we could find at Mr. Knapp's for a reasonable price, and I hope you will not be disappointed in it. Cost: forty-eight dollars.

The visit of Sister and Robert has been very pleasant to us, and my only regret is that they cannot make it convenient to remain longer.

When may we expect the pleasure of seeing you, my dear father and dear mother? Ruth speaks of having little Julia baptized so soon as you can make it convenient to come and administer that rite. We would of course deem it a very great privilege to have her baptized by her dear grandfather.

Ruth is not very well. She needs a change, and I am very anxious that she should leave the city for a while so soon as our guests depart. Dr. Howard, Amanda, Baby, and servants have been with us now for nearly six weeks.

Am glad that my arrangements in Baker meet with your approval. Say to Mother that I shall follow her advice in relation to the land. Regret deeply to hear, Father, that you have not been very well of late, and sincerely hope that you are now feeling better. Will see Captain Anderson in reference to the cotton. Sister and Robert will give you all the town talk. With warmest love to self and dear Mother, in which Ruth and little Julia heartily unite, I am, as ever,

Your affectionate son,
Charles C. Jones, Jr.

Mr. Charles C. Jones, Jr., *to* Rev. *and* Mrs. C. C. Jones[g]

Savannah, *Friday,* January 13th, 1860

My dear Father and Mother,

On yesterday I had the pleasure of seeing Mr. Happersett from Philadelphia. He has changed not a whit since last we met. His inquiries respecting you, Sister, and Brother were of the kindest and most particular character. He is as full of his laughter and good nature as ever. Nothing to trouble him; plenty to amuse; any amount of leisure; no hard study; and a frequent change of scene, just suited to a man of his disposition. And I am sorry to say I think his manner of life and want of study tell not a very favorable tale. How he does *murder* the King's English! I have met no one for a long time who in a short conversation so repeatedly violated the primary rules of grammar—the imperfect tense for the present, plural nouns and singular verbs, the objective for the nominative case, etc.—and all his blunders most unconsciously committed. I could but regret that a church which in so marked a degree may point to an educated clergy should have entrusted one of its most important agencies to one so defectively educated. You would think, however, to hear him talk, that he had the country in a sling. His good nature and *ore rotundo,* I have no doubt, however, are with many very effective. He is a clever man, and one cannot help joking with and liking him. He is off for New Orleans, and when returning this way hopes to come out and see you for a day.

The supreme court is still in session. There are so many cases on the middle-circuit docket that I fear our cases of the eastern district will not be reached at all.

Mr. Anderson tells me that he obtained for the Montevideo cotton twenty-five cents: better than usual. Wish he had a thousand bales and could sell them all at that price!

We are all pretty well; Ruth not as well as we could wish. The little grand-daughter improves every day, and begins to notice and to give the first indications of intelligence. She cuts a figure in her bathing tub. We are full in every room, Ruth having, in addition to Howard and Amanda and child, some Augusta friends with her. Hoping, my dear father and mother, that every blessing will attend you, and that you will let me know whenever I can be of any assistance to you, I am, with warmest love, in which Ruth and the baby unite, as ever

Your affectionate son,
Charles C. Jones, Jr.

Major McIntosh begs me to ask of you, Father, whether you can recommend a competent and reliable young man in Liberty County who for the annual compensation of three hundred dollars would be willing to undertake the education of the children of his son, Judge McIntosh, in Florida. There are three children, all small, and the branches to be taught only those of a plain and elementary English education. Do let me hear from you upon this subject at your early convenience if there be anyone whom you can recommend.

REV. C. C. JONES *to* MR. CHARLES C. JONES, JR.ᵍ

Montevideo, *Saturday,* January 14th, 1860

My dear Son,

Your two last letters have been received. The little matters all came safely and are satisfactory. Am sorry that Ruth is not so well. Too much company and care for one so recently ill is far from being advantageous, and sometimes lays the foundation for protracted debility.

It will suit me any time to go down and baptize the baby that Ruth may appoint, giving us a few days' notice. And should your house be full, it will make no difference: we can stay for the short visit at the Pulaski. Were you to favor us with a visit, and Ruthie might recruit somewhat at the old homestead, little Julia might be baptized in Midway, where her grandparents and father were baptized and pretty much our whole family. You would have all your relations present excepting your brother and Uncle John. This is a mere passing, though a pleasant, thought.

Please say to my friend Major McIntosh that I do not know of a teacher at this moment in the county, but will institute an inquiry and let him know shortly. I presume the salary is three hundred dollars *and board*.

It will gratify me to see Mr. Happersett. He is in the line of qualification you remark upon *sui generis,* but notwithstanding makes an excellent agent. Any man, it matters not what are his attainments in scholarship and intellectual cultivation, if he neglects study and meditation and composition, will inevitably deteriorate. Time should be snatched even from the busiest professional engagements to refresh and invigorate the mind. Excelsior! We know not what positions Providence may call us to occupy. And then the pleasure of knowledge is so great; its acquisition is one of our noblest and purest enjoyments as intelligent beings.

If you get a saving offer for your land, let it go. Mr. Anderson has made a good sale. If we had as many bales as you wish for, and sold at the price, I am afraid we might not meet the responsibility of so great a trust as we should. Hope the Arcadia cotton has sold equally well.

Our political sky is very cloudy! Have you read the Vice-President's speech lately delivered at Frankfort, Kentucky? Excellent. My hope is that He who has so often and so mercifully preserved our country will again show us favor, unworthy as we are, and deliver us from impending evils and grant us peace. He is able to still the tumult of the people.

Mother unites in love to Ruthie and yourself. And kiss the baby for us. I hear she is a sweet little baby.

Your affectionate father,
C. C. Jones.

MRS. MARY JONES *to* MR. CHARLES C. JONES, JR.ᵍ

Montevideo, *Saturday,* January 14th, 1860

Your Aunt Mary, my dear son, has embroidered a *beautiful* sacque for your little daughter, which I will send to Ruth by the first safe opportunity, and which I know you will admire.

Have you called to see our dear old aunt's granddaughters? I know you have but little time for visiting; but if you can do so, for her sake who is entitled to every expression of respect, I would be glad if you would. The young ladies, too, are worthy of attention; they are intelligent and well educated.

If Ruth does not make a change to the up country, I hope she will come out as soon as she possibly can to Montevideo. Although we have but little of interest, I can but hope that rest and freedom from care *at this time* will do her much good.

Our little Mary was perfectly satisfied with "Danpapa" and "Danmama" in her mother's absence. She is a most interesting child. I long to see her and our dear little Julia together. With much love to Ruth and yourself, and kisses for the babe,

Your affectionate mother,
Mary Jones.

Mr. Charles C. Jones, Jr., *to* Rev. *and* Mrs. C. C. Jones[g]
Savannah, *Thursday,* January 19th, 1860
My dear Father and Mother,

Your united and valued favor of the 14th inst. has just been received, and we are truly happy to hear from home. Uncle William left us this morning after (to us) a pleasant visit of two days. He looks remarkably well, and I have never seen him in finer spirits.

We feel obliged to you, Father, for your suggestion in reference to the baptism of our little Julia. It would be to me a pleasure of no ordinary character to know that the consecrated water was administered in the House of God by my own father, and upon the very spot where her grandparents and father were baptized, in the presence of relatives, and in the church with which the earliest impressions of divine worship are associated. The only possible objection in Ruth's mind seems to be—and she does not urge it as such —that none of her sisters or relatives can be present.

Since our marriage Ruth has paid no visit to her relatives. She purposes going to Burke next week to spend a week or two with her friends. Our superior court sitting on Monday next, in case she goes as at present anticipated, my time will be so fully occupied that I can better endure her absence then than at almost any other time. So soon as she returns I wish her to be with you at Montevideo. A change of such a delightful character will, I am persuaded, result in her benefit.

Little Julia will coo her early thanks to Aunt Mary for her kind remembrance. I was so unfortunate as not to meet the young ladies when I called; will go again. We see them every Sabbath, and they are quite well.

It seems so unnatural, Mother, to remove the crib from the old homestead, where it has so long remained, and where we will hope often again to see it and to fill its generous bosom with your children's children, that Ruth and myself will accept your kind present for little Julia from Mr. Morrell. She shall thank you herself with her earliest lip of intelligence, and we will do so in anticipation for her now.

She improves rapidly. Ruth says of her, when conversing with her and folding her to her bosom: "You are just pretty enough for anyone, and the sweetest little thing in this world." I sincerely trust that a kind God will spare her life and give her many days of usefulness and happiness. I will try and do my duty in giving her every advantage.

We all unite, my dear parents, in warmest love. As ever,

Your affectionate son,

Charles C. Jones, Jr.

REV. GEORGE HOWE *to* REV. C. C. JONES[t]

Columbia, *Monday,* January 23rd, 1860

My dear Brother,

Since we have seen each other or heard by letter from one another, another year has closed and a new one commenced. The new has thus far been full of its duties with me, and I have not found time to write to friends, with whom I would gladly exchange kind greetings.

The last part of the year which has closed was to us replete with sorrows. We had just met with one great affliction when we last saw you. In November my aged mother was called away; and my poor boy Walthour about ten days after was released from all his earthly sorrows. In about a week after, we received his remains and consigned them to the narrow house. It was all very sad. My visit to Liberty County and attention to public duties had prevented my usual summer visit to my mother and my afflicted child. Though the one died with her other children at her side, poor Walthour sickened, pined, and died among strangers. We were uninformed of any change in his health, and knew not till a telegraphic message informed us of his death. Though it was better that he should die than live, our minds revert with sadness to the melancholy scene, and with difficulty reconcile ourselves to the fact that there was no hand of relative or friend to minister to him. We do not doubt it would have been a comfort to him to have had us with him, though we could have been to him of no other service. It was three years since his mother and one year since I had seen his face. How mysterious have been the dealings of God with us! How often and how painfully have our hearts been crushed within us! The chastisement is from a Father's hand, and may it work out for us an exceeding and eternal weight of glory!

At last, my dear brother, our *Review* has made its appearance. We have been thrown back by several circumstances: by changes in our printing office, by my own absence in attendance on your synod, and other causes of delay. Your own brief article has given us great satisfaction. I did earnestly wish to put your name to it, but your request that it should be anonymous was so decided that I did not dare do otherwise. I wished it that it might recommend your book, as being a taste of it in advance. Dr. Adger, who is our historian now, expresses his great satisfaction with it, and thinks it augurs highly of the *History* of which it is understood to be an extract. You will see that in my article on abolitionism I am indebted to you for some things in the Scripture argument for slavery. It was easier in my rapid preparation to refer to your article than to hunt up the Scripture points anew, and I hope my reference to your article in the note will not offend you. I wrote on that subject just because I had to write something, and that was the easiest. I intended to have it anonymous, but my coeditors have overruled me in this. I do not think it very fortunate that I, originally from the North, should have written on so Southern a subject. It, however, now belongs to North and South alike.

You will be glad to hear that our numbers have continued to increase in the seminary: fifty-eight this year. . . . The union prayer meeting continues to be kept up in the town daily; the concert of prayer for the world's conversion was held during the second week of this month; and these two meetings have had a manifestly happy effect upon the state of piety in the seminary. . . . You have doubtless seen that Dr. Leland is married again. His children are terribly outraged at it, and the public impression was very unfavorable to the old doctor until he brought home his bride. She is an English lady who has been some twelve years in Saxony, of about twenty-eight or thirty years of age, intelligent and accomplished. She seems to have won golden opinions since her arrival among us, and to be rapidly removing those unfavorable impressions which preceded her coming. The doctor has been much engaged in the union meetings, but I do not think we can reasonably expect that he will continue very long among us. He is seventy-two years old.

But I must stop my loquacious pen. Shall we have another chapter from your book for our next number of the *Review?* Mrs. Howe and the children desire to be kindly remembered by you and Mrs. Jones. Present my best respects also.

Very truly yours,
George Howe.

Mr. Charles C. Jones, Jr., *to* Rev. C. C. Jones[g]
Savannah, *Monday,* February 6th, 1860
My dear Father,

Ruth and myself purpose coming out on Saturday of this week, if you will be so kind as to let the carriage meet us at No. 3 (McIntosh Station). We have two pleasant purposes in view: one to see you and dear Mother and let you see how much your little granddaughter has improved, the other to have her baptized by you at Midway on next Sabbath. Ruth expects soon to visit her friends in Middle Georgia, and is loath to go until her infant is baptized. You may therefore expect us, D.V., on Saturday of this week.

Heard from Brother today. He and Carrie are both quite well. He has sent you a copy of his *Observations on Malarial Fever,* which I will bring with me.

Have been exceedingly busy of late; wish that I could have a little relaxation. All friends well. Cousin Eliza West has a little boy, born on Saturday —her tenth child, if I count correctly. The sober doctor has the good as well as the poor man's blessing. Ruth unites in warmest love to you both, my dear parents. Baby would if she could. We do so for her. As ever,

Your affectionate son,
Charles C. Jones, Jr.

REV. C. C. JONES *to* MR. CHARLES C. JONES, JR.[g]

Montevideo, *Tuesday,* February 7th, 1860

My dear Son,

Mother says she is rejoiced to hear that you will be out on Saturday with Ruthie and the baby, and sends this message, "that if Ruthie and you do not love the baby, to come out prepared *to leave it with her.*" So you can both search your hearts on this point and make up your minds by Saturday. We shall be very glad to see you and to baptize the dear child on Sunday at Midway, God willing. May it please a covenant-keeping God to adopt it into His family and make it an heir of everlasting life!

How would my heart and the heart of your mother rejoice, my dear son, if you could on that occasion present your firstborn in your own personal and precious faith! The hour surely has come for you to take the vows of God upon yourself. Do not put it off. If you are ever saved, there must come a time when you must stop and repent and turn to the Lord; and there is no better time than the present. Your family needs a spiritual head: your duty is not met by attending to its temporal interests; its spiritual interests are infinitely more important. You will give direction to the spirit of that dear little one, who owes, under God, its existence to you *for eternity!* You cannot avoid it. These are considerations to impress and draw you to God.

We are expecting all Aunt's family this week, and hope your sister may be with us also. And maybe she will stay over Sabbath and go with us to Midway. Will send a note to your Aunt Susan and family and your Uncle William and Aunt Julia and Uncle Henry and let them know you hope to be at Midway. You do not remember that you were baptized in this month, February? I think the fourth Sabbath in February 1832, by Rev. Robert Quarterman.

Gilbert will meet you at No. 3 Saturday morning with the carriage, and you will reach home to dinner. . . . Mother requests you to bring out with you from King & Waring's five pounds gunpowder or young hyson tea, four packages of sparkling gelatin, and one bottle quinine. And Father begs you to bring out from Cooper & Company three or four sheets best yellow blotting paper and the work (two volumes) *The Land and the Book,* one of the best modern works on *the* land of all lands, *Palestine.* I wish mine eyes could see that country.

We are having a heavy fall of rain. Still falling. County healthy.

Present our congratulations to Cousins Charles and Eliza; this son, to keep the numbers true, should be called *Decius.* I wrote a letter to little Charles on his going to Princeton by Rev. Mr. Safford. Hope he received it.

One more commission: will you get Messrs. Claghorn & Cunningham to send to your house a box of adamantine candles, *short sixes,* and bring it out with you on Saturday. Mother says: "Let them be *white* and not *yellow.*"

Do not forget to bring your brother's book.

Mother unites in much love to Ruthie and yourself and in many kisses for the baby. We long to see her.

Your ever affectionate father,
C. C. Jones.

Do say to our venerable friend Major McIntosh that there is no teacher to be had within my knowledge in our part of the county. My efforts have failed. Is his daughter-in-law, Mrs. Donald McIntosh from the West, now in Savannah?

Mrs. Mary S. Mallard *to* Miss Mary Jones Taylor[t]
Walthourville, *Thursday,* February 23rd, 1860

My dear Mary,

I was rejoiced to receive your letter day before yesterday—the more so because I was spared the pain of writing you a regular scold. I had been intending to write and inquire if you had entirely blotted me from your memory, but your letter explains all, so we are good friends, and no intentional wrong done on either side. You say that you have not received a letter from me for nearly a year. I have written more recently than that, and you must blame Uncle Sam for my apparent delinquency. I almost began to wonder if you had been in the region of Harpers Ferry, and thought perhaps you might be so occupied with the affairs of the nation that you had no time for correspondence. But I must leave all this alone and proceed to give some account of myself.

Last summer brought its pleasures, and trials too. There were several deaths in our village, and it was my lot to be frequently near the bed of death. I say frequently; it seemed so to me, for there were four or five deaths in families residing near us, and one in our own house. This was a stranger by the name of Henry O. Britton. He came to the county in July and was taken ill at one of the most unhealthy places in it. Mr. Mallard, hearing that he was sick, went to see him and found him extremely ill with the worst form of bilious fever. Thinking that a change to a more healthy situation might save his life, Mr. Mallard invited him to our house; and after lingering ten days he died. There was something mysterious about his whole conduct. He positively refused to give us any definite information respecting his family, although he professed to have several children. He said his wife was dead. We advertised in several papers, and made every effort to discover his relatives, and a few days ago we received a letter from his wife. I have no doubt he had deserted her, though she did not say so. In many respects this illness and death was one of the most distressing I ever heard of. I suppose he was a man from the common walks of life; he was teaching a short method of computing interest. It is quite a relief to us to have heard something of his family.

We remained at home all summer, and enjoyed much health. Mr. Mallard is peculiarly blessed with good health; he has had but one slight attack of fever since our marriage. Our little Mary is much grown, though not a large child. She is very interesting now; says anything, and often surprises us with her use of words. She is the merriest, noisiest little mortal I ever saw. I wish I could show her to you; I think you would say she was worthy to bear the name *Mary Jones*. You ask if she has any companions. Not yet, though I should not be surprised if you heard of an arrival next April. Mary will then be two years old—I think entirely too young to have companions.

So Sarah Ann is engaged! I did not know it before. What is the name of the fortunate gentleman, and when is he to be made happy? Offer her my congratulations—if you approve of the match! (I suppose, of course, she consulted her elder sister.) I hope Sallie will realize all and even more than her present expectations. When persons are happily married, it is a *happy* life. I speak from experience. You say you still cling to your spinster banner and suppose I will say "from necessity." By no means! I am surprised you should think of such a speech coming from one that had listened to Miss Mary Gill's instruction. Don't you recollect how she would occasionally speak to her scholars: "Young ladies, you should always remember that no woman remains single *from necessity* but *from choice;* for I will venture to say every single woman has had at some time offers of marriage." I can never forget this lesson, and often think of it when I see an aged spinster. I should not be at all surprised if you were now engaged. You must tell me all about Sarah Ann's intended. Is he pious? What denomination? Has he a profession? And where will he live?

My brother Joe was married in October to a very lovely young lady—one highly educated and I think well qualified to make him very happy. We all attended the wedding. They are keeping house in Augusta. Brother Joe is still professor in the medical college there; I think I will send you a copy of his introductory address. My brother Charlie's wife has a little daughter about three months old, so you see I am an aunty.

I wish I could tell you of some improvement in my dear father's health, but I cannot. He did seem a little better last summer, but the cold winter seems to have depressed his system. His inaction increases, so that it is with difficulty that he gets about at times. He looks pretty well in face, and in general his spirits are good. He seldom preaches now, and is always compelled to sit while doing so. There is one great comfort: the nervous inaction has never affected his lungs or his head. Mother's health is pretty good.

I am so sorry to hear of Margie Dickson's state of health. What is the matter with her? I know she has been sick a long time, but have never known what her disease was. I am truly sorry for Sue. Do give my love to her when you write, and to Margie too. What have become of John and Le Dickson? . . . I was glad to hear of Miss Sarah Gill once more. Are all of the sisters living in New Jersey? . . . I suppose Paulina is not married yet, as you said nothing about any change of state. Where is Lizzie Paul? Is she still single? I saw Lizzie Grier's marriage in the papers.

Matilda Harden is now in the county on a visit. Her mother moved last fall a year ago to Orangeburg, South Carolina, to be with her two younger daughters while they are completing their education. There is a very excellent school in Orangeburg, and Mrs. Harden thought it would be best for the whole family to reside there until the two girls were educated. The place is rather too quiet for Matilda, though she goes to Columbia to see her uncles, who are professors in the South Carolina College, and then she has a pretty gay time.

I think after receiving this letter you will be assured of my love and good wishes, so please write me very soon and I will return you a speedy answer. Now that a speaker is at last elected, I suppose the Post Office Department will be better regulated and our letters will be better taken care of. We have moved to another and more central portion of the village. The house we are now occupying is much better suited to the size of our family. It is time for the mail to close, so I must say good-bye. Give much love to Sallie and to your mother. Mr. Mallard desires to be presented to you, and I send a kiss from Mamie. Accept much love and assurances of continued friendship from

Your affectionate friend,
Mary S. Mallard.

MRS. MARY JONES *to* MR. CHARLES C. JONES, JR.ᵍ

Montevideo, Tuesday, February 28th, 1860

My dear Son,

We sent dear Marion Glen to the depot on Friday, and by the return of the carriage your boy George came, bearing a most acceptable present of oranges, apples, lemons, and pineapples, for which kind remembrance I am truly obliged to you. We have all enjoyed them. Yesterday they served to decorate our dinner table beautifully, and had ample justice done to them by the eighteen persons who sat down to dinner. I invited all our friends within reach to meet our friends from Marietta, who have now been with us over two weeks. The young ladies went to South Hampton yesterday; and today Aunt, Cousin Mary, Louisa, and Joe have gone to Walthourville to visit your sister and Robert. They will all be with us again next week to remain until they return home.

Our dear and venerable aunt has improved astonishingly in health and strength; but I remark an unusual depression of spirits about her, and believe that her *gray hairs* are going down in sorrow to her grave on account of the conduct and habits of her *only son*. And his poor daughters—oh, what a blight he has cast upon their prospects! What a shadow upon their hearts! Cousin Mary tells me for the *first* time whilst in Savannah they came to a knowledge of his intemperance. It was a dreadful shock to their young and tender hearts. Sometimes they get together and weep as if their hearts would break, and say they feel almost ashamed to lift up their heads in society. And his sisters, kind and generous but dependent women as they are—where is the hand that should protect and support them? And his son, that should now have a father's influence and a father's example to mold and guide his opening manhood—oh, to think his own father can only be held up to him as a *warning!* Poor fellow, for such ruin I know that he is without excuse before God and man; but I can never hear of the misery and disgrace of any friend, especially of those linked by natural ties, without anguish of heart.

Oh, Charles, my son, my own son, if there be any one *sin* embodying all others, it is the sin of intemperance! And where does it begin? None are born drunkards. "The fear of man bringeth a snare." The customs of society cannot be resisted. The social glass, sipped at first in a genteel way, has brought ruin to many souls and sorrow to many hearts. The most hopeless feature of this vice is that it destroys all moral perceptions. Men who drink themselves and invite others to drink are blind to their own danger and the wretched influence they are exerting over others. I never knew a drinking man who did not think he had the habit perfectly under control and knew exactly where to stop, whilst friends around knew the perfect delusion under which he labored. And oh, how easy it is, step by step, to have every principle undermined!

Excuse me, my dear son, if I appear to you unnecessarily decided or solicitous upon this subject. Although you are a man and independent of us in every sense of the term, still a father and a mother's love would seek to throw around you every influence that they can to preserve you in the path of virtue. Yes, "I have no greater joy than to know that my children walk in truth." The *day* will surely come, and it may not be distant, when you and I, mother and son, shall stand before the Judgment Bar of God. Oh, let it not be written against me in that day: "You neglected to do your duty to your own child." I honestly believe that every man who takes a glass, saving in cases of sickness or ill health, or who makes a practice of offering it to his friends, is treading the broad road to ruin himself and drawing others along with him.

Have you read the paper I put into your hands as we parted? Daily does my soul go out to the precious Saviour in anxious cries for your salvation. When, my son, are you going to consider the interests of your immortal soul? Are you daily reading the Word of God? Do you pray? I know that the Holy Spirit alone can enlighten your heart and new create it, but you must "seek if you would find," "knock if you would have the door of mercy opened." Will you not say with the Psalmist: "Create in me a clean heart, O God, and renew a right spirit within me. Wash me thoroughly from mine iniquities. Blot out my sins, and remember no more my transgressions."

Tonight I am alone—free to think, free to weep, free to write. Forgive me if I have said too much. Father has long since retired. It is time to close. Our best love to you, and to dear Ruth when you write her, with kisses for our dear little Julia. God bless and save you, my child!

Your affectionate mother,
Mary Jones.

MR. CHARLES C. JONES, JR., *to* MRS. MARY JONES[t]
Savannah, *Thursday,* March 1st, 1860

My dear Mother,

Your very kind and valued letter of the 28th ult. has just been received. It would be idle for me to say that I only thank you for all your tender expressions of parental solicitude, and for all the good advice which it contains. They will be laid to heart. Every day convinces me more and more that I can never thank God sufficiently for having favored me with such parents as you, my dear mother and father, have ever been and still are. Few indeed have ever been so blessed as I have been, and the fault lies at my own door alone if the privileges have not been improved by me.

I have had a very busy week, and am on the eve of leaving Savannah for Cherokee County. I regret the necessity compelling me to be absent from the office at this time. I write in much haste, but with warmest love to self and Father. As ever,

Your affectionate son,
Charles C. Jones, Jr.

MR. CHARLES C. JONES, JR., *to* REV. *and* MRS. C. C. JONES[g]
Savannah, *Saturday,* March 10th, 1860

My dear Father and Mother,

Yesterday I reached the city, having successfully attended to my engagements in Cherokee Superior Court, and also having had the pleasure of spending a day with Ruth and little Julia in Burke County. They are both very well. Ruth is now with her brother Randolph at the old homestead, where every object is consecrated by some delightful youthful association. You may judge, therefore, that she is enjoying herself very much.

Do say to Brother and Sister Carrie that I very much regret that we were not in the city when they passed through. We will certainly expect a long visit from them upon their return.

I sincerely hope, my dear parents, that you are both well and in the enjoyment of many blessings. There is nothing of interest in the city. Lawyers, poor fellows, are well-nigh in a starving condition; everybody is meeting his engagements, and we consequently have no broken contracts to look after. With warmest love, I am, as ever,

Your affectionate son,
Charles C. Jones, Jr.

MR. CHARLES C. JONES, JR., *to* REV. C. C. JONES[g]

Savannah, *Wednesday,* March 14th, 1860

My dear Father,

I embrace the opportunity of sending you a line by Uncle Henry to convey best love to dear Mother and self, and to beg that you will send me written authority to arrange for the extra dividend in Central Railroad, amounting to some three additional shares of the capital stock, and to receipt for any surplus in cash that there may be after statement of full shares.

Uncle Henry will tell you the outrageous conduct of Joseph W. Robarts. Language and thought fail to express or conceive the depth of infamy into which he has voluntarily plunged himself. I tremble for the effect which a knowledge of his recent alliance, with all its horrid antecedents and concomitants, will cause in the pure bosoms of his venerable mother, high-minded sisters, pure and innocent daughters, and unfortunate son. The heart sickens at thought of such a manifestation of the mean depravity of human nature.

I expect to go to Burke on Saturday to bring Ruth home. I cannot consent for her to remain away any longer, although I doubt not her visit to family and friends proves very pleasant. All well. With warmest love to self and dear Mother, to Brother and Sister Carrie, I am, my dear father, as ever,

Your affectionate son,
Charles C. Jones, Jr.

Captain Anderson tells me he has sold the Island cotton at twenty-eight or twenty-nine cents.

Do be so kind, Father, as to send George in on Monday next. I enclose one dollar to pay his passage.

REV. C. C. JONES *to* MR. CHARLES C. JONES, JR.[g]

Montevideo, *Saturday,* March 17th, 1860

My dear Son,

Your letter of 14th inst., followed soon after it was received by the statements of your Uncle Henry, filled us with astonishment and grief. I say astonishment, for I thought it not improbable that the individual would in the continued indulgence of his intemperate habits besot himself more and more and be cut off by death in some sudden and perhaps horrible manner, as numbers like him are; but that he should sink, despite powerful and opposing influences, to such a depth of degradation and foul infamy, and so openly and impudently, I had not imagined.

But what will not *liquor* do? What blastings of fair prospects; what defeats of high aims and expectations; what losses of business; what consumption of fortune; what corruption of integrity; what pollution of morals; what prostration of honor and character; what reverses in families; what descents in association; what domestic misery; what ruin of dependent wives and helpless children, turned out upon the cold charities of the world; what woundings of the respectability and fair reputation of near relations and ardent friends; what cruel piercings of the hearts of aged and tender parents, sending their gray hairs in sorrow to the grave, has it not accomplished! What infidelity, what irreligion, what Sabbath-breaking, what blasphemies, what murders, what adulteries, what diseases, what deaths, flow from this fountain of evil! What few families have escaped this scourge of intemperance! Some have literally been consumed—name, deeds, reputation—from off the face of the earth! *Ours* has suffered deeply, sadly. . . . There is one bloating in infamous vice near us, and one under your own eye who by his conduct has shocked the vilest of the vile! Some of us are still preserved; may it please God to preserve us unto the end!

Whence comes it all? From the weak-minded, the men of no resolution and of little honor and self-respect? Multitudes of such have fallen. But they are not all. The victims are also the talented, the brave, the honorable; nay, the modest, the virtuous, the very professors of religion itself—men of standing, of station, of influence! Wine overpowers and casts down the mighty. "Let him that *thinketh he standeth* take heed lest he fall." Presumption in this warfare is the precursor of defeat. And how are men so fatally snared? Not in an hour, not in a day, not perhaps in one or two years. Just as they taste now and then, and learn to drink only on occasions, and then keep it, and take it with neighbors and friends and relations, until familiarity fixes the relish, and the relish furnishes the justification. A body acquires momentum as it descends an inclined plane; a single hand may arrest it when it begins slowly to move, but a thousand men avail not for the purpose after it has attained its speed. So with moderate and occasional drinking. No taste is as yet acquired; no longing habit formed. A man may see the danger; he may wisely distrust himself, and he may easily, instantly put by the glass, and remove it from his house, nor offer it to a friend, nor receive it of him. But not so easily after he has fairly begun to slide, and becomes linked in with wine and strong drink, and with men who use one or both, whether genteelly or otherwise. Not so easily after he is known to drink, and people associate him and his house with drink, and his fears are not awakened, nor his conscience stirred.

It is an insidious vice. It is so connected with the social customs of certain classes in society; so identified by them with manly hospitality and good cheer at the social table; so necessary to keep cast with them and to share in their patronage and society; so generous; so much above a stingy, tame association; so rational to use the good gifts of nature; so pleasantly exhilarating; so indicative of refined and good society; and many other like things, that men are drawn into a whirlpool from which they never extricate themselves, but are whirled about until broken to pieces, and their scattered remains serve only to warn the unwary that they approach not within the influence of the dreadful tide. I could, my dear son, with a little effort of memory, recall numbers of citizens of Savannah, professional men like yourself, some of your own profession—men of business, of influence, of family, and of fortune—who began life with as fair and flattering prospects as it has pleased God to bless *you* with; and they have gone down, imperceptibly in the beginning, step by step, from reputation, character, fortune, society, and finally filled a drunkard's grave and, according to God's Holy Word, met a drunkard's doom!

My dear son, I cannot express to you the deep solicitude I feel for you on this whole subject. I well know what at least some of your social connections are; and there is nothing to draw you back, but much to draw you on, in them. You have but very few friends who have your present and eternal interest at heart, to warn you of danger and endeavor to aid you aright; but many who will be your friends so long as you may continue to interest them, even down to your ruin, and never speak one word nor lift one finger to deliver you. I know also your kind, generous, and social dispositions towards your fellow men, and your friends in particular; and they are attractive and noble qualities. But they need to be tempered and exercised with strict regard to temperance, of which we are now more especially speaking, that they prove not a trap and a snare to you. You know what is right; your judgment and conscience approve your education in this matter. Then be a man of resolution. Wine and strong drink are not necessary to a man's reputation, business, family, nor friends, nor religion. Thousands live and prosper and are happy without them. You are our firstborn, and a dear son to your father and mother. You have been in many, many things a great comfort and joy to us. But you know not our solicitude for you that you may escape every danger—the danger of which we have been writing; that you may repent and be converted and make your peace with God, and fill up your days with usefulness, and be gathered—you and your loved ones—at last into the assembly of the saved in That Day.

There are prayers offered for you daily; and often, in the dark and silent hours of midnight, while you are away and lie in unconscious sleep, your ever-anxious and devoted mother is praying for you. Think of this—and think why she prays for you. From close observation through life I have arrived at this settled conclusion: that the man who uses, keeps, and offers intoxicating liquors is in imminent danger of falling a victim to their power—and that before he is aware of it.

Enclosed is written authority for you to arrange for the additional shares accruing from extra dividend in the Central Railroad, and to receipt for the surplus to be paid out, left over the shares.

George has been a useful and good boy. He is a smart boy, and am glad you have one of his age so capable and so reliable.

We shall be happy to hear of your safe return with Ruthie and the baby. Our united love to her, and kisses for the baby. Our aged aunt and daughters are in deep distress; they should receive the sympathy and support of all their relations and friends.

From your ever affectionate father,
C. C. Jones.

If the Central Railroad & Banking Company prefer issuing a new scrip *including* the thirty original shares and the three new ones, I can send the scrip we now hold for the thirty.

Monday Morning, March 19th. All well, D.G.

Mrs. Mary Jones *to* Mr. Charles C. Jones, Jr.^g

Montevideo, *Friday,* March 23rd, 1860

My dear Son,

I have but a moment ere the prayer bell rings to say that we received your affectionate letter yesterday and are glad to know your loved ones are with you again. Will not Ruthie write me a letter and tell me all the sweet things that our little darling can do? Grandmother longs to see her.

On *Monday,* D.V., our dear and distressed aunt and cousins expect to leave us on their way home. They will tarry on *Tuesday* in Savannah to make some business arrangements, and leave on Wednesday. Cousin Mary will, I presume, stop with you. Henry will come down with them. I have seen sorrow in many forms, but never any like unto *this.* God only sustains.

Mrs. King has been and still is very sick: pleurisy. I was with her until late last night, and may have to sit up there tonight. Our united love to Ruth and yourself, and many kisses for our granddaughter.

Ever your affectionate mother,
Mary Jones.

Rev. C. C. Jones *to* Mr. Charles C. Jones, Jr.^g

Montevideo, *Monday,* March 26th, 1860

My dear Son,

Mother begs you to send out the surplus of her dividend by your Uncle Henry, who will hand you this. Aunt and family leave us this morning, and am sorry that she is not as well as she was two or three weeks since, owing to her recent dreadful affliction—enough indeed to bring down her gray hairs with sorrow to the grave.

Mother wrote you a note by last mail. We were happy to receive your last letter and to know that your dear wife and child were safe home with you and all well. We wish to visit you so soon as we can, but cannot fix any day, from having engagements and hindrances of one kind and another ahead.

We are expecting Dr. Stiles in Midway Friday to preach several days. Robert preached for us yesterday and gave us the latest news of you.

The hour for our friends to leave is at hand. Mother unites in much love to Ruthie and yourself, and we send kisses for the baby. We long to see it.

Your ever affectionate father,
C. C. Jones.

MR. CHARLES C. JONES, JR, *to* REV. C. C. JONES[g]

Savannah, *Tuesday,* March 27th, 1860

My dear Father,

I was yesterday afternoon favored at the hands of Uncle Henry with your kind note of the 26th inst. Enclosed please find $86.25, the same being amount paid in cash on account extra dividend by the Central Railroad & Banking Company.

You have also herewith a sealed packet, directed to Mr. Oliver Stevens, containing twenty-seven dollars. John, husband of Uncle William's Louisa, begged me to forward this amount, being his wages, to his master, as he was himself unable to go out and carry the money to him. Will you let me trouble you to send it to Mr. Stevens by some direct and early opportunity? Perhaps Mr. McDonald in going to the Island would oblige me by delivering it.

We are truly happy to know that we will soon have the pleasure of welcoming dear Mother and yourself at our little home here. Your room is always ready, and we will do everything in our power to render your stay pleasant and agreeable. This cool weather will doubtless soon give place to the milder influences of spring. Savannah never looks so beautifully as in early spring.

We were prevented last evening in seeing Aunt Eliza and family, as we purposed, by the coming of visitors. Will call this morning and render any assistance in my power. We deeply sympathize with them.

Ruth and little Julia are both quite well, and unite in warmest love to self, dear Father, and to dear Mother. All friends well. As ever,

Your affectionate son,
Charles C. Jones, Jr.

MR. CHARLES C. JONES, JR., *to* MRS. MARY JONES[t]

Savannah, *Tuesday,* March 27th, 1860

My dear Mother,

Since writing the within to Father, the sad news has reached the office that Mrs. Sorrel, probably in a fit of lunacy, sprang from the second- or third-story window of her residence on Harris Street, next door to the house which was the family mansion for so many years, falling upon the pavement of the yard, and by the concussion terminating her life. Is not the occurrence heartrending in the extreme?

Just next door Miss Gertrude Dunning lies at the point of death, suffering from the effects of an injury upon her head caused by accidentally striking it against a window sash when passing from the piazza into the common parlor.

Uncle Henry will give you all the news about friends, etc. We will be most happy to welcome you and Father so soon as you can make it convenient to come to Savannah. Ruth and little Julia unite in warmest love.

Your ever affectionate son,
Charles C. Jones, Jr.

Mrs. Mary Jones *to* Mr. Charles C. Jones, Jr.[g]

Montevideo, *Thursday,* March 29th, 1860*

My dear Son,

Through your Uncle Henry we received your kind favors and the remittance, which came safely to hand. Also the *hat,* which fits your father finely, for which he says with sundry other dues he is your debtor.

A thought occurs which ought to have been mentioned before. When our new carriage harness was sent out, there were no *breast straps* with them. Gilbert thinks it quite an omission; and as it seems to be a necessary part, please ask Mr. Knapp to send them to you, and we can get them at any convenient time.

It would indeed be very pleasant to your father and myself to make Ruth and yourself a visit, but we cannot at present say when it will be. Independently of our children's association, there is now an additional *charm* to your household in the person of our dear little granddaughter. Precious little ones, how our hearts are waking up to all the interests of a new existence in them! I wish little Mary Jones and little Julia Berrien lived where we could see them every day.

I have not told you what a delightful visit we had from your brother and his wife. It so occurred that she saw nearly all of our immediate relations and friends, and they were all delighted with her. She treated your father and myself with all the confidence, affection, and respect of a daughter. Above all, what gratified us most was the devoted attachment which she seems to feel for Joe—her sympathy in his pursuits and her efforts to advance his professional interests. If there is any one thing in *this life* which brings peculiar joy to our hearts, it is to see our children happily married! I think Carrie possesses charming traits: freedom from selfishness with a cheerful and amiable disposition.

For the two past days we have had delightful weather—a little too cool for the planting interests. Tomorrow a three days' meeting will commence at Midway, attended by Dr. Stiles; and we can but hope and pray as in former days that the divine blessing may rest upon his labors amongst us. It is a great privilege to be instructed in spiritual things by one who has been so eminently useful in the church. You know he is laboring by the appointment of our synod. I wish dear Ruthie and yourself could be with us to enjoy these precious privileges. To Mr. Stiles's preaching I owe some of my deepest religious impressions.

Today week (the 5th of April) I believe the presbytery meets at Walthourville. Your father will have to be there. The week after that *I* expected to go up and make your sister a *long visit*, in anticipation of which, on her account, my heart is filled with anxiety. *But I trust in God* that all will be well with her.

When may we look for your promised visit? We see you so seldom now, if you were not so good to write us frequently, I should think of you as a great way off. Will you not be able to spend a part or the whole of the summer with us at Maybank? We should be so happy to have you do so.

Our friend Mrs. King has been very sick, but is much better. Willie is still with her. Our friends generally are well.

We expect to give the people here and at Arcadia Saturday, that they too may enjoy and reap the benefits of the meeting at Midway. Your brother told you, I presume, of Carolina's death.

I hope our friends have reached their home in Marietta. They left us in the deepest affliction. What an example of the debasing influence of vice is J. W. R.! He has lost even the power to see his own infamy, and *thinks* himself no worse than others who are taken by the hand in society! I have no language to express my horror of his conduct, or to describe the *agony* he has inflicted upon his aged mother, his sisters, and his children. I have gone into their chamber and found them all speechless with grief, and my venerable aunt with her gray head bowed and the heavy tears rolling down to the very hem of her garments!

The death of Mrs. Sorrel was very distressing. I heard some time since that she was subject to great mental depressions. We are not sufficiently grateful for our *preserved reason*. Our commonest blessings are our greatest; we need only to be deprived of them to feel it so.

Your father has come in from the chapel and retired, so I must close this long letter about little or nothing. He unites with me in best love to Ruth and yourself, and kisses for our little Julia. Present us affectionately to all friends, not forgetting my little favorite, Vallie. Excuse my penmanship: your father thinks I will soon forget how to write. Notwithstanding all my domestic duties, I have recently copied fifty pages of his *History* for *The Southern Presbyterian Review*. Do you take it? They are wanting subscribers to enable them to meet expenses. Howdy for the servants.

Ever your affectionate mother,
Mary Jones.

Miss Mary E. Robarts *to* Mrs. Mary Jones[t]
Marietta, *Friday Afternoon,* March 30th, 1860

My dear Cousin,

I write a line by return mail to say that we have reached our home in safety; that my dear mother stood the journey as well as could have been expected, all things considered. In the night at one time she complained of weakness in the back, as she could not recline in the cars on the Central Road; but when we reached Macon she rested an hour, and got through the night tolerably well. We reached Atlanta at seven, remained till half-past ten, then took the train for Marietta, where we arrived in little more than an hour. Our kind Mrs. Ardis and Dr. Stewart had the carriage there to meet us. Suppose Sam had told the doctor we were expected. He met us at the depot and gave us a most cordial greeting. We had not been in the house a half hour before Mrs. Ardis, Mrs. Nesbitt, and Mary Tennent sent us a waiter of lunch—bread, butter, tea, coffee, ham, and beef. We refreshed ourselves on their kind and bountiful supply, and needed no other dinner. Mother went immediately to bed, but got up at five and saw several of our friends who came in to welcome us. Our faithful Sam had everything in point in the yard for us, and Nancy had all the carpets down, beds made up, and fire in Mother's room and parlor. We had an early tea, and my dear mother assembled her afflicted family at prayers, and prayed that God might sanctify our sad trial to us, and that her poor prodigal son might be brought to see the error of his ways and go to Jesus for pardon.

I must now tell you what a sad trial our poor girls passed through in Savannah. On Tuesday morning Mary Sophia wrote me a most touching note entreating me to make arrangements to let them go off in the cars at one o'clock, as she was suffering so, she would give the world to be in Marietta. I did not get the note till too late to let them go, but the next day we left. On Wednesday, after the gentlemen bid us good-bye (our dear cousins Dr. West and Charlie Jones, who had kindly seen us to the cars), the girls handed us a letter to read. It was from their father to each of them and to his son, asking forgiveness of them, his mother, and sisters. The letter would have done very well if it had not contained this clause: "Was it not hard that he should be cast off and treated with contempt when he had done no worse than many men who were taken by the hand by the best society in Savannah, although he had done what perhaps he ought not to have done for their sakes?" I thought from this that he had no idea of the magnitude of his sin or of the wound it had cast upon us.

It seems that he had been taking his meals at Mrs. LaRoche's for a month before his fatal marriage; and when he told her of it, she said she had not the heart to tell him to leave her house—that she and Mr. LaRoche had promised poor Sophia to stick to him and save him from ruin. The girls (nor we) did not know that he was taking his meals there. When he came home to tea at night, little Sophia LaRoche came in from walking and told her mother someone in the streets had told them their cousins were come. Mrs. LaRoche shook her head at her. Joseph then asked if the girls were there. Mrs. La-Roche told him yes, but their grandmother had told them they must not see him; so of course he could not. He did not attempt to go upstairs, but wept bitterly. Came every day to his meals, but the girls kept their room; and when he left the house on Wednesday morning, they looked at his retreating form through the window and saw that he was weeping. Poor girls, it almost broke their hearts. After he left, Mrs. LaRoche's little girl came up and said he had begged her to kiss them for him and say good-bye. He said in his letter that would be the last communication they should receive from him unless they saw fit to answer it. Of course we shall not allow them to write just now.

Mrs. LaRoche gives this version of this dreadful affair. For a fortnight before, he had been drinking so much that Mr. LaRoche told him he was a fit subject for the lunatic asylum; and he was certainly intoxicated the night he was married. (I mention this not as a palliative, but just tell you what they say.) They told the girls that the woman had said she would just as soon have a millstone about her neck as him; that if he would settle her handsomely in New York, she would live with him. (Do not know how they should know what *she* said.) Mr. and Mrs. LaRoche think they have never seen him so subdued; do not think he intends following her. However, Joseph told Henry he had a letter from her on Monday; this looks like he still meant to communicate with her. Of course I do not know. . . . He will never be to me a brother again till he repents and forsakes those two awful sins which caused his downfall.

If Cousin Susan is with you, do show her this; it will be painful to me to write it again. But I wish her and all our near relatives to know exactly what we do. Oh, the misery and disgrace it has brought upon us! I told the girls it was kind in Mr. and Mrs. LaRoche to receive him and try to save him from further ruin, but if she did not have a husband to protect her, she could not do it; that as we were a house of unprotected females, to have such a person in our family would make us forfeit our own position; that they need not expect us to receive him.

Do burn this. Am sorry I had to write it, but wished to conceal nothing from our dear cousins who had so kindly succored us in our distress. Oh, how thankful we are to have a home to come to! And though the scandal will reach here from Savannah, yet the people here cannot know all the disgraceful truth. . . . We thank our friends from our hearts for all their sympathy and prayers. Hope they may be spared such a trial as we have passed through. . . . Please give much love to dear Henry and Abby; will write them soon. . . . Much love from Mother, Louisa, the girls, Joe, and myself to Cousin Charles and yourself. Tell your servants all howdy for us. I am no longer the lady of leisure I have been all winter; have a plenty to do now.

Your ever affectionate cousin,
Mary E. Robarts.

XVII

Rev. C. C. Jones *to* Mrs. Mary S. Mallard[t]
Montevideo, *Thursday,* April 19th, 1860

My dear Daughter,

Mother since coming home has been in a state of constant expectation if not excitement, for she has slept badly, lying awake and thinking and saying: "I wonder how my poor child is now." And all day the barking of the little dogs, or any unusual sounds, keep her constantly on the lookout. Sitting in my study yesterday, I heard James drive up as plain as I ever heard anything in my life; and lo, it proved to be a string of geese with great gravity and industry waddling along barefoot and rustling up the dry leaves!

Mother sends Tom up to know how you are, and he takes you a piece of a young beef killed yesterday—not fat, but fleshy for the season. . . . Yesterday was Little Daughter's second birthday. Her grandmother and grandfather remembered her in their closets and in the family. Dear child, may she grow up an olive plant about your table, and be a pillar in the House of God forever! Kiss her for us, and tell her Grandmother has sent her some strawberries.

Our united love to Robert and yourself. The Lord be with and bless you, my dear child! You must read I Timothy 2:14–15 and the two family Psalms (the 127th and the 128th). You may certainly expect Mother and Father on Saturday afternoon, God willing, if we do not come sooner.

Your ever affectionate father,
C. C. Jones.

Mother makes me write for her this morning, because she had a refreshing and protracted morning nap, and has gone down to fix the things for Tom to carry.

Mrs. Mary S. Mallard *to* Rev. *and* Mrs. C. C. Jones[t]
Walthourville, *Thursday,* April 19th, 1860

My dear Father and Mother,

Tom arrived in due time with the beef, strawberries, and shrubs. Thank you very much. . . . I showed Little Daughter the strawberries and told her Grandmama had sent them to her. She said: "Danma send Mamie tawberries. Tata, Danma, for tawberries; and I send a low courtesy."

I am sorry that I should be the cause of so much anxiety. . . . The text, "Casting all your care on Him, for He careth for you," is seldom out of my mind. We hear almost daily from Dr. Stevens, and I believe he is faithfully keeping at home. We are kept advised of all his calls. . . . We will be so glad to see you on Saturday, and I somehow think we won't send for you before then, so I hope the geese will stop playing horse around the house! . . . Robert unites with me in warmest love to you both. And kisses from your little granddaughter. We will certainly dispatch James to you at our earliest warning.

Your attached daughter,
Mary S. Mallard.

REV. R. Q. MALLARD *to* REV. C. C. JONES[t]

Walthourville, *Friday,* April 27th, 1860

My dear Father,

As I promised to send you word when my dear Mary should be taken sick, I dispatch James for that purpose. We sent for Dr. Stevens between three and four o'clock this morning. He and Mrs. Stevens are both with us. So far everything seems to be taking its natural course, and while my dear Mary suffers, there is no special cause for uneasiness. A kind Providence has provided what I feared might be unavailable at the emergency: the desired medical attendance. May it be an augury of a safe issue from this distress!

By the early freight train I wrote Dr. West for the nurse. I hope that she may be here tomorrow and relieve Mother of the fatigue of nursing. I write this morning that you may come up this afternoon if you see fit. With love from all to you, I remain

Very affectionately your son,
Robert Q. Mallard.

P.S. I send my buggy and horse, which are at your service. If they are here by twelve o'clock tomorrow, it will be in time to send to the depot for Mrs. Smith tomorrow.

REV. C. C. JONES *to* MRS. MARY JONES[t]

Montevideo, *Wednesday,* May 2nd, 1860

My dear Wife,

Pleasant ride down. Met Sister, Laura, and Jimmie shopping at the Boro, just on their way down to Maxwell. All well, and glad to hear the good news from Daughter and the little stranger-boy. Sent Robert's letter to his father direct to Dorchester by them. . . . Saw *West* at Boro in a handsome turnout: buggy and two horses. Has come to look out a permanent place to stay in the county! Gone down to *Sunbury* today!

All *up* at home today, D.G.; but considerable ailing since Friday: effect of sudden cold. . . . Sue out, but complains of the pain in arm and body. Reports last of the youngest "gauslings" died in the cold: four little chickens and one young turkey. All the rest well. . . . Peggy reports her work all done except pockets for one pantaloon and waistband, and one jacket sleeve to make and sew in, and Jack's blue jacket. Thread given out, leaving sleeves to be made and sewed in. She reports no cambric muslin in basket, the basket having been sent up the day the mutton was sent up by Gilbert. . . . The clothing in the bundle is more than you ordered, but as it was put up with commendable zeal and care I thought it not worthwhile to alter it.

Send a part of the strawberries; *the rest will send to Julia this evening.* Also one dozen fresh eggs for Daughter for her breakfasts.

Enclosed is a letter from Miss Clay, and as it was superscribed "For Mrs. Jones," and supposing there might be some important and secret communications between you that I had better know nothing about without special permission, I forbore to break the seal. No other letters. . . . Servants all pleased, and send their congratulations to Missy and the baby. . . . Love to all, and much love to you.

From your affectionate husband,
C. C. Jones.

Will try and be up Saturday sometime, God willing. Thank Robert for the buggy; have refreshed both man and horse.

Rev. C. C. Jones *to* Mrs. Mary S. Mallard[t]

Montevideo, *Thursday,* May 3rd, 1860

My dear Daughter,

I sent Mrs. King last evening some strawberries in the name and with the respects of our grandson, and she returns her congratulations this morning, and a nice piece of beef to me. And I send it up to you with a cup of nice fresh butter in order that you may enjoy a tender steak—if doctor, grandmother, husband, nurse, and company will allow you so great a treat.

Hope you are getting strong, and Baby is good and growing. The Lord be praised for all His mercies to us! Love to Robert, and kisses for the little ones. Kiss Mother for me, with my love. Respects to Mrs. Smith.

Your ever affectionate father,
C. C. Jones.

Mrs. Mary Jones *to* Rev. C. C. Jones[t]

Walthourville, *Thursday,* May 3rd, 1860

My dear Husband,

Tom arrived bright and early. Daughter thanks you for the eggs and butter; says she can eat *them herself* and the fine beef by *proxy,* and enjoyed the strawberries by *word of nose.* She is very comfortable this morning, and I trust through divine mercy will now do well. I think there is no necessity for me to remain longer, and must ask you to send Gilbert and the buggy for me by daylight *or before* on Saturday, so that I can come down in the early part of the day.

Miss Clay's letter is in Joe's envelope. I wrote her this morning saying you would be very happy to see Tom, but might go to Savannah next week. . . . In the cup you will find some sugarplums given by Mrs. Smith to Little Daughter for Grandpapa. . . . Daughter sends kisses to you; so do the babies and your wife. Robert sends love, Mrs. Smith respects.

Your affectionate
Mary.

REV. C. C. JONES *to* MRS. MARY S. MALLARD[t]

Montevideo, Monday, May 7th, 1860

My dear Daughter,

Mother's finger is so rigid that I am now her scribe. I persuaded her to remain quietly at home yesterday, and she is much better for it. The poultice on the finger all day has helped it.

We send Tom to know *precisely how you are, and how Little Daughter is. Write particularly.* If you are all doing well, we may go down to Savannah sometime this week. We must either go or send for supplies; otherwise there may be rebellion in the household, for the people want their clothing and supplies of meat and molasses, etc.

Mother sends you a little *tongue*, which you must keep until you can eat *yourself*. Enclosed is a letter of congratulation from Uncle William. He never got Robert's letter—by some hitch in the transit—until the last of last week. Says he will try and slip up and see you first chance. . . . The eschscholtzia seeds are for Mrs. Smith.

Kiss our little grandson for us. Let us know how he behaves. Kiss Little Daughter for us. Tell her the squirrels are playing before the door. Love to Robert. He must write for you. Respects to Mrs. Smith. Mother sends much love.

Your ever affectionate father,
C. C. Jones.

8 A.M.

REV. R. Q. MALLARD *to* REV. C. C. JONES[t]

Walthourville, Monday, May 7th, 1860

My dear Father,

We have just received your letter and one from Uncle William, together with the seeds. The latter we have given to Mrs. Smith as requested. She desires her thanks to be given to Mother for the same. We are very sorry to hear of Mother's suffering, and hope her invalid finger will soon be convalescent.

I am rejoiced to be able to make a good report touching the health of our household. My dear Mary continues to improve; has had no more return of fever. Young Charles is very well, and is as considerate of his mother's comfort as ever, excepting during about two hours of the night, passed not in crying (he is too manly for that) but in wakefulness. The *cause hopped* out this morning in the shape of a little nondescript. Little Mary, I think, is much better this morning; has no fever; and I have been giving her small doses of quinine. There is nothing, then, in the condition of affairs so far as Walthourville is concerned to keep you from going to the city.

Mary is much obliged to Mother for the tongue. Query: Is the direction "Keep the tongue *until* you get better" symbolical? . . . Mary unites with me in warmest love to yourself and Mother. Kisses from granddaughter and grandson for grandfather and grandmother. By the way, Baby (I'll have to say Daughter now) remarked this morning that "Grandmama was a naughty grandma to leave Mamie." Mrs. Smith sends love and respects to Mother and yourself.

Your affectionate son,
Robert Q. Mallard.

P.S. Mary thinks I have been both too modest and obscure in my account of the cause of Charlie's wakefulness, and fearing misapprehension as to the precise genus, wishes me to say in plain terms it was a *flea*. I give you Webster's definition of it: "An insect of the genus *pulex* remarkable for its agility and troublesome bite."

Mrs. Mary Jones *to* Mrs. Mary S. Mallard[t]

Savannah, *Tuesday,* May 15th, 1860

My very dear Child,

Robert's kind and affectionate favor was duly received, and this perhaps should be an acknowledgment of the same to him; and I truly hope he will receive it as such. It was a great relief to our minds, and I trust you will now continue to improve, and be able to spend the month of June with us at Maybank.

Tomorrow, D.V., we hope to leave at 10 A.M. for Augusta. Joe has been telegraphed to that effect.

Our visit here has been very pleasant. We have seen a great many old friends, and having the buggy has enabled us to move about comfortably, although your dear father is very feeble, and I dread the effect of the dust on the cars tomorrow. Kitty has been twice to see us, and we returned her visit, seeing her venerable grandmother and Miss Sarah Mackay. . . . All of your friends have inquired most affectionately after you, and desire love.

On Friday night after we came in we had the pleasure of hearing an address before the Young Men's Christian Association by Colonel H. R. Jackson. It was noble and elevated and Christian in sentiment, and beautiful and poetic in conception and expression. I consider it one of the finest intellectual treats that I have ever enjoyed.

On Sabbath morning we heard Dr. Axson: a very practical and impressive sermon. The afternoon was devoted to a union Sabbath school celebration, at which our *Mr. Stiles* spoke. *Today* he has left for Macon. His visit to Liberty dwells in his memory, and he was very much delighted with Mr. Buttolph's preaching in McIntosh.

Little Julia Berrien is one of the sweetest and best children. I wish our little *Mary* could see her. Tell her Grandmama will bring her shoes and pretty little stockings and a pair of little mitts and a little shaker hood for her when she comes home, and a little wooden bucket if she will be a good girl and not fret at table or scream in the yard. We long to see our little boy, and hope he is as good as ever.

I was in such straits for a mantua-maker when I first came that I wandered down to Mrs. Smith's friend Mrs. Peck, who was also too busy to serve me. . . . This morning we visited the cemetery and rode around the city and called upon several old friends. . . . It is past ten, and I must close. Father, Brother, and Ruthie unite with me in best love to Robert and yourself, with kisses for the *children*. Respects to Mrs. Smith.

Ever, my dear daughter, your affectionate mother,
Mary Jones.

Your brother says there is no one who can execute the picture at present.

Rev. C. C. Jones *to* Mr. *and* Mrs. Charles C. Jones, Jr.[g]

Augusta, *Saturday,* May 19th, 1860

My dear Son and Daughter,

We arrived 6½ P.M. Wednesday, receiving a hearty welcome from your brother and sister. Both well and happy. Ruthie's bottle of tea and *tumbler* were of essential benefit, as I was threatened with a throat attack between Millen and Augusta.

Mother was taken with a hot fever on Thursday after breakfast, and was in bed until Friday evening. Dr. Ford called in. She is up today, and has had no fever; and hope it will not return. The result of too much fatigue, and heat in the cars. Am thankful she was taken sick after reaching here; medical aid was at hand, and it is good.

God willing, we hope to return to Savannah next week sometime. Do not know what day; all depends upon Mother's health. Your brother looks very thin, but says he is well. Many friends have called. The city looks beautifully in the parts planted with trees. Could preach tomorrow, but have declined doing so.

Your mother, brother, and sister unite in much love to you both, and we all must have a kiss through you for dear little Julia. She is a fine baby, and sensible. We miss the child. Nothing stirring up here more than common. The Lord bless and keep you and yours, is the constant prayer of

Your ever affectionate father,
C. C. Jones.

Mr. Charles C. Jones, Jr., *to* Rev. C. C. Jones[t]

Savannah, *Monday,* May 21st, 1860

My dear Father,

I am this morning in receipt of your kind favor of the 19th inst., and we deeply sorrow to know that dear Mother and yourself have been so unwell. We sincerely trust that you will both be better. Oh, that you were both, my dear parents, restored to that degree of health which you once enjoyed, and which you have so long employed in good deeds and the exercise of the noblest Christian virtues! My heart sinks within me as the ever-present fact recurs that you are daily suffering so much, and are physically precluded from the accomplishment of so many and valuable labors which your cultivated mind, profound theological attainments, sound judgment, matured thought, and generous heart so eminently qualify you to discharge. God's ways are sometimes very strange—as men count strangeness; but the Christian pronounces them all for the best.

We will be most happy to welcome you again when your visit to Brother and Sister Carrie is concluded. We trust that the advice of the medical faculty of Augusta may prove highly beneficial. We are all well, and unite in warmest love to self, dear Mother, Brother, and Sister Carrie. . . . In the midst of our appeal cases, so I must say good-bye.

Your ever affectionate son,
Charles C. Jones, Jr.

Rev. C. C. Jones *to* Mr. Charles C. Jones, Jr.[g]

Augusta, *Tuesday,* May 22nd, 1860

Your favor, my dear son, was received this morning. Glad to hear you are all well. Mother up again, D.G. Only time to say before the mail closes that we hope to be down tomorrow (D.V.) evening. Your brother *goes with* us on a short visit. All send love.

Your affectionate father,
C. C. Jones.

Mrs. Mary S. Mallard *to* Mrs. Mary Jones[t]

Walthourville, *Saturday,* May 26th, 1860

My dearest Mother,

Brother Joe gave us a pleasant surprise this morning. We were heartily glad to see him and to know of your safe return. We were truly sorry to hear of your sickness in Augusta, and Father's indisposition yesterday. We hope you will soon be well again.

I received your letters from Savannah and Augusta, and Mr. Mallard would have acknowledged them for me had he known where you expected to be. Mamie is very much delighted with the many presents you have sent her, and says I must "tell Danma tata." The bucket is her special admiration.

Thank you, dear Mother, for all, and for the beautiful dress you sent me. It is very pretty.

I ate my first meal downstairs today. I have taken several rides. My health is gradually returning. I hope I will have no more fever.

Our dear Charlie is a good little fellow. He never cries; indeed, you would scarcely know there was a baby in the house. . . . I hope Father will be able to baptize the little fellow before you move to Maybank. I think I shall be strong enough tomorrow week, or if Thursday afternoon would be more convenient for you, I think I could go; but I want Father to consult his own health and convenience. . . . I would be glad to have Brother Joe present, and he has partly agreed to remain. It would be a great pleasure to us to have him do so.

Mrs. Smith was very kind in remembering our little ones. She was very attentive to me, and took excellent care of the baby. I do not know what I should have done without her, for Lucy was quite sick for some days and is still rather complaining.

Mr. Mallard sends you a few peas from our garden to let you know how they have grown. He unites with me in warmest love to dear Father and yourself. Mamie is very fond of her little brother; talks to him all the time.

Your attached child,
Mary S. Mallard.

Mrs. Mary S. Mallard *to* Mrs. Mary Jones[t]

Walthourville, *Tuesday,* May 29th, 1860

My dear Mother,

We are truly sorry that Father and yourself are so unwell, and that you will be unable to come up this week. We hoped Father would have been well enough to have baptized our little Charlie before you moved; but it would be a long ride, and I know you will be undergoing a great deal of fatigue this week. As you will not be up on Sabbath, Mr. Mallard will probably go to Savannah and preach for Mr. Porter. He received a note from Mr. Axson this morning requesting him to preach for him on Saturday evening if he came.

I am very anxious, dear Mother, to see and be with you; but I do not think I shall be able to take the long ride so early as next week, for I am not strong, and find I have to be careful even in taking my short morning rides. You know my baby will not be five weeks old until next Friday, and as I now am, I would be afraid to take much exercise. I hope I will be strong enough to go down on Tuesday week, if that time would be convenient to you to send for us. If anything should occur between now and then, I will write. I am very sorry that we cannot come at the time you appointed, but I am sure if you knew all, you would think it imprudent for me to do so.

Lucy is better, though somewhat complaining: a pain in her stomach. We have consulted Dr. Stevens, and he has given her medicine. I think her sickness was the result of a cold, though I was half afraid at one time that she might follow Silvia's example.

I wish you could see Charlie now. He has improved in appearance, and is in our eyes quite a comely boy. He attends faithfully to his legitimate occupation, sleep, though he is beginning to wake up a little.

The mutton is a great treat to us. Thank you for it, dear Mother, and for the raspberries. . . . Tell Brother Joe James was cleaning out the well when Tom came, so I have sent him some earth from the bottom of it. And Mr. Mallard sends him a bug which chirped like a little bird, though he says he does not know that Brother Joe cares about such things at present. Do tell him good-bye for us; I wish we could have seen him again. . . . I have given the beads to Kate, Elvira, and Tenah, and they beg me to "tell Missis they are very much obliged to her". . . . Mr. Mallard unites with me in much love to Father, Brother Joe, and yourself. Kisses from our little ones.

Your affectionate daughter,
Mary S. Mallard.

Mr. Audley King *to* Rev. C. C. Jones[t]
Staten Island, New York, Tuesday, June 5th, 1860

Dear Uncle Charles,

I was sorry to have left home not bidding you good-bye. Aunt and you were then in Augusta, where I hope you enjoyed the visit to your affectionate children and were refreshed thereby. You have ere this returned, and are probably on the Island. May you and our family and good friends at the Point enjoy the coming summer!

I say *coming,* for it seems yet distant from this place. Cold and wet alternately and combined have thus far prevailed. I find the season just two months behind ours. The wild honeysuckles which bloom in March at home are now in full bloom here. Shade trees not all in foliage, and roses still in bud and blooming. Yet a more beautiful place cannot be found. By common consent it is unsurpassed, and the view from the house is exquisite (that within not in question). You know how beautiful the country is in summer: green lawns and ornamental shades; this place possesses water views, and cities in the distance (Brooklyn, New York, Jersey City, Newark, Elizabeth City), and villages innumerable at present. The water filled with sails and swifter steamboats.

The moral characteristics are equally pleasing. Church bells and Sabbath schools are inviting; and the chapel on the water, over which Mr. Irving (nephew to Washington Irving deceased) has pastoral charge, is peculiarly adapted to serious feelings. The impression made is "the Sabbath!" I've not yet heard an oath nor seen an intoxicated person in my ramblings. Mr. Lewis says a drunken man is rarely seen in the streets of New York.

June 7th. Just here I had been interrupted, and again resume my pen after spending yesterday in New York, calling on friends in return for their kindly bestowed attentions. An hour's ride takes us from the lower part of the city to 47th Street, a hundred and fifty of which there are. New York is indeed an enormous place: between six hundred and seven hundred thousand inhabitants, besides visitors and traveling public. That is, New York proper. Brooklyn is a separate city, the third in size of American cities, numbering about three hundred thousand immortal souls.

Political parties are comparatively quiet. The Republican candidates the only ones nominated as yet. Here and there you will see in full the names of Lincoln and Hamlin, but the chances of their election are not brilliant. Conservative men come over almost daily to the Union side. Sumner is denounced as a man beneath the notice of his associates in the Senate, and the *Herald* and *Times* of yesterday both gave him severe and critical remarks. The meetings of the General Assembly (Old School and New School) and conferences of other denominations are duly noticed. The whole national heart seems to beat through this organ (New York) of our republic, and disunion is impossible. Our reason leaves us the day we agree to dissolve so sacred and essential a tie and bond. The South has her *friends* as well as foes in the Northern states; and could the subject in question subside *politically,* peace and harmony would be restored. This, however, is a tempest perhaps necessary to future serenity; but like the storm- and tempest-beaten mariner, we have scarcely aught but hope. Good men must come out. Every good man must put his shoulder to the wheel, and we can roll our car over even this great rock.

With much love to your *entire* family I must bid you adieu. And at your leisure or convenience I would be most pleased to hear from Aunt or yourself.

I am ever yours,
J. A. M. King.

MRS. MARY JONES *to* MR. CHARLES C. JONES, JR.ᵍ

Maybank, *Tuesday,* June 5th, 1860

My dear Son,

Your father has had fever almost every day since our return home, which has prostrated his strength. His appetite is very poor, with a tendency to the old throat affection. I think he must have taken cold in the cars the night we returned from Augusta. High fever came on the day we left you and spent at Richmond. It was a great comfort to have your brother with us; and he did a great deal of good to us both by his skill and kind attentions. I feel very anxious on your dear father's account. My only solace is in looking unto the Great Physician; I know with Him alone are the issues of life and of death! Father says I must tell you he feels better tonight; and I think he is cleared of fever. I hope he will feel better so soon as we have a change of atmosphere. Today the thermometer stood at 92° in our entry. We have never known it higher but once. A dry hot wind *blowing* all day from the west.

Your sister was not strong enough to come down this week. She has appointed next Monday for us to send the carriage for her. She will come to Dorchester on Tuesday. Your father said today how happy we would be to see our little grandchildren all together; and we hope dear Ruth and our little darling Julia and yourself will be able to be with us whilst your sister is here. We will meet any appointment that you make as soon as the carriage returns with your sister.

Should a kind Providence permit you to come out, do be careful that the baby is not exposed to the sun. . . . Father unites with me in best love to Ruth and yourself, and kisses for our little granddaughter.

Ever your affectionate mother,
Mary Jones.

Howdy for the servants.

Mr. Charles C. Jones, Jr., *to* Mrs. Mary Jones[t]

Savannah, Wednesday, June 6th, 1860

My dear Mother,

We are this moment in receipt of your kind favor of the 5th inst., and are deeply pained to learn the severe indisposition of dear Father. Oh, that a good God would restore him to health and strength again!

We are in great distress. I have to convey to you the sad intelligence of the death of Cousin Charles W. West. He died in Newton, Baker County, on Monday morning, whither he had gone on his way to his plantation in Baker County. At Newton he obtained a horse and buggy to drive out to his plantation. The horse took fright while passing through the village, and he was thrown from the buggy, breaking his right arm in the joint, and also receiving an injury upon the head. This occurred on the 1st of June. We heard of his injury by letter. He begged the writer to say to his wife, Sister Eliza, that she must not think of coming to him with her little infant; that the fracture of the arm, although serious, was in no degree dangerous; that he was surrounded by kind friends, and hoped in two weeks to be able to return home. He continued quite well and cheerful until Sunday night, when a change for the worse occurred; and he sank into a stupor and died, we believe, on Monday morning. The immediate cause of his death is believed to have been a suffusion of blood upon the brain.

A dispatch announcing his death arrived last night, and it was made my most painful duty to announce the most heartrending intelligence to her. Never before have I realized the meaning of the expression *a crushed heart.* It is hard to conjecture even the depths of that sorrow into which she has been thus unexpectedly and awfully plunged. Kind friends attend her, and are doing everything to assuage her grief; but the Great Comforter alone can give rest to her weary spirit. And the poor weeping little children, and the little infant in the nurse's arms, unconsciously prattling while others weep! Although bowed in the dust by this saddest of all afflictions, Cousin Eliza's faith is sustained by the promises of that God who has promised to be a Father to the orphan and a Husband to the widow.

Cousin Charles's remains will arrive tonight. The funeral will probably occur tomorrow morning. I am doing everything that I can. I write tonight to Charlie and Willie. I forbear comment, my dear mother, for your kind and sympathizing heart, and that of my dear father, will appreciate everything. . . . With sincerest love to you both, my dear parents, I am, as ever,

Your affectionate son,
Charles C. Jones, Jr.

Mrs. Mary S. Mallard *to* Mrs. Mary Jones[t]

Walthourville, *Thursday,* June 7th, 1860

My dear Mother,

Charles brought the bandbox safely on Saturday night. I am very much obliged to you for the shaker and for the cap. Mamie looks so cunning in her bonnet. I told her her dear "danma" had sent it to her. She said: "No, Mama, Danpa and Danma send Mamie the bonnet." She insisted upon saying her "danpa" had sent it too. The cap *just* fits Charlie.

I think I have improved very much within a few days past, and shall be quite ready to go home on next Tuesday. I have gained strength much faster than I did after Mamie's birth.

We were shocked and grieved to see the death of Cousin Charles West announced in today's paper. What a loss to his family and to the whole city! Poor Cousin Eliza, how I feel for her and for the little children! How perfectly do such bereavements show us our entire dependence upon God and the necessity of preparation for death! I hope this affliction will be sanctified to Brother Charlie. I suppose he has written you particulars. We have seen nothing but the newspaper account. When Mr. Mallard left Savannah on Monday, Cousin Eliza thought of going to Cousin Charles, and Brother Charlie expected to accompany her if she went.

Mr. Mallard preached for Mr. Axson on Saturday evening. The service was preparatory to the Communion; I think there were eight additions. On Sabbath Mr. Mallard preached twice in Mr. Porter's church.

I received a letter from Kitty a day or two since, and in it she sent the enclosed note, which she begged me to read and forward to you. I think from what she says that you would like the Ladd & Webster machine. Mrs. Stiles and Kitty have seen and tried so many machines that I think their judgment can be relied upon. You see from Kitty's note that she rather prefers Grover & Baker.

We have had a refreshing shower this evening. Everything has been burning up; the branches are most of them perfectly dry.

I hope nothing will prevent our going down next week, for it seems so long since I have seen dear Father and yourself. . . . I would write more, but I have a sty upon my eye which is rather painful. . . . Our little Charlie has not waked up yet. He sleeps nearly all the time, and is a very quiet little fellow—much more quiet at night than his sister is. Mr. Mallard unites with me in warmest love to dear Father and yourself. Hoping to be with you soon,

Your affectionate daughter,
Mary S. Mallard.

Rev. C. C. Jones *to* Mrs. Mary S. Mallard[t]
Maybank, *Saturday,* June 9th, 1860
My dear Daughter,

Gilbert leaves with the carriage this afternoon via Montevideo, and thence on Monday afternoon for Walthourville to bring you and Robert and our dear little grandchildren down on a visit to us. You had better make as early a start Tuesday morning as you conveniently can, and take the desert road— the harder and cooler of the two—so as to reach Dorchester as near ten as you can. And it may be best for you to break the long ride—the first you and the little boy have taken—and spend the remainder of the day and night with Mother and Father Mallard, and come down early Wednesday morning to Maybank. But you and Robert must order the journey as you think best. We shall be most happy to see you all, and will kill the fatted calf: not that you are returning prodigals, but beloved children coming home to see Father and Mother. . . .

All friends on the Island and in the vicinity well. Mother unites in much love to yourself and Robert. And kiss the little ones for us. Tell Little Daughter Grandma and Grandpa say she must come soon and see them, and she shall see the river, and she shall see a crab, but we won't let it bite her, but she shall eat some of the crab. And Grandpa has seen two squirrels in the lot. No news from Savannah or Augusta this week. Sent up Tom for the letters today. The Lord keep and bless you and all yours, my dear child!
From your ever affectionate father,
C. C. Jones.

Mrs. Mary Jones *to* Mr. Charles C. Jones, Jr.[g]
Montevideo, *Tuesday,* June 12th, 1860
My dear Son,

On Friday afternoon Sister Susan, Laura, and Mr. Buttolph rode over to Maybank. Your father was walking out at the time of their arrival. As they came in I thought I detected an expression of sadness upon their faces; and when they inquired "when I had heard from *you,*" such a feeling of anguish came over my heart that I replied almost breathlessly: "Tell me, has anything happened to *Charles?*" Mr. Buttolph answered quickly: "No, Aunt Mary; but Dr. Charles West is dead." I cannot describe the shock of such an announcement! Oh, what must it have been to his desolated wife and poor children! The intelligence had been communicated through a letter from Mrs. Lawton.

It was late, and I concluded it best not to inform your father of the fact (as he was so feeble) until the next morning, which would be Saturday, and I knew we would certainly hear from you by the mail. A short time before Tom came from the Boro I told him the sorrowful tidings, and then came your affectionate letter giving us the only satisfactory account that we have had. You may be assured our deeply afflicted relative and her family have our sincerest sympathy. . . . We all mourn the death of one so beloved, so respected, so preeminently useful in the community and in his profession. But his family! None dare speak of their loss! Dear Ruthie, I know how much she loved and respected and confided in him as a brother and physician.

And you, my son—what can I say when the voice of God in this act of His sovereignty is saying to you: "Be ye also ready, for in such an hour as ye think not the Son of Man cometh." Oh, that you would lay this death to heart, and in this the day of merciful visitation, when reason, health, strength, religious privileges, temporal blessings are granted unto you, the *goodness of God, the love of a crucified Saviour* may lead you to repentance and to the exercise of *true saving faith!* "What shall it profit a man if he gain the whole world and lose his own soul? Or what shall a man give in exchange for his soul?"

Thus far, my dear son, I wrote you last night. Today your sister, Robert, and the little ones are with us, and we can but anticipate that dear Ruthie and yourself and our other little one will soon join the family circle at Maybank. We have had no mail this week, and send Tom up tomorrow early for the mail hoping to hear from you. Your father has been better for a few days past, and unites with your sister, Robert, and myself in best love to you both. Kisses for Julia. Our best love and tenderest sympathy with our afflicted relative and family.

Ever your affectionate mother,
Mary Jones.

MR. CHARLES C. JONES, JR., *to* REV. C. C. JONES[g]

Savannah, *Wednesday,* June 13th, 1860
My dear Father,

If you can make it convenient to send Gilbert with the carriage for us to *No. 3, Savannah, Albany & Gulf Railroad (McIntosh Station) on Monday next,* we will, D.V., promise ourselves the pleasure of a visit to yourself and dear Mother.

The supreme court is now in session. I feel this afternoon a little fatigued —the result of an argument before the court this morning of some two hours or more. Tomorrow I have to argue one more cause, and that will conclude our engagements before the court at the present term.

We are all quite well. Ruth and Sallie Berrien are rejoicing in the discovery that our dear little Julia has one *tooth,* and another that promises in a day or two to appear. I presume Mother well remembers the *first tooth* of her firstborn. Sister Eliza and family are all well. The cloud of sorrow hangs heavily above that household. With warmest love to you both, my dear father and mother, in which Ruth and little Julia cordially unite, I am, as ever,

Your affectionate son,
Charles C. Jones, Jr.

Rev. C. C. Jones *to* Mr. Charles C. Jones, Jr.[g]

Maybank, Friday Morning, June 15th, 1860

I have but a moment before Mr. McDonald leaves to catch the mail, my dear son, to acknowledge yours of yesterday and to say that the carriage, D.V., will be punctually at No. 3 for yourself and family on Monday morning, and we shall give you all a most hearty welcome home again. Your sister and Robert are with us, and will be with us next week also. Friends around us all well. Mother is not improving as fast as I could wish, but is up and as active as she usually is. The babies quite well, and there will be a grand time when Julia comes with her two teeth.

Joe prescribes port wine for me as an occasional tonic. Mother thinks it worth a trial. Will you bring out a half-dozen bottles for me if it will not incommode you? Do not get it at Claghorn & Cunningham's, but get it where it is good but not too expensive. Pay for it, and I will hand you the money. My complaint seems to march steadily on, and am not able to see much effect from anything, but am willing to try prescriptions. Your brother is the only physician who has known the case, and his treatment has been of great value in arresting the progress of the disease.

Mother, Sister, and Robert unite in much love to Ruthie and yourself, and say they will be most happy to see you. And we all send kisses for Miss Julia, and congratulate her upon her two teeth so quietly cut. We have sympathized and do sympathize most deeply with Cousin Eliza and her family in the sudden and afflicting death of Cousin Charles. A most impressive providence, and a solemn warning to us all.

Your ever affectionate father,
C. C. Jones.

Rev. C. C. Jones *to* Mrs. Susan M. Cumming[t]

Maybank, Wednesday, June 20th, 1860

My dear Sister,

I am directed to reply to your note, and to say that we will all, God willing, dine with you today, and if possible will bring Brother along with us. Your mutton is fine. May you always have as good to eat and to send to your friends!

Fearing that I may have omitted it, I will embrace this opportunity of giving you the peculiarities of a friendly note: First, it is written on a sufficient quantity of good paper. Second, it is written with ink. Third, it is written most legibly. Fourth, it is fully dated at the place it is written, with the day of the month and year. Fifth, it is fully signed, the name of the writer being written in large letters and entire. Sixth, it is carefully directed, and the conveyance by which it is sent is put in the direction also.

An observation of these rules is of vast importance in life. Notes frequently determine great dates and great events. We may now go to breakfast. All send love to all.

> Your affectionate brother,
> C. C. Jones.

Mrs. Susan M. Cumming *to* Rev. C. C. Jones[t]

> Point Maxwell, *Wednesday,* June 20th, 1860

My dear Brother,

Most happy shall I be to have Sister, Brother, and yourself to dine with us today. The mutton was from the neighborhood of Montevideo; hence its superiority. And may your wish never fail!

In reply to the peculiarities of a friendly note: First, suppose paper scarce. Second, suppose no ink to be had—only pencil. Third, suppose inability to write "most legibly." Fourth, suppose no almanac to determine the date. Fifth, suppose you are ashamed to own the scrawl. Sixth, suppose your messenger, unbeknown to you, takes a mule when you order a horse.

Hope you will have a good appetite for breakfast, and a better one for dinner. With much love from all here to all there,

> Your affectionate sister,
> S. M. Cumming.

XVIII

Mrs. Mary S. Mallard *to* Rev. *and* Mrs. C. C. Jones[t]
Walthourville, *Tuesday,* July 3rd, 1860

My dear Father and Mother,

We left Dorchester at seven this morning and reached home about half-past eleven. We had a delightful breeze and pleasant ride, and found all well. Mr. Mallard was at work in the study, though I expect he had one eye and ear out of the window. As soon as Mamie saw the house, she jumped up and down and called loudly for her father; and she has been in a perfect state of delight, talking to the servants; and every now and then she runs to the dogs and tells them howdy over again.

I found great preparations and improvements going on: the underbrush all cut down in front of our lot, trees trimmed, and a track cleared between Colonel Quarterman's and the Baptist church for the contention. Gentlemen are flying to and fro superintending the making of seats under the grove for the accommodation of ladies; boys busy burning heaps of trash; and carpenters at work erecting a shed in the academy lot for the protection of the dinner. We are just at headquarters; I can see almost everything without going out of the house. The oration will be delivered in the church: Mr. John B. Mallard the orator, and Dr. Stevens the reader. From the number of vehicles I saw this morning I presume many of the guests have arrived already. The young ladies have purchased a silver goblet (thirty dollars) for a prize to be contended for by the two companies. All the citizens seem to have entered into the celebration with more than usual zest. I wish you could be with us.

I hope, dear Father, you feel better and that your fever will not return. It makes me so sad to think my pleasant visit to you is over. . . . Mr. Mallard unites with me in warmest love to you both. . . . Give love to Aunt Susan and Cousin Laura, and to all at Woodville.

Your affectionate daughter,
Mary S. Mallard.

Mr. Charles C. Jones, Jr., *to* Rev. *and* Mrs. C. C. Jones[g]
Savannah, *Wednesday,* July 4th, 1860

My dear Father and Mother,

At six o'clock this morning our ancient and honorable corps assembled at the armory with a view to the celebration of the day. Captain Claghorn being absent, the command devolved upon me. With four guns and some forty-five or fifty uniforms we paraded through some of the principal streets in the city, fired a salute of thirty-three guns on the Bay, and returning to our hall were dismissed. Had the wind been blowing from the north or northwest, I think it very probable you might have heard the faint rumblings of the salute on the Island. By testifying our respect for the day at that early hour, we have been spared the heat of this torrid sun. Other companies have left the city upon excursions, etc., quite ill-timed, I think, at this season. They may deem themselves fortunate if they succeed in escaping severe fevers.

By the last express I received from Europe a copy of Cicero's *Orations* (three volumes), Lucan (one volume), Sallust (one volume), and Curtius (one volume)—all of them original Aldine editions of 1515. They are both interesting and valuable, it being impossible at this date to obtain them except upon the occasion of the sale of private libraries.

Ruth has been much confined to the house for the past few days in consequence of the discharge of Margaret, and our inability as yet to supply her place with a suitable nurse for our dear little Julia. The cause of Margaret's discharge was an impudent manifestation of temper which could not be overlooked. I regretted the occurrence, as she had taken good care of our little infant at all times, and Julia was very fond of her. I wish very much that I could find a competent, reliable nurse. For such an one I am prepared to pay a good price. Very little satisfaction is to be experienced with hired servants.

We are all well, and unite, my dear parents, in warmest love. As ever,

Your affectionate son,

Charles C. Jones, Jr.

I enclose, my dear mother, a few peach stones. The peaches from which they were taken ripened some two weeks since. They were small, but of a delicious flavor, and entirely free from worms. I hope they may grow.

Rev. C. C. Jones *to* Mr. Charles C. Jones, Jr.[g]

Maybank, *Thursday,* July 5th, 1860

My dear Son,

We are glad to receive your letters—the last (of the 4th) this evening—and to hear of your health and the health of Ruthie and the family.

The loss of your *capable* nurse is indeed a great one, and am sorry you have had to dismiss her. She has done better and lasted longer than I anticipated from her exhibitions when she first came into your employ. One's own servants are far preferable to hired ones. We have looked over the places, and there is no one that would suit in our judgment. If there was, we would send her down at once. Could you not secure a *white nurse?* They may sometimes be had in Savannah. Such an one as would not only take good care of Julia but be active also in doing little matters about of one kind and another. There would be no harm in looking around and inquiring. Do not be in too great a hurry. Am sorry we have no one to send Ruthie. It is really a great loss to you. But you must look upon and bear it as one of the crosses of life.

Whenever you are ready to move, Mother says, let us know and she will send *Gilbert* down to help you.

The weather ever since you left has been extremely warm. You were wise to restrain your patriotism to the cool hours of the morning.

The additions to your library of the classic authors and the edition are valuable. When your sister visits you—next week perhaps—will you please get a copy of *The Land and the Book* at Cooper & Company's on my account and present it to her from Father.

All friends well, D.G. Mother, I hope, is improving, and unites in much love to Ruthie and yourself, and in many kisses for little Julia. We missed her and her parents very much, and Daughter and Robert and their little ones. We missed *the little voices* and *the little feet*. The Lord bless and keep you and all yours, my dear son!

Your affectionate father,
C. C. Jones.

Mr. Charles Scribner *to* Rev. C. C. Jones[t]

New York, *Monday,* July 9th, 1860

My dear Sir,

The Rev. Dr. Wilson has put into my hand your letter to him respecting the publication of *A History of the Church of God,* etc., and has requested me to advise with you on the subject. I do not feel prepared at present to make any definite proposals, but if agreeable to you, I would like to look over the work, or a portion of it, and would then advise you of my disposition in the matter of publishing. I think a book covering the period yours embraces is much needed. There are many church histories subsequent to the apostolic times, but I know of none—at least of modern date—which gives a good history of the Bible period. . . .

In reply to your inquiries: First, it is very unusual for the author to incur the entire expense of publication, giving the publisher a commission on the sales for his services. I would not advise such a course.

Second, the usual course is for the publisher to incur the whole expense and to give a per centum on the sales to the author. The usual percentage is ten percent on the retail price of the work. The percentage and time of payment, of course, vary according as the parties may agree. The popularity of the author and the character of the work regulate the matter.

Third, it is not unusual for the author to bear a portion of the expense and receive in consequence a larger percentage. That is, frequently the author stereotypes the work, and the publisher incurs the remaining expense—namely, on paper, printing, binding, advertising, etc., etc. In that case the author owns the stereotype plates and has, of course, more control of the work. He can arrange with the publisher simply for an edition or for a limited time. If these terms (third) would be agreeable to you, you would be more likely to find a publisher; and in case of a large sale you would be better off pecuniarily, as your percentage would be larger—say, fifteen percent on the retail price. I confess I would be more disposed to publish on such terms, as the outlay at first would be less.

Fourth, if the copy is prepared just as you would have it printed, and is legible, there would be no necessity of your seeing the proof, as it would be read by a competent proofreader here. But it is always better for an author to revise the proof. When living at a distance from the printer there is, of course, considerable delay in the transmission of proof. As a substitute we frequently furnish plate proofs—proofs taken after the work is stereotyped and before it is printed. Any error can then be corrected at trifling expense, but no alterations or additions can be made occupying more space. That is, for every new word inserted, an equal amount must be canceled, and vice versa. Such changes are expensive. The printer engages to correct any errors on his part at his own expense.

Fifth, as soon as I receive the copy I can give you an estimate of the number of pages it will make, page and type of any size selected. The page of Hamilton's *Lectures* to which you refer is, I think, rather large. It requires a volume larger than the usual octavo size, and even then does not give sufficient margin. I remain

Very respectfully yours,
Charles Scribner.

REV. J. LEIGHTON WILSON *to* REV. C. C. JONES[t]

New York, *Tuesday,* July 10th, 1860

My dear Sir,

I herewith enclose a letter from Mr. Charles Scribner answering all the questions in your letter to me; and there is occasion for me to add only very little more. Mr. Scribner is an honorable man, and were I going to publish a book again, I would prefer to employ him. My experience with the Harpers is that they are pretty *sharp men* in bargaining. Were I going to advise, I would say throw the whole expense of publication upon the printer. Ten percent upon the retail price is the usual remuneration made to authors. No printer will undertake to publish a book upon his own responsibility without examining the manuscript or a part of it.

If you prefer it, I would see the Messrs. Carter or Harper or any other publisher here you may wish. If you desire it, you can send your manuscript, or part of it, to me, and I will make such use of it only as you direct. Kind regards to Mrs. Jones.

Yours truly and affectionately,
J. Leighton Wilson.

Rev. H. A. Boardman *to* Rev. C. C. Jones[t]

Philadelphia, *Friday,* July 13th, 1860

My dear Dr. Jones,

Our *great* publishing and bookselling house here is that of J. B. Lippincott & Company, and the *character* of the house is unsurpassed. I made several attempts before I found Mr. Lippincott, and I have only within an hour received his reply to my inquiries. It will supply the information you desire.

It will give me pleasure to aid you further in your plans, if in my power. But as I expect, D.V., to leave for Newport next week, the enclosed note may suffice to put you in direct communication with Messrs. Lippincott & Company. Their business facilities are very far beyond those of any other firm here.

I will only add that I am glad to hear you are about giving the church a work like your Biblical history. I wish we might hear that your health was fully reestablished. . . . Remember us to Mrs. Jones and your family. And believe me

Affectionately yours,
H. A. Boardman.

Mr. J. B. Lippincott *to* Rev. H. A. Boardman[t]

Philadelphia, *Friday,* July 13th, 1860

Dear Sir,

In regard to the publication of Dr. Jones's Bible history, respecting which you have been so kind as to call upon us, we would respectfully say that as the work would undoubtedly be of a highly creditable character for any house to issue, it would afford us much pleasure to undertake it.

We beg to submit the following proposition for Dr. Jones's consideration —namely: Provided he will assume the pecuniary expenses of the work, we will agree to superintend its mechanical execution, charging him only the regular prices for the labor performed and the material used in the manufacture of the books. And we will also agree to undertake the circulation and sale of the books for the usual commission of twenty-five percent on the wholesale price of all copies that we may sell—the proceeds of sales *other than our commission* to be paid to Dr. Jones at stated periods.

The cost of stereotyping the work (should it be stereotyped) will be, as near as we judge, from $1.00 to $1.25 per page in style similar to Hamilton's *Lectures on Metaphysics;* and the cost of making the books after the stereotype plates are finished will be, in proper style, from $0.50 to $0.62½ per copy, depending much upon the quality of paper used. The side- and footnotes prevent us from making an accurate estimate of the cost of stereotyping. Should the work, however, not be stereotyped, we judge an edition of 1000 copies would cost from $0.90 to $1.00 per copy. An edition of 2000 copies will probably cost from $0.70 to $0.80 per copy.

We shall be pleased to know that our proposal meets Dr. Jones's approval, or to receive any proposition from him that may be equitable. Should any further information be required, we shall cheerfully furnish it so far as may be in our power. With much respect, we remain

Your obedient servants,

J. B. Lippincott & Company.

MRS. MARY JONES *to* MR. CHARLES C. JONES, JR.ᵍ

Maybank, *Monday,* July 16th, 1860

My dear Son,

It seems scarcely possible that so much time has elapsed since your late delightful visit to us. The merry voices and sweet faces of our dear little grandchildren still linger in our ear and eye. When you all left us—you and Ruth and Julia, Daughter and Robert, little Mary and Charlie—*home* and *father* and *mother* felt desolate indeed. And yet as I said the last farewell my heart responded gratefully: "God bless you all, my children! You are going —in life, in health, in peace, in comfort, in happiness—each to your appointed fields of influence and usefulness." It would be the greatest solace of our declining days if our children were all around us, but it is not ours to "appoint the bounds of your habitations" or order your work and way in life.

On Saturday I received your affectionate favor. Many thanks for the canteloupe seed and Mr. Everett's oration. I am glad you have found comfortable board at Bath, for I am sure Ruth will enjoy herself there. It is very troublesome traveling with an infant, and is almost sure to affect them seriously. Can I do anything for you in the *way of work* or taking care of any of your servants? It would be a good plan if you have no employment for Adeline in your absence for her to learn to wash and iron with some responsible woman. Delia (Alfred's wife) used to be a fine laundress. I felt so anxious about Ruth and dear little Julia that I wished to send you Peggy or someone else as a nurse. But for two weeks Patience has been laid up, and now is so feeble that Flora has to fill her place. Margaret kept the little darling very nicely, but she was a woman of uncommonly bad tempers, and disposed to do as little as possible. I hope you have more than supplied her place. Be sure and call for Gilbert whenever you need him.

On last Thursday we rode to *Maxwell.* A severe storm kept us *all night.* Thunder and lightning—terrific! On our return Friday morning, from the servants' account the lightning rod of our house must have received a stroke. They say it vibrated on the roof, and even the lamp shook upon the table! God's goodness and mercy, protection and love are very great to such sinners as we are. How evident in our preserved lives and that of our servants and our dwelling!

Montevideo, 17th. Left Maybank at five minutes past five o'clock this morning. Arrived at eight o'clock. All well excepting Jackson and Betsy; *she* has been very sick, but is up again. Corn and cotton very good. Rice poor, wanting water; river too salt to flow. Men all moving carriage house beyond the stable, which is nearly done; and a roomy airy building it is.

Father in bed when I left; well as usual. All friends well. When shall we expect you again? I wish every day I could send you the delicious musk- and watermelons we are enjoying. It is now half-past 12 P.M., and I am just starting to meet the mail and return home. Kiss dear Ruthie and my little Julia. Howdy for the servants.

Ever your affectionate mother,
M. Jones.

Mr. Charles C. Jones, Jr., *to* Rev. *and* Mrs. C. C. Jones[t]
Savannah, *Wednesday,* July 18th, 1860
My dear Father and Mother,

Yesterday afternoon we escorted the Republican Blues (John W. Anderson, captain) to the steamship which carries them to New York on a visit similar to that accomplished by the Chatham Artillery a little more than a year since. They took their departure in gallant style, but I fear their appearance this morning is not as fair and joyous as it was on yesterday afternoon. They purpose a sojourn of a week in Gotham, and may extend their excursion to Boston. I am somewhat inclined to doubt the policy of the trip just at this time.

Sister was with us last week. She suffered much at the hands of the dentist, but endured the fatigue and pain with the firmness and resolution of a Spartan matron. I sincerely hope that she will now find relief and renovated health. Cousin Laura is at present at the tender mercies of Dr. Parsons.

We are now *in transiter*—half in our former residence on Harris Street, and half in the house on South Broad Street recently occupied by Dr. West. We hope to be fully moved by Friday noon of this week. A nice room will, my dear parents, be expressly fitted up for you, and we sincerely trust that you will often occupy it.

Ruth and little Julia are not very well. The summer appears to hang very heavily upon them, and a change seems necessary. Ruth is suffering from a severe cold; she can scarcely speak in a whisper. Our present arrangement is to leave the city on Friday night, stop a day or so with Brother and Sister Carrie in Augusta, and then go out to Bath. Having secured very comfortable rooms there at a very reasonable rate, Ruth and little Julia will spend the rest of the summer there. I myself expect for the present to return to Savannah. There are some matters claiming attention here which must be looked after.

Sister Eliza and Charlie West left last night for Bath. She spends the summer with Randolph Whitehead. Beyond this I do not think she has made any definite arrangements.

I heard the other day from a very reliable source a very sad suggestion as to the cause of Dr. West's death. It is this. The probability is that he was poisoned by an improper dose of medicine. This is the belief of his attending physicians, and of those who were about him just before his death. On Sunday he was quite well: had been walking about his room, and only suffering from his arm. In fact, he had been conversing freely with friends in his room, had with his left arm written one or two prescriptions for friends, and bid them good night about ten o'clock. He then retired, and directed the servant in attendance to go over to the village drugstore and procure for him a dose of salts. The boy did so, and mixed it in about a half tumbler of water, which the doctor took at a swallow, and then laid down, telling the boy to permit no one to disturb him, as he desired to have a good night's rest. He closed his eyes and apparently went immediately to sleep. The servant perceived by his unusually labored breathing, however, in a few moments that a change had occurred. He spoke, but received no answer; endeavored to arouse him, but without success; and then immediately summoned the attending physicians, who were in an adjoining room. Their efforts to arouse him were also unavailing, and he continued in a stupor for several hours and then died. It appears that the apothecary had been upon a drunken frolic for several days, from which he was barely recovering; and it is presumed that he must have substituted by mistake some poisonous drug in the stead of the salts ordered. But why did not the physicians examine the tumbler from which the dose had been taken? Whether they did or did not do so I am not informed. At any rate, the impression—and I am told the positive conviction—resting in the minds of those best able to judge is that he was poisoned by that dose, and died in consequence of having taken it. If such be the case, his death becomes the more sad.

A letter this morning received from Brother states that he and Sister Carrie are both quite well. He is now busily engaged in preparing his report for the Planters' Convention in November next. With warmest love, my dear father and mother, to you both, in which Ruth and little Julia unite, I am, as ever,

Your affectionate son,
Charles C. Jones, Jr.

MRS. MARY JONES *to* MR. CHARLES C. JONES, JR.ᵍ

Maybank, *Thursday,* July 26th, 1860*

My dear Son,

We received your affectionate favor written on the eve of your departure for Burke. If a kind Providence has favored your plans, you are again in Savannah and an occupant of your new abode. And a sad, sad one I know it will be to your reflective mind and affectionate heart for a long time to come. I *know* what it is; I passed through it all. When we first lived at Maybank, the *dead* were with me everywhere—their steps, their voices. Has it occurred to you that the two homes you have occupied in Savannah have been rendered vacant by death?

The last sad event increases in sadness. The gloom, the mystery which hangs around the closing scene! Is it possible to have any satisfactory investigation? I view the death of Dr. West as one of the greatest calamities that has befallen the city, ministering as he did especially—with so much skill and kindness—to weak and suffering women and children. Your tribute to him in the *Journal* is very beautiful. Father, Mr. Buttolph, and all think so.

I hope you left dear Ruthie and your sweet little Julia well, and were enabled to procure a good nurse for her.

Providence has opened up a way for your father's having his *History* copied and prepared for publication—the first volume at once. *Mr. ——,* from South Carolina, being on a visit to the Island, expected to return to Columbus, where he now resides, but hearing your father's desire to have the work copied, offered most kindly to do it. He writes well and rapidly, is a good scholar, and your father has engaged him to do the copying. We expect him to be with us on Saturday. (He had to return to Columbus.) He will remain until the last of September, and thinks he can accomplish it in that time. As he is dependent upon his own labor, your father could not think of occupying his time for nought. He becomes an inmate of our family, and copies the first volume for a hundred dollars. He did not wish to take anything, but this we thought just and right.

Will you not be able to spend some of your time with us before you go away for the summer?

Gilbert was quite disappointed you did not call upon him.

I could not think of enjoying our fruit alone. We send to friends around every day, and last week sent up a cart of such as we had to your sister. Gilbert takes a basket to be forwarded to you by the express tomorrow, and I trust they will reach you in good condition. The melons are small compared to those we have had.

Our friends are well, and all desire love to you. Father has retired, and unites with me in best love to you. Patience is better, but Kate suffering and laid by with a sore finger. Howdy for your servants. . . . Good night, my dear child. May the Lord bless and save you!

Your affectionate mother,
M. Jones.

Mr. Charles C. Jones, Jr., *to* Mrs. Mary Jones[t]

Savannah, *Friday,* July 27th, 1860

My very dear Mother,

I am this morning in receipt of your kind letter, so replete with love, and redolent of the sweet perfume of the Island roses.

It is with pleasure that I know that all at home are so well, and that Father will so soon have the benefit of the services of a competent amanuensis. Hope that he may be able to accomplish the task of transcribing within the period designated, and that the work will appear so soon thereafter as possible.

Many inquiries are made here respecting it, and I trust and believe that all that is wished for it will be fully realized.

Reached Savannah on yesterday morning at half-past seven after a comfortable night's ride from Augusta. Left my dear Ruth and little daughter at Bath on Tuesday at 5 A.M. and purposed coming directly through to Savannah. Arrived at Augusta, however, I found an acceptance for me, at the hands of Brother and Sister Carrie, to dine on The Hill. Dr. Davis' carriage was in waiting, and no excuse would be taken. So we all went out and spent a very pleasant day with Dr. Davis and family.

The next day bright and early Brother and myself, taking Titus with us, joined Mr. Phillips, the engineer of the city of Augusta, who very kindly not only accompanied us himself but also placed his boat, hands, and horse at our disposal, in an excursion up the Augusta Canal to examine some interesting ancient monuments in the vicinity of Augusta. The first visited was about four miles from the city. It consists simply of a bluff upon the river, whither, in the fishing season, the Indians must have congregated in great numbers. For about four acres the surface is literally covered with relics—broken pans, pieces of axes, arrow- and spearheads, stone mortars, soapstone ornaments, etc. The addition to my collection there made was extensive and valuable.

We next visited Stallings Island in the Savannah River some eight miles above Augusta. There exists one of the most striking monuments in the state: a mound composed chiefly of the mussel, clam, and snail shells of the river, some three hundred feet in length, and at its greatest width not less than one hundred and twenty feet, with an average altitude of about twenty-four feet, level at the top, and filled with human bones and the various articles of use, ornament, and war usually found in those ancient mounds. It is an enormous sepulchral monument—a matter of profound wonder and astonishment.

I will write and perhaps publish a notice of these remains; and so soon as the sketch is prepared, I will send it to you.

The peaches and melons in delightful order arrived safely. Being by myself, I reserved only a few of them and sent the rest over next door to Mrs. Dr. Harriss, telling her where they came from. She has enjoyed them very much. I sincerely wish that Ruth could have tasted them. Accept my thanks, my dear mother, for your kind remembrance.

Ruth and dear little Julia are delightfully located at Bath in the family of Mr. McNatt: the best of fare, any quantity of excellent servants, kind friends, horses and carriage at her command, and all at a reasonable rate. I sincerely hope that the change of air and the exemption from all care will bring the color again to the cheek of herself and dear little Julia. I expect to see them tomorrow week. . . . With warmest love, my dear father and mother, to you both, I am, as ever,

Your affectionate son,
Charles C. Jones, Jr.

Mrs. Mary S. Mallard *to* Mrs. Mary Jones[t]

Walthourville, *Tuesday,* August 7th, 1860

My dear Mother,

We were rejoiced to receive your letter yesterday telling us that there is a prospect of your coming up on Saturday next. I hope my dear father's health will permit. The ride is so long that I am almost afraid it will be too much for you both; but we shall be so glad to see you, and we are very anxious to have our little Charlie baptized. I don't know why, but Mr. Mallard was so impressed with the idea that you would be with us last Sabbath that he requested the young men if Father should come to meet here on Sabbath night; and I believe he expected you until teatime on Saturday.

I think it is a remarkable providence that Mr. —— should be sent to your very house to copy Father's book. I am truly glad that it is so. Father could scarcely have made a better arrangement, and I expect you find Mr. —— a very pleasant inmate. I did not know that he had consoled himself with a wife. Will he not come up with you on Saturday? We should be very glad to see him. Mr. Mallard is acquainted with him, and I have always had some curiosity to see him. . . .

We have had very pleasant weather for a few days past. I think, taking the whole summer, it is the warmest I ever spent; at least I do not recollect to have experienced more continued warm weather. Do give love to Cousin Laura and Cousin Lyman, and to Aunt Susan and Jimmie, and to all at Woodville. Give love also to Uncle William. For dear Father and yourself accept the united love of your children and grandchildren. Hoping to see you very soon,

Your affectionate daughter,
Mary S. Mallard.

Mrs. Mary Jones *to* Mrs. Mary S. Mallard[t]

Maybank, *Thursday,* August 9th, 1860

My dearest Daughter,

Your father and myself had hoped to be with you on Saturday, but the weather is so hot; and he, feeling unusually feeble this week, will not be able to come up. We will do so as soon as we possibly can, for we long to see you, and realize the importance and duty of as early dedication as possible of your dear little one to our covenant-keeping God and Saviour.

The revision and correction of the *History* is a very laborious work, and keeps your father very closely confined, which is the secret of his recent uncomfortable feelings.

Friends here are all well. Mr. Joseph Maxwell has joined our Island circle, and Willie and Mr. Stewart are also on a visit. Your uncle and friends from Woodville and the Point spent evening before the last with us.

Yesterday I went to Maxwell to commence my work for Carrie on *the machine,* but it was quite a failure on *my part.* If I baste a few tucks in the petticoats, could you run them for me? I think I will buy a Grover & Baker when it is *convenient* to do so. Laura has offered and I know would do any work for me, but she is not able and *ought not*.

Tom is waiting, and I must close. Father unites in best love to Robert and yourself, and kisses for dear Little Daughter and Charlie. The servants all send howdies, and Peggy many thanks for the dress.

Ever your affectionate mother,
Mary Jones.

REV. C. C. JONES *to* MRS. MARY S. MALLARD[t]

Maybank, *Thursday,* August 9th, 1860

My dear Child,

The weather is so hot and dry, and my throat so weak, that I dread the ride to Walthourville this week; and so if you will excuse us we will put it off for a convenient season. I wish the dear little boy had been baptized when we were all down in this region together; but it was thought best to defer it, and no doubt it was better to do so. Kiss him for me, and my dear little granddaughter. I long to see you all, and would enjoy a visit to you highly. The spirit truly is willing in this matter, but the flesh is weak. . . . Write us as often as you can. The Lord bless and keep you, my dear child, and all yours evermore!

From your affectionate father,
C. C. Jones.

MRS. MARY S. MALLARD *to* MISS MARY JONES TAYLOR[t]

Walthourville, *Tuesday,* August 14th, 1860*

My dear Mary,

Your affectionate letter was received at a time when I was too feeble to reply, but it gave me sincere pleasure to hear from you. Thank you for all your good wishes in behalf of myself and family. *Family!* Does not that sound oddly coming from me? But, Mary, I *am* becoming *quite* a matron!

Since I last wrote, a sweet little boy has been added to our number. He made his appearance on the 27th of April and is a noble little fellow; has been blessed with perfect health since his birth, and has a decided talent for sleeping. This being a most desirable thing in a baby, I seek every means of cherishing it. I wish I could let you have a sight of him. He is well grown for his age, has very dark blue eyes, pretty fair complexion, and what little hair he has is very light. As usual, there is a diversity of opinion as to whom he is like. His coloring is that of my family, and the shape of his head, and I think he is a little like my father and brother Charles; but it is difficult to say whom a young infant resembles, the features undergo such constant changes. All I can say is that he is a comely boy in the eyes of his parents. He bears my father's name, Charles Colcock. We have not had him baptized yet, for we have been waiting for Father to do it for us. The weather has been so hot and he so feeble that he could not attempt a ride of twenty-eight miles. I was not so ill at the birth of this child as I was at Mamie's, and his health and quietude have enabled me to regain my strength much more rapidly, though I have not a great deal to boast of—but more than I deserve, and much for which to be thankful.

Little Mary is delighted with her little brother, and often amuses me by the motherly way in which she talks to him. "Laugh, sonny boy! You sweetheart, don't cry! See—Mamie right by you!" etc. She is a child of wonderful life and great activity of mind, so that I have constantly to be on my guard; and she often gets into trouble. It is no easy matter rightly to control a child. A few evenings ago her father reproved her for some misconduct, and she turned and looked at him in the most quizzical way and said: "Oh, darling, don't talk so; you will scare this child into fits!" Native depravity shows itself pretty often, but I hope in a few months more she will be quite an obedient little girl. She is only a few months beyond two years, and her little quaint sayings and conversations are very interesting to her parents. I was amused with her warning one of her little cousins (to whom she had given a hard piece of candy) not to break her teeth on it. She is very much interested in Scripture stories. Moses and Samuel and *"Dolia"* are her favorites. But I have taxed your patience too long with my long discourse on my children; I forget they cannot interest others as they do me.

I spent most of the month of June with Father and Mother. It is always so pleasant to be at home with them, but it grieves me to see my dear father as feeble as he at times is. He still continues to write his church history, and I think it will be a most interesting and valuable work. He has completed the first volume; I won't be certain, but I think this volume extends almost if not quite down to the end of the prophetical writings. It really seems as though Providence were smiling upon the work, for Father has been somewhat concerned to know how he should get the manuscript copied, not feeling able to go from home to employ a regular copyist, and being too feeble to undertake the labor himself. A few weeks ago a gentleman who has taught in this county offered to do it for Father. He is an intelligent man, and takes a great deal of interest in the book. So Father has employed him, and he is now with him at home, busily engaged. Does it not seem a little remarkable in this quiet county one should be sent to the very house in every way qualified for the work? Father finds the revision very wearisome, and I fear it will almost make him sick. I suppose this volume will be published as soon as it can be gotten ready.

I am glad you have found the catechism so useful. I think it one of the simplest and most comprehensive I ever saw. Did I ever tell you that it has been translated into the Chinese, Armenian, and Turko-Armenian languages? At the time our house was burnt (in 1850) Father had another catechism upon the historical portions of the Bible almost ready for the press. The manuscripts were all burnt, and he has never entirely rewritten it. You know the catechism you have is now published by our Presbyterian Board. . . .

So Peery is engaged! I think you are quite enjoying these grievous falls into love which your friends are taking. You had better be mindful of your own steps. Tell Sarah Ann I don't approve of very long engagements, and I want to know what objection she has to my knowing the name of the gentleman to whom she is engaged, for you have never mentioned it in any of your letters. Tell her I hope she is not ashamed of him. Is he handsome? Long or short? Broad or narrow? Pray give me some idea of your future brother!

What is the matter with poor Margie Dickson? Is it spinal disease? I do feel very much for poor Sue. Do give my love to her when you write, and tell her I have not forgotten Margie and herself.

We have had an unusually warm summer. I do not know that I have ever felt more continued warm weather. Although we have suffered from heat, our county has been very healthy.

Tonight I am all alone with my little ones, and they are fast asleep. Not a sound to be heard in the house excepting the ticking of the clock, which is reminding me that my hour for retiring is already here. I have had a quantity of sewing work to do of late, so that I have scarcely been able to do anything else. I do not know how I would accomplish the work of the family if I did not have a Grover & Baker machine. Sewing machines are great inventions.

What are you reading these days? Mr. Mallard has been laughing at me for reading a romance. Perhaps you have read it: *The Marble Faun,* by Hawthorne. It is quite interesting. Have you read Custis' *Recollections of Washington?* I have that on hand, and Mr. Mallard is reading Irving's *Washington* aloud to me. We do not get on very fast in books that we read together, for Mr. Mallard has so much work to do that we are often obliged to make our pleasure yield to more imperative demands. . . .

I must really close this letter. My pen keeps running on and on as if I could not find a stopping place. If Mr. Mallard were here, he would say: "You know you are doing wrong to sit up late." But he is with his mother tonight, eighteen miles off, so I have no one to look after me. Do give much love to Sallie and to your mother. Do write me soon; your letters always refresh me. . . . Believe me, as ever,

Affectionately your friend,
Mary S. Mallard.

Rev. R. Q. Mallard *to* Rev. C. C. Jones[t]

Dorchester, Wednesday, August 15th, 1860

My dear Father and Mother,

As I am nearly twenty miles nearer to you than when at home, and an opportunity of sending a note offers, I write you a few lines from my old home. I came down yesterday morning. . . . I should have been very much pleased to have extended my trip to the Island if I could have come down on Monday. . . . We were disappointed at your not coming up to Walthourville last week, but after hearing of your feebleness were truly glad that you did not venture the ride.

We were truly glad to hear of the arrangement into which you have entered with Mr. ——. It does seem that *the Lord has use for your book,* and I trust will make it a blessing to your fellow men. You must not let our anxiety to have our little Charlie baptized induce you to waste any of the strength so necessary to the completion of the work to which Providence seems to have called you.

I left my dear Mary and the children well. Mary has been somewhat indisposed recently; probably indigestion the cause. Charlie is growing finely, and *we* think is an *uncommonly* fine boy. He takes a great deal of notice, and is a happy-hearted babe. Your little granddaughter is rapidly maturing in mind, and is much more manageable; indeed, is all we could expect in one of her age. She is not obstinate in her tempers, but yields very readily. Her chief difficulty lies in a superabounding and incessant flow of spirits which will sometimes burst over all limits.

My dear old parents are as well as usual, and you may be sure it is a mutual pleasure which my visit confers. Mother and Sister Lou unite in love to you both, in which Father would unite were he present. Mother begs me to say that when you do go to Walthourville, they would be very happy to have you stop overnight at their house, thus dividing the journey. Remember me affectionately to the friends on the Island, and accept the love of your daughter, grandchildren, and son,

Robert Q. Mallard.

Mary has written you of the state of things in our church. Nothing new to add.

REV. C. C. JONES *to* MRS. MARY S. MALLARD[t]

Maybank, *Tuesday,* August 21st, 1860

My dear Daughter,

We were on the eve of leaving for Walthourville last week (Saturday), but were detained by Dinah, who has had a severe injury by a fall and needed our careful attention. She is about the same, and we hope for some good change shortly.

We are all pretty well. Mother has been presuming a little too much in being on her feet and out in the sun, and did not feel so well yesterday and last night.

Mr. —— is moving on and keeping me just ahead. Mother thinks I improve under the "push of poke"—or pen, we should say.

Thank Robert for his kind letter from Dorchester. He can never see his venerable parents too often, nor pay them too much attention. They were all out on Sabbath, and about as usual.

We must put up with our disappointment and wait another opportunity to visit you. Next Sabbath is our Communion at Midway, and we hope, Providence permitting, to be present.

Mother sends you a few quinces more by our good friend Mr. Maxwell. She has had a fine parcel from her trees. There are old works and new going on here in the line of trimming, digging up, transplanting, manuring, and planning. And so life is made happy by mingling all pleasant occupations and useful together.

Mother unites in much love to Robert and yourself. Kiss the children for us. We long to see them. Robert says Little Daughter is a good child. Mrs. King's boy is in a hurry to get back before Mr. Maxwell starts. Prayers and breakfast are waiting. The clock is striking eight: very late. Mother is hurrying with the quinces, and a whole day's work is before Mr. —— and myself, and we are in a hurry to get at it, and the servants are hurrying to get to washing and fixing, and so I must hurry and finish my letter. Every blessing attend you and yours, my dear child!

Your affectionate father,
C. C. Jones.

Mrs. Eliza G. Robarts *to* Rev. C. C. Jones[t]

Marietta, *Saturday,* August 25th, 1860

Dear Charles,

Your very kind letter of the 6th of June ought to have been answered before this, but hearing you were so sick, I would not trouble you. By Mary's letter I was glad to hear you were some better, and sincerely pray that God will continue His mercy and restore you for many years.

The months of June and July were excessively hot and dry: gardens and corn crops burnt up. There will be a great scarcity of grain. And high prices continue. I have never known things so scarce and high in Marietta as this year.

On Thursday night John Jones and your son Charles C. Jones made us a flying visit. They came down from Rome, where Charles had been for a week in search of Indian relics. I believe he has collected many. I was glad to see Charles looking so well and cheerful. He came up with Miss Val Whitehead to Miss Nesbitt's wedding.

Mrs. and Miss Mary Dunwody dined with us on Thursday and went up yesterday with John to Rome. . . . Marion Glen is in Roswell; she wrote the other day and inquired particularly after you and Mary. . . . I have given you all the local news.

The death of our dear cousin Dr. West was a great grief to us. I thought my poor heart was already so filled with sorrow it had no place left for more; but I find yet a spot for others' woe. We feel great sympathy for Eliza and the family. She has written us two letters inquiring about Marietta as a residence. Mary has written her giving her a correct statement of prices for house rent and provisions, but begs she will come up in the fall and look at the place and houses for rent before she decides on a residence; for as much pleasure as it would give us to have them near us, we could not advise her in such an important step; she must decide for herself. Marietta is only a cheap place now in comparison with Savannah and Augusta. Eliza says Bath is too inconvenient a place to live at unless she had a plantation near to get provisions from—poultry, etc. The schools are fluctuating. These and others are her reasons for not wishing to settle at Bath.

I believe I wrote you our servant Hannah had received an injury in her back. She has been laid by for two months, Dr. Stewart attending her. He cupped her on the back several times, which did not relieve; then put a section in her back. She is some better: walks about, but not able to do any work but a little cooking and sewing. This is a drawback to our little income.

Mary sends much love to you and Mary; says she will write Mary soon. . . . Please give our love to Susan's family and Julia. Also Mr. Maxwell; I am glad to hear he is so happy at Springfield. . . . Rev. Mr. Palmer now writes some of his sermons, and we think it has improved his preaching. . . . I was glad to hear you had help in writing your church history. . . . I must now close. Believe me

Ever your affectionate aunt,
Eliza G. Robarts.

Excuse all defects.

REV. JOHN JONES *to* MRS. MARY JONES[t]

Rome, *Monday,* September 3rd, 1860

My dear Sister,

Your last most welcome letter arrived while I was absent from home in response to a Macedonian cry across the mountains of Chattooga County some twenty-five miles to the northwest. . . . The place (Summerville, the county seat of Chattooga) has been honored with a remarkable revival. . . . On my return home I found that my nephew Charles had arrived the Saturday before. I regretted truly my absence, but was pleased to know that he and Dunwody had been very diligent and successful in search of Indian relics.

On Wednesday 22nd of August we visited the house of Major Ridge, one of the former Cherokee chiefs, and now the residence of Judge Wright, an ex-member of Congress. And as he could remain no longer, we made our long-contemplated visit to the celebrated mounds on the Etowah River—at the plantation of Colonel Tumlin of Cass County. The colonel treated us most hospitably, and Charles luxuriated in the past—in exploring and measuring the mounds and making every necessary observation. At the close of this interesting day we returned to Cartersville and took the cars for Marietta, reaching our dear aunt and family and receiving their affectionate welcome about $10\frac{1}{2}$ P.M. I parted with Charles on Friday the 24th. His visit to us was most pleasant, and I feel for him an increasing interest and anxiety that the Spirit of God may make to his heart a saving visit.

And now, dear Sister, I ask a special interest in the prayers of yourself and Brother Charles, that you would remember us and our church during a meeting which will commence on Thursday of this week (the 6th inst.) under supervision of Dr. Stiles and others. Do intercede that salvation may come to our own house in the conversion of our son Dunwody and also our servants, and that our church and town may receive a great blessing.

I congratulate Brother Charles in the good fortune of having with him so fine a copyist and Christian gentleman as Mr. ——. His brother, ———, was my classmate in college. He was a man of remarkably good mind and manners—the most perfect and beautiful translator of the Latin and Greek classics I have ever known. He took the first honor with one or two others. He often spoke to me of his parents, and especially of his mother, who had recently deceased, and who must have been a remarkable lady for piety and talent. Poor fellow, he became intemperate and never fulfilled the bright promise of his youth, and went to the grave in early manhood.

But I must close. My dear Jane and our boys unite in best love to you and Brother Charles, and all at Maxwell and Woodville, and to Mary and Robert and their little ones. Do write soon to
Your affectionate brother,
John Jones.
P.S. I had much more to say, which must be reserved for another letter.

Mr. Charles C. Jones, Jr., *to* Rev. *and* Mrs. C. C. Jones[t]
Bath, Sunday, September 9th, 1860
My dear Father and Mother,

We have just returned to Bath after having enjoyed a very pleasant visit of three days to Brother and Sister Carrie. The Doctor is looking thin and rather badly. He has been taxing himself severely in the preparation of his report upon the marls of Burke, etc. This will make a handsomely executed volume of some two hundred pages filled with analyses, etc., and cannot, I think, fail of proving both of interest and of value to the agricultural interests of our state. But he labors too hard. I sincerely trust that his anticipations, both honorary and pecuniary, may all be fully realized.

We have nothing of interest in this quiet little place. The sojourn here has been of great benefit to Ruth and little Julia. I wish, my dear parents, that you could see your little granddaughter now. Her little mind expands daily, each moment adding new attractions. She has a fine head, and we think is an unusually intelligent and affectionate infant. She is a great favorite here. Both Ruth and herself unite in warmest love. Trusting, my dear father and mother, that every blessing will attend you, I am, as ever,
Your affectionate son,
Charles C. Jones, Jr.

Mr. Charles C. Jones, Jr., *to* Rev. *and* Mrs. C. C. Jones[t]
Bath, *Thursday,* September 13th, 1860

My dear Mother and Father,

We have had no tidings from you for nearly two weeks, and are very anxious to know that our beloved parents are well and in the enjoyment of many blessings. Ruth wrote upon the receipt of your kind letter, Father, and trusts that the reply did not miscarry.

Our dear little Julia has been for the past night or two suffering from a troublesome cold attended with indications of croup, which have caused us no little solicitude. At this time she is far from being well, but we hope that a kind Providence will soon restore her to her wonted health. We have great cause for gratitude to God for the remarkable exemption from disease which she has thus far enjoyed. Her mind expands daily, and her attractions ever increase. She is an intelligent, affectionate infant, and I pray God that she may be spared to her parents and friends to live a life of piety towards her Heavenly Father and usefulness towards her fellow men.

We are now preparing for an approaching concert, to be given by the ladies and some gentlemen of this place, the proceeds of which are to be appropriated towards the building of the First Presbyterian Church in Savannah. We hope to realize some thirty or forty dollars.

I am now busied in writing out my notes of observations in the valleys of the Etowah and Oostanaula. The subject grows upon me. If there be no yellow fever in Savannah, I will expect to return about the 1st of October. Ruth and Julia will be here or in Augusta until frost, as it will not be prudent for them to return before that time. She unites with me in warmest love to you both, my dear parents. Little Julia will soon learn to love her good grandparents and be able to send *her* word of love. As ever,

Your affectionate son,
Charles C. Jones, Jr.

Mr. Charles C. Jones, Jr., *to* Rev. *and* Mrs. C. C. Jones[t]
Bath, *Saturday,* September 15th, 1860

My dear Father and Mother,

We are very anxious to hear from you. Not for many days have we been so long without a kind word from home. Sincerely do we hope that you are both quite well.

Our dear little Julia still suffers much from cold and teething, and causes us no little solicitude. We trust, however, that this precious light of our household will soon be restored to her accustomed health, and be spared to her fond parents many years.

Nothing of interest with us. Fine opportunity for reading. Ruth joins me in warmest love to you both, my dear father and mother. . . . As ever,

Your affectionate son,
Charles C. Jones, Jr.

Rev. C. C. Jones *to* Mr. *and* Mrs. Charles C. Jones, Jr.ᵍ

Maybank, *Thursday,* September 20th, 1860

My dear Son and Daughter,

Your affectionate favors have been received, and in the daily press of writing and correcting to keep ahead of Mr. ——, several mails have passed by without sending you an answer.

We were very sorry to hear by your last of the sickness of dear little Julia, and hope ere this that her cold has left her in her usual good health. You must lay your account with all the joys of parents to meet the cares and sorrows also; and may God spare your dear child to you and grant you every spiritual and temporal blessing along with it! Kiss her for us. We long to see her and her parents also. It is very proper that mother and child remain until frost at Bath. And you, my son, will have to be very careful on your return to Savannah in October. The city is remarkably healthy.

Mr. —— leaves us tomorrow, and has gotten through 800 of my pages of manuscript. There are 536 yet to copy, which he will copy in Columbus and send down to me. It is the only arrangement I can make to have the work done; and he is a scholar and excellent writer and copyist, and is now used to my writing. I shall feel thankful when it is all through with. Will put the first volume to press as soon as Mr. —— finishes it.

Mother has had a terrible bout of toothache, but is relieved and pretty well. Never saw her more fleshy. . . . Your Aunt Susan and Mr. Buttolph and family left last week for Marietta to stay—the family—till frost. . . . Brother Buttolph returns. . . . We are just starting for Montevideo to get Mr. —— off early in the stage in the morning. And we hope to go on to Walthourville and pay Daughter and Robert a visit and baptize our little grandson on Sabbath, D.V. Mother says: "Leave a space for me." Excuse my trembling hand.

From your ever affectionate father,
C. C. Jones.

Mrs. Mary Jones *to* Mr. *and* Mrs. Charles C. Jones, Jr.ᵍ

Montevideo, *Thursday,* September 20th, 1860
Nine o'clock

My dear Children,

From day to day I have been intending to write you both. Your favor, dear Daughter, gave us great pleasure, and I have not told you how much I prize the "little slippers." They stay in my workbasket and remind me daily of the precious little feet whose imprint is so visible.

My heart has been very anxious since receiving your last letter, my dear son. I trust ere this the little darling has been relieved. I used always to give you all when children a simple remedy for colds and hoarseness which never failed to relieve: *linseed oil* and *honey* or syrup. We used to keep it mixed, and if you woke in the night with a croupy cough you were sure to be dosed.

I have never used anything else with white or black. A teaspoonful at a time is enough for an infant. It often acts as a gentle emetic.

We did not reach here until dark. It was so warm the horses became heated, and we came slowly. Sue had a dish of *ricebirds,* which Mr. —— and myself enjoyed. Your father was afraid of the *bones.* Our little Island circle is much diminished by the absence of the family from the Point. We miss them especially at our Tuesday afternoon prayer meeting, which we have recently revived; and we have had some precious meetings.

A letter from our dear Joe by the last mail speaks of your visit as being very pleasant to Carrie and himself. They are charmed with Julia. He says: "She is a lovely babe, and completely won our hearts." Your boy George is doing very well, and often inquires with the other servants after you. Please remember us affectionately to Cousin Eliza and family and to Val and Mrs. Neely and Mr. and Mrs. Dowse. Excuse a tired hand. Good night, my dear children. God bless and save you all! Kisses for my little darling Julia.

Your affectionate mother,
Mary Jones.

Mr. Charles C. Jones, Jr., *to* Rev. *and* Mrs. C. C. Jones[g]
Savannah, *Wednesday,* September 26th, 1860
My dear Father and Mother,

I have only a moment to acknowledge the receipt of your last kind favor, and to say that we thank you both for it. Left Ruth and little Julia at Bath yesterday. Both quite well. Have been very busy all day. Matters in this life go behindhand much more readily than they advance. Saw Brother and Sister Carrie in Augusta last night. Both very well. With warmest love, I am, my dear father and mother, as ever,

Your affectionate son,
Charles C. Jones, Jr.

Please send George in by earliest convenience. One dollar enclosed to pay his expenses.

Mrs. Mary Jones *to* Mr. Charles C. Jones, Jr.[g]
Maybank, *Friday,* September 28th, 1860
My dear Son,

Last evening's mail did not reach us until after nine o'clock—too late to make arrangements for sending your boy George by today's cars. Gilbert and himself are preparing to go up in the buggy to Arcadia, that he may be in readiness for the morning train. I am glad you sent him out. He has been useful and obedient, and I hope will grow up a good servant. He is at the age when boys white and black require steady control and good influences and regular employment. Do, my son, require him to attend the Sabbath school and church. He has a good memory and understands well. When he first came out, I gave him active employment in the lot, which seems to have stretched him several inches. Lately *Flora* has had him in charge, cleaning glasses, paint, etc., etc.—all in the line of his profession.

I am glad you have had a short period of relaxation this summer. Mind and body required it, and I hope you have felt refreshed. The Indian researches must have interested you. We shall look with great interest for your descriptions, etc. Do, my dear child, in returning to the city be careful not to expose yourself to the *hot sun* or *night air*. October has been said by persons of experience to be the most fatally sickly month in the year in Savannah. We were happy to learn that you left Ruth and dear little Julia and Joe and Carrie well. God's mercies to us as a family are very great!

On last Friday Mr. —— left us. We took him up to the Boro, and in the afternoon went to Walthourville. Found your sister and Robert and the little children all well. On Sabbath your father baptized little Charlie. It was of course a time of peculiar interest to us, and I never heard more solemn or appropriate remarks than your father made upon the occasion. I wish you had been present. All the covenant promises and blessings connected with this precious ordinance of God's own appointing were brought forth to strengthen our faith and encourage our fidelity. The dear little babe looked into your father's face; as the water was applied he bowed his little head (*apparently*) to receive it, and then turned and laid it in his father's bosom.

The boys are waiting, and I must close, leaving the last page for your father. Accept the *quinces* for yourself, the *limes* for Ruth; hope you will enjoy the *reds*.

Ever your affectionate mother,
Mary Jones.

Rev. C. C. Jones *to* Mr. Charles C. Jones, Jr.[g]

Maybank, *Friday,* September 28th, 1860

Mother has cautioned you, my dear son, about the hot sun and night air. Use your umbrella in the heat of the day. If you should be sick, write us at once. But I hope you will have good health, God willing. Will write Ruthie soon.

We have not a *bill* in the house. Do order the triweekly *Morning News* sent to me, and pay the subscription from Mr. Anderson for me. I have money in his hands. The *Republican* is below par, and is offensive in its politics. I wish to know how matters are going in the state.

Have read Mr. Bartow's speech with great pleasure. Barring its *egotism*—excusable under the circumstances—it is a capital speech and must do good.

Mother is not as well as I could wish. She is finally riding on horseback with me in the mornings. Very dry. County healthy.

Your affectionate father,
C. C. Jones.

Is Judge Jackson in Savannah?

Mr. Charles C. Jones, Jr., *to* Rev. *and* Mrs. C. C. Jones[g]
Savannah, *Saturday,* September 29th, 1860

My dear Mother and Father,

By the hands of George I am this afternoon favored with your letter of the 28th inst. and the accompanying kind remembrances, for which please accept my sincere thanks. The preserves, my dear mother, are beautiful, and will be highly prized by Ruth. The fish and butter I send to Mrs. Harriss, our next-door neighbor, as I am not now taking my meals at home. To the nice boiled groundnuts I purpose paying especial and personal attention.

On Tuesday night I expect to take the cars for Berzelia. Will, D.V., remain at Bath a few days, and then accompany Ruth and Julia to the Sand Hills near Augusta, where she desires to spend a week or two with her relatives. . . . I myself will return to Savannah.

During my leisure moments I am writing out my notes in reference to the monuments of the Etowah valley. They may prove interesting, and they shall be submitted to you so soon as they are completed. I have employed a son of Mrs. Grant to make accurate drawings of some of the remains in my cabinet, in order that everything may be in readiness for the lithographer when the work which I propose is entirely finished.

Our house here has been newly painted and looks very well. Your room will soon be all ready, and we sincerely hope, my dear parents, that we may often enjoy the pleasure of seeing you in it. . . . I will see that the triweekly *News* is duly sent. The *Republican* is indeed beyond all endurance. With warmest love to you both, my dear father and mother, I am, as ever,

Your affectionate son,
Charles C. Jones, Jr.

Mr. Charles C. Jones, Jr., *to* Rev. *and* Mrs. C. C. Jones[g]
Savannah, *Tuesday,* October 9th, 1860

My dear Father and Mother,

By today's papers you will see that I have been elected mayor of the city of Savannah. This appointment was on my part *wholly unsolicited,* the nomination having been made during my absence from the city. It was also a nomination and ratification by the citizens of Savannah irrespective of party. Under these circumstances I did not feel at liberty to decline, and must admit that the compliment of the election comes home with peculiar effect, conferred as it is by the city of my birth, of my choice—a city, too, whose soil covers the honored dust of Great-Grandfather.

The theory of the citizens' movement in this campaign was *in municipal elections to ignore national politics,* and consult only such questions as concern the interests of our city. Party, factions, and intrigues were ignored, and men of all parties united in the support. The policy pursued by the Breckinridge and Lane party, as represented by the executive committee of this city, was suicidal. Every overture was made to induce them to unite in the general plan of a citizens' ticket irrespective of party, and thus avoid any bias by this election for or against the Presidential candidates. They foolishly refused, and defeat ensued. This is not, however, a test vote of the popularity of Breckinridge and Lane in this city, as many of our citizens had not registered, and the citizens' ticket received the votes of at least three hundred Breckinridge and Lane Democrats.

I trust to see you both soon, my dear parents, and will explain then more fully the theory of this election. I sincerely hope, in view of the important duties thus devolved upon me, that I may receive strength and guidance from above.

Tonight I leave for Augusta. Ruth will return in a week or two. I go to bring her from Bath to Augusta, and will, D.V., come back here myself on Thursday. All friends well. With warmest love, my dear father and mother, to you both, and sensibly alive to the feeling that the chief delight which I experience in this confidence of my fellow citizens arises from the fact that you, my dear parents, and Ruth will be gratified by the result and the course which I have pursued, I am, as ever,

> Your affectionate son,
> Charles C. Jones, Jr.

HON. CHARLES C. JONES, JR., *to* REV. *and* MRS. C. C. JONES[g]

> Savannah, *Monday,* October 15th, 1860

My dear Father and Mother,

The board-elect and the new mayor were this morning "sworn in," to use a common expression, and have entered upon the active discharge of the duties appertaining to our respective offices. I sincerely trust that we may have strength, ability, and honesty fully to meet all the responsibilities devolved upon us.

This cool change has imparted an air of activity to our city. All well. Am expecting Ruth and Julia on Monday of next week. I long to have them home again. Your room, my dear parents, will soon be ready, and we will hope for a long visit from you. As ever,

> Your affectionate son,
> Charles C. Jones, Jr.

REV. C. C. JONES *to* HON. CHARLES C. JONES, JR.[g]

> Maybank, *Monday,* October 15th, 1860

My dear Son,

Your election was unexpected to us, as we had no intimation of your being in nomination until it appeared in the newspaper a day or two before the election took place. It is a high honor, coming unsolicited, and the expression of the confidence of a majority of your fellow citizens; and we esteem it such, and are gratified that your conduct and character have been such as to attract to you their suffrages, which place you in the highest office in their gift. And we sincerely hope that they may not be disappointed in their expectations of you, but that you will conscientiously seek to discharge your very responsible and in many respects difficult duties with all sobriety, industry, impartiality, justice, and integrity, and with kindness and decision and intelligence. I look upon the office as one of very high responsibility, and trust you are of the same impression. Otherwise you may fail in filling it as you ought.

You will, as you remark in your letter, need aid from *above;* and I hope, my dear son, that *you will seek* that aid. Since "the powers that be are ordained of God," and in His providence you have been called to preside as the chief executive officer over a large city, you should acknowledge the Lord's hand in it and seek from Him wisdom to direct and power to stand. "In all thy ways acknowledge Him, and He shall direct thy paths." Elevation to station and influence involves a responsibility which awakens solicitude in the bosom of every right-minded man; and instead of inflation and self-sufficiency he is prompted to humility and watchfulness. And knowing the fickleness of popular favor, and how trivial events cast down those who seem to stand firmest, he will trust but little to it, and take his satisfaction in doing his duty and making himself useful to his friends and country. And such lose not their reward. *Hoc nempe ab homine exigitur, ut prosit hominibus: si fieri potest, multis; si minus, paucis; si minus, proximis; si minus, sibi. Nam, cum se utilem ceteris efficit, commune agit negotium.* So writes Seneca, and his views are just. And may you make yourself useful to others, and so be reckoned a common good, or a benefactor.

Our first desire and prayer for our sons and our daughter has been that you all might be the true children of God, and our second, that your lives might be spent in usefulness to your fellow men. And our advice (and I trust example) has been, never *to seek office,* but let *office seek you.* If it is tendered, and you hope you are qualified to fill it, and it is proper to accept, do so. Honors to be well worn and well borne need to be well merited. You are perhaps the youngest mayor Savannah has ever had; therefore you must so act that no man may despise thy youth.

You are just twice as young as Socrates was when he consented to take public office in Athens. He was fifty-six. You have that to aid you which that great and excellent heathen never had: the knowledge of the living and true God and of His Holy Word. You will let me as your father insist, my son, that you do conscientiously read God's Word carefully *twice* a day. Do not speak or think of the want of time when God gives you all your time and can stop it when He pleases; and you can make no better use of it than by conversing with Him through His Holy Word and by prayer. This will strengthen and enlighten you for all the cares and businesses of life. Try it faithfully, and you will find it so. As you advance and become more and more involved in the affairs of this life, the more anxious your parents feel for your everlasting interests, and pray you *not to neglect them.*

Mother sends much love, and congratulations upon your honors, and her best wishes and prayers for your success under them. Am happy to say she has been better of late. Our kind friend and good neighbor Mrs. King has had a severe fall, and is confined to her bed and suffers much from pain; but the doctor thinks she is not dangerously injured, though her confinement may be protracted. We were glad to hear from Ruthie and Julia and from your brother and Carrie. Love to Ruthie for us when you write, and kisses for Julia. We long to see you all. Weather very cold for the season. God bless and keep you, my dear son!

Your ever affectionate father,
C. C. Jones.

Mrs. Mary Jones *to* Mrs. Mary S. Mallard[t]

Maybank, *Monday,* October 15th, 1860

My dear Daughter,

It has just occurred to me as we were retiring that I might send you a line by Gilbert, who goes to the depot with Joe's box tomorrow. Your beautiful little sacque and gown have been safely deposited with the other articles.

On last Friday week your Aunt Julia was standing in her pantry door when one of the horses she has been in the habit of petting was brought up, and she took hold of the halter whilst the servant drew water for him. She turned around to speak to someone. He threw up his head and jumped off, jerking her out of the door and dashing her upon the ground at least ten feet from the door. She fell upon her left side and was taken up insensible, and has been in bed unable to move ever since, except as she is assisted from one side to the other. I was sent for immediately, and reached her before Dr. Harris, who made (as soon as she could bear it) a thorough examination and said there was neither fracture nor dislocation. But her sufferings continue so great that he now requests a consultation with Dr. Bulloch. I have been as much with her as possible. They are truly a distressed family: Mary and Belle both sick from fatigue and anxiety, and Amy and Phillis laid up.

When may we expect to see Mrs. Stevens and yourself? We have almost winter. You have seen the honor conferred upon your brother; pray for him that he may be found faithful. Father unites with me in best love to Robert and yourself. Kisses for our dear grandchildren.

Ever your affectionate mother,
Mary Jones.

Mrs. Mary S. Mallard *to* Mrs. Mary Jones[t]

Walthourville, *Tuesday,* October 16th, 1860

My dear Mother,

I was just going to get my pen today when the mailbag came, and in it your welcome letter. I am truly sorry to hear of Aunt Julia's injury, and feel very much troubled about her; but I hope our kind Heavenly Father will spare her life. I feel for Cousin Mary and Isabel. And I know the burden of nursing falls upon you, dear Mother; I hope you will not make yourself sick. I wish I were with you to help in some way.

I saw Mrs. Stevens this evening, and if nothing prevents, we hope to be with you on next Tuesday evening. Mr. Mallard expects his father's carriage on Monday next, and we will leave early Tuesday morning, dine in Dorchester, and I will probably take a seat with Mrs. Stevens in her carriage from that place. Mrs. Stevens anticipates a great deal of pleasure in going down, and I have no doubt the change will do her good. She will remain until Friday. I will talk of my arrangements after I get down. I am now thinking a little of going to Savannah with Mr. Mallard, but have not fully determined to do so.

I received a very pleasant letter from Brother Charlie today in reply to one I wrote him offering my congratulations. He expects Ruth next Monday. Julia can say a good many little words.

Last week I had a long, interesting letter from Carrie, in which she sends a great deal of love to Father and yourself and begs me to tell Father that she has written a letter on large paper; and I can testify that every part of it was well filled. Brother Joe sent us quite a flaming placard advertising the Planters' Convention. We intend sending it to the station tomorrow and having it posted there. Perhaps some of the planters may be induced to attend.

What cold weather we have had for several days past! This early cold always carries me back to Maybank. *Well* do I remember the first fires that were kindled in the fall, and how we used to gather around the hearth— Father reading aloud, Mother knitting or sewing, Brother Charlie sitting upon the floor with a bunch of wire grass and ball of flax thread making mats with *Taddy* at his side (or else sinewing arrows), Brother Joe with his paint box and some megatherium skeleton model before him, and I think I used to make mittens or sew my hexagon quilt. Sometimes a hoarded stock of chinquapins would engage the attention of all the children, each one counting his store. I think Father's reading was often interrupted on such evenings by questions as to the *probable* time when frost would come; and if Daddy Jack made his appearance in the room, his opinion was sure to be asked. We all have hearths of our own now, but I do not think any of them will ever burn as brightly or possess the same attractions of that one at Maybank. There was always something peculiar about the first autumn fire. . . .

Our little ones are quite well. Charlie develops daily, and is very good. Mamie often says something about her "danma" and "danpa." Mr. Mallard unites with me in warmest love to dear Father and yourself, dear Mother.

Your affectionate daughter,
Mary S. Mallard.

Book Two
The Edge of the Sword
(1860–1865)

I

Hon. Charles C. Jones, Jr., *to* Rev. C. C. Jones[g]

Savannah, *Thursday,* October 18th, 1860

My dear Father,

I am in receipt of your kind and valued letter of the 15th inst., and sincerely thank you for the same.

No one can form any idea of the multifarious and important duties which devolve upon the mayor of this city until called upon practically to discharge them. The accumulated ordinances of a century and a quarter have to be carefully understood, and administered with firmness and discrimination. Interests varied in their character must be duly considered and protected. Much lies in the discretion and sound judgment of the mayor, and in many things a nice sense of right, of justice and propriety, is his only guide. The summary jurisdiction of the police court, held every morning at ten o'clock, also involves in its proper exercise no little firmness, intelligence, and discrimination. You are aware that over this court the mayor presides every morning at ten o'clock. In fine, he is expected to have a care for every interest and for the every protection of the city at all hours of the day and night. I am feelingly alive to the responsibilities which are thus devolved upon me; and it will be my constant endeavor, with an humble and ever-repeated prayer for assistance from above, to bring to the discharge of the incumbent duties a firm resolution, a clear judgment, and an enlightened perception of right and justice.

Our city, since these recent frosts, improves in health. The broken-bone fever decreases. The summer absentees are returning, and business has received an upward impulse. I must, however, make a special exception in our profession. Legal matters are quite stagnant. The doubt which attends any attempt to conjecture what another month may bring forth in the political and social status of our country exerts in all probability its depressing influence. The election of Lincoln seems now almost a fixed fact, in view of the recent advices received from Pennsylvania, Ohio, and Indiana. The Republicans claim New York by a clear majority of forty thousand. Should Lincoln be elected, the action of a single state, such as South Carolina or Alabama, may precipitate us into all the terrors of intestine war. I sincerely trust that a kind Providence, that has so long and so specially watched over the increasing glories of our common country, may so influence the minds of fanatical men and dispose of coming events as to avert so direful a calamity.

Ruth and little Julia are expected on Monday night next. I shall be truly happy when they return. "It is not good for man to be alone." Especially is this true in the case of a married man.

We have but little of interest with us. I was pained to learn the severe indisposition of Aunt Julia, and sincerely hope for her speedy relief. With warmest love to you, my dear father, and to my dear mother, I am, as ever,

Your affectionate son,
Charles C. Jones, Jr.

MRS. MARY JONES *to* HON. CHARLES C. JONES, JR.[ĸ]

Maybank, *Tuesday,* October 23rd, 1860

My very dear Son,

We are this afternoon in expectation of the arrival of your dear sister and the little ones with Mrs. Dr. Stevens and some of her family to make us a visit; and whilst waiting to receive them I will send you a few lines, as I shall not have the opportunity of writing again this week.

I trust your own fireside has ere this been gladdened by the presence of your dear wife and sweet little daughter. How I long to see you all! Julia's likeness stands open upon the mantelpiece, and we look upon it daily. Precious child, may she long be spared to you, and prove an angel of mercy to direct your heart to the Giver of such a gift!

My feelings of interest and congratulations upon the distinguished position which you have been called to occupy by the voice of your fellow citizens have been already conveyed to you through your good father in his letter of wise and affectionate counsel and advice, which I trust and believe you will reverence and obey. It surely is no common honor for one at your age to be called to preside and direct the interests of fifteen or twenty thousand people! I trust you will realize the high responsibilities which rest upon you. God grant you, my child, *fidelity* in your lot, and uprightness in all your ways! My daily—my *special*—prayer for you is that you may have the teachings and guidance of the Holy Spirit in all that you are called to say or do. I feel that just at this time above all other periods in our national history special grace, wisdom, and decision are needed by all our rulers.

(*Just here* the ladies arrived.)

Yesterday your uncle and Mr. Buttolph spent with us, and we had a pleasant day. Mrs. Stevens has never visited the Island before. She admires both scenery and atmosphere, and yesterday we had a fine display of fish upon the table: sheepshead, young drum, whiting, and yellowtail.

Our good friend and neighbor Mrs. King is more comfortable, but in a very suffering condition, and likely to be so for a great while. If you see Willie, tell him his mother is becoming more accustomed to her confinement, and the family are well, excepting their servant Jaque.

Do you know of any situation in which Mr. John Wells could get business? He is very desirous of obtaining employment; and I feel assured if you could aid him that you would be doing a kindness to one who would be a grateful friend, and faithful and industrious in any business committed to him. He does not wish a sedentary place where there is writing to do. Active outdoor business would suit him best. We have seen a great deal of him this summer, and feel a true interest in his welfare. His industry and attention to business at Woodville could not be surpassed. If you can aid him, please, my son, let him know it as early as convenient.

The coming Sabbath, my dear child, will be your birthday, and Father and Mother now send you our blessing and best wishes upon it. God bless and save you with His everlasting salvation! It would gratify me exceedingly if from that day you would commence and read the Holy Bible, with Dr. Scott's *Practical Observations,* daily. I feel assured you would find it a great means of grace. Enclosed is an order for the railroad dividend, and I wish you to take sixty-five dollars and buy a *desk* or *bookcase* for your nice new study as a *birthday gift from your mother, or any other article* that would be useful and acceptable. The remainder you can send me by any private opportunity.

When shall we see you? Our best love to our dear daughter and little darling Julia, in which Sister unites.

Ever your affectionate mother,
Mary Jones.

October 25th.

Hon. Charles C. Jones, Jr., *to* Mrs. Mary Jones[t]

Savannah, Saturday, October 27th, 1860

My very dear Mother,

I was yesterday favored with your precious letter of the 25th inst., and must thank you for all the kind congratulations and valuable advice which it contains. You never forget my birthday, and each recurrence brings me a message of love and interest, full of the tenderest maternal solicitude and of the purest Christian counsels. How much, my dear mother, do I owe to you and to dear Father! A debt so great, so enduring, ever increasing—one which it shall always be my desire and pleasure sincerely to acknowledge, but one that I can never repay. Not one son of a thousand has so many reasons for earnest thankfulness to Heaven, and scarcely one who has made such few and so poor returns. But whatever be my shortcomings, my dear parents, of this am I confident: that towards you my heart ever goes out with an ever-increasing affection. Time does but consecrate you and all your virtues in my heart of hearts. Amid the varied scenes and phases of life, amid the perplexities and cares which present not infrequently questions in morals hard to be answered by some, I have always some precept of former years, taught by you, which solves the doubt and indicates the path of duty and of honor; while your examples are ever before me—by far the best lesson, the most perfect illustration of the principle. Twenty-nine years of my life have passed away. Solemn thought! And how little have I accomplished! I will remember your request, my mother, in reference to prayer and reading of the Word of God in connection with the commentaries of Dr. Scott.

The duties of the mayoralty are heavy upon me—more particularly so when the present political status of the country is considered, and the further facts which grow out of it—that scoundrels are seen, and suspicious persons found, tampering with our Negroes and attempting to induce them to leave the state. I have now under arrest a crew of Negro sailors—free men of color —who are charged with this offense. The case comes up before me on Monday next. I find also that great laxity has obtained in reference to the conduct of the Negro population. The consequence is that they have forgotten their places—are guilty of gambling, smoking in the streets, drinking, and disorderly conduct generally. To the remedy of this I intend to devote, and am devoting, my every energy. I mean also to bring to justice those offenders of foreign birth, the rum-sellers, who at the corners of our streets in their shops are demoralizing our servants and ruining them in every point of view. Any mayor who is sensibly alive to the duties which are devolved upon him, and who endeavors conscientiously to discharge them, has, I can assure you, his hands full.

I have again to thank you, my dear mother, for your handsome and valued present. It is just what I most coveted. The remainder of the dividend (say, one hundred dollars) is now in my hands, and I will embrace the earliest opportunity for sending it to you.

By the way, Major McIntosh purposes going to Liberty on Thursday or Friday of next week. He will be with Captain Winn at Dorchester. He will let you know when he arrives there, and hopes to spend a day with you on the Island. Should you see Uncle William, please mention this circumstance to him, as I know he will be rejoiced to see his old friend.

Am happy to hear that Aunt Julia improves. Do present us affectionately to her when you next see her, with our best wishes for her early restoration.

In regard to the situation for Mr. Wells, I will be happy to serve him, and will endeavor to obtain for him if possible the situation he desires. I fear, however, for the result. There are so many applicants, and the peculiar character of the engagements he wishes to assume is unusual.

You and Father we will expect and hope to see at least during the meeting of Presbytery if not before. From Mr. Porter we learn that this body convenes here on Thursday the 8th prox. Do, my dear parents, come if you can find it in your power to do so. Ruth has nicely arranged and fitted up her new house. Your room is all ready and waiting for you, and we wish you to see your little granddaughter. You will not be ashamed of her. All well, and unite in warmest love. As ever,

Your affectionate son,
Charles C. Jones, Jr.

Rev. C. C. Jones *to* Hon. Charles C. Jones, Jr.ᵍ

Maybank, *Saturday,* October 27th, 1860

My dear Son,

Your last favors are at hand, and we congratulate you on the return of your dear wife and sweet little daughter. We long to see you all, and will try and pay you a visit after a while.

Enclosed is a draft on Mr. Anderson for two hundred dollars, the amount of my note, which please take up and end the long run. And I hope we may be favored so as to need no more help of the kind. Mr. Anderson has that amount in his hands on my account, which we reserved for contingencies; but as the crop will be going to market, we now use it.

Mother wrote you last mail. Sister and the little ones are on a visit to us. Robert left this morning with Mrs. Dr. Stevens, who has been spending a few days with us. Mrs. King is doing well.

I do not apprehend any very serious disturbance in the event of Lincoln's election and a withdrawal of one or more Southern states, which will eventuate in the withdrawal of all. On what ground can the free states found a military crusade upon the South? Who are the violators of the Constitution? Will the conservatives in the free states make no opposition? If the attempt is made to subjugate the South, what prospect will there be of success? And what *benefit* will accrue to all the substantial interests of the free states? The business world will think very little benefit. Under all the circumstances attending a withdrawal there would be no *casus belli.* Is not the right of self-government on the part of the people the cornerstone of the republic? Have not fifteen states a right to govern themselves and withdraw from a compact or constitution disregarded by the other states to their injury and (it may be) their ruin? But may God avert such a separation, for the consequences may in future be disastrous to both sections. Union if possible—but with it we must have *life, liberty, and equality.*

I pray for your just and prosperous administration of the trusts reposed in you by your fellow citizens. Kiss Ruth and little Daughter for us all. All send much love. Don't hold any courts *Sunday!*

Your ever affectionate father,

C. C. Jones.

Rev. C. C. Jones *to* Hon. Charles C. Jones, Jr.ᵍ

Maybank, *Monday,* November 5th, 1860

My dear Son,

I send by your Cousin Lyman a manuscript volume (the fourth of my *History*) which you will express to Mr. ——, Columbus, Georgia, according to the address, and much oblige me. I wrote Mr. —— that it would be expressed on Thursday of this week, D.V. Some 170 or 180 pages are to follow, and the first volume will be closed, and I shall be grateful. So soon as Mr. —— finishes the copy, will put it to press, D.V.

Also your mother's spectacles: *broken*. Please have the same magnifying power, pebble glasses if to be had, and return them as soon as possible—by mail if you have no direct opportunity out. We have but one available pair of specs between us.

Also my faithful watch: broken in winding up. Please have it well repaired for me.

Sorry to give you so much trouble, as you are so busy.

Moving up this week. Mother worn out gardening and packing. Late, and she has retired. Sends much love to Ruthie and yourself with me, and many kisses for the dear little granddaughter. Must refer you to Cousin Lyman for all the news our way.

Your ever affectionate father,
C. C. Jones.

Mrs. Mary Jones *to* Hon. Charles C. Jones, Jr.[g]

Maybank, *Tuesday,* November 6th, 1860*

Thanks many, my dear son, for your affectionate and valued letter. *Gilbert* begs me to say he can get you eight turkeys at a dollar apiece if you are willing to give it and will send word by *Thursday*. They are very scarce. With much love,

Your affectionate mother,
M. J.

Hon. Charles C. Jones, Jr., *to* Rev. *and* Mrs. C. C. Jones[g]

Savannah, *Wednesday,* November 7th, 1860

My dear Father and Mother,

We are happy today to hear from you so directly. Mr. Buttolph came in while we were at dinner and gave us the latest news from you. The watch and spectacles are already in the hands of the jeweler, and will be repaired so soon as practicable. You shall have them by the earliest opportunity thereafter. The volume is now in charge of the express company, and will be duly forwarded to Mr. ———. In consideration of the fact of my being His Honor the Mayor, the agent refused to receive any pay for the transportation of the same.

The telegrams announce the fact of Lincoln's election by a popular vote! South Carolina has today virtually seceded. Judge Magrath of the U.S. Circuit Court for the District of South Carolina, Hon. William F. Colcock, collector of the port of Charleston, and other government officers have resigned, and we learn that the Palmetto flag will be hoisted on the morrow. A meeting of the citizens here is called for tomorrow evening. We are on the verge of Heaven only knows what.

I write in haste for the mail. You have my congratulations, Father, upon the near completion of your first volume. May you have increasing mind and strength to conclude your most valuable labors! Ruth will, my dear mother, be very happy to get the turkeys at some convenient and early day. Our little Julia is recovering from her attack of broken-bone fever, but my dear Ruth is quite unwell, and has been suffering much for nearly a week. They unite with me, my dear parents, in warmest love to you both. As ever,

Your affectionate son,
Charles C. Jones, Jr.

HON. CHARLES C. JONES, JR., *to* MRS. MARY JONES[g]

Savannah, *Tuesday,* November 13th, 1860

My dear Mother,

We were happy through Sister to hear from you today. She expects, I believe, to be with you on Thursday of this week, unless we can persuade her to remain with us until Robert, who left us this morning, returns from Columbus. My dear Ruth continues quite unwell, and little Julia is not as bright as she might be.

I have my hands completely filled day and night. The duties devolved upon me at this important crisis are many and onerous. Our country needs the prayers of the good and the counsels of the wise. I trust that we may soon see a Southern confederacy. If we are true to ourselves, it may be formed upon a substantial and viable basis.

I have only time to say, my dear mother, that we all unite in warmest love to self and dear Father. As ever,

Your affectionate son,
Charles C. Jones, Jr.

MRS. MARY JONES *to* HON. CHARLES C. JONES, JR.[g]

Montevideo, *Thursday,* November 15th, 1860

My dear Son,

We were happy to receive your affectionate favor by today's mail, and to know that you were well and again at the post of duty. No festive greetings were ever mingled with more elevated feelings of friendship, honor, patriotism, and courage than those recently enjoyed by the citizens of Charleston and Savannah. We were much obliged to you for the *Mercury,* and felt honored that our son bore so high a place. Your opening speech at the Pulaski gave evidently a tone to the meeting.

Be assured, my dear child, of your parents' warmest sympathy at this time, and of our united and special prayer that you may be divinely guided and ever act with wisdom and fidelity in your sacred and responsible station. It is a new era in our country's history, and I trust the wise and patriotic leaders of the people will soon devise some united course of action throughout the Southern states. I cannot see a shadow of reason for civil war in the event of a Southern confederacy; but even that, *if it must come,* would be preferable to submission to Black Republicanism, involving as it would all that is horrible, degrading, and ruinous. "Forbearance has ceased to be a virtue"; and I believe we could meet with no evils out of the Union that would compare to those we will finally suffer if we continue in it; for we can no longer doubt that the settled policy of the North is to crush the South.

But I am wandering quite beyond my object in writing, which is specially to ask if dear Ruth cannot come out with our little granddaughter and spend some time with us until they both recruit. The weather is now delightful, and we would do all in our power to make home pleasant to them. Our little Mary has been a great comfort and source of amusement, and we shall feel lost without her.

Today we sent Gilbert to Sunbury for the turkeys, and tomorrow Sam will take them to Stepney with directions to feed them well, that they may be ready for your use when ordered. They are young birds and not as large as they will be. Poultry is scarce, and we got them as a favor.

Father has just returned from the chapel, and unites with me in best love to Ruth and yourself, and many kisses for our granddaughter.

Ever your affectionate mother,
Mary Jones.

Howdy for the servants.

Rev. C. C. Jones *to* Hon. Charles C. Jones, Jr.[g]

Montevideo, *Thursday,* November 15th, 1860

Your position is a very responsible one. Go calmly and quietly about your duties, and discharge them with integrity and fidelity, and avoid excitements and too frequent speaking on public occasions. I was much gratified with your speech at the dinner to the Charlestonians in Savannah.

The times are remarkable; the questions before the people momentous. The final issues are with Him who rules among the nations. A nation to be born in a day, without a struggle, would be a wonder on earth. If the Southern states resolve on a separate confederacy, they must be prepared for any emergency, even that of war with the free states; as their arrogance and confidence in their power may urge them to attempt our subjugation—although I do not fear it if the Southern states are united. We have a heavy Northern element, and a Southern element Northernized, to contend with in our own borders, and may perhaps lead to some embarrassment; but the majority the other way is so decided that it cannot—at least it is so to be hoped—effect much. Certainly we do need "the prayers of the pious and the wisdom of the wise." Portions of Governor Brown's special message are excellent. Having no access to the leading spirits of the day, I cannot discern the drift of affairs beyond the light of the newspapers, which we read with interest. We have no knowledge of the course which Maryland, Virginia, North Carolina, Tennessee, Kentucky, and Missouri will pursue.

The Lord keep and bless you and yours, my dear son, and give you a place in that Kingdom which cannot be moved, is the prayer of

Your affectionate father,
C. C. Jones.

Rev. C. C. Jones *to* Hon. Charles C. Jones, Jr.[g]

Montevideo, *Monday,* November 19th, 1860

My dear Son,

I shall send, D.V., our shoe measures tomorrow to Messrs. Butler & Frierson to fit and forward by Friday's freight train. Will you do me the favor of calling and selecting the quality and price for me? The first I wish substantial, the second not extravagant. Have notified them that you would do so.

Your sister reached us in safety, and improved by her pleasant visit to you. The little ones pretty well, and very engaging. We want Ruthie and little Julia to come and see us. The change will do them good, and we will do all in our power to make it agreeable in our quiet home.

Preached yesterday at Midway, and do not feel the worse for it today.

Tomorrow the county holds a meeting on Federal affairs. Captain Winn tells me our esteemed friend Judge Law is expected out. We shall be glad to see him; his influence will be good. Shall attend, Providence permitting; and Mother says she will go with me *to represent her father,* being the oldest child of his family now living. You know her patriotism. She has taken possession of your pistol with the shooting apparatus underneath, and Gilbert is ordered to clean and put it in perfect order. And she says she has *caps* for it. I trust the measures of the state will be calmly considered and resolutely taken, and the convention of the people duly called.

Mother and Sister unite with me in love to Ruthie and yourself, and kisses for Julia. I am longing to see the child. The letter of your brother to Mr. Cobb, president of the Cotton Planters' Convention, was a *private* one and never intended for any other eyes than Mr. Cobb's. He should not have published it; and some things your brother ought not to have put in it.

Your affectionate father,
C. C. Jones.

Rev. C. C. Jones *to* Mrs. Ruth B. Jones[g]

Montevideo, *Thursday,* November 22nd, 1860

My dear Daughter,

We were pained to learn through Robert on Tuesday that our dear son, your good husband, was sick with perhaps the broken-bone fever. He said if he should be seriously sick that you would not delay but write and let us know; and as we have heard nothing by mail today, we trust through God's mercy he is doing well if not entirely recovered. Write us, if you please, by return of mail (Saturday's) and let us know the truth. His Honor the Mayor has necessarily a great deal of care and of business, and is obliged to be at least occasionally out at night; and therefore it becomes him to be as careful of himself as he possibly can, and defend himself from the night air when he goes out. And I know you will try like a good wife to relieve him as much as possible from domestic cares, and make his hours at home hours of enjoyment and repose. And so you will do him good and be a helpmeet to him. A cheerful and an affectionate wife is the joy of her husband and the life and light of his home, and I am sure you are such a one. Don't you think a change from town to country would be good for yourself and Julia when you can make it? It will give us great pleasure to have you with us, and we much regret that our son cannot promise to be one of your party.

Robert and Daughter with their little ones left us this morning, and the house has been very silent since. Little Charlie really seemed to verge towards broken-bone, but perhaps it was his teeth. Daughter said she had a most pleasant visit to you, and Joe and Carrie wrote us that they enjoyed your visit to them very much in Augusta.

Mother has been busy all day both without and within the house, and is now measuring off clothing for the plantation to be given out this evening so soon as I return from the chapel; and am expecting the bell to call me over every minute to the lecture. There appears to be some interest in religion among our people, and our hope and prayer is that it may be the work of the Holy Spirit, and result in the saving conversion of some of them. The cases of several are very encouraging.

Our county had its public meeting on Tuesday on Federal affairs, and you will see the proceedings in the papers. Judge Law delivered an excellent address. The substance of the Savannah resolutions was embodied in our resolutions.

Mother unites in much love to our dear son and yourself; and kiss our dear little granddaughter for us many times. Howdy for all the servants. Their families are all well out here.

Your affectionate father,
C. C. Jones.

Bell just ringing. Half-past 7 P.M.

Quarter to nine. Just come back. Full and pleasant meeting.

Mrs. Mary Jones *to* Mrs. Ruth B. Jones[g]

Montevideo, Thursday, November 22nd, 1860

Dear Daughter,

My night's work has just closed, and it is now very late. Father has retired. I have felt anxious and unhappy about my dear child, and expected that you would surely have sent us a line today. Do make him wear his flannel next to his person. May God preserve and bless him!

I trust we shall soon have you and dear little Julia with us. Kiss the little darling over and over for us. With much love to you both,

Ever, believe me, your affectionate mother,
Mary Jones.

Hon. Charles C. Jones, Jr., *to* Rev. *and* Mrs. C. C. Jones[t]
Savannah, *Wednesday,* November 28th, 1860
My dear Father and Mother,

We are all pretty well this evening, and unite in warmest love. The day has been pretty generally observed in the city.

Charlie West has just returned from Princeton. His mother has ordered him home, ostensibly on account of the present political condition of the country. I must say I think she acts without judgment.

Nothing new. The monetary pressure still continues. Governor Brown promises to veto the Alleviation Act, but the legislature will probably pass it by a constitutional majority over his head. As ever, my dear parents,

Your affectionate son,
Charles C. Jones, Jr.

It is rumored that Secretary Cobb and Chief Justice Taney have resigned. Our love to Aunt Susan and cousins.

Mrs. Mary Jones *to* Mrs. Mary S. Mallard[t]
Montevideo, *Friday,* November 30th, 1860
My dear Daughter,

We had a very pleasant visit from your brother and Ruth. Little Julia improved, but Charles was still very unwell when he left. I feel anxious about his state of health.

A letter from Carrie by the last mail. She is bright and well. Joe will deliver his address in the early part of the fair, which commences on Monday the 3rd December. I would be delighted to hear him. Do you know of anyone going up?

Your aunt and cousins came out on Friday to dinner and left us yesterday. Laura was in bed several days with pain in her face. Jimmie is the most wonderfully improved child mentally and physically I ever saw. He says everything, and knows the short questions in the catechism, and a great many little verses. Your Aunt Susan sends the *merino* to Little Daughter and Charlie, and Jimmie sends the little girl to her, and dear old Aunty sends her the book and little sheep, and your Aunt Mary sends you the cake of soap.

Today I rode to Arcadia. Have not been there for a long time. Found all well. I am very tired tonight. In consequence of your father's not feeling able to ride so far this Sabbath, we will not be with you. Remember you are all to come home at Christmas. Charles and Ruth will be with us, *God willing.* We have missed you so much—particularly little Mary. Father has retired, but unites with me in best love to Robert and yourself, and many kisses for our grandchildren.

Ever your affectionate mother,
Mary Jones.

MRS. MARY JONES *to* HON. CHARLES C. JONES, JR.^g

Montevideo, *Tuesday,* December 4th, 1860

My dear Son,

The jars arrived safely yesterday and are very nice, and I am greatly indebted to dear Ruth for selecting them. They could not be better.

One little favor more: I want *two yards* of *very narrow blue* satin ribbon to make a *cockade* for the center of the arrowroot cake designed for the fair. I intend to surround it with a wreath of magnolia and live oak, with sprigs of rice and pods of cotton interspersed, and on the top in some form or other the fifteen Southern states with the cockade in the center. You see I am going to send up a "sentiment" from at least one of the Liberty County ladies—an echo from old St. John's Parish. Will Ruthie send me the ribbon the next time you write in your letter?

A letter from your brother today informs us in consequence of the delay of the European goods that the fair will open a week later than was advertised. It would give us great pleasure to hear his address, but I fear it will not be until Christmas week.

We are very happy to hear of dear little Julia's improvement. Continue the medicine as long as necessary, and be careful of her diet. And do, my dear child, avoid exposure to the night air and overfatigue. Everyone tells me the effects of broken-bone fever are very lasting. . . . It takes but a slight cause, when God so wills it, to lay a strong man low. "*In Him* we live and move and have our being."

If Charlie West is still with you, please say we would be very happy to see him. The removal of a father's influence is a sad loss to a youth about his age. I regret that his course at Princeton was not completed.

Father has long since retired. Excuse this hurried note. Our best love to Daughter and yourself, and kisses for our little Julia. God bless you, my son!

Your affectionate mother,
Mary Jones.

REV. JOHN JONES *to* REV. C. C. JONES^t

Rome, *Monday,* December 10th, 1860

My dear Brother,

Your most welcome letter arrived this morning. The handwriting and all reminded me much of the olden time. We rejoice to see that yourself and Sister are so well.

I write to inform you that we expect to leave Rome, D.V., on day after tomorrow, the 12th inst., and our destination is Montevideo. We thought to stop first on going down and not crowd our visit to Liberty by putting it off as usual to the last. Our plan was to pass Wednesday night in Marietta and, leaving Thursday, to reach Savannah Friday morning, and tarry with Charles and Ruth until Saturday morning, and then come by railroad to No. 3 Gulf Railroad, and thence by stage to Riceboro, where you will please send to meet us. And thus will we do if you and Sister will be at home. But if Sister will have left for Macon, we will continue on in stage to Brother Henry's, and make our visit to you when all are at home. Should you both remain, we should be very happy to meet Mary and Robert and their little ones at Montevideo, if convenient for them to be there. The little Charles we have not seen yet.

I wish much I could hear Joe's speech, but it would be a bad time to stop with one's family in a crowded hotel. If Sister should go up to Macon, I must confess that I should be tempted to turn and go up with her. What day will Joe speak? Could you send me a line to Charles's care in Friday's mail and let us know your plans? If it were not for some arrangements of importance to be made with Henry for 1861, I could linger until next week. We long to see you all around your own fireside. Dunwody is in advance of us; by this he must be with you. Jane and the little boys join in best love to you both.

Your affectionate brother,

J. Jones.

REV. C. C. JONES *to* MRS. MARY S. MALLARD[t]

Savannah, *Thursday*, December 13th, 1860

My dear Daughter,

Mother went up with Brother Joe Monday evening to Macon with her trunk of contributions. Your brother was in waiting. Very thin, but said he was "very hearty," and that Carrie and he had not had "a finger ache" the whole summer. He read me his address, which is to be delivered today, D.V.; and I consider it an excellent one, and hope it may be appreciated and published by the Cotton Planters' Convention and circulated through the state. It will take him an hour and a half to deliver it. You will see in the *Morning News* of this morning a letter written by a lady giving an account of her visit to the fair. You will read it with interest and be glad to know that the fair will be "a decided success." A little energy is a great matter, and what others do we may do. Am so glad Mother went; it will be such a treat and recreation. And Mr. and Mrs. Nisbet will do all in their power to make her stay agreeable. I wish we *all* could have gone. I should have paraded my three little grandchildren and run for the prize at the baby show—if there is such an exhibition at the fair. I could not accompany Mother, fearing the effects of the fatigue, and especially the encumbrance and bother I would have been to the party.

There was a grand secession meeting and nomination here last night. *Vide* the papers. Your brother (His Honor the Mayor) and I went early, and on the opening of the hall he placed Major McIntosh and myself (two old gentlemen) on the front seat. Uncrowded and pleasant location. Hall densely packed; three or four times as many outside. Your brother presided with ease and dignity, and delivered an admirable opening address of eight or ten minutes, rapturously applauded. The speaking followed the nomination from the balconies, the hall emptying itself into the sea of people in the streets. We stayed behind to avoid the crowd, thinking we could stand in the balconies with the speakers—Judge Jackson, Mr. Bartow, and others. But they were so crowded we retired and, taking seats, passed the evening most pleasantly with numerous old friends and acquaintances until, having sent Major McIntosh home, we took our carriage and returned a little before ten. Not a late hour, but we left the meeting when it was at its height.

While the committee was out, Father O'Neill, being called for (he was sitting on the platform), made an entertaining speech, in which he declared himself "a *ra*publican and a *sa*cessionist and *sa*tizen of Georgia; and in case there should be war, he would be the first to *lade* them into battle, he would!" Popery and republicanism make a funny figure together. It was a funny speech altogether, and some good points very well put. I laughed heartily in the progress of it.

When your brother went out on the balcony to put the resolutions and nomination to the multitude in the streets, amidst the universal hurrah of ayes, off went the cannon, and into the sky flew the rockets, illuminating the scene. Then the pause: "Contrary minds, no!" A dead silence—when one man cried out: "There's *narra no, Mayor Jones!*" The meeting was remarkably peaceful and orderly and elevated, with an entire absence of folly and rowdyism.

Mrs. Dr. Harriss and Miss Dowse, the two Mrs. Axson (Edward is down on an exchange with Mr. Porter) and Mrs. Porter and the gentlemen of their families and Mr. Hutchison all made special inquiries after you and Robert and the little ones.

Politics and stringent times and an earnest looking forward to shortly-coming secrets is the order of the day here and everywhere. It is a serious hour, and all the Lord's people must be careful not to be led away from their Bibles and closets, and from Him who rules over all, but be much in prayer for our country and His Church. The aspect of Charleston is impressive. Their theaters and places of public amusement are closed, and seriousness pervades the city. This is the report.

Ruthie and your brother unite in much love to yourself and Robert and to the little ones. Charles is still very unwell from the effects of the broken-bone fever, and has no rest from one day to another. If he does not get better, he will be obliged to take it. Your Uncle John and family are expected down today or tomorrow; and I hope to see Mother back, God willing, tomorrow night. She said she would return home on Saturday. The carriage is ordered to meet us. Much love to Robert. Tell Little Daughter Grandfather sends love and a kiss for her. And kiss Charlie for me. Howdy for all the servants. All well here. The Lord keep and bless you and all yours, my dear child!

Your ever affectionate father,
C. C. Jones.

Hon. Charles C. Jones, Jr., *to* Rev. *and* Mrs. C. C. Jones[t]

Savannah, *Monday,* December 17th, 1860

My dear Father and Mother,

We trust that you reached home safely, and that you have recovered from any fatigue which you may have experienced upon the way.

Our citizens are anxiously awaiting the action of the South Carolina convention, but as yet we have no news. I sincerely trust that there will be no hesitancy or faltering on their part. It is suggested, in consequence of the existence of smallpox in Columbia, that the convention will adjourn to reassemble at once in Charleston.

No movement as yet of a submissive character in this city, although there are intimations to that effect; and there is no doubt of the fact that there are those in our midst who do not sympathize with us upon the question of state action and secession.

A letter from Aunt Mary Robarts states that all in Marietta are well. Ruth and little Julia unite in warmest love. I am, my dear parents, as ever,

Your affectionate son,
Charles C. Jones, Jr.

Dr. John S. Law *to* Rev. C. C. Jones[t]

Cincinnati, *Wednesday,* December 19th, 1860

My dear Friend,

Your highly acceptable letter came to hand on Monday 17th inst. In accordance with your desire I immediately forwarded to your son, the mayor of Savannah, the documents you desired, and wrote him in reference to the subject, saying I would write you in a few days. I saw Mr. William Neff's son, and he informed me it would afford him great pleasure to send you a photograph of his father, and forward the same to your son's address before the week closed. . . . My wife is in Savannah, and will be glad to receive from Mrs. Jones in person the obituary of her brother, and will never forget her kind interest in the matter.

I note your remarks about the fair at Macon. Georgia's progress in internal improvements, etc., has been a subject of considerable boast and pride with me, as one of her native sons, in contact with my fellow citizens here; and as her native son I feel deeply distressed in view of the "stirring and momentous times" to which you allude, and the prospect of a "Southern confederacy." I unhesitantly tell everyone who discusses with me the troubles of the times that the South has just cause for complaint; that she has been grievously wronged; that she has been taunted and insulted on the slavery question sufficiently to drive poor human nature to frenzy; that the press and various organs of the Republican party have laid down an unmistakable program that slavery and slave power must be crushed. But still I do think the South should, in an unbroken body, unite as one man in an endeavor to obtain redress, concessions, and guarantees for the future *in the Union;* and after having resorted calmly to every method a love of country as well as section would suggest to get grievances removed, and failed, then she could adopt the *dernier ressort* and make a manifesto to the world that every argument and appeal had been exhausted.

It is the part of wisdom to estimate in advance the cost of every enterprise in life. The skillful merchant—men of every profession find it necessary to deliberate and carefully measure every step in their business with a view to satisfactory success and ultimate results. And shall a great people, enlightened by the wisdom that is from above, the pure precepts of the gospel, and enjoying such national blessings, and the best form of government upon earth, because of abuses and even serious wrongs rashly embrace an enterprise of such magnitude as the destruction of a republic to whose care seem committed the political destinies and the temporal and spiritual happiness of the human race? Who can estimate even the immediate evils which would be inflicted upon the entire people through the length and breadth of this land? And yet how insignificant would be the first instance of political horror when compared with the fearful tragedies and gloom which would inevitably mark the succeeding scenes of the great drama!

Already we have been treated to a foretaste of pecuniary ruin. Even the impending shadow of disunion has been sufficient to disturb the business of the country from our extreme North to the Gulf and from the Atlantic to the Pacific. In the midst of abundant harvests and the most varied productions of any country, having contributions from the richest gold mines in the world, with a standing army of only twenty thousand men and a population of thirty-one million, the national treasury is bankrupt, and our fiscal agents are beggars in the money markets of the earth. Confidence is deserting the most hopeful of our citizens. The day laborer, who was content with leaving his savings in gold with his banker for interest, rushes to the counter and withdraws it, preferring to sleep with it under his pillow. Unfortunately the great basis of our commerce is credit, and so ramified and reciprocal are our interests that its preservation is vital. A failure of a heavy house in New York or New Orleans precipitates the failure of a half a dozen in our commercial marts. The farmers of the West are now on the Mississippi River trying to sell their rich products, and the planters of the South trying to cash their cotton and sugar. Both have substantial wealth, but it is not available. The manufacturer, in addition to his ordinary expenses, finds liabilities contracted in expectation of a prosperous season, and in the very commencement of winter is obliged to accommodate himself to the crisis by curtailment of his business, discharging a portion of his hands, or placing them on half work. But the present aspect is but a faint representation of the financial gloom which would enshroud the land in the event of a dissolution of the Union.

But what are financial disasters compared to the political, social, and moral effects of a dissolution? Who can contemplate without horror masses of infuriated men arrayed against each other in fratricidal civil war? The most civilized and Christianized nation upon earth in this nineteenth century, regardless of their high responsibilities and their mutual obligations to each other, vilifying and recriminating each other, stubbornly refusing to make concessions and listen to mediation, in ignoble pride and a tempest of passion braving all the dread consequences of threatened calamities which would gladden the hearts of the despots of Europe, astound even the heathen nations of India, China, and Japan, and roll back the tide of civilization and Christianity for centuries!

Let the Christian weigh well the consequences to the Church of Christ! What would be her condition? What influence should she exert? Let every Christian man keep before him his great Pattern for an example, be constant in prayer, keep his eyes steadfastly fixed upon the precepts of his Divine Master, "forbearing one another and forgiving one another if any man have a quarrel against any," remembering the precept: "He that is without sin, let him first cast a stone." We are exalted to heaven above any other nation in point of privileges and blessings. Let us take heed lest we should be cast down to hell for our abuse of them, and our unhallowed lusts and pride, envy and revenge. I am sorry to see the pulpit and religious press, North and South, fanning the flame of discord instead of proclaiming peace and good will to men and exhorting to patience, forbearance, charity, and urging them to exhaust first every effort for redress and reconciliation. Such lose sight of the example and teachings of the meek and lowly Jesus.

I fear, my dear sir, the time is fast arriving when our Old School Presbyterian Church can no longer boast she is a unit. My pastor and I were the other day lamenting over this prospect. He prays most fervently for our country in its present emergency, and spoke at length last Sunday night of the duty of Christians in the present crisis (from the text: "The Lord reigneth; let the people tremble"), saying it was not his province as a minister of the gospel to discuss the question how or by whom the present calamities were brought about, what section or party was responsible, but to present clearly the indication the Lord had a controversy with us, that we had all sinned as a nation and as individuals, that he feared great judgments were in store for us, and it became us to wrestle unceasingly at the mercy seat, and tremble and look to His almighty arm alone for our rescue.

In conclusion I would say so troubled I have been of late by this all-absorbing topic that if it were not that I have responsibilities and obligations on earth that I cannot shake off, some service here yet for my Master, my unceasing prayer would be: "Lord, now lettest thou thy servant depart in peace" to "where the wicked cease from troubling, and the weary are at rest."

The telegraph informed us that the morning of the meeting of the convention of South Carolina at Columbia was ushered in by the densest fog ever was seen. The same morning here at eight o'clock it was so dark that it was necessary to light the gas, and objects were indistinct a half a square off. And yet it seemed neither cloud nor fog. Ever since to this hour the heavens have been weeping. Though I would not pretend to read the teachings of Providence in these phenomena, yet I could not but be struck how emblematic the first was of His frowns, and the second (if good men are permitted to weep in heaven) of the distress of the great and good men who were witnessing deliberations which were calculated to destroy that fair fabric which cost so much blood and treasure and has been the subject of such anxious prayers.

I did promise, my dear friend, when there was railroad communication from here to Savannah to try and visit you. And as a preliminary step I have sent my wife and daughter to spend the winter in the South; and she did hope to extend her visit to good old Liberty. D.V., I hope to visit you in the spring and extend my visit to Florida. But I can form no definite plans at this juncture ahead even for a day. Do remember me and mine affectionately to Mrs. Jones and every portion of your family and all our friends, and call and see my wife, and accept the same regards yourself from me and mine. Believe me to be

Ever sincerely your old friend,
John S. Law.

Hugh insists upon being more specific, and says: "Send definitely my love and my wife's to the Dr. and Mrs. Jones."

20th December. I have delayed my letter to give you some account of the Union meeting yesterday afternoon. Oh, how I did wish those who had mistaken the people of this section could have been present! Not a man of them but would have been made a convert to the sentiment, "These are my brothers." When high compliments were passed upon the South, and brotherly regard expressed, and the sentiments, "They don't understand us is the reason of their feeling and action"; that "if the South Carolina legislature and governor were to visit us now as the Kentucky and Tennessee did last summer, their ovation and cordial reception would even surpass that extended to them"—I say, when such sentiments were uttered, the applause and cry "That's so!" were so stunning and deafening and long-continued that for some time the exercises could not proceed, and it was impossible to stop it. In spite of my efforts the tears rolled down my cheeks; and sturdy men could be seen everywhere wiping their eyes. There were from six to seven thousand persons present, and thousands came and could not get admittance, though the accommodations were so spacious.

I have sent circular papers to your son's address for you; also to my *favorite cousin* Judge Law. You can show him my letter—or any other person—if you think any good will result therefrom. Beg my cousin for me to use his mighty intellect and his weighty Christian influence for the preservation of the Union. Tell him a corrupt press, politicians and demagogues, and desecrated pulpits have done all the mischief. The people are right. There are bad men at the North as well as at the South who are disturbing the country. Is this to be wondered at? It is a rare thing to find a family of ten boys in it without one who disturbs the comfort of the household, and perhaps brings disgrace or dishonor upon the rest. So it is with the people in this section. And I am satisfied if our brethren at the South will only delay and try every legitimate remedy, all will yet be well, and the nation continue to be a blessing to the world.

J. S. L.

Mrs. Mary Jones *to* Hon. Charles C. Jones, Jr.^g

Montevideo, *Thursday,* December 20th, 1860

My dear Son,

We felt disappointed that your letter today gave us no information when we might look for dear Ruth and yourself and our little Julia. I hope she continues to improve, and that you will be with us next week. Your sister and the children are with us, and we have been enjoying the visit of your uncle and Aunt Jane and their noble little boys. They leave us tomorrow.

Our hearts were filled with joy and gratitude at the good tidings received from Augusta on last Tuesday. We have now two granddaughters and two grandsons!

Will you, my dear son, be good enough to draw the dividend and *transmit to your brother* for me (if the present amount of the dividend is the same as the last) sixty-five dollars. I would like the remainder in gold, if you could conveniently obtain it; and you can bring it out when you come.

They are all talking loudly around me, so that I scarcely know what I am writing. This is your father's birthday, and tomorrow will be the thirtieth anniversary of our wedding day! All unite with me in best love to Ruth and yourself, and kisses for our little Julia.

Ever, my dear son, your affectionate mother,
Mary Jones.

Rev. C. C. Jones *to* Hon. Charles C. Jones, Jr.^g

Montevideo, *Monday,* December 24th, 1860

My dear Son,

Niger leaves, D.V., tomorrow on a trip to Savannah to see his daughter Adeline, and Mother embraces the opportunity of sending by him to Ruthie and yourself a piece of fresh beef for your Christmas dinner. We are sorry it is no fatter; our dry fields could afford no better. It may, however, taste like *home.* We regret you could not come out and make part of our circle tomorrow. Small: your sister and Robert and Uncle William, God willing. Your Uncle John and family left us Friday, and the county for McIntosh Saturday of last week.

We dined at Henry's on Friday, the thirtieth anniversary of our wedding day (nearly a generation), and in the same house we were married. It was easy to recall the past and paint in memory the cheerful scenes of the wedding day and evening. I saw the figures, the countenances, the dress, the smiles, and heard the conversation, and saw myself and your mother too, and the wedding party (but four in number), and our venerable friend performing the ceremony, the supper and all things else—a bright and pleasing vision. Since then what changes! I could more than fill my sheet with them. But let me record the mercies of the Lord in one particular, not to mention ten thousand others: he has spared us to rear and educate our dear children, and to see them settled in families, adding *three more* to our children and permitting us to see our *children's children,* and each of you occupying most honored and influential stations in society, and five out of the six members of the Church of Christ! Surely these are special mercies, calling for the greatest gratitude; and we felt that our cup would have been full had our dear *first-born* been added to them. For this mercy we daily and earnestly pray.

Mother received your letter. We all unite in much love to Ruthie and yourself, and kisses for little Julia.

Your affectionate father,
C. C. Jones.

Am obliged for Colonel Jackson's letters; they have been put in circulation.

We were much rejoiced to hear of your brother's blessing, and wrote him and Carrie our congratulations immediately. Please have the enclosed letter mailed to him: to go up by the night train of the *25th.*

Rev. C. C. Jones *to* Hon. Charles C. Jones, Jr.^g

Montevideo, *Thursday,* December 27th, 1860

My dear Son,

Niger arrived just now safely with your note and the basket with its excellent contents, for which Mother expresses her thanks to Ruthie, and will take another opportunity of returning it. You really had a grand affair last night, by the *Republican*'s own showing. Thompson was up too late to send us a paper this morning. Mother illuminated Montevideo house last evening, and it looked beautifully—in honor of South Carolina and to unite with you in Savannah. Abram is waiting. Love from all to all. Kisses for Julia.

Your affectionate father,
C. C. Jones.

Mr. Neff's likeness at hand: excellent.

If you can possibly make time, wish Ruthie and yourself would call and see Mrs. Dr. John S. Law at Mr. William Burroughs'.

Mrs. Mary Jones *to* Hon. Charles C. Jones, Jr.^g

Montevideo, *Thursday,* January 3rd, 1861

My dear Son,

Your affectionate favor was this day received, and from our heart of hearts we respond to your kind wishes—"A Happy New Year!"—although every moment seems fraught with the sad foreboding that it may be only one of trial and suffering. But "God is our refuge and strength, a very present help in trouble. Therefore will not we fear." Read Psalm 46. I trust the Lord of Hosts will be with us!

An indescribable sadness weighs down my soul as I think of our once glorious but now dissolving Union! Our children's children—what will constitute their national pride and glory? *We* have no alternative; and necessity demands that we now protect ourselves from entire destruction at the hands of those who have rent and torn and obliterated every national bond of union, of confidence and affection. When your brother and yourself were very little fellows, we took you into old Independence Hall; and at the foot of Washington's statue I pledged you both to support and defend the Union. *That Union* has passed away, and you are free from your mother's vow.

Your father thinks the occupation of Fort Pulaski will produce more effect than anything that has occurred. How can the South delay united and decided action? . . . The results may be awful unless we are united.

Did your father tell you old Montevideo gave forth her response on the night of the 26th in honor of Carolina and in sympathy with Savannah? Strange to say, as we walked out to view the illumination from the lawn, we discovered that there were thirteen windows on the front of the house, each of which had one brilliant light resembling a star; and without design one of them had been placed far in the ascendant—emblematic, as we hailed it, of the noble and gallant state which must ever be regarded as the polar star of our Southern confederacy.

And now, my dear son, we will look within the home circle. I trust you have regained your accustomed strength, and dear little Julia still improving. Your sister and Robert and the little ones have been with us for two weeks, and left us today. So did your uncle, who spent the day and night with us.

Enclosed I send your brother's letter, with the hope that you may yet help him to obtain the appointment. Would it be possible for you individually, or through Colonel Lawton or anyone else, to see *Governor Brown* whilst he is in Savannah, and if possible to secure the appointment for him? Poor boy, my heart sympathizes very deeply with his disappointments and perplexities. I know you will do all you can to aid him. I believe him worthy of and qualified for the trust, or I would not ask it even for my child.

Your dear father is very unwell from a severe cold. I want to write Ruth a few lines, and my paper is at an end. . . . With love from Father and myself to you both, and kisses for our little darling,

Your affectionate mother,

M. Jones.

Hon. Charles C. Jones, Jr., *to* Mrs. Mary Jones[w]
Savannah, *Monday,* January 7th, 1861

My very dear Mother,

Your kind letter of the 3rd inst., with enclosures as stated, has been duly received, and I sincerely sympathize with you in all your reflections upon the past and present memories of our country.

We are now in a state of very reliable preparation at the fort, and when a few more heavy guns are received, the fortification will be invincible by almost any force that may be sent against it. Everything within its walls is conducted upon strict military principles, and it is truly wonderful what changes the discipline of even a few days has accomplished. My engagements here are of so imperative a character that I am precluded from spending as much time there as I could wish. . . .

I sincerely sympathize with Brother in his disappointment, and had I known the fact earlier would certainly have conversed with Governor Brown on the subject. As it is, I will write the governor and see if something cannot be done for him. While here I saw the governor every day, and upon the most confidential terms. He grew in the esteem of everyone, and received every attention from our citizens. He is a truly honest, strictly upright, pious man, temperate in all things, and is not afraid of responsibilities.

Little Julia is the very picture of health, Ruth quite well, and both unite in warmest love to self and dear Father. I am, my dear mother, as ever,

Your affectionate son,
Charles C. Jones, Jr.

How can I get the hundred dollars to you?

Mrs. Mary C. Nisbet *to* Mrs. Mary Jones[t]
Macon, *Thursday Morning,* January 17th, 1861

Many thanks, my very dear Mrs. Jones, for your kind and charming letter. And allow me—though a little late—to return to you the good wishes you have expressed for us.

I was very sorry when I found that the doctor had not been a candidate, and supposed he considered it unclerical to "assist" in the counsels of the nation—"the empire," I should say, as that is the name claimed for Georgia. (You see how my head turns upon political matters and takes it for granted yours does the same, inasmuch as I speak of "candidates" as though there were but one set in all the commonwealth.) Crowds and crowds of people have gone to Milledgeville. Ten cars full went off from here Tuesday; as many Wednesday. I shall not know how it is today till after this letter is closed. I want to go Saturday. I have never been able to endure Milledgeville for a longer time than a few hours, but it is thought the secession ordinance will be signed and passed that day, and I do want to witness that act. I confess I have no idea that we shall have war; if so, but one or two battles, and then peace we shall have on our own terms. The fact, though, of General

Scott's gathering together his legions against us does ineffably more for us than conciliatory schemes. It makes the South a unit. And he himself then declares coercion and war are absurd.

It must have been a most welcome greeting between your brother's family and yourselves. I think those pleasant surprises—*not* accidental, but granted to us by an indulgent Father in Heaven—bring us nearer to Him and to each other; for love *is* stronger than death. So that "the last seat in the last end of the last car" was, after all, the best of all to you. . . .

I congratulate you upon the little grandson Samuel. Uncle Davis says his father calls the little fellow always "*Little* Samuel," and says that his grandparents Jones think "the omens favorable to his waiting in the sanctuary." I hope he may be a good, great, and useful man in the temple and out. But I hope he will not bring up his sons as badly as some of his namesakes have done. (This for *you,* dear Mrs. Jones; you won't *ruin* me?)

We are expecting Mr. Nisbet's youngest sister, Margaret Nisbet, every day. She comes with some of the families of our returning congressmen. We thought from her last letter that she would have been with us before this time. She says Washington City is utterly gloomy; she never saw the place in the condition it now is. Mr. Nisbet's mother can do nothing with her property there, and thinks the best thing for her to do is to remain to see after it. What times we live in! Our pastor gives us political sermons every Sabbath Day. I am weary of them now, and shall do as I used to do at Dr. Smyth's in Charleston—go to some other church till he gets upon a new theme.

We are all well. Hope you are—that the doctor has recovered from his uncomfortable symptoms. Best love to him and to Mary, to Mother and Laura. Kisses for the dear little ones. Affectionate remembrance to Colonel Maxwell. Hattie desires her love sent separately. She is at school again, though the weather has been so very rainy for some time past. She is tired of being at home, and is willing to take some trouble putting on rubbers, etc., to get back to school. I hope I shall sometimes hear from you, dear Mrs. Jones; it always gives me great pleasure. The love of this family is sent to you—from no one more than

Yours affectionately,
Mary C. Nisbet.

MRS. MARY S. MALLARD *to* MRS. MARY JONES[t]

Walthourville, *Sunday,* January 20th, 1861

My dear Mother,

Niger made his appearance this morning with your note. I was quite surprised to find that matters were to be brought to a focus so soon. I told Niger I did not think the arrangement would suit me at all, for I did not want Tenah to marry. But he seemed to think there could be no valid objections. I do not think I can come down next week, but I will let Lucy and Tenah go down on Saturday morning. I should like to be present, but think I would enjoy a visit more at some other time. . . .

Have you heard that there is a daily prayer meeting in Savannah? It began with the second week in January and will be continued during the period in which the convention will be held, with a direct reference to divine guidance in its deliberations. This is an interesting fact.

Mr. Mallard heard today that his father had been more unwell, so he will probably go down some day this week, and if so will see you. . . . It is Sabbath night, and I must not write more. . . . With warmest love and kisses from us all to Father and yourself,

> Your attached child,
> Mary S. Mallard.

Mrs. MARY JONES *to* Mrs. RUTH B. JONES[g]

> Montevideo, *Tuesday,* January 22nd, 1861

My dear Daughter,

Your kind favor was received by Saturday's mail. . . . We rejoice to know that our dear little granddaughter has entirely recovered. How many teeth has she out? Do tell us all about her when you write.

Mr. Jones has just written Mr. I. W. Morrell that we wished him to furnish a crib for our little grandson in Augusta; and will you, dear Daughter, be so kind as to call at your earliest convenience and select it for me? I wish one *like Julia's;* but perhaps it had best be of *black walnut* to suit Joe and Carrie's bedstead, which is of that material. Mr. Morrell is to forward it as soon as you have selected it.

Our hearts are rejoiced to learn the fact of a daily prayer meeting in Savannah in view of the state of the country and our convention now in session, and to see that on last Sabbath religious services were held in the fort. May God overshadow us all with the guidance and protection of His own Holy Spirit! You and I—a wife and mother—need surely to keep near our Father's throne when we know not what perils are awaiting one who is dear to us as our own life, and who is yet unreconciled to our gracious and Divine Redeemer. I think of him daily—I may say hourly. Oh, that I could be assured that he was the child of God! This one great interest possesses my mind above all others. In all that concerns the honor or welfare of his country in this righteous conflict I know he will be brave and true.

Dear Daughter, do write us often. You know not how anxious we feel when we do not hear from Charles. It is late, and I must close. Father unites with me in much love to you both, and kisses for our dear little Julia.

> Ever your affectionate mother,
> Mary Jones.

Tell Adeline on next Saturday night her sister Judy expects to be married to Sam, and her brother Niger to Tenah, Daughter's nurse, at Montevideo. Howdies for all your servants. *Patience* has a daughter.

Rev. C. C. Jones *to* Hon. Charles C. Jones, Jr.[g]

Montevideo, *Thursday,* January 24th, 1861

My dear Son,

Sam, Abram's brother, expects, D.V., to be married on Saturday evening *the 26th,* and begs me to enclose Abram three dollars (enclosed) to buy him a coat for the occasion. And as the time is very limited, and the case an urgent one, he requests Abram to get his master to write the direction on the coat and to send it out by Adams' Express to Riceboro by railroad and stage *on Saturday morning without fail.* Direct it to me. Sam says the coat that fits Abram will fit him. Please help this cause if you can.

Have just dismissed fourteen (9 P.M.) who have been for religious instruction. A long time since we have had such an awakening on the plantation. May it prove to be a genuine work of the Spirit!

Was not the Missouri Compromise occasioned by the opposition of the anti-slavery North against the reception of Missouri as a slave state? And was not Henry Clay the author of it? I am, at Mother's instigation, engaged in writing an answer to Dr. Hodge's Black Republican article in the last number of *The Princeton Review.* Am sorry to see the doctor so much astray. Hope to finish it in a few days, D.V.

We are all pretty well, and are at the end of a four days' northeaster. More rain fallen than for months.

No special news today. Trust things may remain in forts, etc., *in statu quo* until the convention of the seceding states in February. And then, if on a united application our demands are not responded to, we may go to work. By that time a peaceful solution may be obtained, which is desirable for all parties concerned. Our cooperation members of the convention are acting as well as could be expected in the premises. Wish the convention had more elbow room and we fuller reports.

Mother sends to say she wants room for a *postscriptum.* Love to Ruthie, and a kiss for my little granddaughter. She ought to be walking.

Your affectionate father,

C. C. Jones.

In the judgment of your mother, my dear son, your father's reply will be a twelve-inch columbiad fully charged—and discharged not in offensive but defensive warfare: in the cause of truth and justice!

Mrs. Mary S. Mallard *to* Mrs. Mary Jones[t]

Walthourville, *Friday,* January 25th, 1861

My dear Mother,

What a week of rain we have had! From present appearances I fear the sun will not shine upon the brides tomorrow. Tenah seems quite merry on the occasion. I have been busy getting her dress ready. Her heart was set upon a swiss muslin, so I have given her one. She has been a good, faithful servant to me and always a kind nurse to my children, so I felt she was entitled to a nice dress. Lucy, you know, is labor-saving and self-sparing in her notions, so she preferred to buy bread and cake rather than "bother with the making." She is quite long-faced, as she has had toothache nearly all week. For my own sake I would have been glad if Tenah had been otherwise-minded. I tell her it is a most inconvenient arrangement, and she has taken us by such a surprise that Niger and herself will have to do the best they can until we can provide a place for them to occupy. Little Daughter thinks getting married means having a plenty of cake, for when I was fixing Tenah's cake, she asked: "Mama, can't I get married too? The cake is so nice I want some!"

Mr. Mallard has been waiting all week for fair weather to go and see his father. This afternoon he concluded he would go anyhow, so he went off in the rain. The last time we heard, he was suffering very much and was threatened with another rising.

How do you feel now, dear Mother, that *we* are in a foreign land? Did you illuminate when you heard of Georgia's secession? Savannah does not seem to have made as great a demonstration as when Carolina seceded. What is to be done with those Georgians who unfurled the Stars and Stripes when the news reached them? I think it is a pity the whole county—land and all—could not be transferred immediately to New England. I received a letter from Kitty this week; she is quite stirred up, and rejoices at our freedom. . . .

I was quite amused yesterday morning by some of little Mary's capers. She was playing with a little china doll, and after showing me how she had fixed its dress, she said: "Now, do give me a little basket to shut it up in, so that when the king's daughter comes, she will say: 'Bring me that basket.' And when she opens it, the little baby will cry, and then the king's daughter will say: 'Call somebody to *norse* the baby.'" She told her father today to give her love to Grandma and Grandpa and Grandma's pussy. She often comes to me and says it is time for me to "tell Daddy Dilbud to fix the carriage dood so that we can go to Danma's home."

I am sorry you will have all the trouble of the wedding. It seems Sam had determined to take Elvira if he could not get Judy, and Elvira said if Sam did not marry Judy she would accept him. So Lucy tells me. Accept kisses from the little ones for Father and yourself and the warmest affection of

Your attached child,
Mary S. Mallard.

Mrs. Eliza G. Robarts *to* Rev. C. C. Jones[t]

Marietta, *Saturday,* January 26th, 1861

Dear Charles,

I have been wishing to write you for some time past, but my heart has been so filled with sorrow and care I felt reluctant to put my feelings on paper. And even now, when I think of my poor unfortunate one, I feel as if my heart would burst.

And now I have another trial to bear. Through the kindness of Dr. Stewart, Mary Sophia was offered a place to teach four little girls in his brother's family, Mr. Charles Stewart. The little girls are Mrs. Stewart's nieces. Their mother is dead; their father a Mr. McQuin who lives in New Orleans. They offered Mary Sophia two hundred and fifty dollars, her board and washing. The place is forty miles from Columbus on the Alabama side; the place and post office is called Hardaway, Macon County, Alabama. Sophia seemed anxious to try and do something for herself, and I consented to let her go, although it cost me many bitter pangs and tears to have my poor child go so far from home to teach. Lilla feels the separation to be great, never having been separated before. But I pray God to support us under all our trials and cares. Sophia went to Columbus with Willie Hansell, a son of the general. She wrote me from there; said on the way her heart almost failed. Dear child, her grandmother's heart feels for her. May God protect and guard her from every evil, is my constant prayer.

You must excuse my troubling you with my sorrows. We have many domestic troubles. Poor Hannah is still in her bed, all her limbs paralyzed. She can't walk a step. Provisions of every kind are double price, and we have to economize in every way. We have never wanted bread and meat, and hope the same Heavenly Father will still provide for us.

The winter has not been severely cold, but I have seldom seen more constant or harder rains. Last Tuesday night the wind was very high, with rain. In the morning when we woke, the trees were all covered with sleet and icicles. And it has rained every day since Tuesday night. From constant damp and cold I have already paid fifty dollars for wood.

Last night about seven o'clock we had a cry of fire. Although it was raining, Joe and Sam went off to see where it was, and found it was Dr. Chester's house on fire on the Roswell road. The house was burnt entirely down; most of the furniture saved. It seems it took fire in the upstairs; think a servant must have dropped a spark from a candle in a closet. The roof of the house was all on fire before they discovered it. Dr. Chester's insurance had just run out three days before. The engine went up, but no water except the well being run, the firemen only could save the outbuildings. The loss will be great to the doctor. He has a large family, but I believe he is very well off in pecuniary matters.

Our country is in truly a distressing and fearful state. We can only pray that an overruling and Heavenly Father will avert the great evil of war from our midst. On Monday night there was quite an illumination on the square in honor of the secession of Georgia. All the family went to see it but myself. My cough is daily increasing; I feel my health daily decreasing. It has been such a wet winter I have not walked even in the yard since Christmas.

Tell Mary her cake at Macon must have been beautiful. We were much interested in the description of it. I hope it was eaten by some worthy person. . . . Dr. Cumming was the first to inform us of the birth of Joe's little son. I hope he will live to be a comfort to them. You are greatly blessed in your children. . . . I am glad Julia King is up again, although on crutches. . . . Sam is well; sends kind remembrances to his wife and children. He is an active man for his age. . . . Mary, Louisa, Lilla, Ellen, and Joe all desire love to you and Mary. . . . Write when you are able.

Your ever affectionate aunt,
E. G. Robarts.

HON. CHARLES C. JONES, JR., *to* REV. C. C. JONES[w]

Savannah, *Monday,* January 28th, 1861

My dear Father,

In reply to your query, "Was not the Missouri Compromise occasioned by the opposition of the anti-slavery North against the reception of Missouri as a slave state? And was not Henry Clay the author of it?" I would say yes. Mr. Clay has always had the credit of being the author and the most powerful advocate of that compromise of 1820. During the pendency of the compromise measures of 1850 he alluded to the fact of his position in 1820 and called upon the good and true men of the North to rally to his support then as they had done in 1820. A fatal mistake in both instances. Had we manfully resisted the first aggression, we might have stifled the serpent in its den, and not now have been suffering from the poisonous brood which with hissing tongue and noxious breath are crawling everywhere and polluting the otherwise wholesome air of this once pure and happy country. It is a sad sight to see our national flag lowered, our union of states dissolved, and our unparalleled peace and prosperity interrupted for cause so foul as this. I have long since believed that in this country have arisen two races which, although claiming a common parentage, have been so entirely separated by climate, by morals, by religion, and by estimates so totally opposite of all that constitutes honor, truth, and manliness, that they cannot longer coexist under the same government. Oil and water will not commingle. We are the land of rulers; fanaticism has no home here. The sooner we separate the better.

I really regret the action of our convention in its appointments of delegates to Montgomery. Hill, Kenan, Wright, and Stephens should not have been sent. The convention should have selected representatives not of themselves. Personal ambition and love of preferment, although not so designated by the metaphysicians, should be classed, at least among public men, both as innate and inalienable ideas.

I sincerely trust that you will have health and strength to complete all the most valuable labors in which you are now engaged. Do, Father, let me have a copy of your reply to Dr. Hodge so soon as it is finished. Ruth and Julia, who are both quite well, unite in warmest love to dear Mother and self. Ruth selected the crib for Brother, and it went forward this morning. As ever,

Your affectionate son,
Charles C. Jones, Jr.

II

Rev. George Howe *to* Rev. C. C. Jones[t]

Columbia, *Friday,* February 8th, 1861

My dear Brother,

Your communication on Dr. Hodge was received and read by me with great delight, and is highly spoken of by Brother Porter. The only trouble is its length. It will fill, they suppose, ten columns in the paper; and as they had a press of matter for next week and it should not be delayed, they have resolved to issue an extra—a half-sheet. The arrangement is, I understand, to print your observations on the first page and second page of the paper, and to put their other matter, which cannot otherwise be issued, in the extra.

I had ordered two thousand copies beyond their circulation, understanding that the cost would be less than I learn it will be now. The extra printing and postage is estimated to cost nearly or quite ninety dollars. The wider circulation will be of some advantage to the paper, and I think the concern will be quite content to divide this cost with you. I regret indeed that you should have anything at all to pay after your great labor. But I am acquainted with the concerns of the paper well enough to know that it is far from paying its expenses as yet. There is a great ambition to have a good paper, and on our present scale of expense we need to have its subscription doubled in numbers to make it at all pecuniarily prosperous. . . .

We live tied amidst rumors of wars. May God give peace and quiet to our country! I enclose one among the many testimonies Porter has received of the value set on your paper. With love to all from all,

Yours in Christian bonds,
George Howe.

Rev. A. A. Porter *to* Rev. C. C. Jones[t]

Columbia, *Friday,* February 15th, 1861

Reverend and dear Sir,

I have read and printed your review of Dr. Hodge's article with the utmost gratification, and desire to express my thanks, both personal and *editorial,* to you for it. It is a great service, my dear sir, done to the entire country, to the South, and to the cause of truth and justice. I send it forth to the world with thanksgiving to the Master who has enabled you to write it, and with many prayers that His blessing may go with it.

We have printed two thousand copies additional to the number required for our own subscribers, and desire your advice and instruction as to the disposal to be made of them. I have ordered forty copies to be sent to your own address. You will let us know if you desire more to be forwarded to yourself.

It would gratify me very much if you could *write* for *The Southern Presbyterian* on any subject that interests your own mind and heart. I have a very anxious desire to make the paper a powerful agent for good. Especially under the circumstances of the times it is exceedingly important to have it exert an influence which will be felt on behalf of Christian principle and duty. Can you not help us, my dear sir, to secure this very desirable object?

Please let us hear from you immediately as to your wishes in regard to the distribution of the extra copies. Until we hear from you we propose to go on mailing them to the address of our ministers in this and other Southern states.

Very sincerely and respectfully yours,
A. A. Porter.

Rev. W. M. Cunningham *to* Rev. C. C. Jones[t]

LaGrange, Monday, February 18th, 1861

Many, many thanks to my dear Brother C. C. Jones for his manly and masterly review of Dr. Hodge on "The State of the Country." By this timely and able service you have made the whole South and—what is more—the cause of truth and righteousness your debtors. The cause you defend is the cause of God and of the country, and indirectly of all mankind; and the man you met was a foeman that demanded your steel.

Though a more vulnerable article than that of Dr. Hodge I never read, yet a more *plausible* and *pernicious* one, I verily believe, was never published. Under an air of candor and kindness he disguises a most *bitter* and *blinding* prejudice, of which not even the writer himself was conscious. Behind the cooing of the dove, the poison of the asp is bitter toward the South. In him Black Republicanism has become an angel of light, without one sin *as a party* to confess or one concession of *right* to make; and the Southerners resenting and resisting its rule are perjured covenant-breakers, as reckless of their interests as they are recreant of their duty. And yet we have only to lift the veil that covers this angelic embodiment of candor and kindness and truth and righteousness to see that in thus canonizing and sanctifying the Republican party Dr. Hodge has himself become assimilated to and imbued with the spirit of that foul and fiendish party, whose advocate he has become. The angel, in representing the devil, has, unbeknowing to himself, become a devil.

This seems to be one of the most uniform and deplorable of the consequences of the abolition heresy. It is, as you well say, an *ever-contracting iron band* around the soul that squeezes out and kills all the charity of piety and the humanity of our nature from the heart. How else can we account for it that the naturally mild and prudent and Christian Dr. Hodge should conceive of and compare all the tried patriots of the South who favor secession to Benedict Arnold! And class all the Christian ministers and members in the South—and amongst them his own brethren in the church—who sustain secession, with those who approved and sustained the executions of the Inquisition! How can he maintain Christian fellowship with such traitors and *unnatural monsters*? And what communion can we have with men who so feel and think and speak of us? As much as I deplore it, nothing, I verily believe, will be left for us at the South to do but to separate from the church as well as the state at the North.

In your review you show off finely some of Dr. Hodge's inconsistencies. I would have been gratified if you had remarked upon this in addition. In holding up secession as involving all the crimes of *perjury* and *covenant-breaking* and *treason* and *rebellion*, he yet speaks most *complacently* and *encouragingly* of withdrawing Canada from its allegiance and uniting it by revolution to the Northern confederacy! No sin here! If the North propose to aid in this *awful enormity*, Dr. Hodge thinks it would be a noble achievement, and he would open his arms to receive this perjured and covenant-breaking Canada!

But I did not intend to write a letter, but only to express to you my *gratification and thanks* for your very able and timely review. Without being awed by reverence and conquered by kindness and flattery, *as has been Brown of The Central Presbyterian*, you yet show all that respect and kindness due from one Christian minister to another. And without being quite so bitter and so pungent in your terms as our good Brother Porter, you yet give full expression to your manly indignation and at times *make the truth awfully cutting* and *scathing*. Dr. Hodge will feel it to his innermost soul— as he ought. I only wish it could be read by all the thousands that have read Dr. Hodge's article. Could we not contrive some way to get it into *The New York Observer*, even if it should mean *a supplement to be paid for?* I for one would bear my full proportion of the expense. In haste and in love, I remain,

As ever,

W. M. Cunningham.

REV. JOSEPH R. WILSON *to* REV. C. C. JONES[t]

Augusta, *Tuesday*, February 19th, 1861

Dear Sir,

Having just finished the perusal of your masterly review of Dr. Hodge's late political article, I cannot resist the impulse which compels me to write you my humble word of thanks therefor. You have followed him through all his doublings, have met his arguments at every point, have placed him at your mercy. I am deeply thankful that *you* of all men have undertaken and accomplished this task—you whose whole life has been devoted to the study of the "slavery" subject; you whose reputation is national for wisdom, piety, and learning; you whose official sojourn in the North has made you intimate with the Northern peculiarities of mind.

May I beg of you to have this piece published in pamphlet form and distributed among the ministry of our church at the North? It will do much good. It may indeed have the effect of stopping the prematurely exultant boasting of such abolitionized brethren (of whom there are many at the North) who are, I doubt not, already beginning to hail Dr. Hodge as a leader of their hosts, and his article as an entering wedge to the disruption of our church. Pardon my freedom.

Your brother in Christ,
Joseph R. Wilson.

Hon. Charles C. Jones, Jr., *to* Rev. C. C. Jones[t]

Savannah, *Wednesday,* February 20th, 1861

My dear Father,

I have just finished the perusal of your able and most valuable reply to the article of Dr. Hodge, for the receipt of which I am today indebted to you. You have done the cause of truth and justice great service, and your reply is unanswerable: Dr. Hodge must wince helplessly under it. I trust that he may be brought to realize the error of his ways.

I write this evening to the editor of *The Southern Presbyterian* for several copies of your article. Would it not be well, Father, to have it published in permanent pamphlet form? I wish that you would consent to have this done. All should be in possession of the article, and it ought not to be allowed to remain in its present ephemeral form. Cooper can attend handsomely to the republication, and I will, with your permission, see with pleasure to the correction of the proof sheets.

Did dear Mother and yourself receive copies of my little work upon *The Monumental Remains of Georgia?* I posted to your address the first copies issued, and hope that the perusal may afford you some pleasure.

We are expecting Brother, Sister Carrie, and their little son tonight. Nothing new with us. With our united love to dear Mother and yourself, I am, as ever,

Your affectionate son,
Charles C. Jones, Jr.

Hon. Charles C. Jones, Jr., *to* Rev. *and* Mrs. C. C. Jones[t]

Savannah, *Friday,* February 22nd, 1861

My dear Mother and Father,

D.V., Ruth and little Julia hope to be with you on Thursday next. Will write you again. With our united love,

Your ever affectionate son,
Charles C. Jones, Jr.

Rev. C. C. Jones *to* Hon. Charles C. Jones, Jr.ᵍ

Montevideo, *Tuesday,* February 26th, 1861

My dear Son,

We were happy to learn by yours of last evening that we should have the pleasure of seeing Ruthie and little Julia on Thursday, and will send the carriage for her to the depot (No. 3) on Thursday. The cars, you know, come out in the afternoon, and she will not reach Montevideo until 8 P.M. The pleasure would be increased could you become her escort. Tomorrow, D.V., we send for your sister and little ones, and on Friday Robert hopes to be down, and your Uncle William comes tomorrow. So we have the prospect of having all our children (except yourself) and grandchildren together in the course of the week, which will be a joyful event to us, and one calling for sincerest gratitude. . . .

Your mother and I read your *Monumental Remains* immediately as we received them with great pleasure and instruction. It is written in a graceful and scholarly manner, and is a credit to you and a valuable contribution to the history of the Indian races that once inhabited our country. Your theory of the migration of the Mound Builders from Mexico north up our rivers is new to me and appears reasonable and has facts in its favor. Verily the traces are dim; and the absence of a written language in any character shuts out access to the real history and character of these strange men.

We are passing through historic times, and I have thought some man amongst us should be laying up material for a history of these times—the dissolution of the greatest republic that ever existed, and the formation of two if not more. The work might be appropriately divided into three parts: first, the causes leading to the disruption; second, the disruption and formation of a new confederacy; and third, the settlement of the same: resources and prospects. The material should be laid up of the passing events *ab initio:* many striking facts, speeches, meetings, acts of the people, of governors, legislatures, conventions, Congress (United States and Confederate States), the religious element pervading the whole, and all such like matters. There is much in the newspapers of the day well worth laying by as it comes out, which would save much laborious turning over of leaves afterwards. Patience and perseverance might give us a worthy history of these times.

May it please God so to dispose the hearts of those who have it in their power to plunge us in war to refrain from it! We may be punished for our sins, but my hope is that the confessions and prayers of the true Israel may come up in remembrance before God and that He may grant us peace. I still think we shall have no war—although the prospects are darker.

We all unite in much love to dear Ruthie and in kisses for Julia. We long to hear her prattle. Your brother is devoting himself to exercise and health, which he much needs. The Lord bless and keep you and yours, my dear son! We highly appreciate the inscription of your little work.

Your affectionate father,

C. C. Jones.

9 P.M. A letter from your sister says little Charlie is sick and she cannot come tomorrow. Am sorry for the cause and the fact.

REV. C. C. JONES *to* MRS. MARY S. MALLARD[t]
Montevideo, *Saturday,* March 2nd, 1861

My dear Child,

We were truly sorry to hear of little Charlie's sickness, and that you could not come down. It was a great disappointment to us all. Your brother and family came out on Thursday. He returns this morning; Ruthie and little Julia remain. She is a sweet child, and Little Daughter will be delighted to see her. It would have been so pleasant to have had you all together; but we must be thankful for the mercy we enjoy, and hope the pleasure another time.

Little Stanhope will be baptized, if possible, on Sabbath. Ruthie expects to go back next week—perhaps Thursday; and Miss Davis and Joe and Carrie may go down to the Island. I hope our dear little grandson is better; and not having heard from you, conclude he is better. All are well, D.G., and unite in much love to yourself and Robert, and kisses for the children. Shall ride with Charles this morning as far as Arcadia.

Your ever affectionate father,
C. C. Jones.

You can write us by Niger, who anticipates seeing his family this evening.
C. C. J.

HON. CHARLES C. JONES, JR., *to* MRS. MARY JONES[g]
Savannah, *Saturday,* March 2nd, 1861

My dear Mother,

I forgot to hand you the enclosed chestnuts. They were gathered from a tree which grows very near the tomb of Washington. I thought you might wish to plant and endeavor to rear them. They may grow in our climate if the heat of summer does not prove too severe. The memory of Washington is still as dear, and every association connected with his home and grave as sacred, as ever it was; and I know by no one is that memory more patriotically cherished, or those relics more sincerely valued, than by yourself. The dissolution of this Union cannot silence those consecrated voices of the past; nor can it rob us of the relationship which we bear to, or of the veneration which we shall ever cherish for, the virtues and the great deeds of the Father of our Country. He was of us.

Hoping that under the soft influences of the sweet airs and gentle dews of spring these little seeds may soon burst and expand into a living green, and that among the many beautiful trees which now adorn and render our beloved home so attractive (all of them the offspring of your superintending taste and culture) you may number in a few short years the bright foliage and symmetrical forms of five Mount Vernon chestnuts, I am, with warmest love,

Your ever affectionate son,

Charles C. Jones, Jr.

REV. C. C. JONES *to* HON. CHARLES C. JONES, JR.[g]

Montevideo, *Monday,* March 4th, 1861

My dear Son,

Will you see our friend Major Porter and know if the bank is discounting and if we could be accommodated in some eight hundred dollars if we should need it? I think fully as much as that I will need for a special purpose.

Your brother had his fine little son baptized in old Midway yesterday. The little fellow followed the example of all our grandchildren and never uttered a sound, but displayed unusual good humor. May the outward sign of covenant blessings be followed by the inward blessings themselves, and parents and children all be bound in the sure bundle of life!

Ruth begs you to have the rooms fixed for your Aunt Susan and Cousin Lyman, who will accompany *her down on Thursday.* And so I will defer my visit. Dr. Axson and Brother Buttolph are exchanging pulpits.

I hear little Julia's voice—"Pudna! Pudna!"—prattling in her room, dressing. Ruth sends much love, and intended to write you, but have written for her and myself too. She and Julia quite well. Julia is getting very fond of her grandmother, and is trying to call her *grandma.* I showed her the sheep and told her to say *sheep,* and she made the effort and said *pheep.* All unite in love to you.

Your ever affectionate father,

C. C. Jones.

HON. CHARLES C. JONES, JR., *to* REV. C. C. JONES[t]

Savannah, *Tuesday,* March 5th, 1861

My dear Father,

In reply to your last favor I would say that Major Porter promises the required discount of eight hundred dollars. Whenever you make the note, be pleased to see that it is drawn payable to my order, and at the Bank of the State of Georgia. Enclosed you have receipts for amounts paid, as per statement rendered in my last.

Say to Ruth that the rooms will be all ready on Thursday as desired. I am very sorry to hear you say that you will not come in yourself.

Lincoln's inaugural is before us, and a queer production it is. What does it mean? It means this, and it means that; and then it may mean neither. That sly fox Seward, I expect, has had the shaping of it.

Our large guns are not here as yet. They are, however, daily expected. With warmest love to self, dear Father, dear Mother, Ruth, Julia, Brother, Sister Carrie, and Stanhope, and with respects for Miss Davis, I am, as ever,

Your affectionate son,

Charles C. Jones, Jr.

REV. JOHN JONES *to* REV. *and* MRS. C. C. JONES[t]

Rome, *Tuesday,* March 5th, 1861*

My dear Brother and Sister,

I have been daily meditating a line to you, but many things have to be done after a long absence from home before all matters can be fairly started again. In visiting the flock I am called to sympathize with some who weep for their loved and lost, and to rejoice with others who have been made happy by the addition of newborn joys. These sudden and often painful transitions of feeling are peculiar to the pastor's work.

Last Sabbath I preached for the first time from Isaiah 56:7—"My house shall be called a house of prayer for all people." Does Brother Charles remember that the same was his text when he preached the dedication sermon for Bryan County Church on Saturday, May 1st, 1841? On the 2nd of May 1841 I was ordained and installed pastor of Bryan Church—nearly twenty years ago. . . . But I am running back into the past, and will stop.

Our late visit to the low country will ever remain a green spot in memory's waste. Old Montevideo and all who dwell there seemed dearer to me than ever, and woods and fields and skies all had new charms for me. And I must confess that I felt a yearning and love to native scenes such as I have not known for years—a strong desire to linger and to postpone to the utmost the parting words.

Gilbert, the horses, and carriage were a most substantial help to us in reaching the depot, for just then my purse was well-nigh collapsed. After reaching Savannah, unexpected rain and press of business detained us one day over our appointment. Charles and Ruth were quite well, and little Julia better.

On Wednesday the 13th February, a most lovely day, we went to Augusta. Joseph was in bed, but had a carriage and Titus to meet us at the depot, and our niece Carrie gave us a most affectionate welcome.

On Thursday the 14th I attended with great pleasure the wedding of Colonel Alfred Cumming, Jr., and Miss Davis. The occasion was deeply interesting. The groom and bride were unusually handsome; the ceremony was beautiful, appropriate, and touching; the company and entertainment were charming. Mrs. Davis felt deeply at giving away her daughter; and who would not feel at parting with such a daughter? Dr. Davis is looking remarkably well, and accompanied Niece Carrie and myself to Augusta and visited Joseph.

Our visit to Augusta was truly pleasant, barring only the indisposition of our nephew. We were greatly pleased with his wife; she completely captivated us, children and all. A good wife is from the Lord; I think Joseph may say "Ditto" to this. They have a fine little boy. But you have judged for yourselves before this, as a recent letter from C. C. J., Jr., mentions that Joseph and family had passed through Savannah.

Leaving Augusta at 12 M. on the 14th February, we reached Marietta at 11 A.M. and passed the day and night with our aunt and cousins. All very well, and glad to see us, and we glad to see them and give them all the news from below. On the 16th we reached Rome, and found friends and servants well, and cold freezing weather with a sprinkle of snow. The change from below was powerful.

Last week was most balmy and pleasant, but today it is freezing. We shall have ice tonight. My dear Janey feels these changes most keenly, and a desire for a warmer climate grows on us. Dunwody declares in favor of the low country. I have not been able to secure any business for him. Business is very dull in Rome.

Jane and myself gave Brother Charles's answer to Dr. Hodge a reading together. I think it is a clear, logical refutation of Dr. Hodge's article, and often places the doctor in a ridiculous position. The good temper was maintained throughout, which added great force to the argument. I have loaned the answer to one of our members, and regret that I have not a pamphlet copy. Dr. Hodge has had a number of replies from laymen and ministers.

How do you like our new government, and especially our President, General Davis? Have you any opinion on the subject of war? Mr. Lincoln's inaugural may foreshadow something of the Black Republican policy. His speeches in advancing to Washington were certainly ridiculous.

How long will Joseph remain in Liberty? I trust he will indulge in relaxation and strive to regain his health, or he will be prematurely old and broken down. Do give our best love to him and Niece Carrie, and kisses for the little Stanhope Davis. Remember us in the same manner to Robert and Mary and their little ones. . . . Jane and the boys unite in best love to you both.

Your ever affectionate brother,
John Jones.

P.S. Write soon and give us all the news of the old country.

Mrs. Mary Jones *to* Hon. Charles C. Jones, Jr.[g]

Montevideo, *Thursday*, March 14th, 1861

My dear Son,

The visit of dear Ruth and little Julia was very delightful to us—only far too short. Your sister, too, enjoyed it—especially bringing all our dear little grandchildren under the old roof. I wish it was so in God's providence that we could oftener surround the family altar, the domestic hearth, and the social board together. I dread the alienation which long separations produce even with the nearest and dearest. Your little Julia is a most interesting child: intellectually bright with a loving little heart.

Have you observed the notice of your *Indian Remains* to be found on the last side of *The Southern Presbyterian?*

Should nothing occur in providence to prevent, your brother and myself propose visiting you on Monday of the coming week. But do not look for us until we come, for our old and faithful servant *Sandy* now lies dangerously ill; also our venerable friend Mrs. Mallard. Robert and your sister are both at Dorchester. Very little hope is entertained of her recovery.

Father asks for a little space, so I will close, with the united love of Carrie and Joe and your father and myself to Ruth and yourself, with kisses for our little darling.

> Ever your affectionate mother,
> Mary Jones.

REV. C. C. JONES *to* HON. CHARLES C. JONES, JR.[g]
> Montevideo, *Thursday,* March 14th, 1861

My dear Son,

Your favor advising Major Porter's kind answer has been received, and as your brother hopes to be in Savannah next week, will send the note down by him, and you can get the money and hand to him. . . .

Papers today indicate brightening skies at Washington—if the news be *true*. The sooner *our* convention adjourns the better after ratifying the permanent Constitution of the Confederate States. Some two hundred and fifty or three hundred men (and many raw recruits) kept together for any time are apt to breed either mischief or nonsense.

> Your affectionate father,
> C. C. Jones.

REV. C. C. JONES *to* MRS. MARY S. MALLARD[t]
> Montevideo, *Saturday,* March 16th, 1861

My dear Daughter,

Will you please let us know by Tom how Mrs. Mallard is today, and also Mr. Mallard? We are almost afraid to hear, for from your note our venerable and esteemed friend must be very feeble. Remember your mother and myself particularly and affectionately to her and to Mr. Mallard.

Our old friend and faithful servant Sandy Maybank died at sunset last evening after a most rapid and desperate attack of pneumonia, which came suddenly upon him Tuesday evening. He was death-struck from the beginning. We feel his death, and will miss the cheerful and faithful man always. He has been with us twenty-seven years! Funeral here tomorrow, D.V.

Mother begs me to say that she and your brother design going to Savannah, God willing, on Monday for a few days; and if she can do anything for you,

you must let her know. Aunt Susan is with us. Remember us kindly to all around you. Love to Robert, and kisses for the children.

Your ever affectionate father,
C. C. Jones.

Mrs. Mary S. Mallard *to* Rev. C. C. Jones[t]

Dorchester, *Saturday,* March 16th, 1861

My dear Father,

Mother Mallard passed a most distressing night. She suffered more than she has done during this sickness, and she has been laboring for breath all morning. Her heart is very much affected, and seems to me to be the chief source of distress now. When I wrote you before, we did not think she could survive many hours; but she revived again, and yesterday morning was comparatively comfortable; but now I think she grows hourly weaker, and her breath more labored. . . . It does not seem to me that she can live through the day, though she has revived so often that we hope she may be spared a little longer. I would have been glad to have been with you some of this week, but duty and affection call me here. . . . And then there has been no period at which I could have left expecting to return and find her alive.

Thank dear Mother for me, but I cannot think *now.* What I shall want will depend upon circumstances, and I may write her after she goes to Savannah. . . . Mr. Mallard unites with me in much love to Brother Joe and Carrie. Kiss little Stanhope. . . . I am truly grieved to hear of Daddy Sandy's death. How sudden it must have been! Mr. Mallard unites with me in warmest love to dear Mother and yourself, dear Father.

Your affectionate daughter,
Mary S. Mallard.

Rev. C. C. Jones *to* Mrs. Mary S. Mallard[t]

Montevideo, *Tuesday,* March 19th, 1861

My dear Daughter,

Our last intelligence from Dorchester was that our esteemed mother in Israel had revived, and some hope entertained of her longer continuance with us. On this favorable report Mother and your brother left for Savannah this morning, they having remained over yesterday on Mrs. Mallard's account. Not feeling very well for exposure in this sudden and great change to ride to Dorchester, I send Tom to know how she is today, and what her condition really is. Also how is Mr. Mallard?

Remember me with sincere sympathy and affection and many prayers for them both. I feel confident the Lord will be with and bear them both safely and peacefully through the cup of trial and distress He is now placing before them to drink. Am happy that you are with them, and feel assured you will omit no attentions and no service due from a daughter to so venerable, excellent, kind, and Christian parents. . . . Carrie unites in love to you and to Robert if he is with you. Kiss the little ones for me.

Your ever affectionate father,
C. C. Jones.

MRS. MARY S. MALLARD *to* REV. C. C. JONES[t]

Dorchester, *Tuesday,* March 19th, 1861

My dear Father,

I scarcely know what to write. Yesterday morning we thought Mother Mallard could not live until midday, and last night she was exceedingly weak. And she evidently grows weaker, though her decline is wonderfully gradual. I think myself that nothing but unremitted care and the use of stimulants have kept her alive during the last twenty-four hours. I see very little change since last night saving that her voice is weaker. And she lies asleep nearly all the time, and scarcely notices anything, though her mind is perfect when spoken to. Sometimes when she wakes she is greatly distressed, thinking she is away from home, and longing to rest in her own bed. Today she complains of being so cold. Her pulse is remarkably good for one in her feeble state, and this fact makes Father Mallard hope a little even now. He is deaf, and I think has no idea of her real condition. Dr. Stevens has just come, and he says that he does not see how she has lived. It is a great comfort to us to see that she is not suffering; the only thing she complains of is sore throat when she swallows; and we pray that when the last conflict comes she may be spared all agony. All of her children are here.

I am sorry to hear that you do not feel so well today. The change has been very great and trying. I am glad Mother has gone to Savannah; I hope a little change will do her good. We are all well. Mr. Mallard is here, for there has been no period at which he could have left since we came a week ago. He unites with me in warmest love to you. Much love to Carrie, and a kiss for the baby.

Your affectionate daughter,
Mary S. Mallard.

REV. C. C. JONES *to* HON. CHARLES C. JONES, JR.[g]

Montevideo, *Thursday,* March 28th, 1861

At the close of a day of much fatigue I write you a few lines, my dear son, the purport of which is to say that our kind and good friend Mr. Martin is no more! He died this *morning* at one o'clock and will be buried tomorrow. Your brother and I hope to attend his funeral at Flemington at 11 A.M., God willing. How great a loss to his already afflicted family! What a vanity is all earth as a portion and the only portion of the immortal soul! We hope that he was a Christian in reality. Mr. Buttolph remarked to me that his interview with him was satisfactory, although he was not able to converse a great deal.

Mr. W. E. W. Quarterman has been attending to the business at Arcadia during Mr. Martin's illness. Shall request him tomorrow to continue to do so until you can make some arrangements in respect to it. Meanwhile I will make inquiries and learn what had best be done. Mr. Quarterman is one of the best of men, but I know little of his ability as a planter and manager, and nothing on the point whether he would undertake for you or not. I will make some inquiries tomorrow. The sooner someone is obtained the better, but there is no necessity of being precipitate.

Mr. Mallard's family better. Your sister and Robert went home today, she quite unwell from overfatigue and sore throat. Mother tolerably well, and Carrie also. All unite in love to Ruthie and yourself, and kisses for Julia.

Your affectionate but tired father,
C. C. Jones.

Grist and rice *ordered;* be down next week (Monday or Tuesday).

Mother says: "Tell Charles I had a delightful visit to him and Ruthie."

REV. C. C. JONES *to* HON. CHARLES C. JONES, JR.[g]

Montevideo, *Saturday,* March 30th, 1861

My dear Son,

Your brother and myself attended the funeral of our good friend Mr. Martin yesterday at Flemington Church, the exercises conducted by our pastor, Rev. D. L. Buttolph. And we came down with the body and attended the interment also at Midway. The family requested me to make a brief address and offer prayer at the grave, which I did. Six or seven of the children present—nearly all grown; Mrs. Martin not out. A detachment of the troop, of which he was a member, fired the usual funeral farewell. His daughter, by whose side he lies, had gone to her silent dwelling just one week before him. The plate over the glass of the metallic case was removed in the church, and among many of his friends we took a last look of his face—so altered by the dreadful disease that I should not under other circumstances have recognized him. "Thou prevailest forever against him, and he passeth: Thou changest his countenance and sendest him away" (Job 14). The attendance at the funeral was large, and his sudden death much regretted.

At the grave his son Henry (I think), the oldest, requested me to let the family occupy Arcadia house for some weeks for a change in order that they might have their own home thoroughly cleaned and purified and ventilated, and their own health improved by the change. I told him certainly to do so and welcome. You recollect the house was offered to Mr. Martin early in the winter. None of the family are sick at present, and we hope the seeds of the fever may not be in any of them—which, however, remains to be seen. They will spend a week with their relations at Walthourville, and be at Arcadia the last of next week probably. Stepney has orders to evacuate the yard and keep his people, old and young, over at their quarters—Elsie to go there to attend to her poultry only; and we shall hope no danger from the arrangement. Typhoid fever is slightly contagious, but you must be *with the sick,* in their rooms and nursing, as a general thing to take it.

There are but two persons in the neighborhood that I can think of who might take Mr. Martin's place at Arcadia. Mr. W. E. W. Quarterman, an old friend, a deacon of Midway Church, whose plantation adjoins Arcadia below, and has added to it that part of your Uncle William's place (now Mr. Joseph Stevens') on the right as you go to Midway. He passes Arcadia every other day to visit his place, and has no other business that I know of, and has been in charge of Arcadia since Mr. Martin's illness, and at my request will hold on until we can make arrangements finally. He is an upright and good man; has not been as thrifty as some others, but is now at his new place, I understand, succeeding very well. Should he be employed, he will be conscientious in taking care of the people morally as well as physically, and I doubt not will do his best in cropping and be a pleasant man in business.

The other is Mr. John Mann, a younger man, active, and would be equally attentive and (it may be) more energetic. A pleasant man in business, and said to be an excellent writer of letters on the state of the plantation to his employers. At least, so says Mr. Henry Stevens, who has had him attending to his business in the summers since Mr. Martin gave it up. I have never been on his place near Flemington, but hear that he keeps it in very good order. He is a small planter. Mr. Mann is a member of Midway Church, but am sorry to say he has one tendency which, although it has brought him more than once under the censure of the church (and he *now* is so), he has so far failed to keep under, and of course is a most serious objection, for when most needed he might be most unable to attend to the plantation. Besides, it is a bad example to begin with. Nor could we reasonably hope to bind him to sobriety through motives of interest when those of religion and religious profession fail to do so. In justice, however, to Mr. Mann, towards whom I have the most friendly feelings, I should say that his indulgence is occasional and not habitual. How long it may continue so, no one may predict.

Both are men of family, in good health, and reside at Flemington, a mile or more nearer Arcadia than Mr. Martin did.

Mr. T. Q. Cassels proposed the employment of *his son* under *his supervision.* A youth: whether he has attained his majority or not I do not know. But I told him it was *not* such an arrangement as suited or could suit us. We wished an older man—a man of experience—one who knew about sickness and could attend to the people and take entire charge of the place; as you were in Savannah, and I could not give personal attention to it myself, and your brother was in Augusta, and Robert at Walthourville.

This is as far as I have gone. It will be most convenient to get a manager near the place. Flemington is the nearest permanent residence for one, and he would be in daily communication with Savannah by the railroad—a matter of consequence. On the whole we think—that is, your mother, brother, and I—*that it will be the best plan to employ Mr. W. E. W. Quarterman for the year*. He is now on the place, has the run of the business, and may prove the man we need. That is, if he will accept the offer; and a neighbor of his expressed the opinion that he would. He will be the safer man (to say the least) of the two; and I believe you will find him an agreeable and attentive man, a modest and unpretending man. If this suggestion commends itself to your judgment, you might write him on the subject, and if he is ready, close an agreement without delay.

Carrie is very unwell with a bad cold and cough. The Doctor is prescribing, and she thinks successfully. Rest well, and all unite in love to you and Ruthie, and kisses for Julia.

Your affectionate father,
C. C. Jones.

Monday Morning, April 1st, 1861. Carrie is better. All are taking their morning's nap. Mr. Buttolph preached excellently yesterday. May you and yours awake in the fear and favor of God!

HON. CHARLES C. JONES, JR., *to* REV. C. C. JONES^g

Savannah, Wednesday, April 10th, 1861

My dear Father,

I have to thank you for your kind favor. . . . I write by this mail to Mr. Quarterman, asking him to take charge at Arcadia for the present year. So soon as a reply is received, you shall know it.

All well, and unite in warmest love. We are all busily engaged in getting our defenses in order, in anticipation of hostile demonstrations on the part of the United States. You have seen the telegrams of yesterday. Even at this date we are at a loss to know the purposes of Lincoln. I have only a moment to secure the return post. As ever,

Your affectionate son,
Charles C. Jones, Jr.

MR. CHARLES SCRIBNER *to* REV. C. C. JONES^t

New York, Wednesday, April 10th, 1861

Dear Sir,

Your esteemed favor of 23rd ult. was duly received. I fully appreciate what you say respecting the questions at issue between our two confederacies, and in a great measure sympathize with you in your views. As it regards the work which you proposed to me some time ago for publication, I consider neither of us committed to each other, but free to take any course which may be for our interests. In the present distracted state of our country I do not think it would be wise for you to attempt making arrangements for publication; but you will be able, when North and South come to an amicable understanding with each other, to determine what course you had better take. I remain

Very respectfully yours,
Charles Scribner.

HON. CHARLES C. JONES, JR., *to* REV. *and* MRS. C. C. JONES[w]

Savannah, *Wednesday,* April 17th, 1861

My very dear Father and Mother,

You will, I am sure, excuse me for not oftener writing you when I tell you that in addition to the discharge of the duties devolved upon me in an official, professional, military, and civil way I last week agreed at the request of my company to deliver an address before the Chatham Artillery on the 1st of May next. With such short notice and so little time to devote to its preparation, you may well believe that very few leisure moments are at my command.

Recent telegrams inform us of the probable passage of an ordinance of secession by the Virginia legislature. The North Carolinians are realizing the importance of decided action. A noble reply to Lincoln's demand for troops has been returned by Governor Magoffin of Kentucky. Thus act succeeds act in this wonderful drama. Lincoln has made requisitions upon the Northern states for one hundred and fifty thousand more troops. Every indication points to a prolonged and sanguinary struggle.

We are endeavoring to prepare for the conflict. Colonel Lawton has, as you have observed, been appointed a brigadier general of the Confederate States, and is charged specially with the defense of our city, harbor, and coast. Tybee Island is now occupied by more than two hundred troops. Batteries are soon to be erected there. Near two hundred men from the interior of the state arrived last night, and will take post also upon Tybee. Fort Pulaski is garrisoned by four hundred men, and Fort Jackson by one hundred and twenty. The volunteer corps of the city are at present held as a reserve—subject, however, to orders at any moment. When the plot thickens and the day of battle comes, they will be where stout hearts and brave hands are most needed.

The ladies of Savannah are not idle. They are daily engaged singly and in concert in the preparation of cartridges both for muskets and cannon. Thousands have been already made by them, and the labor is just begun. Others are cutting out and sewing flannel shirts. Others still are making bandages and preparing lint. Their interest and patriotic efforts in this our cause are worthy of all admiration.

We have now three full batteries of field pieces in the city—one in the possession of our company, another in the keeping of the Savannah Artillery, and a third at the barracks. Upon Tybee Island they have two six-pounders and two twelve-pound howitzers. Heavy guns are needed there, and I doubt not but that General Lawton is directing his immediate attention to the preparation of batteries both at the northern and southern extremities of the island. The work of mounting columbiads at Fort Pulaski progresses slowly. Eighteen-pounders have arrived for Fort Jackson, are lying now upon the parade and upon the parapets of that fortification, and will be mounted so soon as carriages can be prepared. The workshops of the Central Railroad are busily occupied with their construction. Our company has been constantly engaged in putting our battery in thorough order, and in the manufacture of fuses (a very delicate and responsible duty) for the forts and for ourselves.

It is today officially announced that our mails are cut off, and that there will be henceforth no further communication through their agency with the Confederate States.

Can you imagine a more suicidal, outrageous, and exasperating policy than that inaugurated by the fanatical administration at Washington? The Black Republicans may rave among the cold hills of their native states, and grow mad with entertainment of infidelity, heresies, and false conceptions of a "higher law"; but Heaven forbid that they ever attempt to set foot upon this land of sunshine, of high-souled honor, and of liberty. It puzzles the imagination to conceive the stupidity, the fanaticism, and the unmitigated rascality which impel them to the course which they are now pursuing. I much mistake the policy of this Confederacy and the purposes of our worthy President (at once soldier and statesman) if in the event of our pure rivers and harbors being blockaded by Northern fleets, a great Southern army is not put in motion, attracting to itself the good and true men of every section, whose object it shall be to redeem the tomb of Washington from the dominion of this fanatical rule, and to plant the standard of this Confederacy even upon the dome of the capitol at Washington. This is a favorite scheme with President Davis, and he has brave men such as Major McCulloch and General Pillow to sustain him in carrying the idea into practical effect.

Nothing from Fort Pickens today. Mr. Ward is daily expected. Colonel Jackson has gone upon professional business to Atlanta, and on Saturday of this week expects to deliver an oration at Marietta commemorative of the virtues and of the character of the late Charles J. McDonald. It will be a finished production.

We are much obliged, my dear parents, for your kind remembrance of us. We enjoyed the strawberries for dinner today. They were the first we had tasted, and were regarded as a great treat.

Robert, who left us yesterday, took with him a package which arrived from Mr. —— for you, Father. I presume it has to do with your work, and will, I hope, reach you safely.

These troubles are seriously interrupting our professional labors, and diminishing our receipts. We will all have soon nothing but war to engage our attention. Ruth and little Julia are both quite well. Ruth is energetically devoting herself every day to the work of cartridge-making. Julia is a sweet child—affectionate, good, and very intelligent. She already takes great delight in her little linen books, and will explain the pictures. We hope, my dear father and mother, that we may soon have the pleasure of welcoming you here. We all unite in warmest love to you both, Brother, Sister Carrie, and little Stanhope. As ever,

Your affectionate son,
Charles C. Jones, Jr.

I have heard nothing as yet from Mr. Quarterman in regard to the management of Arcadia. I wonder at his delay in not answering my letter.

REV. C. C. JONES *to* HON. CHARLES C. JONES, JR.[g]

Montevideo, *Saturday,* April 20th, 1861

My dear Son,

We are aware of your numerous engagements, and never think anything of your not writing as frequently as usual, for we know that you will always write us whenever you can. Your two last came last night with the papers.

A kind Providence seems to watch over our Confederacy. Whoever read or heard of so important and desperate a battle as that of Fort Sumter without the loss of a man on the side of the victors or on the side of the vanquished? And how remarkable that the only men killed were killed saluting their own flag as it was lowered in defeat! May this battle be an earnest of all others that shall be forced upon us in its merciful and glorious success. All honor to Carolina! I hope our state may emulate her bravery and patriotism—and *her self-sacrificing generosity,* in that she has borne out of her own treasury the entire expense of her army and fortifications and all matériel of war, and has not and will not call upon our government for one cent of it. Georgia is well able to do the like for her own seaport and her own territory, and there must be some movement of our chief men to secure so honorable an act. It will relieve our new government, and enable it to appropriate its funds in other directions for our honor and our defense.

We are favored again, in providence, by the belligerent acts and declarations of Mr. Lincoln, which have precipitated the border states upon a decision in our favor precisely at the moment most favorable to us. I never believed we should have war until after Lincoln's inaugural address—and not altogether then, thinking that there were some preventing considerations of interest and self-preservation, and some residuum of humanity and respect for the opinions of the civilized world in the Black Republican party. But in this I have been mistaken. Christianity with its enlightening and softening influences upon the human soul—at least so far as the great subject dividing our country is concerned—finds no lodgment in the soul of that party, destitute of justice and mercy, without the fear of God, supremely selfish and arrogant, unscrupulous in its acts and measures, intensely malignant and vituperative, and persecuting the innocent even unto blood and utter destruction. That party is essentially *infidel!* And these are our enemies, born and reared in our own political family, for whom we are to pray, and from whom we are to defend ourselves!

The conduct of the government of the old United States towards the Confederate States is an outrage upon Christianity and the civilization of the age, and upon the great and just principles of popular sovereignty which we have contended for and embraced for near an hundred years, and brands it with a deserved and indelible infamy. We have nothing left us but to work out our independence, relying, as our good President instructs us, upon "a just and superintending Providence." The ordering out of such large bodies of men is an easy matter; but to *officer*, to *equip*, to *maintain*, and (*more than all*) to *maneuver and bring these forces into safe action with the enemy* —these are the burdens and the arts and realities of war. And we wait Lincoln's success. He is not training and educating the people up to the point of war gradually and familiarizing them with it, but he plunges them up to their necks in it at once. But enough. What is it all for? Are the people of the free states going to attempt *the subjugation* of our Confederacy under the fanatical and brutal lead of Black Republicans? I agree with you fully in your view of the character and conduct of this party. It would be a sublime spectacle to see the conservative portion of the free states uniting with our Confederacy in overthrowing the present government in Washington and installing a better one in its place—not for us, but for themselves. But I fear that portion of the free states have not the decision and daring and patriotism for the effort. *Douglas* leads off for coercion! A miserable politician and patriot he.

No man can even conjecture where this strife is to end. Yet it is under the control of God. He can "still the tumult of the people," and we can but cast this care upon Him and humbly await His interposition. It may be long delayed; it may be immediate. We must maintain our equanimity, go to our daily duties and by His help faithfully discharge them as in times past, and stand ready for emergencies when they arise, and keep in good heart all around us. The Lord keep you, my dear son, and strengthen you to serve Him and to fear His great and holy name, and to discharge your various and responsible duties to your family and country with cheerfulness and self-possession, with purity and integrity, and with intelligence, decision, and kindness. Seek to do all things well, and everything in its proper time.

Am glad you have consented to deliver the address to your company the 1st of May. You may do good by it, and should like to come and hear you.

The package from Mr. —— was his finish of the copy of the first volume of my church history. Arrived safe. . . .

Monday Morning, April 22nd. A pleasant Sabbath yesterday. Our young licentiate Mr. G. W. Ladson preached once for us.

The news from Baltimore and Washington is out here in the form of rumor. The events of the morning are old by the evening. The scenes succeed almost as rapidly as those of a play. Marvelous if Lincoln, who gave us twenty days to disperse, is in less than ten dispersed himself! As our mails North are stopped, send us what news of interest you can spare. Special prayer should be offered for the *life* of our President; I hope he will not expose his person.

Your affectionate father,
C. C. Jones.

III

Rev. David H. Porter *to* Rev. C. C. Jones[t]

Savannah, *Saturday,* April 27th, 1861

Reverend and dear Sir,

Since the last meeting of our presbytery actual hostilities have commenced between the North and South; or rather, the conflict was raging while our presbytery was in session, though we knew it not at the time. Under these circumstances a question has suggested itself to my mind which troubles me no little, and for the solution of which I turn to you, my revered father in the ministry, and one who I know is always ready to give counsel to his younger brethren, though God may not permit him through bodily infirmity to meet with them in presbyterial assembly.

The question is this: ought not our presbytery to have a called meeting to *reconsider* our action in appointing commissioners to the next assembly? We are in a state of war—an unholy, unjust, *brutal* war forced upon us by the North. It has been made painfully evident that many of our brethren of the assembly sympathize with the political principles of our enemies in this contest. And how can we meet with them in General Assembly with a proper self-respect? Is it possible that our delegates could sit with them in counsel or communion when at the very time, perhaps, our brothers and friends were falling in battle? And yet I tremble at the possibility of giving a wrong touch to the Ark. I am anxious that our presbytery should do right in the premises, but I am not able to decide what *is* right.

My own judgment suggests the course I have indicated, but I am afraid to rely upon that judgment alone in a question of so much moment. What do you think? I should be glad to know, and to make up my own mind according to your opinion. I have been hoping to see something from your pen on this question in the columns of *The Southern Presbyterian,* but I fear your bodily strength may not be equal to the labor of writing *in extenso*. If you think it best to let matters remain as they are, I shall be satisfied both in mind and conscience. If you think our action ought to be reconsidered, will you not unite with Brother Mallard or Buttolph (if they coincide) or myself, and the necessary number of elders who may take the same view, in requesting our moderator, Dr. Bowman, to call a meeting of Presbytery at some convenient point and on as early a day as possible?

My dear doctor, I *do* feel very much exercised on this subject, and beg that my anxiety and great desire to be and do *right* may stand as my excuse for troubling you. With Mrs. Porter's and my kindest regards to Mrs. Jones, I am

Very truly yours in Christ,
David H. Porter.

REV. C. C. JONES *to* REV. DAVID H. PORTER[t]

Montevideo, *Tuesday,* April 30th, 1861

Reverend and dear Brother,

Your kind favor of 27th reached me last evening. Brother Mitchel of Darien, one of our commissioners, wrote me last week on the subject of your note, and I answered him that were I a commissioner to our coming assembly under existing circumstances I should not go. The inauguration of war upon the South by the Black Republican government, backed by the entire North, is a sufficient reason.

The church must be divided. There is no help for it, Dr. Hodge in his late article in the last number of *The Princeton Review* to the contrary notwithstanding. Have not read but a few pages of it—enough to make the impression that it is ecclesiastically what the first article on "The State of the Country" was politically. We are two people distinctly and politically now—what we have been in fact for the last ten or fifteen years. To continue the union of the church after we are divided nationally is contrary to the usage of the Church of Christ in all ages. Ecclesiastical connections conform to civil and political. Our political separation is in part upon a subject which will ever remain a tender and vexed question, and be able at any assembly to break up our harmony; and our being citizens of separate confederacies will but tend to bring up the question. The sympathy of the ministers and elders of the Old School in the North and West with the monstrous doctrine of coercion, and their silence in the crisis, will not breed confidence and that charity which fosters union. Our people will not go for a continued union: confidence is measurably destroyed. Union and good feeling will be better promoted by living under our own vine and fig tree and shaking hands across the hedge and sending delegates over to each other to express love and good will.

The boards are all without our territory save one. Foreigners cannot act for us as we can for ourselves. We cannot afford to pay duties for our books to circulate. The present assembly is too large now. The country is large enough to support *two* or more efficient assemblies. An assembly of our own would promise to be continuously harmonious. The powerful influence of Old School Presbyterianism would be promoted in the South by division; we could act more directly upon our people and call out more talent in the conduct of the great work of the church on earth. We can use the assembly's organization in the free states if we desire—for a time, at least. Nor is there division of the assembly but in the sense (if I may so express it) of jurisdictions of government. We remain doctrinally, spiritually, and in organization one: the Old School Presbyterian Church under *two* assemblies—one in the old union of states, the other in the Confederate States. I have no qualms about such a separation. Dr. Hodge is haunted with the notion of *centralization*. He considers division sin, crime, treason—like secession in the state!

But enough. I had written a page or two on the subject for *The Southern Presbyterian,* but when Sumter was bombarded I considered it useless and threw the paper in the fire. Sumter or no Sumter, I believe in division.

The conduct of the old United States government and of the North is a disgrace to the civilization and Christianity of the age, and an outrage on the great principles of political and civil liberty upon which our former government was laid and upon which it has stood for eighty years. We can do no more than humbly commit our cause to God and meet the issue forced upon us unjustly, iniquitously.

Yours very truly in our Lord,
C. C. Jones.

Hon. Charles C. Jones, Jr., *to* Rev. C. C. Jones[w]
Savannah, Saturday, May 4th, 1861

My dear Father,

I am under many obligations to you for your recent kind favor, and am happy to know that all at home are well.

My address is pronounced by my friends and the company to have been a perfect success, although you must excuse me for repeating the compliment. The peculiar circumstances attending its delivery—the state of the country, the presence of several old and respected ex-captains on the stage, and the inspiration growing out of the monuments and the memories of the past, the absorbing questions of the present, and the prospects of the future—all conspired to invest the occasion and the theme with unusual attractions. For the first half hour or more I labored in speaking, and for this reason: my throat had become filled with the dust of the morning parade, and as usual my voice had grown husky from the issuing of orders. It improved, however, as I proceeded. The delivery of the oration occupied about two hours. The stage was filled with army and commissioned officers of our city companies, with ex-members of one company, with clergymen and many prominent citizens. The theater was crowded almost from pit to dome, and heard me one and all with marked attention. The address will be published by the corps, and it will give me great pleasure to send to dear Mother and yourself the first copy issued from the press.

We had on that day ninety-three members in full uniform, and paraded with a battery of six six-pounder guns and two twelve-pounder howitzers and a full brass band. This parade in point of numbers is unprecedented in the history of our company. In the morning a Confederate flag was presented to the corps by the wives and daughters of our noncommissioned officers,

Lieutenant Hartridge making the presentation address and Captain Claghorn responding on behalf of the company. Our exercises in the theater were commenced with a prayer offered to Almighty God by the chaplain of the corps, Private William S. Bogart. The entire proceedings of the day will be published in substantial form, and will constitute, I trust, a pleasant and interesting chapter in the history of our esteemed and time-honored company.

I heartily wish, my dear father, that you could all have been with us upon that occasion. Twenty-five years hence, when the hundredth anniversary will be celebrated, probably but few from out those well-filled detachments will be there to recount the memories of this day. An inexorable past is forever unfolding within its silent embrace the men and the manners of the present, and but few are the memories which escape a shipwreck in the deluge of time.

But a moment since I returned from the Pulaski House, whither I had been summoned in haste. It appears that some of our citizens observed upon the books of the hotel the names of two officers, Miller and Hook by name, connected with the U.S. army. This fact was rapidly circulated, and an excited number of citizens soon assembled there. Immediately upon my arrival at the Pulaski House I requested the proprietor, Mr. Wiltberger, to arrange an interview with them for me in his private parlor. They immediately responded to the call. I found them to be two young lieutenants, recent graduates of West Point, far gone in consumption, who had been upon leave of absence for several months, and had been endeavoring to recruit their enfeebled constitutions in Florida. They were returning home to die, and with them some ladies also sorely burdened with that terrible disease. They were both gentlemanly men. I was touched with some remarks which they made —such, for example, as this: "Why, sir, so far from taking any part in the existing troubles, we have long since ceased to take any interest in anything other than the restoration of health. And now that this appears impossible, we are more nearly concerned about the affairs of a future world than with any excitements of the present. We will neither of us ever see service again," etc. I was fully satisfied with their statements, corroborated as they were by certificates, etc., and by the more emphatic attestation of their consumptive indications, that they were subjects for commiseration rather than for suspicion and hatred. I made a brief statement to the crowd of the result of my interview, and am happy to state that they confessed themselves satisfied therewith, and retired without any noise or acts of violence. The poor fellows will resume their journey, if physically able to do so, on the morrow.

If there is any one thing which I detest more than another, it is any exhibition of mob law. There is always a remedy for almost any evil, and it is a grave reflection upon the good order of any community whenever its citizens disregard the obligations resting upon them first to resort to the exercise of authority provided by the ordinances of the city and the laws of the land and exhaust the remedies therein provided before resorting to lawless and violent manifestations of feeling and act.

It is a proud and enviable peculiarity of our Southern cities that while riots and lawless mobs are perpetrating all kinds of excesses at the North, reminding of the darkest hours of the French Revolution, we have up to this time been law-abiding citizens, preserving the peace, the good order, and the dignity of the community in which we live. Should any disturbances of this character occur, however, many allowances are to be made. Our feelings, our rights, our cherished privileges have all been grossly invaded by a blinded, a malignant, and a fanatical enemy. Daily are we receiving new indications and proofs of their iniquitous policy, and it would not be strange if retaliation should with not a few become the law of the hour.

We have some private intimations today—how reliable we are as yet unable to judge—that several of the companies composing the Volunteer Regiment of this city will soon be ordered to Virginia. We will soon be informed.

I should think that it would be a wise plan for Brother and his family to remain with you this summer. Aside from the pleasure which they would enjoy in being with you, my dear parents, much expense would be spared. He will find that all business matters are most seriously interrupted—that the minds of men are busied with other subjects. And besides, he will enjoy an excellent opportunity for prosecuting his botanical and ornithological studies. Apart from this, the calm quiet rest of the summer will prove most grateful and salutary after several years of unremitting labor and toil. If I were he, I would think twice before I returned to Augusta, at least for the present. A month will demonstrate the probabilities of the future. And, my dear parents, should the war cloud descend along our coast, I may have to commit to your kind keeping Ruth and little Julia.

We are all well, and unite in warmest love. Julia is a perfect gem. As ever,

Your affectionate son,

Charles C. Jones, Jr.

P.S. I almost forgot to say that we will send the tea, etc., by express on Monday, D.V.

Dr. Fraser charged me eighty-five dollars for his attentions to Clarissa. Do you not think the bill heavy? I certainly find it so these "hard times."

Monday Morning, May 6th. All well. A severe storm last night, intermingled with hail.

REV. DAVID H. PORTER *to* REV. C. C. JONES[t]

Savannah, *Tuesday,* May 7th, 1861

Reverend and dear Sir,

I am more obliged to you than I can express for your very kind answer of 30th ult. to my note of a previous date. It has perfectly satisfied and *cleared* my mind on a subject which was occasioning me no little anxiety. And subsequent events have only confirmed the wisdom of your judgment and decision. You have observed the note in the last *Southern Presbyterian* taken from *The American Presbyterian* of Philadelphia on the subject. Does it not amount to a positive *threat?* But I know that the Master loves His Blood-bought Church; and whatever be the wrath and passion and wickedness of man, *He* will see that our beloved Zion "receives no detriment."

You have no doubt heard of our mayor's great oration on the 1st inst. You must excuse me, for I can't help saying that it was the most magnificent effort of the kind I have ever heard. I have never heard anything from him but what was excellent; but this, I think, was the best of all! I am sure if I had not been a minister my *hat* would have suffered seriously; and as it was, I couldn't help joining in the enthusiastic applause which was showered upon him!

Again thanking you, my dear doctor, for your kind attention to my inquiries, I am

Very truly yours,
David H. Porter.

Mrs. Mary Jones *to* Hon. Charles C. Jones, Jr.[g]

Montevideo, *Tuesday,* May 7th, 1861

My dear Son,

After a day of nursing and constant attendance upon the sick I close with a few lines congratulatory upon the success of your late oration. We have heard with no small degree of pleasure—and ought I to say pride?—of the approbation and praise bestowed upon it. I thought a great deal of you on the 1st, and if I had "wings to soar" would certainly have been present to witness the well-earned honor bestowed upon my son. Your dear father and brother, too, deeply regretted that the sickness on the plantation detained them at home.

We have had some cases of critical illness; and whilst I write, your brother is compounding doses for at least a dozen now suffering from violent colds, many of them with pneumonia symptoms. Patience's daughter Miley is very ill, and one poor little infant I scarcely think will live out the night. I never knew as much sickness in all my life. It is a great comfort to have Joe's skill and unwearied attention. No one could do more than he is now doing, and we can but hope that God's blessing will own the means. It all appears the result of an epidemic, and we hear prevails elsewhere. The servants thus far have not had anything of the kind at Arcadia.

Please say to dear Ruth that we are very much obliged to her and yourself for the delightful tea and Chinese fruit, both of which we have already enjoyed. And I shall do my best with the yucca seed.

Margaret has proven herself a great comfort to me, and says if Ruth can spare her she will remain one week longer and not return before week after the next. Please let me know if this will answer.

Your brother thinks it is to his interest to return to Augusta and commence the practice of medicine, and says I must tell you he hopes to see you very shortly. Had it consisted with his interests, we should most happily have kept Carrie and Stanhope and himself with us all summer. And if in God's providence you should commit your loved ones to our care, I hope they will ever receive a father and a mother's welcome. If we had only a good physician within reach at Maybank, and dear Ruth and yourself would consent to such an arrangement, it would be my highest pleasure to have her come home and let me wait upon her in her approaching hour of trial. Please assure her how welcome she would be; and I place the matter before her.

On last Saturday Laura and Mr. Buttolph became the parents of another fine little *boy*. All doing well. We saw your name proposed for the colonelcy; Father says he wants to write you about it. I must close, with the united love of Father, Brother, Sister Carrie, and Mother to Ruth and yourself. Kisses for our little darling. God bless you, my child, and keep you in His fear!

Ever your affectionate mother,
Mary Jones.

REV. C. C. JONES *to* HON. CHARLES C. JONES, JR.ᵍ

Montevideo, Thursday, May 9th, 1861

My dear Son,

Mother wrote you to express our great gratification at your success in your oration. Nothing affords us more sincere pleasure than the fact that our children are filling up their days usefully and honorably on the earth. We endeavored to bring you up to that end, and when we connect with it piety towards God in all, then we can go no higher. Your good friend Rev. D. H. Porter wrote me in the kindest and most complimentary form of the oration. Send us a copy when it comes from the press.

Your brother returns with his family to Augusta next week, God willing. We shall miss them a great deal. He has been for the past week constantly occupied with the sick on this place, and I deem it a special providence in our behalf that he was with us. Since writing the foregoing, today (Saturday the 11th) the sick list has greatly diminished, and all remaining are convalescing. And what contributes to health is the seasonable warm weather. Thermometer 80° in the coolest part of Lyons & Trask's store, Riceboro, this morning.

I do not know how many visits Dr. Fraser paid to Clarissa, but eighty-five dollars strikes me as a large bill. His office cannot be above seven miles from Arcadia. *She was, however, very dangerously ill, and for a considerable time required close attention.* The specific charges, if given on the bill, will best show the justice of it.

Now that your oration is over and everybody is pleased, be grateful for your success and go on as before as though nothing had happened, and stand in your lot to meet the next call, and do the best you can, whatever it may be, for God and your fellow men. The command of the Volunteer Regiment is highly honorable and tempting to one ambitious of military honors, and withal a most useful and *deeply responsible position*. And a man should well understand what he is about who seeks it. It must require a great deal of knowledge of military science (tactics, as they call them) and practice of them—the composition, organization, drill, disposition, movement, and support of large bodies in service. War is both a science and an art, and a man wants an education for such a position. The lives and fortunes of thousands —sometimes the fate of the country—turns upon a single pivot, and that not a very large one. And yet nearly every man thinks he can be a captain, a colonel, and even a general! You have about as much business in the city and in the artillery company as you can well attend to. If you become colonel in these war times, you will have to qualify yourself thoroughly and make a serious business of it. Nothing but an absolute call of duty ought to incline you to accept such an appointment.

I agree with you perfectly in relation to mob law. It is the beginning of the overthrow of justice, mercy, truth, and order. So reads history. Self-preservation should aim every man against it, to go to no higher motive. The law-abiding mass of the American people lies south of Mason and Dixon's line.

Your brother will leave next week for Augusta. He is very anxious to make an effort to get into practice; and although times are deranged, yet sickness comes at all seasons. Besides, Carrie is not acclimated; her family are at a distance, and we know how circumscribed are our associations and privileges on the Island. And your brother at home with his library and laboratory would no doubt do more in a professional way than with us. We appreciate his kind offer to stay with us in these times; yet for that reason alone we could not wish him to do so, especially as we cannot calculate certainly how things are going to turn out. And besides, he has joined our troop, and will come down in case of necessity whenever required to do so.

Our united love to Ruthie and yourself, and kisses for Julia.

Your affectionate father,
C. C. Jones.

Can you let me know what prospect is there of bacon being *higher* or *lower*? And what are clean good sides worth? And what can *good* West Indies molasses be had for by the *tierce*? Ask Aaron Champion among others.

Rev. D. L. Buttolph *to* Rev. C. C. Jones[t]

Point Maxwell, Saturday, May 11th, 1861

My dear Uncle,

Aunt Mary's kind note containing her and your congratulations on the birth of our little one was received last night. Accept our united thanks for the same. May your prayers for it be answered, and your good wishes be fulfilled! Laura still continues to improve. The little stranger keeps well and is doing well. Mother's attentions to it are unwearied.

I regretted to hear of the many cases of sickness you have at Montevideo. Also of George's sickness. I will ride over to Maybank after dinner and see

George. I would have gone yesterday had I known that he was ill. It is a great blessing that you have Cousin Joe with you now. I hope he will not get sick in endeavoring to alleviate and cure the sickness of others.

I was glad to hear that you were able to preach at Pleasant Grove. I hope you have not suffered from it. I have not asked you to preach at Midway because I feared that preaching would injure you. But whenever you have a word to say to the people and feel able to preach, remember that the pulpit at Midway is *always* yours.

I have seen no news for several days. The last news was of great preparations at the North for a hostile invasion upon the South. The present looks dark, but I trust that our Father in Heaven will appear for our deliverance and scatter those who delight in war.

Give our united love to Aunt Mary, Cousins Joe and Carrie, and little Stanhope. Jimmie says that his "illy broder's" name is Stanhope; he will not hear of any other name. With much love, I remain

Your affectionate nephew,
D. L. Buttolph.

P.S. I was in Savannah on the 1st of May. Cousin Charles delivered an anniversary address that day which was complimented on the streets as I never heard a speech complimented before. It was said by all to have been the best speech ever delivered in Savannah. I was too late for it.

Mrs. Susan M. Cumming *to* Mrs. Mary Jones[t]

Point Maxwell, *Saturday,* May 11th, 1861

My dear Sister,

We were very glad to hear from you last evening by Andrew, and sorry to learn you have had so much anxiety about your sick servants. Hope under Dr. Joseph's skillful treatment they will soon be recovered to health.

Am glad to say Laura has been doing very well. . . . Little William does nothing but eat, sleep, cry—and cry, sleep, and eat again. All of his little troubles have been removed. . . . James David insists that the baby's name is Stanhope. *Smyth* or *Lyman* is to be the second name. . . . Brother William has been to see him. . . . He was told the baby was called after him. He seemed pleased, and said he would come soon and see him again when he was more worth seeing.

What troublous times these are! I can only think of the deliverance of Hezekiah and pray it may be ours, for we have no might against this great company. . . . The good Lord watch over and preserve *all*, and especially those near and dear to us, in these times of peril and danger! Laura and Mr. Buttolph unite in much love to you and Brother, Carrie and the M.D. and Stanhope. Jimmie's message to you is: "Kite well."

Your affectionate sister,
S. M. Cumming.

Jimmie has a little Zouave for Stanhope.

Hon. Charles C. Jones, Jr., *to* Rev. C. C. Jones[w]

Savannah, *Tuesday,* May 14th, 1861

My dear Father,

Mr. Robert Hutchison, your old friend and companion in youth, died last night. For some time he has been suffering from debility, and has been looking and feeling badly. The proximate cause of his death I understand to have been a stoppage of the intestinal canal. His funeral took place in a private way this afternoon at five o'clock, and his remains will leave tonight for Virginia.

You have doubtless noticed that the port of Charleston has been blockaded by the *Niagara.* We are daily expecting the arrival of a blockading fleet for this harbor. The clouds thicken, and we know not when the sun of peace will again dawn upon this distracted country. But let them gather as darkly as they may: with a holy cause and manly breasts we can and will fight as bravely and as cheerfully under a shadow as under the brightest skies. We are preparing for the struggle here. Our companies hold themselves in readiness to march upon shortest notice. We have placed ourselves under the command of General Lawton for the defense of this city and the coast of our state.

In reference to the colonelcy, I have determined not to accept the invitation to become a candidate. The responsibilities and the duties involved require more attention and careful consideration than I am able under present circumstances to give to them. The engagements incident to the discharge of the mayoralty and my obligations to my company sufficiently engage my time and attention, and do not allow much opportunity for the consideration of other matters. The office of colonel of this regiment should command and receive at this time the attention of an experienced, efficient man. I trust we may be able to secure the services of such an one.

Bacon is now held at a very high figure. Expectations are entertained that a supply may be soon obtained. I will obtain and send you a statement of the prices of this article and of West Indies molasses.

We are all well, and unite in warmest love to self, dear Mother, Sister Carrie, Brother, and little Stanhope. Robert dined with us yesterday. His mission to the city was of all the most sad; I deeply sympathize with him in his severe bereavement. As ever,

Your affectionate son,

Charles C. Jones, Jr.

P.S. The note matures soon in bank, and I send renewal. Have you the discount, or shall I pay it?

Mrs. Eliza G. Robarts *to* Rev. *and* Mrs. C. C. Jones[t]

Marietta, *Monday,* May 20th, 1861

Dear Charles and Mary,

I must now thank you both for your long and affectionate letter, which gave me much pleasure. I would have answered it before, but the long cold spring increased my cough, which has kept me much debilitated. Even a little walk round the yard tires me much. Added to this, the constant anxiety of mind about our poor servant Hannah depressed me much, with other cares and trouble.

Poor Hannah died on the 29th of April after many months of painful suffering, which she bore with much patience. She was perfectly sensible, and spoke five minutes before she expired. She was perfectly calm and resigned: seemed to have no fear of death. Mr. Palmer spoke with her, and so did your brother John, who was here a few days previous. It was a great comfort to us to see her so happy, and a happy release from her sufferings. I feel as if we had lost a friend in the family, she was such a good servant—so much like poor Clarissa, her aunt, who raised her. If you could have seen with what attention Sam and Peggy nursed her by day and night! Being paralyzed for months, she was lifted like a child. Sam says all his family is gone now. (Hannah was his niece.) I had a neat coffin made for her and got Mr. Palmer to come over and hold the funeral services in the yard, with chairs and benches put out for the Negroes. She was a great loss to us in a pecuniary way, for she was making for us one hundred dollars a year at the time she was taken sick. But I feel her death more as a friend. You both know what that feeling is.

I suppose Henry told you we had sold Henry, Mason, and Clarence (Peggy's three sons). This was a great trial to me—to separate them from their mother so far; but there seemed to be a real necessity, for we could not hire them to advantage to any reliable person; it was a constant change. Knowing Mr. Pynchon to be a kind master (and he says he does not buy to sell), we thought it would be best for them to have a permanent home with a kind master, who has promised to let them come sometimes to see their mother. Better than to sell them to strangers who would not hesitate to sell them again.

All this, with the thoughts of this dreadful war hanging over our once happy land, depresses me much. But my constant prayer is that God will overrule all events of this great evil and turn the hearts of men to an amicable peace. Lincoln—that unwise President—has brought all on themselves. It is indeed a cruel and unjust war. For a month past every car has been filled with soldiers—some going to Pickens, some to Virginia. Mr. Ardis' second son, Payson, has gone with a company from Charleston to Richmond; Mrs. Ardis is much grieved at her son's going. Her daughter, Mrs. Hardy—her husband is gone from North Carolina; Dr. Hardy, she says, is a Christian, and she has given him up to God, and that comforts her; she wrote a beautiful letter to her mother about it. Next week a company from Roswell goes, commanded by Major John Dunwody; Mr. Charlie Dunwody goes with them. Mr. Joseph King left on Saturday to join his company in Savannah. Mr. Irvine Bulloch has come from the North to join the Southern army somewhere. I suppose you have heard of Captain James Bulloch's return; I believe he is in Savannah. I hope all the Southerners will come home. Mrs.

Bulloch says she is true to the South, but her daughters have both married Northern gentlemen, and she is obliged to stay where they are. The gentlemen, I hear, say they will not fight against the South.

About a week ago there was a large company of officers belonging to General Phillips' brigade camped about six miles from here on the Atlanta road. Major Capers went out to drill them every day. Such a large company so near Marietta drained the country of all fresh provisions, such as beef, poultry, eggs, and butter. They have now gone higher up the country. The ladies here gave them a handsome dinner. Their camp ground was a very pretty place, and the ladies were much amused to ride out frequently and see them drilled. Next Thursday some of the ladies here are to have a concert for the wives and children of the soldiers who have gone to the wars.

I have told you all up here about the war. . . . Mr. Buttolph wrote me Laura had another son; I am so glad to hear she is so well over it. . . . I am sorry, Mary, you have been so unwell again. If you could try the sulphur water of Meriwether perhaps it would help you. Can't you and Charles come up to see us in the course of the summer? . . . This letter, I suppose, will find you just about moving to Maybank. When you get settled I shall expect a letter from you if not before. . . . Next Sabbath will be Communion at Midway; I always remember the day and think of my old church and brethren. How many happy and pleasant days I have spent with them! . . . We hear from Mary Sophia every week; she is well and as satisfied as she can be from home. Accept of much love from

Your poor but affectionate aunt,
Eliza G. Robarts.

Mrs. Mary Jones *to* Hon. Charles C. Jones, Jr.^g

Montevideo, Monday, May 20th, 1861

My dear Son,

Tom has just come in from the mail, and I take the earliest opportunity of expressing my great pleasure and gratification at receiving thus early a copy of your oration, which I shall prize most highly, and hope to read early tomorrow, not having leisure tonight, as we are all busy helping to get things in readiness for your brother's departure early in the morning.

We feel very sad at their departure. Joe has been unwearied in his medical attentions to your father and myself, and I know not what we would have done without his skill and attention to the servants. For the past three weeks the plantation has been almost a hospital. We have never known as many cases of sickness, but have great reason to be grateful that their lives have all been spared thus far.

Did you remember that I had your *army glass*—the gift of your old friend Mr. Helm—in possession? *Patience* has taken great pride in brightening it up today, and I send it down to you by the present opportunity. Please let George take the cans, etc., to King & Waring. I must now close, with our united love to dear Ruth and yourself, and kisses many for our little grand-daughter.

Ever your affectionate mother,
Mary Jones.

Hon. Charles C. Jones, Jr., *to* Rev. *and* Mrs. C. C. Jones[g]
Savannah, *Tuesday,* May 21st, 1861

My dear Father and Mother,

We were a few hours since gladdened by the arrival of Brother and his family. I am sorry to see that Sister Carrie is troubled with a very bad cough. As usual they tell us that they can only pay us a flying visit. I must confess I doubt the expediency of Brother's returning to Augusta this summer when he might remain with you upon the Island. My fear is that he will find such a derangement existing in every department, in consequence of the presence of this war, that it will be a very difficult matter to sustain the depressing in-fluences of small fees and poor pay. But of this he must be the best judge.

At his hands, dear Mother, I was favored with your very kind letter, for which you will accept many thanks. Hope that you will not be disappointed upon a perusal of the address. I regret that I did not have the pleasure and honor of delivering it in the presence of yourself and dear Father; for I am well aware that there were many circumstances attendant upon its delivery which conduced no little to the interest and the effect of the occasion. My friend Deitz promises me a bound copy, which I will take great pleasure in sending to you so soon as it is finished.

The news has just reached us from the harbor that the *Harriet Lane* is ly-ing outside blockading the port. A Spanish brig was this morning chased by her, but succeeded in forcing the blockade. The *Harriet Lane* fired at her, but without effect, and the brig is now lying secure from all harm under the guns of the fort. The *Harriet Lane* declined to come within range of the guns of the fort; indeed, she did not dare even an entrance within the sound. The above I give you as the report of a pilot just arrived from below.

Upon Tybee Island we have as yet no battery of heavy guns. Some four hundred troops are stationed there as sharpshooters. The erection of a battery of probably eighteen- and thirty-two-pounder guns is in contemplation. The reason why no very heavy guns will be mounted there is in order that if the battery be taken, there shall be no guns which would be of sufficient size to be turned and used with effect upon the fort.

At Thunderbolt an earthwork has been thrown up mounting one colum-biad and three eighteen-pounder guns. The former is in position, and com-mands the approach for more than two miles. The latter, I believe, are not as yet mounted.

Fort Pulaski is believed to be in a capital state for defense. Some eleven columbiads, I am informed (I have been so much occupied that I really have had no time of late to visit the fort), are in position—most of them *en bar-*

bette, a few in the casemates. These are terrible engines of war, and can be used with fearful effect upon any attacking force. One gun in position in a fixed battery is worth more than a dozen upon a floating battery. The garrison of the fort numbers about six hundred men. The troops have been suffering much from measles, but are now getting better.

The Volunteer Regiment of Savannah are expecting orders for the field early next week. There will then be probably a movement of troops along the coast, with a view to the occupation of exposed points liable to attack. Nothing definite has as yet, however, been determined upon. My own impression is that the troops of this city should not be ordered away from their homes except under a pressing necessity. The avocations of citizen-soldiers who have wives and children dependent upon their daily exertions should not be interrupted until the very latest moment. Distress and want follow at best close upon the heels of war, and it is the part of prudence to postpone their coming as long as possible. The companies here might be drilled every afternoon in regimental and battalion movements to their great advantage without withdrawing them from home and placing them in camp. This may be a long and exhausting war, and the longer we can retain our citizen-soldiery at home—in the bosoms of their own families, engaged in their support and comfort, and thus relieving them from the sad necessity of becoming pensioners upon public charity—the better.

Mr. Hutchison died very quietly and in full possession of his mind. He expressed himself prepared for the last great change, and made every arrangement in reference to his property and worldly affairs. He dismissed all his friends during the night, and died early in the morning with only his servants around him. Major Porter, Mr. Duncan, Colonel Lawton are, I believe, named as his executors.

In consequence of these disjointed times our business engagements are very nearly suspended. We all, my dear parents, unite in warmest love. As ever,

Your affectionate son,
Charles C. Jones, Jr.

Hon. Charles C. Jones, Jr., *to* Mrs. Mary Jones[g]

Savannah, *Saturday,* May 25th, 1861

My dear Mother,

Enclosed please find an ambrotype likeness of General Beauregard, the hero of the battle of Fort Sumter. I thought you might like to have it.

The ladies have concluded their fair for the benefit of the soldiers and of their needy families with considerable success. The profit realized is not yet definitely ascertained, but I presume it will not be less than several thousand dollars. They should now see that this sum is judiciously expended and not wasted in trifles.

Our regiment is under marching orders, and will probably be upon the move early next week, taking post at points most eligible for the defense of the coast. Charlie Whitehead has been elected to the position of major of one of the Georgia regiments in Virginia, and is now stationed at Portsmouth. The present indications are that we shall soon hear of severe and bloody hostilities in that state. The Lincolnites are occupying Alexandria, upon Virginia soil.

Please say to dear Father that the note has been renewed for ninety days, and the order upon Mr. Anderson for forty-five dollars paid, and proceeds deposited to his credit in state bank.

We are all well, and unite in warmest love to self, dear Mother, and to dear Father. Although in much haste, I am, as ever,

Your affectionate son,
Charles C. Jones, Jr.

Mrs. Mary Jones *to* Hon. Charles C. Jones, Jr.^r

Montevideo, *Tuesday,* May 28th, 1861

My very dear Son,

I read your oration with intense interest, and your father and myself regret more than ever that in providence we were not permitted to hear you deliver it. Your father says he was greatly pleased with it, and will write you particularly about it. Accept many thanks for your favor by the last mail enclosing the picture of our gallant hero General Beauregard. All honor to his name!

Our esteemed friend Dr. Howe spent a day with us last week. He was in Charleston on Saturday at the time of the surrender, saw the white flag raised, and heard Major Wigfall give the account of his interview with Major Anderson. He confirmed what the papers stated, that in the center of the fort was placed an immense gun prepared and pointed for shelling the city and destroying defenseless women and children. There were several remarkable providences connected with the engagement and defeat. The barbette gun designed to play upon the iron battery recoiled at the first fire and was rendered useless, and the outer metallic doors to the magazines became so warped that they could not be opened. Dr. Howe says the burning of the officers' quarters was singular, as there was not a particle of wood about them —even marble mantels, and handsomely fitted out. If the truth was known, I would not be surprised to hear that they were fired by Anderson himself. His whole course has been marked by duplicity and falsehood. Our good friends are feeling very deeply for their brave boy Willie. He was stationed on Stono River during the fight, and is now in Virginia in Colonel Kershaw's regiment, which I see by the papers will probably be one of the first to meet the enemy. Here it is that the sword pierces into our own bosoms!

Last Sabbath was our Communion season at old Midway, and a peculiarly precious and solemn time it was. And I doubt not every heart present bore a bleeding country to the Prince of Peace. I trust "The Lord of Hosts is with us; the God of Jacob is our refuge." Do you remember that we *always* close our Communion service with special prayer for the *baptized children* of the church? It seemed to me on last Sabbath that my very heart could empty itself before the Cross on your behalf, my beloved, unconverted child! *I* have no power to win you to Christ, but I do entreat you as I have often done to seek the influences of God's Holy Spirit, that your heart may be changed, and that you may be united to the Divine Redeemer by saving faith. . . . My son, you have no time longer to delay or trifle with your soul's eternal interests. Suffer your mother to remind you of them. And may God preserve you from making shipwreck of your immortal soul! . . . The afternoon service was a prayer meeting especially in view of our present condition, and the church engaged to devote—or rather it was suggested that every evening at sunset we remember our country, our rulers, and those who have gone forth to battle, that God would shield them and crown our arms with victory.

We shall no doubt be soon surrounded by all the horrors of war; and it becomes every heart to be fixed, trusting in God, and every arm to be nerved for the righteous conflict. In my poor way I want to testify my interest in those who are called to defend our homes and firesides, our lives and liberties. I have had all the sage and balm from the garden dried, and if you think it would be acceptable I will send it for the sick. And following out the suggestions of the governor, I would like to prepare clothing for *four* soldiers. I have enough for two suits, and would be much obliged if it does not give you too much trouble to call at Mr. Lathrop's and request him to send me enough for two suits of such material as is used by the army soldiers—thread and buttons, etc., etc.—and materials for four shirts of such as is used in service.

Your father requests you to call at King & Waring's and ask them to send our articles if not already sent, and write us when they do send them. Please ask dear Ruth to send me *by mail six skeins* of linen thread—or by any other way that I can get them soon—*for embroidering flannel.*

Enclosed is a certificate of church membership for Adeline; your father says she must present it to Dr. Axson.

It is late, my dear son, and I must close. Packing all day; begin to move tomorrow, *D.V.* I long to see you and dear Ruth and our darling little granddaughter. What can I do for Ruth? Did you get your army glass? No word from Joe since he left. . . . Father unites with me in best love to you both and kisses for Julia.

Ever your affectionate mother,
Mary Jones.

HON. CHARLES C. JONES, JR., *to* REV. *and* MRS. C. C. JONES[g]
Savannah, *Wednesday,* May 29th, 1861
My dear Father and Mother,

I trust that a kind Providence is dealing mercifully with you, and that all the sick servants are well again. We have not heard from you for some time, and feel very anxious to do so.

Still in the dark as to the true status of affairs in Virginia. Daily anticipating accounts of an engagement between our troops and the Lincolnites. One would think that a collision must inevitably at a very early period ensue. The Fabian policy of our administration may be all for the best, as the Black Republican administration is fast exhausting its resources, and must sooner or later crumble and become the prey of mobs and intestine feuds. You have noticed the heroic death of Jackson in Alexandria—a modern Tell whose name will not be forgotten.

We are adopting measures to provide for the destitute families of our volunteers. A battery is in process of erection on Tybee Island. Our regiment is daily expecting orders from General Lawton. All well, and unite in warmest love to you both, my dear parents. As ever,

Your affectionate son,
Charles C. Jones, Jr.

Rev. C. C. Jones *to* Hon. Charles C. Jones, Jr.[g]
Montevideo, *Thursday Evening,* May 30th, 1861
My dear Son,

Tom has just returned from the office with your letter, and we are thankful to learn that you and Ruthie and our sweet little granddaughter are all well. We are as much so as usual. I think your dear mother has greatly improved under your brother's treatment, and is much better than she was before he came down.

We received a letter from Carrie last night in which she expresses regret that their visit was cut short to you by the sickness of little Stanhope and the invalid condition of the servants. And all three of them have been fairly in bed since they reached Augusta. Stanhope has been unwell too, but is better. We regretted to part with them, but your brother thought he ought to return and see what he might do in the way of practice, unpromising as the times are; and I could not reasonably object. Something may turn up in his favor. And then Carrie is near her own family, which is a great matter in troublous times. I do not know what we should have done without your brother in our late epidemic of colds. He is an excellent physician, and of many resources; and to him I am indebted for great help in my case; and he is the only doctor who seems fully to comprehend it. It is a little remarkable—he left two cases convalescing, and not another has occurred, and our people, D.G., are enjoying their usual health.

I have received a copy of your oration and thank you for it, but had already read Mother's copy. And I must congratulate you on it as an admirable one—well conceived and well written, with some eloquent passages, and adapted to the occasion. And I can well appreciate the praises bestowed upon it well delivered before the audience that honored you with their attendance. I understand some of your best passages were impromptu and do not appear in the text. Please send a copy to Mr. W. F. Colcock; also to *Miss Sarah Jones, Charleston,* and to your Aunt *Sarah Howe, Columbia, South Carolina.*

Robert dined with us today. His family all well. Reported that Captain Lamar's Mounted Rifles were expected in Sunbury this week, to be stationed there till the Liberty Troop is mustered into service. This is all I know about it. Certain it is the Liberty Troop *cannot leave the county* for prudential reasons. The citizens meet at Hinesville on Tuesday next on *public affairs,* Governor Brown's address, etc. Want to attend if possible. Had spasm of throat after preaching on Sabbath.

The Fabian policy is the best for us. Meanwhile our every effort should be put forth thoroughly to arm and equip and ammunition every state in the Confederacy, and put everything in the best state of defense. War or no war, this is the true policy; for if we are to be independent, we must be independent, and ever keep up such a state of preparation for war that the Federal states shall never have us at an advantage. Am glad to know that Lincoln's finances are running low. Did not suppose it, since the cry has been "men and money in abundance—no lack and no stint." I cannot divest myself of the impression that there will be some effectual interposition of a kind Providence in our favor and for our repose. It may be only what I desire; but surely we are right, and whatever be our sins that call for judgment—and *they are many*—yet so far as the North is concerned, we have not sinned against it, and therefore may pray for a blessing.

It is another providence in our favor that Ellsworth, heading those miscreant Zouaves, from whom so much was expected by the Black Republican President and his party, should have been shot dead the first man! Jackson will long be remembered and honored.

What Lincoln and Scott mean to do, time only will show. We can only wait on our arms, trusting in God.

We have now a *third* confederacy—a single one, however. This honor is reserved for *Kentucky!* She has ascended to the pinnacle of state sovereignty and declared herself independent of both the other governments, and warns them both from her soil on penalties most severe to the trespasser.

But enough. Hope Mr. Anderson sold my cotton to go out in that ship that left you last week. Please ask King & Waring if they have sent out our little order of articles. Note all right. We are hoping to be at Maybank Saturday for the summer. Moving this week. . . . Mother says I am writing you a very long letter. She unites in much love to Ruthie and kisses for Julia. May every blessing of God, my dear son, ever rest on you and yours!

Your affectionate father,
C. C. Jones.

Miss Mary E. Robarts *to* Mrs. Mary Jones[t]

Marietta, Friday, May 31st, 1861

My dearest Cousins,

The days and weeks *will* slip away and leave many duties unperformed, and among them is the very pleasant one of writing you.

I received your affectionate and interesting letter just two days after the death of poor Hannah, and thought I would not answer it till I could feel more cheerfully; for you know how one feels when one of their household is removed and laid in the cold and silent grave. Her protracted illness of eleven months engrossed much of our time, and was a constant cause of anxiety. Still I had a hope that she would recover till the last month of her life. She then became decidedly worse, and suffered so much that I despaired of her recovery and became resigned to her death.

In those last weeks her sufferings were acute, and the nursing a painful duty. It took Sam and Peggy two hours in the morning and the same in the evening to attend to her and make her comfortable, and they both began to feel the effects of lifting her, and almost broke down. But they did it cheerfully, and we rewarded them for it. Besides this there was not an hour in the day but she was ministered to by one of us. And I must here mention what an assistance my dear little Ellen was to me. She took charge of the doctor's prescriptions, administered every dose of medicine herself, helped her from the table and carried her some of every nice thing she could get, and read the Bible to her every day and talked to her. Hannah was always cheerful and patient; never complained or murmured. Sometimes she would cry when her sufferings were very great and say: "I can't be with you all much longer!"

On Sabbath morning she was taken worse, so that we did not go to church; but when she heard the bells ringing she said: "Oh, Miss Ellen, you ain't going to leave me?"

I said: "No, Hannah, none of us are going to church. We are all near you; but I hope the Saviour is near you too."

She said: "Yes, ma'am."

I then read her the 51st Psalm, and she would raise her dying head at all the penitential prayers and say: "Oh, yes! Oh, my!"

I prayed with her and then sent for Mr. Palmer. He conversed with her; said: "Hannah, are you afraid to die?"

She said: "Oh, no, sir!"

He then repeated the 23rd Psalm and prayed with her. She thanked him and told him good-bye.

I said: "Hannah, Mother wishes to come and see you, but we persuaded her not."

She said: "Tell Missis I would be glad to see her, but she is old and feeble; she had better not see me now. But I hope we shall soon meet in that happy home where I am going."

She then spoke beautifully to Sam and Peggy, calling them her kind old uncle and cousin who had waited on her "so good." She begged them to meet her in heaven.

She said: "Miss Ellen, I have a new parasol in my trunk; will you take it and keep it to remember me?"

She thanked her again, and all of us, and lingered out the night; and next morning Mother came out to see her. It was touching; and a servant of one of our neighbors was there at the time, and she said to me: "Is it not affecting to see old Mistress take leave of her dying servant and she herself spared?"

Hannah continued sensible to the very last, and could speak till within five minutes. The last thing she said: "All the time you are all doing something for me and giving me something good." In a few minutes after, she died, surrounded by a weeping group, white and black, as we all knelt in prayer at her bedside. Mr. Palmer performed her funeral service the next afternoon, and she was followed to the grave by a large number of good respectable colored people. There was not room for her to be buried by the side of her poor Aunt Clarissa, but as near as possible.

Excuse me, my dear cousin, for this detail, but you have the same sympathies for these members of our household as we have. Hannah was a great favorite with all her colored friends, and they were all very kind to her. When we lose our servants, the loss of their services is the last thing we think of; it is the shadow on our household when an attached faithful one is removed. (We regret the death of your poor old Daddy Sandy; we always thought a great deal of him.)

We heard of the death of our dear and respected friend Mrs. Mallard. I was many years associated with her: our intercourse always so pleasant, she so kind and affectionate. Do give our love and sympathy to Mr. Mallard and all her other children. It makes my heart ache for anyone who loses an aged parent. It is a great mistake to think their children do not feel it a deep bereavement to have them removed.

My dear mother is as comfortable as you could expect: feeble but not in bed, able to read, write, and sew a little. She made a shirt for one of the soldiers on Tuesday, but it fatigued her very much. So does writing. She desires much love to you and Cousin Charles; has written you lately, I believe.

We have this week been engaged working for the soldiers. The ladies have an organization—a committee to purchase, four to cut, and all the others to make garments. It is incredible how many garments can be made by machine and otherwise. We furnished three companies this week, and yesterday morning they all assembled in front of the courthouse. Rev. Mr. Baker addressed them in a most impressive manner, and every soldier was supplied with a Testament from the ladies of Marietta. Poor fellows, they then marched to the depot to the tune of "Dixie," and were followed by an immense crowd. While there they were allowed to leave the ranks to say last words to weeping mothers and sisters and perhaps sweethearts. And you could see them (many of them) with a bouquet in one hand, their other on their arms, and frequently a tear in their eye. It was a sad sight.

John and Charlie Dunwody have gone; so has Major Minton; so has Dunwody. His father and mother feel it deeply, as you may well suppose. Cousin John preached on Sabbath by request to two companies about to leave, and I have been told by those who heard it that it was solemn, affecting, and eloquent. It is to be published.

These are indeed distressing times. Hundreds of soldiers pass here every day, and news from the seat of war is anxiously looked for. Sometimes a telegram comes with startling news which puts the town in a torment, and then it is contradicted the very next day. All eyes are turned to Virginia now, and my constant prayer is that the Lord would turn the edge of the sword before many of our noble sons fall, and that peace may soon be restored to our homes. I feel that we have nothing to expect from the tender mercies of the enlightened North, for they have departed from the worship of the Living God and worship flags and union. So let us and our cause fall into the hands of God, for "great are His tender mercies." If ever a war was unrighteous, it is this. Warring upon a people who would not make an aggression on them —only ask to be let alone and to dwell peaceably in the South country, leaving them to inhabit the North. The country would have been as prosperous, our feelings as fraternal (more so than ever), if this invasion had not been made. But the Lord reigns. We comfort ourselves with this, and humble ourselves under His mighty hand. Oh, that He may enable us to do this, for of ourselves we can do nothing.

Mrs. Ardis, our kind neighbor, is in deep distress; her son Payson is in General Bonham's regiment in Virginia. So is Mrs. Glover's. Mrs. Ardis says her only comfort is that so many prayers are ascending night and day from every closet, from every family altar, from the deep recesses of every mother's heart who has a son in the war.

I feel, my dear cousin, the responsibilities of dear Charles's position, and my constant prayer is that he may be kept from "the evils that are in the world" —its snares, the dangers of position and contact with the world in its most alluring guise: that of its smiles and approval. I return thanks for his gifts, his ability for usefulness; and I can but hope that through integrity of character, sound judgment, and manly courage (moral and physical) it may please God to use him for His own glory as well as the good of his fellow men, and that He will add to those rich gifts His sanctifying grace. These are my wishes—my prayers—for him who is dear to you and to me. . . .

We have had a plenty of nice strawberries. If we had lived in Savannah and had the berries, could have sold enough to buy meat for our family. As we did not, we ate them ourselves and sent them to our neighbors. These are tight times, and our family strictly on a war footing: all superfluities docked off. If we had had the money, could have laid in a fine supply of provisions when they were cheaper. . . .

A lady from Savannah told me that Matilda Jane Harden had left her mother's house to be married to Sumner Stevens; that it was displeasing to Jane, but she told her she might be married at home but she would not witness it. I do not know Sumner Stevens lately; but what a pity the daughter should do anything to separate herself from her mother!

Another thing I heard: that our friend Sarah Maxwell had become a spiritualist. How sorry I am to hear it!

We heard from Mary Sophia yesterday. She is quite well; sends love to all of her friends. . . . Please give much love to Cousin Susan, Laura, and Mr.

Buttolph; and kiss the two sweet little boys. Also Julia's. Some of my friends will have to give me some of their grandchildren; it is a great want in my old age. . . . Love from every member of our household to you and dear Cousin Charles and Cousin William. . . . Tell Patience and all your servants howdy for us. Sam has not been well this week; sends howdy for all.

Your ever affectionate cousin,
Mary E. Robarts.

REV. JOHN JONES *to* REV. *and* MRS. C. C. JONES[t]

Rome, *Friday,* May 31st, 1861

My dear Brother and Sister,

I have unintentionally and unwillingly neglected you. Some time ago I had two attacks of chill and fever, which pulled me down astonishingly and took the red out of my face; and then succeeded the stirring events of April and onward up to the present moment.

I have been and am deeply absorbed in the great subject which commands so much of our thought and time. For the past three Sabbaths I have dwelt chiefly on the war. I first presented a summary of the causes of the war and examined the position of the South. In my second sermon I presented the evidences of God's favor to the South as manifested during the Revolution to the present. And on last Sabbath I preached by their request to the Rome Light Guards and Miller Rifles on the eve of their departure for Virginia.

The day was bright, and an overflowing audience (at least one thousand) were present. They were attracted by the occasion and their deep interest in the soldiers. Many sat in chairs in the aisles, and a number stood up during the service, which was protracted. I never witnessed such solemnity and tenderness in my life. It was a most trying position for a minister and a father. There was my own son among the volunteers, and looking very solemn and attentive. Often did I seek for heavenly wisdom and the Holy Spirit in the preparation of that sermon, that it might be a faithful message to those who might be receiving—at least from me—a final word of warning. And when the closing words were uttered, and the intimation was thrown out that some of us might soon be adopting the lamentations of David over Absalom, and that mothers would be weeping like Rachel and refusing to be comforted, there was a most painful manifestation of distress in the whole audience, and tears fell like drops of morning dew. I trust that some impressions were made by the Holy Spirit upon the unconverted soldiers.

On Monday the 27th the Light Guards left, and the Rifles on Wednesday the 29th; and weeping multitudes followed them to the cars and gave them most affectionate farewells. On Wednesday, as a tall, brawny soldier was parting with his mother, he exclaimed with tears coursing down his cheeks: "Oh, this is the hardest battle we shall fight!"

And now, dear Brother and Sister, we ask a special remembrance of our dear son. He has gone where the battle rages, and he may never return. For without a special providence a bloody war—though it be short—seems inevitable. Rumors of desperate conflicts have already reached us. And our soldiers are now in the heart of Virginia; we have heard from them at Lynchburg through a letter from one of the Light Guards, which is Dunwody's company. They were all well. Their destination is Richmond, where they will be mustered into service and will form a part of the regiment to be commanded by Colonel Bartow of Savannah. My dear Jane is distressed beyond measure. Do unite with us that the Holy Spirit may lay hold of our son and truly and speedily subdue him to Christ.

Do write us soon. It seems a long, long time since we heard from you. Our best love to all at Maxwell and Woodville, and trust they also will remember Dunwody. Love to Cousin William, Robert and Mary, and their little ones when you see them.

Your affectionate brother,
John Jones.

Janey and the little boys unite with me in best love to you both. Howdy for the servants.

J.

Hon. Charles C. Jones, Jr., *to* Rev. C. C. Jones[g]

Savannah, Saturday, June 1st, 1861

My dear Father,

I am today favored with your very kind letter of yesterday, and am truly happy to hear from you and dear Mother. Am deeply pained to know that you have recently suffered from another attack of spasm of the throat.

The knowledge of your favorable opinion of my recent address is most pleasing to me. I did extemporize during its delivery, and could not find time or memory to locate positively the spoken words—the offspring of the moment—which were there given to the passing air. You well know how these sparks are struck from the heated iron.

Ruth and little Julia went to Howard's plantation on Wednesday last on a visit of a few days. I am glad they are gone, and for this reason: the very day after they left, a little Negro of Dr. Harriss' was taken violently ill with scarlet fever and diphtheria, a throat affection which has proven very generally fatal. Neither Ruth nor our little Julia has had either of these diseases, and they are both contagious. While I write, they are momentarily expecting the demise of the poor little Negress. It is impossible for her to live through the night. Were Ruth and Julia here, my anxiety for them would be very great. In these tenement houses the diseases of your next-door neighbor are almost certain to become those of your own yard. Do you know whether any of our servants here have ever had the scarlet fever? In Ruth's present situation I am informed that disease is greatly to be dreaded.

Our regiment, with the exception of one company which is at present held as a reserve corps, has left the city. Lamar's company of Mounted Rifles has, I understand, been ordered to take post for the present at Sunbury. It has not been as yet, however, mustered into service.

Without wishing in any manner to quarrel with the orders of General Lawton, it strikes me his dispositions are to a great extent ill-judged. The theory of his operations is not correct. He has withdrawn from this city between six and seven hundred men at a time when most of all they should be here. Points exist all along the coast where an enemy might readily land. That enemy has command of the sea, and can without let or hindrance transport troops at pleasure, and by means of transports land unmolested at almost any given point. It is unnatural to suppose that Fort Pulaski, strongly built and well fortified, will be attacked when a landing equally effective can be had at other points not far distant, by means of which the fort may be taken in the rear, Savannah attacked from the land, and Pulaski, thus isolated, forced to surrender. The fact is, the Lincolnites, in full force at the Tortugas with a full navy, might any day make a demonstration upon our coast, either by land or by sea. And what at the moment have we to offer as a means of successful resistance to an invading force of four or five thousand men fully appointed and precipitated upon us unexpectedly? As it is now, the regiment is completely scattered—some at Pulaski, other companies at Thunderbolt, others on Skidaway Island, and little or no reserve in the city.

Another mistake of the generals, it appears to me, is this: the companies of our regiment are, *quoad hoc,* pretty well drilled, but there is but little familiarity with battalion and regimental movements. The men rely upon company capabilities and not upon regimental. What we need is a camp of instruction. The regiment should have now while we have the opportunity been ordered into service, and a camp of discipline organized. We would then have learned how to act in concert, and a reserve force of certainly not less than twelve hundred men (than whom no better volunteer troops can anywhere be found) be fully prepared to act promptly and efficiently and in concert wherever and whenever opportunity occurred. As it is, scattered at various points, such general discipline, concert of action, and mutual confidence have all to be subsequently acquired; and it may be that the first lesson will have to be acquired in the face of an invading foe and under the fire of advancing columns. A capital place for brave action, but a poor opportunity for perfection in regimental drill.

An isolated company here and there, with no reserve corps to support it, can do little more than watch the movements of the enemy and report his advance. What we need is a regular system of fortifications at the most accessible points along our coast, with heavy batteries well manned and reserve corps to support in the event of hostile demonstrations.

The withdrawal of a thousand men from our city just at this time gives me no little uneasiness. I am trying to get everything in trim for any emergency.

Tybee Island is now occupied by nearly one thousand regulars, as I am informed, and the battery there progresses rapidly.

We have a telegraphic rumor that fighting has commenced in Virginia. It needs confirmation.

King & Waring say that the articles ordered have already been sent. Willie and Joe Turner are both absent with the Guards.

I forgot to thank dear Mother for the army glass, which came in such admirable condition. It may serve me a good turn before long.

Do let me know, my dear father, whenever I can serve you in any way. When I called at Captain Anderson's counting room to inquire whether the cotton had been sold, I found it shut: all hands gone to the wars. Will endeavor to ascertain, however, on Monday. Our streets have lost many familiar faces by the withdrawal of our regiment. With warmest love, I am, as ever, my dear father and mother,

Your ever affectionate son,
Charles C. Jones, Jr.

A letter from Uncle John, just received, states that Dunwody has gone to Virginia with a company from Rome—as a private, I believe.

REV. C. C. JONES *to* HON. CHARLES C. JONES, JR.ᵍ

Maybank, *Friday,* June 7th, 1861

My dear Son,

We were happy to hear from you last evening that the case had terminated at Dr. Harriss' without spreading. Poor little sufferer! You have had scarlet fever, but I think neither of your servants. Ruthie must be careful; but should she take it, in God's providence, remember that thousands have it, old and young, and are spared, and therefore do not despond. And thousands never take it.

When I think of the *realities* of life, my dear son—sickness and its solemn issues—I long, long for your conversion, that you may be the priest and spiritual stay of your own dear family, and have yourself a God and Saviour to go to and trust in and fear not; for even death is vanquished by our Lord. Let neither business nor pleasure nor cares of any kind cause you to neglect so great salvation. All else is perishing.

We find the change to Maybank very pleasant. Your sister and the children and Miss Kitty Stiles are now with us; and wish all our children and grandchildren were with us. I greatly desired to go down and see you and Ruthie and Julia before moving, but was so unwell that I feared to venture; and you must take the will for the deed. All on the Island well and doing well. And all in the house unite in much love to Ruthie and yourself and kisses for Julia. Embrace an opportunity by Mr. McDonald to send you this hasty line today; may go down tomorrow.

Your ever affectionate father,
C. C. Jones.

P.S. Will you please ask Dr. Axson if he has a copy of Lardner's *Credibility of the Gospel History* in his library? If not, Mr. Porter. If not, is there a copy in their knowledge in the city? It is in eight or ten volumes. My copy was burnt up, and expected to replace it sometime this summer, when I should need to refer to it; but the state of the country forbids it until our ports are open to England. We must import our books direct, and pay no more toll and high tariff.

C. C. J.

Meeting at Hinesville: committee of safety appointed. The assessment of the governor for support of the government and a contingent fund for support of families of such as may go to the war out of the county to be *raised by general tax on the county.* Best way. Nothing done further. Was not able to go to the meeting; report through Rev. D. L. Buttolph.

C. C. J.

MRS. MARY JONES *to* HON. CHARLES C. JONES, JR.[g]

Maybank, Friday, June 7th, 1861

Please say to dear Ruth that I will send the flannels next week. My heart is with her especially at this time, and wish my presence could be also. Nothing but your dear father's extreme feebleness prevents my leaving him. Do advise us constantly of the state of her health. I wish she could be with us in her approaching trial, that we might render her every attention in our power. I hope she will be prudent for the next two or three weeks, living plainly and taking an occasional dose of cooling medicine, looking well to the state of her digestion. Some persons derive great benefit from drinking flaxseed tea daily, taken cold; and to make it palatable she could add lemon juice. (This part of the letter is for her eye.)

We long to see you all. Had you not best send us Julia at least? Did you give my order to Lathrop for the soldiers' garments? With warmest love,

Ever, my dearest son, your affectionate mother,

M. J.

HON. CHARLES C. JONES, JR., *to* REV. *and* MRS. C. C. JONES[g]

Savannah, Monday, June 10th, 1861

My dear Father and Mother,

Ruth has returned after her short visit to Amanda looking pretty well. She suffered one day from an acute attack, but was soon relieved.

I presume you have observed the appointment of Judge Jackson as a brigadier general in the Confederate service. It is a position he has long and most ardently desired, and I doubt not when the hour of combat comes he will do the states no little service.

That hour must soon arrive. Sincerely do I trust and believe that the God of Battles will in that day send the victory where it of right belongs. I cannot bring my mind to entertain even the impression that a God of justice and of truth will permit a blinded, fanatical people, who already have set at naught all rules of equality, of right, and of honor; who flagrantly violate the inalienable right of private liberty by an arrogant suspension of the privilege of habeas corpus, a writ of right than which none can be dearer to the citizen—and that in the face of judicial process issued by the Chief Justice Taney, renowned for his profound legal attainments, respected for his many virtues and high position, and venerable for his many useful labors and constitutional learning; who set at defiance the right of private property by seizing Negroes, the personal chattels of others, without offer of remuneration or consent of the owner; who permit their mercenaries to trifle at will with private virtue; who trample under foot sacred compacts and solemn engagements; who substitute military despotism in the place of constitutional liberty; and who without the fear of either God or man in their eyes recklessly pursue a policy subversive of all that is just and pure and high-minded—to triumph in this unholy war. We have our sins and our short-comings, and they are many; but without the arrogance of the self-righteous Pharisee we may honestly thank God that we are not as they are. Should they be defeated in this fearful contest, how fearful the retribution! Who can appreciate the terrors of this lifted wave of fanaticism when, broken and dismayed, it recoils in confusion and madness upon itself? Agrarianism in ancient Rome will appear as naught in the contrast.

You will observe that I have issued a proclamation requesting the citizens of Savannah to abstain from their ordinary engagements on Thursday next, the day set apart by the President as a day of fasting and prayer, and with one consent to unite in the due observation of the day. You may also notice an anonymous communication in our city papers signed "Citizen," in which I recommend that the suggestion in reference to the taking up of a collection in all places of public worship on that day for the benefit of our army and of our government should meet with a generous, practical, and patriotic adoption. If this plan be pursued generally on that day throughout these Confederate States, the amount received will be large, and the fund thus realized will prove most acceptable to the present finances of the government. The idea is a good one, and should be everywhere carried into effect. I intend myself conscientiously to observe the day. We should all do so.

We are kept very much in the dark with reference to the true movements of our army in Virginia, and it is proper that this should be so. President Davis' presence inspires great enthusiasm and confidence. He appears to be in every respect the man raised for the emergency. At once soldier and statesman, he everywhere acknowledges our dependence upon and our hope in the guiding influence and the protection of a superintending Providence. I regret to know that his health is feeble. In the event of his death, where would we look for a successor?

The Central Railroad Company have declared a semi-annual dividend payable on and after the 15th inst. of five percent. Very acceptable to all stockholders at the present. I send by this post a copy of Judge Jackson's recent eulogy upon the life and character of the Hon. Charles J. McDonald.

We are all well, and unite, my dearest parents, in warmest love to you both. As ever,

Your affectionate son,
Charles C. Jones, Jr.

What was done at Hinesville last Tuesday?

REV. C. C. JONES *to* HON. CHARLES C. JONES, JR.ᵍ

Maybank, *Monday,* June 17th, 1861

My dear Son,

I embrace a moment to write to acknowledge your last favors. Hope your dear wife and child are with you now, and your home is more cheerful and happy. We are all, through divine mercy, in good health. Your sister and Miss Kitty Stiles have been paying us a most pleasant visit; leave us the last of this week. The little children interest us a great deal, and we long to see Julia.

Your responsibilities are very great, and energy and decision and wisdom and justice must characterize your administration. You have been enabled to succeed so far, and I trust the Lord will be with and bring you successfully to the end. It is positively difficult for a man to believe—to realize —the condition of our country. The sun has never shone *on the like before!*

Chief Justice Taney's exposition of the Habeas Corpus Act and Lincoln's usurpation is exceedingly fine. It is as clear as a bell: his style eminently legal. It forms a graceful close to his term of office, if he should go out. Yet the fanatical Northern people will pay no manner of respect to it.

Gilbert has come for the letter, and I must abruptly close. Mother sends much love to Ruthie and yourself, and many kisses for Julia.

Your ever affectionate father,
C. C. Jones.

P.S. Your mother inquires if you ever received her letter enclosing Adeline's certificate of membership and dismission to the Independent Church, Savannah. She fears you never did, as you have never mentioned it.

MRS. MARY JONES *to* HON. CHARLES C. JONES, JR.ᵍ

Maybank, *Tuesday,* June 18th, 1861

My dear Son,

Robin has just arrived bringing the box of books, for which your father is very much obliged; and I embrace the opportunity of sending by him a few little articles of flannel for dear Ruth. There are some other little articles which I hoped to have completed and sent at the same time, but the demands upon time have been so varied and constant I have not been enabled to complete them. The flannel she may want soon. That God will grant her deliverance from protracted sufferings, and make her the joyful mother of a perfect babe, and spare her life and restore her speedily to usefulness in her family, the church, and community is my daily prayer. As soon as possible I hope she will come out and spend some time with us. We long to see our dear little granddaughter, and wish she was here now with her little cousins, who would love and amuse her very much.

We moved down on Saturday two weeks. Miss Kitty Stiles and Daughter came down early the following week, and we have had a delightful visit. Today they are at the Point. . . . In addition to other matters your sister and myself have molded and made up about a hundred and twenty-five or a hundred and fifty bullets and cartridges for Joe's carbine, in case he is called into service with the Liberty Independent Troop, of which corps you know he is now a member. . . . By the last mail we received letters from Carrie and himself. Both she and Stanhope are suffering still from coughs. I feel uneasy about them.

Your father has not recovered from the exhaustion consequent upon preaching at Midway. He is very feeble, and suffers from his throat and pains in his chest. I hope after a while that rest and our sweet Island atmosphere, with God's blessing, will restore him to his usual strength and comfort.

Your father has ridden to see your uncle and consult with him about a singular affair. Last evening we sent Gilbert to Montevideo; he returned early this morning, making the following statement: *Jackson* was sent by Cato very early yesterday morning (Monday) to go throughout the pasture and report if all things were right. As he was going through a piece of brushwood back of Dogwood Swamp he came suddenly upon two white men lying down, two others coming up immediately. They asked him to whom he belonged, where his owner was, who took care of the place—all of which he answered in great alarm. They then told him to pass on his way, but to tell no *white person* that he had seen them. He says he kept on as quietly as he could, but as soon as he was out of their sight he ran home and informed Cato; and they sent immediately for Mr. McDonald, who got one or two men from the Boro and some of our Negroes and made search for them without discovering anyone. Jackson describes them as being dressed in caps and clothes alike and looked somewhat like soldiers. He was so frightened he did not see if they had guns. It certainly is a strange matter, and in these war times must be looked into. We are dealing with an enemy whose aim is our destruction by all or any means. Your father has just come in and reproves me for telling the strange story. I know you will receive it for what it is worth. Some suggest they may be deserters.

I got Mr. McDonald to make trial of the carbine. He stood in the front piazza and sent a ball into the *old cedar tree* (the target tree) upon the lawn *six inches deep*. I had the ball bored out and measured the depth of the hole.

We observed the day of fasting and prayer with our whole household both at Montevideo and Maybank, and presume they did the same at Arcadia. We were very much pleased with your proclamation and the piece signed "Citizen," but do not know if any contributions were taken up in the county.

I do not think you could have received my letter written before leaving Montevideo. It contained a certificate for Adeline of church membership to connect herself with Dr. Axson's. Please let me know if you did do so.

It is time for Robin to start, and I must close this hurried scrawl. Friends are all well on the Island. Your father joins me in best love to Ruth and yourself and kisses for our dear little granddaughter.

Ever, my dear son, your affectionate mother,
Mary Jones.

Our Confederate flag now floats in the Atlantic breeze upon the bay in Sunbury, and "the deserted village" presents a novel sight: white tents upon the plain, all the military arrangements of camp life, officers in command, soldiers on duty, horses ready for service. Two eight-pounders have been taken from the old fort in perfect preservation. They ring like bell metal, and are said to be French pieces. Captain Lamar intends to have them mounted.

I shall feel so anxious about dear Ruth that I hope you will write us as often as you can.

Your father has just written Captain Winn. I presume there will be a thorough search.

Hon. Charles C. Jones, Jr., *to* Rev. *and* Mrs. C. C. Jones[w]
Savannah, Tuesday, June 18th, 1861

My dear Father and Mother,

I am sorry to tell you that our dear little Julia is suffering from scarlet fever. She was very restless all last night with fever, which continues hot and high today. Her little head appears to be unaffected, as she talks and remains quite sensible. Ruth is greatly distressed, and filled with fearful apprehensions. I try to make her look on the bright side of the future. Her heart is so completely bound up in the life, the health, and the happiness of this our dear little daughter that any distress or indisposition affects her very sensibly. I never have seen such devotion as she has and bears for Julia; it has been a marvel to me for many days. The tender love which a mother cherishes for her child—at once so pure, so disinterested, so self-sacrificing—is perhaps the holiest emotion of which this fallen human nature is capable. Dr. Harriss hopes that the attack may not prove very severe. Most of the cases—and there have been many in the city this season—have proved manageable, yielding to treatment. We ardently hope for the best.

I have sent George for Mrs. Hall, that she may be with us and relieve Ruth as much as possible—or rather, as much as she will suffer herself to be relieved. I believe none of our servants have had this fever. Nothing new in the city. With warmest love to you both, my dear parents, in which we all unite, I am, as ever,

Your affectionate son,
Charles C. Jones, Jr.

Did you receive the box of books forwarded yesterday by Stepney?

IV

Mrs. Mary S. Mallard *to* Mrs. Mary Jones[t]

Maybank, *Saturday,* June 22nd, 1861

My dear Mother,

We were rejoiced last evening to hear of your safe arrival and dear little Julia's improvement. I hope she is quite out of danger now, and that she will soon be well. Captain Winn was kind enough to send Brother Charlie's note down last night. The servant came just as we were going to bed. I was very much startled, fearing little Julia was worse; but we were greatly cheered to know she was better. . . .

Yesterday and today have been the warmest I have felt this season. The heat has been intense. The thermometer stood at 95° today, and we heard it was as high as 99° yesterday in Sunbury. I neglected to look here.

Uncle Henry spent last night with us. He had dined with Captain Lamar, and I believe carried a lamb and some vegetables to the soldiers. He says Captain Lamar told him the people of Liberty had been so kind to him that he would love them all the days of his life.

Little Mary has just come in, and says: "Do tell my dear danma that I send my love to her and want her to send me the candy now, and I send my howdy to her." She has made frequent inquiries about you and *chère amie.*

I have been busily engaged in finishing the cartridges, and was very glad my occupation called me in the basement, for it was so much cooler than any other portion of the house. I have finished all—a hundred and twenty-five in number.

Today was so warm that Rex spent a good part of his time in the horse trough.

Father has felt the heat very much, and was very much debilitated by it this morning. I will try and take good care of him, and will stay as long as you wish to be absent.

I feel very anxious about Ruthie, and hope she will be spared the scarlet fever. Do give her much love and my best wishes. I hope she will be spared great and protracted suffering. I know it must be a great comfort to Brother Charlie to have you there. Give much love to him also, and kiss little Julia for me.

Mom Patience has just brought me two dollars and Miley's measure for a pair of shoes. She would like heels; and if any money is left, please bring some hickory stripe. If you are able to go out, will you get for me, dear Mother, some pretty chintz for a bedspread? I would like a light ground and something that can wash. Don't trouble yourself with this unless you feel able to go out, for I know you will have fatigue enough without walking in the sun. We deal at Nevitt's, so please get Mamie's stockings and the calico there.

Pulaski is waiting to go, so I must close, with kisses from your little grandchildren, and love from us all.

Your affectionate daughter,
Mary S. Mallard.

REV. C. C. JONES *to* MRS. MARY JONES[t]

Maybank, Saturday, June 22nd, 1861

My dear Wife,

I had written a page to you, and Daughter sent up her letter to me with this space, and on reading find she has said all I had written and more too. So will add no more. But much love to you and to Ruthie and Charles, and kisses for the dear little patient. Do get something to make me a couple of *thin waistcoats.*

Your ever dear husband,
C. C. Jones.

HON. CHARLES C. JONES, JR., *to* REV. C. C. JONES[w]

Savannah, Sunday, June 23rd, 1861

My dear Father,

Dear Mother suffered from fever last night, but is better this morning, and hopes so soon as the medicine has accomplished its desired effect that she will be entirely relieved.

We trust that our dear little Julia is better, although what the final result will be is known only to Him in whose hands are the issues of life and of death. We hope for the best, and the attending physician thinks that the severity of the attack is well-nigh overpassed.

With our warmest and united love, I am, as ever,

Your affectionate son,
Charles C. Jones, Jr.

HON. CHARLES C. JONES, JR., *to* REV. C. C. JONES[w]

Savannah, Monday, June 24th, 1861

My dear Father,

Mother is quite relieved from her attack of fever, and we trust she will have no return of it. Julia, we hope, is somewhat better this morning. The fever appears to be abating somewhat, leaving the little sufferer very prostrate, however.

In consequence of the amount of electricity along the line of the telegraph between Charleston and Augusta last evening, we received no telegrams, the operators not being able to communicate. We are hourly in anticipation of startling accounts from Virginia. All the indications point to a general and very sanguinary battle. May the God of Battles send us the victory in that day!

All unite in warmest love. As ever,

Your affectionate son,
Charles C. Jones, Jr.

Hon. Charles C. Jones, Jr., *to* Rev. C. C. Jones[w]
Savannah, *Tuesday,* June 25th, 1861

My dear Father,

Ruth was this morning at nine o'clock delivered of a fine little daughter. Her previous sufferings were not protracted, but after the birth of the child she was brought to death's door in consequence of the failure of the womb to contract, and the enormous effusion of blood. This has been stopped, but she lies very weak. Dr. Harriss thinks that the danger is overpassed, but she will have to remain perfectly quiet for hours to come.

Julia, we hope, is better. The febrile action is diminished somewhat, but she continues quite restless. I do not know what we would have done in the absence of dear Mother. She is better this morning, and I sincerely trust that her exertions may not induce a return of her fever.

We all unite in warmest love. As ever,

Your affectionate son,
Charles C. Jones, Jr.

1 P.M.

Rev. C. C. Jones *to* Mrs. Mary Jones[t]
Maybank, *Wednesday,* June 26th, 1861

My dear Wife,

My apprehensions were realized: I feared the long and hot ride, first in the carriage and then in the cars, would prove too much for you. But I am truly happy to learn by Charles's notes of the 23rd, 24th, and 25th that you had had no return of fever. May it please God to restore you speedily!

And so you were just in time to aid in the care of the little patient, and to welcome your third granddaughter! How opportune! Our prayers have been heard. We shall be anxious to know that Ruthie is well over it, for Charles writes she was extremely ill immediately after. I wish Joe was nearer to his brother, though he is distant but a few hours after all. He is a most excellent and prompt physician. Do present Ruthie my hearty congratulations, and many kisses of welcome to my little nameless granddaughter. And say to Mrs. Hall that she must take the same good care of it she did of Julia. Remember: if you have any more fever, I shall come down and nurse you.

The weather has been intensely hot: Saturday 95° and Sunday 99° in the entry—figures I never saw reached at Maybank before. Three showers for three successive evenings; last evening a fine one. Think it was general. Greatly needed.

All well on the Island. Our little ones afflicted with the heat. Daughter is great company and a great comfort to me in your absence. We try to get along as well as we can. I keep the little fry busy within and without doors to let things look cared for when you come back.

We are invited to witness the marriage ceremony of Miss Matilda Jane Harden to Mr. T. Sumner Stevens in Walthourville Presbyterian Church tomorrow evening. And this is the greatest news we have on hand to send you.

Our letters come to Dorchester every evening this week, where we send Tom for them, by an arrangement made with Robert, who is there for the week. His father is no better. . . . Daughter sends a great deal of love to you and to Brother Charlie and Sister Ruthie, with her congratulations on the birth of their little daughter. Shall write to Charles. Kiss Julia for Grandpa. Do write me and let me know how you are, and all in the house. Time for Tom to go. I remain, my dear wife,

Your ever affectionate husband,
C. C. Jones.

REV. C. C. JONES *to* HON. *and* MRS. CHARLES C. JONES, JR.[t]

Maybank, *Wednesday*, June 26th, 1861

My dear Son and Daughter,

I congratulate you both and unite with you in thanksgiving to our Heavenly Father for His great mercy in making you a second time the living parents of a living and a perfect child. Receive it as His gift; and may your lives be spared to train it up for His honor and glory, which will bring the greatest happiness both to parents and child. Your responsibilities are increasing: two precious immortal beings are now committed to your trust. And God only can by His grace enable you to fulfill that trust. May both be spared! What pleasant and happy companions will the two little sisters make for each other! Am so happy Mother is with you; but was distressed to hear she had been sick.

Your Uncle William was exceedingly pleased to hear the good news of the little stranger this morning. Daughter sends her hearty congratulations. Write us daily, and keep us advised how you all are. The recovery from scarlet fever, you know, is generally quite slow, and Julia will require much care. Kiss the two little ones for me, and their mother also, with my love. I am, my dear son and daughter,

Your affectionate father,
C. C. Jones.

Do take *good care* of Mother.

Hon. Charles C. Jones, Jr., *to* Rev. C. C. Jones[w]

Savannah, *Wednesday,* June 26th, 1861

My dear Father,

By God's blessing we hope that Ruth and Julia are both better this morning. The little infant is doing very well. Dear Mother has endured much fatigue, but is resting this morning, and we trust will after a refreshing sleep feel restored. We are more than grateful to her for her great kindness. Her tender attentions to dear little Julia have been unceasing and most valuable.

The presence of these delightful showers will, we hope, produce a beneficial change in the health of the city. We all unite in warmest love. As ever,

Your affectionate son,

Charles C. Jones, Jr.

Hon. Charles C. Jones, Jr., *to* Rev. C. C. Jones[w]

Savannah, *Thursday,* June 27th, 1861

My dear Father,

Little Julia had a more comfortable night than she has had for some time. Her fever has somewhat increased this morning, but we hope that a good God will preserve her precious life. No decided change has as yet occurred. Ruth seems tolerably well—perhaps as well as we might reasonably expect under the trying circumstances. Dear Mother enjoyed an excellent night's rest, and feels quite well this morning. All unite in warmest love. As ever,

Your affectionate son,

Charles C. Jones, Jr.

Ruth calls her little infant (who appears to be getting along very well) *Mary* after her grandmother.

Mrs. Mary Jones *to* Rev. C. C. Jones[t]

Savannah, *Monday,* July 1st, 1861

My dear Husband,

I trust our letter of Saturday may not induce you to come in; I feel that it would be attended with great injury to yourself and could do the sick no good. Charles is much better today; Ruth more comfortable, though still in a very critical condition. Little Julia lies extremely ill: little or no change. If she was not a child of vigorous constitution, I should utterly despair of her recovery. Joe is much worn by nursing and anxiety. The responsibility is now mainly cast upon him, although the *cases* belong to Dr. Harriss, with Drs. Arnold and Sullivan in consultation. Yesterday prayer was offered in both of our churches for this afflicted family. May the Lord in mercy hear and answer!

Do not feel uneasy about me. I must close, with best love for yourself and Daughter, and kisses for the dear children, and howdy for the servants. I should be glad to have a *dozen* chickens (not more) and a few eggs and a little fresh butter sent in. The chickens could be sent in the bird cage. In haste,

Your ever affectionate wife,
Mary Jones.

REV. C. C. JONES *to* MRS. MARY JONES[g]

Maybank, *Monday,* July 1st, 1861

My dear Wife,

Your letter of this morning is just at hand by Gilbert (11 P.M.), and am distressed at the afflictions which lie upon our dear children. We received no letter on Saturday; none ever came. I will send in the morning the chickens in the bird cage and some fresh butter and all the eggs we can collect by the passenger train, with a note to the conductor or express agent to have the things sent immediately up to the house on arrival. Do not fail to write by *tomorrow's mail out in the afternoon,* and we will get the letter from the Boro here at 10 P.M. And whatever you want can be sent down any day.

Am truly glad and thankful to know that our dear son Joe is with you. I have great confidence in his skill and care. And may it please our Heavenly Father to direct the consultations of the physicians aright, and bless the means to the recovery of our dear son and daughter and little granddaughter, and so in mercy hear the prayers of many on their behalf, and on behalf also of you, who have the great care and responsibility of nursing. What may a day bring forth? The Lord is dealing with us, and it is all right, and we can do no more than submit to His hand and wait His will.

Daughter and I want to know what is the matter with Charles, as we did not get your letter. Write us particularly about all tomorrow. Nothing prevents my attempting to go down tomorrow but my *weakness,* which seems to increase, and the fear that I would but add another invalid and increased care to all you now have. I hope through divine mercy there may be no occasion for me to make the attempt.

Daughter unites in a great deal of sympathy and love to dear Ruthie and to our dear son and little Julia. Kiss them all for us. And love to our dear son Joe. Hope he left Carrie and our little Stanhope better if not entirely recovered. Kiss the little stranger for us. And much love to you, my dear wife. I feel in such a time as this my affliction, that prevents me from being with you and helping in time of trouble. May you have strength for the day from on high!

We are getting everything fixed and ready tonight, that Gilbert may be off very early in the morning. It is going on to one o'clock.

Your ever affectionate husband,
C. C. Jones.

Will send all the chickens the bird cage can hold. Fear we shall not be able to get an egg tonight: none on the place. Will get and send some.

Tuesday Morning. Thought the shortest way would be to send Gilbert down and return this evening. Write by him.

MRS. MARY JONES *to* REV. C. C. JONES[t]

Savannah, *Tuesday,* July 2nd, 1861

My dear Husband,

Our little sufferer died this morning about nine o'clock. The physicians decide that there must be an early interment—this evening about seven o'clock. From the nature of the disease and poor Ruth's situation this is necessary. She lies extremely ill—often wandering but mostly unconscious of surrounding objects, but rational when roused, and able to nurse her little babe. Joe thinks her in a very critical situation. She has as yet no symptoms of scarlet fever, but decided ones of puerperal fever. The infant, too, has ulcerated sore throat and a little rash, which we hope may not move into scarlet fever. Charles has been very sick with sore throat and fever—threatened almost with suffocation; can now scarcely speak or swallow. Truly the hand of our God is upon us. Oh, that we may feel and act aright under the rod! We can only have prayer offered ere our dead is removed; Ruth is too ill for any service.

I am thankful you did not come in. And such is the state of the family here I know not when I will be able to leave them. Pray for us: God alone can sustain us. Joe is not well. All unite with me in tenderest love, and kisses for the children.

Ever your affectionate wife,
Mary Jones.

MR. HENRY H. JONES *to* REV. C. C. JONES[t]

Savannah, *Tuesday,* July 2nd, 1861

My dear Brother,

At the request of Sister Mary and my nephew Joseph I write to inform you of the distressed condition of the family of your eldest son Charles Colcock. After a painful illness of the most violent character, the daughter of the latter (little Julia) breathed her last at eight o'clock A.M. of today. The disease was scarlet fever of the most virulent type. Ruth, the mother, is also critically ill with puerperal fever, attended with occasional delirium. At this time she is rather more comfortable, but with no decided change for the better. Your son Charles is up and much better, but greatly distressed in mind. Sister Mary and Joe, though much fatigued, are pretty well, though both have a little sore throat. The babe is quite unwell with sore throat, though no decided symptoms of scarlet fever have developed themselves. Of course poor Ruth is kept in ignorance of her painful bereavement, and kept in a separate chamber to avoid if possible any danger from contagion. Joe's presence is an unspeakable comfort to them all. I have been assisting him in making the necessary arrangements for the funeral and burial. Mr. Porter will perform the services in a private manner sometime this afternoon, and the little remains will be deposited for the present in the Neely family vault.

I regret that intelligence just received through Dr. Stevens of the extreme illness of one of my Negroes, and the indisposition of my dear wife and youngest child, render my return home today indispensable. May a merciful God spare the wife and surviving child of your dear son, and sanctify to the parents the terrible bereavement they have sustained! With much love,

Your affectionate brother,
Henry H. Jones.

Rev. C. C. Jones *to* Hon. Charles C. Jones, Jr.[g]

Maybank, Tuesday, July 2nd, 1861

My dear Son,

Gilbert has just come, and I cannot express to you my sympathy and grief at the loss of dear little Julia and the extreme illness of your affectionate and devoted wife, my dear Ruth.

Sweet child! A child of the covenant, and removed, we trust and believe, to be with God. She is not dead, but sleepeth. We must think of her as with the spirits of the redeemed in heaven. Your heart is torn; you feel what you never felt before. It is a great affliction; I wish I knew how to bear it for you. That sweet child was given you by the Lord, and *He has removed her*. Acknowledge His right, and humbly pray to Him for submission to His will, and that He may bless the stroke to your own eternal welfare. *He* alone can bind up the brokenhearted.

I feel the greatest anxiety for Ruthie, and am so glad your dear mother and brother are with you in this hour of your sorest trial. I am on the point of coming to you, and what to do I know not. Mother says it will be best for me not to do so. Nothing makes me hesitate but my physical weakness and inability to render any aid, and the probability of my adding another care to all. Am not as well as common on account of a recent throat attack, and having it now in an inflamed state. If I do wrong in not undertaking the journey for the reasons given, I hope I may be pardoned. It is my desire to spend and be spent for my dear children, and it adds to my affliction that the ability to do all I desire is no longer mine. Assure yourself, my dear son, of the deepest sympathy and affection of your own father. I am distressed for dear Ruthie. God in mercy to you and to the little one and to us all bring her through this extreme illness! Our hope is alone in Him. You have the best medical attendance and the best nursing, but the issue is with God. You have many prayers ascending for you. Your sister is now writing you, and will express her feelings and Robert's. Our prayers are offered for you all the day and night, that God may be with and bless you and yours.

When you can, kiss my daughter for me, and express to her my true love and sympathy in this dark hour, and my hope that her soul may find peace under all in her gracious Saviour. Kiss the baby for me. God be with and bless you, my dear afflicted son, is the prayer of

Your afflicted and affectionate father,
C. C. Jones.

REV. C. C. JONES *to* MRS. MARY JONES[g]

Maybank, *Tuesday,* July 2nd, 1861

My dearest Wife,

The sad intelligence in your note and Henry's has filled us with deep grief. Alas, the dear little sufferer! It is now all over, and nothing remains of her short pilgrimage but sweet memories of her smiling face and gentle voice and winning ways, and her trying passage through the valley of death to the bright world beyond. How comforting to believe that the Saviour has gathered this little lamb into His fold above!

My dear son! I feel for him in this dark day that has come so unexpectedly upon him, and can but hope and pray that it may be the hand of God leading him to Himself. That hand is upon us all, and with you I pray that we may be made to feel and act aright under it. I am so anxious about dear Ruthie! The Lord spare her life, if it be His holy will!

I do not know what to do. Have just written my dear afflicted son and stated the reason why I have not come down. Still my mind is not satisfied. Daughter thinks I ought not to go. You say you are thankful I did not come.

Daughter says she will come down any time you may need her. She is writing her brother.

We send four dozen eggs in the blue basket and your underclothing in the little black portmanteau by Mrs. King's Cain, who goes in to Savannah tomorrow morning. You did not mention anything about your clothes in your note, or they would have been sent by Gilbert. The articles sent are three chemises, one petticoat, one gown and cape, one pair drawers, two calico dresses, two pair stockings, four handkerchiefs, two aprons, and two collars, and one flannel sacque.

Audley comes out tomorrow, and if you can write by him we will be very glad. If not by him, please write by the mail. *Perhaps you had better write by the mail anyhow* and let us know *particularly* how Ruthie and the baby are.

My dear son Joe, am so happy you are with your brother in his deep sorrows. I know how you feel for him, and trust God may bless your skill and spare his own life and the life of his dear wife. Hope you left Carrie and Stanhope better if not well. Do take care of your sore throat and Mother's. So soon as it may please God to relieve the sick, they should change the air. If you can come out and see us for a day or so, it would be a great happiness to see you. Nothing but my weakness and recent throat attack keeps me from coming down to your brother.

It is going on to one o'clock July 3rd, and I must close and get all ready for Gilbert to go over to Mrs. King's very early. Daughter sends with me love to you and Brother. Do not fail to write, and don't forget to say how you yourself are. The Lord watch over and bless and keep you up in mind and body!

Your ever affectionate husband,
C. C. Jones.

Mrs. Mary Jones *to* Rev. C. C. Jones[t]

Savannah, *Wednesday,* July 3rd, 1861

My dear Husband,

Cain has just arrived with your very acceptable cargo. Thanks to you and Daughter and all the dear friends.

Last evening at five o'clock Mr. Porter came. The doors were closed in the dining room, and prayer offered. We took our precious little body—Joe and Mr. Porter with it in one carriage, Mrs. Harriss, Mrs. Neely, and myself and Susan her nurse in another—and took her to the cemetery, and there laid the remains in Mr. Neely's vault.

But my time for writing is short. Dear Ruth still lies *very ill.* No change for the better; all the symptoms very distressing. The doctors forbid the infant to receive any more nourishment from her; so we must feed the poor little one, which has been more quiet today. Ruth says ask you to pray for her every moment that you are awake.

Charles is exceedingly feeble and cast down. I am very anxious about him. Pray for us. Do not come down: it would only increase our trouble. With best love to Daughter and all friends,

Your affectionate wife,
Mary Jones.

Mrs. Susan M. Cumming *to* Rev. C. C. Jones[t]

Point Maxwell, *Thursday,* July 4th, 1861

My dear Brother,

I have decided to go to Savannah. Mr. Buttolph will go with me to the station. I send Dick to get any note or anything you may wish to send, so as to save the distance and arrive at the station in time. He will meet us at the causeway. I shall tell Charles your great desire was to come, but that we had done all we could to dissuade you from it. With much love to you and Mary,

Your affectionate sister,
S. M. Cumming.

Rev. C. C. Jones *to* Mrs. Susan M. Cumming[g]

Maybank, *Thursday,* July 4th, 1861

My dear Sister,

Am glad you are going down on account of the afflicted ones. Please see that we hear by mail daily. Audley has a boy that comes out today by whom you can write. He will call at Charles's. I do not think I can stand the fatigue. And you see what Mary says. And Joe writes the same. Do tell my dear son how much we sympathize with him, and that my heart is with him and his all the time. Give my love to dear Ruthie. Tell her I will pray for her all the time. . . . May God hear our prayers and spare her life!

I write seeing dimly through tears. Kiss the stranger for me. Thank my dear wife for her letter. The Saturday letter came to hand this morning. Daughter is not awake. Love to Brother Buttolph.

Your ever affectionate brother,
C. C. Jones.

Rev. C. C. Jones *to* Mrs. Eliza G. Robarts[t]

Maybank, *Thursday,* July 4th, 1861

My dear Aunt,

Time has gone rapidly since your valued favor was received, and we have been happy to hear from you through letters received from Marietta lately that you are so well this summer.

It has been so far a summer of much anxiety and of excitement on account of the unnatural, unjust, and infamous war that is waged upon us—so many going, and so much doing, and so much news from all parts of the country to hear and to read. The Lord appears to be on our side, and so far has kept back the advance of the enemy and given us the victory in almost every encounter with him. We are in His hands, and our souls must wait only upon Him. We have been sinning with the Northern people as a nation for seventy or eighty years, and now we have become two nations, and the Lord may use us as rods of correction to each other. While this is so and must be acknowledged in all humility before God, we believe and are confident that in our strife with that people we are in the right, and can commend our cause to His protection and blessing with the assured expectation that we shall eventually triumph.

We are now in affliction. My dear son's family in Savannah is a scene of sorrow. Dear little Julia, after a protracted and distressing illness of two weeks of scarlet fever, died on the 2nd. Ruthie was extremely ill immediately after the birth of her little daughter on the 25th of June, and now lies—and has been so for days—*most critically ill.* The infant not well and taken from her. And poor Charles has been dangerously ill with sore throat and fever, and we hope is better and improving. My dear wife has been down since the 21st June, a day or two after Julia was taken sick; and Joe went down on the 27th. Sister went down today. My weakness and debility of the throat has prevented my going down, and all the family with one voice say I must not attempt it, lest I suffer and add sickness upon sickness and care upon care. So I am here in a state of distress and anxiety, waiting for letters every day to let me know how it is with my dear children. Dr. Harriss is the attending physician, but Drs. Arnold and Sullivan have been called in on consultation. We are in the Lord's hands; He is dealing with us. May we be enabled by his grace to see aright, and to feel and act aright! I can but hope and pray it may please God to spare Ruthie's life and sanctify the affliction to the conversion of our dear son. It is his first affliction in his family. I know you will all sympathize with and pray for us. Daughter and her little ones are staying with me while Mother is away. All on the Island well.

Jack has just handed me this funeral invitation: "The friends and acquaintances of Mr. Thomas Mallard and family are respectfully invited to attend the funeral of the former at Midway Church tomorrow at eleven o'clock A.M. July 4th, 1861." Robert says in a note to Daughter: "My dear father left us this morning (4th) at a quarter past one o'clock, I confidently believe for a better world. He fell into a gentle sleep and yielded up his spirit to his dear Redeemer without a groan or even a sigh." The two aged saints in our Zion— so long lights to us—are now gone, and but a brief period divided from each other! I saw him on last Thursday and on Sabbath. He could not speak much. I put my mouth to his ear and said: "I hope it is all peace and comfort with your soul." He cast his eyes upon me, assented with his head, and gently pressed my hand. And we parted. No rallying place now to their large and worthy family! The Lord prepare us for our great change.

Daughter unites in much love to you, and to Cousin Mary and Lou, and to the young ladies at home, and to Sophia when you write her, and to Joe. . . . I remain, my dear aunt,

Your ever affectionate nephew,
C. C. Jones.

Rev. R. Q. Mallard *to* Mrs. Mary S. Mallard[t]

Dorchester, *Thursday,* July 4th, 1861

My darling Wife,

My dear father left us this morning at a quarter past one o'clock, I confidently believe for a better world. He fell into a gentle sleep and yielded up his spirit to his dear Redeemer without a groan or even sigh. Pray for us that our God may sanctify to us the double stroke which has fallen upon us.

I go to Savannah today to return this afternoon. I am advised against going to see your brother's family. If I could be of any assistance, I would cheerfully encounter the risk; but on account of our little ones I ought not merely for a visit of sympathy to incur the risk. I will communicate with them, however.

Let us know by the bearer of this note when you wish to come to Dorchester, and the carriage will be sent for you.

Your husband,

Robert Q. Mallard.

P.S. The funeral at Midway tomorrow at eleven o'clock A.M.

Hon. Charles C. Jones, Jr., *to* Rev. C. C. Jones[w]

Savannah, *Thursday,* July 4th, 1861

My dear Father,

I know not how to express my heartfelt thanks for your kindest and tenderest sympathies for me in this dark day when the light of life, of hope, and of joy seems wholly withdrawn, and a home of sunshine, of happiness, and of peace converted into the abode of chaos and of black ruin. I pray earnestly to God that I may recognize Him and His will in all this affliction—and that without murmuring or rebellion. Our dear little Julia is in heaven, and in all human probability my dearest wife will not long be separated from her. She never has been made acquainted with the fact of her decease. Her first intimation will be when they are united in the bonds of eternal love around the throne of God.

Just as the precious little sufferer was breathing her last, just as the last breath was escaping from her tranquil little frame, without a single groan, without a single tremor or contortion of her angelic face, I was sitting at her side; and from the eye next to me, as her spirit winged its flight to that holy and happy home where the wicked cease from trembling and the weary are at rest, started one little teardrop, pure as crystal—the only one she had shed during all her lingering and severe illness. It was her farewell to earth, and to her sorrow-stricken parent. It may have been purely accidental, but there was and is in this little circumstance a world of tenderest import which melts my soul to deepest sadness.

My dear Ruth does not improve. Brother tells me that there is little or no hope, and that she must, humanly speaking, soon die. My soul dies within me at thought of the utter wreck of cherished hopes, of present happiness, of future plans, of everything that makes life desirable. I trust that the same God who deals these heaviest blows will enable me in the depths of sorrow to acknowledge His will and to bend in humble submission to the awful dispensations. I know not what will become of me. I feel already like a smitten bark, rudderless and crewless, foundering at noon upon the high seas. I hope I am enabled already to see the error of my ways, and that through the merits of that precious Saviour who died to redeem from destruction even the vilest of sinners, God will accept the penitent prodigal and give me strength to lead a new life.

Dear Mother and Brother have been most tender and unremitting in their kindnesses. I shall never have heart enough to thank them for all their goodness. The Doctor is head and shoulders ahead of his medical brethren here; and it will be a never-failing source of consolation to me to know that my dear Ruth and Julia had the benefit of his superior skill and fraternal attentions.

Today is the anniversary of our original independence, but these weeping skies seem to be bemoaning the distracted condition of our poor country.

Saw Robert Mallard for a moment just now. Poor fellow, he also is passing through deep waters.

I am glad, my dear father, that you have not undertaken the fatigue of a visit to us just at this time. Most glad as I would be to see you now, I know all the sympathies of your generous, Christian, fatherly heart; and most sensibly do I feel them and thank you for them. I pray you, however, do not venture upon the trip. Brother, Mother, all agree in this. We all hope to see you soon. Trusting that God will grant you every needful strength and favor, I am, with warmest love to self, Sister, and little cousins,

Your affectionate and afflicted son,
Charles C. Jones, Jr.

Mother and Brother are quite well. We are truly happy to have Aunt Susan with us. She has always been little less than a mother to me.

REV. R. Q. MALLARD *to* MRS. MARY S. MALLARD[t]

Dorchester, *Thursday*, July 4th, 1861

My dear Mary,

I have just returned from the city, having successfully accomplished the business which carried me. I went with Aunt Susan to Charlie's and saw Mother and both your brothers. Charlie I found reclining in his library, still suffering from sore throat, but able to accompany me down to the front door. Mother did not seem to be well. Brother Joe looked pale, but better than I expected. The little baby is better, but our poor sister I fear will not recover. Brother Joe told me it was a hopeless case. I now almost regret that I did not go in to see her. I did not expect to be asked, and feared that seeing me might injure her.

I told our afflicted brother that I felt for him from my heart, but well knew that he needed a Power higher than man to comfort him. He seems to give Ruthie up. Oh, it is so sad an affliction that I am loath to admit its probability! "Ah, Lord God, thou hast made the heaven and the earth; is there anything too hard for thee?" Poor Charlie, he has no religion to comfort him. It is a severe discipline he is receiving. God grant that it may prove salutary!

I hope to see you tomorrow and talk over our plans. Assure dear Father of my love and heartfelt sympathy with him in his painful and trying position. I am truly glad that he did not go down to Savannah. I have but one living father and one mother now. God bless you all!

My darling, your own
Robert.

Rev. C. C. Jones *to* Mrs. Mary Jones[g]

Maybank, *Thursday,* July 4th, 1861

My dear Wife,

We have just received a note from Robert and a letter from my dear afflicted son, and my heart is sore-broken with his sorrows and the dreadful trial which seems ready to fall upon him. I trust his soul is turned in the right direction—even unto God our Saviour; and from Him I hope he will find salvation and consolation. I am unable to reply to his letter now. Dear, dear Ruthie! All day long Daughter and I have been hoping, hoping for good news of a change for the better tonight. But alas, it is not so. We have been weeping over what has come to hand, and cannot think it will be so. With God all things are possible, and we could but pray again together just now that if it were possible this cup might pass from us. What an affliction! The Lord enable us to understand it, and sanctify us under it!

Am so happy you are all with the chief mourner. He seems filled with comfort that Mother, Brother, and Aunt are with him. Would that I were with him also. Nothing but the positive opinion of all to the contrary has kept me here. If I have done wrong, may I be pardoned for it!

If dear Ruthie can receive it, express to her my fond attachment and sympathy. Kiss her for me. Tell her I have tried to fulfill her request, and we have been praying constantly for her; and I hope that she is resting upon her Saviour, and that all is peace with her. What a trial that I cannot see her! The Lord Jesus receive her spirit! Yet I cannot but hope.

My dear wife, when you do come out let me suggest that you all come out to Walthourville to Daughter's to save a long night's ride from the depot to Maybank. You will reach Walthourville early in the evening. *Should* Daughter not be at home, her key is over at Mr. Samuel Mallard's; and by sending for it everything is open to you, and Lucy and the servants are there. And then at your leisure you can come down afterwards. Daughter begs you to do so. Please write me—someone—*every mail.*

I send Tom up early in the morning with this letter to Riceboro for the mail. The clock strikes twelve. My tenderest love to my dear Ruthie and Charles, to my dear son, and to Sister. And kiss the little one for me. The Lord be with you all!

Your ever affectionate husband,
C. C. Jones.

July 5th. Daughter goes to Mr. Mallard's funeral today. Am feeling so badly, do not think I have heart or strength to go. All well.

Hon. Charles C. Jones, Jr., *to* Rev. C. C. Jones[g]

Savannah, *Friday,* July 5th, 1861

My very dear Father,

Brother tells me that he regards the case of my dear wife as more favorable today. We trust from the bottom of our hearts that God in His infinite mercy will interpose in her behalf. We are endeavoring to do for her all that human skill, care, and attention can suggest or accomplish; and we must leave the result with Him in whose hands are the issues of life and of death. I can but hope that in His great goodness He will spare her precious life.

Her bedding is now being changed, and when everything is again clean and cool, I trust that she will feel better. My heart goes out in thankfulness every hour to my dear mother and brother, and now also to Aunt Susan, for all their unwearied kindness and tender care.

All unite in warmest love. The little infant, who is named Mary after Mother, is pretty well. Hoping, my dear father, that renewed health and strength may be vouchsafed to you from on high, and with united love to Sister and little Nephew and Niece, I am, as ever,

Your affectionate son,
Charles C. Jones, Jr.

REV. C. C. JONES *to* HON. CHARLES C. JONES, JR.^g

Maybank, Saturday, July 6th, 1861

My dear Son,

Yesterday was a day of distress, and as the hours drew near for the coming of the mail, it became more intense. I retired at nine, and lay awake listening for the footsteps of the letter boy. He came; and in a few moments your sister and Robert, who had come home with her from the funeral, I heard running upstairs. The door opened, and your sister with a beaming countenance said: "Father! Good news! Good news, Father, from Sister Ruthie! Brother Joe says her symptoms are more favorable today. Here is Brother Charlie's letter." The letter was read over twice. Oh, what a burden passed off! What a mercy to us! I cannot say it was unexpected, for all day Daughter and I were entertaining *hope* that the Lord, who can quicken even the dead, would hear the many prayers offered and interpose and raise your dear wife up again. We could do no more than rejoice with trembling, and we knelt down and returned thanks to our Heavenly Father for His great mercy to us. . . . And so we retired with this blessing.

My dear son, I do trust—and have a feeling that it is so—that God is dealing mercifully with you in all this dreadful affliction. You now realize to be *true* what before was a vague, inoperative impression—that there is a God, that we are His, that He rules us by His power, that our account is with Him, that all earthly things are weak, helpless, and fading and can never meet all the necessities of our souls, that sin against God is appalling, that judgment and eternity are before us. . . . Despise not thou, my son, the chastening of the Lord. Cultivate these salutary impressions. You deserve nothing. God could take all you have away—your own life—and cast you off forever for your sins! He is calling loudly, mercifully, affectingly to you; and I pray that as you have begun to bow down under His hand and incline your ear to His call, so you will continue never to draw back. . . . I feel deeply for you in the loss of that sweet, blessed child. She cannot return to you, but you can go to her. And if her little tear fell from her eye as she parted from you, those eyes will beam with heavenly light and joy when she throws her arms around you in that better land.

Kiss dear Ruthie for me. Tell her we pray for her constantly, that I hope she is able to cast her all into the Saviour's hands, and that He will raise her up to love Him more and serve Him better all the days of her life. But I must beg her to do one thing: to remember she professes to be God's child. God is her Father; He knows what is best for her; and she must pray and say: "Father, Thy will be done."

Our united love to dear Mother and Brother and Aunt. All friends anxiously send or come every day to know what we hear from you. Robert must soon leave, and I must close. The servants all send howdy, and are much rejoiced to hear that Miss Ruthie is better. Kiss for us your little one. She is now in the place of her sister.

Your ever affectionate father,
C. C. Jones.

HON. CHARLES C. JONES, JR., *to* REV. C. C. JONES[g]
Savannah, *Saturday,* July 6th, 1861

My dear Father,

Dear Ruth is no better this morning. She spent a distressing night, and enjoyed little or no rest. She is at present a little more comfortable, and is quite rational. During her illness her mind has for a good portion of the time wandered. Her strong constitution contests the progress of the poison in her veins inch by inch; a feebler would have yielded long ago. We are doing everything that we can to prolong her precious life, and can only look to God for His blessing. We fear the worst.

The little infant is rather better this morning, and eats heartily. All well, and unite in warmest love to you, my dear father, and to Sister and Nephew and Niece. As ever,

Your affectionate son,
Charles C. Jones, Jr.

REV. C. C. JONES *to* MRS. MARY JONES[t]
Maybank, *Monday,* July 8th, 1861

My dear Wife,

Our dear son arrived at ten this evening, and our fears were all realized! Oh, how I feel for my dear son! How I longed to see that dear child once more! And she died so calmly, so peacefully. What a consolation! I cannot write now.

As you requested, Gilbert leaves very early in the morning with the carriage; but I do not think it advisable for you to attempt coming down tomorrow (the same day) on account of the *heat* and *the ride,* which for the *horses* would be some fifty miles. Your travel would be *slow,* and *very late* in the evening. A day's rest would perhaps benefit you all, and the dear little sufferer in particular. And the next day you could make an early start and get here by eleven or twelve o'clock. I have just sent Joe over with a note to Brother Buttolph to send up the buggy for Sister in the morning. And I think she will have to stay over the day also.

Tom goes up in the morning to Cato to send Peggy down, and she will be here in the afternoon. Daughter stays to see her brother when he comes down, but her little ones will be sent to Dorchester. Our love to my dear son and to Sister. Kiss the baby for us. It is going on to twelve o'clock. I long to see you, my dear wife, and learn all concerning our sad affliction. Love to Robert from us all. His wife and little ones are quite well.

Your ever affectionate husband,
C. C. Jones.

V

Mrs. Mary S. Mallard *to* Mrs. Mary Jones[t]

Walthourville, *Thursday,* July 11th, 1861

My very dear Mother,

We arrived safely today at half-past twelve. Found Mr. Mallard and all quite well. We had a clouded sky and pleasant breeze, so the heat was not at all oppressive. Mamie was so glad to get home and to see the servants that she laughed until she almost cried. She ran over the house trundling her little wheelbarrow and looking at all her toys, riding in turn her babies, marbles, etc. Charlie, seeing his sister's delight, thought there really was something amusing going on, so he "sculled himself" after his sister, laughing merrily and calling out "See da! See da!" to everything she said or did. When he went into the drawing room, he remembered the little girl with the chickens and commenced *shooing* and calling them. . . .

I wish I could have stayed with you this morning, for I feel I scarcely saw you; but my children were both so well I was afraid to have them remain too long in Dorchester, as they would have to make another change in coming here. I have thought of the dear little baby all day, and wish I could take care of it for you. I hope if it is consistent with our Heavenly Father's will its little life may be spared. I wish Brother Charlie could remain out several weeks. What will become of him when he goes back to his lonely home? I do feel so much for him, and think of him all the time. Uncle Henry thinks of going down tomorrow, as he wishes to see him before he returns to Savannah.

I have cut the coat pattern, so don't return this that I send, but please send the coat back by Uncle Henry. I thought you would rather see it on Father before cutting out his coat. If you would send it to me and mark where the buttonholes are to be made, I will make it.

Little Mary says she is so glad for the candy, and says she is "must obiced to Danma" for it. Mr. Mallard and our little ones unite with me in warmest love to Father, Brother Charlie, and yourself, and kisses for the dear little baby. Love to all at Maxwell and Woodville.

Your affectionate daughter,
Mary S. Mallard.

I will fix the mantle and send it as soon as possible. I think your things will come out on Saturday or Monday. If you could send me a skirt to measure by (by Uncle Henry) I could help you make them.

Mrs. Mary Jones *to* Mrs. Mary S. Mallard[t]

Maybank, *Wednesday,* July 17th, 1861

My dear Daughter,

James arrived in good time this morning, and I am very much obliged to you for the things; also for the mantle and collar. I have sent you what I conceive to be the best of the dress patterns; the other one is much worn in holes, but it will answer my purpose, and looks like delaine. Tell my dear little granddaughter Grandma sends a little quilt for her bed. I wanted to have quilted it this summer, but there is no prospect now. I had nothing new to bind it, but send a curtain (not old, but stained with mildew); it will answer very well, and perhaps you could make Lucy quilt it, if not run the two together. The sacque for Charlie I meant to scallop, but I really feel too weak and badly to do anything. My whole system feels prostrated. I am suffering very much from dyspepsia and pain in my side, and am as one struggling to awake from a terrible dream. Oh, for grace to realize through the sanctification of the Holy Spirit all that our Heavenly Father would teach us by these heavy bereavements! I want to live with my own death and coming eternity in view.

Our dear son left us on Monday and returned to his desolate dwelling. He said it was his duty to do so, although he knew not what would become of him. I think he realizes the solemn circumstances into which the Lord has placed him, and whilst with us was engaged in religious reading and frequent conversations with your dear father, who tried to direct his mind to the great work of repentance and faith. I know dear Robert and yourself will remember him constantly. Will not our Redeemer hear and answer us *even now?*

Our dear little babe improves. I think the emaciation has ceased. The nourishment agrees well with her, and she takes a plenty. The discharge still continues from the ear, but in other affections she is better. Sometimes very fretful. We have moved into the rooms below your father (in the smallest), so I am much more comfortably situated, and if I were better, would get pretty good rest at night; but my throat and cough keep me awake.

I have wanted to accept your offer to help me with your father's flannel coat. Have made two attempts to cut it out, but failed. I am too weak at present. I was on the bed all day yesterday.

After tea your father insisted on our riding. We went to inquire after Brother William; I did not get out of the buggy. *Matilda* and *Mr. Stevens* were there, with several of the family from Palmyra.

Your Uncle John writes: "My church have unanimously given me leave of absence for three months to visit our soldiers—particularly the 8th Regiment, to which they belong—to labor as a minister among them. I expect to leave on the 17th inst. for Richmond and Winchester. There is risk in taking my family with me, but I believe it would make Jane ill to leave her. They will return if they should be in danger." I shall feel very anxious about him.

Do return Kitty my best thanks for the things, and enclosed is her change due. . . . Pay Kitty, and buy a hat for Charlie with the rest. Father unites with me in best love to Robert and yourself and many kisses for our dear grandchildren.

Ever your affectionate mother,
Mary Jones.

REV. C. C. JONES *to* HON. CHARLES C. JONES, JR.[g]

Maybank, *Saturday,* July 20th, 1861

My dear Son,

Am happy to inform you that your dear little baby continues to improve. Her complexion is natural, and is assuming the ruddiness of healthy infancy. She has no new eruption; the old has disappeared excepting under one arm, and that is fast healing up. Nurses heartily. Everything right: sleeps soundly, and gives no more trouble at night than is common. Her only affection is that of the ears. The running of the first has much diminished; the second commenced yesterday, but is not excessive; and we hope with Mother's good care and your brother's prescriptions both will soon be well. She enjoys her warm bath every morning, takes quietly the pouring of the water on her little person, which is gaining flesh, and when Mother syringed her ears she held her head still and seemed to feel the comfort of it. We think she is a bright little thing: notices a good deal, and combines a likeness of both her sainted mother and sister, though the shape of the head favors yours. And if, by God's blessing, she continues to improve in time to come as since you left, you will scarcely know her when you see her again. She evidently had scarlet fever; her tongue, her mouth, her surface, and the affection of the ears all prove it; and now the cuticle rubs off in the bath. Your mother thinks so, and I believe it was your brother's impression also. How wonderful that she should have come through so many trials—only three weeks old last Tuesday!

Mother has been very unwell with something of a return of the attack she had in Savannah, but has kept up, and is better today, and—what is specially promising—has had a fair appetite for two days, takes the doctor's prescriptions, slacks off some of her work, and rides out every afternoon. The weather too has been pleasant, with good showers.

You are daily in our thoughts, and are with us in our conversations and in our closets and in family worship. We do feel, my dear son, more for you than we can express; and if "the oppressive silence which reigns around you and the spirit of deep desolation which broods over everything in your once happy home" and your own uncommon sorrows could be removed by your parents, it would so be done. But we are afflicted in your afflictions; and what can we do but to weep with you and for ourselves, and go with you to our Heavenly Father, from whom the afflictions have come, and pray that He who has wounded will heal us, and He that has broken will bind us up. "Is any among you afflicted? Let him pray." God is our only sure and satisfying refuge in times of trouble. . . .

If this affliction, my son, shall lead you to see and to appreciate the fact how you have been living without God, without Christ, and without hope in the world, literally worshiping the creature rather than the Creator, feeling in your prosperity that you could never be moved, and making family and fortune and friends and earthly pleasures your happiness and your trust, looking not beyond the circle of life and regardless of your immortality, making no provision for the life to come; if this affliction leads you to see how for yourself you have lived and not for God, to whom you belong, and who is entitled to and commands your supreme affection and service; if it leads you to do what you have never done before truly and faithfully, to break off all your sins by righteousness, and without the fear or favor of man acknowledge God and your Redeemer, and take Him for your Lord and portion forever; then will the affliction attain the end which I trust and believe God designs in it. And then shall arise out of the darkness and distress of your soul a light divine, peaceful, and eternal! I pray God that by his Blessed Spirit He may so seal it to you, through Jesus Christ our Lord. "The world passeth away and the lust thereof: but he that doeth the will of God abideth forever."

Mother unites in much love to you. We beg you to be careful of your health. Make George sleep near you. Tell all the servants howdy for us. Susan begs that we should "tell her master howdy for her, that she is well, and the baby is well, and sends howdy for the servants."

From your ever affectionate father and mother,
C. C. Jones.
M. Jones.

Mother says be sure and rub your throat with the iodine, and take the quinine every day.

Hon. Charles C. Jones, Jr., *to* Rev. C. C. Jones[g]

Savannah, *Wednesday,* July 24th, 1861

My dear Father,

Amid the heavy engagements which are upon me I have not had an opportunity until this moment for replying to your kind and valued letter of the 20th inst. I thank God that you are all better at Maybank, and that dear little Mary Ruth improves. There is scarcely an hour of the day that my heart does not melt in sincerest gratitude to you both, my dear parents, and rejoice that our precious little motherless infant in the absence of her who gave her birth has been entrusted to the guardian care of those whose hearts will melt in tenderest sympathy for the darling little orphan. Should her life be spared, she will be a standing monument of God's great goodness and mercy.

Our city is filled with mingled exultation and sorrow at the news of the recent triumph of our arms at Manassas—a victory without parallel in the history of this western world, an engagement continental in its magnitude, a success whose influence must be felt and acknowledged not only within the limits of our own Confederacy and of the United States but also throughout the civilized world. Surely the God of Battles is with us.

The price of that victory, however, was great. Colonel Bartow and some of our best young men have fallen, and our city is filled with mourning. A meeting of the citizens last night sent five persons (whose names you will see in the daily journals) to Richmond to attend to our dead and wounded. Colonel Bartow's body will be brought home. The bar had a meeting yesterday afternoon; the resolutions are mine. If the accounts we have of his death are true, he died the death of a hero. None ever for one moment doubted his bravery, and he has left to our army and to his country a signal illustration of true Southern valor.

What a world of heroism in that act of our worthy President—leaving Richmond and in person leading the center column on that fearful battlefield! I presume Dunwody Jones was in the fight. I see in the reports no mention of his being either killed or wounded, but we will not have full details for several days. I have telegraphed the mayor of Richmond for particulars so soon as they can be obtained. He was absent at Manassas when my telegram reached that city.

Mr. Colcock writes me that a miniature of my dear wife can be painted by an artist of Charleston, and I am about sending my locket to him for that purpose. A letter from Brother, this morning received, states that all are well. You will see, my dear parents, that I have written in great haste in my office, and must close for the mail. You have ever the warmest love of

Your affectionate son,
Charles C. Jones, Jr.

Kiss my dear little daughter for me.

MRS. MARY JONES *to* HON. CHARLES C. JONES, JR.[g]

Maybank, Thursday, July 25th, 1861

My dear Son,

Mr. McDonald has just brought your last favor, and as he returns immediately, I have only time to send you a few lines to assure you of our tenderest love and constant remembrance and of the continued improvement of our dear little babe. If the discharge from her ears would cease, I should have every hope of her perfect restoration. Already she looks up into my face and smiles, and is very bright for her *days*—one month old today! What an age of sorrow that one month has brought to our hearts!

My beloved child, do not let the world draw you away from the one great design of this *deep, deep affliction.* Seek and you shall find your long-neglected Saviour! May the Divine Spirit bring you to Him at once! There is no other rest for the weary and heavy-laden.

Our hearts are filled with gratitude to God for our victory over our enemies, and at the same time we weep at the costly sacrifice. I feel especially for Mrs. Bartow, and shall look most anxiously for further accounts. . . . Enclosed we send you twenty dollars. Please forward it as you know best to some official in Richmond for the use of our suffering and wounded soldiers. I wish it was an hundredfold. I thought it best to send it direct to Richmond.

Your father asks you to order *from Richmond* to the office here one of the Richmond *city newspapers,* and he leaves the selection to yourself—either tri-weekly or otherwise. . . . He unites with me in best love to you, and kisses from your little daughter. Susan and the servants beg to be remembered. In haste, my dear son,

Your ever affectionate mother,
Mary Jones.

Hon. Charles C. Jones, Jr., *to* Rev. *and* Mrs. C. C. Jones[g]
Savannah, *Saturday,* July 27th, 1861
My dear Father and Mother,

I have only a moment in which to thank you for your recent kind letters, and to rejoice in the glad tidings of the good health of dear little Mary Ruth.

You cannot imagine the pressure that has been upon me during the past week. We have been in the midst of the greatest excitement consequent upon this glorious victory at Manassas, and last night we received the body of General Bartow. It now lies in the exchange long room under a guard of honor; will be buried tomorrow afternoon.

Judge Fleming's sons both safe. Saw one of them (William O.) this morning; the other (Johnnie) was slightly wounded at Manassas.

It seems to me that I am living in a graveyard. I never have passed through such a period in my life before. The impression will never fade from my memory. Nothing from Dunwody. As ever, my dear father and mother,

Your affectionate son,
Charles C. Jones, Jr.

I will see to it that the generous contribution to the sick and wounded soldiers is forwarded by earliest opportunity.

Hon. Charles C. Jones, Jr., *to* Rev. *and* Mrs. C. C. Jones[w]
Savannah, *Monday,* July 29th, 1861
My very dear Father and Mother,

By the express of today I have the pleasure of sending you herewith box containing:

1. Copies of obituary of my sainted wife. How I wish in its preparation that my pen could have been permitted to shadow forth those feelings of truest love, devotion, and honor for her precious memory which possess me ever! But these emotions belong not to the public but to the sacred recesses of my own heart, where they will ever be most sincerely cherished.

2. Daguerreotype of Ruth, a copy of the one contained in the medallion which I wear—her gift to me during our engagement. It was the best impression that could be obtained by the artist here after repeated trials. This, Father, is for you. I deeply regret that it does not do my dear wife justice. The original I have forwarded to Mr. Colcock, who will place it in the hands of an artist who he assures me will execute for me an accurate and beautiful miniature on ivory. This I am to expect in three weeks. I sincerely trust that he may succeed in his undertaking, for now that the bright original is gone, nevermore to gladden the eye of affection by her coming, never again with her loves to gladden this sorrow-stricken heart, these shadows become sacred beyond expression.

3. A mourning pin for you, my dear mother, containing the commingled hair of Ruth and of our sweet little Julia. You will, I know, accept and preserve it in cherished remembrance of them. Oh, how precious to me every object which speaks of them! For three weeks yesterday has my dear wife been lying in her last long home, and our little Julia a little longer. During that period what I have suffered is known only to my desolate heart. Everything around me appears invested with the habiliments of the grave. And yet amid all these scenes of shadows and of silence there are consecrated associations, happy memories, hallowing by their precious influences every object and every hour.

> Grief fills the room up of my absent ones,
> Lies in their beds, walks up and down with me,
> Puts on their pretty looks, repeats their words,
> Remembers me of all their gracious parts,
> Stuffs out their vacant garments with their forms.
> *Then have I reason to be fond of Grief.*

4. A hair comb for you, Mother. You remember that yours was broken while I was with you on the Island.

5. A mourning pin for Aunt Susan, which I will trouble you to send to her. It also contains the hair of Ruth and Julia.

6. This letter.

Yesterday I attended in an official capacity the funeral of our gallant and lamented fellow townsman, Colonel Bartow. His body lay in state (as they call it in this country, although the application of that term would be inappropriate if we adopt the true European acceptation of the custom) in our city hall (the exchange long room having been draped in mourning and suitably prepared for its reception) ever since Friday night last, until Sabbath afternoon, attended day and night by a guard of honor detailed from Company B of the Oglethorpe Light Infantry, a portion of his former command who did not go to Virginia. The outer box had to be removed, and the metallic case reenclosed in a coffin lined with lead. This was done on Friday night after its arrival, and every unpleasant feature connected with his remains was dissipated. The coffin was covered with the Confederate flag and with numerous tokens of respect, such as chaplets of laurel appropriately entwined, the offerings of the ladies of Charleston and of Savannah. The funeral services were performed by Bishop Elliott from Christ Church, whither the body was transferred from the exchange about four o'clock on Sabbath afternoon. While it lay in the exchange long room hundreds of our citizens paid their farewell respects.

The funeral cortege embraced all the military companies and all the officers of the army, navy, and militia of this city and its vicinity under the command of Colonel Mercer, who was recalled for a day from Fort Pulaski specially for that purpose. It also included, directly and indirectly, the larger portion of the whole population, white and colored, of Savannah. The mayor and city council attended in a body. During the moving of the procession all the bells were tolled, flags displayed at half-staff, a detachment from the Chatham Artillery firing minute guns, and each one rendering every tribute of respect for the memory of the brave departed. The sidewalks and windows of the houses along the line of march were filled with silent spectators. The commons beyond the jail were thronged with Negroes. No noise or confusion: everyone seemed to realize the solemnity of the occasion. Colonel Bartow's name will live in the history of these Confederate States, and his noble daring on the field of Manassas be remembered by all, and especially by those whose state he illustrated in such a signal way by his undaunted courage and chivalrous valor. I have had a most interesting account of the battle from Lieutenants Berrien and Mason, aides to Colonel Bartow, who both passed unharmed through the dangers of that fearful struggle.

Our company will probably during the course of the present week be mustered into service for twelve months. As the first lieutenant of that company I expect to join them so soon as my term of service as the mayor of this city expires, which, D.V., will occur about the 15th October next. Until that time General Lawton will grant me a furlough. I feel it to be my duty, upon a careful comparison of obligations, if I have life and ability, to execute to the end the trust devolved upon me by my fellow citizens of Savannah. I therefore, much as I desire to go with my company, will not resign the mayoralty. But when my term expires, I feel it to be equally my pleasure and my duty, however great the sacrifice, to aid by my own arm in defending these our homes and our national honor. And I trust, and fain would believe, my dear parents, that if the day of battle does come, and I am permitted to share in its dangers and its carnage, you shall not blush at mention of the name of him who owes under the good providence of God his life to you, and all about him that is just and honorable and manly and of good report to your kind teaching and parental example. With my whole heart, from the very inception of the agitation of that question, did I endorse and earnestly advocate our secession movement; and now when it is evident that our national independence can be secured only at the point of the bayonet and at the cannon's mouth, I shall not shrink from testifying even with my blood, if that should in the good providence of Him who doeth according to His pleasure among the armies of heaven and among the inhabitants of earth become necessary, my fixed devotion to the sacred cause of truth, of honor, of religion, of property, and of national independence. A freeman's heart can beat in no nobler behalf, and no more sacred obligations can rest upon any people than those now devolved upon us to protect our homes, our loves, our lives, our property, our religion, and our liberties, from the inhuman and infidel hordes who threaten us with invasion, dishonor, and subjugation.

I have sometimes thought, my dear parents, that my precious Ruth and our darling Julia were taken in the tender mercy of a good God from the evil to come. At least it is most pleasant for me to view their deaths in this light, for even this naked thought robs these dark bereavements of somewhat of their terrors. I now know that it is all well with them. I am assured that they are rejoicing in those happy mansions prepared for the beloved of God Eternal in those heavens where sorrow and strife and dangers enter not, where all is light and love and happiness pure, holy, and unalloyed. In that blessed home they will delight ever in the love, the protection, and the companionship of the Lord of Glory, and of the spirits of the just made perfect. Earth has no more sorrows or trials for them.

My dear little Mary Ruth is rejoicing in that tender care and affection which you alone, my dear parents, can give.

It does seem to me at times that the finger of Providence points me to the path of duty, and bids me stand in my lot upon the tented field with the brave defenders of our country's honor and our country's rights.

My impression is that our company, identified as it has been with the history of our city and state for the past seventy-five years, will be reserved for home and coast defense, and will not be ordered to Virginia. Without doubt, if we may believe the signs of the times, there will be a diversion along our coast during the coming autumn or winter. The two regiments stationed there have been ordered to Manassas, and have already gone. We must therefore from our own firesides furnish the men and materials for our own defense.

Dr. Axson on yesterday morning gave us a remarkably fine thanksgiving sermon, preached in compliance with the recommendation of our Confederate Congress and municipal proclamation. Did your eye rest upon my proclamation? His son was uninjured in the recent battle at Manassas. What a glorious victory! Surely the Lord of Hosts is with us, and it is both proper and pleasant to see the people of these Confederate States, both rulers and the governed, civil and military, referring all our successes to Him, and upon every occasion acknowledging His superintending providence, and imploring His aid and guidance in all our engagements and purposes.

An interesting fact connected with the formation of our Confederate Constitution is that it was born of prayer, and acknowledges in the most emphatic manner the existence and superintending powers of the Living God. The old Federal Constitution was a godless instrument. May it not be the fact that God is now punishing this nation, as He does individuals, for this practical atheism and national neglect in not by organic law, legislation, and in a public manner acknowledging His supremacy? All good governments are ordained of God. Government is a divine institution. It is therefore a fatal error—one which He will not overlook—in the organic act to ignore His existence.

I have sent pins with the hair of my dear Ruth and Julia to Philo, Vallie, Amanda, Mrs. Randolph Whitehead, Sister, Mrs. Harriss, and Sallie Berrien. They will all prize them sincerely.

I trust, my dear father and mother, that I have not wearied you with this long letter. It is so seldom that amid the burdens which are resting upon me I have an opportunity to write you fully, I have embraced this leisure hour for doing so. Kiss little Mary Ruth for me. May God in His great goodness soon restore her to perfect health! With warmest love, my dear parents, I am always

Your affectionate son,
Charles C. Jones, Jr.

Howdies for Susan and for all the servants. Tell Susan the old mama next door says she must hold fast to her profession, and sends her much love.

REV. JOHN JONES *to* REV. *and* MRS. C. C. JONES[t]

Culpeper Courthouse, Virginia, *Wednesday,* July 31st, 1861

My dear Brother and Sister,

I have for days been seeking a quiet place and moment to send you a line and ask you to rejoice with us in God's special mercy in sparing the life of our dear Dunwody. Counting the wounded and dead on both sides, there must have been fifteen to twenty thousand who suffered from shot or shell, bayonet or saber. Amidst this multitude, and in the hottest of the fight connected with that unfortunate 8th Georgia Regiment known as Bartow's, Dunwody was shielded from death. He was struck with two balls in the left foot, one of which pierced his shoe, bruising the side of the heel, and, passing in, lodged in the shoe. He was compelled in the midst of battle to take off his shoe and take out the ball, which he has handed to his mother.

The battle fought on Sabbath the 21st was hard fought and hotly contested and protracted, but it was a signal though dear-bought victory for our Confederacy. The newspaper accounts cannot be relied on; they tell us that our dead are only two hundred and fifty to four hundred and fifty. I learned personally on Wednesday after the battle, and in the immediate vicinity of the battlefield, from two of General Beauregard's aides (Ex-Governor Manning and Mr. John Preston) that our killed was seven hundred to a thousand; and counting the mortally wounded who have died since the battle, we may say a thousand. And I believe that our wounded will not fall under two thousand. There are one thousand at Charlottesville, where the university buildings have been converted into an hospital. There are in this village large hospitals full to overflowing with the wounded. The female college (a large three-story building) and private dwellings without number are full of wounded soldiers. I was for an hour today in the wards of the hospital, and saw the saddest scenes and heard cries, especially from one, that were heart-rending. There must be in this place six hundred wounded. There are hundreds in Richmond, and they are to be found in every village on the railroad from Manassas to Richmond. Three thousand is a moderate estimate for our killed and wounded. I learned also from the above-named aides of General Beauregard that they supposed that the killed and wounded of the enemy would be eight to twelve thousand. This is a moderate estimate. I believe the New York *Herald* says the Federals' loss (killed and wounded) is twenty thousand. And this statement has gone across the water to England, France, etc. This is positively so.

We reached Richmond on Friday the 19th, attended the opening of Congress on the 20th, and heard the reading of the President's message. The message being delivered and Congress opened, our noble President that night prepared for the conflict and left Richmond at 3 A.M. the 21st by special train for Manassas, and arrived in time to mingle in the battle and lead the middle column of our army to the charge. On Sunday the 21st at 9 A.M. it was rumored in Richmond that a battle was going on at Manassas. Rumors multiplied as the day advanced. At 4 P.M. I went out three miles to the camp of instruction and preached to the soldiers (mostly Georgians). On my return to Richmond the news of a battle was confirmed as a dispatch to the War Department, stating that our troops were gaining ground. At 7 P.M. a dispatch from the President to Mrs. Davis announced that we had gained a great but dear-bought victory, that night had closed in with the enemy flying and our troops in full pursuit. All Richmond rejoiced, and the excitement was intense.

We (my dear Jane and myself) rejoiced with trembling, for dispatches arrived announcing the death of Colonel Bartow, and that his regiment was terribly cut up after the most gallant conduct. That night we slept but little. I left in the morning for Manassas, starting in a rain which poured incessantly for twenty hours. Because of many cars crowded with soldiers, incessant rain, we were all day and all night in going one hundred and twenty-five miles, reaching Manassas at sunrise. The sadness and anxiety of that dark rainy night can never be forgotten. In the night we passed trains of wounded men coming down to Richmond and intervening points. I ran out and went from car to car making anxious inquiry. I called out: "Are there any Georgians in this car?" A feeble voice answered: "Nobody here but crippled men." I passed to others with the same inquiry. No Georgians to be found. I asked after the Georgia 8th Regiment (Bartow's); the uniform answer was: "Terribly cut up." That was my satisfaction, and anxiety increased every mile. Arrived at Manassas, and I left the cars to be lost in a wilderness of camps and tents and soldiers. My anxious eyes ran over the thousands of soldiers to recognize one familiar form. After an hour's search I found our boy and ran and threw my arms around his neck and kissed him as one lost and dead suddenly found again. I telegraphed his mother to Richmond and relieved her anxiety, which I knew to be if possible worse than mine.

It was a bloody battle. Charles Dunwody was severely wounded in the hip, Joe King in the side or back, Tom King severely in the foot. Sixteen to twenty were killed or mortally wounded from the Rome companies. Some are still in a critical condition.

We are here with a friend. I am seeking a place for my family, and then expect to join the Georgia 8th Regiment, which has been recruiting after the battle. I could command no ink when I began to write. Do not know where I will be. Love to all on the Island.

Your affectionate brother,
J. Jones.

MRS. MARY JONES *to* HON. CHARLES C. JONES, JR.^g

Maybank, *Friday,* August 2nd, 1861

My very dear Son,

On Wednesday night Tom returned bringing the box containing the precious memorials of our beloved ones and mementos of your own affection, for which we shall ever feel grateful to you.

I cannot express the emotions that fill my heart as I gaze upon the pin. It was my last office to arrange those flaxen locks upon the angelic brow of my precious little granddaughter, and to comb and part the beautiful brown hair of my ever dear daughter upon her calm, pure forehead, where rested the expression of that heavenly peace and joy into which her redeemed spirit had entered. Dear precious Ruth! I received her when you married as my own child, and she was ever such to me in all that was respectful, affectionate, and kind. I knew it not if a shadow ever rested between us, and now day and night the unbidden tears are resting upon my worn face for my loved and departed ones. But most of all for you, my beloved son. They have entered into all the happiness and glory which the Divine Saviour has prepared for His own redeemed ones! But you are left to mourn the withdrawal of all that rendered your life most happy on earth—the sweet affection of one of the most devoted wives, and all the winning loveliness of one of the sweetest children—your bright and happy heart and home suddenly clothed in mourning and silence.

My son, your mother's heart feels for you to its deepest depth. Oh, that I had power to direct you upward to the Divine Redeemer, who now claims the supreme worship and adoration of your sainted wife, your angel child! As you hope and desire to meet them in heaven, "Seek the Saviour, and seek Him at once." God grant that this furnace of affliction may not consume but purify your heart! His Word assures us that "He doth not willingly afflict the children of men"; but when they forget and wander from Him, "in mercy He chastens and afflicts to bring them to Himself." My son, there was a "needs be" for all that God has done; and my constant prayer is that the Holy Spirit may enlighten you to feel and see it all aright, and make it the means of your true conversion to God. We are all pleased with your truthful and beautiful tribute to dear Ruth in the obituary.

The proclamation we saw in a *Daily News* taken at Woodville; our paper did not contain it. It gave us great satisfaction. Your father was delighted with it, and I begged him to cut it out for me, as I wanted to save it. We could hardly wish for you the perplexities of the mayoralty another year. I feel for the past you could have served your fellow citizens in no more important sphere. The courage and *honor* of *my sons* is the *last thing on earth that I could doubt. Assure me* but that they are *Christians,* and I freely yield them up to any service which my Heavenly Father appoints; and none more noble than the defense of truth, honor, religion, and all that we hold dear as a nation.

Father returns grateful thanks for the likeness, and I for the comb, which is very handsome. Some of the copies of the obituary I want to send to some friends.

Did it occur to you to send dear Carrie, *your brother's wife,* some little memento of your dear wife? I think it would be greatly prized by them. Carrie has written me twice since I came home; she seems greatly affected by your deep affliction in the death of Ruth and Julia. She is an affectionate woman and an excellent and devoted wife to Joseph.

Is there anything, my dear son, that I can do for you? Have you got your drawers? It would not give me the least trouble to make them for you if you would select the cloth and send me a pair to cut by. I think they would be stronger than the bought ones. If you go into camp, would it not be best to have some made of flannel? Do send me any work you may have to do, and it shall be immediately attended to. Or if I can render you any assistance in any of your arrangements, I trust you will let me know.

Do you remember to use the *quinine daily,* and to apply the iodine to your throat every now and then? Your father has derived great benefit from the chlorate of potassium as a gargle, and thinks the wine you so kindly sent him has done him good. You and he should both remember and follow Joe's directions.

I am happy, my dear son, to inform you that your dear little babe improves daily. I did not think when we brought her out that she could live many days, but now we have every hope that God will bless and spare her precious life to us. She is very good, especially at night, and begins to notice wonderfully. Your father fancies that she knows my voice. And I must tell you what I know will gratify you—that everyone thinks she will be the image of her dear mother. Susan is very attentive and obedient and fond of her little mistress. She begs to be remembered to you and to Adeline and George and Grace and the old mama at Dr. Harriss'.

My kind remembrances to *Mrs. Harriss.* She was a kind and sympathizing friend, and I shall always remember her affectionately. I trust Mrs. Howard has recovered, and that Mrs. Neely and her family escaped the fever. We have an ill Negro (*Cinda*), which may take your father to Montevideo tomorrow. He has just retired, leaving his best love for you. All the servants desire to be remembered. Your darling little daughter sends her kisses and smiles. That the love of Christ may be shed abroad in your heart ever prays

Your affectionate mother,
Mary Jones.

Have you heard anything of my nephew Dunwody? I feel very anxious about him.

Mrs. Mary Jones *to* Mrs. Mary S. Mallard[t]

Maybank, *Friday,* August 2nd, 1861

My dear Daughter,

We have not heard a word from you since Niger came down, but trust through the mercy of our Heavenly Father that you all continue well. Your father has been improving, and our dear little babe decidedly so, everyone thinks who has seen her. She is filling out, and takes a great deal of notice for one of her age. I have not recovered my strength; took medicine day before yesterday and have commenced tonics.

Mr. McDonald is down for a short time to inform us of Cinda's sickness, and must leave immediately. I write to say that Dr. Parsons (dentist) is now on the Island, and I thought if you wished it and would let us *know before Monday next,* that we would try and get him to return to Savannah by the way of Walthourville and attend to your teeth. It would be such a favorable time, and all at your own home. I would not speak to him, fearing it might not suit you; but if you can let me know if possible by Saturday evening, I would send and engage him to see you on his way home. If he does not come, of course, you will know it did not suit him. He is on a visit to Audley —partly professional; they are enjoying themselves with fruit trees and flowers. They rode over with your aunt and Mr. Buttolph last evening. All well in both families.

Your uncle spent the morning with us; quite well also.

We received this week a letter of twenty-one pages from our dear afflicted child. No heart ever felt its own sorrow and desolation more. Oh, that it might all draw him to the only true source of comfort and peace! An affectionate letter from dear Carrie last week; all well. We have not heard a word from Brother John or of Dunwody since our great battle. I trust the Lord shielded him from harm. Father unites with me in a great deal of love to Robert and yourself, and kisses for our dear little grandchildren. Tell Little Daughter Grandmama has a little sister for her.

Ever your affectionate mother,
Mary Jones.

P.S. I have wanted to send you some of our peaches (such as they are), but we have no cart here, and the carriage horses your father thought not able to go on such an errand; and we hope you have been supplied. Our melons have been poor and sparse. To tell the truth, I have not had the heart since I came home to look after anything outside of the house. And my little babe demands constant care, although she is very good, especially at night, which is a comfort to me, for I do not sleep very well now.

Your mother,

M. J.

Mrs. Mary Jones *to* Mrs. Mary S. Mallard[t]

Maybank, *Saturday,* August 3rd, 1861

My dear Daughter,

James arrived a little before sunset, and immediately I addressed a note to Dr. Parsons and sent Jack over on Lady Franklin. I send you his returned answers to Robert's note and mine; but as they are so faint, you may not be able to read them when they reach you. They contain only the fact that his arrangements will call him to Savannah on Monday, and he cannot call upon you at this time. I am so sorry your horse and servant and buggy have had such a long and fruitless journey. I did not like to speak to him before I knew your feelings.

Sister Susan's cart called here on the way to Lambert, so James has taken a seat in it to Dorchester to spend the night and tomorrow with his relations, and will start early Monday morning. I am so sorry too that our fruit is over. We have had but few melons and not a grape: all eaten by the birds. But I send for my dear little granddaughter and son some nice red potatoes, the first tried for them.

Your dear father is at Montevido tonight. Called this morning to see Cinda, who lost an infant on Monday and is now very ill with pneumonia. Dr. Way attends her. I fear the fatigue and anxiety will make your father sick, but he thought it his duty to go up.

Our dear little babe is very much improved. We think she will look very much like her sainted mother. I wish you could see her now; you could judge of the improvement. She had a severe attack of scarlet fever, and it is a wonder of mercy that she lives—spared, I trust, to love and serve her God and Saviour and to accomplish much good in the world.

How I long to see my little darling granddaughter and dear little Charlie! Hope he will enjoy the potatoes.

This week we received a letter of twenty-one pages from your poor desolate brother. His heart is very sorrowful. He sent both your aunt and myself mourning pins, and your father a daguerreotype of dear Ruth taken from the locket which he wears, and which he has sent to Charleston to have a miniature painted on ivory. I hope it will prove satisfactory.

Your letter was the first tidings we have had of Dunwody, and greatly relieved my anxiety, for in vain have I nearly blinded my eyes looking for tidings of him in the Rome Light Guards, which was one of the most exposed companies. Blessed be the Lord for shielding him in the day of battle! Willie Howe too is safe. Will this suffice these Northern demoniacs? May the Lord give wisdom to our rulers and all in authority over us!

I am glad to know that the ladies of Walthourville have contributed so generously—I must say *nobly*. If I had not already sent on my contribution I would cheerfully send it to them, and will gladly unite still in any way that I can help.

Our friends on the Island are all well. Sister Susan came and spent two days and nights with us. It is late, darling, and I must close, for I did not sleep last night. How I wish I could worship with you tomorrow! Best love for Robert and yourself, and kisses for my little ones. Howdies for the servants. *Niger* will come up next Saturday, D.V.

> Ever your own affectionate mother,
> Mary Jones.

Hon. Charles C. Jones, Jr., *to* Rev. *and* Mrs. C. C. Jones[w]
> Savannah, *Saturday,* August 3rd, 1861

My dear Father and Mother,

Tomorrow morning and one month will have elapsed since the death of my precious Ruth. Our sweet little Julia has lain a little longer in her silent home. Who can measure the griefs which have filled my heart during that period, or appreciate how precious to my soul is the memory of these beloved departed! Each moment in its flight but places an additional seal of consecration upon the cherished recollections of their lives and of their loves. How pure, how spotless their images! Earth has had, and now has, her fair daughters; but fairer than them all in my esteem stands my darling Ruth. Never have I known a heart so free from guile, so pure, so generous, so sincere, so full of tenderest affection. Hers was an affection above that which usually belongs to human breast. Well did I know its happy influence; often have I received its most sacred pledges; and often and again have I been lost in wonder at its purity and constancy. With her, love seemed sublimated into something higher, holier.

Oh, the sad, sad thought that never again will I be permitted to fold that attractive form in these expectant arms; never again press those sweetest lips, so fresh, so full of love; never again listen to the soft accents of that voice, more pleasing to my ear than the sound of the harper harping never so wisely; never again receive from her those pledges of tenderest affection, always so freely given, or turn to her as the sharer of my joys and sorrows in this world of commingled pains and pleasures! The record of her short life, and the still shorter life of our dear little Julia, is as pure and as radiant as though written with a sunbeam. The influence of their loves, and of the many virtues of my sainted Ruth, will be cherished by me so long as this heart can know a generous, a grateful impulse. Oh, my dear parents, what voices dwell in these vacant chairs, this silent piano, this desolate bed, these folded garments, these unused jewels, these neglected toys, these noiseless rooms! God in His infinite mercy grant when life's fitful fever is over a reunion with those dearest departed in that happy world where sin and sorrow enter not, where all tears shall be wiped away, where separations shall be known no more. How have I been brought to see the absolute vanity of earth and the ephemeral nature of the purest human hopes and joys, and to learn and feel that there is nothing true but heaven. My heart is ever full to overflowing, and each day each object which meets my eye serves but to render even more apparent the fearful void caused by these terrible bereavements—a void which nothing but the love of God and a trembling trust in the imputed righteousness of a merciful and precious Saviour can fill.

On Monday last I committed to the care of the express for you, my dear parents, a little box containing a long letter from me and some precious mementos. Not having heard from you during the past week, I have feared that it might have miscarried. I sincerely trust not. . . . How is my dear little daughter? Has she recovered entirely from the effects of her severe illness? If she lives, she will owe her life, under the good providence of God, to your kindest care, my dear parents.

I see by the papers that Dunwody Jones, of the Rome Light Guards, is reported as wounded in the recent engagement at Manassas, but *not severely*. I presume Uncle John is with him.

Our company was mustered into the service of the Confederate States on Thursday afternoon, and went down to Fort Pulaski on Friday morning. I have leave of absence until the expiration of my term of office as mayor of Savannah, which, D.V., occurs about the middle of October next.

Our city is quiet, and by the blessing of God enjoys an unusual degree of health, and as yet evinces but few indications of suffering among the poorer classes. Their wants are being relieved by systematic expenditures of charity.

I will embrace the earliest opportunity of seeing you, my dear parents, and my dear little daughter. Kiss her for me. And believe me ever, my dear father and mother,

Your affectionate son,
Charles C. Jones, Jr.

Howdy for Susan and the servants.

Hon. Charles C. Jones, Jr., *to* Rev. *and* Mrs. C. C. Jones[w]
Savannah, *Tuesday,* August 6th, 1861
My dear Father and Mother,

I am in receipt of your very kind favors of the 2nd and 5th inst., and am truly happy to know that all at home are well, and that precious little Mary Ruth improves daily and bids fair to reflect the features of my sainted Ruth. I sincerely trust that she may, and that her life may long be spared for much usefulness, piety, and happiness. I never will be able, my dear parents, to thank you sufficiently for all your great goodness to me all my days, and for this kindness, so especial in its character, in taking care of my little motherless daughter.

I hope within two weeks to have a miniature painting on ivory of my dear Ruth. My locket for that purpose and also an ambrotype of her are in the hands of Mr. Bounetheau of Charleston, an artist of considerable reputation. Mr. Colcock has been very kind in assisting me in this matter, and I do hope most sincerely that I may be able to secure a truthful picture.

In reference to the mayoralty, I have been pressed to serve for another year, but have declined. I feel that the service of the past year has been sufficient to warrant my declining a second term, especially when I am inclined to believe that a graver duty calls me into the field with my company.

I thank you sincerely, my dear mother, for your kind offer, and if I need anything I will most assuredly let you know.

Dr. Bulloch, who returned today from Virginia, tells me that he saw Dunwody Jones and that he was safe, well, and without a wound. He also saw Uncle John, who was also quite well.

I write in much haste, my dear parents, but with much love to you both, and many kisses for my dear little Mary Ruth. As ever,

Your devoted son,
Charles C. Jones, Jr.

Howdy for Susan and all the servants. Old Mama at Dr. Harriss' says give her best love to Susan, and say to her that all the sisters send love and bid her hold on to her faith.

Hon. Charles C. Jones, Jr., *to* Rev. C. C. Jones[w]

Savannah, *Friday,* August 9th, 1861

My dear Father,

Enclosed please find blank note to be signed and offered in renewal of the one now maturing in the Bank of the State of Georgia, as per enclosed notice. You have funds in bank to your credit, so that you need send no check in payment of the discount.

I hope soon to be able to come out and spend a day or two with you and dear Mother and precious little Mary Ruth. Give them warmest love. And believe me ever, my dear father,

Your affectionate son,
Charles C. Jones, Jr.

Please return the note herewith enclosed at your early convenience.

Rev. C. C. Jones *to* Miss Mary Jones Mallard[t]

Maybank, *Friday,* August 9th, 1861

My dear little Granddaughter,

Don't you know that you have a sweet little cousin, Mary Ruth, at Maybank—Uncle Charlie's and Aunt Ruthie's little baby? And she has got no mother to take care of her. Your dear Aunt Ruthie and Cousin Julia are no longer in this world. They have gone to heaven, where all good people go, and where you will go when you die if you are a good child and love and serve our Saviour Jesus Christ. Do you want to know who takes care of Mary Ruth? Grandmother takes care of her. She sleeps in the little crib every night by Grandmother, and sleeps so good she does not wake at night more than two or three times, and then don't cry, or cries very little, and goes to sleep again. She has gotten 'most well and is gaining every day. Do you want to know who she looks like? She looks like her mother, Aunt Ruthie, and looks like Cousin Julia too. When you come to see Grandma and Grandpa you shall sit down and hold her. Won't that be pleasant? Grandma says you and your brother Charlie must call her Sister, and we must all love her very much and take care of her, for she has no mother. But Grandma will be her mother.

Kiss your mama and papa for Grandma and Grandpa, and your little brother too. Grandpa sends you a roll of peach leather and a piece of candy— all he has in the house. Give Brother some. We heard from Uncle Charlie and Uncle Joe and Aunt Carrie and little Stanhope, and all are well. Uncle William came to see us yesterday, and is well. Jimmie and Willie Buttolph are growing finely. Grandpa and Grandma want to see you and little Brother and Mama and Papa very much, but you know we can't come and leave the little baby. Niger is waiting, and Grandpa can't write any more now. The Lord bless you, my dear child! Give our love to Aunt Lou, and tell all the servants howdy for us.

Your ever affectionate grandfather,
C. C. Jones.

Oh, here is Aunt Susan and Uncle Buttolph and Jimmie just come! And your Aunt Laura sends you a bonnet, and Aunt Susan made it. And send much love.

Miss Mary Jones Mallard *to* Rev. C. C. Jones[t]

Walthourville, *Monday,* August 12th, 1861

My dear Grandpapa,

Mama read your letter to me, and I asked her again and again if you wrote it all for me, and thought you were so good to write a letter to a little girl like me. I will love Cousin Mary Ruth and will call her a sweet little baby; and I want to know if I must take her in my lap when I call her Sister, for you said I must *take* her for my sister. We all want to see her very much.

Uncle Charlie sent me a beautiful necklace last week, and says I must remember my little Cousin Julia in heaven when I wear it. I wanted to wear it now, but Mama has locked it up and will keep it until I grow larger.

I often ask Mama when she is going to take Bubber Charlie and myself to the Island to Maybank to see you and Grandma and Cousin Mary Ruth. Last week Grandma sent us some nice red potatoes, and they were so nice that I begged Mama to let Elvira cook some for breakfast, dinner, and supper; and whenever Mama opened the pantry, Bubber would beg "Ta-a-a" until he got one, and then he would carry it himself to the kitchen. Oh, Grandpa, you don't know how well he can walk! And he says a great many words.

Do tell Aunt Susan I am much obliged to Cousin Laura and herself for the nice bonnet. Mama says it is a little large for me, but she is glad of that, as it will last the longer. . . . Do give my love to Grandma Susan, Aunt Laura, and Cousins Jimmie and Willie. You must kiss Grandma and Cousin Mary Ruth. Mama and Papa send their best love.

Your affectionate little granddaughter,
Mary Jones Mallard.

MRS. MARY S. MALLARD *to* REV. C. C. JONES[t]
Walthourville, *Monday,* August 12th, 1861

The letter I have written you, dear Father, is pretty nearly all in Mamie's own language. We are all quite well, and have much good health for which to be grateful.

Johnnie Fleming has returned wounded in the shoulder, but able to be at church yesterday. Mr. John Baker has also returned. His brother was not well enough to travel, but will come as soon as he can without injury. His wound was very severe, but no bones broken—shot between the elbow and shoulder in the left arm. Mr. Baker saw Uncle John, who was very busy visiting the wounded. Dunwody's wound made him limp a little. Cousin Marion Glen has gone on, and is now in Richmond with her brothers.

The gentlemen that have returned are full of the horrible scenes of the battlefield. Mr. Baker says for miles around the air was awful—so many men either unburied or partially covered, and such numbers of dead horses upon the field. General Beauregard made the prisoners bury the dead, and they would frequently put the bodies in gullies and throw a little earth over them. They represent the New Orleans Zouaves as quite equal to the New York in wickedness. These young men confirm the statement that a Mississippi regiment fired into the Oglethorpes, mistaking them for the enemy; and their fire was quite destructive. They say that the Federals did fight under a Confederate flag. Is not this the most outrageous piece of cowardice you ever heard of?

Our ladies have entered into the soldiers' work with a great deal of zeal. We had a meeting last week. Mrs. E. S. L. Jones was appointed first directress, Mrs. Walthour second, and myself secretary and treasurer; and an executive committee of twelve appointed whose duty it will be to cut out and distribute work. Seventy dollars have been expended, and I have in hand about ninety more. This is doing well, I think. We meet in the upper room of the academy, and a busy scene it is—ladies all at work, some cutting out, some working on machines, others with their needles, etc.

I received a most interesting letter from Kitty on Saturday. She is quite well. Her brother has just gone to Virginia with his company, the Cobb Guards. Mr. Mallard unites with me in warmest love to Mother and yourself and kisses for the baby.

Your affectionate child,
Mary S. Mallard.

Hon. Charles C. Jones, Jr., *to* Rev. C. C. Jones[w]
Savannah, *Thursday,* August 15th, 1861

I have to thank you, my dear father, for your kind favor of the 12th inst. . . . The note was attended to this morning, and has been renewed in its present form for ninety days. There will be no difficulty in renewing until perfectly convenient to pay it. The banks now have little to do, and will have to seek local loans to earn even the seven percent.

Enclosed I send receipt of I. W. Morrell & Company for $17.75 in full of bill rendered, for which they return their acknowledgments.

By this post you will receive, as desired for Uncle William, a copy of the map of the seat of war. Also the New York *Daily Tribune* of the 7th inst. It is a perfect wonder to read now and then issues from that Northern press. I enclose this number that you may judge of the spirit of our quondam brothers as manifested in an article which you will find on the fourth page, marked. Was ever anything more infidel, outrageous, and inhuman? These devils incarnate not only slander the living but endeavor with their polluted tongues to blacken the memory of the dead—and with impious appeals invoke the intervention of a just God.

The "In Memoriam," kindly prepared by Rev. Mr. Porter of this city, I have had printed, and enclose a few copies of the same to you, my dear parents. How earnestly do I desire to show every mark of the profoundest and tenderest respect to the memory of my beloved Ruth! I know she would have done the same for me. I have purchased two lots in Laurel Grove Cemetery, and anxiously desire to have her removed from the vault in which she now lies with dear little Julia (Mr. Neely's vault), and both of them interred in accordance with her request in those consecrated limits. But in consequence of the distracted condition of the country—the absence of laborers and materials—it is at present impossible to compass the fencing of the lots and the erection of a suitable monument. And here, my dear parents, I desire to record it as my *last wish* that in the event of my dying before I am able in person to see to this, that the bodies of my dear Ruth and little Julia be removed as soon as convenient from the vault in which they now temporarily rest and be interred in these lots which I have recently purchased for this purpose. I desire further that these lots be suitably enclosed with a stone and iron fence, and that a monument be erected over my dear wife and child. In case of death (if my body can be identified in the event of my falling in battle) I desire to be laid by the side of my dear wife. It was her dying request, and most sacredly do I desire its fulfillment.

Our city, through the kind providence of God, continues in the enjoyment of much health. I sincerely trust that this great blessing will be continued.

I have just been tendered the captaincy of the Savannah Artillery, and its acceptance is very warmly pressed upon me. My attachment to the Chatham Artillery is, however, so great that I do not feel inclined to separate from my first love—especially when, upon learning the fact at the fort where the Chatham Artillery is now posted, a delegation was sent by that company to urge me by every consideration not to dissolve my connection with the old Chatham. As yet I have given no positive answer. The command tendered is a remarkably fine one, and under ordinary circumstances I would have no hesitancy in accepting the honor.

I am rejoiced to know that dear little Mary Ruth improves daily; and my heart goes forth ever in thankfulness to the Giver of All Good for this His special mercy, and to you, my dear parents, for all your many and great kindnesses. Kiss her for me. And think of me ever as

Your devoted son,
Charles C. Jones, Jr.

Miss Mary E. Robarts *to* Mrs. Mary Jones[t]
Marietta, *Saturday,* August 17th, 1861

My dearest Cousin,

I have not written you for a very long time, though I purposed every day to do so. When the affliction first desolated our dear Charlie's heart and home, I felt as if with all your excitements and troubles I would wait a little while before I wrote you, but I did not expect to defer it so long. So I hope you will excuse me.

We often think of you and Cousin Charles with your dear little baby. I know you consider her a little treasure. I am glad to hear that she is improving in health, and trust she may be spared to bless the hearts and homes of her dear grandparents and her desolate, afflicted father. I have been very much pleased with dear Charles's letters. Besides the tender regrets of losing his beloved wife, the manner of her death and her triumphant faith have made a great impression on him. I pray it may be sanctified to him and bring forth "the peaceable fruits of righteousness." Who nurses the dear little baby? And who does she look like?

This is the week of the convention in Atlanta. I was in hopes of seeing some of our low-country ministers, particularly Mr. Buttolph and Mr. Mallard; but Mr. Ardis has returned from Atlanta and said they were not there. I suppose, of course, the convention made arrangements for the meeting of the General Assembly of the Confederate States. I suppose it will be in Augusta. The synod is to meet here in November; I hope we shall have the great happiness of seeing you and Cousin Charles.

Last Sabbath our minister, Mr. Palmer, announced to the congregation that he had been appointed chaplain of the 14th Georgia Regiment, and requested the views of the congregation on the subject; that he felt a desire to go, and thought it his duty if they would consent; would request the congregation to remain the next afternoon after the prayer meeting for the soldiers, when he would be pleased to hear their views. It took our church quite by surprise. We had the church meeting, and a most interesting one it was. Mr. Palmer stated that he had been elected for the war; that if that was not over by the fall meeting of Presbytery he should request the church to unite with him in asking a dissolution of the pastoral relation. As Mr. Palmer seemed to feel it his duty to go, and at the same time desired so much to go, they would not oppose it, provided he would, after spending several months in the army, resign unless he saw it very plainly his duty to remain there. The church will get a supply till winter. We hope Mr. Baker will preach for us two Sabbaths in the month, as he preaches the other two to churches in the country. We hope our church will not be closed; that would be a sad case. The war has come very near us in feeling. Every family has some member absent in Virginia, and now our minister is going. And one of our elders, Colonel Brumby, already gone.

Oh, this wicked, cruel war! When will it end? The Lord has hitherto helped us. There is news of another victory at Leesburg; another in Missouri. If our enemies could only see the folly of expecting to subjugate the South or reconstruct the broken Union, there might be some prospect of peace. We have not heard a word from Cousin John or his family since they have been in Virginia; have heard of them once in Richmond. Lieutenant Dunwody (Charlie) and Captain Thomas E. King have both been in great danger from their wounds, but are now considered better. Joe King was severely wounded through the hips, but is better; I believe they think of bringing him home. His young bride went to him in Virginia. Indeed, going to Virginia is such a common thing now that it seems very easy; there are persons from here going every day to see their friends. And the ladies are kept quite busy sewing for the soldiers. Whenever you call to see a lady now, you will find her with either a hickory or flannel shirt in her hands, making it or a pair of drawers. Knitting is also very universally done.

Has the war affected the prices of things with you? We feel it here in the high price of bacon, corn, and coffee. Rice is three pounds to the dollar and very scarce. No jars coffee to be had. Sugar we get plentifully from New Orleans, but from the western communication being stopped by the blockade the freight brings it up very high. But if things get no worse, we have great reason to be thankful.

Our dear Mary Sophia returned last night. Mr. and Mrs. Stewart accompanied her. They were delayed in Columbus several days, as Mr. Stewart was taken sick. Mary Sophia is well, but looks tired. She has been so kindly treated by not only Mr. and Mrs. Stewart but by all of their relatives that she feels as happy there as she could be anywhere away from her own home. As one instance of their kindness, Mr. Stewart's father presented his daughter-in-law Mrs. Stewart with a Saratoga trunk in Columbus, and told Mrs.

Stewart that she must go out and buy a handsome dress for Miss Sophia. Mrs. Stewart told him she did not think she needed a summer dress. He said: "Well, go out and buy her a handsome *winter* dress; I respect her grandmother so much I must make Miss Sophia a present." So Mrs. Stewart went out and bought her a handsome poplin. Was not this kind? We feel thankful that she is among such kind people. She says Mr. Stewart's place is the most handsomely settled place she ever saw in her life.

I wish I could hand you some of the beautiful pears and grapes and peaches on the table by me. I suppose as usual, however, you have a plenty of nice fruit at Maybank, owing to your care. . . . Please give our best love to Cousin Susan, Laura, and Mr. Buttolph, and kiss the little boys for me, and your own dear little baby. . . . Mother has been better this summer, but within the last week we have had some damp northeast weather which has caused a return of her cough. The girls are quite well, and rejoicing that they will have their sister several weeks with them. Joe is in Mr. Denmead's warehouse—a very excellent situation for him; suppose they will give him about ten or fifteen dollars per month. He has the war fever dreadfully, but he is so young that we do all we can to keep him at home. . . . Please remember us to your servants. Tell Sam's family he is well and quite fat, and just as faithful as ever. If he were only a Christian! Farewell, my dear cousin. Do write us soon, for we long to hear from you. With love from all, believe me

Your ever affectionate cousin,
Mary E. Robarts.

VI

Rev. C. C. Jones *to* Mr. ————t

Maybank, *Monday,* August 26th, 1861

Sir,

You entered my family on a friendly arrangement for copying my church history, on your own proposal, the 28th of July 1860, and left it on the 20th of the September following, and became first particularly known to me a short time previous when a guest of my neighbors, Rev. D. L. Buttolph and Mr. J. A. M. King. You were introduced as an educated man, the son of a venerable and highly esteemed minister of South Carolina, whose full name you bear; as a married man, having but recently married your second wife, who was then absent at the North for her health; as a prominent member of the Presbyterian church in Columbus, Georgia, the superintendent of the Sunday school, the president of the Young Men's Christian Association, and the principal of a female high school in that city, and recommended on your school circular by names of the first respectability. You had also taught a school within the bounds of our own congregation in Liberty County, and had associated with the active members of the church resident in the village, and taken part in their religious meetings, and I believe aided them in their efforts to give religious instruction to the Negroes. You came to my acquaintance under these favorable circumstances, and were received for what you were considered and professed yourself to be—a gentleman, a married man, and a Christian. You had my confidence as unreservedly as any stranger possibly could have, and enjoyed the kind hospitality of my family from the day you entered to the day you left it. You rendered yourself agreeable, and conducted yourself with every mark of respect and propriety; were always present morning and evening at family worship, and sometimes took part in that worship, and also in our weekly neighborhood prayer meeting. You were the guest of a gentleman, a professing Christian and minister of the gospel, and witnessed from week to week his efforts to instruct religiously the servants of his family and household.

You were under my roof but a short time before you debauched a young Negro girl—a seamstress, and one of our chambermaids. And you continued your base connections with this Negro woman week after week until you took your final leave! Of the hundreds of men of all classes and conditions and professions—men of the church and men of the world, married and unmarried—who have been guests in my house for days, weeks, months, and some for years, you, ————, are the only man who has ever dared to offer to me personally and to my family and to my neighbors so vile and so infamous an insult. You are the only man who has ever dared to debauch my family servants—it being the only instance that has occurred—and to defile my dwelling with your adulterous and obscene pollutions. Had you been detected, I should have driven you instantly out of the house and off the premises, with all the accompanying disgrace which you merited; and I regret that the law affords me no redress under so serious an indignity and injury.

The proof of your criminality is of so clear a character as to remove all doubt. *There is the free, unconstrained confession of the Negro woman herself in full detail; there is the correspondence between the time of your connection with her and the birth of the child—a mulatto, now some time born; and there is a resemblance to you beyond mistake.* In this last proof I do not rely upon my own convictions. I have submitted the child to the inspection of three gentlemen in the county who know you well personally and are familiarly acquainted with your countenance and physiognomy, and they without hesitation declare its resemblance to you to be as striking as possible. And all who have seen it are of the same opinion. The evidence is amply sufficient to warrant the submission of the case to the session of the Columbus church for action.

And now, sir, what are your former Christian friends to think of you? You have sinned under the most forbidding and aggravating circumstances, and it is difficult to conceive of a more degrading and hypocritical course of wickedness and folly, or one which argues a greater destitution of principle or more callousness of conscience! I never have been more deceived in a man in all my life. How have you wounded the Saviour, and brought disgrace upon religion, and given occasion for the ungodly to triumph! What an injury have you done to the soul of the poor Negro! What disgrace and ruin of character have you brought on yourself! I pity you, and try to pray for your redemption. You well know what your duty is both toward God and man, and I hope you may find grace to perform it.

I voluntarily offered you my name on your school circular. I request you to take it off. You have betrayed my confidence and injured me grievously, and I cannot look upon you as I once did nor hold any further intercourse with you.

C. C. Jones.

Hon. Charles C. Jones, Jr., *to* Rev. *and* Mrs. C. C. Jones[g]

Savannah, *Saturday,* September 7th, 1861

My very dear Father and Mother,

After my short but delightful visit to you and to our sweet little Mary Ruth (for whose continued good health and daily improvement I render constant thanks to God and gratitude to you, my dear parents) I left Savannah on Saturday afternoon and spent Sabbath with Brother and Sister Carrie in Augusta. Found them both well, and their interesting little son Stanhope the very picture of health. They are all happy, and are getting along very well. The Doctor as yet has not secured much practice except among the poorer class, where professional services are to be regarded rather as a matter of love and charity. He will not, however, lose his reward.

Arrived in Atlanta on Monday. Governor Brown absent in attendance upon a sick brother. On Tuesday went to Marietta and dined with Aunt Eliza and family. All well. Aunt Eliza is far better than she has been for years; the improvement in her health and strength was marked. Aunt Mary just as fat and good-natured as ever. Cousin Louisa thin, but well. The girls all with them, and Joe employed as a clerk in Mr. Denmead's flour mill. They all desired much love.

Returned to Atlanta that afternoon, and the next day had an interview with Governor Brown. He has given me an order for fifty horses for the use of our company, with a view to placing it upon a war footing as a flying artillery company, and promises an increase at no distant day. He is expected here this evening, and will undertake a tour of inspection along the coast on Monday in company with Commodore Tattnall and General Lawton.

Philo and Amanda were both at Atlanta. The latter, when I left, was suffering much from one of her severe attacks, accompanied with fever. Saw Fred King at his tannery. Please say to Aunt Julia that I spent a pleasant hour with him, and delivered her letter. He is prospering in business. On my arrival at Atlanta, saw our friend Mr. Rogers. He called several times to see me. He is as genial as ever. Philo, Amanda, and myself rode out to his farm, met him there by invitation, enjoyed his fine grapes, and visited his wine cellar. His success in the culture of the vine has been marked. Atlanta is a most thriving place, and already claims a population of sixteen thousand inhabitants, a growth unexampled in the history of our Georgia towns. It bids fair to become the largest city in Georgia.

On my return I stopped for a day at Bath. This little retreat is deserted of the male inhabitants. Most of them are in Virginia. Tarried with Mrs. Randolph Whitehead, with whom Vallie is spending the summer. My visit to Bath was at once pleasant and mournful in its character. Lights and shadows were strangely commingled. And yet as I dwelt upon the pictures which memory evoked from a consecrated past, I found that the shadows rested only upon my own desolate heart, while a pure, a holy, a heavenly light illumined every recollection of the precious lives and loves of my dearest Ruth and our sweet little Julia. How did the recollections of our earliest loves—of those days when the heart throbs almost to bursting with its first, its ardent affections; of the places, the roads, the drives, the walks, the seats, all consecrated by our engagement vows hourly renewed; of that room and hour which gave her to my heart a blushing bride, who never once for even a short moment after ever forgot her vows in married life, or withheld the ready precious offerings of her daily kindnesses and truest loves—come crowding thick and fast, each moment filling my eyes with gushing tears and my heart with sorrow unutterable! Not for her or for our sweet little babe, the tender pledge of our loves, but only for my lone self because they are not. Hard—most hard—is it to contemplate the fact that never again in this life can I joy in their presence, or find accustomed delight in the tender appreciation of their most precious loves. And yet how many the cherished recollections which change not with years, which will be cherished ever while the warm blood pulsates through this beating heart! How precious the legacy in the happy influences of their lives and loves! My heart was very heavy all the time I was at Bath, and a gloom overspread that little community. . . . The death of my dear Ruth and of little Julia weighs very heavily upon all her sisters and relatives.

Leaving Bath on Friday afternoon, I spent that evening with Brother and Sister Carrie, leaving Augusta at midnight and reaching my lonely home this morning. Found all the servants well. All friends desired kindest remembrances to you both, my dear parents. And our kinsman, Mr. Charles Jones Colcock of Charleston, an accomplished and Christian gentleman, whom I met in Atlanta (we traveled from that city towards Augusta together, and passed almost the whole of Wednesday night in the most pleasant conversation), asked me to remember him very especially to you.

I thought while I had the opportunity (it is so seldom that I am able to leave the city) I would improve it by seeing as many friends as I could. They all appeared glad to see me.

I sincerely trust, my dear father and mother, that you are both feeling better, and that little Mary Ruth still continues in the enjoyment of her remarkable health. With warmest love to you both, my dear parents, and kisses for Daughter, I am, as ever,

Your affectionate son,
Charles C. Jones, Jr.

Rev. C. C. Jones *to* Hon. Charles C. Jones, Jr.[g]

Maybank, *Wednesday,* September 11th, 1861

My dear Son,

We were happy to receive your interesting letter last evening, and entered into your feelings on revisiting scenes of your friendship and love towards one now no longer here to cheer and bless you with sweet returns. It is a void never to be filled. The place occupied in the heart is consecrated evermore to her precious memory. And what adds to her right there, above all she was to you as a wife and mother of your children, is that she was God's own child —one sought out and saved by the ever blessed Saviour. And so she lives in happiness; and if you follow the footsteps of her faith, that very one shall be your loving friend and companion forever in a land where sickness and pain and death and parting come no more!

Your dear little daughter, Mother says I must tell you, grows daily, and is developing in mind and body. She has her ups and downs, but sleeps well, and has an excellent appetite, and enjoys her waking hours. She is now on a course of treatment directed by your brother, who sent the medicines prepared by himself by express. Her ear is not yet well, but better.

Mother is better. Your Aunt Abby has been with us for some eight or ten days for the benefit of her little boy, who has been ill with cholera infantum. He is relieved and improving. The ladies ride this morning to Hester's Bluff to see the Liberty Troop, leaving me in charge of the babies.

Am glad you succeeded so well with Governor Brown. You ought to have presented to you by the state a battery of *rifled cannon* from the Rome, Georgia, foundry. They have been sending them on to Virginia. Cannons decide battles. Did you observe that the Hatteras forts were taken by the guns of the ships at long ranges *throwing shell two miles?* Have we any guns to return such salutes *in Fort Pulaski?* If not, General Lawton must look out for the loss of that as well as of the small batteries he is putting out on the coast islands. I have little faith in them. If the enemy are in any force and know what they are about, they may land in two or more divisions in a calm day or clear night at different points on any one of the islands; and what can one or two hundred men do with a thousand or two—and the breastwork open in the rear? We need a camp or camps of six or eight thousand men on the line of the coast that may be gotten together at short notice upon an invasion to attack the enemy instantly; and at different available points on the main, forts that may be holden against any force—at least for a time, to allow succorers to come in, if no more. However, I am only giving my impressions. Our general in command may be doing all he can, but there is much dissatisfaction with him among the people, I understand.

Your Aunt Abby begs to be remembered to you. Mother sends much love. "My love to my dear father." (I held the pen in your dear baby's hand, and she writes you her first little letter. You will be able to read it.) The Lord bless and keep you, my dear son!

Your ever affectionate father,
C. C. Jones.

Hon. Charles C. Jones, Jr., *to* Rev. C. C. Jones[g]

Savannah, *Saturday,* September 14th, 1861

My dear Father,

I am favored with yours of the 11th inst., and am happy to know that all at home are well. Sister left me yesterday morning, after giving me the pleasure of a short sojourn of a few days. I wish that I could have prevailed upon her to have tarried longer, but the claims of a happy home would not admit an additional absence from their duties and their pleasures.

I agree with you fully in your views of the character and efficiency of the batteries erected for the protection of our coast. They may answer the purpose of preventing the ingress of marauding parties in gunboats and vessels of light draught, but they are wholly unable to cope either with a fleet or even with a single ship of the line armed with rifled cannon or with a battery of heavy guns such as those now used on board the U.S. sloops and steamers of war. Should any one of them be taken, and the guns fall into the hands of the enemy, we will be most effectually blockaded by our own batteries. I have just had an interview with Adjutant General Wayne, and he assures me that troops are to be concentrated at once at convenient distances for the defense of the coast, and a system of signals established from the mouth of the Savannah to the mouth of the St. Marys. We need at least ten thousand men in addition to the numbers now in service for the protection of the state. The batteries already erected are to be to a certain extent remodeled, and the garrisons strengthened.

Governor Brown returned last evening from his tour of inspection. The nomination of Judge Nisbet does not carry with it much enthusiasm in this city. On the contrary, I think Governor Brown's chances for reelection have been materially confirmed. In consequence of the smallness of the convention, Mr. Ward refused to allow his name to go before that body for a nomination. I presume from all I can learn that Joseph E. Brown will be our next governor; and if for a third term, why not for life?

I heartily wish that we had some efficient, competent military leader to take in hand and vigorously prosecute this whole matter of our seacoast defenses. Carolina is far ahead of us.

We have not as yet received our horses for the Chatham Artillery. Governor Brown telegraphed to Secretary Walker to know if the Confederacy would pay for one hundred horses with a view to placing the Chatham Artillery upon a war footing as a light battery. The reply was that the expenses would be defrayed by the War Department. Instead of acting at once upon this, he orders the quartermaster here to send on an estimate of the probable expense of the purchase. Nothing has been had in reply, and we are yet without horses, or any reasonable expectation of having them until a further reply is had from Richmond. The delay is very prejudicial and unfortunate at this time, when every moment should be devoted to the efficient drill of men and horses. The drill of a light battery is the most difficult in the service, and we should have been in camp some time since.

The recent intelligence from Kentucky is very unfavorable. Unfortunate people, they will soon experience all the horrors of war without the sympathy of those whom they had not the manliness to acknowledge as friends.

Nothing new in our city. We are enjoying the blessings of health in a remarkable degree. On Tuesday or Wednesday next I hope to send out the crib, etc., for dear little Mary Ruth. Will direct the parcels to No. 3, and will have to trouble you to have a cart sent for them from that point. Mother will find some of Mr. Ward's nice oolong tea, which I send because you, my dear parents, will enjoy it much more than I will. With warmest love, my dear father and mother, to you both, and many kisses for dear little Daughter, who has her father's tenderest thanks for her first remembrance, I am, as ever,

Your affectionate son,
Charles C. Jones, Jr.

MRS. MARY JONES *to* HON. CHARLES C. JONES, JR.ᵍ

Maybank, *Saturday,* September 14th, 1861

My very dear Son,

Your two last favors since your return have been received. We were happy to know that you had the pleasure of seeing so many friends and measurably accomplishing the principal object of your visit. Well does my heart sympathize with you in the melancholy but yet attractive sadness of your visit to Bath, the scene of your early and devoted loves. The recollection of our beloved Ruth and sweet little Julia is ever present with me. What must it be to you in the home once so happy but now so desolate—in your affectionate and generous heart, whose greatest earthly happiness was centered in your wife and child!

When writing or speaking of your heavy sorrows I have no language that can do justice to my feelings. My only relief is when I can pour out my heart before the mercy seat of my God and Saviour and plead that He would bind up the broken heart and heal the wounded spirit of my child; that He would fill with His own love and favor, with holy and heavenly affections, the heart that has been occupied only with frail and perishing objects. Oh, that He would in this solemn season of deepest grief give you a saving sight and sense of your sins forgiven through the imputed righteousness of our Divine Redeemer! My child, I believe that *this* is God's great design in thus blighting your earthly hopes and giving you stroke upon stroke. He means at this time to draw you to Himself. And with what cords of love! Is not heaven itself more to be desired since your loved ones are there? I feel the fearful position which you are now occupying and may soon be called to occupy. God grant that nothing may turn you aside from a due improvement of your afflictions!

Your father wrote you this week, but as Gilbert goes up this afternoon and is now waiting, I send you these hurried lines. Our precious little baby grows every day more and more interesting and intelligent. I am carrying out your brother's directions faithfully, and hope in time that she will be entirely relieved of the affection of her ear. She has had a cold, and today I gave her my old remedy (castor oil), and she appears much better—I may say relieved.

I am glad to know that your sister has been paying you a visit.

Sister Abby and her sick little boy have been with us the past week; he is much better, and I hope the change will do him permanent good.

Yesterday your father performed the funeral service of one of the Mounted

Rifles in Sunbury. He died at Mr. Dunham's. Your father visited him every day; sometimes twice. He was too ill to realize his situation. The morning he died he prayed, and told Mr. Dunham it was the *first time* in his life that he ever did so fervently.

Our friends are all well. I am feeling much better, and think your dear father is no worse. When shall we see you? And what can I do for you? Father unites with me in best love, and Little Sister sends her sweet kisses to her dear papa. God bless and save you, ever prays

Your affectionate mother,
Mary Jones.

Hon. Charles C. Jones, Jr., *to* Mrs. Mary Jones[g]
Savannah, *Wednesday,* September 18th, 1861
My very dear Mother,

I am in receipt of your last kind favor, and sincerely thank you for it, and for your tender sympathy and Christian counsels. I never will be able, the longest day I live, to be sufficiently grateful to you and to dear Father for all your great goodness to me and to my precious little daughter. Regret to know that she still suffers from her ear, and trust that the treatment which she is now undergoing will soon relieve her entirely.

The monotony of our city was on yesterday morning relieved by the arrival of the steamship *Bermuda,* direct from Liverpool, with a cargo consisting among other things of eighteen rifled cannon, some seven thousand Enfield rifles, any quantity of percussion caps, fixed ammunition, blankets, shoes, etc. Her coming is most opportune. She saw nothing whatever of Lincoln's famous blockade. This cargo was brought over in chief, I am informed, for account of the Confederate States. The *Bermuda* came in under English colors, and is an ironclad steamship of some fifteen hundred tons burden. Our Confederacy could not do better than to purchase her and convert her into a sloop of war. She would very easily bear a battery of, say, six or eight guns, and some of the rifled cannon which she brought over might very advantageously be used for that purpose. She is the first of a line of passenger and freight steamships intended for direct communication between Charleston, South Carolina, and Liverpool. We have intelligence that Captain Bulloch and Mr. Edward C. Anderson will soon leave England, each in command of fully appointed steam vessels of war. Were they here, they might very readily levy contribution upon these small fry hovering about our coast.

A letter from Sister, today received, tells me that all are well.

Did you receive the articles sent by Tuesday's train, a list of which I enclosed to Father? I hope they reached you without accident.

Our city, through a kind Providence, still continues in the enjoyment of an unusual degree of health. The dealings with our entire Southern coast during the present season have been remarkable. Myself, Grace, and George have been for some days suffering from colds; mine I contracted at a fire some nights since. With warmest love to you both, my dear parents, kisses for dear little Daughter, and remembrances for Susan and the servants, I am, as ever,

Your affectionate son,
Charles C. Jones, Jr.

MRS. MARY JONES *to* HON. CHARLES C. JONES, JR.[g]

Maybank, *Wednesday,* September 18th, 1861

My very dear Son,

Your last favor was received yesterday. Today your father went to Montevideo and returned, and we were just arranging for Gilbert to go to the depot early in the morning when Robin drove up with the precious memorials of our beloved child in heaven. They opened all the fountains of grief! I shall almost feel as if she is around me. Your father says he realizes more than ever now that he shall see them no more in the flesh. . . .

I hope you will find you have a loving little heart left you in your sweet little daughter. She grows daily more and more interesting, and has the warmest place in her grandparents' hearts. I long for the time to come when you will be with us to enjoy her sweet smiles. She cannot take the place of those who are gone, but she will have her own place in your heart.

When would you like me to come down and assist you in putting away such articles as you would like to preserve for our little one as mementos of her dear mother? Any time you think best will suit me, and I want you to say exactly what you would desire.

I had prepared a bag of dried shrimp, a few sheepshead corned, and red potatoes to send by Gilbert up to the depot, and now forward them by Robin to go by express, hoping you will enjoy them. Father asks you to request Lathrop & Company to send him one piece of Cobb cloth and one piece brown homespun at about nine cents, care of Lyons & Trask, Riceboro. Ask George to take care of the basket with buckets, etc., left in Savannah belonging to Sister Susan with a few articles of my own. You need not send them out. Father is very tired. He unites with me in tenderest love to you, with kisses from your little daughter. Friends all well.

Ever your affectionate mother,
Mary Jones.

HON. CHARLES C. JONES, JR., *to* MRS. MARY JONES[t]

Savannah, *Thursday,* September 19th, 1861

My dear Mother,

I send you herewith a map giving a partial view of the seat of war, which I have just received from one of the officers now on service near Manassas. It may afford you some interest, although it is not as minute as we could wish it.

Mr. Ward left last night for Europe—under the most trying circumstances. He has just heard of a severe accident to his little son Jimmie. Mrs. Ward is in great distress, and he has braved all the dangers of imprisonment, etc., etc., to join them. I feel most deeply for him. He is completely overcome. I sincerely trust that there is some humanity left at the North, and that they will not molest him in passing through the enemy's country. He will bring his family immediately home.

Nothing new in the city. We are better of our colds. Warmest love to you both, my dear parents, and many kisses for dear little Mary Ruth. I am, as ever,

Your affectionate son,
Charles C. Jones, Jr.

Hon. Charles C. Jones, Jr., *to* Mrs. Mary Jones[t]

Savannah, *Sunday,* September 22nd, 1861*

My very dear Mother,

John has just come in for a ticket to go out in the morning, and I embrace the opportunity offered for acknowledging the receipt of your last kind letter and of thanking you for it.

Am happy to know that the articles sent have all been received. They are precious memorials, and it is almost like sundering my heartstrings to part with them; and yet under the circumstances I do it the more cheerfully because they go into the keeping of those who are dearest to me, and are for the use and benefit of that precious little daughter who will never know the tender loves of the mother who made and the sister who gave them. I pray you, Mother, save me one of the dresses—any one which you may deem best—that I may keep it ever near me, although I need no remembrancer of that character to keep the memory of the dear departed in living, cherished recollection. Their bright and loved images, with the thousand associations of purest pleasures and tenderest affections, are ever with me; and the places which they hold in my heart of hearts will always be theirs, come what may. The seal is set, and it will never be broken.

In reference to the disposition of the wardrobe of my dearest Ruth, any day, my dear mother, that you may name as convenient I will be most happy to see you, and will submit the whole matter to your determination.

I saw Messrs. H. Lathrop & Company, and they have executed the commission.

Mr. Ward has left for Europe with a view to bringing his family home. His determination to do so was suddenly formed, and was based upon a letter received last Tuesday in which he received tidings of a severe injury sustained by his little son Jimmie in falling from a swing. Mrs. Ward was in a very distressing condition of mind, and urged him by every consideration to come to her. In obedience to his duties to his family he has braved the dangers of imprisonment, etc., etc., and has entered upon the attempt to reach them.

He had made ample provision for the support of his family in Europe—if necessary for several years. It was a terrible trial to him to leave the country just at this important juncture, when she so much needs the services of every true and loyal son. His own conscience, however, will approve the act, let those who are ignorant of the facts of the case say and think what they may. He has the sincere sympathy of all his friends here. He said he would go—or make the attempt—if it blasted every hope of subsequent profit and preferment, and if he was imprisoned for years. To remain was to refuse to listen to the voice of the most sacred affection. I never saw a strong man more sorely moved than he was upon the receipt of the letter.

We are all better again, through a kind Providence. With warmest love to you, my dear mother, and to dear Father, and with many kisses for my darling little daughter, I am, as ever,

Your affectionate son,
Charles C. Jones, Jr.

HON. CHARLES C. JONES, JR., *to* MRS. MARY JONES[t]

Savannah, *Monday,* September 23rd, 1861

My very dear Mother,

On yesterday evening I wrote in reply to your recent kind letter and stated that I would be most happy to see you any day you might find it convenient to come to the city. I write this evening to say so still, but to suggest that for the present you had better defer your visit, and for the simple reason that the weather is at present very trying, and our city not quite so healthy as it has been. I fear that you might suffer from the exercise of travel and the change of atmosphere. Soon we may hope for more pleasant days, and then I shall eagerly anticipate a visit from yourself and dear Father.

My heart continues very heavy. Time heals not at all the deep wounds which sorrow and desolation have made. The death of those we love does indeed cast a sad, sad gloom over everything earthly, and it is hard to lift the soul from out the shadows which settle ever around and upon me. . . . An honest heart once softened by the touch of holy affection, once refined by the sacred influence of the love of her whom God and companionship have made dearer than life itself, can never forget the hallowed memories which belong to those days of happiness. Earth has nothing to compare with the devotion of a true and loving wife. Honors are vain, empty, unsatisfying; pleasures are evanescent; the opinion of men changing as the breath of April; ordinary friendships fluctuating as the waves of a restless sea. But the love of the wife of your bosom, the mother of your children—how true, how tender, how disinterested, how constant!

Often does my heart cry out in its grief: "Take all else, but oh! give me back the free, the full, the generous, the sincere, the tender, the abiding loves of my precious Ruth!" And yet I would not for worlds recall her if I could to this land of tears, of partial joys, of alternate pleasures and pains. No one can know how sweet, how constant, how pure, how almost heavenly those loves were to me. To me alone she freely gave her virgin loves, and blessed me with the most intimate pledges of her affection.

Her memory, how sacred! Every recollection of her, how precious! Time may bring its changes, and coming years may engraft new buds of affection upon this almost withered stem; but the first, the tenderest loves of this heart were given to her, and hers they will ever be. I love everything that speaks of her, and my constant prayer to a good and merciful God is that He will of His infinite grace grant me a reunion with her and our dear little Julia in that holy world where separations will be known no more, where we may be permitted an eternity of bliss in the enjoyment of all those pleasures which perish not with the using.

I sincerely trust that you, my dear mother, and dear Father and sweet little Mary Ruth are in the enjoyment of many blessings. With a heart full of love for you all, I am, as ever,

Your affectionate son,
Charles C. Jones, Jr.

HON. JOHN JOHNSON *and* MR. A. G. REDD *to* REV. C. C. JONES[t]

Columbus, *Tuesday,* September 24th, 1861

Reverend and dear Sir,

On the 30th ult. —————— of this place showed to the subscribers (members of the session of the Presbyterian church of Columbus) a letter from you dated August 26th, 1861, addressed to said ————, containing a charge against him of a very serious character—namely, adultery—and that, too, under very aggravating circumstances. If the charge be true as stated, we could not be astonished at any degree of indignation and contempt that might be felt and manifested by the injured party.

Your letter bears date 26th ult., but is postmarked 28th. It was shown by Mr. —— to us on the 30th, so that there was no delay after he received it before he made it known to others. He (Mr. ——) most positively, solemnly, and unequivocally denies the charge altogether. He submitted the letter to us as members of the church session (the pastor being absent) for such action in the matter as might be deemed necessary. After some consultation we decided to write to you on the subject, but a severe attack of bilious fever has prevented our writing earlier.

We find stated in your letter, among other things: "The evidence is amply sufficient to warrant the submission of the case to the Columbus church for action." Now, dear sir, the evidence is what the session wants if it takes any action in the matter. And in such cases reliable legal evidence is what is usually most difficult to obtain. You appear to be fully satisfied of the fact. There may be circumstances connected with such cases that may produce conviction in the minds of those well acquainted with them, but it may not be practicable to produce evidence according to established forms and usages sufficient to convince others, or such evidence as would warrant a conviction by an investigating tribunal.

In looking at the evidence so far as appears by your letter, it is: first, the birth of a mulatto child at a time corresponding to the time Mr. —— was in your family; second, the declarations of the mother of the child; and, third, the resemblance of the child to the accused. The first part of the evidence—time—is satisfactory as far as it goes. The second—the mother's declaration—is what usually has to be mainly relied upon in similar cases when the mother is a free white woman; but courts and juries have not always convicted the accused when the mother's declaration upon oath has been positive. The third —to wit, resemblance—is of very doubtful character at best. You can doubtless readily call to mind the very striking resemblance that is often found to exist between persons where there can be no kindred, and then again the absence of resemblance between brothers and sisters, parents and children, where the fidelity of the parents would not be questioned by anyone acquainted with them. Suppose the session should take action in the case upon the state of facts as presented by your letter and should pronounce —— guilty. What would be said of the action by an appellate court?

But let us turn aside a moment and look at the facts of the case and the parties. In a majority of cases that have fallen under our observation tried before the courts of the country for bastardy, the mother, being the complainant and a free white person, has pleaded *promise of marriage*. In this case such plea could not be urged, for in addition to the fact of Mr. ——'s being a married man, the law of the country does not tolerate such marriages. Look at the parties. The woman is a servant—a slave. We have no doubt but that she has been carefully trained and instructed in morals and religion; that she has been taught to observe the strictest rules of chastity. But all this is true of Mr. ——, and in addition thereto he has a character to sustain for himself and his family; and his success in the vocation in which he is engaged must depend in no small degree upon the purity of character he may sustain. He is also much older than the woman—perhaps nearly twice her age; and so far as is known to the subscribers, he has always sustained a fair character.

It is the opinion of some of our ablest legal men who have had much experience in the investigation of cases of bastardy that the propensity in woman is to conceal the true father. The cases that differ from this, they say, are the exceptions, and usually arise from a spirit of revenge for what the woman considers a breach of promise, false pretenses, etc. So strongly impressed have some of our lawyers and judges been with these facts that some effort has been made in the general assembly of the state to have the law so altered as to make the mother incompetent for a witness unless the complaint be made at the time or very soon after the illicit intercourse.

Now, dear sir, the fact is apparent that your woman, the mother of the child, has departed from the rules of chastity. She can plead no breach of promise of marriage. She gave no alarm of any coercive measures having been used. Her own declaration is the only positive evidence. The only corroborative evidence is the coincidence in time and resemblance of the child—that is, so far as the facts appear from your letter. On the other side there is the unequivocal denial of the accused, his former character and position in society, and the interest he must have in maintaining a good moral character. Certainly these are entitled to consideration.

We do not write to you for the purpose of screening Mr. —— from the full measure of any penalty which he may have incurred; but he is a member of the church of which we are officers, and while we grant that it is our duty to look closely to all offenders, yet it is no less our duty to protect and defend innocent members of the church. We make this communication to you in all frankness and candor, with a desire that you reply to us as early as convenient, and if any additional evidence or developments have come to light, that you will inform us. We have given no publicity to this charge, and shall not until time shall have been given to hear from you. The character of Mr. —— is in great jeopardy, and with his character goes his prospects for success even in his secular vocation.

With due consideration and esteem, we are, dear sir,

Truly yours, etc.,
John Johnson
A. G. Redd.

REV. C. C. JONES *to* MRS. ELIZA G. ROBARTS[t]

Maybank, *Friday,* September 27th, 1861

My dear Aunt,

I have been owing you a letter for a long time, and it was my duty to have written before, but my kind relatives and friends will grant me some little grace on account of depressed health.

No longer able to preach regularly, am trying to employ what strength and improve what time I have in the completion of my work on *The History of the Church of God,* which requires a great deal of care and study and time. And it advances at a slower pace than it otherwise would had I usual health and strength to apply myself as many hours a day as formerly. The first volume has been some time completed, and had it not been for this iniquitous and cruel war, would have been published ere this. The second volume, I suppose, is almost half done; and the last half is the most important part of the whole, and will require time and care. It has been a comfort and a consolation in my hope that it may please God to own the work to the edification of His Church and to the advancement of His Kingdom. I try to spend from four to six hours on it daily. More I cannot well do. But there are many interruptions.

The summer has been a remarkably pleasant one in climate, and also very healthy up to this time. . . . Not much stirring down here but matters connected with the war. By the papers it appears our Southern coast is to be invaded, and the coast of Georgia as likely as any. The best thing doing for our protection is establishing a camp or camps of men—some thousands, I hope—at some points on the Savannah, Albany & Gulf Railroad, to be in short reach of Savannah and St. Marys and Brunswick. We are far behind in preparations, so far as I can learn. . . . It is a time of sore judgment over the land, and Christians should live near to God. You have lost your pastor; hope you will not be long without one. You have all been serving your country well in Marietta.

Our dear little charge is growing, everybody says, finely, and interests her grandparents very much. Keeps awake pretty much all day and sleeps pretty much all night, which suits us exactly. Looks like her little sister, but more, we think, like her happy mother. Our dear son sorely afflicted: his letters are on the subject constantly. You have seen him lately. Pray for him, that he may obtain true and everlasting comfort and salvation.

My dear wife has not been well all the summer, but is up and about as usual; and you know what that means. She unites with me in much love to Cousin Mary and Lou and to the young ladies and Joe. It gave us great pleasure to know that your own health had been so good all the summer. Brother is hearty all to his back. Our united love to you, my dear aunt.

Your ever affectionate nephew,
C. C. Jones.

Rev. C. C. Jones *to* Hon. Charles C. Jones, Jr.[g]
Maybank, *Friday,* September 27th, 1861
My dear Son,

Your last favors by mail and by John have been received, and Mother says she will not visit you until she hears particularly from you, as she is ready at any time.

Your afflictions come over me, my son, from time to time with great power. They are very heavy, and what can I do to help you bear them? I recall the persons and the images of my dear daughter and my dear little granddaughter; they are to live in memory only; I am nevermore to see the living and precious ones! The shadows of death cover them; their flesh is now perishing and undergoing a purification by the Holy Spirit for the final quickening at the Resurrection into the fashion of the glorious Body of our Lord and Saviour Jesus Christ. Their spirits have gone to God, who gave them, as I firmly believe; and they are ever with the Lord, and their happiness is complete. This is not imagination, but it is reality. And thanks be to God who makes us know it is so through the gospel of His Son!

You speak of this brighter and purer world, of the happiness of your loved ones there, and of your hope of reunion with them. But you do not speak of your traveling in the way that conducts you there—the way your dear Ruth trod and found unspeakable peace in the end as she passed at death into the fruition of it. There is such a thing as substituting imaginations for realities; and unless you have a real interest in the merits and intercession of the Lord

Jesus Christ, such as your dear wife had, you will never meet her in heaven, and your own immortal soul will be eternally lost! Nothing short of this can satisfy me. I want to see you making a sanctified use of your deep sorrows. God shows you, as you express it in your last letter, the emptiness of pleasure and of honor and of wealth and all else earthly as a portion of the soul and as abiding sources of happiness—what perhaps you would never have so fully realized as by the affliction He has sent upon you. And He has shown you that the religion of Christ is a reality. And the one thing needful—needful, absolutely necessary above all things else—is that we accept Christ as He is freely offered to us in the gospel as our only and all-sufficient Redeemer.

Dear Ruthie in her dying hours told you in all the earnest affection of her soul for you as her own beloved husband "to seek the Lord, and to seek Him now." And she has been lost to your arms in her silent grave these three months, and you have not, so far as we know, done it yet! Oh, if those tender eyes could once more open upon you, and those dumb lips speak and ask you, "*Why, why* have you not done, my husband, what I begged you to do?" you would be speechless! And what His dying disciple said to you, the Saviour Himself has been saying to you now going on some thirty years: "Seek ye the Lord while He may be found. Call ye upon Him while He is near. Let the wicked forsake his way, and the unrighteous man his thoughts. And let him return unto the Lord, and He will have mercy upon him, and to our God, for He will abundantly pardon." And if He should call you before Him (as He can at His pleasure) and ask you why you have not sought Him, you would be speechless!

I cannot but feel that God is dealing very closely with you, my dear son, and am exceedingly anxious that you make your peace with Him, and do it now. Do not postpone so important a matter. He has broken up your precious family by a direct personal affliction; and now your home is to be broken up by a general judgment of a cruel war upon the country, and you are to be thrown into new scenes, and it may be new sorrows. For who knows the issue of war? Do not come out of that home but under the protection and leadership of the Great Captain of our Salvation. And come what will, you will be safe, and saved in Him.

Your dear little daughter is doing as well as possible, and everyone says is growing finely. Mother unites in much love to you. I remain, through God's mercy,

> Your ever affectionate father,
> C. C. Jones.

Hon. Charles C. Jones, Jr., *to* Rev. C. C. Jones[g]

> Savannah, *Tuesday,* October 1st, 1861

My dear Father,

I was two days since favored with your very kind letter of the 27th inst., and have most seriously considered its injunctions, and reflected upon the most important counsels which it contains. I would not have you believe that I am trifling with God's dealings with me, that I am forgetful of the dying request of my precious Ruth, or that I am "substituting imaginations for realities." Those realities are too sacred, too awful, too heartrending, to admit of trifling consideration or of vain imaginations. I am trying to be a better man. I am not endeavoring to shake off the impressions of that holy hour when it was my privilege to watch the triumphant departure of my dearly beloved wife from time into a happy eternity. I am acting not in my own strength. True, I am of all men most weak; and my daily sins, great and numerous, remind me ever that all human righteousness is but vanity. In the free, full, imputed righteousness of the infinitely merciful and all-sufficient Saviour, who died to accomplish the salvation of sinners condemned and dying under the law, is my only hope. I feel that there can be no salvation elsewhere, nor do I desire that there should be any; and my wish is, with every thankfulness and confession of sin, and forsaking unrighteousness, to embrace that salvation and live in the full enjoyment of those inestimable blessings which flow from a sense of sin pardoned and peace made with God. All else is valueless.

I was last evening with Mr. Porter, who has suffered much from several hemorrhages. He is quite weak, and we know not yet what the result will be. He was unable to preach last Sabbath, and is now closely confined to his bed. The doctor hopes that the bleeding comes from the throat and not from the lungs. He is a good man, and I sincerely trust that he may be soon restored to health and usefulness.

The Confiscation Act is being enforced in our city, and I have been busily occupied for several days in drawing returns, etc. A very large amount will be realized in this city and elsewhere.

The fortifications of our coast are progressing more rapidly than they have been at any time heretofore. The question of field fortifications around this city is being considered.

You will see that I have declined a reelection as mayor of this city, and also the appointment as representative from this county in the state legislature. The reasons I will give you in full, for I hope to be with you in a short time. My present term of office expires on the 21st inst.

With every love for yourself, my dear father, dear Mother, and my precious little daughter, I am, as ever,

Your affectionate son,
Charles C. Jones, Jr.

Rev. C. C. Jones *to* Hon. Charles C. Jones, Jr.[g]

Maybank, *Thursday*, October 3rd, 1861
My dear Son,

Your deeply interesting letter of the 1st we received last evening, and your dear mother and father returned thanks to God for what it contained of your views and feelings and purposes in relation to your eternal interests. And we can but hope that the Good Spirit of God is with you. I wrote you with many tears, and your answer filled my heart with gratitude. Your knowledge of the way of salvation is clear; and may you have a true and living faith in the Saviour and enjoy that peace which He alone can give! Our cup will be full when we know and see you to be a true man of God. Write me on this the most interesting of all subjects without any reserve, and let me know the state and progress of your feelings.

We have had a serious affliction this week in the death by typhoid fever of Dinah, Andrew's daughter. She died on Sunday evening at nine o'clock in the washroom, where we removed her for more ready attention. The first case of such a fever we have ever had in our household, and the first I ever saw in my life. Her death has cast a gloom over the place; and it was unexpected to us all, the fever making rapid progress the last two days. She was the life of the place, and a consistent member of the Baptist Church. Another voice of warning to us: "Be ye also ready, for the Son of Man cometh at an hour when ye think not."

Just as your mother and I returned from laying our poor servant in her grave, as the shadows of the evening were deepening into night and we were very sad, your dear sister, Robert, and the children drove up. Their visit seemed a special mercy under the circumstances. They left us on Wednesday.

Your dear little daughter is growing finely, everyone says, and certainly more and more interesting day by day. She is perfectly well all to the ear, which is much better under your brother's treatment. She rode round and round the lot yesterday in the buggy, and when she was brought in, her grandmother put the coconut dipper to her little mouth and she drank heartily like an old person.

Mother wishes to know if you received a bag she sent you some time since containing sundries.

In an interesting letter received from your Uncle John last evening from Manassas, he expresses a most anxious desire to get Dunwody transferred from Virginia to our Georgia coast army, fearing the cold of winter upon his constitution, which has been shaken twice with pneumonia. He asks if he could not be elected in some company a lieutenant and so be transferred, and begs us to do what we can for him. I do not see how such an election could be brought about, nor how the removal can be accomplished. I wish you would make some inquiries on the subject and let me know. Your Uncle John returns this month about the 14th. He asks you in the letter to help him.

Am happy to learn our coast defenses are advancing. There are complaints on that score everywhere. It is past time for it—if the enemy are coming either to Brunswick or Savannah. The defenses of Savannah should not be delayed a single moment, and the city be protected by land as well as by water. I learn Captain Anderson had two or three guns sent him naked as they left the foundry, with not a pound of ammunition, but files ready for spiking!

Mother goes to Montevideo tomorrow and returns immediately. She has a bad cough. She sends much love. Mary Ruth is sleeping sweetly: quarter past 10 P.M. We have had meeting for the people this evening. The Lord bless you, my dear son!

Your affectionate father,
C. C. Jones.

REV. JOHN JONES *to* COL. WILLIAM MAXWELL *and* REV. D. L. BUTTOLPH[t]

Fairfax County, Virginia, *Friday*, October 4th, 1861

To my esteemed relatives Colonel William Maxwell and Rev. D. L. Buttolph I send the most affectionate greeting from this far-off land of the Old Dominion. Often have you both been in my thoughts, and truly do I wish you could have witnessed with me many of the sights and scenes of this summer. It would do my heart good to see Cousin William review the numerous regiments as they march nearer and nearer the enemy. And I should delight to see Brother Buttolph's warm heart kindling and expanding his whole man amidst the present exciting scenes.

I am now with my dear wife and little boys at the house of an old Virginian. On the 23rd September, being unwell and threatened with camp fever, I left our regiment on a short visit to my family in Culpeper Village. On Monday 30th September I left Culpeper on my return to camp, taking my wife and little boys up to see Dunwody, and intending to stop at Fairfax Station (two miles of our encampment). Arriving at Manassas, I ascertained that a battle was daily expected, and an order had been issued forbidding ladies and children to proceed beyond Manassas. I had therefore to seek a home (which is not to be had in Manassas) for my family. I found one after twilight at the house of an interesting old Virginian, who after much persuasion agreed to board us for an indefinite number of days. This house, a fine family mansion of brick, was for six weeks the late headquarters of General Beauregard and staff after the battle of Manassas plains. The house and premises all bear the impress of military occupants, who were here only a few weeks since.

On the 3rd of October I visited for the fourth time the battlefield of the 21st July (Manassas). I took with me my dear wife and little boys—a great day in their lives. Of that battle I shall have *much—very much*—to say when we are permitted to meet again. Every visit to the scene of action impresses me more and more that the Lord won the battle for us—not through the skill of our generals but the indomitable courage and perseverance of our common soldiers, and by timely reinforcements, and particularly by overwhelming the enemy with an uncontrollable panic when they still had more than three to one on our side. But for a mistake of couriers we could easily have captured the entire army of the Federals, estimated (including their reserves) from fifty-five to seventy-five thousand. They were confident of capturing Manassas, and were in a fair way of doing it up to 2 P.M. But I must stop, or I will never end on this fruitful subject.

October 12th, 1861. Having left my family at Mr. Weir's near Manassas, I returned to camp last Saturday the 5th inst. I found our regiment on picket about seven miles distant, our policy being to entice the enemy out from his strongholds. After taking and holding for some weeks Mason's and Munson's Hills, and looking down on the valley of the Potomac and Alexandria and Washington, we have retired back to the neighborhood of Fairfax Courthouse, hoping to entice the Federals out in large numbers. Our regiment (the 8th Georgia) being absent on my return, I went over on Sabbath and preached to the 11th Georgia, which is in our brigade. I preached at the house of a Mr. Brooks, who fled away last May to the North, being a New Yorker, and a resident of Virginia only eight years. His house is now occupied by his tenant and a number of sick South Carolinians. This Brooks house is a hundred years old, and just before it a shady yard, in the midst of which stands a cherry tree a hundred years old. Standing just out of the piazza of this venerable mansion, and literally surrounded with soldiers, I had a most solemn service, and many tears trickled down the sunburnt cheeks of manly faces.

On Monday the 7th I rode over to Fairfax Courthouse—about two miles. At this village lives the widow of the late gallant Jackson of Alexandria, who shot the Zouave chief Ellsworth on the 24th of last May. Rev. Mr. Mullally of Columbia, South Carolina, and myself called on Mrs. Jackson and had a most touching interview. She is about thirty-five years of age, and is an interesting ladylike woman devoted to the memory of her husband. Her description of the heartless cruelties of those Zouaves represented them more as savages than as inhabitants of a Christian land. Fairfax Courthouse is honored as the depository of the original will of General Washington in his own handwriting. I inquired if it could be seen, and found that it had been removed for safekeeping to Warrenton (twenty miles distant) just before the advance of the enemy on Fairfax Courthouse on the 17th of last July.

Our Army of the Potomac, consisting of two grand divisions, is now under the command of Major General Joseph Johnston; and his late division is under General Smith, a Kentuckian; and the other division is under General Beauregard. The position of the army is that of a cross, and the encampments extend four miles each way. The number of the army is about fifty thousand, with only forty-five thousand strong, as we have about five thousand sick and unfit for duty. *But these figures are not for the papers, as our enemy suppose we have many more than we have.* Bennett of the *Herald* lately rated our Army of the Potomac at two hundred thousand. Still more recently he pretended to publish an exact list of all our brigades and the number of our soldiers, and it is supposed that some spy in our midst had been giving him information.

It is impossible for those of us who are not connected with headquarters to know anything certain of our future movements. I think from the fact that all our sick who could travel have been sent down to the hospitals, and all extra baggage removed to Manassas, that an important move is near at hand—either a descent upon Maryland or another great battle in this neighborhood. From the 5th to the 12th October we have daily expected a battle. Cannon often heard day and night. Regiments constantly on picket in advance of the lines, and approaching the enemy from two miles to one. The enemy are about six miles from Fairfax Courthouse and eight miles from our camp. We cannot divine their plans. They come out and then retreat, being careful to keep near their strongholds. Their position is ridiculous: a late army of invasion, subjugation, and occupation were suddenly driven back, repulsed, panic-stricken, and are now acting on the defensive. Some hope that they will yet come out and accept battle. I think that October will be an important month in the campaign. We are lingering to see the crisis passed —either a battle or an entering into winter quarters by our army. (This morning, 14th October, we had frost and ice.) Sometimes I think the policy of our enemy is to protract the war, and worry us, and annoy us on the coast, and in every way test our endurance, and never offer battle (since the Manassas defeat) except when they have vastly superior numbers. General Beauregard is reported to have called this war "a duel of resources," and there is much in his remark.

October 14th. Who do you suppose preached for me yesterday and for our regiment? Guess! Our esteemed friend and elder brother Dr. Joseph C. Stiles. He came to Leesburg some ten days since to see his two sons Robert and Randolph, who are stationed there in an artillery company. (His third son is also in the army in Georgia.) From Leesburg he came to see a brother, Dr. Clifford Stiles, who is a surgeon in the 1st Georgia Regulars, located in this neighborhood. Hearing that I was with the Georgia 8th, he sought me out and called to pass a few hours and return to his brother's camp. But I was lodging in a comfortable mansion, and I persuaded him to remain and pass the Sabbath and preach for us, and also pass Sabbath night, as he found one night in the camp very rough. He preached for us yesterday, and the regiment gave him marked attention. He is a wonderful man in intellect and piety. Today he left for Leesburg, where his sons are, and where he expects to have a protracted meeting and to have in attendance a number of regiments of soldiers.

But I must close my long letter, with my warmest love to you both, and to Cousin Susan, Cousin Laura, and the little boys, to Brother Charles and Sister and all who may be with them, and to all at Woodville.

Your affectionate relative,
John Jones.

P.S. Excuse this joint letter in pencil. I am at a Mr. Watkins' house, three-quarters of a mile from camp. If you answer, direct to Rome, Georgia, as we will leave by the 25th inst.

October 15th, 1861. Last night, or rather this morning at half-past three A.M., there was an alarm that woke up the entire Army of the Potomac. The sentinels were instructed to watch, and if five rockets went up from headquarters at Fairfax Courthouse, they should report them as signals of the enemy's approach. Accordingly, as these faithful men were watching at their posts, up went a rocket, and a second, third, fourth, and fifth; and then the sentinels reported to the colonels, and immediately the long roll was beat in forty regiments or more, and soldiers by thousands sprang to arms and formed in line of battle, ready to meet the enemy. And for one hour it was expected a battle was at hand, until it was ascertained that there was no advance of the enemy. Perhaps some scout from an advanced post mistook in the night some sound or sight for the enemy and so reported. It is well to have our men tried occasionally to make them prompt. I think a great battle is near at hand.

Remember the army continually in your prayers. Dunwody is well, and is reported to have carried himself gallantly through the battle of Manassas. Will Brother Buttolph attend Synod in November?

Affectionately,
J. J.

4 P.M. I have learned that our pickets had a skirmish with the enemy last night and were driven in; and hence the cause of alarm.

HON. CHARLES C. JONES, JR., *to* REV. C. C. JONES[g]

Savannah, *Monday,* October 7th, 1861

My dear Father,

I am much indebted to you for your very kind letter of the 3rd inst., which would have received an earlier reply but for the numerous engagements which are ever pressing upon me.

In addition to the duties of the mayoralty, since the absence of Mr. Ward the entire burden of the office has devolved upon me; and now under the pressure of the Confiscation Act business engagements are greatly multiplied. I presume several hundred thousand dollars' worth of alien enemy property will be sequestrated in this city. The Confederate receiver, Dr. William C. Daniell, is pressing the matter. So intimate have been our business relations with the North that the complications growing out of copartnership trans-actions and joint interests in property owned here are endless. Hardships occur in not a few instances. But the old sore must be soundly probed before the purifying process will begin. The more absolute the separation the better. I have seen an estimate that the alien enemy property at the South will amount in value to some three hundred million dollars. This in our treasury, we will the better be able to prosecute the war and sustain the expenditures incident thereto, although all these sequestrations must eventually be ac-counted for by treaty stipulations—unless, forsooth, we are eventually over-turned, which is simply a matter of impossibility. Even the Lincolnites admit this now, and justify the war upon the plea that it is with them a domestic necessity—that unless public attention be kept away from home, they will suffer from internal dissensions, civil war, and every manner of turmoil, eventuating in absolute destruction.

Kentucky is paying the penalty of her indecision, and reaping the legitimate fruits of her pretended neutrality. The scenes of "the dark and bloody ground" are come again. I regretted to see that two of Governor Helm's sons had been arrested by the Lincolnites and sent for confinement to Lafayette Prison.

Have you noticed the brief account of the recent and successful engagement of General Henry R. Jackson? There is no question of his bravery; I fear for his prudence.

You may observe in the morning papers a proclamation in reference to the immediate defenses of Savannah. The work will commence on Thursday of this week, and the expectation is that it will be completed in ten days. It is expected that three or four hundred hands will report themselves on that day for duty. The principal approaches to the city will be protected by strong earthworks, and these will be connected by a redoubt. The circumvallation will be almost complete. These defenses are constructed in anticipation of a land attack. Captain Gilmer is here, and General Lawton is getting the benefit of his views.

Our military operations have progressed very rapidly during the past two weeks, and troops are being concentrated daily along the coast. Our company is at present stationed at the Isle of Hope, about nine miles from the city. We are busily engaged in getting our horses, men, and drivers in proper training—by no means a light task. My duties here expire about the 22nd of this month, and I expect then to join my company.

There are sundry aspirants for the mayoralty. No nominations by the people have yet been made.

Had the pleasure of a night from Brother on Friday last. Was surprised to find that he was on his way to join the Liberty Troop and serve as a private in the ranks. What do you think of this step? We talked the matter over, and I advised him to ask your judgment of the propriety of the course, all things considered.

I was pained, my dear father, to hear of the death of Dinah. She was a faithful servant, and her loss to her little family and to the circle on the plantation must be severely felt. Her disease was very singular.

In reference to Dunwody, I fear that there will be but little prospect for his obtaining a commission in any of the coast companies. In the formation of companies the officers are those first chosen, and they are men who have the influence necessary to secure the enlistment of the men who are to compose them. It is no easy matter, then, to put aside those who have borne the heat and burden of the day, and who have devoted their time and labor and money in recruiting, for one who has not in any manner contributed "in getting the organization up." You will find that the same is true of regiments. The colonel empowered to raise the regiment confers his field and staff appointments—as many as are at his command—to those whose influence can secure the companies necessary to perfect the organization. I know not of a single commission on our coast which could be secured by Dunwody.

He can act as a private almost anywhere. We can give him a place in our company, but offices we have none. I have just endeavored, but without success, to secure a lieutenancy for Edgeworth Eve, who returned a week since from the Army of the Potomac, where he had been acting as a lieutenant in one of the companies of the 4th North Carolina Regiment.

I am truly happy to hear such good news of my precious little daughter. May God in His great mercy bless her every day! I am trying in weakness, my dear father, to lead a new life, and will remember all your kind counsels and those of my dear mother. I hope to see you both very soon. Mr. Porter is recovering. Our city is not as healthy as it was. It would not be prudent for Mother to come, much as I desire her to do so. Give her my warmest love. Kiss dear little Mary Ruth for me. And believe me ever

Your affectionate son,
Charles C. Jones, Jr.

Did you receive a copy of my annual report?

REV. C. C. JONES *to* HON. CHARLES C. JONES, JR.[g]

Maybank, Wednesday, October 9th, 1861

My dear Son,

We received your two favors of the 7th and 8th this afternoon, and were happy to learn your continued good health. Do be careful of these October *suns* and *dews,* and make use of the preventive recommended by your brother whenever it is needful for you to do so. He thinks it might be a preventive of yellow fever if used in cities liable to that terrible affliction. But it would require a world of quinine, and not now to be had.

Your annual report as mayor of Savannah your brother sat down and read for us so soon as it came to hand, and it gave us great satisfaction. And as far as country folks are capable of judging, we thought it in composition clear, in sentiment admirable, and in suggestions judicious. I wish (had your space permitted) you had recommended the plan we spoke of touching the sewerage of the city. Your brother tells me it is the *plan of Paris.* High example, certainly. I never knew it before. Perhaps you have done so in council. Savannah never can be a healthy city until these intolerable and accumulating nuisances are entirely obliterated. What people would think of tolerating an acre excavated from six to eight feet deep and made a pool of such matter in the heart of their city for public convenience, and the receptacle of tens of thousands of rats, and millions of cockroaches, centipedes, and all manner of vermin! The difference is very little, having the offense to life and comfort put into smaller receptacles and distributed throughout the city. Your reign has been a prosperous one, for which we should be grateful, although from war influences your expenses have exceeded your income.

The Confiscation Act works finely. There will be money enough to pay for all the Negroes stolen and emancipated. Dr. Daniell, my old friend and physician, is an excellent man for carrying out the act; and I agree with you it ought to be carried out *in extremis* and break up the connection totally. The Federals have outwitted themselves for once in the speculation.

May it please God to deliver us from their iniquitous warfare, and enable us on the seacoast to repel their piratical invasions! If we are favored in giving them one or two decided repulses, it would go far to open their eyes; for they would see that our weakest points (in their estimation) are sufficient for their most powerful demonstrations. And on this account particularly I have felt the greatest anxiety that our coast defenses should be as nearly perfect and invulnerable as possible. And it is aggravating to think that golden months have been lost in almost absolute idleness, and that at the last hour things are hurried to preparation. If we are saved in case of an invasion from the sea, it will be a kind Providence over us blessing us when we have not put forth our efforts and done our duty. I apprehend, by all accounts, that the sea and coast defenses of Savannah need overhauling. A poor battery on Tybee with two poorly mounted guns and a force of fifteen hundred raw men! And guns of *limited range* in Fort Pulaski! But I will say no more on this subject; it is an unpleasant one to the people generally.

Your brother felt that he could not reconcile it to his conscience to remain quietly in professional pursuits when his country was imperiled; that the reflection in the future would be disagreeable when all would be over and he never to have borne any part in so good a cause; that he could not call upon up-countrymen to defend his own home and property and he remain behind; that he regards it a duty, and that every true patriot should be willing to make sacrifices; that he is not a military man, nor does he seek position or fame, but opportunity to testify devotion to his country and to aid in achieving her independence; and things being so, there is no better corps for him to serve in—for convenience, for acquaintance, for character—than the Liberty Independent Troop; that the mustering-in will be but for six months to begin with; and he will be, you may say, at home. This is the view he takes, and I do not feel at liberty to interpose any objection when he has made provision for his family for six months or more. And if camp life agrees with him, the relaxation from years of close study and the daily exercise cannot fail to restore his constitution to better health and strength. The truth is, your brother is not liable to military duty at all. You know the weakness of the left arm once broken; he could not carry a musket for any time conveniently, and a horse company is the only arm of service he could well serve in. He has been practicing his fine horse to the use of the pistol and the saber, and he stands fire and the rattle of the scabbard very well. Jerry, mounted by Titus, took part in the practice, but he made a sorry figure under the circumstances as a war horse. . . .

Dunwody would be glad to get a place as a private in our coast army if such a thing can be compassed. He says "he will give all the Confederacy over him and fifty dollars beside to any man who will take his place, and he will serve the Confederacy in the South, and begs his Cousin Charles to help him if he can." His direction is J. Dunwody Jones, care of Captain Magruder, Rome Light Guards, 8th Regiment Georgia Volunteers, Manassas, Virginia. Could he be allowed to get a substitute in Virginia and then come and join here? Do help him if you can.

Waring ought to be closely watched. His property is in Washington; he would be as a surgeon in the very place for a spy.

Your sweet little daughter is growing daily. Took a ride in the little carriage today and was quite delighted. Opens her mouth for you to kiss her, and observes everything. Mother and Brother send much love. May your way be clearer and clearer, my dear son, in the new life in Christ Jesus you are endeavoring to lead! Cast your all into His hands. Am glad to hear Mr. Porter is better.

Your ever affectionate father,
C. C. Jones.

Hon. Charles C. Jones, Jr., *to* Rev. *and* Mrs. C. C. Jones[g]

Savannah, *Thursday,* October 10th, 1861

My dear Father and Mother,

The pleasant change in temperature which this morning brings will, I trust, restore the health of our city. It certainly is delightful, and the warm breath for the first time this fall was cloudy on the early air.

Today I purchased a service horse—a fine animal, bay, six years old, of good action, and I think in every respect reliable. The officers in the flying artillery are required to furnish their own horses, trappings, etc., etc.—quite an item at the present rates. Our battery is still stationed at the Isle of Hope: camps located under those beautiful live oak trees which adorn the old Bulloch lot. With the spot I am familiar, although I have not as yet visited the encampment. The preparation of a mounted battery for efficient service, involving as it does the drill of men and horses, is exceeding onerous. The drill itself is the most difficult and complicated in the service. After frost we will probably be nearer the city. The men having been for more than two months since at Fort Pulaski, it was not deemed prudent to transfer them to open camp on the outskirts of Savannah.

My term of office expires, D.V., on the 21st inst., and I expect so soon thereafter as practicable to join my company. It is quite a sacrifice for me to do so, but I think that I am in the line of duty; and that, ascertained, should be complied with.

I am at quite a loss to know what disposition to make of my furniture. There is no sale for it. To have it boxed and stored is rather an expensive operation; and to store it in a public wareroom without covering would be ruinous. Mr. Morrell says he has no room for it. Today Mr. G. B. Lamar spoke with me about renting the furniture for a year. He did not say definitely whether he would do so or not, and will probably determine on the morrow. It seems to me that if the furniture can be left in the house in the hands of a careful person (as I take Mr. Lamar to be), and thereby the expense and the injury of removal be avoided, that this would be the best disposition that could be made of it. What do you say, my dear mother? It is an utter impossibility for me to retain the house, as I could not afford to pay the rent, all income being at an end.

All friends well. With much love to you both, my dear parents, and to Brother, and many kisses for my dear little daughter, I am, as ever,

Your affectionate son,
Charles C. Jones, Jr.

HON. CHARLES C. JONES, JR., *to* REV. C. C. JONES[g]

Savannah, *Friday,* October 11th, 1861

My dear Father,

I am this afternoon favored with your kind letter of the 9th inst., and rejoice to hear that all at home are well.

Very easily and heartily do I appreciate the feelings which induce Brother to enter the service in the manner he does. The more readily do I sympathize with him in them because my own heart responds to the promptings. How would it do in after years (if in the good providence of God life be spared to attain that age) for the father, when the question is asked by his child just learning the history of his country and studying that chapter, interesting in the extreme, which will be devoted to a record of this eventful period, "Did you fight for our country then?" to answer, "No, my son (or my daughter), I did not." And when the other question, the logical sequence of the first, comes, "Why not, Father?" how awkward and unsatisfactory alike to the parent and the child to respond, "I was too much engaged with private business to do so." A clear record whether in peace or war is the most precious legacy that a parent can leave for a child.

Above all other considerations, however, whether of interest, of inclination, of convenience, or of prudence, rises the desire to stand in one's lot and serve in that capacity in which his services are most needed. I could very easily have avoided active enlistment by consenting to another term of office. Only yesterday (and I say this only at home) a renomination was virtually unanimously tendered to me by the nominating committee appointed at the recent citizens' meeting. They could not agree upon any one of the candidates named, and asked whether I would not allow my name to be used, with a direct assurance that if an affirmative answer were given, no opposition would be made by any of the candidates whose claims were urged before the committee. While sensible of the good feelings of my fellow citizens, and thankful that I commanded their respect and confidence, I could not in all good conscience, and with the apprehensions of duty now resting upon my mind, consent to retain the office for another year.

The truth is, I am weary of the office and its continued routine of duties, which this year have been unusually exacting and important. My heart is heavy, and my mind is weary. I am at times—and especially during the silent watches of the night—so nervous that I spring almost out of the bed when dozing. This is not natural to me. The slightest thing which startles for the moment sets my heart to beating at such a rapid rate that I almost grow faint. This also is not what it should be.

Besides, I regard it as a matter vital to our interests here that the Chatham Artillery should be placed upon a proper footing as a mounted battery. You have, my dear father, no idea of the labor and continued care and study and drill and discipline which are required not only to organize but also to keep in a state of efficiency such a company. The conduct of a regiment of infantry is far easier. The members of the company will not hear to my leaving them, and have waited upon me with committees to protest against my doing so.

Above all, as a matter of personal duty and of private example, I think I ought to render service in the field. Were I to consult my own private inclinations as based upon principles of comfort, considerations of interest, and prospects of gain, I would not go. The service will be arduous, involving sacrifices great in their character; but I am of opinion that my duty requires it, and I will go.

Judging from the morning papers, we are to have several aspirants for the mayoralty. The election occurs on Monday next. I trust a competent and honest man may be secured. It is all-important.

I am happy to know that you were pleased with the annual report. My highest earthly ambition is to secure the approbation in whatever I do of dear Mother and yourself. Your opinions I value more than those of all else.

In my letter of yesterday I mentioned that Mr. G. B. Lamar contemplated renting my house with the furniture and servants. I do not see what better I can do. Today he looked at everything, but will not give a decided answer until next Tuesday or Wednesday. The whole matter is as yet quite open. The furniture, etc., will probably be in as good hands as they could be under similar circumstances. To have everything covered and placed in a store- or wareroom would involve an expense of at least one hundred and fifty dollars. I have not the money to pay for this. And to place everything in store in an open condition would be simply ruinous. What the cockroaches and rats and dust and mold would leave would scarcely be worth retaining.

Adeline tells me that she would be glad to remain with Abram, who is hired at the depot, until January next, and says that she will see that Grace does not fall into any bad habits. In these seasons of financial depression every source of reasonable income should be husbanded.

It makes me very sad to part with the possession—even for the time being —of the furniture so nearly and dearly associated with all the precious memories of my beloved Ruth and sweet little Julia, and to bid farewell to those rooms which are consecrated with all the recollections of their inestimable loves. But though times and places may change, the sweetest influences which belong to their memories will abide with me forever, and at all seasons. In their steads no substitutions can ever be had; a home in the heart —such a home as they had in my heart—can never be occupied by others.

I learn today that Mr. Ward arrived safely in Canada. Before this he has sailed from Quebec. I hope for him a speedy return. Our office will be temporarily closed until he does reach home again.

All friends here are well.

Do, Father, say to dear Mother that I sincerely regret that this (to a certain degree, at least) unhealthy condition of our city has rendered it imprudent for her to come in and select, as she kindly purposed, such articles from the wardrobe of my dear Ruth as should be preserved for my sweet little daughter in precious remembrance of her kind mother, whose loves she never in person can appreciate. When I leave I shall have her wardrobe sent to Philo's house. Would it not be well for me to select and send out some articles? I might bring them with me when I come; for I must see you, my dear parents and my little daughter, before I leave for camp. My duties here expire on the 22nd inst., D.V. I wish also to hand to Mother, to be kept for Mary Ruth, a little box containing some seventy dollars in gold and silver which belonged to her dear little sister Julia. It was her savings bank, and the sweet little thing had learned to take great delight in depositing in it ten-cent pieces, quarters, etc. It will be a matter of great interest to her. I will let you know what day I can come out.

With warmest love to you both, my dear parents, and to the Doctor, and with many kisses for my little daughter, I am, as ever,

Your affectionate son,
Charles C. Jones, Jr.

I will see what can be done for Dunwody.

Mrs. Mary Jones *to* Hon. Charles C. Jones, Jr.[g]

Maybank, *Friday,* October 11th, 1861

My dear Son,

An opportunity occurring to No. 3, I send you a hasty line to say that through divine favor we are all well in our *white* household. One or two cases of autumnal fever with the servants, which we trust will soon yield to your brother's skill, under God's blessing.

Your precious little daughter is very bright and sweet. Every day develops some new charm to her grandpapa and grandmama. Susan takes her walking into the yard, and she is much interested in feeding the chickens. Her Uncle Joe brought me four pairs of socks which he thought had been sent by her aunt Mrs. Howard. If so, please make Baby's and her grandmother's acknowledgments for so seasonable and kind a gift.

I have nearly completed a warm camp blanket for your brother, and would like to make the same for you, as I have another large thick blanket, *if you would like to have it.* It is lined throughout with dark striped Cobb cloth, which makes a very warm covering and relieves the unpleasant contact of the wool from the blanket and does not materially increase the size. You have never sent me your *drawers* to make. I am now perfectly at leisure to do them or any other work you may wish done. Only send the materials and a pair to cut by and they shall be made immediately. Write me if you wish any coarse shirts or pants made for George. I have materials for such in the house.

Many thanks for the delightful tea and gumdrops. Your uncle dined with us yesterday, and I gave him a cup; he said it was superb. We will have to touch such luxuries daintily if the blockade lasts. One thing is certain: we will endure privations joyfully rather than yield an inch to the vile miscreants that are now seeking our destruction.

I am rejoiced to know that active efforts are making for the defense of *Savannah* and our coast. Public feeling has been greatly exasperated by the apparent apathy and neglect of our general in command.

Your brother goes into service on Monday next. Your father has expressed our views of the matter.

Whenever, my dear child, you feel that I can help you in any way, do let me know. Your mother's heart is ever filled with sympathy for you in your deep sorrow. When you think it prudent, I will come down and assist you in any arrangements. Your bedding and carpets I can have put up in such a way as will never be troubled by moths, and you could send them home for safekeeping. Did it ever occur to you to retain the rooms in the third story of your house, where you could store your furniture, and rent out the rest of the building? *The office* itself would be valuable. And in these hard times they ought to reduce your rent at least one hundred dollars. They have done so in other places. I make this suggestion as it may relieve you of the trouble of moving your furniture for the present and save you some expense.

Your father and brother unite with me in much love to you. Many kisses from your little daughter. God bless and save you!

Ever, my dear son, your affectionate mother,
Mary Jones.

HON. CHARLES C. JONES, JR., *to* MRS. MARY JONES[g]

Savannah, *Monday,* October 14th, 1861

My very dear Mother,

I am in receipt of your kind letter of the 11th inst., and am very happy to know that all at home are well, with the exception of one or two cases of fever among the servants, which I trust have before this yielded to treatment.

The delightful sprig of verbena which you were so kind as to enclose in your letter, the perfume of which still lingers about me as I write, is most acceptable to me. I never see or smell this flower without having all the happy associations connected with Maybank revived in all the fullness and freshness of their earliest existence. There is the breath of a pious, generous, quiet, intelligent, beloved home about the perfume of that little flower which is exceedingly precious to me. You know, in eastern lands they talk in flowers; and I can assure you the language of this is soft, sweet, and most attractive.

I am happy to know that my dear little daughter still continues to enjoy health, and that she is daily attracting to herself the renewed loves of her kindest grandparents. I sincerely trust that it may please God to spare her precious life, and that He will at an early age change her heart and cause her to live ever a life of piety and of usefulness. To you, my dear mother, and to dear Father I never can be sufficiently grateful for this renewed proof of your great kindness in thus assuming the especial care of that tender little infant who will never know the sincere loves of her own sainted mother and her sweet little sister.

I much regret, Mother, that the past tendency to ill health in the city has postponed your anticipated visit, which I have so anxiously hoped for. In the event of my leaving the city before you are able to select from the wardrobe of my dear Ruth such articles as you think should be preserved for little Mary Ruth, and such also as you yourself might like to keep, I will have them all packed up and leave them with Mrs. Harriss next door, who will, I know, take every care of them until such time as you may find it prudent and convenient to make the disposition. Philo I have asked to distribute among her sisters the other articles. She was Ruth's favorite sister, and she will faithfully execute this melancholy and sacred trust. It is hard indeed to part with a single memorial of her whom I loved so tenderly; and yet, sad as the parting is, I cannot think of any other more appropriate disposition than the one contemplated.

In my former letters I told you what my anticipated plans were in reference to my furniture, and I hope under the circumstances that they will meet with your approbation. I know not what else can be done; and just now, with all the expenses which are upon me, I do not feel at liberty to decline an arrangement of this character and incur the additional expense of not less than one hundred and fifty dollars for the packing and removal of furniture to a wareroom. I presume by Wednesday of this week I shall hear from Mr. Lamar, who is now in Macon, in reference to the matter. Meanwhile I hope to hear from you.

I would be very much obliged to you, my dear mother, if you would have the blanket made for me. It will be very acceptable, and just at this time it is a matter almost of absolute impossibility to obtain a blanket of any sort or description. My drawers I have had made here (four in number) of white flannel. The coarse shirts and pants for George would be very acceptable.

I expect, D.V., to leave the city for our camp, which for the present is located at the Isle of Hope, some nine miles from the city, about the middle of next week. Before doing so, however, I expect to come out and see you and Father and my dear little daughter.

The probability is that we will be in the vicinity of Savannah for some time to come, unless ordered off upon special duty upon the coast in expectation of an attack from the enemy at some conjectured point. We are promised by the general a prominent position in the first engagement. I hope and trust that the Lord of Hosts will be with us. Him I desire ever as my God and my ever-present help, and desire ever to act in accordance with His will.

There is, Mother, some of that excellent tea left, and you shall have it all. If this blockade continues, we will be almost entirely deprived of these luxuries which in times of peace and plenty came to be regarded as absolute necessaries. For myself, I can very readily dispense with them.

I hope the health of our city is improving. The temperature is very delightful. Give much love to Father. Kiss my precious little daughter for me. And believe me ever, my dear mother,

Your affectionate son,
Charles C. Jones, Jr.

MRS. MARY JONES *to* HON. CHARLES C. JONES, JR.[g]

Maybank, *Tuesday,* October 15th, 1861

My dear Son,

Your affectionate favor, received this afternoon, gives us the delightful assurance that we may hope to see you before long. I cannot bear to think of your going into service without seeing us and your precious little daughter.

Your father and myself fully approve of your renting your house and furniture to Mr. Lamar. He is in every respect a reliable gentleman, and it would be a relief not to make any changes either in your furniture or servants, if he will take Adeline and Grace and allow Abram to be with his family as heretofore. . . . When would Mr. Lamar wish to take possession? I would be glad to come down at any time you thought it prudent, and will probably be compelled to do so as early as is safe.

I write in haste, as Mr. McDonald is waiting to go. This morning your brother was mustered into the Confederate service. We rode down to see him. Henry and himself are in the same tent, but they are very much crowded. I will have the blanket and George's clothes made immediately. What more can I do for you? Unless it is customary I do not think you ought to rent your carpets. Father unites with me in best love to you. Sweetest kisses from your little daughter.

Ever, my beloved child, your affectionate mother,
Mary Jones.

HON. CHARLES C. JONES, JR., *to* REV. C. C. JONES[g]

Savannah, *Wednesday,* October 16th, 1861

My dear Father,

I am in receipt of your kind note at the hands of Titus, and am happy to know that all at home are well.

If you will be so good as to send the buggy for me to No. 3 on Saturday morning next, I will try and be with you and dear Mother and my precious little daughter on that day. I would have been out before, but it has been a matter of utter impossibility for me to escape from the numerous engagements which have been pressing upon me.

As you observe from the daily journals of this city, there has been no election of my successor by the people. In that event it is provided by an act of the legislature that after the board-elect has been fully organized, that they shall at once proceed to select a mayor from the two candidates who shall have received the largest popular vote. I presume from present appearances that Mr. Thomas Purse will be the mayor for the ensuing year, as the board-elect seem to be in his favor. He is a good man in the main, but quite too pliable in his composition and, as I respectfully conceive, unfit for emergencies like the present. Dr. Arnold, his competitor, would possibly on the whole have been more reliable, but even he is not the man for the times.

I am happy to think that in retiring from the office, the duties of which for the past year I have endeavored faithfully and honestly and fearlessly to discharge without favor or affection, that I carry with me the esteem, the confidence, and the approbation of the good men of this community, and withal have preserved my own sense of self-respect and rectitude of purpose. That lost, everything else is of no avail. The annual report is now in the hands of the printer, and will soon appear in pamphlet form. So soon as completed, you shall have copies.

On yesterday a copy of the Richmond *Enquirer* was posted to your address containing the official report of General Jackson's recent engagement on Greenbrier River. The general has made most of the affair, and the report is very characteristic of him. It would have been all the better if he had condensed it into about one-fourth its length.

Successes have crowned our arms in every quarter recently. We are loudly called upon to return earnest thanks to the Giver of All Good for His continued interposition in our behalf. The health of our city is improving; the pleasant change in temperature has exerted a most beneficial influence. . . . All friends are well. Mr. Porter improves, but not very rapidly. . . . With much love, my dear father, to self, dear Mother, and many kisses for my dear little daughter, I am, as ever,

Your affectionate son,
Charles C. Jones, Jr.

Rev. C. C. Jones *to* Hon. John Johnson *and* Mr. A. G. Redd[t]
Maybank, *Wednesday,* October 16th, 1861

My dear Sirs,

Your letter in relation to Mr. —— reached me on the 30th ult., and as you requested, I embrace my earliest convenience to reply to it. You make several points on my letter to him, and I presume with the desire of eliciting some notice of them from me.

Your first point is that "there may be circumstances in a case sufficient to produce conviction in the minds of those well acquainted with them, but it may not be practicable to produce evidence according to established forms and usages sufficient to convince an investigating tribunal." This at times is most unfortunately so—unfortunately so for the innocent, as they must ever lie under suspicion; and unfortunately so for the guilty, as they escape punishment.

Your second point is that "such appears to be the nature of Mr. ——'s case." The first proof submitted in my letter of his guilt was "the free, unconstrained confession of the Negro mother herself." The plea urged by you against it, drawn from the illicit intercourse of whites under promise of marriage, is irrelevant, since no contracts of marriage obtain between whites and blacks. Nor is it essential to the truthfulness of the mother's declaration that she was not forced and gave no alarm. The consent of the woman was all that was required, and her declaration is that she so consented, and that she had repeated criminal conversation with the said ——, and that the mulatto child is his. And she makes the declaration without revenge and without compulsion. Her evidence you allow to be positive evidence. The second proof submitted was "the correspondence of the time of his criminal connection with the Negro and the birth of the child." This you allow to be satisfactory as far as it goes. The third proof submitted was "a resemblance beyond mistake." Your answer to this is that "resemblances may be traced between individuals utter strangers to each other," and that "they are wanting between brothers and sisters, parents and children." These are rare exceptions when you compare man with man, and the members of the same families with each other. And the exceptions prove the rule. The resemblance of progeny to parent is *a law of nature,* and runs through the whole animal kingdom, and can neither be gainsaid nor resisted. The resemblance of the mulatto child to Mr. —— is uncommonly and unmistakably distinct and perfect.

The third point you make is "the character and, by consequence, the credibility of the parties." The party of the first part is the woman—a Negro and a servant, whom you doubt not has been well instructed and morally and religiously brought up. But servants are not always liars, and are particularly slow to father their children upon white men without the best of reasons, and because of their humble and exposed condition are more open to the seductions of their superiors (not in character but in station in society). The careful training of our servant has proved no defense. She says "Mr. —— told her not to make him known if anything should happen." The party of the second part is Mr. ——, who you say has also been well and religiously trained, is respectably connected, has a character to sustain, a family to support, his success in business is dependent upon his good reputation, has always sustained a fair character, and is much older than the woman. Age is too frequently an overmatch for inexperienced youth, and Mr. ——'s age is an immaterial circumstance, for he is in good health and in the prime of life. The circumstances of Mr. —— to which you allude as well calculated to bind him to a life of integrity and virtue are forbidding enough against a life of contrary character, and were all fully drawn out in my letter to him. But in themselves they do not prove him innocent of the charge preferred against him by the Negro girl, although backed by his denial. They afford ground of presumption that he would not perpetrate so vile a crime, but nothing more. Previous good character and standing may mitigate the sentence of condemnation or aggravate it, just as those who try a case are led by the testimony to view it, but can never be admitted of the nature of proof against charges of wrongdoing. Otherwise some of the greatest offenders would escape justice. Our civil and ecclesiastical courts furnish examples of transgressors in high places, and we cannot be forgetful of like examples recorded in the Holy Scriptures for our warning.

You say finally: "So far as is known to us, Mr. —— always sustained a fair character." And your remark obliges me to note the point. So far as was known *to me*, Mr. —— when he came to my house had sustained a fair character. But to my amazement, after he left my house I learned that he had been charged by a Negro girl in the village where he taught school in our county with having had criminal connection with her and with being the father of the child with which she was then pregnant; that he had denied the charge before the trustees of the academy and demanded that the Negro should be punished, which punishment was inflicted previously to the birth of the child; and the trustees acquitted him, there being no evidence but that of the Negro girl against him. Nor did the matter come abroad in our community, so kindly did the people act towards him; at least, it circulated but to a limited extent. The Negro girl, however, persisted under punishment that he was the father of the child. The child was afterwards born, and born a mulatto, and she persists in the charge to this day. And while some in the village believe him innocent, others believe him guilty. Now, here are two Negro women living twenty miles apart, without any knowledge of or correspondence with each other, preferring the same charge against the same man and holding to it. Had I known the first charge when Mr. —— came into our neighborhood, I never would have permitted him to become the inmate of my family without having first assured myself that he was truly an innocent man. And after it came to my knowledge, and before the birth of the mulatto on my own place and the confession of its mother, I had a charitable hope that it might not be true. Nor did I recall this charge to Mr. ——'s remembrance in my letter, for the reason that I did not wish to aggravate his case and go beyond the crime committed in my own household.

When remarking in that letter that "the evidence was amply sufficient to warrant the submission of the case to the Columbus church," I left Mr. —— to act as he chose in the matter; and he has done what he could not well have left undone: he has submitted the case himself.

I have nothing further to add in reply to your letter. You cannot be more surprised nor grieved than I have been, nor more desirous of seeing Mr. ——— cleared—not on technical grounds for want of legal evidence to convict, but upon absolute grounds of innocency, there being no evidence of any kind to convict him. But in my judgment this is impossible. If my servant were a white woman, with the evidence before you, she would carry a prosecution for bastardy against him in any common court of justice. My own belief is settled, which I pronounce with sorrow: that with all the circumstances and evidences before me, he is a guilty man. Nor am I alone in that belief.

I thank you for your Christian letter, and for your kind appreciation of my feelings in so unhappy an affair, and do highly honor the charity and integrity you manifest—charity to protect as far as possible the character of the innocent, and integrity in searching into the matter in order that you may carry out the discipline of the church to the fullest extent necessary without respect of persons, and so preserve the purity and character of Christ's Church, which He has bought with His own Blood, and over which He has set you as rulers. That you may have grace to direct and enable you so to do is the sincere prayer of

Very truly yours,
C. C. Jones.

REV. D. L. BUTTOLPH *to* REV. C. C. JONES[t]

Point Maxwell, *Wednesday,* October 16th, 1861

My dear Uncle,

I have copied your letter to Messrs. Johnson and Redd, and send the copy with the original under envelope. Please look over it to see if any mistakes have been made. I think you have said all that was necessary to be said in reply to their letter, and in a faithful and Christian manner. There is nothing written which you need ever desire should be blotted out. All well, and send love.

Sincerely and truly yours,
D. L. Buttolph.

VII

Lt. Charles C. Jones, Jr., *to* Rev. *and* Mrs. C. C. Jones^g

Camp Claghorn, *Saturday,* October 26th, 1861

My dear Father and Mother,

You will see by the date of this letter that I have joined our battery, and am now fairly entered upon the duties of camp life—a change quite marked from the routine of civil and professional duties which have for many years received my undivided attention. I left the city on yesterday morning, and found our entire command in good health and fine spirits.

Our time is fully occupied with the numerous duties which devolve upon us in preparing our battery for active service. What those duties are, no one can know who is not charged with their constant and faithful discharge. There is, I can assure you, a deal of hard labor in the efficient drill of men and horses, and in the careful conduct of all the details which appertain to a mounted battery. The men, however, who compose our company are unusually efficient. They are gentlemen all, and bring to the discharge of the duties incumbent upon them a degree of intelligence, industry, and cheerfulness quite remarkable. I trust that our shores may never know the pollution of the enemy's presence; but if he does come, I sincerely hope that our battery may be detailed to resist his first attempted landing, and to dispute every inch of ground in his contemplated march of desolation. I am beginning to appreciate the practical entertainment of the *Dulce et decorum est pro patria mori.*

Our camp is advantageously located nine miles from Savannah on the Isle of Hope, upon a bluff overshadowed with some of the noble live oaks which impart such dignity to the forests of our coast region. We occupy the site of the old Bulloch house, a few years since passing from the possession of the former owners and becoming by purchase the property of our present worthy and efficient captain. You would be pleased with the appearance of our encampment. Our pure white tents contrast beautifully with the dark, overhanging foliage of these attractive trees, and our burnished battery gleams brightly in the morning sun. Our garrison flag is floating freely in the quick air, and within a stone's throw of the guard tent a bold river moves onward between its low-lying shores toward the far-off sound. Our reveille is answered by no less than three encampments at distances of several miles above and below us along the coast, while the transmissive wave and the evening air carry to them unimpaired our nightly tattoo.

As I write, the campfires are all dead save that which burns brightly still in front of the guard tent, where "the watchers keep their vigils sharp"; and the stillness is unbroken save by the lazy flap of the tent curtains, the soft ripple of the tide as it gently chafes with the shore, and the occasional note of some waking songbird among the overshadowing branches. All else is hushed. Not a sound from the stables. No challenge from the sentinels. They are keeping their posts, however; for every now and then I can detect the clank of the scabbard against the slings as they come to the about. Even the quiet breathing of the captain, whom I can touch with my hand as he lies sleeping behind me on his camp cot, I cannot hear. And I am holding silent converse with you, my dear parents; and my heart is going forth in warmest love towards you and my sweet little daughter. May a kind Providence prove ever near you to bless and keep you from every harm!

George is with me, and attends well to his duties and to my horse Yorick, who I think will make a very fine parade horse. Did you receive my packages, etc., per Savannah, Albany & Gulf Railroad? With much love to you both, my dear father and mother, and many kisses for dear little Mary Ruth, I am, as ever,

Your affectionate son,
Charles C. Jones, Jr.

Direct to me as usual at Savannah.

Mrs. Mary Jones *to* Lt. Charles C. Jones, Jr.[g]

Maybank, Saturday, October 26th, 1861

My very dear Son,

This is your third night in camp, and my thoughts and heart have dwelt with you, within those thin cloth coverings wet with the dews and rains and swept by the cold northeasters that have been blowing uninterruptedly since you left us. Your couch perhaps has been the damp earth, and sad fears for your health amid such exposures are rising up before me. Oh, this cruel, cruel war! I am every moment forced to feel and realize it has been so from the commencement, in sympathy with my suffering relatives and countrymen; but now it is brought to my own bosom when yielding up our beloved sons.

I feel that you have both acted noble parts in going into active service upon the tented field. You, my son, might have yielded to the solicitations of your fellow citizens in continuing the occupancy of the mayoralty, in the discharge of high and honorable duties, and also in the prosecution of your professional engagements, surrounded by the comforts of home. But it has been your choice to lay these aside and share every hardship and privation with your gallant company, which from its being the most effective arm of service is also the most exposed in the day of battle. I know not one of your men personally, but I pray for them all, from your captain down. I know that the Lord's arm is mighty to protect and save in the day of battle and to make you valiant and victorious. Your brother, too, had every reason to continue his profession, and was exonerated from military duty by the injury in his arm and many considerations.

But it strikes ten o'clock, and I must close. God watch over and bless you this night, and with the light of the coming day grant you the sweet influences and teachings of the Divine Spirit, that you may "Remember the Sabbath Day to keep it holy"!

Monday Morning, October 28th. Yesterday was very dark, damp, and cloudy. Your father worshiped in Sunbury; I remained with my precious charge at home. Your brother from fatigue and exposure was unwell Saturday, but quite recovered and at church.

This is a clear, cool, and I may say brilliant October day—just such an one as thirty years ago was made most memorable in your mother's life when our kind friend Miss Lavender laid a beautiful boy in her arms, and she first felt that new and quenchless fountain of love opened up by her firstborn which will cease only with her existence. Did time permit, I might sketch a pleasant review of these long years, in which the mercy and goodness of God have followed you all your days. And even now, when the heavy hand of sorrow rests upon your heart, I trust you will be made to rejoice in your afflictions, and although the way has been rough and thorny, to know that it has led you to the Cross, where you have found a reconciled God and Saviour. May Jehovah bless and keep and save you through time and in eternity, and add unto your life many, many years of usefulness and happiness; give you true wisdom, the pearl of great price, the "good part" which cannot be taken away from you. Read the 116th Psalm. And may you be enabled to adopt its sentiments as your own!

Mr. McDonald expects to leave in a short time. I have closed hurriedly for want of time. Your sweet babe is very bright and well. Colonel Charles Spalding is keeping our coast guarded: seventeen men from the troop at Can't-Help-It, *couriers* at Riceboro, a guard at Harris Neck, etc., etc. It is very inspiriting to know that we have an active officer in command. Father unites with me in best love and good wishes on your birthday. He remembered you especially this morning. Kisses from your little daughter.

Ever, my dear son, your affectionate mother,

Mary Jones.

Rev. C. C. Jones *to* Mrs. Mary S. Mallard[t]

Maybank, *Saturday,* October 26th, 1861

My dear Daughter,

The past two weeks have been of unusual interest to your mother and father. On the 5th came your dear "Bubber Dodo" to be mustered into service in the Liberty Independent Troop. His summons was one week too early, but none too soon; for the week he spent at home breaking his fine charger to the use of the sword and to the fire of guns and pistols. Carrie has fitted him out handsomely, comfortably, and amply for six months or even more; and he has provided against dews and rains with waterproof coat, and in uniform on his horse accoutered makes a fine-looking trooper. The change of life will be a great advantage to his health, provided it pleases God to avert sickness in camp from him, to which so many fall victims.

On the 14th he joined the troop in Sunbury and went into camp and took quarters in your Uncle Henry's tent, with Prime from Arcadia for his body servant. The old man is vastly pleased, and very attentive, active, and handy, but in a few days lost a nice new blanket and one of his new working shirts your mother gave him. Stolen, of course—although he was very emphatically warned on that common vice of camps. He felt himself perfectly competent to take care of his own blanket, but in this he was mistaken.

On the 15th Mother and I rode down to Sunbury to see the form of mustering the soldiers into service, but we arrived just too late. We understand the form to have been: Forming the line on horse, armed and equipped, the Confederate officer sent for the purpose read the articles of war and the oath, and dispensed with the form of swearing the officers, and then the men in squads; and calling out their names, said every man who answered to his name would be considered *sworn*. And so the thing was done. The other and regular way would have been better, because more direct, personal, and solemn.

Your brother has been on the go, attending the sick here and there, ever since he has been in camp, and on the 21st was appointed surgeon of the post by Captain Winn, which appointment we hope General Lawton will confirm. It is in Joe's line, adds to his comfort and pay, and relieves him from guard duty. The two upper rooms in Mr. Screven's house he has fitted up for his hospital, and I believe occupies one for his quarters, where he keeps also his surgical instruments and medicines, etc. He expects to make some requisitions on the different retreats for hospital bedding and stores. He will have his department all ready and in good order. Mother gave him a cot and mattress and a large blanket lined with Cobb cloth and a camp stool and some candles, etc., so he is pretty well fitted out. He and your Uncle Henry save their flour and send it to Mother, and she has it turned into nice loaf bread and biscuits for them.

Your dear brother Charlie came on the evening of the 19th. He looks thin —through much labor, care, and sorrow. It is wonderful how he has thus far borne his griefs—and all alone. The lonely nights in the desolated home! I feel deeply for him. We hear no complaints, no murmur. We went to church at Dorchester next day, and his brother came and spent the night with him. We sang together some of our old hymns in the evening, and we wished you and yours had been with us. In the afternoon, after our return from church, I had a long and encouraging conversation with him. I can but indulge the pleasing hope that there is a good work begun in him. . . . He is going into camp; but what are all the temptations and trials that can be gathered together against our poor, weak, depraved souls if God be with us? . . . He was much gratified at the growth and improvement of his dear little baby. The little thing seemed to have an instinctive turning to him. Mother made him a double blanket also for camp and a nice gray flannel shirt after Carrie's pattern of Joe's, and trimmed it with some pieces which dear Ruthie gave her, left over from a sacque she used to wear. He recognized it immediately. He had the mayor's office tendered him twice—the last time by the committee of citizens, who could not agree upon a candidate, with the assurance that if he offered, there would be no opposition. Mr. G. B. Lamar takes his house and all his furniture (except the silver) and Adeline and Grace. A great relief, and an excellent arrangement. George becomes his body servant in camp. He was to have gone into camp with his company on the 24th (Thursday) at the Isle of Hope, but soon to be encamped near the city. As in the Doctor's case, so in his—I think the change, provided his throat can stand it, will be very beneficial to his health. He needs change and activity.

Our only sons—and both in the army! They have made great personal sacrifices, and upon a principle of duty. Both could without any reflection upon their patriotism have been usefully employed—and for the public—in important stations; but they preferred to share in the privations, labors, and dangers necessary to their country's independence. There is true nobility in their action. They are conscientious in it. I commend them for it. And we can commend them to God for His care and blessing, and hope He will take care of and bless them.

My physical strength is exhausted; otherwise I should endeavor to find some active employment in my country's service. The Revolutionary struggle was not more important than the one in which we are now engaged. The Lord thus far has evidently been on our side. Let us rejoice with trembling, and pray that His goodness may lead us as a nation to greater and more universal repentance. His countenance will not be turned towards us in full favor until the judgment is removed by Him.

Maybank, Springfield, and Woodville assembled at Maxwell on Thursday in honor of Jimmie Buttolph's third birthday. A squad of troopers on a scout dined with us and fired a salute in Jimmie's honor when they left. The day was closed by united prayer for ourselves and all ours.

Tell Little Daughter Grandma put Little Sister yesterday in a big cotton basket, and she lay like little Moses, but did not cry. And Gilbert and Susan held the pole and swung the basket, and Grandpa weighed her, and she weighed *eighteen pounds*. And she was four months old yesterday.

Tried to get some fish to send to you today, but the northeaster continues to blow, and Niger has had poor luck. Mother unites in much love to Robert and yourself, and in many kisses for our dear little granddaughter and son. All well around us, D.G.

Your ever affectionate father,
C. C. Jones.

Grandmother sends some apples *from Tennessee* for Little Daughter. Her Uncle Charlie brought them out. Her ducks are all well and much grown.

Howdy for the servants. Tell Kate I am glad to hear good news of her. She must watch and pray to the Saviour to give her strength to hold on and to hold out to the end.

Mrs. Mary S. Mallard *to* Rev. C. C. Jones[t]
Walthourville, *Sunday,* October 27th, 1861

My dear Father,

Niger arrived about eleven o'clock Saturday night, bringing your valued letter and the fruit from Mother.

Your letter carried me home and told me just what I wanted to know about all the dear ones there, and particularly about my dear brothers. I read with many tears of joy what you wrote in regard to Brother Charlie's conversation with you, and I could scarcely sleep all night for thinking of him and praying that our Heavenly Father would perfect any good work begun in his heart. I wish he could see his way clear to make a public profession before he fairly enters upon his life in camp. . . . I am sure if Mother and yourself feel that both your sons are soldiers of the Cross, you can cheerfully bid them go forth to fight the battles of our country; and I know they will never be wanting in courage. I regret exceedingly that I did not see Brother Charlie when he was in the county, as I fear it will be long before he has an opportunity to come out again. I hoped he would have taken us in his route. As soon as I can, I will see Brother Joe. Mamie is greatly delighted to hear that he is one of "our Confederate soldiers." She seems to think "our Confederate soldiers" ought to be loved and admired by everyone.

The children are both well, though little Mary is very thin. She charged me to give her love to "Danma" and "Danpa" and to kiss her Little Sister and "beg Danpa please not to leave her when she moved to Montevideo, for she wanted to make her coo and laugh."

Tell Mother I have no idea of going to Synod. Mr. Mallard thinks his going very doubtful: I know he would like to go to the General Assembly, and I don't think he could do both. I suppose he will determine after the meeting of Presbytery. If Mr. Mallard does go to Marietta, I think it would be refreshing to Mother to go with him and see Aunt Eliza. I know a little change would do her good; and perhaps by that time Uncle John will have returned from Virginia, and she can see him too. I will try and take care of Father and Baby, and would be only too happy to have them with me.

I am glad to think you will move so soon. We will come and see you as soon as we can. I shall not be able to go much from home for some weeks to come on Tenah's account. Her mother is so easily frightened by sickness that I would not feel satisfied to leave her. She has always been a kind, good nurse to the children.

Do give much love to all at Woodville and Maxwell and to Uncle William.

Mr. Mallard and our little ones unite with me in warmest love to dear Mother and yourself, dear Father. Howdy for the servants.

Your affectionate daughter,
Mary S. Mallard.

REV. C. C. JONES *to* LT. CHARLES C. JONES, JR.[g]

Maybank, *Wednesday,* October 30th, 1861

My dear Son,

Your two favors of the 24th and 26th reached us this evening, Robin bringing the first with the articles from the depot excepting the champaign basket of sundries which you mention. Have written to Mr. Quarterman to inquire for it at the depot. A trunk, a box, and dear little Julia's chairs were all that came. I thank you for the contents of the box, and will try to make a proper use of them. The paper comes just in time.

Your ambrotype (as we take it to be) is exceedingly fine. It is a handsome picture and fine likeness, and Mother and I greatly prize it. And our hope is that you may be spared in a kind providence, and your brother also, and all your comrades in arms, the perils of battle; and that your likeness may only remind us of your soldier's life and of what you were, by God's help, prepared to do for your country had you been called upon. Not a ray of light relieves our contest with our malignant enemies. We have nothing before us but self-sacrifice and devotion to a cause which exceeds in character that of our first revolution—and an unshaken trust in the righteousness and goodness of God.

Mother wrote you on your birthday, the 28th. On that day thirty years ago I carried your mother from Mr. King's, where we then lived, in Miss Lavender's practicing gig quietly to the entrance into her yard just after breakfast; and at about half-past 2 P.M. we beheld the face of our firstborn—and firstborn son: an uncommonly large and healthy infant. And when I first looked upon him I was as conscious of the flowing of a new affection through my soul towards him as my son as I would have been of a warm stream flowing over the most sensitive part of my person. And that stream has been flowing towards him ever since, and will continue to do so while my heart continues to beat. May God be with and bless you, my dear son, and grant that this year may be your first and a blessed year to you in the Kingdom of our Lord and Saviour Jesus Christ! He can make all grace and consolation abound to you amidst your inward griefs, and all the engagements and distractions and want of quiet and retirement in a life in camp. He is always nigh unto them that call upon Him, and will never leave nor forsake those who put their trust in Him.

Your dear sister, Robert, and the little ones are quite well; and so is your brother now—but had well-nigh made himself sick last week from too much exertion in his calling. I wish his excellent corps was *better officered.*

You know Mr. John Cassels. He sent all the way down from Flemington for your brother—"not that he expected any relief from his disease by his visit, but hoped that he might ease his passage to his grave." He is very low. Your brother went up this morning and returned this evening.

By Colonel Spalding's order seventeen men are stationed at *Can't-Help-It,* relieved every four days, and four couriers at the Boro relieved in the same time. And so the active colonel has all the coast in his command under watch.

Your dear little daughter was weighed by her grandmother on the day she was four months old (the 25th) in a big cotton basket, at the bottom of which she lay perfectly quiet and carefully watching all our operations. Gilbert and Susan swung the basket on a short stick, and she weighed *eighteen pounds*—pronounced by all the neighbors and friends an excellent weight for one of her age. She slept the entire night last night and never woke once. Mother sends much love. Be careful and run no risks in breaking your horse.

Your ever affectionate father,
C. C. Jones.

Mrs. Mary Jones *to* Lt. Charles C. Jones, Jr.[g]

Maybank, *Wednesday,* October 30th, 1861

My dear Son,

I will look over the sacred contents of the trunk and set a seal upon it for our dear little Mary Ruth. If my life is spared, she shall be taught to love and honor her father and her mother. Did you remember to take the wax doll, etc., from the bureau drawer in the third story? It may be ruined if left there. Mrs. Harriss would doubtless take care of it and send it out, to be preserved for Baby when she is old enough to value it. Do write us as often as you can. Many kisses from your little daughter.

Your affectionate mother,
Mary Jones.

Lt. Charles C. Jones, Jr., *to* Mrs. Mary Jones[t]

Camp Claghorn, *Thursday,* October 31st, 1861

My very dear Mother,

I was this morning in receipt of your kind letter of the 28th inst., and am truly happy to know that all at home are well. I have only a moment, after a day of no little fatigue, to send my warmest love and to say that we are all well.

You did not mention the receipt of the packages forwarded to Father's address last week at No. 3. Upon shipping them per Savannah, Albany & Gulf Railroad, I wrote Mr. Quarterman desiring that they be sent immediately down to the Island by Robin. You will excuse my inquiry, but I am solicitous of knowing whether or not they safely reached their destination. I also at the same time penned a letter to you. The trunk contains many precious memorials for my dear little Mary Ruth of her sainted mother, and I would not have them lost or mislaid on any account. I trust that you will approve the selection made.

Our tents are quite comfortable, and both men and horses are daily improving in the drill. Do you ever hear our morning and evening guns? With best love to self, my dear mother, to dear Father, and with many kisses for little Daughter, I am, as ever,

Your affectionate son,
Charles C. Jones, Jr.

I sincerely trust that Brother will have no return of his indisposition.

REV. C. C. JONES *to* LT. CHARLES C. JONES, JR.^g

Maybank, *Monday,* November 4th, 1861

My dear Son,

Yours of the 1st we have just received, and are glad to learn that you are well, and so are all under your command. The cool and rainy weather has for the present closed, and tonight we are expecting under a cloudless sky and still air a little frost for the first time.

Your brother dined with us today. Is looking remarkably well, in good spirits, doing good as usual in his profession, and goes (if nothing prevents) on Friday to see his family in Augusta.

Mr. John Cassels was buried at Midway on Sabbath. Died the death of a Christian. Leaves an interesting wife and one child! His wife told your brother at his bedside that "she would be willing to nurse him all her life if he could only be spared to her as he then was." Who can measure the strength of conjugal affection?

Your ambrotype is exceedingly fine and perfect. Mother and I are greatly pleased with it. Your Uncle William says "it is splendid," and your brother that "it could not be better"; and all your friends express great pleasure at it. You were specially remembered on your birthday; and I trust, my dear son, your resolution to lead a Christian life may spring from the Spirit of God working within you, and that by the grace of the Redeemer you may endure unto the end.

I write this evening particularly to let you know that we are all, through God's mercy, in our usual health. Your dear little daughter is quite well, and grows more interesting every day. She has taken up lately a very affected little cough. Every morning her grandmother puts her little hands together and repeats an infant's prayer for her; and this morning while your mother was repeating it she held her hands together and looked seriously in her face, and when the prayer was finished she put down her hands and drew a long sigh as if she had been engaged in what cost her some effort. Mother says she will write you particularly soon, and sends much love. Mary Ruth is sleeping sweetly in her crib, and Elsie is staying in the room with her.

If it should please God to enable us to repel the invading fleet, it will greatly strengthen our cause. For this we must pray. It will be difficult for the enemy to fit out another such an expedition for some time to come if this should be defeated. Georgia has done her share in the war, and it would be no marvel if they should endeavor to revenge themselves upon us. Surely we desire not to shed their blood, and wish for peace with them and with all mankind; and we must hope and believe that God will not suffer us to fall before their boasted power. We read the report of Captain Anderson's skirmish on Wassaw with interest. The Lord bless and keep you, my dear son!

Your ever affectionate father,
C. C. Jones.

REV. C. C. JONES *to* MRS. ELIZA G. ROBARTS[t]

Maybank, *Monday,* November 4th, 1861

My dear Aunt,

Your welcome letter gave us great pleasure, letting us know your uncommon good health and the health of all your family. By all accounts your patriotism has been at so fervent a heat, and your hands so busy, that you have had but little time or inclination to consider the ills and aches which our poor flesh is heir to.

The whole Confederacy is astir, and none more active than the ladies; and thus far the Lord has mercifully blessed our cause. And we trust that He will give us a happy issue out of so gratuitous and execrable a war as has been forced upon us. The prayers of God's people must not be slackened, and especially that He would restrain our armies and our people, that we may not accumulate our sins and protract His judgments but rather break them off by righteousness, so that His favor may be restored to us. A very considerable force of cavalry and infantry now lies along our coast at different points and in a position for speedy concentration at any given point that may be threatened. No account yet of the invading fleet. If the Lord enables us to repel this boasted invasion, it will greatly establish our cause and dishearten our foes. For this let us pray.

We have no special news in the county. . . . All our relatives and personal friends generally well. . . . We have a vidette of seventeen or eighteen men stationed at Can't-Help-It and four at Riceboro to act as couriers (relieved every four days): both from the Liberty Troop, which is now quartered, as you know, at Sunbury. Dr. Joseph Jones is surgeon of the post, and his hospital and quarters are in the two upper rooms of Mr. Screven's house. He has had his hands full of practice ever since, not so much with the soldiers as with cases in the families of some of them—and some cases severe ones. The active life is doing his general health good. He has long needed relaxation.

His good wife has fitted him out completely in all his camp clothing, and no man is better supplied than he. And you don't know what a fine trooper he makes. His horse is one of the best.

Charles Colcock is now with his company at the Isle of Hope nine miles from Savannah, now made flying artillery; and they are daily practicing men and horses, and accomplishing all for field service. He sent his mother an ambrotype of himself in full uniform as first lieutenant, and it is one of the handsomest pictures I ever saw. We hope you will pray for him. We can but hope that his deep sorrows may be the means appointed of God for his everlasting good.

Daughter and Robert and their little ones were when last heard from in good health. . . . Your good niece sent you up a small barrel of clean rice two weeks or more ago. The railroad would not allow us to prepay the freight, and we fear in consequence what was designed to cost you nothing has come to more than it was worth. Will you please let us know what the charge of freight on it was? . . . Our little granddaughter Mary Ruth is doing well. She weighed eighteen pounds the day she was four months old. Mary unites in much love to you and to Cousin Mary and Lou and to the young ladies and Joe. I remain, my dear aunt,

Your ever affectionate nephew,
C. C. Jones.

Lt. Charles C. Jones, Jr., *to* Rev. *and* Mrs. C. C. Jones[g]
Camp Claghorn, *Tuesday,* November 5th, 1861

My dear Father and Mother,

Environed as we are by the exacting engagements of camp duty and daily drill, and removed from the companionship of those we love and from the pleasant influences and the comforts of home, you cannot think how much enhanced is the joy of receiving letters of kind remembrance from those to whom we are bound by the ties of sincerest affection. I fear my letters may prove at times uninteresting, devoid as they often must be of that variety which is the spice equally of life and of epistolary correspondence; but I can at least tell you that my heart is ever turning to you, my dear father and mother, and to my precious little daughter.

The duties of organizing this battery and of drilling our men and horses have devolved entirely upon Captain Claghorn and myself. Besides the engagements thus incumbent, we have been busily employed in manufacturing fuses, filling shell and cartridges, etc., etc. We know not how soon the hour of battle may come, and we desire to be as fully prepared as practicable for the contest.

The boasted armada of Lincoln is now upon our coast, and we know not at what hour, or where, the attempted invasion may begin. Forty-three sail are today reported off Port Royal in sight of Tybee Island. The attack may be made upon our own coast or upon that of South Carolina or upon both.

We have an inhuman enemy to meet, and in great force in all probability. The struggle may be desperate, but our trust is unshaken in the justice and the manhood of our cause, and our reliance firm in the outstretched arm of Him who is mighty to save, and who has already in such signal manner, and on so many occasions, covered the heads of our brave soldiers in the day of battle. There can be but little doubt but this fleet is quite perfect in all its appointments—except in men: they are at heart, I believe, in the main cowards, for "conscience doth make cowards of us all." Either that, or they are inhuman fanatics, to be classed with mad dogs and shot accordingly. Doubtless every effort will be made to produce a powerful and startling effect upon our coast, but of the result we may rest satisfied. The victory beyond a question must, with the blessing of a kind Providence surely with us, eventuate in our favor. The enemy can never penetrate into the interior.

The Lincoln government is forced to make this demonstration, and in so doing the full power and energy of their navy will be expended. Failing in their present project, their capital besieged, the navigation of the Potomac stopped, defeated at every point, and shut up at home to the workings of their own leaven of unrighteousness, infidelity, rascality, violated faith, broken credit, lawlessness, and corruption, the entire North must sink even lower in the esteem of the world, and remain of all nations the most miserable—and with no one to pity, because with a blind fanaticism and a blackhearted malice, with their own hands they have removed the pillars of the temples of religion, justice, honor, integrity, and common humanity. They have surely worked out their own destruction, and must perish in the ruins which their own hands have made.

I learn from a gentleman that he has received intelligence from a private and reliable source that our independence is in all probability before this acknowledged by England, France, and Spain.

Commodore Tattnall with a portion of his mosquito fleet had a bloodless brush with the enemy off Port Royal last night. We are almost in hearing of the guns. Our battery is located within supporting distance of three batteries on our coast, either one of which we can reach in an hour by a forced march. Their morning and evening drums are answered by ours. Our orders are to support in the event of an attack.

I was here interrupted by tattoo, and have just learned from a member of our company fresh from the city that the fleet which had concentrated to the number of forty-three off Port Royal has gone to sea again, steering south. Brunswick may be the threatened point. Should such be the case, we will in all probability soon be on the move. No arm of the service is more efficient than a light battery in holding an advancing column in check.

Our practice here with six-pounder guns charged with solid shot, and with twelve-pounder howitzers with shell, has been excellent. Our shells explode beautifully, and we are confident that with half a chance we will be able to render effective service and send destruction into the ranks of our enemies.

In our morning drill we fired in battery blank cartridges to practice the men in rapid firing and to accustom our horses to the sound of the cannon. The horses are becoming somewhat accustomed to the discharge. Yorick cannot quite like the sight and sound as yet, but he is manageable. I wish that you could witness our drill. It is imposing, and our proficiency will soon be quite creditable.

I have been for several days suffering from an attack of sore throat, but am glad to say that my throat is better. It was probably induced by the change from close and warm apartments to the airy covering of the canvas. Our men are all well. You have, my dear father and mother, my warmest love. Kiss my sweet little daughter for me. And believe me ever

Your affectionate son,
Charles C. Jones, Jr.

Captain Claghorn, Father, begs that I would convey to you his sincere and respectful regards.

Mrs. Mary S. Mallard *to* Mrs. Mary Jones[t]

Walthourville, *Thursday*, November 7th, 1861

My dear Mother,

I received a message from Aunt Abby today saying that you would send the carriage for me if I would come to the Island. I would like very much to do so, but as I wrote Father, I do not feel that I ought to leave home just now. Little Mary, too, has a very bad cold, which has made her croupy for several nights past. She is, however, much relieved, as I have been giving her linseed oil and molasses constantly. She told me yesterday that "when she coughed the night before, it hurt her throat and made her so *unhappy.*"

Mr. Mallard and his brother Sam started this morning for Darien, but after riding two or three miles heard such heavy and incessant cannonading that they returned to await the arrival of the cars. The only news they brought was that the same firing was heard in Bryan and commenced after they left Savannah. Very many up here heard the guns, though I did not. We are anxiously waiting the news of tomorrow.

I received a letter from Brother Charlie today which was written on the 5th. He says Captain Claghorn and himself have had a most arduous time in drilling the company, and "the probability is they will have a full share in the dangers of any attack the enemy may make." May the Lord cover his head in the day of battle! He was just recovering from "a sharp attack of sore throat." I hope the change to an active life will benefit rather than injure his throat after he gets accustomed to it.

Mr. Mallard left about 2 P.M., and expects to return on Monday.

Brother Joe has sent a list of articles required by the Sunbury hospital, and Mrs. Lowndes Walthour and myself have been around begging. As soon as all the things are sent me, I will pack them and have them sent, which I hope will be on Monday or Tuesday, as I heard yesterday the troop had orders to hold themselves in readiness to march on short notice.

I could but think of Brother Charlie all day, for I knew if an engagement should take place he would surely be exposed. When will this terrible strife cease?

Did you see published a week or two since that Governor Helm of Kentucky had taken the oath of allegiance to the Lincoln government? I was surprised to see it.

It is quite late, so I must close. When will you move? We will come and see you soon after you do, but until Tenah passes through her trouble I feel that I ought not to be long from home. Mamie has just come in and voluntarily kissed me so that I might send it to Grandma and Grandpa, and begs you to kiss Little Sister for her. Do give love to Aunt Susan and Cousin Laura and the little boys. Love to Aunt Julia and family. Tell Cousin Mary Wells I have been expecting her promised visit. Will they move to South Hampton this winter? With warmest love to dear Father and yourself, and a kiss to little Ruthie, I am

Your affectionate daughter,
Mary S. Mallard.

LT. CHARLES C. JONES, JR., *to* REV. C. C. JONES[t]
Camp Claghorn, *Friday,* November 8th, 1861
My dear Father,

I am today favored with your kind letter of the 4th inst., and am more than happy to know that all at home are well.

Today has been a gloomy one with us. Each hour fresh advices arrive of our disaster at Port Royal. The enemy's fleet is represented to be in full possession of everything—forts, islands, and harbor. The batteries seemed to produce no impression upon their men-of-war and ships of the line. From our post every gun was heard yesterday. We had expected—and had confidently anticipated—a successful resistance on the part of our batteries. But so it is: we are repulsed, and this will prolong the war and necessitate much heavy land fighting. I presume the enemy will be occupied several days in landing and entrenching. We learn this afternoon that in Savannah preparations are being made immediately to impede the channel of the Savannah River. A crushing responsibility rests upon the heads of those highest in military authority for the present helpless posture of affairs. We confidently anticipated orders to leave our present position for the support of the batteries at Port Royal, but none arrived. I presume, however, it will not be long before we will be on the move.

These reverses must produce their effect upon the public mind, and that effect should be to gird our loins one and all for the contest, with an earnest prayer that the God of Battles would at an early day grant us a triumphant deliverance from the presence of these violators of public and private peace and happiness, despisers of law, justice, integrity, and truth, and scoffers at the great law of the Living God.

The drill and discipline of our men and horses are excellent, and I trust that whenever the opportunity occurs, you will hear a good account from us. We are in hourly expectation of orders for change of post. I write in great haste, but with warmest love to you, my dear father, to dear Mother, and many kisses for my precious little daughter. As ever,

Your affectionate son,
Charles C. Jones, Jr.

LT. CHARLES C. JONES, JR., *to* REV. *and* MRS. C. C. JONES[g]
Camp Claghorn, *Saturday,* November 9th, 1861
My dear Father and Mother,

Three years ago this very night I led my beloved Ruth, a young, beautiful, and loving bride, to the altar. In your presence those sacred vows were taken, the memory of which will live ever with me. As I look back upon that evening and think of the many joys which that union brought, as I remember the loves which were there cemented and the happy days which succeeded, as I cherish the living recollection of the truest loves of my dear Ruth and dwell upon all the hallowed remembrances of her life and affection, and then turn to these recent days of saddest affliction, of present loneliness and sorrow, my eyes fill with tears, and my heart grows weighty with grief. And yet there is sunlight—bright, holy sunlight—in the midst of this gloom. The sorrows are mine only, but the joy is also mine—to know that she, my dearly beloved wife, and our precious little daughter are both far beyond the reach of all evil, fear, change, and harm; that upon their ear will break no rude alarms of war; that for them an eternal home full of peace and joy and holiness has been securely prepared; and that into it they have already entered. It is thus in the midst of this great sorrow, and amid the depressing influences by which we are surrounded, that my heart, while bowed to the dust, blesses God for the precious deaths which they died, and almost rejoices that they have been taken from the present and the evils which seem soon about to overtake us.

We have nothing new today from the scene of our recent reverse, and have as yet no orders for the removal of our battery. General Lee has, I understand, directed that all the guns be removed from the seacoast islands, with a view to planting them at important points on the main. He is represented as severely condemning the policy adopted by our general. You remember the opinion you expressed in reference to those mantraps. Savannah, I fear, is in rather a precarious condition. We are without the munitions of war requisite for a proper resistance in the event of an attack, and the preliminary labor which should have been accomplished has not been commenced. This will necessitate a desperate resistance on the part of the defenders, fighting as we will have to do under disadvantages.

But the enemy must expect every resistance before success. That success may be temporary, but it will never prove abiding. For one I will most cheerfully give my life in defense of our common and beloved home, and in support of the honor, nationality, and principles for which we are contending. I say this not boastfully, but in all earnestness and calmly. And should it be my lot to fall in this struggle, I will die in the legitimate discharge of the most solemn duty which ever devolves upon a free citizen—the obligation resting upon him to make every sacrifice in support of national honor and in the protection of that soil from which he sprang from the infamous pollution of a lawless and inhuman enemy. I pray God to pardon my many sins, to prepare me for death, and at last to save the poor sinner, of His infinite mercy, through the imputed righteousness of the gracious Saviour who died that we might live.

General Lee, now in South Carolina, is expected very soon in Savannah. That city is in great commotion—many moving away, and more attempting to send forward articles of value. A storm of indignation is reported against General Lawton. Vessels have been sunk in the Savannah River near Fort Pulaski and in Wall's Cut with a view to impeding the passage of the enemy. Mayor Purse is represented as being quite inefficient. He could not be found last night when his presence was greatly needed. The firing of the fleet upon the Port Royal battery is represented as being perfectly awful. Thirteen-, eleven-, and ten-inch guns were used by them, and they completely enfiladed the fort, almost all the guns having been dismounted so soon as position had been taken by them. No impression was made by the batteries. All the talk you see in the papers about Colonel Stiles's having two horses shot under him is simple nonsense. But more of this anon. Randolph Spalding is represented to have been so drunk that he could not take command of his regiment when ordered to the relief of the Port Royal batteries. As yet we have no orders other than notice to hold ourselves in readiness to march at a moment's warning.

The accompanying rough sketch will give you a general idea of the position of the Port Royal batteries, and show how completely the position taken by the fleet enfiladed the fort. It appears that in constructing the fort they never once contemplated the contingency of the enemy's passing Fort Walker and making the attack from the side and rear. They had anticipated that they would be able to prevent all ingress. The fact was that the navy passed in with perfect ease, and by an enfilading fire soon silenced almost every gun in the fort.

I cannot think Savannah in immediate danger. My impression is that they will securely entrench themselves at Port Royal before advancing.

Do, my dear parents, let me know whenever I can be of assistance to you at any time. You have my warmest love. Kiss my dear little daughter for me. And believe me ever

Your affectionate son,
Charles C. Jones, Jr.

Lt. Charles C. Jones, Jr., *to* Rev. C. C. Jones[t]

Camp Claghorn, Monday, November 11th, 1861

My dear Father,

Enclosed please find notice for renewal of note in Bank State of Georgia. On the other page I have sent renewal note, which you will please sign and return.

All well, and nothing new today. We are in the midst of trying times, and must look to Him from whom all our help cometh for our deliverance, and use every exertion to repel this iniquitous invasion. You may, I think, expect a good report from our battery when the occasion occurs. With warmest love to self and dear Mother, and many kisses for my dear little daughter, I am, as ever,

Your affectionate son,
Charles C. Jones, Jr.

Rev. C. C. Jones *to* Lt. Charles C. Jones, Jr.[g]

Maybank, Monday, November 11th, 1861

My dear Son,

Serious events since I last wrote you a week ago! We are to reap the bitter consequences of an imbecile administration of the coast defenses of our state. And to cap the climax, *Pulaski* untenable under a serious attack like that on Hilton Head battery, and the city itself totally at the mercy of the enemy! The best thing now to be done is *to obstruct the channel as in the last war and compel the enemy to come by land,* and we may have a chance. I see nothing before us but a protracted hand-to-hand conflict, and God our hope. The Lord shield your person and life, my dear son! Live close to Him, and lean upon Him.

We are thinking of removing a part of our people up the country—at least for the present. Could you not write your friend Dr. Howard, or any other you have in or about Burke, how many he could take care of or *employ or hire,* so that they might be profitable, and in a safer position; and we can send them up from Arcadia, leaving a part on the plantation.

Unless we can collect twenty or thirty thousand on this side the Savannah and keep the city, our seaboard will be overrun. In Carolina they will need as many more. Georgia can raise speedily thirty thousand men if we can *arm* them. We can pray for *a special interposition of Providence;* without it we shall suffer.

Your dear little daughter, unconscious of the sorrows of life, is in excellent health and full of life. Mother sends much love. We pray for you constantly. Your brother with the troop, now quartered at Riceboro. We leave for Montevideo tomorrow, God willing; your Aunt Susan and family and Uncle William move to Arcadia.

Your ever affectionate father,
C. C. Jones.

Present my very friendly salutations to your excellent captain, and am pleased to be remembered by him.

If the city is to be taken, the banks ought to send their specie away.

LT. CHARLES C. JONES, JR., *to* REV. C. C. JONES[t]

Camp Claghorn, *Wednesday,* November 13th, 1861

My dear Father,

I am today favored with your kind letter of the 11th inst., and am happy to know that all at home are well. I have this moment written to Dr. Howard and to Neely inquiring how many of our Negroes they can accommodate, and upon what terms. I will probably in a few days hear from them.

We have no advices of any movements on the part of the enemy. General Lee is now in Savannah. So is General Walker.

We learn this afternoon that a vessel has arrived and is safely moored at the wharf at Savannah. Her cargo consists of many thousand Enfield rifles, several rifled cannon, sabers, ammunition, shot and shell, blankets, etc., etc. This cargo comes on account either of the State of Georgia or of the Confederate States. This arrival is most opportune, and looks like a direct interposition of Providence in our behalf. Again and again are we called upon to lift up our hearts in earnest gratitude to the Giver of All Good for His continued and most marked interposition in our behalf. These munitions of war will enable us to prepare a determined—and without doubt a successful—resistance in the event of any attempt on the part of the Lincolnites to penetrate in the interior. I doubt very much if any immediate effort is made to advance, unless the attempt be made upon the city of Savannah or Charleston.

Our battery is in excellent order, and our men are ready to expend their every energy in defense of our homes and of all that we hold dear.

Do, Father, let me know if I can serve you in any way. I am pretty well. My throat has been giving me some trouble, but I hope that it will soon be better. With warmest love to self and dear Mother, and many kisses for my dear little daughter, I am, as ever,

Your affectionate son,

Charles C. Jones, Jr.

The name of the vessel, an ironclad propeller, is the *Fingal.* Edward C. Anderson comes in her. She was cleared for "the Island of Madeira and the west coast of Africa."

REV. C. C. JONES *to* LT. CHARLES C. JONES, JR.[g]

Montevideo, *Thursday,* November 14th, 1861

My dear Son,

Your three welcome letters of the 8th, 9th, and 11th came all together last evening, and were read with great interest by your mother, your brother, and myself. I agree with you that the unexpected success of the enemy in carrying the forts on Port Royal Sound will vastly elate the Northern and Western people and serve to protract the war, and *may* give us much hard and hand-to-hand fighting on land.

I say *may*, for the enterprise of their armada carries two faces. The first, to "repossess and hold" (to use President Lincoln's language in his inaugural) all the forts once belonging to the old United States on the coast of the Confederate States, and such other valuable points on the same which might be conquered; and well fortify and garrison the same for the purpose of commanding our available outlets to the sea, and so rendering the blockade perfect and perpetual; and from which forts and points naval and land forces might be sent to make attacks upon the mainland at their pleasure, and keep the seacoast in a state of uneasiness all the time; while their light draft and heavily armed gunboats would, running between and inland, destroy our coasting trade to the last fishing smack. The second face is to do all this, with the addition of "pouring in" (as the enemy terms it) "an overwhelming land force" of horse, foot, and cannon, and carry our great export cities by storm, inflict summary vengeance upon them, desolate the whole seaboard, liberate the great and oppressed "Union party" of the South, and finally "crush out the rebellion"—and perhaps, if it cannot be done otherwise, "proclaim liberty to the captives" and blot out the remembrance of the people from the earth!

All this sounds mighty, and no doubt our enemies would be glad of one or the other, and many of both projects. But the first is perhaps their more probable purpose for the present. The idea of sending large land forces to operate as armies of subjugation and of conquest on the coast of the Southern states, to be fed and clothed by supplies drawn from distances of from three hundred to a thousand miles—and that by sea—and added also their whole matériel of war; and these armies to quit their supply ships and depots and march into a country unfavorable to the movements of large masses of men, difficult to traverse, in the face of a determined resistance of men fighting for their liberties, their property, their homes and firesides—I think it, to say the least, an experiment which none but infatuated men would try with the hope of any permanent success. The capture of the forts, the capture of some of our principal seaports, the occupation of districts on the mainland, would have no power in bringing about our subjugation. Savannah, the seaboard of Georgia, Charleston, the seaboard of South Carolina—nay, all the coasts of the Old Thirteen, and vast portions of their territory—were all under British power in the Revolution; and we are as well able, by the blessing of God, to meet similar calamities, if need be, as our fathers were. We have nothing to do but, relying upon the righteousness of our cause and upon the aid of God, who has thus far left us not without witness of His favor, gather our forces and meet the enemy in every one of his schemes and do our best to convince him of the fruitlessness of his undertakings.

It is certainly matter of devout thankfulness that we have had time allowed us to collect some force and to make some preparations after so miserable an administration and so much absolute exposure to danger and loss. I never hear the name of our commanding general mentioned but with disapprobation, and all rejoice that General Lee has come—we hope in time to save us, under God. A resignation of General Lawton, if not graceful at the present time, would certainly be altogether agreeable to the great body of our people civil and military. I was happy to learn through Judge Fleming, who came from Savannah yesterday, secondhand through Captain Winn, that Savannah was now deemed safe, and that Pulaski could withstand the combined navy of the Federal states—and hope *it is all true.*

You must embrace the opportunity when it offers of making not only the military but the personal acquaintance of General Lee. You know his reputation in the army: he has checkmated Rosecrans in Western Virginia. And he is Miss Kitty Stiles's great friend. Should he make a progress through these regions I should be happy to know and to receive him at our house.

We moved up from Maybank this week. Reached home last evening, and your brother spent the night with us. He is quite well, but full of practice and very popular with all his patients and with his company. He has been attending our old neighbor Mr. John B. Barnard, who is suffering from a severe attack of chill and fever, but is better, but quite feeble. The weather is so warm, sickness may ensue. No frost of consequence yet.

Robert preached for the troop on last Sunday, and your sister came down with him. All well. By invitation of Captain Winn, who called on me this morning, I hope to conduct the religious exercises of the camp tomorrow, D.V., our day of national fast and prayer by order of our good President. Shall have to give them something extempore.

On the 9th your dear mother, who never forgets you, recalled the day as the anniversary of your marriage with one who proved in every respect a blessing to you and a comfort to us. We cherish her precious memory, and think over and over, with gratitude to God, her last sufferings and triumphant death. My dear son, you have the constant sympathy and prayers of your parents in your great sorrows. They will ever have a place in your heart. But we can but hope that you have found a Refuge from sorrow and a Deliverer from sin in the ever blessed Saviour, and have that true consolation which none but the Father of our Spirits can bestow. We read with emotion your remarks on that hallowed wedding day.

Your little one is becoming more and more interesting. Her mind expanding as well as her body; is getting some more use of her voice, and shows some new tricks; takes an interest in all around her; and has been out all the morning amusing herself with the chickens and the ducks and the pigeons and the pig; has a strong will, but pleasant disposition; and all the people say: "She is a little beauty."

Thank you for the sketch of the position of the Hilton Head battery, Fort Henry, and that of the enemy's fleet in the late engagement. The wonder is that the fort held out against such fearful odds and under such disadvantages of construction and guns so long—near six hours. Had the battery been well constructed and well mounted, the fleet might have spent the whole day and done no great harm. The battery guns were of too short range to do much execution. How much was done we shall never know.

Enclosed is the note for the bank signed, and am obliged to you for sending it. The discount—the bank having funds of mine on deposit—can pay itself.

Will you be kept on the Isle of Hope all the winter as an advanced post, or be quartered in Savannah? Have the batteries on Tybee and Green Island been withdrawn by General Lee? Who commands at Fort Pulaski? And what is his value as an officer in that post so important? We feel much anxiety for our commercial emporium.

Mother sends much love. Is very tired, and as I close is lying on the couch in my study enjoying a deep and quiet slumber. And Susan is downstairs making her usual efforts and noises to direct Little Sister. I hear her little voice.

Your ever affectionate father,
C. C. Jones.

Lt. Charles C. Jones, Jr., *to* Rev. C. C. Jones[g]

Camp Claghorn, *Saturday*, November 16th, 1861

My dear Father,

I am this evening in receipt of your very kind and interesting letter of the 14th inst., and am very happy to know that all at home are well, and that peace and quiet still are exerting their sweet influences there.

A moment since, one of our men returned from Savannah bringing with him an extra, by which it appears that the New York *Herald* claims and reports Savannah and Charleston as both in the actual possession of the Lincolnites. This is news to us, and may possibly be accounted for upon the supposition that the wish is father to the thought.

It is indeed a fortunate circumstance for us that the enemy did not immediately advance with the ferryboats and armed steamers of light draft through Wall's Cut up the Savannah River. Had this been done, the city would have been found almost entirely at the mercy of our hated foes. As it is, time has been afforded for arming Fort Jackson and for concentrating troops. While on parade yesterday we heard the garrison practicing with their guns recently mounted upon the ramparts of Fort Jackson.

My own impression, from present indications, is that the Lincolnites purpose a regular siege with a view to the reduction of Fort Pulaski. Nothing prevents their at once occupying Daufuskie Island; and as you are aware, our forces have been withdrawn from Tybee. Nothing would be easier than for them thus to obtain command of the back river, by means of which predatory bands might work their devastations upon the plantations of the Savannah River. To prevent this, batteries should at once be executed below the city capable of beating back their gunboats, etc. Fort Jackson commands the entrance from Wall's Creek, and when put in proper condition will constitute a most valuable fortification, indispensable for the protection of the city.

Fort Pulaski is one of the strongest fortresses on the line of our coast. It is said to be much more powerful than either Sumter or Moultrie or the Mobile and New Orleans forts. Several guns of heavy caliber have recently been added to its armament. In the event of an attack it ought to prove invincible by almost any force which might be sent against it. The enemy will find a vast difference between open sand batteries and regularly constructed casemates. The object of the Lincolnites will probably be to reduce that fortress by getting into the rear; and we should see to it at once that measures are adopted in advance to prevent this.

I have no doubt but that the enemy will advance very cautiously, and be quite circumspect in any attempt to penetrate into the interior. Unless wholly blinded and given over to believe a lie, one would think that at last the fact must find an acknowledgment even from those fanatics that they are now upon a soil where no Union element can lift its friendly arm of protection and of support, but where every bush and swamp has become a fortress bristling with "masked batteries" (which they so much dread), and every man, woman, and child the cannoneers ready and anxious to apply the portfires.

We cannot cope with them upon the sea, for the simple reason that we have not the means for so doing; but when they leave their boasted armada and attempt to penetrate our shores, then, by the blessing of a just and righteous God, they will find that a people armed in the holy cause of liberty, in such a country as this which we possess, are invincible by any force which they may send against us. They may possess themselves of our seacoast; they may desolate our exposed plantations, and to a certain extent compass their cherished plans of theft and lawlessness; but they can no more consummate their avowed designs of subjugation and of annihilation than can the occasional shadows which flit across the sky extinguish forever the bright beams of the risen sun. The lesson which you educe from the history of our own Revolutionary period is conclusive, and of itself, independently of every other consideration, should afford assurances of success of the most satisfactory character.

We have now some eight hundred men on Skidaway Island, within two miles and a half, as the crow flies, from our camp. That post, commanding as it does one of the approaches to Savannah, is to be strengthened; and a battery is in process of construction which when completed will mount some ten or more guns. The bridge which connects this island with the main, a structure passing over a river more than the quarter of a mile wide, is now held by us. Our battery is posted within supporting distance of the commands at Skidaway, at Thunderbolt, and at Green Island. The battery on Green Island will be held, and is the strongest earthwork on the coast. It is garrisoned by the Savannah Volunteer Guards, one hundred and ninety strong, under command of Captain Screven. Although an open battery, in the angles there are casemates, which it is expected will effectually protect the garrison from shell. In the event that any of these commands are compelled to retire, our battery will be essentially requisite to cover the retreat and to oppose a landing of the enemy.

Fort Pulaski is garrisoned at present by six companies—say five hundred men—under command of Major Olmstead of Savannah, a graduate of the Marietta Military Institute and a young officer who is highly esteemed.

Our battery is in good order. We have now some eighty men. Would be glad to recruit up to one hundred and fifty. Are adding daily to our numbers. Our company has lost more than twenty-five members, who are all now in service bearing commissions in other companies. To such an extent has this obtained that it has become a trite remark that the Chatham Artillery has had to officer most of the other companies.

Enclosed, Father, I send a letter this afternoon received from Dr. Howard. Do you think it necessary to remove the Negroes at present?

The renewal note is at hand, and I will endeavor at an early day next week to go to Savannah and have the matter arranged.

We have preaching every Sabbath, and our men attend very generally. The captain and myself always do so. Grace at every meal, and good order, sobriety, and attention to all duties characterize our command. The captain desires his respectful and kind remembrances. He is a brave, high-toned man, fully imbued with our high and holy cause, and will not be found wanting in the day of trial. He enjoys the reputation of being the best-informed and most accomplished artillerist in the state.

Do, my dear father, accept for yourself and my dear mother my warmest love. Kiss my precious little daughter for me. And believe me ever

Your affectionate son,

Charles C. Jones, Jr.

The orderly reports news from the city to the effect that nineteen of the Lincoln armada started from the North, went down in the recent gale at sea, and have not been heard of.

Will be very happy when occasion occurs to form the acquaintance of General Lee. His appointment is a cause for public rejoicing.

As yet we have no orders; for the present we continue in the occupancy of this post.

Hon. John Johnson *to* Rev. C. C. Jones[t]

Columbus, *Monday*, November 18th, 1861

Reverend and dear Sir,

Some time ago the writer of this and A. G. Redd addressed you relative to certain charges made against ———, a member of the Presbyterian church of this place, to which you replied. At that time the pastor of the church was absent. After his return early in October the matter with the correspondence was submitted to him. The pastor, Redd, and myself had several conversations with each other and with ——, he (——) most positively affirming his innocence all the while.

Desiring to do the accused no harm needlessly, the matter has not been laid before the session, nor has it been made known to anyone beyond the above-named persons. —— from the first declared his willingness to swear to his innocence. He has now done so, and a copy of his statement of denial of the charges upon oath is herewith enclosed.

I, being session clerk, have been requested by the pastor to send you this, with a respectful request that you reply as early as convenient, and that from your extensive experience and observation in church judicature you will please suggest what course should be adopted here by session. Will you become prosecutor, or can the case be so made out that the session of this church can take action upon it?

With due consideration and esteem, I am

Yours, etc.

John Johnson.

[Enclosure]

Charges have been made against me by Rev. C. C. Jones embracing adultery and therewith unchristian conduct. I do hereby solemnly deny the truth of such charges and do pronounce them to be utterly false and unfounded.

[signed] ——.

Sworn to and subscribed before me this 9th day of November 1861.

John Johnson, *Ordinary,*
Muscogee County, Georgia.

REV. C. C. JONES *to* LT. CHARLES C. JONES, JR.⁵

Montevideo, *Monday,* November 18th, 1861

My dear Son,

I write to say that your brother *or* myself will, God willing, be in Savannah on Wednesday afternoon at the Pulaski House, where we would be glad to meet you if you could ride in and see us, if only for an hour or two. The visit is one purely of business, and we return next day. Your brother thinks the fatigue will be too much for me, and thinks it will be better for him to make the trip, and you may expect to see him more than myself.

Your aunt and family are with us for a few days while fixing up Arcadia. They unite in love to you. . . . Your dear little daughter is quite well, growing daily, and is a pet for everybody. The Lord bless you, my dear son, ever prays

Your affectionate father,
C. C. Jones.

Lt. Charles C. Jones, Jr., *to* Rev. C. C. Jones[g]

Camp Claghorn, *Saturday,* November 23rd, 1861

My dear Father,

Your kind note of the 18th inst. has been duly received. On Wednesday evening after retreat I left camp for Savannah, expecting the pleasure of seeing you and Brother, thinking that you would both come by the Savannah, Albany & Gulf Railroad. About four miles from the city I was accosted in the darkness of the night by someone on horseback who inquired the way to Captain Claghorn's camp. To my surprise and pleasure I at once recognized the voice of the Doctor, who told me that you had not come. We returned to camp, and he spent the night with us. He will tell you of our camp, etc., etc. I have been quite concerned to know how he endured the fatigue of his return journey, following so closely as it did upon his long ride from Riceboro to Savannah.

I regret, my dear father, that we did not enjoy the pleasure of your company also, and was very sorry to hear from Brother that your recent pulpit exercises had given you considerable uneasiness. From this I sincerely trust you have entirely recovered.

The miniature of my dearest Ruth was received from the artist a day or two since, and is as yet in an unfinished condition. Mr. Bounetheau has sent it to me for suggestions. The painting is exquisite, and the picture beautiful; but it lacks the expression of my precious wife, especially about the mouth. Dear little Mary Ruth will never remember the person of her good mother, and I most earnestly desire to secure for her the best likeness that the art of this Confederacy can afford. I deeply regret that in the present instance the artist has failed to embody a correct shadow of the precious original.

We are all anxiety to know how the battle at Pensacola progresses. It commenced yesterday.

I am tonight the only commissioned officer at this post, and in command. Everything is quiet, and all sound asleep except the guard. Our battery progresses finely, and our men are in an excellent state of drill. Tomorrow will be the Holy Sabbath, a day whose sacred hours I will endeavor to improve. Wishing you both, my dear father and mother, a pleasant night's rest, with warmest love to you both, and with many kisses for my dear little daughter, I am, as ever,

Your affectionate son,
Charles C. Jones, Jr.

Rev. C. C. Jones *to* Lt. Charles C. Jones, Jr.[g]

Montevideo, *Monday,* November 25th, 1861

My dear Son,

Yesterday was the thirty-ninth anniversary of my membership with the church, having united with Midway the fourth Sabbath in November 1822. . . . The congregation of whites and blacks was large, and the day seemed one of interest. Audley had his fine little daughter baptized. We would have wished your dear little Mary Ruth baptized, but thought as you could not be present (neither could her aunts) it ought to be postponed. The dear little thing is quite well and growing, and develops every day. She looks very much like her mother, and reminds us of her daily.

Your brother reached the Boro safely, though he was a little perplexed finding his way out to the Ogeechee road; and when he dismounted, Mr. Barnard's buggy was in waiting to take him out to see him. He took a late tea with us and went on to Mr. Barnard's. He is sent for from all parts of the county, and although kept so much on the go, improves under it. We were happy to hear through him so good accounts of your health and comfort, and of your camp and corps. Your brother's visit to you was very much enjoyed by him.

Look out—if the enemy's gunboats come your way—for Skidaway bridge and the forces on that island. One or two shots will settle the bridge in the river, and neither your battery nor Cumming's horse and foot could stand their broadsides—you having no batteries of any kind on shore, not even such batteries as were put up on the islands and are now to be seen on the Ogeechee road in the outskirts of Savannah!

The supineness and inefficiency of the military commander in Savannah, and *the perfect indifference of the citizens* to the dangers of an attack on the city, amaze every observing man. The attack on Savannah *by water,* the enemy holding Daufuskie and raising the obstructions in the channel in Wall's Cut (is it called?), is the point to be guarded with the greatest care. And it seems nothing is done! Nor is there the first gun mounted on the bluff at either end of the city on the river—positions twenty feet or more above the water which would command the approaches by the river and keep off an attacking force. And nothing is done! The enemy has given full warning, and yet we suffer the city to lie all exposed in this way! It is amazing that no one is awake in the city for its preservation. The cry is: "No danger. No danger. We have forces sufficient to repel any attack." The forces should be a third more, ranging on to twenty thousand men. I confess that I cannot contain my indignation at a condition of things which can be remedied. Our great commercial emporium lies at the mercy of the shot and shell of an enemy.

Send me Mr. Neely's letter so soon as you receive it. . . . Mother sends you much love. And kisses from your sweet baby.

Your ever affectionate father,
C. C. Jones.

Lt. Charles C. Jones, Jr., *to* Rev. C. C. Jones[t]

Camp Claghorn, *Monday,* November 25th, 1861

My dear Father,

Enclosed please find a letter which was this day received from Neely in reply to my inquiries in reference to the removal of the Negroes. Should the necessity arise, I think our Negroes might be accommodated with him and with Dr. Howard. I sincerely trust, however, in the good providence of God, that we may be spared the desolating presence of our enemies.

Nothing new with us. A fire large and bright on Tybee Island (to judge by the eye) last night. All well. With warmest love to dear Mother and yourself, my dear father, and with many kisses for my sweet little daughter, I am, as ever,

Your affectionate son,
Charles C. Jones, Jr.

Lt. Charles C. Jones, Jr., *to* Rev. C. C. Jones[g]

Camp Claghorn, *Wednesday,* November 27th, 1861

My dear Father,

I was yesterday afternoon favored with your kind letter of the 25th inst., and am happy to know that all at home are well.

It would have afforded me the greatest pleasure to have been with you on the past Sabbath, an anniversary filled with such holy memories, and to have had my dear little daughter Mary Ruth baptized. But I found it entirely out of my power to gratify this wish. Captain Claghorn was compelled to absent himself on account of sickness in his family, and the command of this post consequently devolved upon me. Under the circumstances I could not leave. I hope, however, that it may soon be in my power to be with you and my dear little daughter. I am anxious that she should be baptized, and trust that this may be done at the ensuing Communion Sabbath, when I will make every effort to be there. Philo and Vallie are very desirous to be present also.

The plot thickens on our coast. This afternoon twelve vessels are reported off Tybee. The enemy has landed on that island, and it is said a force is upon Wassaw some twelve miles in a direct line east of us. What General Lawton is doing I cannot divine. The Lincolnites with probably not more than seven hundred men landed on Tybee Island last Sabbath afternoon in the face of day, and without the slightest opposition, and have remained there ever since without molestation. The Federal flag flies in sight of Fort Pulaski—and not more than two miles distant. Six thousand men are within less than a half hour of Savannah, ready and desirous of the liberty of attacking these vandals, and yet nothing is done. Five hundred men in the darkness of the night might have driven them in utter consternation into the sea; and there are ten times the number who would have held it a high privilege to have resolved themselves into Spartan bands for the accomplishment of this purpose. But no: General Lawton goes down in a steamboat, takes a look, returns home to a good dinner, and there the matter ends. The enemy meanwhile fortifies and reinforces, and flaunts his flag under our noses—and all forsooth because our general does not think it prudent to attack.

Laocoön tampered idly with the venomous serpent until its powerful folds encircled both him and his sons, confining them in helpless bondage. Nero fiddled while Rome burned. And while these Lincoln troops are thus quietly possessing themselves of our coast, to all appearances there exists a strange indifference or want of action on the part of those who are charged with the conduct of our military affairs. Would that the days of Sumter and Marion were come again! Idle troops are all about us; transportation sufficient can be had at any moment; and yet not the slightest effort is made to repel the invasion! I sincerely sympathize with you in all you have said in your letter in reference to the conduct of our military affairs.

Our battery, which now numbers one hundred and ten men, is in excellent order, and ready for active service.

A few days since, I enclosed T. W. Neely's letter to you.

The idea of the Lincolnites appears to be to establish themselves upon those islands which command the mouths of our rivers, and thus to interrupt all commerce. I do not think that they will venture—at least for the present—away from the range of their guns.

Captain Claghorn desires his respectful remembrances. Am happy to know that the Doctor did not suffer from his long ride. Do give warmest love to my dear mother. Kiss my dear little daughter for me. And believe me ever, my dear father,

Your affectionate son,
Charles C. Jones, Jr.

Since writing the above I have learned that the enemy's forces on Tybee Island are to be attacked tonight, the attack to be conducted by Commodore Tattnall. All success if it be true! It should have been done on last Sabbath night.

VIII

REV. C. C. JONES *to* REV. R. Q. MALLARD[t]

Montevideo, *Saturday,* November 30th, 1861

Dear Robert,

If the Doctor can secure a furlough for a few days, we hope to leave in the cars at No. 3 on Monday for Augusta and the General Assembly. We hope to learn if the furlough will be granted this evening. If not, I feel scarcely able to venture alone.

I write now to request you to be at court at Hinesville on Monday the 2nd. A meeting of the citizens of the county then and there present who are not in military service may be called for the purpose of preferring a request to General Lawton that in case of a necessity for the withdrawment of the forces now in the county to any other point on our coast, that he would leave such a military force behind as will be sufficient to keep our colored population under supervision and control, and so prevent anything like an effort on the part of many or few of them to abandon the plantations and escape to the enemy. And also a force sufficient to give assurance and confidence of protection to our many families who are left without their protectors, fathers and sons having gone off to the war; and in case the Negro population is ordered back into the interior, sufficient to insure their going without giving any trouble. These are important considerations; and although they may be known to General Lawton and to General Lee, yet an expression from the citizens directly will not fail to produce some good result. The county can make this request with a good grace, since two-thirds of her voting population are in the ranks.

Take part in the meeting; and I authorize you to sign my name to the action of the meeting, which will no doubt embody the views here expressed. Should I fail in going to Augusta, will try and be at the meeting. Will you let Messrs. J. B. Mallard, W. Q. Baker, J. McCollough, R. Cay, and others know of the contemplated meeting? We must not request that the Liberty Independent Troop be retained in the county, or any other troop or company, but merely request a military force, and let the commanding general appoint what troop or company *he pleases.*

Mother says Daughter must let her know by Niger upon what day she must send for her next week—Tuesday or Wednesday.

I conversed with your brother, T. Samuel Mallard, and with Mr. S. M. Varnedoe about the meeting, and they thought it proper and good to have it.

Mother unites in love to Daughter and yourself, and many kisses for our dear grandchildren.

> Your affectionate father,
> C. C. Jones.

LT. CHARLES C. JONES, JR., *to* REV. C. C. JONES[g]

> Camp Claghorn, *Saturday,* November 30th, 1861

My dear Father,

By the enclosed letter, received today, you will observe that I am tendered the command of the Oglethorpe Light Infantry from Savannah, now in service for the war, and forming a component part of the Army of the Potomac under Generals Johnston and Beauregard. Although but a few months in service, this company has already lost two captains, Bartow and Couper, and has suffered severely. You remember their conduct upon the plains of Manassas. The application comes upon me unexpectedly. It is highly flattering, and should be considered.

The inclination of my own mind is to decline. My company will not listen for a moment to my leaving them; and I cannot reconcile it with my own ideas of duty for the sake of name and perhaps some military reputation to desert the soil of my native state in this the hour of her immediate peril. But the question is still open, and the letter unanswered; and I write at this early moment to beg that you and my dear mother would give me your views and wishes in the matter.

Can you make it convenient to let Gilbert meet Val Whitehead and myself at the depot on *Thursday* next, the 5th inst., say at No. 3 (McIntosh Station)? She is most anxious to see dear little Daughter, and I hope to be able to spend the night of that day with you, my dear parents, and with her. Such is the nature of my obligations here that I find it almost impossible to leave the camp even for an hour; but I must if practicable see you on the day named, D.V.

We have now mustered into service and belonging to our battery one hundred and twenty-five men—a splendid command. I very much doubt whether a finer can be found within the limits of the Confederate States. With warmest love to you both, my dearest parents, and many kisses for my precious little daughter, I am, as ever,

> Your affectionate son,
> Charles C. Jones, Jr.

MRS. MARY JONES *to* LT. CHARLES C. JONES, JR.[g]

> Montevideo, *Tuesday,* December 3rd, 1861

My dear Son,

Several weeks have passed since I have had leisure to write you a line. Our semi-annual migration brings many additional cares, whose weight I find increases with my own increasing years—to say nothing of the infirmities which must necessarily cluster around advancing age. I can only say that you are constantly in my thoughts and in my poor prayers.

I know that you are now every moment exposed to the attack of our perfidious and merciless enemy; but your sword will be drawn in a righteous cause, and I fervently implore my God and Redeemer to protect and save you in the day of battle, and to encourage your heart and the hearts of your commander and of all your noble company, and to strengthen your arms for the conflict, that in your full measure you may be enabled to repel the infidel invaders who are now at our own doors with their work of ruin and destruction. Their intentions are now openly declared, and nothing but Omnipotent Power will keep them from making this not only a civil but a servile war.

Savannah is still said to be in a defenseless condition! Not a gun on the water approaches! Of course I know nothing about the matter, saving that the *mistakes* of our commanding general have now to be rectified in hot haste at the last moment, and that his name is never mentioned with either respect or confidence as a military leader. Why in such a state of public sentiment and public peril is he not at once superseded and someone of judgment, ability, and tried valor placed in his stead? When General Jackson arrives, will he rank General Lawton?

Your father and brother left yesterday for Augusta—both commissioners to our first General Assembly of the Presbyterian Church in the Confederate States. The meeting will be one of vital interest to our church, and I am glad they are both members. They may not remain longer than Saturday, as Joe's furlough will then be out.

I sent you by them, care of Messrs. Claghorn & Cunningham, a light little mattress for your camp bed, and a pillow. And the mattress I had made long enough to double at the end, thus forming a pillow. I am sorry to send it made of such coarse materials, but I had nothing better in the house, and hope it will add to your comfort.

I was very happy to learn through your brother how pleasantly you were associated. I hope, my dear son, you find time to read your Bible and commune with your God and Saviour. This is the only source of your growth in grace through the Holy Spirit's influence.

Your dear little daughter improves daily. She is the light of our dwelling. Has cut one little tooth without trouble, saving a little restlessness for two nights. Is very bright and playful, delighting herself in the cats and dogs and poultry. Tomorrow, D.V., I expect to send for your sister and the children, to be with me in your father's absence. Little Mary calls the baby "Little Sister," and so do Charlie and Jimmie. They are all in ecstasies with her when they come, and she enjoys seeing them. She sends here kisses for her dear papa. Susan and all the servants send many howdies to you and to George. I write in haste for the mail. God bless and save you, my dear son!

Ever your affectionate mother,
Mary Jones.

Mrs. Mary Jones *to* Lt. Charles C. Jones, Jr.[g]

Montevideo, *Tuesday,* December 3rd, 1861

My dear Son,

Your letter of the 30th November was not received until today. I wrote you this morning before its reception; and failing to reach the mail in time, my letter was handed to Mr. S. S. Barnard, who promised to see that you received it in Savannah.

I am rejoiced to think you will be with us, *D.V.,* on Thursday, accompanied by our friend Val. The carriage will await your arrival at No. 3, and I shall expect you to dinner. It will ever afford me great satisfaction to have the relatives of our beloved daughter visit us and take an interest in our precious little babe, and I hope they will recognize as we do her striking resemblance to her sainted mother. At times it is so marked I wish that I could pick her up and place her with her sweet expression before the artist now painting her likeness.

Your unanimous election by the officers and men of the Oglethorpe Light Infantry, now (it may almost be said) upon the battlefield in Virginia, is indeed a compliment to be valued. As their captain you would doubtless fill a post of distinction much more in the line of military promotion than the one you now occupy. But that, I conceive, would be the only advantage. Your usefulness I do not think would be increased, for I believe you are now occupying one of the most important positions in the most effective arm of service on our coast. It seems to me you are now especially defending your native soil, your own home and servants, your infant daughter, your father, your mother, the graves of your loved ones, the temples where we long have worshiped God. The strong ties which bind you to your present company I know you fully appreciate. I hope that I would not throw even a shadow between you and any post of duty which you may be called in God's providence to occupy, but I must say a change like the present one would grieve me. May the Lord direct you, my dear child, by the unerring influences of His Divine Spirit in this and every other point of duty!

I must close now, as I wish to write your father tonight.

Ever your affectionate mother,
Mary Jones.

Mrs. Mary Jones *to* Rev. C. C. Jones[t]

Montevideo, *Tuesday,* December 3rd, 1861

My dear Husband,

I trust our dear son and yourself had a comfortable journey to Augusta, although I could not but fear that you must have encountered the thunderstorm that seemed to be raging last evening in the northwest. Soon after Gilbert's arrival the rain fell in torrents with us, and all today it has been very cold and cloudy. . . .

Tomorrow I expect to send, D.V., for Daughter and the children; and by a letter received by the mail our dear Charles and Miss Val Whitehead will be with us on Thursday. He did not know of your absence; says he can stay but one night. Enclosed he sent the letter of a committee from the Oglethorpe Light Infantry, now in camp near Centreville, Virginia, stating his unanimous election by officers and men to their captaincy, and urging his acceptance. He wrote for our views. In your absence I could only say what I thought and felt, and told him I did not think it his duty to leave his present post, where he was defending his native soil, his home and servants, his infant daughter, his father and mother, the graves of his loved ones, and the temples where we long have worshiped God—all now invaded by the merciless enemy at our doors.

I hope you have found our dear Carrie and precious little grandson well; and if she thinks it safe, I hope she will accompany you home. I am sure it would greatly increase our pleasure to have her with us.

The weather has become quite cold, and reminds me that our servants are yet unprovided with Negro clothing. Do see about the cloth. And if to be had, bring a pair of light leather shoes (No. 6) for Sue, Flora, and Peggy, and Kate (No. 7), a pair for Jack (a little smaller than for Tom), and a thin pair for Elsie (you can judge of her size by Fanny). *Patience* wears the *largest* woman's size. I would be glad to get for the house servants at least.

I am glad you got off on Monday morning, for that evening Captain Winn received orders not to give a furlough beyond thirty-six hours. . . . I must now close, as it is late. Hoping that the divine blessing will rest upon our first assembly convened in the Confederate States. Best love to Carrie and Joe. Kisses for the dear boy. Respects to Dr. and Mrs. Davis and Julia.

Ever your affectionate wife,
Mary Jones.

Mrs. MARY JONES *to* REV. C. C. JONES[t]

Montevideo, *Wednesday,* December 4th, 1861

My dear Mr. Jones,

I wrote you last night, and now at Robert's desire to say if our son Joe must return on Saturday that you must remain longer, and he will come up on Monday next and accompany you and take care of you on your return home. He appears very anxious to attend our first assembly, and will gladly come and help you back. He begs that you will write without fail so as to inform him by Saturday. Direct to Riceboro: he and Daughter and the children are with me, and all well. Tomorrow, D.V., we send for Charles.

It is very late, and I must close, as I have a little headache. Our united love to Carrie and Joe, and kisses for the dear baby. It is extremely cold tonight; hope you will not suffer from its effects. I trust the divine blessing will rest upon all the acts of our first General Assembly.

Ever your affectionate wife,
Mary Jones.

Rev. C. C. Jones *to* Mrs. Mary Jones[t]

Augusta, *Thursday*, December 5th, 1861

My dear Wife,

Through a kind Providence we reached this city on Tuesday at 5 P.M., having been detained twelve hours by the throwing of the cars off the track sixty miles from Savannah, which Joe will explain to you. No one was injured save a scratch or two upon the baggage master. I refer you to him to describe to you also the case of the sick soldiers who came along with us. We took Carrie upon an agreeable surprise, and found her and little Stanhope in the best of health and spirits. The little fellow is much grown, and is a very fine and interesting and sensible child.

The assembly is more numerously attended than I anticipated. Called to order Wednesday the 4th by Dr. McFarland of Virginia. Dr. B. M. Palmer of New Orleans preached the opening sermon, according to request of the convention last summer, and was elected our moderator. We were in session today some four hours. Business is advancing. Am chairman of the Committee on Domestic Missions. Report on next Tuesday. Gives me opportunity to open the great subject of the religious instruction of the Negroes before the assembly. Do not see how I can return before I fulfill this duty, which is an important one.

And as I am up here, it seemed a good opportunity for me to look at the places in Burke that might be occupied in case of necessity, and learn how a portion of our people might be disposed of favorably. Our kind friend Mr. Gideon Dowse says he thinks he can aid us, and will take me to see several advantageous locations, and says he will do all in his power to help us. I think it may be well to embrace his kind offer, which may keep me a few days longer; for there is no telling what our enemies may venture upon.

The Doctor has secured a deposit of the *History* in the vault of the Bank of Augusta—an excellent place, and as secure as such places usually are.

Will you please tell Cato to start the gin on Monday and handle the cotton for the bag with three or four of the best motors (no more). If Niger wants any buckskin for the bands, you will find it in my black square trunk in the study, and have a strip cut off for him. The dark calico for Susan and the homespun for Martha cannot be bought for less than twenty-five cents per yard. Shall I give that? Please write me by Monday's mail, and your letter will reach here on Tuesday.

Give much love to my dear daughter and Robert, and kiss Little Daughter and Charlie and Little Sister for Grandfather. Howdy for the servants. I write tonight, as tomorrow we may not have the time. I shall be thankful to return home. The days of activity in public assemblies are passing away to me; and after a man becomes too feeble for much locomotion and labor, he had better stand out of the way and let others encounter the labor. Love to Sister and all at Arcadia. . . . I remain, my dear wife,

Your ever affectionate husband,

C. C. Jones.

Rev. C. C. Jones *to* Lt. Charles C. Jones, Jr.[g]

Augusta, *Friday,* December 6th, 1861

My dear Son,

Judge Law informed me of your election to the command of the Oglethorpe Light Infantry on Monday in the cars as we came down to Savannah.

My impression is that Providence has indicated your duty. Your own state is threatened with invasion, and we know not at what moment it will be upon us. You are in a responsible command in the oldest and most respectable artillery company in the state, and perhaps inferior to none in the Confederacy. Your company is already in position for the enemy, and its efficiency in action depends much upon your continuance, and you may serve your country as ably here as in Virginia.

Besides, the climate of Virginia would not be as well suited to your constitution. You are well aware of the difficulties which you experience with your throat even in our own mild and open climate—the best climate perhaps in the world for a winter campaign. And if you should be seriously ill, you will be at home with your own relatives and friends.

If you wish to be in action, there is as great a prospect of having a chance here as in Virginia. It is not military promotion that you would seek in going, for you have had that offered to you abundantly at home. And under all the circumstances I think that your allegiance is due to your own state as a battleground. We cannot afford to lose officers at the present time.

These are my impressions of the call made upon you, and I trust that you may be divinely directed in your decision. The object in life is not to glorify ourselves but to be useful to our fellow men in the fear and love of God; and I think that you are in as useful a position where you are as you would be at Manassas.

Carrie and Joseph unite with me in best love. You see your brother has been my scribe.

Your affectionate father,
C. C. Jones.

Lt. Charles C. Jones, Jr., *to* Rev. C. C. Jones[g]

Camp Claghorn, *Saturday,* December 7th, 1861

My dear Father,

I am this evening favored with your kind letter of the 6th inst., and fully coincide with you in the views therein expressed as to the propriety of my accepting the command of the Oglethorpe Light Infantry, now in Virginia, which has been unanimously tendered to me. Immediately upon the receipt of a communication from that corps expressive of their wishes I wrote you upon the subject, and am happy to find that my own sense of duty agrees with that expressed by you. My own company, hearing of the application, immediately, without my knowledge, held a meeting and passed a series of most complimentary resolutions entreating me not to sever the relationship which exists between us. Those resolutions, as well as all the correspondence in the premises, I will be happy to lay before you at some early day, when I can fully explain the reasons which induce me to remain in the position which I now occupy.

Last Thursday night I had the pleasure of spending at Montevideo with dear Mother and my precious little daughter. Sister and Robert and the little ones and Val Whitehead were there also. I was much disappointed in not seeing you also, and was not aware that you had gone to Augusta until I reached Station No. 3, Savannah, Albany & Gulf Railroad.

I trust, my dear father, that you may find it convenient to visit our camp on your way home. It is only nine miles from Savannah, and a delightful shell road connects it with that place. We will be most happy to welcome you here, and to show you everything connected with our battery. I think you might spend a day with comfort and pleasure. If you did not return from Augusta on Saturday with Brother, Robert intends coming up to Augusta and accompanying you home. . . . Do let me know when you will be in Savannah, and whether you cannot visit our camp. Our parade ground is some five miles from the city, and directly on the shell road leading to camp. We are there almost every morning from half-past 10 A.M. to 1 P.M.

With warmest love to you, my dear father, and kindest remembrances for the Doctor, Sister Carrie, and the little one, I am, as ever,

Your affectionate son,
Charles C. Jones, Jr.

Will you favor me, if practicable, with a report of the proceedings of the General Assembly?

Lt. Charles C. Jones, Jr., *to* Mrs. Mary Jones[g]
Camp Claghorn, *Saturday,* December 7th, 1861
My dear Mother,

I arrived in camp last night about ten o'clock after my short but very pleasant visit to you. For the valuable basket the officers' mess is under many obligations, and Captain Claghorn begs that I will present his especial acknowledgments for your very kind remembrance of him. He begs that you will favor him with the receipt for preparing the Russian sauce.

In consequence of the loss of our mailbag, neither of your kind letters have been received, and the letter of the committee of the Oglethorpe Light Infantry tendering me the captaincy of that corps has been lost.

Received a letter from Father this afternoon in which he fully coincides in the views expressed by you, and acted upon by me, with regard to an acceptance of that command. My letter of acknowledgment and declination has already been written and sent forward.

I trust that Father on his way home may be able to visit our camp. We will be most happy to see him, and I think that he will find somewhat to interest him. Our men are all pretty well. Do remember me affectionately to Sister,

Val, Robert. Kiss my precious little daughter and Sister's little ones for me. And believe me ever, with warmest love, my dear mother,

Your ever affectionate son,
Charles C. Jones, Jr.

REV. C. C. JONES *to* MRS. MARY JONES[t]

Augusta, *Monday,* December 9th, 1861

My dear Wife,

Our dear son left us on Friday afternoon, and it depressed me a great deal to part with him; and I could fully realize the social and other sacrifices he has made for the service of his country. Poor Carrie came back from the depot, where she parted with him, with weeping eyes, and has been about her family duties with her usual cheerfulness since, but feels his absence greatly. Mrs. Cuthbert is staying with her, which is a great relief to her loneliness. Stanhope is a fine, good-natured, lively little fellow, and has got quite acquainted with me. Sits in my lap, but never long, for he is in perpetual motion.

Our assembly has some ninety-three commissioners, and has come into existence full grown, and goes on in its business like an ancient body. We have an excellent representation for talent, especially in the legal line, having several judges of distinction. Dr. Palmer delivered an excellent opening sermon and was elected moderator, which office he discharges with ability and dignity. The debates on various questions have been interesting, and harmony has prevailed throughout. Dr. Thornwell is the author of the assembly's "Address to All the Churches of Christ," which you will read with interest, for it is a paper upon which he has bestowed much labor. I am chairman of the standing Committee on Domestic Missions, and tomorrow we report to the assembly, and propose to have a meeting in the evening to bring forward the colored field for missionary and pastoral labor. And the committee have laid the duty of an address on that subject upon the chairman before the assembly, and, God willing, I shall endeavor to speak. Instead of boards, as under the old General Assembly, our assembly will organize *committees;* and this morning was spent mainly in discussing the mode of organization: to be resumed tomorrow. I took part in the debate today for the first time, having nothing to call me up before.

Have seen many brethren—old acquaintances—who appear as glad to see me as I am to see them. . . . *Mrs.* and *Miss* Eve called to see me on Friday afternoon, and then again on *Sunday* evening, as I was not in at their first call. There is something special in this. . . . Yesterday all the pulpits in town were filled by our ministers. Dr. Palmer preached in the Presbyterian church to an overflowing congregation, but not as ably as I have heard him. . . . I have not been out to preaching at night, as the walk is too much for me; and we are tonight missing a meeting on foreign missions which no doubt will be most interesting. An Indian (full-blooded) from the Choctaws speaks, and I believe he is a minister or exhorter. All the Indian missions are under our care now.

The weather has been mild for two days. The first few days were cold; and suffering from cold at night, Carrie advised me to sleep between blankets, which I did; and have continued to do so, to my great comfort; and consider it a discovery of no mean value to an invalid. It has been an entire relief from all chilly sensations.

Will try and fill your order for shoes if possible, but they are very dear: $2.50 for the commonest kind, and money quite scarce. The express charged $2.50 for the coop of poultry, and $1.00 for your *little* box of sundries for Carrie. War prices!

Hope to see Robert tomorrow. Carrie unites in much love to you and Daughter, and kisses for my dear little grandchildren. I told Mrs. Cuthbert and Carrie about little Mary Ruth's saying her prayers, which interested them very much. Love to my dear son. His family all well, and send much love. Have written Charles about his election to the captaincy of the Oglethorpe Light Infantry. Howdy for all the servants. The Lord bless and keep you, my dear wife!

> Your ever affectionate husband,
> C. C. Jones.

Rev. R. Q. Mallard *to* Mrs. Mary S. Mallard[t]

Augusta, *Wednesday,* December 11th, 1861

My darling Wife,

Through the favor of a kind Providence I arrived in this city in due time and found all our friends well.

As you might have anticipated, I was very cordially welcomed by Sister Carrie; and I believe Father was very much pleased not only to see me but to have my assistance. I arrived too late to assist him in his writing, his report having already been prepared, Mrs. Cuthbert aiding him with her pen. But I have had the pleasure of lending him a helping hand in our walks to the church. Dr. Davis frequently sends his carriage for him, but this is not always convenient at the hour needed. But I do not think the walk at a deliberate speed and with my arm to aid him seems to injure him.

He was looking rather badly last evening—the effect of a long and in some respects exciting morning session; but last night's exercises seem to have refreshed him greatly. He was by a vote of the assembly requested to address the body on one suggestion of the report of the Committee on Domestic Missions touching the religious instruction of the Negroes. His address (one hour long) was simple in language, interesting in the facts related, and powerful in its feeling appeals. It was listened to throughout with profound attention; and the remarks of Dr. McNeill Turner and Dr. Lyon expressive of their gratification and the profit received were no doubt an echo of the feelings of the whole assembly. God grant that the good communicated to my soul and stimulus imparted to my ministry may prove permanent! You may be sure that it is highly gratifying to me to observe the marked and respectful attention with which the assembly listens to him on all occasions.

The assembly is a noble one. All the presbyteries of the South excepting those of Missouri, Kentucky, and Maryland are fully represented. The number of delegates present is ninety-one. In the delegation from the eldership, which is a large one, there is quite an array of judicial talent and learning. There are some distinguished ministers in attendance as visitors. Drs. Howe and Axson are here.

I am enjoying myself very much, and only wish that my beloved Mary was here to participate in the pleasure and profit of an attendance upon the General Assembly. If it had not been for the trouble which our children would have occasioned Mother, I would have insisted more upon your coming up with me. Many inquiries after you have been made by friends. I have had the great pleasure of meeting with Brothers McAllister, Porter, Harris, and Boggs—all fellow seminarians.

Today we are to dine on The Hill at Dr. Davis'. Father has just declined a pressing invitation from Mrs. William Eve to dine with her today. She is *very polite* to *him*, I hear.

Father unites with me in much love to yourself and Mother, and in many kisses for the darling little ones, in which Sister Carrie would join if she were present. Providence permitting, I will give you due notice of my future arrangements. I will probably stay until the close (I mean if the Yankees do not forbid it), and will accompany Father to Burke County if he goes. Would give much for a warm kiss from your sweet lips this morning. God bless you!

Your husband,
R. Q. Mallard.

REV. C. C. JONES *to* MRS. MARY JONES[t]

Augusta, *Wednesday*, December 11th, 1861

My dear Wife,

Robert arrived safely on Tuesday morning to breakfast, bringing the pleasing intelligence that you were all well. The attendance upon the assembly for four or five hours at a sitting, and committee business in addition, and walking generally to the church, has been fatiguing.

By the invitation of the assembly I delivered an address on the religious instruction of the Negroes before that body and such citizens as attended last evening in the Presbyterian church; and although there were but two or three hours to prepare it in, it was well received. And the assembly this morning requested me by resolution to prepare and publish it as delivered before them, and appointed me as chairman to prepare a pastoral address to the churches on the same subject, to be presented at the next assembly. The first I assented to; but on account of health and uncertainty of being at the next assembly, the second was respectfully declined.

The business of the assembly has been conducted with harmony, but slowly, and there will be no adjournment before next week; and I do not feel that I can remain away from home so long at the present time, and under the peculiar circumstances of our country. So Robert and I purpose to leave here, God willing, on Friday, remain over Sabbath in Burke County, and take the cars on Monday for Savannah. Charles begs that I will pay him a visit at his camp, and if we can, will do so for a day and then turn our faces homeward. Should we come out on a mail day, will take the stage to the Boro, and if not, will go on to Walthourville and get Robert's buggy and come down. So you need not send for me to the station, as I can appoint no day.

We dined with Dr. and Mrs. Davis today. Carrie went with us. Mrs. Smith sends her affectionate regards to you particularly and to Daughter. Mr. and Mrs. and Miss Davis also. A pleasant visit. . . . *Mrs. Eve* invited me to dine with her today and meet Mrs. Colonel Cumming, but the engagement at Dr. Davis' prevented. Have returned no calls and paid no visits and accepted no invitations but this one. . . . The weather has been remarkably mild and good, but is changing colder this evening.

We have no news in the papers different from what you have read in the Savannah papers. There is some appearance of returning reason in our enemies. How far it will reach to a peaceful conclusion of difficulties remains to be seen.

A pretty full report of the proceedings of the assembly you will find in *The Southern Presbyterian*. Please keep the numbers for me.

Mrs. Cuthbert, Carrie, and Robert are sitting around me—Mrs. Cuthbert hemming pocket handkerchiefs, Carrie knitting, and Robert giving an account of the meeting of the assembly this evening, from which he has just come in (10 P.M.). And each of them severally and particularly send a great deal of love to you and to Daughter and to the Doctor, and kisses for the dear little ones, in which I join. . . . I am anxious to be with you. Dreamed of you last night. I esteemed the address before the assembly last evening as one of the special occasions granted me of doing good, and hope God will own and bless it. Howdy for the servants. I remain, my dear wife,

Your ever affectionate husband,
C. C. Jones.

REV. R. Q. MALLARD *to* MRS. MARY S. MALLARD[t]

Augusta, *Thursday,* December 12th, 1861

My dearest Mary,

My eyes have just been refreshed by your "counterfeit presentment" in one of the best likenesses of you I have seen. Miss Jones looks, I must admit, a little more youthful than Mrs. Mallard, but very much like her.

We expect to leave tomorrow afternoon for Mr. Gideon Dowse's place. Our business: to look at some places in Burke County. From thence we will, D.V., take the cars on Monday for Savannah. Will you order my horse and buggy to meet me at No. 3 (McIntosh Station) on next Tuesday, so that I may without delay meet my brothers and the appraisers at my father's plantation on Tuesday next? The business that takes me there will carry me to Dorchester on the succeeding day, so that I cannot reach home before Wednesday afternoon at the earliest.

Father, very much to his relief, is now through with his special work. I am thankful that he should have been sustained and enabled to accomplish what he has done. It would have done your heart good to hear the high terms in which Dr. Pryor (the father of Roger Pryor, a prominent secessionist of Virginia) and Mr. Nash of North Carolina spoke of his address. One said it was the best address he had ever heard.

Brothers McAllister and Harris dine with us today. It is the only way to see much of a delegate.

Expecting that you will have returned to Walthourville before Monday, I write to you there. Kiss my little ones a dozen times for their loving father, and accept the same and more from

Your affectionate husband,
Robert Q. Mallard.

REV. R. Q. MALLARD *to* MRS. MARY S. MALLARD[t]

Augusta, *Thursday,* December 12th, 1861

My dearest Mary,

Not knowing whether you have gone to Walthourville or not, I have written one letter to that place, and address this note to Riceboro only to say that I wish my horse and buggy to be sent to No. 3 (McIntosh Station) on Tuesday next. That is the day for the division of the estate. Next day we shall probably go to Dorchester. Love to Mother, and the same and more to our precious little ones and your precious self.

Your own husband,
Robert Q. Mallard.

MRS. MARY S. MALLARD *to* MRS. MARY JONES[t]

Walthourville, *Saturday,* December 14th, 1861

My dear Mother,

I am sorry to hear that you have been unwell for two days past.

Mr. Mallard mentions in his letter that Father and himself will leave Augusta on Monday, and he wishes his buggy to meet him at No. 3 on Tuesday so that he may go immediately to his father's plantation, where he will meet his brothers and the appraisers of the estate. Mr. M. says that Father's address to the assembly was heard with profound attention, and all the ministers have expressed themselves in the most gratifying terms in regard to the benefit received from it. Mr. M., speaking of Father, says it is delightful to observe the marked and respectful attention with which the assembly listens to him on all occasions. He seems to be enjoying the assembly very much, and has seen four of his seminary classmates. Says he hears Mrs. E. is very polite to Father, and he (Father) had just declined a pressing invitation to dinner given by her.

We have in our society here about twenty shirts, the same number of drawers, and twelve pair of socks, which we are thinking of sending to the Mounted Rifles, as we have heard from several sources that they are very needy. No vote has been taken yet, so I don't know what the majority will say. I am sorry the company has left Riceboro, as it will be more difficult for us to send them the clothing; and some are afraid their captain will not trouble himself to find out those most in want.

The receipt for candles I have never tried, but it was given me by Miss Catherine Kallender; and she used it in Limestone and says the candles made from lard were firm and white. I should suppose made from tallow they would be harder. I will send my molds by Niger. The end of one is rather too open, and unless it is carefully fixed the tallow leaks out.

Tenah has not been quite so bright today or tonight, so I hope the end is not many days distant. The children are pretty well. Charlie often tells me: "Gamma carry please." They both send their love and kisses to Grandma and dear Little Sister. Kiss her for me, and accept for yourself, dear Mother, the warmest love of

Your affectionate daughter,
Mary S. Mallard.
For Making Candles

Take twelve pounds lard, one pound saltpeter, one pound alum. Mix and pulverize them, and dissolve in a gill of boiling water. Pour the compound into the lard before it is quite all melted. Stir the whole until it boils. Skim off all that rises. Let it simmer until the water has boiled out, or until it ceases to throw off steam. Pour off the lard as soon as it is done, and clean the boiler while hot. If the candles are to be run, commence immediately; if dipped, let the lard cool to a cake, then treat it as you would tallow.

(I should think tallow would require less saltpeter and alum than lard.)

M. S. M.

Mrs. Mary S. Mallard *to* Rev. R. Q. Mallard[t]

Walthourville, *Monday,* December 16th, 1861

My darling Husband,

You have been gone a long, long time, and it seems too bad that you should be almost two days and a night in the county before returning home. But business must come before pleasure. I shall expect you on Wednesday evening. We are all quite well, and thus far have escaped measles. The children are longing to see you, and Mamie often asks: "How many nights before Papa will come?" Charlie looks into the bed and calls for you in the morning, and then says "Gone!" in a most pitiful tone.

Yesterday we had services part of the day. Mr. McCollough read in the morning. I presume no one could be found to read in the evening, so the church was closed.

I received your letters directed to Montevideo and this place; and as you requested the buggy to be at No. 3 tomorrow morning, I will send James to Arcadia this evening so that he will certainly be in time for you tomorrow. . . . Mamie and Charlie send many kisses and hearts "chock-full" of love to their dear papa. Accept all that is affectionate from

Your loving wife,
Mary S. Mallard.

Mrs. Caroline S. Jones *to* Mrs. Mary Jones[t]

Augusta, *Tuesday,* December 17th, 1861*

My dearest Mother,

If I did not know that you were "the dearest, kindest, and most lenient" of mothers, I should begin my letter with some fear that you would decline reading it when it reaches you and entirely disown me as a correspondent. I have before me a long, delightful letter you wrote me soon after Joe went away, which stirred my heart so at the time of its reception that I did not think a week would go by without my answering it. Yet these many weeks have passed, and I am just now writing! But, dear Mother, I have been in such a vicissitude of *busy-ness* that seemed hardly to leave me time to write, and sadness that quite took away from me the power of writing, that I really think I may plead some excuse.

I hope Joe gave you all my messages of love and thanks for the delightful box you sent me. There was not a thing in it that was not delightful. I do assure you I never received anything more acceptable to *me,* or that met with such unqualified satisfaction from all who shared my good things. Julia desired me to tell you she was exceedingly obliged for your remembrance of her. She intends to perpetuate it by keeping her bottle constantly full.

I hope that this evening Father is comfortably seated at home recounting all the events of his absence. . . . I know well how glad he is to be at home. We all enjoyed his visit to a degree I fear he did not himself. But I hope at all events he will not feel any disadvantage from it. All his friends seemed to have taken so much pleasure in his presence at our first assembly that he ought to feel repaid for all the trouble and fatigue. My only regret was that you and Mary were not with us. I am sure you would have enjoyed it; and as to me, I should have been so delighted I would have gone in the strength of it for many a day. It was very grievous to me to see them going away without me. I had fixed all my hopes on going down under Mr. Mallard's care, but I suppose I must bear it as one more of the many trials of this sad winter.

Last night the assembly was dismissed. Mother had been spending the day with me, and at night Father came down for her, and we all went to the church to be present at the evening services. After reading the minutes of the day there were devotional services which were very interesting. Poor old Dr. McFarland, who had heard that day of the serious illness of two sons belonging to the army, offered a very affecting prayer for the country and prayed most earnestly for peace. After the dismission it was very interesting to witness the leave-takings.

Yesterday was the baby's birthday. I tried to persuade myself that he was brighter and better and *older* than he had ever been before, but I am obliged to confess he did not distinguish himself in any way whatever. He persisted in crawling and making himself just as dirty as he possibly could, was as gay as a lark, ate a great deal, and was very sweet, but no more so than usual. I am trying to teach him to say his prayers, but he is such a perfect little fidget I find it hard to hold his attention. I took a kiss from him to send his dear grandmother, meaning to have written yesterday, but was prevented, so send it now.

Dear Mother, I wish that instead of writing you this poor little letter I were talking with you face to face. I am sure I could make myself much more interesting. At least I may say so, with this forlorn prospect of never having an opportunity of proving the difference to you! Do give a great deal of love to Father. Tell him his departure was so sudden at the last that to this moment I do not know whether he made his visit to Mrs. Eve or whether I am to do it for him along with the others. Take a great deal of love for yourself, and many kisses from Baby and me. God bless you, dear Mother.

Most affectionately your daughter,
Carrie.

Lt. Charles C. Jones, Jr., *to* Mrs. Mary Jones[g]

Camp Claghorn, Wednesday, December 18th, 1861

My very dear Mother,

I have heard for many days neither from yourself nor Father. I trust, however, that all at home are well.

From the report of the proceedings of the General Assembly I observe that many matters of the utmost importance are claiming and have already received the attention of that body. Dr. Palmer's opening sermon, as reported in *The Southern Presbyterian,* I read last Sabbath with great interest. I observe that Father is one of a committee to prepare a report declaring to the world the causes which induced the present separation of the Presbyterian Church of the Confederate States from that of the United States. The report —or circular, as it might properly be termed—will, I doubt not, be a very able paper, and we will anxiously await its coming. Its effect upon all candid minds must be imposing, and in the history of the church it will be regarded as a declaration of independence.

I still hope that we will have the pleasure of a visit from Father at this camp on his way home. Several days since, I addressed a letter to him at Augusta begging this favor. The ride from Savannah will not be fatiguing to him; and he will, I trust, find the visit agreeable in more respects than one.

How is my precious little daughter? Many kisses for her.

A strange inactivity seems to exist on the part of the enemy. One is at a loss to conjecture the plans of our threatened invaders—if indeed any they have. It does seem to me that God has given them over to blindness and madness. Like Ephraim, they are joined to their idols of fanaticism, of infidelity, of lawlessness; and the God of Nations has let them alone to work out their own destruction. The expenditures on the part of the Federalists are said now daily to reach the enormous sum of two million dollars, and yet they are accomplishing literally nothing—defeated in every engagement. The prospects of the United States—political, social, moral, and religious—are of all most miserable.

I rejoice to see that the public voice of England, as reported in the morning's papers, is lifted against the recent outrage offered to their national flag in the matter of the capture of Messrs. Mason and Slidell. If the government sympathizes with the popular feeling, the Yankee government will soon find ample cause for defeat or dire humiliation in the eyes of the world.

We are all pretty well. A heavy rain is greatly needed. With warmest love, I am, as ever, my dear mother,

Your affectionate son,
Charles C. Jones, Jr.

REV. C. C. JONES *to* LT. CHARLES C. JONES, JR.[g]
Montevideo, *Friday,* December 20th, 1861

My dear Son,

I was happy to receive your letter in Augusta and to learn your decision in respect to the Oglethorpe Light Infantry election. I think you reasoned correctly in declining it.

Our meeting of our new General Assembly, independent of the old, was full, every presbytery in the Confederate States being represented (and also from the Indian Territory) except Missouri, from which state in its present agitated condition we looked for none. . . . The occasion was one of deep interest to all the commissioners. It marked an era in our ecclesiastical history, and we were laying foundations which, by God's blessing, we hoped would endure for ages, and prove a blessing to our country and to the world. The address to the churches, of which you speak in your letter to your mother, was drawn up by Dr. Thornwell, and approved by the committee of which he was chairman, and adopted by the assembly; and I think you will be pleased with it, as it is an excellent paper. . . . By request of the assembly I delivered an address before that body, the Tuesday evening after it commenced its sessions, on the religious instruction of the Negroes—one of the rare opportunities granted me of doing good. And although there were but two or three hours to arrange it in my mind, I never spoke with more comfort to myself nor with more acceptance to others. And the assembly requested me afterwards to reduce it to writing and publish it, which I will endeavor to do if I can recall it properly.

The whole meeting was a refreshment. Saw many brethren not seen for years, renewed old friendships, and formed new acquaintances; and indeed I never was received and treated by my brethren with more respect and consideration. But daily walks to the assembly and long sittings began to weary the weak tabernacle; and as Robert, who kindly came up in good part to see me safe home (your brother having returned the week he came up), was obliged to be in Liberty at the division of his father's estate on Tuesday the 17th; and wishing to spend a day in Burke with Mr. Gideon Dowse to look at a place there and make inquiries in view of a removal of our people if it should be necessary, we left Carrie's on Friday (4 P.M.), spent Saturday with Mr. Dowse and his excellent lady and daughters. Sabbath Robert preached in Waynesboro, and in the evening I preached to Mr. Dowse's people. Monday we dined at Mrs. Harlow's, one of the most pleasant old ladies we have met with in a long time. Took the cars at 5½ P.M.; reached Savannah 11½. Night at the Pulaski, and home by 2 P.M. next day, finding all, through God's great mercy, well and doing well.

And no part of my purpose in leaving home was unaccomplished but a visit to my dear son in camp on the Isle of Hope, which I had set my heart upon, and was compelled to forego on account of my fatigued state, and defer for a little time. And I will now say that your Uncle William, who was with us last night, says he will go with me to pay you a visit; and our purpose, God willing, is to do so after Christmas, taking the buggy and driving from home directly to your camp, which will be the most expeditious and agreeable mode of reaching you—of which you shall have due notice. We shall both be greatly gratified with the sight and evolutions of your fine battery.

Saw Dr. Howard and his lady in Waynesboro. He said he could make arrangements for twenty or thirty among his neighbors for their bread and clothing if necessity was laid upon us to remove. Saw nothing favorable at Mr. Dowse's for such a matter. Saw at Waynesboro also Major Charles Whitehead, since gone back to Virginia, and Mr. Randolph Whitehead, and Captain Morris with his wounded hand.

The up country is alive—at least on the lines of travel—with soldiers, many returning home to recruit their wasted constitutions. Disease slays tenfold more than the sword in war, and is invariably attendant upon war. The day we left Liberty for Augusta one poor young man died on the cars between No. 3 and Savannah, and his corpse went up with us on the Central Railroad.

Received calls while in Augusta, and among the rest Mrs. and Miss Eve. They called Friday, and then Sunday afternoon, not seeing me on Friday!

And was invited the week following to dine at Mrs. Eve's—one I never saw nor knew before! And putting one thing with another, I could not divine the intent of these attentions.

Your brother has a fine, noble little boy. Nearly walking. Resembles his mother's family. Carrie bears her separation as well as she can, and is much favored in having Mrs. Cuthbert living with her.

Your brother deposited in the vault of the Bank of Augusta the manuscripts of my first volume of church history and about one-half or two-thirds of the second for safekeeping, and obtained a receipt for the same. Kindly kept for me free of charge.

Am sorry I missed seeing you when you came out. Your sweet baby is quite well, and grows daily more interesting.

What times! The enemy permitted unmolested to occupy and fortify Tybee—in one and a quarter mile of Fort Pulaski—with the avowed design of reducing that fort with heavy ordnance and fleet, and then Savannah afterwards! We shall have another Fort Sumter affair—but not in our favor! Can nothing arouse Savannah and the commander in chief from fatal apathy? The defenses on Green and Skidaway Islands and Thunderbolt will avail nothing when Pulaski falls. And not a gun mounted in the city! It is amazing and distressing to me. We must let England and France and all the world go, and depend upon ourselves, trusting in God.

Do not let camp life nor business nor pleasure nor company nor anything rob you, my dear son, of time daily to read God's Word and meditate thereon and pray to Him in secret. I hope you are coming into clearer and happier views and hopes. Mother wishes to add a line.

Your ever affectionate father,
C. C. Jones.

Respects to Captain Claghorn.

Mrs. Mary Jones *to* Lt. Charles C. Jones, Jr.[g]
Montevideo, *Friday,* December 20th, 1861

I design, my very dear son, to write you at least once a week, but such are my numerous engagements I often fail to do so. I am glad the Russian sauce pleased the captain, and I will send him the recipe as you desired in my next letter.

Will it be possible for you to be with us on Christmas? It would be so delightful to us to have you at home; and I hope your sister and brother will be with us.

Your precious little daughter improves daily. She has now two teeth, and is a perfect specimen of health and cheerfulness. We think she grows more and more like our dear Ruth.

Your father says he will write you particularly about the miniature. I feel that his criticisms may benefit the artist, as he can not only point out defects but their remedy.

We see from the papers that our valued friends the Misses Jones are amongst the sufferers in Charleston, and presume the old family mansion was destroyed by the fire. I have really felt my spirits weighed down in sympathy with the distress in Charleston from that awful conflagration. The defenseless state of our own city and the insulting occupancy of Tybee give us fears that Georgia ere long will be worse off than Carolina. May God in sovereign mercy deliver our beloved country!

This is your dear father's birthday; and if spared to behold the light of tomorrow, it will be the thirty-first anniversary of our marriage. . . . Your father has retired, and I hear the voice of our little darling calling for her nurse. She sends sweet kisses for her papa. *Susan's* lover has not returned; *Old Andrew has not* a very good opinion of him. Father unites with me in best love to you. . . . God bless you, my child!

Ever your affectionate mother,
Mary Jones.

Lt. Charles C. Jones, Jr., *to* Rev. C. C. Jones[g]
Camp Claghorn, *Saturday,* December 21st, 1861

My dear Father,

It is with much regret that I learned from George, who went to Savannah a day since on business, that you had already passed through the city on your way home, and that we would not enjoy the anticipated pleasure of seeing you and Robert at this camp. I had earnestly hoped that you would have found time and convenience to spend at least a day with us, and we were prepared to show you some excellent drill and shell practice. An hour's drive would have conducted you over a capital shell road to this beautiful encampment. I presume, however, that the fatigues attendant upon your recent protracted engagements in Augusta and your anxiety to return home after a considerable absence prevented. I have had no letter from home for more than two weeks, but trust that all are well.

The recent advices from England are most important in their character, and in the event of a refusal on the part of the Federal government to acquiesce in the reported demands of the British government, we may expect comparative quiet here. With the heavy guns of English men-of-war thundering about their ears, they will have but little time and strength and opportunity for stealing Negroes and colonizing sea islands.

The conduct of the Lincolnites in the forcible arrest of Mason and Slidell to my mind involves a gross violation of the laws of neutrality, and a positive insult of the most flagrant character to the British flag. By the law of nations the deck of the *Trent* was as emphatically a portion of British soil, and as exclusively entitled to the protection of the British flag, as any part of the territory of that nation. The *Trent* had violated no blockade. She was an accredited mail steamer plying between neutral ports; and upon the broad highway of nations Messrs. Mason and Slidell, as ordinary passengers, were entitled to the full protection of that flag by the law of common carriers. If they were accredited envoys, they were doubly protected, not only by that law but also by the law of nations. If, on the other hand, they are to be regarded as political refugees and upon British soil, the United States had no right whatever to violate that territory and arrest them by the application of the rule of the *major vis*. In either event the act was lawless in the extreme, and the insult most violent. My only fear is that the United States will, with characteristic Yankee timidity, recede from the position at present taken, and make any apology demanded by England. In that case the unmitigated contempt of the world will be their portion. If a compliance with the demand be refused, then our war is practically at an end. The English and French navies will sweep their blockading squadrons from the coast, our ports will be again open, our staple commodities will go forward, and practical peace and plenty again lie down at every door. To my mind the future of the Lincoln government is of all most gloomy: a God- and man-forsaken people left to work out alone their own destruction.

The health of our camp is excellent, and our men in fine drill. With warmest love to you both, my dear parents, and to my dear little daughter, I am, as ever,

Your affectionate son,
Charles C. Jones, Jr.

Did you receive my letter addressed to you at Augusta? Can I obtain a copy of the proceedings of the General Assembly, and also a copy of the report setting forth the causes which led to a separation of the church? I am very desirous to procure them.

Lt. Charles C. Jones, Jr., *to* Rev. C. C. Jones[w]

Camp Claghorn, Wednesday, December 25th, 1861

My dear Father,

Christmas Day! Many happy returns to you and my dear mother and precious little daughter! And long before the coming of another anniversary may these storm clouds which now hover about us have been succeeded by the pure light of love, of peace, and of righteousness! This is my hope, but whether it will be realized within the time specified, and by whom, is known only to Him who disposes all things in infinite wisdom and according to His own great pleasure. Of the ultimate success of our cause I have no doubt; but I am persuaded that the struggle will be not without privation and (it may be) great personal danger and perhaps death to many into whose immediate keeping is committed the defense of all we hold dear in life and sacred in death.

The enemy with a force of five vessels is now within a few miles of us, threatening the Skidaway battery, an earthwork mounting seven guns. Night before last our company bivouacked on Skidaway Island in supporting distance of the battery, without shelter and to a great extent without food, having moved from our camp at very short notice. A slight skirmish took place that afternoon between a portion of Commodore Tattnall's fleet lying under the guns of the battery and the enemy's vessels, in which several shots were fired but neither man nor vessel injured on either side. Yesterday we returned to our camp. Today heavy firing heard to the seaward, and this afternoon the vessels of the enemy again in the neighborhood of the Skidaway battery. An attack is expected upon the Skidaway battery tomorrow, and we are in expectation of orders to move in the morning. There may be nothing in the present demonstration of the enemy; but everything appears to indicate a contemplated effort to possess themselves of Skidaway Island, which will enable them effectually to cut off our inland navigation, and would also afford additional facilities in the event of any direct operations upon Savannah.

Our bivouac night before last was the first real taste of soldier's life. Our caps were all frosted in the morning, and the canteens of the men sleeping around the fires had ice in them. It was quite cold, but clear, bracing; and no evil effects have been experienced by either men or horses.

George goes home in the morning to see his mother and family, and I send these hurried lines by him. . . . I much regret to see that the Lincolnites are reported prepared to surrender Mason and Slidell in obedience to the demands of the British government, although I must say I fully expected the result. . . . It is late, and I must bid you all good night. My warmest love to self, dear Father, and to my dear mother, with tenderest kisses for my precious little daughter. May a good God continue ever to bless you all at home! As ever,

Your affectionate son,
Charles C. Jones, Jr.

REV. C. C. JONES *to* LT. CHARLES C. JONES, JR.[g]
Montevideo, Wednesday, December 25th, 1861

My dear Son,

With the shadow of God's judgment and displeasure still resting over our beloved country, and no ray of absolute light breaking from any quarter, I do not know that we can greet each other with a "Merry Christmas." But the Apostle bids us to "Rejoice in God always," and this is the privilege of His people. Hoping we are such, we can rejoice that He reigns, that His ways are just and true, that His judgments are right, that we can commit ourselves and all that concerns us into His merciful care, and so rest upon Him to keep and to sustain and bless us. We can rejoice in His mercies to our country in her struggles thus far, in His mercies to us and to ours, and even see His tender mercies mingling in the cup of His severe afflictions put to our lips the past year. We can greet each other with a "Happy Christmas in our ever blessed God and Saviour." What a vanity is all earth without the present favor of God and the hope of glory with Him hereafter!

Our waking eyes have been saluted with the light of as brilliant a sun and as beautiful a day as ever this world saw. Your dear little one put her hands together and said her prayers as the sun arose; and soon after, the servants came with their "Merry Christmas," and our venerable old man wishing us and all ours "peace all the days of our life, without difficulty or trial in the way; the Blessed Jesus was the Lord and Master, in whom was all power and grace, and He was and would be to us the only Giver of all peace." Next followed your sister's two sweet children, rejoicing in their stockings stored with all manner of things pleasing to their eyes and their ears and their tastes. She and Robert are with us. We remembered you at family worship—as we do always in all our prayers—and your brother and all his.

He took tea with us last evening. Is full of occupation in his profession. Said he did not expect that Mr. J. B. Barnard would live out the night. And Cato informed me this morning *that he had died last night*—so reported by a boy from that neighborhood. Do not know that is so from any other source. Your brother has been in almost daily attendance upon him, and without hope from the beginning.

Mr. B. S. Screven gives his man Andrew a character in the following words: "Andrew as far as I know him is honest and of a submissive spirit. He is not what I wish—a Christian." The appearance and conversation of the boy are good. Susan says she wishes to marry him, but only with your and our approbation. Please write on receipt of this and signify your will. I promised Andrew an answer next week—so soon as I heard from you.

We had no mail yesterday, and between nine and eleven this morning we heard cannonading—in direction of Savannah, we thought. It did not continue long, and hope our coast defenses have suffered nothing from the enemy. I cannot say that I am in daily expectation of an attack upon Savannah or the approaches to it, but shall not be surprised to hear of an attack any day. It is to be hoped that all arrangements are perfect for getting our troops off the islands where they are stationed if there shall come a necessity for their withdrawment. The Johns Island retreat in South Carolina should settle the propriety of looking into this matter.

The Liberty Independent Troop have a meeting today of all the families and friends of the troopers, and a contribution dinner, as no one can go home on Christmas to his family. Shall not go on account of a cold, and think none from our house will.

Mr. Barnard is really dead, and his funeral takes place tomorrow at 12 M. The measles have appeared in the troop, and a considerable number have never had them. Your brother is well, but has too much sickness to attend to. Hope it may not last. The *firing* today, I learn, was *south*. Mother, Sister, and Robert and Brother send much love. Little ones quite well. Respects to Captain Claghorn.

Your affectionate father,
C. C. Jones.

Rev. C. C. Jones *to* Hon. John Johnson[t]
Montevideo, *Wednesday,* December 25th, 1861

My dear Sir,

I beg you to excuse my apparent neglect of your note of November 18th in relation to the case of ————. It reached me a few days before I left for Augusta to attend the session of our General Assembly, from which I returned home last week, and embrace the first leisure to reply.

Mr. —— denied from the beginning; his denial under oath makes no change in my own convictions. Acquaintance with persons charged with crimes, and with prosecutions for crime before both ecclesiastical and civil courts, has taught me to rely for the truth more upon the evidence than upon the asseverations of the accused.

It would be highly improper in me at the request of your honored pastor to suggest what course should be adopted by your session, as this would carry me beyond my sphere, being neither prosecutor nor member of your session. And also unnecessary, since in reply to your letter written upon the said ——'s report of his case to you, I have laid pretty fully all the evidence relating to it before you; and upon which, with the first six chapters of our book of discipline in your hands, you are well able of yourselves, independent of all assistance, to decide what course should be pursued without the intervention of any prosecutor at all. I am

Respectfully and very truly yours in our Lord,
C. C. Jones.

IX

Mrs. Mary Jones *to* Lt. Charles C. Jones, Jr.[g]

Montevideo, *Thursday,* January 9th, 1862

My very dear Son,

The clock reminds me that it is hastening on to midnight, and yet if I seize not the waning moments of this day, tomorrow may not with its many cares and interruptions afford me one hour for writing you. I often think of the sweet promise: "There remaineth therefore a *rest* for the people of God." "Blessed are the dead who die in the Lord. Yea, saith the Spirit, for they *rest* from their labors," etc. Not that I imagine for one moment that heaven is the abode of indolent or inactive beings; but I believe all of its employments will be without weariness, and all congenial with the desires of a redeemed, immortal, and glorified spirit.

Your dear father enjoyed his visit to you exceedingly, and Robert and himself have been unsparing in their admiration of the Chatham Artillery, and the truly military appearance of Camp Claghorn, and (though last, not least) the hospitable entertainment extended to them by your honored commander. I quite envied them the visit. God bless you, my very dear child, your captain, your officers, and your brave men! If called to meet our enemies, may the Lord shield you all in the day of battle, and nerve every heart with courage and every hand with strength for the conflict! I feel ever unwavering confidence in asking my Heavenly Father to defend and deliver my suffering country, for I believe our cause is just and right. At the same time I know that we have individual and national sins that merit the displeasure and judgments of a holy God. I pray daily that we may feel them, and so truly repent of them and forsake them that His anger and His wrath may be turned away from us, and the light of His countenance again lifted upon us through our Divine Redeemer!

We have had a delightful visit from your Uncle John, Aunt Jane, and the two little boys. The interesting incidents of the past eventful summer which he has treasured up, and the events of historic moment, would fill a volume. He went upon the battlefield of Manassas the day after the great victory of July 21st, and has lived since then mostly with our Army of the Potomac, acting directly as chaplain to the 8th Georgia Regiment. He has been instrumental in doing great good to our suffering and dying soldiers. Your sister and the children left us on Monday afternoon. Your Uncle John brought an exploded shell from the battlefield, and when showing it little Mary burst into tears and said: "Those Yankees want to kill my Uncle Charlie!"

Your precious little daughter grows more and more interesting every day. When, my dear son, could you spend a Sabbath with us? We desire not to delay her baptism. I want to know that she has been publicly dedicated to her mother's and I trust her father's and her grandparents' God and Saviour. Do write me your wishes; I desire to do nothing contrary to them.

Susan would like to know if you consent to her marrying the man Andrew. I expect it is just as well. I have told her she takes the risk of separation.

Your brother has been quite unwell. We expect Carrie and dear little Stanhope on Saturday. Father has long retired, leaving best love for *you*. With many kisses from your little daughter,

Ever your affectionate mother,
Mary Jones.

The servants all send howdies.

LT. CHARLES C. JONES, JR., *to* MRS. MARY JONES[g]

Camp Claghorn, *Saturday,* January 11th, 1862

My very dear Mother,

I am this moment favored with your kind letter of the 9th inst., and sincerely thank you for it. I am truly happy to know that all at home are well. The very earliest Sabbath that I can be excused from this post shall be named to you as the baptismal day of my precious little daughter. I am exceedingly anxious that this sacred rite should be performed, and that she should in tender infancy be dedicated to the service of that God who is the God of my beloved father and mother, who so signally sustained my dear wife in the hour of her sorest trials, in whose presence she and dear little Julia are rejoicing forevermore, and who, with his Son the Blessed Jesus and the Holy Comforter, is the Author of all truth and righteousness and happiness. It is my daily and fervent prayer to Heaven that she may from childhood be the sincere follower of the Lamb, and that whatever else be denied her she may possess that good part which can never be taken from her. Without this there is nothing valuable.

I have been tendered by General Jackson the judge advocacy of his division, which comprises the brigades of Generals Walker, Capers, and Harrison, with the rank of major, and as chief of artillery. This places me in immediate command of all the artillery in the state service, amounting at present to three batteries numbering in all nineteen pieces. General Jackson regards it—as it is, in fact—the most important position on his staff. The truth is, the position is much superior to that of a colonelcy, and is second in consequence to that of a brigadier general. The duties and responsibilities consequent upon an acceptance will be most responsible. The truth is, the science of artillery and the knowledge of that drill are but little understood as a general rule in our state, and it is no easy matter to find one to fill the position. The only inducement which would influence me in accepting the appointment would be the desire of accomplishing as much good as I could in behalf of my state and country in the present emergency. The labor in preparing these batteries for the field will be great, but must be undertaken by someone.

As yet I have the matter under consideration. Enclosed I send for the perusal of yourself and dear Father the letter of General Jackson, which I must beg that you will preserve and return to me with your views as to the propriety of an acceptance. My mind inclines favorably at present. My greatest regret will be at parting with my own company, to which my attachments are very strong. Do let me hear from you by return mail if practicable.

We have nothing new with us in camp. With warmest love to you both, my dear parents, and many kisses for my precious little daughter, I am, as ever,

Your affectionate son,
Charles C. Jones, Jr.

I have no objections to Susan's marriage if you think it proper.

Rev. C. C. Jones *to* Lt. Charles C. Jones, Jr.[g]

Montevideo, *Monday,* January 13th, 1862

My dear Son,

Yours of the 11th enclosing General Jackson's of the 9th was received by your mother this afternoon, and as she is weary and unwell I undertake to answer for her.

The appointment is tendered you in a frank and kind spirit, is superior to the one you now hold in position, importance, and emolument, and brings you more into service and in the view and knowledge of your own state and fellow statesmen; will certainly give you far more labor and no more exposure in event of your being called into action. To put in good order and efficiency the artillery of the state will be rendering no mean service in such a time as this. We think favorably of the appointment, and your brother, who has read the letters, thinks you ought to accept decidedly. We can well conceive the pain it will give you to separate yourself from the officers and privates of the old Chatham Artillery, from whom you have received so many proofs of their confidence, and to whom you are so much attached. I shall feel it myself, and for your good captain in particular. Mother adds that there will be a great increase of care and of responsibility and also of usefulness, and is an important position. And as we really do not comprehend all involved in it, we feel rather like acquiescing in your decision, believing you will do what you think is right. General Jackson is very candid in his letter; he wants a *working man,* and will expect you to work. Mother says the state has greater claims on you than a single company. Let us know your decision, and if you change, where your quarters will be. We think hotels are miserable places for headquarters for single or married men either. And we are always hoping that your public engagements may not draw off your mind from your higher and immortal interests.

We shall be glad to see you whenever you can come out.

Your dear little daughter has an eruption around her mouth and on her hand which is the effect of her biting my silver pencil and getting on it a little of the iodine ointment which had been rubbed on the back of her ear and on a little sore on her head. At least, that is the supposition. But it is nothing serious, we hope. She sat near me on the sofa this afternoon, playing with the cloth baby her dear mother made for little Julia, of which she is very fond, and for some time was laughing out most heartily with her nurse. She is now in her crib, gone to bed for the night.

Carrie and little Stanhope reached us safely on Saturday. Both in fine health, and it will be a comfort to your brother to have them near him. . . . Mother and Carrie unite in love to you. Our respects to Captain Claghorn. Excuse the blots: they came in some unseen manner. As ever,

Your affectionate father,
C. C. Jones.

Lt. Charles C. Jones, Jr., *to* Rev. C. C. Jones[g]

Camp Claghorn, *Monday,* January 20th, 1862

My dear Father,

I beg at greater length to acknowledge the receipt of your very kind letter of the 13th inst.

Upon reflection I have concluded to decline the appointment tendered by General Jackson. The truth is, I think he acted rather unadvisedly in the matter, and without consulting the organic act of the legislature providing for the raising of the state forces now in the field. By that act it is provided that whenever *four or more* artillery companies should be received and mustered into the service of the state, *a colonel* of artillery should be commissioned by the governor, to be elected by the commissioned officers of the artillery companies, and to be attached to the staff of the commanding general. General Jackson has only *three companies* of artillery in his division. The law makes no provision for a *major of artillery*. The general proposed to fill this hiatus by commissioning me as judge advocate with the rank of major, and assigning me to the specific command of these and of all future batteries which might be mustered into the state service and attached to his command, as *chief of artillery*. I question his right to do this. He certainly finds no warrant for it in the organic act. And besides, Governor Brown has already appointed Colonel Boggs, recently of the Confederate service, and chief of ordnance at Pensacola, as chief of engineers and of artillery for the State of Georgia. You see at once, then, where a conflict of jurisdiction may arise, and the question of rank might lead to difficulty.

Moreover, these batteries attached to the state forces never will be concentrated at any one point so as to be under the immediate direction of a general officer. They are attached to the respective brigades, and in case of an action will in all probability—and in fact, of necessity—be posted with those brigades under the command of their respective officers. The truth is, light batteries always act, and are so regarded, as distinct commands. Seldom in the history of warfare have they been associated together. So that the idea of an intelligent separate command of these batteries upon the field cannot be entertained. There is no field in the vicinity of Savannah where they could be drilled in battalion movements.

The truth is, I very much doubt if Judge Jackson, when he wrote me that letter (which has been already submitted to you) tendering me the appointment, had any very definite idea of what he wished me to do, or of the extent and practical operation of the duties which he desired me to assume. And of this I think I convinced him in a conversation which I had with him. The whole matter, then, resolved itself into a mere appointment upon his staff as judge advocate with the rank and pay of major.

If ease and personal interests were consulted, I would accept the appointment. The emoluments are considerably greater and the labors much less than those devolved upon me in my present position. But I sacrifice personal considerations in my honest endeavor to sustain the efficiency of the Chatham Artillery, a company to which I am attached in no ordinary degree, and in the firm conviction that I will be able in my present subordinate position to render more essential service to the great cause which enlists our every sympathy.

Speaking freely, Hartridge is in very bad health; Davidson is almost crippled with rheumatism; and Captain Claghorn tells me if I should leave the battery he knows not where or how the loss could be supplied. The men urge me not to leave them, and Captain Claghorn has been much depressed at the idea of my doing so. I speak freely because I am writing to you, Father.

All things considered, I believe I am right in remaining where I am. Had the office tendered proved upon examination to be what General Jackson conceived and represented it to be, I would have accepted. But as I said to you before, it resolved itself simply into an appointment upon his staff as judge advocate with the rank of major, with little to do except to conduct causes before a division court-martial. Now, I desire, in as emphatic a manner as possible, to testify my personal devotion to the interests of our young Confederacy, and in common with tens of thousands of our brave soldiers to endure the inconveniences and the privations of actual service. Besides, this desire to hold office merely for the rank and the emoluments, and without discharging any material duties or rendering any essential services, has been and still continues to be a great bane. My idea is that it is a mistake to change a position in which you already are performing valuable services, and where you enjoy the esteem and respect of your associates, unless by that change you can advance the interests of a common cause and enlarge your sphere of usefulness.

We are anxiously awaiting the movements of this Burnside expedition. As yet it has not made its appearance upon our coast. Should a land attack be made upon Savannah, it will probably be attempted in this vicinity. We have now upon the coast of Georgia in both Confederate and state service about sixteen thousand men.

My impression is that along the limits of our Confederacy we will have heavy work during the next three months. The Lincolnites now have ready for the advance an army of four hundred and eighty thousand, exclusive of sick, etc., etc., and of the naval force. With this vast army they propose to overwhelm us by hurling heavy columns upon us simultaneously from different quarters, with the hope (in the language of Seward) to "crush out the rebellion" at once. Vain expectation! But certain it is that we must in meeting the invasions suffer much, and many a brave man surrender his life in the defense of all we hold pure in honor, true in principle, honest in religion, dear in life, and sacred in death. But I earnestly pray, and confidently hope, that the same good and great God who has hitherto so signally interposed in our behalf will continue to bless our exertions and crown our struggle with success. There can be no retreat. The ultimatum with every true lover of his country who is able to bare his breast in support of the principles for which we are contending must be *victory or death*. My daily prayer to God is that He will for Christ's sake pardon my sins and prepare me to stand up fearlessly in my lot when the hour of danger comes. All help is from above.

Our pickets on Skidaway were fired upon by a barge of Lincolnites who approached the island through a creek in Romney Marsh on Saturday night last about eleven o'clock. The shots were distinctly heard at our camp; also the long roll at Stiles's camp, and also at the camp of the Louisiana battalion. None of the picket were wounded, nor are we aware that any of the enemy were killed. One of our company who visited the spot picked out of a tree one of the balls fired by the rascals.

Will you, my dear father, at some leisure moment let me know whether you think the miniature painting of my precious wife can be altered by the artist so as to make it at all a likeness? Where do the defects lie? To me it conveys scarce an idea of my dearest Ruth. Her sacred image is with me ever, and the memory of all her loves is with me morning, noon, and night. Never will love like that kindle again in this breast. It will live alone—pure, separate, ever bright—although other affections may possess the heart. I am especially anxious on account of my dear little daughter to obtain a good likeness of her.

It is late, and I must say good night. Do give warmest love to dear Mother, and many kisses to my precious little daughter. And believe me ever, my dear father,

Your affectionate son,
Charles C. Jones, Jr.
Kindest remembrances to the Doctor, Sister Carrie, and little Stanhope.

Rev. C. C. Jones *to* Lt. Charles C. Jones, Jr.[g]
Montevideo, *Friday,* January 24th, 1862
My dear Son,

Yours of the 20th reached us yesterday. We were aware of the peculiarity of the appointment tendered you by your friend General H. R. Jackson, but presumed that he had secured all the necessary and regular steps thereto, so that you would in accepting be free from every objection and embarrassment. You have done what I was sure you would do—search into the matter and give it proper consideration and then decide; and all your reasons for declining the appointment meet our approbation. There being no law for it settles the question. And what was desirable in the appointment being thereby taken away, and its becoming dwarfed into a mere office of rank and emolument, puts it beneath the consideration of a man who wishes to serve his country in action on the field and in the camp from disinterested and patriotic motives. Changes to meet the approbation of the wise and the good, and especially the approbation of a man's enlightened conscience in the public service at a time like this in our country's need, should be made on the *ascending* scale of *usefulness* in the common cause. In this you are right, and I never wish you to act differently. Your loss to your company I believe would have been a serious one, and much felt by Captain Claghorn.

The *reported armament* of the Burnside expedition, which has been gotten up with much secrecy, is more formidable than that of Sherman's, and if managed with skill and spirit will give us work to do on whatever point on the coast it descends. I cannot comprehend the movement of the selection of the North Carolina coast about Hatteras for that purpose unless that be only *a part* of the program. A flotilla of thirty to fifty vessels carrying hundred-pound rifled cannon and columbiads and other guns proportionally heavy would render an attack on our small sand batteries and short ranges a pretty serious affair. Am happy to learn that there are sixteen thousand men on our coast. Is it true that the lower end of Savannah at the gasworks is now being fortified? And that there is a battery at the lower end of Hutchinson's Island commanding the back river? Ogeechee River should be looked after; a night expedition might destroy the railroad bridge there. The battery on that river is feeble.

There has been a *lull* in Federal war operations for several weeks, preparing, they say, for the grand move of four hundred and eighty thousand men of which you speak on all our borders simultaneously, land and water. Their finances are in a critical condition, as it appears to *outsiders*. But it is not their impression: they are lacking for neither men nor means; and although, through God's mercy towards us, thus far much foiled, they seem as determined as ever to "crush out rebellion" (their favorite phrase); and not one ray of light appears on the horizon indicative of returning peace.

The hope of aid from England or France in our struggle is the faintest possible. The policy of England, indicated months ago, is to "tide over," as they expressed it, the cotton deficit of the present year, 1862, and to put a strain upon her cotton manufacturing interest, and if possible demonstrate their ability to *do without American cottons,* and consequently her independence of us in all time to come. That is, *if it be possible.* The direst necessity alone will force her to interfere in American affairs.

We have nothing to do but humble ourselves under the afflicting hand of

God, and committing our cause to Him, go forward making every arrangement for a protracted and deadly struggle, and doing our best, God helping us, in conquering a peace with as vile and tyrannical enemies as any nation has ever been called to resist. The Lord be with you and bless and keep you, my dear son, from all evil, and unto His Heavenly Kingdom!

Your dear little one has been very unwell with the affection I wrote you about. Is still suffering from it; has lost much flesh; but is in good spirits, and we think better. Your brother is prescribing for her, and sees her almost every day. Mother is somewhat better. All the rest well. And all unite in much love. Will write about the likeness of dear Ruth another time at more leisure. Respects to Captain Claghorn.

Your affectionate father,
C. C. Jones.

Mrs. Mary Jones *to* Lt. Charles C. Jones, Jr.[g]
Montevideo, *Sunday,* January 26th, 1862

I have but a moment to say to you, my very dear son, that through the goodness of God we are all well, and your dear little daughter almost entirely relieved of her cold and the eruption on her face and head. She grows sweeter and sweeter every day.

Please arrange to meet a box or basket at the depot on Thursday evening. I want to send you a few home remembrancers. With our united love, and kisses from your babe,

Ever your affectionate mother,
Mary Jones.

Lt. Charles C. Jones, Jr., *to* Mrs. Mary Jones[g]
Camp Claghorn, *Wednesday,* January 29th, 1862

My dear Mother,

I am this afternoon favored with your kind letter of the 26th inst., and cannot tell you how happy I am to know that all at home are well, and that my dear little daughter is almost entirely relieved from her cold and the eruption on her face and head. I never will be able even to express to you how thankful and more than grateful I am and ever will be to you for this your great kindness in assuming the tender care of my dear little daughter now that she will never know the sympathy and love of my precious Ruth, and while stern necessity prevents me from even seeing her. . . . I long to see you both, my dear parents, and my dear little daughter; but the dangers which environ us preclude the possibility of my leaving this post at this time.

Over twenty Lincoln vessels, war and transports (principally the former), are lying in Wassaw Sound, only a few miles below our batteries. For two days they have been drilling in column, deploying in line of battle, etc., etc., and practicing with their guns. Today they have been testing the currents with floats; and as the tide suits about eight o'clock in the morning, we are expecting an attack upon the Skidaway batteries at that hour. What the result will be is known only to the Sovereign Disposer of all events. From our camp we could distinctly see the shelling from the gunboats behind Wilmington Island.

The convoy of the provision steamboats from Savannah to Fort Pulaski by Commodore Tattnall and his little fleet in the face of the enemy's gunboats on either hand was a most gallant act, and the wonder is that the feat was accomplished. Both from Wall's Cut and from Freeborn's Creek they poured shot and shell upon him from guns of vastly superior metal. One of his vessels, the *Samson,* was struck four times, three shots passing through her and one shell exploding in her storeroom, and, as if by a miracle, no one injured or killed. Commodore Tattnall replied, but with what success is not known. Certain it is that in the face of this opposition he safely convoyed the steamers to Fort Pulaski; and that fortress has now a store of seven months' provisions. Commodore Tattnall's name will live in the grateful remembrance of us all. A truer, nobler, braver man does not breathe. I love him almost as a father, and I believe it is my good fortune to enjoy his positive friendship and esteem, a possession of which I am proud. He stands in strange contrast with some others, high in military preferment, whose names it becomes me not to mention.

General Lee is in Savannah, and every effort is being made to place the city in a state of defense. I learn that the citizens are calm and resolved to meet any emergency which may arise. The enemy are not in possession of Savannah yet by a great deal, and I confidently trust that a kind Providence will continue to vouchsafe His favor to us all.

Our battery is performing laborious picket duty, and now occupies three points. Tonight I bivouac with a section of the battery under my command at the western terminus of the Skidaway bridge for the protection of that structure from a night attack, which is apprehended. The object of the enemy appears to be to get in our rear and to isolate Fort Pulaski and our forces on Skidaway and Green Islands. If this bridge is destroyed, nearly two thousand troops will be cut off. We expect with the rising sun to hear the enemy's guns at the Skidaway batteries. I must mount Yorick and join my command at the bridge.

Many thanks, my dear mother, for your kind remembrance, which I will try and get from the depot. Did you ever receive from Vallie a box containing some articles for Daughter? She asked me some time since if you had received it. With warmest love to you both, my dear parents, and many kisses for my dear little daughter, I am, as ever,

Your affectionate son,
Charles C. Jones, Jr.
Captain Claghorn begs his remembrances to you and Father.

Rev. C. C. Jones *to* Lt. Charles C. Jones, Jr.ᵍ

Montevideo, *Wednesday,* January 29th, 1862

My dear Son,

We were favored with letters last evening from Captain Claghorn and yourself, and were happy to hear from both of you that you were both well and at the post of duty. May God enable you to do your duty; and if called into danger may He preserve you safe in person and in life, and spare you for usefulness to your country and to your families and to His own Heavenly Kingdom! Our kind regards to the captain.

Events are taking the course of which the enemy gave us timely warning very shortly after the Port Royal affair, and about the time that he was beginning to realize the extreme difficulty of operating on Charleston. Savannah is far more accessible from having more approaches by water directly and fewer fortifications, and his attention was turned in that direction. The obstructions in Wall's Cut and Freeborn's Passage have been quietly removed, and our authorities were not aware of it! Pulaski may be considered cut off, and its reduction begun. Next follows the Burnside expedition, and a trial upon our batteries on Green Island and Skidaway, which if carried reduces the seaboard down to St. Simons and Jekyll. And then attempts may be expected there. Our hope is that it may please God to enable us to repel their attacks upon our batteries. If so, we shall do well; if not, we fall back upon the main and repel their advance into the interior and upon the city—which, however, if they approach near enough, may be shelled and damaged. We cannot prevent these naval expeditions: we have no navy. And the taking of our seaboard cities, which cannot be long held, and our coast islands, although subjecting us to great inconveniences and (many of us, perhaps) to pecuniary losses and ruin, will not "crush out rebellion," to use the favorite expression, nor "wipe out the South." The enemy can make no progress inland. Separation from their fleet is starvation and death. And our brave men, fighting for everything dear to men in home and country and in honor and religion, will beat them back inch by inch.

We appear to be at this time, throughout our whole Confederacy and in our foreign relations, at one of the most important periods of our revolution; and I pray that the Lord may pardon our sins and espouse our just cause, as we hope He has heretofore done, and be a wall of fire round about us and a glory in the midst of us. I am obliged to believe that He will hear our prayers ascending from every part of our land and maintain our right. We cannot expect to escape reverses; but they should humble our pride, remove our self-confidence, but increase our courage and resolution in the Lord to meet our cruel and unjust enemies in every battle to the end.

Write us as frequently as you can find time to do so.

Am happy to inform you that your dear little daughter, we hope, is nearly herself again. She is remarkably intelligent, and Mother says "the most *earnest eyes* she ever saw," and very much like dear Ruth. How often does her image and remembrance come up in my mind! Have not had time lately to give the miniature a careful study; will do so early. Your sister and Little Daughter with us. She, Carrie, and Mother unite in much love; and all continually pray for you. All relations, friends, and servants generally well.

Your ever affectionate father,
C. C. Jones.

MRS. MARY JONES *to* LT. CHARLES C. JONES, JR.[g]

Montevideo, *Thursday,* January 30th, 1862

I hope, my very dear son, the basket will reach you in safety and prove acceptable at this time. The weather is so very warm you will have to use the sausages and white puddings at once. The turkey is a present from your sister, and I thought it best to have it roasted.

I need not say how anxiously we are feeling, and hope we will hear as frequently as you can possibly write. God bless and protect you and your whole company and our united army and country! I cannot trust myself to write on this subject. At times I feel that my heart would almost break when I think of what may be the suffering of my own sons and my relatives and countrymen, and the wrongs inflicted by the diabolical enemy upon our country. But God reigns, and I commit all into His just and wise and holy keeping!

Our dear little babe has quite recovered. Your sister left us this morning. Your father, brother, and Carrie unite with me in best love to you. Sweetest kisses from your little daughter. I have received the captain's polite acknowledgment of the recipe, and send you three bottles of the Russian sauce, which I fear is not so good, being prepared of *domestic vinegar* and *mustard*. I must close, or we shall lose the cars.

Ever, my dear son, your affectionate mother,
Mary Jones.

LT. CHARLES C. JONES, JR., *to* MRS. MARY JONES[g]

Camp Claghorn, *Friday,* January 31st, 1862

My very dear Mother,

I am this afternoon in receipt of your note of yesterday and also of your very kind remembrance in the most acceptable basket of sundries, all of them delicious and tempting. You have not only my own but also the hearty thanks of the officers' mess. Such favors are, I can assure you, highly prized, and I promise you the many good things you have sent will be enjoyed with honest appetites. . . . The wax tapers and candles have elicited much praise. One of them is now burning upon the table, and we are admiring its fine light and the slowness with which the material is consumed. Do thank Sister for the turkey. It arrived just in time for dinner, and was greatly enjoyed by us and some officers who dined with us.

The enemy has retired from the immediate vicinity of Savannah, but no less than seventeen vessels remain in Wassaw Sound, only a few miles below our batteries. For what they are waiting, or what their purposes are, we are unable to ascertain with any certainty. This morning, as the tide was favorable, we confidently anticipated an attack. It may have been postponed on account of the dense fog which overshadowed everything until about eight o'clock. Now we have the promise of a regular northeaster, which may further postpone active operations on their part. Every indication points to an attack upon the Skidaway batteries, which have recently been considerably strengthened. The defenses around Savannah and more particularly in the river have received attention.

General Lawton visited our camp today. We are in a state of very creditable preparation, although our battery is at present divided. To us are entrusted Montmollin's Point, the Isle of Hope settlement, and the defense of Skidaway bridge. Tonight I will be on picket duty at the latter point. It is so dark that we will have to keep a very sharp lookout. And the skies promise rain— just the time for an attack. The burning of this bridge will isolate no less than eighteen hundred of our troops at present on Skidaway Island.

We have today a rumor of a desperate battle at Bowling Green, Kentucky, in which we are victorious. I trust and pray that a kind Providence will watch over us and deliver us from the threatened devastations from an inhuman enemy.

With warmest love to you, my dear mother, to Father, to Sister Carrie, the Doctor, and little Stanhope, and many kisses for my precious little daughter, I am, as ever,

Your affectionate son,
Charles C. Jones, Jr.

With the termination of this day six months of our term of service expire. Where we will be at the end of the next six months God only knows. I sincerely hope that before that period elapses we may see the arts of peace restored, our independence established, our honor vindicated, the temples of learning, of justice, and of religion again fully opened, and God acknowledged and fervently worshiped throughout all our borders.

Do thank Father for his valued letter, which I will answer soon, D.V.

LT. CHARLES C. JONES, JR., *to* REV. C. C. JONES[g]

Camp Claghorn, Saturday, February 1st, 1862

My dear Father,

Last night I enjoyed the pleasure of replying to Mother's note and of thanking her for her very kind remembrance, which duly reached us and is sincerely appreciated. Today I write to acknowledge the receipt of your valued favor of the 29th ult. and to express to you my obligations for it and my unqualified acquiescence in all the views therein presented.

The casualties which attended the Sherman expedition to the careless observer might have been referred to the chance effects of an idle wind; but now that forty vessels of the Burnside fleet have been swallowed up and stranded amid the angry billows which guard our coast—vessels freighted with elaborate munitions of war and filled with those who breathed devastation and destruction to our homes and lives—can even the Lincolnites fail of perceiving that there is a God who rides upon the whirlwind and directs the storm? Truly each day—each hour—we are called upon in this, as in everything else, to lift up our hearts and voices in gratitude to the Giver of All Good for His renewed interpositions in our behalf.

We have been in daily expectation of an attack upon our Skidaway batteries. A courier just arrived reports an addition this morning of five vessels. The tide has been favorable, and we are at a loss to conjecture the designs of the enemy, or to explain the reason of this apparent delay. My own impression is that a combined movement is intended against Savannah, both by land and water.

We are now experiencing the realities of the bivouac; nearly fifty members of our company are upon picket duty. Picture a bed of clean pine straw with a couple of blankets and the overarching branches of a generous live oak, and you have my sleeping apartments for the past night—by no means to be despised, even if a regular Scotch mist was settling over everything.

Captain Claghorn desires his especial remembrance. Give warmest love to dear Mother. Kiss my precious little daughter for me. And believe me ever, my dear father,

Your affectionate son,
Charles C. Jones, Jr.

LT. CHARLES C. JONES, JR., *to* REV. *and* MRS. C. C. JONES[g]

Camp Claghorn, *Monday,* February 3rd, 1862

My dear Father and Mother,

I send by express for my precious little daughter a silver cup and spoon which she will accept as a token of the tender love and abiding affection of her absent father.

Heavy firing today on the Carolina shore. As yet we know not the cause. My own impression is that a combined attack is meditated against Savannah. Whether the enemy will have the courage and the ability to consummate their designs time alone will show.

We have a rumor that France and England have entered into an agreement to recognize the Southern Confederacy and raise the blockade. It is quite improbable, and it would be better for us to look less for foreign aid and rely more firmly upon ourselves, by the blessing of Heaven, for the ultimate and favorable solution of our present difficulties.

No change in the disposition of the enemy's forces near Wassaw batteries —or rather I should say Skidaway batteries. As ever, my dear parents,

Your affectionate son,
Charles C. Jones, Jr.

Lt. Charles C. Jones, Jr., *to* Rev. *and* Mrs. C. C. Jones[g]

Camp Claghorn, *Wednesday,* February 5th, 1862

I have only a moment, my dear father and mother, to convey my warmest love to you both and to my precious little daughter. We are all well, and there is no change in the military status of affairs. The Lincolnites appear to be waiting for reinforcements. Their ships are lying idly below our batteries on Skidaway Island, and no new demonstrations are made in our vicinity. This delay is very tedious. The defenses of Savannah have been very materially strengthened during the past few days. Previously the city was, comparatively, at the mercy of the enemy. As ever, my dear parents,

Your affectionate son,
Charles C. Jones, Jr.

Mrs. Mary Jones *to* Lt. Charles C. Jones, Jr.[g]

Montevideo, *Saturday,* February 8th, 1862

My very dear Son,

I have risen a half hour earlier than usual that I might have time not only for my usual family duties but to send you a line of love by today's mail. I am writing in the western wing. The sun in all his glory is just above the trees, and his brilliant rays, darting through the deep green foliage of the old cedar in the yard, fall with fanciful effect all around me. I have just read the 25th and 27th Psalms. They appear this morning possessed of peculiar beauty. I commend them to you at this time. . . . Tomorrow two weeks will be our Communion at Midway. I wish it could be possible for you to be with us and have our dear baby baptized on that day.

It is more than probable that Daughter and myself may come to Savannah on Monday next. I have some dental work which is really necessary to be done by Dr. Parsons. We will stop at the Pavilion, and should I come, will put a line in the mail on Monday for you, hoping you may be able to see us, if only for a moment, on Tuesday.

The beautiful cup and spoon for our little darling was duly received, and she returns her dear papa sweetest kisses for it. She seems to understand that they are her own; stretches out her little hand for the cup, and holds the spoon, upon which already may be traced the print of her little teeth. She is one of the most interesting infants I have ever seen, and the joy of our home.

I wrote Vallie acknowledging the receipt of the box. As she did not write, it was not received as soon as it might have been from the depot.

Your Uncle John is now with us. His account of the battle of Manassas is deeply interesting. He has brought your father a fine map of the battlefield, and myself some valuable relics.

What can I do for you, my dear child? I would be glad oftener to send in articles to you. Would you like to have more of the "Confederate green lights"? I have made quite a supply.

Your father has improved within a few days, but has suffered from a severe cold. Your brother also is better. He has too much to do: *a nurse and surgeon's duty* and a private's reward.

Yesterday we heard of the death of *Willie Howe* at Centreville. He was in Colonel Kershaw's regiment; had been made orderly sergeant; was in the battle of July 21st. A noble, gallant youth. My heart is filled with grief and sympathy for our dear friends Dr. and Mrs. Howe. May God sustain them! Such are the *priceless treasures* this vile enemy demands and receives from our hearts and homes. Father, Carrie, your uncle unite with me in best love to you. Sweetest kisses from your daughter.

Ever your own affectionate mother,
Mary Jones.

REV. C. C. JONES *to* LT. CHARLES C. JONES, JR.ᵍ

Montevideo, *Monday,* February 10th, 1862

My dear Son,

The execution of Mr. Bounetheau's miniature is very fine, but the likeness is not satisfactory. He has copied the larger of the two daguerreotypes, neither of which is satisfactory. The best you have is the one Ruthie gave you before your marriage. I would prefer a copy from that to any other. Mother thinks the one Mr. Bounetheau copied excellent.

It is difficult to point out the variations of the copy from the original on paper. Yet let me say, according to my eye the change of the dress to a low-neck, and a cross to the necklace, is no improvement, while the chest between the arms is too narrow. The entire face and head is more oval than in the original—the top of the head running up more to a point, and the falling of the hair on each side of the forehead and face made to correspond, while there is a considerable flattening of the hair over the left side of the forehead. The face is not as full, looking more *from* you than *to* you or *at* you. The distance between the eyes is less, and the eyes not as deep and earnest in the copy as in the original. The eyebrows rather sharply defined. The nose not as perpendicular, the mouth not as expanded as in the original, and the rounding of the chin too full.

Whether these observations would benefit Mr. Bounetheau I do not know. I am sure if he could hit the *likeness* he would make the *execution* most excellent, and do sincerely hope he may succeed. Your mother showed the daguerreotype to Mary Ruth and told her it was the likeness of her dear mother, and the little thing held it with her hands; and when Mother told her to kiss it, she kissed it two or three times.

Mother has just left for Walthourville, where your sister joins her; and they go on their way to Savannah this afternoon, and put up at the Pavilion to be near Dr. Parsons. She hopes to get a sight of you, if but for a moment, while in town, and if Dr. Parsons finishes her work, will return about Wednesday.

Enclosed is the note duly signed. I think there is enough to my credit in bank to pay the interest and more—*discount,* I should say.

The watermelon seeds I will try and remember to bring up from Maybank when I next go down there. None up here.

Am hopeful that General Lee may put the city and its surroundings in such a state of complete defense that our enemy may be discouraged from making an attack beyond the Green Island and Skidaway batteries, which it is presumed he has made up his mind to attack anyhow. If these batteries are commanded by *brave* and *cool men,* they will find it hard to take them. The defense of the Port Royal battery, manned and worked as it was, ought rather to encourage than discourage us, your brother thinks.

Is it not monstrous that these brutal creatures should come near a thousand miles in gratuitous wrath and cupidity to make war upon us in our very homes and firesides? May the Lord decide for us in the day they come upon us! If Georgia does not do her duty, we shall hang our heads in overwhelming shame and sorrow. Surely if she has fought so gallantly on every field in sister states, will she not fight with equal gallantry in defense of her own sacred soil? I believe, by God's blessing, she will.

We are all pretty well this trying weather. Hope your health is good, and that you are as careful of yourself as you can be, and live in watchfulness and prayer before God. Respects to Captain Claghorn. Love from all, and kisses from your little one.

Your ever affectionate father,
C. C. Jones.

Lt. Charles C. Jones, Jr., *to* Rev. *and* Mrs. C. C. Jones[g]

Camp Claghorn, Monday, February 10th, 1862

My dear Father and Mother,

I sincerely trust that these dark and gloomy days, with their somber shadows and weeping skies, may not be symbolic of the coming fortunes of our young Confederacy for the next few months. I cannot divest myself of the impression, formed as it is with the aid of the best lights at command, that our struggle for national independence and national repose must for some time to come be characterized by unprecedented effort and bloody details. While the Northern armies have been gathering strength, improving in discipline, and recovering from the effect of the reverses to which they were subjected at an early stage of the war, I cannot perceive a corresponding increase of strength on our part, or such an accumulation of the materials of war as will enable us successfully to combat with these barbarian hordes now thronging our borders, except through the continued intervention in our behalf of a gracious superintending Providence and the most desperate exertions of our brave soldiery.

Not only are we sensible of the want of a proper supply of the munitions of war, but we will also soon be forced to recognize in the failure of many whose terms of service are on the eve of expiring to reenlist a prime mistake committed at the outset of our difficulties. That mistake is simply this: in enlisting soldiers for six and twelve months, when they should have been mustered in for the war. The latter could, at the inception of our present contest, have been accomplished without much doubt or difficulty. Men anticipated a short war. They were attracted by the novelties of a soldier's life. They were eager to serve their country and (many of them) to win distinction upon the tented field. They were practically ignorant of the dangers and the inconveniences, the hardships and the privations in store for them. Under such circumstances—the early and strongest tide of patriotism throbbing in their veins—they stood ready to assume any obligations, and to enter with alacrity upon the discharge of all engagements which might have been represented as vital to the best interests of the homes they loved and of the government so recently and so heroically inaugurated. But the opportune moment was permitted to pass unimproved; and the consequence is that we only here and there find a regiment in for the war, while almost entire brigades will soon be disbanded, their terms of enlistment having expired. Wet tents, thin blankets, scanty rations, heavy marches, sleepless nights beneath the canopy of a dripping sky, and long hours of sickness and of pain are the severest tests to which devotion to country can be subjected; and many a soldier with this experience fresh in his remembrance so soon as his term of service expires will return to his home satisfied with past duties, and avoid a repetition of like labors and similar scenes unless forced from his retreat by the searching draft or the near approach of the enemy.

The Lincolnites are evidently watching with great care the result of the expiration of the term of service of many of our troops in April next. I trust that they will freely reenlist, that others will come to the rescue, and that our cause may not suffer repulse or temporary reverse for lack of strong arms and stout hearts upon the field of battle. I have before me a letter from a friend, an officer in the Army of the Potomac, in which, alluding to this question of reenlistment, he uses the following language: "I cannot conjecture how we are to meet the advancing columns of McClellan in the coming spring. Of this grand Army of the Potomac, supposed to number about seventy thousand men, but *twenty regiments,* with a maximum average of five hundred men each, are mustered in for the war. The rest are twelve-months volunteers, whose terms of service will expire in April; and not one of the many whom I have heard express their intentions have any idea of reenlisting. The Georgians all say they will go to the coast of Georgia, the Carolinians to the coast of Carolina, etc. The candidates for home defense are above par. The raging fever to go to Virginia, so prevalent in Savannah and throughout Georgia last summer, has expired at last, and with its dying gasp proclaims the Army of the Potomac, the Army of the Northwest, and the Army of the Peninsula armies composed of fools. Unless the provisional Congress moves vigorously in the matter, Jeff Davis will find himself minus a force sufficient to oppose the advance of McClellan. Great indignation prevails among the higher officers of the army on account of the carelessness of Congress in not providing some remedy for the emergency."

You see, my dear parents, that this picture illustrates rather the dark shadows of West than the bright colorings of Guido.

The Lincoln government foresaw the difficulty and provided against it. It is represented that there are now over six hundred thousand Lincoln troops in service who are in for the war. The only changes, therefore, which can interfere with or diminish this large force are those which result from disease, death, mutiny, etc., etc. Our Congress should at once give to this matter the gravest consideration and devise such remedies as the emergencies of the occasion demand. There is but little philosophy in organizing a grand army, training, arming, and posting the same, with the fact inevitable that at the expiration of a few short months entire brigades will retire to civil life and leave vacancies to be filled with raw recruits, if filled at all.

It sometimes seems to me that our President and those high in authority have misconceived the true theory of the war. We have from its very inception acted solely and exclusively upon the defensive. This has in the main grown out of the peculiar character of our position. But occasions for "carrying the war into Africa" have occurred, which if vigorously improved would have produced good effects and inspired our enemies with a wholesome dread.

One thing is certain: we cannot contend with the enemy on the seas, for the very simple reason that we have no navy. And it has often seemed to me little less than ridiculous, this idea of endeavoring to fortify every avenue by light sand batteries, which must be silenced so soon as the heavy metal of the Lincoln gunboats is brought to bear. The day belongs to the past when open earthworks and palmetto forts can successfully contend with the heavy batteries of modern fleets. And the difficulty is that the rascals will scarcely ever venture beyond the range of their guns. If we could only get them beyond this cover the victory would be ours.

The inaction of the Federals has been most fortunate for us. General Jackson has now large working parties engaged in throwing up a series of earthworks and fortifications which will extend from Causton's Bluff to the Springfield plantation. They will be completed in a few days, and will be very formidable. General Jackson is most sanguine of his ability to defend the city against almost any land force which may be brought. He promises that the history of the defense shall be as famous as that of the success at New Orleans under the veritable "Old Hickory." The river defenses have also progressed very rapidly, and between thirty and forty guns are in position at various points above Fort Pulaski. Live oak is being thrown into Freeborn's Cut and Wilmington River to prevent the passage of gunboats in that direction.

From present indications I have serious doubts whether the enemy really contemplates an attack upon the city. Certainly the requisite force is not present.

Our advices from the West are unfavorable, but we must expect that these open batteries must yield whenever confronted by the heavy guns of the Lincoln gunboats.

I sincerely trust, my dear parents, that you are both well and in the enjoyment of many blessings, and that my dear little daughter has quite recovered. I cannot tell you how anxious I am to see you and her, but it is out of my power to leave this camp at this time. When does Brother's term of enlistment expire? With warmest love to selves, many kisses for my precious daughter, kind remembrances to Sister Carrie, the Doctor, and little Stanhope, and howdy for the servants, I am, my dear father and mother, as ever,
Your affectionate son,
Charles C. Jones, Jr.

Lt. Charles C. Jones, Jr., *to* Rev. *and* Mrs. C. C. Jones[g]
Camp Claghorn, *Thursday,* February 13th, 1862
My dear Father and Mother,

I only write to acknowledge the receipt of your recent favors and to reiterate the thanks for them which I had the great pleasure of expressing in person to you, my dear mother, two days since in Savannah.

No change of any moment in the military status of affairs in our vicinity. The enemy, having landed a considerable force on Wassaw Island, are busily engaged in drilling upon the beach in sight of our batteries. They are reported to be dredging out Wall's Cut and removing the obstacles placed there. An attack upon Savannah is apprehended—and that at no distant day. This is an inference from their apparent movements. I am glad to see that the city council have named tomorrow as a day of humiliation, fasting, and prayer. May a good God hearken in mercy and send us deliverance!

With warmest love to you both, my dear father and mother, many kisses for my precious little daughter, and kindest remembrances for the Doctor, Sister Carrie, and Stanhope, I am, as ever,
Your affectionate son,
Charles C. Jones, Jr.

Lt. Charles C. Jones, Jr., *to* Rev. *and* Mrs. C. C. Jones[g]
Camp Claghorn, *Monday,* February 17th, 1862
My dear Father and Mother,

The news of our recent deliverance in Tennessee fills every patriotic heart with joy and with sincere thankfulness to the God of Battles for sending us the victory. I sincerely trust that the result of our success may be as decided as it is represented to be, although it is very difficult to place absolute reliance upon early telegraphic reports. This victory shows the silver linings of those clouds which seemed to overshadow us so darkly.

There is but little change in the military status of affairs here. Every exertion is being made to render certain the defenses of Savannah. The great neglect was in not effectually preventing, either by batteries or by obstructions of a permanent character, the ingress of the enemy by means of his gunboats through Wall's Cut into the Savannah River. Fort Pulaski is now virtually isolated, and the guns of that strong fortress, which under other circumstances would have proved of such incalculable advantage in defending our city and its approaches from the sea, are entirely valueless. The neglect is an outrageous one, and grievously must condemnation fall upon the guilty one. General Lee, I understand, expresses his belief that the fortifications in the Savannah River located between Venus Point and the city will be able to repulse any force the enemy will be able to bring. Torpedoes and fire rafts will be called into requisition. Several of each are already prepared. General Lawton has taken the field. His headquarters are now upon Skidaway Island. The rivers leading from Wassaw Sound into the Savannah River are being obstructed with live oak trees. We learn that St. Simons and Jekyll Islands have by order of General Lee been abandoned, and the troops withdrawn with the heavy guns to the mainland.

We are all pretty well. Some of our men have colds and sore throats—the effect of exposure upon picket these wet, bleak nights. With warmest love to you both, my dear parents, and many kisses for my precious little daughter, I am, as ever,

> Your affectionate son,
> Charles C. Jones, Jr.

REV. C. C. JONES *to* LT. CHARLES C. JONES, JR.[g]

> Montevideo, *Tuesday,* February 18th, 1862

My dear Son,

We are happy to learn by your last your continued good health, and the continued quiet on the coast.

Professor Brumby's son is just on from Manassas—in not good health—and is staying with us. Your classmate in Columbia. He says that the decided turn in the Army of the Potomac when he left was *for reenlistment for the war,* and the great majority will be found true to the country on that point. This is what I anticipated; and your friend, I hope, who wrote so discouragingly will be happily disappointed. Governor Brown's proclamation in answer to the President's requisition for twelve more regiments from Georgia is a patriotic and excellent one. Our government is thus active, and will forestall the deficiencies of those that will not reenlist. We are engaged in a long and desperate war, and our only hope is in the Lord and in the wise, energetic, and determined use of every means in our power to obtain our independence.

As a country we must disabuse ourselves of any reliance upon *foreign nations.* We ought not to expect them to fight our battles for us. If they choose to go to war with the old United States for their own interests, well and good for us. But after tendering them our friendship and offering them favorable commercial treaties our business with them is at an end. They have treated us not as they did Greece and the South American republics and Belgium and Italy, and we have no reason so far to expect any special favors from them. And I believe if our people are true to themselves we can be free; of course I mean with God's blessing upon our cause, which I believe to be just.

We must disabuse ourselves also of two other notions. The first: that the Federals cannot cope with the Confederates in open and fair battle. Whatever blessing has attended our arms heretofore, we should thank God and take courage, but not presume upon the want of resolution in our foes. To stand firm in battle is much the result of custom; their armies are for the war, and men will fight desperately for interest, for glory, and for their own cause, whatever it be. And the second is that the enemy will exhaust his resources. He will find some way to raise them. There are many ways left. He balks not at the most enormous expenditures. The Federals are displaying the energy of a despotic government laboring to maintain its life. They say "they are fighting for the life of their government." Then we must gird up our loins for the war—develop all our agricultural and manufacturing resources, produce the materials of war, and live as independent of the world as we can. The credit of the government and its existence is with our people. The whole old United States is one workshop of war. The war gives the masses their daily bread and rolls up fortunes for thousands. It is to them now the great pursuit for support and fame, and their furor runs in this channel.

The Fabian policy is and must be ours still. There has been no time in the war that we could safely have departed from it.

The ravaging of our coasts we must submit to for a time, but it goes but a small way to a *conquest*—a *subjugation* of over eight hundred thousand square miles of territory. The expeditions will not accomplish what the enemy anticipates from them. We should withdraw every cannon and soldier from our seaboard islands. They are barren possessions. The enemy commands the entrances already. We cannot afford loss after loss of the men and munitions of war. Small as they may be, the effect is not good.

Excuse my long letter on the all-absorbing subject. Hard fighting in Tennessee! Your dear little daughter is better; three teeth out, one coming. Mother not very well. The Doctor and family well. So is your Uncle John and family, and all others around us. People generally well. Weather very rainy. Take the best care you can of yourself. All send love to you. Do, my dear son, live near to your God and Saviour.

Your ever affectionate father,
C. C. Jones.

Respects to Captain Claghorn. Mail closing.

Lt. Charles C. Jones, Jr., *to* Rev. C. C. Jones[g]

Camp Claghorn, *Friday,* February 21st, 1862

My dear Father,

I thank you for your very kind favor of the 18th inst., which was yesterday received, and I am happy to know that my dear little daughter is so much better. I cannot tell you how anxious I am to see you all at home; but the threatening attitude assumed by our detested enemy, and the necessity existing for the presence at his post of every soldier at this hour of danger, forbid my absenting myself from the battery at this time.

And here I take great pleasure in saying to you that the Chatham Artillery is in a very flourishing condition. We already number some hundred and thirty-five men, and the prospect is that before many days our muster roll will show one hundred and sixty. Every day the application of some good and true man is submitted for membership. You are aware of the peculiar character of our company. No one can be admitted who is not vouched for by at least two members of the company, and then the application is submitted to the corps. If the applicant receives four-fifths of the votes cast, he is admitted; if not, he is rejected. This rule relieves us of the presence of all who are objectionable; and the consequence is, we have a company of companions and of gentlemen—men of true courage and men (many of them) with large private interests at stake. I have often thought that if the Chatham Artillery does not render a good account of itself, by the blessing of God, in the day of battle, then one's faith in character, blood, and social position may well be shaken.

I had the pleasure of seeing at our camp a day or two since Lieutenant Cass of the 1st Georgia Regulars, who has just returned from Manassas. He assures me that the Army of the Potomac will largely reenlist when the terms of service expire—he thinks to the extent of seven-eighths. Our soldiers feel the responsibility resting upon them, and the wants of our Confederacy in this the day of perhaps her greatest peril. Mr. Brumby's views and Lieutenant Cass's are coincident on this subject. You may remember Cass; he studied law in our office. He is a reliable man, and courageous. I have a great attachment for him, and obtained for him a lieutenancy in the service.

The time has emphatically arrived when nearly every man capable of bearing arms within the broad limits of our Confederacy should be in the field. We are pressed on every hand, and by overwhelming forces. Our deliverance is from above, and I feel more and more deeply every day the duty which rests upon every one of us to humble himself before God, to repent of our transgressions, individual and national, and invoke His interposition in our behalf. I believe that the rod will be lifted just so soon as its chastening influences have brought forth the legitimate fruits of penitence, sorrow, and reformation.

Our people must also disabuse themselves of any erroneous impressions as to the inability of our enemy to cope with us upon a fair field. The history of the world shows that the southern race as a general rule triumphs; but it also teaches us that the Puritan stock will fight, and that a feud between kindred races is always the most desperate. We have erred in this particular, and have speculated too much in regard to foreign intervention. I sincerely trust that our recent disasters will inure to our benefit, and that every arm may be nerved for the desperate struggle. We must depend upon ourselves, under God, and upon ourselves alone.

General Lee expresses the opinion that we will be able to resist any attack by water; and I am quite confident that a terrible fate awaits any force attempting an attack by land.

I presume you are aware that St. Simons and Jekyll Islands have been abandoned, and our troops withdrawn upon the main. The guns lately in position there have been brought to Savannah and are being mounted on the river. The delay on the part of the enemy in not advancing at once upon the city when the demonstration was first made was most opportune, and I may say providential.

Yesterday afternoon the enemy struck their tents on Wassaw Island and embarked their troops. This looks like an attack. It may be that they purpose taking possession of the islands recently abandoned by us in the vicinity of Brunswick.

I have settled with Mr. Quarterman for his services for the past year. Arcadia owes nothing except for Negro cloth, the bill of which I have not yet received from Nevitt, Lathrop & Rogers.

Do give warmest love to dear Mother, to my dear little daughter. And believe me ever

Your affectionate son,

Charles C. Jones, Jr.

Kind remembrances to the Doctor, Sister Carrie, and little Stanhope. My respects to Mr. Brumby.

I have directed Messrs. Claghorn & Cunningham to send to you a cask of porter which is said to be very fine. I trust that you and Mother will be benefited by it. The cask will reach No. 3 on Monday next.

Captain Claghorn desires his special remembrance.

X

MRS. MARY JONES *to* LT. CHARLES C. JONES, JR.ᵍ

Montevideo, *Friday,* February 21st, 1862

My very dear Son,

My thoughts have often reverted to the evening we spent together in Savannah. We are living in such solemn and alarming times that we must realize that those who part today may never meet again on earth. God grant you His special care and protection, fidelity in your lot, a holy faith and trust in Him at all times, which will support you in the hour of conflict, deliver you from every fear, and arm you with wisdom and deathless courage!

The hour has arrived when men and women too in the Southern Confederacy must seek to know and to do their duty with fearless hearts and hands. Our recent disasters are appalling. The thought of Nashville, the heart of the country and I may say granary of our Confederacy, falling into the hands of those robbers and murderers casts a terrible gloom over us all. That point in their possession, it really appeared that they might touch every other in North Alabama and Georgia. I trust this day's mail will bring us some encouraging news!

Tomorrow, with the divine blessing, our worthy President will be inaugurated and our government established. Through a suggestion of your father's we are to have religious services and special prayer throughout our county, that God's favor might rest upon the events of the day, upon all placed in authority over us, and upon the whole constitution and government of our beloved country, civil, military, and religious. Your father wrote Mr. Axson upon the subject, and I see there is to be an observance of the day in Savannah. Without the regenerating, sanctifying influences of the religion of our Divine Lord and Saviour we cannot be established in justice, truth, and righteousness.

On last Sabbath your Uncle John preached one of the best-adapted sermons on the present state of things and our duties growing out of them that I ever heard. The place of meeting was the Riceboro hotel, and his audience the Liberty Independent Troop. I wish every camp in the country could hear it. I asked if he could not go and preach it at Camp Claghorn. Would it be practicable?

Next Sabbath will be our Communion. If you could have been present, we wanted to have our precious little Ruth baptized. We are fearing that she will take the measles, as two cases have appeared on the place, and her *nurse* has never had it. Your brother thinks they would not affect the baby seriously, but I would be glad to keep them off. She is now cutting her fourth tooth, and while I am writing is sitting by herself on the carpet. When I reached home from Savannah, Susan met me with her at the gate, when she reached out her little arms with delight and clung to me.

Your letter containing the autograph of our noble old commodore has been received, and I am truly obliged to you, my dear son. I shall prize and preserve it. My relics of war, warriors, and battlefields are increasing. In a letter of much interest recently received from Dunwody he sends me a portion of the nostril of General Bartow's horse. It looks almost like a flake of isinglass.

The day after we saw you Daughter and myself had the pleasure of seeing Commodore Tattnall. He was slowly promenading in the square before the Pulaski House with his son, recently released from the North. We walked up and passed him for a good view, and our hearts went up with the fervent: "God bless and preserve you, noble and bravest of men and patriots! If I had the power, you should command the proudest fleet that ever floated on the ocean." As it is, let us rejoice that our infant navy can claim such a paternity.

Your Uncle John and family are with us. He has a pair of artillery epaulettes from Manassas for you. All unite in best love to you, with kisses from your own babe.

Your affectionate mother,
Mary Jones.

Lt. Charles C. Jones, Jr., *to* Rev. *and* Mrs. C. C. Jones[g]

Camp Claghorn, *Monday,* February 24th, 1862

My dear Father and Mother,

I write to hope that all at home are well, and to send my warmest love. We have nothing of interest with us.

The recent reverses in the West, most severe as they are, will, I trust, bring our people to a nearer trust in God and to a more faithful and energetic use of those means which are placed in our hands for the preservation of our national honor and for the defense of our soil. Every man capable of bearing arms should be in the field; and the country should be thoroughly alive to the sense of the imminent dangers which surround us.

Our battery is receiving almost daily accretions; and we trust, with the blessing of God, to do the state some service when the day of battle comes. Our expectation is, if we can obtain additional horses, to make our battery *an eight-gun battery,* recruiting up to one hundred and seventy-five men.

Give many kisses to my precious little daughter. And believe me ever, my dear parents, with warmest love,

Your affectionate son,
Charles C. Jones, Jr.

LT. CHARLES C. JONES, JR., *to* MRS. MARY JONES[g]
Camp Claghorn, *Thursday,* February 27th, 1862

My very dear Mother,

Many thanks for your very kind and interesting letter, which reached me a day since. I am happy to know that all at home are well. In addition to other duties I have been all the week busily engaged in the capacity of judge advocate in a series of cases at an adjoining encampment.

We can from this camp hear the morning and evening guns from one of the Lincoln batteries recently erected in the Savannah River.

Our recent reverses are exerting a salutary effect, and I trust they will continue to do so. Last evening we admitted thirteen new members, and are expecting many more petitions. Tomorrow is a day of fasting, humiliation, and prayer. This evening at retreat our captain published an order suspending on that day all customary drills and requesting each member of the corps to observe the occasion with becoming solemnity and earnestness. To humble ourselves before God and to repent of our sins, national and individual, and to invoke His interposition in our behalf is now our first duty. And I believe He will hear our cry.

I sincerely wish that I could be at home on Sabbath, but the enjoyment of that privilege does not lie in my power.

There is but little change in our military status. Our defenses are being strengthened daily. General Mercer is now in command of Skidaway Island and of the adjacent forces. Do give much love to Father. Kiss my precious little daughter for me. And believe me ever, my dear mother,
Your ever affectionate son,
Charles C. Jones, Jr.

LT. CHARLES C. JONES, JR., *to* REV. *and* MRS. C. C. JONES[g]
Camp Claghorn, *Monday,* March 3rd, 1862

My dear Father and Mother,

I embrace a moment at this early hour in the morning, while our transportation agent waits with team harnessed and ready for his trip to the city, to send you and my precious little daughter much love. We are all pretty well in camp. The approaching draft has moved the sluggish, and our ranks have materially increased.

The Federal fleet has, with the exception of some four vessels, disappeared from Wassaw Sound. It is rumored that a night attack will soon be made, under the leadership of General Walker of the state forces, upon the batteries recently erected by the Federals in Savannah River. How true this may be time must show. The effect of their capture would be to relieve Fort Pulaski immediately, and indirectly to infuse new spirit and confidence in our troops. The attempt should be made. As ever,
Your affectionate son,
Charles C. Jones, Jr.

Rev. C. C. Jones *to* Lt. Charles C. Jones, Jr.[g]

Montevideo, *Monday,* March 3rd, 1862

My dear Son,

I embrace a moment to let you know that your last notes have been received, and we are happy and grateful to know that you are in good health and spirits, and that your company is so prosperous. I have no doubt that if you are called to the field that both officers and men will do their duty to God and their country. For I consider you as fighting for the cause which our Heavenly Father approves, and that He will give you all courage and strength in that day. My prayer daily for you and for the company is three-fold: first, that officers and men may become the true soldiers of the Cross; second, that you may never see more of war than you now see; and third, if it be ordained otherwise, that the Lord would preserve you in your persons and your lives and bless you with victory.

Our late disasters are arousing our country, and making all a *unit,* and inspiring us with a right spirit. We have been resting on our laurels, and upon the impression of our ability to overcome always. For this good effect we should bless God.

It was indeed fitting that our permanent government should be inaugurated with fasting, humiliation, and prayer; and no doubt the day was devoutly observed throughout the Confederacy. No God was ever acknowledged in the Constitution of the old United States. We have acknowledged "the Almighty God" in our Constitution—the God of the Bible, the only living and true God—as our God; and we take Him as the God of our nation and worship Him, and put our nation under His care as such. This is a blessed fact, and a soul-inspiring fact; and I believe He will own and bless us. And moreover, under the old Constitution of the United States we never had a *Christian President*—never a man who in the Presidential chair openly professed the orthodox faith of the gospel and connected with that profession an open communion with the Lord at His table, and a decidedly Christian walk and conversation. General Washington was a communing member of the Episcopal Church; and while it is hoped and believed that he was a true Christian, yet the evidence is not so clear and satisfactory as we could wish. Our first President is accredited a *Christian man.* We should bless God for this mercy, and pray for him as a brother in Christ as well as our chief magistrate. His proclamation is Christian throughout in language and spirit; and the close of his inaugural address, in prayer to God as the Head of a great nation in such a time as the present, melts into tenderness under a consciousness of weakness and imperfection, and yet rises into the sublimity of faith—the sublimity of an unshaken faith. Oh, for pious rulers and officers! What a healthful influence would flow down from them over our people! Captain Claghorn's order for the day of fasting was an honor to him and acceptable to his companions in arms; and if he will honor the Lord, the Lord will honor him.

Your dear little one is quite bright, full of spirits, intelligent, affectionate;

but is thinner than she was, and troubled with an eruption on her head. It seems hard for her to get over her lingering affection. Yet we hope it is gradually wearing away. She and Stanhope are great friends. It is interesting to see them kiss each other. They ring the bell for family prayers every morning between them, and sometimes stay to prayers; but their patience is not always long enough.

Was with Robert on fast day (Friday); your Uncle John with Mr. Buttolph. All relations and friends generally well. Drop your Uncle William a line sometimes.

Your Uncle John takes this letter down to Savannah with him today, where he expects to stay till Thursday. Puts up at the Pulaski, and hopes if possible to ride out and see you—perhaps on Wednesday.

Mother has just come into the study with Little Sister to show me her head, with iodine put on the little eruptions. She is motioning with her hands like a bird, and with her earnest eyes watching my pen, and in great good spirits, and pulling away at her grandmother's buttons. Do not omit your Bible nor your secret devotions daily; camp life is trying to principle and faith. We pray for you constantly.

Your ever affectionate father,
C. C. Jones.

Lt. Charles C. Jones, Jr., *to* Rev. C. C. Jones[g]
Camp Claghorn, Friday, March 7th, 1862
My dear Father,

I am under many obligations to you for your very kind and valued favor of the 3rd inst., which reached me only last night. Our mail facilities are not as perfect as they might be, and letters are consequently not unfrequently behind their proper seasons.

We have had the pleasure of a visit from Uncle John, which I appreciated and enjoyed, regretting at the same time that he was prevented from extending it. He appeared pleased with our camp and its details. The fact is that it is remarkable for its beauty, cleanliness, and good order. The addition of the tents recently pitched for the recruits has increased the proportions of the encampment almost to those of a regiment.

I have just come in from assisting in dressing the wound of young Samuel S. Law, a son of your esteemed friend Judge Law—a private in our company, and a very exemplary and exceedingly pleasant man. I say *man:* he is about eighteen years old. He was handling his pistol (one of Colt's navy revolvers) with a heavy glove (the day being very cold) when the hammer escaped from his fingers and the cap exploded. The ball passed through the calf of his left leg, barely touching the bone. The wound, although not at present dangerous, is painful, and the accident a sad one.

Today is a day set apart by our governor as a season for humiliation, fasting, and prayer to Almighty God. It is observed as such in our camp.

There is a total suspension of all drills and customary fatigue duties. We cannot regard such occasions too frequently or too solemnly. The nation must be brought to feel their sins and their dependence upon God, not only for their blessings but for their actual salvation from the many and huge dangers which surround us.

I believe that one end of this present punishment is being realized: you may observe signs of penitence and of reform. The last is a most important one. I refer to the exclusion of all intoxicating liquors from our camps, and the prohibition of the manufacture of alcoholic drinks. Could we but rid our armies of the presence of this prime evil, there is no estimating the amount of sickness, immorality, neglect of duty, and false courage which would be removed. Never trust any soldier who drinks habitually. His apparent daring under dangers is, in nine cases out of ten, artificial, and vanishes with the fumes which gave it birth. I have seen illustrations of this. The reform has been begun in earnest in Savannah. The military authorities, acting under the orders of General Jackson, are closing the drinking shops. Were the mayor of the city a man of the right stamp, he would have taken the initiative in this matter long ago. There is a plain way for accomplishing reform.

Our reverses seem to be producing the desired effect. If properly improved, they, instead of being as they seem an injury, will really inure to our great benefit.

I thank you, Father, for the picture of my dear little daughter. I am greatly concerned about that affection of the ear; I fear it may prove permanent in its character. I long to see you all, and hope to be able to do so the latter part of this month. Do give warmest love to my dear mother and little Mary Ruth. Remember me sincerely to the Doctor, Sister Carrie, and little Stanhope. And believe me ever, my dear father,

Your affectionate son,
Charles C. Jones, Jr.

Lt. Charles C. Jones, Jr., *to* Rev. *and* Mrs. C. C. Jones[g]

Camp Claghorn, *Friday,* March 14th, 1862

My dear Father and Mother,

In consequence of the absence of Captain Claghorn I have been so much occupied with the details of the battery that I have not enjoyed an opportunity until this moment of expressing my sincere hope that all at home are well, and of sending my warmest love to you both and to my precious little daughter. In all my often remembrances of home there is a constant and heartfelt regret that I am prevented from enjoying the pleasure which I so much crave of at least an occasional visit. I trust so soon as the captain returns I will be able to come out.

There are so many recruits in our company, and the necessity for drill is so urgent, that we are constantly occupied. The efficiency of the battery is rendered the more requisite now that the guns of the Skidaway batteries are retired, as well as those of Green Island. The troops are still upon those islands. The guns thus retired will be remounted, some at the Thunderbolt and others at the Beaulieu batteries on the main. The withdrawal of those batteries, it seems probable, will necessitate a removal from our present camp, as the gunboats of the enemy can now with but little difficulty find access to this point. A field battery can least of all protect itself at an advanced post. Our line of defenses has been very materially changed. There is now a total abandonment of all the islands. It is astonishing what a vast amount of labor and materials has been wasted in our military operations. And these continued evacuations are exerting a most depressing influence upon the troops. We need some decisive action—let the results be what they may—for a moral effect.

We have a bright ray of sunshine from the *Virginia*. Gallant vessel—and gallant men! They have given us memories which will live in proudest remembrance in the history of our present struggle.

I sat down for a long letter, but am prevented by the coming of General Mercer, who calls upon business and will remain for some hours. The troops from Skidaway and Green Islands will probably be retired to this island and the adjoining main. With warmest love, my dear parents, to you, and many kisses for my dear little daughter, I am, as ever,

Your affectionate son,
Charles C. Jones, Jr.

Rev. C. C. Jones *to* Lt. Charles C. Jones, Jr.[g]

Montevideo, *Friday,* March 14th, 1862

My dear Son,

The week has almost gone, and you have had no letter. Not that your mother and I have not purposed to write, but there has been a succession of family and social events that have remitted the matter from one day to another.

Last Saturday we had an arrival of friends from McIntosh about 6 P.M.—Mrs. and Miss Dunwody and Mrs. Dean Dunwody and five children, ten servants, two carriages and one baggage wagon, and four horses and two mules—en route for the up country, having broken up their plantation on the Altamaha, leaving a small part of the Negroes behind for future disposal, the bulk moving up by steamboat to Doctortown and through Liberty to No. 3 station, part going to Southwest Georgia and part to vicinity of Columbus. The river bottom of the Altamaha has been pretty much abandoned: Negroes moved up the river, and the greater part of the market crop also, the enemy having free access to every part of the river if he chooses to come up. Darien is pretty well deserted.

Satan seems to have taken advantage of the times at Midway last Sunday by sending up a report that the enemy had taken possession of Darien the night before, which threw many people into a nervous state and set nearly everybody talking; and the good seed fell by the wayside, and the fowls of the air devoured them up, and am afraid not much good was done by two very excellent sermons. The war impinges dreadfully upon the Sabbath and upon all the means of grace. War is the most universal of all the divine judgments in its injurious influences upon man and upon his every interest, temporal and eternal. Nothing escapes it. There was, however, no panic on Wednesday, the day of the annual meeting of the Midway Church and Society; for we met, transacted our business quietly, voted the same officers, the same pastor, and the same salaries, and chose pews and went home as if there was no war at all, which was doing just what our duty required.

Our friends the Dunwodys have left us, and your Uncle John went with one party of them to Savannah to assist them in getting through the town with their people and baggage. We expect him home today.

Colonel Spalding has ordered a detachment of twenty-five men from the Liberty Independent Troop to be stationed at Fort Barrington to arrest the ascent of the enemy up the river and so to protect the railroad bridge. The men with their rifles could not do much with a gunboat in rapid motion. Guns of some caliber are required at favorable points below the bridge to do much good. The Ogeechee is equally exposed, and the destruction of either one bridge would seriously incommode us. We hear of Colonel Stiles's killing some Yankees on an oyster bank and of the shelling of Brunswick in revenge by the enemy; of a skirmish towards St. Marys in which we came off very well, taking three prisoners; of the ascent of the St. Johns by the Yankees and of the abandonment of East Florida, etc., etc.

There seems to be a general movement of our armies everywhere, a concentration of forces at given points and a falling back and change of front in others, all foreshadowing warm work and some new line of policy. We are happily waking up from our lethargy and putting off foreign expectations. My own opinion is that we should resort to a system—to a chain of impregnable fortifications: New Orleans, Mobile, Savannah, Charleston, some point in North Carolina, Norfolk, Richmond, and so round through Virginia, North Carolina, and Tennessee to Memphis, and all inland cities that lie in any exposed condition. They would call for heavy forces from the enemy to reduce them, impede their progress, give us more men for active field service, and strengthen our people. Of course we should require more foundries, more powder mills, etc.; but the outlay would be our gain and add to the happy issue of our war.

Mr. Quarterman has consulted me about the amount of cotton to be planted at Arcadia the present season, and showed me your letter. I told him I should not plant above an acre to the hand, if that, and recommended him to inform you of my opinion. We have the present crop on hand, which will be sufficient if sold this or the coming year to pay expenses for two years. If not, why add to it? And if not, our only dependence is upon a provision crop which we may sell for the support of our armies. If peace comes and finds us with a provision crop, we can sell it for something. And then peace will bring some little credit if we need it. But we are to look matters in the face as they are: there is not the faintest prospect in the world now apparent for a peace. Every farmer and planter should see this and feel that he is called upon in duty to his country to raise all the provisions he possibly can for the support of our armies, especially in the cotton states, since Kentucky and Tennessee are not available sources of supply to us now; and when they shall be no one knows.

I say there is not the faintest prospect of peace, for nothing but a demonstration of the utter impossibility of the North's subduing the South will bring about negotiations for peace. If we beat back their six hundred thousand men and they exhaust all their present revenue and plans of revenue, such is the resolution which they aver, and their desire to save themselves from bankruptcy and disgrace, that they will manage to raise another six hundred thousand men and money in some shape to support them. A great necessity, they feel (of their own wretched creation), is laid upon them to go forward; and they say openly they have the power and the money, and they will crush out the South! And we see how they are rousing all their energies for that purpose. We have nothing to do but to meet it; and I believe that if our people are true to themselves and to their principles, by God's help, they cannot conquer us.

Am glad to see more vigor infusing itself into our government—martial law where necessary, suspension of military officers, liquor reforms, etc. Our reverses are doing us good. May it please our God—the Almighty God whom we have acknowledged and taken in our Constitution to be the God of our nation (and it is a source of great comfort to my mind that we have done so, for under the old United States Constitution we acknowledged no God at all, the Constitution being atheistical)—I say, may it please God to hear our prayers, and accept our fasting and humiliation, and cause us to break off our sins by righteousness, and to show us His favor and redeem us from the hand of our enemies! We are not to faint in the day of reverses, but to grasp the sword more firmly and pray more humbly and fervently and fight more manfully.

Mother is very unwell with her cough at nights and her old complaint; and having so many cases, she has not rest enough.

About our arrangements for the summer we will write you another time, D.V. Have sent twenty-five bales cotton and stored it at Arcadia. Mother thinks it would be safer there than on the river here.

Your dear little daughter is looking like herself again, and is full of life; and her little mind is daily expanding, and she begins now to use her voice, and is becoming very decided in her preferences for individuals, and chooses her grandmother above all. She rings the bell for family worship every morning, and as soon as I come down in the parlor and tell her to ring the bell, she looks and leans towards the mantelpiece and carefully takes it by the handle for the purpose. Her nurse thinks she makes special effort to say

"Jack" and "Elsie." But she eschews food, and it is only grains of dry rice that she will pick up in her little fingers and eat.

Carrie and Stanhope are with your sister on a visit; the Doctor is well. Your Aunt Jane and mother unite in much love to you. Thank you kindly for the *porter;* it is an excellent article, with a fine body to it, and agrees with me well; and the Doctor says I must use it daily. You are remembered always in our prayers in our closets and in the family. Our best respects to Captain Claghorn. The Yankees say within thirty days Savannah and Charleston will be laid in ashes by their ironclad steamers that they are waiting for. Hope General Lawton will stop the river before our batteries and bring them to, and that we may be able to disappoint their plans. Has any general been appointed in General Lee's place? Or has he not resigned?

From your ever affectionate father,
C. C. Jones.

Have the Skidaway and Green Island batteries been *abandoned?*

P.S. I mentioned to Mr. Quarterman that perhaps he might be able to sell a few head of stock cattle at Arcadia. He said they were very poor; he had two he was fattening for sale. We have some stock cattle to sell at Maybank (twelve or fourteen head), but there have been no purchasers out for some time. *All stock cattle are poor now.*

Lt. Charles C. Jones, Jr., *to* Rev. C. C. Jones[g]

Camp Claghorn, *Tuesday,* March 18th, 1862

My dear Father,

I am this moment favored with your very kind and valued letter of the 14th inst., for which you have my sincere thanks.

I deeply regret to know that dear Mother has been of late so unwell, and that she still suffers from a return of her old affection. May a good Providence soon restore her to her accustomed health, and keep my dear little daughter in that good health which I am happy to learn she is now enjoying. I long to see you all, and trust so soon as Captain Claghorn returns (which will be certainly within a week from this period, D.V.) that I will be able to obtain from headquarters a furlough of a day or two.

Skidaway and Green Islands have both been entirely evacuated. The guns, provisions, munitions, quartermaster and commissary stores have all been retired, and no advance as yet on the part of the enemy. For some two weeks past only four or five Lincoln vessels have been lying in Wassaw Sound. We have a report today that this number has been increased by the appearance of three more. The evacuation of these islands after the large amount of labor expended in fortifying them, and in the construction of causeways and bridges to facilitate the withdrawal of the troops there stationed in case of actual necessity—when, too, we have no inner line of defenses, except those erected within sight of the city of Savannah, behind which to retire the forces thus removed—seems to me very questionable in a military point of view. The men themselves are sadly disheartened at the necessity which compels them, without firing a single gun, to evacuate forts which they with their own hands had constructed, behind whose ramparts they confidently anticipated a successful combat with the enemy at no distant day.

It does seem to me that all our operations on this coast have been mere military experiments, conceived in ignorance and brought forth none the more wisely—mere jackleg performances. Look at a few of them. Tybee Island evacuated when it should have been heavily fortified and defended by a force of certainly not less than three to five thousand men. Mistake No. 2: attempting to fortify every inlet on the coast with miserable little sand batteries on isolated points, with here and there a thirty-two-pounder and a few rounds of solid shot. Of course labor and time were only idly expended, and the project fell stillborn. Mistake No. 3: fortifications on the inner islands, which, for want of proper forecast and engineering skill in their location, and in the occupation of neighboring points, were soon pronounced untenable. Mistake No. 4: gross and most inexcusable neglect of the water approaches to Savannah and other points on the coast.

And so they may be multiplied at pleasure. The useless expenditure of means, labor, and time on our coast is fearful to contemplate, and the want of proper knowledge and requisite skill on the part of those in authority is most surprising. The reply is: "Our general has done all he could." That is not a proper answer. If he could do no more, then he should have abdicated and permitted someone else to see if he could not have done something more.

I have more confidence in General Mercer than in any of our officers, as at present advised. He is now with his forces on the Isle of Hope. His brigade numbers in all (the forces at Beaulieu, Genesis Point, etc., etc., included) about thirty-five hundred men.

In consequence of this abandonment of our outer line of defenses, this post is thrown quite in advance; and we will have lively work if the enemy moves from this direction. Skidaway Island will still be picketed with mounted men at the most assailable points, such as at the batteries at Waring's Point, Pritchard's plantation, the Indians' Fort, Adams' Point, Modena Point, etc., to give notice of any movements which may be made by the enemy. This brigade is occupied in strengthening the Thunderbolt battery and the battery at Beaulieu, which latter fort commands the approach by Vernon River and will mount ten guns, some of them of heavy caliber.

The defenses of the Savannah River I have never had an opportunity of examining, but I learn that they are numerous and formidable. Great labor has recently been expended in their construction, and we have obtained almost all the guns we need. The condition of our river defenses previous to the arrival of General Lee was horrible. It was said that we could procure no cannon. The forces were scattered about in various camps, doing little else than drilling and loafing. So soon, however, as General Lee assumed command, seconded by the activity of General Jackson of the state forces, everything indicated a most material change for the better. The earthworks thrown up around the city are quite formidable, and siege guns are mounted at intervals. The forests in front have been felled, and determined men behind them can offer a most effectual resistance.

With all due deference to the opinion of General Jackson, I think he errs in risking everything upon these works. I understand his wish is to throw everything open and invite the enemy in, offering no material check to his advance until within reach of these defenses. This is risking too much upon a single cast. We should meet our enemy where his foot first presses the soil, contest every inch, and look to these fortifications as a last resort. You know the enthusiasm of General Jackson. He will lead his forces as gallantly as probably any living man into action, and will fight to the last extremity; but I think he does not calculate sufficiently the chances of reverse. It is a rule as false in war as in logic to presume upon the weakness of our adversary. Of this we have already been guilty on more than one occasion. Recent events fully demonstrate that no such calculations can with safety longer be made. We have to contend against a power numerically vastly stronger than we are, with armies and fleets perfect in all their appointments, men who have and who will fight, and fight desperately, for they are engaged in a desperate enterprise—one in which they either rule or are ruined. We should therefore embrace every chance on our own soil which presents itself for opposing their progress, and not risk the defense of the only place and section we are actually defending upon the issue of a single battle under the very eaves of the houses of our metropolis.

I am inclined to believe that General Jackson had much influence with Generals Pemberton and Lawton in procuring the abandonment of Skidaway Island. I know that he desired it. Better far have held the forts there and taken the chances of the battle. Two causeways would have conducted the forces to the main in the event of defeat. Even a defeat in the face of superior numbers and after a gallant contest is often worth much in giving a moral tone to a contest. General Mercer regrets the step, but of course could do nothing else than obey orders. Evacuation is the order of the day. The sight or sound of that word is now as bad as a dose of hippo.

It appears that all this show of fleets on our coast has hitherto been intended as a demonstration, to keep our forces here while decisive blows were contemplated and actually struck in the West. Every day seems but to tighten the cords around us. The valley of the Mississippi is virtually almost lost, and our entire seacoast and Gulf coast with but few reservations are completely in the power of the enemy. We have nothing to offer on the seas by way of resistance, and the construction of these ironclad steamers has materially changed the value of coast fortifications. Forts are now scarcely of value, and cannot effectually check an advance.

But we are not conquered yet, nor will we be. And most cordially do I say "Amen" to your remark: "We are not to faint in the day of reverses, but to grasp the sword more firmly and pray more humbly and fervently and fight more manfully." McClellan has planned his campaign with great ability, and has already redeemed his pledge that he would compel General Johnston of the Army of the Potomac to evacuate his lines—and that without firing a single gun. But, as the old adage says, that is a long road which has no turning. We have been fighting in the shade very long, but the dawning of new life and light must come. We needed as individuals and as a nation chastisement to bring us to a sense of our sins and of our many and great shortcomings. We are, I trust, being purified as by fire; and my firm belief is that so soon as we are fairly brought to true humility before God and repentance of sin, He will crown our resistance of these lawless, ruthless invaders with quick and absolute success.

Did you observe what the wretches did at New Bern, North Carolina? I want no black flag raised upon a staff, but I wish to see it carried in the breast of every good and true man armed in behalf of our country and of the homes we love. And every Lincolnite found in enmity upon our shores should be put to the sword as an outlaw, outside of the pale of civilization and of humanity.

The concentration of our forces will enable us when the opportunity presents itself to offer more effectual resistance. In concentrating, however, we give up much—very much—that is most valuable. At present an area of ten miles square in extent will embrace about all the soil of Georgia actually defended. This is a most depressing reflection.

I see by the papers that General Lee has been appointed commander in chief of the military of the Confederate States under the provisions of a recent act of Congress. His loss will be severely felt by us. He is succeeded in the command by General Pemberton, an old army officer and a Pennsylvanian by birth. Most of his reputation is, I think, before him.

I fully concur with you, my dear father, as to the character of the crop to be planted the present year. We should all plant largely of provisions. Every bushel of corn and blade of grass will be greatly needed for the support of our armies.

I am happy to know that you enjoy the porter, and trust that it will prove of benefit to you.

We have a report in camp that thirteen thousand stand of Enfield rifles have arrived in Florida for the State of Georgia.

This evening I assisted in laying out an earthwork on this side of Skidaway bridge, designed for the protection of a section of our battery and three hundred infantry to be posted there in case the enemy occupy Skidaway Island and attempt to use that structure in crossing to the main. A courier just arrived from Skidaway reports all the vessels (nine in number) gone. Rumor says our batteries there are to be blown up tonight by our men.

I trust, my dear father and mother, to see you very soon. Meanwhile I am, with warmest love and with many kisses for my precious little daughter, as ever,

Your affectionate son,
Charles C. Jones, Jr.

Lt. Charles C. Jones, Jr., *to* Rev. *and* Mrs. C. C. Jones[g]

Camp Claghorn, *Wednesday,* March 19th, 1862

My dear Father and Mother,

I write to remind you and my dear little daughter of my warmest love and constant remembrance.

We have nothing of interest in our camp or its vicinity. As yet the Lincolnites have made no demonstrations. A report reached us this afternoon that a few troops had been landed from the fleet upon Green Island, but it has been contradicted. The intention of the enemy as expressed by Commodore Du Pont, and illustrated by their acts, seems to be simply to possess our coast and to threaten without attempting an invasion. Another object doubtless is to keep our troops here and prevent heavy reinforcements in the West.

A delightful thunderstorm this afternoon has quite refreshed us, and the falling rain induces quiet thought and a calm of mind and body quite opposed to the turbulent passions and events of the hour. Captain Claghorn has not yet returned. I sincerely hope to see you very soon. As ever,

Your affectionate son,

Charles C. Jones, Jr.

Rev. C. C. Jones *to* Lt. Charles C. Jones, Jr.[g]

Montevideo, *Monday,* March 24th, 1862

My dear Son,

We are in receipt of your two last interesting letters of the 18th and 19th. Mother says you will have to excuse her not writing, as she is not well, and has the constant care of a large family. It has been a long time since we have been alone for a day.

Your dear little daughter is thinner than she was, and has an eruption on her person which Mother thinks may be measles; and your brother has just ordered that she be kept closely housed this very cold, blustering day. She is quite bright, and will not quit her grandmother's arms if she can help it.

Two days ago Peggy took her to nurse, and finding her mumbling something in her mouth, took out a piece of *veritable tobacco* (chewing twist) nearly the size of a quarter of a dollar and somewhat thicker—a piece she got hold of about Susan's person someway, as she uses tobacco (smokes certainly, if she does not chew). It had been in the little thing's mouth long enough to be well moistened; and had she swallowed it, she would have died in a short time and the cause never had been known! It was a special providence, for which we desire to be thankful. Mother has hung the piece of tobacco up by a string in the closet, that Susan may see it morning and evening and at other times when she is washing and dressing the baby. As might be supposed, Susan has not the most remote idea how the baby came by the tobacco.

Last week she was sitting in her grandmother's lap at morning prayers playing with a rose, and several times she plucked off the leaves of the flower, and looking archly into her grandmother's face put them to her lips as if she intended to eat them, and then took down her hand and shook her head. Little Daughter and Charlie and Stanhope and your uncle's boys John and Joseph are very fond of her, and she is delighted with their attentions. Her ear is better. She is somewhat fretful today.

Your sister and family are with us (today at Arcadia), and your brother's family and your Uncle John and family; and if you were with us our little circle would be complete of our children and grandchildren. We bless the Lord for those He spares to us on earth, and we bless Him for those He has taken to Himself in heaven. Dear Ruthie and Julia! How often, how often are they in my mind!

Miss Mary Dunwody and Mr. Howard, who married Carrie Shackelford, are with us, en route to Darien to remove the last of their Negroes from old Sidon up the country.

We have measles both at Montevideo and at Arcadia. Progress very slowly. But no whooping cough as yet. Cold for planting operations. Abundant rains. Planting in hope that we may be permitted to cultivate and harvest.

If the enemy makes no invasion this season and the war continues, arrangements must be made this summer—whoever lives to see it—for a removal back from the coast; for the invasion will come next winter. By present appearances the campaign is to lie westward for the spring and summer, and must prove a heavy one and put our resources to the test. We are changing front from Virginia to Missouri. We are obliged to concentrate and fortify and meet the heavy advancing columns of the enemy. Our people have been ahead of our government. I should like to see more energy and expansion in our government. We have needed and do now need it greatly, although our reverses have had a quickening and salutary effect. We cannot rectify past mistakes except in part. We have to do with the present. If our people are true to themselves, by God's blessing, the issue will eventually be favorable. I tremble for the increasing wickedness of our country. War is the hotbed of iniquity of every kind. The Lord interpose and help us!

Mr. Yancey settles the European intervention! No friend in any government on that civilized continent! This is no news to the historian, nor to the reflecting observer. The republic of America never had any friends in Europe, unless in the Swiss cantons. The forms of government are all opposed to ours. Their wars have been against the power of the people. Opposition to *the form* of our government we have to begin with, then add the dread and abhorrence of revolutions and changes to be found in all despotic and aristocratic governments. And no princes hate revolutions more than those who have risen through revolution into power; to aid revolutionists gives such matters respectability and influence with their own people. All the friendship we shall get is that of interest. Upon this, in the single articles of cotton and tobacco, our government and people have relied most blindly. A kind Providence has so adjusted the provisions for man's necessity that any one product, no matter how largely soever cultivated and used, may be struck out, and after a little temporary inconvenience the world eats, drinks, sleeps, and clothes itself and goes about its business as aforetime. There was a time when the world had neither cotton nor tobacco, and such a time could be again. We are fighting first for our liberty and independence, not for our interests. They certainly are involved, but they are secondary. Give us the first; the second follows surely.

Dr. Axson preached two admirable sermons for us yesterday, adapted to the times.

Mother says I must tell you she is getting on well with her *gunboat fund*. Has killed her stall-fed beef today and says she will corn some up for you, and you must come out and enjoy it. Hope the captain will come soon, so as to give you a chance.

Our men who were sent down to work on the fortifications under General Lawton's requisition have been gone near three weeks. Four have been sent back—one to Arcadia and three to this place.

All unite in much love to you. Our regards to Captain Claghorn. The Lord bless and keep you, my dear son!

Your ever affectionate father,
C. C. Jones.

Lt. Charles C. Jones, Jr., *to* Rev. *and* Mrs. C. C. Jones[g]

Camp Claghorn, *Monday*, March 24th, 1862

My dear Father and Mother,

The recent demonstrations of the enemy on the South Carolina coast, trivial in fact, have by our commanding generals here been magnified into movements of no inconsiderable importance; and the consequence is that we have been for the past week under orders "to march at a moment's notice." The ensuing days, however, on each occasion brought disappointment, and we subsided into the customary status of a fixed encampment. Wright's Legion (eight hundred strong), a band of brave, hardy fellows, yesterday afternoon took up the line of march for Savannah en route for South Carolina. This morning before day they are again in camp. The island resounded with their shouts of joy when moving towards the anticipated field of battle, and the tap of the drum gave impulse to their active tread. This morning in silence they returned to their former camping ground, disappointed and full of regret that the pretended proved not to be a real demonstration on the part of the enemy, and that the day of battle was again indefinitely postponed.

Our limber and caisson chests have all been packed for several days, and we have anxiously hoped that we would soon enjoy the opportunity of rendering essential service to our section and country in the immediate presence of the hated foe; but the prospect for so doing seems at present quite as remote as ever. There is no telling, however, what a day may bring forth, and our duty is to be always in readiness. For one I profess as much disinclination to danger and fighting, abstractly considered, as generally exists; but it is to me a source of deep regret to find day after day of our present term of enlistment expiring, and this fine battery, than which there is said by Generals Lee and Pemberton to be none superior and but one equal (and that one of the companies of the justly celebrated battalion of artillery from New Orleans) in the Confederate service, never allowed the opportunity of testifying its devotion to our immortal cause, and of proving its efficiency and the bravery of each member upon the field of battle.

I am quite sure that it would do your patriotic hearts good to see our proficiency in drill, the order of the company, and to feel the pulse of true courage which throbs in every breast. Our parade ground is visited almost every day by persons from Savannah. So soon as the news reached us of the landing of the Lincolnites at Bluffton, I immediately wrote (Captain Claghorn being still absent) to General Lawton, expressing our preparedness and urging him to send this battery wherever danger seemed most imminent. A flattering reply is before me in which he says that "he highly appreciates the chivalric and patriotic spirit which induced the tender of the services of this battery, and that whenever the emergency arises it will give him great pleasure to afford us the earliest opportunity to exhibit our discipline and efficiency in front of the enemy." From General Mercer, who is in immediate command of this brigade, I have a like assurance.

Nothing but a sense of duty and the honest desire to discharge it and to serve one's country faithfully in this the hour of her greatest need can give satisfaction in camp life, where none of the excitements of an active campaign and of danger actually present exist. You remember Napoleon's rapid movements and remarkable successes in the face of overwhelming forces in the vicinity, I think, of Lake Garda. I have often wondered at the inactivity and slothfulness of many of our officers in command, and have as often wished that some of his spirit, his wonderful enthusiasm, his quickness of perception and activity in execution, could possess them. Price is almost the only one who has any creative genius about him.

Two days since, I rode over to Skidaway Island to our abandoned batteries. They are already to some extent yielding to the disintegrating influences of the winds and rains. Five Lincoln vessels lay in full view. A large sailboat filled with men was amusing itself on the bright waters. The sea gulls and pelicans in large numbers were disporting themselves on easy wing. The first blush of spring was upon the shore, and the waves were gently rising and falling in soothing murmurs beneath the mild sunlight and the evening air. All was perfect stillness—everything emblematic of perfect peace. The antithesis was striking to a degree, and it was difficult to realize the fact that where nature reposed in such sweet, quiet, generous security, peace dwelt not.

For the present I can see in the future no ray of peaceful sunshine. Clouds and darkness are about us. That we shall, if we but prove true to our God and to ourselves, be eventually successful I entertain not the shadow of a doubt; but this consummation will, as matters now stand, be reached only after months and probably years of severe struggle, heroic endurance, and patient patriotism. Foreign intervention is entirely out of the question. I wish our people had thought it so long ago; we would have gone more earnestly about our work. I am glad it is out of the question, and that no foreign power shall attempt to intervene for the supposed settlement of our present difficulties. No compromise can by any possibility be made. We must make ours a self-sustaining government, developing at home resources of every description and remanding ourselves to the days of Roman virtue and Spartan simplicity. Mr. Yancey, I see in a recent speech, suggests that our ministers, now knocking for admission into the cold reception rooms of European palaces, be recalled. I think his idea more than half correct. The time is, I trust, not far distant when the world will feel our power, and in turn itself honored by our friendship and benefited by our commercial alliances.

You see our gallant commodore has left us to assume the command of the *Virginia*. All success to him! We part with him with less regret because he goes to enlarge his sphere of usefulness. We need his example and his services everywhere. . . . I sincerely trust, my dear father and mother, that you both and my precious little daughter are in the enjoyment of many blessings. With warmest love, I am ever

Your affectionate son,
Charles C. Jones, Jr.

Lt. Charles C. Jones, Jr., *to* Rev. *and* Mrs. C. C. Jones[w]

Savannah, *Wednesday,* March 26th, 1862

My dear Father and Mother,

The enemy on yesterday afternoon landed a small force on Skidaway Island, burned our batteries under cover of their steamers, and retired, leaving the United States flag flying from a house recently used by us as a hospital previous to the evacuation of the Island. We had only a few pickets at the battery. Three shell were fired at them from the gunboats, but they did no damage. So soon as the enemy retired, which they did after firing the batteries, the pickets returned and secured the flag. It is now in General Mercer's quarters. I do not think the Lincolnites had any intention in making this trifling demonstration other than the destruction of our abandoned works. All is quiet today, and the vessels are lying at their accustomed anchorage. We could see the smoke of the guns from our camp. If they land in force, General Mercer will, I think, give them a fight upon Skidaway. This I deem quite improbable, as I do not believe that they have in their vessels now lying in Wassaw Sound one thousand men.

I am expecting Captain Claghorn every day. Do kiss my dear little daughter for me. And believe me ever, my dear father and mother, with warmest love,

Your ever affectionate son,
Charles C. Jones, Jr.

I am in the city for an hour or two to attend to our quartermaster and commissary supplies for the next month.

MRS. MARY JONES *to* LT. CHARLES C. JONES, JR.[g]

Montevideo, *Thursday,* March 27th, 1862

My very dear Son,

With my large household it seems impossible to find time for writing you, although my thoughts are ever with you, and we are eagerly looking forward to your promised visit.

Our precious little Ruth has had an eruption all over her person which I have hoped would prove to be measles. Joe does not think it is so. We kept her confined all this week to our chamber. This morning the little bird is released from her cage, and she is delighted to be again in the parlor and playing with the children. They are all devoted to her, showing her every mark of the tenderest love. She has lost flesh, but is bright and cheerful, and every day expands her little mind. I wish she could see you every day, and assure you she is the joy and comfort of her grandparents.

The cases of measles on the place multiply daily; some eight or nine in the house at this time. Several of the men who worked on the entrenchments have returned sick, but a few days' rest I hope will restore them. The measles have also broken out at Arcadia.

Your brother's term of service with the troop ends the 1st of April. Carrie and himself speak of going to Augusta next week, but I want him to rest awhile at home.

I have been making some collections for the gunboat, and will soon forward them to Mr. G. B. Lamar. Mrs. John Barnard and Mr. N. L. Barnard have presented your brother with a silver pitcher and two goblets on a silver waiter—an elegant expression of their kind feelings—each marked "Dr. Joseph Jones." Your father enjoys the porter daily, and takes it not only with relish but benefit. Father, sisters, brother, and Uncle John all unite with me in best love to you, with unnumbered kisses from your own little daughter, and the unfailing love and prayers of

Your affectionate mother,

Mary Jones.

In haste.

LT. CHARLES C. JONES, JR., *to* REV. *and* MRS. C. C. JONES[g]

Camp Claghorn, *Monday,* April 7th, 1862

My dear Father and Mother,

I embrace a moment and an opportunity to the mail this morning to assure you and my dear little daughter of my constant love, and to express my earnest hope that a kind Providence is mercifully restoring to health and strength again the sick at home. How is Tyrone? And are all the measles patients recovering?

I regretted very much that I was compelled to leave you on Saturday, and nothing but a sense of imperative duty compelled me to do so. Arrived at camp Saturday evening. Found everything quiet. Some of our men sick.

Almost all of the troops retired from the Isle of Hope. We now hold the most advanced post. Nothing definite in reference to the movements of the enemy on our coast. Indications point to an early attack upon Fort Pulaski.

The morning papers have just been received, and we are thanking God for our grand victory near Corinth, the Solferino of the war. I trust the accounts as reported are correct. I do not feel entirely confident as yet. We have been so often overwhelmed by numbers that I fear the effect of the advancing reserve columns of Buell. Should this Army of the West be annihilated, the North will feel it most sensibly, and the effect will be great at home and abroad. If the report of numbers be correct, this is the heaviest battle ever fought upon the western continent. Albert Sidney Johnston will have amply established his claim to that regard which ranks him as our best general in the field. I pray God to consummate the victory which He has so auspiciously inaugurated.

I send fifty dollars for Gilbert. In the hurry of leaving at the depot I forgot to hand it to him. Did Brother receive from him one hundred and twenty-five dollars? Mr. Quarterman handed me that sum at the station, and I charged Gilbert with its delivery to Brother, with the request that he would divide it between Sister and himself, sending me receipt for same that I may keep the account of the place correct.

I thank you sincerely, my dear parents, for the volumes. I will read them at the earliest moment, and with care. Pray say to Uncle John that Mr. Lamar promises to meet him and family at the depot on Tuesday afternoon next. I handed the gunboat fund to Mr. Lamar in person on Saturday afternoon. Do kiss my dear little daughter for me. And believe me, my dear father and mother, with warmest love to you both, and with kindest remembrances to all at home,

Your affectionate son,
Charles C. Jones, Jr.

Lt. Charles C. Jones, Jr., *to* Rev. *and* Mrs. C. C. Jones[g]

Camp Claghorn, *Tuesday,* April 8th, 1862

I sincerely wish, my dear father and mother, that we were near enough in person to indulge in mutual congratulations upon the recent glorious success of our arms in the West. Truly we have cause for the proudest exultation and for profoundest thanks to that great God who has in mercy sent us such a signal victory. New Orleans is, for the present at least, safe from any approach of the enemy down the Mississippi valley. Island No. 10 will not now be outflanked. Memphis will remain in undisturbed security. And if the flying legions of the Lincolnites are closely pressed, Nashville may be repossessed and Tennessee delivered from the polluting presence of the insulting invaders, who have of late boasted of the prowess of their arms beneath her beautiful groves, upon her attractive hills, and within the shadow even of her splendid capitol.

We cannot overestimate the importance of this victory, and I trust from the bottom of my heart that the defeat may prove total and awful. The scenes attendant upon the retreat of the British army from Concord and Lexington in the days of the Revolution should be reenacted to the last degree; and every tree, every stone, should be clothed with a voice of thunder. Every man, woman, and child should rise in arms along the line of the retreating foe, and enforce by terrible illustration the lesson to the frightened outlaws how fearful the vengeance of a people armed in the holy cause of liberty, contending upon their own soil for the inalienable rights of life, freedom, religion, and the pursuit of happiness.

Our advices are as yet incomplete, but Beauregard and Polk lead the pursuit. I trust that the reserve columns of Buell may not stay the tide of victory. I do not think they can, with the horrors of defeat in a hostile country resting upon the one army, while the other is jubilant with that enthusiasm which draws its inspiration from such marked, recent, and illustrious success in a struggle whose issues involve all that is sacred in honor, pure in principle, true in religion, and valuable in life. Our troops must have fought with a bravery and a desperation worthy that holy behalf to the support of which they pledged their lives and sacred honors. Think of *eighteen field batteries captured!* This naked fact will give us an idea of the magnitude of the victory, and of the peril and the daring involved in its purchase. They were all probably six-gun batteries of the most approved style, and complete in all their appointments. This would give us, then, 108 field pieces, 3200 men, and at least 2250 horses, as the artillery corps in the "grand army" engaged in the battle, and scattered like the leaves of autumn before the whirlwind of our advancing regiments. The accession of arms, ammunition, camp equipage, and of the general munitions of war thus secured to us by this victory must be enormous and most valuable. The moral effect of this success cannot be overestimated, if we may credit all the accounts we already have. I would most willingly, my dear parents, have given my left arm—yes, both of them, were it necessary—to have been a personal participant in the glories of that day.

But alas, in our garlands of victory the bright and joyous leaves of the laurel are tempered into sadness by the commingled boughs of the mournful cypress. One of our bravest leaders and most accomplished generals, Albert Sidney Johnston, has fallen! And the exultant paeans of victory which rose upon the morning air from ten thousand lips throughout the length and breadth of our Confederacy as the first news of triumph were heralded with lightning speed, melted into strains of genuine sorrow before eveningtide at thought of the great price at which that victory was purchased. And yet I know of no death more grateful to the gallant chieftain—if his peace be made with his God—than to fall, sword in hand, at the head of his victorious legions, sealing by his lifeblood his devotion to country and to the holy cause of her redemption, and consecrating his name for all time upon the living pages of a glorious history as one of the protomartyrs in perhaps the noblest struggle which ever nerved the arms, inspired the energies, and gave impulse to the truest patriotism of man. His labors are ended, and the green grass will soon be growing, the soft airs of spring sighing, and the thoughtless songbirds warbling their accustomed notes of love and joy above the newly made grave of the fallen hero. Although the gleam of his blade shall nevermore amid the smoke and shock of battle point the way to victory, although his brave comrades will not again catch the inspiration of his presence on the field of peril, he will still live in the grateful remembrance of his countrymen; and the valor displayed in his death will prove alike a bright incentive to heroic action and a rich legacy to the record of the triumphs of this momentous struggle for freedom.

The day dawns. God in mercy grant that the rays of the rising sun may shine higher and brighter to the perfect end! . . . Our military status here is unchanged. The enemy, from all that we can gather, seems to be contemplating an attack upon Fort Pulaski at no distant day. The fort, we trust, is prepared to make a formidable and successful resistance. With warmest love to all, I am ever, my dear father and mother,

Your affectionate son,
Charles C. Jones, Jr.

MRS. MARY JONES *to* LT. CHARLES C. JONES, JR.^g
Montevideo, *Thursday,* April 10th, 1862*

My very dear Son,

Your affectionate and interesting letter was received today, and most heartily do we reciprocate the feelings it contains of gratitude to our Divine Master for our recent victory, and of profound grief at the death of our noble and gallant General A. S. Johnston. Our losses from time to time have been very great in our brave leaders, but we must trust in God and never give up our righteous cause.

I and my dear little Ruth are all alone this evening. Your father left after dinner for Walthourville to attend the meeting of Presbytery convened this evening. Joe, Carrie, and Stanhope are taking tea at South Hampton and will be back ere long. Everything around me exhibits a scene of perfect tranquillity. The trees with their deep dark shadows are reposing upon the lawn, which is irradiated with the soft pure light of a half-grown moon; whilst the melodious notes of the whippoorwill, unfailing harbinger of spring returned and winter gone, is echoing from the grove near the house and reechoing from the distant wood. In strange contrast to all that is beautiful and peaceful in this dear home of ours is the "rude sound of war's alarms" as it breaks even now upon my ear from the cannon's slow and measured thunderstrokes. Oh, the agony that comes over me at times! Where is my child? We will await tomorrow's mail with great anxiety. The Lord bless and spare you, my dear child, and preserve your whole company, and if the hour of conflict has arrived, arm you with courage and wisdom and give us the victory over our merciless foe! I trust that Pulaski will stand out against an attack.

The Liberty Troop have not yet reorganized, so we are without their military protection. They will do so in ten days.

Your Uncle John left the county today.

I am thankful to say that our sick are all more comfortable tonight, and Tyrone and Adam and July and Joe slowly improving. . . .

Our dear Little Sister is delighted with her dog. We call him Captain as a remembrancer of his kind donor. She tries to snap her little fingers at him, and he walks and plays with her, and every time she goes up to bed lies down near her crib. I imagine that he still has a "mother want" about him, and try to supply it by frequent feeding; but he has lost flesh. I must find out what is best for him.

Friday Morning. Our sick all better this morning: eight or nine cases up. The firing was heard again this morning, but the wind is so high and blowing from the west that we cannot now hear if it continues. God grant us strength to resist our enemies, and in His own good time entire deliverance from them!

The cargo of the Halifax vessel is fast discharging. I hope we may secure some of the quinine. Some persons suspect that it is a Yankee speculation; if so, I wish it could be proven, for it would nevermore leave our waters.

Your brother unites with me in best love to you, and says as he passes through he will try and see you. Sweetest kisses from your precious daughter, and the love and prayers of

> Your affectionate mother,
> Mary Jones.

Lt. Charles C. Jones, Jr., *to* Rev. *and* Mrs. C. C. Jones[g]
> Camp Claghorn, *Friday,* April 11th, 1862

My dear Father and Mother,

The all-absorbing matter of interest in our immediate neighborhood at present is the bombardment of Fort Pulaski by the Lincoln forces. The fire against the fort is directed mainly from some seven or eight gun- or mortar boats lying to the north and east of the fort, and from the mortar batteries which the enemy has been for some time erecting on Tybee Island. That fire has been continuous ever since a quarter before eight o'clock on yesterday morning. From our camp we can distinctly see the explosion of the shells and the smoke of the discharges. At the commencement of the bombardment Fort Pulaski was provided with about one hundred and thirty rounds of ammunition to the gun. The barbette guns are, I believe, not casemated, although they are to a very great degree protected by traverses. In the casemates are a few eight-inch columbiads, three or four forty-two-pounder guns. The rest are thirty-two-pounder guns. On the barbette are mounted some ten or more heavy eight- and ten-inch columbiads. I understand that a few guns have been placed in position in the demilune which protects the rear of the fort. Several mortars are posted near the south wharf.

With a view to a more accurate observation Captain Claghorn and myself rode over to the abandoned batteries on Skidaway Island yesterday afternoon, and remained there until sunset. The fort is in a direct line from this point not more than (I should judge) six or seven miles, and is clearly discernible with the naked eye. You look across a wide extent of marsh and water without an obstruction of any character. The flag of the fort was flying freely, and every discharge could be noted, whether from barbette or casemate. The fort fired with deliberation—probably not more than twenty-five shots per hour on an average. There was no indication whatever of any injury sustained. In fact, the simple statement that our brave soldiers were working their barbette guns freely will show that no damage had been done. The distance at which the Lincoln batteries are operating forbids the possibility of breaching the fort. The most that can be done—so far, at least, as we were able to judge—will be to sweep the barbettes of the fort by the fragments of exploding shells, and perhaps eventually disable the guns themselves. The batteries on Tybee Island and the gun- or mortar boats fired with great rapidity, and with guns of very heavy caliber. The most of the shells burst high.

While we were at the battery a large steamer which had come in to the south of the fort, and had been engaging the fort for some time, hauled off and crept out to sea very slowly. Our impression was that she was crippled—and that badly. She certainly declined further contest, and moved—or rather crawled—away. We thought with our glass that we could see places where her bulwarks had been considerably shattered, and at one time she appeared to be on fire; but the lights and shadows were so changeful that it was difficult to arrive at any certain knowledge as to her exact condition. Certain it is, however, that she had her fill of the fight, and hauled off with considerable difficulty.

Those rascally gun- or mortar boats lie so low in the water that it will be a difficult thing to strike them at long range. Some very heavy mortars are in position on Tybee Island, and the enemy is using them freely. I have not been over to Skidaway today, but from our camp we can see and hear that the engagement still continues, the enemy firing rapidly, the fort with its accustomed deliberation. At present rate it will be a long time, I think, before any material impression will be made upon the fort. No breach can be effected. Men may be killed at the barbette guns, but all else will be protected. Doubtless as the bombardment continues the enemy will approach nearer, and then the casemate guns will be employed. Olmstead, I think, will do his duty like a man, and offer every resistance. The most painful reflection connected with this affair is that the fort is wholly isolated, and at present we have no means of furnishing reinforcements of men or ammunition. There is no lack of provisions; and powder is there which, if economized, will suffice for many days.

The news has just reached us that the *Virginia* made some captures today in Hampton harbor. Our advices from the West are still unsatisfactory. God help us! We are beleaguered on every hand. But we must only trust in Him, pray more, and fight the harder.

I have written in great haste. I trust all at home are better. With warmest love to you both, my dear parents, many kisses for my dear little daughter, and kindest remembrances for all, I am, as ever,

Your affectionate son,
Charles C. Jones, Jr.

Lt. Charles C. Jones, Jr., *to* Mrs. Mary Jones[g]

Camp Claghorn, *Monday,* April 14th, 1862

My dear Mother,

Let me thank you sincerely for your recent kind letter, perfumed alike with the happy memories of home and the attractive fragrance of flowers I love so much—the first tidings I have had since my recent visit to you.

Since I last wrote, a heavy blow has been struck on our coast in the reduction of Fort Pulaski. I must confess the surrender of that fortification after a bombardment of scarce a day and a half, and with only four wounded, has surprised me beyond measure. It is reported that the effect of the Parrott shot upon the face of the fort looking towards King's landing on Tybee Island was wonderful. Heretofore it has been a military rule, deduced from actual and oft-repeated experiment, that breaching masonry walls of six feet in thickness with solid shot could not be accomplished beyond eleven hundred yards. Remarkable modifications, however, have already occurred during the course of this present war. In the present instance the entire battery of the southern face of the fort was silenced and seven casemates knocked into one by the Parrott guns posted near King's house on Tybee Island, a distance of a mile or more. The projectiles used were pointed with steel and were fired with wonderful accuracy. Knowing perfectly the plan of Pulaski, the enemy concentrated their heaviest fire upon the south magazine and succeeded in breaching even the inner walls of that apparently invulnerable retreat. The world has never known before such perfection in heavy ordnance and in artillery generally as that now possessed by the Lincoln government. Some of the recent improvements in rifled cannon are extraordinary; and each day, with the vast appliances of matériel, skill, and labor at their command, serves but to reveal some new and more terrible engine of war. Our artillery will not compare with theirs, and the consequence is that we are too often compelled to retire beyond the range of their cannon.

It is always a difficult matter to sit in judgment upon the actions of others when we are not fully acquainted with all the attendant circumstances; but it does seem to me, no matter how damaged the condition of the fort, that I never would have surrendered it with magazines well supplied with ammunition and not a member of the garrison killed. Too many similar defenses have been made by us during the existing war—so much so that it has become almost (I should suppose) a matter of pastime for Lincoln gunboats to engage and reduce Confederate batteries. We need more heroic action and sterner resistance to restore a moral tone which has been to some extent, at least, lost. Never did man or officer have a better opportunity of giving a name to history and honor to his country than did Olmstead, and I marvel that he did not improve the chance in a more marked manner. Of course it is but a matter of speculation, but it does seem to me that had I been in his place—in command of the best fort garrisoned by Confederate troops, with the eyes of an agonized country upon me, in sight of the home of my birth, and in immediate protection of all God and nature have rendered most dear upon earth—I should have nailed the color halyards hard and fast, fought every gun until it was thoroughly dismounted beyond redemption, clung to the fortification so long as a single casemate offered its protection, and when further resistance was entirely hopeless, have withdrawn the garrison, or what remained of it, and blown the whole concern to atoms. I never would have been charged with the surrender of a fort in the mouth of the Savannah River. I am afraid Olmstead lacked nerve. But I will not judge of his actions until we know the particulars. He may have done the best in his opinion. Had he perished in the ruins of Pulaski he would have lived a hero for all time. As it is, his reputation is at best questionable.

The enemy may soon move upon Savannah. Every exertion is being made, I understand, to impede the progress of the Lincoln vessels by placing physical obstructions in the channel of the river. No time is to be lost. Physical obstructions and submarine batteries only can offer the requisite resistance. If the heavy masonry walls of Pulaski were of no avail against the concentrated fire of those Parrott guns posted at a distance of more than a mile, what shall we expect from our sand batteries along the river? The great mistake was in the evacuation of Tybee Island, which should have been properly fortified and held at every hazard.

The garrison surrendered at Pulaski numbers, I believe, some 383 men all told. Of this number one company was American (part *Yankee*)—the Oglethorpe Light Infantry, Company B; two companies Irish; one company German; and the fifth company, the Wise Guards, from Western Virginia of late, but composed, I believe, of Georgians. The garrison should have consisted entirely of *Georgians*.

Our location is unchanged. How long we will remain here I know not. I write in haste, but with warmest love to you, my dearest mother, to dear Father, and with many kisses for my precious little daughter. Kindest remembrances to Brother, Sister Carrie, and little Stanhope. I trust the servants are better. Will the Doctor remain at home until we know the issue of our impending dangers?

As ever,

Your affectionate son,
Charles C. Jones, Jr.

MRS. MARY JONES *to* LT. CHARLES C. JONES, JR.[g]

Montevideo, *Wednesday,* April 16th, 1862

My dear Son,

Yesterday I received your most welcome and affectionate letter. We watch with anxious hearts the coming of every mail. Today's was without any tidings—not even a Savannah paper.

The fall of Pulaski after so short a bombardment, and the surrender of the garrison without even an attempt at escape and blowing up of the fort, which certainly could have been done, appears both astounding and humiliating! The state of our long-neglected defenses and the results, now to be fatally realized, of ignorance, imbecility, and neglect make us realize when too late for remedy the ruin and misery brought upon us by the general in command, who has had since this time last year to occupy and fortify the positions taken by our enemies within the past four or five months and now used for our destruction. I see no hope for Savannah but in the special mercy and goodness of God; and my only comfort springs from the hope that He will deliver us in the day of battle from our inhuman foes. If so, it will be all of sovereign mercy bestowed through our compassionate Saviour, for our sins and our presumptuous neglect of duty deserve only His just punishment. How dark the clouds are hanging all over our beloved country! The Righteous Judge alone knows the end from the beginning!

Today another deep sorrow has fallen upon our household in the death of *poor Joe,* another of our young and most active and athletic men. He was one of the three who returned first from the fortifications; and although he looked badly, he went about until a week or ten days since. Your brother has felt very uneasy about him from the first, but did not anticipate his death when he left yesterday. His case has been very peculiar; I never knew any like it. . . . Yesterday afternoon I walked over to see him, and found him sitting up on the side of his bed, and had a conversation with him about the state of his soul. He said "it would have been better for him if he had thought more about it before now." I reminded him that for three years he had been a constant and an attentive attendant upon our Sabbath night school, where I had often spoken to him of our Saviour, and asked him where he was now looking for salvation. He said: "Only to the Lord Jesus Christ." I know your dear father has often and most faithfully warned him. Poor fellow, I wish we could entertain a well-grounded hope of him! All is now over. He has passed to the great Judgment Bar, where we too must sooner or later appear when our summons comes. In these repeated and heavy afflictions your dear father and I desire to say from our hearts: "Thy will be done." He died this morning about ten o'clock.

Our old servant Niger continues very ill; unless relieved shortly I see very little hope for him. Tyrone is still very sick; Adam a little better. Some eight or ten other cases, most of them measles. All the men who worked on the fortifications excepting Pulaski seem to have taken some poison from water, food, or atmosphere into their systems which defies the ordinary remedies.

The effect of this increased anxiety and sorrow upon your father is very evident. The Lord give us grace and strength that we may be patient and submissive under His chastening rod!

Your brother and Carrie left us yesterday. He was to accompany his family as far as Millen and return today or tomorrow.

Thursday. Our sick are more comfortable this morning. God bless and preserve you, my dear child, and your whole company and all our brave soldiers now about to meet our foes! Although they are a mighty host, yet our God has power to destroy them and to give us the victory if we are true to Him and to ourselves. With best respects to Captain Claghorn,

Ever your affectionate mother,
Mary Jones.

Sweetest kisses from your little daughter, love from Father, and howdies from the servants.

LT. CHARLES C. JONES, JR., *to* MRS. MARY JONES[g]

Camp Claghorn, *Saturday,* April 19th, 1862

My dear Mother,

I have only a moment in which to acknowledge the receipt of your kind and valued letter of the 16th inst., this afternoon received, and to thank you most sincerely for it. It is with much sorrow that I learn the death of Joe. The finger of God has indeed been heavily laid upon us at Montevideo; and while we bow in submission, we can but hope and pray that the chastening rod may now be lifted, and that all may in good time be restored to wonted health.

The enemy on yesterday afternoon came in three gunboats opposite the abandoned Skidaway batteries and fired some seven shot and shell at our pickets and upon the island without accomplishing anything save a useless expenditure of ammunition. The gunboats thereupon retired to their former position at the mouth of Romney Marsh, no troops having been landed on Skidaway Island. It is the impression of many that the enemy will make his approaches by the way of Whitemarsh Island. It is of the last importance that he should not be allowed to obtain a foothold there, as in that event batteries could be planted which would soon render our batteries at Thunderbolt and Causton's Bluff and along the Savannah River almost untenable. That island is now held in force by us, and General Smith is energetically engaged in strengthening the river defenses.

The fall of Island No. 10 is severe. We are anxiously anticipating the arrival of recent intelligence from Fort Macon, the forts near the mouth of the Mississippi, the Peninsula, and from Corinth. I understand that Beauregard is unable to advance on account of the want of ammunition. I hope such is not the fact. Ammunition went forward to him and to General Van Dorn from Savannah today.

Only fourteen ounces of quinine were brought by the vessel, and these were sold at fifteen dollars per ounce at public outcry. So soon as I can purchase any, you shall have it. A scarce article. Do give much love to Father. Kiss my dear little daughter for me. And believe me ever, my dearest mother, with warmest affection,

Your son,
Charles C. Jones, Jr.

Lt. Charles C. Jones, Jr., *to* Mrs. Mary Jones[g]

Camp Claghorn, *Monday,* April 21st, 1862

My dear Mother,

We have nothing of special interest in our vicinity today. The enemy appears to be operating quietly down the river, but the exact character and extent of their labors are not, I believe, definitely ascertained. Most of the ships have returned northward, either with a view to returning with reinforcements at some early day, or for the purpose of swelling the immense force which now threatens our army on the Peninsula.

The approaching conflict there will doubtless be terrific. The shock of that battle will be felt in the remotest bounds of our Confederacy, and its results will exert a most material effect upon the duration of this war. If driven from our positions there and discomfited, God alone knows when the war will end; while on the other hand, if He in mercy crowns the valor of our arms with success, the annihilation of that boasted Grand Army of the Potomac under the leadership of McClellan will, at least for the present, in that direction work a practical cessation of hostilities, and may conduce in no small degree to an early and final restoration of peace.

One after another our fortifications and strong places have fallen before the superior forces and untiring industry of our unrelenting enemy. So far our foe is without a permanent check to his general advance, except upon the memorable hills of Shiloh. But I think if we can hold our own until August, we will see more light and somewhat of joy and immediate hope. The present exertions of the Lincoln government are wonderful, and their resources marvelous. All we have to do—now that the mind of the people has at length been happily turned from a morbid consideration of the chances of foreign intervention, and an underestimate of the power of our adversary and the degree of his hate—is to exhaust our every energy, bend every nerve, and develop every Spartan virtue in the resolute defense of all that is holy in religion, dear in honor, valuable in property, true in principle, and sacred in death, at the same time earnestly and constantly invoking divine guidance and the blessings of a just God upon our efforts. Our men must make up their minds to suffer freely, and if need be, to die freely. They must dare all things, and endure all which may become a noble race whose priceless all is placed in imminent peril by an inhuman, powerful, and relentless foe bent upon subjugation and annihilation. So long as many of our generals are afraid of consequences, ignorant of their duties, negligent of imposed obligations—so long as they shrink from attempting deeds even above heroic (for the odds are against us)—we will continue to give back.

I have no fears of our ultimate success; but as matters now stand, and at the rate at which we have been for some time retrograding, the amount of blood, loss, and deprivation to be incurred before that consummation devoutly to be wished for is reached will be enormous. But it is no time to calculate the chances of either pecuniary or vital loss. We are to be saved *as by fire;* and our duty is to go manfully, fearlessly, and persistently about the work of our country's salvation, humbling ourselves for past and present transgressions, as individuals and as a nation, before a just God who will not look upon sin with the least degree of allowance, praying His intervention in our behalf, and using every means to help ourselves while we invoke His aid. If our troops will quit themselves like men and stand bravely to their guns, the enemy will have heavy work in compassing the capture of Savannah. If, on the contrary, the defense be abandoned when only half made, we may expect nothing else than the fall of our beloved city. For one I trust never to see that day.

The existing difficulties about the continuance of the late state forces in service, and the disagreements which recently arose between those in authority, are peculiarly unfortunate just at this time, and would seem to indicate that the Devil is yet at his work, and that true patriotism and the cultivation of the nobler virtues are not uppermost in the minds of at least many of those who are immediately charged with the defense of our sacred rights and liberties. What we greatly need now is artillery of heavy caliber and long range. We are in great want of guns which will enable us to compete successfully with those of our adversary.

But I fear, my dear mother, that I weary you. I trust that all the sick at home continue to improve, and they may all soon be restored to perfect health. Give much love to dear Father. Many kisses for my precious little daughter. And believe me ever

Your affectionate son,
Charles C. Jones, Jr.

Kindest remembrances for the Doctor if he has returned. Howdy for the servants. Did Gilbert ever receive fifty dollars I sent him? And did he hand to Brother one hundred and twenty-five dollars I sent from the depot to him? Do ask the Doctor, if he did receive it, to send me receipt, that I may keep the Arcadia accounts correct.

Rev. C. C. Jones *to* Lt. Charles C. Jones, Jr.[g]

Montevideo, *Monday,* April 21st, 1862

My dear Son,

Your last interesting favors are at hand, and we feel thankful that you are in good health, and your comrades in arms also.

The preservation of the city depends, under God's blessing, upon the wise and energetic and determined action and bravery of our officers and men. No regular approaches should be allowed on the part of the enemy, and nothing left undone to break up and retard their advances. This is fundamental. The loss of Pulaski does not necessarily involve the loss of the city; by no means. It yields the river approach to the enemy, but I see no reason for discouragement in finally repulsing him. Now is the time for General Pemberton and our chief officers to show themselves to be men; and I trust they will, and that God may give us the victory.

The sending our men to work on the Savannah River batteries has been a sad thing to us. Poor Joe died on the 16th with dysentery (river cholera) contracted there, making two of our best men. What is peculiarly affecting in Joe's case is, he died without hope, so far as we have any evidence to the contrary. Tyrone has been extremely ill; is still in bed and something better. Little Adam is just walking about. July has been very sick, and is barely convalescing. Sam was very sick for a short time. And the only one who seems to have escaped the dreadful poison of the place is Pulaski, the youngest of the seven. The plantation, with these extreme cases and the measles with the people, has been going on three weeks *a hospital;* and had not your brother been with us, I do not know what we should have done. Arcadia is suffering also from measles; the men who went to Savannah have suffered much also. Old Niger is suffering from his old chronic complaint and other disorders, and there is little hope of his recovery. But his mind is clear and calm, and his hope in Christ strong and comforting.

You must needs know how much we have been confined at home, and how much care we have had. So has the Lord ordered it, and we are bearing our portion of the judgment of war, for our sicknesses came from the war directly. And we would rather fall in this way into the hands of God than to fall into the hands of man.

Your brother took his family to Augusta on the 15th, stayed a day, and returned kindly for our help on the 18th; and between Montevideo and Arcadia he has had his hands full. I hope it may please God to rebuke our diseases so that he may return to Augusta in a few days. It is a great interruption to him. He has not settled down on any plan for the future, and cannot until he returns to Augusta. The Liberty Independent Troop has split into two companies, neither sufficient in numbers to be mustered in: Lowndes Walthour captain of one and William Thomson of the other. Winn thrown out by both sides.

Mr. Gué, I understand, comes out to No. 3 tomorrow (Tuesday) to purchase cotton for Mr. Molyneaux, who stores it on speculation in Thomasville. Offers twenty-one cents. Am inclined to sell him under these conditions a part of what I have ginned out (one-half the crop here *not* ginned out) at that price—to pay my running accounts and keep a little for contingent expenses. I think it would be well for you to sell a part of the Arcadia crop for the same purposes. Will ask Mr. Gué if he will take a part. If your brother and sister desire it, will sell a part. Your Aunt Susan wishes to sell a part of her crop. The cotton is *not sold to go out of the country*. This I would not do. But if men buy and store on speculation and wait the opening of the ports, and we can afford to sell at their offer, I think we may do so.

Your dear little daughter is quite well, and learning *slowly* to eat. And her little dog, which we call *Captain,* is an unfailing source of amusement to her. Mother and Brother unite in much love to you. We pray for you day by day. Our respects to Captain Claghorn.

Your ever affectionate father,
C. C. Jones.

Lt. Charles C. Jones, Jr., *to* Rev. C. C. Jones[g]
Camp Claghorn, Tuesday, April 22nd, 1862

My dear Father,

Your very kind letter of the 21st inst. was this afternoon received. It finds us under orders to move our encampment in the morning. Whither we know not as yet—probably to some point within a few miles of this beautiful spot, where we have enjoyed an unusual degree of health and quiet for the past seven months. We are loath to leave it, but we are completely deserted by the rest of the brigade, General Mercer in the bargain. It is the first time in my reading or observation that I have ever known or heard of a light battery being kept upon picket week after week at the most advanced post, and for a part of the time, at least, neither cavalry nor infantry to support it in the event of an attack, which might with the utmost ease have been made by the enemy any night. These civilian generals do things in a queer way, and revolutionize all established principles of warfare. While I write, we are the only troops upon this whole island, with the exception of two pickets sent over only an hour since, and at our earnest solicitation. The Isle of Hope will be abandoned by us in the morning—if the enemy does not during the night impel us to a more rapid move. . . . From the very nature of the arm of the service, field batteries with their park of guns and stable of horses are least able to move at a moment's warning, and from the character of camp and weapons least of all capable of self-protection. I think the conduct of General Mercer very reprehensible, but I am forbidden by the articles of war to say so, and I do so knowing that what I say will not be repeated. Our removal will cost trouble and great labor in the preparations of a new camping ground, building stables, etc., etc. This everlasting evacuation, coupled as it is with no apparent disposition on the part of our commanding officers to seek out and check the advance of the enemy, who certainly on our coast have everything their own way, is not only blameworthy in the extreme but also heartily disgusting.

In reference to the cotton, I would sell without hesitancy upon the terms suggested. Do ask Brother to see Mr. Gué if practicable, and to make such arrangements for the disposition of the whole or such part of the Arcadia crop as you may think proper.

I sincerely sympathize with you, my dear father, in all our afflictions at Montevideo, and trust and pray that in the good providence of God the hand of disease may be arrested and all the sick restored to health. The penalty which is exacted by war under the most favorable circumstances is severe. . . . If you do not hear from me for a few days, you will know that we are busily engaged with our change of location and the duties incident thereupon. I have written in great haste, but with much love to self, dear Mother, and many kisses for my precious little daughter. Kindest remembrances for the Doctor. I am ever, my dear father,

Your affectionate son,
Charles C. Jones, Jr.

Captain Claghorn desires his special and respectful remembrances. George well. Howdy for the servants.

XI

Arcadia, *Monday,* April 28th, 1862

My very dear Son,

The news came up from the Island on Friday that two of the enemy's gunboats were in Woodville River at Drum (Timmons') Point below Mrs. King's place; that a part of the troop under Captain W. L. Walthour had gone down to give them a brush should they attempt to land troops or come up the river; and that citizens were going down to aid. Your brother was at Arcadia visiting the sick when he heard it, and posted back to Montevideo, got ready his blanket and camp clothing and waterproofs by the time Mother prepared a hurried lunch; and while he was eating she put up some rations for him; and taking his grandfather John Jones's double-barreled gun with ammunition, he bid us good-bye, and putting spurs to Lewis, hurried away for the fight.

When he arrived at the Island the vessels had passed up and were lying at the Crosstides, and in the midst of divided counsels were not fired on by the small force on the bluffs. He then went with Messrs. Munro McIver and William C. Stevens and George Handley to Carr's Neck, all resolving to fire on anything that should pass, and remained there all night—the rest of the men going, I believe, to Mr. Busby's landing, where the Nova Scotia vessel lay waiting for a cargo. In the morning the gunboats were seen under weigh steaming swiftly, smoothly, and noiselessly up, without a particle of smoke, and out of range. They pushed on for Busby's landing. The Nova Scotia vessel was sunk by the small company there in the channel, and her works above water set on fire. The tide detained the gunboats some hours.

Your brother came on to Montevideo, giving his fine horse a ride that tested his bottom fairly, and reached us about half-past 5 or 6 P.M. He left the gunboats coming up on the flood, and recommended Mother and myself to take the carriage and Little Sister and at once go to Arcadia and be out of the way in case the enemy should either land or shell the plantation.

Mother had that very day sent to Arcadia three or four loads of household furniture, which she had purposed to do, but sickness and interruptions had prevented till then. And Gilbert and the boys were away! There was energetic movement in the house to get things ready on a short notice. The enemy approaching—a complete surprise! You know your mother's energy. Patience, Flora, Elsie, Tom, Sue and Sam, your brother and myself (after a fashion) were all in motion, Susan and Peggy looking after the baby and her outfit in particular, Cook Kate pushing on tea, the horses and carriage getting (and mule-wagon for baggage), Cato called (and Porter) for instructions, Lymus dispatched as a lookout on the lower dam, to run immediately and give notice if he saw or heard the gunboats or any boats at all coming up the river. All astir, but no confusion; and much was accomplished in a very short time. A few principal things out of the house and out of the study, and all the rest left! We had been burnt out once; might be again. We quietly submitted to the will of God. A hasty cup of tea—nothing more.

Just as we were getting into the carriage, Gilbert arrived from Arcadia. The faithful fellow would not let Sam take the box; said "he was fresh and wanted nothing to eat and preferred driving his mistress himself; it was pitch dark, and he knew his horses better than anyone else." It was cloudy and very dark; we took a candle in the carriage, which was a great help in driving, and a comfort. The mule-wagon behind us. Your brother stayed to take care of the people. We had started but a little way when Lymus reported a boat in the river. We had all the lights extinguished, and the people hastened to the brickyard shed, and your brother then went back and reconnoitered. Says it was a boat, but where it went he could not determine; thinks it was a barge sent up on a search and for soundings and then dropped down quietly. (I should have mentioned that he had not reached home fifteen minutes to hurry us off before my neighbor Mr. Calder, managing for Estate J. B. Barnard, sent a boy express to let me know the gunboats were coming up by White's Island not far below the ferry.)

When we reached Arcadia the family had retired; but after some knocking we were let in and welcomed, and after supper and worship went tired to bed.

Your dear brother was up on the watch all night. Gilbert went back to him, and with all the servants packing all night, about daylight the oxcarts were packed with furniture and household matters of every kind and sent off for Arcadia. Meanwhile the carts from Arcadia and Lambert were dispatched. And Sabbath (as it was) we had a stream of carts and wagons running all day between the two places; and by sundown your brother had nearly everything moved out of the house, and nearly all the women and children and some of the sick men moved over also. He says he never saw servants more attentive and active or take a greater interest in the removal and effort to keep clear of the enemy.

When the Negroes ran (on the alarm of the boat) to the brick shed, some-one called for the old patriarch Tony to go along.

Said he: "Where is Massa?"

"Gone."

"Where is Mistress?"

"Gone."

"Well, I am too old to run. I will stay and throw myself into the hands of the Lord."

Your mother and Aunt Susan and Cousins Lyman and Laura went to church, but I was too inactive to go and remained at home with the children. But on the report of the boys with the oxcarts that the enemy were coming up in open barges, that your brother had a detachment of men at Montevideo (and *Robert* among them), and others had gone over to Mr. Barnard's, and they were preparing to attack them, I felt I must go, and ordered the buggy. And your aunt got me a little relish, having taken but one sermon with Mother. And putting your little revolver on the seat by me, refusing to let Mother go with me as she desired to do, I drove off, meeting carriages on the road returning from church. At the Boro I learned that the barges proved to be the yawl of the Nova Scotia vessel coming up to the Boro with the seamen. But the gunboats were lying at the ferry—had not gone up to Busby's landing—and had fired a shell at two of Captain Hughes's men near Mr. J. B. Barnard's settlement, but did no one any damage. Part of Captain Hughes's company had come over to aid from their encampment at South Newport.

Riding up to Montevideo house, the scene was lovely: horses hitched about, others grazing with their saddles on, and little groups of soldiers and men here and there, and the stoop full of them. They all gave me a hearty welcome. Robert there, sure enough; had left his church and come down with others on the alarm, armed.

"But where is Joe?"

"Oh, the Doctor! We have all prescribed him to go and lie down and rest, for he has been up the whole of two nights, and has been riding to and fro all day watching for the enemy on the river."

Not long after, he appeared at the upstairs window in his shirt sleeves, looking like a man just out of a nap. He came down in wet stockings: his boots drying. Had ridden, in reconnoitering along the swamp, into a spring bog which came up to his knees on horseback almost and to the crupper of his saddle. The horse by great exertions got out.

Mr. Edgar Way now arrived and reported that the gunboats had left the ferry and were steaming down to the Colonel's Island, where a part of the troop had gone to fire upon them on their way down. About the time they would reach the Island we heard their cannon. And the firing was continuous, but not very rapid, for half an hour or three-quarters, upon which we concluded our men had fired upon them and they had shelled the woods and Woodville and Maxwell settlements.

Nearly all now started for the Island. Two returned to sick families at Walthourville, leaving Mr. Thomas W. Fleming, Rev. D. L. Buttolph (who had come on after church), Robert, Joe, and myself. The enemy being gone, there was no need of any further guard at this point; and about sundown the three ministers and the planter and the doctor retired in single file—the planter in the lead—to our homes, which we reached near 9 P.M. Robert and Joe came home with Brother Buttolph to Arcadia. Supper; family worship, at which we sang "Come, My Redeemer, Come"; then bed. Such a Sabbath I never spent before—and wish to spend none other like it. We prayed that the enemy might be sent back the way he came; and so it has been done. May all his future visits, if any, prove of like innocent character to our people and their interests!

We have had a hospital at Montevideo for full four weeks. Wally died on the 4th, Joe on the 16th, Old Niger on the 24th, and—last—Cinda on the 25th. (These are the dates, I believe.) Several have been extremely ill. The last case (little James Monroe, George's brother) now better. Three of the Savannah men yet not at work: convalescing. Four deaths and an entire evacuation of house and home for fear of the enemy in four weeks! These are some of the sad changes of life—and all from this unnatural and cruel war. What remains we know not, but ask the presence and blessing of God, and that we may not be hardened under His hand.

All the women have been sent back from Arcadia this morning except those with little children and the little children. We are now hauling and storing the corn from Montevideo in a part of Arcadia cornhouse, and may remove the cotton also. Arcadia is less exposed, we think, than Montevideo. I regret our inability last fall to remove all our people back from the seaboard. We should have been saved much anxiety, and we know not yet what loss. We are planting a crop *in hope* only that we may harvest it. The enemy has for the present everything his own way where he operates with his navy. If he succeeds in the remaining seaboard cities as he has at New Orleans, we may be annoyed in Liberty. But I hope and pray that Savannah may be able to repulse him. General Lovell has done well *not to surrender New Orleans;* he can now attack and retake it as opportunity offers.

I do not know what we should have done without your brother. He has done everything for us he could, and I feel that he has been the means of saving the lives of several of the servants in our recent illnesses. All, thanks to divine mercy, are better. The cotton sold by Mr. Gué for Arcadia and Montevideo is weighing today at No. 3, and Mr. Gué will send you the sale in a few days, I suppose. Jog his memory about it. Your dear little one is quite bright: learning to eat. All in the house unite in much love to you. Write soon.

From your ever affectionate father,
C. C. Jones.

P.S. *Tuesday, April 29th, 1862.* Our citizens and soldiers have had a skirmish at Half Moon (Sellegree's) with the retiring gunboats on Sunday afternoon—the firing we heard at Montevideo. Will write you all the particulars when I learn them. When the men left at the firing, we told them they would be too late. Am glad we fired on the boats. They fired their guns, but the balls and shells went over our men, and we had nobody hurt. They should have been fired upon at the Screven place when they came up. Meet them, fight them at all points, repel them, harass them—keep the war moving. They have a great work to subdue and keep military possession of eight hundred thousand square miles of territory! Conquest! The word can't be found in the dictionary of a people resolute in a good cause, with the Righteous Lord to lean upon.

We are just breakfasting, and there is enough for Captain Claghorn and his military family. Wish you were all here. I think when peace comes we must have the Chatham Artillery—officers, at least—at Montevideo on a picnic. Brother Buttolph goes to the depot this morning to see to the weighing of the cotton. All send much love—old and young. Little Sister is in the best of humors. Received your letter yesterday.

Your affectionate father,
C. C. Jones.

LT. CHARLES C. JONES, JR., *to* REV. C. C. JONES[g]
Camp Claghorn, *Wednesday,* April 30th, 1862
My very dear Father,

I cannot sufficiently thank you for your minute, graphic, and deeply interesting letter of the 28th inst., this afternoon received. It grieves me deeply to know that *home*—a place so peculiarly consecrated to peace, quiet, religion, hospitality, and true happiness, the abode of my honored and beloved parents and of my precious little daughter—should have been ruthlessly disturbed in its security and calm repose by the near approach of those lawless bands of robbers and freebooters who are now infesting our coasts, annoying and murdering our people, pillaging our country, and endeavoring to deprive us of everything which we hold priceless in individual, social, or national existence. I presume the immediate object in the contemplation of the enemy in coming up the river was the destruction of the vessel at Busby's landing. Of the fact of that vessel having passed up the river I imagine the blockading fleet had due notice, as they seem to be apprised of almost everything which transpires along our coast. I do not think the gunboats will return.

The burning of the vessel and the alacrity with which all armed upon the first note of alarm are most praiseworthy. Do offer my congratulations to the Doctor for his energy and most valuable services. I am sorry that he did not enjoy the opportunity of discharging at least both barrels well loaded with buckshot from Grandfather's genuine "Mortimer" (placed in his hands by Mother) full in the face, at easy range of the nefarious rascals. I would have given a great deal to have had a section of our battery at Half Moon and treated the Lincolnites to a dose of shell and canister. A light battery is very effective under such circumstances.

It is a most unfortunate circumstance when the holy quiet of the Sabbath is disturbed by the rude alarms of war; but the obligations of national defense and of the protection of our homes and lives and property from the attacks of an invading foe are as sacred on that as on any other day. When our mothers place the arms in our hands, when our fathers by actual presence counsel, aid, and encourage, and when the ministers of the Living God leave their desks, the sermon half delivered, to hasten to the field of danger, the nation, pressed on every hand though it be, must eventually prove invincible by any force our enemy may send against us. The days of 1776 are come again. The record of the virtues, the courage, the self-denial, and the generous interest of our women in the great cause of our national honor and national defense is as bright, as striking, as it was in the days of Martha Custis, Mrs. Otis, and Mrs. Motte. It remains for our men to prove themselves worthy their mothers, wives, daughters—worthy the cause they espouse.

I could but contrast in my mind the appearance of the river disturbed by the Lincoln gunboats—the trees marred by the iron missiles, and the still air rent by the noise of cannon and of firearms and filled with the strange smell of battle—with that presented of late as, in taking your accustomed morning ride, you halted Jerry as was your wont on the edge of Half Moon Bluff, and uncovering your head beneath the grateful shade of the oak, you enjoyed the calm influences of the scene—nothing to interrupt the perfect harmony of nature, nothing to frighten the songbird from its favorite retreat, nothing to obscure the outlines of the low-lying shores, nothing to hush the voice of the refreshing morning air as it gave life to the forest and a gentle ripple to the waters, nothing to divert the thoughts from those peaceful and happy contemplations which lead the mind and heart through nature up to nature's God. . . . Half Moon Bluff has now become somewhat historical. I hope that the enemy suffered loss and harm in the skirmish, in order that they may be deterred from adventuring a second time.

The hand of affliction has indeed been heavily laid upon us at Montevideo. Am truly happy to know that all the sick are now convalescent, and hope that they may all be soon restored to accustomed health and strength.

The fall of Fort Macon does not surprise, as the work has been isolated for some time, and its surrender was simply a question of time. The age of ordinary fortifications has passed. . . . Alexander telegraphs a battle imminent at Corinth. God grant us a signal victory! Our arms need success to restore confidence and lift the depressing influences caused by our recent disasters.

You see General Lawton has expressed his resolution not to surrender the city of Savannah, and the board of aldermen determine to aid in carrying into effect this determination.

Nothing new in our immediate vicinity. I have written amid a perfect cloud of sand flies, and with both my boots filled with fleas. We lost tonight one of our finest battery horses. Blind staggers: I have never seen a poor animal suffer as it has done for many days. Do give warmest love to dear Mother, many kisses to my precious little daughter, kindest remembrances to the Doctor and all good relatives at Arcadia. And believe me ever, my dear father,

Your affectionate son,
Charles C. Jones, Jr.

Lt. Charles C. Jones, Jr., *to* Rev. *and* Mrs. C. C. Jones^g

Savannah, *Friday,* May 9th, 1862

My dear Father and Mother,

I am still here as judge advocate of this general court-martial. Some very important cases are before us, and the probability is that our sessions will be protracted. For the past few days I have been continuously occupied during not only the hours of light but until two o'clock in the morning; and as I now indite this hurried letter it is the 10th and not the 9th as above dated.

These imperative and uninterrupted engagements must plead my excuse for having delayed Gilbert so long. Each day I have thought that I would have a leisure moment to go to the house and select the volumes I desired packed for removal; but until this morning I did not enjoy the opportunity for doing so, and then only for a very short time. I have sent only a few volumes and the rest of my Indian remains, which I must trouble you, my dear parents, to have placed for me in a safe place. I thank you for the services of Gilbert.

The most outrageous circumstance occurred about midday today in our river. A Federal transport showing a flag of truce at the fore was permitted to ascend the Savannah until she reached within less than a mile of Fort Jackson, and within pistol shot of one of our batteries. She was then not halted by the sentinels but by a captain of one of the steamers lying in the stream opposite Fort Jackson, who steamed down the river to meet her, and succeeded in bringing her to just before she reached the obstructions in the river. The enemy's vessel (unarmed) when halted was so near the city that the stripes in the Federal flag could be distinctly seen with a glass from any part of the city. Generals Lawton and Smith both posted down in the *Ida* to see what was wanted. The object of the flag of truce I do not know; neither am I acquainted with the results, if any, arrived at. The Lincolnites from below were yesterday taking observations from a balloon; I presume wishing to verify these observations they today adopted the ruse of a flag of truce.

I have always been informed that when an enemy is allowed with a flag of truce within the lines, he should be blindfolded so as to be incapable of possessing himself of any information. But in the present case, in the face of a cloudless sunlit sky, this Lincoln transport is permitted to pass our pickets, come within our lines and opposite to one of the river batteries, occupying for two hours a position from which the very men of the city of Savannah could be observed and every fortification along the river accurately viewed and located, and its exact strength and the metal of its guns definitely ascertained. This act does out-Herod Herod, and shows how grossly culpable is the negligence of the officers in charge, and how monstrous the ignorance of our sentinels on the river. That vessel, despite the white flag, should have been brought to just within range of the heaviest guns of our lowest battery. If a shot across the bows would not have accomplished it, the next through her hull would have done it. But uninterrupted in her course by the batteries, those on board the vessel came on and on, and in all probability, unless Captain King of the *St. Johns* had seen fit to stop her, would have steamed clear up to the city. Monstrous to a degree!

We learn this afternoon that the great battle of Corinth commenced today about 12 M., Beauregard making the attack. It is also said that Stonewall Jackson has had another fight, and that the result of the engagement was favorable to us. We have nothing else of interest. With warmest love to you both, my dearest parents, and many kisses for my precious little daughter, I am, as ever,

Your affectionate son,
Charles C. Jones, Jr.

REV. C. C. JONES *to* LT. CHARLES C. JONES, JR.[g]

Arcadia, *Saturday,* May 10th, 1862

My dear Son,

Gilbert has arrived, and we are happy to learn your good estate through his report and your acceptable letter.

Truly we are fallen upon men of ignorance and imbecility! The coming of that transport up Savannah River is a disgrace to the general in command, and sufficient ground for a court-martial, and may result in the overthrow of the city! I must repeat what I have so often said, in view of the lethargy and weakness of the officers in command and the amazing apathy of the citizens, that if Savannah is delivered out of the hands of our enemies, we shall owe it to the immediate and merciful intervention of a kind Providence. And that the city may be so delivered we should daily pray.

The fall of New Orleans is a terrible blow, and the people should demand to know where the responsibility lies. Lost unquestionably through criminal delay and neglect. And so of the fall of our coast fortifications. We are upon the eve of great events; and I agree with you, my dear son, that all who have an interest at a throne of grace should be continually in prayer to our Heavenly Father for a happy deliverance.

We have to add another to our severe afflictions in our household. Poor *Bella,* Agrippa's wife, died the evening of the 7th on this place unexpectedly from an affection of the heart, from which she has been suffering for some time past. Her attack of measles seemed to have pretty much passed away. Your brother said she was liable to sudden death from it. In conversation with her two or three hours before her death she said: "Massa, if the Lord would come for me this night—this *very* night—I would be freely willing to go, for there is nothing to keep me here longer. I can leave all in His hands." *The Lord came,* and my hope is it is well with her. She was a member of Midway Church. Daphne continues very ill, and we fear the result. Rest of the sick on both places better.

Mother has kept up astonishingly. Sends much love. Your dear little one has been steadily improving since we got her to eat, which she now does in a moderate way three times a day. Is full of life and intelligence. Your aunt and Cousins Laura and Lyman send much love. Their little ones well. Very sickly among the Negroes in the county. Whites generally healthy. Seasons good so far. Crops look fair. Have engaged Mr. Calder, managing for Estate J. B. Barnard, to take care of our business at Montevideo, at least for a season. A great relief.

Gilbert is waiting for the letter to go to the depot and bring your things home at once, and they will be carefully put away. Send for him whenever you need him to help you further. Your change to the city is something, if the business is onerous. Praying for you always, I remain, my dear son,

Your ever affectionate father,
C. C. Jones.

LT. CHARLES C. JONES, JR., *to* REV. C. C. JONES[g]

Savannah, Monday, May 12th, 1862

My dear Father,

I am under many obligations to you for your kind favor of the 10th inst.

The telegraphic communications of today cast additional gloom over our prospects: Norfolk evacuated, the navy yard burnt, our vessels, dry dock, and all destroyed, the *Virginia* blown up, the city in the occupancy of the enemy, Commodore Tattnall resigned, and our army in Virginia falling back generally. Add to this that General Beauregard is said to be suffering severely in the Army of the Mississippi for want of provisions; the report that Atlanta is suffering from the supposed Lincoln incendiaries; and the further rumor that both Charleston and Savannah are to be evacuated at no distant day—and we have a chapter of evil tidings which it is almost impossible to consider with composure.

There is no disguising the fact that our country's fortunes are in a most desperate plight, and thus far I see nothing ahead but gathering gloom. Each event but proves more conclusively than the former the power of our enemy, his indomitable energy, consummate skill, and successful effort. General Joseph Johnston, from whom we were led to expect so much, has done little else than *evacuate,* until the very mention of the word sickens one *usque ad nauseam.* There may be a great deal of strategy in all of these movements, but to the eye of the uninitiated there appears but little of real action and determined resistance. This doctrine of evacuation on every occasion robs us of our means of supply, annihilates our ordnance, discourages our troops and people generally, and if persisted in must eventually contract our limits to an alarming extent. Encouraged by an almost uninterrupted succession of decided successes, we cannot wonder that the Northern mind is bent upon a prosecution of the war, and impressed with the idea that the suppression of the rebellion is at hand. Of a mercurial temperament, success works its stimulating influences in a no less marked manner than does defeat exert its depressing effects.

The passage of this conscript law—a law good in itself—just at this time exerts a most disorganizing and deleterious effect upon our armies. The elections thus far evidence the fact that almost all of the good officers have been thrown overboard in the reorganization of companies, battalions, and regiments, and that in their steads men of inferior qualifications—in very many instances mere noses of wax, to be molded and controlled at will by the men whom they should govern—have been entrusted with the command. All the worst phases of low, petty electioneering have been brought to light, and military discipline and becoming subordination are in frequent instances quite neglected. I am sorry to say that in our company there is a strong disposition to depose those officers who have endeavored faithfully to discharge their duties, and to supply their places with men who have not a proper conception of their responsibilities or of the obligations of truth, honor, and of a sacred oath. The election in the Chatham Artillery occurs on Friday or Saturday next. What the result will be I have not inquired. Of one thing you may rest assured: I will compromise neither name nor honor to compass a reelection.

Enclosed I send for your perusal a letter from my friend Cass. Its perusal may interest you. I deeply regret to learn the death of Daphne—*Bella, I mean*—but am truly happy to know that you have hope in her death. . . . The court-martial is still in session. With warmest love to you, my dear father and dear mother, and tenderest kisses for my precious little daughter, I am ever

Your affectionate son,
Charles C. Jones, Jr.

Rev. John Jones *to* Rev. *and* Mrs. C. C. Jones[t]

Rome, *Friday,* May 16th, 1862

My dear Brother and Sister,

I was on the point of writing you again when your deeply thrilling letter arrived. We thank God for your safe escape, and deeply sympathize with you in all the painful emotions and peculiar trials connected with a speedy evacuation of your sweet and valuable home, with the painful apprehension that it might soon be a mass of ruins. I wish I had been there to have assisted you, although you had the best of sons and the trustiest of servants.

And truly do we sympathize with you in the loss by death of so many of your valued servants; truly you have been afflicted. The dying struggles of poor Wally I shall never forget, and shall ever believe that he found pardon and acceptance through a precious Saviour. Did Joe have a good hope for himself? I had a serious talk with him in the woods some six weeks before leaving Liberty.

What an anxious time we now have! Our dear son passed through a terrible skirmish on the 16th of April. He was at Yorktown, greatly exposed in the trenches, sometimes in mud and water to the knees for twenty-four hours, and not a blanket! Every day we expect to hear of a bloody battle near Richmond, and know not when I may be summoned to Virginia. One of my near neighbors lost a gallant son, colonel of the 10th Virginia Regiment, on the 8th inst. at the victory of McDowell under Stonewall Jackson. He was a noble Christian man not quite twenty-nine years old. His parents moved from Virginia to Rome two years since.

Surely our affairs look gloomy. Today we observed in our church as a day of prayer in response to the President's call. Oh, that our Father may hear the prayers that have ascended today from so many anxious hearts! Our condition is not safe here. The news today—and said to be reliable—is that the Yankees are in twelve miles of Chattanooga. If Chattanooga is taken, it is thought Rome will soon be in the hands of the enemy. Henry has just written me suggesting that I ought to be in Liberty for the safety of our servants. What do you think? I would like to come immediately, but am so anxious about Dunwody lest a call should come to summon me to him. I may make a short visit in ten or fifteen days to Liberty. Do write me if you think it necessary.

I am truly thankful to Brother Charles and Brother Buttolph for mentioning to me about the opportunity of selling my cotton, and to Brother Charles for writing to Mr. Gué. Mr. Gué has just written to me and mentioned Brother Charles's letter, and says he will give—or has been authorized to give—twenty-one cents for all of my cotton. Will Brother Charles and Brother Buttolph be kind enough to attend to this sale for me? I will write Mr. Gué tomorrow and request him to inform yourself or Brother Buttolph when he will come out and weigh and settle for the cotton, and give time to have it hauled to No. 3 depot. Will yourself or Brother Buttolph be kind enough to receive the money and keep it for me until you hear from me? It is very possible I may soon come down. I will also write Mr. John L. Mallard, so that you and Brother Buttolph will have as little trouble as possible.

My dear Janey and little boys unite with me in best love to you both and the dear little baby and our dear relatives and their little ones. Do write if possible a line by return mail. Our hearts are very heavy, and we have no relative with us. A recent letter reports all well in Marietta.

Your affectionate brother,
John Jones.

Rev. *and* Mrs. C. C. Jones *to* Lt. Charles C. Jones, Jr.[g]

Montevideo, *Thursday*, May 22nd, 1862

My dear Son,

We were happy to hear of your safe arrival after your short visit, which was so refreshing to us all, and that the election in your company is satisfactory, and consequently there will be no necessity for a transfer of service either to Virginia or to Tennessee. . . . We heard from Little Sister on Monday. Daughter says she is as well and as happy as possible. It was a wise arrangement of Mother's to take her up to Walthourville and wean her at once, for Peggy is just coming out from an attack of the real simon-pure measles.

We removed home on Monday after a delightful visit at Arcadia of three weeks. I believe this is the best way for relatives to visit—go and spend two or three weeks together, old and young, bond and free, and brighten and tighten up all the cords of affection. Real *family* friends are the friends after all.

Montevideo looks beautifully—all day long vocal with the sweet voices of nature bursting from every tree and cover, the little squirrels playing about, the lawn lighted aslant by the evening sun spread with green and covered with sheep and calves and poultry, and Mother's garden looking as if a rainbow had been broken and showered down and its beautiful and varied fragments had caught on all the plants and shrubbery. It is a beautiful world after all, and as Bishop Heber expresses it in his missionary hymn, "Man is only vile."

The plantation is still a hospital. Near twenty cases of sickness, all connected with measles. Better today. And we trust God will give us our wonted health in a short time. . . . We are trying to get up to the Sand Hills this week, but cannot tell if we shall accomplish it: so much sickness. Mother does not wish Dr. Parsons to send out the work, for in that case she cannot return nor have it altered if it does not suit. She will try and come down so soon as we move to Walthourville. The Lord be with and bless you, my dear son, is the daily prayer of

Your affectionate parents,
C. C. and M. Jones.

Lt. Charles C. Jones, Jr., *to* Rev. *and* Mrs. C. C. Jones[t]
Savannah, *Thursday,* May 22nd, 1862
My dear Father and Mother,

I scarcely know whether to direct this note to Montevideo or to Walthourville. All, however, that I desire to do is to assure you, my beloved parents, of my constant love and remembrance.

We have nothing of interest today by telegraph, and the enemy appears to be quiet in the river. Indications seem to point to Charleston as a place of early attack. In that event I presume we will be ordered to South Carolina.

I have just this morning received a check from Mr. Anderson for $1131.41. The session of our court today was so protracted that I did not have an opportunity for paying the bills, but I will endeavor to do so tomorrow, and will then forward account, receipts, etc.

Tomorrow morning we enter upon the consideration of a case involving life and death. The responsibility of a judge advocate under such circumstances is by no means trivial. Do kiss my little daughter for me when you see her. And believe me ever, my dear parents, with warmest love,

Your affectionate son,
Charles C. Jones, Jr.

REV. C. C. JONES *to* LT. CHARLES C. JONES, JR.ᵍ

Walthourville, *Wednesday,* May 28th, 1862

My dear Son,

Enclosed is the note for the bank, signed as requested. I would be glad if you would get a certificate of deposit of the amount you have had placed to my credit in the state bank from the cashier, subject to my check, and send it to me.

Am obliged to you for the memorandum of accounts paid and Mr. Anderson's account current. All right, I think. The memorandum of the investments you have made of Dr. Martin's payment to you of $6778 I will carefully file away with the memorandum of the evidences of your property previously sent me. Your investments, in my opinion, are as good as could be made. If our revolution fails, everything of value in property fails.

Daughter wrote you for me yesterday. We sent for Dr. Stevens this morning to see Little Sister, and he thinks Mother is doing all that is necessary to be done, and that she is getting along very well. She has not slept well for two nights, and has had the fever which accompanies measles; but this morning she plays and laughs, the fever has abated, and the crisis seems to be passing away. It appears to be a genuine attack of measles.

Your sister is not very well today, but is up as usual. Rest pretty well. Much suffering on some plantations, Dr. Stevens tells me, from measles, whooping cough, and dysentery (like cholera), and a tendency to this latter disease more or less in different places. Stepney was ill with convulsions Saturday night last; is better and up. We hope our sickness is abating. Some lingering cases.

Came up for the summer here on Monday the 26th. . . . Hope to get to work now. Tom is unpacking a few cases of books in the nice study Daughter has given me, and Little Daughter is superintending his operations.

James is just in with the morning's *News.* Great and good news from that great and good General Stonewall Jackson. The rout has fallen on the right head this time: Banks. May it be the prelude of what the Lord will do for us at Corinth and at Richmond! If not, collect armies and try it again. Reverses do not indicate in struggles like ours God's final decree concerning our cause; they are often the means He institutes to insure us success. All unite, my dear son, in much love to you. Our respects to Captain Claghorn.

From your ever affectionate father,
C. C. Jones.

If you are passing by the *Morning News,* please order my triweekly sent to *Walthourville.*

LT. CHARLES C. JONES, JR., *to* REV. C. C. JONES[g]

Savannah, *Wednesday,* May 28th, 1862

My dear Father,

I am just favored with your very kind letter of today, and cannot tell you how thankful I am to hear that my dear little daughter is so much better. Since this morning, when I received Sister's letter, I have had nothing but fearful apprehension and ceaseless anxiety; but your welcome assurances of the fact that Mary Ruth is so much better, that she "plays and laughs," and that "she is getting along very well," fills my heart with joy, and gives me the perfect antithesis in feeling to the depression from which I have been suffering. Well do I know how tenderly she will be nursed, and my heart goes out in thankfulness to you both, my dear parents, for your great kindness. . . . Am glad to know that the sickness at Montevideo is abating, and trust that all disease may soon be rebuked.

The enclosed renewal note has been received, and will, D.V., be attended to tomorrow morning. I will endeavor to have it extended until January next so as to avoid the necessity of a renewal every ninety days. The amount which I will deposit to your credit, subject to check, in the Bank State of Georgia at the same time will be $744.53. Besides this amount I will have in hand three hundred dollars to be sent out in current funds by first suitable opportunity, in accordance with your wishes. I will also in the morning attend to the transfer of direction of *Morning News.*

Had a sight of the enemy this morning. Two steamers and one schooner came up the river so near the city that with an ordinary spyglass the stripes (which Butler says we will be made to feel, even if we do not respect the stars) of the United States flag could be distinctly seen. They were careful enough, however, to keep out of range of our batteries. I took a good look at the rascals from the window of the room in which our court-martial is convened, just over Claghorn & Cunningham's store. Reconnoitering, I presume, although the precise character of their mission has not yet transpired.

We have now at the end of the Bay a battery of four guns—two eight-inch columbiads and two long thirty-two-pounder guns; and just to the south of the gasworks, on the brow of the hill, occupying a part of the site of old Fort Wayne, two more guns—eight-inch columbiads. These all have a direct range down the river. These batteries are to be reinforced by some four or six more eight-inch howitzers, I believe, and will form a very valuable addition to the immediate defenses of the city. Thus from the city to Mackay's Point, where St. Augustine Creek enters the Savannah, every available point will present its armament ready to oppose the approach of the enemy by water. On St. Augustine Creek there are two more batteries—one at Causton's Bluff of (I believe) five guns, and a ten- or twelve-gun battery at Thunderbolt. Add to these the battery at Beaulieu and the one at Genesis Point, and you have all our seacoast defenses. I hope in the hour of peril that we will not be found wanting.

General Mercer has been transferred to and put in command of Charleston. General Ripley has been ordered elsewhere. Too much drinking is said to be a besetting sin of both himself and of General Evans.

We will soon be returning the compliment of the enemy by reconnoitering with our own balloon. A member of our company made it, and will make the ascensions. Everything is ready.

To give you an idea of my labors here upon this court-martial, I may state that I today forwarded to General Pemberton two hundred and forty-seven pages foolscap closely written, all in my own handwriting, containing the records of fourteen cases tried and disposed of by this general court-martial. There are some thirty others upon the docket, and new ones coming in every day, so that I cannot tell when we may look forward to a termination of our labors. It is peculiarly unfortunate that I am compelled to be absent from the company just at this time, as Captain Claghorn has been forced on account of ill health to seek and obtain a furlough of thirty days, thus leaving the company in charge of newly elected officers.

I cannot tell you, Father, how happy I am at thought that my sweet little daughter is so much better. Do kiss her for me. Give warmest love to dear Mother, Sister, Robert, and little Niece and Nephew. And believe me ever

Your affectionate son,
Charles C. Jones, Jr.

I will embrace the first opportunity for coming out. Do let me know if my dear little daughter improves. Am sorry to hear that Sister is unwell, and trust that she may soon feel entirely well, and that you, my dear father, may find rest after your many days of anxiety and fatigue.

I am indebted for your letter tonight to the kindness of Mr. Mills, the assistant postmaster, who very kindly kept the office open to me until nearly eight o'clock, and obtained the letter from the bag which would not otherwise have been distributed before half-past nine o'clock tomorrow morning.

MRS. MARY JONES *to* LT. CHARLES C. JONES, JR.ᵍ

Walthourville, Friday, May 30th, 1862

My dear Son,

I am happy and thankful to say that through the loving-kindness of our Heavenly Father our precious little babe is doing as well as she could in the progress of a painful and distressing disease. It has been a genuine case of measles, and aggravated by the scarlet fever influences remaining in her system. At no stage have I felt that there was anything alarming about her; but we have had Dr. Stevens to call twice and see her—first by your sister and once after we came up—to assure ourselves that all was doing that was right and proper in the case. His only suggestion to what we were already using was *young pine-top tea,* which I have found both agreeable and efficacious. And I would commend it especially to our soldiers in all cases of colds, measles, etc. Our dear one is very bright this morning: is up and dressed, playing with her doll; and when her grandpapa came from his study (where he sleeps during her sickness) to bid her good morning, with one little hand she struck him with her baby, and pinched him with the other, and then laughed at the saucy performance! Your brother thought a genuine attack of measles would tend to eradicate the old disease from her system, and I trust it will prove so, in God's mercy.

By a letter received yesterday from your brother, dear little Stanhope was very ill with dysentery. Slightly better when he wrote, but we are very anxious about him, and trust he may be spared to his parents and to us. He is a noble little boy, and wound himself closely around our hearts. . . .

I sympathize deeply with the condition of your company at this perilous juncture, but believe under all circumstances they do good service in their country's cause.

I have a subject of interest on my mind which I wish to mention without delay, although very much hurried now. You know the Halifax brig (after which the enemy invaded our river) was sunk at Mr. Busby's landing. *Captain Thomson* is removing her ropes, etc., etc., and I am told pronounces her a staunch, well-built vessel. Only her upper works were burnt, and she floats at every high tide. Why could we not use her for our coast defense —give her a coat of iron, a lining of cotton bales, a boarding prow, a strong engine, a few big guns; man her with brave hearts; and let her go forth from our quiet little stream (where it seems to me this might be done as well as elsewhere) to make her mark upon our insolent foes? Do, my son, if you think anything can be done to use this vessel for the purpose, speak of the matter to the proper authorities. I am convinced she could be made useful in a short time. Your Uncle Henry expects to go to Milledgeville next week on a visit to the governor, and promises that he will name the subject to him. It would do no harm to have the brig examined. Man, woman, and child in our Confederacy must be up and doing for our beloved country.

With sweetest kisses from your baby, and our united love,

Ever, my beloved child, your affectionate mother,

Mary Jones.

Thanks for the soap, which came safely and is very good—and a bountiful supply.

Mrs. Mary Jones *to* Lt. Charles C. Jones, Jr.[g]

Walthourville, *Sunday,* June 1st, 1862

My very dear Son,

Major Winn has just kindly sent over to say that he expected to see you in the morning, and would take any communication about your precious little one; and I employ a few of the closing moments of this calm and holy day to gladden your heart with the assurance of her continued improvement. She was so well and bright this afternoon that I left her to your sister's care and heard Robert's sermon, an excellent one from Psalm 104:34—"My meditation of Him shall be sweet." The measles eruption is passing off, but the dear little one suffers from small boils over her head and face, which disfigure her completely. But I can but hope, as your brother anticipated, it will eventuate in her permanent benefit. She is cheerful, and her appetite keeps up. She lives in my arms, but amuses herself with the children, who caress her in the tenderest manner. You may rest assured I shall write you of the least change.

Father, Sister, Brother all unite in tenderest love to you, with many kisses from your precious child, now sweetly sleeping in her crib after having enjoyed a warm bath. God bless you, my dear son! May your meditation of Him be sweet!

Ever your affectionate mother,
Mary Jones.

Rev. C. C. Jones *to* Lt. Charles C. Jones, Jr.[g]
Walthourville, Monday, June 2nd, 1862
My dear Son,

Major Winn very politely sent over and gave us the opportunity of writing a line by him which you were to receive in the courtroom at ten this morning. Your dear little daughter had a warm fever during the night, and of course her rest much disturbed; but Mother does not think that she has any fever now, and that we must expect these fluctuations in the disease when it is passing off. The eruption is subsiding. She will not let her grandmother pass her, and almost lives in her arms, and scolds anybody who offers to take her. She holds her porcelain baby carefully which her Aunt Vallie sent, and is much pleased with it. She pulled off my spectacles just now, and gave them up rather reluctantly. She tries to keep up her spirits, and answer caresses with smiles. It is wonderful how she has stood the attack: is no cry-baby with it at all. The eruption over her face and head has been abundant and large, like cat-boils. Mother has taken off her cap and part of her flannel on account of the heat. We hope she will begin to improve. She has fallen away in flesh and strength, but not so much as you would have supposed. We will keep you advised of her state.

We lost another infant on Friday: effect of measles. Patience's last—little Marcia. The first she and Porter have ever lost. Some lingering cases yet.

The papers are just in. We have cause of gratitude to God for the manifest indications of His returning favor. Great has been His blessing upon His servant General Stonewall Jackson. That pious man and able commander has executed one of the most brilliant passages at arms during the war. Every person who has an interest at a throne of grace should be constantly there for our brave Army of the Potomac now in the heat of *the great battle,* perhaps, of the revolution—at least, so far. The Lord be merciful to us and grant us this victory! *Banky* is here; came last week. Says he left the army in excellent condition and in fine spirits, ready for the enemy. Then there is the army of Corinth; by a short notice in the papers of Generals Price and

Van Dorn being ordered to get between the enemy and the river, a battle must be in progress there. My faith is unshaken. Sinners as we are, yet humbly trusting in a just cause and in a just and merciful God, we may confidently hope that He will give us a happy issue.

Mother is much worn by loss of sleep and confinement, but is up, and went to church once yesterday. Daughter stayed with Baby. She is now writing your brother. We feel very uneasy about *little Stanhope*. He was ill with an affection of the bowels last week, and Joe had called in Dr. Ford.

All your boxes came safely and are carefully put away. Mother thanks you for the tea, and says it must be fine to be put up in such nice canisters, and says when Baby gets better she is coming down to see you—and *Dr. Parsons!* The note and your deposit, etc., is all exactly right. All unite in much love to you. And a kiss from your daughter.

Your ever affectionate father,
C. C. Jones.

2 P.M. Your dear little daughter is in her crib, enjoying a sweet sleep.

Lt. Charles C. Jones, Jr., *to* Rev. C. C. Jones[g]

Savannah, Tuesday, June 3rd, 1862
Just before dark

My very dear Father,

It is with great pleasure and thankfulness that I acknowledge the receipt of your very kind letter of yesterday, giving me such a detailed account and so many happy remembrances of my dear little daughter. During the dark hours of this stormy day I have often thought of her and of you all, and have hoped that the change of temperature would not affect her unfavorably. I am this afternoon literally tired out. During the entire day I have been confined to the courtroom with an intermission of scarce half an hour for dinner, having conducted two cases involving life and death, and completed the entire record in them both.

From a private source—how reliable I am unable to say—we have an intimation of the evacuation of Corinth by our forces, who are reported to have fallen back some forty miles. With such generals as Beauregard, Bragg, Price, Van Dorn, and others in command, there must be good cause for the movement; but I confess the intelligence has excited in me no little surprise. Not a word from Richmond, or from that gallant Christian warrior Stonewall Jackson. We are told that the enemy last night made several demonstrations on the South Carolina islands in the vicinity of Charleston. More activity is manifested by the Lincolnites in our immediate vicinity just now than has been exhibited for some time past. I would not be surprised if we are called upon almost any day to meet our foes in a desperate struggle. May we have strength from above in the hour of contest!

I sincerely trust that my dear little daughter may soon be restored to perfect health, and that my dear mother will not suffer from all her kindest care and constant watchings over Mary Ruth. I regret to know that Brother's little boy is so unwell. Will try and write him tonight, and sincerely hope that all may yet be well. When you see Patience, do tell her that I sympathize with her in her recent affliction. With warmest love to all, and many kisses for my precious little daughter, I am ever, my dear father,

Your affectionate son,
Charles C. Jones, Jr.

Rev. C. C. Jones *to* Lt. Charles C. Jones, Jr.[g]

Walthourville, *Wednesday,* June 4th, 1862

My dear Son,

We are happy to hear from you this morning. When will your court be over? It seems to be without end, because transgressions will never cease. You should take a ride on Yorick every day for exercise.

Your dear baby had a pretty good night's rest, and we hope the excitement in her system is passing away. Mother rubbed her all over this morning with *fat bacon* and then gave her a *warm bath;* and she has just waked up after a nap of an hour and a half in which she slept sweetly. She is now (12 M.) taking her butter and hominy, and looks as sober as a judge with her bib on, but cannot repress her smiles when her grandmother speaks to her. The eruption is abundant on her head and face, and it seems she will peel off as in scarlet fever. Little Daughter and Charlie are very fond of her, and she kisses them, and is greatly pleased with their attentions. I now hear her little voice talking to her grandmother: "Da, da, da."

Rode with Robert to the depot to hear the news. The great battle at Richmond yet to come off! Beauregard fallen back! Hope Alexander's statement that it leaves the enemy in possession of the Charleston & Memphis Railroad from Memphis to Chattanooga, and gives him Memphis and Fort Pillow, cannot be true. If true, then the Mississippi is gone from the Ohio to the Gulf, and troops may be forwarded to any point inland whether waters be high or low! General Lee's address not published. Glad of the stand he takes. The truth is, the war has just opened in earnest. All heretofore has been preliminary. We now realize all our enemy designs, and learn his inmost feelings towards us. Butler's proclamation gives us the strength of fifty thousand men. It is victory and honor and independence or defeat and abject humiliation and servitude. I hope General Mercer will be adequate to the position he now holds, and that Charleston will never be surrendered, and that Lawton will fulfill his declaration to hold Savannah to the last extremity. What is to be gained by surrender or evacuation? Let New Orleans speak. If it pleases God to enable us to repulse the enemy in these two cities and in Richmond, it will be a mercy that will produce a mighty effect on the country. If all *fall,* then fall back and renew the contest. Subjugation and submission on the part of the South will still be afar off.

We have been blest with a copious and timely rain: much needed. Another little one has been taken from us—Patience's *grandchild,* Beck's little infant boy. Was well on Saturday when I saw it; taken with fever Sunday evening, and died the same night. Do not know what could have been the cause. This makes the *eighth:* four adults and four infants. May we be made to know why these afflictions are sent, and be sanctified under them! We have prayed that we may fall into the hands of God and not of man, and He may thus be answering our prayer. Mother and Daughter and Robert all unite in much love to you. Hope you will write your brother. No letter from him today.

Your ever affectionate father,
C. C. Jones.

Little Sister is taking an airing in her carriage in the upstairs entry, and seems to enjoy it. 1 P.M.

REV. C. C. JONES *to* LT. CHARLES C. JONES, JR.ᵍ

Walthourville, *Friday,* June 6th, 1862

My dear Son,

Your very interesting favor of yesterday is in by the morning's mail, and I write today because if we defer until tomorrow you will not hear from your dear child until Monday. We still think she is improving, but the eruption on her little head is great and continuous; one pimple does not go before another comes, and they are little boils. And her patience and quiet under all are remarkable. For the first time in two weeks Mother has allowed her to go downstairs; and when her straw bonnet was put on and she understood she was to go out, her countenance exhibited the sincerest delight; neither did she want to come up again. We are looking every day to see the eruption pass off. You must come and see her when you can.

I agree with you fully that our country should not be left to the ravages of the enemy. If government meditates invasion, let a force be kept in the Southwest sufficient to keep the enemy in check, and not allow him to possess and fortify the entire valley of the Mississippi. We private citizens can only conjecture and speculate; we are called upon to exercise patience and to pray for our country. Am sorry for our choice troops to be withdrawn from the coast. Is government going to weaken our defense and play the same game of evacuation or shameful surrender of Charleston and Savannah as of other places? We are weak enough—and our commanders appear to be imbecile enough—as we are.

The condition of things down the Savannah River is simply ridiculous: the enemy's boats *within* our obstructions, and chasing our boy-commanders in open day. They must have a contempt for such management. The next thing we hear will be that they have removed every obstruction, and not a soul in the city or on the river knew when they did it! It is difficult to restrain one's feelings at so much neglect when so many interests are at stake. If I had to go to the wars, I should like to go with such fine troops, but not under an untried commander, and one (as far as known) who has made anything but a favorable impression on the public. But I must not speak evil of dignitaries.

All unite in much love to you, with kisses from the baby, who is downstairs. As ever,

Your affectionate father,
C. C. Jones.

Lt. Charles C. Jones, Jr., *to* Rev. C. C. Jones[w]

Savannah, *Saturday,* June 7th, 1862

My dear Father,

I am under many obligations to you for your last kind favor, which reached me this morning. It rejoices me to know that my precious little daughter is so much better, and I hope that it will please God soon to restore her to perfect health.

We have an intimation this evening—but as yet lacking confirmation—that the enemy has shelled and captured Chattanooga. If this be true, Cherokee Georgia will soon be threatened if the avowed objects of the Lincolnites are further consummated. I believe that the statement that General Beauregard is on his way to Richmond with ten thousand men is incorrect. General Mercer has returned to Savannah, and is in command here, General Lawton having left for Richmond last night. General Smith is in immediate command at Charleston. General Pemberton still remains in command of the Department of South Carolina and Georgia.

I have it from good authority that General Pemberton has telegraphed to the department that in consequence of the withdrawal of such a large portion of the forces from this department, he will be unable to defend both Savannah and Charleston, and submitting which of the two cities shall be evacuated. I trust this is not true. We have already become a laughingstock from our continued and in many instances unwarranted abandonment of important points. It seems to me that all that is necessary to cause an evacuation of a chosen position on our part is the simple fact that it may be hazardous to hold it, or that in the event of its being vigorously attacked by the enemy it may be problematical whether or not a defense under an imagined condition of adverse circumstances could be successfully maintained. Thus it is that we have time and again lost ground without reason. Thus it is that by our own culpable timidity the enemy is induced to attempt enterprises and achieve plans which would not but for our own lack of determination have been seriously undertaken. Thus is the moral tone of our army weakened, the expectations of our countrymen disappointed; and thus the great cause of national honor and national reputation suffers to an unpardonable extent. The time long since has come for desperate enterprises and desperate defenses. It came with the very inception of our present difficulties, when without an army, without a navy, without the appliances of modern warfare we took up arms against a people more than twice as numerous as our own, and with every resource on sea and land to aid them in the unequal contest. Our leaders have in very many instances failed to regard our struggle in its true light, and as a natural and necessary consequence we have lost ground.

We have a report that Stonewall Jackson has met and routed the enemy again at Strasburg under command of General Shields of Mexican notoriety.

George goes out on Monday morning, and to his carriage I commit this letter and the enclosed three hundred dollars, which you desired me to retain and send out by earliest opportunity. Of the balance of the amount received from Mr. Anderson I have already rendered you an account.

I trust, my dear father, that you are feeling better, and that we may all be mercifully spared to hail the return of that day when peace shall again spread her white wings over a land smiling in happiness, in plenty, rejoicing in the assurances of honor vindicated, of national existence and national repose firmly established, confident in the hope of a great and of a good future when we shall indeed be that happy people whose God is the Lord. With warmest love to all, I am ever

Your affectionate son,
Charles C. Jones, Jr.

REV. C. C. JONES *to* LT. CHARLES C. JONES, JR.[g]

Walthourville, Sunday, June 8th, 1862

My dear Son,

As I promised to let you know how your dear little daughter was from time to time, I write today (Sabbath) to say that she was taken with an affection of the bowels yesterday which continued until eleven o'clock last night, when it was checked until five o'clock this morning. It returned, and Dr. Stevens has come and made a prescription which we hope may arrest the affection altogether. The eruption is drying up on her head and person, and renders such an attack unpleasant, and it requires strict attention. She has shrunk in her person a good deal, but her spirits keep up remarkably well, and so far has suffered no pain.

It would afford us great pleasure for you to come out and see her, if it could be done consistently with your engagements. . . . You might come out in the cars in the morning to the Walthourville station, where we will have a buggy in waiting for you, or in any other mode you might choose.

Mother would be glad to have a syringe for *injections for infants*—the common kind, without any pump or India rubber to it. Also a *quart of brandy* for medical purposes. The dear little baby is quietly asleep as I close this note (1 P.M.), but looks languid. All unite in much love to you.

Your affectionate father,
C. C. Jones.

Lt. Charles C. Jones, Jr., *to* Rev. *and* Mrs. C. C. Jones[g]

Savannah, *Monday,* June 9th, 1862

My very dear Father and Mother,

I embrace a moment before retiring to say that I reached the city safely after my most refreshing visit to you, my precious little daughter, and all at home.

The health of my dear little Mary Ruth is ever in my mind, and causes deepest anxiety; but I pray God most earnestly that it may please Him soon to restore her to her accustomed health. I never will be able, my dear parents, to thank you for one tithe of all your great kindness and tender love in this constant care of my motherless infant; but God will reward you, though even your affectionate son cannot.

I trust that Mamie and Charlie will soon be entirely well again.

By the telegraph of today we have the intelligence of another victory by Stonewall Jackson—over Frémont—and an anticipated victory at no distant day over Shields.

It is rumored upon the authority of a gentleman this evening arrived from Florida, whence he came having recently successfully run the blockade with a small steamer, that France has recognized the independence of the Southern Confederacy. He asserts positively that the fact was believed in Havana, and that the news reached that city by steamer *Trent,* arrived in that port the day before he left—namely, the 23rd ult. What degree of credence is to be attached to his statement one cannot judge; it may be, like all of its predecessors on this subject, merely a sensational rumor.

I learn tonight that our battery has been ordered to Causton's Bluff, which will place us within four or five miles of the city. The situation, however, must prove anything else but healthy, exposed as it is directly to the miasmatic influences of the Savannah River and swamp. However, those who are bound must obey. Nothing heard from our detachment in South Carolina.

With warmest love to you both, my dearest parents, many kisses for my precious little daughter, with every prayer and hope for her speedy recovery, and sincere remembrances to Robert, Sister, Mamie, and Charlie, I am ever

Your affectionate son,

Charles C. Jones, Jr.

Rev. John Jones *to* Rev. *and* Mrs. C. C. Jones[t]

Rome, *Tuesday,* June 10th, 1862

My dear Brother and Sister,

Knowing well your anxiety for Dunwody, and supposing as we did for days that he was in the late sanguinary battles near Richmond, I write to say that he is safe, through the tender mercy of God.

The first report that reached Rome represented the 8th as in the battle with other Georgia regiments and as terribly slaughtered. Day after day the reports were unsatisfactory in detail but uniform as to the large number of our killed and wounded. The agony of the past week experienced by my dear Jane and myself was inexpressible; our very bodies became worn and wearied and almost sick. On Friday we felt relieved from some details in which no mention was made of the 8th; and then a dispatch to Macon stated that the 8th was not in either engagement. And yesterday we received a short letter from our dear son from camp, mentioning that a great victory had been won by our troops, but that the 8th Georgia was not in the fight, and that he was in fine health. He gives the reason: the 8th are posted just where the Central Railroad crosses the Chickahominy at Meadow Bridge; their business—a most important one—is to hold that position against the enemy. The battle was fought between the Mechanicsville turnpike and the Williamsburg stage road, and did not reach by a mile or two as far as the position of the 8th, which is in the left wing of our army. Thanks to our merciful Father that there was no call for the 8th in those late battles, which were exceedingly desperate and fatal. I suppose you have read of the gallant charge of our men, and their dear-bought success in storming the batteries of the enemy.

June 11th. I have seen today my good elder and friend Mr. Omberg, just returned from Richmond, having gone there on a short visit to see his son and to accomplish some business. Mr. Omberg saw Dunwody in the camp and reports him in excellent health and spirits. Dunwody never complains, and is uniformly cheerful and buoyant. He has been one of the best campaigners in the army. Except a short recent sojourn in Richmond for rest after the exhausting exposures on the Peninsula, he has never been absent from duty during a year. Surely God has mercifully answered the prayers of his many relatives who remember him without ceasing at a throne of grace. His letters breathe a softened affectionate spirit and a growing acknowledgment of God. Our constant prayer is that the goodness of God may lead him to repentance. He is constantly exposed to death, for we constantly expect the great battle to come off at any day. Mr. Omberg says that we gained a decided advantage over the Federals in the battles of the 31st of May and 1st of June, but that the great battle has yet to be fought. I know you will continue to remember our dear son.

I fully intended a visit to Liberty this week, but had to give it up because of the expected battle before Richmond, not knowing what a day may bring forth, that we may be summoned any day to go to Dunwody. Jane and the little boys join me in best love to you both and Mary, Robert, and the dear little ones. Do write soon to

Your ever affectionate brother,
J. Jones.

P.S. The within rough sketch of the position of our army, and particularly of the 8th Regiment, was made by our little John Carolin from a hasty draft made by a member of the Rome Light Guards (young Black) and sent to his father in this place (Rome). I enclose it, as it may give some idea of the positions of the two armies and the next battlefield.

Lt. Charles C. Jones, Jr., *to* Rev. C. C. Jones[g]

Camp Stonewall Jackson, *Friday,* June 13th, 1862

My dear Father and Mother,

The mails of the past two days have not brought me a letter, and I have passed many anxious moments on account of my dear little daughter. Believing, however, that you would have written me had she not have been improving in health, I have trusted that no news was good news. I pray daily for her, and I hope that it will please God to restore her—and that right early—to her accustomed health.

Our camp is located at Causton's Bluff, just opposite Whitemarsh Island. We are now occupying the ground just vacated by the 47th Georgia Regiment, which, as you have observed by the daily journals, suffered rather severely in the recent engagement on James Island. You cannot imagine how filthy we found everything. The effluvium was horrid, and we have done little else until this morning except police the premises. I am quite confident that much of the ill health of our troops, especially typhoid and fevers of a slow and lingering type, are due to a polluted atmosphere generated by the decaying vegetable and animal matter scattered by the men themselves in the immediate vicinity of their tents, and suffered there to remain and fester in putrid corruption under the influences of a scorching sun. Officers in command cannot be too careful in this particular.

Our section is still in South Carolina, and it is said is attracting much commendation and attention. It was expected that by our rifled gun an action would have been opened today. Read's battery and two regiments infantry have already returned; and I understand that the pledge has been given to Governor Brown that Savannah shall be defended at every hazard, and that at least nine thousand troops shall be kept in its vicinity. Here I can only retail the items of news at second hand. This afternoon I had the battery practiced at shell and solid shot firing, and with very creditable success.

Do kiss my dearest little baby for me. Accept every assurance, my dear parents, of my constant and warmest love for you and for all at home. And believe me ever

Your affectionate son,

Charles C. Jones, Jr.

The mosquitoes are fairly putting out the lamp, and I am covered from ankle to knee with fleas.

Rev. C. C. Jones *to* Lt. Charles C. Jones, Jr.[g]

Walthourville, *Saturday,* June 14th, 1862

My dear Son,

Your two last favors have been received. You have given your new camp a good name. It is a name to inspire the breast of the patriot and nerve the arm of the soldier. Our fine troops have gone to reinforce General Stonewall Jackson; no doubt they will do their duty. By appearances General Pemberton means to hold both *Charleston* and Savannah. He ought so to do—and can do it if he will just go on as he has begun and keep the enemy from *entrenching* on James Island. His first attack badly managed: no reconnaissance, and no support to our brave 47th.

Went to Montevideo yesterday—the reason why you received no letter. A melancholy day. Found *Beck* (Patience's)—that intelligent, fine young woman—*a corpse!* Died about daylight after some ten days' sickness from dysentery consequent upon measles. Dr. Way in daily attendance for a week; says she had pneumonia also, and did his best. A great loss. I never saw her. The message I received was that Mr. Calder had called in Dr. Way and she was mending, which was not true. This, together with the baby's illness, kept me here, and I never knew a word until I went down. This is the seventh case from measles and its consequents, and the *ninth this spring!* It is most affecting and distressing. And the plantation is not over the visitation yet. Little Miley (Beck's sister) is very sick with the same affection, and there is a disposition to it on the place.

Mother has gone down today, from which you may well infer that your dear little daughter is better. The doctor seems to have discharged the case. The affection is checked; her appetite is improving; and she had a fair night's rest last night. But she scolds a good deal more than she has ever done, and it is a sign of a returning sense of her own rights and of a determination to assert them. She will have very little to say to me today. The eruption in the way of little boils here and there (especially about the face and head) continues, but is less a great deal than it has been. We hope she will continue to improve. I called Susan with her and asked her "what I should tell Papa for her"; but she scolded and refused all communication and motioned to withdraw. She was just taking her dinner and stopped to get some water.

Little Daughter has had measles, and is out of bed today for the first time. Lucy, Tenah, Kate, and Elvira—all Daughter's servants but James in the yard —down together with measles. Tenah came out yesterday. Rest still down. We sent down for our cook Kate, and with Flora, Elsie, and Tom are doing very well. . . . Am writing for the mail, and must close. *Lime* is a good disinfecting agent about camps, etc. All unite in much love.

Your ever affectionate father,
C. C. Jones.

Lt. Charles C. Jones, Jr., *to* Rev. *and* Mrs. C. C. Jones[g]

Savannah, *Monday,* June 16th, 1862

My very dear Father and Mother,

I am under great obligations for Father's kind letter of the 14th inst., which relieved me of no little anxiety on account of my precious little daughter. It rejoices me to know that she is so much better, and I thank God for her recovery thus far, and pray that He will restore her fully to her accustomed health. Not a day passes, my dear parents, but brings to my mind and heart a realizing appreciation of the special thanks which I owe to you for your never-tiring care and tender love for my little daughter under the most trying circumstances.

I am shocked and distressed to learn the sad intelligence of the death of Beck, one of the finest and best young women on the place. The hand of God has indeed been most heavily laid upon us, and I am sorry to hear that the progress of disease has not yet been stayed.

Today has been a period of no little anxiety with me. A section of our battery was engaged in the fight on James Island, which has resulted so favorably to our arms. I trust that they have rendered valuable service and suffered no loss. The section numbered thirty-three men, nineteen horses, one Blakely rifled gun, and one twelve-pound howitzer. Everything in the finest order, and the numbers composing the two detachments reliable every way. We will have a good account from them. The day has been unusually propitious for field operations—cool, bracing, and no dust. We should have further particulars tonight. I enclose an extra.

I ought by rights, under ordinary circumstances, to have been in command of that section, and only the peculiar nature of the case prevented. At the time the order was received for the section to move—and that without a moment's delay—Captain Claghorn was absent sick. I was relieved from duty and was in attendance upon general court-martial in Savannah. Lieutenant Wheaton was thus left in command. The order reached camp at night. I knew nothing of it until the section had nearly reached the city en route for Charleston, when I found—as was right and proper under the circumstances—that Lieutenant Askew had been detailed as the officer in charge of the detachments. Although it is all right, I have experienced no little regret that I did not have the opportunity of going in command of the section. It may be, however, that our entire battery may soon have a chance of meeting the enemy, who, although driven back today, if they contemplate a serious demonstration against Charleston will doubtless reinforce themselves and advance again to the attack.

I am happy to know that our defenses on James Island are far more formidable than I had been led to believe. Across the entire island we have entrenchments of strength mounting many siege guns (forty-two-, thirty-two-, twenty-four-, and eighteen-pounders); while at either extremity of our earthworks are protecting forts, located on the streams which respectively wash either side of James Island, mounting considerable batteries containing heavy ten-inch guns and rifle pieces. These forts, it is confidently expected, will be able to resist any advance of the enemy's gunboats. The possession of James Island thus retained by our forces, Charleston may be considered as virtually safe, as I scarcely think an attack will be attempted by way of the harbor—certainly not until the anticipated steel-clad gunboats of the enemy appear upon our coast.

McClellan has, I learn, withdrawn his forces from this side of the Chickahominy. Every day and every account prove more and more forcibly the fact that the recent engagement near Richmond was an important Confederate victory. Its value is enhancing every moment, and I would not be surprised to learn any day—if Stonewall Jackson is sufficiently reinforced, as doubtless he already is—that the boasted modern Napoleon has been compelled to raise the siege of Richmond and consult the immediate safety of the Lincoln capital.

It is difficult to conjecture the cause of Lord Lyons' leaving Washington just at this time. The English fleet is said to be rendezvousing in the vicinity of Fortress Monroe, and the French fleet in New York harbor. A few weeks at farthest will furnish an explanation.

I fear from all that I can learn that General Beaureguard's army is suffering a great deal from sickness. In its present position it appears to be accomplishing little or nothing; and Halleck will hardly pursue, risking the fortunes of a general engagement, when the Mississippi valley is already won.

General Stonewall Jackson is probably awaiting reinforcements. He will not long remain idle. The brigade which General Lawton took with him is one of a thousand, and by God's blessing we may anticipate from their brave deeds results of the most fortunate character.

It appears to me that the Lincoln government is now feeling more than at any previous time the pressure of this war. Although possessed of wonderful resources, it is already a bankrupt government; and a light wind from the wrong quarter may soon send the whole political fabric tumbling about the heads of the misguided race who inaugurated the wretched policy which gave rise to this unholy and most unjust war. The day of retribution, though deferred, must come; and when it does arrive it will be terrible in the extreme. I can imagine no nation with more forbidding prospects in the future than those which look the Lincolnites full in the face. And the most unsatisfactory reflection—if they reflect at all—is that they have themselves made their own destruction sure.

But I fear, my dearest parents, that I tire you, so I will bid you good night, begging that you will kiss my precious little daughter for me. Assure Sister, Robert, and little Niece and Nephew of my kind remembrances. And believe me ever, with warmest love,

Your ever affectionate son,
Charles C. Jones, Jr.

Our court-martial resumed its session in Savannah this morning.

REV. C. C. JONES *to* LT. CHARLES C. JONES, JR.[g]

Walthourville, *Monday,* June 16th, 1862

My dear Son,

Your dear little one did not spend a good day yesterday, nor a good night last night: did not sleep well. She had two large evacuations yesterday—one in the morning, the other in the evening—which exhausted her a good deal;

and the emaciation continues. Called in the doctor again. He lanced her gums for her eyeteeth, which she bore quietly, the operation seeming to be a relief. Mother says if it were not for removing her so far from the doctor and yourself she would take her down to the Island and spend two or three weeks there for the salt-bathing and for the benefit of the change. She intends using a salt bath here. We feel very much concerned for the issue of her complaint, following a severe attack of measles and connected with teething, and in the debilitating heat of summer. We must use every means, and ask a blessing upon them and hope for it.

Your mother left her yesterday morning with your sister and went to church. Your Uncle Henry had me to baptize his last fine infant, five months old. . . . In the evening at family worship we sung in remembrance of you "Come, My Redeemer, Come." And Mother said: "My dear child, I wonder what religious privileges he has enjoyed today."

3 P.M. Our dear baby continues about the same. Is *feeble* today; has little or no appetite. We will write you every day, and should you not hear from us, conclude she is as usual. But her sickness is of such a nature that she might not survive a severe attack of it but a few hours.

Little Daughter has got through the measles wonderfully well, and all the women servants of Daughter's household are up today, all having had the measles *strongly*. We all unite in much love to you. Take care of yourself in this trying northeaster.

> Your ever affectionate father,
> C. C. Jones.

Lt. Charles C. Jones, Jr., *to* Rev. C. C. Jones[g]

Savannah, *Tuesday,* June 17th, 1862

My dear Father,

It is with deep sorrow that I learn through your kind letter of yesterday, this morning received, that my precious little daughter is not as well as when you last wrote. The only consolation I have in my absence from her is that she is in the tender care of you and of dear Mother, and that in your love and kindest treatment she will have the benefit of all that man can do. The issue is with the Father of All Mercies, and I can only pray Him in goodness—if it be His will—to spare her precious life and restore her to many days of happiness and of usefulness. Is there anything in the way of medical advice which I can procure for her here? Or is there anything else I can do to serve you and her in any particular?

I am glad to hear that Sister's little ones and the servants have recovered so soon from the measles. The present attacks of sickness and the unusual prevalence of disease are directly to be referred to the existence of this terrible war.

I feel, this blustering day, for our troops without covering, and often with but scant food, upon the soaked earth; and especially for the section of our battery on James Island. As yet we have no definite intelligence from those detachments, but shall probably know more by the Charleston papers which reach us this afternoon. I am inclined to believe that Captain Claghorn is with that section. No telegraphic reports of any character today. It is thought that the enemy will soon renew the attack on James Island. Hoping, my dear parents, that all will yet be well, I am, with warmest love to you both and to all, and with many kisses for Daughter,

Your ever affectionate son,
Charles C. Jones, Jr.

Mrs. Mary Jones *to* Lt. Charles C. Jones, Jr.[g]

Walthourville, *Tuesday,* June 17th, 1862

My dear Son,

Our precious little babe rested more comfortably last night, and I hope the diarrhea has been arrested; but she continues exceedingly feeble, and suffers from a total loss of appetite. Although we try every imaginable kind of nourishment, she shakes her little head and puts it away with both hands. During the day she is most quiet and patient, often amused with the children. The doctor has commenced giving her tonics, and I would feel encouraged if I could only see the emaciation arrested and a little craving for food.

No one knows how much my heart is bound up in this precious child. It is nearly one year since I received her as a sacred legacy from her dying sainted mother. In that brief period of alternate hope and fear for the young life which I trust I have sought to cherish in every way, she has been to me a precious little comfort, rewarding every care with the affection of a loving little heart. I have often felt that my life was perhaps too much bound up in the life of this little one; and if my Heavenly Father should see fit to remove her from my arms to His own bosom, it would be a crushing blow. . . .

Little Mary Jones has recovered well from the measles. Charlie is just taking them, we think. And all your sister's servants who were taken down at the same time are all out at their accustomed duties. The weather continues very cool and damp. I am sighing for the warm sunshine, that I might take my dear little baby into the fresh air. If it were not for removing her from you so far, and from the care of Dr. Stevens, in whose skill we have confidence, I would take her immediately to the Island for change of atmosphere and salt-bathing, which I feel assured would do her good. Last night I put her into a bath of warm salt and water with beneficial effect.

The bell rings for dinner, and I must close. Be sure and send your clothes as soon as they are cut. Father, Sister, and Robert unite with me in best love to you. Kisses from the children, especially from your own little Mary Ruth. God bless and preserve you, my dear son!

Ever your affectionate mother,
Mary Jones.

Rev. C. C. Jones *to* Lt. Charles C. Jones, Jr.⁸

Walthourville, *Wednesday,* June 18th, 1862

My dear Son,

Your dear baby was very feeble all day yesterday, as Mother wrote you. The doctor is doing his best, and Mother is calling all her experience into practice, and we hope on the whole the little sufferer is no worse today. You would scarcely know her pale and emaciated countenance and form—not above half her size in full health. Understands everything and appreciates all you do for her, but too languid to enjoy anything.

Mother watched with her until four this morning, when I relieved her that she might get some sleep. When Baby woke, she was surprised to see me lying in Mother's place, and did her best to look around me to find her grandmother. She has been very quiet all the morning. The doctor thinks she is no worse, and if we only could get her to eat something we should feel better. But she seems to relish nothing, and Mother has to give her what she thinks best for her regularly.

The only thing we need and which we cannot get out here is some *brandy.* We use it as an external stimulant; and if you could send us a quart bottle of it, care of Mr. Joseph Miller, No. 4, we would be glad to get it. The doctor recommended sponging the baby in whiskey; your mother told him she had been applying the burnt brandy and cloves, and he said it was just as good.

Everybody is interested in the dear child, and everything will be done for her that can be done. And if anything is needed, will let you know. I pray the Lord to spare us the great affliction of her loss, if it be His holy will. Our hearts are very full at times on her account and on yours.

Your two last interesting favors came this morning. The James Island battle was gallant. That is the way: give the wicked enemy no time nor place to entrench; push him everywhere, anyhow. Hope South Carolina will come out yet. A repulse at Charleston and Savannah would be a great blessing. Your not being with your section of your battery on James Island was wholly providential, and so you must consider it. What does General Mercer want with a thousand Negroes? Where is he going to fortify? On a heavy scale, it would seem. The enemy begins to taste a little of the practicability of subjugation by *invasion. We* cannot invade—beyond freeing the border states. The war is now beginning in reality with the Lincolnites. I hope they will find the coveted prize too large for their grasp. We can get along—if true to ourselves—without England or France to help us. My opinion is, McClellan will not fight at Richmond, but siege it out and environ the city with impregnable lines and force General Lee *to evacuate!* This is his design. Will our generals suffer themselves to be whipped in this way? And what a blow the loss of the city would be to us! McClellan is deceiving them with feints— nothing more. . . . All unite in much love to you. As ever,

Your affectionate father,

C. C. Jones.

LT. CHARLES C. JONES, JR., *to* REV. C. C. JONES^g

Savannah, *Friday,* June 20th, 1862

My dear Father,

I am in receipt of your kind favor of yesterday, and cannot express the deepest anxiety which I feel on account of the continued illness of my precious little daughter. It pains me to the bottom of my heart to know that she still continues to be so feeble, and manifests as yet no signs of returning health and appetite; and it costs me many an hour of sincerest regret that I am unable to be with her in this her protracted and severe sickness. I can only pray —and that earnestly and repeatedly—to God that He would bless all the tenderest care and attentions of you, my dear father and mother, to her full and speedy recovery. Has her bowel affection been completely checked? Is there anything in the way of food in Savannah or elsewhere to be procured that you think will tempt her appetite? I send by express one gallon best brandy, which I trust will reach you in safety and without delay. It is directed to you, care of Mr. Miller.

Philo Neely has been here with her children for the past day. She came down to pay her husband a visit, who is connected with the Oglethorpe Siege Artillery stationed at the battery at the foot of the Bay. She desires her special remembrance to you both, my dear parents, and sends many kisses for Mary Ruth.

Our recent victory on James Island appears to increase rather than diminish in its results. I understand today that in their retreat not a few of the Lincolnites were drowned in crossing an intervening creek. Some were also shot in the water. The genuine Yankee was scarcely seen among the dead— mostly foreigners, the Scotch features predominating. Some of the oldest families in Charleston suffered in that battle. That is a misfortune which we have had to encounter during the entire course of this war: our best men are in the field, while we meet in the unequal contest hordes of mercenaries, not one in ten of whom belongs to the race entailing the present miseries, and upon which the avenging rod should descend. Our detachment still remains on James Island. The health of the men is pretty good. Captain Claghorn is expected in this city this afternoon. He has been suffering a great deal of late from dyspepsia, and I understand has had no little sickness in his family at Athens.

If we may credit the reports, a rupture between the U.S. and England appears to be imminent; but I have no question but that the ingenuity of Seward and the cringing policy of that degraded nation will readily afford some apology which, while it disgraces in the eyes of the world, will prevent anybody from "being hurt." For one I desire to see no foreign intervention, and fully concur with you in the conviction that if we are only true to ourselves we will be able, with the blessing of Heaven, to whip our own battles and secure our own freedom. That issue, obtained under such circumstances, will be far more valuable than if secured by the assistance of others. Our national existence will be all the more firm, and the satisfaction and honest pride of victory far greater.

I regret to learn that General Joseph E. Johnston is suffering much from his wound. He has been spitting blood, and a portion of his right lung is involved; but his recovery is anticipated. It is said that G. W. Smith, one of our good generals, is suffering from a stroke of paralysis, which—for the present, at least—incapacitates him from the discharge of active duties.

General Mercer desires the thousand hands, I believe, to strengthen our fortifications on the river and to dam around one or two of the batteries to keep the water out. Our troops on those river battalions are already experiencing the ill effects of their unwholesome locations. . . . With warmest love to you both, my dearest parents, and to all at home, and with tenderest kisses for my precious little daughter, and every hope and prayer for her restoration to health, I am ever

Your affectionate son,
Charles C. Jones, Jr.

MRS. MARY JONES *to* LT. CHARLES C. JONES, JR.[g]

Walthourville, *Friday,* June 20th, 1862

My dear Son,

Through God's mercy I am enabled to say that our precious little one is decidedly better today than she has been since her sickness. So ill has she been that I knew she could not be with us long if the disease was not arrested. Today she notices and will take her boiled milk without constraint. She is still upon the list of topers—a small portion of burnt brandy being necessary three or four times a day. Dr. Stevens has been very attentive in her case, and he is an excellent family physician.

Your father has not been able to leave her until today. He went down to Montevideo; and soon after breakfast we were gratified by the arrival of Sister Susan and Mr. Buttolph to spend the day with us. I have just left them a moment to send you this line. Jimmie and Willie have recovered finely from measles, and so has Little Daughter; but Charlie coughs dreadfully, and they are not fully developed with him. I am uneasy until they do appear. The servants all doing well up here.

Your sister and aunt, Robert and Mr. Buttolph unite with me in best love to you, with sweetest kisses from your own little daughter. We shall look with special interest for tidings of the section of your battery. Daily I implore the deliverance and blessing of Jehovah upon my beloved and suffering country. And I have faith to believe when His wise and just purposes are accomplished —although they may be through great and merited sufferings—that He will own and establish us a free and independent nation.

Ever your affectionate mother,
Mary Jones.

LT. CHARLES C. JONES, JR., *to* MRS. MARY JONES[w]

Savannah, *Saturday,* June 21st, 1862

My very dear Mother,

I cannot express my happiness upon the receipt of your kind letter of yesterday to find that my precious little daughter is so decidedly better. May God in mercy continue the good work of her restoration to perfect health!

During her protracted illness I have often feared, my dear mother, that your continued and unceasing watchings, and the confinement in the sick chamber, united with your tenderest anxieties on her account, must have affected your own health and strength. I trust, however, that you may in her improved health find comfort and rest, and that the nights of apprehension and the days of uneasiness and of hourly ministrations to the every want of the little sufferer may be soon succeeded by periods of quiet with all their refreshing influences. I never will be able to express one moiety of the thanks which I owe to you for all your greatest kindnesses.

Is there any whooping cough on the Sand Hills? I trust not, for if Mary Ruth in her enfeebled state should contract that disease I fear that she would not possess physical strength sufficient to withstand its exhausting effects. As I write, a poor little child not two years old in an adjoining room is laboring and almost suffocating under the influence of that trying affection.

Hope that the gallon of brandy reached you without delay. You will find it a very superior article, and I trust its use will realize every expectation.

We have no telegrams of interest today. There appears to be a general calm for the time being, which in all probability is indicative of a marshaling of forces and a general preparation for future enterprises of moment. General Stonewall Jackson has been heavily reinforced, and will soon with his characteristic energy assume the offensive again.

I regret to find that this question of foreign intervention, which has already proved a source of so much evil to us, is again revived, and that the eyes of not a few are turned to nations beyond the seas to bring deliverance from our present dangers. For one I am loath to indulge in any such expectations, and I am unwilling to believe that in the achievement of our ultimate national existence and political independence we will have to acknowledge our indebtedness to foreign aid. Our future, under such circumstances, will be less honorable, our triumph less perfect, our self-gratulations less pleasing; and it may be that this very intervention may materially involve complications which in after years will inure to our hurt. Rather would I see our redemption from the thralldom of our enemies purchased at the expense of blood and treasure; wrought out by our own strong hands and brave hearts; compassed by our own protracted self-denial and heroic endurance, with no reliance save upon the outstretched arm of Him who ruleth alike amid the armies of heaven and among the inhabitants of earth; assisted by no power save the merciful interposition of the Father of All Strength, who will recognize the right and cover the heads of those who fear Him in the day of danger. We are at all times prepared to hold honorable intercourse with sister nations of the earth. We are ready to enter upon legitimate commercial relations with them, and if they apply in the proper way, their applications will meet with a cheerful response.

Enclosed I send a copy of a lithograph representing in a humble way the first great meeting of the citizens of Savannah when they realized for the first time the necessities for a grand revolution. The occasion has never had a parallel in the history of our city; and as an humble memento of an eventful past this rude lithograph will in after years possess no ordinary interest. The individual "spreading himself" with every conceivable energy and earnestness from the balcony of the clubhouse may be Colonel Bartow or Judge Jackson; or it may be the subscriber, then mayor of the city. We all spoke, using that balcony as a rostrum, on that night to the assembled multitudes, who swayed to and fro on every hand like the sea lifted by the breath of the tornado. We added fuel to the flame; and that meeting, it is said, contributed more to secure the secession of Georgia and to confirm the revolution in adjoining Southern states than almost any other single circumstance of the times. It was followed by similar demonstrations throughout the length and breadth of the cotton-growing states. It evoked unmeasured surprise and condemnation from the Northern press. It stayed the hands of our sister city Charleston, and gave an impulse to the wave of secession which soon swept with a rapidity and a strength, indicating no returning ebb, all over the land. But few copies were struck off—say, a thousand—and they were widely circulated throughout the country.

I hope that little Charlie will soon be up and well again. With warmest love to you both, my dearest parents, kindest remembrances to all, and many kisses for my precious little daughter, I am, as ever,

Your affectionate son,
Charles C. Jones, Jr.

Lt. Charles C. Jones, Jr., *to* Mrs. Mary Jones[t]

Savannah, *Tuesday,* June 24th, 1862

My dear Mother,

I have just taken Mr. Ward by the hand, who returned this afternoon. The vessel in which he arrived from Nassau ran the blockade and got safely into Charleston harbor. I send the Charleston *Mercury,* which gives the particulars. He is looking remarkably well, and I am most happy to see him. He leaves his family in Rome. All well.

Tomorrow will be the birthday of my dear little daughter. May Heaven grant her many years of true piety and happiness upon earth! I sincerely trust that she is regaining her health every hour. . . . As ever,

Your affectionate son,
Charles C. Jones, Jr.

MISS MARY RUTH JONES *to* LT. CHARLES C. JONES, JR.ᵍ

Walthourville, *Wednesday,* June 25th, 1862

My darling Papa,

Do you know that your little daughter is one year old today? I would like to put my little arms around your neck and lay my little head in your bosom and tell you how much I love you. Grandmama hopes that I will be spared to cheer your heart and to be a comfort to you. In the mornings she folds my little hands and teaches me to ask my dear Saviour to bless and keep you from all harm and to save your soul.

Today she has put a short dress upon me of white muslin trimmed with blue which she has made for my birthday. My sleeves are looped with pretty little bracelets that you used to wear at my age, and she has clasped my little blue sacque with your pin which holds the hair of my blessed mother and my angel sister, who have now been in heaven nearly one year.

Dear Papa, God has heard your prayers and made me almost well again. This morning I am very bright. Everybody is so good and kind to your little daughter. My little sister and Bubber Charlie are tender and loving to me, and will give me up their playthings. I cannot talk or walk yet, for I have been a sick baby; but I know a great many little things, play with my doll, and look at the books in Grandpapa's study. I love the birds and flowers and chickens and pussy and my dog Captain, and to walk with Susan in the bright sunshine or under the tall trees, and to ride in the buggy with Sultan.

Grandpapa has gone to see Aunt Susan and Uncle William and to Maybank. When are you coming home to see us? We all send love to you, with sweetest kisses and the true love of

Your own little daughter,

Mary Ruth Jones.

(pen in her hand)

Susan sends howdies for Master and George.

XII

Lt. Charles C. Jones, Jr., *to* Rev. *and* Mrs. C. C. Jones[g]

Savannah, *Saturday,* June 28th, 1862

My dear Father and Mother,

I have just returned from the telegraph office, and rejoice to say that all the reports from the momentous battle near Richmond are most favorable. We are successful at every point. The thorough rout of the Federal army is announced, and it is expected by many that McClellan will capitulate. I earnestly trust that we may not be disappointed in our anticipations. We have on several occasions—just at the heel of our heaviest engagements, and while the cup of absolute success seemed at our lips—had that cup dashed, and failed of the legitimate fruits of our victory, that I am fearful until the final announcements are received. I hope that the annihilation of that proud army may be complete—"horse, foot, and cannon."

Thirty-six hundred prisoners already arrived in Richmond, among them the Federal generals Reynolds, Sanders, and Rankin. Additional batteries captured. We have lost as yet no general officers, but I regret to see it announced that General Elzey is mortally wounded, and the gallant Major Wheat of the Louisiana Tigers killed. The former you will remember as Captain Elzey in command of the Augusta arsenal at the time that it surrendered to the state forces under Governor Brown, and the latter as the brave leader of the Louisiana Zouaves upon the plains of Manassas. The carnage on both sides has doubtless been terrible. Thus is the mournful cypress closely entwined with the laurel in the wreath of victory. So valuable an achievement must have been purchased at great cost.

But if we have in reality overcome, routed, and annihilated this grand army which for more than a year has been furnishing itself forth with every improvement in the munitions of modern warfare, perfecting itself in military art and discipline, proudly boasting of its invincibility and of its ability to crush the beleaguered capital of our young Confederacy under the leadership of "the young Napoleon"—an army which has absorbed the strength of our enemy's forces and stands as the representative of its military power, we may well indulge in congratulations of the most honorable and sincerest character, return our heartfelt thanks to the Lord of Hosts from whom the victory cometh, and with renewed vigor press forward toward the accomplishment of new enterprises until the independence of our Confederacy shall be firmly established. I presume there will be no lack now of a forward movement in following up the victory.

Additional news from Europe indicates the fact that France and England are more seriously than ever contemplating an armed intervention on the basis of a separation between the North and the South. Butler's infamous proclamation has produced no little effect, and given rise to open and emphatic expressions of indignation in Parliament. The cup of Yankee iniquity, already full to overflowing, must run over. A people setting at defiance all the principles of common justice, truth, honor, and ordinary humanity must be regarded finally—although self-interest and accidental circumstances may for a while delay the expression—as a perfect *outlaw* among the nations of the earth, and dealt with as such. Eventually Seward's threats and the *Herald*'s lies, as the Arabian proverb has it, "like chickens will come home to roost."

General Lee's dispatch to the President announcing our successes is perfect.

I am indebted to you, my dearest parents, for a most delightful day. My sincere regret is that I cannot enjoy the privilege of being with you oftener; and I cannot tell you how much it rejoiced my heart to see the evident improvement in the health of my precious little daughter. With warmest love to you both, my dear father and mother, kindest remembrances to Sister, Robert, and the little ones, and many kisses for Daughter, I am, as ever,

Your affectionate son,
Charles C. Jones, Jr.

Rev. C. C. Jones *to* Lt. Charles C. Jones, Jr.[g]

Walthourville, *Monday,* June 30th, 1862
My dear Son,

Your most interesting letter we have just read, and I agree with you that everyone who has an interest at a throne of grace should offer the sincerest thanksgivings to Almighty God our Saviour—and I add, with tears of gratitude—for His blessings which have so far attended our battle of Richmond. If we are made successful in defeating that long-cherished and petted and lauded army, it will be a most direct and signal manifestation of the Lord's approbation of our cause; and the effect in both hemispheres will be great. My faith in the final and favorable issue has never for an instant been shaken. May no delays nor mistakes of the powers that be in the cabinet and in the field deprive us of a victory which seems put within our grasp!

Your dear little one continues to improve. Yesterday at dinner, while a blessing was asking and her grandmother's eyes were closed, being seated in her lap, she stretched out her hand and helped herself to the whole loaf of rusk. I begged she might have a little piece, and it was given her under her grandmother's protest that it would not do her good. And so it fell out, for she passed an unquiet night and was not as well as usual. But she is up and about and interesting herself both in and out of doors. She has just had a nap on the bed in my study, with Elsie to brush off the flies.

Daughter received a letter from Mrs. Thomas Clay (Clarkesville) giving an interesting account of the death of Mrs. Benjamin Stiles, at the request of Miss Kitty, who, as we may well imagine, is in the deepest distress. Dr. Alexander used to say "we had only to live long enough to realize what the sorrows of life are, and what a world we live in." But there is a Balm in Gilead, and there is a Physician nigh.

I write principally to advise you, at Mother's request, of her purpose, God willing, *to take the cars for Savannah tomorrow—Tuesday, July 1st—and to be with you to tea,* and hopes you may be able to meet her at the depot, and that you will please *say to Dr. Parsons that she will see him on Wednesday morning.* All unite in much love to you. I remain, my dear son,

Your ever affectionate father,
C. C Jones.

Lt. Charles C. Jones, Jr., *to* Rev. *and* Mrs. C. C. Jones[g]

Savannah, *Friday,* July 4th, 1862

My dear Father and Mother,

I had hoped that this, the anniversary of our former national independence, would have been rendered memorable in the history of our young Confederacy by the unconditional surrender of McClellan and his boasted army of invasion. It may be that such will be the case before this newly risen sun shall have performed his daily journey. For more than a week have our brave men withstood the shock of this tremendous battle, and by the help of the God of Justice the hostile legions of the aggressor have been driven back, one after another, in consternation and dread confusion. And even now the end is not. The Lincoln forces must have numbered nearly two hundred thousand men. To dissipate, annihilate, or put to flight such an overwhelming army—well appointed in every respect, thoroughly furnished with every appliance of modern warfare, supported by fortifications judiciously selected and erected under the personal supervision of accomplished engineers and bristling with numerous siege guns of recent patent, and capable of ready transportation and rapid concentration at any point of attack—cannot be the work of a day. Add to this the physical difficulties which are met at every step by our advancing columns in the matter of miry roads, deep swamps, thick woods, broken hills, and intervening rivers—and every pass, every obstacle stubbornly held by the slowly retreating enemy, whose rear guard, numerous and powerful, appears to be fighting with a valor worthy of a better cause; and the continued success of our brave men in the face of all these difficulties and dangers, and under such protracted fatigues, seems, as it in reality is, most wonderful. A short time must terminate this most sanguinary struggle, and we have every reason to expect most favorably to us.

If, however, we cannot today rejoice in the unconditional surrender of McClellan and the total annihilation of his army, we can with swelling hearts rejoice in the valor of our men and the success of our arms. We can in all humility and with unbounded thankfulness to Almighty God praise Him for the past, the present, and pray a merciful continuance of His great favor. We can hail with honor and with rejoicing the increasing glories of our young Confederacy, and with one acclaim shout in louder tones of living devotion, of renewed allegiance, and of sterner resolve: *Vivat nova republica!*

The effect of this defeat of their arms before Richmond must exert a most depressing influence upon the Federals. It must teach them the utter impracticability of any theory which looks towards a subjugation. It will strengthen the hands of the peace party in their midst. It will bring desolation to their hearts and sorrow to their eyes. It will completely upset all the boastful schemes, and give the direct lie to all the vain promises, of their corrupt administration. It will deal a blow from which the already shattered finances of that country cannot recover. Credit abroad will be depreciated. You already observe that gold in New York is now quoted at 108—and that when the first whisper of defeat was breathed in her streets and not heeded. Picture the scene when the hurricane of disappointment, rout, and almost annihilation shall lift its fearful voice.

The result in Europe must prove most favorable to us, and we will look with interest for reports from that quarter.

On our part this great victory—while it will cost many a pang to the state who has lost so many brave defenders, while many a sorrowing home will attest the magnitude of the sacrifice, and the voice of loud rejoicing and the paeans of success be hushed before the sounds of lamentation—will nevertheless give to us, one and all, assurance of the favor of God, of the greatness of our cause, of the value of the liberties for which we are contending, and of our absolute invincibility by the proudest force which our enemy may send against us. The tide has indeed turned. I trust that we have been sufficiently punished for our transgressions, and that the avenging rod will be now lifted. You see our successes in Arkansas. James Island has been evacuated by the Lincolnites. Vicksburg still holds bravely out against the thunders of the mortar and gunboat fleet. General T. J. Jackson is by his activity replenishing our commissary stores, etc., etc., by valuable captures from the enemy. Thus the work goes bravely on, and I trust we shall soon hail the return of white-winged peace.

My dear mother, you will, I trust, pardon me for taking the liberty of opening the enclosed letter from Father, which arrived the morning you left. My anxiety to know how all were at home must be my excuse. I trust that you suffered no inconvenience from your ride on the cars, and that you are again feeling much better. The last act of mine in the city is to put this letter in the post. In a moment I will be on my way to camp. With warmest love to you both, my dearest parents, many kisses for my precious little daughter, and kindest remembrances to Sister, Robert, and the little ones, I am, as ever,

Your affectionate son,
Charles C. Jones, Jr.

Rev. C. C. Jones *to* Mrs. Eliza G. Robarts[t]

Walthourville, *Saturday,* July 5th, 1862

My dear Aunt,

I have been owing you a letter for a long time, and you would have received at least forty if all my purposes had gone into effect; but that procrastination which is "the thief of time" (as we used to write in our copybooks at school) has stepped in and stayed proceedings for the moment.

The long spring of affliction and care in our household has passed away, leaving us nine souls less (five adults and four infants), seven from measles and its effects and two not. We have never had such a time of domestic distress before. Now, through divine mercy, our people are up and in the enjoyment of their usual health. I understand on the estate of Mr. G. W. Walthour heired by his family and on Dr. Howe's plantation they have lost upwards of *fifty Negroes* little and big! It is said there never has been so much sickness and mortality among the Negroes in our part of the county before. There has been scarcely any mortality among the whites. County is now enjoying its ordinary health.

We have four companies in service—one infantry and three cavalry, one of which is in Chatham (Captain Thomson), one in Liberty—the Liberty Independent Troop (Captain Walthour), and one in McIntosh (Captain Hughes). The infantry company is in Chatham, and is commanded by the grandson of your old friend Mr. Thomas Bradwell—*Dowse Bradwell,* son of James Sharpe Bradwell.

The war is the all-engrossing subject, as it is everywhere, but the interests of the county are moving on as in ordinary times. Our ministers are faithfully attending to their office, and the people wait on their ministry as usual; but we have no special influences of the Spirit saving a prayerful spirit for God's forgiveness and deliverance in the war.

Some Negroes (not many) have run away and gone to the enemy, or on the deserted sea islands. How extensive the matter may become remains to be seen. The temptation of change, the promise of freedom and of pay for labor, is more than most can stand; and no reliance can be placed *certainly* upon any. The safest plan is to put them beyond the reach of the temptation (as to render it impossible for them to go) by leaving no boats in the water and by keeping guards along the rivers.

We are pleasantly located at Walthourville with Daughter and Robert, and enjoy the nearness to the church and the regularity of the services. Most of our kind friends and good neighbors have been to call on us; and now that our little baby is improving, we can begin to go abroad a little and return their civilities. We have the ladies much in the majority, the gentlemen being off in service.

Yesterday being the 4th of July, the day was celebrated in the afternoon by the parade of the little company of little boys, dressed in red jackets and white pants, armed, and animated by the performance of a little Negro drummer on a small drum. Very little attention was paid, I presume, to the day in the Confederate States—while its observation in the old United States could be nothing but a *desecration*.

Your old friends are pretty well. . . . Brother suffers with his back, but is looking about as usual; and old Springfield is enlivened by the parading of the Liberty Independent Troop every morning before the door, that troop being encamped on Palmyra Bluff. I called over last week to see them, and especially your son *Joseph Robarts, Jr.* He was quite well, and his officers speak well of him and think he will make a good soldier. He has been over to see Sister at Dorchester and over to see Daughter here. . . . Henry went to Baker last week; is expected home perhaps today. His family, including his mother and Helen, well. . . . Banky has a furlough for sixty days. Do not know what he means to do. Is much improved personally by the life in camp. . . . Helen, we hear, is to be married soon. And if common fame is to be trusted, *Cupid* has been an attendant of *May,* for several young ladies are said to have made captives for life of several valiant knights.

Our prayer meeting Thursday afternoon was devoted to prayer for our country, and with special reference to the pending battles before Richmond. They have been wonderful. "The Lord hath done great things for us, whereof we are glad." Such a series of brilliant battles the world has scarcely witnessed. May the consummation come: the defeat and expulsion of that great army so lauded, from which was expected the overthrow of Richmond and of our Confederacy!

Our little baby is very thin: we hope improving slowly. Daughter's little Charlie suffering from effects of measles. Better. She and my dear wife unite in much love to you and to Cousin Mary and to Lou and to the young ladies. . . . Tell Sam his great-grandson (Tenah's) is a fine child, and all his family are well. Please excuse, my dear aunt, my unsteady hand; there are times when I cannot write easily, and it is so now. Mary sends you the enclosed with her love.

From your ever affectionate nephew,
C. C. Jones.

LT. CHARLES C. JONES, JR., *to* REV. *and* MRS. C. C. JONES[g]

Savannah, *Monday,* July 7th, 1862

My very dear Father and Mother,

I am here for an hour or two on business of the company, and am just on my way back to camp. I write to assure all at home of my constant love.

We have a telegram that McClellan has been reinforced by Shields, and with an army of ninety to one hundred thousand men has posted himself very strongly some thirty-five miles from Richmond and offers battle. It is further announced that two of the greatest powers of Europe have officially notified the United States that the war must stop. Exchange in New York is quoted at 120, and gold at 109½. Buell is said to be advancing upon Rome,

Georgia. Sickles' brigade (the brigade of the miserable Dan Sickles of New York notoriety, who you will remember shot District Attorney Key in the streets of Washington, D.C.) went into action in the recent battles before Richmond five thousand strong; and now not five hundred can be found—the rest killed, wounded, and captured! I have for some days felt no little anxiety about the ultimate result of our battles in Virginia. McClellan has doubtless suffered a terrific defeat, accompanied with tremendous losses; but his army has not been annihilated. We will look with the deepest concern for the issues of this the final struggle. We may hear more tonight.

We are all pretty well in camp. Tomorrow will be the anniversary of the death of my dearest Ruth. With warmest love to you both, my dear parents, many kisses for Daughter, and kindest remembrances to Sister, Robert, and the little ones, I am, as ever,

Your affectionate son,
Charles C. Jones, Jr.

The C.S.S. *Nashville* has run into the Ogeechee bringing a cargo of field guns, several fully appointed light batteries, Enfield rifles, etc., etc.—all the property of the Confederate States.

Lt. Charles C. Jones, Jr., *to* Rev. *and* Mrs. C. C. Jones[g]

Camp Stonewall Jackson, Wednesday, July 9th, 1862

My dear Father and Mother,

I trust that all at home are well.

The section of our battery which has been upon James Island for the past month or more returned yesterday—the men completely bronzed, but all well with the exception of two who were left sick in Savannah. The health of our entire command continues thus far to be pretty good. Every care is observed in keeping the encampment well policed, and in the removal as far as practicable of all local causes of disease. Surrounded as we are, however, by the low grounds, brackish marshes, and river swamps of this malarial region, we cannot but expect as the season progresses fevers and other indispositions of a serious character.

I understand that upon the dead Yankees found upon the battlefield on James Island were canteens well filled with water, whiskey, and quinine. Probably no army ever entered upon a campaign as fully equipped or as sedulously provided with every comfort, subsistence, and protection from disease as this Lincoln army of occupation. Everything—even the most trivial —indicates the enormous expenditure of money in its behalf by the Federal government.

The recent successes of our arms, by the blessing of God, have been even more remarkable and encouraging than were our former reverses depressing and unexpected. A degree of rather painful uncertainty still lingers about our final operations in the vicinity of our capital, and the reported reinforcements of McClellan may cost us yet many a brave life. Already is the loud shout of national exultation at thought of our immense victory almost hushed in the universal sorrows of private grief. At such great cost is liberty purchased; at such enormous sacrifices are the rights of personal freedom, national security, and private property secured.

The gallant defense of Vicksburg is rising into the true sublime, and the published order of General Van Dorn has the ring of the true metal about it. A thousand pities that this course had not been adopted in all our beleaguered cities and besieged fortresses long since. Many defeats would have been spared us, and the moral tone of our armies preserved from no little depression. The recapture of Baton Rouge is encouraging. The heavy cloud, dark and threatening although it still is, has lifted; and we already see, I think, through its rent folds the earliest dawn of national life and peace.

The warm days at our camp are succeeded by cool nights. I never have seen such heavy dews: tent as wet on the outside as though drenched with water. The mosquitoes and fleas are ever calling loudly for the exercise of true patience. Our horses have suffered terribly for the want of proper forage. This rice straw will not answer. We have already lost some six; and but for the approach of the time when we can obtain an abundant supply of fodder, I verily believe that they would almost all perish. We are now giving them some marsh grass. The unruly drivers, as a matter of punishment, are made to cut and bring it to the stables.

With warmest love to you both, my dearest parents, many kisses for my precious little daughter, and kindest remembrances to Sister, Robert, Mamie, and Charlie, I am, as ever,

Your affectionate son,
Charles C. Jones, Jr.

REV. C. C. JONES *to* LT. CHARLES C. JONES, JR.[g]
Walthourville, *Thursday,* July 10th, 1862

My dear Son,

Mother has so much to do that the lot of correspondence falls to me; and my only regret is that writing is not so easy and rapid as it once was. The gradual decay of the physical man is seen in the unsteady hand as well as in every other member of the body.

The series of brilliant victories which have been achieved by the Army of Eastern Virginia (as our President terms it in his admirable congratulatory address) has infused new life and energy into our citizens and soldiers; and there are few perhaps who would not desire to be able to say in after times at their own firesides: "We were in the battles before Richmond." But all cannot be the soldiers of our army. We must meet the enemy everywhere he presents himself; and though we never see his columns nor fire a gun, it will be the glory of every soldier that he stood in his lot with the noble patriots of the second and the greater revolution, prepared for battle whenever and however offered. The enemy that dares not set foot on shore for fear of the forces in readiness to receive him is as effectually repelled as if he had landed and been beaten back to his vessels; and the soldier who stands and waits does his duty as effectually as he who marches and fights. And indeed it is the severer part of the trial to the soldier to stand and wait. This has been your lot and that of thousands of brave men and patriots in various positions in the Confederacy. But you must sustain yourself with these reflections. As I said to Captain Claghorn and yourself at Camp Claghorn I say again: I wish you the honor of serving your country as true patriots and good soldiers; that you may never be called into battle; and should you be, that it may please God to give you the victory and preserve your persons and lives and those of your command also.

We long to see the *finale* of McClellan's army. It will be difficult to force his position, and it will require great skill and resolution on the part of our commander in chief and his army. So far it has been a tremendous blow. May it please our Heavenly Father to continue his smiles upon us! The war is now fairly opened. Our malignant, unscrupulous, and determined enemy will call for succor and issue paper currency to defray expenses so long as the people under his despotic rule will respond to his calls and accept his compensation. Ours is the task to demonstrate, by divine aid, to that miserable people the impossibility of subjugation. I am sorry to see the subject of "foreign intervention" in the papers again. But enough for the present.

A public meeting of the citizens was called on the 8th at Hinesville to adopt some measures for suppressing if possible the escape of our Negroes to the enemy on the coast. *Fifty-one* have already gone from this county. Your Uncle John has lost five. *Three* are said to have left from your Aunt Susan's and Cousin Laura's; one was captured, two not; and one of these was *Joefinny!* Such is the report. The temptation of *cheap goods, freedom, and paid labor* cannot be withstood. None may be absolutely depended on. The only preservation is *to remove them beyond the temptation,* or *seal* by the most rigid police all ingress and egress; and this is most difficult. We have petitioned General Mercer to quarter Captain Thomson's company in our county. We need the corps, and trust he may be able to accede to our request. Our people *as yet* are all at home, and *hope* they may continue faithful.

Your dear little baby continues to improve, and is full of good nature; and we hope her ear will be effectually cured. Mother has put her into short clothes, and she is much cooler and more comfortable. Sabbath is Robert's Communion. I wish it were in your power to be here.

Mother has just come in. Your aunt's and cousin's Negroes were Joefinny, his brother Dick, and their nephew *Cato*. Cato is taken; the other two, with others, are said to be on the Island. Little Andrew, who married into the family, knew all about it and has told. I go to Dorchester this afternoon to see Brother Buttolph and family and to consult. My determination is to turn them over to the proper authorities and let them be tried and dealt with as the public welfare may require. Some example must be made of this matter. They are traitors who may pilot an enemy into your *bedchamber!* They know every road and swamp and creek and plantation in the county, and are the worst of spies. If the absconding is not stopped, the Negro property of the county will be of little value. Should you see General Mercer before our petition reaches him, tell him that we have petitioned for Captain 'Thomson's company. Do let me know your opinion on the proper disposition to be made of these absconding Negroes. What would you do with *white men?*

Glad to hear you are all still so well at camp. My kind regards to Captain Claghorn. All unite in much love. And kisses from your little daughter. Here is her love to you marked by her own hand: "Love to Papa." The Lord bless and keep you, my dear son!

Your affectionate father,
C. C. Jones.

Lt. Charles C. Jones, Jr., *to* Rev. *and* Mrs. C. C. Jones[g]

Calhoun, *Monday,* July 14th, 1862*

My very dear Father and Mother,

You will perhaps be somewhat surprised to see this letter located at such a remove from the spot where you suppose I am or should be. Not a case of desertion, however: I am here upon special duty to procure conscripts for our company.

And this is the famous camp of instruction where the unpatriotic are assembled from every part of the state, dragged from their shades of seclusion by the enrolling officers, the terrors and bugbears of the present day. You never saw such a collection of sick men in your life—if you will take the statements of the conscripts themselves. The lung of one "rose some ten years ago and busted," and he has not been a well man since, although even the most practiced eye fails to discover in his stalwart frame the most remote seeds of disease. Another reports himself as ruined by "numony," which "riz in his mouth and fastened his jaw so that he could not chaw good for five years." So soon as the back is turned you see this same fellow devouring most voraciously certainly not less than half a peck of green horse apples. And so they come—each with some woeful disorder which in his own estimation should most certainly exempt him from the operation of the Conscript Act, although these selfsame fellows find ample strength to loaf from year to year and attend to their own interests at home.

Calhoun is located on the state road in Randolph County some forty miles from the Tennessee line. Like all the little towns in Upper Georgia, it is not remarkable either for the cleanliness of its inhabitants or for anything else of an attractive character except the clear, cold water. The evil effects of the existing war are everywhere manifest. All the shops are closed. The sidetrack contains no less than thirteen engines and a number of cars formerly belonging to the Nashville & Louisville Railroad which have been left here for safekeeping and are now rusting in idleness beneath the summer suns and rains.

The trains are daily filled with conscripts and troops—the former reporting at the camp of instruction located three miles from this place, the latter going on to Chattanooga, many of them sick. You cannot imagine the terrible character of the atmosphere in these cars at night. It is enough to make a well man sick. Coming up here I spent the night upon the platform to take advantage of the outside air.

At present there are only a few hundred conscripts in this camp, and Major Dunwody tells me the probability is that the number will fall far short of the expectations of the government. I presume this may be accounted for upon the fact that finding the pressure of the Conscript Act upon them, many have availed themselves of the privilege contained in the act and have recently volunteered, thus accomplishing the objects of the act—to wit, filling up our decimated ranks—although not by men who would be technically known as conscripts. From the character of the men brought into service by the operations of this act, I should say that although our army had gained recruits, it had not been materially benefited by the accretions. However, although they are not the men upon whom a brave leader would rely for energetic, heroic action, they will answer as food for powder and understand how to use the spade.

The Oostanaula River runs in the vicinity of this village, and I am informed that its banks give frequent token of the presence of those ancient tribes who in former years possessed and loved these beautiful hills and valleys. I will not have an opportunity now for examining these monumental remains. Should I have leisure when this war is over, I hope to embrace an early occasion for doing so, and also for investigations in other portions of our state.

When passing through Savannah I met Bishop Elliott, who inquired very specially after your health, Father, and begged me to consent to accept the position of corresponding secretary of the Georgia Historical Society, an office recently vacated by the death of Mr. Tefft. He urged it upon me as the unanimous wish of the society.

In passing through Augusta I had the pleasure of a few hours with Brother and Sister Carrie. They with little Stanhope are all well, and the Doctor appears to be getting along prosperously. He has a very neat little carriage drawn by a fine horse: Titus as charioteer. His hospital engagements are exacting. I noticed in the cars and about the streets of Augusta quite a number of the wounded from Richmond; and singular to state, in almost every instance the wound was in the hand or left arm.

In Madison I saw Amanda and Vallie for a few hours. Amanda is better, but has again suffered from one of her severe attacks.

I am, physically speaking, about as uncomfortable here as one can well be. Slept last night and the night before in a room with nine men—bed full of bedbugs, and the coverlet (here they do not indulge in the luxury of sheets) giving ample token that many days and perhaps weeks had elapsed since it had formed any companionship with the washtub. I will get away as soon as I can.

I hope, my dear parents, that all at home are well. With warmest love to you both, many kisses for my precious little daughter, and kindest remembrances to Sister, Robert, Mamie, and Charlie, I am ever
Your affectionate son,
Charles C. Jones, Jr.

LT. CHARLES C. JONES, JR., *to* REV. *and* MRS. C. C. JONES[g]
Calhoun, *Tuesday,* July 15th, 1862

My dear Father and Mother,

I expect to leave this place in the morning with twenty conscripts en route for Savannah. Have had a pretty laborious time of it, and my success under the circumstances has been somewhat remarkable. The only things pleasant which I will carry away with me are the memories of these beautiful hills, which have for the past few days gladdened the eye, and the recollection of this excellent water, which gushes in cool, generous, refreshing streams on every side. To think of ice would be to exhibit a degree of ingratitude unpardonable in the highest extent.

We are here almost dead to the outside world, and news of three or four days old would possess every imaginable novelty. Today Ex-Governor Foote, who passed in the train from Chattanooga, stated to a gentleman of this place then at the depot that Morgan would tonight burn the bridges across Green River, thus isolating the Federals, while General Bragg was rapidly advancing, and that we would soon hear of most important results.

I forgot to mention in my last a remarkable spring welling up from the solid rock located just at the foot of the hill upon which the conscript camp is pitched. It supplies the every want of four or five hundred men, and you can perceive no abatement whatever in its generous flow. It was famous even in the days of the Indians, and at a remove quite inconsiderable are still seen the traces of a large ball ground. Thus does every object in nature prove a speaking illustration of the truth of the Holy Scriptures: "The places that now know us will soon know us no more." Entire generations fade away as the flower of the field, while the trees which they loved still give back their answering welcome to the changeless air, and lend their refreshing shadows to another and a stranger race. The eagle eye that danced in joy at sight of this attractive spring is dull and glazed in death; and yet its limpid flow, unchecked by the lapse of time, is as pure and bright, as full of life and light, as though born of yesterday. Unclouded by the sad memories of former years, its sweet waters dance in the sheen of the same silver moon which more than a century ago invited the Indian lover and his dusky mate to this quiet retreat; and when shone upon by the beams of the selfsame sun, forgetful of the image of the heated brave with his nodding plumes and bent bow who so often here quenched his ardent thirst, reflect with equal certainty the gangling forms of Georgia conscripts, who loll in numbers upon the broad rocks which environ, voraciously devouring entire baskets of half-ripe horse apples.

Major Dunwody is most zealously discharging his duties here. They are arduous in the extreme, but he is remarkably affable amid a thousand and one questions reiterated by each newcomer, and does everything that he can to further the interests of the Confederacy. He is a brave little man, and most conscientious in the execution of his trust.

Ben Hardin Helm, I am told, is now a brigadier general, and is well esteemed as an officer.

Good night, my dear father and mother. With warmest love to you both, many kisses for my sweet little daughter, and kindest remembrances for Sister, Robert, Mamie, and Charlie, I am ever

Your affectionate son,
Charles C. Jones, Jr.

LT. CHARLES C. JONES, JR., *to* REV. C. C. JONES[g]

Camp Stonewall Jackson, *Saturday,* July 19th, 1862
My very dear Father,

I am only today favored with your very kind letter of the 10th inst., the first intelligence I have had from those I love for many days. It gives me great pleasure to know that all are well, and that my sweet little daughter, by the blessing of a kind Providence, has entirely recovered from her recent and dangerous attack. May it please God in mercy to grant her many years of peace and piety, of usefulness and of true happiness upon this earth of changing joys and sorrows!

I reached camp on Friday morning at two o'clock A.M. with twenty-one conscripts, all able-bodied, active, honest men from Middle Georgia, a valuable acquisition to the strength of our battery. On Monday night next, D.V., I leave again for the camp of instruction at Calhoun to secure some twenty more, which will entirely fill the vacancies in our battery—vacancies to be caused by the discharge from our ranks, by virtue of the operation of the Conscript Act, of all men over thirty-five and under eighteen years of age some ninety days hence. I dread the repetition of the trip, but must perform it for the good of the company. You cannot conceive the change which has occurred in the comfort of travel caused by the present condition of the trains, crowded by troops well, sick, wounded, etc., etc. The atmosphere at night in one of those packed cars is enough to generate typhoid or any other kind of fever—the result of impurities in the atmosphere of the most appalling character.

You have observed our recent success in Tennessee. This, I am led to believe, is but an earnest of a forward movement on the part of our troops, who are heavily massed at and near Chattanooga, which will swell the triumph which now rests upon our arms. May we have the vigor, the courage, and the energy to press the advantages which have so recently and so signally been vouchsafed to us by a kind Providence!

It is a most mortifying reflection that intemperance exerted its baneful influences even in the very midst of our brilliant victories in the vicinity of Richmond; and that we were prevented from reaping the full reward of our achievements, and from compassing the full successes of our plans, by the drunkenness of some of our officers high in command. I do sincerely trust that the President will, instead of relieving them from command, see to it that charges are properly preferred and the delinquents dealt with as their enormous violations of everything true, honorable, patriotic, and right justly demand. The officer who is found indulging in liquor upon the eve of such a battle, or even during the progress of its exciting scenes, is a traitor to his country, a recreant to the high trusts reposed in him, and should be summarily punished—and that in the most public and emphatic manner. I had hoped that the recent orders upon the subject of intemperance in our army would have exerted their legitimate influence upon, and secured prompt obedience from, at least those who are entrusted with rank and authority. But recent events prove that certainly in some instances (let us hope they are but few) they have failed of working the proper results of reformation and of a just recognition of duty.

I deeply regret to learn that the Negroes still continue to desert to the enemy. Joefinny's conduct surprises me. You ask my opinion as to the proper disposition to be made of absconding Negroes, and also inquire what would be done with white men detected in the act of giving over to the enemy. If a white man be apprehended under such circumstances, he would doubtless be hung, and in many instances, if the proof be clear, by an indignant and patriotic community without the intervention of either judge or jury. In the case of a Negro, it is hard to mete out a similar punishment under similar circumstances. Ignorance, credulity, pliability, desire for change, the absence of the political ties of allegiance, the peculiar status of the race—all are to be considered, and must exert their influences in behalf of the slave. If, however, a Negro be found digesting a matured plan of escape and enticing others to do the same; or if, after having once effected his escape to the enemy, he returns with a view to induce others to accompany him, thus in fact becoming an emissary of the enemy; or if he be found under circumstances which indicate that he is a spy, it is my opinion that he should undoubtedly suffer death, both as a punishment for his grave offense and as an example to evildoers. In the case, however, of a Negro endeavoring to effect his escape to the enemy detected in the effort, my opinion is that he should not be put to death, but that he be taken to the county seat of the county in which the offense was committed and there *publicly* and *severely punished*.

I will embrace the earliest opportunity of seeing General Mercer. I think the petition just in all respects, and trust that it will be immediately granted.

I have written in much haste, but with warmest love to self, my dear father, my dear mother, my sweet little daughter, Sister, Robert, Mamie, and Charlie. As ever,

Your affectionate son,
Charles C. Jones, Jr.

REV. C. C. JONES *to* LT. CHARLES C. JONES, JR.[g]

Walthourville, *Monday,* July 21st, 1862

My dear Son,

Your two favors from Calhoun we received last week, and congratulate you on the success of your mission. We could not tell where you were from the ceasing of letters until you turned up so far off. Many of the conscripts will do better in service than they promise for before entering. Good officers go far towards making good men. We need just now all the good men we can get, for our government seems moved to more vigorous action than ever.

Your dear baby is improving daily, getting back her flesh and her voice; and nothing interests her so much as the children. She will sit and play with Little Daughter and Charlie by the half hour, and is also much amused sitting on the matting in my study and scratching upon it with two pencils. Little Charlie is getting better also.

I mentioned in one of my late letters a public meeting held at Hinesville on the state of affairs in the county. Application has since been made to General Mercer to know what shall be done with Negro slaves absconding to the enemy when taken, and we understand he answers that he can do nothing as military commander. Something has to be done by somebody—and that efficiently—or things will grow into a bad condition. Can such Negroes be summarily dealt with under any acts of the state? Could they be taken up under the head of insurrection? Could their overt rebellion in the way of casting off the authority of their masters be made by construction insurrection? They declare themselves enemies and at war with owners by going over to the enemy who is seeking both our lives and property. They are traitors of the worst kind, and spies also, who may pilot the enemy into your bedchamber. It is those caught *going* that we wish to know what to do with; those who are caught *coming back* may no doubt be treated summarily as spies. Please let me hear from you on this point so soon as you are at leisure.

We have lost another child at Montevideo—Little Lymus. Sick some time: inflammatory rheumatism, we think. And our faithful *Sue* is very sick. Mother has gone down today. She went down on Saturday and was very much fatigued by it, the weather has been so warm. I hope she may not be made sick. Robert has gone to his father's plantation today also. Daughter sends much love, and Little Daughter says: "Tell Uncle Charlie howdy for me." "My lo—" Tried to make the baby hold the pen to write her love to you, but she resists *in toto* after the first word, as you see. Hope a kind Providence has brought you safe home again.

Your ever affectionate father,
C. C. Jones.

Lt. Charles C. Jones, Jr., *to* Rev. C. C. Jones[g]
Camp Stonewall Jackson, *Friday,* July 25th, 1862

My dear Father,

I found your favor of the 21st inst. had anticipated my return to camp, which was not accomplished until one o'clock this morning. I have just completed a flying and successful trip to Calhoun, Georgia—the second I have made—bringing with me an additional number of conscripts, sufficient to fill all vacancies in the ranks of the company which will be caused by the operation of the Conscript Act. I have slept and eat but little for the past seventy-two hours, and do not feel very bright this morning.

I had just returned from a similar detail when I was ordered by General Mercer again to repair to the camp of instruction and secure additional conscripts. As there was no examining surgeon at Calhoun, I took our battery surgeon, Dr. J. T. McFarland, with me. (Dr. McFarland was the surgeon at Fort Pulaski when that fortress was captured by the Lincolnites, and was for several months a prisoner in close confinement in the hands of the enemy, having recently been released and returned home under the general order, of late passed, directing that all surgeons shall be unconditionally released— an act of humanity and of simple justice.) Arriving at Calhoun, it was the work of but a few hours to accomplish my mission. I selected twenty-one good men (the complement required), had them duly enrolled, and started with them on Wednesday morning.

In passing the Marietta depot I saw Mr. Bruce of Louisville, a member of our Confederate Congress, the husband of my old friend Lizzie Helm. The cars paused but for a few moments, and I had time only to learn that he and Mrs. Bruce were refugees from Kentucky, and had been spending some time at the Marietta hotel. He pressed me if possible to return and see Mrs. Bruce. With the conscripts in charge I could not then tarry, so I promised to come back that evening if practicable and renew an acquaintance with which I always have had the most pleasant associations. So I ran down to Atlanta and there located my men. The train, according to present schedule, does not connect with the Macon & Western Railroad train, thereby necessitating a delay until 6 A.M. the following morning. This interim I improved by returning in the evening cars, which leave Atlanta at half-past seven and reach Marietta at nine o'clock P.M.

Found Mrs. Bruce expecting me, and most happy to welcome me. She met me, I would say, as a sister; and at once I was carried back to a full realization of all the pleasures which gave such zest to my visit at her father's house in 1854. Time has dealt gently with her, and she is the same lively, kindhearted, attractive Lizzie Helm whom I had seen eight years ago to the day amid the beauties and the comforts of Helm Station. We reviewed minutely all the associations of the past; and but for the dark shadows which had crossed my pathway I could almost imagine that other days were come again. The governor and Mrs. Helm are both well and in Hardin County at their own home, unmolested by the Lincolnites. Miss Jane is dead. Two younger sisters have married. Ben Hardin Helm is a general in the Confederate service, at present stationed at Tupelo. I was very much pleased with Mr. Bruce. He is a refined gentleman of education and of attractive address. He and Ben Hardin were associated in Louisville in the practice of the law, but have been compelled to abandon profession, home, and everything else for the present. Mrs. Bruce has a noble little boy, named after the governor, about eighteen months old. She took me into her room that I might see him, and there the little fellow lay fast asleep, with his fine head and sturdy limbs a miniature of the old governor. She has lost two infants, daughters both. Congress meeting early in August, they expect in a short time to leave Marietta for Richmond.

After spending an hour and a half thus delightfully, I went to see our relatives, old Aunty, Aunt Mary, Cousin Louisa, etc. They had just retired for the night, but soon came down—except Aunt Eliza, whom I saw in her room. They are all perfectly well—Aunt Eliza in the enjoyment of better health than she has had for years, Aunt Mary just as full of good humor as ever, and Cousin Louisa more fleshy than usual. The girls all well. Every inquiry was made after you, my dear parents, and all at home. They have a servant whose death is almost hourly expected—Nancy, Peggy's daughter. Disease: consumption. She is to them a most valuable servant, and her loss will be severely felt. Bid them all good-bye at one o'clock A.M. Thursday morning. Reached Atlanta again at 3 A.M., left with my conscripts at 6 A.M., and reached camp this morning at 1 A.M.

Took tea with Mr. Rogers in Atlanta, and on my way up on a former occasion attended prayer meeting in his church. He and Mrs. Rogers are now keeping house. Her health is restored, and they live in much comfort. I enjoyed the hot rolls and good coffee, waffles and curd prodigiously after my semi-fastings at the rude wayside inns in Cherokee Georgia. He begged me to say to Mother and yourself that nothing would be more gratifying than to welcome you both beneath his own vine and fig tree and enjoy a visit from you this summer. In common with others his church has suffered in consequence of the influences of this gigantic and unholy war.

Atlanta exhibits more signs of life and energy than any other city in Georgia. You would be surprised at the immense quantities of sugars, tobacco, etc., etc., there stored. Real estate has advanced to an enormous extent, and the probability is that when peace and happiness are again restored to our now distracted country, that the future of this city will be very bright. It contains even now a population of some seventeen thousand, and great improvements are constantly progressing. Fine stores with iron and granite fronts. Neat residences meet the eye on every hand. But a few years since, Atlanta was regarded as the home only of speculators, railroad hands, businessmen, demireps, and rowdies; but the tall spires of newly erected churches, frequent schoolhouses, and the increasing comforts of private residences, and the permanency of stores and public buildings give ample token that the rude infancy of this busy place has been superseded by an age of quiet, maturer civilization. It is even rumored that Atlanta may be selected as the future and permanent capital of our Confederacy; but of course this is simply a matter of speculation.

During my recent visit to Upper Georgia and almost to the confines of Tennessee I have seen and conversed with many persons recently from Kentucky and Tennessee. They with one consent represent those states as ripe for a general uprising in behalf of the Southern cause, as thoroughly disabused of those false impressions which the Lincoln government labored to infuse in the public mind, and entirely disgusted with Federal promises, Federal faith, and Federal rule. The mask has been torn from their faces, and the cloud lifted from their eyes. They now see clearly the unhappy results of their own indecision, and the almost fatal consequences of their self-deception, and are prepared with united effort to throw off the galling yoke of the oppressor. Forrest and Morgan have gone to the rescue, and numbers are flocking to their standards. The recent and rapid achievements of these dashing cavalry officers savor of a revival of the days of true chivalry.

Vicksburg still holds the combined fleet of the enemy at bay; and judging from the self-humiliating propositions which have recently been made to General Van Dorn by the commander of that fleet, we must suppose that its vaunted energy and power are fast ebbing away. I have even heard it suggested that the final capture of the entire fleet was by no means uncertain. Hemmed in between Vicksburg and Baton Rouge, which is now being heavily fortified, these hostile vessels, cut off from supplies, their crews dying under the influences of a purely malarial region and suffering every depression from repeated reverses, must, it would seem, unless something unforeseen occurs to prevent, eventually—and that at no distant day—surrender. The ram *Arkansas,* too, has been among them; and though they have seen her but once—and that in not a cloudless sky—they will probably never forget the introduction. Her conduct has added a bright page to our naval history, and her name will be associated with that of the *Virginia.*

Speaking of the *Virginia,* I am happy to see by the morning papers that the recent court-martial convened at Richmond for the trial of Commodore Tattnall have justified the abandonment and burning of that vessel under the circumstances, and have honorably acquitted the old commodore from the charges preferred. While I am glad to know that this has been done, I can never lay aside the regrets which one involuntarily entertains that this gallant vessel, in one day rendered famous for all time, should not have met with a fate more worthy her name and her daring heroism. Had a younger man been in command, her death struggles would in all probability have been encircled by a halo of the moral sublime and accompanied by such an illustration of fearless action that the world would have been amazed at the deed. But if the *Virginia* had lived in the waters which gave her birth, we would probably have had no "Onward to Richmond" on the part of McClellan; and the recent victories near Richmond would not have given to our arms assurance of their prowess, or to our country and the world an earnest, under God, of our ultimate success.

I learned from the agent of the state road that he had orders from the general government to furnish transportation for forty thousand men during the present and the coming week. The Army of the Mississippi is to be moved from Tupelo, Mississippi, to Chattanooga with a view to meeting and overwhelming Buell, who with thirty-five or forty thousand men is now said to be within thirty-five miles of the latter place. Buell whipped, an advance movement through Tennessee will occur, and thus both that state and Kentucky relieved from the hated presence of a detested foe. Twenty thousand of the Army of the Mississippi are said to be ordered on to Richmond. The President seems at last to have determined upon an aggressive policy. Lincolndom will soon feel for the first time the pressure of actual warfare. . . . Our fortunes have never been so prosperous as at this present moment, and if we are but true to ourselves and to the new policy which has been so auspiciously inaugurated, they will grow brighter and brighter unto the perfect end.

On the state road I had a long and interesting conversation with Governor Brown. Among other things he stated to me that that road would this year pay as clear profits into the state treasury the sum of six hundred thousand dollars. The government transportation over that road has been very heavy. The road itself is in capital order.

You ask me, my dear father, in your letter whether Negroes deserting to the enemy can be summarily dealt with by the citizens themselves under the acts of the state. I understand your question to be, whether in such cases the *citizens* can in public meeting condemn to death such offenders and have them summarily executed. A trial by jury is accorded to everyone, whether white or black, where life is at stake; and the trial by jury involves a trial by jury constituted in accordance with the laws of the state and before the judge competent to preside. Any other procedure, although possibly to a certain extent justified by the aggravated character of the offense and upon the grounds of public good, would in a strictly legal sense certainly be *coram non judice,* and would savor of mob law. Any punishment other than that involving a loss of life or limb could be legally inflicted without the intervention of judge or jury.

If General Mercer refuses to take military cognizance of such cases, and they occur during the intervals of the sessions of the courts, I cannot see what can be done except to take the law in one's own hand, and by severe punishment endeavor to prevent the recurrence of an evil whose influence cannot be overestimated. Terrible corporal punishment, accompanied with close and protracted confinement in the county jail, or public punishment followed by banishment from the county and sale in some distant part of the country, seem to me to be proper in cases where the offenders are apprehended under circumstances indicating a purpose on their part to desert to the enemy. If escape be attempted when ordered to halt, they should immediately be shot. No mercy should be shown where the party has once absconded and afterwards returns to induce others to accompany him in his act of desertion to the enemy. Under such circumstances the public good requires, in the absence of legal punishment, that the offender should be summarily dealt with —and that in a public and final manner; and for two simple reasons: first, to prevent effectually a repetition of the offense by the party himself and rid the community of his evil influence; and, second, by the severity of the punishment and the publicity and promptness of its execution, to deter others from attempting the like. If insensible to every other consideration, terror must be made to operate upon their minds, and fear prevent what curiosity and desire for utopian pleasures induce them to attempt. If allowed to desert, our entire social system will be upset if the supremacy of the law of servitude and the ownership of such property be not vigorously asserted in cases where recaptures occur. The main object of the gunboats now lying along our coast doubtless is to encourage the escape of Negroes, and by stealing and reselling them aid in swelling personal wealth and in defraying the expenses of the present war.

I am afraid by this desultory letter that I have already trespassed too long upon your patience. I regret to learn that another death has occurred at Montevideo—another new-made grave added to the many which have so recently been dug in the plantation burial ground. Trust that dear Mother has recovered from her fatigue, and that Sue is better. Do, Father, accept my constant and warmest affection for self and Mother. Kiss my dear little daughter for me. Remember me affectionately to Sister, Robert, Mamie, and Charlie. And believe me ever

Your affectionate son,
Charles C. Jones, Jr.

XIII

Rev. R. Q. Mallard *to* Mrs. Mary S. Mallard[t]

Walthourville, *Saturday,* July 26th, 1862

My dearest Mary,

I reached home safely this morning, and through the blessing of Providence find all well. I hope that you are now quietly domesticated in your brother's home, and trust that your visit will be a very pleasant one. After your close confinement at home for so long a time, you are entitled to a little recreation; and although I shall miss you greatly, I am more than willing to practice that self-denial. Dismiss all cares about home, for I will keep you informed of everything which occurs.

Your father says Charlie has behaved like a little gentleman. When he went to bed he wished to go in Mama's room, but was quieted by his grandmama's telling him that he would sleep near her, where she could put out one hand and touch him and the other and touch Little Sister. About daylight he waked up and "wanted Mama" and cried a little for her; but having also said, "I want candy," this was produced and he was quieted. Dear little fellow, he was very glad to see me. I am so sorry that I could not bring out any candy for him. I walked downtown, but found the doors shut. I opened a little package in his presence, when he said: "Candy in there!"

Your father seems bright, and is hard at work on his book. He received a very interesting letter from Charlie, who has just reached camp with another body of twenty-one conscripts. He had a very pleasant visit to Mr. and Mrs. Bruce (Miss Lizzie Helm), who were refugees and are at the Marietta hotel. He saw the Robartses too. All well in the white family; Miss Louisa fleshier than usual; Nancy is not expected to live. Charlie writes very hopefully about the country; says he has seen a number of persons from Kentucky and Tennessee, and they say that these two states are ripe for a general uprising. He was told by (I think) the superintendent of the state road that he had received orders to provide transportation for forty thousand troops within the course of this and next week. They are a part of Beauregard's army, and are to be massed at Chattanooga to overwhelm Buell, who is marching upon it with some thirty thousand. Twenty thousand of the same army have gone to Richmond. The news from the Mississippi which he gives is better than what the newspapers contain. He says that it is thought that the Yankee fleet may be captured if they remain much longer, being caught between Vicksburg and Baton Rouge, which he says is being heavily fortified.

But I must get to work. Charlie came up a minute or two ago saying:

"Mama come! Mama upstairs!" But he is in a fine humor. . . . Father and
Mother unite with me in sending much love to you. Your little son sends
love and a kiss, which you will find on the left-hand lower corner of this
page.

Your own

Robert Q. Mallard.

Inquire about the price of yarn. Brother John was in Savannah and unsuccessful in getting servants' clothing. Write me what you think. I have just
written Mr. Newton of Athens to make inquiries about price of yarn.

Rev. R. Q. Mallard *to* Mrs. Mary S. Mallard[t]

Walthourville, Monday, July 28th, 1862

My darling Wife,

My heart travels all the way to Augusta many times a day, and this perhaps
makes the time of your absence seem already longer than it really is. I hope
to hear today or at least tomorrow of your safe arrival. You must write me
frequently, if only a few lines at a time. You must not expect always long
letters from me.

Yesterday was a very pleasant day in more respects than one. The temperature was very delightful after our hot July weather. The thermometer stood
between services at only 79°. I wonder if it was as cool in Augusta. I enjoyed
the services very much. My text in the morning was that sweet promise: "I
will not leave you comfortless; I will come to you." Your father seemed to enjoy this service very much, and I think was much pleased (as was also
Mother) with the sermon. My subject in the afternoon was the Parable of
the Marriage Supper. I hope I was assisted from above; the attention of the
people was very solemn and, on the part of more than one, tender. . . . Oh,
that the Good Spirit may deepen these impressions and extend His influence!

Last night I heard some very sweet singing by our servants. I don't know
when I have heard sweeter. They were all assembled in Lucy's house, and
with Flora leading and Niger on the bass and others on the second they
made pleasant music. Niger has a fine bass voice. One of their hymns was
"We Are Passing Away." I told Tenah afterwards how much I enjoyed the
singing and wished that she and her husband were Christians, that they
might make melody in their hearts to God. . . .

But you are impatient to know about your little darling. He is doing very
well, and has substituted me in your place with very good grace. He has not
been quite well today, and your mother has just given him a dose of rhubarb
mixture. Nothing to alarm at all, but I will watch him closely. His appetite
is so good that I think he overtasks his digestion. I lanced a large boil under
his chin this morning, and hope this will give him much relief. He has now
on it a plaster of honey and flour. I hear his little tongue running now in
your room. He has been very sweet. Yesterday evening he went with me to
feed. I had been asking who made and who died for him, which he answered,

and was looking at the little steel buckles on his white slippers when he said: "Papa, God made steel buckle. God made star and sun and moon." I think the star-shaped buckle reminded him of the stars. He went on to say that God made his shoes, etc. I will write you how he is again by next mail, or have it done.

Father and Mother send much love to you and Mamie, Dr. Joseph, Sister Carrie, and Stanhope. Give my love to them also. I wrote in such a hurry before that I forgot to send a kiss even for my dear little daughter. Kiss her lovingly for me, and receive for herself and yourself the tenderest love of your little Charlie and

Your own husband,
R. Q. Mallard.

Mrs. Mary Jones *to* Mrs. Mary S. Mallard[t]

Walthourville, *Thursday*, July 31st, 1862

My dear Daughter,

I have told Robert that I would take the pen this morning and send you a line. He is rubbing down a whipstock for his buggy in the piazza. Little Charlie is merrily laughing and playing by his side, having eaten a bountiful breakfast at his little table, which we set in the dining room, and at which Little Sister and himself preside, but not always in the most harmonious style. She is upstairs, seated in the middle of a wide-spread comforter in my room, with the paper cutter in her hand and Sancho and the India-rubber pussy at her feet. Every now and then she gives Sancho a spank with the cutter and then laughs heartily. Within a few days she tries to creep and say a few words.

I trust you will find the dear little ones much improved. And assure yourself that it is not Charlie that troubles Grandmama, but vice versa. He told his father in the night he did not want Grandmama to sit at the head of the table—he wanted Mama to sit there! Every afternoon, when dressing to ride, he says he is going to meet Mama and Sissy. The ugly fit of "shan'ts" has passed away, and he is again your merry, good-natured little boy.

Duly at the appointed hour your father, Robert, and I repaired to the church. As we turned Mrs. Quarterman's corner the broad lines of light streamed out the open windows. The porch and yard were crowded with groups of boys and servants, and the interior filled with almost the entire village. There were representatives, at least, from every family. Mrs. Jones, Mrs. Harris, and Mrs. Banky Jones occupied the front left-hand seat—on the side you sit upon, but facing the aisle. Behind her sat the mother of the groom-elect with her party. And so the family and friends were intermingled. Perfect decorum was observed in the waiting interval, which must have lasted at least three-quarters of an hour. The arrival of the bridal party was announced by the removal of the table with five candlesticks which occupied the space below the pulpit. The candles were placed upon the desk above, reflecting a soft pretty light upon the party below, who made their entrance up the two aisles. . . . They formed in a circle, the minister and bride and groom forming a part of it, and so arranged as to stand opposite to each other. Six bridesmaids and three groomsmen, all looking very pretty, of course. But the bride really was beautifully dressed in illusion over silk. Her wreath and bunches of orange blossoms on her sleeves and bouquet in front were exquisite; and her veil, while it fell sufficiently over her face for a modest effect, flowed full and free from her person like a shower of pure white mist. And Helen was really a lovely bride. The scene was altogether very interesting—not the least of which was the ceremony pronounced by the young minister in chaste and elegant language and sentiment, with the fervor of one whose espousal was fresh in his own recollection, and with the fidelity of a Christian pastor who was counseling the lambs of his flock for time and for eternity. Robert went to the house and partook of the refreshments; your father and I did not.

As it is so late in the season, if you could find an *alpaca* I think it would do me more service than the thin dress, and I would prefer it. *You can write before buying.* I must close. With our united and best love to you all, dear children and grandchildren, and kisses from your boy,

Ever your affectionate mother,
Mary Jones.

REV. R. Q. MALLARD *to* MRS. MARY S. MALLARD[t]

Walthourville, Saturday, August 2nd, 1862

My dearest Mary,

In the interim between prayers and breakfast I have sat down to commence at least a letter to my darling heart. Can it be possible that one week only has just expired? I will have to quit writing you so frequently if I wish the time shortened.

And now I must tell you that I am requested to consent to your protracting your absence. I received on yesterday a very interesting and touching letter from Miss Kitty, postmarked Savannah. She says: "Edward will take me to Macon next week, and as soon as he finishes his business there, we will go to Clarkesville. His furlough ends in September, and I have promised him to stay in Clarkesville until December, as he will not hear of my going to Virginia. Will you not take pity upon me and bring Mary and the children up there early in September, and stay as long as you can yourself, and then leave them with me until I can come down?" You can give this invitation your consideration and let me know what you think of it by letter.

I am very sorry for Miss Kitty. She writes very sadly, but in a sweet Christian spirit. Edward left Richmond only a few hours before her arrival. She spent several days in the city and then followed him to Savannah. I have not time to tell you all that she wrote, but would only add that Captain Stiles's wound was a severe flesh wound in the hip, and that it is rapidly healing. Poor fellow, he is overwhelmed with grief at his mother's death and cannot speak of it at all.

I am going to the depot to meet Brother Williams and your brother Charlie. This evening I leave for Bryan, and on Monday go to Savannah as chairman of a committee to present your father's memorial (which was adopted by our meeting yesterday) to General Mercer. It is on the subject of the escape of contrabands.

I have written in haste and must now close. Many kisses for your dear self and my little daughter, and love from all to all. Charlie says you must bring him some white candy. I showed him your likeness this morning, and he said immediately: "It's Mama!" He has improved very much.

Your own husband,
R. Q. Mallard.

Mrs. Mary Jones *to* Mrs. Mary S. Mallard[t]
Walthourville, *Tuesday,* August 5th, 1862

My dear Daughter,

Letters from your brother and yourself received yesterday told us of your sickness. I am truly sorry to hear it, but glad, in God's providence, that it occurs where you will have your brother's skill and dear Carrie's kind attentions; and I trust the attack will result in permanent good. Do not forget that one object of your present visit was to consult Joe professionally; and you must tell him candidly how you are. Much suffering may not only be relieved but avoided in the future. Years of weakness and pain is a sad portion for a young mother; and whilst it is the infliction of our Heavenly Father's hand and as such should be borne with patient submission, I believe it to be also as much the divine will that we should do all in our power to promote our health and consequent usefulness.

Thus far I had written, and was about entering upon details about Robert, when the mail arrived. As he has "skedaddled," he may now report himself at headquarters. We will only say his furlough is extended as long as he pleases. Father will take care of the prayer meeting, and I promise to do my best with Charlie and the household. I would not be surprised if Brother Williams would like to occupy the pulpit here next Sabbath. He appears most pastoral in his visitations, and thinks this a choice flock. . . .

Charlie has said a great many funny things about his mama, who seems ever uppermost in his mind. When Mr. Williams came, as Robert was going away and I did not wish to disturb your father, Little Sister and her grandmama moved across the entry. When night came and Charlie discovered the chintz spread from my bed put upon yours, and Little Sister about to be laid in his sissy's bed, he flew into a sad rage, ordered the spread taken off his mama's bed, said it should not stay there, and Little Sister should go out of the room—she should not sleep in his sissy's bed! I tried the usual quietus of a piece of candy, with divers admonitions from Lucy. But all to no purpose. Grandmama and Little Sister should *not* sleep in his mama's bed and his mama's room! He improves daily, and gives not the least trouble; sleeps well at night and eats unsparingly by day.

You need not get either of the dresses at the prices mentioned, for I can do without them. But please send me without fail by Robert two packages of factory yarn for weaving (coarse quality). I hope it can be had reasonably.

Do you think I could get Kitty to have my lamb's wool woven in Habersham into cloth and flannel? And can you not make up your mind to spend the fall with her as she wants you to do? I am sure it would do you great good, and I would take care of Charlie; and if you wish it Patience can serve you as long as you desire and go with you. I hope she makes herself useful to you in every respect. Tell her howdy, and that all her family are well. Gilbert has just come up.

Do thank our dear son for his kind and useful letter; his father will write him soon. Are there any medicinal plants in this region he would like me to gather for him? I could make Tom do so. Would he like more of the bark from the branches?

If you think I could trouble Kitty about the lamb's wool, do let me know. . . . I write in haste, as it is time to send this to the mail and have dinner for Brother Williams, who goes by the train as far as Flemington, where he preaches tonight. . . . Please remember me to Mrs. Smith, Dr. and Mrs. Davis, Julia and Mrs. Cuthbert and Mrs. Cumming. Father unites with me in tenderest love to you and Carrie and Joe, with kisses for our grandchildren, and many sweet ones from your little Charlie and Little Sister. And love to Robert. The Lord bless my dear daughter!

Ever your affectionate mother,
Mary Jones.

REV. R. Q. MALLARD *to* MRS. MARY S. MALLARD[t]

Walthourville, *Friday,* August 8th, 1862

My darling Wife,

After a very pleasant visit to one whose presence constitutes my greatest earthly happiness, I am again, thanks to the kind hand of our Heavenly Father, safely at home.

I find all as well as usual. Your father complains today of great tenderness in his throat, necessitating much care to prevent an attack. (I mention this because I promised to write you particularly.) Charlie is very much improved, and is getting back his flesh very fast, and excepting his opposition to new tenants of Mama's and Sissy's beds, which your father intimates had to be and was removed by stringent means, has been in behavior all that could be desired. Dear little fellow, he met me in the branch at the bridge, and was greatly delighted to see me, and highly pleased with the white candy his dear mama sent him. He was very sweet about it: after I had given him several pieces, which he consumed, he very gently hinted for another supply by saying in somewhat of a singsong way: "White candy!"

Mother will not hear to your returning so early as two weeks hence, and requests me to write to you not to shorten your visit on account of anything at home. I am perfectly willing that you should stay longer.

I write this to go by James, and must now bid you good-bye. Love from all to all. Kiss Mamie for Papa. And believe me

Affectionately yours,

R. Q. Mallard.

P.S. It has been *hot* in Savannah and Walthourville as well as Augusta. Mother says do not get the dress for her.

Mother thinks of having Little Sister baptized on Sabbath. I have offered to stand with her, which she gladly accepted. It is impossible for Charles to be present, and she feels that it should be delayed no longer.

R. Q. M.

Servants all well.

Rev. R. Q. Mallard *to* Mrs. Mary S. Mallard[t]

Walthourville, *Monday,* August 11th, 1862

My dear Wife,

I have just returned from Dorchester. The heat is intense, and Jim manifested a strong disposition to rest and *pant* under almost every good shade. . . . Aunt Susan returned last night from a week's visit to Taylor's Creek. I did not see her, as she returned about ten or eleven o'clock at night. I saw Audley's little girl at Mr. Buttolph's. She is very much of a King in looks; was very sociable and pleasant.

Your old uncle finds the company—or rather the camp followers—a great nuisance. Finding Augustus Quarterman's boy in his cornfield, he administered a correction to him. Presently A. Q. comes over posthaste and desires to know the reason of such a proceeding.

"He was in my cornfield."

"He went there by my orders, sir."

"You had no right to order him there."

"He went by my command, and I assume the responsibility."

"I preferred to assume the responsibility and therefore punished him."

Thereupon the complainant bids him good morning, and was for a time a little offish. The old colonel says he wishes he had moved bag and baggage long ago. Still I have no doubt he is enjoying somewhat the society which the camp gives him.

On my return I found your letter of Saturday. I read it to Father and Mother, and they made various exclamations when I came to the part about "not wishing to run away from them any longer." They say you must not consider that at all in your plans. Mother says Little Sister is so much better that she has no desire to make a change, and will take care of Charlie for you. They seem disposed to favor your going to Habersham; but Father says: "You will have to be a widower for two and a half months." There *is* the rub! I have in hand some six hundred and fifteen dollars, and if the rest of our cotton is sold at a good price, we could perhaps spare a couple of hundred or so for the trip. Do you know of any way of going? Do you wish to go? Write me promptly and freely, my darling. If you should go, you would spend the rest of this month and the whole of September and October, as it would be hardly safe for you to return before frost. Your mother thinks it would be far better for you to leave Charlie here should you determine to make the trip. May a kind Providence guide us in the matter!

And now a word of business. Including James I have eight grown servants and four children. I will therefore need (at the rate of six yards each for the former and three for the latter) in exact measurement sixty yards of the osnaburg. You had better get more. What do you think of getting twice that amount to have some for winter? . . . Enclosed you will find twenty dollars from Sister Lou. She wishes ten yards black delaine like enclosed sample (for a *second* dress), or if that is not to be had, twelve yards of something else suitable for a winter dress. If double width, a less amount will answer. She leaves the price discretionary with you. If anything is over, she wishes half a yard lasting for making shoes. . . . Mother wishes you to inquire whether the wool has been received by the factory.

Charlie is well; in fact, all pretty well. I must now send this. The Lord bless and keep you and my little one in the hollow of His almighty hand! Father and Mother send much love to Brother Joe and Sister Carrie, yourself, and all. I concur. With many kisses for my little daughter, and my best earthly affection to my other self, I am

> Your tenderly attached husband,
> R. Q. Mallard.

REV. R. Q. MALLARD *to* MRS. MARY S. MALLARD[t]

> Walthourville, *Friday,* August 15th, 1862

My dearest Wife,

I have just received and read your kind favor of the 13th inst. You had not at the time of writing received my letter about the cloth. I think you had better get for the house servants too, as it may be very difficult to procure later in the year.

You wish me to write you definitely about my movements, and propose coming home on Thursday next. As I am very anxious to procure as early as possible some gravestones for my dear parents' graves, and may not be able to find any in Savannah; and as the additional expense to Augusta will not be very great; and as you stand in need of my trunk in addition to the ark; and, moreover, as inclination strongly draws me, and my visit before

I count entirely extra; I think I shall, D.V., come for you myself. Providence permitting, I will go to Savannah on Monday afternoon and remain there until the next night. This will give me ample time to visit the marble yard or yards and perhaps the cemetery in that city. I hope by this arrangement to join you in Augusta on Wednesday morning. We could then return on that afternoon. This would give me more time for my pulpit preparations. Or we could return on the next day (Thursday), and that would give me time enough to prepare at least one sermon. Unless, then, you make different arrangements, you may expect me, the Lord permitting, on Wednesday morning next.

I am afraid that I sin in allowing your absence such influence. I know that my work should be so interesting that time should appear too short for its employments, and yet time moves slowly when you are away. You must not, however, let this consideration weigh with you if your brother thinks a trip to Habersham necessary to your complete restoration to health and strength.

Your father is away at present. Your mother well; also the children. Little Sister jabbers constantly, making considerable variety of sounds, and I think will soon begin to talk. Little Charlie is luxuriating in red potatoes, and is now perfectly restored, so that nothing seems to disagree with him. Your peaches will not come amiss to him. The little fellow will be overjoyed to see you. . . . Give our love to all. Kiss for Mamie, and much love to yourself.

Your ever affectionate husband,
R. Q. Mallard.

Mrs. Mary Jones *to* Mrs. Mary S. Mallard[t]

Walthourville, *Friday,* August 15th, 1862

My dear Daughter,

Mrs. *McCollough* asks you to procure two Bibles for her in Augusta. She wishes them as presents for her daughters, and says she would not give over two dollars apiece for them. She requested me to write you.

Do you know if the bale of wool was received by Fleming & Rowland? Please inquire of them how *many yards of cloth one pound of wool will weave.* I do not think we have half enough for the use of both places, and think of ripping up a mattress and sending on the wool if I can only form some just estimate of how many yards of cloth one pound of wool will yield. I would be greatly obliged, my dear daughter, if you would write our old friend *Rev. J. L. Rogers* and ask if a *flying shuttle* for hand looms could be had in Atlanta and at what price; or if there are any carpet looms such as the country people use for rag carpets at the North to be procured there. Tell him from me it would be a great favor conferred if he could help us to any information on the subject. We shall be at our wits' end for clothing and blankets for our people this winter; and if the machinery could be supplied, I think necessity will stir energy enough to accomplish something. After prayer meeting yesterday I called to see your friend Miss Catherine; found her not well, but we had a long talk about looms and spinning wheels, and looked into her barrel of spun wool. I invited her to ride with me and see Mrs. Johns.

You need not get me the dress at all. I will appropriate that sum to better purpose—at least a less selfish one. Will thank you to bring me one or two ounces rutabaga seed and some drumhead cabbage and beet seeds.

Thus far for business. How I long to see you all! Robert tells me our dear little Stanhope says almost everything in his monosyllabic way, and that Carrie and Julia I expect will soon be able to translate Admiral von Chamisso's *Voyages Round the World*. "I do admire" to see ladies keep up their literary tastes, although I am myself a striking example of the opposite practice, and feel to my shame and sorrow the rust and ruin which have accumulated upon a neglected mind. All that I can now do is to warn my daughters and granddaughters, that they may not become as I am. For years and years I had intellectual cravings that made me almost miserable; but starvation has quenched the pangs of hunger, and I am now content with the Book of Books and daily striving to fulfill the ordinary duties of life. I hope none of you will ever pattern after such an example.

Your dear father has felt the *excessive* heat which has prevailed ever since you left us. Some days it has been almost insupportable, and—what is unusual here—many of the nights have been warm. Yesterday we had a cool breeze from southeast, and he went after an early dinner to Dorchester, intending to visit Maybank today. . . . Our servant Porter has been sick; we removed him up here, and he is much better. All Patience's children are well. Tell her she will have to give an *account to me* for Little Daughter's *burning her arm*.

Your dear little boy is as bright and happy as possible, but ever on the look-out for his mama. Little Sister improves daily. Do tell my dear son I hope it will prove as he said it might—that the measles would remove the old affection. Her ear is entirely relieved, and all traces of the eruption passing away. She is still pitted like one who had had smallpox. I wish you could have little Mary vaccinated and bring us the scab.

My dear daughter, I really think it is your duty to accept Kitty's kind invitation. It would not only be a comfort to her but might result in years of benefit to you. You are now halfway there. I could send your warm clothing and take every care of Charlie, who is doing so well it would be wrong to make a change with him. *Your father and I both desire you to do so.*

Do ask my dear son if I can help him in any way. Does he want more arrowroot or herbs? And was the old linen serviceable? It rejoices us to hear his practice is increasing. With warmest love to him and dear Carrie and yourself, and kisses for our grandchildren, and howdies for Patience and the servants, and our kind regards to friends on The Hill,

Ever your affectionate mother,
Mary Jones.

REV. R. Q. MALLARD *to* MRS. MARY S. MALLARD[t]

Walthourville, *Tuesday,* August 26th, 1862

My own Darling,

Through the unmerited goodness of God I have reached home safely. . . . It is with a sad heart that I turn my thoughts to you and remember the sorrowful face of my darling as I drove from the house. It grieved me to my heart that you should be so sorely disappointed. But I am convinced that you have done right. This is also the decided opinion of your father too, to whom I have spoken freely about your state. Much as he desires to see you, he would have disapproved of your coming home under the circumstances. My heart recoiled at the thought of further separation, but my judgment told me that you ought not to remove yourself from your present medical attendants. . . . Please write me frequently and particularly about *your health* and about Mamie.

I find all well as usual. The servants were quite disappointed at your not coming, expressed in ejaculations of "Oh!" Mother is absent at Montevideo. Father hard at work. Addressed the congregation on Sabbath morning, but complains of uncomfortable nights. I shall keep you informed of any changes in him, as I know your anxiety. Your dear little boy is quite well, and too fat for good looks. Delighted to see me. He has been in my study all the time I have been writing, and says I must tell Mama to bring him some candy. He gives little or no trouble now at night, and is pretty much reconciled to change of sleeping arrangements. "Dear Mama, I love you very much. Your son, Charlie." The above is his letter to you. Dear little fellow, if I was rich enough, I would go to see you soon and carry him too.

Enclosed you will find twenty dollars. Three dollars of it is Sister Ann's and two Lizzie's; the balance use as you see fit. Your father unites with me—and your mother were she present would—in much love to all. Charlie sends love to Mama and Sister, and says make haste and come home. Lucy and Tenah both send howdy, and the others would if they knew that I was writing you. Dearest Mary, my heart reproaches me for want of tenderness while with you. God Almighty bless you and comfort you, my own, and spare us to each other!

Your own husband,

R. Q. Mallard.

MRS. MARY S. MALLARD *to* REV. C. C. JONES[t]

Augusta, *Tuesday,* August 26th, 1862

My dear Father,

It was a sore disappointment to me to let Mr. Mallard go home without me, but under the circumstances we thought it best. Brother Joe would rather have me remain under his treatment two weeks longer. He is very kind, and is doing all that a good brother could. . . .

I inquired, as Mother desired, about the wool. Your cloth is woven, and I presume on its way down. Mr. Fleming says one pound of wool will generally weave a yard and a half, though much depends upon the wool. A pound of washed clean wool will weave more, but a yard and a half would be a safe average for unwashed moderately clean wool. Just at this time the factory is so much occupied with government orders that it is difficult for them to fill any private orders certainly. It is the only factory that will weave for private individuals. All the cloth woven by the Augusta factory is sold at auction to the highest bidder, and the other factories sell at a cent or two less, so that the prices are very steadily kept up.

Brother Joe will leave tomorrow to meet the ex-governor of Mississippi and Professor Willet in Atlanta, and from there they will go to Kingston to examine a niter cave in the vicinity, located in Bartow County (formerly Cass). Mr. Mallard can give you the merits of the case. It will be a very pleasant trip to Brother Joe, and while in that region he will inquire about plantations for rent or sale.

I received an interesting letter from Kitty last week, in which she begs me to say she intends writing you very soon, and feels very grateful to you for your kind letter. Her sorrows press more and more heavily upon her. As time wears on she realizes her great loss. Edward treats her with great consideration and affection, and has begged her to live with him. (The farm in Habersham belongs to him.) In many things she says he almost puts her in the place of his mother. His furlough will expire the middle of September, when he will return to his company. They have no overseer upon the farm, so Kitty will look after affairs until December. She will probably spend the winter near Edward. Tell Mother she says the greatest difficulty in the way of having wool woven there is the scarcity of factory thread. She has written to know if it can be obtained in Athens, and will write as soon as she ascertains.

Kiss my dear little son many times for me, and tell him Mama's eyes ache to see him. Carrie and Brother Joe unite with me in warmest love to Mother and yourself, Mr. Mallard, and Little Sister.

> Your affectionate daughter,
> Mary S. Mallard.

Miss Kitty Stiles *to* Rev. C. C. Jones[t]
> *Near* Clarkesville, *Thursday,* August 28th, 1862*

Dear Dr. Jones,

I have been waiting for a quiet time without interruptions to thank you for your kindness in writing to me. It was an honor I did not dare hope for. Thank you for every word you wrote. I trust I may profit by them, and this greatest of sorrows be sanctified to my soul; though Mother's absence can never be anything but a grief to me all my life, and nothing be to me as heretofore.

Edward is still with me, though Sidney has returned to Macon. The former is much exhausted from his wound, which is gradually healing. I do not think he will be able to return to Virginia by the middle of September, though when he hears of any fighting he is impatient to be there. Otherwise he would be content, for he loves his home, and his farm occupies his time.

Ed tells me much of his experience in these eventful times in Virginia, and much of Uncle Joe, who seems to be known and loved by the whole army. His escapes have been miraculous; and he has not only been the means of good to the souls of our men, but his utter fearlessness in battle, and words of encouragement as he accompanies those who are sent into the hottest of the fight, cheer and nerve many whose hearts are trembling. He is hailed as "old fellow," and cheered whenever he goes into camp. Many attend his preaching who will not listen to others. I did not see him when in Richmond, as he had gone into North Carolina to purchase a horse. He had parted with his in battle to expedite an order of General Lee's to some portion of the army, the aide having had his horse shot under him. . . .

I trust the *Nashville* will escape, though that seems almost impossible with so many vessels to head her up if she attempt it.

I wish, my dear friend, you could all be with me in this delightful climate. If it were not for the terrible journey that lies between, I would implore you all to come and stay until the winter. It would do me good in every way, besides being a greater pleasure than anything else could be. And I should like you to know my brother so very much. Responsibility and care came to him early, but he has borne them well, and I trust if spared through this cruel war may be a useful man up here, he has so much influence over his men, and they are all from this neighborhood. His general and colonel both speak highly of him as a soldier and a man, which has pleased me much to hear.

What a loss your church has sustained in the death of Dr. Thornwell! His place cannot be filled. Did you see a small pamphlet he published this spring called "Our Dangers and Our Duties"? It is excellent, and I wish could be read by all in our country. . . . Much love to all the family, not forgetting *chère amie,* Charlie, and Baby. Believe me ever most grateful for your friendship and kindness in writing to me.

Yours sincerely,
K. C. Stiles.

Rev. R. Q. Mallard *to* Mrs. Mary S. Mallard[t]

Wathourville, *Saturday,* August 30th, 1862

My dearest Mary,

I cannot promise you a long letter this time, but feel that I must write, if only a few lines, that too long an interval may not elapse between my letters. . . . It grieves me deeply to hear of your sufferings. . . . May the day not be distant when with restored health you shall be permitted to return!

Your mother says you must give yourself no concern about the house—that we have a plenty to eat and drink. She added that it would be necessary to make a little soap soon. Was your soda intended for that purpose? Shall your mother use it? I find that our flour is out, and our lights. I shall have to try the terebene oil. It is used by some people here, and I want to make some inquiry about it. Can we not do without wheat, or do you think we ought to get at least a sack?

Little Charlie continues fat and hearty. Mother says he is one of the best of children; has not had occasion to switch or even slap him. One day in my absence she threatened to have a "fretting-and-fuming" bench made for his benefit, but the prospect was sufficient. He does not forget Mǎma. Looking at a newspaper this morning, his eye fell on a train of cars. Immediately he thought of you: "Mama gone on cars." He stands up for your individual rights, and would not admit that I had any property in our bed.

I have been reading your copy of Newton's *Memoir* with much interest, and I hope profit. What a wonderful life—so full of remarkable providences! It is pleasant to find your footprints before me. I notice you have marked one striking passage, where Mr. Newton (at sea) accompanies his wife in spirit morning and afternoon to the sanctuary. How tender and deep their attachment for each other! How it was sanctified by religion! Let us endeavor to commune in the same way at our hours of retirement and of public worship. . . .

Father and Mother unite with me in a great deal of love to all. . . . Kiss my dear little daughter for me, and tell her that I hope she is growing good. Love to Doctor, Carrie, and Stanhope. I am, my darling, as ever,

Your loving husband,
R. Q. Mallard.

Rev. R. Q. Mallard *to* Mrs. Mary S. Mallard[t]
Walthourville, *Monday,* September 1st, 1862

Darling Heart,

I thank you for your kind favor of the 29th ult. It is a very great pleasure to me to hear frequently, and particularly from you and my dear little daughter. I am rejoiced to hear that you feel some trifle better than when I left, and trust I am thankful. May the good Lord perfect your recovery! It is certainly very kind in Dr. Ford to insist on furnishing you with some ice, although the pleasure of using it must be in some measure marred by the reflection that it may be needed by our poor soldiers. However, if it is wasting, I do not see that it is your duty positively to refuse. . . .

I understand that Willie Joe Mallard has returned home. His arm, Dr. Walthour says, has been butchered by his surgeon and is in a wretched condition. He does not think, however, that he will lose it. It is his right arm. The Lord spare it to him and to his dependent family! Thomas Gignilliat, Olivius Bacon, and one or more others whose names I forget are in the hospital in Charleston. I am glad of it, for they will enjoy what I fear poor

Madison did not — competent medical attendance. It is the talk in camp that their surgeon was promoted from the humble position of an army nurse. Only twenty-two out of eighty men fit for duty! So write the Bakers. Thus far my nephews have escaped. . . .

Mother at Montevideo. Father hard at work. Very weak yesterday, but had a better night's rest than usual. Tenah says that she has had to put strings to some of Charlie's petticoats. You see from this how well he is. His eyes sparkled with pleasure over the prospect of four big marbles. Little Sister and the servants all well. Love to all. I am sorry to have written in such haste: James waits for my letter. You had better bring another paper of beets; those planted not up yet. I asked Charlie what to send Mama; his reply was either "Dis (just) love" or "Kiss love." Love to all.

Very affectionately your husband,
R. Q. Mallard.

REV. R. Q. MALLARD *to* MRS. MARY S. MALLARD[t]

Walthourville, *Tuesday,* September 2nd, 1862

My darling Wife,

It is a pleasant moonlight evening, and the softened sound of the servants' singing beneath my window falls sweetly upon my ear. God grant that all may learn to make melody in their hearts unto the Lord! Surely these are not the voices of poor downtrodden humanity, looking for its only release from galling servitude in the grave, "where the servant is free from his master." I wish that we could do more for them than is done, and we hope to do in better times. I believe our domestic affairs move on without any extraordinary amount of friction.

Father and Mother are both out this evening on a visit to Miss Claudia Quarterman. They were to have gone this afternoon, but were prevented by calls from Mrs. J. B. Mallard and the Misses McConnell. And as Father had promised to go and hear Miss Claudia sing "Maryland, My Maryland," they concluded to pay their visit after tea.

Your father and in fact all of us are greatly cheered by God's goodness to us in Virginia, of which we have heard tidings today. I trust we feel deeply grateful, and many a fervent and tearful thanksgiving has ascended to Him today. What a beautiful dispatch is General Lee's to the President! Alas, that our joy must be tempered by grief for the many slain, and anxiety for such as we know. The two Flemings, Dunwody, and perhaps Charles Jones were all in these sanguinary conflicts. Have all escaped? May our friends be delivered from the harrowing scenes of the first battle at Manassas! Darwin McConnell is with General Smith in Kentucky; when he wrote last, he was crossing the Cumberland Mountains to get in Morgan's (Federal) rear and cut off his communications and supplies. His sisters seem quite anxious about him—I believe go for the mail themselves every day. Charlie wrote a very beautiful letter today about the news; said that he felt like singing the Song of Moses and Miriam. May a merciful God continue to direct and bless our armies!

I felt so thankful today that I determined to study harder than ever, and had a pleasant morning with Gaussen on inspiration. . . . I wish I had your easy and ready hand to assist me.

Many inquiries are made after you and the time of your return. In regard to the latter I suppose you cannot yet decide. No home consideration, I hope, will be allowed to decide you upon any course which may prejudice your recovery. I hope it is not mere selfishness but my ardent love for you that makes me recoil from the sad prospect of seeing you a confirmed invalid. It is my constant prayer that a merciful God may perfectly restore my own to health. Whenever you make up your mind to return, you must give me timely notice.

Our village is quiet: nothing new or stirring. . . . The bales have not yet arrived. If not out by tomorrow's freight I will write about them to Mr. Gué. Receipts have been taken for them, and are both accessible to me if they should be lost. I presume, however, that they have been simply delayed. . . . I will now close for the night and, D.V., finish in the morning.

Wednesday Morning. Father leaves this morning for the Island. I am sorry that he feels compelled by a sense of duty to go. He says Old Andrew, although a good executive officer, has no arithmetical genius and needs constant directions.

Mother's loom is now in operation, and doing very well. Would you like to have one? James and I could put up one if you give us time. Mother wishes you to inquire if the factory would weave for her thirty pounds of *perfectly clean wool,* and would like to know how much cloth it would make.

Little Charlie was not so well yesterday, and I made up for him by your directions the rhubarb mixture, and it has helped him. I will give him a little quinine today. All the rest well. Mother sends a great deal of love, in which Father would join if aware of my writing. I am, my darling, as ever,

Your own
Robert.

Rev. R. Q. Mallard *to* Mrs. Mary S. Mallard[t]

Walthourville, *Thursday,* September 4th, 1862

My darling Wife,

Extravagant, am I not, to write so frequently when postage is so high? But what is that man's wife worth, for a chat with whom once a day he is not willing—and more—to pay ten cents per diem? Writing is the next best thing to seeing you, but a wide interval lies between them. Your absence is an affliction to me, and I long for it to end, yet would not throw a feather in the way of its prolongation if you should require it to receive the full benefit of a course of medical treatment. . . .

Our prayer meeting was quite full this afternoon, and more than usual feeling was manifested by Christians. Our second prayer is by appointment offered specially for our country, government, and soldiers. We began it a week ago, and I first called upon your father; and oh, what a prayer he made! I wish you could have heard it, it was so comprehensive and feeling and humble and importunate. While we were at prayer the wild uproar of hosts in deadly conflict arose from the ensanguined field twice baptized with the blood of our brave. Who will say that such a prayer was not felt upon that distant field?

Mr. Thomas Fleming offered the special prayer this evening, and it was, as usual with him, a prayer of great feeling and earnestness. . . . The Flemings and Bacons are deeply anxious about their relatives who participated in the recent battles; and the McConnells, I expect, are in suspense until they hear of Darwin, who, I think, is with Kirby Smith in Kentucky. Judge Fleming has gone to Savannah to be near the telegraph office. Thus far they have heard nothing at all beyond the first newspaper accounts. I am greatly concerned to hear the final issue, for it is rumored that the hardest fighting was on Sabbath. God defend the right! Surely we have cause to trust in Him. The news from Kentucky is cheering indeed. We must expect some reverses, however; and they should not discourage us when they come.

Last Sunday night eight Negroes of Mr. Joseph Anderson's took the guard boat at Sunbury and succeeded in making their escape to the Yankees. I have not heard the particulars, but the fact as it stands criminates the picket of most culpable negligence. One of the contrabands had been employed as cook by the picket. The only safety for us is to remove our people into the interior, and this the enormous charges made for plantations seem almost to render impossible.

Mother seems greatly enamored of your machine, and has learned to sew finely on it and to manage it herself. She asked me to fix the lower spool one day, and has quite crowed over me because she detected an oversight on my part. Susan is making her Virginia-acquired talents available, and Little Sister meanwhile takes Elsie for her nurse. Elsie sings her to sleep in the rocking chair with manifest gusto. . . .

I have just received your letter, and am rejoiced to hear that there is a prospect of seeing you so soon. Providence permitting, I will meet you on Monday night at the Central Railroad depot. Love to all from all.

Your affectionate husband,
R. Q. Mallard.

XIV

Mrs. Mary Jones *to* Lt. Charles C. Jones, Jr.^g

Walthourville, *Thursday,* September 4th, 1862

My dear Son,

Your last affectionate favor has been received. We have indeed cause for "profound gratitude" to our Almighty God and Redeemer for the recent discomfiture of our inhuman enemy. I can never rest when such tidings reach us until my knees are bowed in humble praise and thanksgiving to "Him who ruleth in the army of heaven and amongst the inhabitants of earth." Oh, when shall the day of our complete deliverance come? God grant that in that day we shall not only be purged from our former iniquities but be established in righteousness! When we look at the many professedly good men now arrayed against us, some might be led to doubt the truth of religion; but this is not so. Those men have departed from the precepts of the Divine Word, and are illustrating not the falsity of God's truth but their own inherent depravity.

You have doubtless noticed the injury to your friend Brigadier General Helm, and the perilous escape of the Misses Hardin. Were they not the young ladies with whom you visited the Mammoth Cave—nieces of Mrs. Helm?

Your dear father went to the Island yesterday. Our affairs there are necessarily left to Andrew's fidelity. Providence has not yet opened up the way for the removal of our people, and as the time presses on when it may be absolutely necessary to do so, we become anxious, not knowing what distresses await all who live upon accessible points to the enemy the coming winter. I see that these arrangements weigh heavily upon your father, whose increasing feebleness is more and more evident. This summer he has lost both flesh and strength. I know that your brother and yourself will do all you can to relieve him of every care, and I trust the Lord will open up the way and provide a safe and suitable retreat for us and our servants. We have had great sorrows and great losses in their sickness and death this spring, and there are several now in feeble health from their severe illness.

When will you be able to visit us? If you would let us know, we could arrange so as to have our dear little daughter baptized at home, if it is impossible for you to spend a Sabbath with us. I ardently desire the performance of this precious duty and privilege on our part, and feel that it would be in accordance with the faith and wishes of her sainted mother in heaven.

The mail has just arrived, and with it, my dear son, your package, for which accept my sincere thanks. And enclosed you will find ten dollars. Please pay for the awls, etc., and your father's specs (the silver). And will you be so good as to purchase with the remainder for me as many pounds as it will of *washing soda for making soap,* and *bring* the same with you when you come. *You need not send it.* It is usually kept by any of the druggists or grocers.

Gilbert too has just come up with Tyrone, who is quite sick. And your father sends me a note saying that eight of Joe Anderson's Negroes left him on Sunday night, taking three others (making eleven). Their leader was his man James, who was cooking for the picket guard in Sunbury; and while they either slept or ceased to *watch* on Sunday night he took the picket boat and packed it with his own family and friends and left them minus breakfast on Monday morning! What shall be said if this is true of such coast guards! To mend the matter James's daughter went into the house and packed up all Bessie Anderson's best clothes and jewelry in her own trunk and took them away with her!

I observe various notices about Confederate money. Your father has over three hundred dollars in that currency, mostly twenty-, ten-, and five-dollar bills. The whole of the three hundred dollars you sent him from the sale of the cotton remains untouched—*all Confederate money.* And the two twenty-dollar bills you sent me from Lathrop are of the doubtful issue, but look genuine. What shall we do about them?

Your dear daughter is well and very bright. Little Charlie not so well today. I must close for the mail. Would you like me to send you some butter and okra? I have just completed the repairs of your shirts. Would you like buttons *sewed* on the bosoms? If so and you can send me six dozen pearl buttons, I will put them on. With much love from Robert and Charlie, and sweetest kisses from your little Ruth, and sincerest affection of

Your mother,
Mary Jones.

Excuse my trembling hand.

Lt. Charles C. Jones, Jr., *to* Mrs. Mary Jones[g]

Savannah, *Monday,* September 8th, 1862

My dear Mother,

I am favored with your very kind letter of the 4th inst., and would have replied at an earlier date, but have been prevented from doing so in consequence of a severe cut, which almost severed the index finger of my right hand near the first joint. I was fearful at first that the first joint would have to be amputated, but I had the wound dressed soon after the accident, and it is now healing by the first intention. I was endeavoring to lift a large flat-bottomed inkstand, which had not been used for many months, from the table. It stuck hard and fast. I put my forefinger in its mouth to give me a greater purchase upon it, when it broke, and the upper edge of the fracture cut the finger very severely. Being very thick, I think no particles of the glass were given off, and therefore I trust the healing will be rapid and permanent.

The news from Virginia comes in slowly. We have gained a signal but not altogether a decisive victory. The conflict will, I presume, be renewed near Alexandria if our army presses in that direction. Removed as we are from the theater of active operations, and with but partial intimations of the character of the pursuit, we can but speculate as to results. My own impression is that the main body of the army will avoid Alexandria and Arlington heights and, crossing the Potomac higher up, invade Maryland, and, passing in the rear of Washington, subject that city to either a partial or total isolation. An excellent strategic point for occupation would be Harrisburg, Pennsylvania. This in our possession, Pennsylvania would furnish abundant supplies for our army, while Philadelphia, Baltimore, and Washington would be cut off to a very great extent from the rich tributes from the West which have ever furnished them with every necessary.

All we can do, however, in the absence of definite information is to pray for the continued mercies of the Giver of All Good, and repose continued and unshaken confidence in the great leaders and brave troops who have heretofore illustrated every virtue, every daring, and every endurance which belong to the noblest specimens of the truehearted, patriotic soldier contending for everything that is dear to him in principle and in country.

We have cheering news from Tennessee, and we look from that quarter for results even more decisive than in Virginia. Tennessee and Kentucky will soon be entirely relieved from the Lincoln yoke.

I have several letters from various portions of the state in reference to the sale of places, but none can be surrendered before 1st December next, and most of them 1st January—in consequence of the growing crop. I enclose the last received from Colonel Clark. Captain Spencer is now in Southwest Georgia near Thomasville, and has promised me to see if he cannot find a place there. Being perfectly acquainted with the localities, he thinks he may succeed. I am to hear from him in a very few days.

The Confederate money which you now have I do not think is spurious. The issue of which you speak will be at any time received at the customhouse and new bills given instead. So soon as I can come out I will receive the amount which Father and yourself now have and exchange the same for the new issue.

The shirts, I think, have holes in the bosoms for buttons. I do not think I would change them, as I have the studs to wear with them. The spectacles, awls, etc., if I remember, cost about $5.20. The balance of the ten dollars which you enclosed I will invest as you desire in washing soda, if to be procured in the city, and send the same to you by earliest opportunity.

I am sorry to learn that the Negroes of the county still continue to desert to the enemy. I am doing all that I can to ascertain some place of retreat for us. If I could only be relieved for a short time, I think I could succeed in effecting that object. I need some change too. I have had a constant and violent headache now for five days, and no cause for it that I know of. It exerts a very depressing influence, and at some moments almost takes my wits away from me.

I am very sorry to hear that Father is not as well as usual. Do give warmest love to him. Kiss my precious little daughter for me. And accept for yourself, my dearest mother, the constant love and gratitude of

Your affectionate son,
Charles C. Jones, Jr.

Kind remembrances to Robert and Charlie. Howdy for the servants.

REV. C. C. JONES *to* LT. CHARLES C. JONES, JR.ᵍ

Walthourville, *Tuesday,* September 9th, 1862

My dear Son,

Your sister and Robert have reached home in safety, D.G.; and your letter is at hand to Mother, enclosing one from Mr. Richard H. Clark, which is the most promising one we have yet had.

I am much concerned to hear of your *headaches*—in your letter and particularly from Robert. Now, there is a limit to exertion and confinement to business. The weather is hot and trying. You have had a laborious office for months at least, and no assistant allowed you. Headaches occurring with men under your circumstances are premonitions of severer affections and dangerous ones. You must therefore throw down your business for a time on *the score of health,* and relax until the tone of your system is restored to its healthy condition. Necessity knows no law. This is your duty and your right, and General Pemberton cannot deny you. Get a furlough and come out and see us, or take a trip off for your restoration somewhere. I am in earnest in this.

We regret to learn the cut on your finger. It must have been very severe, and hope it will heal "on the first intention." We are not our own keepers. Had you seen forty people put their fingers into that inkstand to disengage it from the table, you would have said: "Don't do that: if the glass breaks, you will ruin your hand."

Please hand the enclosed to Messrs. Claghorn & Cunningham, and present me kindly to Captain Claghorn when you see him.

Do stop and recruit. You do not know how glad we shall be to see you. Little Sister is full of life. Daughter thinks she has fattened very much. I hear her little voice downstairs playing; she has a language of her own. All send love.

Your ever affectionate father,
C. C. Jones.

Lt. Charles C. Jones, Jr., *to* Rev. C. C. Jones[g]

Savannah, *Wednesday,* September 10th, 1862

My dear Father,

I am today favored with your kind letter of the 9th inst. with enclosure to Messrs. Claghorn & Cunningham, which I have duly handed to them.

Do thank Mother for her kind remembrance of me received by Robert. The groundnuts are remarkably large, and are very nice. It is a nut when fresh and well boiled of which I am very fond. Judging from the specimen sent, the yield of the ricefield must be very abundant. There are few grains of richer hue or more attractive view than the rice ready for the harvest. The peppers are very fine, but I am afraid of them. My rule is to eat nothing which may at any future hour remind me of the fact that I have eaten.

This morning I had a conversation with Mr. Gué, the clerk of Mr. Anderson, in reference to a sale of our cotton. He tells me that he thinks he can dispose of the same at forty cents per pound, and bagging can now be purchased at $1.25 per yard. He will have the refusal for some days of nineteen pieces. What do you think of the propriety of disposing of the cotton now in store on the places? Would it not be more prudent to sell than to take the chances of fire and perhaps of graver dangers during the coming winter? We will soon, too, have the addition of the incoming crop. I mention the subject for your consideration, and will abide by your views in the matter.

It is a most difficult matter to secure a place to which the Negroes can be removed. I have corresponded with gentlemen in various portions of the state, and have made every inquiry from the factors here, but without success. You will observe that in almost every instance the places offered in suitable localities are such as are considerably if not badly worn, and are only now exposed for sale with the hope of large profits on the part of the seller. As far as I have been able to judge, Randolph Whitehead's place as a retreat affords more advantages, despite the character of the lands, etc., than any I have yet heard of. It can remain for the present at least as a *dernier ressort*. His price is just what was asked for it before the war—a high figure, however, then. The greatest difficulties connected with the purchase are want of timber for plantation purposes and the exhausted condition of the soil. And yet Randolph tells me that ever since he has planted there he has never made less than five bales of cotton to the hand, and a sufficiency of provisions. A comfortable dwelling house is a great desideratum in the event of our being compelled to abandon the coast.

My own impression is that the principal danger to which we will be subjected will be the voluntary desertion of the Negroes. I very much doubt if the enemy will attempt to penetrate the interior except at strategic points. And the truth is, if God still favors our cause and inspires our armies and leaders as He has done in such a marked manner for some time past, the enemy will be forced to keep his troops for home defense.

The fall campaign opens on our part with a brilliancy and success absolutely wonderful. Contrasted with the position the Confederate States occupied three months since, our present is almost incredible. Already is the promise of our worthy chief magistrate redeemed, and the war is being carried "beyond the outer confines of our Confederacy"—Smith thundering at the gates of Cincinnati; Lee, Jackson, and Longstreet surrounding the beleaguered capital of Lincolndom and pressing to the rescue of Maryland. Ohio and Pennsylvania will both soon feel the presence of actual, present warfare; while a hasty retreat will be all that is left for the scattered armies of our invaders, who linger in uncertainty and fear in our borders, which they of late overran in such pride, strength, and exultation.

Every act in this drama but reveals more and more clearly the wisdom of our rulers, vindicates the energy and the ability of the administration, and affords ever-increasing assurance of the favor of the Ever-Living God, to whom all thanksgivings are due, and are humbly and fervently paid by many a pious heart. Never in the annals of the world has a nation in such short period achieved such a history. Not two years old, and we have already performed such prodigies of valor, given such assurance of greatness, afforded such examples of moral heroism, individual action, and national prowess, and exhibited such proofs of high-toned patriotism, devotion to principle, and love of truth, that we search in vain among the pages of the past for a record to parallel it. Whatever else the nations of the earth may think or say or do, we have already wrested from them unbounded respect and admiration.

Have you noticed one very interesting fact in the history of this war—that the *pious leaders* have been specially blessed in all of their enterprises? If you will only reflect for a moment, the truth of this remark will become most evident. Stonewall Jackson, Lee, Stuart: pious men all—another illustration of the fact that the truly pious man is the best man for every walk and every emergency in life, and for the simple reason that he carries with him the favor of Him from whom alone all success and all strength can come.

As yet today we have no telegrams of interest.

Had the pleasure yesterday of taking by the hand Mr. Charles Jones Colcock, our kinsman, now colonel of a cavalry regiment in South Carolina, one of the most accomplished and agreeable gentlemen one might meet anywhere. He inquired very particularly after you and dear Mother.

Your watch, Father, is repaired and fully regulated, and only awaits a favorable opportunity to be sent home. Had I known of Robert's coming, I would have taken it from the jeweler's hands, but the shop was closed during his sojourn in the city.

Please say to Mother that just now there is no washing soda in the city, but I will secure it for her so soon as any can be had.

My head and finger are both better today. General Pemberton declines to relieve me from the court, and I am not sick enough to procure a physician's certificate. I trust, however, before long to have the great pleasure of seeing you, my dear parents, and my precious little daughter.

The Confederate money which you sent in is all *good*. It will be exchanged at the customhouse here so soon as the government remits new notes with which to call in and redeem the old issue. . . . My paper has all given out, and I must close. With warmest love to you both, my dear parents, with many kisses for my precious little daughter, and kindest remembrances for Sister, Robert, Mary, and Charlie, as ever,

Your affectionate son,
Charles C. Jones, Jr.

Lt. Charles C. Jones, Jr., *to* Rev. C. C. Jones[g]

Savannah, *Monday,* September 22nd, 1862

My dear Father,

I this morning had an interview with Mr. Schley in reference to the purchase of his Buckhead place in Burke County. That plantation contains fourteen hundred and twelve acres, and he asks ten dollars per acre, one-third cash and the balance in one and two years. Will sell corn, peas, fodder, and mules, etc., on the place. Thinks it questionable whether he will be able to give possession much before the 1st January, although he may be able to do so before, in case he sees the opportunity clear for removing his Negroes to Texas. Mr. Schley tells me that one may reasonably calculate upon an average crop of about five bales of cotton per hand, and a yield of from eight to ten bushels of corn per acre. This year his corn crop will average twelve bushels. There are some hundred and fifty or two hundred acres of fine land yet to be cleared. The improvements upon the place are in fair condition. I am to embrace the earliest opportunity for going up and looking at the plantation with him. Health fair—on a par with other places in Burke; some chill and fever. Nine hundred acres cleared land, five hundred and twelve acres wooded land on the place. On the whole I like the prospects of this purchase more than those of any other place of which I have heard. Will be able to speak more definitely when I have seen and examined it, which I will endeavor to do at the earliest practicable moment.

Major Locke tells me that a little later in the season he will be prepared to purchase the cattle, and begs that intermediately they be allowed the benefit of the fields. The difficulty about a present purchase on the part of the government is simply this: there is a large supply now on hand—larger than the stock pastures in the vicinity of the city can conveniently sustain. So soon as that supply is somewhat diminished, the government will be prepared to enter upon new contracts of purchase. Intermediately the cattle fare better if kept upon the pastures and allowed the freedom of the fields upon the plantations. I have not engaged them to him, and will ascertain whether a private sale upon advantageous terms can be effected within a shorter period of time.

From what George tells me I almost fear to inquire how Tyrone is. His case is another illustration of the fearful indirect consequence of this unholy war.

We have most important dispatches from Virginia, but are in a state of painful anxiety in regard to the exact issues of that bloody battle at Sharpsburg, in which our loss is reported by the meager accounts already at hand to have been very heavy. Three brigadier generals killed and several wounded, among the latter our friend General Lawton. We can only hope and pray for the best, relying upon the tried valor of our troops, the known ability of our leaders, and the justice of our cause.

Nothing of local interest. We are still in the midst of this equinoctial, with its somber shadows and dripping skies. With warmest love to dear Mother, little Daughter, and all at home, I am, as ever, my dear parents,

Your affectionate son,
Charles C. Jones, Jr.

REV. C. C. JONES *to* LT. CHARLES C. JONES, JR.[8]

Walthourville, *Wednesday,* September 24th, 1862

My dear Son,

I agree with you that Mr. Schley's plantation is the most promising yet offered, and your personal inspection only can determine the purchase, in which of course you will be careful. It would give me great pleasure to accompany you, but think it would be too great an undertaking for me, as I have been retrograding considerably lately, and my symptoms are peculiar and more than ordinarily weakening.

It will be a question indeed *when* Mr. Schley gets his people off to Texas. The possession of the Mississippi by the enemy, and the regular passes into Texas estopped, will render removals very difficult and hazardous. *This matter,* in case of purchase, must be definitely and distinctly settled. Earlier than January 1st we should be on the ground—in *November early* if possible.

Clear the coast is the order of the day, for the enemy is making his arrangements to capture our remaining seaports and desolate to the utmost the country; and this will be the winter's work. Admitting we are favored in recovering the border states, in them he can do but little in the winter; and his campaign lies south and coast- and river-wise. We are having brilliant times North and West. If *the people* rise in Maryland, Tennessee, and Kentucky, the enemy must retire, and Missouri must follow; and we shall be, humanly speaking, stronger than ever. So may our Heavenly Father decree it for us!

Enclosed is a letter from your brother. I have marked some places. He is doing what he can in his circumstances to help us out. This removal presses heavily upon your dear mother, but I hope it may yet turn out that she need not leave her pleasant and long-cherished home. You can let me know further about the cattle.

Am happy to say Tyrone is much better, though not out of danger. He was not expected to live at one time. Rest of the people at both places well. Busy harvesting.

Your baby is getting as hearty as ever. Begins to display temper, and sets everybody laughing when she essays to enter into conversation on subjects that interest her. Among other accomplishments is learning to kiss: opens her mouth and bites off the kiss from your mouth! . . . Mother, Sister, and Robert send much love, and kisses from your little daughter and niece and nephew.

Your ever affectionate father,
C. C. Jones.

LT. CHARLES C. JONES, JR., *to* REV. C. C. JONES[g]

Savannah, *Saturday*, September 27th, 1862

My dear Father,

I am in receipt of your kind favor of the 24th inst. with enclosed letter from Brother, and thank you for it. I am happy to know that Tyrone is better, and trust that his recovery may prove rapid and permanent.

I hope on next Saturday to be able to go up and examine Mr. Schley's place. The greatest difficulty connected with the purchase is that he will not be able to give possession much before the 1st of January next, in consequence of his having to gather the growing crop, etc. If we resolve upon the purchase of this plantation, we will have to arrange some intermediate disposition of the Negroes. . . . Early possession of any place selected is all-important. Another all-important matter is to secure if possible on the place a sufficiency of provisions and thus avoid the necessity for hauling, etc.

Yesterday we have the sad intelligence of the death of Spalding McIntosh (who married Sis Morris), an aide to General McLaws with the rank of major, and of the fact that both Randolph and Charlie Whitehead are wounded. This at the terrible battle of Sharpsburg. It is said by General Lee that the shock of this battle was more terrific than any which has as yet occurred in the present war. We held the honors of the field, but the long list of killed and wounded which has already reached us attests the severity of the struggle and the heavy price at which the victory was purchased. The present status of our army in Virginia and along the line of the Potomac seems involved in a degree of uncertainty which causes painful anxiety.

It occurs to me that our government ought, upon the termination of a general engagement of such magnitude and unquestioned importance, to furnish at the earliest practicable moment to the country at large at least an announcement of the general result. With the pressure of an active campaign of such proportions upon them our commanding generals of course have not the time to prepare elaborate reports; but a few lines will tell at the moment the fact of success or reverse and thus relieve the public mind. To know the worse, and to realize the true state of things, no matter how unfavorable, is always preferable to a state of disquietude and anxious uncertainty. Our nation has by past acts demonstrated the fact that with astonishing composure it can bear alike the joys of success and the disheartening influences of reverses. It seems scarcely proper, therefore, for our government to withhold authentic information in reference to past occurrences and accomplished facts, and thus to encourage a resort to the uncertain reports of letter-writers and the lying statements of Northern presses to satisfy the laudable desire of the people who are so nearly interested for a knowledge of the true status of affairs. Of course with the future operations of armies and with the anticipated plans of our generals we have no right to be made acquainted, for thus would those operations be often frustrated. I speak only of the duty of the government when the storm cloud has lifted from the battlefield to give the country at an early moment the result of the engagement.

No private dispatches, I believe, have as yet been received announcing the precise character of the wounds of Randolph and Charlie. I still indulge the hope that the report of McIntosh's death may not be correct. I obtained for him his appointment in the army. Until a very recent period he was connected with the 1st Georgia Regulars, and was recently promoted to the staff appointment which he now holds—or held at the time of his reported death. Maria Morris, his wife, was tenderly attached to him, and I feel deeply for her.

The news from the West is cheering. Bragg reported near Louisville; has demanded the surrender of the city.

I sent you on yesterday a copy of an Ohio paper which was handed to me by one of the returned Pulaski prisoners. They suffered much during their captivity, and were subjected to continuous and open insults. Finally all their trunks were broken open, and every article of value taken from them. They were thirteen days on the Mississippi River in returning. Captain Sims tells me that there were eleven hundred crowded on the boat in which he returned, and of that number near nine hundred had the diarrhea. You may imagine the condition of matters. The enemy, it appears, improved the opportunity afforded by the flag of truce used to convey the released Confederate prisoners to Vicksburg to provision several of their posts and garrisons on the line of the river—an act entirely characteristic of the race with which we are at war, devoid alike of everything pertaining to honor or good faith. Those returned officers (many of them) show plainly the effects of harsh usage.

You notice in the morning papers the announcement that Lincoln has issued his proclamation liberating the slaves of all rebels on the 1st January next —the crowning act of the series of black and diabolical transactions which have marked the entire course of his administration. I look upon it as a direct bid for insurrection, as a most infamous attempt to incite flight, murder, and rapine on the part of our slave population. With a fiendish purpose he has designedly postponed the operation of this for a future day in order that intermediately the mind of the slave population may if possible be prepared to realize and look forward to the consummation of the act proposed and thus prepare for the same. Practically, under present circumstances, I do not think the proclamation will have any effect. But this does not in the least detract from the character of the act, or lessen one iota the enormity of its crime.

You observe also that the eleven thousand prisoners lately taken at Harpers Ferry and released upon parole by Stonewall Jackson are to be sent out to the West to repel the threatened uprising of the Indians. The policy is openly avowed of rapine and desolation upon our coast and our borders whenever opportunity occurs.

The question occurs, what are we now to do with future prisoners captured from such an enemy? Are they within the pale of civilization? Are they entitled to consideration as prisoners of war? By the law of England an outlaw could be pursued and captured with hue and cry wherever found in the King's realm and killed at the first crossroad. Shall a less punishment be meted out to these robbers, murderers, plunderers, violators of virtue, and outlaws of humanity? By the statute law of the state anyone who attempts to incite insurrection among our slaves shall if convicted suffer death. Is it right, is it just to treat with milder considerations the lawless bands of armed marauders who will infest our borders to carry into practical operation the proclamation of the infamous Lincoln, subvert our entire social system, desolate our homes, and convert the quiet, ignorant, dependent black son of toil into a savage incendiary and brutal murderer?

Surely we are passing through harsh times, and are beset with perils which humanity in its worst phases has not encountered for centuries. The Age of Gold has yielded to the Age of Iron; and the North furnishes an example of refined barbarity, moral degeneracy, religious impiety, soulless honor, and absolute degradation almost beyond belief. *Omnia vestigia retrorsum.* It does indeed appear impossible to conjecture where all this will end. It does seem that only He who by a word calmed the tempest-tossed sea can bring light and order and peace out of the perfect moral, political, and social chaos which broods so darkly over the Northern states, give to our enemies a better mind, and assure us in the happy possession of our homes and loves and honor and property. Meanwhile we can only make a proper use of those means which He has placed in our power, and with a firm reliance on the justice of our cause, and with earnest supplication of His aid who saves not by many nor by few, offer every resistance to the inroads of this inhuman enemy, and illustrate every virtue which pertains to a brave, God-fearing people engaged in an awful struggle, against wonderful odds, for personal, civil, and religious freedom.

Pray say to Robert that I am in receipt of his favor of the 25th inst., and that I have twice been to the marble yard of Messrs. R. D. Walker & Company, but on each occasion found not even a workman there. I learn that the proprietors are both absent, but that the return of one is anticipated in a few days. Will endeavor at the earliest moment to compass his wishes.

Am happy to hear such favorable news of my dear little daughter. My daily prayer is that God will endow her plenteously with health and intellect and every attraction, but above all things that He will be pleased, even from early infancy, to convert her and acknowledge her as His child. With warmest love to self, my dear father, to dear Mother, Sister, Robert, and Mamie and Charlie, and with kisses for my precious little daughter, I am ever

Your affectionate son,
Charles C. Jones, Jr.

Rev. C. C. Jones *to* Lt. Charles C. Jones, Jr.ᵍ

Walthourville, *Tuesday,* September 30th, 1862

My dear Son,

Your interesting letter of the 27th came yesterday. Would it not be well to make inquiries and see if possible Colonel Seaborn Jones's Tuckahoe plantation, which is offered *for rent,* before seeing or at least before deciding on Mr. Schley's place? Would not the rent of a fair place for a year on reasonable terms be better than a purchase at this time, and give us a further chance of looking out? I do not know how Colonel Jones's place is situated in respect to the railroad. I wish I could go with you, but cannot. You must do the best you can, and in deciding put all the advantages and disadvantages together and strike the balance. I consider the removal pretty much a permanent one, for by the time the war is ended the people will be so well fixed wherever they go that it will be a losing business to break them up again. And the places in this county, if retained, will have to be worked by small forces until increase comes to our aid.

Mr. Schley will find difficulty in taking his Negroes to Texas, unless we succeed in blockading portions of the Mississippi effectually. Our people must be off long before January, for from present appearances it will not be surprising if the enemy begins his campaign on our coasts early in the season. It will be a great relief when our people are *removed.*

It is not without full advisement that Lincoln has issued his Emancipation Proclamation. The conference of the governors sustains him in it, and in the renewal of the war with still greater vigor if possible. There is no other policy in all the old United States but the war policy. The old Northern Democratic party is nothing. Peace party there is none. Military dictatorship is a fancy; and the abolition and anti-South party waxes stronger and stronger. We have nothing but war before us. The enemy considers our subjugation but a question of time only. They can beat us and give us three or four in the game, for they say that they can call out three or four soldiers to our one, and their resources are as many times greater than ours, and consider us well-nigh exhausted now. Wonderful is it how they leave out in their calculations right and justice and God, who rules over the nations—even Him who can save by few as by many; and moreover, that the invader works at a disadvantage of three or four to one. Up to this hour we can say the Lord has been on our side; to Him let us constantly commit our cause.

Am happy to see that this execrable proclamation has been called up to notice in our Congress. I fully agree with you in your views of it. The war has become one for the perpetration of every brutal crime—for robbery, arson, and insurrection; and our government would be justifiable in putting every prisoner taken to instantaneous death, unless the war be wholly altered in its character and the proclamation be withdrawn. The Northern people will uphold the proclamation. England will uphold it, and so will France and every nation in Europe practically. There will be no remonstrances, no protests, unless great changes occur speedily. What Seward threatened them with if they interfered—the abolition of slavery and their loss of cotton, rice, and tobacco—is coming upon them without their interference. We must hope for the best from General Lee's army. A dreadful battle, that of Sharpsburg!

Mother and Sister go down this afternoon on a visit to Dorchester and the Island; also to see your Uncle William, who we hear has been and is still quite sick, but better. Tyrone still critically sick, though the doctor thinks some better. Am confined here on his account all the time.

Your dear baby is quite well. When I poured the water upon her head in her baptism, she meekly bowed it and never uttered a sound! Mr. Samuel Mallard took her in the twilight of the evening from her nurse, and she went and stayed with him and took him for yourself and was not inclined to leave him. She is getting a beautiful set of teeth, and her eyes are the very eyes of her mother. Some mornings she sits quietly through morning worship in the family. Mrs. Cay's tame deer came into the parlor last evening, and she was in an ecstasy.

Mother and Sister and Robert send much love. And kisses from your little one and Mary and Charlie. People generally well.

Your ever affectionate father,
C. C. Jones.

P.S. Did you speak to Mr. Gué to put by two pieces bagging for us—one for Arcadia and one for Montevideo? *Please do it.*

Lt. Charles C. Jones, Jr., *to* Rev. C. C. Jones[g]

Savannah, *Wednesday,* October 1st, 1862

My very dear Father,

I am today in receipt of your kind letter of yesterday, and am happy to hear such good news from home.

I learn upon inquiry that the place of Mr. Jones is located *directly* on the Savannah River. It consists principally of river swamp, the highland being comparatively but little and sadly worn. Place very much out of repair, and the swampland (say, some four or five thousand acres) uncleared and subject to continual overflow. Mr. Jones wishes to *sell,* and asks some sixteen thousand dollars. The place is by no means a desirable one. It is, further, at quite a remove from the railroad.

Night before last, not having seen Brother and Sister Carrie for a long time, I went up to Augusta, breakfasted with them, and returned by the afternoon train, which reached the city last night. Found Sister Carrie and little Stanhope quite well. The Doctor had had a little fever, and was then suffering from headache. He was not looking as well as when I last saw him, but he stated to me that his present indisposition was temporary, and resulted from some night exposure to which he had been recently subjected. He is getting a very clever practice, and tells me he thinks he will be able to make both ends meet without difficulty. Dr. and Mrs. Leyburn were with them, and both desired especial and warmest remembrance to yourself, dear Mother, and Sister. Brother and Sister Carrie united in best love.

I was enabled to enjoy the pleasure of this hurried visit in consequence of the fact that the court-martial was dissolved in the afternoon of the 29th ult. But accompanying the order dissolving that court came another from General Beauregard assembling another, and reappointing me as the *judge advocate*. This court assembled today, and I have been all day trying causes before it. From all indications it appears that this is to be my occupation, at least for the present; and laborious as the duties are, I do not know but they are preferable to the duller engagements of camp life just at this time. It is especially true in military life that those who are bound must obey, and I endeavor to observe the rule that whatever is to be done should always be well done.

A little gunboat has been shelling below—down the river—this afternoon, evidently endeavoring to ascertain whether any new batteries had been erected by us, and whether any additional obstructions had been placed in the river. She has dropped down with the tide, and did not come up as far as the obstructions, or within range of any of our guns.

Randolph and Charlie Whitehead have both returned home. Randolph is badly wounded in the foot, and Charlie wounded in the arm. Poor McIntosh is said to have been horribly mangled, and was buried on the field. His wife is almost deranged. She had concentered all her affections upon him, and her heart, bereft of his loves, is desolate beyond description. I feel very much for her. This is but one illustration of the heavy personal griefs caused by this cruel and unnatural war.

I have seen Mr. Gué in reference to the bagging.

Do give warmest love to dear Mother, Sister, Robert, Charlie, and Mamie, and the tenderest affection and kisses to my precious little daughter. I am ever, my dear father,

Your affectionate son,
Charles C. Jones, Jr.

Rev. C. C. Jones *to* Lt. Charles C. Jones, Jr.[g]

Walthourville, *Thursday*, October 2nd, 1862

My dear Son,

Yours of yesterday is at hand. A few more reappointments will give you a clear right to the judge advocateship. Am glad of it; it is better with its labors, as you say, than the monotony of camp life. You have time to be alone in your chamber morning and evening, and you have the great privilege of quiet Sabbaths and the services of the sanctuary. Those are special mercies in these times of war.

What a judgment is falling upon our country! When we view it in its extent, its ramifications, its intensity, its miseries, and its destruction and mourning and woe, it is enough to sober the most inconsiderate and soften the most obdurate and bring our whole people to humiliation before God, who is thus dealing with us. And while He has most signally and mercifully aided us thus far, yet His hand is still stretched out over us; for the war continues, and the enemy is laying his plans more resolutely and extensively to swallow us up. As we have survived his first great effort, trusting in the Lord may we not hope for a second deliverance? I have faith to believe we may.

The invasion of Maryland and the return of our army to Virginia I look upon *as a special providence in our behalf.* Success began to intoxicate, and incline many to cry out for invasion of the enemy's territory. General Lee was induced to make the experiment in the most favorable moment and upon the most favorable soil—at least one upon which the people were, to a good degree, at least, so friendly as not to rise upon us. He could advance but a little way. The people did not come to his standard. The enemy gathered with energy and promptness an army far outnumbering his and gave him the bloodiest battle (on their own ground, as they deemed it) ever fought on this continent; and nothing saved his army from defeat and ruin but the blessing of God upon his skillful disposition of his forces, and the indomitable courage of his men—men to be annihilated but never defeated! I hope this taste of invasion will be satisfactory—at least for the present. If the enemy with superior numbers and equipments cannot invade our thinly populated territories with large armies without being starved back if not driven back, how can we fare better invading a more densely populated country? The Maryland pear certainly is not ripe yet. When it will be, no one can tell. If we can free the other border states, it will be well. A desperate stand is to be made by the enemy to save both Tennessee and Kentucky. The fighting has not fairly begun there yet.

Will you be able to go up and see Mr. Schley's place on Saturday? Please let me know. I hope it may be in your power, for our time is running short, and we have much to do.

I understand Mr. Millen (brother of Mr. Berrien Millen) has a government contract for beef, and purchases cattle liberally. Do you know him? Am glad you secured the bagging. Will have the gins started in a few days.

Your visit to your brother must have been refreshing to both of you. Am happy to know he is doing so well.

Poor Tyrone still lingers. We had hope of him a few days ago, but he is no better now, and fear he never will rise from his bed! These repeated deaths are most afflicting to us. The doctor has been with him every day as often as he considered it necessary—always once, and most frequently twice, and sometimes three times a day.

Friday, October 3rd. Tyrone died this morning about four o'clock—another death from the sickness contracted on the batteries in Savannah last spring. Three out of the seven men sent have died. The general judgment has been heavy on our household, and of course on us. The last request Tyrone made to me on leaving him about nine or ten was to pray with him—our usual evening's parting. How it is with his immortal soul God only knows.

Robert sends love. Mother and Daughter not returned. Children well. Your dear child now playing in Mother's room.

Your ever affectionate father,
C. C. Jones.

LT. CHARLES C. JONES, JR., *to* REV. C. C. JONES[g]

Savannah, *Friday,* October 3rd, 1862

My dear Father,

We have nothing of interest today except a telegram from Florida announcing that the enemy has landed three thousand strong on the St. Johns River with a view to the capture of our recently constructed batteries, which are seriously interfering with the for some time hitherto unimpeded navigation of that river by Lincoln gunboats. If the hostile force be properly estimated, I fear we have not troops sufficient to offer effectual resistance, as I understand General Finegan has not more than twelve hundred men under his command. But although such a disparity may exist, the fight must only be the harder; for in this contest we cannot expect to meet them once out of a dozen times with forces numerically equal to theirs.

I have my eye upon a place in Jefferson County, but the great difficulty I encounter is that possession cannot be given before 1st January next, which is entirely too late, as the people should be moved this month if practicable. It will be dangerous to let them remain here any longer. I am trying also to effect a temporary arrangement for change of location so as to place them—comparatively, at least—out of direct danger until the 1st of January, when occupancy of a plantation may be had.

The shells of the enemy some afternoons since which exploded near Lee battery down the river produced an amusing stampede among the Negroes at work there. They dropped wheelbarrows, spades, shovels, hods, and many of them upon the parapet and the traverses let go everything, as a large shell burst just over the battery, and came tumbling down head over heels, quitting the battery precipitately, and hiding in the grass of the uncultivated ricefield squares and behind the dams, which they could not be prevailed upon to leave for some time. An eyewitness says it was an amusing sight; and the wonder is that some of them had not broken their necks or legs or arms. Their lives were much more endangered by their lofty and precipitate tumbles than by the projectiles of the enemy.

How much corn, Father, will you have to dispose of at Montevideo? And when will it be ready for market? I am trying to arrange for the sale to the Commissary Department here. In that event I will be able to procure sacks from Major Locke. *This sub rosa.* Just at this time I can make no sale of the cattle. There are over seven thousand head owned by the government in this vicinity, or under purchase; and six hundred have recently been condemned as unfit for present use. Want of pasture.

I hope Tyrone still continues to improve, and that all at home are well. Do give warmest love to dear Mother, Sister, Robert, Charlie, and Mamie. Kiss my precious little daughter for me. And believe me ever, my dear father,

Your affectionate son,

Charles C. Jones, Jr.

LT. CHARLES C. JONES, JR., *to* MRS. MARY JONES[t]

Savannah, *Tuesday*, October 7th, 1862

My dear Mother,

I trust that all at home are well.

You probably noticed in the papers of yesterday morning an announcement of the fact that West had been killed during the recent desperate engagement at Sharpsburg. He was a private in Captain Read's light battery, and has shared the fate of many a brave fellow whose bones lie unmarked, commingled with those of the many slain upon that bloody battlefield. Poor West! With all his deficiencies he had ever an honest heart, and has by his death paid the highest tribute to his country and her cause in this the hour of her extremest peril. It is very sad to think of him away from every relative and every comfort, sharing the nameless grave of the fallen common soldier; and yet if he were prepared for death I know of no better or more honorable way in which he could have met the approach of the Last Enemy. And from the very character of his fate, and the manner of his death, his name will remain all the brighter, and his memory be the more sincerely cherished by his friends and relatives.

We have a floating rumor in the city that General Lawton has died from the effect of his wound, but I have been unable to trace it to any reliable source.

It appears from a recent telegram that our forces before Corinth have had to fall back, and that the inaugurated success of yesterday has not been consummated today. The accounts are, however, so conflicting that it is a difficult matter to ascertain the truth. We will probably have more tonight.

I am still here, and sadly tired of this continued court-martial. The list of cases pending appears to be exhaustless on account of fresh accretions almost every day. We have nothing of interest with us. Do give much love to Father, Sister, Robert, Mamie, and Charlie. Kiss my darling little daughter for me. And accept for yourself, my dearest mother, the truest affection of

Your son,

Charles C. Jones, Jr.

LT. CHARLES C. JONES, JR., *to* REV. C. C. JONES[g]

Savannah, *Wednesday*, October 8th, 1862

My dear Father,

I am today in receipt of your kind favor of the 2nd inst., with postscript of the 3rd inst. announcing the sad intelligence of the death of Tyrone. I had hoped from last advices that although still sick he was nevertheless better, and that reasonable hopes of his recovery were entertained. The hand of affliction has indeed been heavily laid upon us. And where has it not fallen during the past eighteen months? We are in the hands of the Almighty, and it is our duty to acknowledge these His dispensations, and by repentance and in humility seek to make a proper use of them.

The advices from the West are not encouraging, and we appear to have met with a reverse at Shiloh. A battle is regarded as imminent between Bragg and Buell near Louisville, and we are told that Generals Lee and McClellan will soon meet again in deadly conflict. I see no cessation to present hostilities —unless some unlooked-for pressure is brought directly and forcibly to bear —except in absolute exhaustion. The mask is fairly lifted—and by their own hands—from the face of Northern duplicity and Yankee tyranny; and we can now expect from the Lincoln government nothing but renewed attempts and redoubled efforts to effect our annihilation. Their future operations will doubtless be characterized if possible by additional disregard of the commonest principles of justice, humanity, and religion. Devastation, ruin, insult, and barbarity will mark their footsteps. I have, under God, no fear for the final issue; but when our triumph will come, as matters now stand, can be known only to Him in whose hands are the issues of all things. The last victory at Manassas appears to have produced a profounder impression upon the European mind than any of the former which have been won by us.

The *Fingal* here is hastening towards a completion, and will vastly strengthen our river defenses. The guns are being mounted on General Mercer's line of fortifications around the city; and when the attack is made, as seems highly probable at no very distant day, I hope we will be able, by the help of God, to repel the invader with a loss and destruction which will not be soon forgotten. A naval expedition from Port Royal is advertised, but its destination is not given.

Mr. Schley will probably be here tonight, and I hope to be able to go up with him on Friday or Saturday. He has been very kindly assisting me by inquiries in Jefferson and Washington Counties, and tomorrow I will have the result, which you shall know so soon as ascertained.

The bagging is in the store for us, and will be sent out any day you may wish. Cattle ought to be worth from fifteen to twenty dollars. Macpherson B. Millen is captain of commissary; his brother, of whom you speak, I do not know. Mr. Quarterman writes me that he can sell the cattle at Arcadia at fifteen dollars per head. Would it not be well to have at least a portion of the corn crop shelled and sold at once? I think I can make a contract for its sale here to the Quartermaster Department and obtain bags in which to sack it. One dollar per bushel.

By the train of tomorrow, Father, I send you a cask of pale Scotch ale—the only one in the city. I have tried to procure a cask of porter for you in Charleston, Columbus, and elsewhere, but without success. Be pleased to let me know what proportion of the bottles in the cask is good and what defective, as I am to pay only for the good. This can be done without much trouble as they are unpacked and used. If the article sent is not as good as you have had, you will excuse it when I say that it is the only ale which could be had, and was sold to me as a special favor. The *ale* is good, and I trust will do you good.

Do give warmest love to dear Mother, Sister, Robert, Mamie, and Charlie. Kiss my precious little daughter for me. And believe me ever, my dear father,

Your affectionate son,
Charles C. Jones, Jr.

Lt. Charles C. Jones, Jr., *to* Rev. C. C. Jones[g]

Savannah, *Thursday,* October 9th, 1862

My dear Father,

I will try and get off from here so as to examine Mr. Schley's place on Saturday next. From a conversation had with him last night, if the plantation suits I think we will be able to purchase corn, fodder, etc., all on the place, and obtain possession at an early day. But you shall know all about it so soon as I can ascertain by actual examination. You may rely upon my doing the very best I can.

Nothing new here. With warmest love to all at home, I am ever

Your affectionate son,
Charles C. Jones, Jr.

Lt. Charles C. Jones, Jr., *to* Rev. C. C. Jones[g]

Savannah, *Thursday,* October 16th, 1862

My dear Father,

I have just returned from Middle Georgia, and have purchased Mr. Henry J. Schley's Buckhead plantation containing fourteen hundred and twelve acres at ten dollars per acre, and also his present corn crop (say, four thousand bushels) at seventy-five cents per bushel.

The place is situated about one hundred miles, in round numbers, from this city, and is without exception the best place I have seen. It enjoys a fine reputation—none superior in that section. I rode over every foot of it before concluding the purchase. It contains about five hundred acres of as noble forest land as the eye can well discover in our state, is well watered, thoroughly ditched, and generally in fine order as to fences, etc., etc. We will need some four additional Negro houses. A steam sawmill is in the neighborhood where boards, etc., can be procured at a reasonable rate. A gristmill is located only about a mile and three quarters from the settlement, where, as is customary in that section of country, all the grinding can be done for the place. There are a fine overseer's house, ginhouse with gin and running gear in capital order, screw, two corncribs, meat house, kitchen, dairy, four double and two or three single Negro houses—all frame buildings. Two churches in the vicinity—one Baptist, the other Methodist—where preaching is had at present every other Sabbath.

I took the whole of Mr. Schley's corn because I was getting it at a very reasonable figure, because he could not get it away, and because under existing circumstances I think the purchase a valuable one. It will doubtless be much higher as the season advances. It is not all harvested as yet.

The average yield on the place for the past twelve years, as shown by Mr. Schley's books, has been a little over five bales of cotton to the hand, and from ten to twelve bushels of corn to the acre. He has within the past two years taken in, at an expense of six hundred dollars, forty acres of the Buckhead swamp, which this year gives a yield of corn of thirty-five bushels to the acre. It is worth one's while to look at this field—a deep alluvial soil which seems to be almost inexhaustible. The rest of the place is above average, and I think the purchase a valuable one, and that by the blessing of God we may find it a safe, comfortable, and remunerative retreat for our people.

As to the question of possession, Mr. Schley tells me if at any time danger threatens, to send the Negroes up at once, and that they shall be quartered as best they can be with present accommodations. He will be through with gathering his crop by the 1st December, and will if possible complete the harvest and move away by the 15th December. He has promised me to accomplish this at the earliest practicable moment; and he is a gentleman of his word, and with that view will send hands from his lower place to assist.

I think at an early day we had better send the carpenters up and let them commence upon the new buildings which we will require for the accommodation of the people. And the people should be moved so soon as we can conveniently arrange for their removal—say sometime towards the first or middle of November. We cannot well send them at an earlier day, as we have to get out the growing and already matured crop. What Negroes you will send, Father, of course I will leave entirely to you. I expect to take mine from Arcadia, and such as Brother and Sister desire to send. But I will at the earliest practicable moment see you in regard to this matter and receive your wishes and instructions in the premises.

We can send the Negroes either by Central Railroad to No. 9½, where they will have to walk only about twelve miles to the place; or we can send them with wagons, etc., up the Louisville road, the distance of the plantation by that way being only one hundred miles from this city. Or perhaps what would be still better, we can send the women and children, plantation utensils, bedding, etc., by rail, and let the men or a portion of them with a wagon, stock, etc., go up by way of the Louisville road. Your own judgment will indicate what had best be done. The removal will be a matter, I think, of not much trouble.

I propose, Father, to assume the entire responsibility of the purchase of the plantation: $14,120—one-third cash, balance in one and two years. I am unwilling that you should at your time of life, and in your present health, be troubled with any additional moneyed arrangements or new cares. If I live and have health, and these Yankees do not entirely overrun us, by the blessing of God I hope to be able to make the payments. If you can conveniently aid in the purchase of the corn, mules, and meat (which will prove quite an item of expense), I would be glad. And with the cotton which we have on hand, and the corn, etc., which we will be able to sell, I think we can do so without trouble. I am now making inquiries about mules, but will not contract for purchase before seeing you and ascertaining what portion of the stock we can conveniently carry up.

In reference to meat, which will be our greatest trouble, would it not be well at once to see what hogs we can purchase from the Negroes on the places and perhaps on those adjoining? We can then kill and cure below and send up by railroad.

I have this morning secured one keg shingling nails and half-keg flooring or rather weatherboarding nails—all I could find in the city.

In regard to the sale of corn, etc., from home, I can arrange with the quartermaster here to take all the corn we have to spare, if you think best, at one dollar per bushel, delivered at No. 3, Savannah, Albany & Gulf Railroad, the quartermaster furnishing bags in which to sack the corn.

We ought to take to Burke some thirty head of cattle. They can be easily driven up. I can purchase a wagon or two from Mr. Schley, and have also agreed to take his fodder, which is stacked in the field. We can sell our fodder here to the quartermaster, who desired it baled in bundles to weigh, say, three hundred pounds (from that to four hundred).

Mr. Schley's present overseer, a worthy man and a strict member of the Baptist Church, without children and with an excellent wife, represented to be an honest man and attentive to his duties, can be employed by us, I think, for a sum not much to exceed three hundred dollars for the ensuing year. Mr. Schley is pleased with him, and would have retained him had he remained on his plantation another year.

Referring to the conversation which we had at the depot, Father, when I last enjoyed the pleasure of seeing you, I presume Brother and Sister will require their proportion of corn, cattle, cotton, etc., sold from Arcadia, so that only a third of the amount therefrom realized can be appropriated toward the purchase of corn, etc., for the place in Burke.

The health of the place is fair—as good as is found in Middle Georgia—and I should say better than that of our plantations upon the swamps of Liberty. Mr. Schley this year has had to pay no medical bill except for services rendered by a surgeon in the case of one of his Negroes who was run over by a wagon.

I will endeavor, my dear father, to see you at the earliest practicable moment and learn all your wishes in the premises, which it will be equally my duty and pleasure to carry into effect as faithfully and as promptly as I can. I do wish that I could command my own time for about a week or more. I know that I could within that time accomplish much.

In the purchase of the place I have exercised my best judgment, and have done the best I could. If I may believe the opinions of others, I have secured a plantation far above the average. I would not exchange it for any I have seen in Middle Georgia, and I infinitely prefer it to Southwest Georgia. I have asked the blessing of God on the adventure, and trust with His blessing that we may find the investment safe and remunerative. For the present it must be viewed very much in the light of an insurance upon Negroes.

In returning through Waynesboro saw Mrs. Harlow and Cousin Ruth. Both well, and desired kindest remembrance.

I have written in great haste for lack of more time, and must beg you, Father, to excuse the rambling character of this letter. If there are any matters to which I have not alluded, if you will only indicate them I will give you all the information in my possession. Did the cask of ale ever come to hand? And do you find it good? How are all at home? Do give warmest love to dear Mother, Sister, Robert, and the little ones. Kiss my precious daughter for me. And believe me ever, my dear father,

Your affectionate son,
Charles C. Jones, Jr.

A letter from Uncle John says all well at Rome.

Had a glimpse of Uncle Henry and Aunt Abby as the cars left Waynesboro. Why does Uncle Henry wear a uniform? Is he one of Joe Brown's soldiers?

Payments to be made when we take possession. Please let me know at what day you would prefer that the removal of the Negroes should take place, or about what time. I promised Mr. Schley to let him know in order that he might make his arrangements if possible to meet your wishes.

REV. C. C. JONES *to* LT. CHARLES C. JONES, JR.ᵍ

Walthourville, *Saturday,* October 18th, 1862

My dear Son,

Yours of the 16th Mother handed me last evening on my return from Montevideo, where I had been to see Phillis (Niger's wife), who is *quite sick,* Dr. Samuel Way in attendance. The affliction of sickness still continues upon us, and I pray that we may be made to understand and feel it and have it sanctified to us.

Your account of Mr. Schley's place is very satisfactory, and have no doubt that your purchase is a judicious one and as good as could well be made in any part of the cotton districts of our state. And the payment in three installments is more liberal than I had anticipated. And although you so generously offer to assume the whole payment for the place on your own account, yet I shall feel bound to render you every aid in my power to meet the payments as they come to maturity. I agree with you in preferring a location in Middle to one in Southwest Georgia. Am pleased to learn that there are five hundred acres of forest land (a specimen of what Middle Georgia was) and a steam saw- and a gristmill so contiguous. Most desirable advantages are these—and all not far from the Central Railroad. And *two churches* in the immediate vicinity, one of which I should like to have been *Presbyterian*—without intending any reflections whatever upon my brethren of the other denominations, with whom I have always cultivated the best understanding.

The purchase of the corn and fodder was exactly right, and indeed much of a necessity and a great convenience. The rate reasonable; and the surplus (if any) may be sold. Wagons are scarce, and if you can purchase one or two *good,* and on favorable terms, from Mr. Schley, you might do so. And feel the overseer's pulse and retain him, as he is a fixture and has the run of the place, and I presume an *exempt.*

Our corn can be sold at No. 3 depot to Mr. Millen, he furnishing sacks, at $1.25; and the fodder sold there also.

Monday, if the Lord will, I will shut up my beloved study and go to Arcadia and Montevideo and enter upon immediate arrangements to wind up matters, dispatch the carpenters, and prepare as many of the people for removal and at as early a day as we can, of which Mr. Schley shall have due advisement. I will then give you a statement of the whole—corn, cotton, peas, potatoes, rice, mules, cattle, sheep, and hogs.

Daughter has just come in to say the post office will close soon, and I must cease. We all congratulate you on your successful visit and return, and shall be truly glad to see you in person. All send love. Baby hearty and growing. Your Uncle Henry is one of Governor Brown's active and retained aides; hence the uniform.

Return of cask of ale: 4 dozen in good order, $1\frac{1}{2}$ dozen three-quarters full; $1\frac{1}{2}$ ditto half full; and one only broken. If the kindest and most unremitting attentions of the best of wives and the best of children could have made me a well man, I should have been so long ago; and from my heart I appreciate it all, and thank you for it, and hope and pray God will reward you for it.

Mother begs you to send five dollars' worth of *hard* sailor or army biscuit for her. Borchert sometimes makes them if not to be had. She wants to see you very much. "*Insist* upon a furlough," Mother says. Please send out the money sent to be exchanged when you can. As ever,

Your affectionate father,
C. C. Jones.

Five dollars for biscuits enclosed.

Lt. Charles C. Jones, Jr., *to* Rev. C. C. Jones[g]

Savannah, *Tuesday,* October 21st, 1862

My dear Father,

I thank you for your kind letter of Saturday last, which has been duly received, and I am happy to know that all at home are so well—except Phillis, who I trust by this time is better. Am happy to think that my efforts to procure a suitable retreat for our people have been approved by you. Since the purchase my mind has been greatly relieved, and will be more so so soon as we can compass the removal of the people. Do let me know, Father, in what particular I can specifically serve you.

The notes have been exchanged, and Mother's "hard bread" purchased; but the express at present is not running on the Savannah, Albany & Gulf Railroad, so that I am at a loss how to forward them to you. I hope, however, that I may be able to see you on Saturday next, when I will, D.V., bring them out with me and have a full conversation with you in reference to matters and things.

We have nothing of local interest here. General Beauregard is in the city, and the daily journals contain an account of his serenade and speech last evening. He makes a poor out at speaking—not an unusual occurrence among military men, although the records of the past furnish some brilliant exceptions. I learn that he will review all the troops of this district, or as many of them as can conveniently be collected here, on next Friday.

As at present advised, the tenure by which we hold Kentucky appears very uncertain: Bragg said to be in retreat, and before vastly superior forces.

I send you the Charleston *Courier,* containing a synopsis of the recent speech of Van Buren in New York City. Heavy Democratic gains at the North; but what do they signify?

With warmest love to my dear mother, Sister, Robert, and the little ones, and tenderest kisses for my precious little daughter, I am, as ever, my honored and beloved father,

Your attached son,
Charles C. Jones, Jr.

Mrs. Mary S. Mallard *to* Lt. Charles C. Jones, Jr.[g]

Walthourville, *Thursday,* October 23rd, 1862

My dear Brother Charlie,

We are truly glad to know you will be with us on Saturday, and hope no untoward circumstance will prevent your coming. We will all be glad to welcome you; and you will find that the cool weather has brought the roses back to your sweet little daughter's cheeks.

Will you be so kind, my dear brother, as to inquire for a box at the express office in Savannah directed to R. Q. Mallard, and either forward or bring it with you. The box was sent from Marietta, and should have been brought to this station; but as you know, the express has not been running on this road for some weeks past.

We hope to see Uncle John next week, as he will probably leave Rome on the 27th or 28th. Dunwody is still in the county, and will not return for two or three weeks yet. He is very anxious to get transferred to the coast, but that seems almost impossible.

Mr. Mallard went to Dorchester last evening. He is anxious to hire some of his people if possible in a secure part of the state. I think you have been highly favored in your purchase, and we are all under many obligations to you for your kindness. Father will add a postscript to this. With warmest love,

Your affectionate sister,
Mary S. Mallard.

Rev. C. C. Jones *to* Lt. Charles C. Jones, Jr.ᵍ

Walthourville, *Thursday,* October 23rd, 1862

My dear Son,

We are happy to hear that you will be with us, D.V., on Saturday. Try and stay till Monday afternoon.

Our corn and cattle ought to be sold as speedily as possible. Could you see the government officials before you come out? Corn is selling at $1.25 per bushel (sacks furnished) at the depots, weighing so many pounds (fifty-six, I think)—the fairest way to buy and sell all grains. If you furnish sacks and deliver in Savannah: $1.50. Cattle (good stock cattle): about twenty dollars round. The Maybank cattle (between forty and sixty head) were all fat for butchering when I last saw them some three weeks ago. Mr. Quarterman told me he had offered a part of the Arcadia cattle to Mr. George Millen at twenty dollars round. Had received no reply. We might pickle up some beeves for the people if we can get barrels for the purpose.

Could we charter a box car to take up our people (women and children and some men)—take them and all their baggage in at No. 3, *and have the same car go through to Central Railroad and right on* to No. 9½ or wherever they will get out? If this could be done, it would save time, trouble, and exposure. Would be glad to send off the first installment next week with the carpenters if they can be made ready. The car could be brought out the morning of the day, and be all *packed, provisioned,* and *passengered* ready for the afternoon train, which goes in now at 3 P.M.

The people we send up will require much room. Could they not take the place of as many of Mr. Schley's (who might vacate and go to his other place if it suited him) and help finish harvesting his crop?

All send love. Baby well. In some haste for the mail,

Your ever affectionate father,
C. C. Jones.

Lt. Charles C. Jones, Jr., *to* Rev. *and* Mrs. C. C. Jonesʷ

Savannah, *Saturday,* October 25th, 1862

My dear Father and Mother,

I cannot tell you how great my disappointment at not being able to realize my cherished expectation of spending the day with you and all the dear ones at home. My arrangements were all made when a courier arrived announcing that the enemy were about to attack at Coffee Bluff. Our battery, the Guards battalion, and the 4th Louisiana Volunteers were ordered at once to take post there. Mounting Yorick, I reached the scene of anticipated danger, distant from this city some twelve miles, about sunset. Gunboats lying below, but no positive demonstrations made. Attack expected about 10 P.M. on the high tide. Tide falls, hour passes, and no attack. Expectations renewed of an attack at high water today. Another agreeable disappointment, and the declining rays of the sun this afternoon revealed the fact that the abolition boats were again quietly riding at anchor at their former positions in Ossabaw Sound and in Bear River. Slept last night without tent or blanket in an old field. Troop ordered back to their posts tonight, and I have just returned to the city, after a long and somewhat fatiguing ride, to enjoy the quiet and holy privileges of the coming Sabbath.

You have doubtless, my dear parents, noticed the happy accounts of the repulse of the abolition forces along the line of the Charleston & Savannah Railroad. I only wish that we could have surrounded, cut off, and butchered every one of the vile invaders.

I hope to see you some day next week. Do kiss my dear little daughter for me. Give love to Sister, Robert, and the little ones. And believe me ever, my dear parents, with tenderest and most constant affection,

Your son,
Charles C. Jones, Jr.

Mr. Schley consents that we send up the Negroes just when we please, provided they help gather the crop, etc. He will give *working hands* their board, and charge at rate of seventy-five cents per bushel for all corn consumed by nonworkers before the place is finally delivered. A fair proposition.

REV. C. C. JONES *to* LT. CHARLES C. JONES, JR.[g]

Walthourville, *Saturday,* October 25th, 1862

My dear Son,

We were greatly disappointed at not seeing you this morning, but we know you could not help it. Through divine favor we are all well today, and I write now to say that if the Lord will, I will be in Savannah by the cars *on Monday evening* and put up at the Pavilion if it is now open (if not, at the Pulaski) and hope you will still be in town, where I shall be glad to see you on our business matters. All send much love. As ever,

Your affectionate father,
C. C. Jones.

REV. C. C. JONES *to* LT. CHARLES C. JONES, JR.[g]

Walthourville, *Wednesday,* October 29th, 1862

My dear Son,

After my most pleasant visit to you I am again at home, D.G., finding all well, and Mother away on a business expedition at Maybank.

At No. 3 Mr. R. Q. Cassels, who is in charge of that depot, offered to purchase all our corn *for a government agent* at $1.25 delivered at that depot, *he furnishing sacks.* This is better than Major Hirsch's offer at $1.20, which we will be obliged to accept if you have positively engaged with him. I told Mr. Cassels that I would confer with you and let him know, and further that I would not sell one grain to speculators, and if he was in that line we couldn't sell to him. He replied that he was purchasing *for a government agent.* Now, who can he be—to offer five cents per bushel higher than Major Hirsch? Again, Mr. Cassels purchases by *weight*—a bushel rated at fifty-four pounds. Mr. Quarterman says he lost by this mode. You can let me know if you have positively engaged to Major Hirsch, and then I will see Mr. Quarterman before deciding.

Your sweet little baby is quite well, and all unite in much love.

Your affectionate father,
C. C. Jones.

Mrs. Mary Jones *to* Lt. Charles C. Jones, Jr.ᵍ

Walthourville, *Wednesday,* November 5th, 1862

My dear Son,

Your brother gave us a most delightful surprise!

Last week I paid your uncle a short visit. He expressed the wish that yourself and brother would at once take possession of the servants intended for you by your aunt, allowing him a reasonable compensation. Said his will was made, etc., etc., and he was *very anxious* to see you. I asked if he wished me to confer with my sons upon the matter, and regarded what he was saying to me as a business arrangement. He replied yes, and desired me to write you about it. If his will has been legally executed, I should think it well for you to close in with his propositions for various reasons I have not time to name at this time.

By today's mail I received a letter from a *lady* proposing to furnish pork or bacon in payment for salt. Says she has plenty to kill, but no salt to cure. If we could make such an exchange it would aid us in supplying our people with meat. Whilst at Maybank for a day last week (whilst your father was in Savannah) I had a well dug in the salt marsh beyond the first bluff which promises a fine yield of brine, which turns out double the quantity of salt that the river water does. If we had more or larger boilers we could make a good speculation about the bacon. The lady wishes thirty or forty bushels!

Yesterday I turned out the *first blanket* from the loom, and eighty yards of cloth. I am trying with all the energy and means at command to have the people clothed.

Your brother is ready, and I must close. Our respects to Mr. Ward. Your father really enjoyed his visit to Savannah. Our united love. . . . In haste,

Your affectionate mother,
Mary Jones.

Lt. Charles C. Jones, Jr., *to* Mrs. Mary Jones[t]

Savannah, *Thursday,* November 6th, 1862

My very dear Mother,

I sincerely thank you for your kind note of yesterday, received at the hands of Brother, who left this morning for Charleston hoping to be able to return on Saturday next.

A few moments since, I had the pleasure of seeing Uncle John, who goes out to Walthourville tomorrow morning.

On Saturday next the 8th inst. I hope to be able to come out and see you and Father and my dear little daughter and all at home. Vallie Whitehead will probably accompany me; she is very anxious to see dear little Mary Ruth.

We have nothing of special interest here. This gloomy day keeps us within doors; but in a court-martial room we are but little affected by the dripping skies without. I hope the Yankee ironclads are experiencing the benefit of the dangers of the outside navigation, and that many if not all of them now venturing on their nefarious voyage hitherward may never live to tell the tale of their adventures.

Trusting so soon, my dear mother, to enjoy the privilege of seeing you and all the loved ones at home, I will then have the opportunity of congratulating you in person upon the success of your salt-making and cloth manufacture, so all-important under present circumstances. With much love to all, and many kisses for my dear little daughter, I am, as ever,

Your affectionate son,

Charles C. Jones, Jr.

Rev. C. C. Jones *to* Lt. Charles C. Jones, Jr.[g]

Walthourville, *Monday,* November 10th, 1862

My dear Son,

Our missing each other brought about a mutual and real disappointment on Saturday, but we were glad to learn that Miss Whitehead and yourself spent so pleasant a day, and that our sweet little baby interested you so much.

Mother is making every effort to have the people *clothed* who will form the first deportation, and has worked personally very hard, and has gone down today to Montevideo to finish off there and return this evening. Tomorrow, God willing, we purpose moving to *Arcadia* in order to be more immediately *in medias res,* where we hope to entertain Brother and yourself when you come out.

Mother and I appointed *tomorrow week, Tuesday the 18th,* this morning for the people to leave Liberty for their new home, and am glad it is the day that you have also appointed. *Let the 18th, therefore, be the day, if the Lord will.* And we will do all in our power to have everyone and everything ready. The car for us can be left on the track for us at No. 3, and we will have it all packed and ready when the train returns in the afternoon of the 18th. *You will see to the transportation from one depot to the other in*

Savannah, wagons, etc., and that a car be prepared on the Central Railroad so when you arrive on the evening of the 18th there will be no delay.

Mr. R. Q. Cassels declines taking the corn at $1.25. There is no sale for it out here. Major Hirsch is our only chance. *Can you not engage it to him at $1.20 and have the bags sent out at once to No. 3,* and we will begin to deliver forthwith. *The sooner the better.*

Our report from McIntosh County is that the abolition gunboats last week ran up Sapelo River, burnt Captain Brailsford's house, took off *every Negro* belonging to Mr. Reuben King at Mallow, and reduced the aged couple to nothing; and Mrs. Walker's tears alone prevented their carrying the old gentleman off. Captured one of the McDonalds at Fair Hope (the married one) *with a squad of armed Negroes,* and carried him off. His family and household and brother escaped. Burnt Colonel Charles Hopkins' house on the opposite side of the river, where they were fired upon and some of them killed by Captain Octavius Hopkins' company, and made off with themselves. We much need an intelligent, brave, and active commander of the cavalry corps stationed in the three counties to effect concert of action and celerity of movement.

Your Uncle John has just left for his plantation. Robert is at Presbytery in Bryan. We expected your brother today; has not come. Your dear sister sends you much love; and many kisses from the children. Their toys are delighting them now. Your little baby was the coldest infant I ever felt this morning at daylight. Had pushed down her covering, and Mother took her in bed an *icicle.* Half awake, she threw her arms around her neck laughing for the comfort of the change. Your Uncle John preached two admirable sermons for us yesterday. My respects to Mr. Ward; hope he is better. And our kind regards to Miss Val Whitehead.

> Your ever affectionate father,
> C. C. Jones.

Lt. Charles C. Jones, Jr., *to* Rev. C. C. Jones[g]

> Savannah, *Monday,* November 10th, 1862

My dear Father,

Through the kindness of the postmaster I have just received your letter of this morning, and am happy to know that the day named—to wit, the *18th* inst.—meets with your approval.

I leave tonight to arrange with Mr. Schley for the payment of the place, obtain titles, etc., so that in the event of my sudden death or any unexpected casualty there may be no question about title or possession. I propose to pay him ten thousand dollars on account the purchase moneys of the place, which will leave only $4120 due and payable two years hence. To secure this balance I will execute a mortgage upon the plantation to that amount. I will also go on to Augusta and see what can be done in the matter of the purchase of mules. Will probably, D.V., not return before the last of the week. Will hope to be with you on Saturday next. If not, then on Monday morning, stopping at No. 3.

Brother will probably be with you sometime this week. He has doubtless gone to Augusta from Charleston.

You will of course think of all that is necessary for the Negroes to do in order to get them in readiness. I would suggest that all their clothing, pots, etc., etc., be thoroughly washed and put up in bundles of convenient sizes. If they have hogs we will purchase them; and we will have to make the best arrangements we can in reference to their little matters of property. I desire all my Negroes to go, as they are young, and their services will be required at once in putting the place in order. Do, if you can spare Porter and Pulaski, let them go up with William, as the services of the carpenters will be greatly and immediately required. Let them carry their tools. . . . Do not forget a bag or two of salt for the Negroes to take up with them.

I write in much haste. With warmest love to all, I am ever, my dear father,

Your affectionate son,

Charles C. Jones, Jr.

Have notified the railroad companies of the *day*.

I write Major Hirsch offering twelve hundred to eighteen hundred bushels corn at $1.20 delivered at No. 3, Savannah, Albany & Gulf Railroad, he furnishing sacks. If he accepts in my absence, he is to send the sacks out to that station marked "C. C. Jones, Jr., per Arcadia plantation."

XV

Miss Mary E. Robarts *to* Mrs. Laura E. Buttolph[t]

Marietta, *Tuesday,* November 25th, 1862

What is the matter with you, dearest Laura, that I can neither invite nor provoke a word from you or your dear mother? I know you are busy, but don't you know we are anxious—so very anxious—to hear all about our dear friends in Liberty?

We had not heard for weeks till yesterday we had a letter from Joe saying he could see you very seldom now, as you had moved to Taylor's Creek. I am glad you have found a safe retreat so near. Hope you may have a pleasant time—as pleasant as anyone can have who is exiled from their own "Home, Sweet Home." (How earnestly will all the refugees sing who are absent now from all home comforts!) Having your dear Aunt Julia's family so near, it must give you quite a homelike feeling, though you have only the peonies in exchange for the beautiful water and evergreens. But if you only have peace and plenty you will not complain of other losses. Instead of the murmuring wave Mary Wells has the busy loom. Tell her she is indeed a noble woman to use her energies to furnish clothing for her household. I should like to exert mine to the same end if I could, for everything in the Confederacy is so exorbitantly high that nothing seems within our reach but air and water. Do, Laura, write me a description of your new home. Lady Susan, I expect, spends her time as usual (and as I do mine) in washing cups and platters and looking after the fleshpots; you in looking after your little boys, who, I expect, are like the little squirrels gathering acorns and nuts and mash. And their reverend father spends six days out of seven to provide manna for the Sabbath. Wish I could get a little taste of it some Sunday!

Mr. Ardis has just returned from Macon. He stayed with our friend Mary Nisbet; describes her as most fascinating. He saw Mr. Mallard, and tells me our friends are generally well. I know this cannot be true of your dear Uncle Charlie, for everyone we see speaks of his increasing feebleness, which is no doubt aggravated by the excitement and great undertaking of moving. Cousin John is in the low country on the same errand. Dunwody left us on Saturday for the camp of instruction at Macon, where he has an appointment of drill officer. Am glad he is not in a post of danger now. Tell Mr. Buttolph he lost one thing by not being at Synod. The factory presented each minister who attended Synod with a bolt of shirting—a great present these times!

What do you think of the prospects of Savannah?

These times! I think the treatment of the Yankees to our aged friends Mr.

and Mrs. Reuben King and Mr. McDonald was just a specimen of what they would do to all who fall into their hands. We shed tears for old Aunt Abby. . . .

Joe wrote us that Amanda Walker had sent him ten oranges. He gave two to a sick friend, ate two, and sent the other six to his grandmother. She enjoys them very much; eats them at night cut up with sugar for her cough. . . .

Our family are quite well. Louisa is spending the day with Mary Tennent, the girls with their aunt Mrs. LaRoche; so Mother and myself are alone, and both writing letters. Sometimes I have so many interruptions I find it difficult to write. The other day I was in the pantry when one of the girls said: "Aunt Mary, a stranger at the door wishes to see the president of the Ladies' Aid Society." Thinks I to myself: "This sounds very grand to be applied to me!" So, like the widow Walthour, shaking myself into order, I appeared before him in my calico dress and linen collar made before the revolution. He came with an appeal for the hospital at Graysville, where he, an exiled clergyman, was playing the Good Samaritan, and amused me by telling me how he had improvised shirts for the poor soldiers when they arrived there sick, wounded, dirty, and ragged. So of course our society all set to work to get up a box; and even the little schoolgirls are making little bolsters to put under their wounded legs. We had just sent off boxes and bedding to the hospitals at Ringgold, Chattanooga, and Dalton. And now while we are preparing this contribution, the medical director from Knoxville comes to examine the buildings and press them for hospitals; so I expect before another week we shall have six or seven hundred sick soldiers here. Action is the order of the day. I do not think there is a woman or child asleep in the Confederacy. Sometimes I have hardly time to eat.

And now, dear Laura, farewell. Excuse my uninteresting letter. Do write me something that Mary Wells says to cheer my spirits. I dreamed the other night I had a sweet kiss from Audley's little baby. Give it to it for me, and many for your sweet little boys.

Your ever affectionate
Aunt Mary.

I will write a note to your mother. . . . Wish the Yankees were all at home stringing their onions!

MISS MARY E. ROBARTS *to* MRS. SUSAN M. CUMMING[t]

Marietta, *Tuesday,* November 25th, 1862

I know, my dearest cousin, that you have not forgotten us, though you have not written. Busy people are busier now than ever, and there seems little time to parley either on paper or by word of mouth. What would I give to hear one sound from the voice of a beloved relative!

Henry gladdened our hearts by a short visit, which was a treat to us. And Cousin John made us a visit, and we saw him a moment at the depot en route for Liberty. Also James West. Cousin John can tell you more about him than we can, as we saw him only for a moment.

I just heard yesterday that you had moved to Taylor's Creek. Where are your people? Do you intend to move them? I hope your home will be safe and pleasant. You are as much among strangers (except Julia) as if you had moved farther off. Do write us soon all about yourselves and your neighbors.

We are well, and getting along better than last year, as the banks declared a dividend. Still we had last winter to borrow money to live on; and this winter Mother thought it best to sell property and free herself, as she said she did not wish to die in debt. So she sent word to William to choose a master; he went to Mr. Isaac LaRoche and asked him to buy him, which he did at six hundred dollars cash—a very good sale for him, as he was about fifty and rather complaining. We sold him at half price, as we could not warrant him sound. It is painful to us to sell our servants, but when we know they can be better taken care of when they have a good master, it reconciles us to it. We shall now be free of debt and try to keep so; but everything is so high it is almost impossible to live for those who have nothing to sell and everything to buy. Even corn is two dollars per bushel and not to be had. Everything else in proportion. I hope, as the up-country people say, you have "made your own sweetening," as sugar is so high, and molasses not to be thought of at two dollars per gallon.

We spend our time sewing for the soldiers and repairing old garments. Each of the girls has a very neat homespun, which is the only thing we have bought.

Nothing new with us, so do write everything that is going on with you. . . . Everyone I see tells me how badly your dear brother looks. If I knew where I could reach him, I would go to see him once more. Much love to them when you see them. . . . Love to Julia and Mary and all the family.

Your ever affectionate cousin,
Mary E. Robarts.

Col. Charles C. Jones, Jr., *to* Rev. C. C. Jones[g]

Savannah, *Wednesday,* November 26th, 1862

My dear Father,

Major Hirsch has not been in the city today, so that I have failed to see him in reference to the corn. He will, however, D.V., be here on the morrow, and I will then endeavor to effect a sale of, say, twelve hundred bushels or more, and also potatoes if I can.

I have not been assigned to any specific duty as yet, but probably will be on the morrow. Possibly as chief of light artillery on General Mercer's staff. But nothing definite as yet.

I trust, my dearest father, that you will gather strength. I cannot tell you how it pains me to the very bottom of my heart to see you so feeble; and I pray God night and morning that He would in great kindness stay the progress of your wasting disease, and spare your most precious life to us all and to future usefulness in the church and elsewhere.

I hope that my dear little daughter is better today. Regret that I missed Robert last evening. I had left the house, only a moment before he came, to get the syrup of ipecac for Baby. Nothing of interest here. With warmest love to self, dear Mother, Sister, and all, and tenderest kisses for my dear little daughter, I am ever, my honored father,

Your affectionate son,
Charles C. Jones, Jr.

Col. Charles C. Jones, Jr., *to* Rev. C. C. Jones[g]

Savannah, *Friday,* November 28th, 1862

My dear Father,

Will you oblige me by sending by mail the copy of the London *News* which I carried out with me for your perusal, and which I left on the table in the parlor? It belongs to Mr. Ward, and he has promised the loan of it to some parties here.

The *Atlanta* is a perfect success. She dropped down the river last evening to a point near Fort Jackson, where she now lies. It is rumored that we will soon hear from her along the coast—possibly at Port Royal, or at the mouth of the Ogeechee—but with what certainty has not yet transpired. I presume the old commodore will be very anxious to make a demonstration if practicable.

I have been announced by General Mercer as chief of light artillery upon his staff, and have general charge of the light batteries upon the coast. It will require no little time and labor, I fear, to put some of them in good fighting trim.

We have nothing of special interest here. Am endeavoring to arrange for a sale of the corn—by no means a very easy matter. I think I can compass a sale of some potatoes at one dollar delivered at No. 3. Shall I do this? Cotton not yet worth fifty cents; it must go up higher.

I trust, my dear father, that all at home are well, and that my dear little daughter is quite relieved. Do kiss her for me. Give warmest love to Mother. And believe me ever

Your affectionate son,
Charles C. Jones, Jr.

Col. Charles C. Jones, Jr., *to* Rev. C. C. Jones[g]

Savannah, *Monday,* December 1st, 1862

My very dear Father,

I find that I can get for the corn one dollar per bushel delivered at No. 3, sacks furnished. This is offered by Major Locke. I think Major Hirsch will give $1.20. He is to let me know more definitely tomorrow, and I will then communicate the result.

I have fairly entered upon the discharge of my duties, and will be very anxious until I put all the light batteries in good order, some three of which are in not very perfect condition. I hope, however, soon to note a decided improvement.

We have nothing of interest here. Do give warmest love to dear Mother. Kiss my precious little daughter for me. And believe me ever

Your affectionate son,
Charles C. Jones, Jr.

MRS. MARY JONES *to* COL. CHARLES C. JONES, JR.^g

Arcadia, *Monday,* December 1st, 1862

My dear Son,

I am happy to say that our dear baby is much better, and she has been out most of the morning in the sweet sunshine. I hope you received Mr. Ward's London *Times,* for which your father was greatly obliged.

Mr. Millen called today and engaged twenty head of cattle from this place at twenty-five dollars a head, and goes tomorrow to see the Island cattle, now at Montevideo. I hope we shall realize at least fifteen hundred dollars by their sale.

We commenced grinding the cane on Friday, and the mill works so well we will not be occupied with it longer than tomorrow or the day after, which I fear will be too short a time to make it an object to our friends to come out for the purpose of the syrup-boiling. I would insist upon their coming out this week if we were not obliged from the state of the cane to go immediately (as we are done here) over to Montevideo and grind the cane there, where we will be only marooning for a few days. I thought we should be longer at the business, and wish Mrs. Neely and Val and the little folks could have been with us; but you will understand how necessary it is to have the grinding done as soon as possible. And I want to enjoy their visit whenever it will suit them to make it without the hurry which might now attend it. Please remember your father and myself affectionately to them, with many kisses from their little niece. I hope we shall have at least three or four barrels of syrup for plantation use from the two places. Have not yet succeeded in making sugar.

Today at twelve o'clock a concert of prayer was proposed to be observed by the mothers, wives, and daughters of the Southern Confederacy for our beloved country, that we might be delivered from our enemies, and that the Lord would grant us *peace* in all our land. I can but believe that the prayer of faith has this day ascended as from one heart and one voice, although ten thousand knees have bowed in humble supplications at the throne of our Divine Redeemer, Jehovah of Hosts.

Your dear father unites with me in best love. And kisses from your own little darling. Our respects to Mr. Ward. Do when George comes out let him bring the basket and tin bucket. And will you write Mr. Sconyers to ask Stepney if he is willing to sell his poultry or pigs. Robin thinks they will suffer by being kept. I would buy them if he wishes to sell. In haste,

Your affectionate mother,

Mary Jones.

COL. CHARLES C. JONES, JR., *to* MRS. MARY JONES[g]

Savannah, *Tuesday,* December 2nd, 1862

My very dear Mother,

I am in receipt of your kind note of yesterday, and am truly happy to know that all at home are better, and that my precious little daughter is again restored to her accustomed degree of health.

Am also glad to hear that you have been able to effect such a capital sale of the cattle. Cotton, I understand, is worth sixty cents; it will probably be higher. I cannot at present get more than one dollar per bushel for corn. I think by next week it will be worth $1.20 from the government. I can get one dollar for potatoes delivered at the station in small quantities.

I will write to Mr. Sconyers in regard to Stepney's stock and poultry and let you know so soon as I hear from him. I expect to send George out before long, and will see that he carries out the basket and tin buckets.

There seems to be a perfect lull in this fearful contest—doubtless the hush which betokens the advent of a terrible storm. Our enemies are gathering their energies for some heavy demonstration somewhere along our lines. I trust in God that we may be able successfully to meet and repulse them.

My present position gives me a good deal of active exercise, as I visit the batteries on horseback.

It always rejoices my heart when I see and hear of these general assemblages of the people of this Confederacy for humiliation and prayer to Almighty God; and I trust that the fervent prayers of the wives and daughters of our land, offered with one consent on yesterday, may be graciously answered by the Lord of Hosts. War is a national judgment of the severest character; it comes from God, and is sent for wise purposes and to accomplish given ends. Among those objects perhaps the most important is the alienation of the hearts of the people from sin and worldliness, and a return of them to true contrition for past offenses, and the fear and love of God. It seems to me, as I look around me, that we have not even yet learnt the uses or accomplished the objects of this judgment. And this makes me tremble for the future. It does not do to trust in chariots or horses. There is a great Will behind all, over all, and directing all. For one I do try and humble myself before God, in all unworthiness and shamefacedness. And we can but hope and beg of Him that He will soon again lift up the light of His countenance upon us.

We have nothing new or interesting in the city. Do give warmest love to dear Father. Kiss my darling little daughter for me. And believe me ever, my dear mother,

Your affectionate son,
Charles C. Jones, Jr.

REV. C. C. JONES *to* COL. CHARLES C. JONES, JR.^g

Arcadia, *Thursday,* December 4th, 1862

My dear Son,

Your two last letters have been received, from which we learn that you have entered upon your new military duties as lieutenant colonel of light artillery, and hope that you will be able to discharge them intelligently and honorably to yourself and usefully to your country, which I am well assured you will most conscientiously and faithfully endeavor to do.

Your solicitude for the declining state of my health, expressed not only in words but in acts, sensibly affects me. Few men have been more blessed than I with dutiful and affectionate children, and with a wife whose tender kindnesses know no remission; and could relief have come through all your devotion and constant efforts, I should long since have been restored to perfect health. But such has not been the will of God, and to that will it is my desire and prayer to submit cheerfully. My anxiety is that I may not be deceived in my hope of eternal life through Christ Jesus our Lord, but be prepared for eternity when the great change comes.

Your Uncle John left us this morning with the bulk of his people, all in excellent spirits and well stored in a box car. We rode with him to the depot and parted with him there. The exodus of Negroes from the seaboard is large. Abolition raids would scarcely pay expenses, and if the enemy knows this, those who remain on the coast will be the safer for the fact.

Mother informed you of the sale of twenty head of Arcadia cattle at $25 per head = $500: $250 paid, and the rest on delivery of the cattle tomorrow, I suppose. Sold also thirty-two at Montevideo—twenty at $25: 500; and twelve at $12 (small cattle): $144 = $644 delivered and paid for.

Corn is selling in the county at $1.20 to $1.25 to the troop, and *they haul it.* Selling for one dollar and then *hauling* to the depot is rather heavy work; and perhaps by delaying a few days we may secure more favorable terms.

Our old friend Mr. B. A. Busby was buried at Midway on Tuesday. Sick at Taylor's Creek (where he had moved) over two weeks. Typhoid pneumonia. There is reason to believe he died as he lived! Most melancholy! Often, often have I conversed with him and urged immediate attention to his eternal interests; but he believed that he should attain to *great age,* and was seventy-four when he died! I feel his death. Was always a warm friend. Has been under serious impressions. They have special need to fear who grieve away the Holy Spirit upon the passing away of afflictions and a return to the cares and pleasures of life. The Lord may leave them in the undisturbed possession of their choice, and they know nothing more until death is upon them!

Little Sister is getting well again, and is the light of our dwelling. Mother is well. . . . Your Uncle William was here on Tuesday. Stays with Captain Winn at Dorchester. His people at Winn's also. Wish you would write him. Mother sends love. Kisses from your dear baby.

Your ever affectionate father,
C. C. Jones.

COL. CHARLES C. JONES, JR., *to* REV. C. C. JONES[g]

Savannah, Friday, December 5th, 1862

My dear Father,

Mr. Ward and myself are indebted to your kind remembrance for a delightful pair of mallard ducks, which arrived safely and in good order last night. Accept our hearty thanks.

Enclosed I send a letter just received from Mr. Sconyers, the overseer on the Buckhead place. You will be happy to see that all of the people are well. Please let me have the letter when you have completed its perusal.

You said to me that you wished a statement of expenditures already incurred on account Buckhead place. Enclosed you have the same. I have now entirely settled with Mr. Schley, with the exception of one note for $4120, given in payment of balance due upon purchase moneys of the place, which does not mature until 1st January 1865. Everything is now paid for upon the place. I owe in bank between six and seven thousand dollars, but this I hope to pay before very long with proceeds sale of stock and such assistance as you can conveniently give me (say, three thousand dollars) and from my share of articles and crop sold at Arcadia.

Cotton is now worth between fifty and sixty cents. Do not let Anderson sell your cotton unless he promises those figures, as they can be got by other commission merchants on the Bay. I can get one dollar any day for the corn if sold to government, and hope to get more.

Nothing of special interest. I hope, my dear father, that you are feeling better. Do give warmest love to dear Mother. Kiss my precious little daughter for me. And believe me ever, my honored father,

Your affectionate son,
Charles C. Jones, Jr.

COL. CHARLES C. JONES, JR., *to* REV. C. C. JONES[g]

Savannah, Saturday, December 6th, 1862

My dear Father,

I am this morning in receipt of your very kind favor of the 4th inst., and sincerely thank you for it, with every acknowledgment of the good wishes you express for a proper discharge of the new and more important military duties upon which I have just entered. I hope I may have disposition, strength, and ability to perform them aright.

I regret to learn the death of Mr. Busby—although he had enjoyed the threescore years and ten, a period far more extended than that usually allotted to frail, perishing humanity. It is with sorrow that I hear he has left no *good hope* behind.

The sale of the cattle is a fine one. I think with you that we had better delay a sale of the corn for a little while. So soon as the present government restrictions in reference to the conveyance of private freight are removed, my impression is that we will get $1.50 for the corn, and also be able to dispose of peas and potatoes if there are any to be sold.

Yesterday evening I sent you a statement of amounts already expended by me on account Burke plantation as requested by you. I cannot fully express to you, my dear father, what a great pleasure and privilege I have regarded it to have it thus in my power to compass the wishes of yourself and dear Mother in the matter of the removal of and the securing of a new home for our people without subjecting you to any additional trouble or pecuniary risks. I trust that the investment may prove a safe and profitable one.

Am happy to know that dear little Daughter is so well again. Do kiss her for me. Give warmest love to my dear mother. And believe me ever, my honored father,

Your affectionate son,
Charles C. Jones, Jr.

REV. C. C. JONES *to* COL. CHARLES C. JONES, JR.ˢ

Arcadia, *Monday,* December 8th, 1862

My dear Son,

Am obliged to you for the memorandum of expenses for the purchase and stocking of your Buckhead plantation thus far. I will do my best to meet the three thousand dollars you wish, and as much more as we can raise to help you out.

I fear the cotton left over from last year from Montevideo may not turn out as much as we anticipated. We have five bales *upland* packed in *round* bales—fine quality; had no *rope* to put in square bales. Will take your advice about the sale of cotton. If you can negotiate a sale for sixty cents it had better go; and we can get Mr. Anderson to deliver it as usual if *he* cannot do as well.

Kate (*William's* wife) begs to go with her husband. She has three small children, and Mr. Buttolph starts on *Thursday,* D.V., with all their people from Lambert and White Oak save a few left to get out the crop. Your Aunt Susan says she is willing to hire her to you. Please let me know your mind before that day. There will be a year's work on your place for the carpenters to put everything in order, and it would be a great comfort to William to have his wife with him. The only difficulty is house room and *field* room. The force will have to be reduced as soon as the way is opened. As it now is, we are acting under necessity. Would like to draw back some hands for Montevideo—not at all to cripple your operations but to make some ten or twelve to keep up the place and make it profitable. And will do so, God willing, if circumstances admit of it.

But there is no light shining in that direction. Every prospect at home and abroad is for a *protracted struggle*. Lincoln's message breathes the same heartless, cold-blooded, and murderous fanaticism that first began and has marked the war; and he repeats the same false and unjust reasons for it, and winds up by remitting the war until successful from one generation to another! And when successful all the world will approve and God forever bless! The magnitude and transparency of the folly and the wickedness of our enemy estops all comment. I can only repeat our daily prayer that God would take our cause into His own almighty hand, and humble us for our sins and judge between us and our enemy.

Our friends are generally well. The county on the moving order. Your Uncle John off—pleasantly. Your dear baby hearty and very interesting; jabbers and scolds and has a word to say, but in her own tongue. Mother thinks when she begins to talk she will talk all at once.

The notice of your brother in Saturday's *Republican* is highly complimentary, and very strong. We have to take in sail at times, even with a fair wind: it may be too much for our ship and rigging. Hope to write him today.

Syrup crop at Arcadia: two of the large barrels (marked fifty) each filled up, and about ten gallons over. Splendid syrup. Report from Mother, who says she has acted as first directress. We go to Montevideo today to renew the boiling there. When we get through there, will know what we shall have to send up the country. We have lost by the delay in grinding. Mother sends much love.

Your ever affectionate father,
C. C. Jones.

I find a man may write with a *cold hand* but a *warm and cheerful heart*. Much pleased with Mr. Sconyers' letter.

COL. CHARLES C. JONES, JR., *to* REV. C. C. JONES[g]

Savannah, *Friday*, December 12th, 1862

My dear Father,

In consequence of my absence from the city your kind favor of the 8th inst. was not until this morning received. I was sent under orders by General Mercer to Augusta for the purpose of procuring a light battery from the arsenal in that city for one of the artillery companies under my command, at present supplied with guns of an indifferent character. In consequence of this I fear I am too late to reply in time to your inquiry in reference to William's wife and her hire. I can now only say that I heartily endorse any arrangement which you have already made, or which you may see fit and proper to make in the premises.

I have not had an opportunity today to make further inquiries in reference to the prices of corn and cotton, but hope to do so tomorrow, and will let you know the result.

Saw Brother, Sister Carrie, and Stanhope in Augusta. All well. The Doctor went to the Buckhead place at my request to *vaccinate* the Negroes. He is in daily expectation of the receipt of his commission, and thinks it more than probable that he will be ordered to Charleston. In that event he may remove his family to that city, although as yet nothing definite is ascertained.

Have just received a letter from the overseer, Mr. Sconyers. All the people well, and getting along well.

We have nothing of special interest here. Good news—as far as it goes— from Virginia. My throat has been giving me a good deal of trouble lately. I intend getting Dr. Sullivan to examine it for me and place me under treatment. It has always been my weak point. I am most happy to know that dear Mother and my precious little daughter are so well, and sincerely trust, my dear father, that you are feeling better. Today I reviewed and inspected the Chatham Artillery, my old company; found everything in excellent order. In haste, but with warmest love to self, Mother, and little Daughter, I am ever, Father,

> Your affectionate son,
> Charles C. Jones, Jr.

Rev. C. C. Jones *to* Mrs. Eliza G. Robarts[t]

> Montevideo, *Saturday,* December 13th, 1862

My dear Aunt,

We are having moving times in old Liberty, the occurrences of the first revolution coming round in the second. Our young and middle-aged men are in camp, and none but boys and old men and exempts at home. And as a matter of prudence and safety large numbers of our Negro population are carried from the lower to the upper parts of the county, and removed also still further from the coast.

To give you an idea of the extent of these removals, I give you first a list of those who have taken their people from the lower to the upper parts of the county: Dr. Harris, Mrs. J. R. King (from Yellow Bluff and South Hampton both), Thomas J. Dunham, Brother William, Oliver Stevens, Benjamin Screven, B. A. Busby, Edward J. Delegal, Dr. Delegal, R. Cay. And others wish to do so. Second, a list of those who have taken their people up the country, chiefly to Southwest Georgia: H. H. Jones (sold out entirely and removed for good), Estate J. B. Barnard, Solomon Barnard, Randal Jones, Rufus A. Varnedoe (old Liberty Hall), Mrs. S. M. Cumming and Rev. D. L. Buttolph (White Oak and Lambert), C. C. Jones and C. C. J., Jr., Joseph J., and Rev. R. Q. M. (Montevideo and Arcadia), Thomas W. Fleming, Judge

Fleming, Estate Joseph Bacon, Estate R. Quarterman, Rev. John Jones, Captain W. Lowndes Walthour, Russell Walthour, Edward Thomas. And others speak of going. Some have concluded to remain—from necessity or choice.

The effect upon the society remains to be seen. Some will in all probability make permanent settlements and finally remove their families. Others may retain their homes in Liberty and their plantations elsewhere. Persons may purchase and move in and bring in new material for our intellectual, social, and religious advantage—and *may not.* . . . Thus you see God is dealing largely with us and making us feel some portion of the dreadful scourge of war, independent of the wounds and sicknesses of our soldiers in the army and the death of poor West, the only one from our district who has fallen in battle. The Lord's people may say under national as well as private afflictions: "It is good for me that I have been afflicted."

Your grandson makes a good soldier. Is in fine and I may say robust health, though the troop has been all the while stationary and doing nothing but picket duty. The home guard (of old men and boys) will next week dig rifle pits below the ferry and at Half Moon on the Island and perhaps at Carr's Neck and Melon Bluff (Mr. Busby's place) in case the vessels should come up as they did last spring.

You would be astonished to see the numbers from all parts of the state, even from Habersham County, down on the coast, from St. Marys to Savannah, *boiling salt.* Parties come in wagons, bringing their hands and boilers, and locate and boil enough for their use and return. And some companies boil to sell—and at a high figure. Everybody in Liberty, I think, boil their own salt. There has not been so much travel through Liberty for many a day.

Our people do not neglect the House of God, although the church feels the distracting influences of the war. The last Communion in Midway (the fourth Sabbath in November) Mr. Buttolph admitted three whites. . . . I would remind Cousin Mary that it was the *fortieth anniversary* of our membership with Midway Church. I remembered her and others *absent* (and the *dead,* and the *present*) who stood with us and avouched the Lord to be our God the fourth Sabbath in November 1822, more than a generation ago. . . . Brother John preached, and preached admirably; and it was a day of interest. There being no preaching elsewhere in the lower part of the county, there was a large assemblage of Negroes, to whom John preached in the afternoon.

Brother is now living at Dorchester in Captain Winn's family. Sister and family in Mr. John Stacy's house, Gravel Hill (Flemington). Jimmie and Willie have been quite sick. Better. Mr. Buttolph gone this week with the people to Southwest Georgia. Julia and family in Taylor's Creek neighborhood. All well. Audley and Kate for the present below. Robert and Daughter and little ones pretty well. . . . My dear wife works beyond account: has clothed most of the people; is now making *blankets* for the more needy; puts cloth in the loom *herself* and *warps* it too; has been for some days boiling syrup. . . . Our Little Sister neither walking nor talking yet, but a most sensible and interesting baby: Grandmother's pet. The image of her sainted mother, but begins, they say, to look like her father. Sam is well, and seems to have had pleasant times with his pleasing and pleased old spouse.

Mary joins me in love to yourself and Cousins Mary and Lou and the young ladies. As ever,

Your affectionate nephew,
C. C. Jones.

Our post office is McIntosh—No. 3, Savannah, Albany & Gulf Railroad, as we stay at Arcadia.

COL. CHARLES C. JONES, JR., *to* REV. C. C. JONES[g]

Savannah, *Monday,* December 15th, 1862

My dear Father,

The telegraphic intelligence from Virginia and elsewhere, although of a cheering character, does not as yet give assurance of any decided victory.

We are now, in all human probability, just on the verge of that tempest which has for some time been gathering. In view of the paucity of our troops when compared with the immense hosts opposed to us, fortified with all the most approved appliances of modern warfare; in view of the further fact that we are almost entirely unable to procure better arms and more soldiers, it does seem that we can alone in God look for deliverance. It is a time for universal prayer. The recent battle near Fredericksburg, although nobly won, has cost us the loss of valuable lives—Cobb, Gregg, and (more than all) *Hood,* one of the bravest of the brave. Priceless is that liberty purchased at such a cost. Twenty-five hundred of our troops from this military district left the city last night—destination probably North Carolina or wherever else the storm cloud may hang most darkly. We are anxiously expecting tonight more intelligence from Virginia. Our capital is grievously beset. But I have an abiding confidence in the valor and ability of our generals, the almost miraculous courage of our soldiers, and above all in the justice of our cause and the favoring protection of Heaven, and will expect a timely deliverance from all our troubles.

A letter from Mr. Sconyers tells me that all the people are well and getting along without any difficulty. The morning's mail will, I expect, bring me a letter from Brother, which will give his impressions of the place and of the condition of the people.

Will you have the kindness, Father, to have a barrel of rice beaten out at Arcadia and sent to me here in order that I may have it shipped to Mrs. Harlow at Waynesboro? I promised the old lady to send it to her. She is poor, and will esteem the gift. And more than all, she was the aunt of my dearest Ruth and tenderly attached to her.

Has Mother made any arrowroot this year?

I hope to see you and dear Mother and my sweet little daughter very soon. Is there anything in the world that little Mary Ruth needs that can be procured for her? I trust that you are, my dear father, feeling better. Is there any way in which I can serve you? With warmest love to self, dear Mother, and many kisses for my dear little daughter, I am ever

Your affectionate son,
Charles C. Jones, Jr.

Stepney says he wishes his hogs and poultry if practicable sent up.

MRS. MARY JONES *to* COL. CHARLES C. JONES, JR.ᵍ

Arcadia, *Friday,* December 19th, 1862

My dear Son,

We received your kind favor today and the extra, which fills our hearts with humble and adoring gratitude to God for this renewed token of His mercy and goodness to us and our beloved country. I have not words to express the emotions I feel for this signal success in the outset of this last fearful and terrific assault of our enemies, when probably he has arrayed a force five or six to one, armed with all the deadly appliances of modern warfare to overwhelm and destroy us. Surely our strength to resist and overcome is immediately from above and in answer to prayer; and I believe if we trust in our Almighty God and Saviour and strive to perform our duty to our suffering land in His fear and for His glory, that our enemies will never triumph over us. I trust if we are successful in the present repulse that the day of deliverance and the restoration of peace to our bleeding land will not be delayed.

What comfort and encouragement is afforded by the fact that we have so many Christian, true, God-fearing commanders; and that in many regiments of our army amidst the temptations and horrors of war the Blessed Spirit has been poured out for the conviction and conversion of officers and men; and that they who may be said to be treading the courts of death have had opened up to them the gates of everlasting life! Have you read the deeply interesting letters of our esteemed friend Dr. Stiles giving an account of his labors? I feel thankful that in this great struggle the head of our army is a noble son of Virginia, and worthy of the intimate relation in which he stands connected with our immortal Washington. What confidence his wisdom, integrity, and valor and undoubted piety inspire! And Virginia—noble Virginia—although she delayed her action in the offset, has bravely bared her bosom to the storm; and not only her men but her women too have sustained the patriotism and generosity of the state. Oh, that our God would give us true repentance for our many, great, and aggravated sins, which have brought this awful judgment of war upon us, and speedily establish us as a nation in righteousness and peace!

Your father and I took our dear little baby with us and spent the day with your aunt and Laura at Flemington. Found them comfortably located, although the house is small. Mr. Buttolph not yet returned from Baker County. *Kate* (William's wife) was not sent with their people; and your aunt says she is willing to hire her if you desire to have her. I told her we expected to have you with us shortly.

Can you not be with us at Christmas? It would be a great pleasure to us to have all our children with us—not for merrymaking but thanksgiving! I like the good old custom of gathering all under the rooftree at least once a year.

I strive daily, my child, to pray that with your increased responsibilities God would give wisdom and grace to fulfill your high trusts.

Thanks for your brother's letter.

We have now three barrels of superior syrup, and some gallons over, between the two places. Your sister wishes eight gallons for her family's use; you ought (and your brother) to retain the same; and that, with what we shall need on the places below, will leave, I think, two full barrels for Burke. I will this coming week pickle another beef and have a barrel of pork ready, so that you can order them up whenever you please to do so. Your father says there is a crosscut saw here that might go up. Our gins were doing very little, but *Audley very kindly* sent Prophet this week, and he has put them in fine order; so we hope the crop will soon be ready for market and the people to go up with the oxcarts. I am now making the arrowroot. Would you like to have some of it for any of your friends? When are Mrs. Neely and Val coming to visit us?

Do write me if it is impossible for you to be with us next week. If you cannot come, I must send you some sausages, etc. Tell me what day. Write me on Monday, for if you cannot come out, we will send Gilbert in, as I want also to send a box or package to your brother on Tuesday to reach him by Christmas. It is late, and I must close, with best love from Father and Mother. Sweetest kisses from your little Mary Ruth.

Ever your affectionate mother,
Mary Jones.

Col. Charles C. Jones, Jr., *to* Rev. *and* Mrs. C. C. Jones[g]

Savannah, *Saturday,* December 27th, 1862

My very dear Father and Mother,

I have just returned to the city after my delightful Christmas visit to you and to my precious little daughter. I cannot fully express to you, my dear parents, how much I esteem these visits home, with all the quiet loves and pure influences which dwell beneath the paternal roof. I always feel that I am made a better man by reason of the privileges there enjoyed. Never will I be able to answer for one of a thousand of the great kindnesses and unwearied goodnesses, my dear parents, which all my life long you have ever so generously showered upon me, and for all the precious influences of your Christian precepts and examples. But one thing is certain, and that is that you will ever have the warmest thanks, the sincerest love, and the most dutiful obedience of your affectionate son, who will ever esteem it his highest privilege to render you every honor and service that may lie in his power.

Spent Friday night with Arnold, and on Saturday morning reviewed Martin's light battery, and also visited the fixed battery at Genesis Point.

A letter from Eva, just opened, tells me that her father has sunk very perceptibly in the last few days, and that the physicians offer no hope of his bodily or mental recovery. She and Cousin Philo are in great affliction.

I learn nothing new tonight. Mr. Ward desires his especial remembrance, and begs that I convey his hearty thanks to you for your kind remembrance of him and for all the good things sent. Do kiss my little daughter for me. And believe me ever, my dear father and mother, with warmest love,

Your ever affectionate son,
Charles C. Jones, Jr.

The basket for Brother was duly forwarded by George on Friday night.

Miss Mary E. Robarts *to* Mrs. Mary Jones[t]

Marietta, Tuesday, December 30th, 1862

My ever dear Cousin,

It revived my spirit to receive a letter from you once more by our faithful Sam, who arrived safely on Friday week, much to the joy of our whole yard, white and black. He also looked as pleased as Punch to get home. I was standing in the yard in the afternoon, heard a shout from the little Negroes, and there stood the cause of it as large as life, quite well except a cold which he said "took him this side of Macon." After telling us all howdy he said: "Liberty County *done*—the people *'most all gone 'way.*" He then opened his bag, took out the ten oranges Miss Mary sent for Missis. How like old comforts they looked! How nice! How near it brought you to us, as you used sometimes to ride in from Maybank and bring a basket of sweet oranges for us! The little darkies then said: "Daddy, where the sugar cane you promised us?" He then drew out some little roots which he said he had brought to plant—not an inch of cane in which they could get their teeth. They looked so disappointed, I could but think if he had only brought two joints it would have been such a gratification to them. He then walked right out, took up his ax, and went into the woodyard to cut up wood for night and morning, without resting a moment, giving a scold to Will and Willis for breaking the wheelbarrow in his absence. If all servants were like he is, how happy would all masters and servants be! No eye service, no purloining, no answering again; no hard words or blows either.

But we will dismiss the hero of this subject and say how much we thanked you for the oranges. I stole some sugar out of the closet and preserved them for Mother. She enjoys them so—takes them when she coughs. We had a saucer of them on table Christmas Day, and we thought of the dear friends they represented and the now-deserted garden where they grew.

We had one dear relative with us, which made our repast cheerful and pleasant; and we all thought and spoke of the absent—he, poor fellow, with tears in his eyes as he thought of his beloved wife and little ones surrounded by the enemy. Has not heard a word from them, nor does he know when he will. He says his house was surrounded for weeks by Federal pickets watching for him, as he was accused of being a spy of Morgan's, and he had to live in his cornfield; then went and gave himself up, stood his trial, proved himself innocent; was then ordered to leave in ten days with his family, three servants, three trunks, no gold or silver, and just enough money in Kentucky bills to bring him to Georgia. I wish you could see him and hear him talk; I cannot do justice to his interesting narrative. He left us on Friday; has gone to Atlanta for his passport to Murfreesboro, where General Breckinridge is. He reminds me so much of his father—only more sprightly. (I see I forgot to name him; James West is the only relative we had with us.)

We had an excellent turkey raised two years ago, and a ham sent Mother by Mr. George Walker of Pulaski County. He kindly sent her three hams and a bottle of Catawba wine for her Christmas. Was not this kind? We feel that we have had many mercies extended to us. Though we had to borrow money to live on last year, and now had to sell property to pay the debt, still we are thankful that we are able to live at all.

Mr. Russell bought corn in the low country and promised to let us have some. It was ruined. We are not out yet, but our kind friend Dr. Stewart says he will lend us some till Mr. Russell can get more. Corn is $2.50 per bushel up here. The loss of the wheat crop, the drought which injured the corn, and most of all the seizure of the roads by government has brought about this state of things. If there had been transportation, we should not have suffered up here. Sugar is sixty cents, molasses $2.50 per gallon. You may be sure we never taste the latter at that price, and use the former very sparingly—only in our rye coffee.

I have heard of your great and indefatigable industry in clothing your household, and you deserve the encomium awarded to the woman in Proverbs. It is a comfort that you had the energy and the raw material to work upon. We fortunately clothed our servants when homespun was forty cents; they have since been a dollar and $1.25. Our girls each bought a pretty homespun when they were forty cents, and you would be surprised to see how nicely they look since they have made them up. I think more importance seems to be attached to food and clothes now than ever before. It is painful to inquire so much: "What shall we eat, and what shall we drink, and wherewithal shall we be clothed?" For myself I feel thankful for every warm garment I have, and every comfortable meal.

Mary Sophia and Lilla have been for three weeks in Rome. We had pressed Jane to come down here during Cousin John's absence, but she said she could not possibly do so. The girls went up there to keep her company.

On Friday night week Louisa was assisting Mother to bed; Ellen and myself were in the parlor reading. Soon after the cars came we heard a light step on the porch, then a gentle tap at the door. Supposing it was John, I went to the door and said: "Friend or foe? Give the countersign!" "Jeff Davis or Lincoln?" he laughed, and was soon admitted. We then (after he had warmed) adjourned to Mother's room, where we sat up till twelve o'clock. He told us all about his journey to Baker. Arrived there safely with his people, saw Henry, said it looked strange to see his father's portrait in that strange place, and the old bookcase too. (Oh, my heart aches for these changes! My dear uncle was taken from the evil to come.) I think John expects to spend the winter in Baker County, and if he does, I advised him to resign the pastorship in Rome. If it is duty to spend the winter away, it would be injustice to his church to hold on, as there was great dissatisfaction about his long absence last summer. They gave him three months, and he was absent eight. So I advised him to leave the Romans and go to the Corinthians. No doubt he will find an interesting field of labor in Baker among the colored people.

The poor ministers have to scratch hard for a living these times, and I do not blame them for looking after their interest. Our minister has been necessarily absent for two Sabbaths looking after his worldly interest. Mrs. Palmer has got a little property by the death of her father and her brother; and her other brother, John Buchanan, has purchased a place in Alabama on the Coosa River about thirty miles from Rome. I believe Mr. Palmer is interested in it, and I am glad he is; for though his salary is regularly paid, things are so high he finds it hard to make both ends meet. If he were only a better preacher! I feel sometimes as if I were in a spiritual stupor when I come out of church without one idea gained.

Thank my dear cousin for remembering me on the fortieth anniversary of our self-dedication to God. Sometimes I am ready to exclaim: "Oh, that it was with me as in days past!" My mind and heart seemed to receive and retain good impressions better, and religious truth refreshed and sanctified me more than now.

My dear mother is at this time quite feeble. Her cough is very troublesome, and she is very nervous. She is not, however, in bed, though she has to rest every day a long time after dinner and retire to bed early in the evening. Life has been a series of cares and trials with her, though she says many blessings have been mingled in her cup. The last sorrow (the situation of her unfortunate son) has been the bitterest of all. He writes her his health is miserable. She has never given him up; has followed him with her letters, her prayers, her tears and kind offices, supplying his wants as far as she has been able, and has invited him to come up here for a change. You know, of course, it is her house, and she can do as she pleases. Expect if he comes it will be a great trial. And I expect she could hardly stand it herself; any extra excitement tells on her in a few days.

She and Louisa and Ellen desire much love to you and our dear cousin, and a kiss—yes, many kisses—for your sweet little comfort, little Mary Ruth. I hear often from my boy Charlie, who, though lieutenant colonel of artillery, is still Charlie to me. Mother will write Cousin Charles next week if she is able; she is not well enough this week. Please give our love to Cousin Susan and Laura and Mr. Buttolph and their little boys. Will write Cousin Susan soon.

I forgot to tell you that I made a short visit to Mr. and Mrs. Rogers in Atlanta. Went on Saturday so that I could spend the Sabbath there. On Sunday it was extremely cold, so I told him I hoped he would warm us up by his sermon—that a cold hash would never do for such a morning. He left for the Sunday school. Mrs. Rogers, Ellen, and I went at ten, and there sat our excellent friend Rev. J. L. R. in his pulpit, the fresco painting reminding me of an eastern temple. His church is a very handsome one, and he did give us an excellent sermon on the Parable of the Ten Virgins. I really felt edified, and enjoyed the day exceedingly. He told me he saw Patience in Augusta with Mary; I did not know she had been there.

Do give much love to dear Mary and Mr. Mallard and the children. Tell your servants howdy for us.

Your ever affectionate cousin,
Mary E. Robarts.

My heart goes back at this season to the many happy days we have had together at the Retreat and Montevideo. Those beautiful homes abandoned! Oh, how sad—even to us so far away! What must it be to you? . . . Much love to Cousin William. Tell him not to let the Yankees catch his decrepit company; they must hobble off after giving them a plenty of grape. . . . The war news is encouraging today in the West. And what a victory at Fredericksburg! . . . Leading topics up here: political and domestic economy, state of the country, and molding tallow candles, spinning, and weaving.

XVI

Col. Charles C. Jones, Jr., *to* Rev. *and* Mrs. C. C. Jones^g

Savannah, *Thursday,* January 1st, 1863

"Happy New Year," my dearest father and mother and little daughter, trembles upon my lips as I address you; and I find the voices of congratulation upon this the dawn of another twelvemonth almost hushed into the more subdued tones of sympathy as I think of the many shadows which are lengthening all over our land, and of the peculiar sorrows gathering about so many. But although the merry laugh does not ring out as usual upon the calm air of this earliest-born, beautiful day of the new year; although the present is filled with disquietudes, and the clouds of doubt and of apprehension gather about the future; although the year which died last night has left us no rich legacy of peace, no guaranty of happiness; although the harsh sounds of war are abroad in the land, and vandal armies are besieging the very portals of our temple of national liberty; although prosperity has forgotten her accustomed paths, and the white wings of security are no longer hovering about our shores; although the hand of disease is heavily laid upon some whom God and nature and every cherished association of the past have made very near and dear to us; although coming days and future expectations from which we would fain expect only the sweet sunlight of joy and of hope are covered all over by the uncertain shadows of apprehension and of solicitude—we will not yield to fear; we will not forget past blessings; we will not cease to be grateful for present mercies; but will hope on, confiding all things in the hands of Him who doeth all things well, remembering the exhortation of the inspired Preacher: "Let us hear the conclusion of the whole matter: Fear God, and keep His commandments; for this is the whole duty of man."

Although it is New Year's Day, I am and have been very busy.

General Bragg, in command at Murfreesboro, today telegraphs General Beauregard that in the terrific battle which is still raging there between our brave troops and the abolition hosts under their most accomplished General Rosecrans, that we have driven back the right and center of the enemy, capturing four thousand prisoners (among them two brigadier generals), thirty-one pieces of artillery, two hundred wagons, etc., etc. The battle still raging on the left, and with great loss on both sides. I sincerely trust the victory may be complete, decisive. Here is one *bright ray*.

I send the almanac for 1863, and beg pardon for not having done so before. The truth is, my dear parents, I have been of late very busy each day. Nothing more of special interest here. With warmest love to you both, my dearest parents, and many kisses for my precious little daughter, I am ever

Your affectionate son,

Charles C. Jones, Jr.

REV. C. C. JONES *to* COL. CHARLES C. JONES, JR.[g]

Arcadia, *Tuesday,* January 6th, 1863

My dear Son,

As this is my first letter to you in the new year, I must wish you a Happy New Year—happy first in your experience of the forgiving mercy and love of God in Christ Jesus our Lord; next, in your open profession of your Saviour, who endured the Cross, despising the shame, on your account; in the joy you will experience in keeping His commandments and glorifying His name and living submissive to His will; in the accomplishment of all your lawful undertakings; in the realization of your pure and anticipated enjoyments; in the affection and confidence of all your relatives and friends; in a word, in a life of usefulness, illustrating all the virtues and graces which belong to the Christian and which adorn the man. You have the best wishes and prayers of your parents for all these things for you, and for a blessed immortality when life is past.

We had a little family gathering today of your aunt and Cousins Laura and Lyman, your Uncle William and sister, and the little ones (five in number), whose merry voices filled the house all day. We expected Robert, but he did not return by the cars this morning, having gone to James Island to pay a pastoral visit to his church members in Captain Thomson's troop. Our enjoyment would have been greatly increased by the addition also of yourself and your brother and his family.

Your Aunt Susan says she will sell you Kate and her three children to go with William her husband if Kate will consent; and no doubt she will. In determining the price I suggested her choice of a friend and your choice of another, and if they cannot agree, let them call in a third; and if the valuation satisfies you both, then abide by it. She said Mr. Fleming, who knows the family, would be a good person to fix their valuation. If you are still of the same mind to purchase, you can appoint someone to act for you. Your Uncle William would, I imagine, be a very suitable one. You can, however, judge best. He would act for you no doubt with great pleasure. He regrets much that he did not see you in your late visit.

You must let me know how many cattle you wish sent up to Buckhead as early as you can. The crop is ground out at Montevideo, and Pharaoh hopes to run the crop close at Arcadia this week, and the sooner then they are off the better. Am selling corn here and at Montevideo at $1.25 delivered at the cornhouse door. Will sell all shelled up at that price, and then see how much more may be sold now in the ear.

Mr. Buttolph says you wrote to inquire if he would sell his cotton at forty-five cents delivered at No. 3 depot. Do not know what he will do. He speaks of visiting Savannah with samples to see what can be done. Mr. Gué says Floridas fifty cents and over, but Liberty County common cottons forty-five cents. Forty-five cents is an excellent price. Could you include us in a like offer? A part if not the whole we might sell for that price. From Montevideo we have some thirteen or fifteen sea island and five upland in *round* bales.

Have moved Andrew and family from the Island to your Uncle John's to boil salt there. Expect to begin the last of this week or the first of next, and keep on for a year's supply.

Mother has suffered very much from her cold and cough, and is still suffering, although a little better of it. Little Sister well and growing more and more interesting every day. All unite in much love to you. My respects to Mr. Ward.

From your ever affectionate father,
C. C. Jones.

If the cotton purchaser will say fifty cents at the depot, we can make him up an excellent lot. Your Uncle John would come in, I think.

COL. CHARLES C. JONES, JR., *to* REV. *and* MRS. C. C. JONES[g]
Savannah, Wednesday, January 7th, 1863
My very dear Father and Mother,

I sincerely trust, in the absence of any very recent intelligence from home, that all are well—that you, my dear mother, have been relieved of your troublesome cold; that you, Father, are feeling stronger; and that my sweet little daughter is enjoying all the blessings of health.

I cannot say to you how busy I have been of late, and it would be difficult for me to recall a leisure moment during the past two weeks. On Friday of this week I have ordered in five of my light batteries in order that I may give General Mercer an inspection and review. The line will be formed in rear of the Savannah jail fronting north, the right resting on Whitaker Street. I trust the parade and review will be attractive, and assure the general commanding of the efficiency of the light batteries in this command, and of their preparedness at any moment for actual service.

It is a matter of deep regret that General Bragg has not been able to put to flight the army of our abolition enemy in Tennessee. Inspired by such cheering accounts from the battlefield as first greeted our eager ears, it was a sad disappointment to have the cup of general rejoicing so unexpectedly dashed from the expectant lips. I fear General Bragg is not the man for the position he now holds. We cannot afford, under God, to have drawn battles, and a strange want of success appears to have attended from the inception all his military operations. An officer may be a brave man, and what is termed a "fighting" man, and yet be incapable of handling large bodies of men in the field. There may be—and events appear to be demonstrating the fact—a vast difference in the abilities of Captain Bragg commanding with distinction a single light battery and General Bragg with a large army under his control.

The loss of the *Monitor* has been confirmed—another cause for sincerest gratitude to the Giver of All Good, who has so often and so signally turned the counsels of our enemies to nought.

Major William J. McIntosh is dead. He was buried here in Laurel Grove Cemetery on last Sabbath. He simply fell asleep while waiting for his breakfast, and never woke again to the light of this world. He died on board one of the Alabama boats while going from the residence of his son in Florida to visit another son in Alabama.

What do you think, Father, of selling our cotton at fifty cents? I think I can effect a sale at that figure, saving all freight, commissions, etc., etc., upon delivery of it at No. 3. Please let me hear from you on this subject. With warmest love to you both, my dearest parents, and many kisses for my precious little daughter, I am ever

Your affectionate son,
Charles C. Jones, Jr.

Cousin Philo Eve, my dear mother, in a recent letter from Eva begs me to return you her sincere thanks for your delightful arrowroot. It is enjoyed by Mr. Eve in his feeble health more than anything else which has been offered him for many days.

I had the pleasure of seeing Robert last evening.

Col. Charles C. Jones, Jr., *to* Rev. C. C. Jones[t]

Savannah, Thursday, January 8th, 1863

My very dear and honored Father,

It is with sincere gratitude that I acknowledge the receipt of your valued New Year letter of the 6th inst., which reached me only a few moments since. Already have I enjoyed the pleasure of assuring yourself, my dear mother, and my precious little daughter of my earnest and heartfelt wishes and hopes for your every happiness, temporal and spiritual, during the changing seasons of this year upon which we have so recently entered. I beg again, in all sincerity and affection, to renew those assurances, with the fervent aspiration that it may soon please the Supreme Ruler of the Universe to restore the light of His countenance, to grant unto us a speedy, successful, and honorable solution of the present difficulties which surround us, and again assure us in the permanent enjoyment of those blessings social, moral, intellectual, and religious which have in so many instances been almost wholly suspended by the existence of this gigantic and inhuman war.

I trust that dear Mother may soon be entirely relieved from the effects of her protracted and terrible cold. I had hoped that she was before this quite well.

In reference to the cotton, I am authorized to say that *I can get fifty cents for it delivered at No. 3* provided I can make up a good lot. This is above the market value, as I hear of a sale today at forty-five cents. I think it may be best for us to close at this in view of the uncertainties of the future; and you may say to Robert, to Uncle John, to Mr. Buttolph that the offer is open to them. . . . If there are any other parties who wish to be included, I will beg you to mention them to me, and I will endeavor to have the same liberty extended to them. Let come what will, fifty cents is a fine price, and I would rather sell at that than take the uncertain chances of the future.

I will purchase William's wife and children, and will be prepared, Father, to give whatever price you may deem proper, or which may be regarded as fair by anyone whom you may name. I should think, without ever having seen the woman or children, that fifteen hundred dollars would be a fair price if they are all young and healthy. But I leave the matter in your hands to act for me, and will abide any decision in the premises you may deem fair and reasonable.

You do well to sell the corn, I think, at the price named, saving transportation, etc., etc. I presume it would not be well to send more than twenty-five head of cattle to Buckhead plantation, and ten yoke of oxen and two mules if they could be spared. Am glad to hear that Andrew and his family are so profitably employed.

Please, Father, let me know how many bales of cotton can be delivered at No. 3 from all the plantations named, in order that I may at once communicate with the purchasers. By the arrangement proposed we save all the expenses of freight to Savannah, drayage, commissions, etc., which form no small item in the aggregate. If the proposition meets with a favorable consideration, the cotton had best be sent to No. 3 at the earliest convenient day after we have ascertained the probable amount which can be then delivered. One thing I will say to you, Father, in confidence: I would send no more cotton to Gué. I give you this advice *not at random.*

Tomorrow I expect to have a grand review by General Mercer of five of my light batteries. With warmest love to self, my dear father, to my dear mother, and many kisses for my precious little daughter, I am ever

Your affectionate son,
Charles C. Jones, Jr.

REV. C. C. JONES *to* COL. CHARLES C. JONES, JR.[g]

Arcadia, *Friday,* January 9th, 1863
My dear Son,

Yours of the 7th and 8th we have received—the last this morning; and I hasten to say that I will immediately communicate with the parties you have named in relation to their cotton and let you know as soon as possible—by Monday or Tuesday, I hope.

Today is your grand review. Nothing prevented my being present but my weakness and Mother's indisposition. It would have afforded me unfeigned pleasure to have witnessed it. I never saw the like.

Mother, I think, is a little better. She went to Montevideo this morning on business. Your dear child is getting quite hearty again, and her little mind develops daily.

The battles in Tennessee turn out better than expected. Certainly General Bragg has given the invaders a serious check. But without reinforcements what can he do? Rivers rising and railroads open. Stirring times are upon us. We have only to stand the braver and trust in God more perfectly. . . . Mother is pleased that the arrowroot has proved so acceptable to Mr. Eve. Am sorry he is no better. I remain, my dear son,

Your affectionate father,
C. C. Jones.

COL. CHARLES C. JONES, JR., *to* REV. C. C. JONES[g]

Savannah, *Saturday,* January 10th, 1863

My dear Father,

I am favored with your letter of yesterday, and am happy to know that dear Mother is better of her cold, and that little Daughter is so well.

The review and parade of my light batteries were highly praised by everyone. You have probably noticed the comments by the editors. It was the first appearance of a battalion of light artillery in the history of this state. I had on parade about four hundred men, three hundred horses, and twenty-six field pieces (six-pounder guns and twelve-pounder howitzers) with limbers and caissons complete. I desire here to commemorate the fact that during the entire parade, inspection, and review not a piece of harness became deranged and not a horse declined for a second its duty. This was quite remarkable, and is one of the strongest proofs I can give you of the perfect condition of the batteries. When in line of battle for inspection the battalion presented a front of between four and five hundred yards. The display in column of sections was very imposing, and all the movements of the battalion were characterized by precision and rapidity. From General Mercer I received congratulations and compliments. I wish very much, my dear father, that you and Mother could have been present. I think you would have been much pleased with the military display.

The cotton had best be delivered at No. 3 as soon as it is all ready; and when all has been delivered, if you will be kind enough to notify me of the fact, the purchasers will send out an agent and weigh and pay for the same.

The news is encouraging from the West. And Vicksburg, true to her heroic memories, still successfully resists the combined attacks of the enemy. Do give warmest love to dear Mother and my precious little daughter. And believe me ever, my dear father,

Your affectionate son,
Charles C. Jones, Jr.

Mrs. Mary Jones *to* Col. Charles C. Jones, Jr.[g]

Arcadia, *Monday,* January 12th, 1863

My dear Son,

I sent on Saturday to No. 3 to know if there was now an express to Savannah, and found there was none; so I am peculiarly gratified in having an unexpected opportunity of sending Mr. Ward and yourself a few fresh sausages by today's train, and now write a hasty line to assure you of the great pleasure we have felt at the success of your review. It would have given your father and myself great happiness to have been present, but his inability to move about without great effort prevented. I think, however, he continues to improve, and has gone today to see after our salt-boilers. My cold is something better after a day in bed on Saturday.

When will you forward the barrels of pork and syrup and the rice for Mrs. Harlow? Give us a few days' notice, as they are all ready to be packed, and have to be brought over from Montevideo.

I send you two of our Confederate tracts. Please present the one written by Dr. Thornwell to Mr. Ward; I am sure he will recognize in it one of the master minds of the age. The one *for you* your father and I have read with deepest interest; we can never have too much light upon "The Way of Life."

The oranges grew in McIntosh County, and are for your throat; for I am sure you are suffering after the review.

Your precious little daughter is well and very bright, and busy in the sunshine with the poultry and her dog Captain. As you will see, I am writing in great haste, and hope you will be able to read what is written. With kisses from your little Mary Ruth,

Ever, my dear son, your affectionate mother,

Mary Jones.

Col. Charles C. Jones, Jr., *to* Mrs. Mary Jones[g]

Savannah, *Monday,* January 12th, 1863

Upon coming home this evening, my dearest mother, I found your kind letter of this morning with the enclosed tracts and the accompanying package of delightful sausages, etc., etc. For them all please accept my warmest thanks. Major Porter called to see me a few moments since, and as the oranges were so fine, and such a rarity, I gave them to him to take to Mrs. Porter and Mrs. Gilmer, telling him where they came from. The sausages, etc., etc., will be a great treat. Mr. Ward is temporarily absent from the city, but I will keep his tract for him; and he will unite with me, my dear mother, in sincere thanks for your kind remembrance of us. Both of the tracts I have already read tonight with great interest and I trust profit.

Any day that the articles from Arcadia are ready they might be shipped, and I will see that they are reshipped here and forwarded to their proper destination.

I had to give on Saturday seventy-five dollars for a keg of nails weighing a hundred pounds. What think you of that? And fifty dollars per pound for iron!

I am purposing on the morrow a request that General Mercer allow me a leave of absence on Friday and Saturday that I may go up and see how matters are progressing on the place. I trust it will be granted, as I deem it very important that I should see just at this time what they are about and give proper directions, etc., etc.

We have nothing of special interest here. I have been so busy night and day for several weeks past that my head feels this very moment as if it contained a small water mill. . . . I am ever, my dear mother,

Your affectionate son,
Charles C. Jones, Jr.

Did you receive some time since a ten-dollar bank bill—a New Year's present for my dear little daughter?

MRS. MARY JONES *to* COL. CHARLES C. JONES, JR.ᵍ

Arcadia, *Tuesday,* January 20th, 1863

My dear Son,

I thought often of you on Friday night, exposed as I feared you were to all the severity of cold, and prayed that you might be protected from suffering and sickness. As it was a night remembered by me, you may imagine that I felt especially grateful, when yesterday's paper gave an account of the distressing accident on the Central Road, that you were in the up and not the down train.

I trust your visit has been accomplished with satisfaction. I am always anxious to hear from your brother, which we have not done for several weeks. I hope you saw and left him and his family well. He pays so little regard to his own health or comfort that I often fear his constitution will not stand such unreasonable draughts. How did you leave all your friends? Does Mr. Eve improve? Should you wish to send more arrowroot, I have plenty of it.

I hope our servants are doing well. We want to answer their letters very soon. The carts and boys are all ready for going up as soon as someone can be found to go with them. Is there anyone familiar with the route from the up country that could be obtained?

We have just received a letter from my brother, your Uncle John. He will be with us in a few days, and wishes to know if he could purchase Stepney's buggy to take with him to Baker. Stepney on leaving told me he did not wish then to part with it. It is a very good one, and in good repair. Your father says it could go along with the carts, attached or with one of the mules; and as such things are every day more and more scarce, we would like to know what you think about it. Shall it be sold or sent up? Perhaps you know his present wish about it, or might find it useful on the plantation.

Have you succeeded in getting spinning wheels and cards? I see an advertisement for *sheepskins* and offering cotton cards in exchange at the *Milledgeville* factory. I have collected some fine skins, and when the *hides* go up might send them also to Mr. Sconyers to be exchanged. We have reserved all the short staple cotton (five bales and a packet of sixty or seventy pounds and one bale of yellow—long) presuming that the purchasers wanted only *sea island*. As soon as yarn comes down to reasonable prices we must bag *a bale* for weaving. I am just putting in a piece of cloth, but not having my usual strength makes it slow business.

I came from church on Sabbath with a chill; had high fever last night. Your father sent for Dr. Farmer yesterday. He prescribed. I am under the influence of medicine today, and strange to say feel better for the attack of fever. It has at least this effect: confines me to the room.

Your precious little Mary Ruth improves every day, and is as fat and rosy as we could desire.

Your father and myself were much gratified at seeing Mr. Ward, and hope he is feeling better. I had not seen him for many years, and perceived that not even a visit to the "Celestial Empire" had availed to keep off the *snow-flakes* of time.

Your father will meet "the purchaser" at No. 3 tomorrow, and says he will inquire after a Mr. Butler, said to be a suitable person to take the carts, etc., to Burke.

With sweetest kisses from your own little daughter, and thanks to dear Papa for the New Year's gift, safely deposited in the savings bank, and the warmest love of your parents,

Ever your own mother,
Mary Jones.

Col. Charles C. Jones, Jr., *to* Rev. *and* Mrs. C. C. Jones[g]
Savannah, *Tuesday,* January 20th, 1863
My dear Father and Mother,

I found all well at the plantation in Burke, and getting along cleverly: the people content, and busily and cheerfully engaged in the discharge of their accustomed and daily duties. Agrippa had been quite sick with pneumonia, but was up again, and it is hoped will in due time resume his duties. Betty is sorely burdened with the primal sorrow of her sex; I have left specific instructions that she have every attention in the hour of her trial. The nails having arrived, the carpenters will at once complete three houses and proceed with the fourth. Repairs are needed on the old houses; attention will be given to this at the earliest practicable moment. The girls and women are succeeding very well in plowing; Miley is preeminently successful. All are fat and hearty and cheerful. Have prepared some ten or twelve acres for *rice;* and we will want the requisite seed from Arcadia, and also any rice hooks which may be there. Every inquiry was made after you, my dearest parents, and little Daughter, every member of the family, and all of the servants. Adam expects soon to be married. The physical appearance of the people indicates, I think, already decided benefit from the change. Their greatest want is shoes. Mr. Sconyers is busily engaged preparing for the crop of the coming year. The wheat is all up—about twelve acres—and looks very well.

Returned by way of Augusta. Saw Brother and Sister Carrie and Stanhope. All well except Carrie, who had the day I left some fever, but I trust nothing serious. My dear Eva was most happy to see me. Her father grows no better; it is a sad sight to trace in his robust frame the progress of disease. Cousin Philo asked me, my dear mother, to thank you sincerely for the delightful arrowroot, which has been greatly relished by Mr. Eve. Brother wished me to inspect his hospital. I thanked him for the kind invitation, but remarked to him in declining it that I made it a rule never to view humanity in its abnormal conditions except when duty required that I should do so. The next morning he told me he was glad I had pursued the course I did; for upon making his rounds he discovered that a case of confluent smallpox had developed itself in one of the wards during the night. He has sent a pump and some cod-liver oil, which I will ship by tomorrow's train. The pump is for injecting meat with salt water; and he says, Father, that he will be able to procure more oil for you when your present supply is expended. The Doctor is in his usual health. Stanhope a bright, fine little fellow full of health and activity. Brother's position is just the one he desired. His pay as surgeon is ample for his support, and he is able to pursue his studies and investigations.

I forgot to mention that I paid the people for all the corn which they left both at Montevideo and Arcadia. So soon as the meat and molasses and rice are ready for transportation and are sent in, I will see that they are reshipped here.

Your note, Father, matures on the 29th. I send one for renewal, if you desire to run the one in bank for a longer period. If convenient, would it not be wise to pay it? The bank leaves this entirely with you.

How is my dearest little daughter? Do kiss her for me. And believe me ever, my dear father and mother, with best love,

Your ever affectionate son,
Charles C. Jones, Jr.

Howdy for the servants. Will Aunt Susan sell William's wife and family? He is most anxious for me to purchase them so that they can be together.

REV. C. C. JONES *to* COL. CHARLES C. JONES, JR.[g]

Arcadia, *Friday,* January 23rd, 1863

My dear Son,

We were happy to receive yours of the 20th this morning, giving so pleasant an account of your late visit to Buckhead and to Augusta, and of the good health of the people and of your brother and family. Hope Carrie's indisposition may be temporary. Mr. Eve's condition is a sad one, and may last a long time; and his friends can do no more than patiently and affectionately wait upon him and commend him to divine mercy.

The Montevideo and Arcadia cotton has been delivered under my own eye; and enclosed are two checks on the Farmers' & Mechanics' Bank of date by Mr. Rogers—Montevideo: $2780.50 (fifteen bales); Arcadia: $3336.00 (twenty bales)—endorsed over to you. I think with you the note in bank had better be taken up. Please take it up for me; and as the bank has been so accommodating, it will give me pleasure to put it in its power to do me another kindness of the same character should I require it. Send me also a check on your bank in Savannah or on any of the banks in Augusta for $100, which I wish to enclose your brother for Stanhope—a little present for the child which makes him equal with his little cousins, and which I have too long delayed. The balance take and put with the $600 already handed you for moving and plantation expenses towards the $3000. What remains of the $3000 will try and make up shortly.

Have five bales upland in *round* bales—*good*. What is it worth in Savannah?

Have you engaged anyone to go up (white man) with the carts and cattle? Let me know at once. I have spoken to a Mr. Butler, a reliable man in Flemington, who may go for us. You said you wanted *two* yoke of oxen (four). Did you mean *two yoke* (*four only*) or two *sets* (*four to a set*—eight in all)? Twenty head of cattle will be enough to send up, as small cattle cannot be sent, and the large will *calve* this spring.

Shall prepare everything as fast as possible to be sent by the railroad— Negroes' things and all—as *no load* can be sent in the carts. On second thought it seems advisable for the interests of Montevideo to retain *July*, and perhaps will not send him up. Do not forget to answer your mother about *Stepney's buggy*. Will send you a statement in relation to the Negroes' corn, etc., left, that you may compare notes with your payment to them for the same.

Your dear child is growing every day, and begins to say words, and is the light of the house. You must come and see her as soon as you can. Mother has been very unwell for weeks with a cold; hope she is improving now. She unites in much love.

Your ever affectionate father,
C. C. Jones.

COL. CHARLES C. JONES, JR., *to* MRS. MARY JONES[g]

Savannah, *Friday,* January 23rd, 1863

My very dear Mother,

I thank you for your very kind letter of the 20th inst., which reached me yesterday. Previous to its receipt I had given you an account of matters and things at the plantation and of Brother and family in Augusta.

I will endeavor to find someone here who can take charge of the people and wagons, etc., etc., to go from Arcadia. As yet I have been unable to secure a fit person. Men are scarce.

In regard to Stepney's buggy, he does not wish it sold, and it will be a matter of great convenience for me to have it on the place. One of the mules can be driven up in it. Vehicles of all kinds are at present very scarce, and I would suggest that it be reserved and sent up with the carts and cattle.

I am having five spinning wheels made. They will be ready in a very short time, if not already delivered. Cards I have not, but we can exchange skins for them in Milledgeville; and if you will have the kindness, Mother, to send some skins up by the wagons, I will see that the exchange is made.

In reference to shoes for the people, I can have at a tannery on an adjoining place leather tanned upon these terms: send two raw hides to the tannery, and they send you one tanned in exchange. I can then in the county have the leather thus obtained made up into shoes.

If Mr. Butler be deemed by Father a suitable person to take charge of the wagons and cattle and Negroes, and his services can be procured, the sooner the train is started the better. He will have to take the Louisville road, cross over into Burke County (say, at the ninety-five-mile station), and then he will be only twelve miles from the plantation. . . . If Father does not think Mr. Butler a suitable person, I will send for the overseer, Mr. Sconyers, and make him come down and take charge of the people—which, by the way, may be the best plan after all. But the matter is submitted for his and your decision.

I am pained to hear, my dear mother, that you have been suffering so much, and sincerely trust that you are now quite relieved from your severe and protracted cold. Am happy to know that my dear little daughter is so well. Does she walk or talk yet? I trust that Father is feeling stronger. With warmest love to you both, my dear parents, and many kisses for my precious little daughter, I am ever

Your affectionate son,
Charles C. Jones, Jr.

If Daughter has not been vaccinated, will you please have it done? I enclose some choice matter which I wish used for that purpose, as I know where it came from.

If there be any spare old saddles on the places, please have them sent up with the wagons, as they are much needed.

Col. Charles C. Jones, Jr., *to* Rev. C. C. Jones[g]

Savannah, Monday, January 26th, 1863

My very dear Father,

I am in receipt of your kind favor of the 23rd inst., with enclosures as stated: say, check in payment of Montevideo cotton ($2780.50), check in payment of Arcadia cotton ($3336.00), both of which have been paid. In compliance with your request I have today taken up your note in the Bank of the State of Georgia for $800, which is herewith enclosed, and also have purchased check on Augusta payable to your order for $100. Total: $900, which leaves $1880.50 to be applied as you desire to the part payment of corn, etc., etc., on Buckhead place, for which, Father, please accept my warmest thanks. With this sum and my proportion of the Arcadia crop, together with the contributions from Brother and Robert, I will be able so materially to reduce my indebtedness in bank as soon to liquidate the whole amount, if life be spared, D.V.

Please tell me if any portion of the Arcadia cotton sold was owned by Uncle William, as I desire to account with Brother and Robert for their proportions at the earliest practicable day. If any portion be Uncle William's, be pleased at your convenience to let me know the exact amount in order that I may account to him for it.

I think the five bales upland can be sold possibly at the station at from fifteen to eighteen cents. I will inquire and let you know at the earliest practicable moment.

Twenty head of cattle will be ample to send up, and four yoke of oxen— say, eight in all. If an additional yoke could be conveniently spared, I would be very glad if it could be sent up with the others, as I would like to present them to George Owens, who has always been very kind to me, and is now planting not far from the Buckhead place.

I have promised Stepney to let him come down very soon and attend to some matters. He will probably be here next week. I am about to have my fine stallion Red Rover brought to Savannah for me to use as a parade horse. I have now so much riding to do that I am compelled to have two horses, and the price asked for suitable animals is so enormous that I must economize.

We have telegraphic advices of a very heavy demonstration on the North Carolina coast by the Federals. No positive intelligence as yet of any advance from the coast.

We have nothing of special interest in the city. I hope, my dear father, that you are feeling better, and that my dear mother is relieved of her cold. I am rejoiced to hear that my precious little daughter is so well. I trust that I may be able to see you all very soon. With warmest love to all at home, I am ever

Your affectionate son,

Charles C. Jones, Jr.

REV. C. C. JONES *to* COL. CHARLES C. JONES, JR.⁸

Arcadia, *Tuesday,* January 27th, 1863

My dear Son,

Have just received yours of yesterday, enclosing the note for $800 paid in bank and the check for $100 on branch of state bank in Augusta, and memorandum of receipt of drafts for the cotton sold. None of the Arcadia cotton belongs to your Uncle William. He had his cotton hauled and ginned at Captain Winn's, and I believe sold at the same time with ours at fifty cents. The money paid for corn sold *here* I will hand you when you come out—at $1.25; but no more (after what is now sold is delivered) at that price. It is now selling to government out here at $1.50, and if the troops give that to others they may give it to us. Government is buying up the corn in Southwest Georgia at one dollar per bushel—I presume to forestall speculation in the spring and summer.

You said you had paid the people for their corn left at Arcadia and Montevideo. Arcadia I know nothing about. The corn left by them at Montevideo is as follows: Porter 7 bushels; Jackson 12; Betty 12½; Rose 2; Pulaski 7; Peggy 2½; Sam 1. Total: 44. Jackson left 9 bushels rough rice not well winnowed, and Tom some to be winnowed and measured. This I presume you did not pay for. They beg to have it sent up for them. Will have it properly winnowed and measured off.

I think Mr. Butler a reliable man, and would take up the carts and cattle and mules carefully; and will see him, D.V., this week again. The rice for Mrs. Harlow and for your brother has to be put in bags for want of barrels (just as good), and will with the bacon and syrup and other matters belonging to the people be properly marked. The oxcarts can carry *no load* except provisions by the way and some hides and the sail of the *Duck* for a covering on the way. Stepney's buggy may be taken to pieces and put in the carts, or driven up by Mr. Butler with one of the mules or Stepney's mare if she goes up.

Am glad to learn Stepney comes down next week with your horse Red Rover. He can then come out and see after his little matters, and take everything along with him by the cars when he returns. This strikes us as a good plan.

Your Aunt Susan has declined selling Kate and her family on second thought; says she "would much prefer to hire her at a *moderate* rate."

Colonel Joseph Quarterman, about sixty-eight, died at Walthourville on Sunday last. Buried yesterday.

Mother, I hope, is some better of her cold, but the cough still distresses her.

Your dear child grows more and more interesting day by day, and we hope will walk and talk in a little while. Knowing what her early infancy was, she is a wonder of health and progress to us who have had the care of her from the beginning.

I will look out a pair of oxen for your friend Mr. George Owens and send them up with the rest. Mother unites in much love, and Baby sends kisses.

Your affectionate father,
C. C. Jones.

P.S. The pump and cod-liver oil have not come. Did you send them?

Mother's tea is nearly out. Please get a pound from Claghorn & Cunningham on my account of some I see they recently advertise, and send it out by Stepney for me.

I look with great solicitude to the movements in North Carolina. We shall be signally blessed if it pleases God to give us the victory there. And a repulse of the enemy will contribute still to help on a right view of matters North and West.

COL. CHARLES C. JONES, JR., *to* REV. C. C. JONES[g]

Savannah, *Thursday,* January 29th, 1863

My dear Father,

I am today favored with your kind letter of the 27th inst., and am glad to hear that the enclosures of the 26th reached you safely.

I have sent to Brother and Robert checks of *one thousand dollars each* on account their interest in the amount cotton sold. As yet I have not had a leisure moment to make up the Arcadia accounts, or to give them the exact statement of amounts to which they are respectively entitled, or to exhibit the precise sums which they should respectively contribute towards the feeding, clothing, and removal of their Negroes. The margin of corn sold will in all probability cover these expenses, and also the additional item of war taxes, which may, under the contemplated legislation of Congress, prove a very important item for the current year.

I am happy to hear that you will get $1.50 for the corn. It is worth that amount; for all supplies, in consequence of the redundancy and consequent depreciation of the currency, are already—and will be even to a greater degree—appreciated in nominal value. The memorandum of corn furnished in your letter as left by the people at Montevideo corresponds with the amounts for which I have settled with them respectively, paying at the rate of one dollar per bushel.

Bags will answer every purpose for shipping the rice, etc., etc. Stepney's buggy had best be driven up, and his mare might be sent with it. He will himself be down, I hope, early next week—probably before the wagons leave the place. It is the prudent plan, Father, to send no load with the wagons other than the provisions necessary to feed the animals on the way. If you will let me know some days before the articles are shipped per railroad, I will see that arrangements are made here for transshipment from one depot to the other. Let me beg also, Father, that you will furnish me if convenient with a list of articles.

I rejoice to hear that dear Mother is better. Her cold has been one of unusual severity. I am very happy to know that my dear little daughter is so well. I long to see all at home, and will embrace the earliest opportunity for spending a day with you. Do ask Mother if there is anything here which little Mary Ruth needs. I have not sent the box containing the pump and the oil because I feared to commit it to the tender mercies of the freight agent. I trust, however, that I will secure an early opportunity for forwarding it, and will at the same time send the tea.

You have already noticed the fact of the recent effort of the enemy to silence Genesis Point battery. The demonstration was more formidable than any hitherto made, and certainly one ironclad vessel was present and participated in the bombardment. Is it not remarkable that after a bombardment of over five hours no injury was caused either to the fort or the garrison? The object of the enemy evidently is to capture the *Nashville,* now ready for sea, armed as a privateer under the name of the *Rattlesnake,* and lying a few miles above the fort watching her chances for going to sea. A large reward has been offered by the Lincoln government for the capture or destruction of that vessel. We are not credibly informed that the attacking vessels suffered any damage from the fire of the guns of the fort.

The general indications from various quarters point to an increasing and widespread dissension in many parts of the North and West. Let us hope that they will ripen into a political revolution which will produce most important changes in our favor. We are strong in North Carolina, and it is confidently believed that we will be able successfully to repel any advance of the enemy. General Longstreet is there with his army corps.

I regret very much Aunt Susan's determination in reference to *Kate and her family.* The last time I was at the plantation William begged me very earnestly to try and purchase his wife and children, for whom he appears to cherish a strong attachment; and I held out to him the hope that I would be able to do so. I am anxious to purchase them, and still hope—unless Aunt Susan has some special reason to the contrary—that she will agree to sell them to me, in order that they may be with their husband and father. Should you see Aunt Susan at some leisure moment, will you, Father, see if she is positively resolved not to sell?

We have nothing of special interest here. With warmest love to self, my dear father, and to my dear mother and precious little daughter, I am ever
Your affectionate son,
Charles C. Jones, Jr.

COL. CHARLES C. JONES, JR., *to* REV. *and* MRS. C. C. JONES[g]
Savannah, *Sunday,* February 1st, 1863
My dear Father and Mother,

The quiet of the peaceful Sabbath has been disturbed by the sound of the enemy's guns, and the stillness of the sanctuary invaded by the harsh discord of hostile cannon. For the fourth time the battery at Genesis Point has been attacked, and this time again by an ironclad armed with eleven- and fifteen-inch guns. But the fervent prayers which have this day ascended to the Father of Mercies have been heard and answered. The bombardment of the fort lasted five hours, and wonderful to say, resulted in little or no injury to the work. Major Gallie, commanding, was killed, and seven privates slightly wounded. One thirty-two-pounder gun was permanently disabled. Necessary repairs to the earthwork were completed two hours after the bombardment had ceased.

The conduct of the garrison is worthy of the highest commendation. The men and officers behaved most gallantly, fighting hour after hour with the utmost deliberation and with the cool resolve never to surrender the fort, but to stand to their posts until every gun was dismounted, and then, retiring within the bombproofs, to use their small arms in the event the enemy attempted to land. The battery will be held at all hazards. Supporting forces are in the vicinity, besides one light battery and two sections of the "Old Chatham" along the river bank, to contest the passage in case the enemy's vessels pass the fort. The *Rattlesnake* and the steam tug *Columbus,* if the worst comes to the worst, will be sunk in the river above the fort. The armament will also be at once increased by the addition of a ten-inch columbiad.

It is a matter worthy of note that this is the first time that *a fifteen-inch gun* has ever been used in the history of actual warfare. The shells thrown from that gun weigh three hundred and thirty-five pounds. Think of an open earthwork resisting a bombardment from such a monster for five hours, and that enormous gun located in an impenetrable iron turret from whose sides our heaviest solid shot glanced harmlessly away, or when striking them full were broken into fragments. This ironclad was assisted by four gunboats and one mortar boat behaving in the most cowardly manner; for while the ironclad, confident in her invulnerability, approached to within some six or eight hundred yards of the fort, the latter vessels remained at a distance of over two miles—from that point, however, discharging their long-range rifled guns and mortars, which threw their projectiles full into the fort. The flags from the ironclad were all shot away, and not a rascal from within the secure confines of the turret dared show himself to replace them. The upper and back part of Major Gallie's head was all blown off—probably struck by the fragment of a shell.

This afternoon another ironclad appeared within three miles of the Thunderbolt battery accompanied by a gunboat. The former fired a few shell into an island just opposite and retired. We may have an attack upon that battery tomorrow. I went down with General Mercer to that point this afternoon. General Hunter has returned, assuming command of the Federal forces in this vicinity, and promises an early attack upon Savannah. The bombardment of Genesis Point battery will probably soon be renewed by the enemy. I trust that it will please God to give us courage and ability successfully to meet and repulse the invaders.

I send by George for you, my dear parents, two pounds of very excellent tea, which please accept as a little present. I wish that I had something better for you and for my dear little daughter, but I am now *a beggar my-self,* and have told George to ask you to send us *anything to eat* which you can spare from the place. Our market here is miserable, and everything at the most inflated prices. George will carry with him the box from Augusta.

With warmest love to you both, my dearest parents, and many kisses for my precious little daughter, I am ever

Your affectionate son,
Charles C. Jones, Jr.

Ten dollars enclosed for my sweet little daughter.

What gallant deeds in Charleston harbor!

The general would not consent to my going to Genesis Point today, and for the reason that he wanted me in readiness with my light batteries to meet any demonstration of the enemy from the direction of the Isle of Hope, which is not deemed at all improbable.

I hope you will soon hear from the *Atlanta* and Commodore Tattnall.

Rev. C. C. Jones *to* Col. Charles C. Jones, Jr.[g]

Arcadia, *Monday,* February 2nd, 1863

My dear Son,

Your letter of this morning greatly relieved our anxiety. We supposed you had been at Genesis Point. Thanks be to God for His mercy! May our brave men be always so sustained, and those famous ironclads become to fortifications weak as other vessels! We with our state mourn the loss of *Major Gallie!* All honor to his memory, and I hope peace to his soul! How remarkable: but one killed in the action! What news from Charleston! May our *old commodore* be favored with some exploit suitable to his fame and character!

Mother thanks you over and over for sending the delightful tea. She has been as busy as possible to send you what she has *at hand* (as you gave her no notice) as follows: one bag potatoes, one ditto peas and pumpkin, four pieces corned beef, one ham, one gammon, one bag rice, one bag grist, one turkey, three fowls, one bag grist for Abram. Sorry no tanias. And ground-nuts very poor.

A great deal of love to you. And a great deal of haste, for George is loading up and putting the horse in the cart. Baby well. Write every chance.

Your affectionate father,
C. C. Jones.

Col. Charles C. Jones, Jr., *to* Rev. C. C. Jones[g]

Savannah, *Wednesday,* February 4th, 1863

My dear Father,

I was agreeably surprised last evening by the pleasure of Robert's com-pany, and am happy to learn from him that all at home are well. Mr. Ward and myself are under every obligation to you and dear Mother for your kind remembrance of us. The articles, I understand, have arrived by the freight train, and George will have them brought from the depot today. They will be of great assistance to us.

Letters from Augusta and from the Burke place this morning received state that all are well. Agrippa is up, but not strong enough yet to go into the field. I have directed that he be kept from exposing himself until the danger of any relapse seems overpassed. Betty is now in one of the new houses, comfortably located, and she will receive every attention when the day of her confinement arrives. We have ten ploughs running, and more will be going in a few days. Stepney leaves the station (No. $9\frac{1}{2}$) with Red Rover in the freight train of tomorrow; so soon as he arrives I will send him out.

Brother says all are well with him, and that he has just completed and forwarded to the surgeon general an article on tetanus, which I presume will be a valuable contribution to the profession, especially at this time.

The Lincoln ironclads now on our coast are far more formidable than the *Monitor,* which fought with the *Virginia.* Commodore Tattnall has full descriptions of them. It was expected that the attack upon Genesis Point battery would have been renewed today. It has been delayed, however—I presume in consequence of this high northeast wind. We all wish that it would increase to a gale, and send the boasted war vessels disabled wrecks upon our inhospitable sandbars.

Both Savannah and Charleston are liable to be attacked almost any day. If the enemy makes a bold attack upon Charleston with their combined land and naval forces, it will be one of the grandest sights in the history of modern warfare. That city is now as ready with her defenses as she ever will be. We can trust neither in fleets nor numerous armies, but our eyes and hearts will be turned to the God of Battles, who saves not by many nor by few, but by His own omnipotent arm.

With warmest love to dear Mother, Sister, and the little ones, and special kisses for my precious little daughter, I am ever, my dear father,

Your affectionate son,
Charles C. Jones, Jr.

REV. C. C. JONES *to* COL. CHARLES C. JONES, JR.[g]

Arcadia, *Tuesday,* February 10th, 1863

My dear Son,

We hoped for a letter from you this morning, our last intelligence being that you were suffering with cold and fever; but the daily expectation of an attack from the enemy no doubt keeps you employed, and you have few leisure moments to spare. In the event of an attack our united prayer is that God would shield your person and your life, and enable you to do your duty to your country in His fear like a patriot and a Christian man, and in any event that you may be prepared for His will. If ever a people were called upon to put their assured trust in God, and to fight manfully to the last extremity for liberty, for humanity, for civilization and religion, we are the people. And God will bless us. This is my confidence.

Your Aunt Susan accompanies your Uncle John to the city, and have thought it best for you to see her in relation to Kate and her family and know her decision. And I have kept William a day over to assist in getting our shipment ready. And you could let me hear by tomorrow's mail, or by return of your uncle, about Kate; and if she is to go, I will see *her off with William*—the best way for her to go. The baggage or freight train will not go in again until Thursday; and will send everything in on that day.

The oxcarts (two) with ten oxen (eight for Buckhead and two for your friend Mr. Owens, which you can select), together with two mules, Stepney's mare and buggy and harness, bridle and saddle, two lumber chains, two draw chains, five yokes, two reap hooks, one wedge, one ax (Pharaoh's), five and a half cowhides, and one roll sheepskins left on Friday the 6th under charge of Mr. Jesse Butler. Were to have left the day before, but rain and cold prevented. Long and short forage sent along for man and beast. Pharaoh and Dick only sent. Cattle could not be sent: too poor, too cold, country too bare of forage. I give Mr. Butler two dollars per day and pay his expenses. I will settle with him. Gave him fifty dollars at his starting, which hope will be more than enough for everything. Shall write Mr. Sconyers of his coming and give him a list of matters under his hand.

Your affectionate father,
C. C. Jones.

Mrs. Mary Jones *to* Col. Charles C. Jones, Jr.[g]

Arcadia, *Tuesday,* February 10th, 1863

Enclosed, my dear son, is an order for the railroad dividend. When collected please pay for the *sugar mill,* and send me the balance. Also twenty dollars if you can get me some brandy or any good spirit for your father's use. Joe prescribed it; and such is his health that I see it is absolutely necessary for him. I send a nice glass bottle for it. Also $173.75 from the sale of corn at Arcadia. And your Uncle John kindly offers to take a small package which you can send George for to the Pulaski House. . . . Please send the brandy if possible by him.

Many thanks, my very dear son, for your present of the tea. It is delicious, and the only article of luxury I ever crave. Your precious child is well, and growing intellectually and physically. If you will send out the bags by my brother, I could return them filled with grists, etc., when you wish them. These are solemn times. May we all be stayed upon the Everlasting God! And may He guide and arm and shield you, my own dear child!

Ever your affectionate mother,
Mary Jones.

Col. Charles C. Jones, Jr., *to* Rev. *and* Mrs. C. C. Jones[g]

Savannah, *Tuesday,* February 10th, 1863

My very dear Father and Mother,

I had the pleasure of seeing Brother, Sister Carrie, and Stanhope on Saturday last. They were all well. Brother is much interested in the pursuit of his professional engagements, and seems much pleased with his present position as surgeon, which renders him perfectly easy in money matters, and also enables him to carry on uninterruptedly his favorite investigations.

Poor Mr. Eve is failing rapidly, I fear. His eyesight is now seriously impaired, and he lies most of the time in an insensible condition.

It is thought that the enemy contemplates an attack upon Savannah, and we are using every exertion to prepare the city for a successful resistance. Troops are returning from North Carolina. Three regiments have already arrived, and more are expected this evening.

I hope, my dear parents, to be able to see you and my precious little daughter on Thursday of this week. . . . We have nothing of special interest today from the coast. . . . With warmest love to you both, and tenderest kisses for my dear little daughter,

Your ever affectionate son,
Charles C. Jones, Jr.

Col. Charles C. Jones, Jr., *to* Rev. *and* Mrs. C. C. Jones[g]

Savannah, *Saturday,* February 14th, 1863

My very dear Father and Mother,

After my short but most privileged visit to you and to my precious little daughter on Thursday, I returned to Bryan on Friday, inspected the light artillery I now have in that county, visited Fort McAllister, and reached the city Friday evening. Found the artillery in very excellent condition.

The scars caused by the shot and shell fired by the enemy on the 1st inst. are still numerous in and about the fort, and will continue for many days to come. The battery there is now much stronger than it was on the day of the engagement. All damage to the traverses, bombproofs, and parapet has been repaired. In fact, the parapet has been strengthened by the addition of at least three feet of sand, and a ten-inch gun has been added to the armament. An effort is being made to secure torpedoes in the stream below the fort so as to blow up the ironclad when next she takes her position to bombard. I trust the attempt may be successful. One achievement of this character will inspire the abolitionists with a most wholesome dread of our rivers. The memory of the Yazoo torpedo is still quite distinct in their cowardly recollections.

Today, in company with Generals Beauregard and Mercer and other officers, I went down the river on an inspection of our advanced batteries. When at the obstructions, we could with our glasses see several of the enemy's vessels lying above Fort Pulaski. General Beauregard is very pleasant in his intercourse with his officers. I had considerable conversation with him, and he possesses by his manners and deportment the agreeable art of attaching his soldiers to him. He is a man of great physical power, capable of uncommon endurance, plain in his habits, temperate, entirely free from everything savoring of profanity or levity, easy of approach, deferential in his manners, and characteristically polite. Has a rapid, quick eye to positions, and possesses all the qualifications of a first-class engineer. I enjoyed the morning thus spent. He will probably be here for several days.

I sincerely trust, my dear father, that you are feeling better. I cannot tell you how pained I was from the bottom of my heart to see you so weak, and suffering so much from that severe cold. I hope, my dear mother, that you will soon be restored to your accustomed degree of good health, and that my precious little daughter is still so well. I forgot to get a lock of her hair before I left. Will you have the kindness, Mother, to sever one for me and send it to me by some convenient opportunity?

Enclosed are some pistol caps which I promised Uncle John. They are in a separate envelope.

William, Kate, and their children were safely shipped on board the cars, and I doubt not reached home in due season.

We have nothing of special interest today except some telegrams in reference to the condition of matters and things in the West, which if true are very important. But we have long since learned to receive with no little distrust the unsupported statements of even the most "reliable" gentlemen. With warmest love to you both, my dear father and mother, and many kisses for my precious little daughter, I am ever

Your affectionate son,
Charles C. Jones, Jr.

Sunday Afternoon, February 15th, 1863. This morning early Stepney made his appearance. He brings the cheering intelligence that all the people are well and contented; that the boys and wagons have safely arrived; and that William, Kate, and the children reached the station without accident. For this, as well as all other and great mercies, grateful thanks to the Giver of All Good. Stepney goes out in the morning. He will see what hogs he can purchase in the county.

Your affectionate son,
Charles C. Jones, Jr.

Col. Charles C. Jones, Jr., *to* Rev. *and* Mrs. C. C. Jones[g]
Savannah, *Wednesday,* February 18th, 1863

My dear Father and Mother,

We have nothing of special interest here. A review of the troops will probably be had by General Beauregard on Friday and Saturday, if he is not at an earlier day called to Charleston. I have not felt very bright today, but hope, D.V., to be better on the morrow. I write to assure you, my dearest parents, and my precious little daughter of my constant and most affectionate remembrance. The hog and pigs arrived, and were duly forwarded. As ever,

Your affectionate son,
Charles C. Jones, Jr.

Mrs. Mary Jones *to* Col. Charles C. Jones, Jr.^g

Arcadia, *Thursday,* February 19th, 1863

My very dear Son,

Your affectionate favor was received by the morning's mail, and I am up beyond our usual hour to send you assurances of our daily—I may say *now* hourly—remembrances. It is our precious privilege in this dark hour, when we know not where the storm will burst or upon whom the shaft of death will fall, to bear you in the arms of faith to the mercy seat, to the Cross of our Almighty Redeemer. He hath all power in heaven and on earth; and I entreat Him to protect and shield my beloved son, and to give him an assured hope of His love and forgiveness and acceptance, and in the trying and responsible station which you now hold to give you wisdom and prudence and courage, that you may be armed for the conflict and never waver or draw back from duty. I know that you have and will render to your country the fidelity and devotion of a brave man and a true patriot; and my hope and confidence for your safety and protection are in God alone. Above all things may He lift upon you the light of His countenance, and prepare you for life or for death as His sovereign will designs!

What can I do for you? By Stepney, who will not leave before Monday, I will try and send you some poultry, etc. Do let me know whenever I can do anything here for your comfort.

Your dear father has been very much weakened by his recent cold; and the increased anxieties weigh upon him. Today I have packed several trunks with necessary clothing, and shall try and prepare for emergencies; for emphatically we know not what a day may bring forth. . . .

Stepney has been busy every moment since his arrival. The meeting between himself and his father was touching; the old man laid his hands upon him and sobbed aloud.

Next Sabbath will be our Communion at Midway, and wish that you could be with us. Your father and I ardently desire before we "go hence to be no more" that you should join us around the Lord's table.

Your precious child is very bright and well excepting the little eruptions, which result, I hope, from teething. We talk of you daily, and night and morning she folds her little hands to ask God's blessing on her dear papa. It is late, and I must close, with best love from Father, kisses from Daughter, and the constant affection of

Your mother,
Mary Jones.

Rev. C. C. Jones *to* Col. Charles C. Jones, Jr.ᵍ

Arcadia, *Thursday,* February 19th, 1863

Will you put the enclosed piece in the papers if you think it worth publishing?

Dr. Howe writes Robert cotton osnaburgs may be had in Columbia at sixty-two and a half cents per yard for Negro summer clothing. Mother asks if it will be well to engage at that price there.

Did you see the person from the Bainbridge factory?

C. C. J.

Col. Charles C. Jones, Jr., *to* Mrs. Mary Jonesᵍ

Savannah, *Saturday,* February 21st, 1863

My very dear Mother,

I am this morning in receipt of your kind letter of yesterday, and most sincerely thank you for all your precious remembrance of me, for all your best wishes, and also for the sweet lock of hair from my dear little daughter.

I have been pretty sick this week: high fever, cold, and sore throat. The attack reminded me very much of the one from which I suffered when Ruth and our little Julia were both so ill near two years ago. I was taken sick on Tuesday last. Dr. Sullivan has been attending me, and through God's great mercy I am up again, and although somewhat weak, this morning resumed office duties. As a general rule my system very rapidly recovers from any attack, and I trust that I soon will be quite well again.

I have just sent Father's article to Mr. Sneed, editor *Republican,* with the request that he publish and also furnish copy to *News* for publication. I read the communication with much interest, and I fully concur in the views therein presented.

Yesterday General Beauregard had a review of the infantry and cavalry forces in this vicinity. The display is said to have been very creditable, and the general commanding expressed himself as much pleased with the drill and discipline of the troops. In consequence of my illness the light artillery did not appear upon parade. If General Beauregard remains until next week, probably a parade for inspection and review of that arm of the service will be had. Today the general has gone to Genesis Point.

We have nothing of interest from the coast. In fact, the pickets from the lower points report fewer vessels than usual in the vicinity of Port Royal. A remarkable tardiness and indecision appear to characterize all the movements of the enemy. General Beauregard seems confident of our ability, under God, both here and at Charleston to resist successfully any attack which the enemy may make. All we need here is an additional supply of heavy guns and men to make the defenses perfect, or very nearly so.

So soon as the articles are shipped from No. 3 I will have them forwarded from this point. I have just purchased and paid for 1559 pounds cured hogsheads, which have been boxed up and sent to the place. This will be a great assistance; and I have given directions not to have this meat issued until summer, but to have it opened, resalted, hung up, and smoked. Latest advices report all well.

I wish, my dear parents, that I could come out and see you and my dear little daughter; but just at this time it is a difficult matter to leave the city, as it is not known at what moment one's services may be needed. I sincerely trust that Father is better of his severe cold, and that you, Mother, are rapidly regaining your accustomed degree of good health. I am happy to know that my precious little daughter continues so well. With warmest love to you both, my dear father and mother, and many kisses for my sweet little daughter, I am ever

Your affectionate son,
Charles C. Jones, Jr.

I think it would be well to engage the Negro summer clothing at sixty-two and a half cents.

I spoke to Mr. Hamilton about the purchase of the five bales cotton at No. 3, and he promised to let me know whether he would buy, and at what price. Will endeavor to see him again at the earliest practicable moment and learn his determination.

COL. CHARLES C. JONES, JR., *to* REV. C. C. JONES[g]

Savannah, Saturday, February 21st, 1863

My dear Father,

Since writing today I have seen the Messrs. Hamilton, to whom I had spoken in reference to the purchase of your five bales short staple cotton. They tell me that their factory is too far from the railroad to haul the cotton there. I think you can find a market here for the cotton at a reasonable figure—say, eighteen or twenty cents; and I would advise that you send it in, with any stained cotton you may have, to Messrs. Richardson & Martin, who will, I think, effect the best possible sale of it. If unmarketable here, the round bales (short staple cotton) may be shipped to Augusta and sold to the factories there. To them the shape of the bags can be no objection.

Nothing new. I am feeling stronger this evening. . . . With warmest love to self, dear Mother, and my precious little daughter, I am ever

Your affectionate son,
Charles C. Jones, Jr.

I hope to send Mother's tea out by Monday's express.

REV. C. C. JONES *to* COL. CHARLES C. JONES, JR.[g]

Arcadia, Monday, February 23rd, 1863

My dear Son,

Your two favors of 21st came to hand this morning, and we were sorry to learn how sick you have been. May it please God to give you rapid return to health! But do not presume and expose too soon. Better not be present or command at the review and inspection of your arm of service than run serious risks of bringing on a relapse. Your throat needs special care. This is a gentle stroke of God's hand upon you to draw you to Himself, and not put off your open profession of the ever blessed Saviour. Death is doing his ordinary work around us; and many who saw the commencement of the war, and were exposed to its shafts, have been removed quietly and unexpectedly from life to the retributions of the life to come! May that day not find us unprepared!

Yesterday was our Communion at Midway. Six whites admitted. Full congregation of white and black for the times. On our return home found your dear little one, whom we had left in perfect health, with fever and looking wan. No reason for it save cutting teeth that we can divine. She revived her spirits in the evening, and after a pretty comfortable night is without fever and as well as usual this morning; and we hope it will pass off.

The articles for Buckhead after delay got off in Saturday's train: one bag rice, Dr. J. Jones; one ditto, Mrs. Harlow; two bags salt, C. C. J., Jr.; five ditto rough rice, two barrels syrup, one ditto pork, one grindstone, one barrel sundries, two bundles and one box ditto. Stepney has succeeded after some effort in securing some hogs, and will leave, D.V., by the freight train tomorrow (24th) with them and some sundries in charge. His visit in giving such pleasant accounts of the change of the people has been of the nature of a public benefit. My only regret is that they are not *all* removed; for whether we are disturbed or not, we plant in uncertainty, and it becomes a year of anxiety all round.

Mr. J. W. Anderson is my factor, and presume ought to send him the few bales left, unless he gives me no assurance of being able to sell the cotton. If it were in a safe place, would as leave keep as sell it. It is very fine upland.

Your brother in a letter received this morning promises to pay us a visit between Tuesday and Thursday of this week, if the medical director of this division, Dr. Miller, will grant him leave of absence for a few days.

I think I mentioned Mr. Butler's return. Got up all safe. You can select the pair of oxen for your friend Mr. Owens when you go up. Jackson *knows* them all.

Mother says Stepney will *bring in your ducks* tomorrow, and that we will try and supply you with salt so that you need not buy any. Your purchase of the bacon is good. What did you pay? Any more to be had?

Your aunt and Cousin Laura dine with us. All well, and all unite in much love. . . . We were much gratified with your account of General Beauregard, and glad that you had so pleasant an occasion of making his acquaintance. My respects to Mr. Ward.

From your ever affectionate father,
C. C. Jones.

Mother says gargle your throat with *warm salt and water,* and put the *mustard plaster to your throat every night.*

Col. Charles C. Jones, Jr., *to* Rev. C. C. Jones[g]
Savannah, *Friday,* February 27th, 1863

My very dear Father,

I returned today from Augusta, having successfully accomplished the matter of business for which I was detailed. I will soon have here a splendid six-gun battery of twelve-pounder Napoleon guns, the very best field gun which can be employed in our section of the state. I also have notice from Charleston that two very fine rifled guns will be at my disposal tomorrow. Thus I am endeavoring to retire all the light six-pounder guns and to supply their places with weapons of larger caliber, longer range, and of more improved pattern. I will spare neither time nor labor in rendering this arm of the service as efficient as practicable.

Your kind favor arrived during my absence, and I thank you, Father, sincerely for all your kindness. I feel today a little used up by travel, for I am not entirely strong yet; but I expect to be quite refreshed in the morning. My cold is much better, and my throat now gives me no pain.

I deeply regret to hear that my dear little daughter has had fever, and trust that the attack was only temporary, and that she is already quite restored to health.

Saw Sister Carrie and Stanhope in Augusta. Both quite well, and desire sincerest remembrances. Cousin Philo and Eva both well, but Mr. Eve is gradually growing weaker and weaker.

The articles have all been forwarded to No. 9$\frac{1}{2}$. I find today a letter from Mr. Sconyers which reports the safe arrival of Stepney, etc., and also the fact that all the people are well.

We have nothing of special interest from the coast today. Do give warmest love to dear Mother. Kiss my precious little daughter for me. And believe me ever, my dear father,
Your affectionate son,
Charles C. Jones, Jr.

I congratulate you upon the Doctor's visit, and I trust that God will bless his medical skill to your great relief and comfort. Do remember me to him.

I paid fifteen cents for the hogsheads. Would have procured more, but there were no more to be had.

Col. Charles C. Jones, Jr., *to* Rev. *and* Mrs. C. C. Jones[g]
Savannah, *Monday,* March 2nd, 1863

My very dear Father and Mother,

The enemy are lying in force in Ossabaw Sound, and threaten the batteries at Beaulieu and Genesis Point. What their absolute designs are we can only conjecture. We are endeavoring to be thoroughly prepared for any emergency—at least as thoroughly prepared as we can be with the men, arms, and ammunition at command.

We are sadly in need of a greater number of heavy guns. This morning I received two splendid Blakely rifled guns, with harness, limbers, and two hundred rounds to the piece, which I have turned over to my old company. This is a very valuable addition to the efficiency of that battery. I am also in daily expectation of receiving from the Augusta arsenal some twelve-pounder Napoleon guns, and am using every effort to improve, as far as lies in my power, the condition of the light artillery in this military district.

You have seen an account of the destruction of the *Nashville* by the ironclad *Montauk* in the Great Ogeechee River—perhaps in many points of view not an unfortunate affair for us. That vessel, with a drinking captain and a rough crew, has been keeping that neighborhood in hot water for many days.

Dr. Palmer preached twice yesterday in the Independent Presbyterian Church. Both very fine sermons. A letter from Mr. Sconyers tells me that all are well at Buckhead, and matters progressing favorably. I write in much haste, but with warmest love to you both, my dearest father and mother, many kisses for my precious little daughter, and kindest remembrances for the Doctor. As ever,

Your affectionate son,
Charles C. Jones, Jr.

I send per express some of dear little Julia's jewelry for her little sister, and also a pair of shoes.

Howdy for the servants.

COL. CHARLES C. JONES, JR., *to* REV. *and* MRS. C. C. JONES[g]

Savannah, *Tuesday,* March 3rd, 1863

My very dear Father and Mother,

The abolitionists, with three ironclads, four gunboats, and several mortar boats, attacked Fort McAllister this morning. They opened fire about half-past eight, and the engagement continued without intermission until near half-past four o'clock P.M. The last dispatch, which left the fort after the firing had ceased, reports that only two of our men were wounded during the whole of this protracted bombardment, and they only slightly. The carriage of the eight-inch columbiad was disabled by a shot from the enemy. A new one has been sent out; and the gun itself, which was not injured, will be remounted during the night and be all ready for action in the morning. The injury to the parapet of the fort is slight, and will be repaired during the night. The garrison is in fine spirits, and are determined to hold the fort to the last extremity. It is truly wonderful how mercifully and abundantly the good and great God of Battles has encircled our brave men with the protection of His all-powerful arm, shielding them from harm amid dangers imminent and protracted. To Him our hearts ascend in humble, fervent gratitude for the past; from Him we earnestly implore like favor in the future. If the Lord is on our side, as we honestly trust and believe He is, we will not fear what our enemies, with all their boasted strength, can do unto us.

The enemy seems determined to reduce this fort if practicable, probably with a view to the destruction of the railroad bridge. That little fort has thus far so successfully and so bravely resisted every effort on their part for its reduction that they will doubtless use every endeavor, as a matter of pride, to compass its destruction. There is no question of the fact that it is a remarkably well-constructed earthwork—well traversed. The lessons of the past and of the present so demonstrate. It is almost a miniature edition of Vicksburg. In like manner must all our defenses be conducted.

The dispatch to which I alluded above states further that the ironclads, etc., retired, apparently with a view to obtaining an additional supply of ammunition. They dropped down the river only a little way, and a store ship soon joined them and appeared to be serving out ammunition. The attack will doubtless be renewed in the morning; in fact, while I write from my office in the barracks at this $9\frac{1}{2}$ P.M., I hear guns in the direction of Genesis Point. The enemy will probably continue the bombardment at intervals during the night, with a view to wearying our men and preventing the necessary repairs to the fort; and when the morning light again cleverly dawns, the attack will be renewed with vigor. We are supplying the deficiencies in ammunition caused by the expenditures of the day. It is thought that one ironclad was seriously injured. This may be, however, only *conjecture; we hope such is the fact.*

The land force on our side, now in the vicinity of the fort and prepared to resist any effort of the enemy to land, consists of the 29th Georgia Regiment, the sharpshooter battalion, two companies in the fort, our light battery, and some seven or more cavalry companies. With the natural advantages of the country these men, if they do their duty, ought to accomplish a great deal.

We have been reinforced at this point by the arrival of the brave General Walker. General Clingman reached the city today with his brigade of three regiments, and General Taliaferro is expected with his brigade. General Beauregard announces himself prepared to come over at any moment that his services are needed. I trust and confidently believe that we will, with the blessing of Heaven, be able successfully to defend the city from the expected attack, and to teach the enemy a fearful lesson which will not be speedily forgotten.

I am getting my light artillery in capital condition, and hope, when the opportunity presents itself, to render efficient service.

The Doctor came in this afternoon and is staying with us. Mr. Ward also returned by the Charleston train. Many, many thanks, my very dear mother, for your kind and most acceptable remembrance of us.

I am very much pained, my dear father, to hear that you are still so weak. All I can do is to hope and pray that you may soon be better, and that it would please God in tender mercy to us all to prolong your days, so precious to us all. . . . Do, my dear parents, let me know if I can do anything for you at any time, or for my dear little daughter. I wish very much to see you all, but at present it is impossible for me to leave the post of duty, for it is emphatically the fact that we know not what an hour may bring forth. . . . With warmest love to you both, my dear father and mother, and many tender kisses for my dear little daughter, I am ever

Your affectionate son,
Charles C. Jones, Jr.

REV. C. C. JONES *to* COL. CHARLES C. JONES, JR.^g

Arcadia, Wednesday, March 4th, 1863

My dear Son,

Your kind favor of last evening reached us this morning, and afforded us the very information which we were anxious to receive—circumstantial and reliable. No paper from Savannah came.

Surely we have reason to bless God and take courage and fight more manfully than ever. The bombardment of Genesis Point is one of *the events* of this most eventful war. The failure of the vaunted ironclads will have a great moral effect. The enemy will have less confidence, and we stronger assurance, of being able with properly constructed fortifications and good armament, and above all with *brave men,* to repulse them. I look upon it as a special providence—an answer to prayer. Eight hours' bombardment with three ironclads and some six or seven mortar and gunboats, and only two men slightly wounded, one gun carriage injured, and the damage to the breastworks repaired in the night! We learn that the enemy has renewed the attack this morning. May it please God to help us through to the end, that they may be finally repulsed!

The effect of this affair will be most salutary upon our troops in Savannah and Charleston. Right glad am I to learn that you are still receiving reinforcements for the defense of the city, and that an excellent spirit prevails, and that our outposts are to be defended to the last extremity and the enemy fought inch by inch. That is the plan. We heard yesterday that the enemy were to be permitted to land, and the outposts were to be given up, and our forces retired within the line of the city defenses! What an idea! What would be the consequence? A regular siege approach, an accumulation of men and matériel, and the city in all probability captured! Never retire and confine ourselves within our defenses until we are forced to do it.

Am happy to know also that you are so much better, and exerting yourself with energy and judgment and with so much success in putting your batteries in the best order for service. They will no doubt play an important part if the conflict comes, and may determine the fortunes of the day—in which event I trust, my dear son, and pray that God would shield your life and your person and enable you to discharge your duty as a Christian man and as a true soldier and patriot. General Walker is a great accession. Do you observe the *mercy* in the Genesis affair? *Not a man killed;* not one *dangerously* wounded!

The presence of your dear brother with you at this time gives great comfort to Mother and myself, and must be so to you both. The Doctor would not delay, but went down to be with you and on hand with the staff of surgeons if there should be a necessity. I looked at all his fine cases of instruments, and told him I wished they might always be kept in the same capital order, but he never be called to use them on the field of battle. His visit has greatly refreshed us.

Your dear baby is quite well all to the eruption. *She walked alone for the first time Sunday, March 1st, 1863.* Mother, Daughter, Robert, and Miss Kitty Stiles all unite in love and respects to you both. The Lord bless and keep you both!

Your ever affectionate father (with a tired hand),
C. C. Jones.

COL. CHARLES C. JONES, JR., *to* REV. C. C. JONES[g]

Savannah, *Thursday,* March 5th, 1863

My very dear Father,

I am this morning favored with your valued and interesting letter of yesterday.

Have just returned from the vicinity of Coffee Bluff, which commands a view of Genesis Point and Ossabaw Sound. The vessels of the enemy have retired, and are not to be seen. No renewal of the attack since the 3rd, although they presented a menacing front on the 4th; and now on the 5th they appear, for the present at least, to have abandoned any intention of recommencing a bombardment which by the blessing of God proved so futile. The moral effect of the resistance at Fort McAllister must produce a most salutary effect upon the minds of our troops, and dissipates entirely the fearful and terrible ideas with which the abolitionists have sought to invest their proud ironclads. Just now there are no demonstrations apparent on our coast.

A moment since, I had a conversation with Commodore Tattnall. It is his impression that it is not the intention of the enemy seriously to attack either this city or Charleston, but that their purpose is simply to attract attention here by assaulting our outposts, with a view to preventing our reinforcing the armies of the West, where a great battle will probably soon be fought, possibly in the vicinity of Murfreesboro. The news from that section this morning is quite cheering. Van Dorn is redeeming his reputation, which suffered somewhat in the affair at Corinth.

There is no intention on the part of anyone here *to abandon our outposts and retreat within the city lines* except upon an extremity; and the statement made to you to that effect was entirely incorrect. On the contrary, it is the firm resolve to hold every post to the last extremity, and dispute every inch of ground with the enemy; and by the blessing of Heaven, when the hour of battle does come, the abolitionists will find that they have an uphill business in any endeavor to possess themselves of this city.

The Doctor is busily engaged in visiting the camps in this vicinity. He is not at home except at night. He is staying with us. . . . I am sorry to hear that my dear little daughter still suffers from that eruption. The Doctor promises me to prescribe for her. Do kiss her for me. Give warmest love to dear Mother, Sister, and Robert, and the little ones. My special respects to Miss Kitty Stiles. And believe me ever, my honored father,

Your affectionate son,
Charles C. Jones, Jr.

Mrs. Mary Jones *to* Col. Charles C. Jones, Jr.ᵍ

Arcadia, *Saturday,* March 14th, 1863

My dear Son,

Your uncle had walked a mile up the road to meet you, your precious little daughter to the far gate, and Father and Mother in the sunny front piazza awaited your coming, when to our great disappointment Gilbert returned with an empty buggy. I have looked for your visit with peculiar interest, for your dear father has been unusually feeble—more so than he has ever been. This week he has had fever several days and nights, which I hope has been caused by a large boil which has given him great suffering. In his enfeebled condition any additional pain or cause of excitement to his system shows itself immediately. I hope you will be enabled to visit us very soon. I cannot express the anxieties that are weighing on my heart.

Your uncle had been two days and nights with us, and on leaving requested me to send for him at any moment. Night before last I received a note from Robert, but your father was too feeble to be left alone. I wrote Brother William, and he came early in the morning, and has remained today to meet you, thus affording an opportunity for my going up yesterday to see your sister and the newborn granddaughter—a plump little lady, and your sister doing remarkably well. They are very anxious to obtain a nurse, as it is impossible for me to leave your father.

We regret sincerely to learn that Mr. Eve still continues in that distressing and hopeless condition. Such has been your father's and my own sympathy with Mrs. Eve and Eva under this heavy affliction that we have desired to write and express our feelings to them; but his feebleness and many occupations have prevented. Let me ask when you write that you will say how truly we do feel with and for them. And your father has often remembered him in our social devotions. Your brother has often told me what a man of benevolence, industry, and integrity he was. I trust it may be well with him not only for time but also for eternity.

What an admirable account this week's *Republican* contained of the fight at Genesis Point! Who wrote it?

Please, my son, if possible get me some quinine and an ounce of gum camphor. Enclosed ten dollars. If not enough, you must let me know.

Your father and uncle join me in much love, with sweetest kisses from your little daughter and many thanks for the box by express. The rings are her admiration. I have been looking for weeks for that promised visit from Mrs. Howard and Mrs. Neely. My love to them.

Ever your affectionate mother,
Mary Jones.

COL. CHARLES C. JONES, JR., *to* MRS. MARY JONES[t]

Savannah, *Monday,* March 16th, 1863

My very dear Mother,

Your kind letter of the 14th inst. is before me, and it greatly distresses me to know that my dear father continues to be so feeble and so unwell. He is scarcely ever out of my thoughts, and my constant and fervent prayer is that God would graciously stay his declining health and prolong his life, so precious to us all. I hope to be with you on Tuesday the 17th, and regret that I should have disappointed you on last Saturday, although I do not remember to have appointed that day for coming out. Did I do so? That is usually a busy day with me, for all the weekly returns from the batteries have then to be digested and forwarded.

Have written a letter of congratulation to Sister and Robert. I sincerely trust that Sister may soon be restored to her accustomed health, and that the tender life of this little daughter may be prolonged, in the good providence of God, through many years of joy and gladness to her parents and friends, and of usefulness and of piety in her day and generation. I have secured a nurse for Sister in the person of Mrs. Smith, who goes out today prepared to remain the required period of time. Mrs. Hall, on account of previous engagements, could not leave the city.

I will attend to your request, Mother, and bring the quinine and camphor with me when I come.

The description of the recent bombardment of Genesis Point was written, I believe, by Major Locke, formerly the editor of the *Republican,* at present a major in the Commissary Department. It was a very excellent article.

Many thanks for your and Father's kind remembrance of Cousin Philo and Eva in their affliction. I will in my next letter to Eva express your sympathy, for I know how sincerely they will esteem this your remembrance of them.

Aunt Susan left the city on Saturday morning; I accompanied her to the depot.

It is thought that Charleston may be attacked upon the next spring tides —say, on or about the 19th inst. We may, I presume, expect heavy engagements at more points than one during the next sixty days.

Do, my dear mother, give warmest love to my dear father. Kiss my precious little daughter for me. And accept for yourself every assurance of the truest affection of

Your son,
Charles C. Jones, Jr.

Mrs. Mary Jones *to* Col. Charles C. Jones, Jr.[g]

Arcadia, *Monday,* March 16th, 1863

My dear Son,

Your father has passed a very bad night, and I consider him critically ill. I know not if your brother could possibly come, but wish you to telegraph him as early as you can. Your father has objected to sending for the physicians in the county; and I am well aware if his true situation was not understood by them, rash practice would be injurious if not fatal.

Ever your affectionate mother,
Mary Jones.

I wrote this early this morning, intending to send Gilbert immediately. Your dear father insisted I should wait until the cars came, thinking you would be in them. I now send hoping Gilbert will be two hours at least in advance of them. Telegraph Joe immediately: he is evidently growing more and more feeble. May God strengthen and uphold us all!

Your mother, in deep sorrow,
M. J.

Your letter has just come. We still conclude to send Gilbert, that you might telegraph your brother. Your father is very anxious to see him *if* he can possibly come.

XVII

Col. Charles C. Jones, Jr., *to* Rev. George Howe^w

Arcadia, *Thursday,* March 19th, 1863

Reverend and dear Sir,

At the request of my sorrowing mother I write to announce to you the saddest intelligence—of the death of my beloved and honored father. He fell asleep in Jesus on the afternoon of the 16th inst. without the slightest struggle. For several days previous he had been suffering from a severe cold, and was unusually weak. His nights during that period were almost sleepless. Respiration difficult. Amid all his physical infirmities his characteristic composure and cheerfulness never flagged.

On Sabbath morning the 15th inst. he took his usual ride on horseback. On the morning of the 16th, the day upon which he died, he dressed himself, came downstairs, and breakfasted with the family. After breakfast he walked out upon the lawn in front of the house, but soon returned very much fatigued. Retiring to his study, he seated himself in his accustomed chair and read from his favorite Bible. He was then exceedingly feeble. My mother and my aunt (Mrs. Cumming) spent the morning with him in his study. He conversed with difficulty, and although greatly oppressed with restlessness, which induced him frequently to change his position, and also with extreme debility, appeared perfectly calm and happy.

At two o'clock dinner was served in his study. He enjoyed the food prepared, eating with relish. Soon after dinner, addressing my mother, he alluded to some recent published order of General Beauregard as being very encouraging in its character, and referring to the present gigantic efforts made by our enemies to effect our subjugation, added: "The God of Jacob is with us—God our Father, Jehovah, God the Holy Ghost, and God our Divine Redeemer; and we can never be overthrown." My mother repeated some of the promises of the Saviour that He would be present with those who trust in Him, even when called to pass through the dark valley of the shadow of death. To which he responded: "In health we repeat these promises, but now they are realities." My mother replied: "I feel assured the Saviour is present with you." His answer was: "Yes. I am nothing but a poor sinner. I renounce myself and all self-justification, trusting only in the free and unmerited righteousness of the Lord Jesus Christ." Mother then asked if he had any word for his sons. He replied: "Tell them both to lead the lives of godly men in Christ Jesus, in uprightness and integrity."

His feebleness increasing, my mother suggested that it might prove a pleasant change for him to go to his chamber and recline upon the bed, to which he assented. Rising from his rocking chair, he took the arm of Mother and of my aunt. As he was leaving the study he paused for a moment and, smiling, remarked to them: "How honored I am in being waited upon by two ladies!" This was about half-past two o'clock in the afternoon. Reaching the chamber, he reclined upon the bed, suggesting to my mother and aunt the manner in which the pillows should be disposed so as to contribute best to his comfort. My mother commenced rubbing his hands and feet, the circulation in his system being very feeble. He called for his body servant and bade him relieve my mother; and after Tom had rubbed his feet sufficiently, Father said to him: "That will do now; put on my slippers." Which was done. And then: "You can go." Closing his eyes, he rested quietly one foot over the other, as his wont was to lie, and in a few moments—without a groan, without a single shudder, without the movement of a single muscle—fell asleep in Jesus, as calmly as an infant in the arms of a loving mother. He passed away so gently that the devoted watchers at his side scarce perceived when his pure spirit left the frail tabernacle.

In the morning, with the assistance of his body servant, he had dressed himself, as his custom was, in a full suit of black with the utmost neatness. In this habit he died: not a spot upon his pure white cravat, not a blemish or wrinkle upon his vestment. From the bed in his chamber, without a single change in his apparel, a half hour after he breathed his last, his precious body was removed with the utmost tenderness and placed upon the favorite couch in his study. There he lay, surrounded by all the favorite authors whose companionship in life he so much cherished, attended by the precious tokens of his recent labors, in the holy calm of the room he loved so well, until Wednesday morning at eleven o'clock (the 18th inst.), when his honored dust was carried to Midway Church.

In the presence of a large concourse of citizens and of Negroes a funeral sermon was pronounced by the Rev. D. L. Buttolph from the text: "How is the strong staff broken, and the beautiful rod!" After the ceremonies were concluded, his honored remains were interred in the adjoining cemetery near his father and mother and the graves of other near and dear relatives, beneath the solemn oaks which cast their protecting shadows over that consecrated spot.

My father had very evidently been contemplating for months and even years the near approach of death. Not very long ago he said to me: "My son, I am living in momentary expectation of death, but the thought of its approach causes me no alarm. This frail tabernacle must soon be taken down; I only await God's will." The following is the last entry which appears in his journal; it was penned only a few days previous to his death: "March 12th, 1863. Have been very weak and declining since renewal of the cold on the 1st inst. in church. The emaciation continues. Taste scarcely anything; feeling of emptiness but appetite for nothing, and a few mouthfuls suffice.

Throat quiet. Difficulty of throwing off phlegm from the lungs, or rather the bronchial tubes; lungs seem to lack power of expansion so as to take in air enough to oxidate the blood sufficiently; respiration quicker than common. Owing to this cause, sleep badly, being forced every few moments to shift the position. Digestion yet unimpaired. My disease appears to be drawing to its conclusion! May the Lord make me in that hour to say in saving faith and love: 'Into thine hand I commit my spirit: thou hast redeemed me, O Lord God of truth' (Psalm 31:5). So has our Blessed Saviour taught us by His own example to do; and blessed are they who die in the Lord."

Feeling, my dear sir, that you would be deeply interested in an account of the last moments of one who ever held you in such especial regard and friendship—of one so noble in character, elevated in principle, pure in honor, true in affection, generous in thought and act, refined in feeling, cultivated in mind and manners, and exalted in every Christian virtue—I have been thus minute in detail. Were I to attempt a recital of all the holy memories which cluster around his closing hours, were I to repeat all the precious words which fell from his almost inspired lips, time would fail me. His death was little less than a *translation*.

And what shall I say of the delightful, the holy savor of his life? How shall I speak of the loss which has been sustained by the church, by the country, by the community in which he resided, and by his sorrowing family? My honored father was still engaged, as his feeble and declining health would permit, upon his *History of the Church of God,* the great labor of his life. It remains, in the inscrutable providence of Heaven, unfinished, although complete as far as he had progressed with it. A few chapters more and he would have concluded the last page. As it is, it is his last offering to the church—his final labor in the cause of his great Redeemer. So soon as circumstances permit, it will be given to the world just as it came from his trembling hand.

Never through all the years of failing health and of great physical infirmity has Father's intellect been in the least degree impaired. In fact, it appeared to be sublimated in proportion as his feebleness increased, gathering heavenly strength as day after day in his debilitated frame was foreshadowed more and more the image of the grave. To the last moment he preserved to a wonderful degree his characteristic cheerfulness. Time he never wasted. His obligations to his family, to his servants, to the community in which he resided, to nature (whose admiring student he was), to the church, to the country, and to the great God he so faithfully adored, he seemed never for an instant to forget. He lived ever an exalted life, and everyone confessed the purity of his example, the ennobling influences of his walk and conversation.

But, my dear sir, I need not speak thus to you who knew him so well—to you who so truly estimated his virtues. In the warmth of my own feelings I have written much more than I at first intended. You will bear with me, I trust; for I have always loved and honored my father almost to veneration and positive worship.

It is the special request of my dear and bereaved mother that you would at some convenient moment prepare an obituary of Father. We trust that you will be able to do so, knowing as we do your appreciation of his character, assured as we are from your long intimacy, constant association, and close friendship that to you he would with peculiar confidence have entrusted everything touching his life and his labors in his Master's vineyard. With the principal events in Father's life, his responsibilities and engagements, as well as with his characteristic and noble traits, you are quite familiar. Should you desire any facts or dates, or any additional information, my mother or myself will be happy to furnish them at the earliest moment. All expenses connected with the publication of the obituary, in any form you may desire, will of course be gratefully borne by us.

With our sincerest remembrances to Mrs. Howe and each member of your family, I am, dear sir,

Very respectfully and truly yours,
Charles C. Jones, Jr.

Mrs. Eliza G. Robarts *to* Mrs. Mary Jones[t]

Marietta, *Saturday,* March 21st, 1863

My dear Mary,

With a heart overwhelmed with sorrow I attempt to address a few lines to you. This morning brought us Mr. Buttolph's sad letter containing the death of my dear Charles—nay, my son's death. Dear Mary, how can I express my feelings? The anguish of my heart is great, for I have indeed lost a son.

Great is our loss, but we have great consolation. Although a good and great man has been taken from us, we know he is now in glory, freed from all his sufferings, enjoying that eternal rest he was so faithful in seeking. . . . But, dear Mary, your poor aunt can say but little to comfort you; God is our only source in times of trouble, and you know where to go for comfort. I pray God to sustain you under this great affliction. . . . What a consolation to think my dear Charles passed away so easily! How mysteriously to us appears Providence—not one of your children to be with their dear father and you in such a time of trial! Dear Mary Sharpe—what a trial not to see her father! I hope she is doing well in her confinement. . . . My thoughts are often at Midway and the graveyard; and now I have another link there. Last night I dreamed of being there, and saw the longest funeral procession. . . . But dreams are the visions of a diseased body.

Mary is writing you. Louisa and the girls send you much love and the most heartfelt sympathy, for they all loved their cousin. Accept from your poor aunt as much as you can imagine. Excuse my not writing more. When you feel able I shall always be glad to hear from you. Kiss little Ruthie for me. And believe me

Your ever affectionate aunt who loves you much,
Eliza G. Robarts.

Miss Mary E. Robarts *to* Mrs. Mary Jones[t]

Marietta, *Saturday,* March 21st, 1863

And can it be that my paper is before me to write to my dear, my sister-cousin under such solemn, distressing circumstances—that she who was ever a cherished wife is now a sorrowing, desolate widow? Oh, my cousin, what do these words imply? That your dearest earthly friend, the companion of your youth, the solace of maturer years, now sleeps the sleep of death. . . . Earthly friends can weep for and with you, but who can enter fully into your grief? None but your blessed precious Saviour, your "Help in ages past," your "Strength in days to come. . . ." That He will do so we humbly pray.

When Mr. Buttolph's letter came this morning I was at the breakfast table, and hearing my dear mother weep aloud, I ran into her room not knowing what to expect. What new trial had come upon her? But this was not the one I had looked for. Though my dear cousin's failing health had been a matter of daily anxiety with us for months past, still I never realized that we should so soon be called to part with him. So soon! My last word with him was about this time three years ago, as we were bidding him farewell on the porch at Montevideo. As Mr. Buttolph was supporting my dear mother to the carriage, I said to him: "This is the last look you will ever have of your aunty in this world." He said: "Oh, I hope not!" Still I did not think he would be called first. . . . In his last letter to Mother he sent me word that the Sabbath before was the anniversary of our church membership, and that he had remembered me. I immediately retired and prayed for him, and returned thanks to God for giving me such a friend to pray for me. . . . Oh, my cousin, what shall we do now he is gone? . . . As one by one of those with whom I commenced life is taken away, I do not feel as if this is the same world I commenced life in. And if I feel so, how must it be with my aged mother? Oh, how I miss the sympathy and constant, free, unreserved intercourse of beloved relatives—particularly in these times of trial and difficulty! How often have I wished to sit down by your sides at Arcadia and talk over all that oppressed me! . . . Give much love to dear Mary, Charles, and Joe. I grieve that they could not be with you. So has it been with Cousin John and us; but we have all experienced a common sorrow. *Bereavement* better expresses it, for we mourn a treasure lost.

Please give much love to Cousin Susan. How sad she must feel! Her only brother—and such a brother! Love to Laura and Mr. Buttolph. And kiss the dear children for us. Dear little Ruthie I hope will always be with you to comfort you. My dear mother has written you a few lines; she could not write much, she is so much agitated. . . . Tell your servants howdy for us. What a master they have lost! And what a friend the whole race of colored people have lost! Their faithful missionary—one who loved their souls more than the whole host of prating abolitionists. Please thank dear Mr. Buttolph for his letter.

Your ever attached and sympathizing cousin,
Mary E. Robarts.

Rev. John Jones *to* Mrs. Mary Jones[t]

Refuge, Baker County, *Tuesday,* March 24th, 1863

My beloved Sister,

Truly am I with you in your great sorrow! Oh, that I could help you—could more fully share with you the heavy burden which presses on your heart! If there is aught in human sympathy, you have it in many hearts; for my dear brother was like Daniel, "a man greatly beloved." I loved him more than any man on earth; he came very near to my own father. I know that I have lost my best male friend—my ever kind faithful brother, on whom I have leaned with filial confidence from early youth to the present time. But what is my sorrow to yours? The best of husbands, the truest of friends, the companion of your mortal years and brightest days, hath left you to walk alone the path of life! Never were two hearts more perfectly united on this earth! Oh, my sister, my heart yearns to do something, to say some word that may help you. You are seldom absent from my thoughts, and never from my prayers.

Allow me to point you to the disciples of John after his death. "They took up the body and buried it and went and told Jesus." This I know you have done, and that you will continue to do as your trouble comes home in deeper reality by day and in the lone watches of the night. He will not leave you comfortless. . . . Dear Sister, let us not allow our thoughts to dwell too much on the grave; let us think of our beloved and precious one in his Father's house. . . . Often did I pray that you might not be disturbed in the quiet of your home by our ruthless enemies. He is now above and beyond all their malice and evildoings.

My last interview with him was most tender. I left him with very sad feelings. I wrote you both immediately after reaching Baker, and have been looking for a line, not knowing that he was declining. And yesterday evening, as I returned from Mitchell County, where I found some twenty-three Presbyterians and passed the Sabbath and baptized ten children, and was thinking of my dear brother to write him these facts, I passed through Newton. I inquired for letters, and found one from our kind friend and brother Buttolph communicating the sad intelligence. It was most unexpected, for I was continually hopeful that he would be permitted to remain with us for years to come. But he thought otherwise, and lived with his lamps trimmed and burning. Oh, that I could be as ready and willing to depart and be with Jesus as he was!

My dear sister, when you feel able, do send us a line and speak as much of our dear brother as you can. My dear Jane and little boys unite with me in tenderest love to you and dear Mary Sharpe and Robert and their little ones and your dear little baby.

Your ever affectionate brother,

John Jones.

P.S. My dear sister, I cannot omit mentioning that our little boys evinced deep feeling on hearing that their dear uncle was no more. I requested Jane to read to them Brother Buttolph's letter, and had my arms around them; and as they listened, and I told them how much their uncle loved them and prayed for them, they began to weep; and gently slipping away from me, they lay down upon their bed and wept silently and apart, more like grown persons than children. It was really touching to see the little fellows quietly weeping and remaining silent for the rest of the evening. They will never forget their dear uncle.

If Charles and Joseph are with you, do remember us to them most affectionately; and if absent, remember us to them by letter. I direct this letter to Walthourville, thinking you are there.

Your affectionate brother,
John Jones.

P.S. Do give howdy to the servants. Remember us affectionately to Cousin Susan, Cousin David, and Cousin Laura, and Cousin William Maxwell.

COL. HENRY H. JONES *to* MRS. MARY JONES[t]
Malvern, Baker County, *Wednesday,* March 25th, 1863
My beloved Sister,

The intelligence of the sudden yet peaceful end of the dear husband of your youth, my noble brother, was received last night through a letter from Mr. Buttolph to Brother John.

I shall not mock you with any attempt at consolation. This no earthly instrument can bestow, because no *human* power can fill the blank and dreary void left in the heart by the removal of the deceased. But, dear Sister, I can at least *weep* with you and pour forth the full flood tide of my truest, deepest sympathies in your behalf. I mourn for my brother with a sorrow only equaled by the death of our venerated father. Indeed, to *me* he ever stood more in the relation of a parent than a brother; from early childhood he was my counselor and guide, and I can truly add that no mortal man ever wielded such influence over me for good. His kind admonitions, excellent advice, faithful prayers, and *living example* have ever been present with me. . . . But I must cease to recite the long catalogue of his kindnesses to me and mine.

The grave has closed over his loved form, and we are bereft of our brother and friend and benefactor. Alas, we can only fold our hands submissively and exclaim: "*Our loss* is his *gain;* the warfare is ended, the victory won; henceforward there is laid up for him a crown of righteousness beyond the skies; and now, upon the bosom of his Father God, he enjoys the full fruition of the Christian hope."

I had hoped, dear Sister, to have been allowed the sad privilege of waiting around the bedside of my brother in his last moments. It was ordered otherwise. But I thank God to learn that calmly and tranquilly he fell asleep in Jesus without one groan or struggle. Like the full-orbed sun, he sank behind the horizon of life unshorn of a solitary ray, in the full vigor and strength and maturity of that commanding intellect which by *its works,* blessed be God, will continue to work out and perform that mission *for good* which seemed to be the chief end of his existence.

May our Heavenly Father, dearest Sister, vouchsafe unto you that resignation and support which He alone can bestow! Abby fully shares my feelings, and unites with me in tenderest love to yourself, Mr. Mallard, and Mary. I trust the latter and her babe are doing well.

Ever your affectionate brother,
Henry H. Jones.

REV. GEORGE HOWE *to* MRS. MARY JONES[t]

Columbia, *Saturday,* March 28th, 1863

My dear Madam,

How shall I express to you the deep sorrow which takes possession of all our hearts at the loss of our dear friend your lamented husband? And yet *your* loss as far exceeds that of all others as your relation to him was more close and tender, and your knowledge of all that was excellent and endearing in him was more intimate and perfect. That you will no more see his face in the flesh, no more hear his voice uttering words of counsel, wisdom, and affection, be no more stimulated by his daily example and cheered by his presence, no more have the remnant of life's weary journey lightened by his sharing it with you, and the now lonely hours filled no more with those duties you owed him, is a grief into which no heart can ever enter but yours. But you know, my sorrowing friend, where to go for relief. There is One whose heart sympathized when He was upon earth with every form of human suffering, to whom you can now go with all your griefs, and who cannot and will not withhold from you His most precious consolations. That our dear friend should so sicken, and his lovely and useful life be terminated thus, was a part of the eternal plan of Him who is wise in counsel and wonderful in working.

How much will we all miss him—miss his elevated and cheerful piety, his devoted spirit, his active, energetic mind, his friendly greeting, playful humor, and pleasant, instructive talk! How will the church mourn, which he has served so long and well; his brethren in the ministry also, who knew him only to admire and love him! He has been to me always a friend most dear. I have been drawn to him more and more the longer I have known him. Pleasant have been the hours we have spent together, and the memory of them is sweet.

But he is in more blessed society now. The messenger whom God sends to call His people home came noiselessly, and without pain to him terminated his earthly career and opened all at once, without the sorrow of parting with loved ones here, the gate of paradise, and bore him to the presence of that Saviour he loved. His joy how great! His crown how glorious! His eternal house not made with hands how pleasant! Shall we not join him there? And how soon may that happy meeting be? How glorious, too, the morning of the resurrection! "For if we believe that Jesus died and rose again, even so them also which sleep in Jesus will God bring with Him. The dead in Christ shall rise first. Then we which are alive and remain shall be caught up together with them in the clouds to meet the Lord in the air, and so shall we ever be with the Lord. Wherefore comfort one another with these words."

We all feel for you and your dear children, and other friends and relatives to whom your departed husband was so dear. May God multiply to you and them the consolations of His grace now and evermore!

Your friend in affliction and sorrow,

George Howe.

P.S. I am indebted to Mr. Buttolph and your son for their letters, received just as I was leaving home to fulfill an appointment. Will write to them very soon.

Mrs. Mary Jones *to* Col. Charles C. Jones, Jr.[g]

Walthourville, *Monday,* March 30th, 1863

My very dear Son,

I cannot command a pen tonight, and must employ this pencil to send you a line by tomorrow's mail. I am thankful to hear of our dear friends in Augusta, and from our servants. I have wanted to write and tell the latter all about the last days of their honored master. But oh, my son, what language can I find to convey what I would wish expressed? How did they receive the sorrowful tidings?

You know, my son, the desolation which reigns in my heart. I feel at times if it was not (as I humbly hope) for the sustaining grace of God and the presence of my gracious Saviour that I could not longer sustain the weary and heavy-laden burden which life now appears—separated from my head, my guide, my counselor, my beloved husband, to whom my heart has been united in tenderest love for thirty-two years. I ask myself: can there be anything even in the form of duty left to bind me here? God only knows; and also knows how much my foolish, sinful heart deserves His chastening rod in this dark hour. I want to know and do His holy will, and to be comforted only with His love shed abroad in my heart.

I long to return to the solitude of my own home, and to live amid the memorials of our beloved and honored head. If your dear sister is well enough and Robert returns, I want to go to Arcadia the last of this week. She has been graciously sustained under this severe affliction; but for two nights she says it has come over her with such power as to deprive her of sleep; and today she has had a return of the chill, accompanied with fever. I sent for Dr. Stevens; he has just left, saying she needed no medicine. She is very calm now, and I hope will have a good night's rest. The dear baby is perfectly well and quiet, which is a great blessing.

Your own precious child has had an affection of the bowels for two days, but is nearly relieved: the effect probably of teething. The treatment prescribed by your brother has already relieved the eruption, and I hope will do her lasting good.

As soon as I go home, will see that the necessary articles for the women are prepared to go by *Porter* when he returns, which, my dear son, you can direct whenever you think best. On my way down will stop at Montevideo, and if his work is done there will write you so that he may not unnecessarily delay his time here.

When you write, present my affectionate remembrance and tenderest sympathy to Eva and Mrs. Eve. I will write Mrs. Eve as soon as I can command my time. Now it is all taken up in your sister's sick chamber and care of the children. Good night, my dear son! May the example and precepts of your sainted father be ever before you! Follow him, even as he followed Christ, through whom he hath obtained an entrance into everlasting life.

Ever your affectionate mother,
Mary Jones.

My grateful acknowledgments to Mr. Ward for his kind sympathy.

31st. The articles for Aunt (some twelve or sixteen bags—I cannot now remember the number) were shipped last week. Would you let George inquire at the depot if they have gone to Marietta?

By today's express we send a box to Miss Kitty Stiles, who will be a few days longer at the Miss Mackays'. She has in every time of need been the kindest of friends to Daughter and myself, and now offers to do what we require and could not have done. If you have a moment, do call and see her.

Your sister is better this morning, although she did not rest well during the night.

Ever your affectionate mother,
M. Jones.

COL. CHARLES C. JONES, JR., *to* MRS. MARY JONES[g]

Savannah, *Friday,* April 3rd, 1863

My very dear Mother,

I am in receipt of your very kind letter of the 30th ult. and sincerely thank you for it. You are ever present in my thoughts and in my love, and my constant prayer is that you may in this our heaviest affliction experience that consolation which comes only from above. I trust that my dear little daughter is better again, and that Sister has quite recovered.

I had the pleasure of seeing Robert as he passed through the city, and was happy to know that he was so much pleased with Atlanta and the prospects of the church. It strikes me the call is a very important one, and should be *carefully and if practicable favorably considered.* I know of no field in the state which offers equal inducements for extended usefulness.

I hope to be able to see Miss Kitty Stiles this evening. She is a woman for whom I have always entertained the highest esteem. Hers is a friendship which may well be cultivated.

The anticipated attack upon Charleston has not transpired as yet; it was expected on the 2nd inst.

Enclosed, my dear mother, I send you a letter this morning received from Dr. Howe. You will read it with interest. Will you be so kind at some early leisure moment to give me in detail the facts which he there desires, and I will answer his letter fully.

Do, my dearest mother, let me know what your plans are, and if I can serve you at any time. You well know that I will always esteem it not only my highest duty but also my greatest privilege to love and minister to your every comfort. I address this hurried note to Arcadia, as you mentioned in your letter that you expected to return home the latter part of this week. I hope to see you some day next week, and will let you know so soon as I am able to fix the day. With warmest love and tenderest sympathy, I am ever, my dear mother,

Your affectionate son,
Charles C. Jones, Jr.

Many kisses for my sweet little daughter. Howdy for the servants.

Mrs. Mary Jones *to* Col. Charles C. Jones, Jr.ᵍ

Arcadia, Saturday, April 4th, 1863

My dear Son,

Tom has just arrived with your affectionate favor and the enclosed letter of Dr. Howe. I will endeavor at an early day to answer his inquiries as fully as I possibly can.

I know at one time your beloved and honored father had drawn up "family records" which included incidents of his own life and of various members of our family, which if now in existence would be of priceless value to us. But through the inscrutable (to us) but no less wise providence of God they all perished with his other writings in the fire which consumed our dwelling at Columbia, April 18th, 1850. I recollect asking him not long since if he had any memoranda of his early life and labors, to which he replied (as well as I now remember) that he had not. The period of his public services can be easily traced from his various reports; before the church and the world he has been known and read of all men. Full of grace and truth, his life has been one undeviating course of uprightness and integrity. He loved his Master and his Master's work, and sought to advance the Redeemer's Kingdom with all the lofty talents that were so preeminently committed to his trust. "Good and faithful servant," I believe that he has entered into the joy of his Lord.

When I think of him with the Divine Redeemer, so precious to his soul on earth, with saints and angels, with his own dear mother, Sister Betsy, your dear Ruth, and an innumerable company now gathered into the mansions of heavenly peace and rest, I know that our loss is his eternal gain. But oh, when no returning footstep falls upon my listening ear, no voice or touch of love and kindness, no cheerful greeting, no words of counsel or encouragement—that silent study, that empty chair, that vacant sofa where first we plighted our early vows and where he daily rested his weary and enfeebled frame, *that desk* where he labored so perseveringly, his Bible left open upon it, his spectacles just as he laid them down, his hat, his stick just as he placed them on the table in the entry—can you wonder that I longed to be here with all these precious memorials around me?

I left Walthourville at one o'clock yesterday and came immediately down to Midway—my first visit to that consecrated spot. . . . Your dear sister was much better and sitting up when I left. Robert was suffering from a cold taken in Atlanta. So soon as she is strong enough to ride thus far, they will all be with me. . . . I have great reason to be grateful—and trust I am—for my affectionate and dutiful children and many kind friends. You may be assured, my son, I shall call unreservedly upon you at all times. I have received the kindest letters from my brother, from your Uncle Henry, Aunt and Cousin Mary, and Dr. Howe. . . . I will try and acknowledge them when I feel able to do so.

Your precious child is quite well, and almost entirely relieved of the eruption. She is my dear little comforter—my precious one. Seeing me weeping, she cried as if her little heart would break, and when we came here ran into the study and looked all around as if searching for her "papa." Our people are all well, and kind and attentive as they can be. Your dear daughter sends her sweetest kisses. May the Lord bless and save you, ever prays

Your affectionate mother,
Mary Jones.

I had intended to send you Dr. Howe's letter to me, but will reserve it until we meet.

COL. CHARLES C. JONES, JR., *to* MRS. MARY JONES[g]

Savannah, *Saturday,* April 4th, 1863

My very dear Mother,

I am in receipt of your kind letter of this morning, and sincerely thank you for it. So soon as you are able to answer the inquiries suggested in Dr. Howe's letter, if you desire me to do so, I will put them in form and forward them to him. In this I may be able to save you some labor. Do, Mother, add any reflections or incidents which you may deem proper. As soon as practicable, every memory should be made permanent. It is a sad loss to us all, that burning of the autobiographical sketch of my dear and honored father—one which we can never repair and must always most earnestly deplore.

I knew that the sympathy of kind friends would find expression in word as well as in feeling, and it will afford me a great pleasure to read them when we meet. Major Porter wept as I told him of the last hours of Father; and Mrs. Harriss said to me that Dr. Axson on the Thursday following the day of his death, at the prayer meeting, gave a full account of his wonderful and happy demise. Heavy though this affliction be, my dearest mother, dark though the clouds are on that side which looks towards us, we can but rejoice at the happiness upon which he has entered, and with tearful eyes think without sorrow of that great change which has freed his godly and glorious spirit from the frail tabernacle of flesh and translated it to the immortal blessedness of heaven—to the companionship of the saints of all ages whose characters on earth he so much admired; and to an immediate association with that Triune God whom he so dearly loved, whose sacred Word he so much revered and studied, whose sublimated doctrines and laws he so closely observed.

I will be with you, my dear mother, at the earliest practicable day. General Beauregard, I understand, thinks that the attack upon our coast cannot be very long delayed. He expects the demonstration to be made against Charleston, and says that city is prepared for it. We have nothing of special interest here. Do, my dear mother, let me know whenever I can serve you in any particular, no matter how trivial. With many kisses for my sweet little daughter, and much love for you, I am ever

Your affectionate son,
Charles C. Jones, Jr.

Mrs. Mary Jones *to* Col. Charles C. Jones, Jr.[g]

Arcadia, *Wednesday,* April 8th, 1863

My very dear Son,

Tom has just come in with your letter; it is a solace to hear from you thus often.

I am in *the study* today, with aching head, and far more aching heart, trying to gather up the cherished recollections of your honored father, my tenderly beloved husband; my blinding tears every now and then forcing me to stop and ask: "Of whom am I writing? Can it be true that I shall nevermore behold his face on earth?" You have passed through this agony; you know how I feel. But oh, my son, yours was the sundering of young and tenderest ties; our hearts were cemented by thirty-two years of life's companionship. And I can truly say I knew not a moment of unalloyed happiness whenever in that period we were separated.

It is very difficult with no memoranda at hand to write what I desire, but will be faithful in what I do say, and ask of my Heavenly Father guidance and direction. I will try and forward my letter to Dr. Howe to you before it is sent to him. I have found one copy of the tenth report, which is a review of his missionary work among the Negroes, and answers much that the doctor desires to know. I will forward it with the request that it be returned, as I have no other copy excepting the complete set now deposited in the Augusta bank.

I had not until your letter been informed of the attack upon Charleston. I feel the greatest confidence that our just and holy God will hear and answer the prayers of his suffering people at this time, and that our enemies will not prevail against us! But we should humble ourselves and lie low before the Cross. I trust the day of fasting and prayer was observed "in spirit and in truth" throughout our whole Confederacy. Where did you worship on that day? I never doubt the final issue except when I hear of the sin and profanity that prevails, the Sabbath-breaking and immorality which is practiced by men in high places, setting aside the good of society, the welfare of their own souls, and all that is pure and sacred in character and reputation. For all these sins we must receive judgments from the Lord.

I observe by today's paper Mr. Lathrop has *yarn* for sale. What does he ask? I would like to get *if at all reasonable* six bunches, two of them very fine and four medium size. They say it is impossible to obtain it from the factories just now. I shall try and do all we can to clothe the people at home, for I see no other prospect of supplying their wants. When would you like Porter to return?

Your precious child is well and very lively; has been much of the time with me in the study. It is time for the mail, and I must close. What can I do for you? Do you not want a supply of grist or rice? I am thankful *your duties* still keep you in Savannah. May the Lord bless and keep you, and prepare you by His grace renewing and sanctifying your heart for life and for death!

> Ever your affectionate mother,
> Mary Jones.

Col. Charles C. Jones, Jr., *to* Mrs. Mary Jones[g]

> Savannah, *Friday,* April 10th, 1863

My very dear Mother,

I am this evening in receipt of your kind letter to Dr. Howe with the accompanying reports, both of which I will have posted tonight.

I have just been ordered to Charleston, and leave at six o'clock in the morning, D.V. I am sorry, my dearest mother, that I will not have the pleasure of seeing you before I go; but I trust in God, if the enemy does attempt to land, that we may be able to drive the detested invaders back with fearful loss, and that I may be soon restored to your loves and your presence. Heaven bless you and my precious little daughter, and shield you both from every harm!

With warmest love for you, my dearest mother, and many kisses for my little daughter, I am ever

> Your affectionate son,
> Charles C. Jones, Jr.

Mrs. Mary Jones *to* Col. Charles C. Jones, Jr.ᵍ

Arcadia, *Tuesday,* April 14th, 1863

My very dear Son,

Your letter at leaving, with its precious enclosure, although it sent a pang to my heart, was a great comfort to me; and I have been sustained under an abiding conviction that my gracious Redeemer will care for and preserve your life. Oh, my child, in these solemn times, this hour of darkest grief to us, seek to know honestly and truly how stands the great account between God and your own soul. Surely it is time for you to settle this great question and to be decided for your God and Saviour.

I am glad your dear brother is in Charleston. I know in case of an attack he would wish to render every service to his suffering countrymen and to be near to you.

Could I not send you a box of eatables by express? *Write me about it at once,* and *how to direct it,* and I will send it immediately: some hams (boiled if you wish), dried beef, rice, and grist, and whatever I think would reach you in good condition.

There is an interesting state of religion in the Liberty Independent Troop. Many have professed conversion. I am sorry they are going away to Savannah tomorrow. Colonel Millen's battalion is to take their place.

I have had Lymus brought here that I might attend to him, and finding that he did not improve have sent for Dr. Farmer to come and tell me what I had best do for him. I am anxious to omit no attention to the poor fellow. He always appeared attached to your dear and honored father, and is a little younger. The other servants are all well and doing well. Shall I send Porter to Burke as soon as he gets through, which ought to be very shortly?

Mr. Lyons sent a message through Gilbert saying he would give two dollars a bushel for twenty-five bushels of rice. Not knowing anything about the price, I sent a note of inquiry to Mr. Cassels at the depot; his answer this morning is: "There have been no sales here, but it is worth from four to five dollars per bushel if good," and told Gilbert it would bring more in Savannah.

I have received a great many kind and sympathizing letters from friends. One today from General Cocke. . . . Oh, that it was granted you both, my dear sons, to sit as I do in this consecrated study and to talk together of our beloved and honored head, gone from us on earth, but forever with his Lord in glory! Your dear aunt is with me this week, and your sister will be as soon as she is strong enough to ride.

I hope dear Carrie will not feel too anxious about your brother's absence.

Dear little Mary Ruth, my comfort, is well and bright and, Sister Susan says, a very good child. Joseph Robarts has come to bid me good-bye today. Love from your aunt, many kisses from your precious child, and for you both, my beloved sons, the abiding love and prayers of

Your sorrowful mother,

Mary Jones.

Col. Charles C. Jones, Jr., *to* Mrs. Mary Jones^g

Camp W. H. T. Walker, *Friday,* April 17th, 1863

I am this morning, my dearest mother, in receipt of your very kind letter of the 14th inst., and am very happy to know that you and my precious little daughter are both well.

I long to see you both, and wish I could tell when I may expect the pleasure of being with you. Just now we do not know whether we will be returned to Savannah within a short time or not. The impression prevails with many that the real attack upon Charleston has not yet been made, and that the enemy will return to the assault within a few weeks. If such be the belief at headquarters, we will in all probability be retained in our present position for some time. So soon as we ascertain more definitely, I will write you and also answer your kind inquiry whether you shall send the box of good things. It would be very acceptable, and as soon as we know what our movements will be I will write you whether to send it or not.

When Porter completes his work at Montevideo, I would be very glad for you to let him return to Indianola for at least a while.

Rice was worth when I left Savannah from six to eight dollars per bushel; I would not sell it for less than five.

I trust that Lymus may soon be better.

I do wish, my dearest mother, that I could be near and with you to render you every assistance in my power; but you see and appreciate the condition in which I am—the claims which are now upon me. It would indeed prove a great privilege for me again to revisit that home hallowed by such precious loves, and consecrated by memories the purest, the noblest of earth. My beloved and honored father is ever in my most cherished affection and veneration.

May the Good God watch over and preserve you, my dear mother, and my sweet little daughter! Kiss her for me. My love to Aunt Susan. And believe me ever

Your affectionate son,
Charles C. Jones, Jr.

Col. Charles C. Jones, Jr., *to* Mrs. Mary Jones^g

Savannah, *Sunday,* April 19th, 1863

My very dear Mother,

I write only a line for the post in the morning to inform you that I arrived here, through God's mercy, safe this afternoon. My command has (part of it) returned, and the balance will arrive tonight and tomorrow. I sincerely trust that you and my sweet little daughter are both well. Do kiss her for me. And believe me ever, my dear mother, with sincerest love,

Your ever affectionate son,
Charles C. Jones, Jr.

I hope to see you very soon.

Mrs. Mary Jones *to* Col. Charles C. Jones, Jr.^{g}

Arcadia, Tuesday, April 21st, 1863

My dear Son,

I am truly happy to know that your command has been returned to Savannah, and trust you may soon be enabled to visit home.

Yesterday *Dunwody* came out to see me, having obtained a furlough of two days. He appeared to feel deeply; said "if there was a being in a place of happiness, it was your sainted father, for he was the best man he ever knew." He brought the intelligence of poor Cousin Joseph Robarts' death. He arrived in Savannah on Saturday, attended his funeral, which was conducted by Dr. Axson, and followed him to the grave. Dr. Quarterman has been exceedingly kind; had the remains of Cousin Joe removed to his house, where the funeral was held, and attended to all that was necessary. It will be a satisfaction to my dear aunt and cousins to know that her poor son and their father and brother had one to pay him such kind attentions as he received from Dr. Quarterman on his deathbed and after his decease.

Yesterday the Liberty Independent Troop (Captain Walthour), the Liberty Guards (Captain Hughes), the Mounted Rifles (Captain Brailsford) rendezvoused at Midway. . . . Captain Walthour proposed that they should have a parting service. The door of the venerable old church was opened. They all entered with their arms in hand and took their seats, filling every pew below and the galleries above. There were prayers offered, two addresses, closing with the doxology, the whole assembly rising and most of them joining. Mr. Buttolph said during the service perfect stillness was observed, and that the close was sublime. There has been a very interesting state of religion in the troop, and several conversions. I trust the Holy Spirit will abide with them and perfect His blessed work in their hearts.

The removal of this company leaves the entire coast of the county in a defenseless condition. The enemy might now at any moment land troops at Sunbury or the Island or on the North Newport, and there would be nothing but a few pickets to notify the battalion *stationed* thirty miles away in McIntosh County! Meantime they might capture citizens, desolate estates, destroy property, and steal all our servants remaining. I do feel assured if the general commanding knew our exact position we should have a different arrangement. Mr. Quarterman has just called, and says he and Mr. Norman and Colonel Gaulden have been appointed a committee to wait on General Mercer and present our claims; if he fails to answer, the object is to proceed to Charleston and see General Beauregard. The committee will be down in tomorrow evening's train; and Mr. Quarterman would be very glad, he says, of any assistance from you.

I wrote Mrs. Howard last week; have not heard from her. . . . Your precious child is well and very good and bright; she sends her sweetest kisses for her dear papa. Sister Susan unites with me in best love to you.

Ever, my very dear son, your affectionate mother,

Mary Jones.

COL. CHARLES C. JONES, JR., *to* MRS. MARY JONES[g]

Savannah, *Wednesday,* April 22nd, 1863

My very dear Mother,

I am this morning in receipt of your kind letter of yesterday, and am happy to know that you and my dear little daughter are well, and that Aunt Susan has been with you in your hours of deepest loneliness and sorrow. Most sincerely do I wish that I could remain with you, my beloved mother, to relieve you of every anxiety, minister to your requests, and render you every assistance in my power. But the rules of this exacting service are upon me, and I can only respond in heart and not in person to those claims which it will always be my highest pleasure and privilege to recognize and allow.

I was not aware until yesterday of the death of Cousin Joseph Robarts, and communicated the fact, with all the details I could gather touching his demise, to Cousin Mary. If he was prepared for death, it is better as it is.

The parting with the troops at Midway Church must have been an impressive season. I regret to learn the unprotected condition in which our immediate coast is left, and trust that the representations made by the committee may prove effective.

I heard from Indianola yesterday. All well, and getting along well. Martha expects to be confined next week. If the clothes are ready, Mother, they had better be sent up at once.

I hope to be able to spend the day on Friday with you if nothing unforeseen occurs to prevent. Will you please let Gilbert meet me at the depot? I am so happy to know that Sister will be with you; and it will be a great joy for me to see her too.

We have nothing of interest here. With warmest love to you, my dearest mother, and with tenderest sympathy in this our greatest sorrow, with many kisses for my precious little daughter, whom I am very anxious to see, and with affectionate remembrances to Aunt Susan, Sister, and the little ones, I am ever

Your affectionate son,
Charles C. Jones, Jr.

XVIII

REV. JOHN JONES *to* MRS. MARY JONES[t]

Refuge, *Tuesday,* May 19th, 1863

My beloved Sister,

Your precious letter came safely to hand, and I cannot fully tell you how much I prize it and thank you for it. It was just what I longed to see from your own hand. How precious the records of the last days and hours of one so much loved and honored and leaned upon! His closing scenes were remarkable, and yet perfectly becoming. Oh, that it had been my privilege to have been present! When I parted with him—and it was a most tender parting—I thought it might be the last. But I could not realize it, and constantly hoped to meet him again on earth. And now that he is gone, I often feel that "unutterable desolation" mentioned in your letter.

My dear brother left few behind him who leaned more on him than I did. What would I not give for his counsel on a number of important questions now pressing on me! I shall miss him as long as I live, for no joy or sorrow crossed my path which I kept from him. I find a peculiar enjoyment in teaching his catechism both at home and at our little church, and his hymn, "Come, My Soul, to Jesus." And as I reiterate his oft-repeated words, I feel that I am in a measure representing him, and that he still carries on the work he so much loved on earth. And I sometimes think that if permitted to look on us here on earth, he still watches the labors of those who are engaged in his chosen work. Is it not a natural feeling to inquire in our minds after those who have gone to the heavenly home, if they still remember and love us and continue their tender interest in us?

My dear sister, in all your deep affliction I am afflicted, and my heart yearns to administer a drop of comfort to your bereaved heart. And I would have come to you long before this but for the occurrence of circumstances beyond my control. I am now just recovering from a prostrating attack of inflammation and hemorrhage of the bowels, which began on the 12th of this month. I was unable to leave the house on Sabbath, and although recovering am painfully weak. I have been suddenly reduced from excellent health to weakness —occasioned, I think, by overexercise on Monday the 11th inst., a day when ministers ought to rest. . . . And this week, if possible, I am to go to Mitchell County to organize a church next Sabbath.

May 20th. My dear sister, I made many inquiries after summer cloth from the factories at Columbus and Bainbridge, and learned nothing encouraging. I wrote to the proprietor of the Bainbridge factory and learned that cotton sent to him must be delivered at his mill and not in Thomasville. I sent him a sample of your cotton which you gave me, and he was highly pleased with it, but required it to be delivered at Bainbridge. I trust you have before this obtained your summer supply for your people.

And now in reference to Old Mama: I wrote Mr. Mallard some weeks since (and to her also) to talk freely with her and to ascertain if she would be willing to pass the summer at Bonaventure. I have been thrown back in building houses from a want of nails, etc., etc. Have just completed two instead of five, and can put up no more until fall, as the growing crop absorbs all the mulepower. We have been so backward on this place, and are so short of mules, that it has been next to impossible to send off four mules on a journey of some days. And this necessity will continue nearly to August. And in some part of next month, if Rome is considered safe from the Yankees, we shall have to use four to six of the mules in getting to the depot. If you occasionally visit Bonaventure, do see and talk with Mama and ascertain if she would willingly remain for the summer; and if not, then I will send to meet her and George at Thomasville late in July or the first of August. If possible and convenient to you to learn the above for me, please write me at your earliest convenience, as we think of leaving for Rome about the 16th of June. I have written Mr. Mallard, but received no answer; nor have I heard from Mr. Delegal on other matters.

I suppose you have learned how near the Yankees came to Rome, which they would have taken but for a kind Providence through the gallant Forrest. Yesterday we received a letter from our Dunwody informing us that the Yankees were coming again to Rome, and requesting us to send him some trunk keys to enable him to run up to Rome and save his summer clothing and some articles for us. I trust there is a mistake about this matter, but it may be true. I would like to go up myself, but have not strength enough for the journey. I shall write today to Mr. Omberg to know the true state of affairs in Rome, and will regulate our movements accordingly. This terrible war continues, and although victorious on the Rappahannock, we are sorely afflicted in the death of our great and good General Jackson, who in many respects was our first man.

Give our best love and tenderest sympathy to dear Mary Sharpe. I know she is deeply bereaved, for there was a tender tie between her dear father and herself, and he loved those her little ones so fondly. I thank herself and Robert for wishing me to baptize their dear little infant; I esteem it a privilege to succeed my dear brother in such important matters. But contrary to my wishes and plans, my visit to Liberty will be postponed for a long time, especially if we go to Rome next month. And it is not well to postpone too long the dedication of our little ones to Him who says: "Suffer little children to come unto me." Tell Robert that I received his kind answer to my letter. Remember us always affectionately to Charles and Joseph. I wrote Charles some time since. I am glad to know that Joseph and Carrie have a little daughter; our love and congratulations to them both. Our best love to Cousin

Susan and Cousin David and Cousin Laura. How tenderly he writes of my dear brother—as much so as if he were a blood nephew! Brother Buttolph is a dear brother. My dear Janey is not well, and we are lonely. She and the little boys unite in tenderest love to you, my sister, and your dear little baby.

Your devoted brother,

John Jones.

Excuse the blot on the last page, which was the work of some unknown hand after finishing the letter. . . . Do remember us to Cousin William Maxwell most affectionately; also to our friends Mrs. Roswell King and all her family. . . . A kind remembrance to your servants, and our servants if you should see them, and Old Mama.

Mrs. Mary Jones *to* Col. Charles C. Jones, Jr.ᵍ

Arcadia, Tuesday, May 19th, 1863

My dear Son,

Your affectionate favor was this day received, and I will first reply to the business part. Mr. Buttolph will probably be at home the latter part of this week, as it is our Communion Sabbath at Midway, and he ought to be here on Saturday. Next week, I understand, he will go to Baker County. I think, D.V., of riding to see your aunt and cousin tomorrow for the first time in many months, and will write you again particularly when to make the desired arrangements. I ardently wish that you could be with us on Sabbath. We are to have two additions of young soldiers from Captain Thomson's company.

I do not think it possible for me to leave Arcadia next week, as I am overlooking and packing the books, and want to make a catalogue of them. It is now so cool and pleasant from the recent rains that I do not apprehend any danger in staying. Should there appear to be any, I will send the baby up to your sister as she requests me to do. She is so hearty I would not wish to expose her to an unhealthy atmosphere. I have had company so constantly that what I desired to have done is still undone. She speaks of her dear papa every day, and never forgets you.

I believe I told you that Mr. Butler could not take up the cattle. Would it be possible for you to put them upon the cars at the twenty-one-mile station on the Central Road and let Mr. Sconyers meet them at the ninety-five-mile station? They could be driven easily to the twenty-one-mile station in two days, and take the cars that night. The mule-wagon could go along with the forage for the journey from there, and Gilbert knows the route. Syphax will accompany Porter when he returns, and they could take care of them on the cars. If this plan is practicable, you can so arrange for it. The cows are in fine order, and will be a comfort to the people and useful on the place.

Last fall before leaving the Island your dear father had all the fencing put in complete repair and left in the enclosure four cows and four calves and one bull. I thought it proper to send Andrew down this week to see how matters stand, and Gilbert has just returned with the report. (Brother William gave Andrew his pass.) He found the fence to the causeway gate taken down for some distance and removed; the gate propped open; Mr. Dunham's sheep and hogs driven in up to the dwelling house; and the hogs even in the courtyard. Behind the cornhouse a pen was made, into which was put a large hog, which was there fed, probably from the provisions left in the barn, as the doors had been forced and the peas threshed out. Every cellar door to the house had been broken open; also the smokehouse and kitchen doors. Upon Half Moon next to the Cadden hammocks Mr. Delegal, Mr. Anderson, and Mr. King had located themselves, boiling salt and using the wood for that purpose. Audley has recently purchased Dr. Harris's land just over the causeway (known as Dr. McWhir's tract) and located his salt-boilers at the head of the causeway. Andrew saw him and told him of the state of our premises. He sent me word that all he wanted was a note from you or myself, and he would see that our interest was protected in every way, stating that he would be at Midway tomorrow, where I could send it to him. And I have just written the following to him:

Dear Sir:

You are hereby requested and empowered to represent our entire interest on the Colonel's Island, and to forbid all occupation or trespass by any person or persons upon either tract of land known as Maybank and Half Moon. The Half Moon tract joins on to your land recently purchased and is divided from it from Gridiron bridge by a ditch running down to the marsh, the cedar hammocks along the shore from that point being attached to it, and the dividing line between them and the Cadden hammocks being a creek which empties into the Woodville River. Mr. Dunham has a right of way to the Cadden hammocks, which is indicated by the road leading to the causeway to said hammocks.

                                    Respectfully, etc.

I felt that this was just to ourselves, and hope I have acted properly in the matter. This cruel war imposes strange duties upon us all, and I am willing to stand in my lot.

I could but admire the ingenuity of my servants and the protection afforded by them today in the case of a suspicious-looking character who came up and asked for food. They told him their master lived in Savannah, and they could not entertain him. They asked that I would not come down. I told them I could not send him hungry away, and ordered Kate to get some dinner for him. They made him sit in the piazza, and when he attempted to come into the house (as he said, "to see how it looked") Flora and Tom barred the front door. I could see him from the balcony, and when his dinner was ready they sent him by Charles a large plate of rice and pork, a bowl of clabber, and would not even trust him with a knife or fork, but gave him only an iron spoon. The poor fellow eat voraciously—the first, he said, in three days. When he finished, Charles politely told him if he would now start he would put him on the right road. I hope I did not violate any law of charity or humanity, but I had not the courage to let him remain. Charles and Tom managed so well that I gave them each a little reward.

The death of our pious, brave, and noble General Stonewall Jackson is a great blow to our cause! May God raise up friends and helpers to our bleeding country! In what striking contrast stands that of Van Dorn! The one is surrounded by a halo of glory; the other is shrouded in a pall of infamy. There is no man who violates the purity and sanctity of society that will not reap his full reward in the due course of time. He may not always lose his life, and may even be permitted to walk abroad with shameless effrontery and receive the countenance and friendship of those who have not the moral courage, the strength of principle, the fear of God to rebuke his infamous and injurious practices. But he will surely eat of the fruit of his own way.

I will write you again day after tomorrow of Mr. Buttolph's movements. And now, my dear son, good night! Sweetest kisses from your little daughter. May the Lord bless and save you!

Ever your affectionate mother,
Mary Jones.

Robert married Susan and Mac on Saturday night.

Mrs. Mary Jones *to* Col. Charles C. Jones, Jr.[g]

Arcadia, Thursday, May 28th, 1863

My dear Son,

I have been prevented by the rain for two days from going to Montevideo. As there is a prospect of clearing, I will go and spend the night there and have the cattle, sheep, and hogs counted up early in the morning. I wish to do this before leaving for the summer. I am much perplexed at the thought of leaving people and place without some white protection and control. Would it be well to try and get Mr. Calder? Audley is boiling salt at the Island and would not, I fear, undertake it.

Mr. Quarterman advises me that it is time for our *tax returns,* which are now due. How shall they be made out, and will a few days' delay involve anything serious?

Mr. Buttolph is now at home. Will go to Baker before long, but will, I presume, be here all of the coming week. Any arrangements you deem best can be made.

It is not right for me to keep our precious little baby here longer than this week, and if the season had not been so cool and dry, I would have deemed it imprudent to be here to this late period. If you can be out very early next week, I will keep her to see her dear papa. If not, she had best change the air, and I will send her to your sister even if I am compelled to stay. Her little mind expands almost as rapidly now as the unfolding leaves of the evening primrose. She has startled me several times with unexpected developments. She has the warm and loving heart of her own dear mother, and I trust will be as truthful in character. Her perfect remembrance of your beloved father is wonderful for one of her age. She is a great comfort in this period of sorrow and desolation.

I hope you found our friends in Augusta well. I long to see my dear son and Carrie and the little ones; but really these are such troublous times, if one has a quiet and comparatively secure abode I think they ought to be grateful and remain contented without changing.

Mr. Russell, to whom we sent nine sheepskins to be exchanged for cotton cards some four months since, writes that they are not to be had. Can they now be had in Savannah? And at what price? Porter has made me a nice loom, complete all to the blacksmith's part. I have had him repairing house, etc. He is all ready for your orders, and so is the salt. I think we have on hand a year's supply, and had best send it up. Andrew is still boiling. I want him next week to go to Maybank and make up the line fence. Did you get my letter about the cattle?

Hope George arrived safely, and General Beauregard enjoyed the mutton. We feel honored to contribute to his entertainment. Can you get his autograph for me?

These are dark days! How long our cry for deliverance and peace will remain unanswered is known only to our Sovereign Judge, who sees how much our sins deserve His chastening rod! I see no hope or comfort but from on high. With sweet kisses from your little daughter and the love of

Your affectionate mother,
Mary Jones.

Col. Charles C. Jones, Jr., *to* Mrs. Mary Jones[g]

Savannah, *Thursday,* May 28th, 1863

My very dear Mother,

I returned last evening from Indianola, where I spent three days. Found everything suffering very much for want of rain. Corn and cotton both small but healthy. On Tuesday and yesterday generous showers were descending upon the thirsty earth, and this morning the skies are still overcast; so that I trust we will be favored with an abundance of rain, and that the fields will soon rejoice in the life and the vigor of a new existence. All the people were well, and everything appears to be getting along quietly and favorably. The crop was very clean, and seems to be properly attended. I have about six hundred acres planted in corn, and one hundred and thirty in cotton. Am planting heavily in peas. Betty's children—also the infants of Lizzie and Kate—are all well. Peggy had been somewhat sick, but was better. I gave out the Negro cloth on Tuesday night—an abundant supply. The wheat is nearly ready for harvest; hope to make some sixty bushels. Am just about to erect a grain house, and would be very glad, my dear mother, if you would let Porter return to the place to assist in its construction if you have no further use for him. I have made all the tax returns, and have *included*

Porter. I also gave out summer clothing for him, leaving the same in Stepney's charge.

I have seen the railroad agent here, and he tells me that he will have two stock cars at No. 2, Central Railroad, any day I may name, giving him two days' previous notice. So, my dear mother, if you will let me know when it will be convenient for you to have the cattle driven up (say, thirty to forty head), I will see that the cars are ready at that station any day you may name, and also communicate with Mr. Sconyers so that he may have hands in readiness at No. 9½ to drive them to the plantation. Gilbert might take charge of them to No. 2, and Porter go along also. Please see that they are well fed before they start; and if practicable it might be well to send some fodder along with them. Do, my dear mother, if there is an old saddle and bridle not in use on the place, let that accompany Porter. Do not forget to have a *bull* sent with the cattle. Will you please ask Porter whether we have more than one crosscut saw on the places? I cannot get one here, and am using a borrowed one at Indianola. The cattle will be of great advantage to the people, and it would be well to have them sent up at the earliest practicable day.

In regard to the salt, any time you may find it convenient to have it shipped from No. 3 to this city I will attend to its transshipment per Central Railroad.

I find a letter from Mr. Buttolph under date of the 23rd inst., telling me that he expected to go to Baker "on Tuesday next," which was day before yesterday. So soon as he returns we will, my dear mother, attend to the probate of my dear and honored father's will. I write today asking that he will let me know of his return in order that we may arrange this matter as soon as convenient.

Spent a day in Augusta. Eva quite unwell. She and Cousin Philo desired their special remembrance to you and my dear little daughter. Your kind letter of sympathy has been received, and was very sincerely appreciated by them. They begged me to express their deep acknowledgments for your kindness. Brother and Sister Carrie and the little ones were all very well, and united in warmest love. The Doctor had been suffering from a cold, but was better.

When, my dear mother, do you go to Walthourville? Sister writes me that your room is all ready, and that they are very anxious that you should come up as soon as you can. Do you think it prudent for you to remain much longer at Arcadia? I trust that you and my precious little daughter are both quite well, and that a kind Providence is ever near, encircling you with His protection and filling your pathways with many and great blessings, even amid these darkest days of desolation and of severest bereavement. . . . Do, my dearest mother, accept every assurance of my constant and warmest love. . . . Mr. Ward begs me to present his respectful remembrances, and to offer his sincere thanks for your recent kindness. As ever,

Your affectionate son,
Charles C. Jones, Jr.

MRS. MARY JONES *to* COL. CHARLES C. JONES, JR.ᵍ

Arcadia, *Friday,* May 29th, 1863

My dear Son,

On my return this evening found your affectionate favor. I am thankful you found our people all so well and satisfied. After the distressing experience of the past year it always appears a special mercy when I hear "all are well."

Yesterday I took my little companion. We called to see the old people at the salt-boiling and my Old Mama; found them faithfully employed at their post of duty. Thence to Montevideo, where we passed the night, with all the precious memories of the past around me—your beloved and honored father associated with, and I may almost say present in, every spot. Indeed, he is so constantly in my thoughts and affections that I often look around to see if I cannot meet his eye or hear his voice. I often sit at twilight in his lonely study and wish it was given me to behold his precious face and form once more on earth. . . . I have been very much struck by a remark of *Sue's.* Speaking of all the spiritual, the religious instruction given by your father to the Negroes, especially his own, she said: "Our dear master has not left any of us poor; he has given us all our property to live off until our Blessed Saviour calls us home."

It was a new and strange business, but I felt that present circumstances made it a duty to see into the condition of things before leaving for Walthourville, particularly as I feared you might not be able to do so just now. This morning rose early. After family worship had breakfast. *Jerry* was brought to the door. I mounted, rode to the cow pen, counted and took down in memorandum book the number of cattle present, which Cato reported to be all. But there is quite a discrepancy between his account and that of your dear father. I told him they must be brought up and recounted and the pasture thoroughly searched. Thirty-two head were sold last winter; six oxen sent to Indianola. From Montevideo some have died; four or five killed. But still the number is less than it ought to be. Twenty head were sold from this place, and four oxen sent up, which of course diminishes the number. I have directed Prime to have all up here tomorrow. *All told* with Cato's account we have only sixty-four head. This includes Maybank and Montevideo. We had at *Maybank* alone last summer sixty-three. Have left there nine head—which I fear our good neighbor will take care of! I then *reviewed* the hogs. One large one dead; the remainder doing very well. Passed through the corn-fields. Highland very good: putting around seed and plowing; lowland broken. Rice *destroyed* in the largest square from drought and the salt water. A fine rain today, and Cato concluded to replant, as the season is early enough. The sugar cane pretty good; wants work. Close pease good. Cotton just coming up in many places. The month has been so dry it could not sprout; but a heavy crop of weeds.

Everything is wanting work so badly that I do not see how we could spare Gilbert and the mules any time *next* week to drive the cattle. He could do so perhaps the week after, and that would delay Porter another week. Syphax expects to go with him to Burke and visit his family, and could help with the cattle. Mr. Buttolph will be here next week if you could come out in the early part of it.

I took what my own dear father would have called the "grand rounds," and wound up with counting the sheep and a return to my own department in the poultry yard and flower garden. The people are all well, and appear to be faithfully employed; but the whole crop wants work, owing to the peculiarly late and dry season. The rice is so important a crop, although we had not reserved much rice I thought it best to use it for replanting.

I think our dear baby ought not to remain longer here, and will take her up at once and return and remain here next week, if God spares my life. Will ship the salt early next week. And now good night, my son. You may conclude that your mother is tired after such a day's work—*too* much so to sleep.

Ever your affectionate mother,
Mary Jones.

What must I do about the tax returns?

MRS. MARY JONES *to* COL. CHARLES C. JONES, JR.[g]

Arcadia, *Monday,* June 1st, 1863

My dear Son,

I am this moment from Walthourville, and hasten a reply to your letter. Left our little babe not so well from a cold, but thought it prudent she should not return.

I will send up to Mr. Buttolph and ask him to appoint *Thursday* of this week for going to Hinesville, which will give you time for writing the ordinary and also letting us know if you can come out on that day. I could meet you at the cars, and Mr. Buttolph and Laura could meet us at Hinesville.

Providence favored my seeing Mr. Butler this morning. Next Monday, D.V., he will come here and carry the cattle accompanied by Gilbert to his house, start on Tuesday, reach the station (No. 2) on Wednesday, where if you will so arrange, the cars can receive the cattle that night. Porter and Syphax will go down Monday or Tuesday and be ready at the station for the cattle. You will make arrangements with Mr. Sconyers for receiving them.

This afternoon the oxcart will take to McIntosh Station one barrel and three large bags of salt (containing nineteen bushels of salt) for Colonel C. C. Jones; and one sack of salt marked "Mrs. Eliza G. Robarts, Marietta, care of railroad agent." This salt is *more* than a supply for a year hence, bacon curing included; so do charge your manager to be careful of it.

Write particularly what time the cars will be at No. 2. The cattle will be there, Providence favoring, on Wednesday evening. I write in haste.

Ever your affectionate mother,
Mary Jones.

I am all alone.

MRS. MARY JONES *to* COL. CHARLES C. JONES, JR.ᵍ

Arcadia, *Tuesday,* June 2nd, 1863

My dear Son,

The Lord permitting, I will meet you tomorrow as desired at No. 3 (McIntosh Station). I have just written Mr. Calder. . . . Robert leaves for Mount Vernon tomorrow, and kindly offers to take Tom with him, where he will work for four months at tanning and shoemaking, and by fall, I trust, will have gained sufficient knowledge to make the plantation shoes. In haste,

Your affectionate mother,

Mary Jones.

MRS. MARY JONES *to* COL. CHARLES C. JONES, JR.ᵍ

Arcadia, *Friday,* June 5th, 1863

My dear Son,

Mr. Quarterman has just called, and I have handed him twenty dollars to give Mr. Butler, which I presume will be more than sufficient for the expenses of himself and Gilbert and the cattle to the twenty-one-mile station on the Central Railroad. . . . *Thirty* head of cattle will be driven—twenty from this place and ten from Montevideo. Mr. Butler takes them Monday afternoon to Flemington, and Wednesday afternoon they will be at the station ready for the cars. Porter and Syphax will leave this place on Tuesday and meet them at the appointed place.

Enclosed I send Mr. Cassel's receipt for the salt. Please have the sack for our dear aunt, Mrs. Eliza G. Robarts, forwarded to her. It is directed care of railroad agent, and will go right.

Last night I felt the loneliness and isolation of my situation in an unusual degree. Not a white female of my acquaintance nearer than eight or ten miles, and not a white person nearer than the depot! My mind (blessed be God for the mercy) is kept free from all the ordinary fears that distress the unprotected. And surrounded as I am by the precious memorials of your beloved father, and near the spot where his sacred remains repose, I am loath to leave. *Daughter* urges me to do so on the score of health, and perhaps I will go to Walthourville on Saturday.

Should Robert decide for Atlanta, I will then be compelled to think of some resting place for my dear little baby and self during the summer. Your brother and Carrie invite me affectionately to spend it with them. When the time comes, I trust the Lord will provide and lead me in the way that I should go. For thirty-two years I have had a strong arm to lean upon—a wise head to guide, a heart all love and tenderness to bless and make me happy. It is my constant prayer that I may not be permitted to murmur or repine, and that what of life remains to me here may be spent in the discharge of duty, in the love and service of my God and Saviour, and in preparation for the solemn hour of death. Great will be *our condemnation,* my dear son, if after such an example and such precepts we fail through neglect or indifference or the love of sin or the influence of this wicked world to secure eternal life through Jesus Christ our Lord.

Ever your affectionate mother,
Mary Jones.

Many thanks for your coming and all you did yesterday.

Rev. John Jones *to* Mrs. Mary Jones[t]

Refuge, *Tuesday,* June 16th, 1863

My beloved Sister,

Yours of the 2nd was received on the 8th inst., and truly do I thank you for seeing our Old Mama and explaining to her in a satisfactory manner my reasons for postponing sending for her. As we will be absent during the summer, and house room is scant, I believe if she is contented that she will be more comfortable where she is, and especially as she has the company of your servants, and is in a great measure under your care. Tell Daddy Andrew that I am proud to have so good a guardian for my place, people, and stock; and I trust he will remain until the war closes, or as long as will be agreeable to his kind mistress. Do say to Mama—or send her word—that Joe is doing well, is faithful and devoted to his duty, and I will endeavor to carry out her good advice in reference to her family. I sincerely desire to have her with me, and trust her life will be spared to come to this new country and to find a comfortable home in her old age. Enclosed I send five dollars to be appropriated by you for her comfort as you may think best.

You spoke of the promising "herd of swine" at Bonaventure, and expressed a desire to have "a shoat" to improve your own stock. My dear sister, you are welcome not only to a shoat but to a sow and shoats, including the litter born in January or February last, and the present litter also (if there is one), "together with all the future increase." I left at Bonaventure three fine sows (young), and they had seventeen pigs just before I left. Make your selection (or direct Andrew to do it) of one out of these three sows and her shoats and present pigs with her. And let them remain on the place or remove them as you think best. They will have a good range, and plenty of refuse corn was left for them; and I think that under the united care of Andrew and Augustus they will do well and give you a good start. Hogs must be penned every night, and a little food will make them come when called. Did Mama mention receiving a letter sent to her from Joe through Mr. John Mallard? It has been sent two months since.

You mention that Robert has received a call to Atlanta. . . . It will be a sad thing to leave his present charge, and especially to leave them without a shepherd. He may have a larger field, but never a more pleasant and attached people. May the Blessed Master direct him, and ever have him and his dear family in His holy keeping!

I believe I mentioned to you in my last that I organized a little church in Mitchell County on the 24th of May. I visited them again on the 7th of June (first Sabbath of this month) and had a Communion for them—the first Presbyterian Communion ever held in that county. And I saw a strange sight: the table was occupied by colored communicants exclusively, and whites served. How do I wish that my dear brother were where I could tell him all that I have seen and experienced in this new and needy country, and how eagerly the colored people wait on the Word of Life, and especially the teaching of the catechism. He seems very near to me—certainly in thought, in memory, in tenderness and encouragement—every Sabbath. I am greatly pleased with the late obituary of him prepared by Dr. Howe. It is so truthful, affectionate, and fraternal. I have sent for extra copies for our three sons, who will never forget their dear uncle.

My dear sister, may the Holy Spirit, the Blessed Comforter, continue to you His constant supporting presence! I can recall no one whose death is associated with so many happy memories. He has entered into that rest for which he labored and kept constantly in view. When we think of him—his peaceful and quick translation, his present enjoyment, his having attained the great end of life—all seems delightful. But when we look at ourselves, and realize that we shall have his personal presence no more on earth, and feel our need of his counsel, his love, his ever cheerful spirit, then do we feel an unspeakable sorrow. But the Lord hath done it. Blessed be His holy name!

June 17th. My dear sister, as our mail is only triweekly, I add a line today. We expect to start for Rome, D.V., on next Monday the 22nd inst. Some of our friends have admonished us not to go, as Rome is thought to be still in danger. I think we are running a risk, but am under promise to our church to return this month. We shall make diligent inquiry as we go and shape our plans accordingly. It will be a privilege—if it can be enjoyed quietly—to be relieved from present cares and return to the whole duty of the ministry.

Enclosed I send a letter for Mama, which please have forwarded to her at your convenience.

Should Robert respond to the call from Atlanta, would he go up this summer? And where would you pass the summer with your dear little Mary Ruth? The summer climate of Atlanta is delightful. We have not yet suffered from heat in this county, but it must be very warm in midsummer from all accounts. We have had an abundance of rain, and the crops are promising, although they suffered materially from a terrific storm on 5th of June. It lasted only an hour, and thousands of trees were prostrated.

And now adieu for the present, dear Sister. Let us more than ever remember each other at a throne of grace. My dear Jane and little boys unite with me in best love to you and dear Mary Sharpe, Robert, and the four children.

Ever your devoted brother,
John Jones.

P.S. I will write you from Rome.

Brother Henry and Sister Abby and their children are quite well, and will pass the summer in Baker. He has bought in Cuthbert, and will remove his family there in the fall.

Mrs. Mary Jones *to* Col. Charles C. Jones, Jr.^g

Walthourville, *Friday,* June 26th, 1863

My very dear Son,

We were so happy to see you yesterday; and the dear baby calls with increased affection for her papa. I often wish she could make you a daily visit. I trust our Heavenly Father has spared and will continue her precious life for great usefulness on earth. All else but the time we have spent in God's service and doing good will vanish as a dream when we take our last review of life's pilgrimage. . . .

I hope you reached the city without accident. It was my desire to send you the shirts by tomorrow's express, but they are not quite done. They will be forthcoming next week. I would like, if it meets your approval, for *Little Andrew* to return with Syphax and make a short visit to his family.

Today I received the enclosed letter. *Please return it* and give me your views. Ought their use of the wood and occupation to be limited to such a length of time, or shall we allow them to stay as long as they desire? They speak of Mr. *Dunham's consent* to their digging wells. I sent Audley a plot of Half Moon, which includes the hammock where their wells are located; so they are wholly on our land. If you think it best *for me* to answer the letter, I will refer them to that plot in Audley's possession. I feel that what I desired is accomplished by the letter *in part*—a just and respectful recognition of our ownership. They made a request through Audley to be allowed to use the wood cut. I replied that they must communicate by writing, and we would then answer; and if they had been at great expense, I did not object to their doing so at one dollar per cord including what they had and would use.

Your sister and Robert unite with me in best love to you. Kisses from the little ones, especially your own.

Ever your affectionate mother,
Mary Jones.

Will you communicate with Mr. Ward while he is in England? If so, would it be improper to request him to make the inquiry what it would cost to secure the *copyright* and have published your father's *History of the Church of God* in London or any other place in England? It is my fervent desire to give the work as early as possible to the world. We could also take a copyright for the Confederacy to be published here as soon as the state of the country will permit. I should be under great obligations for any suggestions for the accomplishment of this desirable end.

Your mother.

Col. Charles C. Jones, Jr., *to* Mrs. Mary Jones^g

Savannah, *Thursday,* July 2nd, 1863

My very dear Mother,

I am today in receipt of your very kind letter of the 26th inst., and am truly happy to know that all at home are well.

The letter of Messrs. King and Delegal is very respectful, and on the whole is all I think that we can ask of them. I would say to them that they can have the privilege of boiling salt on the premises, paying for all wood already consumed at once and hereafter monthly at one dollar per cord—the privilege to continue until 1st January next, and no oak wood to be cut by them. If you desire me to do so, I will write them for you. Audley would be a very good person, perhaps, on your part to estimate the amount of wood already consumed, if there is any question on that point. If you would prefer my communicating with them, please let me know, and I will do so at once.

Saw all friends at Augusta this week. Left Eva quite unwell, but I trust she soon will be better. Cousin Philo pretty well. The Doctor was looking badly. He purposes a visit to his friend Colonel Johnston at Sparta the ensuing week, and I trust the change will prove beneficial to him. Carrie and the children are well. They all desired sincerest remembrances to you.

Today is the second anniversary of the death of our sweet little Julia. How do all the sorrows of that saddest period come back over my soul with all the realities and freshness of but yesterday! And yet I never think of her otherwise than as a little angel only *lent* to earth, not *given*. How precious the thought that her safety for all time amid the eternal joys of heaven is secure!

General Lee appears to be pressing onward, and with marked success, into Pennsylvania. The enemy will now have a taste of actual warfare. We have a telegram today announcing the exchange of the crew of the *Atlanta*. With much love to all, and kisses for my dear little daughter, I am ever, my dear mother,

> Your affectionate son,
> Charles C. Jones, Jr.

Mrs. Mary Jones *to* Col. Charles C. Jones, Jr.[g]

> Walthourville, *Friday,* July 3rd, 1863

My dear Son,

Your affectionate favor has just been received. This is indeed to us the period of sad memories; and yet what mercy mingles with the bitter cup! We are not mourning without hope. Our beloved ones, although absent from us, are present with the Lord. The Divine Redeemer who washed them in His own Blood, who clothed them in His own righteousness, who accomplished His sovereign will with them on earth, hath now received them into the mansions of everlasting glory and blessedness.

> With us their names shall live
> Through long succeeding years,
> Embalmed with all our hearts can give:
> Our praises and our tears.

It grieves me to hear that my dear Joe looks so badly. I know he is working himself down; I received a letter this week from him telling of his labors.

I hope he will now take a little rest. And dear Eva, I am sorry to learn, is not well. A little change will do her good. You told me she spoke of visiting her friends.

Yesterday I had a long and fatiguing ride. Went both to Montevideo and Arcadia. Servants generally well. Little Andrew asks on account of his wife to remain a day or two over his week. I told him he might stay until Thursday of next week, when he will come in and go to Burke on Friday.

I will be much obliged to you to answer the letter of Messrs. King and Delegal. They speak of getting "Mr. Dunham's consent to dig wells." Please refer them to the *plot* of *Half Moon* which is copied from the original and now in the possession of Mr. Audley King, which will determine the lines.

Our peaceful little village assumed quite a military aspect the first of the week. On Sabbath Captains Hughes's and Walthour's commands arrived en route for the Altamaha. They departed Monday morning; and about one o'clock of the same day the trumpet announced the arrival of the Terrell Artillery, with *whom you are acquainted*. They encamped in the academy yard, around and about us on all sides; and more gentlemanly soldiers I think could not be found. They spoke of their *colonel* in the highest terms; said he was "mightily beliked," and "the boys would die by him"; all they wanted was to meet the enemy. In the afternoon they drilled, much to the admiration of all present. (I did not go out.) Both dinner and supper were provided for them, which they enjoyed, and departed Tuesday morning with their guns and standard decorated with fresh bouquets amid prolonged shouts, leaving behind their assurance that "the Yankees should never reach Walthourville." They excited not only admiration but confidence, and carried away our fervent prayers and best wishes for the divine protection and complete success if called to meet the enemy on the battlefield.

Your shirts, I hope, will *last longer than the war*. Do let me know whenever I can do anything for you. I am writing in great haste for the express. Love from your sister. Sweetest kisses from "Papa's daughter," as she calls herself.

Ever, my dear son, your affectionate mother,
Mary Jones.

Mrs. Mary Jones *to* Col. Charles C. Jones, Jr.[g]

Walthourville, *Tuesday,* July 7th, 1863

My dear Son,

Our mail carrier was unusually late this morning, leaving me but a brief period to say that I will with pleasure attend to the making of the articles, and only wish it was in my power to furnish all you need. From long service and no recent replenishing, the stock of house linen has run low at home; but you may be assured it will give me pleasure to assist you in every way that I can, and I hope you will let me know whenever I can do so. Send the articles, and I will see that they are made as early as practicable.

Our hearts are anxiously looking for tidings from our army, which seems in peril at so many points. "God is our refuge and our strength!" Robert has a prayer meeting every Tuesday night expressly for the country and our army in its present situation. Held at private houses; tonight it meets at Judge Fleming's. The appointments are made at the request of individuals. We can but hope that "He who will be inquired of by His people" will hear and answer their prayers. If ever there was an hour for urgent supplication, it is *now*. . . .

This day is the anniversary of our dear Ruth's death; I should say her peaceful departure to her heavenly rest. I would gladly know, my beloved child, if you have fulfilled her one great desire for you: *"Seek Christ, and seek Him now."* Oh, that He might indeed be formed in your heart—the hope, the foundation, the tried cornerstone of your affections and your happiness for time and for eternity!

I would gladly write more, but must close. You need not buy any more things for Baby unless I write for them. She is amply supplied, and if the shoes do not fit I will return them, for I am going to have some nice little ones made for her here. She sends sweetest kisses to dear Papa. Love from all.

Ever your affectionate mother,
Mary Jones.

I will hand you the bankbook when you come out. When will that be?

Eleven Negroes left this village Saturday night for the enemy; three have been caught.

REV. JOHN JONES *to* MRS. MARY JONES[t]

Rome, *Tuesday,* July 7th, 1863

My dear Sister,

I wrote you not very many days before we left Baker, and promised to write again when we reached Rome. Our brother Henry very kindly loaned us his carriage horses and servant Jack to transport us to Albany—a most substantial favor, as there was no carriage to be hired, and the small hack passing by us eleven miles distant is generally crowded. . . . At Macon we were joined by our son Dunwody, who obtained a furlough of ten days and came with us to Rome.

We passed two nights and a day in Marietta to see our dear aunt and cousins and our dear Mother Dunwody and Sister Mary E. Dunwody and Dean Munro's family. Aunty feels deeply her late affliction, but seems very calm. But she looks more bent with age than I have ever observed before. They had all been unwell with severe colds; and all remember you, dear Sister, with tender love in your deep affliction.

We reached Rome on last Saturday week the 27th of June, and found our servant Harriet had been quite efficient in making ready for us. . . . Since our arrival we have all (including servants) been quite unwell with colds and sore throat. The weather is oppressively warm, sultry, and rainy—so much so that the abundant wheat crops gathered and in the shock are in danger from a tendency to sprout. We have found it much warmer both by day and (especially) night than in Baker. Some of our neighbors have planted a few vegetables in our garden, but the most of it is a wilderness of weeds. Living is ruinous, and exceedingly scarce. We have not had a piece of meat on our table for five days. I left an order with a butcher to bring beef to us, but have had it from him only once, when I brought him up. We have some bacon in the country, but cannot have it hauled in as yet. Milk twenty-five to forty cents per quart.

July 8th. My dear sister, you will have learned before this reaches you that General Bragg with his army has given up Middle Tennessee, moving across the Tennessee River, being thus compelled to abandon to the enemy a vast crop of wheat which had just been harvested; and many noble Confederate citizens have fallen in the lines of the enemy. It was an unavoidable necessity, I am informed. It is thought that this country and place are more exposed than ever to the raids of the enemy by the falling back of Bragg's army. We are packing up some things in order to a move to some safer place—perhaps to Marietta.

How do you feel in Liberty since the burning of Darien? Will the troops be permitted to remain in the county?

Yesterday I found a letter from my dear brother written to cheer me during the severe illness of my dear Jane in January 1848, and also to comfort and cheer her. In reading over and preserving his letters I am more than ever impressed with the spirit of affection which breathes in them, and the hopeful, cheerful words always encouraging to duty and pointing to God as our Father, Saviour, and Almighty Helper. And now that he can speak no more, his letters are peculiarly precious. And all his relatives have such letters; for in the days of his health and strength, when his was the pen of a ready writer, he forgot not one of them.

Has Robert given an answer to the Atlanta church? If he has not, but intends an affirmative, I trust he will be explicit in reference to a competent support. When one has everything to purchase in a city and is in no money-making business to keep up with the times, daily living is ruinous unless the personal income is large. If Robert accepts the call and comes up this summer, will you come up also? Do write us soon. And if we can remain here quiet, we will have a room ready for you and the dear little baby.

Have you heard anything from Bonaventure lately, and Old Mama and our servants there? Will they be safe there this summer? My dear Jane and little boys unite with me in best love to you, Robert, Mary, and your four precious children. Howdy for the servants.

Your ever affectionate brother,
John Jones.

P.S. Our affectionate remembrance to all at Brother Buttolph's, Mrs. King's, and to Cousin William Maxwell.

Mrs. Mary Jones *to* Col. Charles C. Jones, Jr.ᵍ

Walthourville, *Tuesday,* July 14th, 1863

My dear Son,

I have this moment returned from Montevideo, and hasten to send you a basket per express. Hope the lamb will be good. The melon is from your sister, sent to her by Mrs. Fleming. The herbs you can give for the use of the sick soldiers; also the flaxseed. I thought they might be useful, and are just dried from my garden.

The bundle arrived by express, and I will make the articles as you desired. One pair of Baby's shoes she can wear; the other will not fit at all, so I return them at once. Please exchange for fully a size larger. Now that she is so constantly on them, her little feet are not so fairylike as they were.

My dear son, not a moment passes that my thoughts are not with you or my bleeding country in some form. How long will this awful conflict last? And to what depths of misery are we to be reduced ere the Sovereign Judge of all the earth will give us deliverance? It does appear that we are to be brought very low. May the Lord give us such true repentance and humility before Him as shall turn away His wrath and restore His favor, through the merits and intercession of our Divine Redeemer! I do bless God for the spirit of true patriotism and undaunted courage with which He is arming us for this struggle. Noble Vicksburg! From her heroic example we gather strength to hold on and hold out to the last moment. I can look extinction for me and mine in the face, but *submission* never! It would be degradation of the lowest order.

May Jehovah bless and preserve you, my dear child! Love from your sister and the children, with many kisses from your dear daughter and the true affection of

Your mother,
Mary Jones.

Little Mary has just said: "Grandma! Is that an elegant basket! I think Uncle Charlie will ask Beauregard to eat dinner with him."

Will you let George get me two dollars' worth of *black varnish* from the painters and keep it until you come.

Take care of *my basket*.

Col. Charles C. Jones, Jr., *to* Mrs. Mary Jonesᵍ

Savannah, *Wednesday,* July 15th, 1863

My very dear Mother,

It was a sore trial for me to pass so near both this morning and this afternoon without seeing you, my precious little daughter, and the dear ones at home. But my orders were imperative, and I had in their discharge to forego that pleasure. I said to Robert, whom I had the gratification of meeting at the depot, that I might not return before tomorrow; but I was able to compass the object which carried me out in time for the return train.

Many—very many—thanks, my dearest mother, for your kind remembrance of me. I must find some good friend tomorrow to help me enjoy all of these good things. They are indeed a treat. Do thank Sister too for the nice watermelon.

No news from Charleston today. The heavens above us are indeed dark; but although for the present the clouds give no reviving showers, let us look and pray earnestly for His favor who can bring order out of chaos, victory out of apparent defeat, and light out of shadow. All these reverses should teach us our absolute dependence upon a Higher Power, and lead to sincere personal and national repentance.

Daughter's shoes I will, D.V., exchange on the morrow, and will also procure the varnish, not forgetting to take good care of the basket. My head is a little heavy from the hot suns of the Altamaha swamp; but I could not let your kind letter remain unanswered a single night, or sleep until I had returned you, my dear mother, my grateful acknowledgments for your kind and special remembrance of me. Kiss Daughter. Love to all. And believe me ever

Your affectionate son,
Charles C. Jones, Jr.

Tell Mamie I wish General B. was here to enjoy the nice mutton, but that he is so busy fighting the Yankees that he cannot come.

Mrs. Mary Jones *to* Col. Charles C. Jones, Jr.^g

Walthourville, Thursday, July 16th, 1863

My dear Son,

We were greatly disappointed to find we should not see you this afternoon as we had anticipated—and I had promised your little daughter the pleasure of meeting her dear papa at the cars. But I am glad your business did not require you to remain all night at the Altamaha.

She becomes every day increasingly interesting: understands a great deal, and begins to show her own will in many ways. I do not think she will ever be a difficult child to govern. She discovers a decided taste for books, and will amuse herself with them at set times. For instance, as soon as prayers are over in the morning she calls out "Book!" and goes to the table where her favorite book of pictures stands and goes to reading in her own way. I would like a primer or spelling book with pictures for her, as she seems to prefer them to the common picture books. She often reminds me of her father in his infancy. Books were your playthings; at one time you always slept with one.

I fear your mutton was scarcely eatable today, it was so warm.

I am grieved to hear of Adam's illness. He was in feeble health a long time after his return from the fortifications on the Savannah River—was one of the number who were so ill last spring; and I think with God's blessing your brother was the instrument of saving his life at that time.

Will you be so good as to send, or bring me when next you come out, the last dividend from the railroad and the twenty-five dollars recently deposited? I might require them during the summer. Robert will be down before long, and could bring the money if you do not come out.

I would like you to request Audley King to act for us in the salt business, as he could judge of the amount of wood used and receive payment, being on the *spot*. Did the gentlemen say at what time they commenced boiling? They must use over a cord a day. It might be well to understand how they estimate the consumption of wood. Audley has quite a business young man associated with him—Mr. Collins, nephew of Mr. Mitchel of Darien.

Today's paper contained a very handsome acknowledgment from the Terrell Artillery of the hospitalities of Walthourville. . . . The last prayer meeting for the country Robert read the 74th Psalm; look at it. . . . I have felt very sad *today*: it is four months since your beloved father died. I realize every day more and more my desolation. With best love from all,

Ever your affectionate mother,
Mary Jones.

What think you of my idea of printing the *History* in England?

COL. CHARLES C. JONES, JR., *to* MRS. MARY JONES[g]
Savannah, *Saturday,* July 18th, 1863

My dear Mother,

I am this morning in receipt of your kind letter of yesterday, and can but reiterate my sincere regrets that I was unable to stop and see all at home upon my return from the Altamaha. My orders were, however, imperative.

It makes me very happy to hear such good accounts of my precious little daughter. May she be ever a perpetual joy to us all! And may it please God mercifully to surround her with every blessing—social, temporal, and spiritual! Never, my dear mother, will she or I be able to thank you sufficiently for all your great kindness. May the Lord reward and bless you for all your goodness to us!

The dividend from the Central Railroad Bank and the twenty-five dollars received for wood have both been deposited to your credit in the Bank of the State of Georgia, so that you will have to draw a check for what amount you desire. You can make that check payable either to my order or to that of Robert, and the amount will be sent out by the earliest opportunity.

Will you be kind enough, Mother, to send me at your early convenience *a recipe for making Ogeechee limes?* One of Eva's good friends has promised to put up some pickles for her, and also some Ogeechee lime preserves if she can obtain a proper recipe for the latter. And she has requested me at your convenience to obtain the same from you and forward it to her.

I will write Audley in reference to the wood, etc., as you desire. I will read the 74th Psalm. Tell Robert when he comes in that he must stop with me.

It might be well, Mother, under ordinary circumstances to have Father's church history published in England; but it would not now be practicable either to transmit the manuscript in safety or to pay the expenses of the publication. Exchange can only be purchased at a most ruinous rate—say, nine hundred percent. So soon as peace returns, our first duty must be to give this last labor of love of my beloved and honored father to the church, the country, and the world.

It is hard to realize that he has lain more than four months in that silent home prepared for all the living. And yet not *there;* for he is in a far higher, a far happier place, even in the bright heavens above, and in the companionship of the Lord Jehovah, of the Blessed Saviour whom he so much loved, of the Holy Ghost who was ever the Comforter to him, and of the dear departed who have gone before, and of the good and the great, the saints of all ages made perfect in glory. It is hard indeed to think that we will no more here be blessed with his presence. May we be enabled through grace to meet him hereafter!

Nothing new from Charleston. Rain every day. With warmest love to all, and many kisses for my precious little daughter, I am ever, my dear mother,

Your affectionate son,
Charles C. Jones, Jr.

The mutton was a little touched, but we enjoyed and thanked you very much for it.

I will try and procure a primer for Daughter.

Mrs. Mary Jones *to* Col. Charles C. Jones, Jr.[g]

Walthourville, Tuesday, July 21st, 1863

My dear Son,

You have in the above recipe the manner in which I *used* to make Ogeechee limes. I have tried to be explicit, and hope it will be understood. If I only had the sugar I would send you something better than a dry recipe.

These are emphatically times when, "having food and raiment, let us be therewith content." I bless the Lord every day of my life that although I am a refugee from my own pleasant homes, still I am not a houseless wanderer as thousands of my noble countrywomen are, but am still surrounded with the comforts of life. And what is far above all these things, the lives of my beloved children are still spared.

Last evening just before sunset I heard the sound of the bugle, and just under my window two cavalry companies were dismounting—the commands of Captain Walthour and Captain Hughes. Most of them, having friends within reaching distance, dispersed in all directions. Robert and your sister being still away, I had to do the honors of the house. Seven of the friendless soldiers took supper; four stayed all night; and seven had breakfast at five o'clock this morning. A supply of melons, figs, curds, fresh butter, etc., having just come up from the plantation, I placed them at their disposal, and enjoyed the pleasure of seeing them appreciated.

This morning a poor fellow evidently in pain crawled through the paling and laid under the shade of the tree. He was a teamster, and had been injured yesterday in the back. I sent his breakfast and something to relieve the pain. His reply was: "He thanked the Lord there was one friend in the world to care for him." He still lies upon the grass under my window.

One of the melons is so fine I cannot resist sending it to you. With sweetest kisses, and thanks for the primer from your daughter,

Ever your affectionate mother,
Mary Jones.

XIX

Col. Charles C. Jones, Jr., *to* Rev. *and* Mrs. R. Q. Mallard[t]

Savannah, *Tuesday,* August 4th, 1863

My very dear and afflicted Sister and Brother,

Not until a late hour last night did I learn the sorrowful intelligence of the death of your precious little daughter. I did not even know that she had been sick, having returned to the city only last evening after an absence of more than a week. A warm brother's heart sympathizes most tenderly with you in this your hour of special bereavement. I know from sad experience the depths of those shadows which rest upon the parents' heart when the child we love— whose life is knit to that of the fond father and generous mother by the most enduring and intimate ties, cherished by the purest, truest affections—is summoned from our embraces in obedience to the call of an all-wise but inscrutable Providence. I do feel for you most deeply, and my eyes are filled with tears.

And yet is not the loss purely personal? Is not death, to that bright redeemed little spirit, great gain? In this the day of your special bereavement, what a mitigation of the great affliction to feel that all is well with her, that her salvation for eternity is certain, that no matter what rude alarms, what trying ills, may be in store for us in the future, she at least has by a good God been taken from the evil to come! The last entry, you remember, our beloved and honored father ever made in his diary was commemorative of her birth. He never saw her in life, but she is with him now. In that bright world above he has already welcomed her pure spirit; and there, in the living immediate presence of that great Redeemer who while on earth said: "Suffer the little children to come unto me, and forbid them not, for of such is the Kingdom of God," will they joy in the smile of the Lord. She is not lonely there. Ruth and little Julia and all the dear departed who have gone before are with and near her, and the endless companionships and unspeakable privileges of heaven are hers. There is every consolation in the thought that she is saved—an angel in heaven; and thus when we weep, it is only for ourselves, only for the light of the dwelling gone out at early dawn, only for the companionship so dear which can never on earth be renewed. You both are Christians, my dear sister and brother, and have free, full access to the source of all consolation—to the Father of All Mercies, who doth not willingly afflict, and who will bind up the bruised reed. May His sustaining grace be ever present with you to support and to comfort!

Earnestly did I desire to be with you today, but the indications of a possible attack upon this city at no distant day prevented my leaving Savannah. But although absent from you in person, my heart and tenderest sympathies have been and are with you. God bless you both, and the precious little ones who are still spared, and prepare us all to meet the dear ones in that better world where there shall be no more tears or partings or sorrows.

Ever your affectionate brother,
Charles C. Jones, Jr.

COL. CHARLES C. JONES, JR., *to* MRS. MARY JONES[g]

Savannah, Tuesday, August 4th, 1863

My very dear Mother,

I have just written Sister and Robert a letter of sympathy. I was greatly surprised and deeply pained to learn last night of the death of dear little Sarah Burnley. I knew not even of her illness, and great was my regret that I did not enjoy the privilege of being with you today. Do let me know of her sickness and her last moments. For yourself, my dear mother, accept my sincerest sympathies in this new affliction which has come upon us all. . . .

I returned only last night. Yesterday I visited Indianola. Martha's infant better, and all well except Adam, who improves slowly. Crops looking fair. Too much rain for some localities. By the express of yesterday I sent a sack of flour, ground from the wheat made at Indianola, for yourself and Sister. I think you will find it very nice, and hope that you will all enjoy it.

Saw Rev. Mr. Porter on the cars yesterday, who told me that he was going out to Liberty today or tomorrow to dissolve the connection existing between Robert and the Walthourville church in order to permit him to go to Atlanta. He expressed great regret at his leaving. You will doubtless see him while in Walthourville. Robert will, I fear, find it a difficult matter to secure a house, as the city is crowded to overflowing, and rents are at a high figure. His congregation will have to render him essential assistance.

In passing from Augusta to Atlanta I spent a night at General Toombs's with my dear Eva, who is now there on a visit to her friends Mrs. Toombs and Mrs. DuBose. She was pretty well, and very happy thus unexpectedly to see me after our protracted absence. Providence permitting, we will probably be married about the 5th of November. She desired her special remembrance and love to yourself and Sister, and her thanks for the recipe. I know you will love her very dearly, for she is absolutely attractive in every particular, and has a heart as pure and tender and full of affection as dwells in woman's breast. She is as perfectly devoted to me as I am to her, and I trust that Heaven will bless our mutual affections.

We are anxiously anticipating demonstrations on our coast, and are as active as we can be. Dark days are upon us, but we must look to God and gird up our loins. There is a wonderful lack of patriotism in many of our people. The greed of gain is the present curse of the country.

How is my precious little daughter? I am so anxious to see her, and hope to be able to do so before long. God bless her and keep her in His special care, and reward you, my dear mother, for all your kindness to her and to me! Kiss her for me. With best love to all, I am ever

Your affectionate son,
Charles C. Jones, Jr.

Enclosed I send a letter from Betty to you.

Mrs. Mary Jones *to* Major *and* Mrs. Joseph Jones[t]

Walthourville, *Thursday,* August 6th, 1863

My dear Children,

It has pleased our Heavenly Father again to send the Angel of Death into our family circle; and the precious little one who received your beloved and honored father's last blessing on earth has been the first to join him in heaven.

About the middle of the past week our little Eliza Burnley appeared unwell with slight bowel affection. On Friday afternoon fever came on, but she was quiet and apparently free from pain. On Saturday morning the doctor was sent for. . . . He visited her three times a day, but the fever did not abate, although she was frequently drenched in copious perspirations. Sabbath afternoon I felt that her case was hopeless. . . . We sent for Dr. Stevens, and he kindly remained with us until her happy spirit took its departure from your sister's arms below to the bosom of the Divine Redeemer above on the morning of the 3rd at half-past five o'clock.

The little form was beautiful in death. Many kind friends from the village gathered around with tears of sympathy and words of comfort. The children were asleep when she died, and although in the room we did not think it proper to awake them. They were removed and dressed in another room, and when Daughter told them their little sister was dead, Charlie said: "Mama, has God sent for my sister already? And have the angels carried her up to Grandpapa?" He was surprised when he went into the room to find her little body in the crib, and afterwards asked to have it removed into another room, where hung some shades to the windows which he admired. He said they were "so beautiful the angels would like to come in at those windows to carry her away." Little Mary was devoted to the baby; would wait upon her, and was never happier than when permitted to draw her in her carriage. She asked to arrange the flowers about her, and did so. Frequently in life we have gone into the room where the baby was sleeping and found her wreathed around with cedar or flowers by her. Little Sister would insist upon standing at her side and fanning her, saying: "Birdie seeping." She was the center of love and attraction to the whole house.

Your sister bows in submission, but it is a heavy sorrow. Robert says: "I know, O Lord, that in faithfulness Thou hast afflicted me."

The funeral was held by Mr. Buttolph on the morning of the 4th, and we took the precious little form to Midway, where we laid her by the side of your father, in a line with your Uncle John Jones, Jr.'s, grave.

Yesterday by previous appointment Presbytery met here and dissolved Robert's connection with this church as a pastor, declaring it vacant. It was his intention before the baby's death to have preached in Atlanta the coming Sabbath; he will not now leave before next week. It is necessary for him to go up before removing his family and see what arrangements can be made for a house, etc., etc. I do not think they can move before September. When they do leave, if it suits your convenience, I desire very much to come up and see you.

It was one of the sweet anticipations which often crossed my thoughts to have my two darling little granddaughters, so near of an age, in my arms together. May the Lord in mercy spare your loved one to you! Although she was best prepared to go, we shall long miss her. She came in tears, when all were sorrowful around her, but she never added one pang. She was a precious little comforter while she tarried with us.

Your sister and Robert unite with me in best love to you, with many kisses for my dear grandchildren, and love and kisses from the little ones here. Your aunt and her family are well. Howdies for your servants; their families are all well. The Lord bless and keep you and yours, my dear son and daughter!

Ever your affectionate mother,
Mary Jones.

Your letter has this moment come. I hope dear Carrie will write me in your absence. I should think this the best season for going to Virginia.

Mrs. Caroline S. Jones *to* Mrs. Mary S. Mallard[t]

Augusta, Monday, August 10th, 1863

My dearest Sister,

My heart aches as I begin this letter of sympathy to you, for it comes home to me sadly that sympathy nor tears can do anything to heal a heart sore with sorrow so recent as yours. I can only give you what I have: grief and tears for your loss. . . . My heart answers to yours, dear Mary, with a quivering sharp pang of realization as I look at my own precious baby and feel what anguish I too might suffer. And with that realization which only a mother can feel my heart bleeds for you. . . . They say no earthly love is taken away until it has accomplished its work. She has unsealed the fountain of tenderness in all around her, and now she has gone to be another link in the chain that draws you to heaven. . . . A tender and beautiful recollection to your little ones she will always be, and make heaven seem nearer and more real to them. I do not doubt it will make an impression upon Mary's heart that she will never lose, with her quick apprehension and strong feelings.

I hope, dear Mary, you will soon be with us. I have been looking forward to seeing yourself and our dear mother with all the little ones, and now more than ever desire it. You must stay here and recruit while Mr. Mallard makes the necessary arrangements in Atlanta. Your brother left special injunctions with me to add his urgency to mine that you would come at that time. He had left when Mother's letter was received; and how much he will feel with and for you, you know him well enough to understand. Dear Mary, receive my love and sympathy and tears. And believe me

Your ever tenderly attached sister,
Caroline S. J.

Rev. R. Q. Mallard *to* Mrs. Mary S. Mallard[t]

Atlanta, Friday, August 14th, 1863

My darling Mary,

Through God's blessing I arrived safely in this city last evening at six o'clock. The journey was a pleasant one, although the weather was very warm. As far as Savannah we had the company of Mr. and Mrs. Barnard, Mrs. Lowndes and Mrs. Russell Walthour. Mrs. Barnard and Mrs. Russell Walthour and her husband and Mrs. Walthour, Sr., accompanied us as far as Augusta. This added much to our enjoyment.

On the Central Railroad Sister occupied the same seat with a lady who proved to be Miss Kitty Stiles's housekeeper. Her name I have forgotten. She told me that she had been with the family a number of years, and was with them at the time of Mrs. Stiles's death. She had been to Savannah to see her son, who is a member of the Volunteer Guards of Savannah. As she was alone, I offered to take charge of her baggage, etc., for which she seemed quite grateful. I told her to give Miss Kitty a great deal of love for us both and to tell her of our precious baby's death. Dear Eliza Burnley! I saw many children who as infants reminded me by their little motions of her, but none who could compare in loveliness with our sweet babe. I tried to read Flavel's "Visit to the House of Mourning," but did not enjoy it very much, as there were many things to divert my attention. I was enabled to distribute a number of tracts on the cars, which were all pleasantly received. The Lord add His blessing—even though my strange backwardness to do good in this way deserves no such mark of approval.

There are a number of soldiers stationed as a guard on the street in front of the window before which I am writing. I can see them reading the tracts I gave them a few minutes since. You will ask what a guard is doing here. They are a part of Walker's brigade (Bragg's army), who have been sent here for the protection of Atlanta from raids and are engaged in impressing horses for Bragg's artillery. As you may suppose, this creates a great excitement here. Some of the horses have been taken from carriages on the streets, leaving their occupants—even ladies—to make their way home on foot. There was a dray with trunks and without a horse before Mr. Pease's this morning. They have impressed one of Mr. Pease's horses. Many of the people here who would not loan their horses to the organizations formed for the defense of the city a few weeks since are now nicely served. The soldiers seem much amused at their work, and I expect quite enjoy the consternation of some of the citizens. They told me that they had taken some horses out of cellars. Bragg wishes some two hundred and fifty from this city. Fortifications are being now constructed at the different fords of the river for the defense of the city, and it is thought that should a raid be made we could put four or five thousand men in the field.

As for personal matters, I cannot give you any information at present. I am sorry to say that I have found Mr. Pease confined to his house by sickness, and fear I will be able to receive but little outdoor help from him. . . . I am to call at Dr. Logan's office this morning, and he is to take me out this afternoon. I am afraid it will be impossible to get a house, they rent so enormously high; but I believe that if it is the Master's will that I should remove here at once, He will open the way. I wish you were here to enjoy the cool water; it is, I can assure you, most refreshing, and needs no ice.

Dr. Brown, who is, I believe, a member of the Central Presbyterian Church, called to see Mr. Pease this morning. He told me that he had had the pleasure of hearing me preach, and that he sympathizes with me in my affliction. He seemed to feel what he said, having himself lost a child— his only boy. May God sanctify His dealings with us to our eternal good!

Give my love to Mother, and kiss the children all for me. The Lord bless and comfort you, my own darling wife!

Yours in tenderest love,

R. Q. Mallard.

P.S. The band of Walker's brigade is now discoursing sweet music on the street near at hand.

MRS. MARY JONES *to* COL. CHARLES C. JONES, JR.[g]

Walthourville, *Thursday,* August 20th, 1863

My dear Son,

No letter from you since we parted makes me extremely anxious. I hope you are not sick—alone and with no one to write me of the fact. Your sister suggests that you may have been ordered to Charleston; if that was so, I think you would have informed us. . . . Do, my child, let me know if you are still unwell, and if you desire it I will come down any day and nurse you. Make George sleep near your chamber while you are sick in case of needing his services.

I went to Montevideo day before yesterday. All well but Lymus; he continues very feeble. Cato stripping fodder. Our rice a failure from early drought; the river too salt to flow at the proper season. Audley called up and paid me fourteen dollars from Messrs. King and Delegal for July. He is doing well for himself, making, he told me, six hundred dollars per day. . . . I have no doubt the Island will become an attractive point, and whenever you are able to come out I would suggest what I think will benefit ourselves as well as our neighbors. With the exception of that owned by Audley, we own all the wooded land on the western (which is the safe) side of the Island.

I have directed Mr. Jackson to send one of our men to Savannah. Audley told me the requisite number had been received and he did not intend to send. I want to do what is right and aid my country in every way.

Robert did not come today as we expected. Tomorrow will be the day of fasting and prayer appointed by our Christian President. May the Blessed Spirit prepare one and all to come with true repentance, humility, and faith to the throne of mercy, that we may find grace and obtain strength to help in this time of our sorest need! I see no mode of deliverance but by the almighty power of God through the merits and intercession of our Lord Jesus Christ, who is the Prince of Peace.

We received letters from your brother yesterday from Richmond, Virginia. Please, my son, tell George to take the bundle of *flaxseed* over to the Wayside Home, and to send the bowl, etc., when an opportunity occurs. Excuse my trembling hand. Sister unites with me in best love to you. Kisses from the little ones, especially your own.

Ever your affectionate mother,
Mary Jones.

Mrs. Mary Jones *to* Col. Charles C. Jones, Jr.^g

Walthourville, *Saturday,* August 22nd, 1863

My dear Son,

I felt greatly relieved to hear that you had no return of fever, and through Robert that you were looking well again. I can never sufficiently thank and praise the Lord for His goodness and mercy in sparing my dear children to me whilst so many are mourning their loved ones slain upon the battlefield or laid in their graves by the hand of disease!

Robert was in time for his pulpit exercises. We had two services—more in the form of prayer meetings—which were peculiarly appropriate to the due observance of the day. We can but hope from our present circumstances of peril and deep distress that our nation was constrained to keep the fast as unto the Lord, worshiping in spirit and in truth, humbly confessing the sins which have drawn this heavy judgment upon us, and looking to God alone for deliverance. For one I feel that I deserve all and infinitely more than I have ever received of sorrow and affliction on account of my hardness of heart, my want of love and fidelity to my Covenant God and Saviour, and my unfaithfulness in all the relations of life.

A letter from your Uncle John to your sister received today says he has been much engaged in preaching to the Texas Rangers stationed at Rome.

Thirty have professed conversion, and the good work still continues. These revivals in our army are certainly the highest proofs we can possibly desire or receive of the divine favor. I can but regard as the darkest sign of the times this talk about reconstruction and submission, and the spirit of speculation, fattening upon the miseries and wants of a suffering land. We are anxious to know how affairs are in Charleston.

Our dear little Mary Ruth has been quite unwell all the week from cold. She is much better today. Should she not be quite relieved, I will not leave her tomorrow, which will be our Communion season at Midway. Our servant Niger hopes to unite with the church; your beloved father's death, he says, turned his thoughts to God. As our blacks could not bear the journey to and back in one day, I directed Gilbert to bring up the mules, who are good travelers. He will be up this afternoon; and hoping that you may be able to come out on Monday, I will keep him to take you down to the camps and the Island should you come. If prevented, I will hear from you.

I think it will be best for us *not to allow any more* use of the wood at the Island for one dollar per cord, but charge so *much a month*—say, fifty or a hundred dollars according to the use; for it does not appear possible to arrive at an estimate of the consumption. The profits of the consumer are so great they ought to be willing to pay a fair amount for the wood. This, I believe, is the plan adopted, and it appears just and right. If Mr. Collins wants to boil there, we will place a stipulated price per month.

With best love from us all, and kisses from your precious child,

Ever your affectionate mother,
Mary Jones.

You can get the butter at any time. I will send Patience word to have it ready for you.

COL. CHARLES C. JONES, JR., *to* MRS. MARY JONES[g]

Savannah, *Saturday,* August 22nd, 1863

My very dear Mother,

Your kind favor of this date has just been received. I am truly sorry to hear of the indisposition of my dear little daughter, but rejoice to hear you say that she is better. I trust it will please God soon to restore her to her accustomed degree of good health.

The day of fasting and prayer was very generally observed in our city. All places of business were closed, ordinary avocations suspended, and all the churches open. It was a Sabbath in our land. Dr. Axson gave us an excellent sermon, which I would be happy to see published and disseminated throughout the length and breadth of our beleaguered land. I understand the bishop's sermon was full of interest.

I had hoped, my dear mother, to have been out the early part of the coming week, but will be somewhat delayed in equipping and putting in order a light battery which has just reported to me from Florida. So I cannot say on what precise day I can be with you. Will, however, give you notice.

We have nothing of special interest from Charleston except the fact that two enormous Blakely guns recently arrived in Wilmington are on their way thither. These guns are vastly more powerful than any in the possession of the enemy, and when placed in position will most effectually disable any vessel in the attacking fleet. Each gun, independent of the carriage, weighs forty-nine thousand pounds, and throws a solid shot of nearly eight hundred pounds! Think of that! Such monsters are a novelty in the history of warfare. They cost, I understand, seventy-five thousand dollars each. In consequence of their extreme weight it is a very difficult matter to transport them; but every effort is being made to bring them forward at the earliest practicable moment and place them in battery at the most advantageous points. God grant that they may arrive in season to accomplish the safety of the city and the discomfiture of all her enemies!

The abolitionists shelled Charleston from Morris Island—a distance of over four miles—with their Parrott guns on night before last. Several shell fell in the city, and one of them set a house on fire. Can history furnish a parallel to such an act of inhumanity? Think of an enemy in the dead of night, without the slightest intimation, shelling a city filled with women and children and noncombatants! And yet this act is simply characteristic of the infamous race who have upon every occasion insulted our women, murdered our citizens, plundered our homes, robbed our plantations, desolated our fields, and filled the land with enormities such as are not remembered in the annals of savage warfare.

I hope to see Mr. Collins about the wood for his salt, and will act upon the terms suggested by you. Am happy to hear that Uncle John has been so much blessed in his ministrations of the Word to the soldiers. Similar reports come forward from various branches of our armies, and we are called upon to thank God for this evidence of His great favor. With much love to self, my dear mother, and all at home, and many kisses for my sweet little daughter, I am ever

Your affectionate son,
Charles C. Jones, Jr.

MAJOR JOSEPH JONES *to* MRS. MARY S. MALLARD[t]

Richmond, Virginia, *Wednesday,* August 26th, 1863

My dear Sister,

Yesterday I received a letter from Carrie informing me of your recent affliction. This is the first intelligence which I have had of the death of the dear little one; and I deeply sympathize with you, my dear sister and brother, in this severe trial. Notwithstanding that the beautiful little flower has been broken from the parent stem, and the cheerful little light has gone out, and there is a vacant place in the little cradle and in the hearts of the fond parents and of the dear little sister and brother, still the Christian is able to find comfort. At any time—but especially in these times of uncertainty and bloody war—we can but say that these little angels have been removed by their all-wise and merciful Father to His own bosom from the evil to come. The blessing of her sainted grandfather was not long delayed, and now she is with him in perfect peace and happiness, secure forever from all the rude storms and temptations of earth. For our Divine Saviour has said that "in heaven their angels do always behold the face of my Father which is in heaven."

Amidst all our recent afflictions we have great and unnumbered blessings for which to be always thankful. What greater blessing could ever have been bestowed upon children than the kind care, noble example and instruction, and sacred memory of our dear father? And now that he has been removed from us, we can look back upon his life and see at every step the merciful dealings of God with him and his little family. I think that there never was a calmer, more useful and elevated, or more honored life devoted to the service of the Creator. He lived for eternity and not for time, although for others his labors embraced the relations of both; and he was always actuated by the desire to promote the best welfare of his fellow men, temporal and spiritual. What greater blessing than the inheritance of such sacred memories?

I hope, my dear sister, that your health has been entirely restored. You must come up and pay us a long visit. The change will do you good. I am very glad to know that Brother Robert will accept the call to Atlanta. I think that the climate in this elevated region will work a revolution in your health. Besides this, the place is an important and rapidly increasing one, and bids fair to become one of the largest manufacturing inland cities.

Carrie writes me that she will in the course of a few days be in our new rented house. I regret that I am not with her to assist, but in these times of war we cannot command our time as we would.

My present labors are severe and arduous, but they are invested with great interest. I have been greatly struck by the cheerful endurance of our poor sick soldiers. Amongst the thousands which I have visited—many of them, too, with hospital gangrene dissolving their poor limbs and exposing quivering muscles, arteries, and nerves—I have not heard one word of discontent or despondency. Words of submission and complaint are reserved for those who stay at home and enjoy the security afforded by these noble men who stand as a living wall around the homes of the Southern women and children. As long as such noble men compose our armies, we can never be conquered.

If Providence permits, I hope to turn my face homewards in ten days or two weeks. With warmest love to you and Brother Robert and the little ones, I remain

Your affectionate brother,
Joseph Jones.

Col. Charles C. Jones, Jr., *to* Mrs. Mary Jones[g]

Savannah, *Saturday,* August 29th, 1863

My very dear Mother,

Enclosed I have the pleasure of sending you a copy of the letter written by my beloved and honored father to Mrs. Reid in July 1857 descriptive of the passage of the North River through the North Mountain. You expressed a desire to have it. Mrs. Reid will not consent to part with the original, but sent it to me through Cousin Philo that I might have an opportunity of copying it. This, you see, I have done, and have returned the original. It is a very interesting letter, and brings my dear father in every line to my living recollection. What a lover of nature he was! In fact, there was nothing good or great, attractive in nature or art, nothing interesting in the heavens above or in the earth beneath, which failed to engage his attention and enlist his sympathy. If I can assist you, my dear mother, at any time in collecting these precious memorials, I trust you will let me do so.

I am glad to say to you that Colonel Gilmer (whom you know very well, and of whom on one occasion I remember hearing Father make the remark: "Gilmer I like: he is a fine fellow") has received the appointment of major general, and has been ordered to Charleston. While his engineering skill and ability will, under God, prove of vast benefit to our sister city in this the hour of her extreme peril, his upright character and manly virtue must exercise an ameliorating influence upon the demoralized military circles there. We have not a word of news this morning from that city.

Saw Willie King today: on a leave of absence. He is perfectly well, and is fattening.

I have heard nothing from home this week, but hope that all are well, and that my dear little daughter has quite regained her accustomed good health. . . . I hope to see you, my dear mother, sometime next week. With best love to all, and many kisses for my precious little daughter, I am ever

Your affectionate son,

Charles C. Jones, Jr.

Col. Charles C. Jones, Jr., *to* Mrs. Mary Jones[g]

Savannah, *Monday,* August 31st, 1863

My very dear Mother,

I have just been ordered by General Beauregard to Charleston to take command of the light artillery on James Island. I leave in the morning, D.V., not to return, I expect, if God spares my life, until the existing difficulties are settled.

My position is one of great responsibility, and I hope that I may have strength given me from above properly to discharge all the duties which will devolve upon me. All our help cometh from God, and every day do I realize more and more forcibly my every dependence upon Him. May He in mercy watch over and bless with His protecting care and love you, my dear mother, my precious little daughter, Sister, Brother, and all who are near and dear to me! I will hope to do my duty under every circumstance; and you will all remember, whatever may befall me, that I love you all with a true, warm, big heart, and from the bottom of that heart thank you all for your great and never-ceasing kindness and goodness to me all my life. Please let me know if my dear little daughter should at any time need anything.

A detailed statement of my affairs I leave in my tin box in the safe of the Farmers' & Mechanics' Bank in this city.

I regret very much that I did not enjoy the privilege of coming out as I expected to have done, but it was an impracticable matter, and now this order prevents me from accomplishing my contemplated visit this week. I will write you so soon as I can after getting over, and will tell you how to direct your letters to me. Do kiss my precious little daughter for me. Give much love to Sister, Robert, and the little ones. And believe me ever, my dearest mother,

Your affectionate son,
Charles C. Jones, Jr.

Col. Charles C. Jones, Jr., *to* Mrs. Mary Jones[g]
James Island, *Thursday,* September 3rd, 1863
My very dear Mother,

I came over to this island on yesterday under orders from General Beauregard to take command of the light artillery, of which there are here some six light batteries and two siege trains. I am located at the headquarters of General Taliaferro, and am as pleasantly situated as it is possible for me to be under the circumstances. Today I am going to ride around the lines with the general, and when I return I will take the earliest opportunity of giving you an account of the situation of matters. This morning I write simply to tell you that I am well, and to assure you and all at home of my constant love and truest remembrance. Do kiss my precious little daughter for me. Give love to all. And believe me ever, my dearest mother,

Your affectionate son,
Charles C. Jones, Jr.

Do write me as soon as you can, directing your letters to me at Charleston, care of General W. B. Taliaferro.

Col. Charles C. Jones, Jr., *to* Mrs. Mary Jones[g]
James Island, *Friday,* September 4th, 1863
My very dear Mother,

Nothing of an unusual character has occurred in the progress of this siege within the past two days with the exception that the enemy this afternoon paid some attention, with the *Pawnee* and a gunboat, to our southern lines, shelling and then retiring. Heavy firing still continues between the hostile forts on Morris Island; and our batteries at various points on this island are endeavoring to annoy the enemy. As you view Morris Island from the batteries in advance of our quarters and from Secessionville, you can almost imagine that you are looking upon *Staten Island;* there is such an aggregation of shipping of every sort and description, and such a collection of tents, etc., that the island presents the appearance of a continuous village. I have assumed command of the light artillery on this island. If any attack is made by way of James Island, I will have my hands full.

There is not a moment of the day or night but the boom of heavy ordnance, the smoke of our batteries, and the bursting of shells can be seen and heard. I regard the fall of Fort Wagner as a mere question of time, and think the policy of holding it longer a questionable one.

I am well. My thoughts and affections are always with you, my dear mother, with my precious little daughter, and with all at home. May God mercifully preserve you all, surrounding you with His especial favor and blessing!

Our present location is very filthy. You never saw such quantities of flies; and bad smells are everywhere. Should anything unusual occur, I will write you at once. Do kiss my precious little daughter for me. Give love to all. And believe me ever, my dear mother,

Your affectionate son,
Charles C. Jones, Jr.

There is no saying when this siege will end. We hope for the best.

COL. CHARLES C. JONES, JR., *to* MRS. MARY JONES[g]

James Island, *Sunday,* September 6th, 1863

It is Sabbath morning, my dear mother, but it is a very difficult matter to realize the fact. All day yesterday, all last night, and all day up to this hour, Battery Wagner has been subjected to a most terrific bombardment. Over one hundred were killed and wounded within its walls yesterday. No human being could have lived for one moment upon its walls or upon its parade. Against it were hurled the combined projectiles fired from the ironsides and the various mortar and Parrott batteries of the enemy located at different points on Morris Island. As their shells in numbers would explode in the parapet and within the fort, Wagner would seem converted into a volcano. Never was any battery called upon to resist such a bombardment, and I fear that it is now held more as a matter of military pride than anything else. It is very questionable whether this should be done.

In full view of everything on yesterday afternoon, from Battery Haskell, which was firing upon the enemy, I witnessed the progress of the siege. The gunnery of the Federals was wonderful. Wagner could not answer a single shot. The enemy last night assaulted Battery Gregg, which is located on the extreme north point of Morris Island, and were repulsed. God be praised for that; for had Gregg been carried, the entire garrison at Wagner would have been captured. I would not be surprised if the enemy assaulted Wagner tonight. That portion of the parapet looking towards the south of Morris Island has been knocked very much to pieces, and the sand crumbled into the ditch. In the very nature of things it cannot be held very much longer.

As a port of commercial ingress and egress Charleston is gone; but my impression at present is that the enemy will never be able to obtain possession of the city itself. It may be destroyed in whole or in part by the shells of the enemy, but it is questionable whether they can ever hold it as a site. The inner defenses are as yet intact, and the large Blakely gun is nearly mounted. Three ironclad gunboats are in the harbor, ready to attack the enemy in the event of their endeavoring to enter with their fleet.

We know not what a day may bring forth, but I trust that we may all be enabled, by God's blessing, to do our heroic duty under any and every circumstance. This life is a terrible one, but must be endured. Do, my dear mother, kiss my precious little daughter for me. Assure all at home of my sincerest love. And believe me ever

Your affectionate son,
Charles C. Jones, Jr.

COL. CHARLES C. JONES, JR., *to* MRS. MARY JONES[g]

James Island, *Wednesday,* September 9th, 1863

My very dear Mother,

I write simply to assure you and my dear little daughter and all at home of my constant remembrance and truest love.

The enemy yesterday attacked, with the ironsides and four monitors, Fort Moultrie, and were repulsed after a severe and prolonged bombardment. Last night an assault was made by them in barges upon Fort Sumter. The assault was signally repelled. We captured nineteen commissioned officers, one hundred and two noncommissioned officers and privates, and six barges. It is supposed that we killed and wounded and drowned between two and three hundred of the rascals. Our ironclads performed signal service. We captured also the flag which floated from Sumter when that fort was surrendered by Anderson, and which the enemy had brought in the expectation of again planting it upon the walls of that fort.

Day before yesterday I proceeded to the Stono with three light batteries to engage the sloop of war *Pawnee;* but she would not come within range, and after firing a few random shots retired.

Through God's great mercy I am still quite well. I think matters are assuming a rather more favorable aspect, and if the enemy will only delay a little longer any contemplated attack by the way of James Island, we will have completed a new and formidable line of defenses. The enemy will find it a very difficult matter to enter the harbor. What I most fear is the partial destruction of the city by the long-range Parrott batteries of the Federals located on Morris Island. The scoundrels are busy as bees placing them in position, and apparently are training them upon the city and our James Island batteries. Our batteries are always firing, night and day.

Do, my dear mother, kiss my precious little daughter for me. Give best love to all at home. And remember me ever as

Your affectionate son,
Charles C. Jones, Jr.

I have had no letter from home yet.

Mrs. Mary Jones *to* Col. Charles C. Jones, Jr.ᵍ

Walthourville, *Wednesday,* September 9th, 1863

My very dear Son,

Your affectionate consideration in writing is the greatest relief my anxious heart can have. Day and night my thoughts are with you, and my poor prayers ascending to my Covenant God, my Almighty Saviour, for His blessing and protection to my child. Even your little daughter, today at noon, being in the room with me, of her own accord knelt by a little trunk which was yours in infancy and said: "Pray God bless Papa!" Will not this cry enter into the ear of the Lord of Hosts? I believe that it will. And may He enable you savingly to trust in Him with all your heart! And may you be endued with wisdom and courage and strength equal to your day of responsibility and of peril!

I feel that nothing could be more solemn than the circumstances which now surround and the events that may await you. Let me tell you here, my son, that I am prepared to come to you at a moment's warning; and should you suffer in any way by wounds or disease, nothing shall keep me away from you. And I hope you will never deceive me about yourself. I write not thus to depress your spirits; my hope and confidence in God is firm. I know you will do your duty—and that bravely; and I believe He will guard and shield you. Ever look up unto Him, and pray for the unerring guidance of the Holy Spirit. In the basket which I am sending you today I have put a few Testaments and tracts. . . . Can I do anything for you in Savannah in attending to your house or any business which would assist you in any way? I will gladly serve you; only let me know it.

I am trying to do all I can to meet the wants of our people. Owing to the excessive rains our salt-boiling has been almost a failure the three past months. I have about ten or twelve bushels which I will send up before long. If the *boilers* could be had, I would remove *Andrew* back to the Island, where he could do much more at it. Do you know of any boilers that could be purchased?

As all hope of your coming out just now was abandoned, I went down to the Island on Monday, spent that night with your uncle (who has been quite sick with one of his old attacks but is better now), and returned to Walthourville yesterday.

Dr. Harris wrote me a very respectful letter last week proposing, if I would allow him to occupy Maybank house, that he would protect the place and keep things in repair as well as he conveniently could, wishing only planting land for a garden, and saying that he would even furnish firewood from his own land. I have allowed him to do so, and really feel it a kind providence, protecting the house that has been so dear to us from the certain ruin and decay which seemed awaiting it from the outrages of the lawless soldiers, who had commenced to break in glasses, doors, blinds, etc., and who kept it constantly open and exposed to the weather. Dr. Harris says he will vacate whenever I desire it. His family consists only of his wife and himself and a few servants. I reserve the Negro houses beyond the spring, as we may want them if we boil salt there or allow anyone to do so.

Audley has allowed a company of salt-boilers to settle on his land, and for that privilege and the use of the wood on ten acres they pay him six hundred dollars. They are probably making that amount each day. They now want to know if we will sell them wood. I wrote Audley yesterday that our oak wood in ordinary times would bring us, sold at the landing, three dollars a cord; and considering the enormous profits made by them I felt it but just and right that they give us three dollars a cord for oak wood which is just to their hand, and two dollars for the pine; and he might state these as the terms upon which they might have it. Messrs. King and Delegal make, I am told, about five or six bushels a day, ask twenty-five dollars a bushel, and pay us fourteen or fifteen dollars *a month* for the wood which they consume! I told Audley we had not been anxious to locate salt-boilers on the Island, but I felt that it had now been thrown open to them, and I think we may now avail ourselves of the many situations we have for that purpose. Audley was offered three thousand dollars by a gentleman a few days since for a situation on his land; he refused, as he had no room. I told him as we had, he should have referred him to us.

Today I send for you, through the distributing commissary of Savannah, a basket of provisions containing a boiled ham, biscuits, butter, potatoes, green sweet oranges, one dozen candles, and a bottle of blackberry prepared for medicinal use (excellent for all *bowel affections*—prepared with *brandy*, consequently a *strong article*), some horse-radish, etc., etc., which I trust will reach you safely and be acceptable. The potatoes are a present from the little ones. I must now close to get the basket ready. Your sister and Robert unite with me in best love, with the sweetest kisses from your own child. God bless and protect you, my dear son, and make you useful in our just and righteous cause!

Ever your affectionate mother,
Mary Jones.

COL. CHARLES C. JONES, JR., *to* MRS. MARY JONES[g]
James Island, *Sunday,* September 13th, 1863
Accept my sincere thanks, my dear mother, for your very kind remembrance of me. The basket of good things has safely arrived, all in nice order.

Manna in the wilderness was never more gratifying to the famishing children of Israel than are these most acceptable articles to our corn-fed mess. We have not enjoyed such a meal since we have been on the island as that which this morning graced our primitive table beneath the shadow of this large live oak. Contemporaneously with the arrival of your gift came another generous basket from Cousin Philo, so you see for the time being we are in clover. These kind and substantial remembrances from those we love are highly prized at all times; but especially during these montonous periods of "sobby corn dodgers" and antiquated beef do they receive a most hearty and marked welcome. General Taliaferro and all of us are in the best possible condition this morning after our unusually bountiful breakfast.

The tracts and Testaments, too, are most welcome. Already are they in the hands of the mess, and as it is Sunday, several are this moment busy reading them. So soon as I conclude this short note I am going to devote myself to them. I am sorry to say we have no church here today. Persons at home can scarcely realize how grateful and valuable these contributions of Testaments and tracts are to our soldiers in the field. They are eagerly sought after and carefully read, and I doubt not but that many a good seed thus sown springs up and bears fruit an hundredfold.

The enemy has been very quiet for the past two days, but they are without doubt busily engaged in maturing their plans for future and further operations. We will probably hear from their new and altered batteries in a very short time.

We are anxiously expecting the result of that anticipated engagement between our forces and those of Rosecrans. That will be a most momentous struggle for our cause and country, and we cannot overestimate the disastrous results in the event of our defeat. *We must, under God, gain the victory there;* and it becomes us one and all fervently to implore the Lord of Hosts to crown our arms with a signal triumph.

There is no speculating upon the question when or how this siege of Charleston will end. We are being reinforced from General Lee's army. Gillmore is also receiving troops from Meade's army. The Yankees are bent upon the capture of Charleston—if such a thing can be accomplished by a limitless expenditure of men and munitions of war. We are weaker in all respects than they are save in the nature of our cause and the inspiration of our troops and—let us hope—in the favor of a just God.

How is my precious little daughter? Do kiss her for me. Give love to all at home. And remember me ever, my dear mother, as

Your affectionate son,
Charles C. Jones, Jr.

P.S. Under existing circumstances I presume Robert and Sister will hardly be able to go up to Atlanta unless the way is very clear for him to do so. I should think he ought to await the issue of the impending struggle—at least so far as a removal of Sister and family and household is concerned.

MRS. MARY JONES *to* COL. CHARLES C. JONES, JR.ᵍ

Walthourville, *Monday,* September 14th, 1863

My very dear Son,

Your favors of the 9th and 10th have just been received, and I bless the Lord for His mercies to you thus far! The repulse at Sumter was heroic. We should be gratified for the least expression of the divine favor. I am sad to think our men and means so defective; and today a rumor has reached us that the Blakely gun has burst. I trust it will prove false, and that in that gun we will have an effective engine for the destruction of our vile invaders.

Robert is just leaving for Atlanta. I trust "neither bonds nor imprisonment" may await him there; but affairs are assuming a most decided aspect in Upper Georgia. Your sister and the family will not probably leave before the first or middle of October. Should your brother return, I want to make him a visit before frost, *D.V.;* but I am unwilling to be moving about in the present aspect of affairs. Robert preached his farewell sermon yesterday. It was a solemn occasion: seven years of his early ministry closed! He gave a review of his ministerial work and its results in that period. He certainly has been permitted to accomplish much good, which we trust will endure through everlasting ages! It is with great reluctance this tie is severed between him and his people.

Your precious child is as hearty as she can be: all vivacity. Talks of her dear papa daily, enters into the plays with the children, acting her part sometimes as a housekeeper, then a cook, but most frequently as a baby, calling little Mary and Charlie "Mama" and "Papa," which gives them an air of great importance as they undertake her management.

I hope the basket has reached you safely. I write in haste only to assure you of our abiding love and remembrance, in which your sister and Robert unite, and the children, with sweetest kisses from your little daughter. God bless and save you!

Ever your affectionate mother,
Mary Jones.

MRS. MARY JONES *to* COL. CHARLES C. JONES, JR.ᵍ

Walthourville, *Friday,* September 18th, 1863

My dear Son,

For several days we have had weeping skies, and now the rain is falling fast. It *comforts* me to feel that the winds and the waves may be made instruments for our defense by Him who holds them in His almighty hand. Then again I think of my poor boy beneath the thin cloth tent, or exposed upon the open field to the tempest if not to the deadly fire of the inhuman foe.

Today I feel unusually depressed about our future prospects: the occupation of Chattanooga by Rosecrans and his fortifying and making it the base of operations; the various points from which he can draw men and means and supplies; and the devastation which may be inflicted upon our state, like those upon Mississippi, through raids; the giving up of one important point after another by General Bragg, falling back all the time with the delusive expectation of some advantage to be gained; and especially in the present instance, to my plain understanding, he appears to have totally mistaken the designs of the enemy and failed to anticipate his movements. It may all be right; I am of course incapable of judging. But thus it appears. And if we have not the power to prevent the enemy from occupying our strongholds, how are we ever to dislodge them and drive them out when once they have gained possession? And the history of our war has been that whenever they have been allowed a foothold they have maintained it. Their advances upon our territory are fearful!

Do not, my dear son, suppose that my spirit quails beneath the dark clouds which appear to curtain our political horizon on almost every side. No. I believe we are contending for a just and righteous cause; and I would infinitely prefer that *we all* perish in its defense before we submit to the infamy and disgrace and utter ruin and misery involved in any connection whatever with the vilest and most degraded nation on the face of the earth. We cannot pretend to fathom the designs of Infinite Wisdom touching our beloved and suffering Confederacy. It may be our sins will be scourged to the severest extremity—and we deserve it all. But I also believe when that wicked people have filled up the cup of their iniquity, God will take them in hand to deal with them for their wickedness and to reward them according to their transgressions.

I am happy to know that you received the basket in good condition, and that its contents have contributed to your comfort. Next week we will send you another supply. I wish the committee would bring us the basket back; it is so difficult to get anything of the kind. But that, I presume, would not be done. What would you like to have? Would you prefer a ham raw or boiled?

You have never told me who compose your mess. I want to know everything about yourself and situation. General Taliaferro is a Virginian, of course. Your dear father had a friend of that name whom he valued much for his deep piety and many amiable traits. They were classmates in the seminary at Princeton. In 1847, when we visited Virginia and your father was a member of our General Assembly at Richmond, one very charming day we took a trip down the James River, and on board the steamer made the acquaintance of a young U.S. officer of that name. I think he was then on a recruiting service for the Mexican War. We always cherished a very pleasant recollection and impression of him and the kind attentions which he showed us in pointing out the many magnificent estates that then graced the hillsides and beautiful valleys that bordered the river, all of which was perfectly familiar to him. To this day the green heights of Shirley and cultivated fields of Brandon, etc., etc., are before my mind's eye. Alas, for the change which has passed over them! I have a kind of fancy that your general may once have been that young officer.

It is particularly gratifying to me to know that the Testaments and tracts were so kindly received. My dear son, never forget your accountability to the heart-searching, the ever-present God, your Maker, Preserver, and Redeemer. And may God enable you to set an upright and Christian example before all with whom you are associated! What a blessing from above that our army is composed of so many who are truly godly men! The example of our noble Jackson (although some are found envious enough to detract from it) is worthy of imitation by our officers of every grade. He dared to honor the law of his God at all times and in all places and circumstances.

Your precious child is perfectly well. Today she came to my side with a little piece of palmetto which she was stripping with her tiny fingers and said: "I—plait—hat—for—my—papa." She is busy with the children from morning to night, when she is ready for an early supper and a good rest.

All friends are well. *Tom* made his appearance two weeks since, Mr. McRae sending him down with the men who were to work in Savannah—a month earlier than I expected him. He has quite the air of a *graduated tradesman,* and is tanning and making lasts preparatory to making shoes. I hope he will succeed. Could we get leather in Burke? Your sister unites with me in best love. Also Charlie and Mamie. Sweetest kisses from your little Mary Ruth. Howdies from all the servants. How is George?

Ever your affectionate mother,

Mary Jones.

Did you make any positive arrangement with Mr. Cassels about wood? He is on the Island and expects to get it at one dollar. But he ought to pay two dollars, and if you did not agree *positively,* I will charge that.

COL. CHARLES C. JONES, JR., *to* MRS. MARY JONES[g]

James Island, *Saturday,* September 19th, 1863

My very dear Mother,

Your very kind letter of the 14th inst. has been received, and I am very happy to know that all at home are well. The Blakely gun has burst, and is entirely valueless. Its mate will not be brought forward from Wilmington. They are both represented as being exceedingly defective in the theory of their construction.

I am glad to hear that Sister and the children will not go up to Atlanta immediately, and trust by God's help that before the 1st October the enemy will be entirely expelled from our state. Gallant reinforcements have gone forward from General Lee's army.

Eva writes me that Brother's youngest child has been very sick, but that it was better on the 15th and she hoped would recover. The Doctor had been telegraphed for from Richmond. She asks, my dear mother, when she and Cousin Philo are to have the pleasure of seeing you in Augusta, and begs me to remember her affectionately to you. I hope that I may be able to secure a leave of absence the last of October. You know we are, D.V., to be married on the 28th of that month. I hope, my dear mother, that you may be able to be there at that time.

Everything is comparatively quiet here. The enemy appear to be making extensive preparations for the reduction of our batteries on Sullivan's Island, and for that purpose are mounting numerous and heavy guns upon Batteries Wagner and Gregg and at intermediate points. The attack, when made, will probably be a very severe one, and will be sustained by both land and naval batteries of the enemy. Yesterday with two long-range rifled guns I endeavored to annoy the shipping of the enemy in Lighthouse Inlet. I fired some twenty shot at them, but the distance was so great that it was impossible to tell whether any damage was done.

The air is quite chilly this morning, and the sky overcast. We will probably have more rain. I am so happy to hear such pleasant and interesting accounts from my precious little daughter. May a good God have her and you, my dear mother, and all at home in His especial favor! Do kiss her for me. Give love to all. And believe me ever

Your affectionate son,
Charles C. Jones, Jr.

Rev. R. Q. Mallard *to* Mrs. Mary S. Mallard[t]

Atlanta, Wednesday, September 23rd, 1863

My darling Wife,

Your letter of the 21st with its enclosure has reached me safely. . . . The information you give about the shoes is as gratifying as it was unexpected. Did Mr. McRae say that he would make *me* a pair? I hope he will, for everything of that kind is enormously high. What do you think of butter at three dollars per pound? Mr. Pease paid this yesterday in the street before his house. Persons get it cheaper by sending off. If you could get it on anything like reasonable rates, it might be well to purchase and put up for use here. I suppose what Peggy puts up will amount to very little. The truth is, we will probably have to do without it—unless we can make it ourselves in small quantities from our cow. What do you suppose I pay for washing? Three dollars per dozen! You may be sure that I am just as economical of clean linen as decency will permit. Mrs. P. kindly offered to have it done for me, but I knew it would not be convenient.

I have been taking an outside look at Mrs. Dabney's house today, which they hope to get on the 1st of January. It is a neat, plain two-storied house, almost as near the church as Mr. W. Q. Baker's is to the Walthourville church, and in a pleasant neighborhood. I only wish they may be able to get it. Colonel Grant, one of our best members, controls it, and if Mrs. D. should not want it, I hope it may be secured. Atlanta is excessively dusty at present, as there has been no rain, they say, for two months; and the house on Marietta Street is much exposed to the dust. The shrubbery is covered with red clay finely pulverized.

My acquaintance is steadily increasing. Today I had the pleasure of form-ing Dr. Eve's acquaintance. Seeing us approaching on the opposite side of the street, he crossed over (as he said) to obtain an introduction. He attends the Central Presbyterian Church. He has invited me to his hospital; I think I will go tomorrow.

I have been appointed on a committee of thirty to raise funds for the relief of our wounded soldiers. I have done nothing, as my acquaintance is limited; but I met with them this morning. The amount at that time raised was seventeen thousand dollars, and it was thought that it would reach twenty thousand. I am rejoiced at this success; our brave boys should have every comfort.

The wounded are coming in in large numbers today—principally those whose wounds are not serious. I passed through the car shed on my way from a funeral (of which I will again speak) and saw an immense multitude of people (eight or ten thousand perhaps)—soldiers going to Bragg, hundreds of wounded men, from twenty-five hundred to three thousand Yankees ("blue bellies," the soldiers call them), and a vast number of spectators. One poor fellow—and one only—I saw on a stretcher on his way to the distributing hospital; the most of the wounded seem to have been struck in the hand or arm. It is said the proportion of slight wounds is very large. The most seriously wounded, however, are no doubt either on the field or in the nearest points to it. Noble fellows! Dr. Brown bears the highest testimony to their fortitude, and says that they are proud of their wounds. My bosom swelled with joy and pride as I looked from the base hirelings of Lincoln with their regular uniforms to the Confederate guard interspersed among them with their tawny gray or nondescript habiliments—with scarcely anything to show that they were soldiers but their muskets. God abundantly bless them every one!

Truly the news is cheering from the front. May a merciful God deliver the enemy entirely into our hands! Rosecrans has, through God's blessing, re-ceived a crushing defeat. Uniformly successful before and whipped by a general in whom all did not feel confidence, shall we not see in his defeat a signal answer to a nation's prayers?

The funeral of which I spoke above was that of Brigadier General Helm of Kentucky—a son of Ex-Governor Helm—Ben Hardin Helm, I think. . . . The dead hero's coffin was wrapped in what seemed to be a large Con-federate flag. . . . Oh, how that sight brought home to me the fearful reality of war! Mrs. H. is a half-sister of Lincoln's wife. She is boarding at Mrs. Dabney's, and I would call on her did I not fear it might be considered an intrusion in a stranger.

I have made inquiry today about the marble tombstone. Tell Mother that one can be had at about nine hundred dollars, independent of lettering and cost of transportation. (This latter, I understand, can be had via Macon.) Ask Mother to write or telegraph me immediately if she wishes it.

Kiss my dear little ones a dozen times for me. . . . Give much love to Mother; tell her Dr. Logan was glad to get the arrowroot.

Your own
Robert.

Mrs. Mary Jones *to* Col. Charles C. Jones, Jr.^g

Walthourville, *Thursday,* September 24th, 1863

My dear Son,

Yours of the 19th was received yesterday. What suspense hangs upon every hour my anxious heart only could tell. And what a relief when the mailbag reveals a letter in your own handwriting! God be merciful to you, my child, and enable you to do your whole duty to Him and to your country!

I fear I did not thank you as I intended for your deeply interesting account of the bombardment and evacuation of Battery Wagner. It must have been sublimely terrific. I have read it to a great many friends. Mr. Buttolph and Robert thought it ought to be published. You may be assured it shall be preserved. I am keeping all your letters—especially at this period—for your little daughter; if her life is spared I know she will have a head and heart to appreciate them. . . .

I am grieved to hear of the illness of Carrie and your brother's babe. Robert wrote us that Stanhope had been suddenly ill, but was relieved. I have been hoping to make them a visit, but times are so perilous it does not appear prudent to be moving about.

Our friends in Marietta are thrown into very uncomfortable circumstances. Their church at the end of the lot has been converted into a hospital, and the bare necessaries of life scarcely to be obtained.

Do assure Eva of my true affection. I shall love her as a daughter, and hope I may be regarded as her second mother. My best regards to Mrs. Eve. I hope a kind Providence may permit the consummation of your marriage at the appointed time. If I can assist in any of your arrangements, I hope you will let me do so. Gilbert will be at your service. I think your house will need thorough cleansing, with whitewash *in the cellar,* before it is occupied.

I have been hunting for your winter undervests. You must have them in Savannah. Do dress warmly at this season. Are you wanting drawers? I could get some made of *unbleached sheeting* for you—of good quality and warm.

By today's train your sister and myself send a *box*—the largest we could find—with a few things for your comfort. We are puzzled for baskets, etc.; it is not now as formerly. The tracts for distribution we trust will prove little messengers for good to those who receive them. I have a bushel and a half of clean rice for you. Would you like it forwarded to James Island? Write me your wish about it.

I told you *Tom* had come home a month *earlier* than I expected him. We have just received a letter from Mr. McRae stating the reason. He says for several weeks Tom conducted himself so well and learned his trade so fast they were greatly pleased with him, but he commenced going off at nights across the river contrary to orders. Leather was missed from the shop. He was known to have made shoes at night and sold them. Finally several pair of finished shoes were missing from their shop; and suspicion falling on Tom, he thought it best to send him away at once before he got into more serious difficulty from his dishonesty. He says Tom with proper tools can make an excellent shoe. I always knew him to be an unfaithful boy, and one that gave your dear father much trouble. But I felt an interest in him from the fact that he had been his personal attendant, and wanted to make him a tradesman on that account. *Situated as I am,* I could not keep an unprincipled servant about me. Tom is now tanning hides, and some that were commenced in the spring are nearly ready for use. When ready I would like to place him under Mr. Sconyers' eye, where he can be controlled and make the plantation shoes. I have not and will not say a word to Tom about this matter *yet.* I had promised to let him go and visit his mother, and when he does so he can remain.

Peter (Martha's husband) proves to be a great rogue; he married in a few weeks after his return from Indianola. I gave him money to go. *Patrick* also is said to be married.

I am doing all I can in the weaving line. Your sister will provide for her people, so I trust we may make out for the whole. I fear we shall make but little at Montevideo: the rice is pretty much lost; not a pound of cotton picked in yet. I would be glad if you could find time to direct a line to Mr. Jackson. I believe he will try to serve us, but I fear he will rely too much upon *Cato, who I know* must feel himself under authority. I am sorry, my son, amidst the weighty affairs which claim your time and attention to bring any of my little concerns before your mind. I am and will try to accomplish all I can for the good of all concerned. *Clothing, shoes,* and *salt* are *my aims.*

Your sister unites with me in best love to you. Love from the children. Sweetest kisses from your daughter.

Ever your affectionate mother,
Mary Jones.

COL. CHARLES C. JONES, JR., *to* MRS. MARY JONES^g

James Island, *Thursday,* September 24th, 1863

I am this afternoon, my very dear mother, in receipt of your kind and interesting favor of the 18th inst., and am truly thankful to know that all are well at home.

We are rejoicing and thanking the Father of All Mercies for His great favor in having granted us the victory in Upper Georgia. I trust that our triumph is complete. If such be the fact, we cannot overestimate its beneficial results. But as yet I must confess my mind is not clear as to the ultimate results of that immediate struggle. We have a powerful army, an accomplished general, and a rough country to contend against in securing the fruits of the victory. Let us trust, however, that He who has blessed us and inaugurated this good work will continue it even to the perfect end. This He is able to do, and to Him be all the praise and glory given. A decided success just at this time—and in that important direction—will most materially change the whole aspect of our national affairs. That army of Rosecrans is composed of finer material than any other the abolitionists have in the field. They are to a very great extent Western men, descendants of Virginians and Tennesseans and Kentuckians, men in whose veins flows blood at least to some degree kindred with our own. In vanquishing such an army we have to all human appearances overcome our worst enemy.

I read to General Taliaferro, my dear mother, your account of your meeting in 1847 on the James River the young U.S. officer on recruiting service, and of his civilities to you and my beloved father on that occasion. He immediately recalled the circumstance. *It was* our present general; and he begs me to present his respectful regards to you, with his acknowledgments for your kind remembrance of him. My associations with him are of the most pleasant character. Our mess consists of the general; his brother, Captain Taliaferro, A.A.G.; Captain Twiggs, inspecting officer; Lieutenant Cunningham, ordnance officer; Lieutenant Redmond, A.D.C.; my adjutant, Lieutenant Whitehead; and myself. We are all in tents except the general, who sleeps in a room of a partially dilapidated house near our encampment. We eat and sit in the open air beneath a wide-spreading oak tree; and of late, during these cold days and chilly evenings, we have gathered around a cheerful campfire. My associations here are as pleasant as they can be under like circumstances, and I am continually brought into contact with all our generals and prominent officers here on social terms of the most agreeable character. Our encampment is marked by good order and sobriety.

No, my dear mother, neither morning nor night do I ever suffer anything to interrupt my religious exercises—reading the Scriptures and earnest prayer. These I recognize as my first duties and highest privileges. At all times we are liable to death, and the tenure of life is each moment and in every place uncertain; but nowhere else is one brought to realize that fact so forcibly as when he is in the presence of the enemy, and liable at any moment to confront the immediate dangers of the battlefield. The consequence is that with the sober and the reflecting mind a situation of this character, so far from alienating the mind and thoughts from the contemplation of religious subjects, on the contrary induces the calmest thought and the most serious reflection, and leads us practically to realize the fact of our every dependence upon the goodness and the mercy of a superintending Providence.

While I was writing, a nice box of good things arrived from my dearest Eva. She is always so kind, so good to me. I will try, my dear mother, and return the basket to you. I know they are very hard to be procured. You can scarcely realize how sincerely your acceptable remembrance of us was appreciated. We are literally upon short commons, and these good things from home are indeed highly prized. We will look with eagerness for the coming of the other one which you have so kindly promised.

There has been no change in the military status of affairs here since I wrote you this morning. A letter from Augusta tells me that Stanhope is much better. The Doctor has returned, and he and Carrie are anxiously awaiting your coming. Do kiss my precious little baby for me, and thank her for her kind remembrance of her loving papa. I did say to Mr. Cassels that the wood would be one dollar per cord, as in the case of Mr. Delegal; but I have written him herewith a note which, my dear mother, you can enclose him if you think best. Salt is commanding such a high price that two dollars per cord would not be too much; and after the 1st January I would charge Messrs. Delegal and King that price. Do they pay regularly? With warmest love to all, I am ever, my dear mother,

Your affectionate son,
Charles C. Jones, Jr.

Rev. R. Q. Mallard *to* Mrs. Mary S. Mallard[t]
Atlanta, *Wednesday,* September 30th, 1863

My own darling Wife,

I have just written two letters or notes of friendship, and now anticipate the pleasure of spending some moments in epistolary intercourse with you. . . . I have improved the pen which you sent, but as you perceive, the stroke is almost too light for sermon-writing.

I am glad that you have deferred having the tombstone erected over our little Eliza. Sweet babe! I should like to have that pleasure myself. I thought much of her on Sabbath. Precious little darling, I see many children to remind me of, but none *like her.* I see already the design of her death in part. She came and then went to heaven that her father might be fully qualified for his office as comforter as well as guide of God's sorrowing children. I felt this when on Monday I went by request to see a member of our church who had not long lost a child twenty months old. She had heard that I had lost an infant, and there was a common bond of sympathy uniting us. . . . This is the second instance in which I have been called to comfort parents bereaved by the death of little children since I have been in Atlanta this time.

I thank you for your prompt attention to my inquiry; I have filled out and enclosed a check to Walker & Company, Savannah, for the tombstone.

As for the wheat, I have engaged Mr. Pease to get for me five barrels if he can procure it. There are two difficulties: the want of transportation and the disposition in planters to keep back their wheat for higher prices. I do not know whether Mr. Pease could get any for Mother at that price. He has engaged some near Rome, but does not know whether he can get it through. In addition to other difficulties, government may seize it.

I am happy to hear of your success in the cloth manufacture. You will not probably have much more time for that work. . . . Next Wednesday (this day a week hence) Flint River Presbytery is to meet in Griffin; the week after I hope, if the Lord will, to be with you—if there should be any prospect of removal of my family. In fact, should the state of the country not warrant a move, I think I will pay you a visit anyhow and consult over it.

I went up yesterday morning to Marietta and returned this morning. I had a very pleasant time. Found them all as well as usual—busy and cheerful and glad to see me. It was old Aunt Robarts' seventy-eighth birthday. Her continuance in the world to this age must, under Providence, be due to the care which is taken of her. Her cough seems to be troublesome, and she rarely gets out except to church. I found her knitting our little Mary a nice pair of railroad-stitch stockings. They all inquired affectionately after Mother and yourself and the children. The young ladies, I observed, were in mourning—I suppose for their poor father. . . . Marietta is one great hospital. I visited several of the wards in search of men of the 25th Georgia, and distributed a few tracts and conversed with a number of the soldiers. I was much pleased with their appearance and conduct. They seem to be greatly cheered by the consciousness that their wounds have not been received in vain. . . . Your Uncle John was absent in Southwest Georgia, but I called at Mr. Dean Dunwody's and saw your Aunt Jane and the boys, Mrs. Dunwody, Sr., and Miss Mary. Mrs. Jones was with them to remain only during Mr. Jones's absence. They were all well. Mr. John Jones sold his house just in the nick of time. If you have not already heard it, you will be surprised to learn that your Uncle Henry has sold that Elysium in Baker for thirty-seven thousand dollars. Purchaser: Mr. Barrington King of Roswell. Only think of that! It seems that it is too far from Cuthbert. . . . The Robartses received while I was there a letter from J. Audley King announcing the shipment of a sack of salt; and Banky, it seems, upon the reception of the returned bag filled and sent it on again. Mr. Rogers got them some twenty-five bushels wheat in the up country and made it a present to them. I was very glad to hear of these acts of kindness. The Robartses send much love to Mother, yourself, and the children.

I must now close, as I wish to see your Uncle John, who is to come up from Macon this evening. Give my love to Mother and little Ruthie. Kiss the children for me, and tell them that I long to see them. And accept the tenderest and deepest love of

Your husband,
R. Q. Mallard.

Rev. R. Q. Mallard *to* Mrs. Mary S. Mallard[t]

Atlanta, *Tuesday,* October 6th, 1863

My dearest Mary,

Homeward bound! What a pleasant phrase to the mariner at the close of a long voyage! Scarcely less pleasant to me is the thought that tomorrow I shall, D.V., turn my face toward home. Flint River Presbytery convenes tomorrow night at Griffin, which is some fifty miles nearer to you than this city. On next Monday I hope to leave Griffin for Savannah, and you may expect me on the Wednesday following.

Colonel Dabney's house has been sold recently, so that the choice now will lie between the house on Marietta Street and Dr. Calhoun's. The latter has six rooms (but they are small), a fine fruit orchard and vineyard, and several acres of arable land connected with it. In regard to this matter, however, I will postpone its further consideration until I see you.

Last Sabbath was a beautiful day. I preached forenoon and afternoon. The congregation in the morning was quite large, and in the afternoon better than was anticipated. What do you think? I preached both times without notes—but not without careful preparation. The attention was very gratifying and encouraging. . . . There are some very pleasant families connected with the Central Presbyterian Church, and a number of ladies whom I think you will like. Almost all ask when I am going to bring my family to the city. Thus far I must say that I am very much pleased. I have made the acquaintance of nearly thirty families.

Mr. John Jones, Miss Mary Dunwody, and Miss Louisa Robarts (I think) were yesterday in Atlanta shopping. I did not hear of it until too late. Mr. Jones wanted to see me to request me to visit a poor wounded soldier who was very much concerned about his soul. A comrade had gone out of the hospital to seek a minister, and supposing Mr. Jones one, had carried him to the hospital. Yesterday afternoon I accompanied one of the chaplains to the bedside of the poor sufferer. His livid and anxious look seemed to betoken the near approach of death. Poor fellow, I offered to him the gospel and knelt by his side and prayed. I doubt if he is alive today. . . . We distributed a few tracts; spoke a few kind words to the patients, the most of whom seemed quite cheerful. One poor fellow was on his back with a broken leg, but a brighter, more cheery countenance I have not seen in the crowds who walk the streets. There are still between seven and eight hundred wounded upon the field whose wounds are of too serious a character to permit of their removal. Our committee is doing much to minister to their comfort, and its services have been gratefully appreciated both by General Bragg and his army.

At the female institute hospital a soldier wounded through the cheek and at times bleeding alarmingly has been eliciting the deep compassions of the lady visitors and attracting the attention of the attendants. Recently he has been able to speak, and to the question to what regiment he belonged he replied *Indiana!* The ladies have been almost provoked to think that they have been lavishing their sympathies upon a wounded Yankee.

Thank Mother for the sweet little rose. Your letter is still fragrant with its perfume. . . . Give my best love to Mother, and prepare a sweet warm kiss for

Your husband,
R. Q. Mallard.

Mrs. Mary Jones *to* Col. Charles C. Jones, Jr.^g

Walthourville, *Tuesday,* October 6th, 1863

My very dear Son,

Not a line from you for more than a week! My anxieties are so great I fear they run ahead of all reasonable expectations. I fear you may be sick, James Island is admitted to be so unhealthy. The papers give us no accounts of the advance of the enemy, but I know that perils encompass you on all sides. If I could not look up and beyond these dreadful apprehensions which often weigh me down, I should indeed be miserable; but I know that God reigns, and I can commit my dearest ones to Him as a faithful covenant-keeper who will never leave nor forsake them.

We have had colds prevailing, and our dear little daughter has had some fever from hers, but is very bright today. I sent for Dr. Stevens on Sabbath, rather to consult him about a dose of medicine than any uneasiness about her. She is daily expanding in her thoughts and feelings. I often wish she could cheer you with her merry laugh and cheerful prattle. She certainly has a wonderful love for her dear papa; scarcely ever hears the sound of the cars without saying you have come.

Porter and Niger from Indianola arrived on Saturday. Have not seen them yet. They sent me word that *Adam* died last week. I trust he was prepared for the great change; he had been a professor of religion for several years. Was one who contracted that severe disease of which so many died at the fortifications on the Savannah River, and I do not think he has been perfectly well since.

The ladies have just been sending off various supplies today for the sick and wounded in the late battles. I hope you got your box last Saturday week. We want to send you again this week. The mail closes, and I must stop to be in time. Robert returns next week. I want to go to Augusta the third week in this month, but have not decided the day. I am very averse to moving about. Your sister unites with me in best love. Kisses from the little ones.

Ever your affectionate mother,
Mary Jones.

Mrs. Mary Jones *to* Col. Charles C. Jones, Jr.^g

Walthourville, *Wednesday,* October 7th, 1863

My dear Son,

Yours of September 29th was received today and relieves my anxiety, although I am sorry to know that you are not well. Do, my child, use every care to preserve your health. Be sure to *dress* and *sleep warmly.* I have always observed that these cool changes in early fall if not provided against would surely be followed by sickness in our climate.

Your drawers I will cut out and have made as soon as I possibly can get someone to do them. In the meantime I will mend up the old ones and send them to you *next week,* as from various causes I will not be able to send you anything this week as I promised to do. The baby's indisposition and my own will prevent my going below this week to collect the little matters designed for your comfort.

The ladies of Walthourville sent today to our sick and wounded in Atlanta one rice tierce, one barrel, and one box filled with good and useful articles and many delicacies, which I hope our noble and suffering soldiers will enjoy. There is nothing in this world too good for those who are shedding their precious blood and giving their own lives to defend and protect us from ruin and misery. Oh, when will it please our Father in Heaven to hear the cries which ascend from our suffering and afflicted land!

Robert mentions being at the funeral of your valued friend General Helm. The services were conducted by the Episcopal minister. His widow is now in Atlanta, where he was buried. He says he felt inclined to call and see her, but was afraid it would be intrusive. I hope he will do so, for he is "a son of consolation." If I knew where to find his honored mother, Mrs. Helm, I should feel like writing her. Truly does my heart grieve with both of them.

My son, nearly all of your classmates at Cambridge who were your personal friends are no more. One by one they have fallen in manhood's prime. God in love and mercy still prolongs your days. I trust it is that you may yet glorify Him on earth by a consistent and devoted Christian life. It is a great comfort to me to know that you observe your morning and evening devotions, reading the Scriptures and prayer. . . . Every night when I put your baby to sleep she says: *"Sing Jesus Christ."* Already has she learned to lisp that precious name. God grant that it may be engraven on her heart!

I was happy to know that you had made a visit to Augusta, and left dear Eva and all friends well. Gilbert will be at your service when you call for him. Would you desire me to go to Savannah and see about the removal and fixing of your furniture? If so, I will do it with pleasure, and postpone my visit to Augusta until November. I know it is so difficult to get anyone at this time to do such things; and I feel now that my life and time are only valuable as I can make them useful to my children, the church, and those who are dependent upon me. Write and let me know what I can do for you. I hope Mr. Lamar will make good the wear and tear upon your household goods. *Use,* I presume, does not mean *abuse.*

I have not yet seen the servants from Indianola. *Tom* has been doing very well thus far; has made eight pair of shoes for the children, besides mending, and over a dozen lasts of various sizes, all of which display quite a genius in design and execution. I will make him for the present complete the tanning and make up some shoes for the needy ones here. He is certainly a smart boy, and learned well in Mount Vernon.

Do when you write tell me what your command consists of, and what is General Taliaferro's on James Island. Present my respects to the general. I am happy to know that you are associated with a gentleman and officer of whom we formed so pleasant an impression; and the position he now occupies proves his country's estimate of his worth and ability. I do not wonder that he remembered your beloved father, for I think no one could forget his appearance and manners. They strikingly illustrated his noble character.

Time and paper fail. Nearly 12 M. All in bed but your mother. Love from your sister. Kisses from your own child. The servants send many howdies, and are always inquiring after you. God bless and save you, my dear son!

Ever your affectionate mother,
Mary Jones.

Mrs. Mary Jones *to* Col. Charles C. Jones, Jr.[g]

Walthourville, *Thursday,* October 8th, 1863

My dear Son,

Yours of the 5th is just at hand. I will do all in my power to help you. It is now rather late in the week to make arrangements for sending Gilbert, as Sabbath intervenes; but I will go to Montevideo tomorrow, D.V., and direct him to go down to Savannah on Monday accompanied by Tom. I will, if God wills, take Flora and be there on the 15th or 16th, as many hands are said to make light work. I hope all things will be in readiness. Grace and Adeline will, I presume, be there also to assist in washing and cleaning. You had best order a barrel of lime sent to the lot at once for the use of the boys in cleansing the kitchen and servants' rooms and yard. Do you wish the carpets put down? Perhaps Eva would prefer to arrange according to her own taste. I will just see to the purifications.

As I shall be much engaged, I do not care to have any friend know of my being in town, and would prefer to stay quietly at Mr. Ward's, or your own house as soon as it is habitable. Our little ones still have colds. I hope you will soon be well. I will direct Gilbert to go to Mr. Johnson for the keys, etc. With our united love,

Ever your affectionate mother,
Mary Jones.

Col. Charles C. Jones, Jr., *to* Mrs. Mary Jones[g]

James Island, *Monday,* October 12th, 1863

My very dear Mother,

I am today in receipt of your dear letters of the 7th and 8th inst., and am sincerely indebted to you for all your great kindness. Amanda has also promised me to do anything that she can to assist in putting the house in order. Johnson, my clerk at the barracks, will execute any directions which you may give. Your room at Mr. Ward's will be all ready. They will commence moving on the 15th; and I cannot tell you, my dear mother, how grateful I am to you for giving me at this time the invaluable benefit of your kind supervision.

The back parlor Eva wants me to have as a study, and desires all the books arranged there in their respective cases. My cabinet can also stand there. The third room on the first floor we will, D.V., use as a dining room. The front room upstairs I presume Eva will use as her room, and I would be glad if it could be put in order for us, as we expect to come down to Savannah just after our marriage. I would also be glad to have all the carpets put down at once. . . . I have asked Johnson to have all necessary whitewashing done, and I also enclosed him one hundred dollars to defray expenses connected with removal. I will send any more should it be needed. I am very anxious to save all the gas fixtures in my former house. Mrs. Harriss has a complete list of all articles turned over to Mr. Lamar, and Amanda will get it from her and show it to you. Grace and Adeline will be relieved from Mr. Lamar's service on the 15th inst. Do, my dear mother, give just such directions as you may deem best. I am but too happy to think that you will be there.

I hope to be able to spend at least a day in Savannah before going up to Augusta. On what day will you go to Augusta? I trust, my dear mother, that you will not deny us that great pleasure, and I hope that Sister and Aunt Susan will accompany you.

Will you please if convenient have my books and clothing and glass, etc., sent in, and also my boxes of Indian remains, and my cabinet, so soon as the house is ready to receive them. Will you also be good enough to bring in with you my seal and key, that I may place it upon my watch. I am deeply obliged to you for the services of Gilbert. I think that Johnson will prove very valuable to you in carrying out any directions which you may give.

I deeply regret to learn that you and my dear little daughter are still suffering from severe colds, and trust that you both will be soon entirely relieved and restored to perfect health.

My command here consists of six full light batteries of four guns each. I have under my command about six hundred men—a command which I would not exchange for that of any brigadier general on the island. General Taliaferro is the ranking brigadier general on the island. He desires me to present his acknowledgments for your kind remembrance of him.

I am happy to hear that Tom has been behaving himself so well, and trust that he will give no further trouble. . . . Do kiss my precious little daughter for me. Love to Sister and the little ones. And believe me ever, my dear mother,

Your ever affectionate and obliged son,
Charles C. Jones, Jr.

Mrs. Mary Jones *to* Col. Charles C. Jones, Jr.[g]

Walthourville, *Tuesday,* October 13th, 1863

My dear Son,

I am in receipt of your two last favors, and reenclose you Mr. Cassel's letter. As you suggest, perhaps it would be best to allow him to remain until 1864 upon the terms which he considered as agreed upon, cutting pine alone. I did not know that they had been positive; neither did I know that he had anyone associated with him. Did he mention that fact when he applied for a place on the Island? I feel that no individual has a right to secure a privilege for himself apparently when he has associated others in the business whose claims are afterwards urged. We must inform Audley of the permission until 1864. If we allow it, the Island will be denuded by the salt-boilers. I feel that the terms I suggest are just and right. Salt now commands thirty-five dollars per bushel! Audley told me there were others wanting wood, and that the companies on our land gave each of them fifty dollars a month for the *use* of *the water.*

As the gin had to be fixed (trunks, casts, etc.) I have kept Porter back until done. He said William and Niger could go on without him. When he returns I will forward the salt on hand—or earlier if you wish it. I will send what I have, and Mr. Sconyers must use it prudently, but plentifully in curing the bacon. I would be glad if he would collect for me a barrel of black walnuts. He could send them in one of the molasses barrels, and I will return it with syrup. I wrote hoping to secure a barrel of flour in Atlanta, but have failed. Will you be able to let me have a sack from Indianola for winter's use?

A letter yesterday from my dear Joe tells me he would soon be with you. I long to see him and his dear family.

Yesterday Gilbert and Tom left for Savannah with two large trunks and two boxes with all your articles here excepting the cabinet and books, etc., at Arcadia. I gave Gilbert not only a pass for the railroad but one to Mr. Johnson at the barracks and in the city for the removal of your furniture from Mr. Lamar's on the 15th under Mr. Johnson's direction. Tomorrow, D.V., I hope to go down myself with my maid Flora, and will be at the house to receive the articles on the 15th. I am glad you have furnished a list of your household effects. I will take up my abode at Mr. Ward's as you invite me to do, and hope we shall be favored in accomplishing the desired object.

I write in haste for the mail. You can write me in Savannah your wishes about anything you desire. All well today, through divine goodness! Robert expected tomorrow. With our united love, and kisses from your daughter,

Ever your affectionate mother,
Mary Jones.

Wish I could have seen your review.

MRS. MARY JONES *to* COL. CHARLES C. JONES, JR.[g]

Savannah, Monday, October 19th, 1863

My dear Son,

Your favor of the 16th is at hand this morning, and I presume you would like to know the progress of your business affairs. Gilbert and Tom were sent down on Monday the 12th. On Tuesday the 13th *Mr. Johnson* (and here ere I forget let me say no one could be more faithful and attentive to your interest or polite to your mother) commenced moving, so that when I arrived with my maid Flora on the 14th your furniture, etc., was all in your new hired house.

The cars were crowded; the train slow. I did not reach Savannah until after dark. Mr. Wells was in the cars, and obtained a carriage for me at the depot. Mr. Ward's faithful servants were at their posts, and received me hospitably. I went to my room, and having taken a basket of provisions, my tea and breakfast were at hand. That night it rained, thundered, and lightninged. I was sleepless, and after due efforts to forget myself struck a light and read. Rose at drumbeat. Went to the house in Mrs. Howard's carriage, kindly sent, for the streets were swimming. Soon found ample employment. Robert came during the day; and that evening, as all the blankets, quilts, etc., had passed into the washtub, I returned to Mr. Ward's. Your sister unexpectedly came in, and soon after Mrs. Winn, her daughter, and Mrs. McIver. My lunch basket was produced, and a very genteel entertainment drawn from it. They expected additional friends, so I have not returned there, but enjoyed the luxury of quiet and loneliness here. Your sister and Robert went out on Saturday, taking Tom with them. He was very unwell, and I feared might get ill. He has taken to tobacco, and I believe it makes him sick and stupid.

All the carpets are down. . . . Your bookcases, etc., look charmingly in the middle room. Four windows being to the front room and the shades not fitting, I have not put them up. . . . The gas fixtures are in place, but the gas not on yet. I am using candles, for which a patent for running away ought to be obtained.

Has it occurred to your mind that your whole household could not exist very comfortably on the ethereal substance called love? I have sent to Patience to get you some poultry, and ordered in your bag of rice. There is also not a knife or fork or spoon in the house but those of Adeline's.

This afternoon I will send for the oilcloth from Mr. Lamar's and have it put down in the upstairs entry, which is uncovered. Flora and Grace are cleaning and polishing the furniture today. Gilbert and Tom are washing glasses, etc. I hope all things will be ready to answer your expectations.

And above all, my son, may God add His blessing upon your marriage! If He has healed your breaches and again bestowed upon you a beloved companion, your first duty will be to *acknowledge Him in your family*. I do not wish dear Eva and yourself to dwell beneath a shelterless roof.

If, my dear son, circumstances should prevent my going to Augusta, I think you will understand them. I want to return home as soon as your house is in order. I long to see my darling baby. Your sister thinks they will go up very soon to Atlanta. I shall have to help her, and move myself to Arcadia. Many claims from all at home are upon me. It would be a great happiness to see you married, but I could add little to the occasion. Did you inform your Uncles William and John of the event? . . . In haste,

Ever your affectionate mother,
Mary Jones.

XX

Atlanta, *Thursday,* November 12th, 1863

My dear Mother,

I snatch a few moments to tell you of our safe arrival and prosperous journey. We left Savannah on Tuesday morning at half-past five, and after a long day of slow traveling reached Macon at seven o'clock. We spent the night very comfortably at the Brown House. It was so late when we reached Macon that we thought it would be an intrusion to go to Cousin Mary's house; and then there was only one small hack that would take passengers to private houses, and this could not have accommodated ourselves and baggage. I saw Mr. Nisbet at the cars the next morning; he is larger than ever, and said Cousin Mary and Hattie were quite well. I regretted not being able to see them.

We arrived here last evening and went immediately to the Trout House; but Mr. Pease kindly sent his carriage and insisted upon our coming to his house, which we did, leaving all the servants except Tenah at the hotel. We expect to go to Marietta this afternoon. Mr. Pease has made an arrangement by which we will go immediately to Dr. Calhoun's house and thus avoid the necessity of the second move we anticipated. . . . Mr. and Mrs. Pease are very hospitable, and have invited us to remain until our furniture is moved; but I feel this would really be an imposition, for they have had a great deal of sickness among their servants; and now their niece is sick, and they fear it will prove a case of typhoid fever. I thought we had better go to Marietta and remain with Aunty until we could go to the house. I do not yet know what disposition will be made of the furniture until that time. Mr. Mallard has gone out hoping they will allow it to remain in the car.

The children have been quite pleased with the journey, though they begin to feel that they are a long way from Grandmama.

I was very glad Brother Charlie and Eva came from the up country in time for us to see them. I should have been delighted to have seen more of them, but it was impossible for us to remain longer. I think we will all love Eva very much.

Mr. Mallard has improved very much, though he is still very yellow. He is regaining his strength, and has a fine appetite.

Please excuse my writing the first part of this with pencil: I had no ink. The children send much love and kisses to dear Grandmama and Little Sister. Love to Aunt Mary and Ellen if they are with you; also to Aunt Susan and Cousin Laura. Mr. Mallard unites with me in warmest love to you, dear Mother. Howdy for the servants.

Your affectionate daughter,
Mary S. Mallard.

Mrs. Mary S. Mallard *to* Mrs. Mary Jones[t]

Marietta, *Monday,* November 16th, 1863

My dearest Mother,

The children and myself came here on last Friday afternoon. I found Aunty on the bed with a little fever; she looks rather thinner than when we last saw her, but is still cheerful and interested in all passing events. She has knit a pair of stockings for Mamie, and is now knitting a pair of socks for Charlie. . . . I was sorry to bring so large a family here, but we were at a loss to know what to do. I left Lucy with Mrs. Pease, as her servants had been sick and she was glad to have her assistance. Mr. Mallard was to have been installed yesterday, and expects to come here this afternoon.

I came here under Mr. William King's escort. He is perfectly delighted with his daughters' marriages. Says Lizzie's husband is the most eloquent man he ever heard; and Mr. Bowman has a charming parish near Staunton, and his people are unbounded in their kind attentions, regarding their minister as the dispenser of their hospitalities. In one month they received ten barrels of flour, and often find hams and flour rolled in their yard and never know from what source they came. I hope a like spirit may prevail in other congregations: high prices and scarcity are said to prevail to an alarming extent up here.

Yesterday we had a regular war sermon from a Dr. Elliott, a chaplain from Tennessee. His text was the curse of Ham, and his object to show that this was a religious war—the Bible arraigned against infidelity. He had a thorough knowledge of the Yankee character, and anyone that had ever lived among them could testify to the truth of his statements. Some of his ideas were novel. He thought it was a duty binding upon us all to bring the sons of Ham into subjection, and predicted that the day would come when instead of sending missionaries to Africa, overseers and taskmasters would be sent, and when the people were brought into subjection, then they would be Christianized. Another idea advanced was that families who freed their slaves never prospered, because it was a violation of the law of God. Excepting these odd ideas, it was a very good discourse, though not altogether suitable for the Sabbath.

All of the public buildings on the square here are converted into hospitals. It would do your heart good to see how beautifully they are kept. Everything about them is as neat and clean as possible, and very comfortable. I went through a number of the wards with Aunt Lou this morning. We took the children, and they carried little baskets of crackers and were greatly delighted to hand them to the sick soldiers. The cots are provided with very comfortable mattresses, and all have nice sheets and comforts made of homespun. Some wards have calico comforts, and there is a piece of rag carpet spread by the side of every cot. And the men were as clean as possible. The rooms are well ventilated, so that there is no odor of sickness, and the nurses are very attentive. Any want of attention is very severely punished. Last week a nurse was found sleeping, and the surgeon punished him by causing him to lie down with heavy logs of wood placed upon him. Another punishment is to gag them. Miss Lizzie Fraser has entered one of the wards as matron. She has gone in for the war, and receives forty dollars a month. Her business is to see that the food is properly prepared and dispensed. The nurses (men) and physicians attend to the diseases and wounds. She has nothing to do with them. Aunt Lou says I must tell you that if you were only here she could give you more than you could do; says she would give you Wards No. 8 and 10. Amongst the wounded is a Cherokee Indian; the children were very much interested in seeing him. The rooms are all comfortably warmed, and I think all who come to nurse their friends must be delighted to find them so well cared for.

Mamie and Charlie send their love to you, and say I must tell you they have been to the "hossipal" to see our wounded Confederate soldiers. They speak of you every day, and feel it is time for them to be going to see you again. They do not realize how widely we are separated. I do not like to think of this, dear Mother. It is just eight months today since dear Father was taken from us. It seems to me that years have rolled away since then. My thoughts are often with you in that consecrated spot at Midway.

I hope we will be able to return to Atlanta this week, and next week I hope we will be established in our new home. I am very anxious to be settled.

Aunty sends you many thanks for the cow. I presume it will arrive today. Mary Sophia can make feather flowers very prettily, and I think if she had the feathers she might be induced to make them. She is very anxious to get some, and I think if you could send some by Aunt Mary she would be delighted to have them. The small breast feathers and the feathers under the wings are used. Aunty, Aunt Lou, and Mary Sophia all send much love to you, and to Aunt Mary if she is still with you. . . . Do give much love to Aunt Susan and Cousin Laura. The children send many kisses for Grandmama and Little Sister. Tell Little Sister not to forget "Anna." Accept the warmest love of

Your attached daughter,
Mary S. Mallard.

MRS. MARY S. MALLARD *to* MRS. MARY JONES[t]

Marietta, Monday, November 23rd, 1863

My dear Mother,

I have not heard one word from you since we left, but presume letters must be awaiting me in Atlanta. Mr. Mallard left me on last Tuesday for

Synod. He expected to have returned on Saturday to Atlanta in order to fill the pulpit yesterday. . . . I hope we will be able to go to Atlanta tomorrow.

Mr. Mallard made Charles drive the cow up here, for he found it would be delayed some days if he waited to send it by the cars, and it was only twenty-four miles and a plain road. Aunty begs me to return many thanks for it. They have had great difficulty in getting her to eat at all. She is now beginning to eat a little wet straw, but does not take to the washing at all. I hope they will be able to keep her, but unless she improves very much the milk will not pay for the feed. She has improved within a day or two, and now gives a teacup at a milking. The horse and cows all looked very badly after their journey, and I presume it will take them a week or two to recover.

We have all had severe colds; they seem to be prevailing. Charlie had quite a warm fever, and said to me: "Mama, I am afraid I will die." I asked him why he thought so; he said: "Because I am so sick." He had evidently been recalling his dear little sister's sickness and death. He is quite bright today, and I think will have no return of fever. Mamie begs me to tell you Aunt Eliza has promised her brother and herself two beautiful kittens for little pets. . . .

Aunt Mary wrote that a spy had been seen on Colonel's Island, and the salt-boilers had suspended operations for a time. Where did the spy come from—from the blockaders or Savannah? If there seems to be any danger of a raid, you must come right up to us.

Affairs appear rather brighter in the West at present. Some hope we may be able to capture Burnside; and if so, Rosecrans' army may be compelled to evacuate Chattanooga.

One of General Morgan's escaped men called here a few days ago. I did not see him, but Aunt Lou said he was a very handsome young soldier. He made his escape by crawling under the wall when the back of the guard was turned; and he said that any of the guards could be bought with ten dollars, and prisoners frequently escaped.

Do give much love to Aunt Susan and Cousin Laura; also to Aunt Julia's family. Aunt Eliza and Aunt Lou send much love to you. Kiss dear Little Sister for me. Charlie says tell Grandma some little dear pussies are playing with him. Mamie and himself send love and kisses to you. Accept the warmest love of

Your affectionate daughter,
Mary S. Mallard.

Excuse this paper: everything is packed up.

Mrs. Mary S. Mallard *to* Mrs. Mary Jones[t]

Atlanta, *Wednesday,* December 2nd, 1863

My dearest Mother,

I intended to have written you some days ago, but have been so busy and so tired that I could not.

We left Marietta on last Friday morning. On reaching this place we found Mr. Pease at the depot superintending the removal of our furniture, so I came immediately to the house to receive the furniture while Mr. Mallard remained at the depot to load the drays. . . . I presume our furniture would have arrived in almost perfect order could we have removed it ourselves from the car; but unfortunately for us, the government needed the car just two days before we were ready, so they tumbled everything into the ware-room. The result was a terrible scratching of everything and the breakage of one of the mahogany and one of the walnut chairs. I think, however, they can both be mended; and I hope to remove most of the scratches. The marble top of my drawers was broken in half. I will try and have it cemented.

What I grieve for most of all is the loss of my box of candles—that box which I made and put aside in July for Atlanta use. I trust it may come to light yet, though I fear it was stolen from the wareroom. This is a serious loss, for candles are six dollars a pound. Fortunately I had two or three dozen in another box.

I spent Friday here receiving the things. Mrs. Pease sent us a nice dinner and insisted upon our spending the night with her, which we did. Saturday was a most uncomfortable rainy day. However, we came over and have been here ever since. Mrs. Pease kindly sent us dinner again on Saturday, and on Sunday morning two loaves of bread and some butter. Mr. Pease sent some wood the day we arrived, and says he means to see that we are supplied. He has been as thoughtful and kind as possible; no one could have been more so.

Sabbath was a cold, windy, freezing day. We went to church morning and night, but it was so bitterly cold that only a few were out in the evening. The thermometer had fallen to 20°, and the wind blowing a perfect gale, so you can judge how we felt. After the evening service a gentleman remained and sought an introduction to Mr. Mallard, and requested him to call and see him the next day. He wished to see him "particularly for his own personal good." His name is Captain Alphonse Hurtel. Has charge of twelve hundred men, six hundred of whom are deserters, the rest Yankees. Mr. Mallard called at the prison and found that Captain Hurtel had been educated a Romanist, but in Mexico had seen the church in its power and corruption and had renounced the religion of his boyhood and become a skeptic. A few years ago he married a pious Presbyterian. Since then he has been converted, and he says one of Mr. Mallard's sermons has been blessed to him and determined him to make a profession of religion at once. His wife is in Mobile. Mr. Mallard thinks he will join our church at the next Communion. Is not this an interesting case?

Monday morning was even colder than Sabbath. When we woke, every-thing was frozen in our room. It was so cold I suppose our congregation must have been sorry for us, for five loads of wood were sent us during the day. Dr. Logan sent three, Colonel Grant one, and a Mr. Demarest one, directed to "Preacher Mallard." Mrs. Logan sent me a basket of nice Irish potatoes and two pieces of butter done up in Philadelphia style with a thistle stamped upon them. With the potatoes and butter was a pound cake sent by little Joe Logan to the children. Tuesday morning we had more butter sent by a Mr. Cole, and today Mrs. Pease sent me a loaf of bread and some fresh pork. So you see, the first week at the parsonage opens very pleasantly. Truly God has been very good to us, and I trust He will give us grateful hearts. If it were not for this terrible war, I would have more heart about this removal. Sometimes my strength almost fails me.

Mr. Mallard and Charles have been busy whitewashing, and I hope to get pretty well fixed by Saturday; but there is a world of work to be done both in and out of doors. I am on the whole quite pleased with the house. It has six rooms—four in the main building and two in the wing. I shall occupy the two in the wing, and intend to have a door cut between them, as they are very small, being only twelve by eleven feet. The other rooms are very little larger. The parlor is thirteen by fifteen four, and the drawing room a little smaller. They are neat and comfortable rooms, and I think we will find the house a warm one. It is quite near enough to walk to church. The lot is very large; indeed, I may say we have quite a field attached. The basement is very high; in it are two servants' rooms, a kitchen, and another room which I shall use as an open pantry and ironing room. I believe the Calhouns used it as a dining room. Besides these, there is a smokehouse and servants' room under one roof with a washing shed between. In this there is a large pot set in a furnace for washing. The fence around the lot is so dilapidated that the cows cannot be kept out. It will have to be thoroughly repaired before we can plant anything. I have been thus particular in my account of our arrangements, my dear mother, thinking you would like to know everything.

There is no special news from the front today. Fears are entertained for Longstreet's safety, his position being regarded as a very perilous one. Report says General Bragg has been relieved of his command at his own request. Our defeat was shameful and most humiliating. Mr. Bryson, who went to the front just after the battle, told Mr. Mallard it was the most disgraceful defeat of the war; that several regiments threw down their arms without firing a gun and ran when the Yankees advanced. It is said the South Carolinians were among the first to run. It was what we would have called "a regular skedaddle" if it had happened with the Yankees. Some say the army was demoralized before the battle because of insufficient food. I cannot vouch for the truth of this. I presume the men had no confidence in their general. I am glad he has been relieved of his command. It is very difficult to hear anything reliable. Our army is between Ringgold and Dalton, General Hardee commanding until Bragg's place is filled. The last accounts state the Yankees were retreating. I presume they are hastening to support Burnside. If we only had force enough to advance upon them, perhaps we might gain some of the advantages we have lost.

I left Aunt Eliza much better. She had taken several walks, and had missed her fever. Aunt Lou and herself were very kind to us; I do not know what we should have done if they had not kindly taken us in. The cow was improving. When I came here, I found that our own cow had fallen away very much, and does not give one-third as much as she did; but she is improving, and I hope will give as much as she did before.

I forgot to mention that the well is under one corner of the piazza. It seems a queer place to have put it, but it was dug there to be convenient to the kitchen. I would rather have it farther off. Red clay abounds here.

I have reserved the upstairs front room for you, dear Mother, and it is ready for you, and we are all waiting to welcome you. Poor little Charlie made up his mind last night to go to Arcadia this morning to see Grandma and Little Sister, and when I told him it was too far for him to go this morning, he had a cry about it. He said he wanted to go to Arcadia to see Grandma. Mamie says I must tell you she has a new front tooth and had one of the old ones pulled out, which she put under her head, and a heap of nice things came in its place. She says tell you she is learning to unbutton all her own clothes.

I have not seen Mr. Rogers yet. I have thought it charity in the people not to call, and hope none of them will call until next week.

You know how funny Mamie is about getting names wrong. Dr. Calhoun has taken everything away that he possibly could, and yesterday Mamie came to tell me Dr. *Cocoon* had sent for the lock on the chicken coop! Charlie and herself send love and many kisses to their dear grandmama and Little Sister. Mr. Mallard unites with me in warmest love. Howdy for the servants. Do give love to Uncle William, Aunt Susan, and Cousin Laura and Cousin Lyman.

Your affectionate daughter,
Mary S. Mallard.

Rev. John Jones *to* Mrs. Mary Jones[t]

Refuge, Monday, December 7th, 1863

My dear Sister,

For a number of weeks I felt uncertain of your locality, and I wrote to Joseph to know if you had left Augusta. I desired to know certainly when you would be in Liberty. He wrote me about ten days since that you had left for Liberty about two weeks.

I expected fully to have seen you during this month, but having closed with my overseer up to the 1st of this month on last Saturday, I am compelled to remain closely at home until I can obtain another, which will be the 1st of January. I am truly tired of my daily cares; they are without number. To clothe and shoe and properly feed our Negroes and pay our taxes requires more than we make by planting, especially when debts have to be paid. I believe the most pressed people in our Confederacy are the owners of slaves who have no way to support them. Sometimes I think that Providence by this cruel war is intruding to make us willing to relinquish slavery by feeling its burdens and cares.

Our future often looks dark; the enemy draws nearer. If he passes the mountain barriers of Georgia, the whole state will be most probably overrun. And if Georgia is lost, the Confederacy will scarcely survive, for Georgia is the keystone state of our young republic. But the Lord reigns, and into His hands we must commit our hopes and interests.

Providence permitting, I will come to Liberty in January. I long to see you and to visit the scenes and places which will remind me of my dear brother. I desire to stand on the sacred spot where his precious body is sleeping so quietly. The more I think of him and recall his past life, the more am I impressed by his strong character and remarkable piety. He walked with God. Alas, why can I not be more like him? Why do I not love the precious Redeemer as he did? Oh, for his steady piety, his constant pursuit of duty, his unwavering devotion to the Kingdom of the Redeemer!

And now one word about Bonaventure, etc. Do cheer Old Mama up until I come for her. I wrote Mr. Delegal some time ago to deliver to you the hogs whenever you should call for them. And I requested Mr. Delegal to have the hogs fattened that would be fit for bacon this winter. I do not know the number. But after first taking your own for stock, etc., will you have the balance—say, such as are fit for bacon—killed and cured. And for your trouble take one-third of the hogs killed. The salt I will be able to return to you if Mr. Mallard has made any, as he is to give me one-tenth for the privilege of manufacturing on my place.

We are all quite well, through a kind Providence, colds excepted. My dear Jane and little boys unite with me in our best love to you and the dear little baby.

Your ever affectionate brother,
John Jones.

Mrs. Mary Jones *to* Mrs. Mary S. Mallard[t]

Arcadia, Tuesday, December 8th, 1863

My dearest Daughter,

Your long and most interesting letter was received yesterday, and told me your occupations just as I had imagined—putting to rights in all this bitter cold weather. I think of you all constantly, and the fervent prayer of my heart ascends daily for God's blessing upon Robert in his new and at this time very peculiar field of labor and usefulness. . . . I have often wished you could have remained with me until January, as I was anxious for you to have done; and should the situation of Atlanta become more perilous, I hope Robert will consent *at once* to your coming immediately home.

Since the recent fright our coast has been quiet. I wrote you of the abandonment of the Island—although Audley tells me he hopes soon to resume his salt-boiling. I have no doubt the Yankees visit our shore whenever they are inclined. They went recently to Mr. O. Hart's in Bryan and took several of his Negroes away whilst he was at home.

I hope you have received all my letters. I have not written you for the past ten days, as I have during that time been in bed confined to the chamber with a severe cold, and am still keeping my room. The cold was contracted going to Montevideo *very early* an intensely cold morning last week to see a sick Negro (*Delia*). Everything was frozen, and we crushed through ice as the buggy passed on.

I feel so grateful to the good people of Atlanta for their remembrance of you in the *wood,* and especially to Mr. and Mrs. Pease. They have been true friends.

Joe wrote me he had to give thirty-five dollars a cord for most *inferior wood.* I know he must find it hard to supply his family. They have had a great deal of company, and Titus very sick with pneumonia and fearing measles. I shall expect them before long. Our friend Kitty is now with them, and they expected a visit from Edward's wife to see Kitty.

Cousin Mary and Ellen left me on Friday, both looking very well. They speak of a visit to Clifford and Maria before their return home.

Charles and Eva are quite well, and Mrs. Eve and Captain Edgeworth Eve are with them. Eva and her mother were to have come out on Monday, but I was too unwell to receive *Mrs. E.*

The servants, too, have severe colds and sore throats. I have had Phillis trying to cut out the Negro clothes, and she went to her bed yesterday.

On Monday *Rose* resumed her spinning. I thought your wheel, cards, work, etc., would perhaps get on best in the washroom, so she comes there every day and brings me the yarn at night, which I will send as soon as she has enough done. Mrs. Andrews sent by James thirty-one yards of cloth (striped) beautifully woven—the best we have had done. Said she would finish the rest as soon as the yarn came. I will send this up to your people in Burke (as the opportunity offers of doing so) with what I have, which is not half enough for their wants.

I really feel that I can hardly undertake what I have been doing, for my strength and—what is more, I often fear—my nervous system are failing. Oh, my daughter, the desolation of heart which I feel is beyond expression! The death of your beloved father every day presses more and more heavily upon me. To lose such a guide, such a companion, one so tender and sympathizing as a husband, with whom I had never a reserved thought, so wise in all counsel and arrangements—above all, my spiritual guide and instructor in things heavenly and divine! . . . I know that God is able to fill the void I feel within; but I fear the pressing burden of earthly care and occupation, the many and ceaseless calls upon time, all are bowing me down to this earth like a millstone about my neck. If I could only imitate your father's example whilst attending to all earthly duty! His conversation and heart were in heaven.

Tell my darling Mary and Charlie Grandmama loves them dearly and wants to see them every day and will write them a little letter soon. Little Sister talks of them constantly and sends sweetest kisses. She constantly asks where you all are, even to Abram. I must close, as I ought to be in bed. With best love to Robert and yourself, and kisses for the children, and howdies for the servants,

Ever your own affectionate mother,
Mary Jones.

I hope your candles will be recovered. . . . Tell Tenah Niger is quite well. When Robert has time, I would be glad to know if he could be hired to some good man and good work. The servants all send howdies to you and the children and to your servants.

Mrs. Mary S. Mallard *to* Mrs. Mary Jones[t]

Atlanta, *Friday,* December 11th, 1863

My dearest Mother,

I have this evening received your letter written on the 8th. I am truly thankful to receive it, for I was beginning to fear you or Little Sister were sick. This is only the second time that I have heard from you since I left, and I think this is the sixth letter I have written you. I am very sorry you have been suffering from cold, and sincerely hope this attack will not prove as serious as that you had last winter; I remember how much you suffered, and how much flesh you lost. I don't think the climate of Arcadia is as healthy as Montevideo.

I wish, my dear mother, that you could be relieved of care, for I have long seen that your nervous system had more than it could bear. Ah, well do I know that your desolation of heart must increase; and as each month rolls by and brings its precious associations, our hearts are filled with deeper sorrow because our guide and counselor—our light—has been taken away. The 16th of this month will soon be here to remind us that we have passed nine such periods (and oh, how long they have been!) without our loving, sympathizing father. And then come the 20th and 21st—days peculiarly precious to you, filled with many hallowed memories. Pleasant memories and associations they are too; and although there is so much of sorrow when we feel they are gone never to return, still I feel we may have much real enjoyment and cheerful pleasure in recalling them all.

Last Sabbath evening Dr. Stiles took tea with us. I thought so much of my dear father. I wish you could be with us at this time. Dr. Stiles is about to commence a "protracted meeting," which will continue a week or ten days in the Baptist church (Dr. Brantly's). . . . Yesterday was an interesting day here, and I hope it was observed in Liberty, and presume it was; for if ever our people need to humble themselves, it is now. Mr. Mallard preached in our church in the morning. Dr. Stiles preached for Dr. Brantly. Our services closed in time for us to hear a very large fraction of the doctor's sermon. He labored to show that our nation must cry unto God or our cause was lost. In the afternoon there was a union prayer meeting held in our church. . . . I trust great good will grow out of this meeting to be held by Dr. Stiles. Perhaps our city may be saved by it, or in some degree prepared for any trials that may be in store for us.

Our last defeat was most disastrous to our cause. It is said our men did run in a most disgraceful manner. They were completely panic-stricken on the left wing. General Bragg is said to have done his duty bravely, and it is reported that he cut down one officer whom he could not rally. The officer will probably die. The report today is the Yankees have fallen back to Chattanooga and have burned and destroyed everything in the country. Our army is at Dalton. Atlanta is being fortified. Some think the next fall back will be to this place. Very dark days may be in store for us, but I trust God will in His merciful kindness keep the enemy from this place.

If it were not for this cruel war, I think we would find this a pleasant and interesting home. Mr. Mallard's field is extensive, and opens very encouragingly and pleasantly. Next Sabbath we will have Communion. Today two gentlemen called to see Mr. Mallard in his study; both desire to connect themselves with the church. . . . This afternoon an old gentleman called to beg Mr. Mallard to see his son, for whom he felt deeply concerned. The other night after prayer meeting a soldier spoke to Mr. Mallard and asked if he was the pastor of the church and said he wished to connect himself with it. I mention these things to show how encouraging and inviting a field it seems to be.

We have had a number of calls. I have made the acquaintance of some very pleasant people. Mrs. Hull called this afternoon. Mr. Rogers inquired very particularly after and sent his respects to you. I have been introduced to Mrs. Brantly, and she says I shall see her very soon. I think I shall have a very pleasant circle of acquaintances. Today a basket of sweet potatoes came from a Mrs. Gardner—a stranger to both of us, though a member of the church. She sent them a mile by her little son.

Our children have been quite well, and speak of you daily. Charlie cannot understand why I do not take him to Arcadia upon the days he appoints. As soon as your letter came this evening, Mamie ran to me and said: "Do let me kiss you for Grandmama." And Charlie came too, and after kissing me for you he said: "Now kiss me for Little Sister." Enclosed you will find what Mamie says is her letter and a lock of her hair which she promised you, and I think she says she has put in some babies for Little Sister and yourself.

We have had some very cold weather, and a few days of pleasant mild weather.

Charles begs me to say he gives his love to all the people, and tell Niger all are well, and Abram is getting very smart; and he wants Niger to intercede for his corn, which he left with Daddy Robin, and he wants him to sell it when the corn price rises. Charles also sends his best love to Mac. Tenah sends howdy for Niger, and says if he has any small hogs, he had better kill and cure them and bring the meat with him. Mr. Mallard will make inquiries about a place for Niger and write you. Did you ever receive the letter he wrote you about the cow? Kate has just come with her message, and begs to tell her sisters and father howdy for her, and begs her father if he has anything to spare please send it by Niger, and send the shoes she left with Augustus to be soled.

I am very glad to hear that Mrs. Andrews has sent home a part of the cloth. This will nearly clothe the people in the up country. I enclose twenty dollars. Will you be so kind, dear Mother, as to let Henry take it to Mrs. Andrews when she sends her bill? She promised to do these two pieces for money and the others for toll. I am glad it is nicely done. The other piece will be striped too. I think it would be well to send her another bunch of yarn before she completes what she has on hand, as it may secure her weaving it immediately. I wish we could spin by magic. It would assist us very much if we were near a carding factory. I am told there are a plenty around this place, but I do not know what they charge per pound. What do you think of yarn selling from thirty to thirty-five a bunch in Marietta? I priced it myself.

Everything is high. Wood has been sold at fifty dollars per cord here. We have bought some at the rate of forty dollars per cord. I have just engaged some tallow at three dollars per pound. This is much cheaper than candles at six dollars per pound. This is the common price for poor tallow candles. Everything else is in proportion.

The children send many kisses and love to Grandmama and Little Sister. Mr. Mallard unites with me in warmest love to you, dear Mother, and kisses for Little Sister. Howdy for the servants.

Your affectionate daughter,
Mary S. Mallard.

Mrs. Mary Jones *to* Mrs. Mary S. Mallard[t]

Montevideo, *Monday,* December 21st, 1863

My very dear Daughter,

I wrote Robert on the 18th, and on Saturday, feeling that a change was necessary to the recovery of health and strength, which have been failing since this attack of cold, I made the effort and came here—the first time for three weeks that I had been out of the house, I may say, having only walked into the yard once or twice in that time. The change, through divine favor, has been beneficial. Already I feel better, and have more enjoyment of food; and my cough and pain in the chest have greatly diminished. *This first* (after our marriage), this precious home had always peculiar charms for me. Your beloved father often asked if I was conscious of always singing as I came in sight of the house. That was purely an involuntary act; but there was an inward consciousness of emotions of peculiar gratitude and thankfulness to the Giver of every good gift for such an earthly home, and especially for him whose presence and kindness and affection made it all that my heart desired.

Yesterday was the anniversary of his fifty-ninth birthday, today the thirty-third of our marriage! And it was just such a cold, cloudless, brilliant December day as this. It was the first breath of winter upon the beautiful summer and autumn flowers that had lingered in the garden and were gathered to deck the bridal hall. That scene is now almost a vision of the imagination, and yet it is the reality in which I live. Life is now to me an empty shadow with the substance gone. Today I walked *alone* upon the beautiful lawn. I sat upon the blocks where he used to rest and mount his horse. I stood beneath the trees his own hands had trimmed. I listened to the song of the sweet birds he loved so well; saw his squirrels springing from bough to bough; recalled the unnumbered times when, side by side, we have walked together over every foot of ground, talking with unreserved confidence of all our plans for future improvement and usefulness. I could see him gazing up into the beautiful heavens above, or admiring the brilliant sunsets, or the stars as they shone forth in all their glory. He was never tired of contemplating the wonderful works of God. The whole creation was to his capacious mind, to his sanctified heart, the revelation of divine wisdom and goodness. None ever loved or appreciated or enjoyed the beautiful things of earth more than he did. Oh, my child, while grief for him and loneliness of heart must be the portion of my remaining days, I do bless my Lord and Saviour for the mercy and privilege of such a companionship, of such an association—that my lot was cast with such an eminent and godly minister. Oh, that I had been wise—that I had thought less of earthly things and had improved more faithfully his blessed example and his faithful precepts! How different would I now be! How much better prepared for the duties of life and for the solemn and fast-approaching realities of eternity! In view of my whole life all that I can say is: "God be merciful to me a sinner!"

I received today a joint letter from Joe and Carrie. Stanhope, Titus, and Rose have all been sick with measles, and they feared the baby was about to take them. They were only waiting to see if she would take them to come and make me a visit, and will do so as soon as they possibly can, and I hope stay a long time. Kitty was still with them. . . . Charles and Eva wrote me they hoped to be out on Christmas—only perhaps for the day. She is truly a lovely and most affectionate person. How I wish you were all with me!

Little Sister has knelt down several times today in the midst of her play and prayed: "God bless Bubber Sissy." She was delighted with the paper babies, and misses the children a great deal. I am knitting a pair of socks for Charlie, and she comes very often to know if I have "done them for Bubber."

Niger was greatly pleased to hear from his family, and wants to see them. Sends "tousand howdies." The servants all inquire and desire to be remembered. We have had severe colds among them; Patience is now quite unwell. How do you get on with your new cook? The old one is quite in her element—coats tied up at the middle and flailstick in hand, mouth spread from ear to ear.

Our friends at Flemington and in the county are well. Dr. Palmer and family, I am told, are in the county; hope I shall hear him preach. Kiss my precious grandchildren, and tell them not to forget *Grandpapa* nor Grandmama. Little Sister loves them dearly. May the Lord bless and keep you all in peace and safety! With much love to Robert. Howdies for your servants.

Ever your affectionate mother,
Mary Jones.

Mrs. Mary S. Mallard *to* Mrs. Mary Jones[t]
Atlanta, Monday, December 21st, 1863

My dearest Mother,

I did not write you last week, as my time was greatly occupied in attending Dr. Stiles's preaching. He commenced on fast day, preached twice that day and on Friday night; and on Sabbath he began his "protracted meeting," and preached morning and evening every day last week and twice yesterday. He has labored very hard. . . . Whenever I hear Dr. Stiles I feel I am in the presence of a gigantic intellect. I wish everyone could hear him on the necessity of the humbling of the nation before God in order that peace may be secured. He says it is absolute folly for us to say: "We can't be conquered"; for God will overrun and conquer us unless we turn to Him and quit relying upon the valor of our men. . . . On fast day Dr. Stiles gave a full, clear account and justification of secession which is said to have been exceedingly interesting. I did not attend, as we had preaching in our own church.

I must believe the departure of a portion of the enemy from Chattanooga has been in answer to prayer; for if they had chosen to have pressed on, they might have been investing this city; for it is said our army is small and was too much demoralized to have made any desperate resistance.

Last night the government sustained a heavy loss here in the burning of half of the fairground hospital. There were forty buildings in all; about twenty were destroyed, but I believe no lives lost. A valuable bale of blankets was consumed. Dr. Logan told Mr. Mallard he presumed the loss to the government would amount to one hundred thousand dollars.

Mr. Pease's family have been greatly afflicted within a few days by the death of Miss Addie Peck, of whom you may have heard Mr. Mallard speak as having been the pet of the whole family. Her disease was typhoid fever—the fifth case that has occurred in the family. The others were servants; and Mr. Pease thinks he must have had something of the kind. Miss Peck took her bed the day we came up, and has never left it, though the family seemed to have no special concern about her case until within a week of her death. ... Mr. Mallard conducted the funeral exercises in the church. Her body was taken to McIntosh County for interment. ... Mrs. Pease thinks of going to the low country in a few days. I trust she will, for I believe if she does not, the fever will go through the whole family. And she is very much worn by her long nursing.

Mr. Mallard has just received your letter. We are truly sorry to hear that your cold has continued so long. I hoped to have heard you were quite well. I wish so much you could be with us; and if you continue so unwell, do, dear Mother, come up. The weather is very cold, but I think the atmosphere is dry and exhilarating. We have had frequent changes and rainy weather, but we have suffered very little from colds. Those who live here tell us the winter is unusually cold. I have found my thick leather shoes the greatest comfort I ever had, for the soil is red clay and retains the moisture a long time.

A few days ago my box of candles came to light most unexpectedly. James had packed it in the barrel of rice. You may be sure I was rejoiced to see it. The syrup is so little we think it had much better be kept for sickness.

We took tea by invitation with Mr. and Mrs. Rogers. Mr. Mallard spoke to him about Niger, and he said perhaps he would hire him. His work would be cutting wood and hauling it into town for sale. He said he would let us know in a few days, and said there would not be the slightest difficulty about hiring him here at remunerative prices if he came. I hope Mr. Rogers will take him. He seems quite sanguine about his ironworks, and says if the Yankees will only keep away three months he will be able to repay the stockholders. I believe Brother Charlie has some fifty shares in that concern. There is charcoal enough burned to run the furnace three months, and it will be fired this week.

Mr. Mallard says he would be very much obliged to you to let Tom tan the calfskin.

We are expecting Aunt Mary Robarts to spend tomorrow night with us on her way to Marietta. I received a letter from Aunt Lou a few days ago, and she says they are again much disturbed to know what to do about moving away. If they move they will sell their house and lot, for they say everything would go to ruin if left, and if the Yankees ever occupy the place, they will desolate everything. The difficulty is to know where to go. They have begged us to spend Christmas with them, and we think of running up for the day.

This place is being fortified, but unless some reinforcements are sent to our army, we will not be very safe. Our only hope is in God.

Do give much love to Aunt Susan and Cousin Laura; also to Uncle William and Aunt Julia's family. Mr. Mallard and the children unite with me in warmest love to you, dear Mother. I hope you will be quite well before this reaches you. If you should get sick, be sure and send for me, and I will come immediately down. Tenah sends howdy for Niger. Howdy for the servants.

Your affectionate daughter,
Mary S. Mallard.

MRS. MARY S. MALLARD *to* MRS. MARY JONES[t]
Atlanta, *Wednesday,* December 30th, 1863

My very dear Mother,

I received your welcome letter on Monday evening. Mr. Mallard wrote you on Tuesday, so I thought I would delay writing until this evening.

Aunt Mary Robarts came yesterday afternoon and spent last night and today with us. She intended to have gone to Marietta at two o'clock today, and did make the attempt, but the engine ran off the track just by the depot, so she was obliged to wait for this evening's train. We deposited her safely in the cars and bade her good-bye, thinking she would soon be on her journey; but to our surprise she returned soon after, bringing as an escort a refugee from Tennessee—a Methodist minister, most peculiar in his appearance. I suppose he must be an albino: *white—snow-white*—eyebrows and lashes and pinkish eyes. We invited him to tea, as he expected to remain until the next train; and then he had been very kind in assisting Aunt Mary. Mr. Mallard has just returned from the cars; they left in a pouring rain. On the platform Aunt Mary discovered Governor Brown and family, so she introduced herself and Mr. Mallard. The governor had a baby upon his knee trying to shake it into quietude, but failing in his efforts, Mrs. Brown gave it the natural source of comfort. As there was some doubt about the train, Aunt Mary followed in the governor's wake, so I hope she will arrive safely.

We spent Christmas with Aunt Eliza. A quiet, pleasant day: no one there except ourselves. We had agreed to dine together, so I carried up a ham and turkey. The children enjoyed hanging up their stockings, and Mamie said Christmas was a merry, happy day. Charlie carried a small bottle of cream to Aunt Eliza which he told her was to make "sillybubble."

When we returned next day, I found a fat turkey awaiting me—a present from Mrs. Coleman, one of our members. She is a very pleasant lady; I am sorry she is going away. But it is so difficult to get provisions that she is going to LaGrange, where her father resides.

Aunt Eliza told me the history of that little silver acorn you keep in your pocket. Father's father gave it to Grandfather's first wife, and at the same time gave an egg to Aunt Eliza and something of the same description to Mrs. Maybank. So you see, you have a greater right to it than some other members of the family. I have never heard you say where it came from, and felt that its value was greatly enhanced when I heard who the donor was.

We feel quite anxious about Savannah, as reports have come that the Yankees have landed upon Skidaway. Do, dear Mother, if anything should happen to make you feel insecure, come immediately to us. It seems to be rather a general opinion that all the states must be overrun before the people are brought to a proper state of dependence upon God. Many think we must be humbled in this way before peace will dawn upon us.

The gentleman who took tea with us this evening was arrested in Tennessee, and with six bayonets at his breast was ordered to take the oath. He replied: "My life you can take, but my integrity you can't shake." He escaped while the Federals were plundering his father-in-law's house, stealing dresses and everything else; and such clothing as was useless to them they tore in shreds.

We have had very cold weather, but our people are very kind in sending us wood. This is a very great assistance. Mr. Pease says he means to see to it that we are supplied. He is very kind. His youngest child is now quite sick; they thought she would have died on Sabbath, but she is better now, though the fever still continues; and they are beginning to fear she has typhoid fever.

Dr. Stiles's meetings closed last week, and he went to Augusta to preach his sermon on "The State of the Country" in the Baptist church there. His preaching here was not attended with that awakening which we hoped for.

I am glad you are now at Montevideo, and hope the change may entirely restore you. It is certainly a more healthy winter climate; and then there is so much more to interest you there. I know you must feel as though Father were at times almost present with you. Every tree and plant upon that beautiful lawn is associated with him. It was a happy, happy home.

I am very sorry to hear Brother Joe and Carrie have had so much sickness; and yet it is a great relief to them to feel the children and servants have had measles. Kitty Stiles is in Macon now, and I presume she will soon pay us a visit.

The children are quite well; they and Mr. Mallard have enormous appetites and have all fattened. The children speak of you daily, and often appoint a time to go to see Little Sister and yourself. I do want to see her very much. Kiss her many times for us. The children send many kisses for dear Grandmama. . . . Howdy for the servants. The servants here send howdy.

Your affectionate daughter,
Mary S. Mallard.

Mrs. Mary Jones *to* Rev. R. Q. Mallard[t]
Montevideo, *Thursday,* December 31st, 1863
My dear Son,

Your kind favor was received the day before I came here; also that of my precious child, which was so interesting I could not refrain from sending it in for her brother's and Eva's perusal.

I am glad upon the whole that Mr. Quarterman has rendered so favorable a report of the present crop. As regards myself, be assured I have not the slightest claim to prefer to any of the marketable part. The only assistance I would like is in provisioning Kate and Patience, who are fixtures on the place, and Little Ebenezer, employed with the oxcart and gin. For my house and other servants and horses (both long and short forage) I have had all brought from this place ever since I moved down to Arcadia this fall, and find it such a troublesome business that I shall endeavor to remain here as much as possible. Our crop here, with the exception of corn, is exceedingly small. We have made a plenty of provisions for use, but know not if there will be any to sell. The rice was a failure; I will be glad to exchange about ten bushels with you for seed rice. We had no manager here until very late in the season. With the exception of colds the people have been well at Arcadia, and Mr. Quarterman attentive to business. Porter put the gin in order, and it has been doing well until a day or two since; something about it broke, which he is now repairing. Henry appears very cheerful and attentive to all his duties. The fact of your present manager's being compelled to pass this place whenever he visits his own renders it very convenient. You had better be assured of benefiting yourself before you make any change. It is now a most difficult thing to get anyone to take charge of planting. In all this matter you are the best judge, and I know will try to do for the best.

I rode over this afternoon to see Kate and Audley. Their infant is a lovely child; it reminded me of our dear little one now an angel in heaven. It is nearly five months since she joined her sainted grandfather.

This year, so memorable to us, is fast hastening to its close. . . . On last Sabbath Dr. Delegal was reported as dead, but he lived until Monday afternoon. Mr. Buttolph went to see him after church. He has been in a tranquil state of mind for some time, expressing his entire reliance upon the merits and righteousness of our Divine Redeemer and his hope of pardon and acceptance. His bodily sufferings were great; he was wasted to a skeleton. He leaves a widow and eight children, all young.

I am looking for Joe and Carrie very shortly, and for my brother. It will be a great happiness to have them with me.

Say to my grandson Charles Colcock the little socks are for him; and he must send Grandmama word if they fit, so that she may knit him another pair. And if my little granddaughter would like a pair of stockings like them, only ribbed narrower, I will knit a pair for her, and she must let me know. Or would she prefer a pair of red and white mitts?

My paper is out. *A Happy New Year!* May *God's blessing,* which alone can make it so, ever abide with you, my dear children!

Ever your affectionate mother,
Mary Jones.

Kisses from Little Sister. The servants all send howdies. As soon as a place can be found for Niger, I will send him up. Have you tried the tannery?

Mrs. Mary S. Mallard *to* Mrs. Mary Jones[t]

Atlanta, *Wednesday,* January 6th, 1864

My dear Mother,

Mr. Mallard received your letter containing the socks for Charlie last night. They are beautiful, and Charlie says I must say he is "must obliged" to you; that he means to wear the socks you knit to his papa's church, and those Aunt Eliza knit to Dr. Brantly's church! Mamie seems quite undecided which to choose—a pair of stockings or the mitts—so Grandmama will have to decide for her.

We have had intensely cold weather. On New Year's Day the thermometer was as low as six and seven degrees above zero—said to be the coldest weather known here since "the cold Saturday in 1834," when the mercury fell below zero. It was so cold that milk exposed for a short time to the wind froze at midday. I put out a little custard, and it was soon frozen into delightful ice cream. You may know how cold it was when the water remained frozen even in the room where we kept a constant fire. Today icicles are hanging from the houses, and the streets are glazed. I am quite reminded of our winters at the North, except that this climate is far more variable. Thus far we have all kept well.

Our horse and cow mind the cold very much—particularly the latter. Some mornings she will not drink her washing unless it is warmed. She gives us about two quarts a day; sometimes a little more. Everything is so enormously high that I am trying to make her assist in supporting herself and dispose of one quart.

Mr. Mallard is afraid he will have to send Jim back to Liberty, as we are now paying seven dollars per bushel for corn, and it is difficult to obtain it at all. We have not received our corn yet; it has been in Augusta for a month. I shall be very sorry if Mr. Mallard is obliged to give up Jim, for the congregation is so much scattered that it would be exceedingly difficult to visit them without a horse, and it would be impossible to visit those in the country.

Mr. Mallard went this afternoon to the tannery and engaged a place for Niger. Mr. Henderson, the proprietor, offers four hundred dollars a year and will clothe and feed. The tannery is in the city, a little more than a mile from our house. It is a steam tannery; hides can be tanned in sixty days. Niger will have nothing to do with the steam part; his employment will probably be chopping wood. It would be best to send him as soon as possible. Tenah is still well. I trust she will continue so until we have milder weather.

We were very sorry to hear of Dr. Delegal's death, though it was not unexpected. I feel very much for his poor wife. She has a heavy charge—particularly so in these times. And if the conscript age is extended to sixteen, I presume her eldest son will be taken.

The recent abolition of the substitute system will soon make a great upstir in the land. I think some here are quaking. The streets here are crowded with men; I presume many of them are in government employ, but there must be some who ought to be in service.

Our gallant General Morgan's men are gathering at Decatur, six miles below this place. I presume they will fight with good will. We have felt quite anxious about the rumored attack upon Savannah, but I presume the report grew out of the fact that some state troops were ordered down there.

I am afraid we are going to lose Dr. Paul Eve from this place. He will probably get a position in Augusta, and will move his family either to the city or to some place in the country nearby. I am very sorry, for I like Mrs. Eve and think she would have been a very pleasant acquaintance. And Dr. Eve is a regular attendant of our church, not only on Sabbath but our weekly prayer meetings; and he makes a most earnest and feeling prayer. Mrs. Eve is a Baptist, though she is quite regular in attending our church. She is Dr. Eve's second wife.

I find my opposite neighbor, Mrs. Root, quite a pleasant lady. She is a member of Dr. Brantly's church, and I expect her husband is one of its most influential men. He is a large dry goods merchant.

You would be amazed to see how full all the stores are at present. They are flooded with calicoes and light spring worsted goods. The prices are of course high: black calicoes, six dollars; colored, eight dollars. The latter are a yard wide; the others ordinary width.

Charlie says if you will only send Little Sister here, he will play with her. Mamie begs me to tell you she is learning to sweep and put rooms to rights. I was very much amused with her yesterday. A Lieutenant McCoy called, and being extremely diffident, I suppose he must have winked his eyes a great deal. I did not observe him particularly, as other persons were present; but after he went, Mamie said to me with great gravity: "Mama, did you see those things Lieutenant McCoy covers his eyes with when he sleeps? Why, he never let them rest one minute! He kept doing them just so." And then she winked and rolled her eyes just like him. I did not know she was observing anyone specially in the room.

Mr. Pease's little daughter is improving, and the family expect to go to the low country next week if no more of them are taken sick. . . . The children send many kisses for Little Sister and yourself. They speak of you daily, and of dear Father also. Mr. Mallard unites with me in warmest love.

Your attached daughter,
Mary S. Mallard.

MRS. MARY S. MALLARD *to* MRS. MARY JONES[t]
Atlanta, *Thursday,* January 14th, 1864

My dearest Mother,

We have not heard from you this week, but expect a letter tomorrow evening. Mr. Mallard received your letter approving the arrangement contemplated for Niger; you have before this received mine stating the precise terms agreed upon by Mr. Henderson, the proprietor of the tannery.

We have had a great deal of damp, uncomfortable weather for a week past. All our friends tell us this is an unusually severe winter. The icicles hung for days from the trees and houses, so you may imagine how cold it was. I do not know how the poor manage when fuel is so very high. We paid day before yesterday twenty-three dollars for a load of wood; this was at the rate of sixty or eighty dollars per cord. Thus far we have not been obliged to buy a great deal, thanks to the kindness of our people.

This afternoon we were served such a provoking trick by the express that I can hardly get over it. A box of oranges came for us last night, and not knowing it was coming we did not send for it this morning. So the express-man advertised it in the Memphis *Appeal* (an afternoon paper), and an hour or two after the paper was issued sold it as uncalled-for perishable freight. The *Appeal* is issued about two o'clock. We take the *Intelligencer*, but Mr. Mallard heard of the advertisement about five o'clock at Mr. Pease's store and went immediately to inquire for the box; and the man very coolly replied it was their rule to sell all perishable freight that was not immediately called for, and handed Mr. Mallard fourteen dollars. Said he sold the box for twenty. Upon inquiry, an express agent had been the purchaser and had gone to Augusta. The advertisement appeared at two, and I suppose before three the box was sold to the express agent to take immediately to Augusta to speculate upon, for oranges sell here at one dollar. I do feel highly provoked. We hoped if it had been sold to anyone in town we might have recovered it. It is said whenever these express agents want anything, they take it, and when called to account for the missing article, pay the valuation marked upon it. There may have been other things beside oranges in the box; I fear there was. I presume Mrs. Sam Mallard sent the box, and a letter from her, unless it had come directly through, would not have prevented this sale.

Mr. Pease says the express and telegraph are both humbugs and unreliable. Mr. Mallard has had a great deal of trouble trying to get some things through which Aunt Mary expressed from Liberty. The trunk containing wool and yarn has not gone yet, and the barrel of potatoes was sent and brought back and emptied in the streets all decayed. There was some wool in that, but I suppose they will affirm it shared the fate of the potatoes.

I received a note last week from Emily Green (formerly Howe) saying she was now living in Newnan and would come down and pay me a visit. She said she felt so strange among strangers that she longed to see some familiar face, and to see someone she loved. I have been expecting her all week, but presume the cold, wet weather has prevented. As soon as it clears, she will come. I shall be very glad to see her. Mr. Green is post chaplain in Newnan.

Mary Sophia will probably be here the last of this week, and will remain some days on her way to join her sisters in Screven County. Aunt Eliza is again agitating the question of a removal, and has written Uncle Henry to rent a house for her in Cuthbert. But in the meantime she has received a letter from him giving the high prices prevailing there and saying she would not have benefited herself by a removal there. I think there ought to be remarkable inducements that would make them leave their present situation. . . .

We have been trimming our vineyard today, and I hope we will have some nice grapes for you next summer, though the vines have been sadly neglected. I am afraid you could never be induced to cut your vines as unmercifully as they do here; almost everything is cut away except a few buds upon the new wood. Our lot is so dilapidated that unless we are able to put it in better order we will have no garden.

The children are quite well, and speak of you very often. Mamie begged me today "when she died to bury her by her Little Sister so she could be close to her and lie by dear Grandpapa too." Mr. Mallard unites with me in warmest love. Kisses from the children. What is Little Sister after these days?

Your affectionate daughter,
Mary S. Mallard.

MRS. MARY JONES *to* REV. R. Q. MALLARD[t]

Arcadia, *Monday,* January 18th, 1864

My dear Son,

Niger has just left by this afternoon's train for Atlanta. At Savannah I have requested Charles to give him all needful directions, and you will take care of him after he reaches Atlanta, which I trust through a kind Providence he will do safely. Please get for me a written obligation from his employer for his food, clothing, shoeing, hire, and entire care of him in health and in sickness. I hope it may be so that he can be at your yard at night. He is a good man, and I hope will be preserved from evil.

Joe and Carrie and the children have been with me for ten days. He has left this afternoon with Eva and Little Sister on her first visit to her papa and "Mama Eva." I will write Daughter all about it at a leisure hour. With our best love to my dear child and yourself and the children. In haste,

Your affectionate mother,
Mary Jones.

REV. R. Q. MALLARD *to* MRS. MARY S. MALLARD[t]

Arcadia, *Thursday,* January 21st, 1864

My dearest Wife,

Through a kind Providence I have reached this place safely, and find all well. The trip was quite a pleasant one, and unmarked by any incident worthy of record. I was glad that it was in my power to render Mrs. Pease any service; it was highly appreciated. The servants' baggage would have probably given her some trouble if I had not been along. . . . I went as I expected to your brother's, and received a very cordial welcome.

Eva was very pleasant. She acknowledged the receipt of your "sweet" letter (such, I think, she called it); urged her engagements, etc., as a reason why she had not replied sooner. She spoke of having read a beautiful letter from you to your mother which she had sent down for their perusal. We had some pleasant music in the evening. Among other songs she sang for me "Rock Me to Sleep, My Mother" and "Somebody Is Coming." The former was plaintive and very pretty; the latter I styled charming, and such it truly was as sung by her—in a peculiarly arch and merry style, with her eyes on the listener oftener than on the page. Last night her brother Berrien came down. He is very tall, and mind out of proportion. I was pleased with the serious way in which Eva rebuked him for speaking lightly of his former connection with the church. It seems he has given up all his religion. He had not forgotten the "lecture," as he called it, which Father gave him at Mr. Dowse's.

I had expected to have gone up to Walthourville this morning, but Mrs. Pease's friends sent for her to No. 3, so I concluded to get out at the same station. She offered me a seat a part of the way, but as there was a prospect of delay I walked to Arcadia. I found Aunt Susan, Cousin Laura, and the children as well as Carrie with your mother. We all wished for you to be here today. Mother was very glad to get the shoes, as Little Sister was nearly out. Mary Ruth is away on a short visit to Father and "Mama Eva." Mother minded the separation very much. She seems to look upon it (as she expressed it this morning when I told her how fond the child was of Eva) as "the entering wedge." I have handed your package to Aunt Susan.

You will be sorry to hear that two of our Negroes were implicated in the recent attempted stampede—Adam and Tony. Adam is now in military custody, and I suppose being punished by whipping. Tony has not, so far as I can learn, been captured yet. Mr. Delegal's boat was under his house, securely locked, as he supposed, and the pillars too near to admit of its removal. But they dug down one of the pillars; but fortunately it was too wide to pass through the gate, and its creaking as it was drawn over the palings awoke Mr. Delegal. The most of Sister Sarah Quarterman's Negroes were concerned: her man Dickey the ringleader. He induced his wife (Brother John's Esther) to go. They will probably hang Dickey if he is caught.

I expect to go to Brother John's tonight and to Riceboro tomorrow. Your brother advises me to sell in Savannah by a broker, and will make all arrangements for me there. I met Niger in Savannah; he will wait for me until I return. I am anxious to be through and back as soon as possible.

If I can, I will write you again. My thoughts have been much with you. The Lord bless and preserve you and the "wee bairns"! Aunt Susan and Mother and all send much love. Aunt Susan thanks you for the pattern; it was the very thing which she needed, and is using it as I write. She bids me say that I (R. Q. M.) am but half welcome without you. Kiss the children for me.

Your loving husband,

R. Q. Mallard.

Mrs. Mary Jones *to* Mrs. Mary S. Mallard[t]

Arcadia, *Wednesday,* January 27th, 1864

My dearest Daughter,

You may be assured we were happy to see Robert. Would that you could have been with him! Only sorry for the cause of his visit, although I hope it will result in good. He will *explain all.*

I have had a great deal of company for some weeks, and been so busy as not to write you, as I design, every week. And you know how much I have to do, *all* centering in my poor self. The visit of my children has been very cheering. Your brother is now in Florida; I hope to keep them a long time. Your aunt and Laura and the children made me a visit of two days and nights last week. All well and doing well. Also your uncle; only he says you promised and *have not* written him. Miss Clay is now with us.

Eva came for Little Sister, and she has been in Savannah for ten days. You will know how much I must miss my baby and long to have her back. But it was right for her to visit her papa and "Eva Mama," who is as kind and tender to her as possible. She never forgets you and "Bubber Sissy."

Tell my dear little granddaughter I send her a dress. The *skirt* made one for *Mary* and *Ruth* and *Susan.* What three sweet names! . . . I have stolen a few moments to write, and now comes a call. With tenderest love for yourself, and kisses for my dear grandchildren, and much love from Carrie,

Ever your own affectionate mother,

Mary Jones.

Mrs. Mary Jones *to* Mrs. Mary S. Mallard[t]

Arcadia, *Friday,* February 5th, 1864

My dear Daughter,

I ought this moment to be in my bed, for I am nearly sick with a renewal of cold and general inflammation of the throat; but I fear if this leisure evening is not embraced I shall not have another just now. The only period when I have been alone was the three weeks when I was confined to my room and the house; and for the past month friends have been coming and going all the time. And during Robert's brief stay I felt that my time was so much taken up that I did not make half the inquiries I intended.

Yesterday Joe and Carrie left the children with me and dined with your uncle; today they have gone to Taylor's Creek for the day, and will spend the night with your aunt. They only took little Susan.

Dunwody, after a week in the county, returned this afternoon. I expected your Uncle John, but he did not come. This is the fourth time I have been disappointed, and hope nothing has occurred to detain him. Dunwody left quite in a gloomy state; unless he can get some appointment, he will have to return to the ranks as a private, which is not very pleasant to a young lieutenant!

Miss Clay stayed nearly a week with us, and I greatly enjoyed her visit. I never saw her more cheerful. Joe Clay has been very successful in Thomas County, and bids fair to be a great comfort to her, and a very useful Christian man.

I am thankful to hear that Tenah is over her trouble, but am sorry you had so much company when you were so badly prepared for their entertainment. It is really at times a difficult matter to be "given to hospitality" with proper grace, especially when just removed to a new place. I trust your cow will make her appearance. Your brother's was missing several weeks; was finally found, but her milk was gone and has not been restored. I trust Robert's valuable cargo arrived safely, and fear the children's ginger cake in Niger's box was too stale to be eaten.

Carrie and Joe speak of returning to Augusta next week. He has been moving from one point to another; spent a week in South Carolina and another in Florida. I have enjoyed their visit and that of the dear children, and shall feel sad and lonely when they are gone. The baby is a darling *little* creature, and makes one think of our sweet little Eliza.

My baby is still in Savannah, and from all accounts is enjoying her visit. Her "Eva Mama" writes very lovingly of her, and Charles says she is "the light of the household." I hope this may not prove the entering wedge to taking her from me. I do desire that she shall know and love her own father and her mama, who is as kind as possible to her. It really is a great comfort to me to see her kindness and affection to the child.

I received your kind favor with the samples of gingham, and sent them to your aunt and cousin. They did not wish anything of the kind; and as I have been *compelled* to buy a bombazine which cost a price I am ashamed to mention, I could not well add to my wardrobe anything more at present.

I desire if possible to call and see Mrs. Pease, and feel grateful for all her kind attentions to you. Nothing but company or ill health or failure of cavalry, if Providence permits, will prevent.

Robert has given you all the news of the county. . . . Rose is diligent at her spinning, but Mrs. Andrews has not sent home yet the rest of the first pieces. Such a run of company has put a stop to my work in that line. Your brother has dyed me some white homespun a beautiful blue, and I will send Charlie some jackets from it when I send his homespun for pants, which I intended doing by Robert. But my poor head is so forgetful now.

Kiss my precious children many times, and tell them Grandmama longs to see them. With best love to Robert and yourself. Howdies from all the *servants here* and at *Montevideo*. Old Andrew and Sue were very much hurt at not seeing you before you left home. The old man says you know he was always a " 'sponsible man in the family." And now, dear child, good night. . . . May the Lord bless and keep you in His love and fear!

Your affectionate mother,
Mary Jones.

Mrs. Mary S. Mallard *to* Mrs. Mary Jones[t]

Atlanta, *Monday,* February 8th, 1864

My dearest Mother,

I have not written you for a week. Constant company and many occupations have prevented. I have had company constantly for the past three weeks, and in that time have had frequent calls. Although I have returned a great many, I still have about twenty-four ahead.

I was greatly surprised by Cousin Lyman; did not know that he was near until he was in the parlor. We had a delightful visit from him; it was quite a treat to us.

We have all enjoyed the good things you sent us; they all came safely. The marmalade is very nice, and the children have enjoyed their cake. The myrtle wax ornaments have been very much admired. I sent a part of the oranges to Mrs. Logan.

Niger seems quite satisfied and pleased with his work at the tanyard, which consists in hauling bark and cutting wood. He says his employer is "a pretty fine man." He wishes me to send word to his aunty that his baby is named Cinda. Tenah is doing very well; she has really been favored.

We have heard nothing further from our cow, so have concluded she is either closely shut up in somebody's yard or has been killed by the butchers. It is a great loss to us.

I have Kitty with me now, and am enjoying her visit. She looks better than I have ever seen her. Last summer she took the entire charge of the farm in Habersham, and was very active in the management of everything concerning it. She has a black linsey dress which she dyed herself, and it is a beautiful black. She seems to have succeeded remarkably well with her experiments.

Mr. Mallard received a note this evening from Mr. Buttolph in which he mentions Little Sister in connection with Brother Charlie and Eva, so I suppose she is still absent from you. How much you must miss her! I am glad you have had Carrie and her little ones with you during her absence. How I wish I could see them all!

I sent Mamie to Sabbath school for the first time yesterday, and she seems perfectly delighted. Miss Nannie Logan is her teacher, and Mamie says she is *too* pretty. The nice little books which she will have will always be a pleasant inducement to her to go. The Sabbath school is not in a very flourishing condition at present. The number of children who attend is very small, but I presume it will increase as the weather becomes milder. It has been so bitterly cold for several months that children could not be expected to come out. I am very glad to have Mamie go, and hope her interest will increase, for the association with other children will do her good.

Our town was in quite a stir on Saturday, though we knew nothing of it at the time. General Morgan arrived and made a very short speech at the Trout House. He is still here, but I presume will go where his men are collecting near Decatur. I should have liked to have seen him. Have you read the account of his escape written by 290? If not, I will send you a copy; it has been issued here in pamphlet form.

After Aunt Mary Robarts' return to Marietta, Aunt Eliza and all of them became very much exercised about leaving. There was quite a panic in the place, fearing that if the army should fall back, Marietta would be thrown within the Yankee lines. I believe now Aunty has *decided* to remain where she is; and I feel very glad she has, for I do not know where in these times she could be made more comfortable. And then she has so many kind friends there—though a number have moved from the place, amongst others Mr. William Russell. Aunty will miss him very much.

I wrote you week before the last about some ginghams here which are sold at five dollars per yard by the piece. If you would like to have a dress of this kind, I do not think you will be able to get anything cheaper, for many persons think dry goods will be higher. It is more difficult to bring in blockade goods. Mr. Buttolph carried a dress for Aunt Susan and Cousin Laura, and I have gotten three dresses for Miss Louisa. There were four dresses to the piece, but I let Kitty take one. I think I shall get a very black one for myself, and if you would like one of the same, do let me know soon.

Kitty desires much love to you. The children speak of you constantly, and often ask when I am going to take them to see Grandmama. They send love and kisses. Do give love to Brother Joe and Carrie if they are still with you, and kiss the children for us. Mr. Mallard unites with me in warmest love. I long for summer to come so that you may be with us.

Your affectionate daughter,
Mary S. Mallard.

Mrs. Mary S. Mallard *to* Mrs. Mary Jones[t]

Atlanta, Monday, February 22nd, 1864

My dearest Mother,

We have just returned from the country prayer meeting, where a few were assembled to pray for our cause. It is surprising how very few do attend, considering that it is a union meeting.

Mr. Mallard went up to Dalton on last Wednesday, or rather he spent that night in Marietta and went up the next day. It was bitter cold, and the engine became disabled, causing a long delay, which was anything but comfortable, as the windows of the cars were broken and there was no fire to be had. However, he reached Dalton in safety, and the next day walked four miles to the camp of the 25th Georgia. When he wrote, he said he was comfortably and pleasantly fixed and had preached twice that day and expected to continue the services the next day. Major Winn is now commanding that regiment, and Mr. Mallard said he had been very polite in having every arrangement made for preaching. . . . Dr. Stiles was with us a night last week, and he urged Mr. Mallard to go to the front, as he considered it most important that the army should have special religious privileges at this time. So he had come down to get some ministers to go up. It seemed such an imperative call Mr. Mallard felt it his duty to go. There is a great deal of interest on the subject of religion in the army, and unless this opportunity is improved, the time will have passed for doing them any good; for all believe the campaign will soon commence—perhaps in two or three weeks. Troops are daily passing down to reinforce General Polk. I trust he will be successful.

Yesterday afternoon we had a sight of General Morgan and his wife. We were in the Episcopal church, where Bishop Elliott preached and had confirmation; and General Morgan, being one of the congregation, attracted much attention. He was dressed in a handsome suit of black broadcloth, with nothing to indicate the soldier except his cavalry boots and black felt hat turned up on one side with a wreath-around-a-tree worked on it. He is very handsome, and his whole person and bearing is such as you would imagine should become General Morgan. His wife is very pretty, and I can assure you they are a dashing couple. Kitty and I were charmed with the general's dress, it was so unpretending and yet so elegant. I was glad I had Mamie with me. She is in perfect ecstasies at having seen General Morgan.

Dr. Quintard is now preaching in the theater, trying to gather a church; and I presume he will succeed, as he is an interesting preacher, and the people seem much pleased with him. Kitty and I went to hear him, and took Mamie with us. It was the first time she had ever seen the Episcopal service. Kitty asked her how she liked her church. She said: "I did not like it a bit. The people in your church behaved so badly: they looked in books all the time and kept talking, and the minister preached in a dressing gown." She wanted to know if the minister would dress himself in good clothes before he went into the street.

The regular pastor of the Episcopal church here is a very nervous man, and said to be an opium-eater and immoderate snuff-taker. On one occasion a little dog entered the church and so discomposed him that he sailed out of the pulpit and chased it up and down the aisles until he caught it, and then pitched it out and sent it squealing, much to the annoyance of his congregation.

We have had another taste of winter: cold, freezing weather. The apricot in the yard had commenced to bloom, and the flowers are completely killed.

If the spell of warm weather had lasted a little longer, I presume we would have lost all our fruit. I hope we will have some nice grapes for you when you come next summer.

Kitty has been with me for the past three weeks, and will be with me for some time. I am very glad to have her with me during Mr. Mallard's absence. A letter from Brother Charlie mentioned that Little Sister had gone with Eva to Augusta, so I suppose she will not return to you until next week. She has made a long visit. Mamie insists upon putting in some babies which she has made for her. I don't think I told you what Mamie said about the dress you sent her: "Oh, I thank Grandma, and think this is my beautifullest dress!" She is going to Sunday school, and is quite delighted with her teacher, Miss Nannie Logan. Kitty sends love to you. The children unite with me in warmest love and kisses for you.

Your affectionate daughter,
Mary S. Mallard.

Mrs. Mary S. Mallard *to* Mrs. Mary Jones[t]

Atlanta, *Wednesday,* March 2nd, 1864

My darling Mother,

A long time has elapsed since I have heard from you. I have not had a letter for three weeks, and I can't help feeling anxious, thinking you may not be well.

I wrote you that Mr. Mallard had gone to the army—or "the front," as it is called here—to preach to the soldiers. His visit was much shorter than he anticipated, for while in camp the order came for three days' rations to be cooked and the troops to hold themselves in readiness for action. Mr. Mallard returned immediately to Dalton, and had the pleasure of seeing a great portion of General Johnston's army. And a grand sight it was. Mr. Mallard said the sight of the army filled him with hope; the men were all in good spirits and were comfortably clothed and shod. Mr. Mallard preached six times to most attentive audiences, chiefly to the 25th Georgia. He stayed in Willie Winn's hut. (He is now acting colonel of the 25th.) The soldiers all had very comfortable winter quarters.

The result of the forward movement of the enemy you have seen from the papers. They undoubtedly supposed our army would fall back, and they would either gain an easy possession of Atlanta or, if unable to do that, entrench themselves at Dalton. They thought we had sent off so many to reinforce General Polk that we could not resist. Reinforcements had been sent to General Polk, but were speedily returned; and the Yankee prisoners were utterly astounded when they found their captors to be the very men they supposed with General Polk.

Mr. Mallard's visit to the army was very pleasant and refreshing to him. Dr. Stiles did not go up until the day the army commenced to move, so he did not preach at all. There were, however, a number of missionaries who preached.

Mr. Wood, who married Mary Jane Beck, was one of them. He spent a day with us, and told me that Charles Jones Beck had been wounded and taken prisoner at Gettysburg. When he was recovering, a companion and himself requested to be allowed to go upon the field to mark the grave of a friend. The request was granted, and they went out and did not stop until they reached Dixie, passing themselves as members of the 169th Pennsylvania Regiment. They had on hospital clothing, and were obliged to come out in them.

Charlie Pratt has joined Morgan's command. Dr. and Mrs. Pratt were here on last Saturday. They inquired particularly after you, and desired to be remembered to you. Mr. Pratt is looking old. Mrs. Pratt told me that the servant of Mrs. Pynchon who had returned to her owners from the Yankees had again gone to the Yankees, and this time taken all their other house servants. I presume it must have been a Yankee ruse, for the woman returned professing great penitence and loyalty. Said she had been convinced of her duty by reading the Bible and had returned to perform it, and during the months she remained was as humble and faithful as a servant could be. I presume the Pynchons will regret ever having received her.

Have you seen Dr. Stiles's sketch of Captain Thomas King? Kitty and I read it with great interest.

I have just had a delightful visit from Kitty. She has been with me four weeks, and returned this morning to Macon. She would have remained some weeks longer, but Edward had a furlough of thirty days, and she wanted to see him, and as it is will be with him only one or two days, as he went first to Savannah to see his wife and relatives there. Kitty may return to us after a week or two. While here her Aunt Sarah Mackay wrote her that Mrs. Mongin was engaged to Mr. Williams of Bryan. It seems to be a great amazement and amusement to everyone who hears it.

I received a letter from Carrie this evening. She says her children are both well again. She seems to have enjoyed her visit very much.

Where is Brother Charlie now? He wrote me upon the eve of leaving for Florida, but did not say where he was ordered. I presume he was too late for the battle.

How much we have been blessed recently! The enemy seems to have been foiled in all his plans. Oh, that our people would recognize the hand of God in this and not be lifted up in their own strength!

The recent currency bill is making quite a stir in our town. I hope it will reduce the high prices, for I don't know what we are coming to. Think of giving three dollars per pound for ordinary beef, and choice pieces from four to five dollars per pound! It is ruinous.

Do give much love to Aunt Susan and Cousin Laura. I wrote Uncle William last week. Mr. Mallard and the children unite with me in warmest love and many kisses. Has Little Sister returned yet? The servants send howdy. Niger and Tenah have named their baby Cinda. Howdy for the servants.

Your affectionate child,
Mary S. Mallard.

Enclosed $33.35, being Niger's hire for one month.

Mrs. Mary Jones *to* Mrs. Mary S. Mallard[t]

Arcadia, *Saturday,* March 5th, 1864

My dearest Child,

I have not written you, I believe, for four weeks, during which time I have been constantly engaged nursing the sick, and with a continued run of company.

Immediately after Joe and Carrie left, *Fanny* was taken ill with pneumonia. I sent for Dr. Farmer; he thought she would not recover from the first. For twelve days and I may say nights I watched her case, doing all I could; but it was our Heavenly Father's good pleasure to call his servant home, and she departed in perfect peace and full assurance, through the Blood and righteousness of that precious Saviour she had loved and served for so many years. . . . Next, *Patience* has been in bed for two weeks: Dr. Way called in to her. Now improving but very feeble. Kate (cook) laid by for five weeks with a whitlow on her right hand. Still unable to use it. All this while company—sometimes seven or eight whites and three or four servants at a time. *Flora* my only effective servant to cook and wash. And the little "plagues of Egypt" in the house.

My responsibility and fatigue of these cases have issued in great prostration of body and spirit. On last Saturday a chill came on, followed by fever and pain (intense) in one side of my head, face, eyes, and teeth. Yesterday I was almost distracted; today I am up and feel better. Have taken blue pills and quinine, and hope I may not be laid in my bed again, if it be God's will. My eyes are so painful and inflamed I write with difficulty, and use a pencil.

My dear brother paid me a most delightful visit of a month, and returned on last Friday. It was a visit of true consolation and sympathy, and all the time we could command together was given to but one object—your beloved father. Oh, my child, no mortal may know the desolation of heart I feel!

Mrs. Eve and Eva came and brought my baby home. She talks of you all; saw your likeness the other day (the one taken North with Joe) for the first time, and said: "That is my Aunt Mary and my Uncle Joe." She was delighted with the paper babies, and said I must kiss Sissy for them.

Charles has written me but once since he was in Florida; he was in command of the light artillery about ten miles from Jacksonville and about four from the enemy. We cannot hear of any movement. All appears quiet.

I am constantly anxious for my dear child; every movement is one of peril. God only can preserve him. I hope you and Robert remember him constantly.

Edward (Bess's husband) has been sick with a cold here for a week. The rest of the people are well. Henry brought the cloth home on Monday—the rest of the *first pieces.* I handed Robert the twenty dollars and kept ten to pay for it. Thanks for the $33.35; it comes in good time. I had no corn to sell, and have not sold the cotton. When the next month's wages come in, *you must keep them for yourself.*

Kiss my precious grandchildren for me. Best love to Robert and yourself. And howdies for the servants.

Ever, my dear daughter, your affectionate mother,
Mary Jones.

Mrs. Mary S. Mallard *to* Mrs. Mary Jones[t]

Atlanta, Thursday, March 10th, 1864

My dearest Mother,

I hoped yesterday's mail would have brought me a letter, but no tidings yet! I have had only one letter from you since Mr. Mallard was in Liberty. Perhaps I shall get one this evening.

I have been suffering very much this week from severe headache, and yesterday I was obliged to keep my bed, the pain was so severe. I am better today, though rather weak.

I think I wrote you that Kitty had returned to Macon to see her brother. A letter received from her this morning states that Cousin Mary and Mr. Nisbet are in great trouble on account of Hattie's having scarlet fever. One or two of their other children died of this disease, so no wonder they feel very fearful.

I am with you constantly now, dear Mother, as the anniversary of our greatest sorrow draws near. I have been dreaming frequently of my dear father. A few nights ago I thought we were all assembled in some familiar place of worship, whether at Midway or Walthourville I could not tell. A small congregation was assembled. Father was there—yourself, Brother Charlie, Mr. Mallard, and myself. We all seemed impressed with the idea that Father was soon to be taken from us. A hymn was given out to be sung, and we all joined in with trembling voices; but soon the notes died upon the lips of one and another and another until but one was singing, and soon that voice was choked. And there we all sat, weeping and sorrowing that he was so soon to be taken from us. . . . Today, according to the days of the week, is the anniversary of the birth of my dear little baby, though the 12th does not come until Saturday. These are days full of sadness; and yet I seem sometimes almost to hear a voice saying: "Why weep? They are with the redeemed, Blood-washed throng, singing the Song of Moses and the Lamb, and shall be forever with the Lord." I wish I could go to those two precious graves. They are not like ordinary graves; there is an individuality about them which I never thought a grave could possess.

Have you heard from Brother Charlie since he went to Florida? Where is he stationed? Where is Little Sister? Has she returned to you yet? Brother Charlie wrote me she would do so when Eva came from Augusta.

I have been very glad to see through the papers how signally the Yankees have been defeated in Florida. It is wonderful how their whole combined movement has proved a failure. It has turned out that their movement in the front was intended as an attack upon Atlanta—they thinking, of course, General Johnston's army was too much depleted to make any resistance at all.

What a diabolical attempt that was on the part of Colonel Dahlgren to liberate the prisoners, kill our President, and burn Richmond! A General Dahlgren, said to be brother of the commodore, has been attending our church regularly for some Sabbaths past with his family. They are very genteel, attractive persons in their appearance. Mr. Mallard and I intend calling upon them, as we hear they are going to remain here. It is said this brother gave our government the pattern of the Dahlgren guns invented by his Yankee brother.

Mr. Mallard received a letter from Mr. Quarterman day before yesterday telling us of Mom Fanny's death. I am truly sorry to hear of it; she is a great loss to the place, and will be very much missed. She was always so cheerful and so fond of her owners. Was she sick long?

Do tell Daddy Andrew that Charles has seen Abram, poor Dinah's former husband. He was working some miles from this place, and Charles met him once when he came in town. He had not heard of Dinah's death, and said he had never married until pretty recently, for he had always hoped something would turn up and he would be able to go back to Liberty. He sent a great many howdies to Mom Mary Ann and Daddy Andrew.

Our expenses were so heavy that Mr. Mallard has had to give up Jim. One of the army surgeons has him, and Mr. Mallard has the use of him on Mondays. We have never heard from our cow.

I have commenced gardening, and hope I shall succeed, for I see we shall be entirely dependent upon our own resources. One of my neighbors has given me some millet seed; I will enclose you some, for I think you have lost the seed. Mamie says I must tell you "Mrs. Root gave it to me, and she is a Baptist, and a member of Dr. Brantly's church." Mamie says you must be sure to come up, for you will get grapes, peaches, apricots, and cherries to eat.

Mr. Mallard unites with me in warmest love to you. The children send many kisses. Love to Aunt Susan and Cousin Laura.

Your affectionate daughter,
Mary S. Mallard.

Mrs. Mary Jones *to* Mrs. Mary S. Mallard[t]

Arcadia, *Wednesday,* March 16th, 1864

My dearest Daughter,

Yesterday's mail brought me your affectionate letter. I knew that your thoughts would be with me at this time—from last Thursday night (which was in point of day if not of time the anniversary of the birth of your precious babe) to the present moment.

The events which marked that period of the past year have been enacted from hour to hour with a living reality. How sacred is every association with the precious life and death of your beloved and honored father! One year ago and that exalted life on earth was transferred from the duties and toils of earth to the rewards and enjoyments of heaven. Oh, to my desolate heart it appears as if ages had passed since we parted! His hat and stick are lying just as he laid them down on the morning of the 16th, 1863; and although I behold him not with mortal eyes, he is ever present in my tenderest love and recollections. For thirty-two years it pleased the Lord to honor me with his companionship—with his guidance, his support, his spiritual instruction, his wise counsels, his intellectual light and knowledge, his daily example, his prayers and his precepts, and all that tender and affectionate intercourse which as a wife I felt was the cherished boon of my life. Oh, that I had been found worthy of such a blessing!

I could not pass the day without a visit to our precious dead. All was sunlight: no shadows resting on their graves. The wreaths you placed there I have never removed, although I have put fresh flowers around them. But I felt that I could not take them away. I read this afternoon: "Eye hath not seen, nor ear heard, neither have entered into the heart of man the things which God hath prepared for them that love Him." Our beloved ones now see and hear and know. Oh, that we too may by faith in our Divine Lord and Master when our summons comes be made partakers with them of that joy and peace which will be everlasting!

My dear brother's visit was very delightful, and I am glad we were much together in the early part of it, for when Fanny was taken sick I nursed or attended to her medicines day and night for eight days. And then Patience has been down for three weeks, and is still confined to her house, and much of the time to bed. I fear she will be an invalid for a long time. Yesterday I got a vial of iodine for rubbing her pains; it cost eight dollars. Kate is just out at her duties. Edward was quite sick for ten days; I *practiced* for him, and he has returned home. The result has been prostration, with fever and severe neuralgic pains in head, eyes, ear, and teeth; and I have been obliged to keep very close. I want to change to Montevideo as soon as Patience is better. Richard is now very sick with a mild form of pleurisy; Mr. Quarterman called in Dr. Farmer. I have just sent him a bowl of chicken soup and some stimulant, and he says he feels better. I have not been able to see him but twice.

Mr. Quarterman says he wrote you of Elvira's intended marriage; he appears to be very clever, and is very good-looking: a perfect row of ivory. . . .

We have had quite a military change in the county: Colonel Millen's battalion ordered first to Florida, then Virginia; and part of Colonel Colcock's and Major White's regiments have taken their places. Colonel Colcock's son is the acting adjutant to his men. He came last week and spent the evening with me, and I was very much pleased with him.

I hear but seldom from your brother. His last letter was from Camp Baldwin, four miles from the enemy and ten from Jacksonville. You may be assured I am in constant anxiety for him. May the Lord bless and save him, and make him useful in his country's cause!

I have now read with deepest interest Dr. Stiles's sketch of Captain King. *It must* do great good.

I cannot think why you have not received my letters. During the sickness I did not write for three weeks, but know I have written three or four times since Robert was here. I long to see you all. Tell my little grandchildren Little Sister talks constantly of them, and told me the other day: "I have a little baby in heaven." She has outgrown all her clothes, which I must alter. Eva is in Augusta. Kiss my children. Best love to Robert and yourself. Howdy for the servants. I have never been able to call on Mrs. Pease as I wished. . . . God bless you, my dear child, ever prays

Your affectionate mother,
Mary Jones.

Mrs. Mary S. Mallard *to* Mrs. Mary Jones[t]

Atlanta, *Friday,* March 18th, 1864

My dearest Mother,

Your long-looked-for and welcome letter has been received; I cannot tell you what a relief it was to us when we saw your well-known handwriting. I am sorry to know you have been suffering so much from pain in your head and face; I expect it was the result of continued care and anxiety. You must have had a wearisome and trying time when the servants were sick. I am glad Little Sister has returned; she was absent so long I began to fear she was not coming back. Where is Eva? Has she returned to Savannah?

This has been a week of sadness and sorrow. I have thought of my dear father by day and by night. I have longed to be with you, and felt such a yearning towards that consecrated spot at Midway. I think when you come up you may be able to get such a marble tomb as you like. I have recently seen two very good ones in the marble yard, though rather plainer than you would like. I am glad Uncle John was with you so long; it must have been a great comfort.

Mr. Mallard received a letter from Uncle Henry a few days ago requesting him to exchange some bonds for him. He mentions that Aunt Abby has quite recovered, and they have named their little daughter Abby Augusta. Mr. Mallard may possibly go to Cuthbert in April, as the presbytery meets there in that month.

We have had another taste of winter: a great deal of ice and cold winds for several days past. Wood is so expensive that it always grieves us to find the weather getting cold. I am afraid the fruit will be injured. I had lettuce and radishes coming up, but think I have saved the plants by covering. The ground here so soon bakes and becomes hard that it is difficult for small seeds to penetrate the outer crust.

Two days ago we received a note from Mr. Rogers saying that he had shipped us six pieces of hollow ware from his Bellwood furnace. They have not arrived yet, so I do not know what they are. It is a handsome present in these days when iron is so scarce and valuable. I saw a spider and ironstand from his furnace; they were equal and I think better than any I ever saw. He has gone to Columbia now to fill some contract. His whole time and attention is given to these works. I think Brother Charlie has about fifty shares in the furnace. It will very soon pay a handsome percentage.

I look anxiously for the Florida news, and am glad to see the enemy have made no further demonstration, and feel thankful my dear brother has not been exposed in battle.

Mamie has just come in, and begs me to tell you she is going to Sunday school, and says you must write word what you think about it. She says she is making a quilt and growing so fat that you won't know her when you come. She is very much attached to her Sabbath school teacher, Miss Nannie Logan, and in compliment to her has named her doll (a boy) Dr. Logan. Mrs. Logan is a very pleasant lady. I only regret that we live so far apart. There is at least a mile between us, so that it would be impossible for us to be really sociable. I think I wrote you Mr. Mallard had to give up Jim, but still has the privilege of using him on Mondays.

If you have not sent the broken bunch of No. 10 yarn to Mrs. Andrews, please, dear Mother, keep it; for I shall have to knit some flannel shirts next summer for Mr. Mallard, and want Rose to spin me some more wool after the sheep are shorn. I think they are stronger with one thread of cotton, and it saves half the spinning. I have found my flannels great comforts to me this winter, and attribute my freedom from colds to them and the very thick shoes I have been wearing. I wear heavier shoes than I used to get for my housemaids. The finer shoes are so exorbitantly high that many of the ladies wear these heavy shoes. I have found them very necessary in this muddy, rocky country.

I hope you receive all my letters. I write regularly every week. Kitty Stiles will probably return here in a week or two. My last letter from her stated that Hattie Nisbet had genuine scarlet fever, but was doing pretty well. They had a homeopathic physician attending her. Do give much love to Uncle William, Aunt Susan, and Cousin Laura. . . . Mr. Mallard and the children unite with me in warmest love to Little Sister and yourself.

Your affectionate daughter,

Mary S. Mallard.

Mrs. Mary S. Mallard *to* Mrs. Mary Jones[t]

Atlanta, *Thursday,* March 24th, 1864

My dearest Mother,

The days that have elapsed since I last wrote you have been rather eventful, so I will give you a little account of them.

Sabbath evening we had quite a little gust of sleet and rain while the church bells were ringing, and many were detained at home. Mr. Mallard preached to a very small congregation and returned through the rain. The wind blew hard during the night, and the next morning dawned upon us cold, gloomy, and rainy. Mr. Mallard was prevented in his usual pastoral visits. About twelve o'clock Lucy announced that a poor lady with two children wished to speak to me at the door. I found a poor woman shivering with two little children crying with cold, a shabby broken-topped buggy and two poor horses before the door. The woman said she had been trying to find a place to warm and to have her horses fed, and she thought if she could only get to the Presbyterian minister's house, they would take care of her. I brought them in, and the children were soon at home, one in the chimney almost sitting upon the back log, and the other asking for bread, having had nothing to eat all day.

The poor soul began her story. She had come from Alabama (seven miles from Huntsville) with her husband and three children, driven away by the Yankees. They were making their way to the husband's relatives in Cobb County. We did not see Mr. Sullivan (that was the name), as he was engaged with the medical board endeavoring to get a discharge; and he had his eldest child, a girl of seven years, with him to take care of him. Mrs. Sullivan said he had been subject to epilepsy, and his mind was so seriously impaired that he was obliged always to take this child with him. I felt very sorry for her, for she was evidently in no situation to undergo extra fatigues. The Yankees had ripped up their beds, scattered the feathers and carried off the ticking, blankets, and coverings of every description, and had burned her own and her children's clothing. And the Union men had killed their cattle. All their provisions had been taken from them, so they were compelled to find another country. Whenever the Yankee officers were remonstrated with for burning and destroying property which was valuable only to the owners, their universal reply was: "I am sorry for you, but must obey orders."

Mrs. Sullivan said before the war they lived very comfortably in Huntsville, her husband being a lawyer (a pettifogger, I presume); but now, with the exception of a small box which they had sent ahead, they had everything they possessed in their buggy, and no change of clothing for herself or children. I gave her some little things, and when the little girl found there was a dress for her, she insisted upon putting it immediately on; and when I told her she could not put it on then, she raised her hand and would have dealt sundry blows if she had been allowed. Her mother told her she might put it on when she got home. She turned indignantly upon her: "We ain't got no home, and ain't goin' to no home. I want it on now!" (They were regular little crackers.)

After dinner Mrs. Sullivan went out to meet her husband, promising to return if they did not make up their minds to pursue their journey. We heard no more of them. She said that the Union men around Huntsville were faring just as badly as those who had remained true to the South, for the Yankees told them they had no use for men that would not stand by their country. This poor woman excited our compassion very much, and I presume it is one of thousands of instances. I hope they found some hospitable shelter, for it was a fearful night—very dark, and the wind blowing most furiously with gusts of rain and sleet.

The first news we had of our household next morning was from Lucy, who came in early with the announcement: "The robbers has been upon us last night! Forced open the hen house door and carried away all the poultry!" Charles came soon after, saying with rather a tone of triumph that they had left their "howl" (a prodigious pick used here upon the fortifications), and he had it and brought it as a trophy. (Charles must have manufactured the word *howl*.) The thieves had pulled the palings and come in, forced the door (or rather took it off its hinges after removing the board above), and had carried off two fine turkey gobblers, one guinea hen, all the roosters, and some ten or twelve hens, including the servants'. They did not disturb my ducks, I presume either because their hands were too full, or because only English ducks are raised up here. As soon as Charles found the poultry missing, he began looking about to discover where the rogues got in. Upon looking across the street, he found the neighbors examining their broken fence. *All* their poultry had been taken, and a pick similar to that found here was left there, showing that it was a regular thieving party. A neighbor a little farther down the street had everything stolen from their hen houses the same night. How many more suffered I don't know, for not being acquainted with the people, I have no means of ascertaining.

Things are coming to a fearful pass in this city. Mr. Pease says the exceptions are those who have not been robbed. In one instance they entered a smokehouse, opened barrels of wheat flour, emptied them into sacks, and carried off all the bacon. A very nice lady of our acquaintance had her smokehouse opened and all her lard stolen. These things are occurring every night. The night they came here was so fearfully windy and stormy that any amount of noise could not have been heard. It is supposed this kind of rascality is carried on by Negroes hiring their own time and those working upon the fortifications. They are aided, it is supposed, by low white men. Of course our police must be extremely inefficient. There are some soldiers who commit even worse depredations upon the neighboring farms and lots in the suburbs, putting guards around the Negro houses to prevent their giving the alarm and then robbing the hen roosts and taking off even the clothing of the Negroes. A few nights ago a man was knocked down and his boots taken; when he came to himself he was in his stocking feet. The gentlemen consider it unsafe to be much out at night.

I have a few hens left, but no rooster. When meat of all kinds is not to be had except at four and five dollars a pound, and scarce at that, it is a serious loss to have a large number of one's hens stolen, and two turkeys beside.

On Tuesday we had a very heavy snowstorm—as heavy at times as any I ever saw at the North. The whole earth was covered about four inches deep.

I must tell you before I forget of the children's remarks when they heard the robbers had been at the hen house. Mamie said we must get a parrot to stay at the door, and then when any strange person came to open the door, it would scream "Stealing! Stealing!" and then her papa would wake and shoot them with his pistol. Charlie proposed that we should build an iron house, and then "the naughty *India rubbers*" could not get in. They were both quite satisfied with their plans, and finally agreed that the chickens would be perfectly safe with a parrot at the door of Charlie's house built of iron.

March 25th. I commenced this last night, dear Mother, but did not finish. This morning the snow has disappeared from the ground. A number of tender buds and flowers have fallen from the fruit trees. I fear the fruit is seriously injured if not entirely destroyed, for the trees were encased with ice for two days. We indulged in the luxury of a little ice cream; I wished I could have sent you a saucer.

On Tuesday evening, when the ground was covered with snow, Mr. Mallard had to perform a marriage ceremony. He had received a note the day before from a lieutenant saying he was to be *"mared"* and wished him to perform the "serrimony." I received a generous supply of cake.

Last night Mr. Mallard attended a wedding in our church: Miss Mina Barnard to Major Morgan. Dr. Brantly performed the ceremony. The young lady said she must have an organ for the occasion, as the music would cover her embarrassment. The Baptist church has no organ, so they applied for the use of our church. An absurd and funny report was circulated through the town giving the order of exercises. Mr. Root, the Baptist deacon, was to have charge of the music; Dr. Quintard, the Episcopal minister, to perform the ceremony; Mr. Mallard give the bride away; and Dr. Brantly pronounce the benediction! This story was really believed by some.

I have seen very little of Mrs. Brantly, for she went to Augusta a week or two after she called, and will not return until the last of April.

I suppose Little Sister is delighted to be with "Danna" again. Kiss her for all of us. We all want to see you so much. I am sorry to hear Mom Patience is so feeble. Can't you bring her with you this summer? I think the change would do her a great deal of good. Kate has a room, and she could take part with her. Mr. Mallard and the children unite with me in warmest love to you, my dear mother, and many kisses for Little Sister.

Your affectionate daughter,
Mary S. Mallard.

Howdy for all the servants.

Mrs. Mary Jones *to* Mrs. Mary S. Mallard[t]

Arcadia, *Wednesday*, March 30th, 1864

My dearest Daughter,

Your last favor was received yesterday, and greatly interested us in the poor refugees you so kindly relieved. But I felt perfectly incensed at your repeated losses—cow and poultry all gone! If you think it could be done, I could send you up another cow and a few hens and turkeys. They are all very busy at this time laying eggs; not one setting yet. The poor geese, I believe for want of their accustomed feeding, have eaten up their own eggs, so we will have no goslings. I hope the turkeys will do well, as Kate tries her best with them. I despair of doing anything at Montevideo. Hawks and cholera are awful enemies!

Patience continues extremely feeble; I am anxious about her. Richard, after a serious attack of something like pneumonia, is again out this week.

Elvira was married Saturday week, *Henry officiating!* I gave her some substantials and a syrup cake and pone, and today in visiting Patience looked in upon the bridal decorations. Wreaths of China brier were festooned over the doors and around the room, and on the mantelpiece stood two bottles filled with large bunches of dogwood flowers. *Flora* was one of the bridesmaids, and Tom one of the groomsmen. I think she has married well.

I have just had a delightful visit from my dear Marion Glen and her niece Laleah Dunwody. Marion is a lovely Christian woman whose light is not under a bushel. She desired warmest love to yourself and Robert; wants to see you and your little ones.

Mrs. Andrews sent home another piece last week. . . . I will send her the last of the warp this week, and have your woolen yarn spun as soon as the sheep are sheared, which will be the last of April or first of May.

Your aunt and cousins came near being burnt out last Thursday. It was prayer meeting: Mr. Buttolph had walked; the ladies were at home. Whilst speaking, Mr. Cassels called to him: "Your house is on fire!" He closed without waiting for practical observations, benediction, or amen, and started to run home, but was taken up in a buggy. The house caught from a spark on the roof, and but for the mercy of God and the timely help of good neighbors must have been consumed.

Your brother wrote from Florida last week in fine spirits; says they are all fattening on good *pine smoke*. His direction is Lake City, care of Major General Patton Anderson. He is at Camp Milton, near Baldwin; the Liberty Troop with other cavalry are four miles in advance.

I have quite a mind to ask the refusal of the academy at Walthourville. In case the enemy compel you to leave Atlanta, it would be well to have a retreat. The servants all send a thousand howdies for you and your servants; Little Sister many kisses. Best love to Robert and yourself, and kisses for my dear children.

Ever, my darling child, your affectionate mother,
Mary Jones.

Mrs. Mary Jones *to* Miss Mary Jones Mallard[t]
Arcadia, *Wednesday,* March 30th, 1864

My dear Granddaughter,

Do you remember how your dear grandpapa's study looked—where the desk stood, and how the bright warm sunshine used to fall upon it from the windows that opened on the western side of the house in the wintertime; and when the spring came, the two old mulberry trees would spread out their green branches and shade them so beautifully? Do you remember how the books were arranged all around the room, and everything was in such perfect order and neatness? And where the rocking chair stood before the fire, where he used to sit and hold you on his knee when you came in to see him, or give you some pretty book with pictures to look at, or let you take a pencil and mark all over a piece of paper? . . . Grandmama is sitting alone in the study to write you this little letter and tell you how dearly she loves you and Brother Charlie, and longs to see you, and hopes, if God wills, to come and see you this summer.

Little Sister talks of you both; and sometimes in the morning she calls you when she first wakes up, and I think she has been dreaming about you.

I am very much pleased to hear that you go to Sunday school and love your teacher. You must obey all she tells you, and always say your lessons well. Can you read yet? Your Cousin Jimmie is very fond of his book, and comes regularly to his papa to be taught; and he is quite advanced in *The Young Reader*. The other day we went to Flemington, and Willie and Jimmie both repeated a beautiful hymn they had just learned, and did not miss a word of it—the hymn your mother and Uncle Charles and Uncle Joe used to say when they were small; so that Grandmama remembered it, and now writes it from memory for you and Brother to learn to say to me when I come up. Cousin Marion Glen, one of my dear friends, has been a week with me, and her niece Miss Laleah Dunwody, and she said a sweet little grace for Little Sister to learn; and I write it down here for you to say when there is no one to ask a blessing:

> Lord, bless this food which now I take
> To do me good, for Jesus' sake.

And this is the hymn:

> My Heavenly Father, all I see
>   Around me and above
> Sends forth a hymn of praise to Thee
>   And speaks Thy boundless love.
>
> The clear blue sky is full of Thee,
>   The woods so dark and lone.
> The soft south wind, the sounding sea
>   Worship the Holy One.
>
> The humming of the insect throng,
>   The prattling, sparkling rill,
> The birds with their melodious song
>   Repeat Thy praises still.
>
> And Thou dost hear them every one;
>   Thou also hearest me.
> I know that I am not alone
>   When I but think of Thee.

I am sorry my paper is filled up. You must write me a letter very soon. Kiss dear Mama and Papa and Brother for Little Sister and Grandmama. And tell all the servants howdy for us.

Ever your loving grandmama,
Mary Jones.

Little Sister puts in the violets for Sissy.

XXI

Atlanta, *Thursday,* March 31st, 1864

My dearest Mother,

I am all alone tonight, and did I not know that it is a fact that this house is inhabited by tribes of rats, I should imagine myself besieged by robbers both great and small. We have the satisfaction of knowing that some fifty of the thieves and housebreakers who have committed nightly depredations are safely committed to jail.

Mr. Mallard left me on Tuesday for Cuthbert, where he has gone to attend the meeting of Presbytery. Uncle Henry invited him to stay with him, and he expected to do so. He will probably see Uncle John. He will not return until next week. Kitty Stiles will probably return with him from Macon. Hattie Nisbet has so far recovered from the scarlet fever as to be able to sit in the parlor, and thus far has experienced no ill effects. I should have been glad to have had Kitty with me during Mr. Mallard's absence, for in these lawless days it is not pleasant to remain alone.

We have formed General Dahlgren's acquaintance. He commanded the first successful repulse at Vicksburg, and would have continued there; but General Lovell of New Orleans was placed over him, and he would not serve under him, so resigned. He has a son in Virginia who has passed through twenty-three pitched battles and has never received a wound. Is not this a wonderful providence? On several occasions comrades on either side have been killed, and still he was preserved unhurt.

There has been quite an interesting return of a young man in our congregation. His parents had heard nothing of him for nine months, and were almost beginning to mourn him as dead, when one evening, without any intimation, he walked into their sitting room. He had been a prisoner, and had written several times to his parents and bribed the sentinels to mail the letters, but they destroyed them. The young man says when he heard that he had been paroled and was to leave the prison the next day to be sent to the South, he felt as if he were going to heaven. I suppose we can scarcely imagine the relief and joy these poor fellows experience when they are released from those horrible demons.

Our weather continues cold and unpleasant, and some of the wise ones predict more snow in a few days. The cherry and apple trees are now in full bloom, and I hope we will have no more freezing weather, for most of our peaches have been destroyed, and it would be a calamity to have the cherries and apples killed too.

I received a letter from Aunt Lou two days ago; she mentioned that Aunt Eliza had been more unwell, and they had all suffered from colds. The girls had not returned; they are now on a visit to Cousin Clifford Powers and Cousin Maria Gilbert. They will probably stop with me on their way up.

What is the name of the Major Colcock in Liberty? Is he the same we saw in Charleston some years ago?

I have been very much relieved to see everything so quiet in Florida, and I hope my dear brother may not be exposed in battle.

The enemy are very quiet above us. The weather has been such that it would be out of the question to make any forward movement. Many believe that our army will soon fall back to Kingston, owing to the difficulty of transporting provisions. And the country around is entirely eaten out. Of course no one knows anything about it. General Johnston has proverbially been a man of his own counsel, and I presume no one knows what he will do with the army—advance, we hope, when the weather permits.

It is growing late, and I must go to bed, as I have been sewing pretty busily today. I send you a table which may be of some use to you in discounting old currency. It has been in our daily paper for some weeks past. Mamie and Charlie send their love and sweetest kisses to Grandmama and Little Sister. There is a cedar tree growing in the corner of the yard which Mamie says they call "Grandma"; and every day they run to it to get some cake and groundnuts and all sorts of nice things. Do give love to Uncle William. Did you hear him say he had received a letter from me? Good night, dear Mother. I feel that our Heavenly Father watches over us, and in His own good time we shall be united again.

Your loving daughter,
Mary S. Mallard.

Mrs. Mary S. Mallard *to* Mrs. Mary Jones[t]

Atlanta, Thursday, April 7th, 1864

My very dear Mother,

You must excuse a short letter this time, as I am just out of bed, having been very unwell all week. I have suffered severely from headaches this winter; and the last two attacks I have been obliged to go to bed, and have felt quite weak in consequence. Yesterday I sent for Dr. Logan, and he has prescribed, and will put me on a course of tonics which he thinks will relieve me. My headaches are occasioned by nervous exhaustion, and I hope will not return.

Mr. Mallard has been away since last Tuesday week. I felt quite anxious about his not coming at the appointed time, but received a letter this evening saying he had felt it his duty to remain, as there was a precious work going on in Cuthbert. . . . He mentions that quite a number of lads and young men almost ready for the war are concerned. I trust and pray the Holy Spirit will be poured out in large measure, and that Mr. Mallard may receive a blessing which may extend to his church here. It has been in a very cold state. Oh, that it may be revived!

Mamie was delighted with her letter, and will answer it when I get well. Charlie and herself send many kisses for dear Grandmama and Little Sister. With warmest love,

Your affectionate daughter,
Mary S. Mallard.

Mrs. Mary S. Mallard *to* Mrs. Mary Jones[t]

Atlanta, *Friday,* April 15th, 1864

My dearest Mother,

After an absence of two weeks Mr. Mallard returned yesterday afternoon. He had a delightful meeting in Cuthbert, and preached almost every day. . . . The interest was unabated at the close, so that all hope the good work will continue. . . . There is a revival in the Baptist and Methodist churches in Macon; also one in the Methodist church in Americus. And today news has come that a wonderful work is going on at the front near Dalton. What a blessing it would be if this good work could be carried on throughout our whole land!

Whilst Mr. Mallard was in Cuthbert Uncle Henry was elected and ordained elder of the Presbyterian church there. His little baby was baptized by Uncle John just before his ordination. Mr. Mallard says Cuthbert is a very pleasant place, and Uncle Henry is very comfortably located. Aunt Abby is as fat as possible, and the children very hearty. The people in Cuthbert presented Mr. Mallard with a hundred dollars as a token of their appreciation and gratitude for his services. Two of Mr. Hendee's sons (the pastor of the church) were among the converts. I hope Mr. Mallard will bring a blessing back with him.

Kitty Stiles returned on last Tuesday, and will be with me for some time now.

Emily and Mr. Green spent a night with us this week on their way to visit Mr. Green's parents. They will return tomorrow and will take tea with us, as they are detained some four or five hours, the cars not connecting with the West Point train. Emily seems very well, and is pleasantly located in Newnan. They had just come from Marietta, where Mr. Green had been to be ordained.

Aunt Eliza has been very sick with a cold and something like rheumatism. Aunt Mary said if she had continued sick she would have sent down for Mr. Mallard and myself. Our spring is so cold and damp that I am not surprised at its affecting her health.

We have had a great deal of uncomfortable weather, and persons here tell me the season is at least one month later than usual. It is so cold that the seeds that have already come up grow very slowly. I have planted a large bed of Irish potatoes, which are coming up very nicely.

I wrote you such a short letter last week that I did not answer your last to me. You ask if you should send some chickens and turkeys. It is so late in the season that I do not think the turkeys would be very good, as the hens are laying, and I would rather not have my two gobblers sent up. In regard to the cow, unless we could get a *very fine* one from the low country, it would not pay to keep it. The rates on the railroad have risen very much, so that it would probably cost at least fifty dollars to bring a cow here; and then everything upon which we would feed a cow is enormously high. It is almost necessary for us to have a cow, though we do not yet see how we can get one. Butter is ten dollars a pound, and sweet milk from a dollar to a dollar and a half a quart. If we could get a cow that would give milk enough to make butter, it would be a great comfort to us.

You said in your last you thought of applying for the academy in Walthourville in case we should be driven from this point, so that there might be an anchor ahead. A letter which we received from Mr. Sam Mallard mentioned that Mrs. Ben Screven had rented it, and was keeping house there with Mr. Screven's two elder children; and she could only rent it conditionally, as the trustees held it open to a pastor as soon as one should come. I feel, dear Mother, that we are in the hands of Providence, and can only act up to present light. And should this field of labor be closed to Mr. Mallard, then we must trust Him for direction, and I believe He will take care of us. At present this place is in no particular danger, for the indications are towards a battle in Virginia, which all believe will be a most bloody struggle; though of course we none of us know how the tide of war will turn or what point will be most in danger.

I hope we will have a pleasant summer together. Mr. Mallard, the children, and myself are all longing for the time to come for you to be with us. When will you come? I have a sunny *little room* waiting for you. My only regret is that our rooms are so very small. . . . The cold has killed all our peaches, but we shall have cherries and a few apples and some quinces, and I hope our grapes will do well. I should like to try making a little wine if they do well. There are a plenty of Catawba vines here.

Kitty desires much love to you. She will probably return to Habersham this summer. Next Monday will be Mamie's birthday, so Kitty and I have been contriving a cloth head for the big doll as a surprise for her on that day. We locked the parlor doors while we were at work so that she should not find out what we were after, and she has been very curious to know what we could be doing.

Please, dear Mother, send me some pepper seed in your next letter. The paper of peppers I brought with me was entirely eaten up by the rats before I knew anything about it. Kiss Little Sister many times for us all, and accept our united love. Howdy for the servants. Tell Elvira I am glad to hear of her marriage, and wish her much happiness. How is Mom Patience now?

Your affectionate daughter,
Mary S. Mallard.

MRS. MARY S. MALLARD *to* MRS. MARY JONES[t]

Atlanta, Wednesday, April 27th, 1864

My dear Mother,

I wish you could have seen the delight of the children upon the receipt of the nice candy you sent them. It was a great treat to us all. Mamie seemed to enjoy her birthday very much. In commemoration of our own birthdays, which you used to celebrate so pleasantly for us, I made a plate of cake (boys and girls, rabbits, etc.), which gave Charlie and herself the greatest delight. Kitty manufactured a cloth head for my large doll, and this was another great source of pleasure, notwithstanding its ugly face. In addition to this, we were previously engaged to dine with Mr. and Mrs. Rogers, and there Mamie found Maria Whitehead, Mrs. Charles Whitehead's little daughter. The only drawback to her pleasure was a severe blow which she received the night before. She was running very quickly through the door, and struck her forehead just above the eye against the lock (or rather the iron place in which the catch fastens). She was going with a great deal of force—so much so that she was knocked down; and I think the cut went to the bone. It is about three-quarters of an inch long. I felt very much troubled, and we sent for Dr. Logan; but he was unable to come, but sent some sticking plaster, which Kitty and I put on; and I hope the scar will be small. Perhaps it will not show at all, for I put the lips of the wound very closely and carefully together. I cannot tell yet, as the plaster has not yet dropped off. She seemed to suffer no inconvenience whatever afterwards. . . .

You want to know what we think about the safety of this place. I think at present we are as safe here as you are in Liberty, and perhaps a little safer; though of course no one can predict what the changes of war will bring. Persons seem to have ceased fearing for this place, and many think General Johnston will soon make a forward movement into Tennessee. He has a very large army—some fifty thousand effective men—and is being daily reinforced. If we are ever driven from this place, I feel that Providence will direct us where to go; and it does not seem worthwhile for us to provide for that event. It would have been very pleasant for us to have spent a few weeks with you at home, but it was impossible for us to do so, for the season is too far spent. And it is so difficult to take children about at this time, for just now reinforcements are passing on to Virginia and elsewhere, so that the cars are used chiefly for their transportation. And then, dear Mother, you will so soon be with us that I would prefer deferring my visit until next winter, should I live until then.

I have heard from Marietta several times lately. Aunt Eliza has had several very severe attacks, and the last was of so serious a nature they thought she would have died. Hearing this this evening, I have determined to go up tomorrow morning and spend a day with her. She is aged now, and those who have passed their threescore years and ten sometimes pass away very quickly. I will leave the children in charge of Kitty and Mr. Mallard.

We have just succeeded in getting a cow, which we are trying now. I don't know how she will do. Her owners ask four hundred dollars for the cow and calf. This is cheap for this region, as cows command from six hundred to a thousand dollars.

We are all pretty well. Niger has been complaining of headache and cold, but is bright this evening. I gave him a dose of oil, and he has been quiet at home for two days. . . . He does not seem altogether satisfied with his place, because he can't make anything for himself. Says he has no fault to find with Mr. Henderson, as he never meddles with anybody, and there is no kind of work there that would be too hard for him. He says you told him if anything did not please him he must complain to me, and that I might write you about it. His employment seems to have been chiefly job work— hauling tan bark, whitewashing, chopping wood, etc.

Mr. Mallard and the children unite with me in warmest love to Little Sister and yourself.

Your affectionate daughter,
Mary S. Mallard.

I would rather not have my woolen yarn mixed with cotton, as I find it is not so elastic as the all-wool and shrinks more. So please, dear Mother, whenever Rose is ready to spin it, let her put only wool. The rest of the broken bunch might be sent to Mrs. Andrews as we first intended. Yarn is forty to fifty per bunch.

Mrs. Mary Jones *to* Mrs. Mary S. Mallard[t]

Arcadia, *Saturday,* April 30th, 1864

My dearest Daughter,

I did not intend so long a time should pass before writing you, but I have been leading so irregular a life, with so many interruptions, that you must excuse me.

Your brother returned from Florida on last Wednesday week, the campaign having suddenly closed. I received a letter from Eva and himself on Saturday begging that I would come down and bring the baby, which I did on Tuesday, and returned today, having had a very pleasant visit to them. I was thankful to see the state of your brother's feelings, and hope that his thoughts have been specially directed, during the scenes through which he has recently passed, to the great and all-important subject. I know Robert and yourself ever bear him in remembrance at a throne of grace; and I feel more and more the power and efficacy of fervent, believing prayer. What a blessing to our army and our country! God in the outpouring of His Holy Spirit is giving us the highest token of His love and favor. What gratitude should fill our hearts as Christians for all these evidences of divine mercy! And we can but hope the day of our deliverance from our wicked foes is drawing near. I have never despaired of the final issue, but I have never before felt the dawn of hope so near. I trust it is not a presumptuous delusion! I have many interesting relics from the battlefield in Florida.

You will love Eva. She is a most lovable person, and a gifted mind. Her poetical talent is of a high order. She treats me with great affection, and loves Little Sister. It is very pleasant to see the attachment between them.

I received visits from many friends, but went only to the cemetery, where I took the baby. Dear little creature, she appeared to comprehend the object of the visit; gathered all the flowers and green sprigs in the enclosure and laid them on the vault. She looked up into my face and pointing to the door said: "Is my dear papa in there too?" (She never forgets her "dear bessing papa," as she usually speaks of your beloved father.) Oh, my daughter, this afternoon *the truth* that he is not here—that I shall no more behold him in mortal flesh—came over me with awful power as I went to the vacant study! God grant that this may not be the sorrow which worketh death but that which bringeth forth the peaceable fruits of righteousness!

Your brother, although for the present returned to his old command, is in daily expectation of orders to some other point—he thinks either in Virginia or North Carolina. He is looking well, but suffers from rheumatism in the back and down his limbs, and has had neuralgic headaches. In Florida it was very wet, and he often slept in wet clothes on the ground.

I was truly sorry to know you had lost your cow, and that Robert had not the full use of Jim. I hope he has not sold him, but only *let* him out. We have had such a severe winter that the cattle down here could scarcely live. We lost a great many, and about twenty head of sheep and lambs, at Montevideo; here they have done better. But *often* this winter I have not had a drop of milk, and for months not a particle of butter saving an occasional saucer sent me by Sister Susan. As soon as the grass springs and they milk here, I will put up the butter for Joe and yourself, and think during the next month they may accumulate some for me to bring or send you.

Patience has been sick since the first of February, and is still feeble, although about. I want to let her visit her children at Indianola this summer, and will leave Kate in charge here. Rose, I presume, will be confined before long.

I will try and get your wool spun as soon as the sheep are sheared. Mrs. Andrews is now on the last piece. All have had clothing below. About ten yards, I think, was wanting for the children at Indianola. Would you like me to bring up the piece Mrs. Andrews now has—*the dyed warp?* She is an honest woman, and after her toll is taken out sends home more than I got from Mrs. Butler paying her for the whole.

I heard today at the depot of the death of *Julia King* (*Cay* that was). She had been confined, but it was said died of pneumonia. . . . And Mrs. Harden is returning to the county: Anne was married last week to Dr. Adams of Augusta. . . . If dear Kitty is still with you, do give my best love to her. I had hoped if she came to the low country to see her.

Time passes so rapidly I will soon have to be moving. Want to make all my dear children visits, if the Lord permits. Will spend a few weeks with Charles, the same with Joe, and then come up to you, if you are permitted to remain in Atlanta. Dear Aunty I want to see, and friends in Marietta.

Brother William has not been at church for three Sabbaths; he is suffering from his old pain in the back. Sister Susan and Laura are quite well. Mr. Buttolph went down to Savannah with me on his way to Charleston. He goes on invitation to preach to the Guards.

It is Saturday night, a heavy thunderstorm with hail prevailing. Good night, my dear child. May the Lord bless you all, and give you a peaceful and happy day of rest on His Holy Sabbath! With best love to Robert and yourself, and kisses for my grandchildren, and howdies for the servants,

Ever your affectionate mother,
Mary Jones.

Miss Mary Jones Mallard *to* Mrs. Mary Jones[t]

Atlanta, *Thursday,* May 5th, 1864

My dear Grandmama,

I have been wanting to write you ever since your sweet letter came, but Mama has had so much headache that she could not write often, and could not lend me her hands until today. Mama has just read me your letter over again. I remember all about dear Grandpapa's study, and how, when I asked him for pretty books, he would let me go and take them out myself. And I remember how he used to kiss me in the morning.

I long to see you, and I hope the Lord will take care of you, and that you will come up soon this spring to see us. I have some beautiful flowers on the mantelpiece, and the day you come to see us I will have more beautiful flowers for you to see. Tell Little Sister she loves flowers so much she must be sure and come up, because there are a great many more flowers in the woods up here. Apples and cherries are here, and if she will come she can get these. So make haste! Make haste!

I go to Sunday school every Sabbath, and love my teacher very much. She always gives me a pretty book to bring home, and Mama reads it to me. I can say the beautiful hymn you sent for Bubber and myself, and Mama is going to teach me to sing it. I am learning to read, and try to read "The House that Jack Built" and "Dame Trot" by myself; but some of the words are too long: Mama has to tell them to me. Bubber and I learned the grace you wrote for us—I mean the one Little Sister knows; and when Papa was in Cuthbert, Bubber used to put his head down and ask a blessing for Mama and me.

I will put in some beautiful honeysuckles in this letter for Little Sister, so that you may know what kind of flowers we have in our flowerpot. I love you, Grandmama, and send my love to Little Sister. This is all I wish to tell you. Mama, Papa, and Bubber all send love. Tell all the servants howdy for me.

Your loving little granddaughter,
Mary Jones Mallard.

Mrs. Mary S. Mallard *to* Mrs. Mary Jones[t]

Atlanta, *Thursday,* May 5th, 1864

Dear Mother,

I have written almost entirely at Mamie's dictation; the language is her own. She was so full of the flowers, and had so much to say of them, that I should have filled more than one sheet with this suggestive theme. I wish I could put my vase of wild azaleas before you—three varieties of pink and one deep orange. I have never seen any so beautiful.

I received your letter written upon your return from Savannah yesterday, and am glad to know you are well. Your visit to Savannah must have refreshed you very much. I cannot tell you how our hearts rejoiced at such tidings from my dear brother, and trust that He who began the work will carry it on and perfect it and make him a true child of God. This is a time when I think we have every encouragement to pray, for God seems very near and willing to bless our army, and has poured out His Spirit in a wonderful manner upon very many. I think the waking up of the churches at home one of the surest indications of peace we have ever had—or rather the strongest reason for hoping for peace.

We all fear the next terrible struggle, and I trust our people will not be so lifted up by our recent successes as to be led to vainglory and forgetfulness of our merciful Heavenly Father, the source of all these blessings. A battle is daily expected at the front, though some persons think this will be chiefly a diversion to prevent the troops being sent to General Lee. The Yankees are thought to have about eighty thousand men at Chattanooga, and General Johnston has about sixty thousand, all in fine spirits and expecting victory. I trust the battle will be decided very soon. No one seems to apprehend any danger for this place, for falling back is not General Johnston's policy. The committees here are getting ready and preparing themselves to go up to the relief of the wounded should a battle take place.

We were shocked to hear of Julia King's death. She was a fine woman—the flower of the family. Did she profess conversion before her death? It is very sad: a young mother.

I spent a day and two nights in Marietta last week. I found Aunty better than I expected to find her. She was up and engaged in knitting, and was cheerful, though I thought she stooped more than she did a few months ago and looked older and feebler. She had been very ill the week before with cramp and something like rheumatism. Aunt Mary seems to feel very anxious about her. Her friends are exceedingly kind to her; almost every day something is sent to her. The cow you sent them had a calf the day before I went up. They had not seen it, as it was at the house of one of their country friends, where they had put her to board until the calf should be born. They are all delighted, and hope she will give them a plenty of milk now.

I sent some homespun for Rose for diapers and baby shirts, and some spun cloth to make a frock for it. I also sent some homespun to Bess to make a frock for her baby. The bundles were put inside of some bags which Mr. Mallard sent Mr. Quarterman. Will you be so kind, dear Mother, as to ask them if Mr. Quarterman gave them the bundles? They were marked separately.

Mr. Mallard has not sold Jim. I do not think anything but the greatest necessity would compel us to do that. We could not afford to keep him, as corn is from eleven to fifteen dollars a bushel, and difficult to be gotten at that; so Mr. Mallard let one of the surgeons have him to use and keep, Mr. Mallard still having him on Mondays to use in pastoral visitation. Horses are selling from one to three thousand dollars, so any surgeon who wants a horse is glad to get one without having to purchase.

We all look forward to the time when you will be with us, and hope you will not tarry too long by the way. I think I have the best claim upon you. Kitty sends you a great deal of love, and says she is too sorry not to see you this year. She is still with us, and will not return to Habersham for a week or two yet. Thank you, dear Mother, for the pepper seed. My garden is very backward, though I believe not much more so than some of my neighbors'. Mr. Mallard and the children unite with me in warmest love to Little Sister and yourself.

Your affectionate daughter,
Mary S. Mallard.

I think I would like twelve yards of the woolen cloth Mrs. Andrews is weaving sent up here—that is, if all the others above and below have been served. Thank you, dear Mother, for giving it out to them.

Rev. John Jones *to* Mrs. Mary Jones[t]

Refuge, Thursday, May 12th, 1864

My dear Sister,

Your last affectionate letter reached me on the 7th inst., and we thank you for all your tender interest in Dunwody. You and my dear brother were more to him as parents than as uncle and aunt. . . . Our anxiety for Dunwody, which has been very great, has been somewhat relieved by Major General Cobb, to whom I had written in Dunwody's behalf. Major Harris, late commander of conscripts for Georgia, and who had Dunwody ejected as a supernumerary, has himself been superseded by Colonel William M. Browne, aide-de-camp of President Davis. On the arrival of Colonel

Browne, General Cobb presented Dunwody's case to him; and immediately I received a letter from General Cobb stating that Colonel Browne would allow Dunwody to join any command he might select. And the day following the general wrote me again that Colonel Browne authorized him to say that if my son would report immediately for duty at Macon, that he would for the present restore him to his position, and permanently if possible.

On the arrival of these letters (which I answered immediately with my thanks and promise of Dunwody's early appearance) Dunwody was absent on a scout for deserters in Decatur County. A call having been made on the citizens to go in pursuit of deserters, Dunwody volunteered and was put in command of a squad. The party captured seven with arms in their hands, all hearty and strong. As soon as Dunwody rested (one day) we drove to Albany, and thence he went to Macon last Friday, and has written us that he had seen Colonel Browne, who told him to report at camp and he would send him orders in the afternoon. I trust all will be well, although he says that he is not yet out of the woods. His not returning home looks favorable. Oh, if he were only a child of God, what a burden would be removed from our hearts!

I have been very much occupied lately. And a fearful drought, together with a very cold spring, made the prospect of the corn crops exceedingly gloomy. But yesterday we had a special blessing in the shape of a delightful rain for twelve hours more or less at intervals. Today is cool. The wheat crops of this section are very fine, and with rain will be heavy. I hope you will sow a few acres at least this autumn, D.V.

I am truly sorry that you may lose the services of Mr. Jackson. I think you can have him detailed if the case is stated to the secretary of war.

We are passing through a fearful crisis. Oh, the call for prayer and gratitude and humility! Our successes in the Trans-Mississippi Department have been wonderful, and God is helping Generals Lee and Johnston. To His name be praise forever!

My dear Janey (who is almost overcome with warping and weaving) and our boys unite with me in best love to you and unnumbered kisses for dear Little Sister. The dear child, how I do love her! Old Mama is smart; is often at morning prayers, and sends her love to you, and constantly remembers you and talks of you. Howdy for your servants.

Ever your affectionate brother,
J. Jones.

Best love to Charles and Eva when you see them next; the same to Joseph and Carrie and their children, Daughter, Robert, and their little ones.

May 13th. My dear sister, before closing I mention the receipt today of a letter from our old aunt. They have had a distressing winter from excessive cold and scarcity of provisions and high prices. I am distressed about her, but absolutely I have not the money to send, and am very short in the provision line, having made last year only a half-crop, and am feeding by rule. And it is thirty-two miles to the nearest depot if I had anything to send. I am troubled about my old aunty. Mr. William Russell—noble man—has offered to pay their Confederate tax and give them time to return the money to him. He has been more like a son to Aunty than a friend. He lately gave them a bunch of thread and a sack of flour. Oh, that peace may soon come to the relief of many sufferers in the land!

Once more, adieu. Write soon and let me know your summer arrangements.

I hope soon to organize a church at the mill a mile hence.

Mrs. Mary S. Mallard *to* Mrs. Mary Jones[t]
                                        Atlanta, *Saturday,* May 14th, 1864
My dearest Mother,

You are no doubt sharing the universal anxiety felt in regard to the issue of the impending battles. We have had no telegrams from Virginia since the 10th, except one stating that everything has been filed and dispatches will be sent through as soon as practicable. I presume it is necessary to withhold news from the enemy. Kitty is still with me and in much suspense, for her brother is in Longstreet's corps and was most probably in the battle. I do not want her to leave until she hears of his safety. News can reach her so much more quickly here than in Habersham.

We are hourly expecting to hear the battle has commenced on our front, as the enemy are reported as being in full force not far from Resaca, which is sixteen miles this side of Dalton. They came by a circuitous route through Sugar Valley, and their present position has compelled General Johnston to change his whole line of battle. An immense number of wagons and provisions are being sent up, and many think General Johnston will advance if successful. The Yankees are said to have about eighty thousand, and our army is very large—probably seventy thousand. The men are in the best of spirits and very confident of success. We pray God that He will fight the battle for us, and that we may not be given over to vain confidence. The relief committees here are getting ready to go up and attend the wounded, and a portion of them went up yesterday to make arrangements. The hospitals are cleared of sick men, and all are getting ready for the wounded. Some men detailed for the purpose came here yesterday to beg for rags. All these things make us feel what a terrible thing war is. We will be in a dreadful predicament should General Johnston be unsuccessful or be compelled to fall back, but no one seems to contemplate this. All have the utmost confidence in his skill.

Dr. Logan and Mr. Pease took tea with us last evening. Dr. Logan is a perfect gentleman, and very pleasant. I am sorry his family lives so far from me—too far for us to exchange visits often. Mrs. Hull is quite as far; I regret this too, for she has been very polite and kind to us. This place is so scattered that it is difficult to visit without a conveyance.

We have had some strawberries sent us this week, and have enjoyed them very much. Everything is acceptable in these scarce hard times. Think of our paying ten dollars for two pounds of beefsteak! And this is the only thing to be had. I hear occasionally of chickens sold at eight and ten dollars apiece.

Mr. Mallard has had a call to go as chaplain to the 4th Georgia Cavalry, given by Colonel Avery. Of course he would not think of leaving his church. He has a large field among the soldiers who attend his church.

Mary Sophia, Lilla, and Ellen passed through day before yesterday on their way home. Mr. Mallard saw them from the Macon to the Marietta train. Lilla had her arm in a sling, having broken it while visiting Cousin Maria Gilbert. She was on horseback and fell in consequence of some horses' running and frightening her horse.

We are all pretty well except colds, induced by remarkably cold, cloudy weather. Kitty sends much love to you. Mr. Mallard and the children unite with me in much love to yourself and Little Sister. Howdy for the servants. Do, my dear mother, don't stay too late at Arcadia.

> Your affectionate daughter,
> Mary S. Mallard.

Mrs. Mary S. Mallard *to* Mrs. Mary Jones[t]

> Atlanta, *Thursday,* May 19th, 1864

My dearest Mother,

I wrote you late last week telling you we were in daily expectation that the general engagement would commence on our front. We are still in a state of expectation, though all believe it will take place in the next two days. Our army has been steadily falling back for a week past in order to gain good fighting ground and a position that cannot be flanked. The men are in the highest spirits, and express the utmost confidence in General Johnston. They are now at Kingston. Whether they will fall still further back no one knows, though it is conjectured the great battle will be fought at the Etowah River. Our army has had continued skirmishing—or rather it ought to be called a succession of small battles; and in every instance the Yankees have been handsomely repulsed with great slaughter. Our men have fought almost entirely behind breastworks, so that the most of their wounds are slight; that is, the surgeons call them slight, but they all seem terrible. Already about two thousand five hundred wounded have been brought down. Should a general engagement take place, our town will be more than crowded for a time. Those who are able to bear the journey are sent to other points. I trust our merciful Heavenly Father will fight the battle for us and crown our arms with success, for a reverse would be terrible: in all probability this place would go next. Should our army be victorious, it would be disastrous in the extreme to the Yankees, for they are so far from their base of supplies. They are pressing on in very heavy force. Our army numbers over seventy-five thousand effective men, and it is being constantly reinforced.

The relief committees from this place, Macon, Alabama, Florida, and elsewhere have all come up, and are very active in their attentions to the wounded. They seem to be provided with almost everything. I saw one of the gentlemen going around with a haversack full of tobacco distributing it to all who were out of it. Our ladies are very busy preparing and taking food to the depot to give the wounded before they are removed to the distributing hospital. Poor fellows, they seem so glad to get it. I was at the cars day before yesterday when the train came in, and it made my heart ache to see ten men stretched upon litters wounded in all portions of their body, but bearing all their sufferings without a groan. I observed one man particularly who had lost his leg conversing as cheerfully as though nothing had happened. There are comparatively few very severely wounded. Most of them are able to ride in the ambulances, and many of them to walk to the different hospitals. If you have any arrowroot to spare, please send me a little by express. I think by preparing it myself it will be very acceptable. Mr. Mallard went up to the front yesterday to assist in taking care of the wounded. I presume he will be down on Saturday, as the work is so constant and fatiguing they are relieved every day or two. Day before yesterday the lives of forty men were saved by the timely assistance of the committees. Humanly speaking, they would all have died. Mr. Mallard went off with a haversack of eatables, a tin cup, and canteen of whiskey.

A few nights ago, while Mr. Mallard was assisting with the wounded at the depot, a surgeon introduced himself as Dr. Webb, and asked if he had not married Mary Jones; that he had married Mary Castleman, and she had been in Atlanta; but it had not occurred to her that I might be here until after she returned to Forsyth, where Dr. Webb is stationed. At present she has gone North by flag of truce by way of City Point to get her baby, and Dr. Webb is beginning to wonder why she does not return. I cannot imagine what her baby could be doing at the North. I presume when Dr. Webb returns from the front he will call and see me. I should have liked to have seen Mary while she was here, and if she returns I presume I shall see her; but she is such a shrewd, managing person that if Dr. Webb does not mind, she will fix herself comfortably at the North and leave him to take care of himself until after the war.

Kitty has not heard from her brother yet, and of course feels very anxious about him. She will probably go to Habersham next week. I trust she will hear before she leaves.

The children send many kisses and love to dear Grandmama and Little Sister. The weather continues cool. Kitty desires much love. I received a letter from Cousin Laura last week. Give love to Aunt Susan and herself; also to Uncle William. With warmest love to yourself, dear Mother,

Your affectionate child,
Mary S. Mallard.

Mrs. Mary S. Mallard *to* Mrs. Susan M. Cumming[t]

Atlanta, *Friday,* May 20th, 1864

My dear Aunt and Cousin,

I am truly obliged to you for your letters just received. I cannot tell you how much concerned I am about my dear mother. I trust she is better; but if I should receive a letter from you tomorrow saying she is worse, I will take the next train and be with her on Monday. Do, my dear aunt, write me constantly, if only a line, and tell me *exactly what you think* of my dear mother. The communication is very direct now, and if allowed to pass by the military authorities, I could soon be with you. It is a great comfort to me to know that you are with Mother, and I know you will take every care of her. If she expresses any wish that I should go down, do let me know. Your letter came through very quickly—written on the 19th and received this evening (20th).

Mr. Mallard is still with the army attending the wounded. I do not know certainly when he will return, but presume tomorrow, as he expected to be back before Sabbath. It is the impression here that the battle must have commenced today; and if that is the case Mr. Mallard may feel compelled to remain longer. Our last news is that the army has fallen back in the neighborhood of the Etowah, and General Johnston has issued his battle order saying that he will now give battle and will fall back no further. And from all we can gather the army is in line of battle, so I suppose the contest will be decided by tomorrow evening. I scarcely expect Mr. Mallard until after this battle is fought, unless the relief committee insist upon relieving those now engaged with the wounded. It is such heavy work that they send up six or eight new men every day. Of course it is an anxious time with us all, and a time for earnest prayer. If General Johnston is victorious, the Yankees must suffer terribly. All think he is able and will follow up any advantage he may gain.

I wish we had all the old rags from the households in Liberty. There is such a demand for them, and the citizens here have been so frequently called upon that they have very little to give. There is great demand for old sheets to spread over the wounded who are brought down on the cars. You can imagine the necessity for these: when limbs are amputated and the clothing cut off a foot or two above the place, something cooler and lighter than their blankets is necessary to throw over them.

Kitty expects to leave on next Tuesday for Clarkesville. She has heard nothing yet from Edward. His name has not been published in the list of wounded officers, so we conclude he must be safe; though of course nothing short of a letter from him would really be satisfactory.

Do give warmest love to my dear mother, and tell her if she wants me, I will come to her at once; and she must not hesitate to send for me. . . . Much love for yourselves and the children.

Your affectionate
Mary S. Mallard.

Miss Mary E. Robarts *to* Mrs. Mary Jones[t]

Marietta, *Saturday,* May 21st, 1864

My dearest Cousin,

I received your letter a week since, and waited a few days for further developments; but the plot thickened, and the events of this week came crowding upon us so thickly and unexpectedly that I have not had a moment of time scarcely to eat, drink, or sleep.

On Sunday last the surgeons were all ordered up to the front, and a serious engagement (which they called a skirmish) came off on Monday. The wounded came down; several died on the cars. And we were so busy that day working and making bandages and going to the hospitals and sending refreshments to the cars for the wounded that we had no time to bestow a thought on ourselves. Thus it continued for several days. We were told every day that the general battle would come off near Kingston. On Thursday evening General Johnston rode along the lines, and he was cheered. His general order was read at dress parade saying there would be no more falling back: he would lead them into battle confident of victory. With this all went to sleep except pickets. Judge of the surprise when in the morning the army was ordered to fall back! The enemy had attempted to flank him by way of Rome.

The army is now on this side of the Etowah River. The families from above are fleeing before the enemy—the streets filled with all sorts of vehicles, people moving their property of all kinds: cattle, sheep, Negroes. And the stampede has commenced in Marietta: streets filled with movables, neighbors packing and going off. Mr. Rogers came down with his laborers and wagons from the ironworks, took up some of Mr. Ardis' valuables and one trunk for us (containing our quilts and silver) and took them to Atlanta. Mr. Ardis' family will stay till the last moment, then go to Alabama.

You will ask what we are going to do. My dear cousin, we were constantly assured the Yankees would never get here! We tried our best to move to Perry, but could not get transportation; then we were assured that we could not buy provisions there. So, thinking we were in no danger from the enemy, we thought best to stay at home and protect our property; and now we have neither the means to get away nor the place to go to. The relief committees were sent down from the front, and Mr. Mallard stopped to see us for an hour and to know what we meant to do. We asked his advice; he said he could not advise us—that he was at sea himself. The nearest he could come to a conclusion was that if there was a siege, that they would leave Atlanta, but not till the last moment. Thus it is, my dear cousin, the next you hear of us we may be in the Federal lines drawing Federal rations.

You cannot think how miserable I feel. Such a responsibility resting on Louisa and myself! And we are obliged to try and keep calm, as we have our dear mother to account for. Any great excitement or fatigue would be fatal to her. Our dear girls returned a week since. Had been kept away for six months waiting for the battle to come off, and when we thought there was no danger, returned just in time to meet it. If the Yankees really get here, we may send them back to Maria Gilbert's. She was very kind and affectionate to them and invited them to return. We shall have to stay to take care of our property. It is the only home we have, and we are told if we remain it will be protected. But oh, those horrid Yankees! How can I see them enter this place and live? I am so afraid of them!

Please send this to Cousin Susan. Know not when I can write again, I am so broken down with fatigue and excitement. I know our beloved relations pray for us. My confidence in God is unshaken; but when I know how much many better people than I am have been permitted to suffer, my coward heart shrinks from the vandal foe.

Your ever affectionate cousin,
Mary E. Robarts.

If you could see the stir in this place you would think the Yankees were only a mile off. Have you seen Sherman's vile letter?

MRS. MARY S. MALLARD *to* MRS. MARY JONES[t]

Atlanta, *Friday,* May 27th, 1864

My dearest Mother,

I am truly rejoiced to hear through letters from Brother Charlie and Brother Joe that you are decidedly better. I trust our kind Heavenly Father will soon restore you to your accustomed health. I cannot tell you how anxious I was about you; and nothing but my own sickness and the constant apprehension of the approach of the enemy kept me from going immediately to you. I felt very much relieved when I heard that Brother Joe had gone down.

I was quite sick in bed the first of this week, and am still quite weak. I have had a severe cold, which I suppose fell upon my bowels, causing me a great deal of pain and some fever.

We are passing through times of intense anxiety. We hope for a favorable issue, but none know how this campaign will end. The enemy are certainly very near us, McPherson's corps occupying Dallas. It has been a great disappointment to all that they should have proceeded thus far without a battle. General Johnston issued his battle order at Cartersville and undoubtedly intended to have fought there; but the false information brought by his scouts caused him to change his plan and lost him the opportunity. It is said they are laying waste as they come through. We have not heard much from Rome yet.

On Monday night, being restless and wakeful, I was startled by the ringing of our doorbell about two o'clock. I woke Mr. Mallard, and he went in his "disables" to find out who was there. To my astonishment I heard him say: "Yes, ma'am, I will open the door directly." I could not imagine what a lady could be doing there at that hour of the night, but soon found that Mary, Lilla, and Ellen had come down with a gentleman. I was very glad to see them, and we soon had them distributed. I sent Mary up to Kitty's room, spread a bed in the study for the gentleman, sent Mr. Mallard to the sofa in the drawing room and took Lilla with me, and made Mamie give her place to Ellen in the trundle bed. The girls came off without a particle of baggage, as the cars were too crowded for them to bring it. Mr. Bryson remained behind and brought it on Wednesday with the hospital stores. He insisted that the girls should be sent away, and has been as kind as a brother could have been, and went with them on Thursday morning to Fort Valley, and will take them to Perry. They will stay with Cousin Maria Gilbert. I think Mr. Bryson's going all the way with the girls is exceedingly kind, for they have a great deal of baggage, and Nanny with her baby.

I do feel deeply for my dear old aunty, brought to such trials in her old age; though Mr. Bryson, who left them last, says he believes Aunty is bearing it better than Aunt Mary and Aunt Lou. Aunt Mary especially feels it. The girls said Aunt Mary said she believed it would kill her for the Yankees to come to Marietta. "Indeed!" says Aunty. "*I* don't mean to die; it shan't kill *me!*" I was delighted to hear of this spirit, and hope she will be spared through it all. The enemy are moving a little southwest of Marietta, so maybe they will never occupy the place. I know they feel their isolation and desolation terribly now, for the mail has been stopped, and almost every family has left the place: not more than three or four left. They have been so long accustomed to having a number of daily visitors and to being shaken by a half-dozen trains a day that they will feel it terribly. We will watch our opportunities and send them letters whenever we can. The girls—Mary Sophia especially—did not wish to leave, but I think it was very wise to send them away. Their being there might have subjected the family to many more insults and much more trouble; and then they would have been so many more to provide for. They said the panic was very great in Marietta, and the difficulty of getting off very great. Some families waited three days at the depot before they could get off.

A number of persons have left here, though I do not think there has been anything like a panic. We have sent away all of our winter clothing, comforts, carpets, my sewing machine, and most of Mr. Mallard's books to Augusta to Brother Joe, so that if the army does not make a stand at this place, we will not lose everything. We all hope that General Johnston will be successful in driving them away from the city.

Mr. Mallard has been out all morning helping in finding shelters for the poor refugees who have come down here; and he says the last reliable information contradicts the report that McPherson's corps occupies Dallas. Our army is a little beyond that point, and day before yesterday had quite a little battle with the enemy, repulsing them handsomely. The cannonading was heard here. Mr. Mallard conversed with a gentleman who was present and under fire. He says our men behaved most gallantly and repulsed the Yankees in three charges. Our men were behind temporary breastworks. We lost about five hundred killed and wounded, the Yankees two or three thousand. Much of the heavy baggage of the army has been brought to this place, and the town is being quite filled up with army wagons and all the appendages belonging to the rear of an army.

I wish all the ladies in Liberty would send all their rags; they have no idea how much they are needed here, both for the present and the future. They could express the bundle to Mr. Mallard or to Mrs. Winship, president of the Atlanta Hospital Association. There are a great many wounded here now, and of course the number is daily increasing.

Do not feel too uneasy about us, dear Mother. If there is a prospect of the army's falling back to this place or of a battle occurring very near, I will go away with the children. It is a very difficult question to decide what to do. Brother Joe and Carrie have very kindly invited us to go there, but the place where we go must depend upon circumstances. If there is a prospect of a battle that will be decided in a week or two, perhaps I may go there until it is over. But if there should be a prospect of a siege, I think I would have to go to Liberty and take the servants with me. I pray that we may be directed aright and shown what will be best for us. I am living by the light of each day, and have everything so arranged that I could soon pack up my clothing. Of course if the Yankees ever reach this place, we must suffer heavy losses in furniture and everything else; but we are all in good heart and look for victory.

I presume Mr. Rogers' ironworks have been burned, as we know the Etowah works have been.

Kitty left me on Wednesday morning. The same morning Mr. Markham, a classmate of Mr. Mallard's, came here from the army sick, and is still here, though not confined to bed. I have had a full house all week.

I hope yet, dear Mother, that we will enjoy a portion of our summer in peace and quiet, and then we shall hope to have you with us. . . . I wish I could send you a draught of our cool delightful water; we need no ice.

Mr. Mallard and the children unite with me in warmest love. Brother Charlie writes me Little Sister is with them. Love to Aunt Susan, Cousin Laura, and Uncle William. Good-bye, dear Mother.

Your loving daughter,
Mary S. Mallard.

Mrs. Mary S. Mallard *to* Mrs. Mary Jones[t]
Atlanta, *Friday,* June 3rd, 1864
My dearest Mother,

A letter received from Brother Charlie last night mentioned that you would go to Savannah today, so I will direct this letter there. I am truly thankful, my dear mother, to know that you are recovering your strength, and I sincerely hope a removal from care will soon restore you to your accustomed health. Brother Charlie has been very good in writing me, so that I have heard frequently from you.

We are passing through so much anxiety and perplexity that days sometimes seem weeks, and I scarcely realize how time is passing. We have been expecting a general engagement for the past two weeks, and it has not come yet, so that everyone has given up conjecture and now quietly awaits the issue. Our army is about thirty miles from this place, and the Yankees just in front of them. They have made several night attacks recently, and in every instance our men have driven them back with great slaughter. I presume you saw by the papers that seven hundred Yankee dead were left upon the field the night they attacked Cleburne's division. We too are losing many noble lives, though few in comparison with the enemy, for our men fight almost entirely behind breastworks.

Our town is rapidly filling up with the wounded. Some of the hospitals are entirely filled. Stores are being fitted up for hospitals, and I presume the city hall and other buildings will soon be impressed for the same purpose. I have been unable to go to the hospitals myself, as they are very far off, and I have not the strength to walk; but I prepare and send food to them. I have been sending for a week past to a ward filled with Texas men. They often send and beg me to send more arrowroot; sometimes requests come for onions, lettuce, and all manner of things. The bundle of rags and box of arrowroot came quite safely this evening, and will be very acceptable. I will keep the arrowroot and prepare it myself, for it is generally so badly prepared at the hospitals that the men will not eat it.

Mr. Mallard goes down tonight at two o'clock to the cars to assist in having the wounded carried to the various hospitals. There is a great deal of work to be done here now, not only with the wounded but with the refugees, who are here in great numbers. Mr. Mallard works constantly with the committee, and they are doing a great deal of good. They have quite a village of refugees dependent upon them for provisions, and many of them for clothing. The citizens of Savannah have been very generous in sending up rice and corn for them.

A most absurd piece has been published in one of our papers signed "Shadow," which describes a dreadful panic which the author says took place here some ten days ago. He describes the confusion and consternation of the citizens in a most exaggerated manner, and represents the whole population in a state of consternation and all moving off. The whole piece is a falsehood, for no such thing as a panic has ever existed here at all. Some few persons have moved away, and others have sent away articles of value and such things as could not be removed in haste; and this is the extent of the panic. Some of the Jews have removed their possessions, and a few Yankees have gone from our midst; but I believe these are the only men that have deserted the place. Mr. Mallard has been constantly called on the street by his engagements with the committee, and he says everyone seems to him to be earnestly at work trying in every way to alleviate the sufferings of those around.

I hear that the 5th Georgia Cavalry (Colonel Anderson) are to pass through here tomorrow, so I presume they will soon be in battle.

Thus far the enemy have never come to Marietta, and many hope and believe they never will. We heard from Aunty today. They are all well, though Aunt Mary and Aunt Lou say they are very much worn with anxiety. I feel deeply for them. Very few families remain there. The cars still run there, though the mail is stopped. As long as the cars run there and the wounded are brought down that way they will not feel utterly cut off. I have sent them two letters by private opportunity, and if you could write them we can get the letter to them.

I have had Mrs. General Cumming (Sarah Davis) with me since last Saturday. She came up hearing that General Cumming was seriously wounded. Colonel Cumming, his father, came with her, and has gone to the front to see his sons. When she came she expected to have returned in a day or two, but Colonel Cumming is still at the front, and she is awaiting his return. I believe she is almost half disappointed that she did not find the general slightly wounded, for she would then have taken him home with her. The hotels are such abominable places now that I am glad she is with us and not there.

Mr. Markham, the sick chaplain who has been with us recruiting, returned on Tuesday. He was very sick and feeble when he first came, but recovered very rapidly and returned quite well.

I must tell you of the preservation of our dear little children today. Mrs. Rogers called early this morning and begged me to let them spend the day with her; so she took them home, and while there a thunderstorm came up and the house was struck. No one was at all injured. The lightning, striking the bell wire, ran along and then down a portion of the plastering in the parlor. Mrs. Rogers and the children were in a room opposite (an entry between), and did not even feel the shock, though the report was very loud. It was a remarkable providence, and I regard it as such. Their preservation was wonderful. The house is a remarkably small one (only one story), and Mrs. Rogers says it has two rods, so that it is strange that it should have been struck.

I received a letter from Kitty this afternoon. She has reached home in safety. . . . It is growing late, so I must close. I am a great deal better this week; my strength is returning. The weather is delightful: the nights so cool that I always use a quilt. I wish you could have our cool water, it is so refreshing. Do give much love to Brother Charlie and Eva; I will write them in a day or two. Kiss Little Sister for us. Mr. Mallard and the children unite with me in warmest love. I long to have a letter from you once more.

Your affectionate daughter,
Mary S. Mallard.

Mrs. Mary S. Mallard *to* Mrs. Mary Jones[t]

Atlanta, *Tuesday,* June 7th, 1864

My dearest Mother,

Mr. Henderson has just sent home $66.70, amount of Niger's hire for two months (from 1st of April to 1st of June). As Mr. Mallard is absent, I enclose you the amount. Niger was for several weeks at Stone Mountain gathering bark, but is again working at the tanyard.

I hope, dear Mother, that you are quite well again. I wish every day you could come immediately to us; I am sure the change would benefit you, and you would find drinking and bathing in our cool water a tonic in itself. I trust everything will be sufficiently quiet in a few weeks for you to come up.

Our dear old aunty has at last determined to move. Mr. Bryson tells me that the nearer the army comes to Marietta the more Aunt Mary's nerves give way; and he says such is their anxiety and excitement that he does not think it possible for them to remain. He has been a good friend to them, and is now doing all in his power to aid them. Mr. Mallard went up this morning to assist in getting them off, and I expect them tomorrow afternoon to spend some days with me before they pursue their journey. Mr. Bryson ascertained here that their household effects could all be conveyed as far as Macon for three hundred dollars. They have on hand five hundred dollars; and I told Mr. Bryson I knew their relatives would assist them. It is a dreadful trial for them to leave, and yet they begin to feel they could not brook the occupation of the place by the enemy. I do not know whether they have definitely determined where to go. I do feel very much for them. Aunt Lou dislikes leaving very much, for Joe just passed through today on his way to the front, and she feels she would not like to be far from him.

The whole of Colonel Anderson's regiment passed through today—or rather they marched today; they arrived two days ago. Fred King called to see us, and we saw several of the young men at church on Sabbath night. Mr. Porter took tea with us on Sabbath and preached for Mr. Mallard. He appears greatly improved in health, but not much so in figure, being dressed in cavalry uniform, even a round jacket, which exhibited his thin figure very funnily. The young men appear very much attached to him, and he labors very hard amongst them.

In view of the perils of the times our mayor has appointed next Friday a day of fasting and prayer. There are daily union prayer meetings held for the country. They are very interesting, but it is very discouraging to see a small house not half filled. One would suppose that no church in the city could contain those who would attend a union prayer meeting. The religious interest still keeps up in the army, notwithstanding all the fatigues of the retreat.

The children are quite well, and often ask if the summertime, when Grandmama said she would come, has not come yet. Charlie says he thinks it is winter, because if it were summer Grandma and Little Sister would be sure to be here. Good night, dear Mother. Be assured of the warmest love of your grandchildren and affectionate daughter,

Mary S. Mallard.

MRS. MARY JONES *to* MRS. MARY S. MALLARD[t]

Savannah, *Tuesday*, June 7th, 1864

My dearest Child,

Your aunt and myself came to town on last Thursday, and I have designed every day to write you, but my feeble condition and the constant calls from friends have prevented. Through God's mercy I have had no return of fever since it left me, and—what is even more remarkable after such a complicated attack of climate fever and pneumonia—my lungs are free from cough or pain. I presume the inflammation was thrown off. It was a great mercy that your brother was with me. . . .

We have a reported landing of the Yankees on Wilmington and Whitemarsh. No doubt they are enraged at the recent capture of the *Water Witch*. The troops are all withdrawn, and the defense of Savannah would devolve upon the light artillery. We are having most solemn and interesting prayer meetings every afternoon at five o'clock. Churches are crowded. Will not our Almighty Father, our Judge and Deliverer, hear and answer our cries for mercy?

Dear Eva has just come in and says: "Give a great deal of love to Sister." She is as kind and affectionate as possible to me. You will love her tenderly when you know her. Little Sister is quite well and bright.

Your last favor has been received. How thankful I am for the preservation of our dear little children from sudden death! I cannot tell you how anxious I am for you all in Atlanta, and for my dear aunt and cousins. What can I do for them? My heart is weighed down with their situation. Do let me know how I could help them. I pray constantly that you may all be guided by wisdom, and not suffered to remain exposed to that cruel enemy when you might get away. If there is any danger, do send Niger down to Liberty. . . . All unite in tenderest love to you and best love to Robert and the dear children. My heart yearns to see you, my dearest child.

Ever your own mother,

Mary Jones.

MRS. MARY S. MALLARD *to* MRS. MARY JONES[t]

Atlanta, *Saturday*, June 11th, 1864*

My dearest Mother,

I was truly glad and thankful to receive a letter from your own hand day before yesterday. I hope your strength will soon return. If things were only more quiet, I would insist upon your coming immediately to us, for I am sure the change at this time would do you more good than anything else. We are as quiet here so far as the situation of the house is concerned as if we lived in the country.

I wrote you that Mr. Mallard had gone up on Tuesday to assist in packing up Aunt Eliza's furniture. Mr. Bryson and Mr. Mallard packed up everything, and shipped it on Thursday. Mr. Mallard took Charles up to assist, and they were able to bring away everything belonging to themselves and servants. On Wednesday Aunt Mary and Aunt Eliza came here. Aunty bore the journey tolerably well, though she was very much exhausted, having been previously sick from an affection of her bowels. She was quite sick the day after she arrived, but is improving, though so feeble I do not think she will be able to move for a week. She is wonderfully supported under this trial. On Thursday Mr. Mallard came down with all of the furniture and all of the servants, and yesterday Aunt Lou came. The furniture was forwarded to Macon yesterday afternoon, Daddy Sam going with it to see that everything was properly cared for.

When Aunty left Marietta, they thought if no other arrangement could be made that they would go down to Flemington, as they said they had received a pressing invitation from Aunt Susan and Cousin Laura to go to them. They wrote to Mr. George Walker and requested him to receive their furniture and have it stored and if possible rent a house for them, that they might go to housekeeping. Yesterday afternoon they received a letter from Mr. Walker (not in reply to theirs, for he has not yet received that letter) inviting them to go to him should they deem it necessary to leave Marietta. This has determined them to go to Mr. Walker's and remain there at least for a while, until they can make some permanent arrangement. Aunt Mary asked my advice to help her determine, and said Mr. Walker had a very large comfortable house situated in Longstreet (Pulaski County) three miles from the Macon & Brunswick Railroad, that he was a man of large property, abundant means of living from his own plantation, plenty of poultry, butter, etc., and made a great deal of sugar and syrup, for she had seen fifteen barrels of sugar and more than that number of syrup on his place in the winter. Perhaps you had better not say anything about it, but I told her candidly I thought they would all be more comfortable there, and it would be far better to go there than to Flemington, although I knew Aunt Susan would give them as hearty a welcome and do as much for them as any relative they had. And they feel this. Aunt Eliza does not wish to go to Flemington if it can be avoided at this season, for she is so feeble that such a long journey would be exceedingly trying. And then she says it looks like taking her just so much nearer Midway graveyard.

Aunt Mary will leave on Monday for Macon, and from thence to Mr. Walker's to make all necessary arrangements; and when everything is ready and Aunty is strong enough, Aunt Lou and herself with the servants will go on. I do not think Aunty will be able to move for at least a week. I am very glad to think she has the prospect of going where there will be such an abundance of poultry and other things which seem very necessary to her now. It is a great trial to them to break up their pleasant home, for they feel it is a final move, and they do not expect ever to return. It is sad to see such a kind, hospitable family turned out of their own home. Aunt Mary begs me to say to you that the idea of being called by the hated name of *refugees* made them cling to their home until every male friend left the place—even Dr. Stewart, who had determined to remain. But when our army fell back, resting one wing on Kennesaw, they felt the enemy were at their doors; and they did not know to what straits they might be reduced, so got Mr. Bryson to come here and consult Mr. Mallard and Mr. Rogers and determined to move. Almost every family in Marietta has moved.

This move will necessarily be most expensive to Aunty. The expenses of getting the furniture to this place will be about seventy dollars. This Mr. Mallard and myself expect to defray. It will cost about one hundred and fifty dollars to move the furniture to Macon; how much more to the Walkers' I do not know. When there I presume they will be at no expense. They have taken all of their provisions and groceries with them, and will take Peggy, Will, Willis, and Bruce and Daddy Sam with them. Nanny and her child are with the girls at Cousin Maria Gilbert's.

I have been thus particular, my dear mother, for I knew you would want to know everything relative to the move and future plans. I fear Aunty will feel the quiet of the country very irksome, for she finds this place too quiet; thinks if she were in my place she would live more in the heart of the town to see all that was passing. Aunt Mary and Aunt Lou are pretty nearly worn out with fatigue and anxiety.

Our army is about three miles from Marietta, and was in line of battle yesterday; but whether it will result in an engagement it is idle to conjecture, for no one has the slightest idea of General Johnston's plans. I trust the battle will be fought soon, and that our arms will be crowned with success.

Yesterday, in accordance with a proclamation of our mayor, was observed as a day of fasting and prayer. The Baptists, Methodists, and Presbyterians united in the morning, and the services were deeply solemn and interesting. Addresses were made by a colonel from Texas (a minister) who commands in General Cleburne's division, and also by a chaplain from the Virginia army (Longstreet's command). Hearing him speak of Wofford's brigade, I begged Mr. Mallard to inquire if Eddie Stiles had been preserved through the battles. He said he knew him very well, and that he had behaved with distinguished gallantry, and the manner in which he handled his men had won the admiration of all. He had been preserved through all the battles and had been perfectly well. I trust the prayers offered yesterday will be answered, and our city spared.

There is a daily union prayer meeting here, but it is but poorly attended. It is true that many of the ladies and gentlemen are occupied upon various committees ministering to the relief of the sick, wounded, and refugees. Still there is no excuse for a small attendance. I have not attended as many of them as I would like, for they are held a mile from my house, and I am not often able to walk so far.

It would be a great relief to us could we be assured General Johnston would not fall back to the Chattahoochee. Mr. Mallard says if he does, I shall have to go with the children and servants. I trust the necessity will not come. Brother Charlie and Brother Joe have both most kindly invited me to come to them, but I feel that I can form no plans for the future, for I do not know what a day may bring forth. If this place should be given up, of course we will have to seek another home. In that case it would not be right in these times of terrible scarcity and difficulty in living to take a household to anyone in a city; and the expense would be more than we could bear. If there is a prospect of holding this place at all hazards, then the children and myself would go away whilst the battle was undetermined; for we would not remain if there was any prospect of its taking place in or near the town. This is the way I feel about it, my dear mother; and I have tried to commit all these cares and anxieties to my Heavenly Father, and I trust He will make our way plain. The armies may keep their present positions for half the summer. Everyone feels unbounded confidence in General Johnston, and the condition and spirit of the army is as good as could be desired.

I will cut up the pavilion you sent and take it to the hospital early next week. I know the men will be delighted to get pieces to spread over their faces and wounds. I think the flies of Egypt scarcely exceeded the multitude abroad in this town.

Day before yesterday Niger came home discharged from the tannery. Mr. Henderson is breaking up his establishment here, and has no further use for his services. In your letter you say if there is any danger, send him home. We do not think there is any danger now, and write to know what you think best. Shall Mr. Mallard find some other employment for him? He begs to stay; says he would not like to go away as long as we are here. There is a great deal of gardening work to be done at this time, and until we hear from you, will let him employ himself in this way. There is a plenty of job work to be done, so he will not be idle until we hear from you.

Mr. Mallard wrote Mr. Quarterman last night to give out the osnaburgs to the people. I think there will be enough for *all* of the people at Arcadia. I am very glad we happened to have it on hand, for it would be difficult to get it at this time. Roswell factory is threatened, but I hope it will not be destroyed, for it would be a great loss. If the army falls much farther back it will be left exposed.

I have written you a long letter, dear Mother. . . . The children send a great deal of love to you and to Little Sister. . . . I hope you have received my letter enclosing Niger's hire. Aunt Eliza, Aunts Mary and Lou desire best love to you, and to Aunt Susan if she is still in Savannah. Mr. Mallard unites with me in warmest love to you, dear Mother.

Your affectionate daughter,
Mary S. Mallard.

Miss Mary E. Robarts *to* Mrs. Susan M. Cumming[t]

Atlanta, *Monday,* June 13th, 1864

My dearest Cousin,

Your letter and dear Laura's found us in the greatest perplexity and agitation. Day after day we kept hoping that the battle would be over and the enemy not be permitted to invade our homes; but on Sunday night they came nearer, and our army began to fortify Kennesaw Mountain, only two miles from us; and we felt that it would not be safe to stay any longer. Mr. Bryson said he would come to Atlanta and consult Mr. Mallard and Mr. Rogers about our moving; so he came to Atlanta on Monday, and on Tuesday Mr. Mallard returned with him, bringing his man Charles. And in the shortest possible time our carpets were taken up and our house pulled to pieces. Packing went on briskly, so that on Wednesday at two in the afternoon I left with my dear mother, who had been sick in bed four days and was unusually feeble. Three chaplains came down to take care of us; and it was well they did, as they could hardly get her into the car, and when there she had to recline on my shoulder all the way. Dear Mary Mallard was there in a carriage to meet us. Had a cup of tea and a bed ready, so that she went to bed immediately, and slept as well as could have been expected after the excitement she had passed through.

Louisa remained with Mr. Mallard, Mr. Bryson, and the servants to finish packing and send off the furniture. The 5th Georgia Regiment arrived that evening, and Joe was allowed only three hours to stay with us, as they expected marching orders that night. They were, however, ordered to a farm a few miles in the country to refresh themselves and their horses. It was so sad that we had ministered to so many soldiers, fed them at our own table and done all we could for them; and here was this company—the sons of our friends, particularly Julia's and our own boy—that we could not see or do anything for. It seemed hard indeed. Joe slept one night in the cars with our furniture and was taken very sick with cholera morbus, so that he had to come up home to Louisa. He was relieved by morning, and that afternoon Louisa, Mr. Mallard, the furniture, and servants all arrived here safely.

Next day our faithful Sam was sent on to Macon with the furniture (consigned to Mr. Nisbet) to wait till I came. I was to have left this morning, but the rain poured in torrents, and we have to wait till tomorrow.

When we first left, we had expected to accept your kind invitation and go to Flemington, but we received a very kind letter from Mr. Walker insisting on our going there. It really seemed providential, as my dear mother said she was too feeble to undertake so long a journey to Flemington; said I must give her love to you and Laura and Mr. Buttolph, and say if it was winter she would be too glad to come to you, but she could not travel so far in the warm weather. Indeed, my dear cousin, nothing but necessity would make us go a mile further with her. She has been in bed ever since we have been here. Louisa remains a few days longer with her to rest while I go on with the servants to Mr. Walker's. If we can rent a house there, we will go immediately to housekeeping; if not, will get him to store the furniture, and we stay with him till we have time to look about for a house. I am thankful to know that we shall be less of a burden to him than to anyone else, as he has an abundance of everything on his own farm, and a large house. We have been there before, and they are very kind, and always said if we were driven from home to come right to his house. . . . Thank you kindly, my dear cousin, for the sum you and Cousin Mary Jones and Charlie so kindly sent us to help us on our way. Mother said I surely ought to repeat the 23rd Psalm after that new instance of God's goodness in giving us such kind friends.

I cannot tell you what we have passed through in anxiety, fatigue, and distress of mind in giving up our home. It looked more lovely than ever. Just through with a hard winter, we were enjoying a fine garden; the fruits and flowers looked more beautiful than ever. And we clung to it as long as there was a hope that the Yankees would not get there. But every day seemed to bring them nearer, and we heard so much of their treatment to the people of Rome and other places that they have passed through that we were afraid to trust ourselves to their tender mercies. They take all your supplies and compel you to draw rations. Our last male friend had left, and almost every family; and we felt we could stay no longer: would have no one to bury us if we died. Dr. Stewart and Mrs. Stewart have left. On Saturday there was another panic, and the place is now emptied of all who can leave. Mrs. Fraser remains under the protection of the British flag. Louisa went up to see them; found them all well and calm. They have more fortitude than I have! I have been at times so prostrated when the wagons would be falling back that I would feel as if the Yankees were right upon us. Indeed, I have been very ill several times, and sometimes feel so weak and nervous that I can hardly keep up. And I now feel so miserable when I feel that I am a refugee without a home that I shed many bitter tears. We were very comfortable. Though the place was filled with soldiers, they never disturbed us. And the chaplains were very kind to us: they would write us from the battlefield every day; and when Mr. Bryson went down to carry the girls to Perry, every night one would come and sleep at the house to protect us; so that we had a very pleasant time. But this could not last; if the enemy had come, they could not have come, and we would have been desolate.

I cannot tell you more of "the situation" than you see in the papers. Marietta looks like one vast wagon yard; hundreds and hundreds go there. The cars only go as far as Marietta, and these wagons go there to get commissary supplies. The Yankees are moving in the direction of Roswell, and if they are not checked, perhaps in a few days that enterprising village may be in ashes. The Yankees are only eight miles from there now. I fear our army will be worn out marching and countermarching. Would that the great battle could have been fought before they were brought so near us! I do not believe in this falling back; it brings too much misery on those left within the lines. All the crops of corn and wheat have been destroyed. I expect every night to hear that Marietta is in ashes. Mr. Mallard and Mary do not expect to leave unless the army falls back to the Chattahoochee and the battle comes very near Atlanta.

Mary looks better, but is not well. She and Mother and Louisa desire much love to you, Laura, Mr. Buttolph, and Julia's family. . . . Excuse this miserable letter. I write now because I have so much on my mind and hands, and am so unwell I shall not be able to write again directly. Only write to thank you for your kind invitation, and to let you know that we are safely out of Marietta. If it had not been for our kind friend Mr. Bryson, who has done all that a brother or son could do for us, and Mr. Mallard, we never could have got out. Mary's children send love to you, and so do all of us.

Your distressed but affectionate cousin,
Mary E. Robarts.

Tell Julia her boys were well yesterday.

MRS. MARY S. MALLARD *to* MRS. MARY JONES[t]

Atlanta, Thursday, June 23rd, 1864*

My dearest Mother,

This morning Aunt Eliza and Aunt Lou left us for Macon on their way to Pulaski County. Aunty was so sick and feeble that at one time we feared she never would be able to leave us; but her spirit is very firm, and she was determined to reach her journey's end if possible. She has been with us two weeks, and as much as I would have liked to have had her remain longer, we felt it would be wrong to urge her to do so; for if anything like a panic should occur it would be almost impossible to get one so feeble away. I dread the effects of the journey for her, and most of all the seclusion of the country. I do not know how any of them will bear this, for they have so long been in the very center of news that they are very dependent upon it. They have a strong hope that they will be able to rent a very nice cottage of six rooms; there is also a nice vegetable garden all planted, and plenty of servants' accommodation on the lot. The whole town of Marietta has emptied itself: scarcely a family left. Our army is very near, and I believe some of the enemy's shells have already reached those houses next to Kennesaw. The shells now fall entirely over the mountain.

Your last sweet letter reached me on my birthday. Thank you, dear Mother, for it. These are indeed days of darkness and deep anxiety, and I am afraid I shall be among that class of women of whom it is said: "Woe unto them," etc. We have a very unsettled feeling about our future movements; they must depend in great measure upon the movements of the army.

A few days ago officers were impressing Negroes to work upon the fortifications at the Chattahoochee. Charles was of the number impressed. I was glad they did not take Niger, as we are daily expecting to hear from you about him. I wrote nearly two weeks ago to know what you thought best to be done with him, and hope to get an answer tomorrow.

I cut up the gauze you sent into convenient squares, and have given the most of them to the wounded men. You would have been amused to have seen two young crackers with their squares. One of them said he was "mightily proud of it," and the last I saw of him he was alternately covering his face and then folding the gauze to look at it. . . . You would be amazed at the number of wounded in this place. It is a constant source of regret to me that I am unable to walk to the hospitals, and I do not often have an opportunity of riding.

Thus far none of Captain Walthour's company have been wounded, though they have been in a number of skirmishes. Some of Captain Hughes's have been wounded, amongst the number a Mr. John Fennell, son of the person who used to keep a store at Riceboro.

I will direct this to Savannah. I trust, dear Mother, your strength is returning. I wish you would come to us next; I think the change would do you good. I know you would enjoy the cool nights and nice water. Mr. Mallard and the children unite with me in warmest love to you, and love to Brother Charlie and Eva.

Your affectionate daughter,
Mary S. Mallard.

We expect Brother Joe the last of this week.

MRS. MARY JONES *to* MRS. MARY S. MALLARD[t]

Savannah, Saturday, June 25th, 1864

My dear Daughter,

I have been hoping every day for a letter, but I know how much you have to engage your time. I have been scarcely able to write, and now do so in pain from rheumatism or neuralgia in my neck and head, which makes it very stiff, and with difficulty I turn or hold it either up or down. It has been so ever since my illness, and I fear it is becoming a settled affection.

On last Wednesday I made an effort and went home. Spent that night at Montevideo and the next at Flemington with our dear relatives there, who in all my sickness have shown me every kindness and attention. When I left home, Patience had to think of and pack everything; consequently there were some important matters forgotten. And then I wanted to see all the people once more before I left the low country. I found them all well; and all desire to be particularly remembered to Robert and yourself and the children. . . . I had told them on leaving I wanted all the butter at both places sent you as soon as they had enough to make it an object; from the state of the weather they have not made much, but I brought in a jarful done up in shucks which I will express to you on Monday, and hope it may reach you safely. It was all that has been made at both Arcadia and Montevideo since I left. The next gathering I will send to Joe, thus alternating— if you find it worth the while to have it sent up. You must write me about it.

Rose spun your fine wool, which I brought up with me. Mrs. Butler had not sent home the last piece.

If Niger can find employment in Atlanta, I am willing for him to remain as long as you do, and wish you to make him useful to Robert and yourself at any time you may need his services. Please keep the wages that he may make for the present.

My strength returns slowly. If I had only been permitted, in God's providence, to be with you this summer, I know it would have been a great benefit, as well as the greatest happiness I could have had. As it is, the future is all uncertain. I have not appointed any time for going to Augusta. Carrie has had such a spell of nursing I fear to increase her cares. Eva expects to go to her mother, but she wants to delay as long as it is healthy here, for when she goes she cannot return until frost. I would prefer for the *benefit of my health* to go out into the county and board rather than remain in Augusta all summer. I expect certainly to make my dear Joe and Carrie a visit.

Your situation, my dear child, fills me with the greatest anxiety, and I do hope you will not tarry in Atlanta too long. All that I can do is pray for you.

The fearful condition of our armies on the front of our own state and Virginia fills every heart with trembling. Not a day now passes but we receive the sad tidings of some friend or acquaintance slain in battle. Our county is mourning many of her sons slain. Rev. Mr. Andrews and his wife were in deep sorrow for the death of a promising son killed in Virginia. Your Aunt Julia trembles for her boys now upon the battlefield. Colonel Joe McAllister is said to have died bravely. He was surrounded by the enemy, who demanded his surrender. He replied: "Only with life!" and continued to shoot down the enemy until overpowered. His last act was to hurl his pistol at their heads. . . . Major Thomson's remains are expected out in Liberty on Monday.

I have this moment received a letter from Cousin Mary. Aunt had arrived comfortably in Macon on the 23rd, where they would rest awhile and then go to Mr. Walker's. Cousin Mary hopes to rent a house belonging to Mr. Walker's son-in-law. Mr. Walker sent his wagons and had all their furniture moved and stored for them. I feel deeply for them, and rejoice that such friends and helpers are raised up unto them.

Charles and Eva unite with me in best love to Robert and yourself. Kiss my precious children for me. This is Little Sister's birthday. She says: "Tell Sissy and Bubber I send a letter to them."

Ever, my dear daughter, your affectionate mother,
Mary Jones.

MRS. MARY S. MALLARD *to* MRS. MARY JONES[t]

Atlanta, *Friday,* July 1st, 1864

My dear Mother,

The express brought the jar and fans quite safely evening before the last. Nothing could be more opportune than the butter, for I had not a particle, and I am very much obliged to you for it. I have not sent the fans to the hospital yet, but know the men will be glad to have them, and shall get Mr. Dod to distribute them for me.

Brother Joe came up on last Saturday and remained until Wednesday, when Mr. Mallard and himself went to Marietta together. Mr. Mallard went as one of the aid committee to assist with the wounded. . . . Brother Joe was two weeks ahead of his secretary, so he came up to spend a few days with us and to offer his services for ten days in Marietta, where the chief field surgeon has his quarters. I should have been glad to have kept him quietly here, and would have liked to have persuaded him to do nothing for the next two weeks; but you know he must always be at work.

I have had Mr. Dod staying with me for a week past. He is the same who used to teach in Darien, and has recently come from Plaquemine in Louisiana, where he was settled and was living very comfortably, although under Yankee rule. He is quite an interesting man, and has left everything to come and labor in our army. At present chaplains can accomplish but little in the field, so he will probably establish himself in some hospital here; and he bids fair to be an earnest, laborious worker. I am truly glad he will locate here, for ministerial labor is sadly deficient in our hospitals here. Mrs. Dod is in Washington (Wilkes County), and is doing her own cooking. She has a son and daughter with her. I know of no one who has made greater sacrifices; and it has all been a voluntary offering on their part, for they might have remained. I see chaplains quite frequently, and have a weekly visitor in a Mr. Markham, formerly a pastor in New Orleans. Mr. Dod tells me he studied theology under my dear father's direction. He told me that he heard my dear father preach a sermon before the synod in Marietta on a Communion occasion which for beauty, simplicity, and effect upon his audience was unsurpassed; and the theme (as he expressed it) was "a simple narrative of the story of the Cross given by a feeling, loving spectator." Mr. Dod says the impressions made upon him by that discourse will never wear away. It is so pleasant to me to have anyone tell me their recollections of my beloved father. How I miss his counsels now!

Don't you think, dear Mother, you could come first to us and leave your visit to Augusta until later? We do not feel there is any immediate danger; and if there should be after you come, you could easily run down to Augusta. I want you to come while we are enjoying our vegetables; and I am sure a change at once to this climate would do you more good than later. I think even supposing the army falls back to the Chattahoochee, it will not do so for some weeks yet; so do think of it, dear Mother, and come immediately up. The last disaster to Sherman has been a very serious affair, and our cavalry is beginning to operate in the rear. We have had a few torpedoes at work upon the railroad track, so I hope we may yet be permitted to remain here.

I received a letter from Aunt Lou two days ago, and she says Aunty stood the journey remarkably well, and they are comfortably located with Mr.

Walker, but have failed in renting the cottage they hoped to get. Already they begin to realize the utter quiet of the country, and long for a bit of news. I am afraid this will be a dreadful cross to all of them. Aunty misses her cool well of water. Aunt Lou says I must not be surprised to see her very soon, for she feels she must come nearer Joe. It is a time of great exposure to him, being in skirmishes every day. Aunty's house in Marietta has been taken by Bate's division for their hospital. Scarcely a family is left in Marietta.

The attendance upon our daily union prayer meeting is increasing. Some of the meetings are very interesting. . . . Do write soon, dear Mother, and say you are coming. The children send many messages of love. Mr. Mallard would unite with me in much love if he were here. I have written Eva by this mail thanking her for her handsome present.

Your affectionate daughter,
Mary S. Mallard.

REV. JOHN JONES *to* MRS. MARY S. MALLARD[t]

Refuge, *Friday,* July 1st, 1864

My dear Niece,

Your truly interesting letter has been received, and was most welcome from the variety of news it contained, and especially for the information given about our dear aunt and cousins. In the language of your Aunt Jane, your letter was "a great relief" to us. We were in great anxiety about them, and could not tell what had become of them. I do thank Mr. Bryson and Robert for their kindness and great promptitude in aiding our aunt and cousins in making so wonderful and timely an escape from Marietta. We have received a letter from Cousin Mary since yours came to hand, telling us of her entire route from Marietta to Longstreet in Pulaski County, and mentioning most affectionately the kindness of Robert, yourself, Mr. Bryson, and Sister and Cousin Susan and Mr. Walker and others. Surely they have been highly favored, and we do heartily rejoice in their safe removal from a dwelling in the midst of alarms.

And now we shall constantly think of you and yours, with like anxious feelings, until we hear that the enemy is driven back and Atlanta is safe. I have never believed that Atlanta would be taken, but we cannot know certainly anything in this day of uncertain war. The enemy might possibly flank the place and thus compel an evacuation. But I have great confidence in General Johnston as a man of wisdom, prudence, and humanity, and I trust also of piety. When I was in Virginia in 1861, his soldiers had great confidence in him. But what is man? Are we not shut up to God in this great struggle? Is not the whole world against us? Let us daily and hourly commit our cause, ourselves, our all to Him who doeth all things well. Surely we are not to be overwhelmed in utter ruin, poverty, and disgrace! If we are to judge of the future welfare of the colored race by what they have already experienced from the tender mercies of the Yankees, we cannot see that emancipation will be a blessing to them. And certainly subjugation would be utter and hopeless ruin to the South. I therefore believe that our extremity will be God's opportunity to help us and deliver us from the wrath of our wicked, unprincipled foes. Should you have to leave Atlanta, I presume you will go to Augusta. If you cannot go to Augusta, then come to our plain home in Baker. We will be able to give you and the dear children a plenty of milk and butter and corn bread, and some wheat bread too, having just gathered a small crop of wheat. But I hope you will not be compelled to fly from your home, and Robert to leave his church.

I do wish I could have gone with Robert on his late visit to Kennesaw Mountain, and to have enjoyed with him the grand spectacle of two great armies from the same point. Are we not living in a peculiar age? And you who are in the midst of so many stirring and saddening scenes and sights, and in hearing of the war—how trying and eventful is your life! Oh, that we may all live to see an honorable end of this cruel, unparalleled strife!

How wonderful the late testimony of our chaplains and physicians that so many of our mortally wounded die in peace, and seem to go to their everlasting rest! How wonderfully has God the Holy Spirit wrought in our camps, and thus prepared thousands who were appointed to death!

I often desire that I could return to a chaplaincy in our army—that I could do more in this great struggle. And then I know not how I could leave home. I have been compelled to give up my overseer, and to assume in a measure new and most uninviting duties, and distracting and unceasing cares. And then my little churches need fostering care. On the second Sabbath of June, with the help of my good Brother Buttolph, we gathered fifty-six members into a church at Bond's Mills (one mile of our home), baptizing twenty-three recent converts, a part of the fifty-six. . . . In my labors for the country people I often think of my dear brother.

I long to receive a line from my dear sister in her own hand since her illness. Have written her to Savannah. I hope she will be able to come out and pass the most of the summer with you in Atlanta.

You inquired after Dunwody. He has been ordered to Anderson (Sumter County) to drill the guard of the Yankee prisoners, and is very busy. A letter just received from him today says they expected an outbreak of the prisoners very lately and made ready for them, planting artillery and having sharpshooters ready. The Yankees saw the preparation and were quiet.

Excuse my paper, as paper is scarce. Your Aunt Jane and my boys unite with me in best love to you, Robert, and your dear children, and howdy for the servants. Do write again to

Your affectionate uncle,
John Jones.

XXII

Mrs. Mary S. Mallard *to* Mrs. Laura E. Buttolph[t]

Augusta, *Monday,* July 18th, 1864

My dear Cousin,

You have doubtless heard through Cousin Lyman that we have left Atlanta—at least for the present—and are now numbered amongst the numerous throng of refugees. We had hoped to have remained longer in Atlanta, but when the order came to remove all hospitals in a few hours, and the enemy were reported as crossing the river within six miles of us, we thought we had better move our furniture while we could get transportation. And as it was, the granting of a car at that time was a personal favor to Mr. Mallard.

We made up our minds on Thursday morning, and by Friday afternoon everything was packed in the car and the house completely emptied, except one mattress and bedstead left for Mr. Mallard's accommodation. So you may know we worked hard. After everything was packed in the car, a telegram came from Brother Charlie saying expect Mother the next day. We did not know what to do, for everything had gone from the house, and we were compelled to go on ourselves; so Mr. Mallard telegraphed immediately to Mr. Nisbet to say we would leave that night for Augusta, and to stop Mother there. But unfortunately he did not receive it, and Mother had all the fatigue and anxiety of coming on and finding us gone. If we could have had the slightest intimation that she thought of coming, we would have made other arrangements. After a great deal of anxiety in Atlanta and fatigue and detention in coming here, Mother reached this place on Monday morning, we having gotten here the afternoon before.

We were detained in Atlanta by a serious accident which but for the mercy of God might have resulted fatally to some of us. We expected to have left at two o'clock Friday night, and intended to have walked to the depot; but Charles, without our knowledge, had borrowed a dray or four-wheeled wagon from one of the neighbors; and as we were excessively fatigued from the two days' packing, we thought we would ride down with our two trunks. Descending a steep little hill, I think something gave way about the cart, and it ran upon Jim, causing him to start off; and in a few moments we were all thrown out. The children were uninjured saving bruises upon their faces, and the skin was taken off of Mamie's knee. Mr. Mallard's foot caught, and he was dragged for some distance, but sprang back into the cart and disengaged his foot. I was seriously injured, being bruised in every part of my body from my head to my feet, with the exception of a portion of my back and stomach; and my collarbone was dislocated. I discovered something was wrong with it as soon as I was able to rise from the ground, and got Mr. Mallard to draw my shoulder back, which I knew would put the bones in position until a physician could be gotten. I suffered intensely, not only from the dislocation but from the other blows upon my chest, head, hip, knees, etc. But Dr. Logan soon bandaged me up, and advised our leaving at seven with our furniture. So Mr. Mallard opened the bedding and made a bed for me, and fixed a rocking chair so that I could sit down comfortably. It was well we were able to make this arrangement, for I could not have borne the journey in the passenger car. As it was, the bone was dislocated once after we started; and if I had been in a car, where I would have been compelled to have sat up, it would have nearly destroyed me.

Thus you see, my dear cousin, how narrowly our lives were preserved. I feel truly grateful that none of us were more seriously injured. We were two days in getting down here, and received a most affectionate welcome from Brother Joe and Carrie. Brother Joe is taking care of my arm, which will be bandaged up for six weeks, as the bone will not unite before that time. I am obliged to discard dresses, and look like a forlorn old lady sailing around in a sacque with one empty sleeve. I was quite a spectacle coming down on the cars, and often was asked: "Is you wounded?" I suppose they thought I was one of the unfortunate ones that had been caught between the lines when a battle was going on. I still suffer a good deal of pain, but this I must expect. I am truly thankful it was my left and not my right arm. Writing is about the only thing I can do, and that not very long at a time.

Brother Joe kindly let us store our furniture in his house. Mr. Mallard returned to Atlanta on Tuesday, and will abide the issue. If the town is evacuated, he will of course come away. I hope we may be able to return to Atlanta, but of course we will have to be governed by the movements of the army. Should Atlanta be evacuated, I think it probable we would go to Walthourville until some permanent arrangement can be made. I scarcely think yet of any future arrangements, as everything is so uncertain, and all turns upon the condition of affairs in Atlanta.

We found Carrie looking dreadfully, and the children both sick. Stanhope has been very sick, and is so weak that he totters around the house. Susie has been very sick also. Carrie went to The Hill on Saturday to spend a short time with her parents for the benefit of the change both for herself and children. I hope they will be benefited, for they are all very unwell.

I am truly thankful we have such a pleasant retreat. So many poor refugees are thrown out of their home without a shelter.

I think Mother intends enclosing a note in this to Aunt Susan. . . . Accept much love for Aunt Susan and yourself from

Your affectionate cousin,
Mary S. Mallard.

Mrs. Mary Jones *to* Mrs. Susan M. Cumming[t]

Augusta, *Friday,* July 22nd, 1864

My dear Sister,

We were happy this morning to receive dear Laura's letter to Daughter. It is almost the first tidings from Liberty since I left Savannah.

My passage through the state—up one railroad and down the other—was accomplished in such haste that I have been greatly exhausted by three days and nights spent in cars. The last thirty-six hours, between Atlanta and this place, we were detained by four crushed cars, heavily laden with government supplies and furniture of refugees, which could not be removed from the track a night and part of a day beyond the time of arrival. My stock of provisions had been completely exhausted before I left Atlanta. We stopped where not a drop of water could be had. I found a crust of bread in the lunch basket, which was shared with Flora. The most disagreeable part of the whole was walking quite a distance in the middle of the night—up embankments and down in ditches—to reach a relief car. I do not think my strength could have held out for the exertion had not a kind Providence brought to my assistance the strong arm of a young soldier, a lieutenant on furlough, who rendered me every necessary help. In all that journey there was not a human face I had ever seen before, and I felt desolate and lonely beyond expression.

Mr. Buttolph was so kind to me that I enjoyed his society and my trip up greatly. He has doubtless told of our adventures and given you the latest intelligence from the front. Every prospect darkens around us. This place, I fear, will feel next the presence of the enemy. There is so much to invite them in the government works and factories.

My dear daughter improves, but it will be a long time before she will use her wounded arm. Just now it is very painful: in the process of knitting. Her presence of mind and fortitude were wonderful, and it is a great mercy they were not all killed. Robert arrived yesterday, and Carrie and himself have gone today to visit Mr. and Mrs. Porter and Mr. Clarke's family at Beech Island. Carrie's children with Charlie have been quite sick; the boys are better, but little Susan Hyrne looks miserably. She has been threatened with cholera infantum, and is so feeble I would not be surprised if she is removed from this world of sorrow. Daughter and Carrie are both as thin as they well can be. These times of distress are preying alike upon young and old. The *situation* of my poor child makes her present trial peculiarly great.

I received a letter from Cousin Mary today. Aunt had been quite sick with fever, but was restored to her usual health. The girls were going to make a visit to Cuthbert. . . . Aunt and family I think will spend next winter between yourself and myself, and I want to do all in my power to make them comfortable. I expect Daughter and the children of course to be with me, for there is now no prospect of a return to Atlanta. Robert's church members have all removed. What the issue will be is known only to God. The outrages of the enemy at Decatur were awful!

I have not heard a word from Montevideo. Do inquire from Andrew if Mr. Jackson is still there or if he has been removed to the army. I am very anxious about my poor people, left in an unprotected condition, with none to think of or do for them. If my health had permitted and I could have remained in the county, I would not have left them. Those who have food and shelter and quiet homes in a protected region have reason for special gratitude.

Carrie and Joe, Daughter and Robert, with the children, unite with me in best love to yourself and Laura and Mr. Buttolph and the children. Remember us affectionately to Julia and Mary, Belle and Kitty; Audley and Kate when you see them. Love to Brother William from us all; I hope he is feeling better. Do let us hear from you soon.

Ever your affectionate sister,
Mary Jones.

Major Joseph Jones *to* Mrs. Susan M. Cumming[t]

Augusta, Saturday, July 30th, 1864

My dear Aunt,

You will please accept the accompanying picture with the love of Carrie and myself. We regret that it is no better. Carrie's likeness does not, I think, do her justice. We send it to you chiefly on account of the little ones.

Sister and Brother Robert and Mother are now with us, and it gives us great pleasure to have this union of the families after the long separation. Sister's arm is slowly recovering, but still gives her much pain. Stanhope and Susan and Charlie, who have been quite ill, are all better and fast regaining their usual health and strength.

I returned a short time since from the Army of Tennessee, and if Providence permits I will leave for Richmond, Virginia, next Tuesday the 2nd of August. My report (third report to the surgeon general, C.S.A., on typhoid fever) is now completed; and as it contains much matter which would prove of value to our enemies, and as the communication with Richmond is uncertain, it becomes my duty to carry it on and deliver the volume in person to the surgeon general. This volume contains consolidated reports of the diseases, deaths, and mean strength of the Confederate armies from January 1862 to July 1863, and includes about six hundred closely written pages of royal quarto, and also contains a number of plates and maps. The labors have been numerous and continuous, and my health and strength has been greatly taxed. I have been greatly assisted in the manual labors by my secretary, Louis Manigault, of Charleston, South Carolina.

Carrie unites with me in love to you and Cousins Laura and Lyman.

Your affectionate nephew,
Joseph Jones.

Please send the package to Uncle William at your earliest convenience.

Mrs. Mary S. Mallard *to* Mrs. Mary Jones[t]

Walthourville, Monday, August 22nd, 1864

My dearest Mother,

After bidding you good-bye we found the cars so much crowded that I could get no seat for some miles. I made a seat of my large shawls, pillow, and the overcoats, and rode very comfortably until we reached McBean's Station, where a lady got out. I took her place and gave mine to Brother Charlie, and Mr. Mallard sat upon one of the baskets. Lucy and the children located themselves very comfortably in the saloon, and I heard Mamie's little tongue all the way to Millen telling an old lady who shared the saloon with them all about the Yankees and about our living in Atlanta. . . . At Millen we waited an hour and a half. The children thought it fine fun to get up at midnight to play in the moonlight and eat watermelon. From Millen to Savannah we had a very comfortable journey, and I got down with less pain than I anticipated, though I was pretty thoroughly worn out by the time I reached this place. Brother Charlie kindly took us to his house and gave us a hot breakfast, which refreshed us very much.

The family here were all very glad to see us. . . . On Saturday a number of persons called to welcome us back. . . . The committee waited upon Mr. Mallard on Saturday evening, requesting him to preach for the church while he is absent from the Atlanta church. . . . Mrs. Screven thinks of going to her father's when Captain Screven leaves, which will be the 1st of September; so perhaps we may get back to the academy. Mrs. Screven has a little daughter about a month old.

I have heard nothing from Montevideo, as Niger did not come up on Saturday night. . . . I suppose you have seen through the papers that a whole company from Colonel Hood's command were captured in McIntosh. It is even so: thirty-five men and horses captured by marines. (The papers said by cavalry, but that was not so.) The Yankees were on foot, and it is said were exceedingly gentlemanly, allowing the prisoners to communicate with their families and to receive their clothing.

Mr. Mallard omitted one of Colonel Gaulden's acts in his flight from the Yankees in Riceboro, and that was this: being dressed in white clothes, someone suggested the Yankees would be sure to discover him going through the cornfield; so he stopped and smeared his clothing all over with black mud. This is said to be a fact.

I wish it had been so that we all could have remained together this summer, but I think Mr. Mallard did right in coming here. I hope poor little Susie is improving, and that Carrie has more rest. I think of them very often, and wish every day Susie had my piece of chicken. Lucy begs Flora to get her leather belt which she left in Sue's house and bring it for her. Please let Flora get our shoebrushes from Harry and keep them until you come. They were to have been brought, but were left out. Give much love to Carrie and Brother Joe from us all. I will write them very soon. Charlie will not believe he is in Walthourville because we have not gone to the academy. The children and Mr. Mallard unite with me in warmest love to you. Love to Eva and Little Sister.

Your affectionate daughter,

Mary S. Mallard.

I have not gotten over the fatigue of coming down, as I feel quite weak yet.

I forgot to have a pillow put in the small keg of crockery. Will you be kind enough, dear Mother, to take one out the bundle of bedding in the attic and have it put in? The keg is in the basement and contains my finest crockery.

MRS. LAURA E. BUTTOLPH *to* MRS. MARY S. MALLARD[t]

Flemington, *Monday,* August 22nd, 1864

My dearest Cousin Mary,

We are all so glad to hear that you are at Walthourville so near us, and hope to be able to see you before long. It would have given us so much pleasure to have brought you here from the station. Fear the journey fatigued you very much, particularly at this season of the year with your shattered arm. I long to see and know how you are, and to see Mary and Charlie. James, William, and Susie send love and greetings to them particularly.

Mother and Mr. Buttolph have just returned from Dorchester. . . . Mother received a letter today from Mary Nisbet giving the particulars of poor Joe Robarts' death—not from his wound or measles but from diphtheria. . . . It is a heavy affliction. . . . May Aunt Eliza receive strength to bear it as she has received in all her trials and afflictions! Truly the land mourneth!

Colonel Hood has all the militia reporting to him at this church, even Mr. Cassels, Mr. Ezra Stacy, and Mr. Rahn. And an artillery company are now at the station waiting orders—and nothing to eat tonight. Colonel Hood's sick are in the academy, and his men in the arbors. Such is war. What are they expecting so far from the coast? None of my business.

Mother, Mr. Buttolph, and the little ones unite with me in all that is loving and affectionate to you and Cousin Robert, Charlie, and Mary. And our kind remembrances to Mr. and Mrs. Sam Mallard.

Your ever affectionate cousin,

Laura E. Buttolph.

MRS. MARY JONES *to* MRS. MARY S. MALLARD[t]

Augusta, *Monday,* August 22nd, 1864

My dear Daughter,

I have thought of you with great anxiety, and hope you did not wait long for a seat. Your brother wrote me saying you had all breakfasted with him in Savannah, and I trust through divine favor you are safely at your journey's end.

You know how unwell Carrie was for a long time before you left; I am sorry to inform you that she is now quite sick in bed with high fever. . . . Her extremely nervous condition for some time past has made me fear for her a serious attack of illness. . . . I have moved into your spacious apartment, and taken little Susie, crib, and Rose upstairs with me until her mother is restored. She was very good last night, requiring not more than three times to be up with a light. Stanhope is better. . . . Joe is much worn down, and a great deal to do; expected to go to Andersonville next week. Mrs. Cuthbert is sitting with Carrie, and I have left her to write you.

After you left I found a shirt, collar, and cravat of Robert's which I will have washed and bring or send as you desire. I had an affectionate letter from Marion yesterday, and hope soon to visit her in Washington. I must go and give Carrie her medicine. With much love to Robert and yourself, and kisses for the children, and respects to Mr. and Mrs. Mallard,

Ever your affectionate mother,
Mary Jones.

Do send this letter to Mr. Joseph Jackson.

Mrs. Mary S. Mallard *to* Mrs. Mary Jones[t]

Walthourville, Friday, August 26th, 1864

My dearest Mother,

We are anxiously waiting to hear how Carrie is, and trust she is decidedly better ere this. I hope, dear Mother, that you will spare yourself as much as you can, and that your own strength will not give way under nursing. You know you are not as strong as you were previous to your illness. How is the pain in your head? I hope that does not continue severe.

Yesterday we had Aunt Susan with us; she came over with Mr. Buttolph to Jacob Rokenbaugh's funeral. Cousin Laura and the children are quite well. Aunt Susan sends you many thanks for the Testament, and to Brother Joe for the picture; she was very much gratified by his sending it to her.

Aunt Susan has recently received a letter from Aunt Mary Robarts in which she mentioned that Aunt Eliza had not been so well, and she thought she was failing; and if she continued to grow more feeble, she thought of bringing her down in September, that she might end her last days with her friends, as they did not like to trespass too long upon Mr. Walker's hospitality. Aunt Lou had reached Longstreet with the girls.

Aunt Susan saw Uncle William last week. He was quite well, and still at Springfield. Captain Winn's family have moved up here and are occupying old Mrs. Stevens' house. I presume Uncle will miss them very much.

The company captured in McIntosh two weeks ago belonged to Colonel Colcock's regiment, and it is a great source of mortification. The reason assigned for their capture is that they were sent down without any knowledge of the country and were furnished with no competent guides; and as they relieved no pickets, they failed to put out pickets at some important point. A number of Negro men were taken off by the Yankees, but they refused women, children, and old men. They took off two men belonging to Mr. Shepard, and took Mr. Shepard prisoner, but afterwards released him on the ground of his being a noncombatant and over age.

I have not had an opportunity of sending your letter to Mr. Jackson yet, but will do so by Niger when he comes up on Saturday.

Mrs. Mallard is so much delighted with my Bible that she has begged me to enclose you five dollars and ask if you will be kind enough to get one for her. Mr. Mallard brought some of the soldier's Testaments with him, and will have an opportunity of sending some copies to Virginia by Captain Screven, who returns next week.

The children think it very strange we do not move over to the academy. Mamie told Mrs. Lowndes Walthour she was very glad to get back because all her property was here; and when we asked her where it was, she said with the greatest air of confidence: "At the academy lot." They send their love and many kisses to Grandmama, and love to Aunt Carrie, Bubber Joe, and Stanhope. I hope Susie and Stanhope are getting strong again; I wish they were here to run about in this sand. I think Mamie and Charlie have fattened since they came. My shoulder is still very painful at times. Dr. Stevens has recommended me to use a stream of cold water upon it, which I hope will strengthen it. Mr. Mallard unites with me in warmest love to yourself, Brother Joe, and Carrie. Love to Eva and Little Sister.

Your affectionate daughter,
Mary S. Mallard.

The family here desire to be remembered to you.

Please keep the shirt until you come.

Mrs. Mary S. Mallard *to* Mrs. Susan M. Cumming[t]

Walthourville, Wednesday, August 31st, 1864

My dear Aunt Susan,

The evening you left I almost regretted the thunderstorm did not continue long enough to detain you for the night, for I felt that I had not half seen you. I have heard nothing from Mother since you were here, so presume Carrie must be better, or at least no worse. I trust she is recovering.

After you left I wished I had offered you the services of Kate. As one of your maidens is about to disappear for a time, I thought Kate might be useful to you at that time; and if you would like to have her, do say so, and I will send her to you; for I do not need her here, and it would be charity for someone to give her *steady, full* employment.

I see no prospect at present of our keeping house. Mr. Mallard may return to Atlanta sooner than we now anticipate, as some are predicting a speedy retreat for Sherman. It seems to me he is after the Macon & Western Railroad.

The family here are very busy tonight writing to their soldier-boys in Virginia. They will have an opportunity of sending the letters tomorrow by Captain Screven, who leaves to join his command. . . . Do give much love to Cousin Laura, Cousin Lyman, and the children. And accept a great deal for yourself.

Your affectionate niece,
Mary S. Mallard.

Mrs. Mary S. Mallard *to* Mrs. Mary Jones[t]

Walthourville, *Saturday,* September 3rd, 1864

My dearest Mother,

We have heard nothing from you since your letter of last Tuesday week telling us of Carrie's sickness. We hope from not hearing that she is getting quite well again.

I sent your letter to Mr. Jackson by Niger on Saturday. He says the people are all quite well. Daddy Tony continued to grow more feeble after you left until he was confined to bed. His leg swelled very much and gave him a great deal of trouble. Mom Sue attended to his wants and prepared his food for him regularly.

Mr. Mallard rode to Arcadia on Monday. The people are generally well except some fever with two of the children. Tom is now hired to Mr. Edward Delegal at two dollars a day, and found he wants him to make shoes.

We have nothing of special interest in our village. Mr. Mallard has entered upon his labors, and it is quite natural to minister to his old charge again, though he does so to great disadvantage in having no study.

I think we have all improved since coming down. The weather is very cool —quite like fall. I suppose you are enjoying the same change. How is little Susie? The children send love to Stanhope and herself and to Little Sister. Has Brother Joe gone to Andersonville yet? Mr. Mallard unites with me in best love to yourself, Brother Joe, and Carrie.

Your affectionate daughter,
Mary S. Mallard.

Mrs. Mary Jones *to* Mrs. Laura E. Buttolph[t]

Augusta, *Saturday,* September 3rd, 1864

My very dear Niece,

I ought long ago to have thanked you for your loving remembrance of me. My thoughts are daily with you all at Flemington, and I long to see you all. The memory of your kindness in my recent sickness especially dwells with me, and I am thankful to know you all continue so well. And I believe you are as *safely* located as anywhere in the Confederacy.

Augusta has presented a martial appearance today, and it is said fifteen hundred men have left to join the army in its present most critical position. These are from the factories, powderworks, etc., etc. There is a prevailing feeling of depression just at this time, but I trust the Lord will not forsake or deliver us into the hands of our enemies. One thing has greatly astonished me here—the *few* in number who attend the army prayer meeting, which is now held but twice during the week.

Joe has just returned from a visit to Carrie, who with the children has been staying for a week at Beech Island with Mr. Clarke's family. Carrie has been very sick and in most feeble health; I have felt very uneasy about her ever since I came up. And the children also have been very sick.

Mrs. Davis and Mrs. Cuthbert were in today. General Alfred Cumming has been seriously wounded in the hip, and they are daily expecting him home, as his father went on for him.

Colonel Edward Stiles was killed at Front Royal. Dear Kitty, what sorrow this will bring to her heart! And his poor wife!

Carrie and I have been much engaged preparing and taking refreshments to the hospitals. We went at first every day, but now alternate. In her sickness and absence I have gone alone. We are the almoners of Mrs. Smith and Miss Cumming. *Flora* is our cook. We take them among other things the purest and best of coffee; and you would be pleased to see how much good it does them, and to see the eagerness with which they receive and often solicit Testaments. I have distributed a number to them, and if I had them could give away a great many more. The Bible room is now filled with the Word of God for soldiers, and often on Sabbath there is preaching for them at the hospitals. I frequently meet with professors of religion among them, and generally in the morning find them reading their Testaments or see them laid on the pillows at the head of their little beds.

Eva is with her mother at present, and has not been well since she came up to Augusta. My little Mary Ruth is the picture of health and good spirits, and is with me at this time.

Last night Mr. Charles Dunwody spent with us, and returned to Washington this morning. I am hoping to visit dear Marion before long, and to go to Indianola, and just so soon as it may be safe, if the Lord wills, to turn my face homeward. I long to be once more near that consecrated spot, *Midway*. Oh, Laura, this world is all changed to me now! . . .

I have been wanting to write my dear friend Julia, but I do assure you I have been as busy as my time and strength would allow ever since I came here. First one thing and then another, and trying to relieve Carrie all I could. Do give best love to her and Mary and all the family. I often think of them all and of the dear boys in the army, and pray that the Lord would bless and protect them.

I will write my dear sister soon. Do give her our best love, and to Mr. Buttolph. . . . Kiss the precious children for me; and Little Sister sends them a kiss. Please give Brother William much love when you see him. Howdies for the servants, and remembrances to the kind friends around you. Do write soon to

Your ever attached aunt,
Mary Jones.

Mrs. Mary S. Mallard *to* Mrs. Mary Jones[t]

Walthourville, *Monday,* September 5th, 1864

My dearest Mother,

I was truly glad to receive your letter on Saturday and to know that you are pretty well, and Carrie improving. Mr. Mallard received a letter from Mr. Porter today written while Carrie was at Beech Island in which he says they are all improving and Susie sleeping all night "without a whimper," so I hope they will soon be well.

I am very much obliged to you, my dear mother, for the hat for Charlie, and am glad you were able to exchange the cap. Mrs. Mallard thinks she would rather not have the reference Bible if the print is smaller than mine, and wishes you to keep the money until Mr. Mallard goes this week.

Mrs. Morriss has written Mr. Mallard begging him to go to Augusta and preach her sister's funeral sermon on next Sabbath. As he was not in Atlanta when she died, and her parents were members of his church there, he has concluded to go, and will leave on Thursday or Friday. I am sorry he should have to make the journey again.

I scarcely think Colonel Edward Stiles could have been killed, as we have seen no notice of it in the Savannah papers, and I think the family there would have received some intimation of it through the public telegrams. I trust it is not so for poor Kitty's sake. It would be the greatest affliction that could befall her, leaving her almost entirely alone in the world. I know that Mr. Tom Cumming and Eddie were intimate and had promised to take care of each other, so I presume Mr. Cumming's servant must have known Eddie; and this is the only reason why I fear something may have happened.

I see by the papers General Cumming has been badly wounded. Is it a dangerous wound? I presume Mrs. Cumming will now have him at home.

Today we have had the dreadful tidings of the fall of Atlanta. What will go next? It grieves me to think of our beautiful church being desecrated if not destroyed by those horrible creatures. I presume they will endeavor to liberate the prisoners at Andersonville now, or move upon Macon. . . .

Niger came up on Saturday and says the people are all well except Mom Sue and Gilbert, who have had some slight fever. Niger has had a little fever also, but nothing serious. He says you have fine corn and fine rice, but the cotton is rather young to do a great deal before frost. He tells me a jar of honey was sent with the rice and butter. You never received it; neither did Mr. Cassels mention it in his note to you telling of the express charges. Possibly it may not have gone; I will get Mr. Mallard to inquire as he goes along on Thursday. Niger says July put "two *osnaburg* linens" in the bag of rice for his children, and wants to know if you ever saw them. Tell Flora Lucy inquired of Adeline about her clothes, and she says she did not send her new chemise that is now in Savannah. Lucy told her what Flora had received, and she said that was all she sent. So Flora may expect to get the rest of her wardrobe when she goes back to Savannah.

Thus far the Yankees have made no further demonstrations on our coast. Colonel Hood has placed another company in the same place that those were captured in McIntosh. There must have been gross negligence, according to the captain's own acknowledgment, though he was free of blame, being absent at the time.

I am truly sorry to hear Eva is so unwell, and hope she will soon be better. Do give much love to her. Tell Little Sister Sissy and Bubber send love to her and want to see her very much.

You would have been amused to have seen Mamie on Sabbath. As soon as church was out she spoke to Mrs. Judge Fleming, who kissed her and passed to someone else. But Mamie was not to be put off in that way. She pursued her and in a loud voice said: "Mrs. Fleming, Grandma sent her love to you and said I must give it to you." She then peered around but could see none of the other ladies to whom she intended to give your love, so she came out feeling she had not accomplished half as much as she intended.

I hope Mrs. Eve gave you some of her nice pears when she took you out visiting. I have had some very nice ones sent me by Mrs. Cay; she has had an abundance of them.

We are all pretty well here. . . . My arm improves very slowly. I have it out of the close bandages in a sling today for the first time. The bone is by no means firmly united.

How does Mr. Manigault like the idea of going among the smallpox Yankees? I hope Brother Joe will be careful and not make himself sick. It will be a laborious undertaking. Do give love to Carrie and himself, and kiss the children for us. Mr. Mallard unites with me in affectionate love to you.

Your attached daughter,
Mary S. Mallard.

Rev. R. Q. Mallard *to* Mrs. Mary Jones[t]

Augusta, Monday, September 12th, 1864

My dear Mother,

I regret not seeing you, and presume the change in the railroad schedule will prevent your coming today. As the demands of the week will be unusually great, and as both the Doctor and Charlie leave tonight, I have concluded to return by this evening's train as I had originally appointed.

You will be rejoiced to learn that my dear Mary's general health is unusually good. Her appetite I never saw better, if as good, and she has sensibly improved in flesh since we went to Walthourville. She still suffers from her injury. We were very cordially received by my former people. Mary, I believe, has the warm friendship and kindly feeling of all. We are still at my brother's, but have the hope of getting the academy in a few months—at least in January. Having engaged to be their stated supply until return to Atlanta is possible, they promise to supply me with a house and to pay me at the rate of fifteen hundred dollars per annum. I am truly thankful that the Master continues me as an active worker in His cause. Our children are—or were when I left—in the enjoyment of perfect health and abundant flow of animal spirits.

Mary made inquiry according to your request about Mrs. Jones's house. She replied that she did not wish to dispose of it or to rent it, but expected to put it in repair. She was kind enough to offer it to me to store my furniture until I went to housekeeping, but I have concluded not to remove it at present. In fact, I could not, for transportation was not to be had.

I will send the parcel of seed to its destination as soon as possible; also the sacks. Flora delivers your message to me about the crockery and the hat. . . . If I can serve you in any way in the county, please call upon me without hesitation. And remember, Mother, that as Mary's husband I shall always consider myself as your debtor.

Affectionately your son,
R. Q. Mallard.

P.S. I have used Jerry once, and find him in good condition. The crop generally at Arcadia is better than last year. When we get a house we shall be happy to have you with us. Of this we will give you due notice.

Rev. John Jones *to* Mrs. Mary Jones[t]

Refuge, Friday, September 23rd, 1864

My dearest Sister,

Your last affectionate letter, long looked for, was truly welcome; and I was also anxious to hear from dear Mary and her family. Robert might have answered my last letter to Mary, as she was unable. It was indeed a sad accident occurring at such a time. I am glad to learn that Mary and Robert have found so pleasant and useful a refuge as Walthourville. I fear it will be a long time before they will return to their Atlanta home.

The loss of Atlanta is the greatest blow of the war. Our prospects are exceedingly dark to me, and without special divine interposition we are a ruined people. The militia who have just returned home report much drunkenness among the higher officers of our army. Sad evil to exist when we are suffering from exhaustion of men, and need the best of officers to lead and husband our feeble armies! Oh, for a General Lee at the head of every *corps d'armée!* But regrets and reproaches are unavailing, and we must roll our great burden on our Heavenly Father and both hope and wait *for the salvation of the Lord*.

My dear sister, my heart is ever with you in your great affliction. How much and constantly do I miss my dear brother! What should I not give for one hour's interview with him as in past days, that I might obtain his counsel and receive his words of encouragement! But how would his noble spirit be grieved, if he were now on earth, for his country which he loved so truly! He is specially in my thoughts on the Sabbath, and when I hold his book in my hands and teach the truths he taught. The last Sabbath I was out, I thought particularly of one feature of my dear brother's ministry: its faithfulness. He prepared faithfully; he preached faithfully, sparing neither body nor mind, slighting nothing and doing nothing slothfully, ever doing his best, and with more delight in the work of the ministry than any man I have ever known. It was his exceeding thoroughness and faithfulness which overtasked his strength and consumed his vital energies and superinduced premature age and infirmity. But he has gone to his eternal rest; he died in the Lord, and his works do follow him. Oh, for the death of those who slumber in the Lord!

September 24th. My dear sister, I am just recovering from a severe attack of fever, brought on by fatigue and unusual exposure in the sun, and occasionally at night. During the absence of the militia the few of us left at home had to perform double duty. I had also in charge the people of Mr. Barnard and others interested; and a number of sick Negroes called for an unusual amount of attention. I am very feeble, but improving. My dear wife and boys continue well, but look pale: the sun shines hot in this latitude at this season. But we have—servants and all—been remarkably blessed with health.

Dunwody is well, and still at Anderson. He felt the death of our dear young Cousin Joseph Robarts deeply, and wrote me a touching letter on the subject. Oh, how sad and mysterious! Janey and the boys unite in best love to you and Joseph, Carrie, and the children.

Your ever affectionate brother,
John Jones.

Mrs. Mary Jones *to* Mrs. Mary S. Mallard[t]

Augusta, *Saturday,* September 24th, 1864

My dear Daughter,

I returned from Indianola a very short time after Robert and your brothers had left for the cars. It was a great disappointment to find I had missed them. And I had hastened back particularly on Monday hoping to meet Robert. His note, which I received, and for which please thank him kindly, explained the necessity for his early return. I rejoice that he has found a field of labor amongst his old and well-known former charge, and upon such agreeable terms. The Lord has dealt mercifully with him and his, although you have been called to personal sufferings and disappointment where you hoped for a permanent and pleasant home.

I had a most gratifying visit to the people, barring my own indisposition induced by the long hot ride and some other causes. I feared at one time I would be ill while there. Tell Little Daughter and Charlie while I was on my journey an old lady and gentleman—Mr. and Mrs. Partridge—were taking their large family of little ones across the broad road. I made Daddy Titus get down and catch me three of the pretty little creatures and put them into a tin bucket, where I gave them some crumbs of bread and sprinkled in some water, in which they dipped their little bills and drank. As evening came on, they missed their kind mother and began to cry. I made Daddy Titus get me some straw and tried to make a little nest, but with all my skill I could not weave it half as well as Mrs. Partridge would have done. But I wound it round and round, and then put them all into it and put my warm hand over them; and they put their little heads together and drew up close to one another and went fast asleep. They reminded me of the verse in your little hymn:

> Birds in their little nests agree;
> And 'tis a shameful sight
> When children of one family
> Fall out and chide and fight.

I did not have to put a "polster" between these little birds to keep them from "popping" into one another and getting angry when one touched the other, as some little children with sense and reason sometimes do. I sent them to Augusta the next day for Little Sister and Stanhope, but the journey was so long (and I was not there to take care of them) that one or two died, and I do not know what became of the other.

I am thankful, my dear child, to hear of your improved health. Carrie has returned greatly benefited from Beech Island; also the children. I am trying to persuade her to spend next week on The Hill. I expect, a kind Providence permitting, to visit Marion Glen at Washington week after next, going about the 3rd of October and returning about the 8th. And as soon after as practicable I will turn my face homeward. Eva is now on a visit to her friends in Sparta.

Last week our friend Kitty Stiles arrived very unexpectedly. She walked immediately to my room. She had just come from a visit to her sister in Carolina and was going down to see Sidney, who is very ill with typhoid fever—so ill that she has not been informed of Edward's death. Dear Kitty is looking well in bodily health, and bears her grief with great fortitude and Christian submission; but it is a heartrending blow to her. She feels most tenderly for Mrs. Edward Stiles, who she says is crushed. I presume she will write you of her plans.

I do so long to be once more at home. Dear Carrie is as kind and attentive as possible, but I feel it is best for me to have a home and to try to do my duty to those now dependent on me. Do write me all about yourself and the news of the county—I mean so far as the safety, etc., of the inhabitants is concerned. Carrie unites with me in much love to Robert and yourself, with kisses for the dear children, and from Mary Ruth, Stanhope, and Susie. Howdies for the servants.

Ever your affectionate mother,
Mary Jones.

Mrs. Mary S. Mallard *to* Mrs. Mary Jones[t]

Walthourville, *Tuesday*, September 27th, 1864

My dearest Mother,

I was rejoiced to receive your welcome letter yesterday and to know that your fatiguing trip to Indianola had not made you sick. The children were greatly interested in Mr. and Mrs. Partridge and their family; Charlie seemed to think you had sent one of the little ones for him to pet. I am glad to hear that Carrie and the children were improved by their visit to Beech Island, and hope the cool weather will brace them all and restore them to perfect health.

You will no doubt enjoy a visit to Washington very much. I have always heard it was a delightful place, and it will be so pleasant to see Cousin Marion. Do give love to her for us; and if you should see Mrs. Hull, give much love to her. She was very kind to us while we were in Atlanta. It must be a sore trial to her to think of her nice house being occupied by Yankees.

No one gained anything by remaining in Atlanta. I should like to know how much the exiles were allowed to bring with them; the newspaper accounts are so conflicting it is difficult to get at the truth. I hope our beautiful church will be spared, but I suppose it will share the fate of those in other places. Mr. Mallard received a letter from Mrs. Pease yesterday in which she mentions they are now living in the female college in Macon. . . . We have not gotten our horse yet, as Mr. Pease has been unable to get transportation for him. The cars have been so much taken up with government transportation that it is impossible for them to take private freight.

At this time everything is very quiet in the county. Last week one or two families moved away from Jonesville because the troops were temporarily withdrawn from McIntosh County and sent up to the Altamaha bridge; but they have been returned again, and all feel safe. The militia is disbanded at present so that the planters may have an opportunity of harvesting their crops.

Mr. Jackson was at Montevideo last week. All well there. Mr. Jackson's case will come before Judge Fleming on Saturday week, and everyone thinks he will be able to get out of service, as he has so many places in charge. There are really very few men to go into the militia, and several of them should be exempt for the sake of the many widows and orphans under their care. And then there would be so many Negroes left without a single white man to look after them if they are taken away; I mean such men as Mr. McCollough, Mr. Jackson, and Mr. John Mallard, all of whom have from six to ten places to look after.

Colonel Hood's regiment is still in these regions. Colonel Gaulden is still fussing about the militia, and is in command, and says when they meet again he intends offering them to General McLaws on *certain conditions*. Most persons think it will result in their being permanently disbanded;

or at least they will retain their organization but not remain in camp, so that the planters will have an opportunity of attending to their business. . . .

Mrs. Mallard is weaving, and gets along very well. She does her own warping and putting in. Having a friend in Mr. Gignilliat, they were able to supply themselves with yarn; and you know the Roswell yarn runs more evenly than any other.

I still have my arm in a sling, and it is only by comparing it with what it was a month ago that I can perceive the slightest improvement. My work is accumulating so much that I am obliged to use it some, although I never take it out of the sling. My other aches are very great at times. I have been hoping to be able to spend a little time with Aunt Susan and Cousin Laura, and I think I shall do so in a week or two.

Mr. Mallard's sisters, Mrs. Bacon and Miss Louisa, are now in Augusta, having been called there to see Mrs. Bacon's eldest son, who was taken ill on his way to Virginia. I do not know in what hospital he has been placed. He is quite young, and this is the first time he has left home for service. He was returning with Olivius Bacon to Captain Screven's company. I trust his life will be spared, for that family has been so much afflicted. Quarterman Bacon, who died this summer, was as affectionate as if he had been Mrs. Bacon's own child, and she leaned upon him very much. . . .

The children are looking forward with great eagerness to the time when we will all be with Grandmama at Arcadia. They send love and many kisses to you and to Little Sister; love to Aunt Carrie, Stanhope, and Susie. Mr. Mallard unites with me in love to Carrie. Love to Eva too. With warmest love and a kiss for yourself, dear Mother,

Your affectionate daughter,
Mary S. Mallard.

Mrs. Mary Jones *to* Mrs. Susan M. Cumming[t]

Augusta, Thursday, September 29th, 1864

My dear Sister,

We were very happy to hear directly of you this week through Mr. Clay, who had recently made you a visit, the pleasure of which, so far as your family intercourse was concerned, seemed to have impressed him very pleasantly. I am thankful to know you have been so well, and that the children are so fat and hearty. I do long to see you all. And these cool nights give me hope of soon being at home, which after all is the best place for old people. My dear children here have been as kind as possible, showing me every attention in their power; but I often fear I have added a great deal to Carrie's cares, for she has been not only very sick at one time but extremely feeble, and the little girl so fretful and sick nearly all summer that she has had no opportunity of improvement. If they would allow it, I would take her home with me.

Joe has been at Andersonville several weeks investigating the most dreadful diseases amongst those infamous Yankees—smallpox, gangrene, etc. I do trust it will result in good to our own poor soldiers. He is now at Macon. Has his tent pitched near the female college, where he has access to the hospitals both in town and at Vineville. Has *Titus* as his cook and man-of-all-work, and Mr. Louis Manigault as secretary. I wish you could see the beautiful style in which Mr. Manigault prepares all the reports for the surgeon general at Richmond. I should say *transcribes,* as he only does the writing. Joe is most highly favored in this gentleman. He is also allowed two other assistants in his investigations, one a Mr. Ives and the other a son of Dr. Ford's.

I presume you heard of General Alfred Cumming's being severely wounded. He is still unable to move, and suffers very much. . . . Mrs. Smith and Miss Cumming are looking very well. Mrs. Cuthbert and her children are also on The Hill.

Eva has been visiting her friends at Sparta for several weeks, and I hope will return quite improved in health.

I had thought of making Marion Glen a visit next week, and wrote her to that effect. But on Monday she sent us by Major Minton her box of silver and valuables, saying they were apprehending a raid upon Washington. The bitter experience of going to Atlanta in the face of the enemy is too fresh in my recollection for me to attempt again either to embarrass my friends or expose myself, and particularly as I intended to take my little Ruth with me. So I have declined the pleasure of the visit for the present.

Carrie and I have been much interested in the sick and wounded in the hospitals here, and went to them near two months—as long as our supplies lasted. On last Sabbath Mrs. Bacon and Miss Louisa Mallard came up to see Mrs. Bacon's eldest son. We went with them to several hospitals before we found him and his brother Olivius, both sick. The ladies have just left with Mallard on sick leave for twenty days; Olivius is better and goes on to join his regiment in Virginia. Yesterday as I went in to see them in the morning I observed a poor soldier lying near them, evidently near his end. I gave him some blackberry wine, which he took from a spoon; and although he could not converse, I shall long remember the expression of his dying eyes as he would fix them intently on me. After dinner I went back. Only the narrow, naked pine bedstead remained. The poor soldier had been removed to the dead room to await interment, or perhaps to be sent home to his sorrowing friends.

Carrie unites with me in best love to you, dear Sister, to Laura and Mr. Buttolph, with kisses for the dear children. Stanhope and Little Sister send their love and kisses. . . . Howdies for your servants, and my own when you see them. Believe me

Ever your affectionate sister,
Mary Jones.

Mrs. Laura E. Buttolph *to* Mrs. Mary Jones[t]

Flemington, *Wednesday,* October 5th, 1864

My dearest Aunt,

Mother has received your last letter, and says I must answer it immediately for her; and it is needless for me to assure you of the pleasure it gives me so to do.

We are to send for Cousin Mary Mallard to make us a visit next week; would have sent this week, but she desires to remain to their Communion on Sabbath and then come. . . . I have had my loom taken down, and Mother has furnished the room; so *we will still have a spare room,* and you must be sure and come to us just when you feel inclined. *A great plenty of room and a longing in our hearts to see your own precious self.* Do *not* tarry in Savannah: the yellow fever has been there for some time and seems to be on the increase. . . . If you could avoid Savannah entirely in coming home, *I* think it would be a good plan. Cannot your carriage meet you at some station? Sarah Jones reports its being *very sickly* in Savannah. I notice the number of deaths is double the number of last week. There are so many refugees there that a pestilence would be terrible.

Last week we were distinguished by a call from Colonel C. C. Jones and General McLaws. They were in the house before I knew they were at the gate, and found me in a simple white dress bearding palmetto. I was so glad to see the colonel that sometimes I forgot the presence of the distinguished general. And his quiet manner helped me to forget him more than once. Mother ordered a lunch for them, and while they were refreshing us we hope they were refreshed for their afternoon's inspection of militia, troops, etc. In the afternoon Colonel Jones delivered an impromptu address to the militia and the ladies on the part of the general—the most eloquent I have heard since I heard my dear sainted uncle near Riceboro address the soldiers. And Charlie looked so very like him: the fire of true eloquence gleaming from his eyes, every gesture grace, and all hearers spellbound—all wishing that nothing might break the silence. But the occasion was too grand for Colonel Gaulden not to deliver an address he had evidently prepared, and delivered in his own style and manner, wearing an old uniform that looked as if it had been in many a hard battle, and a red sash. He made the ladies and boys laugh and his men look *wilder* than ever, and as Cousin Mary Wells said, "drew a very *encouraging picture* for them of their gray hairs being laid beside their dead sons already in the grave." They were all drawn up in line fronting the church, the ladies sitting upon the church steps. You can imagine the scene. Strange that I was to hear my noble cousin speak for the first time under such circumstances! That one so gifted should be exposed to the bullets of the enemy! May Heaven shield his head in battle! And may God cover his head in all battles he may be called to pass through!

Dear Cousin Joe! While he is devoting his time to the sick and investigating diseases, I trust he will not wear self out. It will do Cousin Carrie good to come home with you, and we will all be so glad to see her and the children. Seeing one's friends is a pleasure the war must not deprive us of, it is such a great comfort. . . . I am sorry you have given up your trip to Washington; I wished to enjoy it through you.

Aunt Julia, Cousin Mary, Kate, and all send you their love. They heard today from Will and Mr. Wells in Virginia, and all the boys in Upper Georgia, whither Cain was dispatched with money and clothing. Bayard went through with General Wheeler; had two shots—one in his thigh and doing well, the other carrying off his boot heel.

Little ones are well, and send love to little Mary Ruth, and say you must bring her with you to see them. And love to Stanhope and Susie. Mother and Mr. Buttolph unite in all that is affectionate.

Your ever attached niece,
Laura E. Buttolph.

Andrew reported all of your servants well on Sabbath, and Mother and Mr. Buttolph report all well on Monday as they returned from Dorchester, where he preached. They went to see Uncle William; he is also well, and sends love.

Mrs. Mary Jones *to* Mrs. Mary S. Mallard[t]

Augusta, Wednesday, October 5th, 1864

My dear Daughter,

Your last kind favor has been received, and I am thankful you all continue so well.

Yesterday *Mr. Ives* (a stranger to me, but now writing in Joe's office) called and inquired if I was in. Said he wished to know if *Dr. Mallard* had not married a member of my family. I told him the Rev. Mr. Mallard had —that he was not a "Dr." He said: "Oh, they call him so up here!" He had been sent by some of the Atlanta church members (a Mr. and Mrs. Whitner amongst others), as I understood him, to inquire if the report was true that *Mrs. Mallard* had died soon after she left Atlanta from the wounds she received when she was thrown out of a wagon. I told him we were very much obliged to the friends for their kindness in sending; and I was happy to inform them that although Mrs. Mallard had suffered and was still a sufferer from the injuries received, her life had been spared; and as she had recently been heard from, I hoped she was improving. I readily detected (as the gentleman's name would indicate) one of regular Puritan descent, so I thought I would end the conference by leaving him a little room for "guessing" what relation I bore to "Dr." and Mrs. Mallard.

Mrs. Bacon and Miss Louisa returned on last Thursday evening, taking Mallard home on sick leave for twenty days. The other brother, who was quite sick also but missed his fever, has, I presume, gone on to Virginia. Carrie, but for the state of her own health and the children and the illness of Sue's husband in the yard, would have insisted that the ladies should stay with her. But it really was impossible under the circumstances.

Carrie, I think, is completely worn down. She has been at The Hill since Saturday with her children. I am alone here with my dear little Mary Ruth, and in charge of Ralph, who continues very ill with typhoid fever. Flora and Harry have gone on a visit to Indianola; only Sue and Fanny and Susan constitute the household, and Sue has to be most of the time nursing her husband.

If a kind Providence favors my plans, I hope soon to return home. I had appointed this week to visit Washington, but Marion sent over her silver and valuables by Major Minton to Joe and Carrie's care, fearing there would be a raid upon Washington. The Atlanta *experience* was too fresh in my memory either to embarrass my friends or expose myself again, so I wrote declining the visit at present. I should have gone earlier, but I was feeling so feeble and sad I had no heart or strength for any extra effort, and now long to be at home.

Eva has been visiting her friends in Sparta for some weeks; her mother sent me word she would return on Thursday.

Mr. Manigault has been here removing his family to a house on this street; returns to Macon tomorrow. And Joe, I hope, will be with us on Saturday. I hope he will return before I leave.

I wrote Sister Sarah Jane some time since, but she has never replied. My letter was directed to *Mrs. James N. Jones.* Please, Daughter, when you write, direct my letters *Mrs. C. C. Jones;* then I am sure of them.

Things are going up every day. Calicoes (narrow) twelve dollars; wide, sixteen dollars a yard. Tea fifty and sixty cents a pound. And so it goes—up, up, up. It is wonderful how people live at all here. Wood eighty-five dollars a cord in the streets!

With much love for Robert and yourself, and kisses for my dear grand-children, and from Little Sister. Remembrances to all inquiring friends.

Ever, my dear child, your affectionate mother,

Mary Jones.

Howdies for the servants.

Mrs. Mary S. Mallard *to* Mrs. Mary Jones[t]

Walthourville, *Friday,* October 7th, 1864

My dear Mother,

I had thought of you as spending this week with Cousin Marion Glen; but a note from Cousin Laura received yesterday mentioned that you had given up all idea of going. I am very sorry you have been unable to do so, for it would have refreshed you very much.

Uncle Henry called to see me two afternoons ago. He is now engaged in Savannah on some of Governor Brown's business, attending court-martial.

He left Aunt Abby and the children quite well. Aunt Mary Robarts and the girls were with them at present, they having gone down to see if they could make any arrangement by which they could make a home in Cuthbert. Uncle Henry said they had partly perfected an arrangement by which they could get a portion of a large comfortable house. If they succeeded in making this arrangement, they would all come immediately down and go to housekeeping. If not, Aunty, Aunt Mary, and Aunt Lou expected to come to Flemington and remain some time in the county. The girls would go to Screven County to their aunt. Cousin Laura mentioned that they were expecting Aunty on the 10th of this month.

I expected to go over early next week and spend ten days or two weeks with Aunt Susan, and will do so if Aunty does not come. I would have done so this week, but our Communion takes place on next Sabbath, and I did not like to be absent. And then I have been constantly nursing Tenah's baby, who has been ill for nearly two weeks past. I am still exceedingly anxious about the child, and do not know yet how it will terminate. She has had very high fevers and apparently some great difficulty in the chest, causing a most distressing and racking cough. Dr. Stevens blistered her chest two days ago. It has been a complicated case: I suppose partly climate fever. Charlie has been quite unwell this week from dysentery, but is quite bright again.

We are again debating whether we shall make an effort to get our furniture down. It is impossible to get transportation for Jim, so Mr. Mallard thinks of sending a servant to Macon and having him ridden across the country. The route would lay through Mount Vernon in Montgomery County. I thought I had brought down all of our clothing, but now that the time draws nigh for us to need them, I find a portion of our winter underclothing has been left. I think they are in the trunk of crockery in the attic. If we conclude not to bring the furniture, I shall be obliged to send for that trunk, though I fear it is scarcely strong enough to bear the journey in anything but a chartered car. I could not have the clothing taken out of the trunk, for there would then be nothing to pack the crockery with.

We are having frequent showers now, which interferes with the harvesting. I hear that Mr. Jackson has succeeded in getting exemption papers. He was at Montevideo last week. All well there.

Miss Louisa Mallard came up last evening. She seems to feel very grateful to you for your kindness to her sister and herself; says she does not know what they would have done if you had not assisted them. Mallard came home with her much better.

Do give a great deal of love to Carrie from all of us. Mrs. Mallard desires love to you. Mr. Mallard and the children unite with me in warmest love to you, my dear mother. When do you think of coming down? Love to Eva and Little Sister.

Your affectionate daughter,
Mary S. Mallard.

Mrs. Mary S. Mallard *to* Mrs. Mary Jones[t]

Flemington, *Wednesday,* October 19th, 1864

My very dear Mother,

Mr. Mallard came over night before last bringing your note. I am truly glad to know that you are well and that Carrie has improved so much.

Our furniture has not yet arrived. The cost of a chartered car from Savannah to this place is *two hundred and eighty-eight* dollars, so Mr. Mallard concluded it would be best to have the furniture come by freight. He would have remained in Savannah until the car came down, but it was so uncertain when it would arrive that he did not consider it safe to remain, as there was so much yellow fever and sickness in Savannah. I will take good care of the things put in the bureau. We hope to be able to take the furniture directly to the academy.

Mr. Quarterman has gone to Virginia to look after his brother, Mr. Stewart Quarterman, who is severely wounded. As it was so uncertain when he would return, I took the liberty of opening your note to him, as there seemed to be a key in it, and I thought you might want something special done. Mr. Mallard went to Arcadia today to get the dress and shawl; so they will be sent by express tomorrow, and I hope they will reach you safely.

The weather is cool, and some persons saw frost ten days ago. There seems to be more sickness than usual in the county, though no serious illness that I know of. We are all anxious to see you, and longing to be with you, but feel it would be very imprudent for you to come down too soon. . . .

I came here a week ago, and have enjoyed my visit exceedingly. . . . The children are enjoying being with Jimmie and Willie very much. They all play very pleasantly together. Aunt Julia and Cousin Mary Wells spent today with us; they are looking remarkably well. Cousin Mary is really fat, and so is Aunt Julia. I enclose a letter from Aunt Julia which she gave me today. She is extremely anxious about Clarence, not knowing where he is.

Everything seems very dark with us now, and we are anxiously awaiting the next telegraphic intelligence, for continued silence seldom indicates favorable news on our side. We have a rumor today from some "reliable gentleman" that General Hood's army has been surrounded, and our loss very great. We wait with sorrowful hearts to hear the truth. I hope it may prove only an idle rumor, for if we lose our army, our state is at Sherman's mercy.

Aunt Susan and Cousin Laura unite with me in warmest love to you, and kisses for Little Sister. Much love to Brother Joe and Carrie. The children all send love. . . . I received a letter from Aunt Lou Robarts this week. They are all probably in Cuthbert by this time, as they expected to leave on the 11th of this month. Good night, dear Mother.

Your affectionate daughter,

Mary S. Mallard.

Miss Louisa J. Robarts *to* Mrs. Laura E. Buttolph[t]

Cuthbert, *Thursday,* October 20th, 1864

My dear Laura,

I have delayed writing you thus long, hoping to have something definite to write about our movements. We thought certainly that we would have been with you and our dear relatives in Liberty. After considering the matter and the expense of the journey and having in the spring again to look for a home, Sister went to Cuthbert to look for a house. At first she despaired of getting one, but a lady kindly let us have four of her rooms. The house is very large, but not finished. Her married daughter and two children are to remain in the house, they furnishing their own provisions; and we are to do the cooking for both families. We furnish all the servants for housework and firewood. We will not have any rent to pay. We hope to have a quiet and comfortable winter.

It is a great disappointment to me not to see you all, but I hope after we get settled to persuade Mother to come and make you all a visit. She is very anxious to see her dear relatives; often speaks of you with great affection. You would be astonished to see with what fortitude and submission she bears her great troubles. Her health has improved somewhat since the cool weather set in. She stood the journey to this place; since we arrived has had fever for a few days, but is now much better, sitting up knitting a little pair of socks for Helen. She sends a great deal of love to you and Cousin Susan and Lyman, and thanks you very much for your kind invitation. Says she thanks you just as much as if she had accepted your kind offer of a home for the present; but she wanted before she died to have her family all with her. We hope Cuthbert will prove a pleasant refuge until we can get to Marietta again. All are anxiously looking for the time when the Yankees will be driven from our soil. Reports are more favorable.

We have heard several times from Marietta. Our friends the Frasers have suffered very much. They hoisted the British flag; the Yankees tore it down; said they would just as leave fight the British as us. Rebecca had been arrested, but was released. They have had to sell their clothes to buy food. Mrs. Hansell has also suffered much. Other families have been well treated, but all have to board the Yankees. We have not heard from our house. . . .

I sent to Mr. Mallard's care a short time since some of my dear child's clothes to Mr. Buttolph, which I hope he will accept and wear for his sake. I wish you could see some of the many beautiful letters of sympathy I have received; they are such a comfort. I know I have great cause of gratitude, and I do thank God for all His mercies in this dreadful affliction. "His ways are not as our ways." I try to bear the yoke that my Heavenly Father has laid upon me.

Please give our united love to dear Cousin Susan, Lyman, and kisses for the dear little ones. I wish I could see them and hear some of their baby talk.

Your affectionate cousin,

Louisa Robarts.

I hope you will write us soon. We are always delighted to hear from our dear relatives in Liberty. I suppose by this time Cousin Mary has returned to Arcadia. Mary Mallard has, I hope, by this time entirely recovered from her injuries. I suppose for the present Mr. Mallard is preaching at Walthourville. . . . I will have to go to Longstreet again to try and get our furniture brought. The cars are all working for government, and it is very difficult to procure any accommodation on any of the roads. . . . Sister will write as soon as we get settled.

Miss Mary E. Robarts *to* Mrs. Susan M. Cumming[t]

Cuthbert, *Monday,* November 28th, 1864

My dear Cousin,

I have not written you for a very long time. Having left Longstreet for this place a day or two after I missed my chills, I felt so unwell for several weeks that I did not feel like writing. Then I was so much occupied in trying to get a house for ourselves that I kept waiting till that was accomplished.

And now I must spare this morning to make a report, and to tell you that a kind Methodist lady consented to rent us a part of her house—a large mansion which she had commenced building before the war but had not finished, so that the last coat of plastering was not put on till just before we moved in, and the doors and windows were not hung till after we were in the house. . . . Mrs. Duncan consented to rent me her rooms only on condition that I would board her family, which I agreed to do. As I had thought we should be obliged to take some boarders to help us out, I thought we might as well take the family who kindly shared their dwelling with us as anyone else; so we entered into the following arrangement: Mrs. Duncan occupies the four rooms upstairs and we the four below, with piazza all round and entry at the side, like the Savannah houses. Her family consists of six: herself and a little niece about twelve years old, her married daughter and her husband, and two nice little children. Their board is paid in provisions (a very liberal supply), and we sup together, so that I have a family of twelve to keep house for. Do not, however, find it much more trouble than to keep house for one family, as they are very pleasant, kind, and polite. In consideration of my keeping house and furnishing wood and servants, do not pay any rent. They of course do their own washing and chamber work; furnish their own lights.

So much for our household. Now for the town of Cuthbert. It is a pretty little place—not so pretty as Marietta, though some say it is larger. It possesses no particular attraction to tempt refugees except that it is safer than other places—more remote from the line of Yankee travel. Provisions are scarce and high, but not more so than in other places. Of the society I know very little, as they are not very sociable with strangers. But we have five families of Marietta refugees here, who with Henry's family and Mrs.

Morris make a pleasant society for us. There are three churches, so that we have preaching every Sabbath. Mr. Hendee preaches in the Presbyterian church, and is a very good preacher; and it is a comfort to us to hear the sound of the "church-going bell" once more after being without all summer.

I have now given you the sunny side of our prospects in Cuthbert. The shadows no doubt will come, but I will not anticipate. Life has lost its bright anticipations, but we can only live up to present duty. We feel farther off from Liberty than we used to do in Marietta, though it is the same distance and not on the direct line of travel.

And now I am writing you, my dear cousin, with scarcely a hope that this may reach you. I send it via Thomasville; for alas, we hear that Sherman is en route for Savannah. Times look dark, and the news is sad indeed. I never could understand the policy of Hood's going off to Tennessee and leaving the Yankees in our midst to make their way undisputed to our seaport cities. We feel the deepest anxiety, and know not what to expect. It seems vain to put confidence in man, and we must try to wait quietly for deliverance from on high. Do write me as soon as you can and let me know all that is going on below; for our news here is very meager.

Henry and Abby left for their place in Baker two weeks since, but Henry had to leave his sugar-boiling and come back in a week to attend to what he calls his "official business." You know he is one of Governor Brown's aides, and thinks him the greatest man in the world. He is here busy from morning till night; sometimes comes over and takes dinner or tea with us. He hopes to return to Baker in a few days to remain till January.

We have not yet seen Cousin John. Heard he is well. Mrs. Dunwody is there at present; no doubt it is a great comfort to Jane to have her mother with her. . . .

Our dear Joe is a great loss to us, and it will be impossible to say how much he is in our thoughts. And often I find myself recalling incidents of his childhood; so many pleasant memories cluster around him. Sometimes we think he cannot be gone—that he is still in the army. Then we comfort ourselves by thinking of him in heaven before his life was sullied by the sins which mark the career of some young men.

Life seems to be more full of sorrows than ever, for in addition to our private grief we have all the burdens of this terrible war to bear. A gentleman of our acquaintance intends trying to get into Marietta next week to look after his possessions there, so we intend getting him to look at our lot and to find out how Mrs. Fraser and her family are. Every account is that they have been hardly treated: their front yard a hospital, and the piazza a place for amputation. And frequently when they wake in the morning, several dead bodies are in the piazza. I heard they called Mrs. Fraser "a damned old rebel." No doubt they have suffered very much. So has Mrs. Hansell. At first she thought she would fare very well, but the Yankees encroached more on her every day, and were very insolent. . . . I trust

Savannah and Charleston may withstand the attack of the enemy, and that they may be repulsed at every point.

I am glad Cousin Mary Jones reached home safely. Hope she and little Ruthie are well. Do give our best love to her, and say that I will write her very soon. Much love to dear Laura, Mr. Buttolph, and the children. Hope he will take Cuthbert in his way whenever he goes to Baker. Much love to Julia and her family. . . . Farewell, my dear cousin. Do write me soon. Give our love to Cousin William when you see him, and any of our friends. Mother, Louisa, and the girls all desire love.

Your affectionate cousin,
Mary E. Robarts.

Louisa begs you will get one of the Kings to inquire what became of our dear Joe's horse. She wrote Captain Walthour but received no answer.

Mrs. Mary Jones *to* Mrs. Susan M. Cumming[t]

Arcadia, *Friday,* December 9th, 1864

My dear Sister,

Will you be kind enough to send my candle molds if you are not using them, as I must try and prepare for nights of darkness. My lights have almost gone out.

My dear child left me on Tuesday. I did all that I could prudently to keep her, but she felt that she must be near Dr. Stevens. My anxieties for her are more than I can express. They will keep a horse on hand to send for me at a moment's warning.

God's dealings with me and mine at this time are very solemn. . . . You know Daughter's situation. Charles stands before a murderous foe, every moment exposed to death if called into battle; of this there can scarcely be a doubt, for their cannon are already firing at intervals. Joseph and his family are I know not where. Desolation has swept over Indianola; if any of our people are spared, they must be in great distress; not one word has been heard from them. And here I am alone with my dear little baby.

I am perplexed about this house. Ought the furniture to be removed? Books, etc.? *All* that I have is here. What arrangements do you think of making if the enemy advance upon the railroad and take possession of this section? . . . If the river did not run at our door, I would move back to Montevideo; for I will be constantly exposed here to stragglers. I try to be calm and hopeful, to trust in God and do the best I can; but sometimes my heart almost dies within me.

With best love to dearest Laura and yourself and Mr. Buttolph. Kiss the children for Little Sister and Aunt Mary. If convenient do let your cart call for the demijohns; I have no means of sending them.

Ever your affectionate sister,
Mary Jones.

Mrs. Susan M. Cumming *to* Mrs. Mary Jones[t]

Flemington, *Saturday,* December 10th, 1864

My dearest Sister,

These are days of darkness, and if we could not call upon a merciful God we should be overwhelmed. God help and pity us! Your dear children, may they be under the shadow of the Almighty! Dear to me as my own, they are constantly on my heart. We must commit *all* to our God and pray Him to choose for us in all things. How I wish you were with us! I would come to you if I could help you.

We have been in great excitement here. Expect the enemy. We cannot go anywhere, but must stay and take whatever comes. Mr. Buttolph speaks of going into service. He is just going to see you. We heard you were at Montevideo.

Sorry you had to send for the molds. Many thanks for their use. The good Lord keep you and yours in perfect safety! With all love. Jimmie has just said: "Let us go to Arcadia; we will have no trouble there."

Your ever affectionate sister,

S. M. Cumming.

Mrs. Laura E. Buttolph *to* Mrs. Mary Jones[t]

Flemington, *Saturday,* December 10th, 1864

My precious Aunt,

These are times when we can alone trust in God. And He is a *mighty Deliverer,* and will hear the cry of the widow and the orphan. . . . Captain Gignilliat told Aunt Julia it was an advantage to her being on the road; that the Yankee officers would station guards around the private residences while the army passed if requested. If it is God's will, I hope we may fall in with the best of them. They do not destroy ministers' houses and private houses.

Mrs. Brooks, writing from Milledgeville, says their army numbers seventy-five thousand, and they expect a fleet from New York to meet them, and speak confidently—say we cannot stand a cross fire. She told them she hoped they would get whipped at Savannah. They came into her yard, killed her hogs, ducks, etc. The cook ran out, caught up three, and killed them. They stole one after she had picked it, but they saved two. She put provisions in all her closets—some here and some there—and packed up all her things as if she was to move out at a moment's warning. . . . She had to cook for some of them, and told them they must furnish all their own meat, as they had taken all of hers, which they did. Their music was splendid, but her heart below zero. And all the time in such great anxiety and distress, not sleeping or taking off her clothes for ten days. . . . Mrs. Brooks's servant told many a party her master was a good man, a poor man, and they must not trouble him. . . . They said they could not feed the Negro; they had no love for the Negro. And yet they tried to persuade her to go off with them —which she refused to do. Faithful old soul!

The waste of provisions, starvation staring us in the face, is what I dread. Many have gone to Thomasville; but the crowd is so great there, and board a hundred dollars a day, we might as well die of want in one place as another.

Make Gilbert take care of and hide your horses. They kill all of those; and our men are now impressing horses, mules, and men. (Some of Wheeler's men were here yesterday.) They don't take oxen, so our oxen are to bring us provisions.

Mr. Buttolph says he will see you today. He must hide if they surprise us, and be on hand to take care of us. Cousin Robert must do the same for Mary. I hope they will get whipped at Savannah. May God shield my beloved cousin from death, and take care of us and all of our loved ones! . . . Kate went to South Hampton yesterday to be near Cousin Audley, and said if she only had someone with her, she would not feel afraid. . . . I hear most of the young girls have gone to Thomasville; Wallace Cumming has gone there with his family. . . . Mr. Buttolph says let house and all go, and come here and let us all be together. Willie said: "I will tell you what to do. Let us give the Yankees some of our little things, and then they will love us and not kill us." May we be able to stand in our lot, with the blessing of God!

Your own niece,
Laura.

Mrs. Mary Jones *to* Mrs. Susan M. Cumming[t]

Montevideo, *Monday,* December 12th, 1864

My dear Sister and Niece,

Your note has this moment been received. *I fear* your being cut off from your supplies. If you will come to us, and can get down to the station, I will send to meet you there whenever you appoint, or send our buggy all the way for you. We came here yesterday afternoon, and are trying to get some of our things over from Arcadia. One cart broke down. With our buggy and yours could you not come down at once?

Daughter is in bed today: overfatigue and anxiety. Robert is just leaving for No. 3; this goes by him. *God be merciful to us sinners!* For my poor child here, and my son in Savannah, my heart aches—and my bleeding country!

Ever yours, in warmest love,
Mary Jones.

XXIII

Mrs. Mary S. Mallard *in her Journal*[t]

Montevideo, *Tuesday,* December 13th, 1864

Mother rode to Arcadia this morning to superintend the removal of household articles and the remainder of library, etc., believing that the Yankees were no nearer than Way's Station, and lingered about the place until late in the afternoon, when she started to return to Montevideo. It was almost sunset, and she was quietly knitting in the carriage, fearing no evil. Jack was driving, and as they came opposite the Girardeau place, now owned by Mr. W. E. W. Quarterman, a Yankee on horseback sprang from the woods and brought his carbine to bear upon Jack, ordering him to halt. Then, lowering the carbine, almost touching the carriage window and pointing into it, he demanded of Mother what she had in the carriage.

She replied: "Nothing but my family effects."

"What have you in that box behind your carriage?"

"My servants' clothing."

"Where are you going?"

"To my home."

"Where is your home?"

"Nearer the coast."

"How far is the coast?"

"About ten miles. I am a defenseless woman—a widow—with only one motherless child with me. Have you done with me, sir? Drive on, Jack!"

Bringing his carbine to bear on Jack, he called out: "No! Halt!" He then asked: "Where are the rebels?"

"We have had a post at No. 3."

Looking into the carriage, he said: "I would not like to disturb a lady; and if you will take my advice you will turn immediately back, for the men are just ahead. They will take your horses and search your carriage, and I cannot say what they will do."

Mother replied: "I thank you for that," and ordered Jack to turn. Jack saw a number of men ahead, and Mother would doubtless have been in their midst had she proceeded but a few hundred yards. (This must have been an officer; he was a hale, hearty man, well dressed, with a new blue overcoat, and well appointed in every respect.) Jack then drove through by Colonel Quarterman's, and not very far beyond met our picket guard.

It was now quite dark. When she came to the junction with the Walthourville road, there she met a company of cavalry commanded by Captain Little.

She informed them of the position of the Yankees, and entreated that he would give her an escort if but for a few miles. She told him the distressing circumstances of her family, and that she was compelled to reach her home and her daughter that night. He replied they were ordered to that point, and if she would stay with them or go with them they would protect her, but they could not send anyone with her. She again urged her distressing circumstances. He said: "The Boro bridge is burnt, and you may not go a mile before you meet the enemy. I cannot help you."

"Then I will trust in God and go forward!"

Meeting a servant of Captain Randal Jones's who had been with him in Virginia, he ran along with the carriage. He had been sent from the depot to inform his young mistress of the presence of the enemy. He rendered her very kind service, acting as a scout. He would dart forward, take an observation, and encourage her to proceed. Every moment she expected to meet the Yankees.

Passing from the public road, Mother turned up the crossroad by Tranquil Hill. At the avenue our picket was stationed, who informed her that the bridges on the causeway had been taken up, and her carriage could not cross over. Mother replied: "Then I must get out and walk, for I must reach home tonight if my life is spared!" She rode up to the dwelling house; Dr. and Mrs. Way came to the carriage and pressed her very kindly to remain all night. She had resolved to walk home when Mr. William Winn, one of the picket guard, rode up and informed Mother the bridges had been fixed so as to allow the carriage to pass over.

She hastened forward and met a picket near the crossroads by the Baptist church; saw no one again until reaching the hill above the Boro. Under the crack of the door she discovered a dim light, and taking the reins sent Jack in to inquire if the enemy was near. The reply was: "Yes, the Boro is full of Yankees." Turning up the Darien road, she made her way through an obscure and very rough road through the woods which had been used as a wood road, just back of our encampment. Jack was unacquainted with the way. The old horses completely tired out, so that with difficulty she passed into the old field back of the Boro into the road leading to our enclosure, reaching home after nine o'clock.

I was rejoiced to hear the sound of the carriage wheels, for I had been several hours in the greatest suspense, not knowing how Mother would hear of the presence of the enemy, and fearing she would unexpectedly find herself in their midst at the Boro.

Late in the evening Milton came running in to say a boy had met the oxcarts going to Arcadia and told them they could not pass, for the Yankees were in the Boro. It was a perfect thunderclap. In a few moments the boy was at the door confirming the intelligence; he was sent by Mr. Audley King and Mr. McCollough. Fearing a raiding party might come up, immediately I had some trunks of clothing and other things carried into the woods, and the carts and horses taken away and the oxen driven away, and prepared to pass the night alone with the little children, as I had no idea Mother could reach home.

After ten o'clock Mr. Mallard came in to see us, having come from No. 3, where a portion of Colonel Hood's command was stationed. Upon consultation the trunks were brought back. Mr. Mallard stayed with us until two o'clock A.M. and, fearing to remain longer, left to join the soldiers at No. 4½ (Johnston Station), where they were to rendezvous. He had exchanged his excellent horse Jim with Cyrus Mallard for a mule, as Cyrus was going on picket and he thought he would need a swifter animal. This distressed us very much, and I told him I feared he would be captured. It was hard parting under this apprehension, and he lingered as long as possible, reading a part of the 8th Chapter of Romans and engaging in prayer before leaving. It was moonlight, and Jack was sent forward to see if there was any advance of the enemy upon the place, as there was much open space to be passed over before he could reach the woods. Before parting he went up and kissed his children, charging me to tell them "Papa has kissed them when asleep." I had a fearful foreboding that he would be captured, and we stayed as long as prudence would permit in the front porch.

Wednesday, December 14th. Although it had been much past midnight when we retired, Mother and I rose early, truly thankful no enemy had come near us during the night. We passed the day in fearful anxiety. Late in the afternoon Charles came into the parlor, just from Walthourville, and burst into tears.

I asked what was the matter.

"Oh," he said, "very bad news! Master is captured by the Yankees, and says I must tell you keep a good heart."

This was a dreadful blow to us and to the poor little children. Mamie especially realized it, and cried all the evening; it was heartrending to see the agony of her little face when told her papa was taken prisoner. Mr. Mallard was standing in the porch of his own house at Walthourville when Kilpatrick's cavalry rode up and hailed him, demanding his horse. Supposing they were our own men (it being early and a very misty morning), he asked by what authority, when to his surprise he found himself a prisoner. The servants were all in the yard, and say he was dreadfully cursed by his captors, their language being both profane and vulgar. He was taken off upon the mule he had been riding. The servants then took the mules and wagon and in fear and trembling came down here. Mr. Mallard was captured before sunrise.

Mother sent Niger to South Hampton to ask Mrs. King to come to us immediately and to say the enemy was in the county. She was too unwell to come.

Thursday, December 15th. About ten o'clock Mother walked out upon the lawn, leaving me in the dining room. In a few moments Elsie came running in to say the Yankees were coming. I went to the front door and saw three dismounting at the stable, where they found Mother and rudely

demanded of her: "Where are your horses and mules? Bring them out!"—
at the same instant rushing by her as she stood in the door. I debated whether
to go to her or remain in the house. The question was soon settled, for in a
moment a stalwart Kentucky Irishman stood before me, having come
through the pantry door. I scarcely knew what to do. His salutation was:
"Have you any whiskey in the house?"

I replied: "None that I know of."

"You ought to know," he said in a very rough voice.

I replied: "This is not my house, so I do not know what is in it."

Said he: "I mean to search this house for arms, but I'll not hurt you." He
then commenced shaking and pushing the folding door and calling for the
key.

Said I: "If you will turn the handle and slide the door you will find it
open."

The following interrogatories took place:

"What's in that box?"

"Books."

"What's in that room beyond?"

"Search for yourself."

"What's in that press?"

"I do not know."

"Why don't you know?"

"Because this is my mother's house, and I have recently come here."

"What's in that box?"

"Books and pictures."

"What's that, and where's the key?"

"My sewing machine. I'll get the key."

He then opened the side door and discovered the door leading into the old
parlor. "I want to get into that room."

"If you will come around, I will get the key for you."

As we passed through the parlor into the entry he ran upstairs and commenced searching my bedroom. "Where have you hid your arms?"

"There are none in the house. You can search for yourself."

He ordered me to get the keys immediately to all my trunks and bureaus.
I did so, and he put his hands into everything, even a little trunk containing
needle books, boxes of hair, and other small things. All this was under cover
of searching for arms and ammunition. He called loudly for *all* the keys;
I told him my mother would soon be in the house and she would get her
keys for him.

While he was searching my bureau he turned to me and asked: "Where
is your watch?"

I told him my husband had worn my watch, and he had been captured
the day before at Walthourville.

Shaking his fist at me, he said: "Don't you lie to me! You have got a
watch!"

I felt he could have struck me to the floor; but looking steadily at him, I replied: "I have a watch and chain, and my husband has them with him."

"Well, were they taken from him when he was captured?"

"That I do not know, for I was not present."

Just at this moment I heard another Yankee coming up the stair steps and saw a young Tennessean going into Mother's room, where he commenced his search. Mother came in soon after and got her keys; and there we were, following these two men around the house, handing them keys (as they would order us to do in the most insolent manner), and seeing almost everything opened and searched and tumbled about.

The Tennessean found an old workbox, and hearing something rattling in it, he thought it was coin and would have broken it open. But Dick, the Kentuckian, prevented him until Mother got the key, and his longing eyes beheld a bunch of keys.

In looking through the bureaus, to Mother's surprise, Dick pulled out a sword that had belonged to her deceased brother and had been in her possession for thirty-one years. Finding it so rusty, they could scarcely draw it from the scabbard, and concluded it would not kill many men in this war and did not take it away.

The Tennessean found a large spyglass which had belonged to Mr. Mallard's father, and brought it out as quite a prize.

I said to him: "You won't take that!"

"No," said he, "I only want to look through it. It's of no use to me."

Dick went into the attic, but did not call for the keys to the two locked rooms. He took up the spyglass, and winking at me said: "I mean to take this to Colonel Jones." (Susan had told him Mary Ruth was Colonel Jones's child.)

Mother said to him: "Is your commanding officer named Jones?"

He laughed and said he meant to take the glass to Colonel Jones.

I said: "You won't take that, for I value it very much, as it belonged to my father."

Said he: "It's of no use to you."

"No, none whatever beyond the association, and you have much finer in your army."

He did not take it, though we thought he would have done so if we had not been present. He turned to Mother and said: "Old lady, haven't you got some whiskey?"

She replied: "I don't know that I have."

"Well," said he, "I don't know who ought to know if you don't!"

Mother asked him if he would like to see his mother and wife treated in this way—their house invaded and searched.

"Oh," said he, "none of us have wives!"

Whilst Mother walked from the stable with one of the Yankees from Kentucky he had a great deal to say about the South bringing on the war. On more than one occasion they were anxious to argue political questions with her. Knowing it was perfectly useless, she would reply: "This is neither the time nor place for these subjects. My countrymen have decided that it was just and right to withdraw from the Union. We wished to do it peaceably; you would not allow it. We have now appealed to arms; and I have nothing more to say with you upon the subject."

Mother asked him if he would like to see his mother and sisters treated as they were doing us.

"No," said he, "I would not. And I never do enter houses, and shall not enter yours."

And he remained without while the other two men searched. They took none of the horses or mules, as they were too old.

A little before dinner we were again alarmed by the presence of five Yankees dressed as marines. One came into the house—a very mild sort of a man. We told him the house had already been searched. He asked if the soldiers had torn up anything. One of the marines (as they called themselves) came into the pantry and asked if they could get anything to eat. Mother told them she had only what was prepared for our own dinner, and if they chose they could take it where it was—in the kitchen. They said they preferred to take it there, and going to the kitchen, they cursed the servants awfully, ordered milk, potatoes, and other things. They called for knives and forks, and having no others Mother sent out those we used; but they ordered Milton to take them immediately back and to tell his mistress to put them away in a safe place, as "a parcel of damned Yankees" would soon be along, and they would take every one from her.

We hoped they would not intrude upon the dwelling; but as soon as they finished eating, the four came in, and one commenced a thorough search, ordering us to get him all the keys. He found some difficulty in fitting the keys, and I told him I would show them to him if he would hand me the bunch.

He replied: "I will give them to you when I am ready to leave the house."

He went into the attic and instituted a thorough search into every hole and corner. He opened a large trunk containing the private papers of my dear father, and finding a tin canister, he tried to open it. Mother could not immediately find the key, and as he spoke insolently to her about getting the key, she told him he had better break it, but she could assure him it contained only the private papers of her husband, who was a minister of the gospel.

"Damn it," he said, "if you don't get the key I will break it. I don't care!"

In looking through the trunk he found a beautiful silver goblet which had been given to Mother by her dear little granddaughter Julia, and which she had valued as a keepsake. His eyes sparkled as he held it up and called out: "Here's something pretty, boys!"

Mother looked at him scornfully and said: "And would you take it?"

He said no, and put it quickly down, although we believe only our presence kept him from pocketing it.

One of the party came in with a secession rosette which Brother Charlie had worn at the great meeting in Savannah when he was mayor of the city. Mother had given it to Jack with a few letters to put away. As they were riding up he took it from Jack, and we were quite amused to see him come in with it pinned on the lapel of his jacket. This one was quite inclined to argue about the origin of the struggle.

One of them had an old cap—the helmet-shaped cap with horsehair plume belonging to the Liberty Independent Troop, and the jacket also, as we afterwards understood were those formerly used by the troop. Being blue with bell buttons, they could very well pass for sailors' jackets. They had rigged themselves from some house they had searched before coming here.

After spending a long time in the search, they prepared to leave with all the horses. Mother told them they were over seventeen years old and would do them no service. They took away one mule, but in a short time we saw it at the gate: they had turned it back.

After they left I found that my writing desk had been most thoroughly searched and everything scattered, and all little articles of jewelry, pencils, etc., scattered. A gold pen was taken from my workbox.

Mother felt so anxious about Kate King that she sent Charles and Niger in the afternoon to urge her coming over to us, and told them if she was too unwell to walk or ride, they must take her up in their arms and let someone help to bring the little children. But they did not reach South Hampton, as they met a Yankee picket which turned Niger back and took Charles with them to assist in carrying horses to Midway, promising to let him return.

Friday, December 16th. Much to our relief, Prophet came over this morning with a note from Kate to know if we thought she could come to us. Mother wrote her to come immediately, which she did in great fear and trembling, not knowing but that she would meet the enemy on the road. We all felt truly grateful she had been preserved by the way.

About four in the afternoon we heard the clash of arms and noise of horsemen, and by the time Mother and I could get downstairs we saw forty or fifty men in the pantry, flying hither and thither, ripping open the safe with their swords and breaking open the crockery cupboards. Fearing we might not have a chance to cook, Mother had some chickens and ducks roasted and put in the safe for our family. These the men seized whole, tearing them to pieces with their teeth like ravenous beasts. They were clamorous for whiskey, and ordered us to get our keys. One came to Mother to know where her meal and flour were, insisted upon opening her locked pantry, and took every particle. They threw the sacks across their horses. Mother remonstrated and pointed to her helpless family; their only reply was: "We'll take it!"

They flew around the house, tearing open boxes and everything that was closed. They broke open Mother's little worktable with an andiron, hoping to find money or jewelry; it contained principally little mementos that were valuable only to herself. Failing to find treasure, they took the sweet little locks of golden hair that her mother had cut from the heads of her angel children near a half century ago, and scattering them upon the floor trampled them under their feet. A number of them rifled the sideboard, taking away knives, spoons, forks, tin cups, coffeepots, and everything they wished. They broke open Grandfather's old liquor case and carried off two of the large square gallon bottles, and drank up all the blackberry wine and vinegar which was in the case. It was vain to utter a word, for we were completely paralyzed by the fury of these ruffians.

A number of them went into the attic into a little storeroom and carried off twelve bushels of meal Mother had stored there for our necessities. She told them they were taking all she had to support herself and daughter, a friend, and five little children. Scarcely one regarded even the sound of her voice; those who did laughed and said they would leave one sack to keep us from starving. But they only left some rice which they did not want, and poured out a quart or so of meal upon the floor. At other times they said they meant to starve us to death. They searched trunks and bureaus and wardrobes, calling for shirts and men's clothes.

We asked for their officer, hoping to make some appeal to him; they said they were all officers and would do as they pleased. We finally found one man who seemed to make a little show of authority, which was indicated by a whip which he carried. Mother appealed to him, and he came up and ordered the men out. They instantly commenced cursing him, and we thought they would fight one another. They brought a wagon and took another from the place to carry off their plunder.

It is impossible to imagine the horrible uproar and stampede through the house, every room of which was occupied by them, all yelling, cursing, quarreling, and running from one room to another in wild confusion. Such was their blasphemous language, their horrible countenances and appearance, that we realized what must be the association of the lost in the world of eternal woe. Their throats were open sepulchres, their mouths filled with cursing and bitterness and lies. These men belonged to Kilpatrick's cavalry. We look back upon their conduct in the house as a horrible nightmare, too terrible to be true.

When leaving they ordered all the oxen to be gotten up early next morning.

MRS. MARY JONES *in her Journal* [t]

Montevideo, *Saturday,* December 17th, 1864

About four o'clock this morning we were roused by the sound of horses; and Sue, our faithful woman, came upstairs breathless with dismay and told us they had come upon the most dreadful intent, and had sent her in to tell me what it was, and had inquired if there were any young women in my family. Oh, the agony—the agony of that awful hour no language can describe! No heart can conceive it. We were alone, friendless, and knew not what might befall us. Feeling our utter weakness and peril, we all knelt down around the bed and went to prayer; and we continued in silent prayer a long time. Kate prayed, Daughter prayed, and I prayed; and the dear little children, too, hearing our voices, got up and knelt down beside us. And there we were, alone and unprotected, imploring protection from a fate worse than death, and that our Almighty God and Saviour would not permit our cruel and wicked enemies to come nigh our persons or our dwelling. We rose from our knees and sat in darkness, waiting for the light of the morning to reveal their purposes, but trusting in God for our deliverance.

New squads were arriving. In the gray twilight of morning we looked out of the window and saw one man pacing before the courtyard gate between the house and the kitchen; and we afterwards found he had voluntarily undertaken to guard the house. In this we felt that our prayers had been signally answered.

MRS. MARY S. MALLARD *in her Journal* [t]

Montevideo, *Saturday,* December 17th, 1864

As soon as it was light Kate discovered an officer near the house, which was a great relief to our feelings. Mother and I went down immediately, when she said to him: "Sir, I see that you are an officer; and I come to entreat your protection for my family, and that you will not allow your soldiers to enter my dwelling, as it has been already three times searched and every particle of food and whatever they wanted taken." He replied it was contrary to orders for the men to be found in houses, and the penalty was death; and so far as his authority extended with his own men, none of them should enter the house. He said he and his squad (there were many others present) had come on a foraging expedition, and intended to take only provisions.

Upon Mother's inviting him to see some of the work of the previous evening he came in and sat awhile in the parlor. Before leaving he discovered a portable desk on a table and walked up and opened it. She said: "That is my private property; it is here for my own use, and has only a little paper in it." He closed it immediately. (It had previously escaped observation and removal.)

The Yankees made the Negroes bring up the oxen and carts, and took off all the chickens and turkeys they could find. They carried off all the syrup from the smokehouse. We had one small pig, which was all the meat we had left; they took the whole of it. Mother saw everything like food stripped from her premises, without the power of uttering one word. Finally they rolled out the carriage and took that to carry off a load of chickens. They took everything they possibly could.

The soldier who acted as our volunteer guard was from Ohio, and older than anyone we had seen; for generally they were young men and so active that Mother called them "fiery flying serpents." As he was going Mother went out of the house and said to him: "I cannot allow you to leave without thanking you for your kindness to myself and family; and if I had anything to offer I would gladly make you some return."

He replied: "I could not receive anything, and only wish I was here to guard you always."

It was not enough that they should insult us by converting our carriage into a chicken-cart and take it away drawn by our own carriage horses; but they sent in to tell Mother if she wanted her carriage to send for it, and when they were done with it she might have it. We afterwards learned it was broken to pieces and left beyond Midway Church.

They took off today June, Martin, George, Ebenezer, Little Pulaski, our house servant Jack, and Carpenter Pulaski. Seeing the two last-named going away, Mother called to the soldier who had them in charge: "Why are you taking my young men away?"

He said: "They need not go if they do not want to."

She then asked: "Boys, do you wish to go or stay?"

They immediately replied: "We wish to stay."

She then said: "Do you hear that? Now, by what right do you force them away?"

They had Pulaski laden down with our turkeys, and wanted Jack to drive one of the carts. So they were all carried off—carriages, wagons, carts, horses and mules and servants, with food and provisions of every kind—and, so far as they were concerned, leaving us to starvation.

A little while after this party started, Mother walked to the smokehouse and found an officer taking sugar that had been put to drip. He was filling a bag with all that was dry. He seemed a little ashamed of being caught in the act, but did not return the sugar, but carried it off on his horse. He was mounted on Mr. Audley King's pet horse, a splendid animal which he had just stolen, and as he rode off said: "How the man who *owns* this horse will curse the Yankee who took him when he goes home and finds him gone!" He had Mr. King's servant mounted on another of his horses, and no doubt knew Mrs. King was with us and would hear the remark.

Immediately we went to work moving some salt and the little remaining sugar into the house; and while we were doing it a Missourian came up and advised us to get everything into the house as quickly as possible, and he would protect us while doing so. He offered to show Mother how to hide her things. She said: "We need instruction from Yankees, for we have never been accustomed to any such mean business." He said he had enlisted to fight for the *Constitution;* but since then the war had been turned into another thing, and he did not approve this abolitionism, for his wife's people all owned slaves. He told us what afterwards proved false—that ten thousand infantry would soon pass through Riceboro on their way to Thomasville.

Soon after this some twenty rode up and caught me having a barrel rolled toward the house. They were gentlemanly. A few only dismounted; said they were from various of our Confederate States. They said the war would soon be over, for they would have Savannah in a few days.

I replied: "Savannah is not the Confederacy."

They spoke of the number of places they had taken.

I said: "Yes, and do you hold them?"

One of them replied: "Well, I do admire your spunk."

They inquired for all the large plantations.

Squads came all day until near dark. We had no time to eat a mouthful. The remaining ox-wagons were taken to the cornhouse and filled with corn.

Sabbath, December 18th. We passed this day with many fears, but no Yankees came to the lot; though many went to Carlawter and were engaged carrying off corn, the key of the cornhouse having been taken from Cato the day before and the door ordered to be left open. A day comparatively free from interruptions was very grateful to us, though the constant state of apprehension in which we were was distressing.

In the afternoon, while we were engaged in religious services, reading and seeking protection of our Heavenly Father, Captain Winn's Isaiah came bringing a note from Mr. Mallard to me and one from Mr. John Stevens to Mother, sending my watch. This was our first intelligence from Mr. Mallard, and oh, how welcome to us all; though the note brought no hope of his release, as the charge against him was taking up arms against the U.S. Captain Winn had been captured but released. We were all in such distress that Mother wrote begging Mr. Stevens to come to us. We felt so utterly alone that it would be a comfort to have him with us.

Monday, December 19th. Squads of Yankees came all day, so that the servants scarcely had a moment to do anything for us out of the house. The women, finding it entirely unsafe for them to be out of the house at all, would run in and conceal themselves in our dwelling. The few remaining chickens and some sheep were killed. These men were so outrageous at the Negro houses that the Negro men were obliged to stay at their houses for the protection of their wives; and in some instances they rescued them from the hands of these infamous creatures.

Tuesday, December 20th. A squad of Yankees came soon after breakfast. Hearing there was one yoke of oxen left, they rode into the pasture and drove them up, and went into the woods and brought out the horse-wagon, to which they attached the oxen. Needing a chain for the purpose, they went to the well and took it from the well bucket. Mother went out and entreated them not to take it from the well, as it was our means of getting water. They replied: "You have no right to have even wood or water," and immediately took it away.

Wednesday, December 21st. 10 A.M. Six of Kilpatrick's cavalry rode up, one of them mounted on Mr. Mallard's valuable gray named Jim. They looked into the dairy and empty smokehouse, every lock having been broken and doors wide open day and night. They searched the servants' houses;

then they thundered at the door of the dwelling. Mother opened it, when one of them presented a pistol to her breast and demanded why she dared to keep her house closed, and that "he be damned if he would not come into it."

She replied: "I prefer to keep my house closed because we are a helpless and defenseless family of women and little children. And one of your officers informed me that the men were not to enter private dwellings. And it is also contrary to the published orders of your general."

He replied: "I'll be damned if I don't come in and take just what I want. Some of the men got wine here, and we must have some."

She told them her house had been four times searched in every part, and everything taken from it. And recognizing one who had been of the party that had robbed us, she said: "You know my meal and everything has been taken."

He said: "We left you a sack of meal and that rice."

Mother said: "You left us some rice; but out of twelve bushels of meal you poured out a quart or so upon the floor—as you said, to keep us from starving."

She then entreated them, on account of the health of her daughter, not to enter the house. With horrible oaths they rode off, shooting two ducks in the yard.

About half an hour after, three came. One knocked in the piazza and asked if Mother always kept her doors locked. She said she had recently done so by the advice of an officer; and Kate King said: "We have been compelled to do so since the house has been so repeatedly ransacked."

He said: "Well, I never do that and did not come for that." Asked if we knew Mrs. S—— of Dorchester, for he had turned some men out of her house who were ransacking it. He demeaned himself with respect, and did not insist upon coming in.

Upon one occasion one of the men as he sat on the bench in the piazza had his coat buttoned top and bottom, and inside we could plainly see a long row of stolen breast pins and jewelry—gallant trophies, won from defenseless women and children at the South to adorn the persons of their mothers, wives, sisters, and friends in Yankeeland!

One hour after, five came. Mother and Kate trembled from head to feet. It appeared as if this day's trials were more than they could bear. They knelt and asked strength from God; went down and found that three had already entered the pantry with false keys brought for the purpose. They immediately proceeded to cut open the wires of the safe and took all they wanted, amongst other things a tin kettle of eggs we had managed to get.

Mother said to them: "Why, you have entered my house with false keys!"

With demoniacal leer they said: "We want none of your keys," and tried to put in one of those they brought into the pantry door.

She told them: "Your soldiers have already broken the key in that lock, and it cannot be opened; but everything has already been taken." When they insultingly insisted the door should be opened, Mother told them: "Very well, break it open just as soon as you please."

She remonstrated against their coming over the house, and told them of the order of the officers. They replied none of their officers prohibited them from coming in, and they would be damned if they would mind any such orders, would be damned if they did not go where they pleased, and would be damned if they did not take what they pleased. Mother remonstrated, and in her earnest entreaty placed her hand upon the shoulder of one of them, saying: "You must not go over my house." Strange to say, they did not go beyond the pantry, and appeared restrained, as we afterwards believed, by the hand of God. They said they wanted pots and buckets, for they were in camp and had nothing to cook in. One asked for whiskey. To our amusement the man who stole the eggs stumbled and fell as he went down the steps and broke them all—but carried off the bucket. (Psalm 27:2—"When the wicked, even mine enemies and my foes, came upon me to eat up my flesh, they stumbled and fell.")

At dinner time twelve more came—six or seven to the door asking for flour and meal. Mother told them she was a defenseless widow with an only daughter on the eve of again becoming a mother, a young friend, and five little children dependent on her for food and protection. They laughed and said: "Oh, we have heard just such tales before!" They wanted to know why the house was kept locked; said it would only make it worse for us. (This had proven false, for when the doors were open it was impossible to keep them out.) Kate observed a large cravat upon the neck of one made of a black silk dress of hers which had been taken by one of them a few days before. Every species of men's clothing in our trunks and bureaus and portmanteaus was taken, but none of our personal apparel, for we generally stood by when they were searching our wardrobes. They took every piece of jewelry they could find. Twelve sheep were found shot and left in the pasture—an act of wanton wickedness.

Late in the afternoon more came and carried off the few remaining ducks. Going to the Negro houses, they called Cato, the driver, and told him they knew he was feeding "that damned old heifer in the house," and they would "blow out his damned brains" if he gave her another morsel to eat, for they meant to starve her to death. Pointing to the chapel, they asked what house that was. Cato answered: "A church which my master had built for the colored people on the place to hold prayers in the week and preach in on Sunday." They said: "Yes, there he told all his damned lies and called it preaching." And with dreadful oaths they cursed him. To Patience, when they were taking good and valuable books from his library (as they said, to send their old fathers at home), they said, when she spoke with honor of her master and his labors for the good of the colored people: "He was a damned infernal villain, and we only wish he was now alive; we would blow his brains out." To Sue they said, when she spoke of his goodness to the people: "We wish he was now here; we would cut his throat." They stole two blankets from July, and attempted to steal his hat. They took a piggin of boiled potatoes from Sue, and threw the piggin in the marsh when they had eaten them.

After all the day's trials, late at night came Kate's servant Prophet bringing her some clothing and chickens. We were rejoiced to see anyone. He reported South Hampton had been visited by a hundred and fifty men, who had taken all the corn given to the Negroes (three months' allowance), killed forty or fifty hogs and taken seven beef cattle, stolen all the syrup and sugar from the Negroes, and taken their clothing, crawling under their houses and beds searching for buried articles.

MRS. MARY JONES *in her Journal* [t]

Montevideo, *Thursday,* December 22nd, 1864

Several squads of Yankees came today, but none insisted upon coming into the house. Most of the remaining geese were killed by them. One attempted forcibly to drag Sue by the collar of her dress into her room. Another soldier coming up told him to "let that old woman alone"; and while they were speaking together she made her escape to the dwelling, dreadfully frightened and thoroughly enraged. The horrible creature then went to old Mom Rosetta; and she told him he had "no manners," and after awhile got him away. Sue's running into the house sent a thrill of terror into Kate and myself, for we were momentarily expecting them to enter the house. My heart palpitates with such violence against my side that with pain I bear the pressure of my dress.

If it was not for the supporting hand of God we must give up and die. His precious Word and prayer sustains our fainting souls. Besides our morning and evening devotions Kate, Daughter, and I observe a special season every afternoon to implore protection for our beloved ones and ourselves and deliverance for our suffering country. I have often said to the enemy: "I pray not for revenge upon you, but I pray daily for deliverance from you"; and always felt amid my deepest distresses: "Oh, if my country was but free and independent, I could take joyfully the spoiling of my goods!"

MRS. MARY S. MALLARD *in her Journal* [t]

Montevideo, *Thursday,* December 22nd, 1864

About midday the two little boys Mac and Pulaski made their appearance, having escaped from the Yankees at Midway. One of the officers told Pulaski Mr. Mallard was at the Ogeechee bridge, and had been preaching for them and walking at large. They had put no handcuffs on him, and he was walking at large, and they gave him plenty to eat. We are all thankful to hear from him.

Pulaski says he asked for the well chain. They cursed him and said his mistress should do without it.

One squad who came to the house asked Mother when she had seen any rebels, and if there were any around here. She told them her son-in-law had been captured more than a week before, and he was the only gentleman belonging to our household.

Looking fiercely at her, he said: "If you lie to me I will—" The rest of the sentence Mother did not quite understand; it was either "I'll kill you" or "I'll blow your brains out."

She immediately stepped out upon the little porch, near which he was sitting on his horse as he spoke to her, and said to him: "In the beginning of this war one passage of Scripture was impressed upon my mind; and it now abides with me: 'Fear not them which kill the body and after that have no more that they can do. But fear Him who, after He hath killed, hath power to cast into hell.' I have spoken the truth, and do you remember that you will stand with me at the Judgment Bar of God!"

There were quite a number around. One man said: "Madam, if that is your faith, it is a good one."

She replied: "It is my faith, and I feel that it has power to sustain me."

One of these men threatened Cato with a pistol at his breast that if he did feed his mistress they would kill him; called her an old devil, and applied other dreadful epithets such as are used by the lowest and most profane.

Early in the afternoon the same officer called who had previously been in the house. He immediately inquired if the men had done any injury within since he was here last. Whilst he conversed with Kate and Mother his men were firing and killing the geese in the lot and loading their horses with them.

Before leaving he asked for a glass of water. Mother handed him a glass, saying: "I regret that I cannot offer a glass of fresh water, for you have taken even the chain from my well bucket."

He replied very quickly: "I did not do it. Neither did my men do it."

Having heard nothing from Mr. Stevens, Mother sent Charles to Captain Winn's (where he was staying) to ask him to come to us, as we were all in much distress. Charles returned saying Mr. Stevens would come, but was waiting for Uncle William, who had left Springfield the day before and walked to Dorchester; and they expected him the next day at Captain Winn's.

Friday, December 23rd. A day of perfect freedom from the enemy at our dwelling. Five or six rode through the pasture, but none came to the house or Negro houses.

Mrs. Mary Jones *in her Journal* [t]

Montevideo, *Saturday,* December 24th, 1864

As we were finishing our breakfast, which we always had to take in the most hurried manner with every window tightly closed upstairs in my chamber, five Yankees made their appearance from different approaches to the house. Kate and I went down, as usual, with beating hearts and knees that smote together, yet trusting in our God for protection.

One knocked at the door next the river. I requested him to go around to the front door, and—most amazing—he answered "Yes, ma'am" and went around. When the door was unlocked he said: "We have come to search for arms."

I told him the house had again and again under that plea been thoroughly searched; not the minutest drawer or trunk but had been searched.

He replied: "I would not like to do anything unpleasant to you."

A Dutchman said: "I have come to search your house, mistress, and I mean to do it. If you have two or three thousand dollars I would not touch it; but I am coming into your house to search it from top to bottom."

I told him the officers had said the soldiers must not enter private dwellings.

He replied: "There is no officer; we are independent scouts and do as we please." He looked up at the windows, and went around the front of the house, remarking in the most cruel manner: "This house will make a beautiful fire and a great smoke."

I said: "Surely you would not burn a house that was occupied!"

He replied: "Your soldiers would do it. I came here to fight, and I mean to do it." Then he insisted upon coming in.

I told him of my daughter's situation and entreated him not to come in, for she was daily expecting to be confined.

"Tell her to go to her room; we will not disturb her. We have not come to insult ladies."

I said: "If you are determined to search, begin your work at once." For they were pushing into the rooms, and with them an insolent little mulatto boy, who commenced running about the parlor. I called to the Dutchman and said: "Order that boy out of my house!"

He immediately stamped his foot and said: "Get out of this house and stay by the horses!"

They searched from the attic down. One of the party wanted to take a comforter, but the Dutchman said: "Let it alone." Another of them emptied out all my spools for weaving and took the bag.

They insisted two rebels had been here the night before, for a man had told them so. I assured them it was false. They then asked if I knew Mr. King, and insisted that he did come to the house, as his wife stayed here, and she knew where he was.

Kate told them she did not know.

The Dutchman said: "It's no use for a woman to tell me she does not know where her husband is."

Kate told him she was a member of the church and trusted a Christian, and would tell a lie to no man, even if he was an enemy. They then showed a pistol and blankets and wanted Kate to say they were her husband's, and gave her to understand he had been captured or killed.

Again they surveyed the house, asked if I knew North and South Hampton, said they had just burnt both places, that my house would be a beautiful flame, and that night they would return and burn it down. They then rode to the Negro quarters and spoke with Cato; told him to tell his mistress they would return and burn her house that night, and she had better move out.

My mind is made up not to leave my house until the torch is put to it.

About two o'clock Jack and Pulaski made their appearance, having been away just one week. They had been driving cattle for the Yankees. They met the same squad of men as they returned on the Boro bridge, and told the boys to come and tell Mrs. Jones they intended to return that night and burn her house down.

Our agony and distress are so great I sent Cato to Captain Winn and Mr. Stevens this afternoon to tell them our situation. We received a note signed "S," saying they did not think the threat would be executed, and that it was reported by the enemy that Savannah was evacuated two days ago, our forces going into Carolina and the Yankees capturing two hundred cars and thirty thousand bales of cotton and nine hundred prisoners.

We have all spent a miserable day, but have committed ourselves to Him who never slumbers nor sleeps. We are completely cut off from all creature helps, from all human sympathy. Helpless—oh, how utterly helpless! And yet blessed be God! We feel that we are in the hollow of His almighty hand. It is a precious, precious feeling that the omnipotent, omnipresent Jehovah is with us, and that Jesus, our Divine Redeemer and Advocate, will be touched with our sorrows.

The darkness of night is around our dwelling. We are all upstairs in one room with closed windows and a dim light. Our poor little children have eaten their supper. We have dressed them warmly, and they have been put to bed with their clothes on, that they may be ready to move at an instant's warning. My poor delicate, suffering, heart-weary child I have forced to lie down, and persuaded Kate to do so also.

Kept watch alone until two o'clock, and then called Kate, who took my place, and I threw myself on the bed for an hour.

May God keep us safe this night! To Him alone do we look for protection from our cruel enemies.

MRS. MARY S. MALLARD *in her Journal* [t]

Montevideo, *Sunday,* December 25th, 1864

With great gratitude we hailed the light this morning, having passed the night. And no enemy has come nigh our persons or our dwelling; although there are appearances of horse tracks, which we have observed before, and believe they are often around at night to try and detect any gentlemen ("rebel," as they call them) coming here.

We were much alarmed towards morning by Sue's calling to have the house opened; Prophet had come bringing Kate some beef and meal.

At breakfast two Yankees rode around the lot, but seeing nothing to take went away; and we were not further interrupted.

George and June came back, saying the ox-wagon had been cut to pieces and the oxen killed. They were carried to the Ogeechee, where George saw Mr. Mallard and says he preached to the Yankees.

Monday, December 26th. Saw no one all day. Towards evening we ventured out with the poor little children, and as we were returning saw one at a distance.

Tuesday, December 27th. No enemy today. Bless the Lord for this mercy!

Wednesday, December 28th. Another day without the appearance of the Yankees. Could we but know we should be spared one day we would breathe freely, but we are in constant apprehension and terror. Everyone that comes has some plea for insult or robbery. Was there ever any civilized land given up for such a length of time to lawless pillage and brutal inhumanities?

Thursday, December 29th. Free from intrusion until afternoon, when three Yankees and one Negro came up. Lucy ran into the house and locked the door after her, which seemed to provoke them. Three came to the door, and after knocking violently several times one broke open the door. Mother and Kate went down as soon as they could, and when he saw them he cursed awfully. They insisted upon coming in, and asked for that "damned wench" that had locked the door, threatening to "shoot her damned brains out," using the Saviour's name in awful blasphemy.

Nothing seemed to keep them from going over the house but Mother's telling them the officers had advised the locking of the doors, and the men had no right to enter the house, under General Sherman's orders. She told them the situation of her family and her daughter. One went into the parlor and pantry and into one or two other rooms; and one went into the room we are compelled to cook in, and crouched like a beast over the fire. He was black and filthy as a chimney sweep. Indeed, such is the horrible odor they leave in the house we can scarcely endure it.

The cook, seeing the party, locked herself into the cooking room; but they thundered at the door in such a manner I had to call to her to open it, which when she did I could scarce keep from smiling at the metamorphosis. From being a young girl she had assumed the attitude and appearance of a sick old woman, with a blanket thrown over her head and shoulders, and scarcely able to move. Their devices are various and amusing. Gilbert keeps a sling under his coat and slips his arm into it as soon as they appear; Charles walks with a stick and limps dreadfully; Niger a few days since kept them from stealing everything they wanted in his house by covering up in bed and saying he had *"yellow fever"*; Mary Ann kept them from taking the wardrobe of her deceased daughter by calling out: "Them dead people clothes!"

Friday, Saturday, Sabbath, and Monday. No enemy came to the dwelling. They sometimes are at the cornhouse and do not come over. We view them from our upper windows taking the provisions and see them killing the sheep and hogs and cattle. We regard it as a great mercy when we are delivered from their presence within the house.

MRS. MARY JONES *in her Journal* [t]

Montevideo, *Tuesday,* January 3rd, 1865

Soon after breakfast three Yankees rode up and wanted to search for rebels and arms. They dismounted and sat upon the front porch. With much entreaty, and reminding them of the orders of their commander and the feeble condition of my daughter, they refrained from coming in.

One said to Kate and myself: "I guess you are too great rebels to go North, but if you will take good advice you will do so," and offered to get us a pass to Savannah if we would go.

I replied: "We prefer to remain in our own home and country."

Four others rode up and proceeded to search the outhouses. In the loft to the washroom they found some ear corn that we had concealed there to sustain our lives. They immediately commenced knocking off the shingles, and soon broke a large hole in the roof, those within hallooing and screaming and cursing to those without to come and see what they had found.

The one who had been speaking to us assured us they would do us personally no harm. I asked him to prevent their breaking down the house.

He called out: "Stop, boys!"

They replied: "We have found a lot of corn!"

"Well, you must let it alone." (I had told him we put it there to keep ourselves and the servants from starving.)

After this they ceased knocking off the shingles.

Seeing there was some trace of humanity in him, I related Mr. Mallard's capture, and that he was a minister of the gospel.

He asked: "What denomination?"

I replied: "Presbyterian," and asked if they had any professors of religion in their army.

He said: "Yes—many when they left their homes; but I do not know where you will find them now."

He was a Methodist, but had many friends who were Presbyterians; his parents Baptist. I asked him to stay and protect us while this lawless squad remained; but he said they must go, and rode off, while the others proceeded to gather all they wanted from the people's houses, making the Negroes fill the bags and take them out.

Sue in her kindness had hid away a few potatoes for the little children. She entreated for them, but they took every one, and tore a breadth from her new woolen dress which she was making and had sewing in her hands to make strings to tie up their bags of plunder. They have stolen even the drawers and petticoats of the women for that purpose; and sometimes they have taken their nether garments and put them on, leaving in their stead their filthy crawling shirts.

Having one ham, I had given it to Sue to keep for me. They found it; and being an old one they chopped it up and flung it to the dogs, Sue exclaiming: "Massa! You do poor Niggers so?" This was the only morsel of meat we had left.

They stayed a long while and finally rode off.

Wednesday, January 4th. At daylight my daughter informed me she was sick. She has been in daily expectation of her confinement for two weeks. I sent immediately for the servants and ordered my little riding pony, Lady Franklin, which the Yankees had taken and dragged several miles by the neck (because she would not lead) and finally let go, when she returned. And we have tried to keep her out of sight for this very purpose, saddled with my sidesaddle. Prepared a yellow flag for Charles (in case he met the Yankees) and wrote to Dr. Raymond Harris, three miles off and the only physician I know of in the county: "I entreat you to come to the help of my suffering child." Charles started before sunrise, going through the woods.

My heart was filled with intense anxiety and distress, especially as my child had an impression something was wrong with her unborn infant—the consequence of injuries received from a severe fall from a wagon, breaking her collarbone and bruising her severely, as they were making their retreat from Atlanta on the approach of General Sherman.

Dr. Harris, with a kindness and courage never to be forgotten, came without delay and in the face of danger; for the enemy was everywhere over the county. He looked very feeble, having been recently ill with pneumonia. Soon after being in her room he requested a private interview, informing me that my child was in a most critical condition, and I must be prepared for the worst. For if he did not succeed in relieving the difficulty, her infant at least must die.

I replied: "Doctor, the mother first."

"Certainly," was his answer.

He returned to her room and with great difficulty and skill succeeded in effecting what he desired. God, our compassionate Saviour, heard the voice of faith and prayer; and she was saved in childbearing, and at eleven o'clock gave birth to a well-formed infant—a daughter.

During these hours of agony the yard was filled with Yankees. It is supposed one hundred visited the place during the day. They were all around the house; my poor child, calm and collected amid her agony of body, could hear their conversation and wild halloos and cursing beneath her windows. Our dear friend Kate King had to meet them alone. She entreated that they would not come in or make a noise, for there was sickness in the house.

They replied: "We are not as bad as you think us. We will take off our spurs and come in." And one actually pushed by her and came in.

She stepped upon the porch and implored if there was one spark of humanity or honor about them that they would not come in, saying: "You compel me to speak plainly. There is a child being born this very instant in this house, and if there is an officer or a gentleman amongst you I entreat you to protect the house from intrusion."

After a while they left, screaming and yelling in a most fiendish way as they rode from the house.

Dr. Harris returned with Charles as a guide and reached his home safely, having met only one of the enemy.

In the afternoon a very large party rode up; said they wanted to know the meaning of the yellow flag which was placed over the front porch. Had we sick soldiers, or was this a hospital? I told them it indicated sickness in my family: my daughter was ill. One asked for matches; I had none to give. And taking Carpenter Pulaski, they rode to the neighboring plantations. They searched all the Negro houses, within and without and under, taking whatever they wanted. They have taken Gilbert's knife and watch and chain, July's pants and blankets, George and Porter's blankets and clothes, the women's pails, piggins, spoons, buckets, pots, kettles, etc., etc.

Thursday, January 5th. Three Yankees rode up in the forenoon and asked for me. I met them at the front porch. They wished to know if there were sick soldiers in the house.

"No, my daughter is sick."

They propounded the usual questions. I told them of the capture of my daughter's husband, and as they were Kilpatrick's men, asked if they would take a letter to him. They said they would; and I wrote telling him of the birth of the baby; and Daughter sent him her Greek Testament, Kate sent a letter North, and Mrs. King one to Clarence.

This man told me he was from Indiana; was a Virginian by birth. Said there was great dissatisfaction in the army on account of the present object of the war, which now was to free the Negroes.

Looking at me, he said: "Have you sons in the army?"

I replied: "Could you suppose I would have sons who would not defend their country and their mother?"

He said: "If your sons are now in that house I would not take them."

Understanding his trickery, I bowed and said: "I am happy to say you will not have the opportunity. If my sons are alive, they are far away and I hope at the post of duty."

We gave him the letters, which he put in one pocket, and the Greek Testament in the other, and rode off; but lingered a great while on the plantation, making the Negroes shell and grind corn for them, shooting down the sheep in the fields, some of which they skinned and carried away.

This man said his name was James Y. Clark, and was the only one of all we saw whose name we heard. A mere youth with him said he had a brother who had been a prisoner in Georgia, and when sick had been taken into a family and nursed; and whenever he met a Georgian he would treat him as well as his own men. They spoke more kindly than any we have conversed with.

Before going to bed—about twelve o'clock—Driver John came to say a letter sent to my brother in Southwest Georgia and letters sent by Kate to Mrs. King and a letter to my sister Mrs. Cumming had all been found on the person of Lewis, a most faithful man, who had come late the previous night to receive them. Flora had ripped up his sleeve and sewed them in. On account of his fidelity some of his own color informed the Yankees that he carried letters for rebels. They put him in custody, and while in their hands he managed to send the old man John to us to say they had taken our letters, and he wanted us to know it and be prepared for them if they came to trouble us. My letter contained only a truthful account of our present condition. These very men that spoke so fair to us this morning had our letters then in their possession and read them aloud at the Negro houses. Where will all this perfidy, insult, and injury to the helpless, the fatherless, and the widow end?

As night closes in upon us I place my darling little Ruthie in bed. Kate sees her little ones at rest; and Daughter with the baby is sleeping, and so are little Mary and Charlie. I often walk alone up and down the front piazza, to mark the light against the sky of the low lingering flame of the last burnt dwelling or outhouse. I can locate them all around on the neighboring plantations. I look with fear and trembling in the direction of our venerable old church at Midway. We hear the Baptist church in Sunbury has been consumed—burnt as a signal fire to indicate by the troops on this side the safe arrival of this portion of the army to that on the opposite shore in Bryan County.

Bless the Lord for the great mercy of nights free from the presence of the enemy! We would certainly go deranged or die if they were here day and night.

Friday, January 6th. No enemy appeared here today, but we have heard firing around on different places.

The people are all idle on the plantations, most of them seeking their own pleasure. Many servants have proven faithful, others false and rebellious against all authority or restraint. Susan, a Virginia Negro and nurse to my little Mary Ruth, went off with Mac, her husband, to Arcadia the night after the first day the Yankees appeared, with whom she took every opportunity of conversing, informing them that the baby's father was Colonel Jones. She has acted a faithless part as soon as she could. Porter left three weeks since, and has never returned to give any report of Patience or himself or anyone at Arcadia. Little Andrew went to Flemington and returned. I sent him back to wait on our dear sister and family and to be with his own. I hope he will prove faithful. Gilbert, Flora, Lucy, Tenah, Sue, Rosetta, Fanny, Little Gilbert, Charles, Milton and Elsie and Kate have been faithful to us. Milton has been a model of fidelity. He will not even converse with the Yankees, and in their face drives up and milks the cow, without the milk of which little

Julia would fare badly, for she is just weaned. His brother, Little Pulaski, refused even to bring a pail of water, and took himself off a week since.

Saturday, January 7th. Forenoon. No enemy thus far. God be praised for His goodness and mercy! Our nights have been free from intrusion.

A keen northwester is sweeping over the lawn and whistling among the trees, from the branches of which the long gray moss is waving. The pall of death is suddenly thrown over our once cheerful and happy home. Not a living creature stirs in garden or yard, on the plain or in the grove. Nature wears a funereal aspect, and the blast, as it sweeps through the branches, is sighing a requiem to departed days.

As I stand and look at the desolating changes wrought by the hand of an inhuman foe in a few days, I can enter into the feelings of Job when he exclaimed: "Naked came I out of my mother's womb, and naked shall I return thither; the Lord gave, and the Lord hath taken away: blessed be the name of the Lord." All our pleasant things are laid low. Lover and friend is put far from us, and our acquaintance into darkness. We are prisoners in our own home; we dare not open windows or doors. Sometimes our little children are allowed under a strict watch and guard to run a little in the sunshine, but it is always under constant apprehension. The poor little creatures at a moment's warning—just let them hear "Yankee coming!"—rush in and remain almost breathless, huddled together in one of the upper rooms like a bevy of frightened partridges. To obtain a mouthful of food we have been obliged to cook in what was formerly our drawing room; and I have to rise every morning by candlelight, before the dawn of day, that we may have it before the enemy arrives to take it from us. And then sometimes we and the dear little ones have not a chance to eat again before dark. The poor servants are harassed to death, going rapidly for wood or water and hurrying in to lock the doors, fearing insults and abuse at every turn. Do the annals of civilized—and I may add savage—warfare afford any record of brutality equaled in extent and duration to that which we have suffered, and which has been inflicted on us by the Yankees? For one month our homes and all we possess on earth have been given up to lawless pillage. Officers and men have alike engaged in this work of degradation. I scarcely know how we have stood up under it. God alone has enabled us to "speak with the enemy in the gates," and calmly, without a tear, to see my house broken open, entered with false keys, threatened to be burned to ashes, refused food and ordered to be starved to death, told that I had no right even to wood or water, that I should be "humbled in the very dust I walked upon," a pistol and carbine presented to my breast, cursed and reviled as a rebel, a hypocrite, a devil. Every servant, on pain of having their brains blown out, is forbidden to wait upon us or furnish us food. Every trunk, bureau, box, room, closet has been opened or broken open and searched, and whatever was wanted of provisions, clothing, jewelry, knives, forks, spoons, cups, kettles, cooking utensils, towels, bags, etc., etc., from this house taken, and the whole house turned topsy-turvy.

Their conduct at Arcadia and our losses there I will tell at some other time.

Monday, January 9th. Yesterday the 8th was the Holy Sabbath Day. No enemy came nigh our dwelling. As has been my custom, the servants assembled—not in the chapel as formerly, that being rather far from the dwelling, but in the kitchen, which is large and comfortable. Seats were arranged around. My audience was composed mostly of women and children; a few men and boys and some strangers had called in. I read the Scriptures and one of my honored husband's sermons. We engaged in singing and prayer. To me it was a season of solemn worship. Also catechized the children. I have tried during this season of distress to remember God in the family and household.

About noon Dr. Harris sent his driver, Caesar, over with a kind note of inquiry after my daughter, saying they had been again treated most shamefully by the Yankees. They had robbed them of bedclothes, provisions, etc. I asked the doctor's acceptance of an Oxford edition of the New Testament and Psalms which I had preserved, "with grateful recollections of his kindness, courage, and skill in an hour of great peril and deep distress."

We understand that Colonel Hood has come in from beyond the Altamaha under flag of truce, and that a number of ladies and children with a few of their personal servants have left the county and gone south towards Thomasville. Although we see no way of relief to ourselves, we rejoice that others are delivered from this dreadful captivity.

No enemy today.

Tuesday, January 10th. We have been free from the presence of the enemy thus far today, although in great apprehension for several hours, as Sue came in at dinner time and advised us to hasten the meal, as she heard firing in the woods between this and White Oak, which is not much over a mile distant. It was reported they would return today with a large forage train of several hundred wagons going on to the Altamaha.

One thing is evident: they are now enlisting the Negroes here in their service. As one of the officers said to me, "We do not want your women, but we mean to take the able-bodied men to dredge out the river and harbor at Savannah, to hew timber, make roads, build bridges, and throw up batteries." They offer twelve dollars per month. Many are going off with them. Some few sensible ones calculate the value of twelve dollars per month in furnishing food, clothing, fuel, lodging, etc., etc. Up to this time none from this place has joined them. I have told some of those indisposed to help in any way and to wander off at pleasure that as they were perfectly useless here it would be best for me and for the good of their fellow servants if they would leave and go at once with the Yankees. They had seen what their conduct was to the black people—stealing from them, searching their houses, cursing and abusing and insulting their wives and daughters; and if they chose such for their masters to obey and follow, then the sooner they went with them the better; and I had quite a mind to send in a request that they be carried off.

Wednesday, January 11th. Our little babe is one week old today. Bless the Lord for His abounding mercy to mother and child—and to me, their only nurse (excepting the attendance of Lucy, who is very faithful by day and night). The precious little one gives no trouble, and the very care she brings calls my thoughts away from surrounding scenes of distress.

We have had another day of freedom from the enemy.

Our servants keep up communication with their neighbors around; and today it is reported (with what truth we have no means of ascertaining, for we never behold a human being) that the enemy nine thousand strong have gone down the Albany & Gulf Road to Thomasville; from thence will send out a raid on Southwest Georgia. This would prove a most disastrous move to our cause, as that is our great grain-growing and meat-raising region, the Commissary Department of our army in Georgia depending upon that section for supplies.

In our captivity we are in utter ignorance of all without. We know not the state of our cause or the condition of affairs in the Confederacy. Clouds and darkness are round about us; the hand of the Almighty is laid in sore judgment upon us; we are a desolated and smitten people. What the divine decrees concerning us are remain with Infinite Wisdom. We see not; we know not. But we cling to the hope that when our Heavenly Father hath sufficiently chastened and humbled us as individuals and as a nation in wrath, He will remember mercy, and that we shall be purged and purified in this furnace of affliction and brought out a wiser and a better people, to His honor and His glory. At present the foundations of society are broken up; what hereafter is to be our social and civil status we cannot see.

The workings of Providence in reference to the African race are truly wonderful. The scourge falls with peculiar weight upon them: with their emancipation must come their extermination. All history, from their first existence, proves them incapable of self-government; they perish when brought in conflict with the intellectual superiority of the Caucasian race. Northern philanthropy and cant may rave as much as they please; but *facts* prove that in a state of slavery such as exists in the Southern states have the Negro race increased and thriven most. We would point to the history of the British West India Islands, and to New England, with her starved and perished blacks. Not that we have done our duty to them here; far from it. I feel if ever we gain our independence there will be radical reforms in the system of slavery as it now exists. When once delivered from the interference of Northern abolitionism, we shall be free to make and enforce such rules and reformations as are just and right. In all my life I never heard such expressions of hatred and contempt as the Yankees heap upon our poor servants. One of them told me he did not know what God Almighty made Negroes for; all he wished was the power to blow their brains out.

Thursday and Friday, January 12th and 13th. We have had days of quiet, no enemy appearing.

The weather is charming, and has been so for four weeks. The atmosphere is brilliant and bracing: nights cold, mornings frosty, the noonday delightfully warm and balmy. I never saw more resplendent nights; the light of the moon is as the light of the sun.

Our dear little children have ventured out and are luxuriating in the sunshine. Sue, like a presiding genius, has them all around her and variously occupied. Some are making traps to catch the little sparrows, others plaiting rush baskets, arranging mimic gardens and houses. Their sports are all of a rustic order, and their little spirits soon react. I never saw them more cheerful and happy than they now are. But only let the watch cry be heard—"Yankee!"—and how soon they would turn pale and flee into the house for protection!

We see no living sign of animal or poultry saving one poor pigeon that taps at our window for food, one little frightened chicken that dodges at every sound under the shrubs in the flower garden, and one old goose who, faithful to her trust, keeps up her nightly watch and with shrill call rings out the hourly changes.

Mr. D—— called to see us, and confirmed the reported advance upon Thomasville and Baker County.

Kate received a letter, and Daughter one from Robert. He has been paroled for ten days, and is now staying with our kind friends Rev. and Mrs. Axson. Efforts are being made for his release. My poor child has had a sorrowful time, but she has borne her troubles with great fortitude and submission.

Zadok brought me a letter: everything confirms the raid south. The enemy are in full possession of Savannah; Negroes in large numbers are flocking to them. We fear our poor army is in a bad way. General Hood is reported almost annihilated, and supplies for General Lee's army greatly diminished. But our God is in the heavens, and we look unto Him. We wait for Thy salvation, Lord!

I know not where my own beloved sons are. May God protect and bless them!

At sunset I was sitting with the baby in Daughter's room. One of the servants came up and said an officer had called, and he looked like one of our men. Kate and myself went below immediately, and to our inexpressible joy found Colonel Hood. He had come under flag of truce to carry any of the inhabitants beyond the Altamaha, or to take them within the Yankee lines if they so preferred. He kindly expressed much sympathy with our situation, and offered to come and take us out as soon as my daughter could move, or to take Mrs. King into Savannah; also to take charge of letters to or from our friends. It was very touching to see the feeling of our little children to him; they evidently regarded him as a deliverer, and crowded into his lap and around his knees. It so happened we had ventured to make a little raised ginger cake, and had a little piece of corned beef in the house; so we insisted he should share it with us, and we put up the remainder for his journey. He told us the reported advance of the enemy upon Thomasville and Southwest Georgia was false, but gave us a gloomy view of our prospects in other parts of the Confederacy. He offered to forward letters to my son Colonel C. C. J. through General Cobb at Macon.

Sabbath, January 15th. We have had a day of rest. All the women and young people assembled in the kitchen, and we had a pleasant religious service, singing, reading the Scriptures, and prayer and a selected piece on true faith. They were all respectful and attentive. I strive to keep up the worship of God in the family, and believe that true and undefiled religion alone is the great controller and regulator of men's actions. And especially at this time do I see the absolute necessity for all the restraints and influences which can be brought to bear upon the ignorance and perversity of this poor deluded people.

Monday, January 16th. Twenty-two months today since my beloved and honored husband entered into his everlasting rest. I bless my Heavenly Father that he is spared our present distresses. And yet oh, how desolate we are without him! My counselor, my earthly support, my spiritual guide removed when most needed! If this deepest, greatest of all sorrows was necessary to be laid on me, all that I can pray is: "Lord, perfect that which concerneth me, and let not my will but Thine be done."

Before Kate and myself had risen from dinner table Mr. Buttolph came. With joyful hearts we welcomed him, and rejoiced to hear from my dear sister and Laura and the children and friends at Taylor's Creek. He had walked from Flemington, and was greatly fatigued. He gave us many particulars of the infamous conduct of the enemy.

Soon after retiring there was a gentle knock at the front door. Throwing up the sash, we recognized J. A. M. K. He gave us cheering news of our army. General Lee has repulsed General Grant in several of his recent attacks, and General Sherman's advance upon Charleston has been met and driven back. We hear that the inhabitants of Savannah are straitened for food and support, and many of the most respectable ladies are compelled to make cakes and corn bread and sell to the Yankees to enable them to live. He told us negotiations for Robert's release had been successful, and he would soon return home via South Carolina. God grant that it may be so!

Audley remained but a short time and left, as it was unsafe for him to be here, although we believe the enemy have generally left the county.

Tuesday, January 17th. As Mr. Buttolph could escort and protect Kate, she concluded to leave us for Taylor's Creek. The oxcart came over from South Hampton and took her baggage, and she and Mr. Buttolph, with her children and nurse, rode in a little jersey wagon drawn by a mule. We are grieved to part with her; our mutual trials and afflictions, our mingled prayers and tears at a throne of grace, have all drawn us very near to each other.

It has been our custom to have a season of reading the Scriptures and prayer morning, noon, and night. Sometimes, when our hearts have fainted and our strength failed as we were surrounded by our foes, we have knelt and prayed together, and God has given us strength to meet and "speak with the enemy in the gates." I never knew before the power or calming influence of prayer. From the presence of our Heavenly Father we feared not to meet the face of man. We must have died but for prayer. However agitated or distressed when we approached the mercy seat, we always had strength given us for our day.

In all my intercourse with the enemy I have avoided conversation or any aggravating remarks, even when I felt a sword pierced through my soul. For instance, when they reviled the memory of my beloved and honored husband, or taunted me with the want of courage on the part of my countrymen (charges which I knew to be as base and false as the lips that uttered them), they always addressed me as an uncompromising rebel, and I never failed to let them know that before High Heaven I believed our cause was just and right. The isolated and utterly defenseless condition of my poor family compelled me often to use entreaties; but after the day was over I frequently inquired of Kate and Daughter: "Tell me, girls, did I act like a coward?"

Every development of the enemy but confirms my desire for a separate and distinct nationality.

Saturday Night, January 21st. On Thursday Mr. L. J. Mallard visited us. He is now with his family. Gave us various accounts of the enemy. They encamped near his house; at one time on his premises over a thousand. They entered his dwelling day and night. They were forced to obtain a guard from the commander of the post, who was stationed at Midway, to protect his family. The house was repeatedly fired into under pretense of shooting rebels, although they knew that none but defenseless women and children were within. And Mrs. Mallard, who is almost blind, was then in her confinement. They rifled the house of every article of food or clothing which they wished. Mr. Mallard had nothing left but the suit of clothes he wore.

On Friday Mr. Richard Axson sent a short note from Robert. His exchange had not been effected, but he was hopeful of success. Mr. Axson had walked to Savannah and obtained a horse from the Yankees.

Kate, Daughter's servant who has been cooking for us, took herself off today—influenced, as we believe, by her father. Sent for Cook Kate to Arcadia; she refuses to come.

Their condition is one of perfect anarchy and rebellion. They have placed themselves in perfect antagonism to their owners and to all government and control. We dare not predict the end of all this, if the Lord in mercy does not restrain the hearts and wills of this deluded people. They are certainly prepared for any measures. What we are to do becomes daily more and more perplexing. It is evident if my dwelling is left unoccupied, everything within it will be sacrificed. Wherever owners have gone away, the Negroes have taken away all the furniture, bedding, and household articles.

Monday, January 23rd. Sabbath was so inclement, had no services for the people. The house servants were all in attendance at family worship.

Today sent again for Kate, and she has come, apparently with her free consent.

Tuesday, January 24th. At sunset walked to the Negro houses and met our good minister, Rev. D. L. Buttolph. He had walked from Flemington, a distance of fourteen and a half miles. As water to a thirsty soul, so is the presence of a friend to us now in our captivity. The family were well, but he gives a deplorable account of their social condition. Nearly all the house servants have left their homes; and from most of the plantations they have gone in a body, either directly to the enemy or to congregate upon the large plantations in Bryan County, which have been vacated and upon which a plenty of rice remains.

Thursday, January 26th. Porter brought his wife, Patience, and their three boys over. She appears glad to return, although the outer pressure is so great it is difficult for anyone to stand up for duty and their owners.

Friday, January 27th. A clear, cold day. The wind was sweeping around the house and drifting the dried and fallen leaves into heaps. I looked out and saw two bending forms passing around to the front door. They looked like time-worn pilgrims. Who can they be? We discovered our friends in adversity, Captain Winn and Mr. John Stevens. They had walked four miles to spend the day with us.

We asked them up into Daughter's chamber, where we recounted our sufferings and trials. Mr. Stevens said he had read the Scriptures and Jay's *Exercises* daily to the captain, and they had been a great comfort. His mother when dying had given him her gold spectacles and her Testament and Psalms; and now in the night of sorrow they had been the means of light and consolation to them. May God sanctify their losses and distresses and convert them unto Himself!

We had a little coffee for sickness that we had hidden. I had a good cup drawn for them, and they left before sunset.

XXIV

Montevideo, *Friday,* February 10th, 1865

My dear Aunt and Cousin,

Our hearts have been greatly cheered this afternoon by letters from Brother Joe and Eva, the first that we have received. Eva wrote for Brother Charlie, as his arm was very much inflamed with symptoms of erysipelas. He had been sent by General Hardee to reorganize General Wheeler's cavalry, and had been detained by his arm in Augusta. Brother Joe says Sherman's main army is at Springfield in Effingham County and in Robertville in Carolina, thus controlling the railroads to Augusta and Branchville. It is thought he will make a simultaneous attack upon both places. Large bodies of troops are being collected to resist the attack, and they hope Augusta may yet be saved. Eva and her cousin, Miss Bird, left Savannah the Sabbath before the evacuation upon a few hours' notice, taking only their trunks with them and all the servants. Library and everything else were left behind, and Eva has heard that the house is occupied by Yankee officers. Brother Charlie had heard of Mr. Mallard's capture, and General Hardee promised to do all he could to facilitate his exchange. But I despair, for both flags of truce have failed, and the Yankees have specified a particular person—a Mr. Dickson, brother of Major Dickson, U.S.A.

Uncle William came here on Wednesday in a little wagon like that Kate rode to the Creek in. We were truly rejoiced to see him, and are most happy to have him stay with us.

February 11th. I had my note partially written last evening when I was interrupted by the arrival of company: Eva and Bessie Anderson, with Tommy Gignilliat. The girls walked almost all the way from Dorchester, and will spend some days with us.

I am very much obliged to you, my dear aunt, for your kind offer of household goods, and *if* I ever have a home and house to keep, they will be most acceptable. Everything now turns upon the release of my poor captive. I have heard ever since the first of January that he was soon to be released, and you know the effect of hope deferred.

My little baby has been remarkably healthy, and gives as little trouble as could be expected for so young a baby. I have never desired to call her Louisa, but have always wanted her called Susan for you, my dear aunt, unless you preferred naming her Georgia Maxwell. We call her by the latter name, as that seems to be your choice. She is a pretty little thing, and Mother says reminds her of your little Georgia. Her brows are quite dark and rather heavy for an infant. I do not know that Mr. Mallard has heard of her birth, for he has never alluded to her in any of his letters. The opportunities are becoming very rare now, and I dread all communication being cut off. Should you hear of anyone going down to Savannah at any time, please write Mr. Mallard a few lines and send it to Dr. Axson, for he would always know where he could be found. I presume he is again in prison, as his parole was out.

How I wish we could all be together, if only for a little while! There is so much to be talked over. What is our future to be? Brother Joe says they are hoping something from our peace commissioners (Stephens, Hunter, and Campbell) now in Washington.

Several families are starting today for the Altamaha: Mrs. Cyrus Mallard's and Mrs. Delegal's. Mr. Delegal's Negroes, Captain Winn's, and Mr. Cay's are being removed. I hope the enemy will not return upon us, and that Sherman's proclamation will not be carried into effect.

Our children have been remarkably well, and blessed with wonderful appetites. Mother and all the little ones unite with me in warmest love to you both and Cousin Lyman. Kisses for the children. Georgia sends many thanks for the shoes, sacque, and flannel.

Affectionately yours,
Mary S. Mallard.

Mrs. Mary Jones *to* Mrs. Susan M. Cumming[t]

Montevideo, *Saturday,* February 11th, 1865

My dear Sister,

Many thanks for your kind remembrance of us. The pork was delicious. I sliced it daily for Daughter, and the weather was so cool it lasted a great while. The children and myself would eat the sauce as butter for our bread.

Our dear old brother is badly off for pants and vests and shirts; we have tried to supply these articles. He appears to feel the sadness of the times very much, but has the consolations of religion as his support.

Daughter has written you all the news. We have heard nothing until yesterday. I am deeply concerned for Charles. . . . Oh, that he were truly and professedly a child of God! My dear child grows more and more anxious about her husband.

William, your driver, wishes to have your oxcart. Shall I send it there? We have been unable to find our oxen until yesterday. They are perfectly wild. We have now a cart, and are most grateful for your having loaned us yours, although we have been able to use it very little for want of oxen.

Andrew tells me if you were in trouble he would wish to be with you; but as you now have Augustus he wishes to stay below, as he can do more for his family. Please let me know your wishes. If you can do without him, he is very necessary to us if we plant, being the plowman if we get a horse or mule.

With our united and best love,

Ever your affectionate sister,
Mary Jones.

Ask dear Laura to send my *manuscript book* by Andrew.
Brother William is minus tobacco.

MRS. CAROLINE S. JONES *to* MRS. MARY JONES[t]

Augusta, *Tuesday,* February 14th, 1865

My dearest Mother,

We have today received your third letter, and are grateful for the intelligence of your welfare, though deeply distressed at the thought of yours and our dear Mary's sufferings. I can never express to you how we have suffered in the thought of your situation. Joe has been ill with anxiety about you and the impossibility which has up to this existed of reaching and helping you. I trust this will not much longer exist. He and his brother, who is here for a few days, have been consulting and trying to devise plans for visiting you and making the arrangements you desire.

I hope you have before this received letters from both of them. Ever since the receipt of your first they have been writing, hoping that the same kind Providence which guided your letter to us would permit you to receive theirs. Joe doubtless told you of the many and vain efforts he had made to obtain a horse after his poor Lewis died at Indianola upon the occasion of his visit there immediately after Kilpatrick's raid upon Burke. He has tried in every direction, but what with the thefts of the Yankees and the necessities of Wheeler's men, there are no horses to be had. And as each effort has ended in failure, poor Joe has sunk deeper into his distress and depression about you.

My dear, dear mother, how can I tell you of our sympathy with you and our grief for your sufferings? Words and time would fail me to tell you, and it is so aggravated by the thought of how helpless we are to aid you. We have been constantly threatened with the approach of the enemy. Only last night it was rumored that two corps were marching upon the city. This morning it is reported they have struck their tents and are marching in the direction of Columbia, so that we do not know from day to day—hardly from hour to hour—what may be the result. The terrors of your position, though, it seems to me perfectly unequaled: alone in a remote place, surrounded by insurgents. It seems to me too dreadful, and it convinces me more and more of what I have always known: that my dear mother is a wonderful woman to have borne it as she has. And poor Mary—to have been called to suffer what is always such a trial to her under such terrible circumstances! I am rejoiced to hear that she and the baby are doing well.

Lest you should not have received Charlie's letters, I will tell you of Eva and himself. Eva came up from Savannah three days before the evacuation, and has been here ever since. She is tolerably well, though not in strong health. Charlie was on a tour of inspection and reorganizing Wheeler's men, and stopped here on his way, intending to leave the following day. But he has been detained by a troublesome boil on his bridle arm, which prevents his riding. So he has been in town, but occupying his time in writing reports on his previous inspections, principally in the Doctor's office. So I have had the pleasure of seeing him frequently. He has probably conveyed to you some idea of his indignation at the conduct of a former member of his household, and threatens condign punishment when a fitting time arrives, as it surely will, *he* thinks; and so do I.

Sherman's movements in Carolina are veiled in the same mystery as when he passed through Georgia. For many days past Kilpatrick has been threatening this place from the neighborhood of Aiken, and a large force of cavalry has been within sixteen miles of the town. We have not known at any moment whether the next intelligence would not be that the enemy were in sight. I have determined to stay and abide the issue. It seems to be the general impression that a populous town is safer than anywhere else; and then at this inclement season, if I went out, I should not know under what roof I and the children would find a shelter. Today for the first time in weeks there seems to be the impression that for the present at least they will not attack Augusta. But if they get the other places, I suppose they have only to come and take it when they are ready. Oh, for a victory! But that seems to be a forgotten word with us.

Joe is buoying himself up greatly on the thought of getting to you; and as he is a determined man and finds a *way* when he has a will (though he may have great *difficulty* in finding it), I should not be surprised if he rode in some fine morning through the gates of his beloved home and brought rescue to his mother and sister. And then my dear mother and sister must come to us and make their home with us (if the Yankees spare us) until the end of the war, and as much longer as they will.

I am too grieved about Mr. Mallard's capture. Oh, that he were free and with you! From time to time we have heard of him through persons coming from Savannah, and that he is well and bears his great trial with an effort at cheerfulness. A few days ago we heard a rumor that he was released. I hope it may be true—or a *presage* of coming release.

We would give a great deal to hear of Aunt's welfare and Cousin Laura's, and something about Uncle William Maxwell. How has he, at his age and with his infirmities, fared through this terrible time?

We both rejoice greatly in hearing of Gilbert's noble conduct. Joe has always said he knew he would prove faithful, and I used to say last year that I thought there was something really touching in his manner to you ever since the death of his master. He seemed to feel that he was specially responsible for looking after your interests, and there was almost a tenderness in his respect to you. I am sure Joe will never forget his faithfulness.

Little Stanhope listens with eyes full of wonder and dismay at the story of the Yankee outrages at Arcadia (which he remembers with the deepest interest), and how they stole everything from his "dear grandmother and Charlie Mallard." If he had the body, he has the soul to fight them to the death for these atrocities. He is very well, and told me only today I must let him go back to Arcadia and play with Ruthie and Captain. Susie, too, is very well, except that she is suffering from dreadful chilblains contracted on this damp ground. Her feet are very sore; but she is otherwise perfectly well and full of spirits.

Mary's baby ought to turn out a wonderful woman, having had the temerity to come in such adverse times. I want to hear all about it and what its name is. How is little Ruthie? Charlie and Eva are very anxious to hear about her. Little Mary, I can readily believe since all the experiences of the past months, is progressing rapidly in womanliness. Do, dear Mother, give my dearest love to Mary, kiss all the children, and take for yourself all the affection and devotion of

Your attached daughter,
Caroline S. Jones.

Joe sends a great deal of love. He is pretty well, only overworked. He has been working double-tilt for some time past, expecting to be broken up by the Yankees. He hopes he will soon be with you. Good-bye, dearest Mother.

C.

Mrs. Mary S. Mallard *to* Mrs. Mary Jones[t]

Doctortown, *Wednesday,* March 8th, 1865

My dearest Mother,

After leaving you on Thursday morning we rode slowly along until we reached the foot of the Sand Hills. Soon after we got fairly into the sand our horses refused to go; however, with much urging and great difficulty we reached Mr. David Miller's. Mr. and Mrs. Miller were very glad to see us, and entertained us very kindly. They both desired me to beg that Uncle and yourself would stop with them on your way to Baker. In the afternoon we met some young men who had just come across the Altamaha, and they brought a most unfavorable report both of the river and the ford over Jones Creek near Mrs. Johnston's. Mr. Miller told us we could avoid this ford by going near Captain Hughes's and crossing what is called the Parker Ford, so we determined to try that route.

On Friday morning Captain Walthour called at Mr. Miller's and said he understood there was a flat at Captain Hughes's landing, and we could cross there and thus avoid the Doctortown route altogether; that he meant to make further inquiries and go that way, as he had a great deal of furniture to move. As we intended to go near Captain Hughes's in order to cross the ford at Jones Creek, this seemed a most pleasing arrangement.

Soon after starting on Friday morning our horse took stands again just by Mr. Cay's. At this moment Tommy Gignilliat rode up, and Uncle John asked him if he could give us any assistance, as there was no prospect of making our broken-down horse carry us to our journey's end. He very promptly said his brother had a mule at Mrs. Hart's and he would get him for us. In this he failed, but got one of Brother Sam's for us. It so happened our horse soon began to draw very well, but after a while Mr. Dunham's mule began to limp and fail so much we had to use the extra mule in the wagon. Our team was altogether so poor that we did not reach Captain Hughes's until dark— a distance of fifteen miles.

We were most hospitably received and entertained. They inquired most particularly concerning Uncle and yourself, and sent a most cordial invitation to you to stop with them should you take that route. We crossed Jones Creek on a bridge about a mile and a half from Captain Hughes's. Greatly to our disappointment we learned there was no flat at Captain Hughes's and no way of crossing there, so he advised us to go about twenty miles higher up and cross at Tillman's Ferry, where he felt sure there was a good flat and there would be no difficulty.

Accordingly we started on Saturday morning, hoping to reach Mr. Edwards', a good place to pass the night. But owing to our poor teams we did not get farther than Messrs. Hall's, two bachelor brothers about twelve miles off. They entertained us in true bachelor style, welcome to all their house afforded. They had a huge number of Negroes, but everything showed the absence of a lady's hand. Here again we were completely foiled in our plans, as Mr. Hall said he thought it doubtful if we could get a flat at Tillman's, and we might have to wait for it several days, as the ferryman lived across the river. But he said Mr. Edwards knew more about it than he did, so Uncle John wrote a note of inquiry, and he kindly sent it over for us. Mr. Edwards replied we might cross if we could get the wagons into the flat, but he was of the opinion we had better go to Nail's Ferry for safety, thirty-eight miles farther on. Our teams were so poor, and Mr. Hall said there was no prospect of buying forage on either side of the river, so Uncle John concluded to return to Captain Hughes's, as we seemed shut up to the Doctortown route. Mr. Hall fed our mules and oxen abundantly, and would not accept any pay.

We returned to Captain Hughes's on Sabbath evening, feeling it was really an imposition upon their hospitality; but they received us very kindly and seemed as if they could not do enough for us. Captain Hughes gave me a bottle of nice scuppernong wine of his own make, and Mrs. Hughes a bottle of wild honey for our journey. The captain had put up a large quantity of it.

On Monday we commenced our journey again, and were directed by a Mr. Chapman to a ford not far from his house where we could cross Jones

Creek on a batteau, and the water there was not so deep as at either of the other fords. When we reached the ford, Uncle John sent Jack ahead on horseback to ascertain the depth. He found it would come into the front of the buggy, but the bottom was hard and free from holes. Uncle John, Ruthie, the baby, and myself went over in the buggy; Charles, Lucy, with my two children, went ahead on the batteau. We had to unload a part of the ox-wagon and take the things in the boat, which occasioned a delay of several hours. The oxen were so worn that they refused to go after traveling a few miles, so we had the prospect of being delayed within four miles of the river.

When within a half mile of the railroad (the point where we expected to dismiss the wagons and take a boat), we were most suddenly brought to a dead halt. Uncle John found to his utter amazement that a branch which was dry when he came was overflowed. A freshet had come down and the water was rising. This was indeed a new development, and bid fair to end our journey just here. Uncle John sent Jack ahead to ascertain the depth, and found it was so deep as to run over the back seat of the buggy, so that it would be impossible to get over dry. The oxen had given out a mile back, so the mules had to be sent back to assist them. There was no alternative: we could not cross, so we made up our minds to camp out.

My kind uncle went to work and soon had a nice little tent constructed and covered with the wagon sheet. The mattress was spread upon some green pine boughs, and the bundle of comforters and blankets opened. The four children and myself slept under the tent, and Uncle John in the buggy. Saving the rolling of the children upon the ground several times during the night, we passed a tolerably comfortable night in front of a regular campfire. My little baby took no cold. She has stood the journey very well.

On Tuesday morning Uncle John thought the water had risen three feet and was still rising, so he took Gilbert and rode to the railroad, hoping to flank this branch. But to his dismay he found it extended to the railroad; and as there was a trestle ahead, there was no way of reaching our destination from that side; so you may imagine our perplexed, puzzled state. At length Uncle John remembered the batteau at Chapman's Ford five miles back, and sent the mules for that.

In the meantime Brother Sam rode up, and soon after Captain Walthour, and in a little while his wagon loaded with furniture. It was a large wagon, and the captain offered to take the children and myself across; so we mounted upon the furniture and fodder and passed over safely, though most of the things in the body of the wagon got thoroughly wet. Brother Sam then brought us over to this place. We came in a small boat across Back Swamp, then walked from there to this place. The walking is heavy a part of the way, but I was agreeably disappointed in the trestles; they are floored, and the walking very good and not dangerous. The water is rising very rapidly— about eight feet in three days. My dear uncle remained on the other side with the servants and baggage in order to move today. It has been raining so hard this morning I fear he will be able to do but very little. (I suppose we had to walk about two miles. The baggage will not be carried so far, as wagons will meet it at the bridge.)

The children have all behaved very well and given as little trouble as could be expected of children of their ages. Your baby has been very good and happy, and walked the greater part of the distance over the railroad yesterday. Charlie and Mamie walked all of it. Ruthie and Charlie were so tired that they have slept all morning. I have borne the journey very well, though I am pretty tired today. I am thankful we have all kept well.

I will not say anything about our movements until Uncle John comes over. There are no letters here for you, and it is impossible to get a newspaper. Colonel Hood's men have been ordered to the next station, and unless they receive further orders will go on to Florida, as the Yankees twenty-two hundred strong are reported to have been moving upon Tallahassee; and it is also reported that they have been repulsed. If the last is true, Colonel Hood's men will not go off. It is reported that we have gained a victory in North Carolina, killing three thousand Yankees and General Kilpatrick. This needs confirmation, though it is said General Early of Virginia attacked in front and Beauregard in the rear. Colonel Hood told me this morning he did not credit Kilpatrick's death. He said the last paper, dated the 4th, states that Kilpatrick's cavalry had met a much larger force than they had anticipated, and had given Charlotte the go-by and were moving towards Wilmington. (Captain Walthour told me Kilpatrick was just such a man in appearance as Uncle Charles Berrien, and had just such a pompous manner.)

My thoughts are with you all the time, my dear mother. I hope we will soon be united again. Do make haste and come out. I feel more anxious than ever about Uncle William and yourself. . . . Nothing of Uncle John yet. The river is rising; I fear he will find it almost impossible to get over. If I hear nothing from him this evening, I will give this to Captain Screven, who is going to Liberty tomorrow; and if your buggy has not already returned, he will go in that. . . . If possible I will get Captain Screven to call and tell you what he knows of the route. The freshet here is a tremendous one, and there is no knowing when the river will be down. It is steadily rising, and I fear Uncle John will be waterbound on the other side of the river. Everything will probably get wet from the heavy rain.

Thursday. Last night was most inclement: tremendous rain accompanied with thunder and lightning. I fear my dear uncle must have suffered very much, for I know it must have been impossible for him to keep dry.

Should you come this way it will be necessary for you to bring some bedding, as nothing but an empty room can be had here. I applied yesterday for rations and am faring pretty well.

Captain Screven thinks of leaving this morning, and I will send this by him, and request Uncle John to add a line indicating the road he thinks best for you to take.

Clarence and Bayard King arrived last night. They were taken to Point Lookout in Maryland, and have been paroled. I saw Clarence.

I hope, my dear mother, you will be supported in your loneliness and that you will soon come out to us. I know how desolate you must feel, but I know the same kind Heavenly Father who has led us all along this dark path will abide with you and with my dear uncle. Ruthie says: "Tell Mama I send a love to her."

I fear you will hear nothing from Mr. Mallard through Zadok, for I hear the black pickets will not allow any Negroes to return. . . . None of the Negroes sent down recently have returned. They are becoming very strict in Savannah.

Mamie and Charlie and Ruthie unite with me in warmest love to Uncle and yourself. Baby Georgia sends sweet kisses to her dear grandmama. One of the soldiers sent her a little milk this morning. Love to all in Flemington and at the Creek. Captain Screven thinks he will not be able to call and see you, as he is now on his way to join his command. Howdy for all the servants. I have Lucy and Elsie with me; the rest are over the river.

Your affectionate daughter,
Mary S. Mallard.

Saturday Morning. The contents of my large yellow trunk are now being brought up thoroughly wet, and I fear many things entirely ruined—a beggarly account of my bonnet, and the children's hats all went under the water. I do not know the condition of the other trunks, as they have not been brought up yet. They did not fall in the water, so I hope things are not all ruined. Am I not unfortunate!

Uncle John tells me he has written you of all that happened at the river. He thinks this route altogether impracticable for you, and thinks it will be best for you either to come by Nail's Ferry or by Barrington. If you come through the country, then go by Taylor's Creek and from there to Mr. Henry Edwards' and from there to Nail's Ferry. Mr. Fennell has a map of Georgia, and you can trace the route upon that. If you wish to strike this railroad, then send Gilbert to Barrington and ascertain whether the waters are low. There is a good flat there and ferryman, and it is not very far to No. 7; and we understand the cars will be running to that station for some time to come. It is a great undertaking by whatever route you may choose. The embankment here is washing away so rapidly that it is almost impossible to come this way.

I have lost my box of candles, the children's tin tub, and some smaller articles.

Gilbert has come for the letter, so I must close. The children all speak of you daily, and send their best love and kisses. The servants are all well. Good-bye, dear Mother.

Your loving daughter,
Mary S. Mallard.

Mrs. Mary S. Mallard *to* Mrs. Mary Jones[t]

No. 7, Albany & Gulf Railroad, *Wednesday,* March 15th, 1865

My dearest Mother,

We left Doctortown yesterday morning in the government wagons (two for the baggage and one for the family), and reached this station in the evening, having traveled about eighteen or twenty miles. We were very fortunate in getting these wagons, for if we had hired them, they would have cost us about two hundred dollars. Colonel Hood was not at Doctortown when we came away, but he had left directions that Uncle John should be furnished with transportation whenever he needed it, so we are indebted to him for it. To our great joy we saw the cars coming down this afternoon, and they are here tonight and expect to return in the morning; so we hope to be off by seven o'clock, and trust we will meet with no further detention.

We have been delayed a long time in our journey, but the causes have all been providential, and I trust we have not been impatient. We have all been blessed with health. The servants have stood the journey remarkably well. Mom Patience has walked all the way, and I have been surprised to see her bear the fatigue so well.

We are staying with a Mrs. Pettigrew, who has furnished us house room, and we do our own cooking. We managed in the same way at Doctortown. Should you come here, you might make the same arrangement, as it is a great saving of expense. This house is very open: large cracks in the floor and no sashes to the windows; but the fireplace is most ample, and lightwood abounds. It is so mild I do not think the children will suffer at all. My little baby continues bright and well, developing every day.

I heard through Tommy Gignilliat that Zadok had returned. Please let me know if possible whether he took my letter to Mr. Mallard; and send a copy of any letter he may have written. A servant of Uncle Banky's will take this to you; and if he returns before you come out, he might bring letters and mail them in Thomasville.

I wrote you from Doctortown telling you of my dreadful loss of silver. Perhaps you may not receive that letter, so I will repeat that portion of it. The silver trunk was one that went under the water, and when I opened it to have it dried, I missed all of my teaspoons (twenty-two in number), my gilt-lined gravy ladle, pickle knife and spoon, mustard spoon, and napkin ring. Did you have any teaspoons in your box? If so, they are all gone; not a teaspoon in the trunk. All of your dessert spoons are safe. The tacks in the hasp of the trunk looked as if they had been drawn, as they were so loose that Uncle John took some of them out with his fingers. He thinks the things were taken by one of the ferrymen (a soldier); for the trunk was alone with them an hour or two, and one of the men deserted the night after. Five deserted, and it is thought some of them made their way to the Yankees. It is bad enough to lose the silver, but worse to think of its being carried into Yankeeland! My bonnets went under and are pretty much ruined, and I have lost the box of candles in the same way. So you see, my losses have been very heavy. I cannot think that any of these articles were left out in packing the silver, though I would be glad if you would look into the teapot I left. And possibly these things may have been abstracted before we left, though I do not think this at all probable. Uncle John submitted the whole affair to Major Camp, and he promised to use every effort for their recovery.

I forgot to bring my woolen yarn. If you can find a place for it, please bring it.

Notwithstanding our many detentions, we have met with a great deal of kindness during our journey, and have been much blessed. If all are able to go through to Thomasville tomorrow, we will leave next morning. Uncle John will be just in time to fill his appointment in Mitchell County. I shall probably be obliged to go directly on, owing to the difficulty of procuring forage, and will reach Baker on Sabbath evening.

Tomorrow will dawn upon us filled with sad memories. How I wish, dear Mother, we could go together and spend the day by that sacred spot where sleeps our precious dead! Perhaps you may have this privilege, but I can be with you only in spirit. Two years have passed away, and oh, how long they have been! . . . Ruthie is quite well, and begged me to write you a letter this morning and say she wanted to kiss you. The children all unite with me in warmest love to Uncle and yourself. Howdy for all the servants.

Your affectionate daughter,
Mary S. Mallard.

I will write you by every opportunity, and will write my brothers as soon as I reach Baker. Good night. Do come soon. We are so anxious about you. You will need some cooking utensils by the way.

Mrs. Mary Jones *to* Mrs. Mary S. Mallard[t]

Montevideo, *Wednesday,* March 22nd, 1865*

My beloved Daughter,

God be praised that my dear brother and yourself and the little ones and servants were preserved amid your many perils and exposures! I hope my brother will not suffer from the wettings and sleeping in the night air. I have suffered intense anxiety for you all, and could not hear one reliable word until Bayard came to see me.

To my inexpressible joy your dear brother arrived late Saturday night in his buggy, and Harry on horseback. He would have gone immediately on the next day to your succor, but was so tired from his own exposures he waited until Monday morning. And I had made every preparation for your relief in food, etc., and he left after breakfast, but to his great relief met Charles and Gilbert and George returning with the horse and mules. One ox died, and they were starving, and had to leave the buggy and wagons in the swamp. They were in great peril. Your brother is just starting this morning back with them, hoping to construct a raft and bring them over; for we must leave this country as soon as possible. Every day perils life and animals. God alone knows the end of all this trouble; every day it becomes worse with us. We have abandoned all hope of going as you did, and will try and make our way through the country. If we are foiled, will write whenever we can.

I gave you every piece of silver I have in the world to pack in the trunk, so if my spoons are missing also, they have been stolen. God's sovereignty appears in the minutest events of life. Truly, my child, you have had sorrow upon sorrow.

Zadok came the week after you left and said he had delivered your letter; that dear Robert was well and would be out the following week. Said also he saw *Clarence and Bayard* in Savannah. I was rejoiced to see him, and believed him and gave him a reward for his fidelity. It all turns out a falsehood, and I do not believe he ever went to Savannah. He has since left the place—it is supposed by water—taking two young women with him and a young man, two plows, and a grindstone. I presume he will settle in Bryan.

Your aunt and cousin will start as soon as they can get transportation. Hope we may all go together the last of this week or first of next. I want Joe out of this country. The Lord bless and reward my dear brother for all his kindness to me and mine! Best love to them all, and kisses for my precious little ones. Tell Ruthie "Danna" hopes to see all soon, and she must not forget to pray for her as she promised.

Ever your own mother,
Mary Jones.

In haste. God willing, I will bring an excellent horse and the old mule and my buggy.

Mrs. Mary Jones *to* Mrs. Susan M. Cumming[t]

Montevideo, Saturday, March 25th, 1865

My dear Sister,

Joseph went on Wednesday to the Altamaha with Charles, Gilbert, and Andrew. He constructed a raft on Thursday; brought over the buggy and wagons on Friday. Was unable to bring over the oxen on the raft; one had died. Consequently the wagons were left, and he returned with the buggy this afternoon.

His life and time are so precious, and horses so valuable, we have concluded to leave this place on Wednesday of the coming week, stay Wednesday night with Julia on Taylor's Creek, *D.V.* We hope most fervently you will all be able to move at the same time, and that we may be permitted to go together. We will have only our buggies, *and a one-horse cart* to help us with our baggage, provisions, etc., and *six* servants, one of them an infant.

This is a very short notice and very limited conveyance, but we can do no better. I cannot even take Mr. Jones's papers that I value above all things. My heart is very sad. But God reigns!

Do let me know your plans. I would rejoice if you could go along now, and we would do all in our power to assist you on the journey. Have heard incidentally that my dear child and brother and the little ones have all arrived safely. With our united and very best love to yourself, Laura, and Mr. Buttolph and the children, believe me

Ever your affectionate sister,
Mary Jones.

MRS. SUSAN M. CUMMING *to* MRS. MARY JONES[t]

Flemington, *Saturday,* April 15th, 1865

My dear Sister,

You can scarce imagine the pleasure your letter gave us. John King met Charles on his return from South Hampton and brought it to us—that is, Mr. Buttolph and myself; for Laura and Susan Mary have been at Julia's since Monday. I feel most thankful that amid the perils and dangers of the way you had progressed so far, and trust you are safely lodged in Cousin John's hospitable mansion ere this, and recovered from the fatigues of the journey, and enjoying the society of the loved ones there.

You will be surprised to hear that our contemplated trip has been postponed, D.V., for six months. Mr. Buttolph's congregation have had a meeting and have proposed to furnish him subsistence, and are so earnest and urgent about it that it seemed to be a plain duty to remain—at least for that length of time—and then see what Providence may determine. In the event of Mr. Buttolph's being compelled to remove, transportation is to be furnished him. We had engaged transportation, and packing commenced, with the intention of leaving on Monday the 17th, and with the understanding that provisions must be carried for sixteen persons and eight horses, leaving very little space for anything else. We expected to go to housekeeping soon after our arrival; consequently were not a little perplexed what we should carry. But I feel that Providence has decided for us, and trust that we may abide safe under the shadow of His wing. And oh, that peace and His blessing may be vouchsafed us ere the time expires!

Mr. Buttolph, the boys, and self dined on Wednesday (Audley's birthday) at Julia's. All well with the exception of Mary: the usual headache. Brother seemed very feeble, and very glad that he did not go with you; said it would have been impossible for him to have gone on with you. He was suffering from the ride on Sunday to church in the wagon. The Lord's Supper was celebrated here for the first time, and your heart will thrill with joy when you hear that Isabel King united with the church. . . . It was a most interesting occasion. . . . Gilbert was up; reported all well.

Andrew came on Wednesday preparatory to our removal. All well, and at work as usual. I hope it will meet with your approval for us to keep Andrew up here; he can go down whenever needed. Augustus is to go on Monday with Mr. Fraser to No. 7 on his way to Southwest Georgia. I overheard him say he was going if it cost him five thousand dollars. Judge Fleming owns his wife, and he has behaved so well that we are under promise that he shall go. Sarey thinks if we stay she will drop a few seeds, and she and Andrew have been busy today planting a little of everything. They are willing to go or willing to stay; their minds are made up at present to stay with us. They have been such comforts and helps to us I hope no temptation will lead them astray.

Now that we are here, remember there is *room* in our *house* and room in our *hearts* for *you* and *yours*. Julia will take every care of the trunks. I saw them in her bedchamber. I have Mary's teapot and sugar bowl. Your bedstead at Arcadia I shall have brought here, and Mr. John Norman has moved up your piano. Mr. Fennell is to look after our affairs; and if I hear or know of anything that I think will make it necessary, and send Mr. Fennell word to that effect, he is to move valuable things here or elsewhere as circumstances may show.

A Mr. Smith has just come here from Savannah, and says Richmond has fallen on the 5th after heavy loss on both sides. Mr. Rahn's son William was killed in North Carolina on the 8th of March. Mr. Grest's Swiss nephew and Mrs. Spencer's son Captain Spencer are dead. Oh, that these days of suffering affliction may be shortened for the elect's sake! . . .

There must have been a most joyful reunion between Mr. Mallard and his dear family. . . . Tell Mary I hoped to be able to bring the little dress for my name-child, but will try and get it to her by a safe hand—perhaps by her father. I feel so sad to think you are all so far from us; but I always felt that I could not go and leave you here, and am glad that Dr. Joseph came and arranged for you. . . . Our children talk very often of their cousins and meeting them in Baker. . . . Brother William seems quite satisfied at Julia's; says he suspects he has come to die with her. . . . Give my warmest love to dear Mary, Mr. Mallard, Cousins Jane and John, Mrs. Dunwody and Mary. Kiss all the little ones for Aunt Susan. Accept of a large share for yourself. And believe me, dear Sister,

Your affectionate sister,
S. M. Cumming.

Mrs. Laura E. Buttolph *to* Mrs. Mary Jones[t]
Taylor's Creek, *Sunday,* April 16th, 1865

My dearest Aunt,

We were so glad to hear from your dear self and Cousin Robert and Cousin Joe yesterday. Truly your journey was eventful and perilous! We had heard of the fight of which you spoke, but wanted faith to believe it until your letter came. We can only be safe in God's keeping. May *He* choose all of *our changes!*

We came here—I with Daughter and Willie—on my way to join you in Southwest Georgia; but Mr. Buttolph's people came forward and promised to feed his family for six months, and then if he desired it to give him transportation without cost over the river to the railroad. They seemed so grieved at the idea of his leaving, and so anxious to keep him, that he has determined to remain with them six months longer. He has suffered with them, and is willing to toil in his Master's vineyard and submit to His will. . . . Last Sabbath Mr. Buttolph administered the Communion in the Flemington church. . . . It was a most solemn occasion. Uncle William was there in Aunt's wagon, which was filled with rocking chairs. We all walked from our house. Mr. Buttolph preached but one sermon, as persons do not like to be absent long from home, all of their servants gone.

We heard threats of a raid last week from Savannah, and then heard that the expedition was ordered back. They would not have gained much in this eaten-out county. May our kind Heavenly Father watch over us and keep us all!

Uncle William says I must tell you he thought of you a great deal, and was afraid you would meet with a great deal of trouble and fatigue in accomplishing the journey. He sends you all a great deal of love. He seems very happy and contented here.

Do write us whenever you can. We are cut off from all that is going on in the world. Aunt Julia says do write and tell her if you hear anything of the 5th Georgia Regiment and the 18th Georgia Battalion. She has heard from Willie; but now that we hear that Richmond has been evacuated, she does not know where they are or at what point a letter can reach them. May this cruel war soon end! Willie seemed to think that it would end by spring. Soldiers are so hopeful, and they know so little of what is going on. Do not take it for granted that we know anything, as we neither get letters nor papers, and a stray letter surprises us.

Do give much love to dear Mary and her little ones, and kiss little Georgia and Little Sister, Mary, and Charlie. Love to Cousin Jane and Mrs. Dunwody and Miss Mary Dunwody and the little boys. How we long to see them all!

Mrs. John Norman is taking care of my piano and also taking care of your piano; and Mr. Trask has some of my best furniture, and may take care of your bedstead left at Arcadia.

Jane returned to Arcadia, but as she has been to Savannah and returned before, I fear she may have come to steal. The Negroes are still flocking to Savannah. May some of the most faithful remain until the end to comfort and warn!

The recent news makes me fear going to Southwest Georgia just now; and your advice seems to come in time. No place seems safe. *I* feel houseless and homeless. Our beautiful Island home I never expect to see again, and when we go hence, feel it will be a final move. . . . All unite in love to you—each and all—from this household. How we miss and long to see you, my precious, precious aunt! May the Lord keep you and your loved ones and bring us all together in peace!

Your ever attached niece,
Laura E. Buttolph.

Miss Mary E. Robarts *to* Mrs. Mary Jones[t]

Cuthbert, *Thursday,* April 20th, 1865

My dearest Cousin,

We were so glad to hear of your safe arrival in Baker. Cousin John's place must have been named Refuge prospectively, for surely it is such now to many beloved relatives.

Give our affectionate love to Mr. Mallard, and tell him we return thanks for his release, and congratulate him and Mary on their reunion. What a happiness to see once more his loved ones! Ask him if he felt as that Methodist minister who walked up with me to his house in Atlanta and told us about his being taken prisoner. He was not too scared to think in poetry: "My person you may take, but my integrity you can't shake."

Ah, me! How much I have passed through since I laughed at that good brother! I have almost forgotten how to laugh now. If we had known the danger we should have been in here at this time, I think we should have made strenuous efforts to have returned to our desolate home this spring. But we have been deterred by the great expense of transportation and the scarcity of food up there. General Hansell wrote me last week I had no idea how hard they had to labor for a meager support, and that a courier had reported the day before that the Yankees several thousand strong were within twelve miles of Rome; had made a raid into Cass County the week before. So it is not considered exactly safe to return there just yet.

I hope Mr. Mallard may be able to go back to Atlanta to gather up his scattered flock. How glad they will be to see him! Hope he may finish the good work he began there. The people of Cuthbert esteem him very highly.

I hope you may not be disappointed in going to Augusta. Report here is that a force is marching on Augusta from Charleston, and expects to take that city and Macon simultaneously. Our present is dark, for the enemy seems to accomplish all he wishes to. If God would make bare His omnipotent arm for our deliverance, how grateful we should be! I trust a raid may not overtake you in Baker, or us here; for as Mary knows, it is sad to fly from the Yankees in one place to be overtaken in another.

You did not tell me what you did with your furniture and things in Liberty. Who did you leave to take care of Montevideo? Sam is very anxious to know where Rosetta and his children are. Do write me all about yourself.

And do, if you can find a quadruped of any description in Baker, do come and see us. And tell Mary we are perfectly in earnest about wishing her to come and stay some time with us. Baker County is a long and wearisome journey; I never expect to get there. Louisa asked Henry to take her when he went to Baker the last time, hoping to see Mary there; but he said the roads were so bad his horse could not possibly pull two people.

My dear mother is much better this week than she was last; then her cough was very severe, and she was most of the time on the bed. This week she has walked over to Henry's twice to see the Savannah exiles. She desires much love to you, and says if you leave this part of the country without seeing her, she is afraid she will never see you again. So do take Cuthbert in your way—you and Mr. Mallard too.

Give our love to all around you. Hope Cousin Susan's family may get out safely if they come. What place is safe now? Kiss dear little Mary Ruth for me; I have not heard from Charlie since November. Our dear girls are not at home now. A terrible time for families to be separated! . . . Farewell, my dear cousin. Do write me very soon, and I will by every opportunity if the mail is stopped.

Your affectionate cousin,
Mary E. Robarts.

Please tell Patience, Lucy, and Tenah howdy for us and for Sam.

Mrs. Mary Jones *to* Col. William Maxwell[t]

Refuge, Saturday, April 22nd, 1865

My dear Brother,

We left Liberty on the 31st of March and reached the home of my dear brother on the 13th of April, where we received the warmest welcome. But as Robert and myself got out of the buggy everyone exclaimed in disappointment: "Where is Uncle? Where is Cousin William?" When I told them you had changed your mind at the last moment, they were all grieved to hear it. Brother John and Sister Jane had already placed a couch for you in a cool place in the entry. Even the little children felt it. Johnnie and Josie asked why Uncle Maxwell had not come; and the next morning the first question Ruthie asked on waking was: "Is Uncle drowned?" (I suppose she remembered the flood of waters through which they came.)

Much as I regretted your not coming with us at this time, I often rejoiced that you were spared the fatigue and exposure of the journey. We had to camp out several nights, and traveled often from daylight to dark, not making over sixteen or twenty miles. . . . After crossing the river at Nail's Ferry, we struck the railroad at Blackshear. Here my dear son Joseph, with Charles and the wagon, retraced their journey together as far as the Altamaha, when Joe took the road via Mount Vernon to Augusta, and Charles the river road to Liberty. You may be assured Daughter and the children were *rejoiced* to see Robert. She had been informed of his release through a letter from Charles.

At Thomasville I saw Mrs. Winn and family. They all inquired particularly after you, and are hoping to return to Liberty in the fall.

On Wednesday of this week we were all thrown into great distress. The Yankees were reported within ten miles of us and advancing with cannon. I thought of your remark: "Mary, I fear you are going into trouble." We have every reason to apprehend their raid through this country now that Columbus is in their hands. And God alone knows what will become of this land if they should desolate it as they did ours. Want and misery of every form must prevail. Corn is now selling here at fifteen and twenty dollars per bushel. The lateness of the season will prevent the hiring of any people, so that I am compelled to keep them here; and while my kind brother will do all in his power for us, his own provision crop last year was very short.

My dear brother, I am deeply concerned for my poor servants, and for the fate of my home, containing everything of value that I have in the world. Do if possible send an occasional message to my people. And say to Mr. Fennell if *there is the least necessity* I wish him to move *my carpets and trunks,* and the *large box* in the closet upstairs, and the box of pictures, and the books, and my bedding, to any point Audley and yourself might think safe. . . . If God spares my life and it is possible, I hope to return early in the fall to Liberty. Do ask Audley to do me the favor of writing me the condition of things at home and on the coast. Have you any soldiers scouting Bryan and Liberty? If you do not find it too great a tax, please send me a line to say how you are. We are expecting daily to hear of Mr. Buttolph's arrival and our dear sister and Laura and the children. *This is a far-off land;* I think a whole continent lies between Liberty and Baker.

Daughter and all the family here unite in warmest love to you and to Julia and every member of her family. Believe me

Ever your affectionate sister,
Mary Jones.

MRS. MARY JONES *to* COL. CHARLES C. JONES, JR.[g]

Refuge, *Tuesday,* April 25th, 1865

My dear Son,

Mrs. Randolph Whitehead called to see us this morning and mentioned that her husband would make an effort to reach Augusta. Through him I trust you will receive this communication. I hope, through the good providence of God, your brother has arrived safely.

We reached my brother's home on Thursday the 13th, where we received the warmest welcome. It was my intention so soon as I was rested from the fatigues of the journey to take your dear child with Susan your servant and proceed immediately on to Augusta, hoping that I would find uninterrupted communication by railroad from Albany to Augusta. The recent developments of the enemy have disappointed these plans, and I will have now patiently to await the turn of coming events. I would be very glad to know your will and wishes about our dear child. I have made every effort for her comfort and safety. *The report* of an armistice for ninety days has reached us; but in this *far-off land* it seems very difficult to obtain any reliable information of the state of the country. We have been in great fear of an inroad upon this section. God in mercy grant us protection and deliverance from such suffering!

I have brought with me twelve servants and Susan. The lateness of the season makes it very difficult if not *impossible* to hire them. *Jack* is the only one I have been able to hire as yet—for twenty-five dollars per month. Corn is now selling for twelve and twenty dollars per bushel, and I will have to purchase provisions for them at that price. Your uncle's provision crop last year was so short that he will not be able to furnish what I will need. In addition will be your sister's servants. But we will try and make some suitable arrangement for them all. We have failed to hire Susan as a weaver. Your uncle has kindly offered the use of a place distant about five miles (if the war continues) that our people might plant; but as we are without mules, plows, or hoes, that would not be practicable. I must depend on hiring.

Your aunt and Mr. Buttolph are expected this week with Laura and the children to make their home in Baker, probably for the war. I am thankful they have a home of their own to come to.

Your dear child said two mornings since: "I dreamed my dear papa had come for me." She speaks constantly of you and of her mama, and sends her sweetest kisses to you both. She is well and happy, and makes the eighth child in this family. They have a merry time. Daughter unites with me in best love to Eva and yourself and to Mrs. Eve. Your Aunt Jane is in *extremely feeble health.* Your uncle desires much love to you both.

Your affectionate mother,
Mary Jones.

Mrs. Caroline S. Jones *to* Mrs. Mary Jones[t]

Augusta, *Sunday,* April 30th, 1865

My dearest Mother,

Finding that Tom Clay is going down to Albany, I think it the most feasible plan for getting a letter to you that has yet offered itself to me, so I hasten to avail myself of it; for I fear the Yankees came between us just in time to intercept our last letter, and you may still be in ignorance of Joe's safe return home. He arrived here just a fortnight ago today, showing great benefit from his visit to you and his various journeyings, forming so desirable a relief from his usual labors and sedentary life. His spirits were lighter, I know, from the moment of being able to make arrangements for reaching you and doing all in his power to aid you in leaving the county. He wrote you the day of his return, and I wrote you twice, I think.

How my heart sank within me when I heard of the successive capture of Selma, Montgomery, and Columbus, fearing it was but a prelude to the devastation of the rich and coveted acres of Southwest Georgia, and that my dear mother and sister might again be called to pass through the trying scenes they have just passed! It was one great consolation among so many painful aspects of the subject that at least fighting and conquest were over for a time.

We are almost paralyzed here by the rapid succession of strange and melancholy incidents that have marked the last few weeks—the sudden collapse of our tried and trusted General Lee and his army, about which, sad as it is, I can feel no mortification, for I know he did all that mortal man could do; then the rumors of peace, so different from the rapturous delight of a *conquered peace* we all looked forward to; then the righteous retribution upon Lincoln. One sweet drop among so much that is painful is that he at least cannot raise his howl of diabolical triumph over us. The rumors of peace-terms negotiations are constantly being repeated, with now and then rumors of armed intervention from abroad, which somebody says is like medical attendance to a man whose throat is cut. It seems to be a very general impression that there is a strong outside pressure and threatened foreign complications which may account first for the armistice and then for these terms of peace of which we hear so often without knowing anything definite. Have we not fallen upon sad, sad times? At least, though, I will take comfort in the thought that you are safe from invasion where you are.

I trust you were well during your long and tedious journey, and that you had a happy reunion with Mary and the children. Tom Clay tells me he met you at some point on the road after the Doctor parted from you. We were rejoiced to receive intelligence of you of that date. How did Uncle William bear the journey? Do give much love to him from both of us.

Dr. Quarterman (Helen Jones's husband) has been spending several days with us on his way to Cuthbert. The cutting off of Macon has embarrassed the movements of all travelers in that direction very much. I should have sent letters to you by Dr. Quarterman, but he started unexpectedly, hearing suddenly of a party going in the same direction. We found him a very pleasant gentleman indeed.

We are suffering here extreme embarrassment from the derangement of the currency consequent upon the war—or rather peace—news. Days ago Confederate money, according to the *government* gold standard, was 100 to 1. Today gold is 300. We got rid of all of ours speedily, the Doctor investing six months' pay in bacon and flour. You will be grieved to hear that our storeroom was broken into and one-third of our flour and every vestige of bacon we owned in the world stolen from us a few nights ago. It is our first misfortune of the kind, and but that now it is irreparable we should not feel it so much, so many others having suffered much more severely. I have taken the hint and moved what little I had left upstairs into the garret.

If you received my letter written just after Joe's return, you received my thanks for your many kind remembrances by him. For the sugar I was very grateful, having given that up some time since. The children were delighted with the groundnut cake, and Stanhope values his tin plate as if it were silver, and eats from it at every meal. . . . Dear Mother, you are in our thoughts and speech every day and many times a day. I hope the time is not distant when you will come to *this* home of yours. We shall be so glad to see you. I am writing late at night, having just heard of Tom's design of leaving in the morning; so being very limited in time, I am obliged to be very hurried. Give a great deal of love to Mary, Mr. Mallard, and the children. What a shock of pleasure Mr. Mallard's return must have been to Mary! Give much love to Uncle John, Aunt Jane, and Uncle William. With a great deal of love from both of us,

Most affectionately your daughter,
Caroline Jones.

Book Three
The Night Season
(1865–1868)

I

Mrs. Eva B. Jones *to* Mrs. Mary Jones[t]
Augusta, *Tuesday,* June 13th, 1865

Dear Mother,

It is with sad and heavy hearts we mark the dark, crowding events of this most disastrous year. We have seen hope after hope fall blighted and withering about us, until our country is no more—merely a heap of ruins and ashes. A joyless future of probable ignominy, poverty, and want is all that spreads before us, and God alone knowing where any of us will end a life robbed of every blessing and already becoming intolerable. You see, it is with no resigned spirit that *I* yield to the iron yoke our conqueror forges for his fallen and powerless foe. The degradation of a whole country and a proud people is indeed a mighty, an all-enveloping sorrow.

I have uninterruptedly sought forgetfulness, or rather *temporary* relief, from these present griefs in a most earnest application to study. Some fourteen volumes of history have claimed my recent attention. And yet the study of human nature from the earliest epochs affords one little comfort. How vice and wickedness, injustice and every human passion runs riot, flourishes, oftentimes going unpunished to the tomb! And how the little feeble sickly attempts of virtue struggle, and after a brief while fade away, unappreciated and unextolled! The depravity of the human heart is truly wonderful, and the moiety of virtue contained on the historic page truly deplorable. How often have these same sorrows and unmerited punishments that we are now undergoing been visited upon the brave, the deserving, the heroic, and the patient of all ages and in all climes! . . . Virtue, like the violet, modest and unnoted, blossoms in silence and fades softly away; the fragrance it threw on the morning breeze was very sweet and very rare; but the breeze died away, and the memory of the virtuous dies too. I fear you will think I am growing very allegorical, but really "the common course of events" is so out-of-date that it needs a few extra flourishes on everything we do at present to mark this most unnatural era. Had it not been for my dear books, the one comfort as yet unmolested (I do not refer to those we left in Savannah), I am inclined to believe I should have been constrained to apply for a suite of apartments in some lunatic asylum—if they too have not vanished with other national comforts!

Charles, thank Heaven, is very well and just the same immaculate darling he always was, but just now so deeply and exclusively busy at the plantation, earning his daily bread "by the sweat of his brow," that I only am occa-

sionally enchanted with a flying visit. He received a week or two ago a
letter from you which we were both rejoiced to receive, and which, by the
way, he immediately answered, I enclosing a note. But after having written,
some farther developments of Yankee policy being foreshadowed, he waited
to see the results, and as he was suddenly called away, left me with directions "not to send the letter." I do not feel at liberty to do so until I hear
more from him.

I suppose you have learned even in the more secluded portions of the
country that slavery is entirely abolished—a most unprecedented robbery,
and most unwise policy. So it must appear even to the ignorant. I know it
is only intended for a greater humiliation and loss to *us*, but I should think
that even the powerful and unconscientious conqueror would reap the ill
effects of so unguarded a movement. However, it *is* done; and we, the
chained witnesses, can only look on and draw inferences and note occurrences—"only this and nothing more." There has been a great rush of the
freedmen from all families in the city and from neighboring plantations.
Adeline, Grace, and Polly have all departed in search of freedom, without
bidding any of us an affectionate adieu. All of Dr. Joe's servants have left
save Titus and Agrippa and children, I think he told me. . . . We have lost
many of our servants, but a sufficient number have remained to serve us,
and as yet these appear faithful and anxious to please. On our plantation
everything is "at sixes and sevens." One day they work, and the next they
come to town. Of course no management of them is allowed. Our Yankee
masters think that *their* term of slavery having expired, that the shackles
they have abandoned, more firmly riveted, will do for us their former
owners. And we meekly bow the head, receive chains and insults, and observe a mute and most submissive demeanor. Veritably like lambs we are
led to the slaughter, and like sheep before the shearers we are dumb. And
they *shear* ahead—in a manner most wonderful to behold.

Very shortly I will, D.V., leave "these scenes so charming" to forget in a
summer sojourning among my best-loved friends some of these present
miseries. After the annual delight of a Sparta trip I hope to visit some
friends in Athens; and from thence I spend the remainder of the summer
in the mountain breezes of Clarkesville with my dear aunt. I trust I'll find
both health and flesh in the delightful summer retreat of my aunt, for I
need both sorely—although I am a little stronger for the past few days, or
rather *two days.*

I fear I am quite wearying you with my unusual volubility. My dearest
mother unites with me in warm love to yourself and Ruthie. I suppose the
little lady is grown entirely beyond one's recollection. Kiss her for me. I
know her papa would send a very affectionate one for her were he here.
Dismayed at the divers accumulations of great poverty, hopeless and in the
depths of an abyss of despair, faintly I reiterate:

> Affectionately yours,
> Eva.

Mrs. Mary Jones *to* Mr. Charles C. Jones, Jr.ᵍ

Atlanta, *Monday,* June 26th, 1865

My dear Son,

I wrote you on the eve of our departure from Baker, and forwarded the letter by express from Macon. I hope you have received it. As it was necessary for your sister and Robert to precede me, I remained—first with my friend Mrs. Mitchel and then with Mr. and Mrs. Nisbet—until Friday morning, when I came up with our dear little Mary Ruth. *Susan* was with me, and so far as I observed appeared as usual; but the night before I left, when I called for her at bedtime to attend upon the baby, she was missing, and I saw nor heard anything more of her. It was useless to delay my plans or make any inquiries after her, so I came up with Mary Ruth as I had designed doing. I wrote requesting you to meet her here, as I was unable to take her to Augusta myself and then to return immediately. Neither funds nor health would permit.

Your sister and Robert are living in Mrs. Coleman's house fronting Mc-Donough Street. . . . We live in a *very, very* small cottage on the slope of the hill, with a vegetable garden in front. It has two rooms below and two small ones in the roofing. One answers to parlor and dining room; the other they have given to me; and your sister and Robert have the upper rooms. Our furniture is as primitive as possible: not even a bedstead as yet, and a little borrowed bedding.

Robert has just called for my letter, and I must close. Yesterday our precious child entered her fifth year. No doubt you remembered it. Soon after she entered the church she whispered gently: "Danna, are you going to baptize me again today?" God grant to her young heart the true baptism of the Holy Spirit!

I wish we had some sweet comfortable place to invite dear Eva to share this healthful climate with us. (The word *home* has died upon my lips.) I hope it will suit your convenience to come up shortly. Your sister and Robert unite with me in warmest love to Eva and yourself, with sweetest kisses from your child. Our love to your brother and Carrie, and affectionate regards to Mrs. Eve. Mary and Charlie send love to Uncle Charlie and Aunt Eva.

Your affectionate mother,
Mary Jones.

Mrs. Eva B. Jones *to* Mrs. Mary Jonesᵗ

Augusta, *Tuesday,* June 27th, 1865

Your last letter to Charlie, dear Mother, reached here some few days after I had written you quite an epistle, and while he was still at Indianola. He had been hard *at work* while there, his hands hard and burnt like a common laborer's. Yet he scarcely had a breathing space before, mounting cotton bales in a wagon, he started down to Savannah to try and make a little money, which article he is totally without and greatly in need of. He begged I would write you immediately and let you know the urgency of the case and say he would try if *possible* to get out to Montevideo. The reason of this great haste was, he had invested some of his Confederate money in two bales of domestics; and hearing he could get ten cents advance on the price here in Savannah—or rather, the market being overstocked here with that sort of goods and there being a dearth of them in Savannah—he, fearing a tumble in the price in that market so soon as these flatboats now building commence to carry freight, wisely seized this probably *best* opportunity, and is now on his way to Savannah in a most primitive style.

Of course you know there is no way for him, or anybody else scarcely, to make money now. He will not be allowed to practice his profession until he is permitted to take the oath. His wheat crop has utterly failed, and we are all as poor as church mice. The Negroes at Indianola wanted to give a little trouble during his last visit, but he soon straightened them up, and now they are behaving very well. We here have been most unfortunate, for being so near to the city, our Negroes are under all the baleful influences of the vile abolitionists (of which the worst specimens are in our midst); and they (the Negroes) work or not just as it best suits their convenience and pleasure. We have only a third-crop planted (that not worked); and our most promising fields are now under water.

Besides this, the Negroes and Yankees have broken into our smokehouse and swept it of *every piece* of meat. Not content with this great and to us terrible robbery, they have even entered with false keys our storeroom here, and have not left us a single ham. So we are now dependent on the market, and have to purchase every bit of meat we eat. Constant depredations are being made on the place, and we can obtain no *redress,* and are entirely at the mercy of the merciless.

I grow so wearied with all these troubles that I long so for the quiet of the up country, where I trust before long to be. I will now wait until my cousin, Miss Casey, is strong enough to accompany me. She has been dangerously ill with typhoid fever, which is spreading all over the city. I have heard that the Yankee surgeon mentioned a few days since a case of black vomit, which sounds something like yellow fever. Indeed, I should be surprised at nothing, for the city is kept fearfully filthy, and the cellars (many of them) continue filling with water from the springs in them caused by last month's great freshet.

Charlie will go to Atlanta so soon as he returns from Savannah. Another great reason for his going so immediately was that a friend had written us if he would go down *directly* he might be able to save *some* of his furniture, which was a great consideration to people who have now to earn their daily bread. It is pitiable the state in which we all find ourselves.

I saw the Doctor yesterday; he said Carrie and the children were quite well. All of their servants but Titus left them.

Do give my warm love to Mr. and Mrs. Mallard and the children. I trust they are all quite well. I know the pleasant climate of Atlanta will invigorate you all. Mother sends kind remembrances. We both send a warm kiss to Ruthie. I saw her aunt, Philo Neely, the other day. She came up for some *new things,* having just received from her father-in-law forty thousand greenbacks. But tell Ruthie she did not remember her, I fear.

Affectionately yours,
Eva.

I directed my last letter to Atlanta. I think it, however, reached that city before you did.

Have you taken the oath yet?

MRS. LAURA E. BUTTOLPH *to* MRS. MARY JONES[t]

Flemington, *Friday,* June 30th, 1865

My dearest Aunt and Cousins,

We received your letter long after Mr. Barnard's wagons had left, and have been cut off and shut up from all news except an occasional letter or paper from Savannah by someone *recently* coming this way. (Returning prisoners were not permitted to bring letters.) The railroad will soon be completed, I hear, to Augusta; and I now send you this by Cousin Kate, who goes to Savannah with Cousin Audley and the children on their way to New York. Cousin Kate expects to spend the winter with her father and mother, and Cousin Audley stays as long as things remain quiet here.

A Yankee company from Maine are now at Walthourville to keep the county in order—particularly the colored population. People are taking the oath and forming contracts with their servants, to which they sign their mark. Rev. Dr. Palmer and Dr. Howe have taken the oath. Dr. Howe spent the night with us on his way from Savannah, and his account of the destruction of Columbia by the Yanks was most thrilling. Dr. Howe says it is so hard to obtain subsistence there he has thought of coming here (Liberty) to live. Dr. Howe says he was advised in Savannah to form a contract with his people to save his lands from confiscation.

I presume you know that your Maybank houses (every one except the little dairy) were burned on the 17th of April. Aunt Julia's and ours were all burned the Saturday before. *Not one house left.* They were intentionally set on fire—some say by a party from St. Catherines, others that an interested person or persons destroyed them. Dr. Harris says he hopes to live long enough to find out who burned all of his houses on the Island.

Cousin Audley has been advised in Savannah to erect a small house and plant a patch of corn, etc., to prevent our lands from falling into the hands of the enemy as abandoned lands, and to save litigation. He wishes to do the same for you, and wishes you and Cousin Joe to write him on the subject, or to appoint an agent to do so. He says he may have a note from you showing him to have the power to act for you. He has always acted for us.

Mr. Fennell says he has a very good crop for you and has gotten on pretty well, making allowances for the new order of things and the unsettled state of affairs. This population are still going to Savannah on *the slightest pretext,* and great prudence and forbearance has to be exercised with regard to them for the present.

Mother would write to you now, but she has broken her glasses and cannot see. She has not had an opportunity before, and this is a very uncertain one. Still you may get this.

The railroads, Mr. S. Fraser says, have all been handed over to their companies by the Yanks, and that this Gulf Road is almost finished to the Altamaha, and will soon be put in order from Savannah. Forty days is the time given, and he doubles it.

So soon as you can come to us, my dear aunt, we will be more than glad to see you. Your room is ready and waiting, and it will be healthy for you if you will stay with us. We get on remarkably well in the eating line, so you need have no care about that. We will have to give up this house to Mr. Stacy on the 1st of November—to go wherever Providence directs. We are without a shelter. . . .

Uncle William sends love to you. He is very feeble, and has only been here to attend church since you left. He is very happy and satisfied at Aunt Julia's, and they do all they can for him. He says "when Mary comes home he is going to stay with her."

I heard yesterday that Mr. Arnold from Bryan had turned off all of his people from Mount Vernon and told them to go to the Yanks: he would feed them no longer; and that some of Mr. Alexander's people had returned, saying they were done with the Yankees forever. William carried off all of our people from Lambert plantation except Joe's sister Bella and Old Jacob; they are on a farm near Savannah, I hear. . . . They all say they have fine crops—and Cousin Audley says the corn is yellow and the fennel higher than the corn. Fine crops! . . . Cousin Audley speaks of rebuilding on the Island and planting, hiring hands and selling South Hampton or resettling it in the fall. A string of log houses for the family they now speak of. . . . Cousin Mary's Virginia maid has gone to Savannah and has gotten married. Good riddance: all parties quite *relieved.*

Dear Cousin Willie's death was a great shock to them all. Fred and Ross feel very bitter; Belle is completely crushed by it; Aunt Julia is very sad. And we all miss his cheerful voice, and feel that the most promising and most loved has fallen. But he was sincere in his love for his Saviour, and ready to meet death even in the shock of battle. . . .

Mr. Buttolph has received a letter from his father (in his eighty-sixth year); and Mr. B.'s health is so bad I wish he could go North and see him. Has not seen him for six years, and has not had a line or heard from him for four years until recently through Dr. Axson. But the war has taken away all our means of transportation. . . .

There are to be *no more bondsmen and no more whippings,* the Yanks tell the Negroes here. A Yankee officer told the servants at the Creek this week that they were to stay at home and work harder than they had ever done in their lives, and not run about and steal; that they had come to see that they behaved themselves. They (the Nigs) were quite disgusted. . . .

Neighbors all well and send love. Mother, Mr. B., and the children unite with me in love to you and Cousins Joe and Carrie, Cousins Mary and Robert; and all the little ones kisses.

Your attached niece,
Laura E. Buttolph.

MRS. MARY JONES *to* MR. CHARLES C. JONES, JR.[g]

Atlanta, *Sunday,* July 9th, 1865

My dear Son,

A gentleman going directly to Augusta informs me that he will take this letter to you and see that it is safely delivered. I have written you three times since I left Baker and twice since my arrival here two weeks since, informing you and asking you to meet your precious child here, as it was not in my power to bring her to Augusta. I have not received an answer to either, and feel convinced they never reached you. One was by express and directed to Mrs. William J. Eve; the other two by mail.

Knowing through your last letter your great desire to have Ruthie with you, and fearing also to expose her longer to the climate of Baker, I left my dear brother's for the purpose of bringing her thus far to you. She will be a precious little comforter to Eva and yourself in these dark days of sorrow. I would bring her to you, but I have not the means to go to Augusta and return here, where I expect to remain until fall if I am then able to go to Liberty. *Of my present situation or future plans I will not now speak, hoping to see you as soon as is convenient for you to come to Atlanta.* I wish your sister was so situated that she could invite dear Eva to accompany you; but we are with the most limited accommodations, and in the smallest house you could well imagine. Robert's church was untouched, and the congregation fast filling up.

I have not received a line from your brother since we parted on the railroad. I know he has written. Have received one letter from Carrie and yours with a note from Eva.

Robert and your sister unite with me in much love to Eva and yourself, and to your brother and Carrie. Your precious child says: "Tell Papa and Mama I send my love, and kisses too." She grows daily more lovely and interesting. God bless you, my son, with the comforts of a true and living faith!

Ever your affectionate mother,
Mary Jones.

Mrs. Eva B. Jones *to* Mrs. Mary Jones[t]

Augusta, *Friday,* July 14th, 1865

How very much have I been surprised, my dear mother, to learn that so few of our letters to you have been received! I have within the last three weeks written you two long letters.

In the last I told you of Charlie's going to Savannah in order to make a little money before leaving for Atlanta; for of funds we *too* were utterly *destitute*. He went down in a most primitive style, mounted upon some bales of cotton, of which our estate owned *six*—a mere pittance. But we were glad to have even that forlorn quantity. Charlie returned from Savannah on yesterday, and left this morning for his plantation to attend some urgent business. He will return very soon in order to go to Atlanta. I suppose he will leave the first of next week. I assure you he would have gone to see you and get Ruthie two weeks since but that we have *not* a *greenback*. And strange to say, the Yankees won't take our Confederate money!

Well, we are all down here as poor as poverty can make us. Besides the freeing of our Negroes (which deprives us of the greater part of our property, of course), the Yankees and Negroes together have stolen every piece of meat we had (about one hundred and seventy pieces), and we have not a *ham* even left. Then a variety of mules, sheep, and hogs; so altogether we are in a forlorn condition. I expect before long to become a very efficient chambermaid and seamstress, though the latter comes very hard to my poor unused fingers. Our ménage has been frightfully reduced; and of our numerous throng there remains a seamstress (who has had to lay aside her old calling to become cook, washer, and chambermaid) and one who attends to everything else about this unfortunate establishment. Adeline, Grace, and Polly were the first to assume freedom. To crown my misfortunes, which persistently attack me from all sides, Charlie and I had been laying aside carefully every few cents of specie that we could gather; and most tenderly did I keep it locked and laid away. To no one would I breathe of my few gold and silver dollars, when what was my surprise and despair the other day to find that my wardrobe had been *entered with a false key* and my forty-three dollars in specie gone—vanished, abstracted!

> 'Twas ever thus from childhood's hour:
> I've seen my fondest hopes decay.

One of our freedwomen expects shortly to enter the holy estate of matrimony, and has therefore indulged in some extravagancies and petty fineries. The question arises: Whence came the "filthy lucre" to purchase these indulgences? And my empty wardrobe echoes emphatically: *"Where?"*

Charlie will soon be with you and tell you all the news of Augusta and Savannah; also Indianola. I have been expecting to go up the country this whole summer, and my friends have been writing constantly for me; but I fear my recent loss will preclude my traveling to any extent. . . . I have some pretty little dresses for Ruthie, but will send nothing I have for her, as you say Charlie will bring her back with him, and it will be merely giving you additional trouble and take up more room in her trunk. I will try to get a servant to attend her, but I suppose as she is growing so fast I will *almost* be able to attend her myself.

Your letters coming this way have been more fortunate in reaching their destination than ours. Both of my last had Yankee stamps and were put in the post office. I saw Dr. Joe this morning; he told me he would try to find some reliable person who would see that you received this.

Charlie never looked better than he does now, and is if anything more adorable than ever. I fear I have spoiled him a little bit, though for *my life* I can't see that I have! We are both going to hard work and try to gain a livelihood some way.

My poor brother Edgeworth feels his glory departed, and lays aside the captaincy with a sigh as he opens an up-country store. He goes bravely to work, and says he'll gain an honest livelihood; and many of his best friends here are delighted with his independence and energy. But these times try men's souls—and women's too!

Tell Ruthie I have sent word to her "new mama," Sallie Casey, that I would wait until she came and carry her up to see her at her sweet cool country home.

Augusta is very unhealthy just now; there is a great deal of typhoid fever here. . . . Sallie Casey came quite near leaving this terrestrial a few weeks since; she had merely come down on a visit. . . . There were twelve Negroes interred yesterday; the city is crowded with them.

Do give my warm love to Mr. and Mrs. Mallard and the children. My mother sends her kind regards to all of you. With love for yourself and Ruthie,

Affectionately yours,
Eva.

REV. JOHN JONES *to* MRS. MARY JONES[t]

Refuge, Wednesday, July 26th, 1865

My dearest Sister,

Day by day I have been meditating letters to you, hoping that some opportunity would arise to send you a remembrance. The opportunity came. Our young kinsman, Adjutant William West, a gallant youth who has just passed through four years' Confederate service (the oldest son of our lamented Cousin Charles West, Jr.), called to see us yesterday afternoon and informed us that he and his Uncle Randolph and family would start for Bath via Atlanta on Friday of this week. Sister Mary Dunwody and myself immediately determined to improve the opportunity and prepare our letters today. And a new impulse was added to our resolution just as we rose from breakfast by the arrival of Brother Henry's faithful servant Lambright's

Ben, bringing letters for us sent by Henry from Cuthbert. Oh, what a treat we have had! All were common stock, and we read letters from William J. Dunwody, our brother in McIntosh County; Kate Dunwody, the wife of Brother Dean M. Dunwody; and then your most welcome letters from yourself and dear Mary. A letter or a newspaper is a great incident to us in this remote and solitary home.

We congratulate you all on your safe arrival and pleasant location in Atlanta, and wish we had wings of doves to fly and come and see you in your new home. You alluded (both of you) to the time spent under our humble roof, and spoke so kindly of us that my heart was touched. I shall ever be thankful for those days when we were all together. But I often regretted that we could do no more for your comfort; and when I look back, I wish that I had been more attentive and tender to you both. But it was a time of great anxiety and pressure upon us all; our cherished government was dissolving, and all that we were seemed to be passing away.

July 27th. And now a word from us all. I regret to say that my dear Jane has been seriously—critically—unwell since you left; a continued and increased hemorrhage forced her to bed for a week. I called in a physician who seemed to understand her case; she is somewhat better, but far, far from well. . . . Mother Dunwody is quite well, though somewhat prostrated by the weather. She has enjoyed very much our fine watermelons. . . . Sister Mary Dunwody is the factotum of the family—ever cheerful, hopeful, and affectionate, and relieving my dear Jane of many cares. She looks forward without flinching from coming troubles, determined to labor and support herself and mother. . . . Johnnie and Josie are studying very well, and I can give them more time, as Mr. Irvin has greatly relieved me from field duties. They have become great fishermen. They lately met with a great misfortune in the loss of their strong box containing a number of fine lines and forty-three hooks accumulated with great care for months. They were fishing on the Nochaway and removed to another point, leaving the box. Some freedmen passed and gobbled it up. . . . Dunwody is well, but much at a loss about the future. . . . I am well, but debilitated by the heat. Have been doing a little study, reading, and writing. . . . The future with me is dark. If I am not called to some church, necessity will compel our remaining here for a part of the year; and we will have to cultivate the soil with the freed Negroes if a sufficient number remain. Ours are quiet and orderly.

Our whole neighborhood received lately a most mystifying quietus. (But you must keep secret what I relate.) The wave of emancipation coming nearer and nearer, a restlessness was perceived almost universally. Insubordination began to crop out. It was reported at Albany; and two Federals, in blue uniforms and armed, came out, visited the said places, and whipped every Negro man reported to them, and in some cases unmercifully. They came almost in sound of this place. Another party visited Colquitt (sixteen miles south) and punished by suspending by the thumbs. The effect has been a remarkable quietude and order in all this region. The Negroes are astounded at the idea of being whipped by Yankees. (But keep all this a secret, lest we should be deprived of their services. I have not called on them yet, but may have to do so.)

Old Mama is quite well, and often inquires after you, and has received your message, and sends you much love. Porter and William have finished some time since their workshop, and are now making cooperware for trade. No money in this country; and Negro labor is a drug.

Rescue has improved. He needed rest after his repeated long trips. He has not plowed in all six days.

I heard lately through Dr. Stevens that the Federals were posting companies along the seaboard for the protection of the inhabitants from runaways and marauders, etc. One company is stationed in Liberty County. Mr. Barnard is absent; he left before your letter was received; I requested him to learn all he could of your affairs. Your letter to Mr. Fennell I will forward by first opportunity, perhaps by Mr. H. M. Stevens, who is daily expected. By the way, his people received a special visit from the Yankee whipping-masters.

Some weeks since, a letter came to you from Thomasville; thinking it was from Liberty from some of our relatives, I opened and read it. It was from Miss Eliza Clay; and I enclose it, as you will prize it from that noble lady and true friend of yours.

My dear sister, I fully respond to all your feelings and anxieties for the memory of your dear husband, my dear honored brother; and most willingly will I rewrite and expand in some measure the hurried estimate I drew up of him when my heart was full to overflowing and every lineament of body and mind and heart were fresh and vivid. And I will forward to you to Atlanta.

Your servants are all well and apparently contented; and all through Patience send love to you and all, and are glad to hear from you. And now, dear Sister, may the Holy Spirit bless and comfort you and enable us to recognize God's hand in changing our affairs so wonderfully! Our best united love from all to you all, and kisses for each of the dear children.

Ever your devoted brother,
John Jones.

Howdy for your servants. I know the house where you live. Say to Robert that I would be glad to know how his future promises. Tell Daughter when I write again I will answer her letter.

Mr. Charles C. Jones, Jr., *to* Mrs. Mary Jones[t]

Augusta, *Friday*, July 28th, 1865

My very dear Mother,

Daughter and myself safely reached Augusta yesterday afternoon at six o'clock. Eva met us at the depot. We had a long and hot ride, but Mary

Ruth is as bright as a new little button this morning after a long and refreshing night's sleep.

This morning at one o'clock Sister Carrie again became a mother: a fine little boy whom they call Charles Colcock Jones after our beloved and honored father. The Doctor is in the best of humors, and both mother and child are doing, I learn, very well. Your kind remembrance came just in time, and for it all are very grateful. The Doctor thinks that the birth of this little stranger was hastened by Carrie's fall from the buggy, of which I told you. The little ones are both well.

Mrs. Eve has been sued by three of her house servants for wages—a most unwarrantable procedure. The truth is that unless something is done here, great annoyance will occur. We will all have to recognize the fact at once that our former slaves have been set free, that we have no further legal claim upon their services, and that if they continue with us we must pay for services rendered. The amount of the compensation will of course depend upon each particular case. I am just writing Mr. Fennell a full letter on the subject.

Eva returns her sincere thanks for your beautiful present, and unites with me in warmest love. Little Daughter sends her sweetest kisses for her dear "danna," to whom, under God, she owes everything, and to whom we can never be sufficiently grateful all our lives. Mrs. Eve desires kindest remembrances. She still suffers much from her cough. I trust, my dear mother, that you may be preserved from many annoyances during this distressing period, and that God will richly endow you of His great grace. Give our best love to Sister, Robert, and the little ones. Do, my dear mother, let me know whenever and in what way I can serve you. As ever,

Your affectionate son,
Charles C. Jones, Jr.

I send a few postage stamps.
I hope to get the letters of attorney, etc., off today.

MRS. MARY JONES *to* GEN. JAMES H. WILSON, U.S.A.[t]

Atlanta, *Tuesday,* August 1st, 1865

General,

Through the Rev. Mr. Wills I was favored with an introduction to you in his own house, at which time I made an unsuccessful application to you for transportation for myself and family to this place. This would perhaps deter me from again troubling you; yet such is the nature and urgency of my present request that I cannot but flatter myself that if it comports with your authority it certainly will with your clemency to grant it.

That you may understand my true situation, pardon me for a moment in referring to the necessities which lead me to ask assistance. A part of General Sherman's army—among them General Kilpatrick's cavalry—in their advance upon Savannah occupied my native place, Liberty County, for four weeks. Most of the inhabitants left their homes at the approach of the army; in good faith I received the published orders of General Sherman and determined to remain in mine. I did not anticipate immunity from distress or from the common losses and spoliations of war. I expected to suffer with my suffering country, but I did believe through those orders I would be protected in my own home from private invasion and pillage.

During those four weeks (excepting two days) my plantation and dwelling were visited three and four times a day by numbers of soldiers varying from forty to two and three at a time. In every possible way they entered my house. When it stood open, they would rush into every part of it. When closed to protect my helpless family—which consisted of my daughter (who became a mother during their occupation) and her three little children, a friend in delicate health with her two little children (who had sought protection under my roof after her own was burned), and myself, a widow with one little granddaughter—they would sometimes burst open the doors or enter them by false keys. Under every imaginable pretext they searched our most private apartments. Not the minutest box or trunk escaped scrutiny; and all that was deemed valuable in furniture, library, household effects, clothing, knives, forks, silver, crockery, or jewelry, etc., was subtracted or injured. Fearing my family might suffer for food—as we often did, preparing and cooking it only by rising at the dawn of day—I had brought twelve bushels of meal and other articles into my pantry. In the face of a starving family of helpless women and little children, and amid entreaties that our circumstances would be considered, they took every particle of our meat and meal, and answered our entreaties with: "You deserve to starve to death, and we mean you shall do it. You have no right even to have wood or water. We will *crush* and humble you in the dust." On the plantation our cotton was entirely destroyed, and with the exception of some corn in the ear and unthreshed rice, every particle of food, sugar, and syrup was taken, even to seed potatoes. My carriage, wagons, carts, and harness and conveyances of every description were taken; hogs, cattle, and sheep taken or destroyed. I lost six horses, two mules, and fourteen head of oxen. Poultry of every kind was taken; not one allowed to remain. In a few days over my once cheerful home was cast the pall of death. Our summer home with every building has been laid in ashes, not even fences remaining. Such desolation and ruin pervaded my native county as might satisfy the deepest revenge.

After the advance of the army and occupation of Savannah, although left in great destitution, I still hoped to remain with the servants at home and do the best we could to sustain life, but found myself and them in such circumstances of peril from marauding bands of Negroes (that had occupied the adjoining counties and sea islands and were continually returning to steal the little that remained) that we were finally compelled to leave, and did so through the assistance of kind friends from abroad, upon whose kindness and charity they have subsisted to the present time.

These people are now desirous of returning to their former home, and I am desirous of aiding them to do so; but as you will see from the above recital, I am powerless to do so. I am reduced from affluence to penury, so far as any available support for them or for myself remains; and if I cannot obtain assistance, they too must be numbered among the millions suddenly made homeless and friendless. My distress is not more for myself than for them. My honored husband, Rev. C. C. Jones, D.D., expended his talents, his energy, his fortune, his exalted piety in devoted efforts to benefit the Negro race. His record is on high, and the good he accomplished in their elevation and true conversion to God will meet an eternal reward. These servants have composed our household, and I would gladly do something to promote their future welfare. But as I have said, I am without the means of assisting them.

The request I prefer is twofold. Will you give me transportation for two families of Negroes, or as many as desire to return (they will be from fifteen to twenty in all, many of them children), from Thomasville on the Savannah, Albany & Gulf Road to No. 3 (McIntosh Station), Liberty County, in the month of October, when I understand the road will be completed? The government have repeatedly aided the destitute or those who applied for agricultural purposes. Can you assist me in obtaining either horses or mules for plantation use, or direct me to any source by which they can be thus secured?

General Wilson, if you have favored my letter with a reading, I fear I have overtaxed your courtesy. I trust your forbearance will be exercised.

Very truly yours,
Mary Jones.

MRS. MARY JONES *to* MRS. EVA B. JONES[g]

Atlanta, Saturday, August 5th, 1865

My dear Daughter,

I have been so unwell since Charles left as scarcely to be out of bed, and our little Georgia is now really sick with an affection which the doctor tells us is now prevailing here among children of her age. I hope my little darling child will not suffer from the change. I have asked her papa if anything prevents your contemplated visit and she is affected by climate or any other cause, to let her return to me here. Do write me *particularly* how she bore the journey up that long hot day, and if she found any kind female friend on the cars.

I marked her catechism as far as she had learned—to "Good Angels." My life has been so irregular, and so many cares and perplexities the past six or eight months, that I have not confined her at all to her book. Indeed, she is quite too young unless it is made a source of pleasure. I think she has a great regard for her catechism, and often think with what delight her beloved grandfather would have listened to her little voice repeating the heavenly truths arranged by him for his own grandchildren and children, as he often told me.

I put in her books and toys, as far as they survived destruction; and her dolls are quite a source of pleasure. She was only favored now and then with the wax doll: it is frail. When I was alone, she became quite independent of society with her books and playthings around her.

Her little cousins here are very much attached to her, and grieved at her going away. Tell her Bubber and Sissy say "she must come back soon; they want to see her."

Her wardrobe is ample for her summer wants: twenty dresses, etc., etc. I put in her winter things, for it will soon be cool weather. The two winter dresses I made so large that they will answer for another season. In the bottom of the trunk is a dress which we thought would be useful in making a cloak or dress. I have not seen anything new or pretty or I would have made it up. I have a dark calico dress and two flannel petticoats which I will send when made. The bonnet you gave her I thought you might like to have altered according to your own taste, so did not trouble it. Among her dresses is one with inserting trimming, nearly worn out. I have some special associations with that and the *pointed* dress, and would like to preserve them after she has worn them out. The *elegant cape* of cashmere and satin presented by her Aunt Vallie got slightly stained at the Altamaha. As I am living only in trunks, I thought you could take better care of it. If her life is spared, she can use it sometime hence.

I was rejoiced to hear you had secured the services of a good *white woman;* they are greatly to be preferred. Ours have not left us yet, but we are preparing for surprises. I truly regret to know that your mother's servants have given her so much trouble. We cannot but feel such ingratitude. They are instituting such revengeful measures that I hope my dear son will not be drawn into trouble by or with them. I think in future he will have to be more prudent. . . .

Do write me some *little* particulars of my baby. I want to know what she *says* and *does,* and if she loves and remembers her "danna." Please remember *us* affectionately to your mother. With a hundred kisses for my baby,

Your affectionate mother,
Mary Jones.

Mr. CHARLES C. JONES, JR., *to* Mrs. MARY JONES[t]
Augusta, *Wednesday,* August 9th, 1865

My dear Mother,

I have just returned from Indianola, where I left all pretty well, and everything progressing as favorably perhaps as might under the circumstances be expected. Am now busily engaged harvesting fodder. The people all inquire very particularly after you, and send special howdies for all.

Eva expects to leave with Ruthie for Sparta on Tuesday next, there to remain, D.V., for a month or more. Brother is now in Burke County, where he has gone to perform a postmortem in a poison case. Sister Carrie and the little ones are all well.

Dear little Daughter has been very well, and is the light of all our hearts. At present she is suffering somewhat from a cold. We have nothing of special interest here. Stepney has not returned as yet. I trust, my dear mother, that you are feeling better, and that all are well. Do give our united love to Sister, Robert, and the little ones, and accept for yourself every assurance of our warmest love. Daughter speaks daily of you, and says: "Tell Danna I send a love to her, and to Anna and Uncle Robert too, and Bubber and Sissy and Cousin Georgia." Do, Mother, let me know whenever I can serve you in any way. And believe me ever

Your affectionate son,
Charles C. Jones, Jr.

MRS. MARY JONES *to* MR. CHARLES C. JONES, JR.^g

Atlanta, Thursday, August 10th, 1865

My dear Son,

Yours of the 28th July did not reach me until the 3rd inst., and confirmed the happy announcement which had been previously made by Mrs. Smith and Miss Cumming of the birth of another son to your brother and sister Carrie. I feel truly grateful to God for this renewed mercy to my children, and have a peculiar love and drawing to my little grandson who is to bear the sacred and honored name of his grandfather. . . . Nothing but the state of my own health prevented my being with them.

For some time I have been conscious of a general failure, and since you were here have had two attacks of fever which confined me to bed. Robert, without my knowledge, brought Dr. Logan to see me, and I am now under his treatment. I am better, but feeble; hope there will be no return of fever. There has been recently a terrible *night atmosphere* around us, owing in part to proximity to camps and an enclosure with hundreds of condemned horses. And there is that universal pressure upon head and heart which all must feel.

I rejoiced to know that you arrived safely with my precious little Ruth. Tell her "Danna" misses her by day and by night, and is constantly listening for her sweet voice and her little step; and when she was sick she wanted her baby to rub her head and bring her a cup of cold water as she used to do. I trust she is well, and I doubt not very happy. No one can ever know what that child has been to me; but I wish her also to know and love her own dear father and her affectionate mama. I repeat what I have already said: she will be welcome to share the last morsel her "danna" has. Do, if Eva is not able to carry out her plans of going into the country, and you find she is likely to suffer from the change to Augusta—do let her return immediately to me here.

If able, I will try to visit Augusta before I return to Liberty. I want to see all my dear ones there, and if practicable would like to go to Indianola and see the people. I want to know their feelings. We have had a conversation with those of our household; *they are all expecting to return to their old home.* Tell Tom Daughter and I were very much pleased with the slippers, and I hope to see him before long. If an arrangement can be made for getting the leather, I will be glad if you will direct Tom to make for me eighteen or twenty pairs of plantation shoes. The people below are in great want. I sent nearly all I had made last year up to Indianola. If the piece of *calfskin* is suitable, he can make me a pair of walking gaiters. Do you think, my son, there is any prospect of recovering those hides put into the steam tannery at Savannah? The bull's hide was superior; I am entirely without a harness, and if it can be recovered, will use it for that purpose. Please tell all the people howdy for me, and that I want to see them all, and that we will try and do all in our power for them. Do let me know whenever you hear from below. When will Stepney return?

I trust we may be guided to those plans and arrangements that will be just and right in God's sight and for our own benefit. I desire under all troubles and trials and changes not to lean upon my own understanding, but to ask the guidance and direction of God's Holy Spirit. I trust, my dear child, heavenly wisdom and prudence will be given to you. We are passing through fearful times. How I often long for the presence of my sons!

Your sister's babe is better. She and Robert join me in much love to Eva and yourself. The children send kisses, and say Little Sister must come back soon. Many, many kisses for my darling child. And she must write and tell me what she is doing, and if she wants to see her "danna." I had a package prepared to send her by Mr. Cumming, but he did not call as he promised. My kind regards to Mrs. Eve. The Lord bless and save you, my son!

Your affectionate mother,
Mary Jones.

MRS. MARY S. MALLARD *to* DR. JOSEPH JONES[t]

Atlanta, *Thursday,* August 10th, 1865

My dear Brother Joe,

We were truly rejoiced to hear through Mrs. Smith and Miss Cumming of the birth of your dear little son. Another Charles Colcock! I know it is a great pleasure to you to have him bear our dear father's full name. And to wish that he may be like him in every respect is the greatest we could desire for him. I am thankful dear Carrie has passed through this great trial without serious illness, for we were very anxious about her. We have been hoping to receive a letter from you, and presume you have written; but all letters from Augusta are very much delayed.

Our dear mother has been quite sick. Her liver is very much disordered, and she has had a great deal of fever—not high, but a low prostrating feverishness, even when actual fever was not on. She coughs very much at night, and complains of constant debility. Dr. Logan prescribed for her two days ago, and I hope she will feel better.

I wish it were in your power to come up and see her. Whenever you can do so, you know we shall be most glad to welcome you; and you must bring Stanhope with you. I begged Brother Charlie to tell you if he appeared at all delicate to send him up to us. A change might do him good. Has he entirely recovered from the effects of his fall?

My baby has not been well; I think she is beginning to teethe.

Miss Cumming told us you would probably lose your servants. I trust you will be able to supply their places with good ones again, as you seemed to have been favored in the first arrangement. Thus far our domestics remain, but I feel a change will come in due time.

Aunt Eliza's family is quite well, and I think have much to encourage them. I have no doubt of their success. They have been only a few days without boarders since their first opening.

We have recently had the perusal of papers containing the minutes of the General Assembly, which met at Pittsburgh. They are deeply interesting, and disclose plainly the views of the church. Henceforward no one will be sent to labor, or permitted to do so, in this missionary field except *loyal men*. If you can get any of the papers from Dr. Wilson or any of your friends, you had better read them carefully.

Do write us soon and tell us all about the baby and Carrie. I suppose Stanhope and Susie had a welcome for their little brother. Mother begs me to say to you she feels much better this morning. Mother wrote expecting to send by Mr. Tom Cumming; but he did not call, and Mr. Mallard could not find him, as he had changed his boarding place. With much love from all of us,

Your affectionate sister,
Mary S. Mallard.

MRS. MARY JONES *to* MR. CHARLES C. JONES, JR.ᵍ

Atlanta, *Friday,* August 18th, 1865
My dear Son,

Your last letter was not received until yesterday. It had evidently been *torn* open either in this or the office in Augusta. This, I am told, is now frequently done to ascertain the sentiments of the people, so we will have to use great prudence. Alas, for our humiliated and degraded condition!

Robert has taken the oath; and as I have several interests to represent, would it not be well for me to do so at once before I go to the low country, where I may not have the opportunity of doing so, and yet might be put to some trouble about our landed property there if there should be any attempt at confiscation? Do write me about this if you can get a reliable *private* opportunity of doing so. I am suspicious of all communications *by mail*.

I have made a written contract with Flora to remain with me until the end of the year, and your sister and Robert have made contracts with their servants. They *all* design returning to Liberty, but will wait until the railroad to Savannah is finished. I am distressed at the thought of Lucy's leaving, for I fear your sister and her little children will miss her sadly. I would do anything in my power to retain her, but your sister thinks if she stays against her will she would be worse than useless. Tenah and her increasing family would be a burden in town. I mean to inform them plainly if they come below it must be to labor and be subject to control, either at Montevideo or Arcadia. I think they have an idea of possession. With regard to cultivating Montevideo, I will be compelled to increase the force there to do so successfully; and if I can do so from those who have lived there and are now at Indianola, I would prefer it to strangers. But of this we can arrange when you come down. Do write me what report Stepney brings when he returns.

I am anxious to visit the people at Indianola, but the time is drawing near for my return, *D.V.,* to Baker, which I hope to do the last of September or first of October. I cannot obtain any information of either the Central or Albany & Gulf Roads. Are they rebuilding? And when will they be in operation?

I wrote Eva and yourself letters last week, which I hope have reached you. I now send two worked flannels for my little darling. Do get them to her as soon as you can, for she will need them in early fall. I have been unable to get any flannel here; would like to have sent her four instead of two. My heart aches to see my precious child. . . . Kiss her again and again for "Danna," and tell her I will write her a letter for herself; and Bubber and Sissy and little Baby send kisses to her. Daughter and Robert unite with me in best love to Eva and yourself. Our kind regards to Mrs. Eve. . . . I have had no fever this week, and feel better under Dr. Logan's treatment.

Ever your affectionate mother,
Mary Jones.

REV. JOHN JONES *to* MRS. MARY JONES[t]

Refuge, *Monday,* August 21st, 1865

My dearest Sister,

On Friday of last week (the 18th inst.) Brother Henry's Jack handed me your last of the 20th of July, brought from Atlanta by Henry and detained unintentionally in Cuthbert, as it was in the hats. Your other letters from yourself and Mary came safely to hand, and were immediately acknowledged by our young relative Willie West, son of Cousin Charles West, Jr.

I trust you received that letter, as I wrote you at length, and enclosed a letter to Aunty, and another to you from Miss Eliza Clay, and one to you from our Joseph. I have lost no opportunity of sending you a letter, as opportunities are scarce.

My dear sister, I wish I could see you more and confer freely with you about our present and future, both alike uncomfortable and dark. I fear we both are laying too much to heart our troubles, and dwelling too much on secondary causes and human agents, and clinging too much to a race who are more than willing to let us go, and to a property which has never been very profitable, and which *has passed its best days* for ease and profit. However we may be able to prove the wickedness of our enemies, we must acknowledge that the providence of God has decided against us in the tremendous struggle we have just made for property rights and country. The hand of the Lord is upon us! Oh, for grace to be humble and behave aright before *Him* until these calamities be overpassed! I confess that I often feel brokenhearted, and tempted sometimes to rebel and then to give up in hopeless despair. Either extreme is wicked, and the antidote for each is a refuge in the sovereignty and righteousness of God.

You spoke in your letter of the quietude of our Refuge home. Some great changes have come over us since you left. The dark, dissolving, disquieting wave of emancipation has broken over this sequestered region. I have been marking its approach for months and watching its influence on our own people. It has been like the iceberg, withering and deadening the best sensibilities of master and servant, and fast sundering the domestic ties of years.

About the 20th July there was an evident restiveness generally throughout this region. Two of our own servants openly rebelled in the field—one at a time on different days—against Mr. Irvin, the overseer; but his prompt action, courage, and strength overcame them. They were both brought under good discipline. A few days after, some Kentuckians and others from Maine at Albany and Bainbridge were sent for to regulate certain plantations. They came promptly, and by use of the strap and sometimes a leather trace they restored order generally. The Negroes were mystified—thunderstruck that they should receive such treatment (and in some cases very severe, even cruel) at the hands of their friends. Very soon they began to whisper that the said Yankees were only Southern men in blue clothes—that the true Yankee had not come yet.

Soon after, the Kentuckians were removed and their places supplied by Illinoisans, and then there went abroad a rumor that the true Yankee, the deliverer of the Negro, had come. And immediately commenced an exodus of hundreds into Albany—a stream which has scarcely stopped, although the main current has been forced back to its fountain. The shock reached this place. On the 5th of August one of our young men left for Albany, and on the 8th inst. (or night before) nine more took up the line of march, carrying our house boy Allen and a girl sixteen years old (Amelia, the spinner). This girl had been corrected for being out the most of Saturday night previously. She was corrected by Joe, the foreman, under Mr. Irvin's eye, and had been somewhat bruised by the strap, which I knew nothing of and never allow. But this girl was taken to Albany into the provost marshal's office and stripped and exhibited—a bold attempt to bring either myself or the overseer or both into trouble. And I looked for trouble. But the provost marshal told them all to return home, and wrote me inquiring why I had turned my servants away. (They had absolutely represented that I had driven them off.) All have come back but Allen, who is said to be waiting on the Yankees at their camps.

Thus you see we have had and will have emancipation trials. I have made a contract with our people to last until the 25th December, at which time I trust that one-half at least will leave, for I am now overburdened supporting them. They will not pay expenses this year. My heart pities them, for I know they will miss their home. They generally seem bent upon returning to Liberty County.

Your people here are well and behaving well, and will gladly go with you to Liberty. I have failed—though constantly applying—to find work for Porter. Elsie is doing finely, and already weaves well.

I sent your letter to Mr. Fennell by Mr. H. M. Stevens. Mr. Barnard has just returned from Liberty; saw Mr. Fennell and reports all well at Montevideo and a promising crop. Mr. Fennell was to have sent a letter, but Mr. Barnard did not bring it. I requested Mr. Barnard to bring a letter from Mr. Fennell, but it was omitted. Mr. Barnard reported Cousin William Maxwell at Cousin Susan's, and all of them well. The lower part of Liberty has been troubled by Negroes from abroad, but steps were taking to remove them.

I have not said near all I wish to say. I will attend to your request about my dear brother; have for a month been in poor condition to compose anything beyond a few short sermons. Our best united love for you all, including Aunt and family.

Ever your affectionate, devoted brother,
J. Jones.

Mr. CHARLES C. JONES, JR., *to* Mrs. MARY JONES[t]
Augusta, *Saturday,* September 2nd, 1865
My very dear Mother,

I am just in receipt of your kind letter of the 18th ult. and of the package for little Ruthie, for both of which please accept warmest thanks. I am rejoiced to know that you are feeling so much better, and I pray God that you may be speedily restored to perfect health.

I have been for a week past under the weather, but I am, thank God, better now. Returned only today from Indianola, where I have been for more than two weeks past trying to harvest the crop of provisions. Very little is done there when I am away, and even while I am there. No one hurts himself by hard work. People all well. Harriet and Miley both lost their infants. All the people are, I think, very anxious to return to Liberty in the fall. As yet I have not conversed generally with them on the subject. Now that they are all free, there are several of them not worth the hiring. Please name, Mother, which of them you wish at Montevideo, and I will try and get them for you. I would have gone to Montevideo before, but I have not been strong enough to undertake the journey.

You had better take the oath at once. You do not come under any of the excepted classes, and it is well as a matter of precaution that you pursue this course.

Stepney says all are well at Montevideo and at Arcadia, and that the crop looks very well. Mr. Fennell writes me that the Negroes are doing very little work.

The Central Railroad is completed to the forty-five-mile station, and I understand that they hope to have the Albany & Gulf Railroad in running order by the 1st October. In consequence of the fact, however, that no dependence can be reposed in the consecutive labor of the hands employed in the reconstruction, no definite time can be assigned for the completion.

Daughter and Eva are still in Sparta. Both quite well. I do not expect them back for two weeks. Eva writes me under date of the 27th enclosing warmest love from herself and Ruthie for you. Brother better. His family quite well. Mrs. Eve desires her special remembrance. I have failed thus far in securing a house in Savannah. Every place crowded. Do, my dear mother, let me know in what I can assist you. With warmest love for yourself, Sister, Robert, and little ones, I am, as ever,

Your affectionate son,

C.

Mrs. Mary Jones *to* Mr. Charles C. Jones, Jr.ᵍ

Atlanta, *Wednesday,* September 6th, 1865

My dear Son,

This is your brother's birthday, and as we always have done, I have been thinking a great deal of him, and trying to commend him in all his interests for time and for eternity to our Covenant God and Saviour, who I trust is not only the God of his father but his own God and Saviour by a true and living faith and an open profession.

Oh, that you too, my dear child, could be so convinced of your own lost condition, and so moved by the infinite love and power of the Blessed Redeemer, as to give your heart to Him and to dedicate your life a willing offering in God's holy service! You have been mercifully preserved through this fearful struggle, and are just entering, as it were, upon the pledges of a new life. May you be truly enabled to decide for God and not for the world!

Evening before the last I asked Robert to walk with me to the graveyard; I wanted to find the grave of your friend General Helm, which was pointed out to us by the old sexton, who bears the significant name of *Pilgrim*. He is buried on the slope of the hill, and his grave marked by a marble head- and footpiece with this inscription:

Ben Hardin Helm
of Kentucky
Fell at Chickamauga
September 20th, 1863
aged 32 years.
He giveth His beloved sleep.

The hand of affection had evidently planted some flowers around the cherished spot, and a long-withered bunch of buds and evergreens lay decaying upon the grave, now overrun with wild vines. I had carried a beautiful bunch of flowers with me, and in his mother's name I laid it on his grave, and brought away a little sprig which I would like to send her if I had the heart to write her. How much I thought of poor George and the pleasant visit he made us on the Island, and the desolating changes that have passed over hearts and homes since then! Whilst my tears were falling upon the grave of the hero, I could not but remember the goodness and mercy of the Lord in sparing the lives of my two sons. Not far off in innumerable graves lay the remains of our noble and unrecorded dead, grown over by rank forest weeds: no name, no date, no place in history, no memorial but the undying love and remembrance of bereaved hearts.

My dear son, your sister has been quite sick for two weeks with severe neuralgic pains in head and back; has now two blisters, which have afforded relief, and just submitted to the extraction of four jaw teeth, and is much better today. I have been of course occupied with the little ones, and but little time for replying earlier to your last favor.

I hope dear Eva and my own little Ruth will enjoy the visit to Sparta. No tongue can tell how much I want to see my child. The children talk every day of her, and love her as a sister.

I expect, *D.V.,* to leave Atlanta on Monday the 2nd of October via Macon for Cuthbert, where I hope your Uncle John will send the buggy to meet me. After remaining a few days in Baker, or until suitable arrangements can be made, I will return to Liberty with those of our people who wish to go back. I hope the road will be in a condition for me to go from Thomasville to No. 3, but I can hear nothing of it. I could not undertake to go overland in a buggy for any consideration, but wish to carry the horse and buggy back on the railroad, and hope to get transportation for the Negroes. How I am to accomplish *all this alone I cannot now see;* but such is my plan. Flora and Milton will return with me from this place. I hope you will be able to meet me at Montevideo as you proposed doing, and organize some plan for the future. I have no home but that, and no means of support but what must come from planting; but my heart sinks at the thought of such an undertaking by myself and under such distressing circumstances.

Through Mr. Barnard I learn that large numbers of Negroes have returned to the county—six hundred, it is said, already; and that, *instigated* by *Cato*, the people at Montevideo had behaved in such a way that Mr. Fennell had been forced to call in the Yankees. They were doing better, and the corn crop was promising. Cato has been to me a most insolent, indolent, and dishonest man; I have not a shadow of confidence in him, and will not wish to retain him on the place. If I am to live there, I would like to have Stepney with me, if he wishes to do so, and a few others of my former servants: Sam and his wife and Hannah; if Patience remains, and Porter, I suppose they will want their children; and I would like to have Peggy with me, and William, and Tom if he will be obedient and industrious. But I feel that I cannot make any arrangements until we meet at Montevideo and see what is best to be done for the interest of all concerned. I must employ those who will be useful, but would prefer those I have known, provided they will be faithful.

I wrote General Wilson, and through General *Wild* he replied that as soon as the *bureau* was opened in Atlanta he thought I would have no difficulty in getting transportation. It has not yet been opened. About mules and horses he referred me to the quartermaster at Atlanta. How would it do for me to apply in Savannah? This place is too far off; I have made no application, as it would be useless.

Should you determine to return to Savannah, I hope it will be in my power to aid you in some articles for housekeeping. . . . Do write me very soon and tell me all you know of the Albany & Gulf Road. Your sister and Robert unite with me in best love to Eva and yourself and my dear baby. Howdy for the servants, and respects to Mr. and Mrs. Sconyers.

Your affectionate mother,
Mary Jones.

Mrs. Mary Jones *to* Hon. Daniel Pittman[t]

Atlanta, *Friday,* September 8th, 1865

I do solemnly swear or affirm, in the presence of Almighty God, that I will henceforth faithfully support, protect, and defend the Constitution of the United States and the union of the states thereunder, and that I will in like manner abide by and faithfully support all laws and proclamations which have been made during the existing rebellion with reference to the emancipation of slaves. So help me God.

Mary Jones.

Sworn to and subscribed before me at Atlanta this 8th day of September 1865.

Daniel Pittman, *Ordinary,*
Fulton County, Georgia.

Mrs. Mary Jones *to* Mr. Charles C. Jones, Jr.[g]

Atlanta, *Tuesday,* September 26th, 1865

My dear Son,

Your affectionate favor of the 21st did not reach me until yesterday, too late for a reply by the return mail; and as you spoke of going to Indianola, this will meet you on your return.

I am grieved to learn that our dear Eva continues so feeble in health; and my fervent prayer is that God would bless her in soul and body, deliver her from every form of suffering, and bestow health and strength in large measure. . . . I am really happy to know that Eva has for herself the services of so skillful a physician, and one in whom she so fully confides; and I trust she will be materially benefited. She always appears to enjoy her visits to Sparta exceedingly. I feel greatly disappointed at the thought of not seeing her and my precious child as I pass through Augusta. I hope they will soon come down and join me at Montevideo, if I am permitted to remain there.

Providence favoring my present arrangements, I hope to be with your brother on Friday the 6th of October, and we can then determine what day of the week following on which to leave for Savannah. I feel it very important to be at home as early as practicable. Would have liked to visit the people at Indianola, but can form no plans until we go below and see the condition of things and what provision crop has been made. Dear as my sweet home has been, if suitable arrangements cannot be made for my remaining there and having it under cultivation and the care of some reliable person, *I may be compelled to part with it.* I will speak of these matters fully when we meet. . . . I have thought as I passed through Savannah I might take the liberty of stopping with my friends Dr. and Mrs. Axson, and could write them to that effect from Augusta. Your sister and Robert unite with me in much love. Please send the enclosed to Eva.

Ever your affectionate mother,

Mary Jones.

Mrs. Mary Jones *to* Mrs. Eva B. Jones[g]

Atlanta, *Tuesday,* September 26th, 1865

My dear Daughter,

I would have written you again long ere this, but heard there were no mail communications between this and Sparta. I hope you received my last letter, and must thank you for your favor written just before leaving Augusta. What a comfort it would have been to me in this long interval to hear from you and of my precious child! I sometimes fear you are scarcely strong enough to take charge of her, and hope if I am permitted to return to Montevideo that you will be with me a great deal this winter.

I am grieved to learn that your health has not improved, and wish it was in my power to promote your comfort in any way. All that I can do is to point you to our Heavenly Father, who doth not willingly afflict His children, but with every chastisement has the gracious design of leading us unto Himself. When he withholds the blessing of health and strength, it is that we might feel our entire dependence upon Him. We are but frail dying creatures, and if our hopes and happiness are centered supremely upon the objects of time, they will surely bring us disappointment and grief.

Charles writes me charming accounts of the improvement intellectually of my darling child. I am happy to know that she commends herself to the kind friends with whom you are. Oh, how I long to see her! She must not forget her "danna." We talk of her every day, and her kind "anna" and Uncle Robert and Sissy and Bubber and little Georgia all want to see her. I am grieved to hear she has suffered from her ear; it has been over eighteen months since she has had the least suffering from it, and I now hope it is only the result of sudden cold. My son, who has ever watched her case with the tenderest solicitude, has always directed me to the use of such external applications and alteratives as, with God's blessing, have relieved her.

For five weeks my daughter has been confined to the house, and much of that time suffering severely. I do not think she has ever recovered from the fatigues of that terrible journey from Liberty. These are peculiar times of trial and suffering to all; we need great faith and patience under them.

Do your mother and yourself still contemplate a visit to Europe?

If I can do anything for you as I pass through Savannah, do write and let me know. And if you go again to housekeeping there, I will be glad to share what I may have remaining with Daughter and yourself. She was robbed of every particle of bedding. How much remains to you?

Mr. Mallard and Daughter unite with me in best love to you, and the children send love to Aunt Eva. Kiss my darling child for *us all*. Tell her to kiss Mama for "Danna." I rejoice to know you have had such a delightful visit to your dear friends in Sparta. Believe me ever

Your affectionate mother,
Mary Jones.

Excuse my pen.

Mrs. Mary Jones *to* Mrs. Caroline S. Jones[g]

Atlanta, *Tuesday,* October 3rd, 1865

My dear Daughter,

I am in distress and perplexity, and write to ask your help. The authorities here promised me transportation for the freedmen who wish to go from this to Savannah. Now, on the eve of leaving, they inform us that it can only be obtained through the bureau in Augusta. Will you be kind enough to obtain from General Tilson the necessary papers for me? These people are really in distressing circumstances. They are without means, and wish to return home where they can obtain an honest livelihood.

Robert leaves for Americus in the morning, and Daughter is anxious for me to stay until he returns on next Tuesday. And as I have not heard a word from Charles, and not yet obtained transportation for the freedmen, I have concluded, my dear daughter, not to be with you until Wednesday of next week, the 11th inst. . . . Do drop me a line, and do your best to get the transportation and forward it to me immediately. Daughter unites with me in best love. Do let Charles know that I will not be in Augusta until Wednesday the 11th.

Ever your affectionate mother,
Mary Jones.

In haste. As I am myself a needy refugee, could you not get transportation for *myself* as well as the freedmen?

Mrs. Mary Jones *to* Mrs. Mary S. Mallard[t]

Savannah, Monday, October 16th, 1865

My beloved Child,

Through the goodness of God your brother Charles and myself arrived safely here on last Saturday night, and I am with our dear friends Mr. and Mrs. Axson. Mr. Axson expects to attend Synod, and it gives me an opportunity of writing you. Carrie promised she would write for me from Augusta.

In consequence of cars off the track I did not arrive at Augusta until between ten and eleven o'clock at night. Charles had waited at the depot until nine; was taken with a chill and had to leave. But Titus was there to meet me, and I found Carrie with a bright fire and hot cup of tea and a most warm welcome. She and the dear children are looking better than I ever saw them, and Charles Colcock Jones, Jr., is a precious boy—fat and amiable: the best baby, she says, they ever had. She has heard but once from Joe since he reached Washington, and nothing of the trial yet.

Charles and I and the freedmen left Augusta Friday night at seven o'clock. Soon as we reached the Waynesboro depot, the rain came down in torrents and continued until we got to Waynesboro, where we took hacks twelve o'clock at night and rode until one o'clock the next day—a distance, I think, of fifty-five miles—when we took the car again. This was a car with a wooden seat running on two sides: no cushions and very rough. To transport our *baggage alone* cost thirty-seven dollars from Augusta to Savannah, and fifteen dollars apiece for passage money. Charles had to dispose of some of his Southwestern Railroad stock to enable me to get down. Flora and Milton had transportation for themselves but not their baggage. If the river had been up we would have taken the boats. We will go out to Liberty as soon as we can get a conveyance. . . .

Do thank Mrs. Hull for the delightful rolls; I ate nothing else coming down. And tell my dear cousin Joe's little children were delighted with her wafers. And your bountiful supply was shared with General Hardee and his daughter, who were our traveling companions from Augusta to Savannah. The railroad will not be finished probably before January.

I do not care about Niger's plans, and had not a chance to talk with him.

Be sure you charge him room rent, and make him cut your wood. Adeline and Grace are here. Adeline is cooking for Mrs. Harriss, and Grace sewing for her living. Alfred has just called to see me, and says he has Dunwody's trunk safely. Do let him know it.

Tuesday. Last night, to my surprise, Dunwody came in and reported all well when he left. I was rejoiced to hear from my dear brother and family. Patience and Porter still in Baker. Dunwody brought on the buggy and horse.

We are hoping to get transportation in a U.S. wagon to Liberty. If so, will try on its return to send in your bale of bedding and Robert's box of books as far as Savannah. Dr. Howard offers to give them house room; and at any time that you order them up, he will forward them to you. He says the river will not rise before January, and by that time the Central Railroad via Augusta will be finished. As it will cost you nothing to get these things to Savannah, it bethought me a good plan for helping to get them thus far on the way to Atlanta. Dr. and Mrs. Howard live in Jones Street between Whitaker and Barnard. He intends moving to Atlanta another year, and says as Robert is to be his pastor, he must take care of your things.

Reports from Liberty are very dreadful. I can only go and see for myself; and if I am endangered by staying, I must seek a home elsewhere. . . . Oh, how I shall miss you all! Sometimes that dreadful loneliness seems more than I can bear. . . . Your letters to me had best come directed to Rev. I. S. K. Axson, D.D., *for Mrs. C. C. Jones,* until we get a mail to Liberty. . . . Kiss my precious children over and over for me. And the best of love for yourself and Robert, with grateful recollections of all your love and kindness. . . . Do write me all about yourself and the children, and take care of your health.

Ever, my dear daughter, your affectionate mother,
Mary Jones.

Mrs. Mary Jones *to* Rev. R. Q. Mallard[t]
Savannah, *Tuesday,* October 17th, 1865

My dear Son Robert,

Dr. Axson and Charles and all with whom I have conversed think the *History* ought not, and probably cannot, be printed under four dollars per volume: eight dollars for the two volumes. *So please fix the price at that rate. If printed otherwise, you could take your pen and alter the circulars before they are distributed, making four dollars per volume, eight dollars for the two.* I must trouble you to distribute the circulars, if ready, both at Synod and the assembly if you are there. If you fail to go, perhaps some friend would interest themselves to do so. I would be glad to receive some of them, but shall be so isolated it will not be possible for me to do much. Do keep an account of any expense you may be at, and I will see that you are refunded.

If you see or hear from Joseph, do let him know that Mr. Rogers has

kindly offered to furnish the paper for the first edition, and wishes to know
how large it will be and when required, that he may order the paper. I
have written Joseph on the subject, but fear he may not have received it.
. . . I write in haste, but with much love.

Ever your affectionate mother,

Mary Jones.

Give much love to dear Carrie and the children. Ask her to send the package for Eva to Mrs. Eve. And you must take the other to little Mary for me.

Mrs. Mary Jones *to* Mrs. Mary S. Mallard[t]

Montevideo, *Wednesday,* October 25th, 1865

My dearest Daughter,

After many days' delay in waiting for transportation your brother succeeded in getting a carriage and wagon, and we reached home on the evening
of the 20th. The road was exceedingly rough. We expected the buggy to
meet us at the courthouse, but Gilbert did not get the message in time, so
we had to take the carriage all the way.

We stopped at Midway and stayed as long as we possibly could. I felt
grateful that I was permitted once more to kneel by that precious grave.
Everything within was untouched, only much overgrown with weeds and
bushes. But it was distressing to see the condition of the church: doors and
windows open, shutters off; and the sheep had evidently taken shelter in the
aisles. Every house around the church was destroyed.

We reached home about dusk, and found the servants apparently glad to
see us. But Mr. Fennell soon informed us that freedom had done its work
here as elsewhere. We found George, July, and young Gilbert had left for
the Albany & Gulf Railroad; and Jack, who had just arrived a day or two
before, had left for Savannah in company with Dick and Anthony from
Indianola. Mr. Fennell reports not one-fourth work done in months, and a
system of stealing here and at Arcadia regularly carried on. At Arcadia
the whole of the cotton had been stolen, and all from here, although we had
scarcely any.

I wrote you that I would send in the bedding and books; but as we failed
to get a U.S. wagon, I was unable to do so, but sent by return of the small
wagon which brought our baggage two mattresses and one feather bed. I
did not send pillows and bolster, as the bundle was large, and I knew you
could do without them.

Charles begs me to say to Lucy he sends best love to her, and wants to
see her, and will come up as soon as the way is open and he has the means.
At the present rates and mode of conveyance it is very difficult and very
expensive to get along. It cost me over one hundred dollars to get out here,
and had also transportation for the servants. You have no idea how expensive
traveling is. Your brother has advanced me the means, or I could not get
along.

I find everything in good preservation here, but a great deal to put to rights. Do not know when Patience and Porter will come. Sue, Flora, and Milton compose my household. We have not yet made any arrangements for another year. I hope you insist on Niger's paying for his room. I am not at all anxious to have him or his family, but if they come and will attend to their work, I will do the best I can by them. If not, they will find no home either here or at Arcadia.

Charles will see about renting Arcadia when he returns from Savannah. He goes in tomorrow, D.V., to meet Mr. Ward and determine his future arrangements.

Mr. Buttolph and your aunt spent last night and dined with us today. All well, and send much love to you all. Mr. Buttolph will preach Willie King's funeral sermon next Sabbath at Flemington. As I will have no buggy, Mr. Buttolph calls for me on Saturday. . . . I have seen no one to inquire of Robert's family. . . . I wish, my darling child, you and your precious children were here with me. Everything is charming to the eye. . . . I think constantly of you and pray God to bless and keep you all and provide for you.

As usual, I write in haste. It is after twelve o'clock at night, and I must close. Will write our beloved relatives as soon as I have seen a few friends and heard the news. Give my warmest love to them. Best love for yourself and Robert, and many kisses for my dear grandchildren. . . . Good night, my darling child. The Lord ever bless and keep you!

Your affectionate mother,
Mary Jones.

Do write me *when* our assembly meets.

REV. JOHN JONES *to* MRS. MARY JONES[t]

Refuge, *Tuesday,* October 31st, 1865

My dearest Sister,

I am truly glad to hear from you today by Dunwody and through your letter to me. Oh, for the privilege of an interview with you!

I am grieved to think of the cruel disappointment that awaits you touching those two servants Porter and Patience, in whom you have trusted so much, and from whom you expect so much. I wrote you most fully (via Atlanta, enclosed to Robert) of my entire failure to induce Porter to enter into any contract at all for 1866 for himself and family. I would have sent them to Thomasville and have given them the transportation you sent for them; but I was bound to follow your directions in the matter, and believe your views are right. I would not allow them to live with me unless they gave unmistakable evidences of repentance and came fully to my terms. I am astonished and vexed at their conduct; and yet I cannot say any more of my own servants. Not one can I depend on to remain with us another year. I believe

William would remain, but his stupid wife will not listen to any counsel on the subject.

Alas, our future is dark—and grows darker! . . . And the health of my dear wife is wretched. She is no better: she is reduced sadly, and those exhausting hemorrhages still continue. . . . I am often very miserable. No prospect of a church before me, and no school for our boys. . . . My crop is not a third-crop. My having to plant so late exposed, the crop to the drought, and there was no recovery. It is impossible for me to keep all of our people, even if they should stay. And to turn them off—although they seem so indifferent to me—will be painful. Oh, let us remember each other continually at a throne of grace!

My dear Jane, Mother, dear Sister Mary, and the boys unite with me in best love to you.

Your devoted brother,
J. Jones.

What shall I do with the transportation you sent me?

Mrs. Mary Jones *to* Mrs. Mary S. Mallard[t]

Montevideo, *Tuesday,* November 7th, 1865

My dear Daughter,

Hearing that Mrs. Winn would go to Savannah day after tomorrow, I embrace the opportunity of sending you a line. We have still no mails, and I have not had a line from you since I left Atlanta. Have written you several times. Robert's kind favor from Augusta has just reached me, but not the circulars, or the letter with information of my brother. I have been exceedingly anxious to hear from him and to know if I may expect Porter and Patience.

The past has been quite a week of trial. *Sam* (Sue's husband) came from Savannah and announced his intention of taking her to a *farm* near Savannah. I spoke with Sue and reminded her of Sam's want of fidelity to her, and the unjust and unkind manner in which he had often treated her. She, however, decided to go; and I told her if so, I preferred she should go at once; whereupon she withdrew Elizabeth in the midst of our last rice-cutting, and they have been for a week beating rice and grinding and washing and walking about at large. I told Sue if she was ever in want or ill-treated, she must return to me. She replied: "No, ma'am, I'll never come back, for you told me to go," thus in a saucy way perverting my remark. As Sam's farm was not exactly ready for their reception, today a cart drove up, and they left to remain at Mr. Lyons' at Riceboro for the present. Although Sue has been disrespectful to me and shown a very perverse spirit, I do remember all her former fidelity; and I am truly sorry for her, for I believe she will feel the loss of her comfortable home. Flora announced if her aunty went she would not stay by herself, so I presume when it suits her convenience she too will go. Even Gilbert (through his wife Fanny) has the matter of change under consideration. What is Charles's ultimate design I cannot tell. I spoke with him soon after I came home and advised him as strongly as I could to go to Atlanta, and he told me he would do so. I hope he will on Lucy's account. But I am thoroughly disgusted with the whole race. I could fill my sheet with details of dishonesty at Montevideo and Arcadia, but my heart sickens at the recital, and a prospect of dwelling with them. For the present it appears duty to do so.

It is a great comfort and support to have your brother with me. He will go to Augusta very soon, and meet Mr. Ward in Savannah. I am told they are proposing to run him for Congress. When last in Savannah he was approached on the subject by some of his friends, *but declined*. I should regret very much to see him enter political life at this juncture of *his life* and the disturbed condition of the country, to say nothing of pecuniary considerations. We are all bankrupt, and only industry and economy will enable us, with God's blessing upon us, to earn a support.

My precious child, I think of you constantly, and wish you had one-half of this large and comfortable home and furniture. When you will ever be able to get anything from here is uncertain, as they are so slow in completing the Central Railroad. The Albany & Gulf Road is done to No. 4 from Doctortown, and I believe they are working also from the Savannah side. I have not had time to examine your crockery, but from the view taken hope the most of it is saved. I have no doubt many things could be sold if people could pay for them.

Your brother sent all his furniture to auction and sold it. Only a very small part remained, and that very much abused. With the proceeds he has bought me a pair of mules and wagon. His library and Indian remains are saved.

We have been trimming up, and the garden and lawn are looking beautifully. Tomorrow we begin to grind cane, and I wish the children were here to enjoy it. I will have some nice stalks saved to send them if possible.

Last Sabbath we took the mule and buggy and attended church at Flemington. It was Communion, and a full attendance. Mr. Buttolph preaches but once, as many persons walk, and they cannot begin before twelve o'clock. They have organized a Presbyterian church, and only await the meeting of Presbytery to have it regularly constituted. . . . Julia and her family and your uncle were out. . . . They are all coming down very soon to South Hampton, and then your uncle will be with us. I hope I may only have someone left to cook and wash!

Sabbath week Mr. Buttolph preached Willie's funeral sermon. It was very interesting, and I asked him to throw the facts into the form of a tract, believing it would do good.

Do give warmest love to our dear relatives at the Stone House; I will try and write them a long letter very soon. We are now going to dine and ride to see Mrs. Winn and get her to take our letters into Savannah. Kiss my precious children for Grandmother. Oh, how I have missed you all! . . . *Milton* has been a comfort to me since I returned; hope I may keep him. . . . Mr. Alexander and our dear Marion Glen are to be married! . . . Remember me to Mrs. Hull and all inquiring friends. With best love for Robert and yourself, my darling child, and remembrances for Ellen and the servants,

Ever your affectionate mother,
Mary Jones.

MRS. MARY JONES *to* MRS. MARY S. MALLARD[t]

Montevideo, *Monday,* November 13th, 1865

My dearest Daughter,

Although I have been on my feet all day, and it is now near twelve o'clock at night, I must send you a line by your brother, who expects to leave in the morning in company with Mr. Owens, who arrived night before the last. And Audley has been with us all day and is spending the night. And tomorrow I expect your uncle.

Your letter was handed me on Sabbath, and I was rejoiced to hear from you, but sorry to know that you are still suffering from your teeth. I wish they were all removed and you had a painless set.

The conduct of Patience and Porter is strange, but I am not surprised. I am glad you wrote your dear uncle not to send any of the people from Baker. I do not wish them, and will probably be able to hire very few, and expect by January I may not have one of my old servants about, unless Gilbert remains. This is very sad *and* perplexing, but I trust the Lord will provide for me. Your brother will write your uncle for me about Patience and Porter. I think Robert will find a very sorry account of Mr. Quarterman's management at Arcadia and the conduct of the people.

I hope to write my dear aunt and cousins very soon; I have been so busy, have not had time. Tell my dear little granddaughter I will be very proud of her letter, and she must certainly send it. Tell Lucy Charles and her mother and all the people send howdies for her and Tenah. I think you ought to make "Mr. Niger" pay like a "gentleman" for his many privileges. Do look if I left my knitting. And would be glad if when Robert comes down he would bring my quilt patches and scraps from the trunk. I wrote asking that he would not receive any more money, but only get subscriptions. I am very much obliged for his interest and efforts. Good night, my darling child. With much love to Robert, and kisses for my dear children, and howdies for the servants,

Ever your affectionate mother,
Mary Jones.

II

Mr. Charles C. Jones, Jr., *to* Mrs. Mary Jones[t]

Savannah, *Wednesday,* November 15th, 1865

My very dear Mother,

We safely arrived in Savannah after a wet and rough ride between five and six o'clock P.M. Found Mr. Ward here. Gilbert did not return today; I thought it best to let Rescue rest for the day, as the trip had been fatiguing. He will, D.V., go out in the morning, and will carry the salt, which, being Liverpool, I hope you will find excellent. I have given Gilbert $5.00 and a pair of shoes ($2.50), and send a pair of shoes for Charles ($2.00); also for Mr. Fennell two handkerchiefs ($1.00). I mention these amounts so that you may, if you please, make a memorandum of them, so as to see exactly how we stand with them in case of any settlement.

Broughton was not open when we passed through the Boro. I write him by Gilbert in reference to the syrup.

Amanda thanks you very sincerely for the syrup and butter, both of which were most acceptable to her. Mrs. Axson also desires her sincere thanks for your very kind remembrance of her.

Letters from Eva. Ruthie is the picture of health and happiness, but Eva has been suffering very much, and I fear is no better. The attending physician advises a colder climate and an early change if practicable.

Mr. Ward will not resume practice in Savannah. He has made every arrangement for opening an office in New York, and has offered me a full copartnership with him. The prospects for success, under God, appear flattering. It seems a providential opening for me in more respects than one. I believe that if I go, I will be able better to provide for your comfort, my dear mother, than I otherwise could. I would also be able to meet the desired change for the benefit of Eva's health. I believe that your health would be greatly benefited by a change of air next summer, if not sooner. I will see Eva on the subject, and will prayerfully ask advice from above. It is a great change—a grave undertaking. I want to do what is best for you, my dear mother, and my dear wife and our sweet little daughter. The more I see of Savannah, the more am I convinced that there is—for the present, at least —but little prospect for aught else than a living. If practicable, I must try and do more. If I do conclude to go to New York, it will, D.V., not be before the middle or last of December.

A letter from Mr. Sconyers tells me that matters are progressing at Indianola only tolerably well. I will go there and see what can be done in reference to the Negroes. I am also making inquiries in reference to the sale of our plantations.

I told Gilbert to look around and see for himself the condition of things. He tells me he has been doing so, and that from all he can see and learn, he feels that home is the best place for him and his family. He will tell you all, and has promised me to do all that he can for you.

Dined with George Owens today, and took tea with Major and Mrs. Porter. All friends well, and unite in much love. I expect to leave for Augusta on Friday morning. Do, my dear mother, let me know if you need anything. God knows that my highest human wishes, hopes, and desires are to conduce to the comfort and happiness of yourself and my precious wife and child. To this I will sacrifice everything; and for the attainment of this end I am prepared now and always as He gives me strength to attempt all, to endure all, and to labor without ceasing. I hope to see you again, D.V., within three weeks. Remember me to all friends. Do not forget to prepare that biography of dear Father. With warmest love, I am ever, my dearest mother,
Your affectionate son,
Charles C. Jones, Jr.
May the good God have you ever in His special favor and protection!

Mr. Charles C. Jones, Jr., *to* Mrs. Mary Jones[t]
Savannah, *Thursday,* November 16th, 1865
My very dear Mother,

I have offered Montevideo plantation for sale (exclusive of furniture, crop, animals, and farming utensils) at thirty thousand dollars in specie, Arcadia tract at fifteen dollars in specie per acre, Maybank tract for eight thousand dollars in specie. In case any of the parties desiring to purchase come out, you will thus know the terms proposed. The places should not be sacrificed. If they can be sold for what we conceive their full value, it may be well to let them go. The descriptions, etc., are in the hands of Messrs. W. H. Burroughs & Company of this city. They will communicate with me before anything is definitely determined upon.

I leave, D.V., in the morning for Augusta. With warmest love, I am ever
Your affectionate son,
C.
Gilbert tells me that he will do his whole duty, and stand by you to the last. He says Anthony and Dick have gone back to Indianola.

Mrs. Mary Jones *to* Mrs. Mary S. Mallard[t]
Montevideo, *Friday,* November 17th, 1865*
My darling Child,

I wrote you this week by your brother, but hearing that Fred was going to Atlanta, I could not miss the opportunity of sending you a letter. I have been busy the most of the week grinding cane, but we have been much interrupted by rain, which has fallen in torrents. The day your brother went into Savannah it poured all day. Gilbert has just returned, having slept on the road last night, the situation of the roads and bridges preventing his reaching home.

Your brother will doubtless write you of his future plans and prospects. I trust the Lord will guide him aright. If he were only a truly converted man —a Christian—my heart would be at rest for him. I hope you do not forget to pray for him; God's Spirit can and I hope will regenerate his heart. He has in his life been called to deep sorrows, and is now enduring an entire prostration of pecuniary means after having acquired an independent support. It is very painful to me to know that I have it not in my power to aid either of my dear children, and that they have all to struggle hard to maintain their families. It is with peculiar sorrow that I think, my dear child, of your uncomfortable situation—not even a carpet on your floor or a pair of andirons in your chimney, and the severe winter soon to set in.

The Albany & Gulf Road, I am told, will not be in running order before February, and the roads to Savannah are almost laid aside. But I see by today's paper brought by Gilbert (for we have no mails) that Captain Charlie will soon be running to Riceboro, and also that freights up to Augusta via the boats have been reduced. Have you received your bedding sent to Savannah by return of the wagon in which we came? I sent two mattresses and one feather bed. The bundle was so large I had to remove the bolsters and pillows I had put in for you, but I knew you were supplied in pillows. Do write and let me know if you wish anything shipped at any time by the vessel.

The military authorities have been sending out a squad of soldiers to detect stolen articles from the crackers and recover them. I wish your things could be recovered. And I would be glad to get all my chairs and kitchen things back.

As I wrote you, Sue had left. She is still at the Boro, and I am told has hired Elizabeth to work at Dr. Samuel Jones's. Flora is in a most unhappy and uncomfortable condition, doing very little, and that poorly. . . . I think Flora will certainly leave when she is ready. I overheard an amusing conversation between Cook Kate and herself: they are looking forward to gold watches and chains, bracelets, and *blue veils* and silk dresses! Jack has entered a boardinghouse in Savannah, where I presume he will practice attitudes and act the Congo gentleman to perfection. Porter and Patience will provide for themselves. I shall cease my anxieties for the race. My life long (I mean since I had a home) I have been laboring and caring for them, and since the war have labored with all my might to supply their wants, and expended everything I had upon their support, directly or indirectly; and this is their return.

You can have no conception of the condition of things. I understand Dr. Harris and Mr. Varnedoe will rent their lands to the Negroes! The conduct of some of the citizens has been very injurious to the best interest of the community. At times my heart is so heavy I feel as if it would give way, and that I cannot remain. But I have no other home, and if I desert it, everything will go to ruin. Mr. Fennell has done all he could to protect my interest; but he is feeble physically, and I do not know that he has any special gift at management. I believe him to be an honest and excellent man. We planted only a half-crop of provisions here, and they did not work one-fourth of their time. Judge the results: not a pod of cotton planted, and all I had stolen, and the whole of that at Arcadia gone. You know I wished Little Andrew to return to Montevideo after Mr. Buttolph decided not to go to Baker, as he was our best plowman. He did not do so. Wanting help at this time in grinding cane, I wished him to come down. He did so, stayed part of a day, and walked off. I have not heard of him since. This is a specimen of their conduct. It is thought there will be a great many returning to the county; I do not believe so.

I have mentioned all the news I could collect in Aunty's letter, and refer you to that.

I hope Robert received your brother's letter in reference to the circulars. All we want at present is to obtain subscribers. The work probably cannot be published under a year. I have requested Joseph to confer with Mr. Rogers about the paper he so generously and kindly offered to give for printing the first edition. Do let him know where Mr. Rogers is.

I have just called Charles and asked if he had any messages. "He sends love to Lucy and Tenah, and begs to be remembered to you, and says he will make an opportunity to come and see them before long." This is the sum and substance of his message. It is impossible to get at any of their intentions, and it is useless to ask them. I see only a dark future for the whole race. . . . Do write me all about yourself and the dear children and Robert and the church. . . . Kiss my precious grandchildren. If they were here they should eat sugar cane all day and boil candy at night. . . . The Lord bless you, my dear child!

Ever your affectionate mother,
Mary Jones.

MR. CHARLES C. JONES, JR., *to* MRS. MARY JONES[t]

Augusta, *Sunday,* November 26th, 1865

My dear Mother,

Before leaving Savannah I wrote you a letter telling you of the proposition which had been made me by Mr. Ward to join him in New York in the practice of the law. I have had the matter under very careful consideration, and have concluded to accept. I find Eva's health very delicate; and her physicians advise as necessary a change at the earliest practicable moment to a colder climate. We hope to sail from Savannah by the 20th prox. if possible, and expect to be with you within the next two weeks. I trust thus, my dear mother, if God spares my life, to be able to secure a home and a support for you. And you know, wherever I go and whatever I do, that I am always your devoted son, ready and most anxious at all times to do all in my power for your comfort and happiness; and further, that my house is always your home.

I called up all the Negroes at Indianola, and the only ones who expressed a willingness to go to Montevideo were: Clarissa and her children (May, Chloe, John, and Jane), Sam and his wife, Big Miley and her girls (Phillis and Lucy), and Silvia and her husband (Billy). All the rest say that they are going they do not know where exactly, but all nearly decide upon a return to Liberty. The women are the controlling spirits. Stepney and Pharaoh are very desirous of going to Arcadia, there to work upon any terms imposed. They were all greatly staggered when I told them I expected to sell Arcadia. Little Tom has ever since my absence been working on his own account upon the adjoining plantations. He says he is going with his father to Liberty, and his father expects to return to White Oak with Martha and the rest of his children. William, Kate, and family expect to go to Liberty, but not to Montevideo or to Arcadia. Abram purposes the same thing. Robert and family, Niger and family, Pharaoh and family, and Hannah expect to do the same thing. Maria is going to hunt for Dick. Rose says she is going with Cato. Little Miley goes with her husband. Mary goes with her husband. Elsie and family go to Syphax. Hannah goes with Pharaoh. Peggy wishes to go with Sue. Dick and Anthony have already left the plantation. You thus have all their expectations. The very best of them are those who wish to go to you at Montevideo. I will make all necessary arrangements. Tom says he will go down to Montevideo in two weeks, and will then make the shoes for the people—that he cannot do so without measures. This, I think, is merely an excuse. I have for you about a hundred yards of cloth, and all the Negroes who come down to you have received shoes and clothing. Will be able, I think, to supply you with corn from Indianola.

Will write you again very soon. Ruthie is very well, and sends sweetest kisses to her dear "danna." Eva unites in warmest love. Brother and family all well. Have attended to all your commissions, and will explain everything when I come. I am ever, my dear mother,

Your affectionate son,
Charles C. Jones, Jr.

Mr. Charles C. Jones, Jr., *to* Mrs. Mary S. Mallard[t]

Augusta, *Thursday,* November 30th, 1865

My very dear Sister,

Upon my return from Liberty I posted for you a letter from Mother which you have doubtless received before this. I remained about three weeks with her at Montevideo, and did all that I could to make her comfortable and repair the damages which had been caused by the enemy. Everything was progressing pretty well when I left, and the servants were orderly, respectful, and at their work. The use of this free labor is an absolute experiment; and while I hope that by March next we may be able to control it to at least a limited extent, I very much fear that for some time to come there will result but little profit from its employment. Poverty and severe legislation can alone render it available. At Arcadia I found everything at loose ends. I think it best for all concerned that this place be sold at the earliest practicable moment, if such sale can be negotiated upon advantageous terms. I am offering it at fifteen dollars in gold per acre, but very much doubt if such a sum can be realized. The Negroes on the place have done nothing for the past year, and Mr. Quarterman has been of little service. All the cotton has been stolen.

Eva's health for four or five months past has been very delicate, and the physicians advise a radical change of scene and air at the earliest practicable moment. Mr. Ward and myself expect to open a law office in New York City on the 1st of January next, and I expect to sail for New York with Eva and Ruthie from Savannah by the 20th December. The condition of Eva's health urges me mainly to the move. I find also in the depressed condition of affairs in Savannah that there is a chance there only for a bare subsistence. I utterly failed also in securing a house. It is a grave change; and it is with a heavy heart, my dear sister, that I contemplate an absence from all who are nearest and dearest to me, and from my native state. I go to New York also as a pauper upon borrowed money. But I hope that the motives which impel me there are correct. I have endeavored to seek guidance from above in determining the grave matter; with God's blessing I trust that we will succeed. Every energy will be devoted to the prosecution of the duties which will devolve upon me, and I hope that I may be able to secure there a home for Mother, where you will always find your room ready, and warm hearts waiting to welcome you.

I am sorry that we will not probably see you before we leave. Did you receive the bundle of bedding? I shipped it from Savannah. We leave here by the 10th to spend a week with Mother. Enclosed please find a photograph of our beloved and honored father; it is one of a number which I had taken in Savannah. I trust, my dear sister, that you are better, and that God will deal graciously with you and yours. Eva and Ruthie unite with me in warmest love to self, Robert, and the little ones. Brother and family well. The doctor is as usual laboring too hard. God bless you, my dear sister! Wherever I go, remember that I am always, in tenderest love and affection,

Your own brother,
Charles C. Jones, Jr.

Mrs. Mary Jones *to* Mrs. Mary S. Mallard[t]
Montevideo, Saturday, December 9th, 1865*

My dearest Daughter,

I feel even at a late hour that I cannot close the record of the past week without sending you a line before retiring; and think I will adopt the plan of writing you daily if I can, so as always to have a letter on hand for the opportunity that may offer through friends of sending it to you.

The past has been a troublous week, and yet one of mercies too. In the midst of perplexities I have had friends to counsel and to cheer me. Your aunt and Jimmie have been with me for two weeks, and your uncle came on last Tuesday. Mr. Buttolph has been here frequently, and Emily and Mr. Green spent a day with me last week. Yesterday Sister Susan left, and Mr. Buttolph today.

On Monday of this week Anne and Dr. Adams came and brought your last letter. Your aunt and I were just going over to the Retreat at the time. They did not tarry long. We started as soon as they left, and had just reached the turn of the road by the chapel when, discovering Sam (Sue's husband), we stopped and hailed him. He came up and presented a *yellow* letter marked "Official Business," addressed to your brother. I opened it and found an order from the bureau stating that as we had refused to pay Sue and her niece wages, we were now ordered to do so or show reason at that bureau for refusing—at fifteen dollars per month for the two from August 1st! We returned to the house, and I replied in full to Colonel Sickles, and made Sam take the reply immediately back with him to Savannah. What the result will be I cannot imagine.

We then proceeded to the Retreat and spent the day until sunset cleaning out the graveyard, which was a perfect wilderness. We cut away the trees which were injuring the tombs, and put the yard in complete order. I hired two axmen that did good service, as there was much to do.

I believe I have written you that we spent a day the week before at Midway, and put our precious enclosure there in perfect order. I have been thankful to show this mark of respect and affection to our beloved ones who are in their peaceful graves. Oh, how peaceful when compared to our days of sorrow and perplexity! When I had finished I went alone into our old church and knelt before the pulpit and there pled with the God of our Fathers that He would not forsake His ancient heritage, but remember the desolations of His own Zion; and although parted and scattered He would once more be favorable unto us, send us help from the sanctuary, and strengthen us out of Zion. I prayed that the prayers and tears of the pious dead might come up in remembrance before the throne; but above all that He who had given His precious Blood for the life of the Church would once more lift upon us the light of His countenance and arise with healing in His wings to our bleeding and desolated church. When I rose from my knees I felt an assurance that God would not cast us off.

And I am happy to tell you when Mr. Buttolph came this week he put a paper into my hands. It was an invitation to renew his work at Midway and preach two Sabbaths in the month, for which they give four hundred dollars; and I presume will give quite as much at Flemington. They now furnish a most liberal supply of every kind of provisions—meats, corn, flour, syrup, potatoes, butter, etc., etc.

I will here close until Monday, D.V.

Monday Night, December 11th. I resume, my dear child, this letter. We spent a quiet Sabbath at home reading to your uncle, and had five boys in the Sunday school in the afternoon.

To return to the record of the past week. On Thursday morning Flora informed me she wished to leave immediately for Savannah. I asked the object of her visit. After some hesitation she said it was to meet Joe, but she would return. I gave her some money, and she left as soon as she had eaten her breakfast. Today I hear she did not go to Savannah, but is still in the county. About midday Patience appeared at the Negro house, and came over and attended to the rooms until Saturday morning, when she went off by sunrise, since which time only Kate and Milton are about me, and Gilbert at the stable. I am doing all the chamber work with Kate's assistance. Patience evidently designs setting up for herself, and has settled herself at Arcadia. She complains that during all the summer old Daddy Robin never received any allowance; and when the crop was shared, although strangers were brought in, he did not get a particle of corn and rice. The management on the place *has truly been astonishing!* Mr. Quarterman told me he believed *Henry* was the person who stole the cotton. The sooner that nest is broken up the better. My heart is pained and sickened with their vileness and falsehood in every way. I long to be delivered from the race. And yet if it be God's will that I remain here, I pray that He would give me a spirit of submission. You can have no idea of their deplorable state. They are perfectly deluded—will not contract or enter into any engagement for another year, and will not work now except as it pleases them. I know not from day to day if I will have one left about me or on the place. Several of them refuse positively to do any work.

December 25th. I would be glad to write the usual "Merry Christmas" to my dear children in Atlanta. I can truly say: "With God's blessing may you ever have many and happy ones!" I have just a moment to send off this sheet.

Yesterday we had preaching at our venerable old church, and are to have it every other Sabbath. All of Robert's family were there and well excepting Mrs. John and Mrs. Cyrus Mallard. The latter has been quite sick.

Steamers are now running three times a week to Sunbury, connecting by a line of hacks to Walthourville via Riceboro. If you wish, I can send your carpets or anything you wish in that way; but there must be someone in Savannah to receive and forward them. . . . We have now a company of Yankees at Riceboro, and I hope they will keep order.

Your brother has not yet arrived. I have been so anxious about him I have not slept for ten days more than a few hours at night. . . . Your uncle is very feeble; sends you his best love. My warmest love for Robert and yourself, and many kisses for my dear grandchildren. Write often. Best love to all at the Stone House. In haste,

Your ever affectionate mother,
Mary Jones.

Mrs. Eva B. Jones *to* Mrs. Mary Jones[t]

Augusta, December 1865

As Charlie tells us it will be, he thinks, almost impossible to take Ruthie out, in the present condition of the roads and derangement of all traveling facilities, to see her dear grandmama, I must write to tell her of the health, sayings, doings, progress, and arrangements made for the comfort of the little one that I know is so dear to her grandmama. She is and has been the picture of health ever since you sent her to me in August last, and I think as merry and happy a little child as I ever saw. She is at present full of going to "New Yark," as she calls it, and cannot be bought out of the fancy for going there.

We both sincerely regret that you cannot see Ruthie before she leaves. I think you would be very proud of the way in which she says her little verses. She repeats eight pieces of poetry, among them all the kings and queens of England down to the reigning monarch, Queen Vic, whose name she pronounces with great gusto—quite beautifully for such a *young personage*. Then I always tell her historical stories, and only a very few at a time, lest her little mind would be confused in hearing too many different ones. I endeavor to inculcate the greatest veneration for truth, to the exclusion of the quantities of foolish fiction prepared for the *injury* (*I* think) of infant minds of the present day. She knows the stories of "The Little Princes," "Richard the Hunchback," "Columbus and His Discovery of America," of "Alfred the Great," "Romulus and Remus," and the mythological tales of "Pyramus and Thisbe" and "Narcissus" (which she will always tell you are "not true"), and tells many of them *very well*. I wish her to know how to use good language, and so always make her tell me the last *old* story before I tell her a new. She says her catechism very well, and also her psalm and hymn. She knows quite a number of Bible stories. She has already made quite a reputation for herself, and talks quite learnedly of kings and queens. At the same time you must not fear, as I hear Mrs. Battey does, that her mind is being overburdened; for I assure you no one would take more care of that than I—the difference between her and other children being merely that she has been taught in the form of stories a *little history*, and they generally hear only of "Jack the Giant-Killer" and other equally silly tales of the nursery.

I am trying in every way possible to do my duty in *every respect* towards this little one that *you sent* to me and her father *brought;* and I trust I am succeeding. She has a clear, bright mind, a most lovely disposition; and although I am a "cruel stepmother," she is remarkably fond of me, and thinks I am quite an *institution,* although *I* say it who should not.

I have her little wardrobe all fixed up splendidly, and did it all myself; and everybody says it is beautiful. I have braided and made for her a dress and cassock of magenta delaine, all lined, the covering wadded. Then she has a reps alpaca gray paletot, lined and wadded, that I also made; three beautiful little braided sacques (my work again) lined warmly for New York; her buff suit; and an embroidered merino, a present from my dear cousin, Mrs. Bird. I have made her a pretty little balmoral, over which she wears a looped-up dress; balmoral boots coming high over the ankles; worsted stockings and leggings. She will be warmly provided for on the steamer. Everything has been made with an eye to the New York winter. Her two hats, which I trimmed myself, are *beauties,* and so pronounced by everybody. One is a beautiful leghorn I *had,* fixed over in the latest shape and trimmed with the new blue real lace and a *gold* buckle, also the inevitable *plumes.* Her other, a traveling hat, is like a little boy's cap trimmed *à la napoléonne,* and is very becoming. I have also a warm little worsted bonnet for her to wear on deck. I have dwelt on her wardrobe at some length, knowing that whatever other people might think, this would be interesting to you, as it is to me. I think if Ruthie could read what I have written, she would beg me to mention the fact of her having two standing collars and some cuffs to which she is greatly devoted.

She is beginning to use a great many big words and old-fashioned phrases, and *patronizes* people to some extent. The other day she was standing in my light, and I said, in the regular "cruel stepmother" style: "My dear, I *know* your head is empty, but it is not in the *least* transparent." She slowly moved away, pulled up a rocking chair, and said, looking at me quite steadily: "No, Mama, my head is *not* empty; it is *full* of *sense*—and of all that *poetry* you taught me *too!*" Triumphantly she concluded this phrase, and all a poor "cut-up" individual could do was to succumb and kiss her gracefully.

I trust that when you join us in New York in the spring you will find her *greatly* improved in every respect. There are the faintest indications only of her yearly eruption, and I think the Northern winter and a summer sea-bathing must certainly cure that entirely.

I wish it were possible for you to meet us in Savannah so you could see the child; she is so sweet and smart, I regret that you cannot see how much she is improved. Notwithstanding all my ill health, I keep her constantly with me. We are rarely separated. She has, however, made little or no progress in her letters, or rather, spelling. I teach her only orally, but she can count to fifty in French and to one hundred in English. I intend to teach her some French verses soon, so as to accustom her to the pronunciation and accent. So much can be done towards removing from study the hardship and lack of interest that most children discover. I want to make learning a pleasure and a pastime to Ruthie if my health permits. I never will allow her to repeat her verses if she shows the least want of interest in them.

I believe you may well rest content on the subject of her being prepared for the cold winter. She has plenty of warm blood, fine health; and if clothes can keep people warm, she *has them* of every sort and description.

I regretted so much that Charlie was unable to see Mrs. Mallard. She only came down for one day, and had left her baby to say good-bye to him. She is entirely lovely and lovable, I think. And with such a daughter and *such a son* as Charlie is, you must be a very happy mother. I have no doubt that Carrie would here announce to you and the public *generally* that the Doctor was of all the brightest and the best. But I allow no such thing. Nobody—not even his brother—shall come near him when I speak of his perfections. He is quite an angel—though I believe I am the only one that has found *that out!*

With warmest kisses from your sweet little grandchild, kind remembrances from Mother, I am

Affectionately yours,
Eva.

Mr. Charles C. Jones, Jr., *to* Mrs. Mary Jones[t]

New York, *Friday,* December 29th, 1865

My dearest Mother,

I embrace the earliest opportunity of announcing the fact of our arrival in this city, through God's mercy, in safety. As I wrote you, we sailed in the *San Salvador,* leaving Savannah on the 23rd inst. In consequence of unusually rough weather and continued fogs, our passage was protracted, and during a considerable portion of the time quite uncomfortable. To escape the violence of the storm we ran into Port Royal harbor and remained at anchor there one night. We reached the city last evening. Found our rooms at 132 East 16th Street all ready for us, through Mr. Ward's kindness. And now, in our office for the first time this morning, I write my first letter to you.

Eva and Ruthie stood the voyage pretty well. Eva is so feeble that she suffered not a little; but Ruthie, with the exception of a few hours during the violence of the first storm, was as well and lively as she could be. She made friends with everyone, and laid everybody and everything under contribution for her amusement and pleasure. She won the hearts of all, and made the captain of the steamer her special playmate.

We are comfortably located, at least as much so as our present means will allow. Our office is on Broadway near Trinity Church. We hope to do a good business, and will, God helping us, bring to the discharge of all duties devolving upon us our every energy and attention. I hope, my dear mother, soon to be able to provide a home and a support for you. Come to me whenever you can, and let me know if I can serve you in any way.

Eva, who will write you very shortly, and Ruthie unite in tenderest love and kisses. And I am ever

Your affectionate son,
Charles C. Jones, Jr.

Direct your letters to me care of Ward & Jones, 119 Broadway, New York.

Mr. Charles C. Jones, Jr., *to* Mrs. Mary Jones[t]

New York, *Saturday,* January 6th, 1866

My very dear Mother,

I am just out of a sickroom, where I have been confined for a week past. Although still quite feeble, I am better, and hope, God willing, soon to be well again. Eva still continues quite unwell, but she has scarcely yet been enabled to derive any advantage from the change, as we have had clouds and snow almost daily. Ruthie is the picture of good health. We are as comfortable as our means will allow, and have rooms at 132 East 16th Street.

I am all anxiety, my dear mother, to know how you are, and how you are getting along. Please let me know all about your precious self and your plans, and the exact posture of affairs. Let me know what you want, and you shall have it. We hope that our prospects are encouraging; we are, however, but beginners. I am trying to see if I can get a good offer for Arcadia. You will have to make the conveyance as executrix, as the deed of gift was never recorded. This will be the simplest plan. Under the will you have the power, you know, to change the investment of any or all of the property by sale or otherwise, so that there will be no difficulty in your making titles at any time to any of the property should you deem it best to sell and change investment. Messrs. Jackson & Lawton in Savannah will at any moment prepare any papers you may desire.

Miss Clay called to see Eva yesterday. She was quite well. She was in for a day from Newark, New Jersey.

I pray God, my dearest mother, to be ever near and bless you, preserving you from every fear and harm. Do write us as soon as you can and let me know what I can do for you. Eva and Daughter unite in tenderest love and kisses. And I am ever

Your affectionate son,
Charles C. Jones, Jr.

Love to all relatives, and kind remembrances to friends. Did you receive the package I sent you from Savannah? The cloth and leather I left at Dr. Howard's for you. Do not be in too great a hurry to sell your rice unless you get a fair price for it. Seed rice will be very scarce, and you ought to get a high price for it—say, three to three and a half to four dollars a bushel for it. I would put everything I could in cotton.

REV. JOHN JONES *to* MRS. MARY JONES[t]

Refuge, Tuesday, January 9th, 1866

My dearest Sister,

Some ten days since, I asked our friend Mr. S. S. Barnard to inform me in good time of his leaving, that I might write you at length. He promised to do so. Yesterday I returned from Whitney, having preached for the people on Sabbath. Today I crossed the creek on foot to inquire into Mr. Barnard's movements, and to know if he could take some sausages and lard for you to Liberty (jar and contents about fifty pounds). I was astonished to find himself and Mr. E. Thomas packed up almost in all their wagons and expecting to leave as soon as possible. But they were in a most distressed condition. The gentleman who had promised to rent their place had not come, and it was doubtful if he could obtain hands. And they were about to leave their stock of cattle and hogs and their corn in a most unprotected condition. I advised them to pause at least until tomorrow; and I seize an hour to write you. They seemed to be so troubled that I barely mentioned to one of them that I came over to see if they could carry a jar of lard and sausages for you to Liberty. But as he made no response, I said no more. Dunwody has gone over to see them this afternoon, and I told him to touch upon the lard again. The sausages are just put up by Mother and Sister Mary and my dear Janey, and all of us are so anxious to get them to you. Oh, that I had something else worth sending you! But alas, we are in a poor condition.

I sent you a line from Atlanta when I went up to see dear Mary. I have responded to the Griffin call, and promised to preach there the first Sabbath of February, D.V. I go in advance to commence my work and arrange for the location of my family, to board if possible this year. My dear wife cannot possibly go up now, she is so feeble. . . . Mother Dunwody says she will not leave Jane until she is better. We are trying to have her and Sister Mary go with us to Griffin, and I think they will if it is possible. Their worldly means are greatly reduced; if we can get a house eventually in Griffin and all live together and share expenses, we may be mutual helps.

My dear sister, I know you will remember me, as you have always done, in my passing into a new field of labor. I feel that my time for usefulness is growing short, and that I must be exceedingly diligent. I am fifty years of age. Well do I remember the solemn emphasis of my dear brother as he said to me in the winter of 1854: "John, I am fifty years old!" Oh, to feel like him so dearly to the precious Redeemer, and to be in some measure as faithful as he was! I thank you for his photograph; it is excellent. Charles Colcock had also sent me one. I have put it in my family Bible, where I can see it every day and think of him.

Dear Sister, shall we ever be near to each other again? I trust you will go to Atlanta, and then we will be in a few hours of each other. Dear Sister, may God help us to bow to His will in these wonderful revolutions and humbling circumstances! My dear Jane, Mother Dunwody, and Sister Mary and our boys all unite with me in best love to you.

Ever your affectionate brother,
J. Jones.

I must send you a special letter about our late servants, the most of whom have left me. Joe and his family and Old Mama all gone.

If the jar reaches you, the good lard is on the top and the sausages below.

Mrs. Mary Jones *to* Mrs. Mary S. Mallard[t]

Montevideo, Wednesday, January 17th, 1866

My dearest Daughter,

I write a line hastily, having just completed the "week's wash" with the use of the machine, and Kate and Milton to help, and Pulaski to bring water. The boys worked cheerfully to the tune of "I'll Away, Away." Try it: it goes finely to the up-and-down motion of a washing machine.

Since Flora left I have had Elsie waiting on me, but I think her mother influenced her to leave on last Sabbath. Porter wanted her to stay with me. Patience has acted very badly; and no one has done more to keep the servants away than Sue, as I believe.

Charles informs me he wishes to go as soon as possible to Atlanta, and Lucy must be looking for him. As he goes via Augusta and could take charge of your things, write me immediately what you would like sent up. Captain Charlie is expected daily, and he might go to Savannah on board his vessel and take charge of books or any articles sent, and at Savannah they could come up on the steamer to Augusta. The only trouble is the means. *If I had them,* you should not be without your furniture. But I am penniless.

Charles writes me from New York he hopes to sell Arcadia. I presume he has corresponded with your brother and Robert and yourself on the subject. I think as you are all away from the county, it would be best to do so, for the place has been running down very fast and is becoming very dilapidated. As landed property there is none more valuable in Liberty County. The Negroes have ruled there entirely this year.

Do *write immediately* if I shall send any things by Charles. . . . Give much love to our dear relatives at the Stone House. Your uncle is quite feeble, and I have to watch over him daily. . . . Audley has written Robert about Dr. Wells: he was a surgeon in the Federal army! I feel that we want our own men to fill posts of honor and profit, not those who have brought us to grief and ruin. . . . Kiss my precious children. And best love to Robert and yourself from

Your ever affectionate mother,
Mary Jones.

Many thanks for the delightful coffee.

MR. CHARLES C. JONES, JR., *to* MRS. MARY JONES[t]

Savannah, Wednesday, January 17th, 1866

My beloved Mother,

I am here on a matter of business which I hope to be able to conclude in time to be with you on Monday next. If not on Monday, then on Wednesday. I will come, D.V., by way of Sunbury.

I left Eva, I trust, improving, and Ruthie in perfect health. She has sent you her likeness, which I forward in advance.

I will probably bring out with me a German, who goes out to look at the plantations. I hope that I will be able to lease or sell Arcadia to him. He will also look at Montevideo and the Island if you desire it.

With tenderest love, and overjoyed at the prospect, God willing, of being so soon with you, I am ever, my dear mother,

Your affectionate son,
Charles C. Jones, Jr.

MR. CHARLES C. JONES, JR., *to* MRS. MARY JONES[t]
                    New York, *Sunday,* February 11th, 1866

My very dear Mother,

Enclosed is a photograph of your dear little Ruthie, which she sends with warmest love to her dear "danna." I think you will agree with us that the likeness is excellent; and I am persuaded that Eva deserves great credit for the artistic design of the picture.

I reached New York only yesterday after a most tedious journey by land. On my return I stopped for two days at Indianola and found matters progressing there much more favorably than I had expected. I have about twenty hands under contract, and they appeared to be working well and in good spirits. Silvia and Billy, Pharaoh and Lizzie have concluded to remain in Burke for the present year and have entered into the contract. They are the only ones of our former Negroes who remain with me, all the rest being strangers. I trust by this time that you have received the corn. I directed Mr. Sconyers immediately upon the receipt of the cotton seed to have the bags filled and shipped. Should you need more, my dear mother, just send the sacks back again, and they shall be replenished. I have lost heavily in hogs by the colera—or *cholera,* as the word is generally spelled.

Brother I found in Augusta looking badly. Sister Carrie and the children were all well. Spent a day in Atlanta with Sister, and was very glad to see that she was looking much better than when we parted. The little ones were all in perfect health. All anxious for Robert's return.

I returned by the way of Knoxville and Lynchburg—a long, tedious route with many interruptions and much discomfort. I find Eva looking better. I trust that this change of scene and air will very materially conduce, by the blessing of Heaven, to the early and complete restoration of her health.

I hope, my dear mother, that everything is progressing as favorably as could be expected, and that God is dealing mercifully with you. Do let me know whenever I can serve you in any way. . . . Eva and Ruthie unite in warmest love to yourself and Uncle William.

                    Your ever affectionate son,
                    Charles C. Jones, Jr.

MR. CHARLES C. JONES, JR., *to* MRS. MARY JONES[t]
                    New York, *Saturday,* February 24th, 1866

My very dear Mother,

I have had not a line from you since bidding you good-bye at Montevideo. You may imagine, therefore, how very anxious we are to hear of and from you, and to know that you are well, and that God is graciously favoring you. Please write us as soon as you can and tell us of everything at home, and particularly of your precious self.

Through God's favor I have thus far been able to sustain my family here in comparative comfort, for which we desire to be very grateful. Eva, I hope, is gradually becoming stronger, although she is not as well as I could wish. Little Ruthie is the picture of life, health, and happiness. She improves in her lessons, and is beginning to spell very well. She repeats a great many little pieces of poetry, psalms, etc., and does not forget her catechism. She often speaks of her dear "danna," and sends sweetest kisses. . . . We are confidently expecting that you will come on and spend the summer with us; and if Providence favors us, I hope to make such arrangements as will secure your comfort and happiness. Do, my dear mother, let me know if there is anything you need. At all times call upon me for anything, and you know I will always esteem it my highest pleasure and privilege to respond.

How are matters progressing at Montevideo? Mr. Sconyers writes me that the fifty-seven bushels of corn were duly shipped from Indianola. I trust that they reached you safely. Whenever you need more, send and get it. Were Messrs. John W. Anderson & Sons able to sell the rice at a good price? I saw them on the subject while in Savannah. How is it with Rescue? I hope he recovered, although I feared from your note, received while at the Pulaski House, that it was all over with him. I trust that you received in due time the package left by me with Messrs. John W. Anderson & Sons in Savannah, to be forwarded to you by earliest opportunity. It contained two pounds of the best tea I could find in the city for you, my dear mother, a pipe and tobacco for Uncle, a suit of clothes and a watch for Gilbert, and a vest for Niger. I trust that Gilbert still remains faithful. I wrote requesting you on his account to let Old Andrew and Mary Ann have allowances of corn, and that I would respond for the amount thus expended. Did Mr. Broughton make his appearance in good season, and are you pleased with him? Pharaoh and Lizzie, Old Billy and Silvia concluded to remain at Indianola for the present year. Have you been able to procure as much cotton seed as you require? Do, my dear mother, let me know if I can advise or serve you in any way. I ardently wish that I was nearer, where I could enjoy the privilege of seeing you often and of relieving you of every burden.

What we have to do is, as far as practicable, to make the Negroes content and happy, and induce them in the present change in their status to realize the obligations devolved upon them. The President's veto message has been fully endorsed here by large and enthusiastic meetings. I send you a copy of the *Times* giving a full account of everything. I do not think that Congress will be able to pass the bill over his veto. This veto is a great matter for the South, and we ought to honor the President for the manner in which he has discharged his duty.

On my way back to New York I had the pleasure of seeing Brother and family in Augusta and Sister in Atlanta. It was a great satisfaction to me to enjoy the opportunity of doing this.

We have nothing of special interest here. The weather is delightful, and reminds us of the pleasant airs and bright suns of our loved Georgia. . . . Eva and Ruthie unite in tenderest love and kisses. Remember us affectionately to Uncle William and to any inquiring friends. And believe me ever, my dear mother,

Your affectionate son,
Charles C. Jones, Jr.

Mr. Charles C. Jones, Jr., *to* Mrs. Mary Jones[t]

New York, *Monday,* February 26th, 1866

My very dear Mother,

Some two days since, I wrote you a long letter, and now add a line simply to enclose you a not very good likeness of a certainly not very handsome fellow. Well, if the picture is not as handsome as it might be (and for this the original is far more to blame than the artist, although the latter has painted the right eye of a Tipperary bully after an Irish wake instead of the mild, reflective optic of an anxious attorney), this counterfeit presentment will at least remind you of one who loves you very dearly, and earnestly prays for your every success and happiness.

I have thus far tried in vain to persuade Eva to have hers taken; but she, indulging in a little display of mock vanity, says: "Wait, Charlie, until I grow a little prettier." As this consummation so devoutly to be wished is, however, very near at hand, I think you may expect her likeness very shortly.

She and Ruthie unite in warmest love and tenderest kisses, with our love for Uncle. I am ever, my dear mother,

Your affectionate son,
Charles C. Jones, Jr.

I hope you received the likeness of Ruthie sent some two weeks since. Please forward the enclosed to Aunt Susan.

Mrs. Mary Jones *to* Mrs. Mary S. Mallard[t]

Montevideo, *Monday,* February 26th, 1866

My dear Daughter,

The whole plantation was astir at the dawn this morning—men and women moving lighter articles on their heads, and the carts carrying the heavier. Captain Charlie lies in the stream, and will move ashore this afternoon and take all aboard; and I hope they will all reach you in safety. I had a jug of syrup all prepared to send the children, but it commenced fermenting, so I concluded as the people had worked so cheerfully to share the greater part to them. And there was little prospect of its reaching you in such a disturbed condition. And if I live, D.V., will fill and send the jug full of syrup in the fall.

I had to boil all the marmalade hastily over; and Kate being sick, it was done by Lucy and badly burnt, but hope you and the children will enjoy it. Your aunt has sent you a wool mattress, and I have also sent you one, and a pair of pillows and bolster. The children's little mattress was too black and worn to send. I would have sent a trundle bedstead, but Robert thought it not worth the expense of carrying. The only articles left which could not be packed are some jars, a few kitchen things, and some chairs badly broken. You will see what I have sent you. I would have sent the entire dozen of chairs, but you know I lost two dozen of my chairs at Arcadia, and some of my bedding, and during the war used up four wool mattresses for the Negroes. The bedding which was sent you I directed Flora to put up last spring, and had not time to see what was in the bundle. We arrived late at night, and it went off by daylight the next morning, and I believe you did not get it for months. I thought Flora had put up a hair mattress, but find she did not. I have sent you a piece of new carpeting for your entry. My own carpets begin to be worn, having been fourteen years in use—all but the one bought in Augusta. And two were cut up for the *ingrates.*

Robert will tell you of my domestic affairs. I sometimes feel that nothing but stern necessity keeps me here, to which is added the abiding desire and aim to be enabled to publish your father's work. I will be much obliged to Robert to send me a list of persons to whom he has sent circulars; and I wish he would send me some more of them, as there are friends to whom I wish to send them.

Lucy was very much troubled to hear Georgia had missed her so much. She has had quite a time nursing Charles, who has not done a full day's work since he *contracted* this year. She has a bad cold, she says *contracted* by being up so much with Charles. Could you not write to Augusta and get Sue to cook and wash for you? She is a good servant, and I think as Niger is in Atlanta would like to be with you, and be permanent. If you favor the idea, *write at once,* for her scamp-brother Pulaski wants to bring her down on Mr. Lyons' plantation. I believe after all it is best to keep the old ones if they will serve, and think you would like Sue.

I must close. Your uncle unites with me in much love to you and Robert and all friends, and kisses for the children.

Ever your affectionate mother,

Mary Jones.

Thank you, my dear child, for the stamps and the breakfast shawl—a perfect comfort to me, and I live in it.

III

Miss Mary E. Robarts *to* Mrs. Mary Jones[t]

Atlanta, *Monday,* February 26th, 1866

My dearest Cousin,

We were rejoiced to welcome Mr. Mallard back and to receive your kind, affectionate, and deeply interesting letter. The past with its pleasant memories causes a pang in contrast with the present, and yet I feel thankful that amid the general ruin that has befallen us we all have some remaining mercies. Let us think on these and keep our hearts from despondency if possible. Hard is the struggle, I know; still we must make the effort.

My heart and hands are full of care all the time. My dear mother has been unusually feeble. Never leaves her room now, because our dining room is in the basement, and Mrs. Gabbett occupies our drawing room as a bedroom. We have had few transient boarders this winter, which has curtailed our income considerably. Still we have lived very comfortably, though we have to deny ourselves in clothing. I have not a solitary resource to draw a dollar from. The rent of our house in Marietta goes to the repairs; we have as yet received nothing over. I am glad to say that the Southwestern Railroad has declared a dividend of four percent, which will give Mother some money; for it is hard for one who has always had the disposal of her own money to be without any. Am thankful we have been and are able and willing to procure her such comforts as her age and delicate appetite require. We got a nice shad for her the other day at $2.50, and it did me good to see how much she enjoyed it. But I must not entertain you with a mourning among the fleshpots. Suffice it to say we are getting along just as you left us. Are trying to get a larger house in a more central part of the city, but have not yet succeeded.

I must now confide to you a secret which you must keep till you receive the wedding cards. My baby Ellen, the darling of my heart, is to be married to Dr. Brumby the last of April. You remember I told you I had objections which I thought too serious ever to be waived; but when he addressed Ellen and she referred him to me, I had a plain conversation with him, and he gave me such assurances that I felt it my duty to withdraw them, as I have seen so much trouble come from opposing young people when their affections are engaged. Then an acquaintance of six months with him, in which there has been nothing wrong, but everything that was gentlemanly and noble-minded besides warmhearted and affectionate, has led me to think he will make Ellen a devoted husband. Of course he has come out of the war (like the rest of us) penniless; but he has fine talents, a fine school here, and will, I hope, make his mark in the literary world.

I told him I meant to write you today. He desired his kind regards and grateful acknowledgments for so kindly taking him to your house when he was sick at Riceboro. He retains a lively impression of it, though he had to get Ellen to express it for him. Thus it is: life is a wheel within a wheel. And while you thought you were only doing your duty as a patriotic woman in taking care of one of our brave soldiers (drawn more particularly to him by having known his parents), you were actually benefiting me by taking care of my future son-in-law.

I know he will be an affectionate one to me. What else I do not know. I trust my health and strength may hold out and always enable me to support myself, so as not to be a burden to anyone. They will continue to board with us for the present year and as much longer as they wish. I am willing for them always to live with me, but *not* willing to live with *them*. An old maiden aunt would be quite a burden for a young couple to commence housekeeping with.

The wedding will be private: only his parents, sisters, and brothers invited, and Mary and Mr. Mallard; of course you and Cousin Susan's family, John and Jane. These are serious times, and my baby's outfit limited. Their little school is small, but yields them a little, which is a comfort. I have just made her six chemises, and commence working the bands for them today.

Oh, my cousin, you who had to give up your only daughter will know what a trial it is to me to give away my baby! How forlorn I shall feel! Still I believe it will promote her happiness to marry. Few know the trials of a single woman when they get to my age, feeling in everybody's way and scoffed at generally. Pray for me, my dear cousin, that my baby be happy and useful, and he be soon converted.

Dr. Brumby and Ellen were invited a few weeks since to wait on Miss Glover, who married Rev. Charles Grant (son of Cornelia Bond that was) of Savannah. Ellen made quite an impression at the wedding: said to be the most beautiful and graceful young lady in the room. Everyone said how much honor such a young lady reflects on her aunty.

His parents and sisters received her most cordially. They were acquainted before, but of course felt a new interest in her. I wish you could see a letter his father, Professor Brumby, wrote him in answer to one he wrote informing him of his engagement. After complimenting him on winning such a young lady, he presses his responsibilities on him by urging him to devote himself to her domestic happiness, his success in life, and their standing in society.

Excuse my writing you all this, but you know what feelings fill a mother's heart at such a time. Would that we were nearer, so that we could talk face to face of these things! . . . The other two girls are busy sewing for Ellen. I think they are three as affectionate, self-sacrificing sisters as I ever knew.

When I feel sad at giving up my baby, I think of what a trial poor Louisa had in losing her dear boy. She is looking badly this winter. Sleeping with Mother I know does not agree with her, but it cannot be avoided. She is as indefatigable as ever.

Felix is still with us, and we have a nice chambermaid and washer. . . . When my rolls and buckwheat are very nice and my boarders all in good humor, I think I have an easy time. But I must stop talking of myself. Am the same good-for-nothing, inefficient woman I ever was, always trying to do right, but not bringing much to pass.

We were glad to see Charlie, and glad to hear from you that he had done all he could for your comfort. He received a beautiful little picture of little Ruthie while here—not the one in the muff. It was lovely. Do you go on next summer? I hope you will come here first.

Am glad you have dear Julia's family so near you. Tell them they are examples to their countrywomen in industry and cheerfulness. Please assure them of our sympathy; Willie was a great favorite of mine. Tell her I wish she would switch Fred for me; I have invited him every time I have seen him to come up and take dinner with us, and he won't come.

Do give our love to our dear Cousin William for us. Am thankful he is with you. Know you will do all you can for his comfort. How changed all his prospects—as well as the rest of us! Tell him Mother is in bed today, but Louisa has been downtown and bought her a fine shad for her dinner, after which we will give her some whiskey to prevent its swimming about too much. Wish he was here to partake of both.

Am sorry you have no mails yet to Liberty. Mr. Woodward goes to Savannah; takes these and promises to get them to you. . . . Tell our faithful Sam howdy many times for us, and tell him all the servants are well. . . . Love, love, love from all of us. Do write and console me about my baby.

Your ever affectionate cousin,
Mary E. Robarts.

MRS. MARY JONES *to* MR. CHARLES C. JONES, JR.[g]

Montevideo, *Monday,* February 26th, 1866

My dear Son,

I have been most anxiously hoping to hear of your safe arrival in New York, but as yet we have no mails, and it is only occasionally I hear of an opportunity to Savannah. One is this moment presented to send you a hasty line of love and remembrance.

Do not let my child forget her "danna." Every day I am missing her more and more, and only the fact that she is contributing to your happiness reconciles me to my loss. I hope you returned Eva my warmest thanks for the likeness, which stands upon my table, where daily I look upon it. She is so much grown, and has assumed such an air of girlhood, that I can scarcely recognize my baby. I hope it may never be necessary to cut her beautiful hair.

By Captain Charlie we last week received your most valuable gifts. Accept my sincere thanks for the delicious tea, and your uncle's for the beautiful pipe and tobacco. You never saw anyone in your life more delighted than he is with the pipe. No stranger even can be any time in the house but he goes and brings it out and shows it with the greatest admiration. He says I must tell you he never smoked anything to equal it, and never saw as beautiful a one. And Gilbert is the proudest fellow in the world of his watch and suit of clothes. Says he means to *"hang to you to the last."* He desires me to give you a "tousand tanks." You may be assured I shall not suffer his parents to want, and have told him to call for any assistance they need.

Niger was very much pleased, and thanks you for his vest. *Today* he returned from Arcadia with a load of pistol shot in his left hand. Coming home he was in company with a man who had a pistol, which Niger attempted to fire at a wildcat, and put the load in his own hand. I sent him immediately over to Dr. William Wells, now at South Hampton; and he has just returned with a note saying the injury might cause him much trouble, and he would not be able to work for some time. He extracted the load and some shot; Niger would not consent to the use of the knife, so other shot remain. So much for their use of firearms!

Charles also has been laid up for some time, but upon the whole we are, I am thankful to say, moving quietly on. Mr. Broughton has arrived, and so far pleases me well. He appears to know his business, and attends to it, which is saying much for any man. He has just called for my letter, so I must close. . . . Warmest love to dear Eva and yourself, and my best wishes and prayers for her entire restoration to health. . . . Tenderest love and kisses for my child, and much love from your uncle, and remembrances from the servants.

Ever, my dear son, your affectionate mother,
Mary Jones.

Mr. Charles C. Jones, Jr., *to* Mrs. Mary Jones[t]
New York, *Thursday,* March 8th, 1866

My very dear Mother,

I cannot express to you our happiness upon the receipt of your kind letter of the 26th ult.—the first we have had since I bade you good-bye. We are rejoiced to hear of your good health, and that everything at Montevideo is progressing so quietly and pleasantly. May God in mercy watch over and protect you and favor you in all things! I am glad that the bundle from Savannah reached you safely, and that the articles contained gave pleasure to those for whom they were intended.

You must make up your mind to come on and spend the summer with us. Brother will probably be coming on about the 1st of June, and he will be your escort.

I write in great haste, and will write you more fully very soon. When will the Albany & Gulf Railroad be opened? Is there anything, my dear mother, that I can do for you? Eva is not so well today; her general health, however, I think is better. Daughter is very well. They both unite in tenderest kisses and love. Remember us affectionately to Uncle. And believe me ever, my dear mother,

Your affectionate son,
Charles C. Jones, Jr.

Mrs. Mary Jones *to* Mrs. Eva B. Jones[g]

Montevideo, *Friday,* March 16th, 1866

My dear Daughter,

This is the return of our sorrowful anniversary, and with the indulgence of my own grief come very special remembrances of yourself and your dear mother. I think it a remarkable coincidence that both your father and my dear Charles's father were removed on the same day. How sadly it presses upon my heart that my dear children have now no one on earth to pray for them and influence them by example and by precept as their devoted and godly father did! I have often heard the petition from his lips: "Let us not forget the dead." God grant that it may be answered in the case of his own children, that they may "not forget the dead." I see in my dear son the noble, generous, and affectionate traits of his beloved father, but my heart yearns to see the decided evidences of Christian character and principle. Would that as a family we were all united to Christ, and had the love and service of God as the great end and aim of our lives! Then could we indulge the blessed anticipation of a joyful reunion in a brighter, better world. *Do when you write tell me where you worship on the Sabbath.*

I had spent the day mostly in my room, reviewing not only my afflictions but God's many undeserved mercies to me, when at its sorrowful close three letters were brought me, all from my very dear son—one containing his own most excellent likeness, and another the precious little picture of my darling child. It is perfectly lovely. Your conception and arrangement is admirable, and you must have practiced even the expression of her little face to have succeeded so admirably. I do thank you for it, my dear daughter, more than I can express, and for all your tender love and care of that sweet child. And I ever pray that you may be rewarded for it. It may be the fruit of my love and partiality, but I have always felt she was an unusually lovely child. Charles does not mention your ever having received either of my letters, or my letter to Ruthie. I hope she will soon write to her "danna" a long sweet letter and tell me all she does. I have a great deal to tell her, and will write very soon. Tell her Mom Lucy and Daddy Gilbert were delighted to see her picture. Mom Kate exclaimed: "Missis, is that your baby that you raised? Do give me one to keep in my *bus-som!*"

Did Charles carry the calico dress I sent her? And did it fit? I had my fears that he did not think it worth carrying. If it reached you, you saw it was unfinished. Although I sat upon the doorsteps in the broad light, I could not see to put on the braid or make the buttonholes. My eyes failed me entirely. Do let me know what work I could do for her. If you would send me her length, I would make her some chemises and pantalets. I have nothing of the kind as a guide. I doubt not you can in every respect do far more and better than I could for her; but if there is anything I could do to promote her comfort, it would give me happiness to do it. God bless her! How I should like once more to fold my child in my arms, and to know that she still loves me!

We have as yet no mails or post office in our county. This week the Gulf Road was opened, but we have no one loyal enough to be entrusted with the *U.S.* mail. I think the Scripture is literally fulfilled in our case: "Because of swearing the land mourneth." Without an oath we cannot have a mail or a post office, a railroad conductor, express agent, or any civil officer. How long will this continue? The Northern clergy who are so active in political affairs had best take that text, using for their illustrations Federal oaths, and for their practical inferences Southern wrongs and oppressions. It is only as some kind friend brings me a letter do I hear from my children. Not one word until this day had I heard from my son Charles since he reached New York. And not a line from Atlanta and Augusta for a month! I have learned to live without newspapers, but I cannot without hearing from my children.

It rejoices my heart to hear that your general health improves, and I pray it may be restored and established. Charles does not mention his own health; I hope he has quite recovered. I was very uneasy about him when he left me. Please do not let him use much tobacco; I cannot resist the impression that it will undermine his health if he uses it to excess.

Sister Susan is quite well, and always desires love. So does my friend Mrs. King. . . . With best love from Uncle and myself to you and Charles, and many, many kisses for my darling child, ever believe me

Your affectionate mother,
Mary Jones.

I shall *confidently* look for *your picture. Do not disappoint me.* Why did you not send it?

MRS. MARY JONES *to* MR. CHARLES C. JONES, JR.^g

Montevideo, *Monday,* March 19th, 1866

My dear Son,

You may judge of our isolation when I tell you I had not heard a word from you since you reached New York until this past week. But your affectionate letters have all come at once, and now I feel like a starving person made happy and comfortable by a warm, hearty meal. This abominable *oath-taking* still embarrasses all our political and social arrangements; in dear Eva's letter I send a text for Dr. Spring or Dr. Tyng or any other Federal D.D. I have also not heard excepting through your letter a word from your brother or sister, and I feel assured they have written. I wrote you acknowledging the valuable presents to your uncle and myself and to Gilbert and Niger, with which all are delighted, and grateful to you for. The tea is delicious, and often refreshes my weary spirit.

And now I must thank you especially for the likenesses. Yours is excellent, although I still fancy as I look at it that you are not entirely well. Do, my child, watch the influence of tobacco upon your constitution. Literary and sedentary men confined to studies and offices cannot indulge the habit as those who lead active lives in the open air. You see *mother-like* I cannot feel that *a word* is sufficient for the wise; where the heart rules it has to speak many and often. . . . The picture of my little darling delights my eye, and I think I can hear her saying, as her little hand lies extended: "See my mother's little crooked finger." The expression of her face is exactly what it should be, listening to the voice of the seashell in her hand. And why did not Eva send me hers too? I shall not feel that the compliment is complete until she does so; and I shall be anticipating its coming in every letter. I will accept her as she is, without waiting for additional charms.

I am thankful, my dear son, to know that your business has been such as to enable you to support your family, and that the desire of your heart is granted in the improved health of your dear wife. I trust and pray that it may be God's will to restore her to perfect health. You made some allusion to housekeeping. Would not such a step be premature, involving increased care to Eva and heavy expense in furnishing, etc.? I know it is far more comfortable to have your own home, and often houses ready furnished may be obtained at moderate rates.

You most kindly speak of my visiting you this summer. It would be a great pleasure, but I do not indulge the anticipation for a moment, and you must not for the present year think of it. If God spares my life and you ever have a home there at some future day, I know it would give me great happiness to see you in it. I have at present no plans for the summer. Shall stay here as long as possible—perhaps the whole of it. Everyone should now conform to their circumstances. My great desire is, if my life is spared, to see your father's work given to the church and to the world, that it may accomplish its mission of good, and to have the means of erecting a suitable monument at Midway.

Your aged uncle, too, requires not simply attentions but *watchful care.* I was so long accustomed to the fluctuations of your beloved father's health, and got so accustomed to observing the least change, that it is perfectly natural for me to watch over the old gentleman—to see just when he ought to rest or retire, or needs a cup of tea or a glass of *milk toddy;* or when I should sit by him and stir up the old fires of memory, talking of Sister Betsy and past days of happiness, or throwing forward some comforting anticipation of brighter and never-changing, never-ending ones to come. Now that my precious baby is no longer with me, it is of God's mercy that one object is left to claim my daily care and attention, so that what others might regard differently I do as a blessing, as it makes me feel I am not living entirely for self.

We are getting along pretty well on the plantation. *So far* we have never had a manager that in all respects suited me so much as Mr. Broughton. He would have planted corn ten days since, but waiting for coal tar, he has commenced today. . . . The people have worked well, but Niger was two weeks out of the field from the pistol wound in the left hand, and Charles has not done a full day's work this year, his ear and head still affected. . . . Thus our little number has been materially reduced. Sam does well as foreman, and Gilbert is as faithful as ever. I have told him your wish about his father and mother, and he will have the corn whenever he wishes. Andrew is preparing a fine crop for himself, and you may be assured they shall not want. Under a new system I am trying to inaugurate such measures as will regulate the future, and in my performances try to exceed my promises. I would be glad if I could give them meat, but have it not. They get syrup weekly as a gift, and have had beef once, and things cooked occasionally for them.

My faithful friend *Rescue* died the third day after he was taken. We are now unable to leave home excepting on Sabbath.

It will grieve you to know that Peggy, the faithful and devoted nurse of our little Mary Ruth, died recently of smallpox in Savannah, and I am told in circumstances of great want and neglect on the part of her husband Henry. She was in Sue's house; but she too, I am told, was afraid to go near her. She told me herself she came from Burke to be with me here, but her aunt and sister were the means of keeping her away. You know she came to see you, and you told her when you got a house in New York you would send for her. The servants tell me she repeated to them what you had said, and told them as soon as you sent she was going to New York to be with her "little missy." I think she was as devotedly attached to the baby as any nurse I have ever seen. Do tell her all about poor Peggy's death, and how much she loved her and wanted to come and take care of her. Poor thing, she told me when you sent for Silvia if she had been able, she would not have let her go to wait on "Little Missy," but would have gone to Augusta herself. I do not know where her little child Eva Lee is, but presume Flora or Sue has her.

Yesterday after an illness of two weeks *Rosetta* died from pneumonia. Her children were devoted to her; her old husband Sam has been with her since Robert came; and all her children but Abram were around her dying bed. She has long been a member of the Baptist Church, and expressed to me a good hope that through her Saviour her peace was made with God.

I tried to do all I could for her, and her life has probably been prolonged by nourishment and stimulants.

Yesterday also Dr. Samuel Way died at Jonesville of confluent smallpox. His whole family have it, and I am told are in a distressed condition. He was truly a good man, and his end was peace. I feel that I have lost a friend.

Mr. Smith Hart died some two weeks since, and Mr. Joseph Anderson lies extremely ill. I received a distressing letter from him, written at the hand of someone, making a request which I cannot well refuse.

My brother Henry spent Saturday night with us; is doing well in Baker. Your Uncle John has accepted the call to Griffin. I must close. Do ask Eva to write me all about Ruthie. Our respects to Mr. Ward. . . . Your uncle unites with me in best love to Eva and yourself and Ruthie, for whom tenderest love and kisses from "Danna." Gilbert and the servants desire to be remembered. God bless and save you, ever prays

Your affectionate mother,
Mary Jones.

Mr. Charles C. Jones, Jr., *to* Mrs. Mary Jones[t]

New York, *Friday,* March 30th, 1866

My very dear Mother,

Your kind and welcome letter of the 19th inst. has just been received, and you can scarcely imagine the delight which it gives us to know that you are well and unharmed amid the changes of this transition period.

I am very sorry to hear of the deaths of Dr. Way, of Mr. Hart, of Peggy, and of Rosetta. I am peculiarly touched by the sad fate of Peggy. She well knew that I was prepared to do all I could for her comfort, and that I offered her a home for life. I never can remember except with the deepest gratitude her kindest attentions to little Ruthie, and her absolute devotion to her in the darkest hours. My effort was to persuade her either to remain at Indianola or come down to you at Montevideo. She would have done the one or the other, but was influenced to a contrary course by her friends. Poor thing, freedom brought sad fates to her door. What will become of her child!

I am glad to hear that everything is getting along so well at Montevideo, and hope that as the period of transition wanes, matters will become better suited. Have you a mail yet to Riceboro? I have heretofore sent my letters to the care either of Dr. Axson or of Messrs. John W. Anderson & Sons.

We have nothing of special interest here. . . . Eva and Ruthie are both quite well. . . . I will try and get Eva to have her likeness taken. She has a great aversion to sitting; she says she never can get a good picture.

Enclosed, my dear mother, I send you a check for one hundred dollars. It is my individual check on the National Bank of the Republic payable to your own order. I think you will have no difficulty in using it. All you will do is to endorse it by writing your name on the back, and either of the storekeepers in Riceboro will cash it for you. Please let me know whenever I can serve you in any way.

Give our love to Uncle, and accept for yourself, my dear mother, our united love and tenderest remembrances. Remember me to all the servants. And believe me ever

Your affectionate son,
Charles C. Jones, Jr.

Mr. Charles C. Jones, Jr., *to* Mrs. Mary Jones[t]

New York, *Monday,* April 9th, 1866

My very dear Mother,

On the 30th ult. I had the pleasure of enclosing to you, under care to Rev. Dr. I. S. K. Axson, my check for one hundred dollars, which I trust reached you in due course of mail and will prove serviceable. In the absence of any information on the question whether or not the post offices at Riceboro and at No. 3, Albany & Gulf Railroad, have been resumed, I send this as usual to the care of our reverend and dear friend.

I deeply regret to learn, through a letter just received from Sister, that her little ones have of late been suffering so severely from whooping cough. Little Georgia especially has been critically ill, and I judge from Sister's account of her present condition that she is still in no little danger. I sincerely trust that they may all soon be restored to perfect health.

Brother writes me that he will soon be with you. I hope that you will make him stay a long time, for I am quite satisfied that he is sadly in need of rest and recreation. I frequently indulge the hope of being able myself to see you, perhaps the last of the present month or during the next. We have some matters of business which may require my presence in Savannah about that time, and I am awaiting developments; so that I may kill two birds with one stone. Every arrangement as yet, however, is uncertain.

Eva and Ruthie are both quite well. Daughter is becoming quite interested in her little books, and begins to spell quite well in words of one and two syllables. She speaks often and tenderly of her dear "danna," and prays for her night and morning. Eva's health, I think, is decidedly improving, and little Ruthie is as well as she can be. I think, under God, this change of climate and scene has been of great benefit to them both. Yesterday we had snow all day, and the weather today, although bright, is quite cool.

We are somewhat at a loss in regard to our plans for the summer. Our landlady goes out of town on the 1st May up the Hudson, increasing her rates, and making it a condition precedent that her rooms there be engaged from May 1st to November 1st. This we are not inclined to comply with. There is a great tendency of the New York population to the country through fear of the cholera, which, it is believed, will prevail here during the summer months. The consequence is, all the country houses within accessible distances for business purposes within the city are commanding very high rents.

We have nothing of special interest. We are getting along pretty well in our business, and we have great cause for gratitude to the Giver of All Good. I trust, my dear mother, that you are well, and that everything at Montevideo continues to move on smoothly. Do let me know if at any time I can serve you in any way. Eva and Ruthie unite in warmest love to self and Uncle. And I am ever, my dear mother,

Your affectionate son,
Charles C. Jones, Jr.

Kind remembrances to relatives and inquiring friends.

MR. CHARLES C. JONES, JR., *to* MRS. MARY JONES[t]

New York, *Monday,* April 23rd, 1866

My very dear Mother,

I often wonder whether my letters reach you regularly. They are written certainly every week, and are usually directed to the care of Dr. Axson. Enclosed is a letter from Eva which will tell you of herself and our precious little Ruthie. It is with the deepest gratitude that I report them both well. Ruthie is as bright and as rosy as possible; her health has never been better. Eva, too, has grown much stronger, and is better than she has been for years. The change, through God's blessing, has been most beneficial to them both.

I have just rented a house on 84th Street opposite the Central Park. It is quite in the country and yet in the city. The Eighth Avenue cars pass every five minutes within one square of the dwelling, and the time from the house to my office is just one hour. The house is a pleasant one, and I hope the locality will prove healthy. It will certainly be much cooler than in the city. In Central Park, too, Ruthie will have ample room for play and for fresh air. Eva is very busily engaged securing furniture, and we hope to get into the house by the 7th of May.

And now, my dear mother, I must insist upon your coming on and spending the summer with us. This is the *very least* you can do, for you know your room will be always ready, and we will be only too happy to welcome you. Brother will be coming on, I expect, in June, and he will be your escort. Now, you will not deny us this pleasure. I am quite sure, under God, that the change will be very beneficial to you. Let me know what you want at any time, and so far as I am able, you shall have it.

Our business matters are progressing favorably. I have been very hard at work ever since I saw you. I hope to see you during the next month if business arrangements will permit. All unite in tenderest love to self and kind remembrances to Uncle. And I am, my dearest mother, as ever,

Your affectionate son,
Charles C. Jones, Jr.

Mrs. Mary Jones *to* Mr. Charles C. Jones, Jr.ᵍ
Montevideo, Friday, May 18th, 1866

My very dear Son,

For over three weeks my longing eyes and heart have waited to welcome your coming. As weeks wear away I fear you may not be able to leave New York, and particularly as you have just gone to housekeeping. . . . For three successive weeks I have had a noble wild turkey hung up in the dairy for you. The last was so fine I kept it four days hoping you would be here to enjoy it. During your brother's visit and since we have had five as fine as you ever saw. I have requested that no more be killed this season *unless* you come. Mr. Broughton says he has two gobblers waiting for you. I have preserved the feathers to some of the finest, and intend having a large fan made for the firm at 119 Broadway to fan *"Southern claims."*

Hoping still to see you, I will not even begin the endless details of plantation life. We have had it very dry, and the season is unusually late. Cotton just fairly up, and rice not all planted. I have had some severe trials with the people here, but trust through divine strength and guidance matters will go right in future. Saw the crop at Arcadia day before yesterday; it looked well, and Robert said they were working well.

Did you get my letter asking you to bring me three padlocks? . . . And we are entirely without scales or steelyards for weighing. I saw Fairbanks (or some such name) very highly recommended; it was said they were not expensive, and yet would weigh a bag of cotton.

I do not propose, *D.V.,* leaving here before the middle or last of June, when I will go to Augusta. Your sister writes to say my room is all ready in Atlanta. And I am truly grateful, my dear son, to Eva and yourself for your kind invitation to pass the summer with you. Holding so large a part of my heart as you do, you place a great temptation before me in such an invitation. Your brother goes on in July.

I am so desirous to have your father's *History* published at once, fearing some accident might occur to the manuscripts, that I wish to dispose of so much of Central Railroad stock as will meet the expense of publication. This can be done either in Savannah or Augusta when I go up. Your brother says he will have time to attend to the publication while he is at the North, and we will try and get Dr. Howe to correct the proof sheets.

Your uncle requests you to try and effect a sale of his plantation near the Island (Springfield). There are three hundred and twenty-five acres, a most healthy and desirable place of residence, fish, oysters, etc., etc. Says you know all about it. He will take ten dollars per acre. It would be a great matter for the old gentleman if you could sell it.

He unites with me in best love to Eva and yourself. Kiss my precious child for me. The Lord bless and keep you, ever prays
Your affectionate mother,
Mary Jones.

Mrs. MARY JONES *to* MISS MARY RUTH JONES[g]

Montevideo, *Friday,* May 18th, 1866

My darling Child,

"Danna" has just come in from the garden, where she found this sweet spring rose, almost the last of the season. It looked so beautiful and was so fragrant it made me think of the precious flower I have blooming far away in New York. So I thought I would sit down and write you a little letter, and put the sweet rose in it, and send it to remind you of your Southern home.

You have not forgotten *Monte-willio-way,* have you? There are no wicked Yankees here now to torment us as they did last winter, when for one month we were all prisoners in our own home. The doors and windows stand wide open now; and the bright sunshine peeps in, and the cool breezes filled with perfume from the tea-scented olive and the sweet roses and flowers of the garden come freely through the entry and halls. The avenue of oaks, the grove, the lawn are all beautiful; the laurels in full bloom. The little squirrels are once more cheerful and happy, and all day long are chasing each other round and round and up and down the trees. Day and night the sweet little birds are singing their songs of praise and thanking God for His kind care of them. You know we had but one old goose left from our flock of seventy. She was very lonely until about two months since we got another; and now they have two little "doozé," as you used to call them. The father and mother take them out walking and picking grass upon the lawn, and are so proud of them. They will not let dog or cat or duck or chicken come near them. The only pigeon left by the Yankees that used to tap at the window for corn and pease flew away and brought home another, and now they have a fat little squab just fledged.

Your dog Captain faithfully guards the house at night. He sleeps sometimes in front on a bed of dried leaves; and when "Danna" hears a noise she throws up the glass and calls, "Captain! Captain!" and he answers with a loud, hoarse bark. His fierce voice makes people afraid of him, but he never bites, for he belongs to an amiable family. Little *Hero,* the colt, grows finely, although he has had to take care of himself since his mother, Lady Franklin, was stolen this winter from the pasture. But he is a brave little fellow, and can whip the largest mule in the stable whenever he fancies the corn and fodder. We have a merry set of calves and little lambs, and Daddy Gilbert is now taking off the warm winter jackets of the old sheep.

Your dear papa has no doubt told you that your nurse Peggy was dead. She took care of and nursed you for the first year of your life, and loved you very dearly. She wanted to go to New York to wait on you, but it is the will of our Heavenly Father that she should not live even to take care of her own child. I hope poor Peggy was a Christian and has gone to heaven.

My darling, "Danna" misses you every day of her life. She keeps your little chair by the side of hers in the parlor, and often wishes you were here to fill it. But I daresay you are better off where you are, your kind mama takes such good care of you, and teaches you so many pretty and smart things, and you live in such a great city, and see so many beautiful things. And then I know you are a great comfort to your dear papa, who is working hard to support Mama and his little daughter, and "Danna" too. You must never forget when he comes home weary and tired to run and meet him with a happy face and a warm, loving kiss, and to do all you can to obey and make him and Mama happy. You must put your little arms around them and kiss them both for me.

You will think this a dull letter, but I hope it will remind you of your home. Never forget, darling, to love the Blessed Saviour and to pray that He would love you and make you His own dear child. May God ever bless you! You must write soon to

Your own loving "danna,"
Mary Jones.

Mom Kate and Daddy Gilbert send you howdies.

Mr. Charles C. Jones, Jr., *to* Mrs. Mary Jones[t]

New York, *Monday,* May 28th, 1866

My very dear Mother,

I am this morning in receipt of your precious favor of the 18th inst. with its sweet enclosure to little Ruthie, which I have also read with the deepest pleasure and interest, and which she will not hear read until I get home tonight. She will at that time, however, be up; and her loving little heart will be very thankful to her dear "danna" for her kind and special remembrance, for all the bright and calm views of that blessed home consecrated by so many memories of happiness and comforts and privileges, and for the sweet rose, redolent of those delightful perfumes which always linger with peculiar richness and delicacy about the garden at Montevideo. She will write you very soon and thank you sincerely for this pleasure. Only last evening she came to me and said: "Papa, hold my hand and let me write a little letter to Danna."

She is the only one (except Eva's wild Irish girl) in the entire household who has not been sick within the past few weeks. Eva and Mrs. Eve are both now quite unwell, and Polly has been very sick. Yesterday I was badly used up with my old enemy. But I hope we are all on the mend. The spring has been a very unpropitious season, abounding in chill winds and cold rains. As I write I am reminded by the whistling winds and cloudy skies more of the dark days of September than the mild hours of May. I presume, however, that summer will soon be upon us in good earnest, for the changes here are, when they occur, very decided.

I have been very hard at work since I have been in New York. We breakfast a little after seven. I reach my office about nine o'clock or a little before, and never leave it until half-past six, which brings me home to dinner about half-past seven.

We are pretty well fixed in our new home; and again, my dear mother, let me urge your coming on and spending the summer with us. Your room is all ready. It is designated as your room, and all you have to do is to come on with the Doctor and occupy it. You well know what a hearty welcome awaits you, and I am quite confident that a change of scene and climate will be most beneficial to you. Remember, we are confidently expecting your coming.

I still hope to be able to come to Georgia during the month of June. My movements have been delayed in consequence of the nonpassage of a law of Congress which will facilitate the transaction of some business of importance committed to our care. If the bill passes, I will go at once to Savannah, and will then enjoy the great pleasure, which my heart craves so sincerely, of being with you.

I regret deeply to hear that you have been subjected to "severe trials" at Montevideo, and heartily unite with you in the hope that they are now overpassed. The transition in the status of the Negro has been such a marked and violent one that we cannot wonder that he does not at once adapt himself rationally and intelligently to the change. He has always been a child in intellect—improvident, incapable of appreciating the obligations of a contract, ignorant of the operation of any law other than the will of his master, careless of the future, and without the most distant conception of the duties of life and labor now devolved upon him. Time alone can impart the necessary intelligence; and the fear of the law, as well as kindness and instruction, must unite in compelling an appreciation and discharge of the novel duties and responsibilities resting upon him.

My advices from Indianola are of an unfavorable character. The season has been cold and wet. Cotton seed has been scarce and of an unreliable quality. The consequence is that everything is backward, and the stand of cotton very irregular and bad. So far as I can learn, the Negroes have behaved pretty well, although on this point Mr. Sconyers has not written me particularly for several weeks. I wish very much that I could visit the place. Have had to furnish bacon, which has been and will continue to be a heavy expense.

In reference to the sale of the Central Railroad stock, my dear mother, for the purpose of publishing Father's manuscript, if you will allow me to suggest, I would advise against its present sale, and for two reasons. First, I am in possession of facts which lead me to believe that a dividend will be declared before very long which, while it will benefit you very much, will also materially enhance the value of the stock. We have just compromised a very heavy claim in favor of the road, which I think will enable the company to declare a dividend. Second, now is not as favorable a season to sell as we may reasonably expect a little later; nor is it a favorable season to have printing done here. Labor and materials are both high. I think next winter we shall see the rates of labor and materials more reasonable. I would be loath also, Mother, to part with that stock, the annual income from which you will need, and which is the very best security in Georgia. By next fall, also, I hope I may be able to *assist* in the expenses of the publication, if not wholly defray them. No one can be more anxious than I am to see the valued labors of my beloved and honored father given to the world, and I would not for one moment suggest any hindrance in the consummation of that most desirable object. But my impression is, unless there be some special reason in the case unknown to me, that it would be more advantageous to delay the publication until next fall. At all events, do not sell the stock now, as it can be done at any time by power of attorney, which I can prepare for you at any moment. The longer the sale is delayed the better.

I hope, my dear mother, that you have found leisure and strength this past winter and spring to prepare Father's biography, or at least to collect and arrange the materials and note your own specific recollections, which will of course be far more valuable than those of anyone else. This I deem a very important matter, and I hope that you will have strength and leisure to accomplish it.

I have promised the Georgia Historical Society to prepare an account of the fortifications erected around, and of the military operations connected with, the city of Savannah during the last war. Have you any journal or newspaper or written accounts or memoranda with the loan of which you could favor me? I have thought that perhaps my letters to yourself and Father from 1860, or say 1859, to the close of the war would prove of some value to me, and enable me to fix certain dates which otherwise I might find trouble in doing. May I ask the favor of you at some early leisure moment to gather up those letters and memoranda of every sort and kind in your possession and send them on to me by express at your early convenience? I will be greatly obliged to you if you would do so. The express freight on the package I will pay here.

Please say to Uncle that I will do the best I can for him in the matter of the sale of his plantation, but that the season is so far advanced that I doubt whether a sale can be effected before fall. Assure him, however, that I will do all that I can.

The scales and padlocks I will look after. Do, my dear mother, let me know if you want anything, and if I can do anything for you. You know my highest pleasure and privilege are to serve you in every way in my power. All unite in tenderest love. Hoping, my dear mother, that every blessing will ever attend you, I am ever

Your affectionate son,
Charles C. Jones, Jr.

MRS. MARY JONES *to* MR. CHARLES C. JONES, JR.[g]

Montevideo, *Monday,* May 28th, 1866

My very dear Son,

Your valued favors by General Lawton reached me last week. They were sent by Captain Charlie Thomson, who delivered them faithfully; and I am most grateful to you, my dear child, for the enclosure of fifty dollars. You have done everything that it was possible for a son to do for a mother, and you really must not continue to make such drafts upon your hard-earned resources. I know you must now have calls for all you make, and it distresses me to feel I may be increasing your cares. I have always tried to make my personal wants as few as possible; and if the Lord is mercifully pleased to prosper us with anything of a crop, I trust I shall be able with economy to make a support from the plantation another year.

Sometimes I am *encouraged; never* very hopeful, from the unreliable character of the laborers. To give you an illustration: Several weeks since, when I thought all things prosperous, Gilbert came and informed me that July and Jesse were going that morning to Savannah with a copy of the *contract,* which they had requested and I had furnished them. Soon after, *Sam* came up on the mule, saying the people one and all had declared they would not strike another lick with the hoe; they were dissatisfied with the contract, and thought I meant to deceive them. I told him to go into the field and order them every one—men and women—to come to me. They did so. I met them on the front steps and inquired kindly but decidedly into the cause of such conduct. They had one and all evidently been poisoned by someone, and July and Jesse were ringleaders in the affair. I was extremely weak at the time, as it was soon after my sickness; but I felt it important to act promptly in the presence of the people. So I told July and Jesse immediately to take up the line of march for Walthourville, where the agent of the bureau lives; and directing Gilbert to get the buggy, I asked Brother William if he would accompany me, as he had been a witness to the contract. The old gentleman was so incensed at their conduct he said he would go a hundred miles with me.

I arrived, of course, before the men, and laid the case and the contract before Mr. Yulee, the agent. He made some shifting remarks about "public opinion" and its being customary to give "half of the crop," etc. I told him the provisions of my contract had been suggested by a Federal officer then acting as a bureau official, and endorsed and approved by him as such. I then asked if he would furnish me a legal standard for contracts. He said they had none.

"Is my contract, then, a legal one?"

"Yes, madam."

"Are the people, then, not bound to comply with its terms?"

"Certainly."

"I now, then, sir, appeal to you as the agent of the bureau to restore order upon my plantation!"

He then rose and wrote a summons for July and Jesse to appear before him, and told me if the people did not return to their duty he would put the instigators into irons; and if that did not answer, he would send them to Savannah and have them put to work with a ball-and-chain upon the streets. I told him I desired nothing of the kind—only the return to order and duty on the place. Soon after we left, July and Jesse arrived, and I received by their return a note saying they professed perfect satisfaction with the contract and promised to return to their duty.

Since this outbreak things have moved on very well. I have told the people that in doubting my word they offered me the greatest insult I ever received in my life; that I had considered them friends and treated them as such, giving them gallons of clabber every day and syrup once a week, with rice and extra dinners; but that now they were only laborers under contract, and only the law would rule between us, and I would require every one of them to come up to the mark in their duty on the plantation. The effect has been decided, and I am not sorry for the position we hold mutually. They have relieved me of the constant desire and effort to do something to promote their comfort.

I am not only satisfied but much pleased with Mr. Broughton. He understands his business and attends to it, and is an excellent planter and manager, especially for these times, commanding respect and obedience in a quiet but decided way. Gilbert has maintained his fidelity on all occasions, and Kate and Lucy are great comforts to me. . . . We are now suffering from a most protracted and distressing drought, and if we do not have rain within a few days, the provision crop must be greatly injured. We have been able to plant but one square of rice, and that is very slim. We are now planting the inland swamp as you cross in going to the Darien road. The Negroes in this county have suffered for want of food, and many are now working simply for provisions. If it had not been for the corn you have sent me, I would too have been in great distress. Mr. Sconyers writes me he has sent me thirty bushels of corn and two of pease, which I am glad to get for planting. . . . Our stock of cattle is carefully watched by Mr. Broughton. Your uncle took a look at them this evening and says they are very fine. I wish I could send you a plate of fresh butter every morning. Do write me if there is anything I can send you from home; and if I can help Eva in any household articles (bedding, etc.) it will be my greatest pleasure to do so. I wrote you of the crop at Arcadia; it is doing well. Last week I made our tax returns.

On Saturday night I received your most affectionate letter, my dear son. It would indeed rejoice my heart to see you and dear Eva and my precious child. I am thankful you are once more in your own hired house. May God's blessing rest upon you in it, and make it to you the abode of peace and happiness! Tell dear Eva she does me too much honor in selecting for me her best chamber; that must not be. I do long to see you, but I do not know how to write about coming on until I reach Augusta. Does Mrs. Eve expect to spend the summer in New York with Eva and yourself?

Mrs. John Barnard told me on Saturday that Adeline was very much inclined to go to New York to cook for you. Do you wish to have her? I think she would be a comfort to you. I cannot get over the feeling of confidence in those born and raised with us. If I can do anything in that line for you, let me know it. I have no doubt you could secure black servants here if you wish them.

Tom is now in the county. I have seen him but for a short time. He came down with a fine double-barreled gun, and is helping his father at Lyons'. *Anthony* has left for *New York*. Tom tells me both *George and Jack* are dead, which makes three gone of our personal servants. Tom is now a carpenter. Did you allow him to keep all the shoemaker's tools you bought for him? Or are they still yours, although his possession?

As I have written you, my dear son, I wish to sell so much of my Central Railroad stock as will enable us to print your father's *History* at once. The way seems providentially opened for your brother to attend to the printing this summer. I am so much more familiar with his handwriting than anyone else, I have thought if I am permitted to visit you this summer and the work is printed in New York, if there was any obscurity I might make it plain.

We are still without any regular mails to Riceboro.

Your uncle has been very feeble recently, and expects to leave this week for Dorchester. *D.V.*, I expect to leave either the 14th or 19th of June for Augusta. He desires you to sell his place if possible, as I wrote you, saying if a purchaser can be found, he will name titles, etc. He feels leaving Montevideo; says there is no other place where he will be so comfortable or so much spoiled. I am sure there is nothing on earth I would not do for him.

Please do not forget the padlocks, etc.; and I will be glad to have seven pounds rutabaga turnip seed and some drumhead cabbage. You must be tired of this scrawl. Best love to dear Eva and yourself. Kisses for my baby. God bless you, my child, ever prays

Your affectionate mother,
Mary Jones.

The servants send many howdies.

MR. CHARLES C. JONES, JR., *to* MRS. MARY JONES[g]

New York, Monday, June 4th, 1866

My very dear Mother,

Your last kind favor has just reached me, and we are truly happy to hear from you and to know that you are well. I am distressed to learn that you were some time since so much troubled and annoyed by the misconduct of the people at Montevideo, but rejoice with you that you have of late found them more obedient and attentive to their duties.

The accounts which I receive from Indianola are very unsatisfactory—only a half-crop of cotton planted, and that in very inferior condition. Late spring, cold rains, and bad seed have united in causing a very indifferent stand, even in the small quantity planted. Some of the Negroes work pretty well, some very well, and some again very indifferently. And so the story runs generally.

I will send on the padlocks and garden seeds by express, D.V., in a day or two. The package will be directed to you, No. 3, Albany & Gulf Railroad, as I presume the express has resumed its carriage on that route.

I am truly sorry to hear of the death of George and of Jack. They were both good servants, and I would have been glad to have assisted them all their lives by every means in my power. I had hoped to have gotten George here. We are anxious that Adeline should come on and cook for us; and some two days since I wrote Amanda Howard requesting her to see Adeline and induce her if she could to come on at the earliest practicable moment. I hope that she will succeed in doing so. We expect to hear from her on the subject very shortly. She will, I think, be a great comfort to us; and I believe with her and Polly, who has proven herself a very treasure, that we will get along very well, D.V.

I have already written you in relation to the sale of the Central Railroad stock. If you conclude to sell a portion of it, I would postpone the sale as long as possible, and would not sell at any rate until definite arrangements had been made with the publishers as to price, time of payment, etc. The payments would in all probability not have to be made until after you had received one dividend. I beg to refer on this subject to my letter of the 28th ult.

I think I let Tom have some tools. He had a great many of his own. I do not think he has any to which he is not entitled.

Enclosed, my dear mother, please find a check in your favor on the Bank of the Republic in this city for fifty dollars. I wish that it was for an hundred times that amount. You will have no difficulty in negotiating it. It is, as you will perceive, payable to your order.

And now, my dear mother, you must let us again renew our earnest entreaty that you come on and spend the summer with us. Your room is all ready, and we are depending upon your acceptance. We can take no refusal, and shall after your arrival in Augusta expect you to let us know exactly when it will suit you to come on.

On the 28th ult. I begged you to send me all my letters addressed to dear Father and yourself since 1859 that you can conveniently find. My object in desiring them is this: I am preparing for the Georgia Historical Society a brief history of Savannah for the past five years, and also for the Chatham Artillery an account of the part borne by that battery in the struggle for Confederate independence. Those letters, as they probably from time to time referred to passing events, will in all probability furnish me with a thread for the respective narratives. If you have also, my dear mother, any printed or written notices or documents touching the local history of the company or of Savannah during the period alluded to, I would be very glad to receive them. Please forward to me, 119 Broadway, New York, care of Ward & Jones, at your early convenience.

Through God's mercy we are all up again. Nothing of special interest. Pray, my dear mother, let me know if you wish anything, or if there is any way in which I can serve you. Tell Uncle that I will do all that I can to compass the sale of his place. All unite in tenderest love and warmest kisses. And I am ever, my dear mother,

Your affectionate son,
Charles C. Jones, Jr.

Kindest remembrances to Uncle and all relatives and friends. Howdy for Gilbert and all the servants.

Mrs. Mary Jones *to* Mrs. Mary S. Mallard[t]

Augusta, Wednesday, June 20th, 1866

My very dear Daughter,

I left Montevideo on Thursday morning in the wagon (the buggy being fairly worn out and laid by for repairs) to No. 3, where I dined with Mr. Augustus Fleming; and under the kind escort of Mr. Buttolph we reached Savannah about six o'clock. Accepting the invitation of our valued friends Dr. and Mrs. Axson, I stopped with them, receiving most hospitable entertainment. In yours and Robert's name I gave them a pressing invitation to visit you this summer, knowing what sincere pleasure it would afford you to entertain friends so valued, and to whom you are under so many obligations for kindness to Robert. Laura had been in Savannah about a month with her numerous friends, and was greatly improved.

I saw Major and Mrs. Porter and all their connection, and was to have gone up in company with Marion Alexander and Dr. and Mrs. Robson on Friday night to this place; but a disappointment in the hack caused me to remain until Saturday morning, when I came up *alone,* your brother meeting me with a hearty welcome at the cars. And Carrie and the children did so at the house. I felt grateful to find them all so bright and well—excepting your brother: he is very thin and *worked down;* looks very badly. Carrie very busy and full of work. We have *hired* a sewing machine, and I am going to try and help her, but do not know how I shall manage without you to arrange it for me.

Carrie and Joe are much disappointed that Kitty passed through Augusta without their seeing her. It would be a great pleasure to me to see her. You know I have always considered her one of my loved and valued friends.

I have thought, my dear child, constantly of the call to New Orleans, and made it a subject of daily prayer that *God* would direct Robert at this time by the special influences of the Holy Spirit, that no false motives may influence his feelings or blind his judgment, but the glory of Christ's cause and Kingdom may be the grand and ultimate aim of his life in this and all other decisions. I can but have a preference for the climate of Atlanta when I think of you and the dear children; and then too I shall feel if you go to New Orleans that I shall hardly ever see you, if I am spared to live longer in Liberty. But this is all personal. There can be no doubt of the importance of his present location and the growing influence of Atlanta. New Orleans must be a trying climate to the constitution, although Randolph Axson tells me the summer is delightful, winter damp and sometimes very cold. Says the church to which Robert is called is beautifully located in the American part of the city. Says living is about as expensive as Savannah, and he prefers New Orleans to any other place. But I presume Robert has ere this written you fully of all things.

Your brother Charles has given me a most pressing invitation to visit him when Joe goes on, and seems to feel hurt at the thought of my not accepting it. Joe thinks of going on now not before August or September. My mind is perplexed about it. I do long to see my dear baby so much.

Carrie and your brother unite with me in best love to you and to Kitty and the dear children, and to Aunt and Cousins Mary and Lou and Sophia and Lilla and Ellen. All friends send much love to you and them. I left your uncle at Dorchester for the present. Excuse my miserable writing.

Ever, my dear daughter, your affectionate mother,
Mary Jones.

Mrs. Mary Jones *to* Rev. R. Q. Mallard[t]

Augusta, *Wednesday,* July 11th, 1866

My dear Son,

I am greatly indebted to you for your affectionate and interesting letter this day received, and thankful to find that you are through God's good care again with your dear family.

You will be assured that I have felt the deepest interest in the result of your visit to New Orleans, and ever since I knew of the call to the church have made it a subject of daily and earnest prayer, that the Divine Spirit might guide and influence your heart and conduct and final decision. Very grave and solemn issues are at stake in such a change. Atlanta, in its present enterprise and prospective influence, its delightful climate and location in your native state, has great claims; and when I think of the health of the two places, the decision must certainly be in favor of Atlanta. I can also believe that New Orleans would be very attractive as a wide field of usefulness. And socially it has all the advantages of organized and established and polished society. . . . To myself the thought of such a change brings with it many sad feelings. This perpetual unsettling of one's home brings much domestic trouble and perplexity to your wife at least, for she has had to move almost every year of her married life. And I well know that her good sense and fortitude have sustained her where others would have failed. This is looking at the matter in a private way. I know as a minister you are bound to obey the Great Head of the Church. New Orleans has always appeared at a great distance, but Joe tells me he thinks there will be direct communication opened up by the Albany & Gulf Road.

It was my wish and intention to be with you in Atlanta this week, but a letter from Charles saying he expected to be on shortly has induced me to delay *until Monday,* when, D.V., I hope for the great happiness of being with my dear children in Atlanta. Say to my precious child her letters have been received, but I have been so busy helping Carrie with her sewing there has been little or no time for writing. . . . The weather is very hot, and plenty of mosquitoes. I shall indeed enjoy the refreshing water, and remember well how great a blessing it appeared to me last summer. . . . Carrie and Joe unite with me in best love to Daughter and yourself and the children and to our relatives. . . . Believe me ever

Your affectionate mother,
Mary Jones.

IV

Mrs. Laura E. Buttolph *to* Mrs. Mary S. Mallard[t]

Flemington, *Tuesday,* July 17th, 1866

My dearest Cousin Mary,

A long time has transpired since a line passed between us, and I think it is now time to make up for lost time. Of course your engagements have been so varied and numerous that I am the only one to blame, and my seeming neglect has been neither willful nor voluntary.

I long to hear directly from you and your loved ones, who have ever been cherished in my warmest affections. I trust dear little Georgia has entirely recovered, and that you feel like yourself again. I hope Cousin Robert may remain in Atlanta, as the place is so healthy, and destined to be the greatest city in the state. New Orleans seems so far off that although the advantages may seem greater, still the climate in summer must be depressing. I have felt the heat of the few past days very much here.

Mr. Buttolph has gone to the North to see his aged father. He sailed in the *Tonawanda* on Saturday for Philadelphia, and expects to be absent two months. And I trust that he will enjoy himself extensively and derive all the advantage he can from the trip. The Yanks have clipped my wings, so I could not accompany him. Mr. W. J. Way took daguerreotypes of the children for their grandfather to see. . . . What do you think of our going to Williamstown, Massachusetts, to live? It seems to me I would stagnate there; but the children will have to be educated, and *if* Mr. Buttolph is called there, I don't know what the result *might* be.

We had a few showers last week, which may save the corn crop in a measure; but it is very dry. The swamps are all dry, and the vegetables all dried up. Gilbert came for Mr. Buttolph's horse and took him on Saturday to Montevideo. He said all the people there were well, but the starving people who had no work were "very plenty."

Mr. Buttolph saw Uncle William in Dorchester the last Sabbath but one. Quite well. . . . Uncle is to make Dr. Robson and Cousin Audley a visit on the Island and then come to us. His room here is nicely fitted up with Mother's cottage furniture and waiting for him with a warm welcome.

If you go to New Orleans, Aunt Mary's children will be scattered, and it will require time to journey from one to the other. I presume by this time she is with you; do give her our warmest love. . . .

I enclose you a photograph colored by Mrs. Cheves of Savannah. They were so poorly taken and the paper so miserable that the paint blotted, and you may not recognize the lady with red hair and red eyelashes! It is the best I have to send. Annie said: "You can't make me believe that is Miss Laura—*the eyes is dreadful!*" And Mother thought it was one of the Pratts.

Mother, James, Willie, and Susie unite with me in much love to Aunt Mary, yourself, and Cousin Robert, Mary, Charlie, and Georgia. Love to Kitty Stiles.

Your ever affectionate coz,
Laura E. Buttolph.

Much love to Aunt Eliza, Aunt Mary, Cousin Lou, Lilla, and Ellen.

Mrs. Mary S. Mallard *to* Mrs. Laura E. Buttolph[t]

Atlanta, Saturday, July 28th, 1866

My dear Cousin,

Your letter containing yourself was received with great joy, and I must return you many thanks for it.

I have done very little letter-writing for some months past. My poor little Georgia has required such undivided attention that I have done little else than mind her. She has been improving for a week past. She had a severe attack of cholera infantum about six weeks ago which reduced her very much and brought her very near death. Dr. Logan has despaired of her life three or four different times, but through the mercy of our kind Heavenly Father she is improving, and we hope will get well. She is very interesting, though the most timid child I ever saw in my life. She will allow no one to touch her except Mr. Mallard and myself and the children. I have only been waiting for her to lose the invalid look to have her photograph taken for Aunt Susan and yourself. She says any single word and begins to connect them. Yesterday she put her little foot in my bed and said: "Mama, scratch it." She is too weak to walk much alone.

I have placed your photograph in my album, though I do not think it does you justice. I think the blotting of the colors and the peculiar color of the hair must change the expression, though I think it like you and am very glad to have it. Mamie knew it immediately. I want one of Cousin Lyman now.

We spent last evening with Aunt Eliza. None of the younger members at home: Mary in Roswell, Ellen and Lilla in Marietta. Mary Sophia seems perfectly happy and delighted with her choice, and the whole family are extremely gratified. Aunt Lou says Mr. Adams is a man of means. He has one child at the North. They are going to the North the middle of August to spend a few weeks in traveling, then visit Mr. Adams' relatives and bring the child home with them. Mr. Adams has purchased Mr. Bayard's house in Roswell, and is adding to it and fitting it up handsomely so that they may go to housekeeping in the fall.

I wish you could have gone North with Cousin Lyman. The change would have done you good. I can't say I would like to think of you living in such a far-off Yankee place as Williamstown!

Our New Orleans arrangements are in uncertainty. Mr. Mallard accepted the call, and requested this church to unite with him in requesting the presbytery to dissolve the pastoral relation existing between them. They refused to do this, dissenting from him in the correctness of their conclusion. He immediately wrote the Prytania Street Church informing them of the action of this church, and received an answer saying they would prosecute the call with all energy. As Presbytery does not meet until the 27th of September, the matter cannot be decided until then; though Mr. Mallard still thinks it his duty to go to New Orleans, as no new facts have been developed to change his decision. New Orleans has always seemed to me a long way off, though it is, in fact, only forty-eight hours from this place. And if the Gulf Railroad is ever completed, we will be just as near Liberty from that point as from this. The greatest drawback is the yellow fever; and I feel that is to be greatly feared. Dr. Palmer sent me word yellow fever was a humbug, but I cannot be induced to believe any such idea as that.

My dear mother is here now, and looks remarkably well. She expects to go North with Brother Joe the middle of August. This arrangement will cut short her visit to us very much. I am so sorry she is going, though I know she is most anxious to see Brother Charlie and Ruthie. . . . Mother and Mr. Mallard unite with me in warmest love to Aunt Susan, Uncle William, and yourself, and many kisses for the children. We really must write each other often.

Your affectionate cousin,
Mary S. Mallard.

Mrs. Mary Jones *to* Mrs. Mary S. Mallard[t]

New York, *Friday,* August 17th, 1866

My dearest Daughter,

I would have written you before this, but the fatigue consequent upon our long journey has almost laid me aside. Think of it: at least thirteen or fourteen hundred miles accomplished in four days and a half—day and night in the cars!

We reached Chattanooga at six o'clock and left at 9 P.M. for Nashville, where we arrived a little after sunrise and enjoyed a nice breakfast at the St. Cloud Hotel, which is served entirely by white servants; and everything was clean and nice and arranged in the eating line after the present approved style of separate tables and ordering whatever you wish, which comes up hot and in a variety of small dishes. Your brother after breakfast went out to see Dr. Eve; I laid down after a bath and took a refreshing nap. After Joe came in we walked to the capitol, a magnificent structure, not much injured by the Yankees, although the grounds around were entrenched and fortified; but almost every tree has been cut down by them, which makes it excessively hot and glaring. Dr. Eve called after dinner (Mrs. Eve prevented by an injured finger); expressed himself much pleased at the prospect of having your brother in the medical college. And by the by, they had already announced him upon their catalogue, which was taking time by the *forelock*. *Despairing* of the *vacancy* they had *anticipated,* to secure his services they had created a new professorship, which he will fill. I do not at this time remember what it is. We were much pleased with the appearance of Nashville, and I trust it will prove a wise and judicious move for my dear son and his family.

We left Nashville at six o'clock, traveled all night, and reached Cincinnati at one o'clock on Friday, expecting to make a close connection and go immediately on to arrive on Saturday in New York, but found to our great disappointment we would be detained ten hours. And what was most distressing, the whole place was pervaded by the cholera panic, which disease had that day taken off forty-nine. The first object I saw from the window of the great saloon of the depot (which is also a kind of hotel) was an open wagon with eight coffins. And the dining room where we went to take our dinner was filled with the odor of chloride of lime; and the presence of disinfectants was evident all over the building, where several fatal cases had occurred. Not far off, in the same street, an entire family had died; and a friend who went to nurse them had been so frightened that he almost had the cholera and was speechless: probably something like paralysis had been induced. The horror which sat upon the countenances of wives parting from their husbands, parents from children, friend from friend, now that the king of terrors was in their midst, I thought might bring home to them some conception of the distress and misery they had brought upon us, fleeing from our beloved homes and friends, and writhing beneath their desolations of all we hold dear. The whole city appeared awe-stricken: not a smile, not a word, as they passed up and down in solemn silence. The whole atmosphere appeared tainted; and one of the waiters told me beef killed overnight was unfit for market the next morning.

We left Cincinnati a few minutes before eleven at night, taking the Great Erie & Western Road. The cars are of magnificent proportions, and sleeping cars all curtained and arranged with every comfort. But we did not go into them; your brother thought in case of cholera it would more likely be there than the open cars. We traveled uninterruptedly day and night, changing, I think, but once—a distance of eight hundred miles through a country cultivated, rich, and beautiful. The scenery at times was very fine.

As I mentioned, the ten hours' detention in Cincinnati threw us into the Sabbath, and we did not reach your brother's door until about one o'clock. He gave us a most hearty welcome, as did Eva; and my little Ruth was delighted to see me. She could not express her joy for excitement. She has been around me all the time. Asks constantly about Bubber and Sissy. Said: "Danna, what made you cut Bubber's hair off? It was so beautiful!" She evidently thought they would come with me. Tell Charlie she reads beautifully in easy reading, and is a remarkable speller. She sits down and studies her lessons entirely alone, then comes up and recites them. I find her much grown and much improved: a little lady in her manners. She undertakes the entire care of me when we walk out, showing and explaining everything and warning me of all danger.

I found Mrs. Eve and Eva all prepared for a trip to Newport for the benefit of sea-bathing, especially to Eva. Tomorrow will be one week since they left. Your brother saw them safely down and returned the next day. They are enjoying themselves; Eva, I trust, has the prospect of permanent benefit to her health. . . . I am now in charge of the house until her return.

Your brother has a delightful house. It is as quiet as the country: beautiful views from every window, and Central Park (that wonder of this country) near enough to walk every day in it—if I only had the strength. But I feel completely used up by the journey, and never in my life more inactive. I cannot walk a square without the most distressing sensations. I hope it will be better with me soon.

We are a great way off from the stores, which I have been but once to; and finding some warm winter skirts (balmoral), I bought *one for you* and *one for myself*. Goods, so far as I see, are as cheap in Atlanta as here.

Your brother Joseph found it impossible to stay this far, as he had to meet the doctors at night, and has put up at the St. James Hotel. He will probably visit Philadelphia and confer with the publishers there about the *History*.

On Sabbath we attended Dr. Scott's church, and your brother has taken a pew and will worship there. I am greatly delighted at this. Dr. Scott is a most earnest and engaged and godly minister. I was greatly moved and interested in all the pulpit exercises. I wish that Robert could hear him and see the manner—so solemn and earnest. He preaches long sermons, and makes great use of the Scriptures, requesting the congregation to read along with him, explaining the chapter at the same time. Yesterday he *called* to see me, and I greatly enjoyed his visit. He spoke with so much respect and affection of your beloved father. I told him of Robert's call to New Orleans; he says it is a noble field, and excellent people in that church. Says you need not have the first fear of the climate. The more I hear and see, the deeper is the impression that Robert has made a wise decision. I do hope the presbytery will not embarrass his move.

Your brother unites with me in best love to Robert and yourself and the dear children. Ruthie sends love and kisses. Your dear letter and the enclosures have been received. Am truly sorry Tenah's baby is dead. . . . Much love to dear Aunty and Cousin Mary and Lou, Ellen and Lilla.

Ever your affectionate mother,
Mary Jones.

Mrs. Laura E. Buttolph *to* Mrs. Mary Jones[t]

Flemington, *Tuesday,* August 21st, 1866

My beloved Aunt,

My heart fails me when I think of the pain you will feel on the reception of the sad bereavement which is pressing like lead upon my heart. Dear Uncle William was called to his heavenly home yesterday the 20th at one o'clock. . . . The funeral services are to be held today at Captain Winn's house at two o'clock, and the interment at Midway this evening. His most *ardent* wish and desire has been accomplished; he said: "I am afraid I am too anxious to die."

He was three weeks on the Island with Cousin Audley and Kate. Today is two weeks since his return to Dorchester. He was looking remarkably well, and enjoyed his visit very much, and had appointed last Wednesday to come to Flemington to remain with us. On Friday he complained of being sick. Was up on Saturday; had it in contemplation to attend church on Sunday at Midway (Communion Sabbath). But Mrs. Winn told him he was not well enough, and when Cousin Audley came for him, he declined going and said he was not able. He got up and dressed Monday and Tuesday, but returned each day to bed. On Wednesday he took his bed and never left it again, though on Thursday he seemed very bright and ate heartily. On Friday he changed for the worse; and Mrs. Winn thought he would not live out the day, and sent for Aunt Julia and Mother. . . . He lacked nothing; Mr. Winn's family did everything for him, and all the Dorchester gentlemen and friends sat up and nursed him. Every night one or two stayed; the last night Mr. Delegal, Mr. Alexander, Mr. Varnedoe, and Mr. John Stevens were with him, and William Stevens and Willie Winn. He could not have been among kinder persons—and among those he loved. Cousin Audley came early on the morning of the 20th, and was there to assist in performing the last sad offices. He then went to South Hampton to make his coffin. It was Uncle William's particular desire that he should do so, and he directed that he should be buried in a suit of clothes Aunt Julia made for him. . . . We mourn for him, but it is his unspeakable gain. He wanted to die under the roof where dear Aunty breathed her last ten years and one month ago. . . . How pleasant the memory of my last visit to Montevideo—the last time I saw him! . . . He loved you particularly, and your children; he was proud of them. Indeed, all of his relatives had a warm place in his heart, and his face would light up as he spoke of each one. . . . Mr. Buttolph will feel so sorry that he was absent; but his visit to his aged father (who is eighty-seven) was a duty, and I hope he will remain as long as he can, as it may be their last meeting on earth.

Expect my dear mother tomorrow. She sends her love to you and Cousin Charlie and Cousin Eva; also Cousin Joe and Mary Ruth.

Your own niece,

Laura E. Buttolph.

Mrs. Mary S. Mallard *to* Mrs. Mary Jones[t]

Atlanta, *Tuesday,* August 21st, 1866

My dear Mother,

Tomorrow will be two weeks since you left us, and still we have no tidings of your arrival. I hope the fatiguing journey has not made you sick. I presume Brother Joe has accepted the call to Nashville, as his name has been announced in the papers as professor of pathology. His name is placed first in the list of professors.

I received a note from Kitty Stiles sending the cholera prescription, which I enclose; but trust none of you will have any use for it. This is the remedy used by Mrs. Tattnall when she had the disease.

I can write only a few lines, as I am myself very feeble. On last Wednesday I had my teeth extracted—nine in all. Six were taken out while I was under the influence of nitrous oxide gas; and had I stopped there, I do not think I would have suffered a great deal. But the three roots had to be extracted without the gas, as it was too tedious and difficult an operation. It was a tremendous shock to my nervous system; but Dr. Logan was with me, and with the aid of brandy and chloroform (taken internally) I got through, but soon after became insensible, and continued so for fifteen or twenty minutes. Mr. Mallard was very much alarmed, though the doctor told him he did not think there was any danger. It proceeded from nervous exhaustion and loss of blood. After an hour or two Mr. Mallard put me in a carriage and brought me home. The poor little children were frightened to see me lifted out and brought into the house in their father's arms. I thought I had more strength for the operation than I really had. I feel a kind Providence has been very merciful to me in watching over and preserving me thus far. I am glad you were not here: I know you would have suffered so much anxiety. I am taking muriate of iron, and hope gradually to recover my strength. I have been up most of every day since, and all of yesterday and today.

All of Aunt Eliza's family well; they have an increase of boarders. . . . How is Eva's health? I hope improving. Much love to Brother Charlie and herself and Ruthie. . . . Mr. Mallard and the children unite with me in warmest love to you, dear Mother. Mamie says to bring Little Sister back with you. Love to Brother Joe. Tell him he must not work too hard.

Your affectionate daughter,

Mary S. Mallard.

Mrs. Mary Jones *to* Mrs. Mary S. Mallard[t]

New York, *Thursday,* August 30th, 1866

My dearest Daughter,

Your last affectionate favor has reached me, filling my heart with gratitude for God's mercy in *sparing your life* under such suffering and (as I believe) direct exposure to death. You must have been in a most critical situation. I hope your health will be improved in the end.

By the time this reaches you, your brother will have returned through Atlanta and given you accounts of himself and of us, and above all of the prospect we now have of your beloved father's work going immediately to press. I have written Dr. Howe asking the great favor of his revision and correction as a Biblical scholar and divine. Your brother here will receive and correct the proofs, and then forward them to Dr. Howe. I trust he will be able to accede to our request. I feel very happy in the prospect of its publication, and trust I shall be able to meet the liabilities involved. It will probably cost twenty-five hundred dollars to stereotype the work.

Day before yesterday I received a letter from your Cousin Laura informing me of the death of our beloved and aged relative, your Uncle William. . . . I presume they have certainly written you all the particulars. There is no one left to mourn for him as I will—no one else whose desolation and loneliness was cheered and protected by his presence and companionship. I had hoped —selfishly, I acknowledge—that God would spare his life on earth many years to come; although he told me before I left home: "Mary, you will never see me again; when you return, it will be to shed a silent tear on my grave." Oh, how I shall miss him—from his place on the sofa and around the hearth, from the family altar and the head of the table—miss his counsel and protection in that sad and lonely home where the very care and attention he claimed at my hands was a blessing! God alone knows what my future will be. I commit my way to Him, and pray and believe that all things will be ordered for me.

I have been very unwell since being here—at times greatly depressed in mind and body. Joe returned in so short a time I did not have the strength to accompany him back. *Do, if Mr. Pease or any of your personal friends come on to New York, let me know it.* I shall be anxious for an opportunity of returning in a few weeks hence, and know of no one here going South. Mrs. Eve speaks of returning, but I do not know any of their arrangements. She and Eva are expected by the boat from Newport in the morning. I hope Eva will return improved in health and strength.

My dear little Ruthie has been my roommate since her mama went away. She has improved in every respect, and spells wonderfully well and reads very correctly. Tell Charlie she is ahead of both Stanhope and himself; studies her lessons by herself and stands up and reads and spells right off. She speaks with great affection of the children, and always says I ought not to have cut her bubber's hair off, it was so pretty. When I showed her the likenesses, she pointed at the right one and said: "That is Uncle Robert."

Have you heard anything more from New Orleans? My dear child, I feel that I must return by way of Atlanta; for when we part this time, I know not when or where the next meeting will be.

I have thought a great deal of my dear old aunt. How much she will feel Brother William's death! Do give her and my dear cousins much love. . . .

Your brother unites with me in warmest love to Robert and yourself and the dear children. Kiss them all for Grandmother and Little Sister, who loves them dearly and talks of them. Do write soon. God bless you, my child!

Your affectionate mother,
Mary Jones.

Mrs. Laura E. Buttolph *to* Mrs. Mary S. Mallard[t]

Flemington, *Thursday,* August 30th, 1866

My dearest Cousin Mary,

Your last affectionate letter should not have remained so long unanswered but that I have felt troubled and anxious.

Dear Uncle William's death was a great shock to me, for I had hoped that he would recover as he had last summer; and he had appointed the day and all to come to us, and I anticipated so much enjoyment in his society. . . . He had climate fever, and suffered greatly from nausea; and his tongue was as white as a piece of linen. Had he called in a physician and used prompt measures the case might have terminated differently. This he refused to do, Mrs. Winn said; and he seemed so anxious to die. Ever since Aunty's death he has seemed like the man at Bethesda, *waiting to go;* and the Angel of Death has at last touched him and taken him away. . . . A piece has come out in the Savannah papers, written by Judge Law, *I presume;* but there are two mistakes. They said Uncle died on the 19th; he died on the 20th at one o'clock in the day at Mr. Abial (and not Abel) Winn's. And then he was born in Carolina and not in Georgia, though he came to this state with his mother when quite a boy. How we shall all miss our dear old uncle! I have only one uncle now left on earth, and I think you too have only one.

Is it true that Cousin John Jones is going to Lexington, Kentucky, having accepted a call to a church there? So Mr. Buttolph writes me from the North as news all the way from Toronto. . . . Mr. Buttolph says the South is the home of his choice, and he shall return better satisfied than ever to live and labor here. After preaching in Norwich an old gentleman came up and said: "You are from secessiondom, but you do preach the pure gospel." And in one of their papers they say: "He preached a very sound and eloquent sermon." The people are *hungering* after the Bread of Life, and fed on *strange* spiritual food. He avoids politics and has gotten on very well.

We have had rain almost constantly for ten days; but in the region of South Hampton you may walk through the swamp, it is so dry. And the crops will be shortened—although the freedmen say they are *splendid.* . . . Mother, James, William, and Susie unite with me in warmest love to you and Cousin Robert, Mary, Charlie, and dear little Georgia. Write soon to

Your devotedly attached cousin,
Laura E. Buttolph.

Love to Cousin John and Cousin Jane when you write. . . . Remembrances to your old servants—if any have returned to their allegiance.

Mrs. Mary S. Mallard *to* Mrs. Susan M. Cumming[t]

Atlanta, *Friday,* August 31st, 1866

My dear Aunt,

A few days ago Aunt Eliza sent us Cousin Laura's letter containing the sad intelligence of Uncle William's death. How remarkable that he should have been permitted to spend his last days where Aunty died ten years ago! I doubt not this was very pleasant to him. It makes us very sad to feel we shall never see him again. He was at Montevideo the last weeks I spent there, and I shall never forget the submissive, quiet spirit that characterized those days. It was really touching to see his gentleness. I think he has longed to depart for some years past. I pray that we may all be ready when the summons comes.

I have heard once from Mother since her arrival in New York. She was much fatigued by the journey, but was delighted to see Brother Charlie's family. Says Ruthie is much grown and improved: "a perfect lady in her manners." Says Brother Charlie has a very nice house beautifully located. Eva and Mrs. Eve left very soon after her arrival for Newport for the benefit of the sea-bathing. Mother does not mention it, but I have heard from Augusta that Mrs. Eve is reported to be married to a Mr. Haywood of Carolina. I do not vouch for the truth of the report.

Brother Joe has accepted the call to the medical college in Nashville, and will commence his lectures there the 1st of October. I presume he will return very soon from the North, as he will have to move his family. I hope it is a wise move. He will have the prospect of a more certain and ample support in Nashville, and the climate is better than that of Augusta. In these days of pecuniary prostration the question of support for a young and increasing family becomes a very serious one.

Our New Orleans movements are still undecided, and will not be determined until the meeting of Presbytery, which takes place the 26th of this month in Griffin. I am most anxious for the matter to be decided, for the uncertainty is very painful to me. The church here will use every effort to have the presbytery retain Mr. Mallard.

Uncle John is with us tonight. Aunt Jane's health continues as feeble as possible, and last week they feared she would hardly live. She still suffers from constant and violent hemorrhages—of course much greater at times. I do not know what she would do without Miss Mary and Mrs. Dunwody; Miss Mary is a host in herself. Uncle John is just on his way to Newnan, where he expects to assist Mr. Stacy at his Communion season.

Aunt Eliza has been more unwell of late, but still keeps up her interest in life and things around. Think of it—she is now knitting socks for her great-grandchildren! Two in prospect; I trust she may live to see them. Mary and Mr. Adams have gone to the North for a small tour, and to bring Mr. Adams' child home. She seems very happy in her marriage, and the match is in every respect satisfactory to the family.

My little Georgia has been improving quite rapidly for the past three weeks. I am now able to get sweet potatoes for her, and they seem to have done her digestion good. She runs all about, and says anything she pleases. If Mamie attempts to control her in anything, she says in the most positive manner: "Now, Mamie, hush!" It has been a struggle for life with her since February, but I begin to hope now that her little life will be spared to us.

If you should see Gilbert or anyone from Montevideo, please tell them to say to Lucy that Tenah and Niger have lost their baby, little Lucy. She was sick about a week. They felt it very much, for she was a remarkably fine child. . . . Please write soon. Mr. Mallard and the children unite with me in much love to Cousin Laura and yourself and kisses for all the children. How I wish I could come down and see you!

Your affectionate niece,
Mary S. Mallard.

Mr. Charles C. Jones, Jr., *to* Mrs. Mary Jones[t]

New York, *Monday,* October 22nd, 1866

My dear Mother,

I have been anxiously observing the heavens, and am very glad to think that you enjoyed a pleasant and smooth passage. Please let me know how you stood the voyage, and whether you have entirely recovered from the fatigue, and whether there is anything which I can do for you. I am very desirous of knowing also how you found matters at Montevideo. Do let us hear from you as soon as you can.

I returned from Washington this morning after a fatiguing sojourn of three days in that unpleasant city. Found Eva better and little Ruthie quite well, but with her face somewhat swollen from toothache. Eva is to take her to the dentist to have it filled. They both unite with me in warmest love.

We have nothing of special interest. The skies are becoming overcast, and I am glad to think that you are safely on terra firma again. Do, my dear mother, let me know whenever I can serve you. As ever,

Your affectionate son,
Charles C. Jones, Jr.

Mr. Charles C. Jones, Jr., *to* Mrs. Mary Jones[t]

New York, *Monday,* November 5th, 1866

My very dear Mother,

I am in receipt of your esteemed favor of the 26th ult., and sincerely rejoice to know of your safe arrival at home, and of your good health. We sincerely trust that you have quite recovered from the fatigues of the sea voyage, and that in the end you will derive benefit from its effects.

Am sorry to hear of the influences of the severe drought; but a dry season as a general rule is, I believe, favorable for the cotton in the marsh, and I hope that what has been lost on the high ground may be made up there. Those best advised are of opinion that cotton will during the coming season command a high price, so that it is all-important that every pound should be saved.

Before I forget it, let me say that from all I can learn of the present status of the commission merchants in Savannah, I think you will find *John L. Villalonga* perhaps the best person to whom you can commit the sale of the cotton. If you conclude to send to him, you can enclose the accompanying letter. I know that he will be glad to serve you, and I believe that he will faithfully and efficiently attend to any business entrusted to his care.

All that can be done for the mules with the distemper is to have them well cared for and have their noses smoked with the fumes of tar and burnt feathers. It is a severe affection, and will reduce them greatly; but as a general rule they will recover. They should have a plenty of forage.

In reference to the sale of the cattle, I think that you would do well to reduce the stock, retaining what you may deem necessary for the supply of the table, etc., etc. They should now command a fine price—or rather a little later in the autumn.

Please let me know Mr. Broughton's determination for another year so soon as he lets you know it.

Have you, my dear mother, heard from Miss Kitty Stiles yet? I do hope that she will come and spend the winter with you. . . . Eva, I hope, is gradually growing better. Little Ruthie is the picture of good health. They both unite with me in warmest love. . . . As ever, my dear mother,

Your affectionate son,
Charles C. Jones, Jr.

Howdy for the servants, and kind remembrances for all relatives and friends. Remember me to Mr. Broughton.

Mr. Charles C. Jones, Jr., *to* Mrs. Mary Jones[t]

Washington, D.C., *Saturday,* November 10th, 1866

My very dear Mother,

Here I am again, a petitioner in favor of the plundered Confederate. The hindrances and procrastinations attendant upon all efforts to bring the matters in question to an early and favorable adjudication are even more frequent and annoying than the famous "law's delays." I am hoping, however, for at least partial success.

I write now simply to assure you of my constant love and remembrance, and indulging the hope that God is mercifully preserving you from every harm. I hope to hear fully from you at your early leisure. I expect to be in Georgia soon after the 20th of December.

Just before I left New York on Thursday last, Mr. Scribner exhibited to me a sample page of Father's *History.* I think you will be greatly pleased with it. So soon as I return, I will commence, D.V., correcting the proof sheets, and will do all in my power to see that this is faithfully and accurately done. I will send you the first specimen page I can. . . . I hope to get back to New York the coming week.

Do, my dear mother, let me know if there is anything you wish, or anything that I can do for you. With warmest love, I am ever

Your affectionate son,
Charles C. Jones, Jr.

Howdy for the servants, and kindest remembrances for all friends and relatives.

MR. CHARLES C. JONES, JR., *to* MRS. MARY JONES[t]

New York, *Tuesday,* November 20th, 1866

My dearest Mother,

I am this morning in receipt of your kind favor of the 13th inst., and am very glad to know that you are well.

I assure you that I feel most deeply for you in your present loneliness, and I would esteem it the greatest privilege if you would come and make your home with us. You know your room is always ready; and all you have to do is to come on and occupy it. I think in justice to yourself and to your children that you ought to divest yourself of all these cares and spend your time with us, where you have every right, and where you ought to know everything will always be done for you that can be done.

I regret to hear of the death of the mule, and must try and supply its place for you at an early day.

In reference to Mr. Broughton, I think that his services for another year should be secured at whatever reasonable price he can be induced to take. Under the circumstances five hundred or even six hundred dollars would not be above the value of his services, and I would engage him at once. So long as we retain the place we must have a competent man there; and you need a prompt, responsible, and reliable man. His presence is an absolute necessity, and I would not hesitate for a moment. He would probably be able also to command labor, and that will be a very important matter. . . . Have you spoken with him in reference to giving him an interest in the crop, he furnishing the labor and managing the place? . . . I hope to be with you in December, and will then put in proper shape all business matters. Meanwhile whatever arrangements, my dear mother, you may deem advisable can be carried into effect.

I will do the best I can here to find a purchaser for Montevideo and Arcadia, but I fear that there will be little chance at present for effecting an advantageous sale. The Island also I will try and sell.

I leave for Washington again tomorrow morning. My business there requires great attention, but is most unsatisfactory. Any dealings with the departments are subject to numerous annoyances and vexatious delays.

In reference to a factor, I believe that Mr. Villalonga or Messrs. Tison &

Gordon or the Andersons will do you justice. Tison & Gordon are excellent factors and very responsible men. Villalonga is a Floridian and an energetic factor. I would sell such of the cattle as you do not need whenever a good price could be obtained; and you will be sure to get this in the present scarcity.

The Central Railroad and Banking Company of Georgia will, we are informed, declare a dividend by the 15th prox. Do not part with that stock: it is the best investment we have.

Father's *History* is in the hands of the stereotyper, and I am correcting the proof sheets. I do not think that he could ever have read over the manuscript after Mr. —— copied it. Mr. ——'s copy is very defective: sometimes words and even portions of sentences left out, and at other times the sentences so confused that I am at a loss to know the meaning. But I will do the best I can, and give all my nights to the task of correcting the proofs and making the work as perfect as I can under the circumstances. The manuscript should have had a thorough revision before it was placed in the hands of the publisher. I hope, however, to get along with the publication without serious difficulty. You may rely upon the fact that I will do all in my power, and in doing this will feel that I am discharging a sacred privilege and duty.

Eva has again been quite unwell. Ruthie is the picture of good health. Both unite in tenderest love. And I am ever, my dear mother,

Your affectionate son,
Charles C. Jones, Jr.

Mr. Ward desires his special remembrance.

V

Miss Louisa J. Robarts *to* Mrs. Mary Jones[t]
Atlanta, *Wednesday,* November 28th, 1866

My dear Cousin,

I cannot let Tenah and her family leave without writing you a few lines to say that we often think of you and our dear relatives and friends in old Liberty. I wish Providence had cast our lot nearer them.

We have just parted with dear Robert and Mary and their interesting children. They left this morning at eleven o'clock. It had rained very hard all night, and this morning Mr. Pease sent his carriage to take them to the depot. This move has given me personally great sorrow. Theirs was the only house in Atlanta that I ever went to. I shall miss them everywhere every day. I feel their leaving on Mother's account. I had hoped when God in His providence called her home, they would have been with us. This is a sad, sad day with us.

Mother is very feeble—sick nearly all the time. She still tries to knit and read every day. She wrote Cousin John a short note the other day. Sister has been quite sick with an inflammation in her eyes; is now in bed: has had some chills and fever. We are in Judge Lyon's large house. Have a good many boarders, and hope it will pay for all the trouble. It is a hard life, and I dread this winter. If I only could take a peep at all my friends in Liberty once more, how rejoiced I would be!

Do give our united love to Cousin Susan, Laura, Mr. Buttolph, the children, and Mrs. King's family, Ann Barnard, Louisa Winn, Jane Harden in particular if in the county. I have written her several times but received no answer.

I send by Tenah a bag for Sam. Tell him howdy for us. He must get Lucy to make his shirt for Christmas. We want to see him very much. Tell him Peggy left us last August and tried to live to herself and hire out the boys. She broke right down and went into galloping consumption and died two weeks ago. I had to pay every expense of her; sent her body with her children to Marietta for burial. She said she wanted to lie by Nancy. I have Willis and Bruce with me; Will is hired out; Clarence also. I am sorry for the boys; they have no one to take them. . . .

Mother says: "Tell Mary do write me. I long to see her and Susan, but fear I never will again." She is extremely anxious to return home. Lilla and Ellen are quite well. Sophia, we hope, will be with us at Christmas. She regretted not seeing you in New York; she was so sick while there that she could never go even to meals. They are going to housekeeping in a few months. . . . I write in haste. With much love,

Your attached cousin,
L. J. Robarts.

Do write soon. Tell Laura to write me a good long letter. Mother says: "Susan has forgotten me."

Mr. Charles C. Jones, Jr., *to* Mrs. Mary Jones[t]

Washington, *Friday,* November 30th, 1866

My very dear Mother,

I have been here for the past ten days attending to some important business, in the transaction of which I have been subjected to the most constant and perplexing delays. Aside from every other consideration, it is a matter of great annoyance to me to be here at this time, and yet I cannot help myself. I hope to get away by the middle of next week, and I hope to get away from New York for my trip home by the 20th of December.

I sincerely trust, my dear mother, that you are well. I long to be with you. Do let me know if there is anything in which I can serve you. . . . My absence from New York delays the correction of the proof sheets of Father's *History.* This I very much regret, but I cannot help it, and upon my return will do all I can to make up for lost time.

There is nothing of special interest here. Members of Congress are flocking in. This is the last place one can visit for anything like pleasure. With warmest love, my dear mother, and hoping soon to see you, I am ever

Your affectionate son,
Charles C. Jones, Jr.

Mr. Charles C. Jones, Jr., *to* Mrs. Mary Jones[t]

Washington, *Monday,* December 3rd, 1866

My very dear Mother,

I am this evening favored with your very kind and interesting letter of the 24th ult., forwarded to me from New York, and am most happy to know that you are so well.

In consequence of my engagements here for the past two weeks, I have been unable to correct any more of the proof sheets of Father's church history. I think upon examination it is quite evident that Father never read over—at least carefully—the copy made by Mr. ———; and that copy is in many respects very carelessly done. I never saw the manuscript. It was placed by Brother in the publisher's hands, and contracts made for publication. It is probably too late now to withdraw the work. I can probably make all the requisite corrections, although the amount of care, attention, time, and responsibility involved will be very great. But this I will endeavor to assume, and will do the very best I can. You may rest assured that I will not allow any imperfections other than such as absolutely inhere in the work (if any there be) to appear. I will correct the proof sheets with reference books at hand. Brother was so urgent in the matter, and had had the manuscript so long in his possession, and seemed so absolutely confident that it was in all respects ready for the press, and was withal so imperative in the matter, that I said nothing after expressing to him my sober, sound convictions of what was proper in the premises. The sequel has thus far fully justified the propriety of the views then expressed—at least to my mind. But, Mother, you must not let the matter trouble you, either pecuniarily or otherwise. I have assumed the responsibility of everything, and if I live and have health and strength, I will endeavor to present the manuscripts in a truthful and proper manner to the public. There are many alterations in style which I think should be made, but as these affect to a certain extent the genuineness of the publication, I will leave the manuscript as I find it, confining my corrections to manifest clerical errors. I will see the printer so soon as I return to New York, and will then write you fully. I think that I will be able to manage matters.

By all means *deny consent* to the establishment of a schoolhouse upon Arcadia land. It would, in the present condition of things, be but an opening to complications, losses, etc., etc. If Stepney will assume the planting of Arcadia upon proper terms, I think with you that there will be no use for the intervention of Mr. Mann. It would only detract from any profits which might be realized to give him any interest in the matter. I do not believe that his overlooking them would do any good to the laborers on the place. Stepney is familiar with Arcadia and knows how to cultivate the place; and if he will act with his former fidelity, I do not see that we could do better for the present than to employ him for this purpose. If he will furnish the labor, seed, etc., he should respond to us for one-third of the crop, he and the laborers assuming all expenses. In other words, the land should earn at least one-third of the crop produced. He will probably see you on the subject, and when I come out in December I can put everything into shape. At present I would make no agreement with Mr. Mann.

Uncle William's estate will, in the absence of a will, go to his next of kin; and someone will have to take out letters of administration. Captain Winn would be a good person to do this. I do not know who his next of kin are. He could find them out, I presume, without difficulty by advertising after he had been qualified as administrator.

Last Thursday I went to Mount Vernon and paid my respects to the home and tomb of General Washington for the second time in my life. The first time, you will remember, was when we all visited the sacred spot in 1839. I could recall the very spot where Father stood and made those lifelike sketches, the loss of which we can never cease to deplore. Everything remains unchanged, and the object of the association is to keep the house, outbuildings, and premises generally in precisely the same form and condition as that in which they were left by the general. Miss Cunningham was there.

She had suffered vastly in the travel, but had had quite a satisfactory meeting of a number of the vice-regents. Efforts are to be made to make collections in behalf of the association, which is sadly in need of funds. She inquired most affectionately and particularly after you, and desired her kindest remembrances. I spent an hour in her chamber. She was in bed, and evidently very weak. Enclosed I send you a sprig from the flower garden at Mount Vernon. The box from which it was plucked is said to have been planted by the general himself.

I am tired to death of this place, and I hope to get away by the middle of the week, or by the last at furthest. Do, my dearest mother, let me know if there is anything in which I can serve you. By last advices Eva and Ruthie were pretty well. With warmest love, I am ever

Your affectionate son,
Charles C. Jones, Jr.

I enclose an order upon Mr. Mann, which can be presented if there is any need.

If you have not already decided upon your factor, I think you will find that Messrs. *Tison & Gordon* would do you ample justice. They are excellent factors and responsible men.

Mr. Charles C. Jones, Jr., *to* Mrs. Mary Jones[t]

New York, *Tuesday,* December 11th, 1866

My very dear Mother,

I am just in receipt of your recent kind favor, for which I sincerely thank you. I am just leaving for Philadelphia upon a matter of business, but hope to be back tomorrow or the next day. I long to see you, my dear mother, and, God willing, shall expect that pleasure about the 27th of December. I expect to return to Washington next Monday, and so soon as I end my engagements there, go South by the way of Augusta.

God bless and preserve you from all harm! Eva has just heard of the death of Mrs. Reid of Augusta. I am happy to say that the manuscript of Father's *History* grows better as it proceeds; and I have now a better proofreader, so that matters are progressing more favorably. Eva is quite feeble. Daughter is the picture of good health. Both unite with me in warmest love. And I am ever, my dear mother,

Your affectionate son,
Charles C. Jones, Jr.

Mrs. Mary Jones *to* Mrs. Mary S. Mallard[t]

Montevideo, *Wednesday,* January 2nd, 1867

A Happy New Year to you, my darling child, and to Robert and the dear children! May our Divine Lord ever abide with and bless you all! The skies with us are very dark: no ray of sunshine since *last year*. It is all in sympathy with our national and domestic gloom. Everything is dark within and without.

Your brother reached Montevideo on Friday last, giving me a most agreeable surprise. It has been raining ever since his arrival, yet he has been hard at work doing all he could with this wicked and perverse generation. This evening, we trust, they have consented to some terms of agreement.

Your brother went to Arcadia yesterday and was most pleasantly received. Stepney is coming back to take charge of the place, and they all engage to do their best the coming year. The place is well filled up with many valuable laborers, and it is hoped they will do better this year than the last. Mr. Mann makes a return of about a *bag and a half* coming to the place, with about twenty-five bushels of corn and a little rice, which I will try to sell. Also the cotton as soon as it can be ginned. I have paid all the taxes on the place, and the corn will meet them.

The most of the people on this place will remain, and Niger and Tenah go in with them. Gilbert will stay as last year, but puts his son to a trade; and Fanny retires as an invalid. Mr. Broughton with great reluctance consents to stay, but begs even now to be released.

My dear child, the anxiety and distress experienced about these people and my situation here cannot be told. Sometimes I feel in utter despair and desperation, and I would rejoice to sell the place tomorrow if I could. Only *one sacred tie* to Liberty would then be left. I feel that my way is gradually hedged up, and I daily ask my Heavenly Father to lead me in "the right way." I forgot to say that Kate announced today that she must go with her husband next year. I hope to persuade her to the contrary. Lucy is very faithful, but they often groan being burdened with freedom. The changes which surround me are marvelous.

Last week I made a visit to your aunt, and found her on the eve of a domestic "January Revolution": Anne gone, and Matilda going, to Savannah. They hoped to secure a good cook and washer. Mr. Buttolph's relative Lyman has presented him with a marvelous washing machine and a wringer. The clothes (from a blanket to a cambric handkerchief) will pass through and come out nearly dry. The cylinders are covered with gutta-percha, and you can sit at the machine and wash and read. Laura has improved in health, but is not strong. Your aunt is quite well, and always busy.

I do so wish you could get a call for Mr. Buttolph in New Orleans. How happy we should all be if only permitted to live near each other! Think of it—I have not been once on Sabbath to dear old Midway since I came back. No way of getting out! Two of the mules dead, and the third too poor to use!

I must close, as I am completely exhausted with the day's excitement. Our best love for Robert and yourself. Many kisses for my dear little grandchildren. Affectionate regards to Dr. and Mrs. Palmer and their family. I heard from Dr. Howe last week. All well.

> Ever, my dearest child, your affectionate mother,
> Mary Jones.

Mr. Charles C. Jones, Jr., *to* Mrs. Mary S. Mallard[t]

Montevideo, *Wednesday,* January 2nd, 1867

My very dear Sister,

You see I am here with Mother in our dear old home—now, alas, so changed. The disastrous influences of this recent war have wrought sad vicissitudes, and where peace and order and content once reigned there are little else than disquietude, turmoil, and desolation.

After a very perplexing day the freedmen here have at length come to terms, which, if not absolutely desirable, are at least the best which could be secured, and, everything considered, may be regarded as tolerably fair, if fully carried into effect. I have endeavored to persuade Mother not to bother herself with the ingrates, but to shut up shop and make her home with her children. But she is loath to do this, and concludes to try free labor another year. Stepney is to return to Arcadia and plant the place with some thirty hands, we to receive one-third of what is made, and to supply nothing. This is the best I could do; and I hope, with the blessing of Providence, that we may find the arrangement at least tolerably remunerative. I regard the whole matter as an experiment in behalf of the free Negro. Labor in this county is in a very demoralized condition, due in a great degree to the inefficiency of the white men, who are led by the Negroes instead of endeavoring to direct and control their services.

Have not seen Eva and Ruthie for more than two weeks. Hope that the next week will find me on my way back, for I long to see them.

Enclosed I send two letters of introduction for Robert, one to General Beauregard and one to General Wheeler. Upon my return to New York, D.V., I will send some circulars of our new firm, which I will feel greatly indebted to Robert if he will distribute as he may think proper among the influential businessmen of his acquaintance and congregation in New Orleans. I hope, my dear sister, that you are already comfortably and pleasantly located in your new home, that you have been kindly welcomed, and that every blessing will attend you, and that Robert's ministry will be sanctified to great good.

Father's *History* is in the hands of the printer, and I hope the first volume will be out in the spring. The correction of the proof sheets occupies all of my time. The manuscript was never corrected by Father, and is in many respects very defective; but I will do the best I can.

All friends here are well, I believe, although the weather has been so inclement during my visit that I have been nowhere except to Arcadia. Mother still has Lucy and Kate and Gilbert with her. Niger and Tenah are here. Mother unites with me in warmest love to self, Robert, and the little ones. And I am ever, my dear sister,

Your affectionate brother,
Charles C. Jones, Jr.

My address is: P.O. Box 6049, New York City.

Our new firm will probably be *Ward, Jones & Whitehead,* the latter member a New York lawyer of probity, character, and considerable distinction. Now, if you have any good cases you wish thoroughly "ventilated," just send them on.

I have just made up and entered for Mother in the family Bible the entire family record; and I deem it but an act of simple justice to apprise you of the fact at this the earliest moment that the space allotted for *births* is *entirely filled, and there is no room for a single further entry.*

Miss Mary E. Robarts *to* Mrs. Mary Jones[t]

Marietta, *Monday,* January 7th, 1867

My dearest Cousin,

We received your welcome letter some weeks since in Atlanta, and would have answered it sooner, but Mother was very ill at the time, and I very sick with intermittent fever. I was confined to bed almost entirely for five weeks, and could not leave my room for six weeks, which depleted me considerably. Mother's illness and my sickness so increased Louisa's care that it almost broke her down, as she not only had her share of the business to attend to but mine, which last she found no trifle when she had it to do, though she used to think I had a very easy time.

Then our dear mother day by day would plead with us to take her home to die among her friends. This induced us to give up our business in Atlanta and come to our own home here. The ground was covered with snow, and it was with fear and trembling that we made the attempt, fearing that my dear mother might not reach here alive. I came up in the morning train. Our kind friends Dr. Stewart and Dr. Dunwody met me at the depot and brought me to my once loved and lovely home. A fire was soon kindled; a hired man, Dr. Brumby's brother, and Willie Dunwody put down the carpet and put up the bedsteads; and the house soon assumed an appearance of comfort. My dear mother and Louisa arrived in the afternoon train. Our kind neighbors sent over dinner and tea, and we had reason to record the goodness of God in bringing us safely through.

Mother had selected our former drawing room as her bedroom, and she is as comfortable as we can make her. But her return home has not afforded her the satisfaction and comfort we expected. She begins to show the restlessness of age; says she does not know the house and wants to move to a milder climate. Great are the trials of extreme age. Well may the Scripture say "If by reason of strength they be fourscore, yet is their strength labor and sorrow." So it is with our dear mother. She can neither rise up nor sit down without assistance; is as helpless as an infant in all respects. We have to feed her, and she moans and complains of great weariness. . . . She converses very little, and seems to take very little interest in things around her.

Sometimes she shows that her mind is failing a little. On Saturday she received a letter from your brother saying he had heard from you, and that our relatives in Liberty were all well. She said: "I have no relatives there."

I said: "Why, Mother, have you forgotten Cousin Mary and Cousin Susan and Laura?"

She said: "Oh, no! I love them dearly, but they don't live in Liberty; they live in Flemington."

I read the questions you asked her about Cousin William. . . . I tried to get Mother to recall the first time she had ever seen him. She said he lived in Bryan, then broke right off and told about Abby Austin's telling him there was to be a dance in Sunbury, and his coming over in a canoe against tide, found all dark in the village, and how "Abby laughed." Thus she can recollect incidents in the early days of her contemporaries, but her mind gets very confused when you go further back. . . . Ask Cousin John Jones all the questions you have asked; he is the best genealogist in the family. . . . Mother really does not know. . . . Her mind is clear about incidents of her own life, but confused about others.

My dear cousin, can we be the same persons who commenced life so differently? Your devoted husband laid in the grave; all your children scattered; you in solitude, with scarce enough to live on left. I feel like Naomi: went out full, came home empty. The dear young faces that used to give light to our dwelling are not with us: one in heaven, the others just beginning life for themselves.

My precious baby went to housekeeping the very day we left Atlanta. That city is extending to what they call West End. A number of Dr. Brumby's patrons live out there, and he was invited to take charge of an academy out there; and I hope he will have a very large school. . . . They rented a little cottage, and are quite delighted at having a home of their own. Lilla remains with them for a little while—till 1st February, when I go down to make Ellen a special visit. . . . Sophia, Mr. Adams, and his little son (five years old) spent Christmas with us. She is very happily married. They go to housekeeping this week in Roswell. She also expects to be sick in the spring.

We feel now as if our time of trial was come. Though we had many cares resting on us in Atlanta, still we lived in comfort and had a plenty. Now we just expect to keep from starving till summer, then expect to take boarders for our support. This place looks desolate indeed, and Louisa feels it particularly. She misses our dear Joe so much here. Our friends are very kind to us in coming to see us, but no one is able to help another now. We felt completely broken up when Mr. Mallard and dear Mary left Atlanta. Mother would keep saying: "I have no little children to come and see me now." And she says a dozen times a day: "I wonder Mary Jones don't write." Am glad Mary is so comfortably fixed in New Orleans.

Bruce is our only little servant with us; the others all remained in Atlanta. We hired Mrs. Nesbitt's Lambert and his wife to stay in our yard. He cuts our wood for his room rent; she cooks and washes for us at five dollars per month.

John wrote us dear Jane had been extremely ill and was still very feeble. I fear she cannot live long if she does not get better soon.

Mother and Louisa and I send three hearts full of love to you, Cousin Susan and Laura, Mr. Buttolph, and children. Will write her soon; am still so weak writing tires me very much. Write soon to

Your ever affectionate cousin,
Mary E. Robarts.

Do tell Sam we got his letter, and were glad to hear from him. Howdy for all his family.

Mrs. Mary Jones *to* Mrs. Mary S. Mallard[t]

Montevideo, *Tuesday,* January 8th, 1867

My dearest Daughter,

Your last affectionate favor has been received. You know not how your letters cheer and comfort my heart in this utter loneliness. Your brother's visit of a week was very precious, and our parting very sad. It rained incessantly whilst he was here. Yesterday we had a glimpse of the sun, but today the heavens are darkened with clouds: every now and then a scud of cold rain, and every evidence of continued bad weather. All is gloom without, and not much light within.

I sometimes feel I must sink under the various perplexities of this situation, and know that if God should withdraw the hope and confidence which I trust He permits me to entertain in His infinite wisdom and special guidance, that I should be truly desolate and miserable. I have struggled hard to bear up under the severe losses, the sad reverses, and I may almost say pecuniary ruin of our temporal prospects. I have tried to live here that I might protect and not sacrifice this our home from any feeling of loneliness or isolation, or from motives of ease and deliverance from care. I have labored to preserve it as my only home, and what might in God's providence be a home to my dear children. And even now I am not willing, if I can prevent it, to have it sacrificed. But I feel that God is hedging up my way here; and I have come to the determination that if a purchaser can be found, we must part with our beloved, our long-cherished home. I do not see how I can keep it up, dependent as I am upon a manager for the oversight and upon the false and faithless freedmen as laborers. If there was hope of improvement in the future, I could endure any temporary trials; but I am convinced the condition of things will grow worse and worse. There is nothing to make it better— at least with the present generation; and by what means the Negro is to be elevated to an intelligent and reliable laborer I cannot see. The whole constitution of the race is adverse to responsibility, to truth, to industry. He can neglect duty and violate contracts without the least compunction of conscience or loss of honor; and he can sink to the lowest depths of want and misery without any sense of shame or feeling of privation which would afflict a sensitive Caucasian.

As I wrote you, I have not even had the means of going once to church to Midway this winter, and I do not feel that I ought to incur the expense of a horse, for I am trying to do all in my power to defray the expense of publishing your beloved father's work. Although your brother has found business in New York, his expenses are very heavy, *and he is in debt;* so that I feel he is unable to bear the pecuniary expense and also to give his entire evenings to the corrections, which he says are so very great that he is employed every night from the time he reaches home until twelve and one o'clock in correcting the proofs. He has to look out the references and often supply sentences, as he finds the manuscripts of *that Mr.* —— exceedingly defective. Your brother Joe has sent him the original copy, and he thus hopes to have it finally in order, but is convinced your father never read the copy over as it came from Mr. ——'s hand. Of this I cannot say, as the year following we had to leave our home, and your father deposited the manuscripts in the bank in Augusta for safekeeping, and there has been no opportunity since of reviewing them. Both Charles and myself desired Dr. Howe to see them before they went into the publisher's hands, but Joe opposed delay, and we yielded. I wrote Dr. Howe from New York, but received no reply until a few weeks since. It would evidently be a great demand upon his time; and although he did not refuse, I could see it would be a great consumption of his time and attention. I will write him soon. Your brother Charles hopes he will be able to make out and get the first volume in print by the spring. If Dr. Palmer fills his appointment from the General Assembly to Europe, I would like to ask the favor of him to take a copy of the work with him.

From the excessive drought our crop here, although better than our neighbors', *will not meet the expenses of this place the past year,* all things taken into consideration. Mr. Broughton has consented to remain another year, but I have to increase his salary to four hundred dollars, and as yet no increase of laborers, and a decreased system of labor. But there was no alternative: the place must be protected until disposed of.

I wish it were so that the furniture and books could be divided and sent to you and your brothers as you each needed and desired. Do write me what you would like to have, and also what would be the probable cost of transportation in a vessel from Savannah to New Orleans. There are certain things I would like to retain if possible; and I would not like to see the library sold. Many persons in this county need furniture, but they are too poor to pay for it.

I have not yet made a formal contract with the people. Gilbert will stay on his old terms, but withdraws Fanny and puts Harry and Little Abram in her place and puts his son Gilbert out to a trade. Cook Kate wants to be relieved of the heavy burden of cooking for two and wait on her husband. Lucy sighs and groans. But I presume these old damsels will remain with me for the present. I have no young ones about even to pick chips; and having walked out, I have just returned with the end of my sack filled with cedar and live-oak chips, which are giving out their fragrance and warmth.

Do write me your views and feelings on all these points. I have really so little to write of beyond my own troubles that I seldom think it profitable to be thus disturbing even my own children. During all my life it has given me pain to make drafts upon the sympathy of anyone.

I hope your black and white help will dwell in peace and not leave you. I would value Kate for her attachment to you and try to keep her. . . . Can you not get a little girl from some orphan asylum bound to you for a certain period that would nurse Georgia? It will injure your arm seriously to carry her so constantly.

Kiss the dear children for Grandmother. Best love to Robert and yourself. Lucy, Kate, Tenah, and Gilbert all desire remembrances, and Gilbert sends many thanks for Robert's gifts to him. . . . Do write soon and often to

Your ever affectionate mother,
Mary Jones.

Mr. Charles C. Jones, Jr., *to* Mrs. Mary Jones[t]
New York, *Tuesday,* February 5th, 1867
My very dear Mother,

Today we see the earth for the first time since my return. It is very like the first blush of Spring, although I very much fear that we will still have many fierce struggles before Winter fairly resigns his scepter. . . . We have nothing of special interest here. Everything is dull, and the future appears uncertain. Business matters are not as flourishing as they might be.

Father's work is being as rapidly printed as the nature of the case will permit. You have no idea how defective the manuscript is. The manuscript was in no respect ready for the printer, and I am quite certain that Father never read it over. I am doing the best I can, but the style and construction of sentences are often so involved and faulty that it is hard to preserve the original. Frequently, too, wrong citations occur (owing to the negligence of the amanuensis) which have to be corrected, and omissions of important words which have to be supplied. Father appears rather to have *noted* what his thoughts were than to have embodied them in finished sentences. How deeply we deplore the fact that his life and health were not spared to perfect what he began! The first volume will, I hope, if the printer does not delay, be out sometime in the spring or summer.

With warmest love, I am, my dear mother,
Your ever affectionate son,
Charles C. Jones, Jr.

Mr. Charles C. Jones, Jr., *to* Mrs. Mary Jones[t]
New York, *Friday,* February 22nd, 1867
My very dear Mother,

I am very anxious to know that you are well, and that God is dealing kindly with you. How are matters progressing at Montevideo? And is there anything that I can do for you?

Everything here is covered with snow to the depth of more than a foot. Eva and Ruthie are completely housed. They are both pretty well, and unite in tenderest love and remembrance. Ruthie is reading in her Bible, and gets along very well.

Over two hundred pages of the first volume of Father's church history is in type, and I hope that the whole will be stereotyped within the next month. The labor of correcting the manuscript and the proof sheets consumes three to four entire evenings each week. My impression is, in view of the cost of publication and the condition of the manuscript, the second volume of which I fear will be in worse condition than the first, that we had better wait awhile after the publication of the first volume until we see whether there will be any demand for it, and until the manuscript of the second volume has been properly read and corrected. I hope there will be ready sale for the work, although I fear from the impoverished condition of the South, and the nature of the work, that the sale will be more limited and tardy than we could wish. I trust, however, that in this apprehension I may be mistaken. Mr. Scribner will do all that he can, I believe.

We have nothing of special interest. Our business has not been very brisk of late, but we hope for better days.

After I left Indianola the Negroes grew tired of picking cotton, and consequently instead of gathering the fine crop of over one hundred bales which was produced, not much more cotton was picked than sufficed to pay expenses. And I have meat and corn to buy for the present year. I am planting this year with about sixteen hands, and will sell so soon as I can get anything like a fair offer.

With our united love, my dearest mother, and hoping that you will let me know if there is anything I can do for you, I am ever

Your affectionate son,
Charles C. Jones, Jr.

Love to all friends.

Mr. Charles C. Jones, Jr., *to* Mrs. Mary Jones[t]

New York, *Sunday,* March 3rd, 1867

My very dear Mother,

I am this moment in receipt of your favor of the 25th ult., and am thankful to God for His merciful preservation of you in health and from every harm.

I regret to hear that the freedmen are not working as you could wish. There is no redress in the matter except to discharge them, and this leaves one in a worse condition than before. Under the present legislation of Congress I look forward to no stability in this labor, at least for the present. I hope that Mr. McDonald will not disappoint you in the care and attention which we have a right to expect of him. Your purpose to plant an additional amount of corn with Gilbert and Andrew is very good.

All reports we have from the South are gloomy. I have endeavored in vain to effect a sale of our real estate. Parties here do not wish to invest at the South when so many better lands, and at cheaper rates, are offered in the West. The passage of this Reconstruction Bill over the President's veto also complicates matters very materially.

In reference to Tom Dunham's conduct, I see no redress except a prosecution for damages; and such a step I would regard as fraught with more expense and annoyance than profit. I wish the Devil had him.

The first volume of the church history will be stereotyped during the present month. The cost of stereotyping will be about twelve hundred and fifty dollars. Could you spare five hundred of this amount from the sale of the crop at Montevideo without inconvenience to yourself? If you can, I will make up the remaining seven hundred and fifty. The stereotypers will probably expect pay within two or three weeks. If the sum named will inconvenience you, Mother, let me know, and I will make an effort to borrow the whole amount here. . . . I would not mention the subject to you, but I have not now more money than I know what to do with; and it is about all that I can do to meet my expenses. The failure of the Negroes in Burke to gather in my crop has disappointed my calculations; and we find great difficulty in collecting the debts due us for services rendered to the South.

All my evenings are employed in passing Father's *History* through the press, and I have spared no pains to make the edition as accurate as possible.

Eva and Ruthie are both quite well, and unite in tenderest love and remembrance. Eva will not go South this spring. In her delicate state of health she could not stand the travel. We are expecting her mother on during the present or the coming month. We are snowbound again: everything completely covered.

Do, my dearest mother, let me know if there is anything I can do for you, or if there is anything you need. I will write you again fully very soon. Many thanks for the sweet tea olive. Its delicate perfume brings back so vividly all the dear memories of "Home, Sweet Home." Love to Aunt Susan and Cousins Laura and Buttolph and the little ones. I am so glad that they have been with you.

Ever your affectionate son,
Charles C. Jones, Jr.

Mrs. Mary Jones *to* Mrs. Mary S. Mallard[t]

Montevideo, *Monday,* March 4th, 1867

My dearest Daughter,

To think over three weeks have passed since I wrote you a line! Your precious letters are a great comfort to me. They cheer my spirits and divert my thoughts from the daily pressure of care and perplexity, which I do assure you do not diminish.

I have felt at times that I must give way. The contract made is of the simplest kind and at the lowest rate—one acre to the women and two to the men, and the ground plowed, only corn and cotton planted; and yet they dispute even the carrying out and spreading the manure, and wanted a plowman extra furnished. And the fences are not yet made up, or the land prepared for planting. Mr. Broughton, too, appears very unwilling to give himself any trouble to enforce their contract. I sometimes feel that things cannot continue at their present rate, and this morning had a decided talk with him. He has accumulated business and not added one to the force here, but asked for higher wages. I have to give four hundred dollars, with no increase of force and diminished quantity of labor. I could do no better. The contract was at his suggestion, and I presume he thought it would save him trouble, of which he is evidently afraid. Gilbert is very faithful, and so is Charles. They are the exceptions. . . . But we will turn to a more pleasing subject.

Your dear aunt and Jimmie have made me a visit of over three weeks, which I greatly enjoyed. It was a time of great perplexity, and her presence and company greatly cheered me. Your aunt is very well and cheerful, and speaks soon of going to Savannah and probably to Macon.

Your Aunt Julia has just spent two days with me, and we had a pleasant time living in the past and talking of our dear children. She has given up all care, and lives with Rossie and Kitty at Walthourville; expects to spend the summer with Fred and Clarence.

Last week I went to Maybank, and called upon Mr. and Mrs. Lewis, and spent the night at Woodville. Kate and Audley are trying to make themselves comfortable. They occupy three houses, and hope soon to have their dwelling put up; but labor is very high and very scarce. He has two white men laboring on the farm; no Negroes yet excepting day laborers. . . . Our dear old home would almost break your heart. As I rode up, Mr. Dunham's sheep were eating down the beautiful flowers as they were putting out; and the whole place, wooded and cleared, has been burnt. Indeed, if our *enemy* is not removed, the forest on the Island will be entirely destroyed by his repeated burnings. And he is making free use of our lumber—cedar, oak, and pine.

Did I write you Stepney has charge of the planting at Arcadia? But all under contract.

My dear child, I have been deeply pained to hear of Robert's continued suffering from his head. I am the more uneasy knowing that he is so uncomplaining. Do try repeated use of tincture of iodine, and then cold bathing after the surface is well from the iodine. Perhaps coffee disagrees with him; it always affects my head and nerves. I believe green tea much better for a student.

And my precious little Georgia—to think she remembers me! Tell her "Danma" has braided her a beautiful gold-colored cambric with black, and will send it by express as soon as she goes to Savannah. I am so thankful she has recovered from pneumonia. I wish you had Tenah in New Orleans.

I am going to write Mary, and will close, with warmest love to Robert and yourself and the dear children. I *think* Mr. Buttolph *would* accept a call to New Orleans.

Ever, my darling child, your affectionate mother,
Mary Jones.

Send me your likeness and Georgia's.
Dunwody is planting at Bonaventure.

Mrs. Mary Jones *to* Miss Mary Jones Mallard[t]

Montevideo, *Monday,* March 4th, 1867

My very dear Granddaughter,

I received your letter a few weeks since while Cousin Jimmie was with me, and it gave me great pleasure to see how well you could write. And Cousin Jimmie read it, and his grandmother told him he must learn at once to write.

He is a good boy and a smart one at his books. Every morning while he was here he read a chapter in the New Testament and a psalm and said a reading and a geography lesson. In the afternoon he always drove up and penned the sheep and cows. One afternoon we heard him calling loudly, and the oxen had penned him up, and he was afraid they would hook him. He was very useful to me, and liked playing with the sheep and lambs and in the garden and under the grove so much that he did not want to go back to Flemington.

Little Sister has just written me a letter through her mama, and she tells me of six or seven books she has read through. And she is now able to read in her Bible, and studies and reads by herself. She sends her love to all her cousins, and I know you will always remember and love each other.

I am happy to hear that Brother and yourself go to school and have so excellent a teacher. You must love and respect her and try to improve by all she teaches you. I want you to tell her Mama has written me about her, and I desire my best respects to her and feel very grateful to her for the kind interest she takes in my little grandchildren.

I wish, my darling, you and Brother were here now. The hand of our kind Heavenly Father seems stretched out in so many beautiful objects around. The trees have put on their new robes of green, and the bright and beautiful flowers are smiling in the sunshine and generously throwing out their sweet odors to every passing breeze. The two pigeons are here still, and come at my call to eat their breakfast and dinner from a little shelf at the pantry door. There is a remarkable chanticleer in the yard who is very proud of his gay feathers. One half of his plumage is bright red and black, and the other half mottled and striped, and he looks as though two different birds had been cut in two and stuck together.

Poor Captain died from eating part of a diseased mule that had died in the pasture.

Your good old nurse, Mama Lucy, asks constantly after you and Charlie, and says you must love your books and study hard. And Tenah wants to see you all, and Abram told me today he wanted to see "Marse Charlie" and "Miss Mamie." You must never forget these servants that were so kind to you all. Tell Kate her mother has been very sick, but she is better now, and all the rest of her family are well; and all they with the people here send many howdies for her. And Daddy Gilbert thanks Papa for what he sent him, and sends many howdies for you all. And so does old Daddy Andrew.

I hope you will write me again soon. . . . Kiss your precious mother and father and brother and Georgia for Grandmother; and know that she loves you all tenderly and longs to see you.

Your affectionate grandmother,
Mary Jones.

MRS. MARY JONES *to* MRS. MARY S. MALLARD[t]

Montevideo, *Friday,* March 15th, 1867

My darling Child,

I have just returned from a very hurried business visit to Savannah, weary and feeling very sad. All things conspire to make me so, especially the return of this most sorrowful period of my life. Oh, how long, how long it has been since your dear father was taken from us! I feel at times as if I must die from the weight of grief which presses on my heart. The unshared burden! Here I am utterly alone. The goodness of God alone comforts and sustains my poor soul with a conviction that for the present I am in the path of duty, and hoping to accomplish the cherished wish of my heart.

Your brother writes me the first volume of the *History* will be through the press this spring, but Mr. Scribner is uncertain whether to give it now to the public or withhold it until fall. The cost of stereotyping that volume will be twelve hundred and fifty dollars. I have just sent all I had from the sale of the cotton over and above what I am at present owing.

The Arcadia cotton (one bale) was sold in the seed to Mr. Mann and realized one hundred and sixty-eight dollars. You request your part sent to your brother to aid in the publication, which I will do. We made here ten light bales of white cotton for *all* concerned and two of stained. Could it have been gotten early to market it would have commanded a good price, but it is now very dull. But I was obliged to sell, fearing also that it would be no better. You know I lost all my mules, even to the little colt (Dove's last representative). I will not by a great deal meet my last year's expenses, and our provision crop was so short I fear many on this place will soon be in want. The freedmen—nearly all of them—went to Savannah for their money; and although they need *bread,* almost all of them, Gilbert tells me, bought either a musket, double-barreled gun, or revolver! They all bear arms of some sort in this county. Such is the limited nature of my contract on this place for the present year—with no increase of laborers, but great increase of the manager's salary, and evident *decrease* of effort on his part—that

I have really very little hope of realizing anything from the place the present year. The only advantage is the protection of the place in view of sale; but such is the state of the country even *that* may not be advisable, although if a good offer presented, I do not think I would hesitate.

While in Savannah I saw Kitty. She is looking remarkably well and cheerful, and will make me a visit before long if possible. I stayed with *our dear* and *tried* friends Dr. and Mrs. Axson. All sent warmest love to Robert and yourself. Randolph was married on the 12th of February to Ella Law. She is a lovely daughter in their family.

March 16th. An opportunity presents itself of sending this immediately to the office at No. 3, and I close hastily this morning. In Savannah I sent by express a little dress for my dear little Georgia. "Danma" braided it for her. I am grieved to hear of her ill health. Do use constant rubbings of sweet oil, camphor, and hartshorn over her little chest and lungs and spine. I am greatly troubled about Robert's state of health. *Do make him rest all you can.* I hope the blisters will help him. Let him use the liniment also down the spine and give up drinking coffee and use tea. . . . Your letters are a great comfort to me, and cheer my heart in this far-off wilderness. God bless you, my beloved child, and your dear husband and precious children! . . . Servants all send howdies.

Ever your own loving mother,
Mary Jones.

MISS MARY E. ROBARTS *to* MRS. MARY JONES[t]

Marietta, *Thursday,* April 11th, 1867

My dearest Cousin,

We received your kind letter last week giving us the account of our faithful Sam's last days, for which—and your kind attentions to him—please accept our united thanks. His was the darkest mind I ever came in contact with. If after so many years of faithful service he had died without my having told him of the Saviour, I should reproach myself without ceasing; but whenever I could, I tried to impress it upon him that his soul must be saved. . . . As you say, we can only leave him in the hands of God. If all servants were as faithful as he was, slavery would have been a pleasant thing to master and servant.

We were agreeably surprised to see our dear Cousin Susan and her little boys coming up the walk a fortnight since. She had written us that she was in Macon but could not come here. We were lamenting over it, when lo, she walked in on Tuesday afternoon! We were truly glad to see her; and it was a peculiar gratification to Mother.

She is always talking about you and Cousin Susan, and says every day: "Mary, do write to Susan and Mary, and ask why they don't write."

I will say to amuse her: "Mother, they are bad girls; I would not write to them."

She says: "Why, Mary, how can you speak so of your cousins?"

Cousin Susan will tell you exactly how she is. Some days she has a hot fever and does not say anything; expectorations very bad. Then again she converses a great deal, particularly about her relatives and former associates; her mind perfectly clear on most subjects. She sits up very little now.

Louisa is completely wilted down from confinement to the sickroom, for on days when she might have gone out to take a little exercise in the yard, it has rained. She looks miserably.

I have not had a comfortable day in a month. First a severe pain in my face which has resulted in what Dr. Stewart calls fungus; says it will have to be cut out and burned with a hot iron. Added to this I have acute rheumatism in my shoulder. And even if not well, necessity is laid upon me. I should often like to lie in bed and be nursed—if I had anyone to do it.

Sophia has been with us a month. Her little baby is now two weeks old. She calls it Lil Ellen (after Lilla and Ellen), but I do not think the name a pretty one.

The doctor and Ellen and their little baby spent a week with us. Ellen looks thin and worn, but her baby is very fat and sweet; has black eyes and a fair complexion. She seems very dear to me, and it is a trial to be separated from her and Ellen; but I fear I never will be much with them, as I have to scuffle for my daily bread, and never expect to make more than that. Ellen received the little dress; it is very pretty, and I saw the baby wear it several times. I hope she wrote and thanked you for it. You were kind to make it for my dear child. The doctor has a fine school; is quite steady and devoted to his wife and baby.

Clifford Powers came up a few weeks since and boarded her daughter Evelyn with us to go to school. We expect to take a few boarders this summer, but only enough to help us to live, for the difficulty of getting servants is so great, and Louisa and myself so unwell, we could not take charge of a very large family. If our health should fail, what would become of our dear mother? Good health and strength are more important to us now than ever, with so much depending on us.

We heard from dear Mary last week. She sent us her likeness, Mr. Mallard's, and Georgia's—all excellent. Why don't you go there and live with Mary instead of tilling the soil with freedmen? You surely cannot make much at it, and it wears away your life to be so separated from your children. . . . And now, my dear cousin, I must say farewell. Louisa and I did receive your letter, and nothing but hands full of daily care prevented our answering them. Do write again. Do tell Lucy, Kate, Gilbert, and any of your old servants howdy for me.

> Your ever affectionate cousin,
> Mary E. Robarts.

Yesterday Bruce broke open a letter we sent to the office, stole the money, and ran away to Atlanta. This is the third time he broke open letters. I tremble to think what is to become of one so young doing such a thing.

Mrs. Mary Jones *to* Mrs. Mary S. Mallard[t]

Montevideo, *Monday, April 22nd, 1867*

My darling Daughter,

This is the tenth anniversary of your marriage, and I am too weary to do more than assure Robert and yourself of my warmest wishes for many happy returns. I have thought a great deal of you today, and sought in a special manner at the throne of grace for the divine blessing upon you both and upon your dear children. May the Lord make you conscientious and faithful and wise in training them up! It is a great and responsible work to educate a family. Habits and manners formed in childhood generally abide through life; and certainly the principles of faith taught in youth will shape the conduct and character for time and for eternity.

I am greatly delighted with the likenesses. Robert's is excellent. Everyone says you look *broken*. Dear little Georgia's is a sweet picture, and "Danma" loves to look at her dear little baby sitting up like a little lady. *Tenah* was delighted to see it. I do long to see you all, but *when* is known only to Him who ordereth all our ways.

23rd. Yesterday was a great mass meeting (political) of the freedmen at Newport Church. I am told there never was such a turnout in this county. They were addressed by Rev. Campbell, the former governor of St. Catherines, now owner of Belleville plantation (McIntosh County), where he has a colony of his own color (black). . . . They erected a stage under the trees near Mr. Law's monument, and had three flags (U.S.) displayed over their heads. Campbell urged them to hold fast to the Radicals and give the Democrats a wide berth. This is the onward progress to (I fear) a war of races.

And yet I am more hopeful than I have been for a long time. I think the bill of our governor, and that of the governor of Mississippi, will test if we have any semblance of a constitution or any law in the land. I believe the whole government to be nothing more nor less than a great stranded whale, whose flounderings are just beginning to appear. I must believe that He who ruleth in the army of heaven and among the inhabitants of earth is about to defeat the counsels of the wicked and bring to confusion the iniquity of this nation. I do feel at times a *strange hopefulness.* . . .

Your brother has sent me the printed title page to your dear father's *History,* and the first volume will soon be stereotyped. I sent him all the money (one hundred and sixty-eight dollars) that came from Arcadia—yours and Joe's and Charles's part—to aid in the publication. I will try and defray the whole expense. Your brother says he has given his entire winter to the work, generally being engaged until one o'clock in the morning.

Your Uncle John writes very sadly of Sister Jane's health. Your aunt has just returned from her visit to Savannah, Macon, Marietta, and Griffin. I must close. Tomorrow, *D.V.,* we meet to clean out the graveyard. Miss Clay spent last week with me, and sends love. Remember me to Dr. and Mrs. Palmer. Tell little Mary I am looking for a letter from her. Do encourage her to write. Kiss the dear children for Grandmother, and best love to Robert and yourself. If *possible* do influence Kate to marry and keep her; she certainly is attached to you. Lucy, Kate, and Gilbert all send howdies.

Ever, my dear child, your affectionate mother,
Mary Jones.

Sam (Lucy's father) died in March.

Mrs. Mary Jones *to* Mrs. Mary S. Mallard[t]

Montevideo, *Wednesday*, May 15th, 1867

My dearest Daughter,

Your last kind favor, with the letter of my dear granddaughter, has been received. You cannot know how precious and acceptable your letters are to me. I hear nothing, see nothing, but as my children write or send me papers. Recently I have, however, been favored with visits from many friends.

Did I write you that Miss Clay spent a week with me? She was so cheerful, so delightful in every respect, that I was greatly refreshed by her society. If God spares our lives next winter, I think if I am here she will be much with me. She says she wants to write a book, and I tell her this is the place to do it in. She really has not even the comfort of a chamber to herself at Richmond, where they have built a rough house which has been more than filled. I do not think at her time of life that she is called upon to make sacrifices that involve entire personal ease and quiet. All but one—and he a man—of their former servants have left. . . . When she came, she brought me half a dozen bottles pure London ale and some nice black tea (about half a pound). Feeling the need of some tonic, I have taken a little of the ale, and thought it did me good. But I cannot bear—and do not like—anything stronger than *tea*. I may not leave here just now, and if I stay will take some kind of tonic to give me a little strength.

Sabbath week was our Communion at Midway, and Rev. Mr. Comfort from Valdosta preached for us all day. . . . He is a Virginian, and a regular F. F. V.—that is, he belongs to the best aristocracy in the world, one of those noble and pious old Presbyterian families of Virginia. . . . Mr. Buttolph brought him and spent the night with me. I was greatly interested in his visit. Being acquainted with many friends whom he knew, and having traveled over the mountains and valley and visited the springs of Virginia, we had many subjects of conversation. He was in Princeton Seminary when the war broke out. Was closely watched; had to leave secretly; made his way through much difficulty; arrived in Alexandria at the very time *Jackson* killed Ellsworth; reached our forces and entered as a private, in which capacity he served until he was licensed and became a chaplain. His health is very feeble; has rheumatism—owing, I presume, to exposure in the army. . . . The day Mr. Buttolph and Mr. Comfort left, Mrs. Alexander and Mr. Alexander and Miss Calhoun with little Hattie came over, and Mrs. Alexander with the baby remained a day and night. She then sent Baby home and stayed with me until Saturday. So you see I have been favored with company.

On Sabbath morning I went to Flemington and worshiped; it was also their Communion. . . . I stayed all night with your aunt and cousin. . . . Your aunt was absent about six weeks with James and Willie; visited our relatives in Marietta and Griffin. Sister Jane continues in very ill health; my brother writes very gloomily of her condition. She has been sick for two years, and is now most of the time in bed. Mary Sophia had just been confined at Aunt's and had a little daughter. They have several boarders, and hope for as many as they can accommodate in summer.

Sister Susan and Laura and Mr. Buttolph have very kindly invited me to spend the summer with them, and so have Joe and Carrie. I am really at a loss what to do. It would be a great happiness to see my dear children, and I know they would do all in their power for me; but I really feel as if the expense of traveling is more than I ought to incur—and cannot unless I am able to raise the means.

I have tried to live as economically this winter as possible, that every means might be furnished to the publication of the *History*. The first volume will cost thirteen hundred dollars; I have been only able, with the hundred and sixty-eight dollars contributed by your brothers and yourself, to send on seven hundred and fifty dollars. I have been making every effort to sell my cattle and sheep to raise the money, but without success.

Last week your brother sent me the first clear stereotype pages of the work, and my eyes rested upon them with feelings of devout gratitude to God. My first impulse was to fall upon my knees and render thanks that I had been permitted to see the desire of my beloved husband accomplished, and to know that the valuable labor of the last ten years of his life would be given to the church and the world.

Your brother Charles has labored very hard to prepare the work for the press. His entire evenings have been given until one o'clock in the morning before he could retire. Says he has not been able this winter to open a law book at night. My constant prayer has been that God would bless these efforts to the good of his own soul. In his last letter he says it has been a hard struggle to support his family. The most of their business is from the South; consequently a great difficulty in collecting.

A friend tells me *Eva* is to be *confined* in July, and said she supposed I knew all about it. But not a *hint* even has been given to me. I understand she wishes only her particular friends informed. If they mean to surprise me, I ought not to anticipate the information; and if designedly withheld, it certainly would not be very pleasant to make inquiries. So the matter must rest with themselves. There are wounds in life very painful.

I am glad you have taken off black. Your dear father did not approve of wearing it for a long season of years.

You do not write me what your plans are for the summer. Do let me know if Dr. Palmer thinks of going to England. I would like so much to place your father's work in his hands if he does go. I hope it may have a European as well as American circulation.

Last night there was a large meeting and registering of names at Riceboro. A Yankee Negro the speaker. Assurances given that the coming year forty acres of land would be given to each, and our lands confiscated and given to them, to whom they justly belonged. All here were present. A fearful state of things! Where will it end?

Tell Kate her family are all well and send howdies. Her father and mother say they want her to come home to them. I am really grieved she has acted so. Tell her I hope if possible she will marry the man and try and lead a better life; that I wish her well, and she can never prosper in sin. . . . Kiss the dear children. Best love to Robert and yourself.

Ever, my dearest child, your affectionate mother,
Mary Jones.

Mrs. Mary Jones *to* Miss Mary Jones Mallard[t]

Montevideo, *Wednesday,* May 15th, 1867

My dear Granddaughter,

I was delighted to receive your letter and to know through Mama that you had composed and written it yourself.

You ask about dear Grandpapa's pets. They are all here, in the grove and on the lawn, just as funny and merry as ever, running up and down the trees and springing from limb to limb with their bushy tails curled over their backs, sometimes sitting up on their hind legs and holding a nut or berry in their forepaws, which they eat like a monkey. When I walk into the grove, they sometimes chatter in the trees overhead and run about and look and act as if they would give battle. But I believe it is all in sport, for the only mischief they do is to steal all the pecan nuts; and what they do not eat on the spot they hide away in winter quarters. They have become so numerous that I have given Mr. Broughton leave to kill them when I go away; I mean some of them.

The garden and trees are filled with pretty, merry birds that are constantly singing praises all day long. And tonight, while the moon is shining almost as bright as day, the great owls have come in from the swamp— I was going to say to give me a serenade upon their bass viols, but I verily believe it is to gather a good supper from my fat little chickens in the poultry yard. I shall keep a sharp eye upon them, for I have no idea of feasting them in these hard times. They had best be off with their music and take for their supper a rabbit or wildcat, for if they stay much longer I shall have their wings for a fan, and Pussy will take the rest!

You know Grandmama lost all her mules and horse this fall. She has been obliged to buy two mules. They are very small. The white one I call Hope, and the yellow one Faith. Week before last the citizens all met to clean out our old graveyard at Midway. When I was coming home, Daddy Gilbert thought he could drive over a bridge that was broken on Lambert causeway. I had walked over, and just as the mules and buggy got on the bridge (one side-sleeper of which was gone, and the bridge leaning) Hope stumbled and fell, which threw Faith into the deep canal. The plank flew up, and away went buggy and mules! Hope lay prostrate on her side, entangled in the harness and plank. She could not move, and submitted quietly. But little Faith just drew herself out of all entanglements; and there she stood in the deep waters and broken fragments perfectly erect, with her little nose and ears just above the water. Gilbert sprang out and cut the harness from Hope and helped her to rise, and swam then out to the bank. The pole of the buggy was broken, but it was kept up in a wonderful way by one hind wheel. Two men and two boys seemed sent at this moment by our Heavenly Father to our relief, and by great effort they pushed the buggy up. All this while the rain fell in torrents, with wind and thunder and lightning. I was soaked from my bonnet all over, and Gilbert and Harry the same. Do not my little mules deserve their names? When Hope was prostrate amid the troubles, she lay submissive and quiet; but little Faith stood erect and never moved, although the waters of the deep canal were almost running over her. It taught me this lesson: my hope may be cast down, but my faith never. She says: "Although He slay me, I will trust Him."

Kiss your precious mother and father and dear little sister and brother for me, and write soon to

Your loving grandmama,
Mary Jones.

Mom Lucy and Tenah and Little Abram and Gilbert and Mom Kate all send howdies to you.

Mrs. Mary Jones *to* Mrs. Mary S. Mallard[t]

Montevideo, *Wednesday,* June 5th, 1867

My darling Child,

I was thinking of your birthday and dated *the 12th,* which, when it arrives, if your mother is alive you may be assured she will be thinking of you and praying for you and wishing you every good and happiness for time and for eternity.

I have been suffering intensely over a week with pain in the arm and shoulder that was injured *ten years* ago. It has caused me to think of your sufferings, which have been so extreme, and which I doubt not you will always feel in your broken bone. On Sabbath I was in bed all day, and am now suffering so much I can scarcely write. It has been owing to sewing very steadily and brushing out the dining room with too much energy. I really fear I have injured some of those old ligatures that were ruptured. I am not at ease in any posture night or day.

For weeks we have had most trying weather: excessive rains and hot sultry atmosphere. The planters are complaining of grass and injury to the crops. One night last week we had a terrible thunderstorm that struck two trees, almost touching the cattle and sheep pens, just back of Sue's and near to Caesar's house. But God mercifully shielded man and beast and shivered only a cedar and a pride-of-India.

My dear child, my heart will be very anxious for Robert and yourself and the dear children this summer. I fear especially as those floods have deluged the land around New Orleans. If yellow fever should appear, you and the children would not certainly remain; and yet how could I counsel you to leave your husband? May God protect, guide, and preserve you all!

It rejoices my heart to hear of Robert's encouragement in the church. He has a wide field of influence. May the Great Shepherd enable him to fill it to divine acceptance!

You have never told me if Dr. Palmer goes to Europe this summer. Please let me know in your next, and remember me to them.

Tell my dear granddaughter I am waiting for her next letter, and look for one from *Charlie also*. I send enclosed one written to me from my little Ruthie with her own hand, and the first she ever wrote. I want Charlie to see it, and *then please send it carefully back, for I value it very much*. You can keep it until I reach Nashville, *D.V.*, where I feel I will be much nearer to you.

I have two pair of linen sheets that I want to send you, and thought it might be best to take them on to Nashville. Write me at once what would be the best way of getting them to you. If you *write immediately*, I will get your letter before I leave. I am anxious to go up the last of this week to Flemington and visit your aunt, and make arrangements for leaving the middle or last of June, if my arm gets better. Laura is in Macon with Susie on a visit to Mrs. Nisbet.

Tell Kate her family are all well. I have never told them a word of her situation. She ought to write them.

In any allusion to Eva's situation, *I must request you not to say a word of my having written you,* as I am not informed by her or Charles. I presume it is her wish to keep it thus. I sent her on a bed and mattress, and your brother has recently sent me a barrel of various nice and useful things in housekeeping. Business is dull with them, and he finds it hard, as everybody else does, to meet expenses. Mrs. Eve is with them, and I have heard would make her home in New York.

I have written in scraps, resting my arm. The servants all send many howdies for yourself, Robert, and the children. Tenah longs to see them, and seems ready to cry whenever she speaks of you or them. *She is huge!* With warmest love to Robert and yourself, and kisses for the dear children, and howdy for Kate. God bless you, my child!

Your own mother,
Mary Jones.

I wrote you your dear father's *History* would be out in the fall. Charles has sent me specimens of the stereotyping. The size of the printing is excellent. Does it not rejoice your heart?

Mrs. Mary Jones *to* Mrs. Mary S. Mallard[t]

Montevideo, *Monday,* June 24th, 1867

My darling Child,

Kind Providence favoring my plans, I will leave home in the morning and go down in the freight train to avoid night riding through the swamps, as the passenger train leaves at four o'clock in the morning.

By the express tomorrow I will send you two pair of linen sheets *for your own use,* which will add to your comfort in that hot climate; one of your old books for Charlie and one for Mary; a lace *crazy Jane* for Georgia; and Bloomfield's Greek Testament (which was your dear father's) for Robert. I trust it will prove useful to him in his study of the Scriptures.

Your kind favor with the valuable enclosure from Robert and yourself has been received, and I am truly grateful to you both for your kind and generous remembrance of me. My great grief is that I can do nothing for my children now, and am only a trouble and expense, although I desire to be as little burdensome as possible.

Much as my heart yearns to see you, my dear child, my judgment is against your coming to Nashville and returning to New Orleans in July. I fear it would be dangerous to do so, and might induce severe illness. If our lives are spared, the General Assembly meets in Nashville in November, and then perhaps you could come up. You know not, my dear child, how I long to see you; but I dread your exposure this first year in that climate.

Did you know that Carrie had *expectations* during the summer or fall? So she writes me. And your brother in his last letter for the first time tells me Eva expected to be sick the middle of July or first of August.

I forgot to say the chemise is for you. I bought it in New York. Hope it will fit you. You will see the sheets are marked, and you can alter to your own name. When your uncle was leaving last summer, I handed him fifteen dollars and told him I had sold his linen sheets (which he did not want) for that amount. He was much pleased, but did not know who bought them. I am told Mr. William Stevens, your old teacher, has administered on his estate.

By the by, it just occurs to me to ask if Robert has any remembrance of having paid whilst Arcadia was in his charge a medical bill to Dr. Farmer for attendance upon *Fanny,* who died. It was in February 1864. He has recently sent me the account, and as he was always very prompt in collecting his bills, I thought this might have been paid. Please let me know when you write about this matter if Robert has any recollection of it.

Tenah has been very sick, and looks badly. She is in a family way. Lucy also is not well. She has just come in, and says she wants to see you and the children "worse than bad." I think Niger has his fill of planting. She and Tenah send many thanks for the presents. They have not come yet.

For six weeks we have had floods of rain. Crops almost lost. Until yesterday the sun had not shone for ten days.

I spent over a week with your aunt. Mr. Buttolph was not well: something of erysipelas. . . . Sister Susan and I went to Walthourville. . . . *Belle* is engaged to be married to *Mr. Tunno* of Carolina, a son of Julia's old friends. It appears to give great pleasure to your Aunt Julia, but disappoints some other persons.

I must close, with much love to Robert and yourself, and kisses for my dear grandchildren. I will look for Charlie's letter. And send me Ruthie's.

Ever your affectionate mother,
Mary Jones.

VI

Mrs. Mary Jones *to* Mrs. Mary S. Mallard[t]

Nashville, *Saturday,* July 20th, 1867

My dearest Child,

I have been one week in this place. Found your brother and Carrie and the children all well and looking well; the children much grown. I had a pleasant journey on, with kind friends meeting me at every point.

Spent a week with your uncle and family. Sister Jane much improved, with prospect of permanent recovery; looked, I thought, as well as usual. Your uncle very thin, and looking much older; perplexed with the uncertain prospect of support from his church. Whilst in Griffin the examinations in the college where Johnnie and Josie attend occurred, and I was highly delighted with their standing and proficiency. In Josie's department he was the only scholar who stood *perfect* in everything (studies, deportment, etc.) They were the best speakers, and the vice-president said they were model boys. I felt truly proud of my nephews, and trust they will be great comforts to their parents. . . .

In Atlanta I was met by Dr. Wilson. . . . Your uncle had sent a sketch of your dear father's missionary labors to Dr. Wilson at my request; and since being here I have been diligently occupied making such extracts from his reports to the Association for the Religious Instruction of the Negroes as would illustrate his life and labors as a missionary. I am especially anxious that this period of his life should appear in its true light and importance. Feeling not very well from the fatigue of a long journey and writing so constantly since my arrival makes me feel good-for-nothing.

I spent three days with our relatives in Marietta. Our dear old aunt enjoyed my visit. Had no fever, and was up all day excepting her usual nap, and sat until some time after dark in the porch. Our cousins well. Ellen and Dr. Brumby with them in vacation. They have a sweet little baby. Spent a day with Mr. and Mrs. Rogers.

I thought a great deal of you in Atlanta. The place much improved: all life and bustle, and population larger than before the war. Marietta rebuilding slowly.

My dear child, I am filled with pressing anxieties for you and Robert and the dear children. Oh, that the Lord would shield you all from that dreadful disease! Do write me constantly, if but a line. I am thankful to feel if you should be taken sick I could come to you.

A letter received today from your aunt says Mr. Buttolph is much better, though still suffering pain in his feet and ankles. She mentions the sudden death from congestive fever of *Mr. John Wells* at Walthourville, and the drowning of poor Mr. Ross in Sunbury. He jumped from a schooner that lay in the river into a canoe which upset, and in attempting to right the boat he sank to rise no more. His father came, and has taken Eva and her child home with him. I went down in the freight train with Mr. Wells, and said to him: "You ought to take care of yourself this summer, it is so wet." He replied: "Oh, nothing hurts me!" He has been *very sad* since Belle's engagement; has loved her since she was fourteen. He was a Christian and therefore ready. But alas for the other!

Your brother and Carrie unite with me in best love to Robert and yourself and to the dear children. I am looking for Charlie's letter, and he must send me Ruthie's. The Lord bless and preserve you all!

Ever your affectionate mother,
Mary Jones.

Mr. Charles C. Jones, Jr., *to* Mrs. Mary Jones[t]

New York, *Sunday,* July 28th, 1867

My very dear Mother,

You have room enough in your warm, generous heart for another little grandson, and here he is. I present him to you: a little stranger not two days old, by name Edgeworth Casey. He was born yesterday morning at ten minutes past one o'clock, so you see he just escaped hangman's day. He is indeed a bouncing boy, weighing full eleven pounds, and measuring around the head fifteen inches and a half, and around the shoulders sixteen inches. He looks very much like himself at present, but before very long we think he will readily be acknowledged by everyone not only as a very fine but also as a very handsome boy. He is called for Eva's mother. Eva herself suffered severely; and, under God, but for the superior attentions of Dr. Taylor, consequences of the most serious character might have ensued. She is doing very well; and we hope that it will please God to grant her a speedy recovery, and to make this little one pious from his earliest infancy, and a man of honor, probity, and marked usefulness.

Eva and the babe have an excellent and experienced nurse, and the doctor is very assiduous in his attentions. Little Ruthie is quite delighted with her little brother, and thinks he is "a very cunning little fellow." She does not quite understand, however, how he got here, where he came from, and why we got him the very night that she went over to spend with Edith Hatch.

Eva desires her warmest love, Ruthie sends to her dear "danna" many kisses, and you must accept also the early kisses of your new little grandson, who, I trust, will always make your heart very happy. Mrs. Eve desires her kindest remembrances. Our united love to the Doctor, Sister Carrie, and the little ones. And I am ever, my dear mother, with truest wishes for your every blessing,

Your affectionate son,
Charles C. Jones, Jr.

Eva had a hard time, but behaved most heroically.

Mrs. Mary S. Mallard *to* Mrs. Susan M. Cumming[t]

New Orleans, Saturday, August 3rd, 1867

My dear Aunt and Cousin,

A letter received from Kate King yesterday mentioned incidentally that Cousin Lyman had been ill. She "supposes I know dear Mr. Buttolph has been ill for weeks." I had not heard anything about it, and am grieved to hear of it, and hope he has quite recovered. She also mentioned Mr. John Wells's sudden death. Aunt Julia must have a sad household. No doubt Dr. Wells's death is all brought back to Cousin Mary. I suppose Mr. Wells must have contracted his sickness on the plantation.

Thus far we have had a healthy summer, though many have constantly predicted an epidemic; and I have heard the remark many times: "This is yellow fever weather." There are a few cases every week and also some cholera, but really nothing to speak of. I think the highest number of deaths that have occurred in one week from yellow fever have been five. This, you see, is proportionately very small. I have known of only one case within my acquaintance, and that was a young man living near us. He had it very lightly, and is quite well again. Still we are very watchful; and if anyone should be unwell about the house, I should put them to bed and send for the doctor, as everyone has impressed it upon us that everything depends upon taking the fever in time.

The last ten days of July were very warm. Now we are again enjoying pleasant breezes and agreeable nights.

Two weeks ago Mr. Mallard preached at Pass Christian, one of the retreats on the Gulf shore. One of our deacons owns a place over there, and invited Mr. Mallard to come over and take a week of rest and preach to the Presbyterians spending the summer there. The houses at Pass Christian are strung along the beach for five or six miles, one house deep. Everyone has a bathhouse in front of their lot, and the water is so shallow that they have to be put a quarter of a mile and more into the water in order to have it deep enough. Mr. Mallard says you can wade a hundred yards and then be not more than waist deep in the water. This makes it particularly safe for the children.

The gentleman with whom Mr. Mallard stayed is one of the wealthiest in our church. He is chief partner in the leading jewelry establishment here, and his family enjoy all the comforts of wealth. I must tell you of a conversation that Mamie and his little daughter had at a party. Mamie had carried a shabby little brown fan to the party. (I did not know she had taken it with her.) Katie Griswold said to her: "What made you bring such a fan? Suppose you were going to a wedding; would you carry that fan?"

"Yes," says Mamie, "for I have no other."

"Well! You ought to be ashamed of yourself. I would get a nice white satin fan and carry that. Why don't you buy one?"

Says Mamie: "I haven't the means."

"Why don't you get your father to buy you one?"

"Because my father has no money to spend on fans."

"Well! Why don't you get somebody to get you one? Ask some of your relations to buy you one!"

Says Mamie: "My relations and friends are all poor, and they could not give it to me."

Katie, not knowing what to say, said: "You ought to be ashamed of yourself to carry such a fan; and you ought to get another."

"Well," says Mamie, "if you are so anxious for me to have a fine fan, why don't you get one yourself and give it to me?"

Thus ended the conversation. Imagine Mamie's telling the child of the wealthiest people in the church her father had no money to spend on fans, and all her relations were poor! It was very funny.

While I write, Georgia has twice put her hands in the soot of the chimney, so that she might have an excuse for playing in the water under pretense of washing them. She requires a great deal of management, and has been sick so much of her life that we feel she is almost a baby yet. . . . I have a little strap which I find very useful as a regulator, and took it to the breakfast table the other morning. Mr. Mallard asked her what it was brought there for. She replied instantly: "To whip Papa."

I suppose all of your children have grown very much. I long to see all of you, but when we shall all meet I cannot tell.

Recently some of the gentlemen of the church have had six large-sized photographs taken of Mr. Mallard, and they were kind enough to send us one. It is very handsomely finished in India ink, and is a most pleasant and satisfactory likeness. I would give anything if I had one as good of my dear father.

I do not know whereunto the expenses of this place will grow. Think of small pods of okra being sold at fifteen cents per dozen, four tomatoes for ten cents, peaches a dollar and a half per dozen, watermelons (not large) for seventy-five cents and upward without limit, five or six small sweet potatoes for ten cents. Don't you wish you could dispose of a hundred bushels at that rate?

We are quite on the progressive order here. The last improvement made by our military master, Phil Sheridan, took effect yesterday. The city council was removed, and several colored aldermen appointed. It is beyond endurance. I never felt as I do now how desirable it would be to be beyond the rule of these wretches. I tell Mr. Mallard I hope if he gets a call from this place it will be to Canada or somewhere out of Yankee bounds. For the present it is our duty to await the issue, and I only hope they will hasten on their schemes and by this means bring an end of some sort.

Do write me soon. While Mother was in the county I did not write you as often as I ought, for I knew you heard of us through her; but now I will write more frequently. Love to Aunt Julia's family, and sympathy, too, in their troubles. Mr. Mallard and the children unite with me in best love to you both and to Cousin Lyman and the children.

Your affectionate niece and cousin,
Mary S. Mallard.

We have no news from Eva yet.

Mrs. Laura E. Buttolph *to* Mrs. Mary S. Mallard[t]

Flemington, *Saturday,* August 10th, 1867

My dearest Cousin Mary,

We were so glad to hear of you and your loved ones and to know that the fever was not raging in New Orleans as the papers reported.

I am sorry to see that you are progressing the wrong way in New Orleans as we are here. No redress in cases of difficulty with the freedmen here; and stealing seems to be the order of their day, until people find it next to impossible to live. Stock of all kinds killed. No meat, no butter, very little meal. Negroes starving with laziness. Military paralyzing all efforts to make them work. Country ruined: South has no future! Things worse and worse. No help as far as I can see. People generally dissatisfied with their homes; too poor to go away. Seasons unfavorable; too poor to live at home! . . . We have no potatoes, corn, or anything else. We rented out our places, and the crops having all failed, we will realize nothing. The people have no money to pay Mr. Buttolph's salary, and as it is impossible to live on air, of course, I do not know what we shall do. Hope Mr. Buttolph will get a call where those who preach the gospel can live of the gospel. . . . Cousin Audley has recently had a difficulty trying to get some of Ben's sons to work, and been heavily fined. The Nigs get the best, and are in the majority in this county. . . . Mr. William Norman intends removing his large family to Florida; says it is impossible to live here, the Negroes steal so and kill his stock. . . . And things must get worse and *worse here*. Sorry to send you so black a picture of the reality of things!

Cousin John's death is a sad affliction to Aunt Julia's family. Cousin Mary feels it most deeply, and indeed every member of the family. I feel that I have lost a near and dear relative. . . . He looked very handsome even in death, and did not look like a corpse, his face retaining its color. . . . Mr. Ross, Eva's husband, was drowned in the Sunbury River sometime about the last of June. His body was not recovered for five days, and could hardly be identified. He was an admirable swimmer, but had on thick clothing and heavy boots. He jumped from the deck of a schooner into a canoe, and it upset, and he tried to right it; and when a rope was thrown, presume he was too much exhausted to take it and sank. They then got out their boat, but the anchor dropped over, and the man rowing had to drag that, and only neared him as he rose for the last time. . . . His body floated up into a creek and was discovered by the birds. . . . He was drowned opposite the old fort in Sunbury.

I suppose you have heard that Charlie's Eva has a son, and Charlie is greatly delighted. He does not say what his name is to be. He was born on the 27th of July. . . . Mother, Mr. Buttolph, and the children unite with me in *best* love to you and Cousin Robert, Mary, Charlie, and Georgia. . . . Mother says she is so much obliged to you for little Georgia's likeness; also for yours and Cousin Robert's. How much pleasure these shadows give us! Write soon to

Your own cousin,
Laura E. Buttolph.

MRS. MARY JONES *to* MRS. MARY S. MALLARD[t]

Nashville, August 1867

My dearest Daughter,

Last night I had a dream that caused me great anguish in sleep, and I woke up shivering as though I had a chill. I thought your dear father had died, and they were taking him away without permitting me to look upon his face!

Soon after breakfast your letter came, telling me of dear little Georgia's illness from yellow fever. My heart has been so sad, so heavy, all day I could scarcely occupy myself. I told your brother I wanted to go immediately to you. He said what my own reason approved—that I might only increase your trouble; for in all probability, going at this season into New Orleans, I would more readily contract the disease and be only an additional trouble. . . . I can but hope that the disease may not extend in the family, and if it does, as it is not prevailing in an epidemic form, that this may prove a favorable period for that terrible acclimation which I believe all must undergo who live in New Orleans. Darling little Georgia, she had a sorrowful birth and has had a suffering life. I hope you are enabled to supply Kate's place, as this is about the time for leaving.

Carrie is far from well, and is often cast down at her coming day of trial. And my dear Joe looks and is truly very feeble; I am seriously concerned for his health. I have been constantly busy since I reached Nashville. The weather has been excessively hot, but the city is thus far free from cholera, which prevailed so fatally here at this time last year—which is due, as their best citizens acknowledge, *under God,* to your brother's unwearied efforts for the health of the city.

Many thanks for Laura's letter. She gives a dark picture of our once happy home. I really think Mr. Buttolph would do well to remove North, where his father still lives, and he has a large circle of excellent relatives. But it would ruin our church in Liberty. He has sold out their interest in Baker to Mr. Thomas Fleming. . . . Good night, my dear child! I will write Mary and Charlie soon, and am very proud of their letters. Your brother and Carrie unite with me in warmest love and sympathy to Robert and yourself and the children. Kiss them all for me. God bless and protect you all!

Ever your affectionate mother,
Mary Jones.

Miss Mary E. Robarts *to* Mrs. Mary Jones[t]

Marietta, Monday, August 26th, 1867

My dear Cousin,

We have been expecting and expecting to hear from you ever since you left us, but have not heard one word. I sincerely hope neither you nor any of dear Joe's family have been sick. Do write, for we are truly anxious to hear. Tell us all about how Joe is situated there, how you like Nashville; and tell me something new, for I feel pretty well rusted out. . . .

Dr. Brumby, Ellen, and sweet little Baby left us about three weeks since for West End. They are well. Louisa was in Atlanta last week and saw them; says the baby is smarter and prettier every day. It is a great trial to me to be separated from them, but I do not know if it will ever be any different. My duty binds me to my dear mother; then I shall have to support myself as long as my health and strength last. We expect Sophia on Wednesday for a few days; I long to see her and her dear little baby. Lilla has been with us for a month past. Mr. Adams goes North for goods; takes his little boy to see his aunts.

Julia King and Johnnie spent several days with us the first of the month. Johnnie had been quite sick; was so here; looked miserably. They went to Fred's at Spring Place. She wrote me from there; is delighted with the place and the pleasant home of her boys.

I had a letter from Charlie a month since announcing the birth of a fine son. Hope he may be a comfort and blessing to them, and that by the time he reaches manhood may have something better to look forward to than any of us have!

The chains seem to be tightening every day. General Pope issued an order to withdraw the appropriation by the state to Franklin University on account of a speech delivered by one of the students. Threatened to close the college or convert it into a barracks, but this has not been done. Exercises will be resumed, faculty supported by pay of the students.

Louisa is quite busy assisting Miss Meigs with her bridal outfit; has been to Atlanta twice to purchase it; is at Mrs. Meigs's for the day and night to assist with the wedding cake. Mrs. Meigs is Dr. Stewart's sister, a particular friend of ours. . . . A fine new bell was hung in our church on Saturday, and when I heard it ring, I lifted up my heart in thanksgiving that there were some able to "strengthen the things that remain and are ready to die"—to care for our Zion in these hard times. . . . The season has been short for boarders this summer, and how we shall get through the winter without them I do not know. . . . Did you hear before you left that Eva Ross's husband had been drowned in the Sunbury River? His father and brother went immediately down and took her and her little boy home. She is expecting another, poor child. . . . Much love to you, Dr. Joseph, and Carrie. Kiss the children for me. . . . Have not heard from dear Mary Mallard since you left. Have you?

Your ever affectionate cousin,
Mary E. Robarts.

Excuse me for not writing before, but I am so engrossed by the fleshpots, can think of nothing else. Rather, can only think of my friends; have not much time for anything else.

REV. JOHN JONES *to* MRS. MARY JONES[t]

Griffin, Thursday, September 5th, 1867

My dearest Sister,

Your last came to hand on last Friday, just before leaving home on that day for an appointment in the country, from which I returned on Monday last.

We are all distressed about Mary, Robert, and the children, and are very anxious to hear again. I wrote them three weeks since, and am looking for a letter every day. Yesterday I saw Dr. Tebault of New Orleans, who is passing some weeks here with his wife, formerly Miss Bailey. His last letters from New Orleans are favorable. Do write very soon and inform us all about Mary and all hers.

A letter from Cousin Mary Robarts yesterday mentions that Robert and family, if compelled to leave New Orleans this summer, will come to them in Marietta. I trust they will leave for a month or six weeks and thus refresh them after the summer. Cousin Mary writes that Brother Palmer has resigned his pastorship in Marietta, having been elected to a professorship in a college in Louisiana, and that Brother Buttolph would be called to Marietta with the promise of a salary of twelve hundred dollars and a parsonage. I trust he will come. And then you must sell out in Liberty and buy that Nevitt cottage in Griffin. Liberty will be too lonely for you if Cousin Susan and all should leave. And Griffin will be so convenient for your children to visit you.

Did you receive my letter addressed to you at Marietta? It was written two days after you left us.

My dear sister, since writing a portion of this letter, I have seen by today's papers that the fever at New Orleans has been pronounced epidemic, though of a mild type. Do write and urge Robert and Mary to leave as soon as possible.

Charles wrote us a special letter announcing the birth of his noble little boy. I wrote him immediately congratulating him and Eva. I do rejoice with him.

I am truly happy to say that my dear Jane has greatly improved since you left. It seems a wonder, and is a cause of constant joy to look upon her and realize what she has passed through. I know you will also rejoice that I have at last bought a home—the Ufford cottage, from the recent purchasers. I have paid down two thousand dollars, and am to pay the balance (six hundred and fifty dollars) on or before 1st January 1868. We get possession 1st of November. I got also in the bargain a cow, two bureaus, a dining table, book case, three bedsteads, six mahogany chairs, six ditto cane-bottom, three small tables, some crockery, two sows, etc., etc., etc. It is considered a good bargain. Our new railroad is now to be built, and property is already looking up. . . . Our united love to Joseph, Carrie, and their dear little ones, and very much of the same to you. Do write soon to

Your ever affectionate brother,
J. Jones.

Mrs. Mary S. Mallard *to* Mrs. Susan M. Cumming[t]
New Orleans, *Thursday,* September 12th, 1867
My dear Aunt,

I take it for granted you are anxious to hear from us at this time. I know you see reports of the epidemic here and know that we are exposed.

We have had no new cases of fever since Georgia's attack, though we are surrounded by it on every side. The yellow fever increases, but not rapidly, and thus far the deaths have been chiefly confined to foreigners. . . . Our most experienced physicians pronounce this a very mild epidemic. The cases, though very decided, yield easily to treatment. The weather has been so pleasant and the skies so beautiful that it has been almost impossible to believe there could be poison in the air.

I received a letter from Aunt Mary Robarts this week in which she mentions Cousin Lyman had been invited to preach for their church with a view to a call. I do hope the way will be open for you to move. Aunt Mary says Marietta has revived very much. Liberty County is hopelessly ruined, and I cannot see anything to make a continuance there desirable. And then there is another phase of the up country: it can be made a white man's country, which the coast will not be—at least for many years. If you get established there, perhaps you may have to entertain some New Orleans friends occasionally!

Brother Charlie has written begging us to go to New York until winter, but at this time it would be far more dangerous to leave than to remain;

for the fever would almost certainly be developed, and it might be where we could not procure either competent medical attendance or good nurses. Most of the nurses here are colored, and some of them very efficient. We have a man engaged should Mr. Mallard take the fever. Our friends here are very kind in offering their services. There is a great deal of kindness and hospitality among these people, and a certain degree of freedom in calling upon each other in time of need that is very pleasant. I trust we will be preserved.

I will write you when I can. We are all very cheerful and hopeful. You must pray that we may be kept in faith and our minds stayed upon God. Mr. Mallard and the children unite with me in much love to yourself, Cousin Lyman, and Cousin Laura and the children. If Kate King's father still thinks of coming here, I hope he will not think of doing so at this time: it might prove fatal. Love to Aunt Julia's family.

Your affectionate niece,
Mary S. Mallard.

MRS. MARY JONES *to* MRS. MARY S. MALLARD[t]

Nashville, *Wednesday,* September 18th, 1867

My darling Child,

I cannot sleep—have been lying awake thinking of you all, and now rise and light the gas, that I may send you a line by the morning's mail. Oh, the goodness and mercy of the Lord to you and to me, that He should be keeping you in perfect peace amid "the pestilence that walketh in darkness and that wasteth at noonday"! Only dear little Georgia has been smitten, and her disease has been healed, so far as I now know. And yet fearfulness and trembling often seizes me as I think: "Perhaps this moment my children are laid upon a bed of sickness." Fearful and distressing! I am so thankful that a cheerful, hopeful spirit is granted to sustain you from day to day. . . .

Carrie still keeps up, and is working bravely. She has a woman in the house who works the sewing machine, and this week we hope to do wonders. She had not made the first preparation when I came, and *nothing* over from Charlie, and has had all her own underclothes to make up; so you may imagine there was plenty of work to be done. Yesterday I took Stanhope to a tailor and had a winter suit cut for him, and today, D.V., I am to cut another by it for him, that he may be prepared for cold weather. The children all look well and have improved much. Susie is very pretty and interesting, and is much more manageable. Stanhope reads very well, and is anxious to go to school.

I fear little Casey cannot be well, or is spoiled. Charles writes: "He has no mercy day or night." I am sorry to hear it, for it will be a great drawback to Eva.

Your last favor has been received. It is my only relief to receive your letters. Nashville continues healthy, but oh, so hot! Plenty of mosquitoes at night, with certain other little *night robbers,* who as I lit my gas scampered away in every direction. *God be with you all, my dear child!* Carrie and Joe always unite in best love to Robert and yourself, and the children speak of you all constantly. Kiss my dear grandchildren.

Ever, my dearest child, your affectionate mother,
Mary Jones.

I am glad to know Kate is with you. *Tell* her *howdy.* I was sorry she acted so wickedly, but I never told any of her family, or anyone at home.

Mrs. Mary Jones *to* Mrs. Laura E. Buttolph[t]
Nashville, Monday, September 23rd, 1867

I did not intend, my dearest niece, that one day should pass without replying to your last dear favor, and yet over a week has done so.

You can scarcely imagine how busy I have been all the time. I found Carrie with all her preparations to make, and we have been trying to get all the little ones prepared for winter. I have been making various new and refitting old garments. The past week Carrie was taken so unwell I thought it would all be over in a short time, but she is up again, and it may be deferred for two weeks.

Above all this is my constant anxiety for my beloved children in New Orleans, from whom I hear three or four times a week. Heard on the 16th and 18th. Dear little Georgia quite recovered, but Robert and Charlie were both sick with the fever. My precious child yet preserved, and little Mary. She writes that Robert and Charlie were both doing well. . . . They were surrounded by kind and efficient friends and nurses, who did not allow her to sit up at all; and day and night a gentleman was in the house to procure medicines and attend to the wants of the family. . . . Robert was taken on last Saturday week, and when it was announced to the congregation by one of the elders on Sabbath, they immediately called a prayer meeting on his behalf; and the elder told the congregation that none of them were to call at the minister's house unless they went as nurses, that they must not go to ring the doorbell and disturb the family, that not even Dr. Palmer would be permitted to see Mr. Mallard unless he went to nurse, and there would be people enough to inform them of his situation. She says if she desired it, one of the ladies would come and relieve her of housekeeping. I never heard of greater kindness than they have received. They have an excellent physician, and the epidemic is pronounced of a mild type. But oh, to think I am not permitted to be with my precious child in this season of sorrow and suffering! Nothing but the assurance on her part and that of Joe that I would only be increasing their distress keeps me away. I dread to hear that Daughter has taken the fever. I am sure in her situation it must go very hard. . . . It is prevailing generally with great fatality throughout Texas.

Thus far Nashville continues healthy, and in providence it is ascribed to the efforts of the health officer in removing all causes of disease. It has been very hot recently, and very dry; and just now mosquitoes abound. I greatly miss the cold delightful water of Upper Georgia.

Daughter enclosed your last letter, and the news about Marietta filled my heart with *sorrow* and with joy. Should our good pastor leave Liberty, the church would be utterly broken; and yet I know the people do not by any means support him. Mr. Buttolph has set us all a noble example of suffering patience under trials and reverses; and I have felt in God's own time and way a door of relief would be opened to a wider field of influence and a surer prospect of support. For myself, if you move away, *my precious dead* will be the only tie remaining to bind me there with a desolated home. I fear there will not be enough made this year at *Montevideo* to pay the manager!

I am glad to hear good tidings from Kate and Audley. Do give Mary and Belle and Kitty much love. I have been intending to write and tell Mary how truly my heart has wept for her great sorrow in the death of our lamented friend Mr. Wells. . . . Joe and Carrie unite with me in best love to my dear sister and niece and Mr. Buttolph, to Jimmie and Willie and Susie. And their little cousins here send love and kisses. I long to hear from you all. Your letters are a great comfort to me, and my heart is with you in warmest love. Do write soon to

Your ever attached aunt,
Mary Jones.

Politically things are in a dreadful condition here.

Mrs. Laura E. Buttolph *to* Mrs. Mary Jones[t]
Flemington, *Wednesday,* October 2nd, 1867
My dearest Aunt,

Your valued letter came day before yesterday, and was like cold water to our thirsty souls! Even the children danced around me when I said: "A letter from my precious Aunt Mary!" And containing so much good news!

May our Heavenly Father bless and spare all of our loved ones in New Orleans and bring them safely through that terrible disease the yellow fever! So glad Cousin Robert and Charlie were better, and the good people so efficient and kind. I do like that elder who gave such sensible directions. Truly they are *warmhearted Christian* people, and no mistake. . . . It would only be feeding the fever if you were to go, and might at this season prove fatal to you, besides increasing their *anxiety and care.* I have heard that one in Mary's case usually has it light. I only trust it may prove so with her, and that little Mary's case may be as light as Charlie's.

Mother gives her very best love to Cousin Joe, and says she congratulates him on removing everything that was *usual* or *unusual,* and hopes that he will receive ample remuneration for finding out all those noxious vapors and preserving life in Nashville; that she considers honor an empty puff these days; that Solomon is wise in saying: "Money answereth all things"; but don't think she is getting to be a "flighty, worldly-minded woman."

Mr. Buttolph returned mentally and physically refreshed by his trip to Marietta. He was officially informed that so soon as the pastoral relation was dissolved between Mr. Palmer and the church, he would receive a call to it. The presbytery will meet on the 10th of this month, and so soon as the door of this cage is opened, D.V., these birds will, I think, fly out. Aunt Eliza says she will live two years longer if we go there. She completed her eighty-second year on Sunday. . . .

The crops are worse this year than the last, and the caterpillars are eating the cotton left by the rain. The person who rented Lambert will make nothing there, so that prospect of income has been cut off. Rossie will not clear expenses at South Hampton; speaks of trying it one year longer, hoping to make money enough to buy a farm in the up country. . . .

Mother, Mr. Buttolph, and the children, who talk of you every day, unite with me in love to you, dear Carrie and Joe and Stanhope and Susie and Charlie. Mother says this is her letter to you.

Your affectionate niece and sister,
Laura E. Buttolph
S. M. Cumming.

Miss Mary E. Robarts *to* Mrs. Mary Jones[t]

Marietta, *Thursday,* October 3rd, 1867

My very dear Cousin,

I cannot tell you how often we have thought of you and shared your anxiety since hearing of the yellow fever in our dear Mary's family. Our last letter was dated 24th; all had had it then except Mary and little Mary, and were doing well. May our Heavenly Father preserve her and all hers and bring them safely through this terrible scourge! It is hard to say: "Thy will be done, not mine" when such precious lives are at stake—a minister, husband, father; a wife, mother, daughter. Darling relatives, how much is bound up in them! How many fond hopes and sweet associations! I can but trust they may all recover, be acclimated and spared for many days of usefulness and happiness. Dear Mary has kindly written her Uncle John and ourselves every week, and we appreciate highly the effort it cost her to write under such circumstances. We are glad to hear from her how kindly they are treated; no doubt if their lives are spared they will come out with a rich experience of His grace and sing of mercy and goodness.

When are you coming home, my dear cousin? Be sure to stop and see us, for we will have much to talk about.

Hope dear Carrie is safely through her trial, and that you have all had a pleasant and happy summer. Hope Dr. Joseph is prosperous in his business. Charlie also. I had a letter from him enclosing dear little Ruthie's likeness, and I have never had time to thank him for it. If you write, please do so for me, and ask him to excuse his delinquent godmother. How long it is since his infant lips learned that word! How much we have all passed through since!

My dear mother was eighty-two on Sunday, and verifies the Scripture: "If by reason of strength they be fourscore, yet is their strength labor and sorrow." She is in bed half of every day with fever. Is sitting up this morning.

Our pastor, Mr. Palmer, has received a call to the chaplaincy and professorship of moral philosophy and English literature in a college near Alexandria, Louisiana, which he has accepted, and therefore resigned his charge. Our session had a meeting and invited Mr. Buttolph to come up and preach in view of a call. . . . He came up and preached four sermons; stayed from Friday till Tuesday. . . . The final meeting takes place on Monday, and it seems pretty clear that they will give him a call, which will be presented as soon as Cherokee Presbytery dismisses Mr. Palmer, which will be next week. . . . I used to wish that Mr. Buttolph might get a call to Charleston or some city church; never dreamed of Marietta in its best days for him. . . . I need not say how glad we should be to have him as a pastor, and our dear relatives near us. Hope you will go to New Orleans so you would not be there to miss them.

Do write me soon when you will be down, so that we can meet you at the depot. Our boarders have all left, and if I do not get some more, or rent our rooms, do not know how we shall weather the winter. Love from all to all of your household.

Your affectionate cousin,
Mary E. R.

REV. JOHN JONES *to* MRS. MARY JONES[t]

Griffin, *Tuesday,* October 8th, 1867

My dearest Sister,

Your last affectionate letter, received about two weeks since, was most welcome. I have often thought of you lately, and of the constant and painful anxiety which you must feel for your dear children in New Orleans. Dear Mary wrote to us repeatedly, and to our relatives in Marietta, and by forwarding to each other her letters, we were informed of the condition of Robert and the children. I also wrote to our relatives in Liberty, sending an extract from Mary's last letter. But we have not heard from her for a week or more. We feel therefore very anxious, fearing that dear Mary herself has been seized by the fever. I therefore write to inquire of you, dear Sister, and ask you to write us by return mail. Also let me know if they have an idea of leaving New Orleans for a little time to recruit, that we may write for them to pay us a visit.

We surely expect a visit from you on your return to Liberty. Write in time, that I may know when to meet you at the cars. I heard very lately from Charles Colcock through a gentleman of Griffin whom I introduced to C. C. by letters and who saw him in New York. He was quite well. A letter today from Dunwody mentions that the caterpillar was destroying the cotton left by the rains. My dear Jane continues to improve. She, Mother, and Sister Mary and the boys unite with me in best love to you, Joseph, and Niece Carrie and the children.

Ever your affectionate brother,
J. Jones.

Rev. R. Q. Mallard *to* Mrs. Mary Jones[t]
New Orleans, *Thursday,* October 17th, 1867
My dear Mother,

About this hour ($3\frac{1}{2}$ o'clock P.M.) Mary was taken sick on Monday last. She has therefore just completed the *third day* of twenty-four hours, considered one of the crises of the disease, perhaps the principal one. Her attack has not been of a severe character, and her symptoms have been favorable with one exception. No nausea, no obstruction of natural functions; she has, however, been suffering very great pain in her back, hips, and limbs (principally the latter two). It is pronounced neuralgic in character, and I fear it will not be entirely subdued until she is able to change her posture and sit up. I have today heard of a case similar to hers in this particular of a lady now convalescent. Her pains prevented sleep last night and this morning, with the exception of a few naps. As soon as the doctor could be had, he administered a remedy which has given her ease. It will have to be repeated probably in the course of the afternoon and night if the pains return with severity. Thus far there have not been, so far as we know, any tendencies to a danger peculiar to her situation. I hope that she may have a quiet night. Of course I feel, and must continue to feel, deeply anxious about one who has grown every year if possible more precious to me. Mary is in good spirits and is hopeful of recovery, through God's blessing.

Charlie has had a slight attack of fever—the result of some unknown imprudence. Mamie and Georgia well. . . . Mamie is quite thin and pale but in fine spirits.

My dear Mary unites with me in warmest expressions of love to yourself and the other members of the household. Continue to pray for us that a merciful God may continue to deal tenderly with us, His undeserving servants.

Affectionately your son,
R. Q. Mallard.

Friday Morning. I did not get an opportunity for mailing this yesterday, and I therefore add a postscript one day later. Mary suffered some pain again last night, but has been quiet since midnight and has had considerable *refreshing* sleep. The doctor was here in the evening and was much gratified at the effect every way of the opiate administered, and directed its repetition if the pain returned. Its effects have now died away, and as she is quiet and almost free of pain, I hope that she will escape further suffering. Charlie bright and waiting for breakfast.

R. Q. M.

Rev. R. Q. Mallard *to* Mrs. Susan M. Cumming[t]

New Orleans, *Saturday,* October 19th, 1867

Dear Aunt Susan,

I rejoice that I have the glad news to communicate of my dear Mary's convalescence. She was taken sick with the yellow fever on Monday last, and the doctor pronounces her today "through the attack" and (to use his language) "well." Every soul on the premises—Addie, Lucy, Kate, Catherine, the children, Mary, and I (nine cases in all)—have been carried safely through. Have we not infinite cause for gratitude to God for His great mercy? Oh, magnify the Lord with me, and let us exalt His name together!

Yours affectionately,
R. Q. Mallard.

Mr. Charles C. Jones, Jr., *to* Mrs. Mary Jones[t]

New York, *Wednesday,* October 30th, 1867

My very dear Mother,

Your last kind favor has been duly received, and I thank you sincerely for it. We have indeed cause for the greatest gratitude to our good Father in Heaven for His special kindness to our dear ones in New Orleans. Well do I know how heavily anxieties on their account must have pressed upon you. Now, however, that the sunshine of returning health appears once more settling upon the household, I hope that you will feel quite well again.

I cannot bear, my dear mother, the thought of your returning to Montevideo to remain any time there. The county is in entirely too unsettled a condition; your position will be altogether too lonely and isolated; and, in a word, I would not subject myself to the discomforts and uncertainties of even a temporary residence there. You may also rest assured that no profit will, under existing circumstances, be realized from planting operations in Liberty County. The decline in cotton and the uncertain nature of the labor cut off all hope—at least for the present—of remunerative adventures in this behalf. At the best estate, profits will not pay you for the disagreeabilities of a residence there.

I have endeavored in vain to interest a single purchaser. Parties will not buy, and for very good reason. Who does wish to buy in a county in such an unhappy condition as that in which our beloved South now is, and in a climate far from healthy during the warm months of the summer? I must confess my heart is very heavy when I think of the present and the future of the South. I have no doubt but that Reason, at present dethroned, will eventually resume her sway; but intermediately what commotions may come before the white race regains its suspended supremacy? Who can tell? No one will wish to be there who can reside elsewhere. My impression is, my dear mother, that it would be best to sell out all the stock and perishable property at Montevideo and rent the place if a responsible party presents himself. Negroes and Negro labor are so entirely unreliable that a sum certain is far better than a speculative interest in the results of labor. I hope to be with you the last of December or early in January, and will do all I can to assist you. Meanwhile, if you have any offers, please consider them.

I am at a loss to know what to do with my Burke place. It is under mortgage for five thousand dollars, and if sold it would not probably pay the mortgage. The only resources I have are from my profession, and our receipts have been very limited of late. I must confess the prospect seems very dark. But all we can do is to do the best we can and trust to a kind Providence.

Do, my dear mother, give up all intention to remain at Montevideo during the coming winter, and come and divide your time with your children, who will be only too happy to welcome you, and will esteem it the highest privilege to have you with them. Let me know if I can do anything for you. The Central Railroad will declare a dividend of five percent in December. This will help you.

Eva is badly pulled down with her little boy, and is not very strong and well. She does not get rest enough. Ruthie and Casey are both pictures of good health. . . . Eva expects to go to Augusta in December. . . . All unite in tenderest love. And I am ever, my dear mother,

Your affectionate son,
Charles C. Jones, Jr.

Mrs. Mary S. Mallard *to* Mrs. Mary Jones[t]

New Orleans, *Thursday,* October 31st, 1867

My dearest Mother,

I am thankful to be able to write you once more. Great have been our mercies: nine cases of that terrible fever in our household, and all recovered, while so many mourn the loss of one or more members of their families. . . . Persons living here say there never has been so sad an epidemic as this. In previous years the mortality has been comparatively small among the natives and higher classes; but this season it has fallen heavily upon the most respectable, and numbers of natives have died, and a remarkable number of children have fallen. We have lost ten by the fever out of our congregation, and now a young lady of seventeen is dangerously ill.

I was taken sick so late that Mr. Mallard has been kept from taking any trip abroad. If possible he will spend a few days across the lake next week. . . .

We will probably have to move from this house next week or the week after, as this with the furniture will be sold on the 15th of November. We will have to furnish for ourselves, and will be able to do so on a very small scale and by degrees, getting only what is absolutely necessary. I am sorry to give up this house, as it is very convenient, though rather far from the church. The other house is pleasantly located in the midst of our people, and I think we shall like it very much.

We are all anxiously looking for the time to come when you will come to us; and we hope, dear Mother, nothing will prevent your coming as soon as possible. I wish it could have been arranged so that Mr. Mallard could have met you in Atlanta. He is writing you in regard to the *History;* I long to see a copy of it.

I would write more, but have not strength. Until day before yesterday I had not been out of my room. I am rejoiced to hear Carrie is doing so well. Give a kiss of love and welcome to the little stranger for us all. The children all unite with me in much love to Brother Joe, Carrie, and the children, and warmest love for yourself. . . . Tomorrow will be All Saints' Day, one of *the days* of interest in New Orleans. The cemeteries will be visited and tombs decorated. I regret I shall be unable to see any of them. The whole city will be given up to the duties of the day.

Your loving daughter,
Mary S. Mallard.

Mrs. Mary S. Mallard *to* Mrs. Mary Jones[t]

New Orleans, Thursday, November 7th, 1867

My dear Mother,

I write you once more to Nashville, not knowing the time you expect to leave.

We have had delightful cool weather for a week past, and some say a little frost. The return of cool weather is doing much for the restoration of our invalids. I am improving slowly, and hope to be able to go to church next Sabbath, which will be our Communion. . . . The yellow fever has almost disappeared from the city, and persons are returning. In a few weeks the city will be full of the summer birds, and I feel we shall have a population totally out of sympathy with the suffering and afflicted ones who have been here during the epidemic.

Mr. Mallard went to Pass Christian on Monday to spend a few days with Mr. Griswold, and will return tomorrow. Even a few days out of the city will be beneficial. Pass Christian is about six hours' run by steamer on the lake shore.

We expect to move on next Tuesday, and then I shall make a change in my household. Kate said to me a few days ago: "I wish to tell you if you will give me twelve dollars per month I will stay with you; but if not, I have had good offers and I will find another place. I had twenty-five dollars offered me to wet-nurse, but I won't nurse for anybody."

"Very well," I said, "if you have had these fine offers, you had better take them. I cannot afford to give you twelve dollars for what you do and support Catherine too."

"Well," said she with a very impertinent air, "I will find another place."

Ever since we came here we have paid her nine dollars a month, and she had not been here two weeks before she incapacitated herself for her work, which was cooking and washing; and the greater part of the time I have had to hire a woman two days every week at a dollar a day to wash and iron; so that I have really paid all the time from thirteen to seventeen dollars per month on her account, besides having the annoyance of her situation and dirt and the screaming of her child. After her confinement I allowed her to return before she was able to work. Then I nursed her child and herself through yellow fever; so that altogether she has been a very expensive servant to me. I have had the comfort of having her here without change, and she did very well while we were sick; though I am now convinced that her *situation* had a great deal to do with her remaining, and I am pretty certain she is entering upon the same life again, which of course would forbid my retaining her. It is too bad. I have warned her and dealt faithfully with her, but she will follow her own evil ways. I have seen for some weeks that she was becoming disaffected and surly, so that it did not surprise me when she gave notice she would leave. Since then she has not found the fine offers she spoke of, and I think she is quite miserable; but I shall make no effort to retain her, although I feel very sorry for her, and shall continue to do what I can for her.

As far as I can judge, Adeline, my white woman I took care of while she had yellow fever, seems truly grateful; and she has offered to do my cooking and washing with the assistance of a woman one day whom she offers to pay out of her own wages. This will be a great relief to me, for she seems to be a quiet, honest woman and says "she don't want me to distress myself." I hope she will prove what I think she is. It will be easier for me to get someone about the house. Adeline is now doing my washing and most of the housework. Kate does the rest and cooks. I am very glad Adeline has offered to cook, for I feel always comfortable when that department is filled. I don't feel able to go into the kitchen, and that is something that has to be attended to. Housework can be postponed. I tell the family the day I have no cook they will all eat lightly! I will make a cup of tea or coffee on the gas, and they can have that with bread and cheese and milk and crackers. I shan't consider hot soups, etc., healthy.

We received a letter from Mr. Mallard's brother John a few days ago giving a deplorable account of the poverty of the people in Liberty. He says many of the sick have continued weak from the want of nourishment, and no prospect of matters improving. They are all very sad about Mr. Buttolph's leaving, but he (Mr. Mallard) says he feels he is in the path of duty, as they cannot support him. Do, my dear mother, remain as short a time as possible in the county. It is even more desolate than last year. Make your arrangements as soon as possible to come to us. Can't you come by the middle of December? We all long to see you.

The children are getting strong again. I let them run in the square and yard as much as possible to try and get their health as quickly as they can, as I want them to begin school again as soon as we move. They send love and kisses to dear Grandmama. Good-bye, dear Mother.

Your loving daughter,
Mary S. Mallard.

MRS. MARY JONES *to* MRS. MARY S. MALLARD[t]

Montevideo, Tuesday, November 19th, 1867

My darling Child,

Here I am, through God's mercy, once more at our dear old home.

I arrived on Friday week and went up to Flemington. The following Monday your aunt, Willie, and Susie and myself, driven by Gilbert, went to the Island. Audley is filling up the Island with white laborers, and is encouraged. Kate has the wife of one of the workmen as her cook; but she has been often doing her own cooking, and has no nurse for her infant, an uncommonly fine babe (*Robert Lewis*).

Last Sabbath was a deeply solemn and sorrowful day at Midway. Our beloved and faithful pastor, connected with us for thirteen years and four months, broke to us the emblems of our Redeemer's love for the last time. Now perhaps for the first time in the history of our venerated sanctuary the living teacher is withdrawn. So far as we are concerned, silence will reign within those consecrated walls, or even a more deplorable end may await them. And our precious, our beloved, our sainted dead must sleep in the solitude and neglect of a wilderness. My heart felt as if it would burst at this last great affliction which it has seemed best for the Great Head of the Church to send upon us.

Mr. Buttolph and his aged father, now eighty-eight, came home and spent the night with me. They will leave the county on Tuesday the 26th. Through Major Wallace they have cars direct to Atlanta and free tickets for all the family; and I know it will cheer your heart to hear that kind Mrs. Smith, now in Canada, has given your good aunt this year one thousand dollars in greenbacks. Mr. Fleming bought their place and has sold profitably all their stock, etc., etc.

It is true, my child, this county is in ruins. The people are becoming poorer and poorer; I know not what is to become of them. My situation here is just this: one bale of cotton and about twenty bushels of corn made by the freedmen employed. Gilbert, whom I hired, has made me some more corn, but one-third is rotten. No rice at all, nor potatoes to speak of. And a salary of four hundred dollars to pay the manager! I had a talk with him last night and offered to turn everything into his hands, but he will not hear to it; and although I have furnished everything besides for his support and comfort in health and sickness, and he has really done nothing so far as labor is concerned on the place, he has not the honor or conscience to say he is willing to share in any degree the total loss of the year. I am totally at a loss what to do with the place, and am trying to sell cattle and sheep to meet expenses.

And now you must write me the best way of going to New Orleans, and what it will cost to take me there. If I only had the means, would send you just what you need to furnish your house. I must send you the Brussels carpet and a bedroom carpet and some bedding if no more. Would you be willing to pay the express on the carpets? Write me candidly and at once and tell me, my precious child, *when* you expect to be sick. I must bring on your father's papers; I could not leave them. All else—books, pictures, bedding, etc., etc.—must remain. Charles will be here 1st of January, and I could not leave before he comes. I am so much perplexed and distressed at my situation, and leaving the place unprotected (for Mr. Broughton will not manage for us again); and if I can get Mr. Alexander, I will do so. *Do write immediately; I have not a moment to spare.*

Bless the Lord for His mercy in your spared lives! Saw all of Robert's sisters and his brother on Sabbath. All looking well. Warmest love for Robert and yourself, and many kisses for my grandchildren.

Ever your loving mother,
Mary Jones.

Mrs. Mary S. Mallard *to* Mrs. Mary Jones[t]
New Orleans, *Tuesday,* November 26th, 1867
My dear Mother,

Your letter written from Montevideo is at hand, and I hasten to reply without waiting for Mr. Mallard to go to the railroad office to inquire the best route here, etc. He will do so this afternoon, and then I will write all particulars. You must not trouble about your expenses here, for we had intended expressing you the amount, and will do so soon. We are truly grateful to you for the carpets and bedding, and will gladly pay the express. All that will be necessary will be to direct to Mr. Mallard, Third Street between Coliseum and Chestnut Streets, and take a receipt. We will pay at this end. The carpets will be the greatest help to us, and the bedding; for such things are above the purse of common people.

I am truly sorry to hear of the deplorable condition of affairs at Montevideo. Would Mr. Alexander be willing to rent the place? Even a small rent would be better than planting yourself and finding things at the end of the harvest worse than nothing. Such is the demoralized condition of the Negroes in Liberty that until half of them die of starvation they will not realize the necessity of earning their bread in the sweat of their brows. Would Audley like to extend his white colony to Maybank? If some of the outbuildings had been spared, something might be done there with white labor; for the climate is so healthy, and the advantages of the salt water so great.

The condition of Midway is distressing. I often think of our dear ones sleeping in the graveyard there, and thought how desolate it would be when there was none to minister in the sanctuary. I feel thankful the sainted ones whose bodies rest there were spared all knowledge of the future. And now they enjoy perfect rest and joy; and "their ashes our Father's care will keep."

I feel anxious, my dear mother, you should leave the county as soon as possible. Now that Aunt Susan and all the family have left, it is too desolate for you to remain; and yet I know it is a tremendous trial to leave so comfortable a home. Still there is nothing but the house. Everything else is changed—and *permanently* changed while our political condition remains what it is. You must make our house your home, and we will try and do all that we can to make you happy. I think you will like this place; the only objection to it is the want of a more invigorating climate.

How did the Negroes appear when you returned this time? Do they still seem to retain any of their former attachment? At this time the "Black-and-Tan" Convention is holding its sessions in this city. One of the papers calls them the "Bones-and-Banjo" Convention. A black Negro occupies the chair, and white and black are sprinkled alternately through the house. These are the men to frame a new constitution for the state! I think the sooner the Radicals run their race the better.

What time in January will Brother Charlie probably come South? I hope early, so that you can make your arrangements before the winter is too far advanced.

I am rejoiced to hear of so much assistance being given Mr. Buttolph in transporting his family. Major Wallace is a Presbyterian and a noble man. Mrs. Smith's gift to Aunt Susan is most generous. I have always thought she was a noble woman, and wholly unappreciated by the Davis family. I do not believe there is another member of the family that would ever think of recognizing Aunt Susan's connection with them. This gift will be a great help to the family. When will Cousin Laura be confined?

I think I shall be sick about the 11th of February—certainly not later than the 15th. I feel sometimes as though it might be nearer, for I have never recovered my activity since the yellow fever, and suffer a good deal at times from those horrible cramps. You know what they are.

My white servants seem quite cheerful and contented in my service, and if they will only remain so, I shall be satisfied. My young German house girl requires constant supervision, but she is so pleasant-tempered and respectful that I hope to make something out of her. She is too new a broom for me to know yet; it is common for all of them to run well for a month.

Mamie and Charlie commenced school today. In a short time the school will be moved within two squares of us, for which I am very glad, as the children are not entirely strong and very susceptible to colds, and we have a great deal of wet weather after January.

I wish you could come on before Christmas. The stores of New Orleans are worth seeing on Christmas Eve, and the crowd that throngs Canal Street is as interesting as the articles on exhibition. . . . Love to Aunt Julia's family. Mr. Mallard and the children unite with me in tenderest love for yourself. Howdy for the servants.

Your affectionate daughter,
Mary S. Mallard.

MRS. MARY JONES *to* MRS. MARY S. MALLARD[t]

Montevideo, Thursday, November 28th, 1867

My darling Child,

Not one word from you since your letter directed to Nashville! I wrote you fully before I left that place, sending two blue merino sacques for Mary and Georgia. Have they ever arrived? My heart aches to hear from you.

If I only had the means of transportation, here is a house full of furniture that could be so useful to you, but it is utterly out of my power. One bag of cotton and forty-two bushels of corn made on this place. And no work done by the manager—not even the spring work. And yet, although he has been cared for and supported, he claims his salary as though he had done his duty and made a crop. I never saw less *true* feeling on the part of a man. At Arcadia they will make about half a bag and some corn and fodder for sale. How much I cannot tell; perhaps enough for taxes. I will tell you as soon as sold. It has been the most disastrous year I ever knew.

I have made no positive arrangements yet for this place; will probably get Mr. Alexander to take charge, and let Gilbert be the foreman. Charles and Lucy promise to move over to the lot and take charge of the house and lot.

Do write me fully the route to New Orleans and the expense of getting there. And write me the time you are expecting to be sick. Do write at once —and *particularly*.

Next week I will try and express the Brussels and one other carpet to you, which will, I hope, be a help to you. Write me what bedding or anything else you want that could come by express without being too expensive. I am trying to pack and arrange the books, furniture, etc., so that if I never am permitted to return, they can be sent to those who will wish them. There is no sale for anything of the kind here. It is the poorest community, and becoming worse and worse. The rod of affliction is still heavy in temporal affairs, and that heavy stroke of losing our beloved pastor is now added.

Day before yesterday (Tuesday) I went up and dined in company with your dear aunt, Mr. Buttolph and his father, and the two boys and Susie. At one o'clock the cars came; and it was an affecting sight to see them leaving, and a long line of weeping and sorrowing ladies, gentlemen, young men, and children left at the side of the vacant track, now sheep without a shepherd. For the first time in its history I believe our venerated church has none to break the Bread of Life. I feel that I am more utterly alone than any being in the county; I am linked only to my beloved and kindred dust. Being unable to do more, I am going to put up the brickwork of a tomb at Midway. It will not prevent a monument as soon as I am able.

I have risen at three o'clock to write, as I do not usually sleep beyond that hour now. *Do write me at once the route and cost of journey to New Orleans,* and time of getting there. And above all write me of yourself. . . . With warmest love for Robert and yourself and the dear children. I am provoked at Kate's ungrateful conduct; she deserves to be sent away. Hope if she stays she will do better. If she could see the ragged and starving ones here, she would value her place.

Ever your own affectionate mother,
Mary Jones.

Mrs. Mary Jones *to* Mrs. Mary S. Mallard[t]

Montevideo, *Sunday,* December 1st, 1867

My darling Child,

I wrote you fully before leaving Nashville; have written you twice since I reached home. Was rejoiced to receive your last on Saturday night; had not heard so long from you.

Before leaving Nashville I wrote to little Mary and sent through the mail two blue French merino sacques that I had cut and embroidered on the machine—one a walking sacque for her, and a house sacque for Georgia. You do not mention getting them. Robert had best inquire particularly at the office. They were put in the very last of October or first of November. If they do not come to light, I will write on to Nashville about them.

Do write me at once the *best route* to New Orleans, and *the expense of getting there,* and *when you expect to be sick.* I long to be with you, and am doing my best to arrange business here so as to leave early in January. I will send you the Brussels and a bedroom carpet, and if the expense of transportation was not too great, would send you furniture *complete* for your drawing room, etc., etc. Would you be willing to pay the express on the Philadelphia sofa and the six chairs to match those you have? It is impossible to sell here: people are too poor to buy. I will send on a bed and mattress with the carpets if the express is not too high.

I write in haste this morning, hoping for a chance to the mail. Do answer these inquiries one and all *immediately,* for my arrangements depend on your reply. With best love to Robert and yourself, and kisses for the dear children,

Ever your affectionate mother,

Mary Jones.

Mrs. Mary S. Mallard *to* Mrs. Mary Jones[t]

New Orleans, *Saturday,* December 7th, 1867

My darling Mother,

Your last letter, dated December 1st, has just arrived, and I hasten to reply. Mr. Mallard opened your letter at the office, and finding you had sent the parcel by mail, he inquired particularly, but the postmaster said nothing had ever come. I am truly sorry, for I fear the pretty sacques are lost. Neither they nor your last letter from Nashville have ever been received. It is too bad.

Mr. Mallard inquired about the routes here. There are two, and the expense from Savannah here is about the same by either. One is by way of Macon, Columbus, Montgomery, and Mobile; thus far by railroad. At Mobile you take a steamer to this place, or rather to the Pontchartrain Railroad, which is only half an hour's run from the city. Sometimes the passage from Mobile is very rough, and persons are made very seasick. When it is calm it is very pleasant to those who enjoy water carriage. The boats are very fine. The other route is entirely by railroad, via Chattanooga, where you will take the Memphis & Charleston Railroad to Grand Junction; from there to Canton, and on to New Orleans. The time occupied is three days and six hours. This is considered by the general ticket agent here the best route, as there are fewer changes; and when they do occur, you only step from one car to another; and there are sleeping cars all the way. The fare by either route is forty dollars from Savannah. There you could obtain a through ticket. We expect to express on the first or second day of January forty-five dollars, which we will direct to you, No. 3 (McIntosh Station). I am sorry we cannot do it at once. Whenever you fix the time for leaving, write us some days previous so that Mr. Mallard can meet you at the depot. Or else telegraph from Savannah.

We are truly obliged to you for the carpets and bedding, and will gladly pay the express on them. Thus far we have not been able to form any idea of the cost of bringing furniture, as the clerk here says there are so many ways of estimating express freight—sometimes by weight and sometimes by bulk. I do not think we could pay the express on the furniture in the next six weeks; but if you could leave the chairs and sofa so that they could be sent afterwards, we would be very glad to have them. The very association would make them valuable. Should anything occur, in the meanwhile, and we can find out definitely about the cost, I will write immediately; or if you should see the express agent at the other end and he could give any idea, we would like to know. Having to furnish from the beginning, anything is acceptable. I tell Mr. Mallard I wish he could be called upon to perform some wedding ceremonies; but I despair, as he has had only one since coming to the city.

Mr. Mallard is under the impression you can check your baggage by the Grand Junction route all the way through. This would be a great relief, as it is the greatest source of trouble to a lady.

I think I shall be sick about the 11th or 15th of February—not later. I do long for the time to come when you will be with us. It is so long since I have seen you, I think I have grown old in the meantime.

I wish I could get the pictures. Could you fix them so that they might be sent for? We can get them after a while, I know. I only wish we had the means to bring everything that would make you comfortable and remind you of home.

It is Saturday night and growing late. All are in bed except myself, so good night, my dear mother. Tenderest love from us all. I have written you three times since knowing you had left for Liberty; hope you will receive the letters. I hope your last from Nashville will yet come to light. Howdy for the servants. I have not seen or heard a word of Kate for nearly three weeks, so don't know whether she succeeded in getting a place or not.

The citizens here hope much from our new commanding general—Hancock. He is said to be a gentleman, and opposed to the Radicals. He has just assumed command, and has already removed the Negroes from the jury. Many of our best men have called upon him, feeling he was, as it were, on a common platform in favor of justice to the South and opposed to Radicalism.

Your loving daughter,
Mary S. Mallard.

REV. JOHN JONES *to* MRS. MARY JONES[t]

Griffin, *Wednesday,* December 11th, 1867

My dearest Sister,

I was so much disappointed in missing you as you passed through Griffin. According to your letter that you would leave Nashville on the 5th November at 5 P.M., I knew you would pass through here at half-past ten at night on the 6th. Accordingly I went down with my boys and a bottle of choice blackberry wine to cheer you, and we looked through the cars. No sister! I went again at 10 A.M. with my bottle, and again on the night of the 7th at half-past 10 P.M., and again at 10 A.M. on the 8th, taking the bottle and a letter written in pencil and a likeness of Johnnie and Josie and Mary in a trio, and after all did not see you, and concluded you had gone by Augusta. But Joe explained that you left Nashville at 6 A.M. on the 5th November, and thus I missed you. It was a great disappointment, I assure you.

My visit to Nashville was delightful. Dr. Joseph and Carrie gave me a most affectionate welcome, and entertained myself and Edward Axson and many others by day in a sumptuous manner. What fine hearty children they have! And the dear little baby is so sweet. I baptized it on the 27th November. Dr. Leighton Wilson made the first prayer, then remarks and baptism, Dr. Buist holding the water. Then prayer by Dr. Plumer and benediction by Dr. Buist. Dr. Buist said it was a royal baptism. Nashville is a great city, and when delivered from Radical rule will become a most desirable place. I trust Joe will be able to rise above the Radical influence; they have poorly rewarded all his diligence in cleaning the city. The meeting of the assembly was charming. Many spoke most affectionately of my dear brother; and Dr. Moore, the moderator, to whom Joe gave a copy of the *History*, commended it publicly to the assembly. I will enclose you the remarks of Dr. Stuart Robinson on the *History*, for which I thanked him personally.

My dear sister, do send for Dunwody and counsel with him; he writes to me in great trouble. I am in trouble also; the man that rented my place in Baker is about swindling me out of two thousand dollars. My dear Janey is not nearly as well as she was. The future is very dark! My dear Jane and Mother Dunwody and Sister Mary and the boys and little Mary all join in best love to you.

Your ever affectionate brother,
J. Jones.

Miss Mary E. Robarts *to* Mrs. Mary Jones[t]
Marietta, *Thursday*, December 12th, 1867
My dearest Cousin,

Your letter from Nashville arrived while I was in Atlanta. Louisa went to the depot to meet you on Wednesday, but you were not there, so presume you passed in the night. So it was with Cousin John in Griffin.

Our dear relatives arrived safely bag and baggage. I was quite shocked to see such a feeble old man as Judge Buttolph; had expected to see him quite robust. He improved very much last week, but is complaining again today of his throat and difficulty of breathing. He sits in the drawing room all the time by a good fire, Mr. Buttolph and the children with him, the rest of us visiting him occasionally. I have not much time to discourse with anyone; am all the time thinking of the fleshpots. Have had fourteen in family; but Colonel Brumby's family, who have been boarding with me six weeks, have left, and I have only ten in number now.

Laura is not sick yet. If she could only wait till the second week in January, she could be settled at the parsonage, as Mrs. Palmer's little boy is now three weeks old, and she will be able to leave in about three more. But we have to take these things as they come. Cousin Susan, Laura, and Susie occupy the room above our dining room that was when you were here. Mr. Buttolph, his father, and the boys occupy the room above the dining room with two beds in it. One corner is nicely arranged for a study, with table and his writing apparatus.

He has been visiting his people; is nearly through with his introductory visits. He has made a very fine impression, and I only hope they may be able to prove their appreciation of him in dollars and cents. But this is the darkest time our church and country have ever passed through. Except the woodshed we are all worse off than in the war. God knows how it will end—our poor distressed country, our afflicted people.

I shall be glad when I hear that you are safely in New Orleans with dear Mary. What a season they have passed through! . . . May God spare their precious lives and bless them in all respects!

My dear mother has been more feeble lately, and quite sick for several days. Has little appetite. . . . Louisa went to Roswell and spent a week with Sophia, and spent a pleasant time. Says she is a nice housekeeper, and has everything in style; is quite disgusted with my establishment. . . . I went to Atlanta to see my dear Ellen; she and Baby were quite well. The doctor doing well; works hard, has a large school, but finds it hard to collect.

They are coming up to spend Christmas with us, and I am going to have a little Christmas tree for Mary Brevard and the little Buttolphs. Nothing splendid, but a little treat to them. The spirit of hilarity has forever departed from me, but I live not for myself, but try to do my duty and make others happy as long as I am in the world.

Cousin Susan is still quite *painful,* as the old Negroes say, but better than when she first came up. Farewell, my ever dear cousin. I hope this is the last letter I shall direct to you in Liberty.

Your ever affectionate cousin,
M. E. Robarts.

Mrs. Susan M. Cumming *to* Mrs. Mary Jones[t]

Marietta, *Friday,* December 20th, 1867

My dear Sister,

Three weeks have passed since our arrival here and since we bade you farewell. It seems months. I was confined to bed for several days, but am better now; hope soon to be as well as usual.

How I long to hear that you have arranged all your business in Liberty, and that you are ready to leave for New Orleans to be with your dear children! My heart aches to think of you separated from all who love you so dearly. Troubles and gloom seem to encompass us on every side. Our only ray of hope and comfort is from above. "The Lord reigneth," and He can restrain the wrath of man.

Our dear aunt is very feeble. Some days she scarcely eats, and is indisposed to rise; at other times takes an interest in passing events. Mr. Buttolph the elder has been very much indisposed since he came up. The cough is exceedingly troublesome. Dr. Stewart has prescribed for him. He has been constantly in the house. The weather has been very damp and cold; we have had but three or four days of sunshine. Mr. Buttolph has been much occupied in making the acquaintance of his church and congregation; and his preaching, I hear, is most acceptable. Mrs. Palmer will leave the parsonage next week, and we expect to move in, D.V. Laura is very well today. Her usual calculation has failed, so we do not know—or rather guess—when to look for the expected guest.

Whatever arrangement you desire you can make respecting White Oak. I will not have anyone there to annoy or trouble you. Prince and Tom can return, and any others you may see fit to have there. July and his family must leave; he has no claim whatever on the place. In the event of your selling Montevideo, I shall be glad to have White Oak included.

Ellen and Baby and Dr. Brumby are here on a visit. Sophia and Lilla are expected from Roswell for a day or two. . . . Aunt, Cousin Mary and Louisa, and Laura and Mr. Buttolph unite with me in best love to you; also the children. Dr. Joseph has sent Mr. Buttolph a copy of my dear brother's book. . . . Believe me, dear Sister,

Your affectionate sister,
S. M. Cumming.

Mrs. Laura E. Buttolph *to* Mrs. Mary Jones[t]

Marietta, *Friday,* December 20th, 1867

My precious Aunt,

We all long to see your dear face and enjoy your society. Mr. Buttolph, Mother, Susie, and all this household speak of you daily.

How I would enjoy a trip to New Orleans and a visit to Mary Mallard in her new home! I do trust she is entirely restored to health and feels no ill effects from the yellow fever, and that Cousin Robert and the children have been benefited by the cold weather. I long to hear from them. . . . Aunt Mary Robarts sends her best love, and wishes you were here at Christmas. Not that we expect any jollification; only that we might be together. . . . Present us very kindly to all inquiring friends. . . . Believe me

Your affectionate niece,
Laura E. Buttolph.

Mrs. Mary S. Mallard *to* Mrs. Mary Jones[t]

New Orleans, *Friday,* December 20th, 1867

My dearest Mother,

This is my dear father's birthday, and tomorrow will be the anniversary of your wedding day. Days full of tender and pleasant memories! I wish you were here to spend them with us.

Little Georgia speaks of your coming constantly, and is making her arrangements. She says "she is going to buy a pretty bed for her dear grandmother, and she will sleep with her downstairs and love her all times." She is still a peculiarly shrinking child, and I think her early fright of Yankees has left a distrust of all her fellow men. She imagines she will have the entire charge of your room, and says you "will come tomorrow day right in the cars."

Thus far our winter has been exceedingly mild, and the weather perfectly charming.

The entire loss of crops throughout the state has depressed and (the businessmen say) almost paralyzed all trade in the city. They say there never has been such a financial distress since the city was built. Very little cotton to be bought, and no price to be gotten for what is produced. I think the Radicals will be convinced of their folly. I see by the papers there are fifty thousand workmen out of employment in New York. Only such home arguments can appeal or affect the Northern politicians.

Mr. Edward Palmer passed through the city last week on his way to Alexandria. His family will not come on until January, as he has just had a son added to his little number—the only *son* in the connection. I did not see Mr. Palmer, but he told Mr. Mallard Mr. Buttolph and family had arrived safely, and Aunt Eliza was enjoying her usual health.

Last evening Mr. Mallard was called upon to perform a wedding ceremony for two of the colored citizens. In this state the legal forms are very peculiar, and accompanied with a good deal of trouble. The marriage certificates have to be signed by the bride and groom and at least three witnesses. Mr. Mallard said it was very amusing to see these Negroes. Of course he had to explain to them the nature of the document. Two of the attendants could write, so they were greatly puffed up by their attainments, and with quite a condescending air brought the bride and her husband to make their marks. The colored ladies and gentlemen are entitled to all the privileges of full citizenship, though it did not occur to them the minister ought to receive a fee!

We have a commander here now—General Hancock—who is disposed to refer all cases to the proper civil authorities, and thus far promises to do justice. He has received much attention from the citizens, and is disposed to take counsel of prudent, sensible, prominent citizens of the place.

I hope, dear Mother, you have received my letter telling you the opinion of the railroad agent here that the best route to New Orleans from Savannah is by Chattanooga, where you take the Memphis & Charleston Railroad to Grand Junction, and then on to Canton and down to New Orleans—railroad all the way. The expense is the same by either route: forty dollars. The changes are less frequent by the Grand Junction route and more easily made by a lady, as there is merely a change of cars. The other route (by Columbus and Mobile) is a very pleasant one, but you are a part of a day and night on steamboat. The boats between Mobile and this place are very fine, and considered safe boats. The difference in time is only a few hours. You must write or telegraph from Savannah which way you will come and at what time you will leave, so that we can know when to meet you. Mr. Mallard will send you by express on the 1st of January forty-five dollars directed to No. 3.

The children are well except colds. I think you will find them grown. Think of it, dear Mother—eighteen months have nearly elapsed since we have seen you. . . . Mr. Mallard and the children unite with me in warmest love. Love to Aunt Julia's family when you see them. Howdy for the servants.

Your loving daughter,
Mary S. Mallard.

Mrs. Mary S. Mallard *to* Mrs. Mary Jones[t]

New Orleans, *Thursday,* December 26th, 1867

My dearest Mother,

Your letter and the bales by express arrived on Christmas Eve. The bales were apparently in good order, but when we opened the bedding we found the whatnot completely crushed, much of it broken into inch pieces; and the table legs are also completely broken. Not one shelf even of the whatnot remains; nothing but the top boards of the tables are safe. Yesterday being a holiday, nothing could be done; but this morning Mr. Mallard will go to the express and see if anything can be done—though we fear not, as the receipt was given for a bale of bedding and one of carpets, and to all appearances they were delivered in good order. The express freight upon the two bales was nearly forty-five dollars. I am so sorry the whatnot and tables were broken, for aside from their being such pretty pieces of furniture, the association made them so valuable. We are truly obliged to you, dear Mother, for the carpets and bedding. I have not opened the carpets yet, as I could not put them down for some days. Mr. Mallard will inquire at the express and then add a postscript to this at the office. There are so many changes in the route here that I scarcely think it would be worthwhile to risk any more furniture or perishable articles. I presume the bale of bedding was put at the bottom, and the weight of freight upon it crushed the whatnot.

I had intended writing a long letter this morning; but just here I have been stopped by company, so I cannot write more and have this in time for the mail.

If the box of pictures could wait until February, we could then be better able to pay the freight upon it. We are obliged to do things by degrees in these days of cash transactions.

Yesterday was as mild as summer, and if it were not for the general financial gloom resting upon the city, I suppose it would be a "merry" Christmas. . . . There seems to be a general apprehension that there will be serious trouble with the Negroes in the country, many of whom are roaming around like Indians. Having made nothing, they are living upon the cattle, and it is thought they will soon make inroads upon the scantily filled barns of the planters. I fear there will be a like condition of things in Liberty, and I am so anxious for you to come away as soon as possible.

The children are well except Charlie, who has an attack of jaundice, which makes him uncomfortable and gives him very yellow eyes. All unite with me in tenderest love for yourself.

Your affectionate daughter,
Mary S. Mallard.

Rev. R. Q. Mallard *to* Mrs. Mary Jones[t]
New Orleans, *Thursday,* December 26th, 1867
My dear Mother,

I have seen the agent of the express, and learn from him that the company are not responsible for the damage done to the whatnot. As the receipt called for a bale of bedding, they are only accountable for the safe delivery of it as such. He says it would have come safely even unpacked, and for no higher freight. I am very sorry that it should have been broken, as it was a memento of happier days.

I send you by express today to No. 3, Albany & Gulf Railroad, forty-five dollars, which I hope will reach you safely. Wish that it was a hundred. I hope that you will come on as soon as possible.

Your affectionate son,
R. Q. Mallard.

Coming via Chattanooga, Grand Junction, and Jackson, you can check your baggage all the way through.

R. Q. M.

Rev. R. Q. Mallard *to* Mrs. Mary Jones[t]
New Orleans, *Friday,* December 27th, 1867
My dear Mother,

I had carried to the express office and left to be forwarded to you a package of forty-five dollars when the dreadful tidings came of the calamity which has befallen your son in Nashville. I know that you will appreciate my motive in diverting this amount, which I had intended for your expenses hither, to the more pressing necessities of my afflicted brother. I am sorry that the expense of moving and furnishing has so straitened me as to forbid my doing what I should like for both.

Lest by any accident the letters from Nashville have not reached you, I would say Carrie writes that they were burned out on last Friday, barely escaping with their lives.

Yours affectionately,
R. Q. Mallard.

Mrs. Mary S. Mallard *to* Mrs. Mary Jones[t]

New Orleans, *Thursday,* January 2nd, 1868

My darling Mother,

A Happy New Year to you from your children and grandchildren! Yesterday was bright and beautiful, and I hope it may be an omen of the coming year. It is customary for the gentlemen to pay their respects to the ladies on New Year's Day. Not deeming it very becoming in me to be sitting up (for shapes), I excused myself yesterday. I really was not well enough to be dressed all day.

I received a letter from Aunt Mary Robarts yesterday announcing the birth of another son on Christmas morning—Cousin Laura's fourth boy. She also mentioned the death of Mrs. Charlie Alexander, whom you wrote me you were nursing. I fear you have had some sad moments and much fatigue, as I suppose you were with her to the end. I never saw her, but always understood she was very delicate. Has she left more than one child?

The box containing one hundred copies of my dear father's *History* arrived day before yesterday; and next week our indefatigable little sexton will commence his labors. He will undertake the sale of them, as we think nothing can be done except by special agency. The book would be entirely buried and lost sight of if it were placed in the bookstores. Mr. Mallard has sent a circular to almost every member of his church, and I hope some copies will be sold. If it were not for the extreme poverty of the people, I have no doubt that a number could be disposed of; but for many here, formerly wealthy, the struggle is for daily bread.

I hope, dear Mother, your next letter will tell us you have appointed the day for leaving Liberty. We long to have you with us. The children are daily expecting and talking of your coming. Georgia thinks she is to have the sole management of everything concerning her "danmother". . . . All unite with me in warmest love.

Your affectionate child,
Mary S. Mallard.

Mrs. Mary Jones *to* Mrs. Mary S. Mallard[t]

Montevideo, *Monday,* January 6th, 1868

My darling Child,

Robert's and your last two favors have been received. I was truly gratified at his disposition of the forty-five dollars, and I know how much good it will do in aiding your poor brother and his family. I am sorry to think you were at so much expense for the articles sent by express, and that what I intended as good proved to be such a loss in the whatnot and tables. But keep the pieces: I am a great hand to *repair;* and perhaps they can be glued, as it is only for ornament.

What shall I say of your dear brother's and Carrie's losses? I am almost cast down beyond measure on their account. Unless Carrie's family can help them, I do not see what they are to do! I have sent them all the money in my power, and as soon as I can hear their plans, will send them some bedding and household matters (sheets, towels, etc., etc.). And there are the good books here which I have desired to share with you all, as I have repeatedly written and said. Furniture is out of the question; it is too expensive to send. I have been making a catalogue of the books and packing them in boxes, which has been a fatiguing business, as it all passes through my own hands.

And two weeks of this busy time has been given to nursing my friend and neighbor Mrs. Alexander. December 10th I was sent for at midnight and went to her. She was confined with a daughter, and was to all appearances doing well until about the fourth day, when she had a chill, which was the precursor of the fatal termination. She had puerperal fever, and died on the 22nd, leaving her little infant. (Doing well at present, and has a black nurse.) I was with her as constantly as my strength would allow; and what with anxiety and distress with and for my bereaved friends and sitting up and nursing, in connection with the cares and perplexities that surround me here, I have been almost laid in bed. Indeed, I had to go to bed for a day and two nights.

Your brother came on Christmas Day and stayed with me until the following Tuesday. Eva and her mother and the children were in Augusta, and would spend the winter South. He returns immediately to New York.

He writes me from Savannah saying the route via Mobile was considered the best. I was also told so yesterday by a gentleman whom I saw at Walthourville as I went to worship there. Grand Junction, he said, would be quite out of the way. Oh, how I *dread* the undertaking! It seems so strange! And yet will not God provide for me as He has done in days that are past? In almost every other journey I seemed to have friends or places that I knew ahead of me. Now I am going to entirely strange places until I reach New Orleans. If I only knew someone to call upon in *Mobile* in case of trouble, and to see me on the steamer! Traveling *alone* becomes more and more unpleasant to me, and no one knows how I feel my lonely and desolate situation.

If possible I wish to leave this county on the 14th, and Savannah as soon as I can arrange my business there. The cars run every other day from No. 3, so that if I do not go, *D.V.*, on the 14th, I may not do so until that day week. But I will write on the eve of leaving.

Miss Louisa called and dined with me on last Thursday. . . . She brought a bag of pecan nuts for the children, which I will *try* to get in the trunks. . . . The pictures are all ready for transportation; I will take and leave them at No. 3 if they cannot go before I leave. . . . Do, my precious child, take care of yourself. I long to be with you, and am anxious every moment on your account. The Lord be with you and bless you and yours! With tenderest love for you and all the family,

Ever your affectionate mother,
Mary Jones.

Dr. Joseph Jones *to* Rev. *and* Mrs. R. Q. Mallard[t]

Nashville, *Wednesday,* January 8th, 1868

My dear Brother and Sister,

You will please accept my thanks for your affectionate and valued favor and generous gifts. The package containing forty-five dollars and the valuable bundle of clothes reached me safely by express. The presents of dear little Mary as well as Charlie's kind prayers and good wishes are gratefully remembered. I fear, my dear sister and brother, that you have robbed yourselves; for I know that your expenses, especially after the past season of protracted and dangerous illness, must be very heavy.

Through a kind Providence the future looks bright. As soon as my dear wife and children could be comfortably clad and prepared for the journey, I carried them to Augusta, where they will remain for the present during the cold weather. If Providence permits, I will perfect the necessary arrangements for their return in the spring. Carrie suffered from cold and high fever during the journey down, but when I left Augusta on the 2nd she was much better. She has borne the distressing calamity with Christian resignation and wonderful cheerfulness. Her calm, uncomplaining conduct has elicited universal admiration from her numerous friends.

After parting with Carrie in Augusta, I rested last Thursday in Marietta with my dear relatives. Aunt Susan was suffering severely from the effects of her labors in moving: a rheumatic affection of the muscles of the neck and back. I prescribed for her, and in accordance with my advice she went to bed. Cousin Laura was doing well, and her last baby is a fine healthy boy. Cousin Lyman's father is still with him—an aged gentleman of near ninety years. I am told that the Presbyterian congregation is delighted with our good cousin, and the people have exerted themselves to make the family happy and comfortable. The parsonage is being renovated, and as soon as the repairs are completed, they will move from Aunt Eliza's, where they are now staying. My dear old aunt is feeble but cheerful. She is confined to her bed most of the time. Cousins Mary and Lou still continue cheerful, charitable, and kind, and the best of daughters and housekeepers. Our dear friends and relatives in Marietta gave me a most hearty welcome, and sincerely sympathized with us in our recent calamity. It gave me great comfort and pleasure to meet with them.

I have rented an office in Church Street near the corner of High Street. Through the noble exertions of my kind friend Dr. Eve, many of my most valuable works were preserved. The library was on the lower floor, immediately in the rear of the store which was burnt. We lost all the furniture, wearing apparel, and all my surgical instruments. Nothing was saved except from my library and a small room back. I am truly thankful that the manuscript of my honored father was not with me at the time of the fire, as it would certainly have been destroyed. The box in which it had been placed was consumed, together with many of his letters and memorials. I would rather have lost everything in the world than this manuscript. I am thankful beyond measure for this great mercy.

The fire appears to have been the work of an incendiary—of one of the tenants of the store immediately beneath our sleeping apartment. As the individual was unknown to us even by sight, and as the goods had been insured for at least four times their value only four days before the fire, it is thought that the sole object was money! Whilst our losses have been heavy, and whilst it was a terrible experience to my precious wife and little ones to flee in their nightdresses from the burning house at the dead hour of night in the rain and wade in the cold mud of the streets in their bare feet, at the same time we have abundant cause for rejoicing in the salvation of our lives. We should all have perished but for the fact that I was aroused immediately upon the first alarm of fire. I had been up until a late hour arranging my library and office, and had just fallen into a gentle sleep when the alarm was sounded. It would be impossible to express the anxiety of my dear wife when we found that our dear little Susie was missing. I left Carrie standing in the street and rushed into the house and rescued her from the suffocating smoke. My feelings have always been peculiarly tender towards Susie since her extreme illness.

Our friends in Nashville have been most kind and sympathizing. Dr. and Mrs. Eve have done everything in their power for our comfort. We feel more attached to Nashville than ever. My hearty consent was given to the present visit, although it breaks up my cheerful home and leaves me very lonely, because I hoped that it would give Carrie a season of comparative freedom from care, in which she might prepare her dresses and the clothing of the children.

I trust that this affliction may be blessed to our spiritual good. "The judgments of the Lord are true and righteous altogether." "Except the Lord build the house, they labor in vain that build it. Except the Lord keep the city, the watchman waketh but in vain. It is vain for you to rise up early, to sit up late, to eat the bread of sorrows, for so He giveth His beloved sleep." We feel that we have every cause for the most devout gratitude. With warmest love, I remain

Your affectionate brother,
Joseph Jones.

Mrs. Mary Jones *to* Mrs. Mary S. Mallard[t]

Savannah, *Saturday,* January 18th, 1868

Thus far, my darling child, am I spared on my way to you. The closing up of my life at home has been very painful. I am here with our ever kind and dear friends Dr. and Mrs. Axson, and expect to leave in the evening train of Monday the 20th via Macon, Columbus, Mobile. I trust God for a safe and prosperous journey. You will know when I ought to arrive, and I know Robert will meet me at the depot. Your friends here all send warmest love. Kiss my dear little children for Grandmother. And with best love for Robert and yourself,

Ever your own affectionate mother,
Mary Jones.

I thought it best to attend to the box of pictures, and have shipped that and two trunks of my own from No. 3. Mr. Fleming thought I had best pay for them at the other end of the road, and said he had no doubt if Robert would say they were private papers of a minister and ask it, they would grant a reduction. They weigh heavily, and I will pay for them when I come.

I have engaged a slab, and leave an inscription to be placed upon it. Wish I could have consulted you all, but I could not leave your father's grave un-cared for, and have done the best I could.

Ever your mother,
Mary Jones.

Epilogue

So ENDED the Georgia world of Mrs. Mary Jones—"a skeleton world," she had called it three years before, where "the bright prisms of hope which once encircled every object and gilded every scene have faded tint by tint, until dark shadows are resting where sunbeams played. Of earthly possessions and enjoyments I have seen an end; riches have taken to themselves wings and flown away; I am a captive in the home I love, and soon must wander from it—an exile in my native land." In those bitter days of March 1865, isolated at Montevideo and still recovering from the ordeal of Kilpatrick's raid, Mrs. Jones had sought consolation in calling up a happier past:

Memory's buried stores lie all exhumed before my eye. My husband brought me to this his home a young and happy wife—happy, oh, no mortal tongue can tell how happy in his love and confidence, how blessed beneath his influence and with his guidance and companionship. The thrilling joys of those bright days do even now affect this withered heart: his precious words of love, his smile of approbation or encouragement as toils and cares came thronging up the way of life, his godly example, his pious teachings, his tenderest sympathy, his unwearied efforts to alleviate every sorrow, to supply every want, to anticipate and gratify every wish. The most refined, confidential, and affectionate intercourse of thirty-two years made my existence blessed beyond the common lot.

Beloved children were the gift of God to us, and in the sanctuary of home they were nurtured and trained. We were enabled to secure the best of teachers for their intellectual and moral education, and received our reward in their improvement and appreciation of those advantages; whilst their obedience and affection crowned our earthly happiness. The chapel where they passed their schooldays is still standing in the bright sunshine; the twigs they planted have grown to lofty trees; the garden where they reaped their little golden harvests, although grass-grown, is still upon the gentle slope; the museum where so diligently were gathered their scientific spoils, their stuffed birds of varied species (all the songsters of our native forest), their Indian remains, and nameless curiosities, is overgrown with rose vines. Fragments of their well-worn books are scattered upon the shelves, and in the drawers are treasured specimens of drawing and early composition. Their little chairs are with me still, to image up their infancy and childhood. The plain, the grove, the woods are here, but they no longer echo to their cheerful voices; their prayers, their songs, their youthful sports all are hushed. . . .

When first we came to this now beautiful home, it was a rough and uncultivated field. A few large live oaks and small trees dotted here and there the rude enclosure. The spacious dwelling has been built and every improvement has been made under our own eye; every tree and flower planted by our own hand. And now that I see them stretching in shady avenues, or grouped in thickly wooded groves waving their lofty branches above our heads, or blooming in rare beauty or with exquisite perfumes, they are all to my heart more than the common forest trees or garden plants. I have loved and cherished them; they speak to me as with living voices of the ever-present past. That cedar of beautiful proportions in front of the dwelling was planted by my husband with his own hands. I see him bending to the task, and daily look upon it as the chronicler of thirty years. Those magnolias in the rear were named Charles and Joseph. Traces of Daughter's mimic garden still remain in sweet mistle and rose bushes, in bulbs that annually spring from their hiding places. That magnificent live oak, from which a twig was never cut, was set out by our faithful house servant Jack before his own cottage door. Old Daddy Jupiter planted that leaning oak at the turn of the avenue "to be remembered by."

These living memorials remain, but the hands that placed them there are moldering where "no work nor device is found." The halls of this mansion no longer echo to the master's step. The chair is vacant at the board and around the hearthstone. The precious study consecrated to spiritual and intellectual toil is closed, the desk unused and the books all packed. The chapel bell no longer rings out its welcome invitation to saint and sinner. The voice of the priest in his own household no more is heard in prayer and praise or unfolding the mysteries of divine revelation. The servants that used so faithfully and pleasantly to wait around us are (many of them) dead or scattered or sadly and willfully changed. All things are altered. "Abroad the sword bereaveth; at home there is as death." "The adversary hath spread out his hand upon all our pleasant things." The enemy has destroyed every living thing; even the plainest food is made scanty. His robberies and oppressions force me from my beloved home, where it is no longer safe or prudent to remain. And I must leave it in my advancing years, knowing not where the gray hairs which sorrow and time have thickly gathered will find a shelter, or the fainting heart and weary body a resting place, or any spot that I may ever again on earth call home.

These gloomy words Mrs. Jones had written in her journal in March 1865, on the eve of her departure from Montevideo for her brother's place in Baker County, the "far-off land" from which she feared she might never return. As we have seen, she did return the following October, but only to struggle for two disastrous years against well-nigh impossible odds, until in November 1867 it became obvious that she must abandon the home she had cherished so long—"smiling Montevideo," to which she had come as a young wife more than three decades before.

I have risen at midnight and thrown wide the closed shutters of my chamber window, that I might look upon my beautiful earthly home. The clear bright moon is approaching its full-orbed proportions; it has passed its meridian in the heavens, and its declination is towards its diurnal repose in the west. From the diadem of night is reflected the magnificent light of countless brilliant stars, some of greater, some of lesser magnitude. Jupiter sits unrivaled upon his imperial throne. Orion displays his martial belt of peerless gems. Sweet Pleiades have paled beneath the moonbeams, whilst the polar star gives out its cold unchanging rays of white. Beautiful Venus still veils her matchless charms behind the orient sky, waiting to harbinger the coming moon.

Nature below is in perfect repose. Not the faintest zephyr stirs the sleeping forest leaves. Not a waving shadow breaks the entire outline of houses and groves. The giant oaks and lofty pines are perfectly daguerreotyped upon the lawn, whose even surface, still thickly strewed with autumnal leaves, reflects a golden tint; whilst the pure white walks of the garden stand out like silvery highways. Not a sound is heard to break the profound stillness of midnight, saving an occasional tinkle of the bell as Pretty Maid shakes her head or changes her place in the cow pen, or our faithful gander, who keeps his sentry watch in the poultry yard, calls out the passing hour.

I alone seem awake in the vast universe around and above. And yet I know that I am not alone: I feel encompassed by countless evidences of an omnipotent, omniscient, omnipresent Deity. Oh, the sweet and precious consolations that have often flowed into my soul—far from living friends and kindred and all the joys and supports and sweet sympathy of my beloved children! Yes, here in this utter solitude my Heavenly Father hath given me songs of rejoicing even amid the utter loneliness and desolation of a widow's heart and a widow's home.

So Mrs. Jones had mused in her journal on December 9th, 1867, only a few weeks before her departure for New Orleans. Small wonder that she found the "closing up" of her "life at home" so "very painful." Despite "the sweet and precious consolations" of "an omnipotent, omniscient, omnipresent Deity" she grew increasingly despondent as the fateful day approached; and her final Sabbath in Liberty County was inexpressibly sad. "I have felt that it might be the very last I should ever spend at my once happy and privileged home, which now appears more like the grave of my buried hopes and affections than as the dwelling place of living and attractive associations. The scenes of the past have been coming up in rapid review. They are so painful in contrast with the great changes that are now upon my heart and life!"

It was not, to be sure, a homeless fate to which Mrs. Jones was destined in January 1868; but it was a fate to which, understandably, she was never to become fully reconciled. Removed in her sixtieth year from the world she had known from childhood, set down in a world that must have seemed to her exotic indeed, she survived but fifteen months, secure though she was in the warmth and affection of her daughter's New Orleans home. Once, in December 1868, she returned briefly to Liberty County, where she saw completed the work on her husband's tomb at Midway—"the most beautiful marble slab I ever saw: very thick, without spot or blemish. . . . As the clear sunlight of heaven fell upon it without stain or shadow, I thought how emblematic of the glorified spirit washed white in the Blood of the Lamb and clothed in the spotless robe of a Saviour's righteousness." But her plantation affairs she found in wretched condition: "Everybody and everything," she wrote Mrs. Mallard on January 8th, 1869, "is at the lowest ebb in Liberty —due, I think, to want of decision and energy on the part of the men. No concert of action, no public sentiment. . . . The place is beautiful—but oh, how sad! And every day some new perplexity. My child, be thankful your lot has been cast elsewhere." Late in January 1869 she returned to New Orleans; her health steadily declined, and on Friday morning, April 23rd, 1869, after an illness of less than forty-eight hours, she died peacefully at her daughter's home. Scarcely two weeks had passed since the death of Robert Holt Mallard, born on March 3rd, 1868; and Mrs. Jones was buried beside her infant grandson in the family vault in Lafayette Cemetery.

On her deathbed Mrs. Jones had been questioned by her daughter: "Mother, have you any wish in regard to resting at Midway? If you have, it could easily be done." Mrs. Jones had replied: "I have always said, 'Where I die, there let me be buried'; for 'at the last day we shall all be raised in a moment, in the twinkling of an eye.'" And so it came to pass that Mrs. Jones's body remained in New Orleans. For several months her children debated the wisdom of sending her back to be buried beside her husband at Midway; but the removal was evidently judged to be impracticable. In a letter written to his sister from New York on January 19th, 1870, Charles Colcock Jones, Jr., speaking of "our dear and sainted mother," virtually settled the question for all time:

With reference to the removal of her remains, I think this ought not to be done at present. She lies now in your own tomb, with her own precious grandchild, whom she loved so tenderly, by her side. Under all circumstances it seems to me that this is a most fitting resting place. You will agree the more readily with me, I think, in this particular when you reflect upon the almost deserted condition of Midway burial ground. My own wish would be, one of these days, to remove Father from that graveyard and inter him in the Savannah cemetery. Private burial grounds and country churchyards are not the best places wherein to deposit the dust of those we love most. They are, in the country, so liable to change and neglect that in nine cases out of ten, under the eyes even of the second generation, they fall into decay and desolation. The absence of the law of primogeniture, the want of local attachment in the American mind, the facility with which alienations of real property are accomplished, the shifting nature of our population, seeking new homes as inclination, ambition, or interests may suggest, all unite in rendering these private burial grounds and cemeteries of small country churches unstable. . . . I think, my dear sister, that Mother had better remain where she is, in your own tomb, for the present at least. At some future day the removal may be made; but I question the expediency of carrying her back to Midway churchyard.

When one recalls the months and years of unremitting toil which Dr. Jones devoted to *A History of the Church of God,* and the veritable obsession with which his widow pursued the arduous task of seeing her husband's manuscript through the press, it is peculiarly affecting to note that the first volume, published by Charles Scribner late in 1867, enjoyed little favor with the book-buying public and hence was never followed by a second. From the beginning the work seemed strangely ill-starred: as we have seen, the box containing one hundred copies which reached New Orleans on the last day of 1867 was entrusted to the "special agency" of the "indefatigable little sexton" of Prytania Street Presbyterian Church, since, as Mrs. Mallard observed, "the book would be entirely buried and lost sight of if it were placed in the bookstores." During the spring of 1868 few copies were sold; by July 14th Mrs. Jones herself reluctantly conceded that "the sale has been so limited I do not know when we will be able to put out the second volume; times are very hard, and it is difficult to interest friends in good books." Eighteen months later, on January 19th, 1870, Charles Colcock Jones, Jr., wrote his sister opposing further publication:

More than a year has elapsed since the first volume was issued. An edition of five hundred copies was printed, and the larger portion of it remains unsold, with little or no inquiry for the work. Due advertisement has been made, and efforts used to give circulation to the work; but even *at home* and where Father was best known there is literally no inquiry for the work, and the copies on hand remain upon the shelves of the booksellers unsought. Even the immediate members of the family, and clergymen who were in personal communication with Father, have not purchased copies. . . . My own judgment has always been averse to the publication; but as a matter of respect to Mother, and in deference to her wishes, I did what I could in passing the first volume through the press.

Now and then a copy of the *History* was sold during the succeeding decade; then, on August 19th, 1881, nearly fourteen years after its publication, Mrs. Mallard wrote her daughter Mamie from New Orleans:

I received a letter from your Uncle Charles three days ago saying he had received $132 from Scribner (proceeds of the sale of your grandfather's book); and he sent me a check for the whole amount, as he desired to relinquish his portion in my favor, and wrote your uncle here desiring him to do so also, which he did this evening. . . . This was a wonderful surprise, for I had no idea there ever would be anything realized upon the book; and your uncle thinks this will be all, as there are a number of copies on hand and no call for them. I feel that the book accomplished one good end in giving occupation and interest to your dear grandfather's invalid life.

The death of Mrs. Jones was a fundamental shock to her children. A link with the past had been broken: no near relative remained in Liberty County to preserve the family places from decay and ruin; and distance made it difficult if not impossible for the children to return. It is a poignant fact that Mrs. Mallard never again saw her native county after her flight from Montevideo on March 2nd, 1865. Bound to New Orleans by the responsibilities of a growing family, she enjoyed the respect and love of her husband's congregation and set an example of Christian benevolence for the whole community. In 1875 she suffered an attack of pleurisy from which she never fully recovered; some six years later a serious relapse left her a semi-invalid. In November 1888 she was prostrated by an attack of pneumonia, after which she was almost continuously confined to her bed; the following May, at her physician's advice, she was carried to Marietta, Georgia, where at the home of Miss Louisa Robarts she died on August 31st, 1889, aged fifty-four, surrounded by numerous relatives and lifelong friends. Her body was returned to New Orleans and placed in the family vault in Lafayette Cemetery. Meanwhile her husband had continued his New Orleans ministry; from 1866 to 1877 he had served as pastor of the Prytania Street Presbyterian Church; from 1879 till his death twenty-five years later he served as pastor of the Napoleon Avenue Presbyterian Church. On January 19th, 1893, he married Amarintha Mary Witherspoon, daughter of a Presbyterian clergyman. Three years later he was elected moderator of the General Assembly of the Southern Presbyterian Church meeting at Memphis in 1896. From 1891 to 1904 he was editor of *The Southwestern Presbyterian*. His two books, *Plantation Life Before Emancipation* (1892) and *Montevideo-Maybank: Some Memories of a Southern Christian Household in the Olden Times* (1898), describe scenes and incidents of life in coastal Georgia immediately prior to the Civil War. He died in New Orleans on March 3rd, 1904, aged seventy-three, and was buried beside his first wife.

Both of the Mallard daughters continued to reside in New Orleans; the son, Charles Colcock Mallard, a civil engineer associated with the Southern Pacific Railroad, held prominent administrative posts at various points in the West throughout a distinguished career of thirty-five years. He died unmarried in New Orleans on November 24th, 1914, aged fifty-four. His elder sister, Mary Jones Mallard, for some years conducted a school for small children in New Orleans. She never married, and after her father's death she lived in the household of her younger sister, Georgia, who had become the wife of William Kimsey Seago on November 17th, 1896. Mary Jones Mallard died in New Orleans on May 7th, 1917, aged fifty-nine; Mrs. Seago, born during a Yankee raid at the height of Sherman's march through Georgia, lived to be nearly eighty-eight. After a long and active career in church and charitable work, during which she served as editor of the Woman's Auxiliary Department of *The Christian Observer*, official organ of the Southern Presbyterian Church, from 1924 to 1939, she died in New Orleans on December 7th, 1952, survived by four children.

Neighbors of the Mallards almost from the beginning of their New Orleans residence were the family of Mrs. Mallard's brother, Dr. Joseph Jones. who in the summer of 1868 was elected professor of chemistry and clinical medicine in the Medical Department of the University of Louisiana (later the Tulane University School of Medicine), a post he held till his retirement in 1894. Through his researches and publications, particularly in tropical medicine and general hygiene, Dr. Jones gained an international reputation;

in addition to scores of articles in technical and professional journals he published, in four enormous volumes, his monumental *Medical and Surgical Memoirs* (1876–1890), embracing the chief investigations of a long career. He was a member of numerous societies, both scientific and historical; and he held many distinguished and responsible posts: he was visiting physician to the New Orleans Charity Hospital (1870–1894), president of the Louisiana Board of Health (1880–1884), and president of the Louisiana Medical Society (1885–1886); in 1889 he was appointed surgeon general of the United Confederate Veterans. A few weeks after his removal from Nashville to New Orleans his wife Carrie died suddenly, on December 4th, 1868, leaving four small children; eighteen months later, on June 21st, 1870, he married Susan Rayner Polk, daughter of the Rt. Rev. Leonidas Polk, bishop of Louisiana and lieutenant general in the Confederate army. Three children were born of his second marriage: Hamilton Polk Jones, Frances Devereux Jones, and Laura Maxwell Jones. In 1892 the University of Georgia conferred on him the honorary degree of doctor of laws. At the time of his death on February 17th, 1896, in his sixty-third year, he was regarded as one of the leading professors of medicine in the United States and one of the profoundest scientific men of his generation. He was buried in the family vault in Lafayette Cemetery, New Orleans.

His eldest son, Stanhope Jones, was also a physician, receiving his degree from the Medical Department of the University of Louisiana in 1883. After a brief period of medical practice in association with his father he died prematurely on July 24th, 1894, in his thirty-fourth year, leaving three motherless children. His younger brother, Charles Colcock Jones III, a mining and metallurgical engineer, graduated in mechanics from Louisiana State University in 1884 and in mining and metallurgy from Lehigh University in 1887. In 1902 he removed to California, where he became prominent in the development of the iron and steel industry; he died in Los Angeles on April 28th, 1953, in his eighty-eighth year. His sister, Caroline Susan Jones (formerly Susan Hyrne Jones), left New Orleans soon after the death of her father in 1896, joining her stepmother and two half-sisters in Chestnut Hill, Pennsylvania, where she taught at Springside School until her death on June 14th, 1921, aged fifty-eight. The younger sister, Mary Cuthbert Jones, married Dr. Julien Trist Bringier on January 21st, 1896, resided at Tezcuco, her husband's plantation on the Mississippi River near Donaldsonville, Louisiana, and died aged seventy-one on May 27th, 1939.

Meanwhile in distant New York Charles Colcock Jones, Jr., had risen to considerable distinction in the profession of law. In the spring of 1877 he returned with his family to Georgia and fixed his residence at Montrose, a fine antebellum mansion in the village of Summerville (now part of Augusta). Here he continued his legal practice and pursued his literary career; as biographer, historian, and archaeologist he gained nationwide recognition, and a substantial series of publications established his fame as one of Georgia's most prolific and successful writers. His longer works illuminate the history of his native state: *The Monumental Remains of Georgia* (1861), *Historical Sketch of the Chatham Artillery* (1867), *Antiquities of the Southern Indians* (1873), *The Siege of Savannah in December 1864* (1874), *The Dead Towns of Georgia* (1878), *The History of Georgia* (1883), published in two large volumes, and *Negro Myths from the Georgia Coast* (1888), beautifully dedicated to the family servants he had known as a youth. In addition he published essays and discourses on a variety of subjects, including some dozen annual addresses delivered before the Confederate Survivors' Association, an organization which he founded in 1879 and of which he was till the time of his death the only president. His archaeological and historical collections were accounted among the most complete of his day. He was twice complimented with the degree of doctor of laws: by New York University in 1880 and by Oxford University (Georgia) in 1882. His wife Eva died suddenly on October 25th, 1890, two weeks before her forty-ninth birthday; three years later, on July 19th, 1893, he followed at the age of sixty-one. He died universally respected and greatly lamented, and was buried with signal honors beside his second wife in Summerville Cemetery.

Both of his children survived. Ruth Berrien Jones (formerly Mary Ruth Jones) had become the wife of the Rev. Samuel Barstow Carpenter, an Episcopal clergyman, on February 13th, 1890. For some years he served as rector of the Church of the Atonement and the Church of the Good Shepherd in Augusta; and after his death in 1912 his widow continued to occupy the family residence, Montrose, until her death on July 17th, 1934, aged seventy-three. Her half-brother, Charles Edgeworth Jones (formerly Edgeworth Casey Jones), inherited his father's taste for literature; he graduated from the University of Georgia in 1885 and later studied Greek and Latin at Johns Hopkins University without receiving a degree. He was the author of several tracts, including *Education in Georgia* (1889) and *Georgia in the War* (1909); he also published a memorial essay on his father in 1893. After a quiet and studious life he died unmarried in Augusta on October 30th, 1931, aged sixty-four.

Of the Marietta branches of the Jones connection little need be said: the lives of the Buttolphs and the Robartses moved pleasantly forward through the latter years of the century with but few winds to ruffle the surface of their peaceful days. The Rev. David Lyman Buttolph continued as pastor of the Marietta Presbyterian Church till 1887, when for reasons of failing health he resigned; in appreciation of his twenty years' service the church erected and presented to him a house, which he occupied with his family until his death on August 7th, 1905, aged eighty-two. His wife Laura had died on October 28th, 1903, aged seventy-nine. Both lie buried in Episcopal Cemetery, Marietta, together with her mother, Mrs. Susan M. Cumming, who had died on September 16th, 1890, a few weeks before her eighty-seventh birthday. The two younger Buttolph children, both unmarried, also rest in Episcopal Cemetery: Wallace Stewart Buttolph, a bank clerk, who died tragically of typhoid fever on August 26th, 1899, when only thirty-one; and Susan Mary Buttolph, who after graduating with distinction from Shorter College in 1881 devoted her time chiefly to art, studied sculpture in Paris, and died in Marietta on August 21st, 1913, in her fiftieth year. James David Buttolph, a businessman, married Elizabeth Barnwell Elliott, grandniece of Bishop Stephen Elliott, in April 1880; he was first associated with flour mills in Marietta, then with an ice company in Chattanooga; in 1895 he went to New York, where for thirty-five years he sold lots for Woodlawn Cemetery. After his retirement in 1930 he wintered in Waycross, Georgia; and there he died on December 21st, 1939, aged eighty. William Smyth Buttolph, a cotton buyer for the Eagle & Phoenix Mills of Columbus, Georgia, married Sallie Peabody in June 1887; he met a violent death at the age of thirty-five when his body was caught and crushed in the driving gear of one of the mills on June 23rd, 1896.

In view of the precarious health of Mrs. Eliza G. Robarts and the solicitude repeatedly expressed for her welfare by anxious relatives, it is remarkable that she lived to see her eighty-third birthday and died quietly in her bed surrounded by family and friends on November 12th, 1868. Her death was a heavy blow to her daughters: she had been their chief care for many years. "I feel sometimes as if my mission on earth was ended," wrote Miss Louisa a few weeks later; "life for the future appears a blank." The two sisters continued to live in the Marietta house which had been their home, with a three-year interval in Cuthbert and Atlanta, since 1853; on December 2nd, 1878, Miss Mary Eliza died in her seventy-fourth year; Miss Louisa outlived her sister eighteen years and died during the night of January 29th, 1897, aged eighty-three. They were buried beside their mother in Citizens Cemetery, Marietta. Meanwhile their nieces had gone their several ways. Following her marriage to Theodore Dwight Adams, a businessman, on June 13th, 1866, Mary Sophia lived first in Roswell, then in Atlanta, and finally in Pensacola, Florida; there, on January 12th, 1901, her husband dropped dead on the street of a heart attack in his seventy-second year. She continued to reside in Pensacola for more than a decade; her son, Theodore Dwight Adams, Jr., was electrocuted at the age of thirty-seven when he fell on a live wire in Mobile, Alabama, on May 23rd, 1912; her sister Lilla, a schoolteacher and something of a poet, shared her Pensacola house after 1910 and died there unmarried on March 22nd, 1914, in her seventy-fourth year. Later Mary Sophia joined the household of her daughter Lil Ellen (Mrs. Francis Burgess Bruce) in Savannah, where she died on October 30th, 1921, one month before her eighty-third birthday; she was buried in St. John's Cemetery, Pensacola, along with her husband, her son, and her sister Lilla. Her younger sister Ellen, following her marriage to Alexander Brevard Brumby, a schoolmaster, on April 25th, 1866, lived first in Atlanta, then in Newton County, then in Lawrenceville, and finally in Athens; here her husband, a scholarly man unfortunately addicted to drink, died on October 25th, 1879, in his forty-eighth year, leaving his widow with six small children and a meager support. Some thirty years later, on January 30th, 1911, she died in Ocala, Florida, in her sixty-eighth year, and was buried beside her husband in Oconee Hill Cemetery, Athens.

The Rev. John Jones, after four years as pastor of the Presbyterian church in Griffin, removed in 1870 to Atlanta, where he labored as evangelist of the Atlanta Presbytery for twenty-three years and attained considerable prominence in public life. From 1872 to 1882 he served as chaplain of the House of Representatives of Georgia; from 1882 to 1893 he served as chaplain of the Senate of Georgia. In 1876 he received the honorary degree of doctor of divinity from his alma mater, the University of Georgia. His latter years were saddened by total loss of sight, but he continued to preach and to act as chaplain of the Senate. He died in Atlanta on November 26th, 1893, aged seventy-eight; the state legislature, then in session, adjourned to attend his funeral in a body. He was buried in Oakland Cemetery, Atlanta, beside his wife ("my dear Janey"), who had died almost ten years before, on March 20th, 1884, aged sixty-three. Their eldest son, Dunwody, after abortive attempts to plant in Liberty County after the war, settled in Atlanta in 1871 and remained there, engaged in various commercial pursuits, until his death on February 19th, 1904, in his sixty-second year. His wife, the former Mary Cornelia Ashley, whom he had married on November 2nd, 1870, died on August 14th, 1924, aged seventy-five, and was buried beside her husband in Oakland Cemetery. According to the Atlanta *Constitution* at the time of his death, "Major Jones was one of the few remaining 'unreconstructed rebels,' and death alone canceled his fealty to the nation that went down in defeat but not in disgrace. . . . With his long and flowing hair, wide-brimmed hat and high-top boots, he presented upon his gray horse a picture of the times of chivalry." His younger brothers both practiced law. John Carolin Jones graduated from Oglethorpe University in 1872; Joseph Henry Jones graduated from Mercer University in 1874; later the two brothers removed to Orlando, Florida (John in 1881, Joseph in 1893), where they established the firm of Jones & Jones. John died in Orlando on March 4th, 1933, aged eighty, survived by his wife, the former Fannie McGoffin, and three children; Joseph died unmarried in Orlando on July 25th, 1935, aged eighty-one.

On her final visit to Liberty County a few months before her death Mrs. Mary Jones spent much time with her old neighbor Mrs. Julia King, one of the few friends of the Jones connection who remained in Liberty to suffer the "hard labor and vexations and trials" of a shattered world. "It would grieve and depress you, as it does me," Mrs. Jones wrote Mrs. Mallard, "to see the children of my friend Julia looking so wretchedly and struggling so hopelessly to support their little families. . . . She has broken since I last saw her, and feels the situation of her sons." In March 1867 Mrs. King had "given up all care" and settled with her son Rossie and his wife Kitty in Walthourville; her eldest daughter, Mary Wells, had joined her. "Mary Wells lives with Ross and does everything for the children; says she never was happier in her life, although she has not a dollar she can command of her own; works hard, sleeps well, has no headaches now; and God blesses her with a grateful, cheerful spirit." Mrs. Wells died on November 6th, 1871, aged forty-three, and was buried beside her husband at Midway. Rossie's wife died the next year, leaving six small children to the care of Audley and Kate; the Walthourville household was broken up, and Mrs. King returned with Rossie's children to live on the Island. "They have a hard life of it, there are so many little mouths to feed," wrote Clarence King on a visit in 1878; "and with the hardest kind of manual labor they barely manage to get on." Mrs. King died on November 25th, 1892, aged eighty-four, and was buried at Midway. Rossie never remarried; after planting briefly in the up country he returned to Liberty County, where he died in obscurity on September 17th, 1911, aged seventy-five, survived by two families, one white, one black. He was buried at Midway with his father, his mother, his sister, and his wife. His brother Audley died on Colonel's Island on February 29th, 1920, aged ninety; a few weeks later, on April 8th, his beloved Kate followed at the age of eighty-one. They were buried together in Dorchester Cemetery, where their tombstone reads: "Lovely and pleasant were they in their lives, and in their death they were not divided."

The rest of the King children left Liberty County and pursued their fortunes elsewhere. Soon after the war Fred King gave up his tannery in Atlanta and established another in Spring Place, Murray County, where he was joined for a time by his brother Clarence and later by his brother Bayard. Fred King never married; at the turn of the century he was living quietly on a small farm in Baker County, where he supplemented his Confederate pension by collecting and selling reptiles; there he died in poverty and infirmity in 1914, aged eighty-three. His sister Isabel married Mathews Robert Tunno, a Savannah cotton broker, on May 20th, 1868; he died on December 5th, 1916, aged eighty-one, and she followed five years later, on December 27th, 1921, aged seventy-nine; they were buried in Bonaventure Cemetery, Savannah. Clarence King conducted a cotton business in Savannah; on January 11th, 1877, he married his cousin, Georgia Barrington Anderson; he died at Pineora, Georgia, at the house of his sister Isabel, on October 18th, 1901, aged fifty-seven; his wife lived till 1948; they were buried in Laurel Grove Cemetery, Savannah. Bayard King engaged in mining and construction; after eight years with the Texas Rangers he married Fernanda Madrill of Mexico City in the late 1880s; she died soon after the birth of a daughter, and in August 1892 he returned with his motherless child to Baker County, where he lived for a time on a Confederate pension with his brother Fred; early in the new century he removed to Fort Meade, Florida, where he undertook phosphate mining; he died there on September 10th, 1929, aged eighty-three, and was buried in Pleasant Grove Cemetery. The youngest of the Kings, John Butler King, a businessman, married Mary Agnes Battey, daughter of Dr. Robert Battey of Rome, Georgia, on March 10th, 1875; they lived in Macon, where he died on November 14th, 1904, aged fifty-six; his wife died on September 2nd, 1934, aged seventy-nine; they were buried in the Battey vault, Myrtle Hill Cemetery, Rome.

"Our affairs here are in sad condition," wrote Mrs. Jones from Montevideo during her final visit in January 1869. "It is well we came, and it will be necessary—painful and expensive as these visits are—for the protection and preservation of the house, etc., to be here at least once a year." Mrs. Jones never again saw her "dear but desolate home"; she died in New Orleans in April 1869, leaving the care and responsibility of the plantations in Liberty County to her eldest son, Charles Colcock, who administered affairs as best he could till his death twenty-four years later. In December 1869 he made the first of many annual visits to Montevideo; he described his experience in a letter from New York on January 5th, 1870:

I returned from Georgia yesterday. My visit to Montevideo was very pleasant but very sad. My beloved mother was not there, and my dear father—he too was gone! Lucy and Charles and Niger have all been very faithful, and have done their best. Everything was in much better order than I expected to find it. The people were delighted to see me, and I left them all in good heart and promising to do their best. Lucy is still in charge of the house, Charles of the lot and oxen, and Niger of the plantation. Stepney is in charge of Arcadia, and I have requested Audley King to do the best he can with Maybank.

Mrs. Mallard, we have seen, never returned to Montevideo after leaving it in March 1865, though for a time, at least, she evidently entertained some expectation of a reunion there with her brothers. "I hope if you visited Georgia that you spent some time at Montevideo," wrote Charles Colcock from New York on April 15th, 1871; "do not forget our plan to spend a month or two there next winter." Unfortunately the happy plan did not work out; and with the passage of the years the likelihood of a reunion at Montevideo steadily decreased. On January 2nd, 1882, Charles Colcock wrote his wife of his annual visit:

Here we are at the old homestead, sadly marred by the disintegrating influences of time, disfigured by the devastations wrought by the recent hurricane, and yet beautiful under the beams of this calm moon and filled with memories pure and consecrated. Overshadowing all is a cloud of sadness each year growing deeper and darker as the influences of inexorable decay become more and more apparent. The garden long since has become a wild. The dwelling, once so bright and cheerful, has already grown discolored, and is in parts sadly out of repair. Even the trees are growing old, and some of the largest, which the tempest has spared, are dying. The entire region is strangely changed. It is peopled only with the phantoms of things that were, and present images are a mockery of the blessed idols once here enshrined. The lesson is repeated everywhere: "The places which now know us will soon know us no more forever." Earthly visions—the truest and loveliest—endure but for a season, and then evanish into the realm of shadows. Everything grows insubstantial with the flight of years, and in the end lapses into something near akin to nothingness. The true, the beautiful, the good alone survive in divine revelations; these we cherish, and they alone amid the general wreck savor of immortality.

In June 1880 the Mallards' former manservant James died leaving a family of nine; early in 1885 Tenah, beloved nurse of the Mallard children, died leaving four girls and one boy. Charles Colcock wrote his sister from Augusta on January 11th, 1886:

Upon my recent visit to Liberty I was sorely distressed at the desolation which had been caused by the floods and the continued rains of last fall. The entire rice crop had been swept away, and the cotton and much of the corn rotted in the fields. The consequence of all this was that I did not collect enough to pay taxes and defray the cost of the extensive repairs which I have found it necessary to put upon the old homestead. At Arcadia the same cause brought about like results, and I was disappointed in realizing the small balance due on account of the sale of lots. . . . Lucy is growing older, but seemed pretty well. Niger has consoled himself with another wife—a widow with some five children. These, added to what Tenah left, are sufficient to people a small plantation. He wisely keeps the two families apart.

And so time continued to take its toll. On his annual visit early in 1888 Charles Colcock found "everything in a situation more depressed and impoverished than usual. . . . Lucy has been crippled up with rheumatism, and although now somewhat better, is scarcely able to move about. The visit was a sad one to me."

For a few more years, until his death in 1893, Charles Colcock continued to maintain the house; thereafter it quickly fell prey to the depredations of the neighboring poor, white and black, who tore out mantels, seized cornices and moldings, carried off stair rails and floorboards, and eventually so despoiled the house that little was left for the winds and the rains to destroy. Montevideo was said to be the last antebellum plantation house in Liberty County to survive the ravages of war and time. Shortly after the turn of the century the place was sold out of the family, and the elements soon completed what the vandals had begun. Today there is no house at all: nothing remains of the splendid mansion that once knew human laughter and human tears; and little in the surrounding wilderness suggests that this was once the seat of wealth, refinement, and learning. To the visitor who knows the past it is a heartbreaking spot. In the tangle of forest growth he traces the rough lines of a brick foundation; in mimosa and magnolia and holly, now monstrously overgrown, he sees vestiges of a garden once laid out with affection and taste. A mile distant the plantation gates still stand, mute evidence of a day that is dead; and streamlined trains, chrome-plated in the sunlight, streak past bound for New York. The rest is silence. The North Newport River still glides on, thoughtless that a way of life has vanished from the earth.

The fate of Midway Church promised for a time to be no less disastrous. Near the end of the war Kilpatrick's cavalry, encamped at the church for six weeks, penned their horses and cattle in the cemetery, appropriated the church as a slaughterhouse, used the melodeon as a meat block, and rifled the cornerstone of its contents. During the succeeding years the church shared the ruin and desolation of the surrounding area; in October 1865 Mrs. Jones found it "distressing to see the condition of the church: doors and windows open, shutters off; and the sheep had evidently taken shelter in the aisles." After the removal of the Rev. Mr. Buttolph in November 1867 and the virtual dissolution of the church, the white membership reluctantly withdrew to worship at the various retreats. Churches were established at Walthourville in 1855, at Flemington in 1866, and at Dorchester in 1871; after the war the fourth retreat, Jonesville, disappeared altogether from the scene. Midway Church was leased to its Negro members, who agreed in return to keep the building in repair and the cemetery in order; some six hundred Negroes organized a separate congregation under the pastorate of the Rev. Joe Williams, a clergyman of their own race, and continued to worship at Midway for twenty years. Mr. Lazarus John Mallard, selectman of Midway Church from 1854 to 1867 and also clerk of the session, described the condition of the church in a letter to his former pastor on October 9th, 1868:

We have not worshiped at Midway since you left, but still consider ourselves members of the old church, and are loath to give up the idea that we will yet some day return to that sacred spot hallowed by so many associations. . . . The old church is still used by the Negroes. The graveyard is now in unusually good order—kept so by the colored people as some compensation to us for the use they have of the church.

Last week I was permitted to visit the much-loved spot. It so happened that Simon the old bell-ringer was passing along the causeway, on which I had just finished some public work. I invited him to a seat in my wagon, with the request that he would go up with me to the old church and ring the bell for me, that I might hear it as in former days. You could hardly imagine—and I could hardly describe—my feelings to you. I stood upon the steps and listened. Where are all those who obeyed that bell and once came at its call into the House of the Lord? I walked up and down the aisles, marking the pews where once a solemn and worshiping assembly sat. Where are they now? All gone—some one way and some another, and many to their long last home. Shall the like of what we have seen never again be witnessed within these walls? Shall that *sacred* desk, made so by the faithful who have there stood, never again be occupied by another who shall break unto us the Bread of Life? Here in this house hundreds received their first serious impressions, and hundreds were built up in their most holy faith; saints have been strengthened, and sinners converted to God. Many and such like thoughts flashed across my mind, and I could have wept over the desolations which have been visited upon our ancient Jerusalem. How unsearchable are the judgments of God, and His ways past finding out!

Although Midway Church was never formally dissolved, the removal of Mr. Buttolph marked its practical extinction as a place of public worship for whites; the last annual meeting of the Midway Church and Society was called in December 1865, and the last entry recorded in the session book was dated October 1867. Ten years later an attempt to sell the building failed: the white membership had hoped to invest the proceeds and apply the income to maintenance of the cemetery, then rapidly falling into decay. Finally, on March 9th, 1887, after a lapse of more than twenty years, the Midway Church and Society resumed its annual meetings; and it has continued to meet annually ever since.

At the meeting in March 1888 it was resolved that the cornerstone of the church, laid at the centennial celebration of 1852 and later rifled of its contents by the Federals, should be relaid with appropriate ceremonies at the next annual meeting. Accordingly Colonel Charles Colcock Jones, Jr., then living in Augusta, was invited to deliver an address at the old church on March 13th, 1889. The day appointed proved to be so rainy that hardly a score of persons appeared; but the address was delivered, and the Savannah *Morning News* next day pronounced it "one of the noblest efforts of the orator-historian." After vividly sketching the centennial celebration of 1852 Colonel Jones paid tribute to "the sterling patriotism, heroic devotion to principle, and great sufferings" of the Midway colonists during the Revolutionary War; he then detailed "the overwhelming ruin and sad changes" which prostrated "this once noble and happy community" during the late struggle for Confederate independence.

Although the tide of active, intelligent life appears in large measure to have receded from this long-accustomed shore; although shadows still gather about us, and the gloom of disaster hangs heavily above plantation and highway; although the voice of the pastor is seldom heard within the porches of this almost deserted temple, and the dust of silent Sabbaths settles noiselessly upon altar and pew; we will nevertheless here set up a column in remembrance of all that has been, in praise of those who sleep within the ivy-mantled walls of this churchyard, in commemoration of the deeds and virtues of our ancestors, and in confident expectation of the rehabilitation of this now wasted community. . . . In relaying this cornerstone let us express and cherish the hope that no untoward events or undue procrastination will delay the consummation of our laudable design, but that the purpose which we this day inaugurate may be speedily accomplished. Thus by a physical embodiment of the exalted memories and valuable traditions of this people, and by symbolizing the general gratitude, will we stimulate a fuller, a prouder recognition of the virtues and the valor of the days that are gone, and encourage nobler efforts for the rehabilitation of a region formerly so favored, and for so many years the abode of refinement, of industry, of morality, of patriotism, and of civilization. [*Address Delivered at Midway Meetinghouse in Liberty County, Georgia, on the Second Wednesday in March 1889* (Augusta, 1889), pp. 18–20]

In view of the pitiless rain on the ceremonial occasion and the consequent thinness of the audience present, it was thought advisable to postpone the actual relaying of the cornerstone until a more propitious day; thus on May 8th, 1889, the people reassembled and the cornerstone was laid by William Augustus Fleming, captain of the Liberty Independent Troop, after a sermon by the Rev. James Stacy, then pastor of the Presbyterian church at Newnan, Georgia:

And though the former order of things may never be restored, and this building, hoary with age and rich in historic renown, as well as sacred memories, may tumble in ruins, and even these tombs and monuments, which mark the last resting places of many loved ones, whose moldering bodies lie slumbering in this camping ground of the dead, be completely obliterated, yet if the descendants of this people, conscious of the mighty responsibility resting upon them, and inspired with fresh vigor and zeal from the monuments of the past, instead of spending the time glorying over bygone achievements, or indulging gloomy forebodings about the future, would diligently and laboriously apply themselves to the task before them, they may yet continue the work so gloriously begun by their forefathers and even make the record of the old church still more illustrious. And it is possible, in some way unknown to us, that God may in the future raise up even here, out of these moldering ruins, another church and clothe it with the vigor and freshness of former years. But if this be not His will, if the time of her active life be past and she is to live only in history and story, then let the influence of her embalmed life continue ever to linger like holy fragrance around this sacred spot, a silent witness of the past and a source of inspiration for the future; in either case a benediction to the world, and to all who shall come after. [*History of the Midway Congregational Church* (Newnan, Georgia, 1899), p. 260]

In his now classic *History of the Midway Congregational Church* Stacy gave a graphic account of the early fortunes of the Midway settlement, reproduced numerous records of the old church, and summarized her astonishing contribution, past and present, to the intellectual and spiritual life of America. On the threshold of its second century the original structure was, he wrote, in a state of remarkable preservation, partly because it had been, according to contract, "built of the best wood," and partly because it had been solicitously maintained and repaired throughout the years.

But time has commenced doing its work. It fills the heart with intense sadness to visit the old spot and see the decay that is going on. For twenty years the old church building was given the colored people, the only compensation required being that they should care for the cemetery. During that time the yard became very much neglected. Many of the monuments were allowed to fall; others were upturned by trees growing up beside them. In the burning of limbs and rubbish and grass many of the monuments were smoked and greatly marred, insomuch that at the end of that time the contract was rescinded and the church used only by the whites at the annual reunions in March. The cemetery now presents much of a neglected appearance, many of the inscriptions being wholly illegible on account of a covering of moss which has been accumulating upon them. No one, however, can visit the place and look upon the old church, standing solitary and alone at the junction of two roads, without a single home in view, her worshipers all gone, her doors closed, her careening steeple still pointing heavenward, with the tops of her faded monuments silently lifting up their heads from underneath an arch of pendant moss and peering over the massive brick wall which encircles the resting place of her dead, without feeling that he is standing upon sacred ground. [pp. 219–220]

This distressing picture of the old church was not long in prompting its friends to action. In 1905 a subscription committee was appointed and a letter of solicitation was addressed to every known descendant of the Midway community; among the contributions received was a personal check from President Theodore Roosevelt, great-grandson of General Daniel Stewart. Soon a sum was raised sufficient to restore the cemetery to order, straighten the "careening steeple," and secure the walls of the church from total collapse. For fifty years these restorations checked further decay; then in 1956, when it became necessary to widen the highway separating the church from the cemetery, the church was moved forty-two feet to the east and at the same time meticulously restored inside and out. The Georgia Department of Highways bore the cost of moving the church and part of the cost of restoration; the balance of the cost was met by voluntary contributions of friends.

Meanwhile in 1946 the Midway Museum Society had been organized under the sponsorship of the St. John's Parish Chapter of the Daughters of the American Colonists, with the participation of the Liberty County Chapter of the United Daughters of the Confederacy; its objective was "to perpetuate for posterity the memory of the Midway colonists through the medium of a museum." A nationwide campaign realized sufficient funds to purchase a museum site directly behind the church; this site was donated to the State of Georgia, and on it a commodious fireproof structure in the style of a typical antebellum plantation house was erected by the Georgia Historical Commission to preserve records and relics associated with Midway history. The museum was dedicated on November 29th, 1959; it is operated and maintained by the State of Georgia under the supervision of the Georgia Historical Commission; it is regularly open to visitors, and a small admission fee contributes to its maintenance.

And so the spirit of Midway Church lives on today, not only in the beautifully restored house of worship built by stalwart Calvinists in 1792, not only in the handsome museum established to perpetuate a glorious history for the instruction and delight of generations to come, but also in the countless sons and daughters of the early communicants, now scattered far and wide across the nation and the world, who cherish the memory of a worthy past and everywhere occupy positions of honor and trust. The church is no longer open for regular services; but each year the Midway Church and Society meets on the second Wednesday in March; and each year on April 26th, the day celebrated as Confederate Memorial Day in Georgia, Florida, Alabama, and Mississippi, hundreds of loyal descendants of the Midway community gather at the church for what is known as the Midway Celebration. In the morning a distinguished clergyman, not necessarily a son of Midway, preaches a sermon and administers Communion from the original service; later a basket lunch is spread in the neighboring grove, where friendships are renewed and ancestral deeds are recalled; in the afternoon a memorial service is held in the cemetery across the way, and flowers are placed on the graves of the honored dead. In April 1954 the annual reunion celebrated the bicentennial of the settlement of the Midway colony and the formal institution of Midway Church on August 28th, 1754. The address of the day was delivered by the Hon. Richard Brevard Russell, United States senator from Georgia, a direct descendant of the Midway colony, and a grandson of William John Russell, the "noble man" who in 1864 offered to pay Aunt Eliza Robarts' Confederate tax and was in many ways "more like a son to Aunty than a friend." After lunch on the grounds a cast of three hundred persons, most of them descendants of original settlers, presented *A Charge to Keep,* a pageant written and directed by Josephine Bacon Martin, a daughter of Charles Jones Martin, who was named for the Rev. Dr. Charles Colcock Jones, a friend of the Martin family, in 1849, and was pronounced by Dr. Jones to be "a fine little fellow" on March 15th, 1858.

Long after his pilgrimage to the old church, long after his scrutiny of treasured heirlooms in the adjacent museum, today's visitor is disposed to linger in the peaceful moss-draped cemetery across the highway to the west. Here, surrounded by a solid brick wall six feet high and eighteen inches thick, the forefathers sleep in the shadow of majestic live oaks more venerable than the church itself. Perhaps no other spot of equal size encompasses the dust of as many men and women who have shaped the destiny of the state and the nation. In less than two acres of ground lie the remains of at least twelve hundred persons, among them Nathan Brownson, delegate to the Continental Congress, member of the Federal Constitutional Convention, and governor of Georgia; John Elliott, United States senator; John Elliott Ward, first United States minister to China; and Louis LeConte, eminent botanist, father of Professors John and Joseph LeConte of the University of California. A tall shaft in the center of the yard, erected by the Congress of the United States and unveiled in 1915, honors the memory of two Revolutionary heroes, General Daniel Stewart and General James Screven. And here and there, in tombs of varying design and elegance, lie the ancestors of

the Mallards, the Quartermans, the Bakers, the Ways, and the Winns—
heroic men and women who braved the perils of the wilderness and risked
the tomahawk of the savage to enjoy the blessings of civil and religious
liberty. Their touching inscriptions tell the story of frail humanity for more
than two hundred years. One such inscription, cut in a marble slab sur-
mounting a bricked-up tomb, evokes a peculiar interest:

Sacred
to the memory of
Revd Charles Colcock Jones D.D.
Born in Liberty County, Georgia
December 20th 1804,
Departed this Life at Arcadia Plantation
March 16th 1863

———

Twice a Professor of Ecclesiastical History
and Church Polity in the Theological
Seminary at Columbia, South Carolina.
Three years the corresponding Secretary of
the Board of Domestic Missions
of the Gen. Assembly of the Presbyterian Church.
His life was employed in Self-denying and
devoted Labors for the evangelization of the
Colored population of his native
County and State;
and in awakening in behalf of this great work
the sympathies and efforts of the South.

———

The devoted Husband and Father, the firm friend &
Kind Master, the public Benefactor, the zealous
Evangelist, the profound Theologian, the learned
Author, the pure Patriot, and the exalted Christian.
In his Character
were combined all those virtues and traits
which dignify, ennoble, and benefit mankind.

———

He walked with God and was not, for God took him.
How is the strong staff broken, and the beautiful rod!

Who's Who

ABORN, SARAH JANE (born 1829) was the daughter of Joseph Rhodes Aborn, who early in the 1820s removed from his native Providence, Rhode Island, to Savannah, Georgia, where he married Sarah W. Frith on May 29th, 1822. Shortly thereafter Sarah Rhodes Aborn (1802–1879) came from Providence to visit her brother Joseph in Savannah, where she married the Hon. Charles Seton Henry (1797–1864) on May 31st, 1827. In 1850 Sarah Jane Aborn was living in the Savannah household of her paternal aunt, Sarah Rhodes (Aborn) Henry, whose sister-in-law, Charlotte Elizabeth Henry, wife of George Washington McAllister, was the stepmother of Emma, Rosella, and Clementina McAllister, of Strathy Hall, Bryan County, Georgia. Sarah Jane Aborn was thus intimately associated with the McAllisters, and she frequently stayed in the New Haven, Connecticut, summer residence of Matilda Willis McAllister, wife of Thomas Savage Clay, and elder sister of Emma, Rosella, and Clementina McAllister. On June 3rd, 1857, Sarah Jane Aborn became the wife of Charles Averill Barlow, of Waynesville, Ohio.

ADAMS, ALVIN (1804–1877), pioneer expressman, son of Jonas Adams and Phoebe Hoar, was born in Andover, Vermont, on June 16th, 1804. His father died of spotted fever on February 19th, 1813, and his mother died of the same disease one week later, on February 26th, 1813. Young Alvin lived with elder brothers until 1820, when he left home to seek employment for himself. For twenty years he was variously engaged; he worked in several hotels and finally entered the produce business, in which he twice failed. In 1840, in association with Ephraim Farnsworth, he established Adams & Company, express agents; he purchased two season tickets on the New York & Boston Railroad, and he and his partner began shuttling between the cities, contracting to carry small bundles for delivery to either city; one day Adams would travel from Boston to New York while Farnsworth traveled from New York to Boston; the next day the two men would reverse their routes. The business flourished and rapidly expanded. Adams soon arranged service between New York and Philadelphia, and thence to Baltimore, Washington, Pittsburgh, Cincinnati, Louisville, St. Louis, New Orleans, and intermediate points. He accumulated a vast fortune. In 1854 the Adams Express Company was incorporated, with Adams as president and William B. Dinsmore as secretary-treasurer. During the Civil War the company's business was enormous. Adams died on his beautiful estate in Watertown, Massachusetts, on September 1st, 1877.

ADAMS, CORNELIUS BERRIEN (1837–1875), physician and cotton broker, was born in South Carolina in 1837. After graduating from Oglethorpe University in 1858 he attended medical lectures in Augusta and Philadelphia. During the Civil War he was assistant surgeon in the Confederate army, with rank of captain. On April 26th, 1864, he married Anne Eliza Harden (1842–1924), of Walthourville, Liberty County, Georgia, daughter of Dr. John Macpherson Berrien Harden (1810–1848) and Jane LeConte (1814–1876), and younger sister of Matilda Jane Harden (1837–1932). After the war he settled in Augusta, where he engaged in the cotton business until his accidental death by drowning in a canal at Graniteville, South Carolina, on the night of January 1st, 1875. Anne Eliza (Harden) Adams died in Augusta on July 10th, 1924, survived by three children, and was buried beside her husband in Magnolia Cemetery.

ADAMS, HAMILTON SEAGRAVE (1861–1894), lawyer, son of Theodore Dwight Adams (1829–1901) and his first wife, Ellen Hamilton Seagrave (1836–1864), was born in Roswell, Georgia, in December 1861. After his mother's death on August 12th, 1864, and his father's marriage to Mary Sophia Robarts (1838–1921) on June 13th, 1866, he lived for some years with his father and stepmother in Roswell and Atlanta. In early manhood he removed to Sanford, Florida, where he rose to prominence as an attorney, a school commissioner, a justice of the peace, and a member of the state legislature. On November 7th, 1891, finding himself in desperate financial straits, he attempted suicide by asphyxiation at the Morton House in New York City; on November 17th, 1894, he died in Sanford from a self-administered overdose of morphine. In 1883 he married Jeannie Berry, of St. Louis, Missouri; his wife and nine-year-old daughter survived.

ADAMS, JAMES HOPKINS (1812–1861), legislator and governor, only son of Henry Walker Adams and Mary Goodwyn, was born in Richland County, South Carolina, on March 15th, 1812. He graduated from Yale College in 1831. Returning to South Carolina, he was a member of the state house of representatives (1834–1837; 1840–1841; 1848–1849) and the state senate (1850–1853). In 1832 he supported the doctrine of nullification; in 1851 he demanded secession. In December 1856, near the close of his two-year term as governor (1854–1856), he shocked the public by proposing to reopen the African slave trade; the state legislature refused to endorse his recommendation. At the state secession convention in December 1860 he favored immediate secession; he was later elected one of three commissioners to visit Washington and negotiate with President James Buchanan for the transfer of United States property in South Carolina to the ownership of the state. He died near Columbia, South Carolina, on July 13th, 1861.

ADAMS, LIL ELLEN (1867–1941), daughter of Theodore Dwight Adams (1829–1901) and his second wife, Mary Sophia Robarts (1838–1921), was born in Marietta, Georgia, on March 24th, 1867. She was named for her two maternal aunts, Elizabeth (Lilla) Walton Robarts and Ellen Douglas Robarts. After her father's death in 1901 she lived with her widowed mother in Pensacola, Florida, where, on June 5th, 1916, in her fiftieth year, she became the second wife of Francis Burgess Bruce (1863–1944), son of Dr. William Henry Bruce and Constance Tudor, of Charles County, Maryland. She died in Savannah on January 1st, 1944, survived by her husband and by one sister, Sarah Douglas (Zaidee) Adams (1869–1958), and was buried in Bonaventure Cemetery.

ADAMS, THEODORE DWIGHT (1829–1901), merchant, son of Edwin Adams and Lydia Fuller, was born in Frankfort, Herkimer County, New York, on March 10th, 1829. In 1857 he removed to Georgia, first to Atlanta, then to Roswell, where he became a clerk in the factory of Barrington King. On March 6th, 1861, in Brooklyn, New York, he married Ellen Hamilton Seagrave (1836–1864), only daughter of Josiah Seagrave (1811–1861) and Phoebe Hamilton Brackett (1811–1865), of Providence, Rhode Island. She died in Cincinnati, Ohio, on August 12th, 1864, leaving one child, Hamilton Seagrave Adams (1861–1894). During the Civil War Adams served briefly as lieutenant of a company organized for home defense. After the war he settled in Roswell, where he was for some years postmaster and storekeeper. On June 13th, 1866, he married Mary Sophia Robarts (1838–1921), eldest daughter of Joseph William Robarts (1811–1863) and Sophia Louisa Gibson (1814–1847), and granddaughter of Eliza Greene (Low) (Walker) (Robarts) Robarts, with whom he was then living in Atlanta. There were three children: Lil Ellen Adams (1867–1941), Sarah Douglas (Zaidee) Adams (1869–1958), and Theodore Dwight Adams (1875–1912). In 1900 the family removed to Pensacola, Florida, where, three months later, on January 12th, 1901, Adams dropped dead on the street of a heart attack while walking with his wife. He was buried in Perdido Bay Cemetery; in 1921 his remains were removed to St. John's Cemetery to rest beside those of his wife and son.

ADGER, JAMES (1777–1858), merchant and banker, son of James Adger and Margaret Crawford, was born in Moneynick, Northern Ireland, in 1777. He migrated in 1794 to New York, and thence in 1802 to Charleston, South Carolina, where he prospered in banking and shipping. At one time he was ranked fourth richest man in the United States. On September 6th, 1806, he married Sarah Elizabeth Ellison; there were nine children, among them Margaret Milligan Adger (1807–1884), wife of the Rev. Thomas Smyth (1808–1873), pastor of the Second Presbyterian Church, Charleston; and the Rev. John Bailey Adger (1810–1899), Presbyterian missionary, pastor, educator, and translator. Sarah Elizabeth (Ellison) Adger died in Charleston on October 18th, 1856, and was buried in the Second Presbyterian Churchyard. James Adger died in the St. Nicholas Hotel, New York City, on September 24th, 1858, and was buried beside his wife on November 27th, 1858. He left substantial bequests to each of his children and grandchildren.

ADGER, JOHN BAILEY (1810–1899), Presbyterian clergyman, eldest son of James Adger (1777–1858) and Sarah Elizabeth Ellison, was born in Charleston, South Carolina, on December 13th, 1810. He graduated from Union College (Schenectady, New York) in 1828 and from Princeton Theological Seminary in 1833. On June 29th, 1834, he married Elizabeth Keith Shrewsbury, of Charleston. He was missionary at Constantinople and Smyrna (1834–1847); pastor of Zion Church (Negro) in Charleston (1847–1851); professor of ecclesiastical history and church polity at Columbia Theological Seminary (1857–1874); and pastor of various churches in South Carolina (1874–1894). While in the Near East he translated *A Catechism of Scripture Doctrine and Practice,* by the Rev. Dr. Charles Colcock Jones, as well as the New Testament, the Shorter Catechism, and *Pilgrim's Progress,* into Armenian and Turko-Armenian. He was author of *My Life and Times* (1899) and coeditor (with John Lafayette Girardeau) of *The Collected Writings of James Henley Thornwell* (4 vols., 1871–1873). He received the honorary degree of doctor of divinity from the College of Charleston in 1853. He died at Pendleton, South Carolina, on January 3rd, 1899, and was buried beside his wife, who had died on October 11th, 1890.

ALBRO, JOHN ADAMS (1799–1866), Congregational clergyman, was born in Newport, Rhode Island, on August 13th, 1799. After graduating from the Litchfield (Connecticut) Law School in 1821 he practiced law briefly in Mansfield, Connecticut. In 1824 he determined to become a clergyman and entered Andover Theological Seminary, where he was the fellow student of Charles Colcock Jones. For thirty years (1835–1865) he was pastor of the First Congregational Church, Cambridge, Massachusetts. He received the honorary degree of master of arts from Yale College (1827) and the honorary degree of doctor of divinity from Bowdoin College (1848) and Harvard College (1851). He died in West Roxbury, Massachusetts, on December 20th, 1866. Charles Colcock Jones, Jr., upon his arrival in Cambridge, wrote his parents on September 5th, 1853: "Dr. Albro has been exceedingly kind and attentive to us. . . . My anticipation is to attend regularly upon his ministry. Regular pews are assigned to the law students in his church—an arrangement quite desirable, and also creditable to the college, which pays the pew rents."

ALEXANDER, ADAM LEOPOLD (1803–1882), planter, son of Adam Alexander (1758–1812), a native of Inverness, Scotland, and Louisa Frederika Schmidt (1777–1846), a native of Stuttgart, Germany, was born in Sunbury, Liberty County, Georgia, on January 29th, 1803. After graduating from Yale College in 1821 he read law in the office of the Hon. John Macpherson Berrien, of Savannah, but he never practiced his profession. On April 29th, 1823, he married Sarah Hillhouse Gilbert (1805–1855), of Washington, Wilkes County, Georgia; she died on February 28th, 1855, and ten years later, on December 5th, 1865, he married Jane Marion Dunwody (1821–1885), widow of the Rev. Stanhope Erwin and Dr. William Glen. After his first marriage he made his residence in Washington, Wilkes County, with intermittent visits to Hopewell, his plantation in Liberty County; in 1872 he removed to Augusta, where he resided until his death on Easter morning, April 9th, 1882. He was buried beside his first wife in the Alexander family cemetery in Washington. A man of wealth and cultivation, he was the progenitor of one of Georgia's most illustrious families. His ten children all survived him: Louisa Frederika Alexander (1824–1895), wife of Jeremy Francis Gilmer; Sarah Gilbert Alexander (1826–1897), wife of Alexander Robert Lawton; Harriet Virginia Alexander (1828–1910), wife of Wallace Cumming; Mary Clifford Alexander (1830–1914), wife of George Gilmer Hull; William Felix Alexander (1832–1907); Edward Porter Alexander (1835–1910); Charles Atwood Alexander (1838–1907); James Hillhouse Alexander (1840–1902); Marion Brackett Alexander (1842–1901), wife of the Rev. William Elliott Boggs; and Alice Vanyeverine Alexander (1848–1902), wife of Alexander C. Haskell.

ALEXANDER, ARCHIBALD (1772–1851), Presbyterian clergyman and educator, third son of William Alexander and Ann Reid, was born in Augusta (now Rockbridge) County, Virginia, on April 17th, 1772. After a brief period as an itinerant clergyman he served as president of Hampden-Sydney College (1796–1807) and pastor of the Pine Street Church, Philadelphia (1807–1812). On April 5th, 1802, he married Janetta Waddel, daughter of the celebrated blind preacher, James Waddel (1739–1805), of Louisa County, Virginia; of their seven children three became eminent Presbyterian clergymen: James Waddel Alexander (1804–1859), Joseph Addison Alexander (1809–1860), and Samuel Davies Alexander (1819–1894). When Princeton Theological Seminary was established in 1812 he became its first professor, a post he held for thirty-nine years. "Dr. Alexander's lectures are very superior, and will be a great help to me," wrote the Rev. Dr. Charles Colcock Jones, one of his students, on August 25th, 1830. "I like the old gentleman more and more." Alexander was author of *A Brief Outline of the Evidences of the Christian Religion* (1825), *The Canon of the Old and New Testaments* (1826), *The*

Lives of the Patriarchs (1835), *Thoughts on Religious Experience* (1841), and *Outlines of Moral Science* (1852). He was moderator of the General Assembly of the Presbyterian Church in 1807. He died in Princeton on October 22nd, 1851; Charles Colcock Jones, Jr., then a senior in the College of New Jersey (Princeton), detailed the funeral in a letter to his parents on October 25th, 1851: "It was one of the largest funerals I have ever witnessed. The strictest decorum and propriety were maintained throughout the entire exercise. The college students in their best suits and with badges and crepe, the uniform black of the clergy and seminarians, all conspired to render the scene very impressive, solemn, and becoming."

ALEXANDER, CHARLES ATWOOD (1838–1907), planter, son of Adam Leopold Alexander (1803–1882) and his first wife, Sarah Hillhouse Gilbert (1805–1855), was born in Washington, Wilkes County, Georgia, on November 4th, 1838. For several years prior to the Civil War he resided at Hopewell, his father's plantation in Liberty County, where he was the "kind friend and neighbor" of the Rev. Dr. Charles Colcock Jones. He married first (on April 8th, 1862) Ida Calhoun (1841–1867), daughter of Edward Calhoun and Frances Middleton, of South Carolina. He married second (on November 4th, 1880) Rosa Calhoun (1848–1912), younger sister of his first wife. During the Civil War he served four years in the Liberty Independent Troop (Company G, 5th Regiment Georgia Cavalry). In 1865 he returned to Liberty County, where he continued for some years to plant. Later he settled in Washington, Wilkes County, where he died on January 30th, 1907, mourned as "a citizen of the highest and truest type of manhood" (Augusta *Chronicle*, February 2nd, 1907). At his death he was one of the largest planters in Wilkes County and senior elder of the Washington Presbyterian Church. He was buried in the Alexander family cemetery in Washington.

ALEXANDER, PETER WELLINGTON (1824–1886), lawyer, editor, and war correspondent, was born in Elberton, Georgia, on March 21st, 1824. After graduating from Franklin College (Athens) in 1844 he was admitted to the bar in 1845 and practiced law at Thomaston, Georgia, for several years. From 1848 to 1856 he was editor of the Savannah *Republican;* later, as war correspondent for this paper, he gained international distinction for his graphic letters, signed "P. W. A." After the war he settled in Columbus, where he practiced law in partnership with James Milton Smith; when Smith became governor of Georgia in 1872 Alexander served as his private secretary (1872–1877). In 1877 he removed to Marietta, where he died on September 23rd, 1886, survived by his wife, Maria Theresa Shorter, of Columbus, whom he had married on September 27th, 1870.

ALEXANDER, ROBERT SPREUL CRAWFORD AITCHESON (1819–1867), stock-raiser, son of the Hon. Robert Alexander (1767–1841), was born in Frankfort, Kentucky, on October 25th, 1819. His father, a native of Scotland, had migrated to America in the 1780s and purchased a large estate, Woodburn, in Woodford County, Kentucky, in 1791. A man of wealth, cultivation, and influence, he represented Woodford County in the state legislature (1795–1802), served as president of the first Bank of Kentucky (1807–1820), and in 1814, in his forty-seventh year, married Eliza Richardson Weiseger, of Frankfort. Robert Aitcheson Alexander matriculated at Trinity College (Cambridge) in 1840 and graduated in 1846. In 1842, while still in England, he inherited the vast Scottish estate of his uncle, Sir William Alexander; to hold the estate he retained his British citizenship all his life. Returning to Woodford County in 1849, he proceeded to develop Woodburn into one of the most famous stock farms in the world. He never married. He died at Woodburn on December 1st, 1867.

ALLEN, BENJAMIN WASHINGTON (1812–1856), planter and overseer, was born in Beaufort, South Carolina, in 1812. In early manhood he settled in Liberty County, Georgia, where he married first (in 1836) Margaret Smylie and second (in 1843) Caroline Elizabeth Fuller. He joined the Liberty Independent Troop in 1837. On January 1st, 1853, he succeeded Thomas Jane Shepard as manager of Montevideo plantation during the absence of the Rev. Dr. Charles Colcock Jones in Philadelphia—"the best *we* could do," wrote Dr. Jones on December 29th, 1852, "and believe he will endeavor to do *his* best for us." Allen continued to manage Montevideo plantation until forced by "continued illness" to retire early in 1856; during the same period he also managed White Oak plantation for Mrs. Susan M. Cumming. He died at his residence in Dorchester on March 25th, 1856, survived by his wife and five young children, and was buried in Midway Cemetery with military honors by the Liberty Independent Troop. As Dr. Jones observed (March 27th, 1856), "He was a very public-spirited and useful and pleasant man in the sphere in which he moved, and is a loss to our little community."

ANDERSON, EDWARD CLIFFORD (1815–1883), planter and Confederate agent, ninth child of George Anderson (1767–1847) and Elizabeth Clifford Wayne, was born in Savannah, Georgia, on November 8th, 1815. At an early age he was sent North to attend school, one of his teachers being George Bancroft. In 1834 he entered the United States navy as a midshipman and rose to the rank of lieutenant before retiring in 1850. He was mayor of Savannah (1855–1856; 1865–1869; 1873–1876). He entered Confederate service in April 1861; later in the same year, as government agent, he went to England, where he purchased the *Fingal,* an ironclad propeller, loaded her with arms, successfully ran the Federal blockade off the Georgia coast, and anchored her safely at Savannah. As colonel of artillery he commanded all the batteries on the Savannah River until the evacuation of the city in December 1864. After the war he served as director of the Atlantic & Gulf Railroad, the Central Railroad of Georgia, and the Southern Bank. On February 10th 1841, he married Sarah Williamson (1816–1884), daughter of John Postell Williamson (1778–1843) and his first wife, Sarah Williamson McQueen. He died in Savannah on January 6th, 1883, and was buried in Laurel Grove Cemetery. Sarah (Williamson) Anderson died on January 31st, 1884, and was buried beside her husband.

ANDERSON, ELIZABETH (BESSIE) MARY EMMA (1844–1879), elder daughter of Joseph Andrew Anderson (1820–1866) and Evelyn Elouisa Jones (1822–1849), and hence half-niece of Mary Jones, wife of the Rev. Dr. Charles Colcock Jones, was born in Dorchester, Liberty County, Georgia, on January 24th, 1844. She was author of a number of unpublished poems, among them "Grandmother's Drawer," in which she recounted the history of her maternal grandmother, Elizabeth Screven Lee Hart (1801–1870), wife of Joseph Jones: "It represents her as looking over the contents of an old drawer, and giving the history of various mementos and relics contained therein, thus unconsciously sketching the events and vicissitudes of her own life." On January 29th, 1874, having just turned thirty, she became the second wife of Dr. Raymond Harris (1799–1888), then in his seventy-fifth year; she died five years later, on January 31st, 1879, and was buried in Walthourville Cemetery. Her gravestone reads: "Here lies the casket of a pearl of great price, tender and true in all the relations of life. A loving daughter and sister, a devoted wife, and an humble, hopeful believer. She sleeps in Jesus."

ANDERSON, EVELYN (EVA) JOSEPHINE (1848–1930), younger daughter of Joseph Andrew Anderson (1820–1866) and Evelyn Elouisa Jones (1822–1849), and hence half-niece of Mary Jones, wife of the Rev. Dr. Charles Colcock Jones, was born in Dorchester, Liberty County, Georgia, on September 27th, 1848. She married first (in Dorchester, on June 19th, 1865) James Columbus Ross (1837–1867), who drowned in the Sunbury River on July 3rd, 1867, leaving his wife pregnant with her second child. She married second (in Cuthbert, on August 6th, 1870) John Odingsell Hart (1844–1903), her mother's first cousin, by whom she had four children. Following her husband's death on July 4th, 1903, she resided with her son, Thomas Screven Hart, in Jacksonville, Florida; she died there on March 26th, 1930, in her eighty-second year and was buried beside her husband in Lott's Cemetery, Waycross, Georgia.

ANDERSON, GEORGE WAYNE (1796–1872), banker, eldest child of George Anderson (1767–1847) and Elizabeth Clifford Wayne, was born in Savannah, Georgia, on May 3rd, 1796. After serving as major in the War of 1812 he returned to Savannah, where he rose to prominence in business and finance.

For forty years he was president of the Planters' Bank. Like his younger brother, John Wayne Anderson (1805–1866), he was long associated with the Independent Presbyterian Church as ruling elder. On May 11th, 1820, he married his first cousin, Eliza Clifford Stites (1805–1865); there were two children. He died in Savannah on April 25th, 1872, and was buried beside his wife in Laurel Grove Cemetery. His only son, Edward Clifford Anderson (1839–1876), a Savannah lawyer, was colonel of the 7th Regiment Georgia Cavalry during the Civil War; his death in the yellow fever epidemic of 1876 was described by the Savannah *Morning News* (December 20th, 1876) as "a great municipal calamity."

ANDERSON, JAMES PATTON (1822–1872), Confederate soldier, was born near Winchester, Franklin County, Tennessee, on February 16th, 1822. After graduating from Jefferson College (Canonsburg, Pennsylvania) in 1842 he practiced law in Hernando, Mississippi, for four years. During the Mexican War (1846–1848) he served as lieutenant colonel of the 2nd Battalion Mississippi Rifles. In 1853 he was appointed United States marshal for Washington Territory and settled in Olympia; he was territorial delegate to Congress (1853–1855). In 1857, declining appointment as governor of Washington Territory, he removed to his plantation, Casabianca, near Monticello, Florida. During the Civil War he served briefly in the Confederate Congress and later became colonel of the 1st Regiment Florida Infantry; he was appointed brigadier general on February 10th, 1862, and fought at Shiloh, Murfreesboro, and Chickamauga. On February 17th, 1864, he was promoted to major general and placed in command of the military district of Florida. After the war he settled in Memphis, Tennessee, as collector of delinquent taxes for Shelby County. He died in Memphis on September 20th, 1872, and was buried in Elmwood Cemetery.

ANDERSON, JOHN WAYNE (1805–1866), planter and merchant, fifth child of George Anderson (1767–1847) and Elizabeth Clifford Wayne, was born in Savannah, Georgia, in 1805. After graduating from Union College (Schenectady, New York) in 1825 he returned to Savannah, where he soon rose to prominence as a cotton factor and commission merchant. Throughout a long and varied career he served as alderman of Savannah, member of the state house of representatives, and member of the state senate; he was one of the original directors of the Central Railroad of Georgia and for some time its acting president; he was long associated with the Independent Presbyterian Church as ruling elder and superintendent of the Sunday school. For many years he served as cotton factor and general financial agent of the Rev. Dr. Charles Colcock Jones, of Liberty County, Georgia. During the Civil War he was captain of the Republican Blues (Company C, 1st Regiment Georgia Infantry) until disability forced him to resign on December 3rd, 1862.

He died in Macon, Georgia, on August 22nd, 1866, and was buried in Laurel Grove Cemetery, Savannah; he was survived by his wife, Sarah Ann Houstoun (1814–1868), whom he had married on October 8th, 1834.

ANDERSON, JOSEPH ANDREW (1820–1866), planter, son of William Anderson, was born in Walthourville, Liberty County, Georgia, on September 22nd, 1820. He graduated from Franklin College (Athens) in 1841. On January 24th, 1843, he married Evelyn Elouisa Jones (1822–1849), daughter of Joseph Jones (1779–1846) and his third wife, Elizabeth Screven Lee Hart (1801–1870), and half-sister of Mary Jones, wife of the Rev. Dr. Charles Colcock Jones. His wife died on November 21st, 1849, leaving two young children: Bessie (aged five) and Eva (aged one). For years Joseph Anderson was something of an inebriate and a ne'er-do-well. As early as August 7th, 1854, his sister-in-law, Mary Jones, declared him "a lost man: intemperance is a hydra, producing *every vice*." Six years later, on March 17th, 1860, the Rev. Dr. Charles Colcock Jones alluded to him as "one bloating in infamous vice." After months of suffering from "dropsy" he died in Sunbury early in April 1866; according to Mrs. Susan M. Cumming (April 12th, 1866), "he was in such agony of body you could hear his screams over the village; consequently large doses of anodyne had to be administered and then he slept; at the last he died so easily that those who were by did not know the time." He was buried in Midway Cemetery. As Charles Colcock Jones, Jr., observed on April 30th, 1866, "His was a life decidedly worse than thrown away."

ANDERSON, ROBERT (1805–1871), Union soldier, son of Richard Clough Anderson and Sarah Marshall, was born near Louisville, Kentucky, on June 14th, 1805. He graduated from the United States Military Academy in 1825 and was commissioned in the 3rd Artillery. In 1857 he was promoted to major. Late in 1860, secession being imminent, he was ordered to take command of the forts in Charleston harbor; he remained at Fort Moultrie for some five weeks, and then on December 26th removed his troops to Fort Sumter, which he surrendered on April 13th, 1861, after a defense of thirty-five hours. As the Rev. Dr. Charles Colcock Jones observed in his journal (April 15th, 1861), "Anderson was the first man who committed *the first belligerent act against the Confederate States* when he abandoned Fort Moultrie, and he is the first man beaten in battle!" He was appointed brigadier general in May 1861, but his health soon collapsed, and on October 27th, 1863, he retired from active service. He was brevetted major general of volunteers in 1865, and was sent to raise the Federal flag over Fort Sumter on April 14th, four years after he had lowered it. He died at Nice, France, on October 26th, 1871.

ANDERSON, ROBERT HOUSTOUN (1835–1888), Confederate soldier, eldest son of

John Wayne Anderson (1805–1866) and Sarah Ann Houstoun (1814–1868), was born in Savannah, Georgia, on October 1st, 1835. He graduated from the United States Military Academy in 1857 and at the outbreak of the Civil War was serving in Washington Territory as second lieutenant of the 9th Infantry. He resigned his commission and entered the Confederate army as first lieutenant of the 2nd Regiment Georgia Regulars. After serving as aide-de-camp to General W. H. T. Walker he became major of the 1st Battalion Georgia Sharpshooters (1862) and colonel of the 5th Regiment Georgia Cavalry (1863). In 1864 he was commissioned brigadier general. According to the Savannah *Morning News* (February 9th, 1888), "General Anderson was, more than most men, a born soldier; he was in every sense a military man." After the war he returned to Savannah and entered his father's commission business; he later established his own insurance firm. In 1866 he was elected chief of police, a post he held for twenty-two years. He died in Savannah on February 8th, 1888, and was buried in Bonaventure Cemetery; he was survived by his wife, Sarah Clitz (1835–1906), whom he had married on December 3rd, 1857.

ANDREWS, EDWARD QUARTERMAN (1800–1880), planter and Methodist clergyman, son of Micajah Andrews (1774–1843) and Ann Quarterman (1775–1815), was born in Liberty County, Georgia, on March 31st, 1800. Although born a Presbyterian, he later joined the Methodist Church and became a local minister of great usefulness; for some years he was employed by the executors of the Lambert estate to preach and minister to the Negroes of Liberty County. On February 28th, 1822, he married Margaret Beasley (1805–1881). Two of his sons served in the Confederate army: Edward G. Andrews (1827–1892), a private in the Liberty Volunteers (Company H, 25th Regiment Georgia Infantry); and Samuel J. Andrews (1834–1864), a private in the Liberty Mounted Rangers (Company B, 20th Battalion Georgia Cavalry). Samuel J. Andrews, described by Mrs. Mary Jones as "promising," was killed at Trevilian's Station, near Louisa Courthouse, Virginia, on June 11th, 1864. Edward Quarterman Andrews died on May 5th, 1880, and was buried in Flemington Cemetery. Margaret (Beasley) Andrews died on June 5th, 1881, and was buried beside her husband.

ARDIS, DAVID (1804–1872), planter, was born in Edgefield District, South Carolina, in 1804. He married Eliza C. Gray (1804–1867), daughter of John Jammieson Gray (1774–1838), of Beech Island, Edgefield District, in 1827. In 1850 he removed with his family to Marietta, Georgia, where for fourteen years he was active in the affairs of the Presbyterian church. He became elder and clerk of the session in 1854, treasurer in 1855, and superintendent of the Sunday school in 1863; he continued to serve in each capacity until the church was closed in the summer of 1864. He was a prominent Presbyterian layman: in May 1857

he was commissioner to the General Assembly of the Presbyterian Church meeting in Lexington, Kentucky; in December 1861 he was commissioner to the first General Assembly of the Southern Presbyterian Church meeting in Augusta, Georgia. He was also a trustee of the Georgia Military Institute (Marietta). Three of his sons served in the Confederate army: John Jammieson Gray Ardis (1838–1865), a graduate of Davidson College (1860), was a private in the Savannah Volunteer Guards (Company C, 18th Battalion Georgia Infantry) and died in prison at Point Lookout, Maryland, on June 23rd, 1865; Payson L. Ardis (1840–1903) enlisted in May 1861 as a private in the Palmetto Guards (Company I, 2nd Regiment South Carolina Infantry), transferred in August 1862 to Phillips' Legion Georgia Volunteers, and became in June 1863 first lieutenant in the 3rd Battalion Georgia Sharpshooters; David E. Ardis (1843–1882) was a private in the Savannah Volunteer Guards (Company C, 18th Battalion Georgia Infantry). At Sherman's approach in the spring of 1864 Ardis and his family continued in Marietta until the last possible moment, then fled in early June to Alabama—first to Macon County, later to Elmore County. Eliza (Gray) Ardis died in Tallassee, Alabama, on January 30th, 1867, and was buried in Citizens Cemetery, Marietta. David Ardis died in Tallassee on June 24th, 1872, and was buried beside his wife. Ardis Street in Marietta was named in his honor.

ARDIS, PAYSON L. (1840–1903), clerk, second son of David Ardis (1804–1872) and Eliza C. Gray (1804–1867), was born in Beech Island, Edgefield District, South Carolina, in 1840. At the age of ten he removed with his family to Marietta, Georgia, where he remained until May 1861, when he enlisted in Charleston as a private in the Palmetto Guards (Company I, 2nd Regiment South Carolina Infantry). He subsequently became a private in Company L (Infantry Battalion), Phillips' Legion Georgia Volunteers (August 1862) and first lieutenant in Company E, 3rd Battalion Georgia Sharpshooters (June 1863). In August 1864 he was taken prisoner at Front Royal and sent to Fort Delaware, from which he was released on June 17th, 1865. After the war he joined his parents in Tallassee, Alabama, where he was clerk in a store; by 1877 he had settled in Atlanta, where he continued as clerk until his death on June 1st, 1903. He was buried near his parents in Citizens Cemetery, Marietta.

ARNOLD, BENEDICT (1741–1801), Revolutionary patriot and traitor, son of Benedict Arnold and Hannah (Waterman) King, was born in Norwich, Connecticut, on January 14th, 1741. Prior to the Revolutionary War he was a bookseller and druggist in New Haven. On February 22nd, 1767, he married Margaret Mansfield, of New Haven, who bore him three sons before her death on June 19th, 1775. Meanwhile in 1774 he was elected captain of a militia company; on May 10th, 1775, together with Ethan Allen, he effected the capture of Fort Ticonderoga. Later in the same year, at

Washington's command, he marched through the Maine wilderness in an unsuccessful attempt to take Quebec. In recognition of his bravery Congress promoted him to brigadier general. After further demonstrations of valor he was placed in command of Philadelphia following the British evacuation in 1778. There, on April 8th, 1779, he married Margaret (Peggy) Shippen (1760–1804), with whom he soon made treasonable overtures to the enemy. In 1780 he assumed command of West Point, which he plotted to surrender to the British in return for twenty thousand pounds. When the scheme failed and the British go-between, Major John André, was hanged by the Americans as a spy, Arnold fled to the British, by whom he was made brigadier general and sent on raiding expeditions in Virginia and Connecticut. After the war he went to England, where he was disappointed in his expectations of military preferment and monetary reward. He died in London, scorned and embittered, on June 14th, 1801.

ARNOLD, RICHARD DENNIS (1808–1876), physician and politician, son of Joseph Arnold and Eliza Dennis, was born in Savannah, Georgia, on August 19th, 1808. He graduated from the College of New Jersey (Princeton) in 1826 and from the Medical College of the University of Pennsylvania in 1830. Returning to Savannah, he married Margaret Baugh Stirk (1813–1850), daughter of John W. Stirk, in 1832. Early in his medical practice he became owner and editor of the Savannah *Georgian* and turned to politics; he was a member of the state house of representatives (1839) and the state senate (1842); he also held various municipal posts and served five terms as mayor between 1842 and 1865. He surrendered the city to Sherman in December 1864. Meanwhile he maintained a large private practice and contributed frequently to medical journals. In 1846 he helped organize the Medical Association of Georgia; in the same year he helped found the American Medical Association and became its first secretary. In 1852 he was one of eight founders of the Savannah Medical College, and he was for some years its professor of medicine. He was universally esteemed in Savannah for his heroism during the yellow fever epidemic of 1854; he himself died of yellow fever on July 10th, 1876. He was buried in Bonaventure Cemetery beside his wife, from whose untimely death on April 21st, 1850, he had never fully recovered.

ARNOLD, THOMAS CLAY (1836–1875), planter, son of Richard James Arnold (1796–1873) and Caroline Gindrat (1804–1871), was born at Whitehall, his father's plantation in Bryan County, Georgia, on September 10th, 1836. The Arnold family, long settled in Rhode Island, was distinguished for its wealth, cultivation, and philanthropy; Richard James Arnold, a graduate of Brown University in 1814 and a trustee from 1826, summered in Providence and wintered on his Georgia plantation. At the outbreak of the Civil War he determined to remain in the North, entrusting his

plantation to the supervision of his son. Thomas Clay Arnold entered Brown University in 1855 but withdrew after one year without graduating. During the Civil War he served briefly as a private in Company B, Oglethorpe Siege Artillery. On December 1st, 1870, he married Elizabeth Woodbridge Screven (1852–1936), daughter of John Screven (1827–1900) and his first wife, Mary White Footman (1827–1863), of Savannah. He died at Whitehall on December 23rd, 1875, and was buried in Laurel Grove Cemetery, Savannah. Elizabeth Woodbridge (Screven) Arnold died in Nassau on December 25th, 1936, and was buried beside her husband.

ASHMORE, JOSEPH (1819–1889), planter and magistrate, son of Joseph Ashmore (1791–1832), was born in Liberty County, Georgia, on April 15th, 1819. He was thrice married. As magistrate of Liberty County he officiated at the trial of Lucy, Negro slave in the custody of the Rev. Dr. Charles Colcock Jones, in December 1859. Later he was elected county ordinary, a post he held for many years. He died in Hinesville, Georgia, on December 14th, 1889, and was buried in Flemington Cemetery. "For uprightness of conduct, devotion to duty, and sterling character he had few peers; he was one of the old landmarks" (Savannah *Morning News,* December 16th, 1889). He was survived by two sons, both of Liberty County: Joseph S. Ashmore (1838–1907), clerk of the superior court; and Charles W. Ashmore (1851–1925), judge of the county court.

ASKEW, THOMAS H. (1832–1899), merchant, son of Thomas Askew and Louisa M. Hogg, was born in Savannah, Georgia, on May 1st, 1832. From boyhood he was active in the Savannah dry goods business, associated with such established firms as Nevitt, Lathrop & Rogers and Eckman & Vetzburg. On December 22nd, 1856, in Robertville, South Carolina, he married Emeline E. Jaudon (1837–1912). During the Civil War he served as lieutenant in the Chatham Artillery; in June 1862 he was detailed as officer in charge of detachments sent to Charleston. After the war he resumed his mercantile career; while on a business trip he died in New York City on December 25th, 1899. He was buried in Laurel Grove Cemetery, Savannah. According to the Savannah *Morning News* (December 26th, 1899), "He was a man of genial manners, of excellent business capacity, and although quiet and unostentatious, the world was better for his having lived in it." Emeline (Jaudon) Askew died on May 28th, 1912, and was buried beside her husband.

AUSTIN, ABIGAIL (1783–1863), daughter of Joseph Austin and his second wife, Sarah Ann Pritchard, was born at Melon Bluff plantation, Liberty County, Georgia, in 1783. From childhood she was associated with the family of the Rev. Dr. Charles Colcock Jones, and once, in April 1854, she told him: "I put the first clothing on you that you ever wore in this world." On December 17th, 1812, she became the second wife of Reuben King (1779–1867), a planter in McIntosh County, son of Timothy King and Sarah Fitch; of their seven children only two survived infancy: Sarah Amanda King (1817–1876), wife of James A. Walker; and Elizabeth Aurelia King (1824–1892), wife of Octavius Caesar Hopkins. In 1839 Reuben King purchased Mallow plantation on the Sapelo River at Pine Harbor Bluff; there he resided with his wife and widowed daughter, Mrs. Walker, until November 1862, when the Federals raided the plantation from a gunboat anchored in the river. Abigail (Austin) King died on July 13th, 1863, and was buried in the family cemetery at Mallow. Reuben King died in 1867 and was buried beside his wife.

AVERY, ISAAC WHEELER (1837–1897), Confederate soldier and journalist, son of Isaac Wheeler Avery and Mary Moore King, was born in St. Augustine, Florida, on May 2nd, 1837. After graduating from Oglethorpe University in 1854 he taught school for one year, read law, and commenced practice in Savannah in 1860. At the outbreak of the Civil War he enlisted as a private in the Oglethorpe Light Infantry (Company B, 8th Regiment Georgia Infantry); he fought throughout the war, reaching the rank of colonel and the command of a brigade. In July 1864, as colonel of the 4th Regiment Georgia Cavalry, he was desperately wounded in the battle of New Hope Church; as a result he walked on crutches for many years. After the war he practiced law in Dalton, Georgia, home of his first wife, Sally H. Morris, whom he had married on November 26th, 1863. He married second (on January 1st, 1868) Emma Bivings. In 1869 he settled in Atlanta, where he resided for the rest of his life. He was editor of the Atlanta *Constitution* for several months (1869–1870) and owner of the Atlanta *Herald* for one year (1875–1876). His *History of the State of Georgia from 1850 to 1881* (1881) is largely political. From 1887 to 1889 he was chief of the public debt division of the United States Treasury. In 1890 he became associate editor for Georgia of *The National Cyclopedia of American Biography*. In 1892 he began the movement for the establishment of direct trade between the Southern ports and foreign countries. He died in Atlanta on September 8th, 1897, and was buried in Oakland Cemetery.

AXSON, ISAAC STOCKTON KEITH (1813–1891), Presbyterian clergyman, son of Samuel Edward Axson and Sarah Ann Palmer, was born in Charleston, South Carolina, on October 3rd, 1813. He graduated from the College of Charleston in 1831 and from Columbia Theological Seminary in 1834. On October 28th, 1834, he married Rebecca Longstreet Randolph (1815–1887), daughter of Isaac Randolph, of Charleston. In 1836, after a year as pastor of Dorchester Church, Summerville, South Carolina, he became co-pastor of Midway Church, Liberty County, Georgia, where he continued until forced by ill health to resign in 1853. Thereafter for four years he served as president of Greensboro Female College, Greensboro, Georgia. In December 1857

he became pastor of the Independent Presbyterian Church, Savannah, where he remained for the rest of his life. His wife died in Savannah on September 22nd, 1887, and was buried in Laurel Grove Cemetery. He died much esteemed on March 31st, 1891, and was buried beside his wife. "As a preacher and thinker Dr. Axson was the fulfillment of Chaucer's ideal parson: 'gladly would he learn and gladly teach.' He was one who cared little for the praise of men or the emoluments of life. His chief aim was to devote his talent to his Master's service, to work in that portion of the vineyard allotted to him" (Savannah *Morning News,* April 1st, 1891). A son of Dr. Axson, the Rev. Samuel Edward Axson (1836–1884), was the father of Ellen Louise Axson (1860–1914), first wife of Thomas Woodrow Wilson (1856–1924), twenty-eighth president of the United States (1913–1921); it was in the manse of the Independent Presbyterian Church that Dr. Axson officiated at his granddaughter's marriage on June 24th, 1885.

AXSON, RANDOLPH (1838–1902), merchant, second son of the Rev. Dr. Isaac Stockton Keith Axson (1813–1891) and Rebecca Longstreet Randolph (1815–1887), was born in Liberty County, Georgia, on October 1st, 1838. Early in his career he lived and worked in New Orleans. At the outbreak of the Civil War he enlisted as a private in the Washington Artillery and proceeded at once to Virginia; he was at First Manassas, Yorktown, Second Manassas, Fredericksburg, Chancellorsville, Gettysburg, and Petersburg. In October 1862 he was detailed to hospital duty, where he remained till the close of the war. On February 12th, 1867, he married Ella Law (1840–1901), daughter of the Hon. William Law (1793–1874) and his third wife, Alethea Jones Stark (1810–1872), of Savannah. In his later years he headed the Savannah firm of Randolph Axson & Sons, cotton factors and commission merchants, and served as elder of the Independent Presbyterian Church. His wife died in Savannah on July 18th, 1901, and was buried in Bonaventure Cemetery. He died in Summerville, South Carolina, on May 9th, 1902, and was buried beside his wife.

AXSON, RICHARD F. (born 1807), planter, was the eldest son of Dr. Samuel J. T. Axson (1761–1827), of Liberty County, Georgia, and his second wife, Ann Lambright (1781–1854), widow of David James Dicks. He never married. After his father's death in 1827 he continued to live with his mother until her death in 1854, after which he lived alone on the family place. Later, while teaching school, he lived for a time with his sister, Olivia Tuckerman Axson (1819–1902), following the death of her husband, Dr. Samuel Way, in 1866. He died in the 1870s.

AXSON, SAMUEL EDWARD (1836–1884), Presbyterian clergyman, eldest son of the Rev. Dr. Isaac Stockton Keith Axson (1813–1891) and Rebecca Longstreet Randolph (1815–1887), was born in Liberty County, Georgia, on December 23rd, 1836. He graduated from

Oglethorpe University in 1855 and from Columbia Theological Seminary in 1858. On November 16th, 1858, he married Margaret Jane Hoyt (1838–1881), daughter of the Rev. Dr. Nathan Hoyt and Margaret Bliss, of Athens, Georgia. He served churches in Beech Island, South Carolina (1858–1860); McPhersonville, South Carolina (1860–1862); Madison, Georgia (1863–1866); and Rome, Georgia (1866–1883). For eleven months (November 1862–October 1863) he was chaplain of the 1st Regiment Georgia Infantry. In the autumn of 1883 his mind became affected and he was sent to the Milledgeville State Hospital, where he died on May 28th, 1884. He was buried beside his wife in Myrtle Hill Cemetery, Rome. A year later, on June 24th, 1885, his eldest child, Ellen Louise Axson (1860–1914), became the wife of Thomas Woodrow Wilson (1856–1924), twenty-eighth president of the United States (1913–1921), at the manse of her grandfather, the Rev. Dr. Isaac Stockton Keith Axson, pastor of the Independent Presbyterian Church, Savannah.

AYTOUN, WILLIAM EDMONSTOUNE (1813–1865), Scottish poet, was born in Edinburgh on June 21st, 1813. Although he was called to the Scottish bar in 1840 his preference was poetry; from 1839 until his death he was a member of the staff of *Blackwood's Magazine,* and in 1845 he became professor of rhetoric and belles lettres at Edinburgh University. His many volumes of poetry include *The Lays of the Scottish Cavaliers* (1848), *Bothwell: A Poem* (1856), and *The Ballads of Scotland* (1858). He died in Blackhills, near Elgin, on August 4th, 1865.

BACON, JOSEPH MADISON (1838–1862), Confederate soldier, eldest son of Joseph Richard Bacon (1814–1860) and his first wife, Olivia Fleming (1818–1845), was born in Liberty County, Georgia, in 1838. When he was seven years old his mother died, leaving three sons; two years later his father married Harriet Newell Mallard (1823–1889), sister of the Rev. R. Q. Mallard; she reared her stepsons as affectionately as if they were her own children. On December 27th, 1860, Joseph Madison Bacon (called "Madison" by his family) married Rebecca Eliza Busby (born 1840), daughter of Bartholomew Austin Busby (1788–1862) and Mary Emeline Mallard, and niece of the Rev. R. Q. Mallard. In October 1861, together with his younger brother, Quarterman Way Bacon, he enlisted as a private in the Liberty Independent Troop (Company G, 5th Regiment Georgia Cavalry), then encamped at Sunbury, for a period of six months; in May 1862, together with his two younger brothers, Quarterman Way Bacon and Olivius Fleming Bacon, he enlisted as a private in the Liberty Mounted Rangers (Company B, 20th Battalion Georgia Cavalry) for a period of three years. He died from the effects of measles at James Island, near Charleston, South Carolina, on August 24th, 1862, and was buried in Midway Cemetery.

BACON, JOSEPH RICHARD (1814–1860), planter, son of John Bacon and Susannah Quarterman, was born in Liberty County, Georgia, on December 25th, 1814. He married first (in 1837) Olivia Fleming (1818–1845), daughter of William Fleming (1778–1822) and his first wife, Anna Winn (1782–1823), widow of Edward Quarterman and William Elliott Way. She died in childbirth on April 15th, 1845, leaving three sons: Joseph Madison Bacon (1838–1862), Quarterman Way Bacon (1842–1864), and Olivius Fleming Bacon (1845–1918). He married second (in 1847) Harriet Newell Mallard (1823–1889), daughter of Thomas Mallard (1778–1861) and his second wife, Rebecca Eliza (Burnley) Baker (1789–1861), and sister of the Rev. R. Q. Mallard; there were four children. He died on January 6th, 1860, and was buried in Midway Cemetery. All three of his sons by his first wife saw service in the Liberty Mounted Rangers during the Civil War, and two of them died of disease; Thomas Mallard Bacon (1848–1878), his eldest son by his second wife, entered Confederate service in September 1864 and went to Virginia with his only surviving half-brother, Olivius Fleming Bacon. Harriet Newell (Mallard) Bacon died on January 7th, 1889, and was buried beside her husband.

BACON, MARY (WINN) (OSGOOD) (1784–1859): *Mrs. Jonathan Bacon,* daughter of Peter Winn and Mary Farley, was born in Liberty County, Georgia, on October 29th, 1784. She was a childhood friend of Eliza Greene Low (1785–1868) and a schoolmate of William Maxwell (1785–1866). She married first (on February 9th, 1802) John Osgood; she married second (on January 8th, 1818) Jonathan Bacon. Both marriages were childless. For many years she resided in Walthourville, where she was affectionately known as "Aunt Polly"; her generosity to the Rev. R. Q. Mallard once prompted him to write: "I have a good friend in this old lady." She died much regretted on July 12th, 1859, and was buried in Midway Cemetery.

BACON, OLIVIUS FLEMING (1845–1918), Confederate soldier, third son of Joseph Richard Bacon (1814–1860) and his first wife, Olivia Fleming (1818–1845), was born in Liberty County, Georgia, on April 8th, 1845. A week after his birth his mother died, leaving three sons; two years later his father married Harriet Newell Mallard (1823–1889), sister of the Rev. R. Q. Mallard; she reared her stepsons as affectionately as if they were her own children. Early in May 1862, together with his two elder brothers, Joseph Madison Bacon and Quarterman Way Bacon, he enlisted as a private in the Liberty Mounted Rangers (Company B, 20th Battalion Georgia Cavalry) for a period of three years. His two brothers both died of disease in the war: Joseph Madison Bacon on August 24th, 1862, and Quarterman Way Bacon on July 19th, 1864. Olivius Fleming Bacon was wounded at Haw's Shop on May 28th, 1864, and spent the following summer on furlough recuperating in Walthourville;

he returned to Virginia with his half-brother, Thomas Mallard Bacon, in September 1864. He was again wounded in December 1864 near Savannah. After the war he married Lilla Gignilliat (1851–1887), daughter of Norman Gignilliat (1809–1871) and Charlotte Trezevant (1819–1910), of Marietta, Georgia. She died in Marietta on June 6th, 1887, and was buried in Episcopal Cemetery. He died in Seneca, South Carolina, on December 25th, 1918, and was buried beside his wife.

BACON, QUARTERMAN WAY (1842–1864), Confederate soldier, second son of Joseph Richard Bacon (1814–1860) and his first wife, Olivia Fleming (1818–1845), was born in Liberty County, Georgia, in 1842. When he was three years old his mother died, leaving three sons; two years later his father married Harriet Newell Mallard (1823–1889), sister of the Rev. R. Q. Mallard; she reared her stepsons as affectionately as if they were her own children. In October 1861, together with his elder brother, Joseph Madison Bacon, he enlisted as a private in the Liberty Independent Troop (Company G, 5th Regiment Georgia Cavalry), then encamped at Sunbury, for a period of six months; in May 1862, together with his two brothers, Joseph Madison Bacon and Olivius Fleming Bacon, he enlisted as a private in the Liberty Mounted Rangers (Company B, 20th Battalion Georgia Cavalry) for a period of three years. He never married. He died of disease in a hospital near Petersburg, Virginia, on July 19th, 1864, and was buried in Midway Cemetery.

BACON, THOMAS MALLARD (1848–1878), Confederate soldier, eldest son of Joseph Richard Bacon (1814–1860) and his second wife, Harriet Newell Mallard (1823–1889), was born in Liberty County, Georgia, in 1848. He entered Confederate service in September 1864 and went to Virginia with his half-brother, Olivius Fleming Bacon. After the war he married Louisa Ward Winn (1848–1873), daughter of Abial Winn (1815–1874) and Louisa Vanyeverine Ward (1818–1892), of Liberty County; she died in childbirth on October 1st, 1873. In the same year he removed to Valdosta, Georgia, where, according to *The Southern Presbyterian* (July 4th, 1878), "his force of character quickly manifested itself, and he soon became a citizen whose influence was felt throughout the whole community. . . . The strictest integrity, a high sense of honor, and indomitable energy rendered him a successful businessman. As a member of the town council there was none more efficient than he. As a son, husband, and father he was affectionate and devoted; and his remarkable tenderness in the quiet scenes of home stood out in pleasing contrast with the graver manners he wore in the active scenes of a business career." On January 25th, 1877, he married Sarah Louisa Varnedoe, daughter of Samuel McWhir Varnedoe and Caroline Fraser Law, of Valdosta. He died of typhoid fever on June 7th, 1878, leaving his wife pregnant with his only child, Mallie Bacon (1878–1911).

BAILIE, JAMES GLOVER (1820–1893), merchant, fourth son of Robert Bailie (1784–1857) and Elizabeth Glover (1792–1882), was born near Randalstown, County Antrim, Northern Ireland, on June 20th, 1820. In 1847 he removed to Charleston, South Carolina, whence, early in 1849, he set out for California in search of gold. For two years he remained in California, where he was successful in mining and merchandising. In 1851 he settled in Augusta, Georgia, and joined his younger brother, George Alexander Bailie (1834–1912), newly arrived from Ireland, in the grocery and carpet business. He married first (on September 30th, 1851) Nancy Courtney, second daughter of Thomas Courtney (1794–1860) and Caroline Miller (1804–1865), of Augusta, formerly of Randalstown, Northern Ireland; he married second (on August 6th, 1860) Margaret Courtney (1830–1911), younger sister of his first wife. For many years he was a prominent merchant in Augusta. He died after a protracted illness on May 10th, 1893, and was buried in Magnolia Cemetery, Augusta.

BAKER, CAROLINE AMANDA (1824–1888), eldest daughter of William Quarterman Baker (1800–1877) and his first wife, Ann Lydia Mallard (1804–1843), was born in Liberty County, Georgia, on January 4th, 1824. On March 1st, 1855, aged thirty-one, she became the second wife of Peter Winn Fleming (1807–1882) then captain of the Liberty Independent Troop, a widower with four children. Her husband died in Walthourville on January 6th, 1882, and was buried beside his first wife in Sunbury Cemetery. Caroline Amanda (Baker) Fleming died on February 13th, 1888, and was buried in Walthourville Cemetery.

BAKER, JOHN ELIJAH (1833–1906), educator, son of William Quarterman Baker (1800–1877) and his first wife, Ann Lydia Mallard (1804–1843), was born in Liberty County, Georgia, on March 23rd, 1833. After graduating from Oglethorpe University in 1852 he taught school for some years in his native county, making his home in Walthourville. On December 18th, 1856, he married Mary Elizabeth Baker (1835–1882), daughter of Thomas Baker (1806–1837) and Sarah Margaret Shaffer (1807–1881), and thus half-niece of the Rev. R. Q. Mallard, who performed the ceremony and described the wedding in his letter of December 24th, 1856. In October 1861 he enlisted for six months as a private in the Liberty Independent Troop (Company G, 5th Regiment Georgia Cavalry), then encamped at Sunbury; in May 1862 he enlisted for three years as first sergeant in the Liberty Mounted Rangers (Company B, 20th Battalion Georgia Cavalry); on November 6th, 1862, he was brevetted second lieutenant. After the war he removed to Thomasville, Georgia; in 1866 he opened the Fletcher Institute, where he taught successfully for three years; in 1869 he became president of Young Female College, a position he continued to hold until failing health forced him to retire. From 1870 to 1906 he served as elder of the First Presbyterian Church, Thomasville. Mary Elizabeth (Baker) Baker died in Thomasville on July 21st, 1882, and was buried in Laurel Hill Cemetery. John Elijah Baker died in Thomasville on December 28th, 1906, and was buried beside his wife.

BAKER, JOHN FABIAN (1827–1885), Presbyterian clergyman, son of John Osgood Baker and Frances Adeline Fabian, was born in Liberty County, Georgia, on September 26th, 1827. He was an elder brother of the Rev. William Elliott Baker (1830–1906). He graduated from the College of New Jersey (Princeton) in 1846. After a period of teaching (1846–1849) and private theological study (1849–1852) he served for two years as stated supply of Presbyterian congregations in Beaver Meadow and White Haven, Pennsylvania. In 1854 he returned to Georgia, spending the winter in Roswell without pastoral charge; in the spring of 1855 he visited his native county, where Mary Sharpe Jones reported on March 1st, 1855: "He is a most excellent preacher, and Father says he possesses uncommon talents. . . . He is awfully stiff, and shows in every action, word, and look from what portion of the country he came." From March 1855 to March 1856 he served as assistant to the Rev. David Lyman Buttolph, pastor of Midway Church. He married first (on November 29th, 1855) Frances Lorinda Pratt, daughter of the Rev. Nathaniel Alpheus Pratt and Catherine Barrington King, of Roswell, Georgia; she died in childbirth on January 26th, 1857. He married second (on September 28th, 1858) Phoebe Steele, of Lexington, Virginia. Throughout a long career he served as pastor of churches in Virginia, Illinois, Missouri, and Arkansas. He died in Austin, Texas, on May 9th, 1885, survived by two sons, both Presbyterian clergymen: William Steele Baker and Adolph Elhart Baker.

BAKER, JOHN ST. LEONARD (1829–1861), druggist, son of Edward Bright Baker and Frances Leonard Jurdine, was born in McIntosh County, Georgia, in 1829. His father, a planter, was for many years an elder of the First Presbyterian Church, Darien. By 1850 John St. Leonard Baker was established in Darien as a druggist. On May 13th, 1856, he married Mary Georgia Dunham (1836–1904), daughter of George C. Dunham (1798–1881) and Martha Pilcher (1812–1865), of McIntosh County. For a time the young couple lived in the Savannah house of the wife's aunt and the husband's half-aunt, Susan Caroline Adams (1812–1891), widow of Charles Dunham, managing her household affairs during her absence in Screven County; early in 1860 they returned with their two infants to McIntosh County, where Baker became "city officer" in Darien. He died of yellow fever on August 26th, 1861, leaving his wife pregnant with her third child, and was buried near Darien in an unmarked grave. In 1868 his widow married Willis A. Burney.

BAKER, JOHN WICKLIFFE (1811–1901), Presbyterian clergyman and educator, son of

William Jeans Baker (1763–1819) and his second wife, Elizabeth Way (1772–1836), was born in Liberty County, Georgia, on January 24th, 1811. He graduated from Franklin College (Athens) in 1832 and from Princeton Theological Seminary in 1835. On February 16th, 1837, he married Charlotte Woodville Shepherd (1817–1897), of Washington, Wilkes County, Georgia. From 1836 to 1854 he was pastor of the Presbyterian church in Milledgeville, with a seven-year interval (1845–1852) as professor of ancient languages at Oglethorpe University. In 1857 he became professor of ethics and English literature at the Georgia Military Institute (Marietta), where he taught and preached until the institute suspended classes in 1864. From January 1858 he also maintained a school for boys and girls, attended by Joseph Jones Robarts. After the war he continued to teach in Marietta; he died there on December 12th, 1901, and was buried in Citizens Cemetery beside his wife, who had died on October 1st, 1897.

BAKER, WILLIAM ELLIOTT (1830–1906), Presbyterian clergyman, son of John Osgood Baker and Frances Adeline Fabian, was born in Liberty County, Georgia, on February 20th, 1830. He was a younger brother of the Rev. John Fabian Baker (1827–1885). He graduated from the College of New Jersey (Princeton) in 1850, and after a year's study at Columbia Theological Seminary he graduated from Princeton Theological Seminary in 1853. On July 17th, 1856, he married Catherine Evelyn King (1837–1923), daughter of Barrington King and Catherine Margaret Nephew, of Roswell, Georgia; they departed immediately for Sacramento, California, where he served for one year as stated supply of the Presbyterian church. From 1857 to 1884 he was pastor of the First Presbyterian Church, Staunton, Virginia; in 1884 he resigned for reasons of health and returned to Roswell, Georgia, where he died on January 5th, 1906. Catherine Evelyn (King) Baker, who in her youth had been a bridesmaid at the wedding of Martha (Mittie) Bulloch and Theodore Roosevelt, father of the President, on December 22nd, 1853, survived her husband almost eighteen years; she died in Roswell on December 25th, 1923, and was buried beside her husband in the Presbyterian Cemetery.

BAKER, WILLIAM EMERSON (1828–1888), sewing machine manufacturer, was born in Boston, Massachusetts, on April 16th, 1828. After graduating from the Roxbury High School he entered a dry goods store, where he became acquainted with a merchant tailor, William O. Grover (1822–1895), who had patented a new sewing machine with an improved stitch. Together they formed a stock company for the manufacture and sale of the Grover & Baker sewing machine, which proved so enormously popular that both men were soon able to retire with vast fortunes. Baker devoted his later years to developing and maintaining the gardens and pleasure grounds of Ridge Hill, his estate in Wellesley; he was also a staunch supporter of the Massachusetts Institute of Technology and the Boston Museum of Fine Arts. He died in Boston on January 5th, 1888, and was buried in Forest Hills Cemetery. A typical notice of "Grover & Baker's celebrated family sewing machine" appeared in the *Kentucky Statesman* (Lexington) on March 8th, 1859: "These machines are now justly admitted to be the best in use for family sewing, making a new, strong, and elastic stitch which will NOT rip, even if every fourth stitch be cut."

BAKER, WILLIAM QUARTERMAN (1800–1877), planter, son of Elijah Baker and Rebecca Baker, widow of William Norman, was born in Liberty County, Georgia, on December 11th, 1800. He married first (on February 13th, 1821) Ann Lydia Mallard (1804–1843), daughter of John Mallard and Lydia Quarterman, who bore him thirteen children; he married second (on April 25th, 1844) Sarah Jane Varnedoe (1820–1852), daughter of Nathaniel Varnedoe and his first wife, Ann T. Jones, who bore him six children; he married third (on May 6th, 1856) Jane Amarintha Quarterman (1813–1874), daughter of Thomas Quarterman and his second wife, Elizabeth Yonge Peacock, and widow of John Sidney Fleming, who bore him one child. For some years he was active in local politics. He outlived all three of his wives and five of his nineteen children. He died on January 29th, 1877, and was buried in Walthourville Cemetery.

BANKS, NATHANIEL PRENTICE (1816–1894), congressman, governor, and Union soldier, eldest child of Nathaniel Prentice Banks and Rebecca Greenwood, was born in Waltham, Massachusetts, on January 30th, 1816. He studied law but never practiced his profession. After some years as inspector in the Boston customhouse and three years as proprietor and editor of the *Middlesex Reporter,* a weekly newspaper, he was a member of the state house of representatives (1849–1852), a member of Congress (1853–1857), and governor of Massachusetts (1858–1861). Early in 1861 he removed to Chicago to become vice-president of the Illinois Central Railroad. On May 16th, 1861, he entered the Union army as major general of volunteers; he served throughout the war, receiving the thanks of Congress on January 18th, 1864, "for the skill, courage, and endurance which compelled the surrender of Port Hudson, and thus removed the last obstruction to the free navigation of the Mississippi River." After the war he was a member of Congress (1865–1873; 1875–1879), United States marshal for Massachusetts (1879–1888), and again a member of Congress (1889–1891). In March 1847 he married Mary I. Palmer. He died in Waltham, Massachusetts, on September 1st, 1894, and was buried in Grove Hill Cemetery.

BARNARD, AMELIA (MINA) WASH (1838–1919), second daughter of Dr. Timothy Guerard Barnard (1809–1849), Savannah physician, and Mary Ann Naylor Mongin, was born on Wilmington Island, Chatham County, Georgia, in 1838. Her father died in May 1849, leaving a widow and four young children. On the evening of March 24th, 1864, in the Central Presbyterian Church, Atlanta, Mina Barnard became the wife of Major John L. Morgan, chief quartermaster on the staff of General Howell Cobb; Mrs. Mary S. Mallard described the wedding in a letter to Mrs. Susan M. Cumming (March 31st, 1864): "It is said she spent eight thousand dollars upon her wardrobe, and had about thirty thousand dollars' worth of diamonds presented her by her husband. . . . Whenever we hear of large sums being expended, the question is always asked: 'Is he a quartermaster? Or is she a quartermaster's wife?' And an affirmative answer always solves the mystery." John L. Morgan died shortly after the war; his widow continued to live in Atlanta in the household of her sister, Anna Barnard, wife of the Rev. William Henry Hunt. On June 23rd, 1886, Mina (Barnard) Morgan became the second wife of Bayard McIntosh Hunter (1840–1896), son of William Presstman Hunter (1799–1869), president of the Savannah Marine Bank. Her husband, formerly of Savannah, had recently been appointed general agent of the Penn Mutual Insurance Company in Atlanta. After his death on November 13th, 1896, she returned to the house of her sister, whose husband had died on March 10th, 1895. Mina (Barnard) (Morgan) Hunter died in Atlanta on May 25th, 1919, and was buried in Westview Cemetery.

BARNARD, JOHN BRADLEY (1807–1861), planter, son of Timothy Barnard and his first wife, Amelia Guerard, was born on Wilmington Island, Chatham County, Georgia, on October 12th, 1807. After graduating from Franklin College (Athens) in 1828 he read law in the office of the Hon. Richard Wylly Habersham, of Savannah, but feeble health forced him to the more active pursuits of planting. For some years he resided at Bruton Hill, his plantation on Wilmington Island; in 1841 he represented Chatham County in the state legislature. In 1846 he removed to North Hampton, his plantation on the North Newport River in Liberty County, where he continued to reside until his death, influential in county affairs and active as a selectman of Midway Church (1848–1857). The Barnards, the Kings, and the Joneses were neighbors, and their children attended a "union school" established expressly for the three families and superintended by the Rev. Dr. Charles Colcock Jones. John Bradley Barnard married first (on May 4th, 1829) Martha J. Law, daughter of Nathaniel Law; he married second (on July 22nd, 1837) Ann P. Law (1819–1891), sister of his first wife. From 1858 to 1861 he was a trustee of the University of Georgia. All three of his sons attended Franklin College (Athens): John Daniel Barnard (1830–1860), class of 1850; Nathaniel Law Barnard (1832–1910), class of 1851; and Timothy Rowland Barnard (1834–1853), who died in his senior year. After a protracted illness John Bradley Barnard died at North Hampton on December 25th, 1861, and was buried in Laurel Grove Cemetery, Savannah. The Savannah *Republican* printed an obituary on May 1st, 1862: "Intelligent and well-informed, a gentleman by nature and education, courteous and even courtly in his manners, he made his impress on all who came within his reach. In domestic life no man more beautifully illustrated the virtues that illumine and make happy the circle of home. He was a devoted husband and father, a faithful friend, and a most kind and humane master. Abundantly blessed with this world's goods, he used them to the comfort and enjoyment of all around him, whilst the poor ever found him a friend in need. With this he was a true patriot, ever ready to aid his country with all the influence and means at his command." Ann (Law) Barnard died in Savannah on December 17th, 1891, and was buried beside her husband.

BARNARD, JOHN DANIEL (1830–1860), physician, eldest son of John Bradley Barnard (1807–1861) and his first wife, Martha J. Law, was born in Savannah, Georgia, on August 17th, 1830. He graduated from Franklin College (Athens) in 1850 and from the Medical College of the University of Pennsylvania in 1854. In the same year he married Harriet Moore, of Huntsville, Alabama. After practicing medicine briefly in Savannah he settled in Huntsville, where he died on April 2nd, 1860, leaving a wife and three young children. He was buried in Laurel Grove Cemetery, Savannah.

BARNARD, NATHANIEL LAW (1832–1910), planter, lawyer, and railroad executive, second son of John Bradley Barnard (1807–1861) and his first wife, Martha J. Law, was born on Wilmington Island, Chatham County, Georgia, on April 15th, 1832. He graduated from Franklin College (Athens) in 1851. He married first (on October 5th, 1853) Frances Elizabeth Dougherty, only daughter of the Hon. Charles Dougherty, of Athens, Georgia; he married second (in August 1888) Augusta Walthour (1834–1908), daughter of George Washington Walthour, of Walthourville, Georgia. For some years "Natty" was in the service of the Central Railroad of Georgia, first in Athens, later in Savannah. He died in Savannah on June 28th, 1910, survived by two daughters, and was buried in Laurel Grove Cemetery beside his second wife, who had died on January 21st, 1908.

BARNARD, SOLOMON SHAD (1821–1875), planter, son of Timothy Barnard and his second wife, Catherine Shad, was born on Wilmington Island, Chatham County, Georgia, on February 19th, 1821. He graduated from Franklin College (Athens) in 1841. On May 7th, 1846, he married Ann Mary Walthour (1827–1901), daughter of George Washington Walthour and Mary Amelia Ann Russell, of Walthourville, Georgia, and settled at Oak Hill, his plantation in Liberty County adjoining North Hampton, the plantation of his half-brother, John Bradley Barnard. In April 1856

he succeeded Benjamin Washington Allen as manager of White Oak, the plantation of Mrs. Susan M. Cumming; in the summer of 1857 he undertook the management of Montevideo plantation during the absence of the Rev. Dr. Charles Colcock Jones in Kentucky and Virginia. Although overage for military service, he enlisted in the Liberty Independent Troop, of which he was a member, at the outbreak of the Civil War and served eight months on the Georgia coast; in 1864 he fought in the trenches at Atlanta. After the war he settled permanently in Walthourville, where he died on February 14th, 1875, survived by his wife, two sons, and three daughters. He was buried in Walthourville Cemetery. As his lifelong friend, Henry Hart Jones, observed at the time of his death, "Mr. Barnard possessed a genial, gentle spirit. . . . Few persons were more uniformly cheerful, even under the most depressing circumstances, and a constant flow of humor and hilarity rendered him one of the most delightful and companionable of men." Ann Mary (Walthour) Barnard died in Walthourville on April 16th, 1901, and was buried beside her husband.

BARNWELL, ROBERT WOODWARD (1801–1882), lawyer, legislator, and educator, son of Robert Barnwell (1761–1814) and Elizabeth Wigg Hayne, was born near Beaufort, South Carolina, on August 10th, 1801. His father, a Revolutionary soldier, was a member of the Continental Congress (1788–1789) and a member of Congress (1791–1793). Robert Woodward Barnwell graduated from Harvard College with first honor in 1821, studied law, and commenced practice in Beaufort in 1824. On August 9th, 1827, he married his second cousin, Eliza Barnwell. He was a member of the state house of representatives (1826–1828); a member of Congress (1829–1833); president of the South Carolina College (1835–1841); and United States senator (1850). He was a member of the state secession convention meeting in Columbia in December 1860 and a delegate to the convention of seceding states meeting in Montgomery, Alabama, in February 1861. Throughout the war he was a member of the Confederate States Senate (1861–1865). After the war he was chairman of the faculty of the University of South Carolina (1866–1872); principal of a girls' school in Columbia (1872–1877); and librarian of the University of South Carolina (1877–1882). He died in Columbia on November 24th, 1882, and was buried in St. Helena's Churchyard, Beaufort.

BARTOW, FRANCIS STEBBINS (1816–1861), lawyer and Confederate soldier, son of Dr. Theodosius Bartow (1773–1856) and Frances Lloyd Stebbins, was born in Savannah, Georgia, on September 6th, 1816. He graduated from Franklin College (Athens) with first honor in 1835. After reading law in the office of the Hon. John Macpherson Berrien and the Hon. William Law, of Savannah, he attended the Yale Law School without receiving a degree. Returning to Savannah in 1837, he was admitted to the bar and rose rapidly to prominence in local and state politics. He was several times a member of the state house of representatives and the state senate; he was also a member of the state secession convention meeting in Milledgeville in January 1861; and he was subsequently elected a member of the Confederate Congress. On May 21st, 1861, he left for Virginia as captain of the Oglethorpe Light Infantry (Company B, 8th Regiment Georgia Infantry); on June 1st, 1861, he was elected colonel. On July 21st, 1861, he was killed while gallantly leading his command at Manassas. In a letter to Governor Joseph E. Brown he had written: "I go to illustrate Georgia." On the battlefield, a moment before his death, he exclaimed to his comrades: "They have killed me, boys, but I never gave up." His body was returned to Savannah and buried with military honors in Laurel Grove Cemetery. He was survived by his wife, Louisa Greene Berrien, daughter of the Hon. John Macpherson Berrien, whom he had married on April 18th, 1844; there were no children. In December 1861 Cass County, Georgia, was renamed Bartow County in his honor.

BATCHELDER, JAMES (1830–1854), Boston truckman, temporarily employed as a police officer by the United States marshal, was fatally stabbed in the left groin by an unknown hand on Friday evening, May 26th, 1854, in Courthouse Square, Boston, when a mob of abolitionists, inflamed to riot after a mass meeting at Faneuil Hall, sought access to the courthouse in order to release Anthony Burns, a fugitive slave, from custody within. The episode aroused intense feeling in Boston. Batchelder was buried from the Free Chapel in Charlestown on Sunday, May 28th. As the Boston *Post* observed, "He was a young man, kind and devoted to his family, quiet and almost always at home, and never engaged in police duty before the night he was murdered. He was a worthy citizen who fell in discharging a citizen's duty" (May 29th, 1854). Happily "A subscription paper for the relief of the widow of the murdered Batchelder was started on Monday afternoon by one of our most patriotic and liberal merchants, and received a large number of names immediately with generous amounts affixed to them" (May 31st, 1854).

BATE, WILLIAM BRIMAGE (1826–1905), lawyer, legislator, Confederate soldier, and governor, son of James Henry Bate and Amanda Weathered, was born at Bledsoe's Lick (now Castalian Springs), Sumner County, Tennessee, on October 7th, 1826. During the Mexican War (1846–1848) he was a private in a Louisiana company and later first lieutenant in Company I, 3rd Regiment Tennessee Volunteer Infantry. After serving as a member of the state house of representatives (1849–1851) he graduated from the Lebanon Law School (now part of Cumberland University) in 1852 and commenced practice in Gallatin, Tennessee. In 1856 he married Julia Peete, of Huntsville, Alabama. During the Civil War he

served as private, captain, colonel, brigadier general, and major general in the Confederate army; he fought at Shiloh, Murfreesboro, Chattanooga, and Missionary Ridge; he later participated in the Atlanta campaign and the Tennessee campaign; he was thrice wounded. In June 1863 he declined the nomination for governor of Tennessee. After the war he resumed the practice of law in Gallatin. He was a member of the Democratic National Convention in 1868 and a member of the Democratic national executive committee for twelve years (1868–1880). He was governor of Tennessee (1882–1886) and United States senator (1887–1905). He died in Washington, D.C., on March 9th, 1905, and was buried in Mount Olivet Cemetery, Nashville, Tennessee.

BATTEY, EMILY ANNE (VERDERY) (1826–1912): *Mrs. George Magruder Battey,* second child of Augustus Nicholas Verdery (1802–1880) and Susan Hampton Burton (1806–1877), was born in Belair, Georgia, on November 18th, 1826. From early youth she was distinguished for her intelligence, social charm, fluency of speech, and versatility of pen. She became the wife of George Magruder Battey (1830–1856), son of Cephas Battey and Mary Agnes Magruder, and resided with her husband, a physician, in Rome, Georgia, until his death in 1856. At the outbreak of the Civil War she was conducting a girls' school in Montgomery, Alabama; in 1867, seeking treatment for eyestrain, she removed to Atlanta, Georgia, where, together with her younger sister, Susan Hampton Verdery (1840–1928), wife of John Smith Prather (1837–1920), she conducted a seminary for young ladies. In 1873 Charles A. Dana offered her a permanent post on the editorial staff of the New York *Sun*; she removed to New York City, where she remained for twenty-three years, rising to national prominence as a contributor to the *Sun*, the *Telegram*, and the *Herald*, as well as to *Harper's, Scribner's,* and the *Century*. Leaving New York, she lived for a time with her sister, Adelaide Anna Verdery, wife of Dr. Dudley Robinson, in Robinson Springs, Lowndes County, Alabama; in 1906 she returned to Atlanta, where she died on November 2nd, 1912. She was buried in the Prather family plot in Decatur Cemetery. She was a devout Roman Catholic. Two of her brothers fought in the Civil War: Thomas Jefferson Verdery (1828–1862) was killed at Fredericksburg on December 13th, 1862; George Thomas Verdery (1837–1894) was severely wounded at Gettysburg on July 2nd, 1863, and never fully recovered.

BAYARD, NICHOLAS JAMES (1799–1879), merchant and planter, son of Dr. Nicholas Serle Bayard (1774–1821) and his cousin, Ann Livingston Bayard, was born in New York City on January 7th, 1799. From infancy he lived in Savannah, Georgia, where his father, an eminent physician, practiced successfully for a quarter of a century until his death on November 21st, 1821. Nicholas James Bayard was for some years a banker in Savannah. He married first (on June 25th, 1829) Sarah E. Harris; he married second (on May 23rd, 1833) Sarah Glen. Following his third marriage—to Eliza Barrington King (1808–1883), daughter of Roswell King and widow of Bayard Hand—he settled in Roswell, Georgia, in the circle of his wife's family. At the outbreak of the Civil War he removed to Rome, Georgia; in 1866 he sold his Roswell house to Theodore Dwight Adams, husband of Mary Sophia Robarts. In April 1875 he took up residence in Florida. He died in Maitland, Florida, on June 6th, 1879, and was buried in Upper Mill Cemetery, McIntosh County, Georgia. Eliza Barrington (King) (Hand) Bayard died on January 13th, 1883, and was buried beside her husband.

BAYNE, PETER (1830–1896), Scottish journalist and theological writer, son of the Rev. Charles John Bayne and Isabella Jane Duguid, was born in Fodderty, Ross-shire, Scotland, on October 19th, 1830. After receiving his master's degree at Marischal College (Aberdeen) in 1850 he undertook to prepare for the ministry at New College (Edinburgh); but considerations of health turned him to writing, and his published essays soon brought him an international reputation. *The Christian Life, Social and Individual,* one of his best-known books, was published in Edinburgh and Boston in 1855. He was editor of *The Witness* (1856–1860), *The Dial* (1860–1862), and *The Weekly Review* (1862–1865). In 1858, on a visit to Germany, he met and married Clotilda Gerwein, who died in childbirth in 1865; he was subsequently married twice. He received the honorary degree of doctor of laws from Aberdeen University in 1879. He died in Norwood on February 19th, 1896, and was buried in Harlington Churchyard, Middlesex.

BEAUREGARD, PIERRE GUSTAVE TOUTANT (1818–1893), Confederate soldier, was born of French ancestry near New Orleans on May 28th, 1818. He graduated from the United States Military Academy in 1838, second in his class. After several years of fortification work, chiefly in Louisiana, he went to Mexico in 1846 as an engineer on the staff of General Winfield Scott. In 1860 he was appointed superintendent of West Point, but on his arrival in January 1861 he served only five days; his openly expressed intention of siding with the South in the event of secession induced the secretary of war to direct his transfer. He resigned his commission on February 20th, 1861, and was immediately appointed brigadier general in the Confederate army. Seven weeks later, at Charleston, he demanded the surrender of Fort Sumter; when Major Robert Anderson refused, Beauregard ordered the bombardment that opened the Civil War. At Manassas (July 21st, 1861) he was second in command to Joseph E. Johnston; for distinguished service he was promoted to full general. Early in 1862 he was sent to the West, where he commanded the Army of Tennessee after the death of Albert Sidney Johnston at Shiloh (April 6th, 1862). In June 1862 illness forced him to surrender

his command to Bragg; after his recovery he commanded the defense of the South Carolina and Georgia coast. In the spring of 1864 he was again in Virginia; in September 1864 he returned to the West; in the spring of 1865 he was in the Carolinas, again second in command to Joseph E. Johnston. After the war he was president of the New Orleans, Jackson & Mississippi Railroad and (after 1888) commissioner of public works in New Orleans. He was twice married: in 1841 to Laure Villère, in 1860 to Marguerite Caroline Deslonde. He died in New Orleans on February 10th, 1893, and was buried in Metairie Cemetery.

BECK, CHARLES JONES (1842–1921), Confederate soldier, son of Charles Beck (1792–1861) and Ann Herron (1804–1874), was born in Columbia, South Carolina, on January 28th, 1842. His father, a resident of Columbia since 1820, was a staunch supporter of Columbia Theological Seminary and named his son for one of its professors, the Rev. Dr. Charles Colcock Jones. In 1861 Charles Jones Beck enlisted as a private in the 2nd Regiment South Carolina Infantry; later he became first sergeant. He saw service at Fort Sumter, Manassas, Seven Pines, and Chancellorsville; at Gettysburg he was wounded and taken prisoner, but he made his escape and rejoined his company. He was again wounded near Richmond in June 1864. After the war he returned to Columbia, where he served for a time as conductor on the Charlotte & Augusta Railroad and later engaged in the drayage business. He was a member of the volunteer fire department for thirty-five years. On December 6th, 1871, he married Mary Esther Squier (1844–1924), daughter of Abraham C. Squier, of Columbia; there were no children. He died in Columbia on January 14th, 1921, and was buried in the First Presbyterian Churchyard. Mary Esther (Squier) Beck died on October 15th, 1924, and was buried beside her husband. Mary Jane Beck (1839–1889), elder sister of Charles Jones Beck, became the wife of the Rev. Myron Doty Wood (1834–1913), a Presbyterian clergyman, in 1857.

BEECHER, HENRY WARD (1813–1887), Congregational clergyman, son of the Rev. Dr. Lyman Beecher (1775–1863) and Roxana Foote, was born in Litchfield, Connecticut, on June 24th, 1813. He was a younger brother of Harriet (Beecher) Stowe (1811–1896), author of *Uncle Tom's Cabin* (1852). He graduated from Amherst College in 1834 and from Lane Theological Seminary (Cincinnati, Ohio) in 1837. On August 3rd, 1837, he married Eunice White Bullard, of West Sutton, Massachusetts; there were ten children. From 1839 to 1847 he was pastor of the Second Presbyterian Church, Indianapolis; in 1847 he took charge of the newly organized Plymouth Church, Brooklyn, New York, where through a long pastorate he became one of the most prominent and influential clergymen in America. His later years were clouded by scandal. He published many volumes of sermons and addresses; *Star Papers; or, Experiences of Art and Nature*

(1855) contains some of his contributions to *The Independent*. He died in Brooklyn on March 8th, 1887.

BEMAN, CARLISLE POLLOCK (1797–1875), Presbyterian clergyman and educator, son of Samuel Beman and Silence Douglas, was born in Hampton, Washington County, New York, on May 5th, 1797. He graduated from Middlebury College with first honor in 1818. Two years later he became a teacher in the Mount Zion Academy, Hancock County, Georgia, where his elder brother, the Rev. Nathan Sidney Smith Beman (1785–1871) was principal and also pastor of the Presbyterian church. The elder brother returned to the North in 1823; the younger brother remained in Georgia; under his direction the Mount Zion Academy became one of the leading classical schools in the South. On December 30th, 1823, he married Avis De Witt. From 1836 to 1840 he was principal of the Manual Labor School (Midway, Georgia), which developed into Oglethorpe University; from 1840 to 1844 he was rector of the LaGrange High School. In 1846 he founded the Villa High School, two miles west of Mount Zion; it was here that Dunwody Jones, son of the Rev. John Jones, studied from 1854 to 1857. The school was discontinued in 1857, but Beman remained in Mount Zion, where he was pastor of the Presbyterian church from 1861 to 1875. In 1853 he received the honorary degree of doctor of divinity from Oglethorpe University. He died in Mount Zion on December 12th, 1875, and was buried beside his wife, who had died on November 28th, 1863.

BENGEL, JOHANN ALBRECHT (1687–1752), Lutheran clergyman and scholar, was born in Winnenden, Württemberg, Germany, on June 24th, 1687. After graduating from the University of Tübingen he entered the ministry in 1707. From 1708 to 1713 he was tutor in theology at the University of Tübingen; from 1713 to 1741 he was master of the Klosterschule, a seminary for ministerial candidates at Denkendorf. He received the honorary degree of doctor of divinity from the University of Tübingen in 1751. His reputation as a Biblical scholar and critic rests chiefly on his edition of the Greek New Testament (1734) and his *Gnomon Novi Testamenti* (1742), a series of exegetical annotations which has passed through many editions in Latin, German, and English and is still highly valued by expositors of the New Testament.

BENNETT, JAMES GORDON (1795–1872), journalist, was born in Newmill, near Keith, Banffshire, Scotland, in 1795. In 1819 he migrated to America, and in 1823, having supported himself for four years as teacher, copyholder, and translator in Halifax, Nova Scotia, Boston, New York, and Charleston, he settled in New York, where he commenced his long, stormy, and successful career as journalist. He was associate editor of the New York *Enquirer* (1827–1829) and associate editor of the combined *Courier & Enquirer* (1829–1832). On May 6th, 1835, he issued the first number of the New York *Herald,* a four-page paper with four columns to the page, sold for a penny a copy or three dollars a year. "We shall support no party," he announced in the first number, "be the organ of no faction or coterie, and care nothing for any election or any candidate from President down to constable. We shall endeavor to record facts on every public and proper subject, stripped of verbiage and coloring, with comments when suitable, just, independent, fearless, and good-tempered." At first Bennett was his own editor, reporter, proofreader, and cashier, but his paper enjoyed immediate success, and through his industry, originality, and boldness the enterprise expanded and flourished. He was the first newspaper editor to employ European correspondents (1838) and the first to secure a full report of a speech by telegraph (1846); during the Civil War he maintained a staff of sixty-three correspondents in the field. In 1840 he married Henrietta Agnes Crean; their son, James Gordon Bennett (1841–1918), succeeded his father as editor in 1866 and later established a daily edition of the *Herald* in London and Paris. Bennett died in New York City on June 1st, 1872, and was buried in Greenwood Cemetery, Brooklyn.

BENNING, HENRY LEWIS (1814–1875), jurist, statesman, and Confederate soldier, son of Pleasant Moon Benning and Matilda Meriwether White, was born on his father's plantation in Columbia County, Georgia, on April 2nd, 1814. After graduating from Franklin College (Athens) in 1834 he settled in Columbus, Georgia, where he resided for the rest of his life. In 1835 he was admitted to the bar, and in 1837 he was appointed solicitor general. On September 12th, 1839, he married Mary Howard Jones, daughter of Seaborn Jones; there were ten children. In 1853 he was elected by the state legislature an associate justice of the supreme court of Georgia; at the expiration of his term in 1859 he was not reelected. An ardent secessionist, he participated actively in the state secession convention meeting in Milledgeville in January 1861. At the outbreak of the Civil War he became colonel of the 17th Regiment Georgia Infantry; he was soon promoted to brigadier general. He fought at Sharpsburg, Chickamauga, and Gettysburg; he was severely wounded in the Wilderness. After the war he resumed the practice of law. He died in Columbus on July 10th, 1875, survived by five daughters, and was buried in Linwood Cemetery.

BERRIEN, JOHN MACPHERSON (1781–1856), statesman, eldest son of John Berrien (1759–1815) and his first wife, Margaret Macpherson (1763–1785), was born in Rocky Hill, near Princeton, New Jersey, on August 23rd, 1781. After graduating from the College of New Jersey (Princeton) in 1796 he studied law in Savannah, Georgia, and soon rose to prominence in local, state, and national politics. He was judge of the eastern circuit of Georgia (1810–1821); state senator (1822–1823); United States senator (1825–1829); attorney general of the United States under President Andrew Jackson (1829–1831); and United States senator (1841–1852). He was president of the American ("Know-Nothing") party convention meeting in Milledgeville in December 1855. He received the honorary degree of doctor of laws from the College of New Jersey (Princeton) in 1829. He married first (on December 1st, 1803) Eliza Anciaux (1776–1828), daughter of Nicholas Anciaux and Lydia Richardson; there were nine children. He married second (on July 8th, 1833) Eliza Cecil Hunter (1810–1852), daughter of James Hunter and Eliza Tuten Cecil; there were six children. He died in Savannah on January 1st, 1856, and was buried in Laurel Grove Cemetery. "Few professional men die with so few enemies and so few faults," wrote the Rev. Dr. Charles Colcock Jones to his son Charles on January 7th, 1856; "your grandfather and he for many years were very intimate and warm friends."

BERRIEN, JOHN MACPHERSON (1841–1875), Confederate soldier, son of the Hon. John Macpherson Berrien (1781–1856) and his second wife, Eliza Cecil Hunter (1810–1852), was born in Savannah, Georgia, on October 27th, 1841. He was a younger half-brother of Louisa Greene Berrien, wife of Francis Stebbins Bartow, in whose Savannah household he was living at the outbreak of the Civil War. As second lieutenant in the Oglethorpe Light Infantry (Company B, 8th Regiment Georgia Infantry) and aide-de-camp to Captain Bartow, he accompanied his brother-in-law to Virginia in May 1861; when Bartow was killed at Manassas on July 21st, 1861, Berrien returned to Savannah with Bartow's body for burial in Laurel Grove Cemetery. In September 1862, as captain in the regular army, he was appointed to the staff of General Thomas R. R. Cobb; at Fredericksburg, on December 13th, 1862, Cobb was killed and Berrien was desperately wounded in the right hip. Although he recovered sufficiently to resume military service, he remained a cripple for life. After the war he returned to Savannah, where he was appointed justice of the peace by the governor. He never married. He died of typhoid fever on July 8th, 1875, and was buried in Laurel Grove Cemetery.

BERRIEN, SARAH (SALLIE) LOWNDES (1837–1872), daughter of the Hon. John Macpherson Berrien (1781–1856) and his second wife, Eliza Cecil Hunter (1810–1852), was born in Savannah, Georgia, on December 15th, 1837. After the death of her mother on February 2nd, 1852, and of her father on January 1st, 1856, she lived in the Savannah household of her elder half-sister, Louisa Greene Berrien, wife of Francis Stebbins Bartow. There she was the intimate friend and daily companion of Ruth Berrien Whitehead, first wife of Charles Colcock Jones, Jr. On October 4th, 1864, she became the wife of Dr. Alexander Jenkins Semmes (1828–1898), son of Raphael Semmes and Mary Matilda Jenkins, and first cousin of Raphael Semmes (1809–1877), admiral in the Confederate navy. Her

husband, a graduate of Georgetown College (1850) and the Medical Department of Columbian College (1851), was a surgeon in the Confederate army. There were no children. She died in Savannah on February 28th, 1872, and was buried beside her father in Laurel Grove Cemetery. Her husband subsequently gave up a distinguished medical practice to become a Roman Catholic priest; for some years he was professor of English literature at Pio Nono College for students of the priesthood in Macon, Georgia. He died in New Orleans on September 21st, 1898.

BIRD, SAIDA BAXTER (1848–1922), daughter of William Edgeworth Bird (1825–1867) and Sarah C. J. Baxter (1828–1910), was born near Sparta, Hancock County, Georgia, in December 1848. Through both her father and her mother she was a cousin of Eva Berrien Eve (1841–1890), second wife of Charles Colcock Jones, Jr., who prized "the annual delight of a Sparta trip . . . sojourning among my best-loved friends." It was with Saida Bird that Eva Berrien (Eve) Jones fled to Augusta when Savannah was evacuated in December 1864, and after the war Saida Bird and her mother often stayed with the Joneses in New York City. William Edgeworth Bird died in 1867, and his widow removed with her two children to Baltimore, Maryland, where on November 16th, 1871, Saida Bird married Victor Smith (1848–1915), a young lawyer, a fellow-Georgian, and son of Martin Luther Smith, Confederate general. According to the Baltimore *Sun* (June 19th, 1922), "The home of Mr. and Mrs. Smith at 22 East Mount Vernon Place was a social center of Baltimore for forty years." Victor Smith died at his residence on September 28th, 1915; as the *Sun* (September 29th, 1915) observed, "Mr. Smith was well known to the children who play in Mount Vernon Place, for he delighted to amuse them with stories of the war, and to bring them candy and other good things; and while his health was good he was often seen on the grass plot in front of his home surrounded by a crowd of boys and girls." Saida Baxter (Bird) Smith died at the residence of her son, Edgeworth Bird Smith, in Kew Gardens, Long Island, New York, on June 18th, 1922, and was buried near her husband, her mother, and her brother in Greenmount Cemetery, Baltimore.

BIRD, SARAH C. J. (BAXTER) (1828–1910): *Mrs. William Edgeworth Bird,* was born in Hancock County, Georgia, on March 26th, 1828. On February 24th, 1848, she became the wife of William Edgeworth Bird (1825–1867), son of James Wilson Bird (1787–1868) and Frances Pamela Casey, of Sparta. There were two children: Saida Baxter Bird (1848–1922) and Wilson Edgeworth Bird (1850–1910). Together with Mrs. Mary Jones of Liberty County and Mrs. Philoclea Eve of Augusta she was for some years active in the work of the Mount Vernon Ladies' Association of the Union. In 1867, soon after the death of her husband, she removed with her son and daughter to Baltimore, Maryland, where for forty years her house in Mount Vernon Place was an intellectual and artistic center. In her youth she had known the Southern poets Henry Timrod and Paul Hamilton Hayne, and during her Baltimore residence she numbered among her intimate friends the poet Sidney Lanier, the humorist Richard Malcolm Johnston, the scientist Joseph LeConte, and the statesmen Robert Toombs and Alexander H. Stephens. She died in Baltimore on February 28th, 1910, and was buried in Greenmount Cemetery.

BLACK, JOHN JOYCE (1844–1896), Confederate soldier, son of George Seaborn Black and Mary Ralls, was born in Cass (now Bartow) County, Georgia, on June 7th, 1844. When a small boy he removed with his parents to Rome, where at the age of seventeen, on May 18th, 1861, he enlisted as fourth corporal in the Rome Light Guards (Company A, 8th Regiment Georgia Infantry). At Manassas he was captured, but he soon made his escape. After serving in the Peninsula campaign of 1862 he was absent on sick leave at Chimborazo Hospital, Richmond, with "chronic diarrhea" from July 8th, 1862, to December 19th, 1862. Toward the end of the war he served in the Ordnance Department. Returning to Rome, he sold insurance and engaged in bookkeeping; in 1876 he was elected tax collector of Floyd County, a post he held for the rest of his life. In 1879 he was one of the founders and original directors of the Young Men's Library Association, from which the Carnegie Library of Rome later developed. He married first (in 1865) Belle Findlay (1849–1885), who bore him four children; he married second (in 1887) Ella Bailey (1859–1895), who bore him three children. He died in Rome on July 30th, 1896, and was buried near his two wives in Myrtle Hill Cemetery.

BLACK, RACHEL ANNICE (1809–1886), seventh child of William Black (1774–1838) and Sarah Hanson Reid (1783–1815), was born in Beaufort District, South Carolina, in 1809. She later described her mother as "the unparalleled of her sex in natural talent, education, accomplishments, and personal appearance"; her father was "a gentleman of fortune, but lost a part of it by an unfortunate security-debt, and in consequence for economy's sake moved his family and planting interest to Barnwell District." Here she spent her early years. A nephew, George Robison Black, remembered her as "a large, handsome, talented, and accomplished lady of fine conversational powers and engaging manner. . . . An uncommon woman in the high order of her endowments and her cultivation of heart, mind, and manner." She never married. Her elder brother, Edward Junius Black (1806–1846), was congressman from Georgia (1839–1845); her elder sister, Joanna Clementina Black (1807–1834), became (in 1828) the third wife of George Washington McAllister (1781–1850) and the mother of Rosella Rachel McAllister (1830–1914) and Clementina Hanson McAllister (1832–1907). As aunt of the McAllister sisters Rachel Black was their fre-

quent companion, not only at Strathy Hall, their plantation residence in Bryan County, Georgia, but also in New Haven, Connecticut, where their half-sister, Matilda Willis McAllister, widow of Thomas Savage Clay, summered with her five children. Rachel Black died on October 12th, 1886, and was buried in the Black family cemetery near Millettville, Allendale County, South Carolina.

BLAKE, ELIZA (EDWARDS) (1802–1878): *Mrs. Joseph Blake,* Cambridge landlady, daughter of John Edwards and Sarah Norwood, was born in Concord, Massachusetts, in 1802. In February 1854 Charles Colcock Jones, Jr., and his friend George Helm, both students at Dane Law School, Harvard, took a room in her house in Main Street, Cambridge, some half a mile from the university, where Jones wrote his parents on March 8th, 1854: "Am more and more pleased with my new room, and the quiet retirement which it affords." After Helm left Harvard late in April 1854 Jones occupied the room alone until July. On May 15th, 1854, he wrote his parents: "In consequence of George Helm's leaving me sole possessor of the premises, which we had jointly engaged, the expense on my part is increased. I would not, however, exchange my present quarters for any in Cambridge. The room is retired, and we have in the way of kindness fallen among good Samaritans. I feel as if I were somewhat of a gentleman—treated as such, and living among gentlemen and ladies." Eliza (Edwards) Blake died in Cambridge on February 2nd, 1878; her husband died on June 15th, 1879.

BLOOMFIELD, SAMUEL THOMAS (1784–1869), English Biblical scholar, received his bachelor's degree at Sidney Sussex College (Cambridge) in 1808. From 1814 to 1869 he served as vicar of Bisbrooke, Rutland; from 1854 to 1869 he was also honorable canon of Peterborough Cathedral. His most distinguished scholarly work, *The Greek Testament with English Notes, Critical, Philological, and Exegetical* (London, 1832; Boston and Philadelphia, 1837), reached its twelfth English edition in 1870. He died at Hone House, Wandsworth Common, near London, on September 28th, 1869.

BOARDMAN, HENRY AUGUSTUS (1808–1880), Presbyterian clergyman, was born in Troy, New York, on January 9th, 1808. He graduated from Yale College in 1829 and from Princeton Theological Seminary in 1833. On November 8th, 1833, he was ordained pastor of the Tenth Street Presbyterian Church, Philadelphia, where he continued until his retirement in 1876, when he became pastor emeritus. For forty years he enjoyed wide influence in Presbyterian affairs; in 1853 he was elected professor of pastoral theology at Princeton Theological Seminary, a post he declined; in 1854 he was elected moderator of the General Assembly of the Presbyterian Church. Many of his books and sermons were published by J. B. Lippincott of Philadelphia. He died in Philadelphia on June 15th, 1880, and was buried in Laurel Hill Cemetery beside his wife, Eliza Beach (1810–1874), who had died on August 19th, 1874.

BOGART, WILLIAM SCHENCK (1819–1892), educator, was born in Princeton, New Jersey, on April 8th, 1819. After graduating from the College of New Jersey (Princeton) in 1836 he taught school in Portsmouth, Virginia, until considerations of health determined him to move farther south. In 1853, having taught briefly in South Carolina and Florida, he settled in Savannah, Georgia, where he opened a school for boys, and where, in 1854, he was elected principal of the Chatham Academy. There he continued until 1861, when he served briefly in the Chatham Artillery at Fort Pulaski. Failing health prevented his continuing service in the field, although in 1864 he was for a time in the trenches around Atlanta. After the war he resumed his post as principal of the Chatham Academy; in 1871 he was elected principal of the Savannah Girls' High School; and in 1889 he was elected assistant superintendent of the Savannah Public Schools. A man of deep piety, he was active in St. John's Episcopal Church, first as vestryman (1860), later as senior warden (1865). He was for thirty years treasurer of the Georgia Historical Society; he was also for many years historian of the Chatham Artillery. He married first (in 1849) Jane H. Dickson, of Portsmouth, Virginia; he married second (in 1869) Florence G. Jordan, also of Portsmouth. He died in Savannah on September 22nd, 1892, leaving a large and valuable library of rare books, manuscripts, and autograph letters, and was buried in Portsmouth, Virginia.

BOGGS, DAVID CHALMERS (1829–1901), Presbyterian clergyman, son of Thomas G. Boggs, was born in Pickens County, South Carolina, on March 18th, 1829. He graduated from Oglethorpe University in 1854 and from Columbia Theological Seminary, where he was a fellow student of Robert Quarterman Mallard, in 1857. For ten years he served various pastorates in South Carolina. On March 13th, 1867, he married Camilla Isabella Brogdon (1846–1924), of Sumter District, South Carolina; and the following year he removed with his bride to Arkansas, where he was pastor in Jacksonport (1868–1873) and Bentonville (1873–1901). He died in Bentonville on July 25th, 1901, and was buried in the City Cemetery. Camilla Isabella (Brogdon) Boggs died in Fayetteville on February 5th, 1924, and was buried beside her husband.

BOGGS, JOHN (1785–1848), Presbyterian clergyman and educator, was born in Virginia in 1785. Although educated in the North he removed early in life to Georgia, where in 1813 he was conducting a school in Sunbury, Liberty County. By 1819 he was pastor in Boundbrook, Somerset County, New Jersey; in 1823 he received an honorary master's degree from the College of New Jersey (Princeton). Returning to Georgia, he was for a time pastor of the First Presbyterian Church, Savannah, after which he taught and preached in Wash-

ington, Wilkes County, and Waynesboro. From 1832 to 1838 he resided in South Carolina, where he was teacher and stated supply in Spartanburg and Greenwood; there he wrote and published his one book, *The Southern Christian, Exemplified in the Memoirs of Anthony Jefferson Pearson* (1835). After teaching and preaching for several years in Louisiana and Virginia he returned to South Carolina in October 1847 to become principal of a girls' high school in Greenwood. He died in Greenwood on August 13th, 1848, and was buried in Rock Presbyterian Churchyard, some three miles north of the town. According to the Rev. James H. Saye, in his manuscript history of Rock Presbyterian Church, "Mr. Boggs was certainly a remarkable man. . . . In person small and emaciated, his face cadaverous, his eyes black and piercing, one would have thought he could perform little or no labor and endure no hardship. Yet he performed an amount of work of which few men in the vigor of manhood would be thought capable. He not only preached often but with great effect. . . . He was alive to the importance of education and stirred up the people on this subject wherever he went. . . . He lived a roving life, perhaps because the Master had use for him in many places" [George Howe, *History of the Presbyterian Church in South Carolina* (Columbia, 1870–1883), II, 527].

BOGGS, WILLIAM ROBERTSON (1829–1911), Confederate soldier, son of Archibald Boggs and Mary Ann Robertson, was born in Augusta, Georgia, on March 18th, 1829. He graduated from the United States Military Academy in 1853. Prior to the Civil War he filled various military posts in New York, Louisiana, Texas, and Pennsylvania. On March 16th, 1861, having resigned his commission, he entered Confederate service as chief of ordnance at Pensacola; on December 23rd, 1861, he was promoted to colonel and appointed chief of engineers and artillery for the State of Georgia. A year later, on November 4th, 1862, he was promoted to brigadier general in recognition of his services on the staff of General Kirby Smith in Kentucky. In 1863 he became chief of staff to General Kirby Smith in the Department of the Trans-Mississippi. After the war he engaged in architecture and engineering and for five years served as professor of mechanics at the Virginia Polytechnic Institute. On December 19th, 1855, he married Mary Sophia Symington, of Troy, New York. He died in Winston-Salem, North Carolina, on September 15th, 1911.

BOND, CORNELIA VANDERVEER. *See* Grant, Cornelia Vanderveer (Bond)

BONHAM, MILLEDGE LUKE (1813–1890), Confederate soldier, legislator, and governor, eighth child of James Bonham and Sophie Smith, was born in Red Bank, Edgefield District, South Carolina, on December 25th, 1813. After graduating from the South Carolina College in 1834 he commenced the practice of law. On November 13th, 1845, he married Ann Patience Griffin (1829–1894).

During the Mexican War (1846–1848) he served as lieutenant colonel of the 12th Infantry. He was a member of the state legislature (1840–1844); solicitor of the southern district of South Carolina (1848–1857); and a member of Congress (1857–1860). At the outbreak of the Civil War he was appointed brigadier general in the Confederate army; he commanded the first troops to arrive in Virginia. Early in 1862 he resigned his commission and served briefly in the Confederate Congress; late in 1862 he was elected governor of South Carolina for a two-year term. In February 1865 he was reappointed brigadier general of cavalry. After the war he resumed the practice of law, engaged in planting, represented Edgefield District in the state legislature (1865–1867), and served as delegate to the Democratic National Convention (1868). In 1878 he was appointed state railroad commissioner. He died at White Sulphur Springs, North Carolina, on August 27th, 1890, and was buried in Elmwood Cemetery, Columbia, South Carolina. Ann Patience (Griffin) Bonham died in Columbia on October 11th, 1894, and was buried beside her husband.

BORCHERT, ANTON (1804–1870), baker, was born in Strelitz, Mecklenburg, Germany, on January 17th, 1804. In 1835 he migrated to the United States and settled in Savannah, Georgia, where he prospered in the bakery business and participated actively in civic affairs. For many years he was a member of the Savannah Board of Health, a director of the Chatham Mutual Loan Association, a foreman of the German Fire Company, and a trustee of the German Lutheran congregation. On November 2nd, 1836, he married Louisa M. Spann (1818–1895), who bore him numerous children. His bakery at the corner of Bryan and Jefferson Streets was "justly celebrated" for its Passover bread; a typical notice appeared in the Savannah *Morning News* on March 24th, 1862: "The undersigned is prepared to furnish Passover bread to the city as well as to the country. I would also give notice that I have no boxes, and nobody to attend to the forwarding department of my business, in consequence of all my sons being in service; therefore country orders can only be received where the parties will have some person here who will attend to the forwarding. A. Borchert." Three of his sons fought in the Civil War: Charles Frederick Borchert was corporal in the Oglethorpe Light Infantry; William Victor Borchert, also corporal in the Oglethorpe Light Infantry, died of disease in Petersburg, Virginia, in August 1862; George Anton Borchert, captain in the Confederate navy, was murdered in South America in September 1867. Anton Borchert died in Savannah on October 4th, 1870, and was buried in Laurel Grove Cemetery. As the Savannah *Morning News* (October 6th, 1870) observed, "He leaves a name which will be remembered in the annals of our city." Louisa (Spann) Borchert died on October 13th, 1895, and was buried beside her husband.

BORROW, GEORGE (1803–1881), English author, was born in East Dereham, Norfolk, in 1803. After a childhood and youth spent in many places in England, Scotland, and Ireland, he lived briefly in London before setting out on his extensive travels (1835–1840) through England, France, Spain, Germany, Russia, and the East. In all these countries he acted as agent of the British and Foreign Bible Society. Returning to England, he married Mary Clarke in 1840 and settled on an estate on Oulton Broad, where he wrote *Lavengro: The Scholar, the Gypsy, the Priest* (1851), an autobiographical work, and its sequel, *The Romany Rye* (2 vols., 1857). His high place in literature rests chiefly on *The Zincali; or, An Account of the Gypsies in Spain* (2 vols., 1841) and on *The Bible in Spain; or, The Journeys, Adventures, and Imprisonments of an Englishman in an Attempt to Circulate the Scriptures in the Peninsula* (3 vols., 1843). He was an accomplished linguist, and in his translations he demonstrated his fluency in Russian, Turkish, and Danish as well as in Manchu, the court language of China. He died at Oulton in August 1881.

BOUNETHEAU, HENRY BRINTNELL (1797–1877), portrait miniaturist, was born of French Huguenot ancestry in Charleston, South Carolina, on December 14th, 1797. After a brief mercantile career he followed his natural gift for drawing and soon became widely known for his skill in painting portrait miniatures. In the words of the Charleston *News & Courier* (February 1st, 1877), "The life of Mr. Bounetheau was unusually uneventful, and yet he made an impression wherever he went by the serenity and amiability of his character. Painting was not his only accomplishment. A man of taste and culture, he was passionately fond of music, and played his favorite instrument, the flute, with remarkable skill and expression. In all things he was temperate and moderate; there was nothing extreme in his character or habits. To the natural evenness of his disposition and the regularity of his manner of living may be traced in a large degree the vigor which, in even his later years, made him as erect and active as when in the prime of life." He died in Charleston on January 30th, 1877. It was in July 1861 that Charles Colcock Jones, Jr., acting on the recommendation of Charles Jones Colcock, of Charleston, commissioned Bounetheau to paint a portrait miniature of his deceased wife, Ruth Berrien Whitehead. Two years later the matter was still unsettled; on August 25th, 1863, Bounetheau wrote Jones acknowledging receipt of his check for seventy-five dollars in full payment of miniature and case: "I will cheerfully hold myself in readiness at your convenience to make any alterations that may be suggested in the hope of improving and making the picture more satisfactory to both parties."

BOWEN, MARY ELIZABETH (1822–1910), eldest child of William Parker Bowen (1800–1859) and Anne Elizabeth Wilkins (1802–1861), was born in Savannah, Georgia, in 1822. She spent almost all of her eighty-eight years in Savannah; her father, a merchant, was something of a ne'er-do-well, and the daughter, often finding herself homeless, divided her time among her friends. Her father died on November 15th, 1859; her mother died less than two years later, on May 14th, 1861. Early in July 1860 she became the second wife of John Joseph Robertson (1819–1873), a physician practicing in Washington, Wilkes County, Georgia, where she resided until her husband's death on May 3rd, 1873. Returning to Savannah, she became an active member of the Independent Presbyterian Church; according to the Savannah *Morning News* (December 28th, 1910), she was "deeply interested in religious matters." She died in Savannah after a long illness on December 26th, 1910, and was buried beside her husband and near her father and mother in Laurel Grove Cemetery.

BOWEN, WILLIAM PARKER (1800–1859), merchant, was born in Savannah, Georgia, in February 1800. In July 1821 he married Anne Elizabeth Wilkins (1802–1861), daughter of Samuel Wilkins, of Sunbury, Liberty County, Georgia; there were five sons and two daughters. For many years he was an active member of the Georgia Hussars, the Savannah Volunteer Guards, and other local military companies. He was evidently something of a ne'er-do-well; as Charles Colcock Jones, Jr., wrote on September 17th, 1859, "He is a drunken vagabond, and the only wonder is that he is permitted to live—an annoyance to his family and a miserable incubus upon society." He died in Savannah on November 15th, 1859, and was buried in Laurel Grove Cemetery. As the Savannah *Republican* (November 16th, 1859) observed, "He was a devoted friend, and in sentiment and bearing partook of the chivalry of other days. He possessed many noble traits, and if faults, they are the common lot of all things human, and we would bury them in the grave to which he has gone." Anne Elizabeth (Wilkins) Bowen died in Savannah on May 14th, 1861, and was buried beside her husband.

BOWMAN, ANNA RICE (1840–1922), daughter of the Rev. Francis William Bowman (1795–1875) and Harriet Byron Minor (1800–1865), was born in Greensboro, Georgia, on June 6th, 1840, the younger sister of John Rice Bowman and Francis Henry Bowman. In 1857 her father, a Presbyterian clergyman, became pastor of Bryan Neck Church, Bryan County, Georgia; at the same time her brother Francis Henry Bowman was co-pastor of Midway Church, Liberty County; she was thus introduced into coastal society, and by February 1858 she was rumored to be engaged to William Henry King (1833–1865), Savannah druggist. But on July 17th, 1860, she became the wife of her first cousin, John Blair Morton (1836–1867), teacher and planter, son of Dr. William Smith Morton and Clementine Minor, and settled at High Hill, the Morton plantation on the Appomattox River, Cumberland County, Virginia; there were four children.

Following her husband's death on September 4th, 1867, she married (on January 10th, 1872) another cousin, the Hon. Isaac Hudson, of Dublin, Pulaski County, Virginia; there were five children. In her later years she resided with her two daughters, Edith Morton and Annie Hudson, in Montreat, North Carolina, where she died on November 6th, 1922. She was buried beside her second husband in Dublin, Virginia.

BOWMAN, FRANCES McLEOD (1858–1920), daughter of the Rev. Francis Henry Bowman (1833–1873) and his first wife, Mary McLeod King (1837–1864), was born in Liberty County, Georgia, early in September 1858. In infancy she removed with her parents to Greensboro, Alabama, and thence to Mount Sidney, Augusta County, Virginia, where her mother died on December 23rd, 1864. Less than two years later, on November 22nd, 1866, her father married Rosalie Freeland Benson, of Charlottesville, Virginia; in 1868 the family removed to Memphis, Tennessee, where the father died of yellow fever on October 6th, 1873. Frances McLeod Bowman graduated from the University of Chicago in 1903. For some years she was teacher of Latin and Greek and assistant principal of Glendale College, Glendale, Ohio; in 1917 she became principal of Montreat Normal School, Montreat, North Carolina, where she died unmarried on October 31st, 1920. She was buried in Hollywood Cemetery, Richmond, Virginia.

BOWMAN, FRANCIS HENRY (1833–1873), Presbyterian clergyman, younger son of the Rev. Francis William Bowman (1795–1875) and Harriet Byron Minor (1800–1865), was born in Charlottesville, Virginia, on July 9th, 1833. In early childhood he removed with his parents to Greensboro, Georgia, where his father, a Presbyterian clergyman, was pastor for nineteen years (1837–1856). He graduated from Oglethorpe University in 1851. After teaching for one year at the Mount Zion Academy he attended the University of Virginia (1852–1854) and Union Theological Seminary, Hampden-Sydney, Virginia (1854–1855); he then proceeded to Princeton Theological Seminary, where he graduated in 1856. From 1856 to 1859 he served as co-pastor with the Rev. David Lyman Buttolph of Midway Church, Liberty County, Georgia. On April 22nd, 1857, he was groomsman at the marriage of the Rev. Robert Quarterman Mallard and Mary Sharpe Jones; on November 5th, 1857, he was himself married to Mary McLeod King (1837–1864), daughter of William King (1804–1884) and Sarah Elizabeth McLeod (1807–1891), of Savannah, with Charles Colcock Jones, Jr., as groomsman. Leaving Liberty County, he served churches in Greensboro, Alabama (1859–1861); Mount Sidney, Augusta County, Virginia (1861–1868); and Memphis, Tennessee (1868–1873). His wife died at Mount Sidney on December 23rd, 1864, leaving three young children; he married second (on November 22nd, 1866)

Rosalie Freeland Benson, of Charlottesville, Virginia, who bore him four children. He died in Memphis of yellow fever on October 6th, 1873, and was buried in Elmwood Cemetery. Meeting Bowman in Philadelphia, Mrs. Mary Jones wrote her husband (July 13th, 1853): "I cannot say when I have ever met a brighter, more intelligent and gentlemanly young man." Hearing him preach in Bryan County, Georgia, Eliza Caroline Clay reported (May 11th, 1858): "Everyone was much pleased—said it was excellent, beautiful, *splendid*." Describing his pastorate at Mount Sidney, Virginia, the Rev. J. N. Van Devanter observed: "He possessed a personal magnetism and an ideal pulpit manner or delivery which gave him wonderful power over all who came in touch with him" [*Augusta Church, 1737 to 1900* (Staunton, Virginia, 1900), p. 51].

BOWMAN, FRANCIS WILLIAM (1795–1875), Presbyterian clergyman, was born in Westford, Vermont, on February 27th, 1795. He graduated from the University of Vermont in 1817 and from Princeton Theological Seminary in 1822. From 1824 to 1826 he was pastor in Charlottesville, Virginia, where he married Harriet Byron Minor (1800–1865) on May 9th, 1825. There were two sons: John Rice Bowman (1826–1897) and Francis Henry Bowman (1833–1873), both Presbyterian clergymen; and one daughter: Anna Rice Bowman (1840–1922). Leaving Charlottesville, he served churches in Greensboro, Georgia (1837–1856) and in Bryan County, Georgia (1857–1862), after which he lived in retirement in Virginia and Tennessee until his death in Dublin, Pulaski County, Virginia, on April 26th, 1875. He received the honorary degree of doctor of divinity from Hampden-Sydney College in 1852.

BOWMAN, JOHN RICE (1826–1897), Presbyterian clergyman, elder son of the Rev. Francis William Bowman (1795–1875) and Harriet Byron Minor (1800–1865), was born in Charlottesville, Virginia, on March 22nd, 1826. He graduated from the College of New Jersey (Princeton) in 1844 and from Columbia Theological Seminary in 1851. From 1851 to 1854 he was stated supply in Madison, Georgia; from 1854 to 1859 he was pastor in Eutaw, Alabama, where he married first (on November 27th, 1855) Mary Virginia Crawford (1830–1857) and second (on October 24th, 1859) Mary Jane Hubbard (1838–1900). Removing to Virginia, he served churches in Buckingham County (1859–1866) and Harrisonburg (1867–1884), after which he was pastor in Gainesville, Texas (1884–1886); Pomona, California (1887–1889); San Angelo, Texas (1889–1890); and Hueneme, California (1890–1892). In 1892 he retired in Los Angeles, California, where he died on October 11th, 1897. He was buried in Rosedale Cemetery.

BRADSHAW, JAMES NEAL (1818–1895), Presbyterian clergyman, son of Eli Givens Bradshaw and Sallie Neal, was born in Maury County, Tennessee, on January 31st, 1818. He was largely self-educated. On May 13th, 1840, in Giles County, Tennessee, he married Anna Jane Brown, sister of Neill S. Brown and John C. Brown, both later governors of Tennessee. From 1845 to 1855 he was evangelist at various points in Middle Tennessee. In 1855 he became pastor of the New School Presbyterian church in Chattanooga, where he remained until 1861, when he became pastor and president of the female college in Cleveland. There he continued until forced to flee at the approach of the Federal army in 1864. For the rest of the war he preached and assisted at army hospitals, first at Griffin, Georgia, later at Perry. After the war he preached and taught in various communities in the vicinity of Macon. Subsequently he served churches in Darien, Georgia (1885–1889) and Madison, Florida (1889–1894). He died in Madison on January 21st, 1895, and was buried in Covington, Georgia.

BRADWELL, SAMUEL DOWSE (1840–1903), educator and Confederate soldier, son of James Sharpe Bradwell and Isabella Fraser, was born near Hinesville, Liberty County, Georgia, on January 5th, 1840. He graduated from Oglethorpe University in 1859. On August 27th, 1861, he was elected first lieutenant of the Liberty Volunteers (Company H, 25th Regiment Georgia Infantry), and in May 1862 he succeeded William Sanford Norman as captain. He fought at James Island, Chickamauga, Resaca, Dallas, Kennesaw Mountain, and Peachtree Creek, where he was wounded on July 22nd, 1864. After the war he served for twenty years as principal of the Bradwell Institute in Hinesville, described by the Savannah *Republican* (July 13th, 1872) as "a fine and prosperous place of learning . . . patronized by young ladies and gentlemen (sixty in number) from all parts of the state." On January 2nd, 1868, he married Elizabeth Clifton (1845–1898), daughter of William Clifton. In 1871 he founded the Hinesville *Gazette*, described by the Savannah *Republican* (April 12th, 1871) as "a small but well printed sheet published at one dollar per year," containing "a variety of miscellany" and "numerous suggestions on farming and education." He was state senator (1888–1889) and state school commissioner (1891–1895); in 1895 he was elected president of the state normal school in Athens, where he died on May 15th, 1903. He was buried in Flemington Cemetery, Liberty County, beside his wife, who had died on November 27th, 1898. His lifelong friend Henry Hart Jones described him as a "courtly gentleman" and an "erudite scholar." The present Bradwell Institute High School, Liberty County, was named in his honor.

BRAGG, BRAXTON (1817–1876), Confederate soldier, son of Thomas Bragg and Margaret Crossland, was born in Warrenton, North Carolina, on March 22nd, 1817. He graduated from the United States Military Academy in 1837. Nineteen years later he resigned his commission and settled on a plantation in Louisiana, native state of his wife,

Elisa Brooks Ellis, whom he had married in 1849. At the outbreak of the Civil War he was commissioned brigadier general in the Confederate army and placed in command of the Gulf coast between Mobile and Pensacola. In April 1862, following his success at Shiloh, he was promoted to general, and in June 1862 he assumed command of the Army of Tennessee. In October 1862 he met Buell in Kentucky; in December 1862 he met Rosecrans in Middle Tennessee; in September 1863 he met Rosecrans again at Chickamauga. In each campaign he was energetic but not persistent: he failed to exploit the advantages he had won. On December 2nd, 1863, after much criticism, he surrendered his command to Joseph E. Johnston and withdrew to Richmond, where he was nominally commander in chief but in effect military adviser to President Davis. In May 1865 he accompanied Davis in his flight to Georgia and was captured and paroled. After the war he practiced civil engineering in Mobile, Alabama, and later in Galveston, Texas, where he died suddenly on September 27th, 1876.

BRAILSFORD, WILLIAM (1826–1887), planter and Confederate soldier, son of Daniel Heyward Brailsford (1797–1833) and Jane Martin Leake Spalding, was born in McIntosh County, Georgia, in 1826. He was a grandson of Thomas Spalding (1774–1851), of Sapelo Island, and a nephew of Charles Harris Spalding (1808–1887) and Randolph Spalding (1822–1862). His father, a graduate of Harvard College (1817), was murdered on August 22nd, 1833, by his overseer, John Forbes, allegedly in response to Brailsford's attentions to Forbes's wife. Before the Civil War William Brailsford was one of the wealthiest cotton planters in coastal Georgia; he was also something of a sportsman, and together with James Hamilton Couper, C. A. L. Lamar, and Randolph Spalding he was active in the Savannah Aquatic Club. As the Savannah *Morning News* (July 2nd, 1887) observed, "He was probably the last of his class in Georgia. Money with him was made only to spend, not in his own enjoyment but in contributing to the enjoyment of others. Ready at all times to serve a friend, even at the risk of his life, he was often identified with affairs of honor in the days when men were called upon by public sentiment to recognize the code *duello*." On June 7th, 1861, he enlisted as first lieutenant in the Savannah Mounted Rifles, then encamped at Sunbury; on September 1st, 1861, he succeeded C. A. L. Lamar as captain. On September 6th, 1864, he was captured by the Federals near Murfreesboro, Tennessee, and was confined on Johnson's Island, Ohio, until released on May 30th, 1865. Returning to Georgia, he settled at the Retreat, his plantation in Bryan County, where he died on June 29th, 1887, survived by his natural daughter, Catherine Brailsford, a mulatto servant, to whom he bequeathed all his property. He was buried in the family cemetery at the Retreat.

BRANTLY, WILLIAM THEOPHILUS (1816–1882), Baptist clergyman, son of the Rev. William Theophilus Brantly (1787–1845), distinguished churchman, and Anna McDonald, was born in Beaufort, South Carolina, on May 18th, 1816. His mother, a sister of Charles James McDonald, governor of Georgia (1839–1843), died when the boy was two years old. In 1826 his father became pastor of the First Baptist Church, Philadelphia; the son was thus educated in the North, graduating from Brown University in 1840. He was pastor of the Greene Street Baptist Church, Augusta, Georgia (1840–1848); professor of belles lettres, history, oratory, and the evidences of Christianity at Franklin College (1848–1856); pastor of Tabernacle Baptist Church, Philadelphia (1856–1861); pastor of the Second Baptist Church, Atlanta (1861–1871); and pastor of the Seventh Baptist Church, Baltimore (1871–1882). On September 7th, 1841, in Danville, Virginia, he married Mary Ann Turpin (1824–1866). He died in Baltimore on March 6th, 1882, survived by his second wife, Martha Marston, whom he had married in 1870, and was buried in Greenmount Cemetery. He received the honorary degree of doctor of divinity from Franklin College (Athens) in 1854.

BRECKINRIDGE, JOHN CABELL (1821–1875), statesman, only son of Joseph Cabell Breckinridge and Mary Clay Smith, was born near Lexington, Kentucky, on January 16th, 1821. He graduated from Centre College (Danville, Kentucky) in 1839. After a brief period at the College of New Jersey (Princeton) he returned to Lexington, where he studied law at Transylvania University and commenced practice. During the Mexican War (1846–1848) he was major of the 3rd Regiment Kentucky Volunteers. After one term in the state legislature (1849) he was a member of Congress (1851–1855), where he established his leadership in national politics. He was vice-president of the United States under President James Buchanan (1857–1861). In December 1861, having served nine months in the United States Senate, he returned to Kentucky, where he was appointed brigadier general in the Confederate army. After Shiloh he was promoted to major general and saw service at Vicksburg, Murfreesboro, and Chickamauga. In 1864 he succeeded John Hunt Morgan in command of the Department of Southwest Virginia; he remained in Virginia until President Davis appointed him secretary of war on February 4th, 1865. After Appomattox he made his way to Cuba and thence to Europe; in 1868 he went to Canada, and in March 1869 he returned to Lexington, Kentucky, where he resumed the practice of law. He died in Lexington on May 17th, 1875, and was buried in Lexington Cemetery. He was survived by his wife, Mary Cyrene Burch (1826–1907), whom he had married on December 12th, 1843.

BRENT, WILLIAM (1818–1862), planter and merchant, son of William Brent (1783–1848) and his cousin, Winifred Beale Lee, was born at Richland, his father's plantation on the Potomac River at Aquia Creek, Stafford County, Virginia, in 1818. The Brent family, long settled in Northern Virginia, had been prominent in social and political life since the seventeenth century. William Brent (1783–1848), a graduate of the College of William and Mary (1800), was a member of the Virginia house of delegates (1810–1811). William Brent (1818–1862) married Caroline Matilda Pleasants, daughter of Archibald Pleasants, of Stafford County, in 1841; there were four children. Until 1850 he resided on his plantation in Stafford County, twenty miles south of Alexandria; for many years he was a near neighbor and intimate friend of Charles F. Suttle (1815–1881), also a planter, from whom he hired Anthony Burns, a Negro slave, from 1846 to 1848. In 1850 Brent removed with his family to Richmond, where he entered the grocery commission business; there, acting as agent for Suttle, he hired out Burns to a third party in 1853 and 1854, remitting Burns's wages to Suttle, who was then living in Alexandria. Burns escaped to Boston in the spring of 1854, and his subsequent extradition as a fugitive slave became an international *cause célèbre*. William Brent died of typhoid fever in Richmond on September 20th, 1862, survived by his wife and four children, and was buried in Hollywood Cemetery.

BRITT, WILLIAM JOHN (1834–1908), wheelwright, was born in Greenville, North Carolina, in 1834. In December 1858 he removed to Riceboro, Liberty County, Georgia, where he plied his trade until August 1861, when he enlisted as a private in the Liberty Volunteers (Company H, 25th Regiment Georgia Infantry). Throughout the war he was detailed for special duty at the Macon arsenal. By 1870 he had settled with his family in McIntosh County, where he continued to ply his trade until infirmity and increasing blindness forced him to retire about 1900. He died at Crescent, McIntosh County, on the night of December 29th, 1908. He was thrice married: Mary E. Britt died of typhoid fever in August 1859 after only a few months of marriage; Martha Wallace Britt died of puerperal fever in March 1870; Leonora Britt survived her husband. One of his sons, Jesse Alexander Britt (1864–1939), a Darien merchant, was ordinary of McIntosh County for thirty-five consecutive years.

BROADBENT, SAMUEL (1811–1880), daguerreotypist and photographer, was born in Weathersfield, Connecticut, in 1811. In early manhood, after a brief mercantile career, he evinced a taste for art and undertook portrait and miniature painting with success. Subsequently, through his friend Samuel F. B. Morse, he learned daguerreotypy, which he practiced first in the South, later in Wilmington, Delaware, and finally in Philadelphia, where for thirty years he was prominently known for his energy and skill. By 1870 he was associated in business with Henry C. Phillips (Broadbent & Phillips), and by 1878 with W. Curtis Taylor (Broadbent & Taylor). He died in Philadelphia on July 24th, 1880, and was buried in Mount Moriah Cemetery.

BROADUS, JOHN ALBERT (1827–1895), Baptist clergyman, son of Edmund Broadus, was born in Culpeper County, Virginia, on January 24th, 1827. In 1850 he graduated from the University of Virginia, where he was assistant professor of ancient languages (1851–1853) and university chaplain (1853–1855); he was also pastor of the Baptist church in Charlottesville (1851–1859). In 1859 he was instrumental in founding the Southern Baptist Theological Seminary in Greenville, South Carolina, where he became professor of homiletics and New Testament interpretation; during the Civil War, when the seminary was forced to suspend, he was first secretary of the Baptist Sunday School Board and missionary to Lee's army in Virginia. After the war he resumed his two professorships, removing with the seminary to Louisville, Kentucky, in 1877; in 1888 he was unanimously elected president. He was a profound Greek scholar and New Testament critic, a versatile linguist, an eloquent orator, and a brilliant conversationalist; he published numerous reviews, sermons, textbooks, and exegetical works. He married first (on November 13th, 1850) Maria Carter Harrison, who bore him three daughters; he married second (on January 4th, 1859) Charlotte E. Sinclair, who bore him five children. He died in Louisville, Kentucky, on March 16th, 1895.

BROOKS, JACOB (1805–1875), farmer, was born in Dutchess County, New York, in 1805. In 1853 he removed with his wife Freeborn, his daughter Sarah Ellen, and his two sons Henry T. and Clarke J., both farmers, to Fairfax County, Virginia, where in April 1854 he purchased the farm of John Devereux on Braddock Road a mile and a half from Fairfax Courthouse. There he resided in a century-old house until May 1861, when he fled to the North to escape the hazards of war. Returning to Virginia in 1865, he continued to live on his Fairfax County farm until his death there on September 14th, 1875. He was survived by his wife, his daughter, and one son.

BROOKS, MARY ROGERS (WORSHAM) (1819–1885): *Mrs. Nicholas Beauchel Brooks*, was born in Putnam County, Georgia, on August 7th, 1819. In 1845 she removed with her widowed mother to Milledgeville, where on July 13th, 1848, she married Nicholas Beauchel Brooks (1821–1878), an architect recently arrived from Forsyth County. Of their five children three died in infancy and two, Anna Nicholas Eve Brooks (1855–1950) and Adam Beauchel Brooks (1860–1946), lived to an advanced age. During the Civil War Nicholas Beauchel Brooks remained in Milledgeville, then the state capital, assigned to local defense; in November 1864, at the approach of Sherman, he and several friends fled with the state seal, official papers, and gold to the safety of the swamps near Savannah. After the war he engaged in the grocery business. He died in Milledgeville on June 13th, 1878, and was buried in Memory Hill Cemetery. Mary Rogers (Worsham) Brooks died on November 15th, 1885, and was buried beside her husband.

BROUGHTON, DANIEL J. E. (1829–1868), plantation overseer, son of Daniel S. Broughton and Elizabeth S. Williams, was born in McIntosh County, Georgia, in 1829. After overseeing various plantations in his native county he enlisted as a private in the McIntosh Cavalry (Company K, 5th Regiment Georgia Cavalry) on May 21st, 1862. He served throughout the war. For two years (1866–1867) he managed Montevideo plantation in Liberty County for Mrs. Mary Jones. At first she was "not only satisfied but much pleased." "He appears to know his business, and attends to it," she wrote on February 26th, 1866, "which is saying much for any man." *"So far,"* she continued on March 19th, 1866, "we have never had a manager that in all respects suited me so much." On May 28th, 1866, she described him as "an excellent planter and manager, especially for these times, commanding respect and obedience in a quiet but decided way." But by November 19th, 1867, her attitude had changed: "Although I have furnished everything besides for his support and comfort in health and sickness, and he has really done nothing so far as labor is concerned on the place, he has not the honor or conscience to say he is willing to share in any degree the total loss of the year." And on November 28th, 1867, she added: "I never saw less *true* feeling on the part of a man." He died in Liberty County in the autumn of 1868, survived by a brother, Samuel W. Broughton (1832–1894), a storekeeper in Riceboro, who administered his estate.

BROWN, HENRY WYER (1827–1907), physician, was born in Savannah, Georgia, on October 10th, 1827. After studying at the Mount Zion Academy in Hancock County he attended lectures at the College of Physicians and Surgeons in New York and subsequently graduated from the Medical Department of the University of the City of New York in 1848. For seven years he practiced medicine in Griffin, Georgia; in 1855 he removed to Atlanta, where he helped establish the Atlanta Medical College and served as professor of chemistry and general and descriptive anatomy. From 1861 to 1865, as surgeon in the Confederate army, he superintended military hospitals in Georgia. After the war he settled in Texas, first in Belton County, later in McLennan County. In 1868 he removed to Waco, where he died on November 26th, 1907. He was vice-president of the American Medical Association in 1874 and president of the Texas State Medical Association in 1875.

BROWN, JAMES ALFRED (1828–1893), grocer, son of William Coggeshall Brown and Sallie Kenyon, was born in Peace Dale, Rhode Island, on October 17th, 1828. Leaving school at an early age, he went to Stonington, Connecticut, to work in the butchering business of his elder brother Alanson Brown. Early in the 1850s he removed to Savannah, Georgia, where he established himself as a dry goods merchant and, a few years later, as a wholesale and retail grocer. On August 20th, 1855, he married Lucy Maria Brown, daughter of Pardon Brown and Sarah Sanford, of Newport, Rhode Island. At the outbreak of the Civil War he returned to Newport, where he continued his grocery business until 1888, when he retired, moved his Middletown residence across Newport harbor to Jamestown, and converted it into a summer hotel. He died in Lynn, Massachusetts, on April 12th, 1893, survived by three daughters and a son, and was buried in Newport beside his wife, who had died on April 11th, 1868.

BROWN, JOSEPH EMERSON (1821–1894), lawyer and governor, son of Mackey Brown and Sallie Rice, was born in Pickens District, South Carolina, on April 15th, 1821. In early boyhood he removed with his parents to Union County, Georgia, where he acquired a rudimentary education while working as a day laborer on his father's farm. He graduated from the Yale Law School in 1846 and settled in Canton, Georgia, to practice his profession. On July 13th, 1847, he married Elizabeth Grisham (1826–1896), daughter of the Rev. Joseph Grisham, a Baptist clergyman of West Union, South Carolina. Two years later he was elected state senator, and his political career was launched. He was judge of the superior court (1855–1857); governor of Georgia for four successive terms (1857–1865); chief justice of the state supreme court (1868–1870); and United States senator (1880–1891). From 1870 to 1890 he was president of the Western & Atlantic Railroad; he undertook the mining of coal and iron, invested largely in Atlanta real estate, and accumulated considerable wealth. He died in Atlanta on November 30th, 1894, and was buried in Oakland Cemetery. Elizabeth (Grisham) Brown died on December 26th, 1896, and was buried beside her husband.

BROWN, WILLIAM (1811–1894), Presbyterian clergyman and editor, son of the Rev. Samuel Brown and Mary Moore, was born in Rockbridge County, Virginia, on September 11th, 1811. He graduated from Washington College (Lexington, Virginia) in 1830, and after teaching school for two years he attended Princeton Theological Seminary from 1832 to 1836. For twenty-four years (1836–1860) he was pastor of Augusta Church, Mount Sidney, Virginia. In 1860 he removed to Richmond, where he was editor of *The Central Presbyterian* from 1860 to 1879, when failing eyesight forced him to retire. He spent his later years in Fredericksburg, Virginia (1879–1883) and in Bayview, Florida (1883–1894). He married first (on May 19th, 1836) Elizabeth Hill Smith, of Frederick, Maryland; he married second (on May 15th, 1882) Lucy Gray Wellford, of Fredericksburg, Virginia. He received the honorary degree of doctor of divinity from Hampden-Sydney College in 1857. He died in Bayview, Florida, on April 23rd, 1894.

BROWNE, WILLIAM MONTAGUE (1827–1883), Confederate soldier, was born in County Mayo, Ireland, on July 7th, 1827, son of the Rt. Hon. D. Geoffrey Browne, member of Parliament for thirty-five years. He was educated at Rugby under the famous Dr. Thomas Arnold and later attended Trinity College (Dublin).

After several years in diplomatic service he removed to New York in 1851 and became political editor of the New York *Journal of Commerce*. In 1857, at the request of President James Buchanan, he removed to Washington to become editor in chief of the *Constitution,* organ of the administration. A Southern sympathizer, he was an intimate friend of Howell Cobb of Georgia, then secretary of the treasury, and at the outbreak of the Civil War Browne accompanied Cobb to Georgia and established his residence in Athens. At the convention of seceding states meeting in Montgomery in February 1861 Browne met Jefferson Davis, and a lifelong intimacy began. As aide-de-camp to President Davis, with rank of colonel of cavalry, he remained in Virginia from 1861 to 1864; in April 1864 he succeeded Charles Jenkins Harris as commandant of conscripts for the State of Georgia. After the war he settled in Athens, graduated in law from the University of Georgia in 1866, practiced law briefly, and then returned to planting and journalism. For several years he edited *Farm and Home,* a popular agricultural journal; he was political editor of the Macon *Star* in 1874 when he was elected professor of history and political science at the University of Georgia. He held this chair until his death on April 28th, 1883. He was buried in Oconee Hill Cemetery, Athens.

BRUCE, HORATIO WASHINGTON (1830–1903), lawyer and legislator, son of Alexander Bruce and Amanda Bragg, was born near Vanceburg, Lewis County, Kentucky, on February 22nd, 1830. After three years as a salesman in a general store (1846–1849) he studied law, was admitted to the bar in 1851, and became one of the foremost lawyers in Kentucky. He represented Fleming County in the state legislature (1855–1856). On June 12th, 1856, he married Elizabeth Barbour Helm (1836–1913), daughter of Ex-Governor John Larue Helm and Lucinda Barbour Hardin, of Elizabethtown, Kentucky. In December 1858 he removed to Louisville, where he practiced law in partnership with his brother-in-law, Ben Hardin Helm (1831–1863), until the outbreak of the Civil War. He represented Kentucky in the Confederate Congress (1862–1865). After the war he resumed the practice of law in Louisville. From 1872 to 1880 he was professor of law in the University of Louisville; in 1880 he became chief attorney of the Louisville & Nashville Railroad, a position he held until his death on January 22nd, 1903. He was buried in Cave Hill Cemetery, Louisville. His son, Helm Bruce (1860–1927), the "noble little boy" whom Charles Colcock Jones, Jr., saw in Marietta, Georgia, in July 1862, graduated from Washington and Lee University in 1879 and became, like his father, grandfather, and great-grandfather, one of the foremost lawyers in Kentucky.

BRUMBY, ALEXANDER BREVARD (1831–1879), educator and Confederate soldier, third child of Richard Trapier Brumby (1804–1875) and Mary Isabelle Brevard (1806–1875), was born at the Forge, his mother's ancestral home in Lincoln County, North Carolina, on December 27th, 1831. After a childhood in Tuscaloosa, Alabama, where his father was professor at the University of Alabama, he attended the South Carolina College, where he was a classmate of Charles Colcock Jones, Jr., from 1848 to 1850, and where he graduated both in law and in medicine in 1851. He practiced neither profession, preferring to teach in his own private schools. At the outbreak of the Civil War he enlisted as a private in the Columbia Artillery; from October 1861 to June 1862 he was sergeant major of the 14th Regiment Georgia Infantry; in May 1863 he enlisted as a private in Company B, 3rd (Palmetto) Battalion South Carolina Light Artillery. He was seriously wounded in the last battle of the war, at Fort Tyler, West Point, Georgia, on April 16th, 1865. After the war he established a private school in Marietta, Georgia, where his father had been professor at the Georgia Military Institute since 1856. On April 25th, 1866, he married Ellen Douglas Robarts (1843–1911), third daughter of Joseph William Robarts (1811–1863) and Sophia Louisa Gibson (1814–1847), and granddaughter of Eliza Greene (Low) (Walker) (Robarts) Robarts, with whom she was then living in Atlanta. For the next ten years he conducted schools in Atlanta, Conyers, and Lawrenceville before settling in Athens in 1876; there he died on October 25th, 1879, survived by his wife and six young children. He was buried in Oconee Hill Cemetery. A brilliant scholar, he was addicted to drink and never realized his full potential. Prior to his marriage Mary Eliza Robarts, aunt and guardian of Ellen Douglas Robarts, found in him "everything that was gentlemanly and noble-minded besides warmhearted and affectionate," and hoped that he would "make Ellen a devoted husband" and "make his mark in the literary world." But three years later, on April 30th, 1869, she confided to a cousin that "the trials I have had from him have told on my health, my nervous system, and my spirits."

BRUMBY, ARNOLDUS VANDERHORST (1808–1877), educator and Confederate soldier, younger son of Thomas Brumby (1764–1811) and Susannah Greening (1774–1842), was born in Sumter District, South Carolina, on December 12th, 1808. He graduated from the United States Military Academy in 1835. After serving in the Seminole War he resigned from the army in 1836; practiced civil engineering in Alabama (1836–1838); served as tutor in mathematics and instructor in civil engineering at the University of Alabama (1838–1840); practiced law in Alabama (1840–1846); and superintended the Alabama Military Institute (1846–1849). In 1851, after a brief return to Sumter, South Carolina, he founded the Georgia Military Institute (Marietta) and became its first superintendent; in 1859 he resigned his post and took up planting and manufacturing. Meanwhile he was ruling elder of the Marietta Presbyterian Church (1854–1867) and aide-de-camp, with rank of colonel, to Governor Howell Cobb (1851–1853) and to Governor Herschel V. Johnson (1853–1857). From July 17th, 1861, to November 21st, 1861, he was colonel of the 14th Regiment Georgia Infantry. In 1867 he removed to Atlanta. He died in Cartersville, Georgia, on November 2nd, 1887.

BRUMBY, MARY BREVARD (1867–1940), eldest child of Alexander Brevard Brumby (1831–1879) and Ellen Douglas Robarts (1843–1911), was born in Atlanta, Georgia, on January 28th, 1867. In early childhood she lived successively in Atlanta, Conyers, Lawrenceville, and Athens, where her father conducted private schools. She completed her education in Athens and taught in the public schools there until her marriage (at the home of her aunt, Mary Sophia Robarts, wife of Theodore Dwight Adams, in Roswell, Georgia, on June 29th, 1893) to William Henry Quarterman (1867–1934), son of Dr. Keith Axson Quarterman (1838–1900) and Helen Louisa Jones (1841–1911), half-sister of Mrs. Mary Jones. Her husband, a graduate of the University of Georgia (A.B. 1888, LL.B. 1890), was a prominent lawyer and judge in Winder, Georgia, for forty years. After his death on January 8th, 1934, she removed to Atlanta, where she died on April 7th, 1940, survived by three children. She was buried beside her husband in Rose Hill Cemetery, Winder.

BRUMBY, RICHARD TRAPIER (1804–1875), educator and scientist, elder son of Thomas Brumby (1764–1811) and Susannah Greening (1774–1842), was born in Sumter District, South Carolina, on August 4th, 1804. He graduated from the South Carolina College with first honor in 1824. After studying law under the Hon. William Campbell Preston he practiced as Preston's partner for six years. On April 22nd, 1828, he married Mary Isabelle Brevard (1806–1875), daughter of Alexander Brevard, of Lincoln County, North Carolina; there were twelve children. In 1831 he removed to Montgomery, Alabama, and thence to Tuscaloosa, where he edited *The Expositor,* a nullification journal. From 1834 to 1849 he was professor of chemistry, mineralogy, and geology at the University of Alabama; from 1849 to 1856 he occupied a similar post at the South Carolina College. During his academic years he assembled and catalogued a remarkable collection of minerals, rocks, fossils, and shells, said to be one of the most complete and valuable of its kind, now preserved at Davidson College. Forced by ill health to retire, he removed in 1856 to Marietta, Georgia, where his younger brother, Arnoldus Vanderhorst Brumby (1808–1877), was then superintendent of the Georgia Military Institute. He was an ardent secessionist; although too feeble for active service in the Civil War, he enlisted in a company for home defense; and all three of his sons, the youngest but fifteen years old, fought at the front. During his long residence in Marietta (1856–1873) he was active in the affairs of the Presbyterian church; on December 4th, 1865, he was unanimously elected elder, a position he held until 1873, when he removed

to Athens. He died in Athens on October 5th, 1875; his wife died the following day; they were buried in the same grave in Oconee Hill Cemetery. His son, Alexander Brevard Brumby (1831–1879), married Ellen Douglas Robarts (1843–1911), granddaughter of Eliza Greene (Low) (Walker) (Robarts) Robarts, of Marietta, on April 25th, 1866.

BRUNNER, ISAAC (1801–1874), plasterer, was born in Alexandria, Virginia, in December 1801. In early youth he removed to Beaufort, South Carolina, and thence in 1852 to Savannah, Georgia, where in association with his son Valentine Brunner (1826–1900) he prospered in the construction business and participated actively in civic affairs, serving variously as alderman, city councilman, and clerk of the market. He died in Savannah on March 18th, 1874, survived by his second wife and eight children, and was buried beside his first wife in Laurel Grove Cemetery. According to the Savannah *Morning News* (March 19th, 1874), "Mr. Brunner was a modest, unassuming gentleman of unimpeachable integrity, and in every respect a most worthy and exemplary citizen."

BRYAN, JOSEPH (1812–1863), navy purser, police chief, and real estate broker, younger son of Joseph Bryan (1773–1812) and Delia Forman, was born in Chatham County, Georgia, on January 25th, 1812. From 1836 to 1853 he was purser in the United States navy, spending most of his time at sea; during the Mexican War (1846–1848) he served in the Gulf squadron and participated in the siege of Vera Cruz. Retiring from the navy in 1853 with rank of lieutenant, he returned to Savannah, where in June 1854 he was appointed chief of the newly organized mounted police. According to the Savannah *Republican* (December 18th, 1863), "he brought the system to perfection, and organized an institution which gave unexampled security to the lives and property of his fellow citizens." In 1857 he resigned his post and entered the brokerage business, in which he continued until "an excruciating and incurable malady" forced him several years later to retire. He died in Savannah on December 5th, 1863, and was buried in Bonaventure Cemetery. He was survived by his wife, Jane Bourke (1812–1892), whom he had married on December 10th, 1834, and four children. As the Savannah *Republican* (December 18th, 1863) observed, "In the death of Captain Bryan Savannah has lost an active and useful citizen, society one of its rarest ornaments, and his family a friend whose affection can never be replaced. A man of the nicest honor, he was one whom a large number of the young selected as their guide and example in life."

BRYCE, CAMPBELL ROBERT (1817–1867), planter, son of John Bryce (1789–1855) and Sarah F. Campbell (1795–1872), was born in Columbia, South Carolina, on October 6th, 1817. His father, a native of Glasgow, Scotland, had migrated to South Carolina in early boyhood; at the time of his death on November 24th, 1855, he had been a resident of Columbia for more than fifty years. Campbell Robert Bryce graduated from the South Carolina College in 1837. In 1841 he married Sarah Margaret Henry (1824–1901), daughter of William D. Henry, of Yorke, South Carolina; there were two sons and six daughters. During the Civil War his wife was active in hospital work, and in 1862 she was one of the founders of the Wayside Hospital for sick and wounded soldiers. Campbell Robert Bryce died suddenly in New York City on August 14th, 1867, having just returned from Brazil, and was buried in the First Presbyterian Churchyard, Columbia. Sarah Margaret (Henry) Bryce died in Philadelphia on February 15th, 1901, and was buried beside her husband.

BRYSON, JOHN HENRY (1831–1897), Presbyterian clergyman, son of the Rev. Henry B. Bryson, was born in Fayetteville, Tennessee, on April 3rd, 1831. After attending Erskine Theological Seminary in South Carolina and Newburgh Theological Seminary in New York he was ordained in 1855. During the Civil War he served as chaplain of the 9th Regiment Kentucky Mounted Infantry, devoting much time to hospital work in the Atlanta area. In 1863 and 1864 he was regularly stationed in Marietta, where on many occasions he rendered essential service to the family of Mrs. Eliza G. Robarts, doing (as Mary Eliza Robarts wrote) "all that a brother or son could do." After the war he was pastor in Shelbyville, Tennessee (1867–1872), and, following a year's study at the University of Virginia, pastor of the First Presbyterian Church, Columbia, South Carolina (1873–1876). From 1877 to 1881 he traveled and studied in the Holy Land; returning to America, he was pastor in Huntsville, Alabama (1881–1896). He died in Shelbyville, Tennessee on February 1st, 1897, and was buried in Maple Hill Cemetery, Huntsville.

BUCHANAN, JAMES (1791–1868), fifteenth president of the United States, son of James Buchanan (1761–1821) and Elizabeth Speer (1767–1833), was born near Mercersburg, Pennsylvania, on April 23rd, 1791. He graduated from Dickinson College in 1809 and was admitted to the bar in 1812. He was a member of the state house of representatives (1814–1815); a member of Congress (1821–1831); United States minister to Russia (1832–1834); United States senator (1834–1845); secretary of state under President James Knox Polk (1845–1849); and United States minister to Great Britain (1853–1856). Returning to America in April 1856, he was nominated by the Democrats as compromise candidate for President against John C. Frémont (Republican) and Millard Fillmore (American, or "Know-Nothing"). Buchanan's term as President (1857–1861) ended with the outbreak of the Civil War. He opposed slavery as morally wrong, but he recognized the duty of the Federal government to protect slavery where it existed. When Lincoln was elected President in November 1860, Buchanan exerted his personal influence to effect a peaceful settlement between the North and the South; but with

the secession of the Southern states and the resignation of the Southern members of his cabinet his administration disintegrated. After Fort Sumter he wrote (April 19th, 1861): "The present administration had no alternative but accept the war instigated by South Carolina or the Southern Confederacy. The North will sustain the administration almost to a man; and it ought to be sustained at all hazards." In 1861 he retired to Wheatland, his country estate near Lancaster, Pennsylvania, where he died unmarried on June 1st, 1868. He was buried in Woodward Hill Cemetery, Lancaster.

BUCHANAN, JOHN MILLICAN (1821–1903), lawyer and planter, eldest son of John Buchanan (1790–1862) and Harriet Yongue (1791–1875), was born in Winnsboro, South Carolina, on February 12th, 1821. His father, a graduate of the South Carolina College (1811) and for many years a trustee, was a prominent lawyer known for his scholarly attainments and support of higher education; during the War of 1812 he was promoted to major general. After preparing at the Mount Zion Institute, Winnsboro, John Millican Buchanan graduated from the South Carolina College in 1842 and returned to Winnsboro to read law in his father's office. On September 20th, 1849, in Orangeburg, South Carolina, he married Eugenia M. Felder (1822–1898), niece of the Hon. John Myers Felder (1782–1851), congressman from South Carolina (1831–1835). In 1862, following the death of his father, he purchased a plantation in Alabama on the Coosa River some thirty miles southwest of Rome, Georgia. After the Civil War he refused to take the oath of allegiance to the United States government; in 1867 he removed with his family to Chapel Hill, Washington County, Texas. He died there on April 14th, 1903, survived by five sons and one daughter, and was buried beside his wife in the Masonic graveyard one mile north of Chapel Hill and nine miles southeast of Brenham. He was christened John Millican Buchanan, but the name on his tombstone is John Madison Buchanan. His sister, Ann Buchanan (1827–1877), became the wife of the Rev. Edward Porter Palmer in November 1850; his brother, William Creighton Buchanan (1831–1862), adjutant of Company C, 12th Regiment South Carolina Infantry, was killed at Second Manassas on September 1st, 1862. One of his sons, James Paul Buchanan (1867–1937), was congressman from Texas (1913–1937); the Buchanan Dam in the Colorado River in Burnet County, Texas, was named in his honor.

BUELL, DON CARLOS (1818–1898), Union soldier, son of Salmon D. Buell and Eliza Buell, was born near Marietta, Ohio, on March 23rd, 1818. He graduated from the United States Military Academy in 1841. He fought in the Seminole War and the Mexican War, and at the outbreak of the Civil War he was lieutenant colonel in the adjutant general's department. He subsequently became brigadier general of volunteers (May 17th, 1861) and major general of volunteers (March 21st, 1862). After aiding in organizing the Army of the Potomac he was sent to Kentucky in November 1861 to assume command of the Army of the Ohio. In the spring of 1862 he supported Grant at Shiloh; in the summer he advanced toward Chattanooga but was stopped by Morgan; in the autumn he met Bragg in Kentucky at the indecisive battle of Perryville. Buell's failure to pursue Bragg led the Washington authorities to relieve him of command; following an official investigation he resigned his regular commission on June 1st, 1864. After the war he settled in Kentucky, where he engaged in mining and served (1885–1889) as pension agent in Louisville. He died near Rockport, Kentucky, on November 19th, 1898.

BUIST, EDWARD TONGÉ (1809–1877), Presbyterian clergyman, son of the Rev. George Buist and Mary Somers, was born in Charleston, South Carolina, on March 1st, 1809. He attended Princeton Theological Seminary from 1828 to 1831 but did not graduate. After serving as pastor of various churches in South Carolina he was president of Laurens Female Seminary (1857–1861); the remainder of his life he spent in Greenville, South Carolina, where he was pastor of the Washington Street Church (1862–1877). He married first (on December 18th, 1832) Margaret Robinson, of Charleston; he married second (on July 8th, 1841) Mrs. Emma H. Lowndes, of Greenville; he married third (on May 23rd, 1867) Flora McNeill, of Greenville. He died in Greenville on November 10th, 1877, survived by his third wife and three young children, and was buried in Springwood Cemetery.

BUKER, EDWARD W. (1818–1864), commission merchant, was born in Gorham, Maine, in 1818. In early manhood he migrated to Savannah, Georgia, where he engaged in mercantile pursuits and where, on November 14th, 1844, he married Mary Ann Thompson, a native of Nottinghamshire, England. For many years he was a prominent member of the Masonic fraternity. He was also captain of the 1st Regiment Georgia Militia; in April 1859 he was elected lieutenant colonel, a post he continued to hold during the early months of the war. After a protracted illness he died in Savannah on January 16th, 1864, survived by his wife and one daughter, and was buried in Laurel Grove Cemetery.

BULLOCH, ANNA LOUISA (1833–1893), eldest child of James Stephens Bulloch (1793–1849) and his second wife, Martha Stewart (1799–1864), widow of the Hon. John Elliott, was born in Savannah, Georgia, on September 15th, 1833. Through her mother she was a granddaughter of General Daniel Stewart (1761–1829), Revolutionary hero of Liberty County, and through her father she was a great-granddaughter of Archibald Bulloch (1730–1777), first president of the provincial congress of Georgia. In 1840 she removed with her parents to Roswell, Georgia, where her father died on February 18th, 1849, leaving a widow, two daughters, and a son. After the

marriage of her sister, Martha (Mittie) Bulloch, to Theodore Roosevelt, of New York, on December 22nd, 1853, her mother sold her Roswell house and removed to Philadelphia with her daughter Anna and her son Irvine to live in the household of Susan Ann Elliott, wife of Dr. Hilborne West, eldest daughter of Mrs. Bulloch by her first husband. It was in Philadelphia that Anna Bulloch met Sue Dickson and Mary Jones Taylor, schoolmates of Mary Sharpe Jones at the seminary of the Misses Gill. In 1856 Mrs. Bulloch and her two children joined the Roosevelt household at 28 East 20th Street, New York City, where Theodore Roosevelt, twenty-sixth president of the United States and nephew of Anna Bulloch, was born on October 27th, 1858. In his *Autobiography* (1913) President Roosevelt recalled his childhood: "My Aunt Anna, my mother's sister, lived with us. She was as devoted to us children as was my mother herself, and we were equally devoted to her in return. She taught us our lessons while we were little. She and my mother used to entertain us by the hour with tales of life on the Georgia plantations." On June 5th, 1866, in her thirty-third year, Anna Bulloch became the wife of James King Gracie (1840–1903), a New York investment broker seven years her junior. She died at Gracewood, their summer home on Oyster Bay, Long Island, on June 9th, 1893, and was buried in Greenwood Cemetery, Brooklyn. James King Gracie died in his town house, 15 East 48th Street, New York City, on November 23rd, 1903, and was buried beside his wife.

BULLOCH, IRVINE STEPHENS (1842–1898), Confederate midshipman and cotton broker, youngest child and only son of James Stephens Bulloch (1793–1849) and his second wife, Martha Stewart (1799–1864), widow of the Hon. John Elliott, was born in Roswell, Georgia, in 1842. Through his mother he was a grandson of General Daniel Stewart (1761–1829), Revolutionary hero of Liberty County, and through his father he was a great-grandson of Archibald Bulloch (1730–1777), first president of the provincial congress of Georgia. His father died on February 18th, 1849, leaving a widow, two daughters, and a son. After the marriage of his sister, Martha (Mittie) Bulloch, to Theodore Roosevelt, of New York, on December 22nd, 1853, his mother sold her Roswell house and removed to Philadelphia with her daughter Anna and her son Irvine to live in the household of Susan Ann Elliott, wife of Dr. Hilborne West, eldest daughter of Mrs. Bulloch by her first husband. In 1856 Mrs. Bulloch and her two children joined the Roosevelt household at 28 East 20th Street, New York City, where Theodore Roosevelt, twenty-sixth president of the United States and nephew of Irvine Bulloch, was born on October 27th, 1858. At the outbreak of the Civil War Irvine Bulloch returned to Georgia, where on August 29th, 1861, he became a midshipman in the Confederate navy. He fired the last gun discharged from the Confederate cruiser *Alabama* before she was sunk on June 19th, 1864, in the harbor of Cherbourg, France, after a naval duel with the United States corvette *Kearsage*. He was subsequently navigating lieutenant of the Confederate steamer *Shenandoah* on her predatory cruise among the whalers in Bering Strait. After the war he settled in Liverpool, England, where he was for many years a cotton broker, and where (in November 1873) he married Ella Clitz Sears (1849–1911), daughter of Henry Beaufort Sears and Harriet Louisa Clitz, Americans living in England. He died in Liverpool on July 14th, 1898, and was buried in Toxteth Park Cemetery. Ella Clitz (Sears) Bulloch died on April 20th, 1911, and was buried beside her husband.

BULLOCH, JAMES DUNWODY (1823–1901), naval officer and Confederate agent, only son of James Stephens Bulloch (1793–1849) and his first wife, Esther Amarintha Elliott, daughter of the Hon. John Elliott, was born near Savannah, Georgia, on June 25th, 1823. Through his father he was a great-grandson of Archibald Bulloch (1730–1777), first president of the provincial congress of Georgia. In 1839 he entered the United States navy as a midshipman; in 1854 he resigned as a lieutenant and entered private mail service in New York. At the outbreak of the Civil War he returned to Georgia, where he was immediately appointed naval agent of the Confederate States, with rank of commander, and sent abroad with almost unlimited powers to buy or build ships and equip them. The story of his wartime struggle with the governments of England and France is recounted in his book, *The Secret Service of the Confederate States in Europe* (1884). After the war he settled in Liverpool, England, where he lived a retired life for thirty-five years, engaged in shipping cotton. He married first (in 1851) Elizabeth Euphemia Caskie, daughter of John Caskie, of Richmond, Virginia; he married second (in 1857) Harriott Cross, daughter of General Osborne Cross, of Maryland, and widow of Joseph Foster. He died in Liverpool on January 7th, 1901, and was buried in Toxteth Park Cemetery beside his second wife, who had died on July 3rd, 1897. His half-nephew, President Theodore Roosevelt, son of his half-sister, Martha (Mittie) Bulloch, recalled his "Uncle Jimmy" in his *Autobiography* (1913): "Uncle Jimmy Bulloch was a dear old retired sea captain, utterly unable to 'get on' in the worldly sense of that phrase, as valiant and simple and upright a soul as ever lived, a veritable Colonel Newcome."

BULLOCH, MARTHA (STEWART) (ELLIOTT) (1799–1864): *Mrs. James Stephens Bulloch,* daughter of General Daniel Stewart (1761–1829) and Susannah Oswald, was born in Liberty County, Georgia, in March 1799. Her father had joined the Revolutionary army at the age of fifteen; after the Revolution he had been made a brigadier general in recognition of his service in the Indian Wars; and for many years he had represented Liberty County in the state legislature. Martha Stewart was christened "Patsy" in Midway Church on August 15th, 1799. On January 6th, 1818, she became the second wife of the Hon. John Elliott (1773–1827), United States senator from Georgia (1819–1825); three of their five children survived infancy: Susan Ann Elliott (1820–1895), Georgia Ann Elliott (1822–1848), and Daniel Stewart Elliott (1826–1862). On May 8th, 1832, she became the second wife of James Stephens Bulloch (1793–1849); three of their four children survived infancy: Anna Louisa Bulloch (1833–1893), Martha (Mittie) Bulloch (1834–1884), and Irvine Stephens Bulloch (1842–1898). James Stephens Bulloch was deputy collector of the port of Savannah, major of the Chatham Battalion, president of the Savannah branch of the United States Bank, and a director of the company under whose auspices the steamship *Savannah* was the first vessel to cross the Atlantic Ocean on her own steam (1819). In 1840 he removed with his family to Roswell, Georgia, where he built Bulloch Hall, participated actively in the affairs of the Presbyterian church, and died on February 18th, 1849. A month earlier, on January 25th, 1849, Susan Ann Elliott, eldest daughter of Mrs. Bulloch by her first husband, had become the wife of Dr. Hilborne West (1818–1907), of Philadelphia; on December 22nd, 1853, Martha (Mittie) Bulloch, second daughter of Mrs. Bulloch by her second husband, became the wife of Theodore Roosevelt (1831–1878), of New York. In October 1854, having sold her Roswell house, she removed with her daughter Anna and her son Irvine to join the Philadelphia household of the Wests; two years later she removed with her daughter and son to join the New York household of the Roosevelts. There, on October 27th, 1858, she attended the birth of her grandson, Theodore Roosevelt (1858–1919), twenty-sixth president of the United States, who recalled her thus in his *Autobiography* (1913): "My grandmother, one of the dearest of old ladies, lived with us, and was distinctly overindulgent to us children, being quite unable to harden her heart towards us even when the occasion demanded it." At the outbreak of the Civil War she remained in the North; as her lifelong friend, Mrs. Eliza G. Robarts, wrote on May 20th, 1861, "Mrs. Bulloch says she is true to the South, but her daughters have both married Northern gentlemen, and she is obliged to stay where they are. The gentlemen, I hear, say they will not fight against the South." She died in Madison, New Jersey, on October 30th, 1864, and was buried in Greenwood Cemetery, Brooklyn.

BULLOCH, WILLIAM GASTON (1815–1885), physician, son of John Irvine Bulloch and Charlotte Glen, was born in Savannah, Georgia, on August 3rd, 1815. He was a great-grandson of Archibald Bulloch (1730–1777), first president of the provincial congress of Georgia. He graduated from Yale College in 1835 and from the Medical College of the University of Pennsylvania in 1838. After studying surgery in Paris for eighteen months he returned to Savannah in 1840 and commenced practice. For many years he was one of the most distinguished physicians and surgeons in Georgia. In 1852 he was one of eight founders of the Savannah Medical College, and he was for some years its professor of surgery. He was at one time president of the Georgia Medical Society. During the Civil War he served as surgeon, with rank of major, in Richmond; as member of the medical examining board in Charleston; and as superintendent of the Broughton Street Hospital in Savannah. He was also active in municipal affairs, serving from time to time as alderman and city councilman. On November 6th, 1851, he married Mary Eliza Adams Lewis (1828–1902), daughter of John Lewis and his second wife, Margaret (Adams) King, of Savannah; there were six children. He died in Savannah on June 23rd, 1885, and was buried in Laurel Grove Cemetery. Mary Eliza Adams (Lewis) Bulloch died on December 17th, 1902, and was buried beside her husband.

BURNS, ANTHONY (1834–1862), Negro slave, was born in Stafford County, Virginia, on May 31st, 1834. From 1846 to 1848 he was hired out by his owner, Charles F. Suttle (1815–1881), of Stafford County, to William Brent (1818–1862), also of Stafford County. In 1853 he was hired out to a third party by Brent, then living in Richmond and acting as agent for Suttle, to whom Brent remitted Burns's wages. Late in March 1854 Burns escaped to Boston, where he lived undetected until his arrest on the evening of May 24th, 1854. His subsequent extradition as a fugitive slave became an international *cause célèbre*. The Fugitive Slave Act of 1850, enabling owners of runaway slaves to secure their property wherever found within the borders of the United States, was upheld and enforced; but the conscience of the North was stirred, and the law was not tested again. As the Richmond *Whig* observed, "We rejoice at the recapture of Burns, but a few more such victories and the South is undone." Soon after Burns was remanded to his owner, Suttle sold him to a North Carolina planter, from whom he was purchased with money raised by the Twelfth Baptist Church, Boston, of which Burns had been a member. In 1855 he secured a scholarship to Oberlin College, where he studied from 1855 to 1856 and again from 1857 to 1862. Early in 1862 he became pastor of Zion Baptist Church, St. Catharines, Ontario, where he died of consumption on July 27th, 1862. He was buried in the local cemetery. A contemporary clergyman, the Rev. R. A. Ball, observed that "He was a fine-looking man, tall and broad-shouldered, but with a slight stoop, indicating a weak chest. His color was light brown. He was a fine speaker, and was considered to be well educated. He was unmarried, and very popular with both the white people and the people of his own race" [Fred Landon, "Anthony Burns in Canada," *Ontario Historical Society Papers and Records*, XXII

(1925), 165]. A flood of pamphlets, booklets, sermons, and poems, most of them sentimental and impassioned, commemorated Burns's trial in 1854. *Anthony Burns: A History*, by Charles Emery Stevens (Boston, 1856), is said to have aided Burns in financing his education at Oberlin.

BURNSIDE, AMBROSE EVERETT (1824–1881), Union soldier, son of Edgehill Burnside and Pamelia Brown, was born in Liberty, Indiana, on May 23rd, 1824. He graduated from the United States Military Academy in 1847. On April 27th, 1852, he married Mary Richmond Bishop, of Providence, Rhode Island. At the outbreak of the Civil War he organized the 1st Regiment Rhode Island Volunteer Infantry and was its colonel at Manassas. He was commissioned brigadier general on August 6th, 1861, and after a successful naval expedition off the coast of North Carolina he was commissioned major general on March 18th, 1862. He fought at Sharpsburg and Fredericksburg, and on September 2nd, 1863, having been assigned to command the Army of the Ohio, he entered Knoxville. Returning to the east in 1864, he commanded the Ninth Corps at the Wilderness, Spottsylvania, and Cold Harbor. At Petersburg the Ninth Corps lost heavily in killed, wounded, and captured, and a military court of inquiry blamed Burnside, who shortly thereafter took leave and subsequently resigned his commission. After the war he was governor of Rhode Island (1866–1869) and United States senator (1875–1881). He died in Bristol, Rhode Island, on September 13th, 1881, and was buried in Swan Point Cemetery.

BURROUGHS, WILLIAM HOWE (1805–1885), commission merchant, son of Benjamin Burroughs (1779–1837) and Catherine Eirick, was born in Savannah, Georgia, in 1805. His father, a native of Newtown, Long Island, New York, had settled in Savannah in 1796 and prospered in the cotton and commission business; with his partner, Oliver Sturges, he had owned a third interest in the steamship *Savannah*, which in 1819 was the first vessel to cross the Atlantic Ocean on her own steam. William Howe Burroughs was educated in the North; upon his return to Savannah he read law in the office of the Hon. James Moore Wayne. After a brief period in Florida, where he was a successful planter, he settled in Savannah and followed mercantile pursuits until failing health forced him to retire. He died in Savannah on March 19th, 1885, survived by his wife, Ann A. McLeod (1811–1886), and was buried in Laurel Grove Cemetery. His sister, Elizabeth Reid Burroughs (1812–1884), became the second wife of Dr. John Stevens Law (1800–1877) on November 24th, 1831.

BUSBY, BARTHOLOMEW AUSTIN (1788–1862), planter, was born in Orangeburg District, South Carolina, on August 10th, 1788. In early manhood, already a wealthy landowner with more than a hundred slaves, he migrated to Liberty County, Georgia, and settled at Melon Bluff, a plantation on the north bank of the North Newport River, a short distance below Montevideo, later the plantation of the Rev. Dr. Charles Colcock Jones. He was active in county affairs: in 1822 he joined the Liberty Independent Troop; in 1834 he represented Liberty County in the state legislature; in 1856 he was president of the Liberty County Agricultural Society. On November 14th, 1839, at the age of fifty-one, he married Mary Emeline Mallard (born 1813), eldest daughter of Thomas Mallard (1778–1861) and his second wife, Rebecca Eliza (Burnley) Baker (1789–1861), and elder sister of the Rev. R. Q. Mallard; three of their four daughters lived to maturity. When the village of Dorchester was established in 1843, he became one of its first settlers; his widow was one of fourteen "incorporating members" of the Dorchester Presbyterian Church at its organization in 1871. In the autumn of 1862, fearing Yankee raids, he removed with his family from Dorchester to Taylor's Creek in the upper part of Liberty County. He died there of "typhoid pneumonia" on December 1st, 1862, having resided in Liberty County for more than fifty years, and was buried in Midway Cemetery. To his neighbor, the Rev. Dr. Charles Colcock Jones, Busby was "a warm personal friend whose loss I sincerely regret." The Rev. Thomas Sumner Winn, reminiscing in 1878 of former days in Dorchester, recalled affectionately "the somewhat blunt but straightforward sincerity and candor of old man Busby."

BUTLER, BENJAMIN FRANKLIN (1818–1893), lawyer, Union soldier, congressman, and governor, son of John Butler and Charlotte Ellison, was born in Deerfield, New Hampshire, on November 5th, 1818. His father died in 1828, and his mother removed to Lowell, Massachusetts, where she ran a factory boardinghouse. After graduating from Waterville (now Colby) College in 1838 he taught school, studied law, and commenced practice in Lowell in 1840. On May 16th, 1844, he married Sarah Hildreth, of Lowell. He was a member of the state house of representatives (1853) and the state senate (1859). On April 17th, 1861, he entered the Union army as a brigadier general; on May 16th, 1861, he was promoted to major general and placed in command of the Department of Eastern Virginia. In the spring of 1862 he headed the land forces accompanying Farragut's expedition against New Orleans. He entered the city on May 1st, 1862, and for eight months ruled it with a high hand. His sensational Order No. 28 provoked a storm of indignation not only in the Confederacy but throughout Europe: "When any female shall, by word or gesture or movement, insult or show contempt for any officer or soldier of the United States, she shall be regarded and held liable to be treated as a woman of the town plying her avocation." Learning of this "infamous proclamation," Charles Colcock Jones, Jr., wrote from Savannah, Georgia, on May 20th, 1862: "How any woman, child, or intelligent Negro can permit the monster to live an hour I cannot understand. . . . If a private Roman citizen could devote his life—and that

without a single hesitation—to the destruction of a hated tyrant, what shall we say of the citizens of New Orleans if such a wretch is permitted to have his being for a short hour in the public streets of the Crescent City? *Quem Deus vult perdere prius dementat.* I trust that quick and certain destruction awaits this vile madman." "Beast Butler" was removed on December 16th, 1862, and placed in command of the Army of the James. After the war he was a member of Congress (1867–1875; 1877–1879) and governor of Massachusetts (1883–1884). He died in Washington, D.C., on January 11th, 1893, and was buried in the Hildreth Cemetery, Lowell, Massachusetts.

BUTLER, JESSE (1812–1880), farmer, son of John Butler, was born in Georgia in 1812. On June 29th, 1836, he married a widow twelve years his senior, Mrs. Margaret R. Mikell. She was the mother of five children, two by her first husband and three by her second. Butler lived near Flemington; although poor, he was "a reliable man," as the Rev. Dr. Charles Colcock Jones observed in January 1863 when engaging him to superintend a party of Negroes traveling overland to Burke County. He died in Liberty County in 1880 and like many Butlers was buried in an unmarked grave in Taylor's Creek Cemetery.

BUTLER, WORTHINGTON CHAUNCEY (1812–1887), shoe merchant, was born in Connecticut on January 28th, 1812. In early manhood he removed to Savannah, Georgia, where he established himself in the shoe business and resided for the rest of his life. By 1850 he was associated with W. H. S. Verstille and Matthew Lufburrow in the firm of Verstille, Lufburrow & Butler, Savannah's leading shoe house. Several years later Lufburrow established his own store, leaving the firm of Verstille & Butler. When Verstille migrated to Texas in 1855 Butler joined George Smith Frierson in the firm of Butler & Frierson, which was dissolved at Frierson's death in 1862. After the war Butler continued the business alone until advancing age caused him to retire. He died in Savannah on December 14th, 1887, and was buried in Laurel Grove Cemetery beside his wife, Elizabeth Miller (1820–1886), a native of Rothesay, Island of Bute, Scotland.

BUTTOLPH, CHARLES EDWARD MAXWELL (1857–1858), eldest child of the Rev. David Lyman Buttolph (1822–1905), a Presbyterian clergyman, and Laura Elizabeth Maxwell (1824–1903), was born in Savannah, Georgia, on March 21st, 1857. An account of his birth appears in a letter written by Mary Eliza Robarts the following day: "The baby is really a fine large infant—a sturdy Scotch Presbyterian, a ruddy complexion, and a real Maxwell." He was named for his maternal uncle, Charles Edward Maxwell (1826–1852), who had died suddenly in Morristown, New Jersey, on April 3rd, 1852, while a student at the Medical College of the University of Pennsylvania. He was baptized in Midway Church on Sunday afternoon, November 22nd, 1857, by his great-uncle, the Rev. Dr. Charles Colcock Jones. On Saturday, May 15th, 1858, he took a severe cold; the next day he grew much worse; late in the evening he was taken with convulsions, which terminated in his death early in the morning of May 17th, 1858. He was buried in Midway Cemetery. Returning from the funeral, the Rev. Dr. Charles Colcock Jones wrote in his journal: "I never knew a child to receive more affection and unceasing care and attention and more the devotion of the whole family and household than he did in his own immediate family! He was an uncommonly fine child, just fourteen months old!"

BUTTOLPH, DAVID (1779–1868), lawyer, was born in North East Township, Dutchess County, New York, on October 28th, 1779. He graduated from Williams College in 1803. After studying law in Poughkeepsie, New York, he removed in 1808 to Norwich, where he successfully practiced law for some thirty years. In May 1818 he married Urania Lyman (1792–1827), of Middlefield, Connecticut; two of their five children lived to maturity: David Lyman Buttolph (1822–1905) and Jane Buttolph (1827–1875). Urania (Lyman) Buttolph died on April 3rd, 1827; David Buttolph soon married Esther Kelso (1783–1859), widow of Joseph Kelso. In 1838 he retired to a small farm a mile or so above Norwich, where he engaged in agricultural pursuits until 1867, when he joined the household of his son in Marietta, Georgia. He died in Marietta on July 27th, 1868, and was buried in Citizens Cemetery.

BUTTOLPH, DAVID LYMAN (1822–1905), Presbyterian clergyman, son of David Buttolph (1779–1868) and his first wife, Urania Lyman (1792–1827), was born in Norwich, New York, on December 24th, 1822. His mother was a cousin of the Rev. Dr. Lyman Beecher (1775–1863), father of Harriet (Beecher) Stowe (1811–1896) and the Rev. Henry Ward Beecher (1813–1887); she died on April 3rd, 1827, when David was four years old, and his father soon married Esther Kelso (1783–1859), widow of Joseph Kelso. David Lyman Buttolph graduated from Williams College in 1845; after conducting a private school in Bluffton, South Carolina, for one year, and a seminary for young ladies in Charleston for three years, he entered Columbia Theological Seminary in 1849 and graduated in 1852. For two years he served as assistant to the Rev. Dr. Thomas Smyth, pastor of the Second Presbyterian Church, Charleston; in July 1854 he became pastor of Midway Church, Liberty County, Georgia, where he continued until the dissolution of the church in November 1867. On June 10th, 1856, he married Laura Elizabeth Maxwell (1824–1903), daughter of James Audley Maxwell (1796–1828) and Susan Mary Jones (1803–1890), and niece of the Rev. Dr. Charles Colcock Jones, of Liberty County. There were five children: Charles Edward Maxwell Buttolph (1857–1858), James David Buttolph (1858–1939), William Smyth

Buttolph (1861–1896), Susan Mary Buttolph (1863–1913), and Wallace Stewart Buttolph (1867–1899). From 1867 to 1887 he was pastor of the First Presbyterian Church, Marietta, Georgia. He died there on August 7th, 1905, and was buried in Episcopal Cemetery beside his wife, who had died on October 28th, 1903. He received the honorary degree of doctor of divinity from the University of Georgia in 1879. (Members of the Buttolph family stressed the second syllable of their surname.)

BUTTOLPH, HORACE A. (1815–1898), physician, son of Warren Buttolph and Mary McAllister, was born in North East Township, Dutchess County, New York, on April 6th, 1815. Through his father he was a first cousin of David Lyman Buttolph. He graduated from the Berkshire Medical College, Pittsfield, Massachusetts (the Medical Department of Williams College) in 1835. After practicing briefly in Norwich, New York, and Sharon, Connecticut, he served on the medical staff of the newly established Utica Lunatic Asylum from 1842 to 1847. In 1847 he was appointed superintendent of the New Jersey State Lunatic Asylum in Trenton, where he continued until 1876, when he became superintendent of the New Jersey State Asylum for the Insane in Morristown, then the largest single mental asylum in the world. In 1885 he retired and settled in Short Hills, New Jersey, where he died on May 21st, 1898. He was buried in Riverview Cemetery, Trenton. For many years he was recognized in America and Europe as an authority on the care and treatment of the insane. In 1872 he received the honorary degree of doctor of laws from Princeton University. He married first (in 1838) Catharine King, daughter of George King, of Sharon, Connecticut; he married second (in 1854) Mrs. Maria Ridgely Gardner, daughter of Dr. John Syng Dorsey, professor of anatomy in the Medical College of the University of Pennsylvania. She died in East Orange, New Jersey, on December 30th, 1900, and was buried beside her husband.

BUTTOLPH, JAMES DAVID (1858–1939), businessman, second child of the Rev. David Lyman Buttolph (1822–1905), a Presbyterian clergyman, and Laura Elizabeth Maxwell (1824–1903), was born at Point Maxwell, Colonel's Island, Liberty County, Georgia, on October 24th, 1858. A vivid account of his birth appears in a letter written two days later by his great-uncle, the Rev. Dr. Charles Colcock Jones. He was named for his two grandfathers: James Audley Maxwell (1796–1828) and David Buttolph (1779–1868). At the age of nine he removed with his parents to Marietta, Georgia, where he attended a school conducted by the Rev. John Wickliffe Baker. In April 1880 he married Elizabeth Barnwell Elliott (1862–1960), daughter of the Rev. James Habersham Elliott, an Episcopal clergyman, and Catherine Sadler. For several years after his marriage he engaged in the manufacture of flour and ice in Marietta and Chattanooga; in 1895 he removed to New York, where for thirty-five years he sold lots for Woodlawn Cemetery. After retiring in 1930 he became a winter resident of Waycross, Georgia, where he died on December 21st, 1939, survived by his wife, four sons, and a daughter. He was buried in Woodlawn Cemetery, New York. Elizabeth Barnwell (Elliott) Buttolph died in Atlanta, Georgia, on January 23rd, 1960, three days before her ninety-eighth birthday, and was buried in Myrtle Hill Cemetery, Rome.

BUTTOLPH, LAURA ELIZABETH (MAXWELL). *See* Maxwell, Laura Elizabeth

BUTTOLPH, SUSAN MARY (1863–1913), artist, fourth child and only daughter of the Rev. David Lyman Buttolph (1822–1905), a Presbyterian clergyman, and Laura Elizabeth Maxwell (1824–1903), was born in Flemington, Liberty County, Georgia, on October 18th, 1863. She was named for her maternal grandmother, Susan Mary (Jones) (Maxwell) Cumming. From childhood she was known for her keen wit and unusual memory. At the age of four she removed with her parents to Marietta, Georgia, where she attended local schools. In the autumn of 1879 she entered Shorter College, Rome, Georgia, from which she graduated with honors in June 1881. She became mentally ill in the summer of 1882 and was sent to the New Jersey State Asylum for the Insane in Morristown, where her cousin, Dr. Horace A. Buttolph, was superintendent; later in the same year she was removed to the Milledgeville State Hospital in Georgia. On July 20th, 1885, Mrs. Mary S. Mallard, visiting in Marietta, observed that "Susie is almost herself again, and is a very sweet-looking girl." At Shorter College she had won a gold medal for drawing; for some years she devoted herself to her pencil and her brush. After the death of her brother Wallace in 1899 she assumed the care of her aged parents; her mother died on October 28th, 1903, her father on August 7th, 1905. She then returned to her art; in 1911 she studied sculpture in Paris. She never married. She died in Marietta on August 21st, 1913, and was buried near her parents in Episcopal Cemetery.

BUTTOLPH, WALLACE STEWART (1867–1899), bank cashier, fifth child of the Rev. David Lyman Buttolph (1822–1905), a Presbyterian clergyman, and Laura Elizabeth Maxwell (1824–1903), was born in Marietta, Georgia, on December 25th, 1867. He spent his entire life in Marietta, where he was assistant cashier and bookkeeper of the First National Bank and elder of the First Presbyterian Church. He never married. After his father's retirement in 1887 he shared with his sister Susie the care of his aging parents. He died suddenly of typhoid fever on August 26th, 1899, and was buried in Episcopal Cemetery in the lot of Dr. Theophilus S. Stewart, a family friend for whom he was named. His cousin, Georgia Maxwell Mallard, wife of William Kimsey Seago, later wrote that "Such was the nobility of his character that the whole town mourned his death, and the stores closed at the hour of his funeral." As the Marietta *Journal* (August 31st, 1899) observed, "If he had an enemy, he is not known. His gentle, kind, loving disposition, his gentlemanly demeanor and courteous words made him friends. He was truly a model young man, and Marietta is poorer by his death."

BUTTOLPH, WILLIAM SMYTH (1861–1896), cotton buyer, third child of the Rev. David Lyman Buttolph (1822–1905), a Presbyterian clergyman, and Laura Elizabeth Maxwell (1824–1903), was born at Point Maxwell, Colonel's Island, Liberty County, Georgia, on May 4th, 1861. At the age of six he removed with his parents to Marietta, Georgia, where he attended a school conducted by the Rev. John Wickliffe Baker. In 1881, after several years of business in Savannah and Atlanta, he settled in Columbus, Georgia, where he became cotton buyer for the Eagle & Phoenix Mills, and where, on June 8th, 1887, he married Sallie Peabody (1861–1952), daughter of John Peabody. Nine years later, on June 23rd, 1896, he met a horrible death when his body was caught and crushed in the driving gear of one of the mills. He was buried in Linwood Cemetery, Columbus. Sallie (Peabody) Buttolph died on March 7th, 1952, and was buried beside her husband.

CALDER, JAMES RICHEY (born 1820), plantation overseer, was the son of James Calder and Jane Myers, of McIntosh County, Georgia. In 1849 he married Sarah Ann Elizabeth Sandiford (1830–1873), of Savannah; there were two sons and a daughter. For some years he managed plantations in McIntosh County; by 1859 he had settled in Liberty County, where he managed North Hampton, the plantation of John Bradley Barnard, and where (from May 1862 to June 1863) he managed Montevideo, the plantation of the Rev. Dr. Charles Colcock Jones. ("A great relief," wrote Dr. Jones on May 10th, 1862.) His brother, Stephen Alexander Calder (1827–1902), was for many years a dentist in Hinesville. James Richey Calder died in Liberty County shortly after the Civil War. His widow returned with her three children to Chatham County, where she continued as keeper of the toll gate on the White Bluff road until her death on April 27th, 1873.

CALHOUN, EZEKIEL NOBLE (1799–1875), physician, eldest son of William Calhoun and Rebecca Tonnyhill, was born in Abbeville District, South Carolina, on October 23rd, 1799. His father, a planter, was a first cousin of the statesman John Caldwell Calhoun (1782–1850). After attending Jefferson Medical College (Philadelphia) he practiced medicine for one year in Elbert County, Georgia. In 1825 he married Lucy B. Wellborn (1803–1884), of Wilkes County; there were three sons (John Caldwell, Edward Livingston, and Pickens Noble) and seven daughters (Carolina, Georgia, Virginia, Indiana, Louisiana, Missouri, and Florida). In 1826 he settled in Decatur, DeKalb County, where he became one of the most prominent physicians in the state. He removed to Atlanta in 1854. Although he opposed secession, he actively supported the Confederate cause: in 1861 he was surgeon of the 4th Battalion Georgia Infantry on Skidaway Island until failing health forced him to retire; and one of his sons, Pickens Noble Calhoun (1840–1862), a private in the Fulton Dragoons, died of disease in camp near Richmond, Virginia, on August 9th, 1862. His younger brother, James Montgomery Calhoun (1811–1875), was mayor of Atlanta for four years (1862–1865) and surrendered the city to General Sherman on September 2nd, 1864. The Calhouns were active in the affairs of the Central Presbyterian Church. Ezekiel Noble Calhoun died in Atlanta on March 13th, 1875, and was buried in Oakland Cemetery. Lucy (Wellborn) Calhoun died on February 11th, 1884, and was buried beside her husband.

CALHOUN, JOHN CALDWELL (1782–1850), statesman, son of Patrick Calhoun and his second wife, Martha Caldwell, was born near Calhoun Mills, Abbeville District (now Mount Carmel, McCormick County), South Carolina, on March 18th, 1782. After graduating from Yale College in 1804 and from the Litchfield (Connecticut) Law School in 1806 he commenced practice in Abbeville, South Carolina, in 1807. In January 1811 he married Floride Calhoun, daughter of his cousin, John Ewing Calhoun, United States senator from South Carolina (1801–1802). He was a member of the state house of representatives (1808–1809); a member of Congress (1811–1817); secretary of war under President James Monroe (1817–1825); vice-president of the United States under President John Quincy Adams (1825–1829); vice-president of the United States under President Andrew Jackson (1829–1832); United States senator (1832–1843); secretary of state under President John Tyler (1844–1845); and United States senator (1845–1850). He was an unyielding defender of Southern rights and opposed the compromise measures of 1850; he favored union but predicted secession within ten years. He was one of the outstanding leaders of the United States prior to the Civil War; according to the Rev. Dr. Charles Colcock Jones (June 12th, 1857) he was one of "the first three," the other two being Daniel Webster (1782–1852) of Massachusetts and Henry Clay (1777–1852) of Kentucky. Calhoun died in Washington, D.C., on March 31st, 1850, and was buried in St. Philip's Episcopal Churchyard, Charleston, South Carolina.

CALHOUN, ROSA (1848–1912), daughter of Edward Calhoun and Frances Middleton, was born in Abbeville, South Carolina, on February 10th, 1848. Her elder sister, Ida Calhoun (1841–1867), married Charles Atwood Alexander (1838–1907), of Liberty County, Georgia, on April 8th, 1862; she died of puerperal fever on December 22nd, 1867, and was buried in Laurel Grove Cemetery, Savannah. She left a daughter, Harriet Virginia Alexander (1866–1882), and an infant who did not

survive. Thirteen years later, on November 4th, 1880, Rosa Calhoun married her sister's widower, then living in Washington, Wilkes County; there were two daughters: Ida Calhoun Alexander and Carlotta Rosa Alexander. Rosa (Calhoun) Alexander died in Washington, Wilkes County, on February 23rd, 1912, and was buried in the Alexander family cemetery beside her husband, who had died on January 30th, 1907.

CAMP, RALEIGH SPINKS (1829–1867), Confederate soldier, was born in Walton County, Georgia, on June 26th, 1829. He graduated from the Georgia Military Institute (Marietta) and subsequently served there for several years as professor of mathematics. On December 15th, 1859, he married Laura Clifford Jones (1832–1911), daughter of Moses Liberty Jones (1805–1851) and Sacharissa Elizabeth Axson (1811–1850), of Liberty County, Georgia. There were two children: Augustus Jones Camp (1861–1912) and Rosa Leigh Camp (1867–1953). At the outbreak of the Civil War he was living in Texas; on October 2nd, 1861, he was mustered into service at Camp Clark, Marshall, Texas, as captain of Company B, 7th Regiment Texas Infantry. On March 19th, 1862, he was commissioned major in the 40th Regiment Georgia Infantry. He was commended for gallantry at Vicksburg in July 1863; in May 1864 his left arm was amputated after a severe gunshot wound sustained in battle in Northwest Georgia. After the war he settled in Atlanta. In the summer of 1867 he returned to Texas on business, leaving his wife and children in Georgia; he had scarcely rejoined his family in Atlanta when he died suddenly of meningitis ("congestion of the brain") on November 24th, 1867. He was buried in Oakland Cemetery, Atlanta; in 1901 his remains were removed to Oak Hill Cemetery, Birmingham, Alabama, where his wife was also buried after her death on July 16th, 1911.

CAMPBELL, JAMES (1812–1893), postmaster general, son of Anthony Campbell and Catharine McGarvey, was born in Southwark (now part of Philadelphia), Pennsylvania, on September 1st, 1812. He studied law and was admitted to the bar in 1833. He was appointed school commissioner in 1840, judge of the court of common pleas in 1842, and attorney general in 1851. As postmaster general under President Franklin Pierce (1853–1857) he energetically promoted the efficiency of postal service; he introduced new methods and negotiated with railroad and steamship companies for better rates. In 1857 he returned to Philadelphia, where he passed the remainder of his life in the quiet practice of his profession. He was trustee and director of various educational and charitable institutions, among them Girard College and Jefferson Medical College. He died in Philadelphia on January 27th, 1893, and was buried in St. Mary's Cemetery.

CAMPBELL, JOHN ARCHIBALD (1811–1889), statesman and jurist, son of Duncan Green Campbell and Mary Williamson, was born in Washington, Wilkes County, Georgia, on June 24th, 1811. After graduating from Franklin College (Athens) in 1825 he studied law and commenced practice in his native town in 1829. A year later he removed to Alabama, where he practiced law, first in Montgomery, later in Mobile, until March 1853, when he was appointed associate justice of the supreme court of the United States by President Franklin Pierce. Prior to the Civil War he opposed secession and favored compromise, but with the outbreak of hostilities he resigned his seat on the supreme bench and returned to the South. In October 1862 he became assistant secretary of war in charge of administering the conscription law. On February 3rd, 1865, he was one of three commissioners (with R. M. T. Hunter and Alexander H. Stephens) representing the Confederacy at the Hampton Roads Conference; they returned to Richmond without the armistice they desired. After the war Campbell settled in New Orleans, where he enjoyed a large and lucrative practice and became one of the leading lawyers in the country. He married Anna Esther Goldthwaite. In 1884 he removed to Baltimore, Maryland, where he died on March 12th, 1889. He was buried in Greenmount Cemetery.

CAMPBELL, TUNIS GULIC (1812–1891), Negro clergyman, son of John Campbell, a blacksmith, was born in Middlebrook, New Jersey, on April 1st, 1812. Through the agency of a white man he was sent at the age of five to a school in Babylon, Long Island, New York, where he was kindly treated, though he was the only Negro child in the school. There he remained until he was eighteen, when he returned to his father's home in New Brunswick, New Jersey, and began his career as an antislavery lecturer. From 1841 to 1846 he was active in establishing schools for Negro children in New York, Brooklyn, and Jersey City; in the 1850s he helped fugitive slaves escape to the North. At the height of the Civil War, in 1863, he sent to President Lincoln "a plan by which the freed people could be educated and made self-supporting, and prepared to exercise the duties of citizens, and relieve the general government from the guardianship which, in my view, they would have to keep over them as a protection against bad men from the North and bad men from the South who would use them for their own purposes." In reply he was ordered to report to General Rufus Saxton at Hilton Head, South Carolina; and after the fall of Charleston he was sent as military governor to the sea islands of Georgia, where he remained until removed from office in 1865 by General Davis Tilson, assistant commissioner in charge of the Freedmen's Bureau (the Federal Bureau of Refugees, Freedmen, and Abandoned Lands) in Georgia. Campbell then purchased Belleville, the plantation of Charles Horrie Hopkins on the mainland in McIntosh County, and established there a colony for freedmen. Under the Reconstruction Act of Congress he was appointed registrar for the second district of Georgia (Liberty,

McIntosh, and Tattnall Counties); he was subsequently a delegate to the state constitutional convention, after which he was elected state senator from the second district. Thereafter for several years he was in constant difficulty with the courts, the legislature, and the white citizens of Georgia; in January 1875 he was convicted by the superior court of McIntosh County of malpractice in office as justice of the peace and sentenced to jail; in January 1876 he was removed to a prison camp in Washington County. Upon his release in January 1877 he removed with his wife and daughter to the District of Columbia, where he worked for several years in support of a scheme to colonize Negroes in different portions of the United States. In 1881 he settled in Boston, Massachusetts, and engaged in missionary work for the African Methodist Episcopal Church. He died in Boston on December 4th, 1891, and was buried in Woodlawn Cemetery.

CAPERS, FRANCIS WITHERS (1819–1892), educator and Confederate soldier, second son of the Rev. William Capers, Methodist Episcopal bishop, and Susan McGill, was born in Savannah, Georgia, on August 8th, 1819. He graduated from the College of Charleston with first honor in 1840 and commenced a long and distinguished career as a teacher. He was tutor in mathematics at the College of Charleston (1840–1843); professor of mathematics at the newly organized South Carolina State Military Academy (1843–1847); professor of ancient languages at Transylvania University, Lexington, Kentucky (1847–1853); superintendent (with rank of major) of the Citadel Academy, Charleston (1853–1859); and superintendent (with rank of major) of the Georgia Military Institute, Marietta (1859–1864). At the outbreak of the Civil War he became captain of the Kennesaw Dragoons, the first military unit organized in Cobb County, Georgia, for war service. When General William Phillips, commanding the Fourth Brigade Georgia Volunteers, organized a camp of instruction (Camp Brown) at Smyrna, six miles south of Marietta, in April 1861, Major Capers and his cadets helped with the drilling; when General Phillips organized another camp of instruction (Camp McDonald) at Big Shanty, seven miles north of Marietta, in June 1861, Major Capers served as instructor in tactics. In the winter of 1861 he was appointed brigadier general and assigned to command the Second Brigade Georgia State Troops. Later he was ordered on engineer service in Northwest Georgia, where he constructed the fortifications in the vicinity of Resaca. In 1864 he saw service at Atlanta, Milledgeville, and Savannah. After the war he taught briefly in a private school in Augusta; in 1867 he became professor of mathematics at the College of Charleston, where he remained until his retirement in 1890. He married first (on August 24th, 1848) Hannah Hawk Bascom, daughter of the Rev. Henry B. Bascom, Methodist Episcopal bishop; there were six children. After her death on February 20th, 1862, he married second (on January 1st, 1863) Susan Rose Rutledge, daughter of John Rutledge, of Charleston. He died in Charleston on January 11th, 1892, survived by his second wife and five children.

CARPENTER, WILLIAM BENJAMIN (1813–1885), English naturalist, fourth child of Dr. Lant Carpenter (1780–1840) and Anna Penn, was born in Exeter, England, on October 29th, 1813. He entered University College (London) as a medical student in 1833 and received the surgeon's and apothecary's diplomas in 1835. He then commenced, at the Edinburgh Medical School, the researches in physiology which led to his great work, *The Principles of General and Comparative Physiology* (1839). In 1844 he removed to London, where he was Fullerian professor of physiology at the Royal Institution, lecturer in physiology at the London Hospital, professor of forensic medicine at University College, examiner in physiology and comparative anatomy at the University of London, and Swiney lecturer in geology at the British Museum. He was also a fellow of the Royal Society. He was editor of *The British and Foreign Medico-Chirurgical Review* (1847–1852) and principal of University Hall, residence for students at University College (1851–1859). In 1856 he resigned his lectureships and devoted himself to the development of the University of London until his resignation in 1879. He died on November 19th, 1885, survived by five sons.

CARTER, ROBERT (1807–1889), publisher, son of Thomas Carter and Agnes Ewing, was born in Earlston, Berwickshire, Scotland, on November 2nd, 1807. The son of a weaver, he was obliged at an early age to work at the loom beside his father; but he studied Greek and Latin at night, became an assistant teacher in a grammar school, and devoted his meager earnings to study at Edinburgh University. In 1831 he migrated to New York, where after teaching school for three years he opened a small bookstore in Canal Street. There he began publishing religious books; his business flourished, and in 1848 he was joined by his two brothers, Peter and Walter, in the firm of Robert Carter & Brothers, which until its dissolution in 1890 was one of the leading publishers of religious books in New York. He was a devout Presbyterian. He died in New York on December 28th, 1889.

CARUTHERS, LOUISA CATHERINE (GIBSON) (1805–1858): *Mrs. William Alexander Caruthers,* daughter of Robert Stewart Gibson and Sarah Turner, was born on her father's plantation on Whitemarsh Island, ten miles east of Savannah, Georgia, in 1805. Early in July 1823 she became the wife of William Alexander Caruthers (1802–1846), who had graduated from the Medical College of the University of Pennsylvania the preceding month; the young couple settled in Lexington, Virginia, where Caruthers practiced medicine for six years. From 1829 to 1835 they lived in New York, and by April 1837 they had settled in Savannah with their five children. There

Caruthers continued to practice medicine, and for four years (1841–1844) he served as alderman. Meanwhile two of his novels, *The Kentuckian in New York* (1834) and *The Cavaliers of Virginia* (1835), had been published in New York; his third and finest novel, *The Knights of the Horseshoe,* published serially in a local magazine in 1841, appeared in book form in 1845. He died of consumption in Marietta, Georgia, on August 29th, 1846. His widow, finding herself in financial straits, opened her Savannah house to boarders; there Charles Colcock Jones, Jr., lived from May 1856, when his aunt, Mrs. Susan M. Cumming, closed her doors in Savannah to return to Liberty County, until October 1856, when he and his brother Joseph rented a house of their own. Louisa (Gibson) Caruthers died in Savannah early in April 1858, survived by three sons and two daughters; she was buried from St. John's Episcopal Church on April 4th, 1858; the place of her burial is not known. Her younger brother, Richard Turner Gibson (1809–1872), resided on his father's plantation on Whitemarsh Island.

CARY, PRESTON M. (1816–1891), daguerreotypist and photographer, was born in Auburn, Massachusetts, on October 12th, 1816. By 1849 he was established in his "daguerreau rooms" in Savannah, Georgia, where he continued until the close of the Civil War. He was widely known for the excellence of his work. According to the Savannah *Republican* (February 5th, 1859), "Artists and the best judges acknowledge his daguerreotypes to be superior to any ever executed in the country. Every person should have one of these pictures, as they are the most permanent as well as the most truthful mementos in the world." An innovation from Cary elicited special notice in the Savannah *Morning News* (May 9th, 1861): "One of the prettiest things we have seen in the way of a visiting card is the new style of picture lately introduced by Cary. Just think of sending in, in the way of a visiting card, an elegant full-length photograph, instead of a bit of pasteboard with your name written or printed on it. Those gotten up by Cary are real gems of art, and must take among those of taste and fashion." On April 16th, 1864, Cary enlisted as a private in Captain W. H. C. Mills's Company (Chatham Siege Artillery), 1st Battalion Georgia Reserves. After the war he became a clerk in Bridgeport, Connecticut, where he died on October 14th, 1891, survived by his wife, Adelia Maria Barnum (1825–1899). He was buried in Mountain Grove Cemetery, Bridgeport.

CARY, SAMUEL FENTON (1814–1900), lawyer, legislator, and temperance reformer, son of William Cary and Rebecca Fenton, was born in Cincinnati, Ohio, on February 18th, 1814. He graduated from Miami University in 1835 and from the Cincinnati Law School in 1837. After eight years of successful practice he abandoned law in 1845 and devoted himself to temperance reform. For twenty-one years he edited newspapers and magazines, wrote tracts, and delivered addresses, not only in all the principal cities in the United States but also in England, Ireland, Scotland, Wales, and Canada. Meanwhile he was active in politics, participating in Presidential campaigns from 1840; in 1864 he was a delegate to the Republican National Convention meeting in Baltimore. He was a member of Congress (1867–1869) and the only Republican to vote against the impeachment of President Andrew Johnson. In 1836 he married Maria Louisa Allen, of Cincinnati; after her death in 1847 he married Lida S. Stilwell, of Oxford, Ohio. He died in College Hill, Cincinnati, on September 29th, 1900, and was buried in Spring Grove Cemetery. He was a cousin of the poets Alice Cary (1820–1871) and Phoebe Cary (1824–1871).

CASEY, SARAH BERRIEN (1846–1931), daughter of Dr. Henry Rozier Casey (1814–1884) and Caroline Rebecca Harriss (1822–1856), was born in Augusta, Georgia, in 1846. Through her father she was a niece of Philoclea Edgeworth Casey (1813–1889), wife of William Joseph Eve, and hence a first cousin of Eva Berrien Eve (1841–1890), second wife of Charles Colcock Jones, Jr. Through her mother she was a niece of Dr. Juriah Harriss (1825–1876), in whose Savannah house she often stayed after her mother's death in 1856. She married Thomas Saunderson Morgan, of Augusta, in 1866; there were four children. After her husband's death she became active in social, civic, and philanthropic movements; she was organizer and first president of the Association for the Education of Georgia Mountaineers, honorary president of the trustees of the Tallulah Falls Industrial School, and organizer and state regent of the Georgia Daughters of the American Revolution. In later life she resided with her son, Berrien Tyrrel Morgan, in Savannah, where she was appointed the city's only woman alderman in 1922. She died in Savannah on June 28th, 1931, and was buried in Magnolia Cemetery, Augusta. According to the Savannah *Morning News* (June 29th, 1931), "Mrs. Morgan was truly a brilliant woman. Her presence was one of striking individuality. . . . She was a gifted conversationalist and a persuasive speaker. . . . She was a delightful hostess and a warm friend, was courageous in her opinion and able as an executive, and her interest in young people never faltered."

CASS, MICHAEL L. (1840–1864), lawyer and Confederate soldier, son of John Cass, was born in Savannah, Georgia, in August 1840. His parents, both natives of Ireland, had migrated in early life to Savannah, where John Cass was for some years a baker, and where in 1858 he became proprietor of the City Hotel. After his death on February 1st, 1859, his wife continued to operate the City Hotel until April 1862, when the furniture and the lease were sold. Michael L. Cass read law in the office of Ward, Jackson & Jones, where Charles Colcock Jones, Jr., found him to be "a reliable man" and formed "a great attachment for him"; in June 1860 he was admitted to the Savannah bar. At the outbreak of the Civil War he was a private in the Chatham Artillery; on February 1st, 1861, Charles Colcock Jones, Jr., "obtained for him a lieutenancy" in the 1st Regiment Georgia Regulars. After six months' absence from the army on sick furlough he died in Savannah of "general debility" on June 27th, 1864, and was buried in the John Cass family tomb in Cathedral (Catholic) Cemetery. He never married.

CASSELS, JOHN (1834–1861), commission merchant, son of Thomas Quarterman Cassels (1808–1879) and Mary Amarintha Mallard (1810–1874), was born in Liberty County, Georgia, on April 4th, 1834. In early manhood he settled in Savannah, where he entered the commission business, and where (on June 23rd, 1859) he married Mary Cook Holcombe (1836–1919), eldest daughter of Thomas Holcombe (1815–1885) and his first wife, Eliza Gale (1815–1853). After a protracted illness he died of consumption at the residence of his parents in Flemington, Liberty County, on November 2nd, 1861, leaving a widow and one son, Thomas Holcombe Cassels (1860–1890). He was buried in Midway Cemetery beside his sister, Valeria Augusta Cassels (1832–1861), wife of the Rev. Donald Fraser; she had died of consumption only two months before. On September 25th, 1866, Mary (Holcombe) Cassels became the second wife of Cormack Hopkins (1832–1885), of Savannah.

CASSELS, MARY TALLULAH (1837–1855), daughter of the Rev. Samuel Jones Cassels (1806–1853) and Mary Eliza Winn, was born in Georgia in 1837. Her father, a native of Liberty County, was a Presbyterian clergyman; he served churches in Washington, Georgia (1832–1837), Macon, Georgia (1837–1841), and Norfolk, Virginia (1841–1846); he was principal of the Chatham Academy, Savannah, Georgia, from 1846 until his death on June 15th, 1853. His widow settled in Liberty County, where Mary Tallulah Cassels died of consumption on May 13th, 1855, early in her nineteenth year, and was buried beside her father in Midway Cemetery. Her epitaph bears the following tribute from her brothers and sisters: "Affection's silken cord was early snapped, but love's golden chain yet links us in a sweet and lasting union."

CASSELS, ROBERT QUARTERMAN (1842–1900), railroad agent and storekeeper, son of Thomas Quarterman Cassels (1808–1879) and Mary Amarintha Mallard (1810–1874), was born in Liberty County, Georgia, on May 21st, 1842. During the Civil War he served as agent of the Savannah, Albany & Gulf Railroad in his native county, handling baggage and shipments at Depot No. 3 (McIntosh Station). After the war he operated a general store at Flemington for many years; the Savannah *Morning News* (December 7th, 1894) described him as "one of the best financiers and economists in the county." He died on March 26th, 1900, survived by his wife, Alice Gordon (1844–1912), and was buried in Flemington Cemetery.

CASSELS, THOMAS QUARTERMAN (1808–1879), planter, son of Elias Cassels and Sarah Jones, was born in Liberty County, Georgia, on January 11th, 1808. On April 14th, 1831, he married Mary Amarintha Mallard (1810–1874), daughter of John Mallard and Lydia Quarterman; there were nine children. He represented Liberty County in the state legislature in 1833, 1835, and 1839. For many years he was active in the affairs of Midway Church, of which he was selectman (1842–1864) and deacon (1857–1865); when the Flemington Presbyterian Church was organized in April 1866 he was elected one of its four ruling elders, a position he held until his death on June 12th, 1879. He was buried in Flemington Cemetery beside his wife, who had died five years before. According to the Rev. David Lyman Buttolph, his former pastor, writing in *The Southern Presbyterian* (August 14th, 1879), "His large and commanding person, his grave and reverend appearance, and his deep-toned voice, which could melt into tenderness or break forth in power, rendered him conspicuous among the leaders of the church." Two of his brothers became Presbyterian clergymen: Samuel Jones Cassels (1806–1853) and John Baker Cassels (1811–1838).

CASSIDEY, HUGH EMMET (1825–1879), Baptist clergyman, son of Hugh Cassidey, was born in Savannah, Georgia, early in January 1825. His father, a native of Ireland, had settled in Savannah soon after the War of 1812. The son completed his junior year at Franklin College (Athens) in 1848; after studying briefly at Dane Law School, Harvard University, he returned to Savannah, where he practiced law for several years before entering the Baptist ministry. Throughout an active career he served numerous churches in Southeast Georgia, among them Walthourville, Brunswick, Sunbury, Springfield, and Guyton. In 1850 he married Ann Eliza Beurquine, of Springfield. During the Civil War he served for a time as chaplain; in 1876–1877 he was a member of the state legislature. He died in Savannah of consumption on November 24th, 1879, and was buried in Laurel Grove Cemetery.

CASTLEMAN, MARY ANN (1836–1902), sixth child of David Castleman (1786–1852) and his second wife, Virginia Harrison, was born at Castleton, her father's stock farm a few miles north of Lexington, Kentucky, on May 10th, 1836. In July 1853, shortly after her father's death, she entered boarding school in Philadelphia, where through the introduction of James Nephew West, a Kentucky cousin of the Rev. Dr. Charles Colcock Jones, she became acquainted with the Jones family, then living in Philadelphia. As Mrs. Mary Jones observed on July 15th, 1853, "She has an intelligent and pleasing face and a fine and commanding figure, with all the good sense and high tone of old Kentucky." Early in August 1853 she accompanied the Joneses to Sharon, Connecticut, where Dr. Jones found her "most sensible, very much a lady in all respects, and most agreeable." Later in the

same month she accompanied Mary Sharpe Jones to Niagara Falls; and in January 1854 she stayed with the Joneses for several weeks at Maybank, their plantation in Liberty County, Georgia. Shortly thereafter the friendship evidently cooled: on June 12th, 1854, Mrs. Jones wrote her son Charles on the eve of his departure for Kentucky: "You will remember our caution about a certain *young lady*, should you see her; I assure you when you know all you will feel as much surprised as we have been at her treatment of your brother, but it would not do to say more till we meet." On October 2nd, 1856, she became the wife of William C. Webb (1825–1914), a physician, and settled in St. Louis, Missouri, where except for a brief absence during the Civil War she resided for the rest of her life. She died in Buck Hill Falls, Pennsylvania, on August 13th, 1902, survived by her husband, four daughters, and one son, and was buried in Bellefontaine Cemetery, St. Louis. William C. Webb died in St. Louis on January 21st, 1914, and was buried beside his wife.

CAY, JULIA ELIZABETH (1836–1864), eldest daughter of Raymond Cay (1805–1883) and Elizabeth Ann Stetson (1811–1896), was born in Walthourville, Liberty County, Georgia, on October 3rd, 1836. On December 31st, 1856, she became the wife of McLeod King, Savannah commission merchant, eldest son of William King (1804–1884) and Sarah Elizabeth McLeod (1807–1891); the Rev. R. Q. Mallard, who performed the ceremony, described the wedding in a letter to his fiancée the following day: "The wedding seemed to pass off very pleasantly with one exception—there was too much wine accessible and too many manifestations of its presence where it should not have been. Several of the guests were so much under its influence as to have very little consciousness of the nature of their acts." Julia Elizabeth (Cay) King died in childbirth at her father's residence in Walthourville on April 26th, 1864, survived by her husband and three young children, and was buried in Midway Cemetery. Her girlhood friend, Mary Sharpe Jones (Mrs. Mary S. Mallard) was "shocked" by news of her death: "She was a fine woman," she wrote on May 5th, 1864: "the flower of the family. . . . It is very sad: a young mother."

CAY, RAYMOND (1805–1883), planter, was born in Baracoa, Cuba, in 1805. In early manhood he settled in Walthourville, Liberty County, Georgia, where he married Elizabeth Ann Stetson (1811–1896), a native of New Bedford, Massachusetts, on November 20th, 1834, the Rev. Dr. Charles Colcock Jones performing the ceremony. There were four sons and four daughters. He was a prosperous planter; in addition to his house in Walthourville he maintained a plantation on Cay Creek near Dorchester; passing regularly between Dorchester and Walthourville he often carried letters for members of the Jones family. After the Civil War he kept a country store. He died on August 23rd, 1883, and was buried in Walthourville Cemetery. On January 23rd, 1858, he had written thus to the Rev. Dr. Jones: "When I look back on the picture of my life (I have panted to gain its summit; that summit I have gained), how different the prospect on the other side! I sigh as I contemplate the waste before me. Life is like a portentous cloud fraught with danger; but religion, like those streaming rays of sunshine, will clothe it with light as with a garment and fringe its shadowy skirts with gold." Elizabeth Ann (Stetson) Cay died on January 11th, 1896, and was buried beside her husband.

CHAMISSO, ADELBERT VON (1781–1838), German poet and botanist, was born at the chateau Boncourt, Champagne, France, on January 30th, 1781. During the French Revolution his family fled to Berlin, where he became page-in-waiting to Queen Louise, attended the Französische Gymnasium, entered an infantry regiment, and studied philology and philosophy. His most famous work, *Peter Schlemihls Wundersame Geschichte* (1813), the story of a man who sold his shadow to the devil, was widely translated. From 1815 to 1818 he accompanied Otto von Kotzebue on a scientific voyage around the world; his diary, *Reise um die Welt mit der Romanzoffischen Entdeckungs-Expedition* (1821) became a classic. Most of his later poems (ballads, song cycles, and narrative verses) were published in the *Deutscher Musenalmanach,* of which he became editor in 1832. He died in Berlin on August 21st, 1838. (In her letter of August 15th, 1862, Mrs. Mary Jones was mistaken in referring to von Chamisso as "admiral.")

CHAMPION, AARON HENRY (1829–1889), wholesale grocer and commission merchant, son of Dr. Moses Champion (1792–1838) and Elizabeth Gazilda Holland (1806–1856), was born in Monticello, Georgia, on July 18th, 1829. In early manhood he removed to Savannah, where he became associated in business with his father's twin brother, Aaron Champion (1792–1880), a prominent banker and merchant. In 1854 he established his own wholesale grocery business. During the Civil War he served as a private in Captain John B. Gallie's Company (Savannah Artillery) and later as a private in Captain John F. Wheaton's Company (Chatham Artillery). After the war he established his own commission business. He married first (on March 20th, 1854) Georgia Ann Davis (1834–1869), daughter of William Henry Davis, of Savannah; he married second (on December 23rd, 1875) Julia E. Smith (1841–1928), daughter of William Henry Smith, of Savannah. He died in Savannah on December 3rd, 1889, and was buried in Laurel Grove Cemetery. Two of his sons, William Davis Champion and Henry Champion, succeeded to his business.

CHAPMAN, ELIJAH (1814–1867), planter, was born in South Carolina in 1814. In early manhood he settled near Riceboro, Liberty County, Georgia, where he married Amanda Mara on February 2nd, 1842. There were nine children: Florence, Morgan, Charles, Benjamin, Amanda, David, Winkler, Rosa, and James. As neighbors of the Jones family at Montevideo the Chapmans received frequent pastoral as well as social calls from the Rev. Dr. Charles Colcock Jones. Elijah Chapman died in September 1867.

CHAPMAN, SHELDON M. (1829–1911), planter and stock-raiser, younger son of Francis John Chapman (1779–1852) and Mary Leigh (1789–1866), was born in Liberty County, Georgia, on January 25th, 1829. In 1855 he married Charity Baggs (1832–1906) and settled on the Chapman place half a mile from Jones Creek and a mile and a half from the house of his elder brother John Chapman (1810–1895) on the Macon-Darien road. Both men were prosperous planters, stock-raisers, and lumbermen. During the Civil War Sheldon Chapman hired a substitute. John Chapman organized a vigilante group composed of men too old for military service and sought to defend communities in lower Liberty County and in McIntosh County from Yankee depredations; in 1864 he was captured and sent to New Jersey, where he spent the last year of the war in a prison camp. It was Sheldon Chapman who directed Mrs. Mary S. Mallard and her party to a ford in Jones Creek during their flight to Baker County in March 1865. He died on July 8th, 1911, and was buried beside his wife in Jones Creek Baptist Churchyard.

CHARLESS, JOSEPH (1804–1859), druggist, banker, and philanthropist, son of Joseph Charless (1772–1834) and Sarah (Jordan) McCloud, was born in Lexington, Kentucky, on January 17th, 1804. His father, a native of Ireland, had migrated to the United States in 1796; after a brief period in Philadelphia he had settled in Lexington, Kentucky; in 1808 he removed to St. Louis, Missouri, set up the first printing press west of the Mississippi River, and founded the *Missouri Gazette.* Joseph Charless (1804–1859) graduated from the law school of Transylvania University but never practiced his profession; in 1828 he returned to St. Louis and joined his father in a thriving wholesale drug business. For many years he was prominent in the commercial and cultural growth of St. Louis; he was president of the State Bank of Missouri and later president of the Mechanics' Bank; he also served as city alderman and as director of the public schools. He was a trustee and devoted friend of Westminster College, a Presbyterian institution in Fulton, Missouri, from its chartering in 1853. On June 3rd, 1859, he was shot in Market Street, St. Louis, by Joseph W. Thornton, against whom he had once been compelled to testify in court; he died the next day and was buried in Bellefontaine Cemetery. In 1831 he had married Charlotte Blow, daughter of Captain Peter Blow; their only daughter, Elizabeth Charless (1832–1881), wife of L. S. LeBourgeois, endowed the Charless professorship of physical science at Westminster College in memory of her father.

CHESTER, NORMAN L. (1803–1876), physician, was born in Groton, Connecticut, on January 21st, 1803. After studying briefly at Yale College he came South in 1820, graduated from Franklin College (Athens) in 1823, studied medicine in Augusta, and settled to practice in Gainesville. In 1830 he married Elizabeth Lydia Mary Davant (1811–1904), daughter of James Davant, formerly of Hilton Head, South Carolina, then living in Greene County, Georgia. From Gainesville he removed in 1837 to Marietta, where he continued to practice medicine until his death on November 27th, 1876. He was buried in Citizens Cemetery. He was a ruling elder of the First Presbyterian Church, Marietta, from its dedication in 1854.

CHEVES, CHARLOTTE LORRAINE (McCORD) (1819–1879): *Mrs. Langdon Cheves,* eldest daughter of David James McCord and Emeline Wagner, was born in South Carolina in 1819. On December 25th, 1839, she married Langdon Cheves (1814–1863), sixth son of Langdon Cheves (1776–1857), for some years president of the United States Bank, and Mary Elizabeth Dulles. Her husband, a graduate of the South Carolina College (1833), was a lawyer in Columbia and state reporter of the court of appeals; in 1841 he became a rice planter on the Savannah River in St. Peter's Parish, Beaufort District. During the Civil War he served as an engineer at Hilton Head and Morris Island; he was killed by the first shell fired at Battery Wagner, Morris Island, on July 10th, 1863. His wife and children took refuge for a time in the house of her kinsman, Charles T. Haskell, in Abbeville; after the war she settled in Savannah, where she resided until her death on June 30th, 1879. According to the Savannah *Morning News* (July 4th, 1879), "Few possessed in such a remarkable degree as she did the faculty of drawing friends to her and keeping them. Of a most genial, kindly nature, she was easily interested in those who came in her way, and through life formed friendships which were rarely broken." Her only son, Dr. Langdon Cheves (1854–1878), died in the Memphis yellow fever epidemic of 1878, "victim of the scourge he so valiantly fought." She was buried beside her husband and her son in Magnolia Cemetery, Charleston.

CHURCH, ALONZO (1793–1862), educator, son of Reuben Church and Elizabeth Whipple, was born near Brattleboro, Vermont, on April 9th, 1793. After graduating from Middlebury College in 1816 he migrated to Georgia, where he headed an academy in Eatonton, Putnam County, and married Sarah J. Trippe, daughter of a Putnam County planter. In 1819 he was elected professor of mathematics at the University of Georgia, and in 1829 he succeeded the Rev. Moses Waddel (1770–1840) as president. For thirty years (1829–1859) he shaped the destiny of a growing university and brought it to a position of influence not only in Georgia but throughout the Southeastern states. After his resignation in 1859 he resided in the country near Athens until his death on May 18th, 1862.

CLAGHORN, JOSEPH SAMUEL (1817–1879), grocer and ship chandler, son of Samuel Claghorn (1787–1840) and Philura Paine Spaulding (1793–1844), was born in Norwich, Connecticut, on January 22nd, 1817. In early childhood he removed with his parents to Savannah, Georgia, where his father joined Thomas Bradley and Orlando A. Wood in the firm of Bradley, Claghorn & Wood, grocers and ship chandlers. After 1828 the firm operated as Claghorn & Wood, and in 1840, at the death of Samuel Claghorn, his son, having attended Yale College from 1835 to 1838, entered commercial life as junior partner in the firm of Wood & Claghorn. Eight years later Joseph Samuel Claghorn joined John Cunningham in the firm of Claghorn & Cunningham, which continued in business from 1848 to 1877. (When Mrs. Mary Jones referred to "Wood & Claghorn" on June 30th, 1857, she was inadvertently recalling the former name of the firm.) On April 23rd, 1846, Claghorn married Sarah Campbell Hunter (1825–1886), daughter of William Presstman Hunter (1799–1869), president of the Savannah Marine Bank; there were ten children. In 1856 he was elected captain of the Chatham Artillery, a post he held until he resigned in December 1862 when his first lieutenant, Charles Colcock Jones, Jr., became chief of artillery for the District of Georgia, with authority to inspect and control his former company. "I regret exceedingly," Claghorn wrote to James A. Seddon, secretary of war, on December 2nd, 1862, "that I am forced to this step at so critical a period in the struggle for our independence; but there are circumstances connected with the promotion of Lieutenant Colonel Jones that render my position extremely embarrassing and disagreeable, and I feel compelled to tender my resignation." Claghorn was succeeded by John Francis Wheaton, who continued as captain until the end of the war. In the 1850s Claghorn had purchased "the old Bulloch house" on the Isle of Hope, nine miles from Savannah; there the Chatham Artillery encamped during the winter of 1861–1862. On November 16th, 1861, Charles Colcock Jones, Jr., praised his captain without reserve: "He is a brave, high-toned man, fully imbued with our high and holy cause, and will not be found wanting in the day of trial. He enjoys the reputation of being the best-informed and most accomplished artillerist in the state." Claghorn died in Savannah on April 8th, 1879, survived by his wife and eight children, and was buried in Laurel Grove Cemetery. Sarah Campbell (Hunter) Claghorn died on March 23rd, 1886, and was buried beside her husband.

CLARK, JAMES Y. (1842–1865), Union soldier, youngest son of Stephen J. Clark, was born in North Carolina in 1842. After his father's death on February 17th, 1852, his mother, Letitia Clark, removed to Saltville, Washington County, Virginia, where she and her five children squatted on mountain lands owned by Boss Litchfield. According to James Henderson, a neighbor, who answered the questions of a pension examiner in 1886, "they were a hard, worthless family who lived in the most abject poverty and shame." The mother was "a thief and an abandoned woman of the worst character" who "made her living, as was generally understood, by the lewd practices of herself and daughters." James Y. Clark was "a drunken, worthless fellow who drifted along as best he could without an effort." Prior to the Civil War he worked sporadically as a teamster for the salt furnace at Saltville. On June 20th, 1861, at Abingdon, Virginia, he enlisted as a private in Captain Milton White's Company (the Campbell Guards), 48th Regiment Virginia Infantry. After three years' service in the Confederate army he deserted and made his way to Richmond, Indiana, where he enlisted on August 26th, 1864, as a private in the 8th Regiment Indiana Cavalry. He was killed in the battle of Averysboro, North Carolina, on March 16th, 1865.

CLARK, RICHARD H. (1824–1896), jurist, son of Josiah Hayden Clark, was born in Springfield, Effingham County, Georgia, on March 24th, 1824. After studying law he was admitted to the bar in 1844 and settled in Albany, Georgia, where he practiced his profession for more than twenty years. He was a delegate to the state secession convention meeting in Milledgeville in January 1861. In 1862 he was appointed judge of the Southwestern circuit. Four years later he removed to Atlanta, where he continued for the rest of his life, serving for a time as judge of the city court and later as judge of the Stone Mountain circuit. He married first Harriet G. Charlton, who bore him two children; he married second Anna Maria Lott, who bore him six children. He died in Atlanta on February 24th, 1896, and was buried in Rose Hill Cemetery, Macon. At the request of Governor Joseph E. Brown he collaborated with Thomas R. R. Cobb and David Irwin in preparing *The Code of the State of Georgia* (1861). His *Memoirs* (1898) contain delightful reminiscences and reveal strong literary gifts. According to his biographer, Bernard Suttler, "His temperament was poetic, sentimental, and kindly. Partial to genealogical research, with an extraordinary memory, he became an authority upon all matters pertaining to family trees and genealogical records of prominent Georgians. Tormented for years with ill health, oppressed by many sorrows, he refused to be soured, and up to the last days of his life was cheerful, genial, kindly, and carried sunshine into every circle where he went" [*Men of Mark in Georgia,* ed. William Northen (Atlanta, 1907), III, 418].

CLARK, WILLIAM PEARSON (1793–1872), hotel proprietor, was born in Union County, New Jersey, on December 15th, 1793. In early manhood he removed to Savannah, Georgia, where for many years he was proprietor of the Pavilion Hotel. On January 27th, 1859, he offered the house for sale "on the most favorable terms to a reliable purchaser";

the Savannah *Republican* carried the following notice: "The house is located in a central position, and encompassed by two of the widest and most beautiful streets in the city, thus securing a free circulation of air and a commanding view. . . . The Pavilion is now in complete order, with all necessary appliances of comfort and convenience, and can accommodate sixty boarders. . . . To anyone disposed to engage in this branch of business, a good opportunity is now offered for investment." After the sale of the Pavilion Hotel Clark conducted a grocery business until his death on October 31st, 1872. He was buried in Laurel Grove Cemetery. He married first (in March 1817) Mrs. Winifred Tucker, widow of Henry Tucker; he married second (in April 1839) Sarah B. Anderson, who survived her husband eleven years.

CLARKE, SAMUEL (1791–1869), planter, was born in South Carolina in 1791. From early manhood he resided in Beech Island, Edgefield District, South Carolina, where he was for many years ruling elder of the Presbyterian church and leader in the affairs of the Charleston Presbytery. His wife, Ann Helena Clarke (1800–1850), died on May 25th, 1850, leaving four children, among them Mary Burney Clarke (1835–1875), who on December 11th, 1855, became the wife of the Rev. David H. Porter, pastor of the First Presbyterian Church, Savannah. The Clarke family were intimate friends of Dr. and Mrs. Joseph Jones, of Augusta, who often stayed with the Clarkes in Beech Island. Samuel Clarke died on June 13th, 1869; his funeral was conducted by the Rev. Dr. Joseph Ruggles Wilson and the Rev. Dr. Samuel Stanhope Davis, both of Augusta.

CLAY, ANNE (1845–1921), third child of Thomas Savage Clay (1801–1849) and Matilda Willis McAllister (1818–1869), was born at Tivoli plantation, Bryan County, Georgia, on April 18th, 1845. After her father's death on October 24th, 1849, her paternal aunt, Eliza Caroline Clay, assumed the guardianship of his five children; the family summered in New Haven, Connecticut, and wintered at Richmond-on-Ogeechee, their plantation in Bryan County, Georgia. Anne Clay was evidently precocious: her aunt, writing from New Haven on June 2nd, 1853, reported that "Anne has lately commenced school, and is much interested. She is an independent, energetic, bright child, and I think will make a fine woman." Two months later, on August 4th, 1853, Mary Sharpe Jones described a visit to New Haven: "Anne is quite a bright girl, but I think she is too conscious of it—though she is a pleasant child." By June 1858 she was five feet eight inches tall. On March 9th, 1871, she became the wife of Ingersoll Washburn (1842–1922), son of Joseph Washburn (1796–1862), of Savannah; four of their children survived infancy. She died in Savannah on December 2nd, 1921, and was buried in Laurel Grove Cemetery. Ingersoll Washburn died on March 14th, 1922, and was buried beside his wife.

CLAY, ELIZA CAROLINE (1809–1895), youngest child of the Hon. Joseph Clay (1764–1811) and Mary Ann Savage (1770–1844), was born at Tranquilla plantation, Bryan County, Georgia, on April 2nd, 1809. Her father, a graduate of the College of New Jersey (Princeton) in 1784, had studied law in Williamsburg, Virginia, under George Wythe and had returned to his native Savannah to become a distinguished jurist; an Episcopalian by birth and training, he had become a Baptist in 1803, and from 1807 until his death in 1811 he had served as pastor of the First Baptist Church in Boston, Massachusetts. It was the family custom to divide the year between the North and the South, visiting the North for health and society during the summer months and returning to their Georgia plantation for the promotion of their business interests during the winter and spring. It was on one of these returns to Georgia that Eliza Caroline Clay was born. After her father's death her mother retired to Medford, near Boston, where she remained until the three children (Anne, Thomas Savage, and Eliza Caroline) were educated; in 1825 she returned to Georgia and purchased Richmond-on-Ogeechee, a plantation in Bryan County, where the family continued to reside, with frequent intervals in the North, until the house was destroyed by Sherman's army in 1864. On May 17th, 1836, Thomas Savage Clay (1801–1849) married Matilda Willis McAllister (1818–1869), eldest daughter of George Washington McAllister (1781–1850) and his second wife, Mary Bowman (1792–1825); five children survived infancy: Joseph Clay (1838–1914), Thomas Carolin Clay (1841–1897), Anne Clay (1845–1921), Emma Josephine Clay (1847–1928), and Robert Habersham Clay (1849–1924). The mother was a semi-invalid; when the father died on October 24th, 1849, the responsibility of his five children fell largely on his younger sister, Eliza Caroline Clay, who devoted herself to their education with energy and enthusiasm. One by one the children married: Tom in 1864, Joe in 1865, Anne in 1871, and Habbie in 1880; Emma, who never married, continued to live with her aunt at Three Gables, a small house in Bryan County built after the war, until Miss Clay's death there on October 18th, 1895. She was buried in Bryan Neck Presbyterian Churchyard beside her brother and his wife. "I shall never cease to feel the highest admiration for her high traits of character." So wrote her "old flame," General John Hartwell Cocke, on February 4th, 1856. A witty, outspoken spinster with a fluent pen and an ear trumpet, she was a great favorite among her friends. "Our dear Eliza Clay was with us for a few hours," wrote Mrs. Anne Elizabeth (Cumming) Smith from Philadelphia on January 14th, 1854: "too short a time to be with such an one as she is, but I am most thankful for that."

CLAY, EMMA JOSEPHINE (1847–1928), fourth child of Thomas Savage Clay (1801–1849) and Matilda Willis McAllister (1818–1869), was born in Clarkesville, Georgia, on August 27th, 1847. After her father's death on October 24th, 1849, her paternal aunt, Eliza Caroline Clay, assumed the guardianship of his five children; the family summered in New Haven, Connecticut, and wintered at Richmond-on-Ogeechee, their plantation in Bryan County, Georgia. Emma Josephine Clay never married. After her mother's death on September 18th, 1869, she continued to live with her aunt at Three Gables, a small house in Bryan County; after her aunt's death on October 18th, 1895, she lived with her brother, Robert Habersham Clay, and his wife and family at Strathy Hall, the McAllister plantation on the Ogeechee River in Bryan County; and after her brother's death on December 23rd, 1924, she removed to Savannah, where she died on December 29th, 1928. She was buried in Laurel Grove Cemetery. According to the Savannah *Morning News* (December 30th, 1928), "Miss Clay, although she had passed her eightieth birthday, had the gaiety and courage of youth, and her lively good humor and wit never flagged. It made contact with her a delight to all her friends and acquaintances. She had suffered in late years the handicap of extreme deafness, but she never allowed this to hamper her intercourse with her friends. . . . Tall and of stately presence, with bright color in her cheeks, her friends were fond of calling her 'the grand duchess' and of saying that she looked and acted the part."

CLAY, HENRY (1777–1852), statesman, son of John Clay, a Baptist clergyman, and Elizabeth Hudson, was born in Hanover County, Virginia, on April 12th, 1777. After studying law in Richmond, Virginia, he commenced practice in Lexington, Kentucky, in 1797 and soon rose to prominence as a criminal lawyer. In 1799 he married Lucretia Hart, daughter of Thomas Hart; there were eleven children. He was a member of the state house of representatives (1803, 1808, 1809); United States senator (1806–1807; 1810–1811); a member of Congress (1811–1814; 1815–1821; 1823–1825); speaker of the house (1811–1814; 1815–1820; 1823–1825); secretary of state under President John Quincy Adams (1825–1829); and United States senator (1831–1842; 1849–1852). His championship of the Missouri Compromise of 1820 won him prominence as "the great pacificator," and thirty years later he fought with equal determination for the Compromise of 1850. He was one of the outstanding leaders of the United States prior to the Civil War; according to the Rev. Dr. Charles Colcock Jones (June 12th, 1857) he was one of "the first three," the other two being Daniel Webster (1782–1852) of Massachusetts and John C. Calhoun (1782–1850) of South Carolina. Clay died in Washington, D.C., on June 29th, 1852, and was buried in Lexington Cemetery.

CLAY, JAMES BROWN (1817–1864), lawyer and congressman, fourth son of Henry Clay (1777–1852) and Lucretia Hart, was born in Washington, D.C., on November 9th,

1817. After attending Kenyon College he studied law at Transylvania University and practiced with his distinguished father in Lexington, Kentucky. He was a member of Congress (1857–1859); early in 1861 he was a member of the peace convention held in Washington in an effort to avert war. He warmly supported the Southern cause, and he was on his way to join the Confederate army when he was arrested and exiled to Canada, where he died of consumption on January 26th, 1864. His wife, Susan M. Jacob (1823–1905), survived. He was buried in Lexington Cemetery.

CLAY, JOSEPH (1838–1914), rice planter, eldest child of Thomas Savage Clay (1801–1849) and Matilda Willis McAllister (1818–1869), was born in Bryan County, Georgia, on December 10th, 1838. After his father's death on October 24th, 1849, his paternal aunt, Eliza Caroline Clay, assumed the guardianship of his five children; the family summered in New Haven, Connecticut, and wintered at Richmond-on-Ogeechee, their plantation in Bryan County, Georgia. From 1852 to 1855 Joseph Clay attended the Collegiate and Commercial Institute of New Haven, conducted by William Huntington Russell; from 1855 to 1856 he attended the Hopkins Grammar School in New Haven; from 1856 to 1860 he attended Yale College. After graduation in 1860 he returned to Georgia and undertook rice planting at Richmond-on-Ogeechee; in the summer of 1862 he purchased a plantation near Boston, Thomas County, to which he removed with his mother and family for safety from Yankee raids. During the Civil War he was drafted, but he hired a substitute and never saw military service. On November 13th, 1865, he married Mary Eliza Herndon (1843–1878), youngest daughter of Dr. Brodie Strachan Herndon (1810–1886) and Lucy Ellen Hansbrough (1813–1880), of Fredericksburg, Virginia. In 1866 he resumed rice planting at Richmond-on-Ogeechee, where he remained until 1893, when he took a position in Savannah as engineer for the United States government. In 1909 he retired and settled in Brunswick, Georgia, where he died on March 26th, 1914, survived by two children. He was buried in Laurel Grove Cemetery beside his wife, who had died on February 1st, 1878.

CLAY, MATILDA WILLIS (McALLISTER) (1818–1869): Mrs. *Thomas Savage Clay*, eldest daughter of George Washington McAllister (1781–1850) and his second wife, Mary Bowman (1792–1825), was born at Strathy Hall, her father's plantation in Bryan County, Georgia, on April 17th, 1818. On May 17th, 1836, she married Thomas Savage Clay (1801–1849), son of the Hon. Joseph Clay (1764–1811) and Mary Ann Savage (1770–1844), and removed to Richmond-on-Ogeechee plantation in Bryan County. Five children survived infancy: Joseph Clay (1838–1914), Thomas Carolin Clay (1841–1897), Anne Clay (1845–1921), Emma Josephine Clay (1847–1928), and Robert Habersham Clay (1849–1924). Her youngest child was born on May

27th, 1849; her husband died suddenly on October 24th, 1849, at the age of forty-eight; her father was thrown from a horse and died on March 18th, 1850. The shock and strain of these events, all occurring within ten months, led her to relinquish much of the responsibility of her children to her unmarried sister-in-law, Eliza Caroline Clay, who devoted herself to their education with energy and enthusiasm. But the mother remained attentive and discriminating; as Miss Clay wrote on October 5th, 1858, she "never loses sight of their best interests, never varies from her high-toned inflexible sense of right and propriety. I think her judgment *very superior,* and her sense of what is *truly refined* very remarkable. . . . I try to impress it on the children that they can't have a better guide than their mother's standard." It was the family custom to divide the year between the North and the South, visiting the North for health and society during the summer months and returning to their Georgia plantation for the promotion of their business interests during the winter and spring. On her Northern visits she was often accompanied by her sister Emma McAllister, her brother Joseph Longworth McAllister, and her two half-sisters Rosella and Clementina McAllister. She was always something of an invalid. She died in Athens, Georgia, on September 18th, 1869, and was buried beside her husband in Bryan Neck Presbyterian Churchyard, Bryan County.

CLAY, THOMAS CAROLIN (1841–1897), commission merchant, second child of Thomas Savage Clay (1801–1849) and Matilda Willis McAllister (1818–1869), was born in Bryan County, Georgia, on January 21st, 1841. After his father's death on October 24th, 1849, his paternal aunt, Eliza Caroline Clay, assumed the guardianship of his five children. The family summered in New Haven, Connecticut, and wintered at Richmond-on-Ogeechee, their plantation in Bryan County, Georgia. From 1852 to 1855 Thomas Carolin Clay attended the Collegiate and Commercial Institute of New Haven, conducted by William Huntington Russell; from 1855 to 1857 he attended Hopkins Grammar School in New Haven; from 1857 to 1859 he studied under a private tutor; from 1859 to 1860 he attended the classical school of the Rev. Henry Martyn Colton in Middletown, Connecticut. In September 1860 he entered Yale College, but when Georgia seceded from the Union in January 1861 he returned to Bryan County, where he enlisted as a private in the Liberty Independent Troop on June 20th, 1862. For some months he was detailed for duty in the signal corps. At the height of the war, on November 1st, 1864, he married Caroline Matilda Law (1842–1909), daughter of the Hon. William Law (1793–1874) and his third wife, Alethea Jones Stark (1810–1872), of Savannah; there were five sons and three daughters. After the war he undertook rice planting in Bryan County with his brother-in-law, Ebenezer Stark Law (1835–1907); in 1867 he settled in Savannah, where he resided for the rest of his life, engaging first in the commission business and later in real estate. He died in Savannah on August 11th, 1897, survived by his wife and six children, and was buried in Laurel Grove Cemetery. Caroline Matilda (Law) Clay died on October 12th, 1909, and was buried beside her husband.

CLEBURNE, PATRICK RONAYNE (1828–1864), Confederate soldier, son of Joseph Cleburne, was born in County Cork, Ireland, on March 17th, 1828. Having failed to pass his entrance examinations at Trinity College (Dublin), he migrated to the United States in 1849; and after six months as a druggist's clerk in Cincinnati, Ohio, he settled in Helena, Arkansas, where he was admitted to the bar in 1856 and practiced law until the outbreak of the Civil War. In 1861 he became captain, then colonel, of the 1st (later the 15th) Regiment Arkansas Infantry; early in 1862 he was promoted to brigadier general, and late in 1862 he became major general. After serving with distinction at Shiloh, Perryville, Murfreesboro, Chickamauga, and Missionary Ridge, he followed Johnston to Atlanta and later retreated with Hood to Tennessee, where he was killed in the battle of Franklin on November 30th, 1864. He was known as "the Stonewall Jackson of the West." He never married. Cleburne, Texas, was named in his honor.

CLINGMAN, THOMAS LANIER (1812–1897), legislator and Confederate soldier, was born in Huntsville, Surry (now Yadkin) County, North Carolina, on July 27th, 1812. He graduated from the University of North Carolina with first honor in 1832. After representing Surry County in the state legislature in 1835 he removed to Asheville, where he continued for sixty years, devoting his life to politics and the development of Western North Carolina. He was a member of the state senate (1840); a member of Congress (1843–1845; 1847–1858); and United States senator (1858–1861). He was a delegate from North Carolina to the convention of seceding states meeting in Montgomery, Alabama, in February 1861. In August 1861 he was appointed colonel of the 25th Regiment North Carolina Volunteers; on May 17th, 1862, he became brigadier general. After the war he returned to Asheville, where he resided for the rest of his life, exploring and measuring mountain peaks in Western North Carolina. He never married. He died in Morganton, Burke County, North Carolina, on November 3rd, 1897, and was buried in Riverside Cemetery, Asheville.

CLINTON, DE WITT (1769–1828), statesman, second son of James Clinton (1733–1812) and his first wife, Mary De Witt, was born in Napanock, Ulster County, New York, on March 2nd, 1769. After graduating with first honor from Columbia College in 1786 he studied law and commenced practice in New York City in 1790. For five years (1790–1795) he was private secretary to his uncle, George Clinton (1739–1812), governor of New York (1777–1795). He was a member of the state assembly (1798), the state senate (1798–1802; 1806–1811), and the United States Senate (1802–1803). As mayor of New York (1803–1807, 1810, 1811, 1813, and 1814) he organized the New York Historical Society (1804) and the Academy of Fine Arts (1808). He was regent of the University of New York (1808–1825); lieutenant governor of New York (1811–1813); and governor of New York (1817–1821; 1825–1828). He was an ardent proponent of the Erie Canal, linking Lake Erie and the Hudson River (362 miles), from its first projection in 1809 until its completion in 1825. He married first (on February 13th, 1796) Maria Franklin, daughter of Walter Franklin, a New York Quaker merchant; there were ten children. After her death in 1818 he married second (on May 8th, 1819) Catharine Jones, daughter of Thomas Jones, a New York physician. He died in Albany, New York, on February 11th, 1828, survived by his second wife, and was buried in Clinton Cemetery, Little Britain, Orange County, New York.

COBB, HOWELL (1815–1868), statesman and Confederate soldier, elder son of John Addison Cobb and Sarah Robinson Rootes, was born at Cherry Hill, his father's plantation in Jefferson County, Georgia, on September 7th, 1815. He graduated from Franklin College (Athens) in 1834, studied law, and was admitted to the bar in 1836. On May 26th, 1835, he married Mary Ann Lamar, of Athens. He was a member of Congress (1843–1851); governor of Georgia (1851–1853); again a member of Congress (1855–1857); and secretary of the treasury under President James Buchanan (1857–1860). He strongly favored secession, and he was unanimously elected president of the convention of seceding states meeting in Montgomery, Alabama, in February 1861. On July 15th, 1861, he became colonel of the 16th Regiment Georgia Infantry; on February 13th, 1862, he was promoted to brigadier general; on September 9th, 1863, he was promoted to major general and placed in command of the military district of Georgia. After the war he opposed reconstruction; he resumed the practice of law in Macon with his relative and close friend James Jackson. He died suddenly at the Fifth Avenue Hotel, New York City, on October 9th, 1868. As Charles Colcock Jones, Jr., wrote from New York the following day, "He was in our office only a day or two since, looking remarkably well, and at the time of his death was walking with his wife and daughter down the stairs of the main entrance of the hotel to take a carriage and come out and see Eva and Mrs. Eve."

COBB, LYMAN (1800–1864), educator and author, son of Elijah William Cobb and Sally Whitney, was born in Lenox, Massachusetts, on September 18th, 1800. Throughout the nineteenth century his textbooks in spelling, reading, and arithmetic were favorably received and widely used. In 1831 his "critical review" of Noah Webster's spelling books provoked a reply from Webster: *To the Friends of American Literature*, an eight-page pamphlet; during the ensuing debate each man pointed out numerous errors in the work of the other. Cobb was editor of *The North American Reader* (1836), "containing a great variety of pieces in prose and poetry from very highly esteemed American and English writers." In *The Evil Tendencies of Corporal Punishment as a Means of Moral Discipline in Families and Schools* (1847) he discussed "objectives," "substitutes," and "preventives" of "the use of the rod." His abridgment of *A Critical Pronouncing Dictionary and Expositor of the English Language,* by John Walker (1732–1807), was first published in 1829 and ran through many editions. In 1822 Cobb married Harriet Chambers, of Caroline, Tompkins County, Pennsylvania. He died in Colesburg, Pennsylvania, on October 26th, 1864, and was buried in an unmarked grave in the local cemetery.

COBB, THOMAS READE ROOTES (1823–1862), jurist and Confederate soldier, younger son of John Addison Cobb and Sarah Robinson Rootes, was born at Cherry Hill, his father's plantation in Jefferson County, Georgia, on April 10th, 1823. He graduated from Franklin College (Athens) with first honor in 1841, studied law, and was admitted to the bar in 1842. On January 9th, 1844, he married Marion Lumpkin, daughter of the Hon. Joseph Henry Lumpkin (1799–1867) and Callender C. Grieve, of Athens. As reporter of the state supreme court (1849–1857) he edited some twenty volumes; he also published *A Digest of the Statute Laws of the State of Georgia* (1851) and *An Inquiry into the Law of Negro Slavery in the United States of America; to which is prefixed, An Historical Sketch of Slavery* (1858). At the request of Governor Joseph E. Brown he collaborated with Richard H. Clark and David Irwin in preparing *The Code of the State of Georgia* (1861). Like his elder brother, Howell Cobb, he strongly favored secession, and he was a delegate, together with his brother, to the convention of seceding states meeting in Montgomery, Alabama, in February 1861. On August 28th, 1861, he was commissioned colonel of Cobb's Georgia Legion; on November 1st, 1862, he was promoted to brigadier general. A few weeks later, on December 13th, 1862, he was killed in the battle of Fredericksburg. He was an elder of the Athens Presbyterian Church and, together with William Letcher Mitchell, superintendent of the Sunday school. He was also a trustee of the University of Georgia and founder of the Lucy Cobb Institute in Athens, named for a daughter who died at fourteen. For genius, knowledge, industry, and personal influence he was unsurpassed among lawyers in his native state.

COCHRAN, ARTHUR EMMET (1820–1865), legislator and jurist, was born in Georgia in 1820. He was the first judge of the superior court of the Brunswick circuit, serving from 1856 to 1859 and again from 1861 to 1865. He represented Glynn County in the state legislature in 1861, 1862, and 1863. He

was a trustee of the University of Georgia (1858–1865). From its inception he was president of the Macon & Brunswick Railroad, and was instrumental in developing the area of Middle Georgia lying between the two cities. Cochran, the county seat of Bleckley County, was incorporated in 1869 and named in his honor. His first wife, Rebecca M. Cochran, died in Irwinton, Georgia, on July 25th, 1858, leaving one child, Arthur Emmet Cochran, Jr. On December 4th, 1861, he married Eugenia Tucker (1834–1928), eldest daughter of Dr. Nathan Tucker, of Lowndes County; she was a graduate of Wesleyan College (1852) and founder and first president of Alpha Delta Pi Sorority. He died in Macon on July 25th, 1865.

COCKE, JOHN HARTWELL (1780–1866), planter and publicist, son of John Hartwell Cocke and Elizabeth Kennon, was born in Surry County, Virginia, on September 19th, 1780. He attended the College of William and Mary from 1794 to 1799. After his marriage to Anne Blaus Barraud, of Norfolk, on December 25th, 1802, he settled to the life of a country gentleman at Bremo, his plantation in Fluvanna County, where he built a superb classical mansion according to plans drawn by his friend Thomas Jefferson. During the War of 1812 he rose in eighteen months from captain to brigadier general. In his range of interests and active support of public causes he was one of the most remarkable Virginians of his day. He opposed slavery, duelling, and indulgence in alcohol and tobacco; he supported popular education, and together with Thomas Jefferson and Joseph C. Cabell he founded the University of Virginia, of which he was for thirty-three years (1819–1852) a member of the board of visitors. He was a warm friend of the Rev. Dr. Charles Colcock Jones from their first meeting in Richmond in 1847. As Mrs. Mary Jones wrote from Bremo on June 11th, 1847, "Universally is it said of him: '*General Cocke lives to do good.*' His heart and hand and purse is engaged in every work of benevolence." He died at Bremo on July 1st, 1866, having outlived his wife and all his children.

COLCOCK, CHARLES JONES (1820–1891), cotton factor, financier, and Confederate soldier, son of Thomas Hutson Colcock (1797–1839) and Eliza Mary Hay (1803–1844), was born near Boiling Springs, Barnwell District, South Carolina, on April 30th, 1820. He was a second cousin once removed of the Rev. Dr. Charles Colcock Jones. After a brief period as a planter he settled in Charleston, where he prospered as a cotton factor, served as director of the Bank of South Carolina and of the Memphis, Chattanooga & Charleston Railroad, and founded the Charleston & Savannah Railroad. Early in the Civil War he became colonel of the 3rd Regiment South Carolina Cavalry, which he commanded throughout the war, serving on the South Carolina and Georgia coast; in June 1864 he became commander of the third military district of South Carolina. His son, John Colcock (1843–1877), also saw service throughout the war and was for a time acting adjutant in his father's regiment. Charles Jones Colcock married first (in 1842) Mary Caroline Heyward; he married second (in 1851) Lucy Frances Horton; he married third (in 1864) Agnes Bostick. He died at Elmwood plantation, Hampton County, South Carolina, on October 22nd, 1891. In the words of his kinsman, Charles Colcock Jones, Jr., he was "one of the most accomplished and agreeable gentlemen one might meet anywhere."

COLCOCK, WILLIAM FERGUSON (1804–1889), lawyer and legislator, son of the Hon. Charles Jones Colcock (1771–1839) and Mary Woodward Hutson (1774–1851), was born in Beaufort District, South Carolina, on November 5th, 1804. He was an uncle of Charles Jones Colcock (1820–1891). After graduating from the South Carolina College in 1823 he studied law and commenced practice in Coosawhatchie, near Beaufort. He was a member of the state legislature (1831–1848); a member of Congress (1849–1853); and collector of the port of Charleston (1853–1865). After the Civil War he resumed the practice of law. He died in McPhersonville, Hampton County, South Carolina, on June 13th, 1889, having outlived two wives: Sarah Huguenin, daughter of Abram Huguenin, and her sister, Emeline Huguenin. According to the Charleston *News & Courier* (June 14th, 1889), "He was of that class of public men the whole political creed of whose lives could be summed up in one commandment: 'Love South Carolina'; and to none, then, surely, could the term 'gentleman of the old school' more fitly apply. He was loyal to his state, devoted in his domestic relations, preeminent in his affection for and observance of the Christian religion, and of charming manners and esprit."

COLE, MOSES (1836–1885), nurseryman, was born in Dorchester, New Brunswick, Canada, on September 5th, 1836. In boyhood he removed with his parents to Atlanta, Georgia, where he resided for the rest of his life. He was a charter member of the Central Presbyterian Church at its organization in 1858, and he became one of its four ruling elders in January 1866. He married first (on June 6th, 1861) Amelia Randall Clarke (1841–1863); he married second (on September 5th, 1866) Maria D. Winship (1838–1905), widow of John H. Burr. During the Civil War he served as private in the 3rd Battalion Georgia State Guards, organized in Atlanta for home defense. After the war he prospered as a nurseryman. He died in Atlanta on December 6th, 1885, survived by his wife and six children, and was buried in Oakland Cemetery.

COLEMAN, SARAH HARRIET (COOPER) (1832–1915): *Mrs. Francis H. Coleman,* daughter of William H. Cooper and Eliza Fall, was born in LaGrange, Georgia, in 1832. On July 9th, 1857, she became the wife of Francis H. Coleman (1829–1861), of Atlanta, wholesale and retail grocer. She was a charter member of the Central Presbyterian Church at its organization in 1858. After her husband's death on August 3rd, 1861, just as he was leaving for Virginia, she remained in Atlanta until early 1864, when the difficulty of securing provisions induced her to remove to her father's house in LaGrange. In 1865 she returned with her two daughters (Carrie and Julia) to Atlanta, where she operated a boardinghouse until her marriage (on April 29th, 1869) to Dr. Charles S. Newton (1825–1899), a druggist. After his death on April 19th, 1899, she resided with her daughter Julia, wife of William H. Burnett, in Madison, Georgia, where she died on August 27th, 1915. She was buried near her two husbands in Oakland Cemetery, Atlanta.

COLLINS, WILLIAM Z. (born 1840), son of Stephen Z. Collins and Sarah Ann McCay, was born in McIntosh County, Georgia, in 1840. His father, a merchant, was a native of Massachusetts; his mother was a sister of Mary Jane McCay, wife of Alexander Mitchel. In 1860 William Z. Collins was a law student living with his widowed mother in the Mitchel household in Darien. For several months in 1863 he was associated in business with James Audley Maxwell King on Colonel's Island, Liberty County. On February 1st, 1864, he enlisted as a private in Company D, 2nd Battalion Kentucky Cavalry; he was captured at Cynthiana, Kentucky, on June 14th, 1864, confined for eight months at Rock Island, Illinois, and exchanged at Point Lookout, Maryland, in February 1865. After the war he joined his younger brother, Stephen M. Collins, on a farm near Americus, Sumter County, Georgia, where he was still living in December 1879.

COMFORT, DAVID (1837–1873), Presbyterian clergyman, son of David Comfort, was born near Charlotte Courthouse, Virginia, on July 29th, 1837. He graduated from Hampden-Sydney College with first honor in 1858. After teaching school for two years he entered Princeton Theological Seminary in the autumn of 1860; in the spring of 1861, after the outbreak of the Civil War, he returned with much difficulty to Virginia, where he enlisted as a private in Company G, 20th Regiment Virginia Infantry. In July 1861 he was taken prisoner and sent to Camp Chase, Ohio, where he contracted the disease from which he later died; after his exchange he was discharged as unfit for further military service. He then entered Union Theological Seminary, Hampden-Sydney, Virginia, hoping to complete his studies; but the war again interrupted his course and he withdrew to become a chaplain in the Confederate army. Ill health forced him to seek the milder climate of Georgia; in the autumn of 1864 he became pastor of churches in Boston and Valdosta, where he remained until his death in Boston on January 22nd, 1873. He was survived by his wife, Charlotte Catherine McIntosh (1841–1908), whom he had married on December 20th, 1865, and three young children.

COOPER, JOHN (1821–1887), grocer, was born in Birmingham, England, on August 6th, 1821. At the age of six he removed with his parents to Savannah, Georgia, where he resided for the rest of his life. For many years he engaged in the grocery and dry goods business, and in his last decade he became a real estate agent. In October 1857 he ran against the Hon. John Elliott Ward for a seat in the state senate; he received 533 votes to Ward's 1191. During the Civil War he was captain of the Washington Volunteers (Company K, 1st Regiment Georgia Volunteers) and served with his command in Upper Georgia, Tennessee, and the Carolinas. He married first (on March 1st, 1849) Caroline Wisenbaker (1828–1872), of Effingham County; he married second (on November 6th, 1873) Susan E. Wright, of Chatham County. He died in Savannah on January 17th, 1887, survived by his second wife, two sons, and three daughters, and was buried in Laurel Grove Cemetery.

COOPER, JOHN McKINNEY (1814–1877), stationer, bookseller, and printer, was born in Augusta, Georgia, in August 1814. In infancy he removed with his parents to Savannah, where he was for many years senior member of the firm of John M. Cooper & Company, "wholesale and retail dealers in school and miscellaneous books and foreign and domestic stationery. Also law and medical books. Books rebound; blankbooks manufactured to order; paper ruled to any pattern." In 1850, in association with William Tappan Thompson (1812–1882), he founded the Savannah *Morning News*; he was publisher from its first issue on January 15th, 1850, until March 1855. He printed a number of booklets for the Rev. Dr. Charles Colcock Jones, among them his *Historical Address Delivered to the Liberty Independent Troop upon Its Anniversary, February 22nd, 1856*. The Joneses dealt regularly with Cooper; on one occasion (April 24th, 1856) Dr. Jones had to ask for his bill: "He is so lenient that one is inclined to think he either needs no money or refuses to charge his friends." Cooper never married. He died in Savannah on June 12th, 1877, after a lingering illness and was buried in Laurel Grove Cemetery beside his mother, Salome (Gugle) Cooper, who had died on September 8th, 1862, in her seventy-seventh year.

COUPER, HAMILTON (1829–1861), lawyer and Confederate soldier, son of James Hamilton Couper (1794–1866) and Caroline Georgia Wylly (1811–1897), was born at Hopeton plantation, Glynn County, Georgia, on January 11th, 1829. After graduating from Yale College in 1849 he studied law in Cambridge, Massachusetts, and New York City and commenced practice in Savannah, Georgia, in 1853. In January 1860 he was appointed United States district attorney for the southern district of Georgia. At the outbreak of the Civil War he became second lieutenant in the Oglethorpe Light Infantry (Company B, 8th Regiment Georgia Infantry); he was subsequently promoted to first lieutenant (July

3rd, 1861) and captain (September 1st, 1861). He died of typhoid fever in camp at Centreville, Virginia, on November 8th, 1861, and was buried at Frederica, St. Simons Island, Glynn County, Georgia.

COUPER, WILLIAM AUDLEY (1817–1888), planter, son of John Couper (1759–1850) and Rebecca Maxwell (1775–1845), was born in Rhode Island on August 15th, 1817. He was a younger brother of James Hamilton Couper (1794–1866) and Ann Sarah Couper (1796–1866), wife of John Fraser. His father, a native of Scotland, had migrated to Georgia in 1775 and become a wealthy landowner in Glynn County. William Audley Couper attended Franklin College (Athens) with the class of 1838 but did not graduate. On January 15th, 1845 he married Hannah Page King (1825–1896), eldest daughter of Thomas Butler King and Anna Matilda Page, of Retreat plantation, St. Simons Island, Glynn County. For some years he divided his time between his house in Marietta, Georgia, and Carteret, his plantation in Glynn County. After 1875 he resided permanently in Marietta, where he died on September 27th, 1888. He was buried in Episcopal Cemetery. Hannah Page (King) Couper died on November 12th, 1896, and was buried beside her husband.

COZBY, JAMES SMITH (1837–1894), Presbyterian clergyman, son of the Rev. James Cooper Cozby (1810–1837) and Hannah Maria Randolph (1805–1858), was born in St. Marys, Georgia, on September 1st, 1837. His father, a Presbyterian clergyman, died on November 27th, 1837, when the boy was less than three months old, and his widowed mother became the second wife of Nathaniel Varnedoe (1790–1856), a wealthy planter of Liberty County, in whose household James Smith Cozby spent his boyhood and early youth. He graduated from Oglethorpe University in 1857 and from Columbia Theological Seminary in 1862. After teaching school for eighteen months he became a chaplain in the Confederate army and served until the close of the war. On January 26th, 1864, he married Mary Louisa Law, daughter of the Hon. William Law (1793–1874) and his third wife, Alethea Jones Stark (1810–1872), of Savannah. He was pastor in Cuthbert, Georgia (1868–1873); Sumter County, South Carolina (1873–1886); and Newberry, South Carolina (1886–1894). He died in Clarkesville, Georgia, on September 10th, 1894, survived by two daughters and two sons, both studying for the ministry. He received the honorary degree of doctor of divinity from Newberry College in 1889.

CRANE, HEMAN AVERILL (1809–1879), merchant, was born in New Milford, Connecticut, on October 1st, 1809. In early manhood he migrated to Darien, Georgia, where he became agent for a line of steamers plying between Savannah and Darien, and where he married Julia R. Underwood (1810–1884), of St. Marys, Georgia, in 1834. Ten years later he removed to Savannah and entered the wholesale grocery business, in which he continued until 1870, when he became a commission merchant. Throughout his long career he was associated variously with Thomas Holcombe (Crane & Holcombe), James Gustavus Rodgers (Crane & Rodgers), and George H. Johnston (Crane, Johnston & Company). From 1844 to 1879 he was active in the affairs of the First Presbyterian Church; he was for many years superintendent of the Sunday school, and in 1847 he was elected ruling elder. He died in Savannah on May 26th, 1879, and was buried in Laurel Grove Cemetery beside his son, William Henry Crane (1839–1861), who had fallen in the battle of Manassas. Julia (Underwood) Crane died on March 10th, 1884, and was buried beside her husband.

CRANE, JOSEPH SIDNEY (1821–1906), physician, son of Sidney Crane (1791–1850) and Catherine Hequembourg, was born in Columbia, South Carolina, on June 10th, 1821. His father, a native of Newark, New Jersey, was ruling elder of the First Presbyterian Church, Columbia, from 1835 until his death in 1850. After attending the South Carolina College Joseph Sidney Crane graduated from the Medical College of the University of Pennsylvania in 1844 and returned to Columbia to practice his profession. On June 9th, 1853, he married Harriet Draper, daughter of William Whiting Draper (1794–1881) and Eliza Greene Chandler (1800–1880), of Greenfield, Massachusetts; there were four children. Shortly before the Civil War he removed to New York City, where he resided for the rest of his life. He died in New York on May 20th, 1906, and was buried in Federal Street Cemetery, Greenfield, Massachusetts.

CRAWFORD, JOHN A. (1797–1876), banker, was born in Ireland on February 12th, 1797. At an early age he migrated to Columbia, South Carolina, where he was for many years president of the Commercial Bank and ruling elder of the First Presbyterian Church. He died in Columbia on December 10th, 1876, survived by his only daughter, Jane Christina Crawford (1823–1904), and was buried in the First Presbyterian Churchyard beside his wife, Sophia Margaret Crawford (1802–1870). "With the grave and serious pursuits of life he blended a strong relish for the amenities of society and a conscientious regard for the duties of friendship." So commented the Columbia *Register* on December 12th, 1876. "He was a man of indomitable energy, of unflagging industry, of buoyant hope, and of unfailing Christian faith. Among his minor tastes and fancies were conspicuous a love of horses and a great fondness for flowers, for the cultivation of which he was known throughout the state."

CRITTENDEN, JOHN JORDAN (1787–1863), statesman, son of John Crittenden and Judith Harris, was born in Woodford County, Kentucky, on September 10th, 1787. After graduating from the College of William and Mary in 1807 he settled in Logan County, Kentucky, where he soon rose to prominence as a criminal lawyer; he later practiced in Frankfort. He was a member of the state house of representatives (1811–1817); United States senator (1817–1819; 1835–1841); attorney general of the United States under President William Henry Harrison (1841); United States senator (1842–1848); governor of Kentucky (1848–1850); attorney general of the United States under President Millard Fillmore (1850–1853); and United States senator (1855–1861). He strongly supported the Union, and in December 1860 he proposed the famous compromise which bears his name; after its defeat he returned to Frankfort to oppose the secession of Kentucky. He was a member of Congress (1861–1863). He died in Frankfort on July 26th, 1863, survived by his third wife. His son George Bibb Crittenden (1812–1880) was a major general in the Confederate army; his son Thomas Leonidas Crittenden (1815–1893) was a major general in the Union army.

CROGHAN, JOHN (1790–1849), physician, eldest son of William Croghan (1752–1822) and Lucy Clark, was born near Louisville, Kentucky, on April 14th, 1790. His father, a native of Ireland, had migrated to Virginia, fought gallantly in the Revolutionary War, accompanied his friend George Rogers Clark to Kentucky in 1784, and married Clark's sister on July 14th, 1789. John Croghan graduated from the College of William and Mary in 1809 and from the Medical College of the University of Pennsylvania in 1813. For some years he practiced medicine in Louisville, where he became, like his father, an extensive landowner. He never married. On October 8th, 1839, he purchased Mammoth Cave, then a property comprising 1610 acres, from Franklin Gorin for ten thousand dollars. During the following decade he spent large sums developing the cave, improving its buildings, grounds, and roads; in 1843 he built cottages in the cave for the benefit of consumptives, but the project was unsuccessful. In April 1840 he inherited his father's house, Locust Grove, near Louisville; he died there on January 11th, 1849, and was buried in the family cemetery; in 1916 his remains, together with those of his parents and other members of the family, were reinterred in Cave Hill Cemetery, Louisville. By the terms of his will Mammoth Cave was devised to trustees to be held for his nine nephews and nieces until the death of the last heir; the cave was thus controlled and operated by trustees until 1926, when it was purchased by the Mammoth Cave National Park Association and turned over to the government. John Croghan's younger brother, George Croghan (1791–1849), won national acclaim for his defense of Fort Stephenson, Ohio, on August 1st, 1813.

CRUMP, WILLIAM (1819–1868), physician, son of Dr. William Crump and Maria Moody, was born in Powhatan County, Virginia, on August 3rd, 1819. After graduating from Jefferson Medical College (Philadelphia) in 1849 he practiced medicine in Culpeper County,

Virginia, and later in Albemarle County. From 1851 to 1860 he spent his summers as resident physician at Hot Springs, Bath County, Virginia, where on June 6th, 1855, he married Alice Goode (1831–1903), daughter of Dr. Thomas Goode, proprietor of Hot Springs, and his wife Mary A. Knox. By 1860 Crump had settled at Ivy Depot, Albemarle County, where he died on September 21st, 1868. He was buried in St. Paul's Episcopal Churchyard. Alice (Goode) Crump died in Richmond, Virginia, on June 12th, 1903, and was buried beside her husband.

CUMMING, ALFRED (1829–1910), soldier, eldest son of Henry Harford Cumming (1799–1866) and Julia Anne Bryan (1803–1879), was born in Augusta, Georgia, on January 30th, 1829. He graduated from the United States Military Academy in 1849. As captain in the 10th Infantry he served in the Utah Expedition (1857–1858) commanded by Albert Sidney Johnston. On February 14th, 1861, he married his first cousin, Sarah Matilda Davis (1830–1910), daughter of the Rev. Samuel Stanhope Davis (1793–1877) and Mary Cuthbert Cumming (1797–1876). At the outbreak of the Civil War he was commissioned lieutenant colonel of the Augusta Volunteer Battalion and assumed command of the Augusta arsenal; preferring service in the field, he soon became lieutenant colonel, later colonel, of the 10th Regiment Georgia Infantry. He was seriously wounded at Sharpsburg, and in October 1862 he was promoted to brigadier general. At Jonesboro, near Atlanta, on August 31st, 1864, he was disabled for further service. After the war he planted in Floyd County, Georgia; from 1880 to 1896 he resided in Rome; in 1896 he returned to his former home in Augusta. He died in Rome at the residence of his only surviving son, Julian Cumming, on December 5th, 1910, and was buried in Summerville Cemetery, Augusta, beside his wife, who had died less than a month before.

CUMMING, EMILY (EMMA) HARFORD (1834–1911), daughter of Henry Harford Cumming (1799–1866) and Julia Anne Bryan (1803–1879), was born in Mount Zion, Hancock County, Georgia, on November 16th, 1834. Her father, a lawyer residing in Augusta, was a son of Thomas Cumming (1765–1834), first mayor of Augusta after its incorporation as a town (1798) and president of the Bank of Augusta from its organization in 1810 until his death in 1834. On November 22nd, 1859, she became the wife of James Henry (Harry) Hammond (1832–1916), son of James Henry Hammond (1807–1864), governor of South Carolina (1842–1844) and United States senator from South Carolina (1857–1860). Her husband, a graduate of the South Carolina College (1852) and the Medical College of the University of Pennsylvania (1855), never practiced medicine; after serving as quartermaster in the Confederate army he retired to Redcliffe, his residence in Beech Island, South Carolina, where

he lived a quiet life, planting and writing, until his death on January 7th, 1916. He was author of *A Report on the Cotton Production of the State of South Carolina* (1884) and *South Carolina: A Primer* (1904). Emily Harford (Cumming) Hammond died in Beech Island on September 4th, 1911, leaving three sons and two daughters, and was buried in the family cemetery at Redcliffe.

CUMMING, HENRY HARFORD (1799–1866), lawyer, son of Thomas Cumming (1765–1834) and Anne Clay (1767–1849), was born in Augusta, Georgia, on October 15th, 1799. His father, head of one of the most distinguished families in Georgia, was the first mayor of Augusta after its incorporation as a town (1798) and president of the Bank of Augusta from its organization in 1810 until his death in 1834. Henry Harford Cumming was identified with the history of Augusta all his life; he was one of the ablest lawyers in Georgia, and in 1845 he conceived and vigorously promoted the construction of the Augusta Canal, completed in 1847. According to the Augusta *Chronicle* (April 18th, 1866), "He was the soul of chivalry, sacrificing convenience and interest and lending the influence of name, wealth, and position to succor the weak and aid the friendless." On the morning of April 14th, 1866, "under the influence of mental alienation, which had been observed to be growing upon him day by day for months, he committed suicide at his office." He was buried in Summerville Cemetery, Augusta; his marker reads: "Dear to his family as the devoted husband, the tender father; honored in this community as the distinguished lawyer, the good citizen, the faithful friend, the fearless defender of the right, the peerless gentleman." He was survived by his wife, Julia Anne Bryan (1803–1879), whom he had married in 1824.

CUMMING, MONTGOMERY (1824–1870), planter and commercial agent, son of Joseph Cumming (1790–1846) and his first wife, Matilda Ann Poe (1795–1827), was born in Savannah, Georgia, on August 25th, 1824. From early manhood he was active in the civic and business affairs of Savannah; he served variously as justice of the inferior court, as alderman (1849–1851; 1853–1854), and as chief of the Savannah Fire Company (1856–1860). Through his stepmother, Mrs. Susan M. Cumming, he was intimately associated with the family of her brother, the Rev. Dr. Charles Colcock Jones; for some years he and his brother, Wallace Cumming (1827–1877), were agents of Dr. Jones in Savannah, and Charles Colcock Jones, Jr., declared Montgomery Cumming to be "one of my best friends in this city." He was the sole manager of the vast Georgia estate of William Heyward Gibbons (1830–1887). During the Civil War he was lieutenant colonel of the 2nd Battalion Georgia Cavalry and served as aide-de-camp to General Alexander Robert Lawton. On September 10th, 1868, aged forty-four, he married Rosalie Melvina Wade (1847–1885), daughter of the Rev. Peyton Lisby Wade, a Methodist clergyman. ("She is very pretty, intelligent, and affable," wrote his stepmother on September 24th, 1868; "Monty has been greatly favored in winning so fair a lady; he has not waited in vain.") Less than two years later, on June 22nd, 1870, he died suddenly at Red Clay, his summer retreat in Whitfield County, Georgia, and was buried in Laurel Grove Cemetery, Savannah, beneath the following inscription: "Stern in integrity; tender in affection; faithful to every trust; unalterable in friendship; the valuable citizen; the honorable man of business; beloved in all the relations of life." On February 13th, 1878, his widow became the wife of Robert Hayne Martin (1847–1928).

CUMMING, SARAH MATILDA (DAVIS) (1830–1910): *Mrs. Alfred Cumming,* second daughter of the Rev. Samuel Stanhope Davis (1793–1877) and Mary Cuthbert Cumming (1797–1876), was born in Augusta, Georgia, in January 1830. Her father, a Presbyterian clergyman, was a graduate of Middlebury College (1812) and Princeton Theological Seminary (1815); on January 5th, 1825, he had married a daughter of Thomas Cumming (1765–1834), first mayor of Augusta after its incorporation as a town (1798) and president of the Bank of Augusta from its organization in 1810 until his death in 1834. Sarah Matilda Davis and her three sisters (Anne Mary, Caroline Smelt, and Julia Cuthbert) spent much of their girlhood in Augusta, where they were known for their remarkable intellect, taste, and charm. On February 14th, 1861, Sarah Matilda Davis became the wife of her first cousin, Alfred Cumming (1829–1910), son of Henry Harford Cumming (1799–1866) and Julia Anne Bryan (1803–1879). During the Civil War her husband rose to the rank of brigadier general and was seriously wounded at Sharpsburg (September 1862) and at Jonesboro (August 1864). After the war he planted in Floyd County, Georgia; from 1880 to 1896 he resided in Rome; in 1896 he returned to his former home in Augusta, where Sarah Matilda (Davis) Cumming died on November 10th, 1910, and Alfred Cumming died less than a month later, on December 5th, 1910. They were buried in Summerville Cemetery. One son, Julian Cumming, survived.

CUMMING, SARAH WALLACE (1807–1895), youngest daughter of Thomas Cumming (1765–1834) and Anne Clay (1767–1849), was born in Augusta, Georgia, on February 16th, 1807. Her father, head of one of the most distinguished families in Georgia, was the first mayor of Augusta after its incorporation as a town (1798) and president of the Bank of Augusta from its organization in 1810 until his death in 1834. Sarah Wallace Cumming never married. All her life she resided in Augusta, where she enjoyed the company of her brothers, William Clay Cumming (1788–1863) and Henry Harford Cumming (1799–1866), both distinguished lawyers; her sister Mary Cuthbert Cumming (1797–1876), wife of the Rev. Samuel Stanhope Davis (1793–1877); and her sister Anne Elizabeth Cumming (1805–1883), widow of General Peter Skenandoah Smith (1795–1858). Her brother Joseph Cumming (1790–1846) was the second husband of Susan Mary Jones (1803–1890), widow of James Audley Maxwell and sister of the Rev. Dr. Charles Colcock Jones. Sarah Wallace Cumming died in Augusta on December 6th, 1895, and was buried in Summerville Cemetery.

CUMMING, SUSAN MARY (JONES) (MAXWELL) (1803–1890): *Mrs. Joseph Cumming,* daughter of John Jones (1772–1805) and his second wife, Susannah Hyrne Girardeau (1778–1810), was born at Liberty Hall, her father's plantation in Liberty County, Georgia, on October 22nd, 1803. Her father died on March 28th, 1805; her mother, a woman of singular piety, died on July 1st, 1810. Susan Mary Jones and her younger brother, Charles Colcock Jones (1804–1863), were reared by kind relatives: their half-aunt, Eliza Greene Low (1785–1868), widow of David Robarts; their half-sister, Elizabeth Jones (1794–1856), wife of William Maxwell; and their uncle, Joseph Jones (1779–1846), younger brother of their deceased father. After mastering the rudiments of an English education under the Rev. Dr. William McWhir at the Sunbury Academy, Susan Mary Jones boarded for eighteen months (1818–1819) at a school for young ladies in Charleston. Returning to Liberty County, she became the wife of James Audley Maxwell (1796–1828), son of Audley Maxwell (1766–1840) and Mary Stevens (1772–1850), in September 1823. There were three children: Laura Elizabeth Maxwell (1824–1903), Charles Edward Maxwell (1826–1852), and Georgia Maxwell (1828–1829). On November 21st, 1838, she became the second wife of Joseph Cumming (1790–1846), son of Thomas Cumming (1765–1834) and Anne Clay (1767–1849), a widower with four children: William Henry Cumming (1820–1893), Mary Cuthbert Cumming (1823–1893), Montgomery Cumming (1824–1870), and Wallace Cumming (1827–1877). Although she owned two plantations in Liberty County (Lambert and White Oak) she preferred to live much of the time between her first and second marriages in the household of her brother; after the marriage of her daughter, Laura Elizabeth Maxwell, to the Rev. David Lyman Buttolph (1822–1905) on June 10th, 1856, she lived permanently with the Buttolphs, first in Liberty County and after 1867 in Marietta, Georgia, where she died on September 16th, 1890. She was buried in Episcopal Cemetery.

CUMMING, THOMAS WILLIAM (1831–1889), civil engineer and Confederate soldier, son of Henry Harford Cumming (1799–1866) and Julia Anne Bryan (1803–1879), was born in Mount Zion, Hancock County, Georgia, on October 14th, 1831. His father, a lawyer residing in Augusta, was a son of Thomas Cumming (1765–1834), first mayor of Augusta after its incorporation as a town (1798) and president of the Bank of Augusta from its organization in 1810 until his death in 1834. Thomas William Cumming was by profession a civil engineer. During the Civil War he was adjutant, with rank of lieutenant, in the 16th Regiment Georgia Infantry, of which his intimate friend, Benjamin Edward Stiles, was lieutenant colonel. Stiles was killed near Front Royal, Virginia, on August 16th, 1864, the same day on which Cumming was taken prisoner and sent to Fort Delaware. On June 12th, 1866, Cumming married Mary Morgan Hazen (1842–1870), daughter of Gideon Morgan Hazen, of Knoxville, Tennessee; after her death on December 24th, 1870, he traveled extensively in Europe, remaining long enough to educate his only son, Henry Harford Cumming, in Geneva. Returning to Augusta, he lived a quiet life, indulging his taste for reading and scholarly pursuits. He died at Redcliffe, the home of his sister Emily (Mrs. James Henry Hammond) in Beech Island, South Carolina, on September 11th, 1889, and was buried in Summerville Cemetery, Augusta.

CUMMING, WALLACE (1827–1877), banker, youngest son of Joseph Cumming (1790–1846) and his first wife, Matilda Ann Poe (1795–1827), was born in Savannah, Georgia, on March 16th, 1827. For many years he was prominently identified with the business and social interests of his native city. He was an original member of the Savannah Fire Company and for several years served as chief. He was president of the Augusta & Savannah Railroad and an honorary member of the Georgia Hussars. Although he studiously avoided politics, he was elected one of twelve aldermen in October 1859; he and Charles Colcock Jones, Jr., led the count with 907 votes each. As banker he was known for his willingness to accommodate mechanics and tradesmen. Through his stepmother, Mrs. Susan M. Cumming, he was intimately associated with the family of her brother, the Rev. Dr. Charles Colcock Jones; for some years he and his brother, Montgomery Cumming (1824–1870), were agents of Dr. Jones in Savannah. On January 12th, 1853, he married Harriet Virginia Alexander (1828–1910), daughter of Adam Leopold Alexander (1803–1882) and his first wife, Sarah Hillhouse Gilbert (1805–1855), of Washington, Wilkes County, Georgia; there were five children. He died in Savannah on February 6th, 1877, and was buried in Laurel Grove Cemetery. Harriet Virginia (Alexander) Cumming died in Baltimore, Maryland, on March 6th, 1910, and was buried beside her husband.

CUMMING, WILLIAM HENRY (1820–1893), physician, eldest son of Joseph Cumming (1790–1846) and his first wife, Matilda Ann Poe (1795–1827), was born in Savannah, Georgia, in 1820. After attending Franklin College (Athens) he studied medicine in Paris and graduated from the Medical College of Georgia (Augusta) in 1841. For five years (1842–1847) he served as medical

missionary in China. Ill health forced him to return home, where on November 30th, 1847, he married Elizabeth Reid McDowall (1820–1895), daughter of Thomas McDowall and Ann Reid, of Augusta. From 1853 to 1860 he lived in Williamstown, Massachusetts, where he practiced medicine, attempted to recover his health, and considered entering the Presbyterian ministry. At the outbreak of the Civil War he returned to Georgia, where he served as medical director on the staff of General Lafayette McLaws. After the war he practiced medicine for several years in Toronto, Canada; returning South in 1871 he lived for six years in Atlanta and then settled in Marietta, home of his lifelong friend, Dr. Theophilus S. Stewart (1818–1901), who had married Susan McDowall (1822–1893), sister of Elizabeth Reid McDowall. He died in the house of Dr. Stewart on August 21st, 1893; Susan (McDowall) Stewart died in the same house the next day; there was a double funeral on August 23rd and a double burial service in Episcopal Cemetery. Elizabeth Reid (McDowall) Cumming died in Marietta on July 1st, 1895, and was buried beside her husband.

CUNNINGHAM, ANN PAMELA (1816–1875), founder and first regent of the Mount Vernon Ladies' Association of the Union, was born at Rosemont plantation, Laurens County, South Carolina, on August 15th, 1816, daughter of Robert Cunningham and Louisa Bird. In 1853 she founded the Mount Vernon Ladies' Association of the Union, established for the purpose of raising two hundred thousand dollars for the purchase of Mount Vernon, home of George Washington, from the owner, John Augustine Washington. As the Rev. Dr. Charles Colcock Jones wrote on February 21st, 1854, "The Washington family, in asking *two hundred thousand dollars* for the home and grave of Washington, are abominable! Selling his remains! Had they *donated* Mount Vernon to either Congress or Virginia, they would have been more than compensated. They appeal to the patriotism of the country; but pray where is *their* patriotism—or even *family veneration*—in the transaction? Yet if it can be taken out of their hands and secured to the country, let it be done." After much disappointment and discouragement Miss Cunningham succeeded in realizing her goal, and the purchase was completed on February 22nd, 1859. After the Civil War, from 1868 to 1874, she resided at Mount Vernon to oversee the estate. She died at Rosemont on May 1st, 1875, and was buried in the First Presbyterian Churchyard, Columbia, South Carolina.

CUNNINGHAM, HENRY CUMMING (1842–1917), lawyer and Confederate soldier, son of Dr. Alexander Cunningham and Anna Frances Mayhew, was born in Savannah, Georgia, on April 5th, 1842. After graduating from the South Carolina College in 1861 he enlisted as a private in the Savannah Volunteer Guards; a year later he was commissioned first lieutenant of artillery and assigned to ordnance duty on the staff of General William

B. Taliaferro, then stationed in Savannah. In the spring of 1863 he accompanied General Taliaferro to Charleston, where he continued to serve as ordnance officer, first on Morris Island, later on James Island, until the evacuation of the city. After the war he returned to Savannah, worked briefly for the Central Railroad of Georgia, and in 1872 commenced the practice of law. In 1881 he joined Alexander Robert Lawton and his son in the firm of Lawton & Cunningham; when Lawton was appointed United States minister to Austria by President Grover Cleveland in 1887, Cunningham became senior member of the firm. From 1880 to 1887 he was corporation attorney for Savannah. He married first (on December 19th, 1867) Virginia Waldburg Wayne (1845–1878), daughter of Dr. Richard Wayne (1804–1858) and Henrietta Jane Harden (1809–1880); there were four children. He married second (on April 7th, 1886) Nora Lawton (1855–1943), daughter of Alexander Robert Lawton (1818–1896) and Sarah Gilbert Alexander (1826–1897); there was one daughter. He died in Savannah on May 9th, 1917, and was buried in Bonaventure Cemetery. Nora (Lawton) Cunningham died on April 4th, 1943, and was buried beside her husband.

CUNNINGHAM, JOHN (1817–1903), grocer and ship chandler, son of John Cunningham (1772–1851) and Sarah Galloway (1780–1850), was born in Rutherglen, near Glasgow, Scotland, in 1817. At the age of fifteen he accompanied his parents to Savannah, Georgia, where he joined Orlando A. Wood and Joseph S. Claghorn in the firm of Wood & Claghorn, wholesale grocers and ship chandlers. In 1848, when Wood retired, Cunningham joined Claghorn in the firm of Claghorn & Cunningham, which continued in business until 1877, when Claghorn retired and William H. Hewes joined Cunningham in the firm of Cunningham & Hewes. During the Civil War Cunningham was captain of Company B, 1st Battalion Georgia Reserves. For many years he was a director of the Central Railroad & Banking Company of Georgia and virtual manager of its bank, then the strongest financial institution in Savannah; but in 1884, having suffered business reverses, he was compelled to accept a position as receiving clerk in the Savannah warehouse of the Central Railroad of Georgia. Two years later he was transferred to Atlanta, where he continued to work for the railroad until forced by old age to retire. He died at his home in Decatur, Georgia, on November 21st, 1903, and was buried in Decatur Cemetery. He was thrice married: first (on November 15th, 1849) to Christina Rettie (1825–1852); second (on July 25th, 1857) to Mrs. Matilda (Broadfoot) De Lara (1830–1860); and third (on October 9th, 1862) to Martha Isabella Gould, who survived her husband. For many years he was active in the St. Andrews Society of Savannah; after joining in 1837 he served as secretary (1839–1850), second vice-president (1861–1863), first vice-president (1863–1865), and president (1865–1874).

CUNNINGHAM, WILLIAM MADISON (1812–1870), Presbyterian clergyman, was born in Jonesboro, Tennessee, on June 28th, 1812. After graduating from Washington College (Greeneville, Tennessee) in 1829 he attended Princeton Theological Seminary for three years (1831–1834). From 1835 to 1840 he was pastor in Lexington, Virginia; in January 1841 he removed to LaGrange, Georgia, where he continued as pastor until his death there on March 3rd, 1870. He was buried in Hillview Cemetery. Hearing of his death, the Rev. David Lyman Buttolph wrote on March 7th, 1870: "It is the heaviest loss our church could sustain in this state. Dr. Cunningham had been elected president of Oglethorpe College, and had accepted the place provided the college would be removed to Atlanta. He was a strong man intellectually and spiritually, and possessed the confidence and love of all who knew him."

CURRY, CALVIN A. (1820–1867), planter, fifth child of Duncan Curry and Sarah Smith, was born in Telfair County, Georgia, on May 8th, 1820. At the age of three he removed with his parents to Decatur County, Georgia, where he resided for the rest of his life. On February 9th, 1843, he married Jane E. Gregory, of Quincy, Florida; there were ten children. Although interested in politics and an ardent Whig, he never held public office; he devoted much of his time and energy to the affairs of the Presbyterian Church. He was a pioneer of Presbyterianism in Decatur County, serving as ruling elder of his local church for fifteen years. In May 1857 he was commissioner from the Florida Presbytery to the General Assembly of the Presbyterian Church meeting in Lexington, Kentucky. He died at his residence in Decatur County on April 21st, 1867. As *The Southern Presbyterian* (June 20th, 1867) observed, "We know of scarcely one in our community whose loss will be more severely felt. . . . With enlarged and liberal views, and with a heart overflowing with generous emotions, he was ever to be found among the first and foremost in every effort for the public good and in every charitable and benevolent work."

CUSHING, LUTHER STEARNS (1803–1856), author and jurist, eldest son of Edmund Cushing and Mary Stearns, was born in Lunenburg, Worcester County, Massachusetts, on June 22nd, 1803. He graduated from Harvard College in 1826 with the degree of bachelor of laws. For several years, in association with Charles Sumner and George S. Hilliard, he edited *The American Jurist and Law Magazine,* published in Boston. He was clerk of the Massachusetts house of representatives (1832–1844); judge of the city court of common pleas (1844–1848); and reporter of the supreme court of the commonwealth (1848–1853). He was also lecturer on Roman law in Dane Law School, Harvard University (1848–1849; 1850–1851); in 1851 he declined a professorship for reasons of health. Among his numerous books the best known is *A Manual of Parliamentary Practice* (1844), providing "rules of proceeding and debate in deliberative assemblies." Cushing's *Manual* became an international classic, running into many editions, and still enjoys widespread use. He married first (on May 19th, 1840) Mary Otis Lincoln; there were three children. He married second (on October 29th, 1853) Elizabeth Dutton Cooper. He died in Boston on his fifty-third birthday, June 22nd, 1856.

CUSTIS, GEORGE WASHINGTON PARKE (1781–1857), author, son of John Parke Custis (stepson of George Washington) and Eleanor Calvert (a descendant of Lord Baltimore), was born at Mount Airy, Maryland, on April 30th, 1781. Six months later, on November 5th, 1781, his father, aide-de-camp to General Washington at Yorktown, died in his twenty-eighth year, leaving the boy to be reared by his stepgrandfather at Mount Vernon. After studying briefly at the College of New Jersey (Princeton) he married Mary Lee Fitzhugh in 1804 and settled at Arlington, his estate on the Potomac River opposite Washington. He wrote several plays, among them *Pocahantas; or, The Settlers of Virginia,* produced in Philadelphia in 1830 and published in the same year. He died at Arlington on October 10th, 1857, survived by his daughter Mary, wife of Robert E. Lee. His *Recollections and Memoirs of Washington,* contributed in installments to *The National Intelligencer* over a period of thirty years and published in book form in 1860, was widely read and remains an important source for biographers and historians.

CUSTIS, MARTHA (DANDRIDGE) (1731–1802): *Mrs. Daniel Parke Custis,* eldest daughter of John Dandridge and Frances Jones, was born in New Kent County, Virginia, on June 2nd, 1731. In 1749 she became the wife of Daniel Parke Custis (1711–1757), of Williamsburg, and removed with her husband to White House plantation on the Pamunkey River. Two of their four children survived infancy: Martha Parke Custis (1755–1773), called "Patsy," and John Parke Custis (1754–1781), called "Jack." After her husband's death on July 8th, 1757, she met George Washington (1732–1799) on March 16th, 1758, and became his wife on January 6th, 1759. She and her two young children settled at Mount Vernon, over which she presided with dignity, amiability, and prudence. During the Revolutionary War she wintered with General Washington in camp, where she was the delight of all, and returned to Mount Vernon when fighting resumed in the spring. She died at Mount Vernon on May 22nd, 1802, and was buried in the family vault.

CUTHBERT, ANNE MARY (DAVIS) (1828–1912): *Mrs. Alfred Cuthbert,* eldest daughter of the Rev. Samuel Stanhope Davis (1793–1877) and Mary Cuthbert Cumming (1797–1876), was born in Camden, South Carolina, on July 12th, 1828. Her father, a Presbyterian clergyman, was a graduate of Middlebury College (1812) and Princeton Theological Seminary (1815); on January 5th, 1825, he had married a daughter of Thomas Cumming (1765–1834), first mayor of Augusta

after its incorporation as a town (1798) and president of the Bank of Augusta from its organization in 1810 until his death in 1834. Anne Mary Davis and her three younger sisters (Sarah Matilda, Caroline Smelt, and Julia Cuthbert) spent much of their girlhood in Augusta, where they were known for their remarkable intellect, taste, and charm. On November 11th, 1856, she became the wife of her cousin, Alfred Cuthbert (1826–1880), son of the Hon. Alfred Cuthbert (1786–1856), United States senator from Georgia (1835–1843), and Sarah Gibbons Jones (1789–1834). Her husband, a graduate of the College of New Jersey (Princeton) in 1847, spent much of his life in the North; in the spring of 1861 he returned with his wife and two young children to Georgia, where he enlisted as a private in the Georgia Hussars (Company E, 6th Regiment Virginia Cavalry; later designated Company F, Jeff Davis Legion Mississippi Cavalry) on September 17th, 1861, leaving his wife in Augusta with her sister Caroline, wife of Dr. Joseph Jones. He died in Morristown, New Jersey, on December 5th, 1880, and was buried in Evergreen Cemetery. His widow survived him thirty-two years, residing in Augusta with her two children, Alfred Cuthbert (1856–1932) and Mary Cumming Cuthbert (1860–1933), until her death on December 2nd, 1912. She was buried in Summerville Cemetery, Augusta.

CUYLER, RICHARD RANDOLPH (1796–1865), lawyer, banker, and railroad official, son of the Hon. Jeremiah La Touche Cuyler and Margaret Elizabeth Clarendon, was born in Savannah, Georgia, on October 19th, 1796. On December 22nd, 1819, he married Mississippi Gordon (1799–1833), daughter of Ambrose Gordon and Elizabeth Meade, and sister of William Washington Gordon (1796–1842), founder and first president of the Central Railroad & Banking Company of Georgia (1836–1842). At Gordon's death in March 1842 Cuyler succeeded him as president, a position he held for twenty-three years (1842–1865); he was also president of the Southwestern Railroad for ten years (1855–1865). A man of unusual enterprise and vision, he promoted the construction of railroads throughout Georgia and made the Central Railroad of Georgia one of the most profitable investments in the state. He also promoted the establishment of a line of steam packets between Savannah and New York in 1847. At the outbreak of the Civil War his son, Richard Matthei Cuyler (1825–1879), for twenty years an officer in the United States navy, resigned his post and became colonel in charge of ordnance at Macon, Georgia. R. R. ("Railroad") Cuyler died in Macon on April 19th, 1865, and was buried in Rose Hill Cemetery; in February 1867 his remains were reinterred in Laurel Grove Cemetery, Savannah, where a monument erected by the Central and Southwestern Railroads commemorates his name. On June 8th, 1865, the directors of the Southwestern Railroad unanimously adopted resolutions regretting his death:

"As a railroad man no one had a better reputation; as a financier none exercised more influence amongst commercial classes; as a businessman no one possessed more energy, fidelity, and honor; as a citizen none excelled him in all the qualities that adorn the gentleman; as a friend no one had a more noble heart or a more liberal hand. The death of such a man is truly a loss to the world." As a rising lawyer in Savannah Cuyler drew up the marriage settlement of the Rev. Dr. Charles Colcock Jones and Mary Jones in December 1830.

DABNEY, WILLIAM HARRIS (1817–1899), lawyer, son of Anderson Dabney and Hannah Bennett, was born near Shady Dale, Jasper County, Georgia, on July 17th, 1817. After graduating from Franklin College (Athens) in 1839 he studied law under James Montgomery Calhoun (1811–1875), of Decatur, husband of his sister, Emma Elizabeth Dabney (1810–1860), and mayor of Atlanta (1862–1865). On December 8th, 1842, he married Martha B. Williams (1825–1885), daughter of Ammi Williams (1780–1864) and Laura Loomis (1790–1873), of Decatur; her sister, Laura Loomis Williams (1820–1879), became the first wife of Lemuel Pratt Grant (1817–1893), distinguished Atlanta citizen, in 1843. From 1840 to 1850 he practiced law in DeKalb County as copartner with James Montgomery Calhoun; in 1850 he removed to Calhoun, Gordon County, where he continued to practice law, with a brief interval in Atlanta during the Civil War, until 1873; he then practiced law in Rome. He was an eminent lawyer; he represented Gordon County in the state legislature in 1854 and in the state secession convention in 1861. During the Civil War he was colonel of the 1st Regiment Georgia Infantry (State Guards), organized for local defense. He died in Calhoun on September 29th, 1899, and was buried beside his wife in Oakland Cemetery, Atlanta. One of his sons, William Anderson Dabney (1845–1927), was a Presbyterian clergyman.

DAHLGREN, CHARLES GUSTAVUS (1808–1888), planter and Confederate soldier, elder son of Bernard Ulric Dahlgren and Martha Rowan, was born in Philadelphia, Pennsylvania, in 1808. His father, a Swedish political refugee, had landed in New York in 1806 and settled in Philadelphia as first Swedish consul to the United States. Charles Gustavus Dahlgren entered banking as private secretary to Nicholas Biddle (1786–1844), president of the Bank of the United States (1823–1839). After a brief period in New Orleans he served as cashier of the Bank of the United States in Natchez, Mississippi (1830–1842); thereafter he undertook cotton planting near Natchez and accumulated a large fortune. At the outbreak of the Civil War he raised and equipped the 3rd Regiment Mississippi Infantry and was commissioned brigadier general; he fought at Vicksburg, Corinth, Chickamauga, and Atlanta. After the war he settled in Brooklyn, New York, and practiced law with great suc-

cess. He married first (in 1840) Mary M. Routh, widow of Thomas Ellis and daughter of Job Routh, one of the largest slaveholders and cotton planters in the South; after her death in 1853 he married second (in 1860) Mary E. Vannoy, of Nashville, Tennessee. He died in Brooklyn on December 18th, 1888, survived by his second wife, and was buried in Natchez, Mississippi. His younger brother, John Adolphus Bernard Dahlgren (1809–1870), was an officer in the United States navy before, during, and after the Civil War. His son, Charles R. Dahlgren, was a private in the Jeff Davis Legion; after passing through twenty-three pitched battles unharmed he was wounded in Virginia early in 1864 and hospitalized in Richmond for six months.

DAHLGREN, JOHN ADOLPHUS BERNARD (1809–1870), naval officer, younger son of Bernard Ulric Dahlgren and Martha Rowan, was born in Philadelphia, Pennsylvania, in 1809. His father, a Swedish political refugee, had landed in New York in 1806 and settled in Philadelphia as first Swedish consul to the United States. John Adolphus Bernard Dahlgren entered the United States navy as a midshipman in February 1826. In 1833 he was assigned to the United States naval station in Philadelphia, and in the following year he was assigned to the coast survey. From 1847 to 1863 he devoted his energies to developing the Bureau of Ordnance in Washington; in July 1862 he was appointed chief, with rank of commander. Subsequently he was promoted to captain (August 1862) and rear admiral (February 1863). Requesting active service, he was placed in command of the South Atlantic blockading squadron on July 6th, 1863, succeeding Commodore Du Pont. He led an expedition up the St. Johns River in February 1864, supported General Sherman at Savannah in December 1864, and entered Charleston with General Schimmelfennig in February 1865. After the war he returned to Washington, where he became chief of the Bureau of Ordnance in 1868 and assumed command of the Washington navy yard in 1869. He married first (on January 8th, 1839) Mary C. Bunker, of Philadelphia; there were seven children. He married second (on August 2nd, 1865) Mrs. Madeleine Vinton Goddard, of Washington; there were three children. He died in Washington on July 12th, 1870, and was buried in Laurel Hill Cemetery, Philadelphia.

DAHLGREN, ULRIC (1842–1864), Union soldier, second son of John Adolphus Bernard Dahlgren (1809–1870) and Mary C. Bunker, was born in Bucks County, Pennsylvania, on April 3rd, 1842. He spent his childhood and youth in Washington, D.C., where his father was associated with the Bureau of Ordnance from 1847 to 1863. He began the study of civil engineering in 1858 and the study of law in 1860. During the Civil War he distinguished himself at Second Manassas, Fredericksburg, Chancellorsville, and Gettysburg. Retreating from Gettysburg he led the charge into Hagerstown and was severely wounded in the foot;

his leg was amputated, but he recovered and, though obliged to use crutches, returned to active service. For his gallantry he was promoted to colonel. On March 2nd, 1864, he was killed in the swamps of King and Queen County, Virginia, in a daring attempt to capture Richmond and release the Union soldiers confined in Libby Prison and Belle Isle. His remains, temporarily buried in a secret grave in Virginia, were reinterred in Laurel Hill Cemetery, Philadelphia, with appropriate ceremonies on November 1st, 1865. A substantial *Memoir,* written by his father and revised and edited by his stepmother, Madeleine Vinton (Goddard) Dahlgren, was published in Philadelphia in 1872.

DANA, RICHARD HENRY (1815–1882), lawyer and author, son of Richard Henry Dana and Ruth Charlotte Smith, was born in Cambridge, Massachusetts, on August 1st, 1815. After studying two years at Harvard College (1831–1833) he withdrew because of eye trouble and in August 1834 embarked as a common sailor on a voyage around Cape Horn to California. Returning to Boston in 1836, he joined the senior class at Harvard and graduated with first honor in 1837. Three years later he was admitted to the bar. Although never an abolitionist, he became deeply absorbed in the antislavery movement: in 1854 he served with Charles Mayo Ellis (1818–1878) as counsel for Anthony Burns, fugitive slave apprehended in Boston; and in 1855 he served as counsel for the Hon. Edward Greely Loring, the judge who had remanded Burns to slavery, on his removal from the office of judge of probate. Dana was United States district attorney for Massachusetts (1861–1866), and he served with William M. Evarts as counsel for the United States in the proceedings against Jefferson Davis for treason (1867–1868). His enthusiasm for travel bore fruit in his books, among them *Two Years Before the Mast* (1840) and *To Cuba and Back* (1859). He died suddenly in Rome, Italy, on January 6th, 1882, and was buried in the Protestant Cemetery. He was survived by his wife, Sarah Watson, whom he had married on August 25th, 1841, and six children.

DANIELL, WILLIAM COFFEE (1793–1868), physician and planter, was born in Greene County, Georgia, on January 12th, 1793. In early manhood he settled in Savannah, where he practiced medicine, "a profession for which he was well fitted," according to the Savannah *Republican* (December 29th, 1868), "by a mind of great natural sagacity, improved by all the advantages of a polite and thorough education." He represented Chatham County several terms in the state legislature, and he once served as mayor of Savannah. As a rice planter he amassed a considerable fortune, much of which he lost during the Civil War. He was an ardent secessionist, and in 1861 he became Confederate receiver under the Sequestration Act. He married first (on April 18th, 1822) Martha Screven; he married second (on March 8th, 1836) Elizabeth Mary Screven, who

survived him eight years. He died in Walthourville, Georgia, at the home of his daughter, Mrs. Julius Caesar LeHardy, on December 27th, 1868, and was buried in Laurel Grove Cemetery, Savannah.

DARSEY, BENJAMIN (1812–1901), planter and magistrate, son of James Darsey (1777–1879) and Amelia Strother (1772–1855), was born in Liberty County, Georgia, on January 15th, 1812. For many years he was justice of the peace of Liberty County, and in his later years he served also as school commissioner. During the Civil War he was first lieutenant of the Liberty Guards (Company D, 5th Regiment Georgia Cavalry). He married first (on June 26th, 1865) Mrs. Eliza Ann (Williams) Miller (1811–1868); he married second (on September 26th, 1869) Mrs. Loanza E. Harnage, from whom he was divorced; he married third (on December 16th, 1880) Susan Jane Zoucks (1839–1916). He died at his residence near Hinesville, Liberty County, on August 9th, 1901, and was buried in Taylor's Creek Cemetery.

DAVIDSON, HENRY GAMBLE (1824–1884), physician, son of the Rev. Andrew Baker Davidson (1779–1861) and Susan Dorman, was born in Rockbridge County, Virginia, in 1824. His father, a Presbyterian clergyman, was a graduate of Washington College (1807) and a trustee (1815–1857). Henry Gamble Davidson attended Washington College (1843–1844) and taught school for five years; he graduated from the Medical Department of the University of Virginia in 1850 and from Jefferson Medical College (Philadelphia) in 1851. Prior to the Civil War he practiced medicine in Richmond. On July 1st, 1861, he was appointed surgeon of the 5th Regiment Virginia Infantry; by December 1862 he was surgeon at a hospital in Richmond; and in February 1864 he became surgeon in charge of the general hospital in Danville. After the war he returned to Richmond, where he served briefly as president of the Southern Insurance Company. By 1870 he had settled in Lexington, where he died in January 1884, survived by his wife, Kate B. Taylor, whom he had married in 1858. He was buried in the Stonewall Jackson Memorial Cemetery.

DAVIDSON, WILLIAM MURRAY (1821–1894), wine merchant, was born in Sandy Bank, near Dunfermline, Fifeshire, Scotland, on November 11th, 1821. In early manhood he settled in Savannah, Georgia, where he prospered in the wholesale liquor business. On December 9th, 1851, he married Sarah Ann McIntire (1833–1866). On August 1st, 1861, he enlisted as senior second lieutenant in the Chatham Artillery (1st Volunteer Regiment Georgia Artillery), in which Julian Hartridge was junior first lieutenant and Charles Colcock Jones, Jr., was senior first lieutenant; he resigned on May 17th, 1862, for reasons of health. In April 1864 he reenlisted as captain of Company C, 1st Battalion Georgia Reserves. His view of the war appeared in a letter written to his wife on April 13th, 1862: "I must *fight* for our country; it will *not* do to let these people run roughshod over us. . . . What son of auld Scotland can sit tamely in his chair or lay down in his downy couch at night with such thoughts hanging over his morning slumbers! He that can do this is no countryman of mine. Away with him!" He died in Savannah on October 24th, 1894, survived by one son, William Murray Davidson (1862–1918), and was buried in Laurel Grove Cemetery.

DAVIS, ANNE MARY. *See* Cuthbert, Anne Mary (Davis)

DAVIS, CAROLINE SMELT (1832–1868), third daughter of the Rev. Samuel Stanhope Davis (1793–1877) and Mary Cuthbert Cumming (1797–1876), was born in Camden, South Carolina, on March 25th, 1832. Her father, a Presbyterian clergyman, was a graduate of Middlebury College (1812) and Princeton Theological Seminary (1815); on January 5th, 1825, he had married a daughter of Thomas Cumming (1765–1834), first mayor of Augusta after its incorporation as a town (1798) and president of the Bank of Augusta from its organization in 1810 until his death in 1834. Caroline Smelt Davis and her three sisters (Anne Mary, Sarah Matilda, and Julia Cuthbert) spent much of their girlhood in Augusta, where they were known for their remarkable intellect, taste, and charm. On October 26th, 1859, she became the wife of Dr. Joseph Jones (1833–1896), second son of the Rev. Dr. Charles Colcock Jones (1804–1863) and Mary Jones (1808–1869), of Liberty County, Georgia. Her husband, a graduate of the College of New Jersey (1853) and the Medical College of the University of Pennsylvania (1856), was professor at the Savannah Medical College (1856–1857), the University of Georgia (1857–1858), the Medical College of Georgia, Augusta (1858–1866), the Medical College of Nashville (1866–1868), and the University of Louisiana (1868–1894). She died suddenly in New Orleans on December 4th, 1868, survived by her husband and four children: Samuel Stanhope Davis Jones (1860–1894), Susan Hyrne Jones (1863–1921), Charles Colcock Jones (1865–1953), and Mary Cuthbert Jones (1867–1939). She was buried in the family vault in Lafayette Cemetery, New Orleans. Her husband married second (on June 21st, 1870) Susan Rayner Polk (1842–1921), daughter of the Rt. Rev. Leonidas Polk (1806–1864), bishop of Louisiana and lieutenant general in the Confederate army.

DAVIS, JEFFERSON (1808–1889), statesman, son of Samuel Davis and Jane Cook, was born in Christian (now Todd) County, Kentucky, on June 3rd, 1808. After studying at Transylvania University he graduated from the United States Military Academy in 1828. For seven years he served in Wisconsin and Illinois as a second lieutenant in the United States army; resigning in 1835, he became a planter in Mississippi (1835–1845). After a brief period as congressman (1845–1846) he commanded the Mississippi Rifles in the Mexican War (1846–1847) and subsequently returned to

Washington as United States senator from Mississippi (1847–1851). He was secretary of war under President Franklin Pierce (1853–1857) and again United States senator (1857–1861). At the outbreak of the Civil War he hoped to be commander in chief of the Southern forces, but instead he was elected president of the Confederate States (1861–1865). With the collapse of the Confederacy he fled southward with his cabinet; he was captured by the Federals at Irwinville, Georgia, on May 10th, 1865, and was imprisoned at Fortress Monroe for two years. In May 1867 he was released on bond. After visiting Europe he lived in retirement and wrote *The Rise and Fall of the Confederate Government* (2 vols., 1881). He married first (in 1835) Sarah Knox Taylor, daughter of Zachary Taylor, who died within three months of her marriage; he married second (in 1845) Varina Howell (1826–1906). He died in New Orleans on December 6th, 1889, survived by his second wife and two daughters, and was buried in Hollywood Cemetery, Richmond, Virginia. In February 1868 Mrs. Mary Jones met Davis in New Orleans; her son, Charles Colcock Jones, Jr., commented from New York: "You doubtless enjoyed your visit to this great and good man, toward whom our hearts turn with a fondness and an admiration which neither the misfortunes of the hour nor the calumnies of our enemies can ever impair."

DAVIS, JULIA CUTHBERT (1834–1918), fourth and youngest daughter of the Rev. Samuel Stanhope Davis (1793–1877) and Mary Cuthbert Cumming (1797–1876), was born in Augusta, Georgia, in 1834. Her father, a Presbyterian clergyman, was a graduate of Middlebury College (1812) and Princeton Theological Seminary (1815); on January 5th, 1825, he had married a daughter of Thomas Cumming (1765–1834), first mayor of Augusta after its incorporation as a town (1798) and president of the Bank of Augusta from its organization in 1810 until his death in 1834. Julia Cuthbert Davis and her three elder sisters (Anne Mary, Sarah Matilda, and Caroline Smelt) spent much of their girlhood in Augusta, where they were known for their remarkable intellect, taste, and charm. On December 3rd, 1864, she married Paul Henry Langdon (1826–1911), son of Samuel Langdon and Mary Halsey, of Wilmington, North Carolina. Her husband, a financier, was director of several corporations and for some time president of the Bank of Augusta. He died in Augusta on October 8th, 1911, and was buried in Summerville Cemetery. Julia Cuthbert (Davis) Langdon died on February 25th, 1918, and was buried beside her husband.

DAVIS, SAMUEL STANHOPE (1793–1877), Presbyterian clergyman, son of Samuel Davis and Mary Dunham, was born in Ballston Centre, New York, on July 12th, 1793. He graduated from Middlebury College in 1812 and from Princeton Theological Seminary in 1815. Removing to Georgia, he served churches in Darien (1821–1823) and Augusta (1823–1827); on January 5th, 1825, he married Mary

Cuthbert Cumming (1797–1876), daughter of Thomas Cumming (1765–1834), first mayor of Augusta after its incorporation as a town (1798) and president of the Bank of Augusta from its organization in 1810 until his death in 1834. There were five children: Thomas Cumming Davis (1827–1897); Anne Mary Davis (1828–1912), wife of Alfred Cuthbert; Sarah Matilda Davis (1830–1910), wife of Alfred Cumming; Caroline Smelt Davis (1832–1868), wife of Dr. Joseph Jones; and Julia Cuthbert Davis (1834–1918), wife of Paul Henry Langdon. Davis was stated supply in Camden, South Carolina (1827–1833); church financial agent in Augusta (1833–1841); professor at Oglethorpe University (1841–1842); stated supply in Ballston, New York (1842–1845); and pastor in Camden, South Carolina (1845–1851). He received the honorary degree of doctor of divinity from Franklin College (Athens) in 1845. From 1851 to 1877 he resided without pastoral charge in Summerville (The Hill), a suburb of Augusta, where his four daughters were known for their remarkable intellect, taste, and charm. Charles Colcock Jones, Jr., visiting the Davis family in June 1855, noted that "The young ladies are all well educated, intelligent, and studious in their habits, with fine conversational powers." Mary Cuthbert (Cumming) Davis died in Augusta on November 2nd, 1876, and was buried in Summerville Cemetery. The Rev. Samuel Stanhope Davis died on June 21st, 1877, and was buried beside his wife.

DAVIS, SARAH MATILDA. *See* Cumming, Sarah Matilda (Davis)

DAWSON, ANDREW HUNTER HOLMES (1819–1898), lawyer, son of Joseph Dawson and Wilhelmina Creswell, was born in Cynthiana, Harrison County, Kentucky, on November 26th, 1819. As a young man he accompanied Kit Carson, frontier scout, on an expedition to the West. After studying law under Thomas F. Marshall in Versailles, Kentucky, and Joseph C. Stevens in Madison, Indiana, he was admitted to the bar in 1841 and practiced successfully in St. Louis, Missouri (1842–1846); Warrenton, Georgia (1846–1854); Savannah, Georgia (1854–1860); and Mobile, Alabama (1860–1861). From 1861 to 1863 he resided chiefly in Richmond, Virginia, in order to be near his son, Joseph Story Dawson, a private in the Confederate army; later he lived as a refugee in various Southern states. In July 1865 he removed to New York City, where he practiced law and served for a time as assistant district attorney, and where, according to the New York *Tribune* (March 20th, 1898), "his erratic ways won him more or less newspaper attention." In later life he assumed the name Andrew Hannibal Humboldt Dawson. On July 4th, 1841, he married Lucy Ann Wickersham (1818–1902), daughter of Ambrose Wickersham and Catharine George, of Louisville, Kentucky. He died in New York City on March 17th, 1898, and was buried in Cypress Hills Cemetery. His *Oration on the Origin, Purposes, and Claims of the Ladies'*

Mount Vernon Association (55 pp.) was published in Savannah in 1858; an enlarged edition (70 pp.) was issued later in the same year. After hearing Dawson's oration Mrs. Cornelia V. Grant wrote her friend Mrs. Mary Jones on March 18th, 1858: "It appears to me that there must be some loose screws in his pericranium almost amounting to insanity or monomania or something. . . . It was never my lot before to meet with a person so aspiring, and with really so much intellect, but with such excessive vanity and total want of good breeding as to make the very *slightest association* with him a trying bore."

DEITZ, JOHN GITLING (1823–1898), bookbinder, son of William Deitz, was born in Philadelphia, Pennsylvania, on May 11th, 1823. In early manhood he removed to Savannah, Georgia, where from 1853 to 1861 he was foreman of the bindery of John M. Cooper & Company, stationers and booksellers. On July 29th, 1853, he married Rose Anna McHugh, ward of Robert Raiford, of Savannah. During the Civil War his sympathies were Southern; on August 1st, 1861, he enlisted as a private in the Chatham Artillery, and for the next twelve months he was detailed on special printing service for the Quartermaster Department in Savannah. After his discharge as a nonconscript on August 1st, 1862, he removed to Macon, where in 1863 he served briefly as a private in the 14th Battalion Georgia Infantry (State Guards). He resided in Macon for the rest of his life. He was a volunteer fireman for thirty years and at one time chief of the city fire department; he was also a member of the city council. For many years he was prominent in the Odd Fellows and Freemasons. He died in Macon on October 27th, 1898, survived by his wife and two sons, and was buried in Rose Hill Cemetery. According to the Macon *Telegraph* (October 28th, 1898), "He was a man of fine presence, possessing in his young manhood a magnificent physique. He was of a benevolent and jovial disposition and carried sunshine wherever he went."

DELEGAL, EDWARD J. (1815–1892), physician, elder son of David Delegal, was born in Liberty County, Georgia, in 1815. Although he never received a medical degree, he was for many years a practicing physician in his native county; he was also copartner of William John King (1823–1885) in the firm of King & Delegal, salt-boilers, during the Civil War. In 1836 he married Mary W. Thomson (1820–1896), daughter of William Thomson and Susan Jane Goulding, and sister of William Goulding Thomson (1822–1864), major of the 20th Battalion Georgia Cavalry. There were three children: Jeannette Thomson Delegal (1837–1926), wife of William James Martin; Ann Eliza Delegal (1841–1921), wife of the Rev. Robert Quarterman Baker; and Edward William Delegal (born 1844), who served as a private in the Liberty Mounted Rangers (Company B, 20th Battalion Georgia Cavalry), married Matilda F. Mallard in 1871, and became a justice of the peace in Liberty County. Edward J. Delegal was one of the first settlers in Dorchester in 1843; he died there in 1892 and was buried in Dorchester Cemetery. A correspondent in the Savannah *Advertiser* (October 2nd, 1874) spoke of "E. J. Delegal, whose vivacity time nor adversity can abate."

DELEGAL, HENRY HARKLEY (1816–1863), physician, younger son of David Delegal, was born in Liberty County, Georgia, in 1816. After graduating from Jefferson Medical College (Philadelphia) in 1839 he practiced medicine in his native county, where he was also a successful planter. On December 10th, 1846, he married Louisa Stevens; there were eight children. Early in the Civil War he served briefly as a private in the Liberty Independent Troop, then encamped at Sunbury. He died in Dorchester after a protracted illness on December 28th, 1863, and was buried in Midway Cemetery.

DEMAREST, DAVID (1811–1879), builder, son of Lawrence Demarest (1772–1829) and his second wife, Margaret Romine (1781–1836), was born in Saddle River, Bergen County, New Jersey, on July 31st, 1811. As a young man he migrated to Georgia, where he worked as a carpenter in Athens before settling in Atlanta in 1854. On November 6th, 1860, the day of Lincoln's election, he enrolled as a "minuteman" in his adopted city; and on August 1st, 1863, he enlisted for six months in Captain J. F. Alexander's Cavalry Company mustered for local defense. In Atlanta directories after the war he was listed variously as "carpenter," "contractor," "builder," and "architect." He died in Atlanta on November 21st, 1879, survived by his second wife, and was buried beside his first wife in Oakland Cemetery.

DENMEAD, EDWARD (1813–1891), contractor, banker, and merchant, was born in Baltimore, Maryland, on March 13th, 1813. Early in 1838 he migrated with his wife Mary (1815–1898) and infant daughter Mary Jane (1837–1838) to Marietta, Georgia, where he was a prominent citizen for more than fifty years. In 1842 he was instrumental (with others) in organizing St. James's Episcopal Church. When the Western & Atlantic Railroad was constructed in the 1840s he was one of its leading contractors, leasing and purchasing extensive tracts of woodland in Northwest Georgia. In 1855 he established the first banking facilities in Cobb County when he opened in Marietta an agency of the City Bank of Augusta. In 1856 he built the Kennesaw mills. Much of his fortune was lost during the Civil War. In 1876 he was elected mayor of Marietta and served for eleven successive years with the exception of one term. He died in Marietta on December 20th, 1891, and was buried in Episcopal Cemetery.

DICKSON, JAMES NEWTON (1807–1866), banker, was born in Philadelphia, Pennsylvania, on August 4th, 1807. In 1831 he married Beulah Clark Allen (1806–1841), daughter of Solomon Allen; there were five children: John Dickson (1832–1878), Susan Allen Dickson (1834–1893), Margaretta Dickson (1837–

1902), James Newton Dickson (1839–1875), and Levi Dickson (1841–1883). The mother died on December 14th, 1841, five days after the birth of her youngest child. For some years James Newton Dickson was president of the Bank of North America; he was also a director of the Princeton Theological Seminary (1844–1866). From 1850 to 1853, when the Rev. Dr. Charles Colcock Jones and his family resided in Philadelphia, Mary Sharpe Jones was a schoolmate of "Sue" and "Margie" Dickson, who, despite feeble health, outlived their father and brothers many years. James Newton Dickson died in Philadelphia on July 5th, 1866; John, James Newton, and Levi, copartners in the firm of Dickson Brothers, brokers, died within eight years of each other (1875–1883); the two sisters, both spinsters, continued to occupy the family residence at 1108 Spruce Street. Susan Allen Dickson, born on November 23rd, 1834, died in Philadelphia on December 29th, 1893; Margaretta Dickson, born on June 18th, 1837, died in Philadelphia on February 16th, 1902. All five children were buried near their parents in Laurel Hill Cemetery.

DIDLAKE, ROBERT JAMES (1811–1859), hotel proprietor, tenth and youngest child of Robert Didlake and Mary Baker, was born in Clark County, Kentucky, on October 30th, 1811. On January 31st, 1833, he married Elizabeth Catharine Ware (1813–1868), daughter of George Ware, of Fayette County; there were six daughters and three sons. For many years he was proprietor of the Broadway Hotel, Lexington, endorsed by the Lexington *Kentucky Statesman* (February 25th, 1859) as "one of the most comfortable hotels in the West." He died on February 20th, 1859, after a long and painful illness and was buried in Lexington Cemetery. His wife continued to operate the Broadway Hotel until May 1865, when her only surviving son, George Ware Didlake (1835–1895), one of "Morgan's Men," returned from Pittsburgh, where he had been imprisoned with his Confederate comrades for eleven months. She died on July 4th, 1868, and was buried beside her husband.

DOD, CHARLES SQUIRE (1814–1872), Presbyterian clergyman, son of Daniel Dod, was born in Elizabeth, New Jersey, on May 15th, 1814. After graduating from the College of New Jersey (Princeton) in 1833 he was principal of the Darien Academy, Darien, Georgia (1834–1837; 1839–1844), and professor of mathematics and modern languages at Jefferson College, Canonsburg, Pennsylvania (1837–1839). On April 11th, 1838, he married Jane E. Harrison, of Darien. In 1849 he was ordained a Presbyterian clergyman; subsequently he was pastor at Holly Springs, Mississippi (1849–1854); president of West Tennessee College (1854–1861); pastor at Plaquemine, Louisiana (1861–1867; 1868–1870); professor of Latin and modern languages at Washington and Lee University (1867–1868); and teacher at Shreveport, Louisiana (1870–1872). He died in Centerville, Louisiana, on November 23rd, 1872.

DOUGLAS, STEPHEN ARNOLD (1813–1861), statesman, son of Dr. Stephen Arnold Douglas and Sarah Fiske, was born in Brandon, Vermont, on April 23rd, 1813. In 1834 he was admitted to the bar and commenced practice in Jacksonville, Morgan County, Illinois. He was a congressman (1843–1847) and United States senator (1847–1861). Between August 21st, 1858, and October 15th, 1858, he engaged in seven debates with Abraham Lincoln, rising leader of the Republican party. In 1852 and 1856 he was an unsuccessful candidate for Presidential nomination; in 1860 he was Democratic nominee for President and received twelve electoral votes. After Lincoln's election he worked wholeheartedly to preserve the Union and conspicuously supported the new President. He married first (on April 7th, 1847) Martha Denny Martin, daughter of Robert Martin, a large slaveholder of Rockingham County, North Carolina; after her death in 1853 he married second (on November 20th, 1856) Adele Cutts, daughter of James Madison Cutts, of Washington, D.C., and great-niece of Dolley Madison. He died in Chicago on June 3rd, 1861, and was buried in Douglas Monument Park.

DOWSE, GIDEON (1814–1881), planter, son of Samuel Dowse (1786–1856) and his second wife, Mary Whitehead (1794–1822), was born in Burke County, Georgia, on September 25th, 1814. He was a half-brother of Sarah Berrien Dowse (1824–1855), wife of William Parker White; Abigail Sturges Dowse (1828–1897), wife of Henry Hart Jones; Susan Clinton Dowse (1833–1886), wife of Dr. Juriah Harriss; and Laura Philoclea Dowse (1835–1899). After attending Franklin College (Athens) he engaged in cotton planting in Middle Georgia, wintering on his plantation in Burke County and summering at Bath, Richmond County, sixteen miles from Augusta. On February 8th, 1843, he married Sarah Almira Morrison (1822–1886), daughter of John Morrison and Rosa Anderson, of Bath. He was ruling elder of the Waynesboro Presbyterian Church from 1852 until his death. In May 1857 he was commissioner to the General Assembly of the Presbyterian Church meeting in Lexington, Kentucky. He died near Atlanta on August 5th, 1881, and was buried in Bath Presbyterian Churchyard. His wife died in Cleburne, Texas, on November 15th, 1886, and was buried in Cleburne Cemetery. A letter of Gideon Dowse, addressed to the Rev. Dr. Charles Colcock Jones on October 15th, 1854, and preserved in the Jones collection at Tulane University, projects "a plan by which we may have our own Negroes more carefully instructed in religious truth than they have ever been" and solicits Dr. Jones's opinion "in this *vitally* important matter."

DOWSE, LAURA PHILOCLEA (1835–1899), daughter of Samuel Dowse (1786–1856) and his fifth wife, Elizabeth Martha Walker (1794–1854), was born in Richmond County, Georgia, on June 8th, 1835. She never married. After the marriage of her elder sister, Susan Clinton Dowse (1833–1886), to Dr. Juriah Harriss on October 27th, 1853, she made her home with the Harriss family in Savannah; after the death of her sister on July 9th, 1886, she removed to Atlanta. She died there on November 13th, 1899, and was buried in Laurel Grove Cemetery, Savannah, in the Harriss family plot. She was a half-sister of Gideon Dowse (1814–1881); Sarah Berrien Dowse (1824–1855), wife of William Parker White; and Abigail Sturges Dowse (1828–1897), wife of Henry Hart Jones.

DuBOSE, SARAH ANN (SALLIE) (TOOMBS) (1835–1866): *Mrs. Dudley McIvor DuBose,* daughter of Robert Toombs (1810–1885) and Julia Ann DuBose (1813–1883), was born in Washington, Wilkes County, Georgia, on December 18th, 1835. Her father, a congressman (1845–1853) and United States senator (1853–1861), served as secretary of state (1861) under President Jefferson Davis, as brigadier general in the Army of Northern Virginia (1861–1863), and as inspector general of the 1st Division Georgia Militia (1864). She spent much of her girlhood in Washington, D.C., where on April 15th, 1858, she became the wife of Dudley McIvor DuBose (1834–1883), a lawyer, of Memphis, Tennessee. In 1860 he removed to Augusta, Georgia, where he practiced law until the outbreak of the Civil War, during which he served as colonel of the 15th Regiment Georgia Infantry until commissioned brigadier general in November 1864. After the war he settled in Washington, Wilkes County, where his wife died on October 27th, 1866, survived by her parents, her husband, and four young children. She was buried in Rest Haven Cemetery. Dudley McIvor DuBose continued to practice law in Washington, Wilkes County, served as congressman (1871–1873), and died on March 2nd, 1883. He was buried beside his wife.

DUBUAR, JAMES (1812–1886), Presbyterian clergyman, was born in Aurora, New York, in 1812. After graduating from Union Theological Seminary he served as pastor of churches in New York and Indiana; for nearly two years (1841–1842) he was teacher of the children of the Rev. Dr. Charles Colcock Jones in Liberty County, Georgia. In 1851 he became pastor of the Presbyterian church in Northville, Wayne County, Michigan, where he resided for the rest of his life. He died in Northville on December 6th, 1886, "widely and sincerely loved as a man of sound reason, warm heart and impulse, and one whose influence was incalculable for the lasting good" [Robert B. Ross and George B. Catlin, *Landmarks of Wayne County and Detroit* (Detroit, 1898), p. 276 (second pagination)].

DUKE, ALEXANDER MORTIMER (1809–1860), physician, son of Henry Duke and Elizabeth Brown, was born in Hanover County, Virginia, in 1809. After attending the University of Virginia (1833–1835) he taught school and planted for some years in his native state. On October 12th, 1835, he married

Evelina Kennon Garrett (1813–1843), daughter of Alexander Garrett (1778–1860) and Evelina Bolling (1789–1863), of Albemarle County, Virginia. In 1851, at the age of forty-two, he undertook the study of medicine; two years later he graduated from the Medical College of the University of Pennsylvania. In May 1854 he removed to Liberty County, Georgia, and practiced medicine until February 1855, when he settled in Savannah; in the autumn of 1859 he removed to Memphis, Tennessee, where he died suddenly in his office on February 7th, 1860. He was buried in Winchester Cemetery. He was survived by his only daughter, Susan Johnson Duke, who on September 1st, 1858, had become the wife of Horace Walker Jones (1834–1904), prominent Virginia educator. General John Hartwell Cocke described his "old acquaintance," Alexander Mortimer Duke, in a letter addressed to the Rev. Dr. Charles Colcock Jones on October 2nd, 1854: "The doctor has tried many things by turns, but nothing long. He first set out, after a respectable but not a distinguished course at our university, as a teacher. He then tried farming, and lately betook himself to physic. . . . To you I am in duty bound to say: 'I do not believe in him.' Nevertheless, far be it from me to say he is not worthy of the respect of any society where he may be, so long as his walk and conversation is equal to his knowledge."

DUNCAN, CATHERINE H. (McNAIR) (1817–1871): *Mrs. George M. Duncan*, was born in Houston County, Georgia, in 1817. On November 1st, 1836, she became the wife of George M. Duncan, son of Robert Duncan, of South Carolina. After residing for some years in Houston County they removed to Cuthbert, Georgia, where George M. Duncan served as financial agent of Andrew Female College and his wife served as matron. On July 2nd, 1861, their only daughter, Mary Virginia Duncan (1845–1871), a graduate of Andrew Female College (1861), became the wife of Joseph H. Taylor, a lawyer, of Cuthbert; there were two children: William Taylor (born 1862) and Anna Ree Taylor (born 1863). The four Taylors were living in the Duncan household in October 1864 when Mrs. Eliza G. Robarts and her family arrived in Cuthbert and rented the downstairs of the newly completed Duncan house. Catherine (McNair) Duncan died in Cuthbert in 1871 and was buried in an unmarked grave in Greenwood Cemetery.

DUNCAN, WILLIAM (1799–1879), insurance agent and commission merchant, was born in Aberdeen, Scotland, on August 4th, 1799. He came to America in 1818 and settled in Augusta, Georgia, where he engaged in steamboat transportation business on the Savannah River. Later he removed to Savannah, where he prospered as copartner of James H. Johnston, his son-in-law, in the firm of Duncan & Johnston, cotton factors, insurance agents, and commission merchants. For many years he was president of the Savannah Hos-

pital. He married first (on February 20th, 1834) Elizabeth McClellan (1809–1840), mother of his three children; he married second (on December 18th, 1861) Martha Deloney Berrien (1818–1896), widow of Dr. Hugh O'Keefe Nesbitt. He died in Savannah on March 20th, 1879, and was buried beside his first wife in Laurel Grove Cemetery. His second wife returned to her former home in Marietta, Georgia, where she died on July 13th, 1896. She was buried in Episcopal Cemetery, Marietta.

DUNHAM, SUSAN CAROLINE (ADAMS) (1812–1891): *Mrs. Charles Dunham*, second living daughter of Edmund Adams (1780–1817) and Mary (Blacksell) Baker, was born in Bryan County, Georgia, on March 8th, 1812. On December 8th, 1831, she became the second wife of Charles Dunham (1794–1834), son of John Dunham (1742–1817) and Sarah Clancy, of McIntosh County. After the marriage of her only daughter, Mary Elizabeth Dunham (1832–1896), to Horace Joseph Royall (1825–1883) on November 15th, 1849, Susan Caroline Dunham resided in the Royall household in Savannah. A few years later she acquired her own house on Gordon Street near the corner of Drayton, and after the marriage of her niece, Mary Georgia Dunham (1836–1904), to John St. Leonard Baker (1829–1861) on May 13th, 1856, she entrusted the management of her household affairs to Baker. She died in Savannah at the residence of her daughter on May 24th, 1891, and was buried in Walthourville Cemetery beside her two sisters, Mary and Jane.

DUNHAM, THOMAS J. (1810–1885), rice planter, son of the Rev. Jacob Hendricks Dunham (1774–1832) and Mary Baisden (1784–1864), was born in Liberty County, Georgia, on July 31st, 1810. His father, a Baptist clergyman, had devoted much of his time and energy to serving the underprivileged Negroes of Liberty and McIntosh Counties. Thomas J. Dunham married Anne Harris (1815–1854), daughter of John Harris, on January 19th, 1834, and settled on the Dunham place in lower Liberty County near Springfield. During the Civil War one of his sons, Thomas Hendricks Dunham (1840–1870), went to Virginia as orderly sergeant of the Georgia Hussars (Company E, 6th Regiment Virginia Cavalry; later designated Company F, Jeff Davis Legion Mississippi Cavalry); on December 4th, 1861, near Burke Station, Fairfax County, he received a bullet wound in his head from which he never fully recovered. Thomas J. Dunham died in Liberty County on September 9th, 1885, and was buried in Sunbury Cemetery beside his wife, his mother, and two of his sons.

DUNHAM, WILLIAM (1786–1856), rice planter, son of John Dunham (1742–1817) and Sarah Clancy, was born in Liberty County, Georgia, on February 2nd, 1786. "From his early youth he exhibited a passionate fondness for agricultural pursuits," *The Southern Presbyterian* observed on August

16th, 1856, "and it is believed that few men have carried the art of farming to greater perfection." He exhibited "a wealth of character not possessed by many, consisting of honesty in the most eminent degree; the most refined and delicate sense of propriety, both in speech and deportment; a total disregard of everything merely artificial; and an uncommon devotion to the welfare of his children, illustrated throughout a long life of self-denial and toil for their sake." He died in Liberty County on July 19th, 1856, survived by his wife Ann and ten of his fourteen children, and was buried in Jones Creek Baptist Churchyard beneath the inscription: "An honest man." His brother, Charles Dunham (1794–1834), married Susan Caroline Adams (1812–1891) on December 8th, 1831.

DUNNING, GERTRUDE RUSSELL (1824–1890), gentlewoman, daughter of Sheldon C. Dunning (1779–1858) and Gertrude Russell (1781–1833), was born in Savannah, Georgia, on September 5th, 1824. Her father, a native of Bethel, Connecticut, had migrated to Savannah in 1799, married Gertrude Russell, a native of New York, in May 1812, and engaged in steamboat transportation business on the Savannah River. Gertrude Russell Dunning spent much of her girlhood in Savannah, where she studied music and painting, translated *Paul and Virginia* from the German, and enjoyed the friendship of Laura Elizabeth Maxwell and Mary Sharpe Jones. After her father's death on April 2nd, 1858, she traveled extensively in the North; she later removed to Darien, Connecticut, where she lived in the household of her sister, Sarah Maria Dunning, wife of Henry D. Weed. She died in Darien on October 1st, 1890, and was buried in Spring Grove Cemetery.

DUNWODY, CHARLES ARCHIBALD ALEXANDER (1828–1905), merchant, youngest child of John Dunwody (1786–1858) and Jane Bulloch (1788–1856), was born in Liberty County, Georgia, on June 6th, 1828. He graduated from Franklin College (Athens) in 1848. On May 6th, 1852, he married Ellen J. Rice (1827–1895), daughter of the Hon. William Rice and Rosaline M. Jackson, of Charleston, and settled in Roswell, Georgia, where he engaged in manufacturing until the outbreak of the Civil War. On May 31st, 1861, he was commissioned first lieutenant of the Roswell Guards (Company H, 7th Regiment Georgia Infantry); at Manassas (July 21st, 1861) he sustained a severe hip wound from which he never fully recovered. He resigned his commission on September 25th, 1861. In the spring of 1862 he was appointed commanding officer, with rank of major, at the camp of instruction at Calhoun, Georgia; as Charles Colcock Jones, Jr., observed (July 15th, 1862), "He is a brave little man, and most conscientious in the execution of his trust." Despite his wound he enlisted the following year, on June 28th, 1863, as a private in the Roswell Battalion Georgia Cavalry, but on December 8th, 1863,

he was again compelled to resign for reasons of health. He died in Roswell in 1905 and was buried in the Presbyterian Cemetery beside his wife, who had died on January 19th, 1895. His elder brother, Henry Macon Dunwody (1826–1863), major in the 51st Regiment Georgia Infantry, was killed at Gettysburg on July 2nd, 1863.

DUNWODY, DEAN MUNRO (1825–1878), planter, fifth child of James Dunwody (1789–1833) and Elizabeth West Smith (1794–1879), was born in Darien, McIntosh County, Georgia, on March 19th, 1825. He was a younger brother of Mary Elizabeth Dunwody (1818–1884); Jane Adaline Dunwody (1820–1884), wife of the Rev. John Jones; and William James Dunwody (1823–1873). He attended Franklin College (Athens) with the class of 1846 but did not graduate. In 1849 he married Catherine Elizabeth McDonald (1826–1889), daughter of the Hon. Charles James McDonald (1793–1860), governor of Georgia (1839–1843), and his first wife, Anne Franklin (1801–1835). For most of his life he resided on his plantation in McIntosh County; after March 1862 he lived for some months in Marietta. He died in Darien on February 5th, 1878, survived by his wife and eight children, and was buried in St. Andrew's Cemetery. Catherine Elizabeth (McDonald) Dunwody died on May 12th, 1889, and was buried beside her husband.

DUNWODY, ELIZABETH WEST (SMITH) (1794–1879): *Mrs. James Dunwody*, only living daughter of James Smith (1766–1854) and Jane Seymour Munro (1774–1857), was born in Sunbury, Liberty County, Georgia, on April 25th, 1794. On February 8th, 1811, she became the wife of James Dunwody (1789–1833), younger son of Dr. James Dunwody (1751–1809) and Esther Dean (1746–1812), widow of Edward Splatt. For half a century she resided on her husband's two plantations in McIntosh County, wintering at Hopestill and summering at Brighton. Six children lived to maturity: Caroline Seymour Dunwody (1816–1838), wife of Francis Robert Shackelford; Mary Elizabeth Dunwody (1818–1884); Jane Adaline Dunwody (1820–1884), wife of the Rev. John Jones; William James Dunwody (1823–1873); Dean Munro Dunwody (1825–1878); and Sarah Ann Dunwody (1827–1849). After the Civil War she and her unmarried daughter Mary Elizabeth lived in the household of the Rev. John Jones, first in Baker County, later in Griffin, and after 1870 in Atlanta, where she died on June 30th, 1879. She was buried beside her mother in Citizens Cemetery, Marietta. As *The Southern Presbyterian* (August 28th, 1879) observed, "Her love of the beautiful, developed in early youth, has been crystallized in her exquisite paintings, running through seventy years; some of the best were executed in her eighty-fifth year!" She was survived by two daughters, Mary Elizabeth Dunwody and Jane Adaline (Dunwody) Jones.

DUNWODY, JAMES BULLOCH (1816–1902), Presbyterian clergyman, eldest child of John Dunwody (1786–1858) and Jane Bulloch (1788–1856), was born in Washington, Wilkes County, Georgia, on September 24th, 1816. After graduating from Yale College in 1836 and from Columbia Theological Seminary in 1841 he served churches in Pocotaligo, South Carolina (1845–1855) and Washington, Georgia (1860–1865). During the Civil War he served briefly as chaplain in the Confederate army. After the war he taught school in Washington, Georgia (1866–1873) and served as pastor of Stoney Creek Church near Yemassee, South Carolina (1873–1902). He married first (in 1842) Laleah Georgiana Wood Pratt (1823–1853), of Tuscaloosa, Alabama; he married second (in 1856) Ellen Galt Martin (1823–1857), of McPhersonville, South Carolina; he married third (in 1859) Caroline I. Haygood, of Barnwell, South Carolina. He died in Walterboro, South Carolina, on June 26th, 1902.

DUNWODY, JOHN (1786–1858), planter, elder son of Dr. James Dunwody (1751–1809) and Esther Dean (1746–1812), widow of Edward Splatt, was born in Sunbury, Liberty County, Georgia, on January 13th, 1786. After studying at Yale College he settled as a planter in his native county, where on June 7th, 1808, he married Jane Bulloch (1788–1856), daughter of James Bulloch and Anne Irvine. Six children lived to maturity: James Bulloch Dunwody (1816–1902), John Dunwody (1818–1903), Jane Marion Dunwody (1821–1885), William Elliott Dunwody (1823–1891), Henry Macon Dunwody (1826–1863), and Charles Archibald Alexander Dunwody (1828–1905). In 1837 John Dunwody removed with his family to Cobb County, Georgia, where he was one of fifteen who joined in 1839 to organize the Roswell Presbyterian Church, of which he was for seventeen years superintendent of the Sunday school and ruling elder. His house in Roswell, rebuilt after a disastrous fire and named Phoenix Hall, was later renamed Mimosa Hall. He died in Roswell after protracted suffering on June 6th, 1858, and was buried in the Presbyterian Cemetery beside his wife, who had died on June 30th, 1856. His brother, James Dunwody (1789–1833), was a planter in McIntosh County; his sister, Esther Dunwody (1775–1815), became in 1795 the first wife of the Hon. John Elliott (1773–1827), United States senator from Georgia (1819–1825).

DUNWODY, JOHN (1818–1903), Confederate soldier, second child of John Dunwody (1786–1858) and Jane Bulloch (1788–1856), was born in Hartford, Connecticut, on November 6th, 1818. His father was a rich planter in McIntosh County, Georgia. In early manhood he resigned a cadetship at the United States Military Academy and served eight years (1838–1846) in the Georgia militia as chief of staff under General Walter Echols. He fought in the Mexican War (1846–1848) and later served as government surveyor in

Kansas. On May 31st, 1861, he was elected major of the 7th Regiment Georgia Infantry; on December 23rd, 1861, he was promoted to lieutenant colonel. At the expiration of his commission (May 12th, 1862) he became disbursing agent of the Confederate States Niter and Mining Bureau, with rank of major; he continued in this post until the close of the war, often carrying important dispatches and large sums of money from Richmond to the West. After the war he resided in Atlanta, where he died on September 2nd, 1903. He was buried in Oakland Cemetery beside his wife, Elizabeth Clark Wing (1825–1898), whom he had married on June 11th, 1849.

DUNWODY, LALEAH GEORGIANA (1844–1919), daughter of the Rev. James Bulloch Dunwody (1816–1902) and his first wife, Laleah Georgiana Wood Pratt (1823–1853), was born in Tuscaloosa, Alabama, on September 24th, 1844. Her father, a Presbyterian clergyman, was pastor of churches in Pocotaligo, South Carolina (1845–1855) and Washington, Georgia (1860–1865); after the death of his first wife on October 25th, 1853, he married Ellen Galt Martin (in 1856) and Caroline I. Haygood (in 1859). Laleah Georgiana Dunwody thus spent much of her girlhood in the household of her stepmothers; she was also much in the company of her paternal aunt, Jane Marion Dunwody (1821–1885), widow of the Rev. Stanhope Erwin and Dr. William Glen. In 1869 she joined the faculty of the Augusta Female Seminary in Staunton, Virginia, where she resided for the rest of her life. On December 5th, 1890, she became the second wife of Joseph Addison Waddell (1823–1914), distinguished lawyer, legislator, and journalist; graduate of Washington College (1841) and the University of Virginia (1844); member of the state house of delegates (1865–1867) and the state senate (1869–1870); editor of the Staunton *Spectator;* and author of *Annals of Augusta County* (1886). For many years he was secretary of the board of trustees of the Augusta Female Seminary (renamed Mary Baldwin College in 1895); in his *History of Mary Baldwin Seminary* (1905) he spoke of his second wife: "Miss Dunwody's specialty was history, and she was considered by her pupils 'a born teacher.'" She died in Staunton on May 21st, 1919, and was buried beside her husband in Thornrose Cemetery.

DUNWODY, MARION. *See* Glen, Jane Marion (Dunwody) (Erwin)

DUNWODY, MARY ELIZABETH (1818–1884), second child of James Dunwody (1789–1833) and Elizabeth West Smith (1794–1879), was born in Darien, McIntosh County, Georgia, on August 14th, 1818. She spent much of her girlhood in McIntosh County on the two family plantations, Hopestill and Brighton. She never married. After the Civil War she and her widowed mother lived in the household of the Rev. John Jones, first in Baker County, later in Griffin, and after 1870 in Atlanta, where she died on

March 13th, 1884, exactly one week before the death of her sister, Jane Adaline Dunwody (1820–1884), wife of the Rev. John Jones. She was buried beside her mother and her maternal grandmother in Citizens Cemetery, Marietta. "Miss Mary Dunwody is indefatigable," Mrs. Mary S. Mallard once wrote; she is "a host in herself." Her brother-in-law, the Rev. John Jones, once called her "Mary *the excellent.*" "Sister Mary Dunwody," he wrote on July 26th, 1865, "is the factotum of the family—ever cheerful, hopeful, and affectionate, and relieving my dear Jane of many cares."

DUNWODY, MARY JANE (1862–1889), sixth child of Dean Munro Dunwody (1825–1878) and Catherine Elizabeth McDonald (1826–1889), was born in Marietta, Georgia, on June 11th, 1862. At the age of five she was living as an "adopted daughter" in the household of her aunt, Jane Adaline Dunwody, wife of the Rev. John Jones, in Griffin, Georgia; in 1870 she removed with the Jones family to Atlanta, where on October 26th, 1887, she became the wife of Samuel Barnett (1850–1943), who was, according to the Atlanta *Constitution* (October 30th, 1887), "a gentleman of high culture, in the enjoyment of a fine law practice." A graduate of the University of Georgia (1869), he had studied for one year at Edinburgh University, served as professor of mathematics at Davidson College, served as professor of physics at the University of Louisiana, and practiced law in Atlanta since 1881. Mary Jane (Dunwody) Barnett died in Atlanta on March 1st, 1889, less than two years after her marriage, and was buried in Rest Haven Cemetery, Washington, Wilkes County. According to the Atlanta *Journal* (March 1st, 1889), "she was the idol of her devoted husband, who did all that human power could do to arrest the sad end."

DUNWODY, WILLIAM ELLIOTT (1823–1891), physician, fourth child of John Dunwody (1786–1858) and Jane Bulloch (1788–1856), was born at Cedar Hill, Liberty County, Georgia, on November 6th, 1823. In his fourteenth year he removed with his parents to Roswell, Cobb County, Georgia, where his father was for seventeen years superintendent of the Sunday school and a ruling elder of the Presbyterian church. He graduated from the Medical Department of the University of the City of New York in 1845. Returning to Georgia, he practiced medicine in Roswell (1845–1848), Marietta (1848–1875), and Macon (1875–1891). He wished always to be known as a "homeopathic" physician. On March 12th, 1846, he married Ruth Ann Atwood (1826–1899), daughter of Henry S. Atwood, Darien manufacturer. He died in Macon on June 15th, 1891, survived by his wife and two sons, and was buried in Riverside Cemetery. A eulogy written by the Rev. John Jones appeared in *The Southern Presbyterian* (August 13th, 1891): "Firm in his friendships and undisguised in his opinions, he left many devoted friends. He was a man of generous nature, with a tender heart and a helping hand. Many of the sick and wounded who have survived our late war will never forget his kind and efficient surgical attentions." One of his sons, William Elliott Dunwody (1848–1890), married Aimee Taylor LaRoche (1850–1934), daughter of Isaac Drayton LaRoche, of Savannah.

DUNWODY, WILLIAM JAMES (1823–1873), lawyer and planter, fourth child of James Dunwody (1789–1833) and Elizabeth West Smith (1794–1879), was born in Darien, McIntosh County, Georgia, on April 15th, 1823. He was a brother of Mary Elizabeth Dunwody (1818–1884); Jane Adaline Dunwody (1820–1884), wife of the Rev. John Jones; and Dean Munro Dunwody (1825–1878). He attended Franklin College (Athens) with the class of 1842 but did not graduate. For the rest of his life he planted and practiced law in his native county, living first in the household of his mother and after the Civil War in the household of his younger brother, Dean Munro Dunwody. He was a member of the state senate (1853). He died unmarried on June 6th, 1873, and was buried in St. Andrew's Cemetery.

Du PONT, SAMUEL FRANCIS (1803–1865), naval officer, son of Victor Marie du Pont (1767–1827) and Gabrielle Joséphine de la Fite de Pelleport, was born in Bergen Point, New Jersey, on September 27th, 1803. His father, a French diplomat, had settled permanently in the United States in 1800; after heading the importing house of V. du Pont de Nemours & Company in New York for several years he removed in 1809 to Wilmington, Delaware, where he managed the woolen mills of his younger brother, Éleuthère Irénée du Pont (1771–1834), proprietor of E. I. du Pont de Nemours & Company, manufacturers of gunpowder. Samuel Francis du Pont was appointed midshipman in the United States navy in 1815. He rose to lieutenant (1826), commander (1842), and captain (1855). In 1845 he was instrumental in organizing the United States Naval Academy in Annapolis. In September 1861 he was designated flag officer (with courtesy title of commodore) and placed in command of the South Atlantic blockading squadron. His victory at Port Royal, South Carolina (November 7th, 1861) earned him the thanks of Congress (February 22nd, 1862) and promotion to rear admiral (July 30th, 1862). His unsuccessful attack on Charleston (April 7th, 1863) was the most serious naval defeat of the war. On June 17th, 1863, two of his ships, the *Weehawken* and the *Nahant,* captured the Confederate ironclad *Atlanta* in Charleston harbor. Three weeks later, on July 6th, 1863, he was succeeded in command by Rear Admiral John A. Dahlgren. His last years were spent in retirement at his residence on the Brandywine River near Wilmington, Delaware. On June 27th, 1833, he married his first cousin, Sophie Madeleine du Pont, youngest daughter of

Éleuthère Irénée du Pont. He died in Philadelphia on June 23rd, 1865. In 1882 the circle at the intersection of Massachusetts and Connecticut Avenues in Washington, D.C., was named in his honor; a memorial statue by Launt Thompson, erected in 1884, was replaced in 1921 by a memorial fountain, the work of Daniel Chester French.

EARLY, JUBAL ANDERSON (1816–1894), Confederate soldier, son of Joab Early and Ruth Hairston, was born in Franklin County, Virginia, on November 3rd, 1816. He graduated from the United States Military Academy in 1837 and fought in the Seminole War. Resigning from the army in July 1838, he studied law and practiced his profession in Rocky Mount, Virginia, with occasional interruptions, from 1840 to 1861. He represented Franklin County in the state house of delegates (1841–1842) and served as major of the 1st Regiment Virginia Infantry in the Mexican War (1847–1848). Although he opposed secession he entered the Confederate army as colonel of the 24th Regiment Virginia Infantry, and after First Manassas he was appointed brigadier general, serving continuously with the Army of Northern Virginia. He subsequently became major general (January 1863) and lieutenant general (May 1864). From June 1864 until the end of the war he was in independent command in the Shenandoah Valley of Virginia, where his raids obstructed Federal communications and threatened Maryland and Pennsylvania. When his force was almost annihilated at Waynesboro in March 1865 he was relieved from duty. After the war he resumed the practice of law in Lynchburg, Virginia, where he died on March 2nd, 1894.

ECKMAN, SAMUEL H. (1824–1901), dry goods merchant, was born in Bavaria, Germany, in 1824. In early manhood he migrated to Savannah, Georgia, where in July 1846 he associated himself with Abraham Einstein (1817–1875), also of Bavaria, Germany, in the firm of Einstein & Eckman, destined to become the leading wholesale dry goods house in the Southeast. In 1870 Abraham Vetzburg, also of Bavaria, Germany, joined the firm; and after Einstein's death in 1875 the firm became Eckman & Vetzburg, with business extending throughout South Carolina, Georgia, Florida, and Alabama. For the last twenty years of his life Eckman resided in New York City, where he represented his Savannah firm as buyer, and where he died on November 27th, 1901, survived by his wife, Fanny Meyer, and five daughters, all married and living in the North. Charles Colcock Jones, Jr., roomed in the Eckman house in Savannah from November 1857, when his brother Joseph left Savannah for Athens, until November 1858, when he himself married and settled in his own house. "My rooms I find quite comfortable," he wrote on November 6th, 1857, "and the house and inmates very quiet, orderly, and cleanly."

EDGAR, JOHN TODD (1792–1860), Presbyterian clergyman, was born in Sussex County, Delaware, on April 13th, 1792. Three years later his father migrated to Kentucky. After attending Transylvania University he graduated from Princeton Theological Seminary in 1816. Returning to Kentucky, he served as pastor of churches in Flemingsburg, Maysville, and Frankfort. In 1833 he accepted a call to the Presbyterian church in Nashville, Tennessee, where he became so generally beloved that when he died on November 13th, 1860, business was suspended in the city, by proclamation of the mayor, and the chancery court, then in session, was adjourned.

EDMUNDS, NICHOLAS WILLIAM (1831–1907), Presbyterian clergyman, younger son of Robert R. Edmunds and Ann Vaughan Marshall, was born in Richland County, South Carolina, on September 23rd, 1831. After preparing at the Mount Zion Institute, Winnsboro, he graduated from the South Carolina College in 1852 and from Columbia Theological Seminary in 1855. For eight years he taught school in Limestone and Barhamville; during the Civil War he was a chaplain in the Confederate army. After the war he served as pastor of churches at Cheraw, Ridgeway, and Hartsville; in 1876 he removed to Sumter, where he was president of Sumter Female Institute (1876–1880) and pastor of the Presbyterian church (1880–1905). On May 23rd, 1855, he married Mary Claudia Leland (1833–1902), daughter of the Rev. Aaron Whitney Leland and his first wife, Eliza Hibben; there were nine children. He died in Sumter on April 17th, 1907, and was buried beside his wife in Sumter Cemetery. As the Charleston News & Courier (April 18th, 1907) fittingly observed, "No man who has ever lived in Sumter was more respected and beloved. His life was an exemplification of the truest Christian character, and his example was a sermon more eloquent than words." He received the honorary degree of doctor of divinity from Davidson College in 1892.

EDWARDS, WILLIAM HENRY (1797–1872), farmer, son of Willis Edwards and Elizabeth O'Neill, was born in Georgetown District, South Carolina, on January 14th, 1797. His father died a few months after his birth, and his widowed mother removed to Bryan County, Georgia, where she and her son lived in the household of her parents. In early manhood William Henry Edwards purchased seven thousand acres of the best farm land in Tattnall County, Georgia, and settled there with his wife, Sarah J. Sands, of Screven County. There were ten children. On March 23rd, 1872, while driving in his buggy, he was instantly killed by the falling of a tree. He was buried on his farm.

ELLIOTT, COLLINS D. (1810–1899), educator and Confederate chaplain, son of Arthur Elliott and Mary Pierce, was born in Butler County, Ohio, on December 20th, 1810. After graduating from Augusta College (Kentucky) in 1829 he taught Greek and

Latin at LaGrange College (Alabama) for ten years; in 1839 he joined the faculty of the Nashville Female Academy, of which he was principal from 1844 to 1861. During his administration enrollment increased from 194 to 513. Although born in the North he was a staunch defender of the South; when the Federals entered Nashville after the fall of Fort Donelson he was one of three men arrested and sent to Camp Chase, Ohio, where he was confined for nearly a year. After his exchange on December 17th, 1862, he served as chaplain of General George Maney's brigade from April 1863 until his voluntary resignation in November 1864. A man of means, he suffered heavy losses during the war; his house in Nashville, used briefly as a Confederate hospital, later fell into Union hands. Returning to Nashville in 1865, he struggled bravely for thirty-four years to adjust himself to Southern defeat. He died in Nashville on July 28th, 1899, and was buried in City Cemetery beside his wife, Elizabeth Porterfield, whom he had married on August 13th, 1837. According to William Thomas Hale and Dixon L. Merritt, "Dr. Elliott was in countless ways a builder of character, a molder of opinions, a strong voice and arm to the whole South in its crisis, and altogether one of Tennessee's great men" [*A History of Tennessee and Tennesseans* (New York, 1913), VII, 2082].

ELLIOTT, DANIEL STEWART (1826–1862), banker, son of the Hon. John Elliott (1773–1827) and his second wife, Martha Stewart (1799–1864), was born in Liberty County, Georgia, on November 20th, 1826. His father was United States senator from Georgia (1819–1825); his maternal grandfather, General Daniel Stewart (1761–1829), for whom he was named, was a hero of the Revolutionary War. After a youth spent in Roswell, Georgia, in the home of his mother's second husband, James Stephens Bulloch (1793–1849), he settled in Savannah, where he was for a time assistant teller in the Bank of the State of Georgia. During the summer of 1856 he traveled in Europe with his friend Robert Hutchison, of Savannah. On February 16th, 1857, after a quarrel in a billiard room, he killed Thomas S. Daniell, son of Dr. William Coffee Daniell, in a duel at Screven's Ferry, on the South Carolina bank of the Savannah River. ("God grant that it may be a warning to the young men of the community," wrote Mrs. Mary Jones three days later: "commencing in a gambling saloon and ending in eternal death!") On June 1st, 1858, he married Lucinda Ireland Sorrel (1829–1903), daughter of Francis Sorrel (1793–1870), of Savannah. ("Were I a lady," wrote Charles Colcock Jones, Jr., the day before, "I would certainly be very loath to marry one who had the guilt of homicide upon his skirts.") During the Civil War he served briefly as a private in Captain Charles Du-Bignon's Company, Phillips' Legion Georgia Volunteers; on October 30th, 1861, he was discharged as "unfit to perform the duties of a soldier in consequence of pulmonary disease with repeated hemorrhages." He died in Marietta, Georgia, on August 3rd, 1862, survived by his wife and two young children, and was buried in the Presbyterian Cemetery, Roswell. Of his funeral sermon Mary Eliza Robarts wrote from Marietta on January 31st, 1863: "Though he died a real penitent, yet I think living the life he was known to have lived here, Mr. Palmer should have guarded his remarks more for the sake of the effect on the living. They might have been led to think no matter how they lived it might be well with them at the last." Daniel Stewart Elliott was a groomsman at the wedding of his half-sister, Martha (Mittie) Bulloch, and Theodore Roosevelt, father of the President, on December 22nd, 1853.

ELLIOTT, STEPHEN (1806–1866), Protestant Episcopal bishop, son of Stephen Elliott (1771–1830), an eminent naturalist, was born in Beaufort, South Carolina, on August 31st, 1806. After graduating from Harvard College in 1824 he studied law and practiced in Beaufort and Charleston from 1827 to 1833. In 1836 he was ordained a priest in the Protestant Episcopal Church, and in 1840 he was elected first bishop of the Diocese of Georgia. Throughout his career as bishop (1840–1866) he also served as rector of St. John's Church, Savannah (1840–1845), president of the Montpelier Female Institute (1845–1853), and rector of Christ Church, Savannah (1853–1866). He was president of the Georgia Historical Society (1864–1866). Together with the Rt. Rev. James Hervey Otey, bishop of Tennessee, and the Rt. Rev. Leonidas Polk, bishop of Louisiana, he founded the University of the South at Sewanee, Tennessee, in 1860. He married first (in 1828) Mary Gibbs Barnwell (1808–1837), a cousin; he married second (in 1839) Charlotte Bull Barnwell (1810–1895), also a cousin. He died suddenly in Savannah on December 21st, 1866, and was buried in Laurel Grove Cemetery. After his death his widow settled with her family in Sewanee, Tennessee, where she died on June 27th, 1895. His son, Stephen Elliott (1832–1866), a brigadier general in the Confederate army, died on March 21st, 1866, from the effects of a wound received at Petersburg in 1864.

ELLIS, CHARLES MAYO (1818–1878), lawyer, son of Charles Ellis and Maria Mayo, was born in Boston, Massachusetts, on December 23rd, 1818. After graduating from Harvard College in 1839 he practiced law successfully in Boston and rose to prominence as an abolitionist. In 1854 he served with Richard Henry Dana (1815–1882) as counsel for Anthony Burns, fugitive slave apprehended in Boston. He supported the Rev. Theodore Parker (1810–1860) and regularly attended his preaching. He was author of *The History of Roxbury Town* (1847). He died at his home in Brookline, Massachusetts, on January 23rd, 1878, survived by his second wife and four children.

ELLSWORTH, ELMER EPHRAIM (1837–1861), Union soldier, son of Ephraim D. Ellsworth and Phoebe Denton, was born in Malta, New York, on April 11th, 1837. After attending public schools in Mechanicsville, New York, he was disappointed in his hope of entering the United States Military Academy and pursuing a military career; instead he removed to Chicago, where he studied law and drilled a volunteer military company, later known as "the United States Zouave Cadets," to a high state of discipline. In 1860 he read law in the office of Abraham Lincoln in Springfield, and in 1861 he accompanied Lincoln to Washington. At the outbreak of the Civil War he recruited a regiment of volunteer firemen in New York and brought it to Washington, where it was mustered into service as one of the first three regiments of the war. When Alexandria was occupied by the Federals on May 24th, 1861, he saw the Confederate flag flying over the Marshall House, went to the roof and tore it down, and as he descended the stairs was shot to death by James William Jackson (1823–1861), proprietor of the hotel, who was himself immediately shot to death by one of Ellsworth's men. Ellsworth's death, the first of the war, created a national sensation; his body lay in state in the White House, was taken to New York by special train, and was buried in Mechanicsville with military honors.

ELZEY, ARNOLD (1816–1871), Confederate soldier, son of Arnold Elzey Jones and Anne Wilson Jackson, was born at Elmwood, his father's residence in Somerset County, Maryland, on December 18th, 1816. After graduating from the United States Military Academy in 1837 he dropped the name *Jones* and adopted his middle name, *Elzey*, as his surname. He served with distinction through the Seminole War and the Mexican War. In 1845 he married Ellen Irwin, of Baltimore. At the outbreak of the Civil War he resigned his commission and entered Confederate service as lieutenant colonel of the 1st Regiment Maryland Infantry. After his brilliant charge at Manassas (July 21st, 1861) he was promoted to brigadier general by President Davis on the field. At the battle of Port Republic (June 9th, 1862) he was slightly wounded, but he was not (as Charles Colcock Jones, Jr., mistakenly reported on June 28th, 1862) killed. At Cold Harbor (June 3rd, 1864) he was desperately wounded; after his recovery he was promoted to major general and ordered to Richmond, where his "local defense brigade" rendered useful service in the autumn of 1864. He later served as chief of artillery in General Hood's Army of Tennessee. After the war he retired with his wife and son to a small farm in Anne Arundel County, Maryland. He died in Baltimore on February 21st, 1871.

ENGLISH, JOHN A. (1831–1878), bookseller, was born in Philadelphia, Pennsylvania, in 1831. In 1853 he joined Samuel B. Smith (1821–1856) in the firm of Smith & English, publishers, booksellers, and importers, at 36 North 6th Street. After Smith's death in 1856 English continued the firm in association with Elias D. Collom and Gerard Buckman. He died in Philadelphia on October 1st, 1878, survived by his wife, Amanda Evans (1830–1912), and was buried in the Odd Fellows Cemetery, subsequently removed to Mount Peace Cemetery, and finally laid to rest in Lawnview Cemetery, Rockledge, Montgomery County, Pennsylvania. The Rev. Dr. Charles Colcock Jones became a patron of Smith & English during his residence in Philadelphia (1850–1853); after returning to Georgia he continued to order books from his old friends. "While in Philadelphia," he wrote his son Charles on November 14th, 1854, "if you think of it, call at Smith & English's and stir them up about my books." Letters from Smith & English often bore personal messages; the following lines from John A. English, written on October 8th, 1859, were typical: "I am glad, dear sir, to hear that your son Dr. Joseph is to be married —and to 'a lovely young lady,' as Rev. Dr. Axson informed me a few days ago when here. I hear such accounts of his great devotion to science that I could hardly expect him to take time to get married. But he is *sensible:* some scientific men are not!" On January 26th, 1861, English wrote once more: "We hope, notwithstanding secession, to have other orders from you. We deeply regret the course adopted by your (and other) states, but hope God will overrule for good our present troubles and preserve our country from war and desolation. . . . Our business is very much depressed by these hard times."

EVANS, NATHAN GEORGE (1824–1868), Confederate soldier, third son of Thomas Evans and Jane Beverly Daniel, was born in Marion, South Carolina, on February 6th, 1824. After attending Randolph-Macon College (Boydton, Virginia) he graduated from the United States Military Academy in 1848. Prior to the Civil War he saw service in the West and was promoted to first lieutenant (1855) and captain (1856). In 1860 he married Ann Victoria Gary, daughter of Dr. Thomas Reeder Gary and Mary Anne Porter, of Abbeville County, South Carolina. At the outbreak of the Civil War he resigned his commission, served as major and adjutant general at Fort Sumter, and entered the regular army of the Confederate States as captain of cavalry. At Manassas (July 1861) he rendered essential service, and after Ball's Bluff (October 1861) he won a vote of thanks from the Confederate Congress, a gold medal from South Carolina, and promotion to brigadier general. Early in 1863 his fortunes shifted: he was tried on charges of intoxication and acquitted; he was tried on charges of disobedience of orders and acquitted; he was temporarily deprived of command for reasons of incompetence; in the spring of 1864 he was injured when he fell from his horse. After the war he was principal of a high school in Midway, Bullock County, Alabama, where he died on November 30th, 1868.

EVE, EVA BERRIEN (1841–1890), daughter of William Joseph Eve (1804–1863) and Philoclea Edgeworth Casey (1813–1889), was born in Augusta, Georgia, on November 9th, 1841. Through her mother she was a great-niece of the Hon. John Macpherson Berrien. After attending schools in Bethlehem, Pennsylvania, and Washington, D.C., she returned to Augusta and settled to a life of cultivated leisure, indulging her taste for art and books. On November 9th, 1858, she was bridesmaid at the marriage of her first cousin once removed, Ruth Berrien Whitehead (1837–1861), to Charles Colcock Jones, Jr. (1831–1893), eldest son of the Rev. Dr. Charles Colcock Jones (1804–1863) and Mary Jones (1808–1869), of Liberty County, Georgia; on October 28th, 1863, she became his second wife. In December 1865 she accompanied her husband to New York City, where their only child, Edgeworth Casey Jones (later called Charles Edgeworth Jones) was born on July 27th, 1867. Returning to Georgia in 1877, she and her husband and son settled in Summerville, a suburb of Augusta, where she died on October 25th, 1890. She was buried in Summerville Cemetery. "She is a most lovable person," wrote Mrs. Mary Jones on April 30th, 1864, "and a gifted mind. Her poetical talent is of a high order." "She is absolutely attractive in every particular," wrote her fiancé on August 4th, 1863, "and has a heart as pure and tender and full of affection as dwells in woman's breast."

EVE, FRANCIS EDGEWORTH (1844–1908), Confederate soldier, son of William Joseph Eve (1804–1863) and Philoclea Edgeworth Casey (1813–1889), was born in Augusta, Georgia, on August 15th, 1844. Through his mother he was a great-nephew of the Hon. John Macpherson Berrien. At the outbreak of the Civil War, though not yet seventeen years old, he went to Virginia as acting third lieutenant in the 5th Regiment North Carolina Infantry (not the 4th Regiment, as Charles Colcock Jones, Jr., mistakenly asserted on October 7th, 1861); returning to Georgia in October 1861, he failed in his effort to secure a lieutenancy, and on May 1st, 1862, he enlisted as a private in the Richmond Hussars (Cavalry Company A, Cobb's Legion Georgia Volunteers). On February 10th, 1863, he was elected captain of the Richmond Dragoons (Cavalry Company K, Cobb's Legion Georgia Volunteers), also known as Captain Eve's Company of Cavalry. By November 1864 he was captain of Cavalry Company K, Phillips' Legion Georgia Volunteers. According to his sister, Eva Berrien Eve, wife of Charles Colcock Jones, Jr., writing on April 23rd, 1864, he was "the merriest young captain in Virginia," whose "happy, gleesome letters" were "written in the offhand nonchalant spirit of a gay boy cavalier." After the war, on November 20th, 1866, he married Mary Elizabeth Lamkin (1844–1894), of Columbia County, and settled on his large plantation ten miles southwest of Augusta. In 1877 he became junior partner of his brother-in-law, Charles Colcock Jones, Jr., in

the law firm of Jones & Eve. After his wife's death on January 20th, 1894, he married second (on May 12th, 1897) Katherine Remsen Tutt (1856–1928), daughter of Dr. William H. Tutt, and widow of Thomas H. Ewing, of Tennessee. He had no children by either marriage. He died in Augusta on May 10th, 1908, and was buried in Magnolia Cemetery.

EVE, MACPHERSON BERRIEN (1846–1886), Confederate soldier, youngest son of William Joseph Eve (1804–1863) and Philoclea Edgeworth Casey (1813–1889), was born in Augusta, Georgia, on August 13th, 1846. Through his mother he was a great-nephew of the Hon. John Macpherson Berrien, for whom he was named. At the outbreak of the Civil War, though not yet fifteen years old, he enlisted in the Confederate army; in the spring of 1864 he was appointed major on the staff of General Henry Constantine Wayne. As his sister, Eva Berrien Eve, wife of Charles Colcock Jones, Jr., observed on April 23rd, 1864, "The child is daft, and his uniform is irreproachable. He smiles blandly and tries to affect dignity." After the war he undertook planting in Columbia County. He died there on June 28th, 1886, survived by his wife, Rilla Moise, and four children, and was buried near his parents in Magnolia Cemetery, Augusta.

EVE, PAUL FITZSIMONS (1806–1877), physician and surgeon, son of Oswell Eve and Aphra Ann Pritchard, was born at Goodale, Richmond County, Georgia, on June 27th, 1806. After graduating from Franklin College (Athens) in 1826 and the Medical College of the University of Pennsylvania in 1828 he worked in the clinics of the most famous surgeons of Europe. Returning to America in November 1831, he served as professor of surgery at the Medical College of Georgia (1832–1850), the University of Louisville (1850–1853), the University of Nashville (1853–1868), the Missouri Medical College (1868–1870), and the University of Nashville (1870–1876). During the Civil War he was surgeon general of Tennessee (1861–1862) and, after the fall of Nashville, surgeon of the Gate City Hospital in Atlanta (1862–1864). For many years he stood in the front rank of his profession; in 1858 he was president of the American Medical Association. He married first Sarah Louise Twiggs (1817–1851), daughter of General George L. Twiggs; he married second Sarah Ann Duncan (1818–1897), daughter of the Rev. Hansford Dade Duncan. He died in Nashville on November 3rd, 1877, and was buried beside his first wife in Magnolia Cemetery, Augusta.

EVE, PHILOCLEA EDGEWORTH (CASEY) (1813–1889): Mrs. William Joseph Eve, only daughter of Dr. John Aloysius Casey (1779–1819) and Sarah Lowndes Berrien (1798–1822), was born in Louisville, Georgia, on December 30th, 1813. Through her mother she was a niece of the Hon. John Macpherson Berrien. On October 27th, 1840, in Sparta, Georgia, she became the wife of William Joseph Eve (1804–1863), a planter of Richmond

County; there were three children: Eva Berrien Eve (1841–1890), Francis Edgeworth Eve (1844–1908), and Macpherson Berrien Eve (1846–1886). For many years she was active as first vice-regent of the Mount Vernon Ladies' Association of the Union. Her husband died in Augusta on March 16th, 1863, and her daughter became the second wife of Charles Colcock Jones, Jr., on October 28th, 1863; after the Civil War she made her home with her daughter, first in New York (1866–1877) and later in Augusta (1877–1889). She died at her daughter's residence in Summerville on January 20th, 1889, and was buried beside her husband in Magnolia Cemetery, Augusta.

EVE, WILLIAM JOSEPH (1804–1863), planter, son of Oswell Eve and Aphra Ann Pritchard, was born at Goodale, Richmond County, Georgia, on December 17th, 1804. On October 27th, 1840, he married Philoclea Edgeworth Casey (1813–1889), daughter of Dr. John Aloysius Casey and Sarah Lowndes Berrien, and niece of the Hon. John Macpherson Berrien; there were three children. For many years he resided in Richmond County, where he was a large slaveholder and an extensive planter; in 1857 he settled with his family in Augusta. According to Dr. Joseph Jones, he was widely respected as "a man of benevolence, industry, and integrity." He died at his residence in Augusta after a lingering illness on March 16th, 1863, and was buried in Magnolia Cemetery.

EVERETT, EDWARD (1794–1865), Unitarian clergyman, statesman, and orator, son of the Rev. Oliver Everett and Lucy Hill, was born in Dorchester, Massachusetts, on April 11th, 1794. After graduating from Harvard College with first honor in 1811 he studied theology and became pastor of the Brattle Street Unitarian Church on February 9th, 1814, two months before his twentieth birthday. In 1815 he resigned his charge, accepted a professorship of Greek at Harvard, and spent nearly five years in Europe preparing for his new post. Returning to America, he was successively professor of Greek at Harvard (1819–1825); congressman (1825–1835); governor of Massachusetts (1836–1839); United States minister to Great Britain (1841–1845); president of Harvard College (1846–1849); secretary of state under President Millard Fillmore (1852–1853); and United States senator from Massachusetts (1853–1854). Resigning for reasons of health, he devoted the last ten years of his life to public oratory, in which he was remarkably gifted and successful. His oration on George Washington, delivered all over America in support of the Ladies' Mount Vernon Association of the Union, raised more than one hundred thousand dollars for the purchase and preservation of Washington's home. During the Civil War he delivered twenty-three orations supporting the Union cause, the best known being the oration delivered at Gettysburg, Pennsylvania, on November 19th, 1863, immediately prior to Lincoln's immortal address. His last oration was delivered in Faneuil Hall, Boston, on January 9th, 1865, in behalf of the recent sufferers in Savannah, Georgia. As a result of a cold caught that day he died in Boston on January 15th, 1865.

EWING, PRESLEY UNDERWOOD (1822–1854), lawyer and congressman, was born in Russellville, Kentucky, on September 1st, 1822. After graduating from Centre College (Danville, Kentucky) in 1840 and from the law school of Transylvania University (Lexington, Kentucky) in 1843, he studied theology at the Baptist Seminary in Newton, Massachusetts, traveled in Germany, and returned to Kentucky to practice law in Russellville. He was a member of the state legislature (1848–1849) and a member of Congress from March 4th, 1851, until his death at Mammoth Cave, Kentucky, on September 27th, 1854. He was buried in Maple Grove Cemetery, Russellville.

FABER, JOHN EBERHARD (1822–1879), pencil manufacturer, son of George Leonard Faber and Albertina Frederika Kupfer, was born near Nuremberg, Bavaria, Germany, on December 6th, 1822. After studying jurisprudence at the Universities of Erlangen and Heidelberg, reading widely at the same time in ancient history and literature, he migrated in 1848 to New York City, where he was American agent for the pencil factory in Stein, Germany, with which his family had been associated for three generations. He later acquired vast tracts of cedar-forest land in Florida, from which he supplied European pencil factories with wood. In 1861 he opened his own factory on the East River in New York City; in 1872 he established a larger factory in Brooklyn. His business flourished, and he eventually undertook the manufacture of rubber bands, erasers, and penholders. His pencils were the first to carry rubber tips and metallic point protectors. In 1854 he married Jenny Haag, daughter of Ludwig Haag, of Munich. He died at his residence in Port Richmond, Staten Island, New York, on March 2nd, 1879.

FAIR, SAMUEL (1804–1870), physician, was born in Newberry District, South Carolina, on March 6th, 1804. After studying medicine in Paris he returned to the capital of his native state, where he practiced his profession for more than twenty-five years. He established the first hospital in Columbia, located on Washington Street between Barnwell and Gregg Streets. He died in Columbia on August 16th, 1870, survived by his wife, Mary DeBrul (1819–1891), and was buried in the First Presbyterian Churchyard. According to the Columbia *Daily Phoenix* (August 17th, 1870), "He was a skillful physician and enjoyed a lucrative practice."

FAIRBANKS, THADDEUS (1796–1886), inventor and scale manufacturer, son of Joseph Fairbanks and Phoebe Paddock, was born in Brimfield, Massachusetts, on January 17th, 1796. He suffered from delicate health all his life. In 1823 he and his elder brother, Erastus Fairbanks (1792–1864), established an iron foundry in St. Johnsbury, Vermont, where

Thaddeus Fairbanks invented and developed a platform scale capable of weighing a wagon and its load. His invention was patented on June 13th, 1831. Three years later the two brothers founded the firm of E. & T. Fairbanks & Company for the manufacture of the new platform scale; the business expanded and prospered, and in 1874 the family partnership was incorporated as the Fairbanks Scale Company. Thaddeus Fairbanks eventually secured thirty-two patents for scales and developed numerous other inventions, among them an improved plow, a parlor stove, a cook stove, a hot-water heater, and a feed-water heater. In 1842, together with his brothers Erastus and Joseph, he founded the St. Johnsbury Academy, which he supported substantially during his lifetime and endowed generously at his death. On January 17th, 1820, he married Lucy Peck Barker, of St. Johnsbury; there were two children. He died in St. Johnsbury on April 12th, 1886, survived by one son, Henry Fairbanks (1830–1918), Congregational clergyman (1857–1860), professor of natural philosophy and natural history in Dartmouth College (1860–1869), and thereafter an associate in his father's business, of which he eventually became vice-president. Erastus Fairbanks (1792–1864) was governor of Vermont (1852–1853; 1860–1861).

FALLIGANT, JOHN G. (1810–1859), merchant, son of Louis Painboeuf Falligant (1776–1832) and Sarah Benedict (1790–1874), was born on the island of Martinique on February 11th, 1810. In early childhood he accompanied his parents to Paris, thence to Philadelphia, thence to Norfolk, Virginia, and finally to Savannah, Georgia, where the family settled in 1817. The father engaged in mercantile pursuits until his death on November 13th, 1832; by then the son was already established as an enterprising dealer in building supplies. John G. Falligant married first (on February 4th, 1835) Catherine F. Hedrick, of St. Augustine, Florida; following her death on December 3rd, 1849, he married second (on January 7th, 1851) Mrs. Sarah Ann Dreese (1820–1884), of Norfolk, Virginia. For one year (1858–1859) he served as alderman of Savannah. After a protracted illness he died in Newark, New Jersey, at the residence of his son-in-law, Frederick van Wagner, on September 19th, 1859, and was buried in Bonaventure Cemetery, Savannah. According to the Savannah *Republican* (September 20th, 1859), "He was an active, stirring man, energetic in the performance of duty both private and public, and enjoyed the good fortune to see his labors, in 'most all he undertook, crowned with success." His elder brother, Louis Numa Falligant (1808–1888), was a Savannah grocer for more than sixty years.

FARMER, JOHN WESLEY (1817–1886), physician, lawyer, journalist, merchant, farmer, and Methodist clergyman, was born in North Carolina on October 17th, 1817. By 1850 he had migrated to Liberty County, Georgia, where he married Laura Amanda Hughes (1826–1883), daughter of William Hughes (1793–1880) and Letitia Lane (1800–1883), and launched upon a career of astonishing versatility. "His professions, callings, and accomplishments are multifarious," wrote Eliza Caroline Clay on February 5th, 1863, and "all good and useful." For more than thirty years he resided in Hinesville, where he was frequently called by slaveowners to minister to sick Negroes throughout the county. On August 27th, 1861, he enlisted for twelve months as a private in the Liberty Volunteers (Company H, 25th Regiment Georgia Infantry). He died in Lakeland, Florida, whither he had gone for reasons of health, on March 1st, 1886, and was buried beside his wife in the Hughes family cemetery near Jones Creek in Liberty County.

FENNELL, JOHN N. (1826–1881), farmer and plantation overseer, son of John W. A. Fennell, was born in South Carolina on September 22nd, 1826. In early youth he accompanied his father to Liberty County, Georgia, where he planted for some twenty years. On April 13th, 1848, he married Mary Elizabeth Girardeau (1825–1902), daughter of William Pinckney Girardeau (1798–1874), for many years judge of the court of ordinary of Liberty County. On January 2nd, 1860, he was elected county sheriff. During the Civil War he served briefly as a private in the Liberty Guards (Company D, 5th Regiment Georgia Cavalry); on May 17th, 1862, he enlisted as a private in the Liberty Independent Troop (Company G, 5th Regiment Georgia Cavalry) and served until June 1864, when he was wounded near Atlanta and forced to retire. In March 1865 he undertook the management of Montevideo plantation during Mrs. Mary Jones's absence in Southwest Georgia; upon her return in the autumn she reported (November 17th, 1865) that "Mr. Fennell has done all he could to protect my interest; but he is feeble physically, and I do not know that he has any special gift at management. I believe him to be an honest and excellent man." On December 29th, 1865, she wrote that "Mr. Fennell is so unpopular with the people they will not serve under him; and indeed he *is* physically unable for the exertion I often require in a manager." Late in January 1866 he gave up the management of Montevideo and removed with his family to Savannah. He died there on December 14th, 1881, survived by his wife, and was buried in Bonaventure Cemetery. Mary Elizabeth (Girardeau) Fennell died on July 10th, 1902, and was buried beside her husband.

FILLMORE, MILLARD (1800–1874), thirteenth president of the United States, son of Nathaniel Fillmore (1771–1863) and Phoebe Millard (1780–1831), was born in Locke Township (now Summerhill), Cayuga County, New York, on January 7th, 1800. After reading law in the office of a local judge he was admitted to the bar in 1823 and practiced law in East Aurora for the next seven years; in 1830 he removed his practice to Buffalo. By then he was already active in politics; after serving in the state legislature (1829–1831) and in Congress (1833–1835; 1837–1843) he was elected vice-president of the United States under President Zachary Taylor in 1848, and at Taylor's sudden death on July 9th, 1850, he became President. His outstanding administrative achievement was the compromise bill of 1850, and when nominated for President by the American ("Know-Nothing") party in 1856 he campaigned for preservation of the Union, always preferring conciliation to coercion. In the election he ran a poor third to John C. Frémont and James Buchanan. Retiring to Buffalo, he undertook various civic, educational, and philanthropic enterprises, became one of the founders of the Buffalo Historical Society, and served as first chancellor of the University of Buffalo. He married first (in Moravia, New York, on February 5th, 1826) Abigail Powers (1798–1853), daughter of the Rev. Lemuel Powers, a Baptist clergyman, and Abigail Newland. He married second (in Albany, New York, on February 10th, 1858) Caroline Carmichael (1813–1881), daughter of Charles Carmichael and Temperance Blachley, and widow of Ezekiel C. McIntosh. He died in Buffalo on March 8th, 1874, and was buried in Forest Hill Cemetery. Charles Colcock Jones, Jr., seeing Fillmore in Washington in the summer of 1850, recorded his observations in a letter to his parents (August 3rd, 1850): "The President is one of the finest men in his personal appearance that I have ever seen; in fact, he is what would commonly be called 'a remarkably handsome man.'"

FINEGAN, JOSEPH (1814–1885), statesman and Confederate soldier, was born in Cloonis, Ireland, on November 17th, 1814. At the age of nineteen he migrated to the United States, where, after a year in New York, he settled in St. Augustine, Florida, as a government commissary clerk. Later he engaged successively in sugar planting, lumber, and railroad construction. At the outbreak of the Civil War he was commissioned captain of the Fernandina Volunteers and, later in the same year, colonel of the Florida state troops. In 1862 he was commissioned brigadier general in the Confederate army and placed in command of the military district of Florida; early in 1864, at the battle of Olustee, he won a signal victory when he forced the Federal troops to retreat to Jacksonville. In June 1864 he was ordered to join Lee's army in Virginia; shortly before Appomattox he returned to command the Florida state troops. After the war he represented Nassau County in the state senate (1865–1866). In 1869 he removed to Savannah, Georgia, where he was cotton factor and commission merchant for seven years; in 1876 he retired to Rutledge, Orange County, Florida, where he died on November 3rd, 1885. He was buried with military honors in Old City Cemetery, Jacksonville. He married first (in 1841) Mrs. Rebecca Towers, who bore him five children; after her death on July 31st, 1870, he married (in 1872) Mrs. Lucy C. Alexander, who survived him.

FISHER, JULIA RUSH (1834–1915), only daughter of Edward Heathcote Fisher (1792–1869) and Frances Rebecca Long (1808–1842), was born in Columbia, South Carolina, on February 2nd, 1834. Her father, a native of Greenville County, Virginia, had removed to Columbia in 1818 at the persuasion of his uncle and namesake, Dr. Edward Fisher (1773–1836), also a native of Virginia, who had settled in Columbia in 1806 and commenced the practice of medicine. Edward Heathcote Fisher, a merchant, erected a handsome classical mansion on Hampton Street; there his only daughter was born and reared. His wife died on March 29th, 1842, when Julia was barely eight years old. In 1848, when the Rev. Dr. Charles Colcock Jones resumed his professorship at Columbia Theological Seminary, Julia Fisher and Mary Sharpe Jones became schoolmates and intimate friends. On November 27th, 1855, when Julia Fisher became the wife of William Kunhardt Bachman (1830–1901), Mary Sharpe Jones was a bridesmaid at the wedding. Bachman, son of the Rev. John Bachman (1790–1874), distinguished Lutheran clergyman and naturalist of Charleston, South Carolina, had graduated from the College of Charleston in 1850 and studied at the University of Göttingen for three years; returning to Charleston, he had read law in the office of the Hon. Henry D. Lesesne, eminent jurist, and later became his partner. After his marriage he settled in Columbia, where for forty-six years he was prominently identified with the South Carolina bar. During the Civil War he served as captain of the German Volunteers, later known as Bachman's Battery, Hampton Legion, Army of Northern Virginia; he fought at First Manassas, Second Manassas, Sharpsburg, Fredericksburg, and Gettysburg. In 1865 he resumed the practice of law, represented Richland County in the state legislature (1865–1866), and served as assistant attorney general of the State of South Carolina (1880–1890). After his death on October 29th, 1901, his widow continued to reside in the Hampton Street house, where she died without issue on March 10th, 1915. She was buried beside her husband in Trinity Episcopal Churchyard.

FLAVEL, JOHN (1630–1691), Presbyterian clergyman, eldest son of Richard Flavel, was born in Bromsgrove, Worcestershire, England, in 1630. After attending University College (Oxford) he was pastor at Diptford (1650–1656) and Dartmouth (1656–1691). He was four times married. He died suddenly in Exeter on June 26th, 1691, and was buried in Dartmouth Churchyard. His numerous published works include *A Token for Mourners* (1674), described in its subtitle as "The advice of Christ to a distressed mother bewailing the death of her dear and only son; wherein the boundaries of sorrow are duly fixed, excesses restrained, the common pleas answered, and divers rules for the support of God's afflicted ones prescribed." *A Token for Mourners* went through many editions in England and America.

FLEMING, ELLEN BARRETT (1843–1893), daughter of Peter Winn Fleming (1807–1882) and his first wife, Matilda Law (1810–1853), was born in Liberty County, Georgia, on October 23rd, 1843. When she was not yet ten her mother died (on August 21st, 1853); her father married second (on March 1st, 1855) Caroline Amanda Baker (1824–1888). On November 4th, 1863, Ellen Barrett Fleming became the wife of Joseph Bacon Martin (1841–1912), son of William Graham Martin (1808–1861) and Eliza Sumner Bacon (1815–1889); there were nine children. Before the war Joseph Bacon Martin had attended Oglethorpe University; after the war he settled in Liberty County, where he farmed and conducted a school at Jones Creek; for twenty years (1886–1906) he was superintendent of the Liberty County Public Schools. After his wife's death on September 20th, 1893, he married second (on December 8th, 1897) Mary Alice Mallard (1849–1910), widow of Josiah Law Fleming (1841–1891), elder brother of his first wife. Joseph Bacon Martin died on November 13th, 1912, and was buried near his two wives in Flemington Cemetery.

FLEMING, GEORGE CLAUDIUS (1822–1858), Presbyterian clergyman, was born in St. Augustine, Florida, on October 30th, 1822. After attending schools in South Hadley and Amherst, Massachusetts, he graduated from the Medical College of the University of Pennsylvania in 1846 and practiced medicine for several years in Black Creek, Screven County, Georgia. His first interest being the Christian ministry, he abandoned his practice, attended Princeton Theological Seminary for two years (1851–1853), served as missionary in Woodstock Mills, Florida (1853–1856), and became stated supply of the Presbyterian church in St. Marys, Georgia, in July 1856. There he continued as pastor for less than two years; on February 15th, 1858, he died of consumption in Magnolia, Florida, whither he had gone for medical advice and change of climate. "From all that I have learned," wrote the Rev. R. Q. Mallard on March 24th, 1858, "he was an excellent and laborious servant of God. He was quite young, and has left a wife and four children in very dependent circumstances." He was buried in Oak Grove Cemetery, St. Marys.

FLEMING, JOHN MOULTRIE (1837–1863), engineer and Confederate soldier, younger son of the Hon. William Bennett Fleming (1803–1886) and his second wife, Eliza Ann Maxwell (1801–1871), was born in Walthourville, Liberty County, Georgia, in August 1837. After graduating from the Georgia Military Institute (Marietta) he was appointed engineer of the Savannah, Albany & Gulf Railroad at a salary of fourteen hundred dollars per annum. At the outbreak of the Civil War he resigned his position, enlisted as a private in the Oglethorpe Light Infantry (Company B, 8th Regiment Georgia Infantry), and joined his company in Virginia, where he was severely wounded in the shoulder at Manassas (July 21st, 1861). After sick leave in Georgia he was appointed adjutant in the 50th Regiment Georgia Infantry on March 30th, 1862; returning to Virginia, he fought through the whole of the Maryland campaign; in November 1862, encamped near Winchester, Virginia, he contracted pneumonia, from the effects of which he died in Walthourville, Georgia, on March 22nd, 1863. He was buried in Midway Cemetery. He never married. As the Savannah *Republican* (March 26th, 1863) observed, "Another martyr to the cause of liberty—another victim to its fiendish and implacable foe."

FLEMING, JOSIAH LAW (1841–1891), farmer and Confederate soldier, son of Peter Winn Fleming (1807–1882) and his first wife, Matilda Law (1810–1853), was born in Liberty County, Georgia, on March 25th, 1841. When he was twelve years old his mother died (on August 21st, 1853); his father married second (on March 1st, 1855) Caroline Amanda Baker (1824–1888). He attended Franklin College (Athens) with the class of 1862; at the outbreak of the Civil War he enlisted as a private in the Liberty Independent Troop (Company G, 5th Regiment Georgia Cavalry), of which company he later became corporal. In November 1864 he was taken prisoner. After the war he resumed farming in Liberty County, where on January 1st, 1868, he married Mary Alice Mallard (1849–1910), daughter of Lazarus John Mallard (1820–1877) and Sarah Stewart Mell (1823–1908). For many years he was active in the affairs of the Dorchester Presbyterian Church, of which he was superintendent of the Sunday school (1871–1882), clerk of the session and treasurer (1887–1891), and ruling elder (1878–1891). He died suddenly in Thomasville, Georgia, on May 24th, 1891, while undergoing treatment for cancer of the face, and was buried with military honors in Sunbury Cemetery. In a series of resolutions adopted after his death the session of the Dorchester church paid tribute to "his high and noble character as a citizen, his sympathetic and kindly nature as a friend and relative, exhibited particularly in times of trouble and bereavement, and his zealous and efficient service in the performance of the duties devolving upon him as an officer of the church." On December 8th, 1897, his widow became the second wife of Joseph Bacon Martin (1841–1912), widower of his younger sister, Ellen Barrett Fleming (1843–1893).

FLEMING, MARY CATHERINE (1832–1910), daughter of the Hon. William Bennett Fleming (1803–1886) and his second wife, Eliza Ann Maxwell (1801–1871), was born in Walthourville, Liberty County, Georgia, in 1832. When thirty years old she became engaged to be married to the Rev. Edwin Theodore Williams (1826–1866), a Presbyterian clergyman, a widower recently returned from three years (1856–1859) as missionary in Monrovia, Liberia, and then (1862) stated supply of the Presbyterian church on nearby Bryan Neck. Learning that her fiancé hoped to return to Africa, "Katy" Fleming broke off her engagement; in so doing she enlisted the sympathy of friends. "I think Katy Fleming did wisely to decline going to Africa," wrote Mary Eliza Robarts on January 26th, 1863; "she is too pretty a girl to lay down her life there. If her reverend admirer prefers to preach to the sable sons of Africa, he might find a field in Southwest Georgia quite large enough—where the life of his pretty bride would not be in danger." Evidently the engagement was renewed: on November 12th, 1863, the couple were married. Less than three years later (on August 9th, 1866) the husband died in Quincy, Florida, where he was pastor of the Presbyterian church; he was buried in Quincy, but his remains were removed to Laurel Grove Cemetery, Savannah, in December 1868. Mary Catherine (Fleming) Williams survived for forty-four years; she died in Flemington, Liberty County, Georgia, on November 14th, 1910, and was buried beside her husband.

FLEMING, PETER WINN (1807–1882), planter, elder son of William Fleming (1778–1822) and his second wife, Anna Winn (1782–1823), widow of Edward Quarterman and William Elliott Way, was born in Liberty County, Georgia, on May 1st, 1807. He was a brother of Thomas Winn Fleming (1815–1894) and a half-brother of the Hon. William Bennett Fleming (1803–1886). He married first (in December 1827) Matilda Law (1810–1853), daughter of the Rev. Samuel Spry Law (1775–1837) and his first wife, Rebecca G. Hughes (1782–1817); he married second (on March 1st, 1855) Caroline Amanda Baker (1824–1888), daughter of William Quarterman Baker (1800–1877) and his first wife, Ann Lydia Mallard (1804–1843). From early manhood he was a member of the Liberty Independent Troop; for many years (1833–1837; 1850–1859) he was captain. In 1855 he was one of sixteen citizens instrumental in organizing the Walthourville Presbyterian Church, of which he was an active member for the rest of his life. He died in Walthourville on January 6th, 1882, survived by his second wife and numerous children, and was buried beside his first wife in Sunbury Cemetery.

FLEMING, PORTER (1808–1891), merchant and cotton factor, son of Robert Fleming, was born on his father's plantation in Lincoln County, Georgia, on November 27th, 1808. In 1830, having attained his majority, he settled in Augusta, where he remained for the rest of his life, engaged in the grocery and cotton business. For many years he was associated with Charles Alden Rowland (1833–1902) in the firm of Fleming & Rowland; according to the *Augusta City Directory* (1859), "Fleming & Rowland, wholesale grocers, keep on hand large stocks of sugar, coffee, bagging, rope, salt, nails, molasses, and every description of groceries (liquors excepted)." After a long illness he died in Augusta on September 9th, 1891, survived by his third wife, Catherine Bathsheba Moragné (1823–1903), and was buried in Magnolia Cemetery. Of his eight

children the third, William Henry Fleming (1856–1944), was congressman from Georgia (1897–1903) and one of the leading lawyers of the state.

FLEMING, THOMAS WINN (1815–1894), planter, younger son of William Fleming (1778–1822) and his second wife, Anna Winn (1782–1823), widow of Edward Quarterman and William Elliott Way, was born in Liberty County, Georgia, on September 16th, 1815. He was a brother of Peter Winn Fleming (1807–1882) and a half-brother of the Hon. William Bennett Fleming (1803–1886). He was an orphan at the age of eight; from 1827 to 1834 he was reared in the home of Eliza Wilson (1789–1850), widow of his uncle, John Winn (1779–1820), along with her own children, John Winn (1814–1892) and Thomas Sumner Winn (1820–1900), both destined to become Presbyterian clergymen, and her orphaned niece, Susan Eliza Wilson (1819–1888), destined to become the wife of Thomas Winn Fleming. After attending Franklin College (Athens) with the class of 1837 he returned to Liberty County, where on February 16th, 1837, he married his childhood companion, Susan Eliza Wilson, orphaned daughter of James Wilson and Sarah Bacon. For the next twenty-five years he planted in his native county; when the Savannah, Albany & Gulf Railroad penetrated Liberty County in the 1850s, Depot No. 2 (Fleming Station) was established for the convenience of his plantation. Thomas Winn Fleming was a selectman of Midway Church (1845–1849; 1852–1864). During the Civil War he settled at Pine Grove plantation, near Newton, Baker County, where he remained for the rest of his life. For many years he served as county school commissioner, and after the death of the Hon. Reuben Smith he completed his unexpired term in the state senate. Susan Eliza (Wilson) Fleming died in Baker County on March 6th, 1888, and was buried in Newton Cemetery. Thomas Winn Fleming died on February 7th, 1894, survived by seven children and numerous grandchildren, and was buried beside his wife.

FLEMING, WILLIAM AUGUSTUS (1830–1904), merchant, son of Peter Winn Fleming (1807–1882) and his first wife, Matilda Law (1810–1853), was born in Liberty County, Georgia, on April 24th, 1830. For much of his adult life he was associated with the Liberty Independent Troop, of which his father was captain for many years (1833–1837; 1850–1859); he joined as fourth sergeant in 1851, and during the Civil War he became first lieutenant, serving for a time in 1862 as acting inspector and mustering officer. On September 4th, 1864, he was taken prisoner at Murfreesboro, Tennessee, and sent to Johnson's Island, Ohio; he was released on oath on June 16th, 1865. Returning to Liberty County, he reopened his country store. Early in 1867 he married Addie F. Oatman (1843–1914). From 1872 to 1884 he was captain of the Liberty Independent Troop. For many years he was postmaster and shipping agent at Depot No. 3

(McIntosh Station) in Liberty County. "It has been whispered," wrote Eliza Caroline Clay to Mrs. Mary Jones on February 28th, 1867, "that the postmaster at No. 3 may not be very efficient. . . . So I send this to Savannah, thinking Dr. Axson may know some sure way to forward." William Augustus ("Gus") Fleming died in Flemington on March 26th, 1904, survived by his wife, three daughters, and two sons, and was buried with military honors in Flemington Cemetery. Addie (Oatman) Fleming died on October 28th, 1914, and was buried beside her husband.

FLEMING, WILLIAM BENNETT (1803–1886), jurist, son of William Fleming (1778–1822) and his first wife, Catharine Winn (1782–1803), was born near Flemington, Liberty County, Georgia, on October 29th, 1803. His mother died at his birth; his father married second (on February 5th, 1805) Anna Winn (1782–1823), widow of Edward Quarterman and William Elliott Way. William Bennett Fleming was thus a half-brother of Peter Winn Fleming (1807–1882) and Thomas Winn Fleming (1815–1894). He attended Yale College with the class of 1825; in his senior year he withdrew for lack of funds, but he received a degree in 1829. Meanwhile he returned to Liberty County, taught school, planted, read law, and commenced the practice of his profession. He married first (in 1826) Ann Eliza Stevens (1806–1826), who died without issue. He married second (on November 20th, 1828) Eliza Ann Maxwell (1801–1871); there were six living children: Sarah Margaret Fleming (1829–1868), wife of William Lowndes Walthour; Ann Eliza Fleming (1831–1918), wife of John Thurston Rowland; Mary Catherine Fleming (1832–1910), second wife of the Rev. Edwin Theodore Williams; William Oliver Fleming (1835–1881); John Moultrie Fleming (1837–1863); and Matilda Olivia Fleming (1839–1927), wife of (1) Russell Walthour and (2) the Rev. John Watt Montgomery. William Bennett Fleming represented Liberty County in the state legislature in 1831 and 1835. In 1837 he removed to Savannah and soon rose to prominence as a jurist. He was judge of the city court of Savannah (1844–1845) and judge of the superior court of the eastern circuit (1847–1849; 1853–1868; 1879–1881). He was a member of the state secession convention meeting in Milledgeville in January 1861. Early in 1879 he was elected to Congress to complete the unexpired term of the Hon. Julian Hartridge (deceased); he served from February 10th, 1879, to March 3rd, 1879, after which he resumed his seat on the bench. In 1881 he retired to his home in Walthourville, Liberty County, where he died after a long illness on August 19th, 1886, survived by three daughters, and was buried beside his second wife in Laurel Grove Cemetery, Savannah.

FLEMING, WILLIAM OLIVER (1835–1881), lawyer and Confederate soldier, elder son of the Hon. William Bennett Fleming (1803–1886) and his second wife, Eliza Ann Maxwell (1801–1871), was born in Walthourville, Liberty County, Georgia, on April 2nd, 1835. After attending Franklin College (Athens) with the class of 1856 he settled in Bainbridge, Georgia, where he undertook the practice of law. On January 18th, 1860, he married Georgia Williams. At the outbreak of the Civil War he enlisted in the Bainbridge Independents; in 1862 he became lieutenant, then captain, of Company F, 50th Regiment Georgia Infantry; on July 31st, 1863, he was promoted to lieutenant colonel in recognition of "gallant and meritorious conduct" at Gettysburg. Resigning from the army, he served briefly in the state legislature, but at Sherman's approach he returned to his regiment. After the war he resumed the practice of law in Bainbridge, where he was solicitor general of the Albany circuit (1877–1880), judge of the superior court (1880–1881), and elder of the Presbyterian church. He died in Bainbridge on November 4th, 1881, survived by his wife and a numerous family. His younger brother, John Moultrie Fleming (1837–1863), adjutant in the 50th Regiment Georgia Infantry, died on March 22nd, 1863, from the effects of pneumonia contracted in camp.

FLINT, AUSTIN (1812–1886), physician, grandson and namesake of Austin Flint, surgeon in the Revolutionary army, was born in Petersham, Massachusetts, on October 20th, 1812. After undergraduate study at Amherst and Harvard he received his medical degree from Harvard in 1833. Three years later he settled in Buffalo, New York, where in 1845 he established *The Buffalo Medical Journal* (1845–1855) and in 1847, with F. H. Hamilton and J. P. White, founded the Buffalo Medical College, at which he was professor of medicine (1847–1861). At the same time he was professor of medicine at the University of Louisville (1852–1856) and at the New Orleans Medical College (1859–1861). In 1861 he settled in New York, where he was professor of pathology and practical medicine at Long Island College Hospital and, together with others, founded the Bellevue Hospital Medical College. For the next twenty-five years he was prodigiously active as hospital physician, teacher, and writer; he was also president of the New York Academy of Medicine (1873), delegate to the International Medical Congress in London (1881), and president of the American Medical Association (1883–1884). In all his work he enjoyed the support of his wife, Anne Skillings, and his son, Austin Flint (1836–1915), also a physician. He died suddenly on March 13th, 1886, having established a firm reputation both in the United States and abroad.

FOOTE, HENRY STUART (1804–1880), statesman, son of Richard Helm Foote and Jane Stuart, was born in Fauquier County, Virginia, on February 28th, 1804. After graduating from Washington College (Lexington, Virginia) in 1819 he studied law and was admitted to the bar in Richmond in 1823. Removing to Mississippi, he practiced law in

Jackson, Natchez, Vicksburg, and Raymond; he represented Mississippi in the United States Senate (1847–1852), where, unlike his colleague, Jefferson Davis, he supported the compromise bill of 1850. In 1851 he defeated Davis for the governorship of Mississippi; he served for one term (1852–1854). At the outbreak of the Civil War, although he opposed secession, he took a seat in the Confederate Congress; but he soon left Richmond in disgust, entered Federal territory, and eventually sailed for Europe. In *The War of the Rebellion* (1866) he attempted to justify his role in the Civil War. He married first Elizabeth Winters, of Tuscumbia, Alabama; he married second Mrs. Rachel D. Smiley, of Nashville, Tennessee. He died in Nashville on May 19th, 1880, and was buried in Mount Olivet Cemetery.

FOOTMAN, MARIA HABERSHAM (1822–1895), daughter of Dr. Richard Hunter Footman and his first cousin, Mary Constance Maxwell, was born in Savannah, Georgia, on April 10th, 1822. She never married. By 1850 she was living in the household of her brother-in-law, Wylly Woodbridge, Savannah commission merchant, husband of her deceased sister Elizabeth Footman (1817–1846). By 1870 she was living in the household of her sister Margaret Footman (1824–1879), widow of John Wallace Owens (1821–1862). Her third sister, Mary White Footman (1827–1863), was the first wife of John Screven (1827–1900). Maria Habersham Footman died in Savannah after a long illness on May 6th, 1895, and was buried in Laurel Grove Cemetery.

FORD, LEWIS DeSAUSSURE (1801–1883), physician, son of the Hon. Gabriel H. Ford, was born in Morristown, New Jersey, on December 30th, 1801. After graduating from the College of Physicians and Surgeons (New York) in 1822 he practiced medicine in Bamburg, South Carolina, for five years; in 1827 he settled in Augusta, Georgia, where he was prominent in civic and professional affairs for the rest of his life. He was twice mayor of Augusta and frequently a member of the city council. For many years he was president of the Augusta Board of Health. He was also first president of the Augusta Bible Society and senior warden of St. Paul's Episcopal Church. When the Georgia Medical Association was organized, he was elected first president. For fifty years he was professor of the institutes and practice of medicine at the Medical College of Georgia. During the Civil War he was surgeon in charge of the general hospital in Augusta. After a long and useful career he died in Augusta on August 21st, 1883. His son, Henry W. DeSaussure Ford (1834–1906), a graduate of Franklin College (Athens) in 1855, was a surgeon in the Confederate army and subsequently rose to distinction as a physician and an educator.

FORREST, NATHAN BEDFORD (1821–1877), Confederate soldier, eldest son of William Forrest and Marian Beck, was born in Bedford (now Marshall) County, Tennessee,

on July 13th, 1821. In 1834 his father removed to Mississippi, and in 1837, at his father's death, the eldest son assumed the support of a large family. Gradually, through industry and ingenuity, he accumulated considerable wealth, largely in cotton plantations in Mississippi and Arkansas. In 1845 he married Mary Ann Montgomery, and in 1849 he settled in Memphis. At the outbreak of the Civil War he enlisted as a private in the Confederate army; in July 1862 he was appointed brigadier general and began the series of brilliant cavalry raids against Union communications for which he became legendary. After Chickamauga he was appointed major general, and in February 1865 he was appointed lieutenant general. After the war he returned to his cotton plantations. He died in Memphis on October 29th, 1877.

FOSTER, GURDON ROBERSON (1827–1887), Presbyterian clergyman, was born in Claiborne, Monroe County, Alabama, on February 6th, 1827. After graduating from Oglethorpe University in 1848 and from Columbia Theological Seminary in 1851 he was pastor in Wetumpka, Alabama (1851–1871), evangelist of the East Alabama Presbytery (1871–1880), and superintendent of the orphans' home of the Synod of Alabama (1880–1887). He was a ministerial delegate from the East Alabama Presbytery to the General Assembly of the Presbyterian Church meeting in Lexington, Kentucky, in May 1857. On December 1st, 1858, he married Annie Slaughter, of Dadeville, Alabama. He died in Tuskegee, Alabama, on October 26th, 1887.

FOWLER, ORSON SQUIRE (1809–1887), phrenologist, son of Horace Fowler and Martha Howe, was born in Cohocton, Steuben County, New York, on October 11th, 1809. After graduating from Amherst College in 1834 he settled in New York City, where he joined his younger brother, Lorenzo Fowler, in promoting the cause of phrenology. In 1837 they published *Phrenology Proved, Illustrated, and Applied*; in 1840 they began publication of *The Phrenological Almanac*; in 1842 they assumed editorship of *The American Phrenological Journal and Miscellany*, founded by Nathan Allen in 1838. Through his numerous pseudo-scientific and pseudo-philosophical writings "Professor" Fowler acquired a national reputation; from 1850 to 1870 he devoted himself chiefly to lucrative lecture tours throughout the United States and Canada. In March 1858 he spent two weeks in Savannah, Georgia; his lectures on phrenology were conspicuously featured on the pages of the Savannah *Republican*: "There has been much controversy in regard to this subject. Some claim for it the highest rank among the sciences, while others (those who have never investigated it) discredit its claim to the name of a science. Be it true or false, useful or worthless, the 'Father of Phrenology in America' will give a course of six lectures at Armory Hall this week, commencing tonight" (March 15th, 1858). "Professor Fowler's lecture this evening is on Self-

Improvement and the Management of Children. This lecture expounds those first principles which govern human life. It is both preeminently philosophical and practical. Will revolutionize the family government of all parents who hear it" (March 16th, 1858). "Analysis of the Phrenological Faculties and the Cultivation of the Intellect is Professor Fowler's subject tonight. The most philosophical lecture of the course" (March 17th, 1858). "Love, Courtship, and Married Life are the subjects of Professor Fowler's lecture this evening. The laws of attraction, reciprocation, and of selection will be scientifically and philosophically handled. The secrets and the philosophy of domestic happiness and success will be treated upon" (March 18th, 1858). "Sexuality, or Nature's Creative Economies, by O. S. Fowler, this evening at Armory Hall, to gentlemen only" (March 19th, 1858). "Professor Fowler devotes this evening to private examinations at the Screven House for the accommodation of those whose business confines them during the day" (March 20th, 1858). "Professor Fowler's lectures having been so well patronized, and Armory Hall being inadequate to accommodate all those who desire to attend, he gives another course this week at St. Andrew's Hall commencing this evening. Subject: Courtship, Its Fatal Errors, and the Happy Family" (March 22nd, 1858). Fowler was himself thrice married: on June 10th, 1835, to Mrs. Martha Chevalier, daughter of Elias Brevoort, of New York City; on October 26th, 1865, to Mrs. Mary Poole, daughter of William Aiken, of Gloucester, Massachusetts; on March 21st, 1882, to Abbie L. Ayres, daughter of Ebenezer Ayres, of Osceola, Wisconsin. He died near Sharon, Connecticut, on August 18th, 1887.

FRANCIS, JOHN WAKEFIELD (1789–1861), physician, son of an immigrant German grocer, was born in New York City on November 17th, 1789. After graduating from Columbia University in 1809 and from the College of Physicians and Surgeons (New York) in 1811 he joined the faculty of the College of Physicians and Surgeons, where he was professor of the institutes of medicine and materia medica (1815–1817), professor of medical jurisprudence (1817–1819), and professor of obstetrics (1819–1826). He resigned in 1826 and together with four colleagues founded Rutgers Medical College, where he was professor of obstetrics and forensic medicine until the institution was closed five years later by legislative act. For some years he practiced medicine in New York City in association with Richard Sharpe Kissam (1808–1861). He married Maria Eliza Cutler, a great-niece of General Francis Marion, of South Carolina; two of his sons, Valentine Mott Francis (1834–1907) and Samuel Ward Francis (1835–1886), were also physicians. John Wakefield Francis died in New York City on February 8th, 1861.

FRASER, ALEXANDER MARTIN (1825–1907), physician, son of Simon Alexander Fraser (1787–1856) and Sarah Martin (1797–1885), was born in Liberty County, Georgia, on January 22nd, 1825. He was a brother of the Rev. Donald Fraser (1826–1887). After graduating from the Medical Department of the University of the City of New York in 1852 he returned to his native county, where he practiced medicine until the outbreak of the Civil War. On August 27th, 1861, he enlisted for twelve months as a private in the Liberty Volunteers (Company H, 25th Regiment Georgia Infantry). On November 18th, 1862, he was commissioned assistant surgeon of the Liberty Mounted Rangers (Company B, 20th Battalion Georgia Cavalry). After the war he practiced medicine in the Bickley district of Ware County, Georgia, where he died in the home of George Herndon on May 31st, 1907. He never married. He was buried near his parents in Flemington Cemetery, Liberty County. The birthdate inscribed on his tombstone (November 12th, 1826) is incorrect; it conflicts with the birthdate of his younger brother Donald Fraser (November 26th, 1826); the birthdate given in the records of Midway Church (January 22nd, 1825) is correct.

FRASER, ANN SARAH (COUPER) (1796–1866): *Mrs. John Fraser*, daughter of John Couper (1759–1850) and Rebecca Maxwell (1775–1845), was born at Cannon's Point, her father's plantation on St. Simons Island, Glynn County, Georgia, in 1796. She was a sister of James Hamilton Couper (1794–1866) and William Audley Couper (1817–1888), and a first cousin of Julia Rebecca Maxwell (1808–1892), wife of Roswell King. Her father, a native of Scotland, had migrated to Georgia in 1775 and subsequently became a wealthy landowner in Glynn County. After attending a school for young ladies in Charleston conducted by Miss Julia Datty she returned to St. Simons Island, where in 1815 she became the wife of John Fraser (1791–1839), a Scotsman, who was first lieutenant of the Royal British Marine Artillery for more than thirty-two years. They resided briefly in England and then settled in Georgia, where John Fraser managed Hamilton plantation on St. Simons Island. There the English actress Frances Anne Kemble (1809–1893) lived for several months in the 1830s as bride of Pierce Butler; in her *Journal of a Residence on a Georgian Plantation in 1838–1839* she frequently mentioned Mrs. Fraser, whom she found to be "a kind-hearted, intelligent woman" and "a perfect Lady Bountiful." The death of John Fraser on July 18th, 1839, left his family in financial straits; eventually his wife secured a modest pension from the British government in recognition of his long term of service, but the family was never again financially secure. In 1852 the mother and her five daughters (Rebecca, Susan, Elizabeth, Frances, and Selina) removed to Marietta, Georgia, where they remained, with a brief interval in Brunswick (1856–1859), until after the Civil War. The only living son, John Couper Fraser (1832–1863), a Savannah commission merchant, was killed at Gettysburg on July 3rd, 1863. Two of the daughters, Rebecca and Elizabeth (Lizzie), served for some months as matrons in a military hospital. In the summer of 1864, when Marietta fell into Union hands, the Frasers, unlike most of their neighbors, remained in the town; they were subjected to considerable indignity as well as inconvenience, and found themselves after the war (as Rebecca wrote) "in abject poverty" and "without a protector." In the spring of 1866 the family removed to New Iberia, St. Martin's Parish, Louisiana, to join the household of the youngest daughter, Selina Fraser (1836–1920), wife of George Mortimer Stubinger. There, a few weeks after their arrival, Ann Sarah (Couper) Fraser died on May 9th, 1866, and was buried at Petite Fausse Point. Late in 1869 the four elder sisters returned to Marietta, where they survived until the 1890s, when one by one they went to unmarked graves in Citizens Cemetery.

FRASER, DONALD (1826–1887), Presbyterian clergyman, son of Simon Alexander Fraser (1787–1856) and Sarah Martin (1797–1885), was born in Liberty County, Georgia, on November 26th, 1826. He was a brother of Alexander Martin Fraser (1825–1907). After graduating from Oglethorpe University in 1848 and from Columbia Theological Seminary in 1851 he was pastor of churches in Bryan County, Georgia (1852–1856); Jacksonville, Florida (1856–1860); Madison, Florida (1860–1867); Monticello, Florida (1867–1870); and Decatur, Georgia (1872–1887). He was chaplain of the 2nd Regiment Florida Infantry (1861–1863) and professor of Greek in Oglethorpe University (1870–1872). On December 30th, 1851, he married Valeria Augusta Cassels (1832–1861), daughter of Thomas Quarterman Cassels (1808–1879) and Mary Amarintha Mallard (1810–1874), of Liberty County. He died on a train traveling from Jesup, Georgia, to Atlanta on the night of September 12th, 1887, and was buried in Decatur Cemetery. One of his sons, Chalmers Fraser (1856–1912), was also a Presbyterian clergyman.

FRASER, SIMON ALEXANDER (1816–1870), planter and grocer, son of William Fraser and Mary Ann Osgood, was born in Liberty County, Georgia, on July 23rd, 1816. He was an orphan at the age of six. On November 17th, 1842, he married Mary William Bacon (1825–1884), daughter of John Bacon and Mary J. Hazzard; there were seven living children. For many years he planted in Liberty County and kept a country store. From 1853 to 1860 he was clerk of the superior and inferior courts. Prior to the Civil War he conducted a Sunday school for the instruction of Negroes. When the Flemington Presbyterian Church was organized in 1866 he was ordained one of its deacons and took an active part in the Sunday school. He died on April 8th, 1870, survived by his wife and seven children, and was buried in Flemington Cemetery. Mary William (Bacon) Fraser died on February 28th, 1884, and was buried beside her husband.

FRÉMONT, JOHN CHARLES (1813–1890), explorer, politician, and soldier, son of Jean Charles Frémon, a French émigré schoolteacher, and Ann Beverly Whiting, estranged wife of John Pryor, was born in Savannah, Georgia, on January 21st, 1813. (He later altered the spelling of his surname to *Frémont.*) His father died in 1818 and his mother removed to Charleston, South Carolina, where the son attended the College of Charleston (1829–1831). After accompanying an expedition conducted by J. N. Nicollet for exploring the plateau between the upper Mississippi and Missouri Rivers he returned to Washington, where he won the patronage of the Hon. Thomas Hart Benton (1782–1858), United States senator from Missouri (1821–1851), and married (on October 19th, 1841) his sixteen-year-old daughter Jessie Benton (1824–1902). After three subsequent expeditions to the West (1842; 1843–1844; 1845–1846) "the Pathfinder" became a national hero; in 1856 he was Republican nominee for President. Defeated by Buchanan, he returned to California, where he engaged in mining until the outbreak of the Civil War. In 1861 he served briefly as major general commanding the Department of the West; in 1862 he commanded the Department of Western Virginia. On May 31st, 1864, he was nominated for President by radical Republicans hostile to Lincoln, but on September 22nd, 1864, he withdrew. His subsequent life was an anticlimax to his former exploring career, for which he is justly celebrated. Although he settled in California in 1887, he died on a visit to New York on July 13th, 1890, survived by his wife, and was buried at Piermont on the Hudson River. Jessie (Benton) Frémont was author of numerous travel sketches, historical sketches, and children's stories, first published in periodicals and later republished in *Souvenirs of My Time* (1887), *Far West Sketches* (1890), and *The Will and the Way Stories* (1891). She also assisted Frémont in writing and publishing his *Memoirs* (1887). She died in Los Angeles on December 27th, 1902, and was buried beside her husband.

FRIERSON, GEORGE SMITH (1822–1862), shoe merchant, son of James Smith Frierson and Susan Garvey Stoll, was born in Macon, Georgia, in April 1822. In early youth he settled in Savannah, where he undertook a mercantile career. On February 3rd, 1842, he married Sarah E. Haupt (1820–1886); there were five children. In 1855 he joined Worthington Chauncey Butler in the firm of Butler & Frierson, "dealers in ladies', gentlemen's, and children's boots and shoes," which continued until Frierson's sudden death in Macon on June 27th, 1862. He was buried in Laurel Grove Cemetery, Savannah. Sarah (Haupt) Frierson died on September 24th, 1886, and was buried beside her husband.

FULTON, GASPAR J. (1823–1866), railroad man, was born in Savannah, Georgia, in 1823. By 1850 he was a conductor on the Central Railroad of Georgia; in 1856 he became a conductor on the newly constructed Savannah, Albany & Gulf Railroad, running from Savannah to Thomasville and serving Liberty County. A charming essay entitled "A Trip to Doctortown" appeared in the Savannah *Republican* on September 23rd, 1857: "The conductor holds the reins and manages with an ease and system which tell plainly that he understands his business, thus assuring security as well as courteous attention to the wayfarer. A pleasant trip is always enjoyed with Mr. Fulton." In 1858 he became general superintendent of the Savannah, Albany & Gulf Railroad (later renamed the Atlantic & Gulf Railroad), a post he held until his death. On July 24th, 1850, he married Virginia N. Craig (1830–1899), of Midville, Burke County, Georgia; there was one daughter. His sister, Mary Teresa Fulton (1831–1906), was the wife of William Oscar Charlton (1816–1902), also a railroad man. Gaspar J. Fulton died in Savannah on December 1st, 1866, survived by his wife and daughter, and was buried in Laurel Grove Cemetery. "The G. J. Fulton," a locomotive operating on the Atlantic & Gulf Railroad in the 1870s, was named in his honor.

GABBETT, SARAH ELIZABETH (RICHARDSONE). *See* Richardsone, Sarah Elizabeth

GALLIE, JOHN B. (1806–1863), cotton factor and commission merchant, was born in Dornoch, Scotland, on July 1st, 1806. In early youth he migrated to Nova Scotia, where he remained for seven years; then, after some time in New Orleans, he settled in Savannah, Georgia, where for more than thirty years he was prominent in business and military circles. He was for several years captain of the Chatham Artillery. He married first (on November 8th, 1838) Augusta Borg; he married second (on July 5th, 1849) Jeannette E. Porcher; he married third (on June 11th, 1858) Charlotte Morgan Eagle. At the outbreak of the Civil War he organized and became captain of the Savannah Artillery (1st Volunteer Regiment Georgia Artillery); on November 13th, 1862, he was elected major of the 22nd Battalion Georgia Artillery and assigned to Fort McAllister ("Genesis Point battery") on the Great Ogeechee River below Savannah. He was killed at Fort McAllister during a Federal bombardment on February 1st, 1863, and was buried in Laurel Grove Cemetery, Savannah, beside his first wife.

GARDNER, CAROLINE R. (1813–1877): *Mrs. Horace B. Gardner,* was born in Newark, New Jersey, in 1813. In 1858 she settled with her husband and five children in Atlanta, Georgia, where her eldest son, Horace B. Gardner, was a wheelwright. Late in 1859 her husband died and she opened her house to boarders. After the war she returned to Newark, where she died on October 19th, 1877.

GAUDRY, JAMES EDWARD (1820–1880), bank officer, son of John B. Gaudry (1782–1846), a native of Bordeaux, France, and Anne Catherine Roubillard (1795–1882), a native of Kingston, Jamaica, was born in Savannah, Georgia, on September 15th, 1820. For many years he was a bank cashier, first at the Mechanics' Savings Bank, later at the Merchants' National Bank, and finally at the Southern Bank of the State of Georgia. He was also for a time a director of the Merchants' National Bank. On January 3rd, 1861, he was ordered with his company, the Chatham Artillery, to Fort Pulaski. Subsequently, in 1864, he served for two months as third lieutenant in the Chatham Siege Artillery (1st Battalion Georgia Reserves); he resigned on June 28th, 1864, because, as he wrote, "I suffer severely from attacks of the gout, which are consequent upon the slightest exposure and fatigue." After the war he continued banking until 1877, when he resigned and entered commerce in association with L. J. Guilmartin. He died in Brooklyn, New York, on May 26th, 1880, survived by his second wife, Urania (1831–1895), and five children, and was buried in Cathedral (Catholic) Cemetery, Savannah. As the Savannah *Morning News* (May 31st, 1880) observed, "He lived and died an honest man. No greater eulogy could be pronounced upon him, even though volumes were written in his praise."

GAUL, MARTIN (1830–1884), gentleman, son of Martin Gaul (1799–1842) and Matilda Souder (1800–1851), was born in Philadelphia, Pennsylvania, on October 3rd, 1830. His grandfather, Frederick Gaul, a native of Frankfort on the Main, Germany, had migrated to America before the Revolutionary War and established "The Gaul Brewery" in Philadelphia; by 1830 his two sons, Frederick and Martin, had assumed the management of a flourishing business. In 1853 Martin Gaul (1830–1884) married Mary Carroll (born 1831), daughter of the Rev. Daniel Lynn Carroll (1797–1851), a Presbyterian clergyman, and Anna Turk Halsted (1805–1884). There were two children: Carroll Gaul, who died on July 6th, 1855, aged seven months; and Matilda Souder Gaul, who died on April 28th, 1859, aged two years and eight months. Martin Gaul died suddenly in Saugerties, Ulster County, New York, on August 21st, 1884, and was buried beside his two infants in Laurel Hill Cemetery, Philadelphia.

GAULDEN, WILLIAM BOATNER (1816–1873), planter and lawyer, son of the Rev. Jonathan Gaulden (1776–1853) and Rhoda Paisley (1788–1853), was born at Millhaven, his father's plantation near Hinesville, Liberty County, Georgia, in 1816. He was one of seven living sons, six of whom became lawyers. After attending Franklin College (Athens) he was a member of the state house of representatives (1838), judge of the inferior court of Liberty County (1841), solicitor general of the eastern circuit (1847), and member of the state senate (1863–1865). In 1850 he was a delegate to the Democratic National Convention meeting in Charleston, South Carolina, where he delivered an impassioned speech championing the reopening of the slave trade.

Although he favored slavery he opposed secession; at the outbreak of the Civil War he nevertheless supported the Southern cause. In August 1861 he proposed to raise a regiment for the defense of the Georgia coast; his letter addressed "To the Patriotic of Georgia" appeared in the Savannah *Republican* (September 12th, 1861): "Georgians! Arouse, awake, and let not the vile foot of a Lincolnite pollute our soil." In July 1864, as aide-de-camp to Governor Joseph E. Brown, he became colonel of the Coast Guard Battalion (3rd Regiment Georgia Militia), organized from the reserve militia of Bryan, Liberty, and McIntosh Counties for local defense. After the war he was an outspoken opponent of Reconstruction. Evidently he was something of an eccentric; he was known as "the Roaring Lion of Liberty County." In a letter to the Savannah *Republican* (August 8th, 1868) the Hon. Thomas Quarterman Cassels described a recent Democratic meeting in Hinesville: "Colonel W. B. Gaulden then addressed the meeting at considerable length in his usual style, dealing out his invectives and sarcasms against Grant, Spoon Butler, and the leaders of the mongrel party generally, by the wholesale." He married first (on December 26th, 1837) Harriet A. Mann (1814–1851); their only son, William Fenderwood Gaulden, died in infancy. He married second (on March 1st, 1855) Laura Glenn Brown (1839–1910), daughter of the Hon. Bedford Brown (1795–1870), United States senator from North Carolina (1829–1840); their only daughter, Mary Glenn Gaulden (1869–1900), became the wife of William Zorn Bryan in 1894. William Boatner Gaulden died suddenly at Millhaven on January 3rd, 1873, and was buried in Taylor's Creek Cemetery. On March 25th, 1875, his widow became the wife of his law partner, Theodore Norman Winn.

GAUSSEN, FRANÇOIS SAMUEL ROBERT LOUIS (1790–1863), Swiss Protestant clergyman, son of Georg Markus Gaussen, was born in Geneva on August 25th, 1790. After graduating from the University of Geneva he served as pastor of the Swiss Reformed church at Satigny near Geneva from 1816 to 1831. In 1830 he was censured and suspended by his ecclesiastical superiors for having discarded the official catechism of his church; and in 1831, when he helped organize a society for the establishment of a new theological college, he was deprived of his pastoral charge. From 1834 to 1857 he was professor of systematic theology in the college he helped to establish. His best-known work, *La théopneustie ou pleine inspiration des saintes écritures* (1840), an elaborate defense of the doctrine of "plenary inspiration," was translated into English and enjoyed wide popularity in England and America. He died at Les Grottes, Geneva, on June 18th, 1863.

GIBBONS, WILLIAM HEYWARD (1831–1887), planter, only son of William Gibbons (1781–1845) and Abigail L. Taintor (1791–1844), was born in New York City in May 1831. His father, a millionaire horseman born of a prominent Georgia family, was said at the time of his death to be one of the richest men in New Jersey. William Heyward Gibbons, who inherited the greater part of his father's wealth, divided his time between Madison, New Jersey, where he lived with his sister, Mrs. Isabel Lathrop, and Savannah, Georgia, where he lived with his agent, Montgomery Cumming. Among his Georgia interests was Shaftesbury, one of the largest and most valuable rice plantations on the Savannah River. He never married. During the Civil War he served as major in the Confederate army. He died after a long illness in Madison, New Jersey, on June 9th, 1887, and was buried in Hillside Cemetery. His sister Sarah became the wife of Samuel Ward McAllister (1827–1895), New York society leader, on March 15th, 1853.

GIBSON, RICHARD TURNER (1809–1872), planter and lawyer, son of Robert Stewart Gibson and Sarah Turner, was born on his father's plantation on Whitemarsh Island, ten miles east of Savannah, Georgia, in 1809. After attending Franklin College (Athens) briefly with the class of 1828 he proceeded to Lexington, Virginia, home of his sister, Louisa Catherine Gibson (1805–1858), and her husband, Dr. William Alexander Caruthers (1802–1846). There he attended Washington College from 1826 to 1827 and probably studied law. Returning to Savannah, he soon rose to prominence as a lawyer; for many years he was road commissioner of Chatham County; he was also judge of the inferior court (1849–1853) and member of the state house of representatives (1861–1863). He died suddenly at his plantation on Whitemarsh Island on October 11th, 1872, and was buried in Laurel Grove Cemetery, Savannah. The Savannah *Republican* carried a long obituary the following day: "As a public speaker his abilities were far above the ordinary, and as a gentleman his conversation was polished and entertaining, and his manners elegant and finished. Judge Gibson was a member of the old regime —a noble gentleman of the old school, and a most exemplary and upright Christian. By his death a public loss is inflicted which cannot be easily supplied."

GIGNILLIAT, THOMAS HART (1842–1905), planter, son of William Robert Gignilliat (1814–1882) and Helen Mary Hart (1821–1862), was born at Greenwood, his father's plantation near Darien, McIntosh County, Georgia, on November 15th, 1842. The Gignilliats were Swiss-French Huguenots who settled in South Carolina after the revocation of the Edict of Nantes in 1685. Thomas Hart Gignilliat and his twin brother, Gilbert West Gignilliat (1842–1896), were privately educated by Arthur Mathewson, a tutor from the North; Thomas Hart Gignilliat later attended the Georgia Military Institute (Marietta), from which he graduated in June 1861. On May 15th, 1862, he enlisted as a private in the Liberty Mounted Rangers (Company B, 20th Battalion Georgia Cavalry); he became second lieutenant on September 12th, 1863, and first lieutenant on January 23rd, 1864. On July 15th, 1863, he married Ellen Barbara Mallard (1840–1914), eldest daughter of Thomas Samuel Mallard (1816–1882) and Ann Eliza Screven (1820–1895); four children lived to maturity. After the war he was a rice planter in McIntosh County. He died of heart disease at his plantation, Greenwood, near Darien, in December 1905 and was buried beside his twin brother in St. Andrew's Cemetery. His wife died in Pineora, Effingham County, Georgia, on May 14th, 1914, and was buried in Bonaventure Cemetery, Savannah. Gilbert West Gignilliat never married; during the Civil War he was a private in the Liberty Independent Troop (Company G, 5th Regiment Georgia Cavalry).

GIGNILLIAT, WILLIAM ROBERT (1814–1882), planter, son of Gilbert Gignilliat and his second wife, Mary McDonald, was born at Ardoch, his father's plantation near Darien, McIntosh County, Georgia, on December 10th, 1814. The Gignilliats were Swiss-French Huguenots who settled in South Carolina after the revocation of the Edict of Nantes in 1685. Mary (McDonald) Gignilliat died at the birth of her son; her husband died the following year. After graduating from Franklin College (Athens) in 1838 William Robert Gignilliat settled at Greenwood, his plantation in McIntosh County, where he enjoyed the cultivated life of a rich antebellum rice planter. On September 19th, 1838, he married Helen Mary Hart (1821–1862), daughter of Charles Thomas Hart (1794–1835) and Ann Catherine Dunham (1802–1886). His three living sons all fought in the Civil War: William Robert Gignilliat (1839–1885), a lawyer, was a private in the Chatham Artillery; Thomas Hart Gignilliat (1842–1905), a planter, was a private (later promoted to first lieutenant) in the Liberty Mounted Rangers; Gilbert West Gignilliat (1842–1896), also a planter, was a private in the Liberty Independent Troop. After the death of Helen Mary Hart on June 17th, 1862, William Robert Gignilliat married Janet Elizabeth Slade, who bore him two daughters. He died of heart disease at his summer residence in Marietta, Georgia, on January 19th, 1882, and was buried beside his first wife in St. Andrew's Cemetery, Darien.

GILBERT, MARIA LOUISA (WEST) (1835–1910): *Mrs. Julius Caesar Gilbert,* youngest daughter of Dr. Charles West (1790–1855) and Sarah Evelyn Nephew (1796–1854), was born in Walthourville, Liberty County, Georgia, on January 19th, 1835. She was a sister of Dr. Charles William West (1815–1860); James Nephew West (1823–1875); Clifford Amanda Stiles West (1827–1890), wife of John Hawkins Powers; and Dr. Joseph Jones West (1832–1869). In childhood she accompanied her parents to Perry, Houston County, Georgia, where her father practiced medicine until his death in 1855. On December 8th, 1853, she became the wife of Dr. Julius Caesar Gilbert (1821–1895), a grad-

uate of Jefferson Medical College (Philadelphia) in 1848 and a respected physician of Perry. Mary Sharpe Jones, an attendant at the wedding, wrote to her brother Joseph on December 21st, 1853: "Dr. Gilbert is not at all handsome, but is quite pleasant and no doubt will do everything he can for the promotion of Ria's happiness and comfort. He has a very fine practice, and made two thousand dollars last year by it. . . . It was a very pleasant party, and we all enjoyed ourselves very much; I do not think I ever did as much laughing in one week before." During the Civil War Dr. Gilbert was first lieutenant and surgeon of the 8th Regiment Georgia State Guards, a force organized for local defense; in October 1864 he was stationed at Camp Smith, near Macon. After the war he returned to Perry, where he continued as physician, druggist, and planter until his death on March 17th, 1895. His wife died on March 12th, 1910, survived by five children and numerous grandchildren, and was buried beside her husband in Evergreen Cemetery. According to the Perry *Home Journal* (March 17th, 1910), "Mrs. Gilbert was indeed one of the very best women who ever lived in Perry—or anywhere. . . . Her life was a benefaction to mankind, a constant testimony to the truth of the religion of Jesus Christ."

GILCHRIST, EFFIE (FAIRLY) (1823–1865): *Mrs. John Gilchrist,* daughter of John Fairly, was born near Rockingham, Richmond County, North Carolina, in 1823. On November 21st, 1839, she became the wife of John Gilchrist (1816–1856), a farmer, son of Angus Gilchrist and his second wife, Mrs. Elizabeth (McNeill) Graham. The Gilchrist family had long been prominent in the business and social life of Richmond and Scotland Counties. John Gilchrist died on May 3rd, 1856, leaving a widow and six young children; the eldest daughter, Flora McNeill Gilchrist, died in her fifteenth year on June 11th, 1857, only a few days before Mrs. Gilchrist met the Rev. Dr. and Mrs. Charles Colcock Jones at Hot Springs, Virginia. A son, John Fairly Gilchrist (1845–1861), died of typhoid fever early in the Civil War; another son, James A. Gilchrist (1840–1865), died unmarried in November 1865. In the same year Effie (Fairly) Gilchrist died at the old Gilchrist place on Lumber River, and was buried in the Gilchrist family cemetery near Wagram, Scotland County, North Carolina. She was survived by three children: Angus Gilchrist (1847–1883), William Gilchrist (1850–1928), and Sallie Elizabeth Gilchrist (1854–1935).

GILL, MARY HARVEY (1814–1864), schoolmistress, third daughter of Bennington Gill (1785–1845) and Sidney Paul (1790–1850), was born in Philadelphia, Pennsylvania, on February 5th, 1814. The following year her parents removed to Birmingham, England, where they remained until 1826; in England three more daughters were born: Sarah Ann Gill (1816–1902), Sidney Paul Gill (1818–1880), and Emily Gill (1821–1882). Returning to America, the family lived for some years in New York City and in Albany, New York, before settling once more in Philadelphia in 1840. Meanwhile the two eldest daughters had married two brothers, both Presbyterian clergymen: Elizabeth Paul Gill (1810–1850) became the wife of the Rev. Matthew Wilson (1807–1853); Anna Read Gill (1812–1896) became the second wife of the Rev. James Patriot Wilson (1808–1889). After the death of Bennington Gill on March 24th, 1845, his widow and her four unmarried daughters (Mary, Sarah, Sidney, and Emily) established a seminary for young ladies in their house on Chestnut Street at the corner of Juniper. The mother died on March 27th, 1850; for six years the four daughters continued the seminary in a house on Spruce Street at the corner of Juniper, with Mary Harvey Gill, the eldest, as principal. There Mary Sharpe Jones studied for two years (1850–1852) along with her friends Mary Jones Taylor, Lizzie Paul, Lizzie Grier, Kate Lampkin, Sue Dickson, Margie Dickson, and two nieces of the Misses Gill: Anna Wilson and Maggie Wilson. In 1856 Sidney Paul Gill and Emily Gill removed to Newark, New Jersey, to live with their sister Anna Read Gill, wife of the Rev. James Patriot Wilson; in 1857 Mary Harvey Gill also removed to Newark, and Sarah Ann Gill removed to Belvidere, New Jersey, to live with her uncle, Theodore Sedgwick Paul (1798–1887). Mary Harvey Gill died in Belvidere on June 5th, 1864; Sidney Paul Gill died in Newark on June 12th, 1880; Emily Gill died in Newark on November 22nd, 1882; the three sisters were buried near their parents in Laurel Hill Cemetery, Philadelphia. Meanwhile in 1864 Sarah Ann Gill removed to Newark, where in 1870 she became the second wife of Samuel P. Smith (1805–1883), wealthy Newark merchant; soon after their marriage they settled in Orange, New Jersey, where he died on May 2nd, 1883. Thereafter Sarah Ann Gill lived with her sister in Newark until Mrs. Wilson's death on November 4th, 1896; she then resided with her niece, Margaretta Peery Wilson (1836–1922), wife of Charles McKean Bayard, in Germantown, Pennsylvania, where she died on March 3rd, 1902. She was buried beside her husband in Mount Pleasant Cemetery, Newark.

GILLMORE, QUINCY ADAMS (1825–1888), Union soldier and military engineer, son of Quartus Gillmore and Elizabeth Reid, was born in Black River, Lorrain County, Ohio, on February 28th, 1825. He graduated from the United States Military Academy in 1849, first in his class, and was commissioned second lieutenant of engineers. He subsequently became first lieutenant (July 1st, 1856) and captain (August 6th, 1861). Prior to the Civil War he supervised construction of fortifications at Hampton Roads, Virginia; served as treasurer, quartermaster, and assistant instructor of practical military engineering at West Point; and headed the engineer district of New York City. During the Civil War he was chief engineer of the Port Royal expedition (1861–1862) and saw service at Hilton Head, South

Carolina (November 7th, 1861) and Fort Pulaski, Georgia (April 10th–11th, 1862). He subsequently became brigadier general of volunteers (April 28th, 1862) and major general of volunteers (July 10th, 1863). After commanding for one year (April 1862–April 1863) in West Virginia and Kentucky he was placed in command of the Department of the South and participated in the attacks on Charleston, South Carolina, during the summer of 1863. Early in 1864 he was ordered to Virginia, where he fought at Bermuda Hundred, Drewry's Bluff, and Petersburg. After the war he commanded the Department of the South until his resignation on December 5th, 1865. He was author of numerous professional treatises, among them his *Official Report to the United States Engineer Department of the Siege and Reduction of Fort Pulaski, Georgia* (1862). He died in Brooklyn, New York, on April 7th, 1888, survived by his second wife and the four sons of his first wife, and was buried with high military honors in West Point National Cemetery.

GILMAN, CAROLINE (HOWARD) (1794–1888): *Mrs. Samuel Gilman,* author, daughter of Samuel Howard and Anna Lillie, was born in Boston, Massachusetts, on October 8th, 1794. In December 1819 she became the wife of the Rev. Samuel Gilman (1791–1858), son of Frederick Gilman and Abigail Hillier Somes, of Gloucester, Massachusetts. Her husband, a graduate of Harvard College (1811), was pastor of the Second Independent Church (Unitarian) of Charleston, South Carolina (1819–1858); he wrote numerous poems, the most famous being "Fair Harvard," written for the Harvard bicentennial celebration on September 8th, 1836. As a literary figure in Charleston he was rivaled only by his wife, whose *Recollections of a Housekeeper* (1834), *Recollections of a Southern Matron* (1836), and *The Poetry of Traveling in the United States* (1838) gracefully sketch the modes and manners of contemporary American life. Her poems and children's stories also enjoyed wide popularity. The Rev. Samuel Gilman died suddenly in Kingston, Massachusetts, on February 9th, 1858, and was buried in the Unitarian Churchyard, Charleston. His widow continued to reside in Charleston until 1870, when she returned to Cambridge. She died in Washington, D.C., on September 15th, 1888, and was buried beside her husband.

GILMER, JEREMY FRANCIS (1818–1883), military engineer, son of Robert Shaw Gilmer (1770–1845) and Anne Forbes, was born in Guilford County, North Carolina, on February 23rd, 1818. After graduating from the United States Military Academy in 1839 he was assistant professor of engineering at West Point (1839–1840); assistant engineer in building Fort Schuyler, New York harbor (1840–1844); assistant engineer at Washington, D.C. (1844–1846); and chief engineer of the Army of the West during the Mexican War (1846–1848). Assigned to Georgia, he superintended the improvement of the Savannah River and the construction of Fort Jackson and Fort Pulaski. He was promoted to captain in 1853, after which he was engaged for five years in fortification work and the improvement of rivers throughout the South. From 1858 to 1861 he superintended the construction of defenses at the entrance to San Francisco Bay. At the outbreak of the Civil War he resigned his commission to enter Confederate service. In September 1861 he was commissioned lieutenant colonel and made chief engineer on the staff of General Albert Sidney Johnston. After Shiloh he was promoted to brigadier general, and in August 1862 he was made chief engineer of the Department of Northern Virginia. Two months later he was made chief of the engineer corps of the Confederate States. In August 1863 he was promoted to major general and assigned to the Department of South Carolina, Georgia, and Florida as second in command to General Beauregard; there he rendered valuable service in the defense of Charleston and Atlanta. Returning to Virginia, he continued his duties as chief engineer until the evacuation of Richmond. After the war he was for eighteen years (1865–1883) president and engineer of the Savannah Gas Light Company. He was also for many years a director of the Central Railroad and Banking Company of Georgia and a trustee of the Independent Presbyterian Church. On December 18th, 1850, he married Louisa Frederika Alexander (1824–1895), daughter of Adam Leopold Alexander (1803–1882) and his first wife, Sarah Hillhouse Gilbert (1805–1855), of Washington, Wilkes County, Georgia. He died in Savannah on December 1st, 1883, survived by his wife and two children, and was buried in the family vault in Laurel Grove Cemetery.

GIRARDEAU, JOHN (1796–1873), planter, elder son of William Girardeau and his first wife, Patience Harris, was born in Liberty County, Georgia, on May 27th, 1796. For several months in 1856 he managed White Oak plantation for Mrs. Susan M. Cumming during the illness of the regular manager, Benjamin Washington Allen. In 1870 he was a cripple, living in the household of his nephew, Isaac Axson Girardeau (1838–1873). He never married. He died in Liberty County in 1873, survived by his younger brother, William Pinckney Girardeau (1798–1874), and was buried in Flemington Cemetery.

GIRARDEAU, WILLIAM PINCKNEY (1798–1874), planter and magistrate, younger son of William Girardeau and his first wife, Patience Harris, was born in Liberty County, Georgia, on November 3rd, 1798. He married first (on July 4th, 1822) Jane Elizabeth Nelms (1807–1858); he married second (on December 8th, 1863) Harriet Spry Law (1805–1877), widow of George Thomas Handley. For some years he taught school; in 1855 he was postmaster in Hinesville; from 1857 to 1874 he was judge of the court of ordinary of Liberty County. He died on September 19th, 1874, survived by his second wife, and was buried in Taylor's Creek Cemetery.

GLEN, JANE MARION (DUNWODY) (ERWIN) (1821–1885): *Mrs. William Glen,* third child of John Dunwody (1786–1858) and Jane Bulloch (1788–1856), was born in Liberty County, Georgia, on June 22nd, 1821. She had five living brothers: James Bulloch Dunwody (1816–1902), John Dunwody (1818–1903), William Elliott Dunwody (1823–1891), Henry Macon Dunwody (1826–1863), and Charles Archibald Alexander Dunwody (1828–1905). In the spring of 1840 she became the wife of the Rev. Stanhope W. Erwin, a Presbyterian clergyman, who died on August 18th, 1840, a few months after their wedding. On November 4th, 1851, she became the wife of Dr. William Glen, a Charleston physician, who died on March 27th, 1853. During the Civil War her brother Charles Dunwody was severely wounded at Manassas (July 21st, 1861) and her brother Henry Macon Dunwody was killed at Gettysburg (July 2nd, 1863). Late in 1862 she purchased a house in Washington, Wilkes County, Georgia, to be near her eldest brother, the Rev. James Bulloch Dunwody, pastor of the Presbyterian church in Washington from 1860 to 1865. On December 5th, 1865, she became the second wife of Adam Leopold Alexander (1803–1882), of Washington. "She is very happy," wrote Mrs. Mary Jones on April 22nd, 1867; "her generous and loving heart would not allow her to be otherwise." She died in Washington on August 23rd, 1885, and was buried beside her third husband in the Alexander family cemetery.

GLOVER, JANE PORTER (BOLAN) (1820–1911): *Mrs. John Heyward Glover,* was born in Beaufort District, South Carolina, on August 14th, 1820. In 1838 she became the wife of John Heyward Glover (1816–1859), scion of a wealthy and aristocratic South Carolina family, and settled at Fontainebleau, his rice plantation near Walterboro. In March 1848 she accompanied her family to Marietta, Georgia, where her husband soon became a leading citizen. He was the first mayor of Marietta in 1852. He built a flourishing tannery on the outskirts of the town; established a factory for the manufacture of leather and shoes; founded his own private bank; organized the first telegraph company in Marietta; presented Glover Park to the town; and contributed substantially toward the erection of the Georgia Military Institute (Marietta). He died suddenly on March 26th, 1859, survived by his wife and numerous children. At the outbreak of the Civil War his son, James Bolan Glover (1841–1926), enlisted as a private in the Palmetto Guards (Company I, 2nd Regiment South Carolina Infantry); in 1863 he transferred to the 7th Regiment Georgia Cavalry. His daughter, Jane L. Glover (1850–1889), became the wife of the Rev. Charles A. Grant (1841–1870), an Episcopal clergyman, on February 6th, 1866. Jane Porter (Bolan) Glover died in Marietta on January 20th, 1911, and was buried beside her husband in Episcopal Cemetery.

GOODE, THOMAS (1787–1858), physician, son of Samuel Goode (1756–1822) and Mary Armistead Burwell, was born in Mecklenburg County, Virginia, on October 31st, 1787. About 1825, having practiced his profession for some years in his native county, he removed with his wife, Mary A. Knox, and his young family to the neighborhood of Big Lick, Botetourt (now Roanoke) County, where he resided for seven years. In 1832 he purchased the hotel at Hot Springs, Bath County, then little known as a resort for health and pleasure; for the rest of his life he devoted his energy and professional skill to developing the springs, and at the time of his death Hot Springs enjoyed a national reputation. His book, *The Invalids' Guide to the Virginia Hot Springs* (1831), was several times reprinted. He died at Hot Springs on April 2nd, 1858, survived by his wife and numerous children, and was buried in a small cemetery near the hotel. On June 6th, 1855, his daughter, Alice Goode (1831–1903), became the wife of Dr. William Crump (1819–1868), resident physician at Hot Springs from 1851 to 1860.

GOODRICH, WILLIAM WALLACE (1824–1857), merchant, was born in Hartford, Connecticut, in 1824. In early manhood he settled in Savannah, Georgia, where he lived in the household of his elder sister, Sarah Goodrich (1815–1883), wife of Isaac William Morrell (1793–1865), and for many years conducted a flourishing grocery business. He died in New York City on September 3rd, 1857, and was buried in Hartford, Connecticut.

GORDON, GEORGE ANDERSON (1830–1872), lawyer, elder son of William Washington Gordon (1796–1842) and Sarah Anderson Stites (1806–1882), was born in Savannah, Georgia, on September 26th, 1830. His father, a distinguished lawyer and engineer, was first president of the Central Railroad & Banking Company of Georgia. After graduating from Yale College in 1849 George Anderson Gordon studied law and practiced his profession in Savannah from 1851 until the outbreak of the Civil War. He was solicitor general for the eastern district of Georgia (1855); United States district attorney for Georgia (1856–1857); alderman of Savannah (1856–1857); member of the state house of representatives (1857–1859); and member of the state senate (1860–1861). In September 1859 he was Democratic nominee for the state senate, but when he was charged with bad faith toward his rival, Alexander Robert Lawton, he withdrew his name and Lawton was elected. During the Civil War he was appointed captain in the 1st Regiment Georgia Infantry (May 30th, 1861), elected major of the 13th Battalion Georgia Infantry (May 26th, 1862), and promoted to colonel of the 63rd Regiment Georgia Infantry (December 23rd, 1862). After the war he removed to Huntsville, Alabama, where he practiced law from 1866 to 1869. He married first (on June 5th, 1850) Caroline B. Steenbergen, who died on July 16th, 1851; he married second (on January 12th, 1854) Ellen C. Beirne, who died on August 15th, 1867. He died in Huntsville on October 5th, 1872, and was buried beside his second wife in Maple Hill Cemetery.

GORDON, WILLIAM WASHINGTON (1834–1912), commission merchant, younger son of William Washington Gordon (1796–1842) and Sarah Anderson Stites (1806–1882), was born in Savannah, Georgia, on October 14th, 1834. His father, a distinguished lawyer and engineer, was first president of the Central Railroad & Banking Company of Georgia. After graduating from Yale College in 1854 he became a clerk in the firm of Tison & Mackay, cotton and rice factors; when William Mein Mackay withdrew in 1856 Gordon joined William Hayes Tison in the firm of Tison & Gordon. On December 21st, 1857, he married Eleanor Lytle Kinzie (1835–1917), daughter of John H. Kinzie, of Chicago; there were four daughters and two sons. During the Civil War he was lieutenant, later captain, in the Confederate army and saw service in Northern Virginia and Maryland as well as in Georgia, where he was slightly wounded in 1864 during the Atlanta campaign. After the war Tison & Gordon resumed business and continued as one of the best-known cotton firms in the South until Tison's death in 1877; thereafter the firm was known as W. W. Gordon & Company. Gordon was president of the Savannah Cotton Exchange (1876–1879); member of the state house of representatives (1884–1885; 1886–1887; 1888–1889); and for many years president of the Central Railroad & Banking Company of Georgia. During the Spanish-American War (1898) he was a brigadier general in the United States army. He died at White Sulphur Springs, West Virginia, on September 11th, 1912, and was buried in Laurel Grove Cemetery, Savannah. One of his daughters, Juliette Magill Gordon (1860–1927), wife of William Mackay Low (1860–1905), was founder of the Girl Scouts.

GOUGH, JOHN BARTHOLOMEW (1817–1886), temperance lecturer, was born in Sandgate, Kent, England, on August 22nd, 1817. At the age of twelve he migrated to New York, where he became a confirmed drunkard; reduced to desperate straits, he supported himself for several years as a ballad singer in cheap theaters and concert halls. In 1842 he was persuaded to sign a temperance pledge, and eventually, after several lapses, he became a lecturer in behalf of temperance reform. From the beginning he was remarkably successful, and he continued lecturing for the rest of his life. He died at Frankford, Pennsylvania, on February 18th, 1886. His *Autobiography* (1846) provides insight into his motivation and early career.

GOULDING, FRANCIS ROBERT (1810–1881), Presbyterian clergyman, eldest son of the Rev. Dr. Thomas Goulding and Ann Holbrook, was born in Liberty County, Georgia, on September 28th, 1810. After graduating from Franklin College (Athens) in 1830 and from Columbia Theological Seminary in 1833 he was pastor of churches in Greensboro, Washington, Bath, Augusta, and Charleston. He was agent of the American Bible Society (1839–1842); principal of a boys' school in Kingston, Georgia (1854–1856); and pastor of the Presbyterian church in Darien, Georgia (1856–1862). During the Civil War he was a chaplain in the Confederate army, stationed at Macon. After the war he was physically unfit for further preaching or teaching; he retired to Roswell, where he died on August 22nd, 1881; he was buried in the Presbyterian Cemetery. He married first (in 1833) Mary Wallace Howard, who bore him six children. He married second (in 1855) Matilda Rees, who bore him two daughters. His eldest son, Charles Howard Goulding, having fought at First and Second Manassas, died from disease in camp on December 23rd, 1862. Francis Robert Goulding was author of *Robert and Harold; or, the Young Marooners on the Florida Coast* (1852), which went through many editions, was translated into several European languages, and became a juvenile classic. "In his death," wrote the Rev. John Jones in August 1881, "we have lost a man of genius, of rare attainments, of varied information, of worldwide reputation. His active mind ranged over a vast field with intelligence and marked originality. As a writer for the young he stood in the forefront of the best authors of the age."

GRANT, CHARLES A. (1841–1870), Episcopal clergyman, third son of Charles Grant (1809–1872) and Cornelia Vanderveer Bond (1811–1870), was born in Savannah, Georgia, in 1841. In his eighteenth year he was "most desirous of becoming a physician, and most desirous of a college course," but his parents were unable to provide the means. As his mother wrote to Mrs. Mary Jones on February 12th, 1859, "He is not so *robust* as our other boys, but has been our *angel child* always— a kind of halo resting on him from his gentle, retiring character, unobtrusiveness, and severe illnesses in childhood, when by miracle, as it seemed, he was twice restored to us from the grave. . . . If you would hear what he is from other than a mother's *partial* lips, ask Mr. Tefft, or any member of the Historical Society, who *admired* his steady, active, *neat* attention to all his duties while assistant librarian last winter. . . . Charlie promised me to be a minister—a missionary—and then he could have had a noble education *free* at Kenyon College. But he does not wish it now." Evidently he soon changed his mind: in 1860 he began studies for the Episcopal ministry; he was ordained deacon in 1862 and priest in 1865. He was assistant rector in Athens (1863–1865); missionary in Northwest Georgia (1865–1866); rector in Griffin (1866–1868); rector in Bainbridge and missionary in Thomasville (1868–1869). He was a victim of lung disease; for four months (November 1868 through February 1869) he suffered "a protracted and very serious illness" which forced him to resign from the Bainbridge church in

May 1869 and from the Thomasville church in August 1869. He died in Thomasville on October 16th, 1870, and was buried in the Old Cemetery. On February 6th, 1866, he married Jane L. Glover (1850–1889), daughter of John Heyward Glover (1816–1859) and Jane Porter Bolan (1820–1911), of Marietta, Georgia; he was survived by his wife and one son. According to the Rt. Rev. John W. Beckwith, bishop of Georgia, "He was an humble-minded, laborious man whose heart was in his work; he was taken in the midst of his usefulness." He founded the first Episcopal church in Thomasville.

GRANT, CORNELIA VANDERVEER (BOND) (1811–1870): *Mrs. Charles Grant,* was born in Savannah, Georgia, in March 1811. Her great-grandfather, Dr. Thomas Bond (1712–1784), distinguished Philadelphia surgeon and friend of Benjamin Franklin, founded the Pennsylvania Hospital, the first hospital in the United States, in 1751. Her grandfather, Dr. Thomas Bond (1743–1825), was "purveyor" of the Pennsylvania Hospital during the Revolutionary War. In 1834 Cornelia Vanderveer Bond became the wife of Charles Grant (1809–1870), son of Dr. Robert Grant, a wealthy rice planter of Glynn County, and Sarah Foxworth. A year earlier Dr. Robert Grant had assigned to his son Charles a tract of rice land in Glynn County known as Evelyn, together with over a hundred slaves; but Charles Grant was never successful as a planter, and twice fell so deeply in debt that his elder brother, Hugh Fraser Grant, had to come to his aid. In April 1837 Charles Grant removed to Chatham County and settled at Woodhome, a farm near Savannah, where he resided until the outbreak of the Civil War. Of his seven sons one, William D. Grant, lieutenant in the Savannah Volunteer Guards (Company B, 18th Battalion Georgia Infantry), was killed in the battle of Sayler's Creek on April 6th, 1865. Another son, Robert Grant, the "firstborn and dearest," a Savannah lawyer, died suddenly in his thirtieth year on August 14th, 1865. After the war Charles Grant and his wife settled in Thomasville, Georgia, where two of their sons resided: Miller B. Grant, a civil engineer, and Charles A. Grant, an Episcopal clergyman. There Mrs. Grant projected "a book of deep and abiding interest to mothers": *Our Boys and Their Woodhome Training: A Mother's Tribute of Love to Her Departed Ones* ("I know a work of that kind must take —it will be original, fresh, and earnest."). For many years she was active in the work of the Ladies' Mount Vernon Association of the Union. She died in Thomasville on July 10th, 1870, and was buried in Laurel Grove Cemetery, Savannah. According to the Savannah *Morning News* (July 15th, 1870), "Mrs. Grant was a lady of cultivated tastes and fine conversational powers. She wrote with great ease and facility, and at times contributed to the periodical literature of the day articles of great literary worth and beauty. She was also unaffectedly pious, sincerely a Christian, and illustrated by precept and example that which she believed." One of her sons, James Edward Grant, an artist, produced the drawings for *The Monumental Remains of Georgia* (1861), by Charles Colcock Jones, Jr.

GRANT, LEMUEL PRATT (1817–1893), civil engineer, was born in Frankfort, Maine, on August 11th, 1817. At the age of nineteen he became rodman in the engineer corps of the Philadelphia & Reading Railroad, and thereafter for the rest of his life he was actively engaged in railroad construction and administration. In January 1840 he came South to survey the line of the Central Railroad of Georgia between Madison and Atlanta, then a village known as Marthasville; in 1844, shrewdly sensing the strategic potential of Atlanta as a metropolis, he began purchasing real estate and eventually acquired vast holdings. For many years he was associated with the Atlanta & West Point Railroad, first as chief engineer (1853–1866), then as general superintendent (1866–1881), and finally as president (1881–1887). He played an important part in making Atlanta the railroad center of the South. During the Civil War, as chief engineer of the Department of Georgia, he superintended the construction of the defenses around Atlanta. After the war he was conspicuously identified with the best interests of the city; he was a member of the first board of education (1869), a member of the city council (1872), and county commissioner (1884–1886). In 1883 he presented to the city a tract of one hundred acres which became Grant Park. He married first (in December 1843) Laura Loomis Williams (1820–1879), daughter of Ammi Williams, one of the first settlers of Atlanta; he married second (in July 1881) Jane Louisa Killian (1826–1912), daughter of Daniel Killian, of Madison, Georgia, and widow of James R. Crew (1823–1865). After 1860 he and his family were active members of the Central Presbyterian Church. He died in Atlanta on January 11th, 1893, survived by his second wife, and was buried beside his first wife in Westview Cemetery. His eldest son, John A. Grant (1845–1907), for many years president of the Texas & Pacific Railroad, married (on October 26th, 1869) Ann Payne Logan (1846–1873), daughter of Dr. Joseph Payne Logan (1821–1891), distinguished Atlanta physician.

GRANT, ROBERT (1835–1865), lawyer, eldest son of Charles Grant (1809–1872) and Cornelia Vanderveer Bond (1811–1870), was born in Savannah, Georgia, in 1835. He was named for his paternal grandfather, Dr. Robert Grant (1762–1843), a native of Leith, Scotland, who had migrated during the Revolutionary War to South Carolina and thence by 1800 to Georgia, where he had become a wealthy rice planter on St. Simons Island and the south bank of the Altamaha River. Robert Grant spent his boyhood and youth in Savannah and practiced law there until the outbreak of the Civil War. For a time he was clerk of the state senate and Milledgeville correspondent of the Savannah *Morning News*. On May 21st,

1861, he enlisted as a private in the Oglethorpe Light Infantry (Company B, 8th Regiment Georgia Infantry); on September 18th, 1861, after distinguished service at First Manassas, he was appointed second lieutenant; on July 25th, 1862, he was assigned to Captain Jacob Read's Regular Light Battery Georgia Artillery (Company D, 1st Regiment Georgia Regulars); on August 15th, 1863, he was appointed captain and assistant adjutant general; on May 1st, 1865, he was paroled at Greensboro, North Carolina. He never married. He died suddenly in Savannah during the night of August 14th, 1865; he retired apparently in good health; the next morning his mother found him dead in his bed. "I have lived over with fresh anguish and remorse," she wrote two years later, "all my soul's unfathomed miseries at the death of my firstborn and dearest." He was buried in Laurel Grove Cemetery. The remains of his brother, William D. Grant (1845–1865), killed in the battle of Sayler's Creek on April 6th, 1865, were removed from Virginia the following December and placed by his side.

GRANT, ULYSSES SIMPSON (1822–1885), Union soldier and eighteenth president of the United States, son of Jesse Root Grant (1794–1873) and Hannah Simpson (1798–1883), was born in Point Pleasant, Ohio, on April 27th, 1822. He graduated from the United States Military Academy in 1843 and served in the Mexican War with distinction; in 1854, after eleven years' service, he resigned and entered upon an unsuccessful course as farmer, real estate agent, and customhouse clerk. On August 22nd, 1848, he married Julia Boggs Dent (1826–1902), daughter of Frederick Dent and Ellen Wrenshall. In June 1861 he was appointed colonel of the 21st Illinois Volunteers; in August 1861 he was appointed brigadier general. After taking Fort Henry and Fort Donelson he was appointed major general of volunteers; after a brilliant victory at Vicksburg he was appointed major general in the regular army. Late in 1863 he won a gold medal, the thanks of Congress, and promotion to lieutenant general for his successful strategy at Missionary Ridge; placed in command of the armies of the United States, he moved east to face Lee before Richmond. After the unsuccessful Wilderness campaign he invested and laid siege to Petersburg; on April 2nd, 1865, Lee abandoned Petersburg and Richmond and marched westward; Grant followed, and on April 9th, at Appomattox Courthouse, Lee surrendered the Army of Northern Virginia. After the war Grant served two scandal-ridden terms as president of the United States (1869–1877), toured Europe with his family for two years, then returned home to a life saddened by financial misfortune, calumny, and illness. He died in Mount McGregor, New York, on July 23rd, 1885, and was buried in a granite mausoleum on Riverside Drive, New York City. His *Personal Memoirs* (2 vols., 1885–1886) were widely read and brought his family a substantial fortune.

GREEN, EDWARD MELVIN (1838–1927), Presbyterian clergyman, son of James G. Green and Sarah Ann James, was born in Darlington, South Carolina, on September 10th, 1838. After graduating from Oglethorpe University in 1859 and from Columbia Theological Seminary in 1863 he served for two years (1863–1865) as chaplain in the Confederate army, stationed at the military hospital in Newnan, Georgia. He was pastor in Washington, Georgia (1866–1871); financial agent of Columbia Theological Seminary and editor of *The Southern Presbyterian* (1871–1874); pastor in Washington, North Carolina (1874–1877); and pastor in Danville, Kentucky (1877–1922). He was moderator of the General Assembly of the Southern Presbyterian Church meeting in New Orleans in 1898. On June 24th, 1863, he married Sarah Emily Howe (1843–1890), daughter of the Rev. Dr. George Howe and his second wife, Sarah Ann Walthour, of Columbia, South Carolina; she died on November 13th, 1890, and was buried near her parents in the First Presbyterian Churchyard, Columbia. In 1896 he married Mrs. Frances Wallace Anderson of Atlanta, Georgia. He died in Danville, Kentucky, on September 20th, 1927, survived by his second wife. He received the honorary degree of doctor of divinity from Southwestern Presbyterian University (Clarksville, Tennessee) in 1894.

GREEN, JANE ELIZA (1831–1923), schoolmistress, daughter of Benjamin Green (1797–1861) and Martha E. Marvin (1811–1891), was born in DeKalb County, Georgia, on May 30th, 1831. In 1846 she removed with her parents to Marietta, Georgia, where she and her younger sister, Sarah Green (1835–1916), attended the Kennesaw Female Seminary, an institution founded in 1845 and conducted under the auspices of St. James's Episcopal Church. Her father was principal of the seminary from 1850 to 1858, when the building was sold. Meanwhile in the autumn of 1857 Jane Eliza Green and her sister, Sarah Green, succeeded to the school of Elizabeth P. Taylor (1828–1866), a native of New York and a graduate of the Rutgers Institute, who after teaching eight years in Marietta removed to Montgomery, Alabama. Among the twelve scholars of the Misses Green were Lilla and Ellen Robarts. On May 2nd, 1867, Jane Eliza Green became the wife of Henry Myers (1827–1901), a native of Savannah, a Confederate veteran, and a junior warden of St. James's Episcopal Church. Sometime after 1880 the couple removed to Jacksonville, Florida, where Myers died on March 21st, 1901. His widow spent her last years at the home of her daughter, Mrs. R. R. Turnbull, in Moultrie, Georgia, where she died on March 22nd, 1923. She was buried beside her husband in Episcopal Cemetery, Marietta.

GREENLEAF, SIMON (1783–1853), lawyer, educator, and writer, son of Moses Greenleaf and Lydia Parsons, was born in Newburyport, Massachusetts, on December 5th, 1783.

In 1790 his family removed to New Gloucester, Maine, where Simon read law in the office of Ezekiel Whitman (1776–1866), later chief justice of Maine. On September 18th, 1806, he married Hannah Kingman, daughter of Ezra Kingman, of East Bridgewater, Massachusetts. After practicing law for six months in Standish, Maine, he removed to Gray, where he practiced for twelve years (1806–1818), at the same time reading widely in the source material of common law. In 1818 he settled in Portland, where he was appointed reporter of the state supreme court on June 24th, 1820. His *Reports of Cases Argued and Determined by the Supreme Judicial Court of the State of Maine* (1820–1832) were notable for their conciseness, clarity, and accuracy and became part of the permanent literature of the profession. In 1833 he became Royall professor of law at Harvard, and in 1846 he succeeded the Hon. Joseph Story (1779–1845) as Dane professor of law. Under the dual leadership of Story and Greenleaf the Harvard Law School rose to its preeminent position among the law schools of the United States. Failing health forced Greenleaf to resign in 1848, when he became professor emeritus. His numerous published works include *A Treatise on the Law of Evidence* (1842), to which he added a second volume (1846) and a third volume (1853); *Cruise's Digest of the Law of Real Property, Revised and Abridged for the Use of American Students* (7 vols. in 5, 1849–1850), and *Examination of the Testimony of the Four Evangelists by the Rules of Evidence Administered in Courts of Justice, with an Account of the Trial of Jesus* (1846). He died in Cambridge on October 6th, 1853, and was buried in Mount Auburn Cemetery. A detailed account of his death and funeral was written by Charles Colcock Jones, Jr., then a law student at Harvard, in a letter dated October 11th, 1853, now preserved among the Jones papers at Tulane University.

GREGG, MAXCY (1814–1862), Confederate soldier, son of James Gregg and Cornelia Maxcy, was born in Columbia, South Carolina, in 1814. After studying law with his father he commenced practice in Columbia in 1839. He was an active politician and an ardent secessionist; he was a member of the state secession convention meeting in Columbia in December 1860. On January 3rd, 1861, he was appointed colonel of the 1st Regiment South Carolina Volunteers; after the fall of Fort Sumter he went to Virginia, where he was made brigadier general in December 1861. He fought at Malvern Hill, Second Manassas, and Sharpsburg. He was killed at Fredericksburg on December 13th, 1862, and was buried in the First Presbyterian Churchyard, Columbia, South Carolina.

GRESHAM, JOHN JONES (1812–1891), lawyer, was born in Burke County, Georgia, on January 21st, 1812. After graduating from Franklin College (Athens) with first honor in 1833 he studied law in Augusta, practiced briefly in Waynesboro, and in 1836 settled in

Macon, where he was for many years a successful planter, lawyer, banker, and businessman. He organized the Macon Manufacturing Company, the first steam cotton factory in the South, and was its president from 1851 to 1869. He was twice mayor of Macon (1843; 1847), judge of the inferior court (1860), and state senator (1866–1867). He was a member of the board of trustees of the Macon Free School, the Alexander Free School, the Georgia Academy for the Blind, Columbia Theological Seminary, Oglethorpe University, and the University of Georgia. For nearly fifty years he was an elder of the First Presbyterian Church, and in memory of his deceased wife he largely financed the building of the Second Presbyterian Church; in May 1859 he was commissioner to the General Assembly of the Presbyterian Church meeting in Indianapolis. On May 25th, 1843, he married Mary E. Baxter, daughter of Thomas W. Baxter, of Athens; there were two children. He died suddenly in Baltimore, Maryland, on October 16th, 1891, at the residence of his daughter, Mrs. Arthur W. Machen, and was buried beside his wife in Rose Hill Cemetery, Macon.

GREST, VALENTINE (1805–1872), planter, was born in Switzerland on May 24th, 1805. Sometime before 1840 he migrated to the United States and settled in Savannah, Georgia, where on August 16th, 1840, he married Mary Frederika Kottman. There were no children. In the 1840s he removed with his wife to Liberty County, Georgia, and purchased a tract of land known as Isle of Wight (later called Grest Island); there he resided for the rest of his life, planting, acquiring considerable property, and participating agreeably in county affairs. He was known particularly for his sense of humor. In the 1850s he was joined by his nephew, Josiah Grest (1832–1872), also born in Switzerland, who became his heir. On August 1st, 1861, Josiah Grest enlisted as a private in Company F, 1st (Olmstead's) Regiment Georgia Infantry; on May 15th, 1862, he enlisted for three years as fourth corporal in the Liberty Mounted Rangers (Company B, 20th Battalion Georgia Cavalry). He saw service throughout the war and returned to Liberty County in the spring of 1865; Mrs. Susan M. Cumming was misinformed when she wrote on April 15th, 1865, that "Mr. Grest's Swiss nephew" was "dead." On March 11th, 1868, he married Mary E. Shave (1850–1907), of Liberty County; there were two daughters: Catherine Grest (1869–1959) and Mary Valentine Grest (1872–1957). On October 22nd, 1872, Josiah Grest died of a stomach disorder thought to be a result of the war. Less than a month later, on November 10th, 1872, Valentine Grest died—it is said of a broken heart—and was buried beside his nephew in Fleming Cemetery. His wife survived. In March 1875 Mary (Shave) Grest, widow of Josiah Grest, married Benjamin Stiles Butler (1845–1909), of Liberty County, planter and Confederate veteran; they now lie buried beside each other in Flemington Cemetery.

GRIER, ELIZABETH (1832–1913), daughter of James Grier and Agnes Stewart, was born in Scotland on April 2nd, 1832. At an early age she migrated to the United States with her parents and settled in Philadelphia, Pennsylvania, where she attended a seminary for young ladies conducted by the Misses Gill. On February 24th, 1859, "Lizzie" Grier became the wife of Peter Campbell (1835–1903), a native of Glasgow, Scotland, who migrated to the United States with his parents in 1841 and secured employment in a Philadelphia carpet mill in 1856. At the time of his death on November 4th, 1903, he had been for twenty-nine years a dyer at the Caledonia Carpet Mills. Elizabeth (Grier) Campbell died in Philadelphia after an illness of five months on February 7th, 1913, survived by two sons and three daughters, and was buried beside her husband in Mount Moriah Cemetery.

GRIFFIN, ROBERT H. (1822–1855), lawyer, son of Samuel Griffin (1773–1847), was born in St. Marys, Georgia, in September 1822. In early manhood he settled in Savannah, where he studied law and was admitted to the bar; according to the resolutions of the Savannah bar at the time of his death he was "a man of integrity and a lawyer of distinction." On November 14th, 1850, he married Henrietta Clifford Wayne (1831–1884), eldest daughter of Dr. Richard Wayne (1804–1858) and Henrietta Jane Harden (1809–1880). He died in Savannah on December 14th, 1855, survived by his mother, his wife, and several children, and was buried in Laurel Grove Cemetery. As the Savannah *Republican* (December 15th, 1855) observed, "The deceased had hardly reached the prime of life; young, intellectual, and fortunate in his position and relations, the prospect before him was full of promise. His death at such a period, and under such circumstances, will be received with pain by all who knew him." Henrietta Clifford (Wayne) Griffin died in Savannah on August 8th, 1884, and was buried beside her husband.

GRISWOLD, ARTHUR BREESE (1829–1877), jeweler, was born near Poughkeepsie, New York, on September 9th, 1829. In 1842, when still a boy, he settled in New Orleans, where after a few years at school he became a clerk at Hyde & Goodrich, a well-known firm of jewelers; he later rose to manager, and at the retirement of the elder members of the firm he became senior partner. "A. B. Griswold & Company, Importers of Watches, Jewelry, and Silverware" was for decades a familiar landmark on the corner of Canal and Royal Streets, New Orleans. In March 1855 Griswold joined the Prytania Street Presbyterian Church, where for many years he taught a Bible class and served as treasurer and trustee; for seventeen years (1860–1877) he was a deacon, and in April 1869 he was one of six pallbearers at the funeral of Mrs. Mary Jones, mother of the pastor's wife. His intimacy with the Rev. R. Q. Mallard was cordial and enduring: "Not a day passes in our home circle," he wrote Mallard on March 30th, 1877, "that we do not speak of you and wish for your return." He died near Poughkeepsie, New York, on May 30th, 1877, and was buried in Lafayette Cemetery, New Orleans. He was survived by his wife, Frances S. Newman (1838–1915), daughter of Samuel Brooks Newman (1814–1893), New Orleans commission merchant, and three children: Jane Newman Griswold (1859–1927), Katharine Livingston Griswold (1860–1927), and George Palfrey Griswold (1865–1946).

GRISWOLD, KATHARINE LIVINGSTON (1860–1927), daughter of Arthur Breese Griswold (1829–1877) and Frances S. Newman (1838–1915), was born in New Orleans, Louisiana, on December 10th, 1860. She spent most of her life in New Orleans, where her father was a wealthy jeweler; she lived and died at the family residence, 1424 Second Street, in the Garden District. For many years she was active in the work of the Prytania Street Presbyterian Church, of which she became a member in 1875; she was also a director of the Poydras Asylum, a home for orphaned girls. On January 14th, 1890, she became the wife of James Hardin Deatherage, son of James Hardin Deatherage and California Beeler, of Louisville, Kentucky; it was an unfortunate marriage and did not last. She died on April 10th, 1927, less than three weeks after the death of her elder sister, Jane Newman Griswold (1859–1927), and was buried near her parents and sister in Lafayette Cemetery. When she was a little girl New Orleans was occupied by Federal troops; one day a Federal officer stopped her on the street and asked her who she was. "I'm a rebel!" she exclaimed. "I'm a rebel to my backbone!"

GROVER, WILLIAM O. (1822–1895), sewing machine manufacturer, was born in Boston in October 1822. After working for some years as a merchant tailor he concluded that the sewing machine, crude and impractical as it then was, would eventually revolutionize the tailoring trade; in 1849 he began experimenting to discover an improved stitch. On February 11th, 1851, he patented the double-locked chain-stitch machine; and in the same year he and another merchant tailor, William Emerson Baker (1828–1888), formed a stock company for the manufacture and sale of the Grover & Baker sewing machine, which proved so enormously popular that both men were soon able to retire with vast fortunes. For many years William O. Grover was director of the Five Cent Savings Bank, the Bank of Commerce, and the Old Colony Trust Company; he was also trustee of Boston University and the New England Conservatory of Music. He gave liberally to the Boston Museum of Fine Arts, the New England Conservatory of Music, the Massachusetts Institute of Technology, and Wellesley College. As the Boston *Evening Transcript* observed on the day of his death, "He contributed liberally but without ostentation to innumerable religious, educational, musical, and charitable objects, while his private benefactions have been very large. Although of a retiring disposition, his integrity and good judgment were fully appreciated by his fellow citizens, who invested him with many offices of high trust." He died at his summer residence in Beverly, Massachusetts, on September 5th, 1895; his wife died in Boston on December 14th, 1897.

GUÉ, FRANCIS L. (1830–1870), cotton factor and planter, was born of French ancestry in St. Augustine, Florida, in September 1830. In 1848 he removed to Savannah, Georgia, where he was for many years clerk in the firm of John W. Anderson & Company, cotton factors and commission merchants. In December 1850 he married Mary E. Oliveros (1828–1878), daughter of Bartolo F. Oliveros, Savannah gunsmith. He was several times alderman of Savannah and served one term in the state legislature. In 1867 he undertook cotton brokerage on his own; as the Savannah *Republican* (September 14th, 1867) observed, "Mr. Gué has had an intimate acquaintance with cotton for the last nineteen years, and is one of the best judges of the article to be found." A year later he retired from business, traveled in Europe, and then settled on his plantation some five miles from Savannah. He died suddenly on August 3rd, 1870, and was buried in Laurel Grove Cemetery. Three of his sons, John W. Gué (1857–1876), William H. Gué (1858–1876), and Francis L. Gué (1860–1876), died within four days of each other during the yellow fever epidemic of 1876. Mary (Oliveros) Gué died on September 20th, 1878, and was buried beside her husband and three sons. During the Civil War Francis L. Gué was popularly thought to be a speculator. On January 8th, 1863, Charles Colcock Jones, Jr., advised his father "in confidence" to "send no more cotton to Gué," adding that he wrote "not at random." In the autumn of the same year the following letter signed "Enquirer" appeared in the Savannah *Republican* (October 6th, 1863): "One of the candidates for the legislature, Mr. F. L. Gué, before the war paid taxes on less than *four thousand dollars*. He now pays taxes on over *ninety-seven thousand* dollars. In ordinary times the rapidity with which a man accumulates property does not concern the public. But now, when speculation is the only means by which fortunes are made, and as every speculator is helping to oppress the soldier's family, as well as every poor man and widow and orphan; it is due to the voters of Chatham that some explanation of Mr. Gué's sudden wealth should be made. The soldier who works for eleven dollars a month cannot vote to put any speculator in an office which will exempt him from military service."

GUIDO. *See* Reni, Guido

HABERSHAM, FRANCES ELIZABETH MATILDA (1835–1868), youngest child of Dr. Joseph Clay Habersham (1790–1855) and Ann Wylly Adams (1795–1876), was born in Savannah, Georgia, on September 11th, 1835. On December 1st, 1857, she became the wife of Louis Manigault (1828–1899), of Charleston, South Carolina, distinguished young connoisseur who after attending Yale College (1845–1847) traveled in Europe, Asia, and South America for four years. She died in Charleston on March 12th, 1868, survived by her husband and three children, and was buried in Magnolia Cemetery.

HALE, SMITH D. (born 1827), lawyer, son of Henry Hale, was born in Washington County, Tennessee, in 1827. In early manhood he settled in Huntsville, Alabama, where he was judge of the circuit court from 1856 to 1862. Early in 1862 he was elected colonel of the 49th Regiment Alabama Infantry, but he soon resigned; on January 10th, 1863, he applied for a post as enrolling officer and drillmaster: "I am unable for camp duty," he wrote his congressman, the Hon. Cassius C. Clay, "but could do this duty well, as I know so much of the country and people." Later in the war he removed to Perry County, Alabama, where he was still living in 1872, taking but little part in public affairs. In 1854 he married Sarah Eliza Pynchon (1832–1859), daughter of Edward Elliott Pynchon and Sarah Harriet Lewis, of Marietta, Georgia; she died suddenly in Huntsville on May 10th, 1859, leaving two young sons, and was buried in Maple Hill Cemetery.

HALL, MARGARET (WALL) (1808–1884), Mrs. William Henry Hall, nurse, was born in Ireland in 1808. By 1843 she was living in Savannah, Georgia, where she became the wife of William Henry Hall in December 1843. She attended the birth of Julia Berrien Jones, elder daughter of Charles Colcock Jones, Jr., in November 1859; and the birth of Mary Ruth Jones, younger daughter of Charles Colcock Jones, Jr., in June 1861. She was unable to attend the birth of Eliza Burnley Mallard, daughter of the Rev. R. Q. Mallard, in Walthourville in March 1863. "She is very competent," wrote Mrs. Mary Jones on November 25th, 1859, "and I am now relieved of all care of mother and infant." She died in Savannah on January 14th, 1884, and was buried in Cathedral (Catholic) Cemetery.

HALL, ZACHARIAH (1800–1875), cotton planter, was born in South Carolina. About 1850 he migrated to Georgia with his younger brother, David Hall (1810–1880), and his natural son, William Henry Hall (1836–1911), and settled on a farm in Tattnall County near Philadelphia Baptist Church. Both men were bachelors. In March 1865 Mrs. Mary S. Mallard and her party, traveling overland from Liberty County to Southwest Georgia, stopped for the night with the Halls. "They entertained us in true bachelor style," she wrote on March 8th, 1865, "welcome to all their house afforded. They had a huge number of Negroes, but everything showed the absence of a lady's hand." In 1875 Zachariah Hall was thrown from a carriage when his horse was frightened by a train; his head struck against a stone, and he died a day or so later as a result. He was buried in an unmarked grave on the Hall place. Shortly thereafter David Hall removed

to a farm in Liberty County near Johnston's Station (No. 4½, Atlantic & Gulf Railroad), where he died in 1880. Meanwhile his nephew, William Henry Hall, had married Martha Tootle (1846–1917) on June 19th, 1861, and served throughout the Civil War as a private in the Liberty Independent Troop (Company G, 5th Regiment Georgia Cavalry). After the war he was for some years clerk of the superior court of Tattnall County and pastor of Ebenezer Free Will Baptist Church. He died on September 5th, 1911, survived by his wife and numerous children, and was buried in Jesup Cemetery.

HALLECK, HENRY WAGER (1815–1872), lawyer, writer, and Union soldier, son of Joseph Halleck and Catherine Wager, was born in Westernville, Oneida County, New York, on January 16th, 1815. After graduating from Union College (Schenectady, New York) in 1837 and from the United States Military Academy in 1839 he worked on fortifications in New York harbor until 1844, when a tour of European fortifications led to a series of twelve lectures, *Elements of Military Art and Science,* delivered at the Lowell Institute in Boston, published in 1846, and widely valued as an officer's manual during the Civil War. From 1846 to 1848 he was secretary of state under the military government of California. In 1854 he resigned his commission and commenced the practice of law in San Francisco. On April 10th, 1855, he married Elizabeth Hamilton, granddaughter of Alexander Hamilton; there was one son. On August 19th, 1861, he was commissioned major general in the regular army, and on November 18th, 1861, he was placed in command of the Department of Missouri. On March 11th, 1862, the Departments of Ohio, Kansas, and Missouri were consolidated to form the Department of the Mississippi. Later in the spring (May 30th, 1862) Halleck took Corinth but allowed Beauregard to escape without vigorous pursuit. On July 11th, 1862, he was called to Washington and made general in chief; he continued in this post, enjoying little success, until March 12th, 1864, when he was demoted to chief of staff. After the war he commanded the military division of the Pacific (1865–1869) and the military division of the South (1869–1872). He died in Louisville, Kentucky, on January 9th, 1872, and was buried in Greenwood Cemetery, Brooklyn, New York. His *International Law; or, Rules Regulating the Intercourse of States in Peace and War* (1861) was subsequently reprinted in many editions.

HAMILTON, JOHN FLOYD (1826–1872), cotton factor, son of Everard Hamilton (1791–1847) and Mary Hazzard Floyd (1795–1888), was born in Twiggs County, Georgia, on September 20th, 1826. In early childhood he removed with his parents to Milledgeville, where his father was secretary of state under Governor George Michael Troup, and his younger brother, Marmaduke Hamilton (1830–1896), was born on September 22nd, 1830.

From Milledgeville the Hamiltons removed to Macon, where Everard Hamilton engaged in the cotton business with Thomas Hardeman; from Macon they removed in 1843 to Savannah, riding on the first train ever to run from Macon to Savannah. Everard Hamilton died on January 12th, 1847, leaving a wife and nine children. For some years John Floyd Hamilton and Marmaduke Hamilton held positions of trust in banks and mercantile houses, engaged variously as clerks, bookkeepers, and merchants; during the Civil War they entered the cotton business, and soon after the war they established the firm of J. F. & M. Hamilton. Both men were bachelors. John Floyd Hamilton died in Savannah on January 11th, 1872, and was buried in Laurel Grove Cemetery; Marmaduke Hamilton died in Savannah on January 28th, 1896, and was buried beside his parents and his brother.

HAMILTON, WILLIAM (1788–1856), Scottish metaphysician, son of Dr. William Hamilton, professor of anatomy at the University of Glasgow, was born in Glasgow on March 8th, 1788. After graduating from Balliol College (Oxford) in 1811 he became a member of the Scottish bar. But he soon entered upon a life of study and reflection at Edinburgh University; as professor of civil history (1821–1836) and professor of logic and metaphysics (1836–1856) he exerted considerable influence upon the thought of his generation. Much of his philosophic system appears in his two books, both published anonymously: *Lectures on Metaphysics* (1858) and *Lectures on Logic* (1860). In March 1828 he married his cousin, Janet Marshall. He died in Edinburgh on May 6th, 1856.

HAMLIN, HANNIBAL (1809–1891), statesman, son of Cyrus Hamlin and Anna Livermore, was born in Paris, Oxford County, Maine, on August 27th, 1809. After reading law in the Portland office of Samuel Fessenden (1784–1869) he practiced his profession in Hampden, Penobscot County, Maine, for fifteen years (1833–1848). He was a member of the state house of representatives (1836–1840; 1847); a member of Congress (1843–1847); United States senator (1848–1857); governor of Maine (January 8th, 1857, to February 20th, 1857); and United States senator (1857–1861). He was vice-president of the United States under President Abraham Lincoln (1861–1865). After the war he was collector of the port of Boston (1865–1866), United States senator (1869–1881), and United States minister to Spain (1881–1882). He died in Bangor, Maine, on July 4th, 1891, and was buried in Mount Hope Cemetery.

HAMPTON, MARY (CANTEY) (1780–1863): *Mrs. Wade Hampton,* daughter of John Cantey, was born in South Carolina in 1780. On July 18th, 1801, she became the third wife of General Wade Hampton (1751–1835), colonel in the Revolutionary War, major general in the War of 1812, and leading citizen of Richland County; at the time of his death he was reputed to be the wealthiest planter and slaveowner in the United States. Of their five daughters two made distinguished marriages: Caroline Martha Hampton (1807–1883) married John Smith Preston, of Virginia; Susan Frances Hampton (1816–1845) married John Laurence Manning, governor of South Carolina (1852–1854). For his third wife General Hampton purchased the elegant Hampton-Preston mansion in Columbia, said to be the work of Robert Mills; its gardens, covering a full city block and enclosed within a wall, featured exotic flowers, shrubs, and trees from abroad. Mary (Cantey) Hampton died in Columbia on June 19th, 1863, and was buried beside her husband in Trinity Episcopal Churchyard. Wade Hampton (1818–1892), Confederate general, was a grandson of General Wade Hampton (1751–1835) and his second wife, Harriet Flud.

HANCOCK, WINFIELD SCOTT (1824–1886), Union soldier, son of Benjamin Franklin Hancock and Elizabeth Hoxworth, was born in Montgomery Square, Pennsylvania, on February 14th, 1824. When four years old he removed with his parents to Norristown, where his father practiced law for over forty years. After graduating from the United States Military Academy in 1844 he served two years with the 6th Infantry in Texas and distinguished himself for gallantry in the Mexican War; for the next fourteen years he saw duty in Florida, Kansas, Utah, and California. On January 24th, 1850, he married Almira Russell, of St. Louis. At the outbreak of the Civil War he was made brigadier general of volunteers (September 23rd, 1861) and assigned to organizing and training the Army of the Potomac. His brigade participated in all the battles of the Peninsula campaign; after Sharpsburg he was promoted to major general of volunteers (November 29th, 1862). He fought brilliantly at Fredericksburg, Chancellorsville, the Wilderness, and Spotsylvania; for distinguished service he was made brigadier general in the regular army (August 12th, 1864) and major general in the regular army (July 26th, 1866). In 1867 he was placed in command of the Department of Louisiana and Texas, but his opposition to the Radicals led to his being relieved. In 1880, as Democratic nominee for President, he was defeated by James A. Garfield. He died on Governors Island after a brief illness on February 9th, 1886, and was buried with military honors in Norristown, Pennsylvania.

HANDLEY, GEORGE THOMAS (1827–1906), clerk, younger son of George Thomas Handley and Harriet Spry Law, was born in Leon County, Florida, on March 7th, 1827. His paternal grandfather, Thomas Handley, was governor of Georgia (1788–1789). George Thomas Handley never married. For many years he lived with his widowed mother in Liberty County, Georgia, where he was engaged as a clerk. He became a member of Midway Church in 1842; in 1855 he was one of sixteen citizens instrumental in organizing the Walthourville Presbyterian Church.

During the Civil War he was third lieutenant, later second lieutenant, in the Liberty Independent Troop (Company G, 5th Regiment Georgia Cavalry); early in 1865 he was wounded near Fayetteville, North Carolina. Returning to Georgia, he continued to live in the household of his mother, who had become (on December 8th, 1863) the second wife of William Pinckney Girardeau, for many years judge of the court of ordinary of Liberty County. After his mother's death in 1877 he lived for a time in the household of Matilda Olivia Fleming, widow of Russell Walthour, and later with his niece, Harriet Alethea Law, wife of Fuller Keller; early in 1905 he became an inmate of the Old Soldiers' Home in Atlanta, where he died of paralysis on September 3rd, 1906. He was buried in Westview Cemetery.

HANDLEY, HARRIET SPRY (LAW) (1805–1877): *Mrs. George Thomas Handley,* daughter of Nathaniel Law and Mrs. Mary Walker, a widow, was born in Liberty County, Georgia, in 1805. She was thus a contemporary and lifelong friend of Mary Eliza Robarts (1805–1878), only daughter of James Robarts and Eliza Greene Low, widow of Charles Walker. Her mother died on September 23rd, 1807, and her father married Mrs. Sarah Groves in 1809. On November 21st, 1822, she became the wife of George Thomas Handley, son of Thomas Handley, governor of Georgia (1788–1789); there were four children. For a time the family resided in Florida; after the father's death the mother lived with her two sons, both bachelors, in Liberty County. William Cumming Handley (1825–1864), private in the 3rd Regiment Georgia Infantry, died of typhoid fever at Jackson Hospital, Richmond, Virginia, on September 14th, 1864; George Thomas Handley (1827–1906), second lieutenant in the Liberty Independent Troop (Company G, 5th Regiment Georgia Cavalry), survived the war and returned to his mother's home. On December 8th, 1863, she became the second wife of William Pinckney Girardeau (1798–1874), for many years judge of the court of ordinary of Liberty County. She died in Liberty County in 1877, survived by two children: George Thomas Handley and Mary Eliza Handley, wife of Henry Macon Law.

HANDLEY, WILLIAM CUMMING (1825–1864), plantation overseer, elder son of George Thomas Handley and Harriet Spry Law, was born in Liberty County, Georgia, in 1825. His paternal grandfather, Thomas Handley, was governor of Georgia (1788–1789). William Cumming Handley never married. For some years he lived with his kinsman, Joseph Benjamin Law, in Liberty County, managing the property of his deceased grandfather, Nathaniel Law. On February 26th, 1864, although overage and not liable to military service, he enlisted as a private in the 3rd Regiment Georgia Infantry; he died of typhoid fever at Jackson Hospital, Richmond, Virginia, on September 14th, 1864.

HANSELL, ANDREW JACKSON (1815–1881), lawyer, eldest son of William Young Hansell (1799–1867) and Susan B. Harris (1797–1873), was born in Milledgeville, Georgia, in January 1815. His father, a native of Brunswick County, Virginia, served in the War of 1812; after practicing law in Baldwin County, Georgia, for many years he removed to Marietta in the 1840s. On December 2nd, 1841, Andrew Jackson Hansell married Caroline Clifford Shepherd (1821–1899), of Washington, Wilkes County, Georgia, daughter of Andrew Shepherd and Mary Hillhouse; they settled in Cobb County, where all six of their children were born. The Hansells figured prominently in the growth of Marietta during the years prior to the Civil War. In 1849 they built Tranquilla, a magnificent Greek Revival house which they occupied for eighteen years. During the Civil War Andrew Jackson Hansell was adjutant general of Georgia; he represented Cobb County in the state senate in 1861, 1862, and 1863. In the summer of 1864, when Marietta fell into Union hands, Mrs. Hansell, unlike most of her neighbors, remained in her house, where she was subjected to considerable indignity as well as inconvenience. In 1867 Hansell removed to Roswell, where he served as president of the Roswell factory until November 1874. He died in Roswell on April 24th, 1881, survived by his wife, and was buried in Citizens Cemetery, Marietta.

HANSELL, WILLIAM ANDREW (1843–1907), merchant, son of Andrew Jackson Hansell (1815–1881) and Caroline Clifford Shepherd (1821–1899), was born in Marietta, Georgia on August 10th, 1843. At the outbreak of the Civil War he was attending the Georgia Military Institute (Marietta); he volunteered for service and became adjutant in the 35th Regiment Alabama Infantry. In August 1862 he entered the corps of engineers as second lieutenant; in June 1864 he came to Atlanta to aid in the city defenses. After the war he planted in northern Alabama; in 1879 he settled in Atlanta, where he engaged in the fertilizer business for twenty-five years. He was a vestryman of St. Philip's Episcopal Church from 1895 until his death. He died in Atlanta on January 4th, 1907, survived by his wife, Antonina Jones (1845–1917), and was buried in Oakland Cemetery.

HAPPERSETT, REESE (1810–1866), Presbyterian clergyman, son of Melchi Happersett, was born in Brandywine Manor, Chester County, Pennsylvania, on July 31st, 1810. After graduating from Washington College (Washington, Pennsylvania) in 1836 and from Princeton Theological Seminary in 1839 he was ordained clergyman in 1841. For three years he was pastor in Havre de Grace, Maryland. In 1844 he became associated with the Board of Domestic Missions of the Presbyterian Church, with offices in Philadelphia; he was agent (1844–1850), assistant secretary (1850–1854), associate secretary (1854–1858), and corresponding secretary (1859–1861). Shortly after resigning from the board in 1861 he removed to California, where he was pastor in Stockton (1862–1866). He never married. He died in San Francisco on October 2nd, 1866. He received the honorary degree of doctor of laws from Jefferson College (Canonsburg, Pennsylvania) in 1856. According to *The Encyclopedia of the Presbyterian Church of America,* "Dr. Happersett preached the gospel with simplicity, with earnestness, and greatly to the acceptance of those to whom he ministered. His generosity, amiableness, and frankness made him many friends; and with a heart full of kindness he sought constantly to serve those who needed his aid or were working for the Church of Christ." On June 16th, 1858, the Rev. Dr. Charles Colcock Jones wrote Happersett, his former assistant secretary in Philadelphia, as follows: "I have uniformly expressed the most favorable opinion of you *as an agent* of the board. You have been one among the most successful and acceptable agents in our church. The *agency* I conceived to be your *special calling.*"

HARDEE, WILLIAM JOSEPH (1815–1873), Confederate soldier, was born at Rural Felicity, his father's plantation in Camden County, Georgia, on October 12th, 1815. After graduating from the United States Military Academy in 1838 he served one year in Florida as second lieutenant of dragoons, then went to Europe as first lieutenant to study foreign military organization. Promoted to captain, he fought in the Mexican War (1846–1848) and was brevetted major for gallantry. On January 21st, 1861, he resigned his commission and entered Confederate service as colonel of cavalry; he rose rapidly from brigadier general (June 16th, 1861) to major general (October 7th, 1861) to lieutenant general (October 10th, 1862). He fought at Shiloh, Perryville, Murfreesboro, Missionary Ridge, Corinth, Resaca, Kennesaw Mountain, and Jonesboro. In October 1864 he was placed in command of the Department of South Carolina, Georgia, and Florida; his evacuation of Savannah in December 1864 was considered a military masterpiece. He surrendered with Johnston's army in Durham, North Carolina, on April 26th, 1865. In January 1863 he married Mary T. Lewis, of Greensboro, Alabama. He died in Wytheville, Virginia, on November 6th, 1873, and was buried in Selma, Alabama.

HARDEN, EDWARD JENKINS (1813–1873), jurist, son of Thomas Hutson Harden (1786–1821) and Matilda Amanda Baker (1790–1862), was born at Republican Hall, his father's plantation in Bryan County, Georgia, on November 19th, 1813. His maternal grandfather, Colonel John Baker, for whom Baker County, Georgia, was named, was a Revolutionary hero. At an early age Edward Jenkins Harden settled in Savannah, where he was prominently identified with civic and social affairs for the rest of his life. After teaching briefly at the Chatham Academy he commenced the practice of law in 1834. He

was judge of the city court (1847–1849) and judge of the Confederate States district court (1861–1865). He was president of the Georgia Historical Society (1868–1873) and author of *The Life of George M. Troup* (1859). For many years he was an elder of the First Presbyterian Church. On May 21st, 1840, he married his first cousin, Sophia Helen Maxwell (1820–1912), daughter of John Jackson Maxwell (1784–1855) and Mary Ann Baker (1787–1871), of Belfast plantation, Bryan County. He died at Indian Springs, Georgia, on April 19th, 1873, survived by his wife and numerous children, and was buried in Laurel Grove Cemetery, Savannah. His son William (1844–1936) was librarian of the Georgia Historical Society for fifty-five years.

HARDEN, JANE (LeCONTE) (1814–1876): *Mrs. John Macpherson Berrien Harden,* daughter of Louis LeConte (1782–1838) and Anne Quarterman (1793–1826), was born at Woodmanston, her father's plantation in Liberty County, Georgia, on November 23rd, 1814. Her father, an eminent botanist, enjoyed an international reputation; his gardens at Woodmanston were among the most beautiful in the world. Her two younger brothers, John LeConte (1818–1891) and Joseph Le-Conte (1823–1901), also distinguished scientists, were instrumental in founding the University of California, and John LeConte served for a time as its president. On December 12th, 1833, Jane LeConte became the wife of John Macpherson Berrien Harden (1810–1848), eldest son of Thomas Hutson Harden (1786–1821) and Matilda Amanda Baker (1790–1862), of Republican Hall, Bryan County, Georgia, and brother of Edward Jenkins Harden (1813–1873) of Savannah. John Macpherson Berrien Harden represented Liberty County in the state legislature in 1832; he graduated from the Medical College of South Carolina (Charleston) in 1836. For the next ten years he practiced his profession in Liberty County, where he was an active member of the Liberty Independent Troop and a selectman of Midway Church (1844–1847). He died of consumption at Belair, near Tallahassee, Florida, on February 16th, 1848, leaving a wife and four young children, and was buried in Tallahassee. His widow continued to reside in Liberty County; in 1858 she removed to Orangeburg, South Carolina, to enable her daughters to complete their education. After the Civil War she visited her brothers, then professors at the University of California; she died in San Francisco on October 28th, 1876, survived by four children: Matilda Jane Harden (1837–1932), wife of Thomas Sumner Stevens; John Harden (1839–1902); Anne Eliza Harden (1842–1924), wife of Cornelius Berrien Adams; and Ada Louisa Harden (1845–1930), who never married. From early childhood Jane (LeConte) Harden was a particular friend of Louisa Jane Robarts (1813–1897), daughter of David Robarts and Eliza Greene Low, widow of Charles Walker and James Robarts.

HARDEN, MATILDA JANE (1837–1932), eldest daughter of Dr. John Macpherson Berrien Harden (1810–1848) and Jane LeConte (1814–1876), was born in Liberty County, Georgia, on April 23rd, 1837. Her maternal grandfather, Louis LeConte (1782–1838), was a world-famous botanist; her maternal uncles, John LeConte (1818–1891) and Joseph LeConte (1823–1901), also distinguished scientists, were professors at Franklin College (Athens) and the South Carolina College (Columbia) before the Civil War and professors at the University of California for many years after its establishment in 1868. Her father, a physician, died in 1848, before she was eleven years old. She was a girlhood friend of Mary Sharpe Jones, and a bridesmaid at her wedding on April 22nd, 1857. In the winter of 1854 she "entered society," but "Miss Till" had already acquired a reputation for beauty and vivacity. "Your friend Matilda Jane Harden," wrote Mrs. Mary Jones to Mary Sharpe Jones on December 10th, 1852, "has grown and improved *astonishingly* during the summer, and dresses in the height of fashion—open front, regular vest of white and colored silk and very gay colors. She is very pretty and quite admired." In 1858 she accompanied her mother and two younger sisters, Anne Eliza Harden (1842–1924) and Ada Louisa Harden (1845–1930), to Orangeburg, South Carolina, where Mrs. Harden resided for several years while her daughters completed their education. On Thursday evening, June 27th, 1861, in the Walthourville Presbyterian Church, Matilda Jane Harden became the wife of Thomas Sumner Stevens (1820–1889), a schoolteacher in his forty-first year, son of Oliver Stevens (1783–1853) and Eliza Sumner Winn (1790–1872), of Liberty County. According to Mary Eliza Robarts (May 31st, 1861), the marriage was "displeasing" to the bride's mother, who "told her she might be married at home but she would not witness it." In October 1861 Thomas Sumner Stevens enlisted as a private in the Liberty Independent Troop (Company G, 5th Regiment Georgia Cavalry), but after six months he was pronounced physically unfit for military service. He was principal of the Walthourville Academy (1865–1870); principal of the West Florida Seminary in Tallahassee (1870–1871); president of the Bowling Green Female College in Bowling Green, Kentucky (1871–1880); and teacher at the Silliman Collegiate Institute for Young Ladies in Clinton, Louisiana (1880–1889). After his death in Clinton on October 30th, 1889, his widow divided her time among her daughters; she died in Raleigh, North Carolina, at the residence of her granddaughter, on March 11th, 1932, only a few weeks before her ninety-fifth birthday, and was buried in Midway Cemetery, Liberty County, Georgia.

HARDIN, SARAH AKERS (1837–1862), eldest daughter of James Pendleton Hardin (1810–1842) and Jane Tandy Chinn (1817–1870), was born in Harrodsburg, Kentucky,

on April 9th, 1837. Her paternal grandfather, Ben Hardin (1784–1852), scion of a distinguished Kentucky family, was one of the greatest lawyers Kentucky ever produced. Her father graduated from the United States Military Academy in 1832 but resigned his commission a few months later; he then studied law and practiced his profession brilliantly for six years (1836–1842) in Bardstown, Kentucky, until his promising career was cut short by death on October 26th, 1842. On November 10th, 1835, he married Jane Tandy Chinn, daughter of the Hon. Christopher Chinn (1789–1868) and Sarah White Stull (1787–1864); his wife survived with three small children: Sarah Akers Hardin (1837–1862), Elizabeth Pendleton Hardin (1839–1895), and Jamesetta Hardin (1840–1927). James Pendleton Hardin was a younger brother of Lucinda Barbour Hardin (1809–1885), wife of John Larue Helm (1802–1867), governor of Kentucky (1850–1852), who became legal guardian of the elder Hardin sisters at their father's death. Sarah and Elizabeth Hardin were thus first cousins of Elizabeth and Rebecca Jane Helm; the four were almost exact contemporaries and frequent companions. On July 29th, 1848, in Shelbyville, Kentucky, Jane Tandy (Chinn) Hardin became the wife of the Rev. Dr. Joseph Cross, English-born clergyman, educator, and author; after a journey through Europe they taught school in Spartanburg, South Carolina, where Dr. Cross was president of Spartanburg Female College. Sarah Akers Hardin never married. She died near Nashville, Tennessee, on March 31st, 1862; the place of her burial is not known. In the summer of 1862 her mother and her two younger sisters, released from military prison in Louisville, were "sent over the lines" into Tennessee—the "perilous escape" to which Mrs. Mary Jones referred on September 4th, 1862. Jane Tandy (Chinn) (Hardin) Cross and her two younger daughters were buried in Spring Hill Cemetery, Harrodsburg.

HARDY, JOHN GEDDINGS (1830–1885), physician, son of Dr. James F. E. Hardy (1802–1882) and his first wife, Jane Patton, was born in Asheville, North Carolina, on June 23rd, 1830. His father, a native of Newberry District, South Carolina, attended medical lectures in Charleston and settled in Asheville, where he became one of the most influential physicians and most universally beloved citizens of Buncombe County. John Geddings Hardy was named for Dr. Eli Geddings, once an associate of his father. After graduating from the Medical College of South Carolina (Charleston) in 1851 he practiced his profession briefly in Asheville; in 1853 he removed to Marietta, Georgia, where he practiced for the next five years. On June 6th, 1854, he married Anna Eliza Ardis (1830–1901), daughter of David Ardis (1804–1872) and Eliza C. Gray (1804–1867), of Marietta. He became a member of the First Presbyterian Church, Marietta, on November 18th, 1854;

he was ordained deacon on May 16th, 1858. Early in 1859 he removed with his wife to Asheville. On April 24th, 1861, he volunteered for six months' service as assistant surgeon of the Buncombe Rifles (Company E, 1st Regiment North Carolina Infantry); on October 25th, 1862, he was appointed surgeon of the 64th Regiment North Carolina Infantry (State Troops); on March 1st, 1863, he was transferred to the 6th Regiment North Carolina Infantry. His half-brother, William Henry Hardy (1842–1861), was killed at First Manassas. After the war he returned to Asheville, where he resumed his practice and proved a worthy successor to his distinguished father. He was devoted to reading, and was instrumental in establishing the Asheville Library. He died in Asheville on January 14th, 1885, greatly beloved, and was buried in the Presbyterian churchyard. Anna (Ardis) Hardy died in Morganton, North Carolina, on September 6th, 1901, and was buried in Riverside Cemetery, Asheville; at the same time her husband's remains were removed from the Presbyterian churchyard and reburied by her side.

HARLOW, REBECCA (WALKER) (1790–1865): *Mrs. Southworth Harlow,* daughter of Isaac Walker and Bethiah Whitehead, was born in Burke County, Georgia, in 1790. She was a first cousin of John Whitehead (1783–1857), and hence a first cousin once removed of his daughter, Ruth Berrien Whitehead (1837–1861), who nevertheless called Mrs. Harlow "aunt" rather than "cousin," probably because of the great disparity in their ages. In 1811 Rebecca Walker became the wife of Dr. Southworth Harlow (1781–1832), a physician, of Waynesboro, Georgia. There were nine children; seven died in infancy and were laid out in the order of their death in Waynesboro Cemetery; two lived to maturity: John A. Harlow (1823–1863) and Ruth Southworth Harlow (1830–1877). Dr. Southworth Harlow was one of the five original commissioners of Waynesboro, elected at the time of its incorporation as a town in January 1813. He was also an elder in the Waynesboro Presbyterian Church (1830–1832). After his death on February 23rd, 1832, his widow continued to reside in Waynesboro with her two young children. Years later Charles Colcock Jones, Jr., spoke of her as "poor"; but in December 1861 the Rev. Dr. Charles Colcock Jones found her to be "one of the most pleasant old ladies we have met in a long time." John A. Harlow, a physician, was captain of Company D, 48th Regiment Georgia Infantry, during the Civil War; he saw action at Mechanicsville, Malvern Hill, and Second Manassas, and he was killed at Gettysburg on July 2nd, 1863. Rebecca (Walker) Harlow died in Waynesboro in 1865 and was buried beside her husband in an unmarked grave in Waynesboro Cemetery. Her only surviving daughter, Ruth Southworth Harlow, died on March 14th, 1877, and was buried near her parents.

HARNDEN, WILLIAM FREDERICK (1813–1845), pioneer expressman, eldest son of Ameriah Harnden, a house painter, and Sally Richardson, was born in Reading, Massachusetts, on August 23rd, 1813. In 1834 he commenced work as conductor on the Boston & Worcester Railroad; he later became ticket agent. In December 1835 he married Sarah Wright Fuller, of Newton, Massachusetts. After five years with the railroad Harnden established, in 1839, a regular carriage service between Boston and New York by which small bundles could be delivered to either city and to intermediate points. The business slowly expanded; in 1841 Harnden & Company established branches in Philadelphia and Albany; in the same year Harnden sent Dexter Brigham, his partner, to Europe to establish branches in Paris, London, and Liverpool. The business was never financially successful. Harnden died insolvent on January 14th, 1845, exhausted by strain and overwork, and was buried in Mount Auburn Cemetery, Cambridge, Massachusetts. In 1866 the express companies of the United States erected over his grave a monument on which appears the following Biblical epitaph: "Because the King's business required haste. . . ." Harnden's business was later absorbed by the Adams Express Company, which continued for some time to use the Harnden name. According to the Savannah *Republican* (March 17th, 1859), "Harnden's and Adams' Expresses, which are supposed to be one and the same thing, cover these United States with a network of operations. It is quite impossible for us, without access to the official bureau, even to guess at the number of *men, wagons, and horses* employed by this company. . . . The expressman is an institution. We have studied him a good deal in our travels, and we do verily believe he is a specialty. He is affable, polite, generous, nimble as a cricket, and wide awake. He is withal generally a very good-looking fellow, inspiring confidence and receiving it. . . . We are pleased to know that the success of the office in Savannah is so great that a contract has been made for the erection of a very spacious warehouse on Bay Street, in which offices and officers will all be accommodated."

HARPER, JAMES (1795–1869), printer and publisher, son of James Harper and Elizabeth Kolyer, was born in Newton, Long Island, New York, on April 13th, 1795. At the age of sixteen he was apprenticed to a family friend, Abraham Paul, of the firm of Paul & Thomas, printers, of New York City. In 1817, when his younger brother, John Harper (1797–1875), had completed a printer's apprenticeship with Jonathan Seymour, the two young men established the firm of J. & J. Harper, printers, in Dover Street. They were soon recognized for their prompt and efficient work. In 1818 they published Locke's *Essay on Human Understanding,* the first of some two hundred books issued by J. & J. Harper before the two younger brothers joined the firm— Joseph Wesley Harper (1801–1870) in 1823 and Fletcher Harper (1806–1877) in 1825. In 1833 the firm assumed the name of Harper

& Brothers. The enormous prosperity of the firm was due partly to the loyalty and integrity of the four brothers and partly to their complementary talents. James was an accomplished pressman; John was a skillful compositor and proofreader; Joseph Wesley was an astute literary critic; and Fletcher, perhaps the ablest of the four, was a shrewd editor and an energetic administrator. James Harper originated *Harper's New Monthly Magazine* (1850); Fletcher Harper originated *Harper's Weekly* (1857) and *Harper's Bazaar* (1867). The four brothers now lie side by side in a tomb erected by their descendants in Greenwood Cemetery, Brooklyn.

HARRIS, CHARLES JENKINS (1833–1893), lawyer and Confederate soldier, son of the Hon. Iverson L. Harris and Mary Davies, was born in Milledgeville, Georgia, on November 26th, 1833. After attending Oglethorpe University he studied law with his father and practiced his profession for three years (1857–1860) in Thomasville, Georgia. In 1860 he settled in Macon, with whose interests he was prominently identified for the rest of his life. On May 15th, 1862, he enlisted for three years as captain of the Lockett Volunteers (Company K, 59th Regiment Georgia Infantry); he was elected major on June 16th, 1862, and promoted to lieutenant colonel on December 22nd, 1862. On July 10th, 1863, he was appointed commandant of conscripts for the State of Georgia, but ill health forced him to resign on April 25th, 1864, when he was succeeded by William Montague Browne. He later became colonel of the 3rd Regiment Georgia Reserves under General Howell Cobb, with whom he continued until the close of the war. Returning to Macon, he resumed the practice of law. He was solicitor general of the Macon circuit (1872); representative of Bibb County in the state legislature (1878); and judge of the city court of Macon (1884–1890). On January 13th, 1857, he married Mary Clopton Wiley (1837–1914), who bore him thirteen children. He died in Macon on January 22nd, 1893, survived by his wife and twelve children, and was buried in Rose Hill Cemetery.

HARRIS, JOHN STITT (1832–1864), Presbyterian clergyman, son of Hugh Harris, was born in Mecklenburg County, North Carolina, on August 1st, 1832. After graduating from Davidson College with first honor in 1852 he attended Columbia Theological Seminary for three years. In 1856 he became stated supply of two churches near Guthriesville (now Guthries), York County, South Carolina; in 1857 he became pastor, and there he labored successfully until his untimely death on November 16th, 1864. As the Rev. John Leighton Wilson observed, "Few men have gone down to their graves more honored, beloved, and blessed in the affections of their people; and few have left behind them better evidences of a successful life and work. . . . He was a man of far more than ordinary parts. Weak and delicate physically, and predisposed to consumption (of which, eventually, he died), he

was mentally of great vigor. . . . His death was a shock to the whole community, who felt that his loss was simply irreparable" [*Memorial Volume of the Semi-Centennial of the Theological Seminary at Columbia South Carolina* (Columbia, 1884), pp. 287–289]. He was buried in Bethesda Churchyard. On April 22nd, 1857, he married Agnes Bratton, daughter of Dr. John S. Bratton. His former classmate at Columbia, Robert Q. Mallard, writing to his fiancée, Mary Sharpe Jones, on April 1st, 1857, spoke of a letter just received from "Brother Harris." "I had written pressing him to attend our wedding, and what do you think (the scamp) is his excuse? Why, he expects to get married himself on that very night! Do you think his excuse a valid one?"

HARRIS, RAYMOND (1799–1888), physician, son of Nathan Harris, a native of Brunswick County, Virginia, was born in Columbia County, Georgia, in 1799. He attended school in Eatonton, Georgia, and while still a boy he fought in the War of 1812. He attended Jefferson Medical College (Philadelphia) without receiving a degree. After practicing medicine briefly in Savannah he removed to Bryan County, where he practiced his profession and planted for some twenty years; in 1850 he removed to Hinesville, Liberty County, and in 1852 he removed to Dorchester. There he resided until after the Civil War, when he settled in Walthourville. He married first (on May 17th, 1822) Mary Elizabeth Law (1803–1871), daughter of Joseph Law (1769–1829) and Elizabeth Stevens (1777–1838), and widow of Samuel Jones (1796–1819); he married second (on January 29th, 1874) Elizabeth (Bessie) Mary Emma Anderson (1844–1879), daughter of Joseph Andrew Anderson (1820–1866) and Evelyn Elouisa Jones (1822–1849). For many years he owned a place on the northern end of Colonel's Island, contiguous to Maybank, the plantation of the Rev. Dr. Charles Colcock Jones. He was closely associated with the Jones family through the marriage of two of his sons: Emma Adelaide Jones (1827–1913), daughter of Joseph Jones (1779–1846) and his third wife, Elizabeth Screven Lee Hart (1801–1870), and hence a half-sister of Mrs. Mary Jones, married first (on June 16th, 1846) Stephen Nathan Harris (1823–1854); she married second (on November 10th, 1858) Columbus Starnes Harris (1828–1874). After the death of his second wife in 1874 Dr. Harris resided for some years in the home of his daughter, Susan R. Harris (born 1834), wife of Thomas Coke Howard (1817–1893), at Kirkwood, near Atlanta. He died in the home of his eldest daughter, Cornelia Elizabeth Harris (1826–1900), widow of the Rev. William Edward Screven (1822–1860), in LaGrange, Georgia, on January 8th, 1888. He was buried near his two wives in Walthourville Cemetery. He practiced medicine in Georgia for more than half a century. Two of his sons were also physicians: Stephen Nathan Harris (1823–1854) and Raymond Benjamin Harris (1838–1910).

HARRIS, STEPHEN NATHAN (1823–1854), eldest son of Dr. Raymond Harris (1799–1888) and his first wife, Mary Elizabeth Law (1803–1871), was born in Liberty County, Georgia, on September 11th, 1823. After graduating from Franklin College (Athens) in 1842 he studied at the Medical College of South Carolina (Charleston) and practiced medicine in Savannah for ten years. On June 16th, 1846, he eloped with Emma Adelaide Jones (1827–1913), daughter of Joseph Jones (1779–1846) and his third wife, Elizabeth Screven Lee Hart (1801–1870), of Liberty County. For her rash act the Jones family never forgave the bride—"one who," as Charles Colcock Jones, Jr., wrote on October 27th, 1854, "has already proved the cause of much trouble in our family—one who, if dealt with according to her deserts, will be found to have forfeited all claim of relationship and regard." Stephen Nathan Harris died of yellow fever in Savannah on September 15th, 1854, leaving a wife and four young children, and was buried in Laurel Grove Cemetery. As the Savannah *Republican* (September 16th, 1854) observed, "No man of his age has ever had a larger or more lucrative practice in Savannah, enjoyed more of the confidence of the people in his medical skill, or commanded to a greater extent the esteem of his medical brethren." Four years later, on November 10th, 1858, Emma Adelaide (Jones) Harris became the wife of Columbus Starnes Harris (1828–1874), younger brother of her first husband. He died on October 6th, 1874, leaving a wife and four young children, and was buried in Walthourville Cemetery. His widow survived nearly forty years; she died in Savannah on January 15th, 1913, and was buried in Laurel Grove Cemetery beneath the following inscription: "Her body lies beside the husband of her youth. We have loved in life, and in death we will not be divided."

HARRIS, WILLIAM (1780–1857), farmer, was born in North Carolina on July 6th, 1780. In early manhood he migrated to Jones County, Georgia, which he represented for one term in the state legislature. When Cobb County, Georgia, was organized in 1833 he was one of its pioneer settlers; he was justice of the inferior court (1833–1834) and a grand juror of the first superior court ever convened in the county (September 17th, 1833). When the Georgia Military Institute (Marietta) was incorporated in 1851 he was one of the eleven original stockholders. He was an active member of the Methodist Church. His last years were saddened by numerous family deaths: his elder son, Matthew Harris (1817–1851), a Marietta merchant, died on March 27th, 1851; his younger son, Peter Jefferson Harris (1826–1853), died on March 19th, 1853; his wife, Mary T. Harris (1799–1853), a native of Warren County, Georgia, died on April 5th, 1853; his daughter, Sarah Harris (1830–1855), wife of Ellison A. Dobbs, died on March 23rd, 1855. William Harris died suddenly in Marietta on Christmas Day 1857 and was buried near his wife and children in Citizens Cemetery. According to his tombstone, "He was an emphatically honest man, the noblest work of God."

HARRISON, GEORGE PAUL (1814–1888), planter and Confederate soldier, son of William Harrison, was born in Effingham County, Georgia, on October 19th, 1814. His father, commander of a company of Georgians during the War of 1812, was a lineal descendant of Benjamin Harrison, signer of the Declaration of Independence and distinguished son of the Harrison family of Virginia. George Paul Harrison married Thurza Adelaide Gunn. Prior to the Civil War he engaged in rice planting on the Savannah River, residing at Monteith, a plantation situated on the line separating Effingham and Chatham Counties. He took an active part in military and political affairs, and was major general of the Georgia militia. At the outbreak of the Civil War he was appointed brigadier general of state troops. During Sherman's march to the sea his palatial home and extensive lands were pillaged and he was taken prisoner by General Oliver Otis Howard, of Sherman's staff. Released from prison, he refused to take the oath of allegiance to the Federal government. After the war he represented Chatham County in the state legislature (1867) and served as clerk of the city court of Savannah (1875–1876); for many years he was clerk of the superior court of Chatham County. He was an active member of the Methodist Church. He died on his farm near Savannah on May 14th, 1888, survived by his wife and four children, and was buried in Laurel Grove Cemetery. His only son, George Paul Harrison (1841–1922), a graduate of the Georgia Military Institute (Marietta) in 1861, rose to the rank of brigadier general in the Confederate army before he was twenty-four years old; he was subsequently a member of the Alabama state senate (1876–1884) and a member of Congress.

HARRISON, PEYTON RANDOLPH (1832–1861), lawyer, youngest son of the Rev. Dr. Peyton Harrison (1800–1887), a Presbyterian clergyman, and Jane Carey Carr (1808–1859), was born in Scottsville, Albemarle County, Virginia, on June 17th, 1832. After graduating from the College of New Jersey (Princeton) in 1851 he taught school for one year at Clifton, the family seat in Cumberland County, Virginia. From 1852 to 1854 he read law with his uncle, David Holmes Conrad, in Martinsburg, (West) Virginia, and commenced practice in July 1854. On December 20th, 1854, he married Sarah Forrest Hunter (1833–1926), daughter of Edmund Pendleton Hunter (1809–1851) and Martha Craufurd (1812–1890); there were four children. He was ordained elder of the Martinsburg Presbyterian Church in 1855. At the outbreak of the Civil War he enlisted as third lieutenant in Company D, 2nd Regiment Virginia Infantry. He was killed at First Manassas on July 21st, 1861, and was buried in Norborne Cemetery, Martinsburg. Sarah Forrest (Hunter) Harrison died on January 11th, 1926, and was buried beside her husband. Two of Harrison's brothers also died in the war: Randolph Harrison (1829–1863), a physician, lieutenant in the 15th Regiment Virginia Infantry, died in Richmond of typhoid fever on September 23rd, 1863; Dabney Carr Harrison (1830–1862), a Presbyterian clergyman, captain in the 56th Regiment Virginia Infantry, was killed at Fort Donelson on February 16th, 1862.

HARRISS, JURIAH (1825–1876), physician, son of the Rev. Juriah Harriss (1784–1868) and Elizabeth Thorn, was born in Columbia County, Georgia, on October 28th, 1825. After graduating from the College of William and Mary in 1845, from the Medical College of Georgia (Augusta) in 1848, and from the University of Paris in 1851 he commenced the practice of medicine in Augusta, where he was also adjunct professor of surgery at the Medical College of Georgia (1851–1857). On October 27th, 1853, he married Susan Clinton Dowse (1833–1886), daughter of Samuel Dowse (1786–1856) and his fifth wife, Elizabeth Martha Walker (1794–1854); she was thus a half-sister of Gideon Dowse (1814–1881); Sarah Berrien Dowse (1824–1855), wife of William Parker White; and Abigail Sturges Dowse (1828–1897), wife of Henry Hart Jones. In 1857 Juriah Harriss joined the faculty of the Savannah Medical College, where he was professor of physiology (1857–1861) and professor of the theory and practice of medicine (1865–1876). He was also editor of *The Savannah Journal of Medicine* (1858–1862). He died in Savannah on November 7th, 1876, survived by his wife, and was buried in Laurel Grove Cemetery. Susan Clinton (Dowse) Harriss died on July 9th, 1886, and was buried beside her husband.

HART, ANN CATHERINE (DUNHAM) (1802–1886): *Mrs. Charles Thomas Hart,* daughter of the Rev. Jacob Hendricks Dunham (1774–1832) and Mary Baisden (1784–1864), was born in Liberty County, Georgia, in 1802. Her father, a Baptist clergyman, had devoted much of his time and energy to serving the underprivileged Negroes of Liberty and McIntosh Counties. Ann Catherine Dunham was a sister of Thomas J. Dunham (1810–1885), Liberty County planter. On January 14th, 1819, she became the wife of Charles Thomas Hart (1794–1835), son of John Hart (1758–1814) and Mary Esther Screven (1767–1845). Her husband died in April 1835; her only daughter, Helen Mary Hart (1821–1862), became the wife of William Robert Gignilliat (1814–1882) on September 19th, 1838; thereafter for many years Ann Catherine (Dunham) Hart lived in the Gignilliat household in McIntosh County. She died in 1882 and was buried in the midst of her daughter's family in St. Andrew's Cemetery, Darien.

HART, ODINGSELL WITHERSPOON (1803–1874), planter, eighth child of John Hart (1758–1814) and Mary Esther Screven (1767–1845), was born at Pine Grove Mills, Lexington County, South Carolina, on December 9th, 1803. After attending Franklin College (Athens) he settled at the Retreat, his sea-island cotton plantation on the coast of Bryan County, Georgia, near Sunbury; there he amassed an enormous fortune, most of which he lost during the Civil War. He represented Bryan County four terms in the state senate. After the war he sold his plantation to General Davis Tilson of the Union army and removed to a farm near Quitman, Georgia, where he died on July 17th, 1874. He married first (on June 12th, 1826) Mary Caroline Stevens (1808–1836), daughter of Oliver Stevens and Eliza Sumner Winn; he married second (on March 22nd, 1838) Sarah Eliza Wilson (1812–1858), daughter of Josiah Wilson and Mary Stewart. He was a younger brother of Elizabeth Screven Lee Hart (1801–1870), third wife of Joseph Jones (1779–1846).

HART, SMITH SCREVEN (1806–1866), planter, ninth and youngest child of John Hart (1758–1814) and Mary Esther Screven (1767–1845), was born at Pine Grove Mills, Lexington County, South Carolina, on April 10th, 1806. In 1815, a year after his father's death, he accompanied his mother to Liberty County, Georgia, where he resided for the rest of his life. For some years he planted near Fleming; in 1855 he settled in Dorchester; and in December 1856 he purchased Lodebar, a neighboring plantation, from Henry Hart Jones. For many years he was an elder of the Sunbury Baptist Church. His first wife, Mary Coleman, died within two years of her marriage; his second wife, Elizabeth Fulton, was the mother of five children. Late in 1855 he married Harriet Atwood Newell (1819–1883), only child of the Rev. Samuel Newell (1784–1821), and his second wife, Philomela Thurston; there were three children. Smith Screven Hart died at Lodebar on February 28th, 1866, survived by his third wife, who died in Dorchester on August 24th, 1883.

HARTRIDGE, JULIAN (1829–1879), lawyer, was born in Savannah, Georgia, on September 9th, 1829. After graduating from Brown University in 1848 and from Dane Law School, Harvard University, in 1850 he commenced the practice of law in Savannah. He was solicitor general of the eastern circuit of Georgia (1854–1858); member of the state legislature (1858–1859); and delegate to the Democratic National Convention (1860). On August 1st, 1861, he enlisted as junior first lieutenant in the Chatham Artillery (1st Volunteer Regiment Georgia Artillery), in which William Murray Davidson was senior second lieutenant and Charles Colcock Jones, Jr., was senior first lieutenant; he resigned on March 27th, 1862. He was a member of the Confederate Congress (1862–1865); a delegate to the Democratic National Convention (1872; 1876); and a member of the United States Congress (1875–1879). On May 11th, 1853, he married Mary M. Charlton, eldest daughter of the Hon. Robert Milledge Charlton (1807–1854), distinguished Savannah jurist. He died in Washington, D.C., on January 8th, 1879, survived by his wife and six children, and was buried in Laurel Grove Cemetery, Savannah.

HASBROUCK, JONATHAN (1824–1908), crockery merchant, son of Jonathan Hasbrouck (1785–1855) and Phoebe E. Field (1788–1880), was born in Newburgh, New York, on October 30th, 1824. In early manhood he settled in Savannah, Georgia, where he conducted a thriving business in china, glass, and earthenware. On August 13th, 1851, in New York City, he married his cousin, Elizabeth M. Hasbrouck (1828–1923), daughter of Benjamin Hasbrouck and Elizabeth G. Hatch; there were three sons. At the outbreak of the Civil War Jonathan Hasbrouck left Savannah for Upper New York State, where he remained for seven years. In 1868 he settled in South Orange, New Jersey, and engaged in the hardware business for ten years before retiring. He died in South Orange on December 22nd, 1908, and was buried in Greenwood Cemetery, Brooklyn, New York. Elizabeth (Hasbrouck) Hasbrouck died on January 10th, 1923, and was buried beside her husband.

HATCH, EDITH MARIE GRANT (1864–1895), eldest daughter of Roswell Daniel Hatch (1832–1922) and Sarah Christina Hogan (1831–1897), was born in New York City on January 5th, 1864. Her father, a lawyer, was secretary of the original Committee of Seventy organized in 1871 to break the grip of the Tweed Ring on New York City. Her mother was one of the first women to be admitted to the bar in New York State. The family were Roman Catholics: the mother was born a Roman Catholic; the father became a convert after his marriage. In July 1867 the Hatch family were near neighbors of the family of Charles Colcock Jones, Jr.; both occupied houses on West 84th Street between Ninth and Tenth Avenues. Edith Hatch was educated at the Convent of the Sacred Heart in New York City. She never married. She died in New York on November 5th, 1895, and was buried in Woodlawn Cemetery.

HAVELOCK, SIR HENRY (1795–1857), British soldier, second son of William Havelock (1757–1837), shipbuilder, and Jane Carter, was born at Ford Hall, Bishop Wearmouth, Sunderland, on April 5th, 1795. He attended Charterhouse, studied law briefly, and entered the army on July 30th, 1815, as second lieutenant in the 95th Regiment; he became lieutenant on October 24th, 1821. In 1822, after seven years at various military posts in Great Britain and Ireland, he exchanged into the 13th Regiment and embarked for India. He reached Calcutta in May 1823 and fought in the Burma War (1824–1826). On February 9th, 1829, he married Hannah Marshman, daughter of the Rev. Dr. Joshua Marshman, a Baptist missionary at Serampore. He was promoted to captain on June 5th, 1838. He served with distinction throughout the First Afghan War (1838–1842) and the First Sikh War (1845–1846) and was appointed quartermaster general (1854) and adjutant general (1855) of the Queen's troops in India. In

1857 he participated in Sir James Outram's expedition to Persia. Learning of the mutiny of several native regiments, he returned to India in the early summer of 1857 and gained a series of victories that made his name a household word throughout the world. He was promoted to major general (July 30th, 1857) and made a K.C.B. (September 26th, 1857). He died of dysentery on November 24th, 1857, and was buried at the Alumbagh. On November 26th, 1857, his death still unknown in London, he was created a baronet; news of his death, reaching England on January 7th, 1858, was received with universal mourning.

HAWTHORNE, NATHANIEL (1804–1864), novelist, son of Nathaniel Hathorne (1776–1808) and Elizabeth Clarke Manning, was born in Salem, Massachusetts, on July 4th, 1804. In early manhood he changed his name from *Hathorne* to *Hawthorne*. He graduated from Bowdoin College in 1825; two of his collegemates became lifelong friends: Henry Wadsworth Longfellow (1807–1882) and Franklin Pierce (1804–1869), fourteenth president of the United States. Returning to Salem, he published his first novel, *Fanshawe* (1828), and wrote numerous short stories, collected in *Twice-Told Tales*, published in 1837 and issued in a second, enlarged edition in 1842. On July 9th, 1842, he married Sophia Peabody, of Boston, and settled in the "Old Manse" in Concord, where he was a neighbor of Ralph Waldo Emerson and Henry David Thoreau. In 1845 he removed to Salem, where he was surveyor of the port (1846–1848). *Mosses from an Old Manse* (1846), a second collection of short stories, was soon followed by three novels: *The Scarlet Letter* (1850), *The House of the Seven Gables* (1851), and *The Blithedale Romance* (1852), and by two children's books: *A Wonder Book for Boys and Girls* (1852) and *Tanglewood Tales for Boys and Girls* (1853). Four years in England (1853–1857) as American consul in Liverpool were recorded in his *English Notebooks* (1870); two years in France and Italy (1858–1859) were recorded in his *French and Italian Notebooks* (1871). In 1860, after another year in England, he returned to Concord. *The Marble Faun* (1860), his last novel, sketched in Italy and completed in England, recounts the mysterious fortunes of several art students in Rome. Hawthorne died in his sleep in Plymouth, New Hampshire, on May 19th, 1864, and was buried in Concord.

HAYMANS, STOUTON (1800–1886), planter, born in Georgia in 1800, was one of a numerous family of planters who settled in Bryan and Liberty Counties near Fleming and raised cattle. On Saturday, June 3rd, 1854, at Beard's Creek Baptist Church in Tattnall County, Stouton Haymans stabbed James Moody, his brother-in-law, in the abdomen with a knife; within five minutes Moody was dead. There being "no sufficient jail" in Tattnall County, Haymans was jailed in Liberty County and later in Chatham County; at the April 1855 term of the Tattnall County Superior Court he was declared not guilty and released. His first wife, Elizabeth Moody, died in the 1870s; on March 21st, 1880, in his eightieth year, he married Laura E. Green, aged twenty-three. He died in Liberty County at the home of his son, James H. Haymans, in the early spring of 1886 and was buried in an unmarked grave in the Haymans family cemetery. His second wife died in Savannah on April 3rd, 1886, aged twenty-nine, and was buried in Laurel Grove Cemetery.

HAYS, ISAAC (1796–1879), ophthalmologist and medical editor, son of Samuel Hays and Richea Gratz, was born in Philadelphia, Pennsylvania, on July 5th, 1796. He graduated from the University of Pennsylvania in 1816 and from the Medical College of the University of Pennsylvania in 1820. He specialized in ophthalmology. For fifty-two years (1827–1879) he was editor of *The American Journal of the Medical Sciences;* in 1843 he originated *The Medical News,* a monthly journal which later became a weekly journal and continued until 1906. He also edited numerous books. He was a member of the Academy of Natural Sciences of Philadelphia and served as its president (1865–1869); he was also an active member of the American Philosophical Society. He was a founder of the Franklin Institute and the American Medical Association. In 1834 he married Sarah Minis, daughter of Isaac Minis, of Savannah, Georgia. He died in Philadelphia on April 13th, 1879, survived by his wife and four children.

HEBER, REGINALD (1783–1826), Anglican bishop, son of the Rev. Reginald Heber and his second wife, Mary Allanson, was born at Malpas, Cheshire, England, on April 21st, 1783. After a brilliant career at Brasenose College (Oxford) he traveled for two years (1805–1807) through Germany, Russia, and the Crimea; returning to England, he took holy orders in 1807, married Amelia Shipley, daughter of the dean of St. Asaph, and became a parish priest. He was prebendary of St. Asaph (1812–1815), Bampton lecturer at Oxford (1815–1822), and bishop of Calcutta (1822–1826). He died suddenly at Trichinopoly, India, on April 3rd, 1826, survived by his wife and two daughters, and was buried in St. John's Church. Of his many hymns the best known is his missionary hymn, "From Greenland's Icy Mountains," written at Wrexham on Whitsun Eve, 1819, and sung the following morning at Wrexham Church, where his father-in-law preached in support of the Society for the Propagation of the Gospel. Five years later Mary Wallace Howard (1808–1853), a young soprano returning from England to Savannah, Georgia, requested Lowell Mason (1792–1872), then a Savannah bank clerk, to compose music for Bishop Heber's hymn; Mason's tune (originally called Heber) was first heard in 1824 in the Independent Presbyterian Church, Savannah, sung by Mary Wallace Howard to the accompaniment of the composer, who was also church organist and choirmaster. In the English-speaking world "From Greenland's Icy Mountains" is still the inevitable hymn for missionary occasions. Of the four stanzas the second reads:

What though the spicy breezes
Blow soft o'er Java's isle,
Though every prospect pleases,
And only man is vile:
In vain with lavish kindness
The gifts of God are strewn;
The heathen, in his blindness,
Bows down to wood and stone!

HELM, BEN HARDIN (1831–1863), lawyer and Confederate soldier, eldest son of the Hon. John Larue Helm (1802–1867) and Lucinda Barbour Hardin (1809–1885), was born on June 2nd, 1831, in Bardstown, Kentucky, at the residence of his maternal grandfather, Ben Hardin (1784–1852), distinguished lawyer, for whom he was named. He graduated from the United States Military Academy in 1851 but resigned his commission a year later for reasons of health. After graduating from the law school of the University of Louisville in 1853 he continued his studies at Dane Law School, Harvard University, for six months. Returning to Kentucky, he practiced his profession in Elizabethtown for four years. He represented Hardin County in the state legislature (1855–1856). In 1858 he removed to Louisville, where he practiced his profession in partnership with his brother-in-law, Horatio Washington Bruce (1830–1903), until the outbreak of the Civil War. On March 26th, 1856, he married Emilie Todd (1836–1930), of Lexington, Kentucky, fourth child of Robert Smith Todd (1791–1849) and his second wife, Elizabeth Humphreys; she was a half-sister of Mary Todd (1818–1882), wife of Abraham Lincoln. Early in 1861 President Lincoln offered his brother-in-law the position of quartermaster general in the United States army, but Helm preferred to enter the Confederate army without a commission. From private he soon rose to colonel of the 1st Regiment Kentucky Cavalry; in April 1862 he was made brigadier general. He fought at Perryville, Stone River, Shiloh, and Vicksburg; at Chickamauga he was mortally wounded on September 20th, 1863. He was buried with military honors in Oakland Cemetery, Atlanta; in September 1884 his remains were removed to Kentucky and buried in the family cemetery at Helm Station, Elizabethtown. His wife, who survived him sixty-six years, died on February 20th, 1930, and was buried near her parents in Lexington Cemetery.

HELM, ELIZABETH (LIZZIE) BARBOUR (1836–1913), third child and eldest daughter of the Hon. John Larue Helm (1802–1867) and Lucinda Barbour Hardin (1809–1885), was born at Helm Station, near Elizabethtown, Kentucky, on April 11th, 1836. In her youth she was a famous belle; Charles Colcock Jones, Jr., summering at Helm Station in 1855, found her to be "lively, kindhearted, attractive . . . one of the most agreeable and accomplished young ladies I have seen for many days." On June 12th, 1856, she became the wife of Horatio Washington Bruce (1830–1903), rising young lawyer, then representative of Fleming County in the state legislature, and soon to become law partner of her elder brother, Ben Hardin Helm, in Louisville (1858–1861). During the Civil War her husband served two terms in the Confederate Congress (1862–1865); returning to Louisville, he resumed the practice of law and rose to distinction in the state. After his death on January 22nd, 1903, his widow resided with her son, Helm Bruce (1860–1927), the "noble little boy" whom Charles Colcock Jones, Jr., saw in Marietta, Georgia, in July 1862, who graduated with honors from Washington and Lee University in 1879, and who became, like his father, grandfather, and great-grandfather, one of the foremost lawyers in Kentucky. She died in Louisville on January 14th, 1913, survived by five children, and was buried beside her husband in Cave Hill Cemetery.

HELM, GEORGE (1833–1858), lawyer, second son of the Hon. John Larue Helm (1802–1867) and Lucinda Barbour Hardin (1809–1885), was born on October 31st, 1833, in Bardstown, Kentucky, at the residence of his maternal grandfather, Ben Hardin (1784–1852). After graduating from Centre College (Danville, Kentucky) in 1852 he studied law at the University of Louisville (1852–1853) and at Dane Law School, Harvard University (1853–1854). In Cambridge he shared rooms with Charles Colcock Jones, Jr., who wrote his parents on January 28th, 1854: "We are upon the warmest terms of friendship, and have often been taken for relatives, being nearly always found in company with each other. He is a hard student and one of the kindest, most openhearted, generous men I have ever seen." After leaving Cambridge without a degree George Helm practiced law for a year in Elizabethtown; in the autumn of 1855 he removed to Memphis, Tennessee, where he continued to practice law until his sudden death of typhoid fever on January 27th, 1858. He never married. In the spring of 1855 (from March 26th to May 1st) he stayed with the family of the Rev. Dr. Charles Colcock Jones in Liberty County, Georgia. "My visit there," he wrote Dr. Jones on October 28th, 1855, "was not only delightful but has been since a source of great pleasure to me in recollections. Your quiet yet cheerful and happy life gave me its lesson. My grandfather, father, and uncles have always lived in the excitement of the bar or politics, and of course they have been constantly before me as examples, until that has seemed to me to be certainly the most pleasant life to lead. By a close observance of your habits and feelings during my visit I have seen how unnecessary such excitements are. I hope it will be a lasting lesson, notwithstanding the opinion of the author of Rasselas to the contrary."

HELM, JAMES PENDLETON (1850–1910), lawyer, tenth child of the Hon. John Larue Helm (1802–1867) and Lucinda Barbour Hardin (1809–1885), was born at Helm Station, near Elizabethtown, Kentucky, on January 7th, 1850. His maternal grandfather, Ben Hardin (1784–1852), was one of the greatest lawyers Kentucky ever produced; his father, also a lawyer, was a distinguished member of the state legislature for many years and governor of Kentucky (1850–1852). Born into a family of lawyers, James Pendleton Helm chose the profession of law at an early age. In 1871 he removed to Louisville, where he became one of the leading corporation lawyers in the state. In 1874 he married Pattie A. Kennedy, daughter of Thomas Kennedy. He died in Louisville on March 29th, 1910, survived by his wife and four children, and was buried in Cave Hill Cemetery.

HELM, JOHN LARUE (1802–1867), lawyer and governor, son of George Helm and Rebecca Larue, was born at Helm Station, near Elizabethtown, Kentucky, on July 4th, 1802. After reading law in the office of Ben Tobin he commenced practice in Elizabethtown at the age of twenty-one. He soon rose to leadership in state politics. He was eleven times a member of the state house of representatives between 1826 and 1843, and four times speaker; he was a member of the state senate (1844–1848; 1865–1867), and twice speaker; he was lieutenant governor of Kentucky (1848–1850) and governor (1850–1852). In 1854 he retired from public life and became first president of the Louisville & Nashville Railroad (1854–1860). During the Civil War he bitterly opposed Lincoln's administration and sympathized with the South; his eldest son, Ben Hardin Helm (1831–1863), brigadier general in the Confederate army, was killed at Chickamauga on September 20th, 1863. In Bardstown, Kentucky, on August 10th, 1830, he married Lucinda Barbour Hardin (1809–1885), eldest daughter of Ben Hardin (1784–1852), eminent Kentucky lawyer, and Elizabeth Pendleton Barbour (1787–1852); eleven of their twelve children lived to maturity. He died near Elizabethtown on September 8th, 1867, five days after his second inauguration as governor of Kentucky, and was buried in the family cemetery at Helm Station.

HELM, LUCINDA BARBOUR (HARDIN) (1809–1885): Mrs. John Larue Helm, eldest daughter of Ben Hardin (1784–1852) and Elizabeth Pendleton Barbour (1787–1852), was born in Bardstown, Kentucky, on February 2nd, 1809. She was a beautiful and brilliant woman with the rare intellectual gifts of her father, an eminent lawyer, with whom she was always a great favorite. On August 10th, 1830, she became the wife of John Larue Helm (1802–1867), rising young lawyer destined to a distinguished career as legislator and governor; eleven of their twelve children lived to maturity. At Helm Station, the family residence near Elizabethtown, Kentucky, she presided with firmness and affection; her daughter Mary Helm later recalled the happiness of her girlhood home: "My mother was given to hospitality, entertaining with a grace and dignity that made her an elegant as well as charming hostess. Parties, teas, and dinings of the formal kind were frequent; but what she enjoyed most was the informal coming together for the day of her chosen friends. There were many occasions when, for weeks at a time, the only limit to the guests was when the last bed was full. Her children were also at full liberty to fill the house with their friends; and whether they were old or young she was the center of attraction for them as well as for her own family, and enjoyed all the fun as much as anyone else in the house" [Arabel Wilbur Alexander, *The Life and Work of Lucinda B. Helm* (Nashville, Tennessee, 1898), p. 21]. She died near Elizabethtown on Christmas Day 1885, survived by six children, and was buried beside her husband in the family cemetery at Helm Station.

HELM, REBECCA JANE (1838–1859), fourth child of the Hon. John Larue Helm (1802–1867) and Lucinda Barbour Hardin (1809–1885), was born at Helm Station, near Elizabethtown, Kentucky, on February 17th, 1838. She never married. She died near Elizabethtown on August 23rd, 1859, and was buried in the family cemetery at Helm Station.

HENDEE, HOMER (1817–1881), Presbyterian clergyman, was born in Aldin, New York, on March 7th, 1817. At the age of fourteen he was sent to live with an uncle engaged in business in Charleston, South Carolina. After graduating from Oglethorpe University in 1841 and from Columbia Theological Seminary in 1844 he was pastor of churches in Louisville, Madison, and Greensboro, Georgia; after five years as pastor in Quincy, Florida (1852–1857) he returned to Greensboro, Georgia, where he was professor and later president of Greensboro Female College (1857–1863). He was stated supply in Cuthbert (1863–1865), Macon (1865–1868), Greensboro and Madison (1868–1871), and Louisville, Kentucky (1871–1874). Removing to St. Louis in 1874, he was stricken with paralysis and forced to resign his charge; for six years he lingered as an invalid, though still prominently identified with the church. He died in St. Louis on February 7th, 1881, survived by two daughters, and was buried in Cave Hill Cemetery, Louisville, Kentucky. On June 1st, 1847, he married Frances M. King, of Greensboro, Georgia. Two of his sons, Henry F. Hendee (born 1848) and George N. Hendee (born 1850) were converted at a special meeting conducted by the Rev. R. Q. Mallard in the Cuthbert Presbyterian Church in April 1864.

HENDERSON, ROBERT TERRILL (1811–1866), tanner, fifth child of Thomas Henderson (1781–1846) and Nancy M. Terrill (1781–1826), was born in Boone County, Kentucky, on October 28th, 1811. His father, a Baptist clergyman, had removed from his native Albemarle County, Virginia, to Boone County, Kentucky, in 1810. In 1812 he removed to Great Crossings, near Georgetown, Scott County, where in 1825 he took charge of the Choctaw Academy, a newly organized vocational school

for Indians. During the next sixteen years the academy grew rapidly under Henderson's able management; his son, Robert Terrill Henderson, joined him as a teacher; and in 1841, when the father left the academy, the son continued teaching for several years. In 1842 Robert Terrill Henderson married Cynthia H. Evans, of Crittenden, Kentucky. By 1855 he was living with his wife and two children (Helen and Victor) in New Orleans, where he remained until 1862, when he removed to Atlanta to become agent of the Atlanta Steam Tannery. In 1863 he established his own tannery, which he continued to operate until interrupted by Sherman's approach to Atlanta in June 1864. After the war he returned to New Orleans, where he died in 1866.

HENRY, JOSEPH (1797–1878), physicist, son of William Henry and Ann Alexander, was born in Albany, New York, on December 17th, 1797. After attending the Albany Academy he became professor of mathematics and natural philosophy there in 1826. In 1832 he became professor of natural philosophy at the College of New Jersey (Princeton); fourteen years later, in December 1846, he left Princeton for Washington to become first secretary and director of the Smithsonian Institution, an establishment founded on the bequest of James Smithson, a British subject, "for the increase and diffusion of knowledge among men." Joseph Henry was one of the leading scientific figures of his day. He became a member of the American Philosophical Society in 1835; he was a founder of the American Association for the Advancement of Science in 1849 and its first president; he was an original member of the National Academy of Sciences, its vice-president (1866–1868) and its president (1868–1878). In May 1830 he married Harriet L. Alexander, of Schenectady, New York; four of their six children lived to maturity. He died in Washington on May 13th, 1878, survived by his wife and three daughters. A memorial service in his honor held in the hall of the House of Representatives on January 16th, 1879, was attended by the President and his cabinet, by both houses of Congress, by the justices of the Supreme Court, by the regents of the Smithsonian Institution, and by many distinguished scientists.

HENRY, PATRICK (1736–1799), statesman, son of John Henry and Sarah (Winston) Syme, was born at Studley plantation in Hanover County, Virginia, on May 29th, 1736. After unsuccessfully operating a country store for two years he married, when scarcely eighteen, Sarah Shelton, daughter of John Shelton; five years later, deeply in debt after failures in farming and storekeeping, he undertook the study of law, commenced practice, and enjoyed immediate success. After the death of his first wife he married Dorothea Dandridge, daughter of Nathaniel West Dandridge. He was a member of the colonial house of burgesses (1765); a member of the Continental Congress (1774–1776); and governor of Virginia (1776–1779; 1784–1786). He declined appointment as

United States senator (1794), as secretary of state (1795), as chief justice of the supreme court of the United States (1796), and as United States minister to France (1797). He died at Red Hill, his plantation in Charlotte County, Virginia, on June 6th, 1799, and was buried in Red Hill Cemetery. His revolutionary speeches were fiery and eloquent; he is remembered particularly for his speech on the Stamp Act, delivered before the Virginia legislature in Williamsburg on May 29th, 1765: "Caesar had his Brutus, Charles the First his Cromwell, and George the Third may profit by their example. . . . If this be treason, make the most of it!" His most famous utterance occurred in a speech delivered before the Virginia convention in St. John's Church, Richmond, on March 23rd, 1775: "I know not what course others may take, but as for me, give me liberty or give me death!"

HENTZ, CAROLINE LEE (WHITING) (1800–1856), author, youngest daughter of John Whiting, was born in Lancaster, Massachusetts, on June 1st, 1800. On September 30th, 1824, she became the wife of Nicholas Marcellus Hentz, a native of Metz, France, then teaching in the Round Hill School in Northampton, Massachusetts. After serving four years (1826–1830) as professor at the University of North Carolina he was principal of a girls' school in Covington, Kentucky (1830–1832); in Cincinnati, Ohio (1832–1834); in Florence, Alabama (1834–1843); in Tuscaloosa, Alabama (1843–1845); in Tuskegee, Alabama (1845–1848); and in Columbus, Georgia (1848–1849). His wife assisted him in his teaching, managed her household, reared four children, and engaged in writing. In 1849 Hentz became an invalid; his school was closed, and his wife thereafter supported the family with her pen. A series of novels appeared in rapid succession, among them *The Planter's Northern Bride* (2 vols., 1854), her most ambitious performance. Her tales appeared in several collections, among them *The Victim of Excitement and Other Stories* (1853); *Courtship and Marriage; or, The Joys and Sorrows of American Life* (1856); and *The Banished Son and Other Stories of the Heart* (1856). She also wrote plays: *De Lara; or, The Moorish Bride* (produced in Philadelphia and Boston in 1831); *Constance of Werdenberg* (produced in New York in 1832); *Lamorah; or, The Western Wild* (produced in Cincinnati in 1832). She died of pneumonia in Marianna, Florida, on February 11th, 1856, and was buried in Episcopal Cemetery. Nicholas Marcellus Hentz died the following November and was buried beside his wife.

HILL, BENJAMIN HARVEY (1823–1882), statesman, son of John Hill and Sarah Parham, was born in Hillsboro, Jasper County, Georgia, on September 14th, 1823. After graduating with first honor from Franklin College (Athens) in 1844 he read law and commenced practice in LaGrange in 1845. On November 27th, 1845, he married Caroline Holt, of Athens; there were six children. "Ben" Hill

enjoyed a large and lucrative practice and became one of the best-known lawyers in the state. He was a member of the state house of representatives (1851) and the state senate (1859–1860). Although he opposed secession, he was a member of the state secession convention meeting in Milledgeville in January 1861 and was one of nine delegates elected to represent Georgia at the convention of seceding states meeting in Montgomery, Alabama, in February 1861. During the Civil War he was Confederate States senator (1861–1865). After the war he resumed the practice of law. He was a member of Congress (1875–1877) and United States senator (1877–1882). He died in Atlanta on August 16th, 1882, and was buried in Oakland Cemetery.

HINES, CHARLTON (1785–1864), planter, younger son of James Hines (1750–1799) and Drusilla Lewis, was born in Pitt County, North Carolina, in 1785. In early childhood he accompanied his parents to Effingham County, Georgia, where on April 2nd, 1799, his elder sister, Ann Drusilla Hines (1781–1829), became the third wife of William Way (1750–1808), a planter of Liberty County. Shortly thereafter Charlton Hines followed his sister to Liberty County, where he resided for the rest of his life. He married first (on July 17th, 1806) Mary Quarterman; he married second (on February 9th, 1809) Ann Beard, widow of William F. Bell; he married third (on October 24th, 1855) Sarah Jane Way. Charlton Hines represented Liberty County in the state senate eight times between 1828 and 1843. Hinesville, county seat of Liberty County, was founded during his senatorial term and was named in his honor. He died in Hinesville in February 1864, survived by his third wife and three sons.

HIRSCH, HERMANN (born 1829), Confederate quartermaster, a native of Berlin, Germany, migrated in early manhood to the United States, where for some ten years prior to the Civil War he was connected with various offices of the United States War and Treasury Departments. In 1856 he was stationed in Wilmington, North Carolina; in 1858 he was stationed in Fernandina, Florida. At the outbreak of the Civil War he was living in Savannah, Georgia, engaged as a clerk in the office of the United States Engineers. In May 1861 a meeting of German citizens, of which Hermann Hirsch was president, drew up the following resolution: "Whereas, as inhabitants of the city of Savannah, we owe supreme and unconditional allegiance to the State of Georgia, which has been so happily exempt from every yoke of tyranny, and which has given us prosperous and happy homes; we will cheerfully support this our new government to the fullest extent of our capabilities" (Savannah *Morning News*, May 17th, 1861). On July 19th, 1861, Hermann Hirsch was appointed captain and assistant quartermaster in the Confederate army, with headquarters in Savannah. On May 21st, 1862, he was appointed major and quartermaster, a position he held until the spring of

1865. During the final months of the war he was assigned by General Howell Cobb to duty in Macon, Augusta, and Columbus. After the war he returned to Savannah and took a position with the Atlantic & Gulf Railroad. On November 24th, 1868, his wife, Sarah Hirsch (1835–1868), a native of Glasgow, Scotland, died in Savannah, leaving a husband and three young children. She was buried in Cathedral (Catholic) Cemetery. Three weeks later, on December 12th, 1868, having resigned his railroad position and sold his property in Savannah and Effingham County, Hermann Hirsch left Savannah for his former home in Germany.

HODGE, CHARLES (1797–1878), educator, son of Dr. Hugh Hodge and Mary Blanchard, was born in Philadelphia, Pennsylvania, on December 28th, 1797. He was a younger brother of Dr. Hugh Lenox Hodge (1796–1873). He graduated from the College of New Jersey (Princeton) in 1816 and from Princeton Theological Seminary in 1819. In 1820 he began his lifelong connection with Princeton Theological Seminary; he was instructor in original languages of Scripture (1820–1822); professor of oriental and Biblical literature (1822–1840); professor of exegetical and didactic theology (1840–1854); and professor of exegetical, didactic, and polemical theology (1854–1878). He was moderator of the General Assembly of the Presbyterian Church in 1846. His published works include *A Commentary on the Epistle to the Romans* (1835), *A Constitutional History of the Presbyterian Church in the United States* (1840), and *Systematic Theology* (3 vols., 1871–1873). He also contributed more than a hundred articles to *The Princeton Review*, among them "The State of the Country" (January 1861) and "The Church and the Country" (April 1861), both of which exerted considerable influence both North and South. He died in Princeton on June 19th, 1878. He received the honorary degree of doctor of divinity from Rutgers University in 1834, and the honorary degree of doctor of laws from Washington and Jefferson College in 1864. The Rev. Dr. Charles Colcock Jones studied Hebrew under Dr. Hodge at Princeton Theological Seminary in the summer of 1830; thereafter for many years they were friends and correspondents.

HODGE, HUGH LENOX (1796–1873), physician, son of Dr. Hugh Hodge and Mary Blanchard, was born in Philadelphia, Pennsylvania, on June 27th, 1796. He was an elder brother of the Rev. Dr. Charles Hodge (1797–1878). He graduated from the College of New Jersey (Princeton) in 1815 and from the Medical College of the University of Pennsylvania in 1818. For many years he was a practicing physician in Philadelphia. He was also professor of obstetrics at the Medical College of the University of Pennsylvania (1835–1863) as well as lecturer on the principles of surgery in the Philadelphia Medical Institute. In 1828 he married Margaret E. Aspinwall, daughter of John Aspinwall, a New York merchant;

there were seven sons. He died in Philadelphia on February 26th, 1873. He received the honorary degree of doctor of laws from Princeton University in 1871. From 1850 to 1853 he was the personal physician of the Rev. Dr. Charles Colcock Jones and his family during their residence in Philadelphia. A charming letter written to Mrs. Mary Jones on October 31st, 1855, two years after the family had returned to Georgia, conveys something of his kindness and warmth: "We all know how pleasant it is to be had in remembrance by those whose friendship and good opinion we value. Please, therefore, accept my grateful acknowledgments for your acceptable testimonial that your Philadelphia physician has not been forgotten by you and your family on your return to your Southern home. I am glad to hear good accounts of you and your daughter, and trust that the health of your valued husband will be fully reinstated. I shall endeavor to keep a lookout upon your son, but he is such an enthusiast in science I am afraid he may forget his physical nature. He, however, promises well."

HODGSON, WILLIAM BROWN (1800–1871), oriental scholar, diplomat, and planter, was born in Georgetown, D.C., in 1800. Left fatherless in infancy, he was educated chiefly by the Rev. James Carnahan (1775–1859), president of the College of New Jersey (Princeton) from 1823 to 1854, who taught school in Georgetown from 1814 to 1823 and encouraged young Hodgson's studies in Hebrew and Sanskrit. Sent by the Department of State to the Barbary coast to continue his study of oriental languages, Hodgson served as acting consul in Algiers (1826–1829). He was in Constantinople (1832–1834), Cairo (1834–1836), London (1836–1841), and Tunis (1841–1842). In May 1842 he returned to America and settled in Savannah, Georgia, where he married Margaret Telfair (1795–1874), youngest daughter of Edward Telfair (1735–1807), governor of Georgia (1787; 1790–1793). For the rest of his life he was prominently identified with the cultural interests of Savannah. He was an active member of the Georgia Historical Society and served as curator for twenty-five years (1845–1870). He spoke more than thirty languages and enjoyed an international reputation as an oriental scholar. From the College of New Jersey (Princeton) he received the honorary degree of master of arts (1823) and the honorary degree of doctor of laws (1858). He died in New York City on June 26th, 1871, and was buried in Bonaventure Cemetery, Savannah. Hodgson Hall, present home of the Georgia Historical Society in Savannah, was given to the society by Hodgson's widow as a memorial to her husband. It was commenced in 1873 at the expense of Margaret (Telfair) Hodgson; after her death on March 2nd, 1874, it was continued at the expense of her sister, Mary Telfair; after her death on June 2nd, 1875, it was completed in 1875 and dedicated on February 14th, 1876. On April 1st, 1857, the Savannah *Re-*

publican announced that "William B. Hodgson, our public-spirited fellow citizen, has presented to the Savannah Medical College a collection of specimens from the mineral and floral kingdom." The same issue reprinted Hodgson's letter accompanying the gift: "I now beg to offer for your acceptance a collection of three thousand specimens in mineralogy, and one hundred herbariums, or books of dried plants and flowers. It is a just expectation and hope that the alumni of your school, and the lovers of science in Georgia and other states, will enlarge and enrich this collection by contributing from the teeming wealth of our floral and animal kingdoms. . . . These collections were made, and classified with Latin and German nomenclature, by an eminent naturalist of a German university."

HOGARTH, WILLIAM (1697–1764), English painter and engraver, only son of Richard Hogarth, a schoolmaster, was born in London on November 10th, 1697. After serving an apprenticeship with an engraver of arms on silver plate he set up for himself in 1720, and throughout a long career he produced such brilliant engravings as *A Harlot's Progress* (1732), *A Rake's Progress* (1735), and *Marriage à la Mode* (1743), all derived from original oil paintings, in which his genius for social satire found definitive expression in sets of pictures arranged as scenes in a play. He also painted a number of small portrait groups known as conversation pieces. His finest canvases include a scene from *The Beggar's Opera* (1728), "The Graham Children" (1742), and "The Lady's Last Stake" (1759). In 1729 he married Jane Thornhill, daughter of Sir James Thornhill, whose art school in St. Martin's Lane passed to Hogarth after Thornhill's death in 1734. Meanwhile, in 1733, Hogarth had purchased a house in Leicester Square, which he occupied for the rest of his life. In 1749 he retired to his villa in Chiswick to write his *Analysis of Beauty* (1753), in which he maintained that the three-dimensional serpentine "line of beauty" was the fundamental principle of beauty and grace. He was the first English-born artist to enjoy international reputation, and he exerted an incalculable influence on subsequent generations of artists. He died at his residence in Leicester Square on October 26th, 1764, and was buried in Chiswick.

HOLCOMBE, THOMAS (1815–1885), wholesale grocer, son of Robert Lynn Holcombe and Elizabeth Witter, was born in Beaufort District, South Carolina, on July 27th, 1815. He was a grandson of the Rev. Thomas Holcombe (1762–1824), distinguished Baptist clergyman. In early childhood he accompanied his parents to St. Marys, Georgia, and at the age of eighteen he settled in Savannah, where for more than half a century he engaged in the wholesale grocery business, his firm being successively known as Huntingdon & Holcombe; Crane & Holcombe; Holcombe, Johnson & Company; Holcombe, Hull & Company; Holcombe, Grady & Company. He served several terms as alderman of Savannah, and in 1862 he was elected mayor. His first wife, Eliza Gale (1815–1853), died in Savannah on December 7th, 1853, leaving six young children. On December 19th, 1854, he married Frances Elizabeth Wellborn (1833–1918), of Barbour County, Alabama; there were six daughters and two sons. His eldest son by his first marriage, Josiah Law Holcombe (1838–1864), private in the 8th Regiment Georgia Infantry and later sharpshooter in the 1st Battalion Georgia Cavalry, was killed in the battle of Jonesboro, Georgia, on August 30th, 1864. His two eldest daughters by his second marriage—the "two interesting little children" whom the Rev. R. Q. Mallard observed at the railroad depot in Savannah on May 12th, 1859—were Julia Roxana Holcombe (born December 12th, 1855), who married (on March 16th, 1876) George Meriwether Bacon; and Matilda Bethune Holcombe (born February 5th, 1858), who married (on April 11th, 1876) William M. Edwardy. Thomas Holcombe died at the home of his daughter Julia in Baconton, Mitchell County, Georgia, on December 29th, 1885, and was buried beside his first wife in Laurel Grove Cemetery, Savannah. His second wife, who survived him thirty-three years, died on November 11th, 1918, and was buried in Albany, Georgia.

HOOD, ARTHUR (1827–1886), lawyer and Confederate soldier, was born in Tennessee in 1827. In early manhood he lived for several years in Washington, D.C., where he served briefly as private secretary to Howell Cobb, congressman from Georgia, and in 1848 commenced the practice of law. In 1851 he married Sarah Claire Johnson (1827–1891), of Maryland. Removing to Georgia in 1852, he settled in Cuthbert, where he practiced his profession until the outbreak of the Civil War and became a prominent member of the Constitutional Union party in the state. He attended the state secession convention meeting in Milledgeville in January 1861, and as presidential elector cast the first vote of Georgia for Jefferson Davis. On March 4th, 1862, he entered Confederate service as first lieutenant in the 2nd Regiment Georgia Cavalry; for six months he served as lieutenant colonel. In April 1863 he was appointed judge advocate of the military courts of the Department of South Carolina, Georgia, and Florida. Eight months later he had organized the 29th Battalion Georgia Cavalry, and in December 1863 was appointed lieutenant colonel. During the summer, autumn, and winter of 1864 he commanded the district comprising McIntosh, Liberty, and Screven Counties, Georgia. In December 1864 his men were stationed in Liberty County at Sunbury, Dorchester, Riceboro, and Depot No. 3 (McIntosh Station), where, according to Union officer E. H. Murray, colonel of the 3rd Regiment Kentucky Cavalry, Hood was "greatly discomfited" by the presence of the enemy; his men "were totally demoralized and fled, reckless of organization, to the Altamaha bridge, whenever attacked." After the war Hood resumed his practice in Cuthbert and became one of the leading lawyers in the state. He died in Cuthbert after a lingering illness on April 10th, 1886, survived by his wife, and was buried in Greenwood Cemetery. Sarah Claire (Johnson) Hood died on July 27th, 1891, and was buried beside her husband.

HOOD, JOHN BELL (1831–1879), Confederate soldier, fifth child of Dr. John W. Hood and Theodocia French, was born in Owingsville, Bath County, Kentucky, on June 1st, 1831. After graduating from the United States Military Academy in 1853 he served with the 4th Infantry in California and with the 2nd Cavalry in Texas. In April 1861 he resigned his commission and joined the Confederate army as first lieutenant. On March 2nd, 1862, he became brigadier general, with command of the "Texas Brigade," and fought brilliantly at Gaines's Mill, Second Manassas, and Sharpsburg. On October 11th, 1862, he was promoted to major general. At Fredericksburg he commanded the first division of Longstreet's corps; he was not killed, as Charles Colcock Jones, Jr., mistakenly reported on December 15th, 1862. At Gettysburg he was badly wounded in the arm, but he recovered in time to distinguish himself at Chickamauga. During the following winter he served in Northwest Georgia under Johnston, whom he replaced before Atlanta on July 17th, 1864. Seizing the offensive, Hood struck unsuccessfully against Sherman and was forced to retire late in July to Atlanta, whence he was again forced to retire on September 1st. In October he moved into Tennessee, where he was defeated at Franklin (November 30th) and Nashville (December 15th–16th). Accepting full responsibility for his failure, he asked to be relieved and on January 23rd, 1865, bade his troops farewell. After the war he engaged unsuccessfully in the cotton business in New Orleans. In 1868 he married Anna Maria Hennen. His wife died of yellow fever on August 24th, 1879, and he died of the same disease six days later, on August 30th, 1879, leaving ten orphaned children. As Mrs. Mary S. Mallard wrote from New Orleans on September 17th, 1879, "It seemed so sad that when there were so few cases General and Mrs. Hood should have been among the number. The public seem to be responding to the call in behalf of his infants—ten, the eldest nine. . . . There have been offers from various sections to adopt one or more of the children, but I hear their personal friends will make an effort to raise them all together. It would be a pity to separate them."

HOOK, CORNELIUS (1837–1864), Union soldier, son of Cornelius Hook and Ann W. Spencer, was born in Jacksonville, Illinois, in 1837. After graduating from the United States Military Academy in 1860 he served as second lieutenant in the garrison at Fort Monroe, Virginia, until January 8th, 1861, when he was granted sick leave of absence in Florida; early in May 1861, returning North through Savannah, Georgia, he and his friend Thomas Edwin Miller (1833–1864) were detained briefly for questioning by Charles Colcock Jones, Jr., mayor of Savannah, and then permitted to continue their journey. On May 14th, 1861, he was promoted to first lieutenant in the Union army; he served on Burnside's expedition to North Carolina as acting assistant adjutant general (October 1861–March 1862). After another sick leave of absence (April 1862–November 1862) he served in the Department of North Carolina (November 1862–June 1863) and in the District of Key West, Florida (June 1863–November 1863). He retired from active service on November 4th, 1863; three weeks later, on November 24th, 1863, he married Eliza Warren (1838–1920), of Cold Spring, Putnam County, New York. There were no children. He died of yellow fever in Key West, Florida, on June 19th, 1864.

HOPE, SIR JAMES (1808–1881), British admiral, son of Rear-Admiral Sir George Johnstone Hope, K.C.B. (1767–1818) and first cousin of Admiral Sir Henry Hope, K.C.B. (1787–1863), was born on March 3rd, 1808. He attended the Royal Naval College (1820–1822) and rose to lieutenant (March 9th, 1827), commander (February 26th, 1830), and rear-admiral (November 19th, 1857). In March 1859 he was appointed commander in chief in China. On June 17th, 1859, he anchored his flagship, the *Chesapeake,* in the Gulf of Pecheli and proceeded in a gunboat to the mouth of the Peiho River to inform the Chinese authorities of the approach of the British and French ambassadors; he found the passage of the river formidably blocked. On June 19th the British and French ambassadors arrived off the bar of the Peiho and requested Hope to force a passage. On June 25th, with eleven gunboats and eleven hundred men, he undertook to do so; one gunboat, the *Plover,* carrying the British flag, was sunk; Hope was twice severely wounded and was transferred to the *Cormorant,* where his flag was again hoisted; the *Cormorant* was subsequently sunk, together with the *Lee;* and the rest of his ships were seriously damaged. Hope's effort to force a passage was regarded as a tactical error, but his gallantry roused great enthusiasm in England. In 1863 he was appointed commander in chief in North America and the West Indies, and in 1867 he returned to England. He became vice-admiral (September 26th, 1864) and admiral (January 21st, 1870); and after his retirement in March 1878 he became honorary admiral of the fleet (June 15th, 1879). He died in Linlithgowshire on June 9th, 1881.

HOPKINS, CHARLES HORRIE (1812–1886), lawyer and planter, son of Francis Hopkins (1772–1821) and Rebecca Sayre (1776–1850), was born at Belleville, his father's plantation in McIntosh County, Georgia, on July 6th, 1812. His father, a native of Bluffton, South Carolina, had migrated to Sapelo Island, McIntosh County, Georgia, in 1805 and removed to Belleville, a plantation on the mainland facing the Sapelo River, in 1808. He represented McIntosh County six terms in the state legislature (1808–1813); he was a major in the War of 1812 and a major general of state troops in the Indian Wars. Charles Horrie Hopkins was identified with the interests of McIntosh County for most of his life. He was a large planter; in the Federal Census of 1860 he was recorded as the owner of 106 slaves. He represented McIntosh County in the state house of representatives (1838) and in the state senate (1839). He was several times mayor of Darien. In 1836 he became major in the 2nd Georgia Regiment; in 1838 he became colonel of the 1st Georgia Regiment. He opposed secession, and at the outbreak of the Civil War he aroused considerable hostility when he resigned his military command to make speeches for the preservation of the Union. In November 1862 his house at Belleville was demolished by a Federal gunboat in the Sapelo River; he and his family removed to a neighboring plantation, the Meadows. Shortly after the war he sold Belleville to the Rev. Tunis Gulic Campbell, a Negro clergyman from the North, who established there a colony of freedmen. Hopkins represented Pierce County in the state legislature (1865) and served as delegate to the reconstruction convention (1867–1868). Returning to McIntosh County, he continued to practice law and was for some years county ordinary and assessor of internal revenue. On May 1st, 1834, he married Mary Givens, of Beaufort, South Carolina; there were ten children. He died at the Meadows on November 29th, 1886.

HOPKINS, OCTAVIUS CAESAR (1819–1881), planter, youngest living son of Francis Hopkins (1772–1821) and Rebecca Sayre (1776–1850), was born at Belleville, his father's plantation in McIntosh County, Georgia, on July 9th, 1819. His father, a native of Bluffton, South Carolina, had migrated to Sapelo Island, McIntosh County, Georgia, in 1805 and removed to Belleville, a plantation on the mainland facing the Sapelo River, in 1808. He represented McIntosh County six terms in the state legislature (1808–1813); he was a major in the War of 1812 and a major general of state troops in the Indian Wars. Octavius Caesar Hopkins was identified with the interests of McIntosh County all his life. He was lieutenant of the McIntosh Dragoons (1850) and captain (1853); he was justice of the inferior court for many years; he represented McIntosh County in the state legislature (1859–1860). On April 3rd, 1861, after a protracted courtship, he married Elizabeth Aurelia King (1824–1892), younger daughter of Reuben King (1779–1867) and Abigail Austin (1783–1863), of Mallow plantation, McIntosh County; there were five children. During the Civil War he was captain of the McIntosh Cavalry (Company K, 5th Regiment Georgia Cavalry). He died at Baisden's Bluff, McIntosh County, on March

12th, 1881, survived by his wife and four children, and was buried near his parents in the Hopkins family cemetery at Belleville. His daughter, Abigail Rebecca Hopkins, recalled that her father "inherited his father's splendid physique—tall, broad-shouldered, straight as an arrow: no waste flesh. He was lovable and sweet, and children loved him instinctively."

HOWARD, CHESSLEY BOSTWICK (1829–1904), cotton planter, son of John H. Howard and Caroline Bostwick, was born near Milledgeville, Georgia, on July 30th, 1829. In early childhood he accompanied his parents to Columbus, Georgia, where he spent his boyhood years. After attending Franklin College (Athens) and the College of New Jersey (Princeton) he studied law and was admitted to the bar, but he preferred planting and never practiced his profession. Prior to the Civil War he managed a large plantation on the Flint River in Taylor County, Georgia. On July 18th, 1860, he married Caroline Matilda Elizabeth Shackelford (1835–1927), daughter of Francis Robert Shackelford (1801–1887) and his first wife, Caroline Seymour Dunwody (1816–1838), of McIntosh County, Georgia. During the Civil War he and his family resided in Taylor County; on August 15th, 1863, he enlisted as a corporal in Captain Chapman's Company Georgia Infantry, a unit organized for local defense. After the war he resided briefly in Columbus; following a business failure in New York City he returned in 1870 to Taylor County, where, according to the Rev. John Jones (September 3rd, 1870), he and his family were "very much reduced, and living in the country without church or school." In 1876 he settled in Kirkwood, near Atlanta. He died in Atlanta of pneumonia on January 10th, 1904, only one day after the death of his boyhood companion and lifelong friend, General John Brown Gordon (1832–1904). He was buried in Westview Cemetery. Caroline (Shackelford) Howard died in Atlanta on June 30th, 1927, and was buried beside her husband. According to the Atlanta *Constitution* (January 11th, 1904), "Mr. Howard was one of the most prominent and best-known figures throughout the Empire State of the South. . . . During the Reconstruction period Howard never concealed his opinion of the methods of the carpetbaggers; he became a potent factor in politics, although he never aspired to any political office himself. . . . If there ever was a man who had the courage of his convictions, it was Ches Howard."

HOWARD, JOHN GORDON (1817–1866), physician and planter, son of Benjamin Howard (1792–1820) and Elizabeth Ann Gordon, was born in Savannah, Georgia, on October 10th, 1817. After attending Franklin College (Athens) with the class of 1838 he studied medicine in Paris. Returning to Savannah, he practiced his profession until the outbreak of the Civil War. In 1852 he was one of eight founders of the Savannah Medical College, and he was for seven years (1852–1859) its professor of anatomy; on July 1st, 1856, he was announced as "dean of the faculty." He was elected first chairman of the Savannah Board of Health at its organization in May 1853. He was also a member of the Georgia Medical Society. He married first (on January 2nd, 1843) Margaret Herb Reed (1823–1856), daughter of Elias Reed, of Savannah. After her death on April 10th, 1856, he married second (on April 19th, 1858), Julia Amanda Whitehead (1831–1896), daughter of John Whitehead (1783–1857) and his second wife, Julia Maria (Berrien) Belt (1801–1857), of Bath, Richmond County, Georgia. Julia Amanda Whitehead was a sister of John Randolph Whitehead (1829–1877); Philoclea Edgeworth Whitehead (1833–1892), wife of Thomas William Neely; Charles Lowndes Whitehead (1835–1866); Ruth Berrien Whitehead (1837–1861), first wife of Charles Colcock Jones, Jr.; and Valeria Burroughs Whitehead (1840–1904), wife of Augustus Ramon Salas; she was a half-sister of Eliza Alice Whitehead (1818–1896), wife of Dr. Charles William West. John Gordon Howard had large planting interests in Burke County. On December 23rd, 1862, he was commissioned surgeon of the 63rd Regiment Georgia Infantry, with rank of major; on September 18th, 1864, he was declared unfit for field service and relieved from duty. Two months later he was placed in charge of the "ophthalmic hospital" in Americus, Georgia. After the war he resumed practice in Savannah, with special attention to diseases of the eye. He died suddenly in Savannah on June 26th, 1866, survived by his wife and four children, and was buried in Laurel Grove Cemetery. Julia Amanda (Whitehead) Howard died in Brooklyn, New York, on June 28th, 1896, and was buried beside her husband.

HOWE, GEORGE (1802–1883), Presbyterian clergyman and educator, son of William Howe and Mary Gould, was born in Dedham, Massachusetts, on November 6th, 1802. After graduating from Middlebury College in 1822 and from Andover Theological Seminary in 1825 he was professor of theology at Dartmouth College (1827–1830). In 1830, fearing consumption, he removed to Columbia, South Carolina, where he was professor of oriental literature and Biblical criticism at Columbia Theological Seminary from 1831 until his death. He married first (on August 25th, 1831) Mary Bushnell (1808–1832), daughter of the Rev. Jedediah Bushnell, of Cornwall, Vermont. He married second (on December 19th, 1836) Sarah Ann Walthour (1803–1885), daughter of Andrew Walthour, of Walthourville, Georgia, and widow of Dr. Robert C. McConnell (1788–1826). Four of their six children lived to maturity: Walthour Howe (1840–1859), William Howe (1842–1862), Sarah Emily Howe (1843–1890), and George Howe (1848–1895). In 1865 he was moderator of the General Assembly of the Southern Presbyterian Church. His *History of the Presbyterian Church in South Carolina* (2 vols., 1870–1883) is scholarly and authoritative. He received the honorary degree of doctor of divinity from the University of North Carolina in 1833, and the honorary degree of doctor of laws from Oglethorpe University in 1871. He died in Columbia on April 15th, 1883, survived by his wife and two children, and was buried in the First Presbyterian Churchyard. Sarah Ann (Walthour) Howe died on April 14th, 1885, and was buried beside her husband. The family of the Rev. Dr. George Howe and the family of the Rev. Dr. Charles Colcock Jones were intimately associated from Dr. Jones's first residence in Columbia early in 1837; the Howe children called Mrs. Jones "Aunty Jones," and the Jones children called Mrs. Howe "Aunt Howe."

HOWE, GEORGE (1848–1895), physician, youngest son of the Rev. Dr. George Howe (1802–1883) and his second wife, Sarah Ann Walthour (1803–1885), widow of Dr. Robert C. McConnell, was born in South Carolina, on January 29th, 1848. After graduating from the University of South Carolina in 1869 and from the Medical Department of the University of South Carolina in 1870 he studied for one year in the Medical Department of the University of Louisiana. Returning to Columbia, he commenced the practice of medicine, with special attention to diseases of the eye. In 1873 he married Annie Josephine Wilson (1854–1916), daughter of the Rev. Dr. Joseph Ruggles Wilson, a Presbyterian clergyman, and sister of Thomas Woodrow Wilson, twenty-eighth president of the United States. He died in Columbia on April 20th, 1895, survived by his wife and three children, and was buried in the First Presbyterian Churchyard.

HOWE, SARAH ANN (WALTHOUR) (McCONNELL) (1803–1885): *Mrs. George Howe,* daughter of Andrew Walthour (1750–1824) and his first wife, Ann Hoffmire, was born in Liberty County, Georgia, on October 5th, 1803. She was a younger sister of George Washington Walthour (1799–1859). After attending a seminary for young ladies in Charleston, South Carolina (1818–1819) she returned to Liberty County, where in 1821 she became the wife of Dr. Robert C. McConnell (1788–1826). Her husband, a native of Williamsburg District, South Carolina, had settled in Liberty County in 1812 and had represented the county in the state senate for three consecutive years (1819–1821). There were two children: Mary Augusta McConnell (1822–1888), who became the wife of the Rev. Dr. Benjamin Morgan Palmer on October 7th, 1841; and James Blakely McConnell (1825–1836), who drowned in the Connecticut River near Hartford on May 28th, 1836. After her husband's death on May 24th, 1826, Sarah Ann (Walthour) McConnell continued to reside in Liberty County, where she was an intimate friend of the Rev. Dr. and Mrs. Charles Colcock Jones; it was in her house in Walthourville that their second son, Joseph Jones, was born on September 6th,

1833. On December 19th, 1836, she became the second wife of the Rev. Dr. George Howe (1802–1883), of Columbia, South Carolina, son of William Howe and Mary Gould. Four of their six children lived to maturity: Walthour Howe (1840–1859), William Howe (1842–1862), Sarah Emily Howe (1843–1890), and George Howe (1848–1895). Her husband died in Columbia on April 15th, 1883, after a distinguished career as clergyman, educator, and author. She died two years later, on April 14th, 1885, and was buried beside her husband in the First Presbyterian Churchyard.

HOWE, SARAH EMILY (1843–1890), daughter of the Rev. Dr. George Howe (1802–1883) and his second wife, Sarah Ann Walthour (1803–1885), widow of Dr. Robert C. McConnell, was born in Columbia, South Carolina, on December 30th, 1843. On June 24th, 1863, she became the wife of the Rev. Edward Melvin Green (1838–1927), a Presbyterian clergyman, son of James G. Green and Sarah Ann James, and a graduate of Oglethorpe University (1859) and Columbia Theological Seminary (1863). She died in Danville, Kentucky, where her husband was then pastor, on November 13th, 1890, and was buried near her parents in the First Presbyterian Churchyard, Columbia. In 1896 her husband married Mrs. Frances Wallace Anderson, of Atlanta, Georgia; he died in Danville, Kentucky, on September 20th, 1927, survived by his second wife.

HOWE, WALTHOUR (1840–1859), son of the Rev. Dr. George Howe (1802–1883) and his second wife, Sarah Ann Walthour (1803–1885), widow of Dr. Robert C. McConnell, was born in Columbia, South Carolina, in February 1840. In the autumn of 1855, having "for several years past been subject to fits," he was taken from school and placed on the farm of the Rev. Lyman Matthews, husband of Dr. Howe's sister Rachel, near Middlebury, Vermont. A year later he became "completely deranged" and was confined in an "asylum" in Philadelphia. On December 9th, 1858, Mary Eliza Robarts, visiting the Howes in Columbia, wrote that "He seems to become more and more imbecile, but is quiet and docile." He died in Philadelphia on November 11th, 1859, and was buried in the First Presbyterian Churchyard, Columbia.

HOWE, WILLIAM (1842–1862), Confederate soldier, son of the Rev. Dr. George Howe (1802–1883) and his second wife, Sarah Ann Walthour (1803–1885), widow of Dr. Robert C. McConnell, was born in Columbia, South Carolina, in January 1842. On December 9th, 1858, Mary Eliza Robarts, visiting the Howes in Columbia, observed that "He seems to be a studious, smart boy, and will, I hope, be a credit and comfort to his parents." At the outbreak of the Civil War he was a student at the South Carolina College. On April 8th, 1861, he enlisted as a private in the Columbia Grays (Company C, 2nd Regiment South Carolina Infantry); after seeing service around Charleston he accompanied his unit to Virginia and fought at First Manassas. He was subsequently made orderly sergeant. He died of "typhoid pneumonia" at Camp Camden, near Centreville, Virginia, on February 2nd, 1862, and was buried in the First Presbyterian Churchyard, Columbia. Two weeks later, on February 18th, 1862, Mrs. Mary S. Mallard described to her mother "a most touching letter from Dr. Howe in reference to Willie's death. He reached him the Thursday previous to his death, which occurred on Sabbath night. He found him on his narrow cot in his tent, but so altered by sickness that he did not at first recognize him —though at that time he was considered better, and hopes were entertained of his recovery. But on Saturday evening he was taken with hemorrhage of the bowels and then sank rapidly. . . . The doctor says his comrades bore the highest testimony to his character, and they told him the captain was in the habit of saying: 'Willie Howe did not know how to do wrong.' I learned from the Walthours that Dr. Howe brought Willie's remains and his mother saw him after they reached Columbia. It is a terrible affliction, and oh, how many such there are and will be as long as this horrid war lasts!"

HOYT, NATHAN (1793–1866), Presbyterian clergyman, was born in Gilmanton, New Hampshire, on February 27th, 1793. He studied theology privately and never attended college. On September 14th, 1826, he married Margaret Bliss, of Springfield, Massachusetts. Shortly thereafter he removed to Georgia, where, having served briefly as pastor in Washington, Wilkes County, he was pastor in Athens for thirty-six years (1830–1866). He died there on July 12th, 1866, and was buried in Oconee Hill Cemetery. His epitaph reads: "They that turn many to righteousness shall shine as the stars forever and ever." According to the Atlanta *Daily Intelligencer* (July 17th, 1866), "Dr. Hoyt has long been classed among the leading divines of the South, and as an effective pulpit orator he had few equals. . . . He was the pride and idol of his congregation, and universally respected for his piety and fine abilities." On December 6th, 1831, the Rev. Dr. Charles Colcock Jones recorded a somewhat different view: "Heard Mr. Hoyt of Athens. His sermon was on the whole fair: nothing extraordinary; some things striking. His manner a little peculiar." Two of Dr. Hoyt's sons became Presbyterian clergymen: Henry Hoyt and Thomas A. Hoyt; his daughter, Margaret Jane Hoyt, became the wife of a Presbyterian clergyman, the Rev. Samuel Edward Axson.

HUFF, SAMUEL POINDEXTER (1828–1896), Baptist clergyman, was born in Botetourt County, Virginia, on June 4th, 1828. He was one of eleven children, and he had to struggle to prepare himself for the ministry. He attended the Roanoke Academy, the Western Theological Seminary, and the University of Virginia. In August 1865 he married Bettie

A. Jurey, of Charlottesville. For more than thirty years he devoted himself to the rural churches of the Valley of Virginia; he accomplished much of his best work in Albemarle and Nelson Counties, residing in Batesville and serving as pastor of the churches in Hebron and Mount Ed from 1862 to 1887. After three years as pastor of the Second Baptist Church, Petersburg (1889–1892), he undertook his final charge in Westmoreland and Richmond Counties. He died in Baltimore at the home of his son, Slaughter W. Huff, on January 13th, 1896, and was buried in Culpeper, Virginia. According to L. Peyton Little, "He was a fine specimen of robust and well-proportioned manhood, and his mind resembled his body in its sturdy qualities. Naturally of an argumentative disposition, firm and unyielding in his convictions, he fastened powerfully upon the Scriptures as containing the only way of refuge and salvation for the soul" [*Virginia Baptist Ministers,* 4th Series, ed. George Braxton Taylor (Lynchburg, Virginia, 1913), pp. 287–288].

HUGHES, THOMAS (1789–1862), planter, was born in Virginia on July 20th, 1789. In early manhood he migrated to Fayette County, Kentucky, where he resided for the rest of his life. He was a prosperous planter. His first wife, Julia Ann Hughes (1805–1846), died on March 18th, 1846, leaving four young children; on December 17th, 1852, he married Sarah Rossiter (1811–1870), widow of Hamilton Atchison, and mother of Isabella Atchison, wife of James Nephew West. Thomas Hughes died in Fayette County on March 18th, 1862, and was buried beside his first wife in Lexington Cemetery. Sarah (Rossiter) (Atchison) Hughes died on March 8th, 1870, and was buried beside her first husband in Lexington Cemetery.

HUGHES, WILLIAM (1793–1880), planter and surveyor, son of George Hughes and Elizabeth Osgood, widow of Jonathan Scarth, was born near Sunbury, Liberty County, Georgia, on November 24th, 1793. He was educated by the Rev. Dr. William McWhir at the Sunbury Academy. In 1819 he married Letitia Lane (1800–1883), of Burke County, Georgia. He was a distinguished civil engineer; for half a century he was county surveyor of Liberty County. He resided on a plantation in upper Liberty County near Johnston's Station, where he operated his own still and made his own wine. He died in Liberty County on April 3rd, 1880, survived by his wife and numerous children, grandchildren, and great-grandchildren, and was buried in the family cemetery.

HUGHES, WILLIAM (1820–1887), planter and surveyor, son of William Hughes (1793–1880) and Letitia Lane (1800–1883), was born in Liberty County, Georgia, on September 21st, 1820. At an early age, under his father's instruction, he became a skillful surveyor. On September 16th, 1847, he married Miriam S. Martin (1826–1910), of Liberty County. For many years he was prominent in county politics and represented Liberty

County at numerous district, congressional, and state conventions. Prior to the Civil War he represented Liberty County twice in the state legislature. He joined the Liberty Independent Troop in 1842. In 1857 he was elected captain of the Liberty Guards; throughout the Civil War this company served with distinction as Company D, 5th Regiment Georgia Cavalry. On June 20th, 1864, at the bloody battle of Noonday Church, Georgia, his horse was shot from under him and his leg was badly crushed. He was paroled at Hillsboro, North Carolina, on May 3rd, 1865. In 1872 the Liberty Guards was reorganized under its former commander, who continued as captain for the rest of his life. As Henry Hart Jones wrote in 1886, "It is needless to say that he is almost worshiped by his men, and retains in a remarkable degree the vigor and energy of youth." He died on the Hughes plantation near Johnston's Station, Liberty County, on November 24th, 1887, survived by his wife and numerous children, and was buried in the Hughes family cemetery. His younger brother, the Rev. Andrew Jackson Hughes (1835–1887), a Baptist clergyman and a schoolteacher, died two days later, on November 26th, 1887.

HULL, ASBURY (1797–1866), lawyer, legislator, and planter, son of Hope Hull and Frances Wingfield, was born in Washington, Wilkes County, Georgia, on January 30th, 1797. His father has been called "the father of Methodism in Georgia"; a native Virginian, he settled in Wilkes County, Georgia, organized the Washington Academy, and taught there until 1803, when he removed to Athens and became an active trustee of the University of Georgia, then in its infancy. Asbury Hull graduated from Franklin College (Athens) in 1814. For forty-seven years (1819–1866) he was secretary and treasurer of the University of Georgia; he was also for many years a trustee. He served in the state legislature as both speaker of the house and president of the senate; he was a member of the state secession convention meeting in Milledgeville in January 1861. He was first president of the Southern Mutual Insurance Company. He married first (in 1819) Lucy Harvie, of Virginia; after her death on May 4th, 1859, he married second (in 1861) Mrs. Maria Cook. He died in Athens on January 25th, 1866, and was buried beside his first wife in Oconee Hill Cemetery. As the Athens *Southern Watchman* (January 31st, 1866) observed, "The deceased was distinguished for strong common sense, conservatism, and above all for unbending integrity, lofty patriotism, and unaffected piety."

HULL, GEORGE GILMER (1829–1885), civil engineer, son of Asbury Hull (1797–1866) and Lucy Harvie (1798–1859), was born in Athens, Georgia, on January 25th, 1829. He graduated from Franklin College (Athens) in 1847 and became a civil engineer. After working several years with Edgar Thompson on the Pennsylvania Central Railroad he returned to Georgia, where he was chief engineer of the Western & Atlantic Railroad in 1855. From 1859 to 1866 he was superintendent of the Atlanta & West Point Railroad, with offices in Atlanta. In 1861 he served for some months as volunteer engineer with General Alexander Robert Lawton in Savannah; returning to Atlanta, he organized (on August 3rd, 1863) Captain Gilmer's Company Georgia Infantry, composed of officers and employees of the Atlanta & West Point Railroad, and reserved for local defense. In 1866 he removed to New York, where he engaged in the railroad supply business until his death. On December 7th, 1854, he married Mary Clifford Alexander (1830–1914), daughter of Adam Leopold Alexander (1803–1882) and his first wife, Sarah Hillhouse Gilbert (1805–1855), of Washington, Wilkes County, Georgia. He died in New York City on April 24th, 1885, survived by his wife and two daughters, and was buried in Laurel Grove Cemetery, Savannah. Mary Clifford (Alexander) Hull died in Savannah on April 22nd, 1914, and was buried beside her husband.

HUMBOLDT, FRIEDRICH HEINRICH ALEXANDER, Baron von (1769–1859), naturalist, son of a Prussian nobleman, was born in Berlin, Germany, on September 14th, 1769. He attended the University of Göttingen and the mining academy of Freiburg. He exerted considerable influence on educational and scientific affairs in Europe; at a time when the sciences tended toward specialization he was tending toward universalism. In his *Kosmos* (5 vols., 1845–1862) he sought to present both a graphic description and an imaginative conception of the physical world. He is best known for his work on the oceanic current off the west coast of South America which bears his name. He died in Berlin on May 6th, 1859, and received a state funeral.

HUNT, WALTER (1796–1859), inventor and sewing machine manufacturer, was born in Martinsburg, New York, on July 29th, 1796. From boyhood he was clever and industrious, and his career was marked by numerous inventions, among them an alarm gong for police stations and telegraph offices (1827), a knife sharpener (1829), a fountain pen (1847), and a safety pin (1849). His most important invention was a lock-stitch sewing machine (1834), for which he received practically nothing either in money or in glory because he neglected to obtain a patent. Hunt preceded Elias Howe (1819–1867), who is usually credited with inventing the lock-stitch sewing machine, by twelve years. Later, in association with George A. Arrowsmith, a blacksmith of Woodbridge, New Jersey, Hunt built a few sewing machines; but Arrowsmith, after purchasing Hunt's invention, became otherwise engaged and refused to permit anyone else to exploit Hunt's machine. In 1814 Hunt married Polly Anne Locks; there were four children. He died in New York City on June 8th, 1859.

HUNTER, DAVID (1802–1886), Union soldier, son of the Rev. Andrew Hunter and his second wife, Mary Stockton, was born in Washington, D.C., on July 21st, 1802. After graduating from the United States Military Academy in 1822 he served in the army for fourteen years; in 1836 he resigned and settled in Chicago, where he engaged in business with John H. Kinzie, brother of his wife, Maria Indiana Kinzie. In 1842 he reentered the army as paymaster, with rank of major, and served in the Mexican War. In May 1861 he was appointed brigadier general of volunteers and placed in command of the 2nd Division of McDowell's army. He was severely wounded at First Manassas. In November 1861 he was placed in command of the Department of the West; in March 1862 he was placed in command of the Department of the South. After reducing Fort Pulaski on April 11th, 1862, he issued an order liberating all slaves in Federal hands, followed on May 9th, 1862, by an order liberating all slaves in the Department of the South. On May 19th, 1862, President Lincoln annulled the order, concluding that it exceeded the general's authority. From 1862 to the end of the war Hunter was frequently engaged in court-martial duty. In 1866 he retired from active service, having been brevetted brigadier general and major general for distinguished conduct during the war. For the next twenty years he resided in Washington, where he died on February 2nd, 1886.

HUNTER, ROBERT MERCER TALIAFERRO (1809–1887), statesman, son of James Hunter and Maria Garnett, was born in Essex County, Virginia, on April 21st, 1809. After graduating from the University of Virginia in 1828 he read law in the office of the Hon. Henry St. George Tucker, of Winchester, Virginia, and commenced practice in Lloyds, Virginia, in 1830. On October 4th, 1836, he married Mary Evelina Dandridge, who bore him eight children. He was a member of the state house of delegates (1833), the state senate (1835–1837), Congress (1837–1843; 1845–1847), and the United States Senate (1847–1861). He declined the position of secretary of state under Presidents Franklin Pierce and James Buchanan. During the Civil War he succeeded Robert Toombs as Confederate secretary of state (July 25th, 1861, to February 18th, 1862) and later served in the Confederate States Senate (1862–1865). On February 3rd, 1865, he was one of three commissioners (with John A. Campbell and Alexander H. Stephens) representing the Confederacy at the Hampton Roads Conference; they returned to Richmond without the armistice they desired. After the war Hunter was treasurer of Virginia (1874–1880) and collector of the port of Tappahannock, Virginia (1885–1887). He died at Fonthill, his estate near Lloyds, Virginia, on July 18th, 1887, and was buried at Elmwood, the family cemetery near Loretto, Virginia.

HURTEL, ALPHONSE (1826–1877), lawyer, merchant, and Confederate soldier, son of John Hurtel (1797–1869), was born in Mobile, Alabama, in 1826. His father, a native of New York, had migrated to Alabama in early manhood and settled in Mobile, where he was for many years a successful merchant, affectionately known by old and young as "Uncle John"; he was at one time mayor of Mobile; and in 1839 he founded the "Can't-Get-Away Club," composed of local citizens who were unable to leave the city during an epidemic of yellow fever. At his death the Mobile *Register* (May 23rd, 1869) described him as "a man who, by a long, useful, and charitable life, had endeared himself to all." His son Alphonse Hurtel was educated at Spring Hill College, Mobile. After several years in Texas and Mexico he returned to Mobile and practiced law. On December 6th, 1855, he married Catherine Marianne Gaillard (1835–1869), daughter of John Gaillard and Caroline Gordon, of Claiborne, Alabama; there were five children. After the death of his first wife ("beloved Kate") on January 26th, 1869, he married second (on November 2nd, 1870) her younger sister, Sarah Blakely Gaillard (1844–1914). On October 17th, 1861, he enlisted at Mobile for twelve months' service in the Confederate army; on November 6th, 1861, he was commissioned captain of Company G, 24th Regiment Alabama Infantry; in June 1862 he was detailed for duty as judge advocate in the Department of the West; on January 30th, 1863, he was detailed for guard duty in Atlanta; on September 4th, 1864, after duty in the field near Atlanta, he was placed in command of the military prison at Macon. After the war he returned to Mobile and joined Charles P. Gage in the firm of Gage & Hurtel, ice merchants. He was three times elected mayor of Mobile (1875, 1876, 1877), the third time only a month before his death on August 9th, 1877. He received a public funeral and was buried beside his first wife in an unmarked grave in Magnolia Cemetery. He died a Methodist.

HUTCHISON, ROBERT (1802–1861), merchant, was born in Glasgow, Scotland, on April 5th, 1802. In early youth he migrated to Savannah, Georgia, where he was for several years a clerk in the countinghouse of Andrew Low. He prospered in business and amassed a large fortune. He married first (on January 12th, 1832) Corinne Louisa Elliott (1813–1838), of Liberty County, Georgia, daughter of the Hon. John Elliott, United States senator from Georgia; she died with two children on the steamer *Pulaski*, which sank in mid-ocean on June 14th, 1838; Hutchison escaped on a raft. He married second (on November 2nd, 1848) Mary Edmonia Caskie (1822–1852), of Richmond, Virginia, daughter of John Caskie, president of the Richmond Tobacco Exchange; she died in Richmond of consumption on July 3rd, 1852, leaving one child, and was buried in Shockoe Cemetery. He married third (on April 23rd,

1857) Ellen Laura Caskie (1836–1858), also of Richmond, a first cousin of his second wife, and daughter of James Caskie, president of the Bank of Virginia; she died in Savannah of puerperal fever on March 22nd, 1858, leaving one infant, and was buried in Shockoe Cemetery, Richmond. Robert Hutchison never recovered from the blow of his third wife's untimely death; his health, formerly excellent, declined, and he died in Savannah on May 14th, 1861. That evening his lifelong friend, the Rev. Dr. Charles Colcock Jones, hearing the news, wrote feelingly in his journal: "We commenced the world together—he a clerk in Andrew Low & Company's counting room and I a clerk in Nicholas & Neff's. I performed his first marriage ceremony—to Miss Corinne Elliott. . . . He was a member of the Independent Church, Savannah, and possessed prudence, wisdom, and energy in business, improved himself intellectually, and was confiding, constant, and generous to his friends. We have been much together from first to last." Robert Hutchison was buried in Shockoe Cemetery, Richmond.

HYDE, ANNIE FRANCES (1837–1898), milliner and dressmaker, was born in London, England, on January 14th, 1837. Orphaned in early childhood, she came to Savannah, Georgia, to live in the household of her aunt, Frances Hyde (1820–1895), for whom she was named, wife of James McIntire (1806–1862), grocer and dry goods merchant. In October 1857 Annie Frances Hyde and her sister, Rebecca Hyde, purchased the millinery and dressmaking establishment of Miss S. A. Tennison on Broughton Street, where, according to the Savannah *Morning News* (January 4th, 1858), "country orders are promptly attended to." On October 10th, 1859, Rebecca Hyde became the wife of John Blair, of Ayr, Scotland, leaving her sister to conduct the business alone. On July 3rd, 1861, Annie Frances Hyde married William Henry King (1836–1885) and retired from the business altogether. Her husband, a native of Bucks County, Pennsylvania, son of William King and Emily Duncan, had come to Savannah in 1859, joined the household of his elder sister, Lucy King (1831–1897), wife of Alexander Fawcett, and become a grocery clerk. In 1866 the Kings settled in Adams, Jefferson County, New York, where William Henry King joined his father (William King) and his two brothers (Nahum King and Charles King) in the butchering business. William Henry King died in Adams on January 23rd, 1885, and was buried in Elmwood Cemetery. Two years later his widow returned with her five sons to Savannah, where she died after a lingering illness on November 26th, 1898. She was buried in Bonaventure Cemetery with the family of her husband's sister, Lucy (King) Fawcett. Four of her sons (Charles King, Alfred F. King, Albert M. King, and Percy M. King) were Savannah businessmen; one son (William D. King) was a missionary to China.

IRVIN, JAMES (born 1829), farmer and overseer, migrated in early manhood from his native South Carolina to Georgia, where by 1854 he and his wife Sarah were settled with their growing family in Baker County. On March 12th, 1864, in Bainbridge, Georgia, he enlisted for the duration of the war as a private in Company E, 1st Regiment Georgia Local Troops, organized for home defense. He was later taken prisoner. On May 17th, 1865, he was paroled in Albany, Georgia, whence he returned to his farm in Baker County; he resumed planting, and served for one season as overseer of the plantation of the Rev. John Jones at Refuge, near Newton. He was evidently a decisive man: on one occasion, through his "prompt action, courage, and strength," two unruly Negroes were "brought under good discipline." The Rev. John Jones gave up his place in Baker County early in 1866 and removed to Griffin. James Irvin remained on his farm, where he and his wife were still living with six of their eight children in June 1880.

IRVING, THEODORE (1809–1880), educator and Episcopal clergyman, son of Ebenezer Irving (1776–1868) and Elizabeth Kip (1784–1827), was born in New York City on May 9th, 1809. His mother died on April 19th, 1827, shortly before his eighteenth birthday. For three years (1828–1830) he traveled in Europe, visiting his uncle, Washington Irving (1783–1859), in Madrid in 1828 and studying modern languages and attending lectures in Paris and London. Returning to the United States, he was professor of history and belles lettres at Geneva (now Hobart) College (1836–1848), and professor of history and belles lettres at the Free Academy of the City of New York (1848–1852). In 1856 he was ordained a clergyman of the Episcopal Church; he was rector successively of Christ Church, Bay Ridge, Long Island; St. Andrew's Church, Staten Island; Ascension Church, Staten Island; and the Church of the Holy Trinity, New York City. He was author of *The Conquest of Florida by Hernando de Soto* (1835) and several devotional works: *The Fountain of Living Waters* (1850), *Tiny Footfalls* (1869), and *More Than Conqueror* (1873). He died in New York City on December 20th, 1880, survived by his wife and four children.

IRVING, WASHINGTON (1783–1859), author, son of William Irving, a successful merchant, and Sarah Sanders, was born in New York City on April 3rd, 1783. As a young man he led a life of pleasure and indulgence, drawn particularly to literature, travel, and feminine society; although he studied law his professional practice was desultory. A series of his light satirical essays, signed "Jonathan Oldstyle, Gent.," was published in his brother Peter's newspaper, the *Morning Chronicle*, in 1802–1803. After two happy years in Europe (1804–1806) he returned to New York and collaborated with his brother William and his friend James Kirke Paulding in *Salmagundi;*

or, The Whim-Whams and Opinions of Launcelot Langstaff, Esq., and Others (1807–1808), twenty essays reminiscent of Addison's rendering of the social scene in *The Spectator*. His next work, *Diedrich Knickerbocker's History of New York* (1809), has been called "the first great book of comic literature written by an American." In 1815 he sailed for England, where he wrote *The Sketch Book of Geoffrey Crayon, Gent.* (1819–1820), his greatest success, a collection of essays and stories including the famous "Rip Van Winkle" and "The Legend of Sleepy Hollow." In 1826 he attached himself to the American legation in Spain, where his interest in the Moorish past bore fruit in *The Conquest of Granada* (1829) and *The Alhambra* (1832). He returned to New York in 1832 after an absence of seventeen years. He served as United States minister to Spain (1842–1846). Retiring to Sunnyside, his beloved home on the Hudson River, he wrote *Oliver Goldsmith* (1849), *Mahomet and His Successors* (1850), and *George Washington* (5 vols., 1859). His fiancée, Matilda Hoffman, daughter of the Hon. Josiah O. Hoffman, died of consumption in her eighteenth year, on April 26th, 1809, and he never married. He died at Sunnyside on November 28th, 1859. He has been called "the first American man of letters."

IVES, ADRIAN C. (1829–1871), bank officer, son of Chauncey Ives (1787–1857) and his second wife, Amanda Clark (1807–1864), was born in Hartford, Connecticut, in 1829. In early manhood he joined Rodney Dennis, also of Hartford, in the firm of Dennis & Ives, "dealers in choice family groceries and provisions." In 1853 he removed to Augusta, Georgia, where he became a clerk in the Bank of Augusta, with which he was associated for the rest of his life. On December 12th, 1854, he married Amanda W. Thew, daughter of George M. Thew, a native of England and cashier in the Bank of Augusta. On February 5th, 1864, he enlisted as a private in Captain George T. Barnes's Company Light Artillery, 1st Regiment Georgia Local Troops, organized for home defense. For some months he was a clerk in the office of Colonel George W. Rains; in September 1864 he was an assistant in the office of Dr. Joseph Jones, surgeon with rank of major. After the war he became assistant cashier in the Bank of Augusta. In the spring of 1871 he went to Florida hoping to restore his health; on his return he visited a British ship in the port of Savannah, contracted smallpox, and died in Augusta after a severe illness on March 14th, 1871, survived by his wife and one daughter. He was buried in Summerville Cemetery.

JACKSON, ANDREW (1767–1845), seventh president of the United States, son of Andrew Jackson and Elizabeth Hutchinson, was born in the Waxhaw settlement in South Carolina on March 15th, 1767. At the age of fourteen he was left an orphan. After studying law in Salisbury, North Carolina, he commenced practice in McLeanville, Guilford County, North Carolina, in 1787. In October 1788 he settled in Nashville, Tennessee, where he married Rachel Donelson (1767–1828), daughter of John Donelson and divorced wife of Lewis Robards. In 1795 he and his wife settled at the Hermitage, an estate near Nashville, where he made his home for the rest of his life. He was a member of Congress (1796–1797); United States senator (1797–1798); and judge of the state supreme court (1798–1804). He was major general of volunteers (1812–1814); on April 19th, 1814, he was commissioned brigadier general in the regular army, and on May 1st, 1814, he was promoted to major general. He defeated the British at New Orleans on January 8th, 1815. After another term as United States senator (1823–1825) he served two terms as president of the United States (1829–1837). Returning to Tennessee, he resided at the Hermitage until his death there on June 8th, 1845. He was buried in the Hermitage garden beside his wife, whose tombstone inscription is believed to have been written by the general himself: "Here lie the remains of Mrs. Rachel Jackson, wife of President Jackson, who died the 22nd of December 1828 aged sixty-one years. Her face was fair, her person pleasing, her temper amiable, her heart kind. She delighted in relieving the wants of her fellow creatures and cultivated that divine pleasure by the most liberal and unpretending methods. To the poor she was a benefactor; to the rich an example; to the wretched a comforter; to the prosperous an ornament. Her piety went hand in hand with her benevolence, and she thanked the Creator for being permitted to do good. A being so gentle and so virtuous slander might wound but could not dishonor; even death, when he bore her from the arms of her husband, could but transport her to the bosom of her God." In 1889 the Ladies' Hermitage Association was organized for the preservation of the estate.

JACKSON, HENRY ROOTES (1820–1898), lawyer, diplomat, and soldier, son of Henry Jackson and Martha Jacqueline Rootes, was born in Athens, Georgia, on June 24th, 1820. His father was professor of mathematics at the University of Georgia. After graduating from Yale College in 1839 he returned to Georgia, studied law, and commenced practice in Savannah. In 1843 he was appointed United States district attorney for Georgia. He was colonel of the 1st Georgia Regiment in the Mexican War (1846–1848); judge of the superior court of Chatham County (1849–1853); and United States minister to Austria (1853–1858). Returning to Georgia in 1858, he was offered the chancellorship of the University of Georgia but declined. Early in 1859 he became a member of the Savannah firm of Ward, Jackson & Jones, replacing George Savage Owens, who had retired. In November 1859 he was a member of the government counsel in the unsuccessful prosecution of the captain and owners of the *Wanderer,* a slave ship seized in November 1858 in its attempt to bring African

slaves into Savannah. He was a member of the state secession convention meeting in Milledgeville in January 1861. During the Civil War he was brigadier general in the Confederate army and also judge of the Confederate States district court for the district of Georgia. After the war he resumed the practice of law in Savannah. He was United States minister to Mexico (1885–1887). For twenty-four years (1874–1898) he was president of the Georgia Historical Society. He was author of *Tallulah and Other Poems* (1850). On February 1st, 1844, he married Cornelia Augusta Davenport (1824–1853), only daughter of Isaiah Davenport, of Savannah. She died on July 16th, 1853, leaving four children, and was buried in Laurel Grove Cemetery. Henry Rootes Jackson died in Savannah on May 23rd, 1898, survived by his second wife, Florence Barclay King (1834–1912), daughter of Thomas Butler King, of St. Simons Island, and was buried in Bonaventure Cemetery. He was one of the most distinguished Georgians of his day.

JACKSON, JAMES WILLIAM (1823–1861), hotel proprietor, youngest son of Richard Jackson (1778–1823) and Jane Donaldson (1796–1872), was born at Prospect Hill, his father's plantation in Fairfax County, Virginia, on March 6th, 1823. In 1843, after studying for a time at Georgetown College, he accompanied his brother, Dr. John Jackson, to Kentucky, where he attended Bardstown College, and where he met Susan Maria Adams (1823–1886), daughter of Eli Adams, a wealthy landowner of Lebanon, Kentucky. In 1845 he married Miss Adams and returned with his bride to Virginia. After living for several years with his mother he became proprietor of the Union Hotel in Fairfax Courthouse in 1860; in February 1861 he removed to Alexandria and became proprietor of the Marshall House, a hotel located on the southeast corner of King and Pitt Streets. There, on the morning of May 24th, 1861, he shot and killed Elmer Ephraim Ellsworth (1837–1861), a Union officer, as he descended the stairs after having torn down the Confederate flag flying on the roof. Jackson was immediately shot to death by one of Ellsworth's men. The twin deaths of Ellsworth and Jackson created a national sensation: Ellsworth's body lay in state in the White House, and Jackson became the first martyr to the Southern cause. Jackson was buried beside his mother in the family cemetery at Prospect Hill; his remains were later reburied in an unmarked grave in Fairfax Courthouse Cemetery. His widow and three young daughters survived. Eleven months after his death, while the memory of his martyrdom was still fresh, an anonymous pamphlet was "published for the benefit of the family": *The Life of James W. Jackson, the Alexandria Hero, the Slayer of Ellsworth, the First Martyr in the Cause of Southern Independence: Containing a Full Account of the Circumstances of His Heroic Death, and the Many Remarkable Incidents in His Eventful Life: Constituting a True History, More Like Romance Than Reality* (Richmond, 1862).

JACKSON, JOSEPH (1814–1890), farmer and overseer, was born in Liberty County, Georgia, on October 12th, 1814. All his life he resided at the Jackson place, situated some five miles below Riceboro, near North Newport Baptist Church. In 1840 he married Mary Ann Somersall, who bore him six children. During the Civil War he was a corporal in the Liberty Volunteers (Company H, 25th Regiment Georgia Cavalry) for twelve months (August 1861–July 1862). Returning to Liberty County, he undertook the management of a number of plantations in the absence of younger planters called into military service. From June 1863 to December 1864 he managed Montevideo plantation for Mrs. Mary Jones. "Everyone thinks he will be able to get out of service," wrote Mrs. Mary S. Mallard on September 27th, 1864, "as he has so many places in charge." By October 7th, 1864, he had "succeeded in getting exemption papers," enabling him to continue at Montevideo until forced to withdraw at Sherman's approach. Joseph Jackson died in Liberty County on November 7th, 1890, and was buried near Sunbury.

JACKSON, SAMUEL (1787–1872), physician and educator, son of Dr. David Jackson (1747–1801), a physician in the Revolutionary army, was born in Philadelphia on March 22nd, 1787. After graduating from the Medical College of the University of Pennsylvania in 1808 he engaged in the drug business for seven years before commencing the practice of medicine in 1815. He rose rapidly to prominence, and in 1820 he became chairman of the Philadelphia Board of Health. From 1822 to 1845 he served in the wards of the Philadelphia Hospital, where his lectures attracted many students. He was professor of the institutes of medicine at the Medical College of the University of Pennsylvania for twenty-eight years (1835–1863); among his distinguished students Joseph Jones (1833–1896) was outstanding. Writing to the Rev. Dr. Charles Colcock Jones on July 17th, 1857, Jackson spoke of his young friend's "contemplated application" for a professorship at the University of Georgia: "I mailed to him a letter of recommendation to the board of trustees in which I expressed the opinion I entertain of your son's abilities, qualifications, and future eminence, should nothing occur to interrupt his progress. It will give me sincere gratification should my attestation to my young friend's attainments and talents have weight with the board to whom it is addressed." Samuel Jackson died in Philadelphia on April 4th, 1872. He had met his young friend for the last time eighteen months before. Dr. Joseph Jones, returning from a European honeymoon with his second wife, wrote from New York on October 13th, 1870, of his plan to stop in Philadelphia: "My good old friend Dr. Samuel Jackson is in very feeble health and desires to see me."

JACKSON, THOMAS JONATHAN ("STONEWALL") (1824–1863), Confederate soldier, third child of Jonathan Jackson and Julia (Beckwith) Neale, was born in Clarks-burg, (West) Virginia, on January 21st, 1824. He graduated from the United States Military Academy in 1846, and after distinguished service in the Mexican War, followed by service at Fort Columbus (1848) and Fort Hamilton (1849–1851), he resigned from the army in February 1852 to become professor of artillery tactics and natural philosophy at the Virginia Military Institute. He married first (in 1853) Eleanor Junkin; he married second (in 1857) Mary Anna Morrison; both of his wives were daughters of Presbyterian clergymen. At the outbreak of the Civil War he was sent to Harpers Ferry as colonel of infantry; on June 17th, 1861, he was made brigadier general. At First Manassas he stoutly resisted the Federal onslaught; General Bernard E. Bee, retreating with his troops, cried: "There stands Jackson like a stone wall!" The sobriquet stuck. On October 7th, 1861, he became major general and assumed command in the Shenandoah Valley; his "Valley campaign" of 1862 has been called the most brilliant display of military science in American history. By Second Manassas he had become a Southern hero. His piety was legendary; his frequent resort to prayer and his strict observance of the Sabbath were known throughout the Confederacy. He played a major role in the Maryland campaign and was promoted to lieutenant general on October 10th, 1862. He subsequently distinguished himself at Fredericksburg. At Chancellorsville, returning to camp in the twilight, he was inadvertently wounded by his own men; he died of pneumonia at Guiney's Station, south of Fredericksburg, on May 10th, 1863. After lying in state in Richmond his body was buried in Lexington. Jackson was one of the greatest of American soldiers; his loss was irreparable, and the Army of Northern Virginia was never as strong again. "The death of our pious, brave, and noble General Stonewall Jackson is a great blow to our cause!" wrote Mrs. Mary Jones on May 19th, 1863. "May God raise up friends and helpers to our bleeding country!"

JACKSON, WILLIAM BULLOCH (1829–1875), bookkeeper and cashier, son of Joseph W. Jackson (1796–1854) and Sarah C. White, was born in Savannah, Georgia, on September 11th, 1829. For many years he was head clerk in the firm of John W. Anderson & Company, Savannah cotton factors and commission merchants. On October 13th, 1853, he married Mary Willis Adams (1833–1919), daughter of Nathaniel A. Adams and Mary Mildred Flournoy, of Athens, Georgia; there were four children. He was lieutenant of the Oglethorpe Light Infantry from its organization. On November 23rd, 1861, he enlisted as a private in Company B, 2nd Battalion Georgia Cavalry; on November 25th, 1862, he was detailed for quartermaster duty under Captain Macpherson Berrien Millen, and later (February 8th, 1863) under Major Hermann Hirsch. On February 17th, 1864, he became aide-de-camp to General Henry Rootes Jackson. He was taken prisoner near the end of the war and paroled in May 1865. After the war he became bookkeeper for A. C. Lomelino, dealer in groceries, provisions, wines, and liquors. He died in Savannah of consumption on March 1st, 1875, and was buried with military honors in Laurel Grove Cemetery. Mary Willis (Adams) Jackson died in Waycross, Georgia, at the home of her daughter, Mrs. James Polk Stewart, on April 12th, 1919, and was buried beside her husband.

JAY, WILLIAM (1769–1853), Nonconformist clergyman, son of a mason and stonecutter, was born at Tisbury, Wiltshire, England, on May 8th, 1769. After assisting his father for a time in the erection of Fonthill Abbey for William Beckford, he studied with Cornelius Winter, a Nonconformist clergyman of Marlborough, and in 1788 preached a series of sermons at Surrey Chapel, London. For sixty-two years (1791–1853) he was pastor of Argyle Independent Chapel in Bath, where his simplicity, earnestness, and fine voice drew large crowds. Two of his published works enjoyed wide circulation on both sides of the Atlantic: *Morning Exercises for the Closet* (1829) and *Evening Exercises for the Closet* (1831). He died in Bath on December 27th, 1853. He received the honorary degree of doctor of divinity from the College of New Jersey (Princeton) in 1810.

JEFFERSON, THOMAS (1743–1826), statesman, diplomat, third president of the United States, son of Peter Jefferson (1708–1757) and Jane Randolph (1720–1776), was born at Shadwell, his father's plantation in Goochland (now Albemarle) County, Virginia, on April 13th, 1743. After graduating from the College of William and Mary in 1762 he studied law and commenced practice in 1767. He was a member of the colonial house of burgesses (1769–1774); a member of the Continental Congress (1775–1776); and chairman of the committee that drew up the Declaration of Independence, which he signed on August 2nd, 1776. On January 1st, 1772, he married Martha Wayles (1748–1782), daughter of John Wayles and Martha Eppes, and widow of Bathurst Skelton; two of their six children lived to maturity. He and his wife settled at Monticello, his beloved residence perched atop a mountain in Albemarle County; the house, designed by Jefferson, was commenced in 1770 and required a generation to complete. He was governor of Virginia (1779–1781); a member of the state house of delegates (1782); a member of the Continental Congress (1783–1785); minister plenipotentiary to France (1785–1788); secretary of state under President George Washington (1789–1793); vice-president under President John Adams (1797–1801); and president of the United States (1801–1809). He retired to Monticello, where he died on July 4th, 1826. He was buried beside his wife in the grounds of Monticello beneath his own epitaph: "Here was buried Thomas Jefferson, author of the Declaration of American Independence, of the statute of Virginia for religious freedom, and father of the University of Virginia." Jefferson's *Manual of Parliamentary Practice* (1801), written during his vice-presidency, was subsequently reprinted in many editions.

JENKINS, CHARLES JONES (1805–1883), lawyer, legislator, and governor, only child of Charles Jones Jenkins, was born in Beaufort District, South Carolina, on January 6th, 1805. After attending Franklin College (Athens) he graduated from Union College (Schenectady, New York) in 1824. Returning to Georgia, he read law in the office of the Hon. John Macpherson Berrien, of Savannah, and commenced practice in Sandersville in 1826. In 1829 he removed to Augusta, where in 1832 he joined the law firm of Augustus B. Longstreet and William M. Mann. He was a member of the state legislature (1831) and attorney general of the state (1832). Returning to the state legislature, he served continuously from 1836 to 1850 with the exception of one term (1842). During the Civil War he was judge of the state supreme court. In November 1865 he was unanimously elected governor of Georgia; he served until January 13th, 1868, when he was removed by General Meade. After residing for some months in Canada and Europe he returned to his home in Summerville, a suburb of Augusta, where he died on June 14th, 1883.

JOHNS, MARGARET JANE (NETTELS) (1819–1893): *Mrs. Malachi Johns,* was born in South Carolina in 1819. In January 1842 she became the wife of Malachi Johns (1821–1891), a farmer living near Taylor's Creek, Liberty County, Georgia. There she resided for the rest of her life, rearing a numerous family and devoting herself to spinning and weaving. One of her sons, Mark D. Johns, too young for military service, enlisted as a private in the 1st Regiment Georgia Reserves early in 1864; he was taken prisoner at Taylor's Creek in December 1864 and confined at Charleston, South Carolina, until the end of the war. Malachi Johns died in Liberty County during the summer of 1891; his wife died in January 1893.

JOHNSON, GEORGE OTIS (1827–1873), merchant, son of George Johnson (1796–1849), was born in Lynn, Massachusetts, on June 8th, 1827. In early manhood he removed to Savannah, Georgia, where he became a clerk in the firm of his uncle, Otis Johnson (1802–1870), dealer in boots and shoes. Shortly before the Civil War Otis Johnson retired, entrusting the business to his nephew and namesake, and returned to Lynn, Massachusetts, his birthplace and the home of his youth. George Otis Johnson remained in Savannah. At the outbreak of the Civil War he entered Confederate service as a private in the Chatham Artillery; for some months in 1863 he was engaged at the Savannah barracks as clerk of Colonel Charles Colcock Jones, Jr. After the war he resided for several years in his native state; by 1870 he was once more living in Savannah, associated with Ezra F. Wood in the firm of Wood & Johnson. He never married. He died in Providence, Rhode Island, on March 5th, 1873, and was buried in Pine Grove Cemetery, Lynn, Massachusetts.

JOHNSON, HERSCHEL VESPASIAN (1812–1880), lawyer, judge, legislator, and governor, son of Moses Johnson and Nancy Palmer, was born in Burke County, Georgia, on September 18th, 1812. After graduating from Franklin College (Athens) in 1834 he studied law and commenced practice in Augusta. On December 19th, 1833, he married Mrs. Ann (Polk) Walker, daughter of the Hon. William Polk, of Maryland. In 1839 he settled at Sandy Grove, a plantation near Louisville, Jefferson County, Georgia, where he continued the practice of law. In 1844 he removed to Milledgeville. He was United States senator (1848–1849); judge of the superior court of the Ocmulgee circuit (1849–1853); delegate to the Democratic National Convention (1848, 1852, 1856); governor of Georgia (1853–1857); delegate to the state secession convention (January 1861); and Confederate States senator (1862–1865). After the war he resumed the practice of law in Louisville, where he also served as judge of the middle circuit of Georgia (1873–1880). He died at Sandy Grove on August 16th, 1880, and was buried in the Old Louisville Cemetery.

JOHNSON, JOHN (1801–1874), magistrate, son of Robert Johnson and Nancy Dolvin, was born in Greene County, Georgia, on May 10th, 1801. In 1828 he removed to Columbus, Georgia, with whose interests he was identified for the rest of his life. In June 1830 he was one of the fourteen founding members of the Columbus Presbyterian Church, of which he was also ruling elder (1830–1874) and session clerk (1839–1874). On August 2nd, 1835, he married Hannah Briggs (1802–1878). In 1845 he became clerk of the inferior court of Muscogee County, and in 1847, when the court of ordinary was instituted, he was elected its first judge. He continued to hold this office until August 12th, 1868, when, according to the Columbus *Enquirer* (April 14th, 1874), "Federal bayonets, assisted by the Negroes, elected Mr. J. W. Duer." On August 13th, 1868, the Columbus *Enquirer* hailed him as "an honest and intelligent man, an upright judge, and an officer made thoroughly acquainted with his duties by long experience and close application"; his retirement from "the important position that he had held so long with honor to himself and to the satisfaction and advantage of the people of the county" constituted "a public loss." For the last six years of his life he was county treasurer. He died in Columbus on April 7th, 1874, and was buried in Linwood Cemetery.

JOHNSON, SAMUEL (1709–1784), English poet, essayist, critic, and lexicographer, son of Michael Johnson, bookseller, and Sarah Ford, was born in Lichfield, Staffordshire, on September 18th, 1709. He entered Pembroke College (Oxford) in 1728 but left in December 1729 after four terms. In 1735, at Derby, he married Elizabeth Porter, a widow twenty years his senior. After unsuccessfully conducting his own school at Edial, near Lichfield, for two years, he went up to London, in company with one of his pupils, David Garrick, in 1737. Thereafter his life was intimately associated with the great metropolis. His rise to literary prominence was slow. After *London* (1738) and *The Vanity of Human Wishes* (1749), didactic poems, and *Irene* (1749), a tragedy, he produced three series of periodical essays: *The Rambler* (1750–1752), *The Adventurer* (1753–1754), and *The Idler* (1758–1760). His *Dictionary,* commenced in 1747, was published in 1755. *Rasselas,* a philosophical romance, written in the evenings of a week to defray his mother's funeral expenses, was published in 1759. His edition of Shakespeare, together with his brilliant preface, was published in eight volumes in 1765. *The Lives of the English Poets* (1779–1781) comprises one of the richest collections of literary criticism in the language. On May 16th, 1763, in the back parlor of Thomas Davies' bookshop in Covent Garden, Johnson met James Boswell (1740–1795), whose *Life of Samuel Johnson* (1791) evokes the personality of "the Great Cham." Their journey to the western islands of Scotland in 1773 was recorded in Johnson's *Journey to the Western Islands* (1775) and Boswell's *Journal of a Tour to the Hebrides* (1785). Johnson died in London on December 13th, 1784, and was buried in Westminster Abbey. According to Boswell, Johnson "had, till very near his death, a contempt for the notion that the weather affects the human frame." In the *Life* Johnson says: "How low is he sunk whose strength depends upon the weather!" In *Idler* No. 11 he expresses the same opinion: "Surely nothing is more reproachful to a being endowed with reason than to resign its powers to the influence of the air, and live in dependence on the weather and the wind for the only blessings which nature has put into our power, tranquillity and benevolence. . . . This distinction of seasons is produced only by imagination operating on luxury. To temperance every day is bright; and every hour is propitious to diligence. He that shall resolutely excite his faculties, or exert his virtues, will soon make himself superior to the seasons; and may set at defiance the morning mist and the evening damp, the blasts of the east, and the clouds of the south."

JOHNSTON, ALBERT SIDNEY (1803–1862), Confederate soldier, son of Dr. John Johnston and Abigail Harris, was born in Washington, Mason County, Kentucky, on February 2nd, 1802. After attending Transylvania University, where he excelled in Latin and mathematics, he graduated from the United States Military Academy in 1826. Eight years later he resigned his commission, engaged briefly in farming, and went to Texas, where he was appointed adjutant general of the Texas army on August 5th, 1836, and senior brigadier general on January 31st, 1837. He was secretary of war for the Republic of Texas (1838–1840). During the Mexican War he was colonel of the 1st Regiment Texas Rifle Volunteers. Prior to the Civil War he saw service with the United States army in Texas, Utah, and California. On April 10th, 1861, he again resigned his commission; he was appointed general in the Confederate army and assigned to the Department of the West. Early in 1862, after his loss of Fort Henry (February 6th) and Fort Donelson (February 16th), his critics urged that he be replaced; President Davis replied: "If Sidney Johnston is not a general, I have none." On Sunday, April 6th, 1862, Johnston attacked the Federals at Shiloh Church, near Pittsburg Landing, and drove them back in complete rout; but in his moment of victory he was struck in the leg and bled to death. He was temporarily entombed in New Orleans; in January 1867 he was buried in Austin, Texas. He married first (on January 20th, 1829) Henrietta Preston; after her death on August 12th, 1835, he married second (on October 3rd, 1843) Eliza Griffin, a cousin of his first wife.

JOHNSTON, ALLEN R. (1823–1859), planter, was born in Georgia on October 24th, 1823. He was for many years a cotton planter in upper McIntosh County near the Liberty County line. When the Savannah, Albany & Gulf Railroad penetrated McIntosh County in the 1850s, Depot No. 4½ (Johnston's Station) was established for the convenience of his plantation. He died on September 24th, 1859, survived by his wife, Elizabeth (1826–1874), and eight children, and was buried in the Baggs Cemetery, McIntosh County.

JOHNSTON, JAMES C. (1792–1879), river pilot, was born in Ireland in August 1792. In 1829 he settled in Cincinnati, Ohio, where he was for fifty years a resident and for many years a pilot on steamers plying the waters of the Ohio River. In June 1857 he was pilot of the *A. W. Quarrier*, the "stern-wheel boat" on which the Rev. Dr. and Mrs. Charles Colcock Jones proceeded up the Ohio and Kanawha Rivers to Charleston, (West) Virginia. He died in Cincinnati on November 15th, 1879, and was buried in Wesleyan Cemetery. According to the Cincinnati *Enquirer* (November 16th, 1879), "He was in his eighty-eighth year, and well known along the river between Pittsburgh and St. Louis, in which trade most of his piloting was done. He was married four times, and was the father of twenty-nine children. By his last wife, who is living and is quite youthful, he had two children, whose respective ages are seven and ten years."

JOHNSTON, JOSEPH EGGLESTON (1807–1891), Confederate soldier, eighth son of Peter Johnston and Mary Wood, was born at Cherry Grove, his father's plantation in Prince Edward County, Virginia, on February 3rd, 1807. He graduated from the United States Military Academy in 1829. After eight years' service as second lieutenant in the 4th Artillery he resigned to become a civil engineer but was recommissioned as first lieutenant, topological engineers. He served in the Mexican War as captain (1846) and lieutenant colonel (1847). In 1855 he became lieutenant colonel of the 1st Cavalry, and in 1860 quartermaster general and brigadier general. On April 22nd, 1861, he resigned his commission and was appointed major general in the Confederate army; after First Manassas he was commissioned general and placed in command of the Army of Northern Virginia. He fought in the Peninsula campaign of 1862 and was twice wounded at Seven Pines. In December 1863 he was assigned to the Army of Tennessee, then facing Chattanooga, with orders to assume the offensive. This he never did; during the spring of 1864 he continued to fall back, until on July 17th, 1864, just before Atlanta, he was relieved of command. On February 23rd, 1865, he was reassigned to the Army of Tennessee; he fought several engagements in North Carolina, where he surrendered his command to Sherman on April 26th, 1865. After the war he sold insurance in Savannah, Georgia, served one term in Congress (1879–1881), and finally settled in Washington, D.C., where he died on March 21st, 1891. He was buried in Greenmount Cemetery, Baltimore, Maryland. The Rev. David Lyman Buttolph recorded his impression of Johnston in a letter written from Atlanta on July 16th, 1864: "In passing General Johnston's headquarters I had a good view of the general, who was sitting in the piazza talking with a gentleman. In the afternoon I saw him riding along the lines on horseback. His soldiers cheered him as he rode along, to which he responded by lifting his hat. He is a fine-looking man—the most soldierly in his appearance of anyone I have ever seen."

JOHNSTON, RICHARD MALCOLM (1822–1898), lawyer, educator, author, and lecturer, son of Malcolm Johnston and Catherine Davenport, was born at Oak Grove, his father's plantation near Powelton, Georgia, on March 8th, 1822. After graduating from Mercer University in 1841 he taught school for one year in Mount Zion, Hancock County. He then read law in the office of Henry Harford Cumming, of Augusta, and began practice in Sparta as partner of Eli W. Baxter. On November 26th, 1844, he married Mary Frances Mansfield (1829–1897), daughter of Eli Mansfield, a Sparta merchant born in New Haven, Connecticut. His practice of law from 1844 to 1857 was interrupted by two intervals of teaching; for four years (1857–1861) he was professor of rhetoric and belles lettres at the University of Georgia; for five years (1862–1867) he conducted a boys' school near Sparta. Removing to Baltimore in 1867, he continued his school for several years until encouraged by his friend Sidney Lanier (1842–1881) to write fiction. *Dukesboro Tales* (1871), his first and best-known work, was characteristic of the local color school in its kindly humor and stress on character and setting rather than on plot. A number of books followed, climaxed by his *Autobiography,* published posthumously in 1900. In 1875 he joined his wife and family in embracing the Roman Catholic faith. He died in Baltimore on September 23rd, 1898.

JONES, ABBY AUGUSTA (1864–1943), eighth child of Henry Hart Jones (1823–1893) and Abigail Sturges Dowse (1828–1897), was born in Cuthbert, Georgia, on February 9th, 1864. She was baptized in April 1864 in the Cuthbert Presbyterian Church by her uncle, the Rev. John Jones, just before the ordination of her father as elder of the church. After graduating from Wesleyan College (Macon) "Gussie" studied voice and elocution. She married first (on October 20th, 1885) Edgar Polhill Mitchell (born 1858), son of Andrew P. Mitchell and Rebecca Rucker; she married second (on June 20th, 1900) Cooper David Winn (1857–1913), widower of her elder sister Eliza Low Jones (1858–1891), and eldest son of David Read Evans Winn and Frances Mary Dean. She reared ten children: a son and a daughter by her first marriage, a son and a daughter by her second marriage, and six nieces and nephews who became her stepchildren. "No one was ever more consistently kind to me than she," one of her nieces later observed; "and I was very fond of her." She died in Macon of a heart attack on November 22nd, 1943, and was buried beside her second husband in Rose Hill Cemetery.

JONES, ABIGAIL (ABBY) STURGES (DOWSE) (1828–1897): *Mrs. Henry Hart Jones,* only child of Samuel Dowse (1786–1856) and his fourth wife, Abigail Elizabeth Sturges (1807–1828), was born in Burke County, Georgia, on June 28th, 1828. Her father, a wealthy planter, married five times and fathered seven children; she was a half-sister of Gideon Dowse (1814–1881); Sarah Berrien Dowse (1824–1855), wife of William Parker White; Susan Clinton Dowse (1833–1886), wife of Dr. Juriah Harriss; and Laura Philoclea Dowse (1835–1899). Her mother died in childbirth. On May 21st, 1846, in Bath, Richmond County, Georgia, she became the wife of Henry Hart Jones (1823–1893), son of Joseph Jones (1779–1846) and his third wife, Elizabeth Screven Lee Hart (1801–1870). Six of their eleven children died in infancy. She and her family lived successively in Liberty County (1846–1862), Baker County (1862–1863), Cuthbert (1863–1871), and Macon (1871–1897). Her husband, a planter and journalist, rose to prominence as editor of the Cuthbert *Appeal* (1866–1870) and the Macon *Telegraph & Messenger* (1871–1881). He died in Vineville, a suburb of Macon, on February 13th, 1893, and was buried in Riverside Cemetery. Abigail Sturges (Dowse) Jones died in Vineville on February 15th, 1897, survived by four children, and was buried beside her husband.

JONES, ALFRED E. (1816–1874), constable, was born in Nansemond County, Virginia, in February 1816. In early manhood he settled in Savannah, Georgia, where for twenty-three years (1846–1869) he was constable of Chatham County. On May 22nd, 1850, he married Sarah A. Dell (1833–1889), of Screven County. During the Civil War he was third lieutenant of the Chatham Guerillas, a company organized for local defense. In 1869 he was commissioned notary public and ex-

officio justice of the peace. He died in Savannah on December 15th, 1874, survived by his wife and a numerous family, and was buried in Laurel Grove Cemetery.

JONES, ANDREW MAYBANK (1831–1895), planter and lawyer, eighth child of Joseph Jones (1779–1846) and his third wife, Elizabeth Screven Lee Hart (1801–1870), was born at the Retreat, his father's plantation in Liberty County, Georgia, on October 16th, 1831. He was a half-brother of the Rev. John Jones (1815–1893) and Mary Jones (1808–1869), wife of the Rev. Dr. Charles Colcock Jones. Although actually an uncle of Charles Colcock Jones, Jr., "Banky" was less than two weeks older than his nephew, and the two were always associated as brothers. After graduating with distinction from Franklin College (Athens) in 1842 he studied medicine for one year with Dr. Charles William West, of Savannah; but ill health forced him to abandon hopes of a medical career, and in November 1853 he retired to Laurel View, the plantation which he had inherited on the south bank of the Medway River in Liberty County. In the late summer of 1855 he became involved in an altercation with James David McConnell, a Liberty County lawyer, which almost eventuated in a duel in March 1856. [For details see Thomas Gamble, *Savannah Duels and Duelists, 1733–1877* (Savannah, 1923), pp. 222–227.] On July 30th, 1856, he married Evelyn Anne Harrison (1834–1868), daughter of Robert H. Harrison, of Amelia Island, Duval County, Florida; there were three children. In January 1859 he removed to Jacksonville, Florida, and undertook the study of law; he practiced his profession in Jacksonville until the outbreak of the Civil War. On July 13th, 1861, he was elected lieutenant in Company G, 2nd Regiment Florida Infantry; he fought at Yorktown and Williamsburg, but resigned after a year's service for reasons of health. After the war he continued to reside in Jacksonville. His wife died on April 16th, 1868, leaving three children, and was buried in the Harrison family cemetery on Amelia Island. On December 16th, 1869, he married Mary Electa Dodge (1852–1930), daughter of James S. Dodge, of Cuthbert, Georgia; there were four children. He was for twenty years an elder of the Presbyterian Church. He died in Atlanta after a lingering illness on September 13th, 1895, survived by his second wife and several children, and was buried in an unmarked grave in Oakland Cemetery.

JONES, AUGUSTUS SEABORN (1795–1869), planter, son of Seaborn Jones and his first wife, Sarah Harwood, was born near Millhaven, Screven County, Georgia, in 1795. He was no relation of the Rev. Dr. Charles Colcock Jones. After graduating from Union College (Schenectady, New York) in 1816 he returned to his home in Screven County, where he was prominent and successful in county affairs. He was treasurer of the Screven County Academy, and he served several terms in the state legislature. In 1854 he removed to Savannah, where he resided for the rest of his life, visiting his plantation at intervals and spending his summers at Catoosa Springs. He was an active member of the state secession convention meeting in Milledgeville in January 1861. Tuckahoe, his plantation in Screven County, "located *directly* on the Savannah River" and "at quite a remove from the railroad," was considered for possible rent by the Rev. Dr. Charles Colcock Jones in the autumn of 1862. As a planter Augustus Seaborn Jones accumulated a large fortune, most of which he lost during the Civil War. He died in Savannah on November 13th, 1869, and was buried in the family vault in Laurel Grove Cemetery.

JONES, CAROLINE SMELT (DAVIS). *See* Davis, Caroline Smelt

JONES, CHARLES BERRIEN (1820–1857), lawyer and planter, eldest son of Joseph Jones (1779–1846) and his third wife, Elizabeth Screven Lee Hart (1801–1870), was born at the Retreat, his father's plantation in Liberty County, Georgia, on November 11th, 1820. He was a half-brother of the Rev. John Jones (1815–1893) and Mary Jones (1808–1869), wife of the Rev. Dr. Charles Colcock Jones. After graduating from Franklin College (Athens) in 1841 he read law in the office of the Hon. Matthew Hall McAllister, of Savannah; returning to Liberty County, he practiced his profession in Walthourville until ill health forced him to retire to the more leisurely life of a planter. On January 25th, 1843, he married Marion Susan Anderson (1823–1888), daughter of William Anderson, of Walthourville; on the preceding day (January 24th, 1843) his younger sister, Evelyn Elouisa Jones (1822–1849) had become the wife of Joseph Andrew Anderson (1820–1866), elder brother of Marion Susan Anderson. In 1853 he represented Liberty County in the state senate, where, according to *The Southern Presbyterian* (June 13th, 1857), "his courteous and polished elocution and perspicacity of thought won for him a respect and popularity seldom enjoyed by one of his years." He died in Savannah, where he had gone to seek medical advice, on May 5th, 1857, leaving a wife and six young children. He was buried on his plantation near Walthourville. Two years later, on April 28th, 1859, his widow became the wife of Thomas King (1820–1879), a planter of Liberty County. As Mrs. Mary S. Mallard observed (April 30th, 1859), "She has seen much trouble, but I hope she will have some bright days yet." She died in East Jacksonville, Florida, after a long illness on July 12th, 1888, survived by eight children, and was buried in Evergreen Cemetery.

JONES, CHARLES COLCOCK (1804–1863), Presbyterian clergyman, son of John Jones (1772–1805) and his second wife, Susannah Hyrne Girardeau (1778–1810), was born at Liberty Hall, his father's plantation in Liberty County, Georgia, on December 20th, 1804. His father died on March 28th, 1805; his mother, a woman of singular piety, died on July 1st, 1810. Charles Colcock Jones and his elder sister, Susan Mary Jones (1803–1890), were reared by kind relatives: their half-aunt, Eliza Greene Low (1785–1868), widow of David Robarts; their half-sister, Elizabeth Jones (1794–1856), wife of William Maxwell; and their uncle, Joseph Jones (1779–1846), younger brother of their deceased father. After mastering the rudiments of an English education under the Rev. Dr. William McWhir at the Sunbury Academy, Charles Colcock Jones was a clerk in the Savannah countinghouse of William Neff for four years (1819–1822); he then continued his studies at Phillips Academy, Andover, Massachusetts (1825–1827), Andover Theological Seminary (1827–1829), and Princeton Theological Seminary (1829–1830). On September 27th, 1830, he graduated from Princeton Theological Seminary. Returning to Georgia, he married his first cousin, Mary Jones (1808–1869), daughter of Joseph Jones (1779–1846) and his second wife, Sarah Anderson (1783–1817), on December 21st, 1830. Three of their four children lived to maturity: Charles Colcock Jones, Jr. (1831–1893), Joseph Jones (1833–1896), and Mary Sharpe Jones (1835–1889). A fourth child died at birth on September 7th, 1840. After serving for eighteen months (May 1831–November 1832) as pastor of the First Presbyterian Church, Savannah, he settled in his native county, where he devoted himself to the evangelization of the Negro, the great work of his life. He was twice professor of ecclesiastical history and church polity at Columbia Theological Seminary, Columbia, South Carolina (1837–1838; 1848–1850), and for three years (1850–1853) corresponding secretary of the Board of Domestic Missions of the Presbyterian Church, with offices in Philadelphia. In October 1853 he returned to Liberty County, where he resided for the rest of his life, supervising his three plantations (Arcadia, Montevideo, and Maybank) and continuing his evangelization of the Negro as his declining health permitted. He was commissioner to the General Assembly of the Presbyterian Church meeting in Lexington, Kentucky, in May 1857; he was also commissioner to the first General Assembly of the Southern Presbyterian Church meeting in Augusta, Georgia, in December 1861. He died at Arcadia plantation on March 16th, 1863, survived by his wife and three children, and was buried in Midway Cemetery. His *Catechism of Scripture Doctrine and Practice* (1837) was translated into Armenian and Turko-Armenian by the Rev. John Bailey Adger, missionary at Smyrna, in 1842; it was translated into Chinese by the Rev. John Winn Quarterman, missionary at Ningpo, in 1853. He also wrote *The Religious Instruction of the Negroes in the United States* (1842) and *A History of the Church of God* (1867). He received the honorary degree of doctor of divinity from Jefferson College (Canonsburg, Pennsylvania) in 1846. As Eliza Caroline Clay, a family friend, observed (February 1st, 1858), "Happy is that community, black or white, who has such a shepherd."

JONES, CHARLES COLCOCK, JR. (1831–1893), lawyer, historian, and archaeologist, eldest son of the Rev. Dr. Charles Colcock Jones (1804–1863) and his first cousin, Mary Jones (1808–1869), was born in Savannah, Georgia, on October 28th, 1831. He spent his boyhood in Liberty County, Georgia, where his parents owned three plantations (Arcadia, Montevideo, and Maybank), and in Columbia, South Carolina, where his father, a Presbyterian clergyman, was twice professor at Columbia Theological Seminary (1837–1838; 1848–1850). He attended the South Carolina College (1848–1850), and in 1850, when his father became corresponding secretary of the Board of Domestic Missions of the Presbyterian Church, with offices in Philadelphia, he accompanied his parents North and entered the College of New Jersey (Princeton), from which he graduated in 1852. After reading law for one year in the office of Samuel H. Perkins, of Philadelphia, he entered Dane Law School, Harvard University, in 1853, continued his studies until December 1854, and received his degree with the class of 1855. Returning to Savannah, he practiced law in association with the Hon. John Elliott Ward, later becoming junior partner in the firm of Ward, Owens & Jones (1857–1859) and Ward, Jackson & Jones (1859–1861). He was alderman of Savannah (1859–1860) and mayor of Savannah (1860–1861). On August 1st, 1861, he enlisted as senior first lieutenant in Captain Joseph S. Claghorn's Company (Chatham Artillery), 1st Volunteer Regiment Georgia Artilley. On October 14th, 1862, he was appointed lieutenant colonel of artillery and assigned to duty as chief of artillery for the military district of Georgia, with headquarters in Savannah. He was chief of artillery at the siege of Savannah (December 1864). After the war he continued the practice of law in New York City in association with the Hon. John Elliott Ward (1866–1877). Returning to Georgia in the spring of 1877, he settled at Montrose, a fine antebellum mansion in Summerville, a suburb of Augusta, where he continued his legal practice and wrote history and biography. His numerous published works include: *Indian Remains in Southern Georgia* (1859), *The Monumental Remains of Georgia* (1861), *Historical Sketch of the Chatham Artillery* (1867), *Antiquities of the Southern Indians* (1873), *The Siege of Savannah in December 1864* (1874), *The Dead Towns of Georgia* (1878), *The History of Georgia* (2 vols., 1883), and *Negro Myths from the Georgia Coast* (1888). The historian George Bancroft pronounced *The History of Georgia* the best state history he knew and referred to its author as "the Macaulay of the South." Charles Colcock Jones, Jr., married first (on November 9th, 1858) Ruth Berrien Whitehead (1837–1861), daughter of John Whitehead (1783–1857) and his second wife, Julia Maria (Berrien) Belt (1801–1857), of Bath, Richmond County, Georgia; there were two children: Julia Berrien Jones (1859–1861) and Mary Ruth Jones (1861–1934). He married second (on October 29th, 1863) Eva Berrien Eve (1841–1890), daughter of William Joseph Eve (1804–1863) and Philoclea Edgeworth Casey (1813–1889), of Augusta, Georgia; there was one child: Edgeworth Casey Jones (1867–1931). Eva Berrien (Eve) Jones died in Augusta on October 25th, 1890, and was buried in Summerville Cemetery. Charles Colcock Jones, Jr., died in Augusta on July 19th, 1893, survived by two children, and was buried beside his second wife. He received the honorary degree of doctor of laws from New York University in 1880 and from Oxford University (Georgia) in 1882.

JONES, CHARLES COLCOCK III (1865–1953), engineer, third child of Dr. Joseph Jones (1833–1896) and his first wife, Caroline Smelt Davis (1832–1868), was born in Augusta, Georgia, on July 28th, 1865. He was named for his paternal grandfather, the Rev. Dr. Charles Colcock Jones (1804–1863). After a childhood spent in Augusta (1865–1866) and Nashville (1866–1868) he accompanied his parents to New Orleans, where his father was professor in the Medical Department of the University of Louisiana (later the Tulane University School of Medicine) for twenty-six years (1868–1894). His mother died suddenly in New Orleans on December 4th, 1868, leaving four young children; his father married second (on June 21st, 1870) Susan Rayner Polk (1842–1921), daughter of the Rt. Rev. Leonidas Polk, bishop of Louisiana and lieutenant general in the Confederate army. Charles Colcock Jones III was a mining and metallurgical engineer. After graduating in mechanics from Louisiana State University in 1884 and in mining and metallurgy from Lehigh University in 1887 he held various engineering posts in the East. In 1902 he removed to California, where for many years he played a prominent part in the development of the iron and steel industry. On May 31st, 1898, he married Elizabeth Clayton King, of Augusta, Georgia. He died in Los Angeles, California, on April 28th, 1953, and was buried in Inglewood Park Cemetery.

JONES, CHARLES MARION (1844–1906), lumber inspector, eldest son of Charles Berrien Jones (1820–1857) and Marion Susan Anderson (1823–1888), was born in Walthourville, Liberty County, Georgia, on January 25th, 1844. When he was thirteen years old his father died (on May 5th, 1857); two years later (on April 28th, 1859) his mother married Thomas King, a planter of Liberty County. On May 25th, 1861, he enlisted as a private in Company D, 2nd Regiment Georgia Infantry; on July 2nd, 1864, he was appointed second lieutenant and ensign. He was severely wounded at Second Manassas on August 30th, 1862; returning to Georgia, he remained on sick furlough until January 1863, when he rejoined his command. After the war he accompanied his mother and stepfather to Jacksonville, Florida, where he engaged in the lumber business. He died suddenly in Jacksonville on August 30th, 1906, leaving a wife and five children, and was buried near his mother in Evergreen Cemetery.

JONES, EDGEWORTH CASEY (1867–1931), author, only son of Charles Colcock Jones, Jr. (1831–1893) and his second wife, Eva Berrien Eve (1841–1890), was born in New York City on July 27th, 1867. He was a prodigious child; in his fourth year (on April 15th, 1871) his father described him as "a grand, big fellow with a wonderful memory and quite a head of his own." His aunt, Mrs. Mary S. Mallard, was more objective: "It would do him good," she wrote on August 30th, 1876, "if he could be tossed around by boys, for he is too cautious ever to be very active." In the spring of 1877 he accompanied his parents to Georgia and settled at Montrose, a fine antebellum mansion in Summerville, a suburb of Augusta. He inherited his father's taste for literature. After graduating from the University of Georgia in 1885 he studied Greek and Latin at Johns Hopkins University for two years (1885–1887) without receiving a degree. He then read law in his father's office. His mother died on October 25th, 1890; his father died three years later, on July 19th, 1893. For the rest of his life he resided at Montrose in the household of his half-sister, Mary Ruth Jones (1861–1934), wife of the Rev. Samuel Barstow Carpenter. He was author of several tracts, including *Education in Georgia* (1889) and *Georgia in the War* (1909); he also published a memorial essay on his father (1893) and translated Augustine Prévost's *Journal of the Siege of Savannah in 1779* from the French (1897). For many years he was historian of the Confederate Survivors' Association, of which his father was founder and first president. He never married. He died at Montrose on October 30th, 1931, survived by his half-sister, and was buried near his parents in Summerville Cemetery. (Sometime during his boyhood he changed his name from Edgeworth Casey Jones to Charles Edgeworth Jones; evidently he preferred a combination of his father's first name and his maternal grandmother's middle name to a combination of his maternal grandmother's middle name and maiden surname.)

JONES, EDWIN WEST (1833–1862), ninth child of Joseph Jones (1779–1846) and his third wife, Elizabeth Screven Lee Hart (1801–1870), was born in Sunbury, Liberty County, Georgia, on September 11th, 1833. He was a half-brother of the Rev. John Jones (1815–1893) and Mary Jones (1808–1869), wife of the Rev. Dr. Charles Colcock Jones. He was evidently something of a ne'er-do-well. "Poor West!" wrote his cousin, Charles Colcock Jones, Jr., on October 7th, 1862; "with all his deficiencies he had ever an honest heart." On November 10th, 1857, he married Mary Elizabeth A. Howitt (1841–1906), of Savannah; their only child, Joseph LeHardy Jones, died in infancy. During the Civil War he was a private in Captain J. P. W. Read's Company (Company K, 10th Regiment Georgia Volun-

teers; attached, as Company L, to the 1st Regiment Virginia Artillery); he fought in the Peninsula campaign, and he was killed at Sharpsburg on September 17th, 1862. His first cousin, Thomas Henry Hart (1843–1864), standing at the next gun, saw him fall and reported his death to his family. He was buried beneath a tree by two of his comrades working at night. As the Rev. Dr. Charles Colcock Jones observed in his journal (October 10th, 1862), "His name must be enrolled among the noble martyrs in our second and greater revolution for liberty and independence." His widow subsequently married Marc A. Barié (1843–1889); she died in Savannah on September 19th, 1906, and was buried beside her second husband in Laurel Grove Cemetery.

JONES, ELIZA LOW (1858–1891), fifth child of Henry Hart Jones (1823–1893) and Abigail Sturges Dowse (1828–1897), was born in Walthourville, Liberty County, Georgia, on May 2nd, 1858. She was named for her great-aunt, Eliza Greene Low (1785–1868), widow of David Robarts. She was baptized with her cousin, Mary Jones Mallard, on Sunday morning, June 6th, 1858, in the Walthourville Presbyterian Church by her uncle, the Rev. Dr. Charles Colcock Jones. On April 9th, 1879, in Macon, Georgia, "Lila" became the wife of Cooper David Winn (1857–1913), eldest son of David Read Evans Winn and Frances Mary Dean. Her husband was engaged in the wholesale candy and cracker business. On the day of her marriage the Macon *Telegraph & Messenger,* of which her father was editor and proprietor, commented thus: "Both the youthful parties, in mercantile parlance, are strictly gilt-edged and unexceptionable. The groom is justly regarded as one of the finest young men in Bibb County, and as for Miss Lila, they don't make them any better." There were six children. Eliza Low (Jones) Winn died of pneumonia in Vineville, a suburb of Macon, on May 10th, 1891, and was buried in Rose Hill Cemetery. As the Atlanta *Constitution* (May 11th, 1891) observed, "The world is always better by the lives of such charming and worthy women." Nine years later, on June 20th, 1900, her husband married the younger sister of his first wife, Abby Augusta Jones (1864–1943), widow of Edgar Polhill Mitchell.

JONES, ELIZABETH SCREVEN LEE (HART) (1801–1870): *Mrs. Joseph Jones,* seventh child of John Hart (1758–1814) and Mary Esther Screven (1767–1845), was born in Charleston, South Carolina, on February 25th, 1801. Her father was captain in the 2nd South Carolina Regiment during the Revolutionary War; her maternal grandfather, General James Screven (1744–1778), fell mortally wounded in a skirmish with the British near Midway Church, Liberty County, Georgia, on November 24th, 1778. On January 25th, 1820, she became the third wife of Joseph Jones (1779–1846), a wealthy planter, son of John Jones (1749–1779) and Mary Sharpe (1753–1798), and settled at the Retreat, his plantation in Liberty County. She was the mother of fourteen children, ten of whom lived to maturity: Charles Berrien Jones (1820–1857); Evelyn Elouisa Jones (1822–1849), wife of Joseph Andrew Anderson; Henry Hart Jones (1823–1893); James Newton Jones (1825–1854); Emma Adelaide Jones (1827–1913), wife of (1) Stephen Nathan Harris and (2) Columbus Starnes Harris; Hetty Augusta Jones (1829–1857), wife of George Troup Maxwell; Andrew Maybank Jones (1831–1895); Edwin West Jones (1833–1862); Josephine Elizabeth Caroline Jones (1839–1857), wife of John Jackson Maxwell; and Helen Louisa Jones (1841–1911), wife of Keith Axson Quarterman. She was a stepmother of the Rev. John Jones (1815–1893) and Mary Jones (1808–1869), wife of the Rev. Dr. Charles Colcock Jones. After her husband's death on October 18th, 1846, continued to reside at the Retreat until December 1856, when she sold the family residence to her son, Henry Hart Jones, and settled in Walthourville. After the war she resided in Randolph County, Georgia, with her youngest living daughter, Helen Louisa Jones, wife of Keith Axson Quarterman. There she died on April 7th, 1870, and was buried in Greenwood Cemetery, Cuthbert. As the Savannah *Republican* (April 15th, 1870) observed, "This excellent Christian lady was the mother of fourteen children, four only of whom survive. She was eminently the child of affliction, having lost a devoted husband and ten children, most of the latter of adult age. Superadded to this was the destruction of her private fortune by the issue of the late war. Still an humble yet earnest servant of Christ, as a member of the Presbyterian Church for half a century, her faith never wavered; but by precept and example her life was a beautiful illustration of our blessed religion. Fragrant indeed are the memories connected with the experience and history of this departed saint."

JONES, ELLA STURGES (1851–1854), third child of Henry Hart Jones (1823–1893) and Abigail Sturges Dowse (1828–1897), was born at Lodebar, her father's plantation in Liberty County, Georgia, on March 22nd, 1851. During the hurricane of September 1854 "little Ella" and her mother stayed at Maybank, the house of her uncle, the Rev. Dr. Charles Colcock Jones, on Colonel's Island. She died of croup on November 18th, 1854, in her fourth year. "A sad affliction," wrote Dr. Jones on November 28th, 1854: "The little thing suffered a great deal, but finally died tranquilly." She was buried in Midway Cemetery.

JONES, ELLEN ELIZABETH (1852–1913), only daughter of James Newton Jones (1825–1854) and Sarah Jane Norman (1827–1896), was born at the Retreat, her father's plantation in Liberty County, Georgia, on December 6th, 1852. Her father died on October 8th, 1854, before her second birthday; two years later her mother sold her interest in the Retreat to her husband's brother, Henry Hart

Jones, and returned to her girlhood home in Walthourville. On June 27th, 1872, in Macon, Georgia, Ellen Elizabeth Jones became the wife of George Boyer Dettre (1841–1885), of Norristown, Pennsylvania. After a brief residence in Norristown she and her husband returned in 1877 to Macon, where George Boyer Dettre engaged in the grocery business until shortly before his death on May 5th, 1885. He was buried in Rose Hill Cemetery, Macon. His widow continued to live with her two daughters in Macon; after her mother's death on August 8th, 1896, she returned to Walthourville, where she lived with her unmarried daughter, Sarah E. Dettre, until 1913, when illness forced her to remove to a hospital in Savannah. She died in Savannah on July 12th, 1913, survived by two daughters, and was buried beside her husband.

JONES, EVA BERRIEN (EVE). *See* Eve, Eva Berrien

JONES, HELEN LOUISA (1841–1911), daughter of Joseph Jones (1779–1846) and his third wife, Elizabeth Screven Lee Hart (1801–1870), was born at the Retreat, her father's plantation in Liberty County, Georgia, on September 23rd, 1841. She was a half-sister of the Rev. John Jones (1815–1893) and Mary Jones (1808–1869), wife of the Rev. Dr. Charles Colcock Jones. On October 18th, 1846, when she was five years old, her father died; her elder brother, James Newton Jones, undertook the management of Retreat plantation and assumed the guardianship of his younger brothers and sisters. He died on October 8th, 1854; two years later, in December 1856, her mother sold her interest in the Retreat to Henry Hart Jones and removed with her daughter to Walthourville. There, on July 30th, 1862, she became the wife of Dr. Keith Axson Quarterman (1838–1900), son of Thomas Quarterman (1788–1857) and his third wife, Sarah Ellen (Sanford) Norman (1801–1871), of Walthourville. Her husband, a graduate of Franklin College (Athens) in 1857 and Jefferson Medical College (Philadelphia) in 1861, was assistant surgeon of the 10th Battalion Georgia Cavalry. There were ten children. After the Civil War she and her husband settled in Cuthbert, Georgia, where he practiced medicine, operated a drugstore, and taught school. For two years (1876–1877) he was principal of the Valdosta Institute. Late in 1877 he returned to Walthourville, where he practiced medicine until his death on August 10th, 1900. Helen Louisa (Jones) Quarterman died in Atlanta on March 29th, 1911, and was buried beside her husband in Walthourville Cemetery.

JONES, HENRY HART (1823–1893), planter and journalist, third child of Joseph Jones (1779–1846) and his third wife, Elizabeth Screven Lee Hart (1801–1870), was born at the Retreat, his father's plantation in Liberty County, Georgia, on December 2nd, 1823. He was a half-brother of the Rev. John Jones (1815–1893) and Mary Jones (1808–1869), wife of the Rev. Dr. Charles Colcock Jones. After graduating with distinction from Franklin College (Athens) in 1844 he returned to his native county and engaged successfully in planting until the outbreak of the Civil War. On May 21st, 1846, in Bath, Richmond County, Georgia, he married Abigail (Abby) Sturges Dowse (1828–1897), only child of Samuel Dowse (1786–1856) and his fourth wife, Abigail Elizabeth Sturges (1807–1828). Six of their eleven children died in infancy. He and his family lived at Lodebar plantation (1846–1856) and at Retreat plantation (1856–1862). His interest in politics was lifelong: in 1852 he was elected delegate to the Democratic National Convention meeting in Baltimore; in 1859 he was appointed aide-de-camp to Joseph Emerson Brown, governor of Georgia (1857–1865). On October 1st, 1861, he enlisted as a private in the Liberty Independent Troop, but in February 1862 he was detached to join the staff of Governor Brown as colonel in charge of enrolling militia in seven counties (Bryan, Liberty, Tattnall, Appling, Montgomery, Telfair, and Coffee). In October 1862 he removed with his family to Baker County, Georgia; and in the following year he settled in Cuthbert, where he entered business and served as editor of the Cuthbert *Appeal* (1866–1870). In 1871 he purchased an interest in the Macon *Telegraph & Messenger* and removed to Macon. During the next ten years he served successively as associate editor, managing editor, and editor in chief; in 1881 he sold his interest and retired from the editorial staff. From 1881 to 1891 he planted in Bibb County and traveled as correspondent of the Macon *Telegraph & Messenger* and the Savannah *Morning News*. In December 1891 he retired to his residence in Vineville, a suburb of Macon, where he died on February 13th, 1893, survived by his wife and four children. He was buried in Riverside Cemetery, Macon. He was a distinguished journalist; his editorial work on the Cuthbert *Appeal* and the Macon *Telegraph & Messenger* has permanent value as a commentary on Southern affairs during the critical years of Reconstruction.

JONES, JAMES DUNWODY (1842–1904), Confederate soldier, planter, and salesman, eldest son of the Rev. John Jones (1815–1893) and Jane Adaline Dunwody (1820–1884), was born at Hopestill, the plantation of his maternal grandfather, James Dunwody, in McIntosh County, Georgia, on May 1st, 1842. He spent his early years in the various places where his father, a Presbyterian clergyman, was pastor: Darien (1843–1847), Marietta (1847–1853), Savannah (1854–1855), Walthourville (1855), Washington (1856–1857), and Rome (1857–1863). After attending school for several years in Marietta he studied in the spring of 1854 at the Chatham Academy, Savannah; for three years (October 1854–October 1857) he attended the Villa High School, conducted by the Rev. Carlisle Pollock Beman near Mount Zion, Hancock County; for one year (January 1858–January 1859) he attended the boys' school conducted by the Rev. John Wilson Reid in Philomath, near

Woodstock, Oglethorpe County. He spent his school vacations at Hopestill, his grandfather's plantation in McIntosh County; at Bonaventure, his father's plantation in Liberty County; and at Maybank and Montevideo, the plantations of his uncle, the Rev. Dr. Charles Colcock Jones, in Liberty County. "Dunwody is very fond of a gun, and has many exploits to relate," wrote his cousin, Mary Sharpe Jones, on April 12th, 1854; "and he is really quite a successful little marksman." On May 18th, 1861, he enlisted as a private in the Rome Light Guards (Company A, 8th Regiment Georgia Infantry). "I like this kind of life first-rate," he wrote on July 8th, 1861, from Camp Washington, near Winchester, Virginia; "it suits me, for you know I always wanted to wander about." He fought at First Manassas and through the Peninsula campaign of 1862. "Dunwody never complains, and is uniformly cheerful and buoyant," his father wrote on June 10th, 1862. "He has been one of the best campaigners in the army." In August 1862 he was transferred to Georgia, where on October 31st, 1862, for great gallantry in the Virginia campaigns, he was promoted to second lieutenant and drillmaster, to serve under Colonel John B. Weems, enrolling officer for the State of Georgia. He continued military service in Georgia until the end of the war; in February 1864, promoted to first lieutenant, he was on duty at headquarters of conscription at Camp Cooper, near Macon; in May 1864 he was scouting for deserters in Decatur County; in July 1864 he was drilling the guard at Andersonville Prison. After the war he planted for several years in Liberty County. On November 2nd, 1870, he married Mary Cornelia Ashley (1848–1924), daughter of William Percy Morford Ashley (1827–1888), of Camden County; a year later, in October 1871, he removed to Atlanta, where he engaged in commercial pursuits until his death on February 19th, 1904. He was buried near his parents in Oakland Cemetery. Mary Cornelia (Ashley) Jones died on August 24th, 1924, and was buried beside her husband.

JONES, JAMES NEWTON (1825–1854), planter, fourth child of Joseph Jones (1779–1846) and Elizabeth Screven Lee Hart (1801–1870), was born in Sunbury, Liberty County, Georgia, on September 14th, 1825. He was a half-brother of the Rev. John Jones (1815–1893) and Mary Jones (1808–1869), wife of the Rev. Dr. Charles Colcock Jones. After the death of his father on October 18th, 1846, he undertook the management of Retreat plantation and the guardianship of his younger brothers and sisters. On November 27th, 1851, he married Sarah Jane Norman (1827–1896), daughter of William Norman (1794–1827) and Sarah Ellen Sanford (1801–1871). Three years later, on October 8th, 1854, he died suddenly of yellow fever at Lodebar, the plantation of his brother, Henry Hart Jones, survived by his wife and one daughter, and was buried in the family cemetery at the Retreat. According to *The Southern Presbyterian* (October 26th,

1854), "he filled no common space in usefulness. . . . To a strong, clear mind, remarkable for its precision and accuracy, he added an indomitable energy and perseverance, scarcely if ever equalled and never surpassed. He stepped into his father's place immediately after his death, at the head of a large family of young children, and with eminent ability, though but a youth, conducted their large and varied interests to the day when he was stricken down. . . . A husband, none was more tender; a father, none more fond; a son and a brother, none more devoted; a citizen, none more esteemed and valued." Sarah Jane (Norman) Jones died in Macon, Georgia, at the home of her daughter on August 8th, 1896.

JONES, JANE ADALINE (DUNWODY) (1820–1884): *Mrs. John Jones,* third child of James Dunwody (1789–1833) and Elizabeth West Smith (1794–1879), was born in McIntosh County, Georgia, on October 10th, 1820. She was a sister of Mary Elizabeth Dunwody (1818–1884), William James Dunwody (1823–1873), and Dean Munro Dunwody (1825–1878). She spent much of her girlhood in McIntosh County on the two family plantations, Hopestill and Brighton. On February 18th, 1841, she became the wife of the Rev. John Jones (1815–1893), son of Joseph Jones (1779–1846) and his second wife, Sarah Anderson (1783–1817). There were four children: James Dunwody Jones (1842–1904), Mary Elizabeth Jones (1849–1852), John Carolin Jones (1852–1933), and Joseph Henry Jones (1854–1935). Through her married years she lived successively in Bryan County (1841–1843), Darien (1843–1847), Marietta (1847–1853), Savannah (1854–1855), Walthourville (1855), Washington (1856–1857), Rome (1857–1863), Baker County (1863–1866), Griffin (1866–1870), and Atlanta (1870–1884). "She is truly a lovable woman, and little, and very amusing," wrote Mary Eliza Robarts on May 23rd, 1847; but she suffered from "extreme reserve" and a frail constitution. She died in Atlanta on March 20th, 1884, exactly one week after the death of her sister, Mary Elizabeth Dunwody, and was buried in Oakland Cemetery.

JONES, JOHN (1815–1893), Presbyterian clergyman, son of Joseph Jones (1779–1846) and his second wife, Sarah Anderson (1783–1817), was born at the Retreat, his father's plantation in Liberty County, Georgia, on November 15th, 1815. His mother died on September 8th, 1817, before he was two years old; his father married third (on January 25th, 1820) Elizabeth Screven Lee Hart (1801–1870). His elder sister, Mary Jones (1808–1869), only other surviving child of his father's second marriage, was his particular friend; as he later recalled, she not only proved to be "a kind sister" but also "acted the part of an affectionate mother." On December 21st, 1830, she became the wife of her first cousin, the Rev. Dr. Charles Colcock Jones (1804–1863). John Jones graduated from Franklin College (Athens) in 1836 and from Columbia Theological Seminary in 1839. On February 18th, 1841,

he married Jane Adaline Dunwody (1820–1884), daughter of James Dunwody (1789–1833) and Elizabeth West Smith (1794–1879), of McIntosh County. There were four children: James Dunwody Jones (1842–1904), Mary Elizabeth Jones (1849–1852), John Carolin Jones (1852–1933), and Joseph Henry Jones (1854–1935). He was pastor of churches in Bryan County (1841–1843), Darien (1843–1847), Marietta (1847–1853), Savannah (1854–1855), Walthourville (1855), Washington (1856–1857), and Rome (1857–1863). For six months in 1861 he was chaplain of the 8th Regiment Georgia Infantry in Northern Virginia. After serving rural churches in Southwest Georgia for three years (1863–1866) he was pastor in Griffin (1866–1870) and then settled in Atlanta, where he was evangelist of the Atlanta Presbytery for twenty-three years (1870–1893), chaplain of the state house of representatives (1872–1882), and chaplain of the state senate (1882–1893). His latter years were saddened by almost total loss of sight. He died in Atlanta on November 26th, 1893, survived by three sons, and was buried beside his wife in Oakland Cemetery. He received the honorary degree of doctor of divinity from the University of Georgia in 1876.

JONES, JOHN, JR. (1798–1813), son of John Jones (1772–1805) and his first wife, Elizabeth Stewart (1774–1801), was born in Liberty County, Georgia, in 1798. He was a younger brother of Elizabeth Jones (1794–1856), wife of William Maxwell; he was also a half-brother of Susan Mary Jones (1803–1890) and Charles Colcock Jones (1804–1863). His mother died on February 27th, 1801, when he was two years old; his father married second (on August 4th, 1801) Susannah Hyrne Girardeau (1778–1810). After his father's death on March 28th, 1805, he continued to live in the household of his stepmother until her death on July 1st, 1810, when he became a ward of his uncle, Joseph Jones. He died on November 24th, 1813, aged fifteen, and was buried in Midway Cemetery.

JONES, JOHN CAROLIN (1852–1933), lawyer, second son of the Rev. John Jones (1815–1893) and Jane Adaline Dunwody (1820–1884), was born in Marietta, Georgia, on June 30th, 1852. He spent his early years in the various places where his father, a Presbyterian clergyman, was pastor: Savannah (1854–1855), Walthourville (1855), Washington (1856–1857), Rome (1857–1863), Baker County (1863–1866), and Griffin (1866–1870). He graduated from Oglethorpe University in 1872. After studying law he practiced for several years in Atlanta; in 1881 he removed to Orlando, Florida, where he became one of the leading lawyers in the state. In 1893 his younger brother, Joseph Henry Jones (1854–1935), settled in Orlando and joined him in the law firm of Jones & Jones. John Carolin Jones died in Orlando on March 4th, 1933, survived by his wife, Fannie McGoffin, and three children, and was buried in Greenwood Cemetery.

JONES, JOSEPH (1779–1846), planter, younger son of John Jones (1749–1779) and Mary Sharpe (1753–1798), was born in Jacksonboro, South Carolina, on November 26th, 1779. His father, a native of Charleston, had migrated shortly before the Revolutionary War to coastal Georgia; a few years later, at the siege of Savannah, he had met a patriot's death on October 9th, 1779, seven weeks before the birth of his younger son. Joseph Jones resided almost all his life in Liberty County, Georgia, where he was, according to his grandson, Charles Colcock Jones, Jr. (May 11th, 1888), "a gentleman of large wealth, and a most successful planter. Just, honorable, charitable to the widow and orphan, he was a man of imperious will, of great personal courage, quick in quarrel, impatient of restraint, intolerant of opposition, and of mark in the community." He married first (on January 16th, 1799) Mary Maybank (1781–1804), daughter of Andrew Maybank and Martha Splatt; only one of their four children lived to maturity: Joseph Maybank Jones (1804–1831). He married second (on June 30th, 1806) Sarah Anderson (1783–1817), daughter of David Anderson and Mary McClenning; two of their eight children lived to maturity: Mary Jones (1808–1869), wife of the Rev. Dr. Charles Colcock Jones, and John Jones (1815–1893). He married third (on January 25th, 1820) Elizabeth Screven Lee Hart (1801–1870), daughter of John Hart (1758–1814) and Mary Esther Screven (1767–1845); ten of their fourteen children lived to maturity: Charles Berrien Jones (1820–1857); Evelyn Elouisa Jones (1822–1849), wife of Joseph Andrew Anderson; Henry Hart Jones (1823–1893); James Newton Jones (1825–1854); Emma Adelaide Jones (1827–1913), wife of (1) Stephen Nathan Harris and (2) Columbus Starnes Harris; Hetty Augusta Jones (1829–1857), wife of George Troup Maxwell; Andrew Maybank Jones (1831–1895); Edwin West Jones (1833–1862); Josephine Elizabeth Caroline Jones (1839–1857), wife of John Jackson Maxwell; and Helen Louisa Jones (1841–1911), wife of Keith Axson Quarterman. Joseph Jones was captain of the Liberty Independent Troop during the War of 1812. He died on October 18th, 1846, from injuries sustained when he was thrown from his buggy three days before. He was buried beside his first two wives in the family cemetery at the Retreat. His third wife died near Cuthbert, Georgia, on April 7th, 1870, and was buried in Greenwood Cemetery, Cuthbert.

JONES, JOSEPH (1833–1896), physician and educator, second son of the Rev. Dr. Charles Colcock Jones (1804–1863) and his first cousin, Mary Jones (1808–1869), was born in Walthourville, Liberty County, Georgia, on September 6th, 1833. He spent his boyhood in Liberty County, where his parents owned three plantations (Arcadia, Montevideo, and Maybank), and in Columbia, South Carolina, where his father, a Presbyterian clergyman, was twice professor at Columbia Theological Seminary (1837–1838; 1848–1850). He attended the South Carolina College (1848–1850), and in 1850, when his father became corresponding secretary of the Board of Domestic Missions of the Presbyterian Church, with offices in Philadelphia, he accompanied his parents North and entered the College of New Jersey (Princeton), from which he graduated in 1853. For the next three years he attended the Medical College of the University of Pennsylvania, where he was a private student of Joseph Leidy, Samuel Jackson, and Hugh Lenox Hodge. After graduating in 1856 he returned to Georgia, where he was professor of chemistry at the Savannah Medical College (1856–1857); professor of natural philosophy and natural theology at the University of Georgia, Athens (1857–1858); and professor of chemistry at the Medical College of Georgia, Augusta (1858–1866). For six months (October 1861–March 1862) he was a private in the Liberty Independent Troop (Company G, 5th Regiment Georgia Cavalry), acting as post surgeon. On December 20th, 1862, he was appointed surgeon, with rank of major; for the rest of the war he conducted medical research in Confederate camps under the direction of Surgeon General Samuel Preston Moore. After the war he was professor of pathology at the Medical College of Nashville (1866–1868) and professor of chemistry and clinical medicine in the Medical Department of the University of Louisiana (1868–1894). He was visiting physician to the New Orleans Charity Hospital (1870–1894); president of the Louisiana Board of Health (1880–1884); president of the Louisiana Medical Society (1885–1886); and surgeon general of the United Confederate Veterans (1889–1896). Through his researches and publications, particularly in tropical medicine and general hygiene, he gained an international reputation; his *Medical and Surgical Memoirs* (1876–1890), published in four enormous volumes, embraced the chief investigations of his long career. He married first (on October 26th, 1859) Caroline Smelt Davis (1832–1868), daughter of the Rev. Dr. Samuel Stanhope Davis (1793–1877) and Mary Cuthbert Cumming (1797–1876), of Augusta; there were four children: Samuel Stanhope Davis Jones (1860–1894), Susan Hyrne Jones (1863–1921), Charles Colcock Jones III (1865–1953), and Mary Cuthbert Jones (1867–1939). He married second (on June 21st, 1870) Susan Rayner Polk (1842–1921), daughter of the Rt. Rev. Leonidas Polk (1806–1864), bishop of Louisiana and lieutenant general in the Confederate army; there were three children: Hamilton Polk Jones (1872–1926), Frances Devereux Jones (1876–1941), and Laura Maxwell Jones (1880–1917). He died in New Orleans on February 17th, 1896, and was buried in the family vault in Lafayette Cemetery. He received the honorary degree of doctor of laws from the University of Georgia in 1892. Two of his sons, Stanhope Jones and Hamilton Polk Jones, and his eldest grandson, Stanhope Bayne-Jones, were also physicians.

JONES, JOSEPH HENRY (1854–1935), lawyer, third son of the Rev. John Jones (1815–1893) and Jane Adaline Dunwody (1820–1884), was born at Hopestill, the plantation of his maternal grandfather, James Dunwody, in McIntosh County, Georgia, on April 21st, 1854. He spent his early years in the various places where his father, a Presbyterian clergyman, was pastor: Savannah (1854–1855), Walthourville (1855), Washington (1856–1857), Rome (1857–1863), Baker County (1863–1866), and Griffin (1866–1870). He attended Oglethorpe University (1870–1872) and Mercer University (1872–1874) and graduated from Mercer University in 1874. In 1877 he became Atlanta editor of the Macon *Telegraph & Messenger.* "You don't know how handsome he is now," wrote Mrs. Mary S. Mallard from Atlanta on March 22nd, 1877, "and as considerate as ever." Eight years later, on July 20th, 1885, she observed that he "is looking very well but is very small." After working for several years as teller in the Merchants' Bank of Atlanta he removed in 1893 to Orlando, Florida, where he joined his elder brother, John Carolin Jones (1852–1933), in the law firm of Jones & Jones. From 1914 to 1923 he was state's attorney for the seventh judicial district. He never married. He died in Orlando on July 25th, 1935, and was buried in Greenwood Cemetery.

JONES, JULIA BERRIEN (1859–1861), elder daughter of Charles Colcock Jones, Jr. (1831–1893) and his first wife, Ruth Berrien Whitehead (1837–1861), was born in Savannah, Georgia, on November 18th, 1859. She was named for her maternal grandmother, Julia Maria Berrien (1801–1857), widow of Lloyd Belt and second wife of John Whitehead. She was baptized on Sunday morning, February 12th, 1860, in Midway Church by her paternal grandfather, the Rev. Dr. Charles Colcock Jones. On March 14th, 1861, Mrs. Mary Jones described her as "a most interesting child: intellectually bright with a loving little heart." On April 17th, 1861, her father reported that "she already takes great delight in her little linen books, and will explain the pictures." She died in Savannah of scarlet fever on July 2nd, 1861, five days before the death of her mother, and was buried in the family vault of T. W. Neely in Laurel Grove Cemetery.

JONES, LAURA CLIFFORD (1832–1911), eldest child of Moses Liberty Jones (1805–1851) and Sacharissa Elizabeth Axson (1811–1850), was born at Green Forest, her father's plantation in Liberty County, Georgia, on January 13th, 1832. She was no relation of the Rev. Dr. Charles Colcock Jones. After the death of her mother on October 30th, 1850, and the death of her father on May 28th, 1851, she assumed the guardianship of her five younger sisters (Leonora, Eugenia, Mary, Clara, and Rosa). In the autumn of 1854 she was engaged to be married to the Rev. Francis Henry Bowman (1833–1873), co-pastor of Midway Church (1856–1859); but by December the engagement was broken off: "*They say* because *she* could not be married immediately,

he would not wait." So wrote Mary Sharpe Jones on December 25th, 1854. "I do really think," she continued, "that any young minister who acts in this way and breaks engagements ought to be disciplined in some way." On December 15th, 1859, Laura Clifford Jones became the wife of Raleigh Spinks Camp (1829–1867), professor of mathematics at the Georgia Military Institute (Marietta). There were two children: Augustus Jones Camp (1861–1912) and Rosa Leigh Camp (1867–1953). At the outbreak of the Civil War she and her husband were living in Marshall, Texas; she returned with her infant son to Georgia, and her husband was mustered into service as captain of Company B, 7th Regiment Texas Infantry. In March 1862 he was commissioned major in the 40th Regiment Georgia Infantry; in May 1864 his left arm was amputated after a severe gunshot wound sustained in battle in Northwest Georgia. After the war they settled in Atlanta, where he died suddenly of meningitis on November 24th, 1867. Laura Clifford (Jones) Camp continued to live in Atlanta until 1885, when she removed with her daughter to Birmingham, Alabama, where her son was secretary-treasurer of the Union Transfer Company (1888) and city auditor (1893). On May 31st, 1888, Rosa Leigh Camp became the wife of John Reed Towers, of Richmond, Virginia. Laura Clifford (Jones) Camp remained with her son in Birmingham, where she died on July 16th, 1911, survived by both of her children. She was buried beside her husband in Oak Hill Cemetery.

JONES, MARY (JONES) (1808–1869): *Mrs. Charles Colcock Jones,* daughter of Joseph Jones (1779–1846) and his second wife, Sarah Anderson (1783–1817), was born at the Retreat, her father's plantation in Liberty County, Georgia, on September 24th, 1808. Her mother died on September 8th, 1817; her father married third (on January 25th, 1820) Elizabeth Screven Lee Hart (1801–1870). Her younger brother, John Jones (1815–1893), only other surviving child of her father's second marriage, was her particular friend; as he later recalled, she not only proved to be "a kind sister" but also "acted the part of an affectionate mother." She attended the McIntosh Academy at Baisden's Bluff (1820–1823) and the academy of Abiel Carter in Savannah (1823–1827). On December 21st, 1830, she became the wife of her first cousin, the Rev. Dr. Charles Colcock Jones (1804–1863), a Presbyterian clergyman, son of John Jones (1772–1805) and his second wife, Susannah Hyrne Girardeau (1778–1810). Three of their four children lived to maturity: Charles Colcock Jones, Jr. (1831–1893), Joseph Jones (1833–1896), and Mary Sharpe Jones (1835–1889). A fourth child died at birth on September 7th, 1840. After serving for eighteen months (May 1831–November 1832) as pastor of the First Presbyterian Church, Savannah, her husband settled in his native county, where he devoted himself to the evangelization of the Negro, the great work of his life. He was twice professor at Columbia Theological Seminary,

Columbia, South Carolina (1837–1838; 1848–1850), and for three years (1850–1853) corresponding secretary of the Board of Domestic Missions of the Presbyterian Church, with offices in Philadelphia. In October 1853 he returned to Liberty County, where he resided for the rest of his life, supervising his three plantations (Arcadia, Montevideo, and Maybank) and continuing his evangelization of the Negro as his declining health permitted. He died at Arcadia plantation on March 16th, 1863, and was buried in Midway Cemetery. After the war his widow struggled unsuccessfully to maintain her three plantations in Liberty County; in January 1868 she removed to New Orleans, home of her daughter, wife of the Rev. Robert Quarterman Mallard, where she died on April 23rd, 1869. She was buried in Lafayette Cemetery. She was a woman of remarkable strength of character. Her husband spoke of her "energy" (December 18th, 1856), her "patriotism" (November 19th, 1860), and her "uniform cheerfulness" (May 22nd, 1854). Her daughter spoke of her "active, energetic, independent spirit" (April 24th, 1869). And her friend Cornelia Bond (Vanderveer) Grant spoke of her "strong, sound, sensible mind and good judgment and clear views" (July 8th, 1867).

JONES, MARY CUTHBERT (1867–1939), fourth child of Dr. Joseph Jones (1833–1896) and his first wife, Caroline Smelt Davis (1832–1868), was born in Nashville, Tennessee, on October 3rd, 1867. She was named for her maternal grandmother, Mary Cuthbert Cumming (1797–1876), wife of the Rev. Dr. Samuel Stanhope Davis. She was baptized in Nashville on November 27th, 1867, by her great-uncle, the Rev. John Jones. In early infancy she accompanied her parents to New Orleans, where her father was professor in the Medical Department of the University of Louisiana (later the Tulane University School of Medicine) for twenty-six years (1868–1894). Her mother died suddenly in New Orleans on December 4th, 1868, leaving four young children; her father married second (on June 21st, 1870) Susan Rayner Polk (1842–1921), daughter of the Rt. Rev. Leonidas Polk, bishop of Louisiana and lieutenant general in the Confederate army. On January 21st, 1896, Mary Cuthbert Jones became the wife of Julien Trist Bringier (1862–1922), a physician, son of Louis Amédée Bringier and Stella Tureaud, and settled at Tezcuco, on her husband's plantation on the Mississippi River at Burnside, near Donaldsonville, Louisiana. She died at Burnside on May 27th, 1939, survived by two daughters, Mary Trist Bringier and Suzanne Bringier, wife of Logan McConnell.

JONES, MARY RUTH (1861–1934), younger daughter of Charles Colcock Jones, Jr. (1831–1893) and his first wife, Ruth Berrien Whitehead (1837–1861), was born in Savannah, Georgia, on June 25th, 1861. Her mother died of puerperal fever on July 7th, 1861, and she was reared in the household of her paternal grandparents, the Rev. Dr. and Mrs. Charles Colcock Jones, of Liberty County, Georgia, until she was four years old. "Little Sister" was baptized on Thursday morning, September 18th, 1862, in the Walthourville Presbyterian Church by the Rev. Dr. Charles Colcock Jones. Her father married second (on October 28th, 1863) Eva Berrien Eve (1841–1890), a first cousin once removed of his first wife; in July 1865 Mary Ruth Jones returned to live in her father's household. From 1866 to 1877 she lived with her parents in New York City and Brooklyn; in the spring of 1877 she accompanied them back to Georgia and settled at Montrose, a fine antebellum mansion in Summerville, a suburb of Augusta, where she resided for the rest of her life. On February 13th, 1890, she became the wife of the Rev. Samuel Barstow Carpenter (1851–1912), an Episcopal clergyman, of Detroit, Michigan, for many years rector of the Church of the Atonement and the Church of the Good Shepherd in Augusta. After his death on May 26th, 1912, she continued to occupy the family residence, Montrose, until her death on July 17th, 1934. Two daughters survived. She was buried beside her husband and near her father and stepmother in Summerville Cemetery. (Sometime during her girlhood she changed her name from Mary Ruth Jones to Ruth Berrien Jones; evidently she preferred a combination of her mother's first name and middle name to a combination of her paternal grandmother's first name and her mother's first name.)

JONES, MARY SHARPE (1835–1889), third child and only daughter of the Rev. Dr. Charles Colcock Jones (1804–1863) and his first cousin, Mary Jones (1808–1869), was born at Lodebar plantation, Liberty County, Georgia, on June 12th, 1835. She spent much of her girlhood in Liberty County, where her parents owned three plantations (Arcadia, Montevideo, and Maybank), and in Columbia, South Carolina, where her father, a Presbyterian clergyman, was twice professor at Columbia Theological Seminary (1837–1838; 1848–1850). For three years (1850–1853) she lived in Philadelphia, where her father was corresponding secretary of the Board of Domestic Missions of the Presbyterian Church; she attended a seminary for young ladies conducted by the Misses Gill (1850–1852). Returning with her parents to Liberty County in October 1853, she led the life of a young lady at home until April 22nd, 1857, when she became the wife of the Rev. Robert Quarterman Mallard (1830–1904), a Presbyterian clergyman, youngest son of Thomas Mallard (1778–1861) and his second wife, Rebecca Eliza Burnley (1789–1861), widow of Thomas Baker; there were five children: Mary Jones Mallard (1858–1917), Charles Colcock Mallard (1860–1914), Eliza Burnley Mallard (1863–1863), Georgia Maxwell Mallard (1865–1952), and Robert Holt Mallard (1868–1869). Her husband was pastor of the Walthourville Presbyterian Church (1856–1863); the Central Presbyterian Church, Atlanta (1863–1866); the Prytania Street Presbyterian Church, New Orleans (1866–1877);

and the Napoleon Avenue Presbyterian Church, New Orleans (1879–1904). She died of pleurisy at the home of Louisa Jane Robarts in Marietta, Georgia, on August 31st, 1889, survived by her husband and three children, and was buried in the family vault in Lafayette Cemetery, New Orleans. "Everybody who knew her admired and loved her," wrote the Rev. David Lyman Buttolph on September 12th, 1889. "I never saw one who seemed so well poised in all those qualities which command admiration, respect, and love. She appeared always to say the right word and do the right thing. She came as near perfection as anyone I ever saw." Her husband married second (on January 19th, 1893) Amarintha Mary Witherspoon, daughter of the Rev. Andrew Jackson Witherspoon, a Presbyterian clergyman; he died in New Orleans on March 3rd, 1904, and was buried beside his first wife.

JONES, RANDAL FLEMING (1833–1864), commission merchant and Confederate soldier, only son of Moses Liberty Jones (1805–1851) and Sacharissa Elizabeth Axson (1811–1850), was born at Green Forest, his father's plantation in Liberty County, Georgia, in 1833. He was no relation of the Rev. Dr. Charles Colcock Jones. After graduating from Franklin College (Athens) in 1854 he became a commission merchant in Savannah. On May 13th, 1862, he enlisted as second lieutenant in the 21st Battalion Georgia Cavalry (later part of the 7th Regiment Georgia Cavalry); on April 10th, 1863, he was elected captain. On June 11th, 1864, he was wounded at Trevilian's Station, near Louisa Courthouse, Virginia; returning to Georgia on sick furlough, he died in Savannah on July 27th, 1864. He never married.

JONES, RUTH BERRIEN (WHITEHEAD). *See* Whitehead, Ruth Berrien

JONES, SAMUEL JOHN (1838–1889), physician, son of William Jones (1802–1885) and Mary Jane Robarts (1806–1886), was born near Riceboro, Liberty County, Georgia, on January 3rd, 1838. He was no relation of the Rev. Dr. Charles Colcock Jones. After graduating from Franklin College (Athens) in 1856 and from the Medical College of South Carolina (Charleston) in 1858 he practiced medicine in Liberty County until July 1863, when he enlisted as a private in the Liberty Mounted Rangers (Company B, 20th Battalion Georgia Cavalry). From March 1864 to November 1864 he was nurse in a military hospital in Charleston. After the war he resumed practice in Liberty County. In 1868 he removed to Thomasville, Georgia, where he planted and practiced his profession for twenty years. He married first (on October 13th, 1859) Mary Hayes, of Athens; he married second (on May 28th, 1878) Mary Elizabeth Mueller, of Savannah. He died in Thomasville on January 10th, 1889, survived by five children, and was buried in Laurel Hill Cemetery beside his second wife, who had died on March 22nd, 1887.

JONES, SAMUEL STANHOPE DAVIS (1860–1894), physician, eldest son of Dr. Joseph Jones (1833–1896) and his first wife, Caroline Smelt Davis (1832–1868), was born in Augusta, Georgia, on December 16th, 1860. He was named for his maternal grandfather, the Rev. Dr. Samuel Stanhope Davis (1793–1877); but he seldom used the full name, preferring to be called simply "Stanhope." He was baptized on Sunday morning, March 3rd, 1861, in Midway Church by his paternal grandfather, the Rev. Dr. Charles Colcock Jones. After a childhood spent in Augusta (1861–1866) and Nashville (1866–1868) he accompanied his parents to New Orleans, where his father was professor in the Medical Department of the University of Louisiana (later the Tulane University School of Medicine) for twenty-six years (1868–1894). His mother died suddenly in New Orleans on December 4th, 1868, leaving four young children; his father married second (on June 21st, 1870) Susan Rayner Polk (1842–1921), daughter of the Rt. Rev. Leonidas Polk, bishop of Louisiana and lieutenant general in the Confederate army. After attending Louisiana State University for one year (1879–1880) he entered the Medical Department of the University of Louisiana in 1880 and graduated on March 29th, 1883. He commenced practice in New Orleans in association with his father. He was assistant coroner of New Orleans (1884–1888). On November 15th, 1887, he married Amelia (Minna) Bayne (1867–1893), daughter of Thomas Livingston Bayne, of Mobile, Alabama; there were three children. After the death of his wife on March 2nd, 1893, he joined his younger brother, Charles Colcock Jones III, in a mining venture in Coeburn, Wise County, Virginia. There he died of dysentery on July 24th, 1894. He was buried in the family vault in Lafayette Cemetery, New Orleans. His eldest son, Stanhope Bayne-Jones (1888–1970), a graduate of Yale College (1910) and the Johns Hopkins Medical School (1914), was professor of bacteriology at the Yale Medical School (1932–1935) and dean (1935–1942). In 1942 he was appointed brigadier general of the United States Army Medical Corps; in 1953 he became technical director of research in the surgeon general's office. He held the Distinguished Service Medal of the United States, the Croix de Guerre, and the Order of the British Empire.

JONES, SARAH BARKSDALE (1804–1865), daughter of the Rev. Samuel Barksdale Jones, was born in Charleston, South Carolina, in 1804. For many years she occupied a house in Guignard Street with her two younger sisters, Susan Legare Jones (1808–1894) and Elizabeth Jones (1812–1857). She never married. She died of consumption on July 18th, 1865. The three Jones sisters were no relation of the Rev. Dr. Charles Colcock Jones, but they were "valued friends" of long standing. "They are as kind as ever," he wrote on May 24th, 1852, while staying in their house, "and grow better with time." From his "pleasant third-story room" he enjoyed a sweeping view of Charleston: "A fine sea breeze fans me while I write, looking over the tops of the houses—two church steeples before me and all the rattle and noise of the city beneath."

JONES, SUSAN HYRNE (1863–1921), second child of Dr. Joseph Jones (1833–1896) and his first wife, Caroline Smelt Davis (1832–1868), was born in Augusta, Georgia, on April 28th, 1863. After a childhood spent in Augusta (1863–1866) and Nashville (1866–1868) she accompanied her parents to New Orleans, where her father was professor in the Medical Department of the University of Louisiana (later the Tulane University School of Medicine) for twenty-six years (1868–1894). Her mother died suddenly in New Orleans on December 4th, 1868, leaving four young children; her father married second (on June 21st, 1870) Susan Rayner Polk (1842–1921), daughter of the Rt. Rev. Leonidas Polk, bishop of Louisiana and lieutenant general in the Confederate army. Soon after her father's death on February 17th, 1896, she joined her stepmother and two half-sisters, Frances Devereux Jones (1876–1941) and Laura Maxwell Jones (1880–1917), in Chestnut Hill, Pennsylvania, where she taught at Springside School until her death on June 14th, 1921. She never married. She was buried in the cemetery of St. Thomas' Church, Whitemarsh, Pennsylvania. (Sometime during her girlhood she changed her name from Susan Hyrne Jones to Caroline Susan Jones; evidently she preferred a combination of her mother's first name and her paternal great-grandmother's first name to a combination of her paternal great-grandmother's first name and middle name.)

JORDAN, JOHN WINN (1806–1883), planter, iron manufacturer, and hotel proprietor, third son of John Jordan (1777–1854) and Lucy Winn (1782–1866), was born in Lexington, Virginia, on July 11th, 1806. His father, a native of Hanover County, had migrated in 1802 to Rockbridge County, where for half a century he was prominently identified with the interests of Lexington and the surrounding area. He promoted iron foundries, blacksmith shops, lumber mills, cotton mills, and flour and grist mills; he built roads and canals and numerous public buildings, including those of Washington College. He and his twelve sons owned and operated twelve iron furnaces in Rockbridge, Alleghany, Botetourt, Amherst, and Louisa Counties. In 1818 he built Jordan's Point, a Greek Revival mansion that became a county landmark. John Winn Jordan graduated from Washington College in 1826. For many years he was engaged in the development of the family iron interests. In the 1840s he purchased the Rockbridge Alum Springs and the Rockbridge Baths, both destined to become popular resorts for wealthy invalids from the slave states prior to the Civil War. It was at Rockbridge Baths that Mrs. Mary Jones found John Winn Jordan to be a "kind and attentive landlord" in August 1857. He died in Lexington on February 15th, 1883, and was buried beside his wife, Rachel F. Davis (1813–1865), in the Stonewall Jackson Memorial Cemetery.

KALLENDER, MARY CATHERINE (1814–1863), only daughter of Dr. Thomas M. Kallender (1785–1818) and Jane Robarts (1786–1838), was born in Liberty County, Georgia, in 1814. Her father died on March 11th, 1818, when she was four years old; after her mother's death on August 20th, 1838, she joined the household of George Washington Walthour in Walthourville, where she remained, evidently something of an invalid, for twenty years. In 1860 she was living as housekeeper in the family of William Lowndes Walthour. From time to time she stayed at Limestone Springs, Spartanburg County, South Carolina, where Eliza Amanda Walthour, eldest daughter of George Washington Walthour, resided with her husband, the Rev. William Curtis, a Baptist clergyman. Mary Catherine Kallender was one of sixteen citizens instrumental in organizing the Walthourville Presbyterian Church in 1855; and she was a friend of the pastor's wife, Mrs. Mary S. Mallard, with whom she exchanged recipes for homemade candles and shared her knowledge of spinning wheels and looms. She never married. She died in Walthourville in December 1863, after what Mrs. Susan M. Cumming called a "painful suffering life," and was buried in an unmarked grave near her parents in Midway Cemetery.

KANE, ELISHA KENT (1820–1857), physician, naval officer, and explorer, eldest son of John Kintzing Kane (1795–1858) and Jane Duval Leiper, was born in Philadelphia, Pennsylvania, on February 3rd, 1820. His father, a graduate of Yale College (1814), was a distinguished jurist. Elisha Kent Kane graduated from the Medical College of the University of Pennsylvania in 1842. As assistant surgeon in the United States navy he accompanied Caleb Cushing (1800–1879) on his China mission (1843–1844) and served briefly in the Mexican War (1846–1848). In 1850–1851 he was senior medical officer on a government expedition to the Arctic, organized by Edwin Jesse DeHaven (1816–1865) to search for Sir John Franklin (1786–1847), British explorer missing since 1845, and using ships supplied by Henry Grinnell (1799–1874). Upon his return to New York in September 1851 Kane described the voyage in *The U.S. Grinnell Expedition in Search of Sir John Franklin* (1853). A second Grinnell expedition, with Kane in command, sailed from New York on May 31st, 1853, and returned on October 11, 1855; Kane's account of the voyage, *Arctic Explorations: The Second Grinnell Expedition in Search of Sir John Franklin in the Years 1853, '54, '55* (2 vols., 1856), enjoyed enormous popularity and made its author a national hero. Kane died in Havana, Cuba, on February 16th, 1857; en route to burial in Philadelphia the body lay in state in New Orleans, Louisville, Columbus, and Baltimore.

KEENER, HENRY CLAY (1823–1866), carpenter and butcher, son of William Keener, was born in Augusta, Georgia, on November 11th, 1823. At an early age he became a carpenter. On January 7th, 1849, he married

Elizabeth C. Nance (1831–1905), of Columbia County, Georgia; there were four children. In January 1852 he was elected bailiff of Richmond County. On Sunday night, September 10th, 1854, during an altercation in a brothel kept by one Jane Yarborough, for whose favors the two men were notorious rivals, Henry Clay Keener shot James Reese three times in the breast and abdomen; two of the balls took fatal effect, and the third shattered Reese's watch. Keener escaped, but three days later he voluntarily gave himself up to the law. At the January 1855 term of the Richmond County Superior Court he was declared guilty and sentenced to hang; in June 1855 a motion for a new trial was granted by the state supreme court; at the November 1856 term of the Richmond County Superior Court he was declared not guilty and discharged. By 1860 he was superintendent of the Augusta waterworks. On April 27th, 1861, he enlisted as fifth sergeant in the Confederate Light Guards (Company G, 3rd Regiment Georgia Infantry); he was discharged for disability in September 1862. On September 19th, 1863, he enlisted as a private in the 12th Battalion Georgia Light Artillery; he was again discharged for disability in January 1864. He died in Augusta on December 17th, 1866, leaving three children and a pregnant wife. His widow survived him thirty-eight years; she supported herself as a seamstress until her death on January 24th, 1905. Two daughters survived: Julia Frances Keener (1850–1924), wife of John Cartledge; and Maud Henry Keener (1855–1936), wife of Alexander H. Miller. Henry Clay Keener was buried in Magnolia Cemetery, Augusta.

KENAN, AUGUSTUS HOLMES (1805–1865), lawyer, second son of John Kenan and Amelia Gray, was born in Montpelier, Baldwin County, Georgia, in 1805. His father, a native of Duplin County, North Carolina, had settled in Montpelier, on the Oconee River just opposite the site of the present Milledgeville; he was for twenty years clerk of the court of Baldwin County. Augustus Holmes Kenan was admitted to the bar in 1825 and soon rose to prominence as a criminal lawyer and state politician. He served three terms in the state house of representatives and one term in the state senate. He strenuously opposed secession: "Shut the doors of Congress!" he said. "Hang to the United States flag! Fight there, and only there, for the rights of the South! The South unquestionably has a right to secede. If she does secede, however, the North has an equal right to force her back in the Union." At the state secession convention meeting in Milledgeville in January 1861 he voted against the secession ordinance thirteen times, but in order to preserve an appearance of unanimity he reluctantly signed the ordinance and then threw away his pen. He was one of nine delegates elected to represent Georgia at the convention of seceding states meeting in Montgomery, Alabama, in February 1861. He was a loyal supporter of the Davis administration. He died on June 16th, 1865.

KERSHAW, JOSEPH BREVARD (1822–1894), lawyer and legislator, son of John Kershaw (1765–1829) and Harriette DuBose, was born in Camden, South Carolina, on January 5th, 1822. His father, a lawyer, was four times mayor of Camden (1798, 1801, 1811, 1822), twice member of the state legislature (1792, 1800), and member of Congress (1813–1815). Joseph Brevard Kershaw was admitted to the bar in 1843. He served in the Mexican War as lieutenant in the Palmetto Regiment. He was a member of the state legislature (1852–1856) and a member of the state secession convention meeting in Columbia in December 1860. At the outbreak of the Civil War he recruited a regiment (the 2nd Regiment South Carolina Volunteers) and became its colonel; he was at Fort Sumter and First Manassas. On February 13th, 1862, he was commissioned brigadier general; his command, known as Kershaw's brigade, McLaws' division, Longstreet's corps, Army of Northern Virginia, fought in the Peninsula campaign of 1862 and distinguished itself at Second Manassas, Sharpsburg, and Fredericksburg. Transferred to the West, his brigade fought at Chickamauga and throughout the Tennessee campaign. On May 18th, 1864, he was promoted to major general. Rejoining the Army of Northern Virginia, he fought at the Wilderness, Spotsylvania, Cold Harbor, and Petersburg. He was taken prisoner and confined for several months at Fort Warren, Boston harbor. After the war he resumed the practice of law in Camden, entered the state senate in 1865, and served as judge of the fifth circuit court (1877–1893). He died in Camden on April 13th, 1894, survived by his wife, Lucretia Douglas, whom he had married in 1844, and was buried in the Quaker burial ground.

KEY, PHILIP BARTON (1818–1859), lawyer, eighth child of Francis Scott Key (1779–1843) and Mary Tayloe Lloyd (1784–1859), was born in Georgetown, D.C., on April 5th, 1818. He was named for his great uncle, Philip Barton Key (1757–1815), of Georgetown, with whom his father was for a time associated in the practice of law. His aunt, Ann Arnold Phoebe Charlton Key (1783–1855), was the wife of Roger Brooke Taney (1777–1864), attorney general of the United States (1831–1833), secretary of the treasury (1833–1835), and chief justice of the supreme court of the United States (1836–1864). His father, author of "The Star-Spangled Banner" (1814), was United States attorney for the District of Columbia (1833–1841). On November 18th, 1845, Philip Barton Key married Ellen Swann (1824–1855), daughter of James Swann and Elizabeth Donnell, of Baltimore, Maryland; there were four children. She died on March 20th, 1855. Key was United States attorney for the District of Columbia (1853–1859); he was a popular figure, and was said to be "the handsomest man in all Washington society." On Sunday afternoon, February 27th, 1859, near the southeast corner of Lafayette Square, in full view of the White House, Key was shot and killed by Daniel Edgar Sickles (1819–1914), United States senator from New York, for his attentions to Sickles' beautiful young wife, Teresa Bagioli (1836–1867), daughter of an Italian music master. Key was buried beside his wife in the Presbyterian Cemetery, Baltimore. As the Washington *Star* (March 1st, 1859) observed, "His fine manly figure as he appeared in the courtroom or dashed along the avenue upon his iron-gray horse is in the memory of all." In a famous trial Sickles pleaded temporary insanity, and on April 26th, 1859, he was acquitted.

KILPATRICK, HUGH JUDSON (1836–1881), Union soldier, son of a farmer, was born near Deckertown, New Jersey, on January 14th, 1836. He graduated from the United States Military Academy on May 6th, 1861, and married Alice Nailer, of New York, on the same day. Three days later he was appointed captain in the 5th Regiment New York Volunteers, and after gallant service at Big Bethel on June 10th, 1861, he was promoted to lieutenant colonel of the 2nd Regiment New York Cavalry. Thereafter he saw continuous field service with cavalry until the end of the war. On June 13th, 1863, he became brigadier general of volunteers. After Gettysburg he was placed in command of the 3rd Cavalry Division, Army of the Cumberland, assembling in Northwest Georgia for the Atlanta campaign. He was severely wounded at Resaca and was subsequently brevetted colonel in the regular army. He joined Sherman's march to the sea, and on March 13th, 1865, he was brevetted brigadier general for service at Fayetteville, North Carolina, and major general for service in the Carolina campaign. After the war he resigned from the army, entered politics, and served as United States minister to Chile (1865–1868). In March 1881 he was reappointed minister to Chile; he died in Santiago on October 2nd, 1881.

KING, ANNA CATHERINE (1835–1906), eldest daughter of William King (1804–1884) and Sarah Elizabeth McLeod (1807–1891), was born in Savannah, Georgia, on April 20th, 1835. Her father was a successful cotton factor, commission merchant, and insurance agent. On April 14th, 1857, she became the wife of William Giles Norwood (1830–1886), Savannah lumber merchant, son of the Hon. John W. Norwood, of Hillsboro, North Carolina; there were four children. During the Civil War her husband was a private in the 1st Volunteer Regiment Georgia Artillery; on June 1st, 1863, he was discharged for disability. After the war he lived for ten years in Hillsboro, North Carolina. In 1875 he returned to Savannah, where he was proprietor of the Screven House for one year before removing to Jesup, Georgia, to become proprietor of the Metropolitan Hotel. He resided in Jesup for the rest of his life, engaged chiefly in the lumber business. He died in Savannah on December 26th, 1886, leaving a wife and four children, and was buried in Jesup Cemetery. His wife survived him twenty years; she lived for some time in Savannah, Marietta, and Austell before returning to Jesup, where she died on December 10th, 1906. She was buried beside her husband.

KING, BARRINGTON (1798–1866), rice planter, merchant, and manufacturer, son of Roswell King (1765–1844) and Catherine Barrington (1776–1839), was born in Darien, McIntosh County, Georgia, on March 9th, 1798. His father, a native of Windsor, Connecticut, and a man of great enterprise and energy, had settled in Darien in 1789 and established a flourishing business in lumber, rice, and cotton. When Cobb County, Georgia, was organized in 1833 Roswell King and his son Barrington King were among its pioneer settlers; in 1837 they founded the village of Lebanon, where they established flour mills, and the village of Roswell, where they established cotton mills and took up residence. The Roswell Manufacturing Company was incorporated in 1839 with Barrington King as president; and Barrington Hall, a fine Greek Revival mansion built by Willis Ball, a carpenter from Connecticut, was completed in 1842. The Kings, father and son, laid out the village with wide streets and a park, and gave building sites for an academy and two churches (Presbyterian and Methodist). Six families, all friends from the Georgia coast, formed "the colony" of Roswell: Roswell King (1765–1844), Barrington King (1798–1866), James Stephens Bulloch (1793–1849), John Dunwody (1786–1858), James Smith (1766–1854), and the Rev. Nathaniel Alpheus Pratt (1796–1879). On February 15th, 1844, Roswell King died in the village that bears his name; he was one of the first to be buried in the Presbyterian Cemetery. His children erected a stone to his memory: "A man of great energy, industry, and perseverance, of rigid integrity, truth, and justice, he early earned and long enjoyed the esteem and confidence of his fellow men." On January 30th, 1822, at Ceylon plantation, McIntosh County, Barrington King married Catherine Margaret Nephew (1804–1887), daughter of James Nephew and his first wife, Mary Margaret Gignilliat. Nine of their twelve children lived to maturity. Six of their sons fought in the Civil War; two were killed: Thomas Edward King (1829–1863) at Chickamauga (on September 19th, 1863) and Barrington Simerall King (1833–1865) at Averysboro, North Carolina (on March 10th, 1865); a third son, Joseph Henry King (1839–1917), was severely wounded at First Manassas (on July 21st, 1861) and never fully recovered. Barrington King was one of fifteen original members of the Roswell Presbyterian Church; he was a ruling elder (1839–1866) and for twenty-six years associated with the Sunday school as teacher and superintendent. He died in Roswell on January 17th, 1866, from injuries sustained when he was kicked by a vicious horse. He was buried in the Presbyterian Cemetery. According to *The Southern Presbyterian* (February 22nd, 1866), "He never sought a place in public life. The strifes of political parties were not congenial to his tastes. He deplored the causes which involved our country in war. But as a true patriot he gave his best wishes and his earnest prayers, his money, and his sons to our struggling cause, and when the sun of the Confederacy went down, he welcomed the return of peace and the cessation of the flow of human blood." Catherine Margaret (Nephew) King died on July 7th, 1887, survived by six children, and was buried beside her husband.

KING, BAYARD HAND (1846–1929), mining and construction engineer, eighth surviving child of Roswell King (1796–1854) and Julia Rebecca Maxwell (1808–1892), was born in Roswell, Cobb County, Georgia, on September 4th, 1846. He was privately educated by graduates of Northern colleges engaged to teach within the family. After his father's death on July 1st, 1854, his eldest brother, Audley, assumed the responsibility of the household, including the guardianship of the younger children. On March 17th, 1864, at Camp Finegan, Florida, he enlisted in the Liberty Independent Troop (Company G, 5th Regiment Georgia Cavalry). Three of his brothers (Fred, Rossie, and Clarence) were soldiers in the same company. On November 16th, 1864, he was taken prisoner near Bear Creek Station, Georgia, on the Macon & Western Railroad, and sent to Point Lookout, Maryland, where he was confined for several months; on February 13th, 1865, he was exchanged, together with his brother Clarence, whom he had met at Point Lookout; and on March 8th, 1865, they reached Doctortown, Georgia, en route to their home in Liberty County. For several years after the war he assisted his brother Audley in planting in Liberty County; he then worked for several years in a tannery operated by his elder brother Fred in Spring Place, Murray County. In the 1870s he undertook mining and construction in the West. After eight years with the Texas Rangers he married Fernanda Madrill of Mexico City in the late 1880s; she died soon after the birth of a daughter, and in August 1892 he returned with his motherless child to Baker County, Georgia, where he lived for a time on a Confederate pension with his brother Fred. Early in the new century he removed to Fort Meade, Florida, where he undertook phosphate mining. He died in Fort Meade on September 10th, 1929, and was buried with military honors in Pleasant Grove Cemetery.

KING, CATHERINE MAXWELL (1861–1919), eldest child of James Audley Maxwell King (1829–1920) and Elizabeth Catherine Lewis (1839–1920), was born at South Hampton plantation, Liberty County, Georgia, on April 2nd, 1861. Later that day her paternal grandmother, Julia Rebecca (Maxwell) King, wrote to her neighbors, the Rev. Dr. and Mrs. Charles Colcock Jones: "Our beloved Kate is well over her troubles—the living mother of a well-formed and noble infant. It occurred this morning at six o'clock. . . . Dr. Stevens says he never had a better case in all his practice—or sooner over." Catherine Maxwell King was

baptized on Sunday, November 24th, 1861, in Midway Church by the Rev. David Lyman Buttolph. She spent her girlhood in the home of her parents on Colonel's Island, where she shared with her sister, Julia Rebecca King (1863–1952), and her brothers, Robert Lewis King (1867–1912) and Audley Maxwell King (1870–1935), the "hard labor and vexations and trials" of a shattered postwar world. On January 8th, 1869, Mrs. Mary Jones described to her daughter a recent visit to the Kings on Colonel's Island: "I wish little Mary could see Kate and Julia, they are such fine robust children. Kate takes the entire charge of her little brother by day and night. In the morning they came into our room, and finding no fire, away they flew with their little wagon and brought in a load of fine burrs and chips, as there was no wood cut." Catherine Maxwell King never married. On November 19th, 1891, she became an inmate of the Milledgeville State Hospital; she died there on August 9th, 1919, survived by her two aged parents and her sister Julia, and was buried in Milledgeville.

KING, CHARLES BARRINGTON (1823–1880), Presbyterian clergyman, eldest son of Barrington King (1798–1866) and Catherine Margaret Nephew (1804–1887), was born at Baisden's Bluff, McIntosh County, Georgia, on July 4th, 1823. As a boy he accompanied his parents to Cobb County, Georgia, where his father and paternal grandfather, Roswell King (1765–1844), founded the village of Roswell, organized the Roswell Manufacturing Company, and settled at Barrington Hall, a fine Greek Revival mansion completed in 1842. After graduating from Franklin College (Athens) in 1845 and from Princeton Theological Seminary in 1848, Charles Barrington King returned to Georgia and served as stated supply of Presbyterian churches in Marietta (1848–1849), Sparta (1849–1850), Columbus (1850–1854), Augusta (1854–1855), and Savannah (1855–1856). "I hardly think he will please as minister long," wrote Mrs. Susan M. Cumming from Savannah on March 20th, 1855. For twenty-four years (1856–1880) he was pastor of White Bluff Congregational Church in Chatham County. On May 25th, 1848, he married Anna Wylly Habersham (1827–1915), daughter of Dr. Joseph Clay Habersham (1790–1855) and Ann Wylly Adams (1795–1876), of Savannah. He died in Savannah on November 24th, 1880, survived by his wife, three daughters, and five sons, and was buried in Laurel Grove Cemetery. According to the Savannah *Morning News* (November 25th, 1880), "He was a forcible speaker and a man of true Christian character, energetic and faithful, never indulging himself with a moment of idleness. He had a great penchant for farming pursuits, to the development of which he brought a well drilled and scientific intellect. His energy exceeded his physical strength, and he entered into all undertakings with great vigor." Anna Wylly (Habersham) King died on July 18th, 1915, and was buried beside her husband.

KING, GEORGE FREDERICK (1831–
1914), tanner, third child of Roswell King
(1796–1854) and Julia Rebecca Maxwell
(1808–1892), was born in McIntosh County,
Georgia, on March 12th, 1831. As a boy
"Fred" attended the "union school" in Liberty
County established expressly for the children
of John Bradley Barnard, Roswell King, and
the Rev. Dr. Charles Colcock Jones. In the
summer of 1850 he entered Yale College with
his brother Willie. "We are closely linked together," he wrote his brother Audley; "Willie's
joys are my joys; his sorrows are my sorrows;
and so mine are his." Willie King continued
his studies at Yale until 1853; Fred King withdrew after a few months. In November 1853
he returned to Liberty County; from 1854 to
1856 he operated a tannery in Cobb County,
two miles from Roswell; in November 1856
he again returned to Liberty County; by July
1860 he was settled in Atlanta, operating a
tannery and living in the household of William Priestley Orme (1819–1893), treasurer of
the Atlanta & West Point Railroad. On a
visit to Atlanta early in September 1861
Charles Colcock Jones, Jr., reported that he
"saw Fred King at his tannery. . . . He is
prospering in business." By the spring of 1862
he had returned to Liberty County, where on
May 17th, 1862, he enlisted as a sergeant in
the Liberty Independent Troop (Company G,
5th Regiment Georgia Cavalry). Three of his
brothers (Rossie, Clarence, and Bayard) were
soldiers in the same company. He fought
throughout the war and was paroled at Hillsboro, North Carolina, on May 3rd, 1865. Soon
after the war, in 1866, he gave up his tannery
in Atlanta and established another in Spring
Place, Murray County, where he was joined
for a time by his brother Clarence and later by
his brother Bayard. He never married. At
the turn of the century he was living quietly
on a small farm in Baker County, where he
supplemented his Confederate pension by collecting and selling reptiles. He died near
Mimsville, Baker County, in 1914, aged eighty-
three.

KING, ISABEL COUPER (1842–1921),
sixth surviving child of Roswell King (1796–
1854) and Julia Rebecca Maxwell (1808–
1892), was born in Liberty County, Georgia,
on March 17th, 1842. She was privately educated by graduates of Northern colleges engaged to teach within the family. After her
father's death on July 1st, 1854, her eldest
brother, Audley, assumed the responsibility of
the household, including the guardianship of
the younger children. "Audley exercises a good
influence over them," her mother wrote on
June 27th, 1851. "He is very gentle and kind,
yet they never disobey him. To Isabel 'My
little sister, you must not do so' is always
sufficient, and has the desired effect." On May
20th, 1868, "Belle" King became the wife of
Mathews Robert Tunno (1835–1916), youngest son of Dr. John Champneys Tunno and
Elizabeth Mellichamp Miles, of Charleston,
South Carolina. Her husband, a graduate of

the Western Military Institute, had enlisted as
a private in the Charleston Light Dragoons
at the outbreak of the Civil War; he had
later become aide-de-camp, with rank of captain, on the staff of General Leonidas Polk.
In 1866 he and his brother, William Miles
Tunno (1830–1901), had settled in Savannah,
where they were for many years associated
in the firm of W. M. Tunno & Company, cotton brokers. They also engaged in banking.
Mathews Robert Tunno died in Savannah on
December 5th, 1916, and was buried in Bonaventure Cemetery. Isabel Couper (King)
Tunno died in Savannah on December 27th,
1921, survived by four sons, and was buried
beside her husband.

KING, JAMES AUDLEY MAXWELL
(1829–1920), planter, second child of Roswell
King (1796–1854) and Julia Rebecca Maxwell (1808–1892), was born in Liberty
County, Georgia, on April 12th, 1829. He was
named for his maternal uncle, James Audley
Maxwell (1796–1828), first husband of Susan
Mary Jones (later Mrs. Susan M. Cumming),
and father of Laura Elizabeth Maxwell. He
was universally known as "Audley." On December 25th, 1851, he was reported by Mrs.
Mary Jones to be "an established planter" who
"fills admirably a useful position in the family, not only governing the plantation but all
the little folks at home. His services could not
well be dispensed with. To his mother especially he is a most dutiful and affectionate
son." After his father's death on July 1st,
1854, he assumed the full responsibility of his
mother's household, including the guardianship of the younger children. On June 27th,
1860, he married Elizabeth Catherine (Kate)
Lewis (1839–1920), eldest daughter of Robert Adams Lewis (1813–1906), a Savannah
merchant then living on Staten Island, New
York; there were four children: Catherine
Maxwell King (1861–1919), Julia Rebecca
King (1863–1952), Robert Lewis King
(1867–1912), and Audley Maxwell King
(1870–1935). In 1862 he served for several
months as a private in the Liberty Independent Troop; in January 1863 he secured a substitute and returned to the administration of
his mother's plantations at Woodville and
South Hampton; in the summer of 1864 he
joined the local militia, leaving his wife and
children with his mother at Taylor's Creek.
"He is no doubt in for the war," his mother
wrote Mrs. Mary Jones on October 17th, 1864.
"But for the family he would long since have
gone to the front. I hope and trust he may
be useful nearer home. He wishes to do his
whole duty." In June 1865 his wife went
North with her children to spend the winter
with her parents on Staten Island; she returned in April 1866 and settled with her husband on Colonel's Island, where for many
years they suffered the "hard labor and vexations and trials" of a shattered postwar world.
"They have a hard life of it, there are so
many little mouths to feed," wrote Clarence
King on March 25, 1878; "and with the hard-

est kind of manual labor they barely manage to get on." Audley King died at Maxwellton, his residence on Colonel's Island, on February 29th, 1920, aged ninety; a few weeks later, on April 8th, 1920, his wife followed at the age of eighty-one. They were buried together in Dorchester Cemetery, where their tombstone reads: "Lovely and pleasant were they in their lives, and in their death they were not divided."

KING, JOHN BUTLER (1848–1904), cotton broker, ninth surviving child of Roswell King (1796–1854) and Julia Rebecca Maxwell (1808–1892), was born in Liberty County, Georgia, on November 1st, 1848. He was privately educated by graduates of Northern colleges engaged to teach within the family. After his father's death on July 1st, 1854, his eldest brother, Audley, assumed the responsibility of the household, including the guardianship of the younger children. "Johnnie" King was too young to fight in the Civil War; his six elder brothers (Audley, Fred, Willie, Rossie, Clarence, and Bayard) were all soldiers, and one brother (Willie) was killed at Sayler's Creek, Virginia, on April 6th, 1865. On March 10th, 1875, in Rome, Georgia, he married Mary Agnes Battey (1855–1934), daughter of Dr. Robert Battey (1828–1895) and Martha Baldwin Smith (1831–1922); five of their six children lived to maturity. John Butler King engaged in the cotton business, first in Savannah, then in Sanford, Florida, and finally in Macon, Georgia, where he was for some years connected with the firm of English, Johnston & Company. He died in Macon on November 14th, 1904, survived by his wife and five children, and was buried in the Battey family vault in Myrtle Hill Cemetery, Rome. Mary Agnes (Battey) King died on September 2nd, 1934, and was buried beside her husband.

KING, JOSEPH HENRY (1839–1917), Confederate soldier, tenth child of Barrington King (1798–1866) and Catherine Margaret Nephew (1804–1887), was born in Roswell, Georgia, on October 19th, 1839. In 1837 his father and paternal grandfather, Roswell King (1765–1844), had removed from McIntosh County, Georgia, to Cobb County, where they had founded the village of Roswell, organized the Roswell Manufacturing Company, and commenced to build Barrington Hall, a fine Greek Revival mansion completed in 1842. Early in 1861, at the outbreak of the Civil War, Joseph Henry King married Ellen Palmer Stubbs (1841–1918); there were seven children. On May 31st, 1861, he enlisted in the Roswell Guards (Company H, 7th Regiment Georgia Volunteer Infantry), of which his elder brother Thomas Edward King (1829–1863) was captain; at First Manassas (July 21st, 1861) he was severely wounded through the hips. His young bride went to him in Virginia, along with his elder brother Dr. William Nephew King (1825–1894), who wrote his father from Richmond on August 7th, 1861, that his wound was "entirely a flesh wound, and he will soon be able to go about, though he made a narrow escape. Had the ball gone a quarter of an inch deeper, it would have divided the end of the spinal cord and caused death." Thomas Edward King was severely wounded in the leg, and was unable to resume command of his company. The two brothers returned to Roswell; neither fully recovered from his wound. Thomas Edward King was killed at Chickamauga on September 19th, 1863; Barrington Simerall King (1833–1865), another brother, was killed at Averysboro, North Carolina, on March 10th, 1865. After the war Joseph Henry King removed with his wife and children to Florida, where they lived in poverty for fifty years. He died in Dania, Florida, on June 29th, 1917, survived by his wife, and was buried in Dania Cemetery. Ellen Palmer (Stubbs) King died on February 15th, 1918, and was buried beside her husband.

KING, JULIA REBECCA (1863–1952), second child of James Audley Maxwell King (1829–1920) and Elizabeth Catherine Lewis (1839–1920), was born at South Hampton plantation, Liberty County, Georgia, on November 1st, 1863. She was named for her paternal grandmother, Julia Rebecca Maxwell (1808–1892), wife of Roswell King (1796–1854). She spent her girlhood in the home of her parents on Colonel's Island, where she shared with her elder sister, Catherine Maxwell King (1861–1919), and her brothers, Robert Lewis King (1867–1912) and Audley Maxwell King (1870–1935), the "hard labor and vexations and trials" of a shattered postwar world. On January 8th, 1869, Mrs. Mary Jones described to her daughter a recent visit to the Kings on Colonel's Island: "I wish little Mary could see Kate and Julia, they are such fine robust children. . . . In the morning they came into our room, and finding no fire, away they flew with their little wagon and brought in a load of fine burrs and chips, as there was no wood cut." Julia Rebecca King never married. After the death of her parents in 1920 she continued to live on Colonel's Island until the death of her brother, Audley Maxwell King, on March 18th, 1935. She spent her last years on Merritt Island, Brevard County, Florida, engaged (as she said) in "writing interminable letters largely on genealogical themes." She died on Merritt Island on April 16th, 1952, and was buried near her parents in Dorchester Cemetery, Liberty County, Georgia.

KING, JULIA REBECCA (MAXWELL) (1808–1892): *Mrs. Roswell King,* daughter of Audley Maxwell (1766–1840) and Mary Stevens (1772–1850), was born at Carrickfergus, her father's plantation near Midway Church, Liberty County, Georgia, on June 1st, 1808. On October 20th, 1825, she became the wife of Roswell King (1796–1854), son of Roswell King (1765–1844) and Catherine Barrington (1776–1839). Nine of their eleven children lived to maturity: Mary Elizabeth King (1827–1871), wife of Dr. Charlton

Henry Wells; James Audley Maxwell King (1829–1920); George Frederick King (1831–1914); William Henry King (1833–1865); Roswell King (1836–1911); Isabel Couper King (1842–1921), wife of Mathews Robert Tunno; Julian Clarence King (1844–1901); Bayard Hand King (1846–1929); and John Butler King (1848–1904). The Kings divided their year between Woodville, their summer retreat on the southeast end of Colonel's Island, and South Hampton, their winter residence a few miles east of Montevideo. The Joneses and the Kings were the closest of neighbors and the dearest of friends; as Mrs. Mary Jones observed on June 19th, 1858, "The many, many years of kind intercourse and unbroken friendship we have enjoyed make them all especially near and dear." Julia Rebecca (Maxwell) King was a younger sister of James Audley Maxwell (1796–1828), first husband of Susan Mary Jones (1803–1890). Mrs. King was therefore sister-in-law to Mrs. Susan M. Cumming and aunt to her daughter, Laura Elizabeth Maxwell (1824–1903); and by easy extension she became "Aunt Julia" to the three Jones children, who looked on Laura as a sister. Roswell King died at Woodville on July 1st, 1854, and was buried in Midway Cemetery. After the war his widow remained in Liberty County to suffer the "hard labor and vexations and trials" of a shattered postwar world. For five years (1867–1872) she lived with her son Roswell and his family in Walthourville; then she returned to Colonel's Island, where she lived with her son Audley and his family until her death on November 25th, 1892. She was buried beside her husband.

KING, JULIAN CLARENCE (1844–1901), cotton broker, seventh surviving child of Roswell King (1796–1854) and Julia Rebecca Maxwell (1808–1892), was born in Liberty County, Georgia, on March 17th, 1844. He was privately educated by graduates of Northern colleges engaged to teach within the family. After his father's death on July 1st, 1854, his eldest brother, Audley, assumed the responsibility of the household, including the guardianship of the younger children. On November 14th, 1861, "Clarence" enlisted as a private in the Liberty Independent Troop (Company G, 5th Regiment Georgia Cavalry). Three of his brothers (Fred, Rossie, and Bayard) were soldiers in the same company. He fought throughout the war; on December 14th, 1864, he was taken prisoner near Dorchester, Liberty County, and sent to Point Lookout, Maryland, where he was confined for some weeks; on February 13th, 1865, he was exchanged, together with his brother Bayard, whom he had met at Point Lookout; and on March 8th, 1865, they reached Doctortown, Georgia, en route to their home in Liberty County. After the war he worked for several years in a tannery operated by his elder brother Fred in Spring Place, Murray County, Georgia. Returning to the coast, he settled in Savannah and joined the firm of W. M. Tunno & Company, cotton brokers, in which his

brother-in-law, Mathews Robert Tunno, was a partner. He later conducted his own cotton business in Savannah, and at the time of his death he was an employee of the John Flannery Company. On January 11th, 1877, in Rome, Georgia, he married Georgia Barrington Anderson (1855–1948), his first cousin once removed, daughter of Dr. Henry Mortimer Anderson and Julia J. Hand; there were two daughters. He died in Pineora, Georgia, at the home of his sister, Isabel (King) Tunno, on October 18th, 1901, and was buried in Laurel Grove Cemetery, Savannah. Georgia Barrington (Anderson) King died in 1948, aged ninety-three, and was buried beside her husband.

KING, MARY McLEOD (1837–1864), daughter of William King (1804–1884) and Sarah Elizabeth McLeod (1807–1891), was born in Charleston, South Carolina, in 1837. She spent her girlhood in Savannah, Georgia, where her father was a successful cotton factor, commission merchant, and insurance agent. On November 5th, 1857, she became the wife of the Rev. Francis Henry Bowman (1833–1873), son of the Rev. Francis William Bowman (1795–1875) and Harriet Byron Minor (1800–1865). Her husband, a Presbyterian clergyman, was co-pastor with the Rev. David Lyman Buttolph of Midway Church, Liberty County, Georgia. For two years (1859–1861) her husband was pastor in Greensboro, Alabama; in 1861 he removed with his wife to Mount Sidney, Augusta County, Virginia, where he was pastor of the Augusta Presbyterian Church. There she died of heart disease on December 23rd, 1864, following the birth of her third child, Mary King Bowman (1864–1952), on December 12th, 1864. She was buried in Augusta County. Her husband married second (on November 22nd, 1866) Rosalie Freeland Benson, of Charlottesville, Virginia, who bore him four children. In 1868 he removed to Memphis, Tennessee, where he died of yellow fever on October 6th, 1873. He was buried in Elmwood Cemetery, Memphis.

KING, NICHOLAS (1819–1889), steamboat captain, was born in Belleville, New Jersey, in 1819. In early manhood he removed to Savannah, Georgia, where he became captain of a steamer plying between Savannah and Palatka, Florida. According to the Savannah Morning News (January 8th, 1889), "Captain King was a favorite among travelers, and the boats he commanded were always crowded with passengers. He was the picture of the jolly, openhearted sailor, who looked not only to the care of his steamer but to the comfort and pleasures of those whom he considered his guests as well as his passengers." For many years "Captain Nick King" commanded the St. Johns; in 1869 he commanded the Nick King, newly built and named in his honor. "We take great pleasure," the Savannah Republican (April 9th, 1869) observed, "in writing her down, for the information of the public, as A No. 1. Her accommodations for passengers are spacious, elegant, and entirely new, while her hull and machinery are of the staunchest kind. Captain King, so long and favorably known on the Florida line, is in command, and perfectly familiar with every square foot of water and mud between Savannah and Palatka, and the old traveler always feels safe in his hands. The other officers of the boat are perfect in their respective duties, while among the stewards, waiters, etc., we recognized several old colored friends who have long been catering for the traveling public and are perfectly at home in their business." Nicholas King married Mary A. Thomas on February 10th, 1861. He died in Savannah on January 7th, 1889, and was buried in Laurel Grove Cemetery.

KING, REUBEN (1779–1867), planter, youngest son of Timothy King (1727–1812) and Sarah Fitch (1736–1785), was born in Windsor, Connecticut, on February 13th, 1779. In 1801 he removed to Darien, McIntosh County, Georgia, where his elder brother, Roswell King (1765–1844), a man of great enterprise and energy, had settled in 1789 and established a flourishing business in lumber, rice, and cotton. On December 17th, 1812, he married Abigail Austin (1783–1863), daughter of Joseph Austin and his second wife, Sarah Ann Pritchard, of Melon Bluff plantation, Liberty County; of their seven children only two survived infancy: Sarah Amanda King (1817–1876), wife of James A. Walker, and Elizabeth Aurelia King (1824–1892), wife of Octavius Caesar Hopkins. In 1839 Reuben King purchased Mallow plantation on the Sapelo River at Pine Harbor Bluff; there he resided with his wife and widowed daughter, Mrs. Walker, until November 1862, when the Federals raided the plantation from a gunboat anchored in the river. Abigail (Austin) King died on July 13th, 1863, and was buried in the family cemetery at Mallow. Reuben King died in 1867 and was buried beside his wife. He was an uncle of Roswell King (1796–1854), Barrington King (1798–1866), and William King (1804–1884).

KING, ROBERT LEWIS (1867–1912), lumber merchant, third child of James Audley Maxwell King (1829–1920) and Elizabeth Catherine Lewis (1839–1920), was born at Woodville, Colonel's Island, Liberty County, Georgia, on August 20th, 1867. He was named for his maternal grandfather, Robert Adams Lewis (1813–1906). He spent his boyhood in the home of his parents on Colonel's Island, where he shared with his elder sisters, Catherine Maxwell King (1861–1919) and Julia Rebecca King (1863–1952), and his younger brother, Audley Maxwell King (1870–1935), the "hard labor and vexations and trials" of a shattered postwar world. Robert Lewis King never married. He was for many years prominently identified with the lumber business of South Georgia. Late in the afternoon of June 5th, 1912, returning to his car after inspecting some timber in the woods a mile or so from Dorchester, he was bitten by

a rattlesnake; he died early the next morning from the effects of the bite and was buried in Dorchester Cemetery.

KING, ROSWELL (1796–1854), planter, son of Roswell King (1765–1844) and Catherine Barrington (1776–1839), was born in Savannah, Georgia, on April 2nd, 1796. He was an elder brother of Barrington King (1798–1866) and William King (1804–1884). His father, a native of Windsor, Connecticut, and a man of great enterprise and energy, had settled in Darien, McIntosh County, Georgia, in 1789 and established a flourishing business in lumber, rice, and cotton. For many years the two Roswell Kings, father and son, jointly or separately supervised the vast estates of Pierce Butler (1744–1822) in Glynn County. On October 20th, 1825, Roswell King (1796–1854) married Julia Rebecca Maxwell (1808–1892), daughter of Audley Maxwell (1766–1840) and Mary Stevens (1772–1850), of Liberty County, Georgia. Nine of their eleven children lived to maturity: Mary Elizabeth King (1827–1871), wife of Dr. Charlton Henry Wells; James Audley Maxwell King (1829–1920); George Frederick King (1831–1914); William Henry King (1833–1865); Roswell King (1836–1911); Isabel Couper King (1842–1921), wife of Mathews Robert Tunno; Julian Clarence King (1844–1901); Bayard Hand King (1846–1929); and John Butler King (1848–1904). The Kings divided their year between Woodville, their summer retreat on the southeast end of Colonel's Island, and South Hampton, their winter residence a few miles east of Montevideo. The Kings and the Joneses were the closest of neighbors and the dearest of friends; as Mrs. Mary Jones observed on June 19th, 1858, "The many, many years of kind intercourse and unbroken friendship we have enjoyed make them all especially near and dear." Roswell King died at Woodville on July 1st, 1854, and was buried in Midway Cemetery. His will had not been altered since May 9th, 1840: "My sons I wish well instructed in the English language and mathematics until the age of seventeen, then apprenticed until the age of twenty-one to a merchant, house carpenter, cabinetmaker, machinist, shipwright, millwright, or blacksmith. But should either of my sons prefer a more learned and lazy mode of life, either physic, law, or gospel, and their means will warrant it, my executors are requested to admit it. . . . Wishing my sons to become useful members of the community in which they live, I desire that my executors hereinafter named do retain the property consolidated and undivided until the youngest child shall have attained the age of twenty-one years."

KING, ROSWELL (1836–1911), farmer, fifth surviving child of Roswell King (1796–1854) and Julia Rebecca Maxwell (1808–1892), was born in Farmington, Connecticut, on August 28th, 1836, during his parents' summer residence in the North. He was always known as "Rossie" or "Ross." As a boy he attended the "union school" in Liberty

County, Georgia, established expressly for the children of John Bradley Barnard, Roswell King, and the Rev. Dr. Charles Colcock Jones. He never attended college. From 1854 to 1856 he worked in the tannery of his elder brother Fred in Cobb County, Georgia, two miles from Roswell. On April 24th, 1860, he married Catherine (Kitty) Ashmead (1842–1872), of Philadelphia, Pennsylvania; there were six children. At the outbreak of the Civil War he enlisted as a private in the Liberty Independent Troop (Company G, 5th Regiment Georgia Cavalry). Three of his brothers (Fred, Clarence, and Bayard) were soldiers in the same company. He fought throughout the war and was paroled at Hillsboro, North Carolina, on May 3rd, 1865. After the war he settled with his family in Walthourville, where he undertook farming with disastrous results. "Rossie will not clear expenses at South Hampton," wrote Laura (Maxwell) Buttolph on October 2nd, 1867; he "speaks of trying it one year longer, hoping to make money enough to buy a farm in the up country." Early in 1867 his mother and his sister, Mary (King) Wells, joined his Walthourville household; after the death of his sister in 1871 and the death of his wife in 1872 he sent his six motherless children to live in the household of his brother Audley on Colonel's Island. "They have a hard life of it, there are so many little mouths to feed," wrote Clarence King on March 25th, 1878; "and with the hardest kind of manual labor they barely manage to get on." Rossie King never remarried; after planting briefly in the up country he returned to Liberty County, where he died in obscurity on September 17th, 1911, survived by two families, one white, one black. He was buried in Midway Cemetery near his parents, his sister, and his wife.

KING, THOMAS (1820–1879), planter, was born in Georgia. In the 1850s he settled in Walthourville, Liberty County, where on April 28th, 1859, he married Marion Susan Anderson (1823–1888), daughter of William Anderson and widow of Charles Berrien Jones (1820–1857). "I doubt not Mr. King will do everything in his power to promote her happiness," wrote Mrs. Mary S. Mallard on April 30th, 1859. "She has seen much trouble, but I hope she will have some bright days yet." Six children by her first marriage, together with three by her second, made up a numerous household. For several years the family occupied the mother's house in Walthourville; after the war they removed to East Jacksonville, Florida, where Thomas King worked as a carpenter until his death in 1879. The marriage was not happy: the couple were eventually separated and divorced. Marion Susan (Anderson) (Jones) King died in East Jacksonville after a long illness on July 12th, 1888, survived by eight children, and was buried in Evergreen Cemetery.

KING, THOMAS EDWARD (1829–1863), manufacturer and Confederate soldier, fourth son of Barrington King (1798–1866) and Catherine Margaret Nephew (1804–1887), was born at South Hampton, the plantation of his uncle, Roswell King (1796–1854), in Liberty County, Georgia, on February 26th, 1829. As a boy he accompanied his parents to Cobb County, Georgia, where his father and paternal grandfather, Roswell King (1765–1844), founded the village of Roswell, organized the Roswell Manufacturing Company, and settled at Barrington Hall, a fine Greek Revival mansion completed in 1842. Thomas Edward King attended Franklin College (Athens) with the class of 1848. Prior to the Civil War he and his elder brother James Roswell King (1827–1897) built and operated the Ivory Mills, established in Roswell for the manufacture of woolen goods. On November 30th, 1854, in Huntsville, Alabama, he married Mary Read Clemens, only child of the Hon. Jeremiah Clemens (1814–1865), United States senator from Alabama (1849–1853), and Mary Talbot Locke Read. On May 31st, 1861, he was elected captain of the Roswell Guards (Company H, 7th Regiment Georgia Volunteer Infantry). He was severely wounded in the leg at First Manassas (July 21st, 1861) and was unable to resume command of his company. Returning to Roswell, he walked on crutches for more than a year. In 1863, when Georgia was threatened with invasion by the Federals, he volunteered his services on the staff of General Preston Smith and fell with his general at Chickamauga on September 19th, 1863. His body was borne from the field by his friend the Rev. Dr. Charles Todd Quintard (1824–1898), chaplain of the 1st Regiment Tennessee Infantry and later bishop of Tennessee (1865–1898). He was buried in the Presbyterian Cemetery, Roswell. On February 7th, 1866, his widow became the wife of Dr. William W. Townsend; in 1871 she and her husband and King's three children settled in Macon County, Georgia, on a Flint River plantation purchased by King at the outbreak of the war as a refuge for his slaves. *Captain Thomas E. King; or, A Word to the Army and the Country*, a sketch of fifty-six pages by the Rev. Dr. Joseph Clay Stiles, was published by the South Carolina Tract Society in Charleston early in 1864.

KING, WILLIAM (1804–1884), cotton factor, commission merchant, and insurance agent, son of Roswell King (1765–1844) and Catherine Barrington (1776–1839), was born on St. Simons Island, Glynn County, Georgia, on November 21st, 1804. He was a brother of Roswell King (1796–1854) and Barrington King (1798–1866). His father, a native of Windsor, Connecticut, and a man of great enterprise and energy, had settled in Darien, McIntosh County, Georgia, in 1789 and established a flourishing business in lumber, rice, and cotton. In early manhood William King settled in Savannah, where he was a successful cotton factor, commission merchant, and insurance agent. On July 19th, 1827, in Greenville, South Carolina, he married Sarah Elizabeth McLeod (1807–1891), eldest daughter of Francis Harris McLeod (1784–1864) and Mary Ann Millen (1787–1875); there were eight children. William King was an active Presbyterian. The Rev. Dr. and Mrs. Charles Colcock Jones lived in his Savannah household from May 1831 to November 1832, when Dr. Jones was pastor of the First Presbyterian Church. In September 1864 King acted as intermediary between his personal friend, General William Tecumseh Sherman, and Governor Joseph Emerson Brown; Sherman's proposal to terminate the war at once was not accepted by the Confederate authorities. King's letter detailing the episode appeared in the Atlanta *Constitution* on June 5th, 1879: "I fully believe the failure on the part of Governor Brown to accept General Sherman's invitation for an interview was a sad blunder, and has greatly aggravated the losses and sufferings of the Southern states." In August 1865, at the request of citizens of Boston, Massachusetts, William King went North to present reliable information on postwar conditions in Georgia. Shortly thereafter he retired from his Savannah business and settled in Cobb County, Georgia, two miles from Marietta, where he sold insurance and dealt in real estate. He died of pneumonia on January 12th, 1884, and was buried in Citizens Cemetery, Marietta, in a vault marked "King." According to the Atlanta *Constitution* (January 15th, 1884), "he was never in bed a day except the week preceding his death. Although eighty years of age, he rose at five o'clock, walked four miles to and from his business, and was as active as a boy. He never drank liquor of any sort, coffee or tea, and never used tobacco in any shape. To this he attributed his wonderful health and vigor." Sarah Elizabeth (McLeod) King died near Marietta on December 23rd, 1891, and was buried beside her husband. Two of his daughters married Presbyterian clergymen: Mary McLeod King (Mrs. Francis Henry Bowman) and Sarah Elizabeth King (Mrs. Thomas Wharey). On October 5th, 1871, his granddaughter, Julia King, daughter of Dr. William King and Elizabeth Clayton, became the wife of Henry Woodfin Grady (1850–1889), editor of the Atlanta *Constitution* (1879–1889) and vigorous apostle of "the New South."

KING, WILLIAM HENRY (1833–1865), druggist, fourth child of Roswell King (1796–1854) and Julia Rebecca Maxwell (1808–1892), was born in Glynn County, Georgia, on October 12th, 1833. As a boy "Willie" attended the "union school" in Liberty County established expressly for the children of John Bradley Barnard, Roswell King, and the Rev. Dr. Charles Colcock Jones. He attended Yale College and the Sheffield Scientific School from 1850 to 1853; late in 1853, without graduating, he removed to Philadelphia, where for one year he clerked in the drugstore of Edward Parrish (1822–1872) while attending lectures in pharmacy at the Medical College of the University of Pennsylvania. "Willie is

very attentive to his business and anxious to improve his time to the best advantage," wrote his friend Joseph Jones from Philadelphia on January 9th, 1855; "and I have no doubt that if he continues to pursue his studies with his accustomed diligence he will rise to eminence in his profession." Returning to Georgia early in 1855, he settled in Savannah, where he joined George Houstoun Waring (1833–1902) in the firm of King & Waring, "wholesale and retail dealers in drugs, chemicals, perfumery, toilet articles, oils, etc." According to an advertisement published in the Savannah *Republican* (March 26th, 1859), "Particular attention will be paid to the preparation of physicians' prescriptions. All family, plantation, and physicians' orders will be executed with neatness, accuracy, and dispatch." On May 31st, 1861, he enlisted as first sergeant in the Savannah Volunteer Guards (Company A, 18th Battalion Georgia Infantry); on May 10th, 1863, he was promoted to first lieutenant. For three years his service was confined to the vicinity of Savannah and Charleston; in May 1864 he was ordered with his battalion to Virginia. He was killed in the battle of Sayler's Creek on April 6th, 1865, three days before Lee's surrender at Appomattox Courthouse. As his cousin, Laura (Maxwell) Buttolph, wrote on June 30th, 1865, "we all miss his cheerful voice, and feel that the most promising and most loved has fallen." The Rev. David Lyman Buttolph preached his funeral sermon in the Flemington Presbyterian Church on Sunday, October 29th, 1865; his body was subsequently removed from Virginia and buried in Laurel Grove Cemetery, Savannah, on December 31st, 1865. Although he was frequently the subject of matrimonial speculation, he never married.

KING, WILLIAM JOHN (1823–1885), planter, son of William John King (1790–1861) and Martha Cooper (1795–1860), was born on Harris Neck, McIntosh County, Georgia, on February 7th, 1823. His father, an elder of the Darien Presbyterian Church, represented McIntosh County three terms in the state legislature; according to his pastor, the Rev. Francis Robert Goulding, he was "a man of truth, integrity, and a stern sense of justice." On March 15th, 1854, William John King (1823–1885) married Caroline Beckwith Peck (1832–1910), a native of Litchfield County, Connecticut, who had come to Harris Neck as a governess the preceding year. There were two children. On October 1st, 1861, he enlisted for six months as a private in the Liberty Independent Troop (Company G, 5th Regiment Georgia Cavalry). Retiring to civilian life, he was copartner of Edward J. Delegal (1815–1892) in the firm of King & Delegal, salt-boilers (1862–1863). In December 1863 he enlisted as a private in the 29th Regiment Georgia Cavalry; a year later, on December 14th, 1864, he was taken prisoner near his home in Dorchester, Liberty County, and sent to Point Lookout, Maryland. During his confinement he was continuously ill, and after the war he never fully regained his health. He died in Dorchester on June 15th, 1885, and was buried in Dorchester Cemetery. Caroline Beckwith (Peck) King survived her husband twenty-five years; she continued teaching school until 1900, when illness forced her to retire; she died on January 27th, 1910, and was buried beside her husband. Mary E. King (1824–1861), sister of William John King (1823–1885), was the wife of William Goulding Thomson (1822–1864).

KINGSLEY, CHARLES (1819–1875), Anglican clergyman, author, and educator, eldest son of the Rev. Charles Kingsley and Mary Lucas, was born at Holne Vicarage, Devonshire, England, on June 12th, 1819. After graduating from Magdalene College (Cambridge) in 1842 he was ordained curate of Eversley, Hampshire, where he continued for the rest of his life. Early in 1844 he married Fanny Grenfell. *Hypatia* (1853), the first and strongest of his historical novels, pictures with remarkable validity the intellectual and spiritual life of Alexandria in the fifth century. *Westward Ho!* (1855) and *Hereward the Wake* (1865), though popular and vivid, betray his bias against Roman Catholicism. His unwarranted attack upon the Rev. John Henry Newman in 1864 provoked Newman to write his *Apologia pro Vita Sua.* Kingsley was one of the few Christians to accept and support Charles Darwin's evolutionary theory; *The Water Babies* (1863), a children's story, reflects Kingsley's thoughts on evolution. He was appointed chaplain to the Queen (1859), regius professor of modern history at Cambridge (1860), and tutor to the Prince of Wales (1861). He died in Eversley on January 23rd, 1875.

KISSAM, RICHARD SHARPE (1808–1861), physician, was born in New York City on October 2nd, 1808. After attending Union College (Schenectady, New York) and Washington College (Hartford, Connecticut) he graduated from the College of Physicians and Surgeons (New York) in 1830. For four years he practiced surgery in Hartford; in 1834 he settled in New York City, where for many years he practiced medicine in association with John Wakefield Francis (1789–1861). According to Harry Friedenwald (*Cyclopedia of American Medical Biography*), "Kissam was dignified yet unostentatious, of the most prepossessing manners, scrupulously neat, with a brilliant and sparkling eye, fascinating by his wit and humor in ordinary conversation, or drawing upon the more scientific treasures of his highly cultivated mind as occasion required." He died in New York City on November 28th, 1861.

KNAPP, NOAH BENEDICT (1805–1879), saddler, was born in Danbury, Connecticut, in 1805. At the age of thirty he settled in Savannah, Georgia, where he engaged in the wholesale and retail saddle and harness business and became a wealthy man. He was at various times alderman, judge of the inferior

court, and inspector of the port of Savannah. He was also a director of the Savannah Gas Light Company and the Savannah Hospital. He was a member of the Savannah Volunteer Guards and for some years colonel of the 1st Regiment Georgia Militia. His wife, Eliza C. Knapp, a native of New York, died on September 9th, 1873. Five and a half years later, on January 19th, 1879, he died suddenly of a cerebral hemorrhage at the Fifth Avenue Hotel in New York City. He was buried beside his wife in Patterson, Putnam County, New York. On July 11th, 1867, he adopted Carrie Clifford Knapp (born May 6th, 1862), to whom he left an estate yielding an annual income of twenty thousand dollars.

LADD, WILLIAM GARDNER (1824–1909), sewing machine manufacturer, second child of William Gardner Ladd (1799–1862) and Margaret Goodale Cushing (1799–1883), was born in Fredericksburg, Virginia, on August 14th, 1824. His maternal great-grandfather was the Hon. Thomas Cushing (1725–1788), Revolutionary patriot, member of the Massachusetts provincial assembly (1761–1774), member of the Continental Congress (1774–1776), and lieutenant governor of Massachusetts (1780–1788). In 1849 Ladd settled in Cambridge, Massachusetts, where he joined Samuel J. M. Homer and Charles W. Homer in the firm of Homers & Ladd, hardware merchants. On September 5th, 1850, he married Adeline Dodge Homer, of Cambridge; there were six children. In 1857 he retired from the hardware firm, removed to Boston, and undertook the manufacture of sewing machines in association with Nehemiah Hunt and Andrew S. Webster. The Ladd & Webster tight-stitch sewing machine enjoyed only limited success; for several years Ladd maintained salesrooms in Boston and New York, but by the end of the Civil War he had abandoned the business altogether, removed to New York City, and become a merchant. In 1869 he settled in Brooklyn, where he worked first as a merchant, then as a secretary in Wall Street, and then again as a merchant. He was for forty years a member of St. Ann's Episcopal Church and for twenty years a member of its vestry. He died at his residence in Brooklyn on April 25th, 1909, survived by his wife and two sons, and was buried in Mount Auburn Cemetery, Cambridge, Massachusetts.

LADSON, GEORGE WHITEFIELD (1830–1864), Presbyterian clergyman, son of William Ladson, was born in Liberty County, Georgia, on June 10th, 1830. His father died two months before his birth; his mother died when he was four years old. He was adopted into the family of his kinsman, John Dunwody (1786–1858), who in 1837 removed to Cobb County, Georgia, and became one of the original settlers of the village of Roswell. George Whitefield Ladson studied at the Roswell Academy under the Rev. Nathaniel Alpheus Pratt. After graduating from Oglethorpe

University in 1859 and from Columbia Theological Seminary in 1862 he settled in Columbia, South Carolina, as a home missionary to the Negroes. On April 4th, 1861, he married Mrs. Juliet Ewart Smith, of Columbia; there were two children. He died in Columbia on July 4th, 1864, much lamented by white and black, and was buried in Elmwood Cemetery. Ladson Chapel, erected in Columbia for a congregation of intelligent, prosperous Negroes, was named in his honor.

LADSON, JOSEPH H. (1824–1862), merchant and planter, was born in Liberty County, Georgia, in 1824. In early manhood he settled in Savannah, where he joined John C. Rokenbaugh in the firm of Rokenbaugh & Ladson, dry goods merchants. On December 9th, 1856, he married Ann C. Varnedoe (born 1836), a native of Liberty County, youngest daughter of Nathaniel Varnedoe (1790–1856) and his first wife, Ann T. Jones (1794–1836). In the same month he closed out his business in Savannah and returned to planting in his native county. He died of consumption at Dowse's, his plantation opposite Liberty Hall, on February 11th, 1862, survived by his wife and two sons. He was an active member of the Methodist Church.

LAMAR, CHARLES AUGUSTUS LAFAYETTE (1824–1865), commission merchant, son of Gazaway Bugg Lamar (1798–1874) and his first wife, Jane Meek Cresswell, was born in Savannah, Georgia, on April 1st, 1824. His father, scion of a distinguished Georgia family, was a banker and businessman of great influence. His son Charles was a godson of the Marquis de Lafayette (1757–1834), who was present at his christening in Savannah in 1825. Gazaway Bugg Lamar and his wife and six children were passengers on the steamer *Pulaski*, which sank in mid-ocean on June 14th, 1838; his wife and five children perished; only Lamar and his son Charles survived. In February 1846 C. A. L. Lamar married Caroline Agnes Nicoll (1825–1902), of Savannah; there were five daughters. On December 6th, 1852, he was elected alderman of Savannah. He was an ardent secessionist and an open proponent of the slave trade; he was one of the owners of the *Wanderer*, a slave ship seized in November 1858 in its attempt to bring African slaves into Savannah; and in April 1859 he was charged with "holding and aiding and abetting the holding of African slaves." As Charles Colcock Jones, Jr., wrote on January 3rd, 1859, "Lamar is a dangerous man, and with all his apparent recklessness and lawlessness a cautious one too. . . . The great difficulty in cases of this character is to procure testimony sufficient to procure conviction." According to the Savannah *Morning News* (May 29th, 1860), "The prosecution, finding that under the ruling of the court it would be impossible to sustain the indictment, entered a nolle prosequi." C. A. L. Lamar was captain of the Georgia Hussars for three years (1852–1854). In April 1861 he organized and became captain

of the Savannah Mounted Rifles, which was stationed at Sunbury, Liberty County, from June 1861 until the Liberty Independent Troop could be mustered into service the following autumn. In October 1861, at Brunswick, Georgia, he was elected colonel of the 25th Regiment Georgia Cavalry. He was killed near Columbus, Georgia, on April 16th, 1865 —"the last man," according to the Savannah *Morning News* (June 4th, 1866), "who fell in the organized struggle for Southern independence." He was buried in Laurel Grove Cemetery, Savannah. Caroline Agnes (Nicoll) Lamar died on August 19th, 1902, and was buried beside her husband.

LAMAR, GAZAWAY BUGG (1798–1874), banker and businessman, son of Basil Lamar and Rebecca Kelly, was born in Richmond County, Georgia, on October 2nd, 1798. In early manhood he rose to prominence in business and financial circles in Augusta and Savannah. He married first (on October 18th, 1821) Jane Meek Cresswell; she and five children perished on the steamer *Pulaski,* which sank in mid-ocean on June 14th, 1838; her husband and one son, C. A. L. Lamar, survived. He married second (on July 11th, 1839) Harriet Cazenove (1817–1861) daughter of Anthony Charles Cazenove, a prominent banker of Alexandria, Virginia. In 1846 he removed to New York City, where he engaged in the commission business until the outbreak of the Civil War. In 1851 he helped organize the Bank of the Republic in New York City and became its first president. Resigning in 1855, he became president of the Bank of Commerce in Savannah. His son, C. A. L. Lamar, was an ardent secessionist and an open proponent of the slave trade; the father neither shared nor approved his son's views. In May 1861 he returned to Savannah, where for two years (October 1861– October 1863) he occupied the house of Charles Colcock Jones, Jr., on South Broad Street. He played a prominent role in Confederate banking. After the war he devoted much of his life to suits in state and federal courts to recover something of his lost fortune. He died in New York City on October 4th, 1874, and was buried beside his second wife in Alexandria, Virginia.

LAMPKIN, CATHERINE ELIZABETH BALDWIN (1834–1903), daughter of Edward Lampkin (1803–1854), a hatter, was born in Athens, Georgia, on January 1st, 1834. In the early 1850s she attended a seminary for young ladies in Philadelphia conducted by the Misses Gill. On July 14th, 1854, she became the wife of Dr. Edward Willard Harker (1824–1880), a dental surgeon practicing in Augusta, Georgia. Her husband, a native of Liverpool, England, had come to America in 1836; after a short time in New York City he had settled in Augusta, studied medicine and dentistry at the Medical College of Georgia, and commenced a lucrative practice. He was never naturalized and was not subject to military call; but during the Civil

War he volunteered his services, and after a brief tour of duty in Charleston, South Carolina, he joined the staff of the military hospital in Augusta, where he demonstrated his remarkable skill and orginality throughout the war. He died in Augusta after a lingering illness on November 2nd, 1880, and was buried in Magnolia Cemetery. Catherine (Lampkin) Harker died on September 7th, 1903, survived by six children, and was buried beside her husband.

LANE, JOSEPH (1801–1881), soldier, legislator, and governor, second son of John Lane and Elizabeth Street, was born in Buncombe County, North Carolina, on December 14th, 1801. In 1810 he removed with his parents to Henderson, Kentucky, and thence in 1821 to Vandenburg County, Indiana, where he became conspicuous in local and state politics. He was a member of the state house of representatives (1822, 1823, 1831–1833, 1838, 1839) and the state senate (1844–1846). During the Mexican War he was commissioned colonel of the 2nd Regiment Indiana Volunteers (June 25th, 1846), promoted to brigadier general (July 1st, 1846), and brevetted major general (October 9th, 1847). He was governor of Oregon Territory (1849–1850), delegate from Oregon Territory in Congress (1851–1859), and United States senator from Oregon (1859–1861). In 1860 he was nominated for vice-president of the United States on the ticket of Breckinridge and Lane. As a proponent of secession he lost the support of his state. He died in Roseburg, Oregon, on April 19th, 1881, and was buried in the Masonic Cemetery.

LARDNER, NATHANIEL (1684–1768), Nonconformist clergyman and Biblical scholar, elder son of the Rev. Richard Lardner (1653–1740), was born at the Tall House, Hawkhurst, Kent, on June 6th, 1684. After studying in Utrecht and Leyden for four years (1699–1703) he returned to London, where he studied theology for six years before entering the ministry in 1709. He was domestic chaplain to Lady Treby (1713–1721); assistant to his father in Hoxton Square, London (1721–1729); and assistant to the Rev. William Harris at the Presbyterian meetinghouse in Poor Jewry Lane (1729–1751). His later years were troubled by extreme deafness. He never married. After a lonely old age he died on July 24th, 1768, and was buried in the family vault in Bunhill Fields. In 1723 he commenced a series of lectures from which developed his greatest work: *The Credibility of the Gospel History*; Part I was published in two volumes in 1727; Part II was published in thirteen volumes, with two supplementary volumes, between 1733 and 1757. Portions of the work were translated into Dutch, German, and Latin. Lardner's collected works were published in 1788 (eleven volumes) and reprinted in 1815 (five volumes), 1829 (ten volumes), and 1835 (ten volumes).

LaROCHE, ISAAC DRAYTON (1816–1895), cotton factor and real estate agent, son of Isaac LaRoche (1792–1826) and Eliza Sophia McIntosh Oliver (1794–1859), was born in Augusta, Georgia, on August 21st, 1816. His father, born in South Carolina of French Huguenot ancestry, had settled in Augusta early in life and become a successful lawyer; his maternal grandfather, John Oliver, born in England and a graduate of Oxford University, had migrated to America before the Revolutionary War, settled in Augusta, and equipped a military company at his own expense to defend his adopted country against the British. Isaac Drayton LaRoche was a younger brother of James Archibald LaRoche (1811–1889). At an early age he settled in Savannah, with whose business interests he was prominently identified for the rest of his life. Prior to the Civil War he was one of the leading cotton factors in Georgia and one of the wealthiest men in Chatham County. He owned substantial property in Savannah and on the Isle of Hope, where he made his home. He was a founding member of St. John's Episcopal Church and for many years a member of the vestry. He married first (on December 1st, 1838) Georgianna J. Roberts; after her death on September 14th, 1860, he married second (on November 6th, 1861) Josephine S. Adams; after her death on March 3rd, 1864, he married third (on December 20th, 1864) Maria A. Richards. On April 16th, 1864, he became acting assistant quartermaster, with rank of second lieutenant, of Company C, 1st Battalion Georgia Reserves. After the war he was for many years head of the firm of I. D. LaRoche & Sons, auctioneers and real estate agents. In 1891, after a paralytic stroke, he retired from business. He died in Savannah on June 23rd, 1895, survived by his third wife, five daughters, and three sons, and was buried beside his first wife in Laurel Grove Cemetery. One of his daughters, Aimee Taylor LaRoche (1850–1934) became the wife of William Elliott Dunwody (1848–1890) on January 3rd, 1870.

LaROCHE, JAMES ARCHIBALD (1811–1889), druggist, manufacturer, commission merchant, and farmer, son of Isaac LaRoche (1792–1826) and Eliza Sophia McIntosh Oliver (1794–1859), was born in Augusta, Georgia, in 1811. His father, born in South Carolina of French Huguenot ancestry, had settled in Augusta early in life and become a successful lawyer; his maternal grandfather, John Oliver, born in England and a graduate of Oxford University, had migrated to America before the Revolutionary War, settled in Augusta, and equipped a military company at his own expense to defend his adopted country against the British. James Archibald LaRoche was an elder brother of Isaac Drayton LaRoche (1816–1895). In early manhood he settled in Savannah, where he was engaged variously as a druggist (Savannah Census, 1850), as a manufacturer and brick merchant (Savannah Census, 1860), and as a commission merchant (Savannah Census, 1870). He married first (on January 12th, 1832) Frances

S. Parker, of Savannah. After her death he married second (on July 23rd, 1840) Mary Madeleine Gibson (1810–1887), of St. Marys, Georgia, divorced wife of George P. Fleming, and daughter of William Gibson and Mary Madeleine Fatio. Mary Madeleine Gibson was an elder sister of Sophia Louisa Gibson (1814–1847), first wife of Joseph William Robarts (1811–1863); she was thus an aunt of the four Robarts children (Mary Sophia, Lilla, Ellen, and Joe) and a sister-in-law of their father, who was always something of a ne'er-do-well. It was in the LaRoche house in Savannah that Sophia Louisa (Gibson) Robarts died of lockjaw on July 30th, 1847; on her deathbed, in response to her appeals for her four children and her trifling husband, the LaRoches "promised poor Sophia to stick to him and save him from ruin." Accordingly, before his "fatal marriage" to Ella Sommers on March 12th, 1860, he had been "taking his meals" with the LaRoches for a month, and Mrs. LaRoche "had not the heart to tell him to leave her house." (So wrote Mary Eliza Robarts on March 30th, 1860.) During the Civil War Mary Madeleine (Gibson) La-Roche and her five daughters (Clara, Julia, Martha, Maria, and Sophia) lived for a time in Marietta (1862–1863) and in Screven County (1863–1865). By 1880 James Archibald LaRoche and his wife had settled on a farm on Baisden's Bluff, McIntosh County, Georgia, with their unmarried daughter Martha. Mary Madeleine (Gibson) LaRoche died there in 1887 and was buried in the Atwood family cemetery at Valona. James Archibald LaRoche died on February 26th, 1889, and was buried beside his second wife. Their youngest daughter, Sophia Letitia LaRoche (1851–1930), became the wife of George Elliott Atwood (1849–1914), of Eatonton, Georgia, on January 4th, 1870.

LATHROP, HENRY (1811–1888), dry goods merchant, son of the Rev. Dwight Lathrop and Lora Stebbins, was born in West Springfield, Massachusetts, in September 1811. In early youth he removed to Northampton, Massachusetts, and became a clerk in the dry goods firm of Tappan & Whitney. After working briefly in New York City he settled in Savannah, Georgia, where he established a flourishing dry goods business and accumulated a handsome fortune. He was for many years a director of the Bank of Savannah. In 1876 he retired from business and returned to Northampton, Massachusetts, where he died of apoplexy during the night of November 26th, 1888. He was survived by his wife, Clarissa Stebbins, and three daughters (Clara, Elizabeth, and Susan). According to the *Hampshire Gazette* (November 27th, 1888), "He was a good citizen and lived an honest, upright life, enjoying the esteem of his fellow citizens."

LAVENDER, MARY (1778–1845), midwife and nurse, was born in Georgia in 1778. For many years she resided in Savannah, where in 1827 she was a founding member, along with Joseph Cumming, William King, and Lowell Mason, of the First Presbyterian Church. It was in her house that Charles Colcock Jones, Jr., was born on October 28th, 1831. "I understand you have determined to spend a little time with a Miss Lavender, *a sweet and good old maid,*" wrote Captain Joseph Jones to his pregnant daughter, Mary (Jones) Jones, on October 13th, 1831. "The arrangement I think a prudent one, but I assure you I could desire from my heart for you to be with us if possible." On the morning of October 28th, 1831, as the Rev. Dr. Charles Colcock Jones recalled in a letter to his son on October 30th, 1861, "I carried your mother from Mr. King's, where we then lived, in Miss Lavender's practicing gig quietly to the entrance into her yard just after breakfast; and at about half-past 2 P.M. we beheld the face of our firstborn—and first-born son: an uncommonly large and healthy infant." Two months later (on December 31st, 1831) "our kind friend Miss Lavender" sent the new mother a long letter of injunctions on baby care. "I long to see her," wrote Mary (Jones) Jones on January 23rd, 1832; "I feel towards her the affection of a daughter to a mother." Mary Lavender never married. She died in Savannah on November 19th, 1845. She was long and affectionately remembered by the Jones family. On February 5th, 1863, a month before his death, the Rev. Dr. Charles Colcock Jones recorded in his journal: "Robert returned from Savannah, bringing me a valued present of a copy of Willison's *Afflicted Man's Companion* from the library of our dear friend Miss Lavender: bought at one of the bookstores."

LAW, EMILY MARBURY (1846–1859), daughter of the Hon. William Law (1793–1874) and his third wife, Alethea Jones Stark (1810–1872), was born in Savannah, Georgia, on May 1st, 1846. She died of "inflammation of the bowels" on June 27th, 1859, and was buried in Laurel Grove Cemetery. A tribute signed "B." appeared in the Savannah *Republican* on June 29th, 1859: "Emily was a girl of no ordinary mark. Her intellect was of a high order, just developing under the stimulus of education, and gave the brightest promise of future culture. Her disposition was docile, affectionate, and confiding; her manners were vivacious and animated; while her personal appearance was full of attraction and grace. Three days of sickness, sudden and violent, sufficed, though in the midst of buoyant health, to prostrate this lovely girl. She will be missed from her home by her fond parents and her weeping brothers and sisters; she will be missed from the schoolroom, where her intelligence and docility won her the love and admiration of her teachers; she will be missed from the social circle, where she was the center to which all hearts proudly turned."

LAW, JOHN STEVENS (1800–1877), physician, druggist, and insurance agent, son of Joseph Law (1769–1829) and Elizabeth Stevens (1777–1838), was born at Ramoth Gilead plantation, Liberty County, Georgia, on March 21st, 1800. After graduating from Yale College in 1822 and from the Medical College of the University of Pennsylvania in 1825 he practiced medicine in his native county for three years (1825–1828) and in Savannah for ten years (1828–1838). He then retired from practice. In 1848 he removed to Cincinnati, Ohio, where for several years he operated a drugstore. In 1852 he became agent of the Royal Insurance Company of Liverpool, which, with other English companies, he continued to represent for the rest of his life. In 1861 he purchased a farm in Loveland, twenty-three miles from Cincinnati; in 1862 he settled in Loveland and became ruling elder of the Presbyterian church. He married first (on May 1st, 1828) Jane Elizabeth Elliott (1809–1828), daughter of the Hon. John Elliott (1773–1827) and his first wife, Esther Dunwody. He married second (on November 24th, 1831) Elizabeth Reid Burroughs (1812–1884), daughter of Benjamin Burroughs (1779–1837) and Catherine Eirick. Six of their nine children lived to maturity: John Hugh Law (1836–1918), Benjamin Burroughs Law (1838–1922), William Francis Law (1843–1914), Charles Henry Law (1845–1904), George Wallace Law (1853–1922), and Sarah Elizabeth Law (1855–1942), wife of William H. Kealhofer (1845–1917). John Stevens Law died in Loveland on January 12th, 1877, survived by his wife and six children, and was buried in Spring Grove Cemetery, Cincinnati. He never lost his pride in his native county; on May 25th, 1857, he wrote the Rev. Dr. Charles Colcock Jones in anticipation of Dr. Jones's visit to Cincinnati: "I shall be rejoiced to meet my old friend once more, revive reminiscences of former days of good old Liberty and its people—a people the like of whom as a whole is rarely seen anywhere, so distinguished for moral worth and reliability. In these days of lamentable departures from the good old landmarks and true standards of creed and practice in morals and religion, it is refreshing to review the history of such a staid people."

LAW, SAMUEL SPRY (1844–1868), Confederate soldier, son of the Hon. William Law (1793–1874) and his third wife, Alethea Jones Stark (1810–1872), was born in Savannah, Georgia, on January 24th, 1844. On February 18th, 1862, at Camp Claghorn, he enlisted as a private in the Chatham Artillery (1st Volunteer Regiment Georgia Artillery); Charles Colcock Jones, Jr., senior first lieutenant, writing on March 7th, 1862, found him to be "a very exemplary and exceedingly pleasant man." He never married. On November 3rd, 1868 (election day), he was murdered on the Ogeechee road, three miles from Savannah, by a lawless band of armed Negroes marching on the city. He was buried in Laurel Grove Cemetery. "The death of young Law," observed the Savannah *Republican* (November 4th, 1868), "is a most sad event, and has cast a spell of sorrow over every heart. Young and full of promise, the idol of a large and devoted family, for him to have thus been cut off in the very opening of an honorable and

useful career by a brutal mob is a calamity indeed."

LAW, WILLIAM (1793–1874), jurist, son of Benjamin Law (1771–1827) and Mary (Sandiford) Maybank (1770–1832), was born in Sunbury, Liberty County, Georgia, on March 27th, 1793. In 1812 he removed to Savannah, where he taught at the Chatham Academy while reading law in the office of William Bellinger Bulloch. He was admitted to the bar in 1815 and soon rose to prominence in his profession. He was solicitor general of the superior court of the eastern circuit (1817–1821) and judge of the superior court of the eastern circuit (1829–1834). He represented Chatham County in the state legislature in 1823, 1824, and 1825. He continued to practice law until the summer of 1873, when ill health forced him to retire. For many years he was an elder of the Independent Presbyterian Church. He received the honorary degree of doctor of laws from Oglethorpe University in 1852. He married three times and fathered eighteen children—two by his first wife, Ann Caroline Fabian (1797–1819), six by his second wife, Alethea Anderson (Jones) Call (1796–1832), and ten by his third wife, Alethea Jones Stark (1810–1872). William Law died in Savannah on January 22nd, 1874, and was buried beside his third wife in Laurel Grove Cemetery. As Charles Colcock Jones, Jr., observed in his oration delivered in Midway Church on March 13th, 1889, "No more courteous gentleman, eloquent advocate, profound jurist, and fair-minded judge ever adorned society and maintained the standard of true excellency in this region."

LAWTON, ALEXANDER ROBERT (1818–1896), lawyer, soldier, and diplomat, son of Alexander J. Lawton (1790–1876), was born in St. Peter's Parish, Beaufort District, South Carolina, on November 5th, 1818. He graduated from the United States Military Academy in 1839. In January 1841 he resigned his commission and entered Dane Law School, Harvard University, from which he graduated in June 1842. Returning to South Carolina, he read law for six months in the office of the Hon. William Ferguson Colcock; in January 1843 he settled in Savannah, Georgia, and commenced the practice of his profession. On November 5th, 1845, he married Sarah Gilbert Alexander (1826–1897), daughter of Adam Leopold Alexander (1803–1882) and his first wife, Sarah Hillhouse Gilbert (1805–1855), of Washington, Wilkes County, Georgia; there were four children. He was president of the Augusta & Savannah Railroad (1849–1854); a member of the state house of representatives (1855–1856); and a member of the state senate (1859–1860). On April 13th, 1861, he was commissioned brigadier general in the Confederate army, placed in command of the military district of Georgia, and charged especially with the defense of Savannah and the neighboring coast. His administration provoked general dissatisfaction: "I never hear the name of our commanding general mentioned but with disapprobation," wrote the Rev. Dr. Charles Colcock Jones on November 14th, 1861. "A resignation of General Lawton, if not graceful at the present time, would certainly be altogether agreeable to the great body of our people civil and military." In June 1862 he was ordered to Virginia, where he fought in the Seven Days' Battle around Richmond. He was desperately wounded at Sharpsburg on September 17th, 1862, and remained incapacitated until May 1863. He was quartermaster general of the Confederate States (1863–1865). After the war he resumed the practice of law in Savannah. He was a member of the state house of representatives (1870–1875); president of the American Bar Association (1882–1883); and United States minister to Austria (1887–1889). For many years he and his wife were active in the affairs of the Independent Presbyterian Church. He died in Clifton Springs, New York, on July 2nd, 1896, and was buried in Laurel Grove Cemetery, Savannah. Sarah Gilbert (Alexander) Lawton died in New York City on November 1st, 1897, and was buried in Bonaventure Cemetery, Savannah. Lawton's remains were later removed and buried beside his wife's. The Lawton Memorial, a building dedicated to the use of the public without charge, was left by Sarah Gilbert (Alexander) Lawton in memory of her husband; it was formally opened and dedicated on March 2nd, 1899.

LeCONTE, JOHN (1818–1891), scientist and educator, son of Louis LeConte (1782–1838) and Anne Quarterman (1793–1826), was born at Woodmanston, his father's plantation in Liberty County, Georgia, on December 4th, 1818. His father, an eminent botanist, enjoyed an international reputation; his gardens at Woodmanston were among the most beautiful in the world. After graduating from Franklin College (Athens) in 1838 and from the College of Physicians and Surgeons (New York) in 1841 John LeConte practiced medicine in Savannah, Georgia, for four years (1842–1846). He was professor of physics and chemistry at Franklin College (1846–1855); professor of chemistry at the College of Physicians and Surgeons (1855–1856); and professor of physics at the South Carolina College (1856–1861). During the Civil War he was chief of the Confederate States Niter and Mining Bureau, with rank of major. After the war he was professor of physics at the University of California (1869–1891) and for five years (1876–1881) its president. He received the honorary degree of doctor of laws from the University of Georgia in 1879. Together with his younger brother, Joseph LeConte (1823–1901), he stood foremost among the scientists of his day. On July 20th, 1841, in New York City, he married Eleanor Josephine Graham (1824–1894), a young lady of rare intelligence, character, and beauty. According to the San Francisco Examiner (December 24th, 1894), "She had a grand manner, and her friends were wont to call her 'the Duchess' from her dignified bearing." There were

three children. John LeConte died in Berkeley, California, on April 29th, 1891, and was buried in Mountain View Cemetery. Eleanor Josephine (Graham) LeConte was burned to death on December 23rd, 1894, when her clothing accidentally caught fire from an open grate. She was buried beside her husband.

LeCONTE, JOSEPH (1823–1901), scientist and educator, son of Louis LeConte (1782–1838) and Anne Quarterman (1793–1826), was born at Woodmanston, his father's plantation in Liberty County, Georgia, on February 26th, 1823. His father, an eminent botanist, enjoyed an international reputation; his gardens at Woodmanston were among the most beautiful in the world. After graduating from Franklin College (Athens) in 1841 and from the College of Physicians and Surgeons (New York) in 1845 Joseph LeConte practiced medicine in Macon, Georgia, for several years, after which he became a private student of Louis Agassiz (1807–1873) in geology and zoology at the Lawrence Scientific School, Harvard University. He was professor of zoology and natural history at Oglethorpe University (1852); professor of geology and natural history at Franklin College (1852–1856); and professor of geology and chemistry at the South Carolina College (1856–1861). **During the Civil War he was chemist at the Confederate medical** laboratory in Columbia, South Carolina. After the war he was professor of geology and natural history at the University of California (1869–1896). He received the honorary degree of doctor of laws from Princeton University in 1896. Together with his elder brother, John LeConte (1818–1891), he stood foremost among the scientists of his day. On January 14th, 1847, in Midway, near Milledgeville, Georgia, he married Caroline Elizabeth Nisbet (1828–1915), daughter of Alfred M. Nisbet; there were five children. He died on July 6th, 1901, while on a camping trip in the Yosemite Valley and was buried in Mountain View Cemetery, Berkeley, California. Caroline Elizabeth (Nisbet) LeConte died in Berkeley on October 11th, 1915, and was buried beside her husband. A journal kept by Joseph LeConte during the last three months of the Confederacy was published as 'Ware Sherman (1937); a journal kept by his daughter, Emma Florence LeConte (1847–1932), from December 1864 to August 1865 was published as When the World Ended (1957).

LEE, ROBERT EDWARD (1807–1870), Confederate soldier, fifth child of Henry ("Light-Horse Harry") Lee (1756–1818) and his second wife, Anne Hill Carter, was born at Stratford, Westmoreland County, Virginia, on January 19th, 1807. His father, scion of a distinguished family, had been a cavalry officer during the Revolutionary War and a governor of Virginia (1791–1794). Robert Edward Lee graduated from the United States Military Academy in 1829. On June 30th, 1831, he married Mary Ann Randolph Custis, only daughter of George Washington Parke Custis (grandson of Martha Washington) and Mary

Lee Fitzhugh. He was made first lieutenant of engineers (1836) and captain (1838). He was assistant engineer at Fort Pulaski, Savannah harbor (1829–1831); assistant engineer at Fort Monroe, Virginia (1831–1834); assistant in the chief engineer's office in Washington (1834–1837); superintending engineer of St. Louis harbor and the upper Mississippi and Missouri Rivers (1837–1841); and engineer at Fort Hamilton, New York harbor (1841–1846). For distinguished service during the Mexican War (1846–1848) he was brevetted colonel. He was engineer in charge of construction at Fort Carroll, Baltimore harbor (1848–1852); superintendent of the United States Military Academy (1852–1855); and lieutenant colonel of the 2nd Cavalry (1855–1857). Meanwhile his wife, a victim of chronic arthritis, was becoming an invalid; he was not on active duty for two years (1857–1859) and even contemplated resigning from the army. In October 1859 he was sent to Harpers Ferry to quell the insurrection of John Brown. Lee opposed secession, but when Virginia seceded in April 1861, he cast his lot with the South. From November 1861 to March 1862 he was in Charleston and Savannah, organizing the defenses of the South Atlantic seaboard. On June 1st, 1862, he succeeded Joseph E. Johnston in command of the Army of Northern Virginia. During the next thirty-four months—through Second Manassas, Sharpsburg, Fredericksburg, Chancellorsville, Gettysburg, Spotsylvania, Cold Harbor, Petersburg, and Appomattox—Lee earned his place as one of the greatest soldiers in history. On April 9th, 1865, he surrendered to Ulysses S. Grant at Appomattox Courthouse. After the war he was president of Washington College (Lexington, Virginia) for five years. He died in Lexington on October 12th, 1870. As a tribute to its late president Washington College changed its name to Washington and Lee University. Mourning for Lee was universal; the sorrow shown in New Orleans was typical. "Our city shares in the common grief felt at the death of our noble General Lee," wrote Mrs. Mary S. Mallard on October 23rd, 1870. "All the stores on Canal Street and most of the private houses throughout the city were draped in mourning. Numbers of portraits of General Lee hung from the doors and windows—some hung with crepe and others wreathed with evergreen and flowers. . . . Some of the old soldiers are wearing crepe on their arms, and numbers of the children are wearing badges of his picture on a little black ribbon. . . . Even the Northern press seem constrained to render him homage."

LEIDY, JOSEPH (1823–1891), scientist and educator, son of Philip Leidy and Catherine Mellick, was born in Philadelphia on September 9th, 1823. He graduated from the Medical College of the University of Pennsylvania in 1844 and devoted his life to biological research, especially in human anatomy, comparative anatomy, and vertebrate paleontology. He was professor of anatomy at the Medical College of the University of Pennsylvania (1853–1891).

At the time of his death he enjoyed an international reputation as a mineralogist, a botanist, an anatomist, a zoologist, and a paleontologist. He received the honorary degree of doctor of laws from Harvard University in 1886. According to Charles A. Pfender, he was "a man of most charming personality: he enjoyed the society of his friends, and was universally beloved by his students." In 1864 he married Anna Harden, daughter of Robert Harden, of Louisville, Kentucky. He died in Philadelphia on April 30th, 1891. A statue to his memory stands near the city hall in Philadelphia; Mount Leidy stands on the western slope of the Rocky Mountains; the Leidy Column and the Leidy Stalactite stand in the Luray Caverns of Page County, Virginia. And in Liberty County, Georgia, prior to the Civil War, Joseph Leidy, a Negro servant belonging to the Rev. Dr. Charles Colcock Jones, bore the name of his master's Northern friend. Joseph Jones (1833–1896) was a favorite student of Joseph Leidy from 1853 to 1856; on November 17th, 1854, Leidy wrote Dr. Jones detailing the progress of his son: "Your son is well and pursues his medical studies with zeal. His labors of last summer have excited a good deal of interest among our physiologists, and the paper which he read before the Academy of Natural Sciences, giving the results of his investigations on endosmosis, is considered by the members as of a highly creditable character. I think with his disposition for study he would find as much advantage in living at home in summer as in remaining here, and he will further lay up a store of health for the succeeding winter. I have already advised him to return to you in the spring; and it would please me very much if I could accept his invitation of visiting you and your interesting country."

LELAND, AARON WHITNEY (1787–1871), Presbyterian clergyman, son of the Rev. John Leland and his second cousin, Hephzibah Leland, was born in Partridgefield, Berkshire County, Massachusetts, on October 1st, 1787. After graduating from Williams College in 1808 he removed to South Carolina, where he taught school for several years in Mount Pleasant, a village near Charleston, while he studied theology privately. On May 23rd, 1809, he married Eliza Hibben (1792–1856), eldest daughter of the Hon. James Hibben (1766–1835), of Mount Pleasant; nine of their ten children lived to maturity. He was pastor of the First Presbyterian Church, Charleston, for twenty years (1813–1833). He then joined the faculty of Columbia Theological Seminary, where he was professor of theology (1833–1856) and professor of sacred rhetoric and pastoral theology (1856–1863). Each of his four daughters married a Presbyterian clergyman (each a graduate of Columbia Theological Seminary): Sarah Margaret Leland (1811–1857) married the Rev. Edwin Cater (1813–1882); Hannah N. Leland (1815–1845) married the Rev. Abner Addison Porter (1817–1872); Eliza Hibben Leland (1830–1857) married the Rev. Joseph Bardwell (1828–

1893); Mary Claudia Leland (1833–1902) married the Rev. Nicholas William Edmunds (1831–1907). His first wife died on December 29th, 1856; he married second (on December 21st, 1859) Clara A. Blight (1832–1917), an "intelligent and accomplished" lady forty-five years his junior. "The family are hostile—Mary Leland up in arms," wrote the Rev. R. Q. Mallard on November 30th, 1859; they "say they will not put their feet in the house except to see the doctor when sick." But on January 23rd, 1860, the Rev. Dr. George Howe reported that the bride "seems to have won golden opinions since her arrival among us, and to be rapidly removing those unfavorable impressions which preceded her coming." Leland retired from teaching in October 1863 after a paralytic stroke. He died in Columbia on November 4th, 1871, and was buried in the First Presbyterian Churchyard. Clara (Blight) Leland died on April 21st, 1917, and was buried beside her husband. Leland received the honorary degree of master of arts from Brown University in 1814 and the honorary degree of doctor of divinity from the South Carolina College in 1815. According to the Rev. Joseph Bardwell, his son-in-law, "Dr. Leland was magnificently endowed with natural gifts, both mental and physical. . . . His majestic form, courtly manners, a voice which was harmony itself, and a style cultivated and fervid, made an impression on those who heard him not soon to be forgotten."

LELAND, ELIZA HIBBEN (1830–1857), daughter of the Rev. Aaron Whitney Leland (1787–1871) and his first wife, Eliza Hibben (1792–1856), was born in Mount Pleasant, near Charleston, South Carolina, on August 10th, 1830. Her father, then pastor of the First Presbyterian Church in Charleston, was later professor at Columbia Theological Seminary for thirty years (1833–1863). She spent her girlhood in Columbia, where on April 5th, 1854, she became the wife of the Rev. Joseph Bardwell (1828–1893), a Presbyterian clergyman, son of Dr. Araunah B. Bardwell and Sarah Guion, a graduate of the College of New Jersey (1850) and Columbia Theological Seminary (1854). At the time of his marriage Bardwell was stated supply of the French Protestant Church in Charleston; in 1855 he removed to Aberdeen, Mississippi, where he was pastor of the Presbyterian church for three years. Eliza Hibben (Leland) Bardwell died at the residence of her brother, Professor John Adams Leland (1817–1892), at Davidson College, North Carolina, on August 13th, 1857, and was buried near her mother and maternal grandparents in Cook's Old Field (Hamlin plantation), the family cemetery in Mount Pleasant, South Carolina. According to *The Southern Presbyterian* (September 19th, 1857), "Her character was adorned with rare and exquisite graces, but they were such as found their chief exercise and shed their brightest light in the circle of near friends, the family fireside, and the closet of prayer. . . . She has left a husband to deplore her early departure,

and an only child, her firstborn babe." On November 6th, 1861, in Macon, Mississippi, the Rev. Joseph Bardwell married Annie Eliza Gillespie. He died near Starkville, Mississippi, on September 22nd, 1893, and was buried in Starkville Cemetery.

LELAND, MARY CLAUDIA (1833–1902), youngest daughter of the Rev. Aaron Whitney Leland (1787–1871) and his first wife, Eliza Hibben (1792–1856), was born in Mount Pleasant, near Charleston, South Carolina, on August 27th, 1833. She spent her girlhood in Columbia, where her father was professor at Columbia Theological Seminary for thirty years (1833–1863). On May 23rd, 1855, she became the wife of the Rev. Nicholas William Edmunds (1831–1907), a Presbyterian clergyman, son of Robert R. Edmunds and Ann Vaughan Marshall, a graduate of the South Carolina College (1852) and Columbia Theological Seminary (1855). There were nine children. Her husband taught school in Limestone and Barhamville for eight years; during the Civil War he was a chaplain in the Confederate army. After the war he served as pastor of churches at Cheraw, Ridgeway, and Hartsville; in 1876 he removed to Sumter, where he was president of Sumter Female Institute (1876–1880) and pastor of the Presbyterian church (1880–1905). Mary Claudia (Leland) Edmunds died in Sumter on May 22nd, 1902, survived by her husband and six children, and was buried in Sumter Cemetery the following day—the forty-seventh anniversary of her marriage. The Rev. Nicholas William Edmunds died on April 17th, 1907, and was buried beside his wife. Mary Claudia Leland and Mary Sharpe Jones were girlhood friends during the residence of the Rev. Dr. Charles Colcock Jones in Columbia, South Carolina, from 1848 to 1850; Mary Sharpe Jones was invited to be a bridesmaid at Mary Leland's wedding but was unable to attend. As Dr. Leland wrote Dr. Jones in July 1853, "My Mary will feel utterly alone until she sees your Mary."

LEWIS, ROBERT ADAMS (1813–1906), merchant, second son of John Lewis (1784–1867) and his first wife, Susan Adams, was born in Savannah, Georgia, on July 19th, 1813. On February 28th, 1838, he married Catherine Ann Barrington Cook, daughter of William Cook, an English barrister, and Eliza Barrington. He was for many years a prominent and successful businessman in Savannah, where he was at various times justice of the inferior court, member of the city council, and acting mayor. He represented Savannah at the commercial convention meeting in Charleston in April 1854. In 1855 he removed to New York, where he resided until after the Civil War. It was at his home on Staten Island that his eldest daughter, Elizabeth Catherine (Kate) Lewis (1839–1920), became the wife of James Audley Maxwell King (1829–1920) on June 27th, 1860. He spent his last years at the King residence on Colonel's Island, Liberty County, Georgia, where he died on January 6th, 1906, in his ninety-third year. He was buried in Dorchester Cemetery. His elder brother, John Nathaniel Lewis (1812–1896), was for many years prominently identified with commercial and banking interests in Savannah.

LEYBURN, JOHN (1814–1893), Presbyterian clergyman, son of John L. Leyburn and Jane McDowell, was born in Lexington, Virginia, on April 25th, 1814. After graduating from the College of New Jersey (Princeton) in 1833 and from Columbia Theological Seminary in 1836 he was stated supply in Gainesville, Alabama (1838–1840), and pastor in Petersburg, Virginia (1840–1849). In 1849 he became secretary of the Board of Publication of the Presbyterian Church, with offices in Philadelphia, where for three years he was associated with the Rev. Dr. Charles Colcock Jones, corresponding secretary of the Board of Domestic Missions (1850–1853). Leyburn was editor of *The Presbyterian* (1852–1861). After serving on several committees of the Presbyterian General Assembly he was stated supply (1866–1870) and pastor (1870–1893) of the Independent Presbyterian Church, Baltimore, Maryland. He received the honorary degree of doctor of divinity from Hampden-Sydney College in 1849. He was a trustee of Princeton University (1875–1886). He died in Waynesboro, Virginia, on July 13th, 1893. Leyburn's friendship with the Jones family continued after the Joneses' return to Georgia in October 1853; his letter of March 21st, 1860, was typical of their correspondence: "It has been a long time since we have spoken with each other, but I have not forgotten old times. I write now to ask if you can give me the probable proportion of the slaves who are professing Christians. Is it one out of every six or one out of every ten? . . . I am expecting to go over the water soon, and wish to be armed with a few facts."

LIEBER, FRANCIS (1800–1872), political philosopher, tenth child of Friedrich Wilhelm Lieber, was born in Berlin, Germany, on March 18th, 1800. He received the Ph.D. degree from the University of Jena in 1820. In 1827 he migrated to the United States and settled in Boston, Massachusetts, where he projected and edited *The Encyclopedia Americana* (13 vols., 1829–1833). On September 21st, 1829, he married his former pupil, Matilda Oppenheimer, upon her arrival from England. For twenty-one years (1835–1856) he was professor of history and political economy in the South Carolina College, where he produced the books which brought him international fame: *Manual of Political Ethics* (2 vols., 1838–1839), *Legal and Political Hermeneutics* (1839), and *On Civil Liberty and Self-Government* (2 vols., 1853). He was subsequently professor of history and political science in Columbia College (1857–1865) and professor of constitutional history and public law in the Columbia Law School (1865–1872). During the Civil War he was frequently consulted by the Federal government; he was appointed keeper of Confederate records captured from

the enemy; and he wrote *A Code for the Government of Armies* (1863), which was issued in revised form for use by Federal troops, became a standard work on military law, and provided the basis of the Hague conventions of 1899 and 1907. Two of his sons, Hamilton Lieber and Guido Norman Lieber, fought in the Union army; a third son, Oscar Montgomery Lieber, died from wounds sustained while fighting in the Confederate army. Francis Lieber died in New York City on October 2nd, 1872.

LILLY, ARCHIBALD, slave dealer, commenced business in New Orleans in 1842 as copartner of Robert R. Robinson in the firm of Lilly & Robinson, commission merchants. By 1855 he was engaged as a Negro trader, with headquarters at 15 Perdido Street; by 1857 he was located at 71 Baronne Street. In March 1857 he wrote the Rev. Dr. Charles Colcock Jones, of Liberty County, Georgia, indicating that he had purchased Cassius and his wife and five children, Negroes formerly the property of Dr. Jones, and requesting that money due Cassius from the sale of his personal property in Liberty County be directed to Lilly in New Orleans. Dr. Jones, sensing deception ("a wheel within a wheel"), refused to entrust Cassius' money ($84.75) to Lilly. Hearing of Lilly's letter, Charles Colcock Jones, Jr., expressed on March 28th, 1857, his "hitherto unshaken conviction that no confidence whatever can be placed in the word of a Negro trader. It is the lowest occupation in which mortal man can engage, and the effect is a complete perversion of all that is just, honorable, and of good report among men."

LINCOLN, ABRAHAM (1809–1865), sixteenth president of the United States, son of Thomas Lincoln (1778–1851) and his first wife, Nancy Hanks (1784–1818), was born in Hardin (now Larue) County, Kentucky, on February 12th, 1809. His mother died on October 5th, 1818, and his father married second (on December 2nd, 1819) Sarah Bush (1788–1869), widow of Daniel Johnston and mother of three children. The family removed to what is now Spencer County, Indiana, in 1816, and to Macon County, Illinois, in 1830. For six years (1831–1837) Lincoln lived in New Salem, a village about twenty miles northwest of Springfield, where he worked in a store, managed a mill, served as village postmaster and county surveyor, and read law. In 1837 he settled in Springfield and commenced the practice of his profession. He was a member of the state house of representatives four terms (1834–1841). On November 4th, 1842, he married Mary Todd (1818–1882), daughter of Robert Smith Todd (1791–1849) and his first wife, Eliza Ann Parker (1795–1825). After serving one term in Congress (1847–1849) he became increasingly active in politics. On June 16th, 1858, he addressed the state Republican convention meeting in Springfield: "A house divided against itself cannot stand. I believe this government cannot endure permanently, half slave and half free. I do not expect the Union to be dissolved—I do not expect the house to fall—but I do expect it will cease to be divided. It will become all one thing or all the other." Between August 21st, 1858, and October 15th, 1858, he engaged in seven debates with Stephen A. Douglas, leader of the Democratic party. On November 6th, 1860, he was elected president of the United States; in his first inaugural address (March 4th, 1861) he disclaimed any intention to interfere with slavery in the states and pleaded earnestly for the preservation of the Union. On September 22nd, 1862, he issued the Emancipation Proclamation, freeing all slaves on January 1st, 1863, but pledging compensation to slaveholders. On November 19th, 1863, in dedicating a soldiers' cemetery at Gettysburg, Pennsylvania, he delivered his most famous speech. He was reelected in November 1864. At the Hampton Roads Conference of February 1865 Lincoln and Secretary of State William Henry Seward conferred with three Confederate commissioners (John A. Campbell, Alexander H. Stephens, and R. M. T. Hunter) aboard a warship; Lincoln insisted on reunion and emancipation but was otherwise liberal to the South. His second inaugural address (March 4th, 1865) was again conciliatory: "With malice toward none, with charity for all, let us strive on to finish the work we are in . . . to do all which may achieve and cherish a just and lasting peace." On the night of April 14th, 1865, in Ford's Theater in Washington, D.C., he was shot by John Wilkes Booth, an actor, during a performance of *Our American Cousin*. He died early the next morning. As Secretary of War Edwin M. Stanton observed, "Now he belongs to the ages." He was buried in Oak Ridge Cemetery, Springfield, Illinois.

LINCOLN, WILLIAM WATERMAN (1814–1901), druggist, son of Royal Lincoln (1779–1865) and Harriet McLellan (1779–1847), was born in Portland, Maine, on April 16th, 1814. In early manhood he settled in Savannah, Georgia, where he was for many years a leading druggist. On September 6th, 1852, in Portland, Maine, he married Mary Waite Lewis (1817–1910); there were two sons: George William Lincoln (1854–1927), an Episcopal clergyman; and Frank Thorla Lincoln (1856–1900), a physician. William Waterman Lincoln was for some years a member of the Savannah Board of Health. He was elected vestryman of St. John's Episcopal Church (1856) and vestryman of Christ Episcopal Church (1867). In August 1873 he sold his drugstore to one of his clerks, Osceola Butler, and retired from business. He died in Newark, New Jersey, at the residence of his son George on March 3rd, 1901. His wife died on January 10th, 1910. Lincoln's advertisements in the Savannah *Morning News* provide vivid glimpses of mid-nineteenth-century Georgia life: "Leeches for sale per steamer *Florida*" (August 24th, 1853); "Dr. J. S. Rose's celebrated family medicine" (May 29th, 1855); "Whitman's choice confections" (December

19th, 1870). "I have just received a fresh lot of cream coconut, cream chocolate, candied fruit (of all kinds), gumdrops, marshmallow drops, jujube paste, etc." (January 1st, 1861). "Officers of the army, sick in Savannah, can have prescriptions prepared at the apothecary store of W. W. Lincoln and charged to the government" (June 11th, 1863). "Copies of the sermon, 'Vain is the Help of Man,' preached in Christ Church, Savannah, September 15th, 1864, by the Rt. Rev. Stephen Elliott, D.D., may be obtained at Mr. Lincoln's drugstore" (November 1st, 1864).

LIPPINCOTT, JOSHUA BALLINGER (1813–1886), publisher, only child of Jacob Lippincott and Sarah Ballinger, was born in Juliustown, Burlington County, New Jersey, on March 18th, 1813. In early youth he became a bookseller's clerk in Philadelphia, and in 1836 he opened his own business, J. B. Lippincott & Company, booksellers and publishers, which eventually became the leading publishing house in the city. For a time he specialized in Bibles, prayer books, and religious works; he later imported extensively from Europe, established connections with leading London publishers, and finally (in 1876) opened a London agency. He founded *Lippincott's Magazine* (1868) and *The Medical Times* (1870). He was a director of the Farmers' & Mechanics' Bank, a manager of the Philadelphia Savings Fund Society, a director of the Philadelphia & Reading Railroad Company, a trustee of Jefferson Medical College and the University of Pennsylvania, and president of the Society for the Prevention of Cruelty to Animals. On October 16th, 1845, he married Josephine Craige, who bore him four children. He died in Philadelphia on January 5th, 1886.

LITTLE, WILLIAM AUGUSTUS (1838–1924), lawyer and Confederate soldier, son of Dr. William G. Little (1808–1877) and Martha A. Holt, was born in Talbot County, Georgia, on November 6th, 1838. After attending Franklin College (Athens) with the class of 1857 he graduated from Oglethorpe University in 1858, attended the Yale Law School, and commenced practice in Talbotton, Georgia, in 1860. At the outbreak of the Civil War he enlisted for six months as a private in the Bibb Cavalry, Georgia State Troops; he subsequently joined Company C, 3rd Regiment Georgia Cavalry. On July 29th, 1863, he was elected captain of Company E, 29th Battalion Georgia Cavalry. He participated in all the battles of Bragg's campaign through Kentucky and Tennessee; he was taken prisoner at New Haven, Kentucky, detained for thirty days in Louisville, and then regularly exchanged. He was later transferred to duty on the Georgia coast; in December 1864 he was stationed in Liberty County, with headquarters at Depot No. 5, Savannah, Albany & Gulf Railroad. After the war he resumed the practice of law in Talbotton; he was county solicitor for Talbot County (1866–1868). In 1873 he settled in Columbus, where he rose to prominence in state politics. He was solicitor general of the Chattahoochee circuit (1873–1877); member of the state constitutional convention (1877); member of the state house of representatives (1882–1888) and speaker of the house (1884–1888); attorney general of Georgia (1891–1892); assistant attorney general of the United States (1892–1893); and associate justice of the supreme court of Georgia (1896–1903). In 1903 he resumed the practice of law in Columbus. On November 1st, 1866, he married Jennie Dozier (1846–1912), daughter of John B. Dozier and Emily Huff, of Muscogee County; two of their three children lived to maturity. He died in Columbus on February 27th, 1924, and was buried beside his wife in Linwood Cemetery.

LOCKE, JOSEPH LORENZO (1806–1864), soldier, engineer, editor, and commissary, son of Joseph Locke and Mary Cowen, was born in Bloomfield, Maine, on July 17th, 1806. He graduated from the United States Military Academy in 1828, filled various military posts for eight years, and resigned from the army on August 16th, 1836. Settling in Savannah, Georgia, he was chief engineer of the Brunswick & Altamaha Canal Company (1837–1840) and editor of the Savannah *Republican* (1840–1853). On January 5th, 1843, he married Laura Jane Bulloch, daughter of William Bellinger Bulloch and Mary Young, of Savannah. From 1853 to 1862 he and his wife resided in Europe. Returning to Georgia in 1862 he became chief commissary of the military district of Georgia, with rank of major. He died in Savannah on October 5th, 1864, and was buried in Laurel Grove Cemetery.

LOCKETT, WILLIAM (1822–1859), civil engineer, eldest son of James Lockett (1795–1844) and Rebecca Barron, was born in Jones County, Georgia, on April 12th, 1822. In early manhood he accompanied his parents to Crawford County, Georgia, where he was for several years a planter. On January 2nd, 1848, he married Nancy Frances Tinsley (1825–1892); two children lived to maturity: James William Lockett (1848–1943) and Rebecca Elizabeth Lockett (1855–1895), wife of William Pritchard Coleman. In 1856 William Lockett lived for some months in Liberty County, Georgia, while engaged in railroad construction. "We are gratified to learn," observed the Savannah *Morning News* (January 17th, 1856) "that the work of settling the superstructure and laying down the iron on this end of the Savannah, Albany & Gulf Railroad was commenced on Monday and is now rapidly progressing. The contractors for the superstructure for a distance of sixteen miles are Asa Thompson and William Lockett." In Liberty County Nancy Frances (Tinsley) Lockett attracted considerable notice as "the lady-dancer with spectacles." On August 11th, 1856, the Rev. R. Q. Mallard wrote of her spiritual state: "I scarcely know what to make of her. She said the other day that they are becoming very good over her way, that Mr. L. frequently read his Bible, and that when he put it down, she took it up, and that she had finished Matthew recently. I am

disposed to regard her case with great hope." In 1857 the Locketts returned to Macon, where William Lockett died of pneumonia on April 9th, 1859. He was buried beside his father in Rose Hill Cemetery. His wife survived him thirty-three years; she died at the residence of her son, James William Lockett, in Washington, D.C., on March 2nd, 1892, and was buried beside her husband.

LOGAN, ANN (NANNIE) PAYNE (1846–1873), daughter of Dr. Joseph Payne Logan (1821–1891) and his first wife, Ann Eliza Pannill (1822–1885), was born in Culpeper County, Virginia, on April 7th, 1846. In 1854 she accompanied her parents to Atlanta, Georgia, where her father became a distinguished physician with a large and lucrative practice. She became a member of the Central Presbyterian Church, of which her father was a ruling elder, on December 27th, 1861; for several years "Miss Nannie Logan" served as a teacher in the Sunday school. On October 26th, 1869, she became the wife of John A. Grant (1845–1907), eldest son of Lemuel Pratt Grant (1817–1893) and his first wife, Laura Loomis Williams (1820–1879). Her husband was a civil engineer; he supervised the construction of the Atlanta waterworks (1873–1875) as well as of numerous railway systems in South America, Central America, and the West. He was for many years president of the Texas & Pacific Railroad. Ann Payne (Logan) Grant died in Atlanta on November 10th, 1873, and was buried in Oakland Cemetery. She left one child, Laura Lee Grant, who was reared in the household of Dr. Joseph Payne Logan. John A. Grant subsequently married Carville Stansbury, of New Orleans.

LOGAN, JOSEPH PAYNE (1821–1891), physician, son of the Rev. Joseph D. Logan, a Presbyterian clergyman, was born in Botetourt County, Virginia, on November 9th, 1821. After attending Washington College (Lexington) and the Medical College of Virginia (Richmond) he graduated from the Medical School of the University of Pennsylvania in 1841. For some twelve years he practiced his profession in Culpeper County, Virginia. Early in 1843 he married Ann Eliza Pannill (1822–1885), of Orange County, Virginia; four of their six children survived infancy: Louisa Lee Logan (1843–1857), Ann Payne Logan (1846–1873), Jane Morton Logan (1848–1883), and Joseph Payne Logan (1856–1870). In 1854 he settled in Atlanta, Georgia, where he soon enjoyed a large and lucrative practice. He was a founding member of the Central Presbyterian Church in 1858 and a ruling elder for thirty-three years (1858–1891). He was one of three delegates representing Fulton County at the state secession convention meeting in Milledgeville in January 1861. At the outbreak of the Civil War he became chief surgeon of the military district of Georgia, but ill health forced him to resign in June 1862; he was succeeded by Dr. H. V. M. Miller. After the war he was professor of physiology at the Atlanta Medical College, and for two years (1866–1868) professor of the principles and practice of medicine at Washington University (Baltimore, Maryland). He was at various times president of the Atlanta Academy of Medicine, president of the Georgia Medical Association, and vice-president of the American Medical Association. He was also for some years editor of *The Atlanta Medical and Surgical Journal*. His first wife died on April 18th, 1885; he married second (on June 23rd, 1887) Alice B. Clarke (1844–1922). He died in Atlanta on June 2nd, 1891, having outlived all six of his children, and was buried in Oakland Cemetery beside his first wife. "Both in personal appearance and in courtliness of manner Dr. Logan was an ideal Southerner," wrote Thomas H. Martin, "illustrating the peculiar graces of the old school and charming everyone with whom he came in contact by the gentle chivalry which always marked him in his intercourse with men" [*Atlanta and Its Builders* (Atlanta, 1902), II, 681].

LONGSTREET, JAMES (1821–1904), Confederate soldier, son of James Longstreet and Mary Anna Dent, was born in Edgefield District, South Carolina, on January 8th, 1821. In early childhood he removed with his parents to a farm near Augusta, Georgia, and after his father's death in 1833 he lived with his mother in Somerville, Morgan County, Alabama. He graduated from the United States Military Academy in 1842. He fought in the Mexican War (1846–1848) and continued in the United States army until the outbreak of the Civil War, when he resigned and became brigadier general in the Confederate army (June 17th, 1861). After distinguished service at First Manassas he was promoted to major general (October 17th, 1861), with command of a division under Joseph E. Johnston. He fought in the Peninsula campaign of 1862 and at Second Manassas, where his greatest military defect became apparent: his reluctance to move when he disapproved his commander's course. He fought at Sharpsburg and was promoted to lieutenant general (October 11th, 1862) on Lee's recommendation. After Jackson's death (May 10th, 1863) he became Lee's most important lieutenant. His delay in supporting Lee on the second day at Gettysburg (July 2nd, 1863) resulted in his reassignment; in September 1863 he was sent to Northwest Georgia, where he fought gallantly at Chickamauga. He was ordered back to Virginia in April 1864; he was wounded at the Wilderness but took part in the final defense of Richmond and surrendered with Lee at Appomattox Courthouse. After the war he was for several years a cotton factor in New Orleans. For thirty-five years (1869–1904) he held a series of political appointments. He married first (on March 8th, 1848) Maria Louise Garland; after her death on December 29th, 1889, he married second (on September 8th, 1897) Ellen Dortch. He died in Gainesville, Georgia, on January 2nd, 1904, survived by his second wife. His military autobiography, *From Manassas to Appomattox* (1896), did little to restore the popular favor

he had lost when he espoused the Republican party after the war.

LORING, EDWARD GREELY (1802–1890), jurist, was born in Boston, Massachusetts, on January 28th, 1802. After graduating from Harvard College in 1821 he read law and commenced practice in Boston. He was appointed United States commissioner (1841) and judge of probate for Suffolk County (1847). He was lecturer at Dane Law School, Harvard University (1852–1855). In 1854, acting on constitutional grounds, he remanded Anthony Burns, a fugitive slave apprehended in Boston, to his owner, Charles F. Suttle, of Virginia. Antislavery protest was so strong that Loring was removed from the bench in the spring of 1855 and rejected as a candidate for a professorship at Harvard. In his trial he was defended by Richard Henry Dana, who had been counsel for Burns a year before. On March 2nd, 1855, the Savannah *Morning News* published a "vindication" of Loring written by his former student Charles Colcock Jones, Jr., "I am very much pleased," wrote Mrs. Mary Jones to her son on March 5th, 1855, "that you have openly vindicated his noble and just conduct, and I feel assured that he will appreciate your letter not only as the expression of personal friendship and high regard but as an honorable tribute to his noble and independent action." In 1858 Loring was appointed judge of the court of claims in Washington, where he remained until his retirement in 1877. He died at his summer home in Winthrop, Massachusetts, on June 18th, 1890, survived by his wife and three children.

LOVELL, MANSFIELD (1822–1884), Confederate soldier, son of Dr. Joseph Lovell (1788–1836) and Margaret Mansfield, was born in Washington, D.C., on October 20th, 1822. His father was surgeon general of the United States army (1818–1836). Mansfield Lovell graduated from the United States Military Academy in 1842, fought in the Mexican War (1846–1848), and was brevetted captain for gallantry at Chapultepec in September 1847. In 1849 he married Emily Plympton, daughter of Joseph Plympton. After resigning from the army in 1854 he worked in Cooper & Hewitt's Ironworks, Trenton, New Jersey (1854–1858) and served as deputy street commissioner in New York City (1858–1861). In September 1861 he resigned to join the Confederate army. On October 7th, 1861, he was appointed major general and placed in command at New Orleans. When Farragut approached with his fleet in April 1862 Lovell was not strong enough to resist possible bombardment and withdrew his forces up the Mississippi River. For the loss of New Orleans Lovell was relieved of command in December 1862; he was subsequently absolved of blame by a military court in November 1863. After the war he returned to New York, where he engaged in civil engineering and surveying until his death on June 1st, 1884.

LOW, ANDREW (1813–1886), merchant, son of John Low (1783–1876), was born in

Kincardineshire, Scotland, in 1813. In early youth he came to Savannah, Georgia, at the instance of his uncle, Andrew Low, founder of the firm of Andrew Low & Company, cotton brokers and commission merchants. Andrew Low (1813–1886) was for many years the leading merchant in Savannah and amassed a large fortune. He was a director of the Central Railroad and Banking Company of Georgia and the Merchants' National Bank of Savannah. In 1849 he built a handsome mansion in Lafayette Square, where the novelist William Makepeace Thackeray (1811–1863) was a guest in 1853 and again in 1856. Andrew Low spent a part of each year in England. During the Civil War he sympathized with the South; returning from England in November 1861 with important papers for the Confederate government, he was arrested and detained at Fort Lafayette until June 1862. In 1872 he retired from business and removed with his family to England. He married first (on January 25th, 1844) Sarah Cecil Hunter (1817–1849), daughter of Alexander Hunter; after her death on May 20th, 1849, he married second (on May 17th, 1854) Mary Cowper Stiles (1832–1863), only daughter of the Hon. William Henry Stiles (1810–1865) and Elizabeth Anne Mackay (1810–1867). The second Mrs. Low was a double first cousin of Katherine Clay (Kitty) Stiles, girlhood friend of Mary Sharpe Jones. Andrew Low died in Leamington, Warwickshire, England, on June 27th, 1886, survived by six children, and was buried in Laurel Grove Cemetery, Savannah, near his two wives on November 12th, 1886. His personal estate was valued at more than three million dollars. His only surviving son, William Mackay Low (1860–1905) married Juliette Magill Gordon (1860–1927), daughter of William Washington Gordon (1834–1912) and Eleanor Lytle Kinzie (1835–1917), on December 21st, 1886.

LUMPKIN, JOSEPH HENRY (1799–1867), jurist, son of John Lumpkin and Lucy Hopson, was born in Oglethorpe County, Georgia, on December 23rd, 1799. After attending Franklin College (Athens) with the class of 1816 he graduated with honors from the College of New Jersey (Princeton) in 1819. Returning to Georgia, he read law in the office of Thomas W. Cobb, commenced practice in Lexington, and later settled in Athens, where he resided for the rest of his life. He was a learned, eloquent practitioner. In 1821 he married Callender C. Grieve, a native of Edinburgh, Scotland. He served two terms in the state legislature (1824–1825) and assisted in framing the Georgia Penal Code (1833). When Georgia established a supreme court in 1845 Lumpkin was one of three justices unanimously elected by the state legislature; his two associates, Eugenius A. Nisbet and Hiram Warner, made him their chief. Soon afterwards a law school was established at the University of Georgia and named in his honor; he lectured there until the outbreak of the Civil War. He received the honorary degree of doctor of laws from the College of New Jersey (Princeton) in 1851. He continued to serve as chief justice of the state supreme court until his death on June 4th, 1867. Lumpkin was for many years a friend of the Rev. Dr. Charles Colcock Jones. When he and his wife proposed to visit the Joneses in Liberty County, Georgia, in January 1858, Mrs. Mary Jones wrote her son Charles (January 19th, 1858): "They are amongst our most worthy Christian people. The judge and your father have long been friends, and we shall be happy to entertain them." And Dr. Jones added: "I have a very high esteem of the judge and his excellent lady." Unfortunately the visit did not work out: Lumpkin's plans were changed, as Charles Colcock Jones, Jr., explained, "in consequence of the illness of a member of his family requiring his presence at home." Wilson Lumpkin (1783–1870), elder brother of Joseph Henry Lumpkin, was governor of Georgia for two terms (1831–1835).

LYON, JAMES ADAIR (1814–1882), Presbyterian clergyman, son of Ezekiel L. Lyon and Mary Adair, was born in Jonesboro, Tennessee, on April 19th, 1814. After graduating from Washington College (Greeneville, Tennessee) in 1832 and from Princeton Theological Seminary in 1836 he was pastor in Rogersville, Tennessee (1837–1841) and Columbus, Mississippi (1841–1847). From May 1847 to May 1848 he traveled in Europe. He was pastor in St. Louis, Missouri (1848–1850); principal of a female seminary in St. Louis (1850–1854); pastor in Columbus, Mississippi (1854–1870); and professor of mental and moral philosophy at the University of Mississippi (1870–1881). On March 14th, 1837, he married Adelaide E. Deadrick, of Knoxville, Tennessee. He received the honorary degree of doctor of divinity from Washington College (Greeneville, Tennessee) in 1855. He was moderator of the General Assembly of the Southern Presbyterian Church in 1863. He died in Holly Springs, Mississippi, on May 15th, 1882. According to the Charlotte (North Carolina) *Daily Bulletin* (May 15th, 1864), "He is a noticeable man in any crowd, being tall, well-formed, with an expressive eye and handsome features, looking to be, as he is, 'a prince and a great man in Israel.'"

LYON, RICHARD FRANCIS (1817–1893), jurist, was born in Lincolnton, Georgia, on September 9th, 1817. He never attended college. After reading law in the office of the Hon. Joseph Henry Lumpkin, of Athens, he commenced practice in Starkville, Lee County, Georgia, and soon became one of the most prominent and successful lawyers in the South. For two years (1858–1859) he was mayor of Albany, Dougherty County. In November 1859 he was elected by the state legislature an associate justice of the supreme court of Georgia; in 1866 he retired from the bench and settled in Macon, where he resided for the rest of his life. He was for many years attorney for the Central Railroad of Georgia. He died in Macon after a long illness on May 25th, 1893, survived by his wife, Ruth Youmans, and five children, and was buried in an unmarked grave in Rose Hill Cemetery. According to the Savannah *Morning News* (May 27th, 1893), "He was a man who never sought an office or accepted a place of political preferment during his long and brilliant career, although he had every opportunity to do so with eminent success." Mrs. Eliza G. Robarts and her family occupied Lyon's "large house" on Peachtree Street, Atlanta, for several months prior to their return to Marietta in December 1866.

LYONS, FREDERICK RANSOM (1823–1897), merchant, son of Frederick Ransom Lyons (1798–1881) and Martha B. Stebbins (1800–1873), was born in Greenfield, Massachusetts, on February 5th, 1823. In early manhood he settled in Riceboro, Liberty County, Georgia, where he was associated for many years with William Bates Trask (1811–1880), also a native of Massachusetts, in operating a general store (Lyons & Trask). In 1847 he married Sarah Jane Trask (1822–1873); there were two children: Frederick Stebbins Lyons (born 1848) and Sarah Jane Lyons (1850–1878), wife of Daniel S. Broughton. Frederick Ransom Lyons died at Johnston's Station, McIntosh County, Georgia, on June 20th, 1897.

LYONS, RICHARD BICKERTON PEMELL (1817–1887), second Baron and first Earl Lyons, British diplomat, was born in Lymington, Hampshire, England, on April 26th, 1817, elder son of Edmund, Baron Lyons. After graduating from Christ Church (Oxford) in 1838 he entered diplomatic service in February 1839. He served successively in Athens (1839–1852), Dresden (1852–1853), Florence (1853–1856), and Rome (1856–1858). On November 23rd, 1858, he succeeded his father in the peerage. As British minister in Washington, D.C. (1859–1865) he tactfully averted war between Great Britain and the United States in November 1861, when James Murray Mason and John Slidell, Confederate commissioners to Europe, were seized aboard the British mail steamer *Trent* and confined at Fort Warren, Boston harbor. Failing health forced him to resign in February 1865. Thereafter he was ambassador in Constantinople (1865–1867) and in Paris (1867–1887). He was created Viscount Lyons of Christchurch (1881) and Earl Lyons (1887). He never married. He died in London on December 5th, 1887, and was buried at Arundel.

McALLISTER, CHARLOTTE ELIZABETH (HENRY) (1804–1856): *Mrs. George Washington McAllister,* daughter of Robert R. Henry and Isabella Seton, was born in Albany, New York, on February 4th, 1804. In 1822 she removed with her two younger sisters, Isabella Seton Henry (1806–1890) and Frances Simond Henry (1808–1895), to St. Marys, Georgia, to live with their elder brother, Charles Seton Henry (1799–1864), a graduate of Hamilton College (1817), who had settled in St. Marys in 1820 and commenced the practice of law. In 1824 Isabella Seton Henry became the wife

of Charles Hais Hardee (1803–1835), a physician of St. Marys. The following year Charles Seton Henry removed with his two unmarried sisters (Charlotte and Frances) to Savannah, where he was solicitor general of the eastern circuit of Georgia (1825–1831), judge of the city court of Savannah (1834–1837), and judge of the superior court of Chatham County (1837–1845). On January 21st, 1834, Frances Simond Henry became the wife of John Nathaniel Lewis (1812–1896), Savannah banker and commission merchant. Exactly six years later, on January 21st, 1840, Charlotte Elizabeth Henry became the fourth wife of George Washington McAllister (1781–1850), a wealthy planter of Strathy Hall, Bryan County, Georgia. She thus became the stepmother of McAllister's five children: Matilda Willis McAllister (1818–1869), wife of Thomas Savage Clay; Joseph Longworth McAllister (1820–1864); Emma McAllister (1824–1903); Rosella (Rosa) Rachel McAllister (1830–1914); and Clementina Hanson McAllister (1832–1907). After her husband's death on March 18th, 1850, she lived with her three unmarried stepdaughters (Emma, Rosa, and Clem) at Strathy Hall; the four of them summered in the household of Matilda (McAllister) Clay in New Haven, Connecticut. Charlotte (Henry) McAllister died of cancer in New York City on February 28th, 1856, and was buried in Laurel Grove Cemetery, Savannah. On March 4th, 1856, the Savannah *Republican* published "A Tribute to the Memory of the Late Mrs. G. W. McAl[li]st[e]r," consisting of nineteen octosyllabic couplets signed "M. E. B."

McALLISTER, CLEMENTINA HANSON (1832–1907), daughter of George Washington McAllister (1781–1850) and his third wife, Joanna Clementina Black (1807–1834), was born at Strathy Hall, her father's plantation in Bryan County, Georgia, on September 27th, 1832. She was a sister of Rosella (Rosa) Rachel McAllister (1830–1914) and a half-sister of Matilda Willis McAllister (1818–1869), wife of Thomas Savage Clay; Joseph Longworth McAllister (1820–1864); and Emma McAllister (1824–1903). After her mother's death on July 18th, 1834, her father married fourth (on January 21st, 1840) Charlotte Elizabeth Henry (1804–1856). After her father's death on March 18th, 1850, she lived with her stepmother and her two unmarried sisters (Emma and Rosa) at Strathy Hall; she often summered in the household of her widowed sister, Matilda (McAllister) Clay, in New Haven, Connecticut. On November 20th, 1861, she became the second wife of Charles Manigault Morris (1820–1895), a native of Wilton Bluff, South Carolina, and a great-grandson of Lewis Morris, signer of the Declaration of Independence. There were four children. Prior to the Civil War Charles Manigault Morris had been an officer in the United States navy; on January 29th, 1861, he had resigned his commission, joined the Confederate navy, and become captain of the cruiser *Florida.* After the war the Morrises lived for some years in England; in 1880 they settled in Baltimore, where Charles Manigault Morris died on March 22nd, 1895. Clementina (McAllister) Morris died in Newport, Rhode Island, on August 24th, 1907, and was buried beside her husband in the Morris family crypt beneath St. Anne's Church, Morrisania, The Bronx, New York.

McALLISTER, EMMA (1824–1903), daughter of George Washington McAllister (1781–1850) and his second wife, Mary Bowman (1792–1825), was born at Strathy Hall, her father's plantation in Bryan County, Georgia, on May 18th, 1824. She was a sister of Matilda Willis McAllister (1818–1869), wife of Thomas Savage Clay, and Joseph Longworth McAllister (1820–1864); she was a half-sister of Rosella (Rosa) Rachel McAllister (1830–1914) and Clementina Hanson McAllister (1832–1907). After her mother's death in 1825 her father married third (on October 26th, 1828) Joanna Clementina Black (1807–1834), a first cousin of his second wife; he married fourth (on January 21st, 1840) Charlotte Elizabeth Henry (1804–1856). After her father's death on March 18th, 1850, she lived with her stepmother and two unmarried sisters (Rosa and Clem) at Strathy Hall; she often summered in the household of her widowed sister, Matilda (McAllister) Clay, in New Haven, Connecticut. On October 18th, 1866, at the age of forty-two, she became the second wife of Dr. Richard Dudley Moore (1809–1873), of Athens, Georgia. Her husband, a graduate of Franklin College (Athens) in 1829 and the Medical College of the University of Pennsylvania in 1831, was a distinguished physician, a trustee of the University of Georgia (1851–1873), and senior warden of Emmanuel Episcopal Church (1843–1873). The Moore Building at the University of Georgia was named in his honor. He died in Athens on October 31st, 1873, and was buried beside his first wife, Elizabeth Stockton (1815–1865), in Oconee Hill Cemetery. Emma (McAllister) Moore died in Athens on February 11th, 1903, and was buried beside her husband.

McALLISTER, JOSEPH LONGWORTH (1820–1864), lawyer and planter, son of George Washington McAllister (1781–1850) and his second wife, Mary Bowman (1792–1825), was born at Strathy Hall, his father's plantation in Bryan County, Georgia, on October 9th, 1820. He was a brother of Matilda Willis McAllister (1818–1869), wife of Thomas Savage Clay, and Emma McAllister (1824–1903); he was a half-brother of Rosella (Rosa) Rachel McAllister (1830–1914) and Clementina Hanson McAllister (1832–1907). After his mother's death in 1825 his father married third (on October 26th, 1828) Joanna Clementina Black (1807–1834), a first cousin of his second wife; he married fourth (on January 21st, 1840) Charlotte Elizabeth Henry (1804–1856). Joseph Longworth McAllister attended Amherst College for three years (1837–1840) but did not graduate. Returning to Georgia, he practiced law and planted in

Bryan County until the outbreak of the Civil War. After his father's death on March 18th, 1850, he assumed the management of Strathy Hall. He was a large slaveholder; in the Federal Census of 1860 he was recorded as the owner of 271 slaves. On April 1st, 1862, he enlisted as captain of the Hardwick Mounted Rifles; when his company was consolidated (in January 1864) with the 24th Battalion Georgia Cavalry and four companies of the 21st Battalion Georgia Cavalry to form the 7th Regiment Georgia Cavalry, he was appointed lieutenant colonel. In the spring of 1864 he was ordered to Virginia, where he was killed in his first engagement, at Trevilian's Station, near Louisa Courthouse, on June 11th, 1864. He was buried in the cemetery in Louisa Courthouse. He never married. According to the Savannah *Republican* (June 20th, 1864), "He was an upright, useful citizen, charitable to the poor and kind to all, a sagacious and dashing soldier, and a true patriot." Fort McAllister, situated on the south bank of the Great Ogeechee River near Strathy Hall, was named in his honor.

McALLISTER, ROBERT SAMUEL (1830–1892), Presbyterian clergyman, son of David R. McAllister and Mary McMurtry, was born in Abbeville District, South Carolina, on December 5th, 1830. After attending the University of Mississippi he graduated from Columbia Theological Seminary in 1855; he was a fellow student of David Chalmers Boggs, John Stitt Harris, Robert Quarterman Mallard, and David H. Porter. He was pastor in Thibodaux, Louisiana (1856–1859); Shreveport, Louisiana (1859–1861); Aberdeen, Mississippi (1865–1866); and Liberty, Mississippi (1870–1892). He died in Amite County, Mississippi, on February 5th, 1892.

McALLISTER, ROSELLA (ROSA) RACHEL (1830–1914), daughter of George Washington McAllister (1781–1850), a planter, and his third wife, Joanna Clementina Black (1807–1834), was born at Strathy Hall, her father's plantation in Bryan County, Georgia, on July 23rd, 1830. She was a sister of Clementina Hanson McAllister (1832–1907) and a half-sister of Matilda Willis McAllister (1818–1869), wife of Thomas Savage Clay; Joseph Longworth McAllister (1820–1864); and Emma McAllister (1824–1903). After her mother's death on July 18th, 1834, her father married fourth (on January 21st, 1840) Charlotte Elizabeth Henry (1804–1856). After her father's death on March 18th, 1850, she lived with her stepmother and her two unmarried sisters (Emma and Clem) at Strathy Hall; she often summered in the household of her widowed sister, Matilda (McAllister) Clay, in New Haven, Connecticut. On April 23rd, 1861, she became the wife of Edward Winslow Wyatt (1827–1866), fourth son of the Rev. William Edward Wyatt (1789–1864), rector of St. Paul's Episcopal Church, Baltimore, Maryland, for fifty years (1814–1864). As Eliza Caroline Clay observed on May 2nd, 1861, "Rosa's husband has had business in New

York, but under the anti-Southern rule now prevalent there I doubt if he can retain his office (his salary is all he has), and they may find themselves uncomfortably situated. I believe Rosa has married a *gentleman*—a high-toned, truthful man who is much attached to her. But he is not rich, which is a great offense in some quarters." The Wyatts settled in Savannah. Two of their children survived infancy. Edward Winslow Wyatt died in Savannah of typhoid fever on August 8th, 1866, and was buried in Laurel Grove Cemetery. Rosa (McAllister) Wyatt survived her husband forty-eight years; in 1905 she removed to Memphis, Tennessee, where she resided in the home of her son, Edward Winslow Wyatt, until her death on October 11th, 1914. She was buried in Forest Hill Cemetery, Memphis; in November 1914 her husband's remains were removed from Savannah and buried by her side.

MACAULAY, THOMAS BABINGTON (1800–1859), English historian, essayist, and politician, son of Zachary Macaulay (1768–1838), was born at Rothley Temple, the country house of an uncle, in Leicestershire, on October 25th, 1800. He attended Trinity College (Cambridge) and later became a fellow. His essay on Milton, the first of many essays on literary and historical themes, appeared in *The Edinburgh Review* in August 1825 and catapulted its young author to fame and social success. He entered Parliament in 1830 and participated actively in politics until his retirement in 1847; from 1834 to 1838 he was in India as member of the supreme council. He is best known for his *History of England* (Vols. I–II, 1849; Vols. III–IV, 1855; Vol. V, 1861), which enjoyed enormous success; it went through numerous editions on both sides of the Atlantic and was translated into German, Polish, Danish, Swedish, Hungarian, Russian, Bohemian, Italian, French, Dutch, and Spanish. In 1857 he was elevated to the peerage as Baron Macaulay of Rothley. He never married. He died on December 28th, 1859, and was buried in Westminster Abbey. His complete works, edited by Lady Trevelyan, appeared in eight volumes in 1866. His essays, first published periodically, include Milton (1825), Machiavelli (1827), Byron (1831), Croker's *Boswell* (1831), Bunyan's *Pilgrim's Progress* (1831), Horace Walpole (1833), Lord Chatham (1834), Bacon (1837), Sir William Temple (1838), Clive (1840), Warren Hastings (1841), Frederick the Great (1842), Madame d'Arblay (1843), and Addison (1843).

McCAY, CHARLES FRANCIS (1810–1889), educator, insurance agent, and banker, son of Robert McCay and Sarah Reed, was born in Danville, Northumberland County, Pennsylvania, on March 8th, 1810. He graduated from Jefferson College (Canonsburg, Pennsylvania) in 1829. After teaching school for three years (1829–1832) he was professor of mathematics, natural philosophy, and astronomy at Lafayette College (1832–1833). In 1833 he joined the faculty of the University of Georgia, where he was tutor (1833–1835), professor of civil engineering (1837–1842), professor of philosophy (1842–1846), and professor of mathematics and civil engineering (1846–1853). His career in Athens was stormy: he was a vigorous teacher and an active disciplinarian. In 1853 he joined the faculty of the South Carolina College, where he was professor of mathematics and mechanical philosophy (1853–1855); after a brief and unfortunate regime as president (1855–1857) he resigned in June 1857. Removing to Augusta, Georgia, he conducted an insurance business for twelve years (1857–1869), after which he settled in Baltimore, Maryland, where he engaged in banking and insurance for the rest of his life. He was author of *Lectures on the Differential and Integral Calculus* (1840). He received the honorary degree of doctor of laws from the College of New Jersey (Princeton) in 1857. In 1880 he established the Charles F. McCay Fund for faculty salaries at the University of Georgia: the sum of $20,000 to be compounded until twenty-one years after the death of twenty-five persons designated in the deed of gift. On August 11th, 1840, he married Narcissa Williams (1819–1907), daughter of Professor William Williams. He died in Baltimore on March 13th, 1889, survived by his wife and five children, and was buried in Magnolia Cemetery, Augusta, Georgia. One of his sons, Charles Francis McCay (1846–1864), was killed in battle during the Civil War.

McCLELLAN, GEORGE BRINTON (1826–1885), Union soldier, son of Dr. George McClellan (1796–1847) and Elizabeth Brinton, was born in Philadelphia, Pennsylvania, on December 3rd, 1826. After attending the University of Pennsylvania for two years (1840–1842) he graduated from the United States Military Academy in 1846, second in his class. He served in the Mexican War (1846–1848) and was assistant instructor in military engineering at West Point (1848–1851). During the 1850s he filled various posts as military engineer. On April 23rd, 1861, he was appointed major general of Ohio Volunteers; on May 3rd, 1861, he was appointed major general in the regular army and placed in command of the Department of the Ohio. After McDowell's defeat at First Manassas McClellan was placed in command of the Army of the Potomac. In the spring of 1862 he advanced up the Peninsula of Virginia almost to the gates of Richmond; in late June he was driven back to Malvern Hill, and on August 3rd the Army of the Potomac was withdrawn. After Pope's defeat at Second Manassas he reorganized the army, prepared the defense of Washington, and met Lee at Sharpsburg. On November 7th, 1862, feeling that McClellan was overcautious, Lincoln relieved him of command; he never again saw duty in the field. In 1864 he was Democratic nominee for President, running against Lincoln on a platform demanding immediate cessation of the war. After his overwhelming defeat he spent three years abroad. He declined offers of the presidency of the University of California (1868) and Union College

(1869). He was governor of New Jersey (1878–1881). He died in Orange, New Jersey, on October 29th, 1885, survived by his wife, Ellen Mary Marcy, whom he had married in 1860.

McCLELLAN, ROBERT MILLER (1833–1887), educator, son of Joseph Parke McClellan and Mary Ellis, was born in Parkesburg, Chester County, Pennsylvania, on September 5th, 1833. After graduating in 1854 from Yale College, where he was a classmate of William Henry King (1833–1865), he studied for one year (1854–1855) at Jefferson Medical College (Philadelphia) and served for two years (1855–1857) as private tutor in the family of Roswell King, a planter of Liberty County, Georgia. "The family all seem to be very much pleased with Mr. McClellan," wrote Mary Sharpe Jones on March 13th, 1856; "he looks after the children *out* as well as *in* school—attends to their general deportment." During 1858 he traveled in Europe. Returning to Georgia, he conducted a boys' school in Savannah until the outbreak of the Civil War. In September 1861 he enlisted as a private in the Georgia Hussars; in November 1862 he was appointed assistant quartermaster, with rank of captain, in the Jeff Davis Legion. After the war he conducted a boys' school in Macon, Georgia, for five years (1865–1870). In 1871 he established the McClellan Institute for Boys in West Chester, Pennsylvania, where, according to an advertisement in the Savannah *Republican* (August 28th, 1872), "manners and morals receive as much care as intellect," and "pupils and principal form one family." As the editor of the *Republican* observed, "The principal is too well known to the citizens of Savannah and Macon to need any commendation at our hands. . . . He is a gentleman by birth and by instinct, and as an educator of youth he has few superiors. . . . To his praise be it said that, although a Pennsylvanian, he battled bravely for Southern rights in the late war between the states." On December 21st, 1871, he married Ella Hildrup, daughter of W. T. Hildrup, of Harrisburg, Pennsylvania; she died on June 27th, 1882. In 1878 he closed his school and resumed his studies at Jefferson Medical College, from which he graduated in 1879. He practiced medicine in Philadelphia until his death there on February 16th, 1887. He was survived by three children.

McCOLLOUGH, JAMES SULLIVAN (1810–1883), planter, son of James McCollough (1778–1810) and Elizabeth Findley, was born in Liberty County, Georgia, on April 10th, 1810. His father, a selectman of Midway Church, died on October 6th, 1810, when his son was six months old; in January 1811 his mother married her husband's brother, John McCollough. On March 8th, 1832, James Sullivan McCollough married Hannah Elizabeth Quarterman (1814–1885), daughter of Thomas Quarterman (1788–1857) and his second wife, Elizabeth Yonge Peacock (1794–1826). There were five children: James Thomas McCollough (1834–1916); Mary Elizabeth McCollough

(1836–1922), wife of Joseph Norman Miller; Corinne Eudora McCollough (1839–1859); Laura Yonge McCollough (1843–1925), wife of the Rev. John Way Quarterman, a Presbyterian clergyman; Ellen Ann McCollough (1847–1918), wife of the Rev. Frank Miles, a Methodist clergyman. In 1855 James Sullivan McCollough was one of sixteen founding members of the Walthourville Presbyterian Church; in April 1858 he was ordained deacon. In 1868 he and his wife removed to Mount Vernon, Montgomery County, Georgia, where their son, James Thomas McCollough, a planter and schoolteacher, had settled in 1866 with his wife, Margaret McRae (1832–1898). In 1877 he and his wife removed to Hazlehurst, Appling County, where they lived in the home of their eldest daughter, Mary Elizabeth McCollough, wife of Joseph Norman Miller. James Sullivan McCollough died in Hazlehurst on November 29th, 1883, survived by his wife and four children, and was buried in Hazlehurst Cemetery. Hannah Elizabeth (Quarterman) McCollough died less than two years later, on September 11th, 1885, and was buried beside her husband.

McCONNELL, ANN AMELIA (DICKS) (1803–1877): *Mrs. William Phinizy McConnell,* daughter of David James Dicks (1779–1805) and Ann Lambright (1781–1854), was born in Liberty County, Georgia, on November 24th, 1803. On November 28th, 1822, in Sunbury, she became the wife of Dr. William Phinizy McConnell (1790–1854), physician and representative of Liberty County in the state legislature (1842). There were eight children: Thomas Rush McConnell (1824–1861); Catharine Ann McConnell (1827–1858), wife of Edward William Russell; William Robert McConnell (1829–1904); James David McConnell (1831–1896); Samuel Darwin McConnell (1834–1889); Mary Eloise McConnell (1836–1893); Theodosia Elizabeth McConnell (1839–1884); Ida Rosalie McConnell (1844–1924), wife of (1) Jacob Henry Rokenbaugh and (2) William Spotswood Turner. After her husband's death on October 15th, 1854, Ann (Dicks) McConnell considered removing to Marietta, where her eldest daughter, Catharine Ann McConnell, was living with her husband, Edward William Russell, and where her eldest son, Thomas Rush McConnell, was commandant of the Georgia Military Institute (1855–1859). But she continued to reside in Walthourville with her three younger daughters (Mary, Theodosia, and Ida) until 1872, when she and her three daughters settled in Atlanta with her two sons: Samuel Darwin McConnell and James David McConnell, both lawyers. She died in Atlanta on her seventy-fourth birthday, November 24th, 1877, survived by six children, and was buried in Oakland Cemetery.

McCONNELL, JAMES DAVID (1831–1896), lawyer, son of Dr. William Phinizy McConnell (1790–1854) and Ann Amelia Dicks (1803–1877), was born in Walthourville, Liberty County, Georgia, on November 29th, 1831. He practiced law in Liberty County for many years. In the late summer of 1855 he became involved in an altercation with Andrew Maybank Jones, a Liberty County lawyer, which almost eventuated in a duel in March 1856. [For details see Thomas Gamble, *Savannah Duels and Duellists, 1773–1877* (Savannah, 1923), pp. 222–227.] During the Civil War he was a private in the Liberty Independent Troop (Company G, 5th Regiment Georgia Cavalry). In 1872 he accompanied his mother and three sisters (Mary, Theodosia, and Ida) to Atlanta, where he was attorney, notary public, and ex-officio justice of the peace (1872–1877). On December 20th, 1873, in Fernandina, Florida, he married Matilda Seton (1829–1884), youngest daughter of Charles Seton (1776–1836). He removed to Texas in March 1877; six years later he settled in Ocala, Florida, where he practiced law with his younger brother, Samuel Darwin McConnell. Matilda (Seton) McConnell died in Fernandina on March 12th, 1884, and was buried in Old Town Cemetery. James David McConnell died in Ocala on September 11th, 1896, and was buried beside his wife. According to the *Florida Times-Union* (September 12th, 1896), "Colonel McConnell was a well-informed and well-read man, and as a lawyer stood high. He was entertaining in conversation, and always had a fund of interesting and instructive stories to relate, either from personal experience, for he had traveled extensively, or facts gleaned from generous reading."

McCONNELL, SAMUEL DARWIN (1834–1889), lawyer, son of Dr. William Phinizy McConnell (1790–1854) and Ann Amelia Dicks (1803–1877), was born in Walthourville, Liberty County, Georgia, on January 14th, 1834. After reading law in the office of E. M. L'Engle, of Jacksonville, Florida, he was admitted to the bar in Ocala in November 1860. On August 27th, 1861, near Marietta, Georgia, he married Mary Eloise Brumby (1839–1905), daughter of Richard Trapier Brumby (1804–1875) and Mary Isabelle Brevard (1806–1875); two of their four children died in infancy. On March 8th, 1862, he enlisted as first lieutenant in Company G, 7th Regiment Florida Infantry; on May 24th, 1862, he was elected captain. He fought with the Army of Tennessee under Kirby Smith, Bragg, Johnston, and Hood until he received two severe wounds in his left leg during Hood's Tennessee campaign in 1864. He never fully recovered, and in later years he was forced to walk on crutches. After the war he returned to Ocala and resumed the practice of law. In 1872 he joined his mother, his brother (James David) and his three sisters (Mary, Theodosia, and Ida) in Atlanta, where he practiced law with W. Izard Heyward until 1880. Returning to Ocala, he practiced law for several years with his brother. He died in Ocala on June 8th, 1889. He preferred law to politics, and held only one political office, to which he was elected without his knowledge: he was the first mayor of Ocala.

McCONNELL, THOMAS RUSH (1824–1861), soldier, eldest son of Dr. William Phinizy McConnell (1790–1854) and Ann Amelia Dicks (1803–1877), was born in Sunbury, Liberty County, Georgia, on July 6th, 1824. After graduating from the United States Military Academy in 1846 he fought with distinction in the Mexican War (1846–1848) and was promoted to captain for gallant and meritorious conduct at Molino del Ray and Chapultepec. He resigned his commission in 1855 and was for four years (1855–1859) commandant and professor of engineering at the Georgia Military Institute (Marietta). On September 3rd, 1857, he married Leonora Virginia Jones, daughter of Moses Liberty Jones (1805–1851) and Sacharissa Elizabeth Axson (1811–1850), of Liberty County. On April 20th, 1861, a few days after receiving his commission in the Confederate army, he died suddenly in Mobile, Alabama, leaving a wife and one infant daughter. "I do not know how Leonora will bear it," wrote Mrs. Mary S. Mallard on April 29th, 1861, "for before she went to Mobile any excitement would throw her into a state of insensibility." Thomas Rush McConnell was buried in Midway Cemetery. In 1866 his widow became the second wife of Dr. Robert Quarterman Stacy (1838–1882), a graduate of Jefferson Medical College (1858), who practiced medicine in Atlanta (1865–1873) and New York City (1873–1882).

McCONNELL, WILLIAM ROBERT (1829–1904), soldier, teacher, and Episcopal clergyman, son of Dr. William Phinizy McConnell (1790–1854) and Ann Amelia Dicks (1803–1877), was born in Riceboro, Liberty County, Georgia, on October 31st, 1829. He attended the South Carolina College for one year. After his father's death on October 15th, 1854, he resided with his mother and three unmarried sisters (Mary, Theodosia, and Ida) in Walthourville, where he supervised their planting interests. On March 4th, 1862, he enlisted as a private in Company H, 47th Regiment Georgia Infantry; on June 11th, 1863, he was elected second lieutenant. He later became second lieutenant in Company G, 1st Regiment Georgia Regulars, and was paroled at Greensboro, North Carolina, on May 1st, 1865. On November 17th, 1864, in Columbia, South Carolina, he married Emma Theresa Clarke (1844–1917), of St. Marys, Georgia. After the war he taught school and studied for the ministry. On January 5th, 1879, in St. Philip's Church, Atlanta, he was ordained deacon in the Episcopal Church. After serving as rector of churches in Hawkinsville and Cartersville he took charge of missionary work in South Georgia, preaching at Ogeechee, Pineora, Sylvania, and Pooler. For fourteen years (1887–1901) he was rector of the church in Pooler, where he died of malarial fever on April 12th, 1904, survived by his wife and two sons. He was buried in Laurel Grove Cemetery, Savannah. Emma Theresa (Clarke) McConnell died in Savannah on February 9th, 1917, and was buried beside her husband.

McCULLOCH, BEN (1811–1862), Confederate soldier, son of Alexander McCulloch and Frances LeNoir, was born in Rutherford County, Tennessee, on November 11th, 1811. In 1820 he removed with his family to Alabama, and thence in 1830 to Dyersburg, Tennessee. After fighting in Texas under David Crockett he settled as a surveyor in Gonzales, a frontier town where he distinguished himself by his exploits against the Comanche Indians. During the Mexican War (1846–1848) the brilliance and daring of his "Texas Rangers" made him known throughout the South. From 1849 to 1853 he was in California; returning to Texas, he served as United States marshal for the eastern district for six years (1853–1859). At the outbreak of the Civil War he was commissioned brigadier general in the Confederate army and placed in command of Arkansas troops. On August 10th, 1861, he won an important victory at Wilson's Creek. The next spring he led his brigade at Elkhorn Tavern, where on March 7th, 1862, he rode directly into a concealed company of sharpshooters and was mortally wounded.

McDONALD, CHARLES J. C. (1835–1887), farmer, youngest son of the Hon. Charles James McDonald (1793–1860), governor of Georgia (1839–1843), and his first wife, Anne Franklin (1801–1835), was born at the Lodge, his father's residence near Macon, Georgia, in 1835. His mother died on October 10th, 1835, soon after his birth, and his father married second (on October 12th, 1839) Eliza (Roane) Ruffin (1802–1860), of Virginia. In 1850 Charles J. C. McDonald was living in the Macon household of his elder sister, Catherine Elizabeth McDonald (1826–1889), wife of Dean Munro Dunwody (1825–1878). He was evidently somewhat deranged; in January 1858 he was sent to the "lunatic asylum" in Columbia, South Carolina. By June 1860 he had returned to his father's residence in Marietta. On January 26th, 1861, a few weeks after his father's death on December 16th, 1860, Mrs. Eliza G. Robarts, writing from Marietta, reported that "Charlie McDonald (son of late governor) was married a week ago to a very poor country girl by the name of Maulding. Her parents, I believe, are good honest people." Governor McDonald, she wrote, had "left him equal with his other children," but had left the property in trust to his son's maternal uncle, Leonidas Franklin (1809–1867), of Macon. On August 1st, 1863, in Marietta, Charles J. C. McDonald enlisted for six months as a private in Captain William G. Gramling's Company (Company E, 7th Regiment Georgia State Guards), organized for local defense; on May 9th, 1864, in Macon, he enlisted for the war as a private in Company B, 3rd Regiment Georgia Reserves. After the war he lived with his family on a farm near Marietta; following the death of his first wife he married second (in April 1876) Cynthia E. Henderson, who bore him five children. He died on his farm on June 26th, 1887. As the Marietta *Journal* (June 30th, 1887) observed, "He had been in

failing health for a long time, but managed to walk to town nearly every week, in quest of food for himself and family, until the last few weeks. Inoffensive and kindhearted, with great faith in the religion of Christ, we believe he has entered a new sphere of existence where he will be forever happy. He has gone to that tribunal where all his wrongs will be righted. He leaves a wife and several children to mourn his death."

McDONALD, CHARLES JAMES (1793–1860), lawyer, legislator, and governor, son of Charles McDonald and Mary (Glas) Burn, was born in Charleston, South Carolina, on July 9th, 1793. After graduating from the South Carolina College in 1816 he read law in the office of Joel Crawford, an eminent Georgia lawyer, and commenced practice in Milledgeville in 1817. He soon rose to prominence in state politics; he held office successively as solicitor general (1822–1825) and judge (1825–1828) of the Flint circuit; as member of the state house of representatives (1830) and the state senate (1834–1837); as governor of Georgia (1839–1843); and as associate justice of the supreme court of Georgia (1856–1859). He married first (on December 16th, 1819) Anne Franklin (1801–1835), daughter of Bedney Franklin and Mary F. Cleveland, of Macon; there were five children. He married second (on October 12th, 1839) Eliza (Roane) Ruffin (1802–1860), daughter of the Hon. Spencer Roane, of Virginia. After his resignation from the supreme bench of the state on May 19th, 1859, he returned to his residence in Marietta, where he died on December 16th, 1860. He was buried in Episcopal Cemetery beside his second wife, who had died the preceding April. On April 20th, 1861, Henry Rootes Jackson (1820–1898), distinguished Savannah lawyer, pronounced in Marietta his *Eulogy upon the Life and Character of the Honorable Charles J. McDonald,* published in Atlanta later in the same year.

McDONALD, DANIEL (1811–1893), rice planter, son of William McDonald (1772–1844) and his first wife, Pheriba Farrow (1776–1811), was born on his father's plantation on the South Newport River, McIntosh County, on January 13th, 1811. He and his elder brother, James McDonald (1811–1874), were twins; their mother died at their birth. On December 7th, 1846, Daniel McDonald married Matilda Henrietta Powell (1821–1898), daughter of Allen Beverly Powell and Mary Calder, of Darien. He and his wife resided for a time at Hopeton plantation in McIntosh County; prior to the Civil War they settled at Fair Hope, situated on the Sapelo River south of Mallow, the plantation of Reuben King. In November 1862 the Federals ran up Sapelo River, raided Mallow and Fair Hope, captured Daniel McDonald, and carried him off. His wife and children took refuge in Jonesville. After the war he resumed planting at Fair Hope. James McDonald died unmarried on March 20th, 1874, and was buried in the South Newport Cemetery (the family cemetery of his father, William McDonald, on the Jonesville road ten miles from Townsend). Daniel McDonald died on March 1st, 1893, and was buried in the Powell family cemetery on "the Ridge" near Darien. Matilda Henrietta (Powell) McDonald died on February 10th, 1898, and was buried beside her husband. James and Daniel McDonald were uncles of Elisha McDonald (1826–1893), manager of Montevideo and Maybank plantations in Liberty County (1858–1861).

McDONALD, ELISHA (1826–1893), plantation overseer, eldest son of William McDonald (1800–1879) and Mary Walker (1805–1876), was born in McIntosh County, Georgia, on October 19th, 1826. In early manhood he settled in Liberty County, where from February 24th, 1858, to November 1st, 1861, he managed Montevideo and Maybank, two plantations owned by the Rev. Dr. Charles Colcock Jones. For his services he received the sum of three hundred dollars per annum, plus "the use of the girl Lucy in his family" and "fifty bushels of corn for his horse." As Mrs. Mary Jones reported on June 19th, 1858, "Mr. McDonald is quite attentive to our business." On February 9th, 1859, he married Sarah Virginia Morrison (1836–1923); there were no children, but they later adopted her niece, Alice McDonald (born 1868), daughter of Samuel McDonald and his first wife, Charity Morrison. On December 31st, 1861, having failed to secure a substitute, he enlisted as a private in the Liberty Guards (Company D, 5th Regiment Georgia Cavalry); on May 21st, 1862, he enlisted as a private in the McIntosh Cavalry (Company K, 5th Regiment Georgia Cavalry). After the war he returned to McIntosh County, where he was a planter and a merchant. He died on December 30th, 1893, and was buried in the McDonald family cemetery on "the Ridge" near Darien. Sarah Virginia (Morrison) McDonald died on February 22nd, 1923, and was buried beside her husband. Among the Jones papers preserved at Tulane University is the following letter of Elisha McDonald, addressed to the Rev. Dr. Jones on February 10th, 1858, and reproduced here verbatim et literatim: "By not hereing from you I suppose you think I charge too mutch for my services after consideration you finding me I will manage for you cheaper I am oblige to raise some money by the end of this year and do not know how I am to do it unless I get employment let me here from you soon and if you are yet in want of a manage inform me the most you are willing to give me."

McDOWELL, IRVIN (1818–1885), Union soldier, son of Abram Irvin McDowell and Eliza Selden Lord, was born in Columbus, Ohio, on October 15th, 1818. After receiving his early education in France, at the Collège de Troyes, he returned to America, entered the United States Military Academy in 1834, and graduated in 1838. For three years (1838–1841) he served as second lieutenant on the Canadian frontier, from Niagara to Maine; for five years (1841–1846) he was tactical officer

at West Point, with rank of adjutant. During the Mexican War (1846–1848) he was brevetted captain for distinguished service at Buena Vista. From 1848 to 1861 he served at army headquarters and in various territorial departments; he was made captain in 1856. On May 14th, 1861, he was promoted to brigadier general and placed in command of the Army of the Potomac. After his defeat at First Manassas he was superseded by McClellan and placed in command of a division. He fought in the Peninsula campaign of 1862. After Second Manassas he was severely criticized and relieved of his command; he was ultimately exonerated, but he never again saw duty in the field. He served in San Francisco (1864–1868), in the Department of the East (1868–1872), in the Department of the South (1872–1876), and again in San Francisco (1876–1882). After his retirement in 1882 he remained in San Francisco, where he died on May 4th, 1885, survived by his wife, Helen Burden, whom he had married in 1849.

McEWEN, ROBERT HOUSTON (1831–1873), lawyer, son of Robert Houston McEwen (1790–1868) and Henrietta Montgomery Kennedy (1796–1881), was born in Nashville, Tennessee, in 1831. His father, a prominent merchant, removed from Fayetteville, Tennessee, to Nashville in 1828 and was ruling elder of the First Presbyterian Church for thirty-seven years (1829–1866). Robert Houston McEwen (1831–1873) entered the College of New Jersey (Princeton) with the junior class in 1851 and graduated in 1853; at Princeton he was a fellow student of Charles Colcock Jones, Jr., and a classmate of Joseph Jones. Returning to Nashville, he studied law and was admitted to the bar in 1854. On October 11th, 1855, he married Lucy V. Putnam, daughter of J. W. Putnam, of Nashville; there were three children. His elder brother, John A. McEwen (1824–1858), also a lawyer, was a leader in the establishment of the Nashville public schools, a founding member of the board of education (1854) and its first secretary (1854–1858), and editor of the Nashville *Daily Gazette* (1852–1853). Robert Houston McEwen committed suicide in Nashville on November 29th, 1873, and was buried in Mount Olivet Cemetery. Lucy V. (Putnam) McEwen died on June 25th, 1906, and was buried beside her husband.

McFARLAND, FRANCIS (1788–1871), Presbyterian clergyman, was born in County Tyrone, Ireland, on January 8th, 1788. In early youth he migrated to America, where he graduated from Washington College (Pennsylvania) in 1818 and from Princeton Theological Seminary in 1820, and entered the ministry of the Presbyterian Church. He was home missionary in Indiana and Missouri (1820–1821) and in Georgia (1821–1822). He was corresponding secretary of the Board of Education of the Presbyterian Church (1835–1841). For forty-two years (1823–1835; 1841–1871) he was pastor of Bethel Church in Augusta County, Virginia; he died there on August

10th, 1871. He was moderator of the General Assembly of the Presbyterian Church in 1856 and called to order the first General Assembly of the Southern Presbyterian Church in 1861. He received the honorary degree of doctor of divinity from Washington College in 1839.

McFARLAND, JOHN THEODORE (1836–1888), physician, son of John McFarland (1791–1865) and Harriet Humbert (1801–1873), was born in Savannah, Georgia, on December 23rd, 1836. He graduated from the Savannah Medical College and practiced medicine in the city of his birth. On June 5th, 1861, he was appointed assistant surgeon of the 8th Regiment Georgia Infantry; he saw service at First Manassas. On February 17th, 1862, he was appointed assistant surgeon of the 1st Battery Georgia Sharpshooters; he was one of the officers surrendered at Fort Pulaski, Savannah harbor, on April 11th, 1862; he was taken to Fort Columbus, New York harbor, and released in July 1862. On February 13th, 1863, he was appointed assistant surgeon of the 5th Regiment Georgia Cavalry and placed in charge of hospitals by order of General Beauregard. On June 1st, 1864, he was appointed surgeon, to rank from January 20th, 1863. He was paroled at Hillsboro, North Carolina, on May 3rd, 1865. After the war he resumed the practice of medicine in Savannah, where he was health officer and secretary of the sanitary commission. He was an active member of the Georgia Medical Society. According to the Savannah *Morning News* (February 11th, 1888), "He was a volunteer on several occasions to distant cities afflicted with yellow fever, and he never at any time hesitated when called upon for any service, either in the line of his profession or as a citizen." In 1870 he married Fannie Aldridge (1850–1909), of Brooklyn, New York. He died in Savannah after a lingering illness on February 10th, 1888, survived by his wife and three children, and was buried in Bonaventure Cemetery.

MACFIE, CATHERINE (McGREGOR) (1807–1895): *Mrs. James Macfie*, daughter of James McGregor and Janet Graham, was born in Newcastle-on-Tyne, England, on April 2nd, 1807. On August 27th, 1829, she became the wife of James Macfie (1800–1837), a prosperous merchant of Columbia, South Carolina, and immediately departed with her husband for her new home. James Macfie died in Columbia on April 1st, 1837, survived by his wife and three children: James Pringle Macfie (1830–1890); Mary Jane Macfie (1832–1898), who became (on November 17th, 1852) the wife of Fitz William McMaster; and Catherine Macfie (1835–1881), who became (on February 15th, 1859) the wife of William James Lomax. Catherine (McGregor) Macfie died in Columbia on July 27th, 1895, survived by one daughter, twenty grandchildren, and fifteen great-grandchildren, and was buried beside her husband in the yard of the First Presbyterian Church, of which she had been a member for sixty-six years. According to the Columbia *State* (July 28th, 1895), "Mrs. Macfie was al-

ways known as a woman of strong character and great Christian charity. She was one of the founders of the Ladies' Benevolent Society and a charter member of the Columbia Orphan House. She was the first president of the Ladies' Memorial Association, and under her supervision the Confederate cemetery lot was laid off. When a call was issued for nurses during the war, she was one of the first women of South Carolina to answer the call, spending several months in the hospitals and on the battlefields of Virginia. She returned to South Carolina to be an active worker in the Wayside Hospital in this city, known throughout the South for its treatment of Confederate soldiers."

McGAVOCK, RANDAL WILLIAM (1826–1863), lawyer, fifth child of Jacob McGavock (1790–1878) and Louisa Caroline Grundy (1798–1878), was born in Nashville, Tennessee, on August 10th, 1826. His father, a native of Wythe County, Virginia, had migrated to Nashville in 1807 to attend Cumberland College; he became one of the wealthiest and most influential citizens of Nashville and was for more than fifty years clerk of the county, circuit, and United States court. His mother, a native of Bardstown, Kentucky, was the eldest daughter of the Hon. Felix Grundy (1777–1840), distinguished lawyer and statesman, congressman (1811–1814), United States senator (1829–1838; 1839–1840), and attorney general of the United States (1838–1839). She was a woman of high intellect and cultivation and the mother of thirteen children. Randal William McGavock graduated from the University of Nashville in 1846 and from Dane Law School, Harvard University, in 1849. After traveling extensively on three continents he published an account of his experiences in *A Tennessean Abroad; or, Letters from Europe, Africa, and Asia* (1854). On August 23rd, 1855, he married Seraphine Deery (1835–1918). For one year (October 1st, 1858–September 30th, 1859) he served as mayor of Nashville; visiting the city in June 1859, Charles Colcock Jones, Jr., found him to be "a gentleman of accomplished manners, of travel, of education, of intelligence, and of thought." Despite the solicitation of friends he retired from office without seeking reelection. At the outbreak of the Civil War he became colonel of the 10th Regiment Tennessee Infantry. He was killed in action at Raymond, Mississippi, on May 12th, 1863.

McHENRY, JOHN HARDIN (1832–1893), lawyer, son of John Hardin McHenry (1797–1871) and Hannah Davis (1800–1862), was born in Hartford, Ohio County, Kentucky, on February 21st, 1832. His father, a distinguished lawyer, was a member of the state house of representatives (1840) and Congress (1845–1847). John Hardin McHenry (1832–1893) was a cousin of George Helm and Ben Hardin Helm. He attended Hanover College (Indiana) and Centre College (Kentucky); after three years at the United States Military Academy he returned to Kentucky, studied law, and graduated from the law school of the University of Louisville in 1857. He commenced the practice of law in Owensboro, Kentucky, first with his father and later in partnership with the Hon. W. T. Owen. In 1861 he recruited the 17th Regiment Kentucky Infantry, with which he fought under Grant at Fort Donelson and Shiloh; when his command was later consolidated with the 25th Regiment Kentucky Infantry he was made colonel of the new regiment. When Lincoln issued his Emancipation Proclamation in September 1862, McHenry took issue and was dismissed. After the war he resumed the practice of law and became one of the most successful practitioners in the state. On December 30th, 1868, he married Josephine Phillips, daughter of Joseph Francis Phillips and Elizabeth Sue Simpson. He was appointed postmaster of Owensboro on March 26th, 1891; he died during his term of office, on July 7th, 1893, and was buried in Elmwood Cemetery. His elder brother, Henry Davis McHenry (1826–1890), also a lawyer, was a member of the state house of representatives (1851–1853; 1865–1867), the state senate (1861–1865), and Congress (1871–1873).

McINTOSH, ANNA (1828–1867), daughter of William Jackson McIntosh (1782–1863) and Maria Hillary (1788–1862), was born in McIntosh County, Georgia, in 1828. In 1846, after a girlhood spent in McIntosh and Bryan Counties, she removed with her parents to Savannah, where she was active in the Needlewoman's Friend Society and the Independent Presbyterian Church. Like her three elder sisters (Sarah, Agnes, and Maria) she never married. She died in 1867.

McINTOSH, DONALD McKAY (1829–1859), lawyer, son of William Jackson McIntosh (1782–1863) and Maria Hillary (1788–1862), was born in McIntosh County, Georgia, in 1829. In 1846, after a boyhood spent in McIntosh and Bryan Counties, he removed with his parents to Savannah, where he read law and commenced the practice of his profession. Late in 1850 he settled in Cedar Rapids, Iowa, where in May 1851 he married Harlie Bryan Rutledge, a native of South Carolina. He died suddenly in Davenport, Iowa, where he was attending the sessions of the state supreme court, in June 1859. His widow returned with her three young sons to her native state, where her eldest son, Harleston Rutledge McIntosh (1852–1862), died in Greenville in his eleventh year on November 14th, 1862.

McINTOSH, McQUEEN (1822–1868), jurist, son of William Jackson McIntosh (1782–1863) and Maria Hillary (1788–1862), was born in McIntosh County, Georgia, in 1822. After attending Franklin College (Athens) with the class of 1843 he read law and commenced practice in Jacksonville, Florida. On December 21st, 1847, he married Georgia Fannin (1825–1908), daughter of Abraham Baldwin Fannin (1791–1851) and Jane Williamson, of Savannah, Georgia; three of their four children lived to maturity. For twenty years McQueen McIntosh was conspicuously identified with the political history of Florida. He was judge of the United States district court for the northern district of Florida (1856–1861) and judge of the Confederate States district court for the southern district of Florida (1861–1865). He was a member of the state secession convention meeting in Tallahassee in January 1861. He died in Pensacola, Florida, after a long and painful illness on June 18th, 1868. As the *West Florida Commercial* (June 26th, 1868) observed, "Judge McIntosh was a man of ardent temperament and lofty personal pride, yet of warm, generous, kindly impulses." His widow survived him forty years. Soon after his death she returned to Savannah with her three children (Thomas Hamilton, Henry Sadler, and Jessie). She died in Savannah on April 28th, 1908, and was buried in Bonaventure Cemetery.

McINTOSH, THOMAS SPALDING (1837–1862), lawyer and Confederate soldier, son of William Jackson McIntosh (1782–1863) and Maria Hillary (1788–1862), was born in McIntosh County, Georgia, in 1837. After graduating from the Georgia Military Institute (Marietta) he read law and commenced practice in Savannah. On July 3rd, 1861, he married Maria B. Morris (1841–1925), only daughter of William St. Clair Morris (1812–1871) and Susan Walker (1810–1873), of Bath, Richmond County, Georgia. On May 18th, 1861, he was appointed second lieutenant in Company F, 1st Regiment Georgia Regulars; on July 5th, 1861, he resigned. On October 19th, 1861, he was appointed captain and assistant adjutant general on the staff of General Lafayette McLaws; he fought in the Peninsula campaign of 1862. On July 16th, 1862, he was appointed major and adjutant general and assigned to duty as aide to General McLaws. He was killed at Sharpsburg on September 17th, 1862. "Poor McIntosh is said to have been horribly mangled," wrote Charles Colcock Jones, Jr., on October 1st, 1862, "and was buried on the field. His wife is almost deranged. She had concentered all her affections upon him, and her heart, bereft of his loves, is desolate beyond description." On February 13th, 1868, Maria (Morris) McIntosh became the wife of Dr. James M. Madden (1840–1906), a physician, and settled in Brunswick, Georgia, where she became the mother of three children. The remains of Thomas Spalding McIntosh were removed from Sharpsburg and reburied in Laurel Grove Cemetery, Savannah, on October 25th, 1867. As General McLaws observed in a private letter, "No one can point out hereafter a more noble hero and chivalrous man than Major McIntosh." A full account of his death appeared in the Augusta *Weekly Chronicle & Sentinel* (November 18th, 1862): "Descended from the purest blood of the Revolution, in his brief and brilliant career he has proved himself worthy of a name that upon the red fields of battle has illustrated the history of Southern chivalry, from the struggles of our fathers for independence to the present war, produced by Northern perfidy and arrogance."

McINTOSH, WILLIAM JACKSON (1782–1863), naval officer and customs appraiser, eldest son of John McIntosh and Sarah Swinton, was born in Sunbury, Liberty County, Georgia, in March 1782. He was educated by the Rev. Dr. William McWhir (1759–1851) at the Sunbury Academy, where he was a schoolmate of Mary Winn (1784–1859), Eliza Greene Low (1785–1868), and William Maxwell (1785–1866). On April 30th, 1800, he entered the United States navy as a midshipman; on May 2nd, 1808, he was promoted to lieutenant; on December 9th, 1808, he resigned. In 1810 he married Maria Hillary (1788–1862), of Colleton District, South Carolina; there were eleven children. After living successively in Liberty, McIntosh, and Bryan Counties for some years he removed in 1846 to Savannah, where he was an appraiser in the United States customhouse. He was an ardent secessionist; in 1861, at the age of seventy-nine, he volunteered his services to Commodore Josiah Tattnall when Savannah was threatened by the Federal fleet. His wife died on February 25th, 1862, and his son Thomas Spalding McIntosh (1837–1862) was killed at Sharpsburg on September 17th, 1862; these deaths weighed on his mind and hastened the decline of his health. He died in his sleep on January 1st, 1863, aboard the steamer *Indian* as it sailed up the Chattahoochee River from the residence of his son the Hon. McQueen McIntosh (1822–1868) in Florida to the residence of his son the Rev. William Hillary McIntosh (1811–1890), a Baptist clergyman, in Alabama. He was buried in Laurel Grove Cemetery, Savannah. As the Savannah *Republican* (February 12th, 1863) observed, "The sorrow which the news of his death will carry to many friends will be softened by the knowledge that he died in the firm and comforting faith of our holy religion."

McIVER, AUGUSTUS MUNRO (1828–1881), planter and teacher, son of Alexander McIver and Elizabeth Munro, was born in Liberty County, Georgia, on December 11th, 1828. After graduating from Franklin College (Athens) in 1848 he taught school for several years in Camden County, Georgia, in the household of Dr. Samuel Furman. In 1851 he undertook planting in his native county. On October 14th, 1858, in Middleboro, Plymouth County, Massachusetts, he married Caroline Matilda Sturtevant (1830–1892), daughter of William H. Sturtevant (1800–1838) and Permelia A. Sturtevant (1800–1878), of Providence, Rhode Island; there were four children. During the Civil War he was a private in the Liberty Independent Troop (Company G, 5th Regiment Georgia Cavalry); he was paroled at Hillsboro, North Carolina, on May 3rd, 1865. Returning to Liberty County, he served as local agent of the Freedmen's Bureau (the Federal Bureau of Refugees, Freedmen, and Abandoned Lands) for

some months in 1867 and later as principal of the Walthourville Academy. In 1878 he and his family removed to Jacksonville, Florida, where he died on January 29th, 1881, survived by his wife and three children. Caroline Matilda (Sturtevant) McIver continued to teach seventh grade in the Jacksonville Grammar School until her death on November 8th, 1892. She was buried beside her husband in Old City Cemetery.

MACKAY, ELIZA ANNE (McQUEEN) (1778–1862): *Mrs. Robert Mackay,* daughter of John McQueen and Anne Smith, was born at the Grange, the Savannah River plantation of Basil Cowper, her uncle by marriage, on April 23rd, 1778. Shortly after the Revolutionary War Anne (Smith) McQueen accompanied her four children to London, England, where Eliza Anne McQueen attended school until 1791, when she returned to Georgia. On January 30th, 1800, she became the wife of Robert Mackay (1772–1816), a Savannah merchant, only son of Robert Mackay and Mary (Malbone) Chilcott. Eight of their nine children lived to maturity: Mary Anne Mackay (1802–1862), wife of Benjamin Edward Stiles; William Mein Mackay (1804–1859); John Mackay (1805–1848); Margaret Cowper Mackay (1807–1893), wife of Dr. Ralph Emms Elliott; Elizabeth Anne Mackay (1810–1867), wife of William Henry Stiles; Catherine Mackay (1811–1879); Robert Mackay (1813–1857); and Sarah Mackay (1815–1876). Soon after their marriage the Mackays spent five years (1806–1811) in England, first in London and later in Liverpool, where Robert Mackay managed the foreign business of his Savannah partners, Alexander and William Mein. Returning with his family to Savannah, Robert Mackay suffered increasingly from poor health; he died in New York City on October 6th, 1816, and was buried in Trinity Churchyard. Eliza (McQueen) Mackay continued to occupy the family residence in Savannah (situated on Broughton Street at the southeast corner of Abercorn) with her eight children; in later years she shared the house with her two unmarried daughters, Catherine and Sarah, and her son, William Mein. She died in Savannah on June 13th, 1862, and was buried in Laurel Grove Cemetery. It was at her Savannah residence that Robert E. Lee, West Point classmate and intimate friend of John ("Jack") Mackay, was a frequent visitor during his military service on Cockspur Island in the winter of 1829–1830; and it was there that Lee was again a frequent visitor during his military service on the Georgia coast in the winter of 1861–1862.

MACKAY, ROBERT (1813–1857), eighth child of Robert Mackay (1772–1816) and Eliza Anne McQueen (1778–1862), was born in the town house of his great-uncle, Archibald Smith (1758–1830), in Reynolds Square, Savannah, Georgia, in 1813. He was a younger brother of Mary Anne Mackay (1802–1862), wife of Benjamin Edward Stiles and mother of Katherine Clay (Kitty) Stiles. His father, a Savannah merchant, died in New York City on October 6th, 1816. His mother continued to occupy the family residence in Savannah (situated on Broughton Street at the southeast corner of Abercorn) with her eight children. On April 16th, 1826, Robert Mackay was confirmed at Christ Episcopal Church, Savannah, together with two of his sisters, Margaret and Catherine. Thereafter his life was "a blank," as Charles Colcock Jones, Jr., observed (October 15th, 1857) on hearing the news of his death. "For several years he has suffered from paralysis, having lost the power of speech almost entirely, and being quite feeble. This is all to a very great extent the result of his habits." He never married.

MACKAY, SARAH (1815–1876), ninth and youngest child of Robert Mackay (1772–1816) and Eliza Anne McQueen (1778–1862), was born in Savannah, Georgia, on April 11th, 1815. She was a younger sister of Mary Anne Mackay (1802–1862), wife of Benjamin Edward Stiles and mother of Katherine Clay (Kitty) Stiles. Her father, a Savannah merchant, died in New York City on October 6th, 1816. Her mother continued to occupy the family residence in Savannah (situated on Broughton Street at the southeast corner of Abercorn) with her eight children; after the mother's death on June 13th, 1862, Sarah Mackay and her elder sister, Catherine Mackay (1811–1879), resided there alone. Sarah Mackay was for many years a member of the Needlewoman's Friend Society, the Widows' Society, the Clothing and Fuel Society, and the Wayside Home, all charitable organizations. On July 20th, 1861, she helped organize "a society, the object of which should be to provide suitable winter clothing for all our soldiers who are or may be in active service. It is our sacred duty to see that our soldiers are well prepared to meet the exposure of a winter campaign" (Savannah *Morning News,* August 3rd, 1861). Sarah Mackay never married. She died in Savannah on March 7th, 1876, and was buried in the Mackay-Stiles lot in Laurel Grove Cemetery beneath the inscription: "Always abounding in the work of the Lord." Catherine Mackay died in Bartow County, Georgia, on January 7th, 1879, and was buried near her sister beneath the inscription: "Faithful unto death."

McLAWS, LAFAYETTE (1821–1897), Confederate soldier, son of James McLaws and Elizabeth Huguenin, was born in Augusta, Georgia, on January 15th, 1821. After attending the University of Virginia one year he entered the United States Military Academy in 1838. Soon after his graduation in 1842 he married Emily Allison Taylor (1824–1890), of Jefferson County, Kentucky, daughter of John Taylor and niece of President Zachary Taylor; there were seven children. Following service in Indian Territory, Mississippi, Louisiana, and Florida he fought in the Mexican War (1846–1848); as captain in the 7th Regiment United States Infantry he was a member of the Utah expedition of 1858. At the outbreak of the Civil War he resigned his commission, returned to his native state, and entered Confederate service; he became lieutenant colonel of the 10th Regiment Georgia Infantry (June 17th, 1861) and rose rapidly to brigadier general (September 25th, 1861) and major general (May 22nd, 1862). He fought at Malvern Hill, Sharpsburg, Fredericksburg, Chancellorsville, Gettysburg, Knoxville, and Chickamauga. During Sherman's invasion of Georgia he commanded the military district of Georgia and conducted the defense of Savannah; in March 1865, moving into North Carolina, he commanded a division at Averysboro and Goldsboro. After the war he sold insurance in Savannah; he was collector of the port of Savannah (1875–1876) and postmaster (1876–1884). He died in Savannah after a long illness on July 24th, 1897, survived by four children, and was buried beside his wife in Laurel Grove Cemetery beneath the following inscription: "I fought not for what I thought to be right but for principles that were right."

McNATT, ADAM (1817–1872), planter, was born in Georgia in 1817. His father died when Adam was still an infant; his mother, Mary McNatt (1790–1871), married second (on June 22nd, 1823) the Rev. Joshua Key, a Baptist clergyman. On June 5th, 1839, Adam McNatt married Emeline Teresa Hart, daughter of Thomas Hart and Ann Barnett, of Greene County, Georgia; two of their children survived infancy. Prior to the Civil War Adam McNatt was a rich planter in Burke County, Georgia; he also maintained a summer residence near Bath, Richmond County; and at both places he was known for his princely hospitality. In the Federal Census of 1860 he was recorded as the owner of ninety-five slaves (Burke County) and thirteen slaves (Richmond County). After the war he shared the general financial ruin of the South; on March 18th, 1868, he filed a petition in bankruptcy, and in October 1868 his property was sold at auction at the Burke County courthouse in Waynesboro. He died in 1872, survived by his wife and one daughter, and was buried in an unmarked grave in Bath Presbyterian Churchyard. On July 19th, 1864, his daughter, Georgia Virginia McNatt (1844–1921), became the wife of Michael Phillip Carroll (1841–1920), of St. Marys County, Maryland, a captain in the Confederate army; after the war he practiced law in Augusta. According to the Augusta *Chronicle* (September 11th, 1921), "Mrs. Carroll was a famous raconteur, and especially noted for her celebrated lecture on the old-time Southern darky, 'Echoes from Dixie.' As a delineator of the old-time darky she had no equal in the South, both in her understanding of the character and in her inimitable gift for mimicry of his talk and manner. She received requests constantly from all parts of the country for this lecture, which never failed to please and entertain both North and South." She was buried beside her husband in Magnolia Cemetery, Augusta.

McPHERSON, JAMES BIRDSEYE (1828–1864), Union soldier, son of William McPherson and Cynthia Russell, was born in Green Creek Township, Sandusky County, Ohio, on November 14th, 1828. After graduating from the United States Military Academy in 1853, first in his class, he saw duty for eight years (1853–1861) in river and harbor improvement and seacoast fortification along the Atlantic and Pacific coasts. At the outbreak of the Civil War he was assigned to fortification work in Boston; after serving briefly as aide-de-camp, with rank of colonel, to General Halleck in Missouri he entered the Tennessee campaign in February 1862 as chief engineer under General Grant. He subsequently became brigadier general of volunteers (May 15th, 1862) and major general of volunteers (October 8th, 1862); in recognition of his services before Vicksburg he was made brigadier general in the regular army (August 1st, 1863). When Grant went east in March 1864 to assume command of all the Northern forces, McPherson assumed command of Sherman's Army of the Tennessee; in this position he conducted the Atlanta campaign until his death before Atlanta on July 22nd, 1864. His loss was a heavy blow to the Union forces; his superior abilities were recognized by Grant, who linked Sherman and McPherson as "the men to whom, above all others, I feel indebted for whatever I have had of success."

McRAE, ELIJAH (1825–1904), planter and timber dealer, son of John McRae (1780–1853) and Margaret McRae (1795–1882), was born near Mount Vernon, Montgomery County, Georgia, on December 28th, 1825. He was for many years a prosperous planter in Montgomery County; he also operated a gristmill and a sawmill, and he owned many slaves. It was on his plantation that Tom, a Negro slave owned by Mrs. Mary Jones, of Liberty County, learned the shoemaking trade during the summer of 1863. Elijah McRae was a member of the Mount Vernon Presbyterian Church from its organization on January 19th, 1851; he was ordained ruling elder on July 16th, 1866, and elected clerk of the session on December 7th, 1873; he was superintendent of the Sunday school from 1851 to 1904. He resided at the old McRae family place near Mount Vernon; on August 8th, 1872, in his forty-seventh year, he married Janie Smith (1846–1923), aged twenty-six. He died on May 26th, 1904, and was buried in the cemetery on the McRae family place. Janie (Smith) McRae died on July 28th, 1923, and was buried beside her husband. Farquhar McRae (1817–1883), elder brother of Elijah McRae, donated the land on which the Mount Vernon Presbyterian Church was built.

McWHIR, WILLIAM (1759–1851), Presbyterian clergyman and educator, was born in County Antrim, Ireland, on September 9th, 1759. After attending the College of Belfast he studied theology in Scotland and was licensed to preach the gospel. In 1783 he migrated to America and settled in Alexandria, Virginia, where for ten years he conducted a public academy of which George Washington was a trustee. In 1793 he traveled on horseback to Georgia and settled in Sunbury, Liberty County, where for many years he conducted one of the finest schools in the state. There the Rev. Dr. Charles Colcock Jones acquired the rudiments of an English education and made a lifelong friend of his distinguished teacher. On December 21st, 1830, Dr. McWhir performed the marriage ceremony of Dr. Jones and his first cousin, Mary Jones. Meanwhile Dr. McWhir had married another Mary Jones (1757–1819), widow of Captain Mathias Lapina (died 1783) and of Colonel John Baker (died 1793). After his wife's death in 1819 he traveled extensively in Ireland, Scotland, and England. Returning to Georgia, he continued active for many years in Presbyterian affairs; although he never had a regular pastoral charge he frequently attended Synod and was more than once commissioner to the General Assembly. He died at South Hampton, the plantation of his friend Roswell King in Liberty County, on January 31st, 1851, and was buried beside his wife in Sunbury Cemetery. He left no descendants. In his will he named the Rev. Dr. Charles Colcock Jones as one of three executors and remembered Dr. Jones and his wife with a legacy of three hundred dollars.

MADISON, DOROTHEA (DOLLEY) (PAYNE) (TODD) (1768–1849): *Mrs. James Madison*, daughter of John Payne and Mary Coles, both Virginians, was born in North Carolina on May 20th, 1768, while her parents were on a visit. After a childhood spent in Hanover County, Virginia, she removed with her father in 1783 to Philadelphia, where on January 7th, 1790, she became the wife of John Todd, a lawyer. He died of yellow fever on October 24th, 1793, and in less than a year (on September 15th, 1794) she became the wife of James Madison (1751–1836), secretary of state under President Thomas Jefferson (1801–1809) and fourth president of the United States (1809–1817). As Washington Irving wrote from Washington on January 13th, 1811, "Mrs. Madison is a fine, portly, buxom dame, who has a smile and a pleasant word for everybody. Her sisters, Mrs. Cutts [Anna Payne, wife of Richard D. Cutts] and Mrs. Washington [Lucy Payne, wife of George Steptoe Washington] are like two Merry Wives of Windsor; but as to Jemmy Madison—ah, poor Jemmy!—he is but a withered little applejohn." In 1817 Madison retired with his wife to Montpelier, his home in Orange County, Virginia, where he died on June 28th, 1836. Dolley Madison died in Washington, D.C., on July 12th, 1849, survived by her son, John Payne Todd (1792–1851), and was buried in Congressional Cemetery. Some years later her remains were removed to Montpelier and laid beside those of her second husband. She lived to be more than eighty years old, and she was said to have retained her beauty, grace, and charm to the end.

MAGOFFIN, BERIAH (1815–1885), lawyer, planter, and governor, son of Beriah Magoffin and Jane McAfee, was born in Harrodsburg, Kentucky, on April 18th, 1815. He graduated from Centre College (Danville, Kentucky) in 1835, studied law privately, and graduated from the law department of Transylvania University (Lexington, Kentucky) in 1838. After practicing law for one year in Mississippi he returned to Harrodsburg, where he soon rose to prominence in his profession. He was police judge for Harrodsburg for ten years (1840–1850). He was a member of the state senate (1850–1851) and a delegate to the Democratic National Convention (1848, 1856, 1860). As governor of Kentucky (1860–1862) he opposed secession, favored compromise, and sought to preserve the neutrality of his state. On April 15th, 1861, he refused Lincoln's call for troops, and a week later he refused Davis' call for troops. After much opposition from his legislature, which was strongly pro-Union, he resigned in August 1862 and returned to Harrodsburg, where he resumed the practice of law. He represented Mercer County in the state legislature (1867–1869) and served as honorary commissioner to the Paris Exposition in 1878. In April 1840 he married Ann Shelby (1818–1880), who bore him ten children. He died in Harrodsburg on February 28th, 1885, and was buried beside his wife in Spring Hill Cemetery. A quotation carved on his monument summarizes his position at the outbreak of the Civil War: "What attitude shall Kentucky occupy in this deplorable conflict? Looking to the Constitution of the United States, the nature of our institutions, and the causes of this war, I think Kentucky has a right to assume a neutral position. Let her be a peacemaker, and when opportunity offers, as a mediator, present terms of peace and of settlement alike honorable to both the contending parties. While opposed to the policy of the government and the measures used to preserve the Constitution, we would not exchange the government of our fathers for any experiment on earth. We differ only as to the best means of preserving the Union. May God yet preserve and bless and guide us by His wisdom in this dread hour."

MAGRATH, ANDREW GORDON (1813–1893), jurist and governor, son of John Magrath and Maria Gordon, was born in Charleston, South Carolina, on February 8th, 1813. After graduating from the South Carolina College in 1831 he attended the Harvard Law School for a few months and subsequently read law in the office of James L. Pettigru. For twenty-one years (1835–1856) he practiced law in Charleston, retiring briefly in 1840 and 1842 to serve in the state house of representatives. On March 8th, 1843, he married Emma Camilla Mikell (1826–1860), daughter of Ephraim Mikell, of Edisto Island. In 1856 he was appointed judge of the United States circuit court for the district of South Carolina; on November 7th, 1860, learning of Lincoln's election, he resigned from the bench with the declaration that "The Temple of Justice, raised under the Constitution of the United States, is now closed." He was a delegate to the state secession convention meeting in Columbia in December 1860, and in 1861 he was appointed judge of the Confederate States circuit court for the district of South Carolina. In December 1864 he resigned to become governor of the state. On May 28th, 1865, he was arrested and for six months was imprisoned at Fort Pulaski; while in prison he corresponded with Mary McCord, of Columbia, whom he married after his release. Returning to Charleston, he resumed the practice of law. He died in Charleston on April 9th, 1893.

MAGRUDER, EDWARD JONES (1835–1892), Confederate soldier, was born at Frescati, ancestral home of the Magruders, in Orange County, Virginia, on May 14th, 1835. After graduating from the Virginia Military Institute in 1855 he settled in Rome, Georgia, where he conducted a military school until the outbreak of the Civil War. On May 14th, 1861 (his twenty-sixth birthday) he married Florence Fouché (1840–1910), daughter of Simpson Fouché (1806–1885); two weeks later (on May 27th, 1861) he left Rome with his company, the Rome Light Guards (Company A, 8th Regiment Georgia Infantry) for Virginia, accompanied by his bride, who took up residence with his family in Orange County. He was elected major on January 28th, 1862, and was promoted to lieutenant colonel on December 16th, 1862. He was several times wounded in battle. After the war he returned to Rome, where he served for many years as city marshal and chief of police. He died in Rome on February 26th, 1892, and was buried in Myrtle Hill Cemetery. Florence (Fouché) Magruder died in Rome on November 2nd, 1910, and was buried beside her husband.

MALLARD, CHARLES COLCOCK (1860–1914), civil engineer, second child of the Rev. Robert Quarterman Mallard (1830–1904) and Mary Sharpe Jones (1835–1889), was born in Walthourville, Liberty County, Georgia, on April 27th, 1860. He was baptized on Sunday, September 23rd, 1860, in the Walthourville Presbyterian Church, of which his father was then pastor, by his maternal grandfather, the Rev. Dr. Charles Colcock Jones, for whom he was named. In 1863 the family removed to Atlanta, and in 1866 they settled in New Orleans. After attending Southwestern Presbyterian University (Clarksville, Tennessee) for two years (1877–1879) he became associated with the Southern Pacific Railroad, with which he held prominent administrative posts at various points in the West throughout a distinguished career of thirty-five years. From 1906 to 1914 he was superintendent of the Arizona Eastern Railroad, with headquarters in Globe, Arizona. He never married. He died in New Orleans on November 24th, 1914, survived by two sisters, and was buried in the family vault in Lafayette Cemetery. According to the New Orleans *Times-Picayune* (November 27th, 1914), "There was no employee or official in the Southern Pacific service from New Orleans to San Francisco who enjoyed greater popularity than Mr. Mallard. He had the confidence of the men higher up, and the large force under him considered him with a regard that was close to devotion."

MALLARD, CYRUS W. (1846–1887), soldier, railroad contractor, and salesman, fourth child of Cyrus Stevens Mallard (1818–1853) and Sarah R. Law (1823–1899), was born at Cedar Hill, his father's plantation near Dorchester, Liberty County, Georgia, in 1846. His father died on September 5th, 1853, leaving a widow and nine young children. On May 15th, 1862, when scarcely sixteen years old, he enlisted for three years as a private in the Liberty Mounted Rangers (Company B, 20th Battalion Georgia Cavalry), together with his elder brother William Joseph Mallard (1842–1914); the two brothers served throughout the war. Returning to Liberty County, he worked for a time as a railroad contractor, then as a traveling salesman. In Spartanburg, South Carolina, he met and married Sally Butler, who died young, leaving her three children (Thomas Butler, Eva, and John Lyman) to the care of her brother and his wife. Cyrus W. Mallard spent his later years in Thomasville, Georgia, where he died on July 19th, 1887. He was buried in Laurel Hill Cemetery. Sometime after the war he adopted the full name of his deceased father, Cyrus Stevens Mallard; his tombstone reads: "C. S. Mallard."

MALLARD, ELIZA BURNLEY (1863–1863), third child of the Rev. Robert Quarterman Mallard (1830–1904) and Mary Sharpe Jones (1835–1889), was born in Walthourville, Liberty County, Georgia, on March 12th, 1863, four days before the death of her maternal grandfather, the Rev. Dr. Charles Colcock Jones, whose last journal entry (March 13th, 1863) recorded her birth: "A note from Robert at sunrise this morning informed us of the birth of our dear daughter's *third* infant—*a little girl!* All reported as well, D.G.! Mother went immediately up to Walthourville after breakfast." Dr. Jones's last letter, written on March 14th, 1863, bore his congratulations to the parents and his blessings to the child. Eliza Burnley Mallard died in Walthourville on August 3rd, 1863, when not yet five months old, and was buried in Midway Cemetery.

MALLARD, GEORGIA MAXWELL (1865–1952), fourth child of the Rev. Robert Quarterman Mallard (1830–1904) and Mary Sharpe Jones (1835–1889), was born at Montevideo, the plantation of her maternal grandmother, in Liberty County, Georgia, on January 4th, 1865. Her father, pastor of the Central Presbyterian Church, Atlanta, was at the time of her birth held prisoner in Savannah by Federal forces occupying the city and conducting raids on neighboring seaboard counties. She was named for Georgia Maxwell (1828–1829), deceased infant of her great-

aunt, Mrs. Susan M. Cumming, and her first husband, James Audley Maxwell. In 1866 the Mallards settled in New Orleans, where the father was pastor of the Prytania Street Presbyterian Church (1866–1877) and the Napoleon Avenue Presbyterian Church (1879–1904). After attending the Sylvester Larned Institute until its closing in 1881 she graduated from the Locquet Leroy Institute in June 1882; she then studied French, German, and music. She was an accomplished organist, and played the melodeon regularly each Sunday morning and evening in her church. On November 17th, 1896, she became the wife of William Kimsey Seago (1855–1941); there were five children. For many years she was active in church and charitable work; from 1924 to 1939 she served as editor of the Woman's Auxiliary Department of *The Christian Observer*, official organ of the Southern Presbyterian Church. She died in New Orleans on December 7th, 1952, survived by four children, and was buried beside her husband in Metairie Cemetery.

MALLARD, JOHN BOYD (1808–1877), planter and educator, son of John Mallard and Lydia Quarterman, was born in Liberty County, Georgia, on September 18th, 1808. His father died on October 28th, 1810; his mother married second (in April 1824) Robert Laing. After graduating from Franklin College (Athens) in 1832 he attended Columbia Theological Seminary for one year; withdrawing for reasons of health, he became a teacher at the Chatham Academy in Savannah. Later he conducted an academy in Walthourville and a female seminary in Midway, near Milledgeville; for a short time he was professor of natural philosophy at Oglethorpe University. He was a deacon of Midway Church for twenty-nine years (1838–1867) and delivered the address at the centennial celebration in December 1852; he was also author of *A Short Account of the Congregational Church at Midway* (1840). He was ruling elder of the Walthourville Presbyterian Church from its organization in 1855 until his death. He represented Liberty County in the state senate (1857–1858) and was a member of the state secession convention meeting in Milledgeville in January 1861. After the war he served at various intervals as ordinary of Liberty County and as county school commissioner. He married first (on December 26th, 1839) Eloisa P. Field, a teacher from the North; after her death on February 27th, 1850, he married second (on July 3rd, 1851) Sarah Wilson Way (1830–1896). He died in Walthourville on March 22nd, 1877, and was buried in Walthourville Cemetery. Sarah Wilson (Way) Mallard died on June 24th, 1896, and was buried beside her husband. John Boyd Mallard was a first cousin of the Rev. Robert Quarterman Mallard. His sister Ann Lydia Mallard (1804–1843) was the first wife of William Quarterman Baker; his sister Mary Amarintha Mallard (1810–1874) was the wife of Thomas Quarterman Cassels.

MALLARD, LAZARUS JOHN (1820–1877), planter, fourth surviving child of Thomas Mallard (1778–1861) and his second wife, Rebecca Eliza Burnley (1789–1861), widow of Thomas Baker, was born in Liberty County, Georgia, on November 25th, 1820. He graduated from Franklin College (Athens) in 1841. After teaching school for two years he undertook planting in his native county. On February 12th, 1845, he married Sarah Stewart Mell (1823–1908), daughter of Benjamin Mell and Susan Rebecca Stevens, of Walthourville. He was one of a committee of thirteen men appointed to make arrangements for the centennial celebration of Midway Church in December 1852. From 1854 to 1867 he was a selectman of Midway Church and also clerk of the session. When the Dorchester Presbyterian Church was organized on January 6th, 1871, he was chosen ruling elder and made superintendent of the Sunday school. Too old for active service during the Civil War, he was a member of the "Home Guard" in Liberty County. After the war he served for two years as county tax collector. He died in Dorchester on May 6th, 1877, survived by his wife and five children, and was buried in Midway Cemetery. According to the session minutes of the Dorchester Presbyterian Church, "His presence fell like a benediction on all who knew him, and good thoughts rose spontaneously in the mind when he passed. . . . He was leading a prayer meeting, and making an address to those worshiping with him, when his speech suddenly failed him as the result of paralysis. Thus like a good soldier he fell at his post of duty."

MALLARD, MARY JONES (1858–1917), eldest child of the Rev. Robert Quarterman Mallard (1830–1904) and Mary Sharpe Jones (1835–1889), was born at Montevideo, the plantation of her maternal grandparents, in Liberty County, Georgia, on April 18th, 1858. She was baptized on Sunday, June 6th, 1858, in the Walthourville Presbyterian Church, of which her father was then pastor, by her maternal grandfather, the Rev. Dr. Charles Colcock Jones. In 1863 the family removed to Atlanta, and in 1866 they settled in New Orleans, where Mary Jones Mallard ("Mamie") resided for the rest of her life. She graduated from the Sylvester Larned Institute in 1875, and for some years conducted a school for young children. She never married, and after her father's death in 1904 she lived in the household of her younger sister, Georgia Maxwell Mallard (1865–1952), who had become the wife of William Kimsey Seago on November 17th, 1896. She was an active worker in the church, a King's Daughter, and a member of the board of governors of St. Anne's Home. She died in New Orleans on May 7th, 1917, survived by her sister, and was buried in the family vault in Lafayette Cemetery. She bore the name of her grandmother, her mother, and her eldest niece.

MALLARD, MARY SHARPE (JONES). See Jones, Mary Sharpe

MALLARD, REBECCA LOUISA (1825–1902), sixth surviving child of Thomas Mallard (1778–1861) and his second wife, Rebecca Eliza Burnley (1789–1861), widow of Thomas Baker, was born in Liberty County, Georgia, on June 30th, 1825. She never married. After the death of her parents in 1861 "Sister Lou" made her home with her brother, Thomas Samuel Mallard (1816–1882), in Walthourville; she later resided in the household of her sister, Ann Elizabeth Mallard (1828–1908), wife of Leander Lewis Varnedoe, in Thomasville. She died in Thomasville on April 24th, 1902, and was buried in Laurel Hill Cemetery. She was musical: she played the melodeon in Midway Church and was said to have a beautiful soprano voice.

MALLARD, ROBERT QUARTERMAN (1830–1904), Presbyterian clergyman, eighth surviving child of Thomas Mallard (1778–1861) and his second wife, Rebecca Eliza Burnley (1789–1861), widow of Thomas Baker, was born in Liberty County, Georgia, on September 7th, 1830. After graduating from Franklin College (Athens) in 1850 and from Columbia Theological Seminary in 1855 he was pastor of the Walthourville Presbyterian Church (1856–1863); the Central Presbyterian Church, Atlanta (1863–1866); the Prytania Street Presbyterian Church, New Orleans (1866–1877); and the Napoleon Avenue Presbyterian Church, New Orleans (1879–1904). He received the honorary degree of doctor of divinity from Southwestern Presbyterian University (Clarksville, Tennessee) in 1875. He was moderator of the General Assembly of the Southern Presbyterian Church meeting in Memphis in 1896. From 1891 to 1904 he was editor of *The Southwestern Presbyterian*. His two books, *Plantation Life Before Emancipation* (1892) and *Montevideo-Maybank: Some Memories of a Southern Christian Household in the Olden Times* (1898), describe scenes and incidents of life in coastal Georgia immediately prior to the Civil War. On April 22nd, 1857, he married Mary Sharpe Jones (1835–1889), only daughter of the Rev. Dr. Charles Colcock Jones (1804–1863) and Mary Jones (1808–1869), of Liberty County, Georgia; there were five children: Mary Jones Mallard (1858–1917), Charles Colcock Mallard (1860–1914), Eliza Burnley Mallard (1863–1863), Georgia Maxwell Mallard (1865–1952), and Robert Holt Mallard (1868–1869). After the death of his first wife on August 31st, 1889, he married second (on January 19th, 1893) Amarintha Mary Witherspoon, daughter of the Rev. Andrew Jackson Witherspoon, a Presbyterian clergyman. He died in New Orleans on March 3rd, 1904, survived by his second wife and three children, and was buried beside his first wife in the family vault in Lafayette Cemetery. According to the minutes of the Presbytery of New Orleans (October 19th, 1904), "Dr. Mallard was a man of striking personality, of commanding presence, of dignified, courteous bearing, gentle, refined, affable, winning his way to the hearts of those with whom he was associated. . . . We greatly miss, and shall still feel the loss of, his genial countenance, his cheerful smile, his pleasant voice, his loving spirit, his earnest counsel, his firm stand for every great law of the Kingdom and every truth of the gospel."

MALLARD, THOMAS (1778–1861), rice planter, son of Lazarus Mallard (1748–1814) and his first wife, Mary Boyd, widow of William Norman, was born in Liberty County, Georgia, on April 13th, 1778. He married first (on March 6th, 1800) Sarah Wilson (1783–1808), daughter of James Wilson and Elizabeth Quarterman. After her death on April 3rd, 1808, he married second (on May 2nd, 1811) Rebecca Eliza Burnley (1789–1861), daughter of Samuel Burnley and his second wife, Elizabeth (Baker) Stevens, and widow of Thomas Baker. Eight of their nine children lived to maturity: Mary Emeline Mallard (born 1813), wife of Bartholomew Austin Busby; Thomas Samuel Mallard (1816–1882); Cyrus Stevens Mallard (1818–1853); Lazarus John Mallard (1820–1877); Harriet Newell Mallard (1823–1889), second wife of Joseph Richard Bacon; Rebecca Louisa Mallard (1825–1902); Ann Elizabeth Mallard (1828–1908), wife of Leander Lewis Varnedoe; and Robert Quarterman Mallard (1830–1904). Thomas Mallard represented Liberty County in the state legislature in 1810. He was a lifelong member of Midway Church, of which he was also selectman (1810–1841) and deacon (1820–1861). When the village of Dorchester was established in 1843 he was one of its first settlers. In his later years he was almost totally deaf; his wife was almost totally blind. Rebecca Eliza (Burnley) (Baker) Mallard died in Dorchester on May 12th, 1861, only a few days after the fiftieth anniversary of her second marriage, and was buried in Midway Cemetery. Thomas Mallard died in Dorchester seven weeks later, on July 4th, 1861, and was buried beside his wife. As the Rev. Dr. Charles Colcock Jones observed in his journal (July 4th, 1861): "He lived a most upright and quiet life, and died in the faith, universally respected."

MALLARD, THOMAS SAMUEL (1816–1882), planter and teacher, second surviving child of Thomas Mallard (1778–1861) and his second wife, Rebecca Eliza Burnley (1789–1861), widow of Thomas Baker, was born in Liberty County, Georgia, on May 17th, 1816. He graduated from Franklin College (Athens) with first honor in 1836. In 1840 he married Ann Eliza Screven (1820–1895), daughter of the Rev. Charles Odingsell Screven (1773–1830), a Baptist clergyman, and his second wife, Barbara Rankin Godolpin. He was a selectman of Midway Church (1842–1846; 1850–1853), and was one of a committee of thirteen men appointed to make arrangements for the centennial celebration of Midway Church in December 1852. He was one of sixteen citizens instrumental in organizing a

separate Presbyterian church in Walthourville in 1855, and was one of its two ruling elders from 1855 until his death. He was a prosperous planter; in the Federal Census of 1860 he was recorded as the owner of seventy-two slaves. His two sons fought through the Civil War in the Liberty Mounted Rangers (Company B, 20th Battalion Georgia Cavalry): Charles Odingsell Screven Mallard (lieutenant) and William Samuel Mallard (private). After the war he represented Liberty County in the state legislature (1866) and taught school for some years, first in Thomasville, later in Walthourville. He died on February 8th, 1882 and was buried in St. Andrew's Cemetery, Darien. Ann Eliza (Screven) Mallard died on December 13th, 1895, and was buried beside her husband.

MALLARD, WILLIAM JOSEPH (1842–1914), soldier, insurance agent, and lawyer, second son of Cyrus Stevens Mallard (1818–1853) and Sarah R. Law (1823–1899), was born at Cedar Hill, his father's plantation near Dorchester, Liberty County, Georgia, in 1842. His father died on September 5th, 1853, leaving a widow and nine young children. On October 10th, 1861, he enlisted for six months as a private in the Liberty Independent Troop (Company G, 5th Regiment Georgia Cavalry); on May 15th, 1862, together with his younger brother Cyrus W. Mallard (1846–1887), he enlisted for three years as a private in the Liberty Mounted Rangers (Company B, 20th Battalion Georgia Cavalry). In August 1862 "Willie Joe" was severely wounded in his right arm while on picket duty on James Island near Charleston, South Carolina; he was at home on sick leave from August 29th until December 31st. On March 30th, 1864, he married Clara Elizabeth Jones (1845–1912), daughter of Moses Liberty Jones (1805–1851) and Sacharissa Elizabeth Axson (1811–1850), of Liberty County. After the war he settled with his family in Atlanta, where he was for some years an insurance agent and later practiced law. He died in Atlanta on October 15th, 1914, survived by two sons and two daughters, and was buried in Oakland Cemetery beside his wife, who had died on September 22nd, 1912.

MANIGAULT, LOUIS (1828–1899), traveler and connoisseur, son of Charles Izard Manigault (1795–1874), was born in Paris, France, on November 21st, 1828, of a wealthy and distinguished Huguenot family of South Carolina. After attending Yale College for two years (1845–1847) he traveled extensively through Europe, Asia, and South America, returning to Charleston in 1851. On December 1st, 1857, he married Frances Elizabeth Matilda Habersham (1835–1868), youngest daughter of Dr. Joseph Clay Habersham (1790–1855) and Ann Wylly Adams (1795–1876), of Savannah, Georgia. He did not qualify for military service during the Civil War, but in the summer of 1864 he became the secretary of Major Joseph Jones, of Augusta, Georgia, surgeon in the Confederate army.

"I wish you could see the beautiful style in which Mr. Manigault prepares all the reports for the surgeon general at Richmond," wrote Mrs. Mary Jones on September 29th, 1864; "Joe is most highly favored in this gentleman." For three months (September, October, and November 1864) Major Jones, accompanied by Louis Manigault, inspected the hospitals and prisons at Macon and Andersonville; a letter written by Manigault to his wife detailing the horrors of Andersonville Prison was reproduced in *The Georgia Historical Quarterly*, XXXVIII, 84–85 (March 1954). After the death of his wife on March 12th, 1868, Manigault lived a retired life in Charleston with his brother Gabriel. According to the Charleston *News & Courier* (November 24th, 1899), "They had traveled and studied in Europe together and had many tastes in common, notably a love of art, and their beautiful home in this city had more art treasures than any home in South Carolina." Louis Manigault died in Pinopolis, South Carolina, on November 22nd, 1899, survived by two sons and one daughter, and was buried beside his wife in Magnolia Cemetery, Charleston.

MANN, JOHN ELLIOTT (1813–1888), planter, son of Luke Mann and Margaret McIntosh, was born in Bryan County, Georgia, on February 17th, 1813. On August 1st, 1839, he married Elizabeth G. Martin (1816–1882). He was for many years a small planter in Liberty County, residing on his place near Flemington. He was a member of Midway Church; when the Flemington Presbyterian Church was organized on April 6th, 1866, he and his wife were charter members. In January 1866 he undertook to rent Arcadia plantation from its joint-owners, the three children of the Rev. Dr. Charles Colcock Jones. "Mr. Mann wants to rent it," wrote Mrs. Mary Jones on January 19th, 1866, "but will not come to terms. At the same time he goes upon the place, and has filled it with Negroes without consulting me or having made any arrangements binding himself in any way. He engaged to see me last week, and I sent him a written agreement at the time specified which he did not sign, and afterwards said he would come here on the 18th and enter into writings. This he has again failed to do, and with Brother William's advice I have just written to say I do not consider the place rented to him, as he failed to meet two appointments, and moreover that the place is open for sale at any time. Brother William disapproves highly of the manner in which he has treated me in the matter. If he were master of the place he could not act with more authority." John Elliott Mann died near Flemington on October 8th, 1888, survived by numerous children, and was buried in Flemington Cemetery beside his wife, who had died on February 16th, 1882.

MANNING, JOHN LAURENCE (1816–1889), planter, legislator, and governor, son of Richard Irvine Manning and Elizabeth Peyre Richardson, was born at Hickory Hill, his father's plantation in Clarendon County,

South Carolina, on January 29th, 1816. He attended the College of New Jersey (Princeton) for three years (1833–1836) and graduated from the South Carolina College in 1837. After planting briefly in South Carolina and Louisiana he entered politics, served several terms in the state house of representatives and the state senate, and became thirty-seventh governor of South Carolina (1852–1854). In 1861 he was volunteer aide-de-camp to General Beauregard, with rank of colonel; after First Manassas Beauregard wrote that he was "greatly indebted" to Manning and his other volunteer aides "for manifold essential services in the transmission of orders on the field and in the preliminary arrangements for the occupation and maintenance of the line of Bull Run." In 1865 Manning was elected to the United States Senate, but as a Southerner was not allowed to take his seat. He served one term in the state senate and then retired to Millford, his plantation in Clarendon County. He married first (in 1838) Susan Frances Hampton (1816–1845), daughter of General Wade Hampton (1751–1835) and his third wife, Mary Cantey (1780–1863), of Columbia, South Carolina; he married second (in 1848) Sally Bland, of Warner Hall, Gloucester County, Virginia, granddaughter of Richard Bland, "the Cato of the Revolution." He died in Camden, South Carolina, on October 29th, 1889, survived by two children, and was buried in Trinity Churchyard, Columbia.

MARION, FRANCIS (1732–1795), Revolutionary soldier, youngest son of Gabriel Marion and Esther Cordes, was born at Winyah, Berkeley County, South Carolina, in 1732. Prior to the Revolutionary War he farmed and hunted and served twice (1759; 1761) in campaigns against the Cherokee Indians. In 1775 he was a member of the provincial congress of South Carolina and was made captain of the 2nd (later the 6th) Continental Regiment. He subsequently became major and lieutenant colonel. When the British conquered South Carolina in 1780 he escaped with a band of guerillas to the swamps, where his brilliant harassment of the British led him to be known as the "Swamp Fox." After the war he served several terms in the state legislature and was commandant of Fort Johnson (1784–1790). In 1786 he married his cousin, Mary Esther Videau, a rich and elderly spinster. He died at his residence in St. Johns, Berkeley County, South Carolina, on February 27th, 1795, and was buried at Belle Isle, St. Stephen's.

MARKHAM, THOMAS RAILEY (1828–1894), Presbyterian clergyman, son of William Fleming Markham and Susan Railey, was born in Fayette, Jefferson County, Mississippi, on December 2nd, 1828. He was educated at Oakland College, Mississippi (1846–1849), Princeton Theological Seminary (1849–1852), the Yale Divinity School (summer 1853), and Columbia Theological Seminary (1853–1854). For thirty-seven years (1857–1894) he was stated supply of the Lafayette Street Presbyterian Church in New Orleans, with the exception of three years during the Civil War (1862–1865) when he was chaplain of the 1st Regiment Mississippi Light Artillery. He received the honorary degree of doctor of divinity from Southwestern Presbyterian University (Clarksville, Tennessee) in 1873. On November 30th, 1858, he married Mary E. Searles, daughter of Charles J. Searles, of Vicksburg, Mississippi; all four of their children died in infancy. He never remarried after the death of his wife on August 2nd, 1863. He died in New Orleans on March 12th, 1894, leaving no descendants, and was buried in the family vault of his colleague, the Rev. Dr. Benjamin Morgan Palmer, in Lafayette Cemetery. As the New Orleans *Daily Picayune* (March 13th, 1894) observed, "He had the sweet sympathy which made him the tenderest of consolers. He was cultured and learned, not in books merely but in the wide experience of the world. Few men have united so many traits that command effectually the respect and love of his followers." Markham was a classmate of the Rev. Robert Quarterman Mallard at Columbia Theological Seminary (1853–1854) and for many years (1866–1894) his colleague in New Orleans. He and the Rev. Dr. Palmer conducted the funeral service of Mary Sharpe Jones, wife of the Rev. Robert Quarterman Mallard, in the Prytania Street Presbyterian Church on September 2nd, 1889.

MARSHALL, JOHN (1755–1835), jurist, son of Thomas Marshall (1730–1802) and Mary Randolph Keith (1738–1809), was born in a log cabin near Germantown, Prince William (now Fauquier) County, Virginia, on September 24th, 1755, the eldest of fifteen children. During the Revolutionary War he served as lieutenant and later as captain in the 11th Regiment Virginia Troops. After studying law at the College of William and Mary in 1779 he commenced practice in Fauquier County, Virginia, in 1781 and later settled in Richmond. He was a member of the house of burgesses (1780; 1782–1788) and a member of the executive council (1782–1795). He declined the appointment of attorney general of the United States under President George Washington and the appointment of associate justice of the supreme court of the United States under President John Adams. He was a member of Congress (1799–1800); secretary of state (1800–1801); and chief justice of the supreme court of the United States (1801–1835). On January 3rd, 1783, he married Mary Willis Ambler. He died in Philadelphia on July 6th, 1835, and was buried in Shockoe Cemetery, Richmond, Virginia. He was the founder of the American system of constitutional law. According to the Rev. Dr. Charles Colcock Jones (January 3rd, 1853), his *Life of Washington* (1804–1807) was "*the* life of Washington—and written by one of the greatest minds ever produced in our country. And Judge Marshall, being himself a part of the Revolutionary struggle, and having personal acquaintance with the contemporaries of Washington, and access to the whole generation of patriots and all the necessary papers, was the man for the life."

MARTIN, CHARLES JONES (1849–1933), farmer, youngest son of William Graham Martin (1808–1861) and Eliza Sumner Bacon (1815–1889), was born in Liberty County, Georgia, on August 4th, 1849. He was named for the Rev. Dr. Charles Colcock Jones, an esteemed neighbor and family friend, who on March 15th, 1858, pronounced him "a fine little fellow." He resided in Liberty County all his life; he farmed, manufactured turpentine and rosin, and conducted a timber business. On December 7th, 1887, in his thirty-ninth year, he married Mary Jane Fraser (1862–1925), youngest daughter of Simon Alexander Fraser (1816–1870) and Mary William Bacon (1825–1884). Seven children lived to maturity. He was for many years an elder of the Flemington Presbyterian Church and also superintendent of the Sunday school. He died on April 13th, 1933, and was buried in Flemington Cemetery beside his wife, who had died on March 22nd, 1925. His daughter, Josephine Bacon Martin, a teacher in the Liberty County public schools, was long associated with Midway history; she was author and director of *A Charge to Keep,* a pageant presented at the bicentennial celebration of the settlement of the Midway colony in April 1954; and she was hostess of the Midway Museum for some years subsequent to its dedication on November 29th, 1959.

MARTIN, EDMUND HOWARD (1825–1907), physician, planter, broker, and merchant, son of Edmund Martin (1796–1871) and his second wife, Mary Anna Maner (1806–1847), was born at Woodstock, his father's plantation in Beaufort District, South Carolina, on November 18th, 1825. After graduating from the South Carolina College in 1845 and from the Medical Department of the University of the City of New York in 1848 he settled in Savannah, Georgia, where he commenced practice in association with Dr. H. L. Byrd. In 1852 he was one of eight founders of the Savannah Medical College, and he was for some five years its professor of physiology. On January 6th, 1853, he married Emily Caroline Wellborn (1833–1914), daughter of Alfred Wellborn (1793–1857) and Elizabeth Terry (1801–1848), of Meriwether County, Georgia; on the same day his younger brother, John Marshall Martin (1832–1924) married Willie Elizabeth Wellborn (1831–1858), elder sister of Emily Caroline Wellborn. Shortly before the Civil War Edmund Howard Martin joined John Richardson (1816–1873) in the cotton brokerage business; the firm of Richardson & Martin flourished in Savannah until the partnership was dissolved by mutual consent on May 29th, 1867. During that period Martin was also a director of the Farmers' & Mechanics' Bank and the Merchants' & Planters' Bank. Leaving Savannah in 1867, he spent some years in Memphis, Tennessee, where he engaged in the hardware business, and in Louisville, Kentucky, where he was secretary and general manager of the Ohio Falls Building & Loan Association. In 1900 he retired from business and removed to New York City, where he lived with his daughter, Anne Elizabeth (Bessie) Martin (1859–1943), wife of Dr. James Harvey Dew (1843–1914). He died in New York City on November 3rd, 1907, survived by his wife and three children, and was buried in Woodlawn Cemetery. Emily Caroline (Wellborn) Martin died in New York City on January 16th, 1914, and was buried beside her husband.

MARTIN, HENRY EDWARD (1837–1862), Confederate soldier, third child and eldest son of William Graham Martin (1808–1861) and Eliza Sumner Bacon (1815–1889), was born in Liberty County, Georgia, on February 5th, 1837. He graduated from Oglethorpe University in 1857. On October 1st, 1861, he enlisted for three years as a private in the Liberty Mounted Rangers (Company B, 20th Battalion Georgia Cavalry). He died of typhoid fever on James Island, near Charleston, South Carolina, on September 3rd, 1862; his body was returned to his native county and buried in Midway Cemetery. (The dates carved on his tombstone, 1838–1863, are incorrect.)

MARTIN, NATHANIEL (1787–1859), planter, son of Martin Martin (1732–1812) and Isabel Graham, was born in Liberty County, Georgia, in 1787. He married first (on December 8th, 1817) Elvira Daniel, who bore him many children; he married second (on December 12th, 1856) Mary Shepard, who bore him one son. Nathaniel Martin became a member of Midway Church in 1815. He died of typhoid fever on November 23rd, 1859, survived by his second wife and many children, and was buried in Taylor's Creek Cemetery. Two of his daughters died in the same epidemic: Margaret Martin (born 1829) died on November 30th, 1859; Catherine Martin (born 1837), wife of John Ivey, died on December 12th, 1859.

MARTIN, WILLIAM GRAHAM (1808–1861), planter and overseer, son of John Martin and Jane Martin, was born in Liberty County, Georgia, in 1808. On February 7th, 1833, he married Eliza Sumner Bacon (1815–1889), daughter of Joseph Bacon and Mary Way; there were nine living children. He was one of a committee of thirteen men appointed to make arrangements for the centennial celebration of Midway Church in December 1852. From June 1856 until his sudden death in March 1861 he managed Arcadia plantation for its joint-owners, the three children of the Rev. Dr. Charles Colcock Jones. On March 19th, 1861, his daughter Anna Louisa Martin (1845–1861) died of typhoid fever and was buried in Midway Cemetery. A week later, on March 27th, 1861, William Graham Martin died of the same disease, leaving a widow and eight children. He was buried in Midway Cemetery with military honors by the Liberty Independent Troop, of which he was for many years a member. "A great loss to his family and household and to the community," wrote the Rev.

Dr. Charles Colcock Jones in his journal (March 28th, 1861). "We have lost a personal friend. . . . A quiet, industrious, prosperous, kind man." Two of his sons died during the Civil War: Henry Edward Martin (1837–1862), a graduate of Oglethorpe University (1857), died of typhoid fever on James Island, near Charleston, South Carolina, on September 3rd, 1862; William James Martin (1839–1864), a graduate of Oglethorpe University (1859), was killed in the battle of Cold Harbor, Virginia, on May 30th, 1864. Another son, Charles Jones Martin (1849–1933), was named for the Rev. Dr. Charles Colcock Jones. Eliza Sumner (Bacon) Martin died on March 14th, 1889, and was buried in Flemington Cemetery.

MASON, JAMES MURRAY (1798–1871), legislator and Confederate diplomat, son of General John Mason (1766–1849) and Anna Maria Murray (1766–1857), was born in Georgetown, D.C., on November 3rd, 1798. He was a grandson of George Mason (1725–1792), Revolutionary statesman, of Gunston Hall, Fairfax County, Virginia. After graduating from the University of Pennsylvania in 1818 and from the law department of the College of William and Mary in 1820 he settled in Winchester, Virginia, and commenced the practice of law. On July 25th, 1822, he married Elizabeth Margretta Chew (1798–1874), daughter of Benjamin Chew, of Philadelphia; there were eight children. He was a member of the state legislature (1826–1827; 1828–1832); congressman (1837–1839); and United States senator (1847–1861). At the outbreak of the Civil War he was appointed Confederate diplomatic commissioner to Great Britain as a colleague of John Slidell (1793–1871), Confederate diplomatic commissioner to France. While en route to Europe on the British mail steamer *Trent* the two men were seized by United States authorities on November 8th, 1861, and confined at Fort Warren, Boston harbor, until January 1st, 1862, when they were released and allowed to proceed to Europe. The episode nearly precipitated war between Great Britain and the United States. Mason continued to represent the Confederacy in London until the close of the war, but he was never received officially by the British government. After the war, fearing arrest by the United States government, he resided in Canada for three years. In 1868 he returned to Virginia and settled at Clarens, a country house in Fairfax County, where he died on April 28th, 1871. He was buried in Christ Church Cemetery, Alexandria. Elizabeth Margretta (Chew) Mason died on February 14th, 1874, and was buried beside her husband.

MASON, JOHN (1841–1925), Confederate soldier, son of James Murray Mason (1798–1871) and Elizabeth Margretta Chew (1798–1874), was born at Selma, his father's plantation near Winchester, Virginia, on November 17th, 1841. His father, a grandson of George Mason (1725–1792), Revolutionary statesman, of Gunston Hall, Fairfax County, Virginia, was

United States senator (1847–1861) and Confederate diplomatic commissioner to Great Britain (1861–1865). John Mason was with the Virginia troops when John Brown was captured at Harpers Ferry in October 1859. On April 19th, 1861, he enlisted as a private in the Winchester Rifles (Company F, 2nd Regiment Virginia Infantry). In July 1861 he became aide-de-camp, with rank of lieutenant, to Francis Stebbins Bartow, colonel of the 8th Regiment Georgia Infantry, who was killed at First Manassas (July 21st, 1861); Mason, together with Lieutenant John Macpherson Berrien, also aide-de-camp to Colonel Bartow, accompanied the body to Savannah, Georgia, for burial. In the autumn of 1861 he was made captain of cavalry under General Turner Ashby; in the spring of 1864 he was made adjutant and inspector general to General A. L. Long, chief of artillery under General Jubal Early. After the war he lived in Texas (1865–1867), joined his father in Canada (1867–1868), and farmed in Maryland (1869–1876). From 1876 to 1889 he resided in Fairfax County, Virginia, where he was active in county and state affairs. On August 15th, 1888, in his forty-seventh year, he married Fannie Edwards Fox (1856–1941), daughter of George K. Fox (1832–1872) and Annie H. Littleton (1834–1927), of Leesburg, Virginia. For thirty-two years (1890–1922) he was in the service of the Federal government, first as a timber agent in Denver, Colorado, later as a customs inspector in Richmond, Virginia. In 1922 he retired to Leesburg, where he died without issue on June 6th, 1925. He was buried in Union Cemetery. His wife died on May 12th, 1941, and was buried beside her husband.

MASSIE, PETER (1767–1840), planter and philanthropist, was born in Paisley, Scotland, in 1767. In early manhood he migrated to the United States and settled in Glynn County, Georgia, where he was a successful planter for thirty years. He died at his summer residence near Elizabeth, New Jersey, on August 3rd, 1840. In his will he left, among other bequests, $5000 "for the education of the poor children of the city of Savannah." This sum, aggregating with interest $7515, was paid over to the city in 1849; judicious investment increased the sum to $15,073.13. On April 5th, 1855, the school commissioners of Chatham County ordered that $9000 of the fund be expended in the erection of a building to be known as the Massie School. Construction was begun in December 1855 and completed on October 1st, 1856; the school opened on October 15th, 1856, with Bernard Mallon as principal and one hundred and fifty pupils in attendance. The Massie School constituted the first unit of what later became the Savannah public school system. As the Savannah *Morning News* (September 23rd, 1932) observed, "No public bequest ever made in Savannah has probably reaped a harvest of greater value to the community than that of the Scotchman Peter Massie."

MATTHEWS, LYMAN (1801–1866), Congregational clergyman, son of Dr. Darius Mat-thews and Abigail Porter, was born in Middlebury, Vermont, on May 12th, 1801. His father, a physician, retired from practice in 1809 and settled on a farm in Cornwall. After graduating from Middlebury College in 1822 he taught school in Powelton, Hancock County, Georgia (1822–1823); in Wilmington, Delaware (1823–1824); and in Newark, New Jersey (1824–1825). He then attended Andover Theological Seminary for three years (1825–1828), and was for one year (1829) an agent of the American Education Society. From 1830 to 1844 he was pastor in South Braintree, Massachusetts; in 1844 his health failed and he retired to a farm in Cornwall. He was author of two books: *Memoir of the Life and Character of Ebenezer Porter, D.D.* (1837) and *History of the Town of Cornwall, Vermont* (1862). He was a trustee of Middlebury College. On October 28th, 1830, he married Rachel Dwight Howe, daughter of William Howe and Mary Gould, and sister of the Rev. Dr. George Howe; there were seven children. He died in Cornwall on August 17th, 1866.

MAXWELL, GEORGE TROUP (1827–1897), physician, son of John Jackson Maxwell (1784–1855) and Mary Ann Baker (1787–1871), was born in Bryan County, Georgia, on August 6th, 1827. After graduating from the Medical Department of the University of the City of New York in 1848 he settled in Liberty County, Georgia, where on December 12th, 1848, he married Hetty Augusta Jones (1829–1857), sixth child of Joseph Jones (1779–1846) and his third wife, Elizabeth Screven Lee Hart (1801–1870). In January 1851 he removed to Tallahassee, Florida, where he practiced his profession until April 1857, when he was appointed surgeon at the United States marine hospital in Key West. His wife died of yellow fever in Key West on September 9th, 1857; his three-year-old son, Elliott LeConte Maxwell, died of yellow fever on September 12th, 1857; and his wife's younger sister, Josephine Caroline Elizabeth Jones (1839–1857), wife of his nephew, Dr. John Jackson Maxwell (1835–1898), died of yellow fever on September 15th, 1857. Shortly thereafter George Troup Maxwell returned to Tallahassee, where on April 15th, 1859, he married his third cousin, Martha Ella Maxwell, second daughter of John Stevens Maxwell, of Belair, Florida. During the Civil War he was colonel of the 1st Regiment Florida Cavalry; on November 25th, 1863, he was taken prisoner at Missionary Ridge and confined on Johnson's Island, Ohio, until March 1865. After the war he returned to Tallahassee, where he was elected delegate from Leon County to the state constitutional convention; after five years in Jacksonville (1866–1871) he removed to Delaware, living first in Middletown, later in New Castle, and finally in Wilmington, where his second wife died on March 21st, 1880. Returning South, he practiced medicine briefly in Atlanta before removing to Florida, where he lived in Fernandina, Ocala, and Lake City before settling once more in Jacksonville in 1888. He died of apoplexy in Jacksonville on September 2nd, 1897, survived by three children, and was buried in Tallahassee.

MAXWELL, JAMES AUDLEY (1837–1900), lawyer and civil engineer, son of Joseph Edward Maxwell (1802–1886) and Sarah Martha Holmes, was born near Sunbury, Liberty County, Georgia, on April 30th, 1837. After graduating from Franklin College (Athens) with first honor in 1855 he studied civil engineering privately in West Point, New York, with Professor D. H. Mahan, of the United States Military Academy. Returning to Georgia, he was civil engineer with the Savannah, Albany & Gulf Railroad until the outbreak of the Civil War. On July 19th, 1861, he was appointed second lieutenant and assigned to Company D, 1st Regiment Georgia Regulars (Captain Jacob Read's Regular Light Battery Georgia Artillery); in November 1862 he was appointed first lieutenant and detached for service in the corps of engineers; on June 8th, 1863, he was appointed captain (to take rank February 1st, 1863) and placed in command of Captain Maxwell's Regular Light Battery Georgia Artillery (formerly designated Captain Jacob Read's Regular Light Battery Georgia Artillery); on December 12th, 1864, he was announced as captain and acting chief of artillery and ordnance, McLaws' division, Department of South Carolina, Georgia, and Florida. After the war he studied law and practiced his profession in Boston, Massachusetts. He married Kathleen Cameron, of New York. In later life he retired to Arlington, Georgia, where he died on May 27th, 1900.

MAXWELL, JOHN JACKSON (1835–1898), physician, son of John Pray Maxwell (1811–1866) and his first cousin, Mary Eliza Harden (1815–1866), was born at Bucklin Hall, his father's plantation in Bryan County, Georgia, on January 21st, 1835. He and his brother, Thomas Harden Maxwell (1835–1908), were twins. He was named for his paternal grandfather, John Jackson Maxwell (1784–1855), a rich planter who repeatedly represented Bryan County in the state legislature and was for many years judge of the inferior court of Bryan County. On August 1st, 1857, in Walthourville, Liberty County, Georgia, John Jackson Maxwell (1835–1898) married Josephine Caroline Elizabeth Jones (1839–1857), twelfth child of Joseph Jones (1779–1846) and his third wife, Elizabeth Screven Lee Hart (1801–1870). Shortly thereafter he removed with his bride to Key West, Florida, where he became an assistant to his uncle, Dr. George Troup Maxwell (1827–1897), surgeon at the United States marine hospital. On September 15th, 1857, his wife died of yellow fever in Key West less than a week after the death of her elder sister, Hetty Augusta Jones (1829–1857), wife of Dr. George Troup Maxwell, from the same disease. Returning to Savannah, Georgia, he married second (on December 14th, 1859) Anna Patton (1836–1872), who bore him two children. On April 16th, 1862, he enlisted as a private in Company C,

18th Battalion Georgia Infantry; on December 1st, 1863, he transferred to Company B, Hardwick Mounted Rifles. For most of the war he was a hospital nurse. After the death of his second wife on November 7th, 1872, he resided for some years in Dorchester, Liberty County. He died in Dorchester on January 1st, 1898, and was buried beside his second wife in Tivoli Cemetery, Bryan County.

MAXWELL, JOSEPH EDWARD (1802–1886), planter, son of Audley Maxwell (1766–1840) and Mary Stevens (1772–1850), was born in Liberty County, Georgia, on November 14th, 1802. He was a younger brother of James Audley Maxwell (1796–1828), first husband of Mrs. Susan M. Cumming and father of Laura Elizabeth Maxwell (1824–1903); he was an elder brother of Julia Rebecca Maxwell (1808–1892), wife of Roswell King. After graduating from Yale College in 1823 he studied law but never practiced his profession. Returning to Georgia, he settled on his plantation near Sunbury, Liberty County; on January 26th, 1826, he married Sarah Martha Holmes; there were six children. By 1850 he was planting in Clarke County, Georgia, near Athens. Each summer he returned to his native county to visit his sister, Julia Rebecca Maxwell, wife of Roswell King, at Woodville on Colonel's Island. In December 1867 he suffered a stroke of paralysis affecting one side of his face. During his later years he resided with a married daughter near Groveton, Georgia; he died there suddenly, on March 8th, 1886, while resting from his usual midday walk. He was survived by his wife and five children. His eldest son, Joseph Edward Maxwell (1826–1854), a graduate of the United States Military Academy (1850) and a second lieutenant in the 3rd Infantry, was killed by the Apache Indians in a skirmish near Fort Union, New Mexico, on June 30th, 1854.

MAXWELL, LAURA ELIZABETH (1824–1903), daughter of James Audley Maxwell (1796–1828) and Susan Mary Jones (1803–1890), was born in Liberty County, Georgia, on July 20th, 1824. Her father died on December 1st, 1828, and her mother married second (on November 21st, 1838) Joseph Cumming (1790–1846), a Savannah merchant. After the death of her stepfather on December 5th, 1846, she and her mother lived at intervals in the household of her mother's brother, the Rev. Dr. Charles Colcock Jones (1804–1863), a Presbyterian clergyman residing in Liberty County. On June 10th, 1856, she became the wife of the Rev. David Lyman Buttolph (1822–1905), a Presbyterian clergyman, son of David Buttolph (1779–1868) and his first wife, Urania Lyman (1792–1827). There were five children: Charles Edward Maxwell Buttolph (1857–1858), James David Buttolph (1858–1939), William Smyth Buttolph (1861–1896), Susan Mary Buttolph (1863–1913), and Wallace Stewart Buttolph (1867–1899). David Lyman Buttolph, a native of Norwich, New York, and a graduate of Williams College (1845), was pastor of Midway Church, Liberty

County, Georgia (1854–1867) and the First Presbyterian Church, Marietta, Georgia (1867–1887). Laura (Maxwell) Buttolph died in Marietta on October 28th, 1903, survived by her husband and two children, and was buried beside her mother in Episcopal Cemetery. David Lyman Buttolph died in Marietta on August 7th, 1905, and was buried beside his wife.

MAXWELL, THOMAS HARDEN (1835–1908), merchant and planter, son of John Pray Maxwell (1811–1866) and his first cousin, Mary Eliza Harden (1815–1866), was born at Bucklin Hall, his father's plantation in Bryan County, Georgia, on January 21st, 1835. He and his brother, John Jackson Maxwell (1835–1898), were twins. He was named for his maternal grandfather, Thomas Hutson Harden (1786–1821). In early manhood he settled in Savannah, Georgia, where he worked briefly as a clerk at Claghorn & Cunningham, grocers, and later joined William H. Burroughs in the firm of Burroughs, Flye & Company, cotton factors and commission merchants. On December 22nd, 1862, he was appointed captain and assistant quartermaster of the 1st Regiment Florida Cavalry, of which his uncle, Dr. George Troup Maxwell (1827–1897), was colonel. After the war he returned to Savannah, where he resided with his mother until her death from smallpox on May 19th, 1866. In 1870 he left Savannah and undertook planting in Bryan County. He never married. He died after a long illness at the Park View Sanitarium in Savannah on November 20th, 1908, and was buried near his twin brother in Tivoli Cemetery, Bryan County.

MAXWELL, WILLIAM (1785–1866), rice planter, son of Thomas Maxwell and Elizabeth McCartney, was born in South Carolina on May 1st, 1785. Two years later his father died, and his mother removed with William and his elder brother, Dupree Maxwell (1781–1805), to Sunbury, Liberty County, Georgia, where his mother died on January 6th, 1793. William Maxwell commanded a gunboat during the War of 1812; after his return to Liberty County he served as captain of the Liberty Independent Troop continuously from 1815 to 1832 with the exception of one year (1818–1819). He also served for a time as collector of the port of Sunbury; and he was a selectman of Midway Church from 1842 to 1844. He was a prosperous planter, one of the respected citizens of Liberty County, and (in the words of the Rev. Dr. Charles Colcock Jones) "a most elegant gentleman of the olden time." On June 10th, 1811, he married Elizabeth Jones (1794–1856), daughter of John Jones (1772–1805) and his first wife, Elizabeth Stewart (1774–1801), sister of General Daniel Stewart of Revolutionary fame. She was thus a half-sister of the Rev. Dr. Charles Colcock Jones, who spent part of his orphaned childhood at Yellow Bluff, their retreat on Colonel's Island. "I am indebted to them for unnumbered kindnesses in sickness and in health," Dr. Jones once wrote; and Mrs. Jones

spoke of "Sister Betsy" as a relative "who almost occupied a mother's place in our hearts." The Maxwells were childless; they lived for some years at Laurel View plantation, then at Lodebar plantation, then at Social Bluff (Point Maxwell) on Colonel's Island, and finally at the Cottage near Sunbury. Elizabeth (Jones) Maxwell died at the residence of Abial Winn in Dorchester on July 24th, 1856, after a long and painful illness, and was buried in Midway Cemetery. William Maxwell died in the same house ten years later, on August 20th, 1866, and was buried beside his wife. The Maxwells were beloved by all their friends for their hospitality and gracious manners. "Among the reminiscences of the past," wrote Mrs. Sarah A. Howe on October 24th, 1855, "are pleasant days spent beneath their roof enjoying their society, always so full of sunshine."

MAYBANK, ANDREW (1768–1834), rice planter, son of Andrew Maybank and Martha Splatt, was born in Liberty County, Georgia, on December 26th, 1768. He was a prosperous planter, and for much of his life he resided at Maybank, his plantation on Colonel's Island in his native county. He married first (on January 18th, 1787) Mary Sandiford, from whom he was divorced; he married second (on February 16th, 1794) Elizabeth Girardeau, daughter of John Girardeau and Hannah Splatt, and hence a sister of Susannah Hyrne Girardeau (1778–1810), second wife of John Jones (1772–1805) and mother of the Rev. Dr. Charles Colcock Jones. On January 16th, 1799, his younger sister, Mary Maybank (1781–1804), became the first wife of Joseph Jones (1779–1846). Thus "Uncle Maybank," though no blood relation of the Rev. Dr. Charles Colcock Jones and his wife, was intimately associated with them through marriage: (1) the marriage of his younger sister, Mary Maybank, to Joseph Jones, father of Mrs. Mary Jones; and (2) his own marriage to Elizabeth Girardeau, maternal aunt of the Rev. Dr. Charles Colcock Jones. Andrew Maybank died without issue on January 17th, 1834, and was buried in Midway Cemetery beneath the following inscription: "His Christian life was active and exemplary, and at his death he bequeathed a large portion of his estate to charitable purposes." Among other bequests he left Maybank and some thirty Negro slaves to the Rev. Dr. Charles Colcock Jones and his wife. "We must ever hold Uncle Maybank in grateful remembrance," wrote Dr. Jones in his journal (June 2nd, 1860), "for bestowing upon us this quiet and healthful retreat, where we reared and educated our children until prepared for college, and where we have experienced unnumbered mercies from above."

MEADE, GEORGE GORDON (1815–1872), Union soldier, son of Richard Worsam Meade (1778–1828) and Margaret Coates Butler, was born in Cadiz, Spain, where his father was United States naval agent, on December 31st, 1815. He graduated from the United States Military Academy in 1835, served in the Seminole War, and resigned from the army on

October 26th, 1836. For several years he engaged in railroad construction in the South. On December 31st, 1840 (his twenty-fifth birthday), he married Margaretta Sergeant, daughter of John Sergeant; there were six children. On May 19th, 1842, he rejoined the army as second lieutenant of topographical engineers; he subsequently became first lieutenant (August 4th, 1851) and captain (May 17th, 1856). On August 31st, 1861, he was made brigadier general of volunteers in the Union army. After serving in the defenses of Washington he was transferred to McDowell's army in Northern Virginia (March 1862) and thence to McClellan's army on the Peninsula (June 1862). On June 18th, 1862, he was promoted to major in the topographical engineers. At Glendale he suffered a wound from which he never fully recovered. After distinguishing himself at Second Manassas, Sharpsburg, Fredericksburg, and Chancellorsville he was placed in command of the Army of the Potomac on June 28th, 1863. His victory at Gettysburg (July 1863) won him the thanks of Congress. He was promoted to brigadier general in the regular army (January 28th, 1864) and major general in the regular army (August 18th, 1864). After the war he commanded successively the Military Division of the Atlantic, the Department of the East, and the third military district of the Department of the South (Georgia, Alabama, and Florida). He was commissioner of Fairmount Park, Philadelphia (1866–1872). He died in Philadelphia on November 6th, 1872.

MEADE, WILLIAM (1789–1862), Protestant Episcopal bishop, son of Richard Kidder Meade (1746–1805) and Mary Fitzhugh Grymes, widow of William Randolph, was born in Frederick (now Clarke) County, Virginia, on November 11th, 1789. After graduating from the College of New Jersey (Princeton) with first honor in 1808 he studied theology and was ordained deacon (1811) and priest (1814) in the Protestant Episcopal Church. He was assistant bishop of Virginia (1829–1841) and bishop of Virginia (1841–1862), his diocese including the present states of Virginia and West Virginia. Through his character and ministry he did much to arrest the decline of the Episcopal Church in Virginia following the Revolutionary War. He was particularly interested in the spiritual state of the Negro. Although he opposed secession he supported the Confederate cause; in October 1861 he became presiding bishop of the Episcopal Church in the Confederate States. He was author of numerous devotional works, among them *Conversations on the Catechism* (1849), *Lectures upon the Pastoral Office* (1849), and *The Bible and the Classics* (1861). His best-known work, *Old Churches, Ministers, and Families of Virginia* (2 vols., 1857), is a useful sourcebook for students of Virginia ecclesiastical history. He married first (on January 31st, 1810) Mary Nelson, daughter of Philip Nelson and Sarah Burwell, of Clarke County; after her death in 1817 he married second (on De-

cember 2nd, 1820) Thomasia Nelson, daughter of Thomas Nelson and Frances Page, of Yorktown. He died in Richmond on March 14th, 1862, and was buried at the Virginia Theological Seminary, Alexandria.

MEIGS, HENRIETTA HARGREAVES (STEWART) (1822–1896): *Mrs. Henry Vincent Meigs,* daughter of Charles Dawson Stewart (1781–1872) and Henrietta Hargreaves, was born in Warrenton, Georgia, on December 11th, 1822. In 1829 she removed with her parents to Columbus, where her father prospered in business. On July 6th, 1843, she became the wife of Henry Vincent Meigs (1821–1897), son of Charles Delucena Meigs (1792–1869), professor at Jefferson Medical College (Philadelphia). Her husband, a native of Philadelphia and a graduate of the University of Pennsylvania (1840), settled in Columbus in early manhood; after practicing law briefly he entered the cotton business. For twenty years he was superintendent of the Columbus factory, of which his father-in-law, Charles Dawson Stewart, had been one of the projectors and builders in the 1830s; he was later superintendent of the Eagle & Phoenix Mills. After the war the Meigs family resided for some months in Marietta, where Henrietta (Stewart) Meigs was "a particular friend" of the Robarts family. In August 1867 Louisa Jane Robarts assisted Mrs. Meigs in preparations for the marriage of Henrietta Hargreaves Meigs and Jacob Lyman Cook on September 4th, 1867. Henrietta (Stewart) Meigs died in Columbus on September 19th, 1896, survived by her husband and three children, and was buried in Linwood Cemetery. Henry Vincent Meigs died on August 30th, 1897, and was buried beside his wife.

MELVILL, HENRY (1798–1871), Anglican clergyman, fifth son of Philip Melvill (1762–1811), an army officer, and Elizabeth Carey (1770–1844), was born on September 14th, 1798. He graduated from St. Peter's College, Cambridge (B.A. 1821, M.A. 1824, B.D. 1836) and continued for ten years (1822–1832) as fellow and tutor of his college. During the succeeding years he held various ecclesiastical posts in London: he became chaplain to the Tower of London in 1840, chaplain to the Queen in 1853, and canon residentiary of St. Paul's Cathedral in 1856. He was said to be "the most popular preacher in London." His sermons were published in numerous editions on both sides of the Atlantic. He died in London on February 9th, 1871, survived by his wife, Margaret Alice Dobree (1805–1878), and was buried in St. Paul's Cathedral. According to the Savannah *Republican* (February 16th, 1871), "The admirable sermons of this eminent English divine have been read by successive generations of Americans with warm admiration for the purity of their teachings, the simplicity and beauty of their construction, and the clearness of their exposition of divine truth. Not only may they be found in the libraries of clergymen of almost every denomination, where they remain as models of pulpit eloquence, but they form today the favorite reading of multitudes of Christian laymen, who find in them an almost inexhaustible mine of spiritual wealth."

MERCER, HUGH WEEDON (1808–1877), Confederate soldier, son of Hugh Mercer and Virginia Stuart, and grandson of General Hugh Mercer (1725?–1777) of Revolutionary fame, was born in Fredericksburg, Virginia, on November 27th, 1808. He graduated from the United States Military Academy in 1828. In 1835 he resigned his commission and settled in Savannah, Georgia, where he was first lieutenant of the Chatham Artillery (1835–1845) and cashier of the Merchants' & Planters' Bank (1841–1861). On February 5th, 1834, he married Mary Stites Anderson (1812–1855), daughter of George Anderson (1767–1847), prominent Savannah cotton merchant, and Elizabeth Clifford Wayne. At the outbreak of the Civil War he entered Confederate service as colonel of the 1st Regiment Georgia Infantry; on October 29th, 1861, he was commissioned brigadier general and placed in command of Savannah, where he continued until the spring of 1864, when he joined General Joseph E. Johnston in the Atlanta campaign. He later fought in the Tennessee campaign and in the Carolinas. After the war he lived in Savannah (1866–1869), in Baltimore (1869–1872), and in Baden Baden, Germany (1872–1877). He died in Baden Baden on June 9th, 1877, and was buried beside his wife in Laurel Grove Cemetery, Savannah. On February 27th, 1879, his remains were transferred to Bonaventure Cemetery. "I have more confidence in General Mercer than in any of our officers, as at present advised," wrote Charles Colcock Jones, Jr., on March 18th, 1862. One month later, on April 22nd, 1862, he had changed his mind: "I think the conduct of General Mercer very reprehensible, but I am forbidden by the articles of war to say so, and I do so knowing that what I say will not be repeated."

MILLEN, JOHN M. (1828–1864), lawyer, was born in Chester County, Delaware, in 1828. In early manhood he settled in Savannah, Georgia, where in April 1852 he became associated with the Hon. William Bennett Fleming in the practice of law. On April 20th, 1853, he married Elizabeth A. Hayward (1831–1861), daughter of Richard Hayward, of Tallahassee, Florida; she died on January 19th, 1861, leaving three young children. John M. Millen was ordinary of Chatham County (1852–1855) and judge of the city court of Savannah (1856–1861). On May 18th, 1861, he became first lieutenant in the Pulaski Guards (Company K, 10th Regiment Georgia Infantry) and went to Virginia with his company (attached, as Company L, to the 1st Regiment Virginia Artillery). On March 6th, 1862, he resigned, returned to Georgia, and raised a corps of cavalry—Millen's Battalion Partisan Rangers (Company B, 20th Battalion Georgia Cavalry)—of which he was appointed major on May 15th, 1862. "My present post," he

wrote Colonel Joseph Frederick Waring, then in Virginia, on June 23rd, 1863, "is in Liberty County, having the counties of Liberty and McIntosh under my charge. A most inglorious service, with no foe but marauding parties of Negroes to contend with and no opportunity of punishing them. My heart yearns to be with you, taking a part in the real drama and feeling that I am where I can contribute my aid towards bringing about the end of this inhuman war." By late summer of 1863 he had mustered a command of seven companies, of which he was appointed lieutenant colonel on September 16th, 1863. He continued service on the Georgia coast until the spring of 1864, when he was ordered first to Florida, then to Virginia. He was killed at the battle of Haw's Shop on May 28th, 1864, and was buried in Hollywood Cemetery, Richmond. His younger brother, George Rufus Millen (1829–1892), a graduate of the Medical College of the University of Pennsylvania (1856), was a physician in Savannah until the outbreak of the Civil War, when he was appointed assistant surgeon on the staff of General John Bankhead Magruder on the Peninsula of Virginia. He was murdered by an unknown hand on December 19th, 1892; three days later his body was discovered half buried in the muck of Salt Water Creek Swamp some ten miles from Savannah.

MILLEN, MACPHERSON BERRIEN (1821–1896), railroad executive, lumber merchant, and Confederate commissary, son of Dr. George Millen and Eliza Jane Williams Dennis, was born in Savannah, Georgia, on September 21st, 1821. By 1850 he was a civil engineer with the Central Railroad of Georgia, superintending construction in Burke County; the town of Millen, a railroad junction, was named in his honor. In February 1852 he was appointed superintendent of the Central Railroad of Georgia. On February 15th, 1855, he married Sarah Ann Eliza Bacon (1833–1862), daughter of Edwin Holcombe Bacon and Eunice Louisa Stevens, of Liberty County, Georgia; she died on July 22nd, 1862, leaving one son, Loring R. Millen (1858–1912). On September 1st, 1857, he joined Solomon Zeigler in the firm of Millen & Zeigler, lumber merchants. During the Civil War he was captain and later major of commissary, with headquarters in Savannah. "The stock of bacon and beef for the armies of the Confederate States is now exhausted," he wrote on October 10th, 1863, "and we must depend entirely upon what we may gather weekly. Starvation stares the army in the face; the handwriting is on the wall." After the war he resumed his lumber business in Savannah. He died in Atlanta on September 13th, 1896 (not, as his tombstone indicates, in August 1897) and was buried beside his wife in Oakview Cemetery, Albany, Georgia.

MILLER, DAVID ANDERSON (1810–1876), planter, son of Hugh Miller and Elizabeth Miller, was born in Liberty County, Georgia, on January 1st, 1810. On January 6th, 1831, he married Margaret Rebecca Norman

(1808–1870), eldest daughter of Joseph Norman and Mary Wilson Stacy, and widow of Donald Fraser; there were nine children. David Anderson Miller was one of sixteen citizens instrumental in organizing a separate Presbyterian church in Walthourville in 1855, and he served as one of two deacons of the church for twenty-one years (1855–1876). Two of his sons fought in the Civil War: Elbert W. Miller (1833–1863), his eldest son, was severely wounded below the knee at the battle of Murfreesboro, and following amputation of his leg he died in Northern hands in March 1863. Edward Payson Miller (1840–1910) enlisted for six months as a private in the Liberty Independent Troop (Company G, 5th Regiment Georgia Cavalry) on October 1st, 1861; he enlisted for three years as a private in the Liberty Mounted Rangers (Company B, 20th Battalion Georgia Cavalry) on May 15th, 1862; he was later promoted to fourth corporal and saw service until captured near Petersburg, Virginia, on September 30th, 1864, and confined in a Northern prison. A third son, Joseph Norman Miller (1836–1893), was for many years postmaster of Walthourville and railroad agent at Depot No. 4 (Walthourville Station). After a long and painful illness David Anderson Miller died in Walthourville at the residence of his son Edward Payson Miller on March 26th, 1876, and was buried beside his wife in Walthourville Cemetery.

MILLER, EDWARD, painter and musician, removed to Savannah, Georgia, from his native New York City early in 1852 and remained in Savannah for seven years, teaching music, French, painting, and drawing. In February 1853 he became director of music at St. John's Episcopal Church, and on Christmas Day 1853 he was confirmed by Bishop Stephen Elliott in the Episcopal faith. On October 10th, 1855, he was announced as a member of the faculty of the Chatham Academy. During his residence in Savannah his name appeared frequently in the columns of the local newspapers: "Mr. E. Miller, having accepted the direction of the music at the new St. John's Episcopal Church, would be glad to receive applications from persons willing or desirous to become members of the choir. Compensation will be given where required" (Savannah *Republican,* February 21st, 1853). "In the windows of the drugstore of Mr. W. W. Lincoln, corner of Bull and Congress Streets, are beautiful monochromatic landscape paintings. They are drawn by Mr. E. Miller of this city" (Savannah *Morning News,* February 7th, 1855). "We have received from Mr. E. Miller a copy of the music, 'The Mocking Bird Polka,' composed by himself and published by Horace Waters of New York" (Savannah *Morning News,* January 16th, 1857). "E. Miller, organist of St. John's Episcopal Church, teaches the organ, melodeon, piano, guitar, and singing. Terms, $25 per quarter" (Savannah *Republican,* January 17th, 1857). On December 8th, 1858, his house and lot on Jones Street between Bull and Whitaker Streets were "offered at private sale on ac-

commodating terms," and in April 1859 he returned to New York City.

MILLER, HOMER VIRGIL MILTON (1814–1896), physician, educator, and statesman, son of Major General Andrew Miller, was born in Pendleton District, South Carolina, on April 29th, 1814. After graduating from the Medical College of South Carolina (Charleston) in 1835 he continued his medical studies in Paris and commenced practice in Cassville, Georgia, in 1838. Prior to the Civil War he was for some years professor of obstetrics in the Memphis Medical School and professor of physiology in the Medical College of Georgia (Augusta). On June 5th, 1861, he was appointed surgeon of the 8th Regiment Georgia Infantry; in June 1862 he succeeded Dr. Joseph Payne Logan as chief surgeon of the military district of Georgia; later he served as inspector of posts and hospitals. After the war he was professor of medicine and later dean of the Atlanta Medical College (1867–1896). He was also a trustee of the University of Georgia. Always active in politics, he was elected United States senator from Georgia on July 28th, 1868; he qualified on February 24th, 1871, and served until March 3rd, 1871. In 1835 he married Harriet Perry Clark; she died in Atlanta on January 8th, 1894, and was buried in Myrtle Hill Cemetery, Rome, Georgia. H. V. M. Miller died in Atlanta on May 31st, 1896, and was buried beside his wife.

MILLER, HUGH (1802–1856), geologist and writer, son of Hugh Miller, was born in Cromarty, Scotland, on October 10th, 1802. At the age of seventeen he was apprenticed to a stonemason, and in 1822, at the termination of his apprenticeship, he became a journeyman mason. In his work he was constantly observing and reflecting, and he recorded his observations and reflections in prose evincing a strong devotion to the Christian faith. His *Poems Written in the Leisure Hours of a Journeyman Mason* (1829) attracted favorable attention, and in 1834 he became accountant in the local commercial bank. His first signal work was *Scenes and Legends of the North of Scotland* (1835), recounting the traditions of his native county and reflecting his lifelong interest in geology. On January 7th, 1837, he married Lydia Falconer Fraser (1811–1876), author of numerous stories, chiefly for children. In 1840 he became editor of the *Witness,* a biweekly newspaper advocating a free church for Scotland. *The Old Red Sandstone; or, New Walks in an Old Field* (1841) first appeared on its pages. A visit to England in 1845 resulted in *First Impressions of England and Its People* (1846). In *Footprints of the Creator* (1847) and *The Testimony of the Rocks* (1857) he argued in support of divine creation as opposed to evolution. His autobiography, *My Schools and Schoolmasters* (1852), elicited the praise of Thomas Carlyle: "You have, as you undertook to do, painted many things to us—scenes of life, scenes of nature, which rarely come upon the canvas. . . . There is a right genial fire in the book, everywhere nobly tempered down into peaceful, radical heat, which is very beautiful to see." Exhausted by overwork and strained by illness, Miller died by his own hand on December 23rd, 1856, and was buried in the Grange Cemetery, Edinburgh. *The Cruise of the Betsy; or, A Summer Ramble Among the Fossiliferous Deposits of the Hebrides* was published in 1858.

MILLER, JOSEPH NORMAN (1836–1893), postmaster and railroad agent, son of David Anderson Miller (1810–1876) and Margaret Rebecca Norman (1808–1870), widow of Donald Fraser, was born in Walthourville, Liberty County, Georgia, on June 9th, 1836. He was named for Joseph Norman, his maternal grandfather. In 1855 he became postmaster of Walthourville, and in 1857, when the Savannah, Albany & Gulf Railroad penetrated Liberty County, he became railroad agent at Depot No. 4 (Walthourville Station). On November 23rd, 1859, he married Mary Elizabeth McCollough (1836–1922), eldest daughter of James Sullivan McCollough (1810–1883) and Hannah Elizabeth Quarterman (1814–1885), of Walthourville. "Yesterday morning," wrote Mrs. Mary S. Mallard on November 24th, 1859, "we had quite an early wedding near us— Miss Lizzie McCollough and Mr. Joseph Miller. The hour appointed for the ceremony was eight o'clock, so we were invited to breakfast. Rather a novel arrangement, as the young couple were only going to Mr. Miller's. I believe their idea was to surprise the community." After the Civil War Joseph Norman Miller removed with his family to Hazlehurst, Appling County, Georgia, where he was railroad agent until his death on December 21st, 1893. He was buried in Hazlehurst Cemetery. Mary Elizabeth (McCollough) Miller died on September 19th, 1922, and was buried beside her husband.

MILLER, THOMAS EDWIN (1833–1864), Union soldier, son of Clayton Miller, was born in Adair County, Kentucky, on January 17th, 1833. After graduating from the United States Military Academy in 1856 he served as second lieutenant in the garrison at Fort Independence, Massachusetts, from 1856 to 1861; during that period he was granted sick leave of absence in Florida twice (from November 1st, 1859, to May 9th, 1860; from October 15th, 1860, to April 26th, 1861). Early in May 1861, returning North through Savannah, Georgia, he and his friend Cornelius Hook (1837–1864) were detained briefly for questioning by Charles Colcock Jones, Jr., mayor of Savannah, and then permitted to continue their journey. He was on duty at Fort Jefferson, Tortugas, Florida (May 1861–October 1861), on recruiting service (October 1861–April 1862), on duty as acting adjutant of artillery in the Peninsula campaign (April 1862–June 1862), and on recruiting service (June 1862–August 1862). He retired from active service on August 25th, 1862. Two years later, on November 13th, 1864, he died of consumption in Adair County, Kentucky, survived by his wife, Alice E. Ward, whom he had married on April 29th, 1858,

and two children. Alice (Ward) Miller married Dr. Harvey S. Taft, former surgeon in the Union army, on December 3rd, 1873.

MILLER, WILLIAM SCOTT (born 1815), son of Archibald Miller, was lessee of Mammoth Cave, Kentucky, and proprietor of the cave hotel for a number of years in the middle decades of the nineteenth century. Dr. John Croghan, owner of Mammoth Cave, described Miller's hotel in his *Rambles in the Mammoth Cave During the Year 1844* (Louisville, Kentucky, 1845, pp. 10–11): "Emerging from these beautiful woodlands, you suddenly have a view of the hotel and adjacent grounds which is truly lovely and picturesque. The hotel is a large edifice, two hundred feet long by forty-five wide, with piazzas sixteen feet wide extending the whole length of the building both above and below, well furnished, and kept in a style by Mr. Miller that cannot fail to please the most fastidious epicure." On a visit to Mammoth Cave in August 1854 Charles Colcock Jones, Jr., found Miller to be "a very gentlemanly and obliging person." Miller was still proprietor of the cave hotel in 1880.

MILLS, JAMES (born 1807) was a free mulatto hiring his services in Savannah, Georgia, in the 1850s and 1860s. His wife, Ann Mills, a seamstress, was born in Riceboro, Liberty County, Georgia, in 1811. Neither James nor Ann Mills could read or write. Their family as recorded in the Federal Census of 1860 consisted of four children: Richard Mills (1831–1866), a mason; Catherine Mills (1842–1864), a seamstress; Mary Celia Mills (1846–1866), a seamstress; and James Mills (1858–1874), not employed. In the autumn of 1856 James Mills was hired by the Rev. Dr. Charles Colcock Jones to help in the renovation of Montevideo, his plantation house in Liberty County.

MILLS, NATHANIEL C. (1818–1888), postmaster, son of William C. Mills, was born in Savannah, Georgia, on November 25th, 1818. In early manhood he resided with his widowed mother, Sarah L. Mills (1790–1858), while he earned his living as a clerk. On December 7th, 1854, he married Sarah Rosamonda Parmenter (1820–1901), a native of Beaufort District, South Carolina; there were no children. For many years Mills was assistant postmaster of Savannah; by 1870 he was city treasurer; in later life he sold real estate. He died in Savannah on January 3rd, 1888, survived by his wife, and was buried beside his mother in Laurel Grove Cemetery. According to the Savannah *Morning News* (January 15th, 1888), "Mr. Mills delighted in the study of botany and was an authority not only in the nomenclature of that science but in the medicinal virtues and the nutritive qualities of plants and vegetables. . . . In affairs of business Mr. Mills always enjoyed the confidence of his employers, and was always prompt in the discharge of every duty with strict honor and integrity; and by diligence and economy he amassed a considerable fortune."

MINTON, JOHN (1797–1871), soldier and planter, was born in New York on October

13th, 1797. In early manhood he migrated to Liberty County, Georgia, where on May 31st, 1820, he married Rosina Ladson Fabian (1799–1874). After residing briefly in Washington, Wilkes County, he and his wife returned to Liberty County; by 1850 they had settled with their numerous family in Roswell, Cobb County, where they became part of "the colony" of Kings, Bullochs, Dunwodys, and Smiths who had removed to the "up country" from the Georgia coast ten years before. On May 14th, 1861, "Major Minton," then in his sixty-fourth year, enlisted for the war as a private in the 8th Regiment Georgia Infantry; he was wounded at First Manassas (July 21st, 1861) and was discharged for disability at Centreville, Virginia, on November 6th, 1861. Three of his sons, John, James, and Axson, were privates in the 21st Battalion Georgia Cavalry (later consolidated with other companies to form the 7th Regiment Georgia Cavalry); Axson Minton (1838–1864), his youngest son, died on June 30th, 1864, from wounds sustained at Nancy's Shop six days before. John Minton died in Roswell on March 5th, 1871, after an illness of thirty months and was buried in the Presbyterian Cemetery. A substantial obituary, written by his lifelong friend the Rev. Francis Robert Goulding, appeared in the Savannah *Republican* on March 29th, 1871: "From youth to old age he had been a soldier, not as a member of the regular army but as a volunteer, serving in every accessible war in the United States, in Texas under the Lone Star, and in Mexico, from the age of fifteen to that of sixty-eight. In the year 1817, while yet a stripling, he received from the hands of General Andrew Jackson the sword and epaulettes of a major, in compliment for gallant conduct; and the last of his several wounds was received at Manassas, where he helped to bear General Bartow and other loved ones from the bloody field on which, at the age of sixty-four, he fought as a private at will."

MITCHEL, ALEXANDER (1797–1864), merchant, was born in Morayshire, Scotland, in 1797. In 1823 he settled in Darien, Georgia, then a thriving seaport, and soon prospered in business. In 1835 he married Mary Jane (Mazie) McCay (1810–1877); there were no children. For many years he was an elder in the Darien Presbyterian Church; according to his pastor, the Rev. Francis Robert Goulding, "he was extensively known and most highly esteemed for his sagelike counsels and for his unflagging labors in the church, the prayer meeting, the Sabbath school, and in the community at large, both white and black. No one accustomed to the artless pathos of his prayers, enriched by a slightly foreign accent, will ever think of him as other than a man of God." In the spring of 1861, at the outbreak of the Civil War, he was appointed commissioner to the General Assembly of the Presbyterian Church meeting in Philadelphia in May; acting on the advice of his friend the Rev. Dr. Charles Colcock Jones, he did not attend. On April 22nd,

1861, he wrote Dr. Jones asking his views on the question of separation within the church: "I would deprecate separation were it possible to continue a harmonious union; but I doubt that. Politically separated, I believe Christian fellowship will after a short time be best conserved by speaking across the lines." A few months later he and Dr. Jones represented the Presbytery of Georgia at the first General Assembly of the Southern Presbyterian Church meeting in Augusta in December 1861. When Darien was burned by the Federals in March 1862 Mitchel removed to Macon, where his nephews and executors, George Smith and Robert Smith, were then residing. He died in Macon of typhoid fever on November 11th, 1864, and was buried in Rose Hill Cemetery. Shortly after the war his widow joined her two nephews, William Z. Collins and Stephen M. Collins, on a farm near Americus; in the summer of 1877 she returned to Macon, where she died on August 5th, 1877, at the residence of her physician and lifelong friend, Dr. William Elliott Dunwody. She was buried beside her husband.

MITCHELL, WILLIAM LETCHER (1805–1882), lawyer and educator, was born in Athens, Georgia, in August 1805. All his life he was closely identified with the University of Georgia; after graduating from Franklin College (Athens) in 1825 he served the university as tutor, professor of law, secretary and treasurer, and trustee. He was also superintendent of the Western & Atlantic Railroad and for some time a member of the state legislature. For many years he was an elder of the Athens Presbyterian Church and, together with Thomas Reade Rootes Cobb, superintendent of the Sunday school. He was a devoted friend of the Rev. Dr. Charles Colcock Jones, who considered Mitchell "one of the best of men"; on May 13th, 1858, Mitchell wrote Dr. Jones persuading him to visit Athens: "It would be a real blessing to our community if you would spend some time with us and give us the proper atmosphere in which to live while imparting religious knowledge to our slaves— not so much by preaching as by daily conversations, by detailing your experience, by anecdotes of success as well as of failure, and by familiar illustrations of your modes of teaching." Mitchell was twice married: first (on December 23rd, 1828) to Sarah Neisler; second (on November 21st, 1854) to Lucia L. Bass. He died in Athens, much honored and much lamented, in October 1882 and was buried in Oconee Hill Cemetery. According to Augustus Longstreet Hull, who wrote from personal experience, "Mr. Mitchell might be called intense. He was positive in every phase of his character—a warm friend, a bitter enemy, a hard fighter, a devoted partisan. He hated the Yankees and despised every church but the Presbyterian. He was naturally dogmatic and pitied those who could not agree with him. . . . For years he was a sufferer from asthma" [*Annals of Athens, Georgia, 1801–1901* (Athens, 1906), p. 143].

MOLYNEUX, EDMUND (1790–1864), merchant and British consul, son of Edmund Molyneux of the Hall Sandfield, West Derby, Lancashire, England, was born in Liverpool in 1790. For thirty-three years (1831–1864) he was British consul in Savannah, Georgia, where he was also a prominent and successful merchant. On April 30th, 1834, he married Eliza Herriott Johnston (1805–1872), fifth daughter of James Johnston and Ann Marion Houstoun, of Savannah. In 1861, at the outbreak of the Civil War, Molyneux removed with his wife to Paris, France, where he died on November 19th, 1864. His wife died in Washington, D.C., at the residence of her brother, Dr. William Patrick Johnston, on July 3rd, 1872. His only son, Edmund Molyneux (1835–1898), born in Savannah and educated at Rugby, pursued his early career in India, where he was lieutenant colonel of the 7th Dragoon Guards; he later retired to England, where he was for some years justice of the peace for Berkshire.

MONGIN, ISABELLA RAE (HABERSHAM) (1817–1880): *Mrs. William Henry Mongin,* daughter of William Habersham (1772–1820) and Mary B. Elliott, was born in South Carolina in 1817. Her mother was a sister of the Rt. Rev. Stephen Elliott (1806–1866), bishop of Georgia (1840–1866). Isabella Rae Habersham married first (on January 27th, 1836) William Henry Mongin (1816–1851), a planter residing in Savannah. Some years after his death on September 1st, 1851, she married second (on April 5th, 1864) the Rev. William Clayton Williams (1821–1888), an Episcopal clergyman and a forty-two-year-old bachelor. According to Mrs. Mary S. Mallard, writing from Atlanta on March 2nd, 1864, the marriage "seems to be a great amazement and amusement to everyone who hears it." William Clayton Williams, a graduate of the College of William and Mary (1840) and the Virginia Theological Seminary (1845), devoted himself for nineteen years (1845–1864) to missionary work among Negro slaves on plantations in Chatham County, Georgia, near Savannah. After his marriage he was rector of Grace Church, Clarkesville (1865–1866), St. Peter's Church, Rome (1866–1879), and St. Luke's Church, Atlanta (1879–1884). Isabella (Habersham) (Mongin) Williams died in Atlanta without issue on July 5th, 1880, and was buried in Oakland Cemetery. Her husband died in Cumberland County, Virginia, on April 27th, 1888, and was buried beside his wife.

MONTAGU, LADY MARY WORTLEY (1689–1762), English letter-writer, eldest daughter of Evelyn Pierrepont and Lady Mary Feilding, was born in London in 1689. Her father succeeded as Earl of Kingston (1690) and was created Marquis of Dorchester (1706) and Duke of Kingston (1715). In August 1712 she eloped with Edward Wortley Montagu (1678–1761), British ambassador to Turkey (1716–1718); from Constantinople she wrote fifty-two "Turkish Embassy Letters" (published posthumously in 1763) detailing her impressions with wit and charm. Returning to England, she introduced the practice of inoculation against smallpox and became the leader of a brilliant social world. Her literary friendships included Fielding, Voltaire, Rousseau, and Montesquieu; her relationship with Pope, at first friendly, later became hostile. For many years she lived abroad: in Avignon (1742–1746), in Brescia (1746–1756), and in Venice (1756–1761). Her letters to her daughter, the Countess of Bute, describing her happy life and recording her opinions of men and books, are among her most distinguished contributions to English literature. She died of cancer in London on August 21st, 1762, and was buried in Grosvenor Chapel. A century later Miss Mary Eliza Robarts (1805–1878), of Marietta, Georgia, was playfully called "Lady Mary Wortley Montagu" by her cousin, the Rev. Dr. Charles Colcock Jones, presumably because she was the regular family correspondent, writing, as Dr. Jones once observed (September 27th, 1855), from "her own mansion of hospitality and wit."

MONTMOLLIN, JOHN SAMUEL (1808–1859), real and personal estate broker, was born in Savannah, Georgia, in April 1808. For many years he was copartner in the firm of Wylly & Montmollin, "general commission agents for the purchase and sale of stocks, bonds, real and personal estate." In January 1857 he was elected one of five auctioneers of the city of Savannah. He was also a member of the board of commissioners of the Savannah waterworks and president of the Mechanics' Savings Bank. On January 20th, 1842, he married Harriet M. Rossignol; one of their sons, Louis Henry Montmollin (1846–1884), was an alderman of Savannah and a prominent member of the Savannah bar. On June 9th, 1859, John Samuel Montmollin was instantly killed by a boiler explosion on the steamboat *John G. Lawton,* on which he was traveling to his rice plantation some fourteen miles up the Savannah River. His body was discovered the next day. According to the Savannah *Republican* (June 13th, 1859), "It was imbedded in marsh, head downwards, to the hips, some seventy or eighty yards from the spot where the explosion occurred, showing that it must have been driven very high into the air. A handkerchief, which he had in his hand at the time of the accident, was still tight in his grasp." He was buried in the family vault in Laurel Grove Cemetery.

MOODY, JAMES (1809–1854), farmer, was born in Georgia in 1809. For some years he planted in upper Liberty County near the Bryan County line. On February 14th, 1833, he married Ann Eliza Bradley. On Saturday, June 3rd, 1854, at Beard's Creek Baptist Church in Tattnall County, Stouton Haymans (1800–1886), Moody's brother-in-law, stabbed him in the abdomen with a knife; within five minutes Moody was dead. He was survived by his wife and a numerous family of young children. At the April 1855 term of the Tattnall County Superior Court Haymans was declared not guilty and released.

MOORE, THOMAS VERNER (1818–1871), Presbyterian clergyman, was born in Newville, Pennsylvania, on February 1st, 1818. After graduating from Dickinson College in 1838 and from Princeton Theological Seminary in 1842 he was pastor of the Second Presbyterian Church, Carlisle, Pennsylvania (1842–1845); the First Presbyterian Church, Greencastle, Pennsylvania (1845–1847); the First Presbyterian Church, Richmond, Virginia (1847–1868); and the First Presbyterian Church, Nashville, Tennessee (1868–1871). He was moderator of the General Assembly of the Southern Presbyterian Church meeting in Nashville in 1867. In 1853 he received the honorary degree of doctor of divinity from Dickinson College. He was a voluminous writer on theological subjects. He died in Nashville on August 5th, 1871.

MORGAN, GEORGE WASHINGTON (1820–1893), soldier, lawyer, and legislator, son of Thomas Morgan and Katherine Duane, was born in Washington County, Pennsylvania, on September 20th, 1820. After attending Washington College (Washington, Pennsylvania) he served under his brother, Thomas Jefferson Morgan, in the Texas war for independence. He was a cadet at the United States Military Academy from 1841 to 1843; he then studied law and commenced practice in Mount Vernon, Ohio, in 1843. During the Mexican War (1846–1848) he was commissioned colonel of the 2nd Regiment Ohio Volunteer Infantry (June 23rd, 1846) and colonel of the 15th Regiment United States Infantry (April 9th, 1847); on August 20th, 1847, he was brevetted brigadier general "for gallant and meritorious conduct at the battle of Contreras and Churubusco, Mexico." For seven years (1848–1855) he farmed and practiced law in Mount Vernon, Ohio; he then became United States consul in Marseilles, France (1856) and United States minister in Lisbon, Portugal (1858–1861). At the outbreak of the Civil War he returned home and on November 12th, 1861, was commissioned brigadier general in the Federal army; he commanded the Seventh Division of the Army of the Ohio until his resignation for reasons of health on June 8th, 1863. He was a member of Congress (1867–1868; 1869–1873) and a delegate to the Democratic National Convention in 1876. On October 7th, 1851, he married Sarah H. Hall, of Zanesville, Ohio. He died at Fort Monroe, Virginia, on July 26th, 1893, survived by his wife and two daughters, and was buried in Mount View Cemetery, Mount Vernon, Ohio.

MORGAN, JOHN HUNT (1825–1864), Confederate soldier, son of Calvin Cogswell Morgan and Henrietta Hunt, was born in Huntsville, Alabama, on June 1st, 1825. In 1829 he removed with his parents to a farm near Lexington, Kentucky. After serving in the Mexican War (1846–1848) he returned to Lexington, where he engaged in business until the outbreak of the Civil War. On November 21st, 1848, he married Rebecca Bruce (1830–1861); she was for many years an invalid and died on July 21st, 1861. On September 20th, 1861, Morgan entered Confederate service as captain of his own company, the Lexington Rifles, which he had organized in 1857. Shortly thereafter he was elected captain of a cavalry company, and early in 1862 he commenced the series of brilliant and astounding raids on the Federal lines which made him famous. He was promoted to colonel (April 1862) and brigadier general (December 1862). On December 14th, 1862, he married Martha Ready, daughter of the Hon. Charles Ready, of Murfreesboro, Tennessee. On July 2nd, 1863, he commenced a daring raid through Indiana and Ohio, where he was overwhelmed by superior forces and compelled to surrender; he was confined in the state penitentiary in Columbus, from which he made a romantic escape on November 26th, 1863. The following spring he was placed in command of the Department of Southwest Virginia; in June he swept through Kentucky, regaining possession of Lexington; early in September he pursued the Federals near Knoxville and was killed at Greeneville, Tennessee, on the morning of September 4th, 1864. He was buried in Abingdon, Virginia; he was soon reburied in Hollywood Cemetery, Richmond; on April 17th, 1868, he was buried in Lexington Cemetery with ceremonies appropriate to "the Thunderbolt of the Confederacy."

MORGAN, ST. CLAIR McINTOSH (1831–1863), merchant, son of Samuel Dold Morgan (1798–1880) and Matilda Grant Rose McIntosh (1801–1860), was born in Huntsville, Alabama, in 1831. His parents, both natives of Staunton, Virginia, settled in Nashville, Tennessee, in January 1833; his father prospered in the cotton and iron industries and became an eminent and useful citizen—"the Merchant Prince of Nashville"; through his enterprise the Tennessee state capitol was built, and at his death, in recognition of his services, he was buried within its walls. St. Clair McIntosh Morgan was a first cousin of the Confederate general, John Hunt Morgan (1825–1864). According to his sister, Amanda Morgan, wife of William C. Sherrod, "He was a strikingly handsome man, of strong personality, making friends for himself of all who knew him. . . . He was a soldier by nature, but to gratify his father he gave up his inclination for the army and was made a junior partner in the wholesale mercantile business of Morgan & Company." On May 4th, 1854, he married Maria Percy Pope, youngest daughter of John Pope, of Memphis, Tennessee; there were three children: Louisa, Judith, and Samuel. In May 1861 he became captain of Company F (later Company C), 10th Regiment Tennessee Infantry. The regiment surrendered at Fort Donelson, Tennessee, on February 16th, 1862; Morgan was confined at Camp Chase, Ohio, and (after May 1st, 1862) on Johnson's Island; he was released at Vicksburg, Mississippi, in September 1862. He was killed at Chickamauga on September 19th, 1863. His younger brother, Samuel Dold Morgan (1841–1862), in cavalry service with his cousin, General John Hunt Morgan, was killed at Augusta, Kentucky, on September 27th, 1862, and was buried in Lexington Cemetery.

MORRELL, ISAAC WILLIAM (1793–1865), furniture dealer, was born in Jamaica, Long Island, New York, in 1793. In 1821 he settled in Savannah, Georgia, where he established a thriving business in furniture, pianos, and sewing machines and amassed a handsome fortune. He was a director of the Savannah, Albany & Gulf Railroad; he was also a director of the Mechanics' & Traders' Bank and the Merchants' & Planters' Bank. Soon after the outbreak of the Civil War he retired from business. He died in Savannah on January 23rd, 1865, survived by his wife, Sarah Goodrich (1815–1883), and four children, and was buried in the family vault in Laurel Grove Cemetery. Sarah (Goodrich) Morrell died on January 7th, 1883, and was buried beside her husband. The Savannah *Republican* carried the following notice on March 19th, 1857: "Those who are in want of a fine *pianoforte* at a low price would do well to give Mr. I. W. Morrell a call. He advertises a large assortment and presents testimonials enough to satisfy any caviler. Amongst those he offers for sale we notice a lot built by Chickering & Sons, men who have obtained a worldwide celebrity for the excellence of their instruments—the superiority of their tone and the neatness with which they are finished. . . . While we are on this subject we would take occasion to call the attention of our readers, both in town and country, to the magnificent furniture establishment of Mr. Morrell on Broughton Street. It is worthwhile to look over his large and varied assortment, embracing the latest and costliest styles, and in quantity excelled by no similar establishment south of New York."

MORRIS, MARIA B. (1841–1925), only daughter of William St. Clair Morris (1812–1871) and Susan Walker (1810–1873), was born in Augusta, Georgia, on May 6th, 1841. Her father was a planter near Bath, Richmond County, Georgia. On July 3rd, 1861, Maria ("Sis") Morris became the wife of Thomas Spalding McIntosh (1837–1862), son of William Jackson McIntosh (1782–1863) and Maria Hillary (1788–1862). After his untimely death in the battle of Sharpsburg (September 17th, 1862) she was said to be "almost deranged." As Charles Colcock Jones, Jr., wrote on October 1st, 1862, "She had concentered all her affections upon him, and her heart, bereft of his loves, is desolate beyond description." On February 13th, 1868, Maria (Morris) McIntosh became the wife of Dr. James M. Madden (1840–1906), a physician, and settled in Brunswick, Georgia, where she became the mother of three children. Her husband subsequently gave up medical practice and entered banking, in which he soon amassed a handsome fortune. He died in Brunswick after a long illness on February 19th, 1906, and was buried in the family vault in Oak Grove Cemetery. In 1912 Maria (Morris) (McIntosh) Madden removed to Jacksonville, Florida, to reside with her son,

Dr. James Morris Madden (1874–1937). She died in Jacksonville on April 23rd, 1925, and was buried beside her husband.

MORRIS, WILLIAM ST. CLAIR (1812–1871), planter, was born in Savannah, Georgia, in 1812. He resided most of his life in Bath, Richmond County, Georgia, where he married Susan Walker (1810–1873), daughter of Isaac Walker and Bethiah Whitehead; there was one daughter: Maria B. Morris (1841–1925). On March 28th, 1860, he was elected brigadier general of the Second Brigade, First Division Georgia Militia. At the outbreak of the Civil War he organized the Poythress Volunteers (named for Colonel John C. Poythress, a prominent citizen of Burke County); this company later became Company E (Infantry Battalion), Cobb's Legion Georgia Volunteers. On August 8th, 1861, Morris was elected captain and went with his company to Virginia, where he joined General John Bankhead Magruder on the Peninsula near Yorktown. In November 1861 he returned to Georgia with a wounded hand, from which he was slow to recover; on August 26th, 1862, he tendered his resignation to the secretary of war, "ill health for months past having rendered me unfit for the performance of my official duties; not being well enough to resume my command after an absence of 'sick leave' of over thirty days; and being over forty years of age." He died in Waynesboro, Georgia, in 1871 and was buried in Bath Presbyterian Churchyard. Susan (Walker) Morris died in Brunswick, Georgia, at the residence of her daughter in 1873 and was buried beside her husband.

MORRISS, MARY ANN (ROLL) (1836–1884), daughter of Charles Roll and Mary Roll, was born in Augusta, Georgia, in 1836. Her parents, both natives of New Jersey, had migrated to Georgia soon after their marriage and settled in Augusta, where Luther Roll, elder brother of Charles Roll, was a prosperous merchant. By 1850 Charles Roll was established as a merchant in Marietta; after an interval of five years in Savannah (1851–1856) he resumed business in Marietta; in the summer of 1860 he opened a family grocery in Atlanta. For several years Mary Ann Roll attended the Kennesaw Female Seminary, conducted in Marietta under the auspices of St. James's Episcopal Church. On March 22nd, 1864, she became the wife of a Lieutenant Morriss, then stationed near Atlanta. "On Tuesday evening," wrote Mrs. Mary S. Mallard on March 24th, 1864, "when the ground was covered with snow, Mr. Mallard had to perform a marriage ceremony. He had received a note the day before from a lieutenant saying he was to be '*mared*' and wished him to perform the 'serrimony.' I received a generous supply of cake." A week later (on March 31st, 1864) Mrs. Mallard, writing of the wedding, recalled that "after it was all over, one of the gentlemen pulled a pair of new white kid gloves out of the groom's pocket. He had actually forgotten to put them on. Was not that soldier-like?" Caroline Virginia Roll

(1840–1864), younger sister of Mary Ann (Roll) Morriss, died in Atlanta on June 26th, 1864, and was buried in Oakland Cemetery. Early in September 1864, at the request of Mrs. Morriss, then a refugee in Augusta, the Rev. R. Q. Mallard, then a refugee in Walthourville, went to Augusta to preach her sister's funeral sermon on Sunday, September 11th, 1864, in the First Presbyterian Church. "The Rolls were very thoughtful," he wrote his wife the next day, "and enclosed in a well-written note to me this morning eighty dollars—more than sufficient to pay the costs of the trip." Mary Ann (Roll) Morriss died of pneumonia in April 1884 and was buried in Magnolia Cemetery, Augusta.

MOTLEY, JOHN LOTHROP (1814–1877), historian and diplomat, son of Thomas Motley and Anna Lothrop, was born in Dorchester, a suburb of Boston, Massachusetts, on August 15th, 1814. After graduating from Harvard College in 1831 he studied law and language for two years in Göttingen and Berlin and returned to Boston in 1835. On March 2nd, 1837, he married Mary Benjamin, daughter of Parke Benjamin and Mary Judith Gall; there were four children. In 1841 he served briefly as secretary to the United States legation in St. Petersburg; he later served as United States minister to Austria (1861–1867) and United States minister to Great Britain (1869–1870). After writing two novels, *Morton's Hope* (1839) and *Merrymount* (1849) he turned to the great work of his life, a political and religious history of the Netherlands. *The Rise of the Dutch Republic* (3 vols., 1856), the fruit of ten years' scholarship, enjoyed enormous popularity and became a literary classic. *The History of the United Netherlands* (4 vols., 1860–1867) and *The Life and Death of John Barneveld* (2 vols., 1874) continued the narrative. A fourth unit, treating the Thirty Years' War and bringing the narrative down to 1648, was projected but never completed. Motley died in Dorchester, Dorset, England, on May 29th, 1877, and was buried beside his wife in Kensal Green Cemetery near London. In her letter endorsing *The Rise of the Dutch Republic* as "delightful reading" (September 14th, 1858) Mary Jones Taylor was mistaken in ascribing the work to "Philip Motley."

MOTTE, REBECCA (BREWTON) (1737–1815): *Mrs. Jacob Motte,* daughter of Robert Brewton (1698–1759) and his second wife, Mary Loughton, widow of William Loughton, was born in Charleston, South Carolina, on June 15th, 1737. On June 28th, 1758, she married Jacob Motte (1729–1780), son of Jacob Motte (1701–1770), public treasurer of South Carolina. From her brother, Miles Brewton (1731–1775), she inherited Mount Joseph, a plantation on the Congaree River in St. Matthew's Parish, Orangeburg District. She was living there in 1781 when the British seized the house as a military post; she and her three daughters were permitted to remain in the house until the Americans under General Francis Marion and Lieutenant Colonel Harry Lee invested and laid siege to the post on May 8th, 1781. Her patriotic "self-denial" on May 12th, 1781, was described by her grandson, Charles Cotesworth Pinckney (1812–1899), in a letter published in the Columbia *Carolinian* on September 27th, 1855: "Mrs. Motte was informed by Lieutenant Colonel Lee that the destruction of her house might be necessary. To this she immediately and cheerfully consented, assuring him that the loss of her property was nothing compared with the advancement of their cause; and to facilitate their operations presented them with some combustible arrows with which to set fire to the house. . . . The arrows were discharged from a rifle; the two first did not ignite; the third set the roof on fire, and as the piece of artillery in possession of the Americans commanded the only access to the roof, the British surrendered immediately. The Americans rushed in, extinguished the fire, and saved the house—an act of gratitude to the owner for her patriotic devotion." Rebecca (Brewton) Motte died on January 10th, 1815.

MOUNT-PLEASANT, JOHN (1810–1887), Indian chief, son of William Mount-Pleasant (1779–1854), was born on the Tuscarora Indian reservation in Niagara County, New York, on January 18th, 1810. In 1827 he was elected chief of the Tuscarora tribe. "His administration of the affairs of his people was marked with ability, judgment, and kindness," recalled William Pool in his *Landmarks of Niagara County, New York* (1897). "He successfully cultivated a large farm, and he lived in a large and handsome dwelling house where the most liberal hospitality always prevailed." In 1831 John Mount-Pleasant married Jane Green, of the Tuscarora tribe; after her death he married Caroline G. Parker, of the Seneca tribe, sister of General Ely S. Parker, military secretary of General U. S. Grant. John Mount-Pleasant died on the Tuscarora reservation on May 6th, 1887. According to the Buffalo *Express* (May 8th, 1887), "He had white blood in his veins, was an educated man, had been a chief since he was seventeen years old, and was a member of the Buffalo Historical Society."

MOUNT-PLEASANT, WILLIAM (1779–1854), Indian interpreter, was born on Mackinac Island in 1779. Two years later his father joined the Tuscarora tribe occupying a reservation in Niagara County, New York, some seven miles north of Niagara Falls. During the War of 1812 William Mount-Pleasant was an officer in the British army. For many years he served as interpreter of the Rev. Gilbert Rockwood (1811–1869), pastor of the Presbyterian church on the Tuscarora reservation from 1837 to 1861. He died on the reservation on October 9th, 1854. His son, John Mount-Pleasant (1810–1887), was chief of the Tuscarora tribe for sixty years (1827–1887).

MULLALLY, FRANCIS PATRICK (1834–1904), Presbyterian clergyman, son of Thomas Mullally and Mary Mandeville, was born in

County Tipperary, Ireland, in 1834. His mother was a daughter of Lord Mandeville. In early manhood he migrated to the United States, where he taught briefly at the Villa High School, Mount Zion, Georgia; after attending the law school of Washington College (Lexington, Virginia) he graduated from Columbia Theological Seminary in 1860. For three years he served the First Presbyterian Church, Columbia, South Carolina: first as co-pastor with the Rev. James Henley Thornwell (March 1860–November 1861) and later as pastor (November 1861–June 1863). On December 2nd, 1861, he married Elizabeth Keith Adger (1841–1899), daughter of the Rev. John Bailey Adger (1810–1899) and Elizabeth Keith Shrewsbury, of Columbia. In June 1863 he entered Confederate service both as chaplain and as colonel; on several occasions he preached to the Federals and officiated at the burial of Federal officers. After the war he was pastor of churches in Bolivar, Tennessee (1867–1869); Covington, Kentucky (1869–1874); Sparta, Georgia (1875–1876); and Lexington, Virginia (1876–1882). From 1882 to 1884 he was president of Adger College (Walhalla, South Carolina). He spent his last years in New York City, where he was evangelist from 1891 to 1904. He died in Pelham Manor, New York, on January 17th, 1904, survived by three daughters and five sons, and was buried beside his wife in Greenwood Cemetery, Brooklyn.

MULOCK, DINAH MARIA (1826–1887), English author, daughter of Thomas Mulock, an eccentric clergyman, was born in Stoke-upon-Trent, Staffordshire, on April 20th, 1826. In early womanhood she settled in London, where she wrote novels and children's stories; with the publication of *John Halifax, Gentleman* (1857), a portrait of the ideal middle-class Englishman, her fame was secure. Such later works as *A Woman's Thoughts About Women* (1858) and *Sermons Out of Church* (1875) are frankly didactic. In 1864 she became the wife of George Lillie Craik, a partner in Macmillan & Company, publishers; shortly thereafter she settled at Shortlands, near Bromley, where she died suddenly of heart failure on October 12th, 1887.

NAPOLEON I (1769–1821), emperor of the French (1804–1815), son of Carlo Bonaparte and Letizia Ramolino, was born in Ajaccio, Corsica, on August 15th, 1769. His father, a lawyer, was of ancient Corsican nobility. From the age of nine Napoleon was educated in France, first at the college of Autun, later at the military college of Brienne, and finally at the military academy in Paris. On September 1st, 1786, he completed his studies and was made second lieutenant of artillery in the regiment of La Fère, a training school for young officers, where he continued his education. Through indomitable energy and insatiable ambition he rose rapidly to prominence and power, and by 1799 he was master of France. As consul (1799–1804) he imposed a military dictatorship on France, re-

formed the administration of French government, promulgated the Code Napoleon (1804), and reestablished peace throughout Europe. On December 2nd, 1804, in Notre Dame Cathedral, he was crowned emperor of the French by Pope Pius VII. His campaign to invade England terminated with its decisive defeat by Nelson at Trafalgar (October 21st, 1805). On the continent he was victorious over the Austrians at Ulm (October 30th, 1805), over the Austrians and Russians at Austerlitz (December 2nd, 1805), and over the Prussians at Jena and at Auerstädt (October 14th, 1806). He reached his zenith in 1810. In June 1812 he invaded Russia; after the indecisive battle of Borodino (September 7th, 1812) he entered Moscow on September 14th, 1812. But Emperor Alexander refused to negotiate; and his disastrous retreat from Russia the following winter encouraged the Prussians, Austrians, and Italians to resist his domination. At Leipzig (October 16th–19th, 1813) Napoleon's *grande armée* was overwhelmingly defeated; and on March 9th, 1814, Austria, Russia, Prussia, and Great Britain signed the treaty of Chaumont, by which they bound themselves for twenty years to his overthrow. Napoleon abdicated on April 6th, 1814, and a month later (on May 4th, 1814) he was confined on the island of Elba. On March 1st, 1815, he landed in the Gulf of Juan and proceeded to Paris, the republican peasants flocking to his standard. He reached Paris on March 20th, 1815. At Waterloo (June 18th, 1815) he was decisively defeated by the British under Wellington. On June 22nd, 1815, he abdicated a second time; he was exiled to St. Helena, where he died on May 5th, 1821. In 1840 he was entombed at the Hotel des Invalides in Paris.

NAPOLEON III (1808–1873), emperor of the French (1852–1870), third son of Louis Bonaparte and Hortense de Beauharnais, was born in Paris on April 20th, 1808. His father, brother of Napoleon I, was king of Holland (1806–1810). His original name, Charles Louis Napoleon, was shortened to Louis Napoleon after the death of his brother, Napoleon Louis Bonaparte, in 1831, when he became heir to the claims of his uncle, Napoleon I. He devoted every energy to winning the throne of France. After an abortive attempt at a military *coup d'état* on October 10th, 1836, he was deported to the United States, from which he returned in the spring of 1837 to Switzerland and thence to England, where he confidently asserted in social and political circles that he would someday be emperor of France. In 1840, after a second abortive attempt at a military *coup d'état,* he was tried and sentenced to life imprisonment; on May 26th, 1846, he escaped from prison disguised as a laborer and returned to England. After the revolution of 1848 he was elected a member of the national assembly, and the republican constitution made him president for four years. On December 2nd, 1851, in a brilliant *coup d'état,* he dissolved parliament and arrested its leaders, together with some twenty thousand of his enemies; on

December 20th, 1851, an overwhelming majority voted him dictatorial powers for ten years. In November 1852 he was elected emperor of the French, and on December 2nd, 1852, he assumed the title of Napoleon III and inaugurated the Second Empire. On January 29th, 1853, he married Eugénie de Montijo (1826–1920), a Spanish countess. In the Crimean War (1854–1856), with the support of Great Britain, he successfully stopped Russian expansion to the Mediterranean; but his subsequent international exploits brought him into serious difficulty—in Italy (1859), in Mexico (1862–1867), and in Prussia (1866). His domestic policies were more successful, and his reign was remarkable for its prosperity. In the Franco-Prussian War (1870) he was promptly defeated at Sedan; he surrendered on September 2nd, 1870, and withdrew to England, where he died in Camden Place, Chislehurst, on January 9th, 1873. His widow continued to reside in England. After 1880 she lived at Farnborough, where she erected a church as a mausoleum for her husband and her only son, Napoleon Eugene Louis (1856–1879). She died in Madrid on July 11th, 1920, and was buried beside her husband.

NASH, FREDERICK KOLLOCK (1813–1861), Presbyterian clergyman, son of the Hon. Frederick Nash (1781–1858), chief justice of the supreme court of North Carolina, and Mary G. Kollock (1781–1863), was born in Hillsboro, North Carolina, on February 14th, 1813. After attending the University of North Carolina and studying law he was ordained clergyman in 1838 and served various churches in the Morgan and Concord Presbyteries before becoming stated supply of Centre Church in Gilopolis, Robeson County, North Carolina, in 1846. For fourteen years (1847–1861) he was pastor of Centre Church. He died of "pleuropneumonia" in Hillsboro, North Carolina, on December 31st, 1861, only a few weeks after attending the first General Assembly of the Southern Presbyterian Church in Augusta, Georgia, and was buried in Centre Churchyard, Gilopolis. Two of his sons died of disease in the Civil War: Henry Potter Nash (1842–1863) died at Hillsboro on June 7th, 1863; Frederick Kollock Nash (1844–1864) died at Point Lookout, Maryland, on August 1st, 1864.

NEELY, LOUISA L. (1837–1872), daughter of Amzi Neely (1806–1880) and Levisa E. Gilmore (1809–1858), was born in Chester, South Carolina, in 1837. In early childhood she removed with her family to Columbia, where her elder brother, Thomas William Neely (1829–1867), graduated from the South Carolina College in 1849; later the family settled in Savannah, where her father and her brother were associated in the cotton business. Her mother died on February 24th, 1858. A year later (on January 27th, 1859) she became the wife of Edward Conrad McLure (1834–1889), son of Thomas McLure (1779–1860) and Ann Ferris Canfield, of Chester, South Carolina. Her husband, a native of New Jersey and a graduate of Harvard College (1854), was a

prosperous lawyer; in 1859 he was aide-de-camp to the governor of South Carolina, with rank of colonel. During the Civil War he was captain of the Chester Blues (6th Regiment South Carolina Volunteers); in April 1862 he was promoted to major; in the spring of 1863 he was assigned to duty in the enrolling department, where he continued until the end of the war. Returning to Chester, he resumed his law practice and in 1869 founded the Chester *Reporter*. Louisa (Neely) McLure died in Chester in 1872, survived by her husband and one child: Annie G. McLure (1859–1880). She was buried in Evergreen Cemetery. In June 1873 Edward Conrad McLure married Jane Wylie (1845–1886), daughter of Dr. Alexander P. Wylie and Juliet A. Gill, of Chester; there were six children. For eight years (1873–1881) he practiced law in Dallas, Texas, and edited the Dallas *Herald*; returning to Chester, he practiced law for two years before removing in 1883 to Washington, D.C., where he was private secretary to Matthew Calbraith Butler (1836–1909), United States senator from South Carolina, and later became appointment clerk in the Post Office Department. He died in Washington on February 27th, 1889, and was buried in Evergreen Cemetery, Chester, South Carolina, beside his second wife and near his first.

NEELY, THOMAS WILLIAM (1829–1867), lawyer, merchant, and planter, son of Amzi Neely (1806–1880) and Levisa E. Gilmore (1809–1858), was born in Chester, South Carolina, in 1829. He graduated from the South Carolina College in 1849 and from Dane Law School, Harvard University, in 1852. After engaging in business for two years in New York he settled in Savannah, Georgia, where he was a successful cotton factor and commission merchant in association with his father. He also planted extensively in Burke County, Georgia. On July 19th, 1855, he married Philoclea Edgeworth Whitehead (1833–1892), daughter of John Whitehead (1783–1857) and his second wife, Julia Maria (Berrien) Belt (1801–1857), of Bath, Richmond County, Georgia. "Philo" Neely was the "favorite sister" of Ruth Berrien Whitehead (1837–1861), first wife of Charles Colcock Jones, Jr., and she married her third child John Jones Neely. She was also a sister of John Randolph Whitehead (1829–1877); Julia Amanda Whitehead (1831–1896), wife of Dr. John Gordon Howard; Charles Lowndes Whitehead (1835–1866); and Valeria Burroughs Whitehead (1840–1904), wife of Augustus Ramon Salas; she was a half-sister of Eliza Alice Whitehead (1818–1896), wife of Dr. Charles William West. Prior to the Civil War Thomas William Neely was several times elected alderman of Savannah. On May 14th, 1862, he enlisted as second lieutenant in Company A, Oglethorpe Siege Artillery (later designated Company C, 22nd Battalion Georgia Heavy Artillery). Failing health forced him to resign, and on December 2nd, 1862, he was appointed assistant quartermaster, with rank of captain. After the war he planted in Jefferson County, Georgia. He died at his residence there on May 31st, 1867, survived by his wife and five children, and was buried in Laurel Grove Cemetery, Savannah. Philoclea Edgeworth (Whitehead) Neely lived for some years in Baltimore with her sister, Valeria Burroughs Whitehead; she died at White Bluff, near Savannah, on August 18th, 1892, survived by five children, and was buried beside her husband.

NEFF, WILLIAM (1792–1856), merchant, son of Peter Neff (1764–1804) and Rebecca Scout (1764–1834), was born in Frankford, Pennsylvania, on February 7th, 1792. In 1808 he began his career as office boy in the Philadelphia commission house of Gustavus and Hugh Calhoun. In 1813 he formed a partnership with his elder brother, John Rudolph Neff (1789–1863): John was to remain in Philadelphia, and William was to conduct the business in Savannah, Georgia. For eleven years (1814–1825) William Neff prospered as a cotton factor and commission merchant in Savannah; on May 19th, 1825, he married Elizabeth Clifford Wayne (1803–1864), daughter of Richard Wayne (1771–1822) and Julianna Smyth (1781–1807). In the spring of 1825 John Rudolph Neff took his three brothers, William Neff, Peter Neff (1798–1879), and George Washington Neff (1800–1850), as partners in the firm of Neff & Brothers, a general hardware business to be conducted in Cincinnati, Ohio. Removing to Cincinnati, William Neff continued with the firm until 1836, when he withdrew to conduct his own meat-packing business (1836–1855). His extensive interest in agriculture, horticulture, and stock-breeding extended to his farm in Edgar County, Illinois (1836–1852) and to his farm in Yellow Springs, Greene County, Ohio (1842–1856). He was a director of the United States Bank, an incorporator of Spring Grove Cemetery, a founder of Wesleyan Female College, and one of the first trustees of Ohio Wesleyan University. He died in Cincinnati on November 25th, 1856, and was buried in Spring Grove Cemetery. Elizabeth Clifford (Wayne) Neff died on October 18th, 1864, and was buried beside her husband. In his youth the Rev. Dr. Charles Colcock Jones worked four years (1819–1822) as a clerk in the Savannah countinghouse of Nicholas & Neff. After Neff's departure from Savannah the friendship continued; Dr. Jones visited Neff in Cincinnati on May 11th, 1851; and it was William Clifford Neff, son of William Neff, who sent Dr. Jones a photograph of his father in December 1860.

NESBITT, MARTHA DELONEY (BERRIEN) (1818–1896): Mrs. Hugh O'Keefe Nesbitt, daughter of Richard McAllister Berrien (1795–1820) and Martha Bolling Deloney, was born in Savannah, Georgia, in 1818. On June 23rd, 1839, she became the wife of Dr. Hugh O'Keefe Nesbitt (1814–1855), of Augusta, a physician recently returned from a course of medical study in Paris. There were three children: Robert Taylor Nesbitt (1840–1913); Eliza Bolling Nesbitt (1841–1863), who married (on August 21st, 1860) Bayard Livingston McIntosh (1838–1903); and Mary Eleanor Nesbitt (1844–1883), who married first (on May 28th, 1861) Thomas B. Brown (died 1862), and second (on December 7th, 1865) John Screven (1827–1900). Hugh O'Keefe Nesbitt did not practice his profession; during the sixteen years of his marriage he devoted himself to his own and his wife's planting interests. The family lived successively in Augusta, Savannah, and Athens. In the spring of 1851 they settled in Marietta, where the three children were educated, and where the Nesbitts became close friends of Mrs. Eliza G. Robarts and her family. Hugh O'Keefe Nesbitt died in Early County, Georgia, on October 27th, 1855, and was buried in Summerville Cemetery, Augusta. On December 18th, 1861, Martha (Berrien) Nesbitt became the second wife of William Duncan (1799–1879), of Savannah, insurance agent and cotton factor. After his death on March 20th, 1879, she returned to her former home in Marietta, where she died on July 13th, 1896. She was buried in Episcopal Cemetery.

NEVITT, JOHN WILSON (1814–1888), dry goods merchant, son of John Nevitt (1770–1852) and his first wife, Sarah Stotesbury (1791–1817), was born in Savannah, Georgia, on November 6th, 1814. His mother, a native of Philadelphia, died on November 6th, 1817 (his third birthday), and his father married Louisa Stotesbury (1797–1890), younger sister of his first wife. John Wilson Nevitt was for many years a successful dry goods merchant in Savannah. Shortly before the Civil War he joined Henry Lathrop and John Swift Rogers in the firm of Nevitt, Lathrop & Rogers. He was a vestryman of St. John's Episcopal Church. On December 17th, 1846, he married Mary Eliza Tschudi (1826–1910), daughter of the Rev. John Jacob Tschudi, an Episcopal clergyman, and Mary George Barrington, of Monk's Corner, South Carolina. In 1876 the Nevitts removed to Athens, where John Wilson Nevitt died on October 12th, 1888, survived by his wife, and was buried in Oconee Hill Cemetery. Mary Eliza (Tschudi) Nevitt died on December 26th, 1910, and was buried beside her husband.

NEWELL, HARRIET ATWOOD (1819–1883), only child of the Rev. Samuel Newell (1784–1821) and his second wife, Philomela Thurston, was born in the East Indies early in 1819. Her father, a graduate of Harvard College (1807) and Andover Theological Seminary (1809), had sailed in 1812 for India, where he served as a missionary until his death of Asiatic cholera in Bombay on March 30th, 1821. Shortly thereafter her mother married James Garrett, also a missionary; after his death Philomela (Thurston) (Newell) Garrett returned to America; she died in Poughkeepsie, New York, on September 16th, 1849. By 1851 Harriet Atwood Newell was living in Liberty County, Georgia; late in 1855 she became the third wife of Smith Screven Hart (1806–1866),

a planter, ninth and youngest child of John
Hart (1758–1814), and Mary Esther Screven
(1767–1845); there were three children. Smith
Screven Hart died at Lodebar, his plantation
near Dorchester, Liberty County, on February
28th, 1866. Harriet Atwood (Newell) Hart
died in Dorchester on August 24th, 1883.

NEWKIRK, MATTHEW (1794–1868), merchant, was born in Pittsgrove, Salem County,
New Jersey, on May 31st, 1794. In 1810 he
came to Philadelphia and entered the dry
goods business, from which he retired in 1839,
having accumulated a handsome fortune. He
then projected, promoted, and became president of the Philadelphia, Wilmington & Baltimore Railroad; he was also an incorporator of
the Pennsylvania Steamship Company, a director of the United States Bank, and a trustee
of the College of New Jersey (Princeton). He
was president of the Pennsylvania Temperance
Society, president of the State Sabbath School
Association, and for thirty years an elder of the
Central Presbyterian Church. He was an active member of the Association of the Soldiers
of the War of 1812. He died in Philadelphia
on May 31st, 1868 (his seventy-fourth birthday), and was buried beside his first wife,
Margaret Heberton (1799–1841), in Laurel
Hill Cemetery. He was survived by a son, the
Rev. Matthew Newkirk (1838–1910), a Presbyterian clergyman. To the Rev. Dr. Charles
Colcock Jones the Newkirks were "our nearest
and best friends in all our stay in Philadelphia."
Upon their arrival in Philadelphia in October
1850 they stayed with the Newkirks until they
could locate suitable quarters; and upon their
departure from Philadelphia in October 1853
they stayed with the Newkirks a few days after
closing up their rooms. "Last week," wrote
Dr. Jones on April 28th, 1853, "upon Mr.
Newkirk's invitation I accompanied him to his
coal mines at Tamaqua, ninety-eight miles
from the city, in the mountains. You leave
shortly after 7 A.M. and reach Tamaqua at
12 M., the railroad skirting the Schuylkill
to Port Clinton at the junction of the Schuylkill with the Little Schuylkill or Tamaqua
River; and proceeding by railroad up this
stream we reach our journey's end after running twenty miles. The village—a mining one
altogether, and irregularly built up the valleys
and on the hillsides—contains between four
and five thousand inhabitants. . . . Mr. Newkirk's energy and kindness and benevolence are
seen on every hand, and he is kindly greeted
wherever he goes, and has a kind word for
everybody."

NEWTON, ELIZUR LOWRANCE (1796–
1882), merchant, youngest son of the Rev.
John Newton (1759–1797) and Catharine
Lowrance (1756–1846), was born in Oglethorpe County, Georgia, on February 10th,
1796. His father, a native of Pennsylvania, was
the first Presbyterian clergyman in Georgia;
in 1786 he settled in Oglethorpe County, where
he remained until his death in 1797, one year
after the birth of his youngest son. In 1810
Elizur Lowrance Newton accompanied his

widowed mother to Athens, where he graduated from Franklin College in 1820. On May
14th, 1822, he married Elizabeth Taylor Callier (1802–1881), daughter of Thomas Callier,
of Warren County, North Carolina; there were
ten children. Newton was an enterprising merchant and became a large landholder in Athens.
He erected the first brick building in Athens,
a hotel called the Newton House. He was one
of the founders of the Georgia Railroad and
for many years a director. In Athens he filled
many offices of honor and trust, and for more
than half a century he was an elder of the
Athens Presbyterian Church. He died in Athens
on March 28th, 1882, and was buried in
Oconee Hill Cemetery beside his wife, who
had died less than five months before, on
November 14th, 1881. According to the Atlanta *Constitution* (March 30th, 1882), he was
"one of the oldest, most respected and beloved
citizens of Athens."

NEWTON, SIR ISAAC (1642–1727), English natural philosopher and mathematician,
son of Isaac Newton (1606–1642) and Hannah
Ayscough, was born in Woolsthorpe, near
Grantham, Lincolnshire, on December 25th,
1642. He graduated from Trinity College
(Cambridge) in 1665 and two years later became a fellow of the college. Between 1665 and
1667 he developed the binomial theorem and
the method of fluxions, an early form of differential calculus; he also analyzed the composition of white light and the nature of color,
developed the telescope, and discovered the
principle of gravitation. Much of his subsequent work was based on these early discov-
eries. In 1669 he succeeded Isaac Barrow as
Lucasian professor of mathematics at Cambridge, a post he held until his resignation in
1701. In 1672 he was elected a fellow of the
Royal Society of London, of which he was
later president (1703–1727). He was a member
of Parliament (1689–1690; 1701), warden of
the mint (1695–1699), and master of the mint
(1699–1727). He was knighted in 1705. His
most famous work, *Principia* (1687), bears
the full title *Philosophia Naturalis Principia
Mathematica* (Mathematical Principles of Natural Philosophy); it is the fundamental book
on which all modern science rests. His *Opticks*
(1704) went through three editions in his own
lifetime. Newton died in London on March
20th, 1727, and was buried in Westminster
Abbey. He was one of the greatest scientific
men of all time.

NEWTON, JOHN (1725–1807), Anglican
clergyman, was born in London on July 24th,
1725. After an adventurous seafaring life as an
African slavetrader he experienced an extraordinary spiritual conversion on March 10th,
1748, and was ordained priest on June 17th,
1764. As curate of Olney (1764–1780) he became the sympathetic friend of the poet William Cowper (1731–1800), and from their
lifelong intimacy sprang the *Olney Hymns*
(1779), among which are some of the best
known and most universally loved poems in
the language. Those who know Cowper's "Oh!

for a closer walk with God" and "There is a fountain filled with blood" and "God moves in a mysterious way" are no less familiar with Newton's "Amazing grace (how sweet the sound!)" and "Glorious things of thee are spoken" and "How sweet the name of Jesus sounds." In 1780 he left Olney to become rector of St. Mary Woolnoth, Lombard Street, London, where he labored with unflagging zeal and widespread popularity for twenty-seven years. On February 12th, 1750, he married Mary Catlett, who died of cancer on December 15th, 1790. Newton died on December 21st, 1807, and was buried beside his wife in St. Mary Woolnoth; in 1893 their remains were removed to Olney. Newton's account of his life at sea and of his religious conversion appears in his *Authentic Narrative,* first published in 1764 and subsequently reprinted in many editions. Richard Cecil (1748–1810) continued the narrative from 1763 to 1807. A *Memoir* by Richard Cecil prefaced *The Works of the Rev. John Newton* (1827).

NISBET, ELIZA CLAY (1852–1857), second child of Thomas Cooper Nisbet (1819–1874) and Mary Cuthbert Cumming (1823–1893), was born in Macon, Georgia, on January 29th, 1852. She was named for her mother's cousin, Eliza Caroline Clay (1809–1895), of Richmond-on-Ogeechee plantation, Bryan County, Georgia. On a visit to Macon in December 1854 Mary Sharpe Jones found Eliza Clay Nisbet "one of the most winning and gentle children I have ever seen." Eliza Clay Nisbet died of "gangrene sore mouth" on January 24th, 1857, five days before her fifth birthday, and was buried in Rose Hill Cemetery, Macon, beside her younger brother, Thomas Cooper Nisbet (1855–1857), who had died of "gangrene sore mouth" less than three weeks earlier, on January 7th, 1857.

NISBET, EUGENIUS ARISTIDES (1803–1871), lawyer, jurist, and congressman, son of Dr. James Nisbet (1767–1834) and Penelope Cooper (1776–1834), was born near Union Point, Greene County, Georgia, on December 7th, 1803. After graduating from Franklin College (Athens) in 1821 he attended the Litchfield (Connecticut) Law School and commenced practice in Madison, Georgia, in 1824. On April 12th, 1825, he married Amanda Battle; nine of their twelve children lived to maturity. He represented Morgan County in the state house of representatives (1827–1830) and in the state senate (1830–1837). In 1837 he settled in Macon and resumed the practice of law. He was a member of Congress (1839–1841) and associate justice of the state supreme court (1845–1853). In January 1861 he was a member of the state secession convention meeting in Milledgeville, and he drafted the ordinance of secession of the State of Georgia. For over forty years he was a ruling elder of the Presbyterian Church. He died in Macon on March 18th, 1871, and was buried in Rose Hill Cemetery. As the Savannah *Republican* (March 19th, 1871) observed, "Georgia has lost one of her ablest, purest, and best of men —a man who received the impress of his character in the better days of the republic, when true merit was the measure of reward, and public men had a motive in aspiring to true wisdom and the highest attainment in virtue."

NISBET, HARRIET (HATTIE) (1853–1910), third child of Thomas Cooper Nisbet (1819–1874) and Mary Cuthbert Cumming (1823–1893), was born in Macon, Georgia, on May 13th, 1853. On March 14th, 1877, "Hattie" became the wife of Edward Dilworth Latta (1851–1925), son of James Theodore Latta (1827–1865) and Angela W. Scott, of Pendleton, South Carolina. After engaging in business for four years in New York City Latta removed to Charlotte, North Carolina, where he prospered in the clothing business, acquired vast real estate holdings, and became one of the wealthiest men in the state. Hattie (Nisbet) Latta died in Charlotte of typhoid fever on October 9th, 1910, survived by her husband and three children, and was buried in the Latta mausoleum in Elmwood Cemetery. According to the Charlotte *Observer* (October 10th, 1910), she was "one of this city's most prominent, most talented, and best-beloved women. . . . Intellectual brilliancy of high order added to Mrs. Latta's charm and made her sought for in every company. Conversant with the realm of letters, her literary taste was mature and discriminating and found reflection in numerous historical and similar papers of which she was the author." On August 31st, 1918, Edward Dilworth Latta married Jane Rees Lea, of Vicksburg, Mississippi. He died in Charlotte on July 14th, 1925, and was buried beside his first wife. According to Mrs. Mary S. Mallard (March 30th, 1877), Louisa Jane Robarts spoke "in glowing terms" of Hattie Nisbet's wedding, where she "had the chief direction of the supper" and "iced all the cake" and "saw more diamonds than she had ever seen before in her life."

NISBET, MARGARET JOHNS (1829–1916), youngest daughter of John Nisbet (1781–1841) and Harriet Cooper (1789–1863), was born in Athens, Georgia, in 1829. Her father died when she was twelve years old, and she was sent North to school. She never married. For many years she resided with members of her family: in Washington, D.C., with her mother; in Macon, Georgia, with her brother, Thomas Cooper Nisbet (1819–1874); in Athens, Georgia, with her sister, Mary Ann Nisbet (1817–1885), wife of Dr. Henry Hull (1798–1881); in South Georgia and Florida with her sister, Sarah Evalina Nisbet (1822–1884), wife of General Martin Luther Smith (1819–1866); in Washington, D.C., with her sister, Harriet Nisbet (1823–1892), wife of Louis LeConte (1821–1852). In March 1878 she was boarding in Marietta, Georgia, with the Robartses. In 1880 she purchased a house in Norcross, Gwinnett County, Georgia, where she was "practically a hermit," as she wrote on October 14th, 1912. She died in Norcross in January 1916.

NISBET, THOMAS COOPER (1819–1874), iron manufacturer, only son of John Nisbet (1781–1841) and Harriet Cooper (1789–1863), was born in Statesville, North Carolina, on May 28th, 1819. He was a first cousin of the Hon. Eugenius Aristides Nisbet (1803–1871), distinguished jurist and congressman, who drafted the ordinance of secession of the State of Georgia in January 1861. John Nisbet removed with his family to Athens, Georgia, in 1823. His only son graduated from Franklin College (Athens) in 1839 and soon settled in Macon, where for many years he prospered in the manufacture of iron. On December 28th, 1847, he married Mary Cuthbert Cumming (1823–1893), only daughter of Joseph Cumming (1790–1846) and his first wife, Matilda Ann Poe (1795–1827). There were four children: Joseph Cumming Nisbet (1850–1853), Eliza Clay Nisbet (1852–1857), Harriet (Hattie) Nisbet (1853–1910), and Thomas Cooper Nisbet (1855–1857). Through her stepmother, Mrs. Susan M. Cumming, Mary (Cumming) Nisbet was intimately associated with the family of her brother, the Rev. Dr. Charles Colcock Jones; he performed her wedding ceremony in Savannah in 1847. Thomas Cooper Nisbet died in Macon of consumption on June 22nd, 1874, survived by his wife and one daughter, and was buried in Rose Hill Cemetery. Mary (Cumming) Nisbet spent her later years in Charlotte, North Carolina, in the home of her daughter, Hattie Nisbet, wife of Edward Dilworth Latta. She died in Macon on July 2nd, 1893, and was buried beside her husband. To Mrs. Mary Jones she was always a "special favorite."

NORMAN, JOHN STACY (1815–1885), planter, son of Joseph Norman (1785–1832) and Mary Wilson Stacy (1789–1863), was born in Liberty County, Georgia, on December 31st, 1815. On March 5th, 1839, he married Susan Westbury Quarterman (1822–1890), daughter of John Stewart Quarterman and his third wife, Susannah Myers; there were ten children. John Stacy Norman and his wife were charter members of the Flemington Presbyterian Church at its organization in April 1866. He was one of several "assistant marshals" who helped record the Liberty County Census of 1870. He died on October 22nd, 1885, and was buried in Flemington Cemetery. Susan Westbury (Quarterman) Norman died on December 18th, 1890, and was buried beside her husband.

NORMAN, MARY WILSON (STACY) (1789–1863): Mrs. Joseph Norman, daughter of John Stacy (1761–1818) and Margaret Wilson (1769–1792), widow of Elijah Quarterman, was born in Liberty County, Georgia, on December 23rd, 1789. Her mother died on May 8th, 1792, and her father married second (on November 23rd, 1797) Sarah Quarterman (1778–1826), daughter of William Quarterman and Sarah Stewart. John Stacy represented Liberty County in the state legislature in 1796 and 1797. On March 26th, 1807, Mary Wilson Stacy became the wife of Joseph Norman

(1785–1832), son of John Norman (1754–1793) and Rebecca Quarterman (1758–1825). Eight of their ten children lived to maturity. "Old Lady Norman" attended Mrs. Laura E. Buttolph after the birth of James David Buttolph on October 24th, 1858. She died in Liberty County in November 1863.

NORMAN, WILLIAM SANFORD (1822–1878), lawyer and planter, son of William Norman (1794–1827) and Sarah Ellen Sanford (1801–1871), was born in Walthourville, Liberty County, Georgia, on February 26th, 1822. His father died on April 16th, 1827, and on June 5th, 1828, his mother became the third wife of Thomas Quarterman (1788–1857). After graduating from Franklin College (Athens) in 1841 he studied law and commenced practice in Savannah in 1843. On January 23rd, 1845, he married Susan Lorenna Stacy (1825–1883), daughter of James Stacy and Mary Boon McGowen, of Walthourville; there were ten children. Returning to Liberty County, he settled in Hinesville and practiced law until the outbreak of the Civil War. He also planted extensively. On August 27th, 1861, he was elected captain of the Liberty Volunteers (Company H, 25th Regiment Georgia Infantry); in the spring of 1862 he was not reelected; and on May 11th, 1862, he was relieved from duty. Subsequently he was appointed solicitor of revenue for Liberty and Bryan Counties. After the war he was elected judge of the county court (1866–1870). He then resumed the practice of law. He died of apoplexy at his residence in Flemington on August 15th, 1878, and was buried in Flemington Cemetery. Susan Lorenna (Stacy) Norman died exactly five years later (on August 15th, 1883), and was buried beside her husband.

NORWOOD, WILLIAM GILES (1830–1886), lumber merchant and hotel proprietor, son of the Hon. John W. Norwood, was born in Hillsboro, North Carolina, on January 29th, 1830. In 1849 he removed to Savannah, Georgia, where he engaged in the lumber business until the outbreak of the Civil War. On April 14th, 1857, he married Anna Catherine King (1835–1906), eldest daughter of William King and Sarah Elizabeth McLeod, of Savannah; there were four children. On May 1st, 1861, he enlisted as a private in Captain John B. Gallie's Company (Savannah Artillery), 1st Volunteer Regiment Georgia Artillery. On April 21st, 1862, he enlisted as a private in Captain Joseph S. Claghorn's Company (Chatham Artillery), 1st Volunteer Regiment Georgia Artillery. He was discharged for disability on June 1st, 1863. After the war he lived for ten years in Hillsboro, North Carolina. In 1875 he returned to Savannah, where he was proprietor of the Screven House for one year before removing to Jesup, Georgia, to become proprietor of the Metropolitan Hotel. He resided in Jesup for the rest of his life, engaged chiefly in the lumber business. He died in Savannah on December 26th, 1886, leaving a wife and four children, and was buried in

Jesup Cemetery. According to the Savannah *Morning News* (December 27th, 1886), "He was a man of the strictest integrity and had the respect and confidence of all who knew him." Anna Catherine (King) Norwood died in Jesup on December 10th, 1906, and was buried beside her husband.

OLCOTT, DANIEL G. (1827–1869), stationer and bookseller, was born in Jersey City, New Jersey, in 1827. In early manhood he accompanied his elder brother, William H. Olcott (1825–1868), to Savannah, Georgia, where they engaged for some years in the bookbinding business. On December 13th, 1855, Daniel G. Olcott married Martha Caroline Etheridge (1834–1867), a native of Putman County, Georgia, daughter of William D. Etheridge, a Savannah coal merchant. On July 9th, 1856, he became associated with the firm of John M. Cooper & Company, "wholesale and retail dealers in school and miscellaneous books and foreign and domestic stationery." For many years he was treasurer of the Union Society, a charitable organization. At the outbreak of the Civil War he enlisted as third lieutenant in the Republican Blues (Company C, 1st Regiment Georgia Infantry); on June 1st, 1862, Michael Boyle, a Savannah wood merchant, enlisted as his substitute. In February 1863, at a meeting of "the first company of exempts," he was elected one of twelve officers of "the corps for the defense of the city." In October 1865 John M. Cooper, William H. Olcott, Daniel G. Olcott, and Stephen Farrelly formed a copartnership under the name of Cooper, Olcott & Farrelly, wholesale and retail stationers and booksellers. After Farrelly's withdrawal on August 10th, 1867, the firm continued as Cooper, Olcott & Company, with Daniel G. Olcott as cashier. Martha (Etheridge) Olcott died on December 31st, 1867, leaving a husband and several young children. William H. Olcott died on November 29th, 1868. Less than three months later, on the afternoon of February 17th, 1869, Daniel G. Olcott was found dead in his room above the bookstore. According to the Savannah *Republican* (February 18th, 1869), he had "committed suicide by placing a pistol in his mouth, pulling the trigger, and sending the charge crashing through his brain, producing instant death. . . . It is impossible to assign any other cause for this melancholy event than a fit of temporary insanity, which must have been produced by some sudden and mysterious derangement of his physicial system. He was highly esteemed and respected by all his numerous friends and acquaintances, and his sudden death has filled their hearts with gloom and sorrow." He was buried beside his wife in Laurel Grove Cemetery.

OLMSTEAD, CHARLES HART (1837–1926), commission merchant and banker, son of Jonathan Olmstead (1793–1854) and Eliza Hart (1803–1881), was born in Savannah, Georgia, on April 2nd, 1837. His father, a native of Connecticut, had removed in early manhood to Savannah, where he had settled, married, and for many years prospered in the banking business. Charles Hart Olmstead graduated from the Georgia Military Institute (Marietta) in 1856. Returning to Savannah, he commenced business as a cashier in the firm of Brigham, Baldwin & Company, commission merchants and shipping agents. On January 20th, 1859, he married Florence L. Williams (1838–1909), daughter of Peter J. Williams, of Milledgeville. Late in 1860 he was appointed adjutant of the 1st Volunteer Regiment, and he was serving at Fort Pulaski when it was seized by order of Governor Joseph E. Brown on January 3rd, 1861. After the regiment was reorganized in the spring and mustered into Confederate service he became major (on May 27th, 1861) and colonel (on December 26th, 1861) of the 1st (Olmstead's) Regiment Georgia Infantry. On April 11th, 1862, believing that further resistance would be futile, he surrendered Fort Pulaski to the Federals after a bombardment of a day and a half. Olmstead and his fellow officers were taken prisoner, confined five months on Johnson's Island, Ohio, and exchanged at Vicksburg, Mississippi, on September 20th, 1862. He commanded the 1st Regiment until the end of the war: in the summer of 1863 he was stationed at Battery Wagner, Charleston harbor, and in the spring of 1864 he joined General Joseph E. Johnston in Northwest Georgia. He was wounded near Atlanta on July 22nd, 1864. He later served in Tennessee and North Carolina, and was paroled at Greensboro, North Carolina, on May 1st, 1865. After the war he was a partner in the firm of Brigham, Holst & Company, commission merchants and shipping agents. In 1873 he became treasurer of the Citizens' Mutual Loan Company; he later engaged in private banking. He was for many years active in the affairs of the Georgia Historical Society. Florence (Williams) Olmstead died on June 6th, 1909, and was buried in Laurel Grove Cemetery. Charles Hart Olmstead died on August 17th, 1926, and was buried beside his wife.

OMBERG, NICHOLAS J. (1814–1864), tailor, was born in Norway in 1814. In early manhood he and his two brothers, Peter and Adolph, migrated to the United States and settled in Rome, Georgia. On June 8th, 1837, Nicholas J. Omberg married Sarah C. Fulton (1820–1864), of Clarke County, Georgia; there were ten children. For many years he was ruling elder of the Rome Presbyterian Church. He was by trade a tailor; during the Civil War he directed the work of the Ladies' Benevolent Association of Rome in producing soldiers' garments. On May 18th, 1861, his son, William F. Omberg (1843–1924), enlisted as a private in the Rome Light Guards (Company A, 8th Regiment Georgia Infantry) and went with his company to Virginia; on October 5th, 1863, he was promoted to second lieutenant in Captain H. A. Gartrell's Company, Georgia Cavalry. Sarah (Fulton) Omberg died early in 1864. When Rome was evacuated on May

17th, 1864, at the approach of the Federal army, Omberg stayed behind; when the Federals evacuated Rome on November 11th, 1864, Omberg joined a patrol force of forty Southern men organized to protect the city from marauding scouts. One night late in 1864, running to the defense of a helpless old woman, he was fatally shot by a ruffian, probably one of Colquitt's Scouts. He died the next morning at the residence of his brother-in-law, Thomas J. Perry (1824–1878), and was secretly buried somewhere in Rome.

O'NEILL, JEREMIAH FRANCIS (1790–1870), Roman Catholic clergyman, was born at Lixnaw, County Kerry, Ireland, on October 15th, 1790. After studying for the priesthood he joined one of the educational orders in Dublin. In 1824 he migrated to the United States and settled in Charleston, South Carolina, where he was ordained priest in 1826. For seven years he labored in Charleston and Columbia; in 1833 he removed to Savannah, where he continued as priest till age and infirmity led him to retire. For several years after the Civil War he resided in Baltimore, Maryland, returning to Savannah in 1869. He died at the residence of the bishop of Savannah on July 12th, 1870, and was buried in Cathedral (Catholic) Cemetery. On July 13th, 1870, the Savannah *Republican* printed a long tribute: "It is seldom that we meet in any sphere of life with men of such admirable traits of character as Father O'Neill. Most zealously devoted to the cause of his Divine Master, and counting no personal sacrifice in His service as worthy of a thought, no man was more earnest and happy in his social duties and relations. Ever cheerful, even under the most trying circumstances of life, full of love and sympathy for his fellow men and always ready to make others happy, he was not only a Christian and a gentleman but a most agreeable and entertaining companion. . . . In an acquaintance of many years we have never heard from him an unkind or uncharitable expression toward those who differed from him in religious views, nor have we ever known him to be indifferent to a good or humane cause, whether in or outside his church. In fine, thoroughly unselfish, he lived only to do good, make the world happier and better, and prepare his fellow men for happiness hereafter. Few men who pass from earth can say with stronger assurance: 'I have fought the good fight; I have kept the faith; I have finished my course.'"

OTIS, MERCY (1728–1814), poet, dramatist, and historian, third child of James Otis and Mary Alleyne, and younger sister of James Otis (1725–1783), fiery patriot of the Revolution, was born in Barnstable, Massachusetts, on September 14th, 1728. On November 14th, 1754, she became the wife of James Warren (1726–1808), Massachusetts political leader; there were five sons. The family lived chiefly in Plymouth; for ten years (1781–1791) they lived in Milton. Through her husband and her brother Mercy (Otis) Warren was intimately involved in the major political events of the day, and her taste for literature and politics found expression in numerous plays and books, including *The Adulateur* (1773) and *The Group* (1775), two political satires; *Poems Dramatic and Miscellaneous* (1790); and *History of the Rise, Progress, and Termination of the American Revolution* (3 vols., 1805). She died on October 19th, 1814. In referring to Mercy Otis as "Mrs. Otis" (April 30th, 1862) Charles Colcock Jones, Jr., erred; but his error is understandable, since Mercy Otis was the sister of James Otis, opponent of the writs of assistance and the Stamp Act, and the Otis name is conspicuously linked with Revolutionary zeal.

OWEN, JOHN (1616–1638), Nonconformist clergyman, second son of the Rev. Henry Owen, was born in Stadhampton, Oxfordshire, England, in 1616. He attended Queen's College (Oxford), from which he received his B.A. (1632), M.A. (1635), and D.D. (1653). He served as pastor of many churches throughout his long career and was vice-chancellor of Oxford, by appointment of Oliver Cromwell, from 1652 to 1658. He was one of the most eminent clergymen of his day. His numerous published works include *The Grace and Duty of Being Spiritually-Minded* (1681), subsequently reissued in many editions. He died in London on August 24th, 1683, and was buried in Bunhill Fields.

OWENS, GEORGE SAVAGE (1825–1897), lawyer and planter, son of George Welshman Owens (1786–1856) and Sarah Wallace (1789–1865), was born in Savannah, Georgia, on March 25th, 1825. His father, a graduate of Cambridge University (England), was a distinguished lawyer, mayor of Savannah (1832–1833), and member of Congress (1835–1839). George Savage Owens graduated from Oglethorpe University in 1843. Returning to Savannah, he studied law in the office of Charlton & Ward (Robert Milledge Charlton and John Elliott Ward) and was later admitted as partner of Charlton, Ward & Owens. After the death of Charlton on January 18th, 1854, the firm became Ward & Owens; on January 1st, 1857, when Charles Colcock Jones, Jr., was admitted as partner, it became Ward, Owens & Jones; early in 1859, when Owens retired from the firm and Henry Rootes Jackson was admitted as partner, it became Ward, Jackson & Jones. After the war Owens gave up the practice of law and devoted himself largely to planting. He was a director of the Central Railroad of Georgia. For many years he was president of the Savannah Jockey Club; as the Savannah *Morning News* (June 13th, 1897) observed, he was "known throughout the country by all racing men as one of the best of turfmen." In 1850 he married Elizabeth Gordon Wayne (1825–1903), daughter of William Clifford Wayne and Ann Gordon. George Savage Owens died in Savannah on June 13th, 1897, survived by his wife and nine children, and was buried in Laurel Grove Cemetery. Elizabeth Gordon (Wayne) Owens died on February 28th, 1903, and was buried beside her husband.

PALMER, BENJAMIN MORGAN (1818–1902), Presbyterian clergyman, son of the Rev. Edward Palmer and Sarah Bunce, was born in Charleston, South Carolina, on January 25th, 1818. He was a brother of the Rev. Edward Porter Palmer (1826–1905). After attending Amherst College for two years (1832–1834) and teaching for two years (1834–1836) he graduated from Franklin College (Athens) in 1838 and from Columbia Theological Seminary in 1841. He was pastor of the First Presbyterian Church, Savannah, Georgia (1841–1842); the First Presbyterian Church, Columbia, South Carolina (1842–1856); and the First Presbyterian Church, New Orleans, Louisiana (1856–1902). He was also professor of church history and government at Columbia Theological Seminary (1853–1856). He was moderator of the first General Assembly of the Southern Presbyterian Church meeting in Augusta, Georgia, in December 1861. For many years he was associate editor of *The Southern Presbyterian Review*; he was also author of several theological works. He received the honorary degree of doctor of divinity from Oglethorpe University in 1852, and the honorary degree of doctor of laws from Westminster College (Fulton, Missouri) in 1870. On October 7th, 1841, he married Mary Augusta McConnell (1822–1888), daughter of Dr. Robert C. McConnell (1788–1826) and Sarah Ann Walthour (1803–1885), and hence stepdaughter of the Rev. Dr. George Howe (1802–1883), second husband of Sarah Ann Walthour and professor at Columbia Theological Seminary. He died in New Orleans on May 25th, 1902. He was a brilliant pulpit orator, and at the height of his long career he was, as Charles Colcock Jones, Jr., observed (September 16th, 1889), "the most distinguished divine in the Presbyterian Church."

PALMER, EDWARD PORTER (1826–1905), Presbyterian clergyman, son of the Rev. Edward Palmer and Sarah Bunce, was born in Summerville, South Carolina, on July 3rd, 1826. He was a brother of the Rev. Benjamin Morgan Palmer (1818–1902). After graduating from Franklin College (Athens) with first honor in 1845 and from Columbia Theological Seminary in 1848 he served various rural churches in South Carolina for seven years (1850–1857); he was then pastor of the First Presbyterian Church, Marietta, Georgia (1857–1867); professor of metaphysics at Louisiana State University (1867–1869); pastor of the Jackson Street Presbyterian Church, Mobile, Alabama (1871–1881); and president of Austin College, Sherman, Texas (1882–1884). In his later years he was pastor in Abilene, Texas (1885–1886); New Orleans, Louisiana (1886–1887); Oxford, Mississippi (1887–1892); and Harrisonburg, Virginia (1893–1904). In the spring of 1854 he declined a call as pastor of Midway Church, Liberty County, Georgia. On July 19th, 1861, he was elected chaplain of the 14th Regiment Georgia Infantry; he served until October 13th, 1861. He received the honorary degree of doctor of divinity from

Louisiana State University in 1874. In November 1850 he married Ann Buchanan (1827–1877), daughter of John Buchanan (1790–1862) and Harriet Yongue (1791–1875), of Winnsboro, South Carolina; their only son, Wallace Thornwell Palmer (1867–1935), became a Presbyterian clergyman. Ann (Buchanan) Palmer died in Mobile, Alabama, on May 28th, 1877. In November 1886 Edward Porter Palmer married Mrs. Bessie Kirkland, of Galveston, Texas. He died in 1905. "Rev. Mr. Palmer now writes some of his sermons," observed Mrs. Eliza G. Robarts on August 25th, 1860, "and we think it has improved his preaching." "If he were only a better preacher!" wrote Mary Eliza Robarts on December 30th, 1862. "I feel sometimes as if I were in a spiritual stupor when I come out of church without one idea gained."

PALMER, SAMUEL (1800–1867), hardware merchant, son of Isaac Palmer and Mary Bright, was born in Providence, Rhode Island, on July 30th, 1800. In 1824 he migrated to Darien, Georgia, where he engaged successfully in planting and served many terms as mayor, and where (on February 21st, 1826) he married Caroline Dexter (1807–1871). In 1852 he settled in Savannah, where he joined his eldest son, Samuel B. Palmer (1828–1913), in the firm of Samuel Palmer & Son, hardware merchants. His younger son, Herbert A. Palmer (1833–1917), also a hardware merchant, was employed from 1852 to 1866 in the firm of Henry D. Weed. In 1863 Samuel Palmer suffered a stroke of paralysis. He died in Flemington, Liberty County, at the residence of his daughter, Caroline America Palmer (1841–1878), wife of Thomas Goulding Stacy (1839–1893), on July 29th, 1867, and was buried in Laurel Grove Cemetery, Savannah. As the Savannah *Republican* (July 30th, 1867) observed, "This most estimable man" had "an enlightened judgment, a constant flow of genial spirits, a mind well cultured, and a heart full of noble aims." For several years his wife lived with her two sons in Savannah; she died in Brunswick, Georgia, at the residence of her daughter, Caroline America (Palmer) Stacy, on August 13th, 1871, and was buried beside her husband. In 1866 Samuel B. Palmer and Herbert A. Palmer joined John H. Deppish (1838–1876) in the firm of Palmer & Deppish, wholesale and retail hardware merchants; after the death of Deppish on December 12th, 1876, the business continued for many years under the firm name of Palmer Brothers.

PARKER, THEODORE (1810–1860), Unitarian clergyman, youngest son of John Parker (1761–1836) and Hannah Stearns, was born in Lexington, Massachusetts, on August 24th, 1810. He graduated from the Harvard Divinity School in 1836. On April 20th, 1837, he married Lydia Cabot, daughter of John Cabot, of Newton, Massachusetts. He was pastor of the West Roxbury Unitarian Church (1837–1845) and minister of the new Twenty-Eighth Congregational Society of Boston (1845–1859). Through his passion for social

reform, manifested particularly in his support
of abolitionism, he made ardent friends and bitter enemies. He participated dramatically in efforts to rescue fugitive slaves William and
Ellen Craft (November 1850) and Thomas
Sims (April 1851). When Anthony Burns, another fugitive slave, was arrested in Boston in
May 1854, Parker's plan to storm the courthouse and rescue the prisoner miscarried;
Parker was indicted, but a year later (April
1855) his indictment was dismissed. Illness
forced him to retire from public life in January 1859; he sailed for Europe in February
1859, summered in London and Paris, wintered
in Rome, and died in Florence on May 10th,
1860. He was buried in the Protestant Cemetery. His collected works, edited by Frances
P. Cobbe, were published in London (14 vols.,
1863–1870); they were translated into German by Johannes Zeithen and published in
Leipzig (5 vols., 1854–1861). Parker is said
to be the source of Lincoln's classic phrase:
"government of the people, by the people, and
for the people."

PARRISH, EDWARD (1822–1872), phar-
macist and educator, seventh son of Dr. Joseph
Parrish (1779–1840) and Susanna Cox (1788–
1851), was born in Philadelphia, Pennsylvania,
on May 31st, 1822. At the age of sixteen he
was apprenticed to his elder brother, Dillwyn
Parrish, proprietor of a drugstore at the southwest corner of 8th and Arch Streets. While
serving his apprenticeship he attended the
Philadelphia College of Pharmacy and graduated in 1842. In the following year he purchased a drugstore at the northwest corner of
9th and Chestnut Streets, and six years later,
in 1849, he opened a school of practical pharmacy in the rear of his store for the training
of medical students insufficiently versed in
pharmaceutical aspects of their profession. From
1850 to 1864, in partnership with his brother
Dillwyn, he operated a drugstore and continued
to conduct his school at the corner of 8th and
Arch Streets. In 1864 he joined the faculty
of the Philadelphia School of Pharmacy, where
he was professor of materia medica (1864–
1867) and professor of the theory and practice
of pharmacy (1867–1872). He was largely instrumental in founding Swarthmore College,
of which he was secretary of the board of
managers (1864–1868) and president (1868–
1871). He was a charter member of the American Pharmaceutical Association (1852), secretary (1853), first vice-president (1866), and
president (1868). He was author of *An Introduction to Practical Pharmacy* (1855) and
numerous articles published in *The American
Journal of Pharmacy* and *Proceedings of the
American Pharmaceutical Association*. In 1849
he married Margaret Hunt, of Philadelphia;
there were five children. He died at Fort Sill,
Indian Territory, on September 8th, 1872,
while fulfilling an appointment by the United
States government to visit certain Indian tribes.

PARSONS, ELISHA (1806–1889), dentist,
was born in Northampton, Massachusetts, in
December 1806. After attending Jefferson Med-

ical College (Philadelphia) and the Cincinnati
Medical College he practiced dentistry for some
years in Cincinnati and Cleveland before settling in Savannah, Georgia, in 1843. He was for
many years the leading dentist in Georgia. He
was one of the founders of the Georgia Dental
Association and served as its first president. He
was also an ardent and accomplished horticul-
turalist, and for many years he and his son,
Edward H. Parsons (1832–1914), operated a
nursery at Jasper Springs on the Augusta road
two miles west of Savannah. "Dr. E. Parsons
invites the lovers of the beautiful in the floral
kingdom to visit his gardens at Jasper Springs"
(Savannah *Morning News,* October 19th,
1854). "Jasper Springs Nursery has choice
roses, evergreens, flowering shrubs and grape-
vines, and also a collection of camellias, tomatoes, and peaches" (Savannah *Morning
News,* December 8th, 1856). Elisha Parsons
died in Savannah on August 21st, 1889, survived by two children, and was buried beside
his wife, Mary (1811–1888), in Laurel Grove
Cemetery. Typical is the following "card" appearing in the Savannah *Morning News* (May
2nd, 1870): "Dr. E. Parsons. Those desiring
his services will find him up with the times in
all branches of his profession. Thankful for
former patronage, he will use every available
means to avoid pain in his operations. Try
him."

PARSONS, THEOPHILUS (1797–1882),
lawyer and educator, son of Theophilus Parsons (1750–1813) and Elizabeth Greenleaf, was
born in Newburyport, Massachusetts, on May
17th, 1797. After graduating from Harvard
College in 1815 he read law in the office of
William Prescott, traveled in Europe, and on
his return practiced his profession in Taunton
(1822–1827) and Boston (1827–1848). He
was professor at Dane Law School, Harvard
University (1848–1869). He was author of
three series of *Essays* (1845, 1856, 1862), *The
Law of Conscience* (1853), *Slavery* (1863),
The Infinite and the Finite (1872), *Outlines
of the Religion and Philosophy of Swedenborg*
(1875), and numerous legal works. In 1823 he
married Catherine Amory Chandler, who bore
him seven children. He died in Cambridge
on January 26th, 1882.

PAUL, ELIZABETH STADLEMAN (1833–
1918), daughter of Theodore Sedgwick Paul
(1798–1887) and Elizabeth Cooper (1810–
1879), was born in Belvidere, New Jersey, on
October 29th, 1833. Her father, a businessman,
was one of the founders of the Second Presbyterian Church, Belvidere, and for many years
an elder; he was a brother of Sidney Paul
(1790–1850), wife of Bennington Gill and
mother of the four Gill sisters (Mary, Sarah,
Sidney, and Emily) who conducted a seminary
for young ladies in Philadelphia from 1845 to
1856. "Lizzie" Paul was thus a first cousin of
the four Gill sisters who were her teachers and
chaperones in Philadelphia in the early
1850s. On November 5th, 1857, she became
the wife of her second cousin, Henry Neill Paul
(1835–1899), son of John Rodman Paul

(1802–1877) and Elizabeth Duffield Neill (1809–1866). Her husband, a graduate of the University of Pennsylvania (1853), was a civil engineer engaged in railroad construction; shortly after their marriage they settled in Philadelphia, where he engaged in banking and insurance. He was a director of the Philadelphia Savings Fund and the Mutual Assurance Company. He was an elder of Calvary Presbyterian Church, Philadelphia, for thirty-nine years (1860–1899). He died in Atlanta, Georgia, on April 8th, 1899. Elizabeth Stadleman (Paul) Paul died on June 26th, 1918, survived by one son; three of her four children had died in infancy.

PAYNE, GEORGE (1781–1848), Congregational clergyman, youngest son of Alexander Payne (1741–1819), a Baptist clergyman, and Mary Dyer (1742–1814), was born in Stow-on-the-Wold, Gloucestershire, England, on September 17th, 1781. After graduating from Glasgow University in 1807 he was assistant to the Rev. Edward Parsons in Leeds (1807–1808), coadjutor to the Rev. George Lambert in Hull (1808–1812), and pastor of a congregation of seceders in Edinburgh (1812–1823). He then served as theological tutor of the Blackburn Academy, Lancashire (1823–1829), and of the Western Academy, Exeter (1829–1848). He was chairman of the Congregational Union of England and Wales (1836–1848). His numerous published works include *Elements of Mental and Moral Science* (1828), *The Separation of Church and State* (1834), *The Doctrine of Original Sin* (1845), and *Lectures on Christian Theology* (2 vols., 1850), containing a "Memoir" by the Rev. John Pyer and "Reminiscences" by the Rev. Ralph Wardlaw. He died in Devenport on June 19th, 1848, and was buried in Mount Street Chapel.

PEASE, PHILANDER PITKIN (1821–1900), merchant, son of Noah Pease and Lucinda Russell, was born in Somers, Connecticut, on February 18th, 1821. In 1846, after teaching school for several years in Trenton, New Jersey, he accompanied his brother, Henry Martyn Pease (1832–1854), to Darien, Georgia, where their double first cousin, Theodore Pitkin Pease (1813–1878), was already established in business. In 1851 Philander Pitkin Pease married Emma Cornelia Powell (1829–1894), of Darien, daughter of Allen Beverly Powell and Mary Calder, and sister of Augusta J. Powell (1827–1909), wife of Theodore Pitkin Pease. At the outbreak of the Civil War he removed to Atlanta, where he established the firm of P. P. Pease & Company, "wholesale grocers and commission merchants, and dealers in yarns, domestics, rope, bagging, grain, and fertilizers." On August 3rd, 1863, he enlisted as a private in Company E, Atlanta Fire Battalion (also designated Company E, 3rd Battalion Georgia State Guards), mustered into service for six months for the defense of Atlanta, and not to be called beyond the limits of Fulton County. After the war he resumed his business in Atlanta; on April 11th, 1866, he became a

charter member of the newly organized Atlanta Board of Trade. In 1875 he removed to Louisville, Kentucky, where he continued in the grocery business until 1889, when he settled in Chicago. For several years he was a traveling salesman for eastern grocery houses; in 1895 he established his own firm, Philander P. Pease & Company. Emma Cornelia (Powell) Pease died in Chicago on July 27th, 1894, and was buried in Graceland Cemetery. Philander Pitkin Pease died in Chicago on January 5th, 1900, from injuries sustained in a streetcar accident two days before; he was buried beside his wife. His five children survived.

PECK, ADELINE M. (1842–1863), only daughter of Marcus M. Peck (1817–1861) and his first wife, Adeline S. Powell (1825–1842), was born in McIntosh County, Georgia, in July 1842. Her mother died on July 17th, 1842, from complications in childbirth, and "Addie" became the ward of her maternal grandmother, Mary Calder, wife of Allen Beverly Powell. Later she became an inmate of the household of her maternal aunt, Emma Cornelia Powell (1829–1894), wife of Philander Pitkin Pease (1821–1900), Darien merchant. On June 17th, 1845, her father, a steamboat captain, married Elizabeth M. Speissegger (1824–1878), daughter of Samuel L. Speissegger (1792–1867) and Martha B. Millen (1800–1858), of Savannah. Adeline M. Peck never married. She died of typhoid fever in Atlanta at the residence of her aunt, Emma (Powell) Pease, on December 17th, 1863, and was buried in the Powell family cemetery on "the Ridge" near Darien, McIntosh County. Her eulogy, published in the Savannah *Republican* (December 30th, 1863) and reprinted in *The Southern Presbyterian* (February 4th, 1864), was written by her pastor, the Rev. R. Q. Mallard: "To a character of rare natural loveliness, divine grace, as we humbly believe, added, during her protracted illness, the crowning excellence of true piety; and while her many relatives and friends mourn the death of one so young, so truthful, so affectionate and tenderly beloved, they derive precious consolation from the pleasing testimony she was permitted to give of her preparation for eternity." According to Mrs. Mary S. Mallard she was "the pet of the whole family."

PECK, RACHEL S. (BEALS) (BETTS) (1817–1887): *Mrs. Theodore P. Peck*, dressmaker, was born in Screven County, Georgia, in 1817. In childhood she removed with her parents to Savannah. She married first (on March 18th, 1833) George Betts; after his death she married second (on February 13th, 1851) Theodore P. Peck, an engineer. She was for some years a dressmaker. She died in Savannah on August 11th, 1887, and was buried beside her mother, Ann Beals (1789–1874), in Laurel Grove Cemetery. On January 15th, 1868, the Savannah *Daily News & Herald* carried the following notice: "Mr. Theodore Peck of this city has invented and patented a smoke stack for locomotive, marine, and stationary engines, its peculiarity being the impossibility of the escape of sparks from the boiler furnace, preventing any opportunity of conflagration from this pregnant source. The importance of this invention can only be properly estimated when the combustibility of our Southern products is taken into consideration. The smoke stack is now in use on the Atlantic & Gulf, the Central, and the Southwestern Railroads."

PEIRCE, BENJAMIN (1809–1880), mathematician and astronomer, third child of Benjamin Peirce (1778–1831) and Lydia Ropes Nicholls, was born in Salem, Massachusetts, on April 4th, 1809. His father was librarian of Harvard College (1826–1831) and compiled the last printed catalogue of the Harvard Library (3 vols. in 4, 1830–1831). Benjamin Peirce graduated from Harvard College in 1829. After teaching two years in association with George Bancroft at the Round Hill School, Northampton, Massachusetts, he joined the faculty of Harvard University, where he was tutor in mathematics (1831–1833), university professor of mathematics and astronomy (1833–1842), and Perkins professor of mathematics and astronomy (1842–1880). He was the foremost American mathematician of his time. He was a member of the American Philosophical Society (1842), an associate of the Royal Astronomical Society of London (1850), a fellow of the American Academy of Arts and Sciences (1858), a corresponding member of the British Association for the Advancement of Science (1861), and an honorary fellow of the Royal Society of Edinburgh (1867). He was a founder of the Harvard Observatory (1843), one of five planners and organizers of the Smithsonian Institution (1847), and one of fifty incorporators of the National Academy of Sciences (1863). He was author of numerous mathematical works. On July 23rd, 1833, he married Sarah Hunt Mills, daughter of Elijah Hunt Mills (1776–1829), congressman (1815–1819) and United States senator (1820–1827); there were five children. He died on October 6th, 1880. His eldest son, James Mills Peirce (1834–1906), was associated for forty-five years with Harvard University, where he was assistant professor of mathematics (1861–1869), university professor of mathematics (1869–1885), and Perkins professor of mathematics (1885–1906); he was also dean of the graduate school (1890–1895) and dean of the faculty (1895–1898). His second son, Charles Sanders Peirce (1839–1914), was a distinguished philosopher, logician, and scientist, and the founder of pragmatism. His youngest son, Herbert Henry Davis Peirce (1849–1916), was a diplomat.

PELOT, JOSEPH S. (1791–1833), lawyer, was born in Savannah, Georgia, on January 1st, 1791. On November 6th, 1813, he was commissioned solicitor general of the eastern circuit of Georgia, a post in which he was, according to the Rev. Dr. Charles Colcock Jones (December 18th, 1856), "too lazy and pleasure-loving" to copy out his own writs. In March 1813 he married Jane E. Maxwell. In his later years he was justice of the peace. He died in Savannah on October 16th, 1833, survived by his wife and one son, and was buried in Colonial Cemetery. In the register of Christ Episcopal Church, Savannah, he was recorded as "an excommunicate person."

PEMBERTON, JOHN CLIFFORD (1814–1881), Confederate soldier, second son of John Pemberton and Rebecca Clifford, was born in Philadelphia, Pennsylvania, on August 10th, 1814. After graduating from the United States Military Academy in 1837 he fought in the Florida Indian Wars (1837–1839) and in the Mexican War (1846–1848); he became captain on September 16th, 1850. On January 18th, 1848, he married Martha Thompson, daughter of William Henry Thompson, of Norfolk, Virginia; there were five children. At the outbreak of the Civil War he refused a commission as colonel in the Union army and offered his services to the Confederacy. He rose rapidly from lieutenant colonel (April 28th, 1861) to colonel (May 8th, 1861) to brigadier general (June 17th, 1861) to major general (February 15th, 1862) to lieutenant general (October 13th, 1862). In March 1862 he was placed in command of the Department of South Carolina, Georgia, and Florida. ("Most of his reputation is, I think, before him," wrote Charles Colcock Jones, Jr., on March 18th, 1862.) In October 1862 he was placed in command of the Department of Tennessee, Mississippi, and Eastern Louisiana; on July 4th, 1863, he surrendered Vicksburg to Grant. He then resigned his commission and served as inspector of ordnance, with rank of colonel, for the rest of the war. For eleven years (1865–1876) he lived on his farm near Warrenton, Virginia; in 1876 he returned to Philadelphia to live with his brothers and sisters. He died in Penllyn on July 13th, 1881, and was buried in Laurel Hill Cemetery, Philadelphia.

PETRIE, GEORGE HOLLINSHEAD WHITEFIELD (1812–1885), Presbyterian clergyman, son of George Petrie and Esther Stiles Tucker, was born in Charleston, South Carolina, on May 5th, 1812. He graduated from the College of Charleston in 1831 and from Columbia Theological Seminary in 1834. After serving several rural churches in South Carolina he was pastor in Washington, Georgia (1838–1851); Charleston, South Carolina (1851–1854); and Marietta, Georgia (1854–1857). For twenty-eight years (1857–1885) he was pastor of the First Presbyterian Church in Montgomery, Alabama. On February 16th, 1837, he married Mary Jane Prince (1817–1893), of Cheraw, South Carolina, daughter of Lawrence Prince and Charlotte Benton; there were three children. He received the honorary degree of doctor of divinity from the University of Alabama in 1859. He died in Montgomery on May 8th, 1885, and was buried in Oakwood Cemetery. His only son, the Rev. George Laurens Petrie (1840–1931), a graduate of Oglethorpe University (1859), was pastor of the First Presbyterian Church, Charlottesville, Virginia, for fifty years (1878–1928).

PETTIGREW, MARTHA ROSABELLA (FAHM) (1840–1918): *Mrs. George W. Pettigrew,* was born in Georgia in 1840. On August 29th, 1858, in Brunswick, Georgia, she became the wife of George W. Pettigrew (1839–1862), a teacher in the local school; there were two children. On August 1st, 1861, George W. Pettigrew enlisted as second sergeant in Company A, 26th Regiment Georgia Infantry; he subsequently became first sergeant (September 23rd, 1861), second lieutenant (May 8th, 1862), and first lieutenant (December 3rd, 1862). On December 13th, 1862, he was wounded at Fredericksburg and taken prisoner; he died in a military hospital in Washington, D.C., on December 30th, 1862, and was buried in Old Colonial Cemetery. During his absence in service his wife and children lived in Waynesville, Wayne County, Georgia, with his mother, Ann C. Clark (1809–1878), wife of Elihu Clark. In 1868 Martha Rosabella (Fahm) Pettigrew became the wife of Alfred E. Green (1838–1920), a Brunswick carpenter; there were three children. She died in Brunswick on July 30th, 1918, survived by four of her five children, and was buried in Palmetto Cemetery.

PHILLIPS, WENDELL (1811–1884), orator and abolitionist, son of John Phillips and Sarah Walley, was born in Boston, Massachusetts, on November 29th, 1811. After graduating from Harvard College in 1831 and from the Harvard Law School in 1834 he commenced practice in Boston and soon became prominently identified with the antislavery cause. Abandoning law, he became a lecturer on the lyceum platform, where his eloquence and charm, together with his wealth and social prestige, made him a powerful proponent of abolitionism. On October 12th, 1837, he married Ann Terry Greene; there were no children. His wife was a disciple of William Lloyd Garrison (1805–1879), editor of *The Liberator,* to which Phillips frequently contributed. Like Garrison he assailed the Constitution for its compromises on the slavery issue and preferred disunion to further connection with the slave states. After the war he advocated prohibition, penal reform, labor reform, and woman's suffrage. He died in Boston on February 2nd, 1884, and was buried in the Granary Burying Ground.

PHILLIPS, WILLIAM (1804–1877), civil engineer, was born in South Carolina in 1804. He was identified all his life with Augusta, Georgia. For many years he was city surveyor and architect, and at the height of his career he was engineer in charge of constructing the Augusta Canal. In 1844 the city council, acting on his recommendation, elected a board of commissioners (with Henry Harford Cumming as president) "for the purpose of constructing a canal, from a point in the Savannah River about seven miles above, to the city of Augusta, for manufacturing purposes, and for the better securing of an abundant supply of water to the city." Work on this gigantic enterprise was commenced in May 1845 and completed early in 1847 at a total cost of two million dollars. In 1826 William Phillips married Mary V. Duffy (1808–1863), a native of Hillsboro, North Carolina; she drowned in the Augusta Canal on December 3rd, 1863, and was buried in Magnolia Cemetery. William Phillips died in Augusta on November 11th, 1877, survived by eight children, and was buried beside his wife.

PHILLIPS, WILLIAM (1824–1908), lawyer and Confederate soldier, was born in Asheville, North Carolina, on July 8th, 1824. After a boyhood spent in Habersham County, Georgia, he attended Franklin College (Athens). By 1850 he had settled in Marietta, Georgia, where he studied law in the office of the Hon. Charles James McDonald (1793–1860), governor of Georgia (1839–1843), and became one of the most prominent and successful lawyers in the state. At the outbreak of the Civil War he was appointed brigadier general and placed in command of the Fourth Brigade Georgia Volunteers; he organized two camps of instruction in Cobb County: Camp Brown (at Smyrna) and Camp McDonald (at Big Shanty). On August 1st, 1861, he resigned and formed Phillips' Legion, of which he became colonel; this command, consisting of fifteen companies of infantry, six companies of cavalry, and one company of artillery, fought with distinction from the Seven Days' Battle to Appomattox. After the war Phillips returned to Marietta and resumed the practice of law; he served five terms in the state legislature and was for many years solicitor general of the Blue Ridge circuit. In 1851 he married Catherine Anna Mongin Smith (1830–1853), eldest daughter of James Mongin Smith and Sarah E. Cole; she died in St. Marys, Georgia, on March 25th, 1853. William Phillips died in Marietta on September 24th, 1908, survived by his second wife, Mary Waterman, and five children, and was buried in Citizens Cemetery.

PILLOW, GIDEON JOHNSON (1806–1878), Confederate soldier, son of Gideon Pillow and Anne Payne, was born in Williamson County, Tennessee, on June 8th, 1806. After graduating from the University of Nashville in 1827 he commenced the practice of law in Columbia, Tennessee, where he was for some years a partner of James Knox Polk. He married Mary Martin, who bore him ten children. During the Mexican War (1846–1848) he served as brigadier general, later major general, of volunteers and was twice wounded. Prior to the Civil War he opposed secession and favored compromise, but when hostilities commenced he supported the South and became brigadier general in the Confederate army. At Fort Donelson (February 1862) he and General John B. Floyd escaped before the Confederate surrender; for six months (March–August 1862) he was suspended for "grave errors of judgment in the military operations which resulted in the surrender of the army." He subsequently held no important command. After the war he practiced law for some years in Memphis, Tennessee. He died in Helena, Arkansas, on October 8th, 1878.

PITTMAN, DANIEL (1835–1886), lawyer and magistrate, son of Daniel N. Pittman (1793–1871), was born in Gwinnett County, Georgia, in 1835. His father, a native of Columbia County, Georgia, had spent much of his life in Gwinnett County; in 1851 he removed with his family to Atlanta. In his early teens Daniel Pittman was sent to Dalton, Georgia, to learn the printer's trade; while there he read law, and when he settled in Atlanta in 1853 he entered the law office of M. A. Bell and prepared himself for the bar. He was clerk of the inferior court for four years (1858–1861). On July 2nd, 1861, he married Louisa J. Neal (1840–1918), daughter of John Neal, one of the pioneer settlers of Atlanta. On May 3rd, 1862, he became first lieutenant, second Company C, 1st Confederate Regiment Infantry (Fulton County, Georgia); on September 4th, 1863, he was elected captain. Two weeks later, on September 19th, 1863, he was severely wounded in the right leg at Chickamauga and permanently disabled. He returned to civilian life, and on May 21st, 1864, he was elected ordinary of Fulton County to succeed Robert E. Mangum, deceased. Pittman was the second ordinary in the history of Fulton County, and he served for sixteen years (1864–1880). In 1885 he suffered a stroke of paralysis, and on May 23rd, 1886, he dropped dead on Whitehall Street near Hunter while talking with two friends. His wife and five children survived. He was buried in Westview Cemetery. According to the Atlanta *Constitution* (May 24th, 1886), "Judge Pittman was an active politician all his life. . . . He was equipped with a good lot of jokes, and told them in an entertaining manner. . . . He had a faculty of remembering everybody he met, and made friends without trouble. . . . Judge Pittman was a capable, competent, and honest official, a true friend, a good citizen, a devoted husband, and a loving father."

PLUMER, WILLIAM SWAN (1802–1880), Presbyterian clergyman, son of William Plumer and Catherine McAlester, was born in Greensburg, Pennsylvania, on July 26th, 1802. He graduated from Washington College (Lexington, Virginia) in 1825 and attended Princeton Theological Seminary for one year (1825–1826). After several years as a home missionary in Virginia and North Carolina he was pastor of the Tabb Street Presbyterian Church, Petersburg, Virginia (1831–1834); the First Presbyterian Church, Richmond, Virginia (1834–1847); and the Franklin Street Presbyterian Church, Baltimore, Maryland (1847–1854). For eight years (1854–1862) he was professor of didactic and pastoral theology in Western Theological Seminary (Allegheny, Pennsylvania). He was stated supply of the Arch Street Presbyterian Church, Philadelphia (1862–1865) and pastor of the Second Presbyterian Church, Pottsville, Pennsylvania (1865–1867). For thirteen years (1867–1880)

he was professor of theology at Columbia Theological Seminary. On June 11th, 1829, he married Eliza (Garden) Hassell, of Hillsboro, North Carolina; she died on October 30th, 1878. In 1838 he received the honorary degree of doctor of divinity from three institutions: Washington College (Pennsylvania), Lafayette College (Pennsylvania), and the College of New Jersey (Princeton). In 1857 he received the honorary degree of doctor of laws from the University of Mississippi. He died in Baltimore on October 22nd, 1880.

POLK, JAMES KNOX (1795–1849), eleventh president of the United States, eldest son of Samuel Polk (1772–1827) and Jane Knox (1776–1852), was born in Mecklenburg County, North Carolina, on November 2nd, 1795. In 1806 his father, a farmer, settled with his family in the valley of Duck River, Maury County, Tennessee. James Knox Polk graduated from the University of North Carolina in 1818; returning to Tennessee, he studied law in the office of the Hon. Felix Grundy and commenced practice in Columbia. He soon rose to prominence. On January 1st, 1824, he married Sarah Childress (1803–1891), daughter of Joel Childress, a prosperous farmer near Murfreesboro; there were no children. He was chief clerk of the state senate (1821–1823); member of the state house of representatives (1823–1825); member of Congress (1825–1839); governor of Tennessee (1839–1841); and president of the United States (1845–1849). Returning to Nashville, he purchased the mansion of the Hon. Felix Grundy located at the corner of Vine Street (now Seventh Avenue) and Union Street. He died there on June 15th, 1849. He was buried temporarily in City Cemetery and reinterred on May 22nd, 1850, in a mausoleum erected on the lawn of the Polk residence. His widow continued to occupy the house, living in retirement and receiving the calls of dignitaries and official bodies, until her death on August 14th, 1891. She was buried beside her husband. In 1893 their remains were removed to the grounds of the state capitol.

POLK, LEONIDAS (1806–1866), Protestant Episcopal bishop, son of William Polk (1758–1834) and Sarah Hawkins, and kinsman of James Knox Polk (1795–1849), eleventh president of the United States, was born in Raleigh, North Carolina, on April 10th, 1806. After attending the University of North Carolina for two years (1821–1823) he graduated from the United States Military Academy in 1827; influenced by the Rev. Dr. Charles Pettit McIlvaine (1799–1873), chaplain at West Point, he resigned his commission within six months and entered the Virginia Theological Seminary. He was ordained deacon (April 1830) and priest (May 1831). In May 1830 he married Frances Devereux, of Raleigh. In 1838 he was appointed missionary bishop of the Southwest (Alabama, Mississippi, Louisiana, Arkansas, and a part of Indian Territory); in 1841 he was appointed bishop of Louisiana. Together with the Rt.

Rev. James Hervey Otey, bishop of Tennessee, and the Rt. Rev. Stephen Elliott, bishop of Georgia, he founded the University of the South at Sewanee, Tennessee; he laid the cornerstone on October 9th, 1860. During the Civil War he was commissioned major general (June 25th, 1861) and lieutenant general (October 10th, 1862) in the Confederate army. He fought at Shiloh, Perryville, and Murfreesboro. He was killed at Pine Mountain, near Marietta, Georgia, on June 14th, 1864. He was the only graduate of West Point ever to become a bishop, and the only bishop North or South to fight in the Civil War. His daughter, Susan Rayner Polk (1842–1921), became the second wife of Dr. Joseph Jones (1833–1896), son of the Rev. Dr. Charles Colcock Jones, on June 21st, 1870.

POPE, JOHN (1822–1892), Union soldier, son of Nathaniel Pope (1784–1850) and Lucretia Backus, was born in Louisville, Kentucky, on March 16th, 1822. He graduated from the United States Military Academy in 1842. After serving four years with the topographical engineers he fought in the Mexican War (1846–1848); returning to the topographical engineers, he served six years surveying railway routes in the West. He married Clara Pomeroy Horton on September 15th, 1859. On July 29th, 1861, he was appointed brigadier general of volunteers (to rank from May 17th, 1861) and ordered to General Frémont in Missouri; on March 21st, 1862, he was appointed major general of volunteers and ordered to General Halleck in Mississippi. On June 26th, 1862, he was ordered to Virginia to organize and concentrate the separate Federal forces into the Army of Virginia; while there, on July 14th, 1862, he was appointed brigadier general in the regular army. After his defeat at Second Manassas (August 27th–30th, 1862) he was relieved of command; he spent the rest of the war in the Department of the Northwest. After the war he commanded the Third Military District (Georgia, Alabama, and Florida) in 1867; the Department of the Lakes (1868–1870); the Department of the Missouri (1870–1883); and the Department of California (1883–1886). On October 26th, 1882, he was promoted to major general. He died in Sandusky, Ohio, on September 23rd, 1892.

POPE, MARIA (PRESTON) (1804–1895): *Mrs. John Pope,* daughter of William Preston and Caroline Hancock, was born in Fincastle, Virginia, on September 7th, 1804. In 1814 her father removed with his family to Louisville, Kentucky, where she resided for the rest of her life. On June 3rd, 1824, she became the wife of John Pope (1801–1825), eldest son of William Pope and Cynthia Sturgus; he was a graduate of Harvard College (1821), a promising young lawyer, and scion of a wealthy and distinguished family. He died of consumption on October 31st, 1825, leaving one infant, who died soon after. Maria (Preston) Pope never remarried. She lived with her father until his death in 1849; in 1860 she erected the handsome mansion on Walnut Street in which she died. One of her sisters, Henrietta Preston (1803–1835), was the first wife of Albert Sidney Johnston (1803–1862), noted Confederate general. Her younger sister, Josephine Preston (1809–1842), was the wife of Jason Rogers (1803–1848) and the mother of two daughters, Susan Preston Rogers (1836–1871) and Maria Preston Pope Rogers (1839–1909), who after their parents' death were reared by their aunt, Mrs. Pope. Her only brother, William Preston (1816–1887), was congressman from Kentucky (1852–1853), United States minister to Spain (1858–1861), and major general in the Confederate army. Maria (Preston) Pope died of pneumonia in Louisville on April 15th, 1895, and was buried in Cave Hill Cemetery. According to the Louisville *Courier-Journal* (April 16th, 1895), "Mrs. Pope was personally a queenly-looking woman, belonging to the old school of society women. She was very punctilious in her etiquette and bearing toward her associates. She was a society belle in her young days. Her mind was so retentive and her intellect so vigorous, even in her extreme age, that she was always a delightful companion to both young and old."

PORTER, ABNER ADDISON (1817–1872), Presbyterian clergyman, son of the Rev. Francis H. Porter and Isabella Kilpatrick, was born in Asheville, North Carolina, in 1817. He was a brother of the Rev. Joseph D. Porter, the Rev. Rufus K. Porter, and the Rev. David H. Porter. He graduated from the College of New Jersey (Princeton) in 1838 and from Columbia Theological Seminary in 1842. After serving churches in Greene County, Alabama, for three years (1843–1846) he was pastor of the Second Presbyterian Church, Charleston, South Carolina (1846–1851) and the First Presbyterian Church, Selma, Alabama (1851–1861). During the Civil War he was editor of *The Southern Presbyterian* (1861–1865). Returning to the pulpit, he was pastor of churches in Spartanburg, South Carolina (1865–1868) and Austin, Texas (1869–1872). He married first (on May 10th, 1848) Isabel J. Pratt, of Tuscaloosa, Alabama; he married second (on March 22nd, 1864) Sarah E. Black, of Piedmont, York District, South Carolina. He received the honorary degree of doctor of divinity from Wofford College in 1867. He died in Austin, Texas, on December 8th, 1872.

PORTER, ANTHONY (1788–1869), financier, was born in Greene County, Georgia, on December 8th, 1788. His father, a planter, had fought in the Revolutionary War. In 1813 he was appointed secretary to the Hon. Peter Early (1773–1817), governor of Georgia (1813–1815); in overhauling the public accounts he developed his natural gift for finance, and when the Bank of the State of Georgia was chartered in 1816 he was sent to Savannah to become its first teller. A year later he was promoted to cashier, a post he held until 1846, when he succeeded George Brown Cumming (1796–1878) as president.

He continued as president for nineteen years (1846–1865). On December 16th, 1824, he married Louisa Alexander (1807–1888), a native of Sunbury, Liberty County, Georgia, daughter of Adam Alexander (1758–1812) and Louisa Frederika Schmidt (1777–1846), younger sister of Adam Leopold Alexander (1803–1882), and hence aunt of Mrs. Jeremy Francis Gilmer, Mrs. Alexander Robert Lawton, Mrs. Wallace Cumming, and Mrs. George Gilmer Hull. Anthony Porter died in Savannah on December 1st, 1869, and was buried in Laurel Grove Cemetery. A long obituary appeared in the Savannah *Republican* (December 3rd, 1869): "In the official and private character of Major Porter there was much to admire and hold up for the imitation of others. To an astute knowledge of business and financial affairs he added perfect candor and an exactness and integrity that no temptation could shake. . . . In the financial world no one was better or more favorably known, and the state bank derived much of its popularity and success from his sterling integrity and excellent business management. . . . He was never blessed with children, but was a most exemplary and devoted husband, and had always as sharers of his home those who looked up to and cherished for him a filial reverence and love. . . . His ample means allowed him both to live as a gentleman and do good to others, and in no sphere did he deal out his benefactions with a sparing hand." Louisa (Alexander) Porter survived her husband nineteen years; she died at Rockwood, summer home of her niece, Mrs. Jeremy Francis Gilmer, near Clarkesville, Georgia, on August 5th, 1888, and was buried beside her husband.

PORTER, DAVID H. (1830–1873), Presbyterian clergyman, son of the Rev. Francis H. Porter and Isabella Kilpatrick, was born in Selma, Alabama, on May 13th, 1830. He was a brother of the Rev. Abner A. Porter, the Rev. Joseph D. Porter, and the Rev. Rufus K. Porter. After graduating from the South Carolina College in 1852 and from Columbia Theological Seminary in 1855 he was pastor of the First Presbyterian Church, Savannah, for eighteen years (1855–1873), with an interval of two years (1863–1865) as chaplain of the 5th Regiment Georgia Cavalry. His pastorate was marked by the erection of a church edifice, dedicated on June 9th, 1872. On December 11th, 1855, he married Mary Burney Clarke (1835–1875), daughter of Samuel Clarke (1791–1869), of Beech Island, South Carolina. ("Mrs. Porter, our pastor's wife, is quite a substantial-looking lady," wrote Laura Elizabeth Maxwell on January 19th, 1856; "but Mr. Porter looks as if he might be blown away like foam.") He died in Savannah on December 21st, 1873, survived by his wife and six children, and was buried in Laurel Grove Cemetery. Mary Burney (Clarke) Porter died on March 9th, 1875, and was buried beside her husband. David H. Porter received the honorary degree of doctor of

divinity from Oxford University (Georgia) in 1872. At the South Carolina College he was a classmate of Charles Colcock Jones, Jr., from 1849 to 1850; at Columbia Theological Seminary he was a classmate of the Rev. R. Q. Mallard, to whom he was always "Brother Dave."

PORTER, HELEN CLARKE (1857–1884), eldest child of the Rev. David H. Porter (1830–1873) and Mary Burney Clarke (1835–1875), was born in Savannah, Georgia, in February 1857. She was named for her maternal grandmother, Ann Helena Clarke (1800–1850), wife of Samuel Clarke (1791–1869), of Beech Island, South Carolina. Her father died on December 21st, 1873, when she was sixteen years old; her mother died on March 9th, 1875, when Helen was just eighteen; the responsibility of five dependent children fell largely on the eldest sister. On November 20, 1883, she became the wife of James H. Killough (1853–1919), a New York commission merchant then living in Hoboken, New Jersey. Her husband, a native of Ireland, son of George Killough and Agnes Connell, had accompanied his parents to the United States in 1862 and had lived briefly in Savannah in the 1870s. Helen (Porter) Killough died in Hoboken on November 12th, 1884, less than a year after her marriage, and was buried near her parents in Laurel Grove Cemetery, Savannah. Her husband subsequently married Ella Gertrude Stringham (1864–1918), daughter of Dean Stringham and Mary Jane Bulmer. At the time of his death he was head of the firm of Killough & Company, commission merchants, and was a director of the Irving Savings Institution, the Fidelity Trust Company, and the Merchants' Association of New York. He died in Brooklyn on October 2nd, 1919, and was buried beside his second wife in Greenwood Cemetery.

PORTER, JOSEPH D. (1821–1879), Presbyterian clergyman, son of the Rev. Francis H. Porter and Isabella Kilpatrick, was born in 1821. He was a brother of the Rev. Abner A. Porter, the Rev. Rufus K. Porter, and the Rev. David H. Porter. After graduating from Princeton Theological Seminary in 1848 he was stated supply of rural churches in the South Alabama Presbytery (1852–1868), evangelist in the Central Texas Presbytery (1868–1874), and evangelist in the East Texas Presbytery (1874–1879). He was also chaplain in the Confederate army (1862–1864). On March 27th, 1879, while traveling alone on horseback to a meeting of Presbytery, he died suddenly near Alto, Houston County, Texas, presumably of apoplexy; the next morning he was found lying by the roadside, his horse standing near him, two of his fingers still clasping the bridle rein. He was buried in Alto.

PORTER, RUFUS KILPATRICK (1827–1869), Presbyterian clergyman, son of the Rev. Francis H. Porter and Isabella Kilpatrick, was born at Cedar Springs, Spartanburg District, South Carolina, on January 1st, 1827. He was a brother of the Rev. Abner A. Porter, the

Rev. Joseph D. Porter, and the Rev. David H. Porter. After graduating from the South Carolina College in 1849 and from Columbia Theological Seminary in 1852 he was pastor of the churches at Bath (Richmond County) and Waynesboro (Burke County), Georgia, for fourteen years (1852–1866), with an interval of some months during the Civil War as chaplain of Cobb's Legion. On May 5, 1853, he married Jane S. Johnston, daughter of the Hon. Samuel Johnston, of Winnsboro, South Carolina. Late in 1866 he succeeded the Rev. R. Q. Mallard as pastor of the Central Presbyterian Church, Atlanta. He died in Atlanta on July 13th, 1869.

POWEL, SAMUEL DILLWYN (1811–1887), church treasurer, fourth son of William Powel and Ann Webster, was born in Abington, Pennsylvania, in 1811. In 1818 his parents removed to Norristown, where Powel spent his boyhood and youth. For twenty-three years he was treasurer of the Board of Domestic Missions of the Presbyterian Church, of which the Rev. Dr. Charles Colcock Jones was corresponding secretary from 1850 to 1853. During their residence in Philadelphia the Joneses and the Powels were cordial friends, and their correspondence after Dr. Jones's return to Georgia attests to their continuing friendship. "I am pleased to know," wrote Powel on September 11th, 1856, "that you have left behind you, in the hearts of all in this building, very pleasant remembrances. Thanks, my dear sir, for your many kind words of comfort and encouragement whilst you were with us—and even now, whilst absent from us, as conveyed in your very acceptable letters." On May 13th, 1857, Powel urged Dr. Jones to visit Philadelphia on his return from Kentucky. "It would do you good, I hope, to see your old friends; and I *know* it would do me *very much good* to see your smiling face once more. I would love to look at you once more *behind your old desk*. It would seem so 'kinda natural.' " For many years Powel maintained a residence in Norristown, to which he resorted in summer; in March 1859 he removed permanently to Norristown and thereafter commuted daily to his Philadelphia office. He died in Norristown on August 24th, 1887, and was buried in Montgomery Cemetery. His wife, Catharine F. Jacoby (1813–1906), daughter of Samuel Jacoby, of Norristown, died on February 12th, 1906, and was buried beside her husband.

POWERS, CLIFFORD AMANDA STILES (WEST) (1827–1890): *Mrs. John Hawkins Powers*, daughter of Dr. Charles West (1790–1855) and Sarah Evelyn Nephew (1796–1854), was born in Sunbury, Liberty County, Georgia, on October 26th, 1827. She was a sister of Dr. Charles William West (1815–1860); James Nephew West (1823–1875); Dr. Joseph Jones West (1832–1869); and Maria Louisa West (1835–1910), wife of Dr. Julius Caesar Gilbert. In childhood she accompanied her parents to Perry, Houston County, Georgia, where her father practiced medicine until

his death in 1855. On February 5th, 1848, she became the wife of John Hawkins Powers (1821–1864), of Perry, a lawyer, and ordinary of Houston County (1852–1855). Two of their children lived to maturity: John Hawkins Powers (1849–1910) and Sarah Evelyn West Powers (1851–1933). On March 18th, 1861, her husband enlisted for twelve months as a private in Company C, 1st Regiment Georgia Infantry, and went to Virginia with his company; on August 3rd, 1861, he was discharged for disability. During the war the family resided on a farm near Millwood, Dooly County, where Mary Eliza Robarts visited them in December 1863. "Clifford is very industrious," she wrote on December 23rd, 1863; "she superintends the spinning and weaving done at this place, which is mostly for her house servants, and she puts out the cloth woven for Mr. Powers and Johnnie. . . . They have abundance of everything, and nothing to buy except coffee and tea." On July 22nd, 1864, Mrs. Mary Jones reported that John Hawkins Powers was "very low with dropsy"; he died in the autumn of 1864. After the war Clifford (West) Powers boarded for a time with the Robarts family in Marietta, Georgia, while her daughter Evelyn attended school; her son John was a civil engineer engaged in railroad construction. In 1875 she removed to Macon, where on June 21st, 1883, she became the second wife of Thomas Johnson Cater (1816–1888), of Perry, a dry goods merchant and a widower with thirteen children. He died in Perry on March 15th, 1888. Clifford (West) (Powers) Cater died in Perry on December 4th, 1890, survived by two children, and was buried beside her first husband in Evergreen Cemetery. As the Perry *Home Journal* (December 11th, 1890) observed, "A good woman has been called to her eternal reward."

POWERS, SARAH EVELYN WEST (1851–1933), daughter of John Hawkins Powers (1821–1864) and Clifford Amanda Stiles West (1827–1890), was born in Perry, Houston County, Georgia, on September 9th, 1851. She was named for her maternal grandmother, Sarah Evelyn Nephew (1796–1854), wife of Dr. Charles West (1790–1855). She attended school for some years in Macon and Marietta. On January 20th, 1869, she became the wife of Samuel Talmadge Walker (1840–1879), sixth child of Gollothun Walker (1805–1862) and Elizabeth Lawrence Adams (1812–1887), of Macon. Her husband, a native of Edgefield District, South Carolina, had been reared chiefly in Charleston; at the outbreak of the Civil War he had withdrawn from the College of Charleston to enlist in the Confederate army; as captain in Trenholm's Battalion he had served throughout the war. In 1866 he had settled in Macon, where he had prospered in business. After a lingering illness he died in Macon on August 11th, 1879, survived by his wife and two children: Samuel Talmadge Walker (1869–1900) and Sarah Whittle Walker (1871–1962). He was buried in Rose Hill Cemetery. Sarah Evelyn (Powers) Walker spent her later years in Boston, Massachusetts, at the residence of her daughter, Sarah Whittle Walker, wife of Samuel Henry Cutting (1861–1930); she died in Richmond, Virginia, at the residence of her granddaughter, Margery Cutting, wife of Thomas Foster Wheeldon, on December 14th, 1933, and was buried beside her husband.

PRATT, CHARLES JONES (1842–1924), civil engineer, son of the Rev. Nathaniel Alpheus Pratt (1796–1879) and Catherine Barrington King (1810–1894), was born in Roswell, Georgia, on March 18th, 1842. He was named for the Rev. Dr. Charles Colcock Jones, a respected and valued family friend. Prior to the Civil War he attended the Georgia Military Institute (Marietta). On May 2nd, 1862, he enlisted as a private in the Savannah Volunteer Guards (Company A, 18th Battalion Georgia Infantry); on June 16th, 1862, he was appointed drillmaster with rank of second lieutenant and transferred to the camp of instruction at Macon. Early in 1863 he resigned to work as engineer on the projected Atlanta & Roswell Railroad. On August 11th, 1863, he enlisted as junior first lieutenant in Company B, Roswell Battalion Georgia Cavalry. Early in 1864 he joined Morgan's command as a private in Company B, 11th Regiment Kentucky Cavalry; he was taken prisoner in Greene County, Tennessee, on September 4th, 1864, sent to Chattanooga on September 13th, 1864, and exchanged at Rough & Ready, Georgia, on September 22nd, 1864. After the war he was agent of the Etiwan Phosphate Company in Savannah. He then farmed near Griffin and Cedartown. For three years (1882–1885) he was assistant city engineer of Atlanta. After holding a position for several years with the Louisville & Nashville Railroad he removed to Florida, where he participated in the construction of the oversea extension of the Florida East Coast Railroad from Miami to Key West. He was forced to retire in 1912 following injuries sustained in a fall. On May 15th, 1867, he married Emma Clinton Stubbs, daughter of Baradall Palmer Stubbs and Eliza Hammond, of Milledgeville; there were six children. His wife was a sister of Julia Eliza Stubbs, wife of his elder brother, Nathaniel Alpheus Pratt (1834–1906). Charles Jones Pratt died in Atlanta on May 12th, 1924, survived by five children, and was buried in Decatur Cemetery.

PRATT, NATHANIEL ALPHEUS (1796–1879), Presbyterian clergyman, son of Ezra Pratt and Temperance Southworth, was born in Saybrook, Connecticut, on January 29th, 1796. He graduated from Yale College in 1820 and from Princeton Theological Seminary in 1823. After serving for some months as stated supply in New Brunswick, New Jersey, he removed to Darien, Georgia, where he was pastor of the Presbyterian church for fourteen years (1826–1840). On March 11th, 1830, he married Catherine Barrington King (1810–1894), daughter of Roswell King (1765–1844) and Catherine Barrington (1776–1839); there

were ten children. His wife's father, a native of Windsor, Connecticut, and a man of great enterprise and energy, had settled in Darien in 1789 and established a flourishing business in lumber, rice, and cotton. When Cobb County, Georgia, was organized in 1833 Roswell King and his son Barrington King were among its pioneer settlers; they founded the village of Lebanon, where they established flour mills, and the village of Roswell, where they established cotton mills and took up residence. In 1840 Pratt settled in Roswell as first pastor of the newly established Presbyterian church; he continued as pastor until a paralytic stroke ended his ministry thirty-nine years later. He received the honorary degree of doctor of divinity from Oglethorpe University in 1854. He died in Roswell on August 30th, 1879, and was buried in the Presbyterian Cemetery. One of his sons, Henry Barrington Pratt (1832–1912), was also a Presbyterian clergyman.

PRATT, NATHANIEL ALPHEUS (1834–1906), scientist, son of the Rev. Nathaniel Alpheus Pratt (1796–1879) and Catherine Barrington King (1810–1894), was born in Darien, Georgia, on January 25th, 1834. In early childhood he removed with his parents to Roswell, Georgia, where his father was pastor of the Presbyterian church for thirty-nine years (1840–1879). After graduating from Oglethorpe University in 1852 and from the Savannah Medical College in 1856 he continued his scientific studies at the Lawrence Scientific School, Harvard University. He never practiced medicine, preferring to devote his life to chemistry, geology, mineralogy, and other scientific pursuits. On November 14th, 1855, he married Julia Eliza Stubbs, daughter of Baradall Palmer Stubbs and Eliza Hammond, of Milledgeville; there were seven children. His wife was a sister of Emma Clinton Stubbs, wife of his younger brother, Charles Jones Pratt (1842–1924). He was professor of chemistry at the Savannah Medical College (1858–1861). At the outbreak of the Civil War he was newly installed as professor of chemistry and geology at Oglethorpe University; he organized his own company, the Jordan Grays, but before he saw active service he was made assistant chief of the Confederate States Niter and Mining Bureau, with rank of captain. After the war he organized the Charleston Mining & Manufacturing Company (1867) and the Etiwan Phosphate Company (1868) for the manufacture of commercial fertilizers. He was professor of applied science at Washington and Lee University (1872–1876). He then devoted himself fully to developing the native resources of the South, and engaged successfully in various scientific, commercial, and industrial ventures. For four years (1884–1888) he was chemist of the State of Georgia. In 1900 he settled in Decatur, where on October 31st, 1906, he was instantly killed by a fast-moving train on the Georgia Railroad. He was buried in Decatur Cemetery.

PRESTON, JOHN SMITH (1809–1881), lawyer, legislator, and Confederate soldier, son of Francis Smith Preston (1765–1836) and Sarah Buchanan Campbell, was born near Abingdon, Virginia, on April 20th, 1809. His father was a member of the state house of delegates (1788–1789; 1812–1814), a member of the state senate (1816–1820), and a member of Congress (1793–1797). His elder brother, William Campbell Preston (1794–1860), was United States senator from South Carolina (1833–1842) and president of the South Carolina College (1845–1851). John Smith Preston attended Hampden-Sydney College (1823–1825) and the University of Virginia (1825–1827) and then studied law at Harvard. On April 28th, 1830, he married Caroline Martha Hampton (1807–1883), daughter of General Wade Hampton (1751–1835) and his third wife, Mary Cantey (1780–1863), of Columbia, South Carolina. After practicing law for ten years in Abingdon, Virginia, he removed to South Carolina and thence to Louisiana, where he accumulated a fortune in the sugar business. Returning to South Carolina, he served in the state senate (1848–1856) and rose to prominence as a champion of states rights. He was a member of the state secession convention meeting in Columbia in December 1860. In 1861 he was volunteer aide-de-camp to General Beauregard; after First Manassas Beauregard wrote that he was "greatly indebted" to Preston and his other volunteer aides "for manifold essential services in the transmission of orders on the field and in the preliminary arrangements for the occupation and maintenance of the line of Bull Run." On August 13th, 1861, Preston was commissioned assistant adjutant general, with rank of lieutenant colonel. In January 1862 he returned to Columbia, where he commanded the prison camp (January 1862–April 1862) and the conscript camp (April 1862–July 1863). From July 1863 to March 1865 he was superintendent of the Bureau of Conscription in Richmond. He was promoted to colonel (April 23rd, 1863) and brigadier general (June 10th, 1864). After the war he opposed reconciliation with the North. He died in Columbia on May 1st, 1881.

PRICE, STERLING (1809–1867), congressman, governor, and Confederate soldier, son of Pugh Williamson Price and Elizabeth Williamson, was born near Farmville, Prince Edward County, Virginia, on September 20th, 1809. After attending Hampden-Sydney College (1826–1827) he studied law under Creed Taylor and commenced practice. In 1831 he removed with his parents to Fayette, Missouri, and thence to Keytesville, Chariton County, Missouri, where he resided for the rest of his life. On May 14th, 1833, he married Martha Head, of Randolph County, Missouri. He was a member of the state house of representatives (1840–1844) and served as speaker; he was a member of Congress (1845–1846). During the Mexican War he was appointed colonel of the 2nd Regiment Missouri Infantry (August

12th, 1846) and promoted to brigadier general of volunteers (July 20th, 1847). Returning to Missouri, he served as governor (1853–1857) and state bank commissioner (1857–1861). At the outbreak of the Civil War he became major general in the Confederate army. His victory at Wilson Creek, twelve miles southwest of Springfield, Missouri, in August 1861, won him widespread popularity. After his defeat near Corinth, Mississippi, in the summer of 1862 he withdrew to Arkansas, where he continued until late 1864, when he retreated to Texas. He died in St. Louis, Missouri, on September 29th, 1867, and was buried in Bellefontaine Cemetery. Jefferson Davis declared Price "the vainest man I ever met"; but those who knew Price well believed that he never received the recognition he deserved. He was the most prominent secessionist west of the Mississippi River.

PRYOR, ROGER ATKINSON (1828–1919), congressman, Confederate soldier, and jurist, son of the Rev. Theodorick Bland Pryor (1805–1890) and his first wife, Lucy Eppes Atkinson, was born in Dinwiddie County, near Petersburg, Virginia, on July 19th, 1828. After graduating from Hampden-Sydney College in 1845 he studied law at the University of Virginia (1846–1847) and practiced law briefly in Charlottesville and Petersburg. Prior to the Civil War he was associated successively with the *Southside Democrat* (Petersburg), the Washington *Union*, the Richmond *Enquirer*, and the Washington *States*; in 1857 he founded the *South*, a pro-Southern newspaper published in Washington. In 1859 he was elected to Congress and served until his resignation on March 3rd, 1861. In the Presidential election of 1860 he supported Breckinridge and was said to be the most persuasive secessionist speaker in Virginia. After serving briefly in the Confederate Congress he became colonel of the 3rd Regiment Virginia Infantry; on April 16th, 1862, he was promoted to brigadier general but shortly thereafter resigned his commission, preferring to fight as a private in Fitzhugh Lee's cavalry. In November 1864 he was captured near Petersburg and confined in Fort Lafayette; he was exchanged shortly before Appomattox. In September 1865 he removed to New York, worked on the New York *Daily News,* studied law, and rose to prominence as a journalist and a lawyer. He was appointed judge of the court of common pleas (1890) and justice of the state supreme court (1896). In 1899 he resigned from the bench and resumed private practice. On November 8th, 1848, he married Sara A. Rice; there were seven children. He died in New York City on March 14th, 1919, and was buried in Princeton, New Jersey.

PRYOR, THEODORICK BLAND (1805–1890), Presbyterian clergyman, son of Richard P. Pryor and Anne Bland, was born at Annesville, Dinwiddie County, Virginia, on January 9th, 1805. After graduating from Hampden-Sydney College in 1826 he studied law at the University of Virginia (1826–

1828) and practiced law for two years. He then attended Union Theological Seminary, Hampden-Sydney, Virginia (1830–1832), with six months at Princeton Theological Seminary in 1831. He was pastor of the Presbyterian church at Nottoway, Virginia (1832–1853); the Third Presbyterian Church, Baltimore, Maryland (1853–1854); and the Second Presbyterian Church, Petersburg, Virginia (1854–1863). He was missionary to the Army of Northern Virginia (1864–1865). After the war he returned to his former charge at Nottoway, Virginia, where he continued as pastor for twenty-three years (1867–1890). He received the honorary degree of doctor of divinity from Hampden-Sydney College in 1852. He was moderator of the General Assembly of the Southern Presbyterian Church in 1883. He married first (on October 11th, 1827) Lucy Eppes Atkinson, of Chesterfield County, Virginia; he married second (on November 15th, 1832) Frances Campbell Eppes, of Nottoway County, Virginia; he married third (on October 6th, 1868) Frances Fitzgerald, of Nottoway County, Virginia. He died at his residence in Nottoway County on July 27th, 1890. Roger Atkinson Pryor (1828–1919), congressman, Confederate soldier, and jurist, son of the Rev. Theodorick Bland Pryor and his first wife, Lucy Eppes Atkinson, was a prominent Virginia secessionist prior to the Civil War.

PURSE, THOMAS (1802–1872), merchant and railroad official, was born in Winchester, Virginia, on March 26th, 1802. In early childhood he removed with his parents to Charleston, South Carolina, and at the age of sixteen he settled in Savannah, Georgia, where he resided for the rest of his life. After a brief period as grocery clerk he joined the firm of Purse & Styles, stationers and booksellers, and subsequently became sole proprietor. Together with William Washington Gordon, Richard Randolph Cuyler, and William Remshart he projected and promoted the Central Railroad & Banking Company of Georgia; he was its first superintendent (1837–1847) and for twenty-five years (1840–1865) a member of its board of directors. He represented Chatham County in the state senate (1849–1850). From 1853 to 1861 he was United States appraiser of customs. He served many terms as alderman of Savannah and succeeded Charles Colcock Jones, Jr., as mayor (1861–1862). He married first (in 1824) Eliza Jane Gugle (1809–1860), of Savannah; six of their children died in infancy. He married second (in 1862) Josephine A. Felt (1824–1882), also of Savannah. He died in Savannah on December 18th, 1872, survived by his second wife and six children, and was buried beside his first wife in Laurel Grove Cemetery. One of his sons, Thomas Purse (1843–1861), a private in the Oglethorpe Light Infantry (Company B, 8th Regiment Georgia Infantry) was killed in his eighteenth year at First Manassas (July 21st, 1861). Another son, Daniel Gugle Purse (1839–1908), an engineer, served three years (1861–1864) in the Ordnance Department in

Savannah; after the war he was president of the Savannah Board of Trade for fourteen successive years and president of the Savannah Bank & Trust Company from 1881 to 1885. Josephine (Felt) Purse died in Savannah on July 7th, 1882, and was buried near her husband in Laurel Grove Cemetery.

PYNCHON, EDWARD ELLIOTT (1803–1868), planter, son of Stephen Pynchon (1769–1823) and Sarah Trask (1778–1856), was born in Brimfield, Massachusetts, on March 27th, 1803. He was a descendant of William Pynchon (1590–1662), who founded Springfield, Massachusetts, in 1636. In 1825 he graduated from Yale College, from which his father had graduated in 1789 and his grandfather, Joseph Pynchon, in 1757. After teaching for several years in Windsor, Connecticut, he migrated to Liberty County, Georgia, where he established the Walthourville Academy, an institution soon known throughout the South for its excellence in scholarship and moral discipline. In 1832 his sister, Eliza S. Pynchon, assumed direction of "the female department." As the Savannah *Georgian* (November 7th, 1832) observed, "The commissioners feel great pleasure in being able to offer to the public the services of a lady of so high a rank as an instructress. She has had experience in one of the most flourishing seminaries at the North, and she will introduce into her school the improvements that have been made in female education. To the advancement of the pupils in literature and science, in morality and its attendant virtues, will be added a system of calisthenic exercises, which conduce essentially to health and to grace in manners." Edward Elliott Pynchon later undertook planting, leaving the school in charge of his sister, who for many years maintained its high reputation. On December 31st, 1829, he married Sarah Harriet Lewis (1812–1872), of Liberty County, daughter of Samuel Lewis (1781–1828) and his second wife, Ann Drusilla Hines (1781–1829), widow of William Way; three of their children lived to maturity. By 1850 Pynchon and his family were living in Marietta, Georgia, where Pynchon was a prosperous planter and a large slaveholder. ("His residence is beautifully located," wrote Mary Sharpe Jones on September 11th, 1855, "commanding a fine view of Marietta and the mountain.") In April 1858 he removed with his household to Huntsville, Alabama, where his daughter, Sarah Eliza Pynchon (1832–1859), resided with her husband, Smith D. Hale, judge of the circuit court. Edward Elliott Pynchon died in Huntsville on June 24th, 1868, and was buried in Maple Hill Cemetery. Sarah Harriet (Lewis) Pynchon died on February 14th, 1872, and was buried beside her husband. Their only son, Lewis Charlton Pynchon (1830–1897), a graduate of Jefferson Medical College (Philadelphia) in 1852 and a surgeon in the Confederate army, was for many years a physician in Huntsville and died there on August 20th, 1897.

QUARTERMAN, AUGUSTUS STEVENS (1831–1908), educator, eldest child of Joseph Quarterman (1796–1863) and Harriet Elizabeth Stevens (1811–1887), was born in Walthourville, Liberty County, Georgia, on September 9th, 1831. After attending Franklin College (Athens) for two years (1848–1850) he returned to his native county, where he commenced teaching school in January 1851. On November 3rd, 1852, he married Anna Matilda Moultrie, daughter of Briggs Hopson Moultrie and Mary Ann Baldwin, of Macon, Georgia. During the Civil War he was a private in the Liberty Independent Troop (Company G, 5th Regiment Georgia Cavalry). Returning to Walthourville, he resumed his teaching; and in 1901 he reported that he was "still teaching: it has been the business of my life." His wife died on November 14th, 1896, and was buried in Walthourville Cemetery. He died at the residence of his son, Julian Herbert Quarterman, in Dowling Park, Florida, on July 12th, 1908, and was buried beside his wife.

QUARTERMAN, CAROLINE CLAUDIA (1835–1919), daughter of Thomas Quarterman (1788–1857) and his third wife, Sarah Ellen Sanford (1801–1871), widow of William Norman (1794–1827), was born in Walthourville, Liberty County, Georgia, on February 22nd, 1835. On August 22nd, 1867, in Macon, Georgia, "Claude" became the wife of Robert Wilson Perry (1842–1905), of Norristown, Pennsylvania; her husband, seven years her junior, was a painter and paperhanger and a Union veteran. He died in Norristown on February 24th, 1905, and was buried in Norristown City Cemetery. Claudia (Quarterman) Perry died while on a visit in Savannah, Georgia, on April 28th, 1919, and was buried beside her husband. She was survived by one son, Dr. Robert F. Perry, a captain in the army medical corps.

QUARTERMAN, JOHN WAY (1841–1916), Presbyterian clergyman, son of Edward William Quarterman (1808–1863) and Adeline Way, was born in Jonesville, Liberty County, Georgia, on March 18th, 1841. He was a grandson of the Rev. Robert Quarterman (1787–1849), pastor of Midway Church (1823–1849). After attending Oglethorpe University for two years (1859–1861) he enlisted as a private in the Liberty Independent Troop (Company G, 5th Regiment Georgia Cavalry) and later as third corporal in the Liberty Mounted Rangers (Company B, 20th Battalion Georgia Cavalry). On February 21st, 1864, shortly before leaving with his company for Virginia, he married Laura Yonge McCollough (1843–1925), daughter of James Sullivan McCollough (1810–1883) and Hannah Elizabeth Quarterman (1814–1885), of Walthourville. After the war he studied theology under the direction of the Rev. Richard Quarterman Way (1819–1895); during his long ministry he served a number of churches in South Georgia: Darien (1871–1873), Mount Vernon (1873–1875), Blackshear (1875–1880), Waycross (1880–1895), Marlow and Pooler (1895–

1904), Dawson and Smithville (1904–1914). He died at his residence in Beach, Georgia, on April 4th, 1916. His wife died in Waycross on December 3rd, 1925.

QUARTERMAN, JOSEPH (1796–1863), planter, son of Joseph Quarterman (1764–1806) and his first cousin, Elizabeth Quarterman (1773–1826), was born in Liberty County, Georgia, on April 26th, 1796. He was a member of the state house of representatives (1823–1827) and the state senate (1849–1850). In October 1830 he married Harriet Elizabeth Stevens (1811–1877), eldest daughter of John Stevens (1777–1832) and Amarintha Munro (1785–1859). "Colonel Quarterman" was one of sixteen citizens instrumental in organizing a separate Presbyterian church in Walthourville in 1855. He was a rich planter; in the Federal Census of 1860 he was recorded as the owner of seventy-two slaves. He died in Walthourville on January 25th, 1863, and was buried in Walthourville Cemetery. Harriet Elizabeth (Stevens) Quarterman died on March 15th, 1887, and was buried beside her husband.

QUARTERMAN, JOSEPH MELANCTHON (1828–1858), Presbyterian clergyman, son of the Rev. Robert Quarterman (1787–1849) and his third wife, Mary Jemima Way (1801–1841), was born in Flemington, Liberty County, Georgia, on April 13th, 1828. His father was pastor of Midway Church (1823–1849). After graduating from Oglethorpe University in 1847 and from Columbia Theological Seminary in 1850 he was pastor of the newly organized Presbyterian church in Mount Vernon, Montgomery County, Georgia, for four years (1851–1855). In November 1855 he settled in Palatka, Florida, where he was pastor of the Presbyterian church until his death on March 29th, 1858.

QUARTERMAN, KEITH AXSON (1838–1900), physician, son of Thomas Quarterman (1788–1857) and his third wife, Sarah Ellen Sanford (1801–1871), widow of William Norman (1794–1827), was born in Walthourville, Liberty County, Georgia, on January 12th, 1838. He graduated from Franklin College (Athens) in 1857 and from Jefferson Medical College (Philadelphia) in 1861. During the Civil War he was assistant surgeon of the 10th Battalion Georgia Cavalry. On July 30th, 1862, he married Helen Louisa Jones (1841–1911), daughter of Joseph Jones (1779–1846) and his third wife, Elizabeth Screven Lee Hart (1801–1870); there were ten children. After the war he settled in Cuthbert, Georgia, where he practiced medicine, operated a drugstore, and taught school. For two years (1876–1877) he was principal of the Valdosta Institute. Late in 1877 he returned to Walthourville, where he practiced medicine until his death on August 10th, 1900. He was buried in Walthourville Cemetery. Helen Louisa (Jones) Quarterman died in Atlanta on March 29th, 1911, and was buried beside her husband.

QUARTERMAN, LAFAYETTE STEWART (1827–1900), planter, son of John Stewart Quarterman (1775–1836) and his third wife,

Susannah Myers, was born in Liberty County, Georgia, on December 25th, 1827. He was a half-brother of William Elliott Way Quarterman (1802–1868). His father died on March 5th, 1836, and two years later (on September 17th, 1838) his mother became the wife of John Arthur. After graduating from Oglethorpe University in 1848 Lafayette Stewart Quarterman returned to his native county and engaged in planting until the outbreak of the Civil War. He married first (in 1849) Sarah Rebecca McGowen; he married second (in 1853) Sarah Elizabeth Mann; he married third (in 1862) Julia P. Barnard. On April 1st, 1862, in Bryan County, Georgia, he enlisted as first sergeant in the Hardwick Mounted Rifles (later consolidated with other companies to form the 7th Regiment Georgia Cavalry); he subsequently became first lieutenant (September 17th, 1863) and captain (January 24th, 1864). He was wounded in Virginia on September 29th, 1864. After the war he resumed planting in Liberty County and taught school for some years. Sometime after 1880 he removed to Ocala, Florida, where he died on December 11th, 1900.

QUARTERMAN, ROBERT (1787–1849), Presbyterian clergyman, son of Thomas Quarterman (1738–1791) and his third wife, Rebecca Baker, widow of Samuel Jones and Edward Ball, was born in Liberty County, Georgia, on January 13th, 1787. He was ordained pastor of Midway Church on May 27th, 1823, and continued as pastor for twenty-six years; in 1847, when ill health forced him to resign, his congregation voted him "honorary pastor" with an annuity of four hundred dollars. He died on April 19th, 1849, and was buried in Midway Cemetery. He was the first pastor of Midway Church to be born in Liberty County. He married first (on September 1st, 1807) his first cousin, Rebecca Quarterman (1785–1813); there were four children. He married second (on March 2nd, 1815) Margaret Esther Myddleton (died 1817); there was one child. He married third (on December 3rd, 1818) Mary Jemima Way (1801–1841); there were twelve children. He married fourth (on August 18th, 1842) Sarah Margaret Shaffer (1807–1881), widow of Thomas Baker; there were no children. Four of his sons were Presbyterian clergymen: William Myddleton Quarterman (born 1816), John Winn Quarterman (1821–1857), Joseph Melancthon Quarterman (1828–1858), and Nathaniel Pratt Quarterman (1839–1915). In 1853 the Rev. John Winn Quarterman, missionary at Ningpo, translated *A Catechism of Scripture Doctrine and Practice* (1837), by the Rev. Dr. Charles Colcock Jones, into Chinese.

QUARTERMAN, SARAH MARGARET (SHAFFER) (BAKER) (1807–1881): *Mrs. Robert Quarterman,* daughter of John William Shaffer (1773–1809) and Mary Lawrence, was born in Savannah, Georgia, in 1807. In 1830 she became the wife of Thomas Baker (1806–1837), of Liberty County, Georgia, son of Thomas Baker (1777–1810) and Rebecca Eliza Burnley (1789–1861). There were two chil-

dren: Thomas Shaffer Baker (1833–1851) and Mary Elizabeth Baker (1835–1882). On June 5th, 1837, Thomas Baker was killed in a hunting accident, and five years later (on August 18th, 1842) Sarah Margaret (Shaffer) Baker became the fourth wife of the Rev. Robert Quarterman (1787–1849), pastor of Midway Church (1823–1849). After his death (on April 19th, 1849, she continued to reside in Walthourville, where on December 18th, 1856, her only daughter became the wife of John Elijah Baker (1833–1906). In 1866 the Bakers removed to Thomasville, Georgia, where John Elijah Baker was teacher in the Fletcher Institute and later president of Young Female College. Sarah Margaret (Shaffer) (Baker) Quarterman accompanied the Bakers to Thomasville, where she resided for the rest of her life. She died in Thomasville at the residence of her daughter on January 31st, 1881, and was buried in Laurel Hill Cemetery. (The dates carved on her tombstone, 1816–1879, are incorrect.) Her first husband, Thomas Baker, son of Rebecca Eliza Burnley by her first husband, was a half-brother of the Rev. R. Q. Mallard, son of Rebecca Eliza Burnley by her second husband; hence Sarah Margaret (Shaffer) (Baker) Quarterman was half-sister-in-law to the Rev. R. Q. Mallard, whose correspondence refers frequently to "Sister Quarterman" and "Sister S. M. Q."

QUARTERMAN, THOMAS (1788–1857), planter, eldest son of Thomas Quarterman and Renchie Norman, was born in Liberty County, Georgia, on February 13th, 1788. All his life he resided in Liberty County. He married first (on February 5th, 1807) Elizabeth Osgood (1789–1808); their only child died in infancy. He married second (on January 12th, 1809) Elizabeth Yonge Peacock (1794–1826); five of their six children lived to maturity: Thomas William Quarterman (1810–1863); Jane Amarintha Quarterman (1813–1874), wife of (1) John Sidney Fleming and (2) William Quarterman Baker; Hannah Elizabeth Quarterman (1814–1885), wife of James Sullivan McCollough; Robert Yonge Quarterman (1820–1857); and Mary Susan Quarterman (born 1823), wife of Charles Hickman. He married third (on June 3rd, 1828) Sarah Ellen Sanford (1801–1871), widow of William Norman; four of their six children lived to maturity: Alexander Sanford Quarterman (1829–1907); Harriet Augusta Quarterman (1833–1888), wife of Milo M. Freeman; Caroline Claudia Quarterman (1835–1919), wife of Robert Wilson Perry; and Keith Axson Quarterman (1838–1900). Thomas Quarterman died in Walthourville, Liberty County, on February 5th, 1857, and was buried in Midway Cemetery. According to the Rev. Dr. Charles Colcock Jones (February 6th, 1857), he had been "for three years blind; totally so for two." Sarah Ellen (Sanford) (Norman) Quarterman died at the residence of her youngest child, Keith Axson Quarterman, near Cuthbert, Georgia, on October 24th, 1871, and was buried beside her second husband.

QUARTERMAN, THOMAS WILLIAM (1810–1886), planter, eldest son of Thomas Quarterman (1788–1857) and his second wife, Elizabeth Yonge Peacock (1794–1826), was born in Liberty County, Georgia, on October 20th, 1810. He was for many years a resident of Walthourville, where he was a successful planter. On January 11th, 1838, he married Sarah Louisa Walker (1821–1907), of Eatonton, Georgia; there were six children. He was one of sixteen citizens instrumental in organizing a separate Presbyterian church in Walthourville in 1855, and he was for many years a deacon. He was elder brother of Hannah Elizabeth Quarterman (1814–1885), wife of James Sullivan McCollough; he was half-brother of Caroline Claudia Quarterman (1835–1919) and Keith Axson Quarterman (1838–1900). He died in Darien, Georgia, on March 24th, 1886, and was buried in St. Andrew's Cemetery. His son, Nathaniel Wirt Quarterman (1842–1862), a private in the Altamaha Scouts (Company F, 25th Regiment Georgia Infantry), died in Walthourville on May 23rd, 1862, of typhoid fever contracted in camp.

QUARTERMAN, WILLIAM ELLIOTT WAY (1802–1868), planter, son of John Stewart Quarterman (1775–1836) and his first wife, Ann Way (1778–1811), was born in Liberty County, Georgia, on December 15th, 1802. He represented Liberty County in the state legislature in 1836, 1837, and 1847. In December 1859 he was one of three county magistrates officiating at the trial of Lucy, Negro slave in the custody of the Rev. Dr. Charles Colcock Jones. For forty-four years (1822–1866) he was active in the affairs of Midway Church, of which he was deacon (1836–1866) and selectman (1839–1841; 1848–1849). When the Flemington Presbyterian Church was organized in April 1866 he was one of four elders ordained. From March 1861 until the end of 1865 he managed Arcadia plantation for its joint-owners, the three children of the Rev. Dr. Charles Colcock Jones. In October 1864 he went to Virginia to attend his half-brother, Lafayette Stewart Quarterman (1827–1900), who had suffered a gunshot wound on September 29th, 1864. He married first (on January 27th, 1823) Jane Irene Ferguson (1803–1827); he married second (on January 31st, 1829) Mary Ann Darsey (1807–1857); he married third (on April 8th, 1858) Lydia Quarterman Andrews (born 1815), widow of William Thomas Elliott Baker. He died in Flemington on February 12th, 1868, and was buried in Flemington Cemetery. On April 2nd, 1861, the Rev. Dr. Charles Colcock Jones quoted Thomas Winn Fleming's opinion of W. E. W. Quarterman: "He said he believed, such was the conscientiousness and integrity of the man that he would do better for another than for himself."

QUINTARD, CHARLES TODD (1824–1898), Protestant Episcopal bishop, son of Isaac Quintard (1793–1883) and Clarissa Hoyt, was born in Stamford, Connecticut, on December 22nd, 1824. His father, a man of wealth and education, was of French Huguenot ancestry. After graduating from the Medical Department of the University of the City of New York in 1847 he spent one year at Bellevue Hospital before commencing practice in Athens, Georgia, in 1848. In the same year he married Eliza Catherine Hand, daughter of Bayard Hand and Eliza Barrington King, of Roswell, Georgia. From 1851 to 1854 he was professor of physiology and pathological anatomy at the Memphis Medical College. In January 1854, influenced by the Rt. Rev. James Hervey Otey, bishop of Tennessee, he became a candidate for holy orders; two years later he was ordained to the priesthood and became rector of Calvary Episcopal Church, Memphis. Late in 1856 he became rector of the Church of the Advent, Nashville, where he continued until the outbreak of the Civil War. In 1861 he was elected chaplain of the 1st Regiment Tennessee Infantry and accompanied his regiment to the seat of war. In January 1864 he was commissioned chaplain-at-large to General Joseph E. Johnston's army, and in February 1864 he was ordered to Atlanta. There, on Easter Monday, March 28th, 1864, he organized the original St. Luke's Episcopal Church, Atlanta; a modest wooden structure seating four hundred people was quickly run up, and the new church was consecrated by the Rt. Rev. Stephen Elliott, bishop of Georgia, on April 22nd, 1864. After the evacuation of Atlanta on September 1st, 1864, and the total destruction of the church during the fire of November 14th–15th, 1864, Quintard served as missionary to General Hood's army until April 1865. After the war he was bishop of Tennessee (1865–1898) and vice-chancellor of the University of the South (1866–1873). He died in Darien, Georgia, on February 15th, 1898, survived by his wife and three children, and was buried in Sewanee, Tennessee.

RAHN, IRWIN M. (1806–1891), plantation overseer, son of Matthew Rahn (1754–1822) and his second wife, Hannah Elizabeth (Hoffman) Dolwich, was born in Effingham County, Georgia, on September 28th, 1806. In early manhood he settled in Liberty County, Georgia, where on September 12th, 1837, he married Sarah Ann Norman (1813–1881). From May 1st, 1850, until December 31st, 1853, he managed Arcadia plantation for its owner, the Rev. Dr. Charles Colcock Jones, while Dr. Jones was absent in Philadelphia. Rahn and his wife were charter members of the Flemington Presbyterian Church at its organization in April 1866. Sarah Ann (Norman) Rahn died on January 8th, 1881, and was buried in Flemington Cemetery. Irwin M. Rahn died on April 16th, 1891, and was buried beside his wife. His son, William Joseph Rahn (1841–1865), clerk in a Savannah dry goods store, enlisted on September 17th, 1861, as a private in the Georgia Hussars (Company E, 6th Regiment Virginia Cavalry; later designated Company F, Jeff Davis Legion Mississippi

Cavalry). He was killed in North Carolina on March 8th, 1865.

RAIFORD, ROBERT (1796–1857), magistrate, was born in Jefferson County, Georgia, in 1796. In early manhood he settled in Savannah, where he was for many years justice of the peace. He never married. His ward, Rose Anna McHugh, became the wife of John Gitling Deitz, Savannah bookbinder, on July 29th, 1853. Robert Raiford died in Savannah of apoplexy on May 2nd, 1857, and was buried in Laurel Grove Cemetery. As the Savannah *Republican* (May 20th, 1857) observed, "He had fixed and settled principles of great regularity in all the transactions of life, and thus armed he moved among his fellow men—beloved, admired, and respected."

RANKIN, WILLIAM GALLOWAY (1822–1891), Union soldier, was born in Mercer, Pennsylvania, in 1822. He fought in the Mexican War (1846–1848). At the outbreak of the Civil War he was appointed from Washington Territory as captain of the 13th Infantry, with duty as acting assistant quartermaster; he saw service on the Peninsula, at Sharpsburg, at Chancellorsville, and at Gettysburg. (In reporting on June 28th, 1862, that Rankin was one of three Federal generals recently taken prisoner before Richmond, Charles Colcock Jones, Jr., was mistaken.) From September 1863 to May 1864 he was on mustering and disbursing duty at Hartford, Connecticut; thereafter he was at headquarters of the military district of the Mississippi until April 1865. After the war he was transferred to the 31st Infantry (September 21st, 1866) and subsequently reassigned to the 13th Infantry (July 14th, 1869). On December 31st, 1870, he was honorably discharged at his own request, with rank of brevet major and brevet lieutenant colonel for faithful service during the war. He spent his last years as a clerk in the New York customhouse. He died in New York on May 30th, 1891, and was buried in Mercer, Pennsylvania. Military records show that Rankin was "in arrest" from December 13th, 1867, to May 16th, 1868, "as unfit for the proper discharge of his duties from other causes than injuries received or disease contracted in the line of his duties." According to R. de Tobriand, colonel of the 13th Infantry, writing on July 16th, 1869, "This officer has been known for years as a hard drinker wherever he served. While in my former regiment, the 31st Infantry, I, being in command of the Middle District, Department of Dakota, had to relieve him from the command of Fort Buford after a drunken row in which he had come to blows with his second in command. . . . On the 4th of July, there being a ball given for the celebration of the anniversary of our independence at Corinne, Captain Rankin appeared there in uniform, and in so gross a state of intoxication that he heavily fell down on the floor while attempting to dance with a lady he had invited."

RAPHAEL (1483–1520): *Raffaello Santi,* Italian painter, son of Giovanni Santi, also a painter, was born in Urbino, probably on April 6th, 1483. His mother died in 1491, his father in 1494. For several years he worked under the influence of Leonardo da Vinci and Michelangelo in Florence; in 1508 he was summoned to Rome, where his brilliant work for Pope Julius II at the Vatican soon established him as worthy to rank alongside his former Florentine masters. His first great commission was a cycle of frescoes executed in a series of four rooms (known as the Stanze) in the Castile di San Damaso. In August 1514 he became architect of St. Peter's, succeeding Bramante. A set of ten tapestry cartoons, based on New Testament themes and woven in Brussels, was commissioned by Pope Leo X to hang on the walls of the Sistine Chapel. His noble study of Baldassare Castiglione (1516), now in the Louvre, was one of the earliest modern portraits. His unfinished masterpiece, "The Transfiguration," now in the Vatican, was completed by his pupils after his death. Of his many Madonnas the most famous is the "Sistine Madonna," now in the Dresden Gallery. He died in Rome on Good Friday, April 6th, 1520, and was buried in the Pantheon.

READ, JACOB (1825–1864), Confederate soldier, eldest son of Jacob Read (1794–1830) and his second wife, Ann (Nancy) Williamson (1807–1830), was born at Drakies plantation on the Savannah River, Chatham County, Georgia, on December 9th, 1825. He bore the name of his distinguished grandfather, Jacob Read (1751–1816), lawyer and planter, native of Christ Church Parish, South Carolina, colonel in the Revolutionary army, delegate to the Continental Congress (1783–1785), speaker of the South Carolina House of Representatives (1789–1794), United States senator (1795–1801), and brigadier general of South Carolina state troops (1810–1816). On March 3rd, 1847, Jacob Read was commissioned second lieutenant in the United States marine corps; on August 19th, 1855, he was promoted to first lieutenant; on February 27th, 1861, he resigned his commission and entered Confederate service. Returning to Georgia, he was appointed (on March 5th, 1861) captain of Company D, 1st Regiment Georgia Regulars (Captain Jacob Read's Regular Light Battery Georgia Artillery). During the summer and autumn of 1861 he was in command at Oglethorpe Barracks in Savannah. He was at Hilton Head, near Port Royal, South Carolina, on November 7th, 1861; he was at James Island, near Charleston, South Carolina, in June 1862. He was at the same time captain in the Confederate States marine corps. In December 1862 he was arrested and placed on trial before general court-martial to answer charges of "flagrant neglect of duty," "incompetency," "conduct prejudicial to good order and military discipline," "conduct unbecoming an officer and a gentleman," and "shameful abandonment of his post." On February 1st, 1863, he was found essentially guilty of the first four charges, not guilty of the fifth, and was sentenced to be dismissed from Confederate service. During the trial, on January 7th, 1863, Henry Bryan

(1836–1879), Savannah broker and personal acquaintance of Captain Read, wrote Captain H. R. Chisholm recommending "discriminating clemency": "I earnestly entreat that Captain Read will not be dismissed from the service but will be transferred to some other branch of the service where he can be made useful. I think him best suited for duty in a fort or garrison where strict discipline is observed and much attention is paid to form and ceremony. . . . If he is dismissed, his wounded pride will drive him to the poisoned liquor of a barroom; and finally, bankrupt in reputation and in purse, he will probably die in the gutter. . . . If he had been placed from the first under the direct control of any officer of firmness and discretion—that is, in a position assimilating to the place he so long held in the old service —Captain Read today would have been an ornament instead of an encumbrance to this district." Jacob Read never married. He died of "disease of the heart" in Luray, Page County, Virginia, on May 13th, 1864, and was buried in Cathedral (Catholic) Cemetery, Savannah.

READ, JAMES BOND (1827–1903), physician, second son of Jacob Read (1794–1830) and his second wife, Ann (Nancy) Williamson (1807–1830), was born in Savannah, Georgia, on August 15th, 1827. He was named for his great-uncle, James Bond Read (1766–1841), Savannah physician, author of a dissertation on typhus fever published in Latin in 1795. His paternal grandfather, Jacob Read (1751–1816), lawyer and planter, native of Christ Church Parish, South Carolina, was colonel in the Revolutionary army, delegate to the Continental Congress (1783–1785), speaker of the South Carolina House of Representatives (1789–1794), United States senator (1795–1801), and brigadier general of South Carolina state troops (1810–1816). James Bond Read graduated from the Medical School of the University of Maryland (Baltimore) in 1849. In the same year he married Jane M. Dugan (1829–1908), daughter of Frederick Dugan, prominent Baltimore lawyer; there were no children. He was for half a century one of the leading physicians of Savannah. In 1852 he was one of eight founders of the Savannah Medical College, and for some years he was its professor of pathological anatomy. At the outbreak of the Civil War he organized his own company, the Irish Volunteers (Company A, 1st Regiment Georgia Volunteers); he served as captain for six months (from July 25th, 1861, to January 25th, 1862). On June 10th, 1862, he was appointed surgeon in the Confederate army and placed in charge of Seabrook's Hospital, Richmond; he was subsequently transferred to General Hospital No. 4, the officers' hospital in Richmond. After the war he resumed medical practice in Savannah, where he was for many years active in city and county affairs. When he retired from practice in 1898 he was the oldest physician in Savannah. He died of pneumonia at his residence in Green Cove Springs, Florida, on No-

vember 10th, 1903, and was buried in Cathedral (Catholic) Cemetery, Savannah. "Dr. J. B. Read is one of those men who have a very kind heart but don't hesitate to call a spade a spade when it is a spade." So stated the Savannah Morning News on September 16th, 1892. Jane (Dugan) Read died in Green Cove Springs on February 7th, 1908, and was buried beside her husband.

READ, JOHN POSTELL WILLIAMSON (1829–1884), Confederate soldier, third son of Jacob Read (1794–1830) and his second wife, Ann (Nancy) Williamson (1807–1830), was born in Savannah, Georgia, on April 21st, 1829. He was named for his maternal grandfather, John Postell Williamson (1778–1843), one of the richest planters and landowners in Savannah in the first half of the nineteenth century. His paternal grandfather, Jacob Read (1751–1816), lawyer and planter, native of Christ Church Parish, South Carolina, was colonel in the Revolutionary army, delegate to the Continental Congress (1783–1785), speaker of the South Carolina House of Representatives (1789–1794), United States senator (1795–1801), and brigadier general of South Carolina state troops (1810–1816). On May 18th, 1861, J. P. W. Read became captain of the Pulaski Guards (Company K, 10th Regiment Georgia Volunteers; attached, as Company L, to the 1st Regiment Virginia Artillery). By special order (dated March 27th, 1863) his company was transferred to the light artillery arm of the service and became Captain Read's Battery Georgia Light Artillery (38th Battalion Virginia Light Artillery). On April 4th, 1863, he was appointed major, to take rank March 2nd, 1863; on November 5th, 1864, he was appointed lieutenant colonel of artillery, to take rank October 27th, 1864. He served with distinguished gallantry in the Peninsula campaign, at Sharpsburg, and at Fredericksburg; he lost an arm at Gettysburg. After the war he removed to Huntsville, Alabama, and later settled in Virginia. He never married. He died at his residence in Campbell County, near Lynchburg, Virginia, on September 28th, 1884, and was buried in Cathedral (Catholic) Cemetery, Savannah.

REDD, ALBERT GRESHAM (1822–1888), merchant and planter, was born in Greene County, Georgia, on June 29th, 1822. In early manhood he settled in Columbus, Georgia, where he prospered in business and amassed a considerable fortune. His handsome house of English gothic design, erected on Rose Hill in a park of seventeen acres, was completed in 1859. He was for many years a member of the session of the Columbus Presbyterian Church. Near the close of the Civil War he served as captain of the Columbus City Light Guards; he was captured in the battle fought at Columbus on April 16th, 1865, and was imprisoned for several months in Macon. He died in Columbus after a lingering illness on April 7th, 1888, survived by his wife, Henrietta Euphrasia Redd (1829–1893), and was buried in Linwood Cemetery.

REDMOND, GEORGE S. (1836–1864), Confederate soldier, was born in Ireland, son of an officer in the British army. In early manhood he migrated to the United States and purchased a plantation in Talbot County, Maryland, where he resided until the outbreak of the Civil War. On September 10th, 1861, at Fairfax Station, Virginia, he enlisted as a private in Company H, 1st Regiment Maryland Infantry; he was discharged on June 18th, 1862. On August 18th, 1862, at Orange Courthouse, Virginia, he enlisted as second lieutenant in Captain William F. Randolph's Company of Scouts, Guides, and Couriers (subsequently designated Company B, 39th Battalion Virginia Cavalry), attached to the headquarters of General Richard S. Ewell. On November 1st, 1862, he resigned and went North to dispose of his property then liable to confiscation: he returned to the Confederate States by way of Nassau, arriving at Charleston in June 1863. At Battery Wagner he met General William B. Taliaferro and became aide-de-camp on his staff, with rank of lieutenant of artillery. He was on James Island, near Charleston, in the summer and autumn of 1863; late in February 1864 he accompanied General Taliaferro to the military district of East Florida. On March 1st, 1864, at Cedar Creek, near Jacksonville, he was fatally shot in the stomach; he died on March 6th, 1864, after great suffering and was buried in Lake City. As General Taliaferro wrote in the Charleston *Mercury* (April 26th, 1864), "Captain Redmond was a truehearted and generous gentleman, a brave and gallant soldier. He received no pay for his services; he had no real rank, nor any peculiar interest in the Confederacy. He yielded up his life a martyr to the abstract principle which he espoused and in vindication of the right of an oppressed people to assert its independence."

REID, ELEONORA LOUISA (MILLER) (1813–1866): *Mrs. Robert Alexander Reid,* was born in Savannah, Georgia, on August 23rd, 1813. On February 21st, 1838, she became the wife of Robert Alexander Reid (1799–1876), of Augusta, a rich merchant and an influential Presbyterian layman. His father, David Reid (1768–1814), a native of Stornoway, Scotland, had migrated to the United States in early manhood and settled in Augusta. His sister, Ann Reid, wife of Thomas McDowall, of Augusta, was mother of Elizabeth Reid McDowall (1820–1895), wife of Dr. William Henry Cumming; and Susan M. McDowall (1822–1893), wife of Dr. Theophilus S. Stewart. In 1849 Reid built Montrose, a handsome classical mansion in Summerville, where he resided for the rest of his life. During the summer of 1857 the Reids visited Rockbridge Alum Springs, Virginia, where they met their Georgia friends, the Rev. Dr. and Mrs. Charles Colcock Jones; it was to the Reids that Dr. Jones addressed his vivid account of "the passage of the North River through the North Mountain" (quoted by Mrs. Mary Jones in her letter of August 1st, 1857; transcribed by Charles Colcock Jones,

Jr., and enclosed in his letter of August 29th, 1863). Eleonora Louisa (Miller) Reid died in Summerville on December 3rd, 1866, and was buried in Summerville Cemetery. Robert Alexander Reid died on July 4th, 1876, and was buried beside his wife. In his will he bequeathed a lot and sufficient money to build a Presbyterian church in Summerville: "The plan and style of said building is necessarily left to the discretion of the trustees. But I recommend, if the means be sufficient, that it be of brick, well but plainly finished, with a basement for a Sunday school room." Reid Memorial Presbyterian Church, built of brick, still stands as a monument to the zeal and generosity of its donor. In 1877 Charles Colcock Jones, Jr., purchased Montrose and occupied it until his death in 1893; the house then passed to his daughter, Ruth Berrien Jones, wife of the Rev. Samuel Barstow Carpenter; she occupied it until her death in 1934, when it passed to her two daughters.

REID, JOHN WILSON (1804–1867), Presbyterian clergyman and educator, son of Joseph R. Reid and Margaret Farr, was born in Cabarrus County, North Carolina, in 1804. After studying theology privately he migrated to Georgia, where he taught school for some ten years in Columbia and Lincoln Counties. In 1842 he removed to Woodstock, Oglethorpe County, where he resided for the rest of his life, conducting a flourishing classical school for boys in nearby Philomath (1842–1860) and serving as pastor of the Woodstock Presbyterian Church (1851–1865). He died in Woodstock on July 11th, 1867. James Dunwody Jones (1842–1904), son of the Rev. John Jones, attended Reid's "Philomath school" from January 1858 to January 1859. According to *The Southern Presbyterian* (October 3rd, 1867), "Mr. Reid stood abreast of the first rank of teachers in the state, and wrought an untold amount of good in the preparation of large numbers for advanced positions in the different colleges of the country. . . . His attachment for youth and his desire for their preparation for usefulness burned with wonderful energy, and led him to spend and be spent in the attainment of these lofty ends."

RENI, GUIDO (1575–1642), Italian painter, was born in Bologna on November 4th, 1575. After studying with Denis Calvaert, a Flemish painter, and with Annibale Carracci he joined the guild of painters in 1599 and thereafter divided his time between Bologna and Rome. He painted frescoes in the cloisters of San Michele in Bosco (1604); in the Vatican (1608); in the pontifical chapel in Montecavallo (1610); in the pontifical chapel of Santa Maria Maggiore (1612); and in the church of San Domenico in Bologna (1614). After 1630 he resided in Bologna, where his art reached its highest perfection. In his classicism, inspired by Raphael's frescoes and the archaeological marbles, he stood apart from the baroque art of his contemporaries. He died in Bologna on August 18th, 1642, and was buried in the church of San Domenico.

REYNOLDS, JOHN FULTON (1820–1863), Union soldier, son of John Reynolds and Lydia Moore, was born in Lancaster, Pennsylvania, on September 20th, 1820. He graduated from the United States Military Academy in 1841. During the Mexican War he was brevetted captain for bravery at Monterey (1846) and major for gallantry at Buena Vista (1847). At the outbreak of the Civil War he was stationed at West Point, where he was commandant of cadets and instructor in artillery, cavalry, and infantry tactics. On August 20th, 1861, he was made brigadier general of volunteers and assigned to the Pennsylvania Reserves. He was taken prisoner at the battle of Gaines's Mill (June 27th, 1862) and confined in Libby Prison, Richmond, for six weeks; after his exchange he fought at Second Manassas, Fredericksburg, and Chancellorsville. He became major general of volunteers (November 29th, 1862) and colonel in the regular army (June 1st, 1863). He was killed at Gettysburg by a sharpshooter's bullet on July 1st, 1863, and buried three days later in Lancaster, Pennsylvania. He never married. His elder brother, William Reynolds (1815–1879), commander in the United States navy, was in charge of the naval depot at Port Royal, South Carolina, throughout the war.

RICHARDSON, JOHN (1816–1873), commission merchant, was born in Edgefield District, South Carolina, in 1816. By 1854 he was settled in Savannah, where he prospered as a cotton factor and commission merchant. In March 1856 he was elected vestryman of St. John's Episcopal Church; in October 1859 he was elected alderman of Savannah. He was for some years president of the Farmers' & Mechanics' Bank. Shortly before the Civil War he joined Dr. Edmund Howard Martin (1825–1907) in the cotton brokerage business; the firm of Richardson & Martin flourished in Savannah until the partnership was dissolved by mutual consent on May 29th, 1867. Richardson died at his plantation on Pawleys Island, Georgetown County, South Carolina, on September 11th, 1873, survived by his wife, Elizabeth Phoebe Richardson (1820–1876), and was buried in All Saints Episcopal Churchyard, Waccamaw. His wife died in Savannah on September 15th, 1876, and was buried in Laurel Grove Cemetery.

RICHARDSONE, SARAH ELIZABETH (1833–1911), eldest daughter of Dr. Cosmo P. Richardsone (1804–1852) and Margaret Bailey, was born in Savannah, Georgia, on July 16th, 1833. Her father, born in Edinburgh, Scotland, of an American father and a Scottish mother, had come as a three-year-old child to Savannah, where he had (according to the Savannah *Republican*, February 7th, 1852) "amassed a handsome fortune and established a reputation as a skillful physician and high-minded honorable gentleman." At the time of his death he was a city alderman and captain of the Savannah Volunteer Guards, oldest infantry company in the state. Margaret (Bailey) Richardsone, a native of Hancock County, Georgia, died when Sarah Elizabeth Richardsone was still a child; in June 1839 Dr. Cosmo P. Richardsone married Elizabeth Bailey, sister of his first wife. He died in Savannah on February 6th, 1852. Three years later, in 1855, Sarah Elizabeth Richardsone became the wife of William Gabbett, Jr., son of William Gabbett and Elizabeth Furnell, of Mount Minnett, County Limerick, Ireland; there were no children. For several years the couple made their home in Savannah. During the Civil War William Gabbett, an architect, served in the Confederate army as captain in the corps of engineers; he was for three years superintendent of Confederate States Niter and Mining District No. 9. Shortly after the war his father died at the ancestral home in Ireland; William Gabbett, the eldest son and heir, returned with his wife to Ireland and settled on the family estate, where he died late in the 1870s. After extensive travel in Europe Sarah Elizabeth (Richardsone) Gabbett returned to Georgia and made her home in Atlanta. In her later years she was an active member of the United Daughters of the Confederacy; she is reported to have designed the gold crosses of honor bestowed on Confederate veterans for valorous conduct during the war. She died in Atlanta on July 16th, 1911 (her seventy-eighth birthday), and was buried near her parents in Laurel Grove Cemetery, Savannah.

RIDGE, MAJOR (1771–1839), Indian leader, was born in Hiawassee, Georgia, in 1771; his father was a full-blooded Cherokee and his mother was a half-breed. At the age of twenty-one he became a member of the Cherokee council; he gradually won the confidence of his people and finally became one of the leaders of the Cherokee nation. He fought with distinction under Andrew Jackson at the battle of the Horseshoe. In 1832 Major Ridge and his son, John Ridge, and his nephew, Elias Boudinot, sensing the hopelessness of attempting to keep the Cherokee people in Northwest Georgia in the face of pressure from the state and federal government to resettle them in Indian Territory, began to negotiate for the best possible terms for the inevitable removal; in 1835 they signed a removal treaty which was ratified by the Senate and ruled binding on the Cherokee nation. On May 24th, 1838, General Winfield Scott and his troops commenced rounding up the Cherokees and sending them west; by September 1838 some fourteen thousand Cherokees were on the march to Indian Territory. But the Cherokees never forgave the three men who had signed the treaty effecting their removal. On June 22nd, 1839, Major Ridge, John Ridge, and Elias Boudinot, though widely separated at the time, were systematically and brutally murdered within a few hours of each other. Major Ridge was waylaid in the road near Cincinnati, Arkansas, and shot; John Ridge was seized in his bed at Honey Creek, Cherokee Nation, and mutilated with knives; and Elias Boudinot was lured from his house near Park Hill and set upon with hatchets.

RIPLEY, ROSWELL SABINE (1823–1887), Confederate soldier, son of Christopher Ripley and Julia Caulkins, was born in Worthington, Franklin County, Ohio, on March 14th, 1823. Inspired by his uncle, General James Wolfe Ripley (1794–1870), he entered the United States Military Academy and graduated in 1843. He served with distinction in the Mexican War (1846–1848) and wrote a history, *The War with Mexico* (2 vols., 1849). On March 22nd, 1852, he married Alicia Middleton, of Charleston, South Carolina, daughter of John Middleton and Mary Burroughs, and widow of William A. Sparks. He resigned from the army on March 2nd, 1853, and engaged in business in Charleston until the outbreak of the Civil War, when he became lieutenant colonel of ordnance in command of Fort Moultrie and subsequently of Fort Sumter. In August 1861 he was made brigadier general in command of South Carolina; in February 1862 he was superseded by General John C. Pemberton and placed in command of a brigade. At Sharpsburg he was severely wounded; returning to Charleston, he was placed in command of the first artillery district. Although popular in civilian life, he was the center of serious quarrels in the army. After the war he resided briefly in London and thereafter in Charleston. He died of apoplexy in New York City on March 29th, 1887.

ROBARTS, ELIZA GREENE (LOW) (WALKER) (ROBARTS) (1785–1868): *Mrs. David Robarts*, daughter of Philip Low (1755–1785) and his second wife, Mary Sharpe (1753–1798), widow of John Jones (1749–1779), was born on Colonel's Island, Liberty County, Georgia, on September 29th, 1785, the day after her father's death. She was a half-sister of John Jones (1772–1805), father of the Rev. Dr. Charles Colcock Jones, and a half-sister of Joseph Jones (1779–1846), father of Mrs. Mary Jones. Before she was twenty-eight years old she had been widowed three times. She married first (on January 20th, 1802) Charles Walker (1774–1802), of Sunbury, a planter; there were no children. After the death of her first husband in Sunbury on November 20th, 1802, she married second (on March 1st, 1804) James Robarts (1774–1807), of Sunbury, a merchant; there was one child: Mary Eliza Robarts (1805–1878). After the death of her second husband in Greensboro, Georgia, on April 4th, 1807, she married third (on December 20th, 1810) David Robarts (1783–1813), of Greensboro, a cotton factor and commission merchant, cousin of her second husband; there were two children: Joseph William Robarts (1811–1863) and Louisa Jane Robarts (1813–1897). After the death of her third husband in Greene County, Georgia, in September 1813 she returned to Liberty County with her three young children. For many years she resided in Sunbury; later she joined the household of her half-brother, Joseph Jones, at the Retreat; after his death in October 1846 she lived briefly in Sunbury before removing in May 1849 to Marietta, Georgia, where she resided with her two spinster daughters and her four grandchildren (Mary Sophia Robarts, Elizabeth Walton Robarts, Ellen Douglas Robarts, and Joseph Jones Robarts), motherless children of her son, Joseph William Robarts. She died in Marietta on November 12th, 1868, survived by two daughters and three granddaughters, and was buried in Citizens Cemetery. According to *The Southern Presbyterian* (January 28th, 1869), "She was uniformly cheerful and always courteous and winning in her manners. Little children delighted in her society, and hung around her sickbed. She was a true lady of the old school." To the Rev. Dr. Charles Colcock Jones and his wife "Aunt Eliza Robarts" was a precious relative. "You and Charles I look upon as my children," she wrote Mrs. Mary Jones on August 12th, 1831; "and I hope I shall ever feel willing to render you any service I would one of my own." (Members of the Robarts family stressed the second syllable of their surname.)

ROBARTS, ELIZABETH (LILLA) WALTON (1840–1914), second daughter of Joseph William Robarts (1811–1863) and Sophia Louisa Gibson (1814–1847), was born in Savannah, Georgia, on December 7th, 1840. Her mother died on July 24th, 1847, leaving four young children to the care of their paternal grandmother, Eliza Greene Low (1785–1868), widow of Charles Walker and James Robarts and David Robarts. In May 1849 Mrs. Robarts settled in Marietta, Georgia, with her two spinster daughters and her four grandchildren, leaving her widowed son, always something of a ne'er-do-well, to fend for himself in Savannah. "Lilla looks on nature with a poet's eye; she has a taste for the beautiful," wrote her aunt, Mary Eliza Robarts, on March 18th, 1856, at the same time observing that her sisters, Mary Sophia and Ellen, "are more matter-of-fact, and grass is only green with them, and clothed with no particular or sentimental interest." As early as December 25th, 1854, her grandmother noted that "Lilla has a taste for narrative; she has written a pretty piece on the afflictions of Savannah." Lilla Robarts "completed her term of education" in January 1858. After the death of her grandmother on November 12th, 1868, she made her home with her elder sister, Mary Sophia Robarts (1838–1921), wife of Theodore Dwight Adams, in Roswell, Georgia. For many years she taught school, first in Roswell, later in Atlanta. She was author of a slender volume of verse, *A Sheaf for Winter Birds* (Atlanta, 1886), comprising six short pieces: "One Step from Night to Morning"; "A Woman's Smile"; "Just As My Father Wishes"; "The Glad Surprise"; "One Step at a Time"; and "Wait to be Crowned." In 1910 she joined the household of her widowed sister, Mary Sophia (Robarts) Adams, in Pensacola, Florida; she died in Pensacola on March 22nd, 1914, and was buried in St. John's Cemetery.

ROBARTS, ELLEN DOUGLAS (1843–1911), third daughter of Joseph William Robarts (1811–1863) and Sophia Louisa Gibson

(1814–1847), was born in Savannah, Georgia, on March 12th, 1843. Her mother died on July 24th, 1847, leaving four young children to the care of their paternal grandmother, Eliza Greene Low (1785–1868), widow of Charles Walker and James Robarts and David Robarts. In May 1849 Mrs. Robarts settled in Marietta, Georgia, with her two spinster daughters and her four grandchildren, leaving her widowed son, always something of a ne'er-do-well, to fend for himself in Savannah. "Ellen says she wishes to be a very intelligent young lady," wrote her aunt, Mary Eliza Robarts, on October 13th, 1856; "that she is studying very hard, but thinks traveling would improve her very much, and that I had better send her to Mount Holyoke. I tell her she must make the best use of the opportunities she has and learn domestic duties at home." Ellen was the special ward of her aunt, Mary Eliza Robarts, who spoke of "my baby Ellen, the darling of my heart," as a "daughter," and spoke of herself as a "mother"; later she was to refer to Ellen's husband as her "son-in-law." On April 25th, 1866, Ellen Douglas Robarts became the wife of Alexander Brevard Brumby (1831–1879), a schoolmaster, son of Richard Trapier Brumby (1804–1875) and Mary Isabelle Brevard (1806–1875); she and her husband lived first in Atlanta, then in Newton County, then in Lawrenceville, and finally in Athens. There her husband, a scholarly man unfortunately addicted to drink, died on October 25th, 1879, leaving a wife and six young children with a meager support. Ellen Douglas (Robarts) Brumby died in Ocala, Florida, on January 30th, 1911, and was buried beside her husband in Oconee Hill Cemetery, Athens.

ROBARTS, JOSEPH JONES (1845–1864), Confederate soldier, only son of Joseph William Robarts (1811–1863) and Sophia Louisa Gibson (1814–1847), was born in Savannah, Georgia, in June 1845. He was named for his great-uncle, Joseph Jones (1779–1846). His mother died on July 24th, 1847, leaving four young children to the care of their paternal grandmother, Eliza Greene Low (1785–1868), widow of Charles Walker and James Robarts and David Robarts. In May 1849 Mrs. Robarts settled in Marietta, Georgia, with her two spinster daughters and her four grandchildren, leaving her widowed son, always something of a ne'er-do-well, to fend for himself in Savannah. Joseph Jones Robarts was the special ward of his aunt, Louisa Jane Robarts (1813–1897), who was, her sister wrote, "as devoted to him as an own mother could be, and he as fond of her." On February 3rd, 1854, Mary Eliza Robarts reported that "our little boy is very active and sweet in sawing wood, receiving our things at the depot, paying the freight, and having a dray to haul them up; but he has no love for books, though Louisa is very faithful and regular in teaching him every day." He later attended a local school conducted by the Rev. John Wickliffe Baker (1811–1901), a

Presbyterian clergyman. On November 6th, 1858, he became a member of the Marietta Presbyterian Church. At the outbreak of the Civil War he was engaged as a clerk in the warehouse of Edward Denmead (1813–1891), Marietta contractor and merchant—"a very excellent situation for him," wrote Mary Eliza Robarts on August 17th, 1861. "He has the war fever dreadfully, but he is so young that we do all we can to keep him at home." On May 17th, 1862, he enlisted as a private in the Liberty Independent Troop (Company G, 5th Regiment Georgia Cavalry), then encamped at Palmyra, Liberty County; on December 13th, 1862, the Rev. Dr. Charles Colcock Jones reported that he "makes a good soldier. Is in fine and I may say robust health, though the troop has been all the while stationary and doing nothing but picket duty." He was wounded in the right leg in the battle of Stone Mountain near Decatur, Georgia, in July 1864; several weeks later, on August 12th, 1864, he died near Perry, Houston County— "not," as Mrs. Laura E. Buttolph wrote on August 22nd, 1864, "from his wound or measles but from diphtheria."

ROBARTS, JOSEPH WILLIAM (1811–1863), commission merchant, son of David Robarts (1783–1813) and Eliza Greene Low (1785–1868), widow of Charles Walker and James Robarts, was born in Greensboro, Georgia, in November 1811. His father, a cotton factor and commission merchant, died in September 1813, and his mother, then thrice widowed, returned to her former home in Liberty County, Georgia, with her three young children. On December 21st, 1837, Joseph William Robarts married Sophia Louisa Gibson (1814–1847), daughter of William Gibson and Mary Madeleine Fatio, of St. Marys, Georgia; there were four children: Mary Sophia Robarts (1838–1921), Elizabeth Walton Robarts (1840–1914), Ellen Douglas Robarts (1843–1911), and Joseph Jones Robarts (1845–1864). Sophia (Gibson) Robarts died in Savannah of lockjaw on July 24th, 1847, leaving her four young children to the care of their paternal grandmother. In May 1849 Mrs. Robarts settled in Marietta, Georgia, with her two spinster daughters and her four grandchildren, leaving her widowed son to fend for himself in Savannah. In October 1853 he was elected city treasurer, and by 1860 he was engaged in the commission business. He was always something of a ne'er-do-well; his addiction to drink was a particular source of family concern, and his marriage to Ella Sommers (aged nineteen) on March 12th, 1860, "shocked the vilest of the vile." (As Charles Colcock Jones, Jr., wrote on March 14th, 1860, "Language and thought fail to express or conceive the depth of infamy into which he has voluntarily plunged himself.") On May 9th, 1862, he enlisted as a private in Company B, 1st (Olmstead's) Regiment Georgia Infantry. He died in Savannah of "general debility" on April 17th, 1863, and was buried beside his first wife in Laurel Grove Cemetery.

ROBARTS, LOUISA JANE (1813–1897), daughter of David Robarts (1783–1813) and Eliza Greene Low (1785–1868), widow of Charles Walker and James Robarts, was born in Greensboro, Georgia, on September 1st, 1813. Her father, a cotton factor and commission merchant, died a few weeks after her birth, and her mother, then thrice widowed, returned to her former home in Liberty County, Georgia, with her three young children: Mary Eliza Robarts (1805–1878), daughter of her second husband, James Robarts; Joseph William Robarts (1811–1863), son of her third husband, David Robarts; and Louisa Jane Robarts (1813–1897), younger sister of Joseph William Robarts. For many years Mrs. Robarts resided in Sunbury; later she joined the household of her half-brother, Joseph Jones, at the Retreat; after his death in October 1846 she lived briefly in Sunbury before removing in May 1849 to Marietta, Georgia, where she resided with her two daughters and her four grandchildren (Mary Sophia Robarts, Elizabeth Walton Robarts, Ellen Douglas Robarts, and Joseph Jones Robarts), motherless children of her son, Joseph William Robarts. After her death on November 12th, 1868, her two daughters continued to occupy the family residence. On February 2nd, 1878, Mary Eliza Robarts died, leaving Louisa Jane Robarts dependent on the care of her three nieces. Louisa Jane Robarts, like her elder half-sister, never married. She looked on her nephew, Joseph Jones Robarts (1845–1864), as her own son; and she never became reconciled to his untimely death in the summer of 1864. She died in Marietta during the night of January 29th, 1897, and was buried beside her mother and her half-sister in Citizens Cemetery. In the minutes of the session of the First Presbyterian Church, Marietta, appears the following letter addressed to "Miss Lou Robarts" on May 17th, 1887, by Enoch Faw, clerk of the session: "It is with pleasure the session has learned that the beautiful marble baptismal font which was quietly placed in the Presbyterian church at this place some time ago was a gift from you. The session has directed me to return to you the thanks of the session and of our church, and to enter a copy of the letter on our minutes. Works of charity and good deeds are always beautiful, but to the eye of the Master never brighter than when performed in that quiet spirit of piety which lets not the left hand know what the right hand does. We invoke the blessings of heaven upon you, and pray that multitudes may be brought into the church and receive the ordinance of baptism from the marble font, which at the same time reminds us of your generosity and your devotion to the Redeemer's cause."

ROBARTS, MARY ELIZA (1805–1878), only daughter of James Robarts (1774–1807) and Eliza Greene Low (1785–1868), widow of Charles Walker, was born in Sunbury, Liberty County, Georgia, on February 1st, 1805. Her father, a merchant, died in Greensboro, Georgia, on April 4th, 1807, when she

was two years old; her mother married third (on December 10th, 1810) David Robarts (1783–1813), of Greensboro, a cousin of her second husband; there were two children: Joseph William Robarts (1811–1863) and Louisa Jane Robarts (1813–1897). After the death of her third husband in September 1813 Mrs. Robarts returned to Liberty County with her three young children. For many years she resided in Sunbury; later she joined the household of her half-brother, Joseph Jones, at the Retreat; after his death in October 1846 she lived briefly in Sunbury before removing in May 1849 to Marietta, Georgia, where she resided with her two daughters and her four grandchildren (Mary Sophia Robarts, Elizabeth Walton Robarts, Ellen Douglas Robarts, and Joseph Jones Robarts), motherless children of her son, Joseph William Robarts. After her death on November 12th, 1868, her two daughters continued to occupy the family residence. Mary Eliza Robarts, like her younger half-sister, never married. She looked on her niece, Ellen Douglas Robarts (1843–1911), as her own daughter; and she was godmother to her cousin, Charles Colcock Jones, Jr. She died in Marietta on December 2nd, 1878, and was buried beside her mother in Citizens Cemetery. According to *The Southern Presbyterian* (February 13th, 1879), "Miss Robarts was a remarkable woman—a beautiful combination of mind and heart—one of nature's noble women! A queenly character! Her cultivated intellect and sparkling wit, genial spirit and graceful manners, made her a most charming companion in the domestic circle or drawing room. On points of honor, delicacy, and propriety she was an oracle. In times of sickness the most intelligent and best of nurses. In sorrow and bereavement, oh, what a comforter! The sunlight of her lovely face, her sweet smile, her cheering words ever free of bitterness or slander, will never be forgotten!"

ROBARTS, MARY SOPHIA (1838–1921), eldest daughter of Joseph William Robarts (1811–1863) and Sophia Louisa Gibson (1814–1847), was born in Liberty County, Georgia, on November 29th, 1838. Her mother died on July 24th, 1847, leaving four young children to the care of their paternal grandmother, Eliza Greene Low (1785–1868), widow of Charles Walker and James Robarts and David Robarts. In May 1849 Mrs. Robarts settled in Marietta, Georgia, with her two spinster daughters and her four grandchildren, leaving her widowed son, always something of a ne'er-do-well, to fend for himself in Savannah. Early in October 1856 Mary Sophia Robarts left school and began "the life of a young lady at home." In January 1861 she became governess in the household of Charles Hargreaves Stewart (1815–1864), a rich planter residing near Hardaway, Macon County, Alabama; she returned to Marietta in the summer of 1862. On June 13th, 1866, she became the second wife of Theodore Dwight Adams (1829–1901), son of Edwin Adams and Lydia Fuller, of Frankfort, Herkimer County, New York. There were three children: Lil Ellen Adams (1867–1941), Sarah Douglas (Zaidee) Adams (1869–1958), and Theodore Dwight Adams (1875–1912). She and her husband settled in Roswell, Georgia, where Adams was postmaster and storekeeper; he subsequently commuted to a clerkship in Atlanta. In 1900 the family removed to Pensacola, Florida, where, three months later, on January 12th, 1901, he dropped dead on the street of a heart attack while walking with his wife. She continued to reside in Pensacola for more than a decade. Her only son was electrocuted when he fell on a live wire in Mobile, Alabama, on May 23rd, 1912; her sister Lilla, a schoolteacher and something of a poet, shared her Pensacola house after 1910 and died there unmarried on March 22nd, 1914. Five years later Mary Sophia (Robarts) Adams joined the household of her daughter Lil Ellen Adams, wife of Francis Burgess Bruce, in Savannah, where she died on October 30th, 1921, one month before her eighty-third birthday. She was buried in St. John's Cemetery, Pensacola, near her husband, her son, and her sister Lilla.

ROBERTSON, WILLIAM (1721–1793), Scottish historian and Presbyterian clergyman, son of the Rev. William Robertson, was born in Borthwick, Midlothian, on September 19th, 1721. After attending Edinburgh University he was presented to the living of Gladsmuir, near Edinburgh, in 1743. He was for many years an active and influential leader of the Scottish Presbyterian Church. On August 21st, 1751, he married Mary Nisbet, daughter of the Rev. James Nisbet and Mary Pitcairne. His *History of Scotland During the Reigns of Queen Mary and of James VI Until His Accession to the Crown of England* (2 vols., 1759) won him the praise of David Hume and Edward Gibbon and secured him an appointment as principal of Edinburgh University (1762–1792). *The History of the Reign of the Emperor Charles V* (3 vols., 1769), his masterpiece, won him a European reputation. His *History of America* (2 vols., 1777) was largely superseded by the work of William Hickling Prescott (1796–1859). He died in Edinburgh on June 11th, 1793. Of *Charles V* Dr. Johnson remarked: "I would say to Robertson what an old tutor of a college said to one of his pupils: 'Read over your compositions, and wherever you meet with a passage which you think is particularly fine, strike it out.'"

ROBIDER, LOUIS (1811–1882), shoemaker, was born in Normandy, France, on October 5th, 1811. In early manhood he went up to Paris, where he resided until 1839, when he migrated to the United States. After six years in New York City he settled in Savannah, Georgia, where he worked as a shoemaker for the rest of his life. His wife, Renée Robider (1813–1883), was an upholsterer. His three sons, Alfred Robider (1832–1924), Anthony Robider (1839–1908), and Henry Robider (1849–1925), were carpenters. Louis Robider ("our good friend from France," as the Rev.

Dr. Charles Colcock Jones called him) died in Savannah of apoplexy on February 18th, 1882, and was buried in Laurel Grove Cemetery. Renée Robider died on August 1st, 1883, survived by three sons and two daughters, and was buried beside her husband.

ROBINSON, STUART (1814–1881), Presbyterian clergyman, son of James Robinson and Martha Porter, was born in Strabone, County Tyrone, Ireland, on November 14th, 1814. In 1815 his father, a linen merchant, migrated with his family to the United States and settled in Berkeley County, (West) Virginia. After graduating from Amherst College in 1836 he attended Union Theological Seminary, Hampden-Sydney, Virginia (1836–1837) and Princeton Theological Seminary (1839–1841); he was principal of Mercer Academy, Charlestown, Berkeley (now Jefferson) County, (West) Virginia (1837–1839), and returned for one year (1841–1842) as teacher. On September 5th, 1841, he married Mary Elizabeth Brigham (1823–1909), daughter of Dr. William Brigham, of Charleston, Kanawha County, (West) Virginia; there were six children. He served churches in Malden, (West) Virginia (1842–1847); Frankfort, Kentucky (1847–1852); and Baltimore, Maryland (1852–1856). For two years (1856–1858) he was professor of pastoral theology and church government at Danville (Kentucky) Theological Seminary. In April 1858 he became pastor of the Second Presbyterian Church, Louisville, Kentucky, where he continued until June 1881, with an absence of three years (1862–1865) in Toronto, Canada. He was founder, editor, and publisher of *The Presbyterial Critic* (1855–1856); he was also editor of *The True Presbyterian* (1861–1862), issued later as *The Free Commonwealth* (1865–1868). He was author of *The Church of God as an Essential Element of the Gospel* (1858) and *Discourses of Redemption* (1866). In 1853 he declined the honorary degree of doctor of divinity offered by Centre College (Danville, Kentucky). In 1869 he was moderator of the General Assembly of the Southern Presbyterian Church. He died in Louisville on October 5th, 1881, survived by his wife and two children, and was buried in Cave Hill Cemetery.

ROBSON, JOHN R. (1823–1867), physician, son of John Robson (1797–1880), a native of England, was born in Madison, Georgia, in 1823. In early manhood he was associated in business with his father, a prosperous merchant, and for some years a trustee of Madison Female College. On October 8th, 1844, he married Ann K. Smith, daughter of Guy Smith (1790–1857), a planter in Morgan County; she died shortly before the Civil War, leaving two young daughters (Louisa and Anna) to the care of their widowed grandmother, Jane Smith (1800–1878). Meanwhile John R. Robson had studied medicine privately and become a practicing physician. On September 11th, 1861, he married Susan R. Harris, daughter of Dr. Raymond Harris (1799–1888) and his first wife, Mary Elizabeth Law (1803–

1871), of Liberty County, Georgia. In August 1866 he attended Colonel William Maxwell (1785–1866) in his final illness. On August 29th, 1866, he left with his family for Texas; a few weeks later he died of yellow fever in Galveston. His widow returned to her father's residence in Liberty County, where on February 16th, 1871, she became the second wife of Thomas Coke Howard (1817–1893), prominent editor, lawyer, and politician of Atlanta.

ROCKWOOD, GILBERT (1811–1869), Congregational clergyman, son of John Rockwood and Hannah Upham, was born in Monson, Massachusetts, on August 29th, 1811. He attended Amherst College for one year (1834–1835) with the class of 1838. In September 1837 he married Avis Bowman Hooper, of Braintree, Massachusetts; there were five children. For twenty-four years (1837–1861) he served as missionary to the Tuscarora Indians occupying a reservation in Niagara County, New York, some seven miles north of Niagara Falls. In 1861 he returned to a farm in South Wilbraham (now Hampden), Massachusetts, where he died on September 21st, 1869.

RODGERS, JAMES GUSTAVUS (1827–1862), merchant, second child of George Tyler Rodgers (1799–1869) and Elizabeth Lavinia Pelot (1807–1883), was born in Macon, Georgia, on April 20th, 1827. In early manhood he removed to Savannah and entered the wholesale grocery business, in which he was associated successively with J. M. Kibbee (Kibbee & Rodgers), Thomas Wood (Wood & Rodgers), Heman A. Crane (Crane & Rodgers), James A. Norris, George F. Johnston, and John W. Birch (Rodgers, Norris & Company). In January 1857 he undertook to conduct the business alone, but within a year he had returned to Macon, where he continued his mercantile pursuits until the outbreak of the Civil War. On June 9th, 1861, he was elected captain of Company H, 12th Regiment Georgia Infantry, and left with his company for Virginia. He was killed at Sharpsburg on September 17th, 1862. He was survived by his wife, Lucretia A. Willet, daughter of Joseph Willet (1798–1850) and Margaret McKay, of Macon; they had been married on July 15th, 1848.

ROGERS, ANNA MUNRO (1836–1886), eldest daughter of the Rev. Charles William Rogers (1809–1861) and Caroline Matilda Woodford (1813–1886), was born in Hartford, Connecticut, in 1836. Her father, a Presbyterian clergyman without pastoral charge, was a rich planter and a large slaveholder; the family divided their time between their town house in Savannah and their summer residence at Kilkenny plantation in Bryan County. On July 16th, 1857, Anna Munro Rogers became the wife of Dr. Joseph Jones West (1832–1869), Savannah physician, son of Dr. Charles West (1790–1855) and Sarah Evelyn Nephew (1796–1854). Her husband, a graduate of Oglethorpe University (1851) and the Savannah Medical College (1854), had recently returned from a year's medical study in Paris.

On July 3rd, 1861, he was elected captain of the Oglethorpe Light Infantry (Company B, 8th Regiment Georgia Infantry); after fighting at First Manassas (July 21st, 1861) he returned to Georgia and resigned his captaincy; he later became surgeon of the 22nd Battalion Siege Artillery. He died in Savannah on December 30th, 1869, and was buried in Laurel Grove Cemetery. Anna Munro (Rogers) West died in Nashville, Tennessee, on May 19th, 1886, and was buried beside her husband.

ROGERS, CAROLINE MATILDA (1838–1863), second daughter of the Rev. Charles William Rogers (1809–1861) and Caroline Matilda Woodford (1813–1886), was born in Farmington, Connecticut, on January 18th, 1838. Her father, a Presbyterian clergyman without pastoral charge, was a rich planter and a large slaveholder; the family divided their time between their town house in Savannah and their summer residence at Kilkenny plantation in Bryan County. On March 20th, 1856, Caroline Matilda Rogers became the wife of Samuel Vernon Stiles (1831–1893), Savannah cotton broker, son of Joseph Stiles (1758–1838) and his second wife, Margaret Vernon Adams (1805–1893). Their daughter, Caroline Vernon Stiles (1857–1861), described by the Rev. R. Q. Mallard as "one of the plumpest little mortals I 'most ever saw," died on May 18th, 1861, aged four. Caroline Matilda (Rogers) Stiles died in Savannah on January 1st, 1863, and was buried in Laurel Grove Cemetery. Samuel Vernon Stiles died on June 2nd, 1893, and was buried beside his wife.

ROGERS, CHARLES WILLIAM (1809–1861), Presbyterian clergyman, son of Dr. Charles William Rogers (1780–1842) and Anne West Munro (1787–1857), was born in Liberty County, Georgia, in February 1809. After graduating from Yale College in 1829 he attended Princeton Theological Seminary; but he never settled as pastor of one church, preferring to preach here and there, supplying pulpits during the absence or illness of colleagues, and ministering chiefly to the Negroes of coastal Georgia. He was a rich planter and a large slaveholder; in the Federal Census of 1860 he was recorded as the owner of 153 slaves. In addition to a house in Savannah he maintained a summer residence at Kilkenny, his plantation in Bryan County. On October 2nd, 1834, he married Caroline Matilda Woodford (1813–1886), daughter of Oliver Woodford, of Hartford, Connecticut; there were four children: Anna Munro Rogers (1836–1886), wife of Dr. Joseph Jones West; Caroline Matilda Rogers (1838–1863), wife of Samuel Vernon Stiles; Georgia Woodford Rogers (born 1842), wife of (1) Peyton Wade and (2) Hugh Fraser Grant; and Charles William Rogers (1844–1863). He died in Savannah on May 9th, 1861, survived by his wife and four children, and was buried in Laurel Grove Cemetery. On June 1st, 1861, *The Southern Presbyterian* deplored the death of "one of the purest spirits and truest hearts of a Southern seaboard planter. . . . As a Southerner his feelings were of the warmest and most unquestioned stamp. For many years he would neither go nor take his family North, in consequence of the increasing tide of abolition sentiment, although he had married a Northern lady of numerous and happy family connections. He felt that it became Southern men, and especially Southern Christians and clergy, to keep their money at home, and evince in every way their disapproval of the tide of aggression whose inroads he with prophetic eye saw and deprecated." Caroline Matilda (Woodford) Rogers died in Asheville, North Carolina, on December 8th, 1886, and was buried beside her husband.

ROGERS, JAMES LEA (1823–1891), Presbyterian clergyman and educator, son of Joseph Rogers and Elizabeth Gibson, was born in Connellsville, Pennsylvania, on January 3rd, 1823. After graduating from Jefferson College (Canonsburg, Pennsylvania) in 1846 he taught for two years in the household of the Rev. Dr. Charles Colcock Jones, of Liberty County, Georgia. In 1848 he accompanied the Jones family to Columbia, South Carolina, where Dr. Jones was professor of ecclesiastical history and church polity at Columbia Theological Seminary (1848–1850) and Rogers was a student with the class of 1851. Leaving the seminary in July 1850 without a degree, he was successively pastor in Waynesboro, Georgia (1851); stated supply in Lincolnton, Georgia (1852); professor at the Georgia Military Institute, Marietta (1853–1854); president of Florence Female Academy, Florence, Alabama (1855–1857); and first pastor of the Central Presbyterian Church, Atlanta, Georgia (1859–1863). After the war he was connected with the Geological Survey in Alabama for two years (1866–1868); he then returned to Marietta, where he sold insurance and preached from time to time at rural churches in the neighboring counties. In 1876 he settled in Atlanta. He was for some years professor of moral and natural science in Agnes Scott College. Throughout his long career as clergyman he was associated with many nonclerical enterprises, among them the mining of gold (1854), the cultivation of wine (1861), and the manufacture of iron (1864). "I have always had a very strong natural taste for the physical sciences," he wrote on July 15th, 1858, "and I think more than ordinary fondness for teaching." As Mary Eliza Robarts observed on August 19th, 1853, "I think his forte must be teaching, for he is not a very spirited preacher." On June 5th, 1851, he married Emily A. Gray (1819–1892), daughter of John Jammieson Gray (1774–1838), of Beech Island, Edgefield District, South Carolina; she was a permanent invalid, and there were no children. Three of her sisters resided in Marietta: Eliza C. Gray (1804–1867), wife of David Ardis (1804–1872), a planter; Julia H. Gray (1817–1857), wife of the Rev. John Francis Lanneau (1809–1867), a Presbyterian clergyman, missionary to Syria (1836–1841; 1843–1846), and stated supply in Marietta (1846–1855); and Adeline T. Gray (1825–1862), a spinster. James Lea

Rogers died in Atlanta on November 4th, 1891, and was buried in Citizens Cemetery, Marietta. Emily (Gray) Rogers died on September 30th, 1892, and was buried beside her husband. On May 4th, 1850, Rogers wrote the Rev. Dr. Charles Colcock Jones after four years as inmate in the Jones household: "Allow me to say that to no other man do I feel myself so largely indebted as to yourself. And there is no family circle more dear to me, or to which in after life my thoughts will more frequently and fondly revert. There has been no period of my life since I left my own maternal roof so pleasant or profitable to me as that spent in your family, in which I have esteemed it a great privilege and pleasure to dwell."

ROGERS, JOHN SWIFT (1815–1876), dry goods merchant, son of Penuel Bowen Rogers (1769–1826), was born in Brookfield, Massachusetts, on March 20th, 1815. In early manhood he settled in Savannah, Georgia, where he was for many years a successful dry goods merchant. Shortly before the Civil War he joined John Wilson Nevitt and Henry Lathrop in the firm of Nevitt, Lathrop & Rogers. On November 21st, 1867, he married Mrs. Mary F. Russell. He died in Savannah on October 6th, 1876, and was buried in Laurel Grove Cemetery. According to the Savannah *Morning News* (October 7th, 1876), he was "a staunch and reliable man."

ROGERS, MARIA PRESTON POPE (1839–1909), younger daughter of Jason Rogers (1803–1848) and Josephine Preston (1809–1842), was born in Louisville, Kentucky, on June 17th, 1839. Her father, a native of Newburgh, New York, and a graduate of the United States Military Academy (1821), had retired from military service in 1836 and settled in Louisville, home of his wife's family. Josephine (Preston) Rogers died on November 6th, 1842, and Jason Rogers died less than six years later, on May 4th, 1848, leaving Maria Preston Pope Rogers and her elder sister, Susan Preston Rogers (1836–1871) to the care of their maternal aunt, Maria Preston (1804–1895), widow of John Pope. On January 14th, 1858, Maria Preston Pope Rogers became the wife of Dr. Thomas Palmer Satterwhite (1835–1917), son of Dr. Thomas Palmer Satterwhite and Mary Cabell Breckinridge, of Lexington, Kentucky, and nephew of John Cabell Breckinridge (1821–1875), vice-president of the United States under President James Buchanan (1857–1861). Her husband, a graduate of the Medical Department of the University of Louisville (1857), practiced his profession in Louisville for sixty years (1857–1917). Maria Preston Pope (Rogers) Satterwhite died in Louisville on March 26th, 1909, survived by her husband, two sons, and two daughters, and was buried in Cave Hill Cemetery. Dr. Thomas Palmer Satterwhite died on June 3rd, 1917, and was buried beside his wife.

ROGERS, SUSAN PRESTON (1836–1871), elder daughter of Jason Rogers (1803–1848) and Josephine Preston (1809–1842), was born in Louisville, Kentucky, on September 24th,

1836. Her father, a native of Newburgh, New York, and a graduate of the United States Military Academy (1821), had retired from military service in 1836 and settled in Louisville, home of his wife's family. Josephine (Preston) Rogers died on November 6th, 1842, and Jason Rogers died less than six years later, on May 4th, 1848, leaving Susan Preston Rogers and her younger sister, Maria Preston Pope Rogers (1839–1909) to the care of their maternal aunt, Maria Preston (1804–1895), widow of John Pope. On November 23rd, 1859, Susan Preston Rogers became the wife of John Watson Barr (1826–1907), son of William Barr (1796–1844) and Ann Watson (1808–1829). Her husband, a graduate of the law school of Transylvania University (1847), practiced his profession in Louisville for twenty-six years (1854–1880); for twenty years (1880–1899) he was judge of the United States district court for the district of Kentucky. Susan (Rogers) Barr died in Louisville on Christmas Day 1871, survived by her husband, two sons, and five daughters, and was buried in Cave Hill Cemetery. John Watson Barr died on December 31st, 1907, and was buried beside his wife.

ROGERS, WILLIAM (1817–1908), banker, son of John Rogers, was born in Fifeshire, Scotland, on November 1st, 1817. In 1838 he migrated to the United States and settled in Savannah, Georgia, with whose financial interests he was prominently identified for almost seventy years. He first entered the business of R. & W. King, cotton factors; he later engaged in banking. In 1844 he married Ann C. Beck (1823–1852); their only son, John H. Rogers, lieutenant in the 66th Regiment Georgia Infantry, was killed near Atlanta on July 22nd, 1864. In 1854 he married Mary Eliza Millen (1823–1927), daughter of Dr. George Millen and Eliza Jane Williams Dennis; two of their sons lived to maturity: William White Rogers, cashier of the Merchants' National Bank of Savannah; and Macpherson Millen Rogers, New York agent of the Central Railroad & Banking Company of Georgia. During the Civil War William Rogers was a purchasing agent for the Commissary Department, of which his brother-in-law, Macpherson Berrien Millen (1821–1896), was captain and later major. On April 16th, 1864, he enlisted as a private in Captain John Cunningham's Company (B), 1st Battalion Georgia Reserves; on October 17th, 1864, he was promoted to lieutenant. After the war he was for twenty-one years associated with the Central Railroad & Banking Company of Georgia, first as bookkeeper in the Savannah office (1866–1869), later as general superintendent (1869–1887). In 1887 he retired from the railroad to become chairman of the board of directors of the Citizens' & Southern Bank, a post he held for the rest of his life. He died in Savannah on October 8th, 1908, and was buried in Bonaventure Cemetery. "No man commanded greater respect," observed the Savannah *Morning News* (October 9th, 1908). "He was public-spirited and charitable, exceedingly methodical; and in his long

career as a railroad official he guarded the interests of every man under him as carefully as he did his own." Mary Eliza (Millen) Rogers died in Savannah on April 8th, 1927, aged one hundred and three, and was buried beside her husband. For many years she was the oldest living member of the Independent Presbyterian Church, having joined in 1842. According to the Savannah *Morning News* (April 9th, 1927), "She was a woman of great appreciation of the good things in life, had a lively intellect, was keenly interested in Savannah, was happy and patient in her associations, a staunch friend, and one of the most remarkable women who has ever lived in Savannah."

ROKENBAUGH, JACOB HENRY (1843–1864), Confederate soldier, son of Jacob Rokenbaugh (1799–1871), was born in McIntosh County, Georgia, in 1843. His father, a native of Virginia, was a rich timber merchant in Darien. On May 17th, 1862, he enlisted for six months as a private in the Liberty Independent Troop (Company G, 5th Regiment Georgia Cavalry); on January 30th, 1864, he enlisted for the war as a private in the Liberty Mounted Rangers (Company B, 20th Battalion Georgia Cavalry). On February 29th, 1864, prior to his departure for Virginia, he married Ida Rosalie McConnell (1844–1924), daughter of Dr. William Phinizy McConnell (1790–1854) and Ann Amelia Dicks (1803–1877), of Walthourville. As Mrs. Mary Jones wrote on March 16th, 1864, "Mr. Buttolph officiated—says she was dressed splendidly and was a lovely bride. The groom gave a handsome fee." Six months later, on August 19th, 1864, Jacob Henry Rokenbaugh died of disease in a military hospital at Kittrell Springs, North Carolina. His funeral was held in Walthourville on August 25th, 1864, and he was buried in Midway Cemetery. His only daughter, Ida Henry Rokenbaugh (1864–1895), was born on Christmas Day 1864 in Thomasville, Georgia, whither her mother had fled for safety from Sherman's army. In 1872, with money inherited from her father-in-law at his death on November 28th, 1871, Ida (McConnell) Rokenbaugh removed to Atlanta with her only child, her mother, and her two unmarried sisters. There, on July 5th, 1882, she became the wife of William Spotswood Turner (1836–1892), son of James A. Turner and Mary Payne, of Lynchburg, Virginia.

ROLAND DE LA PLATIÈRE, MARIE JEANNE (PHILIPON) (1754–1793), was born in Paris, France, on March 17th, 1754, daughter of an engraver. From childhood she manifested remarkable intellectual gifts, and she developed into a woman of unusual brilliance and force. On February 4th, 1780, she became the wife of Jean Marie Roland de la Platière (1734–1793), author and statesman, whose political fortunes she largely shaped. As a disciple of Jean-Jacques Rousseau she favored the emancipation of the common people and enthusiastically supported the French Revolution. In 1791 she and her husband became allied with the Girondist party; on March 23rd, 1792, Roland was appointed minister of the interior in the new Girondist government; accused of favoring the king, he resigned on January 23rd, 1793, two days after the king's execution. With the fall of the Girondins in the summer of 1793 Madame Roland was arrested and confined in the Conciergerie, where she wrote her memoirs, *Appel à l'impartiale postérité* (1795). On November 8th, 1793, she was guillotined, her last words being: "O Liberty, what crimes are committed in thy name!" Her husband, hearing of her death, committed suicide near Rouen on November 15th, 1793. The memoirs and letters of Madame Roland subsequently appeared in numerous editions both in French and in English.

ROMAINE, WILLIAM (1714–1795), Anglican clergyman, son of William Romaine, was born in Hartlepool, England, on September 25th, 1714. He attended Hertford College (Oxford) and graduated from Christ Church College (Oxford), receiving his B.A. (1734) and his M.A. (1737). He was for some years curate of Banstead, Surrey, and of Horton, Middlesex; in 1748 he settled in London, where he held lectureships at St. George's, Botolph Lane; St. Botolph's, Billingsgate; St. Dunstan's-in-the-West; and St. George's, Hanover Square. As a disciple of George Whitefield he encountered sharp opposition from the fashionable world; in 1766 he finally found a secure position and a satisfied congregation at St. Anne's, Blackfriars, where he continued to preach for the rest of his life. He died on July 26th, 1795. His theology and evangelical devotion are forcefully presented in his three treatises: *The Life of Faith* (1763), *The Walk of Faith* (1771), and *The Triumph of Faith* (1795).

ROOT, SIDNEY (1824–1897), dry goods merchant, son of Salmon Root and Eliza Carpenter, was born in Montague, Massachusetts, on March 12th, 1824, the seventh of nine children. In October 1843 he removed to Lumpkin, Georgia, and became clerk in the general merchandise business of his brother-in-law, W. A. Rawson, who had married his sister, Julia Root, earlier that year. By 1848 he was a partner in the firm. On April 17th, 1849, he married Mary H. Clarke (1831–1886), daughter of the Hon. James Clarke and sister of the Hon. Marshall Johnson Clarke. In March 1858 he settled with his family in Atlanta, where he invested largely in real estate and joined John N. Beach in the firm of Beach & Root, wholesale and retail merchants. In 1861 he was one of a committee selected to escort Jefferson Davis from Atlanta to Montgomery for his inauguration as President; a strong and permanent friendship developed between the two, and Root was a frequent visitor at the executive mansion in Richmond. During the war the firm of Beach & Root imported supplies for the Confederate government; the firm maintained warehouses in Atlanta, Charleston, and Wilmington and conducted a highly successful business. In 1864, at the request of President Davis, he ran the

blockade and visited Great Britain, France, and Spain on a confidential government mission; he reached Atlanta in July 1865. Finding his vast fortune practically destroyed, he removed with his family to New York in 1866 and remained until 1878; upon his return to Atlanta he gave up business and devoted himself to philanthropy. It was he who in 1883 persuaded Lemuel Pratt Grant to present to the city the tract of one hundred acres which became Grant Park. He was for many years an active member of the Second Baptist Church, where he was leader of the choir, superintendent of the Sunday school, and teacher of a Bible class. He was author of *Primary Bible Questions for Young Children* (Atlanta, 1864). He died in Atlanta on February 13th, 1897, and was buried in Oakland Cemetery beside his wife, who had died on January 9th, 1886.

ROPER, MARY SMITH (GRIMKÉ) (1822–1880): *Mrs. Thomas Roper,* daughter of Dr. John Grimké (1785–1864) and Sophia Caroline Ladson (1797–1863), was born in Charleston, South Carolina, on March 28th, 1822. On December 12th, 1848, she became the wife of Thomas Roper, of Charleston; there was one daughter, Grace Julia Roper (born November 15th, 1849), who on January 8th, 1868, became the wife of James Munro. Mary Smith (Grimké) Roper died in Charleston on March 12th, 1880, and was buried in Magnolia Cemetery.

ROSECRANS, WILLIAM STARKE (1819–1898), Union soldier, eldest son of Crandall Rosecrans and Jemima Hopkins, was born in Kingston Township, Delaware County, Ohio, on September 6th, 1819. He graduated from the United States Military Academy in 1842. After serving one year at Hampton Roads, Virginia, he returned to West Point, where he was assistant professor of engineering and assistant professor of natural and experimental philosophy (1843–1847). On August 24th, 1843, he married Ann Eliza Hegeman, of New York City. He resigned his commission on April 1st, 1854, and returned to civilian life as an engineer and architect in Cincinnati, Ohio. At the outbreak of the Civil War he volunteered as aide-de-camp to General McClellan; in June 1861 he was commissioned brigadier general in the regular army and succeeded McClellan in command of the Department of the Ohio; in June 1862 he succeeded Pope in command of the Army of the Mississippi. He was promoted to major general of volunteers in October 1862 and ordered to Kentucky, where he relieved Buell and reorganized his command as the Army of the Cumberland. In November 1862 he joined Buell at Murfreesboro; on December 29th, 1862, he met Bragg at Stone River. Bragg retreated to Shelbyville; for six months the two armies faced each other; in June 1863 Rosecrans advanced, forcing Bragg back to Chattanooga. At Chickamauga (September 19th–20th, 1863) Rosecrans was through his own error defeated and forced back to Chattanooga and besieged. On October 19th, 1863, he was relieved and placed in command of the Department of the Missouri. After the war he resigned his commission in the regular army (March 28th, 1867), served two years as United States minister to Mexico (1868–1869), and then engaged in mining operations in Mexico and California. He represented California in Congress (1881–1885) and served as registrar of the treasury (1885–1893). Returning to California, he resided on his ranch near Los Angeles until his death there on March 11th, 1898. He was buried in Rosedale Cemetery, Los Angeles; in 1902 he was reinterred in Arlington National Cemetery, Fort Myer, Virginia.

ROSS, JAMES COLUMBUS (1837–1867), lawyer, son of James L. Ross, was born near Cuthbert, Georgia, in 1837. His father, a native of North Carolina, was a farmer in Randolph County; he later settled in Baker County. At the outbreak of the Civil War James Columbus Ross was a lawyer practicing in Thomasville. On July 27th, 1861, in Savannah, Georgia, he enlisted for one year as a private in the Ochlochnee Light Infantry (Company G, 13th Regiment Georgia Infantry; later designated Company E, 29th Regiment Georgia Infantry). On May 7th, 1862, he was elected second lieutenant; from July 23rd, 1862, until March 5th, 1863, he was "in arrest at convalescent camp by sentence of court-martial"; on February 22nd, 1863, he tendered his "unconditional resignation, to take effect immediately"; and on the same day Colonel William J. Young recommended its acceptance: "Lieutenant Ross is under thirty years of age and by reason of his habits of intemperance, in which he cannot or will not control himself, *is wholly unfit and incompetent* to be an officer in the Confederate States army." On March 21st, 1863, in Bainbridge, Georgia, James Columbus Ross enlisted for the war as second sergeant in Captain C. G. Campbell's Independent Cavalry, Georgia Siege Artillery; on September 23rd, 1863, in Decatur, Georgia, he transferred to Company B, 29th Battalion Georgia Cavalry. He was captured in Dorchester, Liberty County, Georgia, on December 13th, 1864, imprisoned at Point Lookout, Maryland, and paroled on February 18th, 1865. Shortly after the war, on June 19th, 1865, he married Evelyn (Eva) Josephine Anderson (1848–1930), younger daughter of Joseph Andrew Anderson (1820–1866) and Evelyn Elouisa Jones (1822–1849), of Dorchester, Liberty County. ("Eva is a sweet, interesting little girl," commented Mrs. Laura E. Buttolph on June 30th, 1865, "and Mr. Ross is said to be a very intelligent, smart young gentleman.") On July 3rd, 1867, Ross drowned in the Sunbury River, Liberty County, while attempting to right a canoe that had upset. He was survived by his wife and one son, Joseph Anderson Ross (born March 24th, 1866); a daughter, named for her father, was born on October 22nd, 1867. For several years Evelyn Josephine (Anderson) Ross lived with her two children in the household of her husband's father in Baker County. On August 6th, 1870, in Cuth-

bert, she became the wife of her mother's first cousin, John Odingsell Hart (1844–1903).

ROWLAND, CHARLES ALDEN (1833–1902), merchant and planter, was born in Augusta, Georgia, on July 26th, 1833. For many years he was associated with Porter Fleming (1808–1891) in the firm of Fleming & Rowland; according to the *Augusta City Directory* (1859), "Fleming & Rowland, wholesale grocers, keep on hand large stocks of sugar, coffee, bagging, rope, salt, nails, molasses, and every descripton of groceries (liquors excepted)." He also had extensive planting interests. On June 13th 1860, he married Catherine Barnes Whitehead (1838–1917); there were four children. During the Civil War he served briefly as sergeant in Company B, 1st Local Troops Georgia Infantry. He was a charter member of the Second Presbyterian Church, Augusta, an elder, a member of its first session, and for many years session clerk. All three of his sons were elders in the Presbyterian Church. In his later years he was extremely deaf. He died in Augusta during the night of December 18th, 1902, survived by his wife and four children, and was buried in Magnolia Cemetery. According to *The Christian Observer* (February 11th, 1903), "Mr. Rowland was every whit a gentleman. . . . With men he was dignified and temperate. With ladies he was gentle and gallant. With little children his eyes sparkled with merry sympathy. . . . He appreciated and loved good literature. He was familiar with the production of the best authors; and when by reason of his infirmity he was denied many of the delights of social intercourse, much of his time was pleasantly and profitably spent in his well-stored library." Catherine Barnes (Whitehead) Rowland died on August 17th, 1917, and was buried beside her husband.

RUCKER, ALEXANDER RANDOLPH (1831–1900), planter and merchant, son of Joseph Rucker (1788–1864) and Margaret Houston Speer (1792–1864), was born in Ruckersville, Elbert County, Georgia, in 1831. His father, a native of Virginia, had settled in 1812 at the headwaters of Van's Creek in Elbert County, where he had founded the village of Ruckersville, amassed a handsome fortune from planting, and conducted his own bank, the Bank of Ruckersville, with phenomenal success. Alexander Randolph Rucker attended Franklin College (Athens) with the class of 1852 but did not graduate; he also attended Dane Law School, Harvard University, in the autumn of 1854. On January 22nd, 1859, he married Aurelia Calhoun, a great-niece of John Caldwell Calhoun. On August 17th, 1861, in Augusta, he enlisted as a private in the Richmond Hussars (Company A, Cobb's Legion Georgia Cavalry); he subsequently became third corporal (January 1863), fourth sergeant (March 1863), and second lieutenant (November 1863). He fought in Virginia throughout the war and was paroled at Charlotte, North Carolina, on May 23rd, 1865. After the war he worked spasmodically as a merchant and a farmer, but he was always something of a ne'er-do-well, and his later years were spent in want and degradation. He died on an old cot in an abandoned room above a store in Elberton, Georgia, on August 16th, 1900, and was buried in City Cemetery. His headstone reads "E. R." (Eleck Rucker), and his footstone reads "C. S. A." As the Elberton *Star* (August 23rd, 1900) observed, "Mr. Rucker had his faults. He was weak and on many occasions gave way to temptations. It is true that he wasted the golden opportunities of his life. But all in all he was his worst enemy. . . . For over a month he eked out a miserable existence in that miserably furnished room, with no one to give him a kind word or to soothe his aching bones save a few faithful friends. . . . The last request made by him was that he be shrouded in the flag of the Confederacy, which request was granted."

RUSSELL, JAMES NEWTON (1830–1916), planter, third son of Edward William Russell (1798–1863) and Susan Sarah Way (1805–1884), was born in Walthourville, Liberty County, Georgia, on October 10th, 1830. His father, a native of the island of San Salvador and a graduate of Oxford University (England), was a large landowner and slaveholder in coastal Georgia. In 1847 James Newton Russell accompanied his family to Marietta, Cobb County, Georgia, where he planted with his father until the outbreak of the Civil War. On January 19th, 1854, he married Mary H. Eve (1832–1873); there were four children. On May 13th, 1862, in Savannah, he enlisted as a private in Company B, 21st Battalion Georgia Cavalry; on August 1st, 1863, he transferred to the Liberty Independent Troop (Company G, 5th Regiment Georgia Cavalry). After the war he resumed farming in Cobb County. On November 17th, 1874, he married his cousin, Anna H. Curtis (1849–1881), daughter of the Rev. William Curtis (1816–1873), a Baptist clergyman, and Elizabeth Amanda Walthour (1823–1913), of Limestone Springs, South Carolina. There were two children; Anna (Curtis) Russell died at the birth of the second child early in 1881, and five years later (on September 9th, 1886) her aunt, Charlotte Caroline Walthour, widow of Augustus S. Morrall, adopted the two children and took them into her Atlanta household. Soon after his wife's death James Newton Russell settled in Seabreeze, Daytona Beach, Florida, where he pioneered as a nurseryman for some thirty years. He died in Seabreeze on June 11th, 1916, and was buried in Pinewood Cemetery, Daytona Beach. Edward (Eddie) Russell (1854–1859), his eldest son by his first marriage, was malformed at birth; he never developed, and he died after an illness of three months on November 8th, 1859.

RUSSELL, JOHN (1811–1881), steamboat captain, was born in Nassau in 1811. In early manhood he settled in Savannah, Georgia, where he resided for the rest of his life. For some years prior to the Civil War he was captain of the *Fort George Packet,* a schooner plying between Savannah and Riceboro in Liberty County; he often docked his vessel at Montevideo, plantation of the Rev. Dr. Charles Colcock Jones on the North Newport River, to deposit or take on cargo. Among the Jones papers preserved at Tulane University is the following letter written by John Russell from Savannah on August 15th, 1855: "Not knowing but that you may wish to ship something by me, as it is the last trip for the season and no other opportunity afforded you, I take this method of informing you that I am coming out again to leave on Saturday next the 18th inst., kind Providence permitting, and would be glad to bring anything you may want." During the Civil War Russell served in the Confederate navy. On October 19th, 1864, he married Mrs. Mary Ann Hickson (1818–1894), of Savannah. He died in Savannah on December 5th, 1881, and was buried in Laurel Grove Cemetery. Mary Ann (Hickson) Russell died on May 23rd, 1894, and was buried beside her husband.

RUSSELL, WILLIAM HUNTINGTON (1809–1885), educator, son of Matthew Talcott Russell and Mary Huntington, was born in Middletown, Connecticut, on August 12th, 1809. He was a descendant in the fifth generation of the Rev. Noadiah Russell, one of the founders of Yale College. After graduating from Yale College in 1833 he taught for two years (1833–1835) at the Edge Hill School in Princeton, New Jersey; returning to New Haven, he attended the Yale Medical School for one year and graduated in 1836. While at Yale he founded the famous Skull & Bones Society. On August 29th, 1836, in Clinton, New York, he married Mary Elizabeth Hubbard, daughter of Dr. Thomas Hubbard (1776–1838), professor of surgery at the Yale Medical School. In the same year he established in New Haven the school with which he was identified for the rest of his life—the Collegiate and Commercial Institute, for many years one of the most distinguished and successful schools in the country. At first the school was literary; in 1853 Russell introduced the military drill and discipline which made it famous. He represented New Haven in the state legislature in 1846 and 1847. He was an ardent abolitionist and a personal friend of John Brown; he was one of the trustees named in Brown's will. At the outbreak of the Civil War he was appointed major general of the Connecticut state militia. In December 1868 he was appointed collector of internal revenue for the second district. He died in New Haven on May 19th, 1885, survived by his wife and six children, and was buried in the Grove Street Cemetery. According to the New Haven *Evening Register* (May 20th, 1885), "He was conscientious to the point of almost extreme sensitiveness, and though in his institute there were able instructors, he gave his personal attention to the studies of the boys entrusted to his care, watching over their morals with an almost parental solicitude and leading them into the cultivation of noble ambitions as much by the absence of precept as by any reiteration of advice. No one ever governed a school with greater success and with less apparent effort."

RUSSELL, WILLIAM JOHN (1825–1897), merchant and manufacturer, eldest son of Edward William Russell (1798–1863) and Susan Sarah Way (1805–1884), was born in Walthourville, Liberty County, Georgia, on February 8th, 1825. His father, a native of the island of San Salvador and a graduate of Oxford University (England), was a large landowner and slaveholder in coastal Georgia. In early manhood William John Russell went to Milledgeville with his mother's uncle, Charlton Hines (1785–1864), state senator from Liberty County, to serve as secretary of the state senate. He later went to Savannah, where he was a clerk in the countinghouse of his mother's brother, William James Way (1803–1888). In 1847 he accompanied his family to Marietta, Cobb County, Georgia, where he was a partner of the Hon. Charles James McDonald (1793–1860), governor of Georgia (1839–1843), in operating the Sweetwater factory, a large cotton mill located southwest of Marietta in Campbell (now Douglas) County. At the same time he was a partner of John Heyward Glover (1816–1859) and Richard Trapier Brumby (1804–1875) in operating a tannery on the outskirts of Marietta. In the early summer of 1864 both factory and tannery were destroyed by Sherman's army, and Russell entered Confederate service, detailed to the Augusta arsenal. After the war he was general agent and manager of the Princeton factory near Athens. On December 29th, 1859, in Marietta, he married Rebecca Harriet Brumby (1829–1902), daughter of Richard Trapier Brumby (1804–1875) and Mary Isabelle Brevard (1806–1875). He died in Atlanta on October 10th, 1897, following an operation to remove a growth in his throat, and was buried in Oconee Hill Cemetery, Athens. Rebecca Harriet (Brumby) Russell died on July 15th, 1902, and was buried beside her husband. Their eldest son, Richard Brevard Russell (1861–1938), was chief justice of the supreme court of Georgia (1923–1938). Their grandson, Richard Brevard Russell (1897–1971), was governor of Georgia (1931–1933) and United States senator from Georgia (1933–1971).

RUTHERFORD, WILLIAMS (1818–1896), educator, son of Williams Rutherford and Eliza Boykin, was born in Midway, near Milledgeville, Georgia, on September 3rd, 1818. After graduating from Franklin College (Athens) in 1838 he taught school and planted on the Flint River for eighteen years. In 1856 he was elected professor of mathematics at Franklin College (Athens), a post he held until 1889, when he resigned and became professor emeritus. On March 23rd, 1841, he married Laura Bataille Cobb (1817–1888), daughter of John Addison Cobb and Sarah Robinson Rootes, and sister of Howell Cobb (1815–1868) and Thomas Reade Rootes Cobb (1823–1862). She died in Athens on October 16th, 1888,

survived by her husband and five children, and was buried in Oconee Hill Cemetery. Williams Rutherford died on August 21st, 1896, survived by three children, and was buried beside his wife. As the Atlanta *Constitution* (August 22nd, 1896) observed, "Professor Rutherford was from youth a consistent member of the Baptist Church, loyal in his friendships, unswerving in the performance of his duty, a fine example to the young, and an exemplification of what the Christian religion can do for one in this world."

SABAL, EMILE TALVANDE (1835–1907), physician, son of Adolphus Sabal, was born in Augusta, Georgia, in 1835. His father, a native of Cuba, had settled in Augusta in early manhood and become a merchant; shortly before the Civil War he removed with his family to Jacksonville, Florida, where he resided for the rest of his life. Emile Talvande Sabal graduated from the Long Island College Hospital (Brooklyn) in 1859 and from the Medical College of Virginia (Richmond) in 1861. On July 13th, 1861, he enlisted in Jacksonville as a private in Company K, 2nd Regiment Florida Infantry; several days later, on July 19th, 1861, he was appointed assistant surgeon and ordered to Richmond, where he served for some months on the staff of General Hospital No. 21. After the war he commenced medical practice in Jacksonville and became one of the leading physicians in the state. He died in Jacksonville on October 11th, 1907, and was buried in St. Joseph's (Catholic) Cemetery. In June 1859 his elder brother, Adolphus M. Sabal, also a physician, married Mary Ophelia Allen, of Liberty County, Georgia, daughter of Benjamin Washington Allen and his second wife, Caroline Elizabeth Fuller. During the Civil War Adolphus M. Sabal was assistant surgeon at Camp Finegan, Florida, from April 1863 until the summer of 1864.

SADLER, CATHERINE ANN (McINTOSH) (1801–1865): *Mrs. Henry Robinson Sadler*, daughter of John Houstoun McIntosh and Eliza Bayard, was born in Camden County, Georgia, in 1801. On December 8th, 1819, she became the wife of Henry Robinson Sadler (1797–1854), of St. Marys, a planter, son of Henry Sadler (1764–1828), an Englishman who had migrated to the United States at the close of the Revolutionary War. Seven of their eight children lived to maturity. Henry Robinson Sadler died of apoplexy at his plantation on the St. Johns River near Jacksonville, Florida, on February 16th, 1854, and was buried near his parents in Oak Grove Cemetery, St. Marys. Shortly after her husband's death Catherine Ann (McIntosh) Sadler removed to Marietta, Georgia, where she resided until the outbreak of the Civil War, sharing the society of her numerous low-country friends and supervising the education of her two younger daughters: Mary A. Sadler (born 1833), who became the wife of Henry Pierce Simms, of Augusta, on August 8th, 1859; and Louisa S. Sadler (born 1839), who became the wife of Edwin Q. Bell, of New York, on September 10th, 1873. A third daugther, Catherine Ann Sadler, became the wife of (1) the Rev. James A. Shanklin, of Charleston, in December 1846, and (2) the Rev. James Habersham Elliott, of Charleston, on February 28th, 1860. Two of her sons fought in the Civil War. Houstoun McIntosh Sadler (born 1831) enlisted in Savannah on November 27th, 1862, as a private in the Savannah Volunteer Guards (Company C, 18th Battalion Georgia Infantry); on January 29th, 1864, he enlisted in Macon as a private in Company C, 12th Battalion Georgia Light Artillery; on February 24th, 1864, he was promoted to quartermaster sergeant; on August 16th, 1864, he was transferred to Company A, South Carolina Siege Train. Nicholas Bayard Sadler (born 1837) enlisted in Savannah on May 24th, 1862, as a private in Captain Joseph S. Claghorn's Company (Chatham Artillery), 1st Volunteer Regiment Georgia Artillery; on October 4th, 1862, he was appointed second lieutenant in Company C, 1st Battalion Georgia Sharpshooters; he was captured at Big Shanty, near Marietta, on June 15th, 1864, and confined on Johnson's Island, Ohio, until released on June 15th, 1865. Catherine Ann (McIntosh) Sadler died in May 1865.

SAFFORD, HENRY (1793–1870), Presbyterian clergyman, son of Jacob Safford and Mary Searle, was born in Royalton, Vermont, on October 8th, 1793. After graduating from Dartmouth College in 1817 and from Princeton Theological Seminary in 1820 he was missionary in New Jersey and Pennsylvania (1821–1822); missionary in Augusta, Georgia (1822–1823); stated supply and teacher in Beech Island, South Carolina (1823–1825); stated supply in Jackson County, Georgia (1825–1826); missionary in Clarence, New York (1826–1831); and stated supply in Louisville, Georgia (1831–1834). From 1834 to 1843 he was a professor at Oglethorpe University. For twenty-one years (1843–1864) he was colporteur, superintendent, and financial agent of the American Tract Society in Georgia and Florida, making his home in Greensboro, Georgia. On December 25th, 1823, he married Eliza Burr (1802–1860), of Beech Island, South Carolina; she died on February 20th, 1860. "I do not think he has quite his usual heart about his work," wrote Mrs. Mary S. Mallard on January 19th, 1861; "the death of his wife and the troubled state of the country cast a shade upon his zeal." After the war he served for several years as Sunday school agent and colporteur of the Presbyterian Board of Publication. He died in Greensboro on October 8th, 1870, his seventy-seventh birthday.

SALE, JOHN SIMMONS (1834–1858), lawyer, son of Peyton W. Sale and Frances E. Simmons, was born in Goshen, Lincoln County, Georgia, in 1834. After attending Franklin College (Athens) with the class of 1853 he entered Dane Law School, Harvard University, where he was roommate of Charles Colcock Jones, Jr., in the autumn of 1854. "He is one of the kindest and most amiable gentlemen I have ever met," wrote Jones on November 4th, 1854. "We became mutual friends soon after our meeting in Cambridge, and the warmest attachment, ripening every day, has grown up between us." After leaving Harvard Sale commenced the practice of law in Augusta, Georgia, where Jones, writing on June 16th, 1855, found him to be "very comfortably located" and predicted that "with his winning ways and general popularity" he would "succeed admirably." In the spring of 1857 Sale was to have married Sarah Ann (Sallie) Toombs (1835–1866), daughter of the Hon. Robert Toombs and Julia Ann DuBose of Washington, Wilkes County, Georgia. A telegram dated "Augusta, April 7th, 1857" is preserved among the Jones papers at Tulane University: "Miss Toombs very ill. Wedding postponed." As Mrs. Mary Jones explained on June 30th, 1857, "It is said that Mr. Toombs, with a father's feelings for a daughter's happiness, could not do otherwise than prevent the marriage. Withal Mr. Sale is spoken of as a young man of *fascinating manners and address.*" His marital hopes thus dashed, Sale removed to Memphis, Tennessee, where he had scarcely commenced practice before illness compelled him to return to his parents' home. He died of consumption in Goshen, Lincoln County, on September 3rd, 1858, as he was "just entering his twenty-fifth year." On April 15th, 1858, Sallie Toombs became the wife of Dudley McIvor DuBose (1834–1883), a lawyer then practicing in Memphis, Tennessee.

SANDERS, WILLIAM PRICE (1833–1863), Union soldier, was born in Lexington, Kentucky, on August 12th, 1833. He graduated from the United States Military Academy in 1856. At the outbreak of the Civil War he became first lieutenant (May 1st, 1861) and captain (May 14th, 1861) of the 6th United States Cavalry. After participating in the Peninsula campaign (1862) and the Maryland campaign (1862) he became colonel of the 5th Kentucky Cavalry (March 1863) and brigadier general of volunteers (October 1863). He died in Knoxville, Tennessee, on November 18th, 1863, from a wound received two days before at Campbell's Station.

SAVAGE, MARIA (1799–1879): *Mrs. John Savage,* was born in New Jersey in 1799. Shortly after her marriage to John Savage (1806–1873), a native of Hudson, New York, she and her husband settled in Savannah, Georgia, where John Savage engaged for many years in the hat business, and where Maria Savage was for nearly half a century proprietor of large boardinghouses. According to the Savannah *Morning News* (November 28th, 1879), "Mrs. Savage was a most estimable lady, and was extensively known." In the late winter of 1857 Mrs. Laura E. Buttolph spent the final weeks of her confinement at "Mrs. Savage's"; her eldest child, Charles Edward Maxwell Buttolph, was born there on March 21st, 1857. "I am glad I am here," she wrote her husband on February 28th, 1857, "because I can see all of my friends who call, and Mrs. Savage is so kind, and everything is so nice, and Mother can go out and leave me sometimes." John Savage died in Savannah on March 27th, 1873, and was buried in Laurel Grove Cemetery. Maria Savage died on November 26th, 1879, survived by four children, and was buried beside her husband. On December 12th, 1868, Mrs. Mary Jones, passing through Savannah en route to New Orleans, "went to Mrs. Savage's. She was just going to market—literally before daylight. Made me most welcome in her own warm chamber. I took a hearty breakfast, for which she would not allow me to pay a cent."

SCHENCK, WILLIAM EDWARD (1819–1903), Presbyterian clergyman, son of John Conover Schenck and Anne Brooks Hutchinson, was born in Princeton, New Jersey, on March 29th, 1819. After graduating from the College of New Jersey (Princeton) in 1838 he studied law for one year in the office of James S. Green, of Princeton, and then entered Princeton Theological Seminary, from which he graduated in 1842. He was pastor of the Presbyterian church, Manchester, New Jersey (1843–1845); the Hammond Street Presbyterian Church, New York City (1845–1848); and the First Presbyterian Church, Princeton (1848–1852). After two years as superintendent of church extension in the Presbytery of Philadelphia he was elected secretary of the Board of Publication of the Presbyterian Church, with offices in Philadelphia, where he continued for thirty-two years (1854–1886), serving also for eight years (1862–1870) as editor of the board. He married first (on April 18th, 1843) Jane Whittemore Torrey, eldest daughter of William Torrey, of New York City, and niece of Professor John Torrey, of the College of New Jersey (Princeton). After her death on March 9th, 1856, he married second (on April 3rd, 1863) Mary Blake Kittle, daughter of the Rev. Andrew N. Kittle, a Dutch Reformed clergyman. He received the honorary degree of doctor of divinity from Jefferson College (Canonsburg, Pennsylvania) in 1859. He became a director of Princeton Theological Seminary in 1865. After his retirement in 1886 he lived in West Philadelphia until 1899, when he removed to the residence of his son in Oakmont. He died in Oakmont on December 14th, 1903, and was buried in Princeton.

SCHLEY, HENRY JACKSON (1825–1893), planter and civil engineer, son of the Hon. William Schley (1786–1858) and his second wife, Mrs. Eliza Sarah Hargrove, was born at Richmond Hill, his father's plantation six miles southwest of Augusta, Georgia, in 1825. The Hon. William Schley, a distinguished lawyer, was a member of the state house of representatives (1830), a member of Congress (1833–1835), and governor of Georgia (1835–1837); Schley County, Georgia, organized on December 22nd, 1857, was named in his honor. Eliza Sarah (Hargrove) Schley died on February 11th, 1845. Henry Jackson Schley attended Franklin College (Athens) with the class of 1845 but did not graduate. In 1846 he married Frances Virginia Miller (1828–1901), daughter of Baldwin B. Miller and his first wife, Rosa Anderson, widow of John Morrison. Frances Virginia Miller was thus a half-sister of Sarah Almira Morrison (1822–1886), wife of Gideon Dowse; and Henry Jackson Schley and Gideon Dowse were brothers-in-law. Prior to the Civil War Schley was a large landholder in Burke and Richmond Counties; one of his plantations, Buckhead, comprising 1412 acres and situated on Buckhead Creek, Burke County, some twelve miles north of Midville, was sold to Charles Colcock Jones, Jr., in October 1862. In 1857 Schley removed to Texas, drawn by the phenomenal success of his elder half-brother, George Hanson Schley (1815–1866), a large planter in Fort Bend County. On December 1st, 1858, Henry Jackson Schley purchased 2630 acres in Wharton County (adjoining Fort Bend County on the west). At the outbreak of the Civil War he returned to Georgia to settle his business affairs; in April 1861 he was captain of the Miller Volunteers, a company from Burke County stationed at Camp Satilla on the Georgia coast near Brunswick. In 1866 he returned to Texas and settled in Wharton, where he resided for the rest of his life. He planted extensively, and in the 1880s he surveyed most of the land in Wharton, Matagorda, Jackson, and Calhoun Counties. On October 20th, 1893, he dropped dead while surveying land in Hungerford, some five miles northeast of Wharton. He was buried in an unmarked grave in Wharton Cemetery. Frances Virginia (Miller) Schley died on July 20th, 1901, and was buried beside her husband.

SCHOMACKER, JOHN H. (1799–1875), piano manufacturer, was born in Germany in 1799. In 1837 he migrated to the United States and settled in Philadelphia, Pennsylvania, where he commenced the manufacture of pianos in 1838. In 1854 he erected an extensive factory at the corner of 11th and Catharine Streets, where J. H. Schomacker & Company prospered for many years as one of the earliest piano manufacturers in the United States. John H. Schomacker died in Philadelphia on January 16th, 1875, and was buried beside his wife in Mount Vernon Cemetery. On August 16th, 1851, the Rev. Dr. Charles Colcock Jones, then residing in Philadelphia, purchased for his daughter, Mary Sharpe Jones, "one superior rosewood pianoforte with stool at $285"; a receipt for "payment in full," signed by J. H. Schomacker & Company, is preserved among the Jones papers at Tulane University: "The above pianoforte purchased by C. C. Jones is manufactured by us, made of good and seasonable materials and with very good workmanship, so that we guarantee said instrument for one year. Should anything to the contrary occur, we are willing to give full satisfaction, either by exchanging the piano for another or refunding the purchase money." Another receipt, dated October 25th, 1853, reads: "To packing a pianoforte ($7.00); tuning and polishing ($2.50); transporting from house to factory ($1.50); from factory to wharf ($1.00). Total: $12.00." A third receipt, dated October 25th, 1853, fixes the cost of shipping the pianoforte via steamship from Philadelphia to Savannah at $7.08.

SCHUBERT, WILLIAM (1803–1871), musician, was born in Germany in 1803. By 1848 he was living in Philadelphia, Pennsylvania, where he continued to teach music until his death on April 4th, 1871. He never married. He was buried in an unmarked grave in Laurel Hill Cemetery. From 1850 to 1853 Mary Sharpe Jones, then residing with her parents in Philadelphia, studied guitar with William Schubert. In the spring of 1854, after her return to Georgia, she was given "a beautiful German canary" by her cousin, Laura Elizabeth Maxwell. "He sings finely and has a remarkable crest or cap of feathers on his head," wrote Mrs. Mary Jones on March 4th, 1854, "and is so strikingly like Mary's guitar teacher in Philadelphia, who you remember was a German, that she calls him *Willie* Schubert. Poor Charlie and Betty both came to tragical ends—he killed by a rat, she decapitated by a loggerhead."

SCONYERS, ELI (1812–1867), plantation overseer, was born in Georgia in 1812. All his life he resided in Burke County, Georgia, where for some years he managed Buckhead, the plantation of Henry Jackson Schley situated on Buckhead Creek some twelve miles north of Midville (Depot No. 9½, Central Railroad of Georgia). When Charles Colcock Jones, Jr., purchased the plantation in October 1862 and changed its name to Indianola, Sconyers was retained as manager—"a worthy man," Jones wrote on October 16th, 1862, "and a strict member of the Baptist Church, without children and with an excellent wife, represented to be an honest man and attentive to his duties." Sconyers continued to manage Indianola until his death there on October 1st, 1867.

SCOTT, THOMAS (1747–1821), English commentator on the Bible, son of John Scott, was born in Braytoft, Lincolnshire, on February 4th, 1747. He was curate of Stoke Goldington and Weston Underwood (1773–1775), Ravenstone (1775–1781), and Olney (1781–1785). In 1785 he removed to London, where he undertook to write a commentary on the Bible in one hundred weekly numbers, for which he was to receive a guinea a number. One hundred and seventy-four numbers were eventually published, the first on March 22nd, 1788, the last on June 2nd, 1792. The commentary was subsequently reprinted in many editions on both sides of the Atlantic. Sir James Stephen called it "the greatest theological performance of our age and country." Scott preached at St. Margaret's, Lothbury, from 1785 to 1801. In 1803 he settled in Aston Sandford, where he died on April 16th, 1821. *A Commentary on the Holy Bible, Containing the Old and New Testaments According to the Authorized Version: With Explanatory Notes, Practical Observations, and Cop-*

ious Marginal References, by Thomas Scott, was published in Philadelphia in three quarto volumes in 1858 "from the last London edition."

SCOTT, THOMAS FIELDING (1807–1867), Protestant Episcopal bishop, was born in Iredell County, North Carolina, on March 12th, 1807. After graduating from Franklin College (Athens) in 1829 he engaged for some ten years in secular business before preparing for the Episcopal ministry. He was ordained deacon in Augusta, Georgia, on March 12th, 1843; he was ordained priest in Macon, Georgia, on February 24th, 1844. He was rector of St. James's Church, Marietta (1844–1851), and Trinity Church, Columbus (1851–1853). On January 8th, 1854, he was consecrated bishop in Christ Church, Savannah; thereafter he served as bishop of Oregon and Washington Territory until his death. In 1867, while traveling from California to New York, he contracted fever in Panama; he died in New York City on July 14th, 1867. He was buried in Trinity Churchyard.

SCOTT, WILLIAM ANDERSON (1813–1885), Presbyterian clergyman, son of Eli Scott and Martha Anderson, was born in Bedford County, Tennessee, on January 31st, 1813. After graduating from Cumberland College (Princeton, Kentucky) in 1833 he attended Princeton Theological Seminary for nine months. He was missionary in Louisiana and Arkansas (1835–1836); principal of the female academy in Winchester, Tennessee (1836–1838); pastor of the Hermitage Church on Andrew Jackson's estate near Nashville, Tennessee (1838–1840); and pastor of the Presbyterian church in Tuscaloosa, Alabama (1840–1842). While pastor of the First Presbyterian Church in New Orleans (1842–1854) he rose to prominence throughout the South and the Southwest; in 1854 he removed on invitation to San Francisco, California, where he founded Calvary Presbyterian Church and continued as pastor until 1861. After some months in England he settled in New York City, where he was pastor of the Forty-Second Street Presbyterian Church, a congregation with Southern sympathies, from 1863 to 1870. He then returned to San Francisco, where he founded St. John's Presbyterian Church and continued as pastor until his death. He also helped establish (in 1871) the San Francisco Theological Seminary, of which he was first professor of logic and systematic theology. In 1858 he was moderator of the General Assembly of the Presbyterian Church. He was author of numerous religious works, among them *Trade and Letters* (1856), *The Bible and Politics* (1859), and *The Christ of the Apostles' Creed* (1867). On January 19th, 1836, he married Ann Nicholson, of Kilkeel, Ireland. He died in San Francisco on January 14th, 1885.

SCOTT, WINFIELD (1786–1866), soldier, son of William Scott and Ann Mason, was born at Laurel Branch, his father's plantation fourteen miles from Petersburg, Virginia, on June 13th, 1786. After attending the College of

William and Mary for a short time he read law in the office of David Robinson and commenced practice in Petersburg. During the War of 1812 he rose to major general; he was twice wounded in the battle of Lundy's Lane (July 25th, 1814). Continuing in military service, he eventually became commanding general of the United States army (1841–1861). During the Mexican War (1846–1848) he captured Vera Cruz (March 1847), won victories at Cerro Gordo, Contreras, Churubusco, Molino del Ray, and Chapultepec, and entered Mexico City on September 14th, 1847. In 1852 he was Whig nominee for President but was defeated by Franklin Pierce. For the rest of his life he was a popular military figure. During the Civil War he commanded the Union army until age forced him to retire in November 1861. On March 11th, 1817, he married Maria D. Mayo, daughter of John Mayo, of Richmond, Virginia; three of their seven children lived to maturity. He died in West Point, New York, on May 29th, 1866, survived by three daughters, and was buried in the West Point National Cemetery beside his wife, who had died in Rome, Italy, in 1862.

SCREVEN, BENJAMIN SMITH (1826–1871), planter and Confederate soldier, younger son of the Rev. Charles Odingsell Screven (1773–1830) and his second wife, Barbara Rankin Godolphin, was born in Sunbury, Liberty County, Georgia, on June 13th, 1826. His father, a son of General James Screven (1744–1778), Revolutionary hero, was a Baptist clergyman and founder of the Sunbury Baptist Church. Benjamin Smith Screven was a younger brother of William Edward Screven (1822–1860) and Ann Eliza Screven (1820–1895), wife of Thomas Samuel Mallard. After graduating from Franklin College (Athens) in 1844 he returned to his native county, settled at Seabrook, his plantation near Dorchester, and planted successfully until the outbreak of the Civil War. On May 13th, 1852, he married Rebecca Ann Baker (1825–1858), daughter of William Quarterman Baker and his first wife, Ann Lydia Mallard; she died on May 3rd, 1858, leaving three small boys. On November 7th, 1861, he enlisted for six months as a private in the Liberty Independent Troop (Company G, 5th Regiment Georgia Cavalry); on May 15th, 1862, he enlisted as second lieutenant in the Liberty Mounted Rangers (Company B, 20th Battalion Georgia Cavalry); he subsequently became first lieutenant (October 30th, 1862) and captain (February 2nd, 1864). "His friends say he is positively engaged to Miss Rosa Jones, his first love," wrote Mrs. Mary S. Mallard from Walthourville on November 13th, 1862. "They think each other much improved by the lapse of years; and the children are no objection, as they always enliven households." On June 25th, 1863, Benjamin Smith Screven married Rosa Jane Jones (born 1829), daughter of William Jones and Mary Jane Robarts; and in April 1864, before leaving with his company for Virginia, he settled his family in the academy in Wal-

thourville. On May 28th, 1864, in the battle of Haw's Shop, Virginia, he was seriously wounded in the trachea; after some weeks in General Hospital No. 9 in Richmond he was sent home on sick furlough extending to September 8th, 1864. After the war he resumed planting in Liberty County. In 1870 he removed to Athens, where he was associated with *The Southern Cultivator,* "a semi-monthly journal devoted to Southern agriculture, designed to improve the mind and elevate the character of the tillers of the soil, and to introduce a more enlightened system of culture." (It was said to be the only periodical in the South that never missed an issue throughout four years of war.) Benjamin Smith Screven died in Athens on August 12th, 1871, survived by his second wife and six children (three by his first wife and three by his second), and was buried in Oconee Hill Cemetery.

SCREVEN, JAMES PROCTOR (1799–1859), physician, planter, and railroad official, son of Major John Screven, was born in Savannah, Georgia, on October 11th, 1799. After graduating from the South Carolina College in 1817 and from the Medical College of the University of Pennsylvania in 1820 he toured Europe for two years before commencing the practice of medicine in Savannah in December 1822. On December 28th, 1826, he married his first cousin, Hannah Georgia Bryan (1807–1887), daughter of Joseph Bryan (1773–1812) and Delia Forman, of Savannah. After the death of his father in 1830 he retired from medical practice to assume the management of his father's large and profitable plantations in South Carolina. For some years he lived in retirement in the country. Returning to Savannah in 1849, he served as alderman (1849–1854), state senator (1855–1856), and mayor (1856–1857); he was projector and superintendent of the Savannah waterworks (1853–1859), and projector and president of the Savannah, Albany & Gulf Railroad (1853–1859). He was also for many years captain of the Savannah Volunteer Guards. He died in Hot Springs, Virginia, on July 16th, 1859, and was buried in Laurel Grove Cemetery, Savannah. To his wife and four children he left an estate of over a million dollars. According to the Savannah *Republican* (July 21st, 1859), "The characteristics of Dr. Screven were not only an acute and comprehensive intellect but an energy and perseverance of industry which made him anywhere and everywhere a man of mark. Cool, resolute, determined, sagacious, he looked at difficulties as nothing, and overcame obstacles by efforts almost superhuman. . . . It is doubtful if any other man would have undertaken what he did; and yet he found time to attend to everything and superintend the smallest details of business." Hannah Georgia (Bryan) Screven, for many years an invalid, died in Savannah on March 18th, 1887, and was buried beside her husband.

SCREVEN, JOHN (1827–1900), planter, lawyer, railroad official, and Confederate soldier, eldest son of Dr. James Proctor Screven

(1799–1859) and Hannah Georgia Bryan (1807–1887), was born in Savannah, Georgia, on September 18th, 1827. He attended Franklin College (Athens) with the class of 1846 but did not graduate. He read law in the office of the Hon. William Law, of Savannah, but soon retired from practice to assume the management of his father's large and profitable planting interests. He married first (on July 3rd, 1849) Mary White Footman (1827–1863), daughter of Dr. Richard Hunter Footman and Mary Constance Maxwell. There were seven children. After her death on July 6th, 1863, he married second (on December 7th, 1865) Mary Eleanor Nesbitt (1844–1883), daughter of Dr. Hugh O'Keefe Nesbitt and Martha Deloney Berrien, and widow of Thomas B. Brown, colonel of the 2nd Regiment Alabama Cavalry, killed at Murfreesboro on December 29th, 1862. There were two children. In 1858 he succeeded his father as captain of the Savannah Volunteer Guards. In 1859 he succeeded his father as president of the Savannah, Albany & Gulf Railroad, a post he held for twenty-one years (1859–1880). He represented Chatham County in the state legislature (1859–1860) and served as judge of the inferior court (1860). At the outbreak of the Civil War he commanded the Savannah Volunteer Guards (Company A, 18th Battalion Georgia Infantry) at the seizure of Fort Pulaski. During the succeeding months his command saw service in and around Savannah. He was elected major (1862) and commissioned lieutenant colonel (1864). In December 1862 he was permanently detached from his command in order to take charge of transportation of supplies and troops on the Savannah, Albany & Gulf Railroad. After the war he resumed his active participation in civic affairs. He was mayor of Savannah (1869–1873) and at the time of his death was president of the Georgia Historical Society and trustee of the University of Georgia. He died in Savannah on January 9th, 1900, and was buried near his two wives in Laurel Grove Cemetery.

SCREVEN, WILLIAM EDWARD (1822–1860), planter, elder son of the Rev. Charles Odingsell Screven (1773–1830) and his second wife, Barbara Rankin Godolphin, was born in Sunbury, Liberty County, Georgia, on August 31st, 1822. His father, a son of General James Screven (1744–1778), Revolutionary hero, was a Baptist clergyman and founder of the Sunbury Baptist Church. William Edward Screven was a brother of Benjamin Smith Screven (1826–1871) and Ann Eliza Screven (1820–1895), wife of Thomas Samuel Mallard. After graduating from Franklin College (Athens) in 1844 he attended Columbia Theological Seminary for one year but was forced to withdraw for reasons of health. On July 17th, 1845, he married Cornelia Elizabeth Harris (1826–1900), daughter of Dr. Raymond Harris (1799–1888) and his first wife, Mary Elizabeth Law (1803–1871), of Liberty County; there were five children. Still hoping to enter the ministry, he devoted himself to literary pur-

suits; in 1847 he published a short work, *The Relations of Christianity to Poetry and Philosophy,* dedicated to the Rev. Dr. George Howe, his former professor at Columbia Theological Seminary. A stroke of lightning in 1849 rendered him a permanent invalid. He died at Seabrook, the plantation of his brother, Benjamin Smith Screven, on February 12th, 1860, and was buried in Midway Cemetery. As the Rev. Dr. Charles Colcock Jones observed in his journal (February 13th, 1860): "Most melancholy end of a man in the prime of life, and not only a professor of religion but spent some time at Columbia Theological Seminary!"

SCRIBNER, CHARLES (1821–1871), publisher, son of Uriah Rogers Scribner and his second wife, Betsey Hawley, was born in New York City on February 21st, 1821. After graduating from the College of New Jersey (Princeton) in 1840 he studied law and practiced his profession until poor health forced him to retire. In 1846 he turned to publishing, with Isaac D. Baker as partner; in 1850, after Baker's death, he continued publishing under his own name. From the beginning he specialized in philosophical and theological works, among them books by such Presbyterian stalwarts as Archibald Alexander, James Waddel Alexander, Noah Porter, and Theodore Dwight Woolsey. In 1867 he published the first volume of *A History of the Church of God,* by the Rev. Dr. Charles Colcock Jones. His wife, Emma L. Blair, was the daughter of John Insley Blair (1802–1899), a capitalist prominent in railroading. Charles Scribner died in Lucerne, Switzerland, on August 26th, 1871.

SEWARD, WILLIAM HENRY (1801–1872), statesman, son of Dr. Samuel S. Seward and Mary Jennings, was born in Florida, Orange County, New York, on May 16th, 1801. After graduating from Union College (Schenectady, New York) in 1820 he read law and commenced practice in Auburn, New York, where he resided for the rest of his life. On October 20th, 1824, he married Frances Miller, daughter of his law partner. Through his intimate friendship with Thurlow Weed he soon rose to political prominence; he was state senator (1830–1834), governor (1838–1842), and United States senator (1849–1861). In the 1850s he shared the growing antislavery sentiment of the North; in a famous speech delivered in Rochester, New York, on October 25th, 1858, he anticipated the "irrepressible conflict" between North and South. As secretary of state under President Abraham Lincoln (1861–1865) he was alert and active, although his famous memorandum, "Some Thoughts for the President's Consideration, April 1st, 1861," advocating immediate war with Europe as a means of unifying the nation, was reprehensible. In the early spring of 1865 he was seriouly injured in a carriage accident; shortly thereafter, on the night of April 14th, 1865, he was brutally attacked in his house at the moment of Lincoln's assassination in Ford's Theater. In 1867 he negotiated the cession of

Alaska. After traveling around the world he returned in 1871 to Auburn, where he died on October 16th, 1872. He was buried in Fort Hill Cemetery.

SHACKELFORD, CAROLINE MATILDA ELIZABETH (1835–1927), only surviving child of Francis Robert Shackelford (1801–1887) and his first wife, Caroline Seymour Dunwody (1816–1838), was born at Hopestill, the plantation of her maternal grandmother near Darien, McIntosh County, Georgia, on May 5th, 1835. Her mother died on August 27th, 1838, and shortly thereafter her father married Eliza Bloom (1820–1896), of New York. "Carrie" Shackelford spent much of her girlhood in her father's household in Charleston (1844–1855) and Savannah (1855–1859); she also stayed frequently with her maternal grandmother, Elizabeth West Smith (1794–1879), widow of James Dunwody (1789–1833), in McIntosh County. On July 18th, 1860, she became the wife of Chessley Bostwick Howard (1829–1904), son of John H. Howard and Caroline Bostwick, of Columbus. Her husband, educated for law, preferred planting and managed a large plantation on the Flint River in Taylor County, Georgia, where he resided with his family during the Civil War. In 1863 he served as a corporal in Captain Chapman's Company, Georgia Infantry, a unit organized for home defense. After the war he resided briefly in Columbus; after a business failure in New York City he returned in 1870 to Taylor County, where he lived for several years in straitened circumstances before settling in Atlanta in 1876. "Carrie is a noble woman," wrote her uncle, the Rev. John Jones, on September 3rd, 1870, "and endures her reverses most cheerfully, and seems more than ever devoted to her husband." Chessley Bostwick Howard became a prominent figure in state politics, although, as the Atlanta *Constitution* (January 11th, 1904) observed, "he never aspired to any political office himself." He died in Atlanta on January 10th, 1904, and was buried in Westview Cemetery. Caroline (Shackelford) Howard died on June 30th, 1927, survived by three children, and was buried beside her husband. "Why, she is not so pretty after all," wrote the Rev. R. Q. Mallard to his wife on November 14th, 1857, "and I don't believe is anything great comparatively." She was almost exactly the age of Mary Sharpe Jones, and they were girlhood friends.

SHACKELFORD, FRANCIS ROBERT (1801–1887), commission merchant and insurance agent, son of Francis Shackelford (1770–1805), was born in Georgetown, South Carolina, in 1801. In early manhood he entered the cotton business in Georgetown. On May 29th, 1834, he married Caroline Seymour Dunwody (1816–1838), eldest child of James Dunwody (1789–1833) and Elizabeth West Smith (1794–1879), of Darien, McIntosh County, Georgia. His wife was a sister of Jane Adaline Dunwody (1820–1884), wife of the Rev. John Jones (1815–1893). Caroline Seymour (Dunwody) Shackelford died in Philadelphia, Penn-

sylvania, on August 27th, 1838, and was buried in Laurel Hill Cemetery; she left one child: Caroline Matilda Elizabeth Shackelford (1835–1927), who became (on July 18th, 1860) the wife of Chessley Bostwick Howard (1829–1904). In 1839 Francis Robert Shackelford married Eliza Bloom (1820–1896), of New York, who bore him seven children. He was for many years a successful cotton factor and commission merchant, first in Charleston (1844–1855), later in Savannah (1855–1859) and Columbus (1859–1866). After the war he sold insurance for some years in Macon and Atlanta. He died in Atlanta on February 25th, 1887, and was buried in Oakland Cemetery.

SHAFFER, JACOB (1820–1880), carpenter, son of Jacob Shaffer (1783–1859), a saddler, was born in Savannah, Georgia, in 1820. He lived in Savannah all his life, hiring his services as carpenter, sometimes in association with his younger brother, John Shaffer (1829–1889), a brickmason. Both were bachelors, and they shared living quarters in Houston Street. Jacob Shaffer died in Savannah on August 26th, 1880, and was buried in Laurel Grove Cemetery. John Shaffer died on May 24th, 1889, and was buried beside his brother.

SHEPARD, THOMAS JANE (1803–1873), farmer and plantation overseer, son of Thomas Shepard and his second wife, Jane Andrews, was born in Liberty County, Georgia, on June 26th, 1803. His mother died on July 14th, 1803, a few days after his birth, and he was named in her memory. On April 12th, 1804, his father married Rebecca Baker; he died in February 1811, when the boy was in his eighth year. In early manhood he removed to Pike County, Georgia, where he was converted at a camp meeting in 1825 and joined the Methodist Church. On October 18th, 1826, he married Susan Patience Leake (1812–1830), a native of Laurens County, South Carolina; several years later he returned to Liberty County, where his wife died on February 26th, 1830. He married second (on April 14th, 1831) Serena Way (1814–1887), daughter of John Way and Rebecca Jones, of Liberty County; seven of their twelve children survived infancy. Thomas Jane Shepard was manager of Montevideo, the plantation of the Rev. Dr. Charles Colcock Jones in Liberty County, from September 11th, 1848, to January 1st, 1853, during Dr. Jones's absence in Columbia, South Carolina (1848–1850) and in Philadelphia, Pennsylvania (1850–1853); he was succeeded on January 1st, 1853, by Benjamin Washington Allen (1812–1856). During the same period Shepard managed White Oak plantation for Dr. Jones's sister, Mrs. Susan M. Cumming. The correspondence of Jones and Shepard during the four years of Shepard's management of Montevideo is preserved among the Jones papers at Tulane University, together with "Thomas J. Shepard's Account Current as Manager at Montevideo from September 11th, 1848, to January 1st, 1853." "Have engaged Mr. Allen to manage at Montevideo," wrote Dr. Jones on December 29th, 1852; "the last administration has not in some important respects been a prosperous one." The Shepards lived at Grassy Glade, a plantation near Jonesville. Serena Shepard's fans, made from curlew feathers, were said to be lovely things. Among the Jones papers preserved at Tulane University is the following note from Serena Shepard to Mrs. Mary Jones, written from Grassy Glade on December 27th, 1851: "I have sent you three fans which I beg you to accept of. The largest I wish you to give to Mr. Jones from me, to use in his study; the other for yourself; and the small white one for your daughter if she will accept of it. They are not very handsome, but they were the best feathers I could get." Thomas Jane Shepard died in Reidsville, Tattnall County, Georgia, at the residence of his daughter, Sarah Jane Shepard, wife of Dr. Abraham B. Daniel, on May 15th, 1873, survived by seven children, and was buried in Taylor's Creek Cemetery. Serena (Way) Shepard died in Tattnall County at the residence of her son, Charles Wesley Shepard, on January 28th, 1887, and was buried beside her husband.

SHERIDAN, PHILIP HENRY (1831–1888), Union soldier, son of John Sheridan and Mary Meenagh, recent emigrants from County Cavan, Ireland, was born in Albany, New York, on March 6th, 1831. He graduated from the United States Military Academy in 1853. At the outbreak of the Civil War he was made captain in the 13th Infantry and assigned to duty as quartermaster and commissary of Federal troops in Southwest Missouri. On May 25th, 1862, he was appointed lieutenant colonel of the 2nd Michigan Cavalry; a few weeks later he was promoted to brigadier general, and on December 31st, 1862, he was promoted to major general of volunteers. He distinguished himself at Perryville, Stone River, Chickamauga, and Missionary Ridge. When Grant was promoted to lieutenant general he placed Sheridan in command of all cavalry in the Army of the Potomac. He fought at the Wilderness, Spotsylvania Courthouse, and Cold Harbor; for more than two weeks (May 9th, 1864, to May 25th, 1864) he conducted devastating raids on Confederate communications around Richmond. In August 1864 he was placed in command of the Army of the Shenandoah, with instructions to dislodge the enemy and lay waste the Valley of Virginia. After defeating Early at Winchester (September 19th) and at Fisher's Hill (September 22nd) he was made brigadier general in the regular army; after his famous "ride" of twenty miles from Winchester to Cedar Creek on October 19th, 1864, to snatch victory from defeat, he was promoted to major general. In 1867 he was appointed military governor of Louisiana and Texas, with headquarters in New Orleans; his repressive policy, although supported by Grant, led to his transfer to the Department of the Missouri. On March 4th, 1869, he was appointed lieutenant general, and on June 1st, 1888, he was distinguished by the rank of general. His *Personal Memoirs* were published in

two volumes in 1888. He died on August 5th, 1888, and was buried with high military and civil honors in Arlington National Cemetery, Fort Myer, Virginia.

SHERMAN, THOMAS WEST (1813–1879), Union soldier, son of Elijah Sherman and Martha West, was born in Newport, Rhode Island, on March 26th, 1813. After graduating from the United States Military Academy in 1836 he fought in the Seminole War and the Mexican War; he was promoted to first lieutenant (1838) and captain (1846). Prior to the Civil War he served in garrison and on the frontier; while in Kansas he married Mary Shannon, daughter of Wilson Shannon (1802–1877), governor of Ohio (1838–1840; 1842–1844), congressman (1853–1855), and governor of Kansas Territory (1855–1856). After the outbreak of the Civil War he rose rapidly to major and lieutenant colonel in the regular army and brigadier general of volunteers. In the autumn of 1861 he headed a naval expedition designed to seize strategic bases on the Southern coast; on November 7th, 1861, he occupied Port Royal harbor in South Carolina. In 1862 he served under Halleck before Corinth and later commanded troops above New Orleans; on May 27th, 1863, he was wounded at Port Hudson, Louisiana, and subsequently lost his right leg. For meritorious service he was brevetted brigadier general in the regular army and major general of volunteers on March 13th, 1865. After the war he commanded the Department of the East until his retirement as major general on December 31st, 1870. He died at his residence in Newport, Rhode Island, on March 16th, 1879, survived by one son.

SHERMAN, WILLIAM TECUMSEH (1820–1891), Union soldier, son of Charles Robert Sherman and Mary Hoyt, was born in Lancaster, Ohio, on February 8th, 1820. His father, justice of the state supreme court, died in 1829, and the boy was taken into the family of Thomas Ewing (1789–1871), a frontier lawyer. He graduated from the United States Military Academy in 1840. On May 1st, 1850, after an engagement of seven years, he married Eleanor (Ellen) Boyle Ewing, daughter of his guardian. After trying law and banking without success he became superintendent of a new military college in Alexandria, Louisiana (now Louisiana State University), in October 1859; there he prospered until compelled to resign at the outbreak of the Civil War. Sherman felt that the Union must be preserved at all costs; at the same time he loved the South. War, he felt, should be averted if possible; once declared, it should be successfully concluded at the earliest possible moment. In May 1861, having declined a high commission in the Confederate army, he was appointed colonel of the 13th Infantry; he commanded a brigade under McDowell at Manassas. He was promoted to brigadier general of volunteers (August 1861), major general of volunteers (May 1862), and brigadier general in the regular army (July 1863). He fought with distinction at Shiloh and Vicksburg. In September 1863 he was placed in command of the Army of the Tennessee, and in the spring of 1864 he succeeded Grant in command of all armies in the West. In his advance upon Atlanta Sherman with one hundred thousand men opposed Johnston with sixty thousand. Beginning early in May, Sherman progressed slowly but steadily until July 17th, 1864, when Johnston, just in front of Atlanta, was replaced by Hood. Sherman laid siege to the city, and Hood evacuated on the night of September 1st, 1864. For his successful campaign Sherman was promoted to major general in the regular army on August 12th, 1864. On November 15th, 1864, he set out with an army of sixty-two thousand on his famous "march through Georgia," designed to split the Confederacy, destroy the source of Confederate supplies, and thus shorten the war. His army was ordered to live off the country and to destroy all public buildings, factories, and railroads; although his orders were strict, they were not strictly enforced, and many acts of lawlessness and pillage occurred. On December 21st, 1864, he occupied Savannah, and early in February he marched northward into the Carolinas, burning Columbia and forcing the evacuation of Charleston. On April 26th, 1865, Johnston surrendered his command, and Sherman granted liberal terms. At Grant's inauguration as President (March 4th, 1869) Sherman was made general commanding the army. He retired on November 1st, 1883, and after three years in St. Louis he settled in New York City, where he died on February 14th, 1891.

SHIELDS, JAMES (1810–1879), legislator and Union soldier, son of Charles Shields and Katherine McDonnell, was born in Altmore, County Tyrone, Ireland, on May 10th, 1810. In 1823 he migrated to the United States and settled in Kaskaskia, Illinois, where he read law and commenced practice. He was a member of the state house of representatives (1836), state auditor (1839), justice of the state supreme court (1843), and commissioner of the General Land Office (1845–1847). During the Mexican War he was commissioned brigadier general of volunteers (July 1st, 1846) and brevetted major general (April 18th, 1847). After serving as governor of Oregon Territory (1848–1849) he was United States senator from Illinois (1849–1855) and United States senator from Minnesota (1858–1859). He then removed to San Francisco, California, where he married Mary Ann Carr in 1861; three children survived infancy. At the outbreak of the Civil War he was managing a mine in Mazatlan, Mexico. From August 19th, 1861, to March 28th, 1863, he was brigadier general in the Union army, serving chiefly in the Shenandoah Valley of Virginia. Resigning his commission in 1863, he returned to San Francisco and thence removed to Carrollton, Missouri, where he was a member of the state house of representatives (1874; 1879), adjutant general of Missouri (1877), railroad commissioner, and United States senator from Missouri (1879).

He died in Ottumwa, Wapello County, Iowa, on June 1st, 1879, and was buried in St. Mary's Cemetery, Carrollton.

SICKLES, DANIEL EDGAR (1819–1914), congressman, soldier, and diplomat, son of George Garrett Sickles and Susan Marsh, was born in New York City on October 20th, 1819. After attending New York University he studied law and commenced practice in New York City. He was a member of the state legislature in 1847. On September 27th, 1852, he married Teresa Bagioli (1836–1867), of New York City, daughter of Antonio Bagioli, an Italian music master, and his wife Maria Cooke. He was secretary of the United States legation in London (1853–1855), member of the state senate (1855–1857), and member of Congress (1857–1861). On February 27th, 1859, in Washington, D.C., he shot and killed District Attorney Philip Barton Key, son of Francis Scott Key, for his attentions to Teresa (Bagioli) Sickles; in a famous trial Sickles pleaded temporary insanity, and on April 26th, 1859, he was acquitted. At the outbreak of the Civil War he organized the Excelsior Brigade (17th Regiment New York Volunteer Infantry) and led it, as brigadier general, through the Peninsula campaign of 1862. He was promoted to major general of volunteers on November 29th, 1862, and fought through the Chancellorsville campaign of 1863. His military career ended with the loss of a leg at Gettysburg on July 2nd, 1863. After the war he was brevetted brigadier general (March 2nd, 1867) "for gallant and meritorious services in the battle of Fredericksburg," and major general (March 2nd, 1867) "for gallant and meritorious services in the battle of Gettysburg"; on October 30th, 1897, he was awarded the Medal of Honor "for most distinguished gallantry in action at Gettysburg, Pennsylvania, July 2nd, 1863, both before and after the loss of a leg." In 1865 Sickles was appointed military governor of the Carolinas; he was recalled in 1867 because of his severely repressive policies. In 1869 he was appointed United States minister to Spain; he resigned in 1873 because of Spanish opposition to "the Yankee King." In 1886 he became chairman of the New York State Monuments Commission; he was relieved in 1912 because of misappropriation of funds. He died in New York City on May 3rd, 1914, and was buried in Arlington National Cemetery, Fort Myer, Virginia. He is perhaps best remembered for his successful effort to secure Central Park for New York City in 1852.

SICKLES, HIRAM FRANKLIN (1818–1892), merchant and soldier, was born in New York City in 1818. After serving for ten years (1838–1848) in the United States navy he settled in Moline, Rock Island County, Illinois, where he conducted a flour mill for some years prior to the Civil War, and was a member of the board of supervisors (1859–1860; 1868). On September 24th, 1861, he was commissioned major in the 9th Regiment Illinois Cavalry; on February 18th, 1862, he was promoted to lieutenant colonel. He saw action in Arkansas, Mississippi, and Tennessee. On January 16th, 1863, he resigned for reasons of health; two years later he reentered the service and on February 21st, 1865, was commissioned colonel of the 147th Regiment Illinois Infantry. On March 13th, 1865, he was brevetted brigadier general of volunteers "for faithful and meritorious service." After the war he continued in service until January 20th, 1866; in the autumn of 1865 he was detached as assistant commissioner of the Freedmen's Bureau (the Federal Bureau of Refugees, Freedmen, and Abandoned Lands) in Savannah, Georgia. Returning to Moline, he was a city magistrate for six years (1866–1872). He subsequently resided in Lake City, Hinsdale County, Colorado (1872–1878). After conducting mineralogical explorations in Mexico, California, and Colorado for one year (1878–1879) he settled in Rio Grande County, Colorado, where he resided for the rest of his life, first in Cornwall, later in Jasper, and finally in Monte Vista. His first wife died in 1870; on July 23rd, 1872, he married Eliza F. Nye (1834–1906), of Manitou, El Paso County, Colorado. He died in Monte Vista on May 23rd, 1892, survived by his second wife, and was buried in the cemetery of the Colorado Soldiers' and Sailors' Home.

SIMS, FREDERICK WILLIAM (1828–1875), editor and cotton merchant, son of Frederick Sims (1796–1849) and his second wife, Katherine Willis Wellborn, was born in Clinton, Jones County, Georgia, in 1828. In early childhood he accompanied his parents to Macon, where his father was mayor in 1842. Entering the offices of the Central Railroad of Georgia, young Sims rose rapidly and soon went to Savannah as chief accountant. In 1856 he became equal partner with James Roddey Sneed (1818–1891) in the Savannah *Republican*; Sneed was principal editor and Sims was commercial editor and business manager. In January 1858 Sims became sole proprietor and Sneed continued as editor; the partnership thus continued until the fall of Savannah in December 1864. On September 12th, 1850, Sims married Catharine M. Sullivan, of Macon; after her death on September 17th, 1858, he married (on December 10th, 1862) Sarah Louisa Munroe (1842–1904), youngest daughter of Nathan C. Munroe, of Macon; two of their six children survived infancy. At the outbreak of the Civil War he was captain of Company B, Oglethorpe Light Infantry (later designated Company H, 1st [Olmstead's] Regiment Georgia Infantry). He was captured at the fall of Fort Pulaski on April 11th, 1862, and confined on Johnson's Island, Ohio, until exchanged at Vicksburg, Mississippi, on September 21st, 1862. On June 2nd, 1863, he was appointed assistant adjutant general and assigned to duty as inspector, agent, and supervisor of railroad transportation for Confederate troops; he subsequently became major (June 7th, 1863) and lieutenant colonel (January 27th, 1864). He was paroled at Charlotte, North Carolina, on May 12th, 1865. After the

war he was associated with John F. Wheaton in the firm of F. W. Sims & Company, cotton factors and commission merchants. In September 1874 he became business manager of the Savannah *Daily Advertiser*. He died in a lodging house in San Francisco, California, from an overdose of morphine, self-administered, on May 25th, 1875. "An honorable man, highly connected and blameless heretofore in every business transaction," observed the Savannah *Daily Advertiser* (June 2nd, 1875): "let us throw over this last sad act of his life the mantle of charity, and believe it done in a fit of desperation, when a *quiet* moment might have made all right." His wife survived him twenty-nine years; she died in Washington, D.C., on July 18th, 1904, and was buried in Laurel Grove Cemetery, Savannah.

SINCLAIR, CATHERINE (1800–1864), novelist, fourth daughter of Sir John Sinclair (1754–1835) and his second wife, Diana Alexander, was born in Edinburgh, Scotland, on April 17th, 1800. From 1814 to 1835 she was her father's secretary; she then devoted herself to authorship, commencing with children's books and continuing with works of fiction and travel. Her novels include *Modern Flirtations*; *or, A Month at Harrogate* (1841); *Jane Bouverie; or, Prosperity and Adversity* (1846); *Sir Edward Graham; or, Railway Speculators* (1849); *Lord and Lady Harcourt*; *or, County Hospitalities* (1850); and *Beatrice*; *or, The Unknown Relatives* (1852). *Scotland and the Scotch*; *or, The Western Circuit* (1840), a travel book, was republished in America and translated into several languages. Catherine Sinclair never married. She died at the vicarage, Kensington, the residence of her brother, Archdeacon John Sinclair, on August 6th, 1864, and was buried in St. John's Episcopal Churchyard, Edinburgh.

SINGER, ISAAC MERRIT (1811–1875), inventor and sewing machine manufacturer, son of a millwright, was born in Pittstown, Rensselaer County, New York, on October 27th, 1811. He early showed a gift for mechanical invention, and for some years he lived here and there, engaged in various mechanical pursuits. In 1851 he invented and patented a sewing machine and organized the I. M. Singer Company to effect its manufacture. In practical efficiency Singer's machine superseded all its rivals, especially for domestic use, and it soon commanded the sewing machine industry. In 1863 Singer and his partner, Edward Clark, formed the Singer Manufacturing Company, and Singer retired to England. He married first, early in life, Catherine Maria Halsey, from whom he was divorced in 1860; he married second (in 1865) Isabella Eugenia Summerville. He died at his residence in Torquay, Devonshire, England, on July 23rd, 1875, survived by his second wife and two daughters. Of Singer's importance in the history of the sewing machine Frederick L. Lewton has written as follows: "To Isaac Singer should be given the credit for developing the first real practical sewing machine for domestic use. While the yielding vertical presser foot to hold the work on the worktable which is in universal use today, and the development of the wheel feed, an important feature of some special machines for factory use, were contributed by Singer in his first machine, his real service was in bringing the sewing machine into general use. When the competition of Singer's machine began to be felt, inventors of machines of an earlier date were compelled to modify their inventions and adapt them to meet practical conditions and to please the public. Later Singer himself was compelled to do the same thing and changed materially the heavy cumbersome form of his earlier type to meet the competition of the smaller, lighter, and easier-running Wheeler & Wilson machine" ["The Servant in the House," *Annual Report of the Board of Regents of the Smithsonian Institution* (Washington, 1929), p. 581].

SLAUGHTER, HARVEY (1808–1878), physician, son of the Hon. James Slaughter and Martha Grey, was born in Cedar Creek, near Bardstown, Kentucky, on June 19th, 1808. He graduated from the Medical Department of Transylvania University in 1828. After practicing for one year in Big Spring, he removed in 1829 to Elizabethtown, where he resided for the rest of his life, enjoying a large and lucrative practice. In 1832 he married Eliza Harrison Wood (1814–1879), daughter of Jesse Wood and Polly Buckner, of Hart County; their only child died in infancy. He was first president of the Hardin County Medical Society. After practicing medicine in Elizabethtown for forty-five years he retired for reasons of health in 1874. He died in Elizabethtown on August 15th, 1878. His wife died a few months later, on January 23rd, 1879.

SLIDELL, JOHN (1793–1871), legislator and Confederate diplomat, son of John Slidell and Margery Mackenzie, was born in New York City in 1793. He graduated from Columbia College in 1810. After a business failure he removed in 1819 to New Orleans, where he practiced law and soon rose to prominence. In 1835 he married Mathilde Deslonde. He was United States district attorney (1829–1833), congressman (1843–1845), and United States senator (1853–1861). At the outbreak of the Civil War he was appointed Confederate diplomatic commissioner to France as a colleague of James Murray Mason (1798–1871), Confederate diplomatic commissioner to Great Britain. While en route to Europe on the British mail steamer *Trent* the two men were seized by United States authorities on November 8th, 1861, and confined at Fort Warren, Boston harbor, until January 1st, 1862, when they were released and allowed to proceed to Europe. The episode nearly precipitated war between Great Britain and the United States. Slidell continued to represent the Confederacy in Paris until the close of the war; he was cordially received by Napoleon III, whose avowed sympathy with

the Confederate cause failed to result in positive action. After the war Slidell remained in Paris until the Second Empire fell in 1870. He died in Cowes, Isle of Wight, England, on July 26th, 1871, and was buried in the private cemetery of the Saint-Roman family at Villejuif, near Paris.

SMETS, ALEXANDER AUGUSTUS (1795–1862), bibliophile, eldest son of Barthelmy Martin Smets and Jeanne Marie Antoinette Masseau, was born in Nantes, France, on October 13th, 1795. After a brief period in the French army he migrated to the United States; on November 20th, 1816, he landed in Savannah, Georgia, where he resided for the rest of his life. On March 29th, 1820, he married Ann Watt (1797–1854), of Savannah; there were nine children. For some years he engaged extensively in the lumber business, and in 1849 he retired with a handsome fortune. He was a director of the Bank of the State of Georgia, vice-consul of France for the district of Georgia, and treasurer of the Georgia Historical Society. His library was said to be one of the most varied and extensive in private hands. According to *The Southern Literary Messenger*, "The library does not rest its claims upon the large number of volumes it contains, of which there are perhaps eight thousand, but upon the choice selection of the authors and the great variety of the editions. It is composed principally of English works in all branches of learning and the fine arts, embracing the earlier and the later poets, the more celebrated novelists, the best historians and biographers—in a word, every author that can be called standard. . . . When we say further that all the volumes are bound in a manner the most elegant known to the trade, and are arranged in rich cases of mahogany, some idea may be formed of the appearance of the library." The entire collection was sold at auction in New York in May 1868. Smets received the honorary degree of master of arts from Oglethorpe University in 1842. He died in Indian Springs, Butts County, Georgia, on May 9th, 1862, survived by seven children, and was buried beside his wife in Laurel Grove Cemetery, Savannah. As the Savannah *Republican* observed at the time of his death, "The man who could, amid all the cares and perplexities of mercantile life, preserve the taste and inclination for books— and those selected from the classics of every country and time—is as much by his example a public benefactor as he who rests upon the laurels of building railroads or opening manufactories."

SMITH, ANNE ELIZABETH (CUMMING) (1805–1883): *Mrs. Peter Skenandoah Smith,* second daughter of Thomas Cumming (1765–1834) and Anne Clay (1767–1849), was born in Augusta, Georgia, on February 8th, 1805. Her father, head of one of the most distinguished families in Georgia, was the first mayor of Augusta after its incorporation as a town (1798) and president of the Bank of Augusta from its organization in 1810 until his death in 1834. Anne Elizabeth Cumming was a sister of William Clay Cumming (1788–1863); Joseph Cumming (1790–1846), second husband of Susan Mary Jones, sister of the Rev. Dr. Charles Colcock Jones; Mary Cuthbert Cumming (1797–1876), wife of the Rev. Dr. Samuel Stanhope Davis; Henry Harford Cumming (1799–1866); Alfred Cumming (1802–1873); and Sarah Wallace Cumming (1807–1895). On December 20th, 1836, in Augusta, she became the second wife of General Peter Skenandoah Smith (1795–1858), a native of Utica, New York, eldest son of Peter Smith (1768–1837) and Elizabeth Livingston, and brother of Gerrit Smith (1797–1874), noted abolitionist. Peter Skenandoah Smith was named for his father, business partner of John Jacob Astor and a man of vast wealth, and for his father's intimate friend, Skenandoah, last chief of the Oneida Indians. "Peter Sken Smith," as he was generally called, was always something of a ne'er-do-well; his reckless expenditures in youth, and his numerous unsuccessful business ventures, gave his father much trouble and anxiety. For several years after his second marriage he resided in St. Augustine, Florida; in 1843 he removed to Philadelphia, where he was active in politics and was admitted to the bar in 1851. On October 17th, 1850, his only daughter, Cornelia W. Smith, child of his first marriage, became the wife of Absalom Baird (1824–1905), a graduate of the United States Military Academy (1849) and major general of volunteers in the Union army during the Civil War. The Smiths were intimate friends of the Rev. Dr. Charles Colcock Jones and his family during their residence in Philadelphia from 1850 to 1853. Peter Sken Smith died in Springfield, Massachusetts, on May 6th, 1858; Anne Elizabeth (Cumming) Smith returned to Augusta, Georgia, where she and her unmarried sister, Sarah Wallace Cumming, lived in the household of their brother, Henry Harford Cumming. She died without issue on October 20th, 1883, and was buried in Summerville Cemetery. According to her nephew, Joseph Bryan Cumming (1836–1922), she was "a handsome and imposing-looking woman . . . generous, high-minded, and, in the best sense, proud." After the Civil War, when she gave her sister-in-law, Mrs. Susan M. Cumming, "one thousand dollars in greenbacks," Mrs. Mary S. Mallard, finding the gift "most generous," confided to her mother on November 26th, 1867: "I have always thought she was a noble woman, and wholly unappreciated by the Davis family. I do not believe there is another member of the family that would ever think of recognizing Aunt Susan's connection with them."

SMITH, CAROLINE ROSINA MARIA (BLAND) (COURTENAY) (1806–1898): *Mrs. Stephen Hayne Smith,* daughter of Richard Bland (1771–1836) and his second wife, Susan Mary Ann Sealy Cook (1780–1830), was born at May River, her father's plantation in Beaufort District, South Carolina, on November 12th, 1806. She was educated in a private school in Elizabeth, New Jersey. On February 12th, 1824, she became the wife of Edward Thomas Courtenay (1799–1835); there were four children. After her husband's death on March 14th, 1835, she resided with her father in Augusta for seven years. In December 1842 she became the wife of Stephen Hayne Smith and settled on his plantation in South Carolina near Savannah; there were two children. After her husband's death she returned to Savannah, where for some years prior to the Civil War she conducted a private school for young ladies. By 1860 she was engaging her services as a nurse; she attended the birth of Charles Colcock Mallard in Walthourville, Georgia, on April 27th, 1860, and also the birth of Eliza Burnley Mallard in Walthourville on March 12th, 1863. "Mrs. Smith was very kind in remembering our little ones," wrote Mrs. Mary S. Mallard on May 26th, 1860. "She was very attentive to me, and took excellent care of the baby. I do not know what I should have done without her." Caroline Rosina Maria (Bland) (Courtenay) Smith died in Savannah on January 3rd, 1898, and was buried in Laurel Grove Cemetery. At the time of her death she was the oldest living communicant of Christ Episcopal Church.

SMITH, EDMUND KIRBY (1824–1893), Confederate soldier and educator, son of Joseph Lee Smith and Frances Marvin Kirby, was born in St. Augustine, Florida, on May 16th, 1824. His father, a native of Connecticut, had fought in the War of 1812 and was a distinguished lawyer and judge. Edmund Kirby Smith graduated from the United States Military Academy in 1845. After serving in the Mexican War (1846–1848) he was assistant professor of mathematics at West Point for three years (1849–1852). From 1852 to 1861 he served in the West; he was promoted to captain (1855) and major (1860). At the outbreak of the Civil War he resigned his commission (March 3rd, 1861) and returned to Florida, where he was commissioned colonel of cavalry and sent to Virginia to organize and equip Confederate troops. In June 1861 he was promoted to brigadier general. He was severely wounded at First Manassas (July 21st, 1861); while recovering in Lynchburg, Virginia, he married (on September 24th, 1861) Cassie Selden (1837–1907), daughter of Samuel S. Selden. In October 1861 he was promoted to major general, and early in 1862 he was placed in command of the Department of East Tennessee, Kentucky, North Georgia, and Western North Carolina. He invaded Kentucky in June 1862, occupied Lexington, and threatened Cincinnati. In October 1862 he was promoted to lieutenant general, and in February 1863 he was placed in command of the Department of the Trans-Mississippi (Texas, Louisiana, Arkansas, and Indian Territory). In February 1864 he was commissioned general. After the war he turned to education; he was president of the University of Nashville (1870–1875) and professor of mathematics at the University of the South (1875–1893). He died in Sewanee, Tennessee, on March 28th, 1893.

SMITH, FRANCIS GURNEY (1818–1878), physician and educator, son of Francis Gurney Smith, a prominent merchant, was born in Philadelphia, Pennsylvania, on March 8th, 1818. After graduating from the University of Pennsylvania (1837) and from the Medical College of the University of Pennsylvania (1840) he entered private practice, specializing in obstetrics and diseases of women; he was the first president of the Philadelphia Obstetrical Society. For nine years he was an editor of the Philadelphia *Medical Examiner*. He was professor of physiology at the Pennsylvania Medical College (1852–1863) and professor of the institutes of medicine in the Medical College of the University of Pennsylvania (1863–1877); he was also attending physician and clinical lecturer at the Pennsylvania Hospital (1859–1865). During the Civil War he had charge of a military hospital. In 1844 he married Catharine M. Dutilh, of Philadelphia; there were four children. He died in Philadelphia on April 6th, 1878. *Principles of Human Physiology*, by William Benjamin Carpenter (1813–1885), was "edited with additions" by Francis Gurney Smith and published in Philadelphia in 1855.

SMITH, GUSTAVUS WOODSON (1822–1896), civil engineer and Confederate soldier, son of Byrd Smith and Sarah Hatcher Woodson, was born in Georgetown, Scott County, Kentucky, on January 1st, 1822. After graduating from the United States Military Academy in 1842 he was assistant engineer in fortification construction in New London, Connecticut (1842–1844) and instructor in civil and military engineering at West Point (1844–1846). On October 3rd, 1844, he married Lucretia Bassett, daughter of Abner Bassett, of New London, Connecticut. During the Mexican War (1846–1848) he was brevetted successively lieutenant, captain, and major for distinguished service. Returning to West Point, he was assistant professor of engineering until his resignation from the army on December 18th, 1854. Prior to the Civil War he supervised construction of the New Orleans marine hospital, became chief engineer of the Trenton Ironworks, and served three years (1858–1861) as street commissioner of New York City. At the outbreak of the Civil War he favored compromise but later entered Confederate service; on September 19th, 1861, despite a stroke of paralysis suffered the preceding April, he was appointed major general and placed in command of one wing of the Army of the Potomac. In the spring of 1862 he participated in the Peninsula campaign until June 2nd, when he suffered a second stroke of paralysis. He resigned his command on February 17th, 1863, and after serving briefly as volunteer aide-de-camp to General Beauregard in Charleston he became superintendent of the Etowah Ironworks in

Northwest Georgia. In June 1864, at Sherman's approach, he was appointed major general in command of the 1st Division Georgia Militia, attached to the Army of Tennessee. He surrendered to the Wilson Raiders at Macon, Georgia, in April 1865. After the war he was general manager of the Southwestern Iron Company, Chattanooga, Tennessee (1866–1870), and first insurance commissioner of Kentucky (1870–1875). Retiring to New York City, he wrote several works on the Civil War: *Confederate War Papers* (1884), *The Battle of Seven Pines* (1891), and *Generals J. E. Johnston and G. T. Beauregard at Manassas* (1892). He died in New York City on June 24th, 1896.

SMITH, JANE SEYMOUR (MUNRO) (1774–1857): *Mrs. James Smith,* daughter of Simon Munro (1741–1790) and Elizabeth West, was born in Liberty County, Georgia, in 1774. In 1793 she became the wife of James Smith (1766–1854), a planter, a native of Dorchester, South Carolina, then resident in Sunbury, Liberty County. Their only daughter, Elizabeth West Smith (1794–1879), became the wife of James Dunwody (1789–1833) on February 8th, 1811. In 1837 James Smith removed with his wife to Cobb County, Georgia, where they became one of six families, all friends from the Georgia coast, to form "the colony" of Roswell, a village newly founded by Roswell King (1765–1844) and his son Barrington King (1798–1866). James Smith died at Brighton, summer residence of his daughter in McIntosh County, Georgia, on May 22nd, 1854, and was buried in Midway Cemetery, Liberty County. Jane Seymour (Munro) Smith then settled in Marietta, home of many friends and family connections; she died there on April 5th, 1857, and was buried in Citizens Cemetery. She was the maternal grandmother of Jane Adaline Dunwody (1820–1884), wife of the Rev. John Jones.

SMITH, SAMUEL B. (1821–1856), bookseller, was born in Philadelphia, Pennsylvania, in 1821. By 1846 he had established a bookshop at the corner of 4th and Mulberry Streets. In 1853 he joined John A. English (1831–1878) in the firm of Smith & English, publishers, booksellers, and importers, at 36 North 6th Street. The Rev. Dr. Charles Colcock Jones became a patron of Smith & English during his residence in Philadelphia (1850–1853). On September 28th, 1853, "Mr. Smith (of Smith & English) presented me with twelve bound volumes of Dr. [Ashbel] Green's *Christian Advocate* (I believe that is the name) published years ago. Very scarce and valuable. The numbers all complete, and the years bound together. Covers an important period in our church history." After returning to Georgia Dr. Jones continued to order books from Smith & English until communication ceased with the Civil War. Samuel B. Smith died in Philadelphia on March 21st, 1856, survived by his wife, Josephine Hoguet (1820–1915), and was buried in Laurel Hill Cemetery. John A. English continued the firm for some years in association with Elias D. Collom and Gerard Buckman.

SMITH, WILLIAM DUNCAN (1826–1862), Confederate soldier, was born in Georgia in 1826. After graduating from the United States Military Academy in 1846 he served as brevet second lieutenant in the Mexican War (1846–1848) and was severely wounded at Molino del Ray. He later saw garrison duty in the West. On January 28th, 1861, at the outbreak of the Civil War, he resigned his commission and entered Confederate service; on March 16th, 1861, he was commissioned captain of infantry, and on July 14th, 1861, he became colonel of the 20th Regiment Georgia Infantry. He was commissioned brigadier general on March 7th, 1862, and ordered to report to General Pemberton, then commanding the Department of South Carolina, Georgia, and Florida. In June 1862 he was placed in command of the military district of South Carolina, with headquarters in Charleston. He participated in the Confederate victory at Secessionville, near Charleston, on June 16th, 1862. He died of fever in Charleston on October 4th, 1862.

SMYTH, THOMAS (1808–1873), Presbyterian clergyman, son of Samuel Smith and Ann Magee, was born in Belfast, Ireland, on June 14th, 1808. After graduating with first honor from Belfast College in 1829 he studied theology at Highbury College (London) for one year. In 1830 he migrated to the United States, attended Princeton Theological Seminary (1830–1831), and settled in Charleston, South Carolina, where he was associated with the Second Presbyterian Church for the rest of his life, first as stated supply (1831–1834), then as pastor (1834–1870), and finally as honorary pastor (1870–1873). In 1850 a stroke of paralysis rendered him a permanent cripple, but he persevered in his work until a second stroke forced him to retire in 1870. He received the honorary degree of doctor of divinity from the College of New Jersey (Princeton) in 1843. He was author of more than thirty works on theological subjects, published in ten volumes as *The Complete Works of Rev. Thomas Smyth, D.D.* (1908–1912). Numerous details of his life and work appear in his *Autobiographical Notes, Letters, and Reflections* (1914). On July 9th, 1832, he married Margaret Milligan Adger (1807–1884), eldest daughter of James Adger (1777–1858), Charleston banker, and sister of the Rev. John Bailey Adger (1810–1899), missionary at Constantinople and Smyrna (1834–1847) and professor at Columbia Theological Seminary (1857–1874). There were ten children. Thomas Smyth died in Charleston on August 20th, 1873. His library, one of the most complete collections of theological works in private hands, became the property of Columbia Theological Seminary.

SNEED, JAMES RODDEY (1818–1891), editor, son of Archibald Henderson Sneed and Abigail Roddey, was born in Richmond County, Georgia, on December 3rd, 1818. In early manhood he settled in Washington, Wilkes County, where he was for many years editor of the local newspaper. On May 27th, 1840, he married Anna M. Hay (1822–1852), daughter of Dr. Felix G. Hay (1797–1828), of Washington, Wilkes County. She died on December 20th, 1852, and was buried in Rest Haven Cemetery. In 1855 Sneed removed to Savannah, where he became equal partner with Peter Wellington Alexander (1824–1886) in the Savannah *Republican*. When Alexander withdrew in 1856, Sneed became equal partner with Frederick William Sims (1828–1875); Sneed was principal editor and Sims was commercial editor and business manager. In January 1858 Sims became sole proprietor and Sneed continued as editor; the partnership thus continued until the fall of Savannah in December 1864. On May 20th, 1862, Sneed married Leonora Cohen (1842–1919), of St. Marys, Georgia. After the war he removed to Macon, where he was for three years associated with the Macon *Telegraph*; returning to Savannah, he resumed the editorship of the *Republican* for four years (1868–1872). In October 1872 he removed to Atlanta and thence to Washington, D.C., where he was postmaster of the United States Senate (1882–1885) and fourth auditor of the United States Treasury (1885–1889). In the spring of 1890 he removed to Chicago to live with his son, Percival C. Sneed, chief clerk to the general manager of the Baltimore & Ohio Railroad. He died of pneumonia in Chicago on March 17th, 1891, survived by his wife, three sons, and three daughters, and was buried in Bonaventure Cemetery, Savannah. Leonora (Cohen) Sneed died in Augusta, Georgia, on March 31st, 1919, and was buried beside her husband.

SOLOMONS, ABRAHAM A. (1816–1899), druggist, eldest son of Israel Solomons, was born in Georgetown, South Carolina, on May 2nd, 1816. After graduating from the Medical College of South Carolina (Charleston) in 1835 he engaged in business at various points in South Carolina. In 1845 he settled in Savannah, Georgia, and established the firm of A. A. Solomons & Company, druggists, which for more than half a century enjoyed a high reputation throughout the Southeastern states for its quality and integrity. Two of his brothers, Joseph M. Solomons and Moses J. Solomons, later joined the firm. In 1884 Abraham A. Solomons retired, entrusting the business to his two brothers and his son, Isaiah A. Solomons. "They carry a complete line of drugs, chemicals, patent medicines, and pharmaceutical preparations, surgical instruments and appliances, and such sundries as pertain exclusively to their business; the stock is large and complete, the transactions being commensurate in magnitude, while twelve assistants are constantly busy attending to the business of the firm" [*Savannah: Her Trade, Commerce, and Industries, 1883–1884* (Savannah, 1884), p. 90]. Solomons' wife, Cecelia Moses (1815–1882), died on April 27th, 1882, and was buried in Laurel Grove Cemetery. Abraham A. Solomons died on August 8th, 1899, survived by three children, and was buried beside his wife. As the Savannah *Morning News* (August 9th, 1899) observed, "Dr. Solomons was throughout his long career here faithful and devoted to the interests of his adopted city. In the yellow fever epidemic of 1854, which was one of the most severe ever known, he remained at his post and rendered valuable assistance, giving freely of his time and means to the relief of the suffering and dying. . . . As was natural to a man of such kindly nature, the deceased was very charitably inclined and aided many in his quiet and unostentatious way. No worthy appeal for assistance was ever refused. He leaves a name which can be treasured by his family and the people of this city as one worthy of honor and emulation."

SORREL, FRANCIS (1793–1870), commission merchant, son of Antoine François Sorrel des Rivières, a civil engineer, was born in San Domingo, West Indies, in 1793. As a child he narrowly escaped massacre during the slave insurrection in San Domingo following the Declaration of the Rights of Man; he fled with his father and eventually reached Baltimore, Maryland, where he was reared in the household of kind relatives. In 1820 he settled in Savannah, Georgia, where he prospered in the commission business until his retirement in 1852. He was for many years a justice of the inferior court of Chatham County and a director of the Planters' Bank of the State of Georgia; he was also chairman of the board of trustees of the Independent Presbyterian Church. On March 27th, 1860, his wife, Matilda A. Sorrel (1806–1860), a native of Virginia, plunged to her death from a second- or third-story window of her Savannah residence. ("I heard some time since," wrote Mrs. Mary Jones on March 29th, 1860, "that she was subject to great mental depressions.") Francis Sorrel died in Savannah on May 5th, 1870, and was buried beside his wife in Laurel Grove Cemetery. His son, Gilbert Moxley Sorrel (1838–1901), has been called "the best staff officer in the Confederate service." He was lieutenant colonel and chief of staff, Longstreet's corps; at twenty-six he was brigadier general in the Army of Northern Virginia. His war experiences are detailed in his *Recollections of a Confederate Staff Officer* (1905).

SORREL, LUCINDA IRELAND (1829–1903), daughter of Francis Sorrel (1793–1870), was born in Savannah, Georgia, on January 28th, 1829. On June 1st, 1858, in her thirtieth year, she became the wife of Daniel Stewart Elliott (1826–1862), son of the Hon. John Elliott (1773–1827) and his second wife, Martha Stewart (1799–1864). "I wish her joy," wrote Charles Colcock Jones, Jr., on the eve of the wedding, "but fear a disappointment. Were I a lady, I would certainly be very loath to marry one who had the guilt of homicide upon his skirts. The marriage is not, I am told, very warmly approved by her parents." Elliott died of "pulmonary disease" on

August 3rd, 1862, leaving a wife and two young children, and was buried in the Presbyterian Cemetery, Roswell Georgia. Lucinda Ireland (Sorrel) Elliott survived her husband forty-one years; she died in Washington, D.C., on July 3rd, 1903, and was buried with her parents and her distinguished brother General Gilbert Moxley Sorrel (1838–1901), in the Sorrel vault, Laurel Grove Cemetery, Savannah.

SPALDING, CHARLES HARRIS (1808–1887), Confederate soldier, son of Thomas Spalding (1774–1851) and Sarah Leake (1778–1843), was born on Sapelo Island, McIntosh County, Georgia, on January 17th, 1808. After attending Edinburgh University he returned to his native county, where he resided until the Civil War. On July 16th, 1834, he married Eliza V. Houstoun (1810–1836), eldest daughter of James Houstoun and Mary Ann Williamson. After her death he married Evelyn West Kell (1820–1898), daughter of John Kell and Margery Spalding Baillie. There were no children by either marriage. At his mother's death in 1843 he inherited Ashantilly, a house on the mainland a few miles from Darien, and made it his winter residence. He was always active in politics; he represented McIntosh County in the state senate three terms (1841–1844); in 1844 he ran unsuccessfully for Congress. "I unite with you," he wrote the Rev. Dr. Charles Colcock Jones on April 22nd, 1861, "in gratitude for the auspicious inauguration of our Southern Confederacy, and hope, and even expect, that the final settlement of our difficulties, and the peaceful acknowledgment of our nationality, will not be very long delayed." On September 27th, 1861, in Riceboro, Liberty County, he was appointed lieutenant colonel, 1st Battalion Georgia Cavalry (later consolidated with the 2nd Battalion to form the 5th Regiment Georgia Cavalry). "It is very inspiriting," wrote Mrs. Mary Jones on October 26th, 1861, "to know that we have an active officer in command." After the war Spalding and his wife lived at the Nook, his residence in Spalding County; he died there on February 4th, 1887, and was buried in St. Andrew's Cemetery, Darien. Evelyn West (Kell) Spalding died in Sunnyside, Georgia, on August 17th, 1898 (her seventy-eighth birthday), and was buried beside her husband. As the Macon *Telegraph* observed at the time of his death, "Charles Spalding was a type of the elegant and cultured Southern gentleman who made the hospitality of the seaboard of Georgia delightful at home and famous abroad in the better and happier days of the South. Well born, well bred, well educated, and supplied with a generous fortune, he filled his allotted sphere from first to last as a brave and honest gentleman and a citizen of whom any country might be proud. . . . There may be new glories, new power, and new fortunes awaiting what is called the New South. She will be happy if her new civilization shall breed such men as Charles Spalding."

SPALDING, RANDOLPH (1822–1862), planter and Confederate soldier, youngest child of Thomas Spalding (1774–1851) and Sarah Leake (1778–1843), was born at Ashantilly, his father's plantation near Darien, McIntosh County, Georgia, on December 23rd, 1822. After attending Franklin College (Athens) briefly with the class of 1842 he graduated from Oglethorpe University in 1841. Returning to McIntosh County, he settled on Sapelo Island, where he prospered in planting; in the Federal Census of 1860 he was recorded as the owner of 252 slaves. On December 7th, 1842, he married Mary Dorothea Bass (1820–1898), daughter of Sterling Bass and Elizabeth Gregory, of Russell County, Alabama. For many years he represented McIntosh County in the state legislature. "As a legislator," observed the Savannah *Republican* (March 18th, 1862), "he was intelligent and conservative, his talents being of a practical rather than showy order." At the outbreak of the Civil War he became colonel of the 29th Regiment Georgia Infantry, serving as aide-de-camp on the staff of General W. H. T. Walker in Savannah. According to W. D. DeSaussure, colonel of the 15th Regiment South Carolina Volunteers, in his report of the engagement with Union forces on Hilton Head Island on November 7th, 1861, "Colonel Randolph Spalding, of Georgia, attached himself to Company B of this regiment and fought throughout the day as a private in the ranks." He died of pneumonia in Savannah on March 17th, 1862, and was buried in Laurel Grove Cemetery in the vault of the Hon. John Elliott Ward; his remains were later removed to St. Andrew's Cemetery, Darien. In the words of the Savannah *Republican* (March 18th, 1862), "He was a true friend, a kind and generous neighbor, and open and truthful in all he thought or did. The soul of honor, he scorned a little or mean action, and was ever ready to defend the right, knowing no such thing as fear. . . . Had he lived to meet the enemy, he would have carried into the field a gallantry which no one has ever thought to question." He was reputed to be a heavy drinker; on July 27th, 1850, Charles Colcock Jones, Jr., described to his parents his recent journey via stagecoach from Liberty County, Georgia, to Savannah: "One of the passengers, Mr. Spalding, appeared quite fond of the regular 'brown stuff' and made no bones about indulging his propensities on every occasion; so that by the time we reached Savannah he was, to use a familiar expression, 'pretty well corned.' " Mary Dorothea (Bass) Spalding died on Sapelo Island on September 19th, 1898, and was buried beside her husband in St. Andrew's Cemetery.

SPEISSEGGER, SAMUEL L. (1792–1867), musician, was born in Charleston, South Carolina, in May 1792. In early manhood he settled in Savannah, Georgia, where for half a century he participated in musical affairs. In the Federal Census of 1850 he was identified as a "pianist"; in the Federal Census of 1860 he was identified as a "professor of music." His services as piano tuner were in demand not only in Savannah but also throughout the neighboring counties. On June 17th, 1819, he married Martha B. Millen (1800–1858), a native of South Carolina. She died in Savannah on July 4th, 1858, and was buried in Laurel Grove Cemetery. Samuel L. Speissegger died on November 15th, 1867, and was buried beside his wife.

SPENCER, MARY BOON (McGOWEN) (STACY) (1806–1870): *Mrs. William Spencer,* daughter of John McGowen and Mary Brown, widow of William Harrell, was born in Liberty County, Georgia, in 1806. In 1824 she became the wife of James Stacy (born 1801), son of John Stacy and his second wife, Sarah Quarterman; there was one daughter: Susan Lorenna Stacy (1825–1883), who became (on January 23rd, 1845) the wife of William Sanford Norman. On December 17th, 1832, Mary Boon (McGowen) Stacy became the third wife of William Spencer (1795–1843), son of Samuel Spencer and Ann Way. After her husband's death in 1843 she continued to reside in Walthourville with her two daughters (Harriet and Almira) and her three sons, all of whom fought in the Civil War. William W. Spencer (1838–1865), a graduate of Oglethorpe University (1859), enlisted on July 27th, 1861, as second lieutenant in the Ochlochnee Light Infantry (Company G, 13th Regiment Georgia Infantry; later designated Company E, 29th Regiment Georgia Infantry); he was commissioned captain on February 27th, 1862, and reelected captain on May 7th, 1862; he died early in 1865. John Q. Spencer (1840–1890), a graduate of Oglethorpe University (1860), enlisted on October 1st, 1861, as a private in the Liberty Independent Troop (Company G, 5th Regiment Georgia Cavalry); he enlisted on May 15th, 1862, as a private in the Liberty Mounted Rangers (Company B, 20th Battalion Georgia Cavalry); he was later promoted to fifth sergeant. Joseph S. Spencer (born 1842) enlisted on August 27th, 1861, as third corporal in the Liberty Volunteers (Company H, 25th Regiment Georgia Infantry); he was later promoted to fifth sergeant; he was captured at Kennesaw Mountain, near Marietta, Georgia, in June 1864 and was paroled at the end of the war.

SPENCER, SAMUEL BACON (1827–1901), lawyer and educator, son of William Spencer (1795–1843) and his second wife, Sarah Bacon (1798–1831), widow of James Wilson, was born in Liberty County, Georgia, on December 26th, 1827. After graduating from Oglethorpe University in 1848 he was for several years principal of a male academy in Lumpkin, Georgia, before settling in 1853 in Thomasville, where he planted and practiced law until the outbreak of the Civil War. On December 13th, 1849, he married Mary E. Baker (1830–1914), sixth child of William Quarterman Baker (1800–1877) and his first wife, Ann Lydia Mallard (1804–1843), of Liberty County. He was captain, later major, of cavalry in the Confederate army. In 1870 he removed to Atlanta, where he rose to prominence in law and served one term (1874) as mayor. For ten years (1886–1896) he was principal of the Chatham Academy in Savannah. He died in Atlanta on October 16th, 1901, survived by three sons, and was buried in Oakland Cemetery. Mary (Baker) Spencer died in Atlanta on December 21st, 1914, and was buried beside her husband.

SPRATT, LEONIDAS WILLIAM (1818–1903), lawyer, was born at Fort Mill, York County, South Carolina on August 30th, 1818. After attending the South Carolina College he removed to Florida, where he taught school for several years in Quincy and later served as judge of probate in Apalachicola. By 1850 he had returned to Charleston, where he practiced law until the outbreak of the Civil War. He represented Charleston several terms in the state legislature. In 1853, as editor of the *Southern Standard,* he launched a campaign to revive the African slave trade; during the succeeding months, hoping to unite slaveholders and nonslaveholders in a demand for a Southern confederacy, he issued numerous pamphlets designed to foment disunion. By December 1856 the issue had assumed such importance that Governor James Hopkins Adams recommended the reopening of the slave trade in his message to the state legislature. Spratt's proposal was discussed in the commercial conventions meeting in New Orleans (1855), Savannah (1856), Knoxville (1857), and Montgomery (1858), but otherwise it attracted little notice outside of South Carolina. Spratt was a member of the legislature that called the state secession convention meeting in Columbia in December 1860. He was also commissioner from South Carolina to the Florida state secession convention meeting in Tallahassee in January 1861; his impassioned speech advocating secession aroused wild enthusiasm. In 1862 he served briefly as commissary on the staff of General Gregg, with rank of major; in December 1862 he was appointed judge advocate on the staff of General Longstreet, with rank of colonel; he continued to serve in this capacity until 1865. After the war he practiced law for some years in Charleston and Richmond. In 1875 he removed to Jacksonville, Florida, where he continued to practice law until 1881, when he retired to devote himself to literary pursuits. His first wife died in Charleston on June 3rd, 1860; in 1862 he married Mary Ann Wadsworth (1832–1881), of Richmond, Virginia; she died in Jacksonville on March 3rd, 1881, and was buried in Evergreen Cemetery. Leonidas William Spratt died on October 4th, 1903, and was buried beside his wife. In his *Speech upon the Foreign Slave Trade,* delivered before the South Carolina legislature on December 13th, 1858, Spratt declared that "The North has seventeen states and sixteen million people; the South has fifteen states and but ten million people; the North has thus the power of legislation, and she has shown that she will use it; she has used it already to the limits of endurance. . . . If slavery stand—

and it must stand, for it is too abundant of blessings and too prodigal of promise to be given up—it must start from its repose; it must take the moral strength of an aggressive attitude. . . . It is time that slavery should be roused to a consciousness of responsibility for its own preservation; that it should become an actor in the drama of its own fate; that it should speak for itself upon this great question. . . . When it does, its first utterance will be, 'We want to be free—free to expand according to our own nature, free of the touch of any hostile hand upon us. We are right in that existence which it has pleased Almighty God to give us, and we can admit no declaration of a wrong in the means to our advancement.' "

SPRING, GARDINER (1785–1873), Presbyterian clergyman, son of the Rev. Samuel Spring (1746–1819), was born in Newburyport, Massachusetts, on February 24th, 1785. After graduating from Yale College in 1805 he taught school in Bermuda for two years (1805–1807); returning to New Haven, he studied law and commenced practice in 1808. In the autumn of 1809 he felt the call to preach and entered Andover Theological Seminary, where he studied for eight months. In 1810 he became pastor of the Brick Presbyterian Church, New York City, then located on Beekman Street at Nassau, and after 1858 on Fifth Avenue at 37th Street. For sixty-three years he held a commanding position in the religious life of New York; and the publication of many of his sermons and addresses won him nationwide recognition. In 1869 the General Assembly convened in his own church; although eighty-four years old and nearly blind, Spring pleaded eloquently for the reunion of the two branches of the Presbyterian Church, the Old School and the New School. He received the honorary degree of doctor of divinity from Hamilton College in 1819, and the honorary degree of doctor of laws from Lafayette College in 1853. He was twice married. He died in New York City on August 18th, 1873.

STACY, EZRA (1807–1878), planter, son of John Stacy (1761–1818) and his second wife, Sarah Quarterman (1778–1826), was born in Liberty County, Georgia, on May 31st, 1807. His father, also a planter, was deacon of Midway Church (1808–1818) and clerk of the session (1798–1818); he represented Liberty County in the state legislature in 1796 and 1797. Ezra Stacy was a brother of John William Stacy (1798–1871) and a half-brother of Mary Wilson Stacy (1789–1863), wife of Joseph Norman. For twenty-eight years (1838–1866) he was a deacon of Midway Church. He was a charter member of the Flemington Presbyterian Church at its organization in April 1866. He married first (on January 4th, 1831) Sarah Ann Winn (1811–1853), daughter of John Winn; there were eight children. After her death on April 16th, 1853, he married second (on March 15th, 1854) Maria Lavender (1817–1873), daughter of William Lavender; there were five children. After her death on

November 2nd, 1873, he married third (on April 28th, 1875) Ann Irene Quarterman (born 1829), daughter of William Elliott Way Quarterman and widow of the Rev. Moses William Way (1825–1859). Ezra Stacy died on December 9th, 1878, survived by his third wife, and was buried beside his second wife in Flemington Cemetery. One of his sons, Thomas Sumner Stacy (1842–1862), a private in the Liberty Mounted Rangers (Company B, 20th Battalion Georgia Cavalry), died on James Island, near Charleston, South Carolina, early in November 1862 and was buried in Midway Cemetery.

STACY, JAMES (1830–1912), Presbyterian clergyman, son of John William Stacy (1798–1871) and Mary Rebecca Bacon (1799–1857), was born in Liberty County, Georgia, on June 2nd, 1830. After graduating from Oglethorpe University in 1849 and from Columbia Theological Seminary in 1852 he supplied various pulpits in Southwest Georgia from 1853 to 1856. For fifty-four years (1857–1911) he was pastor of the Presbyterian church in Newnan, Georgia, at the same time supplying various other pulpits in the surrounding area. He was also first stated clerk of the Synod of Georgia (1876–1908). He was author of *The Published Records of Midway Church* (1894), *History of the Midway Congregational Church* (1899), and *History of the Presbyterian Church in Georgia* (1912). He received the honorary degree of doctor of divinity from Oglethorpe University in 1876. He married first (on April 18th, 1855) Jane Elizabeth Hawley. After her death on June 8th, 1858, he married second (on October 10th, 1860) Mary Jane McIver. After her death on November 18th, 1861, he married third (on October 9th, 1867) Emily Jones, widow of Meredith Kendrick. He died in Newnan on February 27th, 1912.

STACY, JOHN WILLIAM (1798–1871), planter, eldest son of John Stacy (1761–1818) and his second wife, Sarah Quarterman (1778–1826), was born in Liberty County, Georgia, on November 3rd, 1798. His father, also a planter, was deacon of Midway Church (1808–1818) and clerk of the session (1798–1818); he represented Liberty County in the state legislature in 1796 and 1797. John William Stacy was a brother of Ezra Stacy (1807–1878) and a half-brother of Mary Wilson Stacy (1789–1863), wife of Joseph Norman. On January 27th, 1825, he married Mary Rebecca Bacon (1799–1857), daughter of Jonathan Bacon and Mary Foster; there were seven children, among them the Rev. James Stacy (1830–1912), Presbyterian clergyman and author of *History of the Midway Congregational Church* (1899). For forty-four years (1822–1866) John William Stacy was an active member of Midway Church, and for thirty years (1824–1854) he was clerk of the session. He was a charter member of the Flemington Presbyterian Church at its organization in April 1866. He was also for many years judge of the court of ordinary of Liberty County. Mary Rebecca (Bacon) Stacy died in Fleming-

ton of typhoid fever on November 23rd, 1857, and was buried in Midway Cemetery. John William Stacy died on July 23rd, 1871, and was buried beside his wife. According to *The Southern Presbyterian* (October 26th, 1871), he was "a man of fine social qualities, large general information, kind and generous nature, and earnest piety."

STEBBINS, CHARLES (1806–1877), merchant, was born in Greenfield, Massachusetts, in 1806. In early manhood he settled in Riceboro, Liberty County, Georgia, where for many years he operated a general store. His nephew, Frederick Ransom Lyons (1823–1897), son of his sister, Martha B. Stebbins (1800–1873), also resided in Riceboro, where for many years he operated a general store (Lyons & Trask) in association with William Bates Trask (1811–1880). In 1857 Charles Stebbins removed to Savannah, where he and John Jones became copartners in a livery stable and hack business; after the firm was dissolved in July 1858 Stebbins continued the business for several years alone. Meanwhile his wife kept a boardinghouse in Savannah. After the Civil War he planted for some years in McIntosh County. He died in Riceboro of "bilious fever" on August 24th, 1877. His widow, Margaret M. Stebbins (1813–1879), a native of McIntosh County, returned to Savannah, where she died at the residence of her son, Charles Stebbins, on March 28th, 1879. She was buried in Laurel Grove Cemetery. Among the Jones papers preserved at Tulane University is the following letter written by Charles Stebbins to Dr. Jones from Savannah on May 29th, 1860: "I have bought a nice Vermont mare six years old—over fifteen hands high, gentle in harness, free traveler, good wind, and sound in every respect. For a brood mare I would take her in preference to any I have seen. Her price is $250. I would like you to see her; I think you would be pleased with her."

STEPHENS, ALEXANDER HAMILTON (1812–1883), statesman, son of Andrew Baskins Stephens and his first wife, Margaret Grier, was born in Wilkes County, Georgia, on February 11th, 1812. After graduating from Franklin College (Athens) in 1832 he lived for one year (1833) in the household of the scientist Louis LeConte (1782–1838), of Liberty County, where he conducted a small school for the children of Louis LeConte, Nathaniel Varnedoe, and several neighboring families. In 1834 he commenced the practice of law in Crawfordville, Georgia, not far from the place of his birth. He was a member of the state legislature from 1836 to 1843 with the exception of one term (1841); he was a member of Congress from 1843 to 1859. Returning to Georgia, he continued a lucrative professional practice until the outbreak of the Civil War. At the state secession convention meeting in Milledgeville in January 1861 he was elected one of nine delegates to the convention of seceding states meeting in Montgomery the following month; there, on February 9th, 1861, Jefferson Davis was elected president of the

Confederate States and Alexander Stephens was elected vice-president. His four years in office (1861–1865) gave him little satisfaction; he often censured the government, and as presiding officer of the Senate he became in effect leader of the opposition. On February 3rd, 1865, he was one of three commissioners (with R. M. T. Hunter and John A. Campbell) representing the Confederacy at the Hampton Roads Conference; they returned to Richmond without the armistice they desired. Stephens was arrested in Georgia on May 11th, 1865, confined five months at Fort Warren, Boston harbor, and released on parole on October 12th, 1865. After the war he resumed the practice of law. In 1869 he declined a professorship of political science and history at the University of Georgia. He was author of *A Constitutional View of the Late War Between the States* (2 vols., 1868–1870) and *A Comprehensive and Popular History of the United States* (1882). After serving in Congress for nine years (1873–1882) he was elected governor of Georgia in 1882 and died in office on March 4th, 1883.

STEVENS, AMARINTHA (MUNRO) (1785–1859): *Mrs. John Stevens*, daughter of Simon Munro (1741–1790) and Elizabeth West, was born in Liberty County, Georgia, on October 6th, 1785. Her father, a native of Inverness, Scotland, had migrated in early manhood to coastal Georgia, where he had married Elizabeth West, daughter of Charles West, Sr., in 1767. Amarintha Munro was a sister of Jane Seymour Munro (1774–1857), wife of James Smith; and of Anne West Munro (1787–1857), wife of Dr. Charles William Rogers. On February 2nd, 1804, she became the wife of John Stevens (1777–1832), son of John Stevens and Mary McCartney. There were seven children: John Stevens (1804–1877); Henry Munro Stevens (1808–1888); James Dana Stevens (1810–1845); Harriet Elizabeth Stevens (1811–1887), wife of Joseph Quarterman; Joseph Law Stevens (1814–1862); Mary Anna Stevens (1817–1885), wife of Oliver Winn Stevens; and William Crawford Stevens (1820–1887). John Stevens was for some years collector of the port of Savannah, director of the Bank of the State of Georgia, and member of the state legislature. According to the Rev. Dr. Charles Colcock Jones, he was "a man of sense, of remarkable uprightness and independence of character towards all men; had few intimate acquaintances." He died suddenly in Savannah on June 17th, 1832; his wife returned to Palmyra, her plantation in Liberty County, where she resided for the rest of her life. She died in Walthourville, Liberty County, at the residence of her daughter, Harriet Elizabeth (Stevens) Quarterman, early in the morning of September 18th, 1859 (not September 17th, 1859, as indicated on her gravestone), and was buried beside her husband in Midway Cemetery. She was an "early friend and companion" of William Maxwell (1785–1866) and Eliza Greene Low (1785–1868), widow of David Robarts.

STEVENS, EDWARD ABIEL (1814–1886), Baptist missionary, fifth child of Oliver Stevens (1783–1853) and Eliza Sumner Winn (1790–1872), was born in Sunbury, Liberty County, Georgia, on January 24th, 1814. His parents, both members of Midway Congregational Church at the time of his birth, shortly thereafter became Baptists. Edward Abiel Stevens graduated from Brown University in 1833 and from Newton Theological Seminary in 1836. For fifty years (1836–1886) he served as missionary to Burma; he was for many years president of the board of trustees of Rangoon Baptist College, and he was author of *Elements of General History* and *Commentaries on Matthew, Romans, Galatians, and Hebrews*, both written in Burmese and published at Rangoon. He returned to Georgia on furlough in the autumn of 1854 and remained until the spring of 1855. He died at Rangoon on June 19th, 1886, and was buried in the local cemetery. His wife, Elizabeth Lincoln Haven (1816–1898), died at Insein, Burma, on October 25th, 1898, and was buried beside her husband.

STEVENS, ELIZA SUMNER (WINN) (1790–1872): *Mrs. Oliver Stevens*, daughter of Peter Winn and his second wife, Ann Sumner, widow of Charles Carter and Philip Goode, was born in Liberty County, Georgia, on April 2nd, 1790. On February 27th, 1806, she became the wife of Oliver Stevens (1783–1853), son of the Rev. Josiah Stevens (1743–1804), a Congregational minister, and Mary Gray, of Newport, New Hampshire. Oliver Stevens had come South to settle the estate of his elder brother, Edward Stevens, a Sunbury merchant, who was lost at sea in April 1801. Eliza Sumner (Winn) Stevens was the mother of ten children: Ann Eliza Stevens (1806–1826), first wife of William Bennett Fleming; Mary Caroline Stevens (1808–1836), first wife of Odingsell Witherspoon Hart; Eunice Louisa Stevens (1810–1886), wife of Edwin Holcombe Bacon; Oliver Winn Stevens (1812–1882); Edward Abiel Stevens (1814–1886); Sumner Winn Stevens (1816–1819); Josiah Peter Stevens (1818–1897); Thomas Sumner Stevens (1820–1889); Carlos Wilcox Stevens (1823–1866); and Henry John Stevens (1826–1854). In 1815 Oliver Stevens and his wife left the Presbyterian Church and joined the Baptist. Two of their sons became Baptist clergymen: Carlos Wilcox Stevens and Henry John Stevens; a third son, Edward Abiel Stevens, was a Baptist missionary in Burma for fifty years (1836–1886). The Stevens family resided for many years in Sunbury; by 1850 they had settled in Walthourville. Oliver Stevens died of pneumonia in Greensboro, Georgia, on June 16th, 1853, while visiting his two clergyman sons in Middle Georgia; he was buried in Midway Cemetery, Liberty County. Eliza Sumner (Winn) Stevens continued to reside in Walthourville; she died there in 1872 and was buried beside her husband.

STEVENS, HENRY MUNRO (1808–1888), planter and commission merchant, son of John Stevens (1777–1832) and Amarintha Munro (1785–1859), was born at Palmyra, his father's plantation in Liberty County, Georgia, on

March 17th, 1808. His father, for some years collector of the port of Savannah and director of the Bank of the State of Georgia, represented Liberty County many terms in the state legislature. Henry Munro Stevens was a prosperous planter and a large slaveholder; in the Federal Census of 1860 he was recorded as the owner of seventy-nine slaves. He was one of sixteen citizens instrumental in organizing a separate Presbyterian church in Walthourville in 1855. In 1856 he purchased a house in Marietta, Cobb County, where he spent much of his time prior to and during the Civil War. By 1870 he was engaged in the commission business in Thomasville. He married first (in 1830) Jeannette Thomson; he married second (in 1837) Elizabeth Law (1812–1892), daughter of Samuel Spry Law (1775–1837) and widow of Barne McKinnee. He died in Thomasville on November 1st, 1888, and was buried in Laurel Hill Cemetery. Elizabeth (Law) Stevens died on January 8th, 1892, and was buried beside her husband.

STEVENS, JOHN (1804–1877), planter, eldest son of John Stevens (1777–1832) and Amarintha Munro (1785–1859), was born at Palmyra, his father's plantation in Liberty County, Georgia, in December 1804. His father, for some years collector of the port of Savannah and director of the Bank of the State of Georgia, represented Liberty County many terms in the state legislature. John Stevens was a brother of Henry Munro Stevens (1808–1888); James Dana Stevens (1810–1845); Harriet Elizabeth Stevens (1811–1887), wife of Joseph Quarterman; Joseph Law Stevens (1814–1862); Mary Anna Stevens (1817–1885), wife of Oliver Winn Stevens; and William Crawford Stevens (1820–1887). In early manhood John Stevens resided with his parents in Savannah, where he was a bookkeeper in the Bank of the State of Georgia. After his father's death on June 17th, 1832, he resided with his mother and his younger brother, William Crawford Stevens, at Palmyra, Liberty County, until his mother's death on September 18th, 1859. During Kilpatrick's raid on Liberty County in December 1864 and January 1865 Stevens remained in Dorchester with his old friend Abial Winn; in January 1865 he fled to relatives in South Georgia and Florida and did not return to Liberty County until late spring. In 1870 he was teaching school in Quitman, Brooks County, and living in the household of his sister, Mary Anna Stevens, wife of Oliver Winn Stevens. He never married. He died in Valdosta late in 1877 and was buried in Valdosta Cemetery.

STEVENS, JOSEPH LAW (1814–1862), planter, son of John Stevens (1777–1832) and Amarintha Munro (1785–1859), was born at Palmyra, his father's plantation in Liberty County, Georgia, in 1814. His father, for some years collector of the port of Savannah and director of the Bank of the State of Georgia, represented Liberty County many terms in the state legislature. In childhood he resided with his parents in Savannah; after his father's

death on June 17th, 1832, he resided for several years with his mother at Palmyra, Liberty County. He married first (in 1836) Sarah B. Lodge; he married second (in 1849) Mary Jane Goulding (1815–1853), daughter of Palmer Goulding and Jane Graham, and widow of George W. Leonard. He died in Dorchester on May 16th, 1862, and was buried beside his second wife in Midway Cemetery. His elder brother, John Stevens (1804–1877), was named guardian of his two orphaned children: Joseph Goulding Stevens and Mary Jane Stevens.

STEVENS, JOSIAH PETER (1818–1897), physician and planter, seventh child of Oliver Stevens (1783–1853) and Eliza Sumner Winn (1790–1872), was born in Sunbury, Liberty County, Georgia, on November 17th, 1818. After attending Franklin College (Athens) he graduated from the Medical College of South Carolina (Charleston) in 1840. Returning to his native county he practiced medicine in Walthourville for twenty-three years. On June 8th, 1843, he married Anne LeConte (1825–1866), youngest daughter of Louis LeConte (1782–1838) and Anne Quarterman (1793–1826); there were six children. Anne (LeConte) Stevens was a graduate of Wesleyan Female College in Macon; she possessed a fine soprano voice, and when the Walthourville Presbyterian Church was organized in 1855 she became leader of the choir. To Mrs. Mary Jones Dr. Stevens was "an excellent family physician . . . in whose skill we have confidence." Early in 1860 he removed all his Negroes to Baker County in Southwest Georgia; he and his family remained in Walthourville until November 1863, when they settled on a farm near Newton, Baker County. There Anne (LeConte) Stevens died on September 2nd, 1866. In 1873 Stevens removed to a farm near Leesburg, Lee County, where he planted and practiced medicine for six years. From 1879 to 1890 he practiced medicine in Macon; he then retired to his farm in Lee County, where he died on November 7th, 1897, survived by four children. He was buried in Rose Hill Cemetery, Macon, beside his first wife and near his second wife, Louisa A. Ragan (1836–1879).

STEVENS, OLIVER WINN (1812–1882), planter and educator, fourth child of Oliver Stevens (1783–1853) and Eliza Sumner Winn (1790–1872), was born in Sunbury, Liberty County, Georgia, on March 27th, 1812. On March 28th, 1837, he married Mary Anna Stevens (1817–1885), daughter of John Stevens (1777–1832) and Amarintha Munro (1785–1859); they were not related by blood. Prior to the Civil War Oliver Winn Stevens conducted a school and planted cotton in Liberty County; for several years in the 1850s he was president of the Masonic Female College in Lumpkin, Stewart County. In 1863 he removed with his family to Quitman, Brooks County, where he was principal of the Quitman Academy and for several years county treasurer. He died in Quitman on November 20th, 1882, survived by his wife and six children, and was buried in Westview Cemetery. Mary Anna

(Stevens) Stevens died on September 14th, 1885, and was buried beside her husband.

STEVENS, THOMAS SUMNER (1820–1889), educator, eighth child of Oliver Stevens (1783–1853) and Eliza Sumner Winn (1790–1872), was born in Sunbury, Liberty County, Georgia, on October 14th, 1820. After graduating from Franklin College (Athens) in 1840 he taught school for ten years. In April 1850 he entered the military institute in West Point, New York, for a special course in civil engineering; in November 1850 he received his engineering degree and commenced the practice of his profession. While constructing the Central Railroad of Georgia between Millen and Augusta he suffered a broken hip which incapacitated him for active outdoor life; returning to Liberty County, he resumed teaching and resided with his widowed mother. On June 27th, 1861, in his forty-first year, he married Matilda Jane Harden (1837–1932), eldest daughter of Dr. John Macpherson Berrien Harden (1810–1848) and Jane LeConte (1814–1876), of Walthourville. On October 1st, 1861, he enlisted as a private in the Liberty Independent Troop (Company G, 5th Regiment Georgia Cavalry), but after six months he was pronounced physically unfit for military service. He was principal of the Walthourville Academy (1865–1870); principal of the West Florida Seminary in Tallahassee (1870–1871); president of the Bowling Green Female College in Bowling Green, Kentucky (1871–1880); and teacher at the Silliman Collegiate Institute for Young Ladies in Clinton, Louisiana (1880–1889). He died in Clinton on October 30th, 1889, and was buried in Clinton Cemetery. His wife survived him forty-two years; she died in Raleigh, North Carolina, at the residence of her granddaughter, on March 11th, 1932, only a few weeks before her ninety-fifth birthday, and was buried in Midway Cemetery, Liberty County, Georgia.

STEVENS, WILLIAM CRAWFORD (1820–1887), planter, son of John Stevens (1777–1832) and Amarintha Munro (1785–1859), was born at Palmyra, his father's plantation in Liberty County, Georgia, on May 21st, 1820. His father, for some years collector of the port of Savannah and director of the Bank of the State of Georgia, represented Liberty County many terms in the state legislature. In childhood he resided with his parents in Savannah; after his father's death on June 17th, 1832, he resided with his mother and his elder brother, John Stevens (1804–1877), at Palmyra, Liberty County, until his mother's death on September 18th, 1859. He attended Franklin College (Athens) with the class of 1840 but did not graduate. Returning to Liberty County, he was for a time teacher of the three children of the Rev. Dr. Charles Colcock Jones. By 1850 he was practicing law. During the Civil War he served as a private in the Liberty Independent Troop (Company G, 5th Regiment Georgia Cavalry); he was captured in Liberty County on December 15th, 1864, and confined at Point Lookout, Maryland, until his

release on June 19th, 1865. After the war he resumed planting in Liberty County. He was for some years elder of the Dorchester Presbyterian Church. On December 7th, 1871, he married Julia Virginia Winn, daughter of Washington Winn. He died in Dorchester on December 17th, 1887, survived by his wife and two children, and was buried in Dorchester Cemetery.

STEWART, CHARLES DAWSON (1781–1872), planter, merchant, and manufacturer, was born in Brunswick County, Virginia, in 1781. In early manhood he migrated to Georgia, living for some years in Warrenton and Greensboro; in 1829 he became one of the first settlers of Columbus, where he prospered in business. From January 1832 to March 1834 he was one of six commissioners elected to govern the town; from July 1834 to December 1834 he served as superintendent. He was one of the incorporators of the Eagle & Phoenix Mills. During the Civil War he suffered heavy financial losses, some of which he later recovered. Early in life he married Henrietta Hargreaves, of Charles County, Maryland; after her death he married Rebecca Appling. He spent his last years at the residence of his eldest son, the Rev. George Stewart (1814–1878), in Summerville Heights, Alabama, four miles north of Columbus; he died there on June 27th, 1872, and was buried in Linwood Cemetery, Columbus.

STEWART, CHARLES HARGREAVES (1815–1864), planter, second son of Charles Dawson Stewart (1781–1872) and Henrietta Hargreaves, was born in Greensboro, Georgia, in September 1815. In 1829 he removed with his parents to Columbus, where his father prospered in business. For some years Charles Hargreaves Stewart resided on his plantation near Hardaway, Macon County, Alabama, which Mary Sophia Robarts, governess to his four nieces (1861–1862), described as "the most handsomely settled place she ever saw in her life." On March 4th, 1862, he was elected first lieutenant in Company C, 36th Regiment Alabama Infantry, and entered service at Camp Goode, near Mobile; on September 6th, 1862, he tendered his resignation to the secretary of war: "My health is such as to render me unfit for duty, having about four months since had an attack of the measles from which I have not recovered." After the death of his wife Mary (1825–1863) on July 25th, 1863, he removed to Columbus, where he died on September 26th, 1864. He was buried beside his wife in Linwood Cemetery.

STEWART, JAMES (1825–1875), druggist, was born in New York City in 1825. In early manhood he settled in Savannah, Georgia, where he engaged in the drug business for some years prior to the Civil War, and where he became a particular friend of William Henry King (1833–1865), of King & Waring, druggists. In 1858 he joined Osceola Butler (1838–1892) in the firm of Stewart & Butler, druggists. "Messrs. Stewart & Butler have imported a most delicious extract for the handkerchief, 'Bouquet of Savannah' " (Savannah *Morning News,* January 12th, 1860). At the outbreak of the Civil War Butler withdrew from the firm to enter Confederate service, and Stewart continued the business alone. After the war Stewart was clerk of the city council and ex-officio secretary of the board of health for ten years (1865–1875). In his new post he was, according to the Savannah *Republican,* "polite and efficient," "accomplished and vigilant," "affable," and "energetic." He was a member of the St. Andrew's Society, the Hibernian Society, and the Société Française de Bienfaisance. He never married. He died in Savannah after a long illness on March 29th, 1875. For twenty-four hours his body lay in state in the city exchange; after a service in the Cathedral of St. John the Baptist his body was deposited in the reception vault of Cathedral (Catholic) Cemetery to await the orders of his family. According to the Savannah *Republican* (March 31st, 1875), "The procession was one of the longest and most imposing ever seen in Savannah, and was an earnest and sincere tribute to one who was a true friend and a faithful public servant."

STEWART, THEOPHILUS S. (1818–1901), physician, third son of Charles Dawson Stewart (1781–1872) and Henrietta Hargreaves, was born in Greensboro, Georgia, on July 4th, 1818. In 1829 he removed with his parents to Columbus, where his father prospered in business. After studying medicine at the University of Paris he returned to Columbus, where for some years he practiced his profession. On June 5th, 1849, he married Susan M. McDowall (1822–1893), daughter of Thomas McDowall and Ann Reid, of Augusta; on November 30th, 1847, his lifelong friend, William Henry Cumming (1820–1893), also a physician, had married Elizabeth Reid McDowall (1820–1895), sister of Susan M. McDowall. In 1857 Stewart removed to Marietta, where he continued to practice medicine until the outbreak of the Civil War, when he retired from practice. He had large interests in the Eagle & Phoenix Mills of Columbus, the Sibley Mills of Augusta, and the Roswell Manufacturing Company. On January 2nd, 1860, he joined the First Presbyterian Church, of which he was for thirty-seven years (1864–1901) a deacon. He and his wife were active in charitable work and particularly earnest in the cause of foreign missions. His brother-in-law, William Henry Cumming, died in his house on August 21st, 1893; Susan (McDowall) Stewart died in the same house the next day; there was a double funeral on August 23rd and a double burial service in Episcopal Cemetery, Marietta. Theophilus S. Stewart died without issue on April 4th, 1901, and was buried beside his wife. As the Atlanta *Constitution* (April 5th, 1901) observed, "Marietta has indeed lost a model citizen." Wallace Stewart Buttolph (1867–1899) was named in his honor.

STILES, BENJAMIN EDWARD (1836–1864), planter and Confederate soldier, son of Benjamin Edward Stiles (1794–1855) and Mary Anne Mackay (1802–1862), was born in Savannah, Georgia, on April 24th, 1836. His father, a Savannah merchant, planted for some years in Bibb County, near Macon; early in 1855 he returned with his family to Savannah, where he died on April 10th, 1855, leaving a wife, two daughters, and a son. On July 24th, 1861, "Mr. Eddie" was elected captain of the Cobb Guards (Company E, 16th Regiment Georgia Volunteer Infantry) and went to Virginia with his company. He was severely wounded in the hip at Malvern Hill (July 1st, 1862) and was sent to Georgia on sick furlough for three months. "My brother returns to Virginia immediately," his sister Kitty wrote from Clarkesville, Georgia, on October 4th, 1862. "His wound is healing quickly now, and he is altogether better than he was a few weeks since. I am truly thankful he has escaped these last battles. His company was almost annihilated at Harpers Ferry, and the Sharpsburg battle has left him one lieutenant and one private. A few men had been left in hospitals in Virginia; and some who were wounded near Richmond were at home; but in all there cannot be more than twenty men left of the one hundred and thirty-five he led a year ago." On March 24th, 1863, in Clarkesville, he married Clelia E. Peronneau (1840–1887), daughter of Edward C. Peronneau, of Charleston, South Carolina. Returning to Virginia, he was elected major (May 18th, 1863) and promoted to lieutenant colonel (November 29th, 1863). He was killed in action at Guard Hill, near Front Royal, Virginia, on August 16th, 1864. As the Savannah *Morning News* (September 12th, 1864) observed, "The record of Savannah's cherished dead—already, alas, too full—must again be opened for the name of another hero, fallen in the strife." He was buried in Stonewall Cemetery, Winchester, Virginia. His wife died at the residence of her niece, Mrs. B. T. Gordon, in Nelson County, Virginia, on August 5th, 1887, and was buried beside her husband.

STILES, CLIFFORD ADAMS (1834–1912), physician, son of Joseph Stiles (1758–1838) and his second wife, Margaret Vernon Adams (1805–1893), was born in Savannah, Georgia, on December 7th, 1834. He was a half-brother of the Rev. Joseph Clay Stiles (1795–1875), distinguished Presbyterian clergyman, and the Hon. William Henry Stiles (1810–1865), distinguished lawyer and statesman. After graduating from the Savannah Medical College in 1857 he practiced medicine in his native city until the outbreak of the Civil War. On April 27th, 1861, he was appointed assistant surgeon of the 1st Georgia Regulars; on November 13th, 1861, in camp near Centreville, Virginia, he resigned. For some months in 1862 he was acting surgeon of the Savannah Volunteer Guards (Company A, 18th Battalion Georgia Infantry). After the war he practiced medicine for forty years in Atlanta. Late in 1905 he retired to Seville, Florida, where he died on January 22nd, 1912, survived by his second wife, Katharine Livingston Hutchinson, and five children. He was buried in Laurel Grove Cemetery, Savannah, beside his first wife, Anna Wylly Adams, who had died in Atlanta on October 23rd, 1893.

STILES, JOSEPH CLAY (1795–1875), Presbyterian clergyman, second son of Joseph Stiles (1758–1838) and his first wife, Catherine Clay (1775–1823), was born in Savannah, Georgia, on December 6th, 1795. He was a younger brother of Benjamin Edward Stiles (1794–1855), father of Katherine Clay (Kitty) Stiles (1832–1916), and an elder brother of the Hon. William Henry Stiles (1810–1865). After graduating from Yale College in 1814 he attended the Litchfield (Connecticut) Law School and subsequently read law in the office of the Hon. John Macpherson Berrien (1781–1856), of Savannah. For several years he practiced law in Savannah in partnership with William Washington Gordon (1796–1842). On August 14th, 1820, he married Caroline Peck (1802–1821), daughter of Gad Peck and Asenath Osborn, of New Haven, Connecticut; she died on Green Island, near Savannah, late in the summer of 1821. Feeling a call to preach, he attended Andover Theological Seminary for two years (1822–1824), returned to the South, and commenced his long career as evangelist. From 1829 to 1835 he resided in Darien, McIntosh County, Georgia, where on April 2nd, 1828, he married Caroline Clifford Nephew (1810–1879), daughter of James Nephew and his second wife, Sarah (Pelot) Gignilliat. There were six children. He was subsequently evangelist in Woodford County, Kentucky (1835–1844); pastor of the Shockoe Hill Presbyterian Church, Richmond, Virginia (1844–1848); pastor of the Mercer Street Presbyterian Church, New York City (1848–1850); Southern agent for the American Bible Society (1850–1852); and pastor of the South Congregational Church, New Haven, Connecticut (1852–1860). Early in 1860 he was appointed first evangelist of the Synod of Georgia; he again returned to the South, leaving his family in New Haven. At the outbreak of the Civil War he was appointed evangelist by the Synod of Virginia, serving chiefly in the command of Stonewall Jackson, whom he greatly admired. His three sons (Robert Augustus Stiles, Randolph Railey Stiles, and Eugene West Stiles) served in the Confederate army as privates in Captain R. M. Anderson's Company, Virginia Light Artillery (1st Company Richmond Howitzers). After the war he continued to preach with great success in Virginia, Alabama, Florida, Mississippi, and Missouri. According to Chauncey Allen Goodrich (1790–1860), professor of elocution in the theology department of Yale College, he was "the first pulpit orator in America." "When I hear Dr. Stiles I feel I am in the presence of a gigantic intellect," wrote Mrs. Mary S. Mallard on December 21st, 1863. He was author of numerous books, among them *Modern Reform Examined; or, The Union of the North and South on the Subject of Slavery* (Philadelphia, 1858); *The National Controversy; or, The Voice of the Fathers upon the State of the Country* (New York, 1861); *National Rectitude the Only True Basis of National Prosperity* (Petersburg, Virginia, 1863); and *Captain Thomas E. King; or, A Word to the Army and the Country* (Charleston, 1864). He received the honorary degree of doctor of divinity from Transylvania University in 1846, and the honorary degree of doctor of laws from Oglethorpe University in 1860. He died in Savannah on March 27th, 1875, survived by his wife and five children, and was buried in Hollywood Cemetery, Richmond, Virginia. Caroline Clifford (Nephew) Stiles died in New Haven, Connecticut, at the residence of her eldest daughter, Anna Catherine Stiles, wife of Professor Hubert Anson Newton, on March 29th, 1879, and was buried beside her husband.

STILES, JOSEPHINE CLIFFORD (1834–1907), second child of the Rev. Joseph Clay Stiles (1795–1875) and his second wife, Caroline Clifford Nephew (1810–1879), was born in McIntosh County, Georgia, on October 28th, 1834. She never married. Her early years were spent in the various places where her father, a Presbyterian clergyman, was evangelist or pastor: Woodford County, Kentucky (1835–1844); Richmond, Virginia (1844–1848); New York City (1848–1850); and New Haven, Connecticut (1852–1860). After the war she lived principally in Richmond, Virginia, where her brother, Robert Augustus Stiles (1836–1905), resided with his family and practiced law. She died in Roswell, Georgia, on April 19th, 1907, and was buried near her parents in Hollywood Cemetery, Richmond. According to her brother, Josephine Clifford Stiles was "quite intimate with General Lee's family and a great favorite with the general. She is consequently something of an heiress in interesting mementos of him given her by his own hand. She has a lock of his hair and one of Traveler's, a star from his coat collar, the wooden inkstand which he used generally in our war, and, if I mistake not, in the Mexican War also, and the remains of a pound of tea he gave her, asking that we should make tea from it the first time we were fortunate enough to have a family reunion. She has also the general's parade hat, or rather she and I have committed this to the keeping of the Confederate Museum in Richmond. The circumstances connected with this latter gift are strongly characteristic. My sister had been spending the morning at the general's residence, 707 East Franklin Street, Richmond, Virginia, sitting most of the time with the ladies of the family in Mrs. Lee's room. The general was preparing for a trip somewhere, and was leisurely packing his trunk—that is, after the ladies had done what they could to aid him; and every now and then he would enter the room where they were, bringing in his hand something which he thought would interest them. In one of these incursions he brought a wide-brimmed drab or gray-brown felt hat, saying: 'Miss Josie, has your father a good hat?' My sister replied that she really did not know, as we had not seen him for some time. 'Well,' said the general, 'I have two good hats, and I don't think a good rebel ought to have two good articles of one kind in these hard times. This was my dress-parade hat. Take it, please, and if your father has not a good hat, give him this one from me.' Father would not wear the hat, deeming it too sacred a thing for common use; but after the general's death, by permission of his two daughters, who were present, I wore it at two of our great Confederate reunions, with my dear old Confederate jacket; and I need scarcely say I was the object of more intense interest than ever in my life before or since" [Robert Augustus Stiles, *Four Years Under Marse Robert* (New York, 1903), pp. 356–357].

STILES, KATHERINE CLAY (KITTY) (1832–1916), elder daughter of Benjamin Edward Stiles (1794–1855) and Mary Anne Mackay (1802–1862), was born in Savannah, Georgia, on February 1st, 1832. She was a niece of the Rev. Joseph Clay Stiles. Her father, a Savannah merchant, planted for some years in Bibb County, near Macon, early in 1855 he returned with his family to Savannah, where he died on April 10th, 1855, leaving a wife, two daughters, and a son. "Kitty" Stiles and Mary Sharpe Jones became close friends in 1856; Kitty was bridesmaid at the wedding of Laura Elizabeth Maxwell (June 10th, 1856) and of Mary Sharpe Jones (April 22nd, 1857). "Miss Stiles is an excellent and very pleasant lady," wrote the Rev. Dr. Charles Colcock Jones on March 26th, 1857. "She is a woman for whom I have always entertained the highest esteem," wrote Charles Colcock Jones, Jr., on April 3rd, 1863. "I have always considered her one of my loved and valued friends," wrote Mrs. Mary Jones on June 20th, 1866. Kitty Stiles was profoundly saddened by the death of her mother on June 21st, 1862, followed two years later by the death of her only brother, Benjamin Edward Stiles, on August 16th, 1864. After the war she settled in Richmond, Virginia, where her uncle, the Rev. Joseph Clay Stiles, resided with his wife and children. She continued her friendship with Mary Sharpe Jones, wife of the Rev. Robert Quarterman Mallard, until Mrs. Mallard's death on August 31st, 1889. For twenty years (1896–1916) she was vice-regent and custodian of the Georgia Room in the Confederate Museum in Richmond. According to an obituary prepared by the museum, "she gathered portraits of the great men of her state, pictures and histories of the blockade runners, important maps of the battlefields, flags of the Confederate navy. . . . She was instrumental in placing many books on Confederate history in the libraries of Edinburgh, Scotland, and Oxford, England. In the last years of her life she devoted her time to doing justice to the memory of that great pathfinder of the seas, Commodore Matthew Fontaine Maury" [*The Confederate Memorial Literary Society Yearbook: 1916* (Richmond, 1917), p. 140]. She died in Richmond on October 7th, 1916, and was buried in Hollywood Cemetery. On January 20th, 1907, a special section of the Richmond *Times-Dispatch* was devoted to the centennial celebration of the birth of Robert E. Lee. An article entitled "His Associations with Savannah," written by Katherine C. Stiles, included the following account of her "great friend": "The last time I saw General Lee before the war was in a morning visit at Arlington in the fall of 1858. His daughter Annie, who died in 1862, was in her rich dark coloring, character, quiet dignity, and charm of manner very like him. . . . When I was saying good-bye to her, he came down the steps and stood behind us. Putting a hand on each of us, he said: 'No tears at Arlington—no tears.' It is now a place of tears."

STILES, MARY ANNE (MACKAY) (1802–1862): *Mrs. Benjamin Edward Stiles,* daughter of Robert Mackay (1772–1816) and Eliza Anne McQueen (1778–1862), was born in Savannah, Georgia, on August 18th, 1802. On January 25th, 1825, she became the wife of Benjamin Edward Stiles (1794–1855), eldest son of Joseph Stiles (1758–1838) and his first wife, Catherine Clay (1775–1823), of Savannah; there were seven children. Her husband was a merchant, member of the firm of Stiles & Fannin; he subsequently removed to Bibb County, near Macon, where he planted for some years. Early in 1855 he returned to Savannah, expecting to make it his permanent home. He died in Savannah on April 10th, 1855, leaving his wife and three children: Katherine Clay (Kitty) Stiles (1832–1916), Benjamin Edward Stiles (1836–1864), and Sidney Elizabeth Stiles (1840–1925). After her husband's death Mary Anne (Mackay) Stiles continued to occupy the family residence on Broughton Street, next door to the house of her widowed mother situated at the southeast corner of Broughton and Abercorn. She died at her summer residence near Clarkesville, Habersham County, Georgia, on June 21st, 1862, and was buried in the cemetery of the Chapel of the Holy Cross near Clarkesville.

STILES, RANDOLPH RAILEY (1838–1868), seaman and soldier, fourth child of the Rev. Joseph Clay Stiles (1795–1875) and his second wife, Caroline Clifford Nephew (1810–1879), was born in Woodford County, Kentucky, on January 10th, 1838. He never married. His early years were spent in the various places where his father, a Presbyterian clergyman, was evangelist or pastor: Woodford County, Kentucky (1835–1844); Richmond, Virginia (1844–1848); New York City (1848–1850); and New Haven, Connecticut (1852–1860). For several years he attended the Collegiate and Commercial Institute of New Haven, conducted by William Huntington Russell. As Eliza Caroline Clay, a cousin, observed on July 4th, 1855, "Mr. Russell told his father not long since that among the hundreds of boys he had had under his care none ever compared with his son. He will not study —*will not* do anything which he does not choose to. Smart, plausible, gentlemanly, a good deal of a dandy, late at school, can't be found at recitation time. And so it is—something wrong the whole time. . . . They have decided to send him on a long voyage, where he will be obliged to submit to control. . . . He began to say 'I won't' to his mother before he was two years old." By 1860 he was back with his parents in New Haven, recorded in the Federal Census of 1860 as a "seaman." At the outbreak of the Civil War he returned to Virginia, where, on July 20th, 1861, at Manassas, he enlisted, together with his elder brother, Robert Augustus Stiles (1836–1905), as a private in Captain R. M. Anderson's Company, Virginia Light Artillery (1st Company Richmond Howitzers). In June 1864 he was wounded at Cold Harbor. On December 3rd, 1864, he was appointed second lieutenant in the Confederate navy; he was captured on February 24th, 1865, while engaged in an expedition to destroy boats, bridges, and supplies on the **Holston and Tennessee Rivers; he was** released on oath at Camp Chase, Ohio, on **June 14th, 1865. After the war he operated a** sawmill near Christiansburg, Virginia, where he soon became known for his reckless character. He met a violent death near Alleghany Springs, Virginia, on August 31st, 1868. According to the Savannah *Republican* (September 10th, 1868), "A party consisting of about a dozen ladies and gentlemen went on an expedition to the falls not far from the springs. Among them was Mr. Randolph R. Stiles, a son of the Rev. Dr. Stiles. Soon after the party had arrived at the falls, Mr. Stiles, to amuse himself, climbed a tall pine tree which stands on the brink of the stream. Having gone up a distance of probably forty or fifty feet, he went out on a large limb overhanging the rocky gorge beneath, and while there, holding to another limb overhead, he lost his footing and fell to the chasm below, the bed of which is solid rock. Of course the result was instant death. His head was crushed, his right leg shattered, and his body otherwise mangled. Life was extinct almost as soon as he was reached by his friends, who were in a few feet of him. The effect was appalling on those who were present and witnessed the terrible affair." He was buried in Hollywood Cemetery, Richmond.

STILES, RICHARD CRESSON (1830–1873), physician, was born in West Chester, Pennsylvania, on October 3rd, 1830. After graduating from Yale College in 1851 and from the Medical College of the University of Pennsylvania in 1854 he was assistant physician at Kings County Hospital, Flatbush, New York (1854–1855); professor of physiology and pathology in the Medical Department of the University of Vermont (1857–1858); and professor of physiology at the Berkshire Medical College, Pittsfield, Massachusetts (1858–1862). During the Civil War

he was surgeon in the United States army for two years (1862–1864). He then settled in Brooklyn, New York, where he was resident physician at Kings County Hospital (1864–1870), registrar of vital statistics in Kings County (1866–1870), and assistant superintendent of the Kings County Board of Health (1868–1870). In 1870 he suffered a mental collapse from which he never recovered. After traveling in Europe in 1872 he returned to his mother's residence in West Chester, where he died of pneumonia on April 16th, 1873. Early in 1856, while studying medicine in Europe, he had married, in Leghorn, Italy, Maria Clark Wells (1831–1908), daughter of Dr. Thomas Wells (1792–1874) and his first wife, Eliza Ann Clark (1798–1834), of New Haven, Connecticut. After his death his wife returned to New Haven, where she died on January 5th, 1908, survived by her only son Thomas Wells Stiles; she was buried beside her husband in West Chester, Pennsylvania.

STILES, ROBERT AUGUSTUS (1836–1905), lawyer, third child of the Rev. Joseph Clay Stiles (1795–1875) and his second wife, Caroline Clifford Nephew (1810–1879), was born in Woodford County, Kentucky, on June 27th, 1836. His early years were spent in the various places where his father, a Presbyterian clergyman, was evangelist or pastor: Woodford County, Kentucky (1835–1844); Richmond, Virginia (1844–1848); New York City (1848–1850); and New Haven, Connecticut (1852–1860). After graduating from Yale College in 1859 he read law in New Haven for one year and entered the Columbia Law School in 1860. At the outbreak of the Civil War he returned to Virginia, where, on July 20th, 1861, at Manassas, he enlisted, together with his younger brother, Randolph Railey Stiles (1838–1868), as a private in Captain R. M. Anderson's Company, Virginia Light Artillery (1st Company Richmond Howitzers). By 1864 he had become major of artillery. He was captured in the battle of Sayler's Creek, Virginia, on April 6th, 1865, and confined for six months on Johnson's Island, Ohio, and at Fort Lafayette, New York harbor. After the war he completed his study of law at the University of Virginia, and in January 1867 he settled in Richmond, where he enjoyed a large and lucrative practice. On June 24th, 1874, he married Leila Caperton (1851–1889), daughter of the Hon. Allen Taylor Caperton, of Union, West Virginia; there were three children. His wife died in Richmond on January 6th, 1889, from an accidental dose of poison and was buried in Hollywood Cemetery. He died at Bonair, his summer retreat six miles from Richmond, on December 5th, 1905, and was buried beside his wife. His *Four Years Under Marse Robert* (1903), an account of his experiences during the Civil War, was widely read and appreciated. According to the records of the class of 1859, Yale College, "He was conspicuous among his college associates for his splendid physical development, an ideal of manly stature, and he was a great lover of, and expert in, athletic sports of various kinds. He was naturally an orator, and a conversationalist whose spirit of mingled humor and pathos, combined with the deep seriousness of his nature, gave to his narrative uncommon power."

STILES, SAMUEL VERNON (1831–1893), cotton broker, son of Joseph Stiles (1758–1838) and his second wife, Margaret Vernon Adams (1805–1893), was born in Savannah, Georgia, on April 14th, 1831. He was a half-brother of the Rev. Joseph Clay Stiles (1795–1875), distinguished Presbyterian clergyman, and the Hon. William Henry Stiles (1810–1865), distinguished lawyer and statesman. Samuel Vernon Stiles was identified with the business and social interests of Savannah all his life. He was a successful cotton broker. On March 20th, 1856, he married Caroline Matilda Rogers (1838–1863), second daughter of the Rev. Charles William Rogers (1809–1861) and Caroline Matilda Woodford (1813–1886), of Savannah and Bryan County. On June 26th, 1862, he enlisted as a private in the Savannah Volunteer Guards (Company C, 18th Battalion Georgia Infantry); according to military records he was "discharged the same day on his furnishing R. R. Sturtevant as a substitute." Caroline Matilda (Rogers) Stiles died in Savannah on January 1st, 1863, and was buried in Laurel Grove Cemetery. Samuel Vernon Stiles died on June 2nd, 1893, and was buried beside his wife.

STILES, SIDNEY ELIZABETH (1840–1925), younger daughter of Benjamin Edward Stiles (1794–1855) and Mary Anne Mackay (1802–1862), was born in Savannah, Georgia, on February 14th, 1840. Her father, a Savannah merchant, planted for some years in Bibb County near Macon; early in 1855 he returned with his family to Savannah, where he died on April 10th, 1855, leaving a wife, two daughters, and a son. On March 27th, 1862, "Sid" became the wife of her first cousin, Dr. William Henry Elliott (1837–1919), son of Dr. Ralph Emms Elliott (1797–1853) and Margaret Cowper Mackay (1807–1893); there were seven children. Her husband, a graduate of Harvard College (1857), the Medical Department of the University of Virginia (1858), and the College of Physicians and Surgeons in New York (1859), had planted rice on the Ogeechee River, near Savannah, until November 1861, when he entered Confederate service as a medical volunteer. He was commissioned assistant surgeon on February 6th, 1862, and continued to serve until the end of the war. Returning to Georgia, he practiced medicine in Savannah for forty-six years (1867–1913). He became adjunct professor of chemistry in the Savannah Medical College (1867), professor of anatomy (1870), and professor of surgery (1875). He was a member of the Georgia Medical Society and served as president in 1877. From 1891 to 1913 he was chief surgeon of the Central Railroad of Georgia and the Ocean Steamship Company. He died in Savannah on March 31st, 1919, and was buried in Laurel Grove Cemetery. Sidney Elizabeth (Stiles) Elliott was for many years active in the affairs of Christ Episcopal Church, the Florence Crittenden Home, and the United Daughters of the Confederacy. She died in Savannah on September 23rd, 1925, and was buried beside her husband.

STILES, WILLIAM HENRY (1810–1865), lawyer, statesman, and Confederate soldier, fourth son of Joseph Stiles (1758–1838) and his first wife Catherine Clay (1775–1823), was born in Savannah, Georgia, on January 1st, 1810. He was a younger brother of the Rev. Joseph Clay Stiles (1795–1875). After studying at the Yale Law School he commenced practice in Savannah in 1831. Early in January 1832 he married Elizabeth Anne Mackay (1810–1867), daughter of Robert Mackay (1772–1816) and Eliza Anne McQueen (1778–1862), of Savannah; his wife was a younger sister of Mary Anne Mackay (1802–1862), wife of his elder brother, Benjamin Edward Stiles (1794–1855). There were three children: Mary Cowper Stiles (1832–1863), second wife of Andrew Low (1813–1886); William Henry Stiles (1834–1878); and Robert Mackay Stiles (1836–1874). William Henry Stiles was solicitor general of the eastern district of Georgia (1833–1836), United States district attorney for the district of Georgia (1836–1838), member of Congress (1843–1845), and chargé d'affaires in Vienna, Austria (1845–1849). Returning to Savannah, he continued the practice of law until the outbreak of the Civil War, dividing his time between Savannah and Etowah Cliffs, his residence in Cass (now Bartow) County. In 1858 he was a member of the state house of representatives and served as speaker. In 1860 he was a delegate to the Democratic National Convention meeting in Baltimore. On September 19th, 1861, he was commissioned lieutenant colonel in the Confederate army and placed in command of Skidaway Island near Savannah; in November 1861 he organized the 4th Battalion Georgia Infantry (seven companies), which in May 1862 was increased to a regiment (ten companies) and redesignated the 60th Regiment Georgia Infantry. On May 19th, 1862, he was commissioned colonel; he continued to serve until failing health forced him to withdraw in August 1863, when he was detached to organize nonconscripts for the defense of Northwest Georgia. He resigned on April 30th, 1864. His son, William Henry Stiles, captain of Company H, 60th Regiment Georgia Infantry, was shot through the thigh at Second Manassas (August 28th, 1862) and shot through the right side just below the ribs at Fredericksburg (December 13th, 1862); on August 24th, 1863, he was appointed captain and assistant quartermaster. William Henry Stiles was author of *Austria in 1848–1849* (2 vols., 1852). He received the honorary degree of master of arts from Yale College in 1837. He died in Savannah on December 20th, 1865, and was buried in

Laurel Grove Cemetery. His wife died at Etowah Cliffs exactly two years later, on December 20th, 1867, and was buried in Bartow County.

STODDARD, JOHN (1809–1879), planter, son of Solomon Stoddard (1771–1860) and Mary Tappan (1771–1852), was born in Northampton, Massachusetts, on March 11th, 1809. In 1825 he entered the firm of Edwards & Stoddard in Boston; in 1830 he was placed in charge of the branch house located in Paris and Lyons, France, where he continued for seven years, accumulating a handsome fortune. On January 7th, 1836, in Paris, he married Mary Lavinia Mongin (1818–1865), orphaned granddaughter and heiress of John David Mongin, of South Carolina; there were five children. In 1837 he settled in Savannah, Georgia, where he resided for the rest of his life, planting extensively and successfully on Daufuskie Island and the Ogeechee River. On July 13th, 1840, he became a member of the Georgia Historical Society, and for one year (beginning February 12th, 1867) he was its president. He was also for some years president of the board of education. He was an elder of the Independent Presbyterian Church for thirty-five years (1844–1879). Mary Lavinia (Mongin) Stoddard died at Lenamor, Georgia, on February 22nd, 1865, and was buried in Bonaventure Cemetery, Savannah. John Stoddard died in Savannah on July 25th, 1879, and was buried beside his wife. His elder daughter, Mary Helen Stoddard (1837–1914), married John Lewis Hardee (1836–1891), Savannah cotton merchant, on February 5th, 1861. His younger daughter, Isabelle Stoddard (1840–1927), married Benjamin Green (1838–1865) on December 11th, 1860; after his death on February 14th, 1865, she married William Derrickson Waples (1839–1892) on February 6th, 1872.

STORY, JOSEPH (1779–1845), jurist, educator, and writer, eldest son of Elisha Story and his second wife, Mehitable Pedrick, was born in Marblehead, Massachusetts, on September 18th, 1779. After graduating from Harvard College in 1798 he returned to Marblehead and read law in the office of Samuel Sewall (1757–1814), congressman (1796–1800), associate justice of the state supreme court (1801–1813), and chief justice (1813–1814). Through wide reading he acquired the vast erudition later manifest in his voluminous published works. In 1801 he commenced practice in Salem. He was a member of the state house of representatives (1805–1807), congressman (1808–1809), speaker of the state house of representatives (1811), and associate justice of the supreme court of the United States (1811–1845). He was Dane professor of law at Harvard (1829–1845) and was succeeded by his colleague, Simon Greenleaf (1783–1853); under the dual leadership of Story and Greenleaf the Harvard Law School rose to its preeminent position among the law schools of the United States. Story edited Joseph Chitty's *Practical Treatise on*

Bills of Exchange and Promissory Notes (1809), Charles Abbott's *Treatise on the Law Relative to Merchant Ships and Seamen* (1810), and Edward Lawes's *Practical Treatise on Pleading in Assumpsit* (1811). His *Commentaries,* written and published in rapid succession, distinguish him as one of America's foremost legal writers: *Bailments* (1832), *The Constitution* (3 vols., 1833), *The Conflict of Laws* (1834), *Equity Jurisprudence* (2 vols., 1836), *Equity Pleading* (1838), *Agency* (1839), *Partnership* (1841), *Bills of Exchange* (1843), and *Promissory Notes* (1845). He married first (on December 9th, 1804) Mary Lynde Oliver; after her death in June 1805 he married second (on August 27th, 1808) Sarah Waldo Wetmore, who bore him seven children. He died in Cambridge on September 10th, 1845, and was buried in Mount Auburn Cemetery.

STROTHER, JOHN (1782–1862), magistrate, son of Benjamin Strother (1750–1807) and Kittie Price, was born at Park Forest, his father's residence near Charlestown, Berkeley (now Jefferson) County, (West) Virginia, on November 18th, 1782. After serving in the War of 1812 he returned to Berkeley County, where he was for many years clerk of the county court. On September 1st, 1815, he married Elizabeth Pendleton Hunter. He died at Sir John's Run, Berkeley Springs, (West) Virginia, on January 16th, 1862. His son, David Hunter Strother (1816–1888), gained international fame as a writer-artist. A number of his travel pieces dealing with life North and South and illustrated with his own pen sketches were published under the pseudonym "Porte Crayon" in *Harper's New Monthly Magazine* in the 1850s. During the Civil War he was a topographical expert in the Union army, working chiefly in the Valley of Virginia. After the war he contributed to *Harper's* a series of illustrated articles entitled "Personal Recollections of the War, by a Virginian," based on his diary and his sketches made on the battlefield.

STUART, JAMES EWELL BROWN (1833–1864), Confederate soldier, seventh child of Archibald Stuart and Elizabeth Letcher Pannill, was born at Laurel Hill, his father's plantation in Patrick County, Virginia, on February 6th, 1833. After attending Emory and Henry College for two years (1848–1850) he entered the United States Military Academy in July 1850 and graduated four years later. On October 31st, 1854, he was commissioned second lieutenant in the Mounted Rifles, and in December 1854 he joined his command in Texas. Three months later, on March 3rd, 1855, he was transferred to the 1st United States Cavalry; for six years he was stationed principally in Kansas, where on November 14th, 1855, he married Flora Cocke, daughter of Colonel Philip St. George Cocke (1809–1861), and granddaughter of General John Hartwell Cocke (1780–1866), of Bremo, Fluvanna County, Virginia. In October 1859 Stuart served as Lee's aide at Harpers Ferry.

On May 3rd, 1861, he resigned his commission and joined the Confederate army, in which he rose rapidly from lieutenant colonel of Virginia infantry (May 10th, 1861) to captain of Confederate cavalry (May 24th, 1861) to brigadier general (September 21st, 1861) to major general (July 25th, 1862). He fought at First Manassas, Richmond, Second Manassas, Sharpsburg, Fredericksburg, and Gettysburg. His spectacular achievements, heightened by his dramatic personality, won him popularity and fame; his soldiers idolized him, and Lee esteemed him almost as a son. His private life was above reproach; although his camp was alive with music and dancing, he did not countenance drinking, swearing, and loose living. On May 11th, 1864, at Yellow Tavern, while defending the road to Richmond against Sheridan, he was mortally wounded by a dismounted Federal cavalryman. He died in Richmond the next day and was buried in Hollywood Cemetery. Hearing of Stuart's death, Lee said: "He never brought me a piece of false information." An equestrian statue of Stuart was erected in Richmond in 1907.

STUART, THOMAS MIDDLETON (1830–1873), physician, son of John Allan Stuart (1800–1852) and Claudia Smith (1802–1875), was born in South Carolina on June 15th, 1830. In January 1858 he commenced the practice of medicine in Walthourville, Liberty County, Georgia. On December 29th, 1858, he married Josephine Maria Cay (1839–1918), daughter of Raymond Cay (1805–1883) and Elizabeth Ann Stetson (1811–1896), of Walthourville; there were four children. In October 1859 he was the doctor consulted by the Rev. Dr. Charles Colcock Jones in the case of Negro infanticide on Maybank plantation. On April 13th, 1861, the day after the battle of Fort Sumter, Mrs. Mary S. Mallard reported that "Dr. Stuart left this morning to offer his services. If not accepted professionally he expects to enter the ranks." On July 19th, 1861, he was appointed assistant surgeon in the Confederate army, and on August 22nd, 1861, he was assigned to duty with the Army of the Potomac. For several months he did temporary duty with the 24th Regiment Virginia Volunteers at Camp Pickens, Manassas. He resigned on December 10th, 1861. A year later, on December 10th, 1862, he was appointed assistant surgeon of Major Robert Martin's Battalion, Confederate Reserve Artillery, with rank of captain. He was at Columbus (May 1863), Atlanta (August 1864), and Macon (October 1864 through February 1865); he was paroled at Thomasville, Georgia, on May 12th, 1865. Two days later he addressed E. M. McCook, brigadier general commanding: "Sir, I have the honor to apply to you for a horse—a good and sound one—and for the simple reason that I need one to return to my family and to enable me to support myself and family in the pursuit of my profession. If a horse can be spared from the many here or elsewhere, I trust my application will

not fall to the ground." Thomas Middleton Stuart died on September 27th, 1873. His widow subsequently became the wife of John A. Triay, of Jacksonville, Florida.

SULLIVAN, JAMES SWAN (1809–1874), physician, son of the Hon. William Sullivan (1774–1839) and Sarah Webb Swan (1782–1851), was born in Boston, Massachusetts, on February 18th, 1809. His grandfather, the Hon. James Sullivan (1744–1808), an eminent lawyer, was a member of the Continental Congress (1782) and governor of Massachusetts (1807–1808). James Swan Sullivan graduated from the Harvard Medical School in 1832 and commenced practice in his native city. In November 1839 he married Jane Valentine (1817–1899), daughter of Samuel Valentine (1773–1823) and his second wife, Mary Fisk (1783–1861), of Hopkinton, Massachusetts; there were seven children. After a brief residence in Cincinnati he removed to Darien, Georgia, in 1841 and practiced his profession there for ten years. In 1851 he settled in Savannah, where he resided for the rest of his life. His younger sister, Olivia Buckminster Sullivan (1819–1890), was the wife of the Hon. John Elliott Ward, of Savannah. James Swan Sullivan died in Savannah on February 22nd, 1874, and was buried in Bonaventure Cemetery. According to the Savannah *Morning News* (February 23rd, 1874), "His genial presence, which ever brought sunshine in the chamber of sickness, and his kindly voice, which fell so softly upon the ear of sufferers, will be missed by many whose confidence in him as a physician was almost equaled by their love of him as a man and friend." Jane (Valentine) Sullivan died in Savannah on June 27th, 1899, survived by two children, and was buried beside her husband.

SUMNER, CHARLES (1811–1874), statesman, son of Charles Pinckney Sumner and Relief Jacob, was born in Boston, Massachusetts, on January 6th, 1811. After attending the Boston Latin School (1821–1826) he graduated from Harvard College in 1830 and from the Harvard Law School in 1833. For some years he practiced law in Boston. In 1851 he entered the United States Senate, where his opposition to the Fugitive Slave Law and his insistence upon emancipation did much to bring slavery to an end. On May 19th–20th, 1856, in a brutally frank speech on the Kansas-Nebraska Act, he denounced those senators who had "raised themselves to eminence on this floor by the championship of human wrongs." Two days later, alone at his desk in the Senate, he was savagely assaulted by Representative Preston Smith Brooks (1819–1857), of South Carolina, who declared his speech "a libel on South Carolina and Mr. Butler, who is a friend of mine." The incident became a national sensation and throughout the North provoked an outburst of condemnation of Brooks and sympathy for Sumner. Three and a half years later Sumner was sufficiently recovered to resume his seat, determined to renew his assault on slavery "all along the line." No statesman contributed more than he to public approval of Lincoln's Emancipation Proclamation. His later years were troubled with personal illness, alienation of friends, and constant struggles over reconstruction. He died in Washington, D.C., on March 11th, 1874, and was buried in Mount Auburn Cemetery, Cambridge, Massachusetts.

SUMTER, THOMAS (1734–1832), Revolutionary soldier, son of William Sumter, was born in Hanover County, Virginia, on August 14th, 1734. In 1765 he settled on a plantation near Eutaw Springs, South Carolina, where he operated a general store, served as justice of the peace, and married (in 1767) Mary Cantey, widow of William Jameson. During the Revolutionary War he was lieutenant colonel of the 2nd (later the 6th) Continental Regiment; on September 19th, 1778, he resigned with the rank of colonel. When the British conquered South Carolina in 1780 he organized a vigorous resistance; on October 6th, 1780, he was commissioned brigadier general in command of South Carolina militia, and on January 13th, 1781, he received the thanks of Congress for his brilliant and courageous exploits. After the war he was congressman (1789–1793; 1797–1801) and United States senator (1801–1810). Retiring from public life, he lived at South Mount, his plantation near Stateburg, South Carolina, where he died on June 1st, 1832. He was buried in the family cemetery on his estate. Fort Sumter in Charleston harbor was named in his honor.

SUTTLE, CHARLES F. (1815–1881), planter and commission merchant, was born in Stafford County, Virginia, in 1815. For some years he planted in his native county, serving also from time to time as county sheriff and county representative in the state legislature. He was a near neighbor and intimate friend of William Brent (1818–1862), also a planter, to whom he hired Anthony Burns, a Negro slave, from 1846 to 1848. In 1850 Brent removed with his family to Richmond; there, acting as agent for Suttle, he hired out Burns to a third party in 1853 and 1854, remitting Burns's wages to Suttle, who had removed to Alexandria in August 1852. Burns escaped to Boston in the spring of 1854, and his subsequent extradition as a fugitive slave became an international *cause célèbre*. For twenty-seven years (1852–1879) Suttle resided in Alexandria, where he was a commission merchant, a member of the city council, a director of the Farmers' Bank of Virginia, and a director of the Orange, Alexandria & Manassas Railroad. On October 2nd, 1866, in Baltimore, Maryland, he married Emily Lucretia Taliaferro (1822–1903), daughter of Dr. Richard McCulloch Taliaferro (1789–1861) and Mary Hale (1795–1837), and widow of Ferdinand Leigh Claiborne (1817–1863). In March 1879 he removed to Rocky Mount, Franklin County, Virginia, where he was agent of the Virginia Midland Railroad. He died in Rocky Mount after a

lingering illness on February 9th, 1881, and was buried in the local cemetery. As the Alexandria *Gazette* (February 11th, 1881) observed, "Colonel Suttle's death was reported to have occurred on the 19th of last December; but after the publication of the notice, and a short biography of the deceased, the report was found to be incorrect. There is no doubt, however, of the death of the colonel this time, for official information has been received by the railroad authorities to that effect." Emily (Taliaferro) (Claiborne) Suttle died in Rocky Mount on March 9th, 1903, and was buried beside her husband.

TALIAFERRO, WARNER THROCKMORTON (1833–1881), Confederate soldier, son of Warner Throckmorton Taliaferro (1797–1877) and his second wife, Leah Seddon, was born at Belleville, the family residence in Gloucester County, Virginia, in 1833. His maternal uncle, the Hon. James A. Seddon (1815–1880), was Confederate States secretary of war (1862–1865). In early manhood Taliaferro married Martha Paul, daughter of Samuel W. Paul, of Norfolk, and settled at Isleham, a farm in Mathews County, Virginia, where he became a prominent and influential citizen and a member of the state legislature. In April 1861 he was commissioned major in the 40th Regiment Virginia Infantry. After the expiration of his commission on April 23rd, 1862, he served as volunteer aide-de-camp to his half-brother, General William Booth Taliaferro (1822–1898). On October 7th, 1862, he was appointed captain and assistant adjutant general on his half-brother's staff. In February 1863 he accompanied General Taliaferro to Savannah and shortly thereafter to Charleston, where he served on Morris Island and James Island until the autumn of 1863. On November 17th, 1863, he was assigned to the staff of General Raleigh E. Colston, also commanding a brigade at Charleston. In March 1865 he was aide-de-camp to General Daniel H. Hill. After the war he settled in Norfolk, Virginia, where he was associated with the Atlantic, Mississippi & Ohio Railroad for several years before engaging in the real estate business. He was active in local and state politics and represented Norfolk two terms in the state legislature (1876–1879). He died in Norfolk after a long illness on January 12th, 1881, survived by his second wife, Frances Hardy, daughter of William T. Hardy, of Norfolk.

TALIAFERRO, WILLIAM BOOTH (1822–1898), Confederate soldier, only child of Warner Throckmorton Taliaferro (1797–1877) and his first wife, Frances Booth, was born at Belleville, the family residence in Gloucester County, Virginia, on December 28th, 1822. After graduating from the College of William and Mary in 1841 he studied law at Harvard. During the Mexican War (1846–1848) he distinguished himself as captain in the 11th United States Infantry and was discharged with the rank of major. On February 17th, 1853, he married Sarah Nevison Lyons, of Richmond;

there were eight children. From 1850 to 1853 he represented Gloucester County in the state legislature, and in November 1859, following the capture of John Brown, he assumed command of the militia at Harpers Ferry. During the early months of the Civil War he served under Stonewall Jackson in the Valley of Virginia, first as colonel and after March 4th, 1862, as brigadier general. He was severely wounded at Groveton late in August 1862 but was sufficiently recovered to fight at Fredericksburg in December. He was ordered to Savannah in February 1863 and shortly thereafter to Charleston, where he successfully defended Battery Wagner, Morris Island, on July 18th, 1863, and later, commanding on James Island, frustrated for more than a year all Federal efforts to take Charleston. For several months in the spring of 1864 he commanded the military district of East Florida. On January 1st, 1865, he was commissioned major general. After the war he was a member of the state legislature (1874–1879), judge of the Gloucester County Court (1891–1897), and member of the board of visitors of the Virginia Military Institute and the College of William and Mary. He died at Dunham Massie, his residence in Gloucester County, on February 27th, 1898, and was buried in Ware Churchyard.

TANEY, ROGER BROOKE (1777–1864), jurist, son of Michael Taney and Monica Brooke, was born in Calvert County, Maryland, on March 17th, 1777. After graduating from Dickinson College in 1795 he studied law and commenced practice. On January 7th, 1806, he married Ann Arnold Phoebe Charlton Key (1783–1855), daughter of John Ross Key (1754–1821) and Ann Phoebe Penn Dagworthy Charlton (1756–1830), and younger sister of Francis Scott Key (1779–1843), author of "The Star-Spangled Banner." Six of their seven children survived infancy. In 1823 he settled in Baltimore, where he rose to eminence in his profession. By appointment of President Andrew Jackson he served as attorney general of the United States (1831–1833) and secretary of the treasury (1833–1835). On March 15th, 1836, he succeeded John Marshall as chief justice of the supreme court of the United States. His most famous decision was that rendered in the Dred Scott case (1857): that Congress had no power to exclude slavery from the territories. Taney's sympathies were conditioned by his upbringing in a Southern atmosphere; when the Southern states seceded he opposed coercion, and when hostilities commenced he disapproved of the prosecution of the war. He died in Washington on October 12th, 1864, much resented and much scorned; but posterity has taken a more understanding view of his conduct and motives.

TATTNALL, JOHN ROGER FENWICK (1828–1907), naval officer, only son of Commodore Josiah Tattnall (1795–1871) and Harriette Fenwick Jackson, was born in Middletown, Connecticut, in July 1828. After attend-

ing school in France for six years he entered the United States marine corps in 1847. At the outbreak of the Civil War he was lieutenant of marines, commanding a force on the west coast of Africa. Learning that his vessel had been ordered on service against the Confederacy, he threw his sword into the sea and declared that he would not fight against the South. He was thereupon arrested and put in irons; and after his vessel reached Boston he was confined at Fort Warren until February 1862, when through the influence of friends of his father he was exchanged and permitted to go South. On April 19th, 1862, he was appointed colonel of the 29th Regiment Alabama Infantry, then at Pensacola, Florida; after the evacuation of Pensacola he was placed in command of the department comprising Western Florida and Lower Alabama. On December 9th, 1862, he resigned to become captain in the Confederate marine corps, a position he held until the end of the war. At the siege of Savannah in December 1864 he commanded a battalion of marines. After the war he accompanied his parents to Halifax, Nova Scotia, where he engaged in the manufacture of tobacco. In 1869 he returned to Savannah and entered the cotton business; he was for many years secretary and treasurer of the Savannah Cotton Press Association. In 1894 he was appointed treasurer of the Chatham County Board of Education. He never married. He died in Middletown, Connecticut, birthplace of his mother, on August 17th, 1907, and was buried near his parents in Bonaventure Cemetery, Savannah.

TATTNALL, JOSIAH (1795–1871), naval officer, son of the Hon. Josiah Tattnall (1764–1803) and Harriette Fenwick, was born at Bonaventure, the family homestead three miles from Savannah, Georgia, on November 9th, 1795. His father, United States senator (1796–1799) and governor of Georgia (1801–1802), died in Nassau on June 6th, 1803, when his son was in his eighth year. After six years' schooling in London with his maternal grandfather he entered the United States navy as a midshipman on March 10th, 1812; he participated in the War of 1812 and the Algerian War of 1815 and was commissioned lieutenant on April 1st, 1818. He was stationed at the Brooklyn navy yard (1822–1839), the Boston navy yard (1839–1850), and the Pensacola navy yard (1850–1860). He became commander (February 1838) and captain (February 1850). . . . In June 1859, commanding the Toeywan off the coast of China, Tattnall became involved in a fight between the Chinese and the allied forces of Britain and France at the mouth of the Peiho River. Sir James Hope, British admiral commanding, sent Tattnall a message stating his desperate situation and requesting the use of the Toeywan to tow his vessels into action. According to a report published in the Savannah Republican (October 1st, 1859), "The admiral had been twice wounded, had two ships sunk under him, and had transferred his flag to the third, whence, reclining on deck, he issued his orders with the utmost coolness. Commodore Tattnall and Minister [John Elliott] Ward consulted together upon the propriety of rendering the required assistance, and finally concluded that an act of humanity should not be construed into a breach of neutrality. . . . In the thickest of the fight Commodore Tattnall, like a chivalrous Georgian, as he is, went in the open barge through the most exposed positions to pay a visit of sympathy to his wounded brother officer. . . ." On February 20th, 1861, while stationed at Sackett's Harbor, New York, Tattnall resigned his commission to assume command of the naval defenses of Georgia and South Carolina. According to the Savannah *Republican* (June 16th, 1871), "His gallant services in the defense of this city and the South Atlantic coast in the first year of the late war are fresh in the memory of our citizens. With a few small gunboats and steam tugs, too insignificant to be ranked as ships of war, he presented a bold and defiant front to the fleets of the enemy which hovered on our shores. His attempted defense of Port Royal against the formidable fleet of Admiral Du Pont, offering battle to the largest ships of the line in his little steam tug, was an act of heroism verging on temerity, and proved how dangerous he would have been to the enemy with adequate means at his command." In March 1862 he assumed command of the naval defenses of Virginia, with the ironclad *Virginia* (formerly the *Merrimac*) as his flagship. In May 1862, when Norfolk was evacuated, he burned the *Virginia* to prevent her capture; a court-martial convened in Richmond in July 1862 justified his action. Returning to Georgia, he commanded the naval defenses of Savannah until Sherman's occupation of the city in December 1864. He was paroled in May 1865. After the war he retired with his family to Halifax, Nova Scotia, where he resided until 1869, when he returned to Savannah. On September 6th, 1821, he married Harriette Fenwick Jackson, of Middletown, Connecticut. He died in Savannah on June 14th, 1871, and was buried in Bonaventure Cemetery near the place of his birth. Harriette Fenwick (Jackson) Tattnall died on January 15th, 1873, and was buried beside her husband. His only son, John Roger Fenwick Tattnall (1828–1907), was also a naval officer. "Commodore Tattnall's name will live in the grateful remembrance of us all," wrote Charles Colcock Jones, Jr., on January 29th, 1862. "A truer, nobler, braver man does not breathe." *The Life and Services of Commodore Josiah Tattnall,* by Charles Colcock Jones, Jr., was published in Savannah in 1878.

TAYLOR, ISAAC EBENEZER (1812–1889), physician, son of William Taylor, was born in Philadelphia, Pennsylvania, on April 25th, 1812. After graduating from Rutgers College in 1830 and from the Medical School of the University of Pennsylvania in 1834 he removed to New York City, where he engaged in business with his father-in-law, Stuart Mollan, for five years before commencing the practice of medicine in 1839. He was elected physician to Bellevue Hospital in 1851 and was instrumental in reorganizing the various departments under one administration. In 1860 he proposed the establishment of a medical college in association with the hospital, and when the new medical college was opened the following year he was appointed president, treasurer, and professor of obstetrics. In 1867 he became professor emeritus but continued as president. He was a permanent member of the American Medical Association, the New York Medical Society, the New York Academy of Medicine, and the American Gynecological Society. He contributed numerous articles on obstetrics and women's diseases to *The New York Journal of Medicine and Surgery, The American Journal of the Medical Sciences,* and *The New York Medical Times.* He was the first American physician to introduce uterine auscultation and to use the speculum in diseases of women and children. He died in New York City on October 30th, 1889.

TAYLOR, MARY JONES (1834–1919), elder daughter of John Madison Taylor (1807–1886) and Margaretta Jones (1809–1874), was born in Philadelphia, Pennsylvania, on September 27th, 1834. She spent her early years in Philadelphia, where with her younger sister, Sarah Ann Taylor (1837–1899), she attended a seminary for young ladies conducted by the Misses Gill. There she became the close friend of Mary Sharpe Jones (1835–1889), of Liberty County, Georgia, who resided in Philadelphia from 1850 to 1853 while her father, the Rev. Dr. Charles Colcock Jones, was corresponding secretary of the Board of Domestic Missions of the Presbyterian Church. In April 1857 she removed with her family to Winchester, her father's plantation near Berlin, Worcester County, Maryland, where she resided for the rest of her life. She never married. ("I assure you," she wrote on September 14th, 1858, "I am more devoted than ever to spinsterhood.") She died in Berlin of a cerebral hemorrhage on January 23rd, 1919, and was buried near her parents in Buckingham Cemetery. Mary Jones Taylor was no blood relation of her friend Mary Sharpe Jones, although she was amused by the coincidence of their names: "Did you ever hear of one who bore the illustrious cognomen of Mary Jones who was not a blessing to society at large?" Their correspondence ceased with the coming of the Civil War.

TAYLOR, SARAH ANN (1837–1899), younger daughter of John Madison Taylor (1807–1886) and Margaretta Jones (1809–1874), was born in Philadelphia, Pennsylvania, on April 29th, 1837. She spent her early years in Philadelphia, where with her elder sister, Mary Jones Taylor (1834–1919), she attended a seminary for young ladies conducted by the Misses Gill. Through Mary Sharpe Jones, a friend of her elder sister, she was introduced to Matilda Jane Harden (1837–1932), of Liberty County, Georgia, who became a girlhood friend and occasional correspondent. In

April 1857 she removed with her family to Winchester, her father's plantation near Berlin, Worcester County, Maryland. There, late in April 1861, "saucy Sarah Ann" became the wife of Dr. Francis Jenkins Purnell (1828–1896), of Worcester County; there were four children. Her husband, a practicing physician, had graduated from the Medical College of the University of Pennsylvania in 1850. He died in Berlin on May 20th, 1896, and was buried in Episcopal Cemetery. Sarah Ann (Taylor) Purnell died on August 6th, 1899, and was buried beside her husband.

TEBAULT, CHRISTOPHER HAMILTON (1838–1914), physician, son of Edward John Tebault and Caroline Hall, was born in Raymond, Mississippi, on November 12th, 1838. At the age of six he removed with his parents to New Orleans, where he was educated in private schools; after attending Georgetown University, District of Columbia, he graduated from the Medical Department of the University of Louisiana (later the Tulane University School of Medicine) in 1861. Early in the Civil War he became surgeon of the 21st Regiment Louisiana Infantry; when this regiment was later merged with other Louisiana regiments because of its depleted ranks, he became surgeon of the 10th Regiment South Carolina Infantry. From 1863 to the end of the war he served in hospitals of the Army of Tennessee—first at Calhoun, later at Griffin, Albany, and Macon, Georgia. After the war he settled in New Orleans, where he became one of the most distinguished practitioners in the city. He was professor of anatomy in the Medical Department of the University of Louisiana (1865–1867), surgeon general of the United Confederate Veterans (1896–1914), and for many years a member of the staff of Charity Hospital. On December 27th, 1866, he married Sallie Bradford Bailey (1843–1926), daughter of David Jackson Bailey (1812–1897) and Susan Grantland (1821–1897), of Griffin, Georgia; there were three children. His wife came of a family long prominent in law, politics, and finance. Her maternal grandfather, Seaton Grantland (1782–1864), was congressman from Georgia (1835–1839); her father was congressman from Georgia (1851–1855) and colonel of the 30th Regiment Georgia Infantry during the Civil War. Sallie Bradford (Bailey) Tebault was a gifted artist; in her youth she studied for two years at the Philadelphia Academy of Fine Arts, where she excelled in painting and sculpture; according to Mary W. Mount, "only her marriage prevented her becoming one of the greatest sculptors of America" [*Some Notables of New Orleans* (New Orleans, 1896), p. 180]. Christopher Hamilton Tebault died in New Orleans after a lingering illness on May 24th, 1914, and was buried in Metairie Cemetery in the tomb of the Army of Tennessee, Louisiana Division, beside his old friend General Beauregard. His wife died on March 10th, 1926, and was buried in Metairie Cemetery. Christopher H. Tebault, Jr., and Grantland L. Tebault survived.

TEFFT, ISRAEL KEECH (1794–1862), banker and collector, was born in Smithfield, Rhode Island, on February 12th, 1794. He was educated in Boston, Massachusetts. In 1816 he settled in Savannah, Georgia, where in 1821, with Henry James Finn, he became joint editor and proprietor of the Savannah *Georgian*. In 1848 he was elected cashier of the Bank of the State of Georgia, a post he filled with honor and trust until his death. In 1839, with the Rev. Stephen Elliott, later bishop of Georgia, he proposed a scheme for the organization of the Georgia Historical Society, and he subsequently became its first corresponding secretary; he was succeeded in the post by Charles Colcock Jones, Jr., who served from July 14th, 1862, to February 12th, 1866. He was also a member of the New England Historical Society (1859–1862). He died in Savannah on June 30th, 1862, survived by his wife, Penelope W. Tefft (1800–1873), and was buried in Laurel Grove Cemetery. His wife died on September 11th, 1873, and was buried beside her husband. Their three sons, all intelligent, well educated, and promising, died prematurely in early manhood. As early as 1816 Tefft commenced the great business of his life—the collection of autographs and manuscripts. At the time of his death his collection, comprising some thirty thousand items, was perhaps the most remarkable of its kind in existence. "I take it for granted that no collection in this country can well compare with that of my late excellent and much lamented friend," wrote William Gilmore Simms (1806–1870) on October 3rd, 1866. "With him it was indeed a passion—his pleasant study through the day, his dream of pleasure through the night. . . . Never was mortal more avid in the pursuit of gains of letters and manuscripts. His gentleness, tender consideration, mild and grateful manner, and general though unobtrusive intelligence made his way easy to the affections of others, most of whom were at pains accordingly to yield *him* pleasure by ministering to his ruling passion. Day and night would he be found poring over his collection with one or more friends, who sought to gratify mere curiosity or to obtain rare and valuable biographical and historical material." Tefft's collection was dispersed at public auction in New York in March 1867.

TENNENT, GILBERT (1806–1855), physician, second son of William Peter Tennent and Martha Middleton, was born in Charleston, South Carolina, on January 15th, 1806. His grandfather, the Rev. William Tennent (1740–1777), a graduate of the College of New Jersey (Princeton) in 1758, was pastor of the Independent Church, Charleston, from 1772 to 1777. His father, a Charleston lawyer, removed to Abbeville, South Carolina, in 1815 and died there in 1820. Gilbert Tennent received his medical degree from Transylvania University (Lexington, Kentucky) in 1829. After practicing medicine for some years in Edgefield District, South Carolina, he settled in the 1840s in Marietta, Cobb County, Georgia, where he was, according to Mary Eliza Robarts

(January 5th, 1855), "a good physician, in fine practice" and "an honorable and high-minded man" with "a good property (not wealthy)." His wife, Caroline Graves (1809–1851), died in Marietta on May 2nd, 1851, leaving eight children, the eldest seventeen, the youngest not yet three. Early in 1855 he was engaged to be married to Louisa Jane Robarts (1813–1897), daughter of David Robarts and Eliza Greene (Low) (Walker) Robarts, of Marietta; but two months before the wedding, on February 16th, 1855, he died suddenly of "inflammation of the stomach" and was buried beside his wife in Citizens Cemetery. His two eldest daughters, Mary Tennent (1835–1896) and Cornelia Tennent (1839–1893), managed the household and supervised the younger children; his eldest son, Gilbert R. Tennent (1834–1917), a graduate of the Medical Department of the University of Nashville in 1855, practiced medicine in Marietta for many years and provided support for the family. William A. Tennent (1837–1862), another son, private in Company C, Rifle Battalion, Phillips' Legion Georgia Volunteers, was killed in the battle of Fredericksburg on December 13th, 1862.

TERRELL, WILLIAM (1778–1855), physician and statesman, was born in Fairfax County, Virginia, in 1778. After attending the Medical College of the University of Pennsylvania he settled in Sparta, Georgia, where he practiced his profession for many years, accumulated a fortune, and exerted wide influence throughout the state. He was a member of the state legislature (1810–1813) and a member of Congress (1817–1821). Among other benefactions he donated twenty thousand dollars to establish a chair of agriculture at the University of Georgia. He died in Sparta on July 4th, 1855, and was buried in Sparta Cemetery. In the year of his death his only daughter, Lucy Terrell (1833–1910), became the wife of Edgar Gilmer Dawson (1830–1883), of Columbus, Georgia, son of the Hon. William Crosby Dawson (1798–1856) and his first wife, Henrietta Wingfield (1800–1850). William Crosby Dawson, a resident of Greensboro, Georgia, was a distinguished lawyer and judge, a member of Congress (1836–1841) and United States senator (1849–1855). Edgar Gilmer Dawson, a graduate of Franklin College (Athens) in 1849, had settled in Columbus and commenced the practice of law; after his marriage he gave up law and planted extensively in Southwest Georgia. At the outbreak of the Civil War he organized and equipped a battery of artillery which he named the Terrell Light Artillery in honor of William Terrell, his father-in-law, and which he commanded with distinguished gallantry throughout the war. In 1867 he removed to Baltimore, Maryland, where he resided for the rest of his life, supervising his financial interests without engaging actively in business. He died in Baltimore on April 24th, 1883, survived by his wife and four children, and was buried in Greenmount Cemetery. Lucy (Terrell) Dawson died on March 29th, 1910, and was buried beside her husband. On February

16th, 1856, by legislative act, Terrell County, Georgia, was created from Lee and Randolph Counties; the new county was named for the Hon. Dr. William Terrell; the new county seat, Dawson, was named for the Hon. William Crosby Dawson.

THACKERAY, WILLIAM MAKEPEACE (1811–1863), English novelist, only son of Richmond Thackeray and Anne Becher, was born in Calcutta, India, on July 18th, 1811. His father, a civil servant, died in 1816, and his mother later married Henry Carmichael Smyth. Young Thackeray was educated in England; he attended Charterhouse (1822–1828) and Trinity College, Cambridge (1829–1830). He later studied art in Paris, developing his marked talent for caricature. In 1836 he married Isabella Shawe, daughter of Matthew Shawe; there were three daughters. His marriage was clouded by the mental illness of his wife, who survived until 1892. In 1837 he settled in London and pursued a literary career; during the next decade he contributed numerous sketches and stories to *Fraser's Magazine* and *Punch*. His first major work, *Vanity Fair*, was published serially in twenty-four monthly installments in 1847–1848; other novels followed: *Pendennis* (1850), *Henry Esmond* (1852), *The Newcomes* (1855), and *The Virginians* (1859). In 1851 he wrote *The English Humourists of the Eighteenth Century*, a series of lectures, delivered in England in 1851, delivered in the United States in 1852, and published in 1853. In 1855 he wrote *The Four Georges*, another series of lectures, delivered in England in 1855, delivered in the United States in 1856, and published in 1860. Thackeray was editor of *The Cornhill Magazine* for three years (1859–1862). He died in London on December 24th, 1863, and was buried in Kensal Green. A bust was erected to his memory in Westminster Abbey. Thackeray visited Savannah, Georgia, in 1853 and again in 1856; on both visits he stayed at the residence of Andrew Low (1813–1886) in Lafayette Square. In February 1856 he delivered *The Four Georges* in St. Andrew's Hall: George I (Wednesday, February 13th); George II (Thursday, February 14th); George III (Saturday, February 16th); George IV (Monday, February 18th).

THOMAS, EDWARD JONATHAN (1840–1929), civil engineer, eldest son of John Abbott Thomas (1816–1859) and Malvina Huguenin (1816–1890), was born in Savannah, Georgia, on March 25th, 1840. In early childhood he removed with his parents to Peru, the family homestead on the South Newport River in McIntosh County, where his father planted until his death on November 6th, 1859. His mother then removed with the younger children to Walthourville, where they could enjoy the privilege of a school. After graduating from Franklin College (Athens) in 1860 Edward Jonathan Thomas supervised his mother's planting interests until the outbreak of the Civil War. On October 1st, 1861, he enlisted as a private in the Liberty Independent Troop

(Company G, 5th Regiment Georgia Cavalry); he later became quartermaster sergeant and served as such till the end of the war. On April 2nd, 1862, he married Alice Gertrude Walthour (1843–1927), daughter of George Washington Walthour (1799–1859) and Mary Amelia Ann Russell (1806–1890); there were seven children. After the war he settled in Savannah, where he was general agent of the Coastline Railroad until April 30th, 1879; on May 1st, 1879, he became superintendent of the Savannah, Skidaway & Seaboard Railroad. For many years he was surveyor of Chatham County and engineer of the Savannah streetcar system. He was an active Confederate veteran. Alice Gertrude (Walthour) Thomas died in Savannah on December 2nd, 1927, survived by four children, and was buried in Bonaventure Cemetery. Edward Jonathan Thomas died on August 8th, 1929, and was buried beside his wife. At the time of his death he was the oldest living alumnus of the University of Georgia.

THOMAS, JOHN ABBOTT (1816–1859), planter, son of Jonathan Thomas and Mary Jane Baker, was born at Peru, the family homestead on the South Newport River in McIntosh County, Georgia, in January 1816. In early manhood he settled in Savannah, where in 1839 he married Malvina Huguenin (1816–1890), a native of Charleston, South Carolina, daughter of John Huguenin and Eliza Vallard. Shortly thereafter he returned with his family to McIntosh County, where he was for some years a planter. He died in Walthourville on November 6th, 1859, leaving a wife and seven children, and was buried in the family cemetery on the South Newport River. "Another awful warning of the use of spirituous liquors!" observed the Rev. Dr. Charles Colcock Jones in his journal (November 6th, 1859). "A man of many excellent traits of character. . . . What a melancholy end!" After her husband's death Malvina (Huguenin) Thomas removed with her children to Walthourville, where they could enjoy the privilege of a school. Later she returned to Savannah, where she died on July 5th, 1890, and was buried in Bonaventure Cemetery. Her husband's remains were subsequently removed from McIntosh County and reburied by her side.

THOMPSON, WILLIAM TAPPAN (1812–1882), editor, was born in Ravenna, Ohio, on August 31st, 1812. His mother died in 1823, and he removed with his father to Philadelphia, Pennsylvania, where his father soon died, leaving the orphaned boy on his own resources. Entering the office of the Philadelphia *Chronicle*, he commenced the journalistic career that was to continue for half a century. In 1835 he removed to Augusta, Georgia, where he was associated with Augustus Baldwin Longstreet in publishing the *States Rights Sentinel*. On June 12th, 1837, he married Caroline Love Carrié (1818–1886), daughter of Joseph Carrié, of Augusta. In 1838 he established the Augusta *Mirror*, which merged with the Macon *Family Companion* in 1842 to become the *Family Companion and Ladies' Mirror*. There he

printed the first of the famous letters of "Major Jones," a small collection of which was published locally as *Major Jones's Courtship* (1843), subsequently republished in a greatly enlarged edition (1844), and continued in *Chronicles of Pineville* (1845) and *Major Jones's Sketches of Travel* (1847). These volumes brought Thompson national reputation as a humorist. For two years (1843–1845) he published the *Miscellany*, a weekly, in Madison, Georgia; for five years (1845–1850), in association with Park Benjamin, the poet, he published the *Western Continent*, a weekly, in Baltimore, Maryland. In 1850 he settled in Savannah, Georgia, where, in association with John McKinney Cooper, he founded the Savannah *Morning News*, of which he continued as editor for thirty-two years. "Thompson deserves a leather medal for his discernment," wrote the Rev. Dr. Charles Colcock Jones (December 30th, 1858). "I am much disgusted with his ridiculous remarks and excerpts on the slave trade." Charles Colcock Jones, Jr., agreed (January 3rd, 1859): "Thompson is a drunken fool, and that is all I have to say either for him or his paper." William Tappan Thompson died in Savannah after a lingering illness on March 24th, 1882, and was buried in Laurel Grove Cemetery. According to the Savannah *Morning News* (March 25th, 1882), "He achieved a reputation as journalist and author which is not confined to the limits of Georgia but extends throughout the length and breadth of the land. . . . During a period of nearly half a century of well-nigh constant devotion to his chosen profession, he not only acquired an enviable reputation as a thoughtful and prudent yet fearless writer, but—what is infinitely more to be desired—he was universally recognized as a man thoroughly honest and sincere, and of the most stainless integrity." Caroline Love (Carrié) Thompson died on May 25th, 1886, and was buried beside her husband.

THOMSON, CHARLES (1809–1878), steamboat captain, was born in Hanover, Germany, in 1809. In early manhood he settled in Savannah, Georgia, where he resided for the rest of his life. For some years prior to the Civil War he was captain of the *William Totten*, a schooner plying between Savannah and Riceboro in Liberty County; he often docked his vessel at Montevideo, plantation of the Rev. Dr. Charles Colcock Jones on the North Newport River, to deposit or take on cargo. As the Savannah *National Republican* (December 6th, 1865) observed, "Captain Charlie" is "one of the oldest coasters in the trade, and we can recommend him to all concerned." He never married. He died in Savannah on February 4th, 1878, and was buried in Laurel Grove Cemetery.

THOMSON, JANE REBECCA (HART) (1827–1867): *Mrs. John Hrabowski Thomson*, daughter of Benjamin Hart (1766–1853) and his fourth wife, Harriet (Bell) Heron, was born in St. Matthews, South Carolina, on July 14th, 1827. By 1850 she had become the wife of Dr. John Hrabowski Thomson (1827–1904), son of Charles Robert Thomson (1794–1855) and Eleanor Sabb Hrabowski (1800–1885). Her husband, a native of St. Matthews Parish and a graduate of the Medical College of the University of Pennsylvania (1846), was a physician practicing in Columbia. Five of their eight children survived infancy. By 1858 they had removed to Fort George, Duval County, Florida, near the mouth of the St. Johns River; in 1860 they were living in Ellaville, Suwannee County, Florida, on the Suwannee River. At the outbreak of the Civil War Thomson enlisted as a private in Company C, 8th Regiment Florida Infantry; on August 26th, 1863, he was appointed surgeon, to take rank June 8th, 1863; during the succeeding months he served in various hospitals in Florida and South Carolina. He was paroled at Tallahassee, Florida, on May 15th, 1865. After the war he resumed practice in Ellaville, where Jane Rebecca (Hart) Thomson died on December 5th, 1867, leaving five young children. She was buried in a country cemetery near Ellaville. By 1870 her husband was practicing medicine in Quincy, Gadsden County, Florida, where he subsequently married Alice Willard, a widow, who bore him one daughter. His later years were spent in Live Oak and Quincy. He died in Gadsden County on January 7th, 1904, and was buried in the Nicholson family cemetery.

THOMSON, WILLIAM GOULDING (1822–1864), planter and Confederate soldier, son of William Thomson and Susan Jane Goulding, was born in Liberty County, Georgia, on April 6th, 1822. He attended Franklin College (Athens) with the class of 1840 but did not graduate. Prior to the Civil War he planted extensively and successfully in his native county, residing with his widowed mother in Dorchester. On March 30th, 1854, he married Mary E. King (1824–1861), daughter of William John King (1790–1861) and Martha Cooper (1795–1860), of Harris Neck, McIntosh County, Georgia. His wife died in Dorchester after a brief but severe illness on July 24th, 1861; his mother died in the same house six days later, on July 30th, 1861. On May 15th, 1862, he was elected captain of the Liberty Mounted Rangers (Company B, 20th Battalion Georgia Cavalry); on February 12th, 1864, he was promoted to major. In the summer of 1862 the Liberty Mounted Rangers were sent on picket duty to James Island, near Charleston, South Carolina; in 1863 they were ordered back to the Georgia coast; in the spring of 1864 they were transferred to Virginia, where they participated in numerous bloody battles. William Goulding Thomson was severely wounded in the right forearm in the battle of Haw's Shop, near Richmond, on May 28th, 1864. After several days in a Richmond hospital he set out for Georgia, but he became ill en route and was taken from the train at Goldsboro, North Carolina, where he died on June 23rd, 1864 (not, as his tombstone indicates, on June 18th, 1864). He was buried

beside his wife in Midway Cemetery. His only son, Edward Delegal Thomson (1855–1882), was buried near his parents. According to Henry Hart Jones, "Major Thomson was a magnificent specimen, physically, of a soldier, while possessing all of a woman's gentleness." Mary W. Thomson (1820–1896), sister of William Goulding Thomson, was the wife of Dr. Edward J. Delegal (1815–1892).

THORNWELL, JAMES HENLEY (1812–1862), Presbyterian clergyman and educator, son of James Thornwell and Martha Terrell, was born in Marlborough District, South Carolina, on December 9th, 1812. After graduating from the South Carolina College with first honor in 1831 he taught school for two years in Cheraw, South Carolina; in 1834 he studied briefly at Andover Theological Seminary and the Harvard Divinity School. "He is a man of fine talents, and a Christian," wrote the Rev. Dr. Charles Colcock Jones from Columbia on November 3rd, 1838; "and if nothing untoward happens to prevent, he must rise to eminence." After serving as pastor of rural churches for two years (1835–1837) he was professor of logic and belles lettres at the South Carolina College (1837–1840); pastor of the First Presbyterian Church, Columbia (1840–1841); professor of sacred literature and evidences of Christianity at the South Carolina College (1841–1851); pastor of the Glebe Street Presbyterian Church, Charleston (1851); president of the South Carolina College (1851–1855); and professor of didactic and polemic theology at Columbia Theological Seminary (1855–1862). On December 3rd, 1835, he married Nancy White Witherspoon. He was moderator of the General Assembly of the Presbyterian Church meeting in Richmond, Virginia, in 1847—said to be the youngest man ever to hold that office. He received the honorary degree of doctor of laws from Oglethorpe University in 1855. At the outbreak of the Civil War he was conspicuous in the organization of the Southern Presbyterian Church; he was leader of the Atlanta Convention (August 1861) and an influential participant in the first General Assembly in Augusta (December 1861). His "Address to All the Churches of Jesus Christ Throughout the Earth" summarizes brilliantly the viewpoint of the separating Presbyterians. "Our Danger and Our Duty," an address delivered before Confederate soldiers and afterwards published in the spring of 1862, foretold the terrors of Southern life in the event of a Northern victory. Illness and overwork hastened his end; he died in Charlotte, North Carolina, on August 1st, 1862, and was buried in Elmwood Cemetery, Columbia. The *Southern Confederacy* announced his death on August 7th, 1862: "Such an event is a public calamity. One of the greatest intellectual lights of the South has been extinguished. It is the genius and moral power of such men as Thornwell that constitute the strength and glory of a nation; hence his death involves a loss to the entire Confederacy." His eldest son,

Gillespie Robbins Thornwell (1844–1863), a private in the Hampton Legion, died in Alexandria, Virginia, on May 4th, 1863, of wounds received the previous day near Warrenton. *The Collected Writings of James Henley Thornwell*, edited by John Bailey Adger and John Lafayette Girardeau, were published in four volumes in 1871–1873.

TILSON, DAVIS (1830–1896), Union soldier, son of William F. Tilson (1803–1851) and his first wife, Jane Davis, was born in Rockland, Maine, on April 17th, 1830. After attending the United States Military Academy for two years he resigned when an accident necessitated the amputation of one of his legs. Returning to Maine, he was a member of the state legislature (1857) and adjutant general of the state (1858). At the outbreak of the Civil War he was appointed captain of the 2nd Maine Battery and assigned to the Army of the Rappahannock under Mc-Dowell. After the battle of Cedar Mountain (August 9th, 1862) he became chief of artillery on McDowell's staff and fought at Rappahannock Station and Second Manassas. On March 29th, 1863, he was commissioned brigadier general and made chief of artillery in the Department of the Ohio; he was subsequently placed in command of the military district of East Tennessee; early in 1865 he was transferred to the Department of the Cumberland. After the war he was assistant commissioner in charge of the Freedmen's Bureau (the Federal Bureau of Refugees, Freedmen, and Abandoned Lands) in Georgia from September 1865 to January 1867. His administration was generally felt to be enlightened, harmonious, and progressive. Returning to Maine, he bought Hurricane Island, twelve miles from Rockland, and developed its granite interests; he later cultivated oranges on an extensive scale at De Land, Florida. He died in Rockland on April 30th, 1896, leaving an estate of half a million dollars.

TISON, WILLIAM HAYES (1812–1877), commission merchant, was born at Cole Ridge, Glynn County, Georgia, on August 6th, 1812. After attending an academy in Springfield, Effingham County, he became a clerk in a mercantile house in Macon. He then conducted his own business successively in Wayne County, Georgia; Columbus, Georgia; White Springs, Florida; Alligator (now Lake City), Florida; Ocala, Florida; and Clinch County, Georgia. In 1851, entrusting each business to the care of a resident partner, he established himself in Savannah, a convenient center from which to direct them all. On August 4th, 1853, he married Mary Scotia Fenton (1834–1876), daughter of James Fenton, of Columbia, South Carolina. In the same year Elias Reed, president of the Marine Bank, a rich and experienced cotton and rice factor, took Tison into partnership in the firm of Reed & Tison. After Reed's death a few months later Tison conducted the business alone until the autumn of 1854, when he joined William Mein Mackay in the firm of Tison & Mackay. When Mackay withdrew in 1856 Tison joined William Washington Gordon in the firm of Tison & Gordon, which continued for twenty-one years as one of the best-known cotton firms in the South. As Charles Colcock Jones, Jr., wrote his mother on November 20th, 1866, "Tison & Gordon are excellent factors and very responsible men." In 1864, at the age of fifty-two, Tison answered the governor's call for the state militia to join Johnston's army before Atlanta; he endured all the dangers and fatigues of the campaign, first as a private, later as an ordnance officer. After the war he resumed his business in Savannah. He was a director of the Merchants' National Bank from its organization in 1866. He was several times city alderman. His wife died on November 29th, 1876, and was buried in Laurel Grove Cemetery. Tison died in Savannah on November 24th, 1877, and was buried beside his wife. As the Savannah *Morning News* (November 26th, 1877) observed, "Mr. Tison's record furnishes a bright example of what can be accomplished by intelligence, probity, industry, and economy. Without money or influential friends he passed from poverty to wealth solely by his own efforts."

TODD, EMILIE (1836–1930), fourth child of Robert Smith Todd (1791–1849) and his second wife, Elizabeth Humphreys, was born in Lexington, Kentucky, on November 11th, 1836. She was a half-sister of Mary Todd (1818–1882), wife of Abraham Lincoln. On March 26th, 1856, in Frankfort, Kentucky, she became the wife of Ben Hardin Helm (1831–1863), eldest son of John Larue Helm (1802–1867) and Lucinda Barbour Hardin (1809–1885); there were three children: Katherine Helm (1857–1937); Elodie Helm (1859–1953), wife of Walter H. Lewis; and Ben Hardin Helm (1862–1946). Her husband, a graduate of the law school of the University of Louisville (1853), had attended the United States Military Academy and Dane Law School, Harvard University, and was then representative of Hardin County, Kentucky, in the state legislature. In 1858 he removed to Louisville, where he practiced his profession until the outbreak of the Civil War. Early in 1861 he entered Confederate service; in April 1862 he was made brigadier general; and on September 20th, 1863, he was mortally wounded at Chickamauga. He was buried with military honors in Oakland Cemetery, Atlanta; Emilie (Todd) Helm was visiting her sister, Mrs. N. H. R. Dawson, in Selma, Alabama, when she received the news of his death; she reached Atlanta just in time for the funeral rites. Later, by means of a pass from President Lincoln, she returned with her three young children to her mother's home in Lexington, Kentucky. In September 1884 the remains of Ben Hardin Helm were removed to Kentucky and buried in the family cemetery at Helm Station, Elizabethtown. Emilie (Todd) Helm survived her husband sixty-six years; she died near Lexington on

February 20th, 1930, and was buried in the Todd family lot in Lexington Cemetery.

TOOMBS, ROBERT (1810–1885), statesman, son of Robert Toombs and Catherine Huling, was born in Wilkes County, Georgia, on July 2nd, 1810. He attended Franklin College (Athens), from which he was expelled on January 2nd, 1828, and graduated from Union College (Schenectady, New York) in 1828. After studying law for one year at the University of Virginia he commenced practice in Washington, Wilkes County, Georgia, in 1830. On November 18th, 1830, he married Julia Ann DuBose (1813–1883), of Washington, Wilkes County. He was a member of the state legislature (1837–1840; 1841–1844), a member of Congress (1845–1853), and United States senator (1853–1861). At the inauguration of the Confederate States government he was made secretary of state, but in July 1861 he resigned, entered the Confederate army, and was commissioned brigadier general. He was severely wounded at Sharpsburg (September 17th, 1862), and in March 1863 he resigned from the army. In 1864 he served as inspector general of the 1st Division Georgia Militia, attached to the Army of Tennessee. After the war he was one of five men marked by Secretary of War Edwin M. Stanton for seizure and punishment (Jefferson Davis, Alexander H. Stephens, Howell Cobb, John Slidell, and Robert Toombs); but he escaped arrest, fled the country, and reached Paris in July 1865. In January 1867 he returned to Canada and thence traveled south to Georgia. For some years he practiced law in Washington, Wilkes County, in partnership with Dudley McIvor DuBose (1834–1883), who had married his daughter, Sarah Ann (Sallie) Toombs (1835–1866), on April 15th, 1858. Julia Ann (DuBose) Toombs died in Washington, Wilkes County, on September 4th, 1883, and was buried in Rest Haven Cemetery. Robert Toombs died on December 15th, 1885, and was buried beside his wife.

TRASK, WILLIAM BATES (1811–1880), merchant, fifth child of Jesse Trask (1784–1849) and Eunice Bates (1780–1845), was born in Deerfield, Massachusetts, on August 25th, 1811. In early manhood he removed to Richburg, Chester County, South Carolina, and thence after several years to Tattnall County, Georgia, where on January 4th, 1842, he married Jane Margaret Todd (1810–1898). After planting for some years in Tattnall County he removed in the 1850s to Riceboro, Liberty County, where he was associated with Frederick Ransom Lyons (1823–1897), also a native of Massachusetts, in operating a general store (Lyons & Trask). He was postmaster of Riceboro for many years. He died in Riceboro on February 22nd, 1880, and was buried in Flemington Cemetery. Jane Margaret (Todd) Trask died in Dorchester on September 6th, 1898, and was buried beside her husband.

TREZEVANT, DANIEL HEYWARD (1796–1873), physician, son of Peter Trezevant (1768–1854) and Elizabeth Willoughby Farquhar (1772–1848), was born in Charleston, South Carolina, on March 18th, 1796. He graduated from the South Carolina College in 1813 and from the College of Physicians and Surgeons (New York) in 1818. After practicing for several years in Minervaville, South Carolina, he removed in 1821 to Columbia, where he practiced successfully for more than fifty years. According to his kinsman, John Timothée Trezevant, he was "one of the most magnificent specimens imaginable of a dignified, accomplished physician. He was the friend and intimate of all the leading families in Columbia, in which city no man stood higher." He married first (on May 3rd, 1820) Ann Sewell (1795–1838); there were eight children. After her death on August 20th, 1838, he married second (on November 15th, 1841) Epps Goodwyn Howell (1819–1862); there were six children. One of his sons, Daniel Heyward Trezevant (1829–1847), fought with distinction in the Mexican War and was killed at Chapultepec on September 13th, 1847. Two of his sons were killed in the Civil War: Jesse Howell Trezevant (1842–1862), private in Company D, Cavalry Battalion, Hampton Legion, was killed at Gaines's Mill on June 27th, 1862; Willoughby Farquhar Trezevant (1846–1862), a member of the cadet corps of the South Carolina College, was mortally wounded at Sharpsburg and died at Shepherdstown, (West) Virginia, on September 24th, 1862. Four other sons fought throughout the war: James Davis Trezevant (1822–1892), captain of Company E, Cavalry from Fort Motte; George Sewell Trezevant (1834–1884), assistant surgeon, Confederate army; Peter John Trezevant (1844–1909), private in Company H, 2nd Regiment South Carolina Cavalry; and William Howell Trezevant (1847–1902), private in Company C, 4th Regiment South Carolina Cavalry. When Columbia was burned by the Federals in February 1865 the Trezevant house was destroyed. Epps Goodwyn (Howell) Trezevant died on May 2nd, 1862. Daniel Heyward Trezevant died in Columbia on March 17th, 1873, and was buried near his two wives in Trinity Episcopal Churchyard. According to the Columbia *South Carolinian* (March 18th, 1873), "he was a patriotic and high-spirited South Carolinian—refined in his tastes, manly in his sentiments, and in his nature bold, earnest, independent, and self-reliant."

TRIMBLE, WILLIAM W. (1810–1884), Presbyterian clergyman, son of James B. Trimble and Margaret Wilson, was born in Augusta County, Virginia, on December 26th, 1810. After graduating from Washington College (Lexington, Virginia) in 1840 and from Princeton Theological Seminary in 1843 he was pastor of Old Oxford Church, Rockbridge County, Virginia (1843–1848); principal of an academy in Rockbridge County (1848–1853); pastor of Timber Ridge and Bethesda Churches, Rockbridge County (1853–1860; 1863–1866); and principal of a female seminary in Rockbridge County (1860–1863). From 1866 to 1879 he served churches in Missouri. He married first (on August 15th, 1843) Jane Minor McDowell, of Romney, (West) Virginia; he married second (on August 3rd, 1852) Elizabeth Ann Gilkeson, of Augusta County, Virginia. His second wife died on August 1st, 1882. William W. Trimble died in Concord, Missouri, on July 6th, 1884.

TRUMBULL, JOHN (1756–1843), painter and author, youngest child of the Hon. Jonathan Trumbull (1710–1785), governor of Connecticut (1769–1784), and Faith Robinson, was born in Lebanon, Connecticut, on June 6th, 1756. He graduated from Harvard College in 1773. During the Revolutionary War he served as adjutant to General Joseph Spencer of the 1st Connecticut Regiment; as aide-de-camp to General Washington; as deputy adjutant general, with rank of colonel, to General Horatio Gates; and as volunteer aide-de-camp to General John Sullivan. In May 1780 he sailed for London, where he studied art with Benjamin West. Prompted by West, he commenced his famous series of historical paintings, among them "Washington Resigning His Commission," "The Surrender of Cornwallis," "The Surrender of Burgoyne," and "The Declaration of Independence"—all four subsequently repainted in large replica and hung in the rotunda of the capitol in Washington. On October 1st, 1800, he married Sarah (Hope) Harvey, a beautiful Englishwoman said to be his social inferior. He was secretary to John Jay in London (1794–1804); after four years in the United States he returned to London in 1808 and undertook portrait painting without success. In 1815 he settled in New York City, where he maintained a studio (1815–1837) and served as president of the American Academy of Fine Arts (1817–1836). In 1831, at the suggestion of Professor Benjamin Silliman, his nephew by marriage, Trumbull presented much of his best work to Yale College in exchange for an annuity of a thousand dollars. The Trumbull Gallery, designed by the artist, was opened in October 1832—the first art museum in America to be associated with an educational institution. Trumbull died in New York City on November 10th, 1843, and was buried, according to his instructions, beside his wife beneath the Trumbull Gallery. In 1866 the bodies were removed, together with the pictures, to a larger building; in 1928 they were placed in the Yale Gallery of Fine Arts.

TUCKER, JOHN FREDERICK (1812–1885), planter, son of Henry Tucker, was born in Savannah, Georgia, in 1812. His father died when the boy was very young; in March 1817 his mother, Winifred Tucker, became the wife of William Pearson Clark (1793–1872), for many years proprietor of the Pavilion Hotel in Savannah. In December 1831 he married Julia Holcombe, daughter of John G. Holcombe, of Savannah. He was active in politics and finance; he served several terms as alderman of Savannah, and he was a director of the Mechanics' Savings Bank and the Republican Blues Building & Loan Association. For many years he planted extensively at Southfield, his plantation on Ogeechee Neck some ten miles south of Savannah; in the Federal Census of 1860 he was recorded as the owner of 220 slaves. He was an open proponent of the slave trade; he was one of the owners of the *Wanderer*, a slave ship seized in November 1858 in its attempt to bring African slaves into Savannah; and in April 1859 he was charged with "holding and aiding and abetting the holding of African slaves." According to the Savannah *Morning News* (May 29th, 1860), "The prosecution, finding that under the ruling of the court it would be impossible to sustain the indictment, entered a nolle prosequi." In 1879 Tucker retired from business and removed to Baltimore, Maryland, where he died of pneumonia at the residence of his daughter, Mrs. T. B. Eareckson, on February 24th, 1885. He was buried in Loudon Park Cemetery. His second wife, Adeline M. Moore, died in Baltimore on June 5th, 1924, and was buried beside her husband. Among the Jones papers preserved at Tulane University is the following note written by Henry Hart Jones on February 5th, 1857: "Mr. Tucker has acted *most infamously* in reference to the poor Negroes he bought. Alfred tells me they were all brought to town on Saturday night and locked up, and the next day (Sabbath) shipped by the cars for parts unknown in the hands of a *western trader*. Mr. Wright could not or would not tell me *what* was their destination. Do you envy Mrs. Jones her feelings?"

TUMLIN, LEWIS (1809–1875), planter, son of William Tumlin (1775–1856), was born in Gwinnett County, Georgia, on May 9th, 1809. In early manhood he went as a cattle-driver to Cass (now Bartow) County in Northwest Georgia, where he soon became a prosperous landowner and a large slaveholder and an active leader in politics. He was county sheriff (1834–1840) and state senator (1842–1843; 1851–1852). He married first (in 1835) Jane Scott (1815–1849); there were four children. He married second (on May 25th, 1852) Lucie Elizabeth Goldsmith (1832–1859); there were three children. He married third (on December 24th, 1865) Mrs. Mary L. Lee; there was one child. At his plantation on the Etowah River near Cartersville he dispensed hospitality with a lavish hand. On August 23rd, 1860, Charles Colcock Jones, Jr., spent the day there, searching for Indian relics; three days later he reported that "we were entertained most generously and hospitably. The valley of the Mississippi or that of the Ohio contains not more remarkable or stupendous monuments than those there found. I will always recur with pleasure and profit to the day there spent." On July 4th, 1864, Lewis Tumlin enlisted for six months as a private in Captain James W. Watt's Company, Georgia Mounted Infantry (also designated Company C, 10th Battalion Cavalry, Georgia State Guards), a company organized for local defense. After the war he superintended his large plantations in Northwest and Southwest Georgia. He died at his residence in Bartow (formerly Cass) County on June 2nd, 1875, and was buried in the Tumlin family cemetery on the Cassville road. He was later reburied in Cartersville Cemetery.

TUNNO, MATHEWS ROBERT (1835–1916), banker and cotton broker, youngest son of Dr. John Champneys Tunno and Elizabeth Mellichamp Miles, was born in Charleston, South Carolina, on March 23rd, 1835. He graduated from the Western Military Institute. At the outbreak of the Civil War he enlisted as a private in the Charleston Light Dragoons. In the summer of 1861 he joined the Army of the West and served as post ordnance officer at Columbus, Kentucky, until the evacuation of Columbus in September 1861. He later became aide-de-camp, with rank of captain, on the staff of General Leonidas Polk. From August 1863 to August 1864 he was detailed to serve in the Ordnance Department at Columbus, Mississippi. Resigning, he rejoined the Charleston Light Dragoons at Hixford, Virginia, where he continued in active service until the end of the war. In 1866 he and his elder brother, William Miles Tunno (1830–1901), settled in Savannah, where they were for many years associated in the firm of W. M. Tunno & Company, cotton brokers. They also engaged in banking. On May 20th, 1868, he married Isabel Couper King (1842–1921), daughter of Roswell King (1796–1854) and Julia Rebecca Maxwell (1808–1892), of Liberty County, Georgia; there were six children. He died in Savannah on December 5th, 1916, and was buried in Bonaventure Cemetery. Isabel Couper (King) Tunno died in Savannah on December 27th, 1921, survived by four sons, and was buried beside her husband.

TURNER, DUNCAN McNEILL (1812–1897), Presbyterian clergyman, was born in South Carolina, in 1812. He graduated from the College of Charleston in 1832 and from Columbia Theological Seminary in 1837. For sixty years he taught and preached in North Carolina, South Carolina, Florida, Louisiana, Texas, and Arkansas. In his eighty-fourth year he became pastor of the Presbyterian church in Morrillton, Arkansas; he died there on January 17th, 1897. According to *The Christian Observer* (April 7th, 1897), "Dr. Turner was in many respects a remarkable man. . . . As a teacher of youth he was painstaking and laborious, and nothing seemed to afford him so much pleasure as to impart to anxious, inquiring minds the knowledge of his own richly stored mind. . . . An affectionate husband, a devoted father, he nevertheless held the reins of family government well in hand. . . . Handsome, scholarly, and pious, he commanded the admiration and respect of the world, and at the same time challenged the confidence and Christian esteem of all who knew him."

TURNER, JOSEPH McLEOD (1838–1863), druggist, son of Dr. Joseph McLeod Turner (1816–1859) and Williamina Barrington (1818–1871), was born in Savannah, Georgia, in 1838. His parents were both natives of Philadelphia, Pennsylvania; his father, a physician and druggist, was for some years health officer of Savannah. His uncle, Thomas M. Turner (1811–1872), also a druggist, was mayor of Savannah (1858–1859). At the outbreak of the Civil War "Joe Turner" was a clerk in the firm of King & Waring, Savannah druggists. On May 31st, 1861, he enlisted for sixty days as third sergeant in the Savannah Volunteer Guards (Company B, 18th Battalion Georgia Infantry). On September 17th, 1861, he enlisted as fourth sergeant in the Georgia Hussars (Company E, 6th Regiment Virginia Cavalry; later designated Company F, Jeff Davis Legion Mississippi Cavalry); he became successively third sergeant (January 1862), second sergeant (July 1862), and second lieutenant (February 1863). On November 8th, 1863, he was instantly killed by a shot in the forehead while fighting gallantly at Stevensburg, near Culpeper Courthouse, Virginia. Several days later a farm boy delivered to the Confederate camp a package containing all the effects found in his pockets, accompanied by a letter from Edmund Blunt, first lieutenant and aide-de-camp, 1st Brigade, 3rd Division of Cavalry, Army of the Potomac, explaining that after the battle he had had Turner buried "in a small clump of pines south of Stevensburg" and enclosing a diagram indicating the precise place of burial. "Although I am upon the Union side," he wrote, "and nothing but a Yankee, still I admire bravery, even in an enemy." Joseph McLeod Turner never married. On October 19th, 1867, his widowed mother became the wife of Louis Placide Adolphe Thibault (1820–1890), of Versailles, France. She died in New York City on November 21st, 1871, and was buried beside her first husband in Laurel Grove Cemetery, Savannah.

TWIGGS, HANSFORD DADE DUNCAN (1837–1917), lawyer, judge, legislator, and Confederate soldier, son of George W. L. Twiggs and Harriet Eliza Duncan, was born in Barnwell, South Carolina, on March 25th, 1837. He was a great-grandson of General John Twiggs (1750–1816), Revolutionary patriot, for whom Twiggs County, Georgia, was named. He was a nephew of General David Emanuel Twiggs (1790–1862), of the Confederate army. He graduated from the Georgia Military Institute (Marietta) in 1858. After studying law for one year at the University of Pennsylvania he entered the law school of the University of Georgia and received his degree on January 11th, 1861. On February 1st, 1861, he became first lieutenant in Company D, 1st Regiment Georgia Regulars; on June 4th, 1861, when the regiment was consolidated with the 2nd Regiment to form the 1st Georgia Regulars, he was transferred to Company G. On February 6th, 1862, he was promoted to captain. He was wounded at Malvern Hill (July 1st, 1862); he was severely wounded and captured at Sharpsburg (September 17th, 1862) and later paroled and exchanged. Returning South, he reported to General Beauregard at

Charleston and was appointed inspector general, with rank of captain, on the staff of General William B. Taliaferro on Morris Island. He was severely wounded in the assault on Battery Wagner (July 18th, 1863). He later rejoined his regiment, then on duty on the Southern coast, where he remained until the close of the war; he participated in the battle of Olustee, Florida, in the siege of Savannah, and in the battle of Averysboro, North Carolina, where he was promoted to lieutenant colonel. He was paroled at Greensboro, North Carolina, on April 26th, 1865. After the war he remained on the family plantation in Richmond County, Georgia, until January 1868, when he commenced the practice of law in Augusta in association with Alfred P. Aldrich. For three years (1870–1873) he resided in Sandersville, where he was judge of the superior court of the middle district of Georgia. He then practiced law in Augusta (1873–1892), Swainsboro (1892–1897), and Savannah (1897–1917). In 1880–1881 he represented Richmond County in the state legislature and served as speaker pro tem of the house. On May 21st, 1861, he married Lucie E. Wilkins, daughter of Joseph C. Wilkins and Elizabeth Grant, of Liberty County, Georgia. Early in May 1893 they were divorced in Brookings, South Dakota. A few days later, on May 16th, 1893, in Chattanooga, Tennessee, Twiggs married Mrs. Cornelia E. Harrison, of Charleston, South Carolina, a divorcee thirty years his junior, whom Twiggs had recently represented in her divorce suit against her first husband. Twiggs and his second wife were divorced in February 1899, and on July 24th, 1906, he remarried his first wife. He died in Savannah on March 25th, 1917 (his eightieth birthday), survived by one son, and was buried in Summerville Cemetery, Augusta.

TYNG, STEPHEN HIGGINSON (1800–1885), Episcopal clergyman, fourth child of Dudley Atkins Tyng and Sarah Higginson, was born in Newburyport, Massachusetts, on March 1st, 1800. His father, a graduate of Harvard College (1781), was a distinguished lawyer, United States collector at Newburyport, and reporter for the supreme court of Massachusetts (1806–1821). Stephen Higginson Tyng graduated from Harvard College in 1817 and studied theology under the Rt. Rev. Alexander Viets Griswold (1766–1843), bishop of the Eastern Diocese, whose daughter, Anne Griswold, became his wife on August 5th, 1821. He was rector of St. John's Church, Georgetown, D.C. (1821–1823); Queen Anne's Parish, Prince Georges County, Maryland (1823–1829); St. Paul's Church, Philadelphia (1829–1834); the Church of the Epiphany, Philadelphia (1834–1845); and St. George's Church, New York City (1845–1878). He was an eloquent pulpit orator and drew vast congregations; he was reputed to be the greatest preacher in the Episcopal Church. He was a staunch and unyielding low churchman. His numerous published works include *Recollections of England* (1847), *Christ Is All* (1849), *The Rich Kinsman: The*

History of Ruth the Moabitess (1855), and *The Captive Orphan: Esther, Queen of Persia* (1860). He was also editor of *The Episcopal Recorder* (Philadelphia) and *The Protestant Churchman* (New York). His first wife died in 1832; he married second (in July 1833) Susan Wilson Mitchell. His last years were darkened by mental decline. He died in Irvington-on-Hudson, New York, on September 3rd, 1885. His son, Stephen Higginson Tyng (1839–1898), was also a clergyman.

ULMER, JOHN CHARLES (1829–1911), plantation overseer, was born in Georgia on November 10th, 1829. From April 1st, 1853, to December 31st, 1862, he managed Richmond-on-Ogeechee, plantation of Eliza Caroline Clay (1809–1895) in Bryan County, Georgia. "He is a simple-minded and I believe a *good* man," wrote Miss Clay to the Rev. Dr. Charles Colcock Jones on June 2nd, 1853; "knows little or nothing of rice planting, though acquainted with the culture of corn and cotton and care of stock. More of a farmer, I suspect, than a planter. But he seemed the best I could get." A year later (on May 24th, 1854) she reported that "the overseer gains in my confidence." "Mr. Ulmer continues to give satisfaction to me. I believe he manages well and takes good care of the people and is very desirous of gratifying *me* by carrying out my plans about the immediate premises" (December 29th, 1857). "Mr. Ulmer is invaluable to me" (February 1st, 1858). "I have to raise Mr. Ulmer's wages and give him $1200 next year. *I can't afford to lose him*" (November 1st, 1858). *"Strictly between ourselves,* my first lieutenant, who certainly for seven years has been a most valuable officer to me, thinks more of making a crop than of taking care of what the crop purchases; and we lose by want of attention far more than is consistent with good management" (May 2nd, 1861). After the war Ulmer removed to Savannah, where he resided for the rest of his life. He died in Savannah on September 4th, 1911, survived by a numerous family, and was buried beside his wife, Sarah Emily Ulmer (1836–1897), in Laurel Grove Cemetery.

VAN BUREN, JOHN (1810–1866), lawyer and politician, son of Martin Van Buren (1782–1862), eighth president of the United States (1837–1841), and Hannah Hoes, was born in Kinderhook, New York, on February 10th, 1810. After graduating from Yale College in 1828 he read law with Benjamin Butler and later with Aaron Vanderpoel; in August 1831 he sailed to London, where his father was United States minister to Great Britain (1831–1832) and he was attaché of the American legation. Returning to Albany, he commenced the practice of law in 1832. On June 22nd, 1841, he married Elizabeth Vanderpoel, who died in 1844, leaving one daughter. He was an active Democrat, and in 1845 he became attorney general of the State of New York. He supported the compromise bill of 1850, and ten years later, after Lincoln's election, he urged conciliation, proposed guarantees to the slave states, denounced Lincoln for mobilizing troops, and opposed the draft. He supported McClellan for President in 1864. He died on board the *Scotia* en route to New York on October 13th, 1866, and was buried beside his wife in Albany.

VAN DORN, EARL (1820–1863), Confederate soldier, son of Peter Aaron Van Dorn and Sophia Donelson Caffery, was born near Port Gibson, Mississippi, on September 17th, 1820. His father, a graduate of the College of New Jersey (Princeton) in 1795, was a lawyer and judge of the probate court; his mother was a niece of Rachel Donelson, wife of President Andrew Jackson. After graduating from the United States Military Academy in 1842 he fought in the Mexican War (1846–1848) and in the Seminole War (1849–1850); from 1855 to 1861, as captain in the 2nd Cavalry, he served in Texas and Indian Territory. He resigned his commission on January 31st, 1861, offered his services to the Confederacy, and was appointed brigadier general of Mississippi state troops; in September 1861 he was appointed major general in the regular army. In January 1862 he was placed in command of the Department of the Trans-Mississippi; he was defeated in the battle of Pea Ridge, Arkansas (March 1862). Later, operating in defense of Vicksburg, he was defeated in the battle of Corinth, Mississippi (October 1862); he was sharply criticized, but an investigating court upheld his conduct. He was shot and killed by a personal enemy at Spring Hill, Tennessee, on May 8th, 1863. He was survived by his wife, Caroline Godbold, of Mount Vernon, Alabama, whom he had married in 1843.

VAN RENSSELAER, CORTLANDT (1808–1860), Presbyterian clergyman, eldest son of Stephen van Rensselaer (1764–1839) and his second wife, Cornelia Paterson, was born in Albany, New York, on May 26th, 1808. His father, a graduate of Harvard College (1782), was a member of the state legislature (1789–1791, 1798, 1818), the state senate (1791–1796), and Congress (1822–1829); in 1824 he founded the Rensselaer Polytechnic Institute in Troy. Cortlandt van Rensselaer graduated from Yale College in 1827; after studying at Princeton Theological Seminary he graduated from Union Theological Seminary (Hampden-Sydney, Virginia) in 1833. He was missionary to the slaves in Virginia (1833–1835); organizer and first pastor of the Presbyterian church in Burlington, New Jersey (1836–1840); and pastor of the Second Presbyterian Church, Washington, D.C. (1841–1842). For several years he solicited funds for Princeton Theological Seminary. In February 1846 he became corresponding secretary of the Presbyterian Board of Education, with offices in Philadelphia, where he continued for the rest of his life. From 1850 to 1853 he was associated with the Rev. Dr. Charles Colcock Jones, of Liberty County, Georgia, corresponding secretary of the Presbyterian Board of

Domestic Missions. He was editor of *The Presbyterian Magazine* (1851–1859) and author of *Essays and Discourses* (1861), including "Historical Contributions Relative to the Founders, Principles, and Acts of the Presbyterian Church." He was moderator of the General Assembly of the Presbyterian Church meeting in Lexington, Kentucky, in 1857. On September 13th, 1836, he married Catherine Ledyard Cogswell, who bore him seven children. He died at his residence near Burlington, New Jersey, on July 25th, 1860, and was buried in the family vault in Albany, New York. "What a loss he is to the church!" wrote Mrs. Mary S. Mallard on August 14th, 1860.

VARNEDOE, LEANDER LEWIS (1829–1895), planter, son of Nathaniel Varnedoe (1790–1856) and his first wife, Ann T. Jones (1794–1836), was born in Liberty County, Georgia, on May 16th, 1829. After graduating from Oglethorpe University in 1848 he returned to his native county, where he planted until the outbreak of the Civil War. On December 11th, 1849, he married Ann Elizabeth Mallard (1828–1908), daughter of Thomas Mallard (1778–1861) and his second wife, Rebecca Eliza Burnley (1789–1861), widow of Thomas Baker. His wife was thus a sister of the Rev. R. Q. Mallard. Leander Lewis Varnedoe was a selectman of Midway Church (1858–1867). On May 15th, 1862, he enlisted as a private in the Liberty Mounted Rangers (Company B, 20th Battalion Georgia Cavalry); on January 10th, 1863, he was appointed captain and assistant quartermaster, to take rank October 14th, 1862. He was paroled at Thomasville, Georgia, on May 16th, 1865. After the war he removed with his family to a plantation near Thomasville, where he successfully introduced and popularized the LeConte pear— the Chinese sand pear, first cultivated in the South by John LeConte, of Liberty County, prior to the Civil War. He died near Thomasville on July 3rd, 1895, survived by his wife and numerous children, and was buried in Laurel Hill Cemetery, Thomasville. Ann Elizabeth (Mallard) Varnedoe died on January 28th, 1908, and was buried beside her husband.

VARNEDOE, NATHANIEL (1790–1856), planter, was born in South Carolina of French Huguenot ancestry; the original spelling of the name was *Varnedeaux*. In early manhood he settled in Liberty County, Georgia, penniless and meagerly educated, and through industry and energy accumulated a handsome fortune. He was an extensive landowner and a large slaveholder and a generous supporter of education, both public and private. He was for many years associated with Midway Church, of which he was selectman (1834–1841) and deacon (1836–1856). He resided at Liberty Hall. His first wife was Ann T. Jones (1794–1836), daughter of Samuel Jones and Mary Way, of Liberty County; there were ten children. His second wife was Hannah Maria Randolph (1805–1858), daughter of Isaac Randolph, of Charleston, South Carolina, and widow of the Rev. James Cooper Cozby, a Presbyterian clergyman; there were two children. His second wife was a sister of Rebecca Longstreet Randolph, wife of the Rev. Dr. I. S. K. Axson. Nathaniel Varnedoe died in Liberty County on February 12th, 1856, survived by nine children, and was buried beside his first wife in Midway Cemetery. Hannah Maria (Randolph) Varnedoe died on July 11th, 1858, and was buried beside her husband.

VARNEDOE, RUFUS ALONZO (1834–1893), planter, son of Nathaniel Varnedoe (1790–1856) and his first wife, Ann T. Jones (1794–1836), was born in Liberty County, Georgia, on September 14th, 1834. He attended Franklin College (Athens) with the class of 1854 but did not graduate. On November 18th, 1857, he married Anna M. Rokenbaugh (1839–1915), daughter of Jacob Rokenbaugh (1799–1871), of McIntosh County. On May 17th, 1862, at Palmyra, he enlisted as a private in the Liberty Independent Troop (Company G, 5th Regiment Georgia Cavalry); by August 1862 he was "discharged for general disability." In November 1862 he removed his Negroes from Liberty County to Thomasville in Southwest Georgia, "so as to evade our Yankee or abolition enemy," as he wrote the Rev. Dr. Charles Colcock Jones on October 27th, 1862. For several years after the war he was agent for the Southern Express Company in Thomasville, living in the household of his father-in-law. In 1870 he removed to Atlanta to assume control of the business of the Brooklyn Life Insurance Company for South Carolina, Georgia, and Florida. He later worked in the office of the clerk of the superior court of Fulton County. After an illness of three years he died of dropsy at his residence in Atlanta on November 19th, 1893, survived by his wife and seven children, and was buried in Oakland Cemetery. Anna (Rokenbaugh) Varnedoe died on December 29th, 1915, and was buried beside her husband.

VARNEDOE, SAMUEL McWHIR (1816–1870), planter and educator, eldest son of Nathaniel Varnedoe (1790–1856) and his first wife, Ann T. Jones (1794–1836), was born in Liberty County, Georgia, on August 3rd, 1816. He was named for the Rev. Dr. William McWhir (1759–1851), Presbyterian clergyman and educator, for many years principal of the Sunbury Academy. After graduating from Franklin College (Athens) in 1836 he taught school for eighteen years in his native county. At the same time he farmed successfully on his two plantations. On December 13th, 1837, he married Caroline Fraser Law, daughter of Samuel Law, of Liberty County; there were five children. He represented Liberty County twice in the state legislature. In 1856 he was unsuccessful candidate for Congress on the American ("Know-Nothing") party platform. He and the Hon. William B. Fleming were the two delegates representing Liberty County at the state secession convention meeting in Milledgeville in January 1861. His two older sons fought in the Civil War: James O. Varnedoe (born 1842) was a private in the Liberty Independent Troop (Company G, 5th Regiment Georgia Cavalry); Charles C. Varnedoe (born 1844) was a private in the Liberty Mounted Rangers (Company B, 20th Battalion Georgia Cavalry). In 1866 he founded the Valdosta Institute, one of the finest schools in Georgia, and he continued as principal to the end of his life. He was ordained ruling elder of the Valdosta Presbyterian Church on May 19th, 1866. He died in Valdosta on the night of April 22nd, 1870, survived by his wife and five children.

VERSTILLE, WILLIAM HENRY SHELDON (1820–1860), shoe merchant, son of Sheldon Verstille and Margaret Lynch, was born in New York City in 1820. In early manhood he migrated to Savannah, Georgia, where his uncle, Tristram Shandy Verstille, was military storekeeper and member of the board of health. By 1850 W. H. S. Verstille was associated with Matthew Lufburrow and Worthington Chauncey Butler in the firm of Verstille, Lufburrow & Butler, Savannah's leading shoe house. Several years later Lufburrow established his own store, leaving the firm of Verstille & Butler. On January 1st, 1855, the firm was dissolved by mutual consent. Butler joined George Smith Frierson in the firm of Butler & Frierson; Verstille removed to Johnson County, Texas, where in April 1855 he bought extensive tracts of land in the new county seat, Wardville, and became its first merchant. By 1860 he was living in Buchanan, Johnson County, where he was elected county commissioner on August 6th, 1860. He never married. He died in Johnson County on September 9th, 1860.

VICTORIA (1819–1901), queen of the United Kingdom of Great Britain and Ireland (1837–1901) and empress of India (1876–1901), was born at Kensington Palace, London, on May 24th, 1819, the only child of Edward, Duke of Kent, fourth son of George III, and Princess Mary Louisa Victoria of Saxe-Coburg-Gotha. She was christened Alexandrina Victoria. Her father died when she was eight years old, and she spent her girlhood and youth at Kensington Palace with her mother, her half-sister, and her governess. At the death of William IV on June 20th, 1837, she ascended the throne, and on June 28th, 1838, she was crowned queen. On February 10th, 1840, she became the wife of her first cousin, Prince Albert (1819–1861) of Saxe-Coburg-Gotha; there were nine children. It was a blissfully happy marriage, enjoyed at Buckingham Palace, Windsor Castle, Balmoral in Scotland, and Osborne on the Isle of Wight. After Prince Albert's untimely death on December 14th, 1861, the queen was at first inconsolable. "My nature is too passionate," she confessed to a friend, "my emotions are too fervent; he guided and protected me, he comforted and encouraged me." In her later years she was held in affectionate regard by her subjects; the Jubilees of 1887 and 1897 were measures of her popularity. She died at Osborne on January 22nd, 1901, and was buried beside Prince

Albert in the mausoleum at Frogmore near Windsor. Her reign, the longest in English history, had restored dignity and popularity to the British crown.

VILLALONGA, JOHN L. (1817–1880), cotton factor and commission merchant, was born in St. Augustine, Florida, on June 27th, 1817. In early manhood he removed to Camden County, Georgia, where he prospered as a merchant and represented the county two consecutive terms in the state legislature. In 1853 he settled in Savannah, where he joined John Boston in the firm of Boston & Villalonga, cotton factors and commission merchants. During the Civil War he was division commissary, Georgia state troops, with rank of major. After the war he continued his business alone and accumulated a handsome fortune. For some years he was vice-president and director of the Merchants' National Bank. According to the Savannah *Morning News* (October 26th, 1880), "He was recognized as a businessman of rare ability, attaining a high rank in our commercial community, and during several different administrations served as an alderman of the city, holding the high position of chairman of the finance committee." His wife, Jane C. Villalonga (1818–1879), died in Fernandina, Florida, on July 3rd, 1879, and was buried in the Catholic Cemetery adjoining the convent. John L. Villalonga died in Savannah on October 25th, 1880, survived by one daughter, and was buried beside his wife. He left an estate of approximately six hundred thousand dollars.

WALKER, GEORGE (1793–1865), planter, son of George Walker (1763–1830) and Elizabeth Walker (1767–1835), was born in Burke County, Georgia, on August 13th, 1793. His mother was a sister of Charles Walker (1774–1802), first husband of Eliza Greene Low (1785–1868), subsequently wife of James Robarts and David Robarts. Eliza Greene (Low) (Walker) (Robarts) Robarts was thus an aunt by marriage of George Walker (1793–1865). About 1806, shortly before Pulaski County was organized in 1808, George Walker (1763–1830) migrated from Burke County and built his house near Shellstone Creek, just south of the Twiggs County line. Later his four sons (George, David, Charles, and Thomas) built their houses a few miles east of their father's house on a three-and-a-half-mile stretch of road which came to be known as Longstreet. There George Walker (1793–1865) prospered as a planter; in the Federal Census of 1860 he was recorded as the owner of 101 slaves. And there Mary Eliza Robarts visited in December 1863. "The war had not diminished any of their comforts," she wrote on December 23rd, 1863. "They had everything that was good, and Uncle George took me into his wine cellar, where there was on one side barrel after barrel of Catawba and various other wines, and on the other side of the cellar as many barrels of sugar, syrup, and molasses—all made at home. I could not begin to enumerate the

products of his farm. . . . Longstreet is a village something like Flemington, but the houses are handsomer. The people are all related except one or two families. I thought it would be a good place to rent a house in case we were driven from our homes, but there was not a house or farm to rent." In the summer of 1864, having fled from Marietta at the approach of the Federal army, the Robartses stayed in the house of George Walker for several months; in October they moved on to Cuthbert for the winter and spring. George Walker died in Longstreet on August 30th, 1865, and was buried in the Walker family cemetery in Pulaski (now Bleckley) County. His wife, Martha S. Walker (1801–1866), died on August 13th, 1866, and was buried beside her husband.

WALKER, LEROY POPE (1817–1884), Confederate secretary of war, son of John William Walker, was born near Huntsville, Alabama, on July 28th, 1817. He was admitted to the bar in 1838 and was subsequently elected to the state legislature to represent Lawrence County (1843) and Lauderdale County (1847). After serving as judge of the fourth judicial circuit for three years (1850–1853) he practiced law until the outbreak of the Civil War. In February 1861 he was appointed secretary of war in the cabinet of President Jefferson Davis. He continued to serve until September 21st, 1861, when he was commissioned brigadier general in the Confederate army. He resigned in March 1862. After the war he resumed the practice of law in Huntsville, where he died on August 22nd, 1884.

WALKER, ROBERT DOWNIE (1813–1901), stonecutter, was born in Charleston, South Carolina, on October 13th, 1813. On December 18th, 1834, he married Louisa Adaline Pierce (1816–1897), a native of Fairfield, South Carolina, daughter of the Rev. Reddick Pierce, a Methodist clergyman; there were eleven children. Walker was one of the survivors of the steamer *Pulaski*, which sank in mid-ocean on June 14th, 1838. For some years he worked as a stonecutter in Charleston; in 1846 he removed with his family to Savannah, Georgia, where for many years he headed the marble yards of R. D. Walker & Company, dealers in mantels and monuments. He was alderman of Savannah (1848–1854; 1855–1857). For some years prior to the Civil War he was colonel of the 1st Regiment Georgia Militia; he resigned in 1856. In 1861 he became captain and quartermaster of the 1st Volunteer Regiment; he was captured at the fall of Pulaski on April 11th, 1862, and confined on Johnson's Island, Ohio, until the close of the war. Returning to Savannah, he continued active in civic affairs. When the county commissioners were organized in 1872 he became a member of the board, and for nineteen years (1873–1892) he served as chairman. Under his administration county districts were drained, new roads were graded and opened, and two public buildings, the courthouse and the jail, were erected. He was city assessor for twenty-six years. He was an active member of the Savannah Benevolent Association and the Union Society, charitable organizations, and was an honorary member of the Chatham Artillery. His wife died in Savannah on October 31st, 1897, and was buried in Laurel Grove Cemetery. He died on November 1st, 1901, and was buried beside his wife.

WALKER, SARAH AMANDA (KING) (1817–1876): *Mrs. James A. Walker,* daughter of Reuben King (1779–1867) and Abigail Austin (1783–1863), was born in Darien, McIntosh County, Georgia, on July 26th, 1817. On May 23rd, 1839, she became the wife of James A. Walker (1816–1858), son of Elnathan Walker (1780–1820) and Aurelia King (1781–1821); there were five children. Her husband, a native of Homer, New York, had migrated to McIntosh County, Georgia, in early manhood and engaged in planting. He died in Darien on February 21st, 1858, leaving a wife and five children, and was buried in Upper Mill Cemetery, McIntosh County. Sarah Amanda (King) Walker then resided with her parents at Mallow plantation on the Sapelo River at Pine Harbor Bluff; in November 1862 the Federals raided the plantation from a gunboat anchored in the river. Three of her sons served in the Confederate army: Charles Reade Walker (born 1840), Reuben King Walker (born 1842), and James King Walker (born 1845). After the war she lived in Darien in the household of her son James, a timber inspector. She died in Darien on May 18th, 1876, and was buried beside her husband.

WALKER, WILLIAM HENRY TALBOT (1816–1864), Confederate soldier, son of Freeman Walker and Mary Washington Creswell, was born in Augusta, Georgia, on November 26th, 1816. After graduating from the United States Military Academy in 1837 he served as captain in the Mexican War (1846–1848) and was brevetted major (August 20th, 1847) and lieutenant colonel (September 8th, 1847) for distinguished gallantry. He was on sick leave and recruiting service (1847–1852); deputy governor at East Pascagoula, Mississippi (1852–1854); instructor in military tactics at West Point (1854–1856); and again on sick leave (1856–1860). He resigned his commission on December 20th, 1860, and entered Confederate service. He was appointed major general of volunteers (April 25th, 1861) and brigadier general in the regular army (May 25th, 1861). During the winter of 1861–1862 he saw service on the Georgia coast; he later commanded a division at Vicksburg and Chickamauga. He was killed before Atlanta on July 22nd, 1864, and was buried in Summerville Cemetery, Augusta. He was survived by his wife, Mary Townsend, and four children.

WALLACE, CAMPBELL (1806–1895), railroad official, son of Jesse Wallace, was born in Sevier County, Tennessee, on December 7th, 1806. In 1820 he entered the store of C. McClurg & Son, of Knoxville, Tennessee; after three years he returned to his father's home,

but he later returned to Knoxville and became junior partner in the firm. On May 31st, 1831, he married Susan E. Lyon (1813–1893), of Roane County, Tennessee. In 1853 he became president of the East Tennessee, Virginia & Georgia Railroad. During the Civil War he refused a commission as brigadier general, feeling that he could be more useful to the Confederacy as a railroad official. After the war he was for two years (1866–1868) superintendent of the Western & Atlantic Railroad. From 1866 to 1872 he resided in Marietta, Georgia, where he was ruling elder of the First Presbyterian Church and superintendent of the Sunday school; in 1869 he gave the church its first pipe organ. In 1872 he settled in Atlanta, where he organized the Merchants' Bank and served as president until feeble health forced him to retire. As state railroad commissioner (1879–1890) he rendered invaluable service and came to be known as "the Nestor of railroads in the South." According to the Atlanta *Constitution* (November 3rd, 1887), "There is no man in Atlanta who commands to a larger extent the confidence of the people of all classes and in every walk of life than Major Campbell Wallace. His long life, large experience, excellent sense, and great information, with his sterling honesty, entitle his views on any public question to great weight." He was a member of the Central Presbyterian Church for twenty-three years (1872–1895). His wife died in Atlanta on June 12th, 1893, and was buried in Oakland Cemetery. He died on May 3rd, 1895, survived by six children, and was buried beside his wife. As the Atlanta *Constitution* (May 4th, 1895) observed, "His influence for good in Atlanta cannot be measured; it will be felt for a century hence."

WALTHOUR, ALICE GERTRUDE (1843–1927), eighth surviving child of George Washington Walthour (1799–1859) and Mary Amelia Ann Russell (1806–1890), was born in Walthourville, Liberty County, Georgia, on March 16th, 1843. Her father was the richest planter and the largest slaveholder in Liberty County. On April 2nd, 1862, she became the wife of Edward Jonathan Thomas (1840–1929), son of John Abbott Thomas (1816–1859) and Malvina Huguenin (1816–1890); there were seven children. Her husband, a graduate of Franklin College (Athens) in 1860, was quartermaster sergeant of the Liberty Independent Troop (Company G, 5th Regiment Georgia Cavalry) during the Civil War. In 1865 he settled in Savannah, where he was general agent and secretary of the Coastline Railroad until April 30th, 1879; on May 1st, 1879, he became superintendent of the Savannah, Skidaway & Seaboard Railroad. He was also for many years surveyor of Chatham County and engineer of the Savannah streetcar system. Alice Gertrude (Walthour) Thomas died in Savannah on December 2nd, 1927, survived by four children, and was buried in Bonaventure Cemetery. Edward Jonathan Thomas died on August 8th, 1929, and was buried beside his wife.

WALTHOUR, ANDREW (1825–1867), physician, second child of George Washington Walthour (1799–1859) and Mary Amelia Ann Russell (1806–1890), was born in Wathourville, Liberty County, Georgia, in 1825. His father was the richest planter and the largest slaveholder in Liberty County. For some years prior to the Civil War Andrew Walthour practiced medicine in his native village. Early in June 1852 he married Caroline Morton. On December 10th, 1861, he enlisted for six months as third sergeant in the Liberty Independent Troop (Company G, 5th Regiment Georgia Cavalry). On May 17th, 1862, when his brother William Lowndes Walthour became captain, and his brother Russell Walthour became third sergeant, he succeeded Dr. Joseph Jones as surgeon of the post. He resigned on January 2nd, 1863, for "gout and disability." On February 18th, 1863, he signed a contract agreeing "to perform the duties of a medical officer agreeably to the army regulation at Camp Dorchester." His brother, Captain William Lowndes Walthour, appended the following note: "I certify that the number of persons entitled to medical attention agreeably to regulations at Camp Dorchester is one hundred and twenty-five; that no competent physician can be obtained at a lower rate; and that the services of a private physician are necessary for the following reasons: that there is no medical officer in the command whose services can be had, and that it is necessary for the said Dr. A. Walthour to abandon his own business and give his whole time to the public service." Andrew Walthour died in Walthourville late in March 1867, survived by his wife and one child, and was buried in Walthourville Cemetery.

WALTHOUR, AUGUSTA (1834–1908), fifth surviving child of George Washington Walthour (1799–1859) and Mary Amelia Ann Russell (1806–1890), was born in Walthourville, Liberty County, Georgia, in 1834. Her father, a Baptist layman, was the richest planter and the largest slaveholder in Liberty County. For some years "Gussie" attended a female seminary in Limestone Springs, Spartanburg County, South Carolina, owned and conducted by the Rev. William Curtis (1816–1873), a Baptist clergyman, husband of her eldest sister, Elizabeth Amanda Walthour (1823–1913). In August 1888 she became the second wife of Nathaniel Law Barnard (1832–1910), second son of John Bradley Barnard (1807–1861) and his first wife, Martha J. Law. "It is not often," wrote Mrs. Mary S. Mallard (August 2nd, 1888) on hearing the news, "that a young lady of fifty-three or four marries." Augusta (Walthour) Barnard settled with her husband in Savannah, where he was in the service of the Central Railroad of Georgia. She died in Savannah after a long illness on January 21st, 1908, and was buried in Laurel Grove Cemetery. Nathaniel Law Barnard died in Savannah on June 28th, 1910, survived by two daughters, and was buried beside his wife. "Miss Gussie" was a girlhood friend of Mary Sharpe Jones.

WALTHOUR, GEORGE WASHINGTON (1799–1859), planter, son of Andrew Walthour (1750–1824) and his first wife, Ann Hoffmire, was born in Liberty County, Georgia, on May 3rd, 1799. He was of German ancestry; the original spelling of the name was *Waldhauer*. He was an elder brother of Sarah Ann Walthour (1803–1885), second wife of the Rev. Dr. George Howe, of Columbia, South Carolina. His father, a Revolutionary soldier, was a rich planter; in 1795 he settled some fifteen miles southwest of Midway Church in an area known as the Sand Hills, afterwards called Walthourville in his honor. On January 16th, 1823, George Washington Walthour married Mary Amelia Ann Russell (1806–1890), a native of the island of San Salvador, daughter of John Russell and Mary Hogg, and sister of Edward William Russell (1798–1863), of Liberty County. Ten of their children lived to maturity: Elizabeth Amanda Walthour (1823–1913), wife of the Rev. William Curtis, a Baptist clergyman; Andrew Walthour (1825–1867); Ann Mary Walthour (1827–1901), wife of Solomon Shad Barnard; William Lowndes Walthour (1828–1890); Augusta Walthour (1834–1908), second wife of Nathaniel Law Barnard; Charlotte Caroline Walthour (born 1837), wife of (1) the Rev. Augustus S. Morrall, a Baptist clergyman, and (2) Henry Lewis Russell; Russell Walthour (1841–1878); Alice Gertrude Walthour (1843–1927), wife of Edward Jonathan Thomas; Robert H. Walthour (1845–1905); and Zachary Taylor Walthour (1847–1897). George Washington Walthour represented Liberty County in the state house of representatives (1821–1825) and in the state senate (1827, 1833, 1835, 1839, 1841). He was a member of the Baptist Church. At the time of his death he was, according to the Rev. Dr. Charles Colcock Jones (August 17th, 1859), "the largest slaveholder and the richest man in our county." In the Federal Census of 1860 his estate was recorded as the owner of 300 slaves. He died in New York City of paralysis on August 12th, 1859, and was buried in Midway Cemetery, Liberty County. Mary Amelia Ann (Russell) Walthour spent her later years in Atlanta at the residence of her daughter, Charlotte Caroline Walthour, widow of Augustus S. Morrall. She died in Atlanta of pneumonia on October 26th, 1890, and was buried in Walthourville Cemetery, to which her husband's remains were subsequently removed from Midway. A sympathetic appraisal of George Washington Walthour appeared in the Savannah *Republican* on August 24th, 1859: "Though Mr. Walthour's habitual pursuits were those of a planter, he was a man of no common character. He was possessed of a sound judgment in all matters of business, of prudent forecast, of great industry, of indomitable energy, of the utmost promptitude and dispatch in what he undertook. . . . The bereaved widow and orphan looked to him as a kind friend and advisor. . . . The poor man found in him a friend, and to the distressed and unfortunate his charities were constant and unostentatious. . . . He was hospitable to the stranger, kind and obliging to his neighbors, sympathizing and attentive to the sick, and public-spirited in whatever related to the welfare of his neighborhood, his county, the state, and our common country."

WALTHOUR, RUSSELL (1841–1878), planter, seventh surviving child of George Washington Walthour (1799–1859) and Mary Amelia Ann Russell (1806–1890), was born in Walthourville, Liberty County, Georgia, in 1841. His father was the richest planter and the largest slaveholder in Liberty County. On December 19th, 1860, he married Matilda Olivia Fleming (1839–1927), daughter of the Hon. William Bennett Fleming (1803–1886) and Eliza Ann Maxwell (1801–1871). (On November 7th, 1848, William Lowndes Walthour, elder brother of Russell Walthour, married Sarah Margaret Fleming, elder sister of Matilda Olivia Fleming.) On October 1st, 1861, he enlisted for six months as third corporal in the Liberty Independent Troop (Company G, 5th Regiment Georgia Cavalry); on May 17th, 1862, when his elder brother, William Lowndes Walthour, became captain, he became third sergeant; in October 1863 he was appointed color sergeant of the regiment. He was paroled at Greensboro, North Carolina, on April 26th, 1865. He died in Walthourville of "congestion of the brain" on November 23rd, 1878, and was buried in Walthourville Cemetery. On August 9th, 1887, Matilda Olivia (Fleming) Walthour became the second wife of the Rev. John Watt Montgomery (1825–1904), a Presbyterian clergyman. After his death in Giddings, Texas, on January 23rd, 1904, she resided for some years in Montgomery, Alabama; in 1926 she joined the household of her son, Russell Fleming Walthour (1866–1937), in Jacksonville, Florida, where she died of a cerebral hemorrhage on November 14th, 1927. She was buried near her parents in Laurel Grove Cemetery, Savannah.

WALTHOUR, WILLIAM LOWNDES (1828–1890), planter, fourth surviving son of George Washington Walthour (1799–1859) and Mary Amelia Ann Russell (1806–1890), was born in Walthourville, Liberty County, Georgia, in 1828. His father was the richest planter and largest slaveholder in Liberty County. On November 7th, 1848, in Savannah, he married Sarah Margaret Fleming (1829–1868), daughter of the Hon. William Bennett Fleming (1803–1886) and Eliza Ann Maxwell (1801–1871). (On December 19th, 1860, Russell Walthour, younger brother of William Lowndes Walthour, married Matilda Olivia Fleming, younger sister of Sarah Margaret Fleming.) On October 1st, 1861, William Lowndes Walthour became first lieutenant in the Liberty Independent Troop; in May 1862, when Abial Winn resigned as captain, part of the troop reorganized as the Liberty Mounted Rangers under Captain William Goulding Thomson, and part reorganized as the Liberty Independent Troop under Captain William Lowndes Walthour. The Liberty Independent

Troop continued to act as coast guard at Camp Palmyra, near Sunbury, until the spring of 1863, when it became Company G, 5th Regiment Georgia Cavalry, commanded by Colonel Robert Houstoun Anderson. In 1864, when Anderson was commissioned brigadier general, Walthour became inspector general on his staff. After the war he engaged in railroad construction; he was a member of the firm of Papot, Shotter & Company, who built the Vicksburg & Mobile Railroad late in the 1860s. His wife died in Savannah on May 3rd, 1868, and was buried in Laurel Grove Cemetery. He outlived his wife twenty-two years; he died in Savannah on December 6th, 1890, survived by two sons, and was buried beside his wife.

WARD, JAMES MONTFORT (1854–1904), lawyer, son of John Elliott Ward (1814–1902) and Olivia Buckminster Sullivan (1819–1890), was born at Richmond Hill plantation, Liberty County, Georgia, on October 5th, 1854. He was named for Dr. James Montfort Schley (1816–1874), distinguished Savannah physician, husband of his maternal aunt, Marianne Appleton Sullivan (1816–1908). His father, a lawyer in Savannah, was a conspicuous figure in local, state, and national politics. In early childhood "Jimmie" lived in the Orient, where his father was first United States minister to China (1859–1861); during the Civil War he lived with his mother in Rome, Italy; in December 1865 he settled with his parents in New York City, where his father practiced law successfully for thirty years. James Montfort Ward attended Harvard College with the class of 1875 but left during his junior year, entered the Columbia University Law School, and graduated in 1876. After practicing law in New York City for several years he removed to Savannah in 1881 and thence to Washington, D.C., in 1885, where he headed the law department of the Pension Bureau under President Grover Cleveland (1885–1889). In 1890 he became assistant corporation counsel of New York City; he continued in this post until failing health forced him to retire. In 1896 he was stricken with tuberculosis; in 1898 he removed to Red Bank, New Jersey, to benefit his health, continuing his office duties until January 1904. He died in Red Bank on May 31st, 1904. He married first (in 1876) Agnes Sarmiento Biddle, of Philadelphia, who died in 1879, leaving one child. He married second (in 1884) Mariana Hull Johnston, of Baltimore, who died in 1907; there were ten children.

WARD, JOHN ELLIOTT (1814–1902), lawyer, legislator, and diplomat, son of William Ward and his second wife, Sarah Ann McIntosh, was born near Sunbury, Liberty County, Georgia, on October 2nd, 1814. He attended Amherst College with the class of 1835 but did not graduate. Returning to Georgia, he read law in the office of Matthew Hall McAllister (1800–1865), of Savannah. After studying for one year (1835–1836) at the Harvard Law School he commenced practice in Savannah; he was associated through the

years with several distinguished lawyers: Robert
Milledge Charlton, George Savage Owens,
Charles Colcock Jones, Jr., Henry Rootes Jackson, and Charles E. Whitehead. His firm was
known successively as Charlton & Ward
(1840–1845); Charlton, Ward & Owens
(1845–1854); Ward & Owens (1854–1856);
Ward, Owens & Jones (1857–1858); Ward,
Jackson & Jones (1859–1861); Ward & Jones
(1866); and Ward, Jones & Whitehead (1867–
1877). His practice was large and lucrative.
For many years he was a conspicuous figure in
local, state, and national politics. He was
solicitor general of the eastern circuit of Georgia (1836–1838); United States district attorney for the district of Georgia (1838–1839);
member of the state house of representatives
(1839, 1842, 1845, and 1853); mayor of Savannah (1854–1855); president of the Democratic National Convention meeting in Cincinnati (1856); member of the state senate (1857–
1858); and first United States minister to China
(1859–1861). He opposed secession, and during
the Civil War he did not participate actively
in the Confederate cause. ("I wish that Mr.
Ward's course had entitled him to more respect
and confidence in our country," wrote Mrs.
Mary Jones to her son Charles on September
6th, 1865. "No one ever speaks of him as *true
to our cause*.") From September 1861 to June
1862 he was absent in Europe, where his young
son, James Montfort Ward (1854–1904), had
sustained an injury in falling from a swing.
In the fall of 1863 he spent several months in
Europe "on financial business connected with
the government"; he returned to Savannah in
mid-December 1863. After the war he settled
in New York City, where he practiced law
successfully for thirty years. He received the
honorary degree of doctor of laws from Amherst College in 1891. On August 15th, 1839,
in Boston, Massachusetts, he married Olivia
Buckminster Sullivan (1819–1890), daughter
of the Hon. William Sullivan (1774–1839)
and Sarah Webb Swan (1782–1851), and
younger sister of Dr. James Swan Sullivan
(1809–1874), Savannah physician. His wife
died in Morristown, New Jersey, in 1890. Ward
died in Liberty County, Georgia, on November 29th, 1902, survived by two daughters and
one son, and was buried in Midway Cemetery.
Charles Colcock Jones, Jr., read law in Ward's
Savannah office in the spring of 1855; on
March 8th, 1855, Ward wrote the Rev. Dr.
Charles Colcock Jones of his son's progress:
"I would most anxiously avoid any expressions
which you could construe into flattery; yet it
would be unjust to him to say less than that
I regard him as one of the most accomplished
lawyers of his age I have ever met; and that
he will be in the very front rank of his profession is a 'fixed fact.' "

WARD, MATTHEWS FLOURNOY (1826–
1862), author, son of Robert J. Ward, was
born in Scott County, Kentucky, on May 19th,
1826. His family, one of the wealthiest and
most aristocratic in the state, resided in Louisville. He attended Harvard College for one

year (1844–1845) with the class of 1847. For
eighteen months (1849–1850) he traveled
through Europe and the Near East; a series of
letters describing his travels was printed in
the Louisville *Journal* and later published in
book form in *Letters from Three Continents*
(1851). He also wrote *English Items; or,
Microscopic Views of England and Englishmen*
(1853). On the morning of November 2nd,
1853, accompanied by his brother Robert Ward,
he entered the schoolroom of William Hopkins
Gregg Butler (1823–1853), universally respected principal of the Louisville High School,
and shot him in the presence of some sixty
schoolboys, the occasion being Butler's alleged
mistreatment of one of his pupils, William
Ward, younger brother of Matt. F. Ward, the
preceding day. Butler died at one o'clock the
following morning, survived by his wife and
one child. In a celebrated trial, in which the
ablest attorneys of the day (including John
Jordan Crittenden, United States senator, and
John Larue Helm, ex-governor of Kentucky)
were retained for the defense, Ward was acquitted on April 26th, 1854, provoking a
storm of indignation throughout the country.
Matt. F. Ward never married. For some years
prior to the Civil War he planted cotton in
Arkansas. On September 30th, 1862, he was
killed in front of his house in Helena, Arkansas,
by a Confederate soldier who mistook him for
a Federal. At the time of his death he was
writing a book exploiting incidents from the
Butler tragedy. . . . On May 8th, 1854, the
Rev. Dr. Charles Colcock Jones, writing from
Liberty County, Georgia, addressed his son,
Charles Colcock Jones, Jr., then a student at
Dane Law School, Harvard University: "*Ward
has, I see, been acquitted!* An indignation
meeting held in Louisville! And Mr. Crittenden
requested to resign his seat in Congress! I do
not pronounce upon the case, not having all the
facts before me. I trust, my son, that you will
never, if spared to become an advocate, lend
your talents or influence to the screening of
murderers and guilty criminals, however rich
or elevated, from deserved justice. An advocate
may state every extenuating circumstance, but
to use arguments and influences to blind justice,
to pervert evidence, to save the guilty, I conceive in the just judgment of Heaven and earth
is to become associated with the criminal in his
guilt and to become an accomplice with him
in his crime. . . . What a vast injury is inflicted upon society by men distinguished for
talents, eloquence, learning, and standing,
when they exert all their power to screen and
save the guilty! How does such conduct fasten
opprobrium upon the profession, branding it
as heartless and mercenary, and reckless alike
of virtue and justice! . . . The father of your
friend, I believe, was for the defendant! Of
course, in your association with the family you
will be prudent in your observations. Differ-
ences of opinion are consistent with friendly
relations." On May 20th, 1854, Charles Colcock Jones, Jr., replied: "The result of the
Ward trial has caused much astonishment in

every part of our country. Although I do not approve of the abusive epithets and venomous views which have been promulgated by many of the public prints, and also deprecate the prevalence of mob sentiment and demonstrations manifested in several places in Kentucky, and especially in Louisville, still I cannot feel perfectly assured that the result of the trial was in all respects such as the circumstances and evidence of the case would lead us to expect. There may be extenuating circumstances, but these, while they *modify*, do not *remove* the guilt, and the penalty incident thereto. . . . I have carefully read all the evidence as reported, and I think it must be manifest to everyone that every method was used, whether fair or unfair, to *clear Ward*. What was the grand aim of the trial? Not to find out whether or not he really was guilty, but so to arrange matters that in any event he should not be rendered liable to the vigorous execution of the law. . . . A full and accurate report of the evidence and entire proceedings in the case, including the speeches of counsel, will soon be published by Appleton & Company of New York, which I hope to procure and send to you. Whether or not the circumstances of the case will there appear in a more favorable light as regards the conduct of Ward remains to be seen."

WARING, ANNE MARY (1835–1891), fifth child of Dr. William Richard Waring (1787–1843) and Anna Moodie Johnstone, was born in Savannah, Georgia, in 1835. Her father, a graduate of the College of Charleston (1810) and the Medical College of the University of Pennsylvania (1813), was a prominent Savannah physician until his death on January 2nd, 1843. Late in April 1861 Anne Mary Waring became the wife of Hore Browse Trist (1832–1896), son of Nicholas Philip Trist (1800–1874) and Virginia Jefferson Randolph (1802–1881); there were four children. Her husband, a great-grandson of Thomas Jefferson, attended the University of Virginia (1850–1851) and graduated from Jefferson Medical College (Philadelphia) in 1857. Prior to the Civil War he was a surgeon in the United States navy, stationed aboard the *Vandalia*. During the war he was a surgeon in the United States army, stationed in Washington and New York. After the war he practiced medicine in Washington (1865–1870), Baltimore (1870–1879), and Habersham County, Georgia (1879–1888). From 1888 to 1896 he was medical examiner in the Pension Office in Washington. Anne Mary (Waring) Trist died in Clarkesville, Georgia, on January 28th, 1891, and was buried in Laurel Grove Cemetery, Savannah. Hore Browse Trist died in Washington on Easter Sunday, April 5th, 1896, and was buried in Ivy Hill Cemetery, Alexandria, Virginia.

WARING, GEORGE HOUSTOUN (1833–1902), druggist and cement manufacturer, fourth son of Dr. William Richard Waring (1787–1843) and Anna Moodie Johnstone, was born in Savannah, Georgia, on December 22nd, 1833. His father, a graduate of the Col-

lege of Charleston (1810) and the Medical College of the University of Pennsylvania (1813), was a prominent Savannah physician until his death on January 2nd, 1843. After attending Yale College for one year (1851–1852) George Houstoun Waring graduated from the University of Pennsylvania in 1855. Returning to Savannah, he joined William Henry King (1833–1865) in the firm of King & Waring, "wholesale and retail dealers in drugs, chemicals, perfumery, toilet articles, oils, etc." According to an advertisement published in the Savannah *Republican* (March 26th, 1859), "Particular attention will be paid to the preparation of physicians' prescriptions. All family, plantation, and physicians' orders will be executed with neatness, accuracy, and dispatch." On June 2nd, 1858, he married Ella Susan Howard, daughter of the Rev. Charles Wallace Howard (1811–1876), a Presbyterian clergyman, educator, lecturer, and business entrepreneur, of Kingston, Cass (now Bartow) County, Georgia; there were five children. At the outbreak of the Civil War he enlisted as a private in the Georgia Hussars (Company E, 6th Regiment Virginia Cavalry; later designated Company F, Jeff Davis Legion Mississippi Cavalry). On January 2nd, 1862, he enlisted as a private in Captain Joseph S. Claghorn's Company (Chatham Artillery), 1st Volunteer Regiment Georgia Artillery; he was appointed sixth corporal (May 24th, 1862) and detailed for service in the signal corps (October 14th, 1862). He subsequently became major of cavalry and served with his regiment in Georgia and Virginia. After the war he planted briefly in Habersham County. In 1867 he removed to Bartow (formerly Cass) County to join his father-in-law in the Howard Hydraulic Cement Company, located north of Kingston on the Western & Atlantic Railroad. After Howard's death in 1876 Waring continued the business alone, operating successfully at Cement, Georgia, for some twenty years. He erected a handsome house, Annandale, where he resided until his death. In 1896 he was partially paralyzed as a result of a runaway accident in which his wife was killed. He was a member of the Georgia Historical Society, vice-president of the Georgia State Agricultural Society (1870–1884), and president of the Georgia Horticultural Society (1880–1894). He died in Savannah at the residence of his son, George Houstoun Waring, on June 25th, 1902, and was buried beside his wife in the family cemetery at Cement. In 1926 their remains were transferred to Myrtle Hill Cemetery, Rome.

WARING, JAMES JOHNSTONE (1829–1888), physician, second son of Dr. William Richard Waring (1787–1843) and Anna Moodie Johnstone, was born in Savannah, Georgia, on August 19th, 1829. His father, a graduate of the College of Charleston (1810) and the Medical College of the University of Pennsylvania (1813), was a prominent Savannah physician until his death on January 2nd, 1843. James Johnstone Waring graduated from

Yale College in 1850 and from the Medical College of the University of Pennsylvania in 1852. After one year (1852–1853) as resident physician in the Blockley Hospital, Philadelphia, and one year (1853–1854) as resident physician in the Lying-In Hospital, Dublin, and St. Bartholomew's Hospital, London, he traveled in France, Italy, and Switzerland for seven months. Returning to the United States late in 1854, he settled in Washington, D.C., and commenced the practice of medicine. He was professor of physiology and obstetrics in the National Medical College (1857–1859) and surgeon and curator of the Washington Infirmary (1859–1861). On May 23rd, 1856, he married Mary B. Alston, daughter of Thomas Pinckney Alston, of Charleston, South Carolina; there were seven children. Early in 1861 he accompanied his family on an extended visit to Savannah; returning to Washington, he was arrested by the Confederate authorities and sent back on parole to Savannah, where he continued to practice medicine for the rest of his life. In the late summer of 1876 he returned from his summer residence in Saratoga, New York, to serve his native city during a serious epidemic of yellow fever; his younger brother, Joseph Frederick Waring (1832–1876), died in the epidemic on October 5th, 1876. In 1877, as member of the city council, he instituted the drainage of swamps in the southeastern suburbs of Savannah, thereby removing a formidable source of malaria. As the Savannah *Morning News* (January 9th, 1888) observed, "His natural love for scientific and physical studies placed him far in advance of most of his fellow men and caused him to discern more clearly than they the shadows of the future." He died in Savannah on January 8th, 1888, survived by his wife and several children, and was buried in Laurel Grove Cemetery. His remains were transferred to Bonaventure Cemetery in 1893.

WARNER, HIRAM (1802–1881), jurist and congressman, eldest son of Obadiah Warner and Jane Coffin, was born in Williamsburg, Hampshire County, Massachusetts, on October 29th, 1802. In 1819 he removed to Georgia, where he taught school for three years in Sparta and Blountsville, at the same time reading law. In 1825 he commenced practice in Knoxville, Crawford County, where in 1827 he married Sarah (Abercrombie) Staples, who bore him one daughter. He was a member of the state legislature (1828–1831). In 1830 he removed to Talbotton and thence to Greenville. He was judge of the state superior court (1833–1840), associate justice of the state supreme court (1845–1853), member of Congress (1855–1857), judge of the Coweta Circuit Court (1865–1867), and chief justice of the state supreme court (1867–1880). He died in Atlanta on June 30th, 1881, and was buried in Town Cemetery, Greenville, Meriwether County, Georgia.

WASH, WILLIAM D. (1832–1863), mathematician and educator, was born in Mississippi in 1832. After graduating from Franklin College (Athens) in 1855 he remained at the college as tutor in mathematics (1856–1858) and adjunct professor of mathematics (1858–1861). At the outbreak of the Civil War he resigned his post and entered Confederate service. On May 14th, 1862, in Chattanooga, Tennessee, he enlisted for three years as a private in Company F, 2nd (Duke's) Kentucky Cavalry. He was captured at Bradyville, Tennessee, on March 1st, 1863, and confined at Camp Butler, Illinois, where he died on March 24th, 1863. A "tribute of respect" paid by the college faculty on June 8th, 1863, quoted the letter of an unnamed friend: "I have often heard it rumored by his comrades that he knew no fear; nor have I any hesitation in saying that he was the bravest man I ever saw. He was as cool in battle as if he knew not what was going on. . . . I have been intimately acquainted with him and take pleasure in bearing testimony to his Christian integrity, nobleness of purpose, and undaunted bravery. Many a time have I heard his full, rich voice in camp, lifted to Heaven in prayer. The high moral tone of his character won him the respect of all." He never married.

WASHINGTON, GEORGE (1732–1799), first president of the United States, eldest son of Augustine Washington and Mary Ball, was born at Wakefield, his father's estate near Popes Creek, Westmoreland County, Virginia, on February 22nd, 1732. After his father's death in 1743 he resided with his elder half-brother, Augustine Washington, at Popes Creek and later with his brother, Lawrence Washington, at Mount Vernon. In 1751 he was appointed adjutant general of his military district, with rank of major; in 1754 he became lieutenant colonel and served in the French and Indian War as aide-de-camp to General Edward Braddock. On January 6th, 1759, he married Martha Dandridge (1731–1802), widow of Daniel Parke Custis, and settled with his wife and her two young children at Mount Vernon. He was a member of the colonial house of burgesses (1758–1774); a member of the First Continental Congress (1774) and the Second Continental Congress (1775); and commander in chief of the American forces throughout the Revolutionary War (1775–1783). He was president of the constitutional convention meeting in Philadelphia (1787) and was unanimously elected first president of the United States (1789–1797). He died at Mount Vernon on December 14th, 1799, and was buried in the family vault. Martha (Dandridge) (Custis) Washington died on May 22nd, 1802, and was buried near her husband.

WATKINS, DAVID GRIFFITH (1812–1887), farmer, butcher, and miller, was born in Wales in 1812. In early manhood he migrated to the United States and settled in Fairfax County, Virginia, where in 1834 he married Elizabeth Ann Tressler (1814–1900), daughter of Peter Tressler, a large landowner in Fairfax County; ten of their children lived to maturity. Prior to the Civil War he was a butcher; he later joined his brother, James H.

Watkins, in the milling business. In addition to his farm, Strawberry Hill, in Fairfax County, he owned a house in the west end of Alexandria; there his children resided during the Civil War, while he remained on his farm, safeguarding his interests and operating his mill; his wife had a pass from the Federal authorities permitting her to come and go. He died at Strawberry Hill on December 18th, 1887, survived by his wife and numerous children, and was buried in the Methodist Cemetery, Alexandria. Elizabeth Ann (Tressler) Watkins died in November 1900 and was buried beside her husband.

WAY, JOSEPH BACON (1830–1857), physician, youngest son of Moses William Way (1794–1831) and his second wife, Elizabeth Bacon, was born in Liberty County, Georgia, on May 7th, 1830. His father, a deacon of Midway Church, died on February 6th, 1831, and eight years later, on February 19th, 1839, his mother married Simeon S. Moody, sheriff of Liberty County. Fatherless in infancy, Joseph Bacon Way became the ward of William Graham Martin (1808–1861), a planter in Liberty County, husband of his maternal aunt, Eliza Sumner Bacon (1815–1889). After attending lectures at Jefferson Medical College (Philadelphia) he studied medicine in Paris; returning to his native county, he practiced medicine in Dorchester, where his patients called him "Dr. Way the younger" to distinguish him from Dr. Samuel Way (1810–1866), also practicing medicine in Liberty County. On December 27th, 1854, he married Mary Jane Martin (1835–1918), daughter of his guardian, described by Mary Sharpe Jones as "a very pretty girl," and said to be "the belle of Liberty County." There was one child. Joseph Bacon Way died in Dorchester on November 27th, 1857, less than three years after his marriage, and was buried in Midway Cemetery. Mary Jane (Martin) Way returned with her child, Josephine Bacon Way (1856–1879), to her father's household. On May 14th, 1866, she became the wife of John Sidney Fleming (1839–1915), son of John Sidney Fleming (1812–1847) and Jane Amarintha Quarterman (1813–1874). Her husband, a Confederate veteran, was a planter in Liberty County. He died in Flemington on April 8th, 1915, and was buried in Flemington Cemetery. Mary Jane (Martin) (Way) Fleming died on May 26th, 1918, and was buried beside her second husband.

WAY, JOSEPH EDGAR (1835–1902), planter and educator, son of William Norman Way (1782–1854) and his second wife, Sarah Sumner Bacon (1807–1882), was born in Walthourville, Liberty County, Georgia, on December 21st, 1835. After attending Franklin College (Athens) for some months with the class of 1855 he graduated from the South Carolina College in 1856. Returning to Liberty County, he engaged in planting until the outbreak of the Civil War. On April 6th, 1858, he married Almira E. Spencer (1836–1872), daughter of William Spencer (1795–1843) and

Mary Boon McGowen (1806–1870), widow of James Stacy. On October 1st, 1861, he enlisted for six months as fourth sergeant in the Liberty Independent Troop (Company G, 5th Regiment Georgia Cavalry). On May 15th, 1862, he enlisted as second lieutenant in the Liberty Mounted Rangers (Company B, 20th Battalion Georgia Cavalry); he was promoted to first lieutenant on February 2nd, 1864. He was wounded at Trevilian's Station, near Louisa Courthouse, Virginia, on June 11th, 1864, and captured near Stony Creek, Virginia, in October 1864. After the war he resided in Savannah, where he was associated with the public schools for thirty-five years, first as teacher and later as principal of the Massie School. He was also for many years ruling elder of the First Presbyterian Church. In 1872 his wife died, leaving four young children. On September 13th, 1893, he married Anna Elizabeth Quarterman (1868–1950), daughter of Alexander Sanford Quarterman (1829–1907) and his second wife, Ann Caroline Quarterman (1836–1905). Joseph Edgar Way died in Savannah on April 26th, 1902, survived by his second wife, and was buried beside his first wife in Flemington Cemetery, Liberty County. Anna Elizabeth (Quarterman) Way died on May 21st, 1950, and was buried beside her husband.

WAY, RICHARD QUARTERMAN (1819–1895), Presbyterian clergyman, son of John Way (1776–1832) and Rebecca Jones, was born in Liberty County, Georgia, on December 20th, 1819. He was a younger brother of Dr. Samuel Way (1810–1866). After studying medicine for three years (1836–1839) at the University of Georgia he graduated from Columbia Theological Seminary in 1843. On June 6th, 1843, he married Susan Caroline Quarterman (1824–1893), daughter of the Rev. Robert Quarterman (1787–1849), pastor of Midway Church, and his third wife, Mary Jemima Way (1801–1841). Late in August 1843 they left Liberty County as missionaries to Ningpo and Shanghai, China; they sailed from Boston on November 18th, 1843, reaching China in November 1844; they sailed home from China in 1858, reaching Savannah on April 17th, 1859, accompanied by six children, all born in China. From 1859 to 1866 Way was employed by the executors of the Lambert estate to preach and minister to the Negroes of Liberty County. For twenty years (1866–1886) he served various churches in Southeast Georgia; in 1886 he removed to Savannah, where he was pastor of the Anderson Street (later Second) Presbyterian Church until his retirement in 1893. Susan Caroline (Quarterman) Way died in Savannah on May 20th, 1893, and was buried in Bonaventure Cemetery. The Rev. Richard Quarterman Way died on August 6th, 1895, survived by five children, and was buried beside his wife.

WAY, SAMUEL (1810–1866), physician, son of John Way (1776–1832) and Rebecca Jones, was born in Liberty County, Georgia, on July 19th, 1810. He was an elder brother of the Rev. Richard Quarterman Way (1819–1895). He attended Franklin College (Athens) with the class of 1832 but did not graduate. For many years he was a respected physician in his native county; he was frequently summoned to attend the illnesses of Negroes at Arcadia, Montevideo, and Maybank, plantations of the Rev. Dr. Charles Colcock Jones. In 1837 he married Olivia Tuckerman Axson (1819–1902), daughter of Dr. Samuel J. T. Axson (1761–1827) and his second wife, Ann Lambright (1781–1854), widow of David James Dicks. He died in Jonesville of "confluent smallpox" on March 17th, 1866, survived by his wife and numerous young children, and was buried in Midway Cemetery. "He was a truly good man," wrote Mrs. Mary Jones on March 19th, 1866; "I feel that I have lost a friend." Olivia Tuckerman (Axson) Way died on November 27th, 1902, and was buried beside her husband.

WAY, WILLIAM JOHN (1826–1902), planter, daguerreotypist, and miller, son of John Norman Way (1795–1827) and Eliza Quarterman Stacy (1800–1868), was born in Liberty County, Georgia, on October 29th, 1826. Several months later, on February 27th, 1827, his father was killed by a stroke of lightning in his thirty-second year. William John Way was for some years prior to the Civil War a rice planter in Liberty County. He also engaged in daguerreotypy, and he later operated a sawmill. During the Civil War he was a private in the Liberty Independent Troop (Company G, 5th Regiment Georgia Cavalry). For some twenty-five years he was an elder of the Flemington Presbyterian Church. He died in Savannah on November 19th, 1902, survived by eight children, and was buried beside his wife, Jane Spivey (1832–1885), in Flemington Cemetery, Liberty County.

WAYNE, HENRY CONSTANTINE (1815–1883), Confederate soldier, son of the Hon. James Moore Wayne (1790–1867) and Mary Johnson Campbell (1794–1889), was born in Savannah, Georgia, on September 8th, 1815. His father, a graduate of the College of New Jersey (Princeton) in 1808, was a member of the state house of representatives (1815–1816), mayor of Savannah (1817–1819), congressman (1829–1835), and associate justice of the supreme court of the United States (1835–1867). Henry Constantine Wayne attended Harvard College for two years (1832–1834) and graduated from the United States Military Academy in 1838. He became second lieutenant in the 4th Artillery (1838), first lieutenant in the 1st Artillery (1842), and captain and quartermaster (1846). He was assistant instructor in military and cavalry tactics at West Point (1841–1846). After the Mexican War (1846–1848) he was brevetted major for gallant and meritorious service. *The Sword Exercise, Arranged for Military Institutions,* by Henry C. Wayne, was published in Washington, D.C., "by authority of the War Department," in 1850. On December 31st, 1860, he resigned his commission, and early in 1861 he was appointed adjutant and inspector general of Georgia. In this capacity he served efficiently and energetically throughout the Civil War. During the Atlanta campaign he was major general of militia, and he subsequently disputed Sherman's march to the sea. After the war he operated a lumber business in Savannah. He was active in politics and later became a Republican. In 1879 he embraced the Roman Catholic faith. He died in Savannah on March 15th, 1883, survived by his second wife, Adelaide Hartridge (1825–1913), and was buried beside his first wife, Mary Louisa Wayne (1821–1873), in Laurel Grove Cemetery.

WAYNE, JAMES MOORE (1790–1867), jurist, son of Richard Wayne and Elizabeth Clifford, was born in Savannah, Georgia, in 1790. After graduating from the College of New Jersey (Princeton) in 1808 he studied law in Savannah and New Haven and commenced practice in Savannah in 1810. On March 4th, 1813, he married Mary Johnson Campbell (1794–1889), daughter of Alexander Campbell, of Richmond, Virginia, and stepdaughter of her mother's second husband, the Rev. Dr. Henry Kollock, a Presbyterian clergyman, professor at the College of New Jersey (Princeton). Mrs. Mary Jones later (June 30th, 1857) pronounced her "a lady of rare intelligence and dignity of manners." There were three children. During the War of 1812 James Moore Wayne served as an officer in the Georgia Hussars. Returning to Georgia, he was a member of the state house of representatives (1815–1816); mayor of Savannah (1817–1819); judge of the court of common pleas of Savannah (1820–1822); judge of the superior court of Savannah (1822–1828); congressman (1829–1835); and associate justice of the supreme court of the United States (1835–1867). He was also president of the Georgia Historical Society (1841–1854; 1856–1862). He received the honorary degree of doctor of laws from the College of New Jersey (Princeton) in 1849. He died in Washington, D.C., on July 5th, 1867, and was buried in Laurel Grove Cemetery, Savannah. Thereafter his wife resided in Morristown, New Jersey, where she died on July 23rd, 1889. She was buried beside her husband. On July 16th, 1830, the Rev. Dr. Charles Colcock Jones wrote from Washington: "I heard Judge Wayne make a speech—not very long, to be sure. He is a most *miserable* speaker. His voice is on a high key; he labors to get it out; fairly squeaks; very little force." Wayne's charge to the grand jury in the *Wanderer* case (1859) is reprinted in *The Georgia Historical Quarterly,* II, 87–113 (June 1918).

WAYNE, RICHARD (1804–1858), physician, son of Richard Wayne (1771–1822) and Julianna Smyth (1781–1807), was born in Savannah, Georgia, on April 25th, 1804. His mother died in childbirth on April 25th, 1807, his third birthday; his father, a merchant, and foreman of the Savannah Fire Department, died from injuries sustained at a fire late in December 1822 and was buried on New Year's

Day 1823. His father was an elder brother of the Hon. James Moore Wayne (1790–1867), associate justice of the supreme court of the United States (1835–1867). His elder sister, Elizabeth Clifford Wayne (1803–1864), was the wife of William Neff (1792–1856), Cincinnati merchant. Richard Wayne graduated from Union College (Schenectady, New York) in 1825 and attended lectures at Jefferson Medical College (Philadelphia). For some years he was surgeon in the United States army, stationed at Oglethorpe Cantonment in Savannah. He subsequently resigned his commission and entered private practice in his native city. On January 14th, 1830, he married Henrietta Jane Harden (1809–1880), of Savannah; there were three daughters. He held many posts of honor and trust in Savannah: he served three terms as alderman and six terms as mayor; and he also represented Chatham County in the state legislature. He died in Savannah on June 27th, 1858, while holding the office of mayor, and was buried with civil and military honors in Laurel Grove Cemetery. "In his profession he was assiduous alike to the exalted and the humble," observed the Savannah *Republican* (June 28th, 1858), "and we may say with truth, the poor of Savannah have lost in his death a true friend." Henrietta Jane (Harden) Wayne died on October 5th, 1880, and was buried beside her husband.

WEBB, WILLIAM C. (1825–1914), physician, son of Dr. James W. Webb, also a physician, was born in Hillsboro, North Carolina, on September 6th, 1825. After graduating from Jefferson Medical College (Philadelphia) in 1849 he settled in St. Louis, Missouri, where except for an absence of three years during the Civil War he practiced medicine until his retirement in 1904. On October 2nd, 1856, he married Mary Ann Castleman (1836–1902), sixth child of David Castleman (1786–1852), of Castleton farm, Fayette County, Kentucky. During the Civil War he was surgeon of the 12th Regiment Missouri Cavalry; he enlisted at Orange Courthouse, Virginia, on August 18th, 1862, and was assigned to duty on February 7th, 1863; he was stationed at Forsyth, Georgia, in the spring of 1864. After the war he resumed practice in St. Louis. According to the St. Louis *Republican* (January 22nd, 1914), "He achieved distinction in two cholera epidemics and one of smallpox in St. Louis in the late sixties and the early seventies." He was a founding member of the St. Louis Medical Society and served as president in 1856; he was also a member of the American Medical Association. For many years he was an elder in the Grand Avenue Presbyterian Church. Mary Ann (Castleman) Webb died in Buck Hill Falls, Pennsylvania, on August 13th, 1902, and was buried in Bellefontaine Cemetery, St. Louis. William C. Webb died in St. Louis on January 21st, 1914, survived by five children, and was buried beside his wife.

WEBSTER, DANIEL (1782–1852), statesman, son of Ebenezer Webster and Abigail Eastman, was born in Salisbury, New Hampshire, on January 18th, 1782. His father, captain in the militia during the Revolutionary War, subsequently became colonel in the state militia and served in the state legislature. Daniel Webster attended Phillips Exeter Academy and graduated from Dartmouth College in 1801. He studied law and commenced practice in Boscawen, New Hampshire, in 1805, removing to Portsmouth in 1807; he was congressman from New Hampshire (1813–1817). In 1816 he removed to Boston, Massachusetts, where he was elected delegate to the state constitutional convention in 1820. He was congressman from Massachusetts (1823–1827); United States senator (1827–1841); secretary of state under Presidents William Henry Harrison and John Tyler (1841–1843); United States senator (1845–1850); and secretary of state under President Millard Fillmore (1850–1852). Throughout his long public career he advocated national unity; he opposed slavery, but his first loyalty was to the Constitution, which recognized slavery; hence his resolution not to interfere with the institution but to discourage its spread by every constitutional means. He was one of the outstanding leaders of the United States prior to the Civil War; according to the Rev. Dr. Charles Colcock Jones (June 12th, 1857) he was one of "the first three," the other two being Henry Clay (1777–1852) of Kentucky and John C. Calhoun (1782–1850) of South Carolina. Webster married first (in 1808) Grace Fletcher; he married second (in 1829) Caroline LeRoy. He died in Marshfield, Massachusetts, on October 24th, 1852, and was buried in Winslow Cemetery.

WEIR, WILLIAM J. (1792–1867), farmer, was born in Virginia in 1792. His first wife, Harriet Bladen Mitchell (1793–1841), daughter of Robert Mitchell and Priscilla Carter, inherited 1660 acres of the Lower Bull Run Tract in Prince William County, Virginia, originally owned by her grandfather, Councillor Robert Carter of Nomini Hall, Westmoreland County. On this land, about 1825, William J. Weir erected his house, Liberia, "a fine family mansion of brick," situated on the Centreville road a mile or so from Tudor Hall (later Manassas). Harriet Bladen (Mitchell) Weir died at Liberia on July 14th, 1841, survived by her husband and nine of her thirteen children, and was buried in the family cemetery to the west of the house. By 1850 William J. Weir had married Louisa Ball (born 1797), daughter of Spencer Ball and Elizabeth Landon Carter, and granddaughter of Councillor Robert Carter of Nomini Hall. On June 1st, 1861, General Beauregard, arriving in Manassas to assume command of the Army of the Potomac, made Liberia his headquarters; he remained in the house until early September. Subsequently, on September 30th, 1861, the Rev. John Jones, a Presbyterian chaplain from Georgia, seeking accommodation for his wife and two little boys, approached William J. Weir, "an interesting old Virginian, who after much persuasion agreed to board us for an indefinite number of days." In November 1862 General Daniel E. Sickles, commanding a division of the Union army, made Liberia his headquarters; Lincoln, it is said, visited the house twice. After the war William J. Weir settled at Union Hall, a plantation in Fluvanna County, Virginia; he died there on May 8th, 1867, and was buried beside his first wife at Liberia.

WELLS, CHARLTON HENRY (1822–1854), physician, son of Dr. Thomas Wells (1792–1874) and his first wife, Eliza Ann Clark (1798–1834), was born in Columbia, South Carolina, on October 17th, 1822. His father, a native of Walpole, New Hampshire, had settled in Columbia soon after receiving his medical degree from Dartmouth College in 1817. After attending Brown University for two years (1840–1842) Charlton Henry Wells graduated from the College of Physicians and Surgeons (New York) in 1846. Returning South, he practiced his profession in Macon, Georgia (1846–1851) and in Columbia, South Carolina (1851–1853). On November 1st, 1849, he married Mary Elizabeth King (1827–1871), eldest child of Roswell King (1796–1854) and Julia Rebecca Maxwell (1808–1892), of South Hampton plantation, Liberty County, Georgia. In the summer of 1853 he settled in Savannah, where he enjoyed a growing practice until his sudden death of yellow fever on September 12th, 1854. He was buried temporarily in Laurel Grove Cemetery and subsequently removed to Midway Cemetery, Liberty County. From all accounts he was a man of rare qualities. "We have seen a good deal of him this summer," wrote Mrs. Mary Jones on September 14th, 1854, "and a more lovely character is seldom met with: talented and accomplished in his profession, pure-minded, gentle, and affectionate, tender and devoted in all the relations of life, reflecting peace and happiness. Who could fail to love and admire one so truly amiable, accomplished, and gentlemanly? Long will his many virtues be cherished in the hearts of his friends and relatives." His wife returned to Liberty County to live in the household of her newly widowed mother. She died in Walthourville on November 6th, 1871, and was buried beside her husband in Midway Cemetery.

WELLS, J. HORACE (1828–1883), daguerreotypist and photographer, was born in New York City in 1828. He was no relation of Dr. Thomas Wells (1792–1874), physician of New Haven, Connecticut. In early manhood he removed to New Haven, where in association with his brother, Henry M. Wells, he established extensive "daguerreau rooms" in Mitchell's Building in Chapel Street. "We call particular attention to the new style of daguerreotype in oil, with which we have had very great success. We can produce by this process a truthfulness to life that it is hopeless to attempt to obtain by any other style of painting. We at all times execute anything and everything connected with our art, in a manner not to be surpassed and at prices that shall suit; which we invite all to call and prove to their satisfaction and our profit" (*New Haven City Directory*, 1854–1855, p. 297). "Mr. Wells has, during the past six years, fully established the reputation for taking daguerreotypes equal if not superior to those taken by the first artists of our large cities. He has kept pace with every improvement that has tended to elevate the art to its present proud position as the most beautiful, true, and accurate manner by which likenesses of dear friends may be preserved when the original is far away. Mr. Wells would particularly call the attention of the public to the fact that he has lately introduced the new and beautiful science of photography, which in its splendid results is attracting the attention of scientific men of all countries. Pictures taken by this process are without the reflection of a daguerreotype and can be viewed in any light. Daguerreotypes of deceased or absent friends can be enlarged and copied in a perfectly natural manner by this process, and colored either in oil or watercolors. Everybody is invited to call and examine likenesses of our prominent men, now on exhibition at the rooms of the subscriber" (*New Haven City Directory*, 1855–1856, opposite p. 226). According to the New Haven *Union* (August 24th, 1883), J. Horace Wells was the first man to take daguerreotypes by electric light; at "the college laboratory" he and William A. Beers conducted experiments in which, "by using forty batteries and charcoal points, good pictures were for the first time made." In 1855 Henry M. Wells retired from the business; thereafter the firm was known successively as Wells & Collins (David C. Collins), Wells & Delamater (Richard S. Delamater), and Wells & Stevens (Orrin S. Stevens). Evidently the business declined: for some months in 1866–1867 J. Horace Wells worked as a conductor on the Hartford Railroad. In 1870 he removed to Hartford, where he resumed photography but never repeated his former success; in his later years he suffered from want and poor health. He never married. He died in Hartford on August 23rd, 1883. As the New Haven *Union* (August 24th, 1883) observed, "He was a very intelligent man, a great reader, and his manners were exceedingly agreeable. . . . There are many who will learn with regret that the last years of so sensible and pleasant a gentleman were passed without much enjoyment, and that the death was more lonely than is usual in cases of men who have in their best years done well."

WELLS, JOHN ROBESON (1823–1867), planter, son of Dr. Thomas Wells (1792–1874) and his first wife, Eliza Ann Clark (1798–1834), was born in Columbia, South Carolina, in 1823. His father, a native of Walpole, New Hampshire, had settled in Columbia soon after receiving his medical degree from Dartmouth College in 1817. His mother died on August 27th, 1834, and his father married second (in 1836) Jane Elizabeth Bucklin (1814–1898), a native of Rhode Island. In 1846 his father removed with his family to New Haven, Connecticut, which was his principal residence for the rest of his life. In 1850 John Robeson Wells was living in the New Haven household of his father, engaged in manufacturing. His elder brother, Dr. Charlton Henry Wells (1822–1854), died of yellow fever in Savannah, Georgia, on September 12th, 1854; in March 1855 John Robeson Wells removed to Liberty County, Georgia, and became an inmate of the family of Roswell King, whose daughter, Mary Elizabeth King (1827–1871), was his brother's widow. For the rest of his life he made his home with the Kings, managing their business affairs and engaging their affectionate regard. "No friend or brother could be more devoted than Mr. Wells," wrote Mrs. Mary Jones in October 1860. "His industry and attention to business at Woodville could not be surpassed." At the outbreak of the Civil War he enlisted as a private in the Savannah Volunteer Guards (Company A, 18th Battalion Georgia Infantry); he fought with this company throughout the war. In June 1865 he visited his family in New Haven; returning to Georgia, he took a position with the Atlantic & Gulf Railroad in Liberty County. He died in Walthourville, Liberty County, of "congestion of the brain" on July 8th, 1867, and was buried near his elder brother in Midway Cemetery.

WELLS, MARIA CLARK (1831–1908), daughter of Dr. Thomas Wells (1792–1874) and his first wife, Eliza Ann Clark (1798–1834), was born in Columbia, South Carolina, on March 17th, 1831. Her father, a native of Walpole, New Hampshire, had settled in Columbia soon after receiving his medical degree from Dartmouth College in 1817. Her mother died on August 27th, 1834, and her father married second (in 1836) Jane Elizabeth Bucklin (1814–1898), a native of Rhode Island. Maria Clark Wells spent her girlhood in Columbia; in 1846 she removed with her parents to New Haven, Connecticut, which was her father's principal residence for the rest of his life. In August 1854 she sailed with her family to Europe; early in 1856, in Leghorn, Italy, she became the wife of Dr. Richard Cresson Stiles (1830–1873), of West Chester, Pennsylvania, a graduate of Yale College (1851) and the Medical College of the University of Pennsylvania (1854). Her husband was professor of physiology and pathology in the Medical Department of the University of Vermont (1857–1858) and professor of physiology in the Berkshire Medical College, Pittsfield, Massachusetts (1858–1862). During the Civil War he was surgeon in the United States army for two years (1862–1864). He then settled in Brooklyn, New York, where he was resident physician at King's County Hospital (1864–1870). In 1870 he suffered a mental collapse from which he never recovered. After traveling in Europe in 1872 he returned to his mother's residence in West Chester, where he died of pneumonia on April 16th, 1873. Thereafter Maria (Wells) Stiles resided in New Haven, where she died on January 5th, 1908, survived by her only son, Thomas Wells Stiles;

she was buried beside her husband in West Chester, Pennsylvania.

WELLS, MARY ELIZABETH (KING) (1827–1871): *Mrs. Charlton Henry Wells,* eldest child of Roswell King (1796–1854) and Julia Rebecca Maxwell (1808–1892), was born in Liberty County, Georgia, on January 22nd, 1827. According to her girlhood friend, Mary Sharpe Jones (December 14th, 1857), she was "a very amusing person," though "very odd in some things." She was known for her merry laugh and lively repartee, and was said to be "as gay as a lark and at the head of all mischief and fun," even though she had "little health to enjoy anything" and suffered continually from headaches. On November 1st, 1849, at South Hampton plantation, she became the wife of Dr. Charlton Henry Wells (1822–1854), son of Dr. Thomas Wells (1792–1874), of New Haven, Connecticut, and his first wife, Eliza Ann Clark (1798–1834). Charlton Henry Wells, a graduate of the College of Physicians and Surgeons (New York) in 1846, practiced his profession in Macon, Georgia (1846–1851) and in Columbia, South Carolina (1851–1853). In the summer of 1853 he settled in Savannah, where he died suddenly of yellow fever on September 12th, 1854. He was buried temporarily in Laurel Grove Cemetery and subsequently removed to Midway Cemetery, Liberty County. To "his poor afflicted wife" his death was a stunning blow. "I felt deeply interested for her," wrote Mrs. Sarah Ann Howe, a family friend, on October 31st, 1854, "knowing how she loved him with the most uncontrolled affection." Mary Elizabeth (King) Wells returned to Liberty County to live in the household of her newly widowed mother. In March 1867, suffering the "hard labor and vexations and trials" of a shattered postwar world, she and her mother joined the household of her brother, Roswell King (1836–1911), in Walthourville. "Mary Wells lives with Ross and does everything for the children," wrote Mrs. Mary Jones on January 8th, 1869; "she says she never was happier in her life, although she has not a dollar she can command of her own; works hard, sleeps well, has no headaches now; and God blesses her with a grateful, cheerful spirit." She died in Walthourville on November 6th, 1871, and was buried beside her husband in Midway Cemetery.

WELLS, THOMAS (1792–1874), physician, was born in Walpole, New Hampshire, on April 4th, 1792. After receiving his medical degree from Dartmouth College in 1817 he settled in Columbia, South Carolina, where he practiced his profession for nearly thirty years. In 1820 he married Eliza Ann Clark (1798–1834); six children survived infancy. She died in Columbia on August 27th, 1834, and was buried in the First Presbyterian Churchyard. In 1836 he married Jane Elizabeth Bucklin (1814–1898); three children survived infancy. It was during his two-year residence in Columbia (1837–1838) that the Rev. Dr. Charles Colcock Jones became an intimate friend of Dr.

Wells, "in whose opinion we have great confidence," he wrote on January 20th, 1853—especially his opinion "touching the influence of climate." A son of Dr. Wells, born in 1838, was named Charles Jones Wells in recognition of the friendship. Thomas Wells was elected elder of the First Presbyterian Church, Columbia, in 1824. In 1846 he removed with his family to New Haven, Connecticut, which was his principal residence for the rest of his life. On April 15th, 1853, he wrote Dr. Jones: "I am laboring under serious organic lesion of the tissues of the lungs and general debility, and the atmosphere of New Haven does not agree with me. I want a more equable and dryer atmosphere, and may be induced to seek it in a foreign land." In August 1854 he sailed with his family to Europe, where he traveled for four years, living successively in Paris, Heidelberg, and Florence; he returned to New Haven in the summer of 1858. Two of his sons, Charlton Henry Wells (1822–1854) and William Lowndes Wells (1829–1917), were physicians; his daughter, Maria Clark Wells (1831–1908), became a physician's wife. He died in New Haven on September 28th, 1874. Jane Elizabeth (Bucklin) Wells died in New Haven on November 2nd, 1898.

WELLS, WILLIAM LOWNDES (1829–1917), physician, son of Dr. Thomas Wells (1792–1874) and his first wife, Eliza Ann Clark (1798–1834), was born in Columbia, South Carolina, in 1829. His father, a native of Walpole, New Hampshire, had settled in Columbia soon after receiving his medical degree from Dartmouth College in 1817. His mother died on August 27th, 1834, and his father married second (in 1836) Jane Elizabeth Bucklin (1814–1898), a native of Rhode Island. After graduating from the College of New Jersey (Princeton) in 1850 and from the College of Physicians and Surgeons (New York) in 1852 he spent four years (1854–1858) with his parents in Europe, where he continued his medical studies at the University of Heidelberg. During the Civil War he was a surgeon in the Union army. After the war he settled in Liberty County, Georgia, home of John Robeson Wells, his elder brother, and of Mary Elizabeth (King) Wells, widow of Charlton Henry Wells, his eldest brother. "He was a surgeon in the Federal army!" wrote Mrs. Mary Jones on January 17th, 1866. "I feel that we want our own men to fill posts of honor and profit—not those who have brought us to grief and ruin." At the sudden death of John Robeson Wells on July 8th, 1867, he was "overwhelmed with grief." As Mrs. Susan M. Cumming wrote (July 11th, 1867), "He says he has nothing to live for now—he came South to be with John. It was touching to see his demonstrations of affection for him—and the softening of that formal exclusive manner to all." For five more years he remained in the South. "Dr. Wells is still at Walthourville," wrote Mrs. Laura E. Buttolph (July 17th, 1866), "winning golden opinions by his skill in the healing art. And he has been to Savannah to assist in some

difficult cases." In 1872 he removed to New Rochelle, New York, where he practiced medicine for twenty-five years. In 1897 he retired from practice. He died of pneumonia in New Rochelle on August 17th, 1917, survived by his wife, Marion Sturges, of Southport, Connecticut.

WEST, BENJAMIN (1738–1820), painter, youngest son of John West and his second wife, Sarah Pearson, was born near Springfield, Pennsylvania, on October 10th, 1738. After studying briefly at the College of Philadelphia with the class of 1757 he resided in New York City until 1760, when he sailed for Italy. In 1763 he settled in London, where he flourished as a portrait painter, gained the friendship of Sir Joshua Reynolds, and enjoyed the patronage of George III. He never returned to America. On September 2nd, 1764, he married Elizabeth Shewell, daughter of Stephen Shewell, a Philadelphia merchant. He was history painter to George III (1772–1801) and a charter member of the Royal Academy (1768); in 1792 he succeeded Reynolds as president of the Royal Academy, a position he held, with the exception of one year, until 1820. "The Death of Wolfe" (1771), depicting military figures in contemporary dress rather than in classic drapery, revolutionized British historical painting. Elizabeth (Shewell) West died in London on December 6th, 1814. West died in London on March 11th, 1820, and was buried with signal honors in St. Paul's Cathedral. One of his finest historical pictures, "Penn's Treaty with the Indians," now hangs in Independence Hall, Philadelphia.

WEST, CHARLES (1790–1855), physician, son of William West and Hannah Sharpe, was born at Myrtle Grove, his father's plantation in Liberty County, Georgia, on November 19th, 1790. After his father's death he became a ward of his first cousin, Joseph Jones (1779–1846), a rich planter in Liberty County. He graduated from the Medical College of the University of Pennsylvania in 1812. On January 27th, 1814, at Manchester plantation, McIntosh County, Georgia, he married Sarah Evelyn Nephew (1796–1854), daughter of James Nephew and his first wife, Mary Margaret Gignilliat. There were ten children: Charles William West (1815–1860); Hannah Eliza West (1817–1837), wife of David Anderson; Mary Catherine West (1821–1847), wife of Henry Holcombe Tucker; Susan Caroline West (1819–1827); James Nephew West (1823–1875); Elizabeth Munro West (1824–1844); Clifford Amanda Stiles West (1827–1890), wife of John Hawkins Powers; Sarah Evelyn West (1830–1847); Joseph Jones West (1832–1869); and Maria Louisa West (1835–1910), wife of Dr. Julius Caesar Gilbert. After practicing medicine for some years in Liberty County Dr. Charles West removed with his family to Perry, Houston County, Georgia, in the early 1840s. There he practiced medicine for more than a decade. Sarah Evelyn (Nephew) West died in Perry on August 19th, 1854, and was buried in Rose Hill Cemetery,

Macon. Dr. Charles West died in Saratoga Springs, New York, on September 9th, 1855, and was buried beside his wife.

WEST, CHARLES NEPHEW (1844–1900), lawyer, son of Dr. Charles William West (1815–1860) and Eliza Alice Whitehead (1818–1896), was born in Macon, Georgia, on August 31st, 1844. He spent his boyhood in Savannah, where his father was a prominent physician. In February 1860 he entered the College of New Jersey (Princeton) as an advanced sophomore. His father died on June 4th, 1860. In November 1860, after the election of Lincoln, he was called home by his mother in the middle of his junior year; entering Franklin College (Athens), he graduated in 1862. On April 22nd, 1862, he enlisted as a private in the Savannah Volunteer Guards (Company B, 18th Battalion Georgia Infantry); on October 10th, 1862, he was detailed on signal and telegraphic service. He was paroled at Augusta, Georgia, on May 24th, 1865. After the war he taught school and studied law; he practiced his profession in Savannah (1869–1877), Baltimore (1877–1883), and Savannah (1883–1900). On November 29th, 1869, he married Mary C. Cheves, eldest daughter of Langdon Cheves (1814–1863) and Charlotte Lorraine McCord (1819–1879); there were four children. For many years he was a zealous member of the Georgia Historical Society; *A Brief Sketch of the Life and Writings of Sidney Lanier*, an address which he delivered before the society on December 5th, 1887, was published in Savannah in 1888; *The Life and Times of William Harris Crawford*, an address which he delivered before the society on May 2nd, 1892, was published in Providence, Rhode Island, later the same year. He received the honorary degree of master of arts from the College of New Jersey (Princeton) in 1872. He died in Eureka Springs, Arkansas, on June 29th, 1900, survived by his wife and four children, and was buried in Laurel Grove Cemetery, Savannah. "Roman Men of Note," a brief manuscript executed by Charles Nephew West, is preserved among the Jones papers at Tulane University; it is superscribed in the handwriting of the Rev. Dr. Charles Colcock Jones: "C. N. West's Composition on Distinguished Men of Roman and Grecian History, Summer of 1859." A noble letter written by Dr. Jones on January 24th, 1860, directed to young West on the eve of his departure for Princeton, is preserved among the Jones papers at the University of Georgia; the letter, executed in the handwriting of Charles Colcock Jones, Jr., is superscribed: "Copied by me from the original in the possession of C. N. West, who prizes it so dearly that he was unwilling to part with it. January 3rd, 1864."

WEST, CHARLES WILLIAM (1815–1860), physician, eldest son of Dr. Charles West (1790–1855) and Sarah Evelyn Nephew (1796–1854), was born in Savannah, Georgia, on January 19th, 1815. He was a brother of James Nephew West (1823–1875); Clifford Amanda Stiles West (1827–1890), wife of John Hawkins Powers; Dr. Joseph Jones West (1832–1869); and Maria Louisa West (1835–1910), wife of Dr. Julius Caesar Gilbert. After graduating from Franklin College (Athens) in 1835 he practiced medicine for several years in Augusta. On October 22nd, 1840, in Bath, Richmond County, Georgia, he married Eliza Alice Whitehead (1818–1896), daughter of John Whitehead (1783–1857) and his first wife, Abigail Lewis Sturges (1798–1824). Eliza Alice (Whitehead) West was a half-sister of John Randolph Whitehead (1829–1877); Julia Amanda Whitehead (1831–1896), wife of Dr. John Gordon Howard; Philoclea Edgeworth Whitehead (1833–1892), wife of Thomas William Neely; Charles Lowndes Whitehead (1835–1866); Ruth Berrien Whitehead (1837–1861), first wife of Charles Colcock Jones, Jr.; and Valeria Burroughs Whitehead (1840–1904), wife of Augustus Ramon Salas. After his marriage West removed to Savannah, where for twenty years he enjoyed a large and lucrative practice. In 1852 he was one of eight founders of the Savannah Medical College, and he was for eight years (1852–1860) its professor of chemistry. He was an elder of the First Presbyterian Church (1852–1860). He died in Newton, Baker County, Georgia, probably of accidental poisoning, on June 4th, 1860, leaving a wife and nine children, and was buried in Laurel Grove Cemetery, Savannah. "I view the death of Dr. West as one of the greatest calamities that has befallen the city," wrote Mrs. Mary Jones on July 26th, 1860, "ministering as he did especially—with so much skill and kindness—to weak and suffering women and children." Eliza Alice (Whitehead) West died in Asheville, North Carolina, at the residence of her son, William Whitehead West, on December 31st, 1896, survived by eight children, and was buried beside her parents and near her one full sister in Bath Presbyterian Churchyard, Richmond County, Georgia.

WEST, JAMES NEPHEW (1823–1875), planter, son of Dr. Charles West (1790–1855) and Sarah Evelyn Nephew (1796–1854), was born at Ceylon plantation, McIntosh County, Georgia, on April 5th, 1823. He was a brother of Dr. Charles William West (1815–1860); Clifford Amanda Stiles West (1827–1890), wife of John Hawkins Powers; Dr. Joseph Jones West (1832–1869); and Maria Louisa West (1835–1910), wife of Dr. Julius Caesar Gilbert. He graduated from Franklin College (Athens) in 1842. On September 16th, 1846, in Fayette County, Kentucky, he married Isabella Atchison (1828–1888), daughter of Hamilton Atchison (1799–1842) and Sarah Rossiter (1811–1870); there were ten children. After his marriage he resided at Bellevue (formerly and subsequently called Mount Brilliant), a handsome classical mansion situated on an eminence near Russell's Cave, some six miles north of Lexington, Kentucky. The house was built by William Russell (1758–1825), a native of Culpeper County, Virginia, who had settled in Fayette County shortly after the

Revolutionary War. As a Kentuckian with Southern sympathies West was driven from his home early in the Civil War and separated from his family. On April 16th, 1863, he was appointed captain and provost marshal of military courts in the Department of East Tennessee; he was stationed successively at Knoxville, Bristol, and Abingdon. After the war he resumed planting in Fayette County. He died at Bellevue on April 12th, 1875, survived by his wife and ten children, and was buried in Lexington Cemetery. Isabella (Atchison) West died on October 27th, 1888, and was buried beside her husband.

WEST, JOSEPH JONES (1832–1869), physician, son of Dr. Charles West (1790–1855) and Sarah Evelyn Nephew (1796–1854), was born in Walthourville, Liberty County, Georgia, on March 17th, 1832. He was a brother of Dr. Charles William West (1815–1860); James Nephew West (1823–1875); Clifford Amanda Stiles West (1827–1890), wife of John Hawkins Powers; and Maria Louisa West (1835–1910), wife of Dr. Julius Caesar Gilbert. In childhood he accompanied his parents to Perry, Houston County, Georgia, where his father practiced medicine until his death in 1855. After graduating from Oglethorpe University in 1851 he attended lectures at the Medical College of the University of Pennsylvania before returning to Savannah to complete his studies and receive his degree from the Savannah Medical College in 1854. For one year (1856–1857) he studied medicine in Paris. On July 16th, 1857, having already sued unsuccessfully for the hand of his cousin, Mary Sharpe Jones, two years before, he married Anna Munro Rogers (1836–1886), eldest daughter of the Rev. Charles William Rogers (1809–1861) and Caroline Matilda Woodford (1813–1886), of Savannah and Bryan County. He continued medical practice until the outbreak of the Civil War. On July 3rd, 1861, he was elected captain of the Oglethorpe Light Infantry (Company B, 8th Regiment Georgia Infantry); after fighting at First Manassas (July 21st, 1861) he returned to Georgia and resigned his commission; he later became surgeon of the 22nd Battalion Siege Artillery. After the war he resumed medical practice in Savannah. He died suddenly on December 30th, 1869, and was buried in Laurel Grove Cemetery. Anna Munro (Rogers) West died in Nashville, Tennessee, on May 19th, 1886, and was buried beside her husband.

WEST, LAURA MAXWELL (1854–1908), daughter of Dr. Charles William West (1815–1860) and Eliza Alice Whitehead (1818–1896), was born in Savannah, Georgia, on December 3rd, 1854. She was named for her father's cousin, Laura Elizabeth Maxwell (1824–1903), wife of the Rev. David Lyman Buttolph. She never married. She died in Palmetto, Campbell (now Fulton) County, Georgia, on December 2nd, 1908 (not, as her tombstone indicates, on December 3rd, 1908) and was buried the following day (her fiftyfourth birthday) in Rose Hill Cemetery, Macon.

WEST, WILLIAM WHITEHEAD (1842–1923), real estate agent, son of Dr. Charles William West (1815–1860) and Eliza Alice Whitehead (1818–1896), was born in Macon, Georgia, on November 21st, 1842. After a boyhood spent in Savannah, where his father was a prominent physician, "Willie White" entered the Virginia Military Institute in the autumn of 1859. His father died on June 4th, 1860. In November 1860, after the election of Lincoln, he was called home by his mother, and he consequently never graduated. At the outbreak of the Civil War he served for several months as a private in Company C, 1st Regiment Georgia Infantry. On August 1st, 1861, at Waynesboro, Georgia, he enlisted as second corporal in the Poythress Volunteers (Captain W. S. C. Morris' Company), later designated Company E (Infantry Battalion), Cobb's Legion Georgia Volunteers. He subsequently became first corporal (November 1861), first sergeant (December 1862), sergeant major (June 1863), and acting adjutant (December 1864). For several years after the war he resided with his mother in Savannah, engaged as a clerk in a commission house. On October 26th, 1875, in Philadelphia, Pennsylvania, he married Sarah Burd Shippen (1854–1934), daughter of Edward Shippen (1823–1904) and Augusta Twiggs (1825–1909); there were seven children. In 1883 he removed to Asheville, North Carolina, where he resided for more than thirty years, engaging in the real estate business and serving for a time as president of the school board. In 1919 he and his wife returned to Philadelphia. He died in Philadelphia at the residence of his son, Dr. Charles William West, on February 12th, 1923, survived by three sons and two daughters, and was buried in Laurel Hill Cemetery. Sarah Burd (Shippen) West died in Philadelphia on December 20th, 1934, and was buried beside her husband.

WHEAT, CHATHAM ROBERDEAU (1826–1862), Confederate soldier, son of the Rev. John Thomas Wheat, an Episcopal clergyman, and Selina Blair Patten, was born in Alexandria, Virginia, on April 9th, 1826. In early infancy he removed with his parents to New Orleans, where he was educated in the public schools. After graduating from the University of Nashville in 1845 he began the study of law in Memphis. At the outbreak of the Mexican War he became lieutenant of a company of dragoons; he was later detailed as captain commanding the bodyguard of General Winfield Scott, from whom he received commendation. Returning to New Orleans, he completed the study of law and commenced practice in 1849. He soon rose to prominence and in 1853 represented New Orleans in the state legislature. During the 1850s he fought as colonel in the Cuban war for independence, served for a time as general of artillery in the Mexican army, and fought under Garibaldi in the Italian war for independence. At the outbreak of the Civil War he recruited a battalion of cavalry, five hundred strong, known as the

Louisiana Tigers. He fought brilliantly at First Manassas (July 21st, 1861), but he was severely wounded when a ball pierced both his lungs. Once recovered, he rejoined his command, then attached to the army of Stonewall Jackson in the Valley of Virginia. He was killed at the head of his troops in the battle of Gaines's Mill, near Richmond, on June 27th, 1862. "Bury me on the field, boys!" he exclaimed at the moment of death. In 1863 his remains were transferred to Hollywood Cemetery, Richmond. He never married.

WHEATON, JOHN FRANCIS (1822–1898), lumber merchant, Confederate soldier, and insurance agent, son of William N. Whedon (1797–1882), a sea captain, was born in Guilford, Connecticut, on January 22nd, 1822. He later changed his name from *Whedon* to *Wheaton*. In 1848 he married Anna M. Spinning (1828–1906), of Bridgeport, Connecticut. Four years later he removed with his wife and son to Savannah, Georgia, where he resided for the rest of his life. Prior to the Civil War he engaged in the lumber business. On May 1st, 1856, he joined the Chatham Artillery; according to the Savannah *Morning News* (June 1st, 1898), he was "one of its ruling spirits in all the subsequent events and episodes of the corps, in parades, celebrations at home, and excursions and adventures abroad." On July 31st, 1861, he entered Confederate service as sergeant in the Chatham Artillery; subsequently he became orderly sergeant (March 14th, 1862) and junior first lieutenant (May 16th, 1862); on December 18th, 1862, he succeeded Joseph Samuel Claghorn as captain. He continued in command until May 14th, 1865, when the company was disbanded at Hamburg, South Carolina. At the reorganization of the Chatham Artillery on January 19th, 1872, Wheaton was unanimously elected captain, and he continued in command until his resignation for reasons of health on June 3rd, 1895. In 1886 he projected and organized the centennial celebration of the corps—"undeniably the greatest military celebration that has ever occurred in Savannah; and the presence of the late president of the Confederacy, Jefferson Davis, lent luster to the occasion" (Savannah *Morning News,* May 10th, 1898). After the war Wheaton was associated for eight years (1865–1873) with Frederick W. Sims in the firm of F. W. Sims & Company, cotton factors and commission merchants; he later engaged for some twenty-five years (1873–1898) in the insurance business. He served three terms as mayor of Savannah (1876–1882) and was collector of the port of Savannah under President Grover Cleveland (1885–1889). He died in New York City on May 9th, 1898, survived by his wife and two children, and was buried in Bonaventure Cemetery, Savannah. As the Savannah *Republican* (February 24th, 1872) observed, "a more gallant soldier never drew a sword in defense of the South." Anna (Spinning) Wheaton died in Bridgeport, Connecticut, on May 25th, 1906, and was buried beside her husband.

WHEELER, JOSEPH (1836–1906), Confederate soldier, son of Joseph Wheeler and Julia Knox Hull, was born near Augusta, Georgia, on September 10th, 1836. He graduated from the United States Military Academy in 1859. On April 22nd, 1861, he resigned his commission to become first lieutenant of artillery in the Confederate army. On September 4th, 1861, he was appointed colonel of the 19th Regiment Alabama Infantry; during the next three years he became successively brigadier general (October 1862), major general (January 1863), and lieutenant general (February 1865). He participated prominently in the battles of Shiloh, Murfreesboro, and Chickamauga and disputed Sherman's progress from Atlanta to Savannah and finally to Raleigh. General Lee ranked "Fighting Joe" Wheeler and "Jeb" Stuart as the two outstanding cavalry leaders in Confederate service. After the war he was a commission merchant in New Orleans. On February 8th, 1866, he married Daniella (Jones) Sherrod, a widow, daughter of Richard Jones, of Alabama; there were seven children. In 1868 he settled in Wheeler, Alabama, where he planted cotton and practiced law. He later entered politics and served as congressman from Alabama (1881–1882, 1883, 1885–1900). He died in Brooklyn Heights, New York, on January 25th, 1906, and was buried in Arlington National Cemetery, Fort Myer, Virginia.

WHEELER, NATHANIEL (1820–1893), inventor and sewing machine manufacturer, son of David Wheeler and Sarah De Forest, was born in Watertown, Connecticut, on September 7th, 1820. In youth he learned carriage building in his father's shop, and after his father's retirement in 1841 he conducted the business successfully for five years, at the same time engaging in the manufacture of metalware. In 1851 he joined Allen Benjamin Wilson (1824–1888) in the firm of Wheeler, Wilson & Company and commenced the manufacture of Wilson's newly patented sewing machine in Watertown. The enterprise was an immediate success; Wheeler superintended business arrangements while Wilson perfected his invention. Fundamental among Wilson's numerous subsequent improvements was the four-motion feed, patented on December 19th, 1854, and employed on all later machines. In 1854 Wilson withdrew from active participation in the firm for reasons of health; in 1856 Wheeler removed the factory to Bridgeport, Connecticut, where he continued as president until his death. Wheeler, Wilson & Company, reorganized in 1854 as the Wheeler & Wilson Manufacturing Company, was for many years one of the principal manufacturers of sewing machines in the United States. Wheeler was a member of the state legislature (1866, 1868, 1870, 1872–1874) and a director of the New York, New Haven & Hartford Railroad. He married first (on November 7th, 1842) Huldah Bradley, of Watertown, Connecticut; after her death in 1857 he married second (on August 3rd, 1858) Mary E. Crissey, of New Canaan,

Connecticut. He died in Bridgeport on December 31st, 1893.

WHITE, WILLIAM PARKER (1812–1864), lawyer, was born in Savannah, Georgia, in 1812. After graduating from Franklin College (Athens) in 1831 he practiced law in his native city until the outbreak of the Civil War; he was also for some years customs appraiser of the port of Savannah. On November 16th, 1843, at Bath, Richmond County, Georgia, he married Sarah Berrien Dowse (1824–1855), only child of Samuel Dowse (1786–1856) and his third wife, Sarah Berrien. His wife was a half-sister of Gideon Dowse (1814–1881); Abigail Sturges Dowse (1828–1897), wife of Henry Hart Jones; Susan Clinton Dowse (1833–1886), wife of Dr. Juriah Harriss; and Laura Philoclea Dowse (1835–1899). She died in childbirth on the Isle of Hope, near Savannah, on August 30th, 1855, leaving four young children, and was buried in Laurel Grove Cemetery. As the Rev. Dr. Charles Colcock Jones observed (September 6th, 1855), "It is seldom that we are called to witness a sadder spectacle than the death of a young mother, leaving behind her three or four little ones— and not one able to take care of another!" On May 7th, 1862, White was appointed major of White's Battalion of Partisans (Company A, 21st Battalion Georgia Cavalry; later part of the 7th Regiment Georgia Cavalry). On February 12th, 1864, he was appointed colonel, to take rank January 24th, 1864. (Mrs. Mary Jones was mistaken in her reference to White as "major" on March 16th, 1864.) On the night of March 7th, 1864, at Alderly, near Georgetown, South Carolina, White was shot in the knee by Eli G. Grimes, sergeant in Company D, 21st Battalion Georgia Cavalry, a former farm laborer from Lee County, Georgia, who subsequently alleged that C. C. Bowen, captain of Company D, 21st Battalion Georgia Cavalry, had bribed him to assassinate White. Bowen had been in arrest for seven months in 1863 on charges of "absence without leave" and "disobedience of orders in selling a horse out of the company." "I am constrained to believe," White had written to Captain William Greene, assistant adjutant general, on October 16th, 1863, "that since as well as before his arrest his language and conduct are but little calculated to advance the discipline and subordination of the company he commands." Bowen had been court-martialed in December 1863. On April 7th, 1864, Captain Charles Wood, assistant adjutant general, having investigated the case, reported that "there is probably little foundation in facts for the charges preferred, though it is proper to state that Captain Bowen is anxious to have the matter investigated before a court-martial." White died in the general hospital near Georgetown, South Carolina, from the effects of his gunshot wound on April 6th, 1864, and was buried in Georgetown Cemetery. In March 1869 his remains were transferred to Laurel Grove Cemetery, Savannah, and buried beside those of his wife.

WHITEHEAD, CHARLES EDWARD (1827–1903), lawyer, son of the Rev. Charles Whitehead, was born in Hopewell, Dutchess County, New York, on July 4th, 1827. His father, a Dutch Reformed clergyman, was the father of four sons, all of whom became lawyers. In early childhood he removed with his parents to New Brunswick, New Jersey, where he graduated from Rutgers College in 1847 and studied law in the office of John Jay, whose partner he became. In 1867 he joined John Elliott Ward and Charles Colcock Jones, Jr., in the firm of Ward, Jones & Whitehead, with offices at 119 Broadway, New York. There he became much interested in railroads; he was for several years president of the Des Moines & Fort Dodge Railroad until its merger with the Rock Island System, and later president of the New York, Pennsylvania & Ohio Railroad until its merger with the Erie System. In 1876 he withdrew to manage his private railroad interests, and in 1883 he joined Stanley W. Dexter and William Church Osborn in the firm of Whitehead, Dexter & Osborn. He retired from practice in 1899. He was a member of the City, Ohio, and Century Clubs, the Union League, the Downtown Association, the National Academy of Design, the Metropolitan Museum of Art, and the American Museum of Natural History. He was also an enthusiastic sportsman. He was twice married: his first wife, a daughter of William Curtis Noyes, died in 1899; his second wife, Lucy S. Page, of Virginia, was a cousin of Thomas Nelson Page. He died without issue in Aiken, South Carolina, on March 21st, 1903, and was buried in New York City.

WHITEHEAD, CHARLES LOWNDES (1835–1866), son of John Whitehead (1783–1857) and his second wife, Julia Maria Berrien (1801–1857), widow of Dr. Lloyd Belt, was born at his father's summer residence in Bath, Richmond County, Georgia, on June 29th, 1835. Prior to the Civil War he saw extensive military service in Nicaragua. On April 28th, 1861, he enlisted as a private in Company E, 4th Regiment Georgia Infantry; on May 9th, 1861, he was elected major and left with his company for Virginia. On April 28th, 1862, his term of enlistment having expired, he became volunteer aide-de-camp, with rank of captain, on the staff of General Augustus R. Wright. He was taken prisoner on June 28th, 1862, confined at Fort Warren, Boston harbor, and exchanged on July 31st, 1862. At Sharpsburg (September 17th, 1862) he was severely wounded in the arm. Eleven months later (on August 22nd, 1863) he applied to the secretary of war for a colonelcy in the Georgia troops organized for state defense: "The undersigned states that his health has become impaired by a wound received at the battle of Sharpsburg, he having been in service in this state [Virginia] since the commencement of the war, and that he has been recommended by his surgeon to be transferred south." On January 7th, 1864, in Augusta, he married Sarah A. Whaley (1844–1864); she died in childbirth in Savannah on November 18th, 1864, and was buried in Laurel Grove Cemetery. After the war he planted in Burke County. He died on September 25th, 1866, and was buried near his parents in Bath Presbyterian Churchyard.

WHITEHEAD, GEORGE ARTHUR (1836–1899), cotton merchant and railroad agent, was born in Savannah, Georgia, in 1836. For several years prior to the Civil War he engaged in the commission business. In 1861 he entered Confederate service as a private in the Chatham Artillery; in November 1862, when Charles Colcock Jones, Jr., was appointed lieutenant colonel of artillery, Whitehead became his adjutant, with rank of lieutenant. He served with Jones on James Island, near Charleston, South Carolina, during the summer and autumn of 1863. He was later transferred to the staff of General Joseph Wheeler, with whom he enjoyed a continuing friendship after the war. In 1872 he became associated with the Central Railroad of Georgia; he was general agent in Augusta (1872–1880), general freight and passenger agent in Savannah (1880–1887), and general freight agent in Savannah (1887–1892). In 1892 he resigned and became inspector of fertilizers in Savannah. He died in Savannah on May 6th, 1899, survived by his wife, Elizabeth Church Evans (1840–1907), and was buried in Bonaventure Cemetery. Elizabeth Church (Evans) Whitehead died on June 3rd, 1907, survived by two children, and was buried beside her husband.

WHITEHEAD, JOHN (1783–1857), cotton planter and legislator, was born in Burke County, Georgia, on December 14th, 1783. After graduating from Franklin College (Athens) in 1806 he returned to his native county and settled at Forest Hill plantation, where he was for many years a prosperous planter. He also maintained a summer residence in Bath, Richmond County. He was an extensive landowner and a large slaveholder, and he represented Burke County several terms in the state legislature. His first wife was Abigail Lewis Sturges (1798–1824), daughter of Nathaniel Lewis Sturges and Sarah Bulkley. Two of their three children lived to maturity: Eliza Alice Whitehead (1818–1896), wife of Dr. Charles William West; and Mary Dowse Whitehead (1822–1844). His second wife was Julia Maria Berrien (1801–1857), daughter of John Berrien (1759–1815) and his second wife, Williamina Sarah Eliza Moore (1771–1838); she was a half-sister of the Hon. John Macpherson Berrien (1781–1856) and the widow of Dr. Lloyd Belt. Six of their eight children survived infancy: John Randolph Whitehead (1829–1877); Julia Amanda Whitehead (1831–1896), wife of Dr. John Gordon Howard; Philoclea Edgeworth Whitehead (1833–1892), wife of Thomas William Neely; Charles Lowndes Whitehead (1835–1866); Ruth Berrien Whitehead (1837–1861), first wife of Charles Colcock Jones, Jr.; and Valeria Burroughs Whitehead (1840–1904), wife of Augustus Ramon Salas. Julia Maria

(Berrien) (Belt) Whitehead died suddenly of heart disease in Bath, Richmond County, Georgia, on January 8th, 1857, and was buried in Bath Presbyterian Churchyard. John Whitehead died of heart disease on May 31st, 1857, and was buried beside his wife.

WHITEHEAD, JOHN RANDOLPH (1829–1877), planter and soldier, eldest son of John Whitehead (1783–1857) and his second wife, Julia Maria Berrien (1801–1857), widow of Dr. Lloyd Belt, was born at Forest Hill, his father's plantation in Burke County, Georgia, in 1829. He attended Franklin College (Athens) with the class of 1847 but did not graduate; he also attended the College of New Jersey (Princeton) with the class of 1847 but did not graduate. On November 18th, 1851, he married Sarah E. Connelly (1831–1886), of Jefferson County; there were five children. After the death of both his parents in 1857 he occupied the family homestead in Burke County and the family summer residence in Bath, Richmond County; it was in Bath that his younger sister, Ruth Berrien Whitehead, became the wife of Charles Colcock Jones, Jr., on the evening of November 9th, 1858. On August 1st, 1861, in Waynesboro, Georgia, he enlisted as a private in Company E (Infantry Division), Cobb's Legion Georgia Volunteers; on August 8th, 1861, he was elected first lieutenant, and on January 6th, 1862, he resigned. Two months later (on March 22nd, 1862) he was appointed major of the 48th Regiment Georgia Infantry. At Sharpsburg (September 17th, 1862) he was severely wounded in the foot, and on July 17th, 1863, he unconditionally resigned. After the war he removed to Southwest Georgia, where he planted extensively in Miller County. He was twice a member of the state legislature. He died suddenly on his plantation in Miller County on June 5th, 1877. Sarah (Connelly) Whitehead died in Savannah on January 21st, 1886, and was buried in Laurel Grove Cemetery.

WHITEHEAD, JULIA C. (BURNETT) (1823–1897): *Mrs. Charles E. Whitehead*, eldest daughter of James H. Burnett and Sarah C. Tucker, was born in Sparta, Hancock County, Georgia, in 1823. Her father, a native of New Jersey, had settled in Sparta in early manhood and established himself as a merchant. On June 8th, 1841, she became the wife of Charles E. Whitehead (1817–1880), son of Dr. James Whitehead and Ruth Berrien, of Burke County, Georgia. Her husband had attended Franklin College (Athens) with the class of 1836. For some years prior to the Civil War he resided in Baker County; in 1863 he removed to Atlanta, where he served as captain and quartermaster in the Confederate army. After the war he engaged in the insurance business in Atlanta. He was a deacon of the Central Presbyterian Church from 1864 to 1870. In 1878 he returned to Sparta, where on the morning of July 15th, 1880, he was found dead in his bed. He was buried in Sparta Cemetery. Julia (Burnett)

Whitehead died in Atlanta on June 29th, 1897, survived by three children, and was buried beside her husband.

WHITEHEAD, MARIA (1856–1924), daughter of Charles E. Whitehead (1817–1880) and Julia C. Burnett (1823–1897), was born in Baker County, Georgia, on May 10th, 1856. In 1863 she removed with her parents to Atlanta, where her father was captain and quartermaster in the Confederate army. On October 10th, 1878, she became the wife of Macon B. Spencer (1855–1929), son of Samuel Bacon Spencer (1827–1901) and Mary E. Baker (1830–1914). His father, a native of Liberty County, Georgia, was a lawyer and educator; he was for one term (1874) mayor of Atlanta and for ten years (1886–1896) principal of the Chatham Academy in Savannah. Macon B. Spencer was an auditor and bookkeeper in Atlanta from 1875 to 1929; for some years he resided in Hapeville, several miles south of Atlanta, and commuted daily to his work. Maria (Whitehead) Spencer died in Atlanta on October 30th, 1924, and was buried in Oakland Cemetery. Macon B. Spencer died in Atlanta on May 7th, 1929, survived by one daughter, and was buried beside his wife.

WHITEHEAD, RUTH BERRIEN (1837–1861), daughter of John Whitehead (1783–1857) and his second wife, Julia Maria Berrien (1801–1857), widow of Dr. Lloyd Belt, was born at her father's summer residence in Bath, Richmond County, Georgia, on May 31st, 1837. She was a sister of John Randolph Whitehead (1829–1877); Julia Amanda Whitehead (1831–1896), wife of Dr. John Gordon Howard; Philoclea Edgeworth Whitehead (1833–1892), wife of Thomas William Neely; Charles Lowndes Whitehead (1835–1866); and Valeria Burroughs Whitehead (1840–1904), wife of Augustus Ramon Salas; she was a half-sister of Eliza Alice Whitehead (1818–1896), wife of Dr. Charles William West. Her mother died on January 8th, 1857, and her father died a few months later, on her twentieth birthday, May 31st, 1857. She resided in the household of her elder brother, John Randolph Whitehead, until her marriage on November 9th, 1858, to Charles Colcock Jones, Jr. (1831–1893), eldest son of the Rev. Dr. Charles Colcock Jones (1804–1863) and Mary Jones (1808–1869), of Liberty County, Georgia. Her husband, a graduate of the College of New Jersey (Princeton) in 1852 and Dane Law School, Harvard University, in 1855, was a rising lawyer in Savannah, where he was soon to become alderman (1859–1860) and mayor (1860–1861). There were two children: Julia Berrien Jones (1859–1861) and Mary Ruth Jones (1861–1934). Ruth Berrien (Whitehead) Jones died in Savannah of puerperal fever on July 7th, 1861, and was buried in Laurel Grove Cemetery. On October 28th, 1863, Charles Colcock Jones, Jr., married Eva Berrien Eve (1841–1890), of Augusta, a cousin of Ruth Berrien Whitehead and a bridesmaid at her wedding.

WHITEHEAD, VALERIA BURROUGHS (1840–1904), youngest daughter of John Whitehead (1783–1857) and his second wife, Julia Maria Berrien (1801–1857), widow of Dr. Lloyd Belt, was born at Forest Hill, her father's plantation in Burke County, Georgia, on February 10th, 1840. She was named for her first cousin, Valeria Berrien (1806–1883), wife of Joseph Hallett Burroughs, of Savannah, and second daughter of John Macpherson Berrien (1781–1856) and his first wife, Eliza Anciaux (1776–1828). After the death of her sister, Ruth Berrien Whitehead (1837–1861), first wife of Charles Colcock Jones, Jr., she changed her name to Valeria Berrien Whitehead. "Val" was educated at home by tutors and governesses and later attended a French finishing school in New York City. Her parents both died in 1857, and thereafter she made her home with her brothers and sisters in Burke County and Savannah. After the Civil War she lived for some years with her sister, Philoclea Edgeworth Whitehead (1833–1892), widow of Thomas William Neely, in Baltimore. For a short time she worked in the Treasury Department in Washington. In 1884, aged forty-four, she became the wife of Augustus Ramon Salas (1858–1897), aged twenty-six, son of Ramon Salas and Hortense Poujaud. Her husband, a native of Charleston, South Carolina, was engaged in the ship brokerage business in Savannah. In 1890 he removed to New York City, where he was manager of the Harlem branch of the United States Life Insurance Company of New York. He died of alcoholism in a boardinghouse at 16 West 128th Street, New York City, on September 3rd, 1897, and was buried in the Confederate veterans' plot of Mount Hope Cemetery, Westchester County, New York. According to the Savannah *Morning News* (September 5th, 1897), "Everybody who knew him admired and esteemed him for his warmheartedness and geniality." Returning to Georgia, Valeria (Whitehead) Salas resided for some months in Waynesboro in the household of her nephew, John Flewellyn Neely; she later removed to Greenville, South Carolina, where she died on December 10th, 1904. She was for some years an active member of the Daughters of the American Revolution, and from 1891 to 1895 she was regent for the State of Georgia. In her will she bequeathed "Fifty dollars to go to the support each year of my parrot Nita as long as said parrot shall live after my death. . . . It is my desire and will that the money left to my parrot Nita shall at Nita's death be paid annually to St. Michael's Church, Waynesboro, Georgia." Valeria (Whitehead) Salas was buried in Christ Episcopal Churchyard, Greenville, beneath the inscription: "Numbered with the saints in glory everlasting."

WHITESIDE, HARRIET LEONORA (STRAW) (1824–1903): *Mrs. James Anderson Whiteside,* daughter of Leonard Straw, was born near Wytheville, Virginia, on May 3rd, 1824. She was educated in the Moravian school in Salem, North Carolina, and after the loss of her father's fortune she supported herself as a governess and a teacher of music. When she arrived in Chattanooga in 1842 she was, according to Tomlinson Fort, "a most beautiful and accomplished woman; a graceful dancer and a fine musician, with a voice thoroughly trained, of great natural strength, sweetness, and compass; a splendid conversationalist, queenly in her style and capable of filling any station to which she might be called" [William Thomas Hale and Dixon L. Merritt, *A History of Tennessee and Tennesseans* (New York, 1913), VI, 1746]. On February 1st, 1844, she became the second wife of James Anderson Whiteside (1803–1861), son of Jonathan Whiteside (1766–1860) and Thankful Anderson (1775–1859); there were nine children. Her husband, a native of Danville, Kentucky, had settled in September 1838 at Ross's Landing (later Chattanooga), where he became one of the most dynamic and successful businessmen in East Tennessee. He was influential in locating the terminus of the Western & Atlantic Railroad at Chattanooga, and he was one of the projectors of the Nashville, Chattanooga & St. Louis Railroad. Several years prior to the Civil War he purchased most of the north end of Lookout Mountain and widened the Indian trail leading up the mountain sufficiently to accommodate vehicles. In 1856, seeing the necessity for enlarged and improved accommodations for visitors, he commenced work on a splendid hotel facing the eastern bluff above Leonora Spring; on June 1st, 1857, the Lookout Mountain Hotel was opened to the public, together with twenty-five surrounding cottages. James Anderson Whiteside died at his residence, the oldest brick house in Chattanooga, on November 12th, 1861. Leonora (Straw) Whiteside inherited a vast estate, real and personal, and through her excellent management it accumulated substantially; she was reputed to be the richest woman in Tennessee. She died in Chattanooga on February 19th, 1903, survived by seven children and sixteen grandchildren, and was buried beside her husband in Forest Hill Cemetery. According to the Chattanooga *Times* (February 20th, 1903), "She was a woman of reserved manners—gentle, kind, hospitable, tenacious of her rights, and aroused to combativeness by nothing more easily than any attempt to evade or invade them."

WHITNER, JOHN CHARLES (1831–1906), insurance agent, son of Benjamin Franklin Whitner (1789–1864) and Eliza Ann Spann, was born in Edgefield District, South Carolina, on September 23rd, 1831, the youngest of nine children. His father, a graduate of the South Carolina College, practiced law, served in the state legislature, and later entered business in Hamburg, South Carolina. When John Charles Whitner was still a boy he removed with his parents to Madison County, Florida, and thence to Lake Jackson, some eight miles from Tallahassee, where his father was president of the Union Bank until his death in October 1864. John Charles Whitner graduated from Franklin College (Athens) in 1850; his roommate for three years was John Brown Gordon (1832–1904), future Confederate general, with whom he enjoyed a lifelong intimacy. On September 28th, 1853, he married Sarah Martha Cobb (1831–1906), youngest daughter of John Addison Cobb and Sarah Robinson Rootes, of Athens, Georgia; she was a sister of Howell Cobb (1815–1868) and Thomas Reade Rootes Cobb (1823–1862). Prior to the Civil War he managed his plantation some eight miles south of Quincy, Florida (1853–1855); operated a general store in West Point, Georgia (1855–1856); acted as agent of the Georgia Railroad Bank of Augusta (1856–1857); and acted as agent of the Farmers' & Exchange Bank of Charleston (1857–1861). During the Civil War he served as major on the staff of his brother-in-law, General Howell Cobb, in Virginia and North Carolina; in 1863 his health failed and he was stationed in Atlanta as keeper of archives, subject to staff duties as occasion required. After the fall of Atlanta he was stationed from time to time at Columbus, Augusta, and Columbia, South Carolina. In May 1865 he returned to Atlanta, where for more than forty years he prospered in the insurance business. He accumulated a substantial fortune and became one of the best known and most highly respected men in the state. In 1881 he was instrumental in organizing the Southeastern Underwriters' Association. He was for some years ruling elder of the Central Presbyterian Church and superintendent of the Sunday school. At the time of his death he was, according to the Atlanta *Constitution* (January 16th, 1906), "the dean of the Atlanta insurance world." He died in Atlanta after a lingering illness on January 15th, 1906, and was buried in Westview Cemetery. Sarah Martha (Cobb) Whitner died in Louisville, Kentucky, at the residence of her daughter, Mrs. B. C. Milner, on October 30th, 1906, survived by seven children, and was buried beside her husband. As the Atlanta *Constitution* (November 1st, 1906) observed, "In all the relations of life she was a model of the true Southern woman—modest, gentle, reserved, and courteous, but firm in her convictions and candid in her converse and conduct."

WIGFALL, LOUIS TREZEVANT (1816–1873), lawyer, legislator, and Confederate soldier, third child of Levi Durand Wigfall and Eliza Thomson, was born in Edgefield District, South Carolina, on April 21st, 1816. He attended the South Carolina College, and after serving as lieutenant of volunteers in the Seminole War (1838) he attended the law school of the University of Virginia. In 1848 he removed to Marshall, Texas, where he commenced the practice of law. He was a member of the state house of representatives (1849–1850), a member of the state senate (1857–1859), and United States senator

(1859–1861). On March 23rd, 1861, he withdrew to enter Confederate service. At the bombardment of Fort Sumter (April 12th, 1861) he was aide-de-camp to General Beauregard. Seeing that Federal resistance would be futile, he crossed the bay under terrific cross fire to persuade Major Robert Anderson, commanding at Fort Sumter, to surrender. His heroism and humanity won him distinction. On August 28th, 1861, he was commissioned colonel of the 2nd Regiment Texas Infantry; on October 1st, 1861, he was made brigadier general; on February 20th, 1862, he resigned to enter the Confederate Senate. After the war he resided for some years in London, England; in 1873 he returned to the United States and settled in Baltimore, Maryland. While on a lecture tour he died in Galveston, Texas, on February 18th, 1874, and was buried in Episcopal Cemetery. He married his second cousin, Charlotte Maria Cross, daughter of George Warren Cross and his second wife, Frances Maria Halsey.

WILD, EDWARD AUGUSTUS (1825–1891), Union soldier, was born in Brookline, Massachusetts, on November 25th, 1825. After graduating from Harvard College in 1844 and from Jefferson Medical College (Philadelphia) in 1846 he attended medical lectures in Paris and served as medical officer in the Turkish army during the Crimean War. Returning to the United States, he practiced medicine in Brookline until the outbreak of the Civil War. He was successively captain of the 1st Regiment Massachusetts Infantry (April 21st, 1861); major of the 32nd Regiment Massachusetts Infantry (July 24th, 1862); colonel of the 35th Regiment Massachusetts Infantry (August 20th, 1862); and brigadier general of volunteers (April 24th, 1863). He served in the Peninsula campaign (1862) and at the siege of Charleston (1863); he was wounded at Williamsburg and Fair Oaks and seriously wounded in the left arm at Harpers Ferry. In January 1864 he was placed in command of the military district of Norfolk and Portsmouth. After the war he administered the Freedmen's Bureau (the Federal Bureau of Refugees, Freedmen, and Abandoned Lands) in Georgia until January 15th, 1866, when he resigned from military service. He subsequently engaged in mining operations in Nevada and South America. He died in Medellin, Colombia, on September 3rd, 1891.

WILDMAN, PHILO H. (1813–1854), physician, was born in Connecticut in 1813. In early manhood he removed to Gwinnett County, Georgia, where he commenced the practice of medicine. About 1840 he married Priscilla (Hurt) Ingram, of Putnam County, a widow with two young children. For ten years (1842–1852) he practiced his profession in Columbus. In the autumn of 1852 he settled in Savannah, where he and Dr. Charles Ganahl opened the Georgia General Hospital, a private institution established "for the surgical and medical treatment of diseases" and "fitted with all the appliances of hygiene,

good nursing, medical and surgical attendance." In August 1854 the hospital was reorganized and two more doctors were added to its staff: Dr. Easton Yonge and Dr. Stephen Nathan Harris. An advertisement appeared in the Savannah *Republican* on August 19th, 1854: "With large and admirably ventilated wards, airy and pleasant rooms, spacious grounds, a resident undergraduate in medicine, an experienced steward and a highly intelligent, kind, and obliging stewardess, this establishment offers advantages and inducements rarely found in Southern cities, and makes ample provision for all classes of patients." On September 4th, 1854, at the height of the yellow fever epidemic, the Savannah *Republican* carried a letter written by Wildman recommending "muriated tincture of iron" as a cure for the prevailing malady: "I have treated over one hundred and fifty cases of yellow fever since 21st ult., and of that number not one has died who commenced this remedy prior to 'black vomit.' And since 21st ult. *I have not administered five doses of any other medicine.* I give the tincture in doses varying from twenty to sixty drops every *two* hours in a tablespoonful of water for adults, and smaller doses for children. The cure is generally perfected in three days. This preparation of iron acts by medicating the blood and exerting its styptic qualities upon the coats of the stomach. I would respectfully call the attention of the medical profession to this preparation of iron as an invaluable remedy in yellow fever. In conclusion, I would suggest that ten drops of this medicine in a little water be taken by every citizen remaining in Savannah three times daily as a *preventive* of the yellow fever." The Savannah *Republican* endorsed Wildman's note: "We need hardly say we lay it before the public with the greatest pleasure. Should the muriated tincture of iron be established as a specific for this dreadful scourge of Southern latitudes, the discoverer of its efficacy in yellow fever will reap an immortality second to no man living. We would state for the information of those at a distance that we know Dr. Wildman well— that he is a man of truth and ability, and as great an enemy to quackery in all its forms as any physician in the United States." A few days later, on September 10th, 1854, Wildman died of yellow fever and was buried in Laurel Grove Cemetery. "This is a most sad event," observed the Savannah *Republican* (September 11th, 1854), "for the deceased fell a noble sacrifice to his efforts to relieve the sick. He went night and day, in sunshine and storm, sleeping oftener in his carriage than in his bed, and paying sometimes as many as eighty and one hundred visits during a single night. Several times he felt the invasion of yellow fever upon his system, but as he informed us, he succeeded in checking its progress by taking muriated tincture of iron, the remedy which he has applied with so much success to others. Great, however, as his physical powers of endurance were, he overtasked them; and the specific which brought relief to so many others who now survive to mourn him failed when applied to himself."

WILLET, JOSEPH EDGERTON (1826–1897), scientist and educator, son of Joseph Willet (1798–1850) and Margaret McKay, was born in Macon, Georgia, on November 17th, 1826. He was reared on a farm in Bibb County. After graduating from Mercer University in 1846 he studied law for one year in Macon. In 1847 he was elected professor of natural philosophy and chemistry in Mercer University, where he taught continuously, with the exception of one year's scientific study at Yale University (1848–1849) and one year's leave of absence (1871–1872), until 1893, when he became professor of chemistry in the Medical Department of the University of Georgia. In 1896 he resigned for reasons of health. During the Civil War he served as superintendent of the laboratory of the Atlanta arsenal. For two summers (1878–1879) he was a member of the United States commission to investigate the cotton caterpillar and other insects injurious to the cotton plant. He was a popular lecturer on agricultural and horticultural subjects, a frequent contributor to scientific periodicals, and author of *The Wonders of Insect Life* (1871), a children's book which won first prize in a competition sponsored by the American Baptist Publication Society. In January 1851 he married Emily A. H. Sanders, daughter of the Rev. Billington Sanders, a Baptist clergyman, and first president of Mercer University. He died in Atlanta on February 12th, 1897, survived by his wife and four children, and was buried in Rose Hill Cemetery, Macon. As the Atlanta *Journal* (February 12th, 1897) observed, "Thousands of men throughout the state remember him lovingly as a kind and earnest teacher."

WILLIAMS, EDWIN THEODORE (1826–1866), Presbyterian clergyman, youngest son of Richard Farr Williams and Mary Millen, was born in Savannah, Georgia, on March 12th, 1826. He graduated from the College of New Jersey (Princeton) in 1850 and from Princeton Theological Seminary in 1853. On July 13th, 1853, he married Sarah Wells DuPre (1829–1855), of Charleston, South Carolina, daughter of the Rev. Daniel DuPre, a Methodist clergyman. Four months later, on November 8th, 1853, he sailed with his bride for Corisco, West Africa, where he served as missionary only two months before the failure of his wife's health forced him to return to America. She died in Morristown, New Jersey, on June 12th, 1855. On June 7th, 1856, he sailed for Liberia, where he served as teacher and missionary in Monrovia until the failure of his own health forced him to return to America in June 1859. He served as stated supply of Bryan Neck Presbyterian Church, Bryan County, Georgia (1862–1863), and as pastor of the Presbyterian church in Quincy, Florida (1863–1866). On November 12th, 1863, he married Mary Catherine Fleming

(1832–1910), daughter of the Hon. William Bennett Fleming and his second wife, Eliza Ann Maxwell, of Walthourville, Liberty County, Georgia. He died in Quincy on August 9th, 1866, survived by his wife and two children, and was buried in the local cemetery. In December 1868 his remains were removed to Laurel Grove Cemetery, Savannah. Mary Catherine (Fleming) Williams died in Flemington, Liberty County, on November 14th, 1910, and was buried beside her husband.

WILLIAMS, JOHN (1815–1854), steamboat captain, was born in Germany in 1815. In early manhood he settled in Savannah, Georgia, where he resided for the rest of his life. For some years he was captain of a small sloop plying between Savannah and Sunbury in Liberty County. He died in Sunbury of yellow fever on August 22nd, 1854, and was buried in Laurel Grove Cemetery. He was survived by his wife, Mary, a native of England, and one daughter, Sarah, born in Savannah in 1848.

WILLIAMS, JOSEPH MILLARD (1832–1882), physician, son of Singleton Williams and Ann De Bardelaban, was born in Vernon, Autauga County, Alabama, on August 7th, 1832. After attending the University of Alabama for one year (1848–1849) he studied medicine in the office of Dr. William Owen Baldwin and Dr. William McFarland Bolling, of Montgomery, and graduated from the Medical College of the University of Pennsylvania in 1853. Returning to Alabama, he commenced practice with Dr. William Owen Baldwin. Several years before the Civil War he abandoned his practice and engaged in the drug business. In 1861 he entered the Confederate army as surgeon of the 13th Regiment Alabama Volunteers; he served throughout the war, at first in the field, later in hospitals. After the war he resumed practice in Montgomery, where he was alderman (1874) and city councilman (1876–1878). On July 1st, 1857, he married Mary Louise Marks, daughter of William Mathews Marks and Catherine Ann Crain, of Montgomery; there were six children. He died in Elmore County, Alabama, on October 15th, 1882. In speaking of the cough remedy of "a Dr. Williams of Huntsville, Alabama" (January 16th, 1858) Mrs. Eliza G. Robarts was evidently referring to Dr. Joseph Millard Williams, who engaged in the drug business not in Huntsville but in Montgomery. Her mistake was understandable, since the remedy prepared by Dr. Williams was sent to Mrs. Robarts by the Hon. Smith D. Hale of Huntsville.

WILLIAMS, WILLIAM CLAYTON (1821–1888), Episcopal clergyman, eldest son of John Green Williams (1797–1833) and Mary Ann Cringan (1797–1867), was born in Richmond, Virginia, on December 31st, 1821. His father, a distinguished lawyer and for several sessions a delegate to the state legislature, died on December 15th, 1833, two weeks before his son's twelfth birthday. William Clayton Williams graduated from the College of William and Mary in 1840 and from the Virginia Theological Seminary in 1845. For nineteen years (1845–1864) he devoted himself to missionary work among Negro slaves on plantations in Chatham County, Georgia, near Savannah. On April 5th, 1864, he married Isabella Rae Habersham (1817–1880), of Savannah, widow of William Henry Mongin (1816–1851) and niece of the Rt. Rev. Stephen Elliott (1806–1866), bishop of Georgia (1840–1866). There were no children. After serving temporarily as rector of Grace Church, Clarkesville (1865–1866) he was rector of St. Peter's Church, Rome (1866–1879), and St. Luke's Church, Atlanta (1879–1884). His wife died in Atlanta on July 5th, 1880, and was buried in Oakland Cemetery. In October 1884 he retired from active work and returned to Virginia to live with his sister, Alice Burwell Williams (1827–1896), widow of Carter Henry Harrison (1831–1861), at Clifton, the Harrison family seat in Cumberland County. He died at Clifton on April 27th, 1888, and was buried beside his wife. One of his brothers, the Rev. Channing Moore Williams (1829–1910), also an Episcopal clergyman, devoted his life to the Japanese people as missionary and bishop from 1859 to 1908.

WILLIAMS, WILLIAM THORNE (1785–1868), bookseller and publisher, son of James Williams, an officer in the Revolutionary army, was born in Philadelphia, Pennsylvania, on June 24th, 1785. In 1803 he migrated to Georgia, and in 1805 he settled in Savannah, where he established the first publishing house in the state. He was an officer of artillery in the War of 1812 and for ten years captain of the Chatham Artillery. He was mayor of Savannah for several terms and a judge of the inferior court. For fifty years he was treasurer of the Chatham Academy. Prior to the Civil War he was acting president of the Bank of the State of Georgia. He died in Savannah on October 9th, 1868, and was buried in Laurel Grove Cemetery.

WILLS, DAVID (1822–1915), Presbyterian clergyman, was born in Gettysburg, Pennsylvania, on January 7th, 1822. He graduated from Washington College (Greeneville, Tennessee) in 1847 and from Columbia Theological Seminary in 1850. He was pastor of the Presbyterian church, Laurensville, South Carolina (1851–1860); pastor of the First Presbyterian Church, Macon, Georgia (1860–1870); president of Oglethorpe University (1870–1872); pastor of the Western Presbyterian Church, Washington, D.C. (1875–1879); chaplain in the United States army (1879–1886); pastor of North 10th Street Presbyterian Church, Philadelphia (1886–1888); and pastor of the Disston Memorial Presbyterian Church, Philadelphia (1890–1901). He retired in 1901 and settled in Washington, D.C. In 1849 he married Rebecca Frances Watt (1831–1881), a native of Fairfield, South Carolina; she was the sister of the Rev. James B. Watt, a Presby-

terian clergyman; the sister-in-law of the Rev. James R. Castles, a Presbyterian clergyman; the mother of the Rev. David Wills, Jr., a Presbyterian clergyman; and the mother-in-law of the Rev. Thomas W. Hollingsworth, a Presbyterian clergyman. She died in Washington on July 27th, 1881, and was buried in Glenwood Cemetery. The Rev. David Wills died in Washington on December 30th, 1915, survived by four sons and two daughters, and was buried beside his wife. He received the honorary degree of doctor of divinity from Oglethorpe University in 1866 and the honorary degree of doctor of laws from Washington College (Greeneville, Tennessee) in 1888.

WILSON, ALLEN BENJAMIN (1824–1888), inventor and sewing machine manufacturer, son of Benjamin Wilson, was born in Willet, Cortland County, New York, on October 18th, 1824. In 1848, while employed as a journeyman cabinetmaker in Pittsfield, Massachusetts, he prepared full-size drawings of a sewing machine, which he constructed in 1849 and patented on November 12th, 1850. In 1851 he joined Nathaniel Wheeler (1820–1893) in the firm of Wheeler, Wilson & Company and commenced the manufacture of the new machine in Watertown, Connecticut. The enterprise was an immediate success; Wheeler superintended business arrangements while Wilson perfected his invention. Fundamental among his numerous subsequent improvements was the four-motion feed, patented on December 19th, 1854, and employed on all later machines. In 1850 Wilson married Harriet Emeline Brooks, of Williamstown, Massachusetts. In 1854 he withdrew from active participation in the firm for reasons of health. He died in Waterbury, Connecticut, on April 29th, 1888. His importance in the history of the sewing machine is thus explained by Frederick L. Lewton: "Of all the pioneers of sewing machine invention Allen B. Wilson was decidedly the most original in his ideas. His devices were unique and lasting in their usefulness. No sewing machine device except the eye in the point of the needle has come into such universal use as the four-motion roughened-surface feed. . . . It was one of the strongest patents of those held by the famous sewing machine combination, and enabled that famous monopoly to defy all comers until its expiration" ["The Servant in the House," *Annual Report of the Board of Regents of the Smithsonian Institution* (Washington, 1929), pp. 580–581].

WILSON, ANNA GILL (1835–1855), elder daughter of the Rev. Matthew Wilson (1807–1853) and Elizabeth Paul Gill (1810–1850), was born in Philadelphia, Pennsylvania, on March 22nd, 1835. Her father, a Presbyterian clergyman, was the son, grandson, great-grandson, and great-great-grandson of Presbyterian clergymen. Her paternal uncle, the Rev. James Patriot Wilson (1808–1889), also a Presbyterian clergyman, married Anna Read Gill (1812–1896), sister of Elizabeth Paul Gill; two brothers thus married two sisters. In the early 1850s Anna Gill Wilson and her younger sister, Margaretta Peery Wilson (1836–1922), attended a seminary for young ladies in Philadelphia conducted by their four aunts, the Misses Mary, Sarah, Sidney, and Emily Gill. Elizabeth Paul (Gill) Wilson died on March 20th, 1850; the Rev. Matthew Wilson died on April 14th, 1853. Anna Gill Wilson died of consumption on November 27th, 1855, leaving her younger sister "Maggie" the last surviving member of her immediate family.

WILSON, JAMES HARRISON (1837–1925), engineer and Union soldier, fifth child of Harrison Wilson and Katharine Schneyder, was born near Shawneetown, Illinois, on September 2nd, 1837. He graduated from the United States Military Academy in 1860. During the Civil War he served chiefly with the engineers. Early in 1863 he became inspector general, Army of the Tennessee; after Vicksburg he was promoted to brigadier general of volunteers (October 1863); after Missionary Ridge he was appointed chief of the cavalry bureau in Washington (January 1864). In October 1864 he was brevetted major general and appointed chief of cavalry, military division of the Mississippi. After outfitting Kilpatrick's division for the march to Savannah he moved against Hood in Tennessee. In April 1865 he took Selma, Montgomery, and Columbus; on April 20th, 1865, he reached Macon, where he continued for some months in military control. He was appointed lieutenant colonel in the regular army on July 28th, 1866; after four years' engineering service, chiefly on the Mississippi River, he resigned from the army on December 31st, 1870. He then engaged in railroad construction. In 1883 he settled in Wilmington, Delaware, which was his home for the rest of his life. He participated in the Spanish-American War and assisted in suppressing the Boxer uprising. In 1902 he represented the army at the coronation of Edward VII. He was placed on the retired list as brigadier general (1900) and promoted to major general (1915). He was author of several military biographies, the first being *The Life of Ulysses S. Grant* (1868). On January 3rd, 1866, he married Ella Andrews, who died in Cuba on April 28th, 1900, as a result of burns. He died in Wilmington, Delaware, on February 23rd, 1925, and was buried in the Old Swedes Churchyard.

WILSON, JOHN LEIGHTON (1809–1886), Presbyterian clergyman and missionary, son of William Wilson and Jane E. James, was born near Salem, South Carolina, on March 25th, 1809. After graduating from Union College (Schenectady, New York) in 1829 he taught school for one year (1829–1830) near Charleston, South Carolina, and graduated from Columbia Theological Seminary in 1833. On May 21st, 1834, he married Jane Elizabeth Bayard, of Savannah, Georgia, and shortly thereafter sailed with his bride for Africa, where he served as missionary until 1853, when his wife's failing health forced him to return to America. For eight years (1853–1861) he was secretary of the Board of Foreign

Missions of the Presbyterian Church, with offices in New York, where he also edited *The Home and Foreign Record* and published his encyclopedic *Western Africa: Its History, Condition, and Prospects* (1854). At the outbreak of the Civil War he resigned his position and returned South, where he served briefly as chaplain in the Confederate army. For twenty-five years (1861–1886) he was secretary of the Board of Foreign Missions of the Southern Presbyterian Church. He contributed frequently to *The Southern Presbyterian Review* and in 1866 founded *The Missionary*, which he edited for almost twenty years. He received the honorary degree of doctor of divinity from Lafayette College (Easton, Pennsylvania) in 1854. He died near Salem, South Carolina, on July 13th, 1886.

WILSON, JOSEPH RUGGLES (1822–1903), Presbyterian clergyman, youngest son of James Wilson (1787–1850) and Anne Adams, was born in Steubenville, Ohio, on February 28th, 1822. His parents were both natives of Ulster. After graduating with first honor from Jefferson College (Canonsburg, Pennsylvania) in 1844 he studied at Western Theological Seminary (1845–1846) and Princeton Theological Seminary (1846–1847). On June 7th, 1849, he married Jessie Woodrow (1830–1888), daughter of the Rev. Thomas Woodrow, a Presbyterian clergyman, of Chillicothe, Ohio. He was pastor of the Presbyterian church in Chartiers, Pennsylvania (1849–1851); professor of chemistry and natural science at Hampden-Sydney College (1851–1855); pastor of the Presbyterian church in Staunton, Virginia (1855–1857); pastor of the First Presbyterian Church in Augusta, Georgia (1857–1870); professor of homiletics at Columbia Theological Seminary (1870–1874); pastor of the First Presbyterian Church in Wilmington, North Carolina (1874–1885); and head of the Department of Theology at Southwestern Presbyterian University, Clarksville, Tennessee (1885–1893). It was in his church in Augusta that the first General Assembly of the Southern Presbyterian Church met in December 1861. He was permanent clerk of the General Assembly (1861–1865), stated clerk (1865–1898), and moderator (1879). He received the honorary degree of doctor of divinity from Oglethorpe University in 1857. His daughter, Annie Josephine Wilson (1854–1916), became the wife of Dr. George Howe (1848–1895), son of the Rev. Dr. George Howe, professor at Columbia Theological Seminary. His son, Thomas Woodrow Wilson (1856–1924), became the twenty-eighth president of the United States (1913–1921). Joseph Ruggles Wilson died in Princeton, New Jersey, at the residence of his son on January 21st, 1903, and was buried beside his wife in the First Presbyterian Churchyard, Columbia, South Carolina. His tombstone reads: "Pastor, teacher, ecclesiastical leader. For thirty-four years stated clerk of the General Assembly of the Presbyterian Church of the United States. Steadfast, brilliant, devoted, loving, and beloved. A master of serious eloquence. A thinker of singular power and penetration. A thoughtful student of life and of God's purpose. A lover and servant of his fellow men. A man of God."

WILSON, MARGARETTA PEERY (1836–1922), younger daughter of the Rev. Matthew Wilson (1807–1853) and Elizabeth Paul Gill (1810–1850), was born in Philadelphia, Pennsylvania, on August 3rd, 1836. Her father, a Presbyterian clergyman, was the son, grandson, great-grandson, and great-great-grandson of Presbyterian clergymen. Her paternal uncle, the Rev. James Patriot Wilson (1808–1889), also a Presbyterian clergyman, married Anna Read Gill (1812–1896), sister of Elizabeth Paul Gill; two brothers thus married two sisters. In the early 1850s Margaretta Peery Wilson and her elder sister, Anna Gill Wilson (1835–1855), attended a seminary for young ladies in Philadelphia conducted by their four aunts, the Misses Mary, Sarah, Sidney, and Emily Gill. Elizabeth Paul (Gill) Wilson died on March 20th, 1850; the Rev. Matthew Wilson died on April 14th, 1853; Anna Gill Wilson died on November 27th, 1855. "Maggie" Wilson was thus at the age of nineteen the last surviving member of her immediate family. In the summer of 1856 she removed to Newark, New Jersey, where she joined the household of her uncle, the Rev. James Patriot Wilson, pastor of the South Park Presbyterian Church (1853–1889). On October 12th, 1864, "Peery" became the wife of Charles McKean Bayard (1838–1911), eldest son of Charles Pettit Bayard and Adeline J. McKean; there were six children. Her husband was for many years a broker and a member of the Philadelphia Stock Exchange; they resided in Germantown, where Charles McKean Bayard was a warden of Grace Episcopal Church, Mount Airy, and superintendent of the Sunday school. He died in Germantown on January 10th, 1911. Margaretta Peery (Wilson) Bayard died at her summer residence in Seal Harbor, Maine, on September 27th, 1922.

WILTBERGER, WILLIAM H. (1825–1872), hotel proprietor, son of Peter Wiltberger (1791–1853) and Susan Green (1788–1849), was born in Philadelphia, Pennsylvania, on September 17th, 1825. His father was a sea captain connected with the China trade. Soon after the birth of his son he removed to Macon, Georgia, and thence to Savannah, where for several years he commanded a steamer plying between Savannah and Augusta or between Savannah and Charleston. Retiring from the sea, he became proprietor of the City Hotel, a small brick structure located on Bay Street between Bull and Whitaker. He then rented and later purchased the Pulaski House, located on the northwest corner of Bull and Bryan Streets, where he continued as proprietor as long as he lived. He died in Brooklyn, New York, on September 22nd, 1853. According to the Savannah *Georgian* (September 24th, 1853), "Captain Wiltberger was a man of remarkable dignity of appearance, kind and pleasing in his manners, high-toned and honorable in his views, of scrupulous correctness in all his business relations, energetic and faithful in the discharge of his duty. . . . Starting in life with slender means, we find him in his last hour surrounded by every comfort and possessed of a liberal fortune, reared by honorable industry, respected as a man and a citizen, beloved as a master, and sincerely mourned as a friend." William H. Wiltberger succeeded to his father's position as proprietor of the Pulaski House, and with the exception of the war years he continued as proprietor as long as he lived. On November 23rd, 1861, he entered Confederate service as captain of Company D, 2nd Battalion Georgia Cavalry (later Company A, 5th Regiment Georgia Cavalry); on July 26th, 1864, he was promoted to major and placed in command of a convalescent camp at Union Springs, Alabama. He was paroled at Albany, Georgia, on May 6th, 1865. Two years later, on June 24th, 1867, he married Josephine Gregory, youngest daughter of Lewis Gregory, of New York City; there were no children. He died in Savannah on April 27th, 1872, and was buried near his parents in Bonaventure Cemetery. As the Savannah *Republican* (April 28th, 1872) observed, "Major Wiltberger was not only a good landlord but a liberal and most enterprising citizen. Possessed of large means, he entered freely into almost every project that gave promise of good to his native and much-loved Savannah. He was kind and hospitable to all, though never obtrusive, and did much good of which the world knows little. Peace to his ashes!"

WINN, ABIAL (1815–1874), planter, son of Peter Farley Winn (1786–1824) and his second wife, Mary Fleming Osgood (1795–1819), was born in Liberty County, Georgia, on March 28th, 1815. On March 15th, 1838, he married Louisa Vanyeverine Ward (1818–1892), daughter of William Ward and his second wife, Sarah Ann McIntosh, and sister of the Hon. John Elliott Ward (1814–1902). The marriage took place at Lodebar, the plantation of Colonel and Mrs. William Maxwell, lifelong friends of the Winns. It was in the Winn house in Dorchester that Mrs. Maxwell died on July 24th, 1856; it was in the same house that Colonel Maxwell died ten years later, on August 20th, 1866. Abial Winn was a member of the state senate (1855–1856). He was for many years a member of the Liberty Independent Troop, serving successively as sergeant, cornet, and lieutenant; he was captain from 1842 to 1845 and again from 1859 to 1861. For six months during the first winter of the Civil War (October 1861–March 1862) he continued as captain of the troop during its encampment at Palmyra, Liberty County. After the troop was mustered out of service on April 1st, 1862, Winn resigned command, being too crippled with rheumatism to enter active service. A part of the troop continued as the Liberty Independent Troop under the command of Captain William Lowndes Walthour; a part formed the Liberty Mounted Rangers under the command of Captain William Goulding

Thomson. Abial Winn died in Valdosta, Georgia, on October 16th, 1874, and was buried in Midway Cemetery. Louisa Vanyeverine (Ward) Winn died in Dorchester on April 3rd, 1892, and was buried beside her husband.

WINN, HENRY HOLMES (1840–1890), dentist, eldest son of the Rev. John Winn (1814–1892) and his first wife, Mary C. Brown (1813–1873), was born in Walthourville, Liberty County, Georgia, on June 2nd, 1840. His father, a Presbyterian clergyman, was for some years (1851–1858) engaged by the executors of the Lambert estate to preach and minister to the Negroes of Liberty County. In 1858 the Rev. John Winn removed to Illinois, where he was pastor in Henry (1858–1872) and Dunlap (1872–1878). Henry Holmes Winn entered Yale College in 1858 with the class of 1862 but left in his freshman year and settled with his father in Illinois. He subsequently earned the D.D.S. degree and practiced dentistry for some years in Madison, Wisconsin, before removing in 1875 to the Orient, where he practiced his profession successfully in Japan and China for fifteen years. He was said to be the second American dentist to go to Japan. On October 5th, 1864, he married Joanna Westfall, of Fairview, Illinois; there were six children. He died of tuberculosis in Hong Kong, China, on February 8th, 1890, and was buried in Happy Valley Cemetery. His remains were later transferred to Forest Hill Cemetery, Madison, Wisconsin, and buried beside those of his father, who died in Madison on August 26th, 1892. His brother, Thomas Clay Winn (born 1851), and his sister, Harriet Louisa Winn (born 1853), were both missionaries to Japan. According to Eliza Caroline Clay, a family friend, writing on June 29th, 1858, "He is a good, amiable, well-principled youth with ordinary talent, very moderate literary ambition, tolerable industry, and not a strong constitution; and it appears to me four years' such study as will be necessary (with his imperfect early preparation) to take him creditably through Yale will use him up. And after all, some other occupation would suit him better than a profession. He has not his mother's energy. . . . I think it would be wiser in his father to call him to Illinois and let him form his habits where he is to reside."

WINN, JOHN (1814–1892), Presbyterian clergyman, son of John Winn (1779–1820) and Eliza Wilson (1789–1850), was born on Colonel's Island, Liberty County, Georgia, on January 10th, 1814. He was an elder brother of the Rev. Thomas Sumner Winn (1820–1900). He graduated from Amherst College in 1834 and from Columbia Theological Seminary in 1837. He served churches in St. Marys, Georgia (1837–1838); Forsyth, Georgia (1838–1839); Darien, Georgia (1839–1843); and Bryan Neck, Georgia (1843–1851). For seven years (1851–1858) he was engaged by the executors of the Lambert estate to preach and minister to the Negroes of Liberty County. He was subsequently pastor in Henry, Illinois (1858–1872) and Dunlap, Illinois (1872–

1878). After retiring from active ministry in 1878 he settled in Madison, Wisconsin. On December 20th, 1838, he married Mary C. Brown (1813–1873), daughter of Timothy H. Brown and Phoebe Hinsdale, of Monson, Massachusetts; there were six children, two of whom became missionaries to Japan: the Rev. Thomas Clay Winn (born 1851) and Harriet Louisa Winn (born 1853). After the death of his first wife on January 24th, 1873, he married second (on February 10th, 1876) Sarah A. Baker, daughter of John O. Baker, of Wilkes-Barre, Pennsylvania. He died in Madison, Wisconsin, on August 26th, 1892, survived by his second wife and four children, and was buried in Forest Hill Cemetery. As Mrs. Mary Jones observed on January 5th, 1852, "Mr. Winn is a most excellent man."

WINN, THOMAS SUMNER (1820–1900), Presbyterian clergyman, son of John Winn (1779–1820) and Eliza Wilson (1789–1850), was born in Sunbury, Liberty County, Georgia, on February 5th, 1820. He was a younger brother of the Rev. John Winn (1814–1892). He graduated from Franklin College (Athens) in 1841 and from Columbia Theological Seminary in 1846. For fifteen months (1846–1848) he served as domestic missionary in Houston and Patrick Counties, Georgia. Returning to Liberty County, he served for seven years (1848–1855) as assistant pastor of Midway Church. Early in 1855 he removed to Hale County, Alabama, where he was pastor of a group of rural churches for forty years (1855–1895). On March 23rd, 1848, he married Mary Quarterman (1826–1881), daughter of the Rev. Robert Quarterman (1787–1849) and his third wife, Mary Jemima Way (1801–1841). He died at Stewart Station, Hale County, Alabama, on February 24th, 1900.

WINN, WILLIAM JOHN (1838–1906), civil engineer and Confederate soldier, son of James Wilson Winn (1807–1853) and Elizabeth Rebecca Norman (1819–1861), was born in Walthourville, Liberty County, Georgia, on February 9th, 1838. After graduating from the Georgia Military Institute (Marietta) in 1857 "Willie Winn" returned to his native county, where he supervised the plantation of his widowed mother until the outbreak of the Civil War. On February 26th, 1859, he married Mary Eliza Fleming (1837–1928), daughter of John Sidney Fleming (1812–1847) and Jane Amarintha Quarterman (1813–1874). On August 27th, 1861, he was elected second lieutenant of the Liberty Volunteers (Company H, 25th Regiment Georgia Infantry); he subsequently became major (May 1862) and colonel (November 1863). He fought at James Island, Vicksburg, Chickamauga, Resaca, Dallas, Kennesaw Mountain, and Atlanta; he was desperately wounded at Chickamauga (September 19th, 1863) and at Peachtree Creek (July 22nd, 1864). After the war he taught school in Liberty County and engaged in lighthouse construction on the Atlantic coast. He was chief engineer and builder of the Montgomery & Eufaula Railroad (1869) and of the North &

South Railroad linking Columbus and Rome (1870–1872). After five years in Liberty County he removed in 1877 to Savannah, where he was associated with the Atlantic & Gulf Railroad. He subsequently became superintendent of the Savannah streetcar system and served for nineteen years (1887–1906) as city engineer. He died in Savannah on November 25th, 1906 (not November 6th, 1906, as indicated on his tombstone) from a chronic liver affection induced by the wound he sustained at Peachtree Creek. Mary Eliza (Fleming) Winn died on June 20th, 1928, and was buried beside her husband.

WINN, WILLIAM WILSON (1818–1887), planter, son of John Winn (1779–1820) and Eliza Wilson (1789–1850), was born in Sunbury, Liberty County, Georgia, on March 4th, 1818. He was a brother of the Rev. John Winn (1814–1892) and the Rev. Thomas Sumner Winn (1820–1900), both Presbyterian clergymen. He graduated from Franklin College (Athens) in 1840. Prior to the Civil War he was a planter in Liberty County. In 1843 he married Louisa Varnedoe (1824–1857), daughter of Nathaniel Varnedoe (1790–1856) and his first wife, Ann T. Jones (1794–1836). She died on December 2nd, 1857, leaving six young children, and was buried in Midway Cemetery. He married second (on October 26th, 1858) Claudia Varnedoe (1833–1889), younger sister of his first wife. On October 1st, 1861, he enlisted for six months as a private in the Liberty Independent Troop; being over military age, he did not continue in service beyond the enlistment period. In 1864 he reenlisted for local defense and served as picket guard in Liberty County. After the war he taught school. He died on December 9th, 1887, and was buried in Flemington Cemetery. Claudia (Varnedoe) Winn died on May 21st, 1889, and was buried beside her husband.

WINSHIP, MARTHA ANN PEARSON (COOK) (1813–1882): *Mrs. Isaac Winship,* eldest child of Philip Cook and Ann Wooten, was born in Fort Hawkins, near Macon, Georgia, on October 8th, 1813. On May 1st, 1828, in her fifteenth year, she became the wife of Isaac Winship (1802–1885), son of Benjamin Winship and Mary Adams; there were twelve children. Her husband, a native of New Salem, Massachusetts, had accompanied his elder brother, Joseph Winship (1800–1878), to Georgia in 1825; Joseph had settled in Clinton, Jones County, where he engaged in merchandising; Isaac had settled in Forsyth, Monroe County, where he engaged in the boot and shoe trade, established a factory, and operated a tannery. In 1844 he removed to Vineville, near Macon, where he resided until November 1853, when he removed to Atlanta to join his elder brother in the newly established Winship Machine Company, an iron foundry and machine shop located at the intersection of Foundry Street and the Western & Atlantic Railroad. There the Winship brothers manufactured freight cars and later produced guns and other essential military supplies for the Confederate government. In 1864 the foundry was destroyed by Sherman's army, but after the war it was promptly rebuilt. Isaac Winship sold out his interest in 1866 and returned to Macon; Joseph Winship retired in 1869, leaving the business to his sons, Robert and George; the Winship Machine Company continued for many years one of Atlanta's principal industrial establishments. From 1862 to 1864 Martha (Cook) Winship was the indefatigable president of the Atlanta Hospital Association, a women's organization devoted to caring for sick and wounded soldiers. In 1864, when hospital space was exhausted, she converted the upper floor of her house (six rooms) into a hospital, enlisted her daughters as nurses, and acted herself as surgeon in chief. After the Confederate evacuation of Atlanta she continued her work in Griffin. In 1868 she was elected president of the Ladies' Memorial Association of Macon, and through her efforts the Confederate monument in that city was unveiled in 1879. She died in Macon on June 11th, 1882, and was buried in Rose Hill Cemetery. Isaac Winship died on November 23rd, 1885, and was buried beside his wife.

WOFFORD, WILLIAM TATUM (1823–1884), planter, legislator, and Confederate soldier, son of William Hollingsworth Wofford and Nancy M. Tatum, was born in Habersham County, Georgia, on June 28th, 1823. After studying law in Athens he commenced practice in Cassville in 1846. During the Mexican War (1846–1848) he served as captain of volunteer cavalry under General Winfield Scott. Returning to Cassville, he resumed the practice of law, prospered as a planter, and served in the state legislature (1849–1853). He opposed secession, but during the Civil War he loyally supported the Confederate cause, serving as colonel of the 18th Regiment Georgia Infantry; on January 19th, 1863, he was promoted to brigadier general. He fought at Chancellorsville and Gettysburg, in the campaigns around Richmond and Petersburg, and in the Shenandoah Valley; he was wounded at Spotsylvania and the Wilderness. On January 20th, 1865, he was placed in command of the Department of Northern Georgia, where he raised some seven thousand troops to suppress lawlessness. After the war he devoted himself to rehabilitating the devastated South. He married first (in 1849) Julia A. Dwight, of Spring Place, Murray County, Georgia; three of their six children survived infancy. After her death on September 9th, 1878, he married second (in 1880) Margaret Langdon, of Atlanta. He died at his residence near Cassville on May 22nd, 1884, and was buried in Cassville Cemetery.

WOOD, MYRON DOTY (1834–1913), Presbyterian clergyman and government clerk, son of Joseph Wood and Mary Warner Doty, was born in Alabama in April 1834. After graduating from Oglethorpe University in 1853 and from Columbia Theological Seminary in 1856 he served as pastor of churches in Walterboro, South Carolina (1857–1862); Yorkville, South Carolina (1862–1865); and

Decatur, Georgia (1865–1871). In 1857 he married Mary Jane Beck (1839–1889), daughter of Charles Beck (1792–1861) and Ann Herron (1804–1871), of Columbia, South Carolina; there were three daughters. During the Civil War he was chaplain of the 11th Regiment South Carolina Infantry (March 1861–May 1862); private in Company C, 4th Regiment South Carolina State Troops (August 1863–February 1864); and private in Company D, 5th Battalion South Carolina Reserves (April 1864). He also served from time to time as missionary to soldiers at the front. On October 3rd, 1871, following judicial investigation of "scandalous reports" of his conduct by ecclesiastical and civil courts, he was, by a unanimous vote of the Presbytery of Atlanta, "deposed from the functions of the gospel ministry and suspended from the communion of the church until he give evidence of repentance." In April 1889 the sentence of suspension from the communion of the church was removed. Meanwhile Wood resided in Atlanta for several years, teaching school and editing the Atlanta *Herald*. In 1877 he changed his name to Allen Wood and removed to Washington, D.C., where for thirty-six years he was bookkeeper in the Treasury Department. His wife remained in Atlanta, where her three daughters (Mary, Jane, and Anna) taught school; she died in January 1889 and was buried in Westview Cemetery. Allen Wood (formerly Myron Doty Wood) died in Washington on July 1st, 1913, survived by three daughters, and was buried in Atlanta beside his wife.

WOODWARD, PATRICK HENRY (1833–1917), banker and author, son of Ashbel Woodward and Emeline Bicknell, was born in Franklin, Connecticut, on March 19th, 1833. After graduating from Yale College in 1855 he spent three years in Georgia as principal of an academy in Darien (1855–1856) and as private tutor in the families of William Robert Gignilliat and Thomas Samuel Mallard (1856–1858). For several months he attended the Medical College of South Carolina (Charleston) and Dane Law School, Harvard University; early in 1860 he commenced the practice of law in Savannah, Georgia, in partnership with William Robert Gignilliat, Jr. At the outbreak of the Civil War he abandoned law and returned to Connecticut; during the war he served on the editorial staff of the Hartford *Courant* (1862–1865). In September 1865 he was appointed special agent of the Post Office Department and assigned to reorganize postal service in Georgia; he later supervised railroad mail service south of the Ohio and east of the Mississippi Rivers and notably improved the distribution of mail throughout the South. He was chief special agent of the Post Office Department (1874–1876) and chief investigator of the alleged "star route" frauds (1881–1885). Returning to Hartford, he was secretary and treasurer of the Mather Electric Light Company (1886–1887); secretary of the Hartford Board of Trade (1888–1901); vice-president of the Connecticut General Life Insurance Company (1899–1917); and president of the Dime Savings Bank of Hartford (1900–1917). He was also a trustee of Trinity College, which conferred on him the honorary degree of master of arts in 1900. He was author of *Guarding the Mails* (1876), *Hartford: Its Institutions and Industries* (1889), *One Hundred Years of the Hartford Bank* (1892), *Insurance in Connecticut* (1897), and *Manufactures in Hartford* (1897). On September 11th, 1867, he married Mary Smith, daughter of Charles Smith, of South Windham, Connecticut; there were two children. He died in Hartford on September 4th, 1917.

WRIGHT, AUGUSTUS ROMALDUS (1813–1891), lawyer, congressman, and Confederate soldier, son of William Wright and Mary McCall, was born in Wrightsboro, Columbus County, Georgia, on June 16th, 1813. After attending Franklin College (Athens) and the Litchfield (Connecticut) Law School he commenced practice in Crawfordville, Georgia. For nineteen years (1836–1855) he resided in Cassville, where he continued to practice law and served as judge of the superior court of the Cherokee circuit (1842–1849). In 1855 he settled in Rome. He was a member of Congress (1857–1859), a member of the state secession convention meeting in Milledgeville in January 1861, and one of nine delegates elected to represent Georgia at the organization of the Confederate States in Montgomery in February 1861. During the Civil War he organized Wright's Legion, later consolidated with the 25th Battalion Georgia Infantry to form the 38th Regiment Georgia Infantry, of which he was colonel. Resigning his commission, he served as a member of the Confederate Congress. After the war he resumed the practice of law in Rome. He died there on March 31st, 1891, and was buried in Myrtle Hill Cemetery.

WRIGHT, WILLIAM (1817–1860), real and personal estate broker, was born in Bulloch County, Georgia, in February 1817. In early manhood he settled in Savannah, where he dealt for many years in real and personal estate, specializing in the purchase and sale of Negroes. According to his notice in the Savannah *Republican* (February 24th, 1858), "The subscriber is constantly purchasing Negroes, either single or in families. If owners prefer their Negroes sold on commission, I will take them and become responsible against their escape, as I consider my jail and yard the safest, largest, and most comfortable in the city, if not in the state. Liberal advances will be made, if required, on all Negro property placed in my hands for sale." In February 1845 William Wright married Susan Bogardus, of New York. He died in Savannah on December 4th, 1860, survived by his wife and one child, and was buried in Laurel Grove Cemetery.

YANCEY, WILLIAM LOWNDES (1814–1863), lawyer, planter, editor, and legislator, son of Benjamin Cudworth Yancey (1783–1817) and Caroline Bird, was born in Warren County, Georgia, on August 10th, 1814. His father, a distinguished South Carolina lawyer, died in August 1817, and his mother married second (in 1822) the Rev. Nathan Sidney Smith Beman (1785–1871), then principal of the Mount Zion Academy, Hancock County, Georgia. In 1823 the boy removed with his mother and stepfather to Troy, New York, where Beman was pastor of the First Presbyterian Church (1823–1842). After attending Williams College for three years (1830–1833) he studied law in the office of Nathan Sayre, of Sparta, Georgia, and later in the office of Benjamin F. Perry, of Greenville, South Carolina. On August 13th, 1835, he married Sarah Caroline Earle, daughter of George Washington Earle, of Greenville. For a short time he practiced law, engaged in planting, and edited the Greenville *Mountaineer*; in the winter of 1836–1837 he removed to Dallas County, Alabama, where he engaged in planting and edited the Cahaba *Democrat*; in the spring of 1839 he removed to Coosa (now Elmore) County, where he and his brother, Benjamin Cudworth Yancey (1817–1891), edited the Wetumpka *Argus*. He was a member of the state house of representatives (1841), the state senate (1843), and Congress (1844–1846). In 1846 he removed to Montgomery, where he was elected delegate to the Democratic National Convention in 1848, 1856, and 1860. He was an influential member of the state constitutional convention meeting in Montgomery in January 1861, and he was later appointed chairman of the commission sent to England and France to secure recognition of the Confederate States. In the summer of 1862 he returned, having failed in his mission, and took his seat in the Confederate Senate, to which he had been elected on February 21st, 1862. He died on his plantation near Montgomery on July 28th, 1863, and was buried in Oakwood Cemetery.

YULEE, ELIAS LEVY (1804–1878), lawyer, educator, and civil servant, son of Moses Elias Levy (1781–1854), was born on the island of St. Thomas on February 1st, 1804. He was an elder brother of David Levy Yulee (1810–1886), United States delegate from Florida Territory (1841–1845), United States senator from Florida (1845–1851; 1855–1861), member of the Confederate Congress (1861–1865), and president of the Atlantic & Gulf Railroad. Both brothers in middle life adopted the traditional family name of Yulee, dropped by their father before their birth, and said to have been bestowed as a Moorish title on their ancestors, Portuguese Jewish refugees in Morocco. Moses Elias Levy accumulated a large fortune from the lumber business in St. Thomas; in 1816 he removed to Havana, Cuba, and thence in 1821 to St. Augustine, Florida, where he acquired vast tracts of land and became a leading citizen. He devoted much thought and energy to the colonization and development of Florida, and his name was perpetuated in the county of Levy and in the town of Yulee. Elias Levy Yulee entered Harvard College in 1822 but left during his soph-

omore year, in October 1823, to join his father, then residing temporarily in London, England. Returning to Florida, he lived with his younger brother for several years (1827–1831) on their father's plantation in Alachua and then settled in St. Augustine. He married his cousin, Rachel Benjamin (1811–1882), a cousin of the Hon. Judah P. Benjamin (1811–1884), Confederate secretary of war (1861–1862) and secretary of state (1862–1865). Elias Levy Yulee was principal of the preparatory department of Woodward College, Cincinnati, Ohio (1845–1849); receiver of public moneys, Olympia, Washington Territory (1855–1858); and assistant examiner in the Patent Office, Washington, D.C. (1858–1861). At the outbreak of the Civil War he returned to Florida, where he served in the Commissary Department with rank of major. After the war he settled in Walthourville, Liberty County, Georgia, where for some months in 1866 he was local agent of the Freedmen's Bureau (the Federal Bureau of Refugees, Freedmen, and Abandoned Lands). He was author of *An Address to the Colored People of Georgia* (1868), a thirty-two-page booklet furnishing "a course of facts that may be useful in the hands of intelligent whites to present to the colored people in their immediate vicinity." In 1871 he opened a "select school" for boys. A notice in the Savannah *Republican* (March 8th, 1871) stated that "Mr. E. Yulee, residing at Walthourville, forty miles by rail from Savannah, will receive into his family six pupils, to whom he will devote his strict attention, and extend to them all the comforts and freedom of a home." Yulee died in Savannah on March 30th, 1878, and was buried in Bonaventure Cemetery. As the Savannah *Morning News* (April 1st, 1878) observed, "He was a man of excellent intellectual attainments, a close reader and thinker, and a firm believer in the Swedenborgian or New Church doctrine, and was the author of several works on that subject." Rachel (Benjamin) Yulee died on February 17th, 1882, and was buried beside her husband.

ZIMMERMAN, CHARLES C. A. (1800–1867), educator, born in Germany, migrated to the United States in early manhood and settled in Columbia, South Carolina, where "Dr. and Mrs. Zimmerman's school for young ladies, English, classical, and ornamental" enjoyed a discriminating patronage for many years. In the Federal Census of 1860 Zimmerman was recorded as a "teacher of music" and his wife Hannah, born in South Carolina, was recorded as a "teacher of the common school." The Zimmermans were childless. They were neighbors and friends of the Rev. Dr. Charles Colcock Jones and his family during the Joneses' residence in Columbia from 1848 to 1850. Charles Zimmerman died in Columbia on December 13th, 1867, and was buried in the First Presbyterian Churchyard. According to his tombstone, "His life was devoted to literature and useful purposes."

Index

A NOTE ON THE INDEX

Considerations of space necessitate confining coverage to the text of the letters (pp. 35–1423). All personal names are indexed. The principal characters are indexed comprehensively; the lesser characters are indexed exhaustively. Incidental references ("Love to Aunt Susan and Cousin Laura") are rarely indexed. A separate index of slaves follows the index of free citizens; the name of the owner, when known, follows in parentheses the name of the slave.

KEY TO ABBREVIATIONS

ASJ	Abigail Sturges (Dowse) Jones	JJR	Joseph Jones Robarts
CCJ	Rev. Dr. Charles Colcock Jones	JNJ	James Newton Jones
CCJJ	Charles Colcock Jones, Jr.	JOJ	Rev. John Jones
CCJ3	Charles Colcock Jones III	JRK	Julia Rebecca (Maxwell) King
CCM	Charles Colcock Mallard	JWR	Joseph William Robarts
CEMB	Charles Edward Maxwell Buttolph	KCS	Katherine Clay (Kitty) Stiles
CNW	Charles Nephew West	LEM	Laura Elizabeth Maxwell
CSD	Caroline Smelt Davis		(Mrs. Laura E. Buttolph)
	(Mrs. Caroline S. Jones)	LJR	Louisa Jane Robarts
CWW	Dr. Charles William West	MCJ	Mary Cuthbert Jones
DLB	Rev. David Lyman Buttolph	MER	Mary Eliza Robarts
EAW	Eliza Alice (Whitehead) West	MJ	Mary (Jones) Jones
EBE	Eva Berrien Eve	MJH	Matilda Jane Harden
	(Mrs. Eva B. Jones)	MJM	Mary Jones Mallard
EBM	Eliza Burnley Mallard	MJT	Mary Jones Taylor
ECC	Eliza Caroline Clay	MEW	Mary Elizabeth (King) Wells
ECJ	Edgeworth Casey Jones	MRJ	Mary Ruth Jones
EDR	Ellen Douglas Robarts	MSJ	Mary Sharpe Jones
EGR	Eliza Greene (Low) Robarts		(Mrs. Mary S. Mallard)
EM	Elizabeth (Jones) Maxwell	MSR	Mary Sophia Robarts
EWR	Elizabeth Walton Robarts	RBW	Ruth Berrien Whitehead
GH	Rev. Dr. George Howe		(Mrs. Ruth B. Jones)
GMM	Georgia Maxwell Mallard	RK	Roswell King
HHJ	Henry Hart Jones	RHM	Robert Holt Mallard
JAJ	Jane Adaline (Dunwody) Jones	RQM	Rev. Robert Quarterman Mallard
JAMK	James Audley Maxwell King	SHJ	Susan Hyrne Jones
JBJ	Julia Berrien Jones	SMB	Susan Mary Buttolph
JCJ	John Carolin Jones	SMC	Susan Mary (Jones) Cumming
JDB	James David Buttolph	SSDJ	Samuel Stanhope Davis Jones
JDJ	James Dunwody Jones	WHK	William Henry King
JEW	Hon. John Elliott Ward	WM	William Maxwell
JHJ	Joseph Henry Jones	WSB	William Smyth Buttolph
JJ	Dr. Joseph Jones	WWW	William Whitehead West

The Free

Savannah, 266; to read Aytoun's *Bothwell*, 267–68; performs Ladson-Varnedoe wedding, 271–72; delivers sausages to CCJJ in Savannah, 278; delivers MJ's letter to MSJ, 279; takes MSJ's likeness to CCJ and MJ, 282; calls meeting of Presbytery, 297; LEM visits Savannah for confinement, 302–11 passim; attends JJ's lecture, 305; attends birth of CEMB, 308; asked by CCJ to "give an eye" to Maybank during CCJ's absence, 322; rides often to Maybank, 332, 333, 334, 351; CEMB "growing fatter and more lovely and engaging every day," 333; lectures on Romans weekly, 344; resigns Maybank key to JAMK, 351; to exchange pulpits with RQM, 367, 368; neglects to invite RQM to tea at W. Cumming's, 380; notifies CCJ of death of CEMB, 415; CCJJ's shock and grief, 415–16; family's distress, 417, 423; MER's sympathy, 419; worships with Kings and Joneses at Woodville, 423; visits Phillis (JRK) in illness, 433; MER thanks LEM for adding DLB to family, 445; remembered by MSJ on visit to Lookout Mountain, 445–46; to bring home "Old Lady Norman" for LEM's confinement, 454; birth of JDB, 458–60; walks daily with LEM, 464; pronounces RBW "a most capital housekeeper," 467, 471; on *Wanderer* case, 468; brings CCJJ Indian hatchet, 494; learns "all about" sewing machines in the North, 507; CNW to bring mail to Island for, 511; "the bishop of Midway" visits Savannah, 519, 521; has two days' preaching at Midway Church, 522; to attend JJ's wedding, 526; visits EGR, 529; preaches two excellent sermons, 539; to observe Thanksgiving Day, 539; "uncommon turnout" at Midway Church, 540; preaches admirable sermon, 543; J. C. Stiles "delighted" with his preaching, 580; announces CWW's death to MJ, 587–88; accompanies LEM and SMC to Marietta, 610; his presence missed, 611; spends day at Maybank, 622; takes fourth manuscript volume of CCJ's *History* to Savannah, 625, 626; to accompany RBW back to Savannah, 655; to exchange pulpits with I. S. K. Axson, 655; has "satisfactory" deathbed interview with W. G. Martin, 660–61; conducts Martin's funeral, 661; preaches "excellently," 663; to request meeting of Presbytery to reconsider appointing commissioners to General Assembly, 669; birth of WSB, 675, 680; thanks MJ for congratulations, 676; to visit George (CCJJ) in illness at Maybank, 676–77; Midway pulpit always open to CCJ, 677; "the present looks dark," 677; compliments CCJJ's Chatham Artillery oration, 677; reports to CCJ on Hinesville meeting on public affairs, 694; accompanies SMC to station, 708; to send up buggy for SMC, 716; rides over to Maybank with SMC, JAMK, and E. Parsons, 730; rides over to Maybank with SMC and JDB, 735; MER misses him at Atlanta convention, 738; introduces Mr. —— to CCJ, 741; JOJ writes from Virginia, 759–62; copies and approves

CCJ's letter concerning Mr. ——, accused of fathering mulatto child, 776; JOJ with him on fast day, 856; participates in skirmish with Federal gunboats in North Newport River, 885–88; sees to weighing of cotton, 889; assists JOJ in selling cotton, 895; visits Joneses in Walthourville, 917; consults with CCJ about escape of Negroes to enemy, 929; RQM sees "Audley's little girl" at DLB's house, 947; removes to Flemington, 988, 990, 999; absent from Synod, misses bolt of shirting, 988; removes Negroes to Baker County, 996, 998, 999, 1001; admits three whites to Midway Church, 999; joins family gathering at Arcadia, 1008; considers selling cotton, 1009; offer of fifty cents for cotton open to, 1011; conducts CCJ's funeral, 1042; notifies Robartses of CCJ's death, 1044, 1045; MER sends thanks for letter, 1045; notifies JOJ of CCJ's death, 1046, 1047; notifies GH of CCJ's death, 1049; conducts parting service for military companies in Midway Church, 1057; writes tenderly of CCJ, 1061; to conduct Communion at Midway Church, 1061; to go to Baker County, 1061, 1063, 1065; MJ to inform CCJJ further of his plans, 1063; now at home, 1063; to attend probate of CCJ's will, 1065, 1067; to be at home next week, 1067; conducts EBM's funeral, 1084; thinks CCJJ's account of Fort Wagner bombardment should be published, 1103; visits H. H. Delegal in final illness, 1132; visits Mallards in Atlanta, 1140; writes RQM, 1140; brings dress to SMC and LEM, 1141; his house catches fire, 1154–55; teaches JDB to read, 1155; preaches to Liberty Guards in Charleston, 1164; EGR sends love to, 1183; accompanies MJ to Atlanta, 1191, 1193; returns from Dorchester, 1196; conducts J. Rokenbaugh's funeral, 1197; preaches in Dorchester, 1210; MSJ visits, 1213; LJR sends JJR's clothes to, 1214; speaks of entering Confederate service, 1218; must hide from Yankees to care for family, 1219; walks from Flemington to Montevideo, 1246; escorts Kate King and children to Taylor's Creek, 1246; walks from Flemington to Montevideo, 1247–48; pleased to receive MJ's letter, 1261; postpones journey to Baker County, 1261, 1263, 1309; dines with JRK, 1261; administers Communion at Flemington Church, 1263; daily expected in Baker County, 1266, 1267; his houses on Island burned, 1277; receives letter from father, 1278; preaches WHK's funeral sermon, 1302, 1304; visits Montevideo, 1312; invited to renew work at Midway Church, 1312; to be invited to EDR's wedding, 1325; escorts MJ from Montevideo to Savannah, 1344; visits father in North, 1347, 1352; considers possibility of residing in Williamstown, Massachusetts, 1347; Gilbert (CCJ) takes his horse to Montevideo, 1347; sees WM in Dorchester, 1347; MSJ wants photograph of, 1348; MSJ wishes LEM had accompanied him to North, 1349; will re-

Jones, Charles Colcock (continued)

for check, 296; visits sons in Savannah, 298–99; gratified by CCJJ's invitation to SMC, 300; to arrange bank loan, 300–01; preaches at Pleasant Grove, 302–03; his health does not improve, 304; settles account of Cassius (CCJ), 306; Cassius (CCJ) and family on sale in New Orleans, 309–10; CCJJ's response, 310; MJ arranges for MSJ's wedding, 311; friends regret inability to attend wedding, 312–14; attends Presbytery in Bryan County, 315; travels to Kentucky and Virginia, 315–66 passim; Lexington, 316–29 passim; Cincinnati, 329–36 passim; White Sulphur Springs, 336–37 passim; Hot Springs, 337–49 passim; Rockbridge Alum Springs, 354–57; Rockbridge Baths, 357–59; Rome, 359–63; attends General Assembly, 316–24; visits EGR, 317; visits JOJ, 317–18; health feeble, 318; meets J. N. West, 318, 320; meets Vice-President Breckinridge and lady, 320, 325; visits J. N. West, 322–26 passim; describes country around Lexington, 324; attends Alexander's annual sale of cattle, 325; preaches in Horeb Church, 325, 329; visits Ashland, 327–28; visits Lexington Cemetery, 328–29; travels from Lexington to Cincinnati, 329, 335; visits J. S. Law, 329–30, 335–36, 340; describes Cincinnati, 335–36; travels from Cincinnati to White Sulphur Springs, 336, 340; his health *in statu quo,* 336–37, 338, 355–56; renews bank note, 337; pays taxes, 337; concerned for sons' spiritual state, 337; travels from White Sulphur Springs to Hot Springs, 337–38, 342; W. Crump advises temperate bath, 338, 342; converses with W. Meade, 340; converses with J. M. Wayne, 342; his *Catechism* used by JOJ in colored Sunday school, 345; not benefited by baths at Hot Springs, 347; describes life at Hot Springs, 348–49; describes life at Rockbridge Alum Springs, 354–55; misses his children, 355; fears increasing cares on return home, 356; urges MSJ to "omit no attentions" to WM, 356; urges MSJ to write EGR, 356; suggests RQM preach sermon on reverence for aged, 356–67; travels from Rockbridge Alum Springs to Rockbridge Baths, 357–58; takes drive in "pleasure wagon," 358; worships at Bethesda Church, 358–59; hears S. P. Huff preach in hotel ballroom, 359; travels from Rockbridge Baths to Rome, Georgia, 359–60; MJ "decidedly affected" by forty-two miles' staging, 360; on JJ's unanimous election to Athens professorship, 360, 361–63; recommends W. L. Mitchell as "one of the best of men," 363; his travels summarized by MSJ for RQM, 364; fatigues himself putting study in order, 367; misses MSJ, 368; anticipates MSJ's visit with pleasure, 368; falls from horse, 371, 372; attends Presbytery in Savannah, 379; informed of EGR's illness, 389–91; informed of CCJJ's engagement to RBW, 391–92; saddened by news of EGR's illness, 392; records "week of travel," 398; receives "most affecting" let-

ter from L. B. Helm, 399; concerned for CCJJ's spiritual state, 399; a day of interruptions, 399; attends Presbytery in St. Marys, 399–407 passim; engages plantation manager (E. McDonald), 402; congratulated by MER on birth of MJM, 410–11; turns "housekeeper" at birth of MJM, 411; invited by MER for summer visit, 411; MJ gives CCJ medicines sent by JJ, 415; notified of death of CEMB, 415; visits Savannah to meet RBW, 416, 417; suffers throat attack on train, 416, 416–17; "another friend to love and pray for," 417; "very much pleased" with RBW, 417, 418; baptizes MJM and E. L. Jones in Walthourville, 421; remembers MSJ's birthday, 422; on baptism of MJM, 422; removes to Maybank for summer, 422; minor accident en route, 422; very feeble, 423; worships with Kings and Buttolphs at Woodville, 423; CCJJ sends CCJ magazine containing steel engraving and biographical notice of Sir H. Havelock, 427; orders ink from Cooper's, 430–31, 432; will be glad to read *The Cruise of the Betsy,* 431; regrets F. H. Bowman's alleged plagiarism of Melvill's sermon, 431; visits Phillis (JRK) in illness, 433; conducts her funeral, 433; on importance of cherishing the aged, 433; cattle suffering from murrain, 433; urges CCJJ to go immediately to housekeeping after marriage, 438; CCJJ replies, 439; CCJJ wishes he could exchange health with, 439; CCJJ hopes CCJ will perform marriage ceremony, 439; acts as "senior pastor" during RQM's absence, 445; suffers from "tickling in the throat," 449; wishes to attend Synod, 454; wishes to consult GH about *History,* 454; appreciates grand spectacle on causeway at night, 455; attends birth of JDB, 458–60; MJM resembles CCJ and MJ, 465; attends CCJJ's wedding, 466; visits JJ in Augusta, 466–67; abominates reopening slave trade, 468; on L. W. Spratt, 468; on W. T. Thompson, 468; urges CCJJ to exercise daily, 470; sends for J. P. Stevens to attend MJ's hepatitis, 470; orders Negro blankets from Lathrop, 471; orders sundry household goods from Claghorn & Cunningham, 471; hopes to hear CCJJ address Georgia Historical Society, 471, 473; sends kind wishes to JEW on departure for China, 471, 472; wishes to reduce bank note, 472; hires Katy (EGR) and Lucy (EGR) another year, 474; hears CCJJ's address, 475; EGR recommends Saratoga Springs, 475, 476; MER concerned for his health, 476; MJM "very like" CCJ, 478; sends RQM notes of introduction for General Assembly, 479; advises RQM on conduct at General Assembly, 479; on CCJJ's purchase of plantation in Baker County, 487–88; "impossible to be of two professions," 488; MJM "an uncommonly interesting child," 488; welcomes CCJJ and RBW to Maybank, 488, 489; "the great secret of happiness in life," 488–89; endorses Nashville excursion, 489; appreciates CCJJ's account of Nashville ex-

tober *suns* and *dews*," 764; compliments CCJJ's annual report as mayor of Savannah, 764; on Confiscation Act, 764–65; anxious about backwardness of coastal defenses, 765; hopeful of CCJJ's spiritual state, 780; feels CCJJ and JJ have acted nobly in entering active service, 781; the Lord evidently "on our side," 781; MRJ weighs eighteen pounds at four months, 781, 784, 787; MJM's message to, 782; MSJ to keep CCJ and MRJ during MJ's visit to Marietta, 782; prizes CCJJ's ambrotype, 783, 785, 787; remembers CCJJ's birth thirty years ago, 783, 785; prays for repulse of invading fleet, 786; "the whole Confederacy is astir," 786; deplores Confederate "disaster" at Port Royal, 793; considers removing Negroes to up country, 793; CCJJ to inquire of J. G. Howard, 793; moves from Maybank to Montevideo, 793, 796; sends "very friendly salutations" to J. S. Claghorn, 794; on Lincoln's "boasted armada," 795; deplores A. R. Lawton's "miserable" administration, 795–96; urges CCJJ to make personal acquaintance of R. E. Lee, 796; preaches for Liberty Independent Troop, 796; remembers CCJJ's wedding anniversary, 796; on Port Royal reverse, 796–97; returns signed renewal of bank note, 797; feels "much anxiety for our commercial emporium," 797; to visit Savannah on business, 800; notes thirty-ninth anniversary of membership in Midway Church, 801–02; fears destruction of Skidaway bridge, 802; deplores "supineness and inefficiency" of A. R. Lawton, 802; deplores "perfect indifference of the citizens," 802; fears attack on Savannah by water, 802; requests RQM to attend citizens' meeting at Hinesville, 805; authorizes RQM to sign his name to action of meeting, 805; attends first General Assembly of Southern Presbyterian Church, 805–23 passim; detained twelve hours by railroad accident, 810; visits CSD, 810–23 passim; speaks before assembly on religious instruction of Negroes, 810, 813, 814–15, 815, 816, 817, 817–18, 821–22; to look at plantations in Burke County, 810; manuscript of his *History* deposited in vault of Bank of Augusta, 810; Cato (CCJ) to start cotton gin on Monday, 810; to buy cloth for Susan (CCJJ) and Martha (CCJ), 810; will be "thankful to return home," 810; advises CCJJ to decline captaincy of Oglethorpe Light Artillery, 811, 814, 821; invited by CCJJ to visit camp of Chatham Artillery en route home, 812, 816, 820–21, 822, 824; advised by CSD to sleep between blankets, 814; to fill MJ's order for shoes if possible, 814; aided by A. M. Cuthbert with her pen, 814; helped by RQM in walks to church, 814; S. S. Davis frequently sends carriage for, 814; dines with S. S. Davis, 815, 816; General Assembly marks "an era in our ecclesiastical history," 821; preaches to G. Dowse's Negroes, 822; regrets inability to visit CCJJ in camp, 822; to do so after Christmas, 822; "disease slays tenfold more than the sword in war," 822; concerned for

defenses of Savannah, 823; concerned for CCJJ's spiritual state, 823; to write CCJJ about RBW's portrait miniature, 823; Christmas greetings to CCJJ, 826; Christmas at Montevideo, 827; asks CCJJ's will regarding marriage of Susan (CCJJ) and Andrew (B. S. Screven), 827; "shall not be surprised to hear of an attack any day," 827; does not attend "contribution dinner" for Liberty Independent Troop, 827; death of J. B. Barnard, 827; visits CCJJ in camp, 829; CCJJ offered judge advocacy of H. R. Jackson's division, 830–31; CCJ's views, 831; CCJJ declines, 832–33; CCJ's response, 834–35; on Burnside expedition, 835; concerned for coastal defenses, 835, 838; little hope of aid from England or France, 835; anticipates "a protracted and deadly struggle," 836; sends CCJJ bank note duly signed, 844; to bring up watermelon seeds from Maybank, 844; hopes Lee's defenses will discourage enemy from making attack, 844; Georgia must do her duty, 844; Confederate government active in recruiting soldiers, 848; government must cease reliance on foreign nations, 848–49; people should not presume upon want of resolution in enemy, 849; people should not presume upon exhaustion of enemy's resources, 849; favors Fabian policy, 849; ravaging of coast "goes but a small way to a *conquest*," 849; CCJJ sends cask of porter, 851; institutes observance of Davis' inauguration as day of special prayer, 852; his daily prayer for CCJJ and his company, 855; late disasters unifying country, 855; Confederate Constitution acknowledges "the Almighty God"; U.S. Constitution acknowledges no God, 855, 860; J. Davis "accredited a *Christian man*," 855; with RQM on fast day, 856; receives Dunwodys en route from McIntosh to up country, 858; report of enemy's possession of Darien upsets Midway congregation, 858–59; "war is the most universal of all the divine judgments," 859; concerned for defense of Georgia coast, 859; favors system of impregnable fortifications, 859; decreases cotton crop, increases provision crop, 859–60; "not the faintest prospect of peace," 860; glad to see more vigor in government, 860; thanks CCJJ for porter, 861, 864, 870; JJ says CCJ must drink porter daily, 861; wishes "more energy and expansion" in Confederate government, 866; on European intervention, 866–67; his Negroes requisitioned by A. R. Lawton to work on Savannah River fortifications, 867; attends Presbytery in Walthourville, 873; concerned for preservation of Savannah, 881–82; extreme illness (river cholera) of seven Negroes sent to work on Savannah River fortifications, 882; to sell cotton to F. L. Gué, 882–83; recommends selling part of Arcadia crop, 882; records skirmish with Federal gunboats in North Newport River, 885–88; indignant at "most outrageous circumstance" in Savannah River, 892; distressed at fall of New Orleans, 892; regrets death of Bella

issues proclamation establishing day of fasting and prayer, 695; J. Davis "inspires great enthusiasm and confidence," 695; doubtful of finding successor in event of Davis' death, 695; Central Railroad declares dividend, 695; JBJ's illness, death, and burial, 698–711 passim; MJ stays with in Savannah, 699–716 passim; RBW gives birth to MRJ, 701; RBW's illness and death, 701–16 passim; anticipates "startling accounts from Virginia," 701; CCJ congratulates on birth of MRJ, 702; sick with sore throat and fever, 703–12 passim; acknowledges CCJ's letter on JBJ's death, 711–12; JBJ's "farewell to earth," 711; his desolation at probable death of RBW, 711; his contrition, 711; appreciates kindness of MJ, JJ, and SMC, 711–12, 714; urges CCJ not to venture trip to Savannah, 712; sees RQM in Savannah, 712; CCJ grieved at his distress, 713; CCJ sends sympathy to RBW, 713, 715; his "affliction" providential, 714–15; visits Maybank, 717; returns to Savannah, 718; considers his spiritual state, 718; MRJ improves, 719; his parents concerned for his spiritual state, 719–20; grateful for his parents' care of MRJ, 720; "mingled exultation and sorrow" at news of Manassas, 720–21; has portrait miniature of RBW painted, 721, 723, 731, 734, 801, 823, 834, 836, 838–39, 843; feels pressure following Manassas victory, 722; "living in a graveyard," 722; sends MJ obituary of RBW, 722; daguerreotype of RBW, 723, 731; mourning pin containing hair of RBW and JBJ, 723, 731; hair comb, 723; sends SMC mourning pin containing hair of RBW and JBJ, 723, 731; quotes Shakespeare's *King John* on grief, 723; attends funeral and burial of F. S. Bartow, 723–24; to continue mayoralty until October 1861, 724; thereafter to enter service as first lieutenant of Chatham Artillery, 724–25; RBW and JBJ taken "from the evil to come," 725; Chatham Artillery to be reserved for home and coastal defense, 725; "surely the Lord of Hosts is with us," 725; Confederate Constitution acknowledges God; Federal Constitution "a godless instrument," 725–26; sends mourning pin to MSJ, P. E. Neely, V. B. Whitehead, J. A. Howard, S. E. Whitehead, S. C. Harriss, and S. L. Berrien, 726; MJ's emotions on seeing pin, 728; MJ concerned for his spiritual state, 728–29; MJ pleased with obituary, 729; CCJ delighted with his municipal proclamation, 729; MJ grateful for comb, 729; CCJ grateful for RBW's likeness, 729; MJ suggests he send memento of RBW to CSD, 729; MJ offers to attend to any "work" he may send, 729; MJ urges him to "follow Joe's directions," 729; MRJ "improves daily," 729; MRJ "the image of her dear mother," 729, 731; MJ receives his letter of twenty-one pages, 730, 731; MRJ "very much improved," 731; his continuing grief at death of RBW and JBJ, 732–33; Chatham Artillery mustered into service, 733; appreciates parents' kindness to MRJ,

733–34; declines second term as mayor, 734; sends MJM necklace in memory of JBJ, 735; sends WM map of seat of war, 737; sends CCJ copy of New York *Daily Tribune,* 737; prints D. H. Porter's "In Memoriam" of RBW, 737; purchases two lots in Laurel Grove Cemetery, 737; enjoins parents to rebury RBW and JBJ in event of his death, 737; declines captaincy of Savannah Artillery, 738; visits JJ and family in Augusta, 742–43; dines with EGR and family in Marietta, 743; interviews J. E. Brown in Atlanta, 743; Atlanta "a most thriving place," 743; spends day in Bath, 743–44; a visit "at once pleasant and mournful," 743–44, 744, 747; visits JJ and family in Augusta, 744; meets C. J. Colcock in Atlanta, 744; returns to Savannah, 744; has "little faith" in small batteries on coastal islands, 745–46; favors reelection of Brown as governor, 746; War Department delay in supplying horses "prejudicial and unfortunate," 746; unfavorable intelligence from Kentucky, 746, 763; sends MJ "memorials" of RBW and JBJ, 746, 748; MJ's response, 749; his response, 750; sends MJ oolong tea, 746; *Bermuda* reaches Savannah from Liverpool, 748; MJ to assist him in preserving mementos of RBW, 749, 750, 751, 764, 769, 770, 771; sends MJ map of seat of war, 749; his grief continues, 751–52; "sorely afflicted," 755; CCJ concerned for his spiritual state, 755–56; his reply, 756–57; CCJ's reply, 757–58; declines reelection as mayor, 757; declines appointment to state legislature, 757; W. C. Daniell presses Confiscation Act, 762; fears for H. R. Jackson's "prudence," 763; work to commence on immediate defenses of Savannah, 763; Chatham Artillery stationed on Isle of Hope, 763; surprised at JJ's joining Liberty Independent Troop as private, 763; sees little prospect of JDJ's obtaining military commission, 763–64; cautioned by CCJ about "October *suns* and *dews*," 764; his annual report as mayor of Savannah gives CCJ "great satisfaction," 764; recommends sewerage plan of Paris, 764; asked to help JDJ secure place as private, 765–66; buys service horse, 766; drill of mounted battery onerous, 766; soon to join his company in camp, 766, 771; considers renting house and furniture to G. B. Lamar, 766–67, 768, 771, 772; sympathizes with JJ in his reasons for joining Liberty Independent Troop as private, 767; gives his own reasons for entering service, 767–68; several aspirants for Savannah mayoralty, 768; sad to part with house and furniture associated with RBW and JBJ, 768–69; to send RBW's wardrobe to P. E. Neely, 769; to keep JBJ's savings bank for MRJ, 769; to "see what can be done for Dunwody," 769; MJ offers to make camp blanket for, 169–70; MJ offers to do other sewing for, 770; sends MJ tea and gumdrops, 770; MJ suggests he store furniture on third floor and rent rest of house, 770; appreciates sprig of ver-

feeble, 1059; organizes church in Mitchell County, 1059, 1069; unsuccessful in securing summer clothing for MJ's Negroes, 1059–60; solicitous for comfort of Old Mama, 1060, 1069; Yankees approach Rome, 1060; to write N. J. Omberg for "true state of affairs," 1060; "sorely afflicted" in death of T. J. Jackson, 1060; RQM and MSJ wish JOJ to baptize EBM, 1060; unable to do so, 1060; must postpone visit to Liberty County, 1060; wrote CCJJ recently, 1060; congratulates JJ and CSD on birth of SHJ, 1060; offers MJ sow and shoats from Bonaventure, 1069; on RQM's call to Atlanta, 1069; conducts first Presbyterian Communion in Mitchell County, 1069–70; reminded of CCJ in work, 1070; "greatly pleased" with GH's obituary of CCJ, 1070; sympathizes with MJ in loss of CCJ, 1070; to return to Rome, 1070; sends letter to Old Mama, 1070; returns to Rome, 1074–75; visits Marietta, 1074; weather sultry, 1075; living ruinous, 1075; anxious for safety of Rome, 1075; appreciates CCJ's letters, 1075; advises RQM to be explicit about competent financial support, 1075; invites MJ and MRJ to spend summer in Rome, 1075; preaches to Texas Rangers in Rome, 1087–88; CCJJ pleased, 1089; absent in Southwest Georgia, 1107; sells house in nick of time, 1107; requests RQM to visit wounded soldier, 1108; to be informed of CCJJ's wedding, 1114; writes JJ for MJ's whereabouts, 1121; feels pressure of slave ownership, 1121–22; future looks dark, 1122; to visit MJ in January, 1122; recalls CCJ's strong character, 1122; considers plantation matters at Bonaventure, 1122; MJ anticipates his visit, 1132, 1139; visits MJ, 1145, 1148, 1149; will probably attend Presbytery, 1157; baptizes A. A. Jones, 1159; reports JDJ's military status, 1166–67; on crop prospects in Baker County, 1167; military affairs at fearful crisis, 1167; regrets inability to aid EGR, 1167–68; organizes church at Bond's Mills, 1168, 1190; EGR's safe removal from Marietta "a great relief," 1189; anxious for Mallards' safety in Atlanta, 1189; has great confidence in J. E. Johnston, 1189; concerned for future of Confederacy, 1189–90; invites Mallards to take refuge in Baker County, 1190; wishes to have accompanied RQM on visit to Kennesaw Mountain, 1190; rejoices in religious interest in army, 1190; regrets inability to return to chaplaincy, 1190; longs to hear from MJ, 1190; regrets MSJ's recent injury, 1203; glad Mallards have refuge in Walthourville, 1203; loss of Atlanta greatest blow of war, 1203; longs for a Lee at head of every corps, 1203; suffers fatigue and fever, 1204; reported well, 1216; MJ's letter intercepted by Yankees, 1241; escorts MSJ and family from Montevideo to Baker County, 1253–59; spends night with D. A. Miller, 1253; with W. Hughes, 1254; with Messrs. Hall, 1254; with W. Hughes, 1254; camps out near Altamaha River, 1255; suffers from heavy rain, 1255–56; recommends

MJ's route from Montevideo to Baker County, 1257; travels to No. 7 depot, 1258; stays with M. R. Pettigrew, 1258; MSJ's silver stolen at Doctortown, 1258–59; submits affair to R. S. Camp, 1259; MJ grateful for his safe journey, 1259; arrives safely in Baker County with MSJ and family, 1261; MJ arrives safely in Baker County, 1261, 1264, 1265, 1266, 1268; his place named Refuge prospectively, 1264; disappointed at WM's nonappearance, 1265; his provision crop short, 1266, 1267; offers MJ use of place in Baker County, 1267; sends letters to Atlanta by WWW, 1281, 1291–92; receives letters sent by HHJ, 1281–82; remembers visit of MJ and MSJ in Baker County, 1282; sends news of family, 1282; his future dark, 1282; restlessness among freedmen, 1282–83; Negro labor a drug, 1283; Rescue (horse) improves, 1283; concerned for MJ's affairs in Liberty County, 1283; forwards ECC's letter to MJ, 1283; to rewrite "hurried estimate" of CCJ, 1283, 1293; asks RQM's plans, 1283; to answer MSJ's letter, 1283; receives letter from MJ, 1291; sympathizes with MJ in postwar adjustment, 1292; "emancipation trials" in Baker County, 1292–93; overburdened supporting Negroes, 1293; MJ's Negroes behaving well, 1293; gives MJ news of Liberty County, 1293; MJ to visit in Baker County, 1295; MJ rejoices to hear news of, 1300; hears news of MJ through JDJ, 1302; "astonished and vexed" at conduct of Porter (CCJ) and Patience (CCJ), 1302; his own servants undependable, 1302–03; his future dark, 1303; MJ anxious to hear from, 1303; MSJ writes not to send Negroes from Baker County, 1305; CCJJ to write about Porter (CCJ) and Patience (CCJ), 1305; sends MJ lard and sausages, 1317–18; visits MSJ in Atlanta, 1318; accepts call to Griffin, 1318, 1332; fifty years old, 1318; appreciates photographs of CCJ, 1318; sympathizes with MJ in "humbling circumstances," 1318; most of his servants leave, 1318; to be invited to EDR's wedding, 1325; reported moving to Lexington, Kentucky, 1355; visits Mallards in Atlanta, 1356; to assist J. Stacy at Communion, 1356; EGR writes, 1361; writes EGR, 1367; best genealogist in family, 1368; writes EGR of JAJ's illness, 1368; writes sadly of JAJ's health, 1379, 1381; MJ visits, 1387; looks thin and much older, 1387; sketches CCJ's missionary labors for J. L. Wilson, 1387; anxious for safety of MSJ and family, 1394, 1394–95, 1400; urges MJ to settle in Griffin, 1394; writes MJ at Marietta, 1394; informed by CCJJ of ECJ's birth, 1395; buys cottage in Griffin, 1395; MSJ writes every week, 1399, 1400; shares MJ's anxiety for safety of MSJ and family, 1400; invites MJ to Griffin en route home, 1400–01; introduces Griffin gentleman to CCJJ, 1401; misses MJ at train in Griffin, 1412, 1413; visits JJ during General Assembly, 1412–13; baptizes MCJ, 1413; CCJ's *History* commended to General

tion, 1050; in Charleston, 1055; JOJ congratulates on birth of SHJ, 1060; CCJ visits, 1064, 1065, 1072; invites MJ to spend summer in Augusta, 1068; looks badly, 1072; to visit R. M. Johnston in Sparta, 1072; MJ concerned for his health, 1072–73; saves life of Adam (CCJ), 1077; EBM's death and burial, 1081–85 passim; CCJJ sends RQM and MSJ condolences, 1081–82; CCJJ sends MJ condolences, 1082; MJ recounts death to JJ and CSD, 1083–84; CSD sends MSJ condolences, 1084–85; visits Richmond, 1084, 1087; sends MSJ condolences, 1089–90; CCJ's care, example, and instruction a great blessing to his children, 1090; approves RQM's removal to Atlanta, 1090; moves to new rented house, 1090; struck by endurance of sick soldiers, 1090; MJ to visit before frost, 1098; telegraphed of SHJ's illness, 1100; MJ grieved at illness of his children, 1103; returns to Augusta, 1106; anticipates MJ's visit, 1106; soon to be with CCJJ on James Island, 1113; JOJ writes for MJ's whereabouts, 1121; feels financial pressure of war, 1123; having much company, 1123; much illness in family, 1127; MSJ's regret, 1131; MJ anticipates his visit, 1132; visits MJ at Arcadia, 1136–45 passim; leaves with EBE and MRJ on visit to CCJJ and EBE, 1136; now in Florida, 1138; dines with WM, 1138; spends night with SMC, 1138; his cow missing several weeks, 1139; to return to Augusta, 1139; spends time in South Carolina and Florida, 1139; dyes MJ's white homespun blue, 1139; MRJ recognizes MSJ and JJ in likeness, 1145; MJ sends MJM and CCM hymn he said in childhood, 1155–56; MJ to put up butter for, 1163; MJ to visit, 1164; JOJ asks to be remembered to, 1167; informs MSJ of MJ's improvement, 1173; goes to Liberty County to attend MJ in illness, 1173; RQM sends books to Augusta for safety from Yankees, 1174; invites Mallards to Augusta in emergency, 1175, 1182; visits Mallards in Atlanta, 1186, 1188; MJ to send butter to, 1186; MJ to visit, 1187; offers services to chief field surgeon in Marietta, 1188; Mallards take refuge with, 1191–94; MJ visits, 1191–1213 passim; attends MSJ's dislocated collarbone, 1192; sends family picture to SMC, 1194; to take medical reports to Richmond, 1194; assisted by L. Manigault, 1194, 1202, 1208; to go to Andersonville, 1197, 1199; SMC appreciates his family picture, 1197; visits CSD and children in Beech Island, 1200; labors among "smallpox Yankees," 1202; leaves Augusta, 1202, 1204; investigates diseases at Andersonville Prison, 1208; in Macon, 1208; assisted by A. C. Ives, 1208, 1210; M. Glen sends valuables to his care, 1208, 1211; LEM hopes he won't wear himself out, 1209; to return to Augusta, 1211; his whereabouts unknown to MJ, 1217; writes MJ, 1249; reports hopes for success of peace commissioners, 1250; anxious for safety of MJ and MSJ, 1251; devising plans to visit MJ, 1251, 1252; CCJJ writes reports in his

office, 1252; rejoices in noble conduct of Gilbert (CCJ), 1252–53; overworked, 1253; helps MJ arrange for journey to Baker County, 1259–60, 1262; goes to Altamaha River and returns, 1260; LEM glad to hear from, 1262–63; accompanies MJ to railroad at Blackshear, 1265, 1268; MJ hopes he has reached Augusta safely, 1266; reaches Augusta safely, 1267–68, 1269; embarrassed by deranged currency, 1268; storeroom robbed, 1268–69; MJ sends CSD "kind remembrances" by, 1269; most of his Negroes leave, 1274, 1276, 1290; quite well, 1276; JAMK offers to act as agent for, 1277; MJ receives no letter from, 1279; to expedite EBE's letter to MJ, 1281; CSD gives birth to CCJ3, 1284; performs postmortem in Burke County, 1288; MJ on birth of CCJ3, 1288; MSJ on birth of CCJ3, 1289; MSJ invites to Atlanta, 1290; to get news of Pittsburgh General Assembly from J. R. Wilson, 1290; MSJ asks for news of CCJ3 and CSD, 1290; his health improves, 1294; MJ remembers his birthday, 1294; MJ visits en route to Liberty County, 1297, 1299; prescribes for MRJ's ear affection, 1298; attends Henry Wirz trial in Washington, D.C., 1299; to confer with J. L. Rogers about paper for CCJ's *History*, 1300–01, 1309; well, 1310; laboring too hard, 1311; CSD would announce him as "brightest and best," 1315; CCJJ hopes to sell Arcardia, 1319; CCJJ visits in Augusta, 1320, 1321; looking badly, 1320; MJ anxious to hear from, 1329, 1330; to visit MJ, 1333, 1335; to escort MJ to New York, 1334, 1345, 1349; MJ to visit in summer, 1335; to attend to publication of CCJJ's *History*, 1335, 1342; MJ visits, 1344–46; "very thin and worked down," 1344; disappointed at missing KCS, 1344; predicts direct railroad communication between Savannah and New Orleans, 1345; accompanies MJ to New York, 1349–54 passim; visits Nashville, 1349–50; offered professorship at Medical College of Nashville, 1350; observes cholera panic in Cincinnati, 1350; stays at hotel in New York, 1351; to confer with publishers about CCJ's *History*, 1351; announced as professor of pathology at Medical College of Nashville, 1352; MSJ says he must not work too hard, 1353; returns from New York, 1354; accepts Nashville professorship, 1356; places CCJ's *History* in publisher's hands, 1362; urgent about publication, 1363; sends CCJJ original copy of CCJ's *History*, 1370; wishes to divide furniture and books among children, 1370; sends money toward publication of CCJ's *History*, 1379, 1381; invites MJ to spend summer, 1381; MJ visits in Nashville, 1387–1404 passim; opposes MJ's risking yellow fever in New Orleans, 1392, 1397; very feeble, 1392; frees Nashville from cholera, 1392; MER asks MJ about his Nashville situation, 1393; MJ writes MSJ of CSD and children, 1396; SMC congratulates on freeing Nashville from cholera, 1398–99; MER hopes he prospers in business, 1399; CSD

433; enjoys full health, 433; urges CCJJ to go immediately to housekeeping after marriage, 435; CCJJ replies, 437; gives MSJ $50 for up-country trip, 435, 438; fixes up wardrobe of George (CCJJ), 437–38; CCJJ's thanks, 440, 441; prizes likeness of MJM, 448, 449, 454; busy preparing for CCJJ's nuptials, 449, 454; wedding plans undecided, 454; appreciates grand spectacle on causeway at night, 455; attends birth of JDB, 458–60; attends CCJJ's wedding, 466; visits JJ in Augusta, 466–67; dispatches housekeeping articles for CCJJ and RBW, 463; CCJJ and RBW make "delightful visit" to Montevideo, 463, 464; Christmas at Montevideo, 469; thanks RBW for fruit, 469; wishes to hear CCJJ's essay on "Indian Remains," 470; suffers from hepatitis, 468, 469, 470; gradually improves, 471, 472, 473; cheered by visits of MSJ and JJ, 470, 471; hopes to hear CCJJ address Georgia Historical Society, 471, 473; sends oysters to CCJJ and RBW, 472; sends oysters to EGR, 473; enjoys fruit sent by CCJJ, 472, 473; improves under "retrenchment system," 473; hears CCJJ's address, 475; EGR recommends Saratoga Springs, 475, 476; purple spots on her dress MJM thinks flies, 478; wishes CCJJ to visit Hermitage on anticipated Nashville excursion, 485; visits R. Q. Way and wife, 485; visits J. L. Harden, 485; advises CCJJ on care of painful thumb, 485; sends CCJJ chipped beef, 486; "at work upstairs and downstairs," 488; welcomes CCJJ and RBW to Maybank, 489; CCJJ buys cedar dipper made by convict, 491; visits MSJ and RQM, 495–97; appreciates CCJJ's account of Nashville excursion, 496; anticipates visit of CCJJ and RBW, 496; announced as "Lady Manager" of Mount Vernon cause in Liberty County, 496–97; asks P. W. Fleming for contribution from military companies, 497; sends carriage to Walthourville for CCJJ and RBW, 499–500; busy readying JJ for wedding, 504, 514, 520; anxious over health of Savannah, 505; CCJJ and RBW always welcome at Maybank, 505–06; orders panes of glass from Falligant's, 506, 510, 510–11; warns MSJ not to allow MJM to kiss dog, 506; regrets death of G. W. Walthour, 507; visits Walthourville to see Howes and Walthours, 509–10; GH preaches "one of the best sermons I ever listened to," 509; hopes for religious blessings in Liberty County, 509; regrets inability to hear CCJJ's address in Walthourville, 510, 512; anticipates visit of CCJJ and RBW at Maybank, 510; welcomes CNW to Maybank, 510; sends RBW ducks, chickens, eggs, and quince preserves, 513; copies CCJ's piece for *The Southern Presbyterian Review*, 514; promises to attend RBW in confinement, 516; CCJJ expresses thanks, 516; feels "very sadly" at JJ's departure, 516; wishes wood stain from Solomons (druggist), 519; CCJJ replies, 521; prepares "some very pretty *little* work" for CCJJ's expected child, 520; sends CCJ's

"epigram for Monday morning" to CCJJ, 520; receives long letter from ECC, 520; reads Everett's oration on Webster's statue, 520; numbers her "half century," 520, 521–22; sends CCJJ bag of red potatoes, 520–21; to attend JJ's wedding, 525; esteemed by CCJ as model wife, 526; on Harper's Ferry affair, 528; to attend RBW in confinement, 529; attends RBW in confinement, 534–44 passim; describes birth of JBJ, 538; feels responsibility, 538; reports on *Wanderer* trial, 538; urged by CCJ to take rest, 539; to order "house supplies" from Claghorn & Cunningham, 539; considers JOJ's travel plans, 541–42; white nurse (Mrs. Hall) engaged for JBJ, 542, 543; Thanksgiving Day in Savannah, 542; on infanticide of Lucy (EGR), 542; to buy locks from S. Palmer, 543; eager to return to CCJ, 543; proposes "marooning" in kitchen, 543–44; presented silver goblet by JBJ, 544, 1225; asks CCJJ and RBW to read Scott's *Commentary* together, 544; directs CCJJ in disposition of railroad dividend, 545; solicitous for CCJJ's eyes and throat, 545; CCJJ's reply, 546; prefers CCJJ never to plant or manage Negroes, 547; EGR not to bear expenses of trial of Lucy (EGR) for infanticide, 547; presents crib to MJM, 547; presents crib to JBJ, 547; sends RBW jar of yellow orange preserves, 552; her dresses to be altered by A. F. Hyde, 552; advises CCJJ not to "sacrifice" land, 553, 554; asks CCJJ to call on Robarts girls in Savannah, 556; invites RBW to visit Montevideo, 556–57; MJM "perfectly satisfied" with grandparents in MSJ's absence, 557; CCJJ accepts her present of crib for JBJ, 557; orders tea, sparkling gelatin, and quinine from King & Waring, 560; thanks CCJJ for fruit, 563; distressed by "intemperance" of JWR, 563–64; on sin of intemperance, 564; concerned for CCJJ's spiritual state, 564–65, 568; CCJJ replies, 565; asks RBW for details of JBJ, 569; attends JRK in pleurisy, 571; wishes to see MJM and JBJ every day, 571; enjoys visits of JJ and CSD, 571; indebted to J. C. Stiles for "some of my deepest religious impressions," 572; anticipates "long visit" with MSJ, 572; anticipates CCJJ's "promised visit," 572; her "horror" at conduct of JWR, 572; "our commonest blessings are our greatest," 572; copies fifty pages of CCJ's *History* for *The Southern Presbyterian Review*, 572; MSJ gives birth to CCM, 575–79 passim; sends MJM strawberries on second birthday, 575; attends MSJ at birth of CCM, 576–78; suffers invalid finger, 578; visits Savannah and Augusta, 579–81; calls on Mackays, 579; hears H. R. Jackson's address, 579; hears I. S. K. Axson, 580; hears J. C. Stiles, 580; promises MJM clothes and toy, 580; visits mantua-maker, 580; suffers fever in Augusta, 580; sends beads to Kate (MSJ), Elvira (MSJ), and Tenah (MSJ), 583; shocked by announcement of CWW's death, 587–88; informs CCJ of CWW's death, 588; re-

Jones, Mary (Jones) (continued)

enjoys visit at Montevideo, 1375; MRJ writes through EBE, 1375; MJM and CCM attend school, 1375; writes MJM of Montevideo, 1375; Captain (dog) dies, 1375; Montevideo Negroes send messages to MJM and CCM, 1375–76; remembers anniversary of CCJ's death, 1376; sends money toward publication of CCJ's *History*, 1376, 1379, 1381; sells cotton, 1376; feels financial pressure, 1376–77; freedmen bear arms, 1376; sees KCS in Savannah, 1377; visits Axsons, 1377; appreciates MSJ's letters, 1377, 1380; nurses Sam (EGR) in final illness, 1377; EGR always talking of, 1377–78; sends EDR's baby a dress, 1378; MER recommends her removal to New Orleans, 1378; remembers MSJ's tenth wedding anniversary, 1379; appreciates likenesses of MSJ, RQM, and GMM, 1379; reports mass meeting of freedmen at Newport Church, 1379; feels "strange hopefulness" in national affairs, 1379; CCJJ sends printed title page of CCJ's *History*, 1379; to clean out graveyard, 1379; ECC visits, 1379, 1380; anticipates MJM's letter, 379–80; grieved and provoked at misconduct of Kate (MSJ), 1380, 1382, 1384, 1392, 1397, 1410; receives MJM's letter, 1380, 1382; D. Comfort visits, 1380; Alexanders visit, 1380–81; visits SMC and LEM, 1381; perplexed about summer plans, 1381; CCJJ sends first stereotype pages of CCJ's *History*, 1381, 1385; EBE withholds news of pregnancy from, 1381, 1384; reports mass meeting of freedmen at Riceboro, 1382; writes MJM of Montevideo, 1382–83; Faith and Hope (mules) fall in canal, 1382–83; remembers MSJ's birthday, 1383; suffers old pain in arm and shoulder, 1383; excessive rains threaten crops, 1384, 1386; fears yellow fever for Mallards, 1384, 1386; rejoices in RQM's encouragement in church, 1384; anticipates letters from MJM and CCM, 1384, 1388; MRJ writes first letter in own hand, 1384; encloses letter to MJM and CCM, 1384, 1388; sends MSJ linen sheets, 1384, 1385; visits SMC, 1384, 1386; sends EBE bed and mattress, 1384; CCJ's *History* to be published in fall, 1385; to leave Montevideo for summer, 1385; sends presents to Mallards in New Orleans, 1385; appreciates money sent by MSJ and RQM, 1385; opposes MSJ's visiting Nashville in July, 1385; CCJJ writes of EBE's pregnancy, 1385; "sells" WM's linen sheets, 1385; receives J. W. Farmer's bill for services to Fanny (CCJ), 1385; visits JJ and family in Nashville, 1387–1404 passim; reaches Nashville, 1387; visits JOJ and family in Griffin, 1387; prepares account of CCJ's missionary labors, 1387; visits EGR and family in Marietta, 1387; remembers MSJ in Atlanta, 1387; CCJJ informs of ECJ's birth, 1388–89; MSJ to write LEM more frequently, 1391; dreams of CCJ's death, 1392; GMM has yellow fever, 1392, 1395, 1396, 1397, 1401, 1402; appreciates LEM's letter, 1393; appreciates letters of MJM and CCM, 1393;

MER anxious to hear from, 1393; urged by JOJ to settle in Griffin, 1394; anxious for safety of MSJ and family, 1396; assists CSD in preparations for confinement, 1396, 1397; writes MSJ of JJ's children, 1396; fears ECJ is spoiled, 1396; relieved to hear from MSJ, 1396–97; Nashville healthy but hot, 1397, 1398; writes LEM news of MSJ and family, 1397; RQM has yellow fever, 1397, 1398, 1402; CCM has yellow fever, 1397, 1398, 1402; regrets inability to go to New Orleans, 1397; rejoices in DLB's call to Marietta church, 1398; dreads isolation at Montevideo, 1398; remembers King family, 1398; appreciates letters of SMC and LEM, 1398; MJM has yellow fever, 1398, 1401, 1402; invited to visit Marietta en route home, 1399, 1400; MER hopes she removes to New Orleans, 1400; JOJ shares her anxiety for safety of MSJ and family, 1400; invited to visit Griffin en route home, 1400–01; MSJ has yellow fever, 1401–02; CCJJ rejoices in recovery of MSJ and family, 1402; urged by CCJJ not to remain at Montevideo, 1402–03; MSJ anticipates her visit to New Orleans, 1404, 1406; RQM writes of CCJ's *History*, 1404; urged by MSJ not to remain at Montevideo, 1406, 1408; returns to Montevideo, 1406; visits Kings on Island, 1406; heartbroken at DLB's departure from Midway Church, 1406, 1410; DLB and his father spend night with, 1406; Buttolphs to leave Liberty County for Marietta, 1406; Liberty County in ruins, 1406–07, 1409–10, 1429–30; feels severe financial pressure, 1407, 1409; D. J. E. Broughton unwilling to share total loss of crop, 1407; 1409; plans departure for New Orleans, 1407; asks MSJ best route and cost of travel to New Orleans, 1407, 1409, 1410; wishes to send MSJ household articles, 1407, 1409, 1410; hopes C. A. Alexander will manage Montevideo, 1407, 1409; MSJ advises on best route to New Orleans, 1407, 1411, 1412, 1416–17; MSJ grateful for household articles, 1407; MSJ regrets deplorable condition of Montevideo and Midway Church, 1408; MSJ wishes MJ could come before Christmas, 1409; sends sacques for MJM and GMM, 1409, 1410; considers arrangements for Montevideo after her departure, 1409; DLB and family leave Liberty County for Marietta, 1410; hopes to put up brickwork of CCJ's tomb, 1410; asks RQM to inquire at post office for sacques, 1410; to leave Montevideo early in January, 1410; her sacques for MJM and GMM lost in mails, 1411; Mallards to send $45 in January, 1411; Mallards glad to pay express on household articles, 1411–12; MSJ hopes lost letters come to light, 1412; JOJ misses at train in Griffin, 1412; CCJ's *History* commended to General Assembly by T. V. Moore, 1413; CCJ's *History* endorsed by S. Robinson, 1413; asked by JOJ to counsel with JDJ, 1413; MER wishes she were safely in New Orleans, 1414; SMC wishes she were safely in New Orleans, 1414; SMC

bill makes stir in Atlanta, 1144; writes WM, 1144; sends MJ wages of Niger (CCJ), 1145; recognized by MRJ in likeness, 1145; to remember CCJJ in prayer, 1146; must keep wages of Niger (CCJ) next month, 1146; anxious for letter from MJ, 1146; suffers from headache, 1146; remembers first anniversary of CCJ's death, 1146–47, 1149; Yankees signally defeated in Florida, 1147; deplores U. Dahlgren's "diabolical" plot, 1147; to call on C. G. Dahlgren and family, 1147; regrets death of Fanny (CCJ), 1147; commences gardening, 1147; sends MJ millet seed, 1147; relieved to have MJ's letter, 1149; regrets MJ's illness, 1149; glad MRJ has returned, 1149; more winter weather, 1149; receives present of hollow ware from J. L. Rogers, 1150; anxious for CCJJ's safety in Florida, 1150, 1158; regrets inability to be "really sociable" with A. E. Logan, 1150; to knit flannel shirts for RQM, 1150; finds flannels great comforts, 1150; wears heavy shoes, 1150; writes MJ regularly each week, 1150; recounts visit of Sullivans, 1151–52; Mallards' hen house robbed, 1152–53; heavy snowstorm, 1153; receives cake after lieutenant's wedding, 1153; suggests Patience (CCJ) visit Atlanta, 1154; MJ offers to send cow, chickens, and turkeys, 1154; MJ to ask refusal of Walthourville academy for MSJ and family, 1155; MJ sends MJM and CCM hymn she said in childhood, 1155–56; fifty thieves and housebreakers jailed, 1157; RQM attends Presbytery in Cuthbert, 1157–59 passim; forms C. G. Dahlgren's acquaintance, 1157; paroled soldier returns home, 1157; weather cold and unpleasant, 1157–58, 1160; enemy quiet above Atlanta, 1158; sends MJ currency table, 1158; writes WM, 1158; suffers severely from headaches, 1158; KCS visits, 1159–75 passim; may be called to EGR's bedside, 1159; declines MJ's offer of chickens and turkeys, considers offer of cow, 1160; "we are in the hands of Providence," 1160, 1161; anticipates MJ's visit to Atlanta, 1160, 1161; contrives cloth doll for MJM's birthday, 1160; asks MJ for pepper seed, 1160; wishes Elvira (CCJ) happiness on marriage, 1161; celebrates MJM's birthday, 1161; dines with J. L. Rogers and wife, 1161; troubled by MJM's cut forehead, 1161; on safety of Atlanta, 1161; spends day with EGR, 1162, 1165–66; tries new cow, 1162; Niger (CCJ) not altogether satisfied with work, 1162; asks Rose (CCJ) not to mix yarn with cotton, 1162; to pray for CCJJ's spiritual state, 1162; MJ to put up butter for, 1163; her wool to be spun after sheep are sheared, 1163; MJ to visit, 1164; writes MJM's letter to MJ, 1164–65; reads Sunday school books to MJM, 1164; enjoys wild azaleas, 1165; rejoices at news of CCJJ's spiritual state, 1165; grateful for religious interest in army, 1165; anticipates next battle, 1165; regrets death of J. E. Cay, 1165; sends homespun for babies of Rose (CCJ) and Bess (CCJ),

1166; anticipates MJ's summer visit, 1166, 1175, 1178, 1179–80, 1186; thanks MJ for pepper seed, 1166; her garden very backward, 1166; asks twelve yards wool sent to Atlanta, 1166; JOJ asks to be remembered to, 1167; universal anxiety regarding battles in Virginia, 1168; battle hourly expected on Atlanta front, 1168, 1169–70, 1171; J. P. Logan and P. P. Pease take tea, 1168; M. C. Hull kind and polite, 1168; difficult to visit friends in Atlanta without conveyance, 1168; inflationary prices, 1169; relief committees active, 1170; asks MJ to send arrowroot for wounded soldiers, 1170; concerned about MJ's illness, 1171, 1173; asks SMC for old rags from Liberty County, 1171; rejoices to learn MJ better, 1173; sick in bed, 1173; intense anxiety at enemy's approach, 1173; MSR, EWR, and EDR stay with en route to Perry, 1173–74; no panic in Atlanta, 1174, 1176–77; news from front, 1174–75; asks MJ for old rags from Liberty County, 1175; difficult to decide what to do in crisis, 1175; T. R. Markham comes from army sick, 1175; has full house all week, 1175; CCJJ writes of MJ's Savannah visit, 1175–76; passing through much anxiety and perplexity, 1176; Atlanta filling up with wounded, 1176; sympathizes with Robartses, 1177; T. R. Markham returns to army, 1177; MJM and CCM preserved in house struck by lightning, 1177; her strength returns, 1177; delightful weather, 1177; to write CCJJ and EBE, 1177; sends MJ wages of Niger (CCJ) for two months, 1177; EGR determines to move from Marietta, 1178; 5th Georgia Regiment passes through Atlanta, 1178; Atlanta mayor appoints day of fasting and prayer, 1178, 1181; daily union prayer meetings poorly attended, 1178, 1181–82; EBE sends love, 1179; MJ anxious for safety of Mallards, 1179; Robartses move from Marietta to Longstreet, 1178–89 passim; Mallards help defray expenses, 1181; Confederate army three miles from Marietta, 1181; asks RQM to inquire of B. E. Stiles's safety, 1181; considers plans for leaving Atlanta in emergency, 1182, 1184–85; cuts up MJ's gauze for wounded soldiers, 1182, 1185–86; Niger (CCJ) discharged from tannery, 1182; W. E. W. Quarterman to give out osnaburgs to Arcadia Negroes, 1182; appreciates MJ's birthday letter, 1185; unsettled about future movements, 1185; Negroes impressed to work on fortifications at Chattahoochee, 1185; awaiting MJ's wishes concerning Niger (CCJ), 1185; Liberty County Negroes ask to be remembered to, 1186; MJ to send butter, 1186; Rose (CCJ) spins her fine wool, 1186; MJ willing for Niger (CCJ) to remain in Atlanta, 1187; MJ uncertain about Atlanta visit, 1187; MJ anxious about Mallards' situation in Atlanta, 1187; appreciates MJ's butter, 1187–88; to send fans to hospital, 1188; JJ visits, 1188; C. S. Dod visits, 1188; pleased by Dod's recollections of CCJ, 1188; urges MJ to come immediately to

Sue (CCJ), and Elizabeth (CCJ) remain on his plantation, 1303; Pulaski (CCJ) wants to bring Sue (JJ) to his plantation, 1323; father of Tom (CCJ) working on his plantation, 1342
Lyons, Richard Bickerton Pemell, 912

McAllister, Charlotte Elizabeth (Henry), 51, 192
McAllister, Clementina Hanson, 51, 52, 53
McAllister, Emma, 51
McAllister, Joseph Longworth, 1187
McAllister, Robert Samuel, 815, 817
McAllister, Rosella (Rosa) Rachel, 51
Macaulay, Thomas Babington, 443
McCay, Charles Francis, 381
McClellan, George Brinton: J. Davis may find himself "minus a force" to oppose, 845–46; compels J. E. Johnston to evacuate his lines, 863–64; leads Grand Army of Potomac on Virginia Peninsula, 880; withdraws forces from south of Chickahominy River, 911–12; "the boasted modern Napoleon," 912; to force Lee to evacuate Richmond, 915; expected by many to capitulate, 921; his unconditional surrender not yet announced, 923–24; reinforced by Shields, 926; his army not annihilated, 927; reported to be reinforced, 927–28; CCJ longs to see *finale* of his army, 929; "Onward to Richmond," 939; to meet Lee "in deadly conflict," 975
McClellan, Robert Miller, 217, 225–26, 236, 238, 251, 253, 286, 332, 335
McCollough, Hannah Elizabeth (Quarterman), 424–25, 949
McCollough, James Sullivan, 805, 818, 1206, 1221
McConnell, Ann Amelia (Dicks), 251, 252
McConnell, Ida Rosalie, 955, 957
McConnell, James David, 155, 157, 158, 198, 199, 201
McConnell, Mary Eloise, 955, 957
McConnell, Samuel Darwin, 955, 957
McConnell, Theodosia Elizabeth, 955, 957
McConnell, Thomas Rush, 157
McConnell, William Robert, 252
McCoy, Lt., 1134
McCulloch, Ben, 665
McDonald, Charles J. C., 386
McDonald, Charles James, 386, 665
McDonald, Daniel, 986, 988–89
McDonald, Elisha: MER glad CCJ has manager, 402; CCJ hopes he has good rain, 405; "quite attentive to our business," 424; takes tea at Maybank, 430; informs CCJ of illness of H. O. Britton, 499; directed by CCJ to send up Sam (CCJ) to aid in nursing, 499; fears death of kinsman from typhoid fever, 540; to deliver packet of money to O. W. Stevens, 570; leaves to "catch the mail," 589; CCJ sends letter to CCJJ by, 693; conducts search for four strange men encountered by Jackson (CCJ) back of Dogwood Swamp, 697; makes trial of JJ's carbine, 697; brings CCJJ's letter and returns with reply, 721; informs CCJ of illness of Cinda (CCJ), 730; carries MJ's letter

to post office, 772, 779; CCJJ hopes he will not disappoint MJ, 1372
McDonald, James, 986
McDowell, Irvin, 895
McEwen, Robert Houston, 494
McFarland, Francis, 810, 820
McFarland, John Theodore, 936
Macfie, Catherine, 175
Macfie, Catherine (McGregor), 174, 175
McGavock, Randal William, 490, 493, 498
McGavock, Seraphine (Deery), 493
McHenry, John Hardin, 55, 57–58
McIntosh, Anna, 134
McIntosh, Donald McKay, 561
McIntosh, Harlie (Rutledge), 561
McIntosh, McQueen, 555
McIntosh, Maria B. (Morris), 477, 966, 967, 971
McIntosh, Thomas Spalding, 966, 967, 971
McIntosh, William Jackson, 555, 556, 561, 624, 634, 1010
McIver, Augustus Munro, 885–88
McIver, Caroline Matilda (Sturtevant), 1114
Mackay, Catherine, 278, 282, 286, 410, 1050
Mackay, Eliza Anne (McQueen), 278, 280, 286, 292, 410, 579
Mackay, Robert, 376
Mackay, Sarah, 278, 282, 286, 410, 579, 1050, 1144
McLaws, Lafayette, 966, 1206–07, 1209
McNatt, Adam, 600
McPherson, James Birdseye, 1173, 1174
McRae, Elijah, 1100, 1101, 1103–04
McWhir, William, 274, 1062
Madison, Dorothea (Dolley) (Payne) (Todd), 491
Magoffin, Beriah, 664
Magrath, Andrew Gordon, 626
Magruder, Edward Jones, 766
Mallard, Ann Eliza (Screven), 1135, 1196, 1197, 1198, 1201, 1202, 1207, 1212
Mallard, Charles Colcock: birth, 575–79 passim; his wakefulness caused by flea, 579; his baptism proposed, 582; "quite a comely boy," 583; quieter than MJM, 587; reaches Maybank, 588; MJ misses children and grandchildren, 596; to be baptized by CCJ, 601, 602–03, 605; CCJ postpones visit to Walthourville, 601, 602; described by MSJ for MJT, 602–03; "an *uncommonly* fine boy," 605; baptized by CCJ, 610, 612; verges toward broken-bone fever, 630; SMC send merino, 631; JOJ hopes to see, 633; his illness prevents family visit to Montevideo, 654; stays at Maybank with MSJ during MJ's absence in Savannah, 699–716 passim; delighted to return home, 717; MJ sends sacque, 718; MSJ to buy hat for, 718; CCJ asks MJM to share peach leather and candy with, 735; fond of red potatoes, 735–36; walks and says "a great many words," 736; visits Maybank, 758; calls MRJ "Little Sister," 807; "Gamma carry please," 818; longs to see RQM, 818; rejoices in Christmas stocking, 827; very fond of MRJ, 866, 903; visits Montevideo, 866; has measles, 914, 917, 926, 935; plays with MRJ, 935; behaves "like a little gentleman" during

fanticide, 547; expected at Montevideo with family, 560; to attend JBJ's baptism in Midway Church, 560; stays at Montevideo over two weeks, 563; visits MSJ and RQM in Walthourville, 563; distressed by "intemperance" of JWR, 563–64; scandalized by marriage of JWR, 566–74 passim; to leave Montevideo for Marietta, 569; to stop in Savannah with CCJJ, 569; leaves Montevideo, 570; CCJJ deeply sympathizes with, 570; "speechless with grief," 572; suffers "sad trial" in Savannah, 573–74; returns to Marietta, 573–74; hot weather and high prices in Marietta, 606; JOJ and CCJJ visit, 606; grieved at death of CWW, 606; advises EAW on prices in Marietta, 606–07; illness of Hannah (EGR) "a drawback to our little income," 607; sends MJM book and little sheep, 631; MSR becomes governess in family of C. H. Stewart, 647; provisions "double price," 647; constant damp and cold, 647; country in "distressing and fearful state," 647; JOJ and family visit, 657; much depressed by death of Hannah (EGR), 679; sells Henry (EGR), Mason (EGR), and Clarence (EGR) to E. E. Pynchon, 679; much depressed by "this dreadful war," 679–80; M. Bulloch circumstanced in North, 679–80; glad to hear of WSB's birth, 680; recommends Meriwether Springs to MJ, 680; remembers "happy and pleasant days" at Midway Church, 680; visits Hannah (EGR) on deathbed, 687–88; makes shirt for soldier, 688; "far better than she has been for years," 743; MSJ suggests MJ visit, 782; her patriotism fervent, 786; MJ sends barrel of rice, 787; enjoying "better health than she has had for years," 937; receives six oranges from JJR, 989; writes letters, 989; visited by HHJ, 989; by JOJ, 989–90; by J. N. West, 990; sells William (EGR) to settle debts, 990; receives ten oranges from MJ, 1003; receives three hams and Catawba wine from G. Walker, 1004; enjoys JOJ's visit in Marietta, 1004–05; her health feeble, 1005; remains loyal to JWR, 1005; sends MJ condolences on CCJ's death, 1044, 1045, 1052; MJ ships articles to, 1050; JOJ and family visit, 1074; feels deeply JWR's death, 1074; thrown into uncomfortable circumstances by war, 1103; celebrates seventy-eighth birthday, 1107; knits stockings for MJM, 1107; receives sack of salt from JAMK, 1107; receives sack of salt from A. M. Jones, 1107; receives twenty-five bushels of wheat from J. L. Rogers, 1107; MSJ to spend waiting interval with, 1115; MSJ visits, 1116–18; knits stockings for MJM and socks for CCM, 1116; thanks MJ for cow, 1117, 1118; promises MJM and CCM two beautiful kittens, 1118; her health improves, 1120–21; considers leaving Marietta for safer place, 1129; Mallards spend Christmas with, 1130; tells MSJ history of MJ's silver acorn, 1130; given silver egg by John Jones (1772–1805), 1130; CCM to wear her socks

to W. T. Brantly's church, 1133; agitates question of removal from Marietta, 1136, 1141; will miss W. J. Russell, 1141; her health declines, 1158; sick with cold and "something like rheumatism," 1159; MSJ spends day with, 1162, 1165–66; MJ wishes to visit, 1164; JOJ distressed by her straitened situation, 1167–68; W. J. Russell offers to lend her money to pay Confederate tax, 1168; able to bear Marietta panic better than MER and LJR, 1174; MSJ sympathizes with, 1177; moves from Marietta to Longstreet, 1178–89 passim; recovers from fever, 1193; expected by MJ to spend winter in Liberty County, 1193; afflicted by JJR's death, 1196; her health failing, 1197; hopes to find house in Cuthbert, 1212; may spend winter in Flemington, 1212; settles in Cuthbert, 1213–17; rents part of Duncan house, 1214, 1215; anxious to see relatives in Liberty County, 1214; bears troubles with fortitude and submission, 1214; appreciates Buttolphs' invitation to Liberty County, 1214; CSD concerned for her welfare, 1252; her health improves, 1265; encouraged by success of Atlanta boardinghouse, 1290; JOJ writes, 1292; MJ to write after gathering local news, 1302, 1304, 1305; MJ writes, 1309; unusually feeble, 1324; receives four percent railroad dividend, 1324; LJR sleeps with, 1326; LJR buys shad for, 1326; MJ, JJ, and CSD send love, 1345; MSJ and family spend evening with, 1348; her family gratified at MSR's marriage, 1348, 1356; has increase of boarders, 1353; will miss WM, 1354; LEM writes of WM's death, 1356; maintains interest in things around, 1356; will miss Mallards in Atlanta, 1361; very feeble, 1361, 1367; longs to see MJ and SMC, 1361; anxious to return to Marietta, 1361, 1367; longs to hear from SMC, 1362; returns to Marietta, 1367; shows restlessness of age, 1367–68; "completely broken up" by departure of Mallards for New Orleans, 1368; anxious to hear from MJ, 1368; hires M. D. Nesbitt's Lambert and wife, 1368; appreciates letter of Sam (EGR), 1369; enjoys SMC's visit, 1377–78; always talking of MJ and SMC, 1377–78; her daughters' health essential to her care, 1378; receives likeness of MSJ, RQM, and GMM, 1378; MSR confined at her house, 1381; enjoys MJ's visit, 1387; MER feels duty-bound to, 1393; pleased at DLB's call to Marietta church, 1399; passes eighty-second birthday, 1400; Buttolphs stay with, 1413–15, 1421; has little appetite, 1414; very feeble, 1414; enjoys usual health, 1416; feeble but cheerful, 1421. *See also* Robarts, Louisa Jane; Robarts, Mary Eliza

Robarts, Elizabeth (Lilla) Walton: to visit M. M. LaRoche in Savannah, 126, 135; has "taste for the beautiful," 197; hears T. F. Scott preach on missions in Oregon, 262; anxious to visit Savannah, 263; visits Savannah, 278–92 passim; not staying at

The Slaves

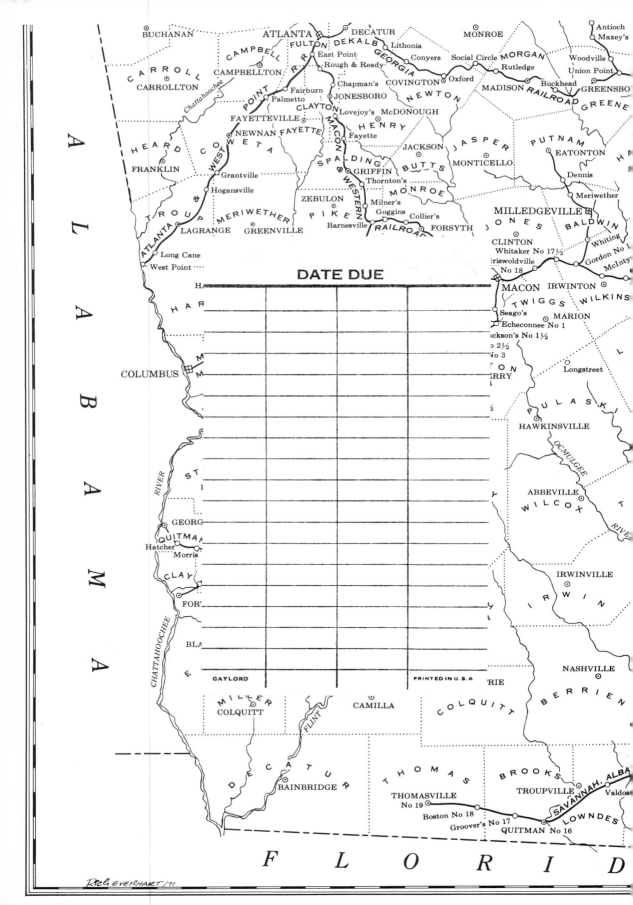